CRIME IN THE UNITED STATES

2009

THIRD EDITION

Published in the United States of America
by Bernan Press, a wholly owned subsidiary of
The Rowman & Littlefield Publishing Group, Inc.
4501 Forbes Boulevard, Suite 200
Lanham, Maryland 20706

Bernan Press
800-865-3457
info@bernan.com
www.bernan.com

ISBN: 978-1-59888-329-9
e-ISBN: 978-1-59888-330-5

♾™ The paper used in this publication meets the minimum requirements of American National Standard for Information Sciences—Permanence of Paper for Printed Library Materials, ANSI/NISO Z39.48-1992. Manufactured in the United States of America.

CONTENTS

SECTION I:
SUMMARY OF THE UNIFORM CRIME REPORTING (UCR) PROGRAM

SUMMARY OF THE UNIFORM CRIME REPORTING (UCR) PROGRAM

Bernan Press is proud to present its third edition of *Crime in the United States*. This title was formerly published by the Federal Bureau of Investigation (FBI), but is no longer available in printed form from the government. This edition contains final data from 2007, the latest data that are currently available.

This section examines the best way of using the publication's data and discusses the history of the UCR Program, which collects the data used in *Crime in the United States*.

About the UCR Program

The UCR Program's primary objective is to generate reliable information for use in law enforcement administration, operation, and management; however, over the course of the program, its data have become one of the country's leading social indicators.

The UCR Program is a nationwide, cooperative statistical effort of more than 17,000 city, university and college, county, state, tribal, and federal law enforcement agencies who voluntarily report data on crimes brought to their attention. During 2007, the law enforcement agencies that were active in the UCR Program represented 94.6 percent of the total population.

Note for Users

It is important for UCR data users to remember that the FBI's primary objective is to generate a reliable set of crime statistics for use in law enforcement administration, operation, and management. The FBI does not provide a ranking of agencies; instead, it provides alphabetical tabulations of states, metropolitan statistical areas, cities with over 10,000 inhabitants, suburban and rural counties, and colleges and universities. Law enforcement officials use these data for their designed purposes. Additionally, the public relies on these data for information about the fluctuations in levels of crime from year to year, while criminologists, sociologists, legislators, city planners, media outlets, and other students of criminal justice use them for a variety of research and planning purposes. Since crime is a sociological phenomenon influenced by a variety of factors, the FBI discourages data users from ranking agencies and using the data as a measurement of the effectiveness of law enforcement.

To ensure that data are uniformly reported, the FBI provides contributing law enforcement agencies with a handbook that explains how to classify and score offenses and provides uniform crime offense definitions. Acknowledging that offense definitions may vary from state to state, the FBI cautions agencies to report offenses according to the guidelines provided in the handbook, rather than by local or state statutes. Most agencies make a good faith effort to comply with established guidelines.

The UCR Program publishes the statistics most commonly requested by data users. More information regarding the availability of UCR Program data is available by telephone at (304) 625-4995, by fax at (304) 625-5394, or by e-mail at <cjis_comm@leo.gov>. E-mail data requests cannot be processed without the requester's full name, mailing address, and contact telephone number.

Variables Affecting Crime

Until data users examine all the variables that affect crime in a town, city, county, state, region, or college or university, they can make no meaningful comparisons.

Caution Against Ranking

In each edition of *Crime in the United States*, many entities—including news media, tourism agencies, and other organizations with an interest in crime in the nation—use reported figures to compile rankings of cities and counties. However, these rankings are merely a quick choice made by that data user; they provide no insight into the many variables that mold the crime in a particular town, city, county, state, or region. Consequently, these rankings may lead to simplistic and/or incomplete analyses, which can create misleading perceptions and thus adversely affect cities and counties, along with their residents.

Considering Other Characteristics of a Jurisdiction

To assess criminality and law enforcement's response from jurisdiction to jurisdiction, data users must consider many variables, some of which (despite having significant impact on crime) are not readily measurable or applicable among all locales. Geographic and demographic factors specific to each jurisdiction must be considered and applied in order to make an accurate and complete assessment of crime in that jurisdiction. Several sources of information are available to help the researcher explore the variables that affect crime in a particular locale. U.S. Census Bureau data, for example, can help the user better understand the makeup of a locale's population. The transience of the population, its racial and ethnic makeup, and its composition by age and gender, educational levels, and prevalent family structures are all key factors in assessing and understanding crime.

Local chambers of commerce, planning offices, and similar entities provide information regarding the economic and cultural makeup of cities and counties. Understanding a jurisdiction's industrial/economic base, its dependence upon neighboring jurisdictions, its transportation system, its economic dependence on nonresidents (such as tourists and convention attendees), and its proximity to military installations, correctional institutions, and other types of facilities all contribute to accurately gauging and interpreting the crime known to and reported by law enforcement.

The strength (including personnel and other resources) and aggressiveness of a jurisdiction's law enforcement agency are also key factors in understanding the nature and extent of crime occurring in that area. Although information pertaining to the number of sworn and civilian employees can be found in this publication, it cannot be used alone as an assessment of the emphasis that a community places on enforcing the law. For example, one city may report more crime than another comparable city because its law enforcement agency identifies more offenses. Attitudes of citizens toward crime and their crime reporting practices—especially for minor offenses—also have an impact on the volume of crimes known to police.

Make Valid Assessments of Crime

It is essential for all data users to become as well educated as possible about understanding and quantifying the nature and extent of crime in the United States and in the more than 17,000 jurisdictions represented by law enforcement contributors to the UCR Program. Valid assessments are possible only with careful study and analysis of the various unique conditions that affect each local law enforcement jurisdiction.

Some factors that are known to affect the volume and type of crime occurring from place to place are:

- Population density and degree of urbanization

- Variations in composition of population, particularly in the concentration of youth

- Stability of the population with respect to residents' mobility, commuting patterns, and transient factors

- Modes of transportation and highway systems

- Economic conditions, including median income, poverty level, and job availability

- Cultural factors and educational, recreational, and religious characteristics

- Family conditions, with respect to divorce and family cohesiveness

- Climate

- Effective strength of law enforcement agencies

- Administrative and investigative emphases of law enforcement

- Policies of other components of the criminal justice system (i.e., prosecutorial, judicial, correctional, and probational policies)

- Residents' attitudes toward crime

- Crime reporting practices of residents

Although many of the listed factors equally affect the crime of a particular area, the UCR Program makes no attempt to relate them to the data presented. **The data user is therefore cautioned against comparing statistical data of individual reporting units from cities, counties, metropolitan areas, states, or colleges or universities solely on the basis on their population coverage or student enrollment.** Until data users examine all the variables that affect crime in a town, city, county, state, region, or college or university, they can make no meaningful comparisons.

Historical Background

Since 1930, the FBI has administered the UCR Program; the agency continues to assess and monitor the nature and type of crime in the nation. Data users look to the UCR Program for various research and planning purposes.

Recognizing a need for national crime statistics, the International Association of Chiefs of Police (IACP) formed the Committee on Uniform Crime Records in the 1920s to develop a system of uniform crime statistics. Establishing offenses known to law enforcement as the appropriate measure, the committee evaluated various crimes on the basis of their seriousness, frequency of occurrence, pervasiveness in all geographic areas of the country, and likelihood of being reported to law enforcement. After studying state criminal codes and making an evaluation of the record-keeping practices in use, the committee completed a plan for crime reporting that became the foundation of the UCR Program in 1929.

Seven main offense classifications, known as Part I crimes, were chosen to gauge the state of crime in the nation. These seven offense classifications included the violent crimes of murder and nonnegligent manslaughter, forcible rape, robbery, and aggravated assault; also included were the property crimes of burglary, larceny-theft, and motor vehicle theft. By congressional mandate, arson was added as the eighth Part I offense category. Data collection for arson began in 1979. Agencies classify and score offenses according to a Hierarchy Rule (with the exception of justifiable homicide, motor vehicle theft, and arson) and report their data to the FBI. More information about the Hierarchy Rule is presented in Appendix I.

During the early planning of the program, it was recognized that the differences among criminal codes precluded a mere aggregation of state statistics to arrive at a national total. Also, because of the variances in punishment for the same offenses in different states, no distinction between felony and misdemeanor crimes was possible. To avoid these problems and provide nationwide uniformity in crime reporting, standardized offense definitions were developed. Law enforcement agencies use these to submit data without regard for local statutes. The definitions used by the program can be found in Appendix II.

In January 1930, 400 cities (representing 20 million inhabitants in 43 states) began participating in the UCR Program.

Congress enacted Title 28, Section 534, of the United States Code that same year, which authorized the attorney general to gather crime information. The attorney general, in turn, designated the FBI to serve as the national clearinghouse for the collected crime data. Since then, data based on uniform classifications and procedures for reporting have been obtained annually from the nation's law enforcement agencies.

Advisory Groups

Providing vital links between local law enforcement and the FBI for the UCR Program are the Criminal Justice Information Systems Committees of the IACP and the National Sheriffs' Association (NSA). The IACP represents the thousands of police departments nationwide, as it has since the program began. The NSA encourages sheriffs throughout the country to participate fully in the program. Both committees serve the program in advisory capacities.

In 1988, a Data Providers' Advisory Policy Board was established. This board operated until 1993, when it combined with the National Crime Information Center Advisory Policy Board to form a single Advisory Policy Board (APB) to address all FBI criminal justice information services. The current APB works to ensure continuing emphasis on UCR-related issues. The Association of State Uniform Crime Reporting Programs (ASUCRP) focuses on UCR issues within individual state law enforcement associations and also promotes interest in the UCR Program. These organizations foster widespread and responsible use of uniform crime statistics and lend assistance to data contributors.

Redesign of UCR

Although UCR data collection was originally conceived as a tool for law enforcement administration, the data were widely used by other entities involved in various forms of social planning by the 1980s. Recognizing the need for more detailed crime statistics, law enforcement called for a thorough evaluative study to modernize the UCR Program. The FBI formulated a comprehensive three-phase redesign effort. The Bureau of Justice Statistics (BJS), agency in the Department of Justice responsible for funding criminal justice information projects, agreed to underwrite the first two phases. These phases were conducted by an independent contractor and structured to determine what, if any, changes should be made to the current program. The third phase would involve implementation of the changes identified.

During the first phase, which began in 1982, the historical evolution of the UCR Program was examined. All aspects of the program, including its objectives and intended user audience, data items, reporting mechanisms, quality control issues, publications and user services, and relationships with other criminal justice data systems, were studied.

Early in 1984, a conference on the future of UCR Program launched the second phase of the study that examined the program's potential and concluded with a set of recommended changes. Phase two ended in early 1985 with the production of a report, *Blueprint for the Future of the Uniform Crime Reporting Program.* The study's Steering Committee reviewed the draft report at a March 1985 meeting and made various recommendations for revision. The committee members, however, endorsed the report's concepts.

In April 1985, the phase two recommendations were presented at the eighth National UCR Conference. Various considerations for the final report were set forth, and the overall concept for the revised UCR Program was unanimously approved. The joint IACP/NSA Committee on UCR also issued a resolution endorsing the *Blueprint.*

The final report, the *Blueprint for the Future of the Uniform Crime Reporting Program,* was released in the summer of 1985. It specifically outlined recommendations for an expanded, improved UCR Program to meet future informational needs. There were three recommended areas of enhancement to the UCR Program:

- Offenses and arrests would be reported using an incident-based system.

- Data would be collected on two levels. Agencies in level one would report important details about those offenses comprising the Part I crimes, their victims, and arrestees. Level two would consist of law enforcement agencies covering populations of more than 100,000 and a sampling of smaller agencies that would collect expanded detail on all significant offenses.

- A quality assurance program would be introduced.

To begin implementation, the FBI awarded a contract to develop new offense definitions and data elements for the redesigned system. The work involved (a) revising the definitions of certain Part I offenses, (b) identifying additional significant offenses to be reported, (c) refining definitions for both, and (d) developing data elements (incident details) for all UCR Program offenses in order to fulfill the requirements of incident-based reporting versus the current summary system.

Concurrent with the preparation of the data elements, the FBI studied the various state systems to select an experimental site for implementing the redesigned program. In view of its long-standing incident-based program and well-established staff dedicated solely to UCR, the South Carolina Law Enforcement Division (SLED) was chosen. The SLED agreed to adapt its existing system to meet the requirements of the redesigned program and to collect data on both offenses and arrests relating to the newly defined offenses.

Following the completion of the pilot project conducted by the SLED, the FBI produced a draft of guidelines for an enhanced UCR Program. Law enforcement executives from around the country were then invited to a conference where the guidelines were presented for final review.

During the conference, three overall recommendations were passed without dissent: the establishment of a new, incident-based national crime reporting system; the FBI as the managing agency for the program; and the creation of an Advisory Policy Board composed of law enforcement executives to assist in directing and implementing the new program.

Information about the redesigned UCR Program, call the National Incident-Based Reporting System, or NIBRS, is contained in several documents. The *Data Collection Guidelines* publication (August 2000) contains a system overview and descriptions of the offense codes, reports, data elements, and data values used in the system. The *Error Message Manual* (December 1999) contains designations of mandatory and optional data elements, data element edits, and error messages. The *Data Submission Specifications* publication is for the use of local and state systems personnel who are responsible for preparing magnetic media for submission to the FBI. The document is available on the FBI's Web site at <www.fbi.gov/ucr/ucr.htm>. Another publication, *Handbook for Acquiring a Records Management System (RMS) that is Compatible with NIBRS,* is also available on that site.

A NIBRS edition of the *UCR Handbook* was published in 1992 to assist law enforcement agency data contributors implementing the NIBRS within their departments. This document is geared toward familiarizing local and state law enforcement personnel with the definitions, policies, and procedures of the NIBRS. It does not contain the technical coding and data transmission requirements presented in the other NIBRS publications.

The NIBRS collects data on each single incident and arrest within 22 crime categories. For each offense known to police within these categories, incident, victim, property, offender, and arrestee information are gathered when available. The goal of the redesign is to modernize crime information by collecting data currently maintained law enforcement records, making the enhanced UCR Program a by-product of current records systems while maintaining the integrity of the program's long-running statistical series.

Implementation of the NIBRS is occurring at a pace commensurate with the resources, abilities, and limitations of the contributing law enforcement agencies. The FBI was able to accept NIBRS data as of January 1989, and to date, the following 31 state programs have been certified for NIBRS participation: Arizona, Arkansas, Colorado, Connecticut, Delaware, Idaho, Iowa, Kansas, Kentucky, Louisiana, Maine, Massachusetts, Michigan, Missouri, Montana, Nebraska, New Hampshire, North Dakota, Ohio, Oregon, Rhode Island, South Carolina, South Dakota, Tennessee, Texas, Utah, Vermont, Virginia, Washington, West Virginia, and Wisconsin. Among those that submit NIBRS data, 8 states (Delaware, Idaho, Iowa, South Carolina, Tennessee, Virginia, West Virginia, and Vermont) submit all their data via the NIBRS.

Suspension of the Crime Index and Modified Crime Index

In June 2004, the Criminal Justice Information Services Advisory Policy Board (CJIS APB) approved discontinuing the use of the Crime Index in the UCR Program and its publications and directed the FBI publish a violent crime total and a property crime total until a more viable index is developed. The Crime Index was first published in *Crime in the United States* in 1960. Congress designated arson as a Part I offense in October 1978, and the UCR Program began collecting arson data in 1979. The FBI adopted the term Modified Crime Index to reflect the addition of arson as a Part I offense. The Modified Crime Index was the number of Crime Index offenses plus arson. However, in recent years, the Crime Index (and subsequently the Modified Crime Index) has not been a true indicator of the degree of criminality. The Crime Index was simply the title used for an aggregation of the seven main offense classifications (Part I offenses) for which data has been collected since the program's implementation.

The Crime Index and Modified Crime Index were driven upward by the offense with the highest number, creating a bias against a jurisdiction with a high number of larceny-thefts but a low number of other serious crimes such as murder and forcible rape. Thus, the sheer volume of those offenses overshadows more serious but less frequently committed offenses. CJIS studied the appropriateness and usefulness of the Crime Index and Modified Crime Index for several years and brought the matter before many advisory groups affiliated with the UCR Program. The consensus was that the Crime Index and Modified Crime Index no longer served their original purpose, and that the UCR Program should suspend their use and develop a more robust index of crime.

SECTION II:
OFFENSES REPORTED

VIOLENT CRIME

- Murder
- Forcible Rape
- Robbery
- Aggravated Assault

PROPERTY CRIME

- Burglary
- Larceny-Theft
- Motor Vehicle Theft
- Arson

VIOLENT CRIME

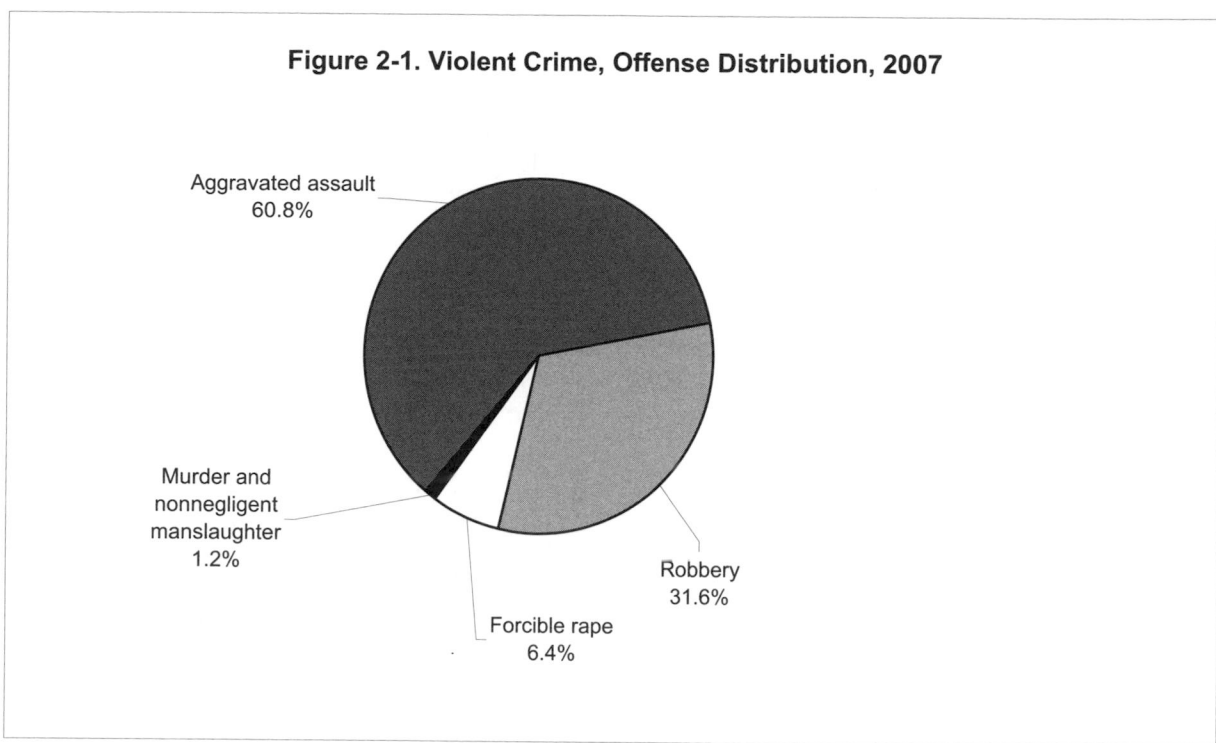

Figure 2-1. Violent Crime, Offense Distribution, 2007

Aggravated assault
60.8%

Murder and
nonnegligent
manslaughter
1.2%

Robbery
31.6%

Forcible rape
6.4%

Definition

Violent crime consists of four offenses: murder and non-negligent manslaughter, forcible rape, robbery, and aggravated assault. According to the Uniform Crime Reporting (UCR) Program, run by the Federal Bureau of Investigation (FBI), violent crimes involve either the use of force or the threat of force.

Data Collection

The data presented in *Crime in the United States* reflect the Hierarchy Rule, which counts only the most serious offense in a multiple-offense criminal incident. In descending order of severity, the violent crimes are murder and nonnegligent manslaughter, forcible rape, robbery, and aggravated assault; these are followed by the property crimes of burglary, larceny-theft, and motor vehicle theft. More information on the expanded violent crime tables (which are available online but not included in this publication) can be found in Appendix I.

National Volume, Trends, and Rate

In 2007, an estimated 1,408,337 violent crimes occurred in the United States. Aggravated assault accounted for 60.8 percent of these crimes, followed by robbery (31.6 percent), forcible rape (6.4 percent), and murder (1.2 percent). (Table 1)

The UCR Program reports data in 2-year, 5-year, and 10-year increments to formulate trend information. From 2006

to 2007, the estimated volume of violent crime in the United States fell 0.7 percent. (The estimated number of property crimes fell 1.4 percent during the same period.) The 5-year and 10-year trend data showed that the estimated number of violent crimes increased 1.8 percent between 2003 and 2007 and decreased 8.2 percent between 1998 and 2007. The rate of violent crime declined in 2007 to 466.9 per 100,000 inhabitants after increasing in 2005 and 2006. (Tables 1 and 1A)

An examination of the volume of individual offenses within the violent crime category showed that in a year-to-year comparison of data from 2006 and 2007, the estimated number of aggravated assaults decreased 0.6 percent, the estimated number of robberies decreased 0.5 percent, and the estimated number of murders decreased 0.6 percent. Forcible rape showed its third consecutive decline, by dropping 2.5 percent from 2006 to 2007. (Tables 1 and 1A)

Among each of the four violent crimes categories, aggravated assault had the highest rate of occurrence. There were an estimated 283.8 aggravated assaults, 147.6 robberies, 30.0 forcible rapes, and 5.6 murders per 100,000 inhabitants in the United States in 2007. (Table 1)

Regional Offense Trends and Rate

The UCR Program divides the United States into four regions: the Northeast, the South, the Midwest, and the West. (More details concerning geographic regions are provided in Appendix III.) The population distribution of the regions is provided in Table 3, and the estimated volume and rate of violent crime by region can be found in Table 4.

The Northeast

The Northeast accounted for an estimated 18.1 percent of the nation's population in 2007 and an estimated 14.5 percent of its violent crimes. (Table 3) Of the four regions, the Northeast had the largest decrease (down 5.1 percent) in the estimated number of violent crimes from 2006 to 2007 The region's population declined by 0.1 percent during this period. In the Northeast, the estimated number of robberies decreased 9.0 percent and the estimated number of murders decreased 7.9 percent, while the estimated number of aggravated assaults decreased 2.4 percent and the estimated number of forcible rapes decreased 4.3 percent. (Table 4)

In 2007, there were an estimated 372.4 violent crimes per 100,000 inhabitants in the Northeast, a 5.0 percent decrease from 2006 figure. By offense, rates were estimated at 210.7 aggravated assaults, 137.8 robberies, 19.8 forcible rapes, and 4.1 murders per 100,000 inhabitants. (Table 4)

The Midwest

With an estimated 22.0 percent of the total population of the United States, the Midwest accounted for 19.4 percent of the nation's estimated number of violent crimes in 2007. (Table 3) The region had a 1.7 percent decrease in violent crime and a 0.3 percent growth in population from 2006 to 2007. The estimated number of aggravated assaults in the Midwest decreased 0.6 percent, the estimated number of robberies decreased 3.2 percent, and the estimated number of murders declined 2.5 percent from 2006 to 2007, while the estimated number of forcible rapes fell 3.6 percent. (Table 4)

The rate of violent crime per 100,000 inhabitants in the Midwest declined 2.0 percent in 2007. There were 244.4 aggravated assaults, 127.5 robberies, 34.4 forcible rapes, and 4.9 murders per 100,000 inhabitants in the region in 2007. (Table 4)

The South

The South, the nation's most populous region, accounted for an estimated 36.6 percent of the nation's population in 2007. An estimated 43.1 percent of the nation's violent crimes took place in this region in 2007. (Table 3) Violent crime in the South increased 1.6 percent from 2006 to 2007, and the region's population grew 1.3 percent during this period. The estimated number of aggravated assaults increased 0.3 percent from 2006 to 2007, while the estimated number of robberies increased 4.9 percent and the estimated number of murders grew 5.3 percent. The estimated number of forcible rapes showed the region's only decline, dropping 1.7 percent from 2006 to 2007. (Table 4)

The estimated rate of violent crime in the South was 549.2 incidents per 100,000 inhabitants in 2007. There were 347.8 aggravated assaults, 162.7 robberies, 31.8 forcible rapes, and 7.0 murders per 100,000 inhabitants. The forcible rape and aggravated assault rates both showed declines between 2006 and 2007, dropping 2.9 percent and 0.9 percent, respectively. (Table 4)

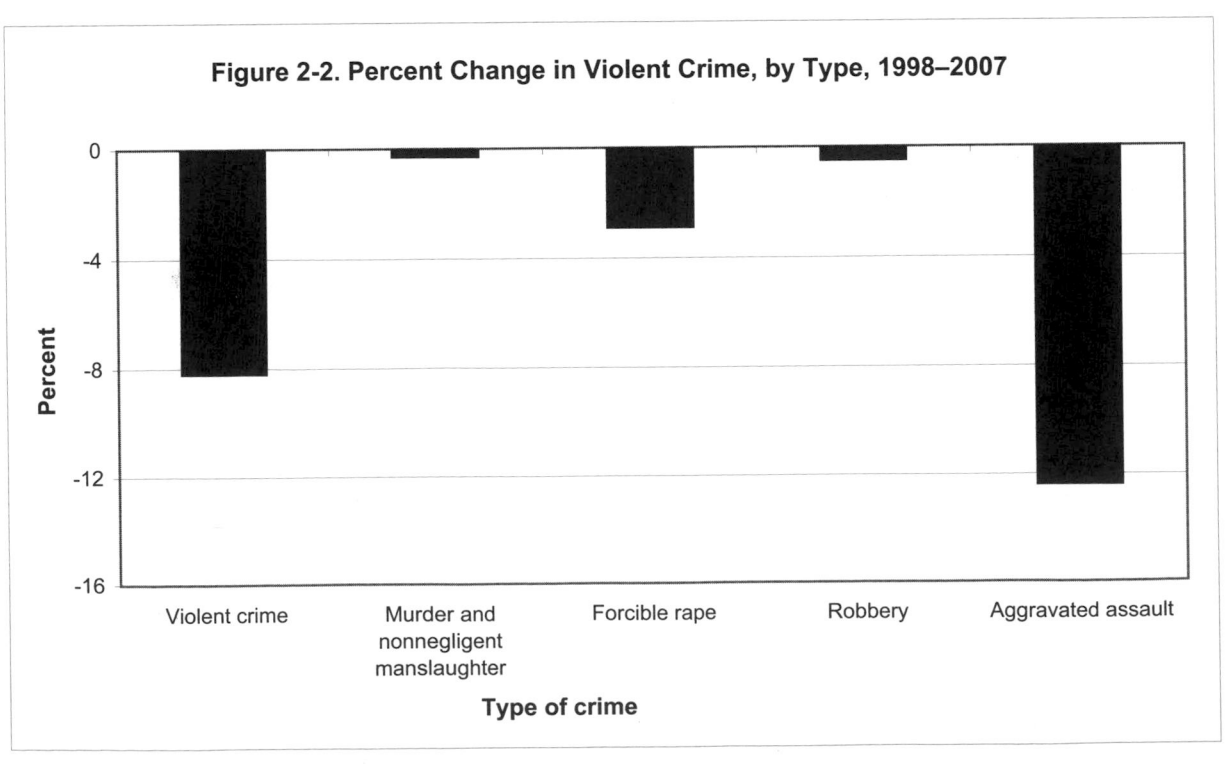

Figure 2-2. Percent Change in Violent Crime, by Type, 1998–2007

The West

With an estimated 23.2 percent of the nation's population in 2007, the West accounted for an estimated 23.1 percent of the nation's violent crime. (Table 3) Violent crime decreased 1.0 percent in this region from 2006 to 2007, while its population grew 1.1 percent. All four violent offense categories decreased in number from 2006 to 2007: murder declined 5.6 percent, forcible rape dropped 1.8 percent, aggravated assault fell 1.2 percent, and robbery decreased by 0.4 percent.

The estimated rate of violent crime in the West in 2007 was 463.7 incidents per 100,000 inhabitants, a 2.1 percent decrease from the 2006 rate. There were 277.1 aggravated assaults, 150.4 robberies, 30.9 forcible rapes, and 5.3 murders per 100,000 inhabitants in this region in 2007. (Table 4)

Community Types

The UCR Program aggregates crime data into three community types: metropolitan statistical areas (MSAs), cities outside MSAs, and nonmetropolitan counties outside MSAs. Appendix III provides additional information regarding community types. Just over 83 percent of the nation's population lived in MSAs in 2007. Residents of cities outside MSAs accounted for 6.7 percent of the country's population, while 10.1 percent of the population lived in nonmetropolitan counties. (Table 2)

An examination of the volume of violent crime by community type showed that 89.8 percent of the estimated number of violent crimes in the United States occurred in MSAs, 5.6 percent occurred in cities outside MSAs, and 4.5 percent occurred in nonmetropolitan counties. By community type, the violent crime rates were estimated at 504.0 incidents per 100,000 inhabitants in MSAs, 395.0 incidents per 100,000 inhabitants in cities outside MSAs, and 209.3 incidents per 100,000 inhabitants in nonmetropolitan counties. (Table 2)

Population Groups: Trends and Rates

In the UCR Program, data are also aggregated into population groups; these groups are described in more detail in Appendix III. The nation's cities had an overall decrease of 1.3 percent in the estimated number of violent crimes from 2006 to 2007. By city population group, cities with over 250,000 inhabitants had the largest percentage decline in the estimated number of violent crimes (2.6 percent), while cities with 10,000 to 24,999 inhabitants were the only group who showed an increase in violent crime (2.4 percent). (Table 12)

The law enforcement agencies in the nation's cities collectively reported a rate of 570.5 violent crimes per 100,000 inhabitants in 2007. Law enforcement agencies in cities subset of 500,000 to 999,999 inhabitants reported the highest violent crime rate, with 989.3 violent crimes per 100,000 inhabitants; the violent crime rate for all cities with 250,000 or more inhabitants was 893.8. Agencies in cities with 10,000 to 24,999 inhabitants reported the lowest violent crime rate (319.5 incidents per 100,000 inhabitants). Law enforcement agencies in the nation's metropolitan counties reported a collective violent crime rate of 338.4 per 100,000 inhabitants, while agencies in nonmetropolitan counties reported a collective rate of 218.4 violent crimes per 100,000 inhabitants. (Table 16)

Weapons Distribution

The UCR Program collects weapons data for murder, robbery, and aggravated assault offenses. In 2007, 68.0 percent of murder weapons were firearms, 14.1 percent were other dangerous weapons, 12.1 percent were knives or cutting instruments, and 5.8 percent were personal weapons such as hands, fists, or feet. Offenders used firearms in 42.8 percent of robberies and 21.4 percent of aggravated assaults. (Expanded Homicide Table 6, Robbery Table 3, and Aggravated Assault Table)

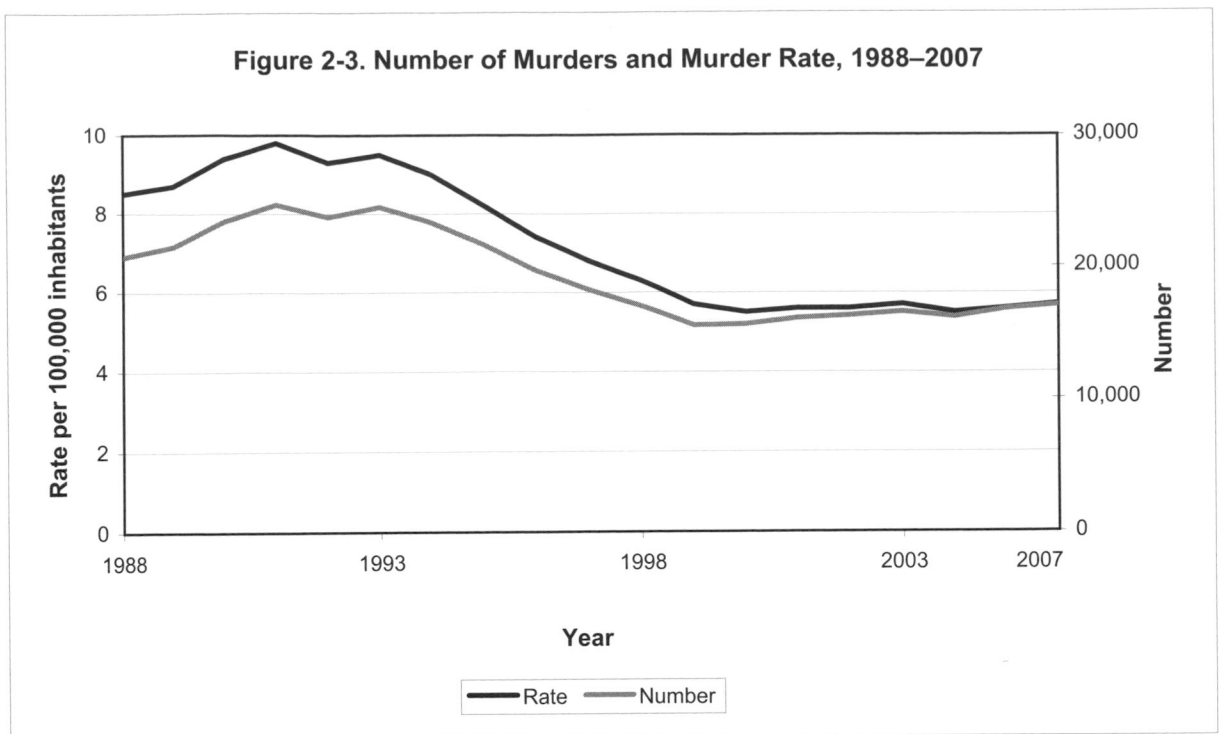

Figure 2-3. Number of Murders and Murder Rate, 1988–2007

MURDER

Definition

The UCR Program defines murder and nonnegligent manslaughter as the willful (nonnegligent) killing of one human being by another. The classification of this offense is based solely on police investigation, rather than on the determination of a court, medical examiner, coroner, jury, or other judicial body. The UCR Program does not include the following situations under this offense classification: deaths caused by negligence, suicide, or accident; justifiable homicides; and attempts to murder or assaults to murder, which are considered aggravated assaults.

Data Collection

The UCR Program's *Supplementary Homicide Report* (SHR) provides information about murder victims and offenders by age, sex, and race; the types of weapons used in the murders; the relationships of the victims to the offenders; and the circumstances surrounding the incident. Law enforcement agencies are asked to complete an SHR for each murder reported to the UCR Program.

National Volume, Trends, and Rates

The UCR Program's homicide data showed a decline in the number of murders in 2007. An estimated 16,929 persons were murdered nationwide in 2007, a decrease of 0.6 percent from the 2006 estimate. An analysis of 5-year and 10-year trend data showed the number of murders increased 2.4 percent during the 2003–2007 (5-year) period, but decreased 0.3 percent from the 1998–2007 (10-year) esti-

mate. Murder accounted for 1.2 percent of the overall estimated number of violent crimes in 2007. (Tables 1 and 1A)

The 2007 data yielded an estimated rate of 5.6 murders per 100,000 inhabitants, a small decline from 5.7 murders per 100,000 inhabitants the previous year. (Tables 1 and 1A)

Regional Offense Trends and Rates

The UCR Program divides the United States into four regions: the Northeast, the South, the Midwest, and the West. (More details concerning geographic regions are provided in Appendix III.) In 2007, the estimated number of murders decreased in three of the four regions. The South, with an increase of 5.3 percent, is the only region that experienced an increase.

The Northeast

In 2007, the Northeast accounted for an estimated 18.1 percent of the nation's population and 13.4 percent of its estimated number of murders. With an estimated 2,261 murders, the Northeast saw a 7.9 percent decrease compared with the 2006 figure. The region's population declined 0.1 percent from 2006 to 2007. The offense rate for the Northeast was 4.1 murders per 100,000 inhabitants, down from 4.5 murders per 100,000 inhabitants in 2006. (Tables 3 and 4)

The Midwest

The Midwest accounted for an estimated 22.0 percent of the nation's total population (the region's population having grown 0.3 percent from 2006 to 2007) and 19.4 percent of the country's estimated number of murders in 2007.

There were an estimated 3,225 murders in the Midwest in 2007, a 2.5 percent decrease from the estimated figure for 2006. The Midwest experienced a rate of 4.9 murders per 100,000 inhabitants in 2007, slightly lower than in 2006. (Tables 3 and 4)

The South

The South, the nation's most populous region, experienced a 1.3 percent growth in population from 2006 to 2007. The region accounted for an estimated 36.6 percent of the nation's population in 2007 and the nation's highest proportion of murders (45.8 percent). The estimated 7,759 murders represented a 5.3 percent increase in the estimated number of murders from 2006 to 2007. The region's estimated rate of 7.0 murders per 100,000 inhabitants represented an increase of 4.0 percent from the estimated rate for 2006. (Tables 3 and 4)

The West

The West accounted for an estimated 23.2 percent of the nation's population and 21.8 percent of the estimated number of murders in 2007. Its population grew 1.1 percent from 2006 to 2007. The West experienced an estimated 3,684 murders, a 5.6 percent decrease from the 2006 estimate. The region's murder rate was 5.3 per 100,000 inhabitants, a 6.6 percent decrease from the 2006 rate. (Tables 3 and 4)

Community Types

The UCR Program aggregates data for three community types: metropolitan statistical areas (MSAs), cities outside MSAs, and nonmetropolitan counties outside MSAs. (See Appendix III for definitions.) In 2007, MSAs accounted for 83.2 percent of the nation's population and 89.9 percent of the estimated total number of murders. With 15,224 estimated homicides, MSAs experienced a rate of 6.1 murders per 100,000 inhabitants in 2007. Cities outside MSAs accounted for 6.7 percent of the U.S. population and (with an estimated 752 murders) accounted for 4.4 percent of the estimated murders in the nation. The murder rate for cities outside MSAs was 3.7 per 100,000 inhabitants. (Table 2)

In 2007, 10.1 percent of the nation's population lived in nonmetropolitan counties outside MSAs. An estimated 953 murders took place in these counties, accounting for 5.6 percent of the nation's estimated total. The murder rate for nonmetropolitan counties outside MSAs was 3.1 murders per 100,000 inhabitants. (Table 2)

Population Groups: Trends and Rates

The UCR Program uses the following population group designations in its data presentations: cities (grouped according to population size) and counties (classified as either metropolitan or nonmetropolitan). A breakdown of these classifications is provided in Appendix III.

From 2006 to 2007, the nation's cities experienced a 2.2 percent decrease in homicides. The city groups with 100,000 to 249,999 inhabitants, 50,000 to 99,999 inhabitants, 25,000 to 49,999 inhabitants, and 10,000 to 24,999 inhabitants all experienced increases in homicides from 2006 to 2007. The city group of 50,000 to 99,999 inhabitants had the largest increase in murders (3.4 percent). Metropolitan counties experienced an increase in homicides of 0.4 percent from 2006 to 2007, while nonmetropolitan counties experienced a decrease of 0.7 percent. (Table 12)

In 2007, cities collectively had a rate of 6.8 murders per 100,000 inhabitants. Cities with 500,000 to 999,999 inhabitants had the highest murder rate (13.7 murders per 100,000 inhabitants) while cities with fewer than 10,000 inhabitants had the lowest murder rate (2.6 murders per 100,000 inhabitants). The homicide rates for metropolitan and nonmetropolitan counties were 4.2 and 3.3 per 100,000 inhabitants, respectively. Suburban areas had a homicide rate of 3.4 per 100,000 inhabitants. (Table 16)

Supplementary Homicide Reports

The UCR Program's *Supplementary Homicide Report* (SHR) provides information regarding the age, sex, and race of both the murder victim and the offender; the type of weapon used in the offense; the relationship of the victim to the offender; and the circumstances surrounding the offense. Of the estimated 16,929 murders that were committed in the United States in 2007, law enforcement agencies contributed data to the UCR Program through SHRs for 14,831 of the incidents. More information on these reports and the expanded homicide tables (which are available online but not included in this publication) can be found in Appendix I. Highlights from these tables have been included below.

Victims

Based on 2007 supplemental homicide data (where the ages, sexes, or races of the murder victims were *known*), 87.7 percent of victims were over 18 years of age, 10.5 percent were under 18 years of age, and the age of 1.8 percent of the victims was unknown. Black victims accounted for 50.1 percent of the victims for whom race was known, followed by White victims (47.6 percent). Male victims made up 78.5 percent of victims for whom sex was known. (Expanded Homicide Tables 1 and 2)

Offenders

For murders where the gender of the offender was known, 90.1 percent were male. Black offenders accounted for 53.9 percent of offenders for whom race was known, followed by White offenders (44.0 percent) and offenders of other races (2.0 percent).

Concerning single victim/single offender incidents, 82.5 percent of White victims were murdered by White offenders and 91.9 percent of Black victims were murdered by Black offenders. In incidents where the age of the offender was known, 93.6 percent of victims were killed by adults. (Expanded Homicide Tables 3, 4, and 5)

Victim-Offender Relationships

For incidents in which the victim-offender relationship was known, 22.2 percent of victims were slain by family members, 24.1 percent were murdered by strangers, and 53.7 percent were killed by other persons such as acquaintances, neighbors, or friends. The 2007 data also showed that among female victims for whom their relationships with their offenders were known, 32.9 percent were murdered by their husbands or boyfriends. (Expanded Homicide Tables 2 and 9)

Weapons

For incidents in 2007 in which the murder weapon was specified, 72.9 percent involved the use of firearms. Handguns made up 87.8 percent of the firearms specified, 5.4 percent involved shotguns, 5.4 percent involved rifles, and 1.4 percent involved other guns. Knives or cutting instruments were used in 13.0 percent of incidents in which the murder weapon was specified; personal weapons such as hands, fist, feet, etc. were used in 6.2 percent of murders where the weapon was specified. Blunt objects, such as clubs and hammers, were used in 4.7 percent of homicides where the weapon was specified. (Expanded Homicide Table 7)

Circumstances

For murders for which circumstances were known, 42.1 percent of the victims were slain during arguments (including romantic triangles), and 23.3 percent were killed in conjunction with a felony (i.e., the victim was slain while being raped, robbed, etc.). Circumstances were unknown for 36.9 percent of reported homicides. (Expanded Homicide Table 9)

Justifiable Homicide

Certain willful killings must be reported as justifiable, or excusable, homicide. In the UCR Program, justifiable homicide is defined as, and is limited to, the following:

- The killing of a felon by a peace officer in the line of duty.

- The killing of a felon, during the commission of a felony, by a private citizen.

Because these killings are determined by law enforcement investigation to be justifiable, they are tabulated separately from murder and nonnegligent manslaughter.

During 2007, law enforcement agencies provided supplemental data for 645 justifiable homicides. A breakdown of those figures revealed that law enforcement officers justifiably killed 391 felons and private citizens justifiably killed 254 felons. Expanded Homicide Tables 13 and 14 provide further details about justifiable homicide but are not published in this text; see Appendix I for more information.

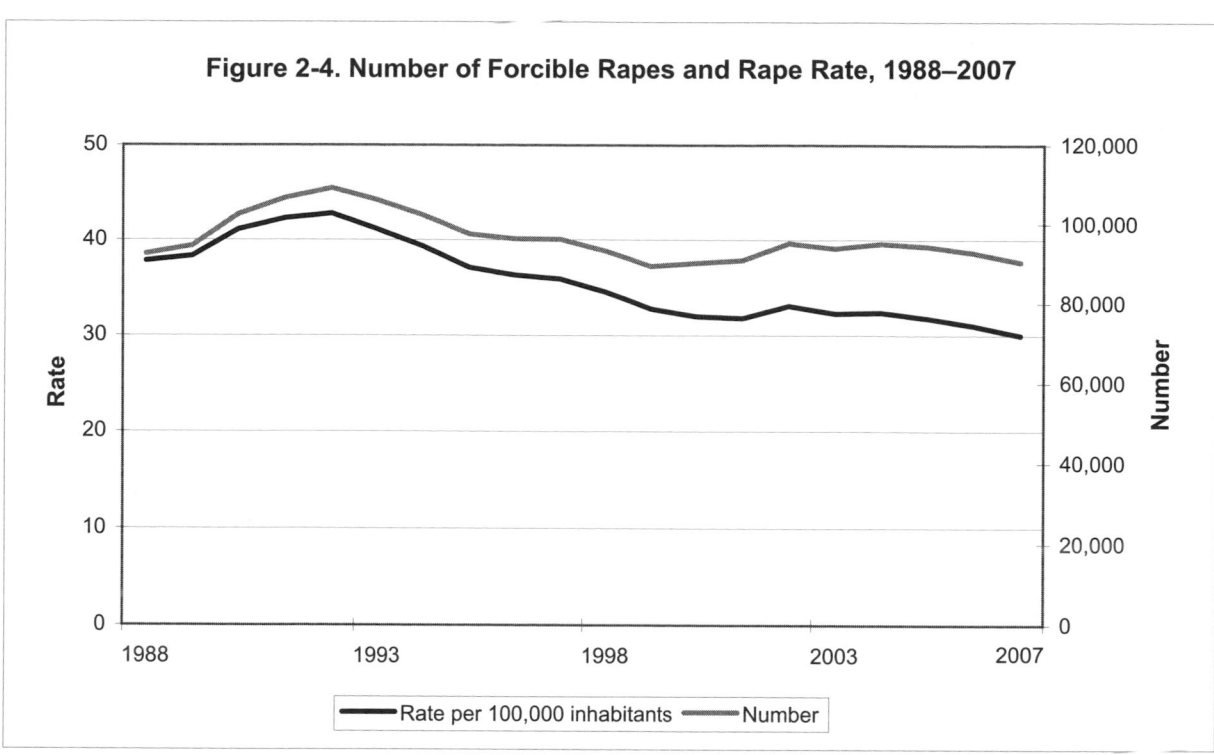

Figure 2-4. Number of Forcible Rapes and Rape Rate, 1988–2007

FORCIBLE RAPE

Definition

Forcible rape is the carnal knowledge of a female forcibly and against her will. Assaults and attempts to commit rape by force or threat of force are included; however, statutory rape (without force) and other sex offenses are excluded.

Data Collection

The UCR Program counts one offense for each female victim of a forcible rape, attempted forcible rape, or assault with intent to rape, regardless of the victim's age. A rape by force involving a female victim and a familial offender is counted as a forcible rape not an act of incest. The Program collects only arrest statistics concerning all other crimes of a sexual nature. The offense of statutory rape, in which no force is used but the female victim is under the age of consent, is included in the arrest total for the sex offenses category. Sexual attacks on males are counted as aggravated assaults or sex offenses, depending on the circumstances and the extent of any injuries.

For this overview only, the FBI deviated from standard procedure and manually calculated the 2007 rate of female rapes based upon the national female population provided by the U.S. Census Bureau.

National Volume, Trends, and Rates

During 2007, approximately 90,427 females nationwide were victims of forcible rape. This estimate represents a 2.5 percent decrease from the 2006 figure and it is the third consecutive year that the number of rapes have declined. The data also showed a 6.0 percent decrease from the 1997 estimated figure. (Tables 1 and 1A)

In preparing rate tables, the UCR Program's computer system automatically calculates offense rates per 100,000 inhabitants for all Part I crimes, which include murder and nonnegligent manslaughter, forcible rape, robbery, aggravated assault, burglary, larceny-theft, motor vehicle theft, and arson. (See Appendix II for more information.) Thus, the rate data are based upon the total U.S. population. However, for this overview, the 2007 rate of female rapes has been recalculated based upon the national female population provided by the Census Bureau. The recalculation resulted in a rate of 59.1 rape victims per 100,000 females, a 3.0 percent decrease when compared with the 2006 estimated rate of 60.9.

Of the forcible rapes known to law enforcement agencies in 2007, rapes by force made up 92.2 percent of reported rape offenses, and assaults to rape attempts accounted for 7.8 percent of reported rape offenses. (Tables 1 and 19)

Regional Offense Trends and Rates

The UCR Program divides the United States into four regions: the Northeast, the South, the Midwest, and the West. (More details concerning geographic regions are provided in Appendix III.) Regional analysis offers estimates of the volume of female rapes, the percent change from the previous year's estimate, and the rate of rape per 100,000 female inhabitants in each region. (Tables 3 and 4)

The Northeast

The Northeast made up 18.1 percent of the U.S. population in 2007 and experienced a 0.1 percent decline in population from 2006 to 2007. In 2007, an estimated 10,821 forcible rapes of females—12.0 percent of the national total—occurred in the Northeast. This was a decline of 4.3 percent from the 2006 estimated figure. (Tables 3 and 4)

The Midwest

The Midwest, which accounted for 22.0 percent of the U.S. population in 2007, experienced a 0.3 percent increase in population from 2006 to 2007. Over one-quarter (25.3 percent) of all forcible rapes in the nation occurred in the Midwest in 2007. The 2007 estimate (22,863 forcible rapes) represented a decline of 3.6 percent from the 2006 estimate. (Tables 3 and 4)

The South

The South, the nation's most populous region, accounted for an estimated 36.6 percent of the nation's population in 2007 (and experienced a population growth of 1.3 percent from 2006 to 2007); the region also accounted for an estimated 38.8 percent of the nation's estimated number of forcible rapes. There were an estimated 35,073 female victims of forcible rape in the South in 2007, down slightly from 35,667 in 2006. (Tables 3 and 4)

The West

The West, which experienced a population growth of 1.1 percent from 2006 to 2007, accounted for 23.2 percent of the nation's population in 2007. The region also accounted for 24.0 percent of the nation's total number of estimated forcible rapes with an estimated 21,670 offenses. The West saw a 1.8 percent decline in forcible rapes from 2006 to 2007. (Tables 3 and 4)

Community Types

Using the U.S. Office of Management and Budget's designations, the UCR Program aggregates crime data by type of community in which the offenses occur: metropolitan statistical areas (MSAs), cities outside MSAs, and nonmetropolitan counties outside MSAs. (Appendix III provides more detailed information about community types.)

MSAs

In 2007, MSAs accounted for 83.2 percent of the nation's population and 83.1 percent of the nation's estimated number of forcible rapes. An estimated 75,114 females were forcibly raped in metropolitan areas. (Table 2)

Cities Outside MSAs

Cities outside MSAs are mostly incorporated areas served by city law enforcement agencies. Though accounting for only 6.7 percent of the U.S. population in 2007, cities outside MSAs accounted for 8.5 percent of the nation's estimated forcible rapes (7,695 offenses). (Table 2)

Nonmetropolitan Counties

In 2007, approximately 10.1 percent of the nation's population lived in nonmetropolitan counties outside MSAs (counties made up of mostly nonincorporated areas served by noncity law enforcement agencies). Collectively, these areas had an estimated 7,618 forcible rapes, representing 8.4 percent of the nation's estimated total. (Table 2)

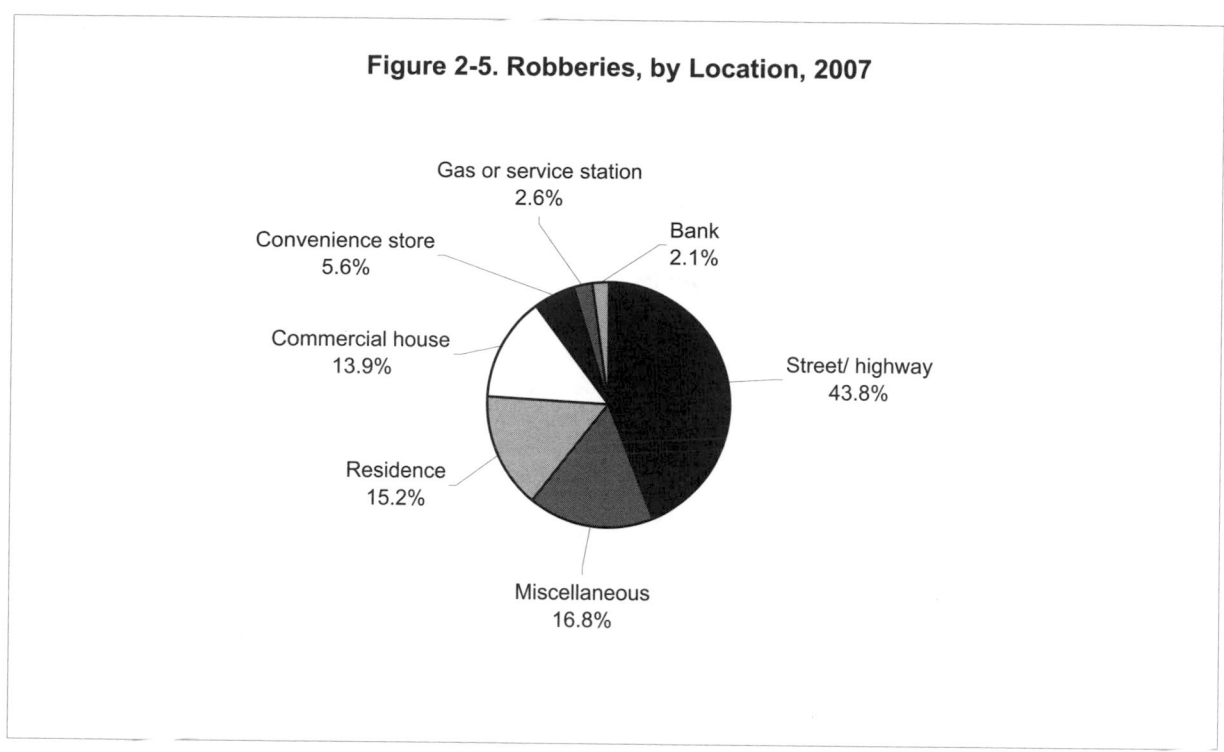

Figure 2-5. Robberies, by Location, 2007

- Gas or service station 2.6%
- Bank 2.1%
- Convenience store 5.6%
- Street/ highway 43.8%
- Commercial house 13.9%
- Residence 15.2%
- Miscellaneous 16.8%

ROBBERY

Definition

The UCR Program defines robbery as the taking or attempting to take anything of value from the care, custody, or control of a person or persons by force or threat of force or violence and/or by putting the victim in fear.

National Volume, Trends, and Rates

While the number of robberies nationwide decreased in 2007, there has been a 7.5 percent increase in robberies since 2003. Estimated offenses totaled 445,125 in 2007, a 0.5 percent decrease from 2006. The rate for robberies was 147.6 per 100,000 inhabitants.

Regional Offense Trends and Rates

The UCR Program divides the United States into four regions: the Northeast, the South, the Midwest, and the West. (More details concerning geographic regions are provided in Appendix III.)

The Northeast

The Northeast, with an estimated 18.1 percent of the nation's population in 2007 (and a 0.1 percent decline in population from 2006 to 2007), accounted for 16.9 percent of its estimated number of robberies. (Table 3) The estimated number of robberies dropped 9.0 percent from 2006, the largest decrease in any region. The rate for this region was 137.8 robberies per 100,000 inhabitants down

from 151.2 robberies per 100,000 inhabitants in 2006. (Table 4)

The Midwest

The Midwest accounted for 22.0 percent of the total population of the United States, and 19.0 percent of its estimated number of robberies, in 2007. The region experienced a 0.3 percent growth in population from 2006 to 2007. (Table 3) There were an estimated 84,674 robberies in the Midwest in 2007, a 3.2 percent decrease from the estimated figure from 2006. The region's robbery rate was 127.5 robberies per 100,000 inhabitants in 2007, a 3.4 percent decrease from the estimated rate for 2006. (Table 4)

The South

The South, the nation's most highly populated region, experienced a 1.3 percent growth in population from 2006 to 2007; in 2007, it accounted for an estimated 36.6 percent of the nation's population and 40.4 percent of the nation's estimated number of robberies. (Table 3) This figure represented a 4.9 percent increase from the 2006 figure. The South was the only region that experienced an increase in robberies from 2006 to 2007. The region experienced the highest rate of robberies per 100,000 inhabitants (162.7), a 3.6 percent increase from the 2006 rate. (Table 4)

The West

The West, having experienced a population growth of 1.1 percent from 2006 to 2007, was home to an estimated 23.2 percent of the nation's population and accounted for 23.7 percent of the nation's estimated number of robberies in 2007. (Table 3) The estimated number of robberies in the region in 2007 represented a 0.4 percent decrease from the 2006 figure. The rate of robberies per 100,000 inhabitants in the West was 150.4, a 1.4 percent increase from the 2006 rate. This was the second highest rate among the four regions. (Table 4)

Community Types

The UCR Program aggregates data for three community types: metropolitan statistical areas (MSAs), cities outside MSAs, and nonmetropolitan counties outside MSAs. MSAs include a central city or urbanized area with at least 50,000 inhabitants, as well as the county that contains the principal city and other adjacent counties that have, as defined by the U.S. Office of Management and Budget, a high degree of social and economic integration as measured through commuting. Cities outside MSAs are mostly incorporated areas, and nonmetropolitan counties are made up of mostly unincorporated areas served by noncity law enforcement.

In 2007, MSAs were home to an estimated 83.2 percent of the nation's population, and 96.1 percent of the nation's estimated number of robberies took place in these areas. Robberies in MSAs occurred at a rate of 170.4 per 100,000 inhabitants. Cities outside MSAs accounted for 6.7 percent of the U.S. population and accounted for 2.8 percent of the estimated number of robberies in the nation. The robbery rate for cities outside MSAs was 61.9 per 100,000 inhabitants. Nonmetropolitan counties made up 10.1 percent of the nation's estimated population and 1.1 percent of the nation's estimated robberies, at a rate of 16.3 robberies per 100,000 inhabitants. (Table 2)

Population Groups: Trends and Rates

The national UCR Program aggregates data by various population groups, which include cities, metropolitan counties, and nonmetropolitan counties. A definition of these groups can be found in Appendix III. All of the population groups except cities with 250,000 inhabitants and over experienced increases in the estimated number of robberies in 2007, compared with the figure for 2006. Robberies in cities as a whole decreased 0.7 percent. Among the population groups labeled *city*, those cities with 10,000 to 24,999 inhabitants had the greatest increase in the number of robberies (2.7 percent), while cities with 1,000,000 or more inhabitants had the largest decline in the number of robberies (2.9 percent). Nonmetropolitan counties had a 2.4 percent increase in the estimated number of robberies, and metropolitan counties showed a 2.0 percent increase. The number of robberies in suburban areas increased 1,6 percent. (Table 12)

Among the population groups, the nation's cities collectively had a rate of 200.7 robberies per 100,000 inhabitants. Of the population groups and subsets designated *city*, those

with 500,000 to 999,999 inhabitants had the highest rate (382.1 per 100,000 inhabitants), while those with fewer than 10,000 inhabitants had the lowest rate (56.1 per 100,000 inhabitants) of robberies. Of the two county groups, metropolitan counties had a rate of 79.7 robberies per 100,000 inhabitants, while nonmetropolitan counties had a rate of 16.4 robberies per 100,000 inhabitants. Suburban areas had a robbery rate of 80.1. (Table 16)

Offense Analysis

The UCR Program collects supplemental data about robberies to document the use of weapons, the dollar loss associated with the offense, and the location types.

Robbery by Weapon

An examination of the 2007 supplemental data regarding the type of weapons offenders used in the commission of the robbery revealed that assailants relied on strong-arm tactics in 39.9 percent of all robberies; they employed firearms in 42.8 percent of robberies. Offenders used knives or other cutting instruments in 8.3 percent of these crimes. In the remainder of the robberies, the offenders used other types of weapons. (Expanded Robbery Table 3)

Loss by Dollar Value

Based on the supplemental reports from law enforcement agencies, robberies cost victims, collectively, an estimated $588 million in 2007. (Tables 1 and 23) The average loss per robbery was $1,321. Average dollar losses were the highest for banks, which suffered an average loss of $4,201 per offense. Gas and service stations lost an average $1,097 per offense. Commercial houses, which include supermarkets, department stores, and restaurants, had average losses of $1,499. An average of $1,516 was taken from residences. An average of $800 was lost in each offense against convenience stores. (Table 23)

Robbery Trends by Location

Among the location types, bank robberies decreased 5.1 percent from 2006 to 2007. Robberies that occurred at residences increased 4.7 percent, and those at commercial houses rose 0.9 percent. The number of robberies on streets and highways decreased 0.2 percent, and robberies at convenience stores increased 0.6 percent. (Table 23)

Percent Distribution

By location type, the greatest proportion of robberies in 2007 occurred on streets and highways (43.8 percent). Robbers targeted commercial houses in 13.9 percent of offenses and residences in 15.2 percent of offenses. Convenience stores accounted for 5.6 percent of robberies, followed by gas and service stations (2.6 percent) and banks (2.1 percent). (Table 23)

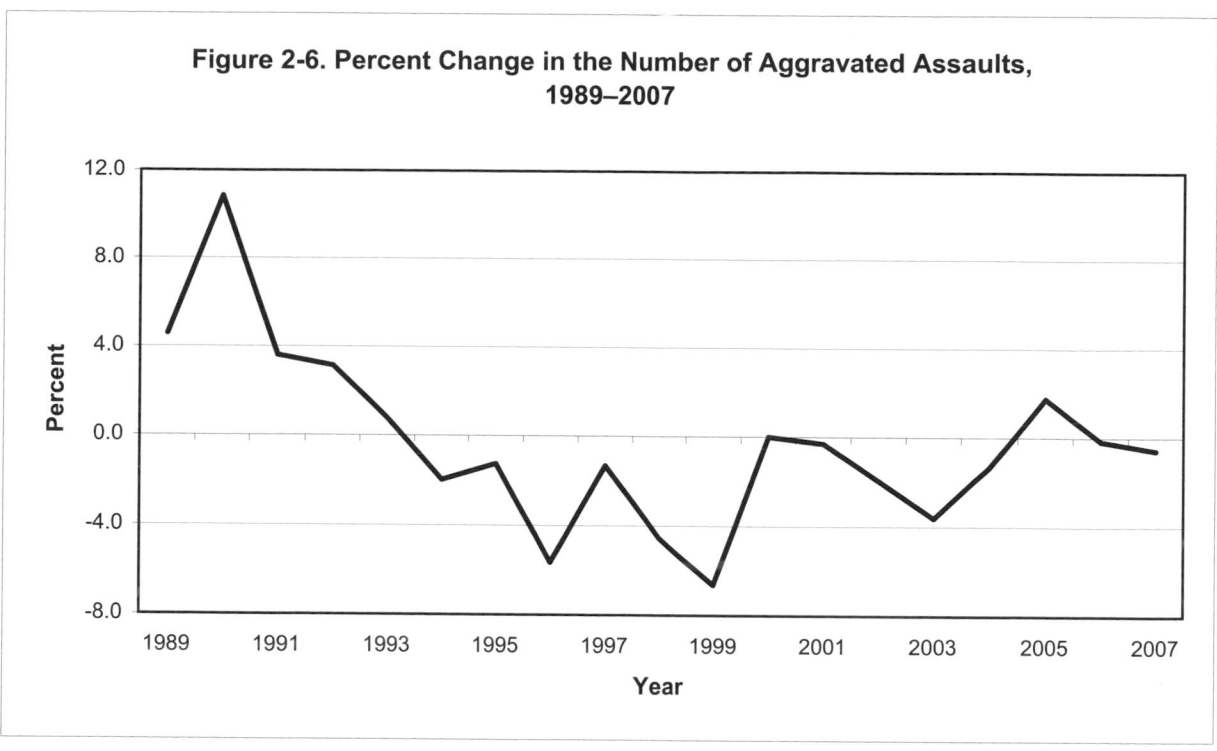

Figure 2-6. Percent Change in the Number of Aggravated Assaults, 1989–2007

AGGRAVATED ASSAULT

Definition

The UCR Program defines aggravated assault as an unlawful attack by one person upon another for the purpose of inflicting severe or aggravated bodily injury. This type of assault is usually accompanied by the use of a weapon or by other means likely to produce death or great bodily harm. Attempted aggravated assaults that involve the display or threat of a gun, knife, or other weapon are included in this crime category because serious personal injury would likely result if these assaults were completed. When aggravated assault and larceny-theft occur together, the offense falls under the category of robbery.

National Volume, Trends, and Rates

In 2007, estimated occurrences of aggravated assaults totaled 855,856, a 0.6 percent decrease from the 2006 figure. The 5-year and 10-year trend data show a 0.4 percent decrease and a 12.4 percent decrease, respectively. The 2007 data also show a decrease for the second consecutive in the rate of aggravated assault per 100,000 U.S. inhabitants. This rate, estimated at 283.8, represents a 1.3 percent decrease from the 2006 rate. However, it also represents a 3.9 percent decrease from the 2003 (5-year trend) rate and a 21.5 percent decrease from the 1998 (10-year trend) rate. (Tables 1 and 1A)

Among the four types of violent crime offenses (murder, forcible rape, robbery, and aggravated assault), aggravated assault typically has the highest rate of occurrence. This

trend continued in 2007 with aggravated assault accounting for 60.8 percent of all violent crime. (Table 1)

Regional Offense Trends and Rates

The UCR Program divides the United States into four regions: the Northeast, the South, the Midwest, and the West. (More details concerning geographic regions are provided in Appendix III.). The South was the only region that experienced an increase in the number number of aggravated assaults from 2006 to 2007. (Table 4)

The Northeast

The region with the smallest proportion of the nation's population (an estimated 18.1 percent in 2007, representing a 0.1 percent population decline from 2006 to 2007) also accounted for the smallest proportion of the nation's estimated number of aggravated assaults (13.5 percent). (Table 3) Occurrences of aggravated assault decreased 2.4 percent from 2006 to 2007, down to an estimated 115,224. The region also had the lowest aggravated assault rate in the nation, at 210.7 incidents per 100,000 inhabitants, a 2.3 percent decline from the 2006 rate. (Table 4)

The Midwest

With 22.0 percent of the nation's total population in 2007—and with a 0.3 percent growth in population from 2006 to 2007—the Midwest accounted for approximately 19.0 percent of the nation's estimated number of aggravated assaults. (Table 3) Occurrences of this offense decreased 0.6 percent from the estimated total for 2006, declining to an estimated 162,256 incidents. The region's aggravated assault rate, at 244.4 incidents per 100,000 inhabitants, represented a 0.9 percent decrease from the 2006 rate. (Table 4)

The South

The South, the nation's most highly populated region, accounted for an estimated 36.6 percent of the nation's population in 2007. (Table 3) From 2006 to 2007, the estimated number of aggravated assaults increased 0.3 percent, reaching a total of 384,107 incidents. However, the region experienced population growth of 1.3 percent during this period, resulting in a slight decline (0.9 percent) in the rate of aggravated assaults, to 347.8 per 100,000 inhabitants. (Table 4)

The West

In 2007, the West was home to an estimated 23.2 percent of the nation's population and experienced a 1.1 percent growth in population from 2006 to 2007. The region accounted for 22.7 percent of the nation's estimated number of aggravated assaults. (Table 3) From 2006 to 2007, the estimated number of offenses decreased 1.2 percent to 194,269 incidents. The rate, estimated at 277.1 offenses per 100,000 inhabitants, decreased 2.3 percent from 2006. (Table 4)

Community Types

The UCR Program aggregates data for three community types: metropolitan statistical areas (MSAs), cities outside MSAs, and nonmetropolitan counties outside MSAs. MSAs include a central city or urbanized area with at least 50,000 inhabitants, as well as the county that contains the principal city and other adjacent counties that have a high degree of social and economic integration as measured through commuting. Cities outside MSAs are mostly incorporated areas, and nonmetropolitan counties are made up of mostly unincorporated areas. (For additional information about community types, see Appendix III.)

In 2007, 83.2 percent of the nation's population lived in MSAs, where the rate of aggravated assault was an estimated 297.6 per 100,000 inhabitants. Cities outside MSAs (with 6.7 percent of the U.S. population) had the next-highest rate of aggravated assault at 291.1 offenses per 100,000 inhabitants. Nonmetropolitan counties accounted for 10.1 percent of the U.S. population and had an offense rate of 164.9 aggravated assaults per 100,000 inhabitants. (Table 2)

From 2006 to 2007, the number of aggravated assaults in four of the six city groups decreased. Cities with 250,000 or more inhabitants experienced the greatest decrease (2.8 percent). Cities with populations of 10,000 to 24,000 experienced an increase of 3.2 percent. In metropolitan counties, the number of aggravated assaults declined 2.1 percent; in nonmetropolitan counties, this number increased 2.9 percent. Aggravated assaults in suburban areas declined 1.1 percent from 2006 to 2007. (Table 12)

Based on reports from agencies submitting 12 months of complete data for 2007, aggravated assault occurred at an estimated rate of 292.6 offenses per 100,000 inhabitants nationwide. The collective rate for cities was 330.0 aggravated assaults per 100,000 inhabitants. Among city population groups, rates ranged from a high of 477.8 offenses per 100,000 inhabitants (in cities with 250,000 inhabitants or more) to a low of 208.8 offenses per 100,000 inhabitants (in cities with 10,000 to 24,999 inhabitants). The aggravated assault rate was 231.0 in metropolitan counties and 172.9 in nonmetropolitan counties. (Table 16)

Offense Analysis

Aggravated Assault by Weapon

The UCR Program collects data about the type of weapons used in aggravated assaults. In 2007, personal weapons were used in 25.7 percent of aggravated assaults for which weapons information was known, firearms were used in 21.4 percent of aggravated assaults, and knives and other cutting instruments were used in 18.8 percent of aggravated assaults. Weapons classified in the "other" category were used in the remaining 34.2 percent of offenses. (Aggravated Assault Table)

An analysis by weapon type showed that the rate of aggravated assaults per 100,000 inhabitants was 73.3 with personal weapons, 61.1 with firearms, 53.6 with knives and other cutting instruments, and 97.6 with weapons in the "other" category. (Table 19)

PROPERTY CRIME

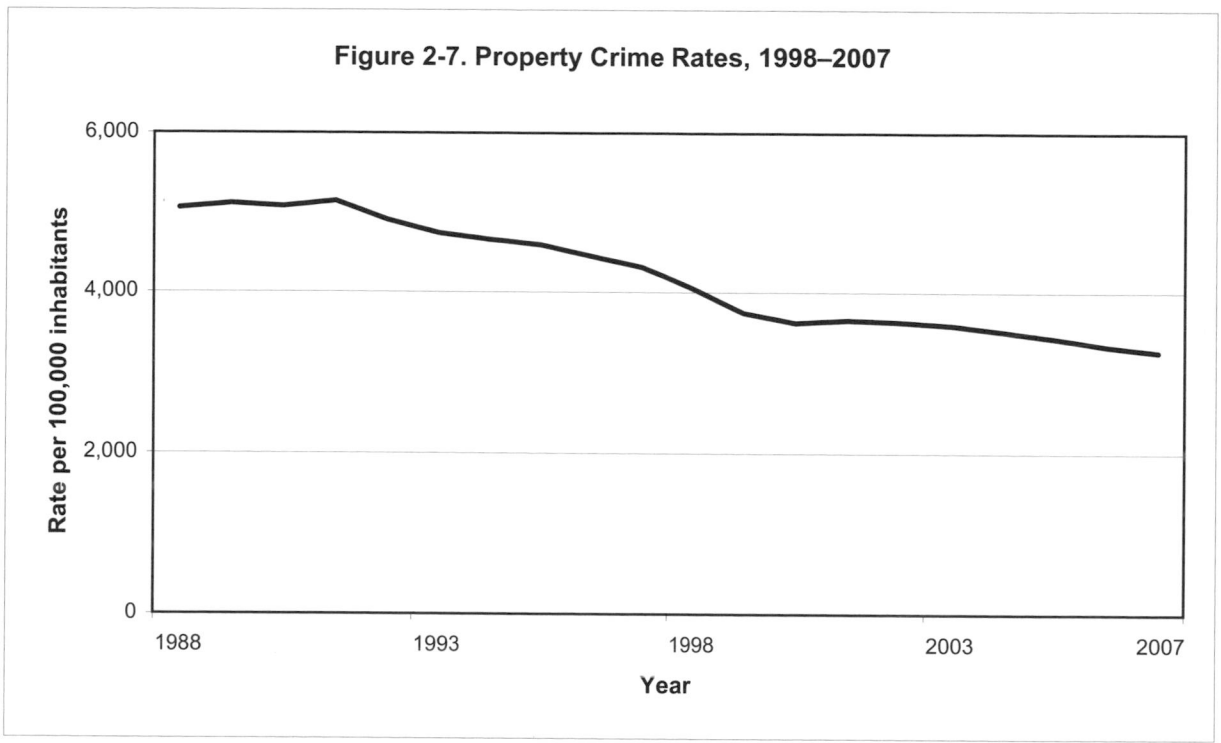

Figure 2-7. Property Crime Rates, 1998–2007

Definition

The Uniform Crime Reporting (UCR) Program's definition of property crime includes the offenses of burglary, larceny-theft, motor vehicle theft, and arson. The object of theft-type offenses is the taking of money or property without the use of force or threat of force against the victims. Property crime includes arson because the offense involves the destruction of property; however, arson victims may be subjected to force. Because of limited participation and the varying collection procedures conducted by local law enforcement agencies, only limited data are available for arson. Arson statistics are included in the trend, clearance, and arrest tables in *Crime in the United States*, but they are not included in any estimated volume data. More information on the expanded arson tables (which are available online but not included in this publication) can be found in Appendix I.

Data Collection

The data presented in *Crime in the United States* reflect the Hierarchy Rule, which counts only the most serious offense in a multiple-offense criminal incident. In descending order of severity, the violent crimes are murder and nonnegligent manslaughter, forcible rape, robbery, aggravated assault; these are followed by the property crimes of burglary, larceny-theft, and motor vehicle theft.

National Volume, Trends, and Rates

An estimated 9,843,481 property crimes were committed in the United States in 2007, representing a 1.4 percent

decrease from the 2006 (2-year trend) estimate, a 5.7 percent decrease from the 2003 (5-year trend) estimate, and a 10.1 percent decrease from the 1998 (10-year trend) estimate. (Tables 1 and 1A)

In 2007, larceny-theft, motor vehicle theft, and buglaries all showed a decline from their 2006 estimates; the number of larceny-thefts was down 0.6 percent and the number of motor vehicle thefts was down 8.1 percent. The number of burglaries decreased 0.2 percent. (Tables 1 and 1A)

The estimated property crime rate per 100,000 inhabitants in 2007 was 3,263.5, a 2.1 percent decrease from the 2006 rate, an 9.1 percent decrease from the 2003 rate, and a 19.5 percent decrease from the 1998 rate. (Tables 1 and 1A)

Regional Offense Trends and Rates

The UCR Program separates the United States into four regions: the Northeast, the Midwest, the South, and the West. (Geographic breakdowns can be found in Appendix III.) Property crime data collected by the UCR Program and aggregated by region reflected the following results.

The Northeast

The Northeast region accounted for 18.1 percent of the nation's population and experienced a 0.1 percent decline in population from 2006 to 2007. The region also accounted for 12.2 of the nation's estimated number of property crimes in 2007. (Table 3) Law enforcement in the Northeast saw a

3.0 percent decrease in the estimated number of property crimes from 2006 to 2007. The property crime rate for the Northeast, estimated at 2,203.7 incidents per 100,000 inhabitants, was 2.9 percent lower than the 2006 rate. (Table 4)

The Midwest

The Midwest, with 22.0 percent of the U.S. population in 2007 and a 0.3 percent growth in population from 2006 to 2007, accounted for 21.3 percent of the nation's estimated number of property crimes. (Table 3) Law enforcement in the Midwest saw a 3.2 percent decrease in the estimated number of property crimes in the Midwest from 2006 to 2007. The rate of property crime in the Midwest in 2007, estimated at 3,157.2 incidents per 100,000 inhabitants, represented a 3.5 percent decrease from the 2006 rate. (Table 4)

The South

The South, the nation's most populous region, accounted for 36.6 percent of the U.S. population in 2007 and experienced a 1.3 percent growth in population from 2006 to 2007. The region also accounted for an estimated 42.7 percent of the nation's property crimes. (Table 3) The South experienced a 1.8 percent increase in its estimated number of property crimes from 2006 to 2007. The 2007 property crime rate, an estimated 3,802.1 incidents per 100,000 inhabitants, was 0.6 percent higher than the 2006 rate. (Table 4)

The West

In 2007, the West accounted for 23.2 percent of the nation's population; the region experienced a 1.1 percent growth in population from 2006 to 2007. The West also accounted for 23.8 percent of the nation's estimated number of property crimes. (Table 3) From 2006 to 2007, the estimated number of property crimes in this region decreased 4.4 percent. The estimated property crime rate in the West in 2007, 3,342.3 incidents per 100,000 inhabitants, was 5.4 percent lower than the 2006 rate. (Table 4)

Community Types

The UCR Program aggregates data by three community types: metropolitan statistical areas (MSAs), cities outside metropolitan areas, and nonmetropolitan counties. (Additional in-depth information regarding community types can be found in Appendix III.) In 2007, 83.2 percent of the U.S. population lived in MSAs. The property crime rate for MSAs was 3,416.5 per 100,000 inhabitants. Cities outside metropolitan areas, which accounted for 6.7 percent of the total population in 2007, had a property crime rate of 3,773.5 per 100,000 inhabitants. Nonmetropolitan counties, with 10.1 percent of the nation's population in 2007, had a property crime rate of 1,667.9 per 100,000 inhabitants. (Table 2)

Population Groups: Trends and Rates

The UCR Program organizes the agencies that contribute data into population groups, which include cities, metropolitan counties, and nonmetropolitan counties. (Appendix III provides further details about these groups.) From 2006 to 2007, law enforcement in the nation's cities collectively reported a 1.9 percent decrease in the number of property crimes. All city groups experienced decreased in the number of property crimes; cities with 250,000 inhabitants or more had the largest declines at 2.3 percent. While metropolitan counties experienced a decline of 0.6 percent from 2006 to 2007; property crime increased in nonmetropolitran counties by 0.2 percent. (Table 12)

The nation's cities collectively had a property crime rate of 3,867.5 incidents per 100,000 inhabitants in 2007. Nonmetropolitan counties had a rate of 1,676.0 incidents per 100,000 inhabitants, and metropolitan counties had a rate of 2,447.7 incidents per 100,000 inhabitants. (Table 16)

Offense Analysis

The estimated dollar loss attributing to property crimes, not including arson, in 2007 was $17.6 billion. Among the individual property crime categories, the dollar losses were an estimated $4.3 billion for burglary, $5.8 billion for larceny-theft, and $7.4 billion for motor vehicle theft. (Tables 1 and 23) Arson had an average dollar loss of $17,289. Arsons of industrial/manufacturing structures resulted in the highest average dollar losses with an average loss of $114,699. (Expanded Arson Table 2)

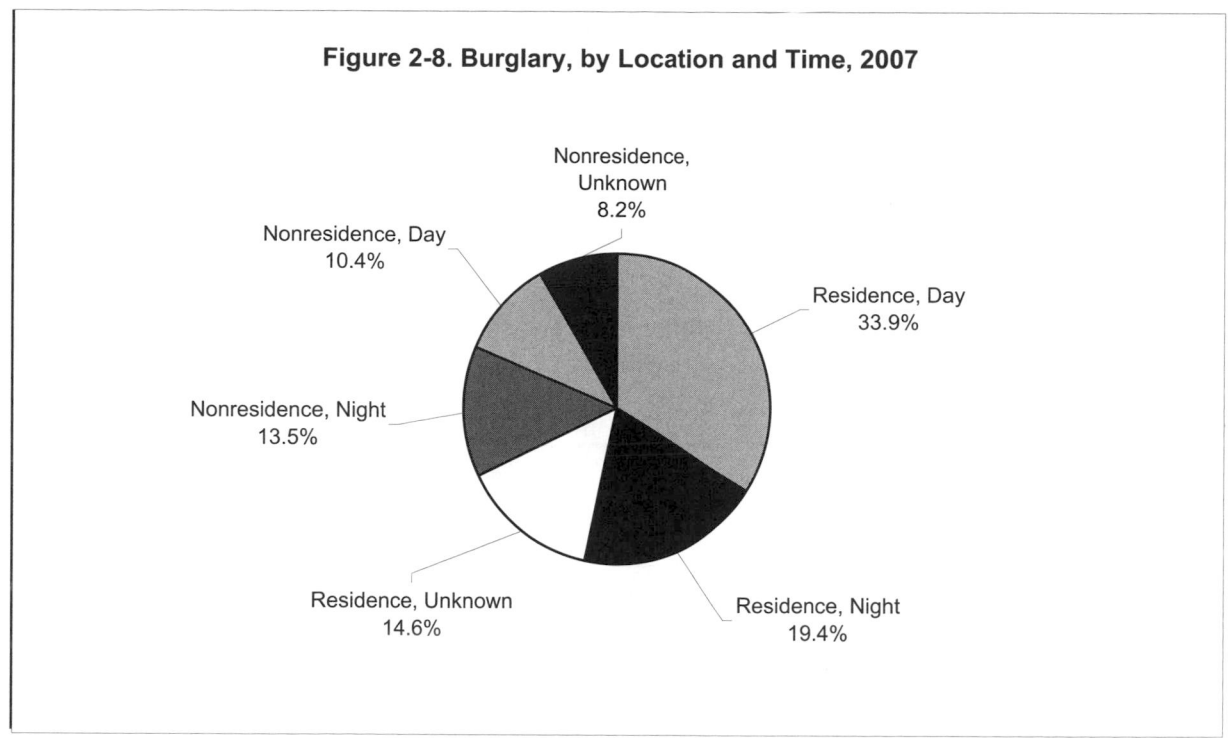

Figure 2-8. Burglary, by Location and Time, 2007

- Nonresidence, Unknown 8.2%
- Nonresidence, Day 10.4%
- Nonresidence, Night 13.5%
- Residence, Unknown 14.6%
- Residence, Night 19.4%
- Residence, Day 33.9%

BURGLARY

Definition

The UCR Program defines burglary as the unlawful entry of a structure to commit a felony or theft. To classify an offense as a burglary, the use of force to gain entry need not have occurred. The program has three subclassifications for burglary: forcible entry, unlawful entry where no force is used, and attempted forcible entry. The UCR definition of "structure" includes, but is not limited to, apartments, barns, house trailers or houseboats (when used as permanent dwellings), offices, railroad cars (but not automobiles), stables, and vessels (i.e., ships).

National Volume, Trends, and Rate

In 2007, an estimated 2,179,140 burglary offenses occurred in the United States. This figure represented a 0.2 percent decrease from the 2006 figure. An examination of 5-year and 10-year trends demonstrated a 1.1 percent increase from the 2003 estimate and an 6.6 percent decrease from 1998 estimate in the number of burglaries. However, the burglary rate for the United States in 2007 was 722.5 incidents per 100,000 inhabitants, a 0.9 percent decrease from the 2006 rate. Burglary accounted for 22.1 percent of the estimated number of property crimes committed in 2007. (Tables 1 and 1A)

Regional Offense Trends and Rates

The UCR Program divides the United States into four regions: the Northeast, the Midwest, the South, and the West. (Details regarding these regions can be found in Appendix III.) An analysis of burglary data by region showed the following details.

The Northeast

In 2007, 18.1 percent of the nation's population lived in the Northeast, which experienced a 0.1 percent decline in population from 2006 to 2007. This region accounted for 10.5 percent of the estimated total number of burglary offenses in the nation in 2007 a decline from 2006 when it accounted for 10.8 percent of the estimated total number of burglary offenses. The region's burglary rate, an estimated 419.1 offenses per 100,000 inhabitants, represented an decrease of 2.5 percent from the 2006 rate. (Tables 3 and 4)

The Midwest

The Midwest accounted for 22.0 percent of the nation's population in 2007 and experienced a 0.3 percent growth in population from 2006 to 2007. This region also accounted for 20.6 percent of the nation's estimated number of burglaries. The estimated number of burglaries in this region decreased 2.2 percent from 2006 to 2007. The Midwest had a burglary rate of 675.0 offenses per 100,000 inhabitants, a 2.5 percent decrease from the 2006 rate. (Tables 3 and 4)

The South

The South, the nation's most highly populated region, had the most burglaries in 2007 (an estimated 1,018,197). With 36.6 percent of the nation's population (and having experienced a 1.3 percent growth in population from 2006 to

2007), this region accounted for 46.7 percent of all burglaries in the United States. The estimated rate of burglary in the South was 921.8 incidents per 100,000 inhabitants, a 2.0 percent increase from the 2006 rate. (Tables 3 and 4)

The West

The West accounted for 23.2 percent of the nation's population in 2007 and experienced a 1.1 percent growth in population from 2006 to 2007. In 2007, this region also accounted for an estimated 22.2 percent of the nation's burglaries. The region's burglary rate was 689.9, a 5.1 percent decrease from the 2006 rate. The total number of burglaries (483,630) represented a 4.1 percent decrease from the 2006 figure. (Tables 3 and 4)

Community Types

The UCR Program aggregates data by three community types: metropolitan statistical areas (MSAs), cities outside MSAs, and nonmetropolitan counties. (See Appendix III for more information regarding community types.) In 2007, 83.2 percent of the U.S. population lived in MSAs, and an estimated 85.3 percent of all burglaries occurred in this type of community. Inhabitants of cities outside MSAs accounted for 6.7 percent of the total population in 2007 and 7.2 percent of the estimated number of burglaries; nonmetropolitan counties, with 10.1 percent of the U.S. population, accounted for 7.5 percent of all burglaries. The burglary rates per 100,000 inhabitants were 740.3 in MSAs, 782.6 in cities outside MSAs, and 535.8 in nonmetropolitan counties. (Table 2)

Population Groups: Trends and Rates

In addition to analyzing data by region and community type, the UCR Program aggregates crime statistics by population groups. Cities are categorized into six groups based on the number of inhabitants; counties are categorized into two groups, metropolitan and nonmetropolitan. (Appendix III offers further details regarding these population groups.)

An examination of data from law enforcement agencies that provided statistics for at least 6 common months in 2006 and 2007 showed that the nation's cities experienced a collective 0.5 percent decrease in burglaries from 2006 to 2007. Burglaries decreased in each city group except cities with a population between 100,000 to 249,999. Cities with

under 10,000 inhabitants experienced the largest decrease (1.3 percent) followed by cities with 25,000 to 49,999 inhabitants (1.1 percent). However, cities with 1,000,000 inhabitants or more—a subset of the city group of cities with 250,000 inhabitants or more—experienced a 4.0 percent increase in the number of burglaries, though the number for the overall group declined by 0.5 percent. The volume of burglaries increased 0.6 percent in metropolitan counties and 0.8 percent in nonmetropolitan counties. (Table 12)

The UCR Program calculates burglary rates for population groups from the information provided by participating agencies that submitted all 12 months of offense data for the year. In 2007, the nation's cities had 801.3 offenses per 100,000 inhabitants. The largest cities (those with 250,000 or more inhabitants) had the highest burglary rate at 948.8 incidents per 100,000 inhabitants. Cities with 10,000 to 24,999 inhabitants had the lowest burglary rate—630.5 incidents per 100,000 inhabitants. Metropolitan counties had a rate of 618.2 per 100,000 inhabitants, and nonmetropolitan counties had a rate of 539.7 per 100,000 inhabitants. (Table 16)

Offense Analysis

The UCR Program requests that participating law enforcement agencies provide details regarding the nature of burglaries in their jurisdictions, such as type of entry, type of structure, time of day, and dollar loss associated with each offense.

An examination of the data revealed, 61.1 percent of all burglaries involved forcible entry, 32.4 percent were unlawful entries (without force), and the remainder (6.5 percent) were forcible entry attempts. (Table 19)

As in the past, burglars targeted residences more often than nonresidential structures. An analysis of data from agencies that provided supplemental burglary data for at least 6 months of 2007 showed that 67.9 percent of burglaries occurred at residences, while 32.1 percent of burglaries occurred at nonresidential structures. (Table 23)

Law enforcement agencies were unable to determine the time of day for 22.9 percent of all reported burglaries. However, of the burglaries for which time of day could be established, most burglaries of residences (63.6 percent) occurred during the day. while most burglaries of nonresidential structures (56.4 percent) occurred at night. The average dollar loss per burglary was $1,991. (Table 23)

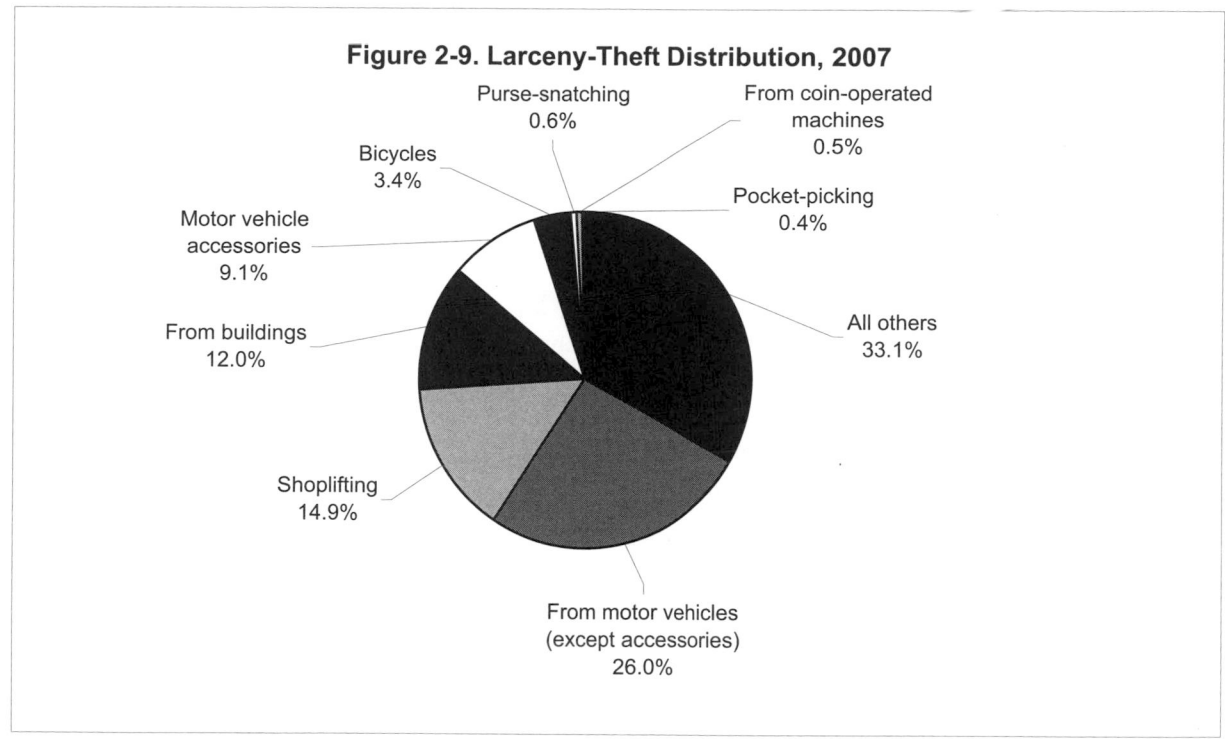

Figure 2-9. Larceny-Theft Distribution, 2007

Purse-snatching 0.6%

From coin-operated machines 0.5%

Bicycles 3.4%

Pocket-picking 0.4%

Motor vehicle accessories 9.1%

From buildings 12.0%

All others 33.1%

Shoplifting 14.9%

From motor vehicles (except accessories) 26.0%

LARCENY-THEFT

Definition

The UCR Program defines larceny-theft as the unlawful taking, carrying, leading, or riding away of property from the possession or constructive possession of another. Examples are thefts of bicycles, motor vehicle parts and accessories, shoplifting, pocket picking, or the stealing of any property or article not taken by force and violence or by fraud. Attempted larcenies are included. Embezzlement, confidence games, forgery, check fraud, etc., are excluded from this category.

National Volume, Trends, and Rates

In 2007, larceny-theft accounted for an estimated 66.7 percent of the nation's property crimes. (Table 1) Trend data showed that the number of larceny-thefts decreased 0.6 percent from 2006 to 2007 (2-year trend data), decreased 6.5 percent from 2003 to 2007 (5-year trend data), and decreased 11.0 percent from 1998 to 2007 (10-year trend data). The trend data also showed decreases in the larceny-theft rates per 100,000 inhabitants during these periods. The larceny-theft rate decreased 1.3 percent between 2006 and 2007, 9.9 percent between 2003 and 2007, and 20.2 percent between 1998 and 2007. (Table 1)

Regional Offense Trends and Rates

The UCR Program defines four regions within the United States: the Northeast, the Midwest, the South, and the West. (See Appendix III for a geographical description of each region.) A comparison of 2006 and 2007 data showed that

both the estimated number and the estimate rate of larceny-theft declined in every region except the South. (Tables 3 and 4) The following paragraphs provide a region overview of larceny-theft.

The Northeast

The region with the smallest proportion (18.1 percent) of the U.S. population in 2007, the Northeast was the only region that experienced a decline in population from 2006 to 2007 (0.1 percent). The region also experienced the fewest larceny-thefts in the country, accounting for only 13.2 percent of all larceny-thefts. (Table 3) The estimated number of offenses in 2007—868,763—represented a 1.8 percent decline from 2006, and the estimated rate—1,588.8 incidents per 100,000 inhabitants—represented a 1.7 percent decline. (Table 4)

The Midwest

With 22.0 percent of the U.S. population in 2007, and a 0.3 percent growth in population from 2006 to 2007, the Midwest accounted for an estimated 22.1 percent of the nation's larceny-thefts. (Table 3) The estimated number of offenses (1,448,457) declined 2.6 percent compared with the 2006 data, and the estimated rate of occurrences (2,181.8 incidents per 100,000 inhabitants) declined 2.9 percent. (Table 4)

The South

With more than one-third of the U.S. population in 2007 (36.6 percent), the South experienced a 1.3 percent growth in population from 2006 to 2007. The region had the nation's highest percentage of larceny-theft offenses: an estimated 42.4 percent. (Table 3) Estimated offenses in this region totaled 2,782,863, a 2.1 percent increase from the 2006 estimate. The South's larceny-theft rate—estimated at 2,519.5 offenses per 100,000 inhabitants—increased 0.8 percent from the 2006 estimate. (Table 4)

The West

In 2007, an estimated 23.2 percent of the U.S. population lived in the West, which experienced a 1.1 percent growth in population from 2006 to 2007. This region was also where 22.4 percent of the nation's estimated number of larceny-thefts took place. (Table 3) Occurrences of larceny-theft declined 2.7 percent from 2006 to 2007, dropping to an estimated total of 1,468,489 offenses. The region's larceny-theft rate, estimated at 2,094.9 offenses per 100,000 inhabitants, declined 3.7 percent from the 2006 rate. (Table 4)

Community Types

The UCR Program aggregates data for three community types: metropolitan statistical areas (MSAs), cities outside MSAs, and nonmetropolitan counties outside MSAs. MSAs include a central city or urbanized area with at least 50,000 inhabitants, as well as the county that contains the principal city and other adjacent counties that share a high degree of social and economic integration as measured through commuting. Cities outside MSAs are mostly incorporated areas, and nonmetropolitan counties are composed of unincorporated areas. (See Appendix III for more information regarding community types.)

In 2007, MSAs were home to an estimated 83.2 percent of the nation's population and experienced 86.7 percent of the nation's larceny-theft incidents. Cities outside MSAs accounted for 6.7 percent of the U.S. population and 8.6 percent of larceny-theft offenses. Nonmetropolitan counties, which were home to 10.1 percent of the nation's population, accounted for 4.6 percent of the estimated number of larceny-theft offenses. (Table 2)

Population Groups: Trends and Rates

In cities, collectively, occurrences of larceny-theft declined 0.9 percent between 2006 and 2007; cities with 10,000 to 24,9999 inhabitants and 500,00 to 900,000 inhabitants, experienced increases of 0.2 and 0.3 respectively. Among the city groups, cities with under 10,000 inhabitants experienced the

greatest decrease (1.7 percent). followed by cities with 100,000 to 249,999 inhabitants (1.4 percent). In both metropolitan and nonmetropolitan counties larceny-theft increased 0.1. (Table 12)

Based on reports of larceny-theft offenses from U.S. law enforcement agencies that submitted 12 months of complete data for 2007, this offense occurred at a rate of 2,221.1 offenses per 100,000 inhabitants. The collective rate for cities was 2,616.4 offenses per 100,000 inhabitants. Among city population groups, cities with 100,000 to 249,000 inhabitants had the highest larceny-theft rate, 2,868.0 incidents per 100,000 inhabitants. Cities with 10,000 to 24,999 inhabitants had the lowest rate at 2,333.9 incidents per 100,000 inhabitants. In metropolitan counties, the rate was 1,550.6 incidents per 100,000 inhabitants; in nonmetropolitan counties, the rate was 1,003.5 incidents per 100,000 inhabitants. (Table 16)

Offense Analysis

Distribution

Thefts from motor vehicles accounted for the majority of larceny-theft offenses in 2007 (26.0 percent). Table 23 provides a further breakdown of larceny-theft offenses, including shoplifting, thefts from buildings, thefts of motor vehicle accessories, thefts of bicycles, thefts from coin-operated machines, purse snatching, and pocket picking. The "all other" category, which includes the less-defined types of larceny-theft, accounted for 33.1 percent of all offenses.

Loss by Dollar Value

Larceny-theft offenses cost victims an estimated $5.8 billion dollars in 2007, up from $5.6 billion in 2006. (Tables 1 and 23) The average value of property stolen was $886 per offense, up from $855 in 2006. Larceny-theft from buildings had the highest average dollar loss per offense at $1,263. Thefts from motor vehicles had an average dollar loss of $722 per offense; thefts of motor vehicle accessories, $554; purse snatching, $402; pocket picking, $728; thefts from coin-operated machines, $363; thefts of bicycles, $273; and shoplifting, $205. (Table 23)

Offenses in which the stolen property was valued at more than $200 accounted for 43.9 percent of all larceny-thefts. Table 23 provides further analysis, including the average dollar value per offense, of all offenses in the overall category of property crime.

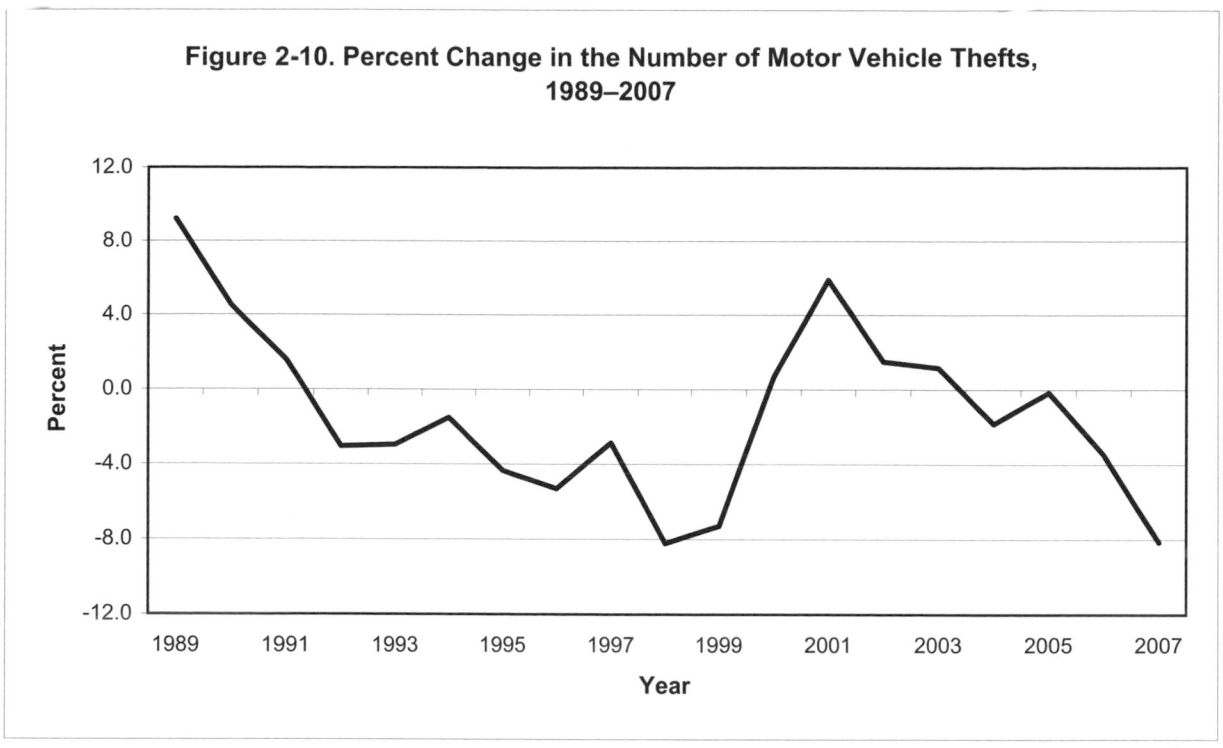

Figure 2-10. Percent Change in the Number of Motor Vehicle Thefts, 1989–2007

MOTOR VEHICLE THEFT

Definition

The UCR Program defines motor vehicle theft as the theft or attempted theft of a motor vehicle. The offense includes the stealing of automobiles, trucks, buses, motorcycles, snowmobiles, etc. The taking of a motor vehicle for temporary use by a person or persons with lawful access is excluded.

National Volume, Trends, and Rates

In 2007, an estimated 1,095,769 motor vehicle thefts took place in the United States. The number of motor vehicles estimated to have been stolen decreased 8.1 percent between 2006 and 2007, decreased 13.1 percent between 2003 and 2007, and decreased 11.8 percent between 1998 and 2007. (Table 1)

The estimated rate of motor vehicle theft in 2007 was 363.3 incidents per 100,000 inhabitants. In the 2-year, 5-year, and 10-year trend data, this rate showed decline: the 2007 rate was 8.8 percent lower than the 2006 rate, 16.2 percent lower than the 2003 rate, and 21.0 percent lower than the 1998 rate. (Table 1)

Regional Offense Trends and Rates

In order to analyze crime by geographic area, the UCR Program divides the United States into four regions: the Northeast, the Midwest, the South, and the West. (Appendix III provides a map delineating the regions.) This section provides a regional overview of motor vehicle theft.

The Northeast

The Northeast accounted for an estimated 18.1 percent of the nation's population in 2007 and experienced a 0.1 percent decline in population from 2006 to 2007. The region also accounted for an estimated 9.8 percent of its motor vehicle thefts. (Table 3) An estimated 107,028 motor vehicle thefts occurred in the Northeast in 2007, representing a 12.0 percent decrease from the 2006 estimate. This was the largest decline among the regions. The estimated rate of 195.7 motor vehicle thefts per 100,000 inhabitants in the Northeast in 2007 represented a 11.9 percent decline from the 2006 rate. (Table 4)

The Midwest

An estimated 22.0 percent of the country's population resided in the Midwest in 2007, and the region experienced a 0.3 growth in population from 2006 to 2007. The region accounted for 18.2 percent of the nation's motor vehicle thefts. (Table 3) The Midwest had an estimated 199,416 motor vehicle thefts in 2007, a 9.5 percent decrease from the previous year's total. The motor vehicle theft rate was estimated at 300.4 motor vehicles stolen per 100,000 inhabitants, a 9.7 percent decrease from the 2006 rate. (Table 4)

The South

The South, the nation's most populous region, was home to an estimated 36.6 percent of the U.S. population in 2007 and experienced a 1.3 percent growth in population from 2006 to 2007. This region accounted for 36.4 percent of the nation's motor vehicle thefts. (Table 3) The estimated

398,589 motor vehicle thefts in the South decreased 3.4 percent from the 2006 estimate. Motor vehicles in the South were stolen at an estimated rate of 360.9 per 100,000 inhabitants in 2007, a rate that was 4.6 percent lower than the 2006 rate. (Table 4)

The West

With approximately 23.2 percent of the U.S. population in 2007, the West experienced a 1.1 percent growth in population from 2006 to 2007. This region accounted for 35.7 percent of all motor vehicle thefts in the nation in 2007. (Table 3) An estimated 390,736 motor vehicle thefts occurred in this region. This number represented a 10.9 percent decrease from the previous year's estimate. The motor vehicle theft rate for the West was also lower in 2007 than in 2006; the 2007 rate of 557.4 motor vehicles stolen per 100,000 inhabitants was 11.8 percent lower than the 2006 rate. (Table 4)

Community Types

The UCR Program aggregates data by three community types: metropolitan statistical areas (MSAs), cities outside MSAs, and nonmetropolitan counties. MSAs are areas that include a principal city or urbanized area with at least 50,000 inhabitants and the county that contains the principal city and other adjacent counties that have, as defined by the U.S. Office of Management and Budget, a high degree of economic and social integration.

The vast majority (83.2 percent) of the U.S. population resided in MSAs during 2007, where approximately 93.1 percent of motor vehicle thefts occurred. For 2007, the UCR Program estimated an overall rate of 406.4 motor vehicles stolen per 100,000 MSA inhabitants. Cities outside MSAs and nonmetropolitan counties made up 6.7 and 10.1 percent of the nation's population, respectively. Cities outside MSAs accounted for 3.2 percent of motor vehicle thefts, and nonmetropolitan counties accounted for 3.7 percent of motor vehicle thefts. The UCR Program estimated a 2007 rate of 175.6 motor vehicles stolen for every 100,000 inhabitants in cities outside MSAs and a rate of 132.0 motor vehicles stolen per 100,000 inhabitants in non-metropolitan counties. (Table 2)

Population Groups: Trends and Rates

The UCR Program aggregates data by various population groups, which include cities, metropolitan counties, and nonmetropolitan counties. (A definition of these groups can be found in Appendix III.)

In cities, collectively, the number of motor vehicle thefts decreased 9.1 percent from 2006 to 2007. Cities with 500,000 to 999,999 inhabitants experienced the greatest decline—10.5 percent. Both metropolitan and nonmetropolitan counties experienced decreases, at 6.4 percent and 1.9 percent, respectively. (Table 12)

In 2007 cities had a collective motor vehicle theft rate of 449.9 per 100,000 inhabitants. Among the population groups, the largest cities, those with 250,000 or more inhabitants, experienced the highest rate of motor vehicle thefts with 730.3 motor vehicle thefts per 100,000 inhabitants. (Within this city group, cities with 500,000 to 999,999 inhabitants had the highest motor vehicle theft rate at 866.1 incidents per 100,000 inhabitants.) Conversely, the nation's smallest cities, those with populations under 10,000, had the lowest rate of motor vehicle theft with 186.0 incidents per 100,000 in population. Within the county groups, metropolitan counties had a rate of 279.0 motor vehicles stolen per 100,000 inhabitants, while nonmetropolitan counties had a rate of 132.8 incident per 100,000 inhabitants. (Table 16)

Offense Analysis

Based on the reports of law enforcement agencies, the UCR Program estimated the combined value of motor vehicles stolen nationwide in 2007 at approximately $7.4 billion. (Tables 1 and 23) Automobiles were, by far, the most frequently stolen vehicle, accounting for 73.4 percent of all vehicles stolen. Trucks and buses accounted for 18.1 percent of stolen vehicles, and other vehicles accounted for 8.6 percent of stolen vehicles. (Motor Vehicle Theft Table)

By type of vehicle, automobiles were stolen at a rate of 279.9 cars per 100,000 inhabitants in 2007. Trucks and buses were stolen at a rate of 68.9 vehicles per 100,000 in population, and other types of vehicles were stolen at a rate of 32.7 vehicles per 100,000 inhabitants. (Table 19)

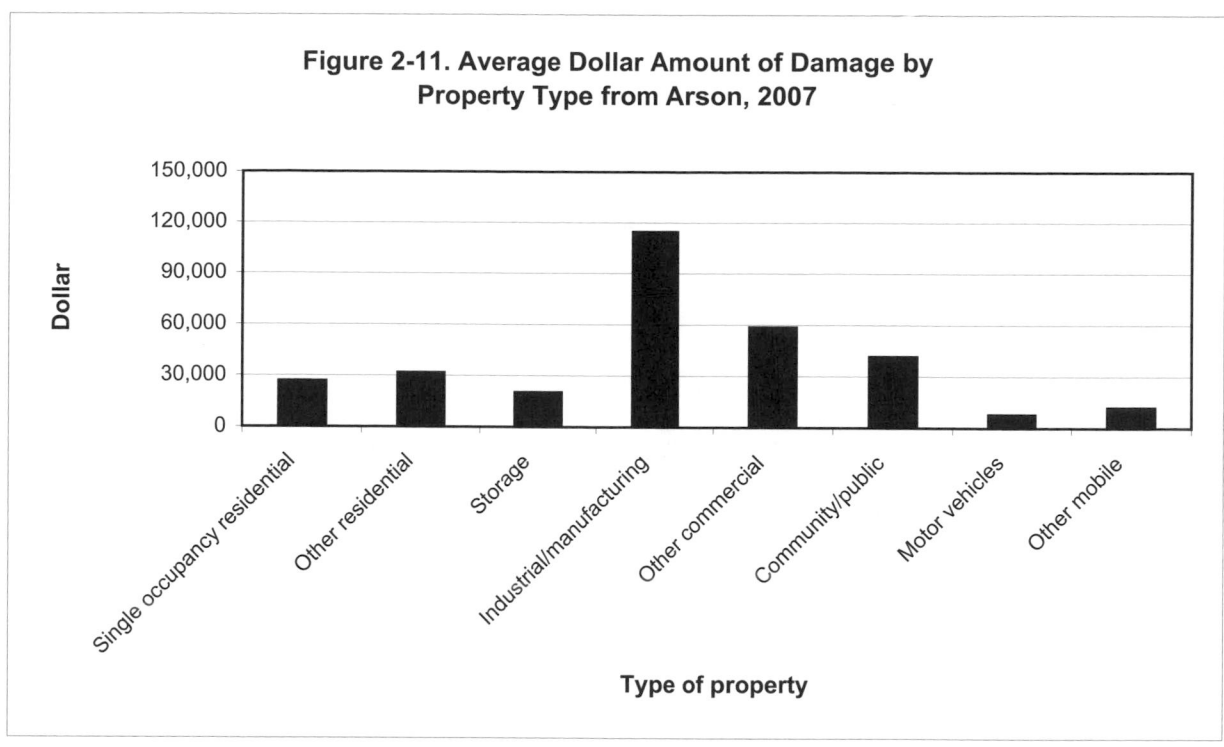

Figure 2-11. Average Dollar Amount of Damage by Property Type from Arson, 2007

ARSON

Definition

The UCR Program defines arson as any willful or malicious burning or attempt to burn (with or without intent to defraud) a dwelling house, public building, motor vehicle, aircraft, personal property of another, etc.

Data Collection

Only fires that investigators determined were willfully set (not fires labeled as "suspicious" or "of unknown origin") are included in this arson data collection. Points to consider regarding arson statistics include:

National offense rates per 100,000 inhabitants (found in Tables 1 through 4) do not include arson data; the FBI presents rates for arson separately. Arson rates are calculated based upon data received from all law enforcement agencies that provide the UCR Program with data for 12 complete months.

Arson data collection does not include estimates for arson, because the degree of reporting arson offenses varies from agency to agency. Because of this unevenness of reporting, arson offenses are excluded from Tables 1 through 7, all of which contain offense estimations.

The number of arsons reported by individual law enforcement agencies is available in Tables 8 through 11. Arson trend data (which indicate year-to-year changes) can be found in Tables 12 through 15, and arson clearance data (crimes solved) can be found in Tables 25 through 28.

National Coverage

In 2007, 14,197 agencies (providing 1 to 12 months of data) reported 64,332 arson offenses. Of those agencies, 14,131 provided expanded offense data about 57,224 arsons. (Unpublished Expanded Arson Table 1; see Appendix I for more information)

Population Groups: Trends and Rates

The number of arsons reported in 2007 decreased 6.7 percent from the 2006 figure. Law enforcement agencies in the nation's cities collectively reported a 6.3 percent decline in the number of arsons from the 2006 figure. The number of arsons declined for all population groups. Among the population groups labeled *city,* those with 50,000 to 99,999 inhabitants had the largest year-to-year decrease in reported arsons, 10.1 percent. Agencies in the nation's metropolitan counties reported a 8.8 percent decrease in the number of arsons, and those in nonmetropolitan counties reported a 5.1 percent decline. (Table 12)

Arson rates were based on information received from 11,590 agencies that provided 12 months of complete arson data to the UCR Program. An examination of data indicated that in 2007, the highest rate among city groups—40.8 arsons per 100,000 inhabitants—was reported in cities with 250,000 or more inhabitants. Among cities with 250,000 or more inhabitants, those with a population of 250,000 to 499,999 had the highest rate at 40.9 per 100,000 inhabitants. Cities with 10,000 to 24,999 inhabitants had the lowest rate of arson at 17.9 per 100,000 inhabitants. Metropolitan counties had 20.0 arsons per 100,000 inhabitants, and nonmetropolitan counties had 16.2 arsons per 100,000 inhabitants, the lowest of all the population groups. (Expanded Arson Table 1)

Offense Analysis

The UCR Program breaks down arson offenses into three property categories: structural, mobile, and other. In addition, the structural property type is broken down into seven types of structures, and the mobile property type consists of two subgroupings. The program also collects information on the estimated dollar value of the damaged property.

Property Type

The number of arsons decreased for all property types in 2007. Arsons for the structural property type decreased 6.2 percent. Arsons for the mobile property type decreased 8.0 percent and arsons of other property types decreased 8.3 percent. (Table 15)

Distributions by Property Type

In 2007, arsons of structures accounted for 42.9 percent of all arsons. Of these arsons, 61.6 percent involved residential properties. Of the residential arsons, most (72.7 percent) were single-occupancy residences, such as houses, townhouses, duplexes, etc. Mobile arsons accounted for 27.9 percent of all arsons. Within this category, 94.5 percent of offenses involved the burning of motor vehicles. Other types of property, such as crops, timber, fences, etc., accounted for 29.2 percent of reported arson offenses. (Expanded Arson Table 2)

Dollar Loss

In monetary terms, the average dollar loss in 2007 for arson was $17,289. The average dollar loss for a structural arson was $32,364. Mobile property had an average dollar loss of $8,112. Other property types had an average dollar loss of $3,918. (Expanded Arson Table 2)

Within the structural arson category, the industrial/manufacturing subcategory had the highest average dollar loss at $114,699. Within that same category, single-occupancy dwellings had an average dollar loss of $26,729. Other residential dwellings had an average dollar loss of $31,642. Storage properties had the lowest average damages at $20,237. (Expanded Arson Table 2)

Table 1. Crime in the United States, by Volume and Rate per 100,000 Inhabitants, 1988–2007

(Number, rate per 100,000 population, percent.)

Year	Population[1]	Violent crime		Murder and nonnegligent manslaughter		Forcible rape		Robbery	
		Number	Rate	Number	Rate	Number	Rate	Number	Rate
1988.............	244,498,982	1,566,221	640.6	20,675	8.5	92,486	37.8	542,968	222.1
1989.............	246,819,230	1,646,037	666.9	21,500	8.7	94,504	38.3	578,326	234.3
1990.............	249,464,396	1,820,127	729.6	23,438	9.4	102,555	41.1	639,271	256.3
1991.............	252,153,092	1,911,767	758.2	24,703	9.8	106,593	42.3	687,732	272.7
1992.............	255,029,699	1,932,274	757.7	23,760	9.3	109,062	42.8	672,478	263.7
1993.............	257,782,608	1,926,017	747.1	24,526	9.5	106,014	41.1	659,870	256.0
1994.............	260,327,021	1,857,670	713.6	23,326	9.0	102,216	39.3	618,949	237.8
1995.............	262,803,276	1,798,792	684.5	21,606	8.2	97,470	37.1	580,509	220.9
1996.............	265,228,572	1,688,540	636.6	19,645	7.4	96,252	36.3	535,594	201.9
1997.............	267,783,607	1,636,096	611.0	18,208	6.8	96,153	35.9	498,534	186.2
1998.............	270,248,003	1,533,887	567.6	16,974	6.3	93,144	34.5	447,186	165.5
1999.............	272,690,813	1,426,044	523.0	15,522	5.7	89,411	32.8	409,371	150.1
2000.............	281,421,906	1,425,486	506.5	15,586	5.5	90,178	32.0	408,016	145.0
2001[2]...........	285,317,559	1,439,480	504.5	16,037	5.6	90,863	31.8	423,557	148.5
2002.............	287,973,924	1,423,677	494.4	16,229	5.6	95,235	33.1	420,806	146.1
2003.............	290,788,976	1,383,676	475.8	16,528	5.7	93,883	32.3	414,235	142.5
2004.............	293,656,842	1,360,088	463.2	16,148	5.5	95,089	32.4	401,470	136.7
2005.............	296,507,061	1,390,745	469.0	16,740	5.6	94,347	31.8	417,438	140.8
2006[3]...........	299,398,484	1,418,043	473.6	17,030	5.7	92,757	31.0	447,403	149.4
2007.............	301,621,157	1,408,337	466.9	16,929	5.6	90,427	30.0	445,125	147.6

Year	Aggravated assault		Property crime		Burglary		Larceny-theft		Motor vehicle theft	
	Number	Rate	Number	Rate	Number	Rate	Number	Rate	Number	Rate
1988.............	910,092	372.2	12,356,865	5,054.0	3,218,077	1,316.2	7,705,872	3,151.7	1,432,916	586.1
1989.............	951,707	385.6	12,605,412	5,107.1	3,168,170	1,283.6	7,872,442	3,189.6	1,564,800	634.0
1990.............	1,054,863	422.9	12,655,486	5,073.1	3,073,909	1,232.2	7,945,670	3,185.1	1,635,907	655.8
1991.............	1,092,739	433.4	12,961,116	5,140.2	3,157,150	1,252.1	8,142,228	3,229.1	1,661,738	659.0
1992.............	1,126,974	441.9	12,505,917	4,903.7	2,979,884	1,168.4	7,915,199	3,103.6	1,610,834	631.6
1993.............	1,135,607	440.5	12,218,777	4,740.0	2,834,808	1,099.7	7,820,909	3,033.9	1,563,060	606.3
1994.............	1,113,179	427.6	12,131,873	4,660.2	2,712,774	1,042.1	7,879,812	3,026.9	1,539,287	591.3
1995.............	1,099,207	418.3	12,063,935	4,590.5	2,593,784	987.0	7,997,710	3,043.2	1,472,441	560.3
1996.............	1,037,049	391.0	11,805,323	4,451.0	2,506,400	945.0	7,904,685	2,980.3	1,394,238	525.7
1997.............	1,023,201	382.1	11,558,475	4,316.3	2,460,526	918.8	7,743,760	2,891.8	1,354,189	505.7
1998.............	976,583	361.4	10,951,827	4,052.5	2,332,735	863.2	7,376,311	2,729.5	1,242,781	459.9
1999.............	911,740	334.3	10,208,334	3,743.6	2,100,739	770.4	6,955,520	2,550.7	1,152,075	422.5
2000.............	911,706	324.0	10,182,584	3,618.3	2,050,992	728.8	6,971,590	2,477.3	1,160,002	412.2
2001[2]...........	909,023	318.6	10,437,189	3,658.1	2,116,531	741.8	7,092,267	2,485.7	1,228,391	430.5
2002.............	891,407	309.5	10,455,277	3,630.6	2,151,252	747.0	7,057,379	2,450.7	1,246,646	432.9
2003.............	859,030	295.4	10,442,862	3,591.2	2,154,834	741.0	7,026,802	2,416.5	1,261,226	433.7
2004.............	847,381	288.6	10,319,386	3,514.1	2,144,446	730.3	6,937,089	2,362.3	1,237,851	421.5
2005.............	862,220	290.8	10,174,754	3,431.5	2,155,448	726.9	6,783,447	2,287.8	1,235,859	416.8
2006[3]...........	860,853	287.5	9,983,568	3,334.5	2,183,746	729.4	6,607,013	2,206.8	1,192,809	398.4
2007.............	855,856	283.8	9,843,481	3,263.5	2,179,140	722.5	6,568,572	2,177.8	1,095,769	363.3

Note: Although arson data are included in the trend and clearance tables, sufficient data are not available to estimate totals for this offense. Therefore, no arson data are published in this table.
[1] Population figures are U.S. Census Bureau provisional estimates as of July 1 for each year except 1990 and 2000, which are decennial census counts.
[2] The murder and nonnegligent manslaughters that occurred as a result of the events of September 11, 2001, are not included in this table.
[3] The 2006 figures have been adjusted.

Table 1A. Crime in the United States, Percent Change in Volume and Rate per 100,000 Inhabitants for 2 Years, 5 Years, and 10 Years

(Percent change.)

Year	Violent crime		Murder and nonnegligent manslaughter		Forcible rape		Robbery		Aggravated assault	
	Number	Rate	Number	Rate	Number	Rate	Number	Rate	Number	Rate
2006–2007..............................	-0.7	-1.4	-0.6	-1.3	-2.5	-3.2	-0.5	-1.2	-0.6	-1.3
2003–2007..............................	+1.8	-1.9	+2.4	-1.3	-3.7	-7.1	+7.5	+3.6	-0.4	-3.9
1998–2007..............................	-8.2	-17.7	-0.3	-10.6	-2.9	-13.0	-0.5	-10.8	-12.4	-21.5

Year	Property crime		Burglary		Larceny-theft		Motor vehicle theft	
	Number	Rate	Number	Rate	Number	Rate	Number	Rate
2006–2007..............................	-1.4	-2.1	-0.2	-0.9	-0.6	-1.3	-8.1	-8.8
2003–2007..............................	-5.7	-9.1	+1.1	-2.5	-6.5	-9.9	-13.1	-16.2
1998–2007..............................	-10.1	-19.5	-6.6	-16.3	-11.0	-20.2	-11.8	-21.0

Note: Although arson data are included in the trend and clearance tables, sufficient data are not available to estimate totals for this offense.

Table 2. Crime in the United States by Community Type, 2007

(Number, percent, rate per 100,000 population.)

Area	Population[1]	Violent crime	Murder and non-negligent manslaughter	Forcible rape	Robbery	Aggravated assault	Property crime	Burglary	Larceny-theft	Motor vehicle theft
United States Total	301,621,157	1,408,337	16,929	90,427	445,125	855,856	9,843,481	2,179,140	6,568,572	1,095,769
Rate per 100,000 inhabitants	466.9	5.6	30.0	147.6	283.8	3,263.5	722.5	2,177.8	363.3	
Metropolitan Statistical Areas	251,045,164									
Area actually reporting[2]	95.7%	1,188,875	14,389	69,828	402,338	702,320	8,121,245	1,766,346	5,375,999	978,900
Estimated total	100.0%	1,265,166	15,224	75,114	427,731	747,097	8,577,047	1,858,602	5,698,194	1,020,251
Rate per 100,000 inhabitants	504.0	6.1	29.9	170.4	297.6	3,416.5	740.3	2,269.8	406.4	
Cities Outside Metropolitan Areas	20,083,243									
Area actually reporting[2]	88.0%	71,138	670	6,633	11,094	52,741	672,408	139,699	500,678	32,031
Estimated total	100.0%	79,335	752	7,695	12,426	58,462	757,846	157,165	565,406	35,275
Rate per 100,000 inhabitants	395.0	3.7	38.3	61.9	291.1	3,773.5	782.6	2,815.3	175.6	
Nonmetropolitan Counties	30,492,750									
Area actually reporting[2]	90.0%	59,066	874	6,644	4,546	47,002	466,163	148,953	279,938	37,272
Estimated total	100.0%	63,836	953	7,618	4,968	50,297	508,588	163,373	304,972	40,243
Rate per 100,000 inhabitants	209.3	3.1	25.0	16.3	164.9	1,667.9	535.8	1,000.1	132.0	

Note: Although arson data are included in the trend and clearance tables, sufficient data are not available to estimate totals for this offense. Therefore, no arson data are published in this table.

[1] Population figures are U.S. Census Bureau provisional estimates as of July 1, 2007.

[2] The percentage reported under "Area actually reporting" is based on the population covered by agencies providing 3 months or more of crime reports to the FBI.

Table 3. Population and Offense Distribution, by Region, 2007

(Percent distribution.)

Region	Population	Violent crime	Murder and non-negligent manslaughter	Forcible rape	Robbery	Aggravated assault	Property crime	Burglary	Larceny-theft	Motor vehicle theft
United States Total[1]	100.0	100.0	100.0	100.0	100.0	100.0	100.0	100.0	100.0	100.0
Northeast	18.1	14.5	13.4	12.0	16.9	13.5	12.2	10.5	13.2	9.8
Midwest	22.0	19.4	19.1	25.3	19.0	19.0	21.3	20.6	22.1	18.2
South	36.6	43.1	45.8	38.8	40.4	44.9	42.7	46.7	42.4	36.4
West	23.2	23.1	21.8	24.0	23.7	22.7	23.8	22.2	22.4	35.7

Note: Although arson data are included in the trend and clearance tables, sufficient data are not available to estimate totals for this offense. Therefore, no arson data are published in this table.

[1] Because of rounding, the percentages may not add to 100.0.

Table 4. Crime, by Region, Geographic Division, and State, 2006–2007

(Number, rate per 100,000 population, percent.)

Area	Year	Population[1]	Violent crime		Murder and non-negligent manslaughter		Forcible rape		Robbery	
			Number	Rate	Number	Rate	Number	Rate	Number	Rate
United States Total[2, 3, 4, 5]	2006..................	299,398,484	1,418,043	473.6	17,030	5.7	92,757	31.0	447,403	149.4
	2007..................	301,621,157	1,408,337	466.9	16,929	5.6	90,427	30.0	445,125	147.6
	Percent change.....		-0.7	-1.4	-0.6	-1.3	-2.5	-3.2	-0.5	-1.2
Northeast[2]	2006..................	54,741,353	214,549	391.9	2,454	4.5	11,303	20.6	82,760	151.2
	2007..................	54,680,626	203,632	372.4	2,261	4.1	10,821	19.8	75,326	137.8
	Percent change.....		-5.1	-5.0	-7.9	-7.8	-4.3	-4.2	-9.0	-8.9
New England	2006..................	14,269,989	45,247	317.1	370	2.6	3,496	24.5	13,940	97.7
	2007..................	14,264,185	43,334	303.8	357	2.5	3,395	23.8	12,225	85.7
	Percent change.....		-4.2	-4.2	-3.5	-3.5	-2.9	-2.8	-12.3	-12.3
Connecticut	2006..................	3,504,809	9,841	280.8	108	3.1	636	18.1	4,241	121.0
	2007..................	3,502,309	8,965	256.0	106	3.0	658	18.8	3,607	103.0
	Percent change.....		-8.9	-8.8	-1.9	-1.8	+3.5	+3.5	-14.9	-14.9
Maine	2006..................	1,321,574	1,526	115.5	23	1.7	339	25.7	384	29.1
	2007..................	1,317,207	1,554	118.0	21	1.6	391	29.7	349	26.5
	Percent change.....		+1.8	+2.2	-8.7	-8.4	+15.3	+15.7	-9.1	-8.8
Massachusetts	2006..................	6,437,193	28,775	447.0	186	2.9	1,742	27.1	8,047	125.0
	2007..................	6,449,755	27,832	431.5	184	2.9	1,634	25.3	7,006	108.6
	Percent change.....		-3.3	-3.5	-1.1	-1.3	-6.2	-6.4	-12.9	-13.1
New Hampshire	2006..................	1,314,895	1,824	138.7	13	1.0	344	26.2	423	32.2
	2007..................	1,315,828	1,807	137.3	15	1.1	333	25.3	432	32.8
	Percent change.....		-0.9	-1.0	+15.4	+15.3	-3.2	-3.3	+2.1	+2.1
Rhode Island	2006..................	1,067,610	2,429	227.5	28	2.6	285	26.7	735	68.8
	2007..................	1,057,832	2,404	227.3	19	1.8	256	24.2	751	71.0
	Percent change.....		-1.0	-0.1	-32.1	-31.5	-10.2	-9.3	+2.2	+3.1
Vermont	2006..................	623,908	852	136.6	12	1.9	150	24.0	110	17.6
	2007..................	621,254	772	124.3	12	1.9	123	19.8	80	12.9
	Percent change.....		-9.4	-9.0	0.0	+0.4	-18.0	-17.6	-27.3	-27.0
Middle Atlantic[2]	2006..................	40,471,364	169,302	418.3	2,084	5.1	7,807	19.3	68,820	170.0
	2007..................	40,416,441	160,298	396.6	1,904	4.7	7,426	18.4	63,101	156.1
	Percent change.....		-5.3	-5.2	-8.6	-8.5	-4.9	-4.8	-8.3	-8.2
New Jersey[2]	2006..................	8,724,560	30,671	351.5	427	4.9	1,237	14.2	13,357	153.1
	2007..................	8,685,920	28,601	329.3	380	4.4	1,050	12.1	12,549	144.5
	Percent change.....		-6.7	-6.3	-11.0	-10.6	-15.1	-14.7	-6.0	-5.6
New York	2006..................	19,306,183	83,966	434.9	921	4.8	3,169	16.4	34,489	178.6
	2007..................	19,297,729	79,915	414.1	801	4.2	2,926	15.2	31,094	161.1
	Percent change.....		-4.8	-4.8	-13.0	-13.0	-7.7	-7.6	-9.8	-9.8
Pennsylvania	2006..................	12,440,621	54,665	439.4	736	5.9	3,401	27.3	20,974	168.6
	2007..................	12,432,792	51,782	416.5	723	5.8	3,450	27.7	19,458	156.5
	Percent change.....		-5.3	-5.2	-1.8	-1.7	+1.4	+1.5	-7.2	-7.2
Midwest[3, 4]	2006..................	66,217,736	277,788	419.5	3,307	5.0	23,715	35.8	87,464	132.1
	2007..................	66,388,795	273,018	411.2	3,225	4.9	22,863	34.4	84,674	127.5
	Percent change.....		-1.7	-2.0	-2.5	-2.7	-3.6	-3.8	-3.2	-3.4
East North Central[3, 4]	2006..................	46,275,645	202,144	436.8	2,565	5.5	16,861	36.4	69,949	151.2
	2007..................	46,338,216	199,337	430.2	2,483	5.4	16,099	34.7	68,120	147.0
	Percent change.....		-1.4	-1.5	-3.2	-3.3	-4.5	-4.6	-2.6	-2.7
Illinois[3, 4]	2006..................	12,831,970	69,498	541.6	780	6.1	4,078	31.8	23,782	185.3
	2007..................	12,852,548	68,528	533.2	752	5.9	4,103	31.9	23,100	179.7
	Percent change.....		-1.4	-1.6	-3.6	-3.7	+0.6	+0.5	-2.9	-3.0
Indiana	2006..................	6,313,520	19,876	314.8	369	5.8	1,835	29.1	7,243	114.7
	2007..................	6,345,289	21,165	333.6	356	5.6	1,742	27.5	7,872	124.1
	Percent change.....		+6.5	+6.0	-3.5	-4.0	-5.1	-5.5	+8.7	+8.
Michigan	2006..................	10,095,643	56,778	562.4	713	7.1	5,269	52.2	14,208	140.7
	2007..................	10,071,822	53,988	536.0	676	6.7	4,579	45.5	13,414	133.2
	Percent change.....		-4.9	-4.7	-5.2	-5.0	-13.1	-12.9	-5.6	-5.4
Ohio	2006..................	11,478,006	40,209	350.3	539	4.7	4,548	39.6	19,149	166.8
	2007..................	11,466,917	39,360	343.2	516	4.5	4,452	38.8	18,260	159.2
	Percent change.....		-2.1	-2.0	-4.3	-4.2	-2.1	-2.0	-4.6	-4.6
Wisconsin	2006..................	5,556,506	15,783	284.0	164	3.0	1,131	20.4	5,567	100.2
	2007..................	5,601,640	16,296	290.9	183	3.3	1,223	21.8	5,474	97.7
	Percent change.....		+3.3	+2.4	+11.6	+10.7	+8.1	+7.3	-1.7	-2.5	+5.5

Note: Although arson data are included in the trend and clearance tables, sufficient data are not available to estimate totals for this offense. Therefore, no arson data are published in this table.

[1] Populations are U.S. Census Bureau provisional estimates as of July 1, 2007, and July 1, 2006.

[2] The 2006 crime figures have been adjusted.

[3] Limited data for 2006 and 2007 were available for Illinois.

[4] The data collection methodology for the offense of forcible rape used by the Illinois and the Minnesota state UCR Programs (with the exception of Rockford, Illinois, and Minneapolis and St. Paul, Minnesota) does not comply with national UCR guidelines. Consequently, their state figures for forcible rape (with the exception of Rockford, Illinois, and Minneapolis and St. Paul, Minnesota) have been estimated for inclusion in this table.

[5] Includes offenses reported by the Zoological Police and the Metro Transit Police.

Table 4.   Crime, by Region, Geographic Division, and State, 2006–2007 *(Contd.)*

(Number, rate per 100,000 population, percent.)

Area	Year	Aggravated assault		Property crime		Burglary		Larceny-theft		Motor vehicle theft	
		Number	Rate	Number	Rate	Number	Rate	Number	Rate	Number	Rate
United States Total[2,3,4,5]	2006	860,853	287.5	9,983,568	3,334.5	2,183,746	729.4	6,607,013	2,206.8	1,192,809	398.4
	2007	855,856	283.8	9,843,481	3,263.5	2,179,140	722.5	6,568,572	2,177.8	1,095,769	363.3
	Percent change	-0.6	-1.3	-1.4	-2.1	-0.2	-0.9	-0.6	-1.3	-8.1	-8.8
Northeast[2]	2006	118,032	215.6	1,241,852	2,268.6	235,348	429.9	884,825	1,616.4	121,679	222.3
	2007	115,224	210.7	1,204,978	2,203.7	229,187	419.1	868,763	1,588.8	107,028	195.7
	Percent change	-2.4	-2.3	-3.0	-2.9	-2.6	-2.5	-1.8	-1.7	-12.0	-11.9
New England	2006	27,441	192.3	341,602	2,393.8	69,727	488.6	236,594	1,658.0	35,281	247.2
	2007	27,357	191.8	337,359	2,365.1	70,828	496.5	235,947	1,654.1	30,584	214.4
	Percent change	-0.3	-0.3	-1.2	-1.2	+1.6	+1.6	-0.3	-0.2	-13.3	-13.3
Connecticut	2006	4,856	138.6	87,764	2,504.1	14,694	419.3	62,680	1,788.4	10,390	296.4
	2007	4,594	131.2	84,052	2,399.9	15,162	432.9	59,723	1,705.2	9,167	261.7
	Percent change	-5.4	-5.3	-4.2	-4.2	+3.2	+3.3	-4.7	-4.6	-11.8	-11.7
Maine	2006	780	59.0	33,286	2,518.7	6,779	512.9	25,167	1,904.3	1,340	101.4
	2007	793	60.2	31,992	2,428.8	6,676	506.8	24,057	1,826.4	1,259	95.6
	Percent change	+1.7	+2.0	-3.9	-3.6	-1.5	-1.2	-4.4	-4.1	-6.0	-5.7
Massachusetts	2006	18,800	292.1	153,913	2,391.0	35,181	546.5	100,771	1,565.4	17,961	279.0
	2007	19,008	294.7	154,246	2,391.5	35,662	552.9	103,592	1,606.1	14,992	232.4
	Percent change	+1.1	+0.9	+0.2	*	+1.4	+1.2	+2.8	+2.6	-16.5	-16.7
New Hampshire	2006	1,044	79.4	24,642	1,874.1	4,358	331.4	18,862	1,434.5	1,422	108.1
	2007	1,027	78.0	24,896	1,892.0	4,986	378.9	18,611	1,414.4	1,299	98.7
	Percent change	-1.6	-1.7	+1.0	+1.0	+14.4	+14.3	-1.3	-1.4	-8.6	-8.7
Rhode Island	2006	1,381	129.4	27,618	2,586.9	5,415	507.2	18,621	1,744.2	3,582	335.5
	2007	1,378	130.3	27,743	2,622.6	5,236	495.0	19,281	1,822.7	3,226	305.0
	Percent change	-0.2	+0.7	+0.5	+1.4	-3.3	-2.4	+3.5	+4.5	-9.9	-9.1
Vermont	2006	580	93.0	14,379	2,304.7	3,300	528.9	10,493	1,681.8	586	93.9
	2007	557	89.7	14,430	2,322.7	3,106	500.0	10,683	1,719.6	641	103.2
	Percent change	-4.0	-3.6	+0.4	+0.8	-5.9	-5.5	+1.8	+2.2	+9.4	+9.9
Middle Atlantic[2]	2006	90,591	223.8	900,250	2,224.4	165,621	409.2	648,231	1,601.7	86,398	213.5
	2007	87,867	217.4	867,619	2,146.7	158,359	391.8	632,816	1,565.7	76,444	189.1
	Percent change	-3.0	-2.9	-3.6	-3.5	-4.4	-4.3	-2.4	-2.2	-11.5	-11.4
New Jersey[2]	2006	15,650	179.4	199,958	2,291.9	39,433	452.0	135,801	1,556.5	24,724	283.4
	2007	14,622	168.3	192,226	2,213.1	37,482	431.5	132,791	1,528.8	21,953	252.7
	Percent change	-6.6	-6.2	-3.9	-3.4	-4.9	-4.5	-2.2	-1.8	-11.2	-10.8
New York	2006	45,387	235.1	396,304	2,052.7	68,565	355.1	295,605	1,531.1	32,134	166.4
	2007	45,094	233.7	381,816	1,978.6	64,857	336.1	288,929	1,497.2	28,030	145.3
	Percent change	-0.6	-0.6	-3.7	-3.6	-5.4	-5.4	-2.3	-2.2	-12.8	-12.7
Pennsylvania	2006	29,554	237.6	303,988	2,443.5	57,623	463.2	216,825	1,742.9	29,540	237.4
	2007	28,151	226.4	293,577	2,361.3	56,020	450.6	211,096	1,697.9	26,461	212.8
	Percent change	-4.7	-4.7	-3.4	-3.4	-2.8	-2.7	-2.6	-2.6	-10.4	-10.4
Midwest[3,4]	2006	163,302	246.6	2,166,146	3,271.2	458,278	692.1	1,487,599	2,246.5	220,269	332.6
	2007	162,256	244.4	2,095,999	3,157.2	448,126	675.0	1,448,457	2,181.8	199,416	300.4
	Percent change	-0.6	-0.9	-3.2	-3.5	-2.2	-2.5	-2.6	-2.9	-9.5	-9.7
East North Central[3,4]	2006	112,769	243.7	1,511,762	3,266.9	330,954	715.2	1,019,828	2,203.8	160,980	347.9
	2007	112,635	243.1	1,456,791	3,143.8	324,218	699.7	989,766	2,136.0	142,807	308.2
	Percent change	-0.1	-0.3	-3.6	-3.8	-2.0	-2.2	-2.9	-3.1	-11.3	-11.4
Illinois[3,4]	2006	40,858	318.4	387,478	3,019.6	77,259	602.1	272,578	2,124.2	37,641	293.3
	2007	40,572	315.7	377,322	2,935.8	75,524	587.6	267,911	2,084.5	33,887	263.7
	Percent change	-0.7	-0.9	-2.6	-2.8	-2.2	-2.4	-1.7	-1.9	-10.0	-10.1
Indiana	2006	10,429	165.2	221,127	3,502.4	46,168	731.3	153,093	2,424.8	21,866	346.3
	2007	11,195	176.4	215,526	3,396.6	46,919	739.4	149,050	2,349.0	19,557	308.2
	Percent change	+7.3	+6.8	-2.5	-3.0	+1.6	+1.1	-2.6	-3.1	-10.6	-11.0
Michigan	2006	36,588	362.4	324,351	3,212.8	76,107	753.9	198,227	1,963.5	50,017	495.4
	2007	35,319	350.7	308,775	3,065.7	75,428	748.9	191,196	1,898.3	42,151	418.5
	Percent change	-3.5	-3.2	-4.8	-4.6	-0.9	-0.7	-3.5	-3.3	-15.7	-15.5
Ohio	2006	15,973	139.2	422,235	3,678.6	104,426	909.8	280,384	2,442.8	37,425	326.1
	2007	16,132	140.7	396,209	3,455.2	98,508	859.1	263,922	2,301.6	33,779	294.6
	Percent change	+1.0	+1.1	-6.2	-6.1	-5.7	-5.6	-5.9	-5.8	-9.7	-9.7
Wisconsin	2006	8,921	160.6	156,571	2,817.8	26,994	485.8	115,546	2,079.5	14,031	252.5
	2007	9,416	168.1	158,959	2,837.7	27,839	497.0	117,687	2,100.9	13,433	239.8
	Percent change	+5.5	+4.7	+1.5	+0.7	+3.1	+2.3	+1.9	+1.0	-4.3	-5.0

Note: Although arson data are included in the trend and clearance tables, sufficient data are not available to estimate totals for this offense. Therefore, no arson data are published in this table.

[2] The 2006 crime figures have been adjusted.

[3] Limited data for 2006 and 2007 were available for Illinois.

[4] The data collection methodology for the offense of forcible rape used by the Illinois and the Minnesota state UCR Programs (with the exception of Rockford, Illinois, and Minneapolis and St. Paul, Minnesota) does not comply with national UCR guidelines. Consequently, their state figures for forcible rape (with the exception of Rockford, Illinois, and Minneapolis and St. Paul, Minnesota) have been estimated for inclusion in this table.

[5] Includes offenses reported by the Zoological Police and the Metro Transit Police.

Table 4. Crime, by Region, Geographic Division, and State, 2006–2007 *(Contd.)*

(Number, rate per 100,000 population, percent.)

Area	Year	Population[1]	Violent crime		Murder and non-negligent manslaughter		Forcible rape		Robbery	
			Number	Rate	Number	Rate	Number	Rate	Number	Rate
West North Central[4]	2006	19,942,091	75,644	379.3	742	3.7	6,854	34.4	17,515	87.8
	2007	20,050,579	73,681	367.5	742	3.7	6,764	33.7	16,554	82.6
	Percent change		-2.6	-3.1	0.0	-0.5	-1.3	-1.8	-5.5	-6.0
Iowa	2006	2,982,085	8,455	283.5	55	1.8	828	27.8	1,298	43.5
	2007	2,988,046	8,805	294.7	37	1.2	904	30.3	1,313	43.9
	Percent change		+4.1	+3.9	-32.7	-32.9	+9.2	+9.0	+1.2	+1.0
Kansas	2006	2,764,075	11,748	425.0	127	4.6	1,238	44.8	1,877	67.9
	2007	2,775,997	12,566	452.7	107	3.9	1,231	44.3	2,016	72.6
	Percent change		+7.0	+6.5	-15.7	-16.1	-0.6	-1.0	+7.4	+6.9
Minnesota[4]	2006	5,167,101	16,425	317.9	125	2.4	1,947	37.7	5,433	105.1
	2007	5,197,621	15,003	288.7	116	2.2	1,873	36.0	4,770	91.8
	Percent change		-8.7	-9.2	-7.2	-7.7	-3.8	-4.4	-12.2	-12.7
Missouri	2006	5,842,713	31,880	545.6	368	6.3	1,764	30.2	7,587	129.9
	2007	5,878,415	29,682	504.9	385	6.5	1,714	29.2	7,165	121.9
	Percent change		-6.9	-7.5	+4.6	+4.0	-2.8	-3.4	-5.6	-6.1
Nebraska	2006	1,768,331	4,983	281.8	50	2.8	548	31.0	1,129	63.8
	2007	1,774,571	5,367	302.4	68	3.8	527	29.7	1,108	62.4
	Percent change		+7.7	+7.3	+36.0	+35.5	-3.8	-4.2	-1.9	-2.2
North Dakota	2006	635,867	813	127.9	8	1.3	193	30.4	72	11.3
	2007	639,715	911	142.4	12	1.9	207	32.4	70	10.9
	Percent change		+12.1	+11.4	+50.0	+49.1	+7.3	+6.6	-2.8	-3.4
South Dakota	2006	781,919	1,340	171.4	9	1.2	336	43.0	119	15.2
	2007	796,214	1,347	169.2	17	2.1	308	38.7	112	14.1
	Percent change		+0.5	-1.3	+88.9	+85.5	-8.3	-10.0	-5.9	-7.6
South[2, 5]	2006	109,083,752	597,279	547.5	7,365	6.8	35,667	32.7	171,394	157.1
	2007	110,454,786	606,667	549.2	7,759	7.0	35,073	31.8	179,728	162.7
	Percent change		+1.6	+0.3	+5.3	+4.0	-1.7	-2.9	+4.9	+3.6
South Atlantic[5]	2006	57,143,670	327,457	573.0	3,859	6.8	16,849	29.5	97,580	170.8
	2007	57,860,260	332,090	574.0	4,097	7.1	16,274	28.1	103,124	178.2
	Percent change		+1.4	+0.2	+6.2	+4.9	-3.4	-4.6	+5.7	+4.4	-0.3
Delaware	2006	853,476	5,817	681.6	42	4.9	400	46.9	1,735	203.3
	2007	864,764	5,960	689.2	37	4.3	336	38.9	1,706	197.3
	Percent change		+2.5	+1.1	-11.9	-13.1	-16.0	-17.1	-1.7	-3.0
District of Columbia[5]	2006	581,530	8,772	1,508.4	169	29.1	185	31.8	3,829	658.4
	2007	588,292	8,320	1,414.3	181	30.8	192	32.6	4,261	724.3
	Percent change		-5.2	-6.2	+7.1	+5.9	+3.8	+2.6	+11.3	+10.0
Florida	2006	18,089,888	128,795	712.0	1,129	6.2	6,475	35.8	34,147	188.8
	2007	18,251,243	131,880	722.6	1,201	6.6	6,151	33.7	38,162	209.1
	Percent change		+2.4	+1.5	+6.4	+5.4	-5.0	-5.8	+11.8	+10.8
Georgia	2006	9,363,941	44,106	471.0	600	6.4	2,173	23.2	15,509	165.6
	2007	9,544,750	47,075	493.2	718	7.5	2,178	22.8	17,340	181.7
	Percent change		+6.7	+4.7	+19.7	+17.4	+0.2	-1.7	+11.8	+9.7
Maryland	2006	5,615,727	38,110	678.6	546	9.7	1,178	21.0	14,375	256.0
	2007	5,618,344	36,062	641.9	553	9.8	1,179	21.0	13,258	236.0
	Percent change		-5.4	-5.4	+1.3	+1.2	+0.1	*	-7.8	-7.8
North Carolina	2006	8,856,505	42,124	475.6	540	6.1	2,495	28.2	13,484	152.2
	2007	9,061,032	42,262	466.4	585	6.5	2,385	26.3	13,548	149.5
	Percent change		+0.3	-1.9	+8.3	+5.9	-4.4	-6.6	+0.5	-1.8
South Carolina	2006	4,321,249	33,078	765.5	359	8.3	1,762	40.8	5,899	136.5
	2007	4,407,709	34,746	788.3	352	8.0	1,739	39.5	6,346	144.0
	Percent change		+5.0	+3.0	-1.9	-3.9	-1.3		-3.2	+7.6
Virginia	2006	7,642,884	21,568	282.2	399	5.2	1,792	23.4	7,749	101.4
	2007	7,712,091	20,798	269.7	406	5.3	1,745	22.6	7,651	99.2
	Percent change		-3.6	-4.4	+1.8	+0.8	-2.6	-3.5	-1.3	-2.2
West Virginia	2006	1,818,470	5,087	279.7	75	4.1	389	21.4	853	46.9
	2007	1,812,035	4,987	275.2	64	3.5	369	20.4	852	47.0
	Percent change		-2.0	-1.6	-14.7	-14.4	-5.1	-4.8	-0.1	+0.2
East South Central	2006	17,754,447	85,218	480.0	1,182	6.7	6,088	34.3	24,932	140.4
	2007	17,944,829	88,127	491.1	1,221	6.8	6,140	34.2	25,355	141.3
	Percent change		+3.4	+2.3	+3.3	+2.2	+0.9	-0.2	+1.7	+0.6

Note: Although arson data are included in the trend and clearance tables, sufficient data are not available to estimate totals for this offense. Therefore, no arson data are published in this table.

[1] Populations are U.S. Census Bureau provisional estimates as of July 1, 2007, and July 1, 2006.

[2] The 2006 crime figures have been adjusted.

[4] The data collection methodology for the offense of forcible rape used by the Illinois and the Minnesota state UCR Programs (with the exception of Rockford, Illinois, and Minneapolis and St. Paul, Minnesota) does not comply with national UCR guidelines. Consequently, their state figures for forcible rape (with the exception of Rockford, Illinois, and Minneapolis and St. Paul, Minnesota) have been estimated for inclusion in this table.

[5] Includes offenses reported by the Zoological Police and the Metro Transit Police.

* = Less than one-tenth of 1 percent.

Table 4.   Crime, by Region, Geographic Division, and State, 2006–2007 *(Contd.)*

(Number, rate per 100,000 population, percent.)

Area	Year	Aggravated assault		Property crime		Burglary		Larceny-theft		Motor vehicle theft	
		Number	Rate	Number	Rate	Number	Rate	Number	Rate	Number	Rate
West North Central[4]	2006	50,533	253.4	654,384	3,281.4	127,324	638.5	467,771	2,345.6	59,289	297.3
	2007	49,621	247.5	639,208	3,188.0	123,908	618.0	458,691	2,287.7	56,609	282.3
	Percent change	-1.8	-2.3	-2.3	-2.8	-2.7	-3.2	-1.9	-2.5	-4.5	-5.0
Iowa	2006	6,274	210.4	83,579	2,802.7	18,017	604.2	60,556	2,030.7	5,006	167.9
	2007	6,551	219.2	78,154	2,615.6	16,941	567.0	56,328	1,885.1	4,885	163.5
	Percent change	+4.4	+4.2	-6.5	-6.7	-6.0	-6.2	-7.0	-7.2	-2.4	-2.6
Kansas	2006	8,506	307.7	103,658	3,750.2	19,992	723.3	74,963	2,712.0	8,703	314.9
	2007	9,212	331.8	102,120	3,678.7	20,263	729.9	73,293	2,640.2	8,564	308.5
	Percent change	+8.3	+7.8	-1.5	-1.9	+1.4	+0.9	-2.2	-2.6	-1.6	-2.0
Minnesota[4]	2006	8,920	172.6	159,119	3,079.5	30,173	583.9	115,567	2,236.6	13,379	258.9
	2007	8,244	158.6	157,829	3,036.6	29,670	570.8	115,633	2,224.7	12,526	241.0
	Percent change	-7.6	-8.1	-0.8	-1.4	-1.7	-2.2	+0.1	-0.5	-6.4	-6.9
Missouri	2006	22,161	379.3	223,570	3,826.5	44,647	764.1	153,490	2,627.0	25,433	435.3
	2007	20,418	347.3	219,759	3,738.4	43,446	739.1	152,529	2,594.7	23,784	404.6
	Percent change	-7.9	-8.4	-1.7	-2.3	-2.7	-3.3	-0.6	-1.2	-6.5	-7.1
Nebraska	2006	3,256	184.1	59,075	3,340.7	9,452	534.5	44,585	2,521.3	5,038	284.9
	2007	3,664	206.5	56,102	3,161.4	9,046	509.8	41,855	2,358.6	5,201	293.1
	Percent change	+12.5	+12.1	-5.0	-5.4	-4.3	-4.6	-6.1	-6.5	+3.2	+2.9
North Dakota	2006	540	84.9	12,719	2,000.3	2,393	376.3	9,314	1,464.8	1,012	159.2
	2007	622	97.2	12,088	1,889.6	2,164	338.3	9,010	1,408.4	914	142.9
	Percent change	+15.2	+14.5	-5.0	-5.5	-9.6	-10.1	-3.3	-3.8	-9.7	-10.2
South Dakota	2006	876	112.0	12,664	1,619.6	2,650	338.9	9,296	1,188.9	718	91.8
	2007	910	114.3	13,156	1,652.3	2,378	298.7	10,043	1,261.3	735	92.3
	Percent change	+3.9	+2.0	+3.9	+2.0	-10.3	-11.9	+8.0	+6.1	+2.4	+0.5
South[2, 5]	2006	382,853	351.0	4,124,293	3,780.8	985,937	903.8	2,725,921	2,498.9	412,435	378.1
	2007	384,107	347.8	4,199,649	3,802.1	1,018,197	921.8	2,782,863	2,519.5	398,589	360.9
	Percent change	+0.3	-0.9	+1.8	+0.6	+3.3	+2.0	+2.1	+0.8	-3.4	-4.6
South Atlantic[5]	2006	209,169	366.0	2,122,337	3,714.0	497,094	869.9	1,399,721	2,449.5	225,522	394.7
	2007	208,595	360.5	2,164,134	3,740.3	516,401	892.5	1,430,636	2,472.6	217,097	375.2
	Percent change	-0.3	-1.5	+2.0	+0.7	+3.9	+2.6	+2.2	+0.9	-3.7	-4.9
Delaware	2006	3,640	426.5	29,171	3,417.9	6,189	725.2	20,166	2,362.8	2,816	329.9
	2007	3,881	448.8	29,143	3,370.1	6,341	733.3	20,486	2,369.0	2,316	267.8
	Percent change	+6.6	+5.2	-0.1	-1.4	+2.5	+1.1	+1.6	+0.3	-17.8	-18.8
District of Columbia[5]	2006	4,589	789.1	27,063	4,653.8	3,835	659.5	15,907	2,735.4	7,321	1,258.9
	2007	3,686	626.6	28,908	4,913.9	3,926	667.4	17,382	2,954.7	7,600	1,291.9
	Percent change	-19.7	-20.6	+6.8	+5.6	+2.4	+1.2	+9.3	+8.0	+3.8	+2.6
Florida	2006	87,044	481.2	721,084	3,986.1	170,873	944.6	473,774	2,619.0	76,437	422.5
	2007	86,366	473.2	746,347	4,089.3	181,833	996.3	490,858	2,689.4	73,656	403.6
	Percent change	-0.8	-1.7	+3.5	+2.6	+6.4	+5.5	+3.6	+2.7	-3.6	-4.5
Georgia	2006	25,824	275.8	364,183	3,889.2	85,117	909.0	235,903	2,519.3	43,163	460.9
	2007	26,839	281.2	372,342	3,901.0	90,690	950.2	239,058	2,504.6	42,594	446.3
	Percent change	+3.9	+2.0	+2.2	+0.3	+6.5	+4.5	+1.3	-0.6	-1.3	-3.2
Maryland	2006	22,011	392.0	195,476	3,480.9	37,457	667.0	127,497	2,270.4	30,522	543.5
	2007	21,072	375.1	192,796	3,431.5	37,095	660.2	127,308	2,265.9	28,393	505.4
	Percent change	-4.3	-4.3	-1.4	-1.4	-1.0	-1.0	-0.1	-0.2	-7.0	-7.0
North Carolina	2006	25,605	289.1	364,960	4,120.8	107,407	1,212.7	227,427	2,567.9	30,126	340.2
	2007	25,744	284.1	370,354	4,087.3	108,800	1,200.7	233,588	2,577.9	27,966	308.6
	Percent change	+0.5	-1.7	+1.5	-0.8	+1.3	-1.0	+2.7	+0.4	-7.2	-9.3
South Carolina	2006	25,058	579.9	183,322	4,242.3	42,772	989.8	124,148	2,873.0	16,402	379.6
	2007	26,309	596.9	188,282	4,271.7	45,214	1,025.8	126,042	2,859.6	17,026	386.3
	Percent change	+5.0	+2.9	+2.7	+0.7	+5.7	+3.6	+1.5	-0.5	+3.8	+1.8
Virginia	2006	11,628	152.1	189,406	2,478.2	31,913	417.6	142,679	1,866.8	14,814	193.8
	2007	10,996	142.6	190,209	2,466.4	31,688	410.9	144,467	1,873.3	14,054	182.2
	Percent change	-5.4	-6.3	+0.4	-0.5	-0.7	-1.6	+1.3	+0.3	-5.1	-6.0
West Virginia	2006	3,770	207.3	47,672	2,621.5	11,531	634.1	32,220	1,771.8	3,921	215.6
	2007	3,702	204.3	45,753	2,525.0	10,814	596.8	31,447	1,735.5	3,492	192.7
	Percent change	-1.8	-1.5	-4.0	-3.7	-6.2	-5.9	-2.4	-2.1	-10.9	-10.6
East South Central	2006	53,016	298.6	630,734	3,552.5	161,791	911.3	413,920	2,331.4	55,023	309.9
	2007	55,411	308.8	635,759	3,542.9	162,688	906.6	421,127	2,346.8	51,944	289.5
	Percent change	+4.5	+3.4	+0.8	-0.3	+0.6	-0.5	+1.7	+0.7	-5.6	-6.6

Note: Although arson data are included in the trend and clearance tables, sufficient data are not available to estimate totals for this offense. Therefore, no arson data are published in this table.

[2] The 2006 crime figures have been adjusted.

[4] The data collection methodology for the offense of forcible rape used by the Illinois and the Minnesota state UCR Programs (with the exception of Rockford, Illinois, and Minneapolis and St. Paul, Minnesota) does not comply with national UCR guidelines. Consequently, their state figures for forcible rape (with the exception of Rockford, Illinois, and Minneapolis and St. Paul, Minnesota) have been estimated for inclusion in this table.

[5] Includes offenses reported by the Zoological Police and the Metro Transit Police.

Table 4.   Crime, by Region, Geographic Division, and State, 2006–2007 *(Contd.)*

(Number, rate per 100,000 population, percent.)

Area	Year	Population[1]	Violent crime		Murder and non-negligent manslaughter		Forcible rape		Robbery	
			Number	Rate	Number	Rate	Number	Rate	Number	Rate
Alabama	2006	4,599,030	19,557	425.2	382	8.3	1,649	35.9	7,059	153.5
	2007	4,627,851	20,732	448.0	412	8.9	1,545	33.4	7,398	159.9
	Percent change		+6.0	+5.3	+7.9	+7.2	-6.3	-6.9	+4.8	+4.1
Kentucky	2006	4,206,074	11,063	263.0	168	4.0	1,297	30.8	3,626	86.2
	2007	4,241,474	12,513	295.0	204	4.8	1,381	32.6	4,069	95.9
	Percent change		+13.1	+12.2	+21.4	+20.4	+6.5	+5.6	+12.2	+11.3
Mississippi	2006	2,910,540	8,691	298.6	223	7.7	1,000	34.4	3,118	107.1
	2007	2,918,785	8,502	291.3	208	7.1	1,040	35.6	2,866	98.2
	Percent change		-2.2	-2.5	-6.7	-7.0	+4.0	+3.7	-8.1	-8.3
Tennessee	2006	6,038,803	45,907	760.2	409	6.8	2,142	35.5	11,129	184.3
	2007	6,156,719	46,380	753.3	397	6.4	2,174	35.3	11,022	179.0
	Percent change		+1.0	-0.9	-2.9	-4.8	+1.5	-0.4	-1.0	-2.9
West South Central[2]	2006	34,185,635	184,604	540.0	2,324	6.8	12,730	37.2	48,882	143.0
	2007	34,649,697	186,450	538.1	2,441	7.0	12,659	36.5	51,249	147.9
	Percent change		+1.0	-0.4	+5.0	+3.6	-0.6	-1.9	+4.8	+3.4
Arkansas	2006	2,810,872	15,506	551.6	205	7.3	1,308	46.5	2,766	98.4
	2007	2,834,797	15,007	529.4	191	6.7	1,268	44.7	3,024	106.7
	Percent change		-3.2	-4.0	-6.8	-7.6	-3.1	-3.9	+9.3	+8.4
Louisiana[2]	2006	4,287,768	29,917	697.7	528	12.3	1,562	36.4	5,729	133.6
	2007	4,293,204	31,317	729.5	608	14.2	1,393	32.4	6,083	141.7
	Percent change		+4.7	+4.5	+15.2	+15.0	-10.8	-10.9	+6.2	+6.0
Oklahoma	2006	3,579,212	17,803	497.4	207	5.8	1,488	41.6	3,133	87.5
	2007	3,617,316	18,072	499.6	222	6.1	1,559	43.1	3,373	93.2
	Percent change		+1.5	+0.4	+7.2	+6.1	+4.8	+3.7	+7.7	+6.5
Texas	2006	23,507,783	121,378	516.3	1,384	5.9	8,372	35.6	37,254	158.5
	2007	23,904,380	122,054	510.6	1,420	5.9	8,439	35.3	38,769	162.2
	Percent change		+0.6	-1.1	+2.6	+0.9	+0.8	-0.9	+4.1	+2.3
West[2]	2006	69,355,643	328,427	473.5	3,904	5.6	22,072	31.8	105,785	152.5
	2007	70,096,950	325,020	463.7	3,684	5.3	21,670	30.9	105,397	150.4
	Percent change		-1.0	-2.1	-5.6	-6.6	-1.8	-2.9	-0.4	-1.4
Mountain	2006	20,845,987	93,590	449.0	1,087	5.2	8,055	38.6	23,975	115.0
	2007	21,360,990	93,652	438.4	1,112	5.2	7,918	37.1	24,252	113.5
	Percent change		+0.1	-2.3	+2.3	-0.2	-1.7	-4.1	+1.2	-1.3
Arizona	2006	6,166,318	30,916	501.4	465	7.5	1,941	31.5	9,226	149.6
	2007	6,338,755	30,600	482.7	468	7.4	1,856	29.3	9,618	151.7
	Percent change		-1.0	-3.7	+0.6	-2.1	-4.4	-7.0	+4.2	+1.4
Colorado	2006	4,753,377	18,616	391.6	158	3.3	2,076	43.7	3,835	80.7
	2007	4,861,515	16,906	347.8	153	3.1	1,998	41.1	3,453	71.0
	Percent change		-9.2	-11.2	-3.2	-5.3	-3.8	-5.9	-10.0	-12.0
Idaho	2006	1,466,465	3,625	247.2	36	2.5	587	40.0	301	20.5
	2007	1,499,402	3,589	239.4	49	3.3	578	38.5	233	15.5
	Percent change		-1.0	-3.2	+36.1	+33.1	-1.5	-3.7	-22.6	-24.3
Montana	2006	944,632	2,397	253.7	17	1.8	269	28.5	164	17.4
	2007	957,861	2,754	287.5	14	1.5	290	30.3	191	19.9
	Percent change		+14.9	+13.3	-17.6	-18.8	+7.8	+6.3	+16.5	+14.9
Nevada	2006	2,495,529	18,508	741.6	224	9.0	1,079	43.2	7,027	281.6
	2007	2,565,382	19,257	750.6	192	7.5	1,096	42.7	6,932	270.2
	Percent change		+4.0	+1.2	-14.3	-16.6	+1.6	-1.2	-1.4	-4.0
New Mexico	2006	1,954,599	12,572	643.2	132	6.8	1,094	56.0	2,105	107.7
	2007	1,969,915	13,085	664.2	162	8.2	1,032	52.4	2,321	117.8
	Percent change		+4.1	+3.3	+22.7	+21.8	-5.7	-6.4	+10.3	+9.4
Utah	2006	2,550,063	5,722	224.4	46	1.8	869	34.1	1,245	48.8
	2007	2,645,330	6,210	234.8	58	2.2	908	34.3	1,420	53.7
	Percent change		+8.5	+4.6	+26.1	+21.5	+4.5	+0.7	+14.1	+9.9
Wyoming	2006	515,004	1,234	239.6	9	1.7	140	27.2	72	14.0
	2007	522,830	1,251	239.3	16	3.1	160	30.6	84	16.1
	Percent change		+1.4	-0.1	+77.8	+75.1	+14.3	+12.6	+16.7	+14.9
Pacific[2]	2006	48,509,656	234,837	484.1	2,817	5.8	14,017	28.9	81,810	168.6
	2007	48,735,960	231,368	474.7	2,572	5.3	13,752	28.2	81,145	166.5
	Percent change		-1.5	-1.9	-8.7	-9.1	-1.9	-2.3	-0.8	-1.3
Alaska	2006	670,053	4,610	688.0	36	5.4	509	76.0	605	90.3
	2007	683,478	4,519	661.2	44	6.4	529	77.4	583	85.3
	Percent change		-2.0	-3.9	+22.2	+19.8	+3.9	+1.9	-3.6	-5.5

Note: Although arson data are included in the trend and clearance tables, sufficient data are not available to estimate totals for this offense. Therefore, no arson data are published in this table.

[1] Populations are U.S. Census Bureau provisional estimates as of July 1, 2007, and July 1, 2006.

[2] The 2006 crime figures have been adjusted.

Table 4.   Crime, by Region, Geographic Division, and State, 2006–2007 *(Contd.)*

(Number, rate per 100,000 population, percent.)

Area	Year	Aggravated assault		Property crime		Burglary		Larceny-theft		Motor vehicle theft	
		Number	Rate	Number	Rate	Number	Rate	Number	Rate	Number	Rate
Alabama	2006	10,467	227.6	181,021	3,936.1	44,571	969.1	121,610	2,644.3	14,840	322.7
	2007	11,377	245.8	183,798	3,971.6	45,331	979.5	124,237	2,684.6	14,230	307.5
	Percent change	+8.7	+8.0	+1.5	+0.9	+1.7	+1.1	+2.2	+1.5	-4.1	-4.7
Kentucky	2006	5,972	142.0	107,023	2,544.5	27,122	644.8	70,658	1,679.9	9,243	219.8
	2007	6,859	161.7	106,813	2,518.3	27,683	652.7	70,455	1,661.1	8,675	204.5
	Percent change	+14.9	+13.9	-0.2	-1.0	+2.1	+1.2	-0.3	-1.1	-6.1	-6.9
Mississippi	2006	4,350	149.5	93,393	3,208.8	27,239	935.9	57,807	1,986.1	8,347	286.8
	2007	4,388	150.3	93,424	3,200.8	27,959	957.9	58,084	1,990.0	7,381	252.9
	Percent change	+0.9	+0.6	*	-0.2	+2.6	+2.4	+0.5	+0.2	-11.6	-11.8
Tennessee	2006	32,227	533.7	249,297	4,128.3	62,859	1,040.9	163,845	2,713.2	22,593	374.1
	2007	32,787	532.5	251,724	4,088.6	61,715	1,002.4	168,351	2,734.4	21,658	351.8
	Percent change	+1.7	-0.2	+1.0	-1.0	-1.8	-3.7	+2.8	+0.8	-4.1	-6.0
West South Central[2]	2006	120,668	353.0	1,371,222	4,011.1	327,052	956.7	912,280	2,668.6	131,890	385.8
	2007	120,101	346.6	1,399,756	4,039.7	339,108	978.7	931,100	2,687.2	129,548	373.9
	Percent change	-0.5	-1.8	+2.1	+0.7	+3.7	+2.3	+2.1	+0.7	-1.8	-3.1
Arkansas	2006	11,227	399.4	111,521	3,967.5	32,042	1,139.9	72,016	2,562.1	7,463	265.5
	2007	10,524	371.2	112,061	3,953.1	32,072	1,131.4	72,979	2,574.4	7,010	247.3
	Percent change	-6.3	-7.1	+0.5	-0.4	+0.1	-0.8	+1.3	+0.5	-6.1	-6.9
Louisiana[2]	2006	22,098	515.4	171,239	3,993.7	44,986	1,049.2	110,613	2,579.7	15,640	364.8
	2007	23,233	541.2	174,991	4,076.0	44,602	1,038.9	115,209	2,683.5	15,180	353.6
	Percent change	+5.1	+5.0	+2.2	+2.1	-0.9	-1.0	+4.2	+4.0	-2.9	-3.1
Oklahoma	2006	12,975	362.5	129,002	3,604.2	34,377	960.5	81,267	2,270.5	13,358	373.2
	2007	12,918	357.1	127,562	3,526.4	34,121	943.3	79,982	2,211.1	13,459	372.1
	Percent change	-0.4	-1.5	-1.1	-2.2	-0.7	-1.8	-1.6	-2.6	+0.8	-0.3
Texas	2006	74,368	316.4	959,460	4,081.5	215,647	917.3	648,384	2,758.2	95,429	405.9
	2007	73,426	307.2	985,142	4,121.2	228,313	955.1	662,930	2,773.3	93,899	392.8
	Percent change	-1.3	-2.9	+2.7	+1.0	+5.9	+4.1	+2.2	+0.5	-1.6	-3.2
West[2]	2006	196,666	283.6	2,451,277	3,534.4	504,183	727.0	1,508,668	2,175.3	438,426	632.1
	2007	194,269	277.1	2,342,855	3,342.3	483,630	689.9	1,468,489	2,094.9	390,736	557.4
	Percent change	-1.2	-2.3	-4.4	-5.4	-4.1	-5.1	-2.7	-3.7	-10.9	-11.8
Mountain	2006	60,473	290.1	794,295	3,810.3	162,688	780.4	506,525	2,429.8	125,082	600.0
	2007	60,370	282.6	763,997	3,576.6	158,301	741.1	495,656	2,320.4	110,040	515.1
	Percent change	-0.2	-2.6	-3.8	-6.1	-2.7	-5.0	-2.1	-4.5	-12.0	-14.1
Arizona	2006	19,284	312.7	285,370	4,627.9	57,055	925.3	173,466	2,813.1	54,849	889.5
	2007	18,658	294.3	279,794	4,414.0	57,825	912.2	173,580	2,738.4	48,389	763.4
	Percent change	-3.2	-5.9	-2.0	-4.6	+1.3	-1.4	+0.1	-2.7	-11.8	-14.2
Colorado	2006	12,547	264.0	164,054	3,451.3	32,422	682.1	110,837	2,331.8	20,795	437.5
	2007	11,302	232.5	146,141	3,006.1	28,751	591.4	100,598	2,069.3	16,792	345.4
	Percent change	-9.9	11.9	-10.9	-12.9	-11.3	-13.3	-9.2	-11.3	-19.2	-21.0
Idaho	2006	2,701	184.2	35,471	2,418.8	7,526	513.2	25,516	1,740.0	2,429	165.6
	2007	2,729	182.0	33,685	2,246.6	6,977	465.3	24,482	1,632.8	2,226	148.5
	Percent change	+1.0	-1.2	-5.0	-7.1	-7.3	-9.3	-4.1	-6.2	-8.4	-10.4
Montana	2006	1,947	206.1	25,387	2,687.5	2,935	310.7	20,704	2,191.8	1,748	185.0
	2007	2,259	235.8	26,489	2,765.4	3,027	316.0	21,707	2,266.2	1,755	183.2
	Percent change	+16.0	+14.4	+4.3	+2.9	+3.1	+1.7	+4.8	+3.4	+0.4	-1.0
Nevada	2006	10,178	407.8	102,036	4,088.8	24,820	994.6	50,255	2,013.8	26,961	1,080.4
	2007	11,037	430.2	96,916	3,777.8	24,840	968.3	49,745	1,939.1	22,331	870.5
	Percent change	+8.4	+5.5	-5.0	-7.6	+0.1	-2.6	-1.0	-3.7	-17.2	-19.4
New Mexico	2006	9,241	472.8	76,956	3,937.2	20,909	1,069.7	46,822	2,395.5	9,225	472.0
	2007	9,570	485.8	73,394	3,725.7	18,992	964.1	45,463	2,307.9	8,939	453.8
	Percent change	+3.6	+2.8	-4.6	-5.4	-9.2	-9.9	-2.9	-3.7	-3.1	-3.9
Utah	2006	3,562	139.7	89,671	3,516.4	14,701	576.5	66,671	2,614.5	8,299	325.4
	2007	3,824	144.6	92,594	3,500.3	15,541	587.5	68,241	2,579.7	8,812	333.1
	Percent change	+7.4	+3.5	+3.3	-0.5	+5.7	+1.9	+2.4	-1.3	+6.2	+2.4
Wyoming	2006	1,013	196.7	15,350	2,980.6	2,320	450.5	12,254	2,379.4	776	150.7
	2007	991	189.5	14,984	2,865.9	2,348	449.1	11,840	2,264.6	796	152.2
	Percent change	-2.2	-3.6	-2.4	-3.8	+1.2	-0.3	-3.4	-4.8	+2.6	+1.0
Pacific[2]	2006	136,193	280.8	1,656,982	3,415.8	341,495	704.0	1,002,143	2,065.9	313,344	645.9
	2007	133,899	274.7	1,578,858	3,239.6	325,329	667.5	972,833	1,996.1	280,696	576.0
	Percent change	-1.7	-2.1	-4.7	-5.2	-4.7	-5.2	-2.9	-3.4	-10.4	-10.8
Alaska	2006	3,460	516.4	24,155	3,604.9	4,136	617.3	17,490	2,610.2	2,529	377.4
	2007	3,363	492.0	23,098	3,379.5	3,682	538.7	16,998	2,487.0	2,418	353.8
	Percent change	-2.8	-4.7	-4.4	-6.3	-11.0	-12.7	-2.8	-4.7	-4.4	-6.3

Note: Although arson data are included in the trend and clearance tables, sufficient data are not available to estimate totals for this offense. Therefore, no arson data are published in this table.

[2] The 2006 crime figures have been adjusted.

Table 4. Crime, by Region, Geographic Division, and State, 2006–2007 *(Contd.)*

(Number, rate per 100,000 population, percent.)

Area	Year	Population[1]	Violent crime		Murder and non-negligent manslaughter		Forcible rape		Robbery	
			Number	Rate	Number	Rate	Number	Rate	Number	Rate
California[2]	2006	36,457,549	194,119	532.5	2,484	6.8	9,212	25.3	70,968	194.7
	2007	36,553,215	191,025	522.6	2,260	6.2	9,013	24.7	70,542	193.0
	Percent change		-1.6	-1.9	-9.0	-9.3	-2.2	-2.4	-0.6	-0.9
Hawaii	2006	1,285,498	3,615	281.2	21	1.6	355	27.6	1,143	88.9
	2007	1,283,388	3,501	272.8	22	1.7	326	25.4	1,105	86.1
	Percent change		-3.2	-3.0	+4.8	+4.9	-8.2	-8.0	-3.3	-3.2
Oregon	2006	3,700,758	10,373	280.3	86	2.3	1,195	32.3	2,689	72.7
	2007	3,747,455	10,777	287.6	73	1.9	1,255	33.5	2,862	76.4
	Percent change		+3.9	+2.6	-15.1	-16.2	+5.0	+3.7	+6.4	+5.1
Washington	2006	6,395,798	22,120	345.9	190	3.0	2,746	42.9	6,405	100.1
	2007	6,468,424	21,546	333.1	173	2.7	2,629	40.6	6,053	93.6
	Percent change		-2.6	-3.7	-8.9	-10.0	-4.3	-5.3	-5.5	-6.6
Puerto Rico	2006	3,927,776	8,929	227.3	739	18.8	118	3.0	5,245	133.5
	2007	3,941,459	8,942	226.9	728	18.5	97	2.5	5,134	130.3
	Percent change		+0.1	-0.2	-1.5	-1.8	-17.8	-18.1	-2.1	-2.5

Note: Although arson data are included in the trend and clearance tables, sufficient data are not available to estimate totals for this offense. Therefore, no arson data are published in this table.
[1] Populations are U.S. Census Bureau provisional estimates as of July 1, 2007, and July 1, 2006.
[2] The 2006 crime figures have been adjusted.

Table 4.   Crime, by Region, Geographic Division, and State, 2006–2007 *(Contd.)*

(Number, rate per 100,000 population, percent.)

Area	Year	Aggravated assault		Property crime		Burglary		Larceny-theft		Motor vehicle theft	
		Number	Rate	Number	Rate	Number	Rate	Number	Rate	Number	Rate
California[2]	2006......................	111,455	305.7	1,156,017	3,170.9	246,464	676.0	666,860	1,829.1	242,693	665.7
	2007......................	109,210	298.8	1,108,660	3,033.0	237,025	648.4	652,243	1,784.4	219,392	600.2
	Percent change......	-2.0	-2.3	-4.1	-4.3	-3.8	-4.1	-2.2	-2.4	-9.6	-9.8
Hawaii	2006......................	2,096	163.0	54,382	4,230.4	8,709	677.5	37,910	2,949.1	7,763	603.9
	2007......................	2,048	159.6	54,228	4,225.4	9,097	708.8	38,416	2,993.3	6,715	523.2
	Percent change......	-2.3	-2.1	-0.3	-0.1	+4.5	+4.6	+1.3	+1.5	-13.5	-13.4
Oregon	2006......................	6,403	173.0	135,895	3,672.1	23,879	645.2	97,556	2,636.1	14,460	390.7
	2007......................	6,587	175.8	132,143	3,526.2	22,821	609.0	94,773	2,529.0	14,549	388.2
	Percent change......	+2.9	+1.6	-2.8	-4.0	-4.4	-5.6	-2.9	-4.1	+0.6	-0.6
Washington	2006......................	12,779	199.8	286,533	4,480.0	58,307	911.6	182,327	2,850.7	45,899	717.6
	2007......................	12,691	196.2	260,729	4,030.8	52,704	814.8	170,403	2,634.4	37,622	581.6
	Percent change......	-0.7	-1.8	-9.0	-10.0	-9.6	-10.6	-6.5	-7.6	-18.0	-19.0
Puerto Rico	2006......................	2,827	72.0	53,197	1,354.4	16,668	424.4	27,936	711.2	8,593	218.8
	2007......................	2,983	75.7	53,937	1,368.5	17,160	435.4	28,955	734.6	7,822	198.5
	Percent change......	+5.5	+5.2	+1.4	+1.0	+3.0	+2.6	+3.6	+3.3	-9.0	-9.3

[2] The 2006 crime figures have been adjusted.

Table 5.   Crime, by State and Area, 2007

(Number, percent, rate per 100,000 population.)

State	Area	Population	Violent crime	Murder and non-negligent man-slaughter	Forcible rape	Robbery	Aggravated assault	Property crime	Burglary	Larceny-theft	Motor vehicle theft
ALABAMA	Metropolitan Statistical Area..........	3,287,653									
	Area actually reporting..................	88.9%	14,985	325	1,031	6,199	7,430	133,325	33,003	89,311	11,011
	Estimated total...............................	100.0%	16,244	348	1,122	6,582	8,192	145,518	35,999	97,554	11,965
	Cities outside metropolitan areas ...	596,064									
	Area actually reporting..................	79.9%	2,701	41	190	588	1,882	22,925	4,915	16,836	1,174
	Estimated total...............................	100.0%	3,355	51	235	724	2,345	28,425	6,100	20,871	1,454
	Nonmetropolitan counties..............	744,134									
	Area actually reporting..................	93.1%	1,055	12	175	86	782	9,175	3,009	5,411	755
	Estimated total...............................	100.0%	1,133	13	188	92	840	9,855	3,232	5,812	811
	State Total....................................	4,627,851	20,732	412	1,545	7,398	11,377	183,798	45,331	124,237	14,230
	Rate per 100,000 inhabitants...........		448.0	8.9	33.4	159.9	245.8	3,971.6	979.5	2,684.6	307.5
ALASKA	Metropolitan Statistical Area..........	337,152									
	Area actually reporting..................	100.0%	2,801	27	308	501	1,965	13,750	1,810	10,414	1,526
	Cities outside metropolitan areas ...	122,393									
	Area actually reporting..................	87.0%	622	5	113	35	469	4,019	509	3,210	300
	Estimated total...............................	100.0%	715	6	130	40	539	4,620	585	3,690	345
	Nonmetropolitan counties..............	223,933									
	Area actually reporting..................	100.0%	1,003	11	91	42	859	4,728	1,287	2,894	547
	State Total....................................	683,478	4,519	44	529	583	3,363	23,098	3,682	16,998	2,418
	Rate per 100,000 inhabitants...........		661.2	6.4	77.4	85.3	492.0	3,379.5	538.7	2,487.0	353.8
ARIZONA	Metropolitan Statistical Area..........	5,866,030									
	Area actually reporting..................	98.1%	27,879	451	1,735	9,398	16,295	262,499	53,089	163,034	46,376
	Estimated total...............................	100.0%	28,272	455	1,763	9,504	16,550	267,026	54,115	165,928	46,983
	Cities outside metropolitan areas ...	200,991									
	Area actually reporting..................	90.3%	915	8	51	73	783	7,155	1,645	4,848	662
	Estimated total...............................	100.0%	1,013	9	56	81	867	7,925	1,822	5,370	733
	Nonmetropolitan counties..............	271,734									
	Area actually reporting..................	75.4%	991	3	28	25	935	3,650	1,423	1,720	507
	Estimated total...............................	100.0%	1,315	4	37	33	1,241	4,843	1,888	2,282	673
	State Total....................................	6,338,755	30,600	468	1,856	9,618	18,658	279,794	57,825	173,580	48,389
	Rate per 100,000 inhabitants...........		482.7	7.4	29.3	151.7	294.3	4,414.0	912.2	2,738.4	763.4
ARKANSAS	Metropolitan Statistical Area..........	1,678,066									
	Area actually reporting..................	97.6%	11,008	142	866	2,556	7,444	77,783	21,267	51,318	5,198
	Estimated total...............................	100.0%	11,146	143	879	2,571	7,553	78,826	21,631	51,923	5,272
	Cities outside metropolitan areas ...	496,464									
	Area actually reporting	97.5%	2,598	28	234	383	1,953	22,372	6,806	14,634	932
	Estimated total...............................	100.0%	2,666	29	240	393	2,004	22,951	6,982	15,013	956
	Nonmetropolitan counties..............	660,267									
	Area actually reporting..................	89.4%	1,068	17	133	54	864	9,193	3,092	5,402	699
	Estimated total...............................	100.0%	1,195	19	149	60	967	10,284	3,459	6,043	782
	State Total....................................	2,834,797	15,007	191	1,268	3,024	10,524	112,061	32,072	72,979	7,010
	Rate per 100,000 inhabitants...........		529.4	6.7	44.7	106.7	371.2	3,953.1	1,131.4	2,574.4	247.3
CALIFORNIA	Metropolitan Statistical Area..........	35,709,515									
	Area actually reporting..................	100.0%	187,861	2,230	8,720	70,239	106,672	1,090,484	231,611	641,384	217,489
	Cities outside metropolitan areas ...	271,704									
	Area actually reporting..................	100.0%	1,413	14	127	179	1,093	9,310	2,372	6,151	787
	Nonmetropolitan counties..............	571,996									
	Area actually reporting..................	100.0%	1,751	16	166	124	1,445	8,866	3,042	4,708	1,116
	State Total....................................	36,553,215	191,025	2,260	9,013	70,542	109,210	1,108,660	237,025	652,243	219,392
	Rate per 100,000 inhabitants...........		522.6	6.2	24.7	193.0	298.8	3,033.0	648.4	1,784.4	600.2
COLORADO	Metropolitan Statistical Area..........	4,187,300									
	Area actually reporting..................	97.8%	14,950	137	1,760	3,309	9,744	128,489	25,660	87,127	15,702
	Estimated total...............................	100.0%	15,191	139	1,794	3,357	9,901	131,549	26,166	89,363	16,020
	Cities outside metropolitan areas ...	304,013									
	Area actually reporting..................	93.8%	1,084	9	140	76	859	10,250	1,609	8,200	441
	Estimated total...............................	100.0%	1,156	10	149	81	916	10,932	1,716	8,746	470
	Nonmetropolitan counties..............	370,202									
	Area actually reporting..................	95.1%	531	4	52	14	461	3,479	826	2,366	287
	Estimated total...............................	100.0%	559	4	55	15	485	3,660	869	2,489	302
	State Total....................................	4,861,515	16,906	153	1,998	3,453	11,302	146,141	28,751	100,598	16,792
	Rate per 100,000 inhabitants...........		347.8	3.1	41.1	71.0	232.5	3,006.1	591.4	2,069.3	345.4
CONNECTICUT	Metropolitan Statistical Area..........	2,824,885									
	Area actually reporting..................	100.0%	8,231	89	536	3,439	4,167	76,390	13,152	54,737	8,501
	Cities outside metropolitan areas ...	159,553									
	Area actually reporting..................	100.0%	247	2	31	74	140	2,861	607	2,019	235
	Nonmetropolitan counties..............	517,871									
	Area actually reporting..................	100.0%	487	15	91	94	287	4,801	1,403	2,967	431
	State Total....................................	3,502,309	8,965	106	658	3,607	4,594	84,052	15,162	59,723	9,167
	Rate per 100,000 inhabitants...........		256.0	3.0	18.8	103.0	131.2	2,399.9	432.9	1,705.2	261.7

Note: Although arson data are included in the trend and clearance tables, sufficient data are not available to estimate totals for this offense. Therefore, no arson data are published in this table.

Table 5.   Crime, by State and Area, 2007 *(Contd.)*

(Number, percent, rate per 100,000 population.)

State	Area	Population	Violent crime	Murder and non-negligent man-slaughter	Forcible rape	Robbery	Aggravated assault	Property crime	Burglary	Larceny-theft	Motor vehicle theft
DELAWARE	Metropolitan Statistical Area..........	680,718									
	Area actually reporting...................	98.4%	4,741	32	246	1,472	2,991	23,010	4,613	16,363	2,034
	Estimated total..............................	100.0%	4,813	32	250	1,492	3,039	23,507	4,703	16,743	2,061
	Cities outside metropolitan areas ...	40,467									
	Area actually reporting...................	100.0%	416	2	25	119	270	2,147	482	1,606	59
	Nonmetropolitan counties...............	143,579									
	Area actually reporting...................	100.0%	731	3	61	95	572	3,489	1,156	2,137	196
	State Total...................................	864,764	5,960	37	336	1,706	3,881	29,143	6,341	20,486	2,316
	Rate per 100,000 inhabitants..........		689.2	4.3	38.9	197.3	448.8	3,370.1	733.3	2,369.0	267.8
DISTRICT OF COLUMBIA[1]	Metropolitan Statistical Area..........	588,292									
	Area actually reporting...................	100.0%	8,320	181	192	4,261	3,686	28,908	3,926	17,382	7,600
	Cities outside metropolitan areas ...	None									
	Nonmetropolitan counties...............	None									
	Total	588,292	8,320	181	192	4,261	3,686	28,908	3,926	17,382	7,600
	Rate per 100,000 inhabitants..........		1,414.3	30.8	32.6	724.3	626.6	4,913.9	667.4	2,954.7	1,291.9
FLORIDA	Metropolitan Statistical Area..........	17,180,667									
	Area actually reporting...................	99.9%	125,870	1,142	5,812	37,477	81,439	715,291	172,079	471,775	71,437
	Estimated total..............................	100.0%	126,008	1,142	5,818	37,524	81,524	716,225	172,284	472,417	71,524
	Cities outside metropolitan areas ...	184,643									
	Area actually reporting...................	97.7%	1,907	9	100	306	1,492	9,030	2,245	6,244	541
	Estimated total..............................	100.0%	1,951	9	102	313	1,527	9,243	2,298	6,391	554
	Nonmetropolitan counties...............	885,933									
	Area actually reporting...................	99.1%	3,887	50	229	322	3,286	20,694	7,187	11,943	1,564
	Estimated total..............................	100.0%	3,921	50	231	325	3,315	20,879	7,251	12,050	1,578
	State Total...................................	18,251,243	131,880	1,201	6,151	38,162	86,366	746,347	181,833	490,858	73,656
	Rate per 100,000 inhabitants..........		722.6	6.6	33.7	209.1	473.2	4,089.3	996.3	2,689.4	403.6
GEORGIA	Metropolitan Statistical Area..........	7,760,436									
	Area actually reporting...................	98.5%	39,218	632	1,748	15,936	20,902	308,050	75,462	193,880	38,708
	Estimated total..............................	100.0%	39,753	638	1,773	16,136	21,206	312,629	76,491	196,926	39,212
	Cities outside metropolitan areas ...	664,213									
	Area actually reporting...................	82.6%	3,955	38	216	802	2,899	29,282	6,022	22,055	1,205
	Estimated total..............................	100.0%	4,788	46	262	970	3,510	35,438	7,285	26,695	1,458
	Nonmetropolitan counties...............	1,120,101									
	Area actually reporting...................	85.8%	2,175	29	123	201	1,822	20,833	5,934	13,248	1,651
	Estimated total..............................	100.0%	2,534	34	143	234	2,123	24,275	6,914	15,437	1,924
	State Total...................................	9,544,750	47,075	718	2,178	17,340	26,839	372,342	90,690	239,058	42,594
	Rate per 100,000 inhabitants..........		493.2	7.5	22.8	181.7	281.2	3,901.0	950.2	2,504.6	446.3
HAWAII	Metropolitan Statistical Area..........	905,903									
	Area actually reporting...................	100.0%	2,613	19	226	943	1,425	37,197	5,777	26,483	4,937
	Cities outside metropolitan areas ...	None									
	Nonmetropolitan counties...............	377,485									
	Area actually reporting...................	100.0%	888	3	100	162	623	17,031	3,320	11,933	1,778
	State Total...................................	1,283,388	3,501	22	326	1,105	2,048	54,228	9,097	38,416	6,715
	Rate per 100,000 inhabitants..........		272.8	1.7	25.4	86.1	159.6	4,225.4	708.8	2,993.3	523.2
IDAHO	Metropolitan Statistical Area..........	979,999									
	Area actually reporting...................	100.0%	2,630	24	442	190	1,974	24,952	5,016	18,229	1,707
	Cities outside metropolitan areas ...	233,900									
	Area actually reporting...................	99.3%	506	7	61	27	411	5,500	1,141	4,084	275
	Estimated total..............................	100.0%	509	7	61	27	414	5,538	1,149	4,112	277
	Nonmetropolitan counties...............	285,503									
	Area actually reporting...................	100.0%	450	18	75	16	341	3,195	812	2,141	242
	State Total...................................	1,499,402	3,589	49	578	233	2,729	33,685	6,977	24,482	2,226
	Rate per 100,000 inhabitants..........		239.4	3.3	38.5	15.5	182.0	2,246.6	465.3	1,632.8	148.5
ILLINOIS[2,3]	State Total...................................	12,852,548	68,528	752	4,103	23,100	40,573	377,322	75,524	267,911	33,887
	Rate per 100,000 inhabitants..........		533.2	5.9	31.9	179.7	315.7	2,935.8	587.6	2,084.5	263.7
INDIANA	Metropolitan Statistical Area..........	4,946,193									
	Area actually reporting...................	88.8%	18,785	312	1,379	7,364	9,730	170,210	37,499	115,911	16,800
	Estimated total..............................	100.0%	19,538	323	1,450	7,560	10,205	181,836	39,817	124,301	17,718
	Cities outside metropolitan areas ...	503,396									
	Area actually reporting...................	84.5%	803	8	120	213	462	18,895	3,355	14,589	951
	Estimated total..............................	100.0%	950	9	142	252	547	22,364	3,971	17,267	1,126
	Nonmetropolitan counties...............	895,700									
	Area actually reporting...................	61.3%	416	15	92	37	272	6,945	1,920	4,588	437
	Estimated total..............................	100.0%	677	24	150	60	443	11,326	3,131	7,482	713
	State Total...................................	6,345,289	21,165	356	1,742	7,872	11,195	215,526	46,919	149,050	19,557
	Rate per 100,000 inhabitants..........		333.6	5.6	27.5	124.1	176.4	3,396.6	739.4	2,349.0	308.2

Note: Although arson data are included in the trend and clearance tables, sufficient data are not available to estimate totals for this offense. Therefore, no arson data are published in this table.

[1] Includes offenses reported by the Zoological Police and the Metro Transit Police.

[2] Limited data for 2007 were available for Illinois.

[3] The data collection methodology for the offense of forcible rape used by the Illinois and the Minnesota state UCR Programs (with the exception of Rockford, Illinois, and Minneapolis and St. Paul, Minnesota) does not comply with national UCR guidelines. Consequently, their state figures for forcible rape (with the exception of Rockford, Illinois, and Minneapolis and St. Paul, Minnesota) have been estimated for inclusion in this table.

Table 5. Crime, by State and Area, 2007 *(Contd.)*

(Number, percent, rate per 100,000 population.)

State	Area	Population	Violent crime	Murder and non-negligent man-slaughter	Forcible rape	Robbery	Aggravated assault	Property crime	Burglary	Larceny-theft	Motor vehicle theft
IOWA	Metropolitan Statistical Area	1,655,199									
	Area actually reporting	98.8%	6,279	26	654	1,130	4,469	54,703	11,219	39,909	3,575
	Estimated total	100.0%	6,317	26	658	1,134	4,499	55,171	11,296	40,279	3,596
	Cities outside metropolitan areas	593,280									
	Area actually reporting	93.1%	1,830	8	176	159	1,487	16,843	3,643	12,349	851
	Estimated total	100.0%	1,966	9	189	171	1,597	18,092	3,913	13,265	914
	Nonmetropolitan counties	739,567									
	Area actually reporting	95.2%	497	2	54	8	433	4,657	1,649	2,651	357
	Estimated total	100.0%	522	2	57	8	455	4,891	1,732	2,784	375
	State Total	2,988,046	8,805	37	904	1,313	6,551	78,154	16,941	56,328	4,885
	Rate per 100,000 inhabitants		294.7	1.2	30.3	43.9	219.2	2,615.6	567.0	1,885.1	163.5
KANSAS	Metropolitan Statistical Area	1,770,487									
	Area actually reporting	99.3%	8,835	82	789	1,747	6,217	71,193	13,336	50,815	7,042
	Estimated total	100.0%	8,877	82	793	1,752	6,250	71,572	13,394	51,111	7,067
	Cities outside metropolitan areas	594,489									
	Area actually reporting	95.1%	2,603	14	299	216	2,074	22,562	4,583	16,975	1,004
	Estimated total	100.0%	2,737	15	314	227	2,181	23,725	4,819	17,850	1,056
	Nonmetropolitan counties	411,021									
	Area actually reporting	98.7%	940	10	122	37	771	6,733	2,023	4,275	435
	Estimated total	100.0%	952	10	124	37	781	6,823	2,050	4,332	441
	State Total	2,775,997	12,566	107	1,231	2,016	9,212	102,120	20,263	73,293	8,564
	Rate per 100,000 inhabitants		452.7	3.9	44.3	72.6	331.8	3,678.7	729.9	2,640.2	308.5
KENTUCKY	Metropolitan Statistical Area	2,413,353									
	Area actually reporting	95.3%	9,349	123	683	3,457	5,086	71,274	17,037	48,239	5,998
	Estimated total	100.0%	9,632	124	714	3,551	5,243	74,138	17,676	50,272	6,190
	Cities outside metropolitan areas	522,435									
	Area actually reporting	88.3%	1,072	10	148	277	637	14,134	3,042	10,343	749
	Estimated total	100.0%	1,215	11	168	314	722	16,013	3,446	11,718	849
	Nonmetropolitan counties	1,305,686									
	Area actually reporting	87.6%	1,467	68	437	179	783	14,595	5,747	7,415	1,433
	Estimated total	100.0%	1,666	69	499	204	894	16,662	6,561	8,465	1,636
	State Total	4,241,474	12,513	204	1,381	4,069	6,859	106,813	27,683	70,455	8,675
	Rate per 100,000 inhabitants		295.0	4.8	32.6	95.9	161.7	2,518.3	652.7	1,661.1	204.5
LOUISIANA	Metropolitan Statistical Area	3,157,645									
	Area actually reporting	97.0%	23,693	526	1,054	5,382	16,731	136,917	34,187	89,571	13,159
	Estimated total	100.0%	24,288	534	1,086	5,466	17,202	141,187	35,024	92,736	13,427
	Cities outside metropolitan areas	386,025									
	Area actually reporting	56.8%	1,883	16	68	214	1,585	9,892	2,437	7,052	403
	Estimated total	100.0%	3,273	28	118	372	2,755	17,312	4,287	12,324	701
	Nonmetropolitan counties	749,534									
	Area actually reporting	85.7%	3,217	39	162	210	2,806	14,126	4,532	8,693	901
	Estimated total	100.0%	3,756	46	189	245	3,276	16,492	5,291	10,149	1,052
	State Total	4,293,204	31,317	608	1,393	6,083	23,233	174,991	44,602	115,209	15,180
	Rate per 100,000 inhabitants		729.5	14.2	32.4	141.7	541.2	4,076.0	1,038.9	2,683.5	353.6
MAINE	Metropolitan Statistical Area	766,722									
	Area actually reporting	100.0%	943	13	208	280	442	20,107	4,001	15,261	845
	Cities outside metropolitan areas	277,589									
	Area actually reporting	100.0%	451	3	127	57	264	8,172	1,463	6,489	220
	Nonmetropolitan counties	272,896									
	Area actually reporting	100.0%	160	5	56	12	87	3,713	1,212	2,307	194
	State Total	1,317,207	1,554	21	391	349	793	31,992	6,676	24,057	1,259
	Rate per 100,000 inhabitants		118.0	1.6	29.7	26.5	60.2	2,428.8	506.8	1,826.4	95.6
MARYLAND	Metropolitan Statistical Area	5,319,855									
	Area actually reporting	100.0%	34,906	546	1,103	13,044	20,213	184,165	35,066	121,111	27,988
	Cities outside metropolitan areas	77,469									
	Area actually reporting	100.0%	506	3	37	130	336	4,236	739	3,369	128
	Nonmetropolitan counties	221,020									
	Area actually reporting	100.0%	650	4	39	84	523	4,395	1,290	2,828	277
	State Total	5,618,344	36,062	553	1,179	13,258	21,072	192,796	37,095	127,308	28,393
	Rate per 100,000 inhabitants		641.9	9.8	21.0	236.0	375.1	3,431.5	660.2	2,265.9	505.4
MASSACHUSETTS	Metropolitan Statistical Area	6,423,818									
	Area actually reporting	98.6%	27,550	183	1,613	6,954	18,800	152,065	35,135	102,096	14,834
	Estimated total	100.0%	27,799	184	1,631	7,003	18,981	153,805	35,570	103,262	14,973
	Cities outside metropolitan areas	24,883									
	Area actually reporting	58.4%	20	0	2	2	16	258	54	193	11
	Estimated total	100.0%	33	0	3	3	27	441	92	330	19
	Nonmetropolitan counties	1,054									
	Area actually reporting	100.0%	0	0	0	0	0	0	0	0	0
	State Total	6,449,755	27,832	184	1,634	7,006	19,008	154,246	35,662	103,592	14,992
	Rate per 100,000 inhabitants		431.5	2.9	25.3	108.6	294.7	2,391.5	552.9	1,606.1	232.4

Note: Although arson data are included in the trend and clearance tables, sufficient data are not available to estimate totals for this offense. Therefore, no arson data are published in this table.

Table 5. Crime, by State and Area, 2007 *(Contd.)*

(Number, percent, rate per 100,000 population.)

State	Area	Population	Violent crime	Murder and non-negligent man-slaughter	Forcible rape	Robbery	Aggravated assault	Property crime	Burglary	Larceny-theft	Motor vehicle theft
MICHIGAN	Metropolitan Statistical Area.........	8,199,839									
	Area actually reporting...................	98.9%	49,735	635	3,397	13,144	32,559	266,389	65,383	160,764	40,242
	Estimated total................................	100.0%	50,027	636	3,427	13,209	32,755	269,119	65,902	162,695	40,522
	Cities outside metropolitan areas ...	645,093									
	Area actually reporting...................	91.9%	1,483	10	344	124	1,005	18,140	2,772	14,824	544
	Estimated total................................	100.0%	1,580	11	366	131	1,072	19,436	2,974	15,874	588
	Nonmetropolitan counties..............	1,226,890									
	Area actually reporting...................	99.3%	2,363	29	780	73	1,481	20,071	6,504	12,534	1,033
	Estimated total................................	100.0%	2,381	29	786	74	1,492	20,220	6,552	12,627	1,041
	State Total......................................	10,071,822	53,988	676	4,579	13,414	35,319	308,775	75,428	191,196	42,151
	Rate per 100,000 inhabitants..........		536.0	6.7	45.5	133.2	350.7	3,065.7	748.9	1,898.3	418.5
MINNESOTA[3]	Metropolitan Statistical Area.........	3,781,574									
	Area actually reporting...................	96.4%	12,106	96	625	4,555	6,830	123,822	22,884	90,385	10,553
	Estimated total................................	100.0%	12,306	98	625	4,623	6,960	128,390	23,555	94,012	10,823
	Cities outside metropolitan areas ...	565,183									
	Area actually reporting...................	99.3%		6		112	688	18,332	2,786	14,736	810
	Estimated total................................	100.0%		6		113	693	18,462	2,806	14,840	816
	Nonmetropolitan counties..............	850,864									
	Area actually reporting...................	99.3%		12		34	587	10,896	3,285	6,731	880
	Estimated total................................	100.0%		12		34	591	10,977	3,309	6,781	887
	State Total......................................	5,197,621	15,003	116	1,873	4,770	8,244	157,829	29,670	115,633	12,526
	Rate per 100,000 inhabitants..........		288.7	2.2	36.0	91.8	158.6	3,036.6	570.8	2,224.7	241.0
MISSISSIPPI	Metropolitan Statistical Area.........	1,274,426									
	Area actually reporting...................	79.0%	3,651	89	382	1,630	1,550	42,370	11,583	26,770	4,017
	Estimated total................................	100.0%	4,181	103	446	1,756	1,876	49,868	13,548	31,666	4,654
	Cities outside metropolitan areas ...	594,355									
	Area actually reporting...................	81.1%	1,924	48	251	641	984	21,902	6,363	14,455	1,084
	Estimated total................................	100.0%	2,371	59	309	790	1,213	26,990	7,841	17,813	1,336
	Nonmetropolitan counties..............	1,050,004									
	Area actually reporting...................	45.3%	884	21	129	145	589	7,512	2,979	3,902	631
	Estimated total................................	100.0%	1,950	46	285	320	1,299	16,566	6,570	8,605	1,391
	State Total......................................	2,918,785	8,502	208	1,040	2,866	4,388	93,424	27,959	58,084	7,381
	Rate per 100,000 inhabitants..........		291.3	7.1	35.6	98.2	150.3	3,200.8	957.9	1,990.0	252.9
MISSOURI	Metropolitan Statistical Area.........	4,306,270									
	Area actually reporting...................	99.9%	24,540	346	1,414	6,833	15,947	178,559	34,641	122,303	21,615
	Estimated total................................	100.0%	24,549	346	1,415	6,835	15,953	178,661	34,657	122,380	21,624
	Cities outside metropolitan areas ...	687,617									
	Area actually reporting...................	98.7%	2,954	18	149	285	2,502	28,311	4,722	22,472	1,117
	Estimated total................................	100.0%	2,994	18	151	289	2,536	28,696	4,786	22,778	1,132
	Nonmetropolitan counties..............	884,528									
	Area actually reporting...................	100.0%	2,139	21	148	41	1,929	12,402	4,003	7,371	1,028
	State Total......................................	5,878,415	29,682	385	1,714	7,165	20,418	219,759	43,446	152,529	23,784
	Rate per 100,000 inhabitants..........		504.9	6.5	29.2	121.9	347.3	3,738.4	739.1	2,594.7	404.6
MONTANA	Metropolitan Statistical Area.........	333,341									
	Area actually reporting...................	99.8%	881	5	83	125	668	12,078	1,215	10,143	720
	Estimated total................................	100.0%	883	5	83	125	670	12,104	1,216	10,167	721
	Cities outside metropolitan areas ...	202,745									
	Area actually reporting...................	93.9%	698	0	88	37	573	7,270	645	6,182	443
	Estimated total................................	100.0%	743	0	94	39	610	7,741	687	6,582	472
	Nonmetropolitan counties..............	421,775									
	Area actually reporting...................	96.4%	1,088	9	109	26	944	6,404	1,083	4,779	542
	Estimated total................................	100.0%	1,128	9	113	27	979	6,644	1,124	4,958	562
	State Total......................................	957,861	2,754	14	290	191	2,259	26,489	3,027	21,707	1,755
	Rate per 100,000 inhabitants..........		287.5	1.5	30.3	19.9	235.8	2,765.4	316.0	2,266.2	183.2
NEBRASKA	Metropolitan Statistical Area.........	1,020,285									
	Area actually reporting...................	100.0%	4,252	52	343	1,037	2,820	39,278	6,325	28,619	4,334
	Cities outside metropolitan areas ...	396,873									
	Area actually reporting...................	88.1%	745	8	124	56	557	11,607	1,672	9,392	543
	Estimated total................................	100.0%	847	9	141	64	633	13,182	1,899	10,666	617
	Nonmetropolitan counties..............	357,413									
	Area actually reporting...................	86.2%	231	6	37	6	182	3,141	709	2,216	216
	Estimated total................................	100.0%	268	7	43	7	211	3,642	822	2,570	250
	State Total......................................	1,774,571	5,367	68	527	1,108	3,664	56,102	9,046	41,855	5,201
	Rate per 100,000 inhabitants..........		302.4	3.8	29.7	62.4	206.5	3,161.4	509.8	2,358.6	293.1
NEVADA	Metropolitan Statistical Area.........	2,298,734									
	Area actually reporting...................	100.0%	18,590	180	989	6,872	10,549	92,055	23,375	46,777	21,903
	Cities outside metropolitan areas ...	46,510									
	Area actually reporting...................	100.0%	150	2	25	15	108	1,273	275	910	88
	Nonmetropolitan counties..............	220,138									
	Area actually reporting...................	100.0%	517	10	82	45	380	3,588	1,190	2,058	340
	State Total......................................	2,565,382	19,257	192	1,096	6,932	11,037	96,916	24,840	49,745	22,331
	Rate per 100,000 inhabitants..........		750.6	7.5	42.7	270.2	430.2	3,777.8	968.3	1,939.1	870.5

Note: Although arson data are included in the trend and clearance tables, sufficient data are not available to estimate totals for this offense. Therefore, no arson data are published in this table.

[3] The data collection methodology for the offense of forcible rape used by the Illinois and the Minnesota state UCR Programs (with the exception of Rockford, Illinois, and Minneapolis and St. Paul, Minnesota) does not comply with national UCR guidelines. Consequently, their state figures for forcible rape (with the exception of Rockford, Illinois, and Minneapolis and St. Paul, Minnesota) have been estimated for inclusion in this table.

Table 5.   Crime, by State and Area, 2007 *(Contd.)*

(Number, percent, rate per 100,000 population.)

State	Area	Population	Violent crime	Murder and non-negligent man-slaughter	Forcible rape	Robbery	Aggravated assault	Property crime	Burglary	Larceny-theft	Motor vehicle theft
NEW HAMPSHIRE	Metropolitan Statistical Area.........	819,370									
	Area actually reporting....................	89.5%	1,035	10	143	320	562	14,238	2,998	10,416	824
	Estimated total.................................	100.0%	1,109	10	158	333	608	15,472	3,252	11,330	890
	Cities outside metropolitan areas ...	448,370									
	Area actually reporting....................	88.6%	582	4	144	88	346	8,115	1,416	6,348	351
	Estimated total.................................	100.0%	658	5	163	99	391	9,163	1,599	7,168	396
	Nonmetropolitan counties..............	48,088									
	Area actually reporting....................	2.3%	13	0	6	0	7	48	11	34	3
	Estimated total.................................	100.0%	40	0	12	0	28	261	135	113	13
	State Total..	1,315,828	1,807	15	333	432	1,027	24,896	4,986	18,611	1,299
	Rate per 100,000 inhabitants..........		137.3	1.1	25.3	32.8	78.0	1,892.0	378.9	1,414.4	98.7
NEW JERSEY	Metropolitan Statistical Area.........	8,685,920									
	Area actually reporting....................	100.0%	28,601	380	1,050	12,549	14,622	192,226	37,482	132,791	21,953
	Cities outside metropolitan areas ...	None									
	Nonmetropolitan counties..............	None									
	State Total..	8,685,920	28,601	380	1,050	12,549	14,622	192,226	37,482	132,791	21,953
	Rate per 100,000 inhabitants..........		329.3	4.4	12.1	144.5	168.3	2,213.1	431.5	1,528.8	252.7
NEW MEXICO	Metropolitan Statistical Area.........	1,295,736									
	Area actually reporting....................	99.6%	9,234	98	692	1,983	6,461	50,393	11,938	31,109	7,346
	Estimated total.................................	100.0%	9,262	98	694	1,985	6,485	50,542	11,976	31,202	7,364
	Cities outside metropolitan areas ...	399,358									
	Area actually reporting....................	88.1%	2,377	32	206	243	1,896	15,584	4,160	10,507	917
	Estimated total.................................	100.0%	2,697	36	234	276	2,151	17,681	4,720	11,921	1,040
	Nonmetropolitan counties..............	274,821									
	Area actually reporting....................	85.5%	962	24	89	51	798	4,419	1,962	2,000	457
	Estimated total.................................	100.0%	1,126	28	104	60	934	5,171	2,296	2,340	535
	State Total..	1,969,915	13,085	162	1,032	2,321	9,570	73,394	18,992	45,463	8,939
	Rate per 100,000 inhabitants..........		664.2	8.2	52.4	117.8	485.8	3,725.7	964.1	2,307.9	453.8
NEW YORK	Metropolitan Statistical Area.........	17,742,225									
	Area actually reporting....................	99.6%	76,431	781	2,454	30,771	42,425	350,043	57,739	265,282	27,022
	Estimated total.................................	100.0%	76,567	782	2,462	30,817	42,506	351,466	57,957	266,422	27,087
	Cities outside metropolitan areas ...	572,570									
	Area actually reporting....................	95.8%	1,379	5	136	204	1,034	15,708	2,767	12,507	434
	Estimated total.................................	100.0%	1,439	5	142	213	1,079	16,391	2,887	13,051	453
	Nonmetropolitan counties..............	982,934									
	Area actually reporting....................	100.0%	1,909	14	322	64	1,509	13,959	4,013	9,456	490
	State Total..	19,297,729	79,915	801	2,926	31,094	45,094	381,816	64,857	288,929	28,030
	Rate per 100,000 inhabitants..........		414.1	4.2	15.2	161.1	233.7	1,978.6	336.1	1,497.2	145.3
NORTH CAROLINA	Metropolitan Statistical Area.........	6,310,791									
	Area actually reporting....................	96.2%	31,040	428	1,688	11,068	17,856	265,631	74,930	169,440	21,261
	Estimated total.................................	100.0%	31,671	437	1,736	11,205	18,293	272,971	77,172	174,050	21,749
	Cities outside metropolitan areas ...	844,934									
	Area actually reporting....................	94.7%	5,690	72	267	1,597	3,754	47,673	12,726	32,599	2,348
	Estimated total.................................	100.0%	5,992	76	281	1,680	3,955	50,228	13,402	34,355	2,471
	Nonmetropolitan counties..............	1,905,307									
	Area actually reporting....................	95.7%	4,400	69	352	634	3,345	45,125	17,441	24,099	3,585
	Estimated total.................................	100.0%	4,599	72	368	663	3,496	47,155	18,226	25,183	3,746
	State Total..	9,061,032	42,262	585	2,385	13,548	25,744	370,354	108,800	233,588	27,966
	Rate per 100,000 inhabitants..........		466.4	6.5	26.3	149.5	284.1	4,087.3	1,200.7	2,577.9	308.6
NORTH DAKOTA	Metropolitan Statistical Area.........	303,244									
	Area actually reporting....................	99.6%	583	5	147	55	376	7,773	1,348	5,846	579
	Estimated total.................................	100.0%	584	5	147	55	377	7,808	1,353	5,873	582
	Cities outside metropolitan areas ...	136,301									
	Area actually reporting....................	90.9%	200	5	38	9	148	2,725	441	2,099	185
	Estimated total.................................	100.0%	220	5	42	10	163	2,996	485	2,308	203
	Nonmetropolitan counties..............	200,170									
	Area actually reporting....................	88.1%	94	2	16	4	72	1,131	287	730	114
	Estimated total.................................	100.0%	107	2	18	5	82	1,284	326	829	129
	State Total..	639,715	911	12	207	70	622	12,088	2,164	9,010	914
	Rate per 100,000 inhabitants..........		142.4	1.9	32.4	10.9	97.2	1,889.6	338.3	1,408.4	142.9
OHIO	Metropolitan Statistical Area.........	9,236,831									
	Area actually reporting....................	86.6%	34,902	458	3,513	16,984	13,947	309,748	79,197	200,917	29,634
	Estimated total.................................	100.0%	36,735	477	3,829	17,647	14,782	341,193	85,587	224,220	31,386
	Cities outside metropolitan areas ...	919,500									
	Area actually reporting....................	79.7%	1,276	17	298	396	565	27,180	5,034	21,260	886
	Estimated total.................................	100.0%	1,601	21	374	497	709	34,122	6,320	26,690	1,112
	Nonmetropolitan counties..............	1,310,586									
	Area actually reporting....................	82.1%	840	15	204	95	526	17,159	5,421	10,686	1,052
	Estimated total.................................	100.0%	1,024	18	249	116	641	20,894	6,601	13,012	1,281
	State Total..	11,466,917	39,360	516	4,452	18,260	16,132	396,209	98,508	263,922	33,779
	Rate per 100,000 inhabitants..........		343.2	4.5	38.8	159.2	140.7	3,455.2	859.1	2,301.6	294.6

Note: Although arson data are included in the trend and clearance tables, sufficient data are not available to estimate totals for this offense. Therefore, no arson data are published in this table.

Table 5.   Crime, by State and Area, 2007 *(Contd.)*

(Number, percent, rate per 100,000 population.)

State	Area	Population	Violent crime	Murder and non-negligent man-slaughter	Forcible rape	Robbery	Aggravated assault	Property crime	Burglary	Larceny-theft	Motor vehicle theft
OKLAHOMA	Metropolitan Statistical Area..........	2,299,419									
	Area actually reporting...................	100.0%	13,667	159	1,111	3,013	9,384	92,267	24,521	56,571	11,175
	Cities outside metropolitan areas ...	698,837									
	Area actually reporting...................	100.0%	3,095	33	324	327	2,411	27,298	6,731	19,064	1,503
	Nonmetropolitan counties..............	619,060									
	Area actually reporting...................	100.0%	1,310	30	124	33	1,123	7,997	2,869	4,347	781
	State Total........................	3,617,316	18,072	222	1,559	3,373	12,918	127,562	34,121	79,982	13,459
	Rate per 100,000 inhabitants..........		499.6	6.1	43.1	93.2	357.1	3,526.4	943.3	2,211.1	372.1
OREGON	Metropolitan Statistical Area..........	2,901,737									
	Area actually reporting...................	99.0%	8,894	48	987	2,569	5,290	105,864	17,377	75,835	12,652
	Estimated total.............................	100.0%	8,941	48	994	2,578	5,321	106,519	17,506	76,291	12,722
	Cities outside metropolitan areas ...	390,400									
	Area actually reporting...................	97.8%	1,188	13	153	217	805	16,936	2,728	13,169	1,039
	Estimated total.............................	100.0%	1,214	13	156	222	823	17,315	2,789	13,464	1,062
	Nonmetropolitan counties..............	455,318									
	Area actually reporting...................	93.7%	582	11	98	58	415	7,783	2,366	4,700	717
	Estimated total.............................	100.0%	622	12	105	62	443	8,309	2,526	5,018	765
	State Total........................	3,747,455	10,777	73	1,255	2,862	6,587	132,143	22,821	94,773	14,549
	Rate per 100,000 inhabitants..........		287.6	1.9	33.5	76.4	175.8	3,526.2	609.0	2,529.0	388.2
PENNSYLVANIA	Metropolitan Statistical Area..........	10,441,953									
	Area actually reporting...................	97.5%	46,597	684	2,714	18,772	24,427	253,280	47,122	181,674	24,484
	Estimated total.............................	100.0%	47,189	688	2,750	18,933	24,818	258,578	47,925	185,860	24,793
	Cities outside metropolitan areas ...	916,386									
	Area actually reporting...................	93.3%	2,258	13	216	336	1,693	18,737	3,176	14,904	657
	Estimated total.............................	100.0%	2,421	14	232	360	1,815	20,087	3,405	15,978	704
	Nonmetropolitan counties..............	1,074,453									
	Area actually reporting...................	100.0%	2,172	21	468	165	1,518	14,912	4,690	9,258	964
	State Total........................	12,432,792	51,782	723	3,450	19,458	28,151	293,577	56,020	211,096	26,461
	Rate per 100,000 inhabitants..........		416.5	5.8	27.7	156.5	226.4	2,361.3	450.6	1,697.9	212.8
PUERTO RICO	Metropolitan Statistical Area..........	3,617,415									
	Area actually reporting...................	100.0%	8,597	709	94	5,001	2,793	50,864	15,744	27,485	7,635
	Cities outside metropolitan areas ...	324,044									
	Area actually reporting...................	100.0%	345	19	3	133	190	3,073	1,416	1,470	187
	Total	3,941,459	8,942	728	97	5,134	2,983	53,937	17,160	28,955	7,822
	Rate per 100,000 inhabitants..........		226.9	18.5	2.5	130.3	75.7	1,368.5	435.4	734.6	198.5
RHODE ISLAND	Metropolitan Statistical Area..........	1,057,832									
	Area actually reporting...................	100.0%	2,393	18	251	751	1,373	27,706	5,233	19,254	3,219
	Cities outside metropolitan areas ...	None									
	Nonmetropolitan counties..............	None									
	Area actually reporting...................	100.0%	11	1	5	0	5	37	3	27	7
	State Total........................	1,057,832	2,404	19	256	751	1,378	27,743	5,236	19,281	3,226
	Rate per 100,000 inhabitants..........		227.3	1.8	24.2	71.0	130.3	2,622.6	495.0	1,822.7	305.0
SOUTH CAROLINA	Metropolitan Statistical Area..........	3,347,369									
	Area actually reporting...................	100.0%	26,854	262	1,410	5,235	19,947	145,771	34,197	97,789	13,785
	Cities outside metropolitan areas ...	271,459									
	Area actually reporting...................	100.0%	3,172	35	93	548	2,496	16,386	3,435	12,165	786
	Nonmetropolitan counties..............	788,881									
	Area actually reporting...................	100.0%	4,720	55	236	563	3,866	26,125	7,582	16,088	2,455
	State Total........................	4,407,709	34,746	352	1,739	6,346	26,309	188,282	45,214	126,042	17,026
	Rate per 100,000 inhabitants..........		788.3	8.0	39.5	144.0	596.9	4,271.7	1,025.8	2,859.6	386.3
SOUTH DAKOTA	Metropolitan Statistical Area..........	354,847									
	Area actually reporting...................	97.6%	858	7	213	86	552	7,491	1,400	5,631	460
	Estimated total.............................	100.0%	870	7	215	86	562	7,592	1,421	5,705	466
	Cities outside metropolitan areas ...	207,296									
	Area actually reporting...................	74.3%	228	1	43	12	172	3,396	479	2,763	154
	Estimated total.............................	100.0%	306	1	58	16	231	4,568	644	3,717	207
	Nonmetropolitan counties..............	234,071									
	Area actually reporting...................	80.9%	138	7	28	8	95	806	253	503	50
	Estimated total.............................	100.0%	171	9	35	10	117	996	313	621	62
	State Total........................	796,214	1,347	17	308	112	910	13,156	2,378	10,043	735
	Rate per 100,000 inhabitants..........		169.2	2.1	38.7	14.1	114.3	1,652.3	298.7	1,261.3	92.3
TENNESSEE	Metropolitan Statistical Area..........	4,485,971									
	Area actually reporting...................	100.0%	38,501	336	1,750	10,334	26,081	198,107	46,896	133,441	17,770
	Cities outside metropolitan areas ...	601,008									
	Area actually reporting...................	100.0%	4,252	24	229	542	3,457	30,089	6,777	21,663	1,649
	Nonmetropolitan counties..............	1,069,740									
	Area actually reporting...................	100.0%	3,627	37	195	146	3,249	23,528	8,042	13,247	2,239
	State Total........................	6,156,719	46,380	397	2,174	11,022	32,787	251,724	61,715	168,351	21,658
	Rate per 100,000 inhabitants..........		753.3	6.4	35.3	179.0	532.5	4,088.6	1,002.4	2,734.4	351.8

Note: Although arson data are included in the trend and clearance tables, sufficient data are not available to estimate totals for this offense. Therefore, no arson data are published in this table.

Table 5. Crime, by State and Area, 2007 *(Contd.)*

(Number, percent, rate per 100,000 population.)

State	Area	Population	Violent crime	Murder and non-negligent man-slaughter	Forcible rape	Robbery	Aggravated assault	Property crime	Burglary	Larceny-theft	Motor vehicle theft
TEXAS	**Metropolitan Statistical Area**	20,890,757									
	Area actually reporting	99.9%	111,650	1,311	7,468	37,746	65,125	909,106	206,760	612,901	89,445
	Estimated total	100.0%	111,671	1,311	7,469	37,752	65,139	909,376	206,816	613,096	89,464
	Cities outside metropolitan areas	1,395,247									
	Area actually reporting	98.3%	6,695	47	622	823	5,203	51,065	12,676	35,888	2,501
	Estimated total	100.0%	6,792	48	632	833	5,279	51,804	12,864	36,407	2,533
	Nonmetropolitan counties	1,618,376									
	Area actually reporting	100.0%	3,591	61	338	184	3,008	23,962	8,633	13,427	1,902
	State Total	23,904,380	122,054	1,420	8,439	38,769	73,426	985,142	228,313	662,930	93,899
	Rate per 100,000 inhabitants		510.6	5.9	35.3	162.2	307.2	4,121.2	955.1	2,773.3	392.8
UTAH	**Metropolitan Statistical Area**	2,351,180									
	Area actually reporting	99.9%	5,755	53	822	1,399	3,481	86,029	14,288	63,301	8,440
	Estimated total	100.0%	5,759	53	823	1,400	3,483	86,095	14,299	63,350	8,446
	Cities outside metropolitan areas	137,076									
	Area actually reporting	86.3%	201	0	43	11	147	3,582	542	2,861	179
	Estimated total	100.0%	233	0	50	13	170	4,153	628	3,317	208
	Nonmetropolitan counties	157,074									
	Area actually reporting	88.7%	193	4	31	6	152	2,081	545	1,396	140
	Estimated total	100.0%	218	5	35	7	171	2,346	614	1,574	158
	State Total	2,645,330	6,210	58	908	1,420	3,824	92,594	15,541	68,241	8,812
	Rate per 100,000 inhabitants		234.8	2.2	34.3	53.7	144.6	3,500.3	587.5	2,579.7	333.1
VERMONT	**Metropolitan Statistical Area**	205,403									
	Area actually reporting	100.0%	365	4	66	42	253	6,311	1,140	4,932	239
	Cities outside metropolitan areas	201,112									
	Area actually reporting	100.0%	226	4	30	24	168	4,992	815	3,971	206
	Nonmetropolitan counties	214,739									
	Area actually reporting	97.0%	176	4	26	14	132	3,032	1,116	1,726	190
	Estimated total	100.0%	181	4	27	14	136	3,127	1,151	1,780	196
	State Total	621,254	772	12	123	80	557	14,430	3,106	10,683	641
	Rate per 100,000 inhabitants		124.3	1.9	19.8	12.9	89.7	2,322.7	500.0	1,719.6	103.2
VIRGINIA	**Metropolitan Statistical Area**	6,604,728									
	Area actually reporting	99.9%	18,776	358	1,506	7,320	9,592	169,781	27,230	129,835	12,716
	Estimated total	100.0%	18,778	358	1,506	7,321	9,593	169,799	27,233	129,849	12,717
	Cities outside metropolitan areas	268,724									
	Area actually reporting	100.0%	774	11	79	152	532	8,252	1,303	6,569	380
	Nonmetropolitan counties	838,639									
	Area actually reporting	100.0%	1,246	37	160	178	871	12,158	3,152	8,049	957
	State Total	7,712,091	20,798	406	1,745	7,651	10,996	190,209	31,688	144,467	14,054
	Rate per 100,000 inhabitants		269.7	5.3	22.6	99.2	142.6	2,466.4	410.9	1,873.3	182.2
WASHINGTON	**Metropolitan Statistical Area**	5,662,399									
	Area actually reporting	100.0%	19,917	160	2,283	5,828	11,646	231,851	45,738	150,499	35,614
	Cities outside metropolitan areas	336,928									
	Area actually reporting	94.9%	904	4	186	162	552	16,540	3,265	12,291	984
	Estimated total	100.0%	953	4	196	171	582	17,436	3,442	12,957	1,037
	Nonmetropolitan counties	469,097									
	Area actually reporting	100.0%	676	9	150	54	463	11,442	3,524	6,947	971
	State Total	6,468,424	21,546	173	2,629	6,053	12,691	260,729	52,704	170,403	37,622
	Rate per 100,000 inhabitants		333.1	2.7	40.6	93.6	196.2	4,030.8	814.8	2,634.4	581.6
WEST VIRGINIA	**Metropolitan Statistical Area**	1,002,071									
	Area actually reporting	94.7%	2,904	30	238	627	2,009	27,771	6,389	19,273	2,109
	Estimated total	100.0%	3,019	31	246	645	2,097	29,090	6,658	20,223	2,209
	Cities outside metropolitan areas	223,371									
	Area actually reporting	80.0%	585	6	29	90	460	5,407	1,086	4,037	284
	Estimated total	100.0%	732	8	36	113	575	6,761	1,358	5,048	355
	Nonmetropolitan counties	586,593									
	Area actually reporting	92.8%	1,147	23	81	87	956	9,191	2,597	5,733	861
	Estimated total	100.0%	1,236	25	87	94	1,030	9,902	2,798	6,176	928
	State Total	1,812,035	4,987	64	369	852	3,702	45,753	10,814	31,447	3,492
	Rate per 100,000 inhabitants		275.2	3.5	20.4	47.0	204.3	2,525.0	596.8	1,735.5	192.7

Note: Although arson data are included in the trend and clearance tables, sufficient data are not available to estimate totals for this offense. Therefore, no arson data are published in this table.

Table 5.   Crime, by State and Area, 2007 *(Contd.)*

(Number, percent, rate per 100,000 population.)

State	Area	Population	Violent crime	Murder and non-negligent man-slaughter	Forcible rape	Robbery	Aggravated assault	Property crime	Burglary	Larceny-theft	Motor vehicle theft
WISCONSIN	**Metropolitan Statistical Area**	4,053,659									
	Area actually reporting	99.9%	14,383	149	930	5,374	7,930	128,314	22,043	94,265	12,006
	Estimated total	100.0%	14,386	149	930	5,375	7,932	128,377	22,051	94,317	12,009
	Cities outside metropolitan areas	627,576									
	Area actually reporting	99.1%	1,128	21	173	75	859	19,356	2,361	16,304	691
	Estimated total	100.0%	1,139	21	175	76	867	19,534	2,383	16,454	697
	Nonmetropolitan counties	920,405									
	Area actually reporting	100.0%	771	13	118	23	617	11,048	3,405	6,916	727
	State Total	5,601,640	16,296	183	1,223	5,474	9,416	158,959	27,839	117,687	13,433
	Rate per 100,000 inhabitants		290.9	3.3	21.8	97.7	168.1	2,837.7	497.0	2,100.9	239.8
WYOMING	**Metropolitan Statistical Area**	158,296									
	Area actually reporting	100.0%	333	5	54	38	236	6,231	1,029	4,886	316
	Cities outside metropolitan areas	213,296									
	Area actually reporting	98.0%	636	6	78	38	514	6,709	877	5,492	340
	Estimated total	100.0%	649	6	80	39	524	6,845	895	5,603	347
	Nonmetropolitan counties	151,238									
	Area actually reporting	100.0%	269	5	26	7	231	1,908	424	1,351	133
	State Total	522,830	1,251	16	160	84	991	14,984	2,348	11,840	796
	Rate per 100,000 inhabitants		239.3	3.1	30.6	16.1	189.5	2,865.9	449.1	2,264.6	152.2

Note: Although arson data are included in the trend and clearance tables, sufficient data are not available to estimate totals for this offense. Therefore, no arson data are published in this table.

Table 6. Crime, by Metropolitan Statistical Area, 2007

(Number, percent, rate per 100,000 population.)

Metropolitan statistical area	Counties/principal cities	Population	Violent crime	Murder and non-negligent man-slaughter	Forcible rape	Robbery	Aggravated assault	Property crime	Burglary	Larceny-theft	Motor vehicle theft
Abilene, TX M.S.A.											
	Includes Callahan, Jones, and Taylor Counties.................	157,713									
	City of Abilene.................	114,644	661	9	89	167	396	4,911	1,324	3,295	292
	Total area actually reporting..........	100.0%	748	10	103	173	462	5,657	1,606	3,708	343
	Rate per 100,000 inhabitants...........		474.3	6.3	65.3	109.7	292.9	3,586.9	1,018.3	2,351.1	217.5
Akron, OH M.S.A.											
	Includes Portage and Summit Counties...........................	699,760									
	City of Akron..............................	208,701	1,567	22	174	730	641	10,494	3,319	5,973	1,202
	Total area actually reporting..........	88.5%	2,046	23	286	899	838	21,164	5,348	14,087	1,729
	Estimated total................................	100.0%	2,191	25	309	955	902	23,494	5,779	15,856	1,859
	Rate per 100,000 inhabitants...........		313.1	3.6	44.2	136.5	128.9	3,357.4	825.9	2,265.9	265.7
Albany, GA M.S.A.											
	Includes Baker, Dougherty, Lee, Terrell, and Worth Counties	164,983									
	City of Albany................................	75,137	637	12	32	205	388	5,503	1,519	3,616	368
	Total area actually reporting..........	99.2%	772	15	39	226	492	7,514	2,089	4,914	511
	Estimated total................................	100.0%	779	15	39	229	496	7,578	2,101	4,960	517
	Rate per 100,000 inhabitants...........		472.2	9.1	23.6	138.8	300.6	4,593.2	1,273.5	3,006.4	313.4
Albany-Schenectady-Troy, NY M.S.A.											
	Includes Albany, Rensselaer, Saratoga, Schenectady, and Schoharie Counties..........................	852,141									
	City of Albany................................	93,916	1,128	3	45	376	704	4,249	965	2,998	286
	City of Schenectady.......................	61,535	606	5	34	265	302	2,947	806	1,851	290
	City of Troy....................................	47,776	345	2	21	131	191	2,203	581	1,449	173
	Total area actually reporting..........	99.9%	2,885	13	180	900	1,792	21,190	4,202	15,874	1,114
	Estimated total................................	100.0%	2,887	13	180	901	1,793	21,209	4,205	15,889	1,115
	Rate per 100,000 inhabitants...........		338.8	1.5	21.1	105.7	210.4	2,488.9	493.5	1,864.6	130.8
Albuquerque, NM M.S.A.[1]											
	Includes Bernalillo, Sandoval,[1] Torrance, and Valencia Counties.....	827,275									
	City of Albuquerque	513,124	5,080	47	307	1,439	3,287	29,293	5,622	18,632	5,039
	Total area actually reporting..........	100.0%		68	436	1,683		37,720	8,281	23,114	6,325
	Rate per 100,000 inhabitants...........			8.2	52.7	203.4		4,559.5	1,001.0	2,794.0	764.6
Alexandria, LA M.S.A.											
	Includes Grant and Rapides Parishes..	150,253									
	City of Alexandria	45,720	1,065	8	16	175	866	4,246	1,099	2,966	181
	Total area actually reporting..........	94.2%	1,342	9	41	192	1,100	6,252	1,655	4,190	407
	Estimated total................................	100.0%	1,403	10	44	201	1,148	6,712	1,740	4,538	434
	Rate per 100,000 inhabitants...........		933.8	6.7	29.3	133.8	764.0	4,467.1	1,158.0	3,020.2	288.8
Allentown-Bethlehem-Easton, PA-NJ M.S.A.											
	Includes Warren County, NJ and Carbon, Lehigh, and Northampton Counties, PA	805,542									
	City of Allentown, PA	107,397	869	20	20	552	277	5,331	1,335	3,462	534
	City of Bethlehem, PA	72,908	270	6	24	100	140	2,288	439	1,721	128
	Total area actually reporting..........	97.1%	2,035	37	111	863	1,024	19,205	3,285	14,742	1,178
	Estimated total................................	100.0%	2,086	37	114	877	1,058	19,668	3,355	15,108	1,205
	Rate per 100,000 inhabitants...........		259.0	4.6	14.2	108.9	131.3	2,441.6	416.5	1,875.5	149.6
Altoona, PA M.S.A.											
	Includes Blair County	125,800									
	City of Altoona	46,609	184	1	20	77	86	1,318	428	824	66
	Total area actually reporting..........	93.3%	353	3	32	93	225	2,636	664	1,847	125
	Estimated total................................	100.0%	372	3	33	98	238	2,807	690	1,982	135
	Rate per 100,000 inhabitants...........		295.7	2.4	26.2	77.9	189.2	2,231.3	548.5	1,575.5	107.3
Amarillo, TX M.S.A.											
	Includes Armstrong, Carson, Potter, and Randall Counties..........	243,547									
	City of Amarillo	187,234	1,834	19	127	431	1,257	11,369	2,585	7,554	1,230
	Total area actually reporting..........	100.0%	1,923	19	140	436	1,328	12,248	2,777	8,168	1,303
	Rate per 100,000 inhabitants...........		789.6	7.8	57.5	179.0	545.3	5,029.0	1,140.2	3,353.8	535.0
Ames, IA M.S.A.											
	Includes Story County.....................	80,075									
	City of Ames....................................	51,622	200	2	18	12	168	1,602	500	1,040	62
	Total area actually reporting..........	100.0%	258	2	26	17	213	2,249	631	1,512	106
	Rate per 100,000 inhabitants...........		322.2	2.5	32.5	21.2	266.0	2,808.6	788.0	1,888.2	132.4

[1] The FBI determined that the agency's data were overreported. Consequently, affected data are not included in this table.

Table 6. Crime, by Metropolitan Statistical Area, 2007 *(Contd.)*

(Number, percent, rate per 100,000 population.)

Metropolitan statistical area	Counties/principal cities	Population	Violent crime	Murder and non-negligent man-slaughter	Forcible rape	Robbery	Aggravated assault	Property crime	Burglary	Larceny-theft	Motor vehicle theft
Anchorage, AK M.S.A.											
	Includes Anchorage Municipality and Matanuska-Susitna Borough	303,996									
	City of Anchorage	284,142	2,405	22	257	453	1,673	11,107	1,454	8,397	1,256
	Total area actually reporting	100.0%	2,526	22	264	458	1,782	12,167	1,548	9,268	1,351
	Rate per 100,000 inhabitants...........		830.9	7.2	86.8	150.7	586.2	4,002.4	509.2	3,048.7	444.4
Anderson, IN M.S.A.											
	Includes Madison County................	130,125									
	City of Anderson	57,189	203	3	27	82	91	2,931	651	2,065	215
	Total area actually reporting	100.0%	236	4	32	88	112	4,179	961	2,937	281
	Rate per 100,000 inhabitants...........		181.4	3.1	24.6	67.6	86.1	3,211.5	738.5	2,257.1	215.9
Anderson, SC M.S.A.											
	Includes Anderson County...............	181,370									
	City of Anderson	26,326	280	1	15	43	221	1,652	361	1,161	130
	Total area actually reporting	100.0%	1,183	5	65	141	972	9,357	2,570	5,890	897
	Rate per 100,000 inhabitants...........		652.3	2.8	35.8	77.7	535.9	5,159.1	1,417.0	3,247.5	494.6
Ann Arbor, MI M.S.A.											
	Includes Washtenaw County	345,430									
	City of Ann Arbor	113,011	298	0	30	66	202	2,777	572	2,046	159
	Total area actually reporting	100.0%	1,159	6	153	263	737	9,179	2,124	6,328	727
	Rate per 100,000 inhabitants...........		335.5	1.7	44.3	76.1	213.4	2,657.3	614.9	1,831.9	210.5
Appleton, WI M.S.A.											
	Includes Calumet and Outagamie Counties......................	220,208									
	City of Appleton	70,169	146	0	26	23	97	2,379	413	1,883	83
	Total area actually reporting	100.0%	232	1	50	36	145	5,673	767	4,704	202
	Rate per 100,000 inhabitants...........		105.4	0.5	22.7	16.3	65.8	2,576.2	348.3	2,136.2	91.7
Asheville, NC M.S.A.											
	Includes Buncombe, Haywood, Henderson, and Madison Counties..	405,975									
	City of Asheville	72,907	505	10	27	229	239	4,249	1,014	2,818	417
	Total area actually reporting	99.5%	1,137	21	84	329	703	11,556	3,373	7,228	955
	Estimated total................................	100.0%	1,147	21	85	332	709	11,671	3,401	7,309	961
	Rate per 100,000 inhabitants...........		282.5	5.2	20.9	81.8	174.6	2,874.8	837.7	1,800.4	236.7
Athens-Clarke County, GA M.S.A.											
	Includes Clarke, Madison, Oconee, and Oglethorpe Counties..	188,310									
	City of Athens-Clarke County	113,389	435	7	38	142	248	5,493	1,306	3,836	351
	Total area actually reporting	84.1%	577	10	45	149	373	6,916	1,535	4,943	438
	Estimated total................................	100.0%	685	12	50	192	431	7,868	1,789	5,515	564
	Rate per 100,000 inhabitants...........		363.8	6.4	26.6	102.0	228.9	4,178.2	950.0	2,928.7	299.5
Atlanta-Sandy Springs-Marietta, GA M.S.A.[1]											
	Includes Barrow, Bartow, Butts, Carroll, Cherokee, Clayton, Cobb, Coweta, Dawson, DeKalb, Douglas, Fayette, Forsyth, Fulton, Gwinnett, Haralson, Heard, Henry, Jasper, Lamar,[1] Meriwether, Newton, Paulding, Pickens, Pike, Rockdale, Spalding, and Walton[1] Counties....................	5,276,703									
	City of Atlanta	497,290	8,075	129	148	3,577	4,221	36,232	8,859	20,353	7,020
	City of Sandy Springs....................	85,830	229	6	24	151	48	3,416	803	2,317	296
	City of Marietta.............................	63,523	479	4	16	297	162	2,579	618	1,553	408
	Total area actually reporting	99.0%		455	1,053	12,205		201,636	51,732	121,090	28,814
	Estimated total................................	100.0%		458	1,066	12,304		203,925	52,217	122,658	29,050
	Rate per 100,000 inhabitants...........			8.7	20.2	233.2		3,864.6	989.6	2,324.5	550.5
Atlantic City-Hammonton, NJ M.S.A.											
	Includes Atlantic County................	270,417									
	City of Atlantic City	39,781	860	6	28	456	370	2,902	545	2,157	200
	City of Hammonton	13,512	20	0	1	4	15	161	36	114	11
	Total area actually reporting	100.0%	1,594	15	65	681	833	9,694	2,020	7,175	499
	Rate per 100,000 inhabitants...........		589.5	5.5	24.0	251.8	308.0	3,584.8	747.0	2,653.3	184.5

[1] The FBI determined that the agency's data were overreported. Consequently, affected data are not included in this table.

Table 6. Crime, by Metropolitan Statistical Area, 2007 *(Contd.)*

(Number, percent, rate per 100,000 population.)

Metropolitan statistical area	Counties/principal cities	Population	Violent crime	Murder and non-negligent man-slaughter	Forcible rape	Robbery	Aggravated assault	Property crime	Burglary	Larceny-theft	Motor vehicle theft
Auburn-Opelika, AL M.S.A.											
	Includes Lee County	127,500									
	City of Auburn	53,160	176	2	25	44	105	2,559	630	1,838	91
	City of Opelika.................	24,600	308	5	36	62	205	1,551	284	1,224	43
	Total area actually reporting	100.0%	617	8	72	137	400	5,275	1,282	3,740	253
	Rate per 100,000 inhabitants...........		483.9	6.3	56.5	107.5	313.7	4,137.3	1,005.5	2,933.3	198.4
Augusta-Richmond County, GA-SC M.S.A.											
	Includes Burke, Columbia, McDuffie, and Richmond Counties, GA and Aiken and Edgefield Counties, SC............	528,421									
	Total area actually reporting	99.4%	2,202	37	223	888	1,054	24,773	5,286	16,695	2,792
	Estimated total..................	100.0%	2,219	37	224	894	1,064	24,915	5,313	16,797	2,805
	Rate per 100,000 inhabitants...........		419.9	7.0	42.4	169.2	201.4	4,715.0	1,005.4	3,178.7	530.8
Austin-Round Rock, TX M.S.A.											
	Includes Bastrop, Caldwell, Hays, Travis, and Williamson Counties............................	1,553,472									
	City of Austin	716,817	3,871	30	328	1,457	2,056	45,453	8,031	34,461	2,961
	City of Round Rock	97,727	112	1	21	23	67	2,400	333	1,997	70
	Total area actually reporting	100.0%	5,345	43	522	1,672	3,108	64,102	12,253	48,005	3,844
	Rate per 100,000 inhabitants...........		344.1	2.8	33.6	107.6	200.1	4,126.4	788.7	3,090.2	247.4
Bakersfield, CA M.S.A.											
	Includes Kern County	792,216									
	City of Bakersfield............	318,743	1,961	15	41	629	1,276	16,058	3,537	9,853	2,668
	Total area actually reporting	100.0%	4,590	50	181	1,132	3,227	32,033	8,200	18,509	5,324
	Rate per 100,000 inhabitants...........		579.4	6.3	22.8	142.9	407.3	4,043.5	1,035.1	2,336.4	672.0
Baltimore-Towson, MD M.S.A.											
	Includes Anne Arundel, Baltimore, Carroll, Harford, Howard, and Queen Anne's Counties and Baltimore City...........	2,652,974									
	City of Baltimore	624,237	10,182	282	146	3,895	5,859	29,939	7,381	16,742	5,816
	Total area actually reporting	100.0%	20,985	355	512	7,139	12,979	92,057	18,977	60,970	12,110
	Rate per 100,000 inhabitants...........		791.0	13.4	19.3	269.1	489.2	3,470.0	715.3	2,298.2	456.5
Bangor, ME M.S.A.											
	Includes Penobscot County............	146,242									
	City of Bangor.................	30,940	46	1	4	24	17	1,905	208	1,655	42
	Total area actually reporting	100.0%	90	3	14	34	39	4,779	775	3,869	135
	Rate per 100,000 inhabitants...........		61.5	2.1	9.6	23.2	26.7	3,267.9	529.9	2,645.6	92.3
Barnstable Town, MA M.S.A.											
	Includes Barnstable County...........	225,323									
	City of Barnstable	47,342	301	2	17	25	257	1,252	439	717	96
	Total area actually reporting	100.0%	859	2	60	71	726	6,054	2,108	3,653	293
	Rate per 100,000 inhabitants...........		381.2	0.9	26.6	31.5	322.2	2,686.8	935.5	1,621.2	130.0
Baton Rouge, LA M.S.A.											
	Includes Ascension, East Baton Rouge, East Feliciana, Iberville, Livingston, Pointe Coupee, St. Helena, West Baton Rouge, and West Feliciana Parishes............	770,283									
	City of Baton Rouge	228,446	2,615	71	72	1,015	1,457	13,643	3,847	8,617	1,179
	Total area actually reporting	95.0%	5,396	135	177	1,382	3,702	32,363	7,995	21,970	2,398
	Estimated total..................	100.0%	5,609	138	189	1,415	3,867	33,857	8,320	23,024	2,513
	Rate per 100,000 inhabitants...........		728.2	17.9	24.5	183.7	502.0	4,395.4	1,080.1	2,989.0	326.2
Battle Creek, MI M.S.A.											
	Includes Calhoun County...............	137,388									
	City of Battle Creek	62,143	818	3	89	130	596	3,591	1,001	2,397	193
	Total area actually reporting	100.0%	1,186	11	133	170	872	5,662	1,457	3,899	306
	Rate per 100,000 inhabitants...........		863.2	8.0	96.8	123.7	634.7	4,121.2	1,060.5	2,837.9	222.7
Bay City, MI M.S.A.											
	Includes Bay County...........	107,654									
	City of Bay City	34,145	164	1	20	50	93	1,170	298	792	80
	Total area actually reporting	100.0%	288	4	59	62	163	2,684	594	1,911	179
	Rate per 100,000 inhabitants...........		267.5	3.7	54.8	57.6	151.4	2,493.2	551.8	1,775.1	166.3

Table 6. Crime, by Metropolitan Statistical Area, 2007 *(Contd.)*

(Number, percent, rate per 100,000 population.)

Metropolitan statistical area	Counties/principal cities	Population	Violent crime	Murder and non-negligent man-slaughter	Forcible rape	Robbery	Aggravated assault	Property crime	Burglary	Larceny-theft	Motor vehicle theft
Beaumont-Port Arthur, TX M.S.A.	Includes Hardin, Jefferson, and Orange Counties	378,783									
	City of Beaumont	109,345	1,073	15	71	309	678	6,643	1,707	4,471	465
	City of Port Arthur	55,481	475	9	47	196	223	2,285	747	1,280	258
	Total area actually reporting	100.0%	2,209	29	189	640	1,351	15,446	4,215	9,940	1,291
	Rate per 100,000 inhabitants		583.2	7.7	49.9	169.0	356.7	4,077.8	1,112.8	2,624.2	340.8
Bellingham, WA M.S.A.	Includes Whatcom County	188,708									
	City of Bellingham	76,290	187	2	29	58	98	5,022	696	4,087	239
	Total area actually reporting	100.0%	441	2	88	81	270	8,167	1,498	6,233	436
	Rate per 100,000 inhabitants		233.7	1.1	46.6	42.9	143.1	4,327.9	793.8	3,303.0	231.0
Bend, OR M.S.A.	Includes Deschutes County	154,723									
	City of Bend	75,185	155	0	20	40	95	2,977	594	2,187	196
	Total area actually reporting	100.0%	342	0	54	61	227	5,302	1,151	3,780	371
	Rate per 100,000 inhabitants		221.0	0.0	34.9	39.4	146.7	3,426.8	743.9	2,443.1	239.8
Billings, MT M.S.A.	Includes Carbon and Yellowstone Counties	150,563									
	City of Billings	101,342	245	1	23	54	167	4,182	435	3,420	327
	Total area actually reporting	99.5%	336	2	39	58	237	5,191	558	4,251	382
	Estimated total	100.0%	338	2	39	58	239	5,217	559	4,275	383
	Rate per 100,000 inhabitants		224.5	1.3	25.9	38.5	158.7	3,465.0	371.3	2,839.3	254.4
Binghamton, NY M.S.A.	Includes Broome and Tioga Counties	246,237									
	City of Binghamton	44,931	214	3	19	67	125	2,100	254	1,809	37
	Total area actually reporting	100.0%	481	4	65	109	303	5,847	853	4,851	143
	Rate per 100,000 inhabitants		195.3	1.6	26.4	44.3	123.1	2,374.5	346.4	1,970.1	58.1
Birmingham-Hoover, AL M.S.A.	Includes Bibb, Blount, Chilton, Jefferson, St. Clair, Shelby, and Walker Counties	1,108,901									
	City of Birmingham	227,686	3,320	86	229	1,609	1,396	19,638	4,864	12,528	2,246
	City of Hoover	69,527	121	0	18	71	32	2,443	372	1,910	161
	Total area actually reporting	88.4%	5,993	121	423	2,517	2,932	45,128	10,873	30,165	4,090
	Estimated total	100.0%	6,461	130	456	2,666	3,209	49,747	11,960	33,349	4,438
	Rate per 100,000 inhabitants		582.6	11.7	41.1	240.4	289.4	4,486.2	1,078.5	3,007.4	400.2
Bismarck, ND M.S.A.	Includes Burleigh and Morton Counties	102,688									
	City of Bismarck	58,648	108	1	25	11	71	1,550	255	1,194	101
	Total area actually reporting	100.0%	172	1	44	14	113	2,197	369	1,673	155
	Rate per 100,000 inhabitants		167.5	1.0	42.8	13.6	110.0	2,139.5	359.3	1,629.2	150.9
Blacksburg-Christiansburg-Radford, VA M.S.A.	Includes Giles, Montgomery, and Pulaski Counties and Radford City	151,219									
	City of Blacksburg	39,250	63	0	8	10	45	656	120	520	16
	City of Christiansburg	17,983	53	0	1	7	45	762	111	622	29
	City of Radford	14,317	40	0	8	5	27	502	120	359	23
	Total area actually reporting	100.0%	316	32	45	41	198	4,240	838	3,234	168
	Rate per 100,000 inhabitants		209.0	21.2	29.8	27.1	130.9	2,803.9	554.2	2,138.6	111.1
Bloomington, IN M.S.A.	Includes Greene, Monroe, and Owen Counties	179,055									
	City of Bloomington	68,918	275	1	24	72	178	2,898	666	2,060	172
	Total area actually reporting	82.6%	389	4	39	91	255	4,373	1,078	3,025	270
	Estimated total	100.0%	431	4	43	102	282	5,022	1,208	3,492	322
	Rate per 100,000 inhabitants		240.7	2.2	24.0	57.0	157.5	2,804.7	674.7	1,950.2	179.8

Table 6. Crime, by Metropolitan Statistical Area, 2007 *(Contd.)*

(Number, percent, rate per 100,000 population.)

Metropolitan statistical area	Counties/principal cities	Population	Violent crime	Murder and non-negligent man-slaughter	Forcible rape	Robbery	Aggravated assault	Property crime	Burglary	Larceny-theft	Motor vehicle theft
Boise City-Nampa, ID M.S.A.											
	Includes Ada, Boise, Canyon, Gem, and Owyhee Counties............	586,066									
	City of Boise	199,104	648	10	122	68	448	6,175	1,018	4,778	379
	City of Nampa	80,397	260	5	55	17	183	2,508	613	1,643	252
	Total area actually reporting	100.0%	1,570	21	278	129	1,142	14,564	3,025	10,433	1,106
	Rate per 100,000 inhabitants...........		267.9	3.6	47.4	22.0	194.9	2,485.0	516.2	1,780.2	188.7
Boston-Cambridge-Quincy, MA-NH M.S.A.[2]											
	Includes the Metropolitan Divisions of Boston-Quincy, MA; Cambridge-Newton-Framingham, MA; and Peabody, MA and Rockingham County-Strafford County, NH......................................	4,460,277									
	City of Boston, MA	591,855	6,837	65	263	2,242	4,267	24,579	3,810	17,351	3,418
	City of Cambridge, MA[2]	101,161	421	0	12	148	261	3,616	662	2,718	236
	City of Quincy, MA	91,382	253	2	16	70	165	1,877	589	1,147	141
	City of Newton, MA	82,731	78	0	8	13	57	1,306	184	1,079	43
	City of Framingham, MA.................	64,482	107	0	3	29	75	1,380	211	1,018	151
	City of Waltham, MA	59,425	125	0	11	19	95	820	172	594	54
	City of Peabody, MA	52,194	128	0	7	16	105	1,235	126	1,002	107
	Total area actually reporting	97.9%	17,096	123	950	4,751	11,272	100,025	20,595	69,908	9,522
	Estimated total.................................	100.0%	17,261	124	969	4,782	11,386	101,681	20,970	71,081	9,630
	Rate per 100,000 inhabitants...........		387.0	2.8	21.7	107.2	255.3	2,279.7	470.2	1,593.6	215.9
Boston-Quincy, MA M.D.											
	Includes Norfolk, Plymouth, and Suffolk Counties	1,839,638									
	Total area actually reporting	98.3%	10,473	93	482	3,215	6,683	48,682	9,192	34,162	5,328
	Estimated total.................................	100.0%	10,565	94	488	3,233	6,750	49,322	9,352	34,591	5,379
	Rate per 100,000 inhabitants...........		574.3	5.1	26.5	175.7	366.9	2,681.1	508.4	1,880.3	292.4
Cambridge-Newton-Framingham, MA M.D.[2]											
	Includes Middlesex County.............	1,466,454									
	Total area actually reporting	99.8%	3,461	13	229	937	2,282	29,693	6,303	21,079	2,311
	Estimated total.................................	100.0%	3,471	13	230	939	2,289	29,758	6,319	21,123	2,316
	Rate per 100,000 inhabitants...........		236.7	0.9	15.7	64.0	156.1	2,029.2	430.9	1,440.4	157.9
Peabody, MA M.D.											
	Includes Essex County.....................	737,494									
	Total area actually reporting	99.5%	2,725	16	153	527	2,029	15,178	3,951	9,709	1,518
	Estimated total.................................	100.0%	2,735	16	154	529	2,036	15,245	3,968	9,754	1,523
	Rate per 100,000 inhabitants...........		370.9	2.2	20.9	71.7	276.1	2,067.1	538.0	1,322.6	206.5
Rockingham County-Strafford County, NH M.D.											
	Includes Rockingham and Strafford Counties	416,691									
	Total area actually reporting	86.4%	437	1	86	72	278	6,472	1,149	4,958	365
	Estimated total.................................	100.0%	490	1	97	81	311	7,356	1,331	5,613	412
	Rate per 100,000 inhabitants...........		117.6	0.2	23.3	19.4	74.6	1,765.3	319.4	1,347.0	98.9
Bowling Green, KY M.S.A.											
	Includes Edmonson and Warren Counties...............................	114,815									
	City of Bowling Green	53,663	348	1	49	87	211	2,739	545	2,072	122
	Total area actually reporting	99.1%	378	1	53	94	230	3,560	782	2,619	159
	Estimated total.................................	100.0%	381	1	53	95	232	3,596	790	2,645	161
	Rate per 100,000 inhabitants...........		331.8	0.9	46.2	82.7	202.1	3,132.0	688.1	2,303.7	140.2
Bradenton-Sarasota-Venice, FL M.S.A.											
	Includes Manatee and Sarasota Counties..	690,730									
	City of Bradenton............................	54,253	530	5	19	156	350	2,476	593	1,674	209
	City of Sarasota................................	52,986	588	6	28	185	369	3,516	806	2,470	240
	City of Venice...................................	21,329	56	0	3	5	48	626	82	517	27
	Total area actually reporting	100.0%	4,571	43	218	1,062	3,248	28,989	6,614	20,452	1,923
	Rate per 100,000 inhabitants...........		661.8	6.2	31.6	153.8	470.2	4,196.9	957.5	2,960.9	278.4

[2] Because of changes in the state/local agency's reporting practices, figures are not comparable to previous years' data.

Table 6. Crime, by Metropolitan Statistical Area, 2007 *(Contd.)*

(Number, percent, rate per 100,000 population.)

Metropolitan statistical area	Counties/principal cities	Population	Violent crime	Murder and non-negligent man-slaughter	Forcible rape	Robbery	Aggravated assault	Property crime	Burglary	Larceny-theft	Motor vehicle theft
Bremerton-Silverdale, WA M.S.A.											
	Includes Kitsap County	241,780									
	City of Bremerton	35,068	336	0	63	60	213	1,652	368	1,185	99
	Total area actually reporting	100.0%	1,049	1	200	105	743	6,259	1,567	4,314	378
	Rate per 100,000 inhabitants		433.9	0.4	82.7	43.4	307.3	2,588.7	648.1	1,784.3	156.3
Bridgeport-Stamford-Norwalk, CT M.S.A.											
	Includes Fairfield County	884,290									
	City of Bridgeport	137,655	1,603	14	77	675	837	6,577	1,201	4,223	1,153
	City of Stamford	119,510	336	3	33	129	171	1,882	332	1,316	234
	City of Norwalk	84,343	343	3	13	120	207	1,872	284	1,378	210
	City of Danbury	79,893	146	2	20	75	49	1,482	275	1,069	138
	City of Stratford	49,440	116	0	3	58	55	1,539	209	1,128	202
	Total area actually reporting	100.0%	2,712	23	166	1,124	1,399	17,692	3,002	12,479	2,211
	Rate per 100,000 inhabitants		306.7	2.6	18.8	127.1	158.2	2,000.7	339.5	1,411.2	250.0
Brownsville-Harlingen, TX M.S.A.											
	Includes Cameron County	395,428									
	City of Brownsville	177,090	880	5	21	207	647	9,474	1,442	7,574	458
	City of Harlingen	64,984	334	7	28	63	236	4,546	1,054	3,241	251
	Total area actually reporting	100.0%	1,616	16	100	317	1,183	19,206	3,965	14,256	985
	Rate per 100,000 inhabitants		408.7	4.0	25.3	80.2	299.2	4,857.0	1,002.7	3,605.2	249.1
Brunswick, GA M.S.A.											
	Includes Brantley, Glynn, and McIntosh Counties	101,687									
	City of Brunswick	16,146	458	8	13	104	333	1,312	354	867	91
	Total area actually reporting	98.9%	830	20	27	165	618	4,585	1,082	3,207	296
	Estimated total	100.0%	836	20	27	167	622	4,637	1,092	3,244	301
	Rate per 100,000 inhabitants		822.1	19.7	26.6	164.2	611.7	4,560.1	1,073.9	3,190.2	296.0
Buffalo-Niagara Falls, NY M.S.A.											
	Includes Erie and Niagara Counties	1,129,953									
	City of Buffalo	273,832	3,490	54	164	1,533	1,739	16,137	4,389	9,477	2,271
	City of Cheektowaga Town	79,164	226	0	20	84	122	2,304	301	1,874	129
	City of Tonawanda	14,971	22	0	4	3	15	431	51	367	13
	City of Niagara Falls	51,897	501	3	38	134	326	2,676	668	1,796	212
	Total area actually reporting	100.0%	5,271	60	331	2,019	2,861	34,365	7,835	23,398	3,132
	Rate per 100,000 inhabitants		466.5	5.3	29.3	178.7	253.2	3,041.3	693.4	2,070.7	277.2
Burlington, NC M.S.A.											
	Includes Alamance County	145,711									
	City of Burlington	48,689	404	3	16	103	282	2,967	763	2,054	150
	Total area actually reporting	98.6%	650	9	33	148	460	5,361	1,442	3,627	292
	Estimated total	100.0%	659	9	34	150	466	5,465	1,467	3,701	297
	Rate per 100,000 inhabitants		452.3	6.2	23.3	102.9	319.8	3,750.6	1,006.8	2,540.0	203.8
Burlington-South Burlington, VT M.S.A.											
	Includes Chittenden, Franklin, and Grand Isle Counties	205,403									
	City of Burlington	38,153	135	0	22	18	95	1,673	359	1,268	46
	City of South Burlington	17,333	20	0	9	2	9	631	27	572	32
	Total area actually reporting	100.0%	365	4	66	42	253	6,311	1,140	4,932	239
	Rate per 100,000 inhabitants		177.7	1.9	32.1	20.4	123.2	3,072.5	555.0	2,401.1	116.4
Cape Coral-Fort Myers, FL M.S.A.											
	Includes Lee County	587,220									
	City of Cape Coral	159,936	402	5	40	97	260	5,574	1,483	3,787	304
	City of Fort Myers	61,810	921	17	26	335	543	3,357	576	2,265	516
	Total area actually reporting	100.0%	3,329	47	177	988	2,117	22,622	6,501	13,983	2,138
	Rate per 100,000 inhabitants		566.9	8.0	30.1	168.3	360.5	3,852.4	1,107.1	2,381.2	364.1
Carson City, NV M.S.A.											
	Includes Carson City	55,713									
	Total area actually reporting	100.0%	206	1	5	21	179	1,103	286	723	94
	Rate per 100,000 inhabitants		369.8	1.8	9.0	37.7	321.3	1,979.8	513.3	1,297.7	168.7

Table 6. Crime, by Metropolitan Statistical Area, 2007 *(Contd.)*

(Number, percent, rate per 100,000 population.)

Metropolitan statistical area	Counties/principal cities	Population	Violent crime	Murder and non-negligent man-slaughter	Forcible rape	Robbery	Aggravated assault	Property crime	Burglary	Larceny-theft	Motor vehicle theft
Casper, WY M.S.A.											
	Includes Natrona County	71,604									
	City of Casper	52,434	152	2	20	22	108	2,595	504	1,935	156
	Total area actually reporting	100.0%	174	4	20	23	127	3,151	646	2,306	199
	Rate per 100,000 inhabitants...........		243.0	5.6	27.9	32.1	177.4	4,400.6	902.2	3,220.5	277.9
Cedar Rapids, IA M.S.A.											
	Includes Benton, Jones, and Linn Counties..................................	250,807									
	City of Cedar Rapids......................	124,730	500	3	34	137	326	6,041	1,083	4,619	339
	Total area actually reporting	96.2%	603	3	51	145	404	7,378	1,450	5,523	405
	Estimated total..............................	100.0%	621	3	53	147	418	7,602	1,487	5,700	415
	Rate per 100,000 inhabitants...........		247.6	1.2	21.1	58.6	166.7	3,031.0	592.9	2,272.7	165.5
Charleston, WV M.S.A.											
	Includes Boone, Clay, Kanawha, Lincoln, and Putnam Counties........	303,537									
	City of Charleston...........................	50,510	572	4	14	131	423	3,051	601	2,235	215
	Total area actually reporting	86.6%	1,183	7	68	218	890	9,185	1,980	6,381	824
	Estimated total..............................	100.0%	1,272	8	75	230	959	10,124	2,185	7,039	900
	Rate per 100,000 inhabitants...........		419.1	2.6	24.7	75.8	315.9	3,335.3	719.8	2,319.0	296.5
Charleston-North Charleston-Summerville, SC M.S.A.											
	Includes Berkeley, Charleston, and Dorchester Counties.................	616,999									
	City of Charleston...........................	109,382	909	15	56	269	569	4,246	746	3,056	444
	City of North Charleston	88,431	1,561	26	92	624	819	6,768	1,195	4,660	913
	City of Summerville.........................	43,985	147	2	13	36	96	1,470	154	1,212	104
	Total area actually reporting	100.0%	5,086	68	278	1,336	3,404	25,262	5,162	17,264	2,836
	Rate per 100,000 inhabitants...........		824.3	11.0	45.1	216.5	551.7	4,094.3	836.6	2,798.1	459.6
Charlotte-Gastonia-Concord, NC-SC M.S.A.											
	Includes Anson, Cabarrus, Gaston, Mecklenburg, and Union Counties, NC and York County, SC	1,635,133									
	City of Charlotte-Mecklenburg, NC...................	733,291	7,233	76	282	3,191	3,684	51,279	12,948	32,313	6,018
	City of Gastonia, NC	70,127	701	5	23	234	439	5,552	1,259	3,842	451
	City of Concord, NC........................	63,284	256	7	21	100	128	3,029	473	2,326	230
	City of Rock Hill, SC.......................	63,388	798	3	20	124	651	2,921	503	2,208	210
	Total area actually reporting	89.1%	11,336	109	482	4,104	6,641	80,865	19,987	52,568	8,310
	Estimated total..............................	100.0%	11,789	116	516	4,200	6,957	86,157	21,628	55,860	8,669
	Rate per 100,000 inhabitants...........		721.0	7.1	31.6	256.9	425.5	5,269.1	1,322.7	3,416.2	530.2
Charlottesville, VA M.S.A.											
	Includes Albemarle, Fluvanna, Greene, and Nelson Counties and Charlottesville City	192,228									
	City of Charlottesville	40,265	273	3	26	93	151	1,938	278	1,524	136
	Total area actually reporting	100.0%	511	5	60	150	296	5,107	783	4,034	290
	Rate per 100,000 inhabitants...........		265.8	2.6	31.2	78.0	154.0	2,656.7	407.3	2,098.5	150.9
Chattanooga, TN-GA M.S.A.											
	Includes Catoosa, Dade, and Walker Counties, GA and Hamilton, Marion, and Sequatchie Counties, TN..................	503,472									
	City of Chattanooga, TN.................	155,043	2,009	11	102	524	1,372	12,484	2,384	9,072	1,028
	Total area actually reporting	100.0%	3,342	18	178	650	2,496	22,399	4,694	15,972	1,733
	Rate per 100,000 inhabitants...........		663.8	3.6	35.4	129.1	495.8	4,448.9	932.3	3,172.4	344.2
Cheyenne, WY M.S.A.											
	Includes Laramie County	86,692									
	City of Cheyenne	55,604	115	1	23	13	78	2,557	261	2,208	88
	Total area actually reporting	100.0%	159	1	34	15	109	3,080	383	2,580	117
	Rate per 100,000 inhabitants...........		183.4	1.2	39.2	17.3	125.7	3,552.8	441.8	2,976.1	135.0

Table 6. Crime, by Metropolitan Statistical Area, 2007 *(Contd.)*

(Number, percent, rate per 100,000 population.)

Metropolitan statistical area	Counties/principal cities	Population	Violent crime	Murder and non-negligent man-slaughter	Forcible rape	Robbery	Aggravated assault	Property crime	Burglary	Larceny-theft	Motor vehicle theft
Chico, CA M.S.A.											
	Includes Butte County	215,992									
	City of Chico	74,288	385	3	59	107	216	2,454	729	1,450	275
	Total area actually reporting	100.0%	977	9	127	176	665	6,666	1,840	3,951	875
	Rate per 100,000 inhabitants..........		452.3	4.2	58.8	81.5	307.9	3,086.2	851.9	1,829.2	405.1
Cincinnati-Middletown, OH-KY-IN M.S.A.											
	Includes Dearborn, Franklin, and Ohio Counties, IN; Boone, Bracken, Campbell, Gallatin, Grant, Kenton, and Pendleton Counties, KY; and Brown, Butler, Clermont, Hamilton, and Warren Counties, OH...................	2,115,244									
	City of Cincinnati, OH	332,388	3,588	63	313	1,961	1,251	20,531	6,200	12,332	1,999
	City of Middletown, OH	51,244	223	3	28	87	105	4,040	874	2,939	227
	Total area actually reporting	82.1%	7,140	94	828	3,133	3,085	62,460	14,263	43,856	4,341
	Estimated total...............................	100.0%	7,702	100	915	3,320	3,367	71,409	16,135	50,393	4,881
	Rate per 100,000 inhabitants..........		364.1	4.7	43.3	157.0	159.2	3,375.9	762.8	2,382.4	230.8
Clarksville, TN-KY M.S.A.											
	Includes Christian and Trigg Counties, KY and Montgomery and Stewart Counties, TN	244,105									
	City of Clarksville, TN....................	114,582	992	9	65	159	759	4,751	1,520	2,907	324
	Total area actually reporting	99.4%	1,386	14	96	240	1,036	8,319	2,482	5,262	575
	Estimated total...............................	100.0%	1,392	14	97	242	1,039	8,373	2,493	5,301	579
	Rate per 100,000 inhabitants..........		570.2	5.7	39.7	99.1	425.6	3,430.1	1,021.3	2,171.6	237.2
Cleveland, TN M.S.A.											
	Includes Bradley and Polk Counties...................................	111,450									
	City of Cleveland............................	38,808	430	1	24	48	357	2,356	465	1,769	122
	Total area actually reporting	100.0%	833	3	36	63	731	3,780	801	2,729	250
	Rate per 100,000 inhabitants..........		747.4	2.7	32.3	56.5	655.9	3,391.7	718.7	2,448.6	224.3
Cleveland-Elyria-Mentor, OH M.S.A.											
	Includes Cuyahoga, Geauga, Lake, Lorain, and Medina Counties...................................	2,104,225									
	City of Cleveland............................	439,888	6,444	90	374	4,022	1,958	27,016	9,050	11,184	6,782
	City of Elyria.................................	55,697	222	1	35	74	112	2,278	602	1,515	161
	City of Mentor................................	51,775	44	1	11	12	20	1,208	135	1,014	59
	Total area actually reporting	79.6%	8,465	121	625	4,862	2,857	51,387	14,869	27,739	8,779
	Estimated total...............................	100.0%	9,184	129	744	5,133	3,178	63,199	17,136	36,624	9,439
	Rate per 100,000 inhabitants..........		436.5	6.1	35.4	243.9	151.0	3,003.4	814.4	1,740.5	448.6
Coeur d'Alene, ID M.S.A.											
	Includes Kootenai County..............	135,581									
	City of Coeur d'Alene.....................	42,324	270	1	35	18	216	1,488	248	1,168	72
	Total area actually reporting	100.0%	466	1	72	29	364	3,218	685	2,328	205
	Rate per 100,000 inhabitants..........		343.7	0.7	53.1	21.4	268.5	2,373.5	505.2	1,717.1	151.2
College Station-Bryan, TX M.S.A.											
	Includes Brazos, Burleson, and Robertson Counties	193,097									
	City of College Station....................	74,997	251	1	38	45	167	2,488	481	1,919	88
	City of Bryan.................................	67,484	596	4	34	96	462	3,542	1,000	2,404	138
	Total area actually reporting	100.0%	1,016	7	88	161	760	7,479	1,849	5,339	291
	Rate per 100,000 inhabitants..........		526.2	3.6	45.6	83.4	393.6	3,873.2	957.5	2,764.9	150.7
Colorado Springs, CO M.S.A.											
	Includes El Paso and Teller Counties...................................	613,181									
	City of Colorado Springs	374,112	1,985	27	285	528	1,145	16,554	3,179	11,888	1,487
	Total area actually reporting	99.5%	2,950	30	365	570	1,985	19,926	3,934	14,162	1,830
	Estimated total...............................	100.0%	2,958	30	366	572	1,990	20,029	3,951	14,237	1,841
	Rate per 100,000 inhabitants..........	482.4	4.9	59.7	93.3	324.5	3,266.4	644.3	2,321.8	300.2	

Table 6. Crime, by Metropolitan Statistical Area, 2007 *(Contd.)*

(Number, percent, rate per 100,000 population.)

Metropolitan statistical area	Counties/principal cities	Population	Violent crime	Murder and non-negligent man-slaughter	Forcible rape	Robbery	Aggravated assault	Property crime	Burglary	Larceny-theft	Motor vehicle theft
Columbia, MO M.S.A.											
	Includes Boone and Howard Counties...............................	157,307									
	City of Columbia............................	95,595	617	3	30	141	443	3,323	594	2,509	220
	Total area actually reporting	100.0%	817	5	37	161	614	4,756	880	3,602	274
	Rate per 100,000 inhabitants...........		519.4	3.2	23.5	102.3	390.3	3,023.4	559.4	2,289.8	174.2
Columbus, GA-AL M.S.A.											
	Includes Russell County, AL and Chattahoochee, Harris, Marion, and Muscogee Counties, GA..........................	290,106									
	City of Columbus, GA.....................	188,944	1,316	24	57	618	617	13,791	2,652	9,367	1,772
	Total area actually reporting	94.8%	1,475	28	70	676	701	15,780	3,165	10,597	2,018
	Estimated total.................................	100.0%	1,531	29	73	698	731	16,268	3,294	10,893	2,081
	Rate per 100,000 inhabitants...........		527.7	10.0	25.2	240.6	252.0	5,607.6	1,135.4	3,754.8	717.3
Columbus, IN M.S.A.											
	Includes Bartholomew County	74,805									
	City of Columbus............................	39,764	53	1	10	16	26	2,593	344	2,116	133
	Total area actually reporting	99.5%	75	2	13	21	39	2,865	361	2,354	150
	Estimated total.................................	100.0%	76	2	13	21	40	2,878	363	2,364	151
	Rate per 100,000 inhabitants...........		101.6	2.7	17.4	28.1	53.5	3,847.3	485.3	3,160.2	201.9
Columbus, OH M.S.A.											
	Includes Delaware, Fairfield, Franklin, Licking, Madison, Morrow, Pickaway, and Union Counties..	1,737,831									
	City of Columbus	735,981	6,269	79	661	3,849	1,680	51,491	14,370	30,893	6,228
	Total area actually reporting	89.4%	7,565	92	907	4,402	2,164	76,479	19,440	49,645	7,394
	Estimated total.................................	100.0%	7,736	94	943	4,449	2,750	80,041	20,330	52,120	7,591
	Rate per 100,000 inhabitants...........		445.2	5.4	54.3	256.0	129.5	4,605.8	1,169.8	2,999.1	436.8
Corpus Christi, TX M.S.A.											
	Includes Aransas, Nueces, and San Patricio Counties......................	417,469									
	City of Corpus Christi	286,269	2,365	17	238	497	1,613	18,713	3,404	14,486	823
	Total area actually reporting	100.0%	2,835	23	298	579	1,935	24,266	4,752	18,486	1,028
	Rate per 100,000 inhabitants...........		679.1	5.5	71.4	138.7	463.5	5,812.6	1,138.3	4,428.1	246.2
Corvallis, OR M.S.A.											
	Includes Benton County	79,314									
	City of Corvallis.............................	49,870	57	1	11	10	35	1,554	226	1,261	67
	Total area actually reporting	100.0%	110	2	19	16	73	2,398	414	1,875	109
	Rate per 100,000 inhabitants...........		138.7	2.5	24.0	20.2	92.0	3,023.4	522.0	2,364.0	137.4
Cumberland, MD-WV M.S.A.											
	Includes Allegany County, MD and Mineral County, WV........................	98,759									
	City of Cumberland, MD	20,654	180	0	7	35	138	1,266	293	935	38
	Total area actually reporting	100.0%	372	1	25	43	303	2,697	656	1,915	126
	Rate per 100,000 inhabitants...........		376.7	1.0	25.3	43.5	306.8	2,730.9	664.2	1,939.1	127.6
Dallas-Fort Worth-Arlington, TX M.S.A.											
	Includes the Metropolitan Divisions of Dallas-Plano-Irving and Fort Worth-Arlington	6,132,121									
	City of Dallas...................................	1,239,104	13,248	200	511	7,222	5,315	83,962	22,472	47,699	13,791
	City of Fort Worth	670,693	4,474	58	335	1,620	2,461	36,681	9,008	24,988	2,685
	City of Arlington.............................	372,073	2,588	13	156	742	1,677	21,079	4,447	14,990	1,642
	City of Plano....................................	259,771	676	2	51	161	462	7,973	1,384	6,168	421
	City of Irving	196,676	729	9	30	240	450	9,030	1,730	6,306	994
	City of Carrollton	123,324	237	5	3	116	113	3,890	893	2,636	361
	City of Denton.................................	113,936	366	2	76	84	204	3,505	718	2,614	173
	City of Richardson...........................	100,933	290	2	22	136	130	3,107	793	2,084	230
	City of McKinney	118,113	255	1	49	44	161	2,626	531	1,949	146
	Total area actually reporting	99.9%	30,904	359	1,937	12,386	16,222	264,138	62,817	173,026	28,295
	Estimated total.................................	100.0%	30,905	359	1,937	12,386	16,223	264,156	62,821	173,039	28,296
	Rate per 100,000 inhabitants...........		504.0	5.9	31.6	202.0	264.6	4,307.7	1,024.5	2,821.8	461.4

Table 6. Crime, by Metropolitan Statistical Area, 2007 *(Contd.)*

(Number, percent, rate per 100,000 population.)

Metropolitan statistical area	Counties/principal cities	Population	Violent crime	Murder and non-negligent man-slaughter	Forcible rape	Robbery	Aggravated assault	Property crime	Burglary	Larceny-theft	Motor vehicle theft
Dallas-Plano-Irving, TX M.D.											
	Includes Collin, Dallas, Delta, Denton, Ellis, Hunt, Kaufman, and Rockwall Counties	4,107,704									
	Total area actually reporting	99.9%	21,174	268	1,164	9,509	10,233	175,648	42,875	111,091	21,682
	Estimated total	100.0%	21,175	268	1,164	9,509	10,234	175,666	42,879	111,104	21,683
	Rate per 100,000 inhabitants		515.5	6.5	28.3	231.5	249.1	4,276.5	1,043.9	2,704.8	527.9
Fort Worth-Arlington, TX M.D.											
	Includes Johnson, Parker, Tarrant, and Wise Counties	2,024,417									
	Total area actually reporting	100.0%	9,730	91	773	2,877	5,989	88,490	19,942	61,935	6,613
	Rate per 100,000 inhabitants		480.6	4.5	38.2	142.1	295.8	4,371.1	985.1	3,059.4	326.7
Dalton, GA M.S.A.[3]											
	Includes Murray and Whitfield Counties	136,405									
	City of Dalton[3]	33,790	140	3	6	30	101		230	1,026	
	Total area actually reporting	99.5%	471	3	26	46	396		917	3,079	
	Estimated total	100.0%	474	3	26	47	398		923	3,100	
	Rate per 100,000 inhabitants		347.5	2.2	19.1	34.5	291.8		676.7	2,272.6	
Danville, VA M.S.A.											
	Includes Pittsylvania County and Danville City	106,432									
	City of Danville	45,114	204	5	9	98	92	2,437	550	1,775	112
	Total area actually reporting	100.0%	269	9	16	122	122	3,041	781	2,088	172
	Rate per 100,000 inhabitants		252.7	8.5	15.0	114.6	114.6	2,857.2	733.8	1,961.8	161.6
Dayton, OH M.S.A.											
	Includes Greene, Miami, Montgomery, and Preble Counties	835,430									
	City of Dayton	155,526	1,597	28	116	749	704	10,465	3,272	5,607	1,586
	Total area actually reporting	80.6%	2,287	37	294	997	959	25,185	5,896	16,779	2,510
	Estimated total	100.0%	2,494	39	332	1,067	1,056	28,932	6,713	19,501	2,718
	Rate per 100,000 inhabitants		298.5	4.7	39.7	127.7	126.4	3,463.1	803.5	2,334.2	325.3
Decatur, AL M.S.A.											
	Includes Lawrence and Morgan Counties	150,246									
	City of Decatur	56,019	251	0	28	105	118	3,624	830	2,584	210
	Total area actually reporting	97.4%	336	0	40	114	182	5,097	1,264	3,526	307
	Estimated total	100.0%	352	0	41	120	191	5,264	1,299	3,646	319
	Rate per 100,000 inhabitants		234.3	0.0	27.3	79.9	127.1	3,503.6	864.6	2,426.7	212.3
Deltona-Daytona Beach-Ormond Beach, FL M.S.A.											
	Includes Volusia County	500,013									
	City of Daytona Beach	64,236	1,063	8	48	323	684	4,612	1,172	2,873	567
	City of Ormond Beach	38,792	107	0	5	30	72	1,278	245	959	74
	Total area actually reporting	99.4%	2,916	20	165	728	2,003	18,239	4,720	11,752	1,767
	Estimated total	100.0%	2,934	20	166	734	2,014	18,361	4,747	11,836	1,778
	Rate per 100,000 inhabitants		586.8	4.0	33.2	146.8	402.8	3,672.1	949.4	2,367.1	355.6
Denver-Aurora, CO M.S.A.											
	Includes Adams, Arapahoe, Broomfield, Clear Creek, Denver, Douglas, Elbert, Gilpin, Jefferson, and Park Counties	2,464,178									
	City of Denver	573,387	3,552	47	296	1,045	2,164	22,409	5,694	11,594	5,121
	City of Aurora	307,621	1,687	14	191	583	899	11,790	2,321	7,750	1,719
	Total area actually reporting	99.9%	9,011	85	1,056	2,320	5,550	77,760	15,788	50,307	11,665
	Estimated total	100.0%	9,016	85	1,057	2,321	5,553	77,818	15,798	50,349	11,671
	Rate per 100,000 inhabitants		365.9	3.4	42.9	94.2	225.3	3,158.0	641.1	2,043.2	473.6

[3] The FBI determined that the agency's data were underreported. Consequently, affected data are not included in this table.

Table 6. Crime, by Metropolitan Statistical Area, 2007 *(Contd.)*

(Number, percent, rate per 100,000 population.)

Metropolitan statistical area	Counties/principal cities	Population	Violent crime	Murder and non-negligent man-slaughter	Forcible rape	Robbery	Aggravated assault	Property crime	Burglary	Larceny-theft	Motor vehicle theft
Des Moines-West Des Moines, IA M.S.A.											
	Includes Dallas, Guthrie, Madison, Polk, and Warren Counties	541,394									
	City of Des Moines	192,948	1,514	4	185	387	938	11,794	2,095	8,631	1,068
	City of West Des Moines	54,988	88	0	15	15	58	1,586	226	1,315	45
	Total area actually reporting	100.0%	2,076	7	256	463	1,350	18,789	3,315	14,003	1,471
	Rate per 100,000 inhabitants		383.5	1.3	47.3	85.5	249.4	3,470.5	612.3	2,586.5	271.7
Detroit-Warren-Livonia, MI M.S.A.[2,4]											
	Includes the Metropolitan Divisions of Detroit-Livonia-Dearborn and Warren-Troy-Farmington Hills	4,451,481									
	City of Detroit	860,971	19,708	394	341	6,575	12,398	58,302	17,767	20,918	19,617
	City of Warren[4]	134,081	840	7	83	216	534		824	2,360	
	City of Livonia	96,261	153	1	27	31	94	2,418	421	1,730	267
	City of Dearborn	91,748	466	1	27	146	292	4,333	581	2,945	807
	City of Troy	81,130	80	1	10	20	49	1,882	272	1,441	169
	City of Farmington Hills	79,475	142	0	13	27	102	1,517	403	949	165
	City of Southfield	75,830	745	2	26	170	547	3,260	755	1,865	640
	City of Pontiac	67,059	1,259	19	44	339	857	3,116	1,287	1,215	614
	City of Taylor	64,048	273	4	25	97	147	2,864	483	1,903	478
	City of Novi	55,127	34	0	5	5	24	1,150	165	939	46
	Total area actually reporting	98.9%	31,430	485	1,381	9,261	20,303		35,833	81,394	
	Estimated total	100.0%	31,591	486	1,398	9,296	20,411		36,117	82,453	
	Rate per 100,000 inhabitants		709.7	10.9	31.4	208.8	458.5		811.3	1,852.3	
Detroit-Livonia-Dearborn, MI M.D.[2]											
	Includes Wayne[2] County	1,951,186									
	Total area actually reporting	97.4%	23,647	428	637	7,688	14,894		24,134	42,374	
	Estimated total	100.0%	23,808	429	654	7,723	15,002		24,418	43,433	
	Rate per 100,000 inhabitants		1,220.2	22.0	33.5	395.8	768.9		1,251.4	2,226.0	
Warren-Troy-Farmington Hills, MI M.D.[4]											
	Includes Lapeer, Livingston, Macomb, Oakland, and St. Clair Counties	2,500,295									
	Total area actually reporting	100.0%	7,783	57	744	1,573	5,409		11,699	39,020	
	Rate per 100,000 inhabitants		311.3	2.3	29.8	62.9	216.3		467.9	1,560.6	
Dothan, AL M.S.A.											
	Includes Geneva, Henry, and Houston Counties	139,475									
	City of Dothan	63,984	411	8	45	187	171	3,294	778	2,333	183
	Total area actually reporting	96.2%	545	14	53	211	267	4,719	1,140	3,263	316
	Estimated total	100.0%	566	14	54	219	279	4,949	1,189	3,428	332
	Rate per 100,000 inhabitants		405.8	10.0	38.7	157.0	200.0	3,548.3	852.5	2,457.8	238.0
Dover, DE M.S.A.											
	Includes Kent County	150,986									
	City of Dover	35,133	277	1	16	62	198	1,861	111	1,625	125
	Total area actually reporting	100.0%	942	5	84	141	712	4,700	922	3,492	286
	Rate per 100,000 inhabitants		623.9	3.3	55.6	93.4	471.6	3,112.9	610.7	2,312.8	189.4
Dubuque, IA M.S.A.											
	Includes Dubuque County	92,749									
	City of Dubuque	57,694	407	1	23	27	356	1,946	610	1,256	80
	Total area actually reporting	100.0%	468	1	25	27	415	2,249	713	1,429	107
	Rate per 100,000 inhabitants		504.6	1.1	27.0	29.1	447.4	2,424.8	768.7	1,540.7	115.4
Duluth, MN-WI M.S.A.[5]											
	Includes Carlton and St. Louis Counties, MN[5] and Douglas County, WI	274,026									
	City of Duluth, MN[5]	83,932		1		111	248	4,292	707	3,358	227
	Total area actually reporting	97.6%		4		150	441	9,471	1,776	7,169	526
	Estimated total	100.0%		4		153	447	9,690	1,808	7,343	539
	Rate per 100,000 inhabitants			1.5		55.8	163.1	3,536.2	659.8	2,679.7	196.7

[2] Because of changes in the state/local agency's reporting practices, figures are not comparable to previous years' data.

[4] It was determined that the agency did not follow national Uniform Crime Reporting (UCR) Program guidelines for reporting an offense. Consequently, this figure is not included in this table.

[5] The data collection methodology for the offense of forcible rape used by the Minnesota state UCR Program (with the exception of Minneapolis and St. Paul, MN) does not comply with national UCR Program guidelines. Consequently, their figures for forcible rape and violent crime (of which forcible rape is a part) are not published in this table.

Table 6. Crime, by Metropolitan Statistical Area, 2007 *(Contd.)*

(Number, percent, rate per 100,000 population.)

Metropolitan statistical area	Counties/principal cities	Population	Violent crime	Murder and non-negligent man-slaughter	Forcible rape	Robbery	Aggravated assault	Property crime	Burglary	Larceny-theft	Motor vehicle theft
Eau Claire, WI M.S.A.											
	Includes Chippewa and Eau Claire Counties	156,492									
	City of Eau Claire	63,472	96	0	12	12	72	1,966	365	1,503	98
	Total area actually reporting	100.0%	157	1	25	15	116	3,574	667	2,732	175
	Rate per 100,000 inhabitants		100.3	0.6	16.0	9.6	74.1	2,283.8	426.2	1,745.8	111.8
El Centro, CA M.S.A.											
	Includes Imperial County	161,766									
	City of El Centro	40,957	266	3	11	31	221	2,072	710	1,115	247
	Total area actually reporting	100.0%	545	4	28	95	418	6,066	1,956	2,950	1,160
	Rate per 100,000 inhabitants		336.9	2.5	17.3	58.7	258.4	3,749.9	1,209.2	1,823.6	717.1
Elizabethtown, KY M.S.A.											
	Includes Hardin and Larue Counties	111,690									
	City of Elizabethtown	23,547	86	1	18	23	44	1,039	173	823	43
	Total area actually reporting	100.0%		3	38	45		1,873	416	1,365	92
	Rate per 100,000 inhabitants			2.7	34.0	40.3		1,677.0	372.5	1,222.1	82.4
Elmira, NY M.S.A.											
	Includes Chemung County	88,057									
	City of Elmira	29,375	134	3	5	28	98	1,266	269	956	41
	Total area actually reporting	88.0%	224	3	14	37	170	2,382	406	1,906	70
	Estimated total	100.0%	244	3	15	44	182	2,583	437	2,067	79
	Rate per 100,000 inhabitants		277.1	3.4	17.0	50.0	206.7	2,933.3	496.3	2,347.3	89.7
El Paso, TX M.S.A.											
	Includes El Paso County	744,171									
	City of El Paso	616,029	2,574	17	258	472	1,827	19,722	2,149	14,545	3,028
	Total area actually reporting	100.0%	2,979	20	289	540	2,130	22,917	2,806	16,848	3,263
	Rate per 100,000 inhabitants		400.3	2.7	38.8	72.6	286.2	3,079.5	377.1	2,264.0	438.5
Erie, PA M.S.A.											
	Includes Erie County	278,948									
	City of Erie	101,812	543	3	75	264	201	3,068	831	2,062	175
	Total area actually reporting	100.0%	801	5	117	313	366	5,995	1,514	4,197	284
	Rate per 100,000 inhabitants		287.2	1.8	41.9	112.2	131.2	2,149.1	542.8	1,504.6	101.8
Eugene-Springfield, OR M.S.A.											
	Includes Lane County	340,482									
	City of Eugene	147,458	426	1	55	181	189	7,804	1,640	5,119	1,045
	City of Springfield	56,201	245	0	10	40	195	3,137	504	2,219	414
	Total area actually reporting	100.0%	1,048	1	94	257	696	13,876	3,096	8,958	1,822
	Rate per 100,000 inhabitants		307.8	0.3	27.6	75.5	204.4	4,075.4	909.3	2,631.0	535.1
Evansville, IN-KY M.S.A.											
	Includes Gibson, Posey, Vanderburgh, and Warrick Counties, IN and Henderson and Webster Counties, KY	351,489									
	City of Evansville, IN	114,985	522	2	56	179	285	5,308	1,108	3,905	295
	Total area actually reporting	82.9%	774	5	82	197	490	8,002	1,491	6,108	403
	Estimated total	100.0%	923	6	97	247	573	9,728	1,843	7,358	527
	Rate per 100,000 inhabitants		262.6	1.7	27.6	70.3	163.0	2,767.7	524.3	2,093.4	149.9
Fairbanks, AK M.S.A.											
	Includes Fairbanks North Star Borough	33,156									
	City of Fairbanks	31,287	258	5	43	42	168	1,358	236	957	165
	Total area actually reporting	100.0%	275	5	44	43	183	1,583	262	1,146	175
	Rate per 100,000 inhabitants		829.4	15.1	132.7	129.7	551.9	4,774.4	790.2	3,456.4	527.8
Fargo, ND-MN M.S.A.[5]											
	Includes Clay County, MN[5] and Cass County, ND	189,580									
	City of Fargo, ND	89,998	241	3	62	26	150	2,745	530	2,018	197
	Total area actually reporting	100.0%		3		37	229	4,537	866	3,338	333
	Rate per 100,000 inhabitants			1.6		19.5	120.8	2,393.2	456.8	1,760.7	175.7
Farmington, NM M.S.A.											
	Includes San Juan County	128,294									
	City of Farmington	44,396	367	8	62	38	259	1,705	582	983	140
	Total area actually reporting	100.0%	744	16	106	50	572	3,052	996	1,777	279
	Rate per 100,000 inhabitants		579.9	12.5	82.6	39.0	445.9	2,378.9	776.3	1,385.1	217.5

[5] The data collection methodology for the offense of forcible rape used by the Minnesota state UCR Program (with the exception of Minneapolis and St. Paul, MN) does not comply with national UCR Program guidelines. Consequently, their figures for forcible rape and violent crime (of which forcible rape is a part) are not published in this table.

Table 6. Crime, by Metropolitan Statistical Area, 2007 *(Contd.)*

(Number, percent, rate per 100,000 population.)

Metropolitan statistical area	Counties/principal cities	Population	Violent crime	Murder and non-negligent man-slaughter	Forcible rape	Robbery	Aggravated assault	Property crime	Burglary	Larceny-theft	Motor vehicle theft
Fayetteville, NC M.S.A.											
	Includes Cumberland and Hoke Counties	345,641									
	City of Fayetteville	167,157	1,320	21	56	500	743	12,614	3,569	8,223	822
	Total area actually reporting	88.3%	2,054	28	85	653	1,288	19,384	5,690	12,474	1,220
	Estimated total	100.0%	2,136	30	92	667	1,347	20,319	6,021	13,005	1,293
	Rate per 100,000 inhabitants		618.0	8.7	26.6	193.0	389.7	5,878.6	1,742.0	3,762.6	374.1
Fayetteville-Springdale-Rogers, AR-MO M.S.A.											
	Includes Benton, Madison, and Washington Counties, AR and McDonald County, MO	432,754									
	City of Fayetteville, AR..................	70,334	362	3	42	55	262	3,236	656	2,435	145
	City of Springdale, AR	65,695	322	2	65	33	222	2,825	621	1,996	208
	City of Rogers, AR	54,223	93	0	44	14	35	2,340	265	2,008	67
	City of Bentonville, AR..................	34,232	79	0	20	4	55	879	128	714	37
	Total area actually reporting	99.4%	1,391	9	256	115	1,011	12,722	2,818	9,241	663
	Estimated total	100.0%	1,403	9	257	118	1,019	12,821	2,847	9,306	668
	Rate per 100,000 inhabitants		324.2	2.1	59.4	27.3	235.5	2,962.7	657.9	2,150.4	154.4
Flagstaff, AZ M.S.A.											
	Includes Coconino County	126,419									
	City of Flagstaff.............................	58,978	316	3	51	63	199	3,678	471	3,087	120
	Total area actually reporting	97.4%	560	3	76	73	408	5,072	721	4,171	180
	Estimated total	100.0%	571	3	77	76	415	5,201	750	4,254	197
	Rate per 100,000 inhabitants		451.7	2.4	60.9	60.1	328.3	4,114.1	593.3	3,365.0	155.8
Flint, MI M.S.A.											
	Includes Genesee County	440,751									
	City of Flint	116,024	2,741	30	109	665	1,937	7,246	3,241	2,965	1,040
	Total area actually reporting	99.7%	3,708	37	223	899	2,549	17,223	5,656	9,687	1,880
	Estimated total	100.0%	3,712	37	223	900	2,552	17,259	5,663	9,712	1,884
	Rate per 100,000 inhabitants		842.2	8.4	50.6	204.2	579.0	3,915.8	1,284.9	2,203.5	427.5
Florence, SC M.S.A.											
	Includes Darlington and Florence Counties......................	201,529									
	City of Florence	31,377	552	5	31	117	399	2,757	586	2,000	171
	Total area actually reporting	100.0%	2,145	30	94	328	1,693	10,933	2,705	7,384	844
	Rate per 100,000 inhabitants		1,064.4	14.9	46.6	162.8	840.1	5,425.0	1,342.2	3,664.0	418.8
Fond du Lac, WI M.S.A.											
	Includes Fond du Lac County	99,825									
	City of Fond du Lac........................	42,349	147	0	29	19	99	1,204	113	1,055	36
	Total area actually reporting	100.0%	211	0	34	21	156	1,872	216	1,578	78
	Rate per 100,000 inhabitants		211.4	0.0	34.1	21.0	156.3	1,875.3	216.4	1,580.8	78.1
Fort Collins-Loveland, CO M.S.A.											
	Includes Larimer County.................	282,097									
	City of Fort Collins.........................	130,935	418	1	70	33	314	4,476	695	3,487	294
	City of Loveland.............................	62,586	114	1	17	17	79	1,734	251	1,408	75
	Total area actually reporting	100.0%	643	4	107	59	473	7,881	1,212	6,168	501
	Rate per 100,000 inhabitants		227.9	1.4	37.9	20.9	167.7	2,793.7	429.6	2,186.5	177.6
Fort Smith, AR-OK M.S.A.[1]											
	Includes Crawford, Franklin, and Sebastian Counties, AR and Le Flore and Sequoyah[1] Counties, OK........................	291,717									
	City of Fort Smith, AR	83,860	787	5	78	143	561	5,474	1,041	4,110	323
	Total area actually reporting	87.8%		7		167		8,669	2,048	6,071	550
	Estimated total	100.0%		8		177		9,554	2,366	6,572	616
	Rate per 100,000 inhabitants			2.7		60.7		3,275.1	811.1	2,252.9	211.2
Fort Walton Beach-Crestview-Destin, FL M.S.A.											
	Includes Okaloosa County	180,091									
	City of Fort Walton Beach	19,245	106	0	11	25	70	826	161	601	64
	City of Crestview	18,753	101	3	13	21	64	770	82	634	54
	Total area actually reporting	100.0%	727	4	61	144	518	5,670	1,182	4,125	363
	Rate per 100,000 inhabitants		403.7	2.2	33.9	80.0	287.6	3,148.4	656.3	2,290.5	201.6

[1] The FBI determined that the agency's data were overreported. Consequently, affected data are not included in this table.

Table 6. Crime, by Metropolitan Statistical Area, 2007 *(Contd.)*

(Number, percent, rate per 100,000 population.)

Metropolitan statistical area	Counties/principal cities	Population	Violent crime	Murder and non-negligent man-slaughter	Forcible rape	Robbery	Aggravated assault	Property crime	Burglary	Larceny-theft	Motor vehicle theft
Fort Wayne, IN M.S.A.											
	Includes Allen, Wells, and Whitley Counties	410,350									
	City of Fort Wayne	248,423	762	24	85	407	246	10,083	2,129	7,312	642
	Total area actually reporting	91.1%	825	25	98	427	275	11,724	2,448	8,508	768
	Estimated total	100.0%	882	26	103	443	310	12,576	2,609	9,132	835
	Rate per 100,000 inhabitants		214.9	6.3	25.1	108.0	75.5	3,064.7	635.8	2,225.4	203.5
Fresno, CA M.S.A.											
	Includes Fresno County	898,391									
	City of Fresno	472,170	3,043	52	99	1,104	1,788	20,969	3,897	13,049	4,023
	Total area actually reporting	100.0%	4,450	73	183	1,430	2,764	35,941	7,159	22,335	6,447
	Rate per 100,000 inhabitants		495.3	8.1	20.4	159.2	307.7	4,000.6	796.9	2,486.1	717.6
Gainesville, FL M.S.A.[3]											
	Includes Alachua and Gilchrist[3] Counties	243,506									
	City of Gainesville	108,289	1,122	5	93	237	787	5,795	1,522	3,837	436
	Total area actually reporting	99.7%	2,291	7	150	410	1,724		3,001		788
	Estimated total	100.0%	2,296	7	150	412	1,727		3,008		791
	Rate per 100,000 inhabitants		942.9	2.9	61.6	169.2	709.2		1,235.3		324.8
Gainesville, GA M.S.A.											
	Includes Hall County	178,408									
	City of Gainesville	34,494	184	2	18	55	109	1,920	293	1,494	133
	Total area actually reporting	100.0%	416	4	37	104	271	4,894	1,023	3,313	558
	Rate per 100,000 inhabitants		233.2	2.2	20.7	58.3	151.9	2,743.2	573.4	1,857.0	312.8
Glens Falls, NY M.S.A.											
	Includes Warren and Washington Counties	129,840									
	City of Glens Falls	14,043	18	1	2	5	10	471	51	413	7
	Total area actually reporting	100.0%	235	5	41	12	177	2,391	376	1,947	68
	Rate per 100,000 inhabitants		181.0	3.9	31.6	9.2	136.3	1,841.5	289.6	1,499.5	52.4
Goldsboro, NC M.S.A.											
	Includes Wayne County	115,119									
	City of Goldsboro	38,053	312	10	6	100	196	2,843	755	1,921	167
	Total area actually reporting	98.1%	526	19	10	132	365	5,394	1,656	3,391	347
	Estimated total	100.0%	536	19	11	135	371	5,505	1,683	3,469	353
	Rate per 100,000 inhabitants		465.6	16.5	9.6	117.3	322.3	4,782.0	1,462.0	3,013.4	306.6
Grand Forks, ND-MN M.S.A.[5]											
	Includes Polk County, MN[5] and Grand Forks County, ND	96,813									
	City of Grand Forks, ND	50,477	120	1	30	11	78	1,762	253	1,379	130
	Total area actually reporting	98.7%		2		11	120	2,541	426	1,938	177
	Estimated total	100.0%		2		11	121	2,576	431	1,965	180
	Rate per 100,000 inhabitants			2.1		11.4	125.0	2,660.8	445.2	2,029.7	185.9
Grand Junction, CO M.S.A.											
	Includes Mesa County	137,907									
	City of Grand Junction	47,235	290	0	36	31	223	2,532	327	2,033	172
	Total area actually reporting	99.7%	473	2	52	51	368	4,111	719	3,067	325
	Estimated total	100.0%	474	2	52	51	369	4,124	721	3,077	326
	Rate per 100,000 inhabitants		343.7	1.5	37.7	37.0	267.6	2,990.4	522.8	2,231.2	236.4
Grand Rapids-Wyoming, MI M.S.A.											
	Includes Barry, Ionia, Kent, and Newaygo Counties	774,927									
	City of Grand Rapids	192,376	1,874	20	69	669	1,116	10,149	2,629	6,931	589
	City of Wyoming	70,243	356	1	42	96	217	2,177	581	1,391	205
	Total area actually reporting	99.1%	3,277	27	355	878	2,017	24,624	5,853	17,471	1,300
	Estimated total	100.0%	3,298	27	357	883	2,031	24,826	5,891	17,614	1,321
	Rate per 100,000 inhabitants		425.6	3.5	46.1	113.9	262.1	3,203.7	760.2	2,273.0	170.5
Great Falls, MT M.S.A.											
	Includes Cascade County	79,880									
	City of Great Falls	56,159	178	1	6	29	142	3,061	235	2,713	113
	Total area actually reporting	100.0%	240	2	8	29	201	3,340	278	2,921	141
	Rate per 100,000 inhabitants		300.5	2.5	10.0	36.3	251.6	4,181.3	348.0	3,656.7	176.5

[3] The FBI determined that the agency's data were underreported. Consequently, affected data are not included in this table.

[5] The data collection methodology for the offense of forcible rape used by the Minnesota state UCR Program (with the exception of Minneapolis and St. Paul, MN) does not comply with national UCR Program guidelines. Consequently, their figures for forcible rape and violent crime (of which forcible rape is a part) are not published in this table.

Table 6. Crime, by Metropolitan Statistical Area, 2007 *(Contd.)*

(Number, percent, rate per 100,000 population.)

Metropolitan statistical area	Counties/principal cities	Population	Violent crime	Murder and non-negligent man-slaughter	Forcible rape	Robbery	Aggravated assault	Property crime	Burglary	Larceny-theft	Motor vehicle theft
Greeley, CO M.S.A.											
	Includes Weld County	247,806									
	City of Greeley	90,707	423	4	50	48	321	3,566	703	2,610	253
	Total area actually reporting	98.1%	753	7	79	63	604	6,507	1,398	4,571	538
	Estimated total	100.0%	765	7	81	65	612	6,664	1,424	4,686	554
	Rate per 100,000 inhabitants		308.7	2.8	32.7	26.2	247.0	2,689.2	574.6	1,891.0	223.6
Green Bay, WI M.S.A.											
	Includes Brown, Kewaunee, and Oconto Counties	302,277									
	City of Green Bay	100,010	616	2	67	89	458	2,843	565	2,094	184
	Total area actually reporting	100.0%	711	4	96	91	520	6,882	1,283	5,225	374
	Rate per 100,000 inhabitants		235.2	1.3	31.8	30.1	172.0	2,276.7	424.4	1,728.5	123.7
Greensboro-High Point, NC M.S.A.											
	Includes Guilford, Randolph, and Rockingham Counties	697,634									
	City of Greensboro	238,122	2,312	40	94	942	1,236	14,778	4,704	8,943	1,131
	City of High Point	97,676	819	13	38	330	438	5,654	1,840	3,401	413
	Total area actually reporting	99.8%	3,914	73	166	1,493	2,182	31,703	9,690	19,797	2,216
	Estimated total	100.0%	3,920	73	166	1,495	2,186	31,768	9,706	19,843	2,219
	Rate per 100,000 inhabitants		561.9	10.5	23.8	214.3	313.3	4,553.7	1,391.3	2,844.3	318.1
Greenville, NC M.S.A.											
	Includes Greene and Pitt Counties	169,150									
	City of Greenville	73,319	663	8	20	275	360	4,928	1,424	3,237	267
	Total area actually reporting	100.0%	1,032	14	46	330	642	8,422	2,596	5,343	483
	Rate per 100,000 inhabitants		610.1	8.3	27.2	195.1	379.5	4,979.0	1,534.7	3,158.7	285.5
Greenville-Mauldin-Easley, SC M.S.A.											
	Includes Greenville, Laurens, and Pickens Counties	613,703									
	City of Greenville	57,595	659	8	26	172	453	3,810	643	2,805	362
	City of Mauldin	20,494	92	1	5	15	71	545	70	427	48
	City of Easley	19,372	103	1	6	20	76	939	126	749	64
	Total area actually reporting	100.0%	4,251	40	247	877	3,087	23,927	6,026	15,611	2,290
	Rate per 100,000 inhabitants		692.7	6.5	40.2	142.9	503.0	3,898.8	981.9	2,543.7	373.1
Hanford-Corcoran, CA M.S.A.											
	Includes Kings County	147,510									
	City of Hanford	49,694	151	0	8	40	103	1,674	244	1,233	197
	City of Corcoran	23,715	45	0	4	5	36	216	65	119	32
	Total area actually reporting	100.0%	441	7	29	92	313	3,439	660	2,214	565
	Rate per 100,000 inhabitants		299.0	4.7	19.7	62.4	212.2	2,331.4	447.4	1,500.9	383.0
Harrisburg-Carlisle, PA M.S.A.											
	Includes Cumberland, Dauphin, and Perry Counties	526,335									
	City of Harrisburg	46,924	734	12	52	443	227	2,297	576	1,556	165
	City of Carlisle	18,317	55	0	12	26	17	663	72	572	19
	Total area actually reporting	99.0%	1,671	21	158	665	827	10,534	1,933	8,124	477
	Estimated total	100.0%	1,683	21	159	668	835	10,644	1,950	8,211	483
	Rate per 100,000 inhabitants		319.8	4.0	30.2	126.9	158.6	2,022.3	370.5	1,560.0	91.8
Harrisonburg, VA M.S.A.											
	Includes Rockingham County and Harrisonburg City	113,967									
	City of Harrisonburg	40,869	150	0	11	37	102	1,240	250	874	116
	Total area actually reporting	100.0%	188	0	20	40	128	1,930	412	1,382	136
	Rate per 100,000 inhabitants		165.0	0.0	17.5	35.1	112.3	1,693.5	361.5	1,212.6	119.3
Hartford-West Hartford-East Hartford, CT M.S.A.											
	Includes Hartford, Middlesex, and Tolland Counties	1,006,947									
	City of Hartford	124,558	1,411	31	58	642	680	7,206	1,168	4,437	1,601
	City of West Hartford	60,644	83	1	2	53	27	1,468	241	1,063	164
	City of East Hartford	48,752	221	3	15	100	103	1,614	349	1,030	235
	City of Middletown	47,743	48	0	0	25	23	1,267	179	966	122
	Total area actually reporting	100.0%	2,936	46	182	1,328	1,380	29,632	5,217	20,804	3,611
	Rate per 100,000 inhabitants		291.6	4.6	18.1	131.9	137.0	2,942.8	518.1	2,066.0	358.6

Table 6. Crime, by Metropolitan Statistical Area, 2007 *(Contd.)*

(Number, percent, rate per 100,000 population.)

Metropolitan statistical area	Counties/principal cities	Population	Violent crime	Murder and non-negligent man-slaughter	Forcible rape	Robbery	Aggravated assault	Property crime	Burglary	Larceny-theft	Motor vehicle theft
Hattiesburg, MS M.S.A.											
	Includes Forrest, Lamar, and Perry Counties	135,875									
	City of Hattiesburg	48,384	234	2	21	135	76	2,588	596	1,821	171
	Total area actually reporting	75.8%	309	2	48	151	108	3,470	931	2,310	229
	Estimated total	100.0%	362	4	54	161	143	4,189	1,129	2,755	305
	Rate per 100,000 inhabitants		266.4	2.9	39.7	118.5	105.2	3,083.0	830.9	2,027.6	224.5
Hickory-Lenoir-Morganton, NC M.S.A.											
	Includes Alexander, Burke, Caldwell, and Catawba Counties	365,896									
	City of Hickory	41,008	368	5	21	116	226	3,398	783	2,338	277
	City of Lenoir	17,988	51	1	1	15	34	768	217	517	34
	City of Morganton	17,183	77	2	8	17	50	713	179	497	37
	Total area actually reporting	99.3%	1,026	19	85	250	672	12,794	3,743	8,087	964
	Estimated total	100.0%	1,037	19	86	253	679	12,923	3,774	8,178	971
	Rate per 100,000 inhabitants		283.4	5.2	23.5	69.1	185.6	3,531.9	1,031.4	2,235.1	265.4
Hinesville-Fort Stewart, GA M.S.A.											
	Includes Liberty and Long Counties	74,369									
	City of Hinesville	29,466	225	4	16	44	161	2,055	479	1,511	65
	Total area actually reporting	100.0%	317	5	26	57	229	2,876	702	2,072	102
	Rate per 100,000 inhabitants		426.3	6.7	35.0	76.6	307.9	3,867.2	943.9	2,786.1	137.2
Honolulu, HI M.S.A.											
	Includes Honolulu County	905,903									
	City of Honolulu	905,903	2,613	19	226	943	1,425	37,197	5,777	26,483	4,937
	Total area actually reporting	100.0%	2,613	19	226	943	1,425	37,197	5,777	26,483	4,937
	Rate per 100,000 inhabitants		288.4	2.1	24.9	104.1	157.3	4,106.1	637.7	2,923.4	545.0
Hot Springs, AR M.S.A.											
	Includes Garland County	96,271									
	City of Hot Springs	38,828	442	7	10	116	309	3,951	848	2,894	209
	Total area actually reporting	100.0%	538	10	24	123	381	6,257	1,784	4,090	383
	Rate per 100,000 inhabitants		558.8	10.4	24.9	127.8	395.8	6,499.4	1,853.1	4,248.4	397.8
Houma-Bayou Cane-Thibodaux, LA M.S.A.											
	Includes Lafourche and Terrebonne Parishes	203,401									
	City of Houma	32,597	340	4	16	65	255	1,489	235	1,182	72
	City of Thibodaux	14,501	120	1	10	21	88	679	126	539	14
	Total area actually reporting	100.0%	997	12	66	134	785	7,104	1,037	5,666	401
	Rate per 100,000 inhabitants		490.2	5.9	32.4	65.9	385.9	3,492.6	509.8	2,785.6	197.1
Houston-Sugar Land-Baytown, TX M.S.A.											
	Includes Austin, Brazoria, Chambers, Fort Bend, Galveston, Harris, Liberty, Montgomery, San Jacinto, and Waller Counties	5,664,249									
	City of Houston	2,169,544	24,564	351	694	11,479	12,040	123,326	29,044	74,817	19,465
	City of Sugar Land	82,402	100	0	17	39	44	1,578	210	1,268	100
	City of Baytown	69,040	324	7	44	113	160	3,098	731	2,048	319
	City of Galveston	57,590	585	7	82	209	287	3,475	757	2,394	324
	Total area actually reporting	99.9%	38,464	496	1,749	15,229	20,990	232,740	56,715	144,760	31,265
	Estimated total	100.0%	38,465	496	1,749	15,229	20,991	232,759	56,719	144,774	31,266
	Rate per 100,000 inhabitants		679.1	8.8	30.9	268.9	370.6	4,109.3	1,001.4	2,555.9	552.0
Huntsville, AL M.S.A.											
	Includes Limestone and Madison Counties	382,202									
	City of Huntsville	169,391	1,379	21	96	586	676	10,731	2,283	7,282	1,166
	Total area actually reporting	83.9%	1,626	25	121	620	860	13,300	2,960	8,847	1,493
	Estimated total	100.0%	1,885	31	138	712	1,004	15,986	3,529	10,778	1,679
	Rate per 100,000 inhabitants		493.2	8.1	36.1	186.3	262.7	4,182.6	923.3	2,820.0	439.3

Table 6. Crime, by Metropolitan Statistical Area, 2007 *(Contd.)*

(Number, percent, rate per 100,000 population.)

Metropolitan statistical area	Counties/principal cities	Population	Violent crime	Murder and non-negligent man-slaughter	Forcible rape	Robbery	Aggravated assault	Property crime	Burglary	Larceny-theft	Motor vehicle theft
Idaho Falls, ID M.S.A.											
	Includes Bonneville and Jefferson Counties	119,795									
	City of Idaho Falls	53,049	222	0	32	16	174	1,927	372	1,432	123
	Total area actually reporting	100.0%	342	1	53	17	271	3,173	680	2,277	216
	Rate per 100,000 inhabitants		285.5	0.8	44.2	14.2	226.2	2,648.7	567.6	1,900.7	180.3
Indianapolis-Carmel, IN M.S.A.											
	Includes Boone, Brown, Hamilton, Hancock, Hendricks, Johnson, Marion, Morgan, Putnam, and Shelby Counties	1,687,197									
	City of Indianapolis	797,268	9,841	114	505	4,046	5,176	50,289	13,385	29,224	7,680
	City of Carmel	62,037	29	1	3	6	19	1,009	123	840	46
	Total area actually reporting	89.6%	10,758	125	588	4,311	5,734	66,567	15,880	41,891	8,796
	Estimated total	100.0%	11,003	130	611	4,375	5,887	70,304	16,620	44,594	9,090
	Rate per 100,000 inhabitants		652.1	7.7	36.2	259.3	348.9	4,166.9	985.1	2,643.1	538.8
Iowa City, IA M.S.A.											
	Includes Johnson and Washington Counties	140,650									
	City of Iowa City	62,700	207	0	18	33	156	1,333	217	1,054	62
	Total area actually reporting	94.8%	362	0	31	45	286	2,841	550	2,167	124
	Estimated total	100.0%	375	0	32	46	297	3,011	578	2,301	132
	Rate per 100,000 inhabitants		266.6	0.0	22.8	32.7	211.2	2,140.8	410.9	1,636.0	93.8
Ithaca, NY M.S.A.											
	Includes Tompkins County	100,687									
	City of Ithaca	29,970	58	0	8	22	28	965	147	805	13
	Total area actually reporting	100.0%	116	0	19	28	69	2,321	343	1,925	53
	Rate per 100,000 inhabitants		115.2	0.0	18.9	27.8	68.5	2,305.2	340.7	1,911.9	52.6
Jackson, MI M.S.A.											
	Includes Jackson County	163,839									
	City of Jackson	34,325	225	1	39	50	135	1,682	281	1,291	110
	Total area actually reporting	98.6%	570	2	98	76	394	4,401	894	3,239	268
	Estimated total	100.0%	578	2	99	78	399	4,469	907	3,287	275
	Rate per 100,000 inhabitants		352.8	1.2	60.4	47.6	243.5	2,727.7	553.6	2,006.2	167.8
Jackson, MS M.S.A.											
	Includes Copiah, Hinds, Madison, Rankin, and Simpson Counties	532,981									
	City of Jackson	175,525	1,512	46	141	862	463	12,465	3,897	6,984	1,584
	Total area actually reporting	79.8%	1,936	60	202	967	707	17,490	5,384	10,217	1,889
	Estimated total	100.0%	2,157	66	229	1,021	841	20,628	6,201	12,280	2,147
	Rate per 100,000 inhabitants		404.7	12.4	43.0	191.6	157.8	3,870.3	1,163.5	2,304.0	402.8
Jackson, TN M.S.A.											
	Includes Chester and Madison Counties	113,807									
	City of Jackson	63,125	681	9	27	266	379	4,606	1,106	2,930	570
	Total area actually reporting	100.0%	953	12	48	283	610	5,891	1,490	3,702	699
	Rate per 100,000 inhabitants		837.4	10.5	42.2	248.7	536.0	5,176.3	1,309.2	3,252.9	614.2
Jacksonville, FL M.S.A.[1]											
	Includes Baker, Clay, Duval, Nassau,[1] and St. Johns Counties	1,290,776									
	City of Jacksonville	797,350	8,146	123	249	3,114	4,660	45,416	11,115	29,484	4,817
	Total area actually reporting	99.5%		139	361	3,480		60,532	14,685	39,968	5,879
	Estimated total	100.0%		139	363	3,494		60,819	14,748	40,165	5,906
	Rate per 100,000 inhabitants			10.8	28.1	270.7		4,711.8	1,142.6	3,111.7	457.6
Jacksonville, NC M.S.A.											
	Includes Onslow County	152,338									
	City of Jacksonville	70,368	278	7	30	65	176	2,297	550	1,614	133
	Total area actually reporting	100.0%	588	11	65	116	396	5,357	1,624	3,389	344
	Rate per 100,000 inhabitants		386.0	7.2	42.7	76.1	259.9	3,516.5	1,066.1	2,224.7	225.8
Janesville, WI M.S.A.											
	Includes Rock County	160,629									
	City of Janesville	63,383	158	0	25	55	78	2,731	431	2,217	83
	Total area actually reporting	100.0%	370	5	47	125	193	5,462	964	4,266	232
	Rate per 100,000 inhabitants		230.3	3.1	29.3	77.8	120.2	3,400.4	600.1	2,655.8	144.4

[1] The FBI determined that the agency's data were overreported. Consequently, affected data are not included in this table.

Table 6. Crime, by Metropolitan Statistical Area, 2007 *(Contd.)*

(Number, percent, rate per 100,000 population.)

Metropolitan statistical area	Counties/principal cities	Population	Violent crime	Murder and non-negligent man-slaughter	Forcible rape	Robbery	Aggravated assault	Property crime	Burglary	Larceny-theft	Motor vehicle theft
Jefferson City, MO M.S.A.[2]											
	Includes Callaway, Cole, Moniteau,[2] and Osage Counties	145,564									
	City of Jefferson City	39,121	286	1	25	30	230	1,484	244	1,186	54
	Total area actually reporting	100.0%	471	3	41	44	383	3,848	731	2,921	196
	Rate per 100,000 inhabitants..........		323.6	2.1	28.2	30.2	263.1	2,643.5	502.2	2,006.7	134.6
Johnson City, TN M.S.A.											
	Includes Carter, Unicoi, and Washington Counties	194,592									
	City of Johnson City	60,488	343	1	22	57	263	3,023	566	2,295	162
	Total area actually reporting	100.0%	814	4	35	77	698	6,034	1,395	4,286	353
	Rate per 100,000 inhabitants..........		418.3	2.1	18.0	39.6	358.7	3,100.8	716.9	2,202.6	181.4
Johnstown, PA M.S.A.											
	Includes Cambria County...............	145,844									
	City of Johnstown	23,609	145	1	3	57	84	864	262	546	56
	Total area actually reporting	91.9%	289	2	9	77	201	2,792	542	2,084	166
	Estimated total...............	100.0%	316	2	11	84	219	3,030	578	2,272	180
	Rate per 100,000 inhabitants...........		216.7	1.4	7.5	57.6	150.2	2,077.6	396.3	1,557.8	123.4
Jonesboro, AR M.S.A.											
	Includes Craighead and Poinsett Counties......................	114,222									
	City of Jonesboro...........................	61,199	333	5	30	92	206	3,526	1,419	1,993	114
	Total area actually reporting	100.0%	477	5	46	102	324	5,060	2,021	2,875	164
	Rate per 100,000 inhabitants..........		417.6	4.4	40.3	89.3	283.7	4,430.0	1,769.4	2,517.0	143.6
Joplin, MO M.S.A.											
	Includes Jasper and Newton Counties..	170,012									
	City of Joplin	48,261	372	1	38	91	242	4,812	845	3,554	413
	Total area actually reporting	100.0%	687	8	65	110	504	8,102	1,563	5,897	642
	Rate per 100,000 inhabitants...........		404.1	4.7	38.2	64.7	296.4	4,765.5	919.3	3,468.6	377.6
Kalamazoo-Portage, MI M.S.A.											
	Includes Kalamazoo and Van Buren Counties	318,778									
	City of Kalamazoo...........................	71,462	835	9	81	302	443	4,472	1,039	3,089	344
	City of Portage	45,287	104	1	20	20	63	2,124	343	1,708	73
	Total area actually reporting	98.9%	1,477	14	219	398	846	12,213	2,796	8,630	787
	Estimated total...............	100.0%	1,487	14	220	400	853	12,318	2,816	8,704	798
	Rate per 100,000 inhabitants...........		466.5	4.4	69.0	125.5	267.6	3,864.1	883.4	2,730.4	250.3
Kennewick-Pasco-Richland, WA M.S.A.											
	Includes Benton and Franklin Counties..	231,368									
	City of Kennewick	63,147	236	1	38	31	166	2,362	341	1,862	159
	City of Pasco.................................	52,761	150	0	29	43	78	1,811	408	1,138	265
	City of Richland...............................	45,555	105	0	13	23	69	1,249	213	960	76
	Total area actually reporting	100.0%	574	4	93	101	376	6,619	1,325	4,704	590
	Rate per 100,000 inhabitants..........		248.1	1.7	40.2	43.7	162.5	2,860.8	572.7	2,033.1	255.0
Killeen-Temple-Fort Hood, TX M.S.A.											
	Includes Bell, Coryell, and Lampasas Counties........................	354,141									
	City of Killeen...............................	104,188	815	12	82	202	519	5,680	2,319	3,098	263
	City of Temple	55,057	203	1	22	76	104	2,973	723	2,107	143
	Total area actually reporting	99.7%	1,399	19	156	344	880	12,981	4,247	8,155	579
	Estimated total...............	100.0%	1,402	19	156	345	882	13,020	4,255	8,183	582
	Rate per 100,000 inhabitants..........		395.9	5.4	44.1	97.4	249.1	3,676.5	1,201.5	2,310.7	164.3
Kingsport-Bristol-Bristol, TN-VA M.S.A.											
	Includes Hawkins and Sullivan Counties, TN and Scott and Washington Counties and Bristol City, VA	305,118									
	City of Kingsport, TN	44,079	335	2	21	57	255	3,064	521	2,395	148
	City of Bristol, TN	25,346	117	0	16	9	92	1,436	207	1,129	100
	City of Bristol, VA	17,484	77	0	11	17	49	764	122	604	38
	Total area actually reporting	100.0%	1,146	8	120	124	894	11,308	2,394	8,185	729
	Rate per 100,000 inhabitants..........		375.6	2.6	39.3	40.6	293.0	3,706.1	784.6	2,682.6	238.9

[2] Because of changes in the state/local agency's reporting practices, figures are not comparable to previous years' data.

Table 6. Crime, by Metropolitan Statistical Area, 2007 *(Contd.)*

(Number, percent, rate per 100,000 population.)

Metropolitan statistical area	Counties/principal cities	Population	Violent crime	Murder and non-negligent manslaughter	Forcible rape	Robbery	Aggravated assault	Property crime	Burglary	Larceny-theft	Motor vehicle theft
Kingston, NY M.S.A.											
	Includes Ulster County	182,932									
	City of Kingston	22,741	67	1	5	38	23	699	122	551	26
	Total area actually reporting	100.0%	456	3	41	66	346	3,003	623	2,251	129
	Rate per 100,000 inhabitants		249.3	1.6	22.4	36.1	189.1	1,641.6	340.6	1,230.5	70.5
Knoxville, TN M.S.A.											
	Includes Anderson, Blount, Knox, Loudon, and Union Counties	682,242									
	City of Knoxville	183,319	2,058	27	109	681	1,241	12,862	2,507	8,984	1,371
	Total area actually reporting	100.0%	3,602	38	202	903	2,459	26,674	6,168	18,024	2,482
	Rate per 100,000 inhabitants		528.0	5.6	29.6	132.4	360.4	3,909.8	904.1	2,641.9	363.8
Kokomo, IN M.S.A.											
	Includes Howard and Tipton Counties	100,734									
	City of Kokomo	45,832	216	1	20	62	133	2,717	450	2,142	125
	Total area actually reporting	100.0%	277	1	24	68	184	3,532	703	2,679	150
	Rate per 100,000 inhabitants		275.0	1.0	23.8	67.5	182.7	3,506.3	697.9	2,659.5	148.9
La Crosse, WI-MN M.S.A.[5]											
	Includes Houston County, MN[5] and La Crosse County, WI	129,892									
	City of La Crosse, WI	50,032	164	1	15	22	126	1,867	305	1,475	87
	Total area actually reporting	95.1%		1		29	162	3,039	472	2,436	131
	Estimated total	100.0%		1		32	168	3,251	503	2,604	144
	Rate per 100,000 inhabitants			0.8		24.6	129.3	2,502.8	387.2	2,004.7	110.9
Lafayette, IN M.S.A.											
	Includes Benton, Carroll, and Tippecanoe Counties	186,687									
	City of Lafayette	61,257	303	0	36	68	199	3,083	610	2,290	183
	Total area actually reporting	95.2%	443	2	57	79	305	5,219	1,157	3,783	279
	Estimated total	100.0%	454	2	58	82	312	5,403	1,194	3,915	294
	Rate per 100,000 inhabitants		243.2	1.1	31.1	43.9	167.1	2,894.1	639.6	2,097.1	157.5
Lafayette, LA M.S.A.											
	Includes Lafayette and St. Martin Parishes	255,453									
	City of Lafayette	114,212	1,293	15	68	319	891	7,118	1,410	5,152	556
	Total area actually reporting	91.7%	1,880	22	104	394	1,360	9,823	2,147	6,884	792
	Estimated total	100.0%	2,029	24	112	416	1,477	10,953	2,357	7,739	857
	Rate per 100,000 inhabitants		794.3	9.4	43.8	162.8	578.2	4,287.7	922.7	3,029.5	335.5
Lake Havasu City-Kingman, AZ M.S.A.											
	Includes Mohave County	199,339									
	City of Lake Havasu City	58,699	134	5	20	8	101	1,813	307	1,388	118
	City of Kingman	28,306	89	1	8	16	64	2,070	415	1,485	170
	Total area actually reporting	100.0%	563	16	34	78	435	8,997	2,242	5,977	778
	Rate per 100,000 inhabitants		282.4	8.0	17.1	39.1	218.2	4,513.4	1,124.7	2,998.4	390.3
Lakeland-Winter Haven, FL M.S.A.											
	Includes Polk County	568,435									
	City of Lakeland	91,009	600	6	39	201	354	5,372	1,093	3,956	323
	City of Winter Haven	31,556	218	2	20	76	120	2,008	507	1,355	146
	Total area actually reporting	99.5%	3,020	31	190	731	2,068	22,251	6,292	14,337	1,622
	Estimated total	100.0%	3,038	31	191	737	2,079	22,368	6,318	14,417	1,633
	Rate per 100,000 inhabitants		534.4	5.5	33.6	129.7	365.7	3,935.0	1,111.5	2,536.3	287.3
Lancaster, PA M.S.A.											
	Includes Lancaster County	496,516									
	City of Lancaster	54,562	515	5	38	241	231	3,252	556	2,441	255
	Total area actually reporting	97.4%	978	12	104	385	477	10,377	1,948	7,779	650
	Estimated total	100.0%	1,007	12	106	393	496	10,636	1,987	7,984	665
	Rate per 100,000 inhabitants		202.8	2.4	21.3	79.2	99.9	2,142.1	400.2	1,608.0	133.9
Lansing-East Lansing, MI M.S.A.											
	Includes Clinton, Eaton, and Ingham Counties	452,907									
	City of Lansing	113,643	1,244	16	92	269	867	4,124	1,252	2,517	355
	City of East Lansing	45,979	201	0	22	34	145	978	231	700	47
	Total area actually reporting	96.9%	1,983	21	247	387	1,328	11,354	2,824	7,853	677
	Estimated total	100.0%	2,028	21	252	397	1,358	11,774	2,904	8,150	720
	Rate per 100,000 inhabitants		447.8	4.6	55.6	87.7	299.8	2,599.7	641.2	1,799.5	159.0

[5] The data collection methodology for the offense of forcible rape used by the Minnesota state UCR Program (with the exception of Minneapolis and St. Paul, MN) does not comply with national UCR Program guidelines. Consequently, their figures for forcible rape and violent crime (of which forcible rape is a part) are not published in this table.

Table 6. Crime, by Metropolitan Statistical Area, 2007 *(Contd.)*

(Number, percent, rate per 100,000 population.)

Metropolitan statistical area	Counties/principal cities	Population	Violent crime	Murder and non-negligent man-slaughter	Forcible rape	Robbery	Aggravated assault	Property crime	Burglary	Larceny-theft	Motor vehicle theft
Laredo, TX M.S.A.											
	Includes Webb County	237,170									
	City of Laredo	221,253	1,281	10	81	325	865	13,949	1,878	10,534	1,537
	Total area actually reporting	100.0%	1,342	13	82	340	907	14,399	2,015	10,800	1,584
	Rate per 100,000 inhabitants		565.8	5.5	34.6	143.4	382.4	6,071.2	849.6	4,553.7	667.9
Las Cruces, NM M.S.A.[2]											
	Includes Dona Ana County	196,085									
	City of Las Cruces[2]	87,958	437	6	40	96	295	4,278	860	3,158	260
	Total area actually reporting	98.9%	860	10	96	125	629	5,802	1,346	4,027	429
	Estimated total	100.0%	873	10	97	126	640	5,868	1,363	4,068	437
	Rate per 100,000 inhabitants		445.2	5.1	49.5	64.3	326.4	2,992.6	695.1	2,074.6	222.9
Las Vegas-Paradise, NV M.S.A.											
	Includes Clark County	1,834,533									
	City of Las Vegas Metropolitan Police Department	1,341,156	13,641	119	723	5,251	7,548	58,897	15,296	27,156	16,445
	Total area actually reporting	100.0%	16,272	157	849	6,185	9,081	75,766	19,784	35,846	20,136
	Rate per 100,000 inhabitants		887.0	8.6	46.3	337.1	495.0	4,130.0	1,078.4	1,954.0	1,097.6
Lawrence, KS M.S.A.											
	Includes Douglas County	114,212									
	City of Lawrence	90,044	409	0	48	63	298	5,030	550	4,283	197
	Total area actually reporting	100.0%	471	2	59	66	344	5,774	688	4,855	231
	Rate per 100,000 inhabitants		412.4	1.8	51.7	57.8	301.2	5,055.5	602.4	4,250.9	202.3
Lawton, OK M.S.A.											
	Includes Comanche County	109,016									
	City of Lawton	86,864	1,075	9	75	184	807	4,638	1,555	2,813	270
	Total area actually reporting	100.0%	1,092	10	80	187	815	4,871	1,619	2,960	292
	Rate per 100,000 inhabitants		1,001.7	9.2	73.4	171.5	747.6	4,468.2	1,485.1	2,715.2	267.9
Lebanon, PA M.S.A.											
	Includes Lebanon County	127,496									
	City of Lebanon	24,144	112	1	13	44	54	768	124	581	63
	Total area actually reporting	96.4%	308	1	37	72	198	2,077	310	1,663	104
	Estimated total	100.0%	319	1	38	75	205	2,169	324	1,736	109
	Rate per 100,000 inhabitants		250.2	0.8	29.8	58.8	160.8	1,701.2	254.1	1,361.6	85.5
Lewiston, ID-WA M.S.A.											
	Includes Nez Perce County, ID and Asotin County, WA	59,973									
	City of Lewiston, ID	31,356	41	1	12	3	25	1,258	239	959	60
	Total area actually reporting	100.0%	75	1	13	8	53	1,883	340	1,445	98
	Rate per 100,000 inhabitants		125.1	1.7	21.7	13.3	88.4	3,139.7	566.9	2,409.4	163.4
Lewiston-Auburn, ME M.S.A.											
	Includes Androscoggin County	107,169									
	City of Lewiston	35,747	97	2	23	34	38	1,117	260	813	44
	City of Auburn	23,150	29	2	6	10	11	817	152	633	32
	Total area actually reporting	100.0%	155	4	39	46	66	2,623	605	1,908	110
	Rate per 100,000 inhabitants		144.6	3.7	36.4	42.9	61.6	2,447.5	564.5	1,780.4	102.6
Lexington-Fayette, KY M.S.A.											
	Includes Bourbon, Clark, Fayette, Jessamine, Scott, and Woodford Counties	441,674									
	City of Lexington	272,815	1,790	16	111	550	1,113	9,349	2,114	6,623	612
	Total area actually reporting	94.4%	2,028	20	151	624	1,233	13,915	3,065	10,009	841
	Estimated total	100.0%	2,070	20	156	636	1,258	14,344	3,170	10,304	870
	Rate per 100,000 inhabitants		468.7	4.5	35.3	144.0	284.8	3,247.6	717.7	2,332.9	197.0
Lima, OH M.S.A.											
	Includes Allen County	105,114									
	City of Lima	37,767	351	1	46	109	195	2,633	773	1,681	179
	Total area actually reporting	91.8%	410	2	61	128	219	4,097	1,047	2,827	223
	Estimated total	100.0%	426	2	64	134	226	4,348	1,093	3,018	237
	Rate per 100,000 inhabitants		405.3	1.9	60.9	127.5	215.0	4,136.5	1,039.8	2,871.2	225.5
Lincoln, NE M.S.A.											
	Includes Lancaster and Seward Counties	286,039									
	City of Lincoln	243,243	1,325	6	113	173	1,033	11,755	1,904	9,428	423
	Total area actually reporting	100.0%	1,358	8	116	175	1,059	12,619	2,063	10,098	458
	Rate per 100,000 inhabitants		474.8	2.8	40.6	61.2	370.2	4,411.6	721.2	3,530.3	160.1

[2] Because of changes in the state/local agency's reporting practices, figures are not comparable to previous years' data.

Table 6. Crime, by Metropolitan Statistical Area, 2007 *(Contd.)*

(Number, percent, rate per 100,000 population.)

Metropolitan statistical area	Counties/principal cities	Population	Violent crime	Murder and non-negligent man-slaughter	Forcible rape	Robbery	Aggravated assault	Property crime	Burglary	Larceny-theft	Motor vehicle theft
Little Rock-North Little Rock-Conway, AR M.S.A.											
	Includes Faulkner, Grant, Lonoke, Perry, Pulaski, and Saline Counties	659,776									
	City of Little Rock........................	184,594	2,987	51	123	1,022	1,791	16,112	3,932	10,915	1,265
	City of North Little Rock	58,680	808	18	39	232	519	5,845	1,537	3,799	509
	City of Conway	57,245	183	1	39	64	79	2,319	465	1,681	173
	Total area actually reporting	99.8%	5,476	87	318	1,503	3,568	36,461	9,459	24,193	2,809
	Estimated total............................	100.0%	5,484	87	319	1,505	3,573	36,520	9,476	24,232	2,812
	Rate per 100,000 inhabitants...........		831.2	13.2	48.3	228.1	541.5	5,535.2	1,436.2	3,672.8	426.2
Logan, UT-ID M.S.A.											
	Includes Franklin County, ID and Cache County, UT......................	114,216									
	City of Logan, UT........................	48,403	27	0	3	3	21	417	60	337	20
	Total area actually reporting	100.0%	85	0	26	5	54	1,525	287	1,184	54
	Rate per 100,000 inhabitants...........		74.4	0.0	22.8	4.4	47.3	1,335.2	251.3	1,036.6	47.3
Longview, TX M.S.A.											
	Includes Gregg, Rusk, and Upshur Counties.............................	204,652									
	City of Longview..........................	75,288	723	5	54	185	479	4,971	1,091	3,415	465
	Total area actually reporting	99.4%	1,237	9	142	245	841	9,840	2,286	6,676	878
	Estimated total............................	100.0%	1,240	9	142	246	843	9,882	2,295	6,706	881
	Rate per 100,000 inhabitants...........		605.9	4.4	69.4	120.2	411.9	4,828.7	1,121.4	3,276.8	430.5
Longview, WA M.S.A.											
	Includes Cowlitz County.................	100,916									
	City of Longview..........................	37,068	134	3	45	39	47	2,341	480	1,662	199
	Total area actually reporting	100.0%	296	3	82	64	147	4,378	953	3,056	369
	Rate per 100,000 inhabitants...........		293.3	3.0	81.3	63.4	145.7	4,338.3	944.3	3,028.3	365.7
Los Angeles-Long Beach-Santa Ana, CA M.S.A.											
	Includes the Metropolitan Divisions of Los Angeles-Long Beach-Anaheim-Glendale and Santa Ana-Anaheim-Irvine	12,929,875									
	City of Los Angeles......................	3,870,487	27,806	395	1,004	13,481	12,926	101,457	19,629	58,304	23,524
	City of Long Beach.......................	473,959	3,426	42	138	1,506	1,740	12,979	2,905	7,214	2,860
	City of Santa Ana	340,223	1,947	23	65	779	1,080	7,797	1,013	4,684	2,100
	City of Anaheim...........................	335,133	1,423	17	96	581	729	8,798	1,827	5,695	1,276
	City of Glendale...........................	200,049	375	2	12	166	195	3,667	611	2,533	523
	City of Irvine..............................	201,872	143	4	19	44	76	3,256	637	2,404	215
	City of Pomona	155,161	1,235	27	32	485	691	5,211	972	3,085	1,154
	City of Pasadena	145,553	744	11	33	303	397	4,304	825	2,993	486
	City of Torrance..........................	142,970	343	2	21	213	107	3,187	476	2,250	461
	City of Orange............................	135,818	266	1	8	116	141	3,049	458	2,158	433
	City of Fullerton	133,855	467	5	41	186	235	4,128	883	2,731	514
	City of Costa Mesa	109,835	258	0	39	77	142	3,336	509	2,426	401
	City of Burbank...........................	104,871	274	3	14	98	159	2,767	487	1,840	440
	City of Compton	95,990	1,623	37	42	466	1,078	2,805	636	1,034	1,135
	City of Carson	94,359	684	16	10	220	438	2,605	429	1,593	583
	City of Santa Monica.....................	88,584	596	2	30	236	328	3,108	682	2,099	327
	City of Newport Beach	80,377	172	1	4	53	114	2,228	645	1,429	154
	City of Tustin	69,945	137	2	17	64	54	1,575	288	1,106	181
	City of Montebello	63,071	242	2	11	116	113	1,948	482	912	554
	City of Monterey Park	62,472	196	2	3	126	65	1,290	273	766	251
	City of Gardena	59,951	448	5	8	287	148	1,428	309	703	416
	City of Paramount	56,508	483	12	11	198	262	1,936	415	843	678
	City of Arcadia............................	56,967	156	2	9	71	74	1,704	375	1,183	146
	City of Fountain Valley	55,973	111	0	8	40	63	1,443	328	991	124
	City of Cerritos	52,462	138	0	4	78	56	1,880	333	1,242	305
	Total area actually reporting	100.0%	71,610	941	2,788	30,737	37,144	331,593	67,583	195,342	68,668
	Rate per 100,000 inhabitants...........		553.8	7.3	21.6	237.7	287.3	2,564.5	522.7	1,510.8	531.1
Los Angeles-Long Beach-Glendale, CA M.D.											
	Includes Los Angeles County	9,929,814									
	Total area actually reporting	100.0%	63,397	864	2,285	27,682	32,566	266,122	55,027	151,414	59,681
	Rate per 100,000 inhabitants...........		638.5	8.7	23.0	278.8	328.0	2,680.0	554.2	1,524.8	601.0

Table 6. Crime, by Metropolitan Statistical Area, 2007 *(Contd.)*

(Number, percent, rate per 100,000 population.)

Metropolitan statistical area	Counties/principal cities	Population	Violent crime	Murder and non-negligent man-slaughter	Forcible rape	Robbery	Aggravated assault	Property crime	Burglary	Larceny-theft	Motor vehicle theft
Santa Ana-Anaheim-Irvine, CA M.D.											
	Includes Orange County..............	3,000,062									
	Total area actually reporting	100.0%	8,213	77	503	3,055	4,578	65,471	12,556	43,928	8,987
	Rate per 100,000 inhabitants...........		273.8	2.6	16.8	101.8	152.6	2,182.3	418.5	1,464.2	299.6
Louisville/Jefferson County, KY-IN M.S.A.											
	Includes Clark, Floyd, Harrison, and Washington Counties, IN and Bullitt, Henry, Jefferson, Meade, Nelson, Oldham, Shelby, Spencer, and Trimble Counties, KY	1,233,503									
	City of Louisville Metro, KY..........	624,030	4,238	71	194	1,910	2,063	29,543	7,588	18,772	3,183
	Total area actually reporting	94.0%	5,200	85	280	2,261	2,574	43,488	10,720	28,524	4,244
	Estimated total..............................	100.0%	5,340	87	291	2,305	2,657	45,424	11,071	29,961	4,392
	Rate per 100,000 inhabitants...........		432.9	7.1	23.6	186.9	215.4	3,682.5	897.5	2,428.9	356.1
Lubbock, TX M.S.A.											
	Includes Crosby and Lubbock Counties..	262,990									
	City of Lubbock	213,988	1,953	15	101	259	1,578	11,684	3,136	7,942	606
	Total area actually reporting	100.0%	2,092	15	115	267	1,695	13,038	3,627	8,707	704
	Rate per 100,000 inhabitants...........		795.5	5.7	43.7	101.5	644.5	4,957.6	1,379.1	3,310.8	267.7
Lynchburg, VA M.S.A.											
	Includes Amherst, Appomattox, Bedford, and Campbell Counties and Bedford and Lynchburg Cities..............................	240,526									
	City of Lynchburg............................	67,932	332	1	23	81	227	2,381	465	1,754	162
	Total area actually reporting	100.0%	562	6	62	123	371	4,854	857	3,664	333
	Rate per 100,000 inhabitants...........		233.7	2.5	25.8	51.1	154.2	2,018.1	356.3	1,523.3	138.4
Macon, GA M.S.A.											
	Includes Bibb, Crawford, Jones, and Monroe, and Twiggs Counties	230,317									
	City of Macon................................	93,205	732	22	43	302	365	7,997	1,979	5,166	852
	Total area actually reporting	99.4%	1,029	30	65	376	558	11,907	2,902	7,783	1,222
	Estimated total................................	100.0%	1,037	30	65	379	563	11,972	2,914	7,830	1,228
	Rate per 100,000 inhabitants...........		450.2	13.0	28.2	164.6	244.4	5,198.1	1,265.2	3,399.7	533.2
Madera, CA M.S.A.											
	Includes Madera County	148,765									
	City of Madera	56,797	415	2	14	97	302	1,272	460	595	217
	Total area actually reporting	100.0%	746	5	31	118	592	3,184	1,078	1,600	506
	Rate per 100,000 inhabitants...........		501.5	3.4	20.8	79.3	397.9	2,140.3	724.6	1,075.5	340.1
Madison, WI M.S.A.											
	Includes Columbia, Dane, and Iowa Counties...........................	550,623									
	City of Madison..............................	225,370	834	8	57	359	410	8,224	2,059	5,658	507
	Total area actually reporting	99.6%	1,304	11	123	444	726	16,146	3,359	11,956	831
	Estimated total................................	100.0%	1,307	11	123	445	728	16,209	3,367	12,008	834
	Rate per 100,000 inhabitants...........		237.4	2.0	22.3	80.8	132.2	2,943.8	611.5	2,180.8	151.5
Mansfield, OH M.S.A.											
	Includes Richland County	126,412									
	City of Mansfield	50,004	163	5	40	63	55	2,886	865	1,945	76
	Total area actually reporting	100.0%	256	7	66	81	102	5,487	1,526	3,826	135
	Rate per 100,000 inhabitants...........		202.5	5.5	52.2	64.1	80.7	4,340.6	1,207.2	3,026.6	106.8
McAllen-Edinburg-Mission, TX M.S.A.											
	Includes Hidalgo County.................	720,595									
	City of McAllen	129,455	372	6	27	114	225	7,908	824	6,537	547
	City of Edinburg	69,708	269	1	20	52	196	3,777	683	2,705	389
	City of Mission...............................	66,216	94	2	8	32	52	2,571	370	1,906	295
	City of Pharr..................................	63,666	249	7	23	64	155	3,696	792	2,586	318
	Total area actually reporting	99.8%	2,454	37	177	520	1,720	32,719	6,711	23,155	2,853
	Estimated total................................	100.0%	2,458	37	177	521	1,723	32,772	6,722	23,193	2,857
	Rate per 100,000 inhabitants...........		341.1	5.1	24.6	72.3	239.1	4,547.9	932.8	3,218.6	396.5
Medford, OR M.S.A.											
	Includes Jackson County	199,631									
	City of Medford	71,969	265	0	30	44	191	3,270	412	2,662	196
	Total area actually reporting	99.8%	500	3	60	62	375	6,016	975	4,656	385
	Estimated total................................	100.0%	500	3	60	62	375	6,029	977	4,666	386
	Rate per 100,000 inhabitants...........		250.5	1.5	30.1	31.1	187.8	3,020.1	489.4	2,337.3	193.4

Table 6. Crime, by Metropolitan Statistical Area, 2007 *(Contd.)*

(Number, percent, rate per 100,000 population.)

Metropolitan statistical area	Counties/principal cities	Population	Violent crime	Murder and non-negligent man-slaughter	Forcible rape	Robbery	Aggravated assault	Property crime	Burglary	Larceny-theft	Motor vehicle theft
Memphis, TN-MS-AR M.S.A.											
	Includes Crittenden County, AR; DeSoto, Marshall, Tate, and Tunica Counties, MS; and Fayette, Shelby, and Tipton Counties, TN.....	1,295,670									
	City of Memphis	669,264	13,055	128	452	4,870	7,605	53,959	14,613	33,146	6,200
	Total area actually reporting	93.9%	15,600	150	588	5,376	9,486	71,775	19,271	44,954	7,550
	Estimated total.................................	100.0%	15,780	154	610	5,424	9,592	74,370	19,933	46,694	7,743
	Rate per 100,000 inhabitants..........		1,217.9	11.9	47.1	418.6	740.3	5,739.9	1,538.4	3,603.8	597.6
Merced, CA M.S.A.											
	Includes Merced County.................	249,018									
	City of Merced	78,186	611	7	28	152	424	3,821	836	2,531	454
	Total area actually reporting	100.0%	1,463	17	79	242	1,125	9,306	2,434	5,608	1,264
	Rate per 100,000 inhabitants..........		587.5	6.8	31.7	97.2	451.8	3,737.1	977.4	2,252.0	507.6
Miami-Fort Lauderdale-Pompano Beach, FL M.S.A.											
	Includes the Metropolitan Divisions of Fort Lauderdale-Pompano Beach-Deerfield Beach, Miami-Miami Beach-Kendall, and West Palm Beach -Boca Raton-Boynton Beach	5,480,920									
	City of Miami	410,252	6,119	78	57	2,537	3,447	21,183	4,829	12,478	3,876
	City of Fort Lauderdale	187,995	1,523	25	56	736	706	9,712	2,266	6,581	865
	City of Pompano Beach	104,989	1,310	10	63	452	785	5,369	1,139	3,603	627
	City of West Palm Beach	101,322	1,158	12	43	574	529	7,255	1,594	4,748	913
	City of Miami Beach	86,742	1,072	4	58	448	562	7,805	1,354	5,607	844
	City of Boca Raton..........................	86,868	236	5	16	83	132	3,441	675	2,596	170
	City of Deerfield Beach..................	76,469	500	4	26	144	326	2,527	571	1,707	249
	City of Boynton Beach....................	69,469	730	6	5	199	520	3,578	798	2,507	273
	City of Delray Beach.......................	65,262	719	3	22	223	471	3,553	753	2,504	296
	Total area actually reporting	100.0%	43,956	429	1,598	16,075	25,854	256,039	54,562	171,808	29,669
	Rate per 100,000 inhabitants..........		802.0	7.8	29.2	293.3	471.7	4,671.5	995.5	3,134.7	541.3
Fort Lauderdale-Pompano Beach-Deerfield Beach, FL M.D.											
	Includes Broward County................	1,795,143									
	Total area actually reporting	100.0%	10,893	105	472	4,051	6,265	68,939	14,183	47,763	6,993
	Rate per 100,000 inhabitants..........		606.8	5.8	26.3	225.7	349.0	3,840.3	790.1	2,660.7	389.6
Miami-Miami Beach-Kendall, FL M.D.											
	Includes Miami-Dade County........	2,401,971									
	Total area actually reporting	100.0%	23,740	228	725	8,872	13,915	131,310	26,713	87,420	17,177
	Rate per 100,000 inhabitants..........		988.4	9.5	30.2	369.4	579.3	5,466.8	1,112.1	3,639.5	715.1
West Palm Beach-Boca Raton-Boynton Beach, FL M.D.											
	Includes Palm Beach County	1,283,806									
	Total area actually reporting	100.0%	9,323	96	401	3,152	5,674	55,790	13,666	36,625	5,499
	Rate per 100,000 inhabitants..........		726.2	7.5	31.2	245.5	442.0	4,345.7	1,064.5	2,852.8	428.3
Michigan City-La Porte, IN M.S.A.											
	Includes La Porte County...............	110,465									
	City of Michigan City.....................	32,008	146	3	14	82	47	1,928	306	1,435	187
	City of La Porte..............................	21,178	31	0	5	15	11	1,462	175	1,217	70
	Total area actually reporting	96.8%	206	7	25	99	75	4,302	736	3,244	322
	Estimated total.................................	100.0%	215	7	26	102	80	4,437	756	3,348	333
	Rate per 100,000 inhabitants..........		194.6	6.3	23.5	92.3	72.4	4,016.7	684.4	3,030.8	301.5
Midland, TX M.S.A.											
	Includes Midland County	125,645									
	City of Midland..............................	102,877	343	4	57	76	206	3,666	833	2,625	208
	Total area actually reporting	100.0%	438	4	68	82	284	4,311	1,036	3,043	232
	Rate per 100,000 inhabitants..........		348.6	3.2	54.1	65.3	226.0	3,431.1	824.5	2,421.9	184.6

Table 6. Crime, by Metropolitan Statistical Area, 2007 *(Contd.)*

(Number, percent, rate per 100,000 population.)

Metropolitan statistical area	Counties/principal cities	Population	Violent crime	Murder and non-negligent man-slaughter	Forcible rape	Robbery	Aggravated assault	Property crime	Burglary	Larceny-theft	Motor vehicle theft
Milwaukee-Waukesha-West Allis, WI M.S.A.											
	Includes Milwaukee, Ozaukee, Washington, and Waukesha Counties............	1,516,093									
	City of Milwaukee	572,938	8,040	105	236	3,529	4,170	38,199	6,203	24,248	7,748
	City of Waukesha	68,162	84	0	12	23	49	1,405	348	990	67
	City of West Allis	58,366	220	2	9	91	118	3,062	584	2,290	188
	Total area actually reporting	100.0%	9,230	110	349	3,974	4,797	60,572	9,365	42,423	8,784
	Rate per 100,000 inhabitants		608.8	7.3	23.0	262.1	316.4	3,995.3	617.7	2,798.2	579.4
Minneapolis-St. Paul-Bloomington, MN-WI M.S.A.[5]											
	Includes Anoka, Carver, Chisago, Dakota, Hennepin, Isanti, Ramsey, Scott, Sherburne, Washington, and Wright Counties, MN[5] and Pierce and St. Croix Counties, WI	3,202,517									
	City of Minneapolis, MN.................	371,240	5,580	47	452	2,520	2,561	22,543	6,164	13,203	3,176
	City of St. Paul, MN.................	271,662	2,327	14	173	777	1,363	11,118	2,696	6,346	2,076
	City of Bloomington, MN[5].............	80,218		0		51	61	3,210	356	2,674	180
	City of Plymouth, MN[5].................	70,737		0		9	32	1,359	304	995	60
	City of Eagan, MN[5]	63,718		0		15	28	1,515	188	1,276	51
	City of Eden Prairie, MN[5].............	61,910		0		13	28	1,475	190	1,254	31
	City of Minnetonka, MN[5].............	49,751		0		14	21	1,014	196	776	42
	Total area actually reporting	96.2%		88		4,302	6,014	108,499	20,226	78,577	9,696
	Estimated total.................	100.0%		90		4,362	6,129	112,527	20,818	81,775	9,934
	Rate per 100,000 inhabitants............			2.8		136.2	191.4	3,513.7	650.1	2,553.5	310.2
Missoula, MT M.S.A.											
	Includes Missoula County	102,898									
	City of Missoula	65,037	218	1	23	36	158	2,935	255	2,541	139
	Total area actually reporting	100.0%	305	1	36	38	230	3,547	379	2,971	197
	Rate per 100,000 inhabitants............		296.4	1.0	35.0	36.9	223.5	3,447.1	368.3	2,887.3	191.5
Mobile, AL M.S.A.											
	Includes Mobile County	405,259									
	City of Mobile[6].............	253,842	1,144	38	23	750	333	14,136	3,650	9,361	1,125
	Total area actually reporting	96.8%	1,764	61	70	946	687	19,380	5,110	12,550	1,720
	Estimated total.................	100.0%	1,818	62	74	965	717	19,939	5,228	12,952	1,759
	Rate per 100,000 inhabitants............		448.6	15.3	18.3	238.1	176.9	4,920.1	1,290.0	3,196.0	434.0
Modesto, CA M.S.A.											
	Includes Stanislaus County.............	517,721									
	City of Modesto	208,067	1,490	11	65	452	962	12,030	2,216	7,850	1,964
	Total area actually reporting	100.0%	3,207	27	139	826	2,215	25,421	5,971	14,712	4,738
	Rate per 100,000 inhabitants............		619.4	5.2	26.8	159.5	427.8	4,910.2	1,153.3	2,841.7	915.2
Monroe, LA M.S.A.											
	Includes Ouachita and Union Parishes.............	172,092									
	City of Monroe.............	51,350	343	1	20	101	221	5,096	1,141	3,792	163
	Total area actually reporting	98.8%	747	4	42	155	546	9,657	2,490	6,796	371
	Estimated total.................	100.0%	761	4	43	157	557	9,768	2,511	6,880	377
	Rate per 100,000 inhabitants............		442.2	2.3	25.0	91.2	323.7	5,676.0	1,459.1	3,997.9	219.1
Monroe, MI M.S.A.											
	Includes Monroe County.................	155,523									
	City of Monroe.............	21,787	70	0	7	23	40	709	125	539	45
	Total area actually reporting	100.0%	293	1	35	63	194	3,270	740	2,263	267
	Rate per 100,000 inhabitants............		188.4	0.6	22.5	40.5	124.7	2,102.6	475.8	1,455.1	171.7
Montgomery, AL M.S.A.											
	Includes Autauga, Elmore, Lowndes, and Montgomery Counties.............	364,491									
	City of Montgomery.............	202,062	1,157	46	54	652	405	12,843	3,317	8,579	947
	Total area actually reporting	83.0%	1,427	49	80	731	567	16,246	4,208	10,870	1,168
	Estimated total.................	100.0%	1,616	52	94	781	689	17,984	4,685	11,982	1,317
	Rate per 100,000 inhabitants............		443.4	14.3	25.8	214.3	189.0	4,934.0	1,285.4	3,287.3	361.3

[5] The data collection methodology for the offense of forcible rape used by the Minnesota state UCR Program (with the exception of Minneapolis and St. Paul, MN) does not comply with national UCR Program guidelines. Consequently, their figures for forcible rape and violent crime (of which forcible rape is a part) are not published in this table.

Table 6. Crime, by Metropolitan Statistical Area, 2007 *(Contd.)*

(Number, percent, rate per 100,000 population.)

Metropolitan statistical area	Counties/principal cities	Population	Violent crime	Murder and non-negligent man-slaughter	Forcible rape	Robbery	Aggravated assault	Property crime	Burglary	Larceny-theft	Motor vehicle theft
Morgantown, WV M.S.A.											
	Includes Monongalia and Preston Counties	115,156									
	City of Morgantown	28,951	99	1	27	29	42	1,025	248	745	32
	Total area actually reporting	96.0%	210	3	40	46	121	2,605	548	1,934	123
	Estimated total	100.0%	220	3	41	48	128	2,748	572	2,044	132
	Rate per 100,000 inhabitants		191.0	2.6	35.6	41.7	111.2	2,386.3	496.7	1,775.0	114.6
Morristown, TN M.S.A.											
	Includes Grainger, Hamblen, and Jefferson Counties	135,710									
	City of Morristown	27,147	264	1	23	65	175	1,905	224	1,572	109
	Total area actually reporting	100.0%	601	5	45	97	454	4,946	1,130	3,504	312
	Rate per 100,000 inhabitants		442.9	3.7	33.2	71.5	334.5	3,644.5	832.7	2,582.0	229.9
Mount Vernon-Anacortes, WA M.S.A.											
	Includes Skagit County	117,546									
	City of Mount Vernon	30,521	77	0	12	30	35	2,324	294	1,866	164
	City of Anacortes	16,948	17	1	2	1	13	568	95	448	25
	Total area actually reporting	100.0%	228	2	42	67	117	6,653	1,201	4,969	483
	Rate per 100,000 inhabitants		194.0	1.7	35.7	57.0	99.5	5,659.9	1,021.7	4,227.3	410.9
Muncie, IN M.S.A.											
	Includes Delaware County	114,292									
	City of Muncie	64,921	375	1	50	60	264	2,652	581	1,932	139
	Total area actually reporting	100.0%	417	1	63	67	286	3,575	756	2,630	189
	Rate per 100,000 inhabitants		364.9	0.9	55.1	58.6	250.2	3,128.0	661.5	2,301.1	165.4
Muskegon-Norton Shores, MI M.S.A.											
	Includes Muskegon County	175,119									
	City of Muskegon	39,562	389	0	35	77	277	2,252	396	1,693	163
	City of Norton Shores	23,567	59	0	7	11	41	958	135	790	33
	Total area actually reporting	100.0%	880	1	113	165	601	7,730	1,291	5,997	442
	Rate per 100,000 inhabitants		502.5	0.6	64.5	94.2	343.2	4,414.1	737.2	3,424.5	252.4
Myrtle Beach-North Myrtle Beach-Conway, SC M.S.A.											
	Includes Horry County	247,229									
	City of Myrtle Beach	29,361	506	2	49	222	233	5,488	1,011	3,998	479
	City of North Myrtle Beach	15,577	57	0	3	17	37	1,576	291	1,264	21
	City of Conway	14,285	219	1	7	54	157	1,412	310	1,012	90
	Total area actually reporting	100.0%	2,344	12	140	480	1,712	17,051	3,604	11,943	1,504
	Rate per 100,000 inhabitants		948.1	4.9	56.6	194.2	692.5	6,896.8	1,457.8	4,830.7	608.3
Napa, CA M.S.A.											
	Includes Napa County	133,808									
	City of Napa	75,266	288	3	16	58	211	2,351	463	1,677	211
	Total area actually reporting	100.0%	460	6	29	82	343	3,723	807	2,550	366
	Rate per 100,000 inhabitants		343.8	4.5	21.7	61.3	256.3	2,782.3	603.1	1,905.7	273.5
Naples-Marco Island, FL M.S.A.											
	Includes Collier County	321,589									
	City of Naples	22,109	49	0	2	9	38	858	126	713	19
	City of Marco Island	16,235	17	1	1	0	15	172	22	142	8
	Total area actually reporting	100.0%	1,363	16	61	242	1,044	6,093	1,485	4,216	392
	Rate per 100,000 inhabitants		423.8	5.0	19.0	75.3	324.6	1,894.7	461.8	1,311.0	121.9
Nashville-Davidson—Murfreesboro—Franklin, TN M.S.A.											
	Includes Cannon, Cheatham, Davidson, Dickson, Hickman, Macon, Robertson, Rutherford, Smith, Sumner, Trousdale, Williamson, and Wilson Counties	1,492,983									
	City of Nashville	564,169	8,513	73	290	2,516	5,634	31,466	6,111	22,729	2,626
	City of Murfreesboro	96,264	691	4	29	137	521	4,186	929	3,028	229
	City of Franklin	57,489	106	2	13	18	73	1,024	125	849	50
	Total area actually reporting	100.0%	12,193	102	553	2,970	8,568	54,818	11,414	39,102	4,302
	Rate per 100,000 inhabitants		816.7	6.8	37.0	198.9	573.9	3,671.7	764.5	2,619.1	288.1

Table 6. Crime, by Metropolitan Statistical Area, 2007 *(Contd.)*

(Number, percent, rate per 100,000 population.)

Metropolitan statistical area	Counties/principal cities	Population	Violent crime	Murder and non-negligent man-slaughter	Forcible rape	Robbery	Aggravated assault	Property crime	Burglary	Larceny-theft	Motor vehicle theft
New Orleans-Metairie-Kenner, LA M.S.A.											
	Includes Jefferson, Orleans, Plaquemines, St. Bernard, St. Charles, St. John the Baptist, and St. Tammany Parishes	1,026,639									
	City of New Orleans.....................	220,614	3,451	209	115	1,154	1,973	15,583	5,039	7,354	3,190
	City of Kenner................................	66,473	388	10	14	124	240	2,760	597	1,859	304
	Total area actually reporting	99.9%	7,933	289	307	2,205	5,132	46,382	12,409	27,422	6,551
	Estimated total..............................	100.0%	7,938	289	307	2,206	5,136	46,419	12,416	27,450	6,553
	Rate per 100,000 inhabitants..........		773.2	28.2	29.9	214.9	500.3	4,521.5	1,209.4	2,673.8	638.3
New York-Northern New Jersey-Long Island, NY-NJ-PA M.S.A.											
	Includes the Metropolitan Divisions of Edison, NJ; Nassau-Suffolk County, NY; Newark-Union, NJ-PA; and New York-Wayne-White Plains, NY-NJ....................................	18,796,306									
	City of New York, NY	8,220,196	50,453	496	875	21,787	27,295	149,488	20,914	115,318	13,256
	City of Newark, NJ	280,158	2,389	104	60	1,101	1,124	10,664	1,914	4,385	4,365
	City of Edison Township, NJ	99,082	225	0	0	86	139	2,239	437	1,578	224
	City of White Plains, NY	57,638	114	0	4	27	83	1,108	45	1,025	38
	City of Union Township, NJ	54,795	144	0	1	69	74	1,331	205	935	191
	City of Wayne Township, NJ	54,606	40	0	0	18	22	1,413	185	1,175	53
	City of New Brunswick, NJ.............	49,950	283	2	25	169	87	1,883	448	1,273	162
	Total area actually reporting	99.8%	77,792	839	1,855	33,784	41,314	343,929	54,835	253,778	35,316
	Estimated total..............................	100.0%	77,864	840	1,859	33,808	41,357	344,687	54,951	254,385	35,351
	Rate per 100,000 inhabitants..........		414.3	4.5	9.9	179.9	220.0	1,833.8	292.3	1,353.4	188.1
Edison-New Brunswick, NJ M.D.											
	Includes Middlesex, Monmouth, Ocean, and Somerset Counties	2,298,551									
	Total area actually reporting	100.0%	3,827	37	198	1,480	2,112	43,083	7,730	32,760	2,593
	Rate per 100,000 inhabitants..........		166.5	1.6	8.6	64.4	91.9	1,874.4	336.3	1,425.2	112.8
Nassau-Suffolk, NY M.D.											
	Includes Nassau and Suffolk Counties....................................	2,792,682									
	Total area actually reporting	99.9%	4,959	54	205	2,005	2,695	45,985	6,471	35,664	3,850
	Estimated total..............................	100.0%	4,962	54	205	2,006	2,697	46,022	6,477	35,693	3,852
	Rate per 100,000 inhabitants..........		177.7	1.9	7.3	71.8	96.6	1,647.9	231.9	1,278.1	137.9
Newark-Union, NJ-PA M.D.											
	Includes Essex, Hunterdon, Morris, Sussex, and Union Counties, NJ and Pike County, PA....................................	2,145,195									
	Total area actually reporting	100.0%	8,129	177	282	3,936	3,734	47,300	9,032	28,349	9,919
	Rate per 100,000 inhabitants..........		378.9	8.3	13.1	183.5	174.1	2,204.9	421.0	1,321.5	462.4
New York-White Plains-Wayne, NY-NJ M.D.											
	Includes Bergen, Hudson, and Passaic Counties, NJ and Bronx, Kings, New York, Putnam, Queens, Richmond, Rockland, and Westchester Counties, NY	11,559,878									
	Total area actually reporting	99.7%	60,877	571	1,170	26,363	32,773	207,561	31,602	157,005	18,954
	Estimated total..............................	100.0%	60,946	572	1,174	26,386	32,814	208,282	31,712	157,583	18,987
	Rate per 100,000 inhabitants..........		527.2	4.9	10.2	228.3	283.9	1,801.8	274.3	1,363.2	164.2
Niles-Benton Harbor, MI M.S.A.											
	Includes Berrien County..................	160,825									
	City of Niles..................................	11,491	52	0	8	14	30	487	73	390	24
	City of Benton Harbor....................	10,567	137	0	6	28	103	285	135	126	24
	Total area actually reporting	97.3%	701	0	97	105	499	4,919	963	3,685	271
	Estimated total..............................	100.0%	714	0	98	108	508	5,046	987	3,775	284
	Rate per 100,000 inhabitants..........		444.0	0.0	60.9	67.2	315.9	3,137.6	613.7	2,347.3	176.6

Table 6. Crime, by Metropolitan Statistical Area, 2007 *(Contd.)*

(Number, percent, rate per 100,000 population.)

Metropolitan statistical area	Counties/principal cities	Population	Violent crime	Murder and non-negligent man-slaughter	Forcible rape	Robbery	Aggravated assault	Property crime	Burglary	Larceny-theft	Motor vehicle theft
Ocala, FL M.S.A.	Includes Marion County	322,272									
	City of Ocala	53,490	633	6	40	178	409	3,444	747	2,503	194
	Total area actually reporting	100.0%	2,163	14	152	275	1,722	9,004	2,489	5,931	584
	Rate per 100,000 inhabitants..........		671.2	4.3	47.2	85.3	534.3	2,793.9	772.3	1,840.4	181.2
Ocean City, NJ M.S.A.	Includes Cape May County	97,291									
	City of Ocean City........................	15,057	28	0	3	19	6	1,153	183	961	9
	Total area actually reporting	100.0%	353	1	26	105	221	4,854	945	3,779	130
	Rate per 100,000 inhabitants..........		362.8	1.0	26.7	107.9	227.2	4,989.2	971.3	3,884.2	133.6
Odessa, TX M.S.A.	Includes Ector County	128,400									
	City of Odessa.............................	95,839	529	6	7	92	424	4,302	870	3,144	288
	Total area actually reporting	100.0%	601	8	17	104	472	5,523	1,142	3,983	398
	Rate per 100,000 inhabitants..........		468.1	6.2	13.2	81.0	367.6	4,301.4	889.4	3,102.0	310.0
Ogden-Clearfield, UT M.S.A.	Includes Davis, Morgan, and Weber Counties	514,786									
	City of Ogden...............................	78,160	501	3	33	136	329	4,914	923	3,466	525
	City of Clearfield	27,419	42	0	11	7	24	867	112	710	45
	Total area actually reporting	100.0%	955	5	150	211	589	15,371	2,649	11,680	1,042
	Rate per 100,000 inhabitants..........		185.5	1.0	29.1	41.0	114.4	2,985.9	514.6	2,268.9	202.4
Oklahoma City, OK M.S.A.	Includes Canadian, Cleveland, Grady, Lincoln, Logan, McClain, and Oklahoma Counties	1,189,823									
	City of Oklahoma City...................	542,199	4,612	58	326	1,397	2,831	31,949	8,110	19,228	4,611
	Total area actually reporting	100.0%	6,151	77	508	1,678	3,888	51,334	12,770	32,533	6,031
	Rate per 100,000 inhabitants..........		517.0	6.5	42.7	141.0	326.8	4,314.4	1,073.3	2,734.3	506.9
Olympia, WA M.S.A.	Includes Thurston County	238,675									
	City of Olympia	44,946	118	0	28	27	63	2,023	296	1,493	234
	Total area actually reporting	100.0%	502	6	68	88	340	7,360	1,530	5,082	748
	Rate per 100,000 inhabitants..........		210.3	2.5	28.5	36.9	142.5	3,083.7	641.0	2,129.3	313.4
Omaha-Council Bluffs, NE-IA M.S.A.	Includes Harrison, Mills, and Pottawattamie Counties, IA and Cass, Douglas, Sarpy, Saunders, and Washington Counties, NE	829,460									
	City of Omaha, NE.........................	431,810	2,578	42	189	818	1,529	20,657	3,345	13,876	3,436
	City of Council Bluffs, IA	60,531	455	2	76	78	299	4,698	878	3,288	532
	Total area actually reporting	100.0%	3,413	47	312	944	2,110	32,267	5,401	22,366	4,500
	Rate per 100,000 inhabitants..........		411.5	5.7	37.6	113.8	254.4	3,890.1	651.1	2,696.5	542.5
Orlando-Kissimmee, FL M.S.A.	Includes Lake, Orange, Osceola, and Seminole Counties	2,020,346									
	City of Orlando.............................	224,417	4,269	39	162	1,534	2,534	19,181	4,164	12,778	2,239
	City of Kissimmee..........................	62,880	576	4	12	188	372	2,786	886	1,658	242
	Total area actually reporting	100.0%	17,074	146	813	5,361	10,754	88,105	23,561	54,653	9,891
	Rate per 100,000 inhabitants..........		845.1	7.2	40.2	265.4	532.3	4,360.9	1,166.2	2,705.1	489.6
Oshkosh-Neenah, WI M.S.A.	Includes Winnebago County	161,620									
	City of Oshkosh	64,183	209	2	10	31	166	2,378	392	1,925	61
	City of Neenah..............................	24,871	56	0	4	1	51	499	92	389	18
	Total area actually reporting	100.0%	373	2	26	40	305	4,146	798	3,224	124
	Rate per 100,000 inhabitants..........		230.8	1.2	16.1	24.7	188.7	2,565.3	493.8	1,994.8	76.7
Oxnard-Thousand Oaks-Ventura, CA M.S.A.	Includes Ventura County	799,872									
	City of Oxnard	186,367	845	9	33	453	350	4,275	866	2,869	540
	City of Thousand Oaks...................	125,196	146	2	19	38	87	1,942	424	1,407	111
	City of Ventura..............................	104,523	368	1	27	151	189	3,827	746	2,733	348
	City of Camarillo	63,238	94	0	8	22	64	1,062	205	794	63
	Total area actually reporting	100.0%	2,120	17	140	821	1,142	17,291	3,436	12,226	1,629
	Rate per 100,000 inhabitants..........		265.0	2.1	17.5	102.6	142.8	2,161.7	429.6	1,528.5	203.7

Table 6. Crime, by Metropolitan Statistical Area, 2007 *(Contd.)*

(Number, percent, rate per 100,000 population.)

Metropolitan statistical area	Counties/principal cities	Population	Violent crime	Murder and non-negligent manslaughter	Forcible rape	Robbery	Aggravated assault	Property crime	Burglary	Larceny-theft	Motor vehicle theft
Palm Bay-Melbourne-Titusville, FL M.S.A.											
	Includes Brevard County................	538,226									
	City of Palm Bay............................	100,666	617	5	28	104	480	2,808	881	1,726	201
	City of Melbourne	77,678	787	2	15	174	596	3,942	926	2,741	275
	City of Titusville............................	44,467	373	5	33	90	245	1,794	475	1,054	265
	Total area actually reporting	100.0%	3,776	32	185	712	2,847	18,637	4,792	12,483	1,362
	Rate per 100,000 inhabitants...........		701.6	5.9	34.4	132.3	529.0	3,462.7	890.3	2,319.3	253.1
Palm Coast, FL M.S.A.											
	Includes Flagler County..................	88,451									
	Total area actually reporting	100.0%	288	4	18	54	212	2,432	608	1,657	167
	Rate per 100,000 inhabitants...........		325.6	4.5	20.4	61.1	239.7	2,749.5	687.4	1,873.4	188.8
Panama City-Lynn Haven, FL M.S.A.											
	Includes Bay County	164,360									
	City of Panama City	36,840	366	7	32	90	237	2,271	399	1,734	138
	City of Lynn Haven	16,110	49	0	10	4	35	460	181	255	24
	Total area actually reporting	100.0%	990	8	106	171	705	6,839	1,569	4,870	400
	Rate per 100,000 inhabitants...........		602.3	4.9	64.5	104.0	428.9	4,161.0	954.6	2,963.0	243.4
Parkersburg-Marietta-Vienna, WV-OH M.S.A.											
	Includes Washington County, OH and Pleasants, Wirt, and Wood Counties, WV	160,687									
	City of Parkersburg, WV.................	31,562	68	1	11	18	38	1,468	286	1,077	105
	City of Marietta, OH	14,128	25	0	10	7	8	536	117	406	13
	City of Vienna, WV.........................	10,667	16	0	3	3	10	291	28	257	6
	Total area actually reporting	97.9%	278	4	44	31	199	3,845	859	2,778	208
	Estimated total...............................	100.0%	284	4	44	33	203	3,948	877	2,857	214
	Rate per 100,000 inhabitants...........		176.7	2.5	27.4	20.5	126.3	2,457.0	545.8	1,778.0	133.2
Pascagoula, MS M.S.A.											
	Includes George and Jackson Counties.....................................	153,177									
	City of Pascagoula	23,555	122	3	17	97	5	1,701	580	932	189
	Total area actually reporting	87.5%	356	12	48	161	135	5,672	1,685	3,318	669
	Estimated total...............................	100.0%	387	13	52	167	155	6,090	1,800	3,577	713
	Rate per 100,000 inhabitants...........		252.6	8.5	33.9	109.0	101.2	3,975.8	1,175.1	2,335.2	465.5
Pensacola-Ferry Pass-Brent, FL M.S.A.											
	Includes Escambia and Santa Rosa Counties.................................	440,445									
	City of Pensacola	52,837	487	3	30	148	306	2,880	608	2,149	123
	Total area actually reporting	100.0%	2,900	24	204	699	1,973	14,907	3,601	10,225	1,081
	Rate per 100,000 inhabitants...........		658.4	5.4	46.3	158.7	448.0	3,384.5	817.6	2,321.5	245.4
Philadelphia-Camden-Wilmington, PA-NJ-DE-MD M.S.A.											
	Includes the Metropolitan Divisions of Camden, NJ; Philadelphia, PA; and Wilmington, DE-MD-NJ	5,821,531									
	City of Philadelphia, PA.................	1,435,533	21,180	392	956	10,258	9,574	61,795	11,524	39,167	11,104
	City of Camden, NJ	78,967	1,755	42	67	781	865	4,600	1,128	2,311	1,161
	City of Wilmington, DE	72,842	1,230	11	30	593	596	3,388	954	1,913	521
	Total area actually reporting	99.6%	36,450	552	1,737	15,351	18,810	167,511	30,624	117,087	19,800
	Estimated total...............................	100.0%	36,543	552	1,742	15,377	18,872	168,198	30,743	117,617	19,838
	Rate per 100,000 inhabitants...........		627.7	9.5	29.9	264.1	324.2	2,889.2	528.1	2,020.4	340.8
Camden, NJ M.D.											
	Includes Burlington, Camden, and Gloucester Counties	1,244,124									
	Total area actually reporting	100.0%	4,349	61	230	1,717	2,341	31,689	6,375	22,186	3,128
	Rate per 100,000 inhabitants...........		349.6	4.9	18.5	138.0	188.2	2,547.1	512.4	1,783.3	251.4

Table 6. Crime, by Metropolitan Statistical Area, 2007 *(Contd.)*

(Number, percent, rate per 100,000 population.)

Metropolitan statistical area	Counties/principal cities	Population	Violent crime	Murder and non-negligent man-slaughter	Forcible rape	Robbery	Aggravated assault	Property crime	Burglary	Larceny-theft	Motor vehicle theft
Philadelphia, PA M.D.											
	Includes Bucks, Chester, Delaware, Montgomery, and Philadelphia Counties	3,880,695									
	Total area actually reporting	99.8%	27,502	456	1,314	12,151	13,581	112,500	19,127	78,799	14,574
	Estimated total	100.0%	27,523	456	1,315	12,157	13,595	112,690	19,156	78,949	14,585
	Rate per 100,000 inhabitants		709.2	11.8	33.9	313.3	350.3	2,903.9	493.6	2,034.4	375.8
Wilmington, DE-MD-NJ M.D.											
	Includes New Castle County, DE; Cecil County, MD; and Salem County, NJ	696,712									
	Total area actually reporting	98.4%	4,599	35	193	1,483	2,888	23,322	5,122	16,102	2,098
	Estimated total	100.0%	4,671	35	197	1,503	2,936	23,819	5,212	16,482	2,125
	Rate per 100,000 inhabitants		670.4	5.0	28.3	215.7	421.4	3,418.8	748.1	2,365.7	305.0
Phoenix-Mesa-Scottsdale, AZ M.S.A.											
	Includes Maricopa and Pinal Counties	4,170,448									
	City of Phoenix	1,541,698	11,159	213	509	4,942	5,495	89,825	19,212	49,754	20,859
	City of Mesa	454,576	2,224	22	175	620	1,407	19,945	2,922	14,063	2,960
	City of Scottsdale	235,243	438	5	41	143	249	8,138	1,523	5,863	752
	City of Tempe	171,320	916	10	63	330	513	11,424	1,866	7,959	1,599
	Total area actually reporting	97.9%	20,169	340	1,157	7,388	11,284	190,616	39,771	115,556	35,289
	Estimated total	100.0%	20,468	343	1,178	7,469	11,478	194,052	40,550	117,752	35,750
	Rate per 100,000 inhabitants		490.8	8.2	28.2	179.1	275.2	4,653.0	972.3	2,823.5	857.2
Pine Bluff, AR M.S.A.											
	Includes Cleveland, Jefferson, and Lincoln Counties	103,240									
	City of Pine Bluff	51,304	889	15	42	265	567	4,422	1,598	2,389	435
	Total area actually reporting	100.0%	1,008	18	55	281	654	5,449	2,006	2,914	529
	Rate per 100,000 inhabitants		976.4	17.4	53.3	272.2	633.5	5,278.0	1,943.0	2,822.5	512.4
Pittsburgh, PA M.S.A.											
	Includes Allegheny, Armstrong, Beaver, Butler, Fayette, Washington, and Westmoreland Counties	2,356,481									
	City of Pittsburgh	312,179	3,455	52	129	1,596	1,678	13,933	3,418	8,977	1,538
	Total area actually reporting	94.7%	8,247	98	464	2,696	4,989	48,992	10,364	34,767	3,861
	Estimated total	100.0%	8,530	101	481	2,773	5,175	51,511	10,745	36,757	4,009
	Rate per 100,000 inhabitants		362.0	4.3	20.4	117.7	219.6	2,185.9	456.0	1,559.8	170.1
Pittsfield, MA M.S.A.											
	Includes Berkshire County	130,630									
	City of Pittsfield	43,194	295	0	43	37	215	1,135	448	608	79
	Total area actually reporting	94.0%	502	1	57	50	394	2,670	903	1,610	157
	Estimated total	100.0%	524	1	59	54	410	2,829	943	1,716	170
	Rate per 100,000 inhabitants		401.1	0.8	45.2	41.3	313.9	2,165.7	721.9	1,313.6	130.1
Pocatello, ID M.S.A.											
	Includes Bannock and Power Counties	87,209									
	City of Pocatello	54,274	132	0	20	9	103	1,706	259	1,360	87
	Total area actually reporting	100.0%	187	0	23	12	152	2,555	339	2,102	114
	Rate per 100,000 inhabitants		214.4	0.0	26.4	13.8	174.3	2,929.7	388.7	2,410.3	130.7
Portland-South Portland-Biddeford, ME M.S.A.											
	Includes Cumberland, Sagadahoc, and York Counties	513,311									
	City of Portland	62,894	231	1	25	103	102	3,079	562	2,356	161
	City of South Portland	23,836	36	0	5	10	21	1,010	114	869	27
	City of Biddeford	22,079	77	0	28	21	28	1,050	160	845	45
	Total area actually reporting	100.0%	698	6	155	200	337	12,705	2,621	9,484	600
	Rate per 100,000 inhabitants		136.0	1.2	30.2	39.0	65.7	2,475.1	510.6	1,847.6	116.9

Table 6. Crime, by Metropolitan Statistical Area, 2007 *(Contd.)*

(Number, percent, rate per 100,000 population.)

Metropolitan statistical area	Counties/principal cities	Population	Violent crime	Murder and non-negligent man-slaughter	Forcible rape	Robbery	Aggravated assault	Property crime	Burglary	Larceny-theft	Motor vehicle theft
Portland-Vancouver-Beaverton, OR-WA M.S.A.											
	Includes Clackamas, Columbia, Multnomah, Washington, and Yamhill Counties, OR and Clark and Skamania Counties, WA	2,171,073									
	City of Portland, OR	538,133	3,701	22	280	1,289	2,110	31,586	4,840	21,978	4,768
	City of Vancouver, WA....................	161,092	646	7	118	166	355	6,557	1,005	4,581	971
	City of Beaverton, OR	91,184	220	0	20	59	141	2,330	337	1,768	225
	City of Hillsboro, OR	90,439	195	0	39	71	85	2,844	456	2,081	307
	Total area actually reporting	98.7%	6,752	47	845	2,174	3,686	75,986	11,751	54,234	10,001
	Estimated total................................	100.0%	6,799	47	852	2,183	3,717	76,628	11,878	54,680	10,070
	Rate per 100,000 inhabitants...........		313.2	2.2	39.2	100.5	171.2	3,529.5	547.1	2,518.6	463.8
Port St. Lucie, FL M.S.A.											
	Includes Martin and St. Lucie Counties................................	400,314									
	City of Port St. Lucie	154,036	421	2	60	53	306	3,595	1,003	2,419	173
	Total area actually reporting	100.0%	2,169	15	146	483	1,525	12,295	3,199	8,338	758
	Rate per 100,000 inhabitants...........		541.8	3.7	36.5	120.7	381.0	3,071.3	799.1	2,082.9	189.4
Poughkeepsie-Newburgh-Middletown, NY M.S.A.											
	Includes Dutchess and Orange Counties................................	676,768									
	City of Poughkeepsie......................	30,074	387	5	15	163	204	1,063	253	704	106
	City of Newburgh	28,340	436	2	14	131	289	1,176	316	791	69
	City of Middletown.........................	26,097	194	1	13	95	85	942	216	690	36
	Total area actually reporting	99.3%	1,934	23	119	573	1,219	13,244	2,208	10,436	600
	Estimated total................................	100.0%	1,943	23	120	576	1,224	13,338	2,222	10,512	604
	Rate per 100,000 inhabitants...........		287.1	3.4	17.7	85.1	180.9	1,970.8	328.3	1,553.3	89.2
Prescott, AZ M.S.A.											
	Includes Yavapai County	214,698									
	City of Prescott	42,674	130	1	7	19	103	1,387	279	1,059	49
	Total area actually reporting	99.8%	806	6	39	42	719	5,368	1,247	3,783	338
	Estimated total................................	100.0%	807	6	39	42	720	5,382	1,250	3,792	340
	Rate per 100,000 inhabitants...........		375.9	2.8	18.2	19.6	335.4	2,506.8	582.2	1,766.2	158.4
Provo-Orem, UT M.S.A.											
	Includes Juab and Utah Counties................................	498,516									
	City of Provo	115,264	168	0	28	35	105	3,298	487	2,526	285
	City of Orem	91,816	67	1	23	15	28	2,835	245	2,455	135
	Total area actually reporting	100.0%	423	2	95	90	236	12,588	1,859	9,998	731
	Rate per 100,000 inhabitants...........		84.9	0.4	19.1	18.1	47.3	2,525.1	372.9	2,005.6	146.6
Pueblo, CO M.S.A.											
	Includes Pueblo County..................	155,852									
	City of Pueblo	103,958	725	6	43	206	470	6,613	1,499	4,526	588
	Total area actually reporting	100.0%	739	7	46	207	479	8,024	1,796	5,583	645
	Rate per 100,000 inhabitants...........		474.2	4.5	29.5	132.8	307.3	5,148.5	1,152.4	3,582.2	413.9
Punta Gorda, FL M.S.A.											
	Includes Charlotte County	154,910									
	City of Punta Gorda	17,522	46	0	0	4	42	399	174	213	12
	Total area actually reporting	100.0%	633	10	28	73	522	4,772	1,149	3,365	258
	Rate per 100,000 inhabitants...........		408.6	6.5	18.1	47.1	337.0	3,080.5	741.7	2,172.2	166.5
Racine, WI M.S.A.											
	Includes Racine County..................	197,757									
	City of Racine	79,285	507	7	27	281	192	3,978	945	2,766	267
	Total area actually reporting	100.0%	594	7	30	332	225	6,303	1,317	4,595	391
	Rate per 100,000 inhabitants...........		300.4	3.5	15.2	167.9	113.8	3,187.2	666.0	2,323.6	197.7
Raleigh-Cary, NC M.S.A.											
	Includes Franklin, Johnston, and Wake Counties........................	1,033,679									
	City of Raleigh	367,120	2,098	23	99	835	1,141	12,762	2,949	8,773	1,040
	City of Cary...................................	114,221	134	1	11	58	64	2,120	448	1,584	88
	Total area actually reporting	99.8%	3,359	37	209	1,169	1,944	28,482	7,209	19,153	2,120
	Estimated total................................	100.0%	3,366	37	209	1,171	1,949	28,568	7,230	19,214	2,124
	Rate per 100,000 inhabitants...........		325.6	3.6	20.2	113.3	188.5	2,763.7	699.4	1,858.8	205.5

Table 6. Crime, by Metropolitan Statistical Area, 2007 (Contd.)

(Number, percent, rate per 100,000 population.)

Metropolitan statistical area	Counties/principal cities	Population	Violent crime	Murder and non-negligent man-slaughter	Forcible rape	Robbery	Aggravated assault	Property crime	Burglary	Larceny-theft	Motor vehicle theft
Rapid City, SD M.S.A.											
	Includes Meade and Pennington Counties.............................	121,126									
	City of Rapid City	63,162	294	4	69	34	187	2,386	443	1,819	124
	Total area actually reporting	100.0%	408	4	108	39	257	3,171	602	2,403	166
	Rate per 100,000 inhabitants...........		336.8	3.3	89.2	32.2	212.2	2,617.9	497.0	1,983.9	137.0
Reading, PA M.S.A.											
	Includes Berks County......................	404,031									
	City of Reading	81,168	752	6	41	385	320	3,818	1,183	1,780	855
	Total area actually reporting	99.1%	1,247	14	72	466	695	9,355	1,966	6,093	1,296
	Estimated total.................................	100.0%	1,256	14	73	468	701	9,431	1,978	6,153	1,300
	Rate per 100,000 inhabitants...........		310.9	3.5	18.1	115.8	173.5	2,334.2	489.6	1,522.9	321.8
Redding, CA M.S.A.											
	Includes Shasta County....................	180,982									
	City of Redding	91,328	455	0	84	100	271	2,645	633	1,730	282
	Total area actually reporting	100.0%	851	11	119	126	595	4,211	1,110	2,629	472
	Rate per 100,000 inhabitants...........		470.2	6.1	65.8	69.6	328.8	2,326.8	613.3	1,452.6	260.8
Reno-Sparks, NV M.S.A.											
	Includes Storey and Washoe Counties...	408,488									
	City of Reno......................................	214,197	1,513	17	95	516	885	9,418	1,835	6,511	1,072
	City of Sparks...................................	86,884	352	3	36	134	179	3,603	832	2,422	349
	Total area actually reporting	100.0%	2,112	22	135	666	1,289	15,186	3,305	10,208	1,673
	Rate per 100,000 inhabitants...........		517.0	5.4	33.0	163.0	315.6	3,717.6	809.1	2,499.0	409.6
Richmond, VA M.S.A.											
	Includes Amelia, Caroline, Charles City, Chesterfield, Cumberland, Dinwiddie, Goochland, Hanover, Henrico, King and Queen, King William, Louisa, New Kent, Powhatan, Prince George, and Sussex Counties and Colonial Heights, Hopewell, Petersburg, and Richmond Cities	1,205,749									
	City of Richmond	191,785	1,837	51	53	973	760	8,966	1,857	5,816	1,293
	Total area actually reporting	99.9%	4,396	104	259	2,033	2,000	34,445	6,676	24,604	3,165
	Estimated total.................................	100.0%	4,398	104	259	2,034	2,001	34,463	6,679	24,618	3,166
	Rate per 100,000 inhabitants...........		364.8	8.6	21.5	168.7	166.0	2,858.2	553.9	2,041.7	262.6
Riverside-San Bernardino-Ontario, CA M.S.A.											
	Includes Riverside and San Bernardino Counties......................	4,115,406									
	City of Riverside	299,312	1,893	12	91	686	1,104	11,154	2,227	7,081	1,846
	City of San Bernardino	200,810	2,150	45	74	862	1,169	10,090	2,129	5,358	2,603
	City of Ontario..................................	175,537	854	15	46	351	442	5,850	970	3,551	1,329
	City of Victorville.............................	104,872	660	9	30	264	357	4,039	1,281	2,099	659
	City of Temecula...............................	93,665	207	5	12	81	109	2,654	667	1,688	299
	City of Chino.....................................	80,699	232	0	7	106	119	2,500	594	1,568	338
	City of Redlands...............................	71,358	303	0	17	114	172	2,505	589	1,554	362
	City of Hemet....................................	71,825	479	3	36	149	291	3,117	815	1,846	456
	City of Colton....................................	51,924	245	9	9	116	111	1,929	498	983	448
	Total area actually reporting	100.0%	19,499	265	1,029	6,466	11,739	132,274	33,725	74,041	24,508
	Rate per 100,000 inhabitants...........		473.8	6.4	25.0	157.1	285.2	3,214.1	819.5	1,799.1	595.5
Roanoke, VA M.S.A.											
	Includes Botetourt, Craig, Franklin, and Roanoke Counties and Roanoke and Salem Cities.......	295,368									
	City of Roanoke................................	90,894	901	4	55	266	576	5,000	1,016	3,637	347
	Total area actually reporting	100.0%	1,205	8	93	308	796	8,223	1,564	6,154	505
	Rate per 100,000 inhabitants...........		408.0	2.7	31.5	104.3	269.5	2,784.0	529.5	2,083.5	171.0
Rochester, MN M.S.A.[5]											
	Includes Dodge, Olmsted, and Wabasha Counties[5]..........................	181,608									
	City of Rochester[5]	98,287		2		76	140	2,556	460	1,928	168
	Total area actually reporting	98.2%		2		81	187	3,588	691	2,672	225
	Estimated total.................................	100.0%		2		83	190	3,697	707	2,759	231
	Rate per 100,000 inhabitants...........			1.1		45.7	104.6	2,035.7	389.3	1,519.2	127.2

[5] The data collection methodology for the offense of forcible rape used by the Minnesota state UCR Program (with the exception of Minneapolis and St. Paul, MN) does not comply with national UCR Program guidelines. Consequently, their figures for forcible rape and violent crime (of which forcible rape is a part) are not published in this table.

Table 6. Crime, by Metropolitan Statistical Area, 2007 (Contd.)

(Number, percent, rate per 100,000 population.)

Metropolitan statistical area	Counties/principal cities	Population	Violent crime	Murder and non-negligent man-slaughter	Forcible rape	Robbery	Aggravated assault	Property crime	Burglary	Larceny-theft	Motor vehicle theft
Rochester, NY M.S.A.											
	Includes Livingston, Monroe, Ontario, Orleans, and Wayne Counties......................	1,032,143									
	City of Rochester	206,686	2,350	50	121	1,032	1,147	11,277	2,582	7,044	1,651
	Total area actually reporting	98.4%	3,337	57	243	1,244	1,793	27,783	5,217	20,295	2,271
	Estimated total.................................	100.0%	3,367	57	245	1,254	1,811	28,096	5,265	20,546	2,285
	Rate per 100,000 inhabitants...........		326.2	5.5	23.7	121.5	175.5	2,722.1	510.1	1,990.6	221.4
Rocky Mount, NC M.S.A.											
	Includes Edgecombe and Nash Counties......................................	148,194									
	City of Rocky Mount	57,132	662	14	21	266	361	4,815	1,354	3,240	221
	Total area actually reporting	99.1%	882	21	34	329	498	6,889	2,126	4,365	398
	Estimated total.................................	100.0%	888	21	34	331	502	6,955	2,142	4,412	401
	Rate per 100,000 inhabitants...........		599.2	14.2	22.9	223.4	338.7	4,693.2	1,445.4	2,977.2	270.6
Rome, GA M.S.A.											
	Includes Floyd County....................	95,960									
	City of Rome	36,233	264	2	17	68	177	2,398	489	1,754	155
	Total area actually reporting	100.0%	421	4	23	75	319	3,822	798	2,760	264
	Rate per 100,000 inhabitants...........		438.7	4.2	24.0	78.2	332.4	3,982.9	831.6	2,876.2	275.1
Sacramento—Arden-Arcade—Roseville, CA M.S.A.											
	Includes El Dorado, Placer, Sacramento, and Yolo Counties	2,091,363									
	City of Sacramento	460,546	5,128	44	194	2,009	2,881	24,399	5,422	12,904	6,073
	City of Roseville	111,497	387	1	31	100	255	3,960	648	2,905	407
	City of Folsom	68,320	98	2	8	27	61	1,594	329	1,146	119
	City of Woodland	51,355	154	1	23	62	68	1,807	467	1,094	246
	Total area actually reporting	100.0%	11,214	101	595	3,902	6,616	69,861	16,218	39,431	14,212
	Rate per 100,000 inhabitants...........		536.2	4.8	28.5	186.6	316.3	3,340.5	775.5	1,885.4	679.6
Saginaw-Saginaw Township North, MI M.S.A.											
	Includes Saginaw County	204,943									
	City of Saginaw	56,989	1,678	17	66	264	1,331	2,764	1,613	825	326
	Total area actually reporting	98.9%	2,186	22	111	361	1,692	7,234	2,943	3,748	543
	Estimated total.................................	100.0%	2,194	22	112	363	1,697	7,301	2,956	3,795	550
	Rate per 100,000 inhabitants...........		1,070.5	10.7	54.6	177.1	828.0	3,562.5	1,442.4	1,851.7	268.4
Salem, OR M.S.A.											
	Includes Marion and Polk Counties......................................	390,689									
	City of Salem	154,484	583	3	58	132	390	7,436	915	5,629	892
	Total area actually reporting	100.0%	1,161	4	131	225	801	14,461	2,103	10,739	1,619
	Rate per 100,000 inhabitants...........		297.2	1.0	33.5	57.6	205.0	3,701.4	538.3	2,748.7	414.4
Salinas, CA M.S.A.											
	Includes Monterey County.............	408,059									
	City of Salinas	145,251	1,154	14	51	378	711	6,878	1,205	3,332	2,341
	Total area actually reporting	100.0%	2,191	29	123	638	1,401	14,427	3,020	8,043	3,364
	Rate per 100,000 inhabitants...........		536.9	7.1	30.1	156.3	343.3	3,535.5	740.1	1,971.0	824.4
Salisbury, MD M.S.A.											
	Includes Somerset and Wicomico Counties......................................	117,891									
	City of Salisbury..............................	27,727	503	2	24	182	295	2,390	583	1,704	103
	Total area actually reporting	100.0%	932	5	48	251	628	4,745	1,272	3,253	220
	Rate per 100,000 inhabitants...........		790.6	4.2	40.7	212.9	532.7	4,024.9	1,079.0	2,759.3	186.6
Salt Lake City, UT M.S.A.											
	Includes Salt Lake, Summit, and Tooele Counties	1,101,656									
	City of Salt Lake City......................	178,449	1,499	17	114	503	865	15,232	2,049	11,196	1,987
	Total area actually reporting	99.8%	4,094	45	527	1,073	2,449	53,108	8,558	38,176	6,374
	Estimated total.................................	100.0%	4,098	45	528	1,074	2,451	53,174	8,569	38,225	6,380
	Rate per 100,000 inhabitants...........		372.0	4.1	47.9	97.5	222.5	4,826.7	777.8	3,469.8	579.1
San Angelo, TX M.S.A.											
	Includes Irion and Tom Green Counties......................................	105,706									
	City of San Angelo	88,285	356	1	46	48	261	4,473	932	3,312	229
	Total area actually reporting	100.0%	378	1	49	49	279	4,855	1,016	3,590	249
	Rate per 100,000 inhabitants...........		357.6	0.9	46.4	46.4	263.9	4,592.9	961.2	3,396.2	235.6

Table 6. Crime, by Metropolitan Statistical Area, 2007 *(Contd.)*

(Number, percent, rate per 100,000 population.)

Metropolitan statistical area	Counties/principal cities	Population	Violent crime	Murder and non-negligent man-slaughter	Forcible rape	Robbery	Aggravated assault	Property crime	Burglary	Larceny-theft	Motor vehicle theft
San Antonio, TX M.S.A.											
	Includes Atascosa, Bandera, Bexar, Comal, Guadalupe, Kendall, Medina, and Wilson Counties	1,975,770									
	City of San Antonio	1,316,882	7,327	122	635	2,445	4,125	84,143	16,750	60,669	6,724
	Total area actually reporting	100.0%	9,053	140	835	2,709	5,369	105,379	21,937	75,572	7,870
	Rate per 100,000 inhabitants		458.2	7.1	42.3	137.1	271.7	5,333.6	1,110.3	3,824.9	398.3
San Diego-Carlsbad-San Marcos, CA M.S.A.											
	Includes San Diego County	2,935,792									
	City of San Diego	1,261,196	6,332	59	296	2,095	3,882	44,167	7,679	23,264	13,224
	City of Carlsbad	95,056	318	2	13	88	215	2,448	528	1,684	236
	City of San Marcos	80,050	287	2	12	101	172	1,669	414	937	318
	City of National City	61,996	424	6	19	180	219	2,169	379	842	948
	Total area actually reporting	100.0%	13,672	107	705	4,388	8,472	89,820	16,720	48,672	24,428
	Rate per 100,000 inhabitants		465.7	3.6	24.0	149.5	288.6	3,059.5	569.5	1,657.9	832.1
Sandusky, OH M.S.A.											
	Includes Erie County	77,695									
	City of Sandusky	25,994	225	1	8	47	169	1,591	398	1,126	67
	Total area actually reporting	98.7%	247	1	9	50	187	2,632	611	1,924	97
	Estimated total	100.0%	249	1	9	51	188	2,663	617	1,947	99
	Rate per 100,000 inhabitants		320.5	1.3	11.6	65.6	242.0	3,427.5	794.1	2,506.0	127.4
San Francisco-Oakland-Fremont, CA M.S.A.											
	Includes the Metropolitan Divisions of Oakland-Fremont-Hayward and San Francisco-San Mateo-Redwood City	4,154,508									
	City of San Francisco	733,799	6,414	100	125	3,771	2,418	34,456	5,079	23,474	5,903
	City of Oakland	396,541	7,605	120	299	3,470	3,716	23,664	4,742	8,954	9,968
	City of Fremont	201,318	606	5	35	232	334	5,173	1,292	3,108	773
	City of Hayward	140,603	881	8	48	538	287	4,667	965	2,021	1,681
	City of Berkeley	101,343	639	5	24	431	179	7,116	1,172	4,949	995
	City of San Mateo	91,441	306	0	19	100	187	2,073	241	1,610	222
	City of San Leandro	77,785	547	0	12	308	227	3,978	791	1,935	1,252
	City of Redwood City	73,435	336	1	22	86	227	1,689	197	1,271	221
	City of Pleasanton	66,707	63	0	8	19	36	1,294	152	1,009	133
	City of Walnut Creek	63,568	90	2	3	36	49	2,586	506	1,875	205
	City of South San Francisco	61,458	177	0	12	73	92	1,567	392	936	239
	City of San Rafael	55,987	280	0	28	80	172	1,763	340	1,103	320
	Total area actually reporting	100.0%	26,746	365	1,049	12,915	12,417	155,539	28,589	91,176	35,774
	Rate per 100,000 inhabitants		643.8	8.8	25.2	310.9	298.9	3,743.9	688.1	2,194.6	861.1
Oakland-Fremont-Hayward, CA M.D.											
	Includes Alameda and Contra Costa Counties	2,474,091									
	Total area actually reporting	100.0%	17,491	251	725	8,245	8,270	99,136	19,690	52,577	26,869
	Rate per 100,000 inhabitants		707.0	10.1	29.3	333.3	334.3	4,007.0	795.8	2,125.1	1,086.0
San Francisco-San Mateo-Redwood City, CA M.D.											
	Includes Marin, San Francisco, and San Mateo Counties	1,680,417									
	Total area actually reporting	100.0%	9,255	114	324	4,670	4,147	56,403	8,899	38,599	8,905
	Rate per 100,000 inhabitants		550.8	6.8	19.3	277.9	246.8	3,356.5	529.6	2,297.0	529.9
San Jose-Sunnyvale-Santa Clara, CA M.S.A.											
	Includes San Benito and Santa Clara Counties	1,780,107									
	City of San Jose	934,553	3,759	33	217	1,068	2,441	24,062	4,449	13,200	6,413
	City of Sunnyvale	130,326	154	2	15	62	75	2,629	372	1,896	361
	City of Santa Clara	109,420	231	3	32	73	123	3,430	553	2,420	457
	City of Mountain View	69,999	238	1	8	56	173	1,519	157	1,224	138
	City of Milpitas	64,498	179	1	10	60	108	2,104	291	1,539	274
	City of Palo Alto	57,696	64	1	1	44	18	1,440	283	1,085	72
	City of Cupertino	53,002	53	0	7	12	34	837	178	618	41
	Total area actually reporting	100.0%	5,831	51	382	1,649	3,749	45,549	8,335	28,270	8,944
	Rate per 100,000 inhabitants		327.6	2.9	21.5	92.6	210.6	2,558.8	468.2	1,588.1	502.4

Table 6. Crime, by Metropolitan Statistical Area, 2007 *(Contd.)*

(Number, percent, rate per 100,000 population.)

Metropolitan statistical area	Counties/principal cities	Population	Violent crime	Murder and non-negligent man-slaughter	Forcible rape	Robbery	Aggravated assault	Property crime	Burglary	Larceny-theft	Motor vehicle theft
San Luis Obispo-Paso Robles, CA M.S.A.											
	Includes San Luis Obispo County	256,373									
	City of San Luis Obispo	42,781	168	3	27	39	99	1,846	312	1,450	84
	City of Paso Robles	28,490	106	0	12	13	81	931	194	659	78
	Total area actually reporting	100.0%	894	5	105	92	692	6,269	1,330	4,516	423
	Rate per 100,000 inhabitants		348.7	2.0	41.0	35.9	269.9	2,445.3	518.8	1,761.5	165.0
Santa Barbara-Santa Maria-Goleta, CA M.S.A.											
	Includes Santa Barbara County	397,342									
	City of Santa Barbara	85,142	445	2	44	96	303	2,277	576	1,536	165
	City of Santa Maria	85,782	604	3	39	139	423	2,616	513	1,622	481
	City of Goleta	29,243	53	0	4	13	36	377	89	255	33
	Total area actually reporting	100.0%	1,644	10	155	311	1,168	8,895	2,013	5,994	888
	Rate per 100,000 inhabitants		413.7	2.5	39.0	78.3	294.0	2,238.6	506.6	1,508.5	223.5
Santa Cruz-Watsonville, CA M.S.A.											
	Includes Santa Cruz County	246,931									
	City of Santa Cruz	54,626	481	1	28	117	335	2,432	410	1,847	175
	City of Watsonville	49,031	397	1	17	110	269	2,276	284	1,770	222
	Total area actually reporting	100.0%	1,239	6	80	275	878	8,866	1,602	6,547	717
	Rate per 100,000 inhabitants		501.8	2.4	32.4	111.4	355.6	3,590.5	648.8	2,651.3	290.4
Santa Rosa-Petaluma, CA M.S.A.											
	Includes Sonoma County	464,218									
	City of Santa Rosa	154,953	771	4	65	136	566	3,732	726	2,634	372
	City of Petaluma	54,624	226	1	14	40	171	1,034	180	765	89
	Total area actually reporting	100.0%	1,974	8	153	270	1,543	9,394	2,154	6,308	932
	Rate per 100,000 inhabitants		425.2	1.7	33.0	58.2	332.4	2,023.6	464.0	1,358.8	200.8
Savannah, GA M.S.A.[3]											
	Includes Bryan, Chatham, and Effingham[3] Counties	324,109									
	City of Savannah-Chatham Metropolitan	208,116	1,319	26	78	743	472	9,851	2,315	6,369	1,167
	Total area actually reporting	99.2%	1,780	28	100	852	800		2,868		1,400
	Estimated total	100.0%	1,794	28	101	857	808		2,891		1,411
	Rate per 100,000 inhabitants		553.5	8.6	31.2	264.4	249.3		892.0		435.3
Scranton—Wilkes-Barre, PA M.S.A.											
	Includes Lackawanna, Luzerne, and Wyoming Counties	548,161									
	City of Scranton	72,444	227	2	26	99	100	2,263	499	1,592	172
	City of Wilkes-Barre	41,050	193	3	19	110	61	1,683	373	1,194	116
	Total area actually reporting	91.5%	1,469	15	110	378	966	11,828	2,301	8,786	741
	Estimated total	100.0%	1,574	16	116	407	1,035	12,766	2,443	9,527	796
	Rate per 100,000 inhabitants		287.1	2.9	21.2	74.2	188.8	2,328.9	445.7	1,738.0	145.2
Seattle-Tacoma-Bellevue, WA M.S.A.[2]											
	Includes the Metropolitan Divisions of Seattle-Bellevue-Everett and Tacoma	3,294,592									
	City of Seattle	585,118	3,667	24	90	1,522	2,031	33,960	5,986	22,192	5,782
	City of Tacoma[2]	196,909	2,059	14	140	647	1,258	14,957	2,628	8,986	3,343
	City of Bellevue	118,984	138	0	29	61	48	4,181	583	3,152	446
	City of Everett	98,845	564	7	61	209	287	8,739	1,405	5,456	1,878
	City of Kent	83,929	525	4	64	174	283	4,873	1,075	2,790	1,008
	City of Renton	59,656	248	1	26	103	118	4,054	677	2,701	676
	Total area actually reporting	100.0%	12,686	101	1,198	4,347	7,040	146,174	28,438	91,625	26,111
	Rate per 100,000 inhabitants		385.1	3.1	36.4	131.9	213.7	4,436.8	863.2	2,781.1	792.5
Seattle-Bellevue-Everett, WA M.D.											
	Includes King and Snohomish Counties	2,518,369									
	Total area actually reporting	100.0%	8,578	76	866	3,250	4,386	109,992	21,005	69,792	19,195
	Rate per 100,000 inhabitants		340.6	3.0	34.4	129.1	174.2	4,367.6	834.1	2,771.3	762.2
Tacoma, WA M.D.[2]											
	Includes Pierce County[2]	776,223									
	Total area actually reporting	100.0%	4,108	25	332	1,097	2,654	36,182	7,433	21,833	6,916
	Rate per 100,000 inhabitants		529.2	3.2	42.8	141.3	341.9	4,661.3	957.6	2,812.7	891.0

[2] Because of changes in the state/local agency's reporting practices, figures are not comparable to previous years' data.

[3] The FBI determined that the agency's data were underreported. Consequently, affected data are not included in this table.

Table 6. Crime, by Metropolitan Statistical Area, 2007 *(Contd.)*

(Number, percent, rate per 100,000 population.)

Metropolitan statistical area	Counties/principal cities	Population	Violent crime	Murder and non-negligent man-slaughter	Forcible rape	Robbery	Aggravated assault	Property crime	Burglary	Larceny-theft	Motor vehicle theft
Sebastian-Vero Beach, FL M.S.A.	Includes Indian River County	131,526									
	City of Sebastian	20,913	64	0	4	5	55	662	198	443	21
	City of Vero Beach	16,840	84	0	6	24	54	707	196	482	29
	Total area actually reporting	100.0%	464	2	36	101	325	4,041	1,046	2,753	242
	Rate per 100,000 inhabitants		352.8	1.5	27.4	76.8	247.1	3,072.4	795.3	2,093.1	184.0
Sheboygan, WI M.S.A.	Includes Sheboygan County	115,407									
	City of Sheboygan	48,291	91	1	21	29	40	2,471	430	1,979	62
	Total area actually reporting	100.0%	144	1	28	34	81	3,485	580	2,817	88
	Rate per 100,000 inhabitants		124.8	0.9	24.3	29.5	70.2	3,019.7	502.6	2,440.9	76.3
Sherman-Denison, TX M.S.A.	Includes Grayson County	119,528									
	City of Sherman	37,985	146	0	6	19	121	1,529	336	1,141	52
	City of Denison	24,130	111	2	5	24	80	1,221	290	879	52
	Total area actually reporting	100.0%	304	4	20	44	236	3,804	975	2,642	187
	Rate per 100,000 inhabitants		254.3	3.3	16.7	36.8	197.4	3,182.5	815.7	2,210.4	156.4
Shreveport-Bossier City, LA M.S.A.	Includes Bossier, Caddo, and De Soto Parishes	387,314									
	City of Shreveport	199,811	2,198	36	112	544	1,506	12,178	2,861	8,216	1,101
	City of Bossier City	61,993	1,146	2	34	88	1,022	2,692	426	2,068	198
	Total area actually reporting	99.0%	4,326	44	174	655	3,453	17,532	3,797	12,176	1,559
	Estimated total	100.0%	4,353	44	176	659	3,474	17,736	3,835	12,330	1,571
	Rate per 100,000 inhabitants		1,123.9	11.4	45.4	170.1	896.9	4,579.2	990.2	3,183.5	405.6
Sioux City, IA-NE-SD M.S.A.	Includes Woodbury County, IA; Dakota and Dixon Counties, NE; and Union County, SD	143,514									
	City of Sioux City, IA	82,942	373	2	40	33	298	2,842	578	2,110	154
	Total area actually reporting	96.9%	429	2	47	36	344	3,348	690	2,483	175
	Estimated total	100.0%	435	2	48	36	349	3,400	701	2,521	178
	Rate per 100,000 inhabitants		303.1	1.4	33.4	25.1	243.2	2,369.1	488.5	1,756.6	124.0
Sioux Falls, SD M.S.A.	Includes Lincoln, McCook, Minnehaha, and Turner Counties	219,627									
	City of Sioux Falls	144,985	381	2	95	44	240	3,780	631	2,881	268
	Total area actually reporting	98.1%	439	3	103	46	287	4,284	789	3,202	293
	Estimated total	100.0%	445	3	104	46	292	4,333	799	3,238	296
	Rate per 100,000 inhabitants		202.6	1.4	47.4	20.9	133.0	1,972.9	363.8	1,474.3	134.8
South Bend-Mishawaka, IN-MI M.S.A.	Includes St. Joseph County, IN and Cass County, MI	317,804									
	City of South Bend, IN	104,437	805	7	67	448	283	6,872	1,945	4,438	489
	City of Mishawaka, IN	49,196	157	1	17	52	87	3,189	342	2,691	156
	Total area actually reporting	100.0%	1,242	13	129	548	552	13,434	3,108	9,493	833
	Rate per 100,000 inhabitants		390.8	4.1	40.6	172.4	173.7	4,227.1	978.0	2,987.1	262.1
Spartanburg, SC M.S.A.	Includes Spartanburg County	276,109									
	City of Spartanburg	38,388	829	6	22	219	582	3,610	919	2,422	269
	Total area actually reporting	100.0%	2,006	25	96	475	1,410	12,684	3,262	8,339	1,083
	Rate per 100,000 inhabitants		726.5	9.1	34.8	172.0	510.7	4,593.8	1,181.4	3,020.2	392.2
Spokane, WA M.S.A.	Includes Spokane County	450,805									
	City of Spokane	198,272	1,322	12	88	414	808	11,376	2,175	7,188	2,013
	Total area actually reporting	100.0%	1,981	14	119	496	1,352	17,167	3,343	11,082	2,742
	Rate per 100,000 inhabitants		439.4	3.1	26.4	110.0	299.9	3,808.1	741.6	2,458.3	608.2
Springfield, MA M.S.A.	Includes Franklin, Hampden, and Hampshire Counties	687,220									
	City of Springfield	151,074	2,068	20	91	690	1,267	7,942	2,027	4,694	1,221
	Total area actually reporting	97.3%	3,912	31	266	927	2,688	19,987	5,229	12,541	2,217
	Estimated total	100.0%	3,966	31	270	938	2,727	20,363	5,323	12,793	2,247
	Rate per 100,000 inhabitants		577.1	4.5	39.3	136.5	396.8	2,963.1	774.6	1,861.6	327.0

Table 6. Crime, by Metropolitan Statistical Area, 2007 *(Contd.)*

(Number, percent, rate per 100,000 population.)

Metropolitan statistical area	Counties/principal cities	Population	Violent crime	Murder and non-negligent man-slaughter	Forcible rape	Robbery	Aggravated assault	Property crime	Burglary	Larceny-theft	Motor vehicle theft
Springfield, MO M.S.A.											
	Includes Christian, Dallas, Greene, Polk, and Webster Counties.............................	412,378									
	City of Springfield......................	150,488	1,051	5	72	294	680	14,315	2,140	11,231	944
	Total area actually reporting	100.0%	1,893	10	100	328	1,455	18,907	3,235	14,442	1,230
	Rate per 100,000 inhabitants..........		459.0	2.4	24.2	79.5	352.8	4,584.9	784.5	3,502.1	298.3
Springfield, OH M.S.A.											
	Includes Clark County	141,098									
	City of Springfield.......................	62,426	461	5	36	241	179	5,407	1,403	3,627	377
	Total area actually reporting	99.8%	505	5	52	256	192	7,240	1,809	4,943	488
	Estimated total................................	100.0%	505	5	52	256	192	7,248	1,811	4,949	488
	Rate per 100,000 inhabitants..........		357.9	3.5	36.9	181.4	136.1	5,136.9	1,283.5	3,507.5	345.9
State College, PA M.S.A.											
	Includes Centre County	141,328									
	City of State College	52,047	43	0	4	15	24	940	104	824	12
	Total area actually reporting	97.9%	136	1	20	33	82	2,681	411	2,198	72
	Estimated total................................	100.0%	142	1	20	35	86	2,739	420	2,244	75
	Rate per 100,000 inhabitants..........		100.5	0.7	14.2	24.8	60.9	1,938.0	297.2	1,587.8	53.1
St. Cloud, MN M.S.A.[5]											
	Includes Benton and Stearns Counties[5]..	184,856									
	City of St. Cloud[5]	67,290			1	48	145	2,943	352	2,466	125
	Total area actually reporting	100.0%			1	52	213	4,751	620	3,929	202
	Rate per 100,000 inhabitants..........				0.5	28.1	115.2	2,570.1	335.4	2,125.4	109.3
St. George, UT M.S.A.											
	Includes Washington County..........	134,726									
	City of St. George	70,579	155	0	13	15	127	2,338	606	1,583	149
	Total area actually reporting	100.0%	221	1	28	20	172	3,536	954	2,341	241
	Rate per 100,000 inhabitants..........		164.0	0.7	20.8	14.8	127.7	2,624.6	708.1	1,737.6	178.9
St. Joseph, MO-KS M.S.A.											
	Includes Doniphan County, KS and Andrew, Buchanan, and De Kalb Counties, MO....................	121,979									
	City of St. Joseph, MO.....................	72,424	216	2	13	66	135	3,857	770	2,814	273
	Total area actually reporting	98.4%	343	2	22	73	246	4,794	1,039	3,427	328
	Estimated total................................	100.0%	350	2	23	74	251	4,853	1,048	3,473	332
	Rate per 100,000 inhabitants...........		286.9	1.6	18.9	60.7	205.8	3,978.6	859.2	2,847.2	272.2
St. Louis, MO-IL M.S.A.											
	Includes Bond, Calhoun, Clinton, Jersey, Macoupin, Madison, Monroe, and St. Clair Counties, IL and Franklin, Jefferson, Lincoln, St. Charles, St. Louis, Warren, and Washington Counties and St. Louis City, MO..........................	2,810,914									
	City of St. Louis, MO......................	348,197	7,654	138	255	2,761	4,500	33,901	7,289	20,330	6,282
	City of St. Charles, MO	63,277	162	1	21	48	92	2,256	309	1,853	94
	Total area actually reporting	75.4%	12,925	182	581	3,879	8,283	85,779	16,206	59,296	10,277
	Estimated total................................	100.0%	15,086	216	582	4,360	9,928	98,410	18,783	68,605	11,022
	Rate per 100,000 inhabitants..........		536.7	7.7	20.7	155.1	353.2	3,501.0	668.2	2,440.7	392.1
Stockton, CA M.S.A.											
	Includes San Joaquin County..........	684,406									
	City of Stockton	297,170	4,216	29	105	1,615	2,467	18,677	4,054	11,783	2,840
	Total area actually reporting	100.0%	6,054	45	165	2,085	3,759	34,415	7,486	21,744	5,185
	Rate per 100,000 inhabitants..........		884.6	6.6	24.1	304.6	549.2	5,028.4	1,093.8	3,177.1	757.6
Sumter, SC M.S.A.											
	Includes Sumter County	105,369									
	City of Sumter.................................	38,955	531	4	9	101	417	2,568	683	1,743	142
	Total area actually reporting	100.0%	1,536	9	42	146	1,339	5,195	1,643	3,104	448
	Rate per 100,000 inhabitants..........		1,457.7	8.5	39.9	138.6	1,270.8	4,930.3	1,559.3	2,945.8	425.2

[5] The data collection methodology for the offense of forcible rape used by the Minnesota state UCR Program (with the exception of Minneapolis and St. Paul, MN) does not comply with national UCR Program guidelines. Consequently, their figures for forcible rape and violent crime (of which forcible rape is a part) are not published in this table.

Table 6. Crime, by Metropolitan Statistical Area, 2007 *(Contd.)*

(Number, percent, rate per 100,000 population.)

Metropolitan statistical area	Counties/principal cities	Population	Violent crime	Murder and non-negligent man-slaughter	Forcible rape	Robbery	Aggravated assault	Property crime	Burglary	Larceny-theft	Motor vehicle theft
Syracuse, NY M.S.A.											
	Includes Madison, Onondaga, and Oswego Counties	648,191									
	City of Syracuse	139,880	1,435	19	67	446	903	5,964	1,785	3,618	561
	Total area actually reporting	100.0%	2,043	26	146	558	1,313	15,297	3,605	10,830	862
	Rate per 100,000 inhabitants..........		315.2	4.0	22.5	86.1	202.6	2,360.0	556.2	1,670.8	133.0
Tallahassee, FL M.S.A.											
	Includes Gadsden, Jefferson, Leon, and Wakulla Counties	335,945									
	City of Tallahassee	159,943	1,813	5	136	568	1,104	8,396	2,588	5,202	606
	Total area actually reporting	97.5%	2,830	8	203	711	1,908	12,975	4,317	7,723	935
	Estimated total..................	100.0%	2,885	8	205	730	1,942	13,350	4,399	7,981	970
	Rate per 100,000 inhabitants..........		858.8	2.4	61.0	217.3	578.1	3,973.9	1,309.4	2,375.7	288.7
Tampa-St. Petersburg-Clearwater, FL M.S.A.											
	Includes Hernando, Hillsborough, Pasco, and Pinellas Counties	2,720,592									
	City of Tampa	337,220	3,575	28	80	1,205	2,262	16,775	4,221	10,390	2,164
	City of St. Petersburg	248,069	3,830	26	103	1,017	2,684	15,189	3,717	9,156	2,316
	City of Clearwater	107,501	868	10	34	240	584	4,678	862	3,469	347
	City of Largo	73,789	564	5	35	128	396	2,875	567	2,105	203
	Total area actually reporting	100.0%	19,138	143	940	4,977	13,078	109,910	26,706	71,986	11,218
	Rate per 100,000 inhabitants..........		703.4	5.3	34.6	182.9	480.7	4,039.9	981.6	2,646.0	412.3
Texarkana, TX-Texarkana, AR M.S.A.											
	Includes Miller County, AR and Bowie County, TX..........	135,211									
	City of Texarkana, TX	36,237	506	9	27	105	365	2,401	507	1,749	145
	City of Texarkana, AR	30,156	447	3	20	64	360	1,548	387	1,043	118
	Total area actually reporting	100.0%	1,155	15	67	187	886	5,531	1,292	3,824	415
	Rate per 100,000 inhabitants..........		854.2	11.1	49.6	138.3	655.3	4,090.6	955.5	2,828.2	306.9
Toledo, OH M.S.A.											
	Includes Fulton, Lucas, Ottawa, and Wood Counties	651,165									
	City of Toledo..............	296,403	3,639	13	151	1,225	2,250	19,826	5,921	12,029	1,876
	Total area actually reporting	94.7%	3,868	13	190	1,291	2,374	28,554	7,285	19,037	2,232
	Estimated total..............	100.0%	3,930	14	200	1,315	2,401	29,550	7,469	19,793	2,288
	Rate per 100,000 inhabitants..........		603.5	2.1	30.7	201.9	368.7	4,538.0	1,147.0	3,039.6	351.4
Topeka, KS M.S.A.											
	Includes Jackson, Jefferson, Osage, Shawnee, and Wabaunsee Counties.......	229,580									
	City of Topeka..............	121,885	719	12	47	308	352	7,774	1,424	5,646	704
	Total area actually reporting	97.1%	935	12	70	324	529	10,402	2,024	7,545	833
	Estimated total..............	100.0%	957	12	72	327	546	10,599	2,054	7,699	846
	Rate per 100,000 inhabitants..........		416.8	5.2	31.4	142.4	237.8	4,616.7	894.7	3,353.5	368.5
Trenton-Ewing, NJ M.S.A.											
	Includes Mercer County	365,977									
	City of Trenton	83,551	1,165	25	15	595	530	2,645	852	1,408	385
	City of Ewing Township	36,753	89	1	5	27	56	685	137	492	56
	Total area actually reporting	100.0%	1,605	26	44	765	770	7,754	1,707	5,324	723
	Rate per 100,000 inhabitants..........		438.6	7.1	12.0	209.0	210.4	2,118.7	466.4	1,454.7	197.6
Tucson, AZ M.S.A.[4]											
	Includes Pima County	963,028									
	City of Tucson[4]	523,299	4,103	49	277	1,432	2,345		4,787		6,767
	Total area actually reporting	100.0%	5,033	74	383	1,717	2,859		7,869		8,921
	Rate per 100,000 inhabitants..........		522.6	7.7	39.8	178.3	296.9		817.1		926.3
Tulsa, OK M.S.A.											
	Includes Creek, Okmulgee, Osage, Pawnee, Rogers, Tulsa, and Wagoner Counties	908,036									
	City of Tulsa..................	381,469	4,552	55	299	1,023	3,175	24,044	6,843	13,522	3,679
	Total area actually reporting	100.0%	5,890	71	450	1,138	4,231	34,626	9,662	20,274	4,690
	Rate per 100,000 inhabitants..........		648.7	7.8	49.6	125.3	466.0	3,813.3	1,064.1	2,232.7	516.5

[4] It was determined that the agency did not follow national Uniform Crime Reporting (UCR) Program guidelines for reporting an offense. Consequently, this figure is not included in this table.

Table 6. Crime, by Metropolitan Statistical Area, 2007 *(Contd.)*

(Number, percent, rate per 100,000 population.)

Metropolitan statistical area	Counties/principal cities	Population	Violent crime	Murder and non-negligent man-slaughter	Forcible rape	Robbery	Aggravated assault	Property crime	Burglary	Larceny-theft	Motor vehicle theft
Tuscaloosa, AL M.S.A.											
	Includes Greene, Hale, and Tuscaloosa Counties	199,823									
	City of Tuscaloosa	83,811	557	10	32	264	251	5,047	1,199	3,569	279
	Total area actually reporting	99.7%	1,125	21	73	412	619	9,824	2,488	6,648	688
	Estimated total	100.0%	1,127	21	73	413	620	9,849	2,493	6,666	690
	Rate per 100,000 inhabitants		564.0	10.5	36.5	206.7	310.3	4,928.9	1,247.6	3,336.0	345.3
Tyler, TX M.S.A.											
	Includes Smith County	197,461									
	City of Tyler	95,596	665	2	59	125	479	4,430	806	3,473	151
	Total area actually reporting	99.0%	1,029	8	106	158	757	7,037	1,578	5,088	371
	Estimated total	100.0%	1,036	8	107	160	761	7,110	1,593	5,141	376
	Rate per 100,000 inhabitants		524.7	4.1	54.2	81.0	385.4	3,600.7	806.7	2,603.6	190.4
Utica-Rome, NY M.S.A.											
	Includes Herkimer and Oneida Counties	296,125									
	City of Utica	58,888	431	5	21	142	263	2,880	752	1,966	162
	City of Rome	34,123	40	1	7	8	24	531	119	383	29
	Total area actually reporting	99.3%	876	11	47	180	638	7,230	1,740	5,205	285
	Estimated total	100.0%	879	11	47	181	640	7,268	1,746	5,235	287
	Rate per 100,000 inhabitants		296.8	3.7	15.9	61.1	216.1	2,454.4	589.6	1,767.8	96.9
Valdosta, GA M.S.A.											
	Includes Brooks, Echols, Lanier, and Lowndes Counties	126,232									
	City of Valdosta	45,712	276	1	33	111	131	2,841	657	2,013	171
	Total area actually reporting	93.3%	535	2	50	138	345	4,684	1,141	3,269	274
	Estimated total	100.0%	582	2	52	155	373	5,085	1,217	3,557	311
	Rate per 100,000 inhabitants		461.1	1.6	41.2	122.8	295.5	4,028.3	964.1	2,817.8	246.4
Vallejo-Fairfield, CA M.S.A.											
	Includes Solano County	410,623									
	City of Vallejo	116,763	1,089	15	26	361	687	6,063	1,455	3,154	1,454
	City of Fairfield	106,098	632	7	36	221	368	4,352	696	2,988	668
	Total area actually reporting	100.0%	2,482	31	121	777	1,553	15,268	3,190	9,307	2,771
	Rate per 100,000 inhabitants		604.4	7.5	29.5	189.2	378.2	3,718.3	776.9	2,266.6	674.8
Victoria, TX M.S.A.											
	Includes Calhoun, Goliad, and Victoria Counties	114,391									
	City of Victoria	62,404	346	1	37	72	236	3,030	670	2,236	124
	Total area actually reporting	99.4%	446	4	45	81	316	4,148	985	2,965	198
	Estimated total	100.0%	448	4	45	82	317	4,174	990	2,984	200
	Rate per 100,000 inhabitants		391.6	3.5	39.3	71.7	277.1	3,648.9	865.5	2,608.6	174.8
Vineland-Millville-Bridgeton, NJ M.S.A.											
	Includes Cumberland County	154,137									
	City of Vineland	58,013	334	5	13	147	169	2,576	589	1,896	91
	City of Millville	28,069	255	4	15	102	134	1,448	343	1,057	48
	City of Bridgeton	24,281	379	1	7	171	200	1,243	376	795	72
	Total area actually reporting	100.0%	1,062	11	36	434	581	6,136	1,566	4,272	298
	Rate per 100,000 inhabitants		689.0	7.1	23.4	281.6	376.9	3,980.9	1,016.0	2,771.6	193.3
Virginia Beach-Norfolk-Newport News, VA-NC M.S.A.											
	Includes Currituck County, NC and Gloucester, Isle of Wight, James City, Mathews, Surry, and York Counties and Chesapeake, Hampton, Newport News, Norfolk, Poquoson, Portsmouth, Suffolk, Virginia Beach, and Williamsburg Cities, VA	1,656,896									
	City of Virginia Beach, VA	435,943	1,089	16	88	555	430	13,030	2,159	10,285	586
	City of Norfolk, VA	227,903	1,924	48	97	910	869	11,518	1,694	8,797	1,027
	City of Newport News, VA	177,550	1,229	28	91	513	597	7,386	1,584	5,132	670
	City of Hampton, VA	144,490	522	6	52	251	213	4,923	764	3,658	501
	City of Portsmouth, VA	101,284	804	17	36	326	425	5,049	1,101	3,646	302
	Total area actually reporting	100.0%	7,289	135	513	3,061	3,580	57,145	9,925	43,232	3,988
	Rate per 100,000 inhabitants		439.9	8.1	31.0	184.7	216.1	3,448.9	599.0	2,609.2	240.7

Table 6. Crime, by Metropolitan Statistical Area, 2007 *(Contd.)*

(Number, percent, rate per 100,000 population.)

Metropolitan statistical area	Counties/principal cities	Population	Violent crime	Murder and non-negligent man-slaughter	Forcible rape	Robbery	Aggravated assault	Property crime	Burglary	Larceny-theft	Motor vehicle theft
Visalia-Porterville, CA M.S.A.											
	Includes Tulare County	424,464									
	City of Visalia	116,766	667	12	38	155	462	5,204	1,109	3,338	757
	City of Porterville	46,621	289	7	14	72	196	2,349	538	1,491	320
	Total area actually reporting	100.0%	2,196	38	128	465	1,565	16,107	3,612	9,808	2,687
	Rate per 100,000 inhabitants		517.4	9.0	30.2	109.5	368.7	3,794.7	851.0	2,310.7	633.0
Waco, TX M.S.A.											
	Includes McLennan County	227,882									
	City of Waco	122,514	1,139	6	95	275	763	8,029	1,987	5,611	431
	Total area actually reporting	100.0%	1,545	9	163	317	1,056	11,584	2,769	8,204	611
	Rate per 100,000 inhabitants		678.0	3.9	71.5	139.1	463.4	5,083.3	1,215.1	3,600.1	268.1
Warner Robins, GA M.S.A.											
	Includes Houston County	130,014									
	City of Warner Robins	59,780	324	3	16	118	187	3,289	922	2,222	145
	Total area actually reporting	100.0%	513	3	28	139	343	4,880	1,255	3,348	277
	Rate per 100,000 inhabitants		394.6	2.3	21.5	106.9	263.8	3,753.4	965.3	2,575.1	213.1
Washington-Arlington-Alexandria, DC-VA-MD-WV M.S.A.											
	Includes the Metropolitan Divisions of Bethesda-Frederick-Gaithersburg, MD and Washington-Arlington-Alexandria, DC-VA-MD-WV	5,348,654									
	City of Washington, DC	588,292	7,924	181	192	3,985	3,566	27,719	3,920	16,476	7,323
	City of Alexandria, VA....................	137,812	370	7	18	162	183	3,280	364	2,557	359
	City of Frederick, MD	59,731	418	5	20	104	289	1,806	275	1,417	114
	Total area actually reporting	100.0%	23,746	412	1,024	11,010	11,300	153,737	21,277	106,084	26,376
	Rate per 100,000 inhabitants		444.0	7.7	19.1	205.8	211.3	2,874.3	397.8	1,983.4	493.1
Bethesda-Frederick-Gaithersburg, MD M.D.											
	Includes Frederick and Montgomery Counties	1,158,220									
	Total area actually reporting	100.0%	3,014	27	168	1,323	1,496	28,371	4,345	21,145	2,881
	Rate per 100,000 inhabitants		260.2	2.3	14.5	114.2	129.2	2,449.5	375.1	1,825.6	248.7
Washington-Arlington-Alexandria, DC-VA-MD-WV M.D.											
	Includes District of Columbia; Calvert, Charles, and Prince George's Counties, MD; Arlington, Clarke, Fairfax, Fauquier, Loudoun, Prince William, Spotsylvania, Stafford, and Warren Counties and Alexandria, Fairfax, Falls Church, Fredericksburg, Manassas, and Manassas Park Cities, VA; and Jefferson County, WV	4,190,434									
	Total area actually reporting	100.0%	20,732	385	856	9,687	9,804	125,366	16,932	84,939	23,495
	Rate per 100,000 inhabitants		494.7	9.2	20.4	231.2	234.0	2,991.7	404.1	2,027.0	560.7
Waterloo-Cedar Falls, IA M.S.A.											
	Includes Black Hawk, Bremer, and Grundy Counties......................	161,918									
	City of Waterloo	65,607	433	4	53	74	302	3,188	952	2,072	164
	City of Cedar Falls..........................	36,995	102	1	16	9	76	821	116	666	39
	Total area actually reporting	100.0%	688	5	87	86	510	4,807	1,286	3,278	243
	Rate per 100,000 inhabitants		424.9	3.1	53.7	53.1	315.0	2,968.8	794.2	2,024.5	150.1
Wausau, WI M.S.A.											
	Includes Marathon County..............	131,265									
	City of Wausau	38,405	111	1	16	31	63	1,113	249	799	65
	Total area actually reporting	100.0%	251	3	18	35	195	2,332	494	1,737	101
	Rate per 100,000 inhabitants		191.2	2.3	13.7	26.7	148.6	1,776.6	376.3	1,323.3	76.9

Table 6. Crime, by Metropolitan Statistical Area, 2007 *(Contd.)*

(Number, percent, rate per 100,000 population.)

Metropolitan statistical area	Counties/principal cities	Population	Violent crime	Murder and non-negligent man-slaughter	Forcible rape	Robbery	Aggravated assault	Property crime	Burglary	Larceny-theft	Motor vehicle theft
Weirton-Steubenville, WV-OH M.S.A.											
	Includes Jefferson County, OH and Brooke and Hancock Counties, WV	123,812									
	City of Weirton, WV	19,095	23	0	0	4	19	215	43	161	11
	City of Steubenville, OH	19,107	79	1	5	40	33	929	167	718	44
	Total area actually reporting	96.7%	213	4	14	45	150	1,965	381	1,467	117
	Estimated total	100.0%	220	4	14	47	155	2,089	403	1,562	124
	Rate per 100,000 inhabitants		177.7	3.2	11.3	38.0	125.2	1,687.2	325.5	1,261.6	100.2
Wenatchee, WA M.S.A.											
	Includes Chelan and Douglas Counties	107,897									
	City of Wenatchee	30,179	92	0	17	20	55	1,549	219	1,243	87
	Total area actually reporting	100.0%	209	3	41	34	131	3,683	603	2,897	183
	Rate per 100,000 inhabitants		193.7	2.8	38.0	31.5	121.4	3,413.4	558.9	2,685.0	169.6
Wheeling, WV-OH M.S.A.											
	Includes Belmont County, OH and Marshall and Ohio Counties, WV	145,995									
	City of Wheeling, WV	29,057	134	1	15	35	83	981	216	693	72
	Total area actually reporting	87.6%	219	2	31	42	144	2,129	507	1,471	151
	Estimated total	100.0%	252	2	36	55	159	2,655	603	1,871	181
	Rate per 100,000 inhabitants		172.6	1.4	24.7	37.7	108.9	1,818.6	413.0	1,281.6	124.0
Wichita, KS M.S.A.											
	Includes Butler, Harvey, Sedgwick, and Sumner Counties	594,974									
	City of Wichita	358,294	3,386	41	269	557	2,519	20,756	4,357	14,263	2,136
	Total area actually reporting	99.5%	4,025	43	346	594	3,042	27,571	5,694	19,366	2,511
	Estimated total	100.0%	4,035	43	347	595	3,050	27,662	5,708	19,437	2,517
	Rate per 100,000 inhabitants		678.2	7.2	58.3	100.0	512.6	4,649.3	959.4	3,266.9	423.0
Wichita Falls, TX M.S.A.											
	Includes Archer, Clay, and Wichita Counties	144,648									
	City of Wichita Falls	98,717	576	4	31	228	313	6,835	1,540	4,797	498
	Total area actually reporting	100.0%	641	6	38	231	366	7,646	1,847	5,244	555
	Rate per 100,000 inhabitants		443.1	4.1	26.3	159.7	253.0	5,285.9	1,276.9	3,625.4	383.7
Williamsport, PA M.S.A.											
	Includes Lycoming County	117,037									
	City of Williamsport	29,701	98	1	10	58	29	1,316	262	970	84
	Total area actually reporting	100.0%	166	3	25	64	74	2,634	597	1,896	141
	Rate per 100,000 inhabitants		141.8	2.6	21.4	54.7	63.2	2,250.6	510.1	1,620.0	120.5
Wilmington, NC M.S.A.[3]											
	Includes Brunswick, New Hanover, and Pender[3] Counties	337,011									
	City of Wilmington	96,913	821	10	58	345	408	5,893	1,637	3,613	643
	Total area actually reporting	98.3%	1,403	19	151	457	776		4,290	8,915	
	Estimated total	100.0%	1,428	19	153	464	792		4,361	9,122	
	Rate per 100,000 inhabitants		423.7	5.6	45.4	137.7	235.0		1,294.0	2,706.7	
Winchester, VA-WV M.S.A.											
	Includes Frederick County and Winchester City, VA and Hampshire County, WV	120,991									
	City of Winchester, VA	25,443	106	1	10	35	60	1,235	169	993	73
	Total area actually reporting	100.0%	251	1	53	48	149	3,139	578	2,314	247
	Rate per 100,000 inhabitants		207.5	0.8	43.8	39.7	123.1	2,594.4	477.7	1,912.5	204.1
Worcester, MA M.S.A.											
	Includes Worcester County	790,004									
	City of Worcester	175,825	1,531	6	93	371	1,061	6,025	1,308	3,815	902
	Total area actually reporting	98.1%	2,953	18	214	534	2,187	15,148	3,735	9,850	1,563
	Estimated total	100.0%	2,995	18	217	542	2,218	15,445	3,809	10,049	1,587
	Rate per 100,000 inhabitants		379.1	2.3	27.5	68.6	280.8	1,955.1	482.1	1,272.0	200.9

[3] The FBI determined that the agency's data were underreported. Consequently, affected data are not included in this table.

Table 6. Crime, by Metropolitan Statistical Area, 2007 *(Contd.)*

(Number, percent, rate per 100,000 population.)

Metropolitan statistical area	Counties/principal cities	Population	Violent crime	Murder and non-negligent man-slaughter	Forcible rape	Robbery	Aggravated assault	Property crime	Burglary	Larceny-theft	Motor vehicle theft
Yakima, WA M.S.A.											
	Includes Yakima County..................	234,592									
	City of Yakima	82,951	561	7	66	136	352	5,705	1,209	3,652	844
	Total area actually reporting	100.0%	899	15	135	214	535	12,676	3,095	7,696	1,885
	Rate per 100,000 inhabitants..........		383.2	6.4	57.5	91.2	228.1	5,403.4	1,319.3	3,280.6	803.5
York-Hanover, PA M.S.A.											
	Includes York County	420,251									
	City of York	40,339	440	11	33	293	103	2,125	499	1,338	288
	City of Hanover	15,079	30	0	3	10	17	614	85	511	18
	Total area actually reporting	99.5%	1,193	16	101	455	621	9,729	1,623	7,412	694
	Estimated total................................	100.0%	1,197	16	101	456	624	9,775	1,630	7,448	697
	Rate per 100,000 inhabitants..........		284.8	3.8	24.0	108.5	148.5	2,326.0	387.9	1,772.3	165.9
Yuba City, CA M.S.A.											
	Includes Sutter and Yuba Counties...	164,006									
	City of Yuba City	61,881	245	2	24	54	165	1,913	322	1,361	230
	Total area actually reporting	100.0%	765	2	57	129	577	4,926	1,383	2,901	642
	Rate per 100,000 inhabitants...........		466.4	1.2	34.8	78.7	351.8	3,003.5	843.3	1,768.8	391.4
Yuma, AZ M.S.A.											
	Includes Yuma County.....................	192,098									
	City of Yuma	88,874	601	6	32	75	488	3,913	888	2,393	632
	Total area actually reporting	87.6%	748	12	46	100	590	5,560	1,239	3,451	870
	Estimated total................................	100.0%	830	13	52	122	643	6,508	1,454	4,057	997
	Rate per 100,000 inhabitants..........		432.1	6.8	27.1	63.5	334.7	3,387.9	756.9	2,111.9	519.0
Aguadilla-Isabela-San Sebastian, Puerto Rico M.S.A.											
	Includes Aguada, Aguadilla, Anasco, Isabela, Lares, Moca, Rincon, and San Sebastian Municipios	336,526									
	Total area actually reporting	100.0%	179	13	3	71	92	1,991	882	997	112
	Rate per 100,000 inhabitants..........		53.2	3.9	0.9	21.1	27.3	591.6	262.1	296.3	33.3
Fajardo, Puerto Rico M.S.A.											
	Includes Ceiba, Fajardo, and Luquillo Municipios	80,545									
	Total area actually reporting	100.0%	171	17	0	73	81	1,021	421	532	68
	Rate per 100,000 inhabitants...........		212.3	21.1	0.0	90.6	100.6	1,267.6	522.7	660.5	84.4
Guayama, Puerto Rico M.S.A.											
	Includes Arroyo, Guayama, and Patillas Municipios...................	84,260									
	Total area actually reporting	100.0%	121	13	2	47	59	375	250	93	32
	Rate per 100,000 inhabitants...........		143.6	15.4	2.4	55.8	70.0	445.1	296.7	110.4	38.0
Mayaguez, Puerto Rico M.S.A.											
	Includes Hormigueros and Mayaguez Municipios	111,219									
	Total area actually reporting	100.0%	209	14	3	99	93	2,407	677	1,620	110
	Rate per 100,000 inhabitants...........		187.9	12.6	2.7	89.0	83.6	2,164.2	608.7	1,456.6	98.9
Ponce, Puerto Rico M.S.A.											
	Includes Juana Diaz, Ponce, and Villalba Municipios	263,352									
	Total area actually reporting	100.0%	706	72	24	306	304	3,395	899	2,239	257
	Rate per 100,000 inhabitants...........		268.1	27.3	9.1	116.2	115.4	1,289.1	341.4	850.2	97.6
San German-Cabo Rojo, Puerto Rico M.S.A.											
	Includes Cabo Rojo, Lajas, Sabana Grande, and San German Municipios........................	145,904									
	Total area actually reporting	100.0%	87	7	3	33	44	898	438	414	46
	Rate per 100,000 inhabitants...........		59.6	4.8	2.1	22.6	30.2	615.5	300.2	283.7	31.5

Table 6.   Crime, by Metropolitan Statistical Area, 2007 *(Contd.)*

(Number, percent, rate per 100,000 population.)

Metropolitan statistical area	Counties/principal cities	Population	Violent crime	Murder and non-negligent man-slaughter	Forcible rape	Robbery	Aggravated assault	Property crime	Burglary	Larceny-theft	Motor vehicle theft
San Juan-Caguas-Guaynabo, Puerto Rico M.S.A.											
	Includes Aguas Buenas, Aibonito, Arecibo, Barceloneta, Barranquitas, Bayamon, Caguas, Camuy, Canovanas, Carolina, Catano, Cayey, Ciales, Cidra, Comerio, Corozal, Dorado, Florida, Guaynabo, Gurabo, Hatillo, Humacao, Juncos, Las Piedras, Loiza, Manati, Maunabo, Morovis, Naguabo, Naranjito, Orocovis, Quebradillas, Rio Grande, San Juan, San Lorenzo, Toa Alta, Toa Baja, Trujillo Alto, Vega Alta, Vega Baja, and Yabucoa Municipios	2,599,997									
	Total area actually reporting	100.0%	6,929	553	53	4,294	2,029	39,737	11,822	20,974	6,941
	Rate per 100,000 inhabitants		266.5	21.3	2.0	165.2	78.0	1,528.3	454.7	806.7	267.0
Yauco, Puerto Rico M.S.A.											
	Includes Guanica, Guayanilla, Penuelas, and Yauco Municipios	124,051									
	Total area actually reporting	100.0%	195	20	6	78	91	1,040	355	616	69
	Rate per 100,000 inhabitants		157.2	16.1	4.8	62.9	73.4	838.4	286.2	496.6	55.6

Table 7. Offense Analysis, 2003–2007

(Number.)

Classification		2003	2004	2005	2006[1]	2007
Murder		16,528	16,148	16,740	17,030	16,929
Forcible rape		93,883	95,089	94,347	92,757	90,427
Robbery:	Total[2]	414,235	401,470	417,438	447,403	445,125
Robbery by location:	Street/highway	179,657	171,812	184,188	199,241	194,772
	Commercial house	60,615	59,006	59,694	61,014	62,026
	Gas or service station	11,385	10,893	11,889	12,075	11,766
	Convenience store	25,826	24,653	23,822	24,921	24,933
	Residence	56,755	55,525	59,207	64,024	67,508
	Bank	9,523	9,775	8,766	9,591	9,252
	Miscellaneous	70,474	69,806	69,871	76,537	74,868
Burglary:	Total[2]	2,154,834	2,144,446	2,155,448	2,183,746	2,179,140
Burglary by location:	Residence (dwelling):	1,418,423	1,409,253	1,417,440	1,445,557	1,478,901
	Residence Night	409,188	405,556	402,881	411,558	421,855
	Residence Day	668,759	666,345	669,579	705,175	738,654
	Residence Unknown	340,477	337,351	344,980	328,824	318,392
	Nonresidence (store, office, etc.):	736,411	735,193	738,008	738,189	700,239
	Nonresidence Night	310,187	307,702	305,729	307,076	293,469
	Nonresidence Day	221,240	223,012	221,183	234,458	227,092
	Nonresidence Unknown	204,984	204,479	211,096	196,655	179,679
Larceny-theft (except motor vehicle theft):	Total[2]	7,026,802	6,937,089	6,783,447	6,607,013	6,568,572
Larceny-theft by type:	Pocket-picking	31,966	29,840	29,221	28,770	27,408
	Purse-snatching	42,181	42,345	42,040	39,997	38,058
	Shoplifting	1,013,265	1,009,214	940,411	872,635	978,978
	From motor vehicles (except accessories)	1,857,619	1,758,241	1,752,280	1,752,432	1,706,979
	Motor vehicle accessories	781,279	749,173	693,225	638,678	599,063
	Bicycles	271,801	249,813	248,792	231,238	224,345
	From buildings	868,621	861,197	852,462	829,756	789,123
	From coin-operated machines	52,373	45,927	40,885	35,264	31,036
	All others	2,107,696	2,191,338	2,184,131	2,178,243	2,173,581
Larceny-theft by value:	Over $200	2,761,752	2,711,560	2,715,997	2,805,338	2,884,126
	$50 to $200	1,586,672	1,562,672	1,522,810	1,474,693	1,471,078
	Under $50	2,678,377	2,662,857	2,544,640	2,326,982	2,213,368
Motor vehicle theft		1,261,226	1,237,851	1,235,859	1,192,809	1,095,769

[1] The 2006 crime figures have been adjusted.

[2] Because of rounding, the number of offenses may not add to the total.

Table 8. Offenses Known to Law Enforcement, by State and City, 2007

(Number.)

State	City	Population	Violent crime	Murder and non-negligent man-slaughter	Forcible rape	Robbery	Aggravated assault	Property crime	Burglary	Larceny-theft	Motor vehicle theft	Arson[1]
ALABAMA	Abbeville	2,955	8	0	1	1	6	105	16	83	6	
	Adamsville	4,771	53	0	1	20	32	416	45	351	20	
	Addison	720	4	0	0	0	4	23	1	21	1	
	Alabaster	28,904	33	1	0	18	14	659	68	545	46	
	Alexander City	15,053	131	2	14	24	91	1,016	182	784	50	
	Aliceville	2,457	3	0	1	1	1	43	11	25	7	
	Andalusia	8,727	40	0	3	7	30	381	63	300	18	
	Anniston	23,736	541	9	20	188	324	2,912	942	1,723	247	
	Arab	7,694	34	0	1	1	32	579	105	445	29	
	Ardmore	1,145	0	0	0	0	0	41	9	27	5	
	Ariton	747	0	0	0	0	0	1	0	1	0	
	Ashford	1,967	2	0	0	0	2	34	10	21	3	
	Ashland	1,856	3	0	0	0	3	26	2	21	3	
	Ashville	2,503	4	0	0	2	2	54	9	40	5	
	Atmore	7,452	83	0	5	19	59	568	131	420	17	
	Auburn	53,160	176	2	25	44	105	2,559	630	1,838	91	
	Autaugaville	885	2	0	0	0	2	27	12	13	2	
	Bay Minette	7,674	54	1	3	9	41	376	73	281	22	
	Bayou La Batre	2,761	25	0	1	4	20	325	70	229	26	
	Bear Creek	1,016	6	0	0	0	6	24	2	19	3	
	Berry	1,212	0	0	0	0	0	4	0	3	1	
	Bessemer	28,217	502	10	34	195	263	3,534	903	2,373	258	
	Birmingham	227,686	3,320	86	229	1,609	1,396	19,638	4,864	12,528	2,246	221
	Blountsville	1,969	3	0	1	0	2	49	18	29	2	
	Boaz	8,175	22	0	3	5	14	554	83	450	21	
	Brantley	906	1	0	0	0	1	47	10	37	0	
	Brent	4,328	3	0	0	2	1	71	17	52	2	
	Brewton	5,304	103	0	2	12	89	254	43	205	6	
	Bridgeport	2,698	2	0	0	1	1	121	27	77	17	
	Brighton	3,358	0	0	0	0	0	1	0	1	0	
	Brilliant	732	3	0	0	0	3	40	14	25	1	
	Brundidge	2,305	21	0	1	4	16	97	13	80	4	
	Butler	1,747	1	0	0	0	1	17	10	7	0	
	Carbon Hill	2,048	7	0	1	1	5	153	28	107	18	
	Carrollton	953	1	0	0	1	0	20	5	15	0	
	Cedar Bluff	1,580	6	0	0	0	6	104	39	59	6	
	Centre	3,411	3	0	1	1	1	166	19	139	8	
	Centreville	2,511	11	0	0	0	11	40	8	28	4	
	Chatom	1,172	5	0	0	0	5	18	1	17	0	
	Cherokee	1,177	1	0	0	0	1	12	6	6	0	
	Chickasaw	6,000	29	0	2	10	17	348	83	242	23	
	Childersburg	4,978	41	0	0	11	30	465	71	383	11	
	Citronelle	3,716	31	2	4	2	23	212	49	142	21	
	Clanton	8,602	57	1	3	11	42	359	68	282	9	
	Clayton	1,383	12	0	0	0	12	39	8	31	0	
	Clio	2,209	0	0	0	0	0	3	0	1	2	0
	Coffeeville	354	2	0	0	0	2	1	0	1	0	0
	Collinsville	1,693	1	0	0	0	1	41	4	33	4	
	Columbiana	3,809	19	0	1	1	17	129	22	106	1	
	Coosada	1,590	2	0	0	0	2	23	2	21	0	
	Cottonwood	1,172	2	0	0	0	2	17	4	10	3	
	Courtland	760	0	0	0	0	0	10	3	3	4	0
	Creola	2,084	6	0	0	1	5	75	9	62	4	
	Crossville	1,463	0	0	0	0	0	2	1	0	1	
	Cullman	14,914	23	0	3	6	14	899	143	704	52	
	Dadeville	3,239	60	0	2	9	49	247	56	179	12	
	Daleville	4,503	12	0	3	4	5	74	32	39	3	
	Daphne	19,352	25	0	3	8	14	583	139	419	25	
	Dauphin Island	1,568	0	0	0	0	0	9	5	3	1	
	Decatur	56,019	251	0	28	105	118	3,624	830	2,584	210	
	Demopolis	7,523	93	0	11	17	65	492	84	395	13	
	Dora	2,441	6	0	2	1	3	103	17	74	12	
	Dothan	64,931	418	8	46	190	174	3,345	790	2,369	186	
	Double Springs	989	4	1	0	0	3	13	2	10	1	
	Douglas	581	9	0	0	1	8	88	34	44	10	
	Dozier	392	0	0	0	0	0	0	0	0	0	
	East Brewton	2,512	3	0	0	1	2	55	7	43	5	
	Eclectic	1,148	1	0	0	0	1	17	2	10	5	
	Elba	4,136	19	0	1	5	13	131	46	82	3	
	Elberta	591	7	0	0	2	5	78	16	54	8	
	Enterprise	24,035	98	1	11	41	45	433	213	184	36	
	Eutaw	3,001	27	0	1	9	17	156	46	109	1	
	Evergreen	3,446	14	0	0	3	11	125	19	104	2	
	Excel	605	1	0	0	0	1	17	2	14	1	

[1] The FBI does not publish arson data unless it receives data from either the agency or the state for all 12 months of the calendar year.

Table 8.   Offenses Known to Law Enforcement, by State and City, 2007 *(Contd.)*

(Number.)

State	City	Population	Violent crime	Murder and non-negligent man-slaughter	Forcible rape	Robbery	Aggravated assault	Property crime	Burglary	Larceny-theft	Motor vehicle theft	Arson[1]
	Fairfield	11,443	209	4	12	84	109	1,212	238	877	97	
	Fairhope	16,735	12	0	2	6	4	344	76	257	11	
	Falkville	1,185	2	0	1	0	1	15	5	9	1	
	Fayette	4,694	11	0	2	4	5	211	36	159	16	
	Flomaton	1,541	4	1	0	0	3	32	4	23	5	
	Florala	1,904	19	0	1	2	16	77	11	63	3	
	Florence	36,784	117	0	8	47	62	1,775	403	1,315	57	3
	Foley	13,463	113	3	6	35	69	1,051	173	803	75	
	Fort Payne	13,889	44	1	3	3	37	691	96	557	38	
	Fyffe	1,045	0	0	0	0	0	3	1	2	0	
	Gadsden	37,066	174	2	15	102	55	2,515	541	1,793	181	10
	Gardendale	13,235	20	1	0	9	10	458	60	380	18	
	Geneva	4,415	17	0	1	4	12	134	31	93	10	
	Georgiana	1,593	13	0	1	2	10	59	13	43	3	
	Geraldine	837	2	0	0	0	2	31	3	24	4	
	Glencoe	5,311	9	0	1	2	6	106	30	71	5	
	Goodwater	1,542	3	0	0	0	3	22	5	15	2	
	Gordo	1,589	4	0	1	1	2	45	11	26	8	
	Grant	692	0	0	0	0	0	9	3	5	1	
	Graysville	2,399	0	0	0	0	0	14	7	4	3	
	Greensboro	2,579	38	1	1	7	29	160	46	104	10	1
	Greenville	7,067	41	1	1	7	32	491	94	380	17	0
	Guin	2,223	3	0	0	1	2	27	9	17	1	
	Gulf Shores	9,486	86	1	8	57	20	450	101	341	8	
	Gurley	850	2	0	1	0	1	29	5	22	2	
	Hackleburg	1,472	1	0	0	0	1	18	5	10	3	
	Haleyville	4,178	46	0	2	2	42	268	57	201	10	
	Hamilton	6,478	15	0	5	2	8	194	47	138	9	1
	Hammondville	545	0	0	0	0	0	5	2	3	0	
	Hanceville	3,261	10	0	1	0	9	165	41	114	10	
	Hartford	2,401	9	0	0	2	7	147	31	110	6	
	Hartselle	13,650	12	0	4	1	7	460	72	376	12	
	Hayneville	1,112	10	0	0	1	9	56	34	19	3	
	Headland	3,864	25	0	1	8	16	132	35	94	3	
	Helena	14,429	15	0	1	0	14	110	24	84	2	
	Henagar	2,560	7	0	1	4	2	45	9	29	7	
	Hobson City	867	0	0	0	0	0	10	6	2	2	
	Hokes Bluff	4,363	11	0	0	2	9	72	19	51	2	
	Hollywood	931	0	0	0	0	0	13	1	11	1	
	Hoover	69,527	121	0	18	71	32	2,443	372	1,910	161	1
	Hueytown	15,816	40	1	3	14	22	430	98	297	35	
	Huntsville	169,391	1,379	21	96	586	676	10,731	2,283	7,282	1,166	49
	Ider	715	0	0	0	0	0	4	1	2	1	
	Irondale	9,471	51	3	1	24	23	564	146	360	58	
	Jasper	14,117	76	1	7	33	35	1,244	182	980	82	
	Killen	1,123	6	0	0	0	6	78	11	67	0	
	Kimberly	2,592	0	0	0	0	0	25	2	18	5	
	Lafayette	3,054	43	0	1	1	41	160	37	117	6	
	Lake View	1,982	2	0	1	1	0	80	25	50	5	
	Leeds	11,169	67	1	2	35	29	569	119	419	31	
	Leesburg	839	3	0	0	0	3	50	7	40	3	
	Leighton	834	8	0	0	1	7	32	7	23	2	
	Level Plains	1,516	13	0	0	0	13	68	17	45	6	0
	Lexington	832	0	0	0	0	0	10	4	6	0	
	Linden	2,326	4	0	0	2	2	34	7	24	3	
	Lineville	2,370	46	0	1	1	44	44	7	33	4	0
	Lipscomb	2,265	0	0	0	0	0	1	0	1	0	
	Littleville	947	1	0	0	0	1	38	4	32	2	
	Livingston	2,961	10	1	2	3	4	126	35	85	6	
	Louisville	569	1	0	0	0	1	9	3	6	0	
	Loxley	1,587	10	1	2	2	5	78	21	52	5	
	Maplesville	686	5	0	0	1	4	33	7	24	2	
	Marion	3,373	35	0	1	1	33	202	40	151	11	
	McIntosh	237	5	0	0	0	5	31	7	24	0	
	McKenzie	612	0	0	0	0	0	9	2	7	0	
	Midfield	5,196	41	0	1	20	20	469	144	296	29	
	Midland City	1,839	15	0	1	5	9	67	20	44	3	0
	Millry	601	1	0	0	0	1	4	0	4	0	
	Mobile[2]	253,842	1,144	38	23	750	333	14,136	3,650	9,361	1,125	134
	Monroeville	6,538	78	1	0	15	62	466	103	329	34	10
	Montgomery	202,062	1,157	46	54	652	405	12,843	3,317	8,579	947	53
	Moody	12,402	5	0	0	5	0	332	56	237	39	0
	Morris	1,910	0	0	0	0	0	33	10	21	2	
	Moundville	2,399	10	0	0	1	9	75	7	60	8	

[1] The FBI does not publish arson data unless it receives data from either the agency or the state for all 12 months of the calendar year.

[2] The population for the city of Mobile, Alabama, includes 61,856 inhabitants from the jurisdiction of the Mobile County Sheriff's Department.

Table 8.   Offenses Known to Law Enforcement, by State and City, 2007 *(Contd.)*

(Number.)

State	City	Population	Violent crime	Murder and non-negligent man-slaughter	Forcible rape	Robbery	Aggravated assault	Property crime	Burglary	Larceny-theft	Motor vehicle theft	Arson[1]
	Mountain Brook	20,952	6	0	0	5	1	395	65	325	5	
	Mount Vernon	821	6	0	0	0	6	15	5	8	2	
	Napier Field	397	0	0	0	0	0	4	1	3	0	
	New Brockton	1,216	0	0	0	0	0	41	8	29	4	
	New Hope	2,709	9	0	0	1	8	61	20	39	2	
	Newton	1,663	5	0	0	2	3	34	7	22	5	
	North Courtland	794	0	0	0	0	0	1	0	1	0	
	Northport	22,201	128	2	5	54	67	1,135	248	798	89	
	Notasulga	833	0	0	0	0	0	25	9	14	2	
	Oakman	945	4	0	1	1	2	21	5	13	3	
	Ohatchee	1,230	0	0	0	0	0	68	32	29	7	
	Oneonta	6,860	21	1	2	1	17	268	21	235	12	
	Opelika	24,600	308	5	36	62	205	1,551	284	1,224	43	
	Opp	6,701	22	1	1	2	18	226	26	198	2	0
	Orange Beach	5,810	8	0	1	4	3	384	66	307	11	
	Oxford	20,396	112	1	11	48	52	1,232	230	936	66	
	Ozark	14,656	118	3	9	19	87	716	147	503	66	
	Parrish	1,260	7	0	1	1	5	48	6	40	2	
	Pelham	21,060	35	0	3	22	10	550	41	475	34	
	Pell City	12,256	78	2	10	13	53	551	106	421	24	
	Pennington	327	0	0	0	0	0	4	3	1	0	
	Phenix City	30,309	113	3	6	52	52	1,286	385	703	198	
	Phil Campbell	1,046	2	0	0	0	2	24	2	21	1	
	Pickensville	646	0	0	0	0	0	10	3	5	2	
	Piedmont	4,998	3	0	1	1	1	263	42	221	0	
	Pine Hill	914	4	1	0	0	3	7	2	4	1	
	Pisgah	702	0	0	0	0	0	2	0	2	0	
	Powell	976	0	0	0	0	0	13	2	11	0	
	Prattville	31,949	90	1	9	33	47	1,301	255	984	62	
	Priceville	2,503	5	0	0	0	5	63	7	50	6	
	Prichard	28,087	255	14	9	98	134	1,353	391	738	224	
	Ragland	2,082	6	1	2	0	3	39	9	27	3	
	Rainbow City	9,079	1	0	0	1	0	239	40	194	5	
	Rainsville	4,923	12	0	0	0	12	142	20	117	5	
	Ranburne	482	1	0	0	0	1	17	1	12	4	
	Red Bay	3,283	5	0	0	0	5	70	12	55	3	
	Red Level	555	0	0	0	0	0	3	3	0	0	
	Reform	1,834	17	0	0	6	11	71	28	43	0	
	Robertsdale	4,976	29	4	3	4	18	152	28	120	4	
	Rockford	396	0	0	0	0	0	0	0	0	0	
	Rogersville	1,190	4	0	0	1	3	60	19	36	5	
	Russellville	8,842	18	0	7	1	10	75	20	47	8	
	Samson	2,027	6	0	1	3	2	17	4	11	2	
	Sardis City	2,101	3	0	0	0	3	65	19	43	3	
	Satsuma	6,032	9	0	0	1	8	112	19	74	19	
	Scottsboro	14,971	28	0	4	6	18	629	15	590	24	
	Selma	19,101	314	4	27	90	193	2,371	694	1,492	185	
	Sheffield	9,176	36	1	8	9	18	533	136	386	11	
	Shorter	338	10	0	0	5	5	16	5	11	0	
	Silas	487	4	0	0	1	3	4	1	2	1	
	Silverhill	704	1	0	0	1	0	33	5	28	0	
	Skyline	842	1	0	0	0	1	4	1	3	0	
	Slocomb	2,040	9	0	0	1	8	24	5	18	1	
	Somerville	471	1	0	1	0	0	32	6	24	2	
	Southside	8,279	10	1	0	1	8	122	26	93	3	
	Spanish Fort	5,619	11	0	1	3	7	162	25	137	0	
	Stevenson	2,140	36	0	1	2	33	115	25	79	11	
	St. Florian	472	2	0	0	1	1	18	9	7	2	
	Sulligent	1,963	1	0	0	0	1	58	3	52	3	
	Sumiton	2,578	4	0	0	4	0	334	40	269	25	
	Summerdale	701	12	0	4	1	7	94	24	68	2	
	Sylacauga	12,946	54	2	3	22	27	844	170	655	19	
	Sylvania	1,267	4	0	0	0	4	24	6	17	1	
	Thomaston	375	0	0	0	0	0	1	0	1	0	
	Thomasville	4,558	31	3	3	3	22	261	76	178	7	
	Thorsby	2,030	0	0	0	0	0	9	2	6	1	
	Town Creek	1,202	0	0	0	0	0	35	4	30	1	
	Triana	482	1	0	0	0	1	5	2	3	0	
	Trinity	1,907	2	0	0	0	2	15	1	7	7	
	Trussville	18,401	53	0	1	37	15	955	63	862	30	
	Tuscaloosa	83,811	557	10	32	264	251	5,047	1,199	3,569	279	
	Tuscumbia	8,235	6	0	1	2	3	233	30	191	12	
	Tuskegee	11,423	130	3	6	28	93	965	368	581	16	
	Uniontown	1,480	34	0	0	0	34	37	9	27	1	

[1] The FBI does not publish arson data unless it receives data from either the agency or the state for all 12 months of the calendar year.

Table 8. Offenses Known to Law Enforcement, by State and City, 2007 *(Contd.)*

(Number.)

State	City	Population	Violent crime	Murder and non-negligent manslaughter	Forcible rape	Robbery	Aggravated assault	Property crime	Burglary	Larceny-theft	Motor vehicle theft	Arson[1]
	Valley Head	653	1	0	0	0	1	1	0	1	0	
	Vernon	1,898	1	0	0	0	1	20	3	16	1	
	Vestavia Hills	31,097	22	0	5	6	11	295	92	182	21	
	Warrior	2,982	0	0	0	0	0	1	1	0	0	
	Weaver	2,620	6	0	0	0	6	73	28	43	2	
	Wetumpka	7,558	20	0	5	6	9	416	73	328	15	
	Winfield	4,711	1	0	0	0	1	139	37	94	8	
	Woodstock	1,018	11	0	0	2	9	45	19	23	3	
	York	2,563	16	0	0	3	13	65	14	48	3	
ALASKA	Anchorage	284,142	2,405	22	257	453	1,673	11,107	1,454	8,397	1,256	145
	Bethel	6,488	61	2	15	0	44	107	25	63	19	2
	Bristol Bay Borough	1,028	8	0	0	0	8	49	11	24	14	1
	Cordova	2,322	9	0	0	0	9	14	1	10	3	0
	Craig	1,186	41	0	0	0	41	18	5	10	3	2
	Dillingham	2,494	76	1	24	3	48	78	18	40	20	0
	Fairbanks	31,287	258	5	43	42	168	1,358	236	957	165	6
	Haines	2,260	16	0	1	0	15	74	24	46	4	0
	Homer	5,629	52	0	2	1	49	220	32	165	23	1
	Houston	1,992	3	0	0	0	3	40	8	24	8	0
	Juneau	30,746	126	1	22	17	86	1,364	174	1,137	53	10
	Kenai	7,620	30	1	2	3	24	318	32	265	21	0
	Ketchikan	7,384	21	0	9	1	11	476	41	407	28	4
	Kodiak	6,242	33	0	5	1	27	209	13	175	21	6
	North Pole	1,869	9	0	1	1	7	116	24	85	7	0
	North Slope Borough	6,569	70	0	15	7	48	149	52	70	27	8
	Palmer	7,931	65	0	4	1	60	282	23	242	17	2
	Petersburg	2,890	1	0	0	0	1	117	6	103	8	0
	Seward	3,054	3	0	1	0	2	146	21	118	7	2
	Sitka	8,932	31	0	9	0	22	290	21	250	19	2
	Skagway	827	1	0	0	0	1	14	1	11	2	0
	Soldotna	4,198	21	0	2	1	18	218	14	189	15	0
	St. Paul	431	6	0	2	0	4	7	6	1	0	0
	Unalaska	4,155	15	0	4	1	10	74	7	59	8	0
	Wasilla	9,931	47	0	2	2	43	553	58	442	53	0
	Wrangell	2,028	1	0	0	0	1	77	5	67	5	0
ARIZONA	Apache Junction	30,925	140	4	18	26	92	1,677	316	1,127	234	5
	Benson	4,913	10	0	1	4	5	240	50	157	33	1
	Bisbee	6,077	41	0	1	2	38	307	44	255	8	0
	Buckeye	34,618	51	1	6	9	35	1,582	560	858	164	6
	Bullhead City	41,209	114	4	2	33	75	1,999	491	1,367	141	10
	Camp Verde	10,780	32	1	1	1	29	327	59	242	26	3
	Casa Grande	35,951	307	2	5	79	221	3,024	968	1,710	346	17
	Chandler	250,868	823	9	51	246	517	7,934	1,231	5,871	832	68
	Chino Valley[3]	10,886		0	2	0		228	42	172	14	0
	Clarkdale	3,904	6	0	1	0	5	65	32	28	5	0
	Clifton	2,285	10	0	0	0	10	75	21	44	10	5
	Colorado City	4,816	1	0	0	0	1	5	2	3	0	0
	Coolidge	7,875	92	1	6	13	72	770	237	457	76	13
	Cottonwood	11,455	52	1	0	8	43	531	72	421	38	3
	Douglas	17,077	30	0	4	7	19	619	94	461	64	3
	Eagar	4,324	12	0	0	0	12	90	23	59	8	0
	Eloy	10,795	90	0	17	17	56	654	168	424	62	15
	Flagstaff	58,978	316	3	51	63	199	3,678	471	3,087	120	70
	Florence	16,964	49	0	0	2	47	173	25	133	15	0
	Fredonia	1,066	1	0	1	0	0	17	2	14	1	0
	Gilbert	206,681	236	1	23	56	156	4,951	996	3,530	425	19
	Glendale	250,444	1,508	15	58	542	893	12,452	2,766	6,719	2,967	67
	Globe	7,097	72	0	5	6	61	414	124	275	15	7
	Goodyear	53,834	143	1	31	27	84	2,497	1,179	996	322	
	Hayden	1,267	18	0	1	1	16	62	28	32	2	6
	Holbrook	5,186	96	0	7	5	84	442	161	259	22	2
	Huachuca City	1,886	3	0	1	0	2	34	10	20	4	0
	Kearny	3,000	15	0	0	0	15	71	34	37	0	1
	Kingman	28,306	89	1	8	16	64	2,070	415	1,485	170	5
	Lake Havasu City	58,699	134	5	20	8	101	1,813	307	1,388	118	10
	Mammoth	2,347	4	0	0	0	4	20	7	8	5	0
	Marana	33,374	65	0	10	16	39	1,149	180	841	128	10
	Mesa	454,576	2,224	22	175	620	1,407	19,945	2,922	14,063	2,960	54
	Miami	1,809	23	0	0	1	22	95	32	57	6	14
	Oro Valley	40,364	24	0	6	5	13	759	134	580	45	11
	Paradise Valley	14,594	7	0	0	1	6	352	204	124	24	1
	Parker	3,211	25	0	0	2	23	237	58	160	19	2
	Peoria	147,223	355	6	41	102	206	5,802	1,329	3,697	776	17
	Phoenix	1,541,698	11,159	213	509	4,942	5,495	89,825	19,212	49,754	20,859	487

[1] The FBI does not publish arson data unless it receives data from either the agency or the state for all 12 months of the calendar year.
[3] The FBI determined that the agency's data were overreported. Consequently, affected data are not included in this table.

Table 8. Offenses Known to Law Enforcement, by State and City, 2007 *(Contd.)*

(Number.)

State	City	Population	Violent crime	Murder and non-negligent manslaughter	Forcible rape	Robbery	Aggravated assault	Property crime	Burglary	Larceny-theft	Motor vehicle theft	Arson[1]
	Pima	1,967	2	0	0	0	2	50	17	30	3	0
	Prescott	42,674	130	1	7	19	103	1,387	279	1,059	49	2
	Prescott Valley	38,204	194	0	14	10	170	851	168	635	48	6
	Quartzsite	3,473	7	0	0	0	7	54	9	44	1	0
	Sahuarita[3]	16,011	29	0	4	4	21			325	42	2
	Scottsdale	235,243	438	5	41	143	249	8,138	1,523	5,863	752	31
	Sedona	11,484	9	0	3	1	5	275	84	180	11	3
	Show Low	11,588	108	0	2	5	101	493	155	299	39	1
	Sierra Vista	43,441	134	4	20	19	91	1,644	283	1,230	131	26
	Snowflake-Taylor	9,448	64	0	0	0	64	250	90	139	21	3
	Somerton	11,370	22	0	0	2	20	220	49	132	39	1
	South Tucson	5,579	186	0	3	88	95	939	145	705	89	1
	Springerville	2,002	5	0	1	0	4	73	21	46	6	0
	Surprise	98,965	154	6	15	34	99	2,493	534	1,719	240	20
	Tempe	171,320	916	10	63	330	513	11,424	1,866	7,959	1,599	69
	Thatcher	4,285	3	0	0	0	3	104	19	83	2	1
	Tolleson	7,121	72	1	2	12	57	911	232	567	112	2
	Tucson[4]	523,299	4,103	49	277	1,432	2,345		4,787		6,767	280
	Wellton	1,898	2	0	0	0	2	36	18	16	2	0
	Wickenburg	6,507	21	0	3	2	16	264	85	134	45	0
	Willcox	3,842	6	0	0	1	5	345	85	213	47	2
	Winslow	10,018	56	3	0	5	48	476	76	378	22	2
	Youngtown	5,062	21	0	0	0	21	118	36	57	25	1
	Yuma	88,874	601	6	32	75	488	3,913	888	2,393	632	30
ARKANSAS	Altheimer	1,143	4	0	0	0	4	31	16	12	3	0
	Arkadelphia	10,418	43	0	5	5	33	324	133	178	13	2
	Arkansas City	538	1	0	0	0	1	19	8	10	1	0
	Ashdown	4,497	20	0	0	5	15	158	21	128	9	4
	Atkins	2,929	1	0	0	0	1	80	30	49	1	0
	Augusta	2,355	17	0	4	1	12	98	17	81	0	0
	Bald Knob	3,364	8	0	0	3	5	201	114	81	6	1
	Barling	4,397	12	0	1	0	11	80	26	51	3	0
	Bay	1,992	0	0	0	0	0	26	10	15	1	0
	Bearden	1,019	6	0	1	1	4	42	23	17	2	0
	Beebe	6,062	27	0	2	5	20	416	109	293	14	3
	Benton	27,758	134	0	14	29	91	1,499	348	1,080	71	2
	Bentonville	34,232	79	0	20	4	55	879	128	714	37	4
	Berryville	5,195	19	0	5	1	13	235	72	156	7	0
	Blytheville	16,161	156	5	8	42	101	1,261	372	780	109	19
	Bono	1,557	2	0	0	0	2	42	21	21	0	0
	Booneville	4,137	16	0	1	1	14	200	57	137	6	1
	Brinkley	3,368	10	1	0	4	5	158	29	123	6	0
	Bryant	14,181	40	0	6	4	30	689	100	551	38	0
	Bull Shoals	2,124	0	0	0	0	0	25	9	15	1	0
	Cabot	23,366	100	2	8	3	87	782	255	491	36	2
	Caddo Valley	622	0	0	0	0	0	12	8	4	0	0
	Camden	11,812	82	0	7	18	57	849	227	600	22	5
	Cammack Village	766	0	0	0	0	0	24	20	3	1	0
	Caraway	1,359	1	0	0	0	1	3	1	1	1	0
	Carlisle	2,451	5	0	1	1	3	70	29	39	2	0
	Cave City	2,074	5	0	1	0	4	39	10	26	3	0
	Cave Springs	1,583	3	0	1	0	2	20	4	16	0	0
	Centerton	7,803	4	0	0	0	4	94	27	67	0	0
	Charleston	3,035	3	0	0	0	3	32	13	19	0	0
	Cherokee Village	4,812	2	0	2	0	0	98	34	59	5	1
	Clarendon	1,766	0	0	0	0	0	0	0	0	0	0
	Clarksville	8,553	40	0	2	6	32	481	45	423	13	0
	Clinton	2,506	1	0	0	0	1	72	7	62	3	0
	Conway	57,245	183	1	39	64	79	2,319	465	1,681	173	6
	Corning	3,403	10	0	5	1	4	30	13	14	3	1
	Cotter	1,074	0	0	0	0	0	32	9	22	1	0
	Crossett	5,623	21	0	3	4	14	266	72	187	7	3
	Danville	2,488	5	0	3	0	2	7	3	4	0	0
	Dardanelle	4,431	21	0	3	1	17	131	114	15	2	5
	Decatur	1,670	2	0	0	0	2	13	6	5	2	0
	De Queen	5,890	36	0	8	3	25	241	50	185	6	0
	Des Arc	1,765	7	0	0	0	7	31	18	10	3	0
	De Witt	3,354	24	0	4	6	14	197	76	117	4	1
	Dierks	1,244	2	0	1	0	1	6	2	2	2	1
	Dover	1,388	2	0	0	1	1	58	35	22	1	0
	Dumas	4,725	25	0	3	11	11	147	38	100	9	1
	Earle	2,835	2	0	0	1	1	132	78	54	0	1
	El Dorado	20,200	207	3	1	46	157	1,276	504	711	61	10
	Elkins	2,463	3	0	0	0	3	13	1	11	1	0

[1] The FBI does not publish arson data unless it receives data from either the agency or the state for all 12 months of the calendar year.

[3] The FBI determined that the agency's data were overreported. Consequently, affected data are not included in this table.

[4] It was determined that the agency did not follow national Uniform Crime Reporting (UCR) Program guidelines for reporting an offense. Consequently, this figure is not included in this table.

Table 8. Offenses Known to Law Enforcement, by State and City, 2007 *(Contd.)*

(Number.)

State	City	Population	Violent crime	Murder and non-negligent man-slaughter	Forcible rape	Robbery	Aggravated assault	Property crime	Burglary	Larceny-theft	Motor vehicle theft	Arson[1]
	England	3,049	15	0	2	3	10	152	43	100	9	2
	Etowah	344	1	0	0	0	1	6	1	5	0	0
	Eureka Springs	2,369	7	0	1	1	5	127	24	99	4	0
	Fairfield Bay	2,527	1	0	1	0	0	40	6	34	0	0
	Farmington	4,801	6	0	1	0	5	74	17	53	4	1
	Fayetteville	70,334	362	3	42	55	262	3,236	656	2,435	145	10
	Flippin	1,407	2	0	1	1	0	61	20	41	0	0
	Fordyce	4,282	21	3	1	3	14	160	63	85	12	1
	Forrest City	13,699	104	2	6	37	59	1,205	206	959	40	6
	Fort Smith	83,860	787	5	78	143	561	5,474	1,041	4,110	323	24
	Gassville	2,083	3	0	0	0	3	35	6	29	0	0
	Gentry	2,688	9	0	2	0	7	19	6	13	0	0
	Glenwood	2,030	3	0	0	0	3	49	31	18	0	0
	Gould	1,171	0	0	0	0	0	0	0	0	0	0
	Gravette	2,465	1	0	0	0	1	39	13	25	1	0
	Greenbrier	3,855	1	0	0	0	1	13	6	7	0	0
	Green Forest	2,876	16	0	2	0	14	52	12	37	3	0
	Greenland	1,195	8	0	0	0	8	36	13	17	6	0
	Greenwood	8,404	15	0	4	0	11	130	35	94	1	1
	Gurdon	2,231	15	0	0	0	15	93	32	59	2	2
	Hamburg	2,770	15	0	4	0	11	58	22	36	0	0
	Hampton	1,493	5	0	1	0	4	38	15	23	0	0
	Hardy	819	0	0	0	0	0	5	3	2	0	0
	Harrisburg	2,142	6	0	2	1	3	132	52	74	6	1
	Harrison	13,097	70	0	12	1	57	638	234	373	31	7
	Hazen	1,502	11	0	1	5	5	40	16	22	2	0
	Heber Springs	7,156	18	0	2	0	16	327	111	213	3	1
	Helena-West Helena	12,800	214	3	12	23	176	1,008	490	466	52	10
	Highland	1,089	0	0	0	0	0	22	11	11	0	0
	Hope	10,467	96	1	10	15	70	672	171	474	27	7
	Horseshoe Bend	2,282	3	0	2	0	1	27	8	18	1	0
	Hot Springs	38,828	442	7	10	116	309	3,951	848	2,894	209	3
	Hoxie	2,635	0	0	0	0	0	20	8	11	1	0
	Jacksonville	30,565	287	5	25	57	200	1,615	360	1,146	109	10
	Jonesboro	61,199	333	5	30	92	206	3,526	1,419	1,993	114	12
	Judsonia	2,145	3	0	1	0	2	22	5	15	2	0
	Kensett	1,717	8	0	2	2	4	46	23	20	3	0
	Lake City	2,022	1	0	0	1	0	14	3	10	1	0
	Lakeview	832	1	0	0	0	1	12	5	7	0	0
	Lake Village	2,552	55	0	5	2	48	57	21	34	2	1
	Leachville	1,813	10	0	1	1	8	32	11	21	0	0
	Lepanto	2,041	4	0	0	0	4	72	32	39	1	0
	Lincoln	1,988	2	0	0	0	2	23	8	14	1	0
	Little Flock	3,179	0	0	0	0	0	18	9	8	1	0
	Little Rock	184,594	2,987	51	123	1,022	1,791	16,112	3,932	10,915	1,265	93
	Lonoke	4,651	18	0	3	5	10	233	87	142	4	1
	Lowell	7,314	12	0	2	0	10	134	62	67	5	0
	Magnolia	10,250	71	0	6	20	45	440	265	149	26	2
	Marianna	4,624	18	0	0	5	13	219	87	132	0	12
	Marion	10,331	59	0	1	18	40	390	132	240	18	0
	Marked Tree	2,666	1	0	0	1	0	67	12	54	1	1
	Marmaduke	1,173	6	0	0	1	5	57	14	41	2	0
	Marvell	1,194	3	0	0	1	2	36	12	23	1	0
	Maumelle	15,613	9	1	1	1	6	346	180	150	16	1
	McCrory	1,616	2	0	0	1	1	11	1	10	0	0
	McGehee	4,105	8	0	0	2	6	138	48	88	2	10
	McRae	695	4	0	0	1	3	53	17	36	0	0
	Mena	5,632	7	0	0	0	7	117	21	95	1	0
	Mineral Springs	1,298	4	0	0	0	4	18	9	9	0	0
	Monticello	9,122	69	0	7	9	53	423	126	267	30	0
	Morrilton	6,558	32	0	5	2	25	502	101	373	28	2
	Mountain Home	12,383	10	0	1	3	6	533	34	490	9	0
	Mountain View	3,079	4	0	0	2	2	79	14	61	4	0
	Mulberry	1,730	3	0	0	0	3	39	16	23	0	0
	Murfreesboro	1,666	1	0	0	0	1	37	17	19	1	0
	Nashville	4,862	18	0	6	1	11	256	131	123	2	2
	Newport	7,129	46	0	5	4	37	504	90	394	20	1
	North Little Rock	58,680	808	18	39	232	519	5,845	1,537	3,799	509	32
	Ola	1,232	3	0	0	0	3	11	10	1	0	2
	Osceola	7,920	155	0	7	10	138	425	127	272	26	5
	Ozark	3,587	11	0	2	0	9	48	27	20	1	1
	Pangburn	671	2	0	0	0	2	14	5	9	0	0
	Paragould	24,562	113	0	18	9	86	1,826	540	1,185	101	7
	Paris	3,674	12	0	0	1	11	146	43	99	4	0

[1] The FBI does not publish arson data unless it receives data from either the agency or the state for all 12 months of the calendar year.

Table 8. Offenses Known to Law Enforcement, by State and City, 2007 *(Contd.)*

(Number.)

State	City	Population	Violent crime	Murder and non-negligent man-slaughter	Forcible rape	Robbery	Aggravated assault	Property crime	Burglary	Larceny-theft	Motor vehicle theft	Arson[1]
	Pea Ridge	4,269	4	0	1	0	3	105	50	51	4	1
	Piggott	3,603	6	0	0	1	5	55	24	31	0	1
	Pine Bluff	51,304	889	15	42	265	567	4,422	1,598	2,389	435	80
	Plummerville	870	4	0	1	0	3	13	4	9	0	0
	Pocahontas	6,893	3	0	0	1	2	100	18	82	0	1
	Pottsville	2,528	17	1	2	3	11	45	25	15	5	1
	Prairie Grove	3,415	12	0	2	1	9	98	32	65	1	0
	Prescott	4,653	53	1	0	2	50	81	21	59	1	0
	Quitman	741	0	0	0	0	0	10	0	7	3	0
	Redfield	1,171	2	0	1	0	1	16	5	9	2	1
	Rison	1,324	2	0	0	0	2	12	7	5	0	0
	Rockport	812	2	0	0	1	1	14	2	10	2	0
	Rogers	54,223	93	0	44	14	35	2,340	265	2,008	67	1
	Rose Bud	453	3	0	1	1	1	4	1	2	1	0
	Russellville	26,319	97	1	14	7	75	1,287	317	895	75	2
	Salem	1,558	0	0	0	0	0	17	11	5	1	0
	Searcy	21,304	58	2	7	7	42	1,110	102	983	25	0
	Sheridan	4,495	4	0	1	0	3	119	46	71	2	0
	Sherwood	23,703	117	0	5	21	91	857	151	633	73	2
	Siloam Springs	14,659	27	0	11	0	16	556	76	431	49	4
	Springdale	65,695	322	2	65	33	222	2,825	621	1,996	208	21
	Star City	2,253	4	0	1	1	2	58	17	41	0	0
	Stuttgart	9,197	53	1	4	9	39	543	196	331	16	2
	Sulphur Springs	676	7	0	0	0	7	13	8	5	0	0
	Swifton	797	0	0	0	0	0	5	1	2	2	0
	Texarkana	30,156	447	3	20	64	360	1,548	387	1,043	118	4
	Trumann	6,821	35	0	5	4	26	493	157	331	5	1
	Tuckerman	1,673	2	0	0	0	2	10	6	4	0	0
	Van Buren	22,238	63	0	7	9	47	831	202	600	29	2
	Vilonia	3,085	5	0	0	0	5	76	22	53	1	0
	Waldron	3,636	50	0	2	2	46	149	106	38	5	3
	Walnut Ridge	4,631	11	0	0	0	11	80	23	52	5	1
	Ward	3,659	17	0	3	1	13	104	25	73	6	0
	Warren	6,182	44	1	6	5	32	135	90	38	7	0
	Weiner	741	2	0	1	0	1	21	6	15	0	0
	West Fork	2,259	1	0	1	0	0	39	18	19	2	0
	West Memphis	28,137	590	3	41	187	359	2,191	882	1,193	116	25
	White Hall	5,196	5	0	0	3	2	140	19	106	15	0
	Wynne	8,481	42	0	3	8	31	377	140	232	5	1
CALIFORNIA	Adelanto	28,719	153	5	7	33	108	758	354	308	96	11
	Agoura Hills	22,966	49	0	3	9	37	348	76	254	18	6
	Alameda	70,445	205	2	9	106	88	1,976	304	1,427	245	17
	Albany	15,889	45	0	3	33	9	776	173	474	129	3
	Alhambra	87,729	285	1	8	192	84	2,120	426	1,301	393	16
	Aliso Viejo	41,691	31	1	5	8	17	526	88	405	33	2
	Alturas	2,924	5	1	0	0	4	90	28	58	4	2
	American Canyon	17,053	51	3	1	14	33	433	100	283	50	2
	Anaheim	335,133	1,423	17	96	581	729	8,798	1,827	5,695	1,276	41
	Anderson	10,629	45	1	4	3	37	438	107	310	21	3
	Antioch	101,973	860	10	27	411	412	3,122	1,027	1,146	949	50
	Apple Valley	71,211	269	2	22	78	167	1,902	535	1,117	250	16
	Arcadia	56,967	156	2	9	71	74	1,704	375	1,183	146	1
	Arcata	16,929	51	0	4	10	37	524	146	353	25	
	Arroyo Grande	16,485	26	0	8	3	15	366	46	300	20	1
	Artesia	16,607	86	1	4	43	38	345	98	183	64	5
	Arvin	15,228	105	0	2	25	78	643	146	397	100	30
	Atascadero	27,465	106	1	11	8	86	565	140	400	25	18
	Atherton	7,307	12	0	0	2	10	205	34	167	4	2
	Atwater	27,762	103	1	8	22	72	1,021	260	681	80	8
	Auburn	13,072	49	0	2	5	42	373	72	260	41	2
	Avalon	3,325	39	0	2	5	32	162	41	82	39	1
	Avenal	17,175	44	0	2	8	34	133	44	76	13	
	Azusa	47,403	206	1	11	56	138	1,273	207	818	248	8
	Bakersfield	318,743	1,961	15	41	629	1,276	16,058	3,537	9,853	2,668	91
	Baldwin Park	78,943	281	8	15	105	153	1,914	392	814	708	16
	Banning	30,163	209	1	11	50	147	769	295	367	107	0
	Barstow	23,957	337	3	21	72	241	1,209	402	621	186	15
	Bear Valley	4,567	1	0	0	0	1	28	13	14	1	0
	Beaumont	30,093	46	0	0	20	26	660	125	415	120	0
	Bell	37,420	175	3	14	82	76	581	171	231	179	
	Bellflower	74,544	507	5	25	244	233	2,524	539	1,297	688	13
	Bell Gardens	45,451	218	6	19	81	112	862	198	322	342	4
	Belmont	24,605	24	0	6	6	12	357	57	260	40	9
	Belvedere	2,065	1	0	0	0	1	22	6	13	3	0

[1] The FBI does not publish arson data unless it receives data from either the agency or the state for all 12 months of the calendar year.

Table 8.   Offenses Known to Law Enforcement, by State and City, 2007 *(Contd.)*

(Number.)

State	City	Population	Violent crime	Murder and non-negligent man-slaughter	Forcible rape	Robbery	Aggravated assault	Property crime	Burglary	Larceny-theft	Motor vehicle theft	Arson[1]
	Benicia	26,544	57	1	5	22	29	475	153	260	62	13
	Berkeley	101,343	639	5	24	431	179	7,116	1,172	4,949	995	29
	Beverly Hills	35,133	157	0	15	81	61	1,169	284	833	52	4
	Big Bear Lake	6,276	42	0	7	4	31	286	95	169	22	1
	Biggs	1,802	22	0	1	1	20	41	11	23	7	0
	Bishop	3,566	30	0	0	4	26	178	40	132	6	0
	Blue Lake	1,110	4	0	1	0	3	61	18	39	4	1
	Blythe	22,696	99	1	6	17	75	593	212	349	32	24
	Bradbury	1,067	0	0	0	0	0	13	5	7	1	0
	Brawley	22,666	64	1	5	23	35	1,162	368	677	117	11
	Brea	39,041	77	0	4	40	33	1,513	207	1,194	112	7
	Brentwood	52,238	124	0	9	44	71	1,271	259	880	132	27
	Brisbane	3,575	10	0	0	3	7	129	22	94	13	0
	Broadmoor	4,345	16	0	1	5	10	77	36	28	13	3
	Buellton	4,345	11	0	1	2	8	100	19	74	7	1
	Buena Park	79,890	317	3	12	131	171	2,058	419	1,122	517	29
	Burbank	104,871	274	3	14	98	159	2,767	487	1,840	440	18
	Burlingame	27,489	57	1	4	21	31	848	127	631	90	6
	Calabasas	22,693	16	2	1	7	6	393	79	286	28	2
	Calexico	38,928	94	0	1	27	66	1,278	365	336	577	7
	California City	13,443	61	1	4	10	46	301	143	143	15	6
	Calimesa	7,528	8	1	0	5	2	204	57	120	27	0
	Calipatria	7,743	0	0	0	0	0	16	8	4	4	0
	Calistoga	5,217	23	0	1	5	17	128	21	101	6	0
	Camarillo	63,238	94	0	8	22	64	1,062	205	794	63	9
	Campbell	37,429	101	1	8	30	62	1,514	232	1,058	224	23
	Canyon Lake	11,544	23	0	1	3	19	170	56	82	32	0
	Capitola	9,432	85	0	9	13	63	811	104	680	27	5
	Carlsbad	95,056	318	2	13	88	215	2,448	528	1,684	236	10
	Carmel	3,905	9	0	0	3	6	158	25	122	11	0
	Carpinteria	13,392	28	0	4	7	17	227	52	165	10	2
	Carson	94,359	684	16	10	220	438	2,605	429	1,593	583	37
	Cathedral City	53,953	204	4	18	49	133	1,787	501	906	380	1
	Ceres	43,427	192	3	7	61	121	2,055	374	1,190	491	
	Cerritos	52,462	138	0	4	78	56	1,880	333	1,242	305	13
	Chico	74,288	385	3	59	107	216	2,454	729	1,450	275	58
	Chino	80,699	232	0	7	106	119	2,500	594	1,568	338	14
	Chino Hills	76,484	74	1	3	25	45	1,111	279	706	126	8
	Chowchilla	18,772	21	2	4	3	12	324	112	194	18	3
	Chula Vista	218,718	921	8	57	396	460	7,279	1,093	3,790	2,396	28
	City of Angels	3,949	20	0	1	1	18	74	25	45	4	3
	Claremont	35,250	87	0	11	41	35	975	269	639	67	9
	Clayton	11,252	9	0	0	6	3	165	37	120	8	0
	Clearlake	15,133	67	2	9	7	49	654	211	345	98	7
	Cloverdale	8,319	28	0	1	5	22	179	28	135	16	1
	Clovis	92,592	133	0	23	48	62	2,843	578	1,964	301	16
	Coachella	38,604	302	2	2	73	225	1,560	380	750	430	8
	Coalinga	17,801	93	0	4	10	79	498	119	342	37	
	Colma	1,436	14	0	1	5	8	373	5	343	25	1
	Colton	51,924	245	9	9	116	111	1,929	498	983	448	5
	Colusa	5,901	14	0	0	5	9	164	63	90	11	0
	Commerce	13,672	149	0	5	67	77	1,137	181	588	368	9
	Compton	95,990	1,623	37	42	466	1,078	2,805	636	1,034	1,135	82
	Concord	122,202	492	3	13	270	206	4,998	816	2,970	1,212	23
	Corcoran	23,715	45	0	4	5	36	216	65	119	32	4
	Corning	7,348	45	0	4	3	38	265	71	170	24	6
	Corona	153,518	340	5	28	187	120	4,022	670	2,659	693	21
	Coronado	26,888	26	1	6	10	9	535	63	378	94	4
	Costa Mesa	109,835	258	0	39	77	142	3,336	509	2,426	401	9
	Cotati	7,272	34	0	0	5	29	154	45	90	19	2
	Covina	47,961	216	6	12	98	100	1,845	408	1,241	196	18
	Crescent City	7,909	29	2	5	4	18	233	67	144	22	1
	Cudahy	24,953	143	4	9	61	69	558	79	280	199	1
	Culver City	39,474	181	2	6	135	38	1,459	214	1,102	143	1
	Cupertino	53,002	53	0	7	12	34	837	178	618	41	22
	Cypress	47,741	96	1	5	38	52	919	206	569	144	8
	Daly City	100,632	293	0	15	186	92	2,111	291	1,410	410	44
	Dana Point	36,051	47	0	3	14	30	552	88	425	39	5
	Danville	41,503	22	1	3	7	11	643	80	509	54	1
	Davis	61,238	169	0	21	57	91	2,121	579	1,436	106	26
	Delano	52,051	282	5	9	42	226	1,863	669	650	544	
	Del Mar	4,365	18	0	2	5	11	217	46	134	37	1
	Del Rey Oaks	1,545	0	0	0	0	0	29	7	19	3	0
	Desert Hot Springs	23,890	276	4	16	61	195	1,718	637	655	426	0

[1] The FBI does not publish arson data unless it receives data from either the agency or the state for all 12 months of the calendar year.

Table 8. Offenses Known to Law Enforcement, by State and City, 2007 *(Contd.)*

(Number.)

State	City	Population	Violent crime	Murder and non-negligent man-slaughter	Forcible rape	Robbery	Aggravated assault	Property crime	Burglary	Larceny-theft	Motor vehicle theft	Arson[1]
	Diamond Bar	57,954	133	3	9	55	66	1,058	362	602	94	6
	Dinuba	19,926	132	1	6	29	96	949	272	503	174	9
	Dixon	17,883	73	1	9	18	45	820	114	624	82	4
	Dorris	851	5	0	0	0	5	11	5	6	0	0
	Dos Palos	5,000	35	0	3	0	32	156	44	93	19	0
	Downey	109,642	516	3	17	289	207	3,896	669	2,175	1,052	13
	Duarte	22,255	84	1	4	29	50	523	120	316	87	4
	Dublin	43,751	76	0	6	18	52	756	117	543	96	7
	Dunsmuir	1,824	9	0	3	0	6	26	5	19	2	0
	East Palo Alto	33,210	261	7	20	66	168	688	263	202	223	1
	El Cajon	91,302	494	4	21	184	285	3,952	584	2,127	1,241	14
	El Centro	40,957	266	3	11	31	221	2,072	710	1,115	247	
	El Cerrito	22,514	177	2	4	114	57	1,145	253	659	233	
	Elk Grove	138,103	505	2	23	154	326	3,683	951	2,186	546	6
	El Monte	124,182	686	6	25	235	420	2,810	625	1,393	792	22
	El Segundo	16,533	36	0	3	17	16	776	154	557	65	5
	Emeryville	9,041	112	1	1	85	25	1,156	144	830	182	0
	Encinitas	59,424	159	0	9	42	108	1,144	306	702	136	7
	Escalon	7,439	21	0	4	1	16	270	86	160	24	0
	Escondido	133,429	657	4	28	280	345	4,329	808	2,428	1,093	23
	Etna	785	0	0	0	0	0	7	7	0	0	0
	Eureka[3]	25,347		1	19	46		1,517	327	993	197	20
	Exeter	10,307	21	0	1	9	11	319	95	174	50	
	Fairfax	7,091	18	0	0	1	17	110	33	64	13	4
	Fairfield	106,098	632	7	36	221	368	4,352	696	2,988	668	30
	Farmersville	10,219	55	0	0	9	46	243	68	129	46	6
	Ferndale	1,398	1	0	0	0	1	18	5	12	1	0
	Fillmore	15,219	52	1	1	8	42	306	51	235	20	3
	Firebaugh	7,036	13	0	0	1	12	213	28	153	32	0
	Folsom	68,320	98	2	8	27	61	1,594	329	1,146	119	13
	Fontana	176,490	896	8	43	292	553	4,152	936	2,067	1,149	13
	Fort Bragg	6,780	42	0	4	3	35	297	66	212	19	4
	Fort Jones	659	1	0	0	0	1	11	2	8	1	0
	Fortuna	11,312	24	1	8	4	11	377	41	307	29	4
	Foster City	28,958	22	0	2	5	15	481	65	375	41	4
	Fountain Valley	55,973	111	0	8	40	63	1,443	328	991	124	5
	Fowler	5,236	9	0	0	0	9	219	31	141	47	1
	Fremont	201,318	606	5	35	232	334	5,173	1,292	3,108	773	18
	Fresno	472,170	3,043	52	99	1,104	1,788	20,969	3,897	13,049	4,023	222
	Fullerton	133,855	467	5	41	186	235	4,128	883	2,731	514	21
	Galt	23,967	94	0	12	26	56	888	202	567	119	7
	Gardena	59,951	448	5	8	287	148	1,428	309	703	416	9
	Garden Grove	166,414	645	8	35	262	340	4,152	866	2,638	648	34
	Gilroy	49,343	251	1	12	74	164	2,016	289	1,431	296	
	Glendale	200,049	375	2	12	166	195	3,667	611	2,533	523	12
	Glendora	50,495	83	1	9	32	41	1,494	218	1,173	103	16
	Goleta	29,243	53	0	4	13	36	377	89	255	33	0
	Gonzales	8,795	38	0	1	9	28	289	86	159	44	0
	Grand Terrace	12,334	22	0	2	2	18	242	73	125	44	5
	Grass Valley	12,525	66	1	3	6	56	368	72	270	26	0
	Greenfield[3]	14,484		2	4	47		540	155	304	81	
	Gridley	5,982	76	0	8	2	66	191	60	109	22	0
	Grover Beach[3]	12,761		0	7	5		276	76	182	18	3
	Guadalupe	6,621	9	0	0	1	8	90	24	53	13	1
	Gustine	5,243	22	0	0	3	19	109	30	63	16	1
	Half Moon Bay	12,370	21	1	2	1	17	256	48	189	19	2
	Hanford	49,694	151	0	8	40	103	1,674	244	1,233	197	33
	Hawaiian Gardens	15,510	149	0	1	75	73	407	81	222	104	
	Hawthorne	85,609	765	10	27	378	350	1,992	451	953	588	5
	Hayward	140,603	881	8	48	538	287	4,667	965	2,021	1,681	60
	Healdsburg	10,955	19	0	2	4	13	279	55	211	13	4
	Hemet	71,825	479	3	36	149	291	3,117	815	1,846	456	18
	Hercules	25,636	51	0	5	24	22	490	129	267	94	4
	Hermosa Beach	19,676	67	0	12	19	36	552	108	410	34	2
	Hesperia	86,750	322	5	27	100	190	2,018	517	1,099	402	25
	Hidden Hills	2,060	0	0	0	0	0	29	9	19	1	0
	Highland	52,582	325	6	18	135	166	1,336	375	582	379	13
	Hillsborough	10,697	2	0	0	0	2	95	27	64	4	0
	Hollister	35,812	194	4	9	47	134	883	300	459	124	13
	Holtville	5,372	6	0	0	0	6	114	49	38	27	1
	Hughson	6,791	1	0	0	1	0	172	40	106	26	0
	Huntington Beach	195,067	376	0	29	102	245	4,035	795	2,825	415	42
	Huntington Park	62,269	603	9	10	379	205	2,777	349	1,326	1,102	19
	Huron	7,301	44	0	0	22	22	194	54	113	27	10

[1] The FBI does not publish arson data unless it receives data from either the agency or the state for all 12 months of the calendar year.

[3] The FBI determined that the agency's data were overreported. Consequently, affected data are not included in this table.

Table 8. Offenses Known to Law Enforcement, by State and City, 2007 *(Contd.)*

(Number.)

State	City	Population	Violent crime	Murder and non-negligent man-slaughter	Forcible rape	Robbery	Aggravated assault	Property crime	Burglary	Larceny-theft	Motor vehicle theft	Arson[1]
	Imperial	12,506	5	0	1	2	2	208	29	144	35	1
	Imperial Beach	26,013	157	0	17	46	94	696	161	267	268	10
	Indian Wells	5,175	3	0	1	2	0	272	109	151	12	1
	Indio	81,909	350	2	32	127	189	2,830	877	1,377	576	2
	Industry	906	112	2	0	60	50	1,708	288	1,026	394	4
	Inglewood	115,223	1,036	19	19	518	480	2,987	851	1,212	924	16
	Ione	7,721	10	0	1	1	8	77	10	60	7	1
	Irvine	201,872	143	4	19	44	76	3,256	637	2,404	215	53
	Irwindale	1,474	28	0	3	16	9	243	86	101	56	
	Isleton	800	14	0	0	1	13	42	26	9	7	0
	Jackson	4,468	24	0	3	3	18	157	43	104	10	2
	Kensington	5,327	4	0	0	2	2	126	15	99	12	0
	Kerman	12,795	28	0	2	3	23	351	47	223	81	4
	King City	11,237	76	1	6	20	49	348	89	189	70	4
	Kingsburg	11,483	14	0	1	2	11	442	92	267	83	4
	La Canada Flintridge	21,079	25	0	1	7	17	431	151	259	21	
	Lafayette	25,007	25	0	2	8	15	433	117	258	58	0
	Laguna Beach	24,215	49	0	10	9	30	495	144	320	31	12
	Laguna Hills	32,172	55	0	6	14	35	643	149	458	36	7
	Laguna Niguel	65,044	47	0	2	13	32	665	134	490	41	4
	Laguna Woods	18,313	3	0	0	1	2	92	8	74	10	0
	La Habra	59,290	209	2	19	66	122	1,451	305	932	214	5
	La Habra Heights	6,004	8	0	1	2	5	90	23	59	8	2
	Lake Elsinore	47,937	184	3	7	51	123	1,657	344	965	348	2
	Lake Forest	76,359	93	1	6	32	54	1,052	209	765	78	25
	Lakeport	5,291	14	0	1	2	11	130	22	98	10	4
	Lake Shastina	2,364	0	0	0	0	0	14	3	10	1	0
	Lakewood	80,138	457	4	17	248	188	2,478	410	1,631	437	8
	La Mesa	52,801	238	0	7	125	106	2,234	380	1,355	499	8
	La Mirada	50,143	115	0	7	39	69	1,080	264	648	168	14
	Lancaster	144,210	1,311	12	59	435	805	5,056	1,612	2,599	845	89
	La Palma	15,821	45	0	1	8	36	296	87	179	30	
	La Puente	41,581	222	1	12	79	130	751	150	388	213	
	La Quinta	44,533	209	1	9	27	172	1,620	555	943	122	6
	La Verne	33,549	82	0	6	39	37	821	155	620	46	5
	Lawndale	32,052	247	1	10	120	116	498	123	214	161	5
	Lemon Grove	23,721	159	1	10	46	102	591	141	233	217	4
	Lemoore	23,461	79	3	9	17	50	733	121	521	91	
	Lincoln	47,236	54	0	7	8	39	456	178	235	43	6
	Lindsay	10,925	75	1	1	12	61	406	91	219	96	1
	Livermore	80,253	169	1	17	68	83	2,069	385	1,518	166	31
	Livingston	13,286	97	0	8	5	84	399	197	146	56	3
	Lodi	63,218	230	1	8	77	144	2,762	501	1,739	522	3
	Loma Linda	21,641	28	0	5	11	12	613	137	330	146	4
	Lomita	20,539	124	2	4	34	84	429	112	265	52	4
	Lompoc	39,697	272	3	22	28	219	871	178	637	56	4
	Long Beach	473,959	3,426	42	138	1,506	1,740	12,979	2,905	7,214	2,860	123
	Los Alamitos	11,725	34	0	2	17	15	340	79	226	35	5
	Los Altos	27,451	18	0	3	8	7	293	147	138	8	1
	Los Altos Hills	8,341	2	0	0	0	2	69	26	40	3	2
	Los Angeles	3,870,487	27,806	395	1,004	13,481	12,926	101,457	19,629	58,304	23,524	2,207
	Los Banos	36,123	142	1	6	20	115	946	241	599	106	0
	Los Gatos	28,320	35	0	4	14	17	625	130	456	39	29
	Lynwood	71,216	721	9	27	274	411	1,847	395	503	949	35
	Madera	56,797	415	2	14	97	302	1,272	460	595	217	0
	Malibu	13,263	29	0	1	1	27	323	77	224	22	6
	Mammoth Lakes	7,449	37	0	3	5	29	241	70	159	12	1
	Manhattan Beach	37,061	54	0	2	29	23	1,027	192	785	50	2
	Manteca	65,857	242	1	14	72	155	2,647	433	1,845	369	28
	Marina	18,048	50	0	5	16	29	586	134	376	76	
	Martinez	35,538	122	1	14	31	76	1,182	251	716	215	0
	Marysville	11,903	167	0	10	29	128	579	157	337	85	1
	Maywood	28,796	175	3	6	88	78	446	90	168	188	1
	Menlo Park	29,867	74	0	5	26	43	560	129	381	50	1
	Merced	78,186	611	7	28	152	424	3,821	836	2,531	454	63
	Millbrae	20,425	39	0	6	12	21	344	120	181	43	4
	Mill Valley	13,280	16	0	2	5	9	184	56	114	14	1
	Milpitas	64,498	179	1	10	60	108	2,104	291	1,539	274	11
	Mission Viejo	95,095	82	0	1	28	53	1,313	205	1,007	101	14
	Modesto	208,067	1,490	11	65	452	962	12,030	2,216	7,850	1,964	129
	Monrovia	38,148	135	2	4	54	75	1,126	187	800	139	4
	Montague	1,485	3	0	0	0	3	25	10	7	8	1
	Montclair	35,893	235	4	12	120	99	2,346	272	1,683	391	4
	Montebello	63,071	242	2	11	116	113	1,948	482	912	554	43

[1] The FBI does not publish arson data unless it receives data from either the agency or the state for all 12 months of the calendar year.

Table 8.   Offenses Known to Law Enforcement, by State and City, 2007 *(Contd.)*

(Number.)

State	City	Population	Violent crime	Murder and non-negligent man-slaughter	Forcible rape	Robbery	Aggravated assault	Property crime	Burglary	Larceny-theft	Motor vehicle theft	Arson[1]
	Monterey	28,674	166	0	17	34	115	1,277	228	962	87	
	Monterey Park	62,472	196	2	3	126	65	1,290	273	766	251	0
	Monte Sereno	3,539	2	0	0	0	2	48	19	26	3	1
	Moorpark	36,255	41	0	4	12	25	579	111	432	36	2
	Moraga	17,034	15	0	4	1	10	255	43	193	19	3
	Moreno Valley	190,248	1,024	13	66	461	484	6,371	1,945	3,237	1,189	16
	Morgan Hill	36,415	84	0	14	23	47	887	165	632	90	
	Morro Bay	10,100	21	0	3	2	16	153	39	97	17	9
	Mountain View	69,999	238	1	8	56	173	1,519	157	1,224	138	12
	Mount Shasta	3,584	8	0	0	0	8	103	22	74	7	0
	Murrieta	98,051	118	3	8	46	61	1,955	483	1,195	277	3
	Napa	75,266	288	3	16	58	211	2,351	463	1,677	211	10
	National City	61,996	424	6	19	180	219	2,169	379	842	948	8
	Needles	5,397	29	0	0	1	28	192	58	115	19	14
	Nevada City	3,014	10	0	1	0	9	61	23	34	4	0
	Newark	41,781	224	0	11	84	129	1,721	311	1,178	232	
	Newman	10,436	36	0	3	5	28	330	80	201	49	0
	Newport Beach	80,377	172	1	4	53	114	2,228	645	1,429	154	9
	Norco	27,469	95	1	9	28	57	942	232	627	83	3
	Norwalk	105,330	607	6	14	211	376	2,631	511	1,340	780	26
	Novato	52,067	157	0	15	38	104	1,192	219	825	148	
	Oakdale	19,890	49	0	5	17	27	1,041	270	665	106	8
	Oakland	396,541	7,605	120	299	3,470	3,716	23,664	4,742	8,954	9,968	287
	Oakley	29,302	117	0	9	24	84	738	191	393	154	10
	Oceanside	166,424	910	3	51	257	599	4,588	839	3,102	647	31
	Ojai	7,861	10	0	2	3	5	253	41	206	6	0
	Ontario	175,537	854	15	46	351	442	5,850	970	3,551	1,329	52
	Orange	135,818	266	1	8	116	141	3,049	458	2,158	433	46
	Orinda	18,449	13	0	2	8	3	308	89	202	17	3
	Orland	7,168	30	0	1	4	25	198	60	120	18	1
	Oroville	13,579	198	1	19	23	155	1,028	270	591	167	3
	Oxnard	186,367	845	9	33	453	350	4,275	866	2,869	540	72
	Pacifica	37,176	74	0	9	23	42	626	100	458	68	7
	Pacific Grove	14,772	23	1	4	4	14	388	146	222	20	0
	Palmdale	142,122	1,043	11	34	360	638	4,302	1,182	2,446	674	46
	Palm Desert	47,903	92	2	16	48	26	2,914	847	1,837	230	11
	Palm Springs	48,542	307	5	15	121	166	3,519	1,128	1,975	416	
	Palo Alto	57,696	64	1	1	44	18	1,440	283	1,085	72	15
	Palos Verdes Estates	13,828	4	0	0	0	4	163	47	108	8	6
	Paradise	26,381	55	0	14	6	35	755	175	531	49	9
	Paramount	56,508	483	12	11	198	262	1,936	415	843	678	16
	Parlier	13,391	124	0	4	29	91	439	95	255	89	19
	Pasadena	145,553	744	11	33	303	397	4,304	825	2,993	486	23
	Paso Robles	28,490	106	0	12	13	81	931	194	659	78	3
	Patterson	19,620	52	0	5	12	35	610	158	350	102	6
	Perris	54,029	338	5	15	125	193	2,270	687	981	602	10
	Petaluma	54,624	226	1	14	40	171	1,034	180	765	89	11
	Pico Rivera	64,452	256	8	10	95	143	1,559	250	839	470	19
	Piedmont	10,478	10	0	0	10	0	207	44	108	55	2
	Pinole	18,844	112	3	2	47	60	792	168	445	179	2
	Pismo Beach	8,369	22	1	4	5	12	355	54	276	25	0
	Pittsburg	63,913	250	8	7	159	76	2,402	456	1,250	696	4
	Placentia	50,428	90	1	1	19	69	710	165	444	101	14
	Placerville	10,142	71	0	7	6	58	235	68	143	24	2
	Pleasant Hill	33,233	125	1	10	48	66	1,607	218	1,187	202	12
	Pleasanton	66,707	63	0	8	19	36	1,294	152	1,009	133	4
	Pomona	155,161	1,235	27	32	485	691	5,211	972	3,085	1,154	22
	Porterville	46,621	289	7	14	72	196	2,349	538	1,491	320	5
	Port Hueneme	21,804	93	1	6	17	69	398	95	237	66	4
	Poway	48,105	102	0	7	19	76	751	183	475	93	3
	Rancho Cucamonga	177,683	376	3	19	118	236	3,930	734	2,637	559	22
	Rancho Mirage	17,293	27	0	3	13	11	1,067	290	703	74	0
	Rancho Palos Verdes	41,845	41	1	3	8	29	537	153	347	37	7
	Rancho Santa Margarit	51,023	30	0	2	8	20	538	103	395	40	1
	Red Bluff	14,111	137	1	8	8	120	676	178	439	59	4
	Redding	91,328	455	0	84	100	271	2,645	633	1,730	282	20
	Redlands	71,358	303	0	17	114	172	2,505	589	1,554	362	25
	Redondo Beach	67,909	205	0	13	85	107	1,634	325	1,165	144	4
	Redwood City	73,435	336	1	22	86	227	1,689	197	1,271	221	4
	Reedley	23,098	136	0	8	17	111	699	127	431	141	20
	Rialto	100,451	747	15	25	288	419	2,281	727	703	851	20
	Richmond	102,471	1,220	47	31	492	650	5,507	1,265	1,933	2,309	45
	Ridgecrest	26,351	152	0	23	16	113	621	221	359	41	4
	Rio Dell	3,174	9	0	1	3	5	65	14	40	11	1

[1] The FBI does not publish arson data unless it receives data from either the agency or the state for all 12 months of the calendar year.

Table 8.   Offenses Known to Law Enforcement, by State and City, 2007 *(Contd.)*

(Number.)

State	City	Population	Violent crime	Murder and non-negligent man-slaughter	Forcible rape	Robbery	Aggravated assault	Property crime	Burglary	Larceny-theft	Motor vehicle theft	Arson[1]
	Rio Vista[3]	7,778		0	0	3		118	44	61	13	0
	Ripon	14,683	36	0	2	5	29	383	42	313	28	
	Riverbank	21,096	64	1	2	23	38	837	198	500	139	
	Riverside	299,312	1,893	12	91	686	1,104	11,154	2,227	7,081	1,846	103
	Rocklin	52,328	101	1	9	24	67	1,096	217	784	95	14
	Rohnert Park	41,043	238	1	16	23	198	953	219	647	87	12
	Rolling Hills	1,941	0	0	0	0	0	9	1	6	2	0
	Rolling Hills Estates	8,136	18	0	1	9	8	183	53	126	4	1
	Rosemead	55,187	252	1	4	140	107	1,393	408	708	277	3
	Roseville	111,497	387	1	31	100	255	3,960	648	2,905	407	9
	Ross	2,296	0	0	0	0	0	20	6	14	0	
	Sacramento	460,546	5,128	44	194	2,009	2,881	24,399	5,422	12,904	6,073	281
	Salinas	145,251	1,154	14	51	378	711	6,878	1,205	3,332	2,341	37
	San Anselmo	11,995	26	0	3	1	22	281	61	212	8	2
	San Bernardino	200,810	2,150	45	74	862	1,169	10,090	2,129	5,358	2,603	81
	San Bruno	39,960	108	0	9	29	70	822	92	583	147	2
	San Carlos	26,902	35	0	1	7	27	451	87	327	37	8
	San Clemente	62,723	83	1	6	21	55	779	195	515	69	12
	Sand City	307	8	0	2	2	4	128	9	118	1	0
	San Diego	1,261,196	6,332	59	296	2,095	3,882	44,167	7,679	23,264	13,224	200
	San Dimas	35,809	82	0	2	23	57	898	215	603	80	9
	San Francisco	733,799	6,414	100	125	3,771	2,418	34,456	5,079	23,474	5,903	232
	San Gabriel	41,186	195	0	5	118	72	770	217	466	87	9
	Sanger	24,769	91	4	4	12	71	697	153	427	117	
	San Jacinto	37,056	158	0	10	49	99	1,215	289	728	198	4
	San Jose	934,553	3,759	33	217	1,068	2,441	24,062	4,449	13,200	6,413	339
	San Juan Capistrano	34,976	67	1	5	17	44	490	116	320	54	9
	San Leandro	77,785	547	0	12	308	227	3,978	791	1,935	1,252	15
	San Luis Obispo	42,781	168	3	27	39	99	1,846	312	1,450	84	
	San Marcos	80,050	287	2	12	101	172	1,669	414	937	318	
	San Marino	13,112	16	0	0	7	9	267	77	184	6	0
	San Mateo	91,441	306	0	19	100	187	2,073	241	1,610	222	20
	San Pablo	31,143	314	6	5	167	136	1,693	348	708	637	5
	San Rafael	55,987	280	0	28	80	172	1,763	340	1,103	320	17
	San Ramon	50,295	54	0	2	15	37	1,052	194	773	85	3
	Santa Ana	340,223	1,947	23	65	779	1,080	7,797	1,013	4,684	2,100	120
	Santa Barbara	85,142	445	2	44	96	303	2,277	576	1,536	165	
	Santa Clara	109,420	231	3	32	73	123	3,430	553	2,420	457	13
	Santa Clarita	170,429	372	1	22	112	237	3,782	764	2,602	416	26
	Santa Cruz	54,626	481	1	28	117	335	2,432	410	1,847	175	33
	Santa Fe Springs	17,207	137	2	5	66	64	1,515	304	879	332	
	Santa Maria	85,782	604	3	39	139	423	2,616	513	1,622	481	12
	Santa Monica	88,584	596	2	30	236	328	3,108	682	2,099	327	13
	Santa Paula	28,518	99	0	7	28	64	717	142	498	77	0
	Santa Rosa	154,953	771	4	65	136	566	3,732	726	2,634	372	21
	Santee	52,465	147	0	12	23	112	1,140	206	662	272	5
	Saratoga	30,067	29	0	2	3	24	300	87	199	14	5
	Sausalito	7,188	5	0	1	0	4	173	39	119	15	0
	Scotts Valley	11,114	11	0	2	1	8	269	51	212	6	3
	Seal Beach	24,383	37	0	2	10	25	406	77	282	47	3
	Seaside	34,204	218	1	11	53	153	712	126	505	81	
	Sebastopol	7,523	7	0	1	3	3	193	34	148	11	3
	Selma	23,175	89	0	5	26	58	1,065	158	680	227	
	Shafter	15,215	68	1	7	4	56	610	221	301	88	32
	Sierra Madre	11,031	23	0	4	0	19	170	30	133	7	0
	Signal Hill	11,270	60	0	3	20	37	455	80	311	64	1
	Simi Valley	122,677	181	2	20	63	96	2,383	432	1,729	222	9
	Solana Beach	12,601	26	0	2	10	14	271	74	146	51	2
	Soledad[3]	28,431		1	1	8		459	174	224	61	3
	Solvang	5,091	12	0	1	2	9	78	33	40	5	0
	Sonoma	9,981	33	0	2	6	25	252	57	182	13	4
	Sonora	4,679	15	0	1	3	11	399	60	316	23	1
	South El Monte	21,696	144	1	2	43	98	641	157	278	206	4
	South Gate	98,701	577	9	17	321	230	2,921	456	1,090	1,375	23
	South Lake Tahoe	23,872	163	1	12	25	125	603	238	313	52	1
	South Pasadena	24,967	36	0	9	24	3	436	167	179	90	4
	South San Francisco	61,458	177	0	12	73	92	1,567	392	936	239	26
	Stallion Springs	1,643	0	0	0	0	0	21	2	15	4	0
	Stanton	37,666	169	2	6	85	76	738	183	409	146	16
	St. Helena	5,899	8	0	0	0	8	89	18	69	2	1
	Stockton	297,170	4,216	29	105	1,615	2,467	18,677	4,054	11,783	2,840	47
	Suisun City	27,010	144	0	11	42	91	733	176	443	114	6
	Sunnyvale	130,326	154	2	15	62	75	2,629	372	1,896	361	16
	Susanville	18,192	68	0	6	8	54	380	93	265	22	2

[1] The FBI does not publish arson data unless it receives data from either the agency or the state for all 12 months of the calendar year.

[3] The FBI determined that the agency's data were overreported. Consequently, affected data are not included in this table.

Table 8.   Offenses Known to Law Enforcement, by State and City, 2007 *(Contd.)*

(Number.)

State	City	Population	Violent crime	Murder and non-negligent man-slaughter	Forcible rape	Robbery	Aggravated assault	Property crime	Burglary	Larceny-theft	Motor vehicle theft	Arson[1]
	Sutter Creek	2,851	16	0	2	0	14	102	27	70	5	0
	Taft	9,198	38	0	3	5	30	404	84	297	23	7
	Temecula	93,665	207	5	12	81	109	2,654	667	1,688	299	6
	Temple City	38,546	85	1	6	35	43	697	276	364	57	4
	Thousand Oaks	125,196	146	2	19	38	87	1,942	424	1,407	111	14
	Tiburon	8,721	6	0	0	1	5	129	15	104	10	0
	Torrance	142,970	343	2	21	213	107	3,187	476	2,250	461	16
	Tracy	84,151	136	2	2	71	61	2,538	352	1,863	323	24
	Trinidad	314	0	0	0	0	0	35	13	22	0	0
	Truckee	16,404	59	0	1	7	51	312	81	213	18	7
	Tulare[5]	53,352	432	7	30	75	320		583	1,469		100
	Tulelake	982	1	0	0	0	1	10	5	4	1	2
	Turlock	70,386	499	0	14	132	353	3,583	827	1,964	792	
	Tustin	69,945	137	2	17	64	54	1,575	288	1,106	181	19
	Twentynine Palms	30,832	96	0	8	15	73	493	177	267	49	9
	Twin Cities	21,050	19	0	2	14	3	555	148	349	58	2
	Ukiah	15,367	134	0	14	20	100	474	174	255	45	4
	Union City	69,769	449	5	19	186	239	2,022	431	1,089	502	22
	Upland	74,049	291	3	15	105	168	2,731	551	1,813	367	8
	Vacaville	93,167	263	5	26	83	149	2,036	289	1,473	274	37
	Vallejo	116,763	1,089	15	26	361	687	6,063	1,455	3,154	1,454	96
	Ventura	104,523	368	1	27	151	189	3,827	746	2,733	348	27
	Vernon	91	46	0	0	32	14	448	70	213	165	2
	Victorville	104,872	660	9	30	264	357	4,039	1,281	2,099	659	16
	Villa Park	6,028	4	0	1	1	2	115	23	91	1	0
	Visalia	116,766	667	12	38	155	462	5,204	1,109	3,338	757	19
	Vista	89,851	526	4	25	170	327	2,149	594	1,038	517	6
	Walnut	31,470	56	2	2	22	30	550	179	308	63	5
	Walnut Creek	63,568	90	2	3	36	49	2,586	506	1,875	205	
	Waterford	9,120	40	0	1	3	36	272	63	177	32	1
	Watsonville	49,031	397	1	17	110	269	2,276	284	1,770	222	11
	Weed	3,050	22	1	6	4	11	127	41	76	10	0
	West Covina	108,097	392	2	21	178	191	3,865	680	2,409	776	4
	West Hollywood	36,604	338	1	19	141	177	1,430	229	1,032	169	7
	Westlake Village	8,613	13	0	1	4	8	168	35	127	6	1
	Westminster	89,700	355	2	22	124	207	2,657	533	1,766	358	25
	Westmorland	2,242	3	0	0	1	2	21	11	9	1	0
	West Sacramento	46,245	371	0	21	76	274	1,386	403	682	301	21
	Wheatland	3,824	5	0	0	1	4	87	34	42	11	0
	Whittier	84,038	340	4	12	145	179	2,328	416	1,489	423	
	Williams	4,895	17	1	2	2	12	99	49	44	6	
	Willits	5,051	45	2	4	7	32	92	44	38	10	
	Willows	6,304	31	0	5	3	23	239	52	175	12	0
	Windsor	25,633	87	0	7	8	72	329	74	221	34	3
	Winters	6,817	13	0	4	1	8	227	37	170	20	0
	Woodlake	7,435	37	0	2	7	28	224	39	126	59	7
	Woodland	51,355	154	1	23	62	68	1,807	467	1,094	246	28
	Yorba Linda	66,252	44	0	7	10	27	1,031	173	802	56	9
	Yountville	3,312	5	0	1	0	4	58	11	46	1	0
	Yreka	7,536	54	1	5	4	44	297	65	218	14	2
	Yuba City	61,881	245	2	24	54	165	1,913	322	1,361	230	10
	Yucaipa	51,624	52	2	9	16	25	914	250	504	160	3
	Yucca Valley	20,865	74	1	4	7	62	563	164	297	102	8
COLORADO	Alamosa	8,714	57	1	11	16	29	565	79	475	11	3
	Arvada	105,197	217	6	29	46	136	2,590	423	1,929	238	25
	Aspen	5,700	27	0	3	1	23	335	34	285	16	0
	Ault	1,419	8	0	0	0	8	63	9	46	8	2
	Aurora	307,621	1,687	14	191	583	899	11,790	2,321	7,750	1,719	83
	Avon	6,517	23	0	1	5	17	204	32	161	11	0
	Basalt	3,093	3	0	0	0	3	8	0	7	1	0
	Bayfield	1,823	1	0	0	0	1	28	9	18	1	1
	Berthoud	5,142	5	0	0	0	5	86	14	68	4	1
	Black Hawk	106	3	0	0	1	2	127	2	123	2	1
	Boulder	91,047	219	1	37	27	154	2,410	404	1,910	96	40
	Bow Mar	807	0	0	0	0	0	11	4	7	0	1
	Breckenridge	2,822	12	0	4	0	8	171	5	157	9	0
	Brighton	31,215	80	0	22	11	47	1,109	145	869	95	5
	Broomfield	46,393	46	0	11	11	24	1,250	135	1,047	68	14
	Brush	5,216	16	0	0	1	15	122	19	101	2	0
	Buena Vista	2,149	2	0	0	0	2	12	1	11	0	0
	Burlington	3,454	9	0	3	0	6	117	17	98	2	0
	Campo	131	0	0	0	0	0	0	0	0	0	0
	Canon City	16,198	120	2	27	1	90	614	88	501	25	2
	Carbondale	6,128	12	0	3	0	9	141	17	114	10	1

[1] The FBI does not publish arson data unless it receives data from either the agency or the state for all 12 months of the calendar year.

[5] The FBI determined that the agency's data were underreported. Consequently, affected data are not included in this table.

Table 8.   Offenses Known to Law Enforcement, by State and City, 2007 *(Contd.)*

(Number.)

State	City	Population	Violent crime	Murder and non-negligent man-slaughter	Forcible rape	Robbery	Aggravated assault	Property crime	Burglary	Larceny-theft	Motor vehicle theft	Arson[1]
	Castle Rock	43,523	20	0	3	2	15	539	137	383	19	7
	Cedaredge	2,270	1	0	0	0	1	35	13	22	0	0
	Centennial	97,746	180	0	34	36	110	1,604	356	1,119	129	36
	Center	2,452	7	0	0	0	7	33	13	18	2	0
	Central City	514	1	0	1	0	0	25	0	23	2	0
	Cherry Hills Village	6,218	8	0	3	0	5	112	29	81	2	0
	Colorado Springs	374,112	1,985	27	285	528	1,145	16,554	3,179	11,888	1,487	109
	Columbine Valley	1,274	0	0	0	0	0	5	2	1	2	0
	Commerce City	42,386	160	3	12	29	116	1,526	377	940	209	6
	Cortez	8,513	21	0	0	0	21	318	20	288	10	0
	Craig	9,262	33	0	5	5	23	231	46	175	10	3
	Crested Butte	1,557	0	0	0	0	0	44	4	39	1	0
	Cripple Creek	1,062	13	0	1	0	12	63	7	52	4	1
	Dacono	3,865	3	0	0	0	3	63	10	42	11	0
	De Beque	485	1	0	0	0	1	22	8	13	1	0
	Delta	8,473	44	1	2	0	41	236	51	170	15	1
	Denver	573,387	3,552	47	296	1,045	2,164	22,409	5,694	11,594	5,121	178
	Dillon	777	1	0	0	0	1	33	1	30	2	1
	Durango	15,785	74	1	24	6	43	916	89	778	49	4
	Eagle	5,275	3	0	1	0	2	121	23	86	12	0
	Eaton	4,281	2	0	0	0	2	36	13	23	0	0
	Edgewater	5,117	14	0	5	4	5	347	34	278	35	2
	Elizabeth	1,509	2	0	0	0	2	47	15	24	8	0
	Empire	332	2	0	0	0	2	5	1	4	0	0
	Englewood	32,362	149	2	7	47	93	2,830	529	2,005	296	9
	Erie	15,759	3	0	1	0	2	109	37	63	9	4
	Estes Park	6,078	1	0	0	0	1	135	23	108	4	2
	Evans	19,420	40	1	2	7	30	430	81	306	43	6
	Federal Heights	11,697	55	0	12	19	24	464	53	333	78	0
	Firestone	8,463	11	0	3	0	8	200	47	137	16	4
	Florence	3,692	13	0	1	0	12	90	11	72	7	0
	Fort Collins	130,935	418	1	70	33	314	4,476	695	3,487	294	23
	Fort Lupton	7,464	13	0	0	1	12	190	33	142	15	6
	Fort Morgan	10,774	27	0	4	4	19	383	71	301	11	6
	Fraser/Winter Park	1,621	15	0	1	1	13	108	25	77	6	2
	Frederick	8,541	42	1	2	1	38	126	27	90	9	1
	Frisco	2,509	6	0	0	0	6	52	9	43	0	2
	Fruita	7,115	30	0	3	3	24	184	33	138	13	6
	Glendale	4,800	32	0	3	17	11	425	34	334	57	0
	Glenwood Springs	8,904	41	1	6	3	31	468	82	360	26	3
	Golden	17,244	25	0	1	1	23	446	50	362	34	7
	Grand Junction	47,235	290	0	36	31	223	2,532	327	2,033	172	35
	Greeley	90,707	423	4	50	48	321	3,566	703	2,610	253	17
	Green Mountain Falls	794	11	0	1	0	10	31	11	19	1	1
	Greenwood Village	13,744	19	0	1	9	9	702	144	520	38	5
	Gunnison	5,296	21	0	3	6	12	394	95	285	14	0
	Haxtun	1,000	2	0	0	0	2	0	0	0	0	0
	Hayden	1,521	2	0	1	0	1	56	7	47	2	3
	Holyoke	2,297	2	0	0	0	2	12	2	10	0	0
	Hotchkiss	1,099	5	0	0	1	4	26	5	20	1	0
	Idaho Springs	1,779	4	0	0	1	3	61	5	53	3	1
	Ignacio	624	6	0	0	0	6	3	2	1	0	1
	Johnstown	9,021	18	1	0	1	16	131	26	92	13	0
	Kersey	1,421	1	0	0	0	1	32	2	24	6	0
	Kiowa	609	2	0	0	0	2	16	5	10	1	0
	Lafayette	24,340	69	1	4	9	55	464	92	349	23	9
	La Junta	7,198	30	0	3	5	22	281	50	218	13	3
	Lakeside	19	0	0	0	0	0	57	5	51	1	0
	Lakewood	139,407	619	1	83	152	383	5,937	954	4,121	862	10
	Lamar	8,287	24	0	1	3	20	411	67	337	7	0
	La Salle	1,927	15	0	1	0	14	44	6	36	2	0
	Las Animas	2,503	3	1	1	0	1	51	8	37	6	2
	La Veta	883	1	0	0	0	1	1	1	0	0	0
	Leadville	2,690	22	0	0	0	22	47	10	36	1	0
	Limon	1,785	1	0	0	0	1	21	2	16	3	0
	Littleton	40,343	67	0	13	20	34	1,253	220	881	152	6
	Log Lane Village	1,009	0	0	0	0	0	8	2	6	0	0
	Lone Tree	9,349	16	0	1	6	9	564	42	494	28	2
	Louisville	18,335	22	0	0	1	21	284	64	203	17	8
	Loveland	62,586	114	1	17	17	79	1,734	251	1,408	75	25
	Mancos	1,242	17	0	0	2	15	26	8	16	2	0
	Manitou Springs	5,085	14	0	1	2	11	199	32	157	10	1
	Meeker	2,309	12	0	0	0	12	40	6	29	5	0
	Milliken	6,380	2	0	1	0	1	89	17	62	10	0

[1] The FBI does not publish arson data unless it receives data from either the agency or the state for all 12 months of the calendar year.

Table 8.   Offenses Known to Law Enforcement, by State and City, 2007 *(Contd.)*

(Number.)

State	City	Population	Violent crime	Murder and non-negligent man-slaughter	Forcible rape	Robbery	Aggravated assault	Property crime	Burglary	Larceny-theft	Motor vehicle theft	Arson[1]
	Minturn	1,141	1	0	0	0	1	15	0	14	1	0
	Monte Vista	4,102	21	0	2	0	19	109	23	83	3	3
	Montrose	17,024	56	0	4	5	47	724	124	579	21	11
	Monument	2,633	6	0	0	2	4	137	31	101	5	2
	Morrison	405	5	0	0	0	5	20	4	16	0	0
	Mountain View	517	4	0	0	2	2	19	7	9	3	1
	Mount Crested Butte	772	2	0	0	0	2	50	3	47	0	0
	Nederland	1,323	10	0	0	0	10	20	7	11	2	0
	New Castle	3,526	11	0	0	0	11	76	8	65	3	0
	Northglenn	33,226	94	3	9	17	65	1,237	215	877	145	2
	Olathe	1,739	2	0	1	0	1	27	4	18	5	0
	Pagosa Springs	1,699	4	0	0	1	3	96	17	78	1	1
	Parachute	1,217	6	0	0	2	4	42	11	26	5	1
	Parker	44,624	35	0	6	9	20	687	120	531	36	12
	Platteville	2,646	21	0	0	0	21	43	8	29	6	0
	Pueblo	103,958	725	6	43	206	470	6,613	1,499	4,526	588	52
	Rangely	2,089	3	0	0	0	3	26	2	22	2	0
	Rocky Ford	4,096	28	0	2	1	25	94	24	67	3	2
	Salida	5,394	15	0	2	0	13	171	11	151	9	2
	Sheridan	5,443	21	0	3	7	11	331	56	226	49	3
	Silt	2,516	15	0	2	0	13	43	13	26	4	2
	Silverthorne	3,812	6	0	2	0	4	84	7	77	0	2
	Snowmass Village	1,732	0	0	0	0	0	59	4	52	3	0
	South Fork	552	0	0	0	0	0	8	4	4	0	0
	Springfield	1,323	0	0	0	0	0	0	0	0	0	0
	Steamboat Springs	9,233	58	1	2	1	54	468	57	391	20	2
	Sterling	12,549	33	0	7	4	22	355	73	260	22	4
	Telluride	2,274	7	0	0	0	7	174	13	155	6	1
	Thornton	113,289	380	2	72	50	256	3,996	740	2,817	439	28
	Trinidad	9,135	51	1	2	2	46	249	82	152	15	2
	Vail	4,622	9	0	0	0	9	281	25	245	11	2
	Victor	419	1	0	0	0	1	9	0	9	0	0
	Walsenburg	3,914	20	0	1	0	19	122	32	85	5	1
	Walsh	661	0	0	0	0	0	0	0	0	0	0
	Westminster	106,383	221	0	22	48	151	3,474	454	2,521	499	19
	Wheat Ridge	30,718	143	0	28	33	82	1,393	225	988	180	12
	Wiggins	960	0	0	0	0	0	0	0	0	0	0
	Windsor	17,031	4	0	2	0	2	310	48	240	22	6
	Woodland Park	6,747	16	1	2	1	12	104	14	87	3	0
	Wray	2,156	0	0	0	0	0	2	0	2	0	0
	Yuma	3,245	5	0	0	0	5	80	8	65	7	0
CONNECTICUT	Ansonia	18,620	38	0	3	21	14	376	38	287	51	0
	Avon	17,526	3	0	0	1	2	190	11	178	1	0
	Berlin	20,380	13	0	1	4	8	410	89	299	22	0
	Bethel	18,670	6	0	2	1	3	108	22	84	2	1
	Bloomfield	20,759	54	0	9	13	32	577	82	440	55	3
	Branford	29,074	31	0	6	9	16	780	98	628	54	6
	Bridgeport	137,655	1,603	14	77	675	837	6,577	1,201	4,223	1,153	43
	Bristol	61,292	187	0	12	65	110	1,548	402	1,046	100	4
	Brookfield	16,498	3	0	0	2	1	170	34	128	8	0
	Canton	10,252	3	0	2	0	1	133	23	105	5	0
	Cheshire	28,868	9	2	1	2	4	271	62	196	13	1
	Clinton	13,695	15	0	5	3	7	256	29	216	11	1
	Coventry	12,292	8	0	1	0	7	156	54	94	8	1
	Cromwell	13,612	20	0	3	10	7	315	42	256	17	2
	Danbury	79,893	146	2	20	75	49	1,482	275	1,069	138	3
	Darien	20,501	3	0	0	1	2	206	31	162	13	0
	Derby	12,465	24	0	2	11	11	471	100	326	45	0
	East Hampton	12,666	3	0	0	2	1	181	26	149	6	0
	East Hartford	48,752	221	3	15	100	103	1,614	349	1,030	235	12
	East Haven	28,755	42	0	6	26	10	743	123	513	107	2
	Easton	7,455	2	0	0	0	2	28	7	18	3	0
	East Windsor	10,650	26	1	4	15	6	357	52	266	39	9
	Enfield	45,229	62	3	9	22	28	997	157	773	67	5
	Fairfield	57,889	33	0	2	14	17	983	174	753	56	2
	Farmington	25,190	19	0	0	12	7	629	73	535	21	2
	Glastonbury	33,179	23	0	2	4	17	404	81	303	20	1
	Granby	11,285	9	0	6	2	1	123	14	104	5	0
	Greenwich	62,196	25	1	1	4	19	446	71	350	25	2
	Groton	9,314	16	0	5	2	9	191	30	151	10	1
	Groton Long Point	669	1	0	0	0	1	11	2	8	1	0
	Groton Town	29,377	21	0	1	9	11	576	168	385	23	2
	Guilford	22,462	19	0	5	2	12	351	52	284	15	0
	Hamden	57,982	121	1	13	63	44	1,396	192	1,067	137	4

[1] The FBI does not publish arson data unless it receives data from either the agency or the state for all 12 months of the calendar year.

Table 8.   Offenses Known to Law Enforcement, by State and City, 2007 *(Contd.)*

(Number.)

State	City	Population	Violent crime	Murder and non-negligent man-slaughter	Forcible rape	Robbery	Aggravated assault	Property crime	Burglary	Larceny-theft	Motor vehicle theft	Arson[1]
	Hartford	124,558	1,411	31	58	642	680	7,206	1,168	4,437	1,601	107
	Madison	18,873	10	0	0	0	10	174	34	130	10	0
	Manchester	55,774	111	1	6	46	58	1,978	218	1,637	123	10
	Meriden	59,607	173	0	6	106	61	2,093	459	1,448	186	9
	Middlebury	7,232	2	0	0	0	2	69	12	56	1	0
	Middletown	47,743	48	0	0	25	23	1,267	179	966	122	0
	Milford	55,404	91	0	4	41	46	1,900	214	1,588	98	6
	Monroe	19,599	6	0	2	2	2	190	36	125	29	0
	Naugatuck	31,994	21	1	2	5	13	621	80	491	50	4
	New Britain	70,630	324	1	6	200	117	3,645	809	2,266	570	2
	New Canaan	20,009	3	0	0	3	0	182	29	150	3	1
	Newington	29,567	21	0	6	15	0	1,046	333	640	73	3
	New Milford	28,890	21	1	3	4	13	309	69	218	22	2
	Newtown	27,262	7	0	4	0	3	161	32	126	3	1
	North Branford	14,527	14	0	0	0	14	200	37	161	2	2
	North Haven	24,168	30	0	1	22	7	593	85	470	38	4
	Norwalk	84,343	343	3	13	120	207	1,872	284	1,378	210	8
	Norwich	36,353	170	0	20	47	103	953	242	626	85	15
	Old Saybrook	10,597	1	0	0	0	1	237	16	220	1	0
	Orange	13,942	8	0	0	7	1	480	43	423	14	0
	Plainfield	15,538	21	1	4	2	14	111	38	60	13	0
	Plainville	17,294	24	0	0	13	11	604	77	495	32	2
	Portland	9,707	4	0	0	4	0	91	21	67	3	0
	Putnam	9,352	22	0	3	6	13	217	29	180	8	6
	Redding	8,990	1	0	1	0	0	49	13	34	2	2
	Ridgefield	24,040	3	0	0	1	2	93	15	76	2	0
	Rocky Hill	18,923	17	0	0	5	12	319	32	257	30	0
	Seymour	16,327	45	0	8	1	36	224	48	161	15	0
	Shelton	40,425	24	0	4	12	8	521	100	363	58	1
	Simsbury	23,674	6	0	0	3	3	241	31	186	24	4
	Southington	42,522	52	0	15	18	19	864	166	648	50	11
	South Windsor	26,214	23	1	5	5	12	516	88	413	15	0
	Stamford	119,510	336	3	33	129	171	1,882	332	1,316	234	11
	Stonington	18,261	3	0	0	0	3	341	6	335	0	0
	Stratford	49,440	116	0	3	58	55	1,539	209	1,128	202	2
	Suffield	15,334	2	0	0	1	1	187	72	107	8	0
	Torrington	35,997	53	0	10	12	31	640	120	485	35	9
	Trumbull	35,055	22	0	3	14	5	634	43	537	54	0
	Vernon	29,843	61	2	4	20	35	331	87	206	38	5
	Wallingford	44,979	33	0	12	7	14	829	119	660	50	5
	Waterbury	107,241	390	3	18	202	167	5,703	872	4,299	532	2
	Waterford	18,780	37	0	4	7	26	557	54	487	16	0
	Watertown	22,419	45	0	0	7	38	360	44	289	27	0
	West Hartford	60,644	83	1	2	53	27	1,468	241	1,063	164	1
	West Haven	52,770	226	1	1	68	156	1,856	233	1,352	271	5
	Weston	10,277	1	0	0	0	1	52	4	48	0	0
	Westport	26,704	17	0	0	7	10	352	58	281	13	0
	Wethersfield	25,977	29	1	3	12	13	580	65	462	53	0
	Willimantic	16,272	51	0	8	34	9	492	144	277	71	0
	Wilton	17,879	11	0	0	6	5	120	16	102	2	0
	Winchester	10,888	13	0	3	3	7	241	61	158	22	5
	Windsor	28,712	24	1	3	9	11	576	45	486	45	1
	Windsor Locks	12,475	20	0	5	1	14	211	38	142	31	0
	Wolcott	16,419	4	0	2	2	0	312	58	238	16	3
	Woodbridge	9,261	1	0	0	1	0	101	9	90	2	0
DELAWARE	Bethany Beach	947	3	0	0	0	3	142	9	133	0	0
	Blades	1,006	0	0	0	0	0	5	2	3	0	0
	Bridgeville	1,597	20	0	0	4	16	64	13	50	1	0
	Camden	2,484	15	0	1	5	9	175	15	157	3	1
	Cheswold	460	3	0	0	2	1	22	6	15	1	0
	Clayton	1,438	4	0	0	0	4	33	6	25	2	0
	Dagsboro	566	0	0	0	0	0	26	4	21	1	0
	Delaware City	1,520	4	0	1	1	2	63	21	36	6	0
	Delmar	1,498	5	0	0	1	4	61	14	47	0	0
	Dewey Beach	313	17	0	1	0	16	53	11	42	0	0
	Dover	35,133	277	1	16	62	198	1,861	111	1,625	125	11
	Ellendale	348	0	0	0	0	0	0	0	0	0	0
	Elsmere	5,721	54	1	2	13	38	190	41	118	31	0
	Felton	857	2	0	0	0	2	14	4	10	0	0
	Fenwick Island	359	1	0	0	0	1	14	1	13	0	0
	Georgetown	4,964	94	1	8	42	43	243	81	152	10	0
	Greenwood	891	2	0	0	0	2	19	7	12	0	0
	Harrington	3,276	28	0	3	4	21	125	46	72	7	0
	Laurel	3,842	72	0	8	22	42	174	26	138	10	1

[1] The FBI does not publish arson data unless it receives data from either the agency or the state for all 12 months of the calendar year.

Table 8.   Offenses Known to Law Enforcement, by State and City, 2007 *(Contd.)*

(Number.)

State	City	Population	Violent crime	Murder and non-negligent man-slaughter	Forcible rape	Robbery	Aggravated assault	Property crime	Burglary	Larceny-theft	Motor vehicle theft	Arson[1]
	Lewes	3,137	2	0	0	1	1	56	24	32	0	0
	Milford	7,995	95	0	3	18	74	487	78	388	21	0
	Millsboro	2,532	24	0	0	1	23	146	26	117	3	0
	Milton	1,803	15	0	2	5	8	94	38	53	3	0
	Newark	30,158	180	0	10	60	110	1,083	200	814	69	7
	New Castle	4,960	23	0	0	5	18	257	35	210	12	0
	Newport	1,106	7	0	0	4	3	51	16	32	3	0
	Ocean View	1,109	4	0	2	0	2	31	12	18	1	0
	Rehoboth Beach	1,562	15	0	0	4	11	245	49	194	2	0
	Seaford	7,121	78	1	2	28	47	414	97	302	15	0
	Selbyville	1,761	8	0	0	1	7	67	22	44	1	0
	Smyrna	8,185	45	0	4	8	33	292	49	231	12	0
	South Bethany	516	1	0	0	0	1	13	1	12	0	0
	Wilmington	72,842	1,230	11	30	593	596	3,388	954	1,913	521	5
	Wyoming	1,311	3	0	1	0	2	25	8	16	1	0
DISTRICT OF COLUMBIA	Washington	588,292	7,924	181	192	3,985	3,566	27,719	3,920	16,476	7,323	63
FLORIDA	Alachua	8,833	68	1	3	10	54	412	80	306	26	1
	Altamonte Springs	40,513	216	4	13	66	133	1,627	289	1,157	181	9
	Altha	516	0	0	0	0	0	6	2	4	0	0
	Apalachicola	2,331	9	0	0	0	9	89	18	68	3	1
	Apopka	36,895	362	2	25	132	203	1,663	465	1,054	144	18
	Arcadia	7,151	73	1	3	15	54	288	106	167	15	4
	Astatula	1,747	0	0	0	0	0	7	5	2	0	0
	Atlantic Beach	13,256	96	0	5	27	64	507	115	364	28	0
	Atlantis	2,131	5	0	0	2	3	33	10	21	2	0
	Auburndale	13,236	84	0	6	30	48	873	253	584	36	1
	Aventura	30,782	77	0	2	49	26	1,888	114	1,711	63	1
	Avon Park	9,135	137	0	2	9	126	332	116	216	0	2
	Bal Harbour Village	3,211	0	0	0	0	0	73	6	65	2	0
	Bartow	16,594	160	1	5	37	117	1,102	266	788	48	0
	Bay Harbor Island	4,996	12	0	0	2	10	84	32	42	10	0
	Belleair	4,149	4	0	0	2	2	62	18	41	3	0
	Belleair Beach	1,611	3	0	1	0	2	36	7	29	0	1
	Belleair Bluffs	2,197	4	0	0	0	4	44	7	36	1	0
	Belle Glade	15,231	471	3	10	121	337	1,402	442	876	84	10
	Belleview	4,074	21	0	1	1	19	323	106	202	15	0
	Biscayne Park	3,049	15	0	0	3	12	57	37	15	5	0
	Blountstown	2,443	10	0	0	2	8	41	8	31	2	0
	Boca Raton	86,868	236	5	16	83	132	3,441	675	2,596	170	2
	Bonifay	2,712	6	0	1	3	2	22	10	9	3	0
	Bowling Green	2,972	18	0	0	5	13	75	22	47	6	0
	Boynton Beach	69,469	730	6	5	199	520	3,578	798	2,507	273	9
	Bradenton	54,253	530	5	19	156	350	2,476	593	1,674	209	13
	Bradenton Beach	1,557	4	0	0	1	3	78	15	62	1	0
	Brooksville	7,651	64	0	4	12	48	332	52	255	25	1
	Bunnell	1,639	56	0	2	9	45	110	23	75	12	0
	Bushnell	2,200	10	0	1	4	5	129	29	96	4	0
	Cape Coral	159,936	402	5	40	97	260	5,574	1,483	3,787	304	15
	Carrabelle	1,290	15	0	2	0	13	60	19	31	10	1
	Casselberry	24,663	178	1	12	54	111	1,038	196	758	84	3
	Cedar Grove	5,201	21	0	4	2	15	102	28	48	26	2
	Cedar Key	1,008	8	0	0	0	8	5	3	2	0	0
	Center Hill	1,009	6	0	0	4	2	18	16	2	0	0
	Chattahoochee	3,807	51	0	2	1	48	118	40	72	6	0
	Chiefland	2,133	27	0	6	3	18	78	24	50	4	1
	Chipley	3,768	15	1	0	0	14	76	20	52	4	0
	Clearwater	107,501	868	10	34	240	584	4,678	862	3,469	347	31
	Clermont	12,385	115	1	9	28	77	739	216	481	42	7
	Clewiston	7,402	60	1	1	22	36	342	63	245	34	3
	Cocoa	16,704	474	4	15	119	336	1,317	447	759	111	8
	Cocoa Beach	12,128	146	0	6	26	114	969	94	829	46	1
	Coconut Creek	51,033	95	0	5	26	64	1,080	172	820	88	3
	Coleman	714	3	0	0	0	3	3	1	2	0	0
	Cooper City	30,182	98	0	1	18	79	702	123	560	19	8
	Coral Gables	42,794	132	1	8	53	70	2,195	404	1,672	119	1
	Coral Springs	131,307	301	3	7	89	202	3,052	478	2,330	244	2
	Crescent City	1,827	26	0	0	4	22	112	31	76	5	0
	Crestview	18,753	101	3	13	21	64	770	82	634	54	11
	Cross City	1,838	12	0	0	4	8	73	20	53	0	0
	Crystal River	3,590	45	0	2	12	31	324	62	246	16	4
	Cutler Bay	40,468	212	1	5	82	124	2,170	303	1,710	157	2
	Dade City	7,079	77	0	7	10	60	432	109	297	26	1
	Dania	29,011	274	1	12	103	158	1,583	331	1,046	206	5

[1] The FBI does not publish arson data unless it receives data from either the agency or the state for all 12 months of the calendar year.

Table 8.   Offenses Known to Law Enforcement, by State and City, 2007 *(Contd.)*

(Number.)

State	City	Population	Violent crime	Murder and non-negligent man-slaughter	Forcible rape	Robbery	Aggravated assault	Property crime	Burglary	Larceny-theft	Motor vehicle theft	Arson[1]
	Davenport	2,056	2	0	0	0	2	89	33	52	4	0
	Davie	87,007	336	1	22	128	185	3,639	578	2,663	398	10
	Daytona Beach	64,236	1,063	8	48	323	684	4,612	1,172	2,873	567	12
	Daytona Beach Shores	5,063	45	1	0	3	41	223	91	98	34	0
	Deerfield Beach	76,469	500	4	26	144	326	2,527	571	1,707	249	3
	De Funiak Springs	4,987	53	0	2	7	44	185	71	109	5	1
	Deland	26,610	167	1	4	46	116	1,442	355	950	137	0
	Delray Beach	65,262	719	3	22	223	471	3,553	753	2,504	296	5
	Doral	21,356	136	0	8	30	98	2,945	353	2,313	279	2
	Dundee	3,148	13	0	1	2	10	191	38	133	20	0
	Dunedin	36,702	118	1	12	27	78	885	187	650	48	3
	Dunnellon	2,016	16	0	2	4	10	106	28	73	5	0
	Eatonville	2,265	44	1	1	13	29	155	38	93	24	0
	Edgewater	21,898	52	0	4	9	39	567	156	377	34	2
	Edgewood	2,084	9	0	0	4	5	131	47	79	5	0
	El Portal	2,384	15	0	0	5	10	99	52	40	7	0
	Eustis	18,685	84	0	5	16	63	518	131	341	46	0
	Fellsmere	4,850	11	0	0	4	7	70	12	42	16	0
	Fernandina Beach	11,423	53	1	7	7	38	409	90	294	25	6
	Flagler Beach	2,874	17	1	1	2	13	139	22	110	7	2
	Florida City	9,704	261	0	4	96	161	1,315	280	962	73	2
	Fort Lauderdale	187,995	1,523	25	56	736	706	9,712	2,266	6,581	865	48
	Fort Meade	5,741	37	0	1	9	27	260	94	156	10	0
	Fort Myers	61,810	921	17	26	335	543	3,357	576	2,265	516	18
	Fort Pierce	39,456	844	4	45	229	566	2,708	818	1,670	220	11
	Fort Walton Beach	19,245	106	0	11	25	70	826	161	601	64	0
	Frostproof	2,915	20	0	3	4	13	138	55	79	4	0
	Fruitland Park	3,983	17	0	0	1	16	120	20	87	13	2
	Gainesville	108,289	1,122	5	93	237	787	5,795	1,522	3,837	436	22
	Golden Beach	893	2	0	0	1	1	16	6	7	3	0
	Graceville	2,432	1	0	0	0	1	62	13	45	4	0
	Greenacres City	33,042	233	1	14	84	134	1,344	362	892	90	2
	Greensboro	610	5	0	0	2	3	29	14	15	0	0
	Groveland	6,519	20	0	2	0	18	152	35	104	13	0
	Gulf Breeze	6,563	7	0	1	3	3	150	27	120	3	0
	Gulfport	12,508	65	0	5	22	38	566	130	361	75	4
	Gulf Stream	751	0	0	0	0	0	10	4	6	0	0
	Haines City	18,172	96	1	5	36	54	632	193	375	64	0
	Hallandale	40,147	444	2	9	116	317	1,665	364	1,131	170	21
	Hampton	453	1	0	0	0	1	11	4	6	1	0
	Havana	1,703	12	0	1	1	10	106	35	65	6	0
	Hialeah	215,853	1,274	7	42	503	722	9,546	1,808	6,044	1,694	28
	Hialeah Gardens	19,705	56	0	2	22	32	944	239	584	121	4
	Highland Beach	4,106	0	0	0	0	0	27	7	19	1	0
	High Springs	4,260	10	0	0	0	10	116	31	74	11	0
	Hillsboro Beach	2,357	1	0	0	0	1	22	0	22	0	0
	Holly Hill	13,510	135	0	5	47	83	820	233	507	80	2
	Hollywood	146,673	827	13	62	433	319	6,713	1,429	4,303	981	5
	Holmes Beach	5,086	8	1	1	0	6	196	29	160	7	0
	Homestead	58,074	890	7	8	375	500	2,593	920	1,358	315	3
	Howey-in-the-Hills	1,274	10	0	1	0	9	26	8	18	0	0
	Hypoluxo	2,680	5	0	1	3	1	38	9	20	9	0
	Indialantic	2,997	6	0	1	2	3	88	22	65	1	0
	Indian Creek Village	39	0	0	0	0	0	2	0	2	0	0
	Indian Harbour Beach	8,516	20	0	3	5	12	188	54	129	5	2
	Indian River Shores	3,488	0	0	0	0	0	49	23	26	0	0
	Indian Rocks Beach	5,227	19	0	6	1	12	148	28	109	11	0
	Indian Shores	4,292	12	0	0	3	9	62	17	39	6	0
	Inglis	1,658	4	0	0	0	4	21	2	11	8	0
	Jacksonville	797,350	8,146	123	249	3,114	4,660	45,416	11,115	29,484	4,817	187
	Jacksonville Beach	21,801	177	2	8	66	101	1,430	282	1,017	131	10
	Jennings	841	3	0	0	1	2	9	3	6	0	0
	Juno Beach	3,395	7	0	2	0	5	130	28	100	2	0
	Jupiter	50,294	236	3	7	73	153	1,739	463	1,190	86	6
	Jupiter Inlet Colony	392	0	0	0	0	0	2	1	1	0	0
	Jupiter Island	653	0	0	0	0	0	19	13	6	0	0
	Kenneth City	4,356	23	0	1	7	15	182	29	146	7	1
	Key Biscayne	9,968	2	0	0	0	2	259	18	227	14	6
	Key Colony Beach	787	0	0	0	0	0	18	2	16	0	0
	Key West	22,968	183	1	26	50	106	1,609	282	1,139	188	0
	Kissimmee	62,880	576	4	12	188	372	2,786	886	1,658	242	11
	Lady Lake	13,838	28	0	6	0	22	310	70	219	21	0
	Lake Alfred	4,280	11	0	2	2	7	170	24	125	21	0
	Lake City	12,257	183	0	8	35	140	982	169	783	30	4

[1] The FBI does not publish arson data unless it receives data from either the agency or the state for all 12 months of the calendar year.

Table 8. Offenses Known to Law Enforcement, by State and City, 2007 *(Contd.)*

(Number.)

State	City	Population	Violent crime	Murder and non-negligent man-slaughter	Forcible rape	Robbery	Aggravated assault	Property crime	Burglary	Larceny-theft	Motor vehicle theft	Arson[1]
	Lake Clarke Shores	3,397	9	0	0	2	7	73	24	41	8	0
	Lake Hamilton	1,440	7	0	0	2	5	99	42	42	15	0
	Lakeland	91,009	600	6	39	201	354	5,372	1,093	3,956	323	9
	Lake Mary	15,234	13	0	1	4	8	280	96	174	10	1
	Lake Park	8,919	119	0	7	48	64	796	100	616	80	0
	Lake Placid	1,867	9	0	2	1	6	94	32	59	3	0
	Lake Wales	14,227	59	4	0	26	29	675	147	504	24	1
	Lake Worth	36,029	556	11	22	300	223	2,426	779	1,354	293	0
	Lantana	10,475	83	0	1	28	54	535	163	321	51	1
	Largo	73,789	564	5	35	128	396	2,875	567	2,105	203	18
	Lauderdale-by-the-Sea	6,010	17	1	2	0	14	136	23	95	18	1
	Lauderdale Lakes	32,003	450	4	19	159	268	1,553	378	984	191	10
	Lauderhill	59,743	683	5	23	222	433	2,768	793	1,664	311	14
	Lawtey	692	7	0	0	0	7	18	12	4	2	0
	Leesburg	20,401	242	2	15	38	187	1,246	349	832	65	1
	Lighthouse Point	11,364	16	0	0	9	7	294	33	239	22	0
	Live Oak	7,100	84	0	0	14	70	316	146	151	19	0
	Longboat Key	7,387	2	0	0	1	1	90	17	71	2	0
	Longwood	13,482	85	0	4	18	63	637	229	375	33	1
	Lynn Haven	16,110	49	0	10	4	35	460	181	255	24	0
	Madeira Beach	4,408	38	0	3	6	29	274	52	206	16	0
	Madison	3,210	50	0	2	7	41	221	54	159	8	0
	Maitland	14,130	39	1	4	21	13	398	109	252	37	3
	Manalapan	342	1	0	0	0	1	26	5	19	2	0
	Mangonia Park	1,259	64	1	1	29	33	292	70	184	38	0
	Marco Island	16,235	17	1	1	0	15	172	22	142	8	0
	Margate	56,261	215	0	7	55	153	966	221	658	87	5
	Marianna	6,293	104	0	3	13	88	296	82	202	12	3
	Mascotte	5,485	22	0	1	0	21	106	31	60	15	2
	Medley	1,043	20	0	1	6	13	401	111	253	37	3
	Melbourne	77,678	787	2	15	174	596	3,942	926	2,741	275	14
	Melbourne Beach	3,208	2	0	0	0	2	52	15	36	1	0
	Melbourne Village	680	0	0	0	0	0	13	4	8	1	0
	Mexico Beach	1,339	1	0	0	0	1	79	18	50	11	0
	Miami	410,252	6,119	78	57	2,537	3,447	21,183	4,829	12,478	3,876	175
	Miami Beach	86,742	1,072	4	58	448	562	7,805	1,354	5,607	844	11
	Miami Gardens	98,762	1,905	24	61	686	1,134	7,606	1,668	4,904	1,034	15
	Miami Lakes	22,139	92	0	0	33	59	1,022	119	755	148	0
	Miami Shores	9,814	65	0	1	39	25	704	212	430	62	1
	Miami Springs	12,860	45	0	3	22	20	511	104	350	57	1
	Milton	8,257	53	0	3	5	45	426	80	339	7	0
	Minneola	9,646	21	0	1	0	20	151	48	91	12	0
	Miramar	114,029	598	7	26	202	363	3,812	1,038	2,274	500	10
	Monticello	2,565	29	0	2	3	24	31	21	7	3	2
	Mount Dora	11,897	121	0	6	33	82	588	162	373	53	2
	Mulberry	3,192	35	1	5	5	24	257	86	149	22	4
	Naples	22,109	49	0	2	9	38	858	126	713	19	2
	Neptune Beach	6,833	33	0	2	12	19	337	61	253	23	1
	New Port Richey	17,393	161	4	9	27	121	967	307	607	53	4
	New Smyrna Beach	23,067	138	1	8	24	105	814	214	548	52	1
	Niceville	12,354	42	0	5	4	33	202	53	140	9	1
	North Bay Village	8,279	10	0	1	4	5	211	36	145	30	0
	North Lauderdale	42,767	308	2	14	101	191	1,004	248	656	100	5
	North Miami	57,368	783	9	30	391	353	4,093	857	2,748	488	11
	North Miami Beach	38,790	465	0	28	225	212	2,292	677	1,478	137	12
	North Palm Beach	12,509	30	0	1	14	15	251	64	161	26	1
	North Port	56,539	119	3	16	20	80	1,730	483	1,190	57	6
	North Redington Beach	1,506	7	0	1	1	5	40	9	31	0	0
	Oak Hill	1,596	18	0	1	0	17	30	16	11	3	0
	Oakland	1,128	10	0	0	2	8	69	30	33	6	0
	Oakland Park	42,486	498	1	18	188	291	2,350	492	1,631	227	3
	Ocala	53,490	633	6	40	178	409	3,444	747	2,503	194	10
	Ocean Ridge	1,678	1	0	0	0	1	58	12	38	8	0
	Ocoee	31,604	199	1	8	58	132	1,545	317	1,062	166	9
	Okeechobee	6,010	22	0	0	3	19	293	40	229	24	0
	Oldsmar	13,656	68	0	12	14	42	669	152	486	31	1
	Opa Locka	15,695	546	12	7	285	242	1,616	745	595	276	1
	Orange City	9,485	80	0	1	26	53	840	102	688	50	1
	Orange Park	9,108	56	0	5	11	40	283	55	199	29	2
	Orlando	224,417	4,269	39	162	1,534	2,534	19,181	4,164	12,778	2,239	60
	Ormond Beach	38,792	107	0	5	30	72	1,278	245	959	74	3
	Oviedo	31,269	68	3	3	11	51	535	121	393	21	2
	Pahokee	6,656	137	1	7	17	112	300	70	207	23	3
	Palatka	11,130	190	3	13	33	141	998	218	739	41	4

[1] The FBI does not publish arson data unless it receives data from either the agency or the state for all 12 months of the calendar year.

Table 8.   Offenses Known to Law Enforcement, by State and City, 2007 *(Contd.)*
(Number.)

State	City	Population	Violent crime	Murder and non-negligent man-slaughter	Forcible rape	Robbery	Aggravated assault	Property crime	Burglary	Larceny-theft	Motor vehicle theft	Arson[1]
	Palm Bay	100,666	617	5	28	104	480	2,808	881	1,726	201	46
	Palm Beach	9,738	7	0	1	1	5	186	28	148	10	0
	Palm Beach Gardens	51,053	129	1	10	45	73	1,652	256	1,276	120	0
	Palm Beach Shores	1,523	5	0	0	2	3	53	10	32	11	0
	Palmetto	14,188	320	1	12	76	231	775	208	513	54	2
	Palmetto Bay	23,287	99	1	4	34	60	1,058	150	822	86	0
	Palm Springs	15,720	94	0	6	43	45	971	286	555	130	5
	Panama City	36,840	366	7	32	90	237	2,271	399	1,734	138	8
	Panama City Beach	14,755	97	0	14	23	60	1,043	257	783	3	2
	Parker	4,613	18	0	2	9	7	170	37	124	9	0
	Parkland	25,062	30	0	1	5	24	307	59	240	8	0
	Pembroke Park	4,991	83	3	2	31	47	373	59	247	67	1
	Pembroke Pines	151,817	390	0	16	146	228	5,343	827	4,100	416	15
	Pensacola	52,837	487	3	30	148	306	2,880	608	2,149	123	11
	Perry	6,801	192	0	3	14	175	257	95	144	18	3
	Pinellas Park	47,419	302	2	24	87	189	2,779	594	2,010	175	14
	Plantation	86,346	306	4	8	149	145	4,139	750	3,098	291	5
	Plant City	31,985	301	3	7	104	187	1,778	274	1,324	180	12
	Pompano Beach	104,989	1,310	10	63	452	785	5,369	1,139	3,603	627	15
	Ponce Inlet	3,294	7	0	0	1	6	45	11	32	2	0
	Port Orange	56,155	83	2	9	22	50	1,209	227	896	86	2
	Port Richey	3,421	16	0	1	5	10	298	59	229	10	0
	Port St. Joe	3,627	15	0	1	0	14	74	42	31	1	0
	Port St. Lucie	154,036	421	2	60	53	306	3,595	1,003	2,419	173	11
	Punta Gorda	17,552	46	0	0	4	42	399	174	213	12	1
	Redington Beaches	1,506	4	0	0	1	3	39	12	23	4	0
	Riviera Beach	36,795	783	13	14	201	555	2,496	773	1,367	356	5
	Rockledge	24,910	78	2	1	20	55	778	164	576	38	4
	Royal Palm Beach	32,441	160	1	12	43	104	1,182	257	850	75	1
	Safety Harbor	17,366	36	0	12	5	19	273	67	200	6	0
	Sanford	50,757	313	4	21	181	107	3,103	668	2,034	401	3
	Sanibel	5,777	0	0	0	0	0	99	24	73	2	0
	Sarasota	52,986	588	6	28	185	369	3,516	806	2,470	240	4
	Sea Ranch Lakes	763	0	0	0	0	0	17	0	16	1	0
	Sebastian	20,913	64	0	4	5	55	662	198	443	21	0
	Sebring	10,749	99	0	7	18	74	534	190	334	10	9
	Seminole	19,330	72	0	3	12	57	644	111	508	25	0
	Sewall's Point	2,035	0	0	0	0	0	31	12	19	0	0
	Shalimar	712	2	0	0	0	2	7	0	5	2	0
	Sneads	1,936	1	0	0	0	1	42	19	23	0	0
	South Bay	4,667	73	2	2	16	53	168	63	92	13	0
	South Daytona	13,529	56	2	5	10	39	474	95	339	40	1
	South Miami	11,071	76	0	0	29	47	740	110	569	61	0
	South Palm Beach	1,501	1	0	0	1	0	5	2	1	2	0
	South Pasadena	5,634	19	0	1	6	12	197	31	156	10	1
	Southwest Ranches	7,449	26	0	1	6	19	174	35	116	23	1
	Springfield	8,963	46	1	3	8	34	355	77	258	20	2
	Starke	5,896	44	1	0	7	36	272	15	233	24	0
	St. Augustine	12,118	125	1	4	21	99	1,027	161	817	49	4
	St. Augustine Beach	6,001	36	0	2	6	28	169	22	141	6	0
	St. Cloud	24,791	180	1	1	21	157	1,155	259	834	62	1
	St. Pete Beach	10,105	46	0	1	7	38	567	196	356	15	1
	St. Petersburg	248,069	3,830	26	103	1,017	2,684	15,189	3,717	9,156	2,316	103
	Stuart	16,385	97	1	6	21	69	884	110	716	58	2
	Sunny Isles Beach	15,190	43	0	3	12	28	638	151	437	50	0
	Sunrise	91,480	428	6	10	196	216	3,824	733	2,821	270	6
	Surfside	4,599	20	0	1	5	14	154	30	113	11	0
	Sweetwater	13,436	49	0	2	11	36	230	45	124	61	2
	Tallahassee	159,943	1,813	5	136	568	1,104	8,396	2,588	5,202	606	62
	Tamarac	61,366	235	4	14	86	131	1,279	351	813	115	5
	Tampa	337,220	3,575	28	80	1,205	2,262	16,775	4,221	10,390	2,164	73
	Tarpon Springs	23,523	239	3	4	41	191	846	217	575	54	5
	Tavares	13,351	39	0	3	4	32	245	58	165	22	0
	Temple Terrace	22,546	114	1	3	55	55	843	195	562	86	1
	Tequesta	6,018	10	0	1	1	8	104	34	67	3	1
	Titusville	44,467	373	5	33	90	245	1,794	475	1,054	265	18
	Treasure Island	7,575	27	0	7	10	10	278	49	219	10	0
	Trenton	1,866	11	0	0	1	10	57	14	40	3	0
	Umatilla	2,812	7	0	1	0	6	74	4	66	4	0
	Valparaiso	6,047	11	0	0	0	11	64	23	37	4	0
	Venice	21,329	56	0	3	5	48	626	82	517	27	2
	Vero Beach	16,840	84	0	6	24	54	707	196	482	29	13
	Village of Pinecrest	19,027	46	0	2	17	27	774	86	658	30	0
	Virginia Gardens	2,221	7	0	0	5	2	56	8	44	4	0

[1] The FBI does not publish arson data unless it receives data from either the agency or the state for all 12 months of the calendar year.

Table 8. Offenses Known to Law Enforcement, by State and City, 2007 *(Contd.)*

(Number.)

State	City	Population	Violent crime	Murder and non-negligent man-slaughter	Forcible rape	Robbery	Aggravated assault	Property crime	Burglary	Larceny-theft	Motor vehicle theft	Arson[1]
	Wauchula	4,517	40	1	7	8	24	212	42	160	10	0
	Webster	865	4	0	1	0	3	31	8	21	2	0
	Welaka	714	1	0	0	1	0	9	1	7	1	0
	Wellington	57,713	158	1	9	36	112	1,864	316	1,403	145	8
	West Melbourne	16,012	32	0	1	6	25	519	264	226	29	2
	West Miami	5,725	25	0	3	3	19	167	61	95	11	0
	Weston	68,230	87	2	2	11	72	965	133	785	47	3
	West Palm Beach	101,322	1,158	12	43	574	529	7,255	1,594	4,748	913	13
	West Park	14,917	118	0	4	44	70	652	142	423	87	4
	White Springs	825	6	0	0	0	6	19	8	11	0	1
	Wildwood	3,211	75	0	4	4	67	202	71	125	6	3
	Williston	2,833	52	0	3	1	48	126	31	87	8	0
	Wilton Manors	12,937	92	0	2	43	47	655	139	460	56	2
	Windermere	2,037	1	0	0	0	1	28	14	12	2	0
	Winter Garden	29,284	235	3	3	59	170	1,271	282	852	137	0
	Winter Haven	31,556	218	2	20	76	120	2,008	507	1,355	146	9
	Winter Park	28,114	130	0	8	63	59	1,133	272	795	66	0
	Winter Springs	32,817	80	0	6	12	62	451	102	313	36	2
	Zephyrhills	12,998	81	0	7	23	51	918	236	627	55	2
	Zolfo Springs	1,693	4	0	0	2	2	46	23	13	10	0
GEORGIA	Abbeville	2,604	1	0	0	0	1	2	1	1	0	
	Acworth	19,646	85	0	0	16	69	518	51	426	41	
	Adairsville	3,199	15	0	0	4	11	244	42	183	19	
	Adel	5,398	42	0	5	13	24	315	89	211	15	
	Albany	75,137	637	12	32	205	388	5,503	1,519	3,616	368	
	Alpharetta	43,909	146	0	10	41	95	1,836	243	1,501	92	
	Americus	16,448	135	2	15	34	84	1,135	383	716	36	
	Aragon	1,071	0	0	0	0	0	23	1	22	0	0
	Athens-Clarke County	113,389	435	7	38	142	248	5,493	1,306	3,836	351	36
	Atlanta	497,290	8,075	129	148	3,577	4,221	36,232	8,859	20,353	7,020	155
	Auburn	7,310	18	0	4	0	14	85	25	46	14	
	Austell	6,976	62	0	2	6	54	266	56	175	35	0
	Avondale Estates	2,817	5	0	0	3	2	104	25	73	6	0
	Baldwin	2,980	0	0	0	0	0	63	7	53	3	
	Ball Ground	910	1	0	0	0	1	25	8	15	2	0
	Barnesville	5,987	38	0	0	5	33	193	45	139	9	
	Barwick	447	0	0	0	0	0	0	0	0	0	0
	Baxley	4,444	36	1	0	4	31	183	35	141	7	1
	Blackshear	3,476	19	1	2	4	12	347	55	280	12	
	Blakely	5,382	26	0	2	5	19	84	21	62	1	
	Bloomingdale	2,644	7	0	0	0	7	70	13	49	8	
	Blythe	802	0	0	0	0	0	12	5	6	1	
	Bowdon	1,991	0	0	0	0	0	91	14	76	1	
	Bremen	5,622	21	0	1	4	16	297	46	234	17	
	Brooklet	1,240	1	0	1	0	0	44	6	37	1	
	Broxton	1,480	17	0	0	1	16	106	18	82	6	
	Brunswick	16,146	458	8	13	104	333	1,312	354	867	91	
	Buchanan	1,010	1	0	0	0	1	48	12	33	3	
	Buena Vista[5]	1,711	5	0	1	1	3	14		2	1	1
	Byron	3,801	15	0	1	6	8	147	34	96	17	0
	Cairo	9,655	34	0	4	14	16	340	109	214	17	
	Calhoun	14,522	47	3	4	15	25	1,024	168	808	48	
	Canton	22,071	62	1	15	10	36	565	49	467	49	
	Carrollton[3]	22,149		1	8	48		1,660	264	1,334	62	
	Cartersville	17,680	99	2	12	30	55	1,295	233	941	121	
	Centerville	7,123	5	0	3	1	1	331	39	265	27	2
	Chamblee	11,038	112	3	1	88	20	711	115	518	78	
	Chatsworth	4,100	12	0	0	2	10	116	8	99	9	0
	Chickamauga	2,535	12	0	0	0	12	91	13	75	3	
	Clarkesville	1,646	3	0	1	0	2	96	12	81	3	0
	Clarkston	7,546	77	0	5	24	48	343	162	102	79	
	Claxton	2,399	7	1	0	3	3	92	12	73	7	
	Cleveland	2,535	41	0	1	0	40	129	21	102	6	
	Cochran	4,788	32	0	3	8	21	278	25	245	8	
	College Park	20,573	379	3	19	181	176	1,936	475	1,165	296	12
	Columbus	188,944	1,316	24	57	618	617	13,791	2,652	9,367	1,772	53
	Commerce	6,189	36	0	3	7	26	256	52	188	16	1
	Conyers	12,704	78	1	4	37	36	938	141	699	98	
	Coolidge	558	2	0	0	0	2	4	1	2	1	0
	Cordele	11,495	108	3	8	36	61	906	211	647	48	
	Cornelia	3,822	14	0	4	1	9	179	16	152	11	
	Covington	14,680	77	0	10	34	33	775	194	528	53	0
	Cumming	6,150	10	0	4	4	2	375	20	332	23	
	Cuthbert	3,481	13	0	0	3	10	69	16	53	0	

[1] The FBI does not publish arson data unless it receives data from either the agency or the state for all 12 months of the calendar year.

Table 8. Offenses Known to Law Enforcement, by State and City, 2007 *(Contd.)*

(Number.)

State	City	Population	Violent crime	Murder and non-negligent man-slaughter	Forcible rape	Robbery	Aggravated assault	Property crime	Burglary	Larceny-theft	Motor vehicle theft	Arson[1]
	Dallas	10,199	151	0	3	16	132	335	68	251	16	
	Dalton[5]	33,790	140	3	6	30	101		230	1,026		
	Darien	1,727	10	1	0	2	7	11	5	4	2	0
	Dawson	4,754	21	0	0	0	21	171	60	111	0	
	Decatur	19,180	64	1	5	35	23	729	125	529	75	
	Donalsonville	2,685	12	1	0	3	8	93	15	73	5	
	Doraville	10,364	98	1	0	46	51	475	66	332	77	
	Douglasville	30,422	169	0	10	55	104	2,247	325	1,735	187	
	Dublin	17,434	192	1	3	32	156	1,330	247	1,020	63	0
	Duluth	26,272	81	3	3	30	45	602	137	403	62	2
	East Dublin	2,738	17	0	0	2	15	129	20	105	4	
	Eastman	5,524	87	0	0	3	84	277	61	205	11	
	East Point	42,497	445	6	14	211	214	2,706	855	1,488	363	
	Elberton	4,655	44	0	0	10	34	497	104	376	17	
	Ellaville	1,824	7	0	0	0	7	23	1	21	1	
	Emerson	1,372	11	0	0	0	11	116	11	100	5	0
	Euharlee	4,190	5	0	3	0	2	41	13	18	10	0
	Fairburn	10,369	48	1	0	18	29	544	190	283	71	8
	Fayetteville	15,603	31	0	1	11	19	550	38	482	30	
	Flowery Branch	3,589	0	0	0	0	0	68	15	52	1	
	Folkston	3,248	19	0	0	3	16	84	11	66	7	
	Forest Park	22,174	185	3	6	119	57	1,349	270	908	171	
	Forsyth	4,174	25	0	3	10	12	229	36	172	21	1
	Fort Oglethorpe	9,809	30	0	3	8	19	675	100	552	23	0
	Fort Valley	8,107	146	2	0	13	131	491	101	371	19	
	Franklin	876	18	0	0	0	18	48	3	43	2	
	Gainesville	34,494	184	2	18	55	109	1,920	293	1,494	133	6
	Garden City	9,387	188	2	5	48	133	537	94	390	53	
	Gordon	2,086	3	0	0	1	2	38	3	29	6	0
	Gray	2,222	6	0	1	0	5	84	9	74	1	0
	Greensboro	3,243	33	0	2	4	27	203	34	165	4	
	Griffin	23,478	170	1	10	64	95	1,708	298	1,356	54	
	Grovetown	8,476	26	0	4	2	20	256	78	156	22	1
	Guyton	1,906	4	0	0	2	2	35	13	20	2	
	Hahira	2,148	2	0	0	0	2	78	18	57	3	
	Hampton	5,167	14	0	0	4	10	126	51	64	11	3
	Hapeville	6,149	78	0	2	46	30	466	52	317	97	
	Hartwell	4,358	15	0	1	1	13	387	45	335	7	
	Hazlehurst	3,819	11	0	0	0	11	213	0	209	4	0
	Helen	791	25	0	0	0	25	98	2	85	11	0
	Hephzibah	4,306	21	0	5	4	12	126	17	97	12	0
	Hiawassee	840	7	0	0	1	6	33	6	26	1	
	Hinesville	29,466	225	4	16	44	161	2,055	479	1,511	65	
	Hiram	1,959	64	0	2	8	54	425	50	345	30	
	Hogansville	2,930	40	0	0	1	39	114	13	97	4	
	Holly Springs	6,897	13	0	0	2	11	121	36	77	8	
	Hoschton	1,586	1	0	0	0	1	33	2	27	4	0
	Irwinton	577	0	0	0	0	0	8	4	4	0	0
	Ivey	1,067	0	0	0	0	0	1	0	0	1	0
	Jackson	4,478	5	0	0	1	4	141	12	127	2	0
	Jefferson	6,906	60	0	0	5	55	340	65	255	20	0
	Jonesboro	3,909	45	1	1	17	26	213	55	132	26	1
	Kennesaw	32,643	34	1	2	10	21	544	94	413	37	
	Keysville	259	0	0	0	0	0	0	0	0	0	0
	Kingsland	12,705	89	0	5	5	79	501	93	393	15	
	Lafayette	6,884	35	0	4	10	21	414	74	319	21	
	LaGrange	27,867	118	2	7	50	59	1,704	375	1,215	114	
	Lake City	2,733	15	0	0	15	0	286	22	221	43	
	Lavonia	2,035	17	0	3	3	11	179	51	118	10	
	Lawrenceville	29,797	129	1	6	86	36	1,026	221	675	130	
	Leesburg	2,939	3	0	1	1	1	119	13	102	4	0
	Lilburn	11,567	59	0	1	37	21	585	111	411	63	
	Lincolnton	1,535	16	0	1	6	9	30	0	27	3	
	Lithonia	2,356	40	0	1	14	25	112	42	47	23	
	Lookout Mountain	1,561	0	0	0	0	0	16	2	14	0	
	Ludowici	1,637	13	0	0	1	12	55	12	39	4	
	Macon	93,205	732	22	43	302	365	7,997	1,979	5,166	852	74
	Madison	3,913	9	0	0	4	5	137	29	97	11	
	Manchester	3,808	26	0	0	5	21	228	64	147	17	
	Marietta	63,523	479	4	16	297	162	2,579	618	1,553	408	
	Maysville	1,639	7	0	0	0	7	37	5	28	4	
	McDonough	18,504	202	0	5	30	167	797	158	570	69	3
	McIntyre	707	3	0	0	0	3	24	3	21	0	0
	McRae	4,492	62	0	1	2	59	116	17	90	9	

[1] The FBI does not publish arson data unless it receives data from either the agency or the state for all 12 months of the calendar year.

Table 8. Offenses Known to Law Enforcement, by State and City, 2007 *(Contd.)*

(Number.)

State	City	Population	Violent crime	Murder and non-negligent man-slaughter	Forcible rape	Robbery	Aggravated assault	Property crime	Burglary	Larceny-theft	Motor vehicle theft	Arson[1]
	Milledgeville	19,896	77	1	6	18	52	1,130	192	897	41	3
	Millen	3,525	44	0	0	2	42	75	47	25	3	
	Molena	492	0	0	0	0	0	0	0	0	0	
	Monroe	12,813	77	3	7	23	44	637	172	414	51	
	Montezuma	3,969	27	0	0	8	19	194	64	127	3	2
	Morrow	5,425	55	0	2	28	25	909	47	770	92	
	Moultrie	15,375	133	6	6	51	70	1,220	261	912	47	17
	Mount Airy	680	1	0	1	0	0	12	1	9	2	0
	Mount Zion	1,549	1	0	0	1	0	20	6	12	2	
	Nashville	4,830	37	1	3	11	22	318	103	204	11	4
	Newnan	29,117	136	3	1	35	97	1,166	219	889	58	3
	Newton	863	0	0	0	0	0	4	3	0	1	0
	Nicholls	2,868	0	0	0	0	0	85	11	74	0	
	Ocilla	3,211	20	1	3	4	12	220	28	177	15	
	Oglethorpe	1,130	7	0	0	0	7	15	9	4	2	
	Oxford	2,480	4	0	0	1	3	27	17	9	1	0
	Palmetto[3]	5,103	17	0	0	11	6		69		24	2
	Peachtree City	35,431	20	0	1	9	10	402	30	292	80	
	Pearson	1,927	12	0	1	2	9	100	19	80	1	0
	Pelham	3,902	41	1	3	6	31	209	39	168	2	
	Pine Mountain	1,276	3	0	1	0	2	66	7	52	7	
	Pooler	12,815	15	0	2	5	8	566	71	462	33	
	Port Wentworth	3,396	4	0	0	1	3	145	25	92	28	0
	Powder Springs	15,285	57	3	2	20	32	365	103	238	24	3
	Reidsville	2,458	7	1	0	3	3	105	14	85	6	
	Richmond Hill	10,324	37	0	2	20	15	221	34	168	19	
	Rincon	7,371	95	0	4	11	80	236	38	184	14	
	Ringgold	2,764	19	0	0	2	17	215	35	167	13	2
	Riverdale	15,977	122	6	8	70	38	919	222	581	116	
	Roberta	771	2	0	0	1	1	42	9	33	0	0
	Rockmart	4,480	17	0	0	3	14	201	40	146	15	0
	Rome	36,233	264	2	17	68	177	2,398	489	1,754	155	12
	Rossville	3,473	16	0	1	4	11	239	46	179	14	
	Roswell	88,879	191	2	17	107	65	2,261	499	1,612	150	0
	Royston	2,730	1	0	0	0	1	85	2	82	1	0
	Sandersville	6,134	47	1	4	19	23	470	97	352	21	
	Sandy Springs	85,830	229	6	24	151	48	3,416	803	2,317	296	
	Savannah-Chatham Metropolitan	208,116	1,319	26	78	743	472	9,851	2,315	6,369	1,167	88
	Senoia	3,213	1	0	0	0	1	30	2	28	0	0
	Shiloh	436	0	0	0	0	0	3	2	1	0	0
	Smyrna	49,259	241	5	9	120	107	1,911	437	1,192	282	
	Snellville	20,414	75	1	5	29	40	847	121	682	44	0
	Statesboro	26,001	459	1	20	30	408	1,254	272	938	44	
	Statham	2,795	13	0	0	1	12	120	20	84	16	
	St. Marys[3]	16,153		2	7	9		529	102	404	23	
	Stone Mountain	7,575	18	1	0	12	5	168	71	50	47	
	Suwanee	14,959	39	1	1	26	11	397	67	308	22	
	Sycamore	529	0	0	0	0	0	0	0	0	0	
	Sylvania	2,522	19	1	1	9	8	130	19	109	2	
	Sylvester	5,874	16	0	1	3	12	290	72	199	19	1
	Talbotton	998	8	0	0	2	6	26	11	14	1	
	Tallapoosa	3,157	5	0	0	1	4	122	31	83	8	0
	Tallulah Falls	157	0	0	0	0	0	1	1	0	0	0
	Temple	4,350	26	0	0	4	22	139	22	109	8	
	Thomaston	9,101	42	0	2	8	32	382	44	329	9	
	Thomasville	19,108	71	0	3	26	42	1,053	212	804	37	
	Thomson	6,922	40	0	4	13	23	411	123	282	6	0
	Tifton	16,803	179	2	9	48	120	1,455	316	1,096	43	
	Trenton	2,399	3	0	0	0	3	36	7	23	6	0
	Trion	2,060	1	0	0	0	1	53	13	38	2	
	Tunnel Hill	1,095	2	0	1	0	1	65	13	47	5	0
	Tybee Island	3,774	12	0	2	3	7	81	7	71	3	1
	Tyrone	6,696	5	0	1	1	3	102	27	69	6	0
	Union City	17,217	219	4	4	59	152	1,680	433	988	259	
	Valdosta	45,712	276	1	33	111	131	2,841	657	2,013	171	
	Vidalia	11,253	117	0	12	44	61	921	244	638	39	0
	Vienna	2,910	24	1	0	6	17	105	16	85	4	
	Villa Rica	12,585	87	2	4	7	74	566	85	448	33	
	Warner Robins	60,116	326	3	16	119	188	3,309	928	2,235	146	14
	Warrenton	1,954	1	0	0	1	0	88	14	66	8	
	Washington	4,093	29	0	4	3	22	109	27	78	4	0
	Watkinsville	2,810	3	0	1	0	2	73	12	59	2	0
	Waverly Hall	808	3	0	0	1	2	8	2	5	1	
	Waycross	14,738	108	1	5	29	73	1,018	166	805	47	

[1] The FBI does not publish arson data unless it receives data from either the agency or the state for all 12 months of the calendar year.

[3] The FBI determined that the agency's data were overreported. Consequently, affected data are not included in this table.

Table 8. Offenses Known to Law Enforcement, by State and City, 2007 *(Contd.)*

(Number.)

State	City	Population	Violent crime	Murder and non-negligent man-slaughter	Forcible rape	Robbery	Aggravated assault	Property crime	Burglary	Larceny-theft	Motor vehicle theft	Arson[1]
	Waynesboro	5,870	54	1	1	22	30	569	87	418	64	0
	West Point	3,349	54	0	3	13	38	398	60	324	14	
	Winder	13,607	146	0	6	24	116	886	180	651	55	
	Wrens	2,251	20	0	0	3	17	97	28	67	2	1
	Zebulon	1,230	2	0	0	1	1	42	11	29	2	0
HAWAII	Honolulu	905,903	2,613	19	226	943	1,425	37,197	5,777	26,483	4,937	407
IDAHO	Aberdeen	1,805	3	0	0	0	3	15	5	8	2	0
	American Falls	4,244	3	0	0	0	3	83	8	72	3	1
	Bellevue	2,238	9	0	0	0	9	19	10	9	0	2
	Blackfoot	11,084	28	0	7	1	20	410	72	319	19	1
	Boise	199,104	648	10	122	68	448	6,175	1,018	4,778	379	80
	Bonners Ferry	2,736	3	0	0	0	3	61	26	33	2	1
	Buhl	4,028	12	0	0	0	12	139	70	57	12	2
	Caldwell	38,713	162	1	19	17	125	1,688	493	1,029	166	20
	Cascade	1,018	4	0	0	0	4	16	2	10	4	0
	Challis	868	1	0	0	0	1	13	5	8	0	0
	Chubbuck	11,039	34	0	3	3	28	559	39	505	15	1
	Coeur d'Alene	42,324	270	1	35	18	216	1,488	248	1,168	72	34
	Cottonwood	1,062	4	0	0	0	4	13	4	9	0	0
	Emmett	6,385	10	0	4	0	6	165	22	137	6	4
	Filer	1,919	3	0	0	0	3	4	0	2	2	0
	Fruitland	4,603	3	0	1	0	2	115	25	86	4	2
	Garden City	11,452	64	0	10	6	48	432	88	305	39	4
	Gooding	3,267	10	0	3	0	7	59	9	42	8	0
	Grangeville	3,171	9	0	2	0	7	76	15	58	3	0
	Hagerman	763	5	0	0	0	5	3	2	1	0	0
	Hailey	7,984	23	0	2	0	21	119	61	57	1	0
	Heyburn	2,749	1	0	0	0	1	25	12	12	1	0
	Homedale	2,585	3	0	0	0	3	17	4	11	2	0
	Idaho City	495	2	0	0	0	2	11	3	8	0	0
	Idaho Falls	53,049	222	0	32	16	174	1,927	372	1,432	123	17
	Jerome	8,778	24	0	2	1	21	330	68	238	24	3
	Kamiah	1,150	3	0	0	0	3	20	5	13	2	0
	Kellogg	2,279	17	1	0	3	13	73	14	55	4	2
	Ketchum	3,258	15	0	2	1	12	123	27	92	4	0
	Kimberly	2,807	1	0	0	0	1	47	13	32	2	0
	Lewiston	31,356	41	1	12	3	25	1,258	239	959	60	5
	McCall	2,644	16	0	2	0	14	141	28	109	4	0
	Meridian	64,294	118	0	26	8	84	1,153	189	897	67	17
	Montpelier	2,460	1	0	0	0	1	37	11	24	2	0
	Moscow	22,503	18	1	2	3	12	507	50	447	10	0
	Mountain Home	11,686	24	0	5	1	18	289	31	242	16	1
	Nampa	80,397	260	5	55	17	183	2,508	613	1,643	252	15
	Orofino	3,103	11	0	4	0	7	54	16	35	3	1
	Osburn	1,448	1	0	1	0	0	16	5	11	0	1
	Parma	1,842	9	0	0	1	8	37	7	26	4	0
	Payette	7,686	9	0	1	0	8	124	29	93	2	0
	Pinehurst	1,608	2	0	0	0	2	15	1	12	2	0
	Pocatello	54,274	132	0	20	9	103	1,706	259	1,360	87	4
	Ponderay	720	1	0	1	0	0	90	10	78	2	0
	Post Falls	25,622	60	0	13	5	42	628	97	483	48	6
	Preston	5,147	9	0	2	0	7	65	10	54	1	0
	Priest River	1,950	5	0	0	0	5	40	13	23	4	0
	Rathdrum	6,551	7	0	1	1	5	158	57	90	11	2
	Rexburg	28,308	9	0	1	0	8	271	64	196	11	2
	Rigby	3,332	7	0	2	0	5	91	14	72	5	1
	Rupert	5,158	17	0	2	0	15	97	16	73	8	1
	Salmon	3,054	3	0	0	0	3	45	17	24	4	0
	Sandpoint	8,413	15	0	2	1	12	258	52	191	15	1
	Shelley	4,249	4	1	0	0	3	53	6	43	4	0
	Soda Springs	3,149	7	0	0	0	7	43	16	26	1	0
	Spirit Lake	1,656	5	0	0	0	5	33	6	24	3	0
	St. Anthony	3,383	6	0	0	0	6	44	7	37	0	0
	St. Maries	2,657	11	0	0	0	11	34	5	24	5	0
	Sun Valley	1,455	6	0	0	2	4	26	9	15	2	0
	Twin Falls	41,236	153	4	21	14	114	1,522	290	1,158	74	11
	Weiser	5,425	5	0	0	0	5	74	12	59	3	0
	Wendell	2,448	4	0	0	0	4	40	8	23	9	1
	Wilder	1,451	7	0	0	1	6	30	8	20	2	0
ILLINOIS[6]	Aurora	174,724		12		172	589	4,507	921	3,321	265	23
	Chicago	2,824,434		443		15,425	17,424	126,298	24,752	82,942	18,604	700
	Elgin	102,960		2		88	104	2,530	508	1,801	221	5
	Joliet	148,484		9		161	400	3,995	885	2,939	171	59
	Naperville	144,933		2		17	76	2,332	250	2,009	73	10

[1] The FBI does not publish arson data unless it receives data from either the agency or the state for all 12 months of the calendar year.

[6] The data collection methodology for the offense of forcible rape used by the Illinois and the Minnesota state UCR Programs (with the exception of Rockford, Illinois and Minneapolis and St. Paul, Minnesota) does not comply with national UCR Program guidelines. Consequently, their figures for forcible rape and violent crime (of which forcible rape is a part) are not published in this table.

Table 8. Offenses Known to Law Enforcement, by State and City, 2007 (Contd.)

(Number.)

State	City	Population	Violent crime	Murder and non-negligent man-slaughter	Forcible rape	Robbery	Aggravated assault	Property crime	Burglary	Larceny-theft	Motor vehicle theft	Arson[1]
	Peoria[7]	113,137		16		390	474	5,216	1,248	3,541	427	47
	Rockford[7]	155,713	2,109	21	113	633	1,342	9,324	2,681	5,983	660	84
	Springfield	117,185		8		329	1,502	7,389	1,543	5,481	365	59
INDIANA	Albion	2,356	1	0	1	0	0	2	2	0	0	0
	Alexandria	5,840	3	0	0	0	3	274	46	215	13	1
	Anderson	57,189	203	3	27	82	91	2,931	651	2,065	215	32
	Angola	7,979	10	0	1	3	6	480	42	433	5	0
	Attica	3,361	12	1	2	3	6	98	32	62	4	1
	Auburn	12,902	18	0	3	12	3	442	78	344	20	0
	Avon	10,197	48	0	2	7	39	550	44	470	36	0
	Bargersville	2,647	1	0	0	0	1	1	0	1	0	0
	Bedford	13,557	21	0	5	1	15	388	62	302	24	5
	Beech Grove	13,975	34	0	4	22	8	476	93	331	52	2
	Berne	4,108	5	0	1	0	4	45	13	24	8	0
	Bloomington	68,918	275	1	24	72	178	2,898	666	2,060	172	14
	Bluffton	9,448	3	0	0	2	1	201	29	172	0	0
	Boonville	6,750	1	0	0	1	0	160	7	148	5	0
	Bremen	4,719	5	0	2	0	3	63	19	43	1	1
	Brownsburg	19,494	19	1	3	5	10	328	44	275	9	1
	Burns Harbor	1,060	2	0	0	1	1	32	3	26	3	1
	Carmel	62,037	29	1	3	6	19	1,009	123	840	46	3
	Cedar Lake	10,350	17	1	0	5	11	415	81	318	16	4
	Charlestown	7,217	11	0	0	6	5	290	56	222	12	0
	Chesterfield	2,755	0	0	0	0	0	83	10	73	0	0
	Chesterton	12,746	7	0	1	1	5	324	75	231	18	2
	Clarks Hill	663	0	0	0	0	0	3	2	1	0	0
	Clarksville	21,295	139	1	9	53	76	2,024	235	1,574	215	5
	Clinton	4,896	2	0	2	0	0	80	7	63	10	3
	Columbia City	8,227	5	0	2	0	3	120	14	101	5	0
	Columbus	39,764	53	1	10	16	26	2,593	344	2,116	133	9
	Connersville	14,099	26	0	4	4	18	1,251	263	963	25	7
	Corydon	2,793	2	0	0	1	1	62	5	54	3	0
	Crawfordsville	15,156	31	0	8	6	17	831	180	625	26	2
	Crown Point	24,072	13	0	7	5	1	684	59	573	52	1
	Culver	1,523	1	0	0	0	1	17	8	6	3	0
	Danville	8,033	14	0	0	1	13	111	16	88	7	0
	Decatur	9,507	1	0	0	0	1	74	22	43	9	0
	Delphi	2,969	1	0	0	1	0	84	30	52	2	0
	Dyer	15,713	11	0	0	6	5	359	19	312	28	1
	East Chicago[7]	30,353	223	14	13	124	72	2,059	388	1,378	293	11
	Elwood	9,013	5	0	1	3	1	418	112	286	20	5
	Evansville	114,985	522	2	56	179	285	5,308	1,108	3,905	295	84
	Fairmount	2,746	8	0	1	0	7	89	8	77	4	1
	Fishers	66,099	28	0	7	12	9	826	73	712	41	1
	Fort Wayne	248,423	762	24	85	407	246	10,083	2,129	7,312	642	72
	Franklin	22,778	86	0	5	7	74	1,210	100	1,080	30	0
	Gary	97,048	669	71	57	324	217	4,667	1,746	2,062	859	
	Gas City	5,774	3	0	0	3	0	176	26	137	13	0
	Georgetown	2,851	5	0	0	1	4	29	7	17	5	0
	Goshen	32,210	53	0	18	28	7	1,156	168	938	50	12
	Greendale[7]	4,391	7	0	1	0	6	57	19	37	1	0
	Greenfield	17,884	24	3	3	6	12	393	64	301	28	3
	Greensburg	10,570	9	0	2	5	2	406	66	320	20	6
	Greenwood	46,063	141	1	2	15	123	1,763	121	1,554	88	5
	Griffith	16,370	43	2	0	13	28	665	76	524	65	1
	Hagerstown	1,646	0	0	0	0	0	34	8	25	1	0
	Hammond	77,662	645	15	25	279	326	3,840	994	2,312	534	50
	Hartford City	6,493	6	0	2	1	3	201	48	148	5	0
	Hebron	3,634	4	0	0	0	4	25	2	20	3	0
	Highland	22,879	43	0	3	19	21	1,000	126	812	62	4
	Hobart	28,428	86	2	8	19	57	1,545	167	1,237	141	6
	Huntingburg	6,107	0	0	0	0	0	106	13	91	2	0
	Huntington	16,767	25	0	5	3	17	386	50	320	16	2
	Indianapolis	797,268	9,841	114	505	4,046	5,176	50,289	13,385	29,224	7,680	336
	Jasper	14,098	9	1	0	1	7	176	36	131	9	1
	Knox[7]	3,699	12	0	2	0	10	249	43	195	11	0
	Kokomo	45,832	216	1	20	62	133	2,717	450	2,142	125	4
	Lafayette	61,257	303	0	36	68	199	3,083	610	2,290	183	16
	La Porte	21,178	31	0	5	15	11	1,462	175	1,217	70	2
	Ligonier	4,470	2	0	0	0	2	71	15	47	9	1
	Logansport	18,995	23	1	8	12	2	847	119	681	47	2
	Long Beach	1,544	1	1	0	0	0	2	2	0	0	2
	Lowell	8,319	13	0	0	3	10	145	9	132	4	0
	Marion[7]	30,288	95	3	19	49	24	1,594	322	1,128	144	7

[1] The FBI does not publish arson data unless it receives data from either the agency or the state for all 12 months of the calendar year.

[7] Because of changes in the state/local agency's reporting practices, figures are not comparable to previous years' data.

Table 8.   Offenses Known to Law Enforcement, by State and City, 2007 *(Contd.)*

(Number.)

State	City	Population	Violent crime	Murder and non-negligent man-slaughter	Forcible rape	Robbery	Aggravated assault	Property crime	Burglary	Larceny-theft	Motor vehicle theft	Arson[1]
	Martinsville	11,805	42	0	1	0	41	936	62	850	24	3
	Merrillville	32,091	89	3	2	42	42	1,065	123	809	133	2
	Michigan City	32,008	146	3	14	82	47	1,928	306	1,435	187	20
	Mishawaka	49,196	157	1	17	52	87	3,189	342	2,691	156	24
	Monticello	5,401	4	0	0	3	1	232	37	185	10	2
	Mooresville	11,639	11	0	3	3	5	331	36	269	26	0
	Muncie	64,921	375	1	50	60	264	2,652	581	1,932	139	52
	Munster	22,467	23	1	0	14	8	472	41	400	31	0
	Nappanee	7,118	1	0	0	1	0	191	12	172	7	1
	New Albany	36,840	137	1	4	56	76	2,507	452	1,871	184	51
	New Castle	18,577	16	0	3	7	6	1,652	341	1,245	66	0
	New Whiteland	5,658	10	0	0	0	10	136	7	126	3	3
	Noblesville	41,927	48	1	14	13	20	1,008	143	813	52	2
	North Liberty	1,351	4	0	1	0	3	6	1	5	0	0
	North Manchester	5,887	9	0	1	2	6	194	20	159	15	0
	North Vernon	6,407	15	0	1	6	8	358	38	310	10	1
	Plainfield	25,722	25	0	4	4	17	921	120	732	69	3
	Plymouth	11,192	12	0	5	2	5	379	34	324	21	1
	Portage	36,701	139	0	5	12	122	1,557	252	1,190	115	2
	Portland	6,149	3	0	3	0	0	284	25	252	7	0
	Rensselaer	6,276	36	0	7	1	28	221	40	173	8	6
	Richmond	37,129	166	0	14	57	95	1,935	453	1,362	120	43
	Rushville	5,570	12	0	0	0	12	192	38	150	4	0
	Salem	6,558	8	0	0	0	8	24	13	11	0	0
	Schererville	29,494	12	0	2	8	2	676	73	536	67	2
	Scottsburg	5,982	22	0	2	1	19	424	83	325	16	0
	Seymour	19,246	89	0	5	4	80	1,198	116	1,001	81	10
	South Bend	104,437	805	7	67	448	283	6,872	1,945	4,438	489	106
	South Whitley	1,865	4	0	0	0	4	28	8	19	1	0
	Speedway	12,357	69	0	1	45	23	597	91	436	70	3
	St. John	12,237	4	0	1	1	2	147	16	118	13	2
	Sullivan	4,481	1	0	0	0	1	79	16	58	5	0
	Tell City	7,561	6	0	2	0	4	195	58	131	6	2
	Terre Haute	56,946	197	4	30	97	66	4,927	992	3,508	427	45
	Tipton	5,181	0	0	0	0	0	163	43	116	4	0
	Valparaiso	29,764	88	0	2	6	80	825	123	673	29	0
	Vincennes	17,905	28	1	1	7	19	1,317	287	954	76	3
	Wabash	11,021	9	0	2	6	1	204	55	132	17	2
	Walkerton	2,186	10	0	0	1	9	70	20	43	7	0
	Warsaw	13,154	16	0	7	9	0	618	74	519	25	6
	Waterloo	2,194	20	0	1	0	19	53	20	30	3	0
	Westfield	14,037	18	0	5	4	9	551	64	461	26	6
	West Lafayette	29,045	49	0	4	3	42	519	96	402	21	0
	Westville	5,194	2	0	2	0	0	82	13	66	3	0
	Whiting	4,793	7	0	1	5	1	207	35	155	17	0
	Winchester	4,705	10	0	2	1	7	208	32	172	4	1
	Winona Lake	4,314	1	0	0	0	1	33	4	27	2	1
IOWA	Adel	4,135	4	0	0	0	4	75	23	49	3	0
	Albia	3,615	7	1	1	0	5	49	8	37	4	1
	Algona	5,443	15	0	1	0	14	58	16	40	2	0
	Altoona	13,882	22	0	4	2	16	485	44	416	25	0
	Ames	51,622	200	2	18	12	168	1,602	500	1,040	62	2
	Anamosa	5,675	3	0	0	0	3	111	22	84	5	1
	Atlantic	6,842	2	0	0	0	2	125	26	94	5	0
	Bettendorf	32,501	43	0	2	4	37	820	150	650	20	7
	Bloomfield	2,575	5	0	1	0	4	9	5	4	0	1
	Boone	12,768	74	0	18	1	55	295	105	185	5	9
	Burlington	25,258	188	0	11	32	145	1,227	270	896	61	17
	Camanche	4,298	1	0	0	1	0	59	7	50	2	0
	Carlisle	3,599	2	0	0	0	2	56	17	36	3	2
	Carroll	9,976	6	1	1	0	4	158	25	123	10	3
	Carter Lake	3,304	21	1	3	2	15	225	41	162	22	2
	Cedar Falls	36,995	102	1	16	9	76	821	116	666	39	7
	Cedar Rapids	124,730	500	3	34	137	326	6,041	1,083	4,619	339	24
	Centerville	5,662	16	0	4	1	11	246	49	181	16	2
	Chariton	4,554	12	0	1	1	10	172	39	125	8	0
	Charles City	7,574	9	0	0	0	9	130	23	99	8	0
	Cherokee	4,911	5	0	0	0	5	89	21	68	0	0
	Clarinda	5,558	11	0	1	1	9	176	45	115	16	4
	Clarion	2,796	8	0	1	0	7	36	8	23	5	0
	Clinton	26,937	188	0	25	22	141	1,270	299	891	80	15
	Clive	14,231	47	0	5	4	38	356	56	271	29	3
	Coralville	18,496	41	0	5	9	27	779	85	674	20	12
	Council Bluffs	60,531	455	2	76	78	299	4,698	878	3,288	532	44

[1] The FBI does not publish arson data unless it receives data from either the agency or the state for all 12 months of the calendar year.

Table 8.   Offenses Known to Law Enforcement, by State and City, 2007 *(Contd.)*

(Number.)

State	City	Population	Violent crime	Murder and non-negligent man-slaughter	Forcible rape	Robbery	Aggravated assault	Property crime	Burglary	Larceny-theft	Motor vehicle theft	Arson[1]
	Cresco	3,763	3	0	0	0	3	73	19	48	6	2
	Davenport	99,631	821	2	40	225	554	6,222	1,211	4,730	281	29
	Decorah	8,066	7	0	0	0	7	106	11	86	9	2
	Denison	7,427	7	0	0	1	6	96	16	76	4	0
	Des Moines	192,948	1,514	4	185	387	938	11,794	2,095	8,631	1,068	90
	De Witt	5,360	7	0	0	0	7	131	44	81	6	1
	Dubuque	57,694	407	1	23	27	356	1,946	610	1,256	80	47
	Dyersville	4,186	4	0	1	0	3	64	8	55	1	0
	Eldora	2,789	3	0	1	0	2	47	3	43	1	0
	Emmetsburg	3,633	1	0	0	0	1	34	11	19	4	0
	Estherville	6,276	30	0	7	0	23	109	14	89	6	0
	Evansdale	4,998	8	0	1	1	6	154	50	95	9	2
	Fairfield	9,354	24	0	4	0	20	247	61	179	7	0
	Forest City	4,202	13	0	0	0	13	18	5	11	2	1
	Fort Dodge	25,330	158	1	8	34	115	1,555	333	1,089	133	19
	Fort Madison	10,841	20	0	3	4	13	284	44	225	15	3
	Garner	2,990	0	0	0	0	0	19	4	13	2	0
	Glenwood	5,816	6	0	1	1	4	121	26	87	8	0
	Hampton	4,226	9	0	0	1	8	12	0	11	1	0
	Hawarden	2,426	5	0	0	1	4	17	10	7	0	0
	Humboldt	4,379	4	0	0	1	3	45	10	28	7	0
	Indianola	14,399	26	0	4	1	21	270	42	209	19	2
	Iowa City	62,700	207	0	18	33	156	1,333	217	1,054	62	10
	Jefferson	4,337	2	0	0	0	2	28	4	22	2	0
	Johnston	15,622	13	0	2	4	7	283	48	227	8	1
	Le Mars	9,375	26	1	5	0	20	250	57	182	11	1
	Leon	1,923	2	0	0	0	2	50	3	44	3	0
	Manchester	4,958	26	0	4	0	22	66	10	50	6	1
	Maquoketa	6,006	12	0	2	0	10	136	49	82	5	0
	Marion	31,772	40	0	5	5	30	510	137	353	20	7
	Marshalltown	25,958	91	0	1	8	82	1,132	248	811	73	4
	Mason City	27,541	60	0	8	18	34	1,141	242	872	27	7
	Monticello	3,738	2	0	0	0	2	35	4	31	0	0
	Mount Pleasant	8,918	33	0	1	0	32	270	61	198	11	1
	Mount Vernon	4,210	4	0	1	0	3	60	7	53	0	0
	Muscatine	22,705	132	1	18	4	109	733	158	551	24	8
	Nevada	6,275	23	0	2	1	20	117	14	87	16	2
	New Hampton	3,464	4	0	2	0	2	52	28	22	2	0
	Norwalk	8,413	6	0	2	1	3	119	20	96	3	5
	Oelwein	6,273	8	0	1	1	6	76	18	53	5	0
	Orange City	5,897	1	0	1	0	0	40	4	35	1	0
	Osage	3,447	7	0	0	0	7	59	13	44	2	0
	Osceola	4,782	8	0	1	0	7	127	24	97	6	1
	Oskaloosa	11,033	31	0	4	4	23	308	62	223	23	2
	Ottumwa	24,822	191	0	12	5	174	1,287	269	951	67	6
	Pella	10,280	26	0	3	0	23	186	61	117	8	3
	Perry	9,001	46	0	1	0	45	143	12	116	15	6
	Pleasant Hill	7,458	10	0	0	2	8	129	44	78	7	1
	Polk City	3,098	0	0	0	0	0	32	3	27	2	0
	Prairie City	1,459	2	0	0	0	2	17	7	9	1	0
	Red Oak	5,907	16	2	5	1	8	219	57	150	12	5
	Sac City	2,157	1	0	0	0	1	29	9	19	1	0
	Sergeant Bluff	4,009	13	0	0	0	13	87	13	73	1	3
	Sheldon	4,863	3	0	1	0	2	91	23	63	5	5
	Shenandoah	5,172	4	0	0	0	4	135	14	109	12	4
	Sioux City	82,942	373	2	40	33	298	2,842	578	2,110	154	19
	Spencer	11,015	1	0	0	1	0	369	64	295	10	0
	Spirit Lake	4,783	4	0	2	0	2	191	25	166	0	0
	State Center	1,356	3	0	0	0	3	29	8	21	0	0
	Storm Lake	9,855	42	0	6	4	32	418	112	298	8	4
	Story City	3,187	0	0	0	0	0	47	13	30	4	1
	Urbandale	38,381	67	0	7	16	44	760	153	571	36	9
	Vinton	5,239	14	0	4	0	10	96	20	73	3	0
	Waterloo	65,607	433	4	53	74	302	3,188	952	2,072	164	29
	Waukee	11,945	21	0	3	0	18	198	53	135	10	1
	Waverly	9,396	73	0	4	2	67	163	28	123	12	1
	Webster City	8,004	35	0	1	1	33	198	49	130	19	3
	West Burlington	3,376	13	0	3	1	9	241	33	203	5	0
	West Des Moines	54,988	88	0	15	15	58	1,586	226	1,315	45	9
	West Liberty	3,695	3	0	1	1	1	71	29	41	1	1
	Williamsburg	2,831	0	0	0	0	0	33	11	21	1	1
	Wilton	2,862	5	0	0	0	5	37	11	26	0	0
	Windsor Heights	4,506	6	0	0	3	3	198	25	164	9	1
	Winterset	4,970	7	0	0	0	7	85	13	71	1	0

[1] The FBI does not publish arson data unless it receives data from either the agency or the state for all 12 months of the calendar year.

Table 8. Offenses Known to Law Enforcement, by State and City, 2007 *(Contd.)*

(Number.)

State	City	Population	Violent crime	Murder and non-negligent man-slaughter	Forcible rape	Robbery	Aggravated assault	Property crime	Burglary	Larceny-theft	Motor vehicle theft	Arson[1]
KANSAS	Abilene	6,419	20	1	6	0	13	271	33	221	17	1
	Andover	9,955	27	0	5	0	22	594	47	539	8	0
	Anthony	2,217	3	0	0	0	3	58	25	28	5	0
	Arkansas City	11,342	78	1	10	1	66	449	82	345	22	7
	Atchison	10,138	32	0	6	4	22	412	67	324	21	3
	Atwood	1,104	1	0	0	0	1	10	1	9	0	0
	Auburn	1,132	0	0	0	0	0	0	0	0	0	0
	Augusta	8,715	20	0	4	0	16	520	52	447	21	0
	Baldwin City	4,255	10	0	0	0	10	76	11	63	2	2
	Basehor	3,742	4	0	0	0	4	61	17	42	2	1
	Baxter Springs	4,164	8	1	0	0	7	149	31	107	11	1
	Bel Aire	6,739	7	0	2	1	4	57	14	38	5	3
	Belle Plaine	1,576	1	0	0	0	1	38	8	25	5	0
	Beloit	3,591	6	0	1	0	5	63	16	44	3	0
	Bonner Springs	7,121	22	0	1	5	16	332	61	233	38	3
	Chanute	8,822	36	0	5	2	29	295	31	251	13	1
	Chapman	1,262	3	0	0	0	3	18	4	14	0	0
	Chetopa	1,227	8	0	1	0	7	33	10	21	2	1
	Clay Center	4,305	17	0	7	0	10	140	47	83	10	0
	Clearwater	2,299	2	0	0	1	1	67	20	45	2	0
	Coffeyville	10,280	74	0	8	14	52	602	181	387	34	4
	Colby	4,854	20	0	1	1	18	194	43	141	10	2
	Columbus	3,216	7	0	2	1	4	86	25	58	3	0
	Colwich	1,380	2	0	0	0	2	7	1	6	0	0
	Concordia	5,229	16	0	5	2	9	235	58	166	11	6
	Derby	21,531	50	0	10	4	36	743	136	560	47	12
	Dodge City	26,236	179	2	15	16	146	993	193	744	56	14
	Edwardsville	4,565	24	0	1	0	23	147	32	101	14	0
	El Dorado	12,693	48	0	3	4	41	621	121	453	47	4
	Elkhart	1,969	9	0	0	0	9	9	2	6	1	0
	Ellis	1,849	1	0	0	0	1	31	3	25	3	0
	Ellsworth	2,869	4	0	2	0	2	51	7	43	1	0
	Elwood	1,144	5	0	3	0	2	59	24	28	7	1
	Erie	1,146	0	0	0	0	0	25	8	17	0	0
	Eudora	6,323	13	0	3	0	10	129	21	99	9	0
	Fairway	3,815	4	0	2	1	1	40	7	24	9	1
	Fort Scott	7,922	33	0	5	5	23	334	66	247	21	4
	Fredonia	2,446	5	0	0	0	5	124	39	82	3	0
	Frontenac	3,134	5	0	1	0	4	73	17	54	2	0
	Galena	3,150	2	0	0	0	2	117	24	83	10	0
	Garden City	26,949	176	0	13	16	147	1,142	196	902	44	9
	Gardner	16,658	38	0	3	4	31	369	61	290	18	0
	Garnett	3,272	6	0	1	0	5	110	31	72	7	0
	Girard	2,645	12	0	0	0	12	66	19	41	6	0
	Goddard	3,836	3	0	0	2	1	131	34	95	2	0
	Grandview Plaza	995	10	0	0	0	10	47	14	30	3	2
	Great Bend[4]	15,562		1	4	4		726	144	560	22	7
	Hays	19,672	57	1	8	6	42	598	123	457	18	5
	Haysville	10,227	28	0	7	0	21	437	100	315	22	1
	Herington	2,459	9	0	2	1	6	101	16	69	16	0
	Hesston	3,666	2	0	1	0	1	73	24	47	2	2
	Hiawatha	3,207	12	0	2	1	9	96	15	76	5	0
	Hill City	1,415	3	0	0	0	3	18	5	11	2	0
	Hillsboro	2,694	3	0	0	0	3	49	11	36	2	0
	Holton	3,364	3	0	0	1	2	72	7	62	3	2
	Horton	1,821	4	0	0	0	4	41	15	22	4	0
	Independence	9,229	69	1	1	12	55	484	116	333	35	7
	Inman	1,189	0	0	0	0	0	10	6	4	0	0
	Iola	5,916	32	0	2	6	24	348	68	267	13	0
	Junction City	15,727	164	1	15	23	125	759	138	590	31	9
	Kansas City	143,371	1,149	20	91	489	549	9,717	2,269	5,431	2,017	
	Kechi	1,645	1	0	0	1	0	19	3	13	3	0
	Kingman	3,072	14	0	1	0	13	93	22	66	5	1
	Lansing	10,861	33	0	2	2	29	230	45	156	29	1
	Larned	3,677	22	0	2	1	19	200	41	156	3	3
	Lawrence	90,044	409	0	48	63	298	5,030	550	4,283	197	23
	Leavenworth	34,918	292	1	15	72	204	1,483	264	1,112	107	7
	Leawood	31,121	72	0	15	9	48	514	88	397	29	7
	Lebo	945	0	0	0	0	0	6	3	3	0	0
	Lenexa	45,059	91	0	8	15	68	1,364	197	1,009	158	14
	Liberal	20,477	182	1	24	21	136	963	222	686	55	2
	Lindsborg	3,282	3	0	2	0	1	87	19	67	1	0
	Louisburg	3,739	3	0	1	0	2	59	8	50	1	0
	Maize	2,717	3	0	0	0	3	49	7	40	2	0

[1] The FBI does not publish arson data unless it receives data from either the agency or the state for all 12 months of the calendar year.

[4] It was determined that the agency did not follow national Uniform Crime Reporting (UCR) Program guidelines for reporting an offense. Consequently, this figure is not included in this table.

Table 8. Offenses Known to Law Enforcement, by State and City, 2007 *(Contd.)*

(Number.)

State	City	Population	Violent crime	Murder and non-negligent man-slaughter	Forcible rape	Robbery	Aggravated assault	Property crime	Burglary	Larceny-theft	Motor vehicle theft	Arson[1]
	Marysville	3,110	9	0	2	0	7	37	12	19	6	0
	McPherson	13,577	20	1	5	4	10	393	84	283	26	3
	Meriden	713	0	0	0	0	0	1	0	1	0	0
	Minneapolis	2,021	2	0	0	0	2	44	6	37	1	0
	Mission	9,691	21	0	2	8	11	434	42	306	86	1
	Mission Hills	3,514	1	0	0	0	1	13	3	8	2	1
	Mulberry	566	2	0	0	0	2	12	4	7	1	1
	Mulvane	5,836	8	0	1	0	7	180	25	149	6	1
	Neodesha	2,635	12	0	2	0	10	107	28	76	3	2
	Newton	18,164	88	0	10	8	70	676	101	558	17	5
	Nickerson	1,160	3	0	2	0	1	22	3	19	0	0
	North Newton	1,574	0	0	0	0	0	12	2	10	0	1
	Norton	2,726	2	0	1	0	1	38	11	25	2	0
	Oakley	1,870	4	0	2	0	2	59	5	53	1	0
	Osage City	2,936	9	0	2	0	7	79	22	55	2	4
	Osawatomie	4,578	24	0	5	2	17	238	52	174	12	0
	Oswego	1,993	4	0	0	0	4	49	7	42	0	0
	Ottawa	12,901	64	0	15	3	46	406	62	335	9	10
	Overland Park	169,224	311	2	35	53	221	4,266	532	3,305	429	44
	Oxford	1,092	0	0	0	0	0	23	10	13	0	0
	Paola	5,378	11	0	3	2	6	168	14	147	7	3
	Park City	7,603	14	0	6	4	4	206	43	152	11	1
	Parsons	11,190	82	0	2	7	73	679	137	516	26	12
	Peabody	1,264	2	0	0	0	2	42	11	29	2	0
	Pittsburg	19,104	101	1	10	10	80	1,153	240	855	58	14
	Pleasanton	1,367	1	0	0	0	1	17	8	7	2	0
	Prairie Village	21,312	28	0	2	5	21	293	45	216	32	8
	Pratt	6,389	16	0	2	0	14	127	26	95	6	1
	Roeland Park	6,916	17	0	5	4	8	274	27	247	0	0
	Rose Hill	4,028	5	0	0	0	5	87	3	81	3	0
	Russell	4,224	11	0	1	0	10	79	27	47	5	2
	Sabetha	2,506	3	0	0	0	3	37	8	25	4	0
	Salina	46,180	168	0	45	15	108	2,753	362	2,291	100	19
	Scott City	3,459	10	0	5	1	4	75	17	58	0	0
	Sedgwick	1,657	5	0	0	0	5	13	5	8	0	0
	Seneca	2,054	0	0	0	0	0	27	9	18	0	0
	Shawnee	60,950	122	0	9	21	92	1,306	164	935	207	18
	South Hutchinson	2,477	8	0	0	0	8	85	11	73	1	1
	Spring Hill	5,203	9	0	1	0	8	86	18	62	6	0
	Stafford	1,041	1	0	0	0	1	22	1	17	4	0
	Sterling	2,537	7	0	0	0	7	32	13	15	4	0
	St. Marys	2,240	6	0	0	0	6	29	5	22	2	0
	Tonganoxie	4,312	8	0	1	1	6	136	12	115	9	1
	Topeka	121,885	719	12	47	308	352	7,774	1,424	5,646	704	10
	Towanda	1,371	0	0	0	0	0	18	4	14	0	0
	Ulysses	5,620	19	0	1	0	18	56	5	48	3	0
	Valley Center	6,044	5	0	0	0	5	106	14	84	8	0
	Valley Falls	1,182	2	0	1	0	1	5	3	1	1	0
	Wa Keeney	1,716	0	0	0	0	0	30	15	15	0	0
	Wamego	4,243	5	0	0	0	5	90	8	78	4	0
	Wathena	1,297	8	0	1	0	7	32	8	22	2	0
	Wellington	7,898	23	0	2	1	20	405	67	319	19	1
	Wellsville	1,694	2	0	0	0	2	52	8	43	1	0
	Westwood	1,832	4	0	0	3	1	85	15	64	6	0
	Wichita	358,294	3,386	41	269	557	2,519	20,756	4,357	14,263	2,136	189
	Yates Center	1,451	2	0	1	0	1	37	4	30	3	0
KENTUCKY	Adairville	937	0	0	0	0	0	4	4	0	0	1
	Albany	2,323	2	0	0	0	2	13	3	9	1	0
	Alexandria	7,948	16	0	0	0	16	168	19	132	17	0
	Anchorage	2,804	3	0	0	0	3	42	10	29	3	0
	Auburn	1,509	3	0	0	0	3	18	4	12	2	0
	Audubon Park	1,568	6	0	0	2	4	35	10	23	2	0
	Barbourville	3,561	2	0	0	1	1	24	6	15	3	0
	Bardstown	11,158	31	0	7	4	20	327	61	250	16	0
	Beattyville	1,135	1	0	0	0	1	10	4	6	0	0
	Bellefonte	846	0	0	0	0	0	4	1	3	0	0
	Benham	547	0	0	0	0	0	1	1	0	0	0
	Berea	13,946	22	0	3	8	11	399	101	274	24	0
	Bloomfield	887	0	0	0	0	0	2	1	1	0	0
	Bowling Green	53,663	348	1	49	87	211	2,739	545	2,072	122	3
	Burnside	681	1	0	0	0	1	22	4	17	1	0
	Butler	648	0	0	0	0	0	3	2	1	0	0
	Cadiz	2,604	8	0	0	2	6	84	20	60	4	0
	Calhoun	803	3	0	0	0	3	6	3	3	0	0

[1] The FBI does not publish arson data unless it receives data from either the agency or the state for all 12 months of the calendar year.

Table 8.   Offenses Known to Law Enforcement, by State and City, 2007 *(Contd.)*

(Number.)

State	City	Population	Violent crime	Murder and non-negligent man-slaughter	Forcible rape	Robbery	Aggravated assault	Property crime	Burglary	Larceny-theft	Motor vehicle theft	Arson[1]
	Campbellsville	10,957	29	0	3	9	17	414	100	298	16	1
	Carlisle	2,133	3	0	0	0	3	14	7	6	1	0
	Carrollton	3,888	16	1	3	4	8	124	27	92	5	0
	Cave City	2,088	6	0	0	2	4	58	13	40	5	1
	Central City	5,763	6	1	0	2	3	40	4	31	5	0
	Clay City	1,365	1	0	0	0	1	43	16	26	1	0
	Clinton	1,331	1	0	0	0	1	7	2	5	0	0
	Cold Spring	5,758	23	0	0	3	20	175	10	159	6	0
	Columbia	4,195	7	0	3	2	2	61	18	38	5	0
	Corbin	8,344	25	0	2	3	20	352	74	254	24	0
	Covington[5]	42,682	385	1	44	191	149		659	1,357		0
	Crescent Springs	3,988	9	0	0	5	4	132	15	110	7	0
	Cynthiana	6,291	16	0	2	3	11	323	70	233	20	0
	Danville	15,377	53	0	7	24	22	507	113	370	24	0
	Dawson Springs	2,947	4	0	3	0	1	32	11	18	3	0
	Earlington	1,593	2	0	1	0	1	7	1	5	1	0
	Edmonton	1,624	0	0	0	0	0	4	2	2	0	0
	Elizabethtown	23,547	86	1	18	23	44	1,039	173	823	43	0
	Elkton	1,962	6	0	5	0	1	30	8	18	4	0
	Elsmere	7,848	16	0	2	8	6	127	31	81	15	0
	Eminence	2,264	4	0	0	0	4	28	4	23	1	0
	Erlanger	16,986	27	0	4	16	7	345	72	258	15	0
	Evarts	1,056	4	0	1	0	3	11	1	9	1	0
	Falmouth	2,129	6	0	1	0	5	68	27	38	3	0
	Flatwoods	7,647	3	0	1	1	1	88	43	32	13	0
	Fleming-Neon	805	0	0	0	0	0	7	0	5	2	0
	Flemingsburg	3,105	2	0	1	0	1	34	10	22	2	0
	Florence	27,405	220	0	13	44	163	1,302	173	1,032	97	3
	Fort Thomas	15,266	11	1	2	2	6	214	38	155	21	0
	Fort Wright	5,379	17	0	1	12	4	283	25	249	9	0
	Franklin	8,101	32	1	7	16	8	268	57	198	13	0
	Fulton	2,435	18	1	3	5	9	116	22	84	10	0
	Georgetown	20,997	48	0	12	12	24	956	176	720	60	0
	Glasgow	14,282	24	2	3	2	17	232	62	163	7	0
	Glencoe	251	0	0	0	0	0	7	1	6	0	0
	Graymoor-Devondale	3,008	4	0	1	1	2	48	11	33	4	0
	Greensburg	2,408	0	0	0	0	0	6	3	3	0	0
	Greenville	4,258	3	0	1	0	2	10	5	3	2	0
	Guthrie	1,441	1	0	1	0	0	9	6	3	0	0
	Hardinsburg	2,466	1	0	0	0	1	0	0	0	0	0
	Harlan	1,893	8	0	0	3	5	115	21	93	1	0
	Harrodsburg	8,164	15	0	2	7	6	161	49	92	20	1
	Hartford	2,685	1	0	0	0	1	41	6	30	5	0
	Hawesville	983	0	0	0	0	0	1	1	0	0	0
	Hazard	4,862	7	0	0	0	7	242	48	185	9	0
	Heritage Creek	1,654	0	0	0	0	0	10	5	4	1	0
	Hickman	2,253	4	0	1	0	3	70	16	49	5	0
	Hillview	7,506	10	1	1	1	7	127	31	84	12	1
	Hodgenville	2,781	?	0	1	0	1	17	6	9	2	0
	Horse Cave	2,345	2	0	0	0	2	10	2	7	1	0
	Independence	21,038	18	0	4	1	13	333	84	227	22	0
	Indian Hills	3,149	2	0	1	1	0	32	9	21	2	0
	Inez	450	0	0	0	0	0	3	1	2	0	0
	Irvine	2,699	9	0	1	2	6	112	38	68	6	0
	Irvington	1,421	0	0	0	0	0	2	0	2	0	0
	Jackson	2,401	0	0	0	0	0	46	16	27	3	1
	Jamestown	1,738	3	0	0	0	3	47	11	35	1	0
	Jeffersontown	25,837	48	1	8	24	15	584	120	385	79	1
	Jenkins	2,288	1	0	0	0	1	21	7	12	2	0
	La Grange	6,238	4	0	2	2	0	183	48	129	6	0
	Lakeside Park-Crestvie	6,205	0	0	0	0	0	94	12	79	3	0
	Lancaster	4,452	5	0	0	1	4	75	21	54	0	0
	Lawrenceburg	9,710	13	0	1	3	9	139	37	101	1	0
	Lebanon	5,980	17	0	2	0	15	244	69	162	13	0
	Lebanon Junction	1,994	2	0	0	1	1	69	23	42	4	2
	Leitchfield	6,561	2	0	0	0	2	77	24	45	8	1
	Lewisburg	924	0	0	0	0	0	2	1	1	0	0
	Lewisport	1,658	3	0	0	2	1	14	4	10	0	0
	Lexington	272,815	1,790	16	111	550	1,113	9,349	2,114	6,623	612	30
	London	7,922	21	0	1	9	11	529	78	415	36	0
	Lone Oak	437	0	0	0	0	0	7	6	1	0	0
	Louisa	2,076	2	0	0	1	1	16	4	11	1	0
	Louisville Metro	624,030	4,238	71	194	1,910	2,063	29,543	7,588	18,772	3,183	214
	Lynch	838	0	0	0	0	0	15	5	10	0	0

[1] The FBI does not publish arson data unless it receives data from either the agency or the state for all 12 months of the calendar year.

[5] The FBI determined that the agency's data were underreported. Consequently, affected data are not included in this table.

Table 8.   Offenses Known to Law Enforcement, by State and City, 2007 *(Contd.)*

(Number.)

State	City	Population	Violent crime	Murder and non-negligent man-slaughter	Forcible rape	Robbery	Aggravated assault	Property crime	Burglary	Larceny-theft	Motor vehicle theft	Arson[1]
	Lynnview	980	0	0	0	0	0	8	2	5	1	0
	Manchester	1,945	6	1	0	0	5	26	4	14	8	0
	Marion	3,022	1	0	0	0	1	51	13	35	3	0
	Maysville	9,205	31	1	6	5	19	583	152	407	24	0
	McKee	864	1	0	0	0	1	10	2	7	1	0
	Millersburg	872	0	0	0	0	0	12	8	4	0	0
	Monticello	6,120	3	0	0	1	2	185	51	128	6	0
	Morganfield	3,365	12	0	3	2	7	114	15	94	5	0
	Mortons Gap	953	0	0	0	0	0	3	1	0	2	0
	Mount Sterling	6,569	21	0	3	6	12	412	68	321	23	0
	Mount Vernon	2,622	2	0	0	2	0	42	11	28	3	3
	Mount Washington	12,334	4	0	1	0	3	136	44	80	12	0
	Muldraugh	1,309	0	0	0	0	0	9	3	6	0	0
	Munfordville	1,624	2	0	1	0	1	27	7	19	1	0
	Murray	15,811	28	0	7	8	13	675	124	532	19	0
	New Castle	932	0	0	0	0	0	12	4	6	2	0
	Newport	15,540	95	3	18	53	21	1,137	168	856	113	5
	Nicholasville	25,495	61	0	11	22	28	1,098	226	810	62	0
	Nortonville	1,250	0	0	0	0	0	2	0	2	0	0
	Oak Grove	7,303	33	0	2	13	18	337	94	220	23	0
	Olive Hill	1,823	2	0	1	0	1	23	14	7	2	0
	Owenton	1,491	0	0	0	0	0	12	3	7	2	0
	Owingsville	1,596	0	0	0	0	0	45	10	33	2	0
	Paintsville	4,176	4	0	0	0	4	98	12	76	10	0
	Paris	9,329	26	1	1	9	15	230	51	168	11	0
	Park Hills	2,748	0	0	0	0	0	16	6	5	5	0
	Pewee Valley	1,598	0	0	0	0	0	8	5	3	0	0
	Pikeville	6,331	11	0	2	3	6	381	32	334	15	0
	Pineville	1,997	3	0	0	2	1	52	7	39	6	0
	Pioneer Village	2,687	0	0	0	0	0	18	6	11	1	0
	Powderly	892	0	0	0	0	0	50	12	38	0	0
	Prestonsburg	3,850	11	0	0	0	11	124	18	101	5	0
	Princeton	6,402	16	0	0	4	12	171	56	104	11	0
	Prospect	5,044	1	0	0	1	0	5	3	1	1	0
	Providence	3,521	3	0	0	0	3	30	14	14	2	0
	Raceland	2,548	0	0	0	0	0	18	4	13	1	0
	Radcliff[4]	21,560		1	18	21		583	155	395	33	1
	Russell	3,598	1	0	0	1	0	127	16	102	9	0
	Russell Springs	2,573	4	0	0	1	3	103	28	70	5	0
	Science Hill	658	0	0	0	0	0	5	3	1	1	0
	Scottsville	4,567	2	0	1	0	1	33	15	14	4	0
	Shelbyville	11,101	46	0	3	22	21	410	107	277	26	0
	Shepherdsville	9,123	14	1	2	4	7	513	90	408	15	0
	Shively	15,621	111	1	3	85	22	754	197	453	104	2
	Silver Grove	1,158	0	0	0	0	0	9	4	5	0	0
	Smiths Grove	741	1	0	0	1	0	7	3	3	1	0
	Somerset	12,344	27	0	6	8	13	572	89	468	15	0
	Southgate	3,291	0	0	0	0	0	38	6	31	1	0
	Springfield	2,845	6	0	1	2	3	63	27	34	2	0
	Stanford	3,467	3	0	0	1	2	20	4	15	1	0
	St. Matthews	17,676	45	0	2	28	15	728	128	562	38	0
	Sturgis	1,967	2	0	1	0	1	20	5	15	0	0
	Taylor Mill	6,682	6	0	1	3	2	77	17	51	9	0
	Taylorsville	1,226	2	0	0	0	2	33	6	20	7	0
	Tompkinsville	2,656	5	0	0	3	2	53	23	25	5	0
	Uniontown	1,046	1	0	0	0	1	5	3	2	0	0
	Vanceburg	1,722	1	0	1	0	0	22	1	18	3	0
	Villa Hills	7,672	1	0	0	1	0	32	3	28	1	0
	Vine Grove	3,915	5	0	0	0	5	73	26	46	1	0
	Warsaw	1,832	9	0	0	0	9	26	10	15	1	0
	West Liberty	3,362	0	0	0	0	0	44	5	35	4	0
	West Point	992	0	0	0	0	0	10	1	6	3	0
	Whitesburg	1,504	0	0	0	0	0	16	0	15	1	0
	Wilder	3,037	2	0	0	1	1	61	7	52	2	0
	Williamsburg	5,192	13	0	2	5	6	77	15	56	6	0
	Williamstown	3,465	2	0	0	0	2	108	35	66	7	0
	Wilmore	5,862	4	0	0	1	3	77	13	61	3	1
	Winchester	16,515	30	1	3	9	17	775	170	582	23	3
	Worthington	1,686	0	0	0	0	0	10	4	6	0	0
LOUISIANA	Addis	3,145	9	0	0	0	9	5	0	4	1	0
	Alexandria	45,720	1,065	8	16	175	866	4,246	1,099	2,966	181	0
	Baker	13,600	51	2	4	12	33	729	151	535	43	3
	Basile	2,392	4	0	0	0	4	15	3	12	0	0
	Baton Rouge	228,446	2,615	71	72	1,015	1,457	13,643	3,847	8,617	1,179	210

[1] The FBI does not publish arson data unless it receives data from either the agency or the state for all 12 months of the calendar year.

[4] It was determined that the agency did not follow national Uniform Crime Reporting (UCR) Program guidelines for reporting an offense. Consequently, this figure is not included in this table.

Table 8. Offenses Known to Law Enforcement, by State and City, 2007 *(Contd.)*

(Number.)

State	City	Population	Violent crime	Murder and non-negligent man-slaughter	Forcible rape	Robbery	Aggravated assault	Property crime	Burglary	Larceny-theft	Motor vehicle theft	Arson[1]
	Bernice	1,677	7	1	0	0	6	15	5	10	0	0
	Berwick	4,312	30	0	0	0	30	37	15	20	2	0
	Bogalusa	12,927	201	3	11	35	152	888	259	550	79	4
	Bossier City	61,993	1,146	2	34	88	1,022	2,692	426	2,068	198	15
	Breaux Bridge	8,047	32	0	2	3	27	31	15	14	2	0
	Clinton	1,907	32	1	0	0	31	72	18	47	7	0
	Coushatta	2,166	12	0	0	1	11	84	22	57	5	0
	Covington	9,745	67	0	1	13	53	320	69	232	19	1
	Crowley	13,992	86	0	8	9	69	680	270	392	18	0
	Denham Springs	10,552	145	0	5	29	111	1,085	226	832	27	0
	De Quincy	3,192	11	0	1	0	10	152	40	107	5	1
	De Ridder	10,143	26	0	1	1	24	172	48	123	1	0
	Elton	1,252	11	0	1	2	8	60	25	35	0	1
	Eunice	11,621	47	0	1	9	37	697	113	548	36	0
	Farmerville	3,567	42	0	3	1	38	188	60	128	0	1
	Franklin	7,794	96	0	2	9	85	526	60	453	13	2
	Franklinton	3,723	48	0	2	8	38	293	52	229	12	0
	French Settlement	1,100	2	1	0	0	1	7	0	7	0	0
	Golden Meadow	2,158	2	0	0	0	2	10	1	8	1	1
	Gonzales	9,067	54	1	3	12	38	376	31	315	30	0
	Gramercy	6,946	33	0	2	2	29	133	14	113	6	2
	Gretna	16,240	165	4	10	52	99	868	215	543	110	0
	Harahan	9,212	21	0	0	4	17	187	37	138	12	13
	Haughton	2,997	22	0	0	0	22	4	0	4	0	0
	Houma	32,597	340	4	16	65	255	1,489	235	1,182	72	7
	Iowa	2,565	15	0	0	1	14	124	28	88	8	0
	Jackson	3,714	31	0	0	0	31	73	11	61	1	0
	Jeanerette	6,015	19	0	1	3	15	105	23	79	3	0
	Jennings	10,577	81	2	3	14	62	512	112	361	39	2
	Kenner	66,473	388	10	14	124	240	2,760	597	1,859	304	24
	Kentwood	2,302	6	0	1	0	5	256	36	214	6	0
	Kinder	2,148	31	0	3	0	28	75	5	64	6	0
	Lafayette	114,212	1,293	15	68	319	891	7,118	1,410	5,152	556	28
	Lake Arthur	2,894	8	0	2	3	3	96	16	74	6	0
	Mamou	3,443	36	0	1	2	33	139	14	117	8	1
	Mandeville	12,346	38	0	4	4	30	426	58	358	10	1
	Monroe	51,350	343	1	20	101	221	5,096	1,141	3,792	163	
	Moreauville	944	5	0	0	0	5	21	7	13	1	0
	Morgan City	11,810	74	0	4	19	51	501	115	356	30	0
	New Orleans	220,614	3,451	209	115	1,154	1,973	15,583	5,039	7,354	3,190	
	Olla	1,352	5	0	1	0	4	38	11	27	0	0
	Pearl River	2,170	21	0	0	2	19	106	14	88	4	0
	Pineville	14,540	58	0	7	8	43	716	170	500	46	0
	Plaquemine	6,627	115	7	1	6	101	353	50	294	9	2
	Ponchatoula	6,244	89	0	2	11	76	651	204	417	30	0
	Port Allen	5,136	31	1	1	4	25	201	43	126	32	2
	Ruston	20,532	100	0	0	26	74	823	211	598	14	0
	Shreveport	199,811	2,198	36	112	544	1,506	12,178	2,861	8,216	1,101	111
	Slidell	28,272	143	0	11	23	109	2,137	285	1,696	156	0
	Sterlington	1,240	1	0	0	0	1	20	4	16	0	0
	Tallulah	7,883	102	4	1	8	89	334	118	210	6	1
	Thibodaux	14,501	120	1	10	21	88	679	126	539	14	0
	Tickfaw	687	1	0	0	0	1	43	4	38	1	0
	Vinton	3,131	21	0	1	1	19	200	38	148	14	1
	Westlake	4,526	20	0	2	0	18	166	26	127	13	0
	West Monroe	12,989	99	0	2	15	82	1,040	193	812	35	3
	Westwego	9,957	43	0	3	7	33	312	74	215	23	2
	Winnfield	5,183	16	0	0	1	15	154	13	141	0	0
	Zachary	13,428	39	1	4	7	27	183	22	144	17	0
MAINE	Ashland	1,460	3	0	0	2	1	4	4	0	0	0
	Auburn	23,150	29	2	6	10	11	817	152	633	32	3
	Augusta	18,572	69	1	15	10	43	1,138	183	931	24	11
	Baileyville	1,593	1	0	0	0	1	72	22	49	1	0
	Bangor	30,940	46	1	4	24	17	1,905	208	1,655	42	3
	Bar Harbor	5,197	4	0	2	0	2	25	7	18	0	1
	Bath	9,175	5	0	3	0	2	284	25	255	4	0
	Belfast	6,866	6	0	1	1	4	268	31	233	4	1
	Berwick	7,603	11	0	6	1	4	105	29	67	9	3
	Bethel	2,671	1	0	1	0	0	32	8	23	1	0
	Biddeford	22,079	77	0	28	21	28	1,050	160	845	45	5
	Boothbay Harbor	2,340	2	0	1	0	1	62	14	44	4	0
	Brewer	9,101	4	0	0	2	2	429	37	381	11	2
	Bridgton	5,325	6	0	0	2	4	140	44	89	7	1
	Brownville	1,306	6	0	1	0	5	45	18	27	0	0

[1] The FBI does not publish arson data unless it receives data from either the agency or the state for all 12 months of the calendar year.

Table 8.   Offenses Known to Law Enforcement, by State and City, 2007 *(Contd.)*

(Number.)

State	City	Population	Violent crime	Murder and non-negligent man-slaughter	Forcible rape	Robbery	Aggravated assault	Property crime	Burglary	Larceny-theft	Motor vehicle theft	Arson[1]
	Brunswick	22,048	18	0	12	1	5	428	59	352	17	8
	Bucksport	4,969	13	0	1	0	12	83	14	69	0	0
	Buxton	8,284	4	0	0	1	3	119	41	72	6	4
	Calais	3,253	26	0	0	0	26	185	18	166	1	0
	Camden	5,327	3	0	0	0	3	109	22	85	2	0
	Cape Elizabeth	8,806	3	0	0	0	3	112	26	75	11	0
	Caribou	8,279	5	0	0	4	1	240	61	169	10	0
	Carrabassett Valley	467	1	0	1	0	0	106	9	97	0	0
	Clinton	3,400	3	0	2	0	1	51	17	33	1	0
	Cumberland	7,728	1	0	1	0	0	37	9	20	8	1
	Damariscotta	1,965	7	0	6	1	0	60	2	58	0	0
	Dexter	3,720	9	0	2	1	6	176	59	111	6	0
	Dixfield	2,564	5	0	2	0	3	58	14	39	5	0
	Dover-Foxcroft	4,391	19	0	3	0	16	166	26	135	5	1
	East Millinocket	3,171	1	0	0	0	1	11	1	10	0	0
	Eastport	1,575	0	0	0	0	0	12	0	10	2	1
	Eliot	6,453	3	0	0	0	3	60	10	47	3	0
	Ellsworth	7,165	4	0	2	1	1	331	23	293	15	0
	Fairfield	6,808	10	1	4	3	2	301	64	222	15	2
	Falmouth	10,591	3	0	1	1	1	146	17	129	0	0
	Farmington	7,603	15	0	8	3	4	246	20	220	6	0
	Fort Fairfield	3,510	11	0	0	0	11	30	5	24	1	0
	Fort Kent	4,202	2	0	0	0	2	51	8	43	0	0
	Freeport	8,190	3	0	2	1	0	159	22	132	5	0
	Fryeburg	3,363	2	0	0	0	2	29	4	25	0	0
	Gardiner	6,174	6	0	3	2	1	107	29	78	0	1
	Gorham	15,593	12	0	1	0	11	201	80	113	8	2
	Gouldsboro	2,040	1	0	1	0	0	12	4	8	0	0
	Greenville	1,759	3	0	1	0	2	47	8	37	2	0
	Hallowell	2,521	1	0	0	0	1	55	22	33	0	0
	Hampden	6,847	4	0	2	1	1	107	11	94	2	0
	Holden	2,961	0	0	0	0	0	63	16	46	1	3
	Houlton	6,258	10	0	5	1	4	154	38	114	2	0
	Jay	4,847	0	0	0	0	0	69	20	47	2	2
	Kennebunk	11,658	4	0	1	1	2	188	30	155	3	0
	Kennebunkport	4,070	2	0	1	0	1	45	4	40	1	1
	Kittery	10,645	8	0	1	4	3	171	32	135	4	1
	Lewiston	35,747	97	2	23	34	38	1,117	260	813	44	9
	Limestone	2,298	4	1	0	1	2	11	10	1	0	0
	Lincoln	5,235	1	0	0	0	1	40	7	30	3	0
	Lisbon	9,474	3	0	1	0	2	161	42	115	4	3
	Livermore Falls	3,200	5	0	3	1	1	78	17	60	1	1
	Machias	2,191	6	0	0	1	5	55	9	45	1	2
	Madawaska	4,402	0	0	0	0	0	51	11	38	2	0
	Madison	4,673	2	0	1	0	1	98	14	83	1	2
	Mechanic Falls	3,256	1	0	0	0	1	50	15	32	3	0
	Mexico	2,932	7	0	2	1	4	113	27	77	9	1
	Milbridge	1,316	1	0	0	0	1	27	4	23	0	0
	Millinocket	4,927	2	0	0	0	2	77	13	61	3	0
	Milo	2,414	30	0	0	0	30	103	25	71	7	3
	Monmouth	3,849	3	0	1	0	2	60	17	40	3	0
	Mount Desert	2,214	0	0	0	0	0	35	1	32	2	1
	Newport	3,106	2	0	0	1	1	121	21	98	2	1
	North Berwick	4,911	0	0	0	0	0	4	2	2	0	1
	Norway	4,846	8	0	6	0	2	138	22	110	6	2
	Oakland	6,239	4	0	1	2	1	113	26	86	1	1
	Ogunquit	1,295	0	0	0	0	0	44	3	40	1	0
	Old Orchard Beach	9,423	13	0	3	3	7	278	62	199	17	4
	Old Town	7,704	2	0	0	1	1	225	35	185	5	0
	Orono	9,737	6	0	2	1	3	174	22	149	3	1
	Oxford	3,954	4	0	3	0	1	163	24	135	4	0
	Paris	5,048	2	0	1	1	0	84	17	62	5	1
	Phippsburg	2,205	0	0	0	0	0	10	4	6	0	0
	Pittsfield	4,296	2	0	0	1	1	106	24	77	5	0
	Portland	62,894	231	1	25	103	102	3,079	562	2,356	161	16
	Presque Isle	9,217	11	0	4	4	3	288	38	241	9	3
	Rangeley	1,168	4	0	1	0	3	32	11	18	3	0
	Richmond	3,440	1	0	0	0	1	25	7	18	0	0
	Rockland	7,582	13	0	5	3	5	406	24	375	7	0
	Rockport	3,590	0	0	0	0	0	26	0	26	0	0
	Rumford	6,405	20	0	11	1	8	215	43	169	3	1
	Sabattus	4,702	7	0	2	1	4	52	18	27	7	0
	Saco	18,509	19	1	8	5	5	588	104	463	21	3
	Sanford	21,648	40	1	14	11	14	798	151	608	39	12

[1] The FBI does not publish arson data unless it receives data from either the agency or the state for all 12 months of the calendar year.

Table 8.   Offenses Known to Law Enforcement, by State and City, 2007 *(Contd.)*

(Number.)

State	City	Population	Violent crime	Murder and non-negligent man-slaughter	Forcible rape	Robbery	Aggravated assault	Property crime	Burglary	Larceny-theft	Motor vehicle theft	Arson[1]
	Scarborough	19,187	12	0	0	5	7	343	60	268	15	2
	Searsport	2,668	1	0	1	0	0	75	20	51	4	0
	Skowhegan	8,876	12	0	6	2	4	320	58	256	6	5
	South Berwick	7,350	4	0	2	1	1	73	18	51	4	0
	South Portland	23,836	36	0	5	10	21	1,010	114	869	27	4
	Southwest Harbor	1,982	0	0	0	0	0	62	3	58	1	0
	Swan's Island	311	0	0	0	0	0	0	0	0	0	0
	Thomaston	4,203	4	0	0	0	4	65	6	57	2	0
	Topsham	10,073	3	0	1	1	1	213	19	187	7	0
	Van Buren	2,520	0	0	0	0	0	8	5	3	0	0
	Veazie	1,873	0	0	0	0	0	21	2	17	2	0
	Waldoboro	5,123	1	0	0	0	1	141	44	93	4	1
	Washburn	1,616	1	0	0	0	1	32	9	23	0	0
	Waterville	15,631	33	0	14	9	10	736	130	588	18	2
	Wells	10,142	6	1	1	1	3	177	36	139	2	3
	Westbrook	16,188	44	1	11	10	22	542	111	411	20	1
	Wilton	4,210	21	0	1	2	18	106	35	69	2	2
	Windham	16,814	16	0	6	1	9	395	80	299	16	3
	Winslow	7,979	9	0	7	0	2	153	46	103	4	0
	Winter Harbor	973	2	0	1	0	1	8	0	7	1	0
	Winthrop	6,514	3	0	0	1	2	84	21	57	6	0
	Wiscasset	3,904	1	0	0	0	1	59	15	43	1	0
	Yarmouth	8,106	5	0	1	2	2	67	9	55	3	3
	York	13,384	8	0	3	0	5	201	41	154	6	1
MARYLAND	Aberdeen	14,187	115	0	4	41	70	702	98	567	37	3
	Annapolis	36,462	448	8	5	186	249	1,787	412	1,180	195	17
	Baltimore	624,237	10,182	282	146	3,895	5,859	29,939	7,381	16,742	5,816	407
	Baltimore City Sheriff	0	0	0	0	0	0	0	0	0	0	0
	Bel Air	10,074	87	0	4	14	69	396	49	326	21	2
	Berlin	3,812	7	0	1	3	3	162	16	145	1	0
	Berwyn Heights	3,045	16	0	0	10	6	101	16	60	25	0
	Bladensburg	7,849	106	1	2	60	43	592	99	314	179	0
	Boonsboro	3,286	2	0	0	2	0	24	7	16	1	0
	Brunswick	5,282	11	0	2	0	9	79	16	60	3	1
	Cambridge	11,479	117	3	2	39	73	702	129	558	15	7
	Capitol Heights	4,259	7	0	2	3	2	47	14	17	16	0
	Centreville	3,099	2	0	0	0	2	64	19	43	2	1
	Chestertown	4,942	39	0	2	9	28	162	37	124	1	1
	Cheverly	6,614	36	0	1	26	9	232	44	122	66	0
	Chevy Chase Village	2,779	2	0	0	2	0	34	5	27	2	1
	Cottage City	1,166	5	0	0	3	2	49	3	32	14	0
	Crisfield	2,804	12	0	1	4	7	147	22	119	6	0
	Cumberland	20,654	180	0	7	35	138	1,266	293	935	38	10
	Delmar	2,590	23	1	2	3	17	132	35	89	8	0
	Denton	3,602	22	0	2	6	14	201	33	155	13	0
	District Heights	6,253	33	3	0	10	20	210	55	115	40	0
	Easton	14,249	74	0	3	15	56	603	85	507	11	1
	Edmonston	1,381	5	1	0	1	3	79	10	46	23	0
	Elkton	15,228	215	1	2	62	150	1,095	279	730	86	10
	Fairmount Heights	1,554	0	0	0	0	0	27	3	15	9	0
	Federalsburg	2,647	22	0	4	3	15	181	56	115	10	0
	Forest Heights	2,656	5	0	0	2	3	54	22	26	6	0
	Frederick	59,731	418	5	20	104	289	1,806	275	1,417	114	29
	Frostburg	7,809	15	0	3	0	12	206	55	146	5	1
	Fruitland	4,193	66	0	0	7	59	237	41	186	10	0
	Glenarden	6,340	6	0	1	3	2	38	10	16	12	0
	Greenbelt	22,090	210	2	10	132	66	1,170	130	768	272	0
	Greensboro	2,016	9	0	0	0	9	46	15	27	4	0
	Hagerstown	39,263	223	2	11	99	111	1,601	270	1,214	117	29
	Hampstead	5,535	1	0	0	0	1	137	14	119	4	1
	Hancock	1,721	6	0	0	0	6	23	1	19	3	0
	Havre de Grace	12,584	60	0	1	9	50	381	64	297	20	2
	Hurlock	2,015	9	0	0	4	5	114	38	66	10	0
	Hyattsville	15,152	173	2	6	124	41	1,721	146	1,392	183	0
	Landover Hills	1,575	6	0	0	3	3	24	10	10	4	0
	La Plata	9,090	50	0	0	13	37	195	50	134	11	1
	Laurel	22,086	166	1	5	80	80	1,150	174	755	221	0
	Lonaconing	1,137	0	0	0	0	0	1	0	1	0	0
	Luke	74	0	0	0	0	0	0	0	0	0	0
	Manchester	3,609	1	0	0	1	0	55	27	24	4	2
	Morningside	1,305	6	0	0	6	0	58	5	34	19	0
	Mount Rainier	8,660	91	2	2	64	23	408	68	211	129	0
	New Carrollton	12,712	68	0	6	41	21	350	70	205	75	0
	North Brentwood	482	2	0	0	2	0	10	0	7	3	0

[1] The FBI does not publish arson data unless it receives data from either the agency or the state for all 12 months of the calendar year.

Table 8. Offenses Known to Law Enforcement, by State and City, 2007 *(Contd.)*

(Number.)

State	City	Population	Violent crime	Murder and non-negligent man-slaughter	Forcible rape	Robbery	Aggravated assault	Property crime	Burglary	Larceny-theft	Motor vehicle theft	Arson[1]
	North East	2,856	18	0	0	6	12	163	20	129	14	5
	Oakland	1,869	1	0	0	0	1	63	7	53	3	0
	Ocean City	7,005	142	0	15	43	84	1,295	189	1,067	39	9
	Ocean Pines	11,134	7	0	2	0	5	163	40	115	8	0
	Oxford	735	0	0	0	0	0	8	1	7	0	0
	Perryville	3,826	17	0	1	4	12	148	21	120	7	6
	Pocomoke City	3,863	29	0	3	6	20	243	36	206	1	0
	Port Deposit	704	1	0	0	0	1	20	4	16	0	0
	Preston	647	1	0	0	0	1	16	4	12	0	0
	Princess Anne	2,934	43	0	2	8	33	159	38	109	12	2
	Ridgely	1,485	5	0	0	0	5	47	5	37	5	0
	Rising Sun	1,821	5	0	0	0	5	85	18	65	2	0
	Riverdale Park	6,584	104	0	1	55	48	371	63	223	85	0
	Rock Hall	1,424	1	0	0	0	1	30	10	18	2	0
	Salisbury	27,727	503	2	24	182	295	2,390	583	1,704	103	13
	Seat Pleasant	5,020	57	0	2	26	29	252	38	143	71	0
	Smithsburg	3,031	5	0	1	0	4	42	7	34	1	0
	Snow Hill	2,278	11	0	2	0	9	43	13	28	2	1
	St. Michaels	1,088	6	0	0	2	4	62	19	42	1	0
	Sykesville	4,499	2	0	1	0	1	44	10	32	2	5
	Takoma Park	18,539	131	1	4	83	43	699	140	432	127	2
	Taneytown	5,533	3	0	1	1	1	122	9	109	4	3
	Thurmont	6,092	16	0	0	1	15	55	6	40	9	0
	Trappe	1,179	2	0	1	0	1	10	0	9	1	0
	University Park	2,379	3	0	0	3	0	55	14	33	8	0
	Upper Marlboro	681	6	0	0	0	6	25	3	20	2	0
	Westernport	1,971	5	0	1	0	4	54	13	41	0	0
	Westminster	18,036	118	0	0	12	106	739	129	572	38	10
MASSACHUSETTS	Abington	16,673	43	0	2	8	33	316	114	181	21	3
	Acton	20,619	30	0	3	4	23	283	34	243	6	0
	Acushnet	10,575	20	0	3	1	16	170	81	77	12	3
	Adams	8,316	37	0	1	4	32	265	65	189	11	0
	Agawam	28,573	41	0	4	8	29	428	138	248	42	3
	Amesbury	16,551	41	0	3	3	35	239	53	175	11	2
	Amherst	33,913	81	0	14	5	62	391	194	163	34	3
	Andover	33,615	21	0	4	1	16	396	52	316	28	4
	Aquinnah	356	0	0	0	0	0	2	1	1	0	0
	Arlington	40,902	64	1	6	11	46	638	231	371	36	15
	Ashburnham	6,065	16	0	3	1	12	68	36	29	3	0
	Ashfield	1,826	5	1	0	0	4	12	5	7	0	
	Ashland	15,818	26	0	5	5	16	84	25	50	9	2
	Athol	11,721	50	0	4	1	45	183	89	88	6	3
	Attleboro	43,474	139	0	8	25	106	962	243	613	106	4
	Auburn[8]	16,445		0	5	7		528	72	418	38	2
	Avon[8]	4,310		0	0	1		181	26	150	5	
	Ayer	7,306	25	0	3	2	20	151	66	81	4	8
	Barnstable	47,342	301	2	17	25	257	1,252	439	717	96	6
	Barre	5,467	15	0	1	2	12	89	18	67	4	1
	Becket	1,804	1	0	0	0	1	48	33	14	1	0
	Bedford	12,862	1	0	0	0	1	179	35	143	1	0
	Belchertown	14,268	21	0	2	0	19	189	68	108	13	1
	Bellingham	15,965	30	0	1	7	22	309	47	244	18	1
	Belmont	23,184	25	0	5	4	16	242	71	156	15	1
	Berkley	6,494	15	0	2	2	11	51	30	18	3	0
	Berlin	2,771	0	0	0	0	0	29	3	26	0	0
	Beverly	39,493	106	0	10	15	81	668	111	521	36	4
	Billerica	41,568	40	0	4	7	29	589	74	478	37	1
	Blackstone	9,067	13	0	1	5	7	121	35	66	20	0
	Bolton	4,517	3	0	1	0	2	37	10	23	4	1
	Boston	591,855	6,837	65	263	2,242	4,267	24,579	3,810	17,351	3,418	
	Bourne	19,308	80	0	3	5	72	674	288	353	33	11
	Boxborough	5,106	8	0	1	0	7	37	6	28	3	2
	Boxford	8,155	1	0	0	0	1	62	17	43	2	0
	Boylston	4,295	0	0	0	0	0	27	4	22	1	0
	Braintree	34,147	107	1	2	25	79	921	115	761	45	1
	Brewster	10,158	19	0	1	0	18	127	25	99	3	1
	Bridgewater	25,767	37	0	5	4	28	186	41	131	14	2
	Brimfield	3,744	5	0	0	0	5	6	0	3	3	0
	Brockton[8]	94,180		11	42	199		3,321	695	2,163	463	22
	Brookline	54,976	129	0	1	36	92	1,008	161	809	38	
	Burlington	24,978	39	0	2	10	27	881	258	595	28	1
	Cambridge[7]	101,161	421	0	12	148	261	3,616	662	2,718	236	9
	Canton	21,890	60	0	5	2	53	261	44	202	15	1
	Carver[8]	11,639		0	1	4		92	41	41	10	2

[1] The FBI does not publish arson data unless it receives data from either the agency or the state for all 12 months of the calendar year.

[7] Because of changes in the state/local agency's reporting practices, figures are not comparable to previous years' data.

[8] The data collection methodology for the offense of aggravated assault used by this agency does not comply with national UCR Program guidelines. Consequently, the figures for aggravated assault and violent crime (of which aggravated assault is a part) are not included in this table.

Table 8.   Offenses Known to Law Enforcement, by State and City, 2007 (Contd.)

(Number.)

State	City	Population	Violent crime	Murder and non-negligent man-slaughter	Forcible rape	Robbery	Aggravated assault	Property crime	Burglary	Larceny-theft	Motor vehicle theft	Arson[1]
	Charlemont	1,381	2	0	0	0	2	7	2	5	0	0
	Charlton	12,765	21	0	0	0	21	134	43	75	16	0
	Chatham	6,811	9	0	0	1	8	161	28	131	2	0
	Chelmsford	33,740	44	1	1	6	36	520	63	438	19	0
	Chelsea	32,439	607	2	19	207	379	1,334	372	756	206	10
	Cheshire	3,335	0	0	0	0	0	9	6	2	1	
	Chicopee	54,414	305	0	32	52	221	1,735	474	1,055	206	3
	Clinton	14,247	11	0	1	1	9	135	39	85	11	0
	Cohasset	7,213	10	0	0	1	9	105	17	82	6	1
	Concord	16,766	13	0	1	0	12	240	58	178	4	1
	Dalton	6,627	20	0	3	0	17	79	20	54	5	2
	Danvers	25,979	58	0	7	11	40	919	65	809	45	2
	Dartmouth	31,465	106	0	7	17	82	1,157	188	907	62	6
	Dedham	23,653	30	0	0	7	23	573	63	481	29	0
	Deerfield	4,763	3	0	0	0	3	102	31	69	2	0
	Douglas	8,093	8	0	2	1	5	29	9	16	4	2
	Dover	5,650	3	0	0	1	2	20	7	13	0	0
	Dracut	29,444	33	0	6	6	21	271	106	152	13	1
	Dudley	10,951	14	2	0	0	12	50	27	21	2	0
	East Bridgewater	14,077	22	0	5	1	16	257	56	190	11	4
	East Brookfield	2,095	0	0	0	0	0	23	7	15	1	0
	Eastham	5,519	4	0	3	0	1	70	12	57	1	0
	Easthampton	16,082	35	0	2	1	32	172	55	99	18	4
	East Longmeadow	15,061	44	0	2	9	33	400	54	332	14	2
	Easton	23,142	14	0	0	3	11	201	54	131	16	0
	Egremont	1,364	5	0	0	1	4	29	9	20	0	0
	Erving	1,574	2	0	1	0	1	32	18	13	1	1
	Everett	36,826	188	1	11	57	119	1,239	289	782	168	1
	Fairhaven	16,268	75	1	1	15	58	564	140	404	20	5
	Falmouth	33,722	151	0	11	10	130	1,113	548	495	70	6
	Fitchburg[8]	40,180		0	21	39		1,015	293	645	77	9
	Foxborough	16,276	37	1	4	2	30	173	72	85	16	
	Framingham	64,482	107	0	3	29	75	1,380	211	1,018	151	
	Franklin	31,478	6	0	1	1	4	99	14	76	9	0
	Freetown	9,042	26	0	0	0	26	182	77	83	22	4
	Gardner	20,813	120	1	6	10	103	497	139	328	30	6
	Georgetown	8,210	5	0	0	0	5	45	14	30	1	
	Gloucester	30,597	28	0	5	4	19	538	82	445	11	1
	Goshen	965	0	0	0	0	0	6	4	2	0	0
	Grafton	17,750	13	1	0	0	12	125	41	73	11	0
	Granby	6,381	15	0	1	1	13	72	19	47	6	0
	Great Barrington	7,423	12	1	2	0	9	143	31	107	5	0
	Greenfield[8]	17,648		3	12	9		438	165	238	35	6
	Groton	10,737	3	0	0	0	3	31	10	21	0	0
	Groveland	6,863	4	0	1	0	3	41	8	31	2	0
	Hadley	4,817	7	0	0	4	3	197	42	146	9	0
	Halifax	7,834	10	0	2	1	7	73	15	51	7	0
	Hamilton	8,262	6	0	1	0	5	85	27	54	4	0
	Hampden	5,349	5	0	1	1	3	46	18	24	4	1
	Hanover	14,266	5	0	0	2	3	302	42	255	5	0
	Hanson[8]	10,054		0	5	3		158	44	103	11	3
	Hardwick	2,670	5	0	0	0	5	40	14	24	2	0
	Harvard	6,062	2	0	0	0	2	31	15	12	4	2
	Harwich	12,573	28	0	3	2	23	292	134	157	1	2
	Hatfield	3,266	0	0	0	0	0	12	4	7	1	0
	Haverhill	60,308	365	0	13	81	271	1,552	720	626	206	17
	Hingham	22,059	16	0	1	1	14	324	67	248	9	1
	Hinsdale[8]	1,782		0	0	0		1	1	0	0	0
	Holbrook	10,724	21	0	6	9	6	252	81	153	18	
	Holden	16,816	12	0	1	0	11	78	11	64	3	3
	Holliston	13,903	7	0	1	0	6	64	19	40	5	2
	Holyoke	39,769	497	2	45	54	396	2,203	421	1,569	213	15
	Hopedale	6,277	11	0	1	1	9	45	23	17	5	1
	Hopkinton	14,294	1	0	0	0	1	62	6	56	0	0
	Hubbardston	4,494	16	0	0	0	16	35	11	23	1	1
	Hudson	19,595	2	0	0	2	0	198	18	165	15	0
	Hull	11,261	40	0	1	3	36	142	56	76	10	4
	Ipswich	13,326	8	0	1	0	7	196	64	125	7	0
	Kingston	12,581	28	0	5	5	18	335	48	263	24	2
	Lakeville	10,770	13	1	0	1	11	188	72	110	6	2
	Lancaster	7,043	9	0	1	0	8	46	22	19	5	2
	Lawrence	70,462	506	4	15	128	359	1,676	451	817	408	
	Lee	5,842	14	0	0	0	14	31	3	25	3	0
	Leicester	11,077	27	0	4	1	22	178	35	128	15	1

[1] The FBI does not publish arson data unless it receives data from either the agency or the state for all 12 months of the calendar year.

[8] The data collection methodology for the offense of aggravated assault used by this agency does not comply with national UCR Program guidelines. Consequently, the figures for aggravated assault and violent crime (of which aggravated assault is a part) are not included in this table.

Table 8. Offenses Known to Law Enforcement, by State and City, 2007 *(Contd.)*

(Number.)

State	City	Population	Violent crime	Murder and non-negligent man-slaughter	Forcible rape	Robbery	Aggravated assault	Property crime	Burglary	Larceny-theft	Motor vehicle theft	Arson[1]
	Lenox	5,169	2	0	0	0	2	64	11	52	1	0
	Leominster[8]	41,602		0	11	28		1,169	204	881	84	5
	Lexington	30,220	16	0	2	1	13	333	65	262	6	1
	Lincoln	7,929	5	0	2	0	3	25	8	17	0	2
	Littleton	8,713	5	0	1	1	3	63	12	46	5	0
	Longmeadow	15,465	10	0	2	3	5	222	89	128	5	4
	Lowell	102,918	875	3	44	241	587	3,326	953	1,891	482	
	Ludlow	22,066	22	0	3	2	17	254	71	161	22	0
	Lunenburg	10,105	10	0	0	0	10	146	46	95	5	0
	Lynn	87,817	931	8	45	192	686	2,697	1,105	1,202	390	3
	Lynnfield	11,429	17	0	0	2	15	217	116	93	8	0
	Malden	55,538	258	1	4	87	166	1,530	387	979	164	0
	Mansfield	23,175	40	0	3	6	31	374	135	226	13	4
	Marblehead	20,194	28	0	1	2	25	241	33	197	11	0
	Marion	5,313	10	0	1	0	9	168	37	120	11	1
	Marlborough	38,227	32	0	4	10	18	609	108	457	44	1
	Marshfield	24,915	12	0	1	4	7	211	38	167	6	1
	Mashpee	14,552	45	0	4	4	37	354	105	232	17	2
	Mattapoisett	6,502	3	0	0	1	2	94	13	73	8	0
	Maynard	10,150	16	0	2	1	13	28	5	20	3	1
	Medfield	12,299	0	0	0	0	0	55	15	38	2	1
	Medford	55,706	70	3	4	42	21	1,556	240	1,210	106	
	Medway	12,867	1	0	1	0	0	62	7	52	3	0
	Melrose	26,549	34	0	4	8	22	409	81	291	37	0
	Mendon	5,837	7	0	1	0	6	36	13	21	2	0
	Merrimac	6,420	4	0	2	0	2	32	12	20	0	3
	Methuen	44,333	106	1	6	20	79	959	166	718	75	4
	Middleboro	21,503	57	0	6	9	42	453	122	281	50	7
	Middleton	9,562	8	0	0	0	8	82	0	79	3	0
	Milford	27,635	85	2	4	9	70	413	78	299	36	6
	Millbury[8]	13,711		1	4	2		176	51	107	18	2
	Millis	7,977	1	0	0	0	1	43	9	31	3	0
	Millville	2,988	1	0	1	0	0	34	12	20	2	0
	Milton	25,888	13	0	0	6	7	238	48	172	18	
	Monson	8,856	17	1	4	0	12	119	41	64	14	0
	Montague	8,359	23	1	3	2	17	151	59	87	5	2
	Monterey	967	0	0	0	0	0	3	2	1	0	0
	Nahant	3,544	9	0	0	1	8	43	5	36	2	0
	Natick	31,854	61	0	7	12	42	648	81	528	39	2
	Needham	28,343	6	1	0	1	4	251	33	215	3	0
	New Bedford	92,373	1,093	2	40	286	765	3,152	900	1,859	393	33
	Newbury	6,992	10	0	0	1	9	48	22	26	0	1
	Newburyport	17,317	12	0	1	2	9	198	34	152	12	2
	New Salem	990	0	0	0	0	0	4	1	2	1	0
	Newton	82,731	78	0	8	13	57	1,306	184	1,079	43	1
	Norfolk	10,596	3	0	1	0	2	43	11	32	0	0
	North Adams	13,738	93	0	6	8	79	507	176	294	37	5
	Northampton	28,550	105	0	8	17	80	959	195	708	56	9
	North Andover	27,271	3	0	0	0	3	284	65	210	9	0
	North Attleboro	28,095	39	0	6	6	27	690	97	552	41	3
	Northborough	14,783	3	0	0	0	3	104	16	84	4	0
	Northbridge	14,596	19	0	3	3	13	265	58	195	12	3
	North Brookfield[8]	4,847		0	0	0		29	8	16	5	0
	Northfield	3,326	8	0	1	0	7	46	13	31	2	0
	Norton	19,423	3	1	0	2	0	125	36	81	8	0
	Norwell	10,466	12	0	0	2	10	124	41	78	5	0
	Norwood	28,336	21	0	1	5	15	524	90	397	37	3
	Oak Bluffs	3,768	8	0	1	0	7	111	24	84	3	0
	Oakham	1,946	7	0	1	0	6	54	28	20	6	2
	Orange	7,762	39	0	2	4	33	203	70	126	7	1
	Orleans	6,412	14	0	1	2	11	190	36	152	2	0
	Oxford	13,760	51	0	3	7	41	113	38	58	17	10
	Palmer	12,991	43	2	4	6	31	202	67	117	18	4
	Paxton	4,591	3	0	0	0	3	21	4	15	2	1
	Peabody	52,194	128	0	7	16	105	1,235	126	1,002	107	4
	Pembroke	18,932	32	0	2	4	26	212	62	133	17	0
	Pepperell	11,454	15	0	2	0	13	130	24	97	9	0
	Pittsfield	43,194	295	0	43	37	215	1,135	448	608	79	6
	Plainville	8,162	12	0	3	1	8	165	55	106	4	2
	Plymouth	56,023	106	0	5	14	87	824	177	611	36	3
	Princeton	3,547	1	0	0	0	1	47	30	15	2	1
	Provincetown	3,411	10	0	0	0	10	181	11	164	6	0
	Quincy	91,382	253	2	16	70	165	1,877	589	1,147	141	12
	Randolph	30,233	149	3	13	30	103	843	125	642	76	2

[1] The FBI does not publish arson data unless it receives data from either the agency or the state for all 12 months of the calendar year.

[8] The data collection methodology for the offense of aggravated assault used by this agency does not comply with national UCR Program guidelines. Consequently, the figures for aggravated assault and violent crime (of which aggravated assault is a part) are not included in this table.

Table 8.   Offenses Known to Law Enforcement, by State and City, 2007 *(Contd.)*

(Number.)

State	City	Population	Violent crime	Murder and non-negligent man-slaughter	Forcible rape	Robbery	Aggravated assault	Property crime	Burglary	Larceny-theft	Motor vehicle theft	Arson[1]
	Raynham	13,975	43	0	1	17	25	432	72	327	33	3
	Reading	23,004	14	0	0	3	11	269	41	219	9	0
	Rehoboth	11,551	10	0	0	1	9	128	48	70	10	1
	Revere	46,658	266	3	19	50	194	1,704	417	1,065	222	9
	Rochester	5,530	7	0	0	1	6	65	31	29	5	0
	Rockland	17,914	26	0	3	11	12	296	79	201	16	
	Rockport	7,677	7	0	2	0	5	18	2	14	2	0
	Rowley	5,927	5	0	0	0	5	31	7	22	2	0
	Royalston	1,399	2	0	0	1	1	14	9	5	0	0
	Rutland	7,800	13	1	4	0	8	48	13	34	1	0
	Salem	41,507	134	0	15	21	98	792	148	614	30	0
	Salisbury	8,506	45	1	5	3	36	168	83	75	10	2
	Sandwich	20,584	41	0	6	4	31	381	91	277	13	1
	Saugus	27,214	94	2	5	18	69	997	248	679	70	1
	Savoy	732	0	0	0	0	0	8	3	3	2	
	Scituate	18,116	12	0	0	0	12	167	50	113	4	1
	Seekonk	13,681	30	0	2	4	24	558	76	449	33	2
	Sharon	17,100	8	0	1	2	5	110	13	93	4	1
	Shelburne	2,045	1	0	0	0	1	9	1	7	1	1
	Sherborn	4,217	0	0	0	0	0	22	7	14	1	0
	Shirley	7,661	7	0	2	0	5	31	7	21	3	0
	Shrewsbury	33,485	13	0	4	0	9	377	40	308	29	0
	Somerset	18,473	47	0	1	6	40	323	48	261	14	2
	Somerville	74,156	289	1	17	119	152	2,252	436	1,533	283	2
	Southampton[8]	6,010		0	1	0		37	9	25	3	1
	Southborough	9,674	0	0	0	0	0	33	13	15	5	1
	Southbridge	17,109	112	0	8	12	92	430	206	199	25	6
	South Hadley	17,011	27	0	0	0	27	266	93	154	19	1
	Southwick	9,719	13	0	1	2	10	161	52	96	13	1
	Spencer	12,153	40	2	2	2	34	141	37	99	5	0
	Springfield	151,074	2,068	20	91	690	1,267	7,942	2,027	4,694	1,221	63
	Sterling	7,927	6	0	0	0	6	69	37	32	0	1
	Stockbridge	2,256	6	0	0	0	6	77	26	46	5	0
	Stoughton	26,814	105	0	4	13	88	423	154	230	39	2
	Stow	6,263	3	0	0	0	3	29	12	17	0	1
	Sturbridge	9,141	18	0	6	1	11	163	31	123	9	3
	Sudbury	17,061	5	1	0	0	4	107	8	96	3	0
	Sunderland	3,778	9	0	1	0	8	29	11	16	2	0
	Sutton	9,154	17	0	1	1	15	103	45	52	6	2
	Swampscott	14,097	6	0	1	2	3	318	28	281	9	0
	Swansea	16,271	50	0	3	5	42	311	47	237	27	0
	Taunton	56,091	290	1	12	71	206	1,230	472	582	176	7
	Templeton	7,812	19	0	2	4	13	111	48	52	11	4
	Tewksbury	29,450	53	0	5	13	35	452	92	329	31	4
	Topsfield	6,128	1	0	0	1	0	78	11	62	5	0
	Townsend	9,343	12	0	2	1	9	108	56	50	2	1
	Truro	2,163	1	0	0	1	0	24	0	24	0	0
	Tyngsboro	11,584	16	0	1	1	14	131	23	94	14	0
	Upton	6,597	8	0	2	1	5	61	13	37	11	0
	Uxbridge	12,818	10	1	2	0	7	126	55	65	6	4
	Wakefield	24,557	49	0	5	6	38	290	49	220	21	3
	Wales	1,853	2	0	0	0	2	8	2	5	1	0
	Walpole	23,199	11	0	2	1	8	300	29	258	13	0
	Waltham	59,425	125	0	11	19	95	820	172	594	54	1
	Ware	10,031	31	0	2	1	28	123	34	81	8	2
	Wareham	21,472	153	1	8	22	122	596	206	354	36	3
	Watertown	32,065	56	0	3	12	41	610	114	464	32	0
	Wayland	12,954	0	0	0	0	0	82	16	65	1	1
	Webster	16,886	76	1	3	11	61	352	74	250	28	1
	Wellesley	26,966	21	0	1	2	18	235	63	169	3	0
	Wellfleet	2,798	9	0	2	0	7	60	6	51	3	0
	Wenham	4,609	5	0	1	0	4	46	18	24	4	0
	Westborough	18,740	20	0	3	2	15	309	95	185	29	1
	West Boylston	7,810	5	0	2	1	2	193	28	152	13	1
	Westfield[8]	40,518		0	11	12		657	274	354	29	4
	Westford	21,624	1	0	0	1	0	95	11	82	2	0
	Westhampton	1,601	1	0	0	0	1	7	3	3	1	0
	West Newbury	4,306	11	0	0	0	11	30	10	18	2	2
	Westport	15,280	29	0	0	0	29	217	114	87	16	3
	West Springfield	27,854	124	1	5	33	85	1,209	218	870	121	1
	West Tisbury	2,673	0	0	0	0	0	6	2	4	0	0
	Westwood	13,790	6	0	0	1	5	149	22	110	17	0
	Weymouth	53,553	112	1	9	22	80	891	203	611	77	
	Whately	1,578	1	0	0	1	0	15	3	11	1	1

[1] The FBI does not publish arson data unless it receives data from either the agency or the state for all 12 months of the calendar year.

[8] The data collection methodology for the offense of aggravated assault used by this agency does not comply with national UCR Program guidelines. Consequently, the figures for aggravated assault and violent crime (of which aggravated assault is a part) are not included in this table.

Table 8.   Offenses Known to Law Enforcement, by State and City, 2007 *(Contd.)*

(Number.)

State	City	Population	Violent crime	Murder and non-negligent man-slaughter	Forcible rape	Robbery	Aggravated assault	Property crime	Burglary	Larceny-theft	Motor vehicle theft	Arson[1]
	Wilbraham...............	14,123	23	0	0	4	19	185	32	133	20	1
	Williamsburg...........	2,440	3	0	0	0	3	38	21	16	1	0
	Williamstown..........	8,159	6	0	2	0	4	165	29	134	2	2
	Winchendon.............	10,221	52	0	1	6	45	170	54	101	15	2
	Winchester...............	21,155	6	0	0	2	4	351	69	276	6	3
	Winthrop..................	17,056	61	0	1	10	50	221	71	145	5	4
	Woburn....................	36,996	116	0	6	17	93	942	110	750	82	4
	Worcester................	175,825	1,531	6	93	371	1,061	6,025	1,308	3,815	902	18
	Wrentham................	11,215	0	0	0	0	0	46	9	36	1	0
	Yarmouth[8].............	24,304		0	6	14		711	269	406	36	8
MICHIGAN	Adrian.....................	21,612	123	0	37	14	72	834	176	638	20	4
	Albion.....................	9,267	99	4	5	18	72	381	86	275	20	4
	Algonac...................	4,585	13	0	1	0	12	42	9	31	2	1
	Allegan...................	4,963	76	0	3	0	73	66	9	54	3	1
	Allen Park...............	27,384	2	0	0	0	2	264	61	158	45	1
	Alma.......................	9,231	17	0	3	0	14	55	32	20	3	0
	Almont....................	2,863	10	0	1	0	9	92	25	62	5	1
	Ann Arbor...............	113,011	298	0	30	66	202	2,777	572	2,046	159	15
	Argentine Township......	7,328	8	0	1	1	6	115	26	83	6	0
	Armada...................	1,640	2	0	0	0	2	13	0	12	1	0
	Auburn...................	2,058	1	0	0	0	1	25	3	20	2	0
	Auburn Hills...........	21,149	85	1	12	21	51	1,111	138	895	78	0
	Bad Axe..................	3,163	2	1	0	0	1	116	15	99	2	0
	Bangor....................	1,881	15	0	4	2	9	97	9	85	3	0
	Baraga....................	1,242	1	0	0	0	1	17	3	14	0	0
	Bath Township.........	11,721	10	0	1	0	9	116	34	76	6	0
	Battle Creek............	62,143	818	3	89	130	596	3,591	1,001	2,397	193	26
	Bay City..................	34,145	164	1	20	50	93	1,170	298	792	80	13
	Belding...................	5,872	22	0	12	0	10	237	33	198	6	0
	Belleville................	3,766	5	0	0	4	1	146	16	122	8	0
	Benton Harbor.........	10,567	137	0	6	28	103	285	135	126	24	1
	Benton Township......	15,626	189	0	18	33	138	1,298	195	1,032	71	3
	Berkley...................	14,906	13	0	4	6	3	186	25	147	14	1
	Berrien Springs-Orono......	9,570	16	0	7	1	8	272	37	227	8	2
	Beverly Hills...........	9,955	15	0	0	3	12	122	24	91	7	0
	Big Rapids..............	10,536	23	0	6	3	14	380	59	311	10	2
	Birch Run................	1,700	5	0	0	2	3	144	6	136	2	0
	Birmingham............	19,149	25	0	1	5	19	392	65	303	24	7
	Blackman Township......	25,461	65	1	11	11	42	633	85	520	28	5
	Blissfield.................	3,251	4	0	1	0	3	59	11	47	1	1
	Bloomfield Hills.......	3,818	2	0	0	1	1	61	14	46	1	0
	Bloomfield Township......	41,231	19	0	3	8	8	683	129	514	40	3
	Bloomingdale...........	504	1	0	0	0	1	25	2	23	0	0
	Bridgeport Township......	11,134	34	0	1	8	25	282	96	171	15	1
	Bridgman................	2,429	0	0	0	0	0	79	8	69	2	2
	Brighton.................	7,326	14	0	2	4	8	264	18	239	7	2
	Bronson..................	2,294	2	0	1	0	1	35	8	27	0	1
	Brown City..............	1,294	0	0	0	0	0	32	0	32	0	0
	Brownstown Township......	30,336	67	1	2	8	56	691	182	403	106	6
	Buena Vista Township......	9,631	179	2	10	33	134	534	238	255	41	8
	Burr Oak.................	759	2	0	2	0	0	8	1	6	1	0
	Burton....................	30,958	131	1	6	40	84	1,507	286	1,101	120	4
	Cadillac..................	10,329	45	0	12	4	29	525	70	437	18	8
	Calumet..................	797	4	0	1	0	3	21	3	16	2	0
	Canton Township......	88,126	110	1	21	19	69	1,562	277	1,165	120	5
	Capac.....................	2,308	1	0	0	0	1	47	8	38	1	0
	Carleton..................	2,947	4	0	1	0	3	47	4	39	4	0
	Caro.......................	4,136	10	0	4	0	6	180	36	139	5	0
	Carrollton Township......	6,128	21	0	1	5	15	325	67	236	22	0
	Cass City................	2,568	2	0	0	0	2	30	2	28	0	0
	Cassopolis...............	1,792	3	0	0	0	3	23	5	17	1	0
	Cedar Springs..........	3,287	14	0	1	0	13	112	18	87	7	4
	Center Line.............	8,209	25	0	4	10	11	248	36	139	73	2
	Charlotte................	9,047	29	0	15	2	12	327	63	254	10	6
	Cheboygan..............	5,114	20	0	7	1	12	189	22	163	4	0
	Chelsea...................	5,014	5	0	2	1	2	135	14	117	4	1
	Chesterfield Township......	45,849	161	0	13	15	133	1,227	175	966	86	13
	Chikaming Township......	3,686	2	0	0	0	2	82	9	73	0	0
	Chocolay Township......	5,989	0	0	0	0	0	30	1	29	0	0
	Clare......................	3,198	18	0	8	0	10	186	14	167	5	3
	Clawson..................	12,175	14	0	1	0	13	152	47	99	6	0
	Clayton Township......	7,885	11	0	2	1	8	107	28	70	9	0
	Clay Township.........	9,848	3	0	1	0	2	170	43	117	10	0
	Clinton...................	2,439	5	0	0	1	4	41	5	35	1	0

[1] The FBI does not publish arson data unless it receives data from either the agency or the state for all 12 months of the calendar year.

[8] The data collection methodology for the offense of aggravated assault used by this agency does not comply with national UCR Program guidelines. Consequently, the figures for aggravated assault and violent crime (of which aggravated assault is a part) are not included in this table.

Table 8.   Offenses Known to Law Enforcement, by State and City, 2007 *(Contd.)*

(Number.)

State	City	Population	Violent crime	Murder and non-negligent man-slaughter	Forcible rape	Robbery	Aggravated assault	Property crime	Burglary	Larceny-theft	Motor vehicle theft	Arson[1]
	Clinton Township	96,948	308	3	24	76	205	2,299	534	1,454	311	17
	Clio	2,606	9	0	1	1	7	92	18	71	3	2
	Coldwater	10,711	34	0	9	2	23	423	60	345	18	1
	Coleman	1,252	0	0	0	0	0	59	9	49	1	0
	Coloma Township	6,662	15	0	3	1	11	236	69	157	10	2
	Colon	1,173	2	0	1	0	1	44	5	36	3	0
	Columbia Township	7,734	4	0	0	0	4	211	33	169	9	1
	Constantine	2,149	11	1	4	0	6	116	7	104	5	1
	Corunna	3,375	5	0	1	0	4	85	15	66	4	0
	Covert Township	3,123	15	0	4	1	10	98	28	57	13	3
	Croswell	2,554	3	0	0	0	3	81	20	55	6	0
	Davison	5,294	5	0	0	1	4	104	22	79	3	0
	Dearborn	91,748	466	1	27	146	292	4,333	581	2,945	807	24
	Dearborn Heights	54,901	212	2	14	63	133	1,534	491	705	338	11
	Decatur	1,872	20	0	4	1	15	175	19	152	4	0
	Denton Township	5,649	7	0	1	0	6	119	45	72	2	0
	Detroit	860,971	19,708	394	341	6,575	12,398	58,302	17,767	20,918	19,617	758
	Dewitt	4,399	6	0	0	0	6	32	5	24	3	0
	Dewitt Township	13,295	23	0	4	4	15	173	67	98	8	1
	Douglas	2,209	4	0	1	0	3	109	32	75	2	0
	Dowagiac	5,913	43	1	5	9	28	293	41	240	12	1
	Dryden Township	4,773	3	0	0	0	3	45	16	26	3	0
	East Grand Rapids	10,309	3	0	1	1	1	134	29	100	5	1
	East Jordan	2,270	0	0	0	0	0	113	7	104	2	0
	East Lansing	45,979	201	0	22	34	145	978	231	700	47	21
	Eastpointe	32,797	243	2	13	50	178	1,116	181	579	356	16
	East Tawas	2,808	10	0	1	2	7	175	27	144	4	1
	Eaton Rapids	5,304	11	0	3	0	8	158	20	137	1	2
	Eau Claire	632	0	0	0	0	0	17	2	15	0	0
	Elk Rapids	1,708	4	0	0	0	4	67	7	60	0	1
	Elkton	783	0	0	0	0	0	31	2	27	2	0
	Emmett Township	12,048	59	0	4	9	46	600	95	493	12	1
	Erie Township	4,780	9	1	2	0	6	63	22	33	8	0
	Escanaba	12,494	5	0	2	0	3	495	88	400	7	2
	Essexville	3,523	0	0	0	0	0	99	15	82	2	0
	Evart	1,717	4	0	1	0	3	55	13	42	0	0
	Farmington	9,930	17	0	2	6	9	192	35	146	11	0
	Farmington Hills	79,475	142	0	13	27	102	1,517	403	949	165	7
	Fenton	12,151	16	0	1	3	12	288	49	218	21	2
	Ferndale	21,207	93	1	6	24	62	735	137	420	178	1
	Flat Rock	9,739	13	0	0	0	13	205	39	149	17	1
	Flint	116,024	2,741	30	109	665	1,937	7,246	3,241	2,965	1,040	240
	Flint Township	32,626	188	3	19	72	94	2,146	471	1,471	204	10
	Flushing	8,014	10	0	3	2	5	173	22	138	13	0
	Flushing Township	10,394	9	0	1	0	8	124	34	82	8	2
	Forsyth Township	4,855	6	0	2	0	4	60	14	38	8	0
	Fowlerville	3,148	7	0	3	0	4	100	13	85	2	0
	Frankenmuth	4,777	7	0	1	1	5	120	36	83	1	0
	Frankfort	1,480	5	0	0	0	5	42	7	33	2	0
	Franklin	2,977	2	0	0	1	1	54	14	39	1	0
	Fraser	15,068	27	0	2	4	21	556	86	437	33	2
	Fremont	4,303	15	0	6	1	8	175	23	151	1	0
	Fruitport	1,080	41	0	6	8	27	774	45	711	18	1
	Garden City	28,282	94	0	1	30	63	645	146	411	88	7
	Gaylord	3,749	13	1	6	0	6	213	32	176	5	1
	Genesee Township	23,961	91	0	10	20	61	681	206	411	64	6
	Gerrish Township	3,198	5	0	2	0	3	52	13	38	1	4
	Gibraltar	5,300	12	0	1	2	9	119	12	105	2	0
	Gladstone	5,252	6	0	2	1	3	143	28	110	5	0
	Gladwin	2,984	11	0	2	0	9	95	16	78	1	1
	Grand Blanc	7,749	17	0	1	4	12	229	53	165	11	0
	Grand Blanc Township	36,319	49	1	4	10	34	765	187	524	54	6
	Grand Ledge	7,708	4	0	2	0	2	185	19	159	7	0
	Grand Rapids	192,376	1,874	20	69	669	1,116	10,149	2,629	6,931	589	119
	Grayling	1,902	1	0	0	0	1	93	14	75	4	0
	Green Oak Township	18,279	23	0	3	2	18	262	46	195	21	3
	Greenville	8,374	37	0	12	4	21	459	63	381	15	1
	Grosse Ile Township	10,455	10	0	0	0	10	93	18	75	0	0
	Grosse Pointe	5,289	15	0	0	4	11	141	15	98	28	0
	Grosse Pointe Farms	9,099	6	0	1	1	4	204	21	141	42	0
	Grosse Pointe Park	11,606	22	0	1	3	18	354	37	243	74	0
	Grosse Pointe Shores	2,644	0	0	0	0	0	4	4	0	0	0
	Grosse Pointe Woods	15,998	23	0	2	6	15	285	29	214	42	0
	Hamburg Township	22,486	8	0	0	0	8	172	44	123	5	0

[1] The FBI does not publish arson data unless it receives data from either the agency or the state for all 12 months of the calendar year.

Table 8.   Offenses Known to Law Enforcement, by State and City, 2007 *(Contd.)*

(Number.)

State	City	Population	Violent crime	Murder and non-negligent man-slaughter	Forcible rape	Robbery	Aggravated assault	Property crime	Burglary	Larceny-theft	Motor vehicle theft	Arson[1]
	Hampton Township	9,827	23	1	4	0	18	350	33	304	13	3
	Hamtramck	21,448	321	3	7	123	188	1,201	328	418	455	18
	Hancock	4,156	5	0	1	1	3	75	22	49	4	0
	Harbor Beach	1,670	9	0	3	0	6	37	6	31	0	0
	Harbor Springs	1,575	1	0	1	0	0	30	4	25	1	0
	Harper Woods	13,284	172	1	9	62	100	1,354	137	894	323	3
	Hart	2,004	8	0	3	0	5	94	13	78	3	0
	Hartford	2,407	13	0	1	0	12	105	18	82	5	0
	Hastings	7,091	21	0	11	1	9	230	23	199	8	0
	Hazel Park	18,211	70	0	6	24	40	618	112	335	171	2
	Hillsdale	7,842	12	0	1	0	11	182	35	138	9	1
	Holly	6,410	20	0	2	1	17	110	26	79	5	0
	Homer	1,785	6	0	3	0	3	41	5	34	2	0
	Houghton	7,017	16	0	2	0	14	118	5	111	2	0
	Howard City	1,615	16	1	6	0	9	81	13	64	4	1
	Howell	9,921	31	0	2	2	27	295	47	239	9	2
	Hudson	2,378	6	0	0	0	6	64	10	53	1	0
	Huntington Woods	5,866	2	0	0	1	1	83	9	67	7	0
	Huron Township	16,354	27	2	3	2	20	319	65	188	66	1
	Imlay City	3,825	6	0	0	1	5	128	29	95	4	0
	Inkster	28,233	379	4	32	86	257	1,133	500	464	169	20
	Ionia	12,595	19	0	9	1	9	301	43	253	5	2
	Iron Mountain	7,963	7	0	2	0	5	159	14	143	2	2
	Iron River	3,085	6	0	3	0	3	97	14	75	8	1
	Ishpeming	6,440	17	0	6	2	9	145	7	130	8	0
	Ithaca	3,074	6	0	1	0	5	81	5	72	4	0
	Jackson	34,325	225	1	39	50	135	1,682	281	1,291	110	10
	Jonesville	2,281	10	0	2	1	7	120	13	107	0	1
	Kalamazoo	71,462	835	9	81	302	443	4,472	1,039	3,089	344	53
	Kalamazoo Township	21,497	50	0	6	13	31	626	193	388	45	7
	Kalkaska	2,207	4	0	1	1	2	134	13	112	9	1
	Keego Harbor	2,848	7	0	0	1	6	40	6	29	5	0
	Kentwood	46,748	205	0	24	35	146	1,738	371	1,297	70	1
	Kingsford	5,426	7	0	2	0	5	102	7	94	1	0
	Laingsburg	1,276	0	0	0	0	0	46	12	34	0	0
	Lake Angelus	312	0	0	0	0	0	4	1	3	0	0
	Lake Odessa	2,281	2	0	1	0	1	35	2	33	0	0
	Lake Orion	2,759	8	0	0	2	6	72	9	59	4	3
	Lakeview	1,120	1	0	1	0	0	51	9	41	1	0
	Lansing	113,643	1,244	16	92	269	867	4,124	1,252	2,517	355	53
	Lapeer	9,372	24	0	4	2	18	400	36	356	8	1
	Lapeer Township	5,214	0	0	0	0	0	24	2	20	2	0
	Lathrup Village	4,112	19	0	1	5	13	72	17	48	7	2
	Laurium	2,001	6	0	0	0	6	35	6	29	0	0
	Lawton	1,839	6	0	0	0	6	51	11	38	2	0
	Lennon	501	0	0	0	0	0	3	1	2	0	0
	Leoni Township	13,889	17	0	2	1	14	210	51	141	18	1
	Lincoln Park	37,294	147	2	7	60	78	1,672	271	1,078	323	5
	Lincoln Township	14,496	19	0	5	3	11	306	42	253	11	0
	Linden	3,560	0	0	0	0	0	26	1	24	1	0
	Litchfield	1,422	2	0	0	0	2	33	5	27	1	0
	Livonia	96,261	153	1	27	31	94	2,418	421	1,730	267	21
	Lowell	4,159	2	0	1	0	1	37	5	29	3	0
	Ludington	8,433	34	1	8	1	24	314	56	249	9	0
	Luna Pier	1,550	4	0	0	0	4	62	9	50	3	0
	Madison Heights	29,901	95	1	4	19	71	1,144	275	697	172	9
	Madison Township	7,977	5	0	0	0	5	40	4	36	0	0
	Mancelona	1,380	3	0	1	0	2	26	5	21	0	0
	Manistee	6,604	8	2	2	0	4	156	17	133	6	1
	Marine City	4,417	8	0	0	1	7	140	30	109	1	1
	Marlette	2,047	8	0	0	0	8	52	10	40	2	0
	Marquette	20,467	22	0	6	3	13	451	57	378	16	1
	Marshall	7,244	31	1	2	6	22	229	39	170	20	2
	Marysville	10,135	14	0	5	0	9	239	35	198	6	1
	Mattawan	2,945	1	1	0	0	0	88	4	82	2	0
	Memphis	1,123	3	0	1	0	2	21	11	9	1	0
	Mendon	922	1	0	0	0	1	21	1	19	1	0
	Menominee	8,537	12	0	3	2	7	316	66	243	7	1
	Meridian Township	37,958	78	0	9	23	46	952	177	749	26	6
	Metamora Township	4,796	4	0	1	0	3	62	24	34	4	0
	Midland	41,540	69	0	13	18	38	1,044	176	844	24	4
	Milan	5,686	11	0	1	2	8	155	22	129	4	2
	Milford	6,629	29	0	3	1	25	127	18	103	6	1
	Monroe	21,787	70	0	7	23	40	709	125	539	45	5

[1] The FBI does not publish arson data unless it receives data from either the agency or the state for all 12 months of the calendar year.

Table 8.   Offenses Known to Law Enforcement, by State and City, 2007 *(Contd.)*

(Number.)

State	City	Population	Violent crime	Murder and non-negligent man-slaughter	Forcible rape	Robbery	Aggravated assault	Property crime	Burglary	Larceny-theft	Motor vehicle theft	Arson[1]
	Montague	2,305	1	0	0	0	1	49	9	38	2	0
	Montrose Township	7,919	11	0	4	0	7	135	36	90	9	3
	Morenci	2,323	5	0	1	0	4	76	14	61	1	0
	Mount Morris	3,308	20	0	1	3	16	156	29	118	9	2
	Mount Morris Township	22,966	184	0	17	49	118	1,073	433	514	126	11
	Mount Pleasant	26,270	57	1	15	4	37	699	138	534	27	6
	Munising	2,350	1	0	0	0	1	24	6	17	1	0
	Muskegon	39,562	389	0	35	77	277	2,252	396	1,693	163	8
	Muskegon Heights	11,698	219	1	15	48	155	916	187	621	108	22
	Napoleon Township	7,148	5	0	2	0	3	73	21	48	4	0
	Nashville	1,697	2	0	0	1	1	48	2	45	1	0
	Negaunee	4,429	4	0	3	0	1	105	17	81	7	0
	Newaygo	1,670	10	0	4	0	6	124	19	99	6	1
	New Baltimore	12,071	13	0	3	3	7	211	35	168	8	3
	New Buffalo	2,429	5	0	2	0	3	42	6	35	1	0
	Niles	11,491	52	0	8	14	30	487	73	390	24	1
	North Branch	1,009	6	0	0	0	6	26	5	19	2	0
	Northfield Township	8,383	33	0	6	0	27	196	37	136	23	3
	North Muskegon	3,968	1	0	0	0	1	100	10	89	1	1
	Northville	6,202	5	0	0	1	4	89	20	68	1	0
	Northville Township	26,528	22	1	2	3	16	427	76	325	26	0
	Norton Shores	23,567	59	0	7	11	41	958	135	790	33	4
	Norway	2,897	1	0	0	0	1	60	4	54	2	0
	Novi	55,127	34	0	5	5	24	1,150	165	939	46	4
	Oak Park	30,771	161	1	10	54	96	1,052	260	596	196	3
	Ontwa Township-Edwardsburg	5,930	31	0	5	2	24	204	38	154	12	3
	Orchard Lake	2,230	2	0	0	0	2	51	5	46	0	0
	Oscoda Township	7,028	31	0	12	2	17	274	73	192	9	3
	Otsego	3,900	9	0	6	2	1	86	15	70	1	0
	Ovid	1,415	0	0	0	0	0	10	2	8	0	0
	Owosso	15,341	75	0	16	4	55	701	104	568	29	9
	Oxford	3,583	4	0	0	0	4	64	9	53	2	0
	Parchment	1,778	9	0	0	1	8	65	8	55	2	0
	Parma-Sandstone	6,902	6	0	0	0	6	52	11	38	3	0
	Paw Paw	3,294	21	0	2	1	18	187	19	158	10	0
	Pentwater	988	1	0	0	0	1	17	4	12	1	0
	Perry	2,084	1	0	0	1	0	40	2	36	2	0
	Petoskey	6,128	7	0	0	0	7	184	17	160	7	1
	Pinckney	2,470	7	0	1	0	6	55	5	48	2	0
	Pinconning	1,327	1	0	0	0	1	56	16	39	1	1
	Pittsfield Township	34,615	57	0	5	18	34	923	144	690	89	2
	Plainwell	3,952	4	0	2	2	0	165	2	159	4	1
	Pleasant Ridge	2,471	3	0	2	0	1	26	3	22	1	0
	Plymouth	9,046	10	0	0	1	9	155	27	116	12	2
	Plymouth Township	26,751	15	1	1	4	9	475	87	353	35	1
	Pontiac	67,059	1,259	19	44	339	857	3,116	1,287	1,215	614	32
	Portage	45,287	104	1	20	20	63	2,124	343	1,708	73	13
	Port Huron	31,166	265	0	28	63	174	1,419	319	1,009	91	15
	Portland	3,793	5	0	1	0	4	66	9	53	4	0
	Prairieville Township	3,553	2	0	1	0	1	23	12	10	1	0
	Raisin Township	7,358	5	0	0	0	5	28	6	21	1	0
	Redford Township	48,489	171	1	1	77	92	1,905	476	977	452	12
	Richfield Township, Genesee County	8,874	12	0	4	0	8	124	54	55	15	0
	Richmond	5,804	33	1	2	1	29	163	15	146	2	1
	Riverview	12,447	8	0	2	1	5	236	16	183	37	1
	Rochester	11,360	19	0	4	1	14	166	17	137	12	4
	Rockford	5,248	24	0	1	0	23	134	20	110	4	3
	Romeo	3,806	6	0	0	0	6	65	6	56	3	0
	Romulus	24,269	138	2	16	29	91	975	210	563	202	9
	Roosevelt Park	3,790	4	0	0	3	1	300	18	276	6	0
	Roseville	47,329	242	0	30	48	164	2,262	313	1,526	423	6
	Royal Oak	57,695	175	0	20	29	126	1,244	226	878	140	5
	Saginaw	56,989	1,678	17	66	264	1,331	2,764	1,613	825	326	230
	Saginaw Township	39,736	75	0	6	29	40	1,195	280	872	43	7
	Saline	8,955	12	0	4	2	6	202	21	177	4	3
	Sandusky	2,676	10	0	2	1	7	174	14	157	3	1
	Sault Ste. Marie	14,279	42	0	11	4	27	643	120	498	25	4
	Schoolcraft	1,482	2	0	2	0	0	69	13	52	4	0
	Scottville	1,263	3	0	0	0	3	55	9	42	4	0
	Shelby Township	71,736	123	1	18	12	92	1,193	210	862	121	3
	Somerset Township	4,767	0	0	0	0	0	49	10	37	2	0
	Southfield	75,830	745	2	26	170	547	3,260	755	1,865	640	6
	Southgate	29,074	71	0	10	18	43	1,313	104	986	223	16
	South Haven	5,182	29	0	9	4	16	254	40	206	8	4

[1] The FBI does not publish arson data unless it receives data from either the agency or the state for all 12 months of the calendar year.

Table 8. Offenses Known to Law Enforcement, by State and City, 2007 (Contd.)

(Number.)

State	City	Population	Violent crime	Murder and non-negligent man-slaughter	Forcible rape	Robbery	Aggravated assault	Property crime	Burglary	Larceny-theft	Motor vehicle theft	Arson[1]
	South Lyon	11,226	38	0	5	3	30	138	23	112	3	1
	Sparta	4,007	6	0	3	2	1	180	37	141	2	1
	Spring Arbor Townshi	8,495	6	0	0	1	5	78	18	58	2	1
	Springfield	5,137	39	0	8	1	30	206	52	146	8	2
	Spring Lake-Ferrysbur	5,347	2	0	2	0	0	160	20	139	1	2
	St. Charles	2,107	3	0	2	0	1	100	17	79	4	3
	St. Clair	5,938	5	0	2	0	3	113	12	101	0	2
	St. Clair Shores	60,900	178	0	13	35	130	1,328	219	891	218	10
	Sterling Heights	128,555	293	2	21	39	231	3,103	390	2,470	243	22
	St. Ignace	2,324	6	0	0	0	6	77	16	55	6	0
	St. Johns	7,329	3	0	1	0	2	151	31	116	4	2
	St. Joseph	8,600	38	0	4	3	31	275	55	218	2	0
	St. Joseph Township	9,827	15	0	0	4	11	149	31	110	8	1
	St. Louis	6,463	6	0	6	0	0	62	7	55	0	0
	Stockbridge	1,274	14	0	1	0	13	60	8	51	1	0
	Sturgis	11,026	42	0	8	11	23	325	55	251	19	3
	Summit Township	22,104	39	0	2	9	28	333	87	229	17	1
	Swartz Creek	5,394	20	1	4	2	13	201	32	162	7	1
	Sylvan Lake	1,654	0	0	0	0	0	17	2	13	2	0
	Taylor	64,048	273	4	25	97	147	2,864	483	1,903	478	26
	Tecumseh	8,878	8	0	2	0	6	145	31	111	3	0
	Thomas Township	12,670	12	1	0	3	8	487	201	280	6	3
	Three Rivers	7,245	73	1	6	14	52	476	65	388	23	4
	Tittabawassee Townsh	9,047	2	0	1	0	1	125	22	99	4	0
	Traverse City	14,406	40	0	11	4	25	502	61	429	12	2
	Troy	81,130	80	1	10	20	49	1,882	272	1,441	169	4
	Tuscarora Township	3,145	2	0	1	0	1	141	7	130	4	0
	Unadilla Township	3,477	4	0	0	0	4	59	17	40	2	0
	Union City	1,737	5	0	2	1	2	93	10	82	1	0
	Utica	5,022	27	0	4	2	21	203	24	165	14	1
	Van Buren Township	28,247	80	0	8	18	54	812	121	581	110	2
	Vernon	813	1	0	0	0	1	0	0	0	0	0
	Walker	23,794	42	1	12	10	19	1,030	117	885	28	1
	Walled Lake	6,988	12	0	3	2	7	133	20	101	12	0
	Warren[4]	134,081	840	7	83	216	534		824	2,360		37
	Waterford Township	71,233	170	1	37	43	89	1,820	383	1,265	172	5
	Waterloo Township	3,035	4	0	1	0	3	44	15	28	1	0
	Wayland	3,906	5	0	1	1	3	100	11	85	4	0
	Wayne	18,203	141	0	16	33	92	616	132	392	92	12
	West Bloomfield Tow	64,616	43	0	10	6	27	823	167	625	31	5
	West Branch	1,875	5	0	1	1	3	98	16	81	1	1
	Westland	84,293	463	2	37	114	310	2,716	684	1,698	334	31
	White Cloud	1,421	13	0	2	0	11	102	16	86	0	0
	White Lake Township	30,412	22	0	0	5	17	534	87	424	23	3
	White Pigeon	1,579	3	0	1	0	2	33	1	31	1	0
	Wixom	13,572	20	0	5	5	10	433	91	311	31	3
	Wolverine Lake	4,307	8	0	0	0	8	31	4	25	2	0
	Woodhaven	13,514	21	0	3	4	14	453	54	356	43	1
	Wyandotte	26,290	55	1	7	11	36	701	95	527	79	7
	Wyoming	70,243	356	1	42	96	217	2,177	581	1,391	205	12
	Yale	1,967	8	0	0	1	7	45	12	33	0	1
	Ypsilanti	21,672	338	1	22	80	235	1,151	364	688	99	7
	Zeeland	5,433	9	0	2	0	7	122	4	116	2	1
MINNESOTA[6]	Albany	2,072		0		0	0	7	1	6	0	0
	Albert Lea	17,663		0		1	19	400	38	335	27	0
	Alexandria	11,029		1		1	9	328	24	299	5	2
	Annandale	3,114		0		2	4	110	12	93	5	0
	Anoka	17,413		0		11	16	818	103	659	56	4
	Appleton	1,929		0		0	4	60	14	42	4	0
	Apple Valley	50,794		0		21	39	1,509	195	1,275	39	2
	Austin	23,300		1		11	31	837	112	682	43	2
	Avon	1,284		0		0	0	16	2	14	0	1
	Baxter	8,243		1		0	8	285	7	274	4	0
	Bayport	3,266		0		0	4	37	6	27	4	0
	Becker	4,294		0		0	0	3	0	2	1	0
	Belgrade	705		0		0	0	0	0	0	0	0
	Belle Plaine	4,998		0		0	8	114	13	97	4	3
	Bemidji	13,448		0		8	43	1,127	130	953	44	2
	Benson	3,096		0		0	4	80	22	55	3	0
	Big Lake	9,852		0		1	12	359	48	300	11	0
	Biwabik	944		0		0	1	4	0	4	0	0
	Blackduck	765		0		0	2	23	2	21	0	1
	Blaine	56,747		3		10	34	2,259	265	1,904	90	8
	Blooming Prairie	1,975		0		0	1	28	8	15	5	0

[1] The FBI does not publish arson data unless it receives data from either the agency or the state for all 12 months of the calendar year.

[6] The data collection methodology for the offense of forcible rape used by the Illinois and the Minnesota state UCR Programs (with the exception of Rockford, Illinois and Minneapolis and St. Paul, Minnesota) does not comply with national UCR Program guidelines. Consequently, their figures for forcible rape and violent crime (of which forcible rape is a part) are not published in this table.

[4] It was determined that the agency did not follow national Uniform Crime Reporting (UCR) Program guidelines for reporting an offense. Consequently, this figure is not included in this table.

Table 8.   Offenses Known to Law Enforcement, by State and City, 2007 *(Contd.)*

(Number.)

State	City	Population	Violent crime	Murder and non-negligent man-slaughter	Forcible rape	Robbery	Aggravated assault	Property crime	Burglary	Larceny-theft	Motor vehicle theft	Arson[1]
	Bloomington	80,218		0		51	61	3,210	356	2,674	180	14
	Blue Earth	3,366		0		0	3	98	19	76	3	0
	Brainerd	13,731		0		2	42	523	79	422	22	6
	Breckenridge	3,325		0		0	1	68	4	62	2	0
	Brooklyn Center	27,118		4		96	81	1,987	246	1,540	201	5
	Brooklyn Park	70,112		3		118	169	3,093	608	2,162	323	11
	Browns Valley	619		0		0	3	7	2	5	0	0
	Brownton	795		0		0	0	6	0	5	1	0
	Buffalo	14,456		0		2	12	462	41	408	13	1
	Caledonia	2,910		0		0	0	54	10	43	1	0
	Cannon Falls	4,038		0		0	1	190	16	166	8	2
	Centennial Lakes	11,454		0		0	11	174	20	148	6	0
	Champlin	23,463		0		6	10	550	61	461	28	0
	Chaska	24,764		1		2	7	339	36	294	9	2
	Chisholm	4,592		0		1	7	159	32	119	8	0
	Cloquet	11,523		0		0	27	497	41	436	20	4
	Cold Spring	3,726		0		0	5	86	8	78	0	0
	Columbia Heights	17,894		0		47	40	1,077	235	762	80	7
	Coon Rapids	62,299		0		23	60	3,096	317	2,663	116	7
	Corcoran	5,698		0		0	2	66	11	50	5	0
	Cottage Grove	33,288		0		3	23	797	148	611	38	1
	Crookston	7,752		0		0	5	37	15	16	6	1
	Crosby	2,232		0		0	9	135	11	124	0	0
	Crystal	21,325		1		22	15	743	108	576	59	6
	Dawson	1,405		0		0	2	35	4	29	2	0
	Dayton	4,620		0		1	2	34	7	9	18	0
	Deephaven-Woodland	4,129		0		0	0	25	6	16	3	0
	Detroit Lakes	8,111		0		1	14	401	39	339	23	0
	Dilworth	3,600		0		0	4	76	7	66	3	0
	Duluth	83,932		1		111	248	4,292	707	3,358	227	10
	Eagan	63,718		0		15	28	1,515	188	1,276	51	5
	Eagle Lake	2,130		0		0	2	23	4	18	1	1
	East Grand Forks	7,896		1		0	12	252	43	204	5	0
	Eden Prairie	61,910		0		13	28	1,475	190	1,254	31	10
	Edina	45,007		1		6	15	1,120	182	901	37	3
	Elk River	23,224		0		4	21	913	127	764	22	6
	Elmore	677		0		0	1	10	8	1	1	0
	Ely	3,565		0		2	0	99	11	83	5	0
	Eveleth	3,577		1		2	14	146	34	101	11	2
	Fairmont	10,337		0		2	6	408	57	334	17	0
	Falcon Heights	5,417		0		0	1	190	24	163	3	1
	Faribault	22,408		0		8	51	851	154	659	38	14
	Farmington	19,276		0		4	3	342	60	273	9	0
	Fergus Falls	13,842		0		3	21	434	78	342	14	5
	Floodwood	493		0		0	2	6	0	6	0	0
	Forest Lake	17,984		0		5	4	563	54	460	49	0
	Fridley	26,124		0		49	54	1,517	159	1,210	148	13
	Gilbert	1,743		0		0	0	33	3	27	3	1
	Glencoe	5,644		0		0	6	164	14	146	4	0
	Glenwood	2,553		0		1	1	22	3	18	1	0
	Golden Valley	19,865		0		11	12	682	141	492	49	2
	Goodview	3,394		0		0	1	68	13	51	4	1
	Grand Rapids	8,297		0		0	10	320	30	279	11	0
	Granite Falls	2,961		0		0	2	28	3	23	2	0
	Hallock	1,051		0		0	0	0	0	0	0	0
	Hastings	21,839		0		2	12	716	113	569	34	10
	Hermantown	9,247		0		2	5	324	53	254	17	0
	Hibbing	16,198		1		2	17	135	43	89	3	0
	Hilltop	749		0		7	6	98	15	74	9	0
	Hokah	582		0		0	0	14	2	12	0	0
	Hopkins	16,613		0		12	14	481	117	317	47	0
	Houston	991		0		0	1	13	0	13	0	0
	Hutchinson	14,050		0		3	17	415	74	328	13	3
	International Falls	6,108		0		0	9	189	30	148	11	3
	Inver Grove Heights	34,060		0		8	24	853	147	651	55	6
	Jackson	3,429		0		0	5	75	19	53	3	1
	Janesville	2,201		0		0	0	29	11	17	1	0
	Kimball	691		0		0	2	7	1	6	0	0
	Lake City	5,409		0		0	2	125	20	103	2	0
	Lake Crystal	2,562		0		1	2	43	5	32	6	0
	Lakefield	1,687		0		0	2	12	6	6	0	0
	Lakes Area	8,333		0		1	16	189	30	148	11	1
	Lakeville	54,565		0		4	9	950	153	763	34	2
	Lauderdale	2,169		0		1	2	62	14	38	10	1

[1] The FBI does not publish arson data unless it receives data from either the agency or the state for all 12 months of the calendar year.

Table 8. Offenses Known to Law Enforcement, by State and City, 2007 *(Contd.)*

(Number.)

State	City	Population	Violent crime	Murder and non-negligent man-slaughter	Forcible rape	Robbery	Aggravated assault	Property crime	Burglary	Larceny-theft	Motor vehicle theft	Arson[1]
	Lester Prairie	1,737		0		0	2	44	6	36	2	0
	Lewiston	1,483		0		0	0	0	0	0	0	0
	Lino Lakes	20,334		0		1	6	240	49	183	8	0
	Litchfield	6,655		0		2	3	183	25	149	9	0
	Little Falls	8,162		0		1	14	242	25	192	25	0
	Long Prairie	2,877		0		0	1	125	13	110	2	0
	Madison	1,605		0		0	1	9	1	8	0	0
	Mankato	35,331		1		25	57	1,911	296	1,535	80	3
	Maple Grove	62,145		0		21	22	1,548	278	1,238	32	5
	Mapleton	1,633		0		0	1	44	7	37	0	
	Maplewood	35,444		1		31	70	2,463	326	1,952	185	19
	Medina	5,033		0		1	2	114	25	86	3	0
	Melrose	3,146		0		0	0	31	2	29	0	0
	Mendota Heights	11,318		0		1	8	315	48	250	17	1
	Milaca	3,073		0		0	7	177	16	158	3	0
	Minneapolis	371,240	5,580	47	452	2,520	2,561	22,543	6,164	13,203	3,176	217
	Minnetonka	49,751		0		14	21	1,014	196	776	42	6
	Minnetrista	8,350		0		0	1	118	25	82	11	0
	Montevideo	5,305		1		0	8	148	28	112	8	2
	Montgomery	3,308		0		0	11	128	25	98	5	0
	Moorhead	35,052		0		7	38	814	132	631	51	6
	Moose Lake	2,622		0		2	3	64	2	57	5	0
	Mora	3,521		0		1	3	185	20	157	8	0
	Morris	5,057		1		1	5	150	27	113	10	0
	Mound	9,404		0		1	8	207	40	159	8	3
	Mounds View	11,921		0		5	18	417	70	310	37	2
	Mountain Lake	1,982		0		0	1	11	4	7	0	0
	New Brighton	20,644		0		10	21	631	72	506	53	7
	New Hope	20,301		0		15	17	693	109	546	38	7
	Newport	3,606		0		2	6	160	38	116	6	0
	New Prague	7,153		0		0	4	212	16	194	2	1
	New Richland	1,155		0		0	0	28	6	21	1	0
	New Ulm	13,369		0		1	8	241	39	193	9	0
	North Branch	10,886		0		0	7	287	27	248	12	1
	Northfield	19,447		0		3	5	557	121	420	16	0
	North Mankato	12,295		0		0	0	198	10	173	15	4
	North St. Paul	11,201		0		4	12	458	52	375	31	4
	Oakdale	27,306		1		10	55	1,255	138	1,021	96	24
	Oak Park Heights	4,097		0		0	4	226	16	195	15	0
	Olivia	2,449		0		0	11	112	19	85	8	0
	Orono	12,212		0		0	3	122	19	92	11	1
	Ortonville	2,003		0		0	0	19	3	16	0	0
	Osakis	1,570		0		0	1	51	9	39	3	0
	Osseo	2,553		0		0	2	17	3	7	7	0
	Owatonna	24,796		0		7	17	695	164	502	29	4
	Park Rapids	3,577		0		0	9	298	52	217	29	1
	Paynesville	2,255		0		0	2	83	21	59	3	0
	Plymouth	70,737		0		9	32	1,359	304	995	60	10
	Princeton	4,885		0		0	2	263	15	243	5	1
	Prior Lake	23,879		0		2	22	530	79	418	33	4
	Proctor	2,771		0		0	4	128	7	116	5	1
	Ramsey	23,617		1		1	12	706	67	606	33	4
	Red Wing	15,705		0		3	23	659	121	506	32	10
	Redwood Falls	5,155		0		0	21	219	35	172	12	1
	Richfield	33,112		2		55	51	1,174	192	898	84	6
	Richmond	1,264		0		0	0	2	1	1	0	0
	Robbinsdale	13,211		0		20	16	509	91	368	50	1
	Rochester	98,287		2		76	140	2,556	460	1,928	168	37
	Rogers	6,802		0		0	3	94	2	88	4	0
	Roseau	2,827		0		0	1	70	9	58	3	0
	Rosemount	21,393		0		4	6	414	72	326	16	1
	Roseville	31,645		0		14	26	1,574	217	1,231	126	5
	Sartell	13,816		0		0	8	258	31	220	7	1
	Sauk Centre	3,906		0		0	1	152	14	132	6	0
	Sauk Rapids	11,768		0		3	4	126	15	93	18	1
	Savage	28,266		1		11	22	882	166	673	43	9
	Shakopee	35,113		0		6	41	896	151	698	47	2
	Silver Lake	814		0		0	1	14	4	10	0	0
	Slayton	1,907		0		1	0	40	12	26	2	0
	Sleepy Eye	3,463		0		0	0	24	3	20	1	0
	South Eastern Faribaul	1,151		0		0	0	0	0	0	0	0
	South Lake Minnetonk	12,066		0		2	7	163	37	121	5	0
	Springfield	2,124		0		0	0	0	0	0	0	0
	Spring Lake Park	6,618		0		8	12	354	48	278	28	0

[1] The FBI does not publish arson data unless it receives data from either the agency or the state for all 12 months of the calendar year.

SECTION II: OFFENSES REPORTED 137

Table 8.   Offenses Known to Law Enforcement, by State and City, 2007 (Contd.)
(Number.)

State	City	Population	Violent crime	Murder and non-negligent man-slaughter	Forcible rape	Robbery	Aggravated assault	Property crime	Burglary	Larceny-theft	Motor vehicle theft	Arson[1]
	St. Anthony	7,680		1		3	3	323	43	271	9	3
	Staples	3,082		0		0	0	105	10	90	5	0
	St. Charles	3,567		0		0	3	35	3	31	1	0
	St. Cloud	67,290		1		48	145	2,943	352	2,466	125	9
	St. Francis	7,744		0		2	14	224	35	172	17	3
	Stillwater	18,116		0		0	18	414	60	336	18	4
	St. James	4,380		0		0	4	120	17	97	6	2
	St. Joseph	5,926		0		0	1	84	11	69	4	0
	St. Louis Park	43,001		0		40	32	1,515	273	1,155	87	7
	St. Paul	271,662	2,327	14	173	777	1,363	11,118	2,696	6,346	2,076	164
	St. Paul Park	5,285		0		1	8	156	31	115	10	0
	St. Peter	10,823		0		3	12	350	41	296	13	4
	Thief River Falls	8,440		0		0	6	218	33	172	13	1
	Two Harbors	3,435		0		0	0	44	11	31	2	0
	Virginia	8,471		0		4	27	662	126	508	28	3
	Wabasha	2,587		0		0	2	107	3	101	3	0
	Wadena	3,981		0		0	9	95	1	93	1	0
	Waite Park	6,795		0		4	12	507	44	454	9	6
	Warroad	1,663		0		0	0	67	5	61	1	0
	Waseca	9,465		0		1	11	254	20	225	9	0
	Wayzata	3,894		0		0	1	153	33	113	7	1
	Wells	2,442		0		0	0	22	2	20	0	0
	West Hennepin	5,671		0		1	2	72	22	46	4	3
	West St. Paul	18,748		0		25	21	1,029	77	883	69	0
	Wheaton	1,463		0		0	2	25	3	22	0	0
	White Bear Lake	23,486		0		9	51	969	205	688	76	11
	Willmar	18,012		0		8	15	675	90	552	33	3
	Windom	4,327		0		0	7	131	34	93	4	0
	Winnebago	1,386		0		0	2	28	13	13	2	0
	Winona	26,464		0		6	14	574	112	430	32	2
	Winsted	2,457		0		0	4	51	11	37	3	0
	Woodbury	55,376		0		8	21	1,417	277	1,074	66	4
	Worthington	11,026		0		1	20	261	97	154	10	2
	Wyoming	3,985		0		0	2	89	11	75	3	0
	Zumbrota	3,050		0		0	2	73	7	60	6	0
MISSISSIPPI	Aberdeen	6,138	17	0	3	3	11	194	66	124	4	0
	Amory	7,332	11	0	1	3	7	346	68	266	12	0
	Batesville	7,767	26	0	6	9	11	481	114	350	17	0
	Bay St. Louis	6,399	22	1	1	6	14	474	88	369	17	6
	Booneville	8,669	9	0	0	3	6	236	60	172	4	0
	Brandon	20,621	8	0	2	5	1	217	59	143	15	2
	Brookhaven	9,991	7	0	0	5	2	284	46	227	11	0
	Byhalia	714	5	0	0	1	4	79	24	50	5	0
	Canton	12,505	81	5	12	19	45	510	280	225	5	0
	Charleston	1,969	18	0	2	3	13	123	39	84	0	0
	Clarksdale	18,650	77	5	11	29	32	920	653	200	67	13
	Cleveland	12,500	65	0	2	20	43	884	143	728	13	2
	Collins	2,788	6	0	2	2	2	166	23	125	18	0
	Columbus	23,968	66	4	8	32	22	1,082	207	817	58	1
	Edwards	1,309	1	0	0	0	1	3	0	3	0	0
	Eupora	2,236	6	0	1	0	5	6	2	2	2	0
	Flowood	7,112	27	0	4	7	16	428	98	313	17	0
	Fulton	4,127	3	0	0	1	2	85	12	68	5	1
	Gloster	1,054	8	0	2	2	4	13	13	0	0	0
	Greenville[7]	37,326	136	6	23	71	36	2,079	624	1,345	110	35
	Greenwood	16,538	92	3	4	32	53	1,149	394	686	69	0
	Grenada	14,487	83	4	5	28	46	666	186	431	49	2
	Gulfport	64,455	286	4	27	165	90	5,199	1,288	3,529	382	24
	Hattiesburg	48,384	234	2	21	135	76	2,588	596	1,821	171	16
	Heidelberg	806	0	0	0	0	0	27	8	18	1	1
	Hernando	11,115	12	0	1	1	10	273	64	191	18	0
	Holly Springs[3]	7,970		0	6	17		328	113	197	18	1
	Horn Lake	23,125	19	0	0	10	9	935	132	719	84	1
	Indianola	11,143	77	2	11	15	49	823	272	523	28	8
	Iuka	2,947	8	0	0	0	8	66	21	42	3	3
	Jackson	175,525	1,512	46	141	862	463	12,465	3,897	6,984	1,584	39
	Kosciusko	7,325	27	3	3	12	9	197	67	127	3	1
	Laurel	18,437	123	4	22	62	35	1,178	415	686	77	0
	Leakesville	993	0	0	0	0	0	0	0	0	0	0
	Leland	5,008	8	0	1	1	6	143	55	87	1	0
	Lexington	1,902	14	0	2	4	8	18	8	10	0	0
	Long Beach	15,371	14	0	0	6	8	378	72	287	19	0
	Louisville	6,671	13	0	1	3	9	69	52	17	0	0
	Lucedale	3,026	9	0	0	3	6	109	15	85	9	0

[1] The FBI does not publish arson data unless it receives data from either the agency or the state for all 12 months of the calendar year.
[3] The FBI determined that the agency's data were overreported. Consequently, affected data are not included in this table.
[7] Because of changes in the state/local agency's reporting practices, figures are not comparable to previous years' data.

Table 8. Offenses Known to Law Enforcement, by State and City, 2007 (Contd.)

(Number.)

State	City	Population	Violent crime	Murder and non-negligent man-slaughter	Forcible rape	Robbery	Aggravated assault	Property crime	Burglary	Larceny-theft	Motor vehicle theft	Arson[1]
	Madison	17,554	14	0	4	2	8	220	17	199	4	0
	Magee	4,314	7	0	0	1	6	131	21	95	15	0
	Magnolia	2,126	10	0	2	0	8	43	15	23	5	0
	McComb	13,583	60	0	1	28	31	748	158	530	60	0
	Meridian	37,954	229	2	38	83	106	1,916	753	1,044	119	19
	Morton	3,421	24	0	1	2	21	36	21	10	5	0
	Moss Point	14,464	77	2	12	39	24	1,036	429	472	135	0
	Natchez	16,930	57	3	4	21	29	971	193	764	14	6
	New Albany	8,113	29	1	0	1	27	120	37	76	7	0
	Newton	3,698	6	0	0	1	5	74	40	33	1	0
	Olive Branch	31,223	77	1	10	30	36	1,651	368	1,189	94	4
	Oxford	14,362	37	1	8	8	20	443	100	323	20	0
	Pascagoula	23,555	122	3	17	97	5	1,701	580	932	189	0
	Pass Christian	6,041	12	0	2	2	8	187	45	130	12	0
	Pearl	24,161	62	2	20	24	16	844	287	489	68	0
	Petal	10,302	13	0	6	2	5	125	73	43	9	4
	Poplarville	2,781	12	0	0	1	11	43	21	18	4	0
	Port Gibson	1,717	6	0	0	1	5	21	5	16	0	0
	Purvis	2,579	1	0	0	0	1	0	0	0	0	0
	Ridgeland	21,701	44	2	2	22	18	654	50	564	40	0
	Ripley	5,680	18	0	1	1	16	90	31	53	6	0
	Roxie	552	0	0	0	0	0	0	0	0	0	0
	Shelby	2,646	11	0	1	1	9	22	17	1	4	0
	Starkville	22,663	46	0	4	15	27	509	129	368	12	1
	Stonewall	1,095	0	0	0	0	0	5	5	0	0	0
	Summit	1,641	2	0	0	2	0	59	11	46	2	0
	Vicksburg	25,610	220	6	26	51	137	1,842	440	1,282	120	9
	Waveland	5,668	26	0	2	2	22	433	87	320	26	0
	Waynesboro	5,655	26	0	0	17	9	110	86	21	3	0
	West Point	11,433	36	2	4	14	16	371	122	249	0	0
	Wiggins	4,774	21	0	2	4	15	263	101	160	2	0
	Winona	4,740	9	0	1	3	5	34	3	27	4	0
MISSOURI	Adrian	1,885	3	0	0	1	2	5	2	2	1	0
	Advance	1,214	0	0	0	0	0	7	4	3	0	0
	Alton	645	1	0	0	0	1	5	2	3	0	0
	Anderson	1,927	15	0	2	0	13	43	13	25	5	0
	Appleton City	1,302	6	0	0	0	6	30	10	20	0	0
	Arbyrd	496	4	0	0	0	4	4	4	0	0	0
	Archie	989	2	0	0	0	2	26	3	21	2	0
	Arnold	20,831	36	0	2	4	30	1,296	68	1,206	22	5
	Ash Grove	1,502	14	0	0	1	13	34	5	28	1	0
	Ashland	2,156	11	0	0	0	11	54	7	45	2	1
	Aurora	7,421	48	0	4	10	34	566	124	410	32	3
	Auxvasse	1,006	5	0	0	0	5	17	5	11	1	0
	Ava	3,124	36	0	0	1	35	114	23	81	10	0
	Ballwin	30,120	17	0	2	2	13	305	63	235	7	0
	Bates City	237	0	0	0	0	0	14	3	9	2	1
	Battlefield	4,148	0	0	0	0	0	77	21	50	6	0
	Bella Villa	642	5	1	0	0	4	4	0	2	2	0
	Belle	1,362	0	0	0	0	0	6	1	5	0	0
	Bellefontaine Neighbor	10,430	79	0	4	18	57	561	204	268	89	4
	Bellerive	257	0	0	0	0	0	4	2	2	0	0
	Bellflower	408	2	0	0	0	2	1	1	0	0	0
	Bel-Nor	1,496	4	0	0	1	3	30	10	20	0	0
	Bel-Ridge	2,924	24	0	1	6	17	184	75	89	20	2
	Belton	24,492	55	2	7	10	36	713	119	546	48	2
	Berkeley	9,460	172	0	8	54	110	614	218	293	103	7
	Bernie	1,803	2	0	0	0	2	22	5	14	3	0
	Bethany	3,078	12	0	0	0	12	75	20	55	0	0
	Billings	1,135	0	0	0	0	0	20	3	16	1	0
	Birch Tree	627	3	0	0	0	3	5	2	1	2	1
	Birmingham	216	1	0	0	0	1	1	0	1	0	0
	Bismarck	1,569	1	0	0	0	1	2	1	1	0	2
	Bland	566	2	0	0	0	2	11	9	2	0	0
	Bloomfield	1,883	1	0	0	0	1	33	11	19	3	0
	Blue Springs	54,718	80	0	12	31	37	1,765	275	1,323	167	7
	Bolivar	10,748	82	1	7	4	70	373	89	270	14	2
	Bonne Terre	7,153	4	0	0	0	4	92	17	65	10	1
	Boonville	8,830	20	0	1	3	16	274	28	241	5	1
	Bourbon	1,415	18	0	0	0	18	26	7	16	3	1
	Bowling Green	5,166	4	0	0	0	4	173	38	135	0	0
	Branson	7,496	139	1	2	19	117	1,138	126	969	43	0
	Branson West	514	3	0	0	0	3	17	0	17	0	0
	Braymer	.963	10	0	1	0	9	8	2	3	3	0

[1] The FBI does not publish arson data unless it receives data from either the agency or the state for all 12 months of the calendar year.

Table 8. Offenses Known to Law Enforcement, by State and City, 2007 (Contd.)

(Number.)

State	City	Population	Violent crime	Murder and non-negligent man-slaughter	Forcible rape	Robbery	Aggravated assault	Property crime	Burglary	Larceny-theft	Motor vehicle theft	Arson[1]
	Breckenridge Hills	4,525	32	0	3	9	20	246	35	186	25	1
	Brentwood	7,238	8	0	2	4	2	404	27	368	9	0
	Bridgeton	15,120	128	2	7	34	85	926	104	740	82	1
	Brookfield	4,371	16	0	1	0	15	115	18	91	6	1
	Bucklin	482	0	0	0	0	0	2	1	1	0	0
	Buckner	2,738	7	0	0	1	6	103	21	77	5	0
	Buffalo	3,143	5	1	0	0	4	134	17	113	4	2
	Butler	4,271	5	0	0	0	5	162	28	131	3	1
	Butterfield Village	426	0	0	0	0	0	4	3	0	1	1
	Byrnes Mill	2,912	2	0	0	0	2	14	1	9	4	0
	Cabool	2,150	3	0	2	0	1	49	15	25	9	0
	California	4,209	11	0	1	4	6	87	11	75	1	0
	Calverton Park	1,286	4	0	0	2	2	31	10	13	8	0
	Camden Point	558	0	0	0	0	0	0	0	0	0	0
	Camdenton	3,226	8	0	1	0	7	166	15	141	10	2
	Cameron	9,015	21	0	0	1	20	195	24	163	8	5
	Campbell	1,853	0	0	0	0	0	36	5	29	2	0
	Canton	2,489	14	0	1	0	13	60	9	48	3	0
	Cape Girardeau	36,754	254	1	10	34	209	2,462	332	2,085	45	9
	Cardwell	739	1	0	0	0	1	13	5	6	2	0
	Carl Junction	7,071	33	0	1	0	32	132	36	91	5	0
	Carterville	1,937	2	0	0	0	2	29	8	19	2	0
	Carthage	13,407	17	0	0	4	13	342	79	250	13	1
	Caruthersville	6,310	21	0	1	7	13	238	58	172	8	0
	Cassville	3,278	4	0	0	0	4	133	15	108	10	0
	Centralia	3,593	17	0	0	3	14	99	21	72	6	0
	Chaffee	2,981	8	0	0	0	8	72	26	43	3	0
	Charlack	1,357	7	0	2	1	4	85	5	76	4	0
	Charleston	5,268	24	0	0	5	19	159	40	112	7	0
	Chesterfield	46,642	55	0	6	12	37	875	122	734	19	6
	Chillicothe	8,700	34	0	0	0	34	369	68	284	17	1
	Clarkton	1,262	3	0	1	0	2	15	4	10	1	0
	Claycomo	1,289	3	0	0	0	3	17	7	10	0	0
	Clayton	16,036	26	0	2	6	18	422	54	351	17	0
	Cleveland	690	1	0	0	0	1	3	1	2	0	0
	Clever	1,321	1	0	0	0	1	1	1	0	0	0
	Clinton	9,523	8	0	0	0	8	414	60	346	8	1
	Cole Camp	1,160	0	0	0	0	0	12	2	10	0	0
	Columbia	95,595	617	3	30	141	443	3,323	594	2,509	220	7
	Concordia	2,409	1	0	0	0	1	63	11	47	5	0
	Cool Valley	1,014	10	0	0	3	7	84	13	59	12	0
	Cooter	430	4	0	0	0	4	7	5	1	1	0
	Cottleville	2,685	6	0	0	0	6	49	3	46	0	0
	Country Club Hills	1,293	6	0	3	3	0	71	28	33	10	0
	Country Club Village	1,977	3	0	1	0	2	22	5	14	3	0
	Crane	1,445	6	0	0	0	6	25	1	23	1	2
	Crestwood	11,545	14	0	0	3	11	631	19	599	13	0
	Creve Coeur	17,028	21	0	1	10	10	331	42	274	15	0
	Crocker	989	2	0	0	0	2	19	2	15	2	0
	Crystal City	4,599	19	1	5	5	8	152	23	122	7	0
	Cuba	3,529	21	0	0	0	21	265	57	203	5	0
	Deepwater	505	2	0	2	0	0	2	0	2	0	0
	Dellwood	4,937	26	0	1	12	13	165	80	62	23	0
	Delta	541	0	0	0	0	0	0	0	0	0	0
	Desloge	5,218	14	0	1	1	12	220	21	195	4	0
	De Soto	6,579	26	0	0	0	26	212	26	175	11	1
	Des Peres	8,626	8	0	0	4	4	359	36	320	3	0
	Dexter	7,658	14	0	3	0	11	201	49	144	8	1
	Diamond	881	1	0	1	0	0	8	2	6	0	0
	Dixon	1,519	2	0	0	0	2	57	11	44	2	0
	Doniphan	1,935	5	0	1	0	4	128	24	100	4	0
	Doolittle	672	3	0	0	0	3	5	3	2	0	0
	Drexel	1,106	7	0	0	0	7	26	7	18	1	0
	Duenweg	1,213	7	0	0	0	7	53	8	40	5	1
	Duquesne	1,708	9	0	0	2	7	49	20	21	8	1
	East Lynne	308	0	0	0	0	0	0	0	0	0	0
	East Prairie	3,145	13	0	0	0	13	102	11	87	4	0
	Edgerton	550	5	0	1	0	4	12	5	4	3	1
	Edmundson	789	7	0	0	1	6	73	5	41	27	0
	Eldon	4,991	14	0	0	1	13	163	24	138	1	2
	El Dorado Springs	3,811	23	0	0	1	22	157	27	126	4	0
	Ellington	999	0	0	0	0	0	28	7	20	1	2
	Ellisville	9,323	7	0	0	1	6	108	12	89	7	1
	Elsberry	2,601	6	0	2	2	2	22	4	18	0	0

[1] The FBI does not publish arson data unless it receives data from either the agency or the state for all 12 months of the calendar year.

Table 8. Offenses Known to Law Enforcement, by State and City, 2007 *(Contd.)*

(Number.)

State	City	Population	Violent crime	Murder and non-negligent man-slaughter	Forcible rape	Robbery	Aggravated assault	Property crime	Burglary	Larceny-theft	Motor vehicle theft	Arson[1]
	Eminence	560	1	1	0	0	0	7	5	2	0	0
	Eureka	9,287	13	0	1	5	7	326	21	296	9	3
	Everton	321	2	0	0	0	2	6	4	2	0	?
	Excelsior Springs	11,747	69	1	2	6	60	389	100	265	24	3
	Exeter	760	1	0	0	0	1	6	0	6	0	0
	Fair Grove	1,331	2	0	0	0	2	19	4	14	1	0
	Fair Play	451	1	0	1	0	0	17	12	3	2	1
	Farber	396	0	0	0	0	0	0	0	0	0	0
	Farmington	15,711	78	0	3	4	71	733	61	650	22	0
	Fayette	2,686	4	0	0	0	4	15	3	11	1	0
	Ferguson	21,142	104	1	9	52	42	1,208	247	766	195	4
	Ferrelview	584	3	0	0	0	3	13	4	9	0	0
	Festus	11,390	103	0	5	3	95	275	36	221	18	3
	Flordell Hills	870	15	0	1	4	10	52	28	17	7	0
	Florissant	51,025	90	0	4	49	37	1,300	234	905	161	3
	Foley	209	0	0	0	0	0	0	0	0	0	0
	Fordland	765	1	0	0	0	1	10	3	6	1	0
	Foristell	330	1	0	0	0	1	67	4	61	2	0
	Forsyth	1,698	2	0	0	0	2	45	2	40	3	0
	Fredericktown	4,057	24	0	2	0	22	146	27	111	8	2
	Freeman	611	0	0	0	0	0	0	0	0	0	0
	Frontenac	3,531	5	0	0	2	3	70	8	60	2	0
	Fulton	12,311	45	1	2	5	37	524	51	451	22	3
	Galena	529	0	0	0	0	0	0	0	0	0	0
	Gallatin	1,761	9	0	0	0	9	22	5	17	0	2
	Garden City	1,694	1	0	0	0	1	16	6	10	0	3
	Gerald	1,242	5	0	1	0	4	33	13	20	0	0
	Gideon	988	0	0	0	0	0	4	1	3	0	0
	Gladstone	27,686	72	1	11	23	37	657	116	477	64	6
	Glasgow	1,194	1	1	0	0	0	9	1	8	0	0
	Glendale	5,526	4	0	0	1	3	43	6	36	1	0
	Glen Echo Park	159	0	0	0	0	0	0	0	0	0	0
	Goodman	1,265	1	0	0	0	1	13	6	7	0	0
	Gower	1,430	4	1	1	0	2	24	3	21	0	0
	Grain Valley	10,225	16	0	1	2	13	262	71	173	18	0
	Granby	2,259	8	0	0	0	8	47	8	36	3	1
	Grandin	238	0	0	0	0	0	0	0	0	0	0
	Grandview	24,322	182	4	12	52	114	1,188	278	707	203	6
	Greendale	698	2	0	0	0	2	7	5	2	0	0
	Greenfield	1,286	5	0	0	0	5	12	6	5	1	0
	Greenwood	4,650	8	0	0	1	7	56	19	36	1	1
	Hallsville	939	1	0	0	0	1	23	2	19	2	0
	Hamilton	1,800	5	0	2	0	3	38	8	30	0	0
	Hannibal	17,612	105	0	20	16	69	1,402	183	1,194	25	1
	Harrisonville	9,935	21	0	1	4	16	414	28	374	12	0
	Hartville	604	0	0	0	0	0	0	0	0	0	0
	Hawk Point	552	1	0	0	0	1	8	3	4	1	0
	Hayti	3,007	16	0	0	6	10	195	36	150	9	0
	Hayti Heights	772	2	0	0	0	2	16	8	8	0	2
	Hazelwood	25,407	82	1	3	26	52	1,128	200	803	125	0
	Henrietta	442	0	0	0	0	0	0	0	0	0	0
	Herculaneum	3,306	3	0	1	1	1	309	6	302	1	2
	Hermann	2,759	11	0	0	0	11	88	20	66	2	0
	Higginsville	4,662	12	0	1	1	10	133	19	109	5	0
	High Hill	222	0	0	0	0	0	1	0	1	0	0
	Highlandville	929	1	0	0	0	1	1	0	1	0	0
	Hillsboro	1,938	10	0	0	0	10	61	6	50	5	1
	Holcomb	691	0	0	0	0	0	2	0	2	0	0
	Holden	2,525	11	0	0	0	11	88	17	65	6	0
	Hollister	3,797	61	1	5	0	55	164	48	108	8	1
	Holt	465	1	0	0	0	1	18	5	11	2	0
	Holts Summit	3,600	18	0	0	3	15	139	21	117	1	0
	Hornersville	674	0	0	0	0	0	0	0	0	0	0
	Houston	2,025	3	0	0	1	2	55	12	41	2	1
	Humansville	1,008	3	0	0	0	3	19	10	9	0	0
	Huntsville	1,641	0	0	0	0	0	6	1	5	0	0
	Hurley	160	0	0	0	0	0	0	0	0	0	4
	Iberia	684	6	1	0	0	5	9	7	1	1	1
	Independence	108,879	837	7	45	154	631	7,933	1,304	5,547	1,082	35
	Indian Point	672	0	0	0	0	0	5	2	3	0	0
	Iron Mountain Lake	707	0	0	0	0	0	11	2	5	4	0
	Ironton	1,353	6	0	0	0	6	66	8	55	3	0
	Jackson	13,431	18	2	3	1	12	342	50	283	9	0
	JASCO Metropolitan	2,802	25	0	1	0	24	26	4	18	4	0

[1] The FBI does not publish arson data unless it receives data from either the agency or the state for all 12 months of the calendar year.

Table 8. Offenses Known to Law Enforcement, by State and City, 2007 *(Contd.)*

(Number.)

State	City	Population	Violent crime	Murder and non-negligent man-slaughter	Forcible rape	Robbery	Aggravated assault	Property crime	Burglary	Larceny-theft	Motor vehicle theft	Arson[1]
	Jasper	1,046	0	0	0	0	0	6	6	0	0	0
	Jefferson City	39,121	286	1	25	30	230	1,484	244	1,186	54	4
	Jennings	14,738	180	3	12	49	116	1,406	475	655	276	4
	Jonesburg	724	6	0	0	0	6	14	2	11	1	0
	Joplin	48,261	372	1	38	91	242	4,812	845	3,554	413	37
	Kahoka	2,185	1	0	1	0	0	43	19	21	3	0
	Kearney	8,262	9	0	0	1	8	133	19	111	3	0
	Kennett	10,909	31	0	0	10	21	663	161	477	25	1
	Keytesville	508	0	0	0	0	0	0	0	0	0	0
	Kimberling City	2,584	4	0	0	0	4	40	11	26	3	0
	Kimmswick	92	0	0	0	0	0	0	0	0	0	0
	King City	910	1	0	1	0	0	5	3	2	0	0
	Kirksville	16,934	107	0	0	1	106	496	57	430	9	2
	Kirkwood	26,875	39	1	3	6	29	784	121	636	27	8
	Knob Noster	3,072	1	0	0	0	1	153	49	101	3	1
	Ladue	8,199	8	0	0	0	8	144	25	116	3	0
	La Grange	934	3	0	0	0	3	8	5	1	2	1
	Lake Lafayette	378	0	0	0	0	0	7	5	1	1	0
	Lake Lotawana	1,945	1	0	0	0	1	37	11	23	3	1
	Lake Ozark	2,022	6	0	0	0	6	60	7	51	2	0
	Lakeshire	1,297	2	0	0	0	2	18	4	12	2	0
	Lake St. Louis	14,325	17	0	0	3	14	227	20	193	14	2
	Lake Tapawingo	795	1	0	0	0	1	10	2	6	2	0
	Lake Waukomis	900	0	0	0	0	0	2	0	1	1	0
	Lake Winnebago	1,130	0	0	0	0	0	10	0	10	0	0
	Lamar	4,649	25	1	6	0	18	158	31	122	5	1
	La Monte	1,076	5	0	0	0	5	19	7	12	0	0
	La Plata	1,438	1	0	0	0	1	1	1	0	0	0
	Lathrop	2,357	6	0	1	0	5	43	12	27	4	1
	Laurie	719	5	0	0	0	5	51	5	43	3	0
	Lawson	2,407	0	0	0	0	0	43	6	34	3	0
	Leadington	220	1	0	0	0	1	4	0	4	0	0
	Leadwood	1,173	3	0	0	0	3	14	3	9	2	0
	Lebanon	13,964	66	2	5	3	56	871	99	712	60	3
	Lee's Summit	83,558	109	0	10	42	57	2,479	390	1,857	232	8
	Leeton	625	0	0	0	0	0	14	4	10	0	0
	Lexington	4,590	13	0	2	0	11	158	43	106	9	1
	Liberal	811	6	0	0	0	6	3	0	3	0	0
	Liberty	30,050	63	1	11	6	45	654	107	499	48	13
	Licking	1,516	2	0	0	0	2	65	9	53	3	0
	Lilbourn	1,205	6	1	0	0	5	18	0	17	1	0
	Lincoln	1,107	2	0	0	0	2	26	10	14	2	0
	Linn	1,432	3	0	0	0	3	9	6	3	0	0
	Linn Creek	301	3	0	0	0	3	3	0	3	0	0
	Lockwood	953	0	0	0	0	0	2	0	2	0	0
	Lone Jack	887	2	0	0	0	2	22	14	8	0	0
	Lowry City	749	6	0	0	0	6	8	3	4	1	0
	Macon	5,446	14	0	1	2	11	161	24	133	4	2
	Malden	4,569	9	0	0	0	9	108	38	70	0	0
	Manchester	18,769	10	0	1	2	7	281	24	247	10	0
	Mansfield	1,359	3	0	0	1	2	22	6	15	1	0
	Maplewood	8,701	36	1	4	10	21	396	43	317	36	1
	Marble Hill	1,515	3	0	0	0	3	53	6	44	3	0
	Marceline	2,331	13	0	3	0	10	35	4	30	1	0
	Marionville	2,177	5	0	0	0	5	76	14	59	3	0
	Marquand	265	0	0	0	0	0	1	0	1	0	0
	Marshall	12,281	20	0	2	4	14	303	53	240	10	0
	Marshfield	7,173	11	0	0	0	11	147	17	121	9	2
	Marston	549	1	1	0	0	0	0	0	0	0	0
	Marthasville	864	0	0	0	0	0	0	0	0	0	0
	Martinsburg	328	3	0	0	0	3	0	0	0	0	0
	Maryland Heights	26,221	34	2	1	13	18	875	135	687	53	4
	Maryville	10,540	13	2	1	0	10	165	19	139	7	0
	Matthews	545	0	0	0	0	0	7	5	2	0	0
	Maysville	1,137	0	0	0	0	0	4	1	3	0	2
	Mayview	292	0	0	0	0	0	0	0	0	0	0
	Memphis	1,995	5	0	0	0	5	24	9	13	2	0
	Mexico	10,965	25	0	0	6	19	220	35	183	2	2
	Milan	1,796	0	0	0	0	0	21	7	13	1	0
	Miller	801	2	0	0	0	2	16	4	11	1	0
	Miner	1,329	26	0	2	1	23	112	20	84	8	0
	Moberly	14,023	22	0	0	3	19	739	92	635	12	1
	Moline Acres	2,540	25	0	1	5	19	187	54	116	17	1
	Monett	8,851	8	0	1	1	6	400	87	293	20	6

[1] The FBI does not publish arson data unless it receives data from either the agency or the state for all 12 months of the calendar year.

Table 8. Offenses Known to Law Enforcement, by State and City, 2007 *(Contd.)*

(Number.)

State	City	Population	Violent crime	Murder and non-negligent man-slaughter	Forcible rape	Robbery	Aggravated assault	Property crime	Burglary	Larceny-theft	Motor vehicle theft	Arson[1]
	Monroe City	2,541	16	0	2	0	14	83	19	60	4	0
	Montgomery City	2,538	11	0	0	0	11	49	10	38	1	0
	Montrose	434	1	0	0	0	1	9	6	3	0	0
	Morehouse	935	3	0	0	0	3	8	4	3	1	0
	Mosby	244	3	0	1	0	2	5	2	1	2	1
	Moscow Mills	2,460	13	0	1	0	12	49	9	37	3	0
	Mound City	1,078	1	0	0	1	0	10	3	6	1	1
	Mountain View	2,605	20	0	0	1	19	105	32	61	12	1
	Mount Vernon	4,511	21	0	1	1	19	273	40	222	11	0
	Napoleon	200	1	0	0	0	1	6	3	2	1	0
	Neosho	11,328	17	3	2	2	10	461	68	371	22	5
	Nevada	8,457	45	0	6	4	35	539	74	425	40	4
	New Bloomfield	749	1	0	0	0	1	3	1	2	0	1
	Newburg	476	5	0	0	0	5	8	0	5	3	0
	New Florence	776	1	0	0	0	1	17	2	15	0	0
	New Franklin	1,107	7	0	0	0	7	5	3	2	0	0
	New Haven	2,014	10	0	0	0	10	61	7	48	6	0
	New London	1,011	1	0	0	0	1	23	6	16	1	0
	New Madrid	3,073	0	0	0	0	0	15	4	11	0	0
	New Melle	286	0	0	0	0	0	4	4	0	0	0
	Niangua	497	0	0	0	0	0	0	0	0	0	0
	Nixa	18,220	15	1	1	0	13	241	43	187	11	2
	Noel	1,562	4	0	0	0	4	11	1	7	3	0
	Norborne	776	1	0	0	0	1	1	0	1	0	0
	Normandy	4,946	66	3	1	12	50	188	39	97	52	1
	North Kansas City	5,619	31	2	1	14	14	493	55	345	93	0
	Northmoor	403	2	0	0	0	2	23	5	13	5	0
	Northwoods	4,353	9	0	2	4	3	151	59	59	33	2
	Oak Grove	7,069	9	1	4	0	4	153	15	135	3	0
	Oakland	1,575	0	0	0	0	0	29	3	26	0	0
	Oakview Village	389	1	0	0	0	1	6	5	1	0	0
	Odessa	4,828	4	0	0	1	3	103	26	64	13	1
	O'Fallon	76,542	58	0	8	12	38	1,823	159	1,620	44	5
	Old Monroe	300	0	0	0	0	0	1	0	1	0	0
	Olivette	7,439	25	0	1	5	19	215	33	167	15	0
	Olympian Village	675	0	0	0	0	0	2	1	1	0	0
	Oran	1,259	17	0	0	0	17	26	10	14	2	1
	Orrick	848	2	0	0	0	2	20	8	11	1	0
	Osage Beach	4,554	33	0	2	0	31	403	50	331	22	0
	Osceola	804	2	0	0	0	2	16	5	10	1	0
	Overland	15,783	69	0	5	17	47	814	116	651	47	1
	Owensville	2,523	0	0	0	0	0	137	9	125	3	0
	Ozark	17,496	57	0	4	8	45	413	71	327	15	0
	Pacific	7,245	28	1	1	2	24	259	15	234	10	0
	Pagedale	3,440	39	0	3	15	21	197	47	115	35	0
	Palmyra	3,443	2	0	0	0	2	47	2	43	2	0
	Park Hills	8,744	5	1	2	0	2	122	13	104	5	1
	Parkville	5,276	4	0	1	0	3	140	11	127	2	0
	Parma	785	7	0	0	0	7	25	10	15	0	0
	Pasadena Park	463	0	0	0	0	0	8	0	7	1	0
	Peculiar	4,495	6	0	0	2	4	183	9	170	4	0
	Perry	668	0	0	0	0	0	1	0	0	1	0
	Perryville	8,062	8	0	1	4	3	231	37	181	13	2
	Pevely	4,442	13	0	0	2	11	131	17	104	10	2
	Piedmont	1,954	3	0	0	1	2	43	7	36	0	2
	Pierce City	1,456	2	0	1	0	1	33	13	19	1	0
	Pilot Grove	748	1	0	0	0	1	12	2	10	0	0
	Pilot Knob	688	0	0	0	0	0	3	0	3	0	0
	Pine Lawn	4,038	85	1	2	8	74	252	63	140	49	1
	Pineville	878	1	0	0	0	1	1	1	0	0	0
	Platte City	4,971	9	0	0	0	9	94	16	74	4	0
	Platte Woods	458	1	0	1	0	0	27	2	23	2	0
	Plattsburg	2,416	6	0	0	0	6	67	16	48	3	0
	Pleasant Hill	7,108	3	0	1	0	2	163	18	143	2	0
	Pleasant Hope	590	0	0	0	0	0	2	2	0	0	0
	Pleasant Valley	3,481	5	0	1	0	4	73	17	47	9	2
	Poplar Bluff	17,054	75	1	4	18	52	1,335	212	1,061	62	17
	Portageville	2,990	12	0	0	0	12	20	6	12	2	0
	Potosi	2,725	9	0	0	0	9	120	11	103	6	0
	Purdy	1,175	6	0	0	0	6	31	15	14	2	2
	Puxico	1,149	2	0	0	0	2	9	7	2	0	1
	Randolph	50	0	0	0	0	0	3	0	3	0	0
	Raymore	17,439	15	1	3	1	10	529	54	453	22	1
	Raytown	28,344	93	0	7	44	42	967	235	558	174	4

[1] The FBI does not publish arson data unless it receives data from either the agency or the state for all 12 months of the calendar year.

Table 8. Offenses Known to Law Enforcement, by State and City, 2007 *(Contd.)*

(Number.)

State	City	Population	Violent crime	Murder and non-negligent man-slaughter	Forcible rape	Robbery	Aggravated assault	Property crime	Burglary	Larceny-theft	Motor vehicle theft	Arson[1]
	Reeds Spring	720	3	0	0	0	3	13	3	9	1	0
	Republic	11,777	43	0	2	0	41	394	83	289	22	0
	Rich Hill	1,510	11	0	1	0	10	68	27	40	1	0
	Richland	1,756	2	0	0	1	1	39	6	31	2	0
	Richmond	6,029	13	0	2	0	11	223	44	162	17	0
	Richmond Heights	9,179	54	0	4	14	36	720	50	633	37	2
	Riverside	2,961	12	1	1	4	6	202	22	158	22	3
	Riverview	2,948	34	1	2	5	26	167	75	57	35	3
	Rockaway Beach	586	12	0	0	0	12	11	2	8	1	0
	Rock Hill	4,641	3	0	1	1	1	95	17	71	7	0
	Rock Port	1,306	8	0	0	0	8	10	0	9	1	0
	Rogersville	2,647	23	0	0	0	23	66	6	58	2	0
	Rolla	18,208	81	0	6	14	61	948	151	746	51	4
	Rosebud	378	0	0	0	0	0	3	1	2	0	0
	Salem	4,860	21	0	0	2	19	167	25	137	5	0
	Savannah	5,118	2	0	1	1	0	115	19	96	0	0
	Scott City	4,571	13	0	1	2	10	3	3	0	0	0
	Sedalia	20,682	189	0	8	23	158	1,402	266	1,081	55	5
	Seligman	924	0	0	0	0	0	0	0	0	0	0
	Senath	1,626	0	0	0	0	0	3	0	3	0	0
	Seneca	2,277	1	0	0	0	1	100	15	79	6	4
	Seymour	2,025	8	0	0	0	8	32	11	19	2	0
	Shrewsbury	6,290	6	0	0	3	3	122	14	101	7	0
	Sikeston	17,188	273	2	4	45	222	862	170	640	52	15
	Silex	288	0	0	0	0	0	0	0	0	0	0
	Slater	1,911	4	0	0	0	4	51	5	41	5	0
	Smithville	7,777	10	0	0	0	10	87	8	73	6	0
	Southwest City	931	6	0	1	0	5	24	4	19	1	1
	Sparta	1,223	6	0	0	1	5	10	7	3	0	0
	Springfield	150,488	1,051	5	72	294	680	14,315	2,140	11,231	944	64
	St. Ann	12,887	95	0	7	17	71	832	107	690	35	1
	St. Charles	63,277	162	1	21	48	92	2,256	309	1,853	94	6
	St. Clair	4,400	43	0	4	2	37	289	36	243	10	4
	Steele	2,136	7	0	1	4	2	105	15	80	10	1
	Steelville	1,454	16	0	0	0	16	30	11	14	5	0
	Ste. Genevieve	4,479	3	0	0	1	2	66	8	56	2	0
	St. George	1,222	4	0	0	0	4	20	1	18	1	0
	St. James	4,110	32	0	1	3	28	234	36	195	3	0
	St. John	6,444	25	1	2	8	14	254	46	178	30	1
	St. Joseph	72,424	216	2	13	66	135	3,857	770	2,814	273	16
	St. Louis	348,197	7,654	138	255	2,761	4,500	33,901	7,289	20,330	6,282	410
	St. Marys	392	0	0	0	0	0	4	1	2	1	0
	Stover	1,045	22	0	3	0	19	66	14	48	4	0
	St. Peters	55,291	106	0	12	19	75	1,352	132	1,166	54	19
	Strafford	2,025	4	0	0	3	1	123	7	111	5	0
	St. Robert	3,319	73	0	4	4	65	261	52	197	12	4
	Sturgeon	897	6	0	0	1	5	6	4	2	0	1
	Sugar Creek	3,506	23	2	0	10	11	205	57	119	29	0
	Sullivan	6,698	18	1	2	3	12	253	43	200	10	0
	Summersville	562	2	0	0	0	2	20	9	9	2	1
	Sunset Hills	8,314	20	0	1	6	13	253	34	206	13	1
	Sweet Springs	1,527	3	0	1	1	1	16	7	9	0	0
	Tarkio	1,823	1	0	0	0	1	6	0	4	2	0
	Thayer	2,166	1	0	0	1	0	8	4	3	1	0
	Tipton	3,125	3	0	1	0	2	27	6	20	1	0
	Town and Country	10,757	6	0	0	0	6	145	14	131	0	0
	Tracy	210	0	0	0	0	0	19	2	16	1	0
	Trenton	6,070	25	0	2	0	23	190	56	126	8	0
	Trimble	481	0	0	0	0	0	2	0	2	0	0
	Troy	11,674	53	0	1	1	51	472	33	422	17	1
	Truesdale	615	0	0	0	0	0	7	1	6	0	0
	Union	9,648	54	0	2	1	51	519	50	451	18	0
	Unionville	1,959	0	0	0	0	0	3	2	1	0	2
	University City	36,743	246	0	11	87	148	2,020	343	1,514	163	6
	Uplands Park	442	1	0	0	0	1	6	1	3	2	0
	Urbana	435	1	0	0	0	1	11	4	4	3	1
	Van Buren	819	0	0	0	0	0	27	7	19	1	0
	Vandalia	4,099	5	0	1	0	4	50	9	39	2	0
	Velda City	1,512	4	0	0	1	3	28	11	11	6	0
	Verona	726	0	0	0	0	0	11	2	7	2	0
	Versailles	2,709	5	0	0	0	5	104	4	93	7	0
	Viburnum	808	5	0	0	0	5	22	17	4	1	0
	Vienna	643	2	0	0	0	2	19	5	12	2	0
	Vinita Park	1,803	8	0	0	3	5	93	20	64	9	3

[1] The FBI does not publish arson data unless it receives data from either the agency or the state for all 12 months of the calendar year.

Table 8. Offenses Known to Law Enforcement, by State and City, 2007 *(Contd.)*

(Number.)

State	City	Population	Violent crime	Murder and non-negligent man-slaughter	Forcible rape	Robbery	Aggravated assault	Property crime	Burglary	Larceny-theft	Motor vehicle theft	Arson[1]
	Walnut Grove	641	0	0	0	0	0	9	3	6	0	0
	Wardell	255	0	0	0	0	0	5	1	3	1	0
	Warrensburg	18,206	36	0	2	7	27	559	112	428	19	10
	Warrenton	7,146	16	0	0	2	14	481	34	425	22	0
	Warsaw	2,273	21	0	1	0	20	99	19	74	6	0
	Warson Woods	1,875	1	0	0	1	0	31	3	28	0	0
	Washburn	480	0	0	0	0	0	0	0	0	0	0
	Washington	14,367	27	0	1	2	24	384	38	328	18	2
	Waverly	802	3	0	1	0	2	7	2	5	0	0
	Waynesville	3,616	8	0	0	0	8	115	19	83	13	0
	Weatherby Lake	1,856	6	0	0	0	6	20	6	13	1	0
	Webb City	11,142	5	0	2	0	3	438	53	350	35	0
	Webster Groves	22,620	19	0	2	8	9	354	65	267	22	0
	Wellsville	1,383	1	0	0	0	1	20	9	11	0	0
	Wentzville	24,137	30	0	8	3	19	652	76	560	16	3
	Weston	1,594	3	0	0	0	3	38	1	31	6	0
	West Plains	11,673	39	0	2	2	35	985	160	787	38	2
	Westwood	295	0	0	0	0	0	0	0	0	0	0
	Wheaton	749	0	0	0	0	0	5	0	5	0	0
	Willard	3,320	9	0	0	1	8	100	20	74	6	0
	Willow Springs	2,145	28	0	0	0	28	56	15	36	5	0
	Winfield	900	6	0	1	0	5	16	2	12	2	1
	Winona	1,343	13	0	2	0	11	36	17	17	2	0
	Woodson Terrace	4,056	8	0	0	3	5	149	28	87	34	0
	Wright City	2,837	5	0	0	1	4	166	16	146	4	0
MONTANA	Baker	1,620	2	0	0	0	2	15	5	10	0	0
	Belgrade	7,552	31	0	5	2	24	246	29	198	19	8
	Billings	101,342	245	1	23	54	167	4,182	435	3,420	327	28
	Boulder	1,468	7	0	1	0	6	9	1	6	2	0
	Bozeman	36,158	88	0	17	15	56	1,583	128	1,333	122	16
	Chinook	1,283	2	0	0	0	2	10	0	9	1	0
	Colstrip	2,342	8	0	0	0	8	93	9	75	9	2
	Columbia Falls	4,826	16	0	1	0	15	125	4	116	5	2
	Columbus	1,954	5	0	0	1	4	39	1	37	1	0
	Conrad	2,556	8	0	1	0	7	43	4	34	5	1
	Cut Bank	3,182	39	0	2	0	37	133	12	116	5	0
	Dillon	4,029	9	0	0	0	9	112	6	102	4	0
	East Helena	2,108	3	0	0	0	3	29	7	19	3	1
	Ennis	1,029	2	0	0	0	2	13	4	8	1	0
	Eureka	1,030	5	0	0	0	5	73	4	68	1	0
	Fort Benton	1,451	6	0	2	0	4	32	6	25	1	0
	Glasgow	2,926	16	0	3	0	13	62	5	56	1	0
	Glendive	4,606	13	0	1	0	12	168	2	164	2	1
	Great Falls	56,159	178	1	6	29	142	3,061	235	2,713	113	27
	Hamilton	4,774	23	0	2	0	21	209	13	187	9	4
	Havre	9,414	47	0	6	2	39	421	31	365	25	4
	Helena	28,128	126	0	16	9	101	1,073	127	889	57	14
	Joliet	617	0	0	0	0	0	4	2	2	0	0
	Kalispell	20,104	69	0	7	6	56	1,311	83	1,168	60	10
	Laurel	6,434	14	0	3	0	11	270	11	251	8	5
	Lewistown	6,047	28	0	6	1	21	104	12	89	3	0
	Libby	2,666	8	0	0	1	7	132	17	111	4	0
	Livingston	7,307	26	0	5	0	21	187	43	123	21	0
	Manhattan	1,503	1	0	1	0	0	21	2	17	2	0
	Missoula	65,037	218	1	23	36	158	2,935	255	2,541	139	17
	Plains	1,272	3	0	0	0	3	56	2	48	6	1
	Polson	5,082	42	0	3	0	39	181	10	156	15	0
	Poplar	900	1	0	0	0	1	2	1	1	0	0
	Red Lodge	2,494	10	0	1	0	9	59	6	53	0	2
	Ronan City	2,033	13	0	1	0	12	102	18	72	12	0
	Stevensville	1,966	11	0	1	0	10	27	2	23	2	1
	St. Ignatius	830	1	0	0	0	1	23	2	15	6	0
	Thompson Falls	1,420	6	0	1	0	5	45	5	38	2	1
	Three Forks	1,865	0	0	0	0	0	32	3	26	3	0
	Troy	996	2	0	0	0	2	13	3	8	2	0
	West Yellowstone	1,240	1	0	1	0	0	5	0	5	0	0
NEBRASKA	Alliance	8,054	31	0	0	1	30	175	34	131	10	7
	Ashland	2,586	0	0	0	0	0	6	3	3	0	0
	Auburn	3,187	1	0	0	0	1	118	15	98	5	1
	Aurora	4,261	0	0	0	0	0	40	3	30	7	0
	Bayard	1,143	0	0	0	0	0	35	10	20	5	1
	Beatrice	12,972	47	1	15	1	30	506	106	381	19	5
	Blair	7,962	4	0	0	2	2	143	12	117	14	0
	Bridgeport	1,478	1	0	1	0	0	24	6	17	1	0

[1] The FBI does not publish arson data unless it receives data from either the agency or the state for all 12 months of the calendar year.

Table 8.   Offenses Known to Law Enforcement, by State and City, 2007 *(Contd.)*

(Number.)

State	City	Population	Violent crime	Murder and non-negligent man-slaughter	Forcible rape	Robbery	Aggravated assault	Property crime	Burglary	Larceny-theft	Motor vehicle theft	Arson[1]
	Broken Bow	3,235	3	0	2	0	1	35	6	28	1	0
	Central City	2,839	3	0	1	0	2	49	5	40	4	0
	Chadron	5,158	6	0	1	0	5	114	22	71	21	1
	Cozad	4,293	3	0	2	0	1	59	9	49	1	0
	Crete	6,345	5	0	0	0	5	199	33	158	8	2
	David City	2,520	0	0	0	0	0	45	16	28	1	0
	Emerson	819	0	0	0	0	0	10	4	6	0	1
	Falls City	4,119	0	0	0	0	0	73	15	53	5	1
	Fremont	25,423	38	0	14	2	22	748	94	619	35	5
	Gering	7,677	9	0	0	0	9	225	32	177	16	1
	Gothenburg	3,748	2	1	1	0	0	47	0	46	1	0
	Grand Island	44,812	124	4	5	16	99	2,112	313	1,662	137	5
	Hastings	25,250	51	0	16	9	26	896	164	685	47	10
	Holdrege	5,281	7	0	1	0	6	134	21	105	8	3
	Imperial	1,833	4	0	2	1	1	14	2	10	2	0
	Kearney	29,652	71	0	6	6	59	960	139	796	25	12
	La Vista	16,816	12	1	5	3	3	316	26	268	22	3
	Lexington	10,262	30	0	2	3	25	384	47	328	9	6
	Lincoln	243,243	1,325	6	113	173	1,033	11,755	1,904	9,428	423	2
	Lyons	887	1	0	1	0	0	7	3	4	0	0
	Milford	2,045	0	0	0	0	0	20	2	16	2	0
	Minden	2,867	1	0	1	0	0	83	18	65	0	0
	Mitchell	1,774	2	0	0	0	2	42	11	30	1	0
	Nebraska City	7,106	3	0	2	0	1	217	29	181	7	0
	Norfolk	23,977	27	0	15	3	9	681	71	584	26	3
	Ogallala	4,585	9	0	5	0	4	178	15	154	9	1
	Omaha	431,810	2,578	42	189	818	1,529	20,657	3,345	13,876	3,436	
	O'Neill	3,391	1	0	0	0	1	14	2	12	0	0
	Papillion	21,748	8	0	2	1	5	358	20	321	17	1
	Plainview	1,254	1	0	0	0	1	11	2	9	0	0
	Plattsmouth	7,070	7	0	4	0	3	178	10	159	9	1
	Ralston	6,144	5	0	0	1	4	155	15	120	20	0
	Scottsbluff	14,719	67	0	12	7	48	853	116	712	25	0
	Seward	6,922	5	0	0	1	4	71	12	54	5	0
	Sidney	6,386	10	0	2	0	8	196	25	166	5	0
	South Sioux City	12,139	4	0	1	1	2	194	25	160	9	0
	St. Paul	2,263	1	0	0	0	1	10	3	7	0	0
	Superior	1,845	0	0	0	0	0	9	5	3	1	0
	Valentine	2,694	6	0	0	0	6	80	15	54	11	0
	Valley	1,868	5	0	1	0	4	68	7	58	3	2
	Wahoo	4,060	3	0	2	0	1	73	20	51	2	0
	Wayne	5,136	9	0	3	0	6	140	35	102	3	0
	West Point	3,446	1	0	1	0	0	35	6	27	2	0
	Wilber	1,804	0	0	0	0	0	9	0	9	0	0
	Wymore	1,612	5	0	1	1	3	22	5	16	1	0
	York	7,921	4	0	0	3	1	247	20	218	9	1
NEVADA	Boulder City	15,028	17	1	0	2	14	179	89	79	11	4
	Carlin	2,121	26	0	2	0	24	31	14	14	3	1
	Elko	16,933	46	0	14	7	25	523	87	392	44	1
	Fallon	8,444	24	0	3	2	19	361	46	296	19	7
	Henderson	251,270	591	9	66	227	289	6,293	1,789	3,215	1,289	65
	Las Vegas Metropolitan Police Department	1,341,156	13,641	119	723	5,251	7,548	58,897	15,296	27,156	16,445	334
	Lovelock	1,886	14	0	3	1	10	54	23	27	4	0
	Mesquite	15,660	21	0	2	2	17	450	32	374	44	0
	North Las Vegas	211,419	1,777	28	53	645	1,051	8,195	2,334	3,631	2,230	33
	Reno	214,197	1,513	17	95	516	885	9,418	1,835	6,511	1,072	21
	Sparks	86,884	352	3	36	134	179	3,603	832	2,422	349	22
	West Wendover	5,128	12	2	0	2	8	137	32	99	6	1
	Winnemucca	8,051	28	0	3	3	22	114	35	67	12	1
	Yerington	3,947	0	0	0	0	0	53	38	15	0	0
NEW HAMPSHIRE	Alexandria	1,524	2	0	0	0	2	12	3	9	0	1
	Alton	5,205	6	0	1	0	5	72	32	32	8	3
	Amherst	11,836	8	0	2	4	2	159	27	128	4	0
	Antrim	2,642	2	0	1	0	1	72	18	47	7	1
	Ashland	2,029	3	0	1	1	1	38	5	27	6	1
	Auburn	5,235	3	0	1	0	2	47	14	31	2	0
	Barrington	8,384	2	0	0	0	2	86	37	45	4	0
	Bartlett	2,945	2	0	0	0	2	36	6	29	1	0
	Bedford	21,389	20	0	1	4	15	224	42	173	9	1
	Belmont	7,365	9	0	3	0	6	135	33	98	4	6
	Bennington	1,488	1	0	0	0	1	41	6	33	2	0
	Berlin	9,909	20	0	5	3	12	152	45	101	6	8
	Bethlehem	2,452	2	0	1	1	0	37	15	21	1	0
	Boscawen	3,930	4	1	0	0	3	35	11	24	0	0

[1] The FBI does not publish arson data unless it receives data from either the agency or the state for all 12 months of the calendar year.

Table 8. Offenses Known to Law Enforcement, by State and City, 2007 (Contd.)

(Number.)

State	City	Population	Violent crime	Murder and non-negligent man-slaughter	Forcible rape	Robbery	Aggravated assault	Property crime	Burglary	Larceny-theft	Motor vehicle theft	Arson[1]
	Bow	8,250	5	0	0	2	3	63	15	44	4	0
	Brentwood	3,866	2	0	0	0	2	51	6	41	4	0
	Bristol	3,145	3	0	0	1	2	69	14	52	3	1
	Campton	3,001	4	0	2	0	2	32	25	3	4	3
	Candia	4,200	3	0	0	1	2	49	13	34	2	0
	Carroll	752	3	0	0	0	3	59	9	43	7	0
	Charlestown	4,987	2	0	0	0	2	42	13	27	2	0
	Chester	4,793	2	0	0	1	1	42	18	22	2	1
	Claremont	13,291	39	0	5	3	31	376	49	309	18	5
	Colebrook	2,406	2	0	1	0	1	32	9	16	7	0
	Concord	42,638	87	0	16	18	53	1,048	166	852	30	16
	Conway	9,300	36	3	5	6	22	346	45	289	12	6
	Dalton	907	2	0	0	0	2	19	11	7	1	0
	Danville	4,425	6	0	0	1	5	48	8	38	2	0
	Deerfield	4,220	1	0	0	0	1	40	4	35	1	0
	Deering	2,070	2	0	0	0	2	28	4	23	1	0
	Derry	34,118	73	1	14	20	38	692	150	488	54	16
	Dover	28,661	20	0	5	3	12	598	68	510	20	7
	Dunbarton	2,641	1	0	1	0	0	18	4	12	2	0
	Enfield	4,890	6	0	0	0	6	45	9	36	0	0
	Epping	6,263	5	0	1	0	4	167	40	123	4	2
	Epsom	4,609	4	0	0	1	3	66	14	43	9	1
	Exeter	14,851	13	0	4	0	9	169	25	140	4	3
	Farmington	6,688	22	0	2	2	18	186	31	142	13	1
	Fitzwilliam	2,321	1	0	1	0	0	9	3	5	1	0
	Franconia	1,052	0	0	0	0	0	14	2	12	0	0
	Fremont	4,156	7	0	0	1	6	49	17	29	3	3
	Gilford	7,569	11	0	1	3	7	156	19	128	9	0
	Gilmanton	3,621	2	0	0	0	2	30	12	14	4	0
	Goffstown	17,810	11	0	2	0	9	265	48	212	5	8
	Gorham	2,914	3	0	1	0	2	35	3	32	0	0
	Grantham	2,578	2	0	0	0	2	13	2	9	2	0
	Greenland	3,409	3	0	0	0	3	35	4	30	1	0
	Hampstead	8,904	4	0	0	0	4	93	24	63	6	0
	Hampton	15,493	10	0	3	2	5	357	56	278	23	3
	Hancock	1,824	2	0	0	0	2	5	0	4	1	1
	Hanover	11,198	14	0	10	0	4	187	17	166	4	1
	Haverhill	4,623	15	0	2	1	12	141	30	104	7	1
	Henniker	5,187	5	0	1	0	4	105	24	78	3	0
	Hillsborough	5,539	16	1	4	2	9	116	41	69	6	3
	Hinsdale	4,219	12	0	5	0	7	68	12	55	1	2
	Hooksett	13,705	7	0	4	2	1	272	31	227	14	1
	Hopkinton	5,651	2	0	2	0	0	33	1	31	1	1
	Hudson	24,996	23	0	3	5	15	409	70	318	21	7
	Jaffrey	5,729	12	0	4	2	6	49	20	25	4	3
	Keene	22,693	54	0	12	9	33	640	86	537	17	7
	Kingston	6,284	4	0	1	0	3	60	14	40	6	1
	Laconia	17,153	47	0	13	8	26	686	100	560	26	4
	Lancaster	3,362	3	0	2	0	1	95	19	70	6	0
	Lebanon	12,589	18	0	5	7	6	427	35	384	8	1
	Lee	4,481	2	0	0	0	2	67	20	38	9	0
	Lincoln	1,322	2	0	0	1	1	80	6	73	1	0
	Lisbon	1,663	1	0	1	0	0	23	3	19	1	1
	Litchfield	8,737	7	0	0	1	6	80	15	59	6	2
	Littleton	6,213	9	0	5	0	4	95	14	77	4	1
	Londonderry	25,121	25	0	5	7	13	348	62	246	40	2
	Loudon	5,215	5	0	2	2	1	82	11	58	13	1
	Madison	2,329	2	0	1	0	1	57	15	40	2	0
	Marlborough	2,107	4	0	2	0	2	26	11	15	0	0
	Meredith	6,780	8	0	3	1	4	128	14	108	6	2
	Merrimack	26,847	2	0	0	1	1	210	43	155	12	2
	Middleton	1,806	1	0	1	0	0	45	20	24	1	1
	Milford	15,271	26	0	7	3	16	213	53	147	13	11
	Milton	4,531	6	0	3	0	3	83	19	58	6	1
	Moultonborough	5,019	3	0	1	0	2	79	15	59	5	2
	New Boston	5,121	3	0	0	0	3	26	9	17	0	0
	Newbury	2,129	0	0	0	0	0	17	2	15	0	0
	New Durham	2,536	2	0	1	0	1	35	3	28	4	0
	Newfields	1,598	4	0	1	0	3	41	7	32	2	0
	New Hampton	2,283	1	0	0	1	0	32	10	21	1	1
	Newington	816	2	0	0	1	1	185	4	175	6	0
	New Ipswich	5,258	0	0	0	0	0	62	15	39	8	3
	New London	4,510	0	0	0	0	0	21	3	16	2	0
	Newport	6,570	11	0	1	0	10	236	30	194	12	0

[1] The FBI does not publish arson data unless it receives data from either the agency or the state for all 12 months of the calendar year.

Table 8.   Offenses Known to Law Enforcement, by State and City, 2007 *(Contd.)*

(Number.)

State	City	Population	Violent crime	Murder and non-negligent man-slaughter	Forcible rape	Robbery	Aggravated assault	Property crime	Burglary	Larceny-theft	Motor vehicle theft	Arson[1]
	Newton	4,544	2	0	0	2	0	30	5	24	1	1
	Northfield	5,257	4	0	0	0	4	130	21	104	5	0
	North Hampton	4,600	1	0	0	1	0	65	4	56	5	0
	Northumberland	2,397	1	0	1	0	0	34	7	26	1	1
	Northwood	4,122	3	0	1	0	2	23	12	10	1	0
	Nottingham	4,564	2	0	0	1	1	30	11	17	2	0
	Ossipee	4,723	4	0	1	0	3	101	36	60	5	2
	Pelham	12,774	5	0	2	2	1	177	57	103	17	5
	Pembroke	7,466	6	0	2	1	3	95	26	62	7	2
	Peterborough	6,127	12	0	3	0	9	294	198	96	0	2
	Pittsfield	4,476	8	0	2	2	4	70	12	56	2	1
	Plaistow	7,702	2	0	0	2	0	158	17	129	12	1
	Plymouth	6,406	18	0	6	3	9	212	30	178	4	1
	Portsmouth	20,584	31	0	11	3	17	675	72	579	24	11
	Raymond	10,256	19	0	6	3	10	201	28	162	11	2
	Rindge	6,541	8	0	1	1	6	88	12	71	5	4
	Rochester	30,355	62	0	9	11	42	987	163	769	55	6
	Rollinsford	2,627	1	0	1	0	0	13	4	8	1	1
	Rye	5,219	2	0	1	0	1	31	7	24	0	0
	Sandown	5,873	5	0	2	1	2	49	6	34	9	1
	Sandwich	1,335	1	0	1	0	0	19	4	15	0	0
	Seabrook	8,588	14	0	1	2	11	196	21	169	6	1
	Strafford	4,084	0	0	0	0	0	21	12	9	0	0
	Stratham	7,293	2	0	1	0	1	64	12	49	3	0
	Sugar Hill	602	0	0	0	0	0	5	0	3	2	0
	Sunapee	3,398	0	0	0	0	0	6	3	3	0	0
	Thornton	2,105	1	0	1	0	0	11	2	7	2	0
	Tilton	3,645	10	0	4	3	3	260	20	232	8	0
	Troy	2,098	3	0	0	1	2	21	11	7	3	0
	Wakefield	5,477	5	0	2	0	3	65	24	37	4	2
	Warner	3,021	2	0	0	1	1	32	9	23	0	0
	Washington	1,084	2	0	0	0	2	11	2	8	1	1
	Waterville Valley	271	0	0	0	0	0	72	0	70	2	0
	Webster	1,900	3	0	1	0	2	19	6	13	0	0
	Wilton	3,946	5	0	1	0	4	81	43	36	2	0
	Windham	13,283	13	0	8	1	4	140	38	93	9	0
	Wolfeboro	6,710	2	0	1	1	0	81	26	47	8	0
	Woodstock	1,181	2	0	0	0	2	12	6	6	0	0
NEW JERSEY	Aberdeen Township	18,301	25	0	1	5	19	251	38	198	15	2
	Absecon	8,029	28	0	2	15	11	268	70	188	10	0
	Allendale	6,683	2	0	0	0	2	57	10	45	2	0
	Allenhurst	698	1	0	0	0	1	28	4	23	1	0
	Allentown	1,839	1	0	0	1	0	24	5	16	3	0
	Alpha	2,426	18	0	0	0	18	28	2	23	3	0
	Alpine	2,418	2	0	0	1	1	8	2	6	0	0
	Andover Township	6,523	20	0	0	0	20	37	8	28	1	2
	Asbury Park	16,473	351	6	11	184	150	717	235	410	72	4
	Atlantic City	39,781	860	6	28	456	370	2,902	545	2,157	200	16
	Atlantic Highlands	4,594	6	0	0	0	6	69	9	60	0	0
	Audubon	8,941	9	0	1	4	4	263	27	226	10	2
	Audubon Park	1,066	0	0	0	0	0	16	1	13	2	0
	Avalon	2,116	4	0	1	0	3	295	48	244	3	1
	Avon-by-the-Sea	2,156	2	0	0	1	1	54	13	41	0	0
	Barnegat Light	829	0	0	0	0	0	12	3	8	1	0
	Barnegat Township	21,098	27	1	1	5	20	181	43	131	7	5
	Barrington	6,973	11	0	2	0	9	41	12	22	7	0
	Bay Head	1,254	0	0	0	0	0	78	13	65	0	0
	Bayonne	58,583	189	1	6	83	99	941	212	626	103	4
	Beach Haven	1,360	5	0	0	0	5	114	8	105	1	0
	Beachwood	10,696	21	0	0	3	18	225	42	181	2	0
	Bedminster Township	8,412	2	0	0	0	2	59	14	44	1	1
	Belleville	34,291	117	1	1	59	56	779	150	448	181	2
	Bellmawr	11,143	17	0	2	4	11	329	78	227	24	0
	Belmar	5,897	16	0	0	2	14	333	70	254	9	0
	Belvidere	2,689	0	0	0	0	0	13	1	12	0	0
	Bergenfield	26,078	30	0	1	11	18	203	39	154	10	2
	Berkeley Heights Tow	13,515	3	0	0	0	3	83	9	68	6	0
	Berkeley Township	42,388	56	2	4	17	33	806	135	647	24	4
	Berlin	7,875	8	0	0	3	5	171	36	128	7	0
	Berlin Township	5,381	10	0	0	5	5	195	18	163	14	4
	Bernards Township	27,020	1	0	0	0	1	159	14	136	9	0
	Bernardsville	7,654	0	0	0	0	0	55	6	48	1	0
	Beverly	2,639	17	0	0	6	11	46	16	25	5	0
	Blairstown Township	5,956	2	0	0	0	2	57	8	47	2	1

[1] The FBI does not publish arson data unless it receives data from either the agency or the state for all 12 months of the calendar year.

Table 8.   Offenses Known to Law Enforcement, by State and City, 2007 *(Contd.)*

(Number.)

State	City	Population	Violent crime	Murder and non-negligent man-slaughter	Forcible rape	Robbery	Aggravated assault	Property crime	Burglary	Larceny-theft	Motor vehicle theft	Arson[1]
	Bloomfield	45,171	124	1	2	82	39	1,283	182	900	201	4
	Bloomingdale	7,570	3	0	0	0	3	51	7	43	1	0
	Bogota	8,072	8	0	0	5	3	75	12	58	5	0
	Boonton	8,562	4	0	1	0	3	47	13	30	4	3
	Boonton Township	4,377	8	0	5	0	3	24	7	17	0	0
	Bordentown	3,935	2	0	0	1	1	58	7	44	7	0
	Bordentown Township	10,423	22	0	1	10	11	165	26	121	18	1
	Bound Brook	10,180	18	0	1	11	6	233	63	160	10	0
	Bradley Beach	4,763	15	0	0	3	12	138	29	108	1	0
	Branchburg Township	14,982	2	0	0	1	1	104	14	86	4	0
	Brick Township	77,886	97	0	3	12	82	1,355	249	1,057	49	4
	Bridgeton	24,281	379	1	7	171	200	1,243	376	795	72	6
	Bridgewater Township	44,620	15	0	1	6	8	706	91	584	31	1
	Brielle	4,831	5	0	0	0	5	75	48	27	0	0
	Brigantine	12,829	12	0	0	5	7	197	49	147	1	0
	Brooklawn	2,284	15	0	0	7	8	196	17	162	17	0
	Buena	3,787	22	0	8	1	13	110	44	62	4	1
	Burlington	9,672	46	2	2	23	19	216	40	157	19	5
	Burlington Township	21,691	31	0	2	14	15	459	55	381	23	1
	Butler	8,038	6	0	6	0	0	130	33	90	7	0
	Byram Township	8,618	2	0	1	0	1	53	6	45	2	1
	Caldwell	7,340	2	0	0	0	2	36	8	25	3	0
	Camden	78,967	1,755	42	67	781	865	4,600	1,128	2,311	1,161	115
	Cape May	3,792	4	0	0	2	2	202	29	172	1	0
	Cape May Point	229	0	0	0	0	0	10	3	7	0	0
	Carlstadt	6,010	14	0	2	4	8	198	22	156	20	0
	Carney's Point Towns	7,946	31	1	4	6	20	151	43	92	16	0
	Carteret	22,165	55	0	4	24	27	359	62	250	47	8
	Cedar Grove Township	12,791	8	0	0	1	7	170	27	137	6	3
	Chatham	8,353	1	0	0	0	1	59	9	50	0	1
	Chatham Township	10,233	1	0	0	0	1	37	3	34	0	0
	Cherry Hill Township	71,269	98	1	3	43	51	2,152	255	1,759	138	1
	Chesilhurst	1,871	5	0	0	1	4	51	16	26	9	0
	Chester	1,644	0	0	0	0	0	28	5	23	0	0
	Chesterfield Township	6,422	0	0	0	0	0	37	3	34	0	0
	Chester Township	7,855	2	0	0	0	2	45	12	31	2	3
	Cinnaminson Township	15,381	19	0	2	8	9	272	48	211	13	1
	Clark Township	14,585	8	0	1	2	5	217	17	195	5	0
	Clayton	7,436	14	0	1	9	4	199	38	152	9	0
	Clementon	4,900	31	0	0	6	25	138	27	102	9	2
	Cliffside Park	22,868	27	0	0	10	17	224	50	163	11	0
	Clifton	79,253	221	0	5	108	108	1,910	389	1,319	202	2
	Clinton	2,593	0	0	0	0	0	13	0	12	1	0
	Clinton Township	14,020	9	0	2	1	6	55	18	36	1	0
	Closter	8,691	2	0	0	0	2	44	7	36	1	0
	Collingswood	13,899	27	0	4	15	8	433	79	305	49	2
	Colts Neck Township	11,536	13	0	0	2	11	97	10	83	4	0
	Cranbury Township	3,882	4	0	1	0	3	39	6	28	5	0
	Cranford Township	22,270	10	0	1	5	4	229	32	191	6	0
	Cresskill	8,400	0	0	0	0	0	67	6	60	1	1
	Deal	1,039	3	0	1	0	2	52	22	29	1	0
	Delanco Township	4,205	5	0	1	0	4	89	31	54	4	0
	Delaware Township	4,709	1	0	0	0	1	22	6	11	5	0
	Delran Township	17,206	21	1	1	11	8	218	36	159	23	0
	Demarest	5,083	0	0	0	0	0	28	4	24	0	0
	Denville Township	16,597	2	0	0	0	2	173	29	137	7	0
	Deptford Township	30,082	151	1	0	58	92	1,298	166	1,052	80	17
	Dover	18,306	66	0	4	39	23	313	53	235	25	2
	Dumont	17,288	13	0	4	0	9	170	16	151	3	0
	Dunellen	6,909	8	0	0	4	4	156	17	133	6	5
	Eastampton Township	6,667	13	0	4	3	6	88	20	62	6	3
	East Brunswick Township	47,438	42	1	9	11	21	830	92	707	31	13
	East Greenwich Township	6,758	10	0	2	0	8	91	24	64	3	1
	East Hanover Township	11,581	4	0	0	2	2	245	16	216	13	0
	East Newark	2,207	5	0	0	0	5	31	4	23	4	0
	East Orange	66,949	525	8	32	239	246	1,813	446	890	477	28
	East Rutherford	8,891	3	0	0	1	2	265	20	219	26	1
	East Windsor Township	26,807	20	0	3	4	13	350	42	299	9	3
	Eatontown	13,960	20	0	0	12	8	575	53	506	16	1
	Edgewater	9,585	9	0	0	1	8	220	9	201	10	0
	Edgewater Park Township	7,933	16	0	0	8	8	172	39	115	18	2
	Edison Township	99,082	225	0	0	86	139	2,239	437	1,578	224	6
	Egg Harbor City	4,434	20	1	1	7	11	99	36	54	9	1
	Egg Harbor Township	38,621	86	0	8	26	52	939	210	676	53	15

[1] The FBI does not publish arson data unless it receives data from either the agency or the state for all 12 months of the calendar year.

Table 8.   Offenses Known to Law Enforcement, by State and City, 2007 *(Contd.)*

(Number.)

State	City	Population	Violent crime	Murder and non-negligent man-slaughter	Forcible rape	Robbery	Aggravated assault	Property crime	Burglary	Larceny-theft	Motor vehicle theft	Arson[1]
	Elizabeth	125,621	939	16	25	612	286	5,253	786	3,115	1,352	14
	Elk Township	3,850	1	0	0	0	1	110	26	72	12	3
	Elmer	1,364	0	0	0	0	0	31	4	27	0	0
	Elmwood Park	18,722	24	1	0	13	10	448	75	337	36	0
	Elsinboro Township	1,068	2	0	0	0	2	25	15	8	2	0
	Emerson	7,286	2	0	0	1	1	40	7	32	1	0
	Englewood	27,701	70	0	1	38	31	418	145	246	27	2
	Englewood Cliffs	5,767	4	0	0	1	3	78	13	61	4	0
	Englishtown	1,833	2	0	0	1	1	24	3	21	0	0
	Essex Fells	2,062	0	0	0	0	0	14	3	11	0	0
	Evesham Township	46,504	34	1	6	8	19	701	78	598	25	4
	Ewing Township	36,753	89	1	5	27	56	685	137	492	56	6
	Fairfield Township, Essex County	7,673	12	0	1	2	9	359	31	314	14	1
	Fair Haven	5,859	0	0	0	0	0	57	0	56	1	1
	Fair Lawn	31,108	34	0	2	7	25	395	62	318	15	0
	Fairview	13,568	72	0	6	23	43	242	64	161	17	0
	Fanwood	7,179	5	0	1	2	2	64	11	51	2	0
	Far Hills	924	0	0	0	0	0	14	4	10	0	0
	Flemington	4,248	14	0	1	3	10	152	21	126	5	2
	Florence Township	11,585	16	0	2	5	9	151	51	89	11	1
	Florham Park	12,549	6	1	1	2	2	97	5	88	4	0
	Fort Lee	36,844	17	0	0	8	9	306	63	237	6	2
	Franklin	5,187	4	0	2	0	2	74	9	58	7	1
	Franklin Lakes	11,290	4	0	0	2	2	128	16	107	5	0
	Franklin Township, Gloucester County	16,778	17	0	3	2	12	335	107	205	23	4
	Franklin Township, Hunterdon County	3,138	1	0	0	0	1	39	3	34	2	1
	Franklin Township, Somerset County	60,006	64	4	8	30	22	959	215	625	119	7
	Freehold	11,344	54	0	5	28	21	247	33	204	10	0
	Freehold Township	33,803	54	0	8	22	24	916	69	825	22	1
	Frenchtown	1,484	1	0	0	0	1	21	8	13	0	0
	Galloway Township	36,045	146	1	11	17	117	850	200	597	53	4
	Garfield	29,515	57	1	2	18	36	402	128	224	50	0
	Garwood	4,214	2	0	0	1	1	59	3	52	4	0
	Gibbsboro	2,440	1	0	1	0	0	38	12	26	0	1
	Glassboro	19,274	85	4	6	37	38	668	148	475	45	10
	Glen Ridge	6,877	11	0	0	8	3	147	21	116	10	1
	Glen Rock	11,346	2	0	0	1	1	60	12	47	1	0
	Gloucester City	11,431	39	0	8	15	16	313	65	219	29	0
	Gloucester Township	65,396	174	0	9	47	118	1,706	439	1,153	114	11
	Green Brook Township	6,824	5	0	2	3	0	137	20	100	17	0
	Greenwich Township, Gloucester County	4,950	7	0	1	3	3	143	32	110	1	0
	Greenwich Township, Warren County	5,206	8	0	3	0	5	112	11	99	2	0
	Guttenberg	10,670	39	0	0	23	16	115	30	74	11	0
	Hackensack	43,478	124	2	0	38	84	1,099	120	898	81	3
	Hackettstown	9,436	16	0	0	0	16	173	24	146	3	1
	Haddonfield	11,464	7	0	0	2	5	255	31	219	5	5
	Haddon Heights	7,332	4	0	1	2	1	115	13	100	2	3
	Haddon Township	14,420	28	0	0	15	13	368	62	269	37	1
	Haledon	8,321	19	0	0	4	15	152	41	81	30	0
	Hamburg	3,538	4	0	1	0	3	46	22	23	1	3
	Hamilton Township, Atlantic County	24,315	64	1	1	24	38	1,131	179	900	52	5
	Hamilton Township, Mercer County	90,158	195	0	7	103	85	1,723	346	1,209	168	8
	Hammonton	13,512	20	0	1	4	15	161	36	114	11	2
	Hanover Township	13,676	11	0	0	2	9	177	21	142	14	0
	Harding Township	3,348	2	0	0	0	2	20	2	18	0	0
	Hardyston Township	8,246	6	0	2	0	4	62	24	33	5	0
	Harrington Park	4,894	1	0	0	0	1	8	0	7	1	0
	Harrison	13,880	44	0	2	28	14	320	94	176	50	0
	Harrison Township	11,797	6	0	0	1	5	163	21	139	3	3
	Harvey Cedars	387	0	0	0	0	0	24	4	20	0	0
	Hasbrouck Heights	11,570	2	0	0	1	1	127	22	103	2	0
	Haworth	3,418	2	0	0	0	2	12	4	7	1	0
	Hawthorne	18,086	9	0	1	2	6	321	35	276	10	0
	Hazlet Township	20,843	7	0	0	5	2	328	42	268	18	8
	Helmetta	2,014	0	0	0	0	0	12	7	5	0	0
	High Bridge	3,746	4	0	1	0	3	45	7	36	2	1
	Highland Park	14,112	10	0	1	4	5	214	47	157	10	2
	Highlands	4,965	2	0	0	0	2	77	25	48	4	1
	Hightstown	5,277	12	0	0	4	8	89	14	70	5	1
	Hillsborough Township	37,941	11	1	4	2	4	349	72	262	15	3
	Hillsdale	10,008	4	0	1	1	2	73	7	66	0	0
	Hillside Township	21,588	97	2	6	67	22	706	141	425	140	5
	Hi-Nella	1,003	1	0	0	0	1	29	15	12	2	1
	Hoboken	39,676	151	0	4	50	97	997	251	640	106	1

[1] The FBI does not publish arson data unless it receives data from either the agency or the state for all 12 months of the calendar year.

Table 8. Offenses Known to Law Enforcement, by State and City, 2007 *(Contd.)*

(Number.)

State	City	Population	Violent crime	Murder and non-negligent man-slaughter	Forcible rape	Robbery	Aggravated assault	Property crime	Burglary	Larceny-theft	Motor vehicle theft	Arson[1]
	Ho-Ho-Kus	4,077	1	0	1	0	0	13	2	10	1	0
	Holland Township	5,286	2	0	1	0	1	21	11	8	2	0
	Holmdel Township	16,759	10	0	1	1	8	209	16	186	7	0
	Hopatcong	15,814	7	0	0	0	7	104	11	88	5	0
	Hopewell	2,013	3	0	0	1	2	26	11	15	0	0
	Hopewell Township	17,888	9	0	0	1	8	121	28	87	6	0
	Howell Township	50,324	57	1	3	15	38	600	101	466	33	5
	Independence Township	5,744	3	0	0	0	3	44	10	32	2	0
	Interlaken	877	0	0	0	0	0	3	0	3	0	0
	Irvington	57,767	1,236	23	29	616	568	3,298	928	1,354	1,016	14
	Island Heights	1,869	0	0	0	0	0	9	0	9	0	0
	Jackson Township	52,073	23	0	2	3	18	571	99	441	31	10
	Jamesburg	6,401	5	0	1	1	3	68	16	45	7	0
	Jefferson Township	21,866	17	0	1	3	13	232	86	141	5	4
	Jersey City	240,718	2,421	20	47	1,248	1,106	6,804	1,504	4,082	1,218	100
	Keansburg	10,526	46	0	4	7	35	269	42	215	12	2
	Kearny	37,840	108	0	6	50	52	1,098	146	760	192	9
	Kenilworth	7,707	1	0	0	0	1	137	7	117	13	0
	Keyport	7,438	13	0	1	5	7	144	37	94	13	9
	Kinnelon	9,638	2	0	0	1	1	64	31	32	1	1
	Lacey Township	26,184	23	0	0	3	20	699	95	598	6	2
	Lake Como	1,744	4	0	0	1	3	38	14	21	3	0
	Lakehurst	2,662	8	0	1	0	7	39	8	30	1	0
	Lakewood Township	69,298	182	3	1	96	82	1,448	462	886	100	10
	Lambertville	3,791	10	0	0	2	8	54	12	41	1	0
	Laurel Springs	1,914	10	0	1	2	7	28	8	18	2	0
	Lavallette	2,740	0	0	0	0	0	71	22	49	0	0
	Lawnside	2,788	22	0	2	6	14	97	9	85	3	0
	Lawrence Township, Mercer County	31,939	55	0	13	21	21	878	96	730	52	4
	Lebanon Township	6,264	1	0	0	0	1	47	15	31	1	0
	Leonia	8,760	10	0	0	4	6	89	16	69	4	0
	Lincoln Park	10,808	5	0	2	0	3	92	20	67	5	1
	Linden	39,697	142	1	6	84	51	1,357	242	904	211	6
	Lindenwold	17,084	179	0	7	96	76	615	205	329	81	9
	Linwood	7,321	8	0	0	1	7	76	22	53	1	0
	Little Egg Harbor Tow	20,193	23	0	3	3	17	481	79	391	11	6
	Little Falls Township	11,777	16	0	0	4	12	454	79	361	14	0
	Little Ferry	10,668	20	0	2	3	15	124	16	92	16	0
	Little Silver	6,062	5	0	0	1	4	106	38	67	1	0
	Livingston Township	28,287	21	0	2	8	11	439	33	382	24	2
	Loch Arbour	273	0	0	0	0	0	8	1	7	0	1
	Lodi	24,202	29	0	0	9	20	346	90	221	35	1
	Logan Township	6,150	2	0	1	1	0	130	20	106	4	0
	Long Beach Township	3,483	6	0	0	0	6	261	23	238	0	0
	Long Branch	32,171	91	0	0	42	49	683	203	450	30	0
	Long Hill Township	8,746	3	0	0	0	3	55	8	47	0	0
	Longport	1,083	1	0	0	0	1	13	4	9	0	0
	Lopatcong Township	8,402	7	0	0	3	4	103	13	83	7	0
	Lower Alloways Creek	1,906	2	0	0	0	2	21	5	16	0	0
	Lower Township	20,693	68	0	1	11	56	459	95	348	16	1
	Lumberton Township	12,276	17	1	2	6	8	316	42	266	8	10
	Lyndhurst Township	19,645	9	1	0	4	4	386	62	283	41	0
	Madison	15,945	9	0	2	1	6	143	20	122	1	0
	Magnolia	4,360	24	0	0	11	13	111	25	79	7	0
	Mahwah Township	24,451	10	0	2	0	8	135	5	113	17	0
	Manalapan Township	37,004	30	0	2	7	21	419	49	355	15	1
	Manasquan	6,172	11	1	1	1	8	165	22	142	1	1
	Manchester Township	41,628	15	0	0	2	13	356	85	256	15	14
	Mansfield Township, Burlinton County	8,011	2	0	1	0	1	126	17	92	17	3
	Mansfield Township, Warren County	8,237	4	0	0	1	3	133	24	99	10	1
	Mantoloking	449	0	0	0	0	0	17	2	15	0	0
	Mantua Township	14,908	20	0	3	7	10	368	78	279	11	3
	Manville	10,435	2	0	1	1	0	156	9	135	12	4
	Maple Shade Townshi	19,454	42	0	6	24	12	399	76	265	58	1
	Maplewood Township	22,658	57	1	0	33	23	399	42	286	71	2
	Margate City	8,563	6	1	0	1	4	154	26	123	5	1
	Marlboro Township	39,667	26	0	1	4	21	398	85	295	18	5
	Matawan	8,742	6	0	1	1	4	96	14	76	6	0
	Maywood	9,332	2	0	0	0	2	89	32	56	1	0
	Medford Lakes	4,143	1	0	0	0	1	27	1	26	0	0
	Medford Township	23,295	14	0	2	2	10	266	62	199	5	8
	Mendham	5,153	2	0	0	0	2	26	1	23	2	0
	Mendham Township	5,571	6	0	0	1	5	27	3	24	0	0
	Merchantville	3,789	3	0	0	3	0	83	13	65	5	0

[1] The FBI does not publish arson data unless it receives data from either the agency or the state for all 12 months of the calendar year.

Table 8.   Offenses Known to Law Enforcement, by State and City, 2007 *(Contd.)*

(Number.)

State	City	Population	Violent crime	Murder and non-negligent man-slaughter	Forcible rape	Robbery	Aggravated assault	Property crime	Burglary	Larceny-theft	Motor vehicle theft	Arson[1]
	Metuchen	13,157	28	0	1	5	22	278	43	233	2	0
	Middlesex	13,685	10	0	0	3	7	134	23	98	13	1
	Middle Township	16,306	82	0	11	22	49	725	163	523	39	9
	Middletown Township	67,279	55	0	8	9	38	833	120	675	38	0
	Midland Park	6,875	4	0	0	0	4	45	3	41	1	2
	Millburn Township	19,068	9	0	0	6	3	615	35	536	44	2
	Milltown	7,007	3	0	1	0	2	120	15	100	5	0
	Millville	28,069	255	4	15	102	134	1,448	343	1,057	48	10
	Mine Hill Township	3,650	0	0	0	0	0	36	10	25	1	0
	Monmouth Beach	3,558	3	0	1	0	2	58	3	55	0	0
	Monroe Township, Gloucester County	31,793	44	2	2	10	30	669	157	465	47	6
	Monroe Township, Middlesex County	34,752	10	0	1	1	8	257	55	190	12	1
	Montclair	37,144	97	2	5	50	40	780	207	496	77	1
	Montgomery Townshi	23,140	4	0	0	1	3	212	61	144	7	0
	Montvale	7,276	2	0	0	0	2	57	7	48	2	0
	Montville Township	21,347	8	0	0	2	6	162	39	119	4	3
	Moonachie	2,785	3	0	0	1	2	90	16	64	10	1
	Moorestown Township	19,907	22	0	4	5	13	424	57	351	16	1
	Morris Plains	5,576	4	0	0	4	0	67	6	58	3	0
	Morristown	18,838	121	0	1	56	64	500	73	410	17	4
	Morris Township	21,279	30	0	4	3	23	130	23	97	10	2
	Mountain Lakes	4,324	3	0	0	0	3	75	22	52	1	0
	Mountainside	6,615	4	0	1	0	3	70	11	54	5	0
	Mount Arlington	5,683	3	0	0	0	3	56	13	43	0	0
	Mount Ephraim	4,417	12	0	1	8	3	189	37	140	12	0
	Mount Holly Township	10,555	41	0	0	21	20	321	54	257	10	1
	Mount Laurel Township	40,147	41	0	11	12	18	828	77	726	25	1
	Mount Olive Township	25,950	6	0	1	0	5	266	38	217	11	0
	Mullica Township	6,053	13	0	0	2	11	108	36	60	12	0
	National Park	3,201	7	0	1	0	6	69	10	56	3	0
	Neptune City	5,127	12	0	1	7	4	209	30	176	3	0
	Neptune Township	28,038	166	3	3	74	86	1,368	261	1,016	91	9
	Netcong	3,277	5	0	1	0	4	77	20	52	5	0
	Newark	280,158	2,389	104	60	1,101	1,124	10,664	1,914	4,385	4,365	93
	New Brunswick	49,950	283	2	25	169	87	1,883	448	1,273	162	7
	Newfield	1,657	3	0	0	0	3	22	14	8	0	0
	New Hanover Township	9,437	0	0	0	0	0	6	3	3	0	0
	New Milford	16,171	3	0	0	1	2	99	15	81	3	0
	New Providence	11,862	6	0	0	1	5	115	26	86	3	1
	Newton	8,300	5	0	0	1	4	117	25	88	4	1
	North Arlington	15,010	15	0	1	2	12	203	22	154	27	0
	North Bergen Township	56,984	109	0	10	55	44	1,010	151	719	140	4
	North Brunswick Township	39,676	90	0	3	39	48	888	203	588	97	2
	North Caldwell	7,175	4	0	1	0	3	45	14	30	1	1
	Northfield	7,968	3	0	0	3	0	123	38	82	3	0
	North Haledon	8,999	13	0	0	0	13	70	11	57	2	0
	North Hanover Township	7,543	1	0	0	0	1	60	13	42	5	1
	North Plainfield	21,642	61	0	3	36	22	545	126	349	70	5
	Northvale	4,542	2	0	0	1	1	36	5	30	1	0
	North Wildwood	4,782	16	0	2	4	10	366	47	317	2	0
	Norwood	6,239	1	0	0	0	1	18	5	13	0	0
	Nutley Township	26,891	48	0	2	16	30	417	58	317	42	11
	Oakland	13,498	6	0	0	0	6	87	6	80	1	0
	Oaklyn	4,062	13	0	0	5	8	123	38	79	6	1
	Ocean City	15,057	28	0	3	19	6	1,153	183	961	9	0
	Ocean Gate	2,121	6	2	0	1	3	40	9	30	1	0
	Oceanport	5,726	1	0	0	0	1	55	3	50	2	1
	Ocean Township, Monmouth County	27,362	41	0	2	18	21	716	89	600	27	0
	Ocean Township, Ocean County	8,205	4	0	0	0	4	104	19	85	0	0
	Ogdensburg	2,611	1	0	0	0	1	14	4	9	1	0
	Old Bridge Township	65,370	41	0	0	15	26	903	145	682	76	5
	Old Tappan	5,986	1	0	0	0	1	20	2	18	0	0
	Oradell	7,922	4	0	1	1	2	41	6	35	0	0
	Orange	31,717	391	5	9	220	157	1,468	447	620	401	5
	Oxford Township	2,610	1	0	0	0	1	29	4	23	2	1
	Palisades Park	19,220	24	1	1	11	11	140	40	83	17	0
	Palmyra	7,564	26	0	1	5	20	151	36	104	11	1
	Paramus	26,430	54	0	1	25	28	1,578	68	1,467	43	9
	Park Ridge	8,905	1	0	1	0	0	43	3	40	0	0
	Parsippany-Troy Hills Township	51,609	42	0	5	10	27	881	356	479	46	2
	Passaic	67,673	695	3	3	313	376	1,587	395	952	240	4
	Paterson	148,049	1,479	14	26	695	744	4,376	1,460	2,004	912	19
	Paulsboro	6,035	27	0	0	4	23	261	40	199	22	1
	Peapack and Gladstone	2,469	0	0	0	0	0	21	8	13	0	0

[1] The FBI does not publish arson data unless it receives data from either the agency or the state for all 12 months of the calendar year.

Table 8. Offenses Known to Law Enforcement, by State and City, 2007 *(Contd.)*

(Number.)

State	City	Population	Violent crime	Murder and non-negligent man-slaughter	Forcible rape	Robbery	Aggravated assault	Property crime	Burglary	Larceny-theft	Motor vehicle theft	Arson[1]
	Pemberton	1,375	5	0	1	1	3	16	4	11	1	0
	Pemberton Township	28,703	76	1	3	30	42	560	182	342	36	2
	Pennington	2,676	1	0	0	0	1	13	5	8	0	0
	Pennsauken Township	35,286	155	0	4	76	75	1,514	362	941	211	7
	Penns Grove	4,776	42	1	1	4	36	173	56	110	7	4
	Pennsville Township	13,274	9	0	0	1	8	391	49	332	10	1
	Pequannock Township	16,248	7	0	0	0	7	179	41	125	13	0
	Perth Amboy	48,392	215	3	1	115	96	1,111	187	775	149	3
	Phillipsburg	14,765	24	2	2	4	16	305	71	213	21	4
	Pine Beach	2,023	1	0	0	1	0	32	5	26	1	0
	Pine Hill	11,225	51	0	1	11	39	247	53	175	19	19
	Pine Valley	23	0	0	0	0	0	1	0	1	0	0
	Piscataway Township	52,425	85	1	2	29	53	845	158	626	61	7
	Pitman	9,158	4	0	0	0	4	125	7	110	8	2
	Plainfield	47,143	485	4	9	240	232	1,370	229	951	190	7
	Plainsboro Township	21,119	10	0	2	4	4	189	21	161	7	1
	Pleasantville	18,898	179	3	3	80	93	634	208	373	53	2
	Plumsted Township	8,086	4	0	0	1	3	93	18	67	8	0
	Pohatcong Township	3,395	23	0	0	2	21	108	10	94	4	0
	Point Pleasant	19,794	18	0	1	3	14	341	33	304	4	0
	Point Pleasant Beach	5,374	9	0	2	6	1	265	35	220	10	0
	Pompton Lakes	11,193	7	0	2	1	4	99	10	88	1	0
	Princeton	13,623	15	0	0	3	12	332	70	261	1	3
	Princeton Township	17,276	9	0	0	0	9	147	27	113	7	1
	Prospect Park	5,695	13	0	0	2	11	129	39	74	16	0
	Rahway	27,720	84	0	1	58	25	656	125	461	70	0
	Ramsey	14,710	16	0	0	5	11	194	25	167	2	0
	Randolph Township	25,622	4	0	0	1	3	212	20	184	8	2
	Raritan	6,399	8	0	0	2	6	118	21	96	1	0
	Raritan Township	22,619	5	0	0	0	5	219	28	185	6	1
	Readington Township	16,223	13	0	4	1	8	117	25	92	0	0
	Red Bank	11,798	40	0	4	19	17	287	61	215	11	3
	Ridgefield	10,947	5	0	2	1	2	103	28	60	15	1
	Ridgefield Park	12,609	18	0	2	7	9	201	32	161	8	0
	Ridgewood	24,530	9	0	0	4	5	244	25	215	4	2
	Ringwood	12,757	7	0	2	0	5	83	13	70	0	0
	Riverdale	2,664	3	0	0	0	3	89	15	68	6	0
	River Edge	10,814	5	0	0	0	5	55	10	44	1	0
	Riverside Township	7,915	10	0	1	8	1	89	23	58	8	0
	Riverton	2,703	2	0	0	0	2	56	12	42	2	0
	River Vale Township	9,708	4	0	0	0	4	50	2	48	0	1
	Rochelle Park Townsh	6,000	6	0	0	0	6	114	24	83	7	1
	Rockaway	6,382	4	0	0	2	2	56	9	46	1	0
	Rockaway Township	25,675	20	0	1	7	12	552	39	499	14	1
	Rockleigh	391	5	0	0	0	5	5	1	4	0	0
	Roseland	5,376	1	0	0	1	0	27	1	25	1	1
	Roselle	21,064	84	0	0	67	17	384	98	230	56	3
	Roselle Park	13,066	29	0	1	17	11	248	47	185	16	0
	Roxbury Township	23,698	17	0	0	5	12	341	57	272	12	0
	Rumson	7,162	0	0	0	0	0	58	10	48	0	1
	Runnemede	8,424	31	0	1	8	22	332	42	275	15	3
	Rutherford	17,792	15	0	0	5	10	296	41	231	24	3
	Saddle Brook Township	13,565	5	0	0	2	3	385	35	328	22	0
	Saddle River	3,769	0	0	0	0	0	19	6	13	0	0
	Salem	5,758	78	1	8	22	47	357	121	212	24	3
	Sayreville	42,372	59	1	5	19	34	693	165	474	54	4
	Scotch Plains Township	23,143	28	0	3	6	19	236	43	186	7	2
	Sea Bright	1,791	2	0	0	0	2	45	3	41	1	0
	Sea Girt	2,035	2	0	1	0	1	49	16	30	3	0
	Sea Isle City	2,936	14	0	0	0	14	293	28	263	2	1
	Seaside Heights	3,228	61	0	3	10	48	189	23	152	14	0
	Seaside Park	2,292	0	0	0	0	0	66	12	51	3	0
	Secaucus	15,493	18	0	0	6	12	647	22	563	62	0
	Ship Bottom	1,421	4	0	0	0	4	76	11	65	0	1
	Shrewsbury	3,701	5	0	0	0	5	72	8	64	0	0
	Somerdale	5,100	14	0	1	5	8	114	24	82	8	0
	Somers Point	11,522	39	1	1	5	32	303	81	220	2	5
	Somerville	12,494	20	0	0	13	7	296	42	237	17	0
	South Amboy	7,830	15	1	0	0	14	107	31	64	12	3
	South Bound Brook	4,504	1	0	0	1	0	28	3	22	3	0
	South Brunswick Township[3]	40,390	21	0	2	4	15			377	33	3
	South Hackensack Township	2,303	9	0	1	4	4	69	8	56	5	3
	South Harrison Township	2,943	5	0	0	0	5	23	5	17	1	0
	South Orange	16,298	56	0	0	31	25	393	69	241	83	0

[1] The FBI does not publish arson data unless it receives data from either the agency or the state for all 12 months of the calendar year.

[3] The FBI determined that the agency's data were overreported. Consequently, affected data are not included in this table.

Table 8.   Offenses Known to Law Enforcement, by State and City, 2007 *(Contd.)*

(Number.)

State	City	Population	Violent crime	Murder and non-negligent man-slaughter	Forcible rape	Robbery	Aggravated assault	Property crime	Burglary	Larceny-theft	Motor vehicle theft	Arson[1]
	South Plainfield	22,694	34	0	0	15	19	429	76	321	32	0
	South River	15,752	25	0	0	5	20	163	38	113	12	7
	South Toms River	3,700	10	0	0	5	5	100	15	76	9	1
	Sparta Township	19,262	5	0	0	0	5	96	9	85	2	0
	Spotswood	8,143	6	0	0	0	6	100	14	82	4	1
	Springfield	14,652	13	0	2	6	5	238	31	190	17	0
	Springfield Township	3,554	1	0	0	0	1	31	6	19	6	0
	Spring Lake	3,460	3	0	1	0	2	80	9	71	0	0
	Spring Lake Heights	5,083	2	0	0	0	2	18	1	17	0	0
	Stafford Township	25,705	20	1	0	3	16	489	51	425	13	0
	Stanhope	3,650	1	0	1	0	0	51	12	38	1	3
	Stillwater Township	4,366	3	0	0	0	3	20	8	10	2	0
	Stone Harbor	1,034	4	0	3	0	1	62	25	34	3	0
	Stratford	7,090	19	0	0	9	10	177	28	137	12	1
	Summit	21,010	10	0	0	4	6	285	14	259	12	0
	Surf City	1,535	1	0	1	0	0	47	8	37	2	0
	Swedesboro	2,034	5	0	0	0	5	54	15	32	7	0
	Tavistock	26	0	0	0	0	0	1	0	1	0	0
	Teaneck Township	39,435	63	0	1	31	31	549	132	373	44	11
	Tenafly	14,326	1	0	1	0	0	97	23	70	4	1
	Teterboro	18	2	0	0	2	0	38	4	27	7	0
	Tewksbury Township	6,061	4	0	2	0	2	22	12	10	0	0
	Tinton Falls	17,006	13	1	4	4	4	308	43	247	18	2
	Toms River Township	94,469	123	0	14	46	63	2,039	327	1,637	75	12
	Totowa	10,587	11	0	3	1	7	272	29	222	21	0
	Trenton	83,551	1,165	25	15	595	530	2,645	852	1,408	385	21
	Tuckerton	3,810	4	0	0	0	4	44	3	39	2	0
	Union Beach	6,602	12	0	0	3	9	88	17	68	3	0
	Union City	63,647	406	1	4	182	219	1,422	332	917	173	7
	Union Township	54,795	144	0	1	69	74	1,331	205	935	191	1
	Upper Saddle River	8,493	2	0	0	0	2	42	8	32	2	0
	Ventnor City	12,508	25	0	1	14	10	403	141	251	11	5
	Vernon Township	25,340	14	0	0	1	13	399	52	339	8	4
	Verona	12,880	8	0	1	0	7	118	28	82	8	0
	Vineland	58,013	334	5	13	147	169	2,576	589	1,896	91	15
	Voorhees Township	29,261	53	1	6	13	33	784	115	645	24	25
	Waldwick	9,578	6	0	0	1	5	72	4	68	0	0
	Wallington	11,379	11	0	0	8	3	167	35	112	20	0
	Wall Township	25,882	25	0	0	1	24	380	85	279	16	0
	Wanaque	11,122	6	0	0	2	4	155	19	131	5	0
	Warren Township	15,746	4	0	1	0	3	132	26	100	6	0
	Washington	6,811	8	1	0	4	3	195	37	151	7	4
	Washington Township, Bergen County	9,627	0	0	0	0	0	26	4	22	0	0
	Washington Township, Gloucester County	51,595	78	0	3	19	56	1,104	227	791	86	14
	Washington Township, Mercer County	11,853	8	0	0	2	6	93	18	73	2	1
	Washington Township, Morris County	18,608	10	0	1	1	8	122	17	104	1	0
	Washington Township, Warren County	6,950	1	0	0	0	1	58	3	53	2	0
	Watchung	6,256	5	0	1	2	2	288	15	266	7	1
	Waterford Township	10,660	13	0	0	3	10	196	44	133	19	6
	Wayne Township	54,606	40	0	0	18	22	1,413	185	1,175	53	1
	Weehawken Township	12,593	29	0	0	19	10	306	51	207	48	0
	Wenonah	2,323	1	0	0	1	0	19	8	11	0	0
	Westampton Township	8,732	17	0	0	6	11	190	21	156	13	4
	West Amwell Township	2,931	4	0	0	0	4	26	10	16	0	0
	West Caldwell Towns	10,749	6	0	0	0	6	90	6	81	3	1
	West Cape May	1,003	1	0	0	0	1	38	7	31	0	0
	West Deptford Townsh	21,667	32	2	1	13	16	451	86	330	35	3
	Westfield	29,811	19	0	2	2	15	352	40	300	12	1
	West Long Branch	8,275	13	0	2	3	8	242	32	205	5	2
	West Milford Townshi	28,019	35	0	6	1	28	355	87	251	17	1
	West New York	46,193	197	4	4	97	92	837	192	543	102	4
	West Orange	43,343	89	2	2	48	37	795	162	501	132	0
	West Paterson	11,184	9	0	0	5	4	332	70	244	18	0
	Westville	4,438	23	0	0	8	15	132	34	78	20	0
	West Wildwood	406	4	0	1	0	3	21	8	13	0	0
	West Windsor Township	26,163	15	0	0	3	12	536	55	453	28	1
	Westwood	10,886	11	0	0	2	9	108	18	84	6	0
	Wharton	6,183	7	0	1	2	4	95	21	67	7	0
	Wildwood	5,285	84	0	4	41	39	690	180	477	33	0
	Wildwood Crest	3,691	14	0	0	0	14	160	42	118	0	0
	Willingboro Township	32,899	107	0	14	51	42	630	143	433	54	5
	Winfield Township	1,479	1	0	0	0	1	10	5	5	0	0
	Winslow Township	38,441	161	0	11	34	116	742	252	433	57	14
	Woodbine	2,497	1	0	0	0	1	9	0	8	1	0

[1] The FBI does not publish arson data unless it receives data from either the agency or the state for all 12 months of the calendar year.

Table 8. Offenses Known to Law Enforcement, by State and City, 2007 *(Contd.)*

(Number.)

State	City	Population	Violent crime	Murder and non-negligent man-slaughter	Forcible rape	Robbery	Aggravated assault	Property crime	Burglary	Larceny-theft	Motor vehicle theft	Arson[1]
	Woodbridge Township	98,769	234	1	14	99	120	2,879	439	2,180	260	23
	Woodbury..........................	10,364	45	0	2	15	28	508	68	392	48	2
	Woodbury Heights	3,017	1	0	0	1	0	71	16	50	5	0
	Woodcliff Lake	5,927	3	0	0	0	3	56	4	49	3	0
	Woodlynne..........................	2,706	24	0	2	13	9	134	37	74	23	2
	Wood-Ridge..........................	7,560	3	0	0	1	2	113	36	73	4	0
	Woodstown..........................	3,318	16	0	1	0	15	61	13	42	6	0
	Woolwich Township	8,574	6	0	0	1	5	52	13	37	2	0
	Wyckoff Township	17,091	13	0	0	1	12	113	20	92	1	0
NEW MEXICO	Alamogordo........................	36,162	110	1	33	4	72	1,082	154	883	45	8
	Albuquerque........................	513,124	5,080	47	307	1,439	3,287	29,293	5,622	18,632	5,039	90
	Artesia..............................	10,563	13	0	4	3	6	526	228	267	31	0
	Aztec................................	7,154	35	0	10	3	22	230	64	145	21	0
	Bayard..............................	2,371	3	0	0	0	3	34	6	28	0	0
	Belen................................	7,128	59	2	1	13	43	583	190	327	66	0
	Bloomfield..........................	7,529	92	0	5	1	86	164	61	99	4	1
	Bosque Farms	3,991	7	0	0	1	6	58	8	38	12	0
	Carlsbad............................	25,360	143	2	10	15	116	1,188	217	916	55	7
	Carrizozo............................	1,099	6	0	2	1	3	22	15	6	1	1
	Clovis................................	33,395	257	2	37	34	184	2,265	514	1,634	117	30
	Corrales............................	7,936	13	0	1	0	12	81	24	53	4	0
	Cuba................................	640	0	0	0	0	0	0	0	0	0	0
	Deming..............................	15,449	28	0	1	6	21	620	251	310	59	1
	Dexter..............................	1,243	7	0	0	1	6	16	8	7	1	0
	Estancia............................	1,545	10	0	0	0	10	34	11	22	1	0
	Eunice..............................	2,636	9	0	1	0	8	68	31	33	4	0
	Farmington........................	44,396	367	8	62	38	259	1,705	582	983	140	19
	Gallup..............................	19,160	272	7	20	35	210	1,260	185	955	120	7
	Grants..............................	9,000	79	0	8	8	63	304	138	132	34	
	Hobbs..............................	29,378	382	4	22	39	317	1,802	348	1,356	98	7
	Jal..................................	2,046	0	0	0	0	0	9	1	7	1	1
	Las Cruces[7]........................	87,958	437	6	40	96	295	4,278	860	3,158	260	8
	Las Vegas..........................	13,797	104	2	9	12	81	601	193	358	50	7
	Los Alamos	19,088	58	1	6	4	47	210	39	168	3	3
	Los Lunas..........................	12,022	45	0	5	10	30	555	85	358	112	0
	Lovington..........................	9,723	48	1	7	1	39	464	238	210	16	0
	Melrose............................	721	1	0	0	0	1	1	0	0	1	0
	Milan................................	2,651	17	0	0	0	17	106	37	64	5	0
	Moriarty............................	1,797	14	1	2	1	10	108	48	53	7	0
	Raton..............................	6,721	37	0	1	4	32	114	38	66	10	2
	Rio Rancho..........................	74,542	253	1	18	18	216	1,728	457	1,043	228	16
	Roswell............................	45,581	386	6	20	49	311	2,500	651	1,715	134	21
	Ruidoso Downs	2,080	1	0	0	0	1	132	41	77	14	0
	Santa Rosa	2,450	80	0	0	1	79	108	42	54	12	2
	Silver City..........................	9,903	84	3	5	9	67	544	154	361	29	3
	Socorro............................	8,570	53	1	2	2	48	246	86	152	8	6
	Springer............................	1,185	1	0	0	0	1	4	4	0	0	1
	Sunland Park[7]	14,364	53	0	5	7	41	176	52	99	25	0
	Taos................................	5,253	49	1	3	3	42	401	109	270	22	0
	Taos Ski Valley	57	0	0	0	0	0	13	5	8	0	0
	Truth or Consequences..........	6,869	32	1	2	0	29	287	84	190	13	0
NEW YORK	Adams Village......................	1,637	0	0	0	0	0	12	0	12	0	0
	Addison Town and Village	2,559	1	0	0	0	1	23	7	16	0	0
	Akron Village......................	3,015	2	0	0	0	2	29	3	26	0	1
	Albany..............................	93,916	1,128	3	45	376	704	4,249	965	2,998	286	15
	Albion Village......................	5,697	34	0	1	7	26	397	75	309	13	0
	Alexandria Bay Village..........	1,083	0	0	0	0	0	12	3	9	0	0
	Alfred Village......................	4,995	4	0	0	0	4	47	9	38	0	0
	Allegany Village	1,795	6	0	1	0	5	36	7	29	0	0
	Altamont Village	1,701	0	0	0	0	0	9	0	9	0	0
	Amherst Town	111,622	137	2	8	47	80	1,808	200	1,558	50	5
	Amity Town and Belmont Village	2,158	0	0	0	0	0	0	0	0	0	0
	Amityville Village..................	9,412	14	0	1	8	5	166	17	141	8	1
	Amsterdam	17,678	80	0	0	0	80	137	53	83	1	1
	Ardsley Village	4,943	3	0	1	1	1	34	3	26	5	0
	Asharoken Village	635	0	0	0	0	0	5	0	5	0	0
	Attica Village	2,464	7	0	1	1	5	29	0	28	1	0
	Auburn..............................	27,662	103	0	11	17	75	1,020	164	824	32	1
	Avon Village	2,955	1	0	0	0	1	50	9	39	2	0
	Bainbridge Village	1,349	1	0	0	0	1	14	2	12	0	0
	Baldwinsville Village..............	7,105	9	0	1	1	7	164	18	142	4	1
	Ballston Spa Village	5,511	7	0	1	0	6	127	15	111	1	0
	Batavia..............................	15,368	23	0	4	5	14	489	76	400	13	2
	Bath Village........................	5,532	19	0	2	4	13	142	19	120	3	0

[1] The FBI does not publish arson data unless it receives data from either the agency or the state for all 12 months of the calendar year.

[7] Because of changes in the state/local agency's reporting practices, figures are not comparable to previous years' data.

Table 8.   Offenses Known to Law Enforcement, by State and City, 2007 *(Contd.)*

(Number.)

State	City	Population	Violent crime	Murder and non-negligent man-slaughter	Forcible rape	Robbery	Aggravated assault	Property crime	Burglary	Larceny-theft	Motor vehicle theft	Arson[1]
	Beacon	14,928	62	1	1	20	40	247	67	154	26	5
	Bedford Town	18,668	5	1	0	2	2	149	18	127	4	0
	Bethlehem Town	33,057	32	0	4	10	18	538	81	446	11	3
	Binghamton	44,931	214	3	19	67	125	2,100	254	1,809	37	8
	Blooming Grove Town	12,396	11	0	0	1	10	116	29	75	12	0
	Bolivar Village	1,126	1	0	0	0	1	26	5	21	0	0
	Bolton Town	2,180	2	0	0	0	2	16	7	9	0	0
	Boonville Village	2,074	1	0	0	0	1	13	5	8	0	0
	Brant Town	1,849	0	0	0	0	0	9	3	6	0	1
	Briarcliff Manor Village	8,034	1	0	0	0	1	51	12	35	4	0
	Brighton Town	34,335	28	0	5	11	12	969	133	800	36	0
	Brockport Village	8,138	17	0	4	6	7	180	30	145	5	1
	Bronxville Village	6,477	3	0	0	1	2	72	8	50	14	0
	Buffalo	273,832	3,490	54	164	1,533	1,739	16,137	4,389	9,477	2,271	109
	Cairo Town	6,689	4	0	0	0	4	45	19	24	2	0
	Caledonia Village	2,191	1	0	0	0	1	72	4	67	1	0
	Cambridge Village	1,843	1	0	0	0	1	59	6	52	1	0
	Camden Village	2,288	11	0	0	0	11	86	15	69	2	0
	Camillus Town and Village	23,350	13	0	1	4	8	208	30	166	12	2
	Canisteo Village	2,256	8	0	0	0	8	68	7	61	0	0
	Cape Vincent Village	768	0	0	0	0	0	3	0	3	0	0
	Carmel Town	34,972	29	1	2	5	21	294	30	256	8	4
	Carroll Town	3,473	3	0	0	0	3	8	4	4	0	0
	Carthage Village	3,717	6	0	2	0	4	112	22	85	5	2
	Catskill Village	4,337	8	0	0	3	5	247	27	214	6	0
	Cattaraugus Village	1,006	0	0	0	0	0	3	1	1	1	0
	Cayuga Heights Villag	3,670	0	0	0	0	0	51	6	45	0	0
	Cazenovia Village	2,717	1	0	0	0	1	28	2	26	0	0
	Central Square Village	1,660	1	0	0	0	1	20	4	15	1	0
	Chatham Village	1,726	8	0	0	1	7	86	28	52	6	0
	Cheektowaga Town	79,164	226	0	20	84	122	2,304	301	1,874	129	5
	Chester Town	9,929	0	0	0	0	0	31	11	19	1	0
	Chester Village	3,616	7	0	1	4	2	132	8	121	3	0
	Chittenango Village	4,936	2	0	0	0	2	103	11	86	6	1
	Cicero Town	28,347	8	0	0	3	5	451	65	374	12	0
	Clarkstown Town	78,909	85	0	8	29	48	1,625	140	1,415	70	3
	Clay Town	54,134	27	0	3	7	17	395	66	318	11	4
	Clifton Springs Village	2,174	1	0	0	0	1	35	12	23	0	0
	Clyde Village	2,133	3	0	0	0	3	67	8	56	3	0
	Cobleskill Village	4,647	13	0	1	1	11	184	16	163	5	2
	Coeymans Town	7,991	35	0	5	3	27	80	13	62	5	0
	Cohoes	14,944	68	0	1	4	63	171	44	114	13	0
	Colchester Town	2,054	2	0	1	0	1	1	1	0	0	0
	Cold Spring Village	2,008	1	0	0	0	1	28	9	19	0	0
	Colonie Town	77,550	86	1	5	21	59	2,369	270	2,046	53	12
	Copake Town	3,331	1	0	0	0	1	17	6	11	0	0
	Corning	10,428	47	0	4	9	34	433	58	366	9	6
	Cornwall-on-Hudson Village	3,094	0	0	0	0	0	19	1	18	0	0
	Cornwall Town	9,763	6	0	0	0	6	129	24	100	5	0
	Cortland	18,382	78	0	8	6	64	383	96	271	16	2
	Coxsackie Village	2,835	2	0	0	0	2	21	4	17	0	0
	Crawford Town	9,540	17	0	1	2	14	261	51	199	11	0
	Cuba Town	3,364	12	0	1	0	11	38	18	20	0	0
	Dansville Village	4,574	8	0	0	1	7	191	10	180	1	0
	Deerpark Town	8,433	8	0	0	1	7	139	31	101	7	0
	Delhi Village	2,745	9	0	0	0	9	6	1	5	0	0
	Depew Village	15,473	27	0	8	8	11	421	90	319	12	4
	Deposit Village	1,605	4	0	0	0	4	4	2	2	0	0
	Dewitt Town	21,606	34	1	3	12	18	547	96	424	27	1
	Dexter Village	1,119	0	0	0	0	0	1	0	1	0	0
	Dobbs Ferry Village	11,206	10	0	0	1	3	6	138	17	118	3	4
	Dryden Village	1,821	4	0	1	1	2	101	5	95	1	0
	Dunkirk	12,190	45	0	3	9	33	365	99	258	8	0
	East Aurora-Aurora Town	13,611	12	0	1	3	8	190	29	154	7	0
	Eastchester Town	18,768	4	0	0	2	2	210	13	184	13	0
	East Fishkill Town	29,535	156	1	0	2	153	350	32	295	23	18
	East Greenbush Town	17,159	13	0	0	4	9	405	31	363	11	0
	East Hampton Town	19,143	26	0	5	2	19	471	98	347	26	1
	East Hampton Village	1,345	1	0	0	0	1	142	6	134	2	0
	East Rochester Village	6,231	9	0	2	1	6	142	33	97	12	0
	East Syracuse Village	3,029	21	0	0	3	18	113	15	94	4	0
	Eden Town	7,789	0	0	0	0	0	69	23	41	5	0
	Ellenville Village	3,914	7	0	0	4	3	124	28	91	5	0
	Ellicott Town	5,294	12	0	0	1	11	240	44	188	8	0

[1] The FBI does not publish arson data unless it receives data from either the agency or the state for all 12 months of the calendar year.

Table 8.   Offenses Known to Law Enforcement, by State and City, 2007 *(Contd.)*

(Number.)

State	City	Population	Violent crime	Murder and non-negligent man-slaughter	Forcible rape	Robbery	Aggravated assault	Property crime	Burglary	Larceny-theft	Motor vehicle theft	Arson[1]
	Ellicottville	1,880	0	0	0	0	0	64	8	54	2	1
	Elmira	29,375	134	3	5	28	98	1,266	269	956	41	2
	Elmira Heights Village	3,931	4	0	0	3	1	90	14	74	2	0
	Elmira Town	5,907	1	0	0	0	1	11	4	7	0	
	Elmsford Village	4,772	8	0	1	3	4	66	10	50	6	0
	Endicott Village	12,499	54	1	8	14	31	570	97	456	17	1
	Evans Town	17,000	17	0	1	0	16	281	64	200	17	3
	Fairport Village	5,467	4	0	0	0	4	56	7	45	4	1
	Fallsburg Town	12,082	23	0	1	2	20	222	67	141	14	2
	Fishkill Town	19,088	12	0	0	4	8	261	20	228	13	2
	Fishkill Village	1,731	8	0	0	1	7	43	5	38	0	0
	Floral Park Village	15,550	11	0	1	8	2	72	17	50	5	1
	Florida Village	2,793	2	0	0	0	2	32	5	27	0	0
	Fort Edward Village	3,074	8	0	0	0	8	26	7	18	1	0
	Frankfort Town	4,933	4	1	0	0	3	25	11	14	0	1
	Franklinville Village	1,741	1	0	0	1	0	20	3	17	0	0
	Fredonia Village	11,192	20	0	0	2	18	223	22	191	10	0
	Freeport Village	43,050	219	2	7	105	105	1,056	147	778	131	3
	Freeville Village	505	2	0	0	0	2	9	6	2	1	
	Friendship Town	1,865	1	0	0	0	1	7	4	3	0	0
	Fulton City	11,404	22	0	4	6	12	494	75	413	6	4
	Garden City Village	21,804	12	0	0	12	0	285	39	237	9	1
	Gates Town	28,396	56	0	7	22	27	1,066	113	911	42	2
	Geddes Town	10,616	5	0	0	3	2	210	24	182	4	0
	Geneseo Village	7,841	8	0	6	1	1	111	14	96	1	1
	Geneva	13,336	27	1	1	6	19	365	83	273	9	1
	Germantown Town	2,015	0	0	0	0	0	2	1	1	0	0
	Glen Cove	26,406	14	0	0	7	7	202	33	160	9	1
	Glen Park Village	491	0	0	0	0	0	2	0	2	0	0
	Glens Falls	14,043	18	1	2	5	10	471	51	413	7	1
	Glenville Town	21,347	7	0	1	0	6	282	34	234	14	0
	Gloversville	15,146	60	0	4	4	52	675	139	509	27	3
	Goshen Town	8,608	3	0	1	0	2	92	16	73	3	0
	Goshen Village	5,527	11	1	1	1	8	77	6	69	2	5
	Gouverneur Village	4,088	10	0	3	0	7	154	30	121	3	0
	Gowanda Village	2,664	11	0	0	1	10	122	32	90	0	1
	Granville Village	2,585	6	0	3	0	3	29	3	26	0	0
	Great Neck Estates Village	2,711	0	0	0	0	0	12	1	11	0	0
	Greece Town	93,123	122	0	8	40	74	2,147	279	1,790	78	0
	Greenburgh Town	43,734	44	1	3	17	23	718	71	617	30	0
	Greene Village	1,683	0	0	0	0	0	0	0	0	0	0
	Green Island Village	2,591	1	0	0	0	1	57	11	41	5	0
	Greenport Town	4,060	2	0	0	1	1	93	3	89	1	0
	Greenwich Village	1,858	1	0	0	0	1	47	6	41	0	0
	Greenwood Lake Village	3,460	11	0	0	0	11	46	6	37	3	0
	Groton Village	2,403	1	0	0	1	0	68	10	55	3	0
	Guilderland Town	33,006	18	0	1	7	10	765	49	701	15	0
	Hamburg Town	44,187	28	0	4	9	15	402	60	336	6	1
	Hamburg Village	9,413	8	0	2	3	3	195	17	172	6	0
	Hamilton Village	3,787	2	0	0	1	1	40	7	32	1	0
	Hancock Village	1,111	11	0	0	0	11	10	3	5	2	0
	Harriman Village	2,274	0	0	0	0	0	33	8	23	2	0
	Harrison Town	26,654	27	0	1	2	24	297	40	244	13	0
	Hastings-on-Hudson Village	7,858	26	0	2	2	22	135	8	124	3	0
	Haverstraw Town	24,515	76	1	2	27	46	446	91	331	24	3
	Hempstead Village	52,430	335	7	12	141	175	909	194	497	218	6
	Herkimer Village	7,117	74	0	5	2	67	409	51	357	1	0
	Highland Falls Village	3,742	4	0	0	0	4	69	17	50	2	0
	Highlands Town	9,106	1	1	0	0	0	12	0	12	0	0
	Hoosick Falls Village	3,289	2	0	1	1	0	57	21	31	5	3
	Hornell	8,662	13	0	2	1	10	139	18	121	0	0
	Horseheads Village	6,256	14	0	2	4	8	214	21	191	2	0
	Hudson Falls Village	6,752	8	0	1	1	6	44	6	38	0	0
	Hunter Town	2,756	1	0	0	0	1	7	6	1	0	0
	Huntington Bay Village	1,472	0	0	0	0	0	2	0	2	0	0
	Hyde Park Town	20,675	9	0	1	5	3	182	33	142	7	0
	Ilion Village	8,187	28	0	0	1	27	105	26	79	0	1
	Independence Town	1,052	0	0	0	0	0	0	0	0	0	0
	Irondequoit Town	50,106	75	2	3	35	35	1,573	242	1,223	108	6
	Irvington Village	6,658	1	0	0	0	1	30	4	26	0	0
	Ithaca	29,970	58	0	8	22	28	965	147	805	13	1
	Jamestown	29,646	167	1	20	30	116	1,151	300	814	37	6
	Johnson City Village	14,807	54	0	7	10	37	680	86	584	10	3
	Johnstown	8,489	9	0	2	2	5	290	36	247	7	0

[1] The FBI does not publish arson data unless it receives data from either the agency or the state for all 12 months of the calendar year.

Table 8. Offenses Known to Law Enforcement, by State and City, 2007 *(Contd.)*

(Number.)

State	City	Population	Violent crime	Murder and non-negligent man-slaughter	Forcible rape	Robbery	Aggravated assault	Property crime	Burglary	Larceny-theft	Motor vehicle theft	Arson[1]
	Jordan Village	1,338	0	0	0	0	0	11	4	7	0	0
	Kenmore Village	15,172	22	0	1	7	14	273	39	222	12	
	Kensington Village	1,181	0	0	0	0	0	0	0	0	0	0
	Kent Town	14,443	1	0	0	0	1	140	25	110	5	0
	Kingston	22,741	67	1	5	38	23	699	122	551	26	0
	Kirkland Town	8,423	3	0	0	0	3	101	12	83	6	0
	Lackawanna	17,775	119	0	6	30	83	459	129	300	30	0
	Lake Placid Village	2,840	0	0	0	0	0	51	11	38	2	1
	Lake Success Village	2,833	1	0	0	0	1	101	25	71	5	0
	Lakewood-Busti	7,455	3	0	0	1	2	221	23	194	4	1
	Lancaster Town	23,342	16	0	2	4	10	489	77	398	14	0
	Larchmont Village	6,535	2	0	0	1	1	101	12	86	3	0
	Le Roy Village	4,226	3	0	0	0	3	144	11	128	5	0
	Lewisboro Town	12,606	0	0	0	0	0	96	12	83	1	0
	Lewiston Town and Village	16,766	17	0	2	1	14	174	26	134	14	1
	Liberty Village	3,973	30	0	1	8	21	204	28	172	4	0
	Little Falls	4,952	36	0	0	2	34	159	39	110	10	1
	Liverpool Village	2,381	1	0	0	0	1	47	12	34	1	0
	Lloyd Harbor Village	3,654	1	0	0	0	1	22	2	20	0	0
	Lloyd Town	10,771	8	0	0	2	6	110	15	88	7	
	Lockport	20,872	70	0	7	35	28	744	157	561	26	8
	Long Beach	35,057	30	0	0	13	17	211	29	181	1	0
	Lowville Village	3,216	4	0	2	0	2	100	13	84	3	0
	Lynbrook Village	19,392	19	0	0	9	10	166	15	142	9	0
	Lyons Village	3,475	21	0	3	5	13	148	17	127	4	0
	Macedon Town and Village	8,963	4	0	1	0	3	43	5	36	2	0
	Malone Village	5,879	13	0	4	0	9	182	29	153	0	0
	Malverne Village	8,725	5	0	0	3	2	26	11	14	1	0
	Mamaroneck Town	11,470	1	0	0	0	1	113	19	90	4	2
	Mamaroneck Village	18,468	19	0	0	9	10	245	39	193	13	0
	Manchester Village	1,434	0	0	0	0	0	0	0	0	0	0
	Manlius Town	25,127	18	0	1	1	16	440	56	372	12	1
	Marlborough Town	8,351	23	0	0	1	22	122	28	85	9	0
	Massena Village	10,747	12	0	4	0	8	206	26	178	2	2
	Maybrook Village	4,185	0	0	0	0	0	32	2	30	0	0
	McGraw Village	963	0	0	0	0	0	2	1	1	0	
	Mechanicville	4,912	36	0	0	3	33	57	11	41	5	1
	Medina Village	6,160	13	0	2	1	10	222	40	179	3	0
	Menands Village	3,782	9	1	1	4	3	176	35	129	12	0
	Middleport Village	1,803	0	0	0	0	0	39	0	39	0	0
	Middletown	26,097	194	1	13	95	85	942	216	690	36	8
	Millbrook Village	1,559	2	0	0	0	2	6	1	5	0	0
	Mohawk Village	2,523	1	0	0	0	1	19	7	11	1	0
	Monroe Village	8,187	30	0	3	9	18	252	20	227	5	0
	Montgomery Town	8,921	16	0	6	1	9	150	27	108	15	1
	Monticello Village	6,654	59	0	1	32	26	301	86	201	14	2
	Moravia Village	1,313	1	0	0	0	1	17	2	15	0	0
	Moriah Town	3,547	2	0	0	0	2	4	1	3	0	0
	Mount Hope Town	7,581	2	0	0	0	2	43	10	28	5	0
	Mount Kisco Village	10,505	5	0	0	3	2	130	14	115	1	0
	Mount Morris Village	2,944	5	0	3	0	2	68	16	50	2	
	Mount Pleasant Town	26,693	9	0	3	2	4	239	40	188	11	1
	Mount Vernon	68,380	600	7	10	266	317	1,844	461	1,200	183	9
	Nassau Village	1,115	3	0	0	1	2	4	3	1	0	0
	Newark Village	9,234	31	1	3	1	26	336	38	289	9	0
	New Berlin Town	1,717	0	0	0	0	0	14	0	12	2	1
	Newburgh	28,340	436	2	14	131	289	1,176	316	791	69	
	Newburgh Town	30,995	47	1	2	28	16	1,172	117	1,006	49	6
	New Castle Town	17,819	0	0	0	0	0	129	21	107	1	1
	New Hartford Town and Village	19,586	23	0	2	9	12	820	58	753	9	0
	New Paltz Town and Village	14,121	75	0	7	4	64	247	29	208	10	
	New Rochelle	73,603	219	1	3	119	96	1,454	234	1,142	78	1
	New Windsor Town	25,320	22	0	1	8	13	456	56	384	16	3
	New York	8,220,196	50,453	496	875	21,787	27,295	149,488	20,914	115,318	13,256	
	New York Mills Village	3,128	5	0	0	2	3	50	5	42	3	1
	Niagara Falls	51,897	501	3	38	134	326	2,676	668	1,796	212	36
	Niagara Town	8,515	13	0	0	3	10	279	43	218	18	1
	Niskayuna Town	21,863	11	0	0	4	7	369	37	321	11	1
	Nissequogue Village	1,458	0	0	0	0	0	4	0	4	0	0
	North Castle Town	12,317	10	0	0	2	8	86	15	70	1	0
	North Greenbush Town	11,837	20	0	1	1	18	233	31	197	5	1
	Northport Village	7,480	4	0	0	4	0	69	6	61	2	0
	North Syracuse Village	6,668	7	1	0	0	6	51	12	38	1	0
	North Tonawanda	31,575	53	0	5	11	37	614	137	441	36	1

[1] The FBI does not publish arson data unless it receives data from either the agency or the state for all 12 months of the calendar year.

Table 8.   Offenses Known to Law Enforcement, by State and City, 2007 *(Contd.)*

(Number.)

State	City	Population	Violent crime	Murder and non-negligent man-slaughter	Forcible rape	Robbery	Aggravated assault	Property crime	Burglary	Larceny-theft	Motor vehicle theft	Arson[1]
	Northville Village	1,162	1	0	0	0	1	24	2	22	0	0
	Norwich	7,183	9	1	7	0	1	273	31	238	4	0
	Ogdensburg	11,213	10	0	0	3	7	588	80	500	8	3
	Ogden Town	19,186	23	0	0	3	20	204	37	161	6	0
	Old Brookville Village	2,254	1	0	0	1	0	106	16	86	4	0
	Old Westbury Village	5,340	0	0	0	0	0	30	7	19	4	1
	Olean	14,485	20	0	1	15	4	678	87	580	11	3
	Olive Town	4,720	1	0	0	0	1	14	2	11	1	0
	Oneida	10,928	16	0	4	1	11	431	85	339	7	0
	Oneonta City	13,239	36	0	5	6	25	347	87	253	7	4
	Orangetown Town	36,171	38	0	0	13	25	470	43	411	16	0
	Orchard Park Town	28,208	20	0	2	3	15	437	85	340	12	5
	Oriskany Village	1,424	1	0	0	0	1	14	2	12	0	0
	Ossining Town	5,755	6	0	0	0	6	46	5	41	0	0
	Ossining Village	23,514	52	1	2	22	27	340	100	227	13	1
	Oswego City	17,573	46	0	2	5	39	482	74	399	9	0
	Owego Village	3,760	7	0	1	1	5	19	7	12	0	0
	Oxford Village	1,566	0	0	0	0	0	32	1	31	0	0
	Oyster Bay Cove Village	2,248	1	0	0	0	1	6	2	4	0	0
	Painted Post Village	1,784	1	0	0	0	1	52	0	52	0	1
	Palmyra Village	3,475	2	0	0	0	2	43	3	40	0	0
	Peekskill	24,910	74	0	1	33	40	216	36	166	14	0
	Pelham Manor Village	5,420	7	0	1	5	1	119	16	94	9	1
	Pelham Village	6,403	8	0	0	8	0	128	25	93	10	0
	Penn Yan Village	5,217	1	0	1	0	0	109	12	96	1	0
	Perry Village	3,743	7	0	0	0	7	143	22	114	7	0
	Phelps Village	1,931	0	0	0	0	0	10	2	8	0	0
	Phoenix Village	2,177	1	0	1	0	0	25	6	19	0	0
	Piermont Village	2,603	1	0	0	0	1	26	4	20	2	0
	Pine Plains Town	2,750	0	0	0	0	0	16	0	16	0	0
	Plattekill Town	10,993	3	0	0	2	1	42	19	18	5	0
	Plattsburgh City	19,365	27	0	5	4	18	646	113	521	12	0
	Pleasantville Village	7,167	0	0	0	0	0	0	0	0	0	0
	Port Byron Village	1,257	2	0	0	0	2	1	0	1	0	0
	Port Chester Village	28,019	88	0	3	46	39	686	114	530	42	0
	Port Dickinson Village	1,605	0	0	0	0	0	15	0	15	0	0
	Port Jervis	9,203	31	0	4	10	17	217	42	169	6	3
	Portville Village	973	0	0	0	0	0	40	2	38	0	2
	Port Washington	18,532	6	0	1	1	4	116	18	90	8	3
	Potsdam Village	9,869	13	1	3	0	9	201	16	177	8	0
	Poughkeepsie	30,074	387	5	15	163	204	1,063	253	704	106	5
	Poughkeepsie Town	44,016	53	1	0	32	20	1,522	101	1,399	22	3
	Pound Ridge Town	5,011	1	0	0	0	1	45	1	44	0	0
	Pulaski Village	2,323	8	0	0	3	5	61	12	48	1	0
	Quogue Village	1,125	2	0	0	0	2	31	12	18	1	0
	Ramapo Town	76,371	64	0	1	13	50	624	98	503	23	1
	Rensselaer City	7,822	29	0	5	9	15	265	60	189	16	0
	Rhinebeck Village	3,107	0	0	0	0	0	67	6	60	1	0
	Riverhead Town	35,087	90	1	3	31	55	864	173	658	33	1
	Rochester	206,686	2,350	50	121	1,032	1,147	11,277	2,582	7,044	1,651	204
	Rockville Centre Village	23,952	8	1	0	5	2	227	19	187	21	2
	Rome	34,123	40	1	7	8	24	531	119	383	29	
	Rosendale Town	6,312	1	0	0	0	1	57	12	43	2	0
	Rotterdam Town	29,547	30	0	0	14	16	812	119	664	29	13
	Rouses Point Village	2,420	1	0	0	0	1	19	4	15	0	0
	Rye	15,127	6	0	0	1	5	218	27	176	15	0
	Rye Brook Village	9,820	2	0	1	0	1	116	15	97	4	0
	Sag Harbor Village	2,363	2	0	0	0	2	55	7	45	3	0
	Salamanca	5,718	26	0	1	3	22	298	65	225	8	1
	Sands Point Village	2,839	0	0	0	0	0	10	1	9	0	0
	Saranac Lake Village	4,895	8	0	2	0	6	124	38	83	3	0
	Saratoga Springs	28,807	41	0	1	4	36	685	149	513	23	1
	Saugerties Town	15,816	9	1	2	0	6	217	63	151	3	5
	Saugerties Village	3,912	13	0	0	2	11	103	5	94	4	0
	Scarsdale Village	17,890	3	0	0	1	2	158	13	136	9	0
	Schenectady	61,535	606	5	34	265	302	2,947	806	1,851	290	48
	Schodack Town	11,374	4	1	0	1	2	127	24	97	6	0
	Scotia Village	8,107	9	0	0	1	8	131	17	110	4	0
	Seneca Falls Village	6,791	10	0	1	0	9	28	5	23	0	0
	Shawangunk Town	12,813	15	0	1	2	12	148	46	97	5	0
	Shelter Island Town	2,471	0	0	0	0	0	44	14	30	0	0
	Sherburne Village	1,443	0	0	0	0	0	49	0	49	0	0
	Sherrill	3,152	0	0	0	0	0	17	5	12	0	0
	Shortsville Village	1,342	0	0	0	0	0	0	0	0	0	0

[1] The FBI does not publish arson data unless it receives data from either the agency or the state for all 12 months of the calendar year.

Table 8.   Offenses Known to Law Enforcement, by State and City, 2007 *(Contd.)*

(Number.)

State	City	Population	Violent crime	Murder and non-negligent man-slaughter	Forcible rape	Robbery	Aggravated assault	Property crime	Burglary	Larceny-theft	Motor vehicle theft	Arson[1]
	Sidney Village	3,809	9	0	2	0	7	190	33	156	1	0
	Silver Creek Village	2,842	10	0	0	0	10	35	17	17	1	2
	Skaneateles Village	2,585	2	0	1	0	1	22	4	18	0	0
	Sleepy Hollow Village	10,262	0	0	0	0	0	0	0	0	0	0
	Sodus Village	1,639	1	0	0	0	1	40	3	36	1	0
	Solvay Village	6,514	8	0	0	1	7	140	31	100	9	0
	Southampton Town	50,284	86	1	12	24	49	969	210	700	59	5
	Southampton Village	4,091	9	0	1	0	8	161	24	131	6	0
	South Glens Falls Village	3,435	6	0	2	1	3	120	18	98	4	0
	South Nyack Village	3,358	7	0	0	0	7	47	10	37	0	0
	Southold Town	19,872	16	0	0	1	15	383	77	301	5	0
	Spring Valley Village	25,397	204	0	12	71	121	450	88	325	37	2
	Stillwater Town	6,501	1	0	1	0	0	25	4	21	0	0
	Stockport Town	2,882	0	0	0	0	0	10	0	10	0	0
	Stony Point Town	15,073	9	0	0	4	5	98	16	81	1	0
	Suffern Village	10,944	6	0	1	4	1	67	13	52	2	0
	Syracuse	139,880	1,435	19	67	446	903	5,964	1,785	3,618	561	48
	Tarrytown Village	11,525	4	0	0	3	1	114	13	92	9	1
	Ticonderoga Town	5,076	11	0	2	0	9	61	10	45	6	3
	Tonawanda	14,971	22	0	4	3	15	431	51	367	13	2
	Tonawanda Town	57,312	119	0	8	33	78	1,181	218	887	76	3
	Troy	47,776	345	2	21	131	191	2,203	581	1,449	173	6
	Trumansburg Village	1,587	1	0	0	0	1	52	1	50	1	0
	Tuckahoe Village	6,311	3	0	0	2	1	53	7	40	6	1
	Tupper Lake Village	3,842	13	0	0	0	13	136	33	93	10	2
	Tuxedo Park Village	726	0	0	0	0	0	0	0	0	0	0
	Tuxedo Town	3,033	0	0	0	0	0	10	0	8	2	0
	Ulster Town	12,877	9	0	1	3	5	239	28	200	11	2
	Utica	58,888	431	5	21	142	263	2,880	752	1,966	162	12
	Vernon Village	1,168	1	0	0	0	1	24	7	17	0	0
	Vestal Town	27,403	8	0	0	0	8	584	25	547	12	1
	Walden Village	6,929	16	0	0	1	15	139	12	123	4	1
	Wallkill Town	27,554	36	0	5	18	13	662	84	545	33	4
	Walton Village	2,880	7	0	0	0	7	79	21	54	4	0
	Wappingers Falls Village	5,181	10	0	1	5	4	135	16	115	4	0
	Warsaw Village	3,717	7	0	4	0	3	92	9	82	1	0
	Warwick Town	20,075	2	1	1	0	0	128	26	100	2	
	Washingtonville Village	6,239	3	0	1	0	2	52	4	46	2	0
	Waterford Town and Village	8,660	0	0	0	0	0	48	11	35	2	0
	Waterloo Village	5,098	6	0	0	0	6	227	18	206	3	2
	Watertown	26,726	123	2	13	27	81	1,167	179	918	70	14
	Watervliet	9,749	37	0	6	10	21	263	64	181	18	3
	Watkins Glen Village	2,092	6	0	0	1	5	54	3	50	1	0
	Waverly Village	4,442	4	0	0	0	4	158	17	136	5	1
	Wayland Village	1,819	0	0	0	0	0	6	0	6	0	0
	Webster Town and Village	41,471	20	0	4	6	10	602	104	484	14	6
	Weedsport Village	1,950	0	0	0	0	0	22	0	22	0	0
	Wellsville Village	4,877	21	0	0	2	19	133	22	103	8	1
	Westfield Village	3,405	2	0	0	0	2	46	16	29	1	0
	Westhampton Beach Village	1,956	3	0	0	0	3	62	10	51	1	1
	West Seneca Town	43,955	77	1	8	19	49	895	166	691	38	1
	Whitehall Village	2,609	4	0	0	0	4	34	4	28	2	0
	White Plains	57,638	114	0	4	27	83	1,108	45	1,025	38	1
	Whitesboro Village	3,823	15	0	0	1	14	63	14	46	3	0
	Whitestown Town	9,348	2	0	1	0	1	48	9	36	3	0
	Windham Town	1,914	0	0	0	0	0	54	17	34	3	0
	Woodbury Town	10,458	4	0	1	3	0	182	15	164	3	0
	Woodridge Village	1,085	3	0	0	0	3	4	1	3	0	0
	Woodstock Town	6,214	4	0	0	0	4	65	19	45	1	0
	Yonkers	198,071	878	10	44	424	400	3,012	642	1,994	376	35
	Yorkville Village	2,593	6	0	0	3	3	158	35	118	5	0
NORTH CAROLINA	Aberdeen	5,337	23	0	1	7	15	298	50	224	24	3
	Ahoskie	4,278	29	0	1	4	24	303	80	215	8	2
	Albemarle	15,355	143	1	13	34	95	1,213	309	837	67	15
	Angier	4,288	48	0	2	8	38	190	78	94	18	3
	Archdale	9,474	32	0	1	10	21	368	78	267	23	2
	Asheboro	24,399	57	0	6	22	29	1,670	349	1,215	106	1
	Asheville	72,907	505	10	27	229	239	4,249	1,014	2,818	417	51
	Atlantic Beach	1,839	27	0	2	2	23	210	39	169	2	1
	Bailey	679	4	0	0	2	2	50	14	35	1	0
	Banner Elk	895	5	0	2	0	3	28	4	21	3	0
	Beaufort	4,326	12	0	0	0	12	216	74	131	11	0
	Belhaven	1,997	9	0	0	0	9	64	25	37	2	3
	Belmont	9,005	64	0	4	17	43	523	95	395	33	2

[1] The FBI does not publish arson data unless it receives data from either the agency or the state for all 12 months of the calendar year.

Table 8. Offenses Known to Law Enforcement, by State and City, 2007 *(Contd.)*

(Number.)

State	City	Population	Violent crime	Murder and non-negligent man-slaughter	Forcible rape	Robbery	Aggravated assault	Property crime	Burglary	Larceny-theft	Motor vehicle theft	Arson[1]
	Benson	3,422	37	0	0	17	20	254	60	175	19	1
	Bethel	1,680	9	0	0	1	8	55	6	46	3	1
	Beulaville	1,117	6	0	0	0	6	58	16	38	4	0
	Biltmore Forest	1,527	0	0	0	0	0	22	5	17	0	1
	Biscoe	1,732	18	0	0	6	12	171	23	144	4	1
	Black Mountain	7,686	7	0	0	2	5	152	48	93	11	1
	Boiling Spring Lakes	4,637	7	0	3	0	4	69	21	43	5	5
	Boiling Springs	3,856	6	0	1	2	3	45	5	38	2	0
	Boone	13,283	21	0	2	4	15	458	69	375	14	0
	Brevard	6,634	33	1	4	3	25	285	65	211	9	1
	Bryson City	1,382	16	0	0	1	15	102	0	100	2	1
	Burlington	48,689	404	3	16	103	282	2,967	763	2,054	150	8
	Butner	6,520	63	0	0	11	52	268	70	182	16	2
	Canton	3,925	22	1	0	4	17	240	84	149	7	4
	Cape Carteret	1,460	5	0	0	0	5	50	3	44	3	0
	Carolina Beach	5,675	21	0	3	11	7	329	86	217	26	3
	Carthage	2,036	12	0	0	2	10	109	24	84	1	0
	Cary	114,221	134	1	11	58	64	2,120	448	1,584	88	13
	Chadbourn	2,071	26	2	1	1	22	188	49	137	2	1
	Charlotte-Mecklenburg	733,291	7,233	76	282	3,191	3,684	51,279	12,948	32,313	6,018	388
	Cherryville	5,533	22	0	3	1	18	186	64	119	3	3
	China Grove	3,723	18	1	1	3	13	145	31	107	7	0
	Chocowinity	730	0	0	0	0	0	34	3	30	1	0
	Claremont	1,127	9	0	1	1	7	98	30	63	5	0
	Clayton	14,843	54	1	3	18	32	404	123	265	16	2
	Cleveland	829	3	0	0	1	2	53	16	33	4	0
	Clinton	8,818	77	0	4	17	56	587	147	415	25	1
	Coats	2,086	4	0	0	1	3	64	17	42	5	1
	Columbus	993	2	0	1	0	1	56	6	47	3	0
	Concord	63,284	256	7	21	100	128	3,029	473	2,326	230	20
	Conover	7,183	26	0	4	8	14	579	93	435	51	0
	Creedmoor	3,472	15	0	4	1	10	109	33	72	4	2
	Dobson	1,506	4	0	0	1	3	78	8	68	2	0
	Drexel	1,900	0	0	0	0	0	41	9	28	4	0
	Dunn	10,072	123	0	5	32	86	853	182	600	71	5
	Eden	15,608	64	1	3	20	40	894	240	606	48	6
	Edenton	4,988	32	0	3	10	19	194	51	137	6	2
	Elkin	4,314	12	0	1	0	11	235	38	190	7	0
	Elon	7,173	9	0	2	0	7	131	40	90	1	0
	Emerald Isle	3,752	10	0	4	2	4	231	115	111	5	0
	Enfield	2,345	42	0	3	20	19	110	66	41	3	1
	Erwin	4,843	21	0	0	3	18	150	46	96	8	0
	Fairmont	2,737	86	0	1	21	64	321	101	197	23	2
	Farmville	4,553	31	0	1	2	28	256	95	155	6	3
	Fayetteville	167,157	1,320	21	56	500	743	12,614	3,569	8,223	822	49
	Forest City	7,277	67	1	3	18	45	612	170	414	28	3
	Four Oaks	1,881	5	0	1	0	4	31	11	13	7	0
	Franklin	3,633	8	0	1	1	6	177	56	115	6	2
	Franklinton	1,948	4	0	1	1	2	92	20	70	2	2
	Garland	841	3	0	0	0	3	17	0	17	0	0
	Garner	24,547	99	0	5	47	47	1,246	204	970	72	0
	Garysburg	1,171	11	0	0	1	10	64	31	32	1	0
	Gastonia	70,127	701	5	23	234	439	5,552	1,259	3,842	451	55
	Gibsonville	4,627	9	1	1	6	1	100	23	74	3	0
	Goldsboro	38,053	312	10	6	100	196	2,843	755	1,921	167	3
	Graham	14,275	81	1	5	19	56	624	142	439	43	3
	Greensboro	238,122	2,312	40	94	942	1,236	14,778	4,704	8,943	1,131	135
	Greenville	73,319	663	8	20	275	360	4,928	1,424	3,237	267	21
	Hamlet	5,715	40	3	2	10	25	362	145	202	15	7
	Henderson	16,165	183	7	3	77	96	1,726	521	1,129	76	13
	Hendersonville	11,863	117	2	4	29	82	964	148	758	58	0
	Hertford	2,135	8	0	0	1	7	82	17	62	3	0
	Hickory	41,008	368	5	21	116	226	3,398	783	2,338	277	26
	Highlands	948	1	0	0	0	1	80	37	43	0	0
	High Point	99,297	832	13	39	335	445	5,746	1,870	3,456	420	42
	Hillsborough	5,380	32	1	1	13	17	475	138	317	20	0
	Holden Beach	863	1	0	0	0	1	91	41	50	0	0
	Hope Mills	12,778	65	0	1	21	43	850	198	612	40	6
	Hudson	3,075	3	0	1	0	2	119	27	87	5	0
	Huntersville	41,018	93	1	3	31	58	1,306	259	983	64	11
	Indian Beach	96	0	0	0	0	0	10	4	4	2	0
	Jacksonville	70,368	278	7	30	65	176	2,297	550	1,614	133	10
	Jefferson	1,368	2	0	0	0	2	15	5	9	1	0
	Jonesville	2,296	9	0	2	2	5	172	52	111	9	0

[1] The FBI does not publish arson data unless it receives data from either the agency or the state for all 12 months of the calendar year.

Table 8.   Offenses Known to Law Enforcement, by State and City, 2007 *(Contd.)*

(Number.)

State	City	Population	Violent crime	Murder and non-negligent man-slaughter	Forcible rape	Robbery	Aggravated assault	Property crime	Burglary	Larceny-theft	Motor vehicle theft	Arson[1]
	Kannapolis	40,554	176	1	13	57	105	1,107	366	604	137	10
	Kenansville	902	0	0	0	0	0	33	1	31	1	1
	Kenly	1,894	11	0	1	3	7	114	29	74	11	1
	Kernersville	22,325	87	0	6	23	58	1,125	250	823	52	1
	Kill Devil Hills	6,718	23	1	4	2	16	454	118	319	17	1
	King	6,639	24	0	3	1	20	261	50	198	13	1
	Kings Mountain	11,003	54	0	4	19	31	571	167	392	12	2
	Kinston	22,568	290	1	12	63	214	1,408	359	995	54	15
	Kitty Hawk	3,391	3	0	0	2	1	130	31	90	9	0
	La Grange	2,782	33	0	1	1	31	150	46	94	10	3
	Lake Lure	1,022	0	0	0	0	0	46	7	38	1	0
	Landis	3,074	0	0	0	0	0	97	5	89	3	1
	Laurel Park	2,123	2	0	1	1	0	18	3	15	0	0
	Laurinburg	15,743	98	3	2	36	57	890	338	503	49	16
	Leland	4,693	20	0	0	5	15	313	135	165	13	1
	Lenoir	17,988	51	1	1	15	34	768	217	517	34	2
	Lexington	20,452	171	0	9	44	118	1,082	409	617	56	6
	Liberty	2,743	6	0	0	4	2	54	12	40	2	0
	Lillington	3,214	4	0	0	1	3	77	16	56	5	0
	Locust	2,562	2	0	0	1	1	61	24	37	0	1
	Long View	4,904	32	0	7	9	16	367	156	174	37	2
	Louisburg	3,813	18	0	2	8	8	167	27	131	9	1
	Lumberton	21,983	365	7	6	135	217	2,828	780	1,844	204	8
	Madison	2,283	39	0	0	3	36	142	51	90	1	2
	Maggie Valley	810	2	0	0	0	2	120	5	110	5	0
	Maiden	3,366	12	0	0	4	8	181	31	138	12	1
	Manteo	1,336	6	0	0	0	6	72	11	59	2	0
	Marion	5,070	38	0	0	9	29	421	136	263	22	4
	Mars Hill	1,821	11	0	1	2	8	37	15	21	1	0
	Matthews	26,693	77	0	5	42	30	1,133	188	879	66	21
	Mayodan	2,624	13	0	1	3	9	126	20	106	0	0
	Maysville	978	2	0	0	1	1	16	4	8	4	0
	Mebane	9,555	55	0	1	13	41	336	67	251	18	2
	Mint Hill	18,810	62	2	4	22	34	407	222	150	35	5
	Mocksville	4,568	18	2	1	3	12	297	51	236	10	0
	Monroe	31,345	253	1	10	73	169	2,350	595	1,579	176	12
	Mooresville	21,143	75	0	9	26	40	1,203	255	878	70	13
	Morehead City	9,501	56	0	7	12	37	593	114	454	25	3
	Morganton	17,183	77	2	8	17	50	713	179	497	37	1
	Morrisville	14,336	8	0	0	2	6	301	58	235	8	0
	Mount Airy	8,448	59	0	6	7	46	764	162	550	52	2
	Mount Gilead	1,406	8	0	0	2	6	69	34	29	6	1
	Mount Holly[3]	9,811	47	0	5	10	32		141		37	3
	Murfreesboro	2,276	12	0	0	5	7	90	18	70	2	1
	Murphy	1,573	17	1	3	1	12	104	22	72	10	0
	Nags Head	3,114	12	0	1	1	10	261	62	196	3	1
	Nashville	4,509	26	0	0	5	21	132	49	76	7	0
	New Bern	28,254	156	1	10	54	91	1,866	433	1,391	42	4
	Newland	663	4	0	3	1	0	25	3	19	3	0
	Newport	4,070	8	0	0	5	3	89	25	62	2	1
	Newton	13,211	46	0	5	21	20	828	210	553	65	1
	North Topsail Beach	874	1	0	0	0	1	56	35	21	0	0
	North Wilkesboro	4,195	21	2	0	7	12	261	77	172	12	0
	Norwood	2,150	13	0	3	1	9	83	24	54	5	1
	Oak Island	8,355	36	2	3	9	22	403	182	208	13	3
	Oxford	8,567	126	0	3	29	94	569	211	337	21	7
	Pembroke	2,677	24	0	1	10	13	212	90	103	19	3
	Pinebluff	1,352	0	0	0	0	0	28	10	18	0	0
	Pinehurst	12,132	2	0	0	2	0	111	1	108	2	0
	Pine Knoll Shores	1,584	3	0	0	0	3	40	10	30	0	0
	Pineville	3,826	83	0	0	35	48	1,143	101	967	75	3
	Pittsboro	2,537	4	0	1	3	0	84	24	58	2	0
	Plymouth	3,930	96	1	0	10	85	182	40	142	0	0
	Raeford	3,646	31	0	0	9	22	235	98	132	5	2
	Raleigh	367,120	2,098	23	99	835	1,141	12,762	2,949	8,773	1,040	72
	Ramseur	1,728	1	0	0	0	1	117	22	90	5	3
	Randleman	3,700	17	1	2	5	9	349	63	280	6	1
	Red Springs	3,518	40	1	5	13	21	313	171	114	28	2
	Reidsville	14,906	89	1	4	39	45	1,087	325	717	45	14
	Richlands	835	2	0	0	1	1	43	6	36	1	1
	Roanoke Rapids	16,407	90	2	6	30	52	861	212	578	71	2
	Robersonville	1,601	16	0	1	7	8	95	27	64	4	0
	Rockingham	9,093	105	2	5	17	81	1,091	209	861	21	7
	Rockwell	1,989	3	0	0	2	1	59	9	50	0	0

[1] The FBI does not publish arson data unless it receives data from either the agency or the state for all 12 months of the calendar year.
[3] The FBI determined that the agency's data were overreported. Consequently, affected data are not included in this table.

Table 8. Offenses Known to Law Enforcement, by State and City, 2007 *(Contd.)*

(Number.)

State	City	Population	Violent crime	Murder and non-negligent man-slaughter	Forcible rape	Robbery	Aggravated assault	Property crime	Burglary	Larceny-theft	Motor vehicle theft	Arson[1]
	Rocky Mount	57,132	662	14	21	266	361	4,815	1,354	3,240	221	16
	Rolesville	1,805	3	0	0	0	3	103	28	74	1	0
	Rose Hill	1,403	4	0	0	2	2	55	17	32	6	0
	Rowland	1,157	5	1	0	2	2	64	28	30	6	0
	Roxboro	8,738	74	0	5	20	49	659	266	375	18	5
	Rutherfordton	4,090	5	0	0	3	2	140	21	115	4	1
	Salisbury	28,449	327	3	10	145	169	2,051	501	1,381	169	12
	Scotland Neck	2,195	31	1	2	3	25	184	76	105	3	3
	Selma	6,877	61	3	6	15	37	499	230	236	33	6
	Shallotte	1,698	14	0	4	7	3	241	81	143	17	4
	Shelby	21,437	177	2	20	69	86	1,190	324	815	51	9
	Siler City	8,636	45	0	3	14	28	396	94	281	21	2
	Smithfield	12,456	112	0	10	34	68	1,121	227	832	62	5
	Southern Pines	12,351	91	1	4	23	63	864	238	589	37	4
	Southern Shores	2,708	0	0	0	0	0	56	20	35	1	0
	Southport	2,960	3	0	0	0	3	137	34	100	3	8
	Sparta	1,767	2	0	1	0	1	39	8	28	3	0
	Spencer	3,355	24	0	0	8	16	231	88	139	4	0
	Spindale	3,916	28	0	1	3	24	265	80	171	14	0
	Spring Hope	1,280	8	0	0	1	7	46	9	36	1	1
	Spring Lake	8,080	55	0	3	15	37	610	212	357	41	2
	Stallings	4,201	24	0	1	3	20	228	104	107	17	1
	Stanley	3,134	14	0	0	6	8	182	74	102	6	0
	Statesville	25,756	275	7	10	84	174	1,794	650	1,013	131	7
	St. Pauls	2,053	14	1	0	9	4	133	59	70	4	0
	Sunset Beach	2,296	3	0	0	2	1	87	46	39	2	0
	Surf City	1,873	15	0	2	0	13	155	74	74	7	0
	Swansboro	1,540	8	0	0	0	8	87	14	66	7	1
	Sylva	2,369	22	0	0	2	20	192	44	138	10	1
	Tarboro	10,463	53	0	5	17	31	423	101	300	22	1
	Taylorsville	1,828	8	0	0	4	4	139	29	103	7	0
	Thomasville	26,437	140	0	4	33	103	1,265	364	838	63	7
	Trent Woods	3,889	1	0	0	0	1	37	8	25	4	0
	Troutman	1,767	11	0	0	5	6	103	33	69	1	0
	Troy	3,408	25	0	2	9	14	168	31	134	3	2
	Tryon	1,745	5	0	0	2	3	42	15	27	0	0
	Valdese	4,525	13	0	1	2	10	101	20	78	3	0
	Vass	778	4	0	1	1	2	42	11	30	1	0
	Wadesboro	5,134	38	0	5	10	23	467	184	251	32	6
	Wake Forest	24,348	49	1	4	12	32	594	120	467	7	4
	Warsaw	3,149	21	0	0	6	15	181	35	137	9	0
	Washington	10,092	105	3	3	43	56	645	121	500	24	4
	Waxhaw	3,505	15	0	2	6	7	167	42	120	5	2
	Waynesville	9,436	19	0	1	3	15	385	118	251	16	3
	Weaverville	2,543	4	0	1	0	3	91	8	81	2	1
	Weldon	1,290	10	1	1	6	2	142	29	112	1	0
	Wendell	4,867	19	0	1	0	18	178	37	127	14	0
	Whispering Pines	2,138	0	0	0	0	0	7	2	5	0	1
	Whitakers	772	5	0	0	1	4	29	16	13	0	1
	White Lake	581	11	0	0	0	11	116	31	84	1	0
	Wilkesboro	3,193	15	0	1	4	10	351	85	255	11	0
	Williamston	5,531	58	1	4	12	41	419	93	309	17	2
	Wilmington	96,913	821	10	58	345	408	5,893	1,637	3,613	643	16
	Wilson	47,727	331	5	5	64	257	2,334	493	1,743	98	20
	Wilson's Mills	1,535	9	0	1	0	8	34	13	17	4	0
	Windsor	2,175	8	0	0	1	7	71	16	55	0	1
	Wingate	3,876	14	0	2	3	9	108	48	57	3	2
	Winterville	4,658	26	1	0	7	18	182	49	128	5	0
	Woodfin	3,335	10	0	1	4	5	107	37	56	14	0
	Wrightsville Beach	2,573	1	0	1	0	0	198	64	129	5	1
	Yadkinville	2,898	17	0	1	3	13	153	23	123	7	1
	Youngsville	738	16	0	0	1	15	67	16	51	0	0
	Zebulon	4,358	33	0	0	7	26	329	39	282	8	0
NORTH DAKOTA	Beulah	2,974	3	0	0	0	3	42	10	29	3	0
	Bismarck	58,648	108	1	25	11	71	1,550	255	1,194	101	5
	Cavalier	1,404	1	0	1	0	0	20	7	12	1	0
	Devils Lake	6,647	13	1	1	2	9	272	36	226	10	1
	Dickinson	15,595	7	0	0	0	7	462	79	349	34	0
	Fargo	89,998	241	3	62	26	150	2,745	530	2,018	197	21
	Fessenden	519	0	0	0	0	0	2	2	0	0	0
	Grafton	4,118	6	0	1	0	5	108	14	84	10	0
	Grand Forks	50,477	120	1	30	11	78	1,762	253	1,379	130	3
	Harvey	1,671	6	0	2	0	4	22	4	18	0	1
	Jamestown	14,696	23	0	7	0	16	298	58	226	14	3

[1] The FBI does not publish arson data unless it receives data from either the agency or the state for all 12 months of the calendar year.

Table 8.   Offenses Known to Law Enforcement, by State and City, 2007 *(Contd.)*

(Number.)

State	City	Population	Violent crime	Murder and non-negligent man-slaughter	Forcible rape	Robbery	Aggravated assault	Property crime	Burglary	Larceny-theft	Motor vehicle theft	Arson[1]
	Mandan	17,521	34	0	7	2	25	436	46	351	39	6
	Mayville	1,919	0	0	0	0	0	9	2	6	1	0
	Minot	34,487	91	3	19	5	64	866	140	656	70	6
	Northwood	853	0	0	0	0	0	4	0	3	1	0
	Portland	562	1	0	0	0	1	0	0	0	0	0
	Rolla	1,451	3	0	1	0	2	43	15	27	1	0
	Rugby	2,606	0	0	0	0	0	12	2	7	3	0
	Steele	676	0	0	0	0	0	7	2	5	0	0
	Valley City	6,325	9	1	1	0	7	89	19	65	5	0
	Wahpeton	7,850	14	0	0	1	13	182	14	164	4	3
	West Fargo	22,462	29	0	5	4	20	487	93	340	54	2
	Williston	12,260	17	0	4	1	12	202	15	160	27	8
OHIO	Akron	208,701	1,567	22	174	730	641	10,494	3,319	5,973	1,202	110
	Alliance	22,703	107	1	18	23	65	1,105	254	822	29	15
	Amberley Village	3,204	1	0	0	0	1	50	25	25	0	0
	Amelia	3,624	1	0	0	1	0	75	13	58	4	0
	Amherst	11,850	13	0	3	8	2	230	47	178	5	1
	Arcanum	2,002	1	0	0	0	1	34	4	30	0	1
	Archbold	4,530	4	0	0	0	4	72	6	65	1	0
	Ashland	21,939	19	0	8	11	0	551	67	473	11	0
	Athens	20,833	40	0	1	6	33	481	72	400	9	3
	Aurora	14,512	13	0	5	3	5	163	16	140	7	0
	Austintown	35,888	19	1	0	17	1	1,684	236	1,366	82	0
	Bainbridge Township	11,334	13	0	1	4	8	327	44	276	7	0
	Barberton	26,942	57	1	7	31	18	1,176	235	879	62	8
	Batavia	1,691	1	0	0	0	1	109	22	83	4	0
	Bath Township, Summit County	10,277	0	0	0	0	0	179	20	151	8	0
	Beachwood	11,239	8	0	1	5	2	447	36	383	28	0
	Beavercreek	39,552	30	1	12	11	6	1,346	143	1,139	64	10
	Beaver Township	6,176	5	0	0	3	2	156	37	117	2	0
	Bedford Heights	10,568	28	0	3	18	7	339	70	216	53	0
	Bellaire	4,674	12	0	2	1	9	51	4	45	2	1
	Bellbrook	6,892	1	0	0	0	1	119	11	107	1	1
	Bellefontaine	12,772	34	0	6	8	20	662	93	548	21	0
	Bellville	1,731	2	0	1	1	0	55	9	45	1	1
	Belpre	6,518	5	0	0	0	5	138	25	105	8	0
	Berea	18,026	14	0	4	3	7	316	63	241	12	3
	Bethel	2,608	6	0	1	0	5	209	30	177	2	0
	Beverly	1,310	0	0	0	0	0	57	6	50	1	0
	Bexley	12,161	27	0	0	16	11	441	124	305	12	2
	Blendon Township	7,561	11	0	2	8	1	285	34	229	22	2
	Blue Ash	11,409	8	0	0	3	5	251	39	208	4	1
	Bluffton	3,992	6	1	2	0	3	94	17	76	1	0
	Bowling Green	29,733	30	0	11	7	12	1,121	119	951	51	3
	Brecksville	13,065	7	0	1	0	6	58	5	53	0	0
	Brimfield Township	7,854	14	0	3	1	10	261	37	216	8	0
	Broadview Heights	17,798	8	0	1	0	7	72	17	47	8	0
	Brooklyn	10,574	44	0	6	21	17	615	53	466	96	0
	Brooklyn Heights	1,474	0	0	0	0	0	44	11	25	8	0
	Brook Park	19,498	21	0	3	4	14	289	20	221	48	2
	Brookville	5,307	1	0	0	0	1	66	10	53	3	1
	Bryan	8,327	6	0	3	0	3	193	27	162	4	1
	Buckeye Lake	3,055	22	0	3	4	15	194	34	149	11	0
	Butler Township	8,208	10	0	3	5	2	299	20	242	37	0
	Cadiz	3,379	8	0	2	1	5	82	20	59	3	0
	Cambridge	11,444	55	0	8	10	37	862	194	630	38	0
	Camden	2,248	1	0	0	0	1	15	8	6	1	0
	Campbell	8,630	48	3	6	18	21	338	176	142	20	0
	Canal Fulton	5,106	8	0	1	0	7	125	30	95	0	3
	Canfield	7,014	0	0	0	0	0	98	18	77	3	0
	Canton	78,653	761	8	61	417	275	6,158	1,768	3,916	474	38
	Cardington	2,011	2	0	0	0	2	61	12	48	1	1
	Celina	10,403	21	0	5	1	15	330	31	289	10	2
	Centerville	23,049	11	0	1	7	3	562	114	429	19	4
	Chardon	5,298	3	0	0	1	2	116	12	98	6	0
	Cincinnati	332,388	3,588	63	313	1,961	1,251	20,531	6,200	12,332	1,999	231
	Circleville	13,648	19	1	3	13	2	1,100	244	822	34	3
	Clay Township, Ottawa County	2,732	3	0	0	0	3	33	12	17	4	0
	Cleveland	439,888	6,444	90	374	4,022	1,958	27,016	9,050	11,184	6,782	516
	Cleveland Heights	46,609	28	1	1	21	5	545	71	398	76	0
	Cleves	2,501	1	0	0	0	1	75	19	53	3	1
	Clinton Township	3,938	26	0	3	21	2	555	103	421	31	2
	Clyde	6,172	3	0	0	3	0	222	48	170	4	2
	Coldwater	4,454	3	0	2	0	1	63	9	49	5	0

[1] The FBI does not publish arson data unless it receives data from either the agency or the state for all 12 months of the calendar year.

Table 8.   Offenses Known to Law Enforcement, by State and City, 2007 *(Contd.)*

(Number.)

State	City	Population	Violent crime	Murder and non-negligent man-slaughter	Forcible rape	Robbery	Aggravated assault	Property crime	Burglary	Larceny-theft	Motor vehicle theft	Arson[1]
	Columbus	735,981	6,269	79	661	3,849	1,680	51,491	14,370	30,893	6,228	638
	Conneaut	12,573	35	0	2	7	26	435	128	287	20	0
	Cortland	6,508	10	0	1	0	9	113	15	85	13	0
	Covington	2,572	0	0	0	0	0	49	15	34	0	0
	Crestline	5,077	7	0	1	1	5	60	16	41	3	1
	Creston	2,132	1	0	0	1	0	58	5	51	2	0
	Cridersville	1,743	3	0	2	1	0	31	8	23	0	0
	Crooksville	2,469	5	0	2	0	3	19	5	13	1	0
	Cuyahoga Falls	50,543	76	0	17	17	42	1,549	167	1,287	95	5
	Danville	1,081	0	0	0	0	0	13	2	11	0	0
	Dayton	155,526	1,597	28	116	749	704	10,465	3,272	5,607	1,586	172
	Deer Park	5,432	9	0	5	4	0	112	17	87	8	0
	Defiance	16,159	35	0	16	8	11	778	82	692	4	4
	Delaware	33,177	95	3	48	16	28	979	219	737	23	16
	Delhi Township	29,808	27	2	4	9	12	359	72	268	19	1
	Delphos	6,794	7	0	5	0	2	132	47	84	1	0
	Delta	2,936	2	0	1	0	1	87	19	67	1	1
	Dennison	2,896	0	0	0	0	0	12	2	9	1	0
	Dover	12,533	15	0	5	4	6	146	36	97	13	0
	Dublin	37,326	25	0	8	12	5	757	139	583	35	4
	Eastlake	19,590	28	1	3	16	8	446	29	377	40	4
	Eaton	8,213	16	0	5	2	9	331	58	264	9	4
	Edgerton	1,997	1	0	0	0	1	52	4	48	0	1
	Elmwood Place	2,343	9	0	4	2	3	49	11	37	1	2
	Elyria	55,697	222	1	35	74	112	2,278	602	1,515	161	13
	Englewood	12,844	18	1	2	5	10	438	38	379	21	2
	Euclid	48,186	200	2	24	106	68	1,631	521	924	186	4
	Fairborn	31,705	111	1	33	39	38	1,151	194	894	63	9
	Fairfield	42,264	223	1	20	42	160	1,487	253	1,126	108	12
	Fairfield Township	17,093	24	0	3	6	15	541	80	452	9	0
	Fairlawn	7,138	15	0	0	10	5	375	25	340	10	0
	Fairport Harbor	3,225	18	0	2	2	14	153	34	115	4	3
	Findlay	38,038	59	1	24	15	19	1,281	222	1,023	36	3
	Forest Park	17,470	55	0	7	47	1	655	103	510	42	5
	Fort Recovery	1,350	1	0	1	0	0	10	4	6	0	0
	Fort Shawnee	3,741	8	0	0	0	8	29	10	19	0	0
	Fredericktown	2,468	0	0	0	0	0	68	9	59	0	0
	Fremont	16,885	49	0	1	19	29	1,079	157	892	30	3
	Gahanna	33,140	120	0	12	17	91	921	130	744	47	12
	Galion	11,093	19	0	6	3	10	565	91	461	13	1
	Garfield Heights	28,221	140	4	11	47	78	897	250	587	60	1
	Gates Mills	2,308	0	0	0	0	0	16	2	13	1	0
	Geneva-on-the-Lake	1,522	1	0	0	0	1	23	7	13	3	0
	Genoa	2,319	0	0	0	0	0	51	6	45	0	0
	Georgetown	3,624	9	0	4	0	5	200	39	161	0	0
	Germantown	5,126	5	0	2	0	3	80	14	66	0	0
	German Township, Clark County	7,359	2	0	1	0	1	251	18	230	3	3
	German Township, Montgomery County	3,255	4	0	1	0	3	62	26	35	1	1
	Gibsonburg	2,478	1	0	0	0	1	89	9	78	2	0
	Girard	10,306	56	0	5	7	44	344	61	249	34	0
	Glendale	2,090	3	0	1	1	1	35	7	27	1	0
	Goshen Township, Clemont County	16,421	12	0	6	3	3	325	72	244	9	4
	Goshen Township, Mahoning County	3,496	10	0	0	0	10	110	35	70	5	1
	Grandview Heights	6,144	12	0	3	3	6	163	40	111	12	1
	Granville	5,306	3	0	0	1	2	66	7	56	3	0
	Greenfield	5,172	8	0	0	4	4	303	72	214	17	2
	Greenville	12,978	48	5	10	5	28	519	101	391	27	5
	Grove City	32,472	66	0	9	44	13	1,192	154	977	61	6
	Groveport	5,087	13	0	3	4	6	212	29	170	13	1
	Hamilton	62,330	501	2	101	193	205	4,144	1,077	2,742	325	25
	Harrison	8,440	7	1	2	2	2	354	22	322	10	6
	Hartville	2,564	1	0	0	0	1	27	5	20	2	0
	Heath	8,936	16	0	3	7	6	551	51	489	11	2
	Hebron	2,165	1	0	1	0	0	90	13	77	0	0
	Highland Heights	8,693	4	0	0	1	3	95	12	78	5	0
	Highland Hills	1,386	1	0	0	1	0	10	1	6	3	0
	Hilliard	27,186	33	0	7	14	12	830	132	654	44	9
	Hillsboro	6,736	3	0	0	3	0	283	34	241	8	2
	Holland	1,274	4	0	0	4	0	167	9	156	2	0
	Howland Township	16,761	22	0	0	8	14	552	114	419	19	0
	Hubbard Township	5,826	11	0	0	0	11	169	43	117	9	2
	Huber Heights	37,588	64	0	19	26	19	1,181	158	917	106	17
	Huron	7,394	0	0	0	0	0	153	16	134	3	0
	Independence	6,760	10	0	2	3	5	188	10	163	15	0

[1] The FBI does not publish arson data unless it receives data from either the agency or the state for all 12 months of the calendar year.

Table 8.   Offenses Known to Law Enforcement, by State and City, 2007 *(Contd.)*

(Number.)

State	City	Population	Violent crime	Murder and non-negligent man-slaughter	Forcible rape	Robbery	Aggravated assault	Property crime	Burglary	Larceny-theft	Motor vehicle theft	Arson[1]
	Indian Hill	5,611	1	0	0	0	1	56	7	45	4	0
	Jackson Township, Mahoning County	2,290	1	0	1	0	0	74	15	51	8	0
	Jackson Township, Montgomery County	3,820	0	0	0	0	0	24	13	10	1	0
	Jackson Township, Stark County	39,149	65	0	7	31	27	1,345	176	1,125	44	2
	Jefferson	3,483	4	0	2	1	1	77	13	59	5	0
	Johnstown	4,037	3	0	1	2	0	37	22	13	2	2
	Kent	27,921	77	0	7	11	59	697	186	478	33	45
	Kenton	8,123	4	0	3	1	0	352	75	273	4	2
	Kettering	54,254	78	1	12	39	26	1,602	245	1,212	145	17
	Kirtland	7,400	0	0	0	0	0	70	10	58	2	1
	Kirtland Hills	793	0	0	0	0	0	8	2	6	0	0
	Lakemore	2,778	3	0	1	1	1	133	31	98	4	2
	Lake Township	7,362	6	0	2	3	1	417	33	368	16	2
	Lakewood	51,606	90	2	5	49	34	1,326	283	889	154	14
	Lancaster	36,735	88	0	16	34	38	1,933	377	1,464	92	16
	Lebanon	20,828	36	0	8	8	20	392	60	305	27	2
	Lexington	4,189	1	0	0	1	0	90	26	62	2	0
	Liberty Township	12,118	23	0	1	16	6	413	117	273	23	1
	Lima	37,767	351	1	46	109	195	2,633	773	1,681	179	32
	Liverpool Township	4,246	0	0	0	0	0	47	10	32	5	0
	Logan	7,426	10	0	6	2	2	437	99	328	10	0
	London	9,603	10	0	4	2	4	333	45	278	10	0
	Lorain	70,861	328	7	16	140	165	2,403	855	1,391	157	43
	Lordstown	3,611	0	0	0	0	0	72	20	49	3	0
	Loudonville	2,995	2	0	2	0	0	73	16	57	0	1
	Lynchburg	1,427	1	0	0	1	0	26	2	23	1	0
	Lyndhurst	14,052	4	0	1	0	3	0	0	0	0	0
	Madeira	8,052	2	0	0	1	1	67	6	58	3	1
	Madison Township, Lake County	16,953	64	0	11	4	49	444	86	338	20	5
	Mansfield	50,004	163	5	40	63	55	2,886	865	1,945	76	10
	Mariemont	3,011	1	0	0	0	1	72	2	69	1	0
	Marietta	14,128	25	0	10	7	8	536	117	406	13	3
	Marion	35,975	97	1	26	31	39	1,741	391	1,302	48	9
	Marysville	17,829	4	0	2	0	2	340	23	313	4	1
	Mason	30,640	14	0	6	3	5	576	67	497	12	4
	Mayfield Heights	17,941	9	2	0	3	4	315	16	275	24	0
	Mayfield Village	3,159	5	0	3	0	2	73	13	59	1	0
	McArthur	2,074	1	0	1	0	0	52	12	38	2	2
	McComb	1,653	3	0	1	0	2	30	9	21	0	0
	Medina Township	8,683	0	0	0	0	0	71	8	59	4	0
	Mentor	51,775	44	1	11	12	20	1,208	135	1,014	59	18
	Mentor-on-the-Lake	8,316	1	0	0	1	0	67	13	53	1	1
	Miamisburg	19,925	27	0	7	8	12	736	135	553	48	10
	Miami Township	40,056	27	0	6	6	15	773	103	657	13	5
	Middlefield	2,437	1	0	1	0	0	47	5	41	1	0
	Middletown	51,244	223	3	28	87	105	4,040	874	2,939	227	2
	Milford	6,323	14	0	2	3	9	213	18	190	5	0
	Millersburg	3,610	4	0	1	0	3	84	16	68	0	0
	Milton Township	2,892	1	0	0	0	1	59	14	40	5	0
	Minerva	3,967	10	0	0	1	9	176	31	136	9	5
	Mingo Junction	3,373	22	0	0	0	22	66	14	46	6	0
	Mogadore	3,952	1	0	1	0	0	84	6	77	1	0
	Monroe	14,327	55	0	9	7	39	687	84	584	19	7
	Montgomery	9,819	1	0	0	0	1	199	22	174	3	1
	Montpelier	4,082	10	1	2	0	7	234	58	170	6	3
	Montville Township	7,410	2	0	1	1	0	73	29	43	1	0
	Mount Gilead	3,532	5	0	0	3	2	115	16	96	3	2
	Mount Orab	2,891	2	0	0	2	0	59	13	45	1	0
	Munroe Falls	5,253	0	0	0	0	0	34	7	25	2	1
	Napoleon	9,092	14	1	3	3	7	406	51	349	6	3
	Navarre	1,424	0	0	0	0	0	23	3	17	3	1
	New Albany	6,776	5	0	1	0	4	71	10	61	0	0
	Newark	47,373	123	3	34	53	33	2,515	587	1,818	110	31
	New Boston	2,161	8	0	1	4	3	322	57	261	4	0
	Newcomerstown	3,916	3	0	0	0	3	111	11	92	8	0
	New Franklin	15,087	7	0	6	0	1	117	41	64	12	3
	New Lebanon	4,150	6	0	3	1	2	68	9	53	6	0
	New Lexington	4,613	15	0	4	4	7	210	31	164	15	0
	New London	2,592	2	0	1	0	1	32	8	23	1	0
	New Philadelphia	17,470	17	0	4	9	4	153	25	118	10	2
	Newtown	3,966	1	0	0	1	0	69	10	56	3	0
	Niles	19,675	79	3	10	27	39	1,221	211	915	95	5
	North Canton	16,761	15	0	4	7	4	259	60	192	7	5
	North Olmsted	31,854	39	1	5	21	12	587	107	419	61	7

[1] The FBI does not publish arson data unless it receives data from either the agency or the state for all 12 months of the calendar year.

Table 8. Offenses Known to Law Enforcement, by State and City, 2007 *(Contd.)*

(Number.)

State	City	Population	Violent crime	Murder and non-negligent man-slaughter	Forcible rape	Robbery	Aggravated assault	Property crime	Burglary	Larceny-theft	Motor vehicle theft	Arson[1]
	North Ridgeville	27,959	12	0	2	0	10	298	96	176	26	1
	Northwood	5,482	9	0	1	1	7	309	39	261	9	0
	Norwalk	16,586	15	1	8	1	5	430	86	334	10	2
	Oberlin	8,247	14	0	2	6	6	153	26	125	2	0
	Olmsted Falls	8,376	8	0	3	0	5	97	21	73	3	2
	Ontario	5,301	9	0	3	4	2	562	29	521	12	0
	Orange Village	3,316	6	0	2	0	4	53	10	41	2	0
	Oregon	19,074	20	0	1	5	14	882	112	750	20	8
	Orrville	8,451	17	0	6	7	4	206	21	175	10	7
	Orwell	1,501	2	0	0	0	2	35	3	31	1	0
	Owensville	836	0	0	0	0	0	25	2	23	0	0
	Oxford	22,457	98	0	14	6	78	609	134	460	15	5
	Parma	79,250	180	3	24	46	107	1,705	526	1,018	161	29
	Parma Heights	20,108	17	0	5	5	7	438	80	317	41	4
	Pataskala	13,002	12	0	3	5	4	300	74	215	11	7
	Paulding	3,390	3	1	1	0	1	23	5	16	2	0
	Pepper Pike	5,698	3	0	1	0	2	59	10	49	0	1
	Perkins Township	12,994	2	0	0	2	0	290	10	279	1	1
	Perry Township, Franklin County	3,595	2	0	1	0	1	43	6	37	0	0
	Perry Township, Montgomery County	3,801	4	0	2	0	2	41	18	21	2	1
	Perry Township, Stark County	28,623	66	1	4	15	46	782	156	567	59	4
	Pickerington	17,854	15	1	1	10	3	361	31	322	8	1
	Pierce Township	11,002	14	0	2	10	2	398	51	339	8	3
	Piqua	20,875	34	0	13	16	5	1,113	194	886	33	21
	Plain City	3,653	1	0	0	0	1	27	5	17	5	0
	Poland Township	11,336	0	0	0	0	0	35	10	25	0	1
	Poland Village	2,724	1	0	0	0	1	22	4	17	1	0
	Port Clinton	6,246	15	0	1	5	9	245	49	191	5	0
	Portsmouth	20,030	125	1	16	58	50	2,138	533	1,537	68	20
	Reading	9,936	29	0	7	15	7	390	67	277	46	0
	Reminderville	2,544	1	0	0	0	1	14	6	7	1	0
	Reynoldsburg	33,210	102	0	9	55	38	1,249	233	923	93	4
	Rittman	6,291	5	0	0	3	2	152	39	100	13	1
	Riverside	22,317	65	1	7	27	30	975	241	610	124	7
	Roaming Shores Village	1,217	0	0	0	0	0	14	4	8	2	0
	Rossford	6,349	6	0	0	5	1	164	24	134	6	2
	Salem	11,915	2	0	0	0	2	156	3	141	12	0
	Saline Township	1,373	2	0	2	0	0	19	6	10	3	0
	Sandusky	25,994	225	1	8	47	169	1,591	398	1,126	67	4
	Sebring	4,587	1	0	0	0	1	34	10	22	2	0
	Seville	2,464	2	0	2	0	0	55	5	50	0	0
	Sharon Township	2,306	0	0	0	0	0	40	5	33	2	0
	Sheffield Lake	9,049	7	0	1	3	3	197	52	136	9	2
	Shelby	9,441	13	0	4	4	5	584	131	448	5	4
	Silverton	4,556	11	2	2	5	2	132	23	95	14	0
	Smithville	1,306	1	0	1	0	0	29	4	25	0	1
	Solon	22,318	20	0	3	4	13	265	29	229	7	1
	South Charleston	1,808	0	0	0	0	0	24	3	19	2	1
	South Euclid	21,559	42	2	8	30	2	580	166	356	58	4
	South Russell	3,982	0	0	0	0	0	12	3	9	0	0
	South Solon	387	0	0	0	0	0	1	0	1	0	0
	Spencer	825	0	0	0	0	0	7	2	5	0	0
	Spencerville	2,180	0	0	0	0	0	23	6	17	0	0
	Springdale	9,520	29	0	2	25	2	800	52	715	33	3
	Springfield	62,426	461	5	36	241	179	5,407	1,403	3,627	377	27
	Springfield Township, Hamilton County	35,051	71	4	11	37	19	688	152	489	47	6
	Springfield Township, Mahoning County	6,116	4	0	1	1	2	153	48	98	7	1
	Springfield Township, Summit County	15,449	38	0	7	21	10	769	156	591	22	3
	St. Bernard	4,364	14	0	2	6	6	169	20	132	17	0
	St. Clair Township	7,805	4	0	0	3	1	29	1	28	0	0
	Steubenville	19,107	79	1	5	40	33	929	167	718	44	0
	St. Henry	2,382	0	0	0	0	0	15	2	12	1	0
	Stow	34,617	24	0	6	15	3	825	119	696	10	9
	Strasburg	2,704	4	0	2	2	0	105	21	79	5	0
	Struthers	10,987	21	0	2	11	8	405	101	287	17	0
	Sugarcreek Township	6,875	12	0	1	2	9	125	7	112	6	3
	Sylvania Township	26,380	9	0	0	5	4	667	91	544	32	0
	Tallmadge	17,506	23	0	4	15	4	399	95	279	25	3
	Tipp City	9,376	13	0	5	6	2	240	51	182	7	1
	Toledo	296,403	3,639	13	151	1,225	2,250	19,826	5,921	12,029	1,876	359
	Twinsburg	17,545	9	0	0	3	6	141	25	111	5	1
	Uhrichsville	5,597	2	0	0	0	2	217	49	157	11	0
	Union	6,345	4	0	0	1	3	69	12	52	5	0
	University Heights	12,865	20	0	2	17	1	252	45	196	11	1

[1] The FBI does not publish arson data unless it receives data from either the agency or the state for all 12 months of the calendar year.

Table 8. Offenses Known to Law Enforcement, by State and City, 2007 *(Contd.)*

(Number.)

State	City	Population	Violent crime	Murder and non-negligent man-slaughter	Forcible rape	Robbery	Aggravated assault	Property crime	Burglary	Larceny-theft	Motor vehicle theft	Arson[1]
	Upper Arlington	31,009	9	0	2	6	1	374	66	293	15	8
	Vandalia	14,171	20	0	7	9	4	427	74	329	24	0
	Van Wert	10,381	29	0	11	3	15	498	99	392	7	3
	Vermilion	10,892	5	0	0	1	4	256	54	187	15	1
	Village of Leesburg	1,345	1	0	1	0	0	48	7	38	3	0
	Wadsworth	20,391	15	0	8	1	6	416	44	341	31	5
	Waite Hill	554	0	0	0	0	0	2	2	0	0	0
	Walbridge	3,077	0	0	0	0	0	67	14	49	4	0
	Walton Hills	2,310	0	0	0	0	0	21	1	17	3	0
	Wapakoneta	9,583	8	0	3	0	5	244	29	204	11	1
	Warren	44,858	508	6	48	191	263	2,492	923	1,370	199	
	Warrensville Heights	13,815	57	0	3	49	5	476	159	204	113	5
	Warren Township	6,173	5	0	0	1	4	94	21	64	9	1
	Washingtonville	762	0	0	0	0	0	20	7	12	1	0
	Waverly	4,430	0	0	0	0	0	109	5	104	0	0
	Waynesburg	974	0	0	0	0	0	16	3	11	2	1
	Wells Township	2,898	0	0	0	0	0	49	13	33	3	1
	West Alexandria	1,328	2	0	1	0	1	31	1	29	1	0
	West Carrollton	12,897	42	0	16	9	17	466	79	307	80	4
	West Chester Township	55,216	78	1	14	35	28	1,701	324	1,334	43	16
	Westerville	34,907	34	0	7	22	5	918	149	753	16	8
	West Jefferson	4,254	4	0	1	0	3	155	33	116	6	0
	Whitehall	17,719	193	1	18	135	39	1,471	305	1,064	102	0
	Willard	6,757	11	0	1	6	4	265	64	191	10	0
	Williamsburg	2,352	3	0	2	1	0	83	17	63	3	1
	Willoughby	22,319	15	0	2	3	10	373	71	276	26	0
	Willoughby Hills	8,430	10	0	3	3	4	131	40	84	7	0
	Willowick	13,804	13	0	2	2	9	196	27	152	17	0
	Wilmington	12,806	28	0	5	6	17	690	65	623	2	2
	Windham	2,711	7	0	1	3	3	113	31	80	2	0
	Wintersville	3,860	0	0	0	0	0	88	7	75	6	0
	Woodlawn	2,492	9	0	0	5	4	131	14	105	12	0
	Wooster	25,914	55	2	15	19	19	982	168	792	22	28
	Worthington	12,941	20	0	0	9	11	352	61	290	1	8
	Wyoming	7,485	6	0	0	4	2	127	22	95	10	1
	Xenia	23,335	43	1	9	25	8	1,130	194	895	41	11
	Youngstown	81,521	812	42	51	277	442	4,101	1,704	1,898	499	296
	Zanesville	25,332	118	0	21	56	41	1,588	350	1,161	77	10
OKLAHOMA	Achille	530	3	1	0	0	2	15	5	9	1	0
	Ada	15,901	137	1	16	7	113	1,011	195	757	59	3
	Altus	19,284	45	0	0	16	29	794	225	547	22	2
	Alva	4,747	10	0	0	0	10	144	20	117	7	0
	Anadarko	6,519	47	0	1	4	42	409	125	266	18	20
	Antlers	2,481	36	0	3	1	32	74	15	55	4	2
	Apache	1,583	9	0	1	0	8	47	20	25	2	0
	Ardmore	24,663	241	3	17	25	196	1,276	341	860	75	2
	Arkoma	2,205	1	0	1	0	0	21	9	11	1	0
	Atoka	3,044	7	0	3	0	4	118	37	75	6	1
	Bartlesville	34,902	114	0	15	18	81	1,333	255	993	85	14
	Beaver	1,378	1	0	0	0	1	18	9	9	0	0
	Beggs	1,374	2	0	0	0	2	22	9	10	3	0
	Bethany	19,456	70	2	13	16	39	724	212	421	91	5
	Bixby	20,303	20	0	4	2	14	276	74	184	18	3
	Blackwell	7,134	19	0	3	2	14	153	52	92	9	3
	Blanchard	6,351	2	0	2	0	0	108	26	64	18	1
	Boise City	1,284	1	0	0	0	1	14	7	6	1	0
	Boley	1,086	2	0	1	0	1	9	6	3	0	2
	Bristow	4,402	14	0	1	3	10	212	46	148	18	2
	Broken Arrow	89,463	187	1	24	27	135	1,961	426	1,397	138	26
	Broken Bow	4,217	25	1	3	1	20	253	105	118	30	0
	Caddo	982	5	0	0	1	4	21	10	11	0	1
	Calera	1,817	3	0	0	1	2	46	16	29	1	0
	Carnegie	1,589	9	0	0	0	9	31	18	11	2	0
	Catoosa	6,789	39	2	2	6	29	149	38	84	27	3
	Chandler	2,876	8	0	3	1	4	99	37	55	7	0
	Checotah	3,520	6	0	0	0	6	134	17	110	7	1
	Chelsea	2,269	1	0	0	0	1	31	14	13	4	0
	Cherokee	1,445	0	0	0	0	0	7	6	1	0	0
	Chickasha	17,346	120	0	6	10	104	779	217	507	55	7
	Choctaw[3]	11,009		0	1	2		230	51	162	17	4
	Chouteau	2,016	7	0	0	1	6	63	22	39	2	1
	Claremore	17,519	53	1	14	3	35	516	122	365	29	0
	Clayton	722	14	0	0	0	14	10	6	4	0	0
	Cleveland	3,230	17	0	2	1	14	116	29	78	9	0

[1] The FBI does not publish arson data unless it receives data from either the agency or the state for all 12 months of the calendar year.
[3] The FBI determined that the agency's data were overreported. Consequently, affected data are not included in this table.

Table 8. Offenses Known to Law Enforcement, by State and City, 2007 *(Contd.)*

(Number.)

State	City	Population	Violent crime	Murder and non-negligent man-slaughter	Forcible rape	Robbery	Aggravated assault	Property crime	Burglary	Larceny-theft	Motor vehicle theft	Arson[1]
	Clinton	8,395	32	1	1	4	26	207	30	160	17	2
	Coalgate	1,836	2	0	1	0	1	18	9	6	3	0
	Colbert	1,115	4	0	1	0	3	21	12	9	0	0
	Collinsville	4,559	12	0	4	2	6	82	29	47	6	1
	Comanche	1,525	4	0	1	0	3	65	21	42	2	1
	Cordell	2,910	9	0	0	0	9	27	1	26	0	0
	Coweta	8,847	21	1	5	1	14	168	44	107	17	0
	Crescent	1,356	4	0	0	0	4	13	2	8	3	0
	Cushing	8,479	27	1	6	0	20	198	40	134	24	1
	Davenport	893	0	0	0	0	0	10	5	5	0	0
	Davis	2,671	1	0	0	0	1	62	14	44	4	3
	Del City	21,872	115	2	15	35	63	1,213	401	713	99	16
	Dewey	3,281	6	0	1	1	4	143	34	108	1	0
	Drumright	2,890	1	0	0	0	1	50	9	37	4	0
	Duncan	22,486	50	0	8	10	32	923	178	702	43	3
	Durant	15,177	54	2	13	4	35	891	203	617	71	5
	Edmond	77,879	92	2	21	31	38	1,845	387	1,377	81	8
	Elk City	11,079	18	0	1	2	15	245	40	192	13	0
	El Reno	16,221	68	2	4	7	55	568	158	381	29	7
	Enid	46,454	155	3	22	22	108	1,990	465	1,452	73	2
	Eufaula	2,797	8	1	1	1	5	141	40	92	9	0
	Fairfax[3]	1,486		0	0	0		59	38	15	6	0
	Fairview	2,592	4	0	1	0	3	69	19	49	1	0
	Fort Gibson	4,328	2	0	2	0	0	48	11	35	2	0
	Frederick	4,113	17	0	1	3	13	134	43	84	7	6
	Geary	1,239	7	0	1	0	6	42	13	28	1	0
	Glenpool	9,251	18	0	2	1	15	173	44	111	18	0
	Goodwell	1,127	2	0	1	0	1	15	7	8	0	0
	Grove	6,141	15	0	1	0	14	161	32	128	1	0
	Guthrie	11,074	26	1	5	5	15	277	73	186	18	2
	Guymon	10,721	47	1	5	6	35	370	69	285	16	2
	Harrah	5,010	7	0	1	0	6	120	41	77	2	0
	Hartshorne	2,072	5	0	0	0	5	46	17	27	2	0
	Haskell	1,781	2	1	0	0	1	8	4	3	1	0
	Healdton	2,772	3	0	1	0	2	73	13	59	1	0
	Heavener[3]	3,274		0	3	0		67	23	40	4	1
	Henryetta	6,090	16	0	3	1	12	175	51	95	29	1
	Hinton	2,172	0	0	0	0	0	26	9	13	4	0
	Hobart	3,741	11	0	1	0	10	51	12	35	4	0
	Holdenville	5,546	13	1	2	0	10	140	38	85	17	0
	Hollis	2,072	5	1	2	0	2	35	9	25	1	1
	Hominy	3,701	20	0	0	1	19	28	13	9	6	4
	Hooker	1,725	1	0	0	0	1	18	9	5	4	0
	Hugo	5,573	12	0	0	4	8	168	52	110	6	1
	Hulbert	530	1	0	0	0	1	3	0	2	1	0
	Hydro	1,034	0	0	0	0	0	25	10	13	2	1
	Idabel	6,906	47	3	11	4	29	309	44	249	16	6
	Jay	3,020	5	0	3	0	2	46	15	31	0	0
	Jenks	14,906	15	0	2	0	13	236	48	170	18	2
	Jones	2,674	2	0	1	0	1	11	2	9	0	0
	Kingfisher	4,515	5	0	1	1	3	88	14	72	2	1
	Kingston	1,561	2	0	0	1	1	16	10	4	2	0
	Konawa	1,417	2	0	0	0	2	26	9	13	4	0
	Krebs	2,137	6	0	0	0	6	42	7	29	6	1
	Lawton	86,864	1,075	9	75	184	807	4,638	1,555	2,813	270	49
	Lexington	2,071	0	0	0	0	0	41	7	33	1	0
	Lindsay	2,918	3	0	0	0	3	47	16	25	6	1
	Locust Grove	1,589	6	0	0	0	6	46	8	34	4	0
	Lone Grove	5,239	11	1	0	1	9	123	30	88	5	0
	Luther	1,098	2	0	1	0	1	10	5	3	2	0
	Madill	3,735	13	0	1	2	10	145	33	99	13	1
	Mangum	2,695	14	0	0	0	14	78	18	58	2	1
	Mannford	2,787	6	0	1	0	5	41	10	28	3	0
	Marietta	2,568	16	0	3	2	11	93	25	62	6	0
	Marlow	4,564	10	0	5	0	5	84	14	66	4	0
	Maysville	1,304	4	0	1	0	3	18	2	12	4	0
	McAlester	18,414	52	0	7	11	34	1,111	194	881	36	1
	McLoud	4,250	12	0	1	2	9	69	25	38	6	0
	Meeker	1,000	3	0	1	0	2	25	8	15	2	0
	Miami	13,622	72	0	5	3	64	603	151	435	17	4
	Midwest City	55,315	257	1	19	54	183	2,365	554	1,645	166	10
	Minco	1,805	0	0	0	0	0	5	3	2	0	0
	Moore	50,548	70	1	9	15	45	1,950	393	1,397	160	5
	Mooreland	1,229	0	0	0	0	0	25	10	14	1	0

[1] The FBI does not publish arson data unless it receives data from either the agency or the state for all 12 months of the calendar year.
[3] The FBI determined that the agency's data were overreported. Consequently, affected data are not included in this table.

Table 8.   Offenses Known to Law Enforcement, by State and City, 2007 *(Contd.)*

(Number.)

State	City	Population	Violent crime	Murder and non-negligent man-slaughter	Forcible rape	Robbery	Aggravated assault	Property crime	Burglary	Larceny-theft	Motor vehicle theft	Arson[1]
	Morris	1,323	0	0	0	0	0	18	7	7	4	0
	Mountain View	816	1	0	0	0	1	10	3	7	0	0
	Muldrow	3,216	5	0	0	0	5	72	16	55	1	1
	Muskogee	40,113	379	3	39	57	280	1,675	604	981	90	14
	Mustang	16,960	49	1	2	5	41	537	78	433	26	6
	Newcastle	6,880	9	0	0	2	7	183	32	140	11	1
	Newkirk	2,128	8	0	0	0	8	83	20	60	3	0
	Nichols Hills	3,981	1	0	0	0	1	48	8	37	3	0
	Nicoma Park	2,371	10	0	0	1	9	53	16	33	4	0
	Noble	5,638	3	0	1	0	2	91	34	53	4	2
	Norman	103,721	177	4	35	52	86	3,615	795	2,549	271	2
	Nowata	4,009	23	0	1	1	21	88	29	49	10	1
	Oilton	1,125	4	0	0	0	4	12	6	6	0	0
	Okemah	2,965	14	0	3	3	8	150	38	104	8	2
	Oklahoma City	542,199	4,612	58	326	1,397	2,831	31,949	8,110	19,228	4,611	173
	Okmulgee	12,805	80	2	5	16	57	516	124	349	43	2
	Oologah	1,163	2	0	0	0	2	24	9	14	1	0
	Owasso	25,974	65	0	15	6	44	591	118	437	36	1
	Pauls Valley	6,175	20	0	4	2	14	416	93	299	24	2
	Pawhuska	3,481	63	0	1	0	62	75	19	49	7	0
	Pawnee	2,222	5	0	1	0	4	32	13	17	2	1
	Perkins	2,251	6	0	2	0	4	45	8	35	2	0
	Perry	5,045	14	0	0	0	14	128	26	93	9	1
	Piedmont	5,233	13	0	3	1	9	40	13	27	0	1
	Ponca City	24,548	210	1	13	24	172	1,410	391	940	79	28
	Porum	735	1	0	0	0	1	12	4	7	1	0
	Poteau	8,347	38	0	2	2	34	152	19	106	27	0
	Prague	2,153	3	0	0	0	3	26	10	16	0	0
	Pryor	9,361	75	0	3	2	70	384	71	274	39	2
	Purcell	6,026	11	0	3	3	5	256	94	147	15	1
	Ringling	1,062	6	0	2	1	3	16	4	7	5	0
	Roland	3,216	5	0	0	0	5	25	8	16	1	0
	Rush Springs	1,349	2	0	0	0	2	32	12	17	3	0
	Sallisaw	8,842	48	0	5	3	40	285	71	194	20	1
	Sand Springs	18,362	40	1	7	8	24	664	123	460	81	1
	Sapulpa	20,960	36	1	6	7	22	672	149	448	75	8
	Sayre	2,743	10	0	1	0	9	77	20	53	4	12
	Seminole	6,960	29	0	1	0	28	280	56	209	15	2
	Shawnee	30,109	232	2	17	30	183	1,734	364	1,219	151	5
	Skiatook	6,486	33	0	5	3	25	293	77	197	19	0
	Snyder	1,430	2	0	0	0	2	2	1	1	0	0
	Spencer	3,943	12	0	1	0	11	101	46	44	11	1
	Spiro	2,336	16	0	0	1	15	51	19	24	8	2
	Stigler	2,825	12	0	5	1	6	111	15	94	2	1
	Stillwater	45,692	115	0	16	15	84	1,243	321	858	64	10
	Stilwell[3]	3,551	7	0	1	1	5				13	1
	Stratford	1,496	1	0	0	0	1	15	6	8	1	0
	Stringtown	413	1	0	0	0	1	7	1	5	1	0
	Stroud	2,777	6	0	0	0	6	87	24	53	10	1
	Sulphur	4,924	5	0	0	0	5	103	42	56	5	1
	Tahlequah	16,491	65	2	10	8	45	726	183	483	60	1
	Talihina	1,250	5	0	0	1	4	45	18	24	3	0
	Tecumseh	6,723	55	1	8	1	45	207	50	148	9	3
	Texhoma	936	2	0	0	0	2	9	2	7	0	0
	The Village	9,719	24	0	1	6	17	352	94	234	24	3
	Tishomingo	3,248	10	0	3	0	7	122	64	55	3	0
	Tonkawa	3,080	8	0	4	0	4	103	26	69	8	0
	Tulsa	381,469	4,552	55	299	1,023	3,175	24,044	6,843	13,522	3,679	255
	Tushka	363	0	0	0	0	0	4	2	2	0	0
	Tuttle	5,935	2	0	0	0	2	63	17	45	1	2
	Valliant	752	8	0	1	0	7	38	6	32	0	1
	Vian	1,483	1	0	0	0	1	16	3	11	2	2
	Vinita	5,982	23	0	1	2	20	212	39	153	20	0
	Wagoner	8,043	85	0	2	5	78	405	100	296	9	0
	Walters	2,548	2	0	0	1	1	33	21	12	0	0
	Warner	1,447	1	0	1	0	0	8	2	6	0	1
	Warr Acres	9,384	53	0	4	24	25	502	121	324	57	0
	Watonga	5,807	7	0	0	0	7	86	25	54	7	0
	Waukomis	1,192	4	0	0	0	4	25	9	15	1	0
	Waurika	1,811	9	0	0	0	9	9	6	3	0	0
	Waynoka	901	2	0	0	0	2	26	4	20	2	0
	Weatherford	9,951	57	1	3	2	51	409	75	312	22	2
	Weleetka	938	2	0	1	0	1	10	3	4	3	0
	Westville	1,687	12	0	0	1	11	64	15	47	2	0

[1] The FBI does not publish arson data unless it receives data from either the agency or the state for all 12 months of the calendar year.

Table 8. Offenses Known to Law Enforcement, by State and City, 2007 *(Contd.)*

(Number.)

State	City	Population	Violent crime	Murder and non-negligent manslaughter	Forcible rape	Robbery	Aggravated assault	Property crime	Burglary	Larceny-theft	Motor vehicle theft	Arson[1]
	Wetumka	1,422	6	0	0	3	3	51	29	19	3	1
	Wewoka	3,368	10	0	0	2	8	121	43	72	6	2
	Wilburton	2,896	10	0	0	2	8	67	12	52	3	1
	Wilson	1,627	21	0	0	0	21	66	29	34	3	2
	Woodward	12,064	31	0	1	3	27	650	164	473	13	1
	Wright City	803	3	0	0	0	3	15	3	12	0	1
	Wynnewood	2,311	4	1	0	0	3	47	23	17	7	1
	Yale	1,284	1	0	0	0	1	0	0	0	0	0
	Yukon	22,457	42	1	2	3	36	659	125	504	30	2
OREGON	Albany	46,999	55	1	6	33	15	2,236	233	1,867	136	33
	Amity	1,462	0	0	0	0	0	35	9	26	0	1
	Ashland	21,068	19	0	7	7	5	606	124	458	24	5
	Astoria	9,935	31	0	3	5	23	353	61	276	16	2
	Aumsville	3,378	18	0	1	1	16	89	8	68	13	1
	Aurora	1,025	0	0	0	0	0	19	2	13	4	0
	Baker City	9,614	41	0	0	1	40	207	30	162	15	1
	Bandon	2,911	1	0	0	1	0	87	16	69	2	0
	Banks	1,631	0	0	0	0	0	22	3	18	1	0
	Beaverton	91,184	220	0	20	59	141	2,330	337	1,768	225	23
	Bend	75,185	155	0	20	40	95	2,977	594	2,187	196	21
	Black Butte		0	0	0	0	0	7	1	6	0	0
	Boardman	3,094	17	0	3	1	13	81	20	57	4	0
	Brookings	6,476	7	0	1	2	4	168	30	132	6	1
	Burns	2,702	21	0	2	1	18	111	32	76	3	0
	Canby	15,725	16	0	5	3	8	350	37	302	11	3
	Cannon Beach	1,740	0	0	0	0	0	26	5	21	0	0
	Carlton	1,523	1	0	0	0	1	22	10	12	0	0
	Central Point	16,701	11	0	6	2	3	323	39	255	29	2
	Clatskanie	1,663	3	0	0	0	3	55	10	42	3	1
	Coburg	1,011	0	0	0	0	0	25	6	16	3	0
	Condon	684	0	0	0	0	0	0	0	0	0	0
	Coos Bay	16,096	30	0	0	9	21	687	146	501	40	10
	Coquille	4,250	1	0	1	0	0	48	10	35	3	1
	Cornelius	11,498	14	0	3	4	7	219	37	156	26	2
	Corvallis	49,870	57	1	11	10	35	1,554	226	1,261	67	15
	Cottage Grove	8,921	16	0	2	7	7	487	71	340	76	10
	Creswell	4,945	20	0	3	1	16	166	61	73	32	2
	Dallas	15,097	35	0	7	2	26	318	45	259	14	4
	Eagle Point	8,547	5	0	1	0	4	198	42	148	8	2
	Enterprise	1,736	1	0	0	0	1	20	5	13	2	1
	Estacada	2,473	4	0	0	1	3	73	18	51	4	0
	Eugene	147,458	426	1	55	181	189	7,804	1,640	5,119	1,045	72
	Fairview	9,753	17	0	3	11	3	357	75	230	52	2
	Florence	8,250	7	0	1	4	2	362	83	254	25	4
	Forest Grove	20,457	23	0	1	3	19	563	51	469	43	5
	Gearhart	1,117	0	0	0	0	0	12	1	10	1	0
	Gervais	2,451	14	0	0	1	13	102	9	72	21	3
	Gladstone	12,256	26	0	3	12	11	380	48	307	25	6
	Gold Beach	1,909	3	0	0	0	3	35	4	28	3	0
	Grants Pass	30,292	67	3	14	21	29	1,667	185	1,328	154	13
	Gresham	98,089	470	1	74	170	225	4,332	627	2,671	1,034	45
	Hermiston	15,148	67	0	5	12	50	972	163	739	70	5
	Hillsboro	90,439	195	0	39	71	85	2,844	456	2,081	307	32
	Hines	1,464	0	0	0	0	0	5	0	5	0	0
	Hood River	6,778	11	0	0	3	8	212	24	168	20	2
	Hubbard	2,624	1	0	0	0	1	52	9	32	11	1
	Independence	9,211	21	0	2	3	16	235	36	191	8	1
	Jacksonville	2,190	0	0	0	0	0	31	4	25	2	0
	John Day	1,555	18	0	1	0	17	27	7	18	2	0
	Junction City	5,378	1	0	0	1	0	28	7	18	3	0
	Keizer	35,423	74	0	6	7	61	926	122	727	77	4
	King City	2,257	5	0	0	4	1	76	14	59	3	2
	Klamath Falls	19,817	92	3	15	27	47	665	119	494	52	13
	La Grande	12,288	23	0	3	1	19	444	82	343	19	7
	Lake Oswego	36,917	31	0	6	8	17	612	110	473	29	30
	Lakeview	2,412	23	1	0	0	22	89	20	62	7	1
	Lebanon	14,620	49	0	8	16	25	789	126	619	44	5
	Lincoln City	7,996	47	2	7	6	32	496	80	394	22	4
	Madras	5,301	24	0	2	6	16	399	122	240	37	1
	Malin	634	1	0	0	0	1	6	4	1	1	0
	Manzanita	640	0	0	0	0	0	22	5	17	0	0
	McMinnville	30,980	47	0	13	11	23	795	113	629	53	1
	Medford	71,969	265	0	30	44	191	3,270	412	2,662	196	53
	Milton-Freewater	6,392	12	0	0	0	12	209	49	151	9	4

[1] The FBI does not publish arson data unless it receives data from either the agency or the state for all 12 months of the calendar year.

Table 8. Offenses Known to Law Enforcement, by State and City, 2007 *(Contd.)*

(Number.)

State	City	Population	Violent crime	Murder and non-negligent man-slaughter	Forcible rape	Robbery	Aggravated assault	Property crime	Burglary	Larceny-theft	Motor vehicle theft	Arson[1]
	Milwaukie	21,060	42	1	8	11	22	656	90	489	77	8
	Molalla	7,210	7	0	2	1	4	172	23	138	11	1
	Monmouth	9,751	23	0	3	1	19	245	52	175	18	2
	Mount Angel	3,429	8	0	1	1	6	142	32	96	14	1
	Myrtle Creek	3,555	2	0	0	1	1	128	6	116	6	1
	Newberg-Dundee	25,209	35	1	10	4	20	622	50	517	55	5
	Newport	9,953	54	0	7	7	40	614	82	496	36	7
	North Bend	9,892	9	0	0	4	5	301	82	201	18	1
	North Plains	1,833	0	0	0	0	0	6	2	3	1	0
	Oakridge	3,127	5	0	1	0	4	114	39	69	6	0
	Ontario	11,100	128	0	6	10	112	747	98	609	40	4
	Oregon City	31,284	58	0	12	26	20	1,048	120	838	90	7
	Pendleton	16,620	101	3	25	21	52	1,043	151	815	77	4
	Philomath	4,206	12	0	0	1	11	150	51	91	8	1
	Phoenix	4,416	3	0	1	1	1	129	14	108	7	0
	Portland	538,133	3,701	22	280	1,289	2,110	31,586	4,840	21,978	4,768	331
	Prairie City	936	0	0	0	0	0	11	5	6	0	1
	Prineville	9,583	86	0	3	0	83	362	84	274	4	6
	Redmond	24,095	84	0	16	16	52	1,227	250	889	88	18
	Reedsport	4,352	3	0	1	0	2	139	20	114	5	0
	Rogue River	1,943	1	0	1	0	0	91	21	65	5	0
	Roseburg	21,128	44	0	18	16	10	1,021	130	844	47	15
	Salem	154,484	583	3	58	132	390	7,436	915	5,629	892	30
	Sandy	8,770	9	0	1	1	7	360	50	285	25	2
	Scappoose	6,222	8	0	0	1	7	192	15	170	7	0
	Seaside	6,229	26	0	5	4	17	502	58	416	28	1
	Shady Cove	2,293	2	0	0	1	1	52	8	44	0	0
	Sherwood	17,957	7	0	2	2	3	237	30	196	11	3
	Silverton	9,200	15	0	4	4	7	229	44	175	10	1
	Springfield	56,201	245	0	10	40	195	3,137	504	2,219	414	23
	Stayton	7,385	29	0	2	2	25	425	64	328	33	10
	St. Helens	12,708	11	0	1	4	6	352	78	252	22	15
	Sunriver		2	0	2	0	0	89	5	82	2	0
	Sutherlin	7,396	18	0	6	1	11	189	46	130	13	5
	Sweet Home	8,659	9	0	2	2	5	424	120	293	11	3
	Talent	6,150	6	0	2	1	3	124	13	104	7	0
	The Dalles	11,900	30	0	3	6	21	624	91	496	37	2
	Tigard	50,087	103	1	9	43	50	1,725	190	1,445	90	16
	Tillamook	4,435	7	0	1	2	4	203	28	168	7	1
	Toledo	3,398	2	0	0	0	2	108	19	79	10	0
	Troutdale	15,212	32	0	6	12	14	582	74	442	66	13
	Tualatin	26,712	50	0	5	13	32	890	132	700	58	1
	Turner	1,689	5	0	0	0	5	62	10	50	2	0
	Umatilla	5,397	16	0	3	0	13	153	35	105	13	0
	Veneta	3,927	27	0	1	1	25	197	73	103	21	3
	Vernonia	2,319	0	0	0	0	0	45	2	41	2	2
	Warrenton	4,438	1	0	0	1	0	225	33	178	14	0
	West Linn	25,636	16	0	8	2	6	262	36	210	16	3
	Wilsonville	16,916	22	0	7	10	5	584	45	494	45	3
	Winston	4,803	6	0	0	0	6	144	40	95	9	5
	Woodburn	22,399	66	1	7	19	39	862	111	673	78	1
	Yamhill	850	0	0	0	0	0	14	3	11	0	0
PENNSYLVANIA	Abington Township	54,413	57	1	4	32	20	1,285	107	1,117	61	0
	Adamstown	1,329	0	0	0	0	0	18	2	14	2	0
	Adams Township, Butler County	8,963	9	0	0	1	8	71	5	64	2	0
	Adams Township, Cambria County	6,113	5	1	0	2	2	46	3	41	2	0
	Akron	4,013	2	0	0	1	1	35	4	31	0	0
	Aldan	4,277	7	1	0	3	3	124	15	105	4	0
	Aliquippa	10,854	59	1	1	18	39	254	73	157	24	0
	Allegheny Township, Blair County	6,907	14	0	1	3	10	158	25	130	3	2
	Allegheny Township, Westmoreland County	8,177	9	0	0	3	6	82	14	66	2	0
	Allentown	107,397	869	20	20	552	277	5,333	1,335	3,462	536	46
	Altoona	46,609	184	1	20	77	86	1,318	428	824	66	24
	Ambler	6,248	7	0	1	2	4	117	11	101	5	1
	Amity Township	11,838	8	0	0	1	7	161	26	123	12	0
	Annville Township	4,717	3	0	0	0	3	27	2	25	0	0
	Arnold	5,301	14	0	2	6	6	75	22	42	11	2
	Ashland	3,121	3	0	0	1	2	69	17	51	1	0
	Ashley	2,691	0	0	0	0	0	26	1	20	5	0
	Ashville	262	0	0	0	0	0	0	0	0	0	0

[1] The FBI does not publish arson data unless it receives data from either the agency or the state for all 12 months of the calendar year.

Table 8. Offenses Known to Law Enforcement, by State and City, 2007 *(Contd.)*

(Number.)

State	City	Population	Violent crime	Murder and non-negligent man-slaughter	Forcible rape	Robbery	Aggravated assault	Property crime	Burglary	Larceny-theft	Motor vehicle theft	Arson[1]
	Aspinwall	2,720	3	0	0	0	3	32	5	24	3	0
	Aston Township	16,853	31	0	2	6	23	290	42	225	23	0
	Atglen	1,378	3	0	1	0	2	7	0	6	1	0
	Athens	3,272	10	0	3	0	7	103	11	90	2	0
	Avondale	1,091	1	0	0	1	0	2	0	2	0	0
	Avonmore Boro	775	0	0	0	0	0	0	0	0	0	0
	Baldwin Borough	18,440	13	1	3	4	5	154	30	115	9	0
	Baldwin Township	2,048	1	0	0	0	1	27	4	22	1	0
	Bally	1,112	0	0	0	0	0	0	0	0	0	0
	Bangor	5,282	8	0	2	2	4	184	17	158	9	0
	Barrett Township	4,387	6	0	0	1	5	40	7	32	1	3
	Beaver	4,447	2	0	0	0	2	131	34	95	2	0
	Beaver Falls	9,189	101	0	3	31	67	467	62	365	40	2
	Bedford	3,011	4	0	0	0	4	90	15	70	5	0
	Bedminster Township	5,681	7	0	1	0	6	63	3	56	4	1
	Bell Acres	1,383	0	0	0	0	0	1	0	1	0	0
	Bellevue	8,023	11	0	1	8	2	83	22	55	6	1
	Bellwood	1,890	0	0	0	0	0	9	1	7	1	0
	Bensalem Township	58,788	120	1	9	60	50	2,639	368	2,065	206	16
	Berks-Lehigh Regional	28,142	10	0	1	2	7	342	42	278	22	1
	Bern Township	7,165	38	0	0	2	36	76	14	53	9	1
	Bernville	887	0	0	0	0	0	1	0	1	0	0
	Berwick	10,246	20	0	12	2	6	362	45	309	8	1
	Bessemer	1,106	1	0	0	0	1	8	2	6	0	0
	Bethel Park	31,669	12	0	2	1	9	296	35	248	13	0
	Bethel Township, Armstrong County	1,214	0	0	0	0	0	0	0	0	0	0
	Bethel Township, Delaware County	10,683	8	0	0	1	7	107	16	90	1	0
	Bethlehem	72,908	270	6	24	100	140	2,288	439	1,721	128	6
	Bethlehem Township	23,960	19	1	0	5	13	437	13	410	14	0
	Biglerville	1,167	1	0	0	1	0	20	0	20	0	0
	Birdsboro	5,224	6	0	2	0	4	108	12	87	9	2
	Birmingham Township	4,273	1	0	0	0	1	17	1	16	0	0
	Blacklick Township	2,096	0	0	0	0	0	4	0	4	0	0
	Blairsville	3,421	2	1	0	0	1	89	5	79	5	0
	Blakely	6,782	3	0	0	0	3	55	7	46	2	1
	Blawnox	1,446	1	0	0	0	1	5	3	2	0	0
	Bloomsburg Town	12,959	12	0	4	2	6	218	29	185	4	0
	Bolivar	472	0	0	0	0	0	0	0	0	0	0
	Braddock Hills	1,836	3	0	0	2	1	66	3	59	4	0
	Bradford	8,501	44	0	4	2	38	258	32	219	7	0
	Bradford Township	4,763	28	0	4	0	24	36	4	29	3	0
	Brandywine Regional	10,045	16	0	1	0	15	106	4	99	3	2
	Brecknock Township, Berks County	4,935	12	0	1	0	11	26	6	20	0	0
	Brentwood	9,574	16	0	0	6	10	174	22	141	11	0
	Briar Creek Township	3,062	3	0	0	0	3	35	3	30	2	1
	Bridgeport	4,404	9	0	2	3	4	172	27	124	21	1
	Bridgeville	4,898	2	0	0	1	1	61	15	44	2	0
	Bridgewater	891	1	0	0	1	0	40	5	35	0	0
	Brighton Township	7,996	9	0	0	1	8	48	7	40	1	0
	Bristol	9,747	40	0	3	14	23	371	39	299	33	1
	Bristol Township	54,096	175	3	6	96	70	1,799	281	1,291	227	7
	Brookhaven	7,805	23	1	1	9	12	185	20	153	12	0
	Brookville	4,037	4	0	0	1	3	95	3	87	5	0
	Brownsville	2,653	9	0	0	1	8	46	6	39	1	0
	Buckingham Township	19,293	2	0	0	1	1	149	31	110	8	0
	Buffalo Township	7,318	23	0	0	0	23	74	13	55	6	0
	Bushkill Township	8,136	17	0	0	0	17	86	7	73	6	0
	Butler	14,258	88	0	2	13	73	545	86	459	0	4
	Butler Township, Butler County	16,894	43	0	4	9	30	359	24	324	11	1
	Butler Township, Schuykill County	5,751	4	0	0	0	4	26	8	17	1	0
	California	6,065	22	0	1	1	20	98	23	74	1	1
	Caln Township	12,283	44	0	0	11	33	315	30	270	15	8
	Cambria Township	6,199	13	0	0	0	13	126	9	110	7	0
	Cambridge Springs	2,260	7	0	1	1	5	37	8	29	0	0
	Camp Hill	7,384	13	0	2	5	6	111	13	94	4	0
	Carbondale	9,256	31	0	0	3	28	163	31	119	13	8
	Carlisle	18,317	55	0	12	26	17	663	72	572	19	5
	Carnegie	8,001	20	0	3	7	10	199	23	161	15	0
	Carrolltown	977	1	0	0	0	1	19	0	19	0	0

[1] The FBI does not publish arson data unless it receives data from either the agency or the state for all 12 months of the calendar year.

Table 8.   Offenses Known to Law Enforcement, by State and City, 2007 *(Contd.)*

(Number.)

State	City	Population	Violent crime	Murder and non-negligent man-slaughter	Forcible rape	Robbery	Aggravated assault	Property crime	Burglary	Larceny-theft	Motor vehicle theft	Arson[1]
	Carroll Township, York County	5,383	5	0	0	2	3	163	35	123	5	1
	Castle Shannon	8,099	20	0	0	3	17	161	23	125	13	1
	Catasauqua	6,562	15	0	0	3	12	195	16	165	14	0
	Catawissa	1,544	1	0	0	0	1	51	8	43	0	0
	Cecil Township	10,456	5	0	0	0	5	38	18	20	0	0
	Center Township	11,804	18	0	1	5	12	337	36	292	9	2
	Centerville	3,242	1	0	0	1	0	18	2	15	1	0
	Central Berks Regional	7,489	5	0	0	3	2	179	30	120	29	1
	Chalfont	4,243	0	0	0	0	0	37	0	37	0	0
	Chambersburg	17,958	104	0	3	41	60	881	143	703	35	7
	Chartiers Township	7,239	5	0	1	1	3	64	4	57	3	0
	Cheltenham Township	36,403	110	0	5	74	31	1,103	190	826	87	1
	Chester	36,799	945	27	25	231	662	1,330	437	635	258	31
	Chester Township	4,594	51	1	3	13	34	23	11	5	7	0
	Cheswick	1,751	0	0	0	0	0	14	4	10	0	0
	Chippewa Township	9,815	0	0	0	0	0	205	35	164	6	1
	Christiana	1,083	2	0	0	0	2	14	4	10	0	1
	Churchill	3,267	37	0	0	1	36	41	3	37	1	0
	Clarion	5,141	3	0	0	1	2	74	11	62	1	0
	Clay Township	5,766	2	0	0	1	1	14	7	5	2	0
	Clearfield	6,240	20	0	3	3	14	374	48	321	5	0
	Cleona	2,104	3	0	2	0	1	9	1	8	0	0
	Clifton Heights	6,586	43	0	1	10	32	197	16	166	15	1
	Coal Township	10,277	29	0	0	1	28	188	27	148	13	0
	Coatesville	11,744	169	0	3	78	88	564	150	344	70	1
	Colebrookdale District	6,462	7	0	1	0	6	160	11	142	7	0
	Collegeville	5,011	7	0	0	3	4	109	9	97	3	0
	Collier Township	6,235	12	0	1	3	8	185	7	169	9	1
	Collingdale	8,440	102	0	4	22	76	267	34	216	17	0
	Colonial Regional	19,420	15	1	2	8	4	518	33	472	13	1
	Columbia	10,034	24	0	4	5	15	236	45	174	17	1
	Colwyn	2,375	13	0	1	7	5	46	18	21	7	0
	Conemaugh Township, Cambria County	2,507	6	0	0	0	6	30	3	25	2	0
	Conewago Township, Adams County	6,184	4	0	3	0	1	92	3	86	3	1
	Conewango Township	3,647	6	0	2	1	3	143	26	117	0	2
	Conneaut Lake Regional	3,539	6	0	0	0	6	90	14	73	3	0
	Connellsville	8,526	28	0	6	11	11	328	55	253	20	0
	Conoy Township	3,288	3	0	0	0	3	37	17	16	4	0
	Conyngham	1,844	0	0	0	0	0	5	0	5	0	0
	Coplay	3,381	2	0	1	0	1	64	6	58	0	0
	Coraopolis	5,610	65	0	1	7	57	134	37	92	5	0
	Cornwall	3,460	1	0	0	0	1	4	2	2	0	0
	Corry	6,451	36	0	2	0	34	79	14	61	4	0
	Covington Township	2,154	4	0	0	1	3	62	10	49	3	0
	Crafton	6,138	15	0	1	4	10	138	16	117	5	1
	Cranberry Township	28,084	51	0	0	11	40	366	39	318	9	3
	Cresson Township	4,239	0	0	0	0	0	14	4	10	0	0
	Croyle Township	2,262	0	0	0	0	0	14	0	13	1	0
	Cumberland Township, Adams County	6,377	4	0	2	0	2	35	22	12	1	0
	Cumberland Township, Greene County	6,492	20	0	0	0	20	121	18	98	5	0
	Cumru Township	17,595	14	1	0	8	5	370	41	292	37	2
	Curwensville	2,505	17	0	0	0	17	82	12	67	3	1
	Dale	1,384	5	0	0	1	4	21	5	16	0	0
	Dallas	2,493	1	0	0	1	0	25	2	21	2	0
	Dallas Township	8,424	14	1	3	1	9	66	21	37	8	1
	Danville	4,530	15	0	2	1	12	222	39	179	4	1
	Darby	9,967	405	0	5	58	342	467	156	244	67	3
	Darby Township	9,615	31	0	0	8	23	107	13	70	24	0
	Darlington Township	2,040	0	0	0	0	0	1	1	0	0	0
	Decatur Township	3,089	4	0	0	0	4	58	3	55	0	0
	Delaware Water Gap	831	0	0	0	0	0	0	0	0	0	0
	Delmont	2,473	1	0	0	0	1	40	3	36	1	0
	Denver	3,700	4	0	0	1	3	51	8	40	3	0
	Derry Township, Dauphin County	21,923	69	0	3	9	57	655	85	547	23	8
	Dickson City	5,916	4	0	0	0	4	445	22	414	9	0
	Donegal Township	2,574	4	0	1	0	3	18	4	13	1	0
	Donora	5,317	37	0	9	2	26	81	13	60	8	1
	Dormont	8,467	54	0	1	6	47	140	20	114	6	0

[1] The FBI does not publish arson data unless it receives data from either the agency or the state for all 12 months of the calendar year.

Table 8. Offenses Known to Law Enforcement, by State and City, 2007 *(Contd.)*

(Number.)

State	City	Population	Violent crime	Murder and non-negligent man-slaughter	Forcible rape	Robbery	Aggravated assault	Property crime	Burglary	Larceny-theft	Motor vehicle theft	Arson[1]
	Douglass Township, Montgomery County..............	10,323	13	0	0	2	11	116	5	101	10	0
	Downingtown	7,924	30	0	2	7	21	320	34	260	26	0
	Doylestown	8,208	19	0	1	4	14	244	18	216	10	1
	Doylestown Township............	18,847	15	0	1	6	8	254	30	205	19	0
	Dublin Borough.....................	2,182	4	0	0	0	4	9	2	7	0	0
	Du Bois..................................	7,757	32	0	6	2	24	319	19	285	15	1
	Dunbar...................................	1,157	0	0	0	0	0	3	1	2	0	0
	Duncannon............................	1,503	2	0	1	0	1	28	2	23	3	2
	Duncansville	1,181	2	0	0	0	2	27	1	25	1	0
	Dupont...................................	2,601	8	0	0	0	8	52	3	46	3	0
	Duquesne	6,705	88	1	5	32	50	397	147	203	47	5
	Earl Township	6,918	1	0	0	1	0	68	30	33	5	3
	East Buffalo Township	5,939	5	0	2	0	3	22	5	16	1	0
	East Cocalico Township.........	10,398	4	0	0	2	2	115	22	82	11	1
	East Conemaugh	1,186	6	0	0	0	6	4	1	3	0	0
	East Coventry Township........	6,236	1	0	1	0	0	44	11	32	1	0
	Eastern Adams Regional........	9,083	0	0	0	0	0	4	0	4	0	0
	East Fallowfield Township......	7,343	18	0	0	0	18	81	22	57	2	2
	East Franklin Township	3,981	0	0	0	0	0	33	1	32	0	0
	East Hempfield Township	23,212	27	0	6	9	12	573	112	436	25	5
	East Lampeter Township........	14,910	30	1	3	14	12	790	61	703	26	1
	East Lansdowne	2,495	41	0	1	18	22	118	34	72	12	0
	East McKeesport...................	2,816	3	0	0	0	3	14	7	7	0	0
	East Norriton Township.........	13,485	10	0	2	6	2	319	24	274	21	0
	East Norwegian Township......	797	0	0	0	0	0	3	0	3	0	0
	Easton....................................	26,207	156	5	14	69	68	1,074	141	826	107	13
	East Pennsboro Township	19,894	16	3	1	8	4	295	45	245	5	2
	East Petersburg.....................	4,327	3	0	1	0	2	91	25	65	1	4
	East Pikeland Township.........	6,849	8	0	1	4	3	152	19	125	8	1
	East Rochester.......................	573	2	0	0	2	0	41	3	37	1	0
	East Taylor Township............	2,571	0	0	0	0	0	0	0	0	0	0
	Easttown Township	10,503	5	0	0	1	4	124	19	97	8	1
	East Vincent Township	6,589	5	0	1	2	2	70	18	46	6	0
	East Washington	1,877	6	0	2	1	3	29	6	18	5	0
	East Whiteland Township.......	10,632	7	0	0	3	4	144	20	118	6	1
	Ebensburg.............................	2,880	1	0	0	1	0	124	9	112	3	0
	Economy................................	9,192	2	0	1	1	0	29	4	25	0	0
	Eddystone	2,361	33	0	1	7	25	247	7	232	8	3
	Edgewood	3,018	7	0	1	5	1	277	15	259	3	0
	Edgeworth.............................	1,582	0	0	0	0	0	1	0	1	0	0
	Edinboro	6,646	6	0	0	1	5	106	25	80	1	1
	Edwardsville	4,688	69	1	2	13	53	195	18	162	15	1
	Elizabethtown........................	11,900	11	0	3	2	6	195	29	160	6	2
	Elizabeth Township................	12,837	48	0	0	1	47	118	18	91	9	0
	Elkland	1,685	3	0	0	0	3	22	8	14	0	0
	Ellwood City	8,064	34	0	2	7	25	241	35	200	6	8
	Emmaus..................................	11,414	9	0	0	2	7	295	33	252	10	8
	Ephrata..................................	13,067	30	0	3	12	15	287	67	199	21	2
	Ephrata Township	9,557	7	0	0	1	6	161	25	126	10	1
	Erie..	101,812	543	3	75	264	201	3,068	831	2,062	175	44
	Etna.......................................	3,578	16	0	0	3	13	146	32	97	17	1
	Everett...................................	1,869	2	0	0	0	2	39	5	25	9	0
	Exeter	5,995	17	1	1	1	14	120	22	90	8	2
	Exeter Township, Berks County..........................	27,080	25	0	1	8	16	557	41	491	25	1
	Exeter Township, Luzerne County......................	2,557	1	0	0	0	1	13	1	8	4	1
	Fairview Township, Luzerne County......................	4,321	8	0	2	1	5	37	5	32	0	0
	Fairview Township, York County..........................	16,630	28	0	3	2	23	325	45	268	12	0
	Fallowfield Township	4,242	11	0	0	1	10	49	16	25	8	2
	Falls Township, Bucks County..........................	34,033	58	1	3	33	21	887	81	720	86	5
	Fawn Township	2,324	8	0	0	0	8	22	6	14	2	0
	Ferguson Township................	16,302	13	0	2	4	7	169	18	139	12	0
	Ferndale.................................	1,685	0	0	0	0	0	1	1	0	0	0
	Findlay Township...................	5,053	9	0	0	0	9	60	7	49	4	0
	Fleetwood..............................	4,029	4	0	0	0	4	70	7	62	1	0
	Folcroft	6,878	42	0	4	2	36	136	18	95	23	0
	Ford City...............................	3,190	7	0	0	1	6	84	6	76	2	1
	Forest City	1,765	1	0	0	0	1	15	3	12	0	0
	Forest Hills............................	6,271	8	1	0	2	5	49	15	32	2	0

[1] The FBI does not publish arson data unless it receives data from either the agency or the state for all 12 months of the calendar year.

Table 8.   Offenses Known to Law Enforcement, by State and City, 2007 *(Contd.)*

(Number.)

State	City	Population	Violent crime	Murder and non-negligent man-slaughter	Forcible rape	Robbery	Aggravated assault	Property crime	Burglary	Larceny-theft	Motor vehicle theft	Arson[1]
	Forks Township	14,452	4	1	1	0	2	151	6	140	5	0
	Forty Fort	4,273	7	0	2	1	4	82	14	66	2	0
	Foster Township	4,304	3	0	1	0	2	28	8	18	2	1
	Fountain Hill	4,602	10	0	1	1	8	116	18	85	13	2
	Fox Chapel	5,144	0	0	0	0	0	29	6	23	0	0
	Franklin	6,758	19	0	1	1	17	203	33	166	4	0
	Franklin Park	11,908	3	0	1	0	2	63	16	47	0	1
	Freedom	1,624	13	0	1	0	12	60	9	43	8	0
	Freemansburg	2,007	0	0	0	0	0	51	4	44	3	0
	Freeport	1,818	3	0	0	0	3	23	5	17	1	0
	Gaines Township	569	0	0	0	0	0	4	1	3	0	0
	Galeton	1,263	8	0	2	0	6	27	0	26	1	0
	Gallitzin	1,908	2	0	0	0	2	28	3	25	0	0
	Gettysburg	8,194	32	0	3	14	15	173	33	134	6	1
	Girard	2,991	7	0	0	1	6	33	2	31	0	0
	Glenolden	7,261	20	0	0	8	12	164	16	145	3	1
	Granville Township	4,915	5	0	0	1	4	122	18	97	7	2
	Greencastle	4,036	11	0	0	3	8	118	20	94	4	0
	Greenfield Township, Blair County	3,779	9	0	3	0	6	155	15	134	6	1
	Greensburg	15,567	26	0	6	4	16	547	64	463	20	0
	Green Tree	4,353	5	0	0	4	1	56	6	45	5	0
	Greenville	6,263	22	0	4	0	18	113	19	94	0	3
	Greenwood Township	2,046	0	0	0	0	0	0	0	0	0	0
	Grove City	7,644	7	0	2	0	5	138	22	115	1	0
	Halifax Regional	4,168	0	0	0	0	0	10	3	6	1	0
	Hamburg	4,209	20	0	1	3	16	110	24	77	9	0
	Hamiltonban Township	2,739	1	0	0	0	1	6	2	2	2	0
	Hampden Township	26,612	14	0	1	4	9	111	22	80	9	0
	Hampton Township	17,139	6	0	0	1	5	221	51	161	9	0
	Hanover	15,079	30	0	3	10	17	614	85	511	18	3
	Hanover Township, Luzerne County	11,060	12	0	3	3	6	316	45	260	11	1
	Hanover Township, Washington County	2,752	27	0	0	0	27	61	5	53	3	0
	Harleton	265	0	0	0	0	0	1	0	0	1	0
	Harmar Township	3,018	5	0	0	0	5	91	8	77	6	0
	Harmony Township	3,111	3	0	0	0	3	99	13	81	5	0
	Harrisburg	46,924	734	12	52	443	227	2,297	576	1,556	165	40
	Harrison Township	10,016	20	1	8	3	8	139	36	94	9	0
	Hastings	1,312	12	0	0	0	12	29	10	16	3	1
	Hatboro	7,177	29	0	2	3	24	149	37	107	5	1
	Hatfield Township	20,241	22	0	4	3	15	251	32	202	17	9
	Haverford Township	48,434	27	0	2	18	7	606	83	505	18	0
	Heidelberg Township, Berks County	1,774	1	0	0	0	1	9	3	6	0	0
	Heidelberg Township, Lebanon County	4,113	0	0	0	0	0	21	3	17	1	0
	Hellam Township	9,139	15	0	3	2	10	97	12	74	11	0
	Hemlock Township	2,214	3	0	1	1	1	178	8	166	4	1
	Hermitage	16,576	22	0	2	9	11	705	72	623	10	3
	Highland Township	1,210	0	0	0	0	0	4	1	3	0	0
	Highspire	2,585	14	0	0	2	12	44	5	38	1	2
	Hilltown Township	13,175	18	0	1	2	15	210	42	153	15	1
	Hollidaysburg	5,563	14	0	0	5	9	106	20	80	6	0
	Homestead	3,476	76	2	4	33	37	342	53	260	29	0
	Honesdale	4,795	13	1	3	0	9	125	13	105	7	1
	Honey Brook Township	7,140	3	0	1	0	2	7	3	4	0	0
	Horsham Township	24,947	17	0	0	8	9	317	40	259	18	0
	Hughesville	2,067	0	0	0	0	0	22	3	19	0	0
	Hummelstown	4,386	7	0	1	2	4	57	6	51	0	0
	Huntingdon	6,815	6	0	0	0	6	109	13	95	1	0
	Independence Township, Beaver County	2,736	0	0	0	0	0	39	7	28	4	0
	Indiana	14,792	36	0	4	6	26	278	66	207	5	1
	Indiana Township	6,947	5	0	3	0	2	86	21	63	2	2
	Industry	1,821	10	1	1	0	8	40	9	27	4	0
	Ingram	3,389	18	0	2	1	15	58	10	44	4	0
	Irwin	4,116	5	0	1	0	4	95	16	79	0	0
	Ivyland	882	0	0	0	0	0	1	0	1	0	0
	Jackson Township, Butler County	3,841	4	0	0	1	3	42	4	38	0	0
	Jackson Township, Luzerne County	4,597	0	0	0	0	0	17	8	7	2	0

[1] The FBI does not publish arson data unless it receives data from either the agency or the state for all 12 months of the calendar year.

Table 8. Offenses Known to Law Enforcement, by State and City, 2007 *(Contd.)*

(Number.)

State	City	Population	Violent crime	Murder and non-negligent man-slaughter	Forcible rape	Robbery	Aggravated assault	Property crime	Burglary	Larceny-theft	Motor vehicle theft	Arson[1]
	Jeannette	10,021	70	1	0	4	65	236	74	162	0	1
	Jenkins Township	4,951	3	0	0	0	3	107	18	83	6	4
	Jermyn	2,230	19	0	0	6	13	53	21	31	1	0
	Jersey Shore	4,360	8	0	4	1	3	137	17	112	8	0
	Jim Thorpe	4,898	7	0	1	0	6	122	16	105	1	1
	Johnsonburg	2,747	2	0	0	1	1	68	34	33	1	0
	Johnstown	23,609	145	1	3	57	84	864	262	546	56	7
	Kane	3,828	2	0	0	0	2	13	0	13	0	0
	Kennedy Township	9,313	35	0	3	4	28	185	20	151	14	0
	Kennett Square	5,294	10	0	1	4	5	136	16	108	12	4
	Kidder Township	1,386	11	0	3	0	8	153	22	129	2	0
	Kingston	13,036	28	0	2	14	12	306	48	240	18	0
	Kingston Township	7,069	13	0	1	0	12	74	10	60	4	1
	Kiskiminetas Township	4,801	4	0	0	0	4	72	9	59	4	0
	Kline Township	1,491	4	0	2	1	1	26	2	23	1	0
	Knox	1,110	27	1	1	0	25	142	9	133	0	1
	Koppel	788	4	0	1	1	2	64	13	50	1	1
	Kutztown	5,075	15	1	1	3	10	190	32	152	6	0
	Laflin Borough	1,503	1	0	0	0	1	25	6	16	3	0
	Lake City	2,985	7	0	1	0	6	40	15	24	1	0
	Lamar Township	2,433	0	0	0	0	0	8	1	6	1	0
	Lancaster	54,562	515	5	38	241	231	3,252	556	2,441	255	32
	Lancaster Township, Lancaster County	14,347	34	0	5	19	10	348	61	256	31	6
	Lansdale	15,669	53	0	7	20	26	415	71	308	36	4
	Lansdowne	10,720	51	1	1	15	34	263	61	186	16	1
	Lansford	4,180	11	0	0	1	10	30	7	19	4	2
	Latrobe	8,504	18	0	0	1	17	233	23	204	6	2
	Lawrence Park Township	3,778	7	0	1	0	6	64	9	53	2	0
	Lawrence Township, Clearfield County	7,613	57	1	1	1	54	237	16	217	4	1
	Lawrence Township, Tioga County	1,712	1	0	0	0	1	20	4	16	0	0
	Lebanon	24,144	112	1	13	44	54	768	124	581	63	6
	Leetsdale	1,122	0	0	0	0	0	0	0	0	0	0
	Leet Township	1,510	0	0	0	0	0	1	0	1	0	0
	Lehighton	5,489	11	0	2	4	5	199	32	154	13	4
	Lehigh Township, Northampton County	10,831	14	0	0	1	13	181	16	155	10	2
	Lehman Township	3,308	8	0	0	0	8	34	13	21	0	0
	Lewisburg	5,572	17	0	0	0	17	73	12	61	0	1
	Liberty	2,447	3	0	0	0	3	31	4	23	4	0
	Liberty Township, Bedford County	1,449	0	0	0	0	0	0	0	0	0	0
	Ligonier	1,633	4	0	0	1	3	24	0	24	0	0
	Limerick Township	17,087	4	0	0	0	4	271	31	229	11	2
	Lincoln	1,125	0	0	0	0	0	10	6	3	1	0
	Lititz	9,029	13	0	2	1	10	137	34	101	2	1
	Littlestown	4,187	35	0	1	3	31	123	21	98	4	1
	Lock Haven	8,584	18	0	4	4	10	330	24	297	9	3
	Locust Township	2,518	6	0	6	0	0	53	5	47	1	1
	Logan Township	11,887	78	2	2	5	69	273	53	217	3	2
	Loretto	1,270	0	0	0	0	0	0	0	0	0	0
	Lower Allen Township	17,701	4	0	3	1	0	236	29	205	2	1
	Lower Burrell	12,315	25	0	2	1	22	138	31	105	2	3
	Lower Frederick Township	4,858	2	0	0	0	2	16	5	9	2	0
	Lower Gwynedd Township	11,368	9	0	0	0	9	178	11	162	5	0
	Lower Heidelberg Township	5,282	3	0	0	0	3	29	4	25	0	0
	Lower Makefield Township	32,550	10	0	1	2	7	361	66	280	15	0
	Lower Merion Township	57,691	66	0	2	42	22	1,002	142	813	47	0
	Lower Milford Township	3,919	1	0	0	0	1	18	4	13	1	0
	Lower Moreland Township	11,894	5	0	1	0	4	167	47	109	11	1
	Lower Paxton Township	44,961	101	1	4	38	58	1,119	144	948	27	9
	Lower Pottsgrove Township	12,240	11	0	3	3	5	256	43	206	7	1
	Lower Providence Township	26,047	6	0	1	3	2	336	76	252	8	1
	Lower Salford Township	14,419	6	0	0	1	5	92	16	71	5	1
	Lower Saucon Township	11,360	15	0	2	1	12	100	13	83	4	1
	Lower Southampton Township	19,189	59	0	4	10	45	424	71	331	22	5
	Lower Swatara Township	8,364	12	1	1	5	5	117	17	94	6	0
	Lower Windsor Township	7,847	5	0	0	1	4	97	9	66	22	0
	Luzerne Township	6,739	0	0	0	0	0	31	11	18	2	2
	Madison Township	1,607	0	0	0	0	0	0	0	0	0	0

[1] The FBI does not publish arson data unless it receives data from either the agency or the state for all 12 months of the calendar year.

Table 8. Offenses Known to Law Enforcement, by State and City, 2007 *(Contd.)*

(Number.)

State	City	Population	Violent crime	Murder and non-negligent man-slaughter	Forcible rape	Robbery	Aggravated assault	Property crime	Burglary	Larceny-theft	Motor vehicle theft	Arson[1]
	Mahanoy City	4,361	2	0	0	2	0	29	13	16	0	0
	Mahanoy Township	3,592	0	0	0	0	0	1	0	1	0	0
	Mahoning Township, Carbon County	4,336	19	0	1	2	16	68	17	48	3	0
	Main Township	1,305	0	0	0	0	0	1	0	0	1	0
	Malvern	3,115	2	0	0	0	2	35	7	26	2	0
	Manheim	4,626	6	0	1	0	5	108	11	92	5	1
	Manheim Township	36,069	49	3	1	21	24	827	119	679	29	12
	Manor Township, Armstrong County	3,968	1	0	0	0	1	5	3	2	0	0
	Manor Township, Lancaster County	18,683	6	0	2	2	2	179	27	146	6	1
	Mansfield	3,245	1	0	0	0	1	11	4	6	1	0
	Marietta	2,587	5	0	3	0	2	56	14	39	3	0
	Marion Center	422	0	0	0	0	0	0	0	0	0	0
	Marion Township, Berks County	1,659	0	0	0	0	0	4	0	4	0	1
	Marlborough Township	3,280	4	0	1	0	3	32	8	21	3	0
	Marple Township	23,579	13	0	2	6	5	330	47	267	16	2
	Marysville	2,454	0	0	0	0	0	18	2	16	0	0
	Masontown	3,424	11	0	1	6	4	80	10	59	11	0
	Mayfield	1,702	0	0	0	0	0	0	0	0	0	0
	McCandless	27,339	14	0	0	3	11	320	47	268	5	0
	McKeesport	22,190	299	6	12	70	211	799	278	453	68	6
	McSherrystown	2,841	3	0	0	1	2	54	3	51	0	0
	Mechanicsburg	8,771	30	0	1	3	26	216	17	196	3	4
	Media	5,445	18	0	1	7	10	23	10	11	2	2
	Mercer	2,253	4	0	0	0	4	35	9	23	3	1
	Mercersburg	1,556	4	0	0	0	4	39	5	34	0	0
	Meyersdale	2,302	1	0	0	0	1	3	1	2	0	0
	Middleburg	1,345	1	0	0	1	0	58	5	52	1	0
	Middlesex Township, Cumberland County	6,868	8	0	3	3	2	234	28	198	8	1
	Middletown	8,806	22	0	5	5	12	160	16	140	4	4
	Middletown Township	47,710	54	0	2	19	33	1,761	182	1,505	74	11
	Midland	2,898	5	0	0	0	5	117	41	73	3	1
	Mifflinburg	3,564	1	0	0	0	1	9	2	6	1	0
	Mifflin County Regional	26,255	69	0	6	3	60	601	73	511	17	2
	Mifflin Township	2,266	0	0	0	0	0	0	0	0	0	0
	Milford	2,945	3	0	0	0	3	23	6	14	3	0
	Millcreek Township, Erie County	52,592	54	0	11	24	19	863	200	629	34	1
	Millersburg	2,454	11	0	0	0	11	46	10	35	1	4
	Millersville	7,204	9	0	5	2	2	83	29	51	3	0
	Millville	950	0	0	0	0	0	2	2	0	0	0
	Milton	6,377	17	0	0	0	17	127	15	111	1	2
	Minersville	4,264	6	0	0	0	6	44	4	37	3	0
	Mohnton	3,111	8	0	0	0	8	14	4	6	4	0
	Monaca	5,833	22	0	1	3	18	145	8	124	13	1
	Monessen	8,159	80	0	2	7	71	299	67	210	22	2
	Monongahela	4,468	17	0	2	3	12	176	44	123	9	1
	Monroeville	27,659	104	1	3	21	79	606	76	481	49	6
	Montgomery Township	24,419	5	0	0	4	1	617	30	574	13	1
	Montoursville	4,630	1	0	0	0	1	24	0	24	0	0
	Moon Township	22,623	26	0	4	9	13	245	34	199	12	0
	Moore Township	9,502	3	0	0	0	3	50	8	39	3	0
	Moosic	5,793	38	0	2	5	31	286	22	249	15	2
	Morrisville	9,706	45	0	1	13	31	215	23	145	47	1
	Morton	2,649	12	0	0	2	10	96	6	85	5	0
	Moscow	1,953	1	0	0	0	1	18	2	16	0	0
	Mount Carmel	5,914	29	0	0	1	28	103	16	83	4	0
	Mount Carmel Township	2,586	3	0	0	0	3	16	3	12	1	1
	Mount Gretna Borough	234	0	0	0	0	0	0	0	0	0	0
	Mount Jewett	1,015	3	0	0	0	3	14	5	9	0	0
	Mount Joy	7,097	6	1	2	2	1	139	20	111	8	0
	Mount Lebanon	30,543	24	0	0	7	17	271	46	215	10	1
	Mount Oliver	3,681	69	1	1	30	37	217	71	108	38	1
	Muhlenberg Township	18,334	19	1	0	16	2	625	59	502	64	2
	Muncy	2,486	0	0	0	0	0	8	0	8	0	0
	Munhall	11,239	16	0	0	10	6	190	49	130	11	0
	Murrysville	19,565	4	0	0	2	2	134	18	111	5	0
	Nanticoke	10,261	45	0	6	7	32	391	99	270	22	2
	Narberth	4,079	4	0	0	0	4	53	9	39	5	0
	Nazareth Area	6,061	10	0	1	1	8	114	14	97	3	0

[1] The FBI does not publish arson data unless it receives data from either the agency or the state for all 12 months of the calendar year.

Table 8. Offenses Known to Law Enforcement, by State and City, 2007 *(Contd.)*

(Number.)

State	City	Population	Violent crime	Murder and non-negligent man-slaughter	Forcible rape	Robbery	Aggravated assault	Property crime	Burglary	Larceny-theft	Motor vehicle theft	Arson[1]
	Neshannock Township	9,369	2	0	0	2	0	151	16	129	6	3
	Newberry Township	15,563	18	0	0	2	16	327	65	239	23	0
	New Brighton	9,493	69	0	1	13	55	573	109	459	5	0
	New Britain	2,292	11	0	0	0	11	51	10	40	1	0
	New Britain Township	10,795	5	0	1	0	4	97	13	82	2	1
	New Castle Township	392	2	0	0	1	1	24	0	24	0	0
	New Cumberland	7,084	1	0	0	1	0	17	1	15	1	0
	New Garden Township	11,699	7	0	0	2	5	215	27	178	10	2
	New Hanover Township	9,267	1	0	0	0	1	63	16	45	2	1
	New Holland	5,152	3	0	0	2	1	148	51	85	12	1
	New Hope	2,296	11	0	0	0	11	83	13	68	2	0
	Newport	1,465	17	0	0	0	17	78	16	62	0	0
	New Sewickley Township	7,722	6	0	0	1	5	98	27	67	4	0
	Newtown	2,247	3	0	0	1	2	29	2	26	1	0
	Newtown Township, Delaware County	11,894	7	0	0	1	6	202	27	169	6	0
	Newville	1,313	0	0	0	0	0	41	5	36	0	0
	Norristown	30,205	408	2	20	214	172	1,451	355	915	181	16
	Northampton	9,818	15	0	3	3	9	194	29	156	9	3
	Northampton Township	41,293	10	0	3	3	4	279	54	216	9	6
	North Belle Vernon	1,987	10	0	0	2	8	123	16	102	5	0
	North Catasauqua	2,861	5	0	0	0	5	58	10	43	5	0
	North Charleroi	1,327	0	0	0	0	0	9	3	5	1	0
	North Cornwall Township	6,526	28	0	1	3	24	95	7	86	2	1
	North Coventry Township	7,698	7	0	1	1	5	286	25	252	9	0
	North East, Erie County	4,268	8	0	1	2	5	138	22	110	6	1
	Northern Berks Regional	12,351	7	0	0	1	6	161	28	122	11	1
	Northern Cambria Borough	3,970	10	0	0	1	9	95	26	61	8	0
	Northern Regional	27,442	8	0	0	1	7	314	30	270	14	0
	Northern York Regional	63,294	42	0	0	14	28	1,223	168	970	85	7
	North Fayette Township	12,998	0	0	0	0	0	296	20	272	4	0
	North Franklin Township	4,681	8	0	0	5	3	146	16	123	7	0
	North Huntingdon Township	29,478	11	0	0	4	7	399	71	301	27	0
	North Lebanon Township	10,896	59	0	0	5	54	279	43	227	9	3
	North Londonderry Township	6,939	7	0	1	0	6	131	7	120	4	1
	North Middleton Township	10,946	4	0	1	1	2	56	10	43	3	0
	North Sewickley Township	5,729	0	0	0	0	0	8	4	4	0	0
	North Strabane Township	12,176	35	0	1	1	33	218	20	193	5	1
	Northumberland	3,517	7	0	5	1	1	85	22	56	7	0
	North Union Township	1,248	0	0	0	0	0	1	1	0	0	0
	North Versailles Township	12,280	37	0	2	8	27	276	24	240	12	6
	North Wales	3,248	2	0	0	0	2	90	11	74	5	1
	Northwest Lancaster County Regional	18,083	9	1	2	3	3	153	3	145	5	0
	Northwest Lawrence County Regional	6,759	10	0	1	3	6	89	35	43	11	2
	Norwood	5,813	19	1	3	3	12	89	7	76	6	1
	Oakdale	1,441	0	0	0	0	0	24	7	16	1	0
	O'Hara Township	9,537	13	0	0	2	11	100	15	83	2	0
	Ohioville	3,654	11	0	2	0	9	59	18	37	4	0
	Oil City	10,762	7	0	1	1	5	115	17	91	7	2
	Old Forge	8,540	12	0	0	0	12	17	1	13	3	0
	Oley Township	3,672	2	0	0	0	2	22	6	16	0	0
	Oliver Township	2,068	2	0	0	0	2	7	1	6	0	0
	Orwigsburg	2,969	0	0	0	0	0	33	2	30	1	1
	Osceola Mills	1,170	1	0	0	0	1	13	1	12	0	0
	Oxford	4,738	28	0	0	3	25	114	20	83	11	1
	Paint Township	3,210	3	0	0	0	3	11	3	8	0	1
	Palmerton	5,261	20	0	0	0	20	158	15	140	3	1
	Palmer Township	19,673	10	0	2	4	4	171	18	152	1	0
	Palmyra	6,944	7	0	0	2	5	87	9	77	1	1
	Parkesburg	3,455	5	0	3	1	1	71	22	43	6	0
	Parkside	2,195	10	0	0	3	7	55	4	48	3	0
	Patterson Area	3,617	0	0	0	0	0	97	9	80	8	1
	Patton	1,883	1	0	0	0	1	24	7	16	1	0
	Patton Township	12,839	10	0	1	5	4	178	21	150	7	2
	Paxtang	1,480	9	0	0	4	5	36	5	27	4	1
	Pen Argyl	3,667	7	0	1	2	4	72	14	54	4	1
	Penbrook	2,891	2	0	1	1	0	1	0	1	0	0
	Penn Hills	43,955	164	6	11	66	81	1,166	348	687	131	20
	Pennridge Regional	10,414	9	0	0	2	7	131	26	96	9	2

[1] The FBI does not publish arson data unless it receives data from either the agency or the state for all 12 months of the calendar year.

Table 8. Offenses Known to Law Enforcement, by State and City, 2007 *(Contd.)*

(Number.)

State	City	Population	Violent crime	Murder and non-negligent man-slaughter	Forcible rape	Robbery	Aggravated assault	Property crime	Burglary	Larceny-theft	Motor vehicle theft	Arson[1]
	Penn Township, Butler County	5,246	1	0	0	0	1	44	10	32	2	2
	Penn Township, Lancaster County	8,201	14	0	0	1	13	111	13	77	21	0
	Penn Township, Perry County	3,222	7	0	3	1	3	75	14	60	1	0
	Penn Township, Westmoreland County	20,476	8	0	0	1	7	23	17	6	0	0
	Penn Township, York County	16,010	17	0	3	1	13	242	35	202	5	0
	Pequea Township	4,492	5	1	0	0	4	51	7	41	3	0
	Perkasie	8,709	15	0	1	4	10	242	26	212	4	0
	Perryopolis	1,735	3	0	0	0	3	19	3	16	0	0
	Peters Township	20,264	11	0	0	2	9	153	37	104	12	2
	Philadelphia	1,435,533	21,180	392	956	10,258	9,574	61,795	11,524	39,167	11,104	
	Phoenixville	15,962	50	0	5	3	42	338	21	308	9	1
	Pittsburgh	312,179	3,455	52	129	1,596	1,678	13,933	3,418	8,977	1,538	79
	Plains Township	10,403	26	0	3	3	20	145	23	108	14	0
	Pleasant Hills	7,767	3	0	0	3	0	105	12	88	5	0
	Plum	26,209	14	0	2	5	7	181	67	109	5	1
	Plumstead Township	11,978	6	0	2	1	3	160	20	129	11	2
	Plymouth Township, Montgomery County	16,260	27	1	5	15	6	759	68	654	37	4
	Pocono Mountain Regional	35,733	98	3	16	27	52	897	400	429	68	8
	Pocono Township	11,468	12	0	0	5	7	381	47	325	9	2
	Point Township	3,827	3	0	0	1	2	37	12	24	1	1
	Portage	2,631	0	0	0	0	0	52	6	42	4	1
	Port Allegany	2,228	0	0	0	0	0	0	0	0	0	0
	Pottstown	21,346	221	3	20	74	124	1,193	191	920	82	23
	Prospect Park	6,402	23	0	0	0	23	144	14	124	6	0
	Punxsutawney	6,046	21	0	5	1	15	197	22	173	2	1
	Pymatuning Township	3,644	3	0	0	0	3	110	20	83	7	0
	Quarryville	2,150	10	0	0	1	9	42	8	32	2	0
	Raccoon Township	3,277	0	0	0	0	0	17	1	16	0	0
	Rankin	2,116	21	1	0	3	17	55	29	18	8	0
	Reading	81,168	752	6	41	385	320	3,818	1,183	1,780	855	49
	Reynoldsville	2,582	4	0	0	0	4	10	2	7	1	0
	Rice Township	2,826	0	0	0	0	0	18	6	12	0	0
	Richland Township, Bucks County	13,027	9	0	4	0	5	316	20	284	12	0
	Richland Township, Cambria County	12,623	15	0	1	5	9	603	31	561	11	2
	Ridgway	4,194	24	0	1	0	23	115	27	87	1	0
	Ridley Park	7,029	14	0	2	1	11	89	9	75	5	0
	Ridley Township	30,055	61	1	3	12	45	541	60	449	32	3
	Roaring Brook Township	1,759	4	0	0	0	4	32	8	24	0	0
	Roaring Spring	2,280	0	0	0	0	0	35	3	32	0	0
	Robesonia	2,074	3	0	2	0	1	16	1	13	2	0
	Robeson Township	7,619	6	0	1	1	4	79	24	44	11	1
	Robinson Township, Allegheny County	13,585	26	0	3	9	14	481	35	421	25	0
	Rochester	3,717	21	0	3	5	13	278	41	214	23	0
	Rochester Township	2,917	5	0	0	1	4	56	11	41	4	0
	Roseto	1,655	0	0	0	0	0	9	2	7	0	0
	Rosslyn Farms	425	1	0	0	0	1	1	1	0	0	0
	Ross Township	30,522	46	0	1	17	28	844	142	678	24	1
	Rostraver Township	11,749	21	4	0	9	8	558	38	501	19	1
	Royersford	4,316	21	0	3	1	17	92	11	70	11	0
	Rush Township	3,567	2	0	1	1	0	50	8	39	3	0
	Ryan Township	2,560	0	0	0	0	0	0	0	0	0	0
	Rye Township	2,511	0	0	0	0	0	10	0	7	3	0
	Salem Township, Luzerne County	4,133	5	0	1	1	3	58	8	48	2	0
	Salisbury Township	14,006	6	0	0	4	2	291	26	254	11	0
	Sandy Lake	708	0	0	0	0	0	8	0	8	0	0
	Sandy Township	11,602	18	0	1	0	17	242	46	190	6	1
	Saxton	761	0	0	0	0	0	0	0	0	0	0
	Sayre	5,554	23	2	6	1	14	207	22	180	5	1
	Schuylkill Haven	5,198	17	0	3	1	13	112	15	93	4	0
	Scottdale	4,488	15	0	0	0	15	97	12	78	7	0
	Scott Township, Allegheny County	15,908	22	1	1	9	11	267	40	214	13	0
	Scott Township, Columbia County	4,976	0	0	0	0	0	49	0	49	0	0

[1] The FBI does not publish arson data unless it receives data from either the agency or the state for all 12 months of the calendar year.

Table 8.   Offenses Known to Law Enforcement, by State and City, 2007 *(Contd.)*

(Number.)

State	City	Population	Violent crime	Murder and non-negligent man-slaughter	Forcible rape	Robbery	Aggravated assault	Property crime	Burglary	Larceny-theft	Motor vehicle theft	Arson[1]
	Scott Township, Lackawanna County	4,932	4	0	0	1	3	13	3	9	1	0
	Scranton	72,444	227	2	26	99	100	2,263	499	1,592	172	28
	Selinsgrove	5,339	69	0	4	3	62	228	73	147	8	4
	Seven Springs	119	3	0	0	0	3	31	1	30	0	0
	Seward	458	0	0	0	0	0	0	0	0	0	0
	Sewickley	3,584	5	0	0	1	4	73	10	60	3	0
	Sewickley Heights	919	0	0	0	0	0	0	0	0	0	0
	Shaler Township	28,042	14	0	1	1	12	268	56	198	14	1
	Shamokin	7,396	33	0	1	2	30	74	12	48	14	1
	Shamokin Dam	1,451	1	0	1	0	0	38	2	35	1	0
	Sharon Hill	5,326	26	1	1	11	13	178	22	136	20	0
	Sharpsburg	3,281	9	0	0	2	7	63	19	28	16	0
	Sharpsville	4,186	18	0	3	1	14	111	6	96	9	0
	Shenandoah	5,199	13	0	0	2	11	203	58	135	10	17
	Shenango Township, Lawrence County	7,680	15	0	0	0	15	204	40	161	3	0
	Shillington	5,047	5	0	1	1	3	102	12	73	17	0
	Shippensburg	5,604	1	0	0	1	0	45	6	39	0	0
	Shippingport	223	0	0	0	0	0	0	0	0	0	0
	Shiremanstown	1,471	2	0	0	0	2	8	2	5	1	0
	Shohola Township	2,479	0	0	0	0	0	18	9	7	2	0
	Silver Lake Township	1,772	0	0	0	0	0	8	3	4	1	0
	Silver Spring Township	13,052	2	0	0	2	0	93	4	85	4	0
	Sinking Spring	3,641	3	0	0	0	3	73	16	50	7	1
	Slippery Rock	3,248	2	0	0	1	1	40	6	32	2	1
	Smethport	1,593	2	0	0	0	2	15	3	11	1	0
	Solebury Township	9,007	7	0	0	0	7	72	17	54	1	1
	Somerset	6,428	12	0	2	4	6	152	27	121	4	1
	Souderton	6,623	29	0	1	3	25	107	10	90	7	0
	South Abington Township	9,646	19	0	2	1	16	164	28	135	1	3
	South Beaver Township	2,875	3	0	0	0	3	38	5	32	1	0
	South Buffalo Township	2,811	0	0	0	0	0	16	4	10	2	1
	South Centre Township	1,917	3	0	1	0	2	117	17	96	4	0
	South Coatesville	1,075	3	0	0	0	3	6	3	3	0	0
	Southern Regional Lancaster County	3,825	2	0	0	0	2	36	6	26	4	0
	Southern Regional York County	9,873	15	0	1	10	4	197	21	169	7	0
	South Fayette Township	13,174	25	0	1	2	22	68	15	50	3	3
	South Fork	1,046	8	0	0	1	7	2	0	0	2	0
	South Heidelberg Township	7,146	10	0	0	0	10	74	7	60	7	3
	South Heights	501	0	0	0	0	0	0	0	0	0	0
	South Lebanon Township	8,622	4	0	0	0	4	129	12	113	4	1
	South Londonderry Township	7,124	3	0	0	0	3	55	5	50	0	0
	South Park Township	13,953	1	0	0	0	1	37	10	23	4	2
	South Pymatuning Township	2,841	0	0	0	0	0	0	0	0	0	0
	South Strabane Township	8,762	18	0	1	5	12	364	21	337	6	0
	Southwestern Regional	17,840	25	0	8	2	15	219	34	175	10	0
	Southwest Greensburg	2,241	3	0	0	0	3	60	5	55	0	0
	Southwest Mercer County Regional	11,421	23	0	3	8	12	130	27	84	19	1
	Southwest Regional	2,180	1	0	0	0	1	0	0	0	0	0
	South Whitehall Township	19,486	30	0	0	14	16	738	66	658	14	2
	South Williamsport	6,064	10	0	0	2	8	146	34	106	6	0
	Spring City	3,410	10	0	2	1	7	110	35	73	2	0
	Springdale	3,507	10	0	0	1	9	28	6	18	4	0
	Springdale Township	1,655	2	0	0	0	2	4	0	3	1	0
	Springettsbury Township	24,663	50	0	6	28	16	1,166	86	1,052	28	10
	Springfield Township, Bucks County	5,099	1	0	0	0	1	48	17	26	5	1
	Springfield Township, Delaware County	22,935	29	0	1	16	12	751	66	652	33	0
	Springfield Township, Montgomery County	19,003	13	0	0	5	8	215	22	181	12	0
	Spring Garden Township	11,876	39	1	0	23	15	392	58	307	27	1
	Spring Township, Berks County	26,659	16	0	2	10	4	345	37	273	35	1
	Spring Township, Centre County	6,720	1	0	0	0	1	81	1	77	3	0
	Spring Township, Snyder County	1,563	0	0	0	0	0	6	1	3	2	0

[1] The FBI does not publish arson data unless it receives data from either the agency or the state for all 12 months of the calendar year.

Table 8. Offenses Known to Law Enforcement, by State and City, 2007 *(Contd.)*

(Number.)

State	City	Population	Violent crime	Murder and non-negligent man-slaughter	Forcible rape	Robbery	Aggravated assault	Property crime	Burglary	Larceny-theft	Motor vehicle theft	Arson[1]
	State College	52,047	43	0	4	15	24	940	104	824	12	11
	St. Clair Boro	3,052	4	1	0	0	3	59	4	55	0	0
	St. Clair Township	1,362	0	0	0	0	0	2	2	0	0	0
	Steelton	5,576	36	0	5	19	12	212	45	153	14	2
	Stewartstown	2,047	2	0	0	2	0	14	2	10	2	0
	St. Marys City	13,614	9	0	2	2	5	248	60	183	5	3
	Stoneboro	1,038	1	0	0	0	1	15	1	14	0	1
	Stonycreek Township	2,959	10	0	0	0	10	46	11	34	1	1
	Strasburg	2,734	0	0	0	0	0	37	0	35	2	0
	Stroud Area Regional	35,211	91	1	9	41	40	1,231	143	1,035	53	9
	Sugarcreek	5,033	5	0	0	0	5	79	2	77	0	0
	Sugarloaf Township, Luzerne County	3,975	3	0	0	3	0	187	5	177	5	1
	Summerhill Township	2,618	1	0	0	0	1	34	4	26	4	0
	Summit Township	2,278	4	0	0	0	4	9	2	7	0	0
	Sunbury	9,855	102	0	14	2	86	259	30	210	19	8
	Susquehanna Regional	6,533	6	0	0	1	5	84	20	59	5	0
	Susquehanna Township, Dauphin County	22,905	41	1	9	20	11	406	50	346	10	2
	Swarthmore	6,148	8	0	0	1	7	82	9	68	5	0
	Swatara Township	22,281	192	0	1	26	165	737	113	603	21	14
	Sweden Township	741	0	0	0	0	0	0	0	0	0	0
	Swissvale	8,811	94	0	0	25	69	260	86	171	3	0
	Swoyersville	7,649	30	0	2	0	28	137	21	107	9	0
	Tamaqua	6,633	8	1	3	0	4	266	23	241	2	2
	Tarentum	4,558	28	0	3	1	24	318	34	269	15	3
	Tatamy	1,106	0	0	0	0	0	12	0	12	0	0
	Telford	4,629	5	0	4	0	1	88	20	63	5	1
	Throop	3,996	5	0	1	0	4	42	7	33	2	0
	Tidioute	732	0	0	0	0	0	11	1	10	0	0
	Tilden Township	3,825	2	0	0	0	2	66	6	58	2	0
	Tinicum Township, Bucks County	4,265	1	0	0	0	1	43	7	35	1	0
	Tinicum Township, Delaware County	4,226	37	0	0	4	33	241	10	205	26	1
	Titusville	5,759	7	0	2	1	4	247	28	210	9	0
	Towamencin Township	17,812	17	0	0	2	15	180	11	162	7	2
	Towanda	2,885	5	0	2	3	0	92	22	65	5	0
	Tredyffrin Township	29,002	22	0	2	4	16	448	61	371	16	1
	Troy	1,479	1	0	0	0	1	23	1	21	1	0
	Tullytown	1,981	7	0	0	1	6	48	6	39	3	1
	Tulpehocken Township	3,588	0	0	0	0	0	14	7	7	0	0
	Tunkhannock	1,801	5	1	1	1	2	26	10	13	3	0
	Tunkhannock Township, Wyoming County	4,332	0	0	0	0	0	63	13	48	2	1
	Turtle Creek	5,569	2	0	0	1	1	4	0	4	0	0
	Ulster Township	1,299	0	0	0	0	0	7	1	6	0	0
	Union Township, Lawrence County	5,102	4	0	0	4	0	138	10	122	6	0
	Upland	2,965	22	0	1	4	17	97	29	64	4	0
	Upper Allen Township	17,802	0	0	0	0	0	1	1	0	0	0
	Upper Chichester Township	17,623	63	1	2	20	40	510	67	402	41	7
	Upper Darby Township	79,020	326	5	18	207	96	2,355	279	1,876	200	9
	Upper Dublin Township	26,138	56	0	5	4	47	304	29	258	17	0
	Upper Gwynedd Township	15,870	9	0	2	2	5	151	22	126	3	4
	Upper Leacock Township	8,449	9	0	1	3	5	122	29	85	8	0
	Upper Makefield Township	8,668	7	0	0	0	7	55	18	37	0	0
	Upper Merion Township	26,680	24	0	2	10	12	1,588	104	1,426	58	1
	Upper Moreland Township	24,398	25	0	0	7	18	458	65	365	28	1
	Upper Nazareth Township	5,669	5	0	0	0	5	77	2	75	0	0
	Upper Perkiomen	6,464	16	0	0	2	14	165	23	126	16	0
	Upper Pottsgrove Township	5,161	8	0	0	1	7	71	13	51	7	0
	Upper Providence Township, Delaware County	11,232	3	0	0	0	3	71	12	57	2	1
	Upper Providence Township, Montgomery County	19,373	2	0	1	0	1	290	42	237	11	0
	Upper Saucon Township	14,725	7	0	1	1	5	218	19	195	4	0
	Upper Southampton Township	15,404	13	0	0	3	10	198	46	137	15	0
	Upper St. Clair Township	18,927	3	0	1	1	1	125	9	111	5	0
	Upper Uwchlan Township	10,022	1	0	0	0	1	86	14	69	3	0

[1] The FBI does not publish arson data unless it receives data from either the agency or the state for all 12 months of the calendar year.

Table 8. Offenses Known to Law Enforcement, by State and City, 2007 (Contd.)

(Number.)

State	City	Population	Violent crime	Murder and non-negligent manslaughter	Forcible rape	Robbery	Aggravated assault	Property crime	Burglary	Larceny-theft	Motor vehicle theft	Arson[1]
	Upper Yoder Township	5,580	2	0	0	1	1	20	1	19	0	0
	Uwchlan Township	18,689	29	0	1	2	26	244	43	193	8	15
	Valley Township	6,445	14	0	0	1	13	19	4	11	4	0
	Vandergrift	5,088	16	0	1	1	14	10	4	6	0	0
	Vandling	705	0	0	0	0	0	0	0	0	0	0
	Vernon Township	5,398	18	0	0	1	17	67	10	55	2	8
	Verona	2,857	7	0	0	3	4	140	14	114	12	0
	Walnutport	2,170	0	0	0	0	0	55	4	51	0	0
	Warminster Township	33,777	47	2	7	18	20	618	116	448	54	3
	Warren	9,519	172	0	2	1	169	242	34	207	1	0
	Warrington Township	23,208	27	0	4	2	21	324	48	270	6	1
	Warwick Township, Bucks County	15,086	2	0	0	1	1	121	22	94	5	1
	Warwick Township, Lancaster County	17,362	7	0	0	2	5	79	13	61	5	0
	Washington, Washington County	14,710	103	1	21	46	35	689	120	471	98	4
	Washington Township, Fayette County	4,186	10	0	0	0	10	45	10	34	1	0
	Washington Township, Franklin County	11,942	12	0	2	5	5	321	43	266	12	5
	Washington Township, Northampton County	4,898	7	0	0	0	7	75	26	43	6	1
	Washington Township, Westmoreland County	7,476	5	0	0	2	3	49	11	35	3	0
	Watsontown	2,100	10	0	0	1	9	61	4	55	2	1
	Waynesburg	4,169	4	0	0	0	4	79	12	67	0	1
	Weatherly	2,608	22	0	0	1	21	87	20	65	2	0
	Wellsboro	3,293	5	0	0	0	5	42	7	35	0	0
	Wernersville	2,504	2	0	0	2	0	45	7	36	2	0
	West Brandywine Township	7,756	2	0	0	0	2	64	11	47	6	1
	West Caln Township	8,237	9	0	0	0	9	53	12	39	2	0
	West Chester	18,276	114	1	18	37	58	429	75	320	34	1
	West Cocalico Township	7,150	1	0	1	0	0	38	9	25	4	1
	West Cornwall Township	1,983	1	0	0	1	0	6	1	4	1	0
	West Deer Township	12,002	15	0	0	0	15	114	33	74	7	0
	West Earl Township	7,465	2	0	0	2	0	97	15	80	2	2
	Westfall Township	2,933	20	0	2	1	17	164	8	145	11	0
	West Goshen Township	21,255	45	2	2	6	35	468	60	390	18	2
	West Hazleton	3,334	6	0	0	3	3	68	27	35	6	0
	West Hempfield Township	16,026	14	0	0	9	5	237	36	189	12	0
	West Homestead	2,008	39	0	1	12	26	63	17	38	8	0
	West Lampeter Township	15,539	8	0	1	4	3	184	37	135	12	0
	West Lebanon Township	840	9	0	0	2	7	99	1	97	1	0
	West Manchester Township	18,181	46	0	2	18	26	688	67	595	26	4
	West Manheim Township	7,178	7	1	1	1	4	56	4	43	9	0
	West Mead Township	5,119	0	0	0	0	0	0	0	0	0	0
	West Norriton Township	14,642	41	0	3	13	25	340	22	300	18	0
	West Nottingham Township	2,799	0	0	0	0	0	0	0	0	0	0
	West Penn Township	4,233	0	0	0	0	0	0	0	0	0	0
	West Pikeland Township	4,113	7	0	0	0	7	32	9	23	0	1
	West Pike Run	1,848	0	0	0	0	0	9	1	8	0	1
	West Pittston	4,883	7	0	0	0	7	95	19	73	3	1
	West Reading	4,086	17	0	0	2	15	182	28	136	18	0
	West Sadsbury Township	2,512	6	0	2	0	4	75	0	73	2	0
	West Salem Township	3,389	1	0	0	0	1	28	8	18	2	0
	West Shore Regional	6,619	6	0	0	3	3	9	2	6	1	0
	Westtown-East Goshen Regional	31,691	49	0	3	4	42	273	35	229	9	2
	West View	6,704	9	0	0	1	8	179	14	158	7	4
	West Vincent Township	4,180	1	0	0	0	1	39	13	26	0	0
	West Whiteland Township	18,480	11	1	3	3	4	516	28	476	12	0
	West Wyoming	2,698	0	0	0	0	0	43	5	37	1	0
	West York	4,219	10	0	0	9	1	81	14	62	5	0
	Whitaker Borough	1,224	6	0	0	4	2	53	13	34	6	0
	Whitehall	13,439	13	0	2	4	7	60	9	50	1	2
	Whitehall Township	26,917	40	0	3	23	14	1,327	87	1,205	35	2
	Whitemarsh Township	17,422	20	0	3	6	11	261	43	213	5	2
	Whitpain Township	18,799	24	1	3	3	17	258	47	195	16	1
	Wiconisco Township	1,102	0	0	0	0	0	4	1	3	0	0
	Wilkes-Barre	41,050	193	3	19	110	61	1,683	373	1,194	116	13
	Wilkes-Barre Township	3,060	17	0	0	10	7	750	18	719	13	2
	Wilkinsburg	17,583	193	2	6	71	114	595	220	262	113	10
	Wilkins Township	6,453	9	0	0	4	5	156	22	126	8	0

[1] The FBI does not publish arson data unless it receives data from either the agency or the state for all 12 months of the calendar year.

Table 8. Offenses Known to Law Enforcement, by State and City, 2007 *(Contd.)*

(Number.)

State	City	Population	Violent crime	Murder and non-negligent man-slaughter	Forcible rape	Robbery	Aggravated assault	Property crime	Burglary	Larceny-theft	Motor vehicle theft	Arson[1]
	Williamsburg	1,260	1	0	1	0	0	27	0	26	1	0
	Williamsport	29,701	98	1	10	58	29	1,316	262	970	84	16
	Willistown Township	10,861	8	0	1	0	7	120	24	95	1	0
	Windber	4,043	10	0	0	2	8	36	7	24	5	2
	Wind Gap	2,815	5	0	0	3	2	66	4	59	3	0
	Womelsdorf	2,823	8	0	0	2	6	42	8	34	0	1
	Wright Township	5,834	0	0	0	0	0	58	5	52	1	0
	Wyoming	3,020	3	0	1	1	1	100	11	89	0	0
	Wyomissing	10,464	8	0	0	5	3	384	27	325	32	0
	Yardley	2,532	2	0	0	1	1	14	0	13	1	0
	Yeadon	11,440	93	0	3	33	57	367	80	227	60	1
	York	40,339	440	11	33	293	103	2,125	499	1,338	288	17
	York Area Regional	57,252	111	0	13	15	83	775	125	619	31	3
	Youngsville	1,689	2	0	0	0	2	27	2	24	1	1
	Zelienople	4,008	16	0	0	1	15	61	3	55	3	0
RHODE ISLAND	Barrington	16,414	3	0	1	1	1	249	35	207	7	4
	Burrillville	16,392	17	1	6	0	10	135	37	86	12	7
	Central Falls	18,818	114	1	17	39	57	430	124	202	104	4
	Charlestown	8,131	6	0	1	0	5	98	29	63	6	3
	Coventry	34,353	30	0	5	2	23	434	120	289	25	0
	Cranston	80,724	111	0	8	42	61	2,041	341	1,481	219	13
	East Greenwich	13,338	5	0	1	1	3	160	36	116	8	0
	East Providence	48,668	59	0	13	10	36	833	126	648	59	25
	Foster	4,467	3	0	0	1	2	47	12	29	6	0
	Glocester	10,498	2	0	1	0	1	58	9	44	5	2
	Hopkinton	7,976	11	0	1	2	8	106	23	74	9	2
	Jamestown	5,484	2	0	0	0	2	153	19	125	9	1
	Johnston	28,585	25	0	2	9	14	594	106	429	59	4
	Lincoln	21,855	21	0	3	9	9	488	56	394	38	1
	Little Compton	3,510	1	0	0	0	1	62	18	44	0	0
	Middletown	16,278	14	0	2	4	8	340	53	272	15	6
	Narragansett	16,552	12	0	0	2	10	341	88	244	9	1
	Newport	24,192	117	0	15	22	80	1,100	267	784	49	34
	New Shoreham	1,023	0	0	0	0	0	65	8	50	7	0
	North Kingstown	26,475	25	0	7	0	18	437	81	338	18	6
	North Providence	32,685	34	1	5	9	19	504	104	329	71	2
	North Smithfield	11,183	4	0	0	1	3	140	32	98	10	0
	Portsmouth	16,853	13	0	3	0	10	231	32	184	15	0
	Providence[7]	173,719	973	11	43	370	549	8,262	1,636	5,063	1,563	26
	Scituate	10,814	0	0	0	0	0	121	35	77	9	1
	Smithfield	21,495	10	0	3	0	7	282	43	220	19	4
	South Kingstown	29,172	15	0	5	2	8	361	82	264	15	3
	Tiverton	15,074	13	0	2	2	9	342	101	212	29	2
	Warren	11,089	22	0	3	3	16	193	27	162	4	0
	Westerly	23,197	30	0	4	2	24	447	72	340	35	1
	West Greenwich	6,371	3	0	0	1	2	79	14	59	6	2
	West Warwick	29,293	55	0	11	6	38	566	98	428	40	3
SOUTH CAROLINA	Abbeville	5,659	93	1	1	2	89	203	65	130	8	1
	Aiken	29,256	159	2	13	26	118	1,284	227	987	70	1
	Allendale	3,781	83	1	0	6	76	161	72	83	6	0
	Anderson	26,326	280	1	15	43	221	1,652	361	1,161	130	8
	Andrews	3,017	37	1	2	2	32	178	31	138	9	1
	Atlantic Beach	385	23	0	2	8	13	40	14	20	6	0
	Aynor	580	31	0	0	0	31	42	3	35	4	0
	Bamberg	3,480	19	0	1	3	15	166	37	123	6	5
	Barnwell	4,847	55	0	2	4	49	327	91	229	7	2
	Batesburg-Leesville	5,620	67	0	3	3	61	323	55	239	29	1
	Beaufort	11,960	146	0	2	35	109	852	140	669	43	1
	Belton	4,607	16	0	0	4	12	182	26	137	19	0
	Bennettsville	10,898	186	1	4	14	167	679	131	525	23	2
	Bethune	367	0	0	0	0	0	5	2	2	1	0
	Bishopville	3,945	23	0	0	5	18	288	60	213	15	1
	Blacksburg	1,899	24	0	0	4	20	178	32	138	8	1
	Blackville	2,888	11	0	0	3	8	57	21	36	0	0
	Bluffton	3,791	51	0	0	10	41	348	52	279	17	4
	Bonneau	338	2	0	0	0	2	11	1	8	2	0
	Bowman	1,163	10	1	0	0	9	25	11	11	3	0
	Branchville	1,037	0	0	0	0	0	0	0	0	0	0
	Brunson	576	0	0	0	0	0	0	0	0	0	0
	Burnettown	2,670	8	0	1	0	7	18	2	15	1	0
	Calhoun Falls	2,231	10	0	2	1	7	82	14	68	0	0
	Camden	7,071	89	1	4	18	66	516	168	323	25	1
	Cameron	416	0	0	0	0	0	0	0	0	0	0

[1] The FBI does not publish arson data unless it receives data from either the agency or the state for all 12 months of the calendar year.

Table 8. Offenses Known to Law Enforcement, by State and City, 2007 *(Contd.)*

(Number.)

State	City	Population	Violent crime	Murder and non-negligent man-slaughter	Forcible rape	Robbery	Aggravated assault	Property crime	Burglary	Larceny-theft	Motor vehicle theft	Arson[1]
	Campobello	584	0	0	0	0	0	0	0	0	0	0
	Cayce	12,659	153	0	13	21	119	745	140	554	51	2
	Central	4,147	16	0	2	3	11	150	34	110	6	0
	Chapin	698	2	0	2	0	0	48	4	43	1	0
	Charleston	109,382	909	15	56	269	569	4,246	746	3,056	444	11
	Cheraw	5,417	42	0	1	9	32	398	39	346	13	2
	Chesnee	1,057	21	0	1	4	16	75	9	62	4	0
	Chester	6,074	97	0	1	12	84	298	92	184	22	2
	Chesterfield	1,321	14	0	0	8	6	57	10	45	2	0
	Clemson	12,532	30	0	8	5	17	334	91	225	18	0
	Clinton	9,018	130	4	6	21	99	486	95	364	27	2
	Clio	740	3	2	0	0	1	16	4	12	0	0
	Clover	4,493	166	0	3	6	157	211	36	166	9	3
	Columbia	120,549	1,542	16	67	345	1,114	6,963	1,267	5,066	630	24
	Conway	14,285	219	1	7	54	157	1,412	310	1,012	90	5
	Cottageville	699	1	0	0	0	1	25	2	18	5	0
	Coward	674	0	0	0	0	0	7	2	3	2	0
	Cowpens	2,364	12	0	0	3	9	114	36	70	8	0
	Darlington	6,525	149	1	4	16	128	650	105	530	15	2
	Denmark	3,052	23	1	1	5	16	96	32	61	3	0
	Due West	1,286	2	0	0	0	2	16	2	13	1	0
	Duncan	3,020	19	0	2	1	16	133	32	91	10	0
	Easley	19,372	103	1	6	20	76	939	126	749	64	3
	Eastover	767	3	0	0	0	3	8	5	3	0	1
	Edgefield	4,529	16	2	0	1	13	58	11	39	8	1
	Edisto Beach	724	1	0	0	0	1	60	12	44	4	0
	Ehrhardt	561	1	0	0	0	1	1	0	0	1	0
	Elgin	1,080	4	0	1	0	3	52	6	45	1	0
	Elloree	698	1	0	0	0	1	10	0	8	2	0
	Estill	2,381	34	0	1	4	29	133	49	70	14	0
	Eutawville	329	4	0	0	0	4	19	3	11	5	0
	Fairfax	3,167	22	1	4	7	10	41	17	21	3	1
	Florence	31,377	552	5	31	117	399	2,757	586	2,000	171	30
	Folly Beach	2,339	6	0	0	2	4	203	20	168	15	1
	Forest Acres	9,818	74	0	3	24	47	680	104	540	36	7
	Fort Lawn	816	14	0	1	1	12	72	18	50	4	0
	Fort Mill	8,709	61	2	0	4	55	256	36	204	16	5
	Fountain Inn	7,261	44	0	2	11	31	178	28	141	9	0
	Gaffney	12,945	158	2	8	39	109	965	218	703	44	3
	Gaston	1,405	0	0	0	0	0	5	2	3	0	0
	Georgetown	8,668	149	2	5	18	124	669	78	562	29	1
	Goose Creek	32,139	85	0	1	26	58	917	150	711	56	5
	Great Falls	2,052	33	0	1	5	27	145	30	110	5	1
	Greeleyville	410	0	0	0	0	0	14	5	6	3	0
	Greenville	57,595	659	8	26	172	453	3,810	643	2,805	362	5
	Greenwood	22,428	300	3	11	35	251	1,554	373	1,112	69	8
	Greer	23,224	69	1	4	25	39	812	185	543	84	2
	Hampton	2,780	26	2	2	4	18	170	42	126	2	0
	Hanahan	13,983	91	4	4	28	55	622	128	434	60	2
	Hardeeville	1,857	28	0	3	8	17	259	30	213	16	2
	Harleyville	694	4	0	1	1	2	9	4	4	1	0
	Hartsville	7,460	234	2	13	41	178	1,174	240	906	28	9
	Hemingway	513	6	0	0	0	6	51	11	39	1	0
	Holly Hill	1,346	6	0	0	3	3	54	19	32	3	0
	Honea Path	3,628	39	0	2	3	34	235	69	150	16	2
	Inman	1,942	13	0	1	3	9	104	19	76	9	0
	Irmo	11,364	42	0	5	10	27	366	52	298	16	1
	Isle of Palms	4,653	4	0	2	0	2	210	22	179	9	0
	Iva	1,188	0	0	0	0	0	13	1	12	0	0
	Jackson	1,650	5	0	1	0	4	57	20	30	7	0
	Jamestown	96	0	0	0	0	0	4	3	1	0	0
	Johnsonville	1,461	4	0	0	0	4	84	11	70	3	0
	Johnston	2,339	18	0	1	3	14	92	22	63	7	0
	Jonesville	914	1	0	0	0	1	34	10	24	0	0
	Kingstree	3,317	21	0	0	6	15	244	34	202	8	1
	Lake City	6,693	94	2	8	15	69	671	126	510	35	2
	Lake View	789	8	0	0	4	4	44	20	21	3	0
	Lamar	1,001	17	0	0	1	16	68	18	45	5	2
	Lancaster	8,393	166	1	7	23	135	733	207	484	42	2
	Landrum	2,554	4	0	0	1	3	67	11	52	4	0
	Lane	533	0	0	0	0	0	0	0	0	0	0
	Latta	1,501	60	0	1	10	49	64	6	52	6	0
	Laurens	9,841	148	2	3	19	124	550	120	405	25	2
	Lexington	14,715	57	0	4	4	49	578	46	518	14	1

[1] The FBI does not publish arson data unless it receives data from either the agency or the state for all 12 months of the calendar year.

Table 8.   Offenses Known to Law Enforcement, by State and City, 2007 *(Contd.)*

(Number.)

State	City	Population	Violent crime	Murder and non-negligent man-slaughter	Forcible rape	Robbery	Aggravated assault	Property crime	Burglary	Larceny-theft	Motor vehicle theft	Arson[1]
	Liberty	3,034	8	0	1	1	6	124	16	103	5	0
	Lincolnville	840	0	0	0	0	0	0	0	0	0	0
	Loris	2,322	13	0	0	4	9	142	34	102	6	0
	Lyman	2,812	10	0	1	2	7	124	16	101	7	0
	Lynchburg	579	1	0	0	0	1	6	4	2	0	0
	Manning	4,016	51	0	1	12	38	275	65	195	15	0
	Marion	6,949	123	3	1	33	86	515	116	369	30	3
	Mauldin	20,494	92	1	5	15	71	545	70	427	48	5
	McBee	713	3	0	1	0	2	18	6	12	0	0
	McColl	2,368	21	0	0	2	19	163	32	125	6	6
	McCormick	2,712	23	0	0	5	18	72	8	57	7	1
	Moncks Corner	6,645	41	0	4	10	27	359	58	270	31	2
	Mount Pleasant	60,746	224	1	7	48	168	1,400	201	1,127	72	3
	Mullins	4,820	68	1	3	15	49	493	97	374	22	1
	Myrtle Beach	29,361	506	2	49	222	233	5,488	1,011	3,998	479	10
	Newberry	10,927	55	0	3	9	43	431	48	376	7	0
	New Ellenton	2,251	11	0	2	3	6	72	23	41	8	0
	Nichols	404	1	0	0	0	1	11	5	5	1	0
	Ninety Six	1,920	13	0	0	0	13	28	4	22	2	1
	North	778	6	1	0	2	3	28	8	17	3	1
	North Augusta	20,270	53	0	7	26	20	950	111	742	97	10
	North Charleston	88,431	1,561	26	92	624	819	6,768	1,195	4,660	913	34
	North Myrtle Beach	15,577	57	0	3	17	37	1,576	291	1,264	21	0
	Norway	363	4	0	0	0	4	21	4	17	0	0
	Orangeburg	13,674	87	0	4	28	55	789	162	558	69	2
	Pacolet	2,756	11	0	1	4	6	69	12	54	3	0
	Pageland	2,539	59	4	2	3	50	193	26	162	5	0
	Pamplico	1,152	6	0	0	1	5	29	15	11	3	1
	Pawleys Island	143	0	0	0	0	0	13	0	12	1	0
	Pelion	599	3	0	0	0	3	46	9	37	0	0
	Pickens	2,990	20	0	0	3	17	171	28	139	4	1
	Pine Ridge	1,760	5	0	0	1	4	51	16	33	2	0
	Port Royal	9,959	20	1	1	10	8	250	31	210	9	0
	Prosperity	1,072	12	0	0	0	12	45	15	29	1	0
	Ridgeland	2,640	37	1	2	11	23	142	18	115	9	1
	Ridgeville	2,075	1	0	0	1	0	10	1	8	1	0
	Rock Hill	63,388	798	3	20	124	651	2,921	503	2,208	210	25
	Salem	132	0	0	0	0	0	0	0	0	0	0
	Salley	415	1	0	0	0	1	10	3	6	1	0
	Saluda	2,979	64	1	0	5	58	84	5	65	14	1
	Santee	714	19	0	0	6	13	121	27	89	5	0
	Scranton	998	0	0	0	0	0	3	1	2	0	0
	Seneca	8,076	70	0	3	8	59	541	67	441	33	1
	Simpsonville	16,211	177	0	9	17	151	818	94	675	49	3
	Society Hill	696	3	0	0	2	1	15	4	8	3	0
	South Congaree	2,413	8	0	0	1	7	88	22	59	7	0
	Spartanburg	38,388	829	6	22	219	582	3,610	919	2,422	269	27
	Springdale	2,956	10	0	0	4	6	99	15	79	5	0
	Springfield	483	0	0	0	0	0	2	1	1	0	0
	St. George	2,124	21	0	0	4	17	122	36	75	11	1
	St. Matthews	1,995	33	0	1	1	31	88	18	63	7	1
	St. Stephen	1,702	8	0	1	2	5	91	20	62	9	0
	Sullivans Island	1,868	5	0	1	2	2	47	6	40	1	0
	Summerton	1,047	21	0	0	6	15	72	16	52	4	0
	Summerville	43,985	147	2	13	36	96	1,470	154	1,212	104	2
	Sumter	38,955	531	4	9	101	417	2,568	683	1,743	142	11
	Surfside Beach	4,846	27	0	2	8	17	354	75	255	24	0
	Swansea	784	15	0	0	2	13	45	6	35	4	0
	Tega Cay	4,612	4	0	0	0	4	44	14	30	0	0
	Timmonsville	2,384	48	0	2	8	38	176	63	104	9	2
	Travelers Rest	4,396	18	0	0	8	10	219	22	188	9	1
	Turbeville	721	4	0	0	0	4	28	11	13	4	0
	Union	8,167	103	1	3	12	87	375	88	275	12	6
	Vance	199	3	0	0	1	2	11	2	6	3	1
	Varnville	2,035	0	0	0	0	0	0	0	0	0	0
	Wagener	878	9	0	1	0	8	31	5	22	4	0
	Walhalla	3,689	31	0	2	7	22	132	26	102	4	0
	Walterboro	5,601	129	3	5	37	84	603	99	463	41	2
	Ware Shoals	2,359	11	0	0	0	11	110	23	80	7	0
	Wellford	2,315	15	1	3	3	8	85	12	67	6	1
	West Columbia	13,729	167	0	11	53	103	885	139	698	48	3
	Westminster	2,675	27	0	0	9	18	94	25	66	3	1
	West Pelzer	905	2	0	0	1	1	9	3	6	0	0
	Whitmire	1,543	4	0	1	0	3	44	6	38	0	0

[1] The FBI does not publish arson data unless it receives data from either the agency or the state for all 12 months of the calendar year.

Table 8. Offenses Known to Law Enforcement, by State and City, 2007 *(Contd.)*

(Number.)

State	City	Population	Violent crime	Murder and non-negligent man-slaughter	Forcible rape	Robbery	Aggravated assault	Property crime	Burglary	Larceny-theft	Motor vehicle theft	Arson[1]
	Williamston	3,914	24	0	1	12	11	141	23	109	9	5
	Williston	3,239	18	1	0	4	13	146	44	100	2	1
	Winnsboro	3,637	45	0	4	4	37	244	29	211	4	1
	Woodruff	4,076	42	0	6	3	33	220	46	168	6	1
	Yemassee	857	4	0	0	1	3	15	3	11	1	0
	York	7,537	108	1	5	12	90	325	61	239	25	1
SOUTH DAKOTA	Aberdeen	23,992	30	0	13	1	16	498	80	389	29	1
	Avon	536	0	0	0	0	0	0	0	0	0	0
	Bonesteel	264	0	0	0	0	0	0	0	0	0	0
	Box Elder	3,112	12	0	8	0	4	69	31	36	2	0
	Brandon	7,956	2	0	0	0	2	59	10	49	0	0
	Bridgewater	579	0	0	0	0	0	0	0	0	0	0
	Burke	590	0	0	0	0	0	0	0	0	0	0
	Canton	3,237	7	0	0	0	7	33	10	22	1	1
	Centerville	856	0	0	0	0	0	0	0	0	0	0
	Clark	1,128	0	0	0	0	0	0	0	0	0	0
	Colman	553	0	0	0	0	0	1	0	1	0	0
	Corsica	601	0	0	0	0	0	0	0	0	0	0
	Deadwood	1,269	2	0	0	1	1	43	1	41	1	0
	Delmont	229	0	0	0	0	0	0	0	0	0	0
	Eagle Butte	950	1	0	0	0	1	17	2	15	0	0
	Estelline	668	1	0	0	0	1	11	1	9	1	0
	Eureka	952	0	0	0	0	0	0	0	0	0	0
	Freeman	1,178	0	0	0	0	0	0	0	0	0	0
	Gettysburg	1,130	0	0	0	0	0	2	0	2	0	0
	Hermosa	360	0	0	0	0	0	0	0	0	0	0
	Hot Springs	4,095	1	0	0	0	1	28	15	13	0	0
	Hoven	421	0	0	0	0	0	0	0	0	0	0
	Irene	403	0	0	0	0	0	2	0	2	0	0
	Jefferson	593	0	0	0	0	0	0	0	0	0	0
	Kadoka	673	1	0	0	0	1	3	3	0	0	0
	Kimball	678	0	0	0	0	0	0	0	0	0	0
	Lead	2,837	6	0	0	0	6	20	0	19	1	0
	Leola	394	0	0	0	0	0	0	0	0	0	0
	Madison	6,221	7	0	0	0	7	92	9	82	1	0
	Martin	1,029	4	0	1	0	3	18	10	8	0	0
	McIntosh	212	0	0	0	0	0	0	0	0	0	0
	McLaughlin[4]	755		0	0	1		16	11	4	1	1
	Miller	1,343	0	0	0	0	0	14	5	8	1	0
	Mitchell	14,894	33	0	3	2	28	487	72	384	31	9
	Mobridge	3,188	5	0	0	0	5	97	6	85	6	0
	New Effington	225	0	0	0	0	0	0	0	0	0	0
	North Sioux City	2,545	0	0	0	0	0	1	0	1	0	0
	Parkston	1,506	0	0	0	0	0	12	7	5	0	1
	Pierre	14,124	34	0	9	1	24	547	80	444	23	5
	Rapid City	63,162	294	4	69	34	187	2,386	443	1,819	124	17
	Rosholt	437	0	0	0	0	0	0	0	0	0	0
	Scotland	816	0	0	0	0	0	0	0	0	0	0
	Sioux Falls	144,985	381	2	95	44	240	3,780	631	2,881	268	39
	Spearfish	9,796	9	0	3	0	6	338	26	308	4	0
	Springfield	1,510	0	0	0	0	0	0	0	0	0	0
	Sturgis	6,090	13	0	1	1	11	154	17	125	12	0
	Tripp	643	0	0	0	0	0	1	1	0	0	0
	Tyndall	1,135	0	0	0	0	0	0	0	0	0	0
	Vermillion	9,810	9	0	1	0	8	86	5	80	1	0
	Viborg	793	4	0	0	0	4	0	0	0	0	0
	Wagner	1,596	4	0	0	0	4	21	3	12	6	0
	Watertown	20,568	37	0	8	2	27	617	76	509	32	1
	Whitewood	810	2	0	1	0	1	7	0	5	2	0
	Wilmot	524	0	0	0	0	0	0	0	0	0	0
	Winner	2,892	4	0	0	0	4	58	3	51	4	0
	Yankton	13,805	26	1	4	4	17	344	54	280	10	0
TENNESSEE	Adamsville	2,122	5	0	1	0	4	34	3	24	7	0
	Alamo	2,349	9	0	0	0	9	48	11	33	4	1
	Alcoa	8,544	107	0	7	11	89	528	96	401	31	6
	Alexandria	870	2	0	1	0	1	16	6	9	1	0
	Algood	3,293	20	1	1	2	16	115	9	106	0	0
	Ardmore	1,142	9	0	0	2	7	34	4	27	3	0
	Ashland City	4,696	11	0	1	0	10	249	51	189	9	2
	Athens	14,183	202	2	10	29	161	1,245	280	880	85	4
	Atoka	6,868	17	0	0	2	15	174	23	147	4	2
	Baileyton	501	3	0	0	2	1	17	3	14	0	0
	Baneberry	459	0	0	0	0	0	0	0	0	0	0
	Bartlett	47,333	150	2	7	23	118	1,137	213	855	69	3

[1] The FBI does not publish arson data unless it receives data from either the agency or the state for all 12 months of the calendar year.

[4] It was determined that the agency did not follow national Uniform Crime Reporting (UCR) Program guidelines for reporting an offense. Consequently, this figure is not included in this table.

Table 8.   Offenses Known to Law Enforcement, by State and City, 2007 *(Contd.)*

(Number.)

State	City	Population	Violent crime	Murder and non-negligent man-slaughter	Forcible rape	Robbery	Aggravated assault	Property crime	Burglary	Larceny-theft	Motor vehicle theft	Arson[1]
	Baxter	1,367	2	0	0	0	2	31	6	24	1	0
	Bean Station	3,043	20	1	3	1	15	154	46	103	5	1
	Belle Meade	3,170	1	0	0	0	1	37	17	19	1	0
	Bells	2,275	12	0	0	1	11	82	33	46	3	2
	Benton	1,080	8	0	0	1	7	47	8	37	2	1
	Berry Hill	690	10	0	0	8	2	105	16	84	5	0
	Bethel Springs	786	1	0	0	0	1	7	3	4	0	0
	Big Sandy	515	5	0	0	0	5	2	1	1	0	0
	Blaine	1,751	3	0	0	1	2	36	7	24	5	0
	Bluff City	1,629	9	0	0	1	8	59	10	46	3	0
	Bradford	1,063	2	0	0	0	2	6	0	5	1	0
	Brentwood	35,019	27	0	4	5	18	511	82	420	9	1
	Brighton	2,664	16	0	0	0	16	48	13	33	2	0
	Bristol	25,346	117	0	16	9	92	1,436	207	1,129	100	6
	Brownsville	10,539	148	0	5	20	123	610	214	363	33	3
	Bruceton	1,469	7	0	0	2	5	24	9	14	1	0
	Burns	1,411	3	0	0	0	3	40	16	19	5	0
	Calhoun	522	6	0	0	0	6	28	7	18	3	0
	Camden	3,693	26	0	1	0	25	189	27	160	2	2
	Carthage	2,234	18	1	0	1	16	81	19	57	5	0
	Caryville	2,400	16	0	2	2	12	103	29	64	10	0
	Celina	1,380	8	0	0	0	8	31	7	23	1	0
	Centerville	4,018	5	0	1	0	4	99	34	62	3	0
	Chapel Hill	1,285	4	0	0	0	4	27	9	18	0	0
	Charleston	654	4	0	0	0	4	8	1	6	1	0
	Chattanooga	155,043	2,009	11	102	524	1,372	12,484	2,384	9,072	1,028	14
	Church Hill	6,644	14	0	0	1	13	155	44	97	14	1
	Clarksburg	374	0	0	0	0	0	2	0	2	0	0
	Clarksville	114,582	992	9	65	159	759	4,751	1,520	2,907	324	22
	Cleveland	38,808	430	1	24	48	357	2,356	465	1,769	122	13
	Clifton	2,684	7	0	0	0	7	15	8	6	1	0
	Clinton	9,516	54	0	1	8	45	463	101	330	32	3
	Collegedale	7,423	19	0	2	3	14	242	20	218	4	0
	Collierville	39,569	59	0	1	12	46	821	129	654	38	4
	Collinwood	1,038	2	0	0	0	2	12	2	9	1	2
	Columbia	33,897	486	5	20	78	383	1,820	384	1,316	120	11
	Cookeville	28,691	127	1	13	28	85	1,715	335	1,281	99	2
	Coopertown	3,324	6	0	1	0	5	51	19	23	9	0
	Copperhill	465	2	0	0	2	0	14	3	10	1	0
	Cornersville	948	0	0	0	0	0	4	1	3	0	0
	Covington	9,193	127	1	3	16	107	502	114	367	21	0
	Cowan	1,758	5	0	0	0	5	42	13	24	5	1
	Cross Plains	1,602	0	0	0	0	0	40	10	26	4	0
	Crossville	11,111	123	0	15	11	97	940	228	656	56	6
	Crump	1,457	22	0	0	2	20	85	30	52	3	2
	Cumberland City	321	0	0	0	0	0	15	7	7	1	0
	Cumberland Gap	205	0	0	0	0	0	9	1	8	0	0
	Dandridge	2,497	13	0	1	0	12	160	8	151	1	0
	Dayton	6,686	32	0	1	7	24	325	50	265	10	1
	Decatur	1,468	5	0	0	2	3	64	9	53	2	0
	Decaturville	825	0	0	0	0	0	6	5	1	0	0
	Decherd	2,164	10	0	0	2	8	99	27	70	2	0
	Dickson	13,171	117	1	9	19	88	791	146	554	91	2
	Dover	1,550	2	0	0	0	2	18	2	15	1	0
	Dresden	2,629	6	0	0	0	6	76	16	50	10	1
	Dunlap	4,891	14	0	1	1	12	140	18	109	13	0
	Dyer	2,422	3	1	0	0	2	29	6	20	3	1
	Dyersburg	17,391	203	5	17	28	153	1,454	366	1,012	76	6
	Eagleville	472	0	0	0	0	0	0	0	0	0	0
	East Ridge	19,641	192	1	8	35	148	1,289	333	875	81	4
	Elizabethton	13,917	78	0	5	3	70	866	169	648	49	8
	Elkton	500	2	0	0	0	2	14	10	3	1	0
	Englewood	1,722	15	0	0	1	14	73	11	52	10	2
	Erin	1,453	11	0	0	1	10	45	13	26	6	0
	Erwin	5,802	12	1	1	2	8	154	26	127	1	0
	Estill Springs	2,285	4	0	0	0	4	38	7	26	5	0
	Ethridge	555	2	0	0	1	1	13	2	9	2	0
	Etowah	3,775	26	0	0	2	24	257	47	195	15	0
	Fairview	7,712	18	0	1	1	16	160	43	104	13	0
	Fayetteville	7,104	93	0	2	9	82	353	72	261	20	5
	Franklin	57,489	106	2	13	18	73	1,024	125	849	50	5
	Friendship	602	3	0	0	0	3	6	2	2	2	0
	Gadsden	547	2	0	0	0	2	6	0	6	0	0
	Gainesboro	845	1	0	0	0	1	41	5	33	3	1

[1] The FBI does not publish arson data unless it receives data from either the agency or the state for all 12 months of the calendar year.

Table 8. Offenses Known to Law Enforcement, by State and City, 2007 *(Contd.)*

(Number.)

State	City	Population	Violent crime	Murder and non-negligent man-slaughter	Forcible rape	Robbery	Aggravated assault	Property crime	Burglary	Larceny-theft	Motor vehicle theft	Arson[1]
	Gallatin	28,419	104	1	5	13	85	576	79	471	26	3
	Gallaway	715	13	0	0	1	12	31	5	21	5	0
	Gates	852	2	0	0	0	2	10	6	4	0	0
	Gatlinburg	5,165	25	0	3	2	20	451	176	258	17	4
	Gibson	406	4	0	0	0	4	16	1	12	3	0
	Gleason	1,402	11	0	0	0	11	33	12	20	1	0
	Goodlettsville	15,854	124	1	5	36	82	962	145	741	76	1
	Gordonsville	1,320	10	0	1	0	9	33	5	28	0	0
	Grand Junction	312	5	0	0	2	3	15	3	11	1	0
	Graysville	1,438	10	0	0	0	10	37	5	27	5	0
	Greenbrier	6,434	29	0	0	3	26	142	39	94	9	1
	Greeneville	15,558	70	0	5	22	43	855	172	637	46	4
	Greenfield	2,028	6	0	0	0	6	30	2	24	4	0
	Halls	2,201	13	0	0	2	11	46	27	15	4	0
	Harriman	6,714	35	0	1	7	27	362	60	281	21	8
	Henderson	6,290	29	1	1	1	26	233	38	179	16	1
	Hendersonville	46,989	163	1	14	19	129	1,236	197	955	84	6
	Henning	1,290	13	0	1	0	12	35	18	12	5	1
	Henry	545	4	0	0	1	3	15	3	12	0	0
	Hohenwald	3,832	14	0	0	1	13	92	40	50	2	2
	Hollow Rock	943	1	0	0	0	1	19	4	15	0	0
	Hornbeak	425	2	0	0	1	1	5	1	4	0	0
	Humboldt	9,213	122	2	3	14	103	486	135	314	37	6
	Huntingdon	4,163	12	0	0	0	12	105	26	76	3	0
	Huntland	882	0	0	0	0	0	8	3	4	1	1
	Jacksboro	2,055	14	0	0	2	12	209	19	180	10	1
	Jackson	63,125	681	9	27	266	379	4,606	1,106	2,930	570	22
	Jamestown	1,907	16	0	1	0	15	110	22	85	3	2
	Jasper	3,086	4	0	0	0	4	94	31	57	6	0
	Jefferson City	8,055	33	0	2	3	28	454	67	367	20	0
	Jellico	2,546	3	0	0	0	3	154	17	128	9	1
	Johnson City	60,488	343	1	22	57	263	3,023	566	2,295	162	12
	Jonesborough	4,803	22	0	1	2	19	96	25	65	6	1
	Kenton	1,306	2	0	0	0	2	12	4	8	0	0
	Kimball	1,380	4	0	0	2	2	73	2	62	9	1
	Kingsport	44,079	335	2	21	57	255	3,064	521	2,395	148	20
	Kingston	5,588	7	0	1	0	6	134	30	95	9	1
	Kingston Springs	2,945	1	0	0	0	1	40	7	30	3	0
	Knoxville	183,319	2,058	27	109	681	1,241	12,862	2,507	8,984	1,371	99
	Lafayette	4,289	16	0	0	1	15	82	21	55	6	1
	La Follette	8,212	59	0	2	4	53	626	191	393	42	3
	La Grange	146	0	0	0	0	0	0	0	0	0	0
	Lakewood	2,403	5	0	1	0	4	52	22	25	5	0
	La Vergne	28,719	153	1	12	10	130	661	155	445	61	3
	Lawrenceburg	10,826	124	0	5	10	109	608	128	446	34	5
	Lebanon	24,219	226	3	10	39	174	1,158	168	893	97	6
	Lenoir City	7,835	68	0	3	8	57	473	117	318	38	4
	Lewisburg	10,866	81	0	4	11	66	333	89	231	13	1
	Lexington	7,829	85	0	8	13	64	496	122	343	31	3
	Livingston	3,518	15	0	2	4	9	131	53	76	2	1
	Lookout Mountain	1,865	0	0	0	0	0	5	0	5	0	0
	Loretto	1,707	3	0	0	0	3	65	13	48	4	0
	Loudon	4,915	18	0	1	2	15	194	35	151	8	0
	Lynnville	338	0	0	0	0	0	0	0	0	0	0
	Madisonville	4,542	29	0	3	2	24	255	39	204	12	6
	Manchester	9,858	63	0	0	9	54	525	70	419	36	3
	Martin	10,043	38	1	6	5	26	359	50	304	5	1
	Maryville	26,941	57	0	6	14	37	647	106	510	31	1
	Mason	1,174	10	0	0	2	8	38	8	27	3	0
	Maury City	705	0	0	0	0	0	9	0	7	2	0
	Maynardville	1,940	0	0	0	0	0	52	18	30	4	0
	McEwen	1,681	3	0	0	1	2	11	4	4	3	0
	McKenzie	5,438	14	1	0	2	11	209	49	153	7	0
	McMinnville	13,378	97	0	8	10	79	594	126	442	26	3
	Medina	1,609	10	0	0	0	10	40	7	31	2	0
	Memphis	669,264	13,055	128	452	4,870	7,605	53,959	14,613	33,146	6,200	147
	Middleton	623	7	0	0	0	7	28	5	22	1	0
	Milan	7,885	48	1	1	8	38	354	59	282	13	2
	Millersville	6,365	19	0	0	1	18	125	49	65	11	0
	Millington	10,323	90	0	2	21	67	599	105	451	43	1
	Minor Hill	450	0	0	0	0	0	14	4	10	0	0
	Monteagle	1,209	4	0	0	1	3	30	8	17	5	1
	Monterey	2,856	1	0	0	1	0	47	4	43	0	0
	Morristown	27,147	264	1	23	65	175	1,905	224	1,572	109	14

[1] The FBI does not publish arson data unless it receives data from either the agency or the state for all 12 months of the calendar year.

Table 8. Offenses Known to Law Enforcement, by State and City, 2007 *(Contd.)*

(Number.)

State	City	Population	Violent crime	Murder and non-negligent man-slaughter	Forcible rape	Robbery	Aggravated assault	Property crime	Burglary	Larceny-theft	Motor vehicle theft	Arson[1]
	Moscow	571	3	0	0	1	2	8	2	4	2	0
	Mountain City	2,389	9	0	3	1	5	57	14	37	6	0
	Mount Carmel	5,436	3	0	0	0	3	99	20	72	7	0
	Mount Juliet	20,259	61	0	1	8	52	419	74	328	17	11
	Mount Pleasant	4,442	40	1	3	2	34	230	50	163	17	0
	Munford	6,268	20	0	1	0	19	168	37	112	19	0
	Murfreesboro	96,264	691	4	29	137	521	4,186	929	3,028	229	13
	Nashville	564,169	8,513	73	290	2,516	5,634	31,466	6,111	22,729	2,626	110
	Newbern	3,134	34	0	0	1	33	116	33	72	11	1
	New Hope	1,025	1	0	0	0	1	9	4	5	0	0
	New Johnsonville	1,993	3	0	0	0	3	70	18	48	4	1
	New Market	1,327	1	0	0	0	1	4	1	2	1	0
	Newport	7,406	79	0	2	7	70	749	82	627	40	6
	New Tazewell	2,896	12	0	2	1	9	148	18	124	6	0
	Niota	805	2	0	0	0	2	8	4	4	0	1
	Nolensville	2,643	2	0	0	0	2	51	8	42	1	0
	Norris	1,468	0	0	0	0	0	18	3	15	0	0
	Oakland	3,821	8	0	0	0	8	72	2	63	7	0
	Oak Ridge	27,682	146	4	9	37	96	1,410	334	1,009	67	12
	Obion	1,100	4	0	0	0	4	28	8	18	2	0
	Oliver Springs	3,322	5	0	1	1	3	136	25	96	15	0
	Oneida	3,685	21	0	1	1	19	206	48	150	8	0
	Paris	10,014	93	0	2	13	78	560	161	380	19	1
	Parsons	2,377	8	0	0	1	7	50	21	25	4	0
	Petersburg	603	2	0	0	0	2	8	2	6	0	0
	Pigeon Forge	6,019	59	0	6	9	44	720	236	430	54	6
	Pikeville	1,890	2	0	0	0	2	43	2	39	2	0
	Piperton	1,001	4	0	0	0	4	13	2	9	2	0
	Pittman Center	622	2	0	0	0	2	14	7	6	1	0
	Plainview	2,135	1	0	0	0	1	6	2	4	0	0
	Pleasant View	3,822	4	0	0	1	3	58	13	41	4	0
	Portland	11,060	92	0	6	3	83	350	82	237	31	4
	Powells Crossroads	1,216	5	0	0	0	5	7	1	6	0	0
	Pulaski	7,869	63	0	7	10	46	417	98	304	15	2
	Puryear	678	2	0	0	0	2	16	4	12	0	0
	Red Bank	11,526	70	1	8	12	49	518	144	344	30	2
	Red Boiling Springs	1,072	3	0	1	0	2	26	8	16	2	0
	Ridgely	1,513	8	1	0	1	6	28	8	18	2	0
	Ridgetop	1,705	0	0	0	0	0	30	9	17	4	0
	Ripley	7,705	159	0	8	14	137	776	232	508	36	2
	Rockwood	5,453	15	0	0	2	13	478	73	393	12	1
	Rogersville	4,327	24	0	0	1	23	310	42	254	14	0
	Rossville	514	2	0	0	1	1	21	4	16	1	0
	Rutherford	1,236	2	0	0	0	2	26	9	15	2	0
	Rutledge	1,282	1	0	0	1	0	62	22	37	3	0
	Savannah	7,281	74	0	1	15	58	569	137	403	29	2
	Scotts Hill	913	0	0	0	0	0	13	5	7	1	0
	Selmer	4,724	28	0	3	2	23	248	60	176	12	0
	Sevierville	16,070	78	0	8	14	56	1,046	174	806	66	2
	Sewanee	2,555	1	0	0	0	1	57	16	40	1	1
	Sharon	908	4	0	0	0	4	20	3	15	2	0
	Shelbyville	19,586	99	0	12	20	67	549	113	392	44	2
	Signal Mountain	7,063	9	0	1	0	8	84	19	64	1	0
	Smithville	4,227	27	0	2	5	20	237	43	186	8	1
	Sneedville	1,309	11	0	0	2	9	70	26	42	2	0
	Soddy-Daisy	12,098	74	0	4	6	64	493	96	363	34	2
	Somerville	2,949	39	0	1	7	31	125	19	101	5	0
	South Carthage	1,301	2	0	0	1	1	53	13	40	0	0
	South Fulton	2,446	12	0	1	0	11	67	21	41	5	0
	South Pittsburg	3,113	26	0	1	2	23	133	28	93	12	1
	Sparta	4,839	19	1	3	2	13	385	92	274	19	3
	Spencer	1,683	1	0	0	0	1	14	3	11	0	0
	Spring City	2,018	0	0	0	0	0	41	5	35	1	0
	Springfield	16,844	228	2	15	39	172	815	123	645	47	4
	Spring Hill	23,774	33	1	6	2	24	228	60	156	12	0
	St. Joseph	859	2	0	0	0	2	2	1	1	0	0
	Surgoinsville	1,777	5	0	3	1	1	26	7	18	1	0
	Sweetwater	6,419	59	1	1	5	52	310	52	239	19	2
	Tazewell	2,158	13	0	1	1	11	126	28	92	6	0
	Tellico Plains	955	7	0	0	0	7	31	6	24	1	0
	Tiptonville	3,998	10	0	0	1	9	77	25	48	4	0
	Toone	356	0	0	0	0	0	1	0	1	0	0
	Townsend	262	2	0	0	0	2	22	11	8	3	0
	Trenton	4,538	20	0	1	1	18	168	33	129	6	0

[1] The FBI does not publish arson data unless it receives data from either the agency or the state for all 12 months of the calendar year.

Table 8.   Offenses Known to Law Enforcement, by State and City, 2007 *(Contd.)*

(Number.)

State	City	Population	Violent crime	Murder and non-negligent man-slaughter	Forcible rape	Robbery	Aggravated assault	Property crime	Burglary	Larceny-theft	Motor vehicle theft	Arson[1]
	Trezevant	889	8	0	0	1	7	31	9	21	1	1
	Trimble	727	0	0	0	0	0	4	0	4	0	0
	Troy	1,241	3	0	0	0	3	29	6	21	2	0
	Tullahoma	19,036	126	0	7	17	102	887	209	631	47	7
	Tusculum	2,260	0	0	0	0	0	19	12	6	1	0
	Union City	10,772	59	0	2	7	50	726	129	577	20	5
	Vonore	1,483	11	0	0	0	11	99	12	80	7	1
	Wartburg	912	2	0	0	0	2	8	3	5	0	0
	Wartrace	570	1	0	0	0	1	4	1	2	1	0
	Watertown	1,408	0	0	0	0	0	40	9	28	3	2
	Waverly	4,215	6	0	0	0	6	58	11	43	4	0
	Waynesboro	2,146	20	0	1	0	19	36	10	23	3	2
	Westmoreland	2,195	8	0	1	1	6	52	20	28	4	0
	White Bluff	2,473	2	0	1	0	1	33	20	12	1	0
	White House	9,464	14	1	4	0	9	114	18	91	5	0
	White Pine	2,099	9	0	1	2	6	175	14	151	10	1
	Whiteville	4,480	15	0	0	0	15	80	23	50	7	0
	Whitwell	1,589	5	0	0	1	4	61	10	45	6	1
	Winchester	7,911	92	0	3	7	82	369	92	260	17	3
	Winfield	999	13	0	0	0	13	57	15	33	9	0
	Woodbury	2,554	14	0	0	1	13	56	12	40	4	1
TEXAS	Abernathy	2,748	9	1	0	1	7	44	8	33	3	0
	Abilene	114,644	661	9	89	167	396	4,911	1,324	3,295	292	31
	Addison	13,764	127	0	8	32	87	1,092	185	798	109	2
	Alamo	16,496	55	0	0	9	46	1,025	105	842	78	9
	Alamo Heights	7,087	17	0	0	5	12	312	52	256	4	0
	Alice	19,850	138	0	5	8	125	2,082	423	1,596	63	14
	Allen	78,630	58	0	10	14	34	1,760	365	1,344	51	2
	Alpine	6,056	11	0	3	1	7	104	56	45	3	3
	Alto	1,152	2	0	0	0	2	62	25	32	5	0
	Alton	7,793	9	0	1	3	5	372	87	234	51	0
	Alvarado	4,200	17	0	3	0	14	124	34	79	11	1
	Alvin	22,542	64	1	8	17	38	715	136	546	33	4
	Amarillo	187,234	1,834	19	127	431	1,257	11,369	2,585	7,554	1,230	70
	Andrews	9,541	53	0	7	1	45	315	82	228	5	2
	Angleton	18,811	99	0	27	11	61	544	105	398	41	7
	Anna	1,811	5	0	2	0	3	105	24	77	4	1
	Anson	2,364	1	0	0	0	1	19	7	11	1	0
	Anthony	4,155	22	0	0	7	15	176	10	157	9	1
	Anton	1,153	2	0	1	0	1	8	1	5	2	0
	Aransas Pass	9,082	63	0	7	14	42	793	146	612	35	0
	Arcola	1,292	4	0	0	0	4	18	8	10	0	0
	Argyle	3,291	0	0	0	0	0	26	6	20	0	0
	Arlington	372,073	2,588	13	156	742	1,677	21,079	4,447	14,990	1,642	64
	Arp	945	1	0	0	0	1	12	5	7	0	0
	Athens	12,742	54	2	9	12	31	600	185	381	34	3
	Atlanta	5,606	32	0	6	5	21	229	40	171	18	0
	Austin	716,817	3,871	30	328	1,457	2,056	45,453	8,031	34,461	2,961	116
	Azle	10,973	31	1	1	9	20	469	66	391	12	7
	Baird	1,668	2	0	0	0	2	7	3	2	2	0
	Balch Springs	19,852	211	1	18	85	107	1,256	161	1,016	79	1
	Balcones Heights	2,969	44	0	1	16	27	712	191	475	46	1
	Ballinger	3,875	8	0	0	1	7	73	13	56	4	0
	Bangs	1,636	1	0	0	0	1	17	2	14	1	0
	Bastrop	7,966	42	1	6	14	21	530	65	446	19	2
	Bay City	18,211	462	0	10	34	418	1,088	235	808	45	1
	Bayou Vista	1,717	0	0	0	0	0	2	0	2	0	0
	Baytown	69,040	324	7	44	113	160	3,098	731	2,048	319	22
	Beaumont	109,345	1,073	15	71	309	678	6,643	1,707	4,471	465	51
	Bedford	48,974	258	1	19	34	204	1,734	289	1,331	114	8
	Bee Cave	2,464	3	0	0	2	1	113	31	81	1	0
	Beeville	13,721	48	0	2	4	42	425	125	285	15	0
	Bellaire	17,879	41	0	1	33	7	303	57	224	22	2
	Bellmead	9,573	131	1	6	20	104	906	92	779	35	2
	Bellville	4,416	15	0	2	2	11	90	13	70	7	0
	Belton	16,191	30	0	1	8	21	505	127	357	21	3
	Benbrook	22,618	31	0	7	5	19	519	123	363	33	3
	Bertram	1,378	3	0	1	0	2	28	13	13	2	0
	Beverly Hills	2,046	4	0	0	1	3	89	11	76	2	0
	Big Sandy	1,360	6	0	0	2	4	24	7	16	1	0
	Big Spring	24,099	197	0	35	26	136	1,616	429	1,112	75	9
	Bishop	3,199	5	0	1	2	2	155	25	129	1	0
	Blanco	1,641	3	0	0	0	3	26	10	15	1	0
	Bloomburg	368	0	0	0	0	0	1	1	0	0	2

[1] The FBI does not publish arson data unless it receives data from either the agency or the state for all 12 months of the calendar year.

Table 8. Offenses Known to Law Enforcement, by State and City, 2007 *(Contd.)*

(Number.)

State	City	Population	Violent crime	Murder and non-negligent man-slaughter	Forcible rape	Robbery	Aggravated assault	Property crime	Burglary	Larceny-theft	Motor vehicle theft	Arson[1]
	Blue Mound	2,354	3	0	0	0	3	60	13	46	1	0
	Boerne	9,090	19	0	0	0	19	246	35	200	11	1
	Bogata	1,318	1	0	0	0	1	16	1	15	0	0
	Bonham	10,756	56	0	1	3	52	387	93	282	12	3
	Borger	13,128	120	1	6	12	101	843	245	560	38	23
	Bovina	1,790	4	0	1	0	3	18	12	5	1	0
	Bowie	5,591	17	0	4	1	12	292	46	221	25	1
	Brady	5,382	24	0	0	3	21	170	44	122	4	2
	Brazoria	2,998	13	0	3	1	9	105	25	71	9	0
	Breckenridge	5,647	11	0	1	4	6	86	22	58	6	0
	Bremond	895	1	0	0	0	1	8	6	2	0	1
	Brenham	14,887	96	1	12	8	75	484	122	322	40	2
	Bridge City	8,735	26	0	2	2	22	214	54	143	17	0
	Bridgeport	5,966	10	1	2	1	6	164	40	110	14	1
	Brookshire	3,734	23	0	1	14	8	169	61	84	24	1
	Brookside Village	2,005	6	0	0	0	6	31	14	15	2	0
	Brownfield	9,110	27	0	0	5	22	127	41	75	11	2
	Brownsville	177,090	880	5	21	207	647	9,474	1,442	7,574	458	20
	Brownwood	19,820	113	0	11	12	90	917	174	700	43	1
	Bruceville-Eddy	1,535	2	0	0	1	1	69	13	52	4	0
	Bryan	67,484	596	4	34	96	462	3,542	1,000	2,404	138	10
	Bullard	1,741	3	0	0	1	2	56	14	42	0	1
	Bulverde	4,662	7	0	1	0	6	107	14	91	2	1
	Burkburnett	10,203	8	0	0	0	8	162	69	90	3	2
	Burleson	33,383	62	1	12	13	36	985	163	750	72	14
	Burnet	5,779	18	0	1	1	16	96	22	69	5	2
	Cactus	2,679	17	0	1	1	15	37	25	11	1	0
	Caddo Mills	1,218	3	0	0	0	3	17	6	8	3	1
	Caldwell	3,807	6	0	0	2	4	28	8	15	5	0
	Calvert	1,401	25	1	0	3	21	35	22	10	3	0
	Cameron	5,883	20	0	5	3	12	290	51	236	3	2
	Canton	3,688	12	1	0	0	11	127	18	97	12	0
	Canyon	13,644	3	0	0	0	3	190	15	170	5	0
	Carrollton	123,324	237	5	3	116	113	3,890	893	2,636	361	8
	Carthage	6,598	25	1	0	2	22	162	28	125	9	0
	Castle Hills	4,148	11	0	1	7	3	328	50	264	14	0
	Castroville	3,080	4	0	0	0	4	93	12	75	6	0
	Cedar Hill	44,629	103	2	8	34	59	1,336	312	890	134	3
	Cedar Park	57,286	42	0	5	8	29	924	187	696	41	5
	Celina	4,789	4	0	0	2	2	98	17	81	0	0
	Center	5,823	54	2	2	9	41	373	109	236	28	4
	Childress	6,631	26	0	0	0	26	94	30	57	7	0
	Chillicothe	721	1	0	0	0	1	6	2	4	0	0
	Cibolo	11,960	8	0	0	1	7	137	31	98	8	1
	Cisco	3,777	10	0	1	0	9	96	18	72	6	0
	Clarksville	3,582	2	0	0	2	0	70	28	42	0	1
	Cleburne	30,174	144	1	29	19	95	1,353	304	962	87	4
	Cleveland	8,081	68	0	13	17	38	713	116	558	39	3
	Clifton	3,654	6	0	0	0	6	81	31	46	4	0
	Clint	990	4	0	0	1	3	9	4	5	0	0
	Clute	10,781	49	0	2	10	37	613	118	443	52	0
	Clyde	3,744	3	0	0	0	3	89	21	60	8	1
	Cockrell Hill	4,291	18	0	0	8	10	168	52	85	31	2
	Coffee City	209	1	0	0	0	1	7	4	3	0	0
	Coleman	4,832	13	2	0	2	9	187	86	90	11	1
	College Station	74,997	251	1	38	45	167	2,488	481	1,919	88	2
	Colleyville	23,743	8	0	0	0	8	272	39	229	4	2
	Collinsville	1,528	2	0	2	0	0	30	16	11	3	0
	Colorado City	3,918	16	0	8	1	7	174	35	132	7	3
	Columbus	3,930	84	0	9	7	68	184	57	121	6	2
	Comanche	4,308	15	0	2	0	13	148	20	126	2	1
	Combes	2,892	16	0	3	0	13	57	16	35	6	0
	Commerce	9,692	72	0	10	16	46	402	109	273	20	0
	Conroe	51,582	252	4	25	67	156	2,424	441	1,792	191	4
	Converse	14,323	32	1	8	18	5	365	84	265	16	0
	Coppell	39,572	40	0	1	10	29	740	134	543	63	2
	Copperas Cove	29,706	115	1	11	21	82	1,136	316	785	35	19
	Corinth	21,054	15	0	3	4	8	287	45	215	27	0
	Corpus Christi	286,428	2,367	17	238	497	1,615	18,732	3,407	14,501	824	98
	Corrigan	1,975	1	0	0	0	1	30	11	16	3	3
	Corsicana	26,696	88	0	14	31	43	1,446	351	1,009	86	1
	Crane	3,028	3	0	0	0	3	23	5	16	2	0
	Crockett	6,960	28	0	1	1	26	293	66	205	22	2
	Crowell	1,055	1	0	0	0	1	13	6	6	1	0

[1] The FBI does not publish arson data unless it receives data from either the agency or the state for all 12 months of the calendar year.

Table 8.   Offenses Known to Law Enforcement, by State and City, 2007 *(Contd.)*

(Number.)

State	City	Population	Violent crime	Murder and non-negligent man-slaughter	Forcible rape	Robbery	Aggravated assault	Property crime	Burglary	Larceny-theft	Motor vehicle theft	Arson[1]
	Crowley	11,618	26	0	10	5	11	239	64	175	0	2
	Crystal City	7,388	6	0	0	1	5	218	74	133	11	0
	Cuero	6,642	25	1	9	3	12	169	34	128	7	0
	Daingerfield	2,462	8	0	0	0	8	123	50	65	8	1
	Dalhart	6,990	30	0	2	2	26	168	55	103	10	0
	Dallas	1,239,104	13,248	200	511	7,222	5,315	83,962	22,472	47,699	13,791	909
	Dalworthington Gardens	2,408	5	0	0	1	4	39	6	26	7	0
	Danbury	1,683	1	0	0	0	1	3	2	1	0	0
	Dayton	7,377	24	1	6	4	13	232	51	168	13	3
	Decatur	6,402	17	0	3	6	8	211	33	156	22	7
	Deer Park	29,971	76	0	6	17	53	866	176	627	63	7
	De Kalb	1,795	9	0	0	2	7	90	43	45	2	0
	De Leon	2,406	4	0	0	0	4	28	7	20	1	0
	Del Rio	36,864	73	0	0	16	57	1,255	230	925	100	4
	Denison	24,130	111	2	5	24	80	1,221	290	879	52	1
	Denton	113,936	366	2	76	84	204	3,505	718	2,614	173	6
	Denver City	4,012	5	0	1	0	4	57	5	51	1	0
	DeSoto	47,253	165	1	9	54	101	1,550	526	877	147	5
	Devine	4,531	7	0	1	0	6	149	31	113	5	0
	Diboll	5,512	12	0	5	0	7	167	43	118	6	0
	Dickinson	18,151	65	0	5	15	45	586	166	363	57	2
	Dilley	4,142	8	0	0	0	8	30	11	17	2	2
	Dimmitt	3,815	11	0	0	0	11	118	28	84	6	0
	Donna	16,662	99	0	8	14	77	1,086	236	771	79	6
	Double Oak	3,199	2	0	0	0	2	15	0	14	1	0
	Driscoll	818	6	0	0	0	6	110	17	91	2	0
	Dublin	3,674	8	0	0	0	8	45	14	30	1	0
	Dumas	14,084	54	0	16	3	35	549	95	438	16	2
	Duncanville	35,512	133	0	10	78	45	1,478	360	949	169	0
	Eagle Lake	3,732	9	0	1	1	7	78	10	67	1	0
	Eagle Pass	26,974	114	1	9	17	87	1,085	218	830	37	1
	Early	2,821	4	0	1	0	3	67	12	55	0	1
	Eastland	3,915	8	0	1	0	7	115	19	88	8	1
	East Mountain	629	3	0	0	0	3	9	8	0	1	0
	Edcouch	4,578	5	0	0	0	5	106	30	75	1	1
	Eden	2,386	6	0	0	0	6	23	9	14	0	0
	Edgewood	1,478	1	0	0	0	1	22	4	17	1	0
	Edinburg	69,708	269	1	20	52	196	3,777	683	2,705	389	20
	Edna	5,854	9	0	2	2	5	131	23	102	6	0
	El Campo	10,799	35	0	13	3	19	330	66	253	11	2
	Electra	2,854	8	0	0	1	7	98	43	43	12	5
	Elgin	9,951	36	1	10	4	21	320	122	181	17	0
	El Paso	616,029	2,574	17	258	472	1,827	19,722	2,149	14,545	3,028	81
	Elsa	6,758	103	0	1	8	94	438	96	307	35	1
	Ennis	19,520	104	0	6	22	76	1,054	230	756	68	3
	Euless	52,899	115	2	0	42	71	1,729	435	1,157	137	9
	Everman	5,739	18	0	1	1	16	171	40	117	14	3
	Fairfield	3,612	7	0	0	2	5	51	15	28	8	0
	Fair Oaks Ranch	6,082	6	0	2	0	4	40	22	17	1	0
	Farmers Branch	26,455	77	0	5	45	27	1,431	239	1,047	145	4
	Farmersville	3,481	1	0	0	0	1	44	16	22	6	1
	Farwell	1,298	0	0	0	0	0	12	7	5	0	0
	Ferris	2,414	10	0	1	5	4	158	48	96	14	1
	Flatonia	1,423	2	0	0	0	2	17	3	13	1	0
	Florence	1,133	0	0	0	0	0	11	5	6	0	0
	Floresville	7,463	16	0	1	1	14	209	48	158	3	1
	Flower Mound	68,191	48	5	4	3	36	620	114	467	39	3
	Floydada	3,214	5	0	0	0	5	56	21	33	2	0
	Forest Hill	13,771	78	0	2	31	45	633	108	460	65	0
	Forney	14,020	22	0	3	5	14	288	69	194	25	0
	Fort Stockton	7,350	12	0	0	2	10	263	88	163	12	0
	Fort Worth	670,693	4,474	58	335	1,620	2,461	36,681	9,008	24,988	2,685	227
	Frankston	1,276	5	0	0	1	4	46	12	30	4	0
	Fredericksburg	11,004	5	1	0	0	4	211	20	185	6	1
	Freeport	12,588	63	1	6	8	48	519	176	306	37	1
	Freer	3,022	9	0	0	0	9	60	17	41	2	0
	Friendswood	34,140	38	0	2	7	29	483	112	335	36	2
	Friona	3,698	11	0	0	1	10	49	25	20	4	0
	Frisco	90,674	90	1	7	21	61	2,688	524	2,100	64	6
	Gainesville	16,710	92	1	15	18	58	915	262	596	57	1
	Galena Park	10,177	26	0	1	7	18	293	91	174	28	0
	Galveston	57,590	585	7	82	209	287	3,475	757	2,394	324	16
	Ganado	1,848	0	0	0	0	0	5	1	4	0	0
	Garland	218,236	763	7	52	323	381	8,243	2,026	5,516	701	34

[1] The FBI does not publish arson data unless it receives data from either the agency or the state for all 12 months of the calendar year.

Table 8.   Offenses Known to Law Enforcement, by State and City, 2007 *(Contd.)*

(Number.)

State	City	Population	Violent crime	Murder and non-negligent man-slaughter	Forcible rape	Robbery	Aggravated assault	Property crime	Burglary	Larceny-theft	Motor vehicle theft	Arson[1]
	Gatesville	15,450	34	0	4	4	26	393	114	260	19	1
	Georgetown	44,834	64	0	15	9	40	743	132	555	56	2
	Giddings	5,517	39	0	2	2	35	170	25	138	7	0
	Gilmer	5,191	25	1	3	3	18	337	61	260	16	2
	Gladewater	6,355	38	0	13	6	19	366	101	236	29	11
	Glenn Heights	10,739	33	1	1	3	28	297	150	119	28	3
	Godley	1,011	1	0	0	0	1	10	6	3	1	0
	Gonzales	7,534	111	0	8	8	95	347	118	225	4	1
	Gorman	1,248	1	0	0	0	1	21	13	6	2	0
	Graham	8,689	17	0	5	0	12	206	44	148	14	3
	Granbury	8,040	17	0	0	0	17	528	38	466	24	3
	Grand Prairie	157,913	608	6	74	225	303	7,330	1,577	4,575	1,178	34
	Grand Saline	3,296	1	0	0	1	0	52	8	42	2	0
	Granger	1,359	1	0	0	0	1	20	3	17	0	0
	Granite Shoals	2,794	6	0	0	0	6	97	51	46	0	2
	Grapeland	1,400	14	0	0	1	13	31	10	20	1	0
	Grapevine	49,498	88	0	11	32	45	1,515	185	1,205	125	2
	Greenville	26,130	189	5	8	51	125	1,454	338	1,023	93	0
	Gregory	2,261	6	1	1	1	3	137	8	127	2	1
	Groesbeck	4,368	7	0	0	2	5	72	32	38	2	1
	Groves	14,610	39	0	3	20	16	532	147	333	52	1
	Gun Barrel City	6,168	48	0	3	4	41	256	56	186	14	0
	Hale Center	2,176	8	0	0	1	7	26	12	13	1	0
	Hallettsville	2,532	7	0	3	1	3	77	6	69	2	0
	Hallsville	2,984	3	0	1	0	2	42	10	29	3	0
	Haltom City	40,114	148	3	15	35	95	2,186	537	1,450	199	12
	Hamlin	1,954	2	0	2	0	0	25	3	17	5	1
	Harker Heights	23,726	51	1	9	21	20	689	207	452	30	0
	Harlingen	64,984	334	7	28	63	236	4,546	1,054	3,241	251	28
	Haskell	2,683	3	0	1	0	2	78	21	55	2	0
	Hawk Cove	617	2	0	0	0	2	14	7	7	0	0
	Hawkins	1,520	2	0	0	0	2	27	5	21	1	0
	Hawley	592	1	0	0	0	1	3	3	0	0	0
	Hearne	4,751	22	1	0	2	19	249	60	183	6	0
	Heath	7,263	9	0	0	0	9	88	15	70	3	0
	Hedwig Village	2,317	9	0	2	4	3	193	43	141	9	0
	Helotes	6,826	2	0	1	0	1	129	40	81	8	0
	Hemphill	1,070	1	0	0	0	1	32	9	22	1	1
	Hempstead	7,188	50	0	3	13	34	301	95	170	36	0
	Henderson	11,633	95	1	10	15	69	745	111	595	39	5
	Hereford	14,528	62	0	2	2	58	437	112	300	25	6
	Hewitt	13,522	28	0	6	4	18	242	58	171	13	0
	Hickory Creek	3,553	10	0	2	4	4	93	8	77	8	0
	Hidalgo	12,008	16	0	1	6	9	194	45	122	27	3
	Highland Park	9,062	8	0	0	6	2	270	45	214	11	1
	Highland Village	16,298	16	0	2	2	12	75	13	60	2	1
	Hill Country Village	1,083	0	0	0	0	0	54	11	38	5	0
	Hillsboro	9,161	40	0	3	11	26	284	43	221	20	6
	Hitchcock	7,389	26	0	3	3	20	255	90	133	32	1
	Holliday	1,821	1	0	0	1	0	15	6	9	0	0
	Hollywood Park	3,276	1	0	0	0	1	92	15	75	2	1
	Hondo	9,089	53	0	10	1	42	284	43	227	14	0
	Hooks	2,934	0	0	0	0	0	15	7	4	4	0
	Horizon City	11,855	13	0	1	4	8	174	52	101	21	2
	Horseshoe Bay	3,822	9	0	1	0	8	75	23	49	3	0
	Houston	2,169,544	24,564	351	694	11,479	12,040	123,326	29,044	74,817	19,465	1,047
	Howe	2,749	5	0	1	0	4	28	9	14	5	1
	Hubbard	1,706	5	0	0	2	3	1	1	0	0	0
	Hudson	4,191	1	0	0	0	1	22	15	7	0	0
	Hudson Oaks	1,944	3	0	1	0	2	75	6	61	8	0
	Humble	14,977	125	0	9	68	48	1,483	145	1,122	216	3
	Huntington	2,099	1	0	0	0	1	25	10	13	2	0
	Huntsville	37,906	168	1	14	44	109	1,048	207	788	53	7
	Hurst	38,452	204	0	16	42	146	2,115	252	1,762	101	5
	Hutchins	3,039	17	0	2	6	9	164	13	123	28	4
	Hutto	12,635	22	0	5	0	17	129	33	93	3	0
	Idalou	2,052	4	0	1	1	2	46	16	27	3	0
	Ingleside	9,355	27	2	11	2	12	203	71	125	7	3
	Ingram	1,886	2	0	0	0	2	59	11	44	4	0
	Iowa Park	6,100	17	0	2	0	15	82	25	49	8	1
	Irving	196,676	729	9	30	240	450	9,030	1,730	6,306	994	34
	Italy	2,124	7	0	0	0	7	37	10	27	0	0
	Itasca	1,655	9	0	0	0	9	14	4	10	0	0
	Jacinto City	9,890	89	0	3	18	68	387	105	231	51	1

[1] The FBI does not publish arson data unless it receives data from either the agency or the state for all 12 months of the calendar year.

Table 8. Offenses Known to Law Enforcement, by State and City, 2007 *(Contd.)*

(Number.)

State	City	Population	Violent crime	Murder and non-negligent man-slaughter	Forcible rape	Robbery	Aggravated assault	Property crime	Burglary	Larceny-theft	Motor vehicle theft	Arson[1]
	Jacksboro	4,653	2	0	0	0	2	64	7	48	9	0
	Jacksonville	14,481	106	1	18	27	60	754	191	528	35	2
	Jamaica Beach	1,127	1	0	0	0	1	19	5	12	2	0
	Jasper	7,435	34	1	0	10	23	365	68	276	21	1
	Jefferson	1,991	16	0	1	0	15	96	17	77	2	1
	Jersey Village	7,176	23	0	0	4	19	280	44	187	49	0
	Johnson City	1,581	1	0	0	0	1	34	7	27	0	0
	Jones Creek	2,120	3	0	2	0	1	7	6	1	0	0
	Jonestown	2,192	14	4	1	0	9	52	10	41	1	1
	Joshua	5,731	16	0	0	1	15	87	38	38	11	0
	Junction	2,647	22	0	0	0	22	60	7	51	2	0
	Karnes City	3,399	15	0	3	2	10	101	24	75	2	0
	Katy	13,830	58	0	1	14	43	680	84	568	28	2
	Kaufman	8,294	18	0	2	7	9	380	128	230	22	1
	Keene	6,301	1	0	1	0	0	104	22	78	4	0
	Keller	38,439	19	1	4	5	9	515	79	424	12	0
	Kemah	2,497	15	0	2	3	10	96	9	80	7	2
	Kemp	1,309	2	0	0	0	2	58	14	38	6	2
	Kempner	1,190	0	0	0	0	0	0	0	0	0	0
	Kenedy	3,363	31	0	0	0	31	72	40	31	1	2
	Kennedale	6,848	45	0	1	14	30	327	87	201	39	2
	Kerens	1,844	12	0	0	1	11	69	32	32	5	0
	Kermit	5,144	11	0	2	1	8	35	10	17	8	0
	Kerrville	22,636	73	0	13	11	49	903	154	717	32	3
	Kilgore	12,152	60	0	12	14	34	850	142	645	63	21
	Killeen	104,188	815	12	82	202	519	5,680	2,319	3,098	263	36
	Kingsville	24,235	243	1	12	17	213	1,113	314	753	46	3
	Kirby	8,560	15	0	0	5	10	169	51	106	12	2
	Kirbyville	2,020	7	0	0	1	6	32	5	22	5	0
	Kountze	2,172	11	0	1	2	8	58	19	37	2	1
	Kress	779	0	0	0	0	0	4	1	3	0	0
	Kyle	24,778	19	0	0	0	19	213	43	168	2	0
	Lacy-Lakeview	5,761	35	0	12	3	20	213	61	130	22	1
	La Feria	6,890	18	0	6	3	9	436	97	334	5	0
	Lago Vista	5,986	4	0	0	0	4	107	33	69	5	1
	La Grange	4,669	8	0	2	3	3	66	18	48	0	0
	Laguna Vista	3,068	6	0	1	2	3	56	12	39	5	0
	La Joya	4,833	1	0	0	0	1	48	25	23	0	0
	Lake Dallas	7,423	18	0	4	4	10	193	36	139	18	0
	Lake Jackson	27,788	56	1	5	18	32	832	148	657	27	4
	Lakeside	1,279	1	0	0	0	1	22	10	12	0	0
	Lakeview	6,477	10	0	0	2	8	64	17	43	4	0
	Lakeway	9,774	13	0	1	0	12	197	39	153	5	2
	Lake Worth	4,732	21	0	0	6	15	538	48	469	21	0
	La Marque	14,081	121	3	21	26	71	610	292	269	49	5
	Lamesa	9,167	50	1	1	2	46	203	60	131	12	2
	Lampasas	7,973	29	0	5	1	23	206	33	164	9	2
	Lancaster	35,090	203	1	18	16	168	1,841	689	925	227	5
	La Porte	34,165	92	0	4	10	78	357	94	218	45	13
	Laredo	221,253	1,281	10	81	325	865	13,949	1,878	10,534	1,537	101
	La Vernia	1,203	4	0	0	0	4	31	10	19	2	1
	Lavon	424	1	0	0	0	1	24	13	11	0	0
	League City	68,743	87	0	18	24	45	1,713	360	1,274	79	6
	Leander	23,175	38	0	0	3	35	432	61	356	15	3
	Leon Valley	9,876	41	0	4	14	23	673	102	515	56	0
	Levelland	12,653	81	0	11	4	66	524	180	335	9	9
	Lewisville	97,184	185	1	21	73	90	2,755	553	1,916	286	4
	Lexington	1,265	4	0	0	0	4	40	18	20	2	1
	Liberty	8,474	30	1	2	6	21	315	82	219	14	0
	Lindale	4,503	13	0	0	3	10	215	21	190	4	0
	Linden	2,181	7	0	2	0	5	49	17	32	0	1
	Little Elm	26,824	28	0	2	2	24	237	48	176	13	0
	Littlefield	6,213	42	0	0	1	41	186	57	121	8	2
	Live Oak	12,117	23	0	3	6	14	615	94	483	38	1
	Livingston	6,567	39	0	5	4	30	356	76	259	21	12
	Llano	3,326	2	0	0	0	2	68	11	55	2	0
	Lockhart	13,946	83	2	7	2	72	362	103	247	12	1
	Lockney	1,802	4	0	1	0	3	61	26	35	0	0
	Lone Star	1,597	11	0	2	2	7	56	19	35	2	0
	Longview	77,003	739	5	55	189	490	5,083	1,116	3,492	475	25
	Lorena	1,656	3	0	0	2	1	40	9	30	1	0
	Lorenzo	1,241	0	0	0	0	0	11	4	7	0	0
	Los Fresnos	5,465	4	0	1	0	3	89	20	69	0	1
	Lubbock	213,988	1,953	15	101	259	1,578	11,684	3,136	7,942	606	34

[1] The FBI does not publish arson data unless it receives data from either the agency or the state for all 12 months of the calendar year.

Table 8.   Offenses Known to Law Enforcement, by State and City, 2007 *(Contd.)*

(Number.)

State	City	Population	Violent crime	Murder and non-negligent man-slaughter	Forcible rape	Robbery	Aggravated assault	Property crime	Burglary	Larceny-theft	Motor vehicle theft	Arson[1]
	Lufkin	33,997	198	3	18	50	127	1,619	457	1,047	115	6
	Luling	5,442	21	0	2	1	18	213	50	152	11	0
	Lumberton	9,853	11	0	4	2	5	318	63	234	21	0
	Lytle	2,733	4	0	0	1	3	114	36	67	11	0
	Madisonville	4,349	38	0	4	9	25	221	62	143	16	2
	Magnolia	1,288	8	0	0	0	8	29	10	16	3	0
	Malakoff	2,374	18	0	2	1	15	120	40	76	4	0
	Manor	2,993	10	0	1	1	8	97	29	66	2	0
	Mansfield	43,901	82	0	7	29	46	1,054	251	749	54	7
	Manvel	4,912	14	0	0	3	11	75	18	49	8	1
	Marble Falls	7,562	40	1	10	9	20	402	46	338	18	1
	Marfa	1,903	3	0	0	0	3	46	16	29	1	1
	Marion	1,135	2	0	0	0	2	23	5	16	2	0
	Marlin	6,097	33	1	3	6	23	75	25	42	8	0
	Marshall	23,978	191	4	27	48	112	1,308	451	798	59	22
	Mart	2,517	6	0	0	0	6	57	14	41	2	1
	Martindale	1,117	1	0	0	0	1	5	2	2	1	0
	Mathis	5,486	20	0	1	5	14	210	59	151	0	2
	McAllen	129,455	372	6	27	114	225	7,908	824	6,537	547	17
	McGregor	4,862	19	0	1	1	17	250	66	178	6	0
	McKinney	118,113	255	1	49	44	161	2,626	531	1,949	146	20
	Meadows Place	6,919	10	0	0	6	4	117	29	78	10	1
	Melissa	3,395	3	0	0	0	3	82	19	57	6	0
	Memorial Villages	11,714	5	0	0	3	2	226	78	141	7	0
	Memphis	2,363	7	0	0	1	6	66	37	27	2	4
	Mercedes	14,879	94	4	1	10	79	796	197	513	86	3
	Meridian	1,510	0	0	0	0	0	0	0	0	0	0
	Merkel	2,587	8	0	2	1	5	48	19	28	1	0
	Mesquite	132,399	577	6	8	199	364	5,543	944	3,916	683	29
	Mexia	6,726	45	1	4	8	32	465	76	379	10	1
	Midland	103,118	343	4	57	76	206	3,673	835	2,630	208	9
	Midlothian	15,600	17	1	2	4	10	269	54	173	42	5
	Milford	748	4	0	1	0	3	11	4	7	0	0
	Mineral Wells	17,083	60	0	14	3	43	775	194	537	44	3
	Mission	66,216	94	2	8	32	52	2,571	370	1,906	295	1
	Missouri City	77,166	163	0	6	63	94	1,163	342	749	72	6
	Monahans	6,340	51	0	2	2	47	171	61	103	7	1
	Mont Belvieu	2,645	7	0	3	3	1	139	23	97	19	1
	Montgomery	593	4	0	0	0	4	11	2	7	2	0
	Morgans Point Resort	4,291	5	0	1	2	2	63	14	45	4	0
	Mount Pleasant	15,360	67	1	2	14	50	462	103	333	26	4
	Muleshoe	4,481	15	0	2	0	13	166	63	91	12	0
	Munday	1,291	1	0	0	0	1	19	6	11	2	0
	Murphy	15,497	7	0	1	2	4	163	27	135	1	0
	Mustang Ridge	931	4	0	0	0	4	14	5	7	2	0
	Nacogdoches	31,300	107	0	19	26	62	1,159	196	909	54	3
	Nash	2,426	1	0	1	0	0	48	5	39	4	0
	Nassau Bay	4,040	7	0	0	3	4	112	18	88	6	0
	Navasota	7,464	39	0	1	7	31	343	75	247	21	3
	Nederland	16,325	52	0	9	11	32	732	155	536	41	3
	Needville	3,585	3	0	0	0	3	21	13	5	3	0
	New Boston	4,630	9	0	0	3	6	342	66	254	22	3
	New Braunfels	51,860	158	1	10	35	112	2,078	322	1,673	83	20
	New Deal	726	1	0	0	0	1	3	1	2	0	2
	Nocona	3,291	5	0	1	0	4	73	28	41	4	1
	Nolanville	2,393	7	0	1	0	6	111	19	88	4	0
	Northlake	1,109	2	0	0	0	2	24	6	18	0	0
	North Richland Hills	63,270	267	2	28	36	201	2,256	482	1,594	180	0
	Oak Ridge	258	1	0	0	0	1	12	6	4	2	1
	Oak Ridge North	3,422	6	0	1	1	4	97	10	69	18	1
	Odessa	95,839	529	6	7	92	424	4,302	870	3,144	288	16
	O'Donnell	966	0	0	0	0	0	6	0	5	1	0
	Olmos Park	2,298	3	0	1	1	1	59	12	45	2	0
	Olney	3,328	5	0	0	0	5	59	14	39	6	0
	Olton	2,232	7	0	0	0	7	27	6	21	0	0
	Onalaska	1,564	3	0	1	0	2	8	3	3	2	0
	Orange	17,793	208	2	10	54	142	1,298	419	768	111	13
	Orange Grove	1,426	4	0	0	0	4	39	15	22	2	0
	Overton	2,337	35	0	2	0	33	52	18	33	1	0
	Ovilla	3,925	7	0	1	0	6	37	8	28	1	0
	Oyster Creek	1,236	5	0	0	0	5	60	30	26	4	0
	Paducah	1,286	0	0	0	0	0	18	13	3	2	0
	Palacios	5,158	40	0	4	6	30	159	71	81	7	1
	Palestine	18,250	121	1	3	22	95	722	145	514	63	10

[1] The FBI does not publish arson data unless it receives data from either the agency or the state for all 12 months of the calendar year.

Table 8.   Offenses Known to Law Enforcement, by State and City, 2007 *(Contd.)*

(Number.)

State	City	Population	Violent crime	Murder and non-negligent man-slaughter	Forcible rape	Robbery	Aggravated assault	Property crime	Burglary	Larceny-theft	Motor vehicle theft	Arson[1]
	Palmer	2,200	2	0	0	1	1	36	10	23	3	0
	Pampa	16,998	114	1	19	3	91	895	215	634	46	1
	Panhandle	2,619	6	0	2	0	4	19	4	15	0	0
	Pantego	2,344	7	0	0	4	3	168	29	131	8	0
	Paris	26,583	140	1	1	21	117	1,561	405	1,115	41	16
	Parker	2,781	1	0	0	0	1	35	5	26	4	0
	Pasadena	145,235	635	2	75	149	409	5,014	1,034	3,507	473	24
	Pearland	73,190	123	2	26	30	65	1,852	420	1,302	130	3
	Pearsall	7,779	17	0	0	0	17	329	102	222	5	0
	Pecos	7,946	20	0	0	4	16	230	56	167	7	0
	Pelican Bay	1,609	2	0	1	0	1	37	15	22	0	0
	Penitas	1,189	5	0	0	0	5	45	31	7	7	10
	Perryton	8,305	7	0	0	1	6	77	16	56	5	1
	Pflugerville	32,157	53	0	17	7	29	786	107	647	32	4
	Pharr	63,666	249	7	23	64	155	3,696	792	2,586	318	7
	Pilot Point	4,293	24	0	3	0	21	50	14	33	3	0
	Pinehurst	2,202	14	0	0	2	12	104	24	75	5	0
	Pittsburg	4,648	22	0	6	5	11	227	59	165	3	0
	Plainview	22,054	87	0	9	19	59	1,203	245	908	50	6
	Plano	259,771	676	2	51	161	462	7,973	1,384	6,168	421	44
	Pleasanton	9,742	36	0	10	1	25	337	55	270	12	3
	Ponder	1,114	2	0	1	1	0	30	8	21	1	0
	Port Aransas	3,812	33	0	3	3	27	388	65	297	26	2
	Port Arthur	55,481	475	9	47	196	223	2,285	747	1,280	258	32
	Port Isabel	5,433	27	0	9	3	15	327	30	294	3	0
	Portland	16,645	20	1	6	2	11	396	68	317	11	1
	Port Lavaca	11,658	20	0	3	1	16	400	90	284	26	1
	Port Neches	12,803	29	1	1	4	23	524	98	395	31	1
	Poteet	3,719	15	0	0	0	15	105	12	90	3	1
	Pottsboro	2,130	2	0	0	0	2	83	34	43	6	0
	Premont	2,822	12	0	0	0	12	62	19	34	9	0
	Presidio	4,939	3	0	0	0	3	43	6	31	6	0
	Primera	3,356	0	0	0	0	0	96	22	69	5	0
	Princeton	5,057	7	0	1	0	6	148	32	109	7	0
	Progreso	5,375	4	0	0	2	2	162	27	125	10	1
	Prosper	5,828	0	0	0	0	0	135	22	111	2	0
	Queen City	1,577	11	0	0	3	8	76	17	57	2	2
	Quinlan	1,466	1	0	0	0	1	75	10	61	4	0
	Quitman	2,273	16	0	1	0	15	28	7	20	1	0
	Ransom Canyon	1,079	0	0	0	0	0	12	2	10	0	0
	Raymondville	9,554	239	1	13	8	217	652	212	427	13	3
	Red Oak	8,538	17	1	1	2	13	271	112	138	21	1
	Refugio	2,760	3	0	0	0	3	28	4	22	2	0
	Reno	3,073	3	0	0	1	2	40	12	25	3	0
	Richardson	100,933	290	2	22	136	130	3,107	793	2,084	230	16
	Richland Hills	8,067	21	0	4	5	12	367	109	212	46	0
	Richmond	13,979	70	0	11	15	44	293	75	186	32	8
	Richwood	3,389	2	0	0	0	2	64	17	43	4	0
	Riesel	1,012	1	0	0	0	1	11	3	8	0	0
	Rio Grande City	14,098	54	1	2	7	44	540	146	313	81	0
	Rising Star	834	1	0	0	0	1	0	0	0	0	0
	River Oaks	6,914	5	0	0	3	2	188	57	116	15	0
	Roanoke	3,758	5	0	0	2	3	91	14	72	5	1
	Robinson	10,011	14	0	8	2	4	196	26	163	7	0
	Robstown	12,361	78	0	3	19	56	689	267	397	25	7
	Rockdale	6,066	15	0	1	4	10	182	49	122	11	0
	Rockport	9,464	13	0	0	5	8	521	92	415	14	1
	Rockwall	34,872	36	0	11	6	19	820	122	651	47	1
	Rollingwood	1,363	0	0	0	0	0	28	5	23	0	0
	Roma	11,394	30	1	10	6	13	194	45	84	65	0
	Roman Forest	3,788	0	0	0	0	0	5	1	3	1	0
	Roscoe	1,260	0	0	0	0	0	5	3	2	0	0
	Rosebud	1,365	5	0	0	2	3	19	6	13	0	0
	Rose City	514	0	0	0	0	0	0	0	0	0	0
	Rosenberg	33,131	96	0	14	28	54	862	201	588	73	6
	Round Rock	97,727	112	1	21	23	67	2,400	333	1,997	70	9
	Rowlett	56,432	72	0	9	7	56	1,171	270	840	61	2
	Royse City	8,086	47	0	3	0	44	116	23	88	5	0
	Runaway Bay	1,409	0	0	0	0	0	10	8	2	0	0
	Rusk	5,173	19	0	4	1	14	101	38	58	5	1
	Sabinal	1,672	9	1	0	1	7	32	11	21	0	1
	Sachse	19,028	21	0	3	3	15	264	77	174	13	2
	Saginaw	19,818	37	0	7	1	29	481	99	350	32	4
	Salado	1,926	2	0	1	0	1	25	6	19	0	0

[1] The FBI does not publish arson data unless it receives data from either the agency or the state for all 12 months of the calendar year.

Table 8. Offenses Known to Law Enforcement, by State and City, 2007 (Contd.)

(Number.)

State	City	Population	Violent crime	Murder and non-negligent man-slaughter	Forcible rape	Robbery	Aggravated assault	Property crime	Burglary	Larceny-theft	Motor vehicle theft	Arson[1]
	San Angelo	88,285	356	1	46	48	261	4,473	932	3,312	229	20
	San Antonio	1,316,882	7,327	122	635	2,445	4,125	84,143	16,750	60,669	6,724	459
	San Augustine	2,429	17	0	0	3	14	44	13	31	0	0
	San Benito	25,150	64	0	5	14	45	1,356	305	1,005	46	3
	San Diego	4,520	24	0	0	1	23	131	64	66	1	1
	Sanger	7,391	13	0	2	0	11	153	24	118	11	3
	San Juan	33,213	101	1	7	21	72	1,648	388	1,155	105	8
	San Marcos	48,979	168	0	15	46	107	1,650	255	1,251	144	5
	San Saba	2,548	2	0	0	0	2	9	2	7	0	0
	Sansom Park Village	4,140	21	0	1	0	20	107	19	69	19	0
	Santa Anna	1,034	1	0	0	0	1	18	6	12	0	0
	Santa Fe	10,735	40	0	10	3	27	280	87	158	35	3
	Santa Rosa	2,995	10	0	1	1	8	74	22	51	1	2
	Schertz	29,519	60	2	8	6	44	626	91	512	23	0
	Seabrook	11,448	38	1	9	2	26	245	49	171	25	1
	Seadrift	1,433	0	0	0	0	0	27	11	13	3	0
	Seagoville	11,452	45	0	3	14	28	596	158	339	99	0
	Seagraves	2,360	14	0	2	0	12	10	2	8	0	0
	Sealy	6,267	9	0	0	0	9	222	70	138	14	0
	Seguin	25,203	64	0	11	12	41	1,226	251	922	53	5
	Selma	3,219	10	1	1	1	7	301	49	239	13	1
	Seminole	6,105	3	0	2	0	1	91	17	71	3	0
	Seven Points	1,274	12	0	0	9	3	59	10	44	5	0
	Seymour	2,639	13	0	5	0	8	74	32	40	2	0
	Shallowater	2,227	1	0	0	1	0	28	10	16	2	0
	Shamrock	1,834	5	1	1	0	3	51	20	26	5	0
	Shavano Park	3,138	0	0	0	0	0	74	8	65	1	0
	Shenandoah	1,954	3	0	0	1	2	205	14	180	11	0
	Sherman	37,985	146	0	6	19	121	1,529	336	1,141	52	0
	Silsbee	6,844	19	0	0	7	12	187	39	142	6	0
	Sinton	5,491	30	0	4	7	19	150	33	112	5	1
	Slaton	5,642	15	0	0	1	14	170	50	114	6	2
	Smithville	4,543	17	0	3	2	12	133	25	107	1	1
	Snyder	10,549	96	0	12	1	83	322	111	199	12	2
	Socorro	31,588	109	0	5	26	78	678	161	456	61	5
	Somerset	1,832	0	0	0	0	0	26	3	22	1	0
	Somerville	1,723	19	0	1	4	14	65	9	54	2	2
	Sonora	3,081	20	0	1	0	19	59	13	41	5	2
	Sour Lake	1,748	2	0	0	0	2	48	13	32	3	0
	South Houston	16,348	106	2	3	54	47	674	126	432	116	0
	Southlake	26,367	12	0	4	2	6	539	88	435	16	0
	South Padre Island	2,747	54	2	13	1	38	687	103	547	37	0
	Southside Place	1,636	1	0	0	1	0	16	7	4	5	0
	Spearman	2,911	4	0	0	0	4	24	5	18	1	5
	Springtown	2,905	22	0	1	3	18	60	13	45	2	1
	Spring Valley	3,717	0	0	0	0	0	110	22	82	6	0
	Stafford	20,460	98	2	13	41	42	947	179	623	145	2
	Stamford	3,175	13	0	1	0	12	88	50	35	3	0
	Stanton	2,229	1	0	0	0	1	20	12	7	1	0
	Stephenville	16,219	51	0	12	3	36	495	83	395	17	0
	Stratford	1,878	2	0	1	0	1	20	9	10	1	0
	Sudan	1,020	12	0	3	0	9	21	7	10	4	0
	Sugar Land	82,402	100	0	17	39	44	1,578	210	1,268	100	6
	Sullivan City	4,466	7	0	1	1	5	85	47	26	12	0
	Sulphur Springs	15,396	30	0	5	3	22	252	70	168	14	4
	Sunrise Beach Village	757	0	0	0	0	0	5	3	2	0	0
	Sunset Valley	798	2	0	0	2	0	153	7	141	5	0
	Surfside Beach	880	7	0	0	0	7	34	17	13	4	1
	Sweeny	3,613	8	0	1	0	7	111	28	75	8	0
	Sweetwater	10,519	100	1	14	10	75	458	155	282	21	2
	Taft	3,435	2	0	1	0	1	138	16	120	2	2
	Tahoka	2,691	2	0	1	0	1	55	16	37	2	0
	Tatum	1,198	4	0	2	1	1	28	11	15	2	0
	Taylor	15,597	13	0	1	7	5	504	104	384	16	1
	Teague	4,785	5	0	1	0	4	57	11	38	8	0
	Temple	55,057	203	1	22	76	104	2,973	723	2,107	143	4
	Terrell	19,302	149	0	15	36	98	1,058	305	640	113	11
	Terrell Hills	5,136	1	0	0	0	1	129	53	73	3	0
	Texarkana	36,237	506	9	27	105	365	2,401	507	1,749	145	11
	Texas City	45,574	301	4	13	105	179	2,410	573	1,663	174	15
	The Colony	42,563	59	1	9	12	37	699	148	496	55	4
	Thorndale	1,335	3	0	0	0	3	9	2	7	0	0
	Thrall	874	4	0	0	0	4	20	1	17	2	0
	Three Rivers	1,707	6	0	0	0	6	53	24	23	6	0

[1] The FBI does not publish arson data unless it receives data from either the agency or the state for all 12 months of the calendar year.

Table 8.   Offenses Known to Law Enforcement, by State and City, 2007 *(Contd.)*

(Number.)

State	City	Population	Violent crime	Murder and non-negligent man-slaughter	Forcible rape	Robbery	Aggravated assault	Property crime	Burglary	Larceny-theft	Motor vehicle theft	Arson[1]
	Tioga	924	0	0	0	0	0	11	3	8	0	1
	Tolar	684	0	0	0	0	0	2	1	1	0	0
	Tomball	10,176	32	2	6	7	17	454	57	372	25	1
	Tool	2,495	6	1	0	0	5	60	22	35	3	0
	Trinity	2,762	33	1	0	3	29	93	39	47	7	0
	Trophy Club	7,836	5	0	1	0	4	57	11	45	1	0
	Troy	1,344	4	0	0	1	3	38	10	28	0	0
	Tulia	4,664	15	0	0	3	12	130	46	79	5	0
	Tye	1,114	4	0	0	2	2	31	2	28	1	0
	Tyler	95,596	665	2	59	125	479	4,430	806	3,473	151	13
	Universal City	18,238	37	0	2	8	27	429	93	313	23	0
	University Park	24,300	11	0	2	5	4	435	75	337	23	3
	Uvalde	16,594	87	1	8	12	66	1,010	218	761	31	8
	Van	2,632	4	0	1	0	3	28	10	16	2	0
	Van Alstyne	2,948	10	0	0	0	10	56	12	42	2	0
	Vernon	11,161	70	2	8	7	53	627	119	477	31	18
	Victoria	62,404	346	1	37	72	236	3,030	670	2,236	124	8
	Vidor	11,158	48	1	9	7	31	491	110	327	54	0
	Waco	122,514	1,139	6	95	275	763	8,029	1,987	5,611	431	14
	Waelder	1,018	0	0	0	0	0	4	4	0	0	1
	Wake Village	5,528	3	0	0	1	2	107	24	81	2	0
	Waller	2,034	22	0	2	7	13	140	30	104	6	1
	Wallis	1,298	1	0	0	0	1	19	8	10	1	0
	Watauga	23,931	69	0	0	18	51	536	138	355	43	3
	Waxahachie	27,500	118	0	10	18	90	1,028	261	702	65	10
	Weatherford	25,500	43	0	10	7	26	769	118	608	43	0
	Webster	10,070	46	0	7	19	20	858	122	658	78	0
	Weimar	2,031	3	0	0	2	1	18	9	9	0	0
	Wells	803	3	0	0	0	3	4	3	1	0	0
	Weslaco	32,707	136	2	15	34	85	2,044	393	1,452	199	4
	West	2,693	1	0	0	0	1	44	16	25	3	0
	West Columbia	4,216	10	1	1	3	5	92	30	59	3	1
	West Lake Hills	3,044	3	0	0	1	2	75	16	59	0	0
	West Orange	3,935	19	0	3	5	11	231	43	181	7	1
	Westover Hills	689	0	0	0	0	0	12	0	11	1	0
	West Tawakoni	1,773	12	0	1	0	11	52	23	22	7	0
	West University Place	15,249	10	0	0	8	2	200	49	143	8	0
	Westworth	3,079	4	0	0	1	3	129	19	108	2	0
	Wharton	9,355	70	0	0	12	58	389	74	304	11	5
	Whitehouse	7,556	4	0	0	1	3	76	10	60	6	2
	White Oak	6,350	5	0	2	1	2	152	18	122	12	0
	Whitesboro	4,054	2	0	1	0	1	82	9	69	4	0
	White Settlement	16,106	39	0	3	12	24	578	159	354	65	1
	Whitney	2,101	5	0	1	1	3	53	7	44	2	0
	Wichita Falls	98,717	576	4	31	228	313	6,835	1,540	4,797	498	39
	Willis	4,298	37	1	2	15	19	196	49	138	9	1
	Willow Park	4,057	9	0	4	0	5	38	4	30	4	3
	Wills Point	3,940	4	0	0	2	2	52	20	25	7	0
	Wilmer	3,616	14	0	1	2	11	116	42	60	14	0
	Windcrest	5,156	12	0	0	7	5	322	21	288	13	1
	Wink	878	0	0	0	0	0	15	5	10	0	0
	Winnsboro	3,901	26	0	2	0	24	52	19	33	0	1
	Winters	2,630	10	0	1	0	9	12	4	8	0	0
	Wolfforth	3,281	4	0	0	0	4	45	12	33	0	1
	Woodville	2,281	6	1	0	2	3	31	14	17	0	0
	Woodway	8,693	22	0	3	0	19	142	26	111	5	0
	Wortham	1,076	5	0	0	1	4	14	3	10	1	0
	Wylie	36,386	45	0	10	5	30	641	145	467	29	3
	Yoakum	5,659	7	0	0	0	7	166	45	115	6	1
	Yorktown	2,222	5	0	2	0	3	13	0	13	0	2
UTAH	Alpine/Highland	24,586	6	0	6	0	0	340	107	213	20	0
	American Fork/Cedar Hills	35,945	34	1	5	5	23	1,029	145	840	44	4
	Blanding	3,161	3	0	0	0	3	21	2	17	2	0
	Bountiful	41,132	45	0	9	10	26	1,065	144	876	45	3
	Brian Head	117	1	0	0	0	1	31	4	27	0	1
	Brigham City	18,609	26	0	5	4	17	553	68	463	22	0
	Cedar City	26,479	37	0	14	3	20	827	154	631	42	1
	Centerville	15,140	13	0	3	0	10	322	40	272	10	0
	Clearfield	27,419	42	0	11	7	24	867	112	710	45	4
	Clinton	19,882	12	0	5	2	5	268	37	211	20	1
	Draper	38,875	29	1	8	1	19	1,030	269	700	61	1
	Farmington	16,078	5	0	1	1	3	200	35	156	9	0
	Grantsville	8,329	6	0	3	0	3	182	34	133	15	0
	Gunnison	2,768	12	0	0	1	11	127	29	87	11	0

[1] The FBI does not publish arson data unless it receives data from either the agency or the state for all 12 months of the calendar year.

Table 8.   Offenses Known to Law Enforcement, by State and City, 2007 *(Contd.)*

(Number.)

State	City	Population	Violent crime	Murder and non-negligent man-slaughter	Forcible rape	Robbery	Aggravated assault	Property crime	Burglary	Larceny-theft	Motor vehicle theft	Arson[1]
	Harrisville	5,514	10	0	0	3	7	238	25	205	8	0
	Heber	10,155	5	0	3	0	2	112	31	67	14	0
	Helper	1,869	7	0	1	0	6	21	7	11	3	0
	Hildale	1,958	1	0	0	0	1	8	4	4	0	0
	Hurricane	12,749	16	0	3	0	13	359	97	225	37	0
	Ivins	7,663	2	0	1	0	1	123	57	62	4	0
	Kaysville	24,050	17	0	6	0	11	410	66	322	22	1
	La Verkin	4,260	5	0	4	0	1	66	21	37	8	0
	Layton	63,284	79	1	21	14	43	2,057	288	1,673	96	17
	Leeds	731	0	0	0	0	0	3	1	2	0	0
	Lehi	39,483	16	0	10	3	3	841	101	678	62	1
	Logan	48,403	27	0	3	3	21	417	60	337	20	3
	Mapleton	7,363	0	0	0	0	0	94	28	66	0	0
	Midvale	27,275	117	0	20	27	70	1,683	236	1,116	331	6
	Moab	4,886	20	0	1	1	18	219	19	193	7	0
	Monticello	1,918	1	0	0	0	1	23	6	17	0	0
	Murray	44,748	174	3	21	51	99	3,085	441	2,323	321	0
	Naples	1,533	3	0	1	0	2	43	5	33	5	0
	Nephi	5,276	8	0	2	0	6	121	36	79	6	0
	North Ogden	17,050	5	0	4	0	1	219	38	173	8	1
	North Park	10,615	3	0	0	0	3	191	25	159	7	0
	North Salt Lake	12,070	10	0	3	1	6	410	183	203	24	1
	Ogden	78,160	501	3	33	136	329	4,914	923	3,466	525	22
	Orem	91,816	67	1	23	15	28	2,835	245	2,455	135	3
	Park City	8,132	8	0	2	1	5	472	86	365	21	0
	Parowan	2,545	13	0	0	0	13	54	5	45	4	0
	Payson	17,378	17	0	3	6	8	528	81	421	26	0
	Perry	3,579	9	0	1	0	8	81	10	69	2	1
	Pleasant Grove/Lindon	41,890	24	0	6	10	8	929	136	754	39	3
	Pleasant View	6,607	4	0	1	0	3	129	22	106	1	0
	Price	7,954	11	0	3	1	7	325	40	272	13	2
	Provo	115,264	168	0	28	35	105	3,298	487	2,526	285	7
	Richfield	7,139	2	0	0	0	2	299	45	245	9	1
	Riverdale	8,023	20	0	2	10	8	484	37	420	27	1
	Roosevelt	4,740	14	0	6	0	8	188	31	151	6	0
	Roy	35,366	41	0	19	4	18	870	96	727	47	10
	Salem	5,790	1	0	0	1	0	90	21	66	3	0
	Salina	2,399	4	0	0	0	4	105	10	93	2	0
	Salt Lake City	178,449	1,499	17	114	503	865	15,232	2,049	11,196	1,987	55
	Sandy	94,975	189	1	27	33	128	3,317	534	2,519	264	17
	Santaquin/Genola	8,367	4	0	1	2	1	99	27	69	3	0
	Smithfield	7,484	3	0	0	0	3	146	28	111	7	0
	South Jordan	46,571	29	0	4	4	21	1,177	207	881	89	1
	South Ogden	15,473	29	0	8	11	10	545	74	450	21	2
	South Salt Lake	21,262	204	3	40	46	115	2,248	326	1,488	434	2
	Spanish Fork	28,950	15	0	1	6	8	625	116	481	28	3
	Springville	26,883	31	0	7	7	17	754	119	602	33	0
	St. George	70,579	155	0	13	15	127	2,338	606	1,583	149	8
	Stockton	593	2	0	0	0	2	9	5	4	0	0
	Sunset	4,870	4	0	0	0	4	142	38	103	1	0
	Syracuse	21,544	19	0	10	0	9	297	38	246	13	0
	Taylorsville City	57,944	231	3	34	61	133	2,900	504	2,060	336	6
	Tooele	30,019	69	0	20	5	44	867	134	663	70	21
	Tremonton	6,383	13	0	3	1	9	217	29	179	9	1
	Vernal	8,231	11	0	3	0	8	245	27	195	23	1
	Washington	16,607	24	0	6	3	15	452	99	324	29	0
	West Bountiful	5,287	7	0	1	0	6	110	25	83	2	0
	West Jordan	96,681	203	1	37	49	116	3,395	559	2,512	324	15
	West Valley	121,447	594	6	92	155	341	6,745	1,106	4,548	1,091	30
	Woods Cross	8,440	11	0	3	4	4	250	50	172	28	0
VERMONT	Barre	9,050	7	0	2	2	3	257	37	207	13	0
	Barre Town	8,146	1	0	0	0	1	74	14	56	4	0
	Bellows Falls	2,957	9	0	0	1	8	56	16	36	4	1
	Bennington	15,297	34	0	6	0	28	535	88	404	43	2
	Berlin	2,875	2	0	0	0	2	31	0	30	1	0
	Bradford	819	0	0	0	0	0	16	1	14	1	0
	Brandon	3,926	7	1	1	0	5	83	28	49	6	1
	Brattleboro	11,706	26	1	4	2	19	351	47	293	11	4
	Burlington	38,153	135	0	22	18	95	1,673	359	1,268	46	4
	Castleton	4,384	1	0	0	0	1	7	1	6	0	0
	Chester	3,092	3	0	1	0	2	50	25	25	0	0
	Colchester	17,201	26	0	6	5	15	648	101	530	17	2
	Dover	1,448	1	0	0	0	1	197	11	183	3	0
	Essex	19,350	17	0	5	3	9	414	75	328	11	2

[1] The FBI does not publish arson data unless it receives data from either the agency or the state for all 12 months of the calendar year.

Table 8. Offenses Known to Law Enforcement, by State and City, 2007 *(Contd.)*

(Number.)

State	City	Population	Violent crime	Murder and non-negligent man-slaughter	Forcible rape	Robbery	Aggravated assault	Property crime	Burglary	Larceny-theft	Motor vehicle theft	Arson[1]
	Fair Haven	2,963	2	0	0	0	2	65	13	47	5	2
	Hardwick	3,271	3	0	1	0	2	74	16	56	2	0
	Hartford	10,892	11	1	1	2	7	127	25	96	6	2
	Hinesburg	4,552	3	0	1	2	0	79	21	56	2	0
	Ludlow	2,736	1	0	0	1	0	64	12	52	0	0
	Lyndonville	1,238	0	0	0	0	0	3	3	0	0	0
	Manchester	4,366	2	0	0	0	2	134	20	107	7	0
	Middlebury	8,194	5	0	2	0	3	269	26	241	2	2
	Milton	10,469	21	0	5	0	16	239	34	197	8	1
	Montpelier	7,944	15	0	2	1	12	343	59	273	11	1
	Morristown	5,606	9	0	1	0	8	116	15	98	3	0
	Newport	5,329	3	0	2	0	1	123	22	100	1	0
	Northfield	5,813	7	0	0	0	7	105	24	78	3	0
	Norwich	3,551	1	0	1	0	0	35	12	23	0	0
	Randolph	5,124	4	0	0	0	4	58	6	49	3	0
	Richmond	4,128	0	0	0	0	0	9	2	6	1	1
	Rutland	19,626	37	1	2	10	24	821	115	683	23	3
	Shelburne	7,071	4	0	0	1	3	103	20	81	2	0
	South Burlington	17,333	20	0	9	2	9	631	27	572	32	1
	Springfield	8,752	20	0	2	3	15	261	60	192	9	0
	St. Albans	7,374	33	0	0	1	32	499	46	444	9	0
	St. Johnsbury	7,553	4	0	0	2	2	91	17	70	4	2
	Stowe	4,822	2	0	1	0	1	243	34	206	3	0
	Swanton	6,508	2	0	0	0	2	91	28	61	2	0
	Thetford	2,836	0	0	0	0	0	3	2	1	0	0
	Vergennes	2,747	0	0	0	0	0	62	5	56	1	0
	Waterbury	5,290	1	0	0	0	1	36	3	32	1	0
	Weathersfield	2,868	0	0	0	0	0	39	10	28	1	0
	Williston	8,363	13	0	5	1	7	308	13	288	7	0
	Wilmington	2,358	3	0	1	0	2	67	25	40	2	0
	Windsor	3,687	5	0	0	0	5	29	10	18	1	0
	Winhall	786	0	0	0	0	0	74	5	66	3	1
	Winooski	6,284	20	0	0	3	17	279	52	216	11	0
	Woodstock	3,174	0	0	0	0	0	74	7	38	29	0
VIRGINIA	Abingdon	7,953	14	0	3	0	11	371	22	332	17	0
	Alexandria	137,812	370	7	18	162	183	3,280	364	2,557	359	4
	Altavista	3,379	11	0	3	1	7	129	12	109	8	0
	Amherst	2,221	2	0	0	1	1	27	1	24	2	0
	Appalachia	1,751	5	0	0	1	4	47	15	28	4	0
	Ashland	7,111	19	0	2	8	9	288	22	247	19	1
	Bedford	6,216	10	0	5	1	4	132	19	101	12	0
	Berryville	3,216	3	0	1	0	2	68	1	61	6	0
	Big Stone Gap	5,689	7	0	1	2	4	164	33	124	7	1
	Blacksburg	39,250	63	0	8	10	45	656	120	520	16	5
	Blackstone	3,526	11	0	3	1	7	133	11	112	10	1
	Bluefield	5,213	12	0	0	1	11	179	19	156	4	1
	Boykins	611	0	0	0	0	0	5	1	4	0	0
	Bridgewater	5,431	1	0	0	0	1	20	6	14	0	0
	Bristol	17,484	77	0	11	17	49	764	122	604	38	5
	Broadway	3,016	1	0	1	0	0	11	3	7	1	0
	Buena Vista	6,456	7	0	2	0	5	69	0	67	2	1
	Burkeville	470	3	0	0	0	3	18	0	16	2	0
	Cape Charles	1,530	5	0	0	2	3	19	9	10	0	0
	Cedar Bluff	1,064	1	0	0	0	1	11	1	10	0	0
	Charlottesville	40,265	273	3	26	93	151	1,938	278	1,524	136	10
	Chase City	2,343	4	0	1	0	3	63	12	43	8	0
	Chatham	1,278	0	0	0	0	0	14	6	7	1	0
	Chesapeake	223,093	979	12	78	326	563	7,216	1,251	5,476	489	27
	Chilhowie	1,771	0	0	0	0	0	37	5	31	1	1
	Chincoteague	4,379	5	0	1	1	3	101	27	68	6	0
	Christiansburg	17,983	53	0	1	7	45	762	111	622	29	3
	Clarksville	1,269	0	0	0	0	0	26	1	25	0	0
	Clifton Forge	4,008	6	0	0	1	5	84	22	61	1	2
	Clinchco	408	0	0	0	0	0	0	0	0	0	0
	Clintwood	1,513	4	0	0	0	4	56	12	42	2	0
	Colonial Beach	3,733	7	1	0	3	3	40	6	30	4	0
	Colonial Heights	17,747	47	0	2	23	22	731	42	641	48	14
	Courtland	1,259	0	0	0	0	0	0	0	0	0	0
	Covington	6,027	13	0	4	1	8	166	28	130	8	3
	Crewe	2,266	16	0	0	5	11	98	19	74	5	0
	Culpeper	13,574	52	0	5	15	32	424	38	364	22	4
	Damascus	1,086	3	0	0	1	2	41	2	35	4	0
	Danville	45,114	204	5	9	98	92	2,437	550	1,775	112	19
	Dayton	1,347	1	0	1	0	0	17	3	12	2	0

[1] The FBI does not publish arson data unless it receives data from either the agency or the state for all 12 months of the calendar year.

Table 8.   Offenses Known to Law Enforcement, by State and City, 2007 (Contd.)

(Number.)

State	City	Population	Violent crime	Murder and non-negligent man-slaughter	Forcible rape	Robbery	Aggravated assault	Property crime	Burglary	Larceny-theft	Motor vehicle theft	Arson[1]
	Dublin	2,206	5	0	0	2	3	50	5	43	2	1
	Dumfries	4,795	16	0	0	6	10	167	40	108	19	1
	Edinburg	877	0	0	0	0	0	3	0	3	0	0
	Elkton	2,597	2	0	0	1	1	25	6	19	0	0
	Emporia	5,607	66	1	1	16	48	370	72	282	16	1
	Exmore	1,381	6	0	0	5	1	40	8	31	1	0
	Fairfax City	22,484	39	1	9	11	18	616	52	522	42	5
	Falls Church	10,831	32	0	2	16	14	347	31	290	26	2
	Farmville	6,908	8	0	4	1	3	97	14	79	4	1
	Franklin	8,856	35	1	1	6	27	399	80	285	34	2
	Fredericksburg	21,521	150	3	14	40	93	1,103	99	932	72	9
	Fries	557	0	0	0	0	0	0	0	0	0	0
	Front Royal	14,700	38	0	10	9	19	373	33	313	27	1
	Galax	6,643	20	1	2	0	17	299	25	260	14	2
	Gate City	2,081	1	0	1	0	0	45	5	40	0	0
	Glade Spring	1,544	1	0	0	1	0	10	3	7	0	0
	Glasgow	1,011	1	0	0	0	1	2	0	2	0	0
	Glen Lyn	167	0	0	0	0	0	7	1	6	0	0
	Gordonsville	1,684	1	0	1	0	0	28	9	19	0	1
	Gretna	1,204	2	0	0	1	1	20	8	11	1	0
	Grottoes	2,178	5	0	0	0	5	39	20	17	2	0
	Grundy	975	0	0	0	0	0	5	0	5	0	0
	Halifax	1,272	2	0	0	0	2	16	2	13	1	1
	Hampton	144,490	522	6	52	251	213	4,923	764	3,658	501	34
	Harrisonburg	40,869	150	0	11	37	102	1,240	250	874	116	5
	Haymarket	1,790	0	0	0	0	0	2	0	2	0	0
	Haysi	179	1	0	0	0	1	1	0	1	0	0
	Herndon	21,892	46	1	4	11	30	430	18	396	16	1
	Hillsville	2,691	11	0	3	1	7	75	16	53	6	0
	Honaker	909	1	0	0	0	1	12	6	6	0	0
	Hurt	1,226	0	0	0	0	0	12	3	8	1	0
	Independence	901	0	0	0	0	0	8	2	4	2	0
	Jonesville	981	1	0	0	0	1	15	2	13	0	0
	Kenbridge	1,315	3	0	1	0	2	15	3	11	1	0
	Kilmarnock	1,195	2	0	0	1	1	9	0	9	0	0
	La Crosse	595	2	0	0	0	2	15	8	5	2	0
	Lawrenceville	1,139	7	0	3	1	3	26	6	20	0	0
	Lebanon	3,185	2	0	0	1	1	105	7	92	6	1
	Leesburg	38,931	70	0	13	21	36	797	60	689	48	4
	Lexington	6,711	6	0	0	1	5	93	15	74	4	0
	Louisa	1,557	8	1	2	0	5	42	11	28	3	0
	Luray	4,879	6	0	1	0	5	133	19	111	3	2
	Lynchburg	67,932	332	1	23	81	227	2,381	465	1,754	162	17
	Manassas	36,735	197	2	16	58	121	1,132	178	838	116	8
	Manassas Park	11,816	27	1	8	6	12	236	21	177	38	2
	Marion	6,100	41	0	1	1	39	192	27	159	6	0
	Martinsville	14,856	51	2	10	11	28	614	94	483	37	5
	Middleburg	954	0	0	0	0	0	18	0	18	0	0
	Mount Jackson	1,799	0	0	0	0	0	26	1	23	2	0
	Narrows	2,189	2	0	0	0	2	14	2	12	0	0
	New Market	1,863	0	0	0	0	0	19	5	13	1	0
	Newport News	177,550	1,229	28	91	513	597	7,386	1,584	5,132	670	79
	Norfolk	227,903	1,924	48	97	910	869	11,518	1,694	8,797	1,027	36
	Norton	3,602	7	0	1	0	6	258	22	234	2	2
	Occoquan	817	0	0	0	0	0	3	0	2	1	0
	Onancock	1,437	4	0	0	2	2	15	2	11	2	0
	Onley	490	1	0	0	1	0	25	1	24	0	0
	Orange	4,597	16	1	1	3	11	115	21	89	5	1
	Pearisburg	2,805	0	0	0	0	0	62	13	49	0	0
	Pembroke	1,190	1	0	0	0	1	15	4	10	1	0
	Pennington Gap	1,753	0	0	0	0	0	46	12	34	0	0
	Petersburg	32,210	499	7	17	212	263	2,332	673	1,375	284	14
	Pocahontas	428	0	0	0	0	0	1	0	0	1	0
	Poquoson	11,939	16	0	1	0	15	155	20	124	11	2
	Portsmouth	101,284	804	17	36	326	425	5,049	1,101	3,646	302	18
	Pound	1,082	1	0	0	0	1	36	5	28	3	0
	Pulaski	9,006	27	0	4	8	15	367	85	260	22	3
	Purcellville	5,048	7	1	3	0	3	64	4	58	2	1
	Quantico	634	1	0	0	0	1	19	3	14	2	0
	Radford	14,317	40	0	8	5	27	502	120	359	23	5
	Rich Creek	692	2	0	0	0	2	24	4	19	1	0
	Richlands	4,083	20	0	2	3	15	236	36	192	8	1
	Richmond	191,785	1,837	51	53	973	760	8,966	1,857	5,816	1,293	49
	Roanoke	90,894	901	4	55	266	576	5,000	1,016	3,637	347	28

[1] The FBI does not publish arson data unless it receives data from either the agency or the state for all 12 months of the calendar year.

Table 8. Offenses Known to Law Enforcement, by State and City, 2007 *(Contd.)*

(Number.)

State	City	Population	Violent crime	Murder and non-negligent man-slaughter	Forcible rape	Robbery	Aggravated assault	Property crime	Burglary	Larceny-theft	Motor vehicle theft	Arson[1]
	Rocky Mount	4,568	10	0	1	1	8	153	18	128	7	0
	Rural Retreat	1,357	0	0	0	0	0	0	0	0	0	0
	Salem	24,774	26	0	3	9	14	700	88	574	38	2
	Saltville	2,256	12	0	1	0	11	47	12	31	4	1
	Shenandoah	1,873	1	0	0	0	1	98	71	26	1	1
	South Boston	8,007	41	2	6	8	25	430	72	338	20	1
	South Hill	4,618	16	0	0	5	11	211	32	170	9	2
	Stanley	1,336	1	0	0	0	1	25	0	25	0	0
	Staunton	23,210	71	0	4	19	48	730	99	600	31	6
	Stephens City	1,463	1	0	0	0	1	37	5	31	1	0
	St. Paul	971	1	0	0	1	0	8	3	5	0	0
	Strasburg	4,348	9	0	0	0	9	137	8	126	3	1
	Suffolk	83,631	333	2	25	84	222	2,514	457	1,930	127	16
	Tappahannock	2,158	16	0	3	6	7	114	8	104	2	1
	Tazewell	4,369	12	0	2	1	9	98	21	74	3	0
	Timberville	1,705	3	0	0	1	2	14	1	12	1	0
	Victoria	1,783	2	0	0	0	2	25	4	20	1	0
	Vinton	7,924	14	1	0	0	13	269	26	240	3	2
	Virginia Beach	435,943	1,089	16	88	555	430	13,030	2,159	10,285	586	171
	Warrenton	9,064	26	0	2	6	18	251	21	220	10	0
	Warsaw	1,364	0	0	0	0	0	8	0	8	0	0
	Waverly	2,194	5	0	0	2	3	28	10	16	2	1
	Waynesboro	21,681	79	1	7	17	54	652	90	524	38	9
	Weber City	1,349	3	0	0	0	3	35	9	25	1	0
	West Point	3,133	1	0	0	0	1	28	8	19	1	2
	White Stone	342	0	0	0	0	0	7	6	1	0	0
	Williamsburg	11,740	30	0	4	20	6	256	18	218	20	1
	Winchester	25,443	106	1	10	35	60	1,235	169	993	73	4
	Wise	3,256	8	0	2	2	4	112	23	87	2	3
	Woodstock	4,303	8	0	0	1	7	49	0	42	7	0
	Wytheville	8,184	9	0	2	0	7	292	42	239	11	0
WASHINGTON	Aberdeen	16,382	33	0	5	13	15	1,085	220	752	113	3
	Airway Heights	4,794	14	1	3	1	9	156	36	108	12	2
	Algona	2,726	7	0	2	1	4	72	14	44	14	0
	Anacortes	16,948	17	1	2	1	13	568	95	448	25	3
	Arlington	16,736	18	0	0	2	16	858	132	590	136	5
	Asotin	1,130	3	0	0	0	3	39	10	26	3	1
	Auburn	49,710	248	1	12	92	143	3,225	590	1,962	673	30
	Bainbridge Island	22,442	24	0	3	2	19	382	86	288	8	8
	Battle Ground	14,149	33	0	11	3	19	385	91	270	24	5
	Bellevue	118,984	138	0	29	61	48	4,181	583	3,152	446	20
	Bellingham	76,290	187	2	29	58	98	5,022	696	4,087	239	31
	Bingen	703	1	0	0	0	1	24	9	14	1	0
	Black Diamond	3,948	5	0	0	0	5	51	12	35	4	1
	Blaine	4,622	5	0	1	0	4	241	24	210	7	2
	Bonney Lake	15,737	31	0	3	4	24	464	81	337	46	4
	Bothell	31,521	21	0	2	12	7	767	150	510	107	8
	Bremerton	35,068	336	0	63	60	213	1,652	368	1,185	99	12
	Brewster	2,124	11	0	3	2	6	119	27	88	4	1
	Brier	6,382	5	0	1	2	2	104	26	59	19	0
	Buckley	5,514	4	0	2	0	2	138	23	99	16	0
	Burien	31,035	191	1	16	83	91	1,710	375	943	392	6
	Burlington	8,921	36	0	2	18	16	1,322	134	1,072	116	1
	Camas	18,256	18	0	3	5	10	396	60	313	23	6
	Carnation	1,827	0	0	0	0	0	11	3	7	1	0
	Castle Rock	2,147	7	0	1	0	6	97	25	65	7	3
	Centralia	15,708	99	1	8	15	75	991	168	764	59	7
	Chehalis	7,249	28	0	5	11	12	695	78	581	36	2
	Cheney	10,597	15	0	5	3	7	247	31	202	14	1
	Chewelah	2,334	2	0	1	0	1	75	16	54	5	0
	Clarkston	7,231	15	0	1	2	12	358	23	314	21	2
	Cle Elum	3,330	4	0	0	2	2	190	32	145	13	1
	Clyde Hill	2,997	1	0	0	0	1	36	20	15	1	2
	College Place	9,148	8	0	3	1	4	251	34	210	7	1
	Colville	5,055	3	0	1	0	2	194	17	167	10	0
	Connell	2,987	2	0	1	0	1	43	4	37	2	0
	Cosmopolis	1,692	2	0	0	0	2	22	2	20	0	0
	Coulee Dam	1,083	0	0	0	0	0	24	11	10	3	0
	Coupeville	1,857	1	0	0	0	1	91	22	64	5	1
	Covington	18,072	25	0	9	9	7	504	91	343	70	5
	Des Moines	28,907	117	2	21	54	40	888	211	450	227	2
	Dupont	6,831	2	0	0	0	2	38	15	22	1	0
	Duvall	6,064	1	0	0	0	1	33	8	24	1	0
	East Wenatchee	9,013	36	0	5	5	26	694	94	578	22	3

[1] The FBI does not publish arson data unless it receives data from either the agency or the state for all 12 months of the calendar year.

Table 8. Offenses Known to Law Enforcement, by State and City, 2007 *(Contd.)*

(Number.)

State	City	Population	Violent crime	Murder and non-negligent man-slaughter	Forcible rape	Robbery	Aggravated assault	Property crime	Burglary	Larceny-theft	Motor vehicle theft	Arson[1]
	Eatonville	2,455	5	0	1	1	3	49	10	39	0	3
	Edgewood	9,860	24	0	1	6	17	195	62	118	15	1
	Edmonds	40,218	60	1	4	22	33	985	247	625	113	13
	Ellensburg	17,033	41	0	14	5	22	893	176	682	35	5
	Elma	3,177	10	0	3	4	3	288	83	172	33	0
	Enumclaw	10,966	7	0	0	2	5	285	41	208	36	16
	Ephrata	7,361	16	0	2	2	12	516	117	378	21	4
	Everett	98,845	564	7	61	209	287	8,739	1,405	5,456	1,878	19
	Everson	2,031	6	0	2	1	3	115	19	94	2	0
	Federal Way	84,026	287	3	48	129	107	4,837	739	3,159	939	19
	Ferndale	10,559	24	0	3	6	15	396	61	303	32	6
	Fife	6,746	47	0	7	11	29	565	74	354	137	0
	Fircrest	6,318	22	0	1	5	16	170	30	118	22	2
	Forks	3,249	21	0	2	1	18	178	44	133	1	0
	Garfield	604	0	0	0	0	0	2	0	2	0	0
	Gig Harbor	6,691	14	1	0	6	7	385	51	297	37	1
	Goldendale	3,758	9	0	0	0	9	228	40	169	19	7
	Grand Coulee	1,950	11	0	1	2	8	85	30	53	2	0
	Grandview	9,222	21	0	6	3	12	621	144	407	70	5
	Granite Falls	2,972	5	0	1	1	3	130	19	100	11	0
	Hoquiam	9,058	26	1	6	6	13	464	106	326	32	5
	Ilwaco	1,004	1	0	0	0	1	56	8	46	2	0
	Issaquah	19,193	9	0	0	5	4	864	77	686	101	0
	Kalama	2,077	2	0	0	0	2	88	6	82	0	1
	Kelso	12,156	81	0	16	19	46	1,000	164	763	73	4
	Kenmore	20,167	30	0	6	12	12	448	101	298	49	3
	Kennewick	63,147	236	1	38	31	166	2,362	341	1,862	159	25
	Kent	83,929	525	4	64	174	283	4,873	1,075	2,790	1,008	29
	Kettle Falls	1,621	1	0	0	1	0	69	16	51	2	0
	Kirkland	46,686	67	0	13	24	30	1,881	336	1,366	179	12
	Kittitas	1,194	2	0	0	2	0	58	13	42	3	0
	La Center	1,944	3	0	0	0	3	25	3	21	1	0
	Lacey	36,037	89	2	6	24	57	1,749	259	1,341	149	6
	Lake Forest Park	12,506	3	0	1	1	1	253	55	163	35	0
	Lake Stevens[3]	8,238	32	1	3	7	21		129			5
	Lakewood	57,465	495	2	47	137	309	3,724	890	2,215	619	17
	Langley	1,035	0	0	0	0	0	56	10	45	1	0
	Liberty Lake	6,399	5	0	0	0	5	94	17	60	17	1
	Long Beach	1,400	2	0	2	0	0	90	26	60	4	0
	Longview	37,068	134	3	45	39	47	2,341	480	1,662	199	11
	Lynden	11,159	9	0	2	0	7	259	35	218	6	2
	Lynnwood	33,663	131	0	11	73	47	2,873	280	2,162	431	13
	Malden	191	0	0	0	0	0	1	1	0	0	0
	Maple Valley	16,798	11	1	5	0	5	365	108	215	42	4
	Marysville	32,623	105	0	8	44	53	1,534	230	925	379	10
	McCleary	1,589	1	0	0	0	1	27	14	7	6	1
	Medical Lake	4,493	2	0	1	0	1	58	19	36	3	0
	Medina	3,561	1	0	0	1	0	77	6	62	9	0
	Mercer Island	23,671	6	0	0	1	5	392	73	289	30	8
	Mill Creek	15,843	22	0	2	5	15	573	98	388	87	0
	Milton	6,836	16	0	2	7	7	281	47	187	47	1
	Monroe	16,505	27	0	0	10	17	615	116	425	74	1
	Montesano	3,556	1	0	0	1	0	98	13	79	6	0
	Morton	1,102	2	0	0	0	2	37	3	34	0	0
	Moses Lake	17,561	82	0	24	20	38	1,801	336	1,365	100	12
	Mountlake Terrace	20,193	31	0	3	12	16	690	138	441	111	15
	Mount Vernon	30,521	77	0	12	30	35	2,324	294	1,866	164	12
	Moxee	2,044	4	0	2	0	2	12	2	10	0	0
	Mukilteo	20,642	27	0	5	10	12	568	136	335	97	5
	Napavine	1,499	3	0	2	0	1	39	0	36	3	0
	Newcastle	9,867	11	0	4	2	5	214	46	142	26	2
	Normandy Park	6,207	4	0	0	0	4	133	33	82	18	0
	North Bend	4,605	13	0	3	1	9	144	19	108	17	0
	North Bonneville	775	1	0	0	0	1	12	1	11	0	0
	Oakesdale	379	0	0	0	0	0	4	4	0	0	0
	Oak Harbor	23,168	35	0	7	5	23	555	104	403	48	7
	Oakville	730	0	0	0	0	0	22	7	13	2	0
	Ocean Shores	4,785	3	0	0	1	2	187	102	80	5	0
	Odessa	931	4	0	1	0	3	27	3	23	1	0
	Olympia	44,946	118	0	28	27	63	2,023	296	1,493	234	12
	Omak	4,745	18	0	3	1	14	251	56	177	18	6
	Oroville	1,588	6	0	2	0	4	66	14	47	5	1
	Othello	6,357	23	1	2	2	18	627	147	434	46	2
	Pacific	5,910	10	0	3	3	4	235	73	120	42	2

[1] The FBI does not publish arson data unless it receives data from either the agency or the state for all 12 months of the calendar year.
[3] The FBI determined that the agency's data were overreported. Consequently, affected data are not included in this table.

Table 8. Offenses Known to Law Enforcement, by State and City, 2007 *(Contd.)*

(Number.)

State	City	Population	Violent crime	Murder and non-negligent man-slaughter	Forcible rape	Robbery	Aggravated assault	Property crime	Burglary	Larceny-theft	Motor vehicle theft	Arson[1]
	Pasco	52,761	150	0	29	43	78	1,811	408	1,138	265	6
	Pe Ell	690	0	0	0	0	0	0	0	0	0	0
	Port Angeles	19,064	76	1	24	12	39	873	135	674	64	14
	Port Orchard	8,026	80	0	12	1	67	378	70	280	28	2
	Port Townsend	9,248	26	0	1	4	21	387	76	306	5	0
	Poulsbo	7,919	28	0	8	1	19	291	51	232	8	6
	Prosser	5,150	5	0	1	1	3	198	39	143	16	2
	Pullman	25,408	31	0	10	5	16	480	131	339	10	5
	Puyallup	37,078	136	1	16	53	66	3,092	389	2,191	512	17
	Quincy	5,659	12	0	6	2	4	332	115	195	22	0
	Rainier	1,637	3	1	0	0	2	30	16	12	2	1
	Raymond	2,976	5	0	1	0	4	82	31	45	6	0
	Reardan	610	0	0	0	0	0	5	1	2	2	0
	Redmond	49,195	78	0	13	19	46	1,685	239	1,292	154	5
	Renton	59,656	248	1	26	103	118	4,054	677	2,701	676	11
	Republic	985	2	0	0	0	2	12	2	9	1	0
	Richland	45,555	105	0	13	23	69	1,249	213	960	76	6
	Ridgefield	4,023	2	0	0	1	1	112	34	66	12	0
	Ritzville	1,714	2	0	1	0	1	78	21	54	3	0
	Rosalia	571	0	0	0	0	0	11	3	5	3	0
	Roy	834	3	0	0	0	3	5	1	3	1	2
	Royal City	1,990	11	0	0	3	8	67	15	48	4	0
	Ruston	882	8	0	0	1	7	7	5	2	0	1
	Sammamish	35,327	9	0	2	3	4	549	143	386	20	7
	Sea Tac	25,320	156	1	24	67	64	1,745	360	878	507	9
	Seattle	585,118	3,667	24	90	1,522	2,031	33,960	5,986	22,192	5,782	183
	Sedro Woolley	10,643	16	0	1	10	5	695	146	491	58	1
	Selah	7,037	4	0	3	1	0	211	22	163	26	1
	Sequim	5,898	12	0	1	2	9	231	32	193	6	1
	Shelton	9,352	72	0	10	22	40	1,087	151	832	104	4
	Shoreline	52,189	121	2	21	53	45	1,679	326	1,152	201	22
	Snohomish	8,838	22	0	2	6	14	404	98	261	45	5
	Snoqualmie	8,403	0	0	0	0	0	134	16	111	7	0
	South Bend	1,840	1	0	1	0	0	38	11	21	6	1
	Spokane	198,272	1,322	12	88	414	808	11,376	2,175	7,188	2,013	88
	Spokane Valley	83,928	290	0	15	56	219	2,851	481	1,957	413	25
	Stanwood	5,685	11	0	5	1	5	225	25	179	21	2
	Steilacoom	6,159	3	0	0	1	2	89	26	50	13	0
	Sumas	1,157	4	0	1	1	2	32	10	19	3	0
	Sumner	9,601	54	1	6	8	39	475	105	285	85	11
	Sunnyside	14,931	52	1	6	3	42	1,151	276	662	213	12
	Tacoma[7]	196,909	2,059	14	140	647	1,258	14,957	2,628	8,986	3,343	90
	Tenino	2,251	1	0	0	0	1	89	27	57	5	2
	Tieton	1,185	0	0	0	0	0	11	3	8	0	0
	Toledo	686	2	0	0	0	2	29	8	17	4	0
	Tonasket	960	0	0	0	0	0	70	7	62	1	0
	Toppenish	9,213	55	3	9	12	31	686	141	430	115	10
	Tukwila	17,103	160	2	13	81	64	2,908	298	1,976	634	5
	Tumwater	13,695	28	0	5	8	15	488	88	340	60	0
	Union Gap	5,702	33	0	11	9	13	747	91	604	52	0
	University Place	30,699	78	0	12	19	47	936	224	571	141	13
	Vancouver	161,092	646	7	118	166	355	6,557	1,005	4,581	971	59
	Walla Walla	31,002	112	0	30	12	70	1,548	285	1,195	68	20
	Wapato	4,609	39	0	2	16	21	296	86	158	52	4
	Washougal	11,769	18	0	0	3	15	291	61	189	41	2
	Wenatchee	30,179	92	0	17	20	55	1,549	219	1,243	87	6
	Westport	2,554	9	0	0	1	8	108	28	73	7	0
	West Richland	10,477	4	0	2	0	2	117	43	65	9	2
	White Salmon	2,373	2	0	0	1	1	58	11	43	4	0
	Wilbur	891	0	0	0	0	0	11	2	8	1	0
	Winlock	1,233	2	0	0	0	2	57	19	36	2	0
	Winthrop	374	1	0	0	0	1	19	4	15	0	0
	Woodinville	10,143	23	0	6	4	13	468	101	313	54	10
	Woodland	4,691	25	0	7	5	13	172	37	116	19	3
	Woodway	1,390	1	0	0	1	0	40	7	31	2	0
	Yakima	82,951	561	7	66	136	352	5,705	1,209	3,652	844	63
	Yarrow Point	1,039	0	0	0	0	0	8	2	3	3	0
	Yelm	5,359	13	0	5	2	6	210	42	152	16	0
	Zillah	2,679	5	0	0	1	4	159	32	117	10	3
WEST VIRGINIA	Anawalt	240	0	0	0	0	0	0	0	0	0	0
	Ansted	1,597	0	0	0	0	0	5	2	3	0	0
	Barboursville	3,276	7	0	0	1	6	419	36	378	5	0
	Bayard	290	0	0	0	0	0	0	0	0	0	0
	Beckley	16,774	151	1	0	29	121	1,235	202	961	72	13

[1] The FBI does not publish arson data unless it receives data from either the agency or the state for all 12 months of the calendar year.

Table 8.   Offenses Known to Law Enforcement, by State and City, 2007 *(Contd.)*

(Number.)

State	City	Population	Violent crime	Murder and non-negligent man-slaughter	Forcible rape	Robbery	Aggravated assault	Property crime	Burglary	Larceny-theft	Motor vehicle theft	Arson[1]
	Belington	1,831	1	0	0	0	1	9	2	6	1	0
	Benwood	1,463	0	0	0	0	0	5	2	3	0	0
	Bethany	977	0	0	0	0	0	0	0	0	0	0
	Bethlehem	2,506	0	0	0	0	0	7	1	6	0	0
	Bluefield	11,000	43	1	4	12	26	305	101	175	29	6
	Bridgeport	7,806	13	0	1	2	10	193	27	164	2	2
	Buckhannon	5,551	18	0	3	1	14	88	8	72	8	0
	Cameron	1,110	4	0	0	0	4	0	0	0	0	0
	Capon Bridge	250	0	0	0	0	0	4	1	3	0	0
	Ceredo	1,607	4	0	0	1	3	49	13	33	3	0
	Chapmanville	1,132	4	0	0	1	3	39	4	34	1	0
	Charleston	50,510	572	4	14	131	423	3,051	601	2,235	215	33
	Charles Town	4,013	9	0	0	2	7	101	19	77	5	1
	Clarksburg	16,420	89	0	9	7	73	767	144	585	38	10
	Clearview	558	0	0	0	0	0	0	0	0	0	0
	Dunbar	7,612	19	0	6	5	8	181	38	115	28	2
	Elkins	7,050	20	1	2	2	15	210	38	170	2	2
	Follansbee	2,893	3	0	0	1	2	26	9	15	2	2
	Glen Dale	1,443	0	0	0	0	0	36	16	18	2	1
	Glenville	1,470	1	0	0	0	1	20	4	15	1	0
	Grafton	5,372	5	0	0	0	5	30	6	22	2	0
	Harpers Ferry/Bolivar	1,413	2	0	0	1	1	19	1	18	0	1
	Hartford City	515	0	0	0	0	0	0	0	0	0	0
	Henderson	311	0	0	0	0	0	0	0	0	0	0
	Hinton	2,622	10	0	0	2	8	48	14	31	3	0
	Huntington	48,669	367	3	47	181	136	3,626	1,268	2,061	297	27
	Hurricane	6,179	8	0	3	1	4	194	27	156	11	1
	Kenova	3,325	10	0	0	2	8	159	22	125	12	1
	Kermit	225	0	0	0	0	0	0	0	0	0	0
	Keyser	5,331	13	0	4	4	5	151	29	115	7	0
	Lewisburg	3,554	1	0	0	0	1	14	1	12	1	0
	Logan	1,525	39	0	1	7	31	280	37	239	4	6
	Mannington	2,080	2	0	0	0	2	6	5	1	0	0
	Marlinton	1,241	0	0	0	0	0	0	0	0	0	0
	Mason	1,044	1	0	0	0	1	11	5	5	1	0
	Masontown	656	0	0	0	0	0	0	0	0	0	0
	Matoaka	302	1	0	0	0	1	0	0	0	0	0
	Monongah	911	0	0	0	0	0	2	1	1	0	0
	Montgomery	1,925	1	0	0	0	1	48	10	33	5	1
	Moorefield	2,432	16	0	1	0	15	46	9	31	6	0
	Morgantown	28,951	99	1	27	29	42	1,025	248	745	32	3
	Moundsville	9,385	17	0	4	3	10	224	55	156	13	9
	New Cumberland	1,021	0	0	0	0	0	0	0	0	0	0
	Northfork	437	0	0	0	0	0	0	0	0	0	0
	Nutter Fort	1,640	2	0	0	1	1	37	8	27	2	1
	Oceana	1,445	10	0	0	0	10	119	13	103	3	0
	Paden City	2,659	2	0	0	0	2	3	3	0	0	0
	Parkersburg	31,562	68	1	11	18	38	1,468	286	1,077	105	17
	Piedmont	925	0	0	0	0	0	2	1	1	0	0
	Point Pleasant	4,459	6	0	0	1	5	210	37	159	14	1
	Princeton	6,178	62	1	1	9	51	522	91	406	25	4
	Ranson	4,067	13	0	0	4	9	36	1	32	3	0
	Ravenswood	3,992	1	0	0	0	1	17	7	10	0	0
	Reedsville	534	0	0	0	0	0	3	2	1	0	0
	Ridgeley	690	0	0	0	0	0	0	0	0	0	0
	Ripley	3,272	13	1	3	1	8	55	3	49	3	1
	Rivesville	915	0	0	0	0	0	0	0	0	0	0
	Ronceverte	1,523	4	0	1	0	3	31	16	14	1	0
	Shinnston	2,238	2	0	0	0	2	31	4	27	0	0
	South Charleston	12,468	55	0	2	20	33	639	81	517	41	7
	Spencer	2,242	8	0	2	1	5	93	37	52	4	0
	St. Albans	10,999	37	2	0	6	29	427	106	279	42	4
	Summersville	3,366	5	0	0	1	4	82	11	65	6	0
	Triadelphia	816	0	0	0	0	0	0	0	0	0	0
	Vienna	10,667	16	0	3	3	10	291	28	257	6	0
	Wardensville	246	1	0	0	0	1	1	0	1	0	0
	Weirton	19,095	23	0	0	4	19	215	43	161	11	0
	Welch	2,283	5	0	0	2	3	59	13	45	1	0
	West Logan	394	0	0	0	0	0	0	0	0	0	0
	West Milford	651	0	0	0	0	0	0	0	0	0	0
	Weston	4,215	1	0	0	0	1	23	1	21	1	0
	Wheeling	29,057	134	1	15	35	83	981	216	693	72	4
	White Sulphur Springs	2,323	0	0	0	0	0	1	0	1	0	0
	Williamson	3,128	5	0	0	1	4	59	15	40	4	0
	Williamstown	2,975	1	0	0	0	1	44	5	37	2	0

[1] The FBI does not publish arson data unless it receives data from either the agency or the state for all 12 months of the calendar year.

Table 8. Offenses Known to Law Enforcement, by State and City, 2007 *(Contd.)*

(Number.)

State	City	Population	Violent crime	Murder and non-negligent man-slaughter	Forcible rape	Robbery	Aggravated assault	Property crime	Burglary	Larceny-theft	Motor vehicle theft	Arson[1]
WISCONSIN	Albany	1,119	4	0	0	0	4	33	3	29	1	0
	Algoma	3,228	2	0	2	0	0	82	5	73	4	0
	Altoona	6,377	3	0	2	0	1	152	22	117	13	0
	Amery	2,846	7	0	0	0	7	40	6	32	2	0
	Antigo	8,225	7	0	0	0	7	604	101	492	11	0
	Appleton	70,169	146	0	26	23	97	2,379	413	1,883	83	8
	Arcadia	2,329	1	0	0	0	1	44	7	35	2	0
	Ashland	8,147	25	0	1	2	22	374	48	307	19	2
	Ashwaubenon	17,033	10	1	2	0	7	933	66	839	28	1
	Bangor	1,343	2	0	1	1	0	15	4	11	0	0
	Baraboo	11,015	40	0	2	1	37	390	28	347	15	0
	Barron	3,145	6	0	2	2	2	51	10	30	11	0
	Bayfield	579	1	0	0	0	1	20	4	16	0	0
	Bayside	4,216	1	0	0	1	0	23	1	22	0	0
	Beaver Dam	15,551	8	0	1	3	4	493	53	437	3	0
	Belleville	2,246	3	0	1	0	2	43	3	40	0	0
	Beloit	36,424	151	2	12	63	74	1,719	283	1,327	109	14
	Beloit Town	7,475	7	0	1	2	4	163	30	124	9	2
	Berlin	5,197	4	0	0	0	4	193	23	164	6	1
	Black River Falls	3,456	6	0	2	0	4	138	14	118	6	0
	Blair	1,276	2	0	0	0	2	33	9	22	2	1
	Bloomer	3,378	1	0	0	0	1	63	4	56	3	0
	Bloomfield	5,990	4	0	3	0	1	100	16	82	2	0
	Boscobel	3,185	10	0	0	0	10	52	10	42	0	0
	Brillion	2,857	2	0	1	0	1	35	4	29	2	0
	Brodhead	3,089	3	0	1	0	2	63	7	56	0	0
	Brookfield	39,738	29	0	2	16	11	1,190	112	1,063	15	2
	Brookfield Township	6,243	13	0	0	2	11	173	23	144	6	0
	Brown Deer	11,507	25	0	1	9	15	462	46	386	30	0
	Burlington	10,599	3	0	0	1	2	328	34	285	9	0
	Burlington Town	6,552	4	0	0	0	4	69	10	55	4	1
	Butler	1,806	6	0	0	0	6	60	13	44	3	1
	Caledonia	25,682	28	0	0	23	5	299	51	226	22	0
	Campbellsport	1,929	0	0	0	0	0	39	4	35	0	0
	Campbell Township	4,437	5	0	0	0	5	51	9	40	2	0
	Cedarburg	11,216	5	0	0	0	5	154	5	148	1	0
	Chenequa	590	0	0	0	0	0	5	1	4	0	0
	Chetek	2,177	2	0	0	0	2	49	20	26	3	0
	Chilton	3,635	1	0	1	0	0	63	9	50	4	0
	Chippewa Falls	13,158	18	0	2	2	14	243	36	201	6	2
	Cleveland	1,401	3	0	1	0	2	8	1	7	0	1
	Clinton	2,261	2	0	0	1	1	55	5	48	2	2
	Clintonville	4,435	16	0	1	0	15	178	16	157	5	1
	Colby-Abbotsford	3,649	3	0	0	0	3	82	5	72	5	0
	Columbus	5,068	2	0	0	0	2	112	6	106	0	0
	Combined Locks	3,121	2	0	0	0	2	19	4	15	0	0
	Cornell	1,424	4	0	0	0	4	34	2	32	0	0
	Cottage Grove	5,530	4	0	1	0	3	150	32	113	5	0
	Crandon	1,880	10	6	0	0	4	60	15	42	3	0
	Cross Plains	3,541	2	0	0	1	1	52	10	41	1	0
	Cuba City	2,052	3	0	1	0	2	58	9	49	0	2
	Cudahy	17,998	68	0	9	28	31	589	115	447	27	4
	Cumberland	2,299	0	0	0	0	0	24	1	18	5	0
	Dane	952	0	0	0	0	0	0	0	0	0	0
	Darien	1,609	2	0	0	0	2	38	5	32	1	0
	Darlington	2,328	9	0	0	0	9	32	3	27	2	0
	DeForest	8,845	7	0	1	0	6	167	26	137	4	0
	Delafield	6,975	14	0	0	2	12	125	12	111	2	0
	Delavan	8,450	21	5	1	1	14	366	27	326	13	0
	Delavan Town	4,906	17	0	0	0	17	117	23	89	5	0
	Denmark	2,124	0	0	0	0	0	9	2	7	0	0
	De Pere	22,781	5	0	2	0	3	413	56	347	10	0
	Dodgeville	4,577	4	0	1	2	1	110	10	99	1	0
	Durand	1,867	0	0	0	0	0	4	2	1	1	0
	Eagle River	1,579	2	0	1	1	0	109	8	97	4	0
	Eagle Village	1,838	3	0	0	0	3	21	5	16	0	0
	East Troy	4,276	6	1	2	1	2	212	15	191	6	1
	Eau Claire	63,472	96	0	12	12	72	1,966	365	1,503	98	2
	Edgar	1,490	1	0	0	0	1	7	2	5	0	0
	Edgerton	5,230	1	0	0	1	0	41	12	28	1	0
	Eleva	656	0	0	0	0	0	11	2	8	1	0
	Elkhart Lake	1,153	0	0	0	0	0	35	3	32	0	0
	Elkhorn	9,354	7	0	6	0	1	240	31	202	7	0
	Elk Mound	805	4	0	0	0	4	6	2	3	1	0

[1] The FBI does not publish arson data unless it receives data from either the agency or the state for all 12 months of the calendar year.

Table 8.   Offenses Known to Law Enforcement, by State and City, 2007 (Contd.)

(Number.)

State	City	Population	Violent crime	Murder and non-negligent man-slaughter	Forcible rape	Robbery	Aggravated assault	Property crime	Burglary	Larceny-theft	Motor vehicle theft	Arson[1]
	Ellsworth	3,112	2	0	0	0	2	77	16	59	2	2
	Elm Grove	6,064	0	0	0	0	0	98	9	88	1	0
	Elroy	1,487	3	0	1	1	1	23	3	20	0	0
	Evansville	5,023	9	0	0	0	9	104	7	94	3	0
	Everest	15,771	56	2	2	4	48	371	66	297	8	3
	Fennimore	2,255	1	0	0	0	1	63	9	54	0	0
	Fitchburg	22,793	64	1	7	17	39	724	74	616	34	4
	Fond du Lac	42,349	147	0	29	19	99	1,204	113	1,055	36	9
	Fontana	1,890	3	0	0	0	3	44	6	38	0	0
	Fort Atkinson	12,023	9	0	0	2	7	357	16	335	6	0
	Fox Lake	1,486	2	1	1	0	0	14	1	13	0	0
	Fox Point	6,663	3	0	0	3	0	53	7	46	0	0
	Franklin	34,449	73	0	9	7	57	804	120	639	45	7
	Frederic	1,220	0	0	0	0	0	9	0	9	0	0
	Geneva Town	4,726	2	0	0	0	2	139	18	120	1	0
	Genoa City	2,911	0	0	0	0	0	34	1	30	3	0
	Germantown	19,491	15	1	4	4	6	413	52	348	13	4
	Glendale	12,736	29	0	0	26	3	759	33	657	69	0
	Grafton	11,712	7	0	0	3	4	230	10	216	4	0
	Grand Chute	20,793	19	0	5	7	7	1,178	60	1,082	36	1
	Grand Rapids	7,741	1	0	1	0	0	53	15	34	4	0
	Grantsburg	1,445	1	0	1	0	0	38	13	24	1	0
	Green Bay	100,010	616	2	67	89	458	2,843	565	2,094	184	11
	Greendale	13,708	17	0	0	9	8	781	17	753	11	0
	Greenfield	35,435	59	0	9	25	25	1,456	169	1,204	83	3
	Green Lake	1,158	1	0	0	0	1	22	0	21	1	0
	Hales Corners	7,538	7	0	1	1	5	157	15	137	5	0
	Hartford	13,611	7	0	0	2	5	332	28	294	10	1
	Hartland	8,793	7	0	1	2	4	126	25	100	1	0
	Hayward	2,330	16	0	6	2	8	206	21	172	13	0
	Hazel Green	1,134	1	0	0	0	1	0	0	0	0	0
	Hillsboro	1,283	0	0	0	0	0	1	0	1	0	0
	Hobart-Lawrence	9,725	0	0	0	0	0	61	10	48	3	0
	Holmen	7,512	5	0	0	0	5	137	22	107	8	0
	Horicon	3,640	4	1	1	1	1	57	2	52	3	1
	Hortonville	2,774	1	0	0	0	1	142	8	132	2	1
	Hudson	12,408	26	0	2	9	15	656	60	580	16	0
	Hurley	1,623	4	0	0	1	3	59	4	49	6	0
	Independence	1,243	2	0	0	1	1	8	0	8	0	0
	Iron Ridge	990	1	0	0	0	1	14	1	12	1	0
	Jackson	6,248	9	0	3	0	6	42	5	35	2	2
	Janesville	63,383	158	0	25	55	78	2,731	431	2,217	83	9
	Jefferson	7,773	32	0	1	1	30	239	18	209	12	1
	Juneau	2,654	1	0	1	0	0	60	14	45	1	0
	Kaukauna	15,405	8	0	2	1	5	324	4	300	20	1
	Kenosha	96,996	357	2	46	144	165	3,395	770	2,368	257	6
	Kewaskum	4,070	5	0	1	0	4	30	3	27	0	1
	Kewaunee	2,877	3	0	1	0	2	34	4	30	0	0
	Kiel	3,518	14	0	1	2	11	91	6	80	5	1
	Kohler	1,992	0	0	0	0	0	60	0	58	2	0
	La Crosse	50,032	164	1	15	22	126	1,867	305	1,475	87	6
	Ladysmith	3,594	2	0	1	0	1	154	10	140	4	0
	Lake Delton	2,973	11	0	2	2	7	543	36	498	9	1
	Lake Geneva	8,209	9	0	4	1	4	418	31	379	8	0
	Lake Hallie	5,959	6	0	0	0	6	233	44	180	9	0
	Lake Mills	5,483	5	0	2	0	3	60	6	53	1	0
	Lancaster	3,869	0	0	0	0	0	53	12	41	0	0
	Lodi	2,947	3	0	0	0	3	81	5	75	1	0
	Luxemburg	2,286	0	0	0	0	0	30	5	23	2	0
	Madison	225,370	834	8	57	359	410	8,224	2,059	5,658	507	68
	Manitowoc	33,541	66	0	5	2	59	789	116	633	40	0
	Maple Bluff	1,286	0	0	0	0	0	34	3	31	0	0
	Marathon City	1,562	4	0	0	0	4	37	7	30	0	0
	Marinette	10,906	12	0	2	4	6	440	54	369	17	2
	Marion	1,232	1	0	0	0	1	10	0	9	1	0
	Markesan	1,332	2	0	0	0	2	29	4	24	1	0
	Marshall Village	3,604	5	0	2	0	3	79	10	67	2	0
	Marshfield	19,175	16	3	3	4	6	504	95	395	14	8
	Mauston	4,329	22	0	1	0	21	158	17	132	9	0
	Mayville	5,430	1	0	0	0	1	14	2	12	0	0
	McFarland	7,663	8	0	1	0	7	195	48	143	4	0
	Medford	4,108	7	0	3	0	4	159	13	145	1	0
	Menasha	16,756	63	0	8	5	50	529	85	428	16	1
	Menomonee Falls	34,612	23	1	0	9	13	631	85	520	26	1

[1] The FBI does not publish arson data unless it receives data from either the agency or the state for all 12 months of the calendar year.

Table 8. Offenses Known to Law Enforcement, by State and City, 2007 *(Contd.)*

(Number.)

State	City	Population	Violent crime	Murder and non-negligent man-slaughter	Forcible rape	Robbery	Aggravated assault	Property crime	Burglary	Larceny-theft	Motor vehicle theft	Arson[1]
	Menomonie	15,367	28	0	1	2	25	337	52	269	16	2
	Mequon	23,736	8	0	3	5	0	123	30	89	4	0
	Merrill	9,860	20	0	7	1	12	420	48	356	16	0
	Middleton	16,710	11	0	1	4	6	451	66	361	24	2
	Milton	5,800	4	0	0	0	4	44	9	32	3	0
	Milwaukee	572,938	8,040	105	236	3,529	4,170	38,199	6,203	24,248	7,748	346
	Mineral Point	2,562	5	0	0	0	5	56	9	46	1	0
	Minocqua	5,026	5	0	1	0	4	155	7	138	10	0
	Mishicot	1,397	0	0	0	0	0	6	1	5	0	1
	Mondovi	2,638	1	0	0	0	1	31	4	26	1	0
	Monona	7,924	10	0	0	6	4	358	30	316	12	0
	Monroe	10,563	13	0	3	1	9	282	23	250	9	3
	Mosinee	4,078	2	0	0	0	2	103	17	79	7	0
	Mount Horeb	6,674	2	0	0	1	1	145	16	126	3	0
	Mount Pleasant	26,237	31	0	1	16	14	804	151	623	30	2
	Mukwonago	6,890	2	0	0	0	2	114	16	91	7	0
	Muskego	22,961	6	0	0	2	4	257	39	207	11	1
	Neenah	24,871	56	0	4	1	51	499	92	389	18	16
	Neillsville	2,615	1	0	0	0	1	82	5	75	2	0
	New Berlin	39,350	24	0	2	9	13	622	122	477	23	5
	New Glarus	2,064	4	0	0	0	4	76	2	74	0	0
	New Holstein	3,166	4	0	1	0	3	77	5	69	3	0
	New Lisbon	2,592	11	0	0	0	11	27	1	26	0	0
	New London	7,008	4	1	0	0	3	124	11	104	9	0
	New Richmond	8,200	3	0	3	0	0	204	12	186	6	2
	Niagara	1,766	4	0	0	0	4	26	6	19	1	0
	North Fond du Lac	4,959	3	0	0	0	3	111	11	87	13	0
	North Hudson	3,800	1	0	0	0	1	17	2	15	0	0
	North Prairie	2,055	0	0	0	0	0	5	2	3	0	0
	Oak Creek	32,896	35	0	6	15	14	1,020	121	850	49	5
	Oconomowoc	14,414	5	0	2	0	3	211	29	175	7	0
	Oconomowoc Town	8,196	3	0	0	0	3	52	17	30	5	0
	Oconto Falls	2,854	1	0	0	0	1	89	11	71	7	1
	Omro	3,316	14	0	0	0	14	25	22	0	3	0
	Onalaska	16,377	12	0	1	5	6	466	44	417	5	1
	Oregon	9,006	8	0	3	1	4	267	53	202	12	0
	Osceola	2,719	10	0	0	0	10	62	9	49	4	0
	Oshkosh	64,183	209	2	10	31	166	2,378	392	1,925	61	17
	Osseo	1,637	2	0	0	0	2	45	4	40	1	0
	Palmyra	1,751	4	0	0	0	4	46	6	37	3	1
	Park Falls	2,425	1	0	1	0	0	47	4	43	0	0
	Pepin	929	0	0	0	0	0	8	1	7	0	0
	Peshtigo	3,276	2	0	0	0	2	104	16	82	6	0
	Pewaukee	12,939	14	0	0	1	13	169	37	127	5	0
	Pewaukee Village	9,125	18	1	0	2	15	136	16	118	2	1
	Phillips	1,530	4	0	1	1	2	34	2	32	0	2
	Platteville	9,711	20	0	10	0	10	117	10	101	6	0
	Pleasant Prairie	19,426	15	0	2	5	8	378	47	324	7	0
	Plover	11,495	12	0	2	1	9	317	46	262	9	0
	Plymouth	8,333	14	0	1	3	10	303	24	272	7	0
	Portage	9,789	43	1	3	2	37	333	15	312	6	0
	Port Washington	11,115	5	0	2	3	0	163	6	152	5	0
	Poynette	2,579	3	0	0	0	3	31	4	27	0	0
	Prescott	4,058	9	0	3	1	5	131	16	112	3	0
	Princeton	1,448	1	0	0	0	1	27	6	21	0	0
	Pulaski	3,528	4	0	0	0	4	73	3	69	1	0
	Racine	79,285	507	7	27	281	192	3,978	945	2,766	267	26
	Readstown	384	0	0	0	0	0	2	1	1	0	0
	Reedsburg	8,629	12	0	6	0	6	165	21	134	10	0
	Rhinelander	7,786	15	0	5	0	10	304	29	266	9	0
	Rice Lake	8,422	13	0	4	2	7	326	46	268	12	6
	Richland Center	5,145	10	0	1	0	9	98	7	90	1	0
	Ripon	7,286	17	0	2	0	15	172	20	151	1	0
	River Falls	13,803	34	0	4	3	27	433	56	361	16	0
	River Hills	1,614	2	0	1	0	1	13	1	11	1	0
	Rome Town	3,015	0	0	0	0	0	55	15	39	1	0
	Rothschild	5,232	3	0	0	0	3	165	9	154	2	0
	Sauk Prairie	4,225	1	0	0	1	0	312	13	291	8	0
	Saukville	4,334	6	0	0	1	5	117	14	102	1	0
	Seymour	3,411	5	0	0	1	4	77	4	73	0	0
	Shawano	8,790	22	1	5	4	12	638	55	574	9	1
	Sheboygan	48,291	91	1	21	29	40	2,471	430	1,979	62	13
	Sheboygan Falls	7,795	1	0	1	0	0	103	21	81	1	0
	Shorewood	13,185	17	0	0	14	3	409	48	343	18	1

[1] The FBI does not publish arson data unless it receives data from either the agency or the state for all 12 months of the calendar year.

Table 8. Offenses Known to Law Enforcement, by State and City, 2007 *(Contd.)*

(Number.)

State	City	Population	Violent crime	Murder and non-negligent man-slaughter	Forcible rape	Robbery	Aggravated assault	Property crime	Burglary	Larceny-theft	Motor vehicle theft	Arson[1]
	Shorewood Hills	1,629	0	0	0	0	0	56	3	53	0	0
	Silver Lake	2,530	1	0	0	0	1	32	2	30	0	0
	Siren	842	5	0	0	0	5	65	8	57	0	0
	Slinger	4,476	2	0	0	0	2	121	14	106	1	0
	Somerset	2,365	2	0	0	0	2	52	3	46	3	0
	South Milwaukee	20,641	46	0	7	17	22	481	68	380	33	1
	Sparta	9,070	36	0	3	3	30	308	55	247	6	0
	Spencer	1,846	0	0	0	0	0	15	2	13	0	0
	Spooner	2,577	2	0	0	0	2	116	16	98	2	2
	Spring Green	1,439	0	0	0	0	0	22	2	20	0	0
	Stanley	3,676	5	0	0	0	5	104	9	94	1	0
	St. Croix Falls	2,192	3	0	0	0	3	64	5	59	0	0
	Stevens Point	24,333	57	0	11	1	45	809	135	656	18	2
	St. Francis	8,899	14	0	1	8	5	193	25	158	10	0
	Stoughton	12,572	10	0	2	0	8	283	41	231	11	1
	Strum	1,038	1	0	0	1	0	8	1	6	1	0
	Sturgeon Bay	9,129	9	0	0	1	8	143	14	125	4	5
	Sturtevant	6,626	4	0	1	2	1	142	31	101	10	0
	Summit	5,155	1	0	1	0	0	34	8	24	2	0
	Sun Prairie	27,366	56	0	5	8	43	712	72	616	24	0
	Superior	26,896	64	0	15	19	30	1,452	209	1,174	69	12
	Theresa	1,326	4	0	0	0	4	16	1	14	1	0
	Thiensville	3,258	8	0	0	1	7	39	7	28	4	0
	Three Lakes	2,266	1	0	1	0	0	30	3	26	1	0
	Tomah	8,764	22	0	3	1	18	402	26	359	17	0
	Tomahawk	3,708	6	1	0	0	5	130	14	107	9	0
	Town of East Troy	3,936	4	0	0	0	4	47	8	34	5	0
	Town of Madison	5,828	57	0	13	23	21	253	34	179	40	0
	Town of Menasha	17,192	12	0	3	1	8	251	55	188	8	0
	Trempealeau	1,532	0	0	0	0	0	2	0	1	1	0
	Twin Lakes	5,580	5	0	1	0	4	165	15	135	15	0
	Two Rivers	11,916	37	0	1	1	35	243	51	181	11	0
	Valders	987	1	0	0	0	1	5	1	4	0	0
	Verona	10,525	12	1	0	0	11	179	21	156	2	0
	Viroqua	4,378	4	0	0	1	3	105	2	101	2	0
	Walworth	2,669	4	0	0	0	4	56	9	46	1	0
	Washburn	2,125	7	0	0	0	7	59	2	54	3	0
	Waterloo	3,252	1	0	0	0	1	32	4	27	1	0
	Watertown	23,334	66	0	6	7	53	604	117	459	28	10
	Waukesha	68,162	84	0	12	23	49	1,405	348	990	67	5
	Waunakee	10,894	6	0	0	1	5	157	10	141	6	0
	Waupaca	5,833	15	0	0	0	15	257	12	239	6	0
	Waupun	10,668	10	0	1	1	8	198	22	170	6	0
	Wausau	38,405	111	1	16	31	63	1,113	249	799	65	12
	Wautoma	2,088	1	0	0	0	1	54	4	48	2	0
	Wauwatosa	44,463	96	0	6	70	20	2,027	289	1,612	126	0
	West Allis	58,366	220	2	9	91	118	3,062	584	2,290	188	20
	West Bend	30,070	27	0	3	2	22	767	57	695	15	3
	Westby	2,166	1	0	1	0	0	25	4	19	2	0
	West Milwaukee	3,977	31	0	1	18	12	439	50	352	37	0
	West Salem	4,725	7	0	0	0	7	99	6	92	1	0
	Whitefish Bay	13,450	5	0	0	4	1	190	20	165	5	0
	Whitehall	1,620	2	0	2	0	0	44	4	39	1	0
	Whitewater	14,147	19	0	9	1	9	317	74	240	3	1
	Williams Bay	2,687	0	0	0	0	0	80	8	70	2	0
	Winneconne	2,490	2	0	0	0	2	10	7	2	1	0
	Wisconsin Dells	2,538	21	0	6	1	14	378	66	304	8	1
	Wisconsin Rapids	17,633	14	0	5	4	5	899	142	727	30	2
	Woodruff	2,036	4	0	0	0	4	45	6	37	2	0
WYOMING	Afton	1,817	2	0	0	0	2	25	10	15	0	0
	Basin	1,242	6	0	1	0	5	32	2	30	0	0
	Buffalo	4,566	28	0	2	0	26	70	6	58	6	1
	Casper	52,434	152	2	20	22	108	2,595	504	1,935	156	7
	Cheyenne	55,604	115	1	23	13	78	2,557	261	2,208	88	11
	Cody	9,266	31	0	3	1	27	247	37	206	4	0
	Diamondville	678	2	0	0	0	2	12	3	9	0	0
	Douglas	5,691	15	0	2	1	12	178	20	157	1	0
	Evanston	11,585	18	0	7	2	9	436	44	375	17	1
	Evansville	2,321	4	0	0	0	4	89	11	73	5	0
	Gillette	24,438	41	1	9	5	26	920	103	773	44	6
	Glenrock	2,393	9	0	2	0	7	45	9	30	6	0
	Green River	11,957	78	0	2	0	76	308	55	235	18	0
	Guernsey	1,118	6	0	0	0	6	11	2	9	0	1
	Hanna	855	0	0	0	0	0	3	0	1	2	0

[1] The FBI does not publish arson data unless it receives data from either the agency or the state for all 12 months of the calendar year.

Table 8.   Offenses Known to Law Enforcement, by State and City, 2007 *(Contd.)*

(Number.)

State	City	Population	Violent crime	Murder and non-negligent man-slaughter	Forcible rape	Robbery	Aggravated assault	Property crime	Burglary	Larceny-theft	Motor vehicle theft	Arson[1]
	Jackson	9,292	42	0	19	0	23	323	25	280	18	4
	Kemmerer	2,508	3	0	0	0	3	25	1	24	0	1
	Lander	7,066	15	0	0	0	15	213	24	178	11	0
	Laramie	25,504	18	0	1	4	13	828	76	690	62	8
	Lovell	2,279	4	1	0	0	3	28	0	28	0	0
	Lusk	1,316	5	0	0	0	5	17	4	13	0	0
	Mills	2,926	9	0	0	0	9	87	13	68	6	1
	Moorcroft	861	1	0	0	1	0	14	8	5	1	0
	Newcastle	3,275	12	0	0	0	12	122	19	96	7	0
	Pine Bluffs	1,142	5	0	1	0	4	20	6	13	1	0
	Powell	5,388	11	0	4	0	7	202	17	179	6	3
	Rawlins	8,572	54	1	5	3	45	377	53	307	17	1
	Riverton	9,795	32	0	7	1	24	417	49	337	31	2
	Rock Springs	19,432	135	3	9	16	107	851	154	643	54	6
	Saratoga	1,721	1	0	0	0	1	22	0	22	0	0
	Sheridan	16,507	9	0	2	3	4	372	58	297	17	4
	Sundance	1,199	0	0	0	0	0	12	4	7	1	0
	Thermopolis	2,912	17	0	0	0	17	81	10	70	1	0
	Torrington	5,446	7	0	0	1	6	170	36	133	1	0
	Wheatland	3,426	7	0	1	0	6	121	17	100	4	1
	Worland	4,857	15	0	0	0	15	43	10	25	8	0

[1] The FBI does not publish arson data unless it receives data from either the agency or the state for all 12 months of the calendar year.

Table 9.   Offenses Known to Law Enforcement, by State and University and College, 2007

(Number.)

State	University/College	Campus	Student enroll-ment[1]	Violent crime	Murder and non-negligent man-slaughter	Forcible rape	Robbery	Aggra-vated assault	Property crime	Burglary	Larceny-theft	Motor vehicle theft	Arson[2]
ALABAMA	Alabama State University		5,565	13	0	0	9	4	136	28	106	2	1
	Auburn University	Montgomery	5,079	0	0	0	0	0	48	3	43	2	
	Jacksonville State University		8,957	5	0	0	1	4	120	36	83	1	1
	Troy University		27,938	2	0	1	1	0	180	17	162	1	0
	University of Alabama	Tuscaloosa	23,838	5	0	1	2	2	509	151	353	5	
	University of Montevallo		2,895	0	0	0	0	0	44	1	43	0	
	University of North Alabama		6,810	1	0	0	1	0	91	35	54	2	
	University of South Alabama		13,090	14	0	2	0	12	171	46	119	6	
ALASKA	University of Alaska:	Anchorage	16,163	5	0	1	2	2	103	5	93	5	1
		Fairbanks	8,340	5	0	0	0	5	88	2	85	1	0
ARIZONA	Arizona State University	Main Campus	51,234	34	0	8	7	19	1,063	138	853	72	3
	Central Arizona College		6,471	3	0	0	0	3	50	17	32	1	0
	Northern Arizona University.		20,555	28	0	6	1	21	396	58	331	7	6
	Pima Community College		32,532	2	0	0	1	1	264	3	213	48	1
	Yavapai College		9,305	1	0	0	0	1	42	5	36	1	0
ARKANSAS	Arkansas State University:	Beebe	4,073	0	0	0	0	0	0	0	0	0	0
		Jonesboro	10,949	3	0	1	0	2	160	69	89	2	0
	Arkansas Tech University		7,038	2	0	1	0	1	82	33	49	0	0
	Henderson State University		3,664	0	0	0	0	0	20	19	1	0	0
	Northwest Arkansas Community College		5,732	0	0	0	0	0	0	0	0	0	0
	Southern Arkansas University		3,113	5	0	0	1	4	40	6	32	2	0
	University of Arkansas:	Fayetteville	17,926	10	0	3	0	7	270	80	185	5	0
		Little Rock	11,905	13	0	0	9	4	210	82	123	5	0
		Medical Sciences	2,435	7	0	0	2	5	215	1	200	14	0
		Monticello	3,179	1	0	1	0	0	26	7	19	0	0
		Pine Bluff	3,128	13	0	1	2	10	97	48	47	2	0
	University of Central Arkansas		12,330	5	0	0	1	4	227	63	159	5	1
CALIFORNIA	Allan Hancock College		12,321	1	0	0	0	1	21	7	14	0	0
	California State Polytechnic University:	Pomona	20,510	2	0	1	1	0	224	26	169	29	1
		San Luis Obispo	18,722	2	0	0	1	1	127	7	115	5	
	California State University:	Bakersfield	7,711	2	0	0	1	1	115	31	74	10	0
		Channel Islands	3,123	1	0	0	0	1	38	4	34	0	0
		Chico	16,250	13	0	5	3	5	255	28	226	1	2
		Dominguez Hills	12,068	10	0	2	3	5	103	18	63	22	0
		East Bay	12,706	3	0	0	2	1	105	15	80	10	0
		Fresno	22,098	10	0	0	4	6	347	59	275	13	1
		Fullerton	35,921	7	0	2	3	2	197	45	128	24	1
		Long Beach	35,574	7	0	1	2	4	200	19	154	27	0
		Los Angeles	20,565	6	0	2	1	3	232	23	175	34	0
		Monterey Bay	3,818	6	1	1	0	4	113	33	71	9	1
		Northridge	34,560	15	0	5	5	5	266	30	223	13	0
		Sacramento	28,529	4	0	2	0	2	252	42	192	18	1
		San Bernardino	16,479	7	0	1	2	4	130	28	91	11	0
		San Jose[3]		12	0	3	7	2	384	35	344	5	3
		Stanislaus	8,374	2	0	0	0	2	54	5	45	4	0
	College of the Sequoias		9,959	0	0	0	0	0	64	34	27	3	0
	Contra Costa Community College		6,870	16	0	0	14	2	198	6	172	20	
	Cuesta College		10,578	0	0	0	0	0	16	4	11	1	0
	El Camino College		23,488	8	0	0	8	0	171	22	116	33	2
	Foothill-De Anza College		39,874	2	0	0	1	1	73	31	41	1	0
	Fresno Community College		22,040	5	0	0	3	2	189	8	146	35	1
	Humboldt State University		7,435	3	0	1	2	0	122	14	107	1	0
	Marin Community College		6,512	2	0	0	0	2	45	6	39	0	1
	Pasadena Community College		25,873	12	0	0	10	2	197	0	181	16	1
	Reedley Community College		11,782	0	0	0	0	0	39	2	37	0	0
	Riverside Community College		29,486	3	0	1	0	2	133	7	118	8	0
	San Bernardino Community College		12,090	5	0	2	1	2	77	21	44	12	0
	San Diego State University		33,441	33	0	9	8	16	585	85	393	107	

Note: Caution should be exercised in making any intercampus comparisons or ranking schools because university/college crime statistics are affected by a variety of factors. These include demographic characteristics of the surrounding community, ratio of male to female students, number of on-campus residents, accessibility of the campus to outside visitors, size of enrollment, etc.

[1] The student enrollment figures provided by the United States Department of Education are for the 2006 school year, the most recent available. The enrollment figures include full-time and part-time students.

[2] The FBI does not publish arson data unless it receives data from either the agency or the state for all 12 months of the calendar year.

[3] Student enrollment figures were not available.

Table 9. Offenses Known to Law Enforcement, by State and University and College, 2007 *(Contd.)*

(Number.)

State	University/College	Campus	Student enrollment[1]	Violent crime	Murder and non-negligent manslaughter	Forcible rape	Robbery	Aggravated assault	Property crime	Burglary	Larceny-theft	Motor vehicle theft	Arson[2]
	San Francisco State University		29,628	10	0	1	4	5	317	59	233	25	1
	San Jose/Evergreen Community College		18,164	0	0	0	0	0	79	10	63	6	2
	Santa Rosa Junior College		24,806	0	0	0	0	0	86	10	72	4	0
	Sonoma State University		8,274	4	0	1	2	1	122	20	101	1	0
	University of California:	Berkeley	33,920	48	0	7	27	14	842	89	737	16	11
		Davis	29,628	10	0	0	0	10	716	85	623	8	3
		Hastings College of Law	1,272	8	0	0	6	2	29	15	13	1	
		Irvine	25,230	7	0	3	1	3	486	54	419	13	1
		Los Angeles	36,611	38	0	5	13	20	955	227	686	42	1
		Medical Center, Sacramento[3]		6	0	0	1	5	185	21	157	7	1
		Merced	1,286	1	0	0	0	1	19	3	16	0	0
		Riverside	16,875	10	0	0	8	2	317	51	247	19	7
		San Diego	26,247	5	0	1	2	2	471	56	373	42	4
		San Francisco	2,943	3	0	0	1	2	404	30	355	19	
		Santa Barbara	21,082	13	0	5	0	8	498	36	459	3	1
		Santa Cruz	15,364	8	0	3	1	4	243	40	198	5	7
	Ventura County Community College District		11,757	2	0	0	1	1	112	1	110	1	2
	West Valley-Mission College		18,740	0	0	0	0	0	66	6	57	3	0
COLORADO	Adams State College		8,442	12	0	5	0	7	50	20	29	1	0
	Arapahoe Community College		6,918	0	0	0	0	0	18	0	18	0	0
	Auraria Higher Education Center[3]			4	0	0	2	2	250	22	219	9	1
	Colorado School of Mines		4,357	2	0	0	0	2	41	4	36	1	0
	Colorado State University:	Fort Collins	27,636	7	0	3	2	2	428	14	407	7	3
		Pueblo	6,205	0	0	0	0	0	49	2	42	5	1
	Fort Lewis College		3,905	3	0	3	0	0	83	20	62	1	1
	Pikes Peak Community College		10,526	2	0	0	0	2	18	0	18	0	0
	Red Rocks Community College		6,727	0	0	0	0	0	18	0	18	0	0
	University of Colorado:	Boulder	31,665	14	0	5	2	7	457	54	398	5	7
		Colorado Springs	8,647	5	0	3	0	2	75	14	60	1	1
		Health Sciences Center[3]		0	0	0	0	0	27	1	25	1	0
		Health Sciences Center, Fitzsimons Campus[3]		0	0	0	0	0	38	2	36	0	0
	University of Northern Colorado		13,363	5	0	4	1	0	207	23	178	6	0
CONNECTICUT	Central Connecticut State University		12,144	0	0	0	0	0	52	7	44	1	0
	Eastern Connecticut State University		5,239	2	0	0	2	0	76	5	64	7	0
	Southern Connecticut State University		12,326	0	0	0	0	0	107	7	98	2	0
	University of Connecticut:	Health Center[3]		1	0	0	0	1	42	2	40	0	0
		Storrs, Avery Point, and Hartford[3]		8	0	0	3	5	267	38	214	15	3
	Western Connecticut State University		6,086	1	0	1	0	0	45	16	28	1	0
	Yale University		11,415	6	0	0	1	5	426	120	299	7	0
DELAWARE	Delaware State University		3,690	10	1	2	3	4	47	13	33	1	0
	University of Delaware		20,380	10	0	0	5	5	330	34	294	2	0
FLORIDA	Florida Atlantic University		25,325	6	0	2	2	2	259	47	191	21	0
	Florida Gulf Coast University		8,279	2	0	0	1	1	34	2	32	0	0

Note: Caution should be exercised in making any intercampus comparisons or ranking schools because university/college crime statistics are affected by a variety of factors. These include demographic characteristics of the surrounding community, ratio of male to female students, number of on-campus residents, accessibility of the campus to outside visitors, size of enrollment, etc.

[1] The student enrollment figures provided by the United States Department of Education are for the 2006 school year, the most recent available. The enrollment figures include full-time and part-time students.

[2] The FBI does not publish arson data unless it receives data from either the agency or the state for all 12 months of the calendar year.

[3] Student enrollment figures were not available.

Table 9. Offenses Known to Law Enforcement, by State and University and College, 2007 *(Contd.)*

(Number.)

State	University/College	Campus	Student enroll-ment[1]	Violent crime	Murder and non-negligent man-slaughter	Forcible rape	Robbery	Aggra-vated assault	Property crime	Burglary	Larceny-theft	Motor vehicle theft	Arson[2]
	Florida International University		37,997	13	0	2	5	6	463	90	342	31	1
	Florida State University:	Panama City[3]		0	0	0	0	0	7	0	7	0	0
		Tallahassee	39,973	28	0	4	15	9	581	82	480	19	4
	New College of Florida		746	1	0	0	0	1	66	4	61	1	0
	Pensacola Junior College		10,208	2	0	0	1	1	65	12	51	2	0
	Santa Fe Community College		14,012	1	0	0	1	0	66	2	62	2	0
	Tallahassee Community College		12,732	0	0	0	0	0	156	0	152	4	0
	University of Central Florida.		46,646	19	0	2	10	7	647	87	524	36	2
	University of Florida		50,912	11	0	2	5	4	551	23	502	26	2
	University of North Florida		15,954	3	0	0	2	1	216	14	197	5	0
	University of South Florida:	St. Petersburg[3]		0	0	0	0	0	40	0	31	9	0
		Tampa	43,636	13	0	2	4	7	427	120	273	34	2
	University of West Florida		9,819	2	0	0	0	2	72	7	61	4	0
GEORGIA	Abraham Baldwin Agricultural College		3,574	5	0	1	1	3	65	14	50	1	0
	Albany State University		3,927	3	0	0	0	3	110	3	107	0	
	Armstrong Atlantic State University		6,713	2	0	0	0	2	43	12	30	1	0
	Berry College		1,841	0	0	0	0	0	48	9	39	0	0
	Clark Atlanta University		4,514	15	0	1	12	2	188	67	101	20	0
	Coastal Georgia Community College		3,051	0	0	0	0	0	8	0	8	0	0
	Columbus State University		7,587	0	0	0	0	0	81	3	78	0	
	Dalton State College		4,348	1	0	0	1	0	15	0	15	0	0
	Emory University		12,338	3	0	2	1	0	357	33	319	5	
	Georgia College and State University		6,040	0	0	0	0	0	23	2	21	0	0
	Georgia Institute of Technology		17,936	15	0	2	6	7	587	85	448	54	
	Georgia Perimeter College		19,955	0	0	0	0	0	147	4	133	10	0
	Georgia Southern University		16,425	2	0	0	2	0	255	14	236	5	1
	Georgia Southwestern State University		2,456	9	0	2	4	3	44	2	42	0	
	Georgia State University		26,135	16	0	0	15	1	229	12	214	3	
	Kennesaw State University		19,844	2	0	0	0	2	176	60	111	5	
	Medical College of Georgia		2,227	3	0	0	2	1	153	4	144	5	0
	Mercer University		7,049	5	0	0	2	3	61	13	47	1	1
	Morehouse College		2,933	8	0	0	6	2	158	23	131	4	
	North Georgia College and State University		4,922	1	0	1	0	0	44	2	42	0	0
	Southern Polytechnic State University		4,206	2	0	1	1	0	74	22	47	5	0
	South Georgia College		1,465	1	0	0	0	1	24	7	16	1	0
	University of Georgia		33,959	6	0	1	0	5	409	16	386	7	
	Valdosta State University		10,888	2	0	1	0	1	180	1	178	1	1
	Wesleyan College		632	0	0	0	0	0	14	0	14	0	
INDIANA	Ball State University		20,030	9	0	5	3	1	316	49	262	5	0
	Indiana State University		10,568	8	0	1	1	6	266	27	234	5	0
	Indiana University:	Bloomington	38,247	18	0	5	8	5	511	100	396	15	0
		Gary	4,819	0	0	0	0	0	26	0	26	0	0
		Indianapolis[3]		6	0	0	0	6	419	99	307	13	0
		New Albany	6,183	0	0	0	0	0	16	0	16	0	0
	Marian College		1,796	2	0	1	1	0	20	5	14	1	0
	Purdue University		40,609	8	0	3	3	2	447	84	362	1	0
IOWA	Iowa State University		25,462	18	0	1	3	14	327	43	275	9	3
	University of Iowa		28,816	9	0	3	1	5	273	30	240	3	1
	University of Northern Iowa		12,327	4	0	2	0	2	112	6	106	0	0
KANSAS	Emporia State University		6,473	1	0	0	0	1	43	4	37	2	0
	Kansas City Community College		5,547	0	0	0	0	0	45	2	41	2	0
	Kansas State University		23,141	8	0	4	1	3	144	36	105	3	0
	Pittsburg State University		6,859	2	0	1	0	1	92	7	84	1	1
	University of Kansas:	Main Campus	26,773	9	0	4	3	2	230	63	164	3	1
		Medical Center	2,150	6	0	0	2	4	211	0	203	8	0
	Washburn University		7,153	1	0	1	0	0	50	17	33	0	0
	Wichita State University		13,964	2	0	1	1	0	142	4	134	4	1
KENTUCKY	Eastern Kentucky University		15,763	7	0	4	2	1	227	47	180	0	0

Note: Caution should be exercised in making any intercampus comparisons or ranking schools because university/college crime statistics are affected by a variety of factors. These include demographic characteristics of the surrounding community, ratio of male to female students, number of on-campus residents, accessibility of the campus to outside visitors, size of enrollment, etc.

[1] The student enrollment figures provided by the United States Department of Education are for the 2006 school year, the most recent available. The enrollment figures include full-time and part-time students.

[2] The FBI does not publish arson data unless it receives data from either the agency or the state for all 12 months of the calendar year.

[3] Student enrollment figures were not available.

Table 9.   Offenses Known to Law Enforcement, by State and University and College, 2007 *(Contd.)*

(Number.)

State	University/College	Campus	Student enrollment[1]	Violent crime	Murder and non-negligent man-slaughter	Forcible rape	Robbery	Aggra-vated assault	Property crime	Burglary	Larceny-theft	Motor vehicle theft	Arson[2]
	Kentucky State University		2,498	1	0	0	1	0	20	4	16	0	0
	Morehead State University		8,958	2	0	2	0	0	46	9	37	0	0
	Murray State University		10,298	2	0	1	0	1	122	18	104	0	9
	Northern Kentucky University		14,617	3	0	1	2	0	124	3	121	0	0
	University of Kentucky		26,382	14	0	3	6	5	573	33	533	7	0
	University of Louisville		20,785	5	0	0	4	1	277	34	235	8	0
	Western Kentucky University		18,660	6	0	2	3	1	232	64	161	7	1
LOUISIANA	Delgado Community College		11,916	3	0	0	1	2	27	1	25	1	0
	Grambling State University		5,065	8	0	1	1	6	173	99	69	5	0
	Louisiana State University	Baton Rouge[3]		19	2	0	9	8	456	55	382	19	1
	McNeese State University		8,327	2	0	0	0	2	91	9	80	2	0
	Nicholls State University		6,804	6	0	1	0	5	36	3	32	1	0
	Southeastern Louisiana University		15,106	7	0	1	1	5	172	29	139	4	0
	Southern University and A&M College:	Baton Rouge	8,624	9	0	2	3	4	179	13	161	5	0
		New Orleans	2,197	0	0	0	0	0	11	0	11	0	0
	Tulane University		10,237	24	0	18	2	4	232	69	156	7	0
	University of Louisiana:	Lafayette	16,302	2	0	1	0	1	139	13	123	3	0
		Monroe	8,576	7	0	0	2	5	153	17	132	4	0
	University of New Orleans		11,747	12	0	0	1	11	87	3	79	5	0
MAINE	University of Maine:	Farmington	2,421	3	0	1	0	2	51	9	42	0	0
		Orono	11,797	1	0	1	0	0	252	20	230	2	25
	University of Southern Maine		10,478	2	0	2	0	0	68	5	63	0	5
MARYLAND	Bowie State University		5,291	15	0	0	4	11	97	46	45	6	2
	Coppin State University		4,104	2	0	0	2	0	35	11	23	1	0
	Frostburg State University		4,910	16	0	2	0	14	130	50	79	1	1
	Morgan State University		6,705	25	0	0	18	7	154	32	121	1	0
	Salisbury University		7,383	2	0	0	0	2	94	5	88	1	0
	St. Mary's College		1,957	2	0	0	0	2	85	6	78	1	0
	Towson University		18,921	13	0	0	0	13	176	53	122	1	5
	University of Baltimore		4,948	2	0	0	2	0	57	5	49	3	0
	University of Maryland:	Baltimore City	5,636	13	0	0	9	4	106	1	105	0	0
		Baltimore County	11,798	0	0	0	0	0	167	27	131	9	0
		College Park	35,102	18	0	0	9	9	568	89	439	40	7
		Eastern Shore	4,130	8	0	1	4	3	175	32	143	0	0
MASSACHUSETTS	Assumption College		2,792	7	0	0	0	7	42	7	35	0	1
	Bentley College		5,555	3	0	0	0	3	77	17	60	0	0
	Boston College		14,661	18	0	10	0	8	161	61	98	2	
	Boston University		31,574	16	0	4	5	7	525	71	450	4	1
	Brandeis University		5,313	1	0	0	0	1	67	10	57	0	
	Bridgewater State College		9,655	6	0	1	0	5	93	21	72	0	0
	Bristol Community College		6,927	0	0	0	0	0	13	1	12	0	
	Clark University		3,071	8	0	0	1	7	59	18	41	0	0
	Dean College		1,315	1	0	1	0	0	26	14	12	0	
	Emerson College		4,324	6	0	2	1	3	48	15	33	0	0
	Fitchburg State College		5,508	3	0	1	0	2	64	0	63	1	0
	Harvard University		25,778	9	0	1	3	5	510	301	204	5	
	Holyoke Community College		6,297	0	0	0	0	0	46	0	42	4	
	Lasell College		1,275	2	0	1	0	1	43	5	38	0	0
	Massachusetts College of Art		2,286	0	0	0	0	0	51	8	43	0	0
	Massachusetts College of Liberal Arts		1,805	3	0	0	0	3	29	3	26	0	0
	Massachusetts Institute of Technology		10,253	4	0	0	0	4	497	115	372	10	1
	Massasoit Community College		6,975	0	0	0	0	0	16	0	16	0	0
	Merrimack College		2,282	3	0	0	0	3	48	14	34	0	0
	Mount Holyoke College		2,153	4	0	3	0	1	103	8	95	0	0
	Northeastern University		23,411	8	0	4	3	1	339	45	293	1	0
	North Shore Community College		6,910	1	0	0	0	1	24	1	23	0	0

Note: Caution should be exercised in making any intercampus comparisons or ranking schools because university/college crime statistics are affected by a variety of factors. These include demographic characteristics of the surrounding community, ratio of male to female students, number of on-campus residents, accessibility of the campus to outside visitors, size of enrollment, etc.

[1] The student enrollment figures provided by the United States Department of Education are for the 2006 school year, the most recent available. The enrollment figures include full-time and part-time students.

[2] The FBI does not publish arson data unless it receives data from either the agency or the state for all 12 months of the calendar year.

[3] Student enrollment figures were not available.

Table 9.   Offenses Known to Law Enforcement, by State and University and College, 2007 *(Contd.)*

(Number.)

State	University/College	Campus	Student enroll-ment[1]	Violent crime	Murder and non-negligent man-slaughter	Forcible rape	Robbery	Aggra-vated assault	Property crime	Burglary	Larceny-theft	Motor vehicle theft	Arson[2]
	Salem State College		10,230	4	0	1	0	3	88	32	55	1	0
	Springfield College..................		4,994	11	0	1	1	9	80	26	52	2	0
	Tufts University:	Medford	9,638	7	0	3	2	2	153	29	123	1	
		Suffolk[3]		1	0	0	1	0	32	0	32	0	0
		Worcester[3]		1	0	0	0	1	3	0	3	0	0
	University of Massachusetts:	Amherst	25,593	23	0	2	3	18	294	71	214	9	1
		Dartmouth	8,756	17	0	1	3	13	268	68	199	1	
		Harbor Campus, Boston	12,362	2	0	0	1	1	111	32	79	0	0
	Wellesley College		2,370	1	0	0	0	1	51	17	34	0	
	Western New England College..............................		3,653	4	0	1	2	1	40	3	35	2	0
	Westfield State College...........		5,426	2	0	2	0	0	58	12	46	0	0
MICHIGAN	Central Michigan University................................		26,710	4	0	2	1	1	197	9	186	2	5
	Delta College		10,149	1	0	0	0	1	42	0	42	0	0
	Eastern Michigan University................................		22,950	9	0	3	1	5	326	100	216	10	6
	Grand Rapids Community College		15,224	3	0	0	2	1	187	3	183	1	0
	Lansing Community College................................		20,394	3	0	0	2	1	134	1	133	0	1
	Macomb Community College................................		21,131	2	0	0	1	1	82	0	82	0	1
	Michigan State University......		45,520	26	0	3	11	12	803	118	676	9	1
	Michigan Technological University................................		6,546	0	0	0	0	0	91	11	79	1	0
	Mott Community College.......		10,038	2	0	0	1	1	77	3	73	1	0
	Northern Michigan University................................		9,689	6	0	5	0	1	113	14	98	1	1
	Oakland Community College................................		24,123	1	0	1	0	0	66	2	63	1	1
	Oakland University.................		17,737	7	0	1	1	5	116	6	106	4	1
	Saginaw Valley State University................................		9,543	4	0	1	0	3	89	43	45	1	1
	University of Michigan:	Ann Arbor	40,025	20	0	3	2	15	864	27	832	5	5
		Dearborn	8,342	0	0	0	0	0	59	1	51	7	0
		Flint	6,527	1	0	0	1	0	76	6	64	6	1
	Western Michigan University................................		24,841	5	0	4	1	0	186	4	177	5	2
MINNESOTA[4]	University of Minnesota:........	Duluth	11,190		0		1	2	86	12	73	1	0
		Morris	1,747		0		0	0	26	0	26	0	0
		Twin Cities	50,402		0		13	8	701	74	617	10	4
MISSISSIPPI	Coahoma Community College................................		1,838	1	0	0	0	1	14	12	1	1	0
	Jackson State University........		8,256	0	0	0	0	0	110	16	88	6	2
	Mississippi State University ...		16,206	6	0	2	0	4	151	11	135	5	0
	University of Mississippi:	Medical Center	1,598	3	0	1	2	0	165	3	155	7	0
		Oxford	15,220	0	0	0	0	0	184	10	173	1	0
MISSOURI	Lincoln University...................		3,224	8	0	2	0	6	38	7	30	1	0
	Mineral Area College		2,926	0	0	0	0	0	4	4	0	0	0
	Missouri Western State University................................		5,276	0	0	0	0	0	77	40	37	0	0
	Northwest Missouri State University................		6,242	1	0	0	1	0	44	12	30	2	0
	Southeast Missouri State University................................		10,454	2	0	0	0	2	79	28	51	0	0
	St. Louis Community College	Meramec	10,887	2	0	0	0	2	18	1	17	0	0
	Truman State University........		5,820	0	0	0	0	0	75	9	64	2	1
	University of Central Missouri		10,711	6	0	0	2	4	92	11	81	0	0
	University of Missouri:	Columbia	28,184	11	0	1	2	8	374	23	351	0	2
		Kansas City	14,213	2	0	0	0	2	126	22	99	5	0
		Rolla	5,858	0	0	0	0	0	53	5	48	0	0
		St. Louis	15,528	9	0	1	2	6	121	21	96	4	0
	Washington University		13,355	1	0	0	1	0	151	12	138	1	1
NEBRASKA	University of Nebraska:..........	Kearney	6,468	0	0	0	0	0	58	11	47	0	0
		Lincoln	22,106	1	0	1	0	0	347	47	294	6	0

Note: Caution should be exercised in making any intercampus comparisons or ranking schools because university/college crime statistics are affected by a variety of factors. These include demo-graphic characteristics of the surrounding community, ratio of male to female students, number of on-campus residents, accessibility of the campus to outside visitors, size of enrollment, etc.

[1] The student enrollment figures provided by the United States Department of Education are for the 2006 school year, the most recent available. The enrollment figures include full-time and part-time students.

[2] The FBI does not publish arson data unless it receives data from either the agency or the state for all 12 months of the calendar year.

[3] Student enrollment figures were not available.

[4] The data collection methodology for the offense of forcible rape used by the Minnesota state Uniform Crime Reporting (UCR) program does not comply with national UCR guidelines. Conse-quently, their figures for forcible rape and violent crime (of which forcible rape is a part) are not published in this table.

Table 9.   Offenses Known to Law Enforcement, by State and University and College, 2007 *(Contd.)*

(Number.)

State	University/College	Campus	Student enroll-ment[1]	Violent crime	Murder and non-negligent man-slaughter	Forcible rape	Robbery	Aggra-vated assault	Property crime	Burglary	Larceny-theft	Motor vehicle theft	Arson[2]
NEVADA	Truckee Meadows												
	Community College		11,556	0	0	0	0	0	22	15	6	1	0
	University of Nevada:	Las Vegas	27,912	8	0	1	1	6	410	60	292	58	2
		Reno	16,663	6	0	1	3	2	160	23	132	5	1
NEW JERSEY	Brookdale Community												
	College		13,745	1	0	0	1	0	39	2	36	1	0
	Essex County College		10,972	1	0	0	1	0	71	1	66	4	0
	Kean University of												
	New Jersey		13,050	4	0	0	0	4	99	17	80	2	0
	Middlesex County College		11,990	0	0	0	0	0	44	0	44	0	0
	Monmouth University		6,399	3	0	2	0	1	73	8	64	1	2
	Montclair State University		16,076	4	0	2	0	2	328	27	299	2	0
	New Jersey Institute of												
	Technology		8,209	17	0	0	8	9	137	3	121	13	0
	Richard Stockton College		7,212	3	0	0	0	3	75	23	52	0	1
	Rowan University		9,578	7	1	1	2	3	147	31	115	1	1
	Rutgers University:	Camden	5,165	2	0	1	1	0	80	14	61	5	1
		Newark	10,203	10	0	0	6	4	196	31	146	19	1
		New Brunswick	34,392	14	0	2	7	5	586	102	481	3	5
	Stevens Institute of												
	Technology		4,829	1	0	0	1	0	38	3	34	1	0
	The College of New												
	Jersey		6,934	0	0	0	0	0	86	15	70	1	0
	University of Medicine												
	and Dentistry:	Camden[3]		1	0	0	1	0	2	0	2	0	0
		Newark	5,677	37	0	0	17	20	249	10	210	29	0
		New Brunswick[3]		3	0	0	3	0	23	0	23	0	0
		Piscataway[3]		0	0	0	0	0	9	0	9	0	0
	William Paterson												
	University		10,599	3	0	0	1	2	91	11	79	1	0
NEW MEXICO	Eastern New Mexico												
	University		4,122	1	0	1	0	0	46	6	40	0	0
	University of New Mexico		25,721	24	0	3	2	19	632	60	505	67	2
NEW YORK	Cornell University		19,639	5	0	0	1	4	321	34	276	11	3
	Ithaca College		6,409	0	0	0	0	0	155	29	126	0	2
	Rensselaer Polytechnic												
	Institute		6,680	0	0	0	0	0	118	13	105	0	0
	State University of												
	New York:	Albany	17,434	3	0	2	0	1	181	17	164	0	0
		Buffalo	27,823	7	0	2	2	3	473	121	347	5	2
		Downstate Medical Center[3]		5	0	0	2	3	68	2	66	0	0
		Maritime College	1,324	0	0	0	0	0	44	7	36	1	0
		Upstate Medical Center[3]		2	0	0	0	2	146	0	146	0	0
	State University of New York Agricultural and												
	Technical College:	Farmingdale[3]		0	0	0	0	0	38	0	37	1	0
		Morrisville[3]		1	0	0	0	1	98	4	93	1	0
	State University of												
	New York College:	Buffalo	11,220	11	0	4	4	3	226	33	184	9	2
		Cortland	6,995	2	0	1	0	1	119	30	89	0	0
		Fredonia	5,406	0	0	0	0	0	111	11	100	0	1
		Geneseo	5,530	1	0	0	0	1	95	11	84	0	0
		New Paltz	7,699	0	0	0	0	0	90	11	79	0	0
		Old Westbury	3,450	2	0	2	0	0	107	8	96	3	0
		Oneonta	5,786	0	0	0	0	0	83	10	73	0	0
		Oswego	8,183	1	0	1	0	0	134	16	117	1	0
		Plattsburgh	6,217	0	0	0	0	0	138	11	127	0	0
		Potsdam	4,332	1	0	0	0	1	103	19	84	0	0
		Purchase	3,891	5	0	2	1	2	138	35	102	1	2
	United States Merchant												
	Marine Academy		949	0	0	0	0	0	44	27	17	0	0

Note: Caution should be exercised in making any intercampus comparisons or ranking schools because university/college crime statistics are affected by a variety of factors. These include demographic characteristics of the surrounding community, ratio of male to female students, number of on-campus residents, accessibility of the campus to outside visitors, size of enrollment, etc.

[1] The student enrollment figures provided by the United States Department of Education are for the 2006 school year, the most recent available. The enrollment figures include full-time and part-time students.

[2] The FBI does not publish arson data unless it receives data from either the agency or the state for all 12 months of the calendar year.

[3] Student enrollment figures were not available.

Table 9.   Offenses Known to Law Enforcement, by State and University and College, 2007 *(Contd.)*

(Number.)

State	University/College	Campus	Student enroll-ment[1]	Violent crime	Murder and non-negligent man-slaughter	Forcible rape	Robbery	Aggra-vated assault	Property crime	Burglary	Larceny-theft	Motor vehicle theft	Arson[2]
NORTH CAROLINA	Appalachian State University		15,117	3	0	1	1	1	162	23	138	1	3
	Duke University		13,373	3	0	1	1	1	698	61	629	8	0
	East Carolina University		24,351	12	0	1	5	6	246	10	234	2	0
	Elon University		5,230	1	0	0	0	1	75	12	63	0	1
	Fayetteville State University		6,301	2	0	1	1	0	138	5	128	5	0
	Methodist College		2,116	0	0	0	0	0	31	2	29	0	0
	North Carolina Agricultural and Technical State		11,098	17	0	0	8	9	270	47	220	3	2
	North Carolina Central University		8,675	14	0	0	4	10	251	40	204	7	0
	North Carolina School of the Arts		845	1	0	0	0	1	32	5	26	1	0
	North Carolina State University	Raleigh	31,130	17	0	3	8	6	390	51	335	4	0
	University of North Carolina:	Asheville	3,639	0	0	0	0	0	47	5	41	1	0
		Chapel Hill	27,717	3	0	0	2	1	428	12	408	8	0
		Greensboro	16,872	9	0	0	4	5	262	3	254	5	0
		Pembroke	5,827	0	0	0	0	0	93	8	84	1	0
		Wilmington	12,098	1	0	1	0	0	281	22	250	9	1
	Wake Forest University		6,739	3	0	0	0	3	132	21	110	1	1
	Western Carolina University		8,861	1	0	1	0	0	164	22	140	2	3
NORTH DAKOTA	North Dakota State College of Science		2,493	0	0	0	0	0	45	13	32	0	1
	North Dakota State University		12,258	0	0	0	0	0	135	12	121	2	0
	University of North Dakota		12,834	3	0	2	0	1	131	6	125	0	0
OHIO	Bowling Green State University		19,108	3	0	0	1	2	300	50	248	2	4
	Cleveland State University		14,807	6	0	0	6	0	164	6	139	19	0
	Columbus State Community College		22,745	1	0	0	1	0	118	2	112	4	0
	Cuyahoga Community College		24,289	2	0	0	2	0	126	4	120	2	0
	Kent State University		22,697	1	0	1	0	0	186	31	153	2	0
	Lakeland Community College		8,649	0	0	0	0	0	26	0	25	1	0
	Marietta College		1,522	0	0	0	0	0	26	20	6	0	0
	Miami University		16,329	10	0	3	1	6	194	21	172	1	0
	Ohio State University		51,818	17	0	8	6	3	976	207	756	13	17
	Ohio University		20,610	7	0	4	2	1	237	42	194	1	2
	Sinclair Community College		19,103	0	0	0	0	0	114	5	108	1	0
	University of Akron		21,882	15	0	6	8	1	367	15	338	14	1
	University of Cincinnati		28,327	8	0	0	5	3	551	51	497	3	2
	Wright State University		16,088	4	0	0	3	1	227	38	179	10	2
	Youngstown State University		13,273	4	0	1	3	0	141	14	122	5	0
OKLAHOMA	Cameron University		5,737	0	0	0	0	0	23	1	20	2	0
	East Central University[5]		4,453	13	0	3	1	9		10		5	0
	Murray State College		2,232	2	0	1	0	1	2	0	2	0	0
	Northeastern Oklahoma A&M College		1,923	0	0	0	0	0	36	19	17	0	0
	Northeastern State University		9,417	7	0	3	3	1	77	17	60	0	0
	Oklahoma State University:	Main Campus	23,499	8	0	1	0	7	199	32	164	3	1
		Okmulgee	3,255	0	0	0	0	0	21	3	17	1	0
		Tulsa[3]		0	0	0	0	0	20	5	5	10	0
	Rogers State University		3,955	0	0	0	0	0	19	4	15	0	0
	Seminole State College		2,038	0	0	0	0	0	16	0	16	0	0
	Southeastern Oklahoma State University		3,830	2	0	0	0	2	47	18	28	1	1

Note: Caution should be exercised in making any intercampus comparisons or ranking schools because university/college crime statistics are affected by a variety of factors. These include demographic characteristics of the surrounding community, ratio of male to female students, number of on-campus residents, accessibility of the campus to outside visitors, size of enrollment, etc.

[1] The student enrollment figures provided by the United States Department of Education are for the 2006 school year, the most recent available. The enrollment figures include full-time and part-time students.

[2] The FBI does not publish arson data unless it receives data from either the agency or the state for all 12 months of the calendar year.

[3] Student enrollment figures were not available.

[5] The FBI determined that the agency's data were overreported. Consequently, affected data are not included in this table.

Table 9. Offenses Known to Law Enforcement, by State and University and College, 2007 *(Contd.)*

(Number.)

State	University/College	Campus	Student enrollment[1]	Violent crime	Murder and non-negligent man-slaughter	Forcible rape	Robbery	Aggra-vated assault	Property crime	Burglary	Larceny-theft	Motor vehicle theft	Arson[2]
	Southwestern Oklahoma State University		5,122	0	0	0	0	0	80	25	55	0	0
	Tulsa Community College		16,632	1	0	0	0	1	51	2	41	8	0
	University of Central Oklahoma		15,588	4	0	2	0	2	136	10	126	0	5
	University of Oklahoma:	Health Sciences Center	3,790	3	0	0	0	3	181	4	173	4	0
		Norman	25,923	0	0	0	0	0	323	38	273	12	0
PENNSYLVANIA	Bloomsburg University		8,723	6	0	1	2	3	77	2	73	2	0
	California University		7,720	1	0	0	0	1	59	4	55	0	0
	Cheyney University		1,667	16	0	0	2	14	105	56	49	0	4
	Clarion University		6,563	5	0	0	0	5	24	6	18	0	0
	Dickenson College		2,400	1	0	0	0	1	40	3	37	0	0
	East Stroudsburg University		7,013	6	0	0	0	6	95	53	42	0	3
	Elizabethtown College		2,329	2	0	0	1	1	21	0	21	0	0
	Indiana University		14,248	26	0	4	0	22	113	24	87	2	1
	Kutztown University		10,193	6	0	3	2	1	121	19	102	0	0
	Lehigh University		6,858	5	0	0	1	4	103	6	95	2	2
	Lock Haven University		5,175	0	0	0	0	0	65	3	61	1	0
	Moravian College		1,965	3	0	0	1	2	28	3	24	1	0
	Pennsylvania State University:	Altoona	3,837	1	0	1	0	0	33	2	31	0	0
		Beaver	730	0	0	0	0	0	8	1	7	0	0
		Behrend	3,839	0	0	0	0	0	26	4	22	0	1
		Berks	2,660	0	0	0	0	0	17	9	8	0	0
		Harrisburg	3,799	0	0	0	0	0	25	8	17	0	2
		Hazelton	1,143	0	0	0	0	0	13	3	10	0	0
		McKees-port[3]		0	0	0	0	0	15	6	9	0	0
		Mont Alto	1,032	1	0	0	0	1	23	5	18	0	0
		University Park	42,914	9	0	1	4	4	545	80	460	5	3
	Shippensburg University		7,516	3	0	1	0	2	97	39	58	0	2
	Slippery Rock University		8,230	1	0	0	0	1	58	0	58	0	0
	University of Pittsburgh:	Bradford	1,333	0	0	0	0	0	17	2	15	0	0
		Pittsburgh	26,860	27	0	0	11	16	379	23	354	2	0
	West Chester University		12,879	6	0	1	1	4	114	46	67	1	3
RHODE ISLAND	Brown University		8,125	4	0	0	1	3	198	54	144	0	2
	University of Rhode Island		15,062	5	0	2	1	2	211	22	182	7	1
SOUTH CAROLINA	Aiken Technical College		2,442	0	0	0	0	0	0	0	0	0	0
	Benedict College		2,531	13	0	0	10	3	248	120	124	4	5
	Bob Jones University[3]			0	0	0	0	0	29	17	12	0	0
	Clemson University		17,309	10	0	1	2	7	256	31	211	14	1
	Coastal Carolina University		8,049	1	0	0	1	0	82	13	66	3	2
	College of Charleston		11,218	4	0	0	2	2	144	22	118	4	2
	Columbia College		1,446	0	0	0	0	0	11	0	11	0	0
	Denmark Technical College		1,377	0	0	0	0	0	0	0	0	0	0
	Erskine College		924	0	0	0	0	0	1	0	1	0	0
	Francis Marion University		4,075	2	0	0	0	2	54	10	43	1	0
	Lander University		2,682	2	0	0	0	2	45	10	35	0	1
	Medical University of South Carolina		2,498	2	0	0	0	2	199	3	194	2	0
	Midlands Technical College		10,849	2	0	0	2	0	33	0	32	1	0
	Presbyterian College		1,224	0	0	0	0	0	0	0	0	0	0
	South Carolina State University		4,384	13	0	0	6	7	187	62	123	2	1
	Spartanburg Methodist College		779	1	0	0	1	0	21	9	11	1	0
	The Citadel		3,306	0	0	0	0	0	7	2	5	0	1
	Trident Technical College		11,808	0	0	0	0	0	49	3	45	1	0
	University of South Carolina:	Aiken	3,380	1	0	0	0	1	34	1	32	1	0
		Columbia	27,390	15	0	3	4	8	395	83	305	7	1
		Upstate	4,608	3	0	1	0	2	39	6	32	1	1
	Winthrop University		6,292	3	0	0	1	2	125	12	107	6	5
SOUTH DAKOTA	South Dakota State University		11,303	0	0	0	0	0	0	0	0	0	0

Note: Caution should be exercised in making any intercampus comparisons or ranking schools because university/college crime statistics are affected by a variety of factors. These include demographic characteristics of the surrounding community, ratio of male to female students, number of on-campus residents, accessibility of the campus to outside visitors, size of enrollment, etc.

[1] The student enrollment figures provided by the United States Department of Education are for the 2006 school year, the most recent available. The enrollment figures include full-time and part-time students.

[2] The FBI does not publish arson data unless it receives data from either the agency or the state for all 12 months of the calendar year.

[3] Student enrollment figures were not available.

Table 9.   Offenses Known to Law Enforcement, by State and University and College, 2007 *(Contd.)*

(Number.)

State	University/College	Campus	Student enroll-ment[1]	Violent crime	Murder and non-negligent man-slaughter	Forcible rape	Robbery	Aggra-vated assault	Property crime	Burglary	Larceny-theft	Motor vehicle theft	Arson[2]
TENNESSEE	Austin Peay State University		9,207	6	0	2	1	3	58	2	56	0	1
	Christian Brothers University		1,779	0	0	0	0	0	42	3	35	4	3
	East Tennessee State University		12,390	5	0	0	2	3	97	17	75	5	3
	Middle Tennessee State University		22,863	16	0	3	3	10	264	73	186	5	2
	Northeast State Technical Community College		5,145	0	0	0	0	0	17	2	15	0	0
	Southwest Tennessee Community College		11,446	1	0	0	1	0	75	0	70	5	0
	Tennessee State University		9,038	7	0	0	3	4	114	4	103	7	0
	Tennessee Technological University		9,733	4	0	0	1	3	120	26	90	4	0
	University of Memphis		20,562	6	1	2	1	2	200	32	159	9	1
	University of Tennessee:	Chattanooga	8,923	7	0	1	2	4	204	62	138	4	1
		Knoxville	28,901	6	0	2	1	3	411	3	402	6	0
		Martin	6,888	3	0	0	2	1	73	16	54	3	0
		Memphis[3]		2	0	0	1	1	66	1	60	5	0
	Vanderbilt University		11,607	41	0	13	4	24	526	51	473	2	3
	Volunteer State Community College		7,370	0	0	0	0	0	24	1	23	0	0
	Walters State Community College		5,738	0	0	0	0	0	8	0	8	0	0
TEXAS	Abilene Christian University		4,777	0	0	0	0	0	80	16	63	1	0
	Alamo Community College District[3]		20	0	1	2	17	317	11	290	16	0	
	Alvin Community College		3,996	0	0	0	0	0	9	0	8	1	0
	Amarillo College		10,356	2	0	0	0	2	29	2	27	0	1
	Angelo State University		6,265	1	0	1	0	0	103	7	95	1	0
	Austin College		1,354	0	0	0	0	0	51	8	42	1	0
	Baylor Health Care System[3]		7	1	0	1	5	501	26	459	16	0	
	Baylor University	Waco	14,040	10	0	0	0	10	258	20	236	2	0
	Central Texas College		17,726	1	0	0	0	1	17	0	17	0	0
	College of the Mainland		3,834	1	0	0	0	1	27	0	26	1	1
	Eastfield College		12,015	1	0	0	0	1	48	20	28	0	0
	El Paso Community College		26,105	0	0	0	0	0	125	3	117	5	0
	Grayson County College		3,720	0	0	0	0	0	24	7	17	0	0
	Hardin-Simmons University		2,367	1	0	0	0	1	36	19	15	2	0
	Houston Baptist University		2,143	1	0	0	0	1	14	1	13	0	0
	Lamar University	Beaumont	9,906	14	0	4	1	9	113	11	101	1	0
	Laredo Community College		8,152	0	0	0	0	0	22	1	20	1	0
	McLennan Community College		7,794	1	0	1	0	0	41	1	40	0	0
	Midwestern State University		6,042	1	0	0	0	1	48	12	34	2	0
	Mountain View College		7,022	0	0	0	0	0	42	0	27	15	0
	North Lake College		9,397	0	0	0	0	0	55	3	52	0	0
	Paris Junior College		4,331	2	0	1	0	1	16	5	11	0	0
	Prairie View A&M University		8,006	7	0	1	0	6	253	98	150	5	1
	Rice University		5,024	5	0	2	1	2	200	22	173	5	0
	Richland College		14,555	3	0	0	2	1	83	7	73	3	0
	Southern Methodist University		10,941	8	0	2	2	4	281	31	244	6	1
	South Plains College		9,045	1	0	0	0	1	28	4	24	0	0
	Southwestern University		1,277	0	0	0	0	0	24	11	12	1	0
	Stephen F. Austin State University		11,756	9	0	2	2	5	303	43	250	10	2
	Sul Ross State University		2,773	1	0	1	0	0	33	15	18	0	0
	Tarleton State University		9,464	1	0	1	0	0	68	22	45	1	0

Note: Caution should be exercised in making any intercampus comparisons or ranking schools because university/college crime statistics are affected by a variety of factors. These include demographic characteristics of the surrounding community, ratio of male to female students, number of on-campus residents, accessibility of the campus to outside visitors, size of enrollment, etc.

[1] The student enrollment figures provided by the United States Department of Education are for the 2006 school year, the most recent available. The enrollment figures include full-time and part-time students.

[2] The FBI does not publish arson data unless it receives data from either the agency or the state for all 12 months of the calendar year.

[3] Student enrollment figures were not available.

Table 9. Offenses Known to Law Enforcement, by State and University and College, 2007 *(Contd.)*

(Number.)

State	University/College	Campus	Student enroll-ment[1]	Violent crime	Murder and non-negligent man-slaughter	Forcible rape	Robbery	Aggra-vated assault	Property crime	Burglary	Larceny-theft	Motor vehicle theft	Arson[2]
	Texas A&M International University		4,917	2	0	1	0	1	51	16	35	0	0
	Texas A&M University:	College Station	45,380	8	0	2	3	3	493	31	453	9	1
		Commerce	8,471	4	0	1	0	3	101	21	80	0	0
		Corpus Christi	8,585	1	0	0	0	1	48	20	28	0	0
		Galveston	1,553	1	0	0	0	1	29	3	26	0	0
		Kingsville	6,728	1	0	0	0	1	100	27	72	1	0
	Texas Christian University		8,865	2	0	0	0	2	165	12	148	5	0
	Texas Southern University		11,224	15	0	1	8	6	239	43	184	12	1
	Texas State Technical College:	Harlingen	4,281	1	0	0	0	1	29	5	24	0	0
		Marshall	626	0	0	0	0	0	9	2	7	0	0
		Waco	4,209	15	0	0	0	15	142	30	109	3	0
	Texas State University	San Marcos	27,485	5	0	4	0	1	245	29	210	6	1
	Texas Technological University	Lubbock	27,996	8	0	3	1	4	286	17	266	3	3
	Texas Woman's University		11,832	1	0	0	0	1	71	4	65	2	0
	Trinity University		2,698	3	0	3	0	0	90	33	48	9	0
	Tyler Junior College		9,423	1	0	0	0	1	110	6	102	2	0
	University of Houston:	Central Campus	34,334	17	0	3	11	3	455	40	399	16	0
		Clearlake	7,706	0	0	0	0	0	6	0	6	0	0
		Downtown Campus	11,449	5	0	1	4	0	85	0	80	5	0
	University of Mary Hardin-Baylor		2,735	0	0	0	0	0	44	2	42	0	0
	University of North Texas:	Denton	33,395	4	0	0	3	1	203	41	156	6	2
		Health Science Center	1,129	0	0	0	0	0	29	2	26	1	0
	University of Texas:	Arlington	24,825	10	0	5	3	2	347	70	272	5	0
		Austin	49,697	5	0	1	3	1	528	20	497	11	3
		Brownsville	15,688	0	0	0	0	0	82	1	73	8	0
		Dallas	14,523	6	0	0	1	5	133	16	114	3	0
		El Paso	19,842	5	0	4	0	1	186	29	140	17	1
		Health Science Center, San Antonio	2,874	0	0	0	0	0	73	8	62	3	0
		Health Science Center, Tyler[3]		0	0	0	0	0	4	0	4	0	0
		Houston[3]		21	0	0	1	20	300	23	272	5	0
		Medical Branch	2,255	2	0	0	2	0	225	2	219	4	1
		Pan American	17,337	2	0	0	0	2	120	3	112	5	0
		Permian Basin	3,462	1	0	0	1	0	40	5	34	1	0
		San Antonio	28,379	8	0	1	1	6	193	9	176	8	0
		Southwestern Medical School	2,434	1	0	0	1	0	243	9	229	5	0
		Tyler	5,926	1	0	1	0	0	48	16	29	3	0
	Western Texas College		1,974	0	0	0	0	0	5	1	4	0	0
	West Texas A&M University		7,412	2	0	2	0	0	51	5	45	1	1
UTAH	Brigham Young University		34,185	1	0	1	0	0	285	18	264	3	2
	College of Eastern Utah		2,262	2	0	1	0	1	8	3	5	0	0
	Southern Utah University		7,029	3	0	1	0	2	46	9	34	3	0
	University of Utah		30,511	4	1	0	1	2	530	26	480	24	0
	Utah State University		14,444	1	0	1	0	0	97	9	88	0	0
	Utah Valley State College		23,305	0	0	0	0	0	74	6	63	5	0
	Weber State University		18,303	2	0	0	0	2	80	15	65	0	0
VERMONT	University of Vermont		11,870	2	0	2	0	0	145	35	108	2	0

Note: Caution should be exercised in making any intercampus comparisons or ranking schools because university/college crime statistics are affected by a variety of factors. These include demographic characteristics of the surrounding community, ratio of male to female students, number of on-campus residents, accessibility of the campus to outside visitors, size of enrollment, etc.

[1] The student enrollment figures provided by the United States Department of Education are for the 2006 school year, the most recent available. The enrollment figures include full-time and part-time students.

[2] The FBI does not publish arson data unless it receives data from either the agency or the state for all 12 months of the calendar year.

[3] Student enrollment figures were not available.

Table 9. Offenses Known to Law Enforcement, by State and University and College, 2007 *(Contd.)*

(Number.)

State	University/College	Campus	Student enrollment[1]	Violent crime	Murder and nonnegligent manslaughter	Forcible rape	Robbery	Aggravated assault	Property crime	Burglary	Larceny-theft	Motor vehicle theft	Arson[2]
VIRGINIA	Christopher Newport University		4,793	3	0	0	0	3	150	3	145	2	1
	College of William and Mary		7,709	0	0	0	0	0	242	21	219	2	0
	Emory and Henry College		1,051	0	0	0	0	0	3	2	1	0	0
	Ferrum College		1,060	1	0	0	0	1	24	3	21	0	7
	George Mason University		29,889	5	0	2	1	2	232	10	218	4	4
	Hampton University		6,152	4	0	0	3	1	102	17	83	2	0
	James Madison University		17,393	3	0	1	0	2	233	10	222	1	0
	Longwood College		4,479	3	0	2	1	0	48	12	36	0	1
	Norfolk State University		6,238	11	1	2	3	5	169	56	107	6	3
	Northern Virginia Community College		38,166	0	0	0	0	0	153	1	152	0	0
	Old Dominion University		21,625	9	0	1	4	4	235	5	227	3	1
	Radford University		9,220	1	0	0	0	1	142	15	127	0	0
	Thomas Nelson Community College		9,718	1	0	0	1	0	13	0	13	0	0
	University of Richmond		4,496	1	0	0	0	1	86	19	65	2	1
	University of Virginia		24,068	15	0	0	7	8	334	44	286	4	2
	University of Virginia's College at Wise		2,043	0	0	0	0	0	1	1	0	0	0
	Virginia Commonwealth University		30,189	34	0	0	17	17	546	18	522	6	0
	Virginia Military Institute		1,397	1	0	1	0	0	18	10	6	2	0
	Virginia Polytechnic Institute and State University		28,470	6	2	2	1	1	282	55	225	2	2
	Virginia State University		4,872	8	0	0	5	3	160	3	154	3	0
	Virginia Western Community College		8,365	0	0	0	0	0	19	1	18	0	0
WASHINGTON	Central Washington University		10,688	1	0	1	0	0	166	12	152	2	0
	Eastern Washington University		11,161	2	0	0	1	1	99	8	88	3	0
	Evergreen State College		4,416	2	0	2	0	0	116	16	97	3	0
	University of Washington		39,524	11	1	0	2	8	587	69	488	30	3
	Washington State University:	Pullman	23,655	3	0	1	1	1	160	18	137	5	4
		Vancouver[3]		0	0	0	0	0	14	3	10	1	0
	Western Washington University		14,035	0	0	0	0	0	260	25	231	4	0
WEST VIRGINIA	Fairmont State University		4,611	2	0	1	0	1	37	12	25	0	0
	Glenville State College		1,381	0	0	0	0	0	16	7	9	0	1
	Marshall University		13,936	2	0	0	0	2	137	8	127	2	2
	Potomac State College		1,485	0	0	0	0	0	12	3	9	0	0
	West Virginia State University		3,502	3	0	0	1	2	43	8	33	2	2
	West Virginia Tech		1,472	0	0	0	0	0	39	18	19	2	1
	West Virginia University		27,115	4	0	1	2	1	205	16	182	7	0
WISCONSIN	University of Wisconsin:	Eau Claire	10,766	0	0	0	0	0	70	0	69	1	0
		Green Bay	5,690	2	0	2	0	0	53	1	52	0	0
		La Crosse	9,849	0	0	0	0	0	57	3	53	1	4
		Madison	41,028	15	0	2	4	9	475	146	319	10	4
		Milwaukee	28,309	6	0	2	3	1	257	29	227	1	0
		Oshkosh	12,530	6	0	2	3	1	66	17	49	0	0
		Parkside	5,007	1	0	0	0	1	97	1	96	0	0
		Platteville	6,813	3	0	0	0	3	72	7	65	0	0
		Stevens Point	9,048	0	0	0	0	0	91	0	90	1	1
		Stout	8,372	3	0	1	0	2	160	19	140	1	0
		Superior	2,924	0	0	0	0	0	32	11	20	1	1
		Whitewater	10,502	2	0	1	0	1	95	13	80	2	0
WYOMING	Sheridan College		3,066	0	0	0	0	0	17	4	12	1	0
	University of Wyoming		13,203	0	0	0	0	0	132	4	128	0	1

Note: Caution should be exercised in making any intercampus comparisons or ranking schools because university/college crime statistics are affected by a variety of factors. These include demographic characteristics of the surrounding community, ratio of male to female students, number of on-campus residents, accessibility of the campus to outside visitors, size of enrollment, etc.

[1] The student enrollment figures provided by the United States Department of Education are for the 2006 school year, the most recent available. The enrollment figures include full-time and part-time students.

[2] The FBI does not publish arson data unless it receives data from either the agency or the state for all 12 months of the calendar year.

[3] Student enrollment figures were not available.

Table 10. Offenses Known to Law Enforcement, by State Metropolitan and Nonmetropolitan Counties, 2007

(Number.)

State	County	Violent crime	Murder and non-negligent man-slaughter	Forcible rape	Robbery	Aggravated assault	Property crime	Burglary	Larceny-theft	Motor vehicle theft	Arson[1]
ALABAMA-Metropolitan Counties	Autauga	28	0	5	4	19	421	138	243	40	
	Bibb	11	0	1	0	10	78	29	46	3	
	Chilton	291	1	8	2	280	454	151	296	7	
	Colbert	170	0	9	6	155	624	137	477	10	
	Geneva	23	3	1	0	19	173	69	85	19	
	Hale	58	1	6	12	39	242	88	134	20	
	Henry	21	0	3	3	15	165	57	86	22	
	Houston	12	3	0	2	7	477	100	319	58	
	Jefferson	557	3	48	221	285	5,320	1,844	2,932	544	30
	Lawrence	39	0	2	4	33	449	143	286	20	
	Limestone	19	0	3	2	14	240	50	150	40	
	Lowndes	28	1	2	7	18	133	103	22	8	
	Madison	216	4	21	31	160	2,176	588	1,311	277	
	Mobile	245	7	29	80	129	2,624	783	1,572	269	
	Montgomery	66	0	4	16	46	719	219	426	74	
	Morgan	24	0	4	4	16	407	196	166	45	
	Russell	21	1	2	4	14	105	50	43	12	
	Shelby	83	0	12	18	53	961	341	545	75	
	Tuscaloosa	280	4	25	58	193	2,278	633	1,388	257	
	Walker	26	0	3	3	20	688	222	442	24	
ALABAMA-Nonmetropolitan Counties	Baldwin	134	0	23	6	105	993	316	610	67	
	Barbour	0	0	0	0	0	2	0	2	0	
	Bullock	31	0	0	2	29	140	64	76	0	
	Chambers	24	0	3	1	20	163	53	107	3	
	Cherokee	8	0	6	0	2	249	66	182	1	
	Clarke	4	0	0	0	4	13	5	6	2	
	Clay	7	0	0	0	7	130	47	82	1	
	Cleburne	24	0	7	3	14	209	76	108	25	
	Coffee	16	0	0	2	14	163	72	89	2	
	Conecuh	0	0	0	0	0	14	4	10	0	
	Coosa	25	1	7	4	13	173	57	107	9	
	Crenshaw	27	0	1	3	23	189	45	118	26	
	Cullman	108	2	24	7	75	1,495	470	908	117	
	Dale	34	0	5	2	27	127	38	88	1	
	De Kalb	112	0	32	1	79	686	187	408	91	
	Escambia	20	0	0	1	19	151	45	91	15	
	Fayette	9	0	1	0	8	132	56	56	20	
	Jackson	64	2	7	7	48	609	190	334	85	
	Lamar	2	0	0	0	2	37	14	18	5	
	Macon	28	0	3	6	19	282	119	119	44	
	Marengo	24	0	6	5	13	174	82	82	10	
	Marshall	35	1	8	1	25	495	152	313	30	
	Monroe	40	0	0	1	39	100	36	51	13	
	Perry	7	0	1	0	6	95	28	57	10	
	Pickens	16	0	3	0	13	66	36	26	4	
	Pike	7	0	1	0	6	98	46	50	2	
	Talladega	62	0	7	14	41	662	210	413	39	
	Tallapoosa	16	1	3	7	5	252	95	122	35	
	Washington	29	0	2	3	24	52	18	32	2	
	Winston	19	0	5	1	13	183	41	132	10	
ARIZONA-Metropolitan Counties	Coconino	161	0	14	4	143	539	144	365	30	16
	Maricopa	989	32	13	129	815	8,081	2,074	4,782	1,225	84
	Mohave	225	6	4	21	194	3,110	1,027	1,734	349	30
	Pima	606	25	80	165	336	13,012	2,439	8,891	1,682	126
	Pinal	290	11	60	41	178	5,065	743	3,405	917	18
	Yavapai	325	3	12	3	307	1,728	527	1,054	147	12
	Yuma	123	6	14	23	80	1,391	284	910	197	16
ARIZONA-Nonmetropolitan Counties	Cochise[2]		2	17	17		1,383	564	656	163	20
	Gila	61	0	3	0	58	396	121	219	56	6
	La Paz	66	0	0	0	66	429	82	317	30	1
	Navajo	65	1	8	4	52	738	393	224	121	5
ARKANSAS-Metropolitan Counties	Cleveland	2	0	0	1	1	101	49	42	10	1
	Craighead	22	0	4	1	17	373	135	211	27	5

[1] The FBI does not publish arson data unless it receives data from either the agency or the state for all 12 months of the calendar year.

[2] It was determined that the agency did not follow national Uniform Crime Reporting (UCR) Program guidelines for reporting an offense. Consequently, this figure is not included in this table.

Table 10. Offenses Known to Law Enforcement, by State Metropolitan and Nonmetropolitan Counties, 2007 *(Contd.)*

(Number.)

State	County	Violent crime	Murder and non-negligent man-slaughter	Forcible rape	Robbery	Aggravated assault	Property crime	Burglary	Larceny-theft	Motor vehicle theft	Arson[1]
	Crittenden	81	2	8	7	64	465	178	256	31	11
	Faulkner	44	0	2	2	40	745	162	526	57	5
	Franklin	21	0	2	0	19	181	63	107	11	5
	Garland	96	3	14	7	72	2,306	936	1,196	174	3
	Grant	38	0	5	1	32	178	63	103	12	0
	Jefferson	69	3	7	9	50	489	202	225	62	5
	Lincoln	18	0	3	0	15	83	45	38	0	0
	Lonoke	122	5	12	4	101	616	209	339	68	5
	Madison	30	1	5	0	24	61	24	31	6	4
	Perry	14	0	1	0	13	64	41	21	2	3
	Poinsett	66	0	3	2	61	112	103	4	5	6
	Pulaski	402	4	17	36	345	2,223	898	1,056	269	11
	Saline	95	0	10	5	80	1,016	315	645	56	3
	Sebastian	66	1	6	5	54	413	150	243	20	2
	Washington	142	1	24	4	113	657	259	354	44	4
ARKANSAS- Nonmetropolitan Counties	Arkansas	7	0	1	0	6	90	32	47	11	1
	Ashley	12	0	2	0	10	149	53	86	10	0
	Baxter	31	1	0	1	29	613	112	464	37	6
	Boone	42	2	12	0	28	301	98	171	32	4
	Bradley	4	0	1	0	3	18	10	4	4	0
	Calhoun	1	0	0	0	1	23	15	5	3	0
	Carroll	27	0	2	0	25	225	53	155	17	6
	Chicot	6	1	1	0	4	80	7	58	15	0
	Clark	18	0	2	0	16	171	87	72	12	1
	Clay	12	0	2	0	10	90	31	56	3	0
	Cleburne	50	1	6	1	42	376	175	170	31	2
	Columbia	30	0	2	3	25	199	60	132	7	0
	Cross	35	0	1	1	33	214	41	164	9	0
	Dallas	0	0	0	0	0	23	5	18	0	0
	Drew	35	1	1	0	33	133	44	75	14	1
	Fulton	11	0	1	0	10	77	38	38	1	0
	Greene	15	0	3	0	12	203	90	106	7	4
	Hempstead	26	0	5	1	20	139	52	74	13	1
	Howard	8	0	3	0	5	107	51	56	0	0
	Independence	101	2	13	6	80	1,258	431	745	82	13
	Izard	12	0	0	2	10	100	52	39	9	4
	Jackson	25	0	7	0	18	164	55	93	16	2
	Johnson	0	0	0	0	0	120	27	89	4	0
	Lafayette	5	0	0	1	4	60	55	2	3	0
	Lawrence	26	0	2	0	24	164	85	79	0	1
	Lee	16	5	1	0	10	14	10	4	0	0
	Little River	2	0	0	0	2	33	7	23	3	1
	Logan	18	0	6	1	11	258	91	145	22	5
	Marion	41	0	3	0	38	169	44	122	3	3
	Mississippi	43	0	8	5	30	400	99	254	47	4
	Monroe	2	0	0	0	2	58	16	26	16	1
	Montgomery[2]		0	3	0		157	38	104	15	0
	Nevada	16	2	1	1	12	32	13	17	2	0
	Ouachita	29	1	2	5	21	215	87	106	22	2
	Polk	31	0	1	2	28	154	66	77	11	1
	Pope	42	0	9	0	33	378	140	209	29	3
	Randolph	7	0	3	0	4	12	5	7	0	1
	Scott	6	0	4	0	2	67	33	32	2	1
	Searcy	1	0	0	0	1	15	11	3	1	0
	Sevier	14	0	3	2	9	144	58	81	5	1
	St. Francis	40	1	2	12	25	401	129	271	1	2
	Stone	3	0	0	0	3	31	13	16	2	1
	Union	25	0	1	6	18	421	68	313	40	3
	Van Buren	21	0	1	0	20	124	26	80	18	0
	White	62	0	14	3	45	789	285	420	84	4
	Woodruff	0	0	0	0	0	14	1	10	3	0
	Yell	52	0	3	1	48	116	71	27	18	6
CALIFORNIA- Metropolitan Counties	Alameda	683	6	27	293	357	2,864	676	1,275	913	33
	Butte	217	5	21	34	157	1,502	565	920	17	50
	Contra Costa	666	11	42	218	395	3,503	1,147	2,336	20	35
	El Dorado	236	3	20	24	189	2,034	652	1,350	32	20
	Imperial	106	0	10	11	85	945	301	616	28	6
	Kern	1,918	28	92	400	1,398	11,001	3,118	6,352	1,531	286
	Fresno	618	17	33	149	419	6,497	1,705	3,812	980	

[1] The FBI does not publish arson data unless it receives data from either the agency or the state for all 12 months of the calendar year.

[2] It was determined that the agency did not follow national Uniform Crime Reporting (UCR) Program guidelines for reporting an offense. Consequently, this figure is not included in this table.

Table 10. Offenses Known to Law Enforcement, by State Metropolitan and Nonmetropolitan Counties, 2007 *(Contd.)*

(Number.)

State	County	Violent crime	Murder and non-negligent man-slaughter	Forcible rape	Robbery	Aggravated assault	Property crime	Burglary	Larceny-theft	Motor vehicle theft	Arson[1]
	Kings	113	4	6	22	81	460	186	262	12	
	Los Angeles	7,784	127	218	2,185	5,254	20,516	5,293	9,516	5,707	455
	Madera	310	1	13	18	278	1,282	505	764	13	2
	Marin	130	1	3	26	100	822	233	586	3	
	Merced	451	8	26	40	377	2,240	820	1,406	14	17
	Monterey	219	7	20	64	128	1,952	599	1,317	36	14
	Napa	79	0	10	4	65	562	194	362	6	6
	Orange	178	1	9	33	135	1,481	296	1,023	162	25
	Placer	255	2	26	28	199	1,997	634	1,329	34	19
	Riverside	2,243	32	112	461	1,638	14,935	3,829	8,226	2,880	61
	Sacramento	3,231	40	172	1,251	1,768	14,912	4,695	9,928	289	111
	San Benito	57	1	6	0	50	327	135	179	13	9
	San Bernardino	1,286	24	69	194	999	6,569	2,178	2,990	1,401	114
	San Diego	1,699	13	99	296	1,291	7,564	2,055	3,625	1,884	58
	San Joaquin	1,081	12	30	234	805	5,269	1,751	3,334	184	26
	San Luis Obispo	239	0	29	16	194	1,356	449	897	10	7
	San Mateo	238	3	9	37	189	1,598	214	1,122	262	4
	Santa Barbara	193	2	35	23	133	1,602	486	1,108	8	6
	Santa Clara	321	3	31	36	251	1,757	430	1,078	249	5
	Santa Cruz	256	4	21	33	198	2,396	710	1,674	12	29
	Shasta	349	10	31	23	285	968	369	547	52	20
	Solano	186	2	8	27	149	518	261	244	13	23
	Sonoma	524	2	44	37	441	1,726	705	997	24	22
	Stanislaus	779	12	36	120	611	3,826	1,738	1,634	454	253
	Sutter	124	0	6	8	110	938	357	521	60	12
	Tulare[3]	488	10	36	97	345		783	2,038		
	Ventura	184	1	13	24	146	1,303	317	891	95	19
	Yolo	30	3	1	7	19	389	145	223	21	10
	Yuba	222	0	17	37	168	1,138	513	606	19	20
CALIFORNIA-Nonmetropolitan Counties											
	Alpine	15	1	1	0	13	74	15	59	0	0
	Amador	104	0	17	8	79	457	160	290	7	0
	Calaveras	48	0	18	9	21	633	254	374	5	3
	Colusa	34	0	2	0	32	310	82	219	9	0
	Del Norte	57	0	21	3	33	225	104	120	1	3
	Glenn	9	2	0	1	6	133	56	73	4	1
	Humboldt	136	1	17	17	101	894	246	626	22	4
	Inyo	104	0	2	0	102	132	5	126	1	2
	Lake	147	3	9	13	122	754	334	411	9	18
	Lassen	36	0	7	2	27	117	50	67	0	3
	Mariposa	31	0	6	1	24	306	101	205	0	0
	Mendocino	319	4	15	34	266	716	318	393	5	13
	Modoc	19	0	2	0	17	104	43	61	0	1
	Mono	14	0	4	0	10	93	40	51	2	0
	Nevada	132	1	7	7	117	597	224	370	3	1
	Plumas[4]		1	14	6		405	164	235	6	
	Sierra	15	0	0	0	15	69	28	37	4	0
	Siskiyou	50	0	6	0	44	217	86	128	3	9
	Tehama	192	0	5	4	183	416	234	182	0	20
	Trinity	21	2	0	5	14	112	69	42	1	0
	Tuolumne	108	1	13	12	82	875	423	449	3	7
COLORADO-Metropolitan Counties											
	Adams	404	1	75	48	280	3,036	641	1,793	602	27
	Arapahoe	225	0	22	27	176	1,548	405	961	182	26
	Boulder	45	0	8	0	37	583	171	362	50	13
	Clear Creek	28	0	4	0	24	88	27	55	6	4
	Douglas	175	2	43	20	110	2,089	474	1,542	73	6
	Elbert	7	0	0	0	7	44	12	27	5	0
	El Paso	856	1	66	32	757	2,104	544	1,303	257	28
	Gilpin	18	0	0	0	18	40	8	31	1	0
	Jefferson	256	2	41	17	196	3,049	615	2,209	225	29
	Larimer	96	2	17	7	70	986	209	663	114	6
	Mesa	152	2	13	17	120	1,365	347	879	139	15
	Park	32	1	4	0	27	108	46	48	14	2
	Pueblo	14	1	3	1	9	1,362	295	1,015	52	3
	Teller	17	1	1	0	15	77	22	49	6	1
	Weld	143	0	13	4	126	924	329	482	113	8

[1] The FBI does not publish arson data unless it receives data from either the agency or the state for all 12 months of the calendar year.

[3] The motor vehicle thefts for this county are collected by the Tulare County Highway Patrol. These data can be found in Table 11.

[4] The FBI determined that the agency's data were overreported. Consequently, affected data are not included in this table.

Table 10.   Offenses Known to Law Enforcement, by State Metropolitan and Nonmetropolitan Counties, 2007 *(Contd.)*

(Number.)

State	County	Violent crime	Murder and non-negligent man-slaughter	Forcible rape	Robbery	Aggravated assault	Property crime	Burglary	Larceny-theft	Motor vehicle theft	Arson[1]
COLORADO- **Nonmetropolitan** **Counties**	Alamosa	9	0	3	0	6	38	6	32	0	1
	Archuleta	14	0	1	0	13	105	36	65	4	1
	Baca	2	0	0	0	2	1	0	1	0	0
	Bent	1	0	0	0	1	30	10	16	4	1
	Chaffee	9	0	1	0	8	90	11	69	10	1
	Crowley	5	0	0	0	5	0	0	0	0	0
	Custer	7	0	0	0	7	38	7	30	1	0
	Delta	7	0	4	0	3	126	24	81	21	0
	Dolores	0	0	0	0	0	16	4	12	0	0
	Eagle	68	0	7	5	56	502	98	400	4	9
	Fremont	29	1	1	0	27	239	64	163	12	2
	Garfield	73	0	6	1	66	289	76	175	38	8
	Grand	10	0	0	0	10	156	30	125	1	0
	Gunnison	13	0	0	0	13	37	14	20	3	0
	Hinsdale	0	0	0	0	0	8	0	8	0	0
	Huerfano	5	0	0	1	4	129	7	107	15	0
	Jackson	2	0	0	0	2	18	2	14	2	0
	Kiowa	1	0	0	0	1	2	1	1	0	0
	Lake	10	0	1	2	7	17	6	6	5	1
	La Plata	28	0	9	0	19	270	107	139	24	0
	Las Animas	4	0	0	0	4	2	0	2	0	0
	Logan	3	0	1	0	2	50	17	30	3	1
	Mineral	0	0	0	0	0	1	0	0	1	0
	Moffat	12	0	0	0	12	27	9	17	1	2
	Montezuma	35	2	0	1	32	161	61	87	13	1
	Montrose	24	1	2	1	20	176	61	100	15	0
	Morgan	0	0	0	0	0	53	9	39	5	0
	Ouray	8	0	0	0	8	29	7	21	1	0
	Phillips	0	0	0	0	0	3	1	2	0	0
	Pitkin	17	0	5	0	12	125	23	95	7	0
	Prowers	5	0	2	0	3	29	5	21	3	0
	Routt	12	0	0	0	12	34	6	22	6	1
	Saguache	8	0	0	0	8	14	7	5	2	1
	San Juan	0	0	0	0	0	26	2	23	1	0
	San Miguel	6	0	0	0	6	50	13	33	4	0
	Sedgwick	2	0	0	0	2	8	2	6	0	0
	Summit	38	0	6	1	31	303	41	258	4	2
	Washington	2	0	0	0	2	39	7	23	9	0
	Yuma	7	0	0	0	7	35	14	16	5	0
DELAWARE- **Metropolitan** **Counties**	New Castle County Police	1,519	9	77	364	1,069	7,084	1,782	4,569	733	9
FLORIDA- **Metropolitan** **Counties**	Alachua	1,041	1	52	156	832	3,812	1,262	2,283	267	23
	Baker	100	3	5	4	88	326	28	277	21	0
	Bay	392	0	41	35	316	2,349	572	1,608	169	6
	Brevard	1,209	14	79	163	953	5,907	1,353	4,172	382	32
	Broward	438	7	29	128	274	1,146	222	826	98	8
	Charlotte	585	10	28	69	478	4,372	975	3,151	246	5
	Clay	819	5	48	100	666	4,161	920	2,953	288	23
	Collier	1,297	15	58	233	991	5,063	1,337	3,361	365	49
	Escambia	2,032	17	120	518	1,377	9,730	2,391	6,493	846	43
	Flagler	214	3	15	43	153	2,186	564	1,474	148	8
	Gadsden	289	1	12	34	242	773	478	223	72	0
	Gilchrist[5]	27	0	0	0	27		67		17	1
	Hernando	653	1	73	70	509	5,080	1,587	3,173	320	20
	Hillsborough	4,799	35	232	1,302	3,230	29,766	6,742	19,817	3,207	107
	Indian River	304	2	26	68	208	2,547	617	1,754	176	6
	Jefferson	112	1	6	6	99	134	68	63	3	1
	Lake	776	2	56	49	669	3,529	1,185	1,986	358	39
	Lee	2,004	25	111	555	1,313	13,303	4,414	7,602	1,287	99
	Leon	380	0	32	69	279	1,666	733	775	158	42
	Manatee	2,160	15	81	458	1,606	10,940	2,467	7,651	822	41
	Marion	1,493	8	109	92	1,284	5,130	1,608	3,152	370	9
	Martin	476	2	11	135	328	3,192	673	2,348	171	11
	Miami-Dade	8,614	84	353	2,679	5,498	52,483	9,737	35,866	6,880	89
	Nassau[4]		1	9	23		1,254	407	719	128	8

[1] The FBI does not publish arson data unless it receives data from either the agency or the state for all 12 months of the calendar year.

[4] The FBI determined that the agency's data were overreported. Consequently, affected data are not included in this table.

[5] The FBI determined that the agency's data were underreported. Consequently, affected data are not included in this table.

Table 10.   Offenses Known to Law Enforcement, by State Metropolitan and Nonmetropolitan Counties, 2007 *(Contd.)*

(Number.)

State	County	Violent crime	Murder and non-negligent man-slaughter	Forcible rape	Robbery	Aggravated assault	Property crime	Burglary	Larceny-theft	Motor vehicle theft	Arson[1]
	Okaloosa	465	1	32	94	338	3,798	863	2,706	229	5
	Orange	7,051	58	354	2,463	4,176	32,116	8,783	18,872	4,461	0
	Osceola	849	11	12	187	639	6,669	2,806	3,402	461	5
	Palm Beach	2,997	32	181	938	1,846	18,858	5,016	11,692	2,150	121
	Pasco	1,582	14	115	295	1,158	13,075	3,738	8,312	1,025	55
	Pinellas	1,305	10	135	228	932	7,607	1,981	5,007	619	9
	Polk	1,676	16	103	301	1,256	10,384	3,461	6,038	885	0
	Santa Rosa	309	4	49	23	233	1,579	476	1,008	95	8
	Sarasota	772	12	58	160	542	8,485	1,908	6,076	501	8
	Seminole	627	8	55	91	473	3,648	978	2,299	371	9
	St. Johns	537	3	15	63	456	3,906	1,164	2,491	251	10
	St. Lucie	326	6	24	45	251	1,853	570	1,148	135	9
	Volusia	943	5	75	171	692	5,632	1,802	3,225	605	20
	Wakulla	99	1	8	6	84	651	229	372	50	6
FLORIDA- **Nonmetropolitan** **Counties**	Bradford	88	0	8	5	75	362	178	150	34	0
	Calhoun	16	1	2	0	13	79	35	37	7	0
	Citrus	366	4	24	29	309	2,420	638	1,634	148	25
	Columbia	236	2	9	23	202	1,702	576	1,018	108	0
	DeSoto	189	3	4	15	167	809	404	357	48	7
	Dixie	73	2	10	1	60	392	144	220	28	4
	Franklin	12	0	0	1	11	106	41	56	9	1
	Glades	48	0	1	7	40	324	115	179	30	5
	Gulf	93	0	4	3	86	233	78	142	13	2
	Hamilton	44	0	4	5	35	226	98	117	11	0
	Hardee	72	2	6	12	52	629	172	402	55	0
	Hendry	263	5	10	42	206	1,111	466	521	124	4
	Highlands	173	5	14	37	117	1,921	769	1,006	146	9
	Holmes	55	2	7	3	43	197	54	125	18	0
	Jackson	220	6	14	11	189	638	218	372	48	1
	Lafayette	18	0	1	0	17	61	29	29	3	1
	Levy	154	0	13	6	135	817	251	494	72	2
	Madison	133	0	6	3	124	367	137	207	23	3
	Monroe	253	3	8	18	224	1,964	406	1,435	123	6
	Okeechobee	218	1	19	9	189	744	329	368	47	3
	Putnam	562	7	30	53	472	2,588	1,166	1,208	214	3
	Sumter	137	3	17	23	94	799	279	469	51	4
	Suwannee	170	3	4	7	156	587	176	321	90	0
	Taylor	107	0	5	0	102	215	101	108	6	3
	Union	66	0	4	4	58	163	73	72	18	1
	Walton	89	0	4	5	80	997	179	756	62	1
	Washington	22	0	1	0	21	221	75	119	27	1
GEORGIA- **Metropolitan** **Counties**	Augusta-Richmond	1,007	24	128	670	185	13,618	2,878	8,956	1,784	132
	Barrow	219	3	6	3	207	879	134	638	107	
	Bartow	248	0	17	27	204	3,028	815	1,880	333	
	Bibb	149	7	11	49	82	2,042	471	1,359	212	
	Brantley	28	1	2	1	24	308	116	155	37	1
	Brooks	84	1	0	5	78	376	134	200	42	4
	Bryan	11	0	2	3	6	244	53	167	24	
	Catoosa	80	2	9	9	60	1,128	225	749	154	
	Cherokee	87	0	1	8	78	1,514	416	1,007	91	2
	Clarke	0	0	0	0	0	0	0	0	0	0
	Clayton County Police Department	1,366	35	77	605	649	8,736	3,241	3,897	1,598	57
	Cobb	6	0	0	0	6	0	0	0	0	0
	Cobb County Police Department	1,402	24	97	624	657	12,466	3,118	7,744	1,604	37
	Coweta	78	0	7	22	49	1,183	311	734	138	10
	Crawford	21	0	0	3	18	305	103	169	33	
	Dade	19	0	2	1	16	191	54	113	24	
	Dawson	19	0	1	2	16	469	96	316	57	1
	DeKalb County Police Department	4,644	108	169	2,804	1,563	34,755	10,069	17,902	6,784	204
	Dougherty	0	0	0	0	0	66	8	47	11	0
	Dougherty County Police Department	32	0	3	13	16	519	195	268	56	0
	Douglas	179	6	9	51	113	2,394	660	1,424	310	8
	Echols	11	0	0	1	10	42	27	9	6	
	Effingham[5]	50	0	0	0	50		108		32	

[1] The FBI does not publish arson data unless it receives data from either the agency or the state for all 12 months of the calendar year.

[5] The FBI determined that the agency's data were underreported. Consequently, affected data are not included in this table.

Table 10. Offenses Known to Law Enforcement, by State Metropolitan and Nonmetropolitan Counties, 2007 *(Contd.)*

(Number.)

State	County	Violent crime	Murder and non-negligent man-slaughter	Forcible rape	Robbery	Aggravated assault	Property crime	Burglary	Larceny-theft	Motor vehicle theft	Arson[1]
	Fayette	33	2	4	10	17	570	148	362	60	2
	Floyd	11	0	0	1	10	2	1	1	0	
	Floyd County Police Department	143	2	6	6	129	1,360	296	958	106	
	Forsyth	121	0	16	28	77	2,043	451	1,502	90	9
	Fulton	9	0	0	0	9	17	0	16	1	
	Fulton County Police Department	909	20	49	387	453	7,307	2,579	3,572	1,156	17
	Glynn County Police Department	265	10	10	53	192	2,525	501	1,880	144	
	Gwinnett County Police Department	1,945	36	73	1,111	725	18,730	5,501	10,848	2,381	123
	Hall	225	2	19	44	160	2,702	683	1,623	396	11
	Harris	2	0	0	0	2	313	67	213	33	0
	Heard	17	0	0	0	17	183	54	104	25	
	Henry	0	0	0	0	0	0	0	0	0	0
	Henry County Police Department	323	2	11	134	176	3,022	881	1,777	364	1
	Houston	138	0	9	10	119	981	241	666	74	
	Jasper	10	0	2	1	7	186	64	110	12	
	Jones	23	1	0	4	18	487	143	289	55	0
	Lamar[4]		0	4	2		279	80	179	20	1
	Lanier	46	0	1	0	45	78	22	48	8	
	Lee	22	0	2	3	17	489	130	336	23	
	Liberty	51	1	6	12	32	557	144	391	22	
	Long	18	0	4	0	14	162	63	89	10	3
	Lowndes	114	0	15	21	78	1,080	280	757	43	
	Madison	76	2	5	4	65	530	74	413	43	
	Marion	8	0	2	1	5	34	1	27	6	0
	McDuffie	17	0	2	5	10	307	71	195	41	0
	Meriwether	31	0	1	6	24	426	114	252	60	
	Monroe	24	0	6	3	15	344	94	212	38	2
	Murray	56	0	8	3	45	792	182	528	82	
	Newton	336	7	5	31	293	1,581	606	765	210	
	Oglethorpe	51	1	0	3	47	355	110	215	30	
	Paulding	191	2	16	25	148	2,341	611	1,469	261	31
	Pickens	72	0	6	1	65	357	66	248	43	
	Pike	3	0	0	0	3	260	72	168	20	0
	Rockdale	293	1	8	53	231	2,064	536	1,290	238	14
	Spalding	154	4	14	24	112	1,681	437	1,112	132	0
	Twiggs	31	0	1	2	28	169	33	128	8	
	Walker	247		3	8	236	1,184	332	790	62	11
	Walton[4]		0	5	3		785	271	445	69	
	Whitfield	260	0	11	10	239	1,835	456	1,251	128	
	Worth	5	1	0	0	4	147	56	74	17	
GEORGIA-Nonmetropolitan Counties	Baldwin	147	1	8	8	130	951	262	650	39	
	Banks	100	1	2	3	94	770	103	610	57	
	Berrien	19	1	2	1	15	232	80	140	12	0
	Bleckley	13	0	2	0	11	99	18	64	17	0
	Bulloch	45	0	1	14	30	778	244	473	61	
	Calhoun	8	0	2	0	6	35	12	17	6	
	Camden	26	0	0	4	22	409	127	248	34	
	Candler	0	0	0	0	0	89	32	56	1	0
	Charlton	6	1	0	0	5	118	26	78	14	
	Clay	6	0	0	0	6	2	0	2	0	0
	Clinch	11	0	1	3	7	77	21	51	5	1
	Coffee	76	2	10	6	58	812	260	527	25	4
	Cook	20	1	0	3	16	100	22	75	3	0
	Crisp	9	0	0	0	9	417	81	304	32	
	Decatur	34	0	6	9	19	346	102	222	22	
	Dodge	9	0	1	1	7	50	15	34	1	
	Dooly	14	0	0	2	12	65	11	49	5	0
	Early	57	1	2	11	43	203	60	135	8	
	Emanuel	17	0	2	7	8	366	179	151	36	
	Fannin	9	0	1	1	7	151	73	76	2	
	Franklin	22	2	1	3	16	259	106	127	26	
	Gordon	43	0	4	2	37	557	137	392	28	
	Grady	23	2	1	6	14	166	82	70	14	
	Greene	18	0	2	3	13	185	51	125	9	

[1] The FBI does not publish arson data unless it receives data from either the agency or the state for all 12 months of the calendar year.
[4] The FBI determined that the agency's data were overreported. Consequently, affected data are not included in this table.

Table 10. Offenses Known to Law Enforcement, by State Metropolitan and Nonmetropolitan Counties, 2007 *(Contd.)*

(Number.)

State	County	Violent crime	Murder and non-negligent man-slaughter	Forcible rape	Robbery	Aggravated assault	Property crime	Burglary	Larceny-theft	Motor vehicle theft	Arson[1]
	Habersham	37	1	4	1	31	381	100	260	21	0
	Hancock	13	0	0	1	12	141	42	70	29	
	Hancock County Police Department	0	0	0	0	0	0	0	0	0	0
	Hart	55	1	1	5	48	316	95	196	25	
	Irwin	3	0	1	0	2	115	27	65	23	2
	Jackson	52	0	4	2	46	872	217	607	48	
	Jeff Davis	24	0	1	1	22	374	68	276	30	1
	Johnson	29	0	0	1	28	67	32	29	6	0
	Laurens	49	0	2	6	41	668	195	409	64	1
	Lincoln	9	0	0	2	7	97	33	52	12	
	Lumpkin	36	0	4	0	32	411	103	260	48	
	Macon	2	0	0	1	1	69	24	39	6	
	Mitchell	55	0	2	3	50	163	32	125	6	
	Peach	26	0	1	7	18	309	85	180	44	0
	Polk	0	0	0	0	0	0	0	0	0	0
	Polk County Police Department	102	3	3	10	86	890	317	457	116	
	Putnam	57	0	1	6	50	315	108	192	15	
	Rabun	17	0	7	0	10	234	61	159	14	1
	Seminole	14	0	1	0	13	62	28	29	5	0
	Stephens	45	0	3	2	40	413	85	286	42	
	Stewart	3	0	0	1	2	22	4	11	7	0
	Tattnall	9	0	0	3	6	197	73	109	15	0
	Taylor	0	0	0	0	0	56	33	12	11	0
	Thomas	57	2	0	2	53	239	43	195	1	2
	Tift	99	7	4	15	73	945	223	633	89	
	Towns	16	1	0	1	14	191	92	89	10	
	Treutlen	22	0	0	3	19	129	41	83	5	0
	Troup	66	0	2	10	54	1,174	153	954	67	
	Upson	72	0	3	2	67	408	142	234	32	0
	Ware	59	2	4	9	44	784	173	540	71	0
	Washington	39	0	0	4	35	315	99	205	11	
	Wheeler	6	0	1	1	4	67	32	26	9	
	White	16	0	2	0	14	243	77	130	36	3
	Wilcox	7	0	4	1	2	39	18	19	2	
	Wilkes	4	0	0	0	4	15	6	7	2	0
	Wilkinson	7	0	0	0	7	51	21	29	1	
IDAHO-Metropolitan Counties	Ada	166	4	21	5	136	1,252	289	894	69	33
	Bannock	18	0	0	0	18	169	26	137	6	0
	Boise	14	0	3	1	10	129	35	85	9	4
	Bonneville	98	1	10	1	86	953	230	644	79	10
	Canyon	77	1	8	3	65	805	234	472	99	6
	Franklin	14	0	2	0	12	34	9	24	1	0
	Gem	13	0	3	0	10	22	5	16	1	0
	Jefferson	15	0	9	0	6	202	64	129	9	0
	Kootenai	124	0	23	5	96	911	277	563	71	11
	Nez Perce	1	0	0	0	1	85	29	52	4	0
	Owyhee	17	0	7	2	8	140	17	112	11	3
	Power	0	0	0	0	0	38	7	28	3	0
IDAHO-Nonmetropolitan Counties	Adams	5	1	0	0	4	45	7	35	3	0
	Bear Lake	3	0	2	0	1	36	12	23	1	1
	Benewah	4	0	1	0	3	20	8	7	5	0
	Bingham	22	0	7	0	15	303	74	208	21	0
	Blaine	26	3	4	0	19	59	28	29	2	2
	Bonner	44	1	4	1	38	420	93	288	39	3
	Boundary	6	0	1	1	4	60	21	35	4	0
	Butte	4	0	0	0	4	13	2	7	4	0
	Camas	0	0	0	0	0	11	2	9	0	1
	Caribou	2	0	1	0	1	28	9	18	1	0
	Cassia	40	0	5	4	31	525	83	402	40	6
	Clark	1	0	0	0	1	14	2	12	0	0
	Clearwater	24	0	4	0	20	99	14	84	1	1
	Custer	3	0	1	0	2	4	3	1	0	0
	Elmore	11	2	1	0	8	136	30	93	13	2
	Fremont	7	0	0	0	7	56	13	39	4	0
	Gooding	18	1	2	0	15	54	15	27	12	0
	Idaho	26	0	1	1	24	88	26	58	4	0
	Jerome	7	0	1	1	5	92	20	61	11	0

[1] The FBI does not publish arson data unless it receives data from either the agency or the state for all 12 months of the calendar year.

Table 10.   Offenses Known to Law Enforcement, by State Metropolitan and Nonmetropolitan Counties, 2007 *(Contd.)*

(Number.)

State	County	Violent crime	Murder and non-negligent man-slaughter	Forcible rape	Robbery	Aggravated assault	Property crime	Burglary	Larceny-theft	Motor vehicle theft	Arson[1]
	Latah	24	1	5	0	18	165	79	80	6	1
	Lemhi	2	0	0	0	2	9	1	7	1	0
	Lewis	6	0	2	1	3	33	10	19	4	1
	Lincoln	3	0	1	0	2	4	1	2	1	0
	Madison	16	0	7	0	9	86	16	69	1	1
	Minidoka	20	0	3	2	15	184	58	117	9	2
	Oneida	4	0	1	1	2	39	6	31	2	1
	Payette	8	0	0	0	8	70	23	37	10	1
	Shoshone	23	3	4	2	14	114	28	77	9	0
	Teton	1	0	0	0	1	22	8	12	2	0
	Twin Falls	43	0	7	2	34	240	88	137	15	6
	Valley	16	0	8	0	8	133	17	100	16	2
	Washington	9	0	1	0	8	23	12	10	1	0
INDIANA-Metropolitan Counties											
	Allen	43	1	9	18	15	1,140	237	802	101	3
	Bartholomew	21	0	3	5	13	272	17	238	17	1
	Boone	23	1	0	3	19	260	83	159	18	2
	Brown	3	0	0	2	1	79	26	53	0	0
	Carroll	34	1	4	1	28	195	81	97	17	2
	Delaware	28	0	8	4	16	589	124	420	45	2
	Elkhart	59	1	12	31	15	1,865	634	1,001	230	20
	Floyd	4	0	0	0	4	844	184	623	37	0
	Gibson	2	0	0	0	2	166	22	140	4	4
	Greene	19	0	1	3	15	168	50	103	15	0
	Hancock	15	0	4	4	7	276	106	152	18	1
	Harrison	15	0	1	7	7	636	171	426	39	0
	Howard	46	0	1	5	40	544	178	351	15	3
	Johnson	6	0	1	5	0	821	136	667	18	0
	Lake	18	1	1	8	8	1,124	167	834	123	0
	La Porte	19	3	4	1	11	754	240	471	43	2
	Madison	11	0	4	3	4	431	135	270	26	3
	Monroe	63	3	5	8	47	721	251	413	57	4
	Newton	6	0	0	0	6	179	71	93	15	0
	Porter	47	1	3	6	37	1,041	208	740	93	0
	Putnam	37	0	4	6	27	431	122	253	56	0
	Shelby	6	0	1	2	3	445	123	287	35	5
	St. Joseph	119	1	18	27	73	1,774	383	1,304	87	7
	Tippecanoe	28	0	7	3	18	819	238	527	54	10
	Tipton	11	0	1	1	9	73	29	40	4	1
	Vanderburgh	83	1	6	7	69	1,153	133	977	43	9
	Warrick	114	1	8	1	104	647	104	516	27	12
	Wells	2	0	1	0	1	102	31	57	14	0
INDIANA-Nonmetropolitan Counties											
	Blackford	1	1	0	0	0	51	8	36	7	0
	Daviess	11	0	0	0	11	90	23	57	10	0
	Fayette	6	0	1	0	5	275	85	181	9	1
	Grant	14	0	5	6	3	380	82	263	35	0
	Henry	9	1	4	2	2	706	249	410	47	0
	Huntington	7	0	4	0	3	113	26	79	8	1
	Jackson	11	1	0	0	10	293	60	221	12	3
	Kosciusko	27	1	6	4	16	759	167	563	29	4
	LaGrange	6	0	3	1	2	251	67	173	11	0
	Lawrence	6	1	2	0	3	347	98	213	36	2
	Martin	3	0	1	0	2	36	9	22	5	0
	Noble[6]	7	0	2	1	4	149	66	64	19	3
	Parke	9	0	2	7	0	233	58	158	17	2
	Pulaski	1	0	0	0	1	165	17	144	4	1
	Randolph	0	0	0	0	0	168	64	102	2	0
	Ripley	0	0	0	0	0	190	44	133	13	0
	Starke	13	0	1	2	10	414	125	238	51	3
	Steuben	13	0	5	1	7	601	142	423	36	3
	Wabash	1	0	0	1	0	130	15	113	2	0
	Wayne	0	0	0	0	0	142	48	85	9	0
	White	0	0	0	0	0	28	27	0	1	0
IOWA-Metropolitan Counties											
	Benton	7	0	1	1	5	102	28	70	4	0
	Black Hawk	43	0	10	0	33	238	104	122	12	0
	Bremer	17	0	1	0	16	42	8	32	2	1
	Dallas	0	0	0	0	0	102	36	63	3	1
	Dubuque	57	0	1	0	56	241	95	120	26	4
	Grundy	5	0	0	0	5	71	20	48	3	0

[1] The FBI does not publish arson data unless it receives data from either the agency or the state for all 12 months of the calendar year.

[6] Because of changes in the state/local agency's reporting practices, figures are not comparable to previous years' data.

Table 10. Offenses Known to Law Enforcement, by State Metropolitan and Nonmetropolitan Counties, 2007 *(Contd.)*

(Number.)

State	County	Violent crime	Murder and non-negligent man-slaughter	Forcible rape	Robbery	Aggravated assault	Property crime	Burglary	Larceny-theft	Motor vehicle theft	Arson[1]
	Guthrie	0	0	0	0	0	41	20	20	1	0
	Harrison	4	0	1	0	3	158	55	95	8	4
	Johnson	69	0	1	0	68	236	107	103	26	4
	Jones	3	0	0	0	3	55	10	39	6	0
	Linn	30	0	6	2	22	368	139	201	28	2
	Madison	7	0	2	2	3	49	13	30	6	0
	Mills	11	0	1	1	9	138	44	80	14	3
	Polk	117	2	17	12	86	929	191	623	115	5
	Pottawattamie	31	0	8	1	22	580	158	366	56	2
	Scott	19	1	6	1	11	234	73	149	12	1
	Story	17	0	5	1	11	156	61	80	15	3
	Warren	37	1	5	5	26	281	72	180	29	5
	Washington	17	0	3	0	14	140	92	44	4	0
	Woodbury	23	0	0	1	22	71	27	41	3	0
IOWA- **Nonmetropolitan** **Counties**	Adair	5	0	0	0	5	52	7	41	4	0
	Adams	4	0	0	0	4	59	29	28	2	0
	Allamakee	0	0	0	0	0	13	1	12	0	1
	Appanoose	6	0	0	0	6	80	22	50	8	2
	Audubon	4	0	1	0	3	24	10	11	3	0
	Boone	17	1	2	0	14	52	15	31	6	3
	Buchanan	2	0	0	0	2	129	25	95	9	3
	Buena Vista	6	0	2	0	4	69	24	41	4	1
	Butler	1	0	0	0	1	40	19	18	3	1
	Calhoun	4	0	1	0	3	96	26	67	3	0
	Cass	6	0	3	0	3	48	13	32	3	0
	Cerro Gordo	7	0	0	0	7	129	50	66	13	0
	Cherokee	5	0	0	0	5	30	7	21	2	1
	Chickasaw	1	0	1	0	0	38	13	22	3	1
	Clarke	2	0	0	0	2	67	25	33	9	2
	Clay	6	0	1	0	5	53	22	29	2	0
	Clayton	9	0	0	0	9	54	23	28	3	0
	Clinton	25	0	3	1	21	133	35	86	12	2
	Crawford	0	0	0	0	0	0	0	0	0	0
	Davis	5	0	1	0	4	8	5	3	0	1
	Des Moines	18	0	2	1	15	147	35	98	14	1
	Fayette	15	0	1	1	13	59	17	34	8	0
	Floyd	1	0	0	0	1	42	25	15	2	0
	Franklin	0	0	0	0	0	8	1	7	0	0
	Hamilton	8	1	0	0	7	85	47	38	0	1
	Hancock	4	0	1	0	3	48	31	16	1	1
	Hardin	2	0	1	0	1	102	45	50	7	1
	Henry	11	0	0	0	11	96	25	62	9	0
	Howard	1	0	1	0	0	70	12	54	4	1
	Humboldt	3	0	0	2	1	44	21	20	3	0
	Ida	8	0	0	1	7	57	25	29	3	0
	Iowa	7	0	1	0	6	67	16	48	3	2
	Jasper	9	0	1	0	8	111	38	63	10	1
	Jefferson	11	0	0	2	9	53	7	41	5	1
	Lee	13	0	1	0	12	73	35	33	5	2
	Louisa	6	0	2	0	4	77	39	30	8	0
	Lucas	5	0	0	0	5	79	21	50	8	2
	Lyon	15	0	2	0	13	78	45	27	6	0
	Mahaska	23	0	2	0	21	94	25	58	11	0
	Marion	16	0	4	0	12	110	45	53	12	2
	Marshall	11	0	0	0	11	68	43	19	6	3
	Mitchell	0	0	0	0	0	19	7	12	0	0
	Monona	0	0	0	0	0	2	0	0	2	0
	Monroe	3	0	0	0	3	34	6	25	3	0
	Muscatine	28	0	8	0	20	143	71	65	7	4
	O'Brien	9	0	0	0	9	99	33	62	4	0
	Osceola	1	0	0	0	1	15	3	11	1	0
	Palo Alto	8	0	0	0	8	79	36	37	6	0
	Plymouth	8	0	1	0	7	42	15	23	4	0
	Pocahontas	2	0	1	0	1	27	9	17	1	1
	Poweshiek	10	0	3	0	7	189	67	102	20	3
	Sac	1	0	0	0	1	40	16	21	3	0
	Sioux	5	0	0	0	5	84	27	53	4	0
	Tama	32	0	0	0	32	154	59	83	12	4
	Union	7	0	0	0	7	43	21	17	5	0
	Van Buren	8	0	0	0	8	112	58	49	5	2
	Wapello	6	0	0	0	6	134	66	62	6	1

[1] The FBI does not publish arson data unless it receives data from either the agency or the state for all 12 months of the calendar year.

Table 10. Offenses Known to Law Enforcement, by State Metropolitan and Nonmetropolitan Counties, 2007 *(Contd.)*

(Number.)

State	County	Violent crime	Murder and non-negligent manslaughter	Forcible rape	Robbery	Aggravated assault	Property crime	Burglary	Larceny-theft	Motor vehicle theft	Arson[1]
	Wayne	9	0	1	0	8	59	16	35	8	0
	Webster	30	0	1	0	29	266	65	168	33	4
	Winneshiek	1	0	0	0	1	19	5	12	2	0
	Worth	3	0	0	0	3	86	16	66	4	0
	Wright	1	0	0	0	1	44	27	17	0	1
KANSAS- Metropolitan Counties											
	Butler	61	1	11	1	48	479	144	302	33	4
	Doniphan	5	0	1	0	4	70	21	47	2	0
	Douglas	30	2	4	0	24	309	43	246	20	3
	Franklin	37	0	7	0	30	204	90	98	16	2
	Harvey	8	0	2	0	6	90	35	53	2	0
	Jackson	27	0	4	0	23	164	40	112	12	5
	Jefferson	19	0	2	0	17	364	121	219	24	6
	Johnson	136	0	17	2	117	240	52	188	0	10
	Leavenworth	57	0	4	2	51	260	101	140	19	20
	Linn	15	0	2	0	13	102	39	55	8	2
	Miami	24	0	3	1	20	220	96	107	17	14
	Osage	19	0	0	4	15	86	33	47	6	2
	Shawnee	102	0	11	7	84	1,535	292	1,167	76	14
	Sumner	15	0	0	1	14	97	33	56	8	0
	Wabaunsee	8	0	0	1	7	84	31	49	4	3
KANSAS- Nonmetropolitan Counties											
	Allen	13	0	1	0	12	63	24	30	9	3
	Anderson	9	0	2	1	6	68	21	41	6	2
	Barber	3	0	1	0	2	24	6	11	7	0
	Barton	22	1	2	1	18	90	35	49	6	
	Bourbon	11	0	0	0	11	74	27	37	10	3
	Brown	13	0	0	0	13	82	36	40	6	1
	Chautauqua	9	0	2	0	7	43	17	22	4	1
	Cherokee	20	1	2	1	16	166	56	95	15	9
	Cheyenne	1	0	0	0	1	18	9	9	0	0
	Clark	2	0	0	0	2	28	18	10	0	0
	Clay	15	0	6	0	9	86	46	34	6	7
	Coffey	10	1	1	0	8	55	27	23	5	1
	Cowley	48	0	3	1	44	222	105	98	19	1
	Crawford	31	0	2	1	28	305	119	166	20	14
	Dickinson	8	0	4	1	3	124	38	81	5	4
	Elk	4	0	1	0	3	55	22	31	2	0
	Ellis	13	0	2	0	11	93	33	56	4	6
	Ellsworth	8	0	0	0	8	47	10	30	7	1
	Finney	44	1	3	3	37	281	89	174	18	7
	Ford	17	0	2	0	15	56	25	25	6	0
	Geary	4	0	0	0	4	34	8	24	2	1
	Grant	3	0	1	0	2	13	5	8	0	0
	Gray	0	0	0	0	0	12	2	10	0	1
	Greenwood	16	0	4	1	11	193	57	129	7	5
	Harper	2	0	1	0	1	20	4	13	3	0
	Haskell	6	0	0	0	6	48	9	35	4	1
	Hodgeman	3	0	0	0	3	40	20	19	1	0
	Kearny	16	0	4	1	11	89	19	66	4	3
	Kingman	6	0	1	0	5	63	18	42	3	2
	Kiowa	8	0	0	1	7	25	6	13	6	0
	Labette	9	0	0	0	9	101	44	52	5	5
	Lane	3	0	0	0	3	15	3	10	2	0
	Lyon	13	0	2	1	10	116	28	77	11	3
	Marion	3	0	0	0	3	32	16	15	1	1
	McPherson	4	0	1	0	3	81	29	45	7	1
	Morris	8	0	0	0	8	54	17	34	3	6
	Morton	5	0	1	0	4	29	3	26	0	0
	Nemaha	11	0	2	0	9	53	21	24	8	0
	Neosho	18	0	0	0	18	78	28	43	7	0
	Norton	1	0	0	0	1	6	3	3	0	0
	Osborne	3	0	0	0	3	24	7	15	2	0
	Ottawa	5	0	3	0	2	62	18	40	4	1
	Pawnee	18	1	2	0	15	32	9	21	2	1
	Phillips	5	0	1	0	4	6	2	4	0	1
	Pottawatomie	43	0	7	3	33	264	60	185	19	3
	Pratt	4	0	0	0	4	49	16	31	2	0
	Rawlins	0	0	0	0	0	16	5	5	6	0
	Reno	18	0	1	0	17	191	76	103	12	0
	Republic	1	0	1	0	0	46	14	28	4	1

[1] The FBI does not publish arson data unless it receives data from either the agency or the state for all 12 months of the calendar year.

Table 10. Offenses Known to Law Enforcement, by State Metropolitan and Nonmetropolitan Counties, 2007 *(Contd.)*

(Number.)

State	County	Violent crime	Murder and non-negligent man-slaughter	Forcible rape	Robbery	Aggravated assault	Property crime	Burglary	Larceny-theft	Motor vehicle theft	Arson[1]
	Rice...........................	11	0	0	0	11	57	17	35	5	0
	Riley County Police Department ...	221	3	42	17	159	1,661	291	1,297	73	19
	Rooks	0	0	0	0	0	8	4	3	1	0
	Rush	3	0	0	0	3	43	28	14	1	0
	Russell...........................	4	1	0	0	3	23	7	16	0	0
	Saline...........................	31	0	4	1	26	146	47	90	9	9
	Seward...........................	6	0	2	0	4	69	17	41	11	1
	Sherman...........................	11	0	1	0	10	20	10	10	0	0
	Stanton...........................	3	0	0	0	3	23	7	16	0	0
	Thomas...........................	5	0	0	0	5	41	8	32	1	2
	Trego	1	0	0	0	1	15	5	10	0	0
	Washington...........................	4	0	0	0	4	9	2	6	1	0
	Wichita...........................	3	0	1	1	1	40	11	28	1	0
	Wilson	3	0	0	0	3	49	22	23	4	3
	Woodson...........................	1	0	0	0	1	41	15	23	3	2
KENTUCKY-Metropolitan Counties											
	Boone...........................	300	1	21	17	261	1,132	279	786	67	4
	Bourbon...........................	1	0	0	0	1	14	8	6	0	0
	Boyd...........................	30	0	6	14	10	308	93	174	41	0
	Bracken...........................	1	0	0	0	1	9	8	1	0	0
	Bullitt...........................	30	1	11	3	15	585	222	315	48	0
	Campbell County Police Department...........................	35	0	13	3	19	268	52	201	15	2
	Christian...........................	17	1	1	5	10	353	139	181	33	0
	Clark...........................	6	0	1	3	2	245	98	135	12	3
	Daviess...........................	27	3	6	1	17	497	112	370	15	6
	Edmonson...........................	1	0	0	1	0	44	18	23	3	0
	Gallatin...........................	3	0	0	0	3	29	7	16	6	0
	Grant...........................	4	0	1	0	3	70	33	29	8	0
	Greenup...........................	5	1	0	1	3	70	28	39	3	0
	Hancock...........................	0	0	0	0	0	12	6	4	2	0
	Hardin...........................	7	1	1	0	5	95	33	57	5	0
	Jefferson...........................	1	0	0	1	0	13	1	11	1	0
	Jessamine...........................	19	0	5	5	9	290	95	164	31	0
	Kenton...........................	1	0	0	0	1	6	1	5	0	0
	Larue...........................	3	0	0	1	2	53	21	27	5	1
	McLean...........................	0	0	0	0	0	22	9	10	3	0
	Meade...........................	14	1	2	1	10	159	67	85	7	0
	Nelson...........................	23	3	5	2	13	245	78	143	24	2
	Oldham...........................	1	0	0	0	1	13	2	10	1	0
	Oldham County Police Department...........................	12	1	4	4	3	422	122	279	21	0
	Pendleton...........................	4	0	0	0	4	96	23	62	11	0
	Scott...........................	25	2	2	7	14	229	69	143	17	0
	Shelby...........................	39	0	4	20	15	504	131	343	30	0
	Spencer...........................	3	1	0	1	1	40	22	16	2	0
	Trigg...........................	1	0	0	0	1	60	25	28	7	0
	Trimble...........................	1	0	0	1	0	6	1	5	0	0
	Warren	22	0	2	2	18	538	152	360	26	1
KENTUCKY-Nonmetropolitan Counties											
	Allen...........................	2	0	0	0	2	33	9	20	4	0
	Anderson...........................	3	0	1	1	1	97	28	65	4	0
	Ballard...........................	8	0	3	0	5	50	21	28	1	1
	Barren...........................	9	0	1	0	8	148	59	79	10	2
	Bell...........................	3	0	0	2	1	96	35	59	2	0
	Boyle...........................	9	0	1	1	7	59	23	32	4	0
	Breckinridge...........................	1	0	0	1	0	22	8	9	5	0
	Butler...........................	0	0	0	0	0	38	17	17	4	1
	Caldwell...........................	2	0	0	0	2	62	29	20	13	0
	Calloway...........................	14	0	2	2	10	396	133	232	31	0
	Carter...........................	2	0	0	0	2	178	78	88	12	0
	Clay...........................	1	0	0	0	1	131	35	75	21	0
	Crittenden...........................	1	0	0	1	0	43	11	32	0	0
	Cumberland...........................	0	0	0	0	0	9	5	2	2	0
	Estill...........................	0	0	0	0	0	22	7	8	7	0
	Fleming...........................	0	0	0	0	0	70	32	30	8	0
	Floyd...........................	4	0	0	1	3	152	32	102	18	0
	Franklin...........................	13	0	3	2	8	162	52	96	14	0
	Fulton...........................	4	0	0	0	4	60	16	42	2	0
	Garrard...........................	4	0	0	0	4	85	16	64	5	0
	Graves...........................	7	0	2	0	5	167	72	79	16	0

[1] The FBI does not publish arson data unless it receives data from either the agency or the state for all 12 months of the calendar year.

Table 10. Offenses Known to Law Enforcement, by State Metropolitan and Nonmetropolitan Counties, 2007 *(Contd.)*

(Number.)

State	County	Violent crime	Murder and non-negligent man-slaughter	Forcible rape	Robbery	Aggravated assault	Property crime	Burglary	Larceny-theft	Motor vehicle theft	Arson[1]
	Grayson	6	0	2	0	4	145	77	57	11	0
	Harlan	17	0	0	2	15	92	28	64	0	0
	Harrison	3	0	0	2	1	179	98	67	14	0
	Hart	0	0	0	0	0	31	23	7	1	0
	Hopkins	14	0	1	1	12	198	74	104	20	0
	Jackson	1	0	0	1	0	32	15	17	0	0
	Johnson	2	0	0	0	2	49	4	36	9	0
	Knott	2	0	0	0	2	67	7	55	5	0
	Knox	8	0	1	0	7	291	112	139	40	0
	Laurel	20	4	1	5	10	822	271	457	94	0
	Lawrence	1	0	0	1	0	26	8	17	1	0
	Lee	0	0	0	0	0	2	0	1	1	0
	Letcher	1	0	0	0	1	67	35	29	3	0
	Lewis	4	0	0	0	4	80	52	23	5	1
	Lincoln	3	0	0	0	3	73	34	34	5	0
	Livingston	6	0	0	1	5	106	35	64	7	0
	Logan	16	0	2	1	13	155	61	82	12	0
	Lyon	4	0	0	1	3	44	20	22	2	0
	Madison	9	0	4	0	5	284	106	160	18	0
	Marion	0	0	0	0	0	105	47	52	6	0
	Martin	1	0	0	0	1	87	42	29	16	0
	Mason	11	0	2	1	8	149	77	57	15	0
	McCreary	3	0	0	1	2	101	33	56	12	1
	Mercer	2	0	0	0	2	70	28	39	3	0
	Metcalfe	3	0	0	0	3	52	17	26	9	0
	Monroe	0	0	0	0	0	4	0	3	1	0
	Montgomery	14	1	0	5	8	460	133	294	33	0
	Muhlenberg	4	0	0	1	3	17	7	8	2	0
	Ohio	14	0	3	3	8	135	61	62	12	1
	Owen	1	0	0	0	1	74	36	26	12	0
	Owsley	0	0	0	0	0	25	8	15	2	0
	Pike	4	0	3	1	0	28	5	22	1	0
	Powell	0	0	0	0	0	15	7	6	2	0
	Pulaski	19	2	3	3	11	649	213	393	43	7
	Rockcastle	3	0	0	1	2	37	13	18	6	0
	Russell	1	0	0	0	1	35	10	18	7	0
	Simpson	7	0	0	2	5	123	46	63	14	0
	Taylor	12	0	1	2	9	197	89	101	7	2
	Todd	2	0	0	0	2	32	14	15	3	0
	Union	12	0	0	2	10	52	14	34	4	0
	Washington	2	0	0	0	2	47	27	16	4	0
	Wayne	8	0	3	1	4	79	44	29	6	0
	Whitley	2	0	0	1	1	113	37	58	18	1
	Wolfe	0	0	0	0	0	20	3	15	2	0
LOUISIANA-Metropolitan Counties	Ascension	407	6	28	37	336	2,890	605	2,018	267	7
	Bossier	254	1	4	3	246	538	57	439	42	2
	Caddo	202	3	22	14	163	993	210	668	115	5
	Calcasieu	280	2	88	87	103	3,640	899	2,480	261	10
	Cameron	71	1	3	0	67	187	29	145	13	1
	East Baton Rouge	925	20	29	189	687	8,927	1,995	6,425	507	50
	Iberville	141	6	5	5	125	460	90	350	20	2
	Jefferson	2,616	44	74	634	1,864	15,090	3,632	9,596	1,862	177
	Lafayette	428	4	14	41	369	1,553	459	898	196	22
	Lafourche	142	0	7	7	128	1,836	129	1,631	76	0
	Livingston	490	8	14	26	442	1,551	593	800	158	0
	Plaquemines	56	2	2	4	48	600	136	409	55	4
	Pointe Coupee	74	4	0	4	66	377	105	252	20	2
	Rapides	189	1	18	9	161	1,042	297	596	149	1
	St. Bernard	110	1	4	15	90	1,706	496	1,018	192	1
	St. Charles	170	2	11	43	114	1,338	460	774	104	20
	St. John the Baptist	194	7	9	93	85	1,731	434	1,109	188	1
	St. Martin	80	2	15	12	51	488	114	369	5	
	St. Tammany	411	10	31	29	341	2,861	790	1,762	309	24
	Terrebonne	387	7	32	41	307	3,054	543	2,274	237	13
	West Baton Rouge	93	2	5	18	68	491	53	398	40	0
	West Feliciana	72	2	2	4	64	140	23	106	11	2
LOUISIANA-Nonmetropolitan Counties	Acadia	16	0	1	1	14	406	81	278	47	0
	Assumption	121	0	5	4	112	400	77	290	33	0
	Avoyelles	16	0	1	0	15	211	172	15	24	0

[1] The FBI does not publish arson data unless it receives data from either the agency or the state for all 12 months of the calendar year.

Table 10. Offenses Known to Law Enforcement, by State Metropolitan and Nonmetropolitan Counties, 2007 *(Contd.)*

(Number.)

State	County	Violent crime	Murder and non-negligent man-slaughter	Forcible rape	Robbery	Aggravated assault	Property crime	Burglary	Larceny-theft	Motor vehicle theft	Arson[1]
	Beauregard	36	3	8	1	24	429	161	232	36	3
	East Carroll	20	0	1	6	13	32	10	22	0	0
	Evangeline	66	1	9	4	52	440	127	269	44	
	Franklin	15	0	0	0	15	203	65	125	13	3
	Jefferson Davis	54	2	6	5	41	417	64	316	37	2
	Lincoln	39	5	3	5	26	247	84	149	14	0
	Madison	61	2	3	4	52	180	79	89	12	1
	Morehouse	32	1	1	2	28	438	93	334	11	1
	Natchitoches	99	0	5	5	89	456	163	244	49	0
	St. James	203	3	6	15	179	697	199	451	47	2
	St. Landry	164	1	8	18	137	1,127	325	697	105	6
	St. Mary	193	2	7	52	132	1,027	226	756	45	0
	Tangipahoa	884	11	41	59	773	3,684	1,515	2,027	142	3
	Vermilion	401	1	7	0	393	218	33	184	1	
	Vernon	233	1	6	5	221	638	136	472	30	8
	Washington	185	3	24	12	146	774	151	534	89	0
	West Carroll	29	0	0	0	29	279	83	179	17	1
MAINE-Metropolitan Counties											
	Androscoggin	7	0	3	0	4	226	59	156	11	2
	Cumberland	36	0	6	8	22	562	273	251	38	1
	Penobscot	5	0	1	0	4	750	200	517	33	0
	Sagadahoc	5	0	0	0	5	179	59	109	11	1
	York	31	0	9	1	21	469	203	224	42	4
MAINE-Nonmetropolitan Counties											
	Aroostook	8	0	0	1	7	81	23	56	2	0
	Franklin	2	0	1	0	1	92	28	62	2	3
	Hancock	4	0	1	1	2	196	49	136	11	0
	Kennebec	16	0	10	1	5	286	84	190	12	1
	Knox	7	0	1	0	6	175	56	110	9	1
	Lincoln	16	0	8	3	5	232	68	157	7	0
	Oxford	21	0	15	0	6	298	122	155	21	1
	Piscataquis	1	0	0	0	1	118	44	73	1	1
	Somerset	15	0	5	0	10	326	104	198	24	0
	Waldo	11	0	7	0	4	115	57	39	19	1
	Washington	7	0	0	0	7	150	62	77	11	0
MARYLAND-Metropolitan Counties											
	Allegany	7	0	2	0	5	115	16	93	6	0
	Anne Arundel	0	0	0	0	0	0	0	0	0	0
	Anne Arundel County Police Department	2,605	12	85	722	1,786	16,489	3,000	12,053	1,436	108
	Baltimore County	0	0	0	0	0	0	0	0	0	0
	Baltimore County Police Department	5,331	36	151	1,786	3,358	26,499	4,868	18,299	3,332	349
	Calvert	191	2	0	16	173	1,279	240	947	92	1
	Carroll	70	0	29	5	36	315	77	231	7	0
	Cecil	127	1	7	20	99	1,118	414	617	87	2
	Charles	787	4	33	184	566	4,003	706	2,875	422	2
	Frederick	286	2	13	18	253	1,446	251	1,109	86	5
	Harford	455	7	35	106	307	2,875	712	1,861	302	18
	Howard	0	0	0	0	0	0	0	0	0	0
	Howard County Police Department	577	5	36	244	292	7,191	1,242	5,421	528	75
	Montgomery	0	0	0	0	0	0	0	0	0	0
	Montgomery County Police Department	2,059	19	129	1,096	815	23,567	3,550	17,534	2,483	275
	Prince George's	128	0	0	7	121	4	1	3	0	0
	Prince George's County Police Department	6,134	123	226	3,092	2,693	35,628	5,940	19,745	9,943	356
	Queen Anne's	84	0	6	11	67	661	149	482	30	3
	Somerset	1	0	1	0	0	33	8	24	1	0
	Washington	217	4	24	27	162	1,276	326	861	89	0
	Wicomico	122	2	10	22	88	867	288	533	46	3
MARYLAND-Nonmetropolitan Counties											
	Caroline	37	0	3	9	25	318	109	198	11	0
	Dorchester	24	2	1	2	19	322	76	221	25	0
	Garrett	28	0	1	1	26	268	81	177	10	0
	Kent	19	0	0	2	17	116	68	42	6	1
	St. Mary's	270	1	13	39	217	2,018	542	1,368	108	6
	Talbot	11	0	1	4	6	168	37	118	13	0
	Worcester	69	0	2	2	65	153	53	82	18	1

[1] The FBI does not publish arson data unless it receives data from either the agency or the state for all 12 months of the calendar year.

Table 10.   Offenses Known to Law Enforcement, by State Metropolitan and Nonmetropolitan Counties, 2007 *(Contd.)*

(Number.)

State	County	Violent crime	Murder and non-negligent man-slaughter	Forcible rape	Robbery	Aggravated assault	Property crime	Burglary	Larceny-theft	Motor vehicle theft	Arson[1]
MICHIGAN-Metropolitan Counties	Barry	42	2	12	4	24	370	95	261	14	2
	Bay	41	1	10	9	21	533	116	374	43	0
	Berrien	134	0	22	14	98	848	188	590	70	7
	Calhoun	82	0	4	5	73	414	131	248	35	2
	Cass	34	2	9	5	18	742	280	413	49	7
	Clinton	12	1	1	1	9	220	78	125	17	3
	Eaton	138	0	24	30	84	1,341	294	954	93	3
	Genesee	56	0	13	6	37	667	161	459	47	3
	Ingham	126	3	44	11	68	1,039	319	650	70	10
	Ionia	28	0	11	1	16	447	165	252	30	10
	Jackson	117	0	18	2	97	643	162	440	41	7
	Kent	345	0	47	52	246	4,182	1,038	2,954	190	28
	Lapeer	51	0	9	1	41	508	139	341	28	1
	Livingston	50	0	6	9	35	1,010	278	683	49	10
	Macomb	390	8	39	57	286	2,829	551	2,029	249	12
	Monroe	171	0	18	33	120	2,079	511	1,399	169	35
	Newaygo	69	1	20	1	47	491	154	308	29	6
	Oakland	417	1	66	53	297	4,055	826	3,038	191	40
	Ottawa	308	1	113	22	172	3,113	785	2,261	67	22
	Saginaw	127	2	12	12	101	780	247	484	49	4
	St. Clair	190	0	39	14	137	1,772	433	1,198	141	21
	Van Buren	82	1	25	3	53	663	188	420	55	4
	Washtenaw	328	5	65	91	167	2,230	732	1,197	301	18
	Wayne[6]	102	3	0	42	57	220	60	81	79	0
MICHIGAN-Nonmetropolitan Counties	Alcona	14	1	0	0	13	187	65	117	5	0
	Allegan	80	4	16	7	53	1,173	294	809	70	5
	Alpena	0	0	0	0	0	38	7	29	2	0
	Arenac	28	0	3	0	25	224	99	112	13	4
	Baraga	2	0	0	0	2	20	5	15	0	0
	Benzie	16	0	6	0	10	159	45	106	8	0
	Branch	26	0	5	0	21	225	61	148	16	3
	Charlevoix	20	0	8	0	12	182	34	140	8	1
	Cheboygan	7	0	4	0	3	111	35	67	9	1
	Chippewa	13	1	1	1	10	121	45	71	5	0
	Crawford	25	0	4	0	21	247	92	136	19	1
	Delta	2	0	0	1	1	65	32	32	1	1
	Dickinson	8	0	6	0	2	94	21	70	3	2
	Emmet	21	0	9	0	12	196	39	144	13	0
	Gladwin	23	0	4	1	18	140	49	83	8	0
	Grand Traverse	119	1	29	5	84	1,026	199	787	40	9
	Gratiot	16	0	11	2	3	194	103	83	8	2
	Hillsdale	43	0	23	0	20	207	74	121	12	2
	Houghton	11	0	0	0	11	101	22	75	4	0
	Huron	12	0	4	0	8	183	62	113	8	2
	Iosco	3	0	1	0	2	17	8	8	1	0
	Iron	6	0	2	1	3	42	14	26	2	1
	Isabella	39	0	14	0	25	456	173	263	20	5
	Kalkaska	56	0	4	0	52	254	59	176	19	0
	Keweenaw	2	0	0	0	2	42	19	22	1	1
	Lake	40	0	7	3	30	312	154	150	8	1
	Leelanau	18	0	3	2	13	147	45	97	5	3
	Lenawee	51	1	11	2	37	404	196	205	3	7
	Luce	4	0	1	1	2	26	7	17	2	0
	Mackinac	6	0	0	0	6	69	33	33	3	0
	Manistee	10	0	2	0	8	92	28	63	1	1
	Marquette	5	0	0	0	5	146	31	109	6	0
	Mason	42	1	11	1	29	525	115	403	7	1
	Mecosta	35	0	10	1	24	471	111	333	27	0
	Menominee	5	0	1	0	4	101	39	56	6	1
	Midland	73	0	30	1	42	507	122	362	23	4
	Missaukee	14	0	3	0	11	132	28	96	8	0
	Montcalm	91	2	35	0	54	623	214	358	51	9
	Montmorency	10	0	0	0	10	83	40	38	5	2
	Oceana	14	0	6	1	7	243	67	165	11	3
	Ogemaw	20	0	4	0	16	243	108	122	13	4
	Ontonagon	4	0	0	0	4	35	11	21	3	1
	Osceola	23	0	2	1	20	177	64	109	4	0
	Oscoda	6	0	1	1	4	200	43	151	6	0
	Otsego	2	0	0	0	2	74	16	55	3	0

[1] The FBI does not publish arson data unless it receives data from either the agency or the state for all 12 months of the calendar year.

Table 10. Offenses Known to Law Enforcement, by State Metropolitan and Nonmetropolitan Counties, 2007 *(Contd.)*

(Number.)

State	County	Violent crime	Murder and non-negligent man-slaughter	Forcible rape	Robbery	Aggravated assault	Property crime	Burglary	Larceny-theft	Motor vehicle theft	Arson[1]
	Presque Isle	0	0	0	0	0	33	18	15	0	1
	Roscommon	25	0	7	1	17	232	47	176	9	2
	Sanilac	24	0	5	0	19	141	49	87	5	0
	Shiawassee	57	0	20	3	34	419	107	290	22	3
	St. Joseph	51	1	10	2	38	301	84	202	15	6
	Tuscola	33	0	11	0	22	327	122	182	23	6
	Wexford	25	0	10	1	14	355	57	280	18	3
MINNESOTA- Metropolitan Counties[7]											
	Benton		0		0	12	245	54	172	19	2
	Carver		0		3	23	1,002	118	841	43	13
	Chisago		0		1	16	563	103	422	38	1
	Clay		0		0	9	104	42	55	7	0
	Dakota		0		2	12	220	66	134	20	2
	Dodge		0		0	9	252	38	208	6	0
	Hennepin		0		0	21	159	33	111	15	0
	Houston		0		0	3	88	25	53	10	0
	Isanti		0		1	14	535	194	290	51	2
	Olmsted		0		5	25	467	156	270	41	18
	Polk		0		0	18	219	74	131	14	2
	Ramsey		1		8	39	1,234	167	909	158	9
	Scott		0		2	12	184	46	118	20	1
	Sherburne		2		1	46	761	160	563	38	0
	Stearns		0		1	34	478	96	359	23	2
	St. Louis		1		2	38	792	304	421	67	7
	Washington		0		5	39	1,085	230	800	55	2
	Wright		1		8	67	2,177	219	1,809	149	7
MINNESOTA- Nonmetropolitan Counties[7]											
	Aitkin	1			0	13	411	132	250	29	1
	Becker	1			2	11	317	143	149	25	2
	Beltrami	0			6	61	522	156	327	39	1
	Big Stone	0			1	2	46	9	34	3	1
	Blue Earth	1			0	5	224	62	130	32	0
	Cass[5]	2			4	27		166		56	0
	Clearwater	0			1	17	171	41	119	11	1
	Cook	0			0	4	134	22	99	13	2
	Cottonwood	1			0	1	48	21	23	4	0
	Crow Wing	1			2	21	426	106	295	25	0
	Douglas	0			1	12	289	65	210	14	3
	Faribault	1			0	2	65	30	29	6	0
	Fillmore	0			1	5	118	41	67	10	0
	Freeborn	0			0	7	108	27	70	11	0
	Goodhue	0			0	10	338	123	190	25	2
	Grant	0			0	1	73	24	47	2	1
	Hubbard	0			1	14	385	147	216	22	1
	Itasca	0			2	31	443	123	278	42	4
	Jackson	0			1	2	30	8	22	0	0
	Kanabec	0			1	22	236	83	128	25	4
	Kandiyohi	1			0	12	280	57	208	15	1
	Kittson	0			0	1	59	4	52	3	0
	Koochiching	0			0	9	166	33	113	20	2
	Lac Qui Parle	0			0	4	45	3	39	3	0
	Lake	0			0	0	80	30	49	1	0
	Lake of the Woods	0			0	5	105	18	82	5	0
	Le Sueur	0			1	8	126	15	104	7	2
	Lyon	0			0	4	65	26	33	6	1
	Martin	0			0	0	34	10	18	6	0
	McLeod	0			1	14	133	48	73	12	2
	Meeker	0			2	8	214	61	142	11	0
	Mille Lacs	0			0	28	406	73	287	46	2
	Morrison	1			0	13	331	60	241	30	2
	Mower	0			1	17	194	56	118	20	2
	Murray	0			0	2	35	15	19	1	0
	Nicollet	0			0	2	61	12	44	5	1
	Nobles	0			0	3	99	58	38	3	0
	Norman	0			0	1	63	14	46	3	2
	Otter Tail	0			1	19	533	185	315	33	1
	Pennington	0			0	0	41	13	24	4	0
	Pipestone	0			0	1	60	8	48	4	0
	Pope	0			0	3	77	14	55	8	1
	Red Lake	0			0	1	12	1	10	1	0
	Redwood	0			0	7	102	19	65	18	2

[1] The FBI does not publish arson data unless it receives data from either the agency or the state for all 12 months of the calendar year.

[5] The FBI determined that the agency's data were underreported. Consequently, affected data are not included in this table.

Table 10.   Offenses Known to Law Enforcement, by State Metropolitan and Nonmetropolitan Counties, 2007 *(Contd.)*

(Number.)

State	County	Violent crime	Murder and non-negligent man-slaughter	Forcible rape	Robbery	Aggravated assault	Property crime	Burglary	Larceny-theft	Motor vehicle theft	Arson[1]
	Renville		0		0	12	163	49	100	14	0
	Rice		0		0	10	288	127	140	21	2
	Rock		0		0	34	103	33	61	9	1
	Roseau		0		0	0	131	39	89	3	0
	Steele		0		0	6	157	60	78	19	0
	Stevens		0		1	1	25	11	13	1	0
	Swift		0		0	3	61	19	38	4	0
	Todd		0		0	6	251	109	127	15	2
	Traverse		0		0	0	15	0	13	2	1
	Wadena		0		0	5	86	34	44	8	0
	Waseca		2		0	3	72	24	45	3	2
	Watonwan		0		0	7	87	34	49	4	1
	Wilkin		0		0	0	46	12	27	7	2
	Winona		0		0	11	106	44	55	7	0
	Yellow Medicine		0		1	5	79	22	50	7	0
MISSISSIPPI-Metropolitan Counties	DeSoto	29	0	4	6	19	604	108	406	90	5
	Jackson	125	6	15	16	88	2,050	533	1,231	286	0
	Lamar	61	0	21	14	26	757	262	446	49	1
	Rankin	64	1	8	5	50	702	280	387	35	5
	Tate	10	1	1	0	8	266	94	128	44	0
	Tunica	99	3	3	29	64	744	112	575	57	
MISSISSIPPI-Nonmetropolitan Counties	Adams	41	2	10	6	23	529	169	310	50	12
	Chickasaw	21	2	0	3	16	38	20	16	2	0
	Claiborne	33	0	6	10	17	188	122	64	2	0
	Coahoma	7	0	0	3	4	146	60	65	21	0
	Grenada	11	1	1	4	5	131	37	63	31	1
	Jefferson	44	0	1	4	39	45	22	22	1	5
	Lauderdale	34	1	13	7	13	569	293	229	47	5
	Leake	0	0	0	0	0	28	15	11	2	1
	Lee	77	0	10	10	57	700	275	351	74	11
	Leflore	132	1	9	6	116	580	244	306	30	0
	Lincoln	14	2	1	1	10	337	71	238	28	2
	Lowndes	89	0	32	18	39	495	126	338	31	2
	Oktibbeha[6]	50	0	2	6	42	158	80	61	17	11
	Panola	55	0	8	12	35	456	202	223	31	4
	Pearl River	24	1	15	5	3	712	319	342	51	5
	Pike	33	2	0	8	23	499	192	269	38	
	Tippah	24	3	1	2	18	44	17	23	4	19
	Union	11	0	1	2	8	211	112	87	12	5
	Warren	15	0	2	2	11	339	118	181	40	0
	Washington	17	3	3	4	7	340	119	194	27	3
	Winston	33	1	1	1	30	25	10	14	1	0
MISSOURI-Metropolitan Counties	Andrew	14	0	0	2	12	198	63	124	11	0
	Bates	20	0	2	0	18	155	45	83	27	1
	Boone	126	0	6	14	106	804	201	562	41	8
	Buchanan	37	0	1	4	32	174	43	113	18	1
	Caldwell	5	0	0	0	5	81	31	37	13	1
	Callaway	31	0	6	1	24	775	186	532	57	5
	Cass	72	0	5	0	67	431	139	243	49	0
	Christian	176	0	2	0	174	273	78	158	37	2
	Clay	20	1	1	2	16	198	80	102	16	4
	Clinton	8	1	1	0	6	112	36	68	8	0
	Cole	29	1	3	1	24	472	131	304	37	3
	Dallas	26	0	2	2	22	217	96	107	14	7
	De Kalb	43	0	1	0	42	82	30	44	8	2
	Franklin	64	1	5	0	58	906	214	623	69	3
	Greene	282	1	9	14	258	1,445	333	1,010	102	0
	Howard	16	1	0	0	15	44	21	21	2	0
	Jackson	70	1	5	17	47	612	192	335	85	0
	Jasper	106	1	12	7	86	772	225	496	51	2
	Jefferson	396	2	36	17	341	3,418	377	2,827	214	36
	Lafayette	12	0	4	0	8	219	88	108	23	0
	Lincoln	71	0	2	1	68	250	86	137	27	3
	McDonald	70	1	7	3	59	368	99	228	41	9
	Moniteau[6]	20	0	1	0	19	47	15	27	5	0
	Newton	78	3	8	4	63	815	180	562	73	9
	Osage	6	0	0	0	6	142	43	83	16	0

[1] The FBI does not publish arson data unless it receives data from either the agency or the state for all 12 months of the calendar year.
[6] Because of changes in the state/local agency's reporting practices, figures are not comparable to previous years' data.

Table 10. Offenses Known to Law Enforcement, by State Metropolitan and Nonmetropolitan Counties, 2007 *(Contd.)*

(Number.)

State	County	Violent crime	Murder and non-negligent man-slaughter	Forcible rape	Robbery	Aggravated assault	Property crime	Burglary	Larceny-theft	Motor vehicle theft	Arson[1]
	Platte	37	0	3	1	33	325	69	247	9	4
	Polk	28	1	0	0	27	271	124	135	12	0
	St. Charles	234	3	10	11	210	1,490	372	1,030	88	36
	St. Louis County Police Department	1,290	15	62	334	879	10,688	2,454	7,186	1,048	89
	Warren	55	0	2	0	53	289	72	188	29	3
	Washington	50	0	1	2	47	242	81	137	24	4
	Webster	43	0	0	0	43	133	25	92	16	2
MISSOURI- Nonmetropolitan Counties	Adair	6	0	0	0	6	18	5	12	1	0
	Atchison	1	0	0	0	1	11	7	3	1	1
	Audrain	16	0	2	3	11	186	48	131	7	1
	Barry	41	2	8	0	31	440	149	266	25	6
	Barton	14	0	3	0	11	80	19	61	0	0
	Benton	35	0	5	0	30	213	84	119	10	2
	Bollinger	7	2	1	0	4	98	27	70	1	0
	Butler	74	0	0	0	74	610	128	438	44	0
	Camden	64	2	1	3	58	460	123	302	35	3
	Cape Girardeau	83	0	3	2	78	283	70	198	15	3
	Carroll	5	0	1	0	4	38	15	20	3	0
	Carter	8	0	0	0	8	41	16	19	6	0
	Cedar	3	0	0	0	3	116	29	82	5	0
	Clark	5	0	0	0	5	51	21	23	7	2
	Cooper	9	0	0	0	9	145	27	100	18	0
	Crawford	100	0	8	0	92	181	79	92	10	0
	Dade	10	0	1	0	9	36	10	22	4	0
	Daviess	7	0	3	1	3	61	32	25	4	0
	Dent	8	1	1	0	6	128	49	72	7	2
	Douglas	26	0	4	0	22	90	35	40	15	2
	Dunklin	19	0	2	1	16	210	53	146	11	2
	Gasconade	36	0	1	0	35	99	47	42	10	3
	Gentry	5	0	0	0	5	43	22	16	5	0
	Grundy	8	0	0	0	8	71	40	28	3	2
	Harrison	3	0	0	0	3	55	26	25	4	2
	Henry	39	1	2	0	36	261	81	164	16	6
	Hickory	2	0	1	0	1	117	44	58	15	2
	Holt	3	0	0	0	3	84	31	43	10	0
	Howell	72	0	3	2	67	410	153	228	29	4
	Iron	11	0	0	0	11	59	33	21	5	0
	Johnson	23	0	2	0	21	314	101	189	24	0
	Knox	7	0	1	0	6	109	25	83	1	1
	Laclede	18	0	1	0	17	389	117	237	35	0
	Lawrence	13	0	1	1	11	291	99	177	15	1
	Lewis	4	0	0	0	4	67	15	46	6	0
	Linn	10	0	1	0	9	56	25	21	10	18
	Livingston	2	0	1	0	1	57	22	26	9	1
	Macon	19	0	0	1	18	57	17	36	4	2
	Madison	5	0	0	0	5	78	23	51	4	1
	Maries	6	0	0	1	5	70	31	33	6	0
	Marion	5	0	0	1	4	91	20	69	2	0
	Mercer	5	0	1	0	4	16	12	2	2	2
	Miller[6]	86	0	5	0	81	221	74	132	15	1
	Mississippi	27	0	0	1	26	82	21	50	11	0
	Monroe	0	0	0	0	0	54	16	31	7	0
	Montgomery	10	0	0	0	10	90	42	47	1	0
	Morgan	163	0	2	1	160	228	90	116	22	0
	New Madrid	45	0	3	4	38	113	27	68	18	1
	Nodaway	2	0	0	0	2	138	63	61	14	0
	Oregon	18	0	1	0	17	36	6	28	2	0
	Ozark	26	1	2	0	23	132	57	63	12	1
	Pemiscot	10	0	2	1	7	131	31	95	5	1
	Perry	10	2	0	0	8	69	12	42	15	0
	Pettis	35	2	0	2	31	249	67	180	2	2
	Phelps	85	0	2	1	82	381	117	223	41	1
	Pike	15	0	1	1	13	97	46	45	6	0
	Pulaski	134	3	19	4	108	234	98	109	27	0
	Putnam	0	0	0	0	0	8	3	3	2	0
	Ralls	34	0	2	0	32	115	33	67	15	1
	Randolph	21	0	2	0	19	127	47	76	4	1
	Reynolds	4	0	1	0	3	31	16	9	6	1
	Ripley	15	0	4	0	11	211	65	124	22	1
	Saline	13	0	5	0	8	111	32	70	9	0
	Schuyler	4	0	1	0	3	10	9	1	0	2

[1] The FBI does not publish arson data unless it receives data from either the agency or the state for all 12 months of the calendar year.

[6] Because of changes in the state/local agency's reporting practices, figures are not comparable to previous years' data.

Table 10. Offenses Known to Law Enforcement, by State Metropolitan and Nonmetropolitan Counties, 2007 *(Contd.)*

(Number.)

State	County	Violent crime	Murder and non-negligent man-slaughter	Forcible rape	Robbery	Aggravated assault	Property crime	Burglary	Larceny-theft	Motor vehicle theft	Arson[1]
	Scotland	0	0	0	0	0	27	5	21	1	0
	Scott	21	0	2	1	18	158	33	110	15	3
	Shannon	5	0	1	0	4	64	10	44	10	1
	Shelby	0	0	0	0	0	63	17	40	6	0
	Ste. Genevieve	21	1	2	0	18	160	52	94	14	0
	St. Francois	60	0	4	1	55	487	130	312	45	4
	Stoddard	28	0	2	0	26	194	72	110	12	0
	Stone	125	1	6	1	117	568	187	334	47	1
	Sullivan	4	0	1	0	3	65	28	30	7	0
	Taney	73	0	4	1	68	463	141	272	50	1
	Texas	38	2	1	2	33	216	86	111	19	10
	Vernon	40	0	2	0	38	260	73	160	27	3
	Wayne	11	0	2	0	9	102	45	46	11	0
	Worth	10	0	2	0	8	29	13	12	4	0
	Wright	40	0	5	1	34	98	49	39	10	0
MONTANA-Metropolitan Counties											
	Carbon	10	0	0	0	10	27	17	9	1	0
	Cascade	62	1	2	0	59	279	43	208	28	2
	Missoula	87	0	13	2	72	612	124	430	58	6
	Yellowstone	57	1	12	4	40	649	87	516	46	4
MONTANA-Nonmetropolitan Counties											
	Beaverhead	4	0	0	0	4	42	8	28	6	0
	Big Horn	65	0	3	0	62	235	10	200	25	2
	Blaine	4	0	0	0	4	25	2	17	6	0
	Broadwater	15	0	0	0	15	162	7	144	11	2
	Carter	0	0	0	0	0	3	0	3	0	0
	Chouteau	5	1	0	0	4	15	1	12	2	1
	Dawson	6	0	3	0	3	76	10	65	1	1
	Deer Lodge	27	0	4	0	23	99	9	79	11	0
	Fallon	1	0	0	0	1	9	0	6	3	0
	Fergus	13	0	2	0	11	15	5	9	1	1
	Flathead	241	2	19	6	214	1,168	225	879	64	6
	Gallatin	70	0	19	1	50	445	59	337	49	14
	Garfield	0	0	0	0	0	1	0	1	0	0
	Glacier	9	0	0	0	9	50	8	35	7	0
	Granite	3	0	0	0	3	47	3	42	2	0
	Hill	28	0	1	0	27	153	10	130	13	2
	Jefferson	21	0	0	0	21	58	14	36	8	1
	Judith Basin	6	0	0	0	6	9	0	8	1	0
	Lake	70	2	10	1	57	348	82	208	58	6
	Lewis and Clark	57	0	10	1	46	350	87	227	36	11
	Lincoln	33	1	5	0	27	240	70	158	12	2
	Madison	8	0	0	0	8	64	17	39	8	0
	McCone	1	0	0	0	1	15	1	14	0	0
	Meagher	6	0	0	0	6	27	2	23	2	0
	Mineral	16	0	1	0	15	29	8	17	4	0
	Musselshell	7	0	2	0	5	83	6	74	3	0
	Park	19	0	2	0	17	94	29	53	12	1
	Phillips	6	0	0	0	6	63	10	49	4	0
	Pondera	1	0	1	0	0	8	2	4	2	1
	Powell	27	0	2	0	25	131	24	99	8	0
	Ravalli	48	0	8	3	37	406	58	327	21	9
	Roosevelt	10	1	0	0	9	32	11	18	3	1
	Rosebud	19	0	1	0	18	66	7	57	2	1
	Sanders	31	0	5	0	26	141	21	114	6	1
	Sheridan	5	1	0	0	4	17	2	12	3	0
	Silver Bow	142	1	7	12	122	1,389	222	1,044	123	4
	Stillwater	18	0	3	0	15	38	22	13	3	1
	Sweet Grass	10	0	0	0	10	39	1	33	5	1
	Teton	15	0	1	0	14	87	6	78	3	1
	Toole	17	0	0	0	17	56	10	41	5	1
	Valley	4	0	0	2	2	56	10	42	4	0
	Wibaux	0	0	0	0	0	3	0	3	0	0
NEBRASKA-Metropolitan Counties											
	Cass	10	0	1	0	9	263	38	207	18	1
	Dakota	1	0	0	0	1	45	13	29	3	0
	Dixon	3	0	3	0	0	65	22	39	4	0
	Douglas	171	1	7	16	147	1,347	361	893	93	0
	Lancaster	23	1	1	1	20	383	88	281	14	6
	Seward	3	1	1	0	1	42	10	24	8	0
	Washington	5	0	0	0	5	92	19	66	7	2

[1] The FBI does not publish arson data unless it receives data from either the agency or the state for all 12 months of the calendar year.

Table 10.   Offenses Known to Law Enforcement, by State Metropolitan and Nonmetropolitan Counties, 2007 *(Contd.)*

(Number.)

State	County	Violent crime	Murder and non-negligent man-slaughter	Forcible rape	Robbery	Aggravated assault	Property crime	Burglary	Larceny-theft	Motor vehicle theft	Arson[1]
NEBRASKA-Nonmetropolitan Counties	Adams	4	0	0	1	3	117	36	74	7	3
	Antelope	1	0	0	0	1	37	14	18	5	0
	Box Butte	0	0	0	0	0	9	1	6	2	0
	Boyd	0	0	0	0	0	13	3	9	1	0
	Brown	2	0	0	0	2	43	9	32	2	0
	Buffalo	13	0	1	1	11	198	46	142	10	0
	Burt	3	0	1	0	2	36	12	21	3	0
	Butler	5	0	0	0	5	45	3	42	0	0
	Cedar	4	0	1	0	3	8	4	4	0	0
	Chase	4	0	0	0	4	19	7	9	3	0
	Cheyenne	2	0	0	0	2	89	21	56	12	0
	Colfax	21	0	0	0	21	58	15	40	3	0
	Cuming	0	0	0	0	0	11	8	2	1	0
	Custer	4	0	2	0	2	42	11	30	1	0
	Dawson	3	0	0	0	3	88	10	73	5	0
	Deuel	0	0	0	0	0	33	3	29	1	0
	Dodge	11	0	0	0	11	157	16	125	16	0
	Franklin	2	0	1	0	1	17	6	9	2	0
	Frontier	2	0	2	0	0	23	6	17	0	0
	Furnas	2	0	0	0	2	22	6	14	2	0
	Gage	4	0	2	0	2	190	46	132	12	3
	Gosper	1	0	0	0	1	37	8	27	2	2
	Hall	12	1	1	0	10	219	54	150	15	0
	Hamilton	2	0	1	0	1	49	11	35	3	1
	Harlan	1	0	0	0	1	2	0	2	0	0
	Hitchcock	3	0	0	0	3	5	2	3	0	0
	Holt	0	0	0	0	0	21	4	17	0	0
	Hooker	0	0	0	0	0	1	1	0	0	0
	Jefferson	4	1	0	0	3	65	23	31	11	2
	Kearney	2	0	2	0	0	49	10	37	2	0
	Keith	3	0	2	0	1	36	6	28	2	0
	Keya Paha	0	0	0	0	0	5	1	4	0	0
	Kimball	1	0	0	0	1	18	0	14	4	0
	Knox	1	0	0	0	1	23	4	19	0	0
	Lincoln	6	0	0	2	4	168	27	135	6	0
	Madison	7	2	1	0	4	53	13	38	2	0
	Merrick	0	0	0	0	0	52	8	41	3	0
	Morrill	1	0	0	0	1	34	5	26	3	0
	Nance	1	0	0	0	1	13	4	8	1	0
	Nemaha	4	0	0	0	4	32	2	30	0	1
	Pawnee	1	0	0	0	1	30	9	14	7	0
	Perkins	2	0	1	1	0	23	4	18	1	0
	Phelps	1	0	1	0	0	31	7	20	4	2
	Platte	6	0	0	0	6	243	45	186	12	0
	Polk	0	0	0	0	0	67	5	62	0	0
	Red Willow	2	0	1	0	1	36	13	21	2	0
	Richardson	3	0	0	0	3	57	24	30	3	0
	Rock	0	0	0	0	0	17	4	13	0	0
	Saline	3	0	1	0	2	69	15	41	13	2
	Scotts Bluff	8	2	1	0	5	106	28	67	11	0
	Sheridan	0	0	0	0	0	56	18	37	1	1
	Sioux	0	0	0	0	0	1	0	1	0	0
	Stanton	4	0	0	0	4	35	7	27	1	0
	Thayer	2	0	0	0	2	61	19	41	1	0
	Wayne	1	0	0	0	1	14	3	10	1	0
	Webster	3	0	1	0	2	20	6	14	0	0
	Wheeler	1	0	0	0	1	1	0	1	0	0
	York	3	0	0	0	3	55	8	41	6	0
NEVADA-Metropolitan Counties	Carson City	206	1	5	21	179	1,103	286	723	94	23
	Washoe	208	2	0	13	193	1,755	563	954	238	3
NEVADA-Nonmetropolitan Counties	Churchill	40	1	8	2	29	266	109	143	14	10
	Douglas	69	0	5	7	57	920	202	663	55	9
	Elko	25	3	8	3	11	195	95	80	20	2
	Esmeralda	1	0	0	0	1	3	1	2	0	3
	Eureka	9	0	0	1	8	26	9	14	3	1
	Humboldt	63	1	0	1	61	58	26	26	6	2
	Lincoln	2	0	0	0	2	36	4	22	10	1

[1] The FBI does not publish arson data unless it receives data from either the agency or the state for all 12 months of the calendar year.

Table 10. Offenses Known to Law Enforcement, by State Metropolitan and Nonmetropolitan Counties, 2007 *(Contd.)*

(Number.)

State	County	Violent crime	Murder and non-negligent man-slaughter	Forcible rape	Robbery	Aggravated assault	Property crime	Burglary	Larceny-theft	Motor vehicle theft	Arson[1]
	Lyon	84	2	3	10	69	777	244	465	68	11
	Mineral	15	0	7	0	8	32	14	14	4	0
	Nye	117	2	18	19	78	989	340	501	148	19
	Pershing	38	0	9	0	29	42	21	21	0	0
	White Pine[5]	13	0	2	1	10		76		7	1
NEW HAMPSHIRE-Metropolitan Counties	Rockingham	36	0	0	0	36	5	1	3	1	0
NEW HAMPSHIRE-Nonmetropolitan Counties	Carroll	3	0	1	0	2	37	10	24	3	0
	Cheshire	0	0	0	0	0	3	0	3	0	0
	Merrimack	10	0	5	0	5	0	0	0	0	0
NEW MEXICO-Metropolitan Counties	Bernalillo	900	7	46	150	697	2,401	710	1,301	390	80
	Sandoval[4]		1	1	0		162	97	63	2	0
	San Juan	250	8	29	8	205	953	289	550	114	6
	Santa Fe	211	0	29	12	170	1,072	735	335	2	12
	Valencia	199	8	14	12	165	1,166	511	408	247	41
NEW MEXICO-Nonmetropolitan Counties	Catron	5	2	0	0	3	39	27	8	4	0
	Chaves	53	2	7	4	40	467	250	175	42	6
	Cibola[6]	9	0	1	1	7	94	56	28	10	0
	Colfax	3	0	0	0	3	7	3	4	0	0
	Curry	11	0	1	0	10	158	80	63	15	0
	Eddy	48	2	10	2	34	371	133	225	13	0
	Grant	13	0	2	0	11	153	98	55	0	0
	Lea	43	0	10	3	30	477	163	274	40	3
	Lincoln	64	1	1	1	61	149	52	90	7	0
	Luna	77	4	0	3	70	359	151	161	47	0
	McKinley	86	0	2	9	75	279	125	125	29	19
	Mora	1	0	0	0	1	5	2	2	1	0
	Otero[4]		1	15	1		269	125	127	17	0
	Quay	4	1	0	1	2	31	9	21	1	1
	Rio Arriba	65	2	4	0	59	113	65	36	12	5
	Roosevelt	5	0	0	0	5	55	14	38	3	0
	Sierra	11	0	3	0	8	48	23	22	3	1
	Socorro	21	0	1	1	19	95	42	47	6	0
NEW YORK-Metropolitan Counties	Albany	23	0	2	0	21	95	22	72	1	0
	Broome	57	0	12	5	40	772	143	601	28	2
	Chemung	17	0	2	1	14	409	52	342	15	0
	Dutchess	66	1	5	11	49	897	186	678	33	3
	Erie	118	0	12	19	87	908	198	671	39	10
	Herkimer	0	0	0	0	0	16	0	16	0	0
	Livingston	24	0	4	1	19	764	99	646	19	1
	Madison	8	0	1	1	6	291	101	186	4	1
	Monroe	213	1	20	44	148	3,853	605	3,087	161	13
	Nassau	1,639	14	71	748	806	13,886	1,807	10,928	1,151	
	Niagara	79	0	15	14	50	1,336	370	914	52	7
	Oneida	66	4	2	2	58	531	173	333	25	7
	Onondaga	174	3	25	34	112	1,785	362	1,333	90	14
	Ontario	38	1	8	5	24	891	201	665	25	6
	Orange	7	0	1	2	4	17	7	9	1	1
	Oswego	45	0	8	9	28	411	134	246	31	0
	Putnam	20	0	5	3	12	300	64	222	14	2
	Rensselaer	40	0	3	4	33	208	56	148	4	2
	Rockland	24	0	1	0	23	40	0	39	1	0
	Saratoga	26	0	9	4	13	977	175	770	32	13
	Schenectady	9	0	0	1	8	35	1	31	3	
	Schoharie	2	0	0	0	2	78	28	48	2	0
	Suffolk	155	0	0	1	154	9	1	2	6	0
	Suffolk County Police Department	2,205	28	89	874	1,214	24,039	3,360	18,583	2,096	301
	Tioga	7	0	1	1	5	161	57	89	15	1
	Tompkins	16	0	7	2	7	404	66	321	17	1
	Ulster	42	0	2	2	38	317	71	235	11	1
	Warren	57	0	12	4	41	850	133	695	22	1

[1] The FBI does not publish arson data unless it receives data from either the agency or the state for all 12 months of the calendar year.
[4] The FBI determined that the agency's data were overreported. Consequently, affected data are not included in this table.
[5] The FBI determined that the agency's data were underreported. Consequently, affected data are not included in this table.
[6] Because of changes in the state/local agency's reporting practices, figures are not comparable to previous years' data.

Table 10. Offenses Known to Law Enforcement, by State Metropolitan and Nonmetropolitan Counties, 2007 *(Contd.)*

(Number.)

State	County	Violent crime	Murder and non-negligent man-slaughter	Forcible rape	Robbery	Aggravated assault	Property crime	Burglary	Larceny-theft	Motor vehicle theft	Arson[1]
	Washington	41	3	7	2	29	348	70	257	21	1
	Wayne	48	0	14	7	27	504	100	389	15	3
	Westchester Public Safety	69	0	1	2	66	289	24	248	17	
NEW YORK-Nonmetropolitan Counties											
	Allegany	0	0	0	0	0	1	0	1	0	0
	Cattaraugus	40	1	5	4	30	421	142	246	33	5
	Cayuga	33	0	6	3	24	300	70	225	5	1
	Chautauqua	49	0	19	5	25	896	238	630	28	8
	Chenango	13	2	1	1	9	353	91	251	11	4
	Clinton	2	0	0	0	2	14	2	11	1	0
	Columbia	26	0	1	2	23	359	92	250	17	1
	Cortland	13	0	4	0	9	328	61	257	10	1
	Delaware	4	0	3	0	1	183	66	109	8	0
	Franklin	0	0	0	0	0	0	0	0	0	0
	Fulton	17	0	9	0	8	388	115	258	15	0
	Genesee	36	0	4	6	26	605	147	437	21	7
	Greene	7	0	0	1	6	36	8	25	3	0
	Hamilton	0	0	0	0	0	11	1	10	0	0
	Lewis	16	0	1	0	15	150	61	86	3	1
	Montgomery	23	1	2	2	18	337	50	268	19	0
	Otsego	14	0	5	0	9	206	90	108	8	1
	Schuyler	8	0	0	0	8	67	23	41	3	0
	Seneca	7	0	2	0	5	136	13	123	0	1
	Steuben	8	0	4	0	4	83	20	63	0	0
	St. Lawrence	15	0	1	0	14	95	18	75	2	0
	Sullivan	41	0	6	0	35	533	168	340	25	3
	Wyoming	14	0	3	1	10	245	70	170	5	0
	Yates	2	0	0	0	2	179	54	120	5	1
NORTH CAROLINA-Metropolitan Counties											
	Alexander	80	3	12	7	58	763	289	423	51	8
	Brunswick	151	5	17	34	95	2,175	787	1,184	204	12
	Buncombe	185	6	19	32	128	2,540	952	1,373	215	12
	Caldwell	72	2	11	7	52	1,384	532	741	111	23
	Cumberland	581	7	24	107	443	4,906	1,606	2,993	307	33
	Currituck	44	1	1	1	41	533	179	334	20	2
	Davie[4]	64	2	1	5	56			350	46	7
	Durham	65	2	0	18	45	1,079	285	712	82	1
	Edgecombe	74	3	5	17	49	681	302	321	58	3
	Forsyth	286	2	25	50	209	2,720	819	1,764	137	25
	Franklin	30	2	3	16	9	653	316	291	46	1
	Gaston	16	0	0	0	16	6	0	6	0	0
	Gaston County Police Department	289	4	22	38	225	1,956	674	1,049	233	32
	Greene	39	0	9	10	20	670	276	342	52	6
	Guilford	202	8	9	52	133	1,973	762	1,074	137	32
	Haywood	103	2	5	5	91	884	300	534	50	3
	Henderson	68	0	18	14	36	1,306	476	709	121	3
	Madison	9	0	4	1	4	223	106	101	16	3
	Nash	48	4	3	18	23	673	256	329	88	14
	New Hanover	222	1	29	42	150	2,723	591	1,929	203	21
	Onslow	294	4	35	50	205	2,785	994	1,592	199	31
	Orange	31	4	3	19	5	895	428	410	57	4
	Pender[5]	75	1	30	2	42		429	588		4
	Person	69	1	10	6	52	624	268	326	30	2
	Pitt	235	3	14	27	191	1,823	698	986	139	18
	Randolph	129	6	4	24	95	2,489	712	1,595	182	6
	Rockingham	105	3	4	24	74	1,422	451	863	108	1
	Stokes	125	0	8	5	112	1,042	376	566	100	6
	Wake	217	6	29	43	139	2,944	1,070	1,559	315	17
	Wayne	163	6	4	24	129	2,097	793	1,135	169	4
	Yadkin	97	2	4	4	87	644	268	314	62	7
NORTH CAROLINA-Nonmetropolitan Counties											
	Ashe	33	0	6	1	26	364	168	182	14	5
	Beaufort	120	1	6	11	102	782	321	399	62	4
	Bertie	19	0	1	11	7	331	163	135	33	2
	Bladen	147	1	1	20	125	1,012	348	607	57	9
	Camden	8	0	3	0	5	92	23	69	0	1
	Caswell	54	3	8	7	36	454	202	224	28	3

[1] The FBI does not publish arson data unless it receives data from either the agency or the state for all 12 months of the calendar year.

[4] The FBI determined that the agency's data were overreported. Consequently, affected data are not included in this table.

[5] The FBI determined that the agency's data were underreported. Consequently, affected data are not included in this table.

Table 10. Offenses Known to Law Enforcement, by State Metropolitan and Nonmetropolitan Counties, 2007 *(Contd.)*

(Number.)

State	County	Violent crime	Murder and non-negligent man-slaughter	Forcible rape	Robbery	Aggravated assault	Property crime	Burglary	Larceny-theft	Motor vehicle theft	Arson[1]
	Chowan	10	2	2	2	4	124	58	64	2	0
	Clay	14	0	1	0	13	197	65	111	21	3
	Craven	138	1	10	12	115	1,367	413	857	97	3
	Dare	36	0	3	3	30	567	171	382	14	1
	Davidson	205	3	2	21	179	2,212	252	1,719	241	20
	Duplin	148	2	5	21	120	1,232	483	638	111	8
	Gates	9	0	2	2	5	128	41	85	2	3
	Granville	101	1	5	18	77	909	290	565	54	6
	Halifax	124	4	6	20	94	1,062	552	441	69	11
	Hertford	48	2	1	18	27	339	117	197	25	1
	Iredell	193	1	15	22	155	1,998	720	1,110	168	19
	Jones	16	1	0	5	10	222	49	166	7	1
	Lee	41	3	7	7	24	607	271	281	55	12
	Lenoir	149	1	11	18	119	997	344	595	58	11
	Lincoln	126	3	12	21	90	1,820	730	1,016	74	8
	Macon	16	0	4	1	11	494	182	281	31	3
	McDowell	31	2	6	4	19	636	279	310	47	8
	Montgomery	34	1	5	4	24	459	163	262	34	1
	Moore	63	2	7	8	46	882	371	447	64	4
	Northampton	47	2	4	5	36	504	271	183	50	1
	Pasquotank	57	0	6	3	48	425	155	239	31	8
	Perquimans	2	1	0	1	0	132	62	64	6	6
	Richmond	143	2	4	37	100	1,264	491	677	96	24
	Robeson	507	2	24	90	391	4,278	2,203	1,631	444	33
	Rutherford	131	0	11	18	102	1,212	440	690	82	16
	Scotland	42	1	11	5	25	630	346	230	54	15
	Stanly	56	0	15	3	38	544	212	299	33	7
	Surry	114	1	21	12	80	1,381	483	666	232	32
	Swain	23	0	1	3	19	234	84	135	15	1
	Transylvania	40	3	3	4	30	335	133	158	44	2
	Tyrrell	12	0	0	3	9	93	11	80	2	1
	Vance	117	1	10	20	86	1,374	617	649	108	5
	Warren	30	0	5	9	16	550	161	359	30	3
	Watauga	16	0	1	1	14	529	222	278	29	3
	Wilkes	171	1	5	18	147	1,221	461	675	85	7
	Wilson	88	2	7	10	69	842	216	559	67	9
	Yancey	20	0	3	0	17	104	54	45	5	1
NORTH DAKOTA-Metropolitan Counties											
	Burleigh	20	0	6	1	13	123	40	75	8	1
	Cass	11	0	3	0	8	176	50	107	19	3
	Grand Forks	6	0	1	0	5	117	32	66	19	0
	Morton	10	0	6	0	4	69	20	43	6	1
NORTH DAKOTA-Nonmetropolitan Counties											
	Barnes	0	0	0	0	0	31	15	13	3	0
	Bottineau	1	0	0	0	1	40	12	22	6	1
	Cavalier	3	0	0	0	3	90	12	72	6	0
	Dickey	1	0	0	0	1	38	5	30	3	0
	Dunn	0	0	0	0	0	0	0	0	0	0
	Eddy	1	0	0	1	0	19	14	5	0	0
	Emmons	0	0	0	0	0	19	2	16	1	0
	Griggs	0	0	0	0	0	5	2	3	0	0
	Hettinger	2	0	2	0	0	13	1	12	0	0
	Kidder	0	0	0	0	0	2	1	1	0	0
	Logan	1	0	0	0	1	2	0	2	0	0
	McHenry	2	0	0	0	2	29	11	17	1	0
	McIntosh	0	0	0	0	0	5	3	2	0	0
	McKenzie	0	0	0	0	0	34	6	25	3	0
	McLean	2	0	0	0	2	122	21	91	10	1
	Mercer	1	0	0	0	1	9	0	8	1	1
	Nelson	3	0	0	0	3	24	9	8	7	0
	Pembina	2	0	0	0	2	18	4	10	4	0
	Ramsey	3	0	1	0	2	22	3	16	3	0
	Renville	2	0	2	0	0	13	2	11	0	0
	Richland	13	0	0	0	13	77	20	51	6	1
	Rolette	5	0	3	0	2	14	5	6	3	3
	Sargent	1	0	1	0	0	23	2	21	0	0
	Stark	4	0	1	0	3	24	2	20	2	0
	Stutsman	3	0	1	0	2	52	13	32	7	2
	Towner	0	0	0	0	0	19	8	8	3	0

[1] The FBI does not publish arson data unless it receives data from either the agency or the state for all 12 months of the calendar year.

Table 10. Offenses Known to Law Enforcement, by State Metropolitan and Nonmetropolitan Counties, 2007 *(Contd.)*

(Number.)

State	County	Violent crime	Murder and non-negligent man-slaughter	Forcible rape	Robbery	Aggravated assault	Property crime	Burglary	Larceny-theft	Motor vehicle theft	Arson[1]
	Traill	7	0	1	0	6	22	7	9	6	1
	Walsh	4	0	0	1	3	71	19	42	10	2
	Ward	20	0	3	0	17	97	29	57	11	1
	Wells	3	2	0	0	1	25	11	11	3	2
	Williams	5	0	0	1	4	70	18	41	11	3
OHIO- **Metropolitan** **Counties**											
	Belmont	15	0	5	1	9	394	99	266	29	6
	Brown	12	1	5	5	1	394	147	229	18	0
	Carroll	2	0	2	0	0	175	40	115	20	1
	Clermont	82	1	43	3	35	1,734	441	1,176	117	14
	Erie	18	0	1	1	16	446	150	278	18	4
	Fairfield	41	2	11	13	15	1,366	359	935	72	3
	Greene	16	1	6	2	7	450	128	310	12	2
	Hamilton	302	4	39	148	111	6,224	1,003	4,911	310	47
	Jefferson	42	1	2	0	39	429	86	310	33	2
	Lawrence	25	0	3	1	21	343	97	214	32	3
	Licking	13	1	1	4	7	965	258	590	117	3
	Lorain	59	3	19	26	11	1,044	571	443	30	23
	Lucas	60	0	6	22	32	1,333	271	975	87	10
	Mahoning	13	0	1	4	8	239	48	179	12	1
	Medina	1	0	0	0	1	37	30	7	0	0
	Miami	11	0	7	1	3	489	152	307	30	9
	Morrow	15	0	7	5	3	445	171	232	42	3
	Ottawa	4	0	0	1	3	370	59	292	19	0
	Pickaway	47	1	5	6	35	1,099	361	699	39	14
	Portage	39	0	16	7	16	1,624	470	1,054	100	8
	Preble	23	2	4	3	14	403	170	215	18	4
	Richland	68	2	18	8	40	1,298	465	794	39	12
	Stark	119	1	23	47	48	2,735	761	1,830	144	32
	Trumbull	27	0	6	3	18	505	148	290	67	2
	Union	21	0	6	0	15	290	80	197	13	5
	Washington	64	0	17	1	46	470	176	273	21	3
	Wood	10	0	2	1	7	550	148	385	17	2
OHIO- **Nonmetropolitan** **Counties**											
	Adams	10	1	6	2	1	494	200	258	36	1
	Ashland	10	0	6	1	3	275	108	148	19	2
	Champaign	20	0	10	2	8	405	128	252	25	12
	Columbiana	22	0	4	2	16	435	106	289	40	3
	Coshocton	25	1	4	3	17	712	175	521	16	6
	Crawford	11	0	1	3	7	289	118	159	12	0
	Darke	30	1	10	0	19	374	148	212	14	6
	Defiance	9	0	5	0	4	165	40	122	3	1
	Fayette	27	0	7	5	15	599	135	450	14	4
	Guernsey	12	0	8	0	4	276	122	138	16	2
	Hancock	7	1	1	0	5	252	74	170	8	4
	Hardin	3	0	2	1	0	278	100	161	17	0
	Harrison	14	0	5	0	9	144	53	72	19	5
	Henry	9	0	4	0	5	261	80	177	4	1
	Highland	11	0	1	0	10	435	178	231	26	4
	Hocking	9	0	2	0	7	335	102	207	26	4
	Holmes	8	0	2	1	5	269	82	166	21	2
	Huron	6	0	1	3	2	479	156	303	20	2
	Marion	21	0	6	12	3	709	163	528	18	3
	Meigs	7	0	1	2	4	314	142	152	20	1
	Mercer	3	0	0	1	2	223	42	166	15	2
	Morgan	7	0	2	2	3	180	71	96	13	1
	Muskingum	45	0	22	8	15	1,166	330	733	103	6
	Paulding	13	1	4	0	8	216	63	153	0	2
	Pike	16	0	5	3	8	500	168	282	50	9
	Ross	40	0	13	6	21	1,788	471	1,207	110	3
	Seneca	6	0	0	4	2	165	53	110	2	0
	Tuscarawas	8	0	2	1	5	346	131	184	31	1
	Van Wert	7	0	6	1	0	216	78	131	7	0
	Wayne	24	0	9	0	15	613	239	330	44	7
	Williams	12	0	7	2	3	301	81	202	18	6
OKLAHOMA- **Metropolitan** **Counties**											
	Canadian	21	0	1	0	20	61	37	15	9	0
	Cleveland	44	1	6	3	34	287	101	163	23	4
	Comanche	17	1	5	3	8	210	63	127	20	1
	Creek	74	1	17	1	55	546	173	319	54	9

[1] The FBI does not publish arson data unless it receives data from either the agency or the state for all 12 months of the calendar year.

Table 10.   Offenses Known to Law Enforcement, by State Metropolitan and Nonmetropolitan Counties, 2007 *(Contd.)*

(Number.)

State	County	Violent crime	Murder and non-negligent man-slaughter	Forcible rape	Robbery	Aggravated assault	Property crime	Burglary	Larceny-theft	Motor vehicle theft	Arson[1]
	Grady	19	0	3	0	16	277	73	176	28	3
	Le Flore	44	1	1	2	40	290	115	147	28	3
	Lincoln	35	0	6	2	27	266	97	134	35	6
	Logan	40	0	2	0	38	177	60	79	38	2
	McClain	34	1	7	1	25	190	58	116	16	2
	Oklahoma	30	0	1	2	27	248	72	147	29	1
	Okmulgee	6	0	2	0	4	192	82	86	24	4
	Osage	31	3	6	2	20	297	121	160	16	10
	Pawnee	29	0	1	1	27	156	60	72	24	1
	Rogers	3	0	0	0	3	240	98	91	51	0
	Sequoyah[4]		0			1	405	166	173	66	13
	Tulsa	269	2	15	17	235	1,080	353	585	142	10
	Wagoner	35	1	3	1	30	345	129	165	51	2
OKLAHOMA-Nonmetropolitan Counties	Adair	58	1	3	0	54	140	65	42	33	8
	Alfalfa	4	0	0	0	4	24	7	13	4	1
	Atoka	18	0	4	1	13	122	29	78	15	0
	Beaver	6	1	3	0	2	41	6	32	3	0
	Beckham	9	0	1	1	7	76	20	47	9	4
	Blaine	6	0	1	0	5	42	8	27	7	1
	Bryan	65	1	6	0	58	366	162	159	45	2
	Caddo	23	1	1	1	20	253	64	148	41	1
	Carter	48	3	1	2	42	167	46	111	10	8
	Cherokee	195	4	7	1	183	341	169	120	52	3
	Choctaw	19	1	2	1	15	159	57	91	11	0
	Cimarron	0	0	0	0	0	3	0	2	1	0
	Coal	8	0	0	1	7	82	17	61	4	0
	Cotton	1	0	1	0	0	19	8	11	0	0
	Craig	18	0	2	0	16	124	46	57	21	4
	Custer	2	0	0	1	1	74	24	47	3	1
	Delaware	72	4	18	2	48	456	211	201	44	11
	Dewey	1	0	0	0	1	19	10	7	2	0
	Ellis	1	0	0	0	1	13	5	7	1	0
	Garfield	11	0	3	1	7	75	25	44	6	3
	Garvin	20	1	4	1	14	212	52	133	27	1
	Grant	25	0	0	0	25	63	11	51	1	1
	Greer	2	1	1	0	0	24	6	18	0	0
	Harmon	2	0	1	1	0	13	3	10	0	1
	Harper	2	0	0	0	2	28	13	13	2	0
	Haskell	42	0	0	0	42	72	23	28	21	1
	Hughes	3	0	0	0	3	126	25	74	27	3
	Jackson	10	0	0	0	10	96	41	46	9	5
	Jefferson	10	0	0	1	9	40	14	21	5	0
	Johnston	23	0	1	1	21	16	8	5	3	0
	Kay	12	2	3	0	7	127	45	75	7	3
	Kingfisher	5	0	0	1	4	62	27	32	3	0
	Kiowa	5	0	0	0	5	39	18	18	3	1
	Latimer	16	0	1	0	15	53	13	33	7	0
	Love	3	0	1	0	2	97	15	68	14	0
	Major	6	1	1	0	4	64	22	38	4	2
	Marshall	38	0	1	0	37	141	38	87	16	1
	Mayes	23	1	1	1	20	270	92	152	26	0
	McCurtain	34	1	5	2	26	493	166	289	38	11
	McIntosh	26	0	3	1	22	340	174	150	16	2
	Murray	6	0	2	0	4	51	20	21	10	1
	Muskogee	58	1	11	4	42	253	97	125	31	10
	Noble	10	1	3	0	6	82	40	37	5	2
	Nowata	22	0	3	0	19	86	32	45	9	0
	Okfuskee	3	0	0	0	3	67	15	43	9	4
	Ottawa	19	0	2	1	16	125	51	55	19	0
	Payne	19	0	0	0	19	220	80	118	22	0
	Pittsburg	26	3	6	2	15	517	175	331	11	18
	Pontotoc[4]		0	2	0		202	95	97	10	8
	Pottawatomie	63	1	8	4	50	477	170	267	40	7
	Pushmataha	13	0	1	0	12	105	49	42	14	3
	Roger Mills	1	0	0	0	1	50	8	40	2	3
	Seminole	39	1	2	0	36	223	67	143	13	3
	Stephens	38	0	2	1	35	157	35	110	12	3
	Texas	5	0	1	0	4	52	13	37	2	0
	Tillman	5	0	3	0	2	45	11	29	5	2
	Washington	27	0	2	0	25	163	64	93	6	8
	Washita	6	0	0	0	6	23	8	12	3	1
	Woods	3	0	0	0	3	16	5	10	1	0
	Woodward	6	0	0	0	6	111	49	46	16	0

[1] The FBI does not publish arson data unless it receives data from either the agency or the state for all 12 months of the calendar year.
[4] The FBI determined that the agency's data were overreported. Consequently, affected data are not included in this table.

Table 10. Offenses Known to Law Enforcement, by State Metropolitan and Nonmetropolitan Counties, 2007 *(Contd.)*

(Number.)

State	County	Violent crime	Murder and non-negligent man-slaughter	Forcible rape	Robbery	Aggravated assault	Property crime	Burglary	Larceny-theft	Motor vehicle theft	Arson[1]
OREGON-Metropolitan Counties	Benton	27	1	5	0	21	277	77	185	15	7
	Clackamas	220	5	42	95	78	5,885	989	4,292	604	16
	Deschutes	97	0	15	4	78	990	298	610	82	15
	Jackson	179	3	10	6	160	1,177	297	778	102	9
	Lane	277	0	15	22	240	1,483	605	693	185	21
	Marion	125	0	32	50	43	2,955	569	2,003	383	12
	Multnomah	33	1	1	11	20	895	132	675	88	2
	Polk	40	0	5	1	34	274	70	182	22	6
	Washington	245	3	50	59	133	3,433	644	2,418	371	36
	Yamhill	36	1	9	6	20	596	127	416	53	9
OREGON-Nonmetropolitan Counties	Baker	3	0	0	1	2	20	6	11	3	0
	Clatsop	16	0	4	2	10	183	41	131	11	0
	Crook	30	0	5	2	23	133	50	80	3	0
	Douglas	59	1	21	4	33	1,139	315	743	81	15
	Gilliam	0	0	0	0	0	27	8	17	2	0
	Grant	0	0	0	0	0	65	20	40	5	0
	Harney	0	0	0	0	0	21	8	11	2	0
	Hood River	13	0	1	4	8	301	46	230	25	3
	Jefferson	29	0	6	3	20	257	85	128	44	6
	Josephine	31	1	4	4	22	844	273	457	114	7
	Lincoln	51	0	8	4	39	499	143	333	23	4
	Linn	21	2	2	5	12	1,175	394	690	91	4
	Malheur	3	0	2	0	1	197	78	107	12	1
	Morrow	18	0	5	0	13	202	51	126	25	1
	Sherman	0	0	0	0	0	39	3	34	2	0
	Tillamook	11	0	3	2	6	308	114	169	25	5
	Umatilla	46	2	9	3	32	445	148	229	68	9
	Union	6	0	2	0	4	181	50	119	12	1
	Wallowa	8	0	2	0	6	52	11	38	3	0
	Wasco	1	0	0	0	1	253	68	139	46	0
	Wheeler	0	0	0	0	0	23	9	13	1	1
PENNSYLVANIA-Metropolitan Counties	Allegheny	19	0	0	0	19	2	0	2	0	0
	Allegheny County Police Department	51	0	11	0	40	253	11	213	29	44
	Beaver	5	0	0	0	5	5	0	5	0	0
	Cumberland	0	0	0	0	0	0	0	0	0	0
	Lycoming	0	0	0	0	0	0	0	0	0	0
	Montgomery	0	0	0	0	0	0	0	0	0	0
	Pike	0	0	0	0	0	0	0	0	0	0
	Washington	3	0	0	0	3	3	1	2	0	0
	York	2	0	0	0	2	0	0	0	0	0
PENNSYLVANIA-Nonmetropolitan Counties	Bradford	1	0	0	0	1	0	0	0	0	0
	Elk	0	0	0	0	0	0	0	0	0	0
	Greene	0	0	0	0	0	0	0	0	0	0
	Snyder	0	0	0	0	0	0	0	0	0	0
	Tioga	0	0	0	0	0	0	0	0	0	0
SOUTH CAROLINA-Metropolitan Counties	Aiken	441	6	51	88	296	3,150	1,008	1,723	419	6
	Anderson	820	4	47	76	693	7,068	2,088	4,263	717	33
	Berkeley	587	7	34	94	452	3,318	956	1,929	433	15
	Calhoun	85	0	1	12	72	297	72	178	47	3
	Charleston	937	7	33	107	790	2,696	797	1,488	411	11
	Darlington	440	15	17	41	367	2,084	697	1,150	237	17
	Dorchester	445	6	29	80	330	2,321	634	1,449	238	10
	Edgefield	32	0	1	3	28	364	84	238	42	1
	Fairfield	210	2	11	12	185	739	256	413	70	5
	Florence	596	5	19	86	486	3,158	827	1,999	332	8
	Greenville	2,252	20	121	524	1,587	11,531	3,467	6,812	1,252	44
	Horry	1	0	0	0	1	38	0	38	0	0
	Horry County Police Department	1,465	9	77	166	1,213	7,875	1,853	5,151	871	24
	Kershaw	157	2	16	14	125	1,236	335	757	144	12
	Laurens	243	3	27	28	185	1,351	472	747	132	5
	Lexington	607	10	60	124	413	4,161	1,036	2,667	458	5

[1] The FBI does not publish arson data unless it receives data from either the agency or the state for all 12 months of the calendar year.

Table 10.   Offenses Known to Law Enforcement, by State Metropolitan and Nonmetropolitan Counties, 2007 *(Contd.)*

(Number.)

State	County	Violent crime	Murder and non-negligent man-slaughter	Forcible rape	Robbery	Aggravated assault	Property crime	Burglary	Larceny-theft	Motor vehicle theft	Arson[1]
	Pickens	247	0	27	12	208	1,906	555	1,139	212	10
	Richland	2,282	23	90	420	1,749	8,715	2,147	5,587	981	34
	Saluda	52	0	8	4	40	223	67	129	27	1
	Sumter	1,005	5	33	45	922	2,624	960	1,358	306	43
	York	602	2	35	57	508	3,323	820	2,193	310	13
SOUTH CAROLINA- **Nonmetropolitan** **Counties**	Abbeville	61	0	1	1	59	320	91	209	20	3
	Allendale	15	0	0	2	13	70	19	44	7	0
	Bamberg	49	0	2	4	43	303	140	124	39	3
	Barnwell	97	2	2	3	90	381	117	236	28	1
	Beaufort	671	7	22	127	515	3,928	1,018	2,643	267	10
	Cherokee	147	0	1	25	121	1,542	467	969	106	4
	Chester	222	1	6	22	193	731	186	482	63	5
	Chesterfield	141	2	2	9	128	893	277	549	67	7
	Clarendon	227	3	18	33	173	933	238	566	129	4
	Colleton	302	2	8	35	257	1,274	332	786	156	14
	Dillon	307	3	16	39	249	1,081	309	634	138	8
	Georgetown	237	3	16	27	191	1,553	360	1,062	131	10
	Greenwood	348	1	10	12	325	1,658	336	1,223	99	6
	Hampton	97	2	2	8	85	342	101	208	33	2
	Jasper	147	3	8	16	120	717	203	422	92	4
	Lancaster	206	3	20	46	137	1,934	590	1,229	115	10
	Lee	90	2	4	4	80	488	132	306	50	8
	Marion	163	2	12	15	134	769	205	496	68	9
	Marlboro	124	0	6	10	108	603	173	371	59	6
	McCormick	24	0	1	1	22	105	30	61	14	3
	Newberry	80	4	8	6	62	445	83	332	30	2
	Oconee	271	0	26	16	229	1,212	374	741	97	7
	Orangeburg	453	9	36	82	326	3,669	1,407	1,753	509	2
	Union	116	1	2	5	108	461	164	266	31	4
	Williamsburg	125	5	7	15	98	687	230	354	103	9
SOUTH DAKOTA- **Metropolitan** **Counties**	Lincoln	7	0	1	0	6	75	28	42	5	0
	McCook	5	0	1	0	4	28	4	24	0	0
	Meade	30	0	6	0	24	130	16	103	11	0
	Minnehaha	20	0	5	2	13	268	96	159	13	1
	Pennington	59	0	24	4	31	432	95	320	17	2
	Turner	6	0	1	0	5	26	8	14	4	3
	Union	11	0	2	1	8	35	9	25	1	1
SOUTH DAKOTA- **Nonmetropolitan** **Counties**	Beadle	2	0	0	0	2	36	3	32	1	0
	Bennett	6	0	0	0	6	2	0	2	0	0
	Bon Homme	1	0	0	0	1	0	0	0	0	0
	Brookings	0	0	0	0	0	36	2	32	2	0
	Brown	5	0	3	0	2	44	21	17	6	0
	Campbell	1	0	1	0	0	4	1	3	0	0
	Charles Mix	6	0	0	0	6	16	7	9	0	1
	Clay	1	0	0	0	1	31	5	25	1	0
	Codington	3	1	1	0	1	32	6	25	1	1
	Corson	0	0	0	0	0	20	6	12	2	0
	Custer	1	0	0	0	1	8	0	8	0	0
	Davison	1	0	0	0	1	15	4	9	2	0
	Deuel	2	0	1	0	1	36	12	21	3	0
	Dewey	4	0	1	0	3	6	1	3	2	0
	Edmunds	0	0	0	0	0	0	0	0	0	0
	Hamlin	2	0	1	0	1	30	19	11	0	1
	Hanson	1	0	0	0	1	9	2	6	1	0
	Harding	0	0	0	0	0	0	0	0	0	0
	Hughes	3	0	2	0	1	9	4	5	0	0
	Hutchinson	0	0	0	0	0	6	6	0	0	0
	Kingsbury	2	0	0	0	2	0	0	0	0	0
	Lawrence	9	0	0	1	8	63	27	30	6	1
	Marshall	4	0	0	0	4	55	22	30	3	1
	McPherson	0	0	0	0	0	1	1	0	0	0
	Miner	1	0	0	0	1	32	20	11	1	1
	Moody	5	0	0	0	5	34	6	28	0	1
	Perkins	0	0	0	0	0	4	2	2	0	0
	Roberts	3	0	0	0	3	1	1	0	0	0
	Spink	4	0	1	0	3	45	13	29	3	0

[1] The FBI does not publish arson data unless it receives data from either the agency or the state for all 12 months of the calendar year.

Table 10.   Offenses Known to Law Enforcement, by State Metropolitan and Nonmetropolitan Counties, 2007 *(Contd.)*

(Number.)

State	County	Violent crime	Murder and non-negligent man-slaughter	Forcible rape	Robbery	Aggravated assault	Property crime	Burglary	Larceny-theft	Motor vehicle theft	Arson[1]
	Sully....................	0	0	0	0	0	2	1	1	0	0
	Tripp....................	0	0	0	0	0	12	1	10	1	0
	Yankton................	3	0	1	0	2	29	11	14	4	0
	Ziebach................	0	0	0	0	0	4	4	0	0	0
TENNESSEE-Metropolitan Counties	Anderson..............	164	1	10	5	148	1,021	387	533	101	13
	Blount..................	300	0	29	18	253	1,661	585	911	165	10
	Bradley................	349	2	11	9	327	1,064	249	725	90	14
	Cannon................	20	0	0	0	20	116	51	48	17	0
	Carter..................	55	1	0	3	51	654	216	389	49	11
	Cheatham.............	100	0	5	2	93	545	148	312	85	1
	Chester................	25	0	2	1	22	131	33	85	13	0
	Dickson...............	124	0	14	4	106	766	267	407	92	11
	Fayette................	131	0	5	10	116	579	182	300	97	4
	Grainger..............	32	1	0	4	27	437	166	234	37	1
	Hamblen..............	116	1	7	16	92	724	284	394	46	10
	Hamilton..............	344	2	24	17	301	1,942	516	1,309	117	4
	Hartsville-Trousdale......	37	0	1	4	32	170	45	114	11	2
	Hawkins...............	93	1	13	6	73	1,104	381	614	109	10
	Hickman...............	60	0	8	4	48	480	172	264	44	4
	Jefferson..............	104	1	8	4	91	827	291	461	75	4
	Knox....................	519	5	22	106	386	5,761	1,515	3,743	503	26
	Loudon................	78	1	2	10	65	681	175	433	73	8
	Macon..................	56	2	1	1	52	223	53	149	21	4
	Madison...............	218	2	18	15	183	920	313	507	100	4
	Montgomery..........	168	2	9	8	149	770	247	462	61	4
	Polk.....................	40	0	1	3	36	289	75	180	34	1
	Robertson............	73	0	9	2	62	482	160	289	33	1
	Rutherford............	216	2	20	11	183	1,309	374	787	148	8
	Sequatchie............	32	0	2	1	29	94	37	48	9	2
	Shelby.................	489	6	32	80	371	3,555	1,122	2,140	293	22
	Stewart................	38	0	1	1	36	156	68	73	15	3
	Sullivan...............	323	2	31	19	271	1,980	623	1,172	185	28
	Sumner................	159	0	31	3	125	744	221	476	47	8
	Tipton..................	219	2	8	10	199	661	214	345	102	5
	Unicoi..................	32	0	0	0	32	107	15	83	9	0
	Union...................	33	0	1	5	27	384	170	174	40	1
	Washington...........	268	1	6	8	253	1,052	364	615	73	22
	Williamson............	61	2	2	4	53	620	166	414	40	2
	Wilson.................	209	1	5	7	196	959	355	507	97	14
TENNESSEE-Nonmetropolitan Counties	Bedford................	51	1	1	1	48	266	78	162	26	4
	Benton.................	45	1	1	1	42	215	80	120	15	0
	Bledsoe................	26	2	2	0	22	91	19	46	26	2
	Campbell..............	83	0	3	6	74	940	275	566	99	10
	Carroll.................	39	0	1	4	34	211	70	121	20	1
	Claiborne..............	108	0	5	7	96	721	292	374	55	9
	Clay....................	4	0	0	0	4	107	40	57	10	2
	Cocke..................	99	2	4	8	85	706	292	337	77	7
	Coffee.................	55	0	0	3	52	490	59	387	44	0
	Crockett...............	13	0	4	2	7	128	25	82	21	0
	Cumberland...........	78	1	4	5	68	1,077	386	588	103	12
	Decatur................	36	0	5	0	31	196	56	114	26	1
	DeKalb................	34	0	0	1	33	367	131	192	44	2
	Dyer....................	38	0	3	3	32	366	122	219	25	0
	Fentress...............	46	1	0	0	45	339	143	165	31	4
	Franklin...............	37	0	2	4	31	310	75	200	35	11
	Gibson.................	57	0	3	3	51	309	112	159	38	2
	Giles...................	68	0	3	0	65	289	134	134	21	0
	Greene.................	219	0	12	15	192	1,158	387	669	102	18
	Grundy................	129	0	4	0	125	142	66	33	43	6
	Hancock...............	7	0	0	1	6	151	65	82	4	2
	Hardeman.............	102	1	5	9	87	421	155	209	57	3
	Hardin.................	98	1	7	2	88	542	214	282	46	3
	Haywood..............	39	2	1	8	28	204	79	96	29	2
	Henderson............	86	3	2	4	77	311	102	177	32	0
	Henry..................	68	1	3	2	62	503	194	274	35	0
	Houston...............	24	0	0	0	24	149	68	71	10	1
	Humphreys............	25	0	1	0	24	155	38	101	16	1
	Johnson...............	89	0	0	1	88	184	81	83	20	11
	Lake....................	6	0	1	0	5	32	2	28	2	0

[1] The FBI does not publish arson data unless it receives data from either the agency or the state for all 12 months of the calendar year.

Table 10.   Offenses Known to Law Enforcement, by State Metropolitan and Nonmetropolitan Counties, 2007 *(Contd.)*
(Number.)

State	County	Violent crime	Murder and non-negligent man-slaughter	Forcible rape	Robbery	Aggravated assault	Property crime	Burglary	Larceny-theft	Motor vehicle theft	Arson[1]
	Lauderdale	51	0	4	2	45	351	115	189	47	6
	Lawrence	154	1	10	4	139	589	217	307	65	8
	Lewis	34	0	3	0	31	150	50	85	15	5
	Lincoln	128	0	2	0	126	505	208	257	40	10
	Marshall	57	0	2	1	54	219	55	148	16	3
	Maury	172	2	18	16	136	900	264	547	89	9
	McNairy	43	2	5	3	33	420	139	242	39	3
	Meigs	42	0	5	0	37	312	118	160	34	0
	Monroe	111	1	4	1	105	655	252	344	59	7
	Moore	11	0	4	0	7	84	13	68	3	1
	Morgan	19	0	1	1	17	271	94	147	30	2
	Obion	27	0	3	3	21	215	47	155	13	2
	Overton	23	1	1	0	21	312	110	181	21	0
	Perry	30	0	1	0	29	165	43	97	25	3
	Pickett	4	0	0	0	4	99	14	83	2	0
	Putnam	105	2	8	3	92	610	132	434	44	2
	Rhea	60	3	8	0	49	411	76	305	30	2
	Roane	152	2	16	7	127	1,078	305	662	111	3
	Scott	127	1	3	1	122	544	142	359	43	4
	Sevier	140	5	12	6	117	2,197	1,119	942	136	1
	Van Buren	3	1	0	0	2	44	5	32	7	1
	Warren	43	0	0	2	41	434	132	263	39	4
	Wayne	29	0	0	1	28	97	38	49	10	2
	Weakley	53	0	2	3	48	236	70	138	28	2
	White	61	0	4	0	57	350	100	211	39	2
TEXAS-Metropolitan Counties											
	Aransas	27	2	6	4	15	562	198	345	19	1
	Armstrong	1	0	1	0	0	6	1	5	0	0
	Atascosa	22	3	0	1	18	298	99	181	18	3
	Austin	15	0	0	0	15	152	53	92	7	0
	Bandera	46	0	7	2	37	302	112	176	14	5
	Bastrop	108	1	2	13	92	981	422	492	67	5
	Bell	74	2	19	7	46	791	259	488	44	9
	Bexar	542	8	62	93	379	6,737	2,126	4,165	446	106
	Bowie	124	3	12	11	98	640	182	369	89	6
	Brazoria	85	3	0	30	52	1,402	522	753	127	0
	Brazos	30	0	3	3	24	367	140	209	18	1
	Burleson	34	0	8	1	25	69	33	22	14	1
	Caldwell	37	0	2	2	33	223	94	122	7	1
	Calhoun	14	0	0	0	14	175	66	97	12	4
	Callahan	2	0	1	1	0	30	21	8	1	1
	Cameron	201	2	12	23	164	1,845	828	858	159	11
	Carson	5	0	1	0	4	16	6	7	3	0
	Chambers	124	2	5	7	110	518	216	270	32	4
	Clay	15	2	5	0	8	207	59	134	14	0
	Collin	73	1	14	1	57	792	338	390	64	3
	Comal	129	0	18	9	102	857	319	490	48	6
	Coryell	18	1	0	0	17	134	69	60	5	0
	Crosby	0	0	0	0	0	0	0	0	0	0
	Dallas	45	0	6	9	30	419	108	255	56	12
	Delta	10	1	0	1	8	124	49	69	6	1
	Denton	115	1	5	11	98	952	258	649	45	7
	Ector	53	2	10	11	30	1,039	250	676	113	0
	Ellis	170	1	5	10	154	1,105	387	597	121	4
	El Paso	226	3	21	29	173	1,282	361	808	113	20
	Fort Bend	784	10	38	136	600	3,009	1,035	1,666	308	23
	Galveston	147	5	15	23	104	900	365	474	61	19
	Goliad	8	0	0	6	2	54	21	28	5	1
	Grayson	26	2	5	1	18	689	251	376	62	3
	Gregg	103	2	27	13	61	943	199	631	113	3
	Guadalupe	107	0	11	8	88	653	234	387	32	1
	Hardin	30	1	9	1	19	404	126	206	72	1
	Harris	6,731	65	354	1,987	4,325	48,319	13,286	28,382	6,651	
	Hays	78	1	25	8	44	744	294	425	25	0
	Hidalgo	833	14	64	150	605	6,598	2,332	3,657	609	149
	Hunt	36	0	0	10	26	1,088	389	590	109	4
	Irion	0	0	0	0	0	13	3	10	0	0
	Jefferson	27	0	5	5	17	479	139	279	61	3
	Johnson	177	1	0	13	163	1,379	469	790	120	20
	Jones	24	1	4	0	19	109	40	63	6	0
	Kaufman	206	3	6	17	180	1,758	678	879	201	23
	Kendall	24	1	7	0	16	178	41	122	15	2

[1] The FBI does not publish arson data unless it receives data from either the agency or the state for all 12 months of the calendar year.

Table 10. Offenses Known to Law Enforcement, by State Metropolitan and Nonmetropolitan Counties, 2007 (Contd.)

(Number.)

State	County	Violent crime	Murder and non-negligent man-slaughter	Forcible rape	Robbery	Aggravated assault	Property crime	Burglary	Larceny-theft	Motor vehicle theft	Arson[1]
	Lampasas	9	1	0	0	8	69	26	41	2	1
	Liberty	184	4	10	11	159	1,191	439	584	168	14
	Lubbock	104	0	10	4	90	742	377	282	83	3
	McLennan	114	2	31	8	73	855	336	444	75	7
	Medina	60	0	8	1	51	320	148	155	17	0
	Midland	88	0	11	5	72	524	188	316	20	2
	Montgomery	841	9	67	131	634	7,424	2,064	4,695	665	30
	Nueces	72	0	13	7	52	394	127	245	22	1
	Orange	112	0	11	12	89	785	301	400	84	3
	Parker	79	3	11	4	61	1,091	333	667	91	0
	Potter	18	0	3	1	14	238	72	141	25	0
	Randall	52	0	4	4	44	328	87	202	39	5
	Robertson	24	0	2	2	20	135	59	68	8	0
	Rockwall	51	0	6	1	44	248	95	143	10	1
	Rusk	86	0	7	2	77	598	231	301	66	3
	San Jacinto	58	3	0	4	51	523	193	259	71	4
	San Patricio	28	0	3	5	20	356	95	229	32	0
	Smith	332	6	46	28	252	1,828	662	961	205	30
	Tarrant	129	1	35	19	74	1,225	391	748	86	0
	Taylor	26	0	4	2	20	182	79	83	20	1
	Tom Green	21	0	2	1	18	266	74	173	19	0
	Travis	262	1	22	40	199	3,435	1,064	2,157	214	13
	Upshur	56	0	10	3	43	773	291	412	70	2
	Victoria	58	3	5	2	48	462	127	307	28	1
	Waller	27	1	8	0	18	261	107	119	35	0
	Webb	56	3	0	14	39	299	111	143	45	1
	Wichita	10	0	0	1	9	135	66	61	8	1
	Williamson	161	1	27	10	123	1,632	422	1,129	81	20
	Wilson	42	1	3	1	37	197	72	108	17	2
	Wise	120	1	5	3	111	582	187	385	10	0
TEXAS-Nonmetropolitan Counties	Anderson	70	3	13	4	50	432	215	186	31	1
	Andrews	4	0	1	0	3	94	18	72	4	0
	Angelina	189	4	9	12	164	458	174	243	41	0
	Bailey	5	0	1	0	4	23	11	10	2	0
	Baylor	0	0	0	0	0	15	5	7	3	0
	Bee	28	1	3	2	22	144	48	90	6	0
	Blanco	8	0	0	1	7	39	16	21	2	0
	Borden	0	0	0	0	0	4	1	3	0	0
	Bosque	22	0	7	1	14	92	29	63	0	0
	Brewster	15	0	0	1	14	20	9	10	1	0
	Briscoe	0	0	0	0	0	5	2	2	1	0
	Brooks	0	0	0	0	0	14	3	10	1	0
	Brown	27	0	4	1	22	169	79	79	11	3
	Burnet	64	0	6	3	55	297	105	164	28	7
	Camp	10	0	0	1	9	192	42	141	9	1
	Cass	22	0	6	4	12	274	113	124	37	1
	Castro	8	0	0	1	7	71	27	35	9	0
	Cherokee	76	1	13	1	61	486	182	249	55	4
	Childress	2	0	0	0	2	15	7	6	2	0
	Cochran	4	0	0	0	4	71	25	44	2	0
	Coke	0	0	0	0	0	10	8	2	0	0
	Coleman	1	0	0	0	1	48	18	29	1	0
	Collingsworth	0	0	0	0	0	3	1	2	0	0
	Colorado	11	0	2	1	8	160	37	114	9	1
	Comanche	3	0	1	0	2	88	26	55	7	1
	Concho	3	0	0	0	3	17	5	9	3	1
	Cooke	51	1	5	2	43	276	122	124	30	1
	Cottle	0	0	0	0	0	1	0	1	0	0
	Crane	1	0	0	0	1	39	9	30	0	0
	Crockett	16	0	3	0	13	29	8	14	7	0
	Culberson	4	0	0	0	4	10	3	7	0	0
	Dallam	4	0	0	0	4	27	12	12	3	1
	Dawson	5	0	0	1	4	30	9	13	8	0
	Deaf Smith	11	0	1	0	10	83	28	50	5	1
	Dewitt	11	0	0	0	11	60	17	34	9	1
	Dickens	2	0	0	0	2	0	0	0	0	0
	Dimmit	34	2	1	3	28	329	130	157	42	1
	Donley	8	0	0	1	7	46	11	31	4	0
	Duval	11	0	0	0	11	135	44	79	12	2
	Eastland	2	0	0	0	2	81	22	52	7	1
	Edwards	7	0	1	0	6	22	10	10	2	1

[1] The FBI does not publish arson data unless it receives data from either the agency or the state for all 12 months of the calendar year.

Table 10. Offenses Known to Law Enforcement, by State Metropolitan and Nonmetropolitan Counties, 2007 *(Contd.)*

(Number.)

State	County	Violent crime	Murder and non-negligent man-slaughter	Forcible rape	Robbery	Aggravated assault	Property crime	Burglary	Larceny-theft	Motor vehicle theft	Arson[1]
	Erath	34	5	3	0	26	147	44	94	9	0
	Falls	23	0	4	2	17	100	33	57	10	0
	Fannin	26	0	4	2	20	256	116	127	13	3
	Fayette	3	0	0	1	2	148	44	95	9	2
	Fisher	9	0	4	1	4	63	28	33	2	0
	Floyd	5	0	0	0	5	19	10	9	0	0
	Foard	0	0	0	0	0	4	2	2	0	0
	Franklin	11	0	3	0	8	140	43	82	15	0
	Freestone	15	1	0	1	13	123	41	71	11	1
	Frio	8	0	0	0	8	54	30	21	3	0
	Gaines	4	0	0	1	3	52	13	28	11	0
	Garza	7	0	2	1	4	75	13	57	5	0
	Gillespie	5	0	1	0	4	110	24	82	4	0
	Glasscock	0	0	0	0	0	0	0	0	0	0
	Gonzales	14	1	1	1	11	46	17	28	1	0
	Gray	9	0	0	1	8	104	27	71	6	0
	Grimes	15	0	0	4	11	354	114	217	23	5
	Hale	11	0	0	0	11	120	46	60	14	0
	Hall	2	0	0	0	2	9	4	3	2	0
	Hamilton	24	0	2	1	21	110	39	65	6	0
	Hansford	3	0	0	0	3	22	12	10	0	2
	Hardeman	6	0	0	0	6	83	40	36	7	0
	Harrison	104	1	3	4	96	806	335	429	42	0
	Hartley	3	0	0	0	3	18	8	9	1	0
	Haskell	4	0	1	1	2	28	14	12	2	0
	Hemphill	7	0	0	0	7	75	17	58	0	1
	Henderson	203	4	3	14	182	1,120	481	527	112	2
	Hill	10	0	2	3	5	286	107	152	27	1
	Hockley	6	0	1	0	5	93	30	61	2	0
	Hood	39	0	0	1	38	621	207	370	44	7
	Hopkins	39	0	2	1	36	207	77	112	18	3
	Houston	14	0	1	1	12	155	68	75	12	3
	Howard	17	1	2	0	14	102	40	53	9	4
	Hudspeth	7	0	0	2	5	41	21	16	4	0
	Hutchinson	12	0	2	1	9	76	26	41	9	0
	Jack	3	0	0	0	3	32	11	12	9	0
	Jackson	15	0	1	0	14	71	12	54	5	0
	Jasper	14	0	1	0	13	84	34	46	4	0
	Jeff Davis	0	0	0	0	0	13	7	6	0	0
	Jim Hogg	12	0	0	0	12	78	26	43	9	0
	Jim Wells	113	1	7	4	101	456	222	199	35	6
	Karnes	13	0	3	0	10	79	22	55	2	1
	Kenedy	2	0	0	0	2	3	0	3	0	0
	Kent	3	0	0	0	3	13	3	8	2	0
	Kerr	24	0	4	2	18	351	117	208	26	0
	Kimble	1	0	0	0	1	11	8	3	0	0
	King	0	0	0	0	0	0	0	0	0	0
	Kinney	5	0	0	2	3	9	1	8	0	0
	Kleberg	22	0	2	0	20	724	25	697	2	0
	Knox	2	0	1	0	1	13	7	6	0	0
	La Salle	9	0	0	0	9	88	21	67	0	0
	Lamar	63	0	4	1	58	347	120	198	29	1
	Lamb	5	0	0	2	3	90	18	63	9	1
	Lavaca	11	0	1	1	9	56	24	29	3	0
	Lee	17	0	4	0	13	86	33	50	3	1
	Leon	27	1	2	2	22	118	39	71	8	0
	Limestone	46	0	4	0	42	226	91	118	17	3
	Lipscomb	3	0	1	0	2	15	7	8	0	0
	Live Oak	4	1	0	0	3	55	19	31	5	0
	Llano	17	0	4	3	10	240	72	154	14	0
	Loving	1	0	0	0	1	19	5	13	1	1
	Lynn	1	0	0	0	1	15	2	13	0	0
	Madison	12	0	0	1	11	120	45	62	13	0
	Marion	41	0	11	3	27	263	134	105	24	1
	Martin	0	0	0	0	0	27	6	21	0	0
	Mason	4	0	1	0	3	34	4	29	1	0
	Matagorda	43	1	0	4	38	284	101	166	17	1
	Maverick	180	0	13	0	167	595	234	327	34	1
	McCulloch	16	0	1	0	15	34	4	26	4	0
	McMullen	2	1	0	0	1	2	0	1	1	0
	Menard	1	0	0	0	1	3	0	2	1	0
	Milam	17	1	1	2	13	149	59	77	13	1
	Mills	7	0	0	1	6	34	7	26	1	0

[1] The FBI does not publish arson data unless it receives data from either the agency or the state for all 12 months of the calendar year.

Table 10. Offenses Known to Law Enforcement, by State Metropolitan and Nonmetropolitan Counties, 2007 *(Contd.)*

(Number.)

State	County	Violent crime	Murder and non-negligent man-slaughter	Forcible rape	Robbery	Aggravated assault	Property crime	Burglary	Larceny-theft	Motor vehicle theft	Arson[1]
	Mitchell	1	0	0	0	1	23	4	18	1	0
	Montague	10	0	0	0	10	190	67	113	10	2
	Moore	4	0	1	1	2	56	24	25	7	0
	Morris	18	0	3	0	15	124	54	54	16	0
	Motley	0	0	0	0	0	12	9	3	0	0
	Nacogdoches	115	2	17	4	92	383	134	215	34	4
	Navarro	29	2	7	2	18	579	242	302	35	7
	Newton	21	1	4	1	15	192	36	142	14	0
	Nolan	5	0	2	0	3	50	20	24	6	0
	Ochiltree	9	0	2	0	7	48	10	32	6	1
	Oldham	5	0	1	0	4	33	5	26	2	0
	Palo Pinto	9	0	0	0	9	123	52	53	18	0
	Panola	67	0	7	3	57	370	95	230	45	0
	Parmer	1	0	0	0	1	52	27	22	3	0
	Pecos	8	3	0	0	5	20	8	12	0	0
	Polk	63	1	20	4	38	829	265	492	72	1
	Presidio	1	0	0	1	0	2	0	2	0	0
	Rains	17	0	4	1	12	131	36	73	22	0
	Reagan	1	0	0	0	1	11	3	7	1	0
	Real	2	0	0	0	2	18	10	7	1	0
	Red River	28	0	0	0	28	116	34	72	10	1
	Reeves	16	0	4	0	12	92	29	61	2	0
	Refugio	18	0	0	1	17	53	14	34	5	0
	Roberts	2	0	0	1	1	27	2	24	1	0
	Runnels	0	0	0	0	0	17	4	12	1	0
	Sabine	47	2	1	1	43	144	50	84	10	0
	San Augustine	14	0	3	1	10	116	45	55	16	2
	San Saba	3	0	0	0	3	19	9	9	1	0
	Schleicher	0	0	0	0	0	11	4	7	0	0
	Scurry	6	0	1	0	5	54	24	26	4	0
	Shackelford	1	0	0	0	1	9	3	5	1	0
	Shelby	38	2	5	5	26	215	83	111	21	1
	Sherman	0	0	0	0	0	0	0	0	0	0
	Somervell	3	0	0	1	2	95	27	63	5	0
	Starr	80	4	13	7	56	362	173	128	61	0
	Stephens	1	0	0	0	1	46	14	29	3	0
	Sterling	1	0	1	0	0	5	1	4	0	0
	Stonewall	5	0	0	0	5	12	4	7	1	0
	Sutton	6	0	2	0	4	19	5	13	1	0
	Swisher	9	0	1	0	8	37	13	20	4	1
	Terrell	1	1	0	0	0	13	8	2	3	0
	Terry	3	0	1	1	1	19	8	9	2	0
	Throckmorton	3	0	2	0	1	4	0	4	0	0
	Titus	62	0	9	2	51	285	99	162	24	4
	Trinity	26	0	4	5	17	139	58	64	17	2
	Tyler	60	0	3	4	53	279	157	99	23	8
	Upton	6	0	0	0	6	13	2	10	1	0
	Uvalde	27	0	7	4	16	175	61	105	9	2
	Val Verde	6	1	1	1	3	149	33	103	13	1
	Van Zandt	79	2	0	4	73	767	293	383	91	2
	Walker	60	1	13	5	41	410	143	233	34	1
	Ward	18	0	1	1	16	117	34	77	6	1
	Washington	32	1	1	0	30	115	49	62	4	1
	Wharton	72	0	0	6	66	479	236	213	30	3
	Wheeler	6	0	0	0	6	50	16	29	5	0
	Wilbarger	4	0	1	0	3	19	7	10	2	0
	Willacy	13	1	2	1	9	134	56	77	1	2
	Winkler	5	0	0	0	5	49	9	38	2	1
	Wood	174	5	0	1	168	514	170	317	27	3
	Yoakum	9	0	2	0	7	50	12	36	2	0
	Young	14	0	1	0	13	76	27	43	6	0
	Zapata	28	1	1	2	24	239	93	114	32	2
	Zavala	15	0	2	0	13	109	58	45	6	2
UTAH- **Metropolitan** **Counties**											
	Cache	28	0	18	2	8	575	146	411	18	1
	Davis	27	0	3	0	24	196	81	99	16	2
	Juab	3	0	1	0	2	97	36	54	7	1
	Morgan	2	0	0	0	2	71	15	54	2	0
	Salt Lake	675	9	91	121	454	9,071	1,856	6,265	950	30
	Summit	13	0	6	4	3	725	102	589	34	0
	Tooele	15	0	7	1	7	243	76	155	12	0
	Utah	18	0	1	0	17	407	121	261	25	3
	Washington	18	1	1	2	14	187	69	104	14	1
	Weber	50	1	7	8	34	1,227	267	888	72	5

[1] The FBI does not publish arson data unless it receives data from either the agency or the state for all 12 months of the calendar year.

Table 10.   Offenses Known to Law Enforcement, by State Metropolitan and Nonmetropolitan Counties, 2007 *(Contd.)*

(Number.)

State	County	Violent crime	Murder and non-negligent man-slaughter	Forcible rape	Robbery	Aggravated assault	Property crime	Burglary	Larceny-theft	Motor vehicle theft	Arson[1]
UTAH- **Nonmetropolitan** **Counties**	Beaver	12	1	2	0	9	95	24	66	5	0
	Box Elder	3	0	2	0	1	222	61	154	7	0
	Carbon	21	0	8	0	13	136	46	74	16	7
	Daggett	0	0	0	0	0	10	6	4	0	0
	Emery	6	0	0	2	4	174	56	110	8	0
	Grand	5	0	0	0	5	60	20	34	6	0
	Iron	23	0	6	3	14	181	65	93	23	1
	Kane	4	1	1	0	2	50	36	14	0	0
	Millard	30	0	2	0	28	247	51	183	13	3
	Rich	8	0	0	0	8	58	21	37	0	0
	San Juan	7	0	0	0	7	24	5	19	0	0
	Sevier	11	0	1	1	9	195	40	141	14	0
	Uintah	33	0	7	0	26	253	52	174	27	2
	Wasatch	6	0	1	0	5	162	23	130	9	0
	Wayne	8	1	0	0	7	42	5	31	6	0
VERMONT- **Metropolitan** **Counties**	Chittenden	0	0	0	0	0	0	0	0	0	0
	Franklin	19	0	3	2	14	218	40	166	12	2
	Grand Isle	1	0	0	0	1	49	9	38	2	0
VERMONT- **Nonmetropolitan** **Counties**	Addison	0	0	0	0	0	0	0	0	0	0
	Bennington	0	0	0	0	0	0	0	0	0	0
	Caledonia	0	0	0	0	0	2	1	1	0	0
	Lamoille	10	0	1	1	8	95	17	73	5	1
	Orange	0	0	0	0	0	29	4	24	1	0
	Orleans	1	0	0	0	1	29	5	24	0	0
	Rutland	2	0	0	0	2	124	3	120	1	0
	Washington	0	0	0	0	0	0	0	0	0	0
	Windham	0	0	0	0	0	5	1	4	0	0
	Windsor	0	0	0	0	0	0	0	0	0	0
VIRGINIA- **Metropolitan** **Counties**	Albemarle County Police Department	152	1	24	45	82	2,034	304	1,639	91	26
	Amelia	17	0	2	1	14	176	42	95	39	1
	Amherst	49	1	10	17	21	463	40	395	28	5
	Appomattox	18	0	2	4	12	130	25	88	17	2
	Arlington County Police Department	328	2	26	150	150	4,208	396	3,520	292	5
	Bedford	56	2	7	8	39	737	129	564	44	4
	Botetourt	21	1	3	5	12	348	55	278	15	3
	Campbell	76	0	12	10	54	825	163	607	55	3
	Caroline	63	4	7	12	40	432	103	328	1	2
	Charles City	8	0	1	1	6	20	10	8	2	0
	Chesterfield County Police Department	683	10	73	327	273	7,261	1,636	5,123	502	105
	Clarke	23	0	2	1	20	187	36	135	16	3
	Craig	3	0	0	1	2	24	10	13	1	13
	Cumberland	20	1	2	1	16	54	20	22	12	1
	Dinwiddie	63	5	12	14	32	408	95	267	46	2
	Fairfax County Police Department	865	15	69	480	301	16,574	1,369	13,988	1,217	136
	Fauquier	76	4	11	5	56	715	131	520	64	8
	Fluvanna	25	0	2	2	21	208	56	135	17	1
	Franklin	34	1	9	2	22	564	92	427	45	0
	Frederick	94	0	40	12	42	1,502	284	1,078	140	4
	Giles	13	0	3	0	10	166	35	116	15	2
	Gloucester	34	1	9	6	18	553	53	476	24	10
	Goochland	65	4	3	1	57	154	26	109	19	2
	Greene	30	0	5	2	23	261	45	204	12	3
	Hanover	49	0	6	20	23	1,085	111	929	45	4
	Henrico County Police Department	568	13	33	331	191	8,557	1,362	6,662	533	123
	Isle of Wight	26	0	2	7	17	466	115	290	61	4
	James City County Police Department	92	2	11	16	63	863	160	653	50	18
	King and Queen	8	0	2	0	6	48	20	23	5	1
	King William	11	1	0	2	8	74	18	55	1	1
	Loudoun	167	0	38	34	95	2,803	273	2,315	215	48

[1] The FBI does not publish arson data unless it receives data from either the agency or the state for all 12 months of the calendar year.

Table 10. Offenses Known to Law Enforcement, by State Metropolitan and Nonmetropolitan Counties, 2007 *(Contd.)*

(Number.)

State	County	Violent crime	Murder and non-negligent man-slaughter	Forcible rape	Robbery	Aggravated assault	Property crime	Burglary	Larceny-theft	Motor vehicle theft	Arson[1]
	Louisa	35	3	8	2	22	442	81	333	28	8
	Mathews	6	0	0	1	5	148	34	107	7	0
	Montgomery	53	0	14	5	34	590	182	374	34	12
	Nelson	13	1	3	1	8	305	55	224	26	0
	New Kent	27	0	3	2	22	234	35	174	25	2
	Powhatan	12	0	4	0	8	250	67	168	15	0
	Prince George County Police Department	56	0	11	16	29	442	71	323	48	8
	Prince William County Police Department	629	10	23	277	319	7,125	1,010	5,496	619	107
	Pulaski	14	0	5	3	6	574	85	471	18	3
	Roanoke County Police Department	194	1	22	24	147	1,109	255	809	45	14
	Rockingham	22	0	6	1	15	315	113	200	2	0
	Scott	26	2	1	1	22	410	116	271	23	11
	Spotsylvania	283	5	28	34	216	1,892	127	1,692	73	12
	Surry	22	0	4	3	15	82	44	36	2	1
	Sussex	23	0	1	5	17	202	87	105	10	1
	Warren	18	1	3	3	11	288	39	228	21	6
	Washington	90	0	20	9	61	1,317	248	1,016	53	6
	York	76	1	11	27	37	1,190	155	991	44	22
VIRGINIA-Nonmetropolitan Counties	Accomack	75	5	8	31	31	601	169	369	63	1
	Alleghany	11	3	1	1	6	97	31	60	6	1
	Augusta	76	1	12	11	52	814	193	556	65	4
	Bland	4	0	0	3	1	69	29	37	3	0
	Brunswick	21	1	0	5	15	132	34	77	21	4
	Buchanan	44	1	3	7	33	541	146	352	43	15
	Buckingham	15	1	0	1	13	163	75	73	15	1
	Carroll	40	4	5	3	28	368	91	241	36	7
	Charlotte	20	0	1	3	16	147	41	88	18	1
	Culpeper	18	0	3	6	9	219	44	156	19	1
	Dickenson	17	4	3	1	9	247	33	204	10	1
	Essex	8	0	1	0	7	83	25	51	7	1
	Floyd	12	0	3	0	9	168	64	89	15	1
	Grayson	14	0	2	2	10	125	39	73	13	2
	Greensville	29	0	3	4	22	287	99	172	16	0
	Halifax	18	2	1	1	14	300	90	189	21	0
	Henry	166	3	18	28	117	1,351	365	878	108	7
	King George	41	0	5	8	28	382	62	290	30	1
	Lancaster	13	0	2	2	9	114	28	81	5	1
	Lee	28	1	0	2	25	508	159	344	5	0
	Lunenburg	12	1	0	3	8	73	21	34	18	2
	Madison	12	0	2	1	9	192	35	133	24	2
	Mecklenburg	47	1	5	4	37	478	125	315	38	8
	Middlesex	9	0	2	1	6	117	30	78	9	2
	Northampton	26	1	3	8	14	173	53	101	19	2
	Northumberland	7	0	0	2	5	123	36	82	5	1
	Nottoway	10	1	1	1	7	108	20	77	11	2
	Orange	32	0	6	2	24	238	50	171	17	2
	Page	27	0	13	1	13	227	90	125	12	7
	Patrick	27	0	6	3	18	447	121	271	55	0
	Rappahannock	3	0	0	1	2	47	19	25	3	0
	Richmond	10	0	2	0	8	54	5	44	5	0
	Rockbridge	14	0	2	1	11	308	63	230	15	0
	Russell	30	0	7	3	20	308	95	184	29	8
	Smyth	36	1	7	4	24	364	69	275	20	7
	Southampton	38	2	2	7	27	346	93	238	15	2
	Tazewell	54	2	11	7	34	501	108	374	19	4
	Westmoreland	18	0	3	2	13	208	35	159	14	3
	Wise	62	1	6	1	54	421	126	257	38	21
	Wythe	24	0	2	2	20	161	28	128	5	1
WASHINGTON-Metropolitan Counties	Asotin	15	0	0	3	12	143	39	94	10	0
	Benton	59	3	7	1	48	647	226	381	40	9
	Chelan	40	1	15	3	21	886	153	698	35	3
	Clark	271	2	76	46	147	4,125	801	2,757	567	57
	Cowlitz	47	0	13	1	33	684	242	371	71	6
	Douglas	41	2	4	6	29	549	135	376	38	4
	Franklin	13	0	2	2	9	192	51	118	23	4
	King	685	16	121	212	336	7,900	2,466	4,170	1,264	158

[1] The FBI does not publish arson data unless it receives data from either the agency or the state for all 12 months of the calendar year.

Table 10.   Offenses Known to Law Enforcement, by State Metropolitan and Nonmetropolitan Counties, 2007 *(Contd.)*

(Number.)

State	County	Violent crime	Murder and non-negligent man-slaughter	Forcible rape	Robbery	Aggravated assault	Property crime	Burglary	Larceny-theft	Motor vehicle theft	Arson[1]
	Kitsap	581	1	114	41	425	3,556	992	2,329	235	36
	Pierce[6]	1,099	6	94	187	812	10,419	2,743	5,824	1,852	82
	Skagit	82	1	25	8	48	1,648	508	1,024	116	18
	Skamania	27	0	8	2	17	254	53	186	15	1
	Spokane	331	1	7	21	302	2,286	576	1,443	267	10
	Thurston	244	3	21	27	193	2,631	778	1,577	276	21
	Whatcom	157	0	45	8	104	1,520	540	857	123	8
	Yakima	119	4	30	29	56	2,747	989	1,289	469	55
WASHINGTON-Nonmetropolitan Counties											
	Adams	16	1	6	2	7	297	87	187	23	7
	Clallam	71	0	24	1	46	696	170	477	49	4
	Columbia	2	0	0	0	2	177	33	138	6	1
	Ferry	3	1	0	0	2	27	9	17	1	0
	Garfield	3	0	0	0	3	48	10	37	1	0
	Grant	86	2	8	13	63	1,634	478	984	172	19
	Grays Harbor	36	1	4	4	27	561	202	292	67	5
	Island	36	0	13	2	21	1,181	374	767	40	1
	Jefferson	51	0	5	2	44	520	157	332	31	1
	Kittitas	15	0	2	2	11	592	174	384	34	1
	Klickitat	4	1	0	0	3	160	113	15	32	0
	Lewis	62	1	11	5	45	847	286	483	78	10
	Lincoln	4	0	2	1	1	199	44	147	8	0
	Mason	137	0	31	13	93	1,747	560	979	208	8
	Okanogan	37	0	11	2	24	470	133	306	31	2
	Pacific	21	0	2	2	17	408	155	218	35	0
	Pend Oreille	6	1	1	1	3	413	93	294	26	0
	San Juan	9	0	2	1	6	220	60	136	24	2
	Stevens	38	1	10	3	24	724	256	403	65	2
	Wahkiakum	9	0	2	0	7	47	19	21	7	0
	Walla Walla	17	0	6	0	11	385	94	266	25	0
	Whitman	13	0	10	0	3	89	17	64	8	0
WEST VIRGINIA-Metropolitan Counties											
	Berkeley	80	3	1	19	57	1,212	270	880	62	15
	Boone	26	0	3	1	22	87	26	46	15	0
	Brooke	27	1	1	0	25	75	23	47	5	3
	Cabell	41	0	6	15	20	810	221	500	89	6
	Hampshire	30	0	0	1	29	127	51	66	10	6
	Hancock	4	0	0	0	4	21	6	14	1	0
	Jefferson	49	0	8	3	38	442	91	295	56	9
	Kanawha	170	0	12	28	130	1,308	473	685	150	24
	Marshall	11	0	1	0	10	219	58	139	22	3
	Mineral	57	1	0	1	55	45	14	25	6	1
	Monongalia	44	0	5	3	36	465	71	370	24	2
	Morgan	13	0	0	2	11	55	20	31	4	0
	Pleasants	1	0	0	0	1	10	7	3	0	0
	Putnam	66	0	13	8	45	930	162	685	83	9
	Wood	72	3	0	2	67	432	110	299	23	10
WEST VIRGINIA-Nonmetropolitan Counties											
	Braxton	13	0	0	0	13	35	7	27	1	1
	Fayette	78	3	9	3	63	391	159	194	38	8
	Greenbrier	9	0	1	0	8	151	58	79	14	1
	Hardy	4	0	0	0	4	40	13	27	0	1
	Harrison	56	2	0	2	52	483	151	287	45	2
	Jackson	9	2	0	1	6	43	4	23	16	0
	Lewis	3	0	0	0	3	29	8	19	2	0
	Mason	9	0	2	0	7	193	6	163	24	1
	McDowell	16	0	0	3	13	80	28	37	15	1
	Mercer	91	2	3	9	77	532	203	282	47	1
	Mingo	2	0	0	0	2	1	0	0	1	0
	Monroe	8	0	0	0	8	36	11	22	3	0
	Nicholas	42	0	7	3	32	418	92	294	32	3
	Pendleton	0	0	0	0	0	0	0	0	0	0
	Pocahontas	3	0	0	0	3	18	6	10	2	0
	Raleigh	107	1	0	16	90	1,219	272	850	97	15
	Randolph	10	0	1	1	8	45	15	27	3	0
	Ritchie	7	1	1	0	5	45	14	27	4	0
	Summers	13	0	0	1	12	55	20	28	7	3
	Tyler	0	0	0	0	0	1	0	1	0	0
	Upshur	6	0	0	1	5	60	23	30	7	3
	Wyoming	7	0	0	5	2	217	152	58	7	0

[1] The FBI does not publish arson data unless it receives data from either the agency or the state for all 12 months of the calendar year.
[6] Because of changes in the state/local agency's reporting practices, figures are not comparable to previous years' data.

Table 10.   Offenses Known to Law Enforcement, by State Metropolitan and Nonmetropolitan Counties, 2007 *(Contd.)*
(Number.)

State	County	Violent crime	Murder and non-negligent man-slaughter	Forcible rape	Robbery	Aggravated assault	Property crime	Burglary	Larceny-theft	Motor vehicle theft	Arson[1]
WISCONSIN- **Metropolitan** **Counties**	Brown	49	0	17	0	32	1,318	234	1,030	54	5
	Calumet	8	0	0	3	5	266	85	174	7	0
	Chippewa	13	1	8	0	4	427	87	310	30	0
	Columbia	32	0	2	1	29	400	123	259	18	0
	Dane	66	0	15	11	40	1,376	324	967	85	7
	Douglas	11	0	2	2	7	258	101	132	25	0
	Eau Claire	11	0	1	1	9	282	98	170	14	2
	Fond du Lac	42	0	3	2	37	285	61	198	26	4
	Iowa	9	0	0	0	9	188	43	138	7	0
	Kenosha	34	1	2	12	19	772	184	554	34	0
	Kewaunee	7	0	2	0	5	97	26	64	7	1
	La Crosse	12	0	2	1	9	178	42	120	16	1
	Marathon	73	0	0	0	73	477	137	323	17	2
	Milwaukee	5	0	2	2	1	48	5	42	1	0
	Oconto	1	0	0	1	0	634	261	307	66	1
	Outagamie	20	1	5	0	14	466	74	376	16	0
	Ozaukee	21	0	2	0	19	126	26	96	4	4
	Pierce	10	0	0	0	10	255	106	136	13	0
	Racine	17	0	1	9	7	683	95	539	49	5
	Rock	38	3	9	3	23	605	187	396	22	4
	Sheboygan	38	0	5	2	31	513	102	395	16	3
	St. Croix	24	0	5	3	16	591	187	365	39	2
	Washington	24	0	6	1	17	567	122	409	36	8
	Waukesha	30	0	5	4	21	493	101	378	14	0
	Winnebago	17	0	0	0	17	409	131	260	18	1
WISCONSIN- **Nonmetropolitan** **Counties**	Adams	11	0	0	0	11	54	29	23	2	0
	Ashland	11	0	1	0	10	49	16	27	6	0
	Barron	4	0	2	1	1	264	111	125	28	4
	Bayfield	29	1	1	2	25	186	54	115	17	2
	Buffalo	0	0	0	0	0	74	18	40	16	0
	Burnett	9	0	0	0	9	432	217	194	21	2
	Clark	12	0	0	1	11	267	47	203	17	1
	Crawford	5	0	4	0	1	154	30	119	5	0
	Dodge	37	1	5	0	31	266	73	177	16	3
	Door	9	0	1	0	8	224	45	172	7	0
	Dunn	31	0	4	0	27	219	61	141	17	1
	Florence	7	0	0	0	7	115	48	62	5	1
	Forest	16	0	0	2	14	204	56	128	20	3
	Grant	33	0	1	0	32	195	94	89	12	1
	Green	10	2	3	0	5	167	46	110	11	1
	Green Lake	4	0	0	0	4	111	31	79	1	0
	Iron	12	0	1	0	11	54	22	32	0	0
	Jackson	15	0	8	3	4	298	70	195	33	1
	Jefferson	51	0	7	1	43	478	167	287	24	6
	Juneau	28	2	4	0	22	280	86	171	23	0
	Lafayette	2	0	1	0	1	165	40	122	3	1
	Langlade	9	0	2	0	7	268	116	145	7	1
	Lincoln	3	0	1	0	2	200	69	115	16	0
	Manitowoc	31	1	4	2	24	285	85	185	15	3
	Marinette	14	3	3	0	8	416	184	205	27	4
	Marquette	17	0	3	0	14	118	11	80	27	0
	Menominee	3	0	0	0	3	89	19	68	2	0
	Monroe	14	1	3	0	10	264	70	164	30	0
	Oneida	12	0	4	1	7	284	119	158	7	36
	Pepin	8	0	1	0	7	24	22	0	2	0
	Polk	81	0	14	1	66	391	153	212	26	4
	Portage	22	0	3	1	18	348	107	229	12	0
	Price	25	0	0	0	25	89	41	43	5	2
	Richland	24	0	0	0	24	151	45	96	10	0
	Rusk	0	0	0	0	0	106	28	72	6	0
	Sauk	33	0	2	6	25	614	88	497	29	0
	Sawyer	27	1	4	0	22	315	93	190	32	0
	Shawano	9	0	0	1	8	531	187	312	32	0
	Taylor	8	0	4	0	4	187	64	112	11	0
	Trempealeau	3	0	3	0	0	100	32	62	6	1
	Vernon	11	0	4	0	7	145	39	97	9	0
	Vilas	18	0	4	0	14	210	57	140	13	0
	Walworth	6	0	5	0	1	407	75	297	35	1
	Washburn	20	0	2	0	18	212	80	128	4	2
	Waupaca	19	0	6	0	13	470	130	298	42	0
	Waushara	11	1	1	0	9	341	66	255	20	0
	Wood	7	0	2	1	4	227	64	145	18	1

[1] The FBI does not publish arson data unless it receives data from either the agency or the state for all 12 months of the calendar year.

Table 10.   Offenses Known to Law Enforcement, by State Metropolitan and Nonmetropolitan Counties, 2007 *(Contd.)*

(Number.)

State	County	Violent crime	Murder and non-negligent man-slaughter	Forcible rape	Robbery	Aggravated assault	Property crime	Burglary	Larceny-theft	Motor vehicle theft	Arson[1]
WYOMING-											
Metropolitan											
Counties	Laramie	39	0	10	2	27	503	116	359	28	2
	Natrona	9	2	0	1	6	380	118	230	32	0
WYOMING-											
Nonmetropolitan											
Counties	Albany	5	0	0	1	4	73	16	49	8	0
	Big Horn	16	0	1	0	15	35	12	20	3	0
	Campbell	35	0	4	2	29	245	41	177	27	1
	Carbon	5	1	1	0	3	48	4	40	4	0
	Converse	12	0	2	0	10	46	6	38	2	1
	Crook	3	0	0	0	3	60	18	38	4	0
	Fremont	17	0	3	2	12	151	25	115	11	0
	Goshen	29	0	2	0	27	80	9	66	5	0
	Hot Springs	4	0	0	1	3	16	4	11	1	0
	Johnson	4	0	1	0	3	35	3	31	1	0
	Lincoln	11	1	0	1	9	183	84	90	9	1
	Niobrara	0	0	0	0	0	14	2	12	0	0
	Park	35	0	2	0	33	76	25	49	2	0
	Platte	1	0	0	0	1	42	19	20	3	0
	Sheridan	6	0	1	0	5	75	18	47	10	0
	Sublette	37	1	3	0	33	244	48	184	12	3
	Sweetwater	25	0	4	0	21	177	58	106	13	4
	Teton	7	0	0	0	7	137	23	104	10	1
	Uinta	4	1	2	0	1	151	2	146	3	0
	Washakie	10	1	0	0	9	13	3	7	3	0
	Weston	3	0	0	0	3	7	4	1	2	0

[1] The FBI docs not publish arson data unless it receives data from either the agency or the state for all 12 months of the calendar year.

Table 11. Offenses Known to Law Enforcement, by State and Other Agencies, 2007

(Number.)

State	State/Other Agency	Unit/Office	Violent crime	Murder and non-negligent man-slaughter	Forcible rape	Robbery	Aggra-vated assault	Property crime	Burglary	Larceny-theft	Motor vehicle theft	Arson[1]
ALABAMA- **State Agencies**	Alabama Alcoholic Beverage Control Board		0	0	0	0	0	1	0	1	0	
ALABAMA- **Other Agencies**	2nd Judicial Circuit Drug Task Force		0	0	0	0	0	0	0	0	0	
	22nd Judicial Circuit Drug Task Force		0	0	0	0	0	1	0	1	0	
	24th Judicial Circuit Drug and Violent Crime Task Force			0	0	0	0	0	1	0	0	1
	Madison-Morgan County Strategic Counterdrug Team ..		0	0	0	0	0	3	0	3	0	
	Marshall County Drug Enforcement Unit		0	0	0	0	0	0	0	0	0	
ALASKA- **State Agencies**	Alaska State Troopers.............		1,003	11	91	42	859	4,728	1,287	2,894	547	65
	Alcohol Beverage Control Board.........................		0	0	0	0	0	0	0	0	0	0
ALASKA- **Other Agencies**	Anchorage International Airport......................................		1	0	0	0	1	82	0	70	12	0
	Fairbanks International Airport......................................		3	0	0	0	3	21	0	19	2	1
ARIZONA- **State Agencies**	Arizona Department of Public Safety		3	0	0	0	3	3	0	3	0	0
ARKANSAS- **State Agencies**	State Capitol Police................		0	0	0	0	0	24	6	18	0	0
CALIFORNIA- **State Agencies**	Agnews Developmental Center		1	0	0	0	1	8	3	5	0	0
	Atascadero State Hospital		97	0	0	0	97	8	1	7	0	1
	California State Fair...............		7	0	0	0	7	81	2	76	3	
	Department of Parks and Recreation:	Angeles	0	0	0	0	0	8	0	8	0	
		Bay Area	0	0	0	0	0	1	0	1	0	1
		Calaveras County	0	0	0	0	0	0	0	0	0	0
		Capital	0	0	0	0	0	11	9	2	0	
		Channel Coast	1	0	0	0	1	37	1	35	1	0
		Colorado	0	0	0	0	0	0	0	0	0	
		Four Rivers District	0	0	0	0	0	15	2	13	0	0
		Gold Fields District	5	1	0	1	3	106	6	98	2	2
		Hollister Hills	0	0	0	0	0	2	0	1	1	0
		Hungry Valley	0	0	0	0	0	1	0	0	1	0
		Inland Empire	1	0	0	0	1	7	0	7	0	0
		Marin County	0	0	0	0	0	6	1	5	0	0
		Mendocino Headquarters	2	0	0	0	2	10	0	10	0	0
		Monterey County	1	1	0	0	0	88	3	84	1	1
		North Coast Redwoods	1	0	0	0	1	37	1	36	0	0
		Northern Buttes	1	0	0	0	1	34	0	31	3	
		Oceano Dunes	15	0	4	0	11	119	5	94	20	0
		Ocotillo Wells	2	0	1	0	1	4	0	0	4	3
		Orange Coast	1	0	0	0	1	75	7	64	4	0
		Russian River	1	0	0	0	1	21	0	20	1	0
		San Diego Coast	3	0	1	1	1	95	2	84	9	1
		San Joaquin	0	0	0	0	0	11	5	6	0	
		San Luis Obispo Coast	0	0	0	0	0	14	3	11	0	0
		Santa Cruz Mountains	1	0	0	0	1	115	3	111	1	1
		Sierra	0	0	0	0	0	9	3	6	0	0
		Silverado	0	0	0	0	0	9	1	8	0	0
		Twin Cities	0	0	0	0	0	4	2	1	1	1
	Fairview Developmental Center		5	0	0	0	5	10	3	7	0	0
	Highway Patrol:......................	Alameda County	3	0	0	0	3	359	0	29	330	0
		Alpine County	0	0	0	0	0	0	0	0	0	0
		Amador County	0	0	0	0	0	38	0	0	38	0
		Butte County	2	0	0	0	2	389	2	53	334	0
		Calaveras County	0	0	0	0	0	78	0	8	70	0
		Colusa County	1	0	0	0	1	29	0	0	29	0
		Contra Costa County	1	0	0	1	0	1,066	0	18	1,048	0
		Del Norte County	0	0	0	0	0	56	1	0	55	0
		El Dorado County	1	0	0	0	1	240	0	51	189	0

[1] The FBI does not publish arson data unless it receives data from either the agency or the state for all 12 months of the calendar year.

Table 11.   Offenses Known to Law Enforcement, by State and Other Agencies, 2007 *(Contd.)*

(Number.)

State	State/Other Agency	Unit/Office	Violent crime	Murder and non-negligent man-slaughter	Forcible rape	Robbery	Aggra-vated assault	Property crime	Burglary	Larceny-theft	Motor vehicle theft	Arson[1]
		Fresno County	0	0	0	0	0	228	0	14	214	0
		Glenn County	0	0	0	0	0	32	0	2	30	0
		Humboldt County	0	0	0	0	0	174	0	15	159	0
		Imperial County	0	0	0	0	0	133	0	9	124	0
		Inyo County	1	0	0	0	1	21	1	4	16	0
		Kern County	2	0	0	0	2	353	1	53	299	0
		Kings County	1	0	0	0	1	220	0	0	220	0
		Lake County	0	0	0	0	0	140	0	18	122	0
		Lassen County	0	0	0	0	0	27	0	3	24	0
		Los Angeles County	41	0	1	3	37	526	13	39	474	0
		Madera County	0	0	0	0	0	305	0	47	258	0
		Marin County	0	0	0	0	0	108	0	0	108	0
		Mariposa County	0	0	0	0	0	24	0	7	17	0
		Mendocino County	2	0	0	0	2	102	2	22	78	0
		Merced County	0	0	0	0	0	574	0	55	519	0
		Modoc County	0	0	0	0	0	8	0	1	7	0
		Mono County	1	0	0	0	1	1	0	0	1	0
		Monterey County	2	0	0	0	2	460	0	26	434	0
		Napa County	1	0	0	1	0	102	0	12	90	0
		Nevada County	0	0	0	0	0	82	0	27	55	0
		Orange County	6	0	0	0	6	46	6	10	30	0
		Placer County	1	0	0	0	1	274	3	73	198	0
		Plumas County	0	0	0	0	0	40	0	13	27	0
		Riverside County	11	0	0	0	11	102	11	11	80	0
		Sacramento County	6	0	0	0	6	5,587	19	412	5,156	0
		San Benito County	0	0	0	0	0	25	0	0	25	0
		San Bernardino County	9	0	0	0	9	58	1	6	51	0
		San Diego County	8	0	0	0	8	125	7	29	89	0
		San Francisco County	0	0	0	0	0	47	0	9	38	0
		San Joaquin County	0	0	0	0	0	1,142	0	258	884	0
		San Luis Obispo County	3	0	0	0	3	137	0	17	120	0
		San Mateo County	1	0	0	0	1	25	0	3	22	0
		Santa Barbara County	3	0	0	0	3	131	0	24	107	0
		Santa Clara County	1	0	0	0	1	85	0	12	73	0
		Santa Cruz County	0	0	0	0	0	323	0	54	269	0
		Shasta County	2	0	0	0	2	154	0	37	117	0
		Sierra County	0	0	0	0	0	4	0	1	3	0
		Siskiyou County	3	0	0	0	3	31	0	2	29	0
		Solano County	0	0	0	0	0	89	2	0	87	0
		Sonoma County	2	0	0	1	1	325	0	77	248	0
		Stanislaus County	1	0	1	0	0	593	1	13	579	0
		Sutter County	0	0	0	0	0	47	0	8	39	0
		Tehama County	4	0	0	2	2	109	0	7	102	
		Trinity County	0	0	0	0	0	25	0	0	25	0
		Tulare County	0	0	0	0	0	1,285	0	293	992	0
		Tuolumne County	0	0	0	0	0	155	0	11	144	0
		Ventura County	3	0	0	1	2	50	0	8	42	0
		Yolo County	1	0	0	0	1	61	3	5	53	0
		Yuba County	0	0	0	0	0	216	0	18	198	0
	Napa State Hospital		5	0	0	0	5	0	0	0	0	0
	Porterville Developmental Center		8	0	0	0	8	3	0	3	0	0
	Sonoma Developmental Center		0	0	0	0	0	0	0	0	0	0
CALIFORNIA-Other Agencies	East Bay Municipal Utility		0	0	0	0	0	18	1	17	0	1
	East Bay Regional Parks:	Alameda County	3	0	1	1	1	141	9	125	7	6
		Contra Costa County	23	3	3	12	5	218	5	209	4	11
	Fontana Unified School District		24	0	0	8	16	322	96	221	5	2
	Grant Joint Union High School		29	0	0	9	20	101	50	49	2	4
	Los Angeles County Metropolitan Transportation Authority		3	0	0	0	3	33	3	30	0	0
	Los Angeles Transportation Services Bureau		445	0	1	291	153	700	32	496	172	2
	Monterey Peninsula Airport		2	0	0	0	2	20	1	11	8	0
	Port of San Diego Harbor		21	0	0	4	17	581	29	549	3	1
	San Bernardino Unified School District		94	0	2	78	14	310	176	105	29	9
	San Francisco Bay Area Rapid Transit:	Alameda County	163	0	1	131	31	1,567	11	1,204	352	2

[1] The FBI does not publish arson data unless it receives data from either the agency or the state for all 12 months of the calendar year.

Table 11.   Offenses Known to Law Enforcement, by State and Other Agencies, 2007 *(Contd.)*

(Number.)

State	State/Other Agency	Unit/Office	Violent crime	Murder and non-negligent man-slaughter	Forcible rape	Robbery	Aggra-vated assault	Property crime	Burglary	Larceny-theft	Motor vehicle theft	Arson[1]
		Contra Costa County	51	0	0	44	7	902	5	627	270	2
		San Francisco County	31	0	0	22	9	200	6	194	0	1
		San Mateo County	9	0	1	7	1	164	0	138	26	0
	Santa Clara Transit District................................		43	0	0	31	12	85	7	67	11	0
	Stockton Unified School District................................		76	0	0	10	66	577	137	429	11	18
	Union Pacific Railroad:	Alameda County	3	0	0	0	3	259	241	18	0	0
		Amador County	0	0	0	0	0	0	0	0	0	0
		Butte County	8	0	0	0	8	17	0	17	0	0
		Calaveras County	0	0	0	0	0	0	0	0	0	0
		Colusa County	0	0	0	0	0	0	0	0	0	0
		Contra Costa County	1	0	0	0	1	4	0	4	0	0
		El Dorado County	0	0	0	0	0	0	0	0	0	0
		Fresno County	0	0	0	0	0	1	1	0	0	0
		Glenn County	0	0	0	0	0	0	0	0	0	0
		Humboldt County	0	0	0	0	0	0	0	0	0	0
		Imperial County	1	0	0	0	1	117	115	2	0	0
		Inyo County	0	0	0	0	0	0	0	0	0	0
		Kern County	0	0	0	0	0	15	14	1	0	0
		Kings County	0	0	0	0	0	0	0	0	0	0
		Lassen County	0	0	0	0	0	2	0	2	0	0
		Los Angeles County	4	0	0	0	4	169	135	34	0	0
		Madera County	0	0	0	0	0	1	1	0	0	0
		Marin County	0	0	0	0	0	0	0	0	0	0
		Mendocino County	0	0	0	0	0	0	0	0	0	0
		Merced County	1	0	0	0	1	6	1	5	0	0
		Modoc County	0	0	0	0	0	0	0	0	0	0
		Monterey County	0	0	0	0	0	2	0	2	0	0
		Napa County	0	0	0	0	0	0	0	0	0	0
		Nevada County	0	0	0	0	0	0	0	0	0	0
		Orange County	0	0	0	0	0	0	0	0	0	0
		Placer County	4	0	0	0	4	14	2	12	0	0
		Plumas County	0	0	0	0	0	1	0	1	0	0
		Riverside County	1	0	0	0	1	196	154	42	0	0
		Sacramento County	14	0	0	0	14	17	8	9	0	0
		San Benito County	0	0	0	0	0	0	0	0	0	0
		San Bernardino County	2	0	0	0	2	88	48	40	0	0
		San Francisco County	0	0	0	0	0	0	0	0	0	0
		San Joaquin County	16	0	0	0	16	150	130	20	0	0
		San Luis Obispo County	0	0	0	0	0	0	0	0	0	0
		San Mateo County	0	0	0	0	0	0	0	0	0	0
		Santa Barbara County	0	0	0	0	0	7	0	7	0	0
		Santa Clara County	0	0	0	0	0	2	0	2	0	0
		Santa Cruz County	0	0	0	0	0	1	0	1	0	0
		Shasta County	0	0	0	0	0	6	1	5	0	0
		Sierra County	0	0	0	0	0	0	0	0	0	0
		Siskiyou County	1	0	0	0	1	1	1	0	0	0
		Solano County	3	0	0	0	3	0	0	0	0	0
		Sonoma County	0	0	0	0	0	0	0	0	0	0
		Stanislaus County	2	0	0	0	2	18	1	17	0	0
		Sutter County	0	0	0	0	0	6	0	6	0	0
		Tehama County	1	0	0	0	1	0	0	0	0	0
		Trinity County	0	0	0	0	0	0	0	0	0	0
		Tulare County	0	0	0	0	0	1	0	1	0	0
		Ventura County	0	0	0	0	0	0	0	0	0	0
		Yolo County	3	0	0	0	3	1	0	1	0	0
		Yuba County	2	0	0	0	2	2	0	2	0	0
COLORADO- **State Agencies**	Colorado Mental Health Institute................................		0	0	0	0	0	0	0	0	0	0
	State Patrol............................		13	0	0	0	13	63	0	20	43	1
COLORADO- **Other Agencies**	Two Rivers Drug Enforcement Team.................		0	0	0	0	0	0	0	0	0	0
CONNECTICUT- **State Agencies**	Connecticut State Police.........		487	15	91	94	287	4,801	1,403	2,967	431	108
	State Capitol Police..............		0	0	0	0	0	14	0	14	0	0
DELAWARE- **State Agencies**	Attorney General:..................	Kent County	0	0	0	0	0	0	0	0	0	0
		New Castle County	0	0	0	0	0	0	0	0	0	0
		Sussex County	0	0	0	0	0	2	0	2	0	0

[1] The FBI does not publish arson data unless it receives data from either the agency or the state for all 12 months of the calendar year.

Table 11.   Offenses Known to Law Enforcement, by State and Other Agencies, 2007 *(Contd.)*

(Number.)

State	State/Other Agency	Unit/Office	Violent crime	Murder and non-negligent manslaughter	Forcible rape	Robbery	Aggra-vated assault	Property crime	Burglary	Larceny-theft	Motor vehicle theft	Arson[1]
	Division of Alcohol and Tobacco Enforcement............		0	0	0	0	0	0	0	0	0	0
	Environmental Control		0	0	0	0	0	1	0	1	0	0
	Fish and Wildlife.....................		1	0	0	0	1	19	3	16	0	0
	Park Rangers		4	0	0	0	4	83	12	70	1	0
	River and Bay Authority		4	0	0	1	3	13	1	9	3	0
	State Capitol Police...............		3	0	0	0	3	26	6	20	0	0
	State Fire Marshal		38	0	0	0	38	21	20	1	0	249
	State Police:............................	Kent County	469	3	56	49	361	1,749	590	1,035	124	3
		New Castle County	767	6	42	285	434	5,847	607	4,872	368	3
		Sussex County	731	3	61	95	572	3,487	1,156	2,135	196	2
DELAWARE- **Other Agencies**	Amtrak Police..........................		0	0	0	0	0	2	0	2	0	0
	Drug Enforcement Administration	Wilmington Resident Office	0	0	0	0	0	2	0	2	0	0
	Wilmington Fire Department............................		1	0	0	0	1	0	0	0	0	16
DISTRICT OF COLUMBIA- **Other Agencies**	Metro Transit Police		394	0	0	276	118	1,168	5	886	277	0
	National Zoological Park		2	0	0	0	2	21	1	20	0	0
FLORIDA- **State Agencies**	Capitol Police..........................		0	0	0	0	0	41	0	41	0	0
	Department of Environmental Protection, Division of Law Enforcement:	Alachua County	0	0	0	0	0	5	0	5	0	0
		Baker County	0	0	0	0	0	0	0	0	0	0
		Bay County	0	0	0	0	0	3	0	3	0	0
		Bradford County	0	0	0	0	0	0	0	0	0	0
		Brevard County	0	0	0	0	0	9	0	8	1	0
		Broward County	0	0	0	0	0	5	0	5	0	0
		Charlotte County	0	0	0	0	0	1	0	1	0	0
		Citrus County	0	0	0	0	0	0	0	0	0	0
		Clay County	0	0	0	0	0	0	0	0	0	0
		Collier County	0	0	0	0	0	0	0	0	0	0
		Columbia County	0	0	0	0	0	0	0	0	0	0
		Dixie County	0	0	0	0	0	0	0	0	0	0
		Duval County	0	0	0	0	0	10	0	10	0	0
		Escambia County	0	0	0	0	0	2	0	2	0	0
		Flagler County	0	0	0	0	0	1	0	1	0	0
		Franklin County	0	0	0	0	0	0	0	0	0	0
		Hamilton County	0	0	0	0	0	0	0	0	0	0
		Highlands County	0	0	0	0	0	1	0	1	0	0
		Hillsborough County	0	0	0	0	0	1	0	1	0	0
		Holmes County	0	0	0	0	0	0	0	0	0	0
		Indian River County	0	0	0	0	0	6	0	6	0	0
		Jackson County	0	0	0	0	0	1	0	1	0	0
		Lake County	0	0	0	0	0	1	0	1	0	0
		Lee County	0	0	0	0	0	4	0	4	0	0
		Leon County	0	0	0	0	0	0	0	0	0	0
		Levy County	0	0	0	0	0	2	0	2	0	0
		Madison County	0	0	0	0	0	0	0	0	0	0
		Manatee County	0	0	0	0	0	0	0	0	0	0
		Marion County	0	0	0	0	0	0	0	0	0	0
		Martin County	0	0	0	0	0	4	0	4	0	0
		Miami-Dade County	0	0	0	0	0	9	0	9	0	0
		Monroe County	0	0	0	0	0	12	0	12	0	0
		Nassau County	1	0	0	0	1	5	0	5	0	0
		Okaloosa County	0	0	0	0	0	2	0	2	0	0
		Okeechobee County	0	0	0	0	0	0	0	0	0	0
		Orange County	0	0	0	0	0	7	0	7	0	0
		Pasco County	0	0	0	0	0	0	0	0	0	0
		Pinellas County	0	0	0	0	0	4	0	4	0	0
		Polk County	0	0	0	0	0	0	0	0	0	0
		Santa Rosa County	0	0	0	0	0	1	0	0	1	0
		Sarasota County	0	0	0	0	0	0	0	0	0	0
		Seminole County	0	0	0	0	0	1	1	0	0	0
		St. Johns County	0	0	0	0	0	2	0	2	0	0
		St. Lucie County	0	0	0	0	0	4	0	4	0	0
		Volusia County	0	0	0	0	0	19	0	19	0	0
		Wakulla County	0	0	0	0	0	0	0	0	0	0
		Walton County	0	0	0	0	0	4	0	4	0	0

[1] The FBI does not publish arson data unless it receives data from either the agency or the state for all 12 months of the calendar year.

Table 11. Offenses Known to Law Enforcement, by State and Other Agencies, 2007 *(Contd.)*

(Number.)

State	State/Other Agency	Unit/Office	Violent crime	Murder and non-negligent man-slaughter	Forcible rape	Robbery	Aggra-vated assault	Property crime	Burglary	Larceny-theft	Motor vehicle theft	Arson[1]
		Washington County	0	0	0	0	0	0	0	0	0	0
	Department of Insurance:	Broward County	0	0	0	0	0	0	0	0	0	0
		Duval County	0	0	0	0	0	0	0	0	0	0
		Escambia County	0	0	0	0	0	0	0	0	0	0
		Hillsboro County	0	0	0	0	0	0	0	0	0	0
		Lee County	0	0	0	0	0	0	0	0	0	0
		Miami-Dade County	0	0	0	0	0	0	0	0	0	0
		Orange County	0	0	0	0	0	0	0	0	0	0
		Palm Beach County	0	0	0	0	0	0	0	0	0	0
		Pinellas County	0	0	0	0	0	0	0	0	0	0
	Department of Law Enforcement:	Duval County, Jacksonville	0	0	0	0	0	0	0	0	0	0
		Escambia County, Pensacola	2	0	1	0	1	1	0	1	0	0
		Hillsborough County, Tampa	0	0	0	0	0	0	0	0	0	0
		Lee County, Fort Myers	0	0	0	0	0	0	0	0	0	0
		Leon County, Tallahassee	1	0	0	0	1	2	0	2	0	0
		Miami-Dade County, Miami	0	0	0	0	0	3	0	3	0	0
		Orange County, Orlando	0	0	0	0	0	0	0	0	0	0
	Florida Game Commission: ...	Alachua County	0	0	0	0	0	0	0	0	0	0
		Baker County	0	0	0	0	0	0	0	0	0	0
		Bay County	0	0	0	0	0	0	0	0	0	0
		Bradford County	0	0	0	0	0	0	0	0	0	0
		Brevard County	0	0	0	0	0	0	0	0	0	0
		Broward County	0	0	0	0	0	0	0	0	0	0
		Calhoun County	0	0	0	0	0	0	0	0	0	0
		Charlotte County	0	0	0	0	0	0	0	0	0	0
		Citrus County	0	0	0	0	0	0	0	0	0	0
		Clay County	0	0	0	0	0	0	0	0	0	0
		Collier County	0	0	0	0	0	0	0	0	0	0
		Columbia County	0	0	0	0	0	0	0	0	0	0
		DeSoto County	0	0	0	0	0	0	0	0	0	0
		Dixie County	0	0	0	0	0	0	0	0	0	0
		Duval County	0	0	0	0	0	0	0	0	0	0
		Escambia County	0	0	0	0	0	0	0	0	0	0
		Flagler County	0	0	0	0	0	0	0	0	0	0
		Franklin County	0	0	0	0	0	0	0	0	0	0
		Gadsden County	0	0	0	0	0	0	0	0	0	0
		Gilchrist County	0	0	0	0	0	0	0	0	0	0
		Glades County	0	0	0	0	0	0	0	0	0	0
		Gulf County	0	0	0	0	0	0	0	0	0	0
		Hamilton County	0	0	0	0	0	0	0	0	0	0
		Hardee County	0	0	0	0	0	0	0	0	0	0
		Hendry County	0	0	0	0	0	0	0	0	0	0
		Hernando County	0	0	0	0	0	0	0	0	0	0
		Highlands County	0	0	0	0	0	0	0	0	0	0
		Hillsborough County	1	0	0	0	1	0	0	0	0	0
		Holmes County	0	0	0	0	0	0	0	0	0	0
		Indian River County	0	0	0	0	0	0	0	0	0	0
		Jackson County	0	0	0	0	0	0	0	0	0	0
		Jefferson County	0	0	0	0	0	0	0	0	0	0
		Lafayette County	0	0	0	0	0	0	0	0	0	0
		Lake County	0	0	0	0	0	0	0	0	0	0
		Lee County	0	0	0	0	0	0	0	0	0	0
		Leon County	0	0	0	0	0	0	0	0	0	0
		Levy County	0	0	0	0	0	0	0	0	0	0
		Liberty County	0	0	0	0	0	0	0	0	0	0
		Madison County	0	0	0	0	0	0	0	0	0	0
		Manatee County	0	0	0	0	0	0	0	0	0	0
		Marion County	0	0	0	0	0	0	0	0	0	0
		Martin County	0	0	0	0	0	0	0	0	0	0
		Miami-Dade County	0	0	0	0	0	0	0	0	0	0
		Monroe County	2	0	0	0	2	0	0	0	0	0
		Nassau County	0	0	0	0	0	0	0	0	0	0
		Okaloosa County	0	0	0	0	0	0	0	0	0	0
		Okeechobee County	0	0	0	0	0	0	0	0	0	0
		Orange County	0	0	0	0	0	0	0	0	0	0
		Osceola County	0	0	0	0	0	0	0	0	0	0
		Palm Beach County	0	0	0	0	0	0	0	0	0	0
		Pasco County	0	0	0	0	0	0	0	0	0	0

[1] The FBI does not publish arson data unless it receives data from either the agency or the state for all 12 months of the calendar year.

Table 11. Offenses Known to Law Enforcement, by State and Other Agencies, 2007 *(Contd.)*

(Number.)

State	State/Other Agency	Unit/Office	Violent crime	Murder and non-negligent manslaughter	Forcible rape	Robbery	Aggravated assault	Property crime	Burglary	Larceny-theft	Motor vehicle theft	Arson[1]
		Pinellas County	0	0	0	0	0	0	0	0	0	0
		Polk County	0	0	0	0	0	0	0	0	0	0
		Putnam County	0	0	0	0	0	0	0	0	0	0
		Santa Rosa County	1	0	0	0	1	0	0	0	0	0
		Sarasota County	0	0	0	0	0	0	0	0	0	0
		Seminole County	0	0	0	0	0	0	0	0	0	0
		St. Johns County	0	0	0	0	0	0	0	0	0	0
		St. Lucie County	0	0	0	0	0	0	0	0	0	0
		Sumter County	0	0	0	0	0	0	0	0	0	0
		Suwannee County	0	0	0	0	0	0	0	0	0	0
		Taylor County	0	0	0	0	0	0	0	0	0	0
		Volusia County	0	0	0	0	0	0	0	0	0	0
		Wakulla County	0	0	0	0	0	0	0	0	0	0
		Walton County	0	0	0	0	0	0	0	0	0	0
		Washington County	0	0	0	0	0	0	0	0	0	0
	Highway Patrol:......................	Alachua County	0	0	0	0	0	1	0	1	0	0
		Baker County	0	0	0	0	0	0	0	0	0	0
		Bay County	0	0	0	0	0	0	0	0	0	0
		Bradford County	0	0	0	0	0	0	0	0	0	0
		Brevard County	1	0	0	0	1	0	0	0	0	0
		Broward County	50	0	0	0	50	156	0	40	116	0
		Calhoun County	0	0	0	0	0	1	0	0	1	0
		Charlotte County	2	0	0	0	2	0	0	0	0	0
		Citrus County	0	0	0	0	0	0	0	0	0	0
		Clay County	0	0	0	0	0	0	0	0	0	0
		Collier County	0	0	0	0	0	0	0	0	0	0
		Columbia County	2	0	0	0	2	1	0	1	0	0
		DeSoto County	0	0	0	0	0	0	0	0	0	0
		Dixie County	1	0	0	0	1	0	0	0	0	0
		Duval County	4	0	0	0	4	3	0	1	2	0
		Escambia County	3	0	0	1	2	1	0	1	0	0
		Flagler County	1	0	0	0	1	0	0	0	0	0
		Franklin County	0	0	0	0	0	0	0	0	0	0
		Gadsden County	0	0	0	0	0	1	0	0	1	0
		Gilchrist County	0	0	0	0	0	0	0	0	0	0
		Glades County	0	0	0	0	0	0	0	0	0	0
		Gulf County	0	0	0	0	0	0	0	0	0	0
		Hamilton County	0	0	0	0	0	0	0	0	0	0
		Hardee County	0	0	0	0	0	0	0	0	0	0
		Hendry County	0	0	0	0	0	0	0	0	0	0
		Hernando County	0	0	0	0	0	2	0	1	1	0
		Highlands County	1	1	0	0	0	0	0	0	0	0
		Hillsborough County	14	0	0	0	14	2	0	1	1	0
		Holmes County	0	0	0	0	0	0	0	0	0	0
		Indian River County	1	0	0	0	1	0	0	0	0	0
		Jackson County	0	0	0	0	0	0	0	0	0	0
		Jefferson County	2	0	0	0	2	0	0	0	0	0
		Lafayette County	0	0	0	0	0	0	0	0	0	0
		Lake County	3	0	0	0	3	1	0	1	0	0
		Lee County	0	0	0	0	0	0	0	0	0	0
		Leon County	1	0	0	0	1	0	0	0	0	0
		Levy County	0	0	0	0	0	0	0	0	0	0
		Liberty County	0	0	0	0	0	0	0	0	0	0
		Madison County	1	0	0	0	1	0	0	0	0	0
		Manatee County	2	0	0	0	2	1	0	1	0	0
		Marion County	0	0	0	0	0	1	0	1	0	0
		Martin County	1	0	0	0	1	1	0	1	0	0
		Miami-Dade County	54	0	0	2	52	79	0	21	58	0
		Monroe County	0	0	0	0	0	0	0	0	0	0
		Nassau County	0	0	0	0	0	0	0	0	0	0
		Okaloosa County	0	0	0	0	0	1	0	0	1	0
		Okeechobee County	0	0	0	0	0	0	0	0	0	0
		Orange County	11	0	0	0	11	12	0	10	2	0
		Osceola County	2	0	0	0	2	6	0	6	0	0
		Pasco County	6	0	0	0	6	3	0	3	0	0
		Pinellas County	3	0	0	0	3	2	0	1	1	0
		Polk County	2	0	0	0	2	1	0	1	0	0
		Putnam County	0	0	0	0	0	0	0	0	0	0
		Santa Rosa County	2	0	0	0	2	0	0	0	0	0
		Sarasota County	7	0	0	0	7	4	0	3	1	0
		Seminole County	3	0	0	0	3	0	0	0	0	0
		St. Johns County	0	0	0	0	0	1	0	1	0	0
		St. Lucie County	4	0	0	0	4	4	0	3	1	0
		Sumter County	3	0	0	0	3	0	0	0	0	0

[1] The FBI does not publish arson data unless it receives data from either the agency or the state for all 12 months of the calendar year.

Table 11.   Offenses Known to Law Enforcement, by State and Other Agencies, 2007 *(Contd.)*

(Number.)

State	State/Other Agency	Unit/Office	Violent crime	Murder and non-negligent man-slaughter	Forcible rape	Robbery	Aggra-vated assault	Property crime	Burglary	Larceny-theft	Motor vehicle theft	Arson[1]
		Suwannee County	0	0	0	0	0	0	0	0	0	0
		Taylor County	0	0	0	0	0	0	0	0	0	0
		Union County	0	0	0	0	0	0	0	0	0	0
		Volusia County	4	0	0	0	4	0	0	0	0	0
		Wakulla County	0	0	0	0	0	0	0	0	0	0
		Walton County	0	0	0	0	0	0	0	0	0	0
		Washington County	0	0	0	0	0	0	0	0	0	0
	State Treasurer's Office	Division of Insurance Fraud	0	0	0	0	0	0	0	0	0	0
FLORIDA-Other Agencies	Duval County Schools		117	0	2	23	92	931	234	651	46	6
	Florida School for the Deaf and Blind		1	0	0	0	1	1	1	0	0	0
	Fort Lauderdale Airport........		5	0	0	2	3	327	2	283	42	0
	Jacksonville Airport Authority		1	0	0	1	0	138	16	92	30	0
	Lee County Port Authority		0	0	0	0	0	251	2	220	29	0
	Melbourne International Airport................................		0	0	0	0	0	1	0	1	0	0
	Miami-Dade County Public Schools		474	0	29	171	274	2,742	941	1,773	28	22
	Miccosukee Tribal		14	0	0	2	12	84	20	49	15	2
	Palm Beach County School District		100	0	4	23	73	683	145	530	8	4
	Port Everglades		4	0	1	0	3	52	0	52	0	0
	Sarasota-Bradenton International Airport		2	0	0	0	2	6	2	3	1	0
	Seminole Tribal		107	0	10	23	74	578	54	471	53	0
	St. Petersburg-Clearwater International Airport		0	0	0	0	0	1	0	1	0	0
	Tampa International Airport................................		5	0	0	0	5	224	26	159	39	0
	Volusia County Beach Management		18	0	0	16	2	230	0	227	3	0
GEORGIA-State Agencies	Department of Natural Resources	Social Circle	0	0	0	0	0	0	0	0	0	0
	Department of Public Safety		1	0	0	1	0	70	6	52	12	0
	Department of Transportation	Office of Investigations	0	0	0	0	0	9	0	9	0	0
	Georgia World Congress		18	0	0	7	11	508	32	468	8	0
	Ports Authority	Savannah	2	0	0	0	2	8	0	7	1	0
GEORGIA-Other Agencies	Bibb County Board of Education		10	0	0	0	10	132	12	119	1	
	Chatham County Board of Education...........................		11	0	1	7	3	248	32	211	5	
	Cobb County Board of Education		13	0	0	2	11	514	44	467	3	6
	DeKalb County School System...................................		285	0	1	6	278	741	163	533	45	0
	Fulton County Marshal		31	0	0	3	28	119	7	101	11	
	Fulton County School System...................................		12	0	0	4	8	203	7	186	10	1
	Gwinnett County Public Schools................................		36	0	0	3	33	437	54	380	3	3
	Hartsfield-Jackson Atlanta International Airport		9	0	0	1	8	348	1	288	59	
	Metropolitan Atlanta Rapid Transit Authority.........		177	0	0	53	124	283	20	209	54	4
	Stone Mountain Park		1	0	0	1	0	48	1	46	1	0
IDAHO-State Agencies	Idaho State Police..................		22	6	1	0	15	10	3	7	0	0
INDIANA-State Agencies	Northern Indiana Commuter Transportation District.....................		3	0	0	1	2	50	0	37	13	0
	State Police:[2]	Adams County		0	0	0		1	0	1	0	0
		Allen County		0	1	0		30	0	26	4	0
		Bartholomew County		1	0	0		0	0	0	0	0
		Benton County		0	0	0		4	3	1	0	0
		Blackford County		0	0	0		0	0	0	0	0

[1] The FBI does not publish arson data unless it receives data from either the agency or the state for all 12 months of the calendar year.

[2] It was determined that the agency did not follow national Uniform Crime Reporting (UCR) Program guidelines for reporting aggravated assault. Consequently, this figure is not included in this table.

Table 11. Offenses Known to Law Enforcement, by State and Other Agencies, 2007 *(Contd.)*

(Number.)

State	State/Other Agency	Unit/Office	Violent crime	Murder and non-negligent man-slaughter	Forcible rape	Robbery	Aggra-vated assault	Property crime	Burglary	Larceny-theft	Motor vehicle theft	Arson[1]
		Boone County		0	0	0		1	0	1	0	0
		Brown County		0	0	0		4	1	3	0	1
		Carroll County		1	1	0		23	9	13	1	0
		Cass County		0	5	1		11	3	8	0	0
		Clark County		0	2	2		190	23	152	15	1
		Clay County		0	0	0		0	0	0	0	0
		Clinton County		0	2	0		17	1	16	0	0
		Crawford County		0	0	0		32	7	18	7	0
		Daviess County		0	2	0		14	4	10	0	0
		Dearborn County		0	1	2		28	7	19	2	0
		Decatur County		0	3	0		17	2	15	0	1
		De Kalb County		1	0	0		9	1	7	1	0
		Delaware County		0	0	0		18	2	16	0	0
		Dubois County		0	4	0		56	7	48	1	0
		Elkhart County		0	1	1		23	2	17	4	0
		Fayette County		0	0	0		6	3	3	0	0
		Floyd County		0	1	2		40	0	34	6	0
		Fountain County		0	2	1		12	2	10	0	0
		Franklin County		1	0	0		13	4	9	0	0
		Fulton County		0	0	0		7	2	3	2	0
		Gibson County		0	1	0		37	6	31	0	0
		Grant County		0	1	0		6	1	4	1	0
		Greene County		0	0	0		27	3	21	3	0
		Hamilton County		0	0	0		7	1	4	2	0
		Hancock County		0	0	0		7	1	6	0	0
		Harrison County		0	2	1		68	29	32	7	2
		Hendricks County		0	0	0		14	1	7	6	0
		Henry County		1	0	0		10	1	8	1	1
		Howard County		0	1	0		27	2	23	2	0
		Huntington County		0	0	0		11	0	10	1	0
		Jackson County		1	0	0		77	12	54	11	3
		Jasper County		0	0	0		9	0	6	3	0
		Jay County		0	0	0		5	1	4	0	0
		Jefferson County		0	2	0		25	13	12	0	0
		Jennings County		0	1	0		21	5	15	1	0
		Johnson County		0	0	0		2	0	2	0	0
		Knox County		1	0	0		31	1	30	0	1
		Kosciusko County		1	0	1		23	5	13	5	0
		LaGrange County		0	0	0		49	14	34	1	0
		Lake County		0	1	0		112	2	54	56	0
		La Porte County		0	0	0		24	0	18	6	0
		Lawrence County		2	0	0		15	3	12	0	0
		Madison County		1	0	0		42	7	28	7	0
		Marion County		0	3	2		70	1	33	36	0
		Marshall County		0	2	0		25	3	17	5	0
		Martin County		0	0	0		9	1	7	1	1
		Miami County		0	4	0		63	17	37	9	1
		Monroe County		0	3	0		35	5	24	6	0
		Montgomery County		0	1	2		18	0	18	0	0
		Morgan County		0	0	0		33	5	21	7	0
		Newton County		0	0	0		5	0	5	0	0
		Noble County		0	0	0		20	7	9	4	1
		Ohio County		0	0	0		1	0	1	0	0
		Orange County		0	5	0		21	5	15	1	0
		Owen County		0	1	0		13	3	8	2	0
		Parke County		0	0	0		1	0	1	0	0
		Perry County		0	2	0		27	3	22	2	0
		Pike County		0	0	0		30	1	29	0	0
		Porter County		0	0	0		35	3	24	8	0
		Posey County		0	3	0		32	8	24	0	0
		Pulaski County		0	1	0		5	0	5	0	1
		Putnam County		0	0	0		31	2	28	1	0
		Randolph County		0	0	0		5	0	5	0	0
		Ripley County		0	1	1		115	23	91	1	0
		Rush County		0	0	0		6	1	4	1	0
		Scott County		1	0	3		55	6	42	7	0
		Shelby County		0	0	1		1	0	1	0	0
		Spencer County		0	0	0		20	6	13	1	1
		Starke County		0	0	0		5	1	4	0	0
		Steuben County		0	3	0		20	6	13	1	0
		St. Joseph County		1	0	1		36	4	30	2	0
		Sullivan County		0	0	0		0	0	0	0	0
		Switzerland County		0	1	2		14	1	12	1	1
		Tippecanoe County		0	2	0		42	4	38	0	0

[1] The FBI does not publish arson data unless it receives data from either the agency or the state for all 12 months of the calendar year.

Table 11.   Offenses Known to Law Enforcement, by State and Other Agencies, 2007 *(Contd.)*

(Number.)

State	State/Other Agency	Unit/Office	Violent crime	Murder and non-negligent man-slaughter	Forcible rape	Robbery	Aggra-vated assault	Property crime	Burglary	Larceny-theft	Motor vehicle theft	Arson[1]
		Tipton County		0	1	0		8	1	7	0	0
		Union County		0	0	0		7	4	3	0	0
		Vanderburgh County		0	2	0		33	0	33	0	0
		Vermillion County		0	0	0		0	0	0	0	0
		Vigo County		0	0	0		3	1	2	0	0
		Wabash County		1	1	0		11	4	7	0	0
		Warren County		0	0	0		2	2	0	0	0
		Warrick County		1	0	0		22	2	20	0	0
		Washington County		1	4	0		33	10	17	6	0
		Wayne County		2	1	1		14	0	12	2	0
		Wells County		0	0	0		3	0	3	0	0
		White County		0	0	0		16	2	13	1	0
		Whitley County		0	0	0		17	0	16	1	0
INDIANA- Other Agencies	St. Joseph County Airport Authority		0	0	0	0	0	17	0	8	9	0
KANSAS- State Agencies	Kansas Alcoholic Beverage Control		0	0	0	0	0	0	0	0	0	0
	Kansas Bureau of Investigation		3	0	1	0	2	4	0	4	0	0
	Kansas Department of Wildlife and Parks		10	0	0	0	10	42	5	35	2	0
	Kansas Highway Patrol		34	1	0	0	33	61	5	43	13	3
KANSAS- Other Agencies	Kickapoo Tribal		0	0	0	0	0	2	0	0	2	0
	Metropolitan Topeka Airport Authority		1	0	0	0	1	10	2	8	0	0
	Potawatomi Tribal		8	0	0	1	7	29	1	28	0	1
	Shawnee Mission Public Schools		0	0	0	0	0	10	0	10	0	0
	Unified School District:	Goddard	2	0	0	0	2	33	1	32	0	0
		Topeka	11	0	1	2	8	79	0	78	1	1
	Wyandotte County Parks and Recreation		5	0	2	1	2	20	0	19	1	0
KENTUCKY- State Agencies	Fish and Wildlife Enforcement		0	0	0	0	0	1	0	1	0	0
	Kentucky Horse Park		0	0	0	0	0	41	0	38	3	0
	Motor Vehicle Enforcement		7	0	0	0	7	8	0	5	3	0
	Park Security		0	0	0	0	0	22	6	16	0	0
	South Central Kentucky Drug Task Force		0	0	0	0	0	6	0	6	0	0
	State Police		1,138	61	398	129	550	6,999	2,939	3,307	753	
	Unlawful Narcotics Investigation	Treatment and Education	0	0	0	0	0	4	0	4	0	0
KENTUCKY- Other Agencies	Buffalo Trace-Gateway Narcotics Task Force		0	0	0	0	0	0	0	0	0	0
	Cincinnati-Northern Kentucky International Airport		1	0	0	0	1	136	1	124	11	0
	FIVCO Area Drug Task Force		0	0	0	0	0	0	0	0	0	0
	Greater Hardin County Narcotics Task Force		0	0	0	0	0	3	1	2	0	0
	Jefferson County Board of Education		44	0	0	0	44	144	86	58	0	0
	Lake Cumberland Area Drug Enforcement Task Force		1	0	0	0	1	6	0	6	0	0
	Louisville Regional Airport Authority		0	0	0	0	0	28	0	6	22	0
	Northern Kentucky Narcotics Enforcement Unit		0	0	0	0	0	3	0	3	0	0
	Pennyrile Narcotics Task Force		1	0	0	1	0	3	0	3	0	0
LOUISIANA- State Agencies	Department of Public Safety	State Capitol Detail	3	0	0	1	2	34	0	33	1	1
MAINE- State Agencies	Drug Enforcement Agency:	Androscoggin County	0	0	0	0	0	0	0	0	0	0
		Aroostook County	0	0	0	0	0	0	0	0	0	0

[1] The FBI does not publish arson data unless it receives data from either the agency or the state for all 12 months of the calendar year.

Table 11. Offenses Known to Law Enforcement, by State and Other Agencies, 2007 *(Contd.)*

(Number.)

State	State/Other Agency	Unit/Office	Violent crime	Murder and non-negligent man-slaughter	Forcible rape	Robbery	Aggra-vated assault	Property crime	Burglary	Larceny-theft	Motor vehicle theft	Arson[1]
		Cumberland County	0	0	0	0	0	0	0	0	0	0
		Franklin County	0	0	0	0	0	0	0	0	0	0
		Hancock County	0	0	0	0	0	0	0	0	0	0
		Kennebec County	0	0	0	0	0	0	0	0	0	0
		Knox County	0	0	0	0	0	0	0	0	0	0
		Lincoln County	0	0	0	0	0	0	0	0	0	0
		Oxford County	0	0	0	0	0	0	0	0	0	0
		Penobscot County	0	0	0	0	0	0	0	0	0	0
		Piscataquis County	0	0	0	0	0	0	0	0	0	0
		Sagadahoc County	0	0	0	0	0	0	0	0	0	0
		Somerset County	0	0	0	0	0	0	0	0	0	0
		Waldo County	0	0	0	0	0	0	0	0	0	0
		Washington County	0	0	0	0	0	0	0	0	0	0
		York County	0	0	0	0	0	0	0	0	0	0
	State Police:................	Androscoggin County	6	0	1	0	5	122	42	72	8	2
		Aroostook County	13	0	2	4	7	215	47	158	10	1
		Cumberland County	19	1	0	2	16	141	50	66	25	0
		Franklin County	4	0	0	0	4	78	35	39	4	1
		Hancock County	4	1	2	0	1	177	56	113	8	2
		Kennebec County	9	1	2	1	5	326	106	211	9	6
		Knox County	3	0	0	0	3	74	18	53	3	1
		Lincoln County	1	1	0	0	0	10	1	9	0	4
		Oxford County	8	0	1	0	7	204	89	104	11	1
		Penobscot County	7	2	2	3	0	428	123	285	20	5
		Piscataquis County	1	0	0	0	1	16	11	5	0	3
		Sagadahoc County	1	0	0	0	1	7	3	3	1	0
		Somerset County	4	1	0	1	2	167	51	100	16	4
		Waldo County	4	1	1	0	2	202	53	142	7	6
		Washington County	1	0	0	0	1	175	48	120	7	4
		York County	6	0	1	3	2	187	57	117	13	5
MARYLAND- State Agencies	Comptroller of the Treasury...................	Field Enforcement Division	0	0	0	0	0	0	0	0	0	0
	Department of Public Safety and Correctional Services...................	Internal Investigations Unit	255	3	0	0	252	0	0	0	0	0
	General Services:................	Annapolis, Anne Arundel County	0	0	0	0	0	15	0	15	0	0
		Baltimore City	3	0	0	0	3	37	1	36	0	0
	Maryland State Police Statewide...................		3	0	0	0	3	0	0	9	0	0
	Natural Resources Police......		9	0	2	0	7	197	10	186	1	124
	Rosewood...................		10	0	0	0	10	15	0	15	0	0
	Springfield Hospital..............		0	0	0	0	0	17	0	17	0	1
	State Fire Marshal.................		0	0	0	0	0	0	0	0	0	0
	State Police:................	Allegany County	39	0	5	0	34	487	109	336	42	8
		Anne Arundel County	15	0	0	2	13	83	0	47	36	1
		Baltimore City	2	0	0	0	2	1	0	1	0	0
		Baltimore County	27	0	0	1	26	71	1	40	30	1
		Calvert County	88	1	1	3	83	338	72	253	13	12
		Caroline County	27	0	4	5	18	138	41	74	23	3
		Carroll County	164	1	0	19	144	1,322	345	903	74	14
		Cecil County	185	3	6	19	157	769	245	464	60	35
		Charles County	9	0	0	1	8	45	0	40	5	45
		Dorchester County	10	0	2	4	4	54	22	26	6	2
		Frederick County	76	0	0	11	65	462	89	338	35	15
		Garrett County	35	0	5	1	29	215	73	129	13	3
		Harford County	216	1	6	42	167	663	174	402	87	43
		Howard County	13	0	0	3	10	46	0	23	23	0
		Kent County	21	0	0	0	21	46	26	17	3	6
		Montgomery County	1	0	0	0	1	22	0	7	15	5
		Prince George's County	19	0	0	3	16	192	0	58	134	0
		Queen Anne's County	56	0	0	7	49	220	52	151	17	14
		Somerset County	58	0	1	5	52	223	102	111	10	4
		St. Mary's County	55	0	2	6	47	246	68	159	19	34
		Talbot County	19	0	2	8	9	115	32	72	11	0
		Washington County	52	0	2	9	41	291	68	194	29	21
		Wicomico County	94	0	6	16	72	288	118	147	23	9
		Worcester County	25	1	3	1	20	218	62	145	11	10
	Transit Administration............		0	0	0	0	0	0	0	0	0	0
	Transportation Authority........		16	0	0	1	15	270	5	216	49	0

[1] The FBI does not publish arson data unless it receives data from either the agency or the state for all 12 months of the calendar year.

Table 11.   Offenses Known to Law Enforcement, by State and Other Agencies, 2007 *(Contd.)*

(Number.)

State	State/Other Agency	Unit/Office	Violent crime	Murder and non-negligent manslaughter	Forcible rape	Robbery	Aggravated assault	Property crime	Burglary	Larceny-theft	Motor vehicle theft	Arson[1]
MARYLAND- **Other Agencies**	Maryland-National Capital Park Police:	Montgomery County	14	0	0	8	6	201	13	181	7	0
		Prince George's County	54	6	3	32	13	253	25	208	20	0
MASSACHUSETTS- **State Agencies**	Massachusetts Bay Transportation Authority:	Bristol County	0	0	0	0	0	14	0	8	6	
		Essex County	3	0	0	1	2	18	0	13	5	
		Middlesex County	30	0	0	14	16	132	0	126	6	
		Norfolk County	14	0	0	5	9	97	0	80	17	
		Plymouth County	2	0	0	1	1	18	1	14	3	
		Suffolk County	226	1	1	142	82	273	8	252	13	
		Worcester County	0	0	0	0	0	1	0	1	0	0
	State Police:	Barnstable County	7	0	0	0	7	0	0	0	0	0
		Berkshire County	4	0	0	0	4	77	37	35	5	0
		Bristol County	32	0	0	1	31	5	1	1	3	0
		Dukes County	0	0	0	0	0	0	0	0	0	0
		Essex County	1	0	0	1	0	1	1	0	0	
		Franklin County	11	0	0	0	11	0	0	0	0	0
		Hampden County	11	0	1	0	10	57	7	22	28	0
		Hampshire County	8	0	1	0	7	4	2	2	0	0
		Middlesex County	3	0	0	0	3	0	0	0	0	0
		Plymouth County	15	0	0	0	15	2	0	1	1	0
		Worcester County	22	0	0	0	22	3	0	3	0	0
MICHIGAN- **State Agencies**	State Police:	Alcona County	3	1	0	0	2	18	10	7	1	0
		Alger County	6	0	5	0	1	70	28	40	2	0
		Allegan County	83	3	26	4	50	410	118	263	29	2
		Alpena County	28	0	11	3	14	166	39	121	6	1
		Antrim County	7	0	1	0	6	22	8	11	3	1
		Arenac County	23	0	8	0	15	29	13	13	3	1
		Baraga County	8	0	1	0	7	40	17	19	4	1
		Barry County	40	1	18	0	21	348	104	214	30	2
		Bay County	57	1	25	3	28	403	112	253	38	2
		Benzie County	5	0	1	0	4	40	8	29	3	0
		Berrien County	50	0	15	4	31	327	92	208	27	2
		Branch County	38	4	9	1	24	217	83	113	21	6
		Calhoun County	52	3	18	1	30	197	48	133	16	1
		Cass County	21	0	7	1	13	114	45	60	9	3
		Charlevoix County	12	0	8	0	4	31	6	22	3	0
		Cheboygan County	21	0	9	1	11	102	43	54	5	1
		Chippewa County	28	2	2	0	24	156	70	73	13	2
		Clare County	8	0	6	0	2	104	66	36	2	0
		Clinton County	5	0	4	0	1	25	11	14	0	0
		Crawford County	6	0	5	0	1	32	14	16	2	0
		Delta County	12	1	2	0	9	105	40	62	3	2
		Dickinson County	2	0	1	0	1	51	17	31	3	0
		Eaton County	14	0	4	0	10	128	41	80	7	2
		Emmet County	14	0	6	1	7	165	31	128	6	2
		Genesee County	47	1	16	2	28	210	74	110	26	3
		Gladwin County	26	1	10	0	15	101	39	59	3	0
		Gogebic County	11	1	6	0	4	31	8	23	0	0
		Grand Traverse County	22	0	9	1	12	199	46	143	10	0
		Gratiot County	29	0	5	3	21	154	48	91	15	2
		Hillsdale County	23	0	7	0	16	213	64	126	23	4
		Houghton County	23	0	13	0	10	169	48	114	7	1
		Huron County	9	0	4	0	5	94	35	54	5	0
		Ingham County	17	1	11	0	5	93	11	78	4	1
		Ionia County	42	0	14	0	28	305	121	169	15	11
		Iosco County	19	0	4	0	15	272	113	149	10	8
		Iron County	10	0	2	0	8	55	24	30	1	1
		Isabella County	23	0	14	1	8	300	137	149	14	0
		Jackson County	82	0	23	2	57	419	128	256	35	3
		Kalamazoo County	6	0	6	0	0	34	10	21	3	1
		Kalkaska County	10	0	4	0	6	91	35	49	7	1
		Kent County	11	0	9	0	2	42	1	37	4	0
		Lake County	11	0	7	0	4	14	7	6	1	0
		Lapeer County	33	0	14	0	19	113	39	65	9	4
		Leelanau County	3	0	1	0	2	5	1	4	0	0
		Lenawee County	16	0	8	0	8	169	54	104	11	4
		Livingston County	40	3	12	3	22	417	84	308	25	9
		Luce County	14	1	6	0	7	67	35	27	5	1
		Mackinac County	18	0	3	1	14	109	46	55	8	2

[1] The FBI does not publish arson data unless it receives data from either the agency or the state for all 12 months of the calendar year.

Table 11. Offenses Known to Law Enforcement, by State and Other Agencies, 2007 *(Contd.)*

(Number.)

State	State/Other Agency	Unit/Office	Violent crime	Murder and non-negligent man-slaughter	Forcible rape	Robbery	Aggra-vated assault	Property crime	Burglary	Larceny-theft	Motor vehicle theft	Arson[1]
		Macomb County	20	1	12	0	7	40	9	28	3	1
		Manistee County	10	0	4	0	6	197	56	135	6	1
		Marquette County	43	0	21	1	21	330	136	179	15	2
		Mason County	15	0	10	0	5	66	21	39	6	0
		Mecosta County	10	0	7	0	3	105	33	68	4	1
		Menominee County	11	0	4	0	7	104	41	54	9	0
		Midland County	11	0	6	0	5	34	12	21	1	0
		Missaukee County	8	0	5	0	3	40	13	23	4	0
		Monroe County	31	0	7	6	18	226	57	138	31	3
		Montcalm County	40	1	24	0	15	256	86	156	14	4
		Montmorency County	4	0	3	0	1	24	3	21	0	0
		Muskegon County	45	0	22	1	22	401	110	263	28	3
		Newaygo County	43	1	16	0	26	388	128	231	29	3
		Oakland County	56	1	9	4	42	324	95	197	32	2
		Oceana County	19	0	10	0	9	112	37	70	5	1
		Ogemaw County	26	0	10	2	14	167	60	95	12	4
		Ontonagon County	3	0	0	0	3	25	9	16	0	0
		Osceola County	28	1	13	1	13	191	81	96	14	0
		Oscoda County	9	0	7	0	2	17	5	10	2	0
		Otsego County	24	0	12	0	12	205	64	131	10	5
		Ottawa County	7	0	3	0	4	44	7	37	0	1
		Presque Isle County	2	0	1	0	1	11	4	7	0	0
		Roscommon County	13	1	5	2	5	166	65	96	5	1
		Saginaw County	39	0	10	4	25	254	70	156	28	3
		Sanilac County	36	0	14	1	21	200	88	94	18	3
		Schoolcraft County	11	0	5	0	6	72	34	34	4	2
		Shiawassee County	25	0	17	0	8	156	45	98	13	1
		St. Clair County	46	0	12	2	32	242	83	124	35	5
		St. Joseph County	41	0	16	3	22	241	90	127	24	0
		Tuscola County	40	0	17	1	22	220	90	109	21	1
		Van Buren County	70	2	18	4	46	516	212	248	56	13
		Washtenaw County	52	0	12	1	39	265	99	136	30	5
		Wayne County	46	1	7	4	34	128	13	65	50	1
		Wexford County	20	0	11	0	9	170	37	130	3	1
MICHIGAN- **Other Agencies**	Bishop International Airport.		0	0	0	0	0	23	1	4	18	0
	Wayne County Airport		13	0	0	0	13	369	4	299	66	0
MINNESOTA- **State Agencies[3]**	Capitol Security	St. Paul		0		1	0	23	0	23	0	0
	Minnesota State Patrol			0		0	0	0	0	0	0	0
	State Patrol:	Brainerd		0		0	0	1	0	0	1	0
		Detroit Lakes		0		0	0	0	0	0	0	0
		Duluth		0		0	0	0	0	0	0	0
		Golden Valley		0		0	0	0	0	0	0	0
		Mankato		0		0	0	0	0	0	0	0
		Marshall		0		0	0	0	0	0	0	0
		Oakdale		0		0	0	0	0	0	0	0
		Rochester		0		0	0	0	0	0	0	0
		St. Cloud		0		0	0	0	0	0	0	0
		Thief River Falls		0		0	0	0	0	0	0	0
		Virginia		0		0	0	0	0	0	0	0
MINNESOTA- **Other Agencies[3]**	Minneapolis-St. Paul International Airport			0		0	0	0	0	0	0	0
	Three Rivers Park District			0		0	1	195	6	189	0	0
MISSOURI- **State Agencies**	Capitol Police..........................		5	0	0	0	5	83	4	79	0	0
	Department of Conservation..........................		1	0	0	0	1	0	0	0	0	0
	Division of Alcohol and Tobacco Control		0	0	0	0	0	0	0	0	0	0
	Gaming Commission...............	Enforcement Division	9	0	0	0	9	328	0	327	1	0
	State Fire Marshal		0	0	0	0	0	0	0	0	0	0
	State Highway Patrol:	Jefferson City	7	0	0	0	7	11	1	5	5	
		Kirkwood	5	0	1	0	4	10	1	6	3	0
		Lee's Summit	13	0	1	0	12	27	1	14	12	0
		Macon	7	0	2	0	5	17	4	7	6	0
		Poplar Bluff	6	1	0	0	5	18	1	9	8	0
		Rolla	4	0	0	1	3	5	0	1	4	0
		Springfield	4	0	0	0	4	7	0	3	4	0
		St. Joseph	10	0	0	2	8	14	2	6	6	0
		Willow Springs	1	0	0	0	1	3	0	1	2	0

[1] The FBI does not publish arson data unless it receives data from either the agency or the state for all 12 months of the calendar year.
[3] The data collection methodology for the offense of forcible rape used by the Minnesota state UCR Program does not comply with national UCR Program guidelines. Consequently, their figures for forcible rape and violent crime (of which forcible rape is a part) are not published in this table.

Table 11. Offenses Known to Law Enforcement, by State and Other Agencies, 2007 *(Contd.)*

(Number.)

State	State/Other Agency	Unit/Office	Violent crime	Murder and non-negligent man-slaughter	Forcible rape	Robbery	Aggra-vated assault	Property crime	Burglary	Larceny-theft	Motor vehicle theft	Arson[1]
	State Park Rangers................		3	0	0	0	3	102	9	85	8	4
	State Water Patrol		10	0	1	0	9	225	1	223	1	0
MISSOURI- **Other Agencies**	Bootheel Drug Task Force		0	0	0	0	0	0	0	0	0	0
	Clay County Drug Task Force		1	0	0	0	1	0	0	0	0	1
	Clay County Park Authority		0	0	0	0	0	15	3	12	0	1
	Jackson County Drug Task Force		0	0	0	0	0	0	0	0	0	0
	Jackson County Park Rangers.................................		0	0	0	0	0	0	0	0	0	0
	Lambert-St. Louis International Airport		15	0	0	1	14	270	3	266	1	0
	Platte County Multi-Jurisdictional Enforcement Group...		0	0	0	0	0	0	0	0	0	0
	St. Charles County Park Rangers.................................		0	0	0	0	0	0	0	0	0	0
	St. Peters Ranger Division		0	0	0	0	0	56	2	54	0	0
NEBRASKA- **State Agencies**	Nebraska State Patrol............		8	0	0	0	8	0	0	0	0	0
	State Patrol:..........................	Adams County	4	0	3	0	1	4	1	0	3	0
		Antelope County	0	0	0	0	0	0	0	0	0	0
		Arthur County	0	0	0	0	0	0	0	0	0	0
		Banner County	1	0	0	0	1	0	0	0	0	0
		Blaine County	0	0	0	0	0	2	1	1	0	0
		Boone County	0	0	0	0	0	0	0	0	0	0
		Box Butte County	0	0	0	0	0	0	0	0	0	0
		Boyd County	0	0	0	0	0	0	0	0	0	0
		Brown County	0	0	0	0	0	0	0	0	0	0
		Buffalo County	1	0	0	0	1	4	1	2	1	0
		Burt County	0	0	0	0	0	0	0	0	0	0
		Butler County	0	0	0	0	0	2	0	2	0	0
		Cass County	2	0	0	0	2	2	0	2	0	0
		Cedar County	1	0	0	0	1	0	0	0	0	0
		Chase County	0	0	0	0	0	0	0	0	0	0
		Cherry County	1	0	0	0	1	0	0	0	0	0
		Cheyenne County	0	0	0	0	0	0	0	0	0	0
		Clay County	0	0	0	0	0	0	0	0	0	0
		Colfax County	0	0	0	0	0	0	0	0	0	0
		Cuming County	0	0	0	0	0	0	0	0	0	0
		Custer County	1	0	0	0	1	1	0	1	0	0
		Dakota County	0	0	0	0	0	0	0	0	0	0
		Dawes County	0	0	0	0	0	0	0	0	0	0
		Dawson County	0	0	0	0	0	1	0	1	0	0
		Deuel County	0	0	0	0	0	0	0	0	0	0
		Dixon County	1	0	1	0	0	0	0	0	0	0
		Dodge County	0	0	0	0	0	0	0	0	0	0
		Douglas County	0	0	0	0	0	7	0	3	4	0
		Dundy County	0	0	0	0	0	1	1	0	0	0
		Fillmore County	0	0	0	0	0	0	0	0	0	0
		Franklin County	0	0	0	0	0	0	0	0	0	0
		Frontier County	0	0	0	0	0	0	0	0	0	0
		Furnas County	0	0	0	0	0	0	0	0	0	0
		Gage County	0	0	0	0	0	0	0	0	0	0
		Garden County	0	0	0	0	0	0	0	0	0	0
		Garfield County	0	0	0	0	0	0	0	0	0	0
		Gosper County	0	0	0	0	0	0	0	0	0	0
		Grant County	0	0	0	0	0	1	1	0	0	0
		Greeley County	1	0	0	0	1	2	1	0	1	0
		Hall County	4	0	0	1	3	4	0	1	3	0
		Hamilton County	0	0	0	0	0	0	0	0	0	0
		Harlan County	1	0	0	0	1	0	0	0	0	0
		Hayes County	0	0	0	0	0	0	0	0	0	0
		Hitchcock County	2	0	0	0	2	0	0	0	0	0
		Holt County	0	0	0	0	0	1	1	0	0	0
		Hooker County	0	0	0	0	0	0	0	0	0	0
		Howard County	0	0	0	0	0	0	0	0	0	0
		Jefferson County	0	0	0	0	0	0	0	0	0	0
		Johnson County	0	0	0	0	0	0	0	0	0	0
		Kearney County	0	0	0	0	0	0	0	0	0	0
		Keith County	1	0	0	0	1	0	0	0	0	0

[1] The FBI does not publish arson data unless it receives data from either the agency or the state for all 12 months of the calendar year.

Table 11.   Offenses Known to Law Enforcement, by State and Other Agencies, 2007 *(Contd.)*

(Number.)

State	State/Other Agency	Unit/Office	Violent crime	Murder and non-negligent man-slaughter	Forcible rape	Robbery	Aggra-vated assault	Property crime	Burglary	Larceny-theft	Motor vehicle theft	Arson[1]
		Keya Paha County	0	0	0	0	0	0	0	0	0	0
		Kimball County	0	0	0	0	0	1	1	0	0	0
		Knox County	0	0	0	0	0	0	0	0	0	0
		Lancaster County	1	0	0	0	1	1	0	1	0	0
		Lincoln County	1	0	0	0	1	1	1	0	0	0
		Logan County	1	0	0	0	1	3	3	0	0	0
		Loup County	0	0	0	0	0	0	0	0	0	0
		Madison County	3	0	0	0	3	3	0	3	0	0
		McPherson County	0	0	0	0	0	1	0	1	0	0
		Merrick County	1	0	1	0	0	1	0	0	1	0
		Morrill County	0	0	0	0	0	0	0	0	0	0
		Nance County	0	0	0	0	0	0	0	0	0	0
		Nemaha County	4	0	4	0	0	0	0	0	0	0
		Nuckolls County	0	0	0	0	0	0	0	0	0	0
		Otoe County	0	0	0	0	0	0	0	0	0	0
		Pawnee County	0	0	0	0	0	0	0	0	0	0
		Perkins County	0	0	0	0	0	0	0	0	0	0
		Phelps County	1	0	1	0	0	0	0	0	0	0
		Pierce County	0	0	0	0	0	2	1	0	1	0
		Platte County	0	0	0	0	0	1	0	1	0	0
		Polk County	0	0	0	0	0	1	1	0	0	0
		Red Willow County	0	0	0	0	0	0	0	0	0	0
		Richardson County	0	0	0	0	0	0	0	0	0	0
		Rock County	0	0	0	0	0	0	0	0	0	0
		Saline County	0	0	0	0	0	0	0	0	0	0
		Sarpy County	1	0	0	0	1	2	0	1	1	0
		Saunders County	0	0	0	0	0	0	0	0	0	0
		Scotts Bluff County	2	0	1	0	1	5	2	3	0	0
		Seward County	0	0	0	0	0	0	0	0	0	0
		Sheridan County	2	0	1	0	1	0	0	0	0	0
		Sherman County	0	0	0	0	0	4	4	0	0	0
		Sioux County	0	0	0	0	0	1	1	0	0	0
		Stanton County	0	0	0	0	0	0	0	0	0	0
		Thayer County	0	0	0	0	0	0	0	0	0	0
		Thomas County	0	0	0	0	0	0	0	0	0	0
		Thurston County	0	0	0	0	0	0	0	0	0	0
		Valley County	1	0	0	0	1	0	0	0	0	0
		Washington County	0	0	0	0	0	0	0	0	0	0
		Wayne County	1	0	0	0	1	0	0	0	0	0
		Webster County	0	0	0	0	0	0	0	0	0	0
		Wheeler County	0	0	0	0	0	0	0	0	0	0
		York County	0	0	0	0	0	0	0	0	0	0
NEVADA- State Agencies	Taxicab Authority[4]		102	0	0	16	86	98	2	95	1	0
NEVADA- Other Agencies	Clark County School District		115	0	4	41	70	1,244	182	1,004	58	57
	Washoe County School District		7	0	0	0	7	142	9	133	0	14
NEW HAMPSHIRE- State Agencies	Liquor Commission		0	0	0	0	0	8	1	7	0	0
NEW JERSEY- State Agencies	Human Services	Woodland Township	4	0	0	0	4	11	0	11	0	0
	Hunterdon Developmental Center		0	0	0	0	0	13	0	13	0	0
	New Jersey Transit Police		106	0	0	42	64	286	6	267	13	0
	Palisades Interstate Parkway		7	0	0	0	7	3	0	3	0	0
	State Police:	Atlantic County	62	1	0	20	41	1,223	95	1,109	19	3
		Bergen County	5	0	0	2	3	90	3	64	23	0
		Burlington County	43	1	2	5	35	488	113	327	48	29
		Camden County	13	1	0	1	11	47	0	37	10	0
		Cape May County	29	1	0	6	22	371	87	263	21	3
		Cumberland County	94	1	1	14	78	869	258	524	87	11
		Essex County	17	1	0	1	15	51	5	41	5	0
		Gloucester County	4	0	0	0	4	13	0	5	8	1
		Hudson County	7	0	0	3	4	17	0	17	0	0
		Hunterdon County	24	1	0	3	20	221	57	146	18	4
		Mercer County	9	0	1	1	7	116	6	106	4	0
		Middlesex County	17	0	0	7	10	88	0	87	1	0
		Monmouth County	32	0	0	3	29	209	38	159	12	2
		Morris County	11	0	2	0	9	28	6	18	4	1
		Ocean County	12	0	0	0	12	117	13	100	4	2

[1] The FBI does not publish arson data unless it receives data from either the agency or the state for all 12 months of the calendar year.

Table 11. Offenses Known to Law Enforcement, by State and Other Agencies, 2007 *(Contd.)*

(Number.)

State	State/Other Agency	Unit/Office	Violent crime	Murder and non-negligent man-slaughter	Forcible rape	Robbery	Aggra-vated assault	Property crime	Burglary	Larceny-theft	Motor vehicle theft	Arson[1]
		Passaic County	3	0	0	0	3	9	0	9	0	1
		Salem County	52	0	1	8	43	404	124	251	29	14
		Somerset County	3	1	0	0	2	7	1	5	1	0
		Sussex County	44	1	0	4	39	476	112	338	26	1
		Union County	6	0	0	1	5	21	0	19	2	0
		Warren County	15	0	0	2	13	201	41	144	16	1
NEW MEXICO-State Agencies	New Mexico State Police........		212	9	32	23	148	1,221	534	482	205	4
NEW MEXICO-Other Agencies	Acoma Tribal...........................		18	0	0	0	18	20	8	11	1	0
	Laguna Tribal...........................		106	1	12	0	93	70	13	56	1	0
	Taos Pueblo Tribal..................		17	0	0	1	16	9	6	3	0	0
	Zuni Tribal..............................		5	0	4	0	1	43	41	0	2	0
NEW YORK-State Agencies	State Park:...............................	Albany County	0	0	0	0	0	3	0	3	0	0
		Allegany County	0	0	0	0	0	0	0	0	0	0
		Bronx County	0	0	0	0	0	10	0	10	0	0
		Broome County	1	0	0	0	1	6	2	4	0	0
		Cattaraugus County	0	0	0	0	0	8	4	4	0	0
		Cayuga County	0	0	0	0	0	5	0	5	0	0
		Chautauqua County	0	0	0	0	0	4	3	1	0	0
		Chemung County	0	0	0	0	0	2	0	2	0	0
		Chenango County	0	0	0	0	0	0	0	0	0	0
		Clinton County	0	0	0	0	0	2	0	2	0	0
		Cortland County	0	0	0	0	0	0	0	0	0	0
		Delaware County	0	0	0	0	0	0	0	0	0	0
		Erie County	0	0	0	0	0	11	1	10	0	0
		Franklin County	0	0	0	0	0	0	0	0	0	0
		Fulton County	0	0	0	0	0	0	0	0	0	0
		Genesee County	0	0	0	0	0	3	0	3	0	0
		Greene County	0	0	0	0	0	0	0	0	0	0
		Herkimer County	0	0	0	0	0	0	0	0	0	0
		Jefferson County	0	0	0	0	0	17	1	16	0	0
		Kings County	0	0	0	0	0	0	0	0	0	0
		Lewis County	0	0	0	0	0	0	0	0	0	0
		Livingston County	0	0	0	0	0	3	0	3	0	0
		Madison County	0	0	0	0	0	1	0	1	0	0
		Monroe County	1	0	0	0	1	7	0	7	0	0
		Montgomery County	0	0	0	0	0	0	0	0	0	0
		Nassau County	13	0	0	0	13	59	0	57	2	0
		New York County	1	0	0	1	0	67	0	67	0	0
		Niagara County	2	0	0	0	2	40	0	40	0	0
		Oneida County	0	0	0	0	0	7	0	7	0	0
		Onondaga County	0	0	0	0	0	4	0	4	0	0
		Ontario County	0	0	0	0	0	0	0	0	0	0
		Orleans County	0	0	0	0	0	3	0	3	0	0
		Oswego County	0	0	0	0	0	2	1	1	0	0
		Otsego County	0	0	0	0	0	4	0	4	0	0
		Queens County	0	0	0	0	0	1	0	1	0	0
		Rennselaer County	0	0	0	0	0	2	0	2	0	0
		Richmond County	0	0	0	0	0	1	1	0	0	0
		Saratoga County	2	0	0	1	1	32	7	25	0	0
		Schenectady County	0	0	0	0	0	0	0	0	0	0
		Schoharie County	0	0	0	0	0	1	0	1	0	0
		Schuyler County	0	0	0	0	0	2	0	2	0	0
		Seneca County	0	0	0	0	0	7	2	5	0	0
		Steuben County	0	0	0	0	0	1	0	1	0	0
		St. Lawrence County	0	0	0	0	0	15	1	14	0	0
		Suffolk County	7	0	0	1	6	55	6	47	2	1
		Taconic Region	0	0	0	0	0	31	7	24	0	0
		Tioga County	0	0	0	0	0	0	0	0	0	0
		Tompkins County	0	0	0	0	0	6	0	6	0	0
		Washington County	0	0	0	0	0	0	0	0	0	0
		Wayne County	0	0	0	0	0	0	0	0	0	0
		Wyoming County	0	0	0	0	0	5	0	5	0	0
		Yates County	0	0	0	0	0	0	0	0	0	0
	State Police:...........................	Albany County	24	0	3	2	19	153	14	131	8	
		Allegany County	43	1	8	0	34	295	122	165	8	
		Broome County	58	0	16	11	31	621	127	480	14	
		Cattaraugus County	55	0	6	1	48	388	120	263	5	0
		Cayuga County	32	0	4	2	26	309	58	247	4	4
		Chautauqua County	28	0	8	0	20	141	39	94	8	2
		Chemung County	54	0	5	1	48	390	46	334	10	3

[1] The FBI does not publish arson data unless it receives data from either the agency or the state for all 12 months of the calendar year.

Table 11.   Offenses Known to Law Enforcement, by State and Other Agencies, 2007 *(Contd.)*

(Number.)

State	State/Other Agency	Unit/Office	Violent crime	Murder and non-negligent man-slaughter	Forcible rape	Robbery	Aggra-vated assault	Property crime	Burglary	Larceny-theft	Motor vehicle theft	Arson[1]
		Chenango County	24	0	10	0	14	185	87	91	7	
		Clinton County	191	1	16	6	168	975	281	663	31	
		Columbia County	71	1	8	6	56	351	100	241	10	
		Cortland County	23	0	2	1	20	283	30	245	8	
		Delaware County	49	1	7	3	38	282	158	120	4	1
		Dutchess County	126	5	19	8	94	699	183	489	27	
		Erie County	38	0	4	5	29	517	82	421	14	2
		Essex County	67	0	9	1	57	342	100	229	13	
		Franklin County	115	1	11	4	99	407	188	201	18	
		Fulton County	42	1	6	0	35	106	32	73	1	
		Genesee County	25	0	2	0	23	112	14	92	6	
		Greene County	154	1	18	2	133	548	162	367	19	
		Hamilton County	2	0	0	0	2	35	13	22	0	0
		Herkimer County	30	0	4	4	22	211	115	92	4	
		Jefferson County	131	0	33	0	98	533	121	398	14	
		Lewis County	45	0	36	0	9	91	39	47	5	
		Livingston County	12	0	1	0	11	103	15	87	1	
		Madison County	35	2	7	3	23	279	82	190	7	3
		Monroe County	31	0	5	3	23	79	2	77	0	
		Montgomery County	10	0	3	2	5	105	19	83	3	1
		Nassau County	6	0	0	2	4	16	0	11	5	
		New York County	4	0	0	2	2	51	0	51	0	0
		Niagara County	15	0	3	4	8	216	32	177	7	0
		Oneida County	95	0	5	4	86	827	267	538	22	
		Onondaga County	47	0	12	8	27	651	141	488	22	
		Ontario County	15	0	2	2	11	245	45	197	3	0
		Orange County	115	2	21	7	85	856	128	689	39	
		Orleans County	15	0	4	0	11	74	10	60	4	0
		Oswego County	36	0	4	3	29	848	216	619	13	4
		Otsego County	48	1	5	1	41	415	150	258	7	
		Putnam County	17	2	3	2	10	118	20	93	5	
		Rensselaer County	39	0	7	1	31	421	118	290	13	
		Rockland County	22	0	4	0	18	11	1	8	2	0
		Saratoga County	85	0	13	9	63	749	118	612	19	
		Schenectady County	14	0	1	2	11	86	10	71	5	1
		Schoharie County	17	0	3	0	14	167	65	97	5	
		Schuyler County	5	0	2	0	3	23	5	18	0	0
		Seneca County	22	0	3	0	19	121	36	81	4	0
		Steuben County	63	2	24	2	35	443	133	290	20	
		St. Lawrence County	116	0	9	2	105	490	172	303	15	4
		Suffolk County	11	0	0	3	8	33	8	20	5	0
		Sullivan County	111	0	11	3	97	530	139	347	44	
		Tioga County	15	0	1	0	14	158	37	116	5	0
		Tompkins County	29	0	3	1	25	189	39	144	6	
		Ulster County	171	1	23	6	141	389	122	238	29	
		Warren County	32	1	4	0	27	183	26	154	3	1
		Washington County	57	0	12	0	45	284	57	216	11	
		Wayne County	51	0	9	1	41	429	145	269	15	
		Westchester County	110	1	5	13	91	544	67	467	10	
		Wyoming County	12	0	2	0	10	31	13	14	4	
		Yates County	10	0	1	1	8	36	3	33	0	0
NEW YORK-Other Agencies	Board of Water:	Delaware County	0	0	0	0	0	1	1	0	0	0
		Sullivan County	1	0	0	0	1	3	1	2	0	0
		Ulster County	4	0	0	0	4	7	3	4	0	0
		Westchester County	1	0	0	0	1	14	0	14	0	0
	Broome County Special Investigations Task Force		0	0	0	0	0	1	0	1	0	0
	CSX Transportation:	Albany County	0	0	0	0	0	10	1	9	0	0
		Bronx County	0	0	0	0	0	70	0	70	0	0
		Cattaraugus County	0	0	0	0	0	0	0	0	0	0
		Cayuga County	0	0	0	0	0	0	0	0	0	0
		Chautauqua County	0	0	0	0	0	0	0	0	0	0
		Columbia County	0	0	0	0	0	1	0	1	0	0
		Dutchess County	0	0	0	0	0	0	0	0	0	0
		Erie County	0	0	0	0	0	13	0	13	0	0
		Genesee County	0	0	0	0	0	0	0	0	0	0
		Greene County	0	0	0	0	0	0	0	0	0	0
		Herkimer County	0	0	0	0	0	0	0	0	0	0
		Jefferson County	0	0	0	0	0	0	0	0	0	0
		Madison County	0	0	0	0	0	1	0	1	0	0
		Monroe County	0	0	0	0	0	2	0	2	0	1
		Montgomery County	0	0	0	0	0	3	2	1	0	0
		Niagara County	0	0	0	0	0	2	0	2	0	0

[1] The FBI does not publish arson data unless it receives data from either the agency or the state for all 12 months of the calendar year.

Table 11.   Offenses Known to Law Enforcement, by State and Other Agencies, 2007 *(Contd.)*

(Number.)

State	State/Other Agency	Unit/Office	Violent crime	Murder and non-negligent man-slaughter	Forcible rape	Robbery	Aggra-vated assault	Property crime	Burglary	Larceny-theft	Motor vehicle theft	Arson[1]
		Oneida County	0	0	0	0	0	0	0	0	0	0
		Onondaga County	0	0	0	0	0	5	0	5	0	0
		Ontario County	0	0	0	0	0	0	0	0	0	0
		Orange County	0	0	0	0	0	0	0	0	0	0
		Orleans County	0	0	0	0	0	0	0	0	0	0
		Oswego County	0	0	0	0	0	0	0	0	0	0
		Queens County	0	0	0	0	0	0	0	0	0	0
		Rensselaer County	0	0	0	0	0	1	0	1	0	0
		Rockland County	0	0	0	0	0	1	0	1	0	0
		Seneca County	0	0	0	0	0	0	0	0	0	0
		St. Lawrence County	0	0	0	0	0	2	0	2	0	0
		Ulster County	0	0	0	0	0	0	0	0	0	0
		Wayne County	0	0	0	0	0	2	0	2	0	0
		Westchester County	0	0	0	0	0	1	0	1	0	0
	New York City Metropolitan Transportation Authority........		93	0	0	50	43	591	18	567	6	0
	Onondaga County Parks		4	0	0	0	4	46	8	38	0	0
	Suffolk County Parks..............		2	0	0	0	2	47	2	44	1	1
NORTH CAROLINA- **State Agencies**	Department of Human Resources[2]............................			0	0	0		13	3	10	0	0
	State Capitol Police...............		2	0	0	1	1	41	5	35	1	0
	State Park Rangers:................	Crowders Mountain	1	0	0	1	0	9	3	6	0	0
		Elk Knob	0	0	0	0	0	0	0	0	0	0
		Eno River	0	0	0	0	0	2	0	2	0	0
		Goose Creek	0	0	0	0	0	0	0	0	0	0
		Jones Lake	0	0	0	0	0	0	0	0	0	0
		Merchants Millpond	0	0	0	0	0	0	0	0	0	0
		William B. Umstead	0	0	0	0	0	0	0	0	0	0
NORTH CAROLINA- **Other Agencies**	Raleigh-Durham International Airport		1	0	0	0	1	142	6	132	4	1
	Wilmington International Airport...................................		0	0	0	0	0	10	1	3	6	0
OHIO- **State Agencies**	Ohio Department of Natural Resources..................		0	0	0	0	0	9	0	0	9	0
	Ohio State Highway Patrol.......................................		252	5	17	10	220	423	12	326	85	8
OHIO- **Other Agencies**	Cleveland Metropolitan Park District.............................		7	0	0	4	3	179	1	170	8	2
	Lake Metroparks....................		1	0	0	0	1	18	1	17	0	1
	Port Columbus International Airport		2	0	0	0	2	106	3	101	2	0
OKLAHOMA- **State Agencies**	Capitol Park Police.................		0	0	0	0	0	22	1	20	1	0
OKLAHOMA- **Other Agencies**	Jenks Public Schools		4	0	1	0	3	19	0	19	0	0
	Madill Public Schools.............		0	0	0	0	0	6	0	6	0	0
	McAlester Public Schools		2	0	0	0	2	2	0	2	0	0
	Norman Public Schools		0	0	0	0	0	51	5	46	0	1
	Putnam City Campus..............		0	0	0	0	0	121	1	116	4	3
OREGON- **State Agencies**	State Police:..........................	Baker County	3	0	1	1	1	5	1	3	1	2
		Benton County	7	0	2	1	4	136	31	103	2	2
		Clackamas County	9	0	5	0	4	14	0	10	4	8
		Clatsop County	7	0	0	0	7	5	1	2	2	7
		Columbia County	3	2	0	0	1	16	2	11	3	1
		Coos County	3	0	0	1	2	19	0	13	6	9
		Crook County	1	0	1	0	0	2	0	2	0	1
		Curry County	1	0	0	0	1	9	0	8	1	2
		Deschutes County	4	0	1	1	2	12	3	6	3	5
		Douglas County	3	0	0	0	3	16	0	10	6	9
		Gilliam County	0	0	0	0	0	1	0	1	0	4
		Grant County	0	0	0	0	0	3	2	0	1	3
		Harney County	2	0	0	0	2	1	0	1	0	
		Hood River County	2	0	0	0	2	1	0	1	0	3
		Jackson County	9	0	2	0	7	15	1	9	5	16
		Jefferson County	1	0	0	0	1	13	1	9	3	1

[1] The FBI does not publish arson data unless it receives data from either the agency or the state for all 12 months of the calendar year.

[2] It was determined that the agency did not follow national Uniform Crime Reporting (UCR) Program guidelines for reporting aggravated assault. Consequently, this figure is not included in this table.

Table 11.   Offenses Known to Law Enforcement, by State and Other Agencies, 2007 *(Contd.)*

(Number.)

State	State/Other Agency	Unit/Office	Violent crime	Murder and non-negligent man-slaughter	Forcible rape	Robbery	Aggra-vated assault	Property crime	Burglary	Larceny-theft	Motor vehicle theft	Arson[1]
		Josephine County	6	0	3	0	3	15	4	7	4	8
		Klamath County	21	2	1	0	18	9	1	6	2	8
		Lake County	2	0	0	0	2	3	2	0	1	1
		Lane County	24	0	6	0	18	73	7	54	12	26
		Lincoln County	3	0	1	1	1	8	0	5	3	2
		Linn County	1	0	0	0	1	9	0	4	5	5
		Malheur County	28	0	2	1	25	6	1	3	2	2
		Marion County	102	0	3	1	98	86	5	64	17	12
		Morrow County	2	0	1	0	1	3	0	3	0	
		Multnomah County	7	0	3	0	4	44	0	35	9	5
		Polk County	2	0	0	0	2	4	0	2	2	
		Sherman County	0	0	0	0	0	1	0	1	0	1
		Tillamook County	1	0	0	0	1	15	3	10	2	1
		Umatilla County	27	0	4	1	22	33	7	22	4	12
		Union County	10	0	0	0	10	5	1	3	1	
		Wallowa County	0	0	0	0	0	1	0	0	1	
		Wasco County	4	0	1	0	3	12	2	5	5	7
		Washington County	4	0	0	0	4	4	0	4	0	6
		Wheeler County	0	0	0	0	0	2	0	2	0	
		Yamhill County	2	0	0	1	1	5	0	2	3	
OREGON-												
Other Agencies		Port of Portland	0	0	0	0	0	506	7	448	51	0
		Siletz Tribal	2	0	0	1	1	43	11	27	5	0
PENNSYLVANIA-												
State Agencies	Bureau of Narcotics:	Allegheny County	0	0	0	0	0	0	0	0	0	0
		Bedford County	0	0	0	0	0	0	0	0	0	0
		Blair County	0	0	0	0	0	0	0	0	0	0
		Bradford County	0	0	0	0	0	0	0	0	0	0
		Cambria County	0	0	0	0	0	0	0	0	0	0
		Cameron County	0	0	0	0	0	0	0	0	0	0
		Centre County	0	0	0	0	0	0	0	0	0	0
		Chester County	0	0	0	0	0	0	0	0	0	0
		Clearfield County	0	0	0	0	0	0	0	0	0	0
		Clinton County	0	0	0	0	0	0	0	0	0	0
		Columbia County	0	0	0	0	0	0	0	0	0	0
		Crawford County	0	0	0	0	0	0	0	0	0	0
		Cumberland County	0	0	0	0	0	0	0	0	0	0
		Dauphin County	0	0	0	0	0	0	0	0	0	0
		Delaware County	0	0	0	0	0	0	0	0	0	0
		Elk County	0	0	0	0	0	0	0	0	0	0
		Erie County	0	0	0	0	0	0	0	0	0	0
		Fayette County	0	0	0	0	0	0	0	0	0	0
		Forest County	0	0	0	0	0	0	0	0	0	0
		Greene County	0	0	0	0	0	0	0	0	0	0
		Huntingdon County	0	0	0	0	0	0	0	0	0	0
		Juniata County	0	0	0	0	0	0	0	0	0	0
		Lackawanna County	0	0	0	0	0	0	0	0	0	0
		Luzerne County	0	0	0	0	0	0	0	0	0	0
		Lycoming County	0	0	0	0	0	0	0	0	0	0
		McKean County	0	0	0	0	0	0	0	0	0	0
		Mifflin County	0	0	0	0	0	0	0	0	0	0
		Montour County	0	0	0	0	0	0	0	0	0	0
		Northumberland County	0	0	0	0	0	0	0	0	0	0
		Philadelphia County	0	0	0	0	0	0	0	0	0	0
		Pike County	0	0	0	0	0	0	0	0	0	0
		Potter County	0	0	0	0	0	0	0	0	0	0
		Snyder County	0	0	0	0	0	0	0	0	0	0
		Somerset County	0	0	0	0	0	0	0	0	0	0
		Sullivan County	0	0	0	0	0	0	0	0	0	0
		Susquehanna County	0	0	0	0	0	0	0	0	0	0
		Tioga County	0	0	0	0	0	0	0	0	0	0
		Union County	0	0	0	0	0	0	0	0	0	0
		Venango County	0	0	0	0	0	0	0	0	0	0
		Warren County	0	0	0	0	0	0	0	0	0	0
		Washington County	0	0	0	0	0	0	0	0	0	0
		Wayne County	0	0	0	0	0	0	0	0	0	0
		Westmoreland County	0	0	0	0	0	0	0	0	0	0
		Wyoming County	0	0	0	0	0	0	0	0	0	0
	Department of Environmental Resources		1	0	0	0	1	9	0	9	0	0
	State Capitol Police		1	0	0	0	1	54	2	52	0	0
	State Park Police	Pymatuning	0	0	0	0	0	47	0	47	0	0
	State Police:	Adams County	56	0	23	7	26	604	191	377	36	6
		Allegheny County	102	0	2	0	100	20	7	10	3	0

[1] The FBI does not publish arson data unless it receives data from either the agency or the state for all 12 months of the calendar year.

Table 11. Offenses Known to Law Enforcement, by State and Other Agencies, 2007 *(Contd.)*

(Number.)

State	State/Other Agency	Unit/Office	Violent crime	Murder and non-negligent man-slaughter	Forcible rape	Robbery	Aggra-vated assault	Property crime	Burglary	Larceny-theft	Motor vehicle theft	Arson[1]
		Armstrong County	28	0	4	3	21	518	191	290	37	8
		Beaver County	23	0	1	3	19	215	77	128	10	15
		Bedford County	76	0	9	6	61	682	221	434	27	17
		Berks County	198	5	13	10	170	731	189	472	70	10
		Blair County	41	0	4	3	34	362	102	228	32	8
		Bradford County	41	3	20	0	18	514	179	305	30	12
		Bucks County	56	0	2	4	50	571	94	443	34	7
		Butler County	49	0	12	7	30	755	179	546	30	12
		Cambria County	36	0	3	5	28	314	109	152	53	7
		Cameron County	6	0	1	0	5	90	43	45	2	0
		Carbon County	60	0	2	6	52	345	120	215	10	16
		Centre County	55	1	11	4	39	578	167	380	31	19
		Chester County	157	2	15	30	110	1,456	436	925	95	28
		Clarion County	43	0	12	0	31	516	130	361	25	9
		Clearfield County	45	0	12	3	30	672	233	395	44	11
		Clinton County	74	1	4	5	64	435	90	325	20	7
		Columbia County	20	0	1	1	18	187	70	100	17	2
		Crawford County	35	1	6	3	25	750	296	385	69	7
		Cumberland County	49	0	12	13	24	719	211	469	39	5
		Delaware County	62	1	4	18	39	1,048	95	892	61	4
		Elizabethville	75	2	15	10	48	659	111	492	56	5
		Elk County	6	0	1	1	4	158	53	98	7	7
		Erie County	111	2	26	20	63	1,423	384	982	57	15
		Fayette County	270	7	32	55	176	1,852	558	1,088	206	98
		Franklin County	351	3	23	35	290	1,213	278	866	69	23
		Fulton County	29	1	5	4	19	187	54	120	13	9
		Greene County	26	0	5	9	12	413	134	242	37	9
		Huntingdon County	66	0	15	13	38	403	131	250	22	8
		Indiana County	105	3	18	6	78	1,122	316	754	52	25
		Jefferson County	44	0	15	2	27	290	80	184	26	5
		Juniata County	25	0	10	5	10	186	58	120	8	5
		Lackawanna County	28	0	5	3	20	215	69	128	18	46
		Lancaster County	88	0	21	19	48	973	337	565	71	29
		Lawrence County	41	1	7	9	24	567	140	396	31	75
		Lebanon County	48	0	4	15	29	341	81	242	18	4
		Lehigh County	57	0	11	13	33	775	171	563	41	9
		Luzerne County	261	5	5	25	226	952	250	625	77	22
		Lycoming County	49	2	11	3	33	903	275	585	43	3
		McKean County	10	0	1	1	8	195	85	95	15	1
		Mercer County	37	0	9	5	23	503	156	303	44	15
		Mifflin County	13	2	0	1	10	111	34	75	2	8
		Monroe County	137	0	26	25	86	1,097	410	603	84	15
		Montour County	7	0	2	1	4	79	25	51	3	0
		Northampton County	23	0	3	4	16	296	73	203	20	12
		Northumberland County	108	0	8	4	96	239	62	162	15	1
		Perry County	60	1	18	5	36	596	184	381	31	4
		Philadelphia County	4	0	0	0	4	5	0	5	0	1
		Pike County	84	3	15	9	57	855	332	471	52	20
		Potter County	140	1	123	0	16	201	81	103	17	1
		Schuylkill County	219	2	27	7	183	670	198	402	70	27
		Skippack	100	1	5	4	90	539	157	354	28	20
		Snyder County	33	0	3	2	28	377	73	287	17	2
		Somerset County	93	1	15	0	77	470	135	286	49	6
		Sullivan County	8	0	5	0	3	155	65	85	5	0
		Susquehanna County	43	0	14	4	25	481	138	297	46	8
		Tioga County	24	0	5	2	17	341	148	170	23	5
		Tionesta	27	0	4	0	23	116	58	55	3	0
		Union County	16	0	6	1	9	183	58	115	10	2
		Venango County	28	1	14	1	12	400	149	231	20	13
		Warren County	44	0	13	2	29	280	104	167	9	6
		Washington County	84	4	17	21	42	806	239	481	86	30
		Wayne County	132	1	15	5	111	525	170	316	39	14
		Westmoreland County	179	2	37	39	101	1,615	390	1,093	132	26
		Wyoming County	25	1	5	2	17	324	81	220	23	4
		York County	259	3	23	17	216	676	238	386	52	36
	State Police, Bureau of Criminal Investigation:	Adams County	0	0	0	0	0	0	0	0	0	0
		Allegheny County	1	0	0	0	1	4	0	1	3	0
		Armstrong County	0	0	0	0	0	1	0	1	0	0
		Beaver County	0	0	0	0	0	2	0	1	1	0
		Bedford County	0	0	0	0	0	0	0	0	0	0
		Berks County	0	0	0	0	0	2	0	1	1	0
		Blair County	0	0	0	0	0	3	0	1	2	0

[1] The FBI does not publish arson data unless it receives data from either the agency or the state for all 12 months of the calendar year.

Table 11. Offenses Known to Law Enforcement, by State and Other Agencies, 2007 *(Contd.)*

(Number.)

State	State/Other Agency	Unit/Office	Violent crime	Murder and non-negligent man-slaughter	Forcible rape	Robbery	Aggra-vated assault	Property crime	Burglary	Larceny-theft	Motor vehicle theft	Arson[1]
		Bradford County	0	0	0	0	0	0	0	0	0	0
		Bucks County	0	0	0	0	0	0	0	0	0	0
		Butler County	0	0	0	0	0	1	1	0	0	0
		Cambria County	0	0	0	0	0	1	0	1	0	0
		Cameron County	0	0	0	0	0	0	0	0	0	0
		Carbon County	0	0	0	0	0	0	0	0	0	0
		Centre County	0	0	0	0	0	0	0	0	0	0
		Chester County	0	0	0	0	0	0	0	0	0	0
		Clarion County	0	0	0	0	0	2	0	0	2	0
		Clearfield County	0	0	0	0	0	0	0	0	0	0
		Clinton County	0	0	0	0	0	0	0	0	0	0
		Columbia County	0	0	0	0	0	0	0	0	0	0
		Crawford County	0	0	0	0	0	0	0	0	0	0
		Cumberland County	0	0	0	0	0	0	0	0	0	0
		Dauphin County	0	0	0	0	0	2	0	2	0	0
		Delaware County	0	0	0	0	0	0	0	0	0	0
		Elk County	0	0	0	0	0	0	0	0	0	0
		Erie County	0	0	0	0	0	0	0	0	0	0
		Fayette County	0	0	0	0	0	4	1	3	0	0
		Forest County	0	0	0	0	0	0	0	0	0	0
		Franklin County	0	0	0	0	0	0	0	0	0	0
		Fulton County	0	0	0	0	0	0	0	0	0	0
		Greene County	0	0	0	0	0	1	0	1	0	0
		Huntingdon County	0	0	0	0	0	0	0	0	0	0
		Indiana County	0	0	0	0	0	0	0	0	0	0
		Jefferson County	0	0	0	0	0	0	0	0	0	0
		Juniata County	0	0	0	0	0	0	0	0	0	0
		Lackawanna County	0	0	0	0	0	1	0	0	1	0
		Lancaster County	0	0	0	0	0	0	0	0	0	0
		Lawrence County	0	0	0	0	0	0	0	0	0	0
		Lebanon County	0	0	0	0	0	0	0	0	0	0
		Lehigh County	0	0	0	0	0	0	0	0	0	0
		Luzerne County	1	0	0	0	1	0	0	0	0	0
		Lycoming County	0	0	0	0	0	0	0	0	0	0
		McKean County	0	0	0	0	0	0	0	0	0	0
		Mercer County	0	0	0	0	0	0	0	0	0	0
		Mifflin County	0	0	0	0	0	0	0	0	0	0
		Monroe County	0	0	0	0	0	0	0	0	0	0
		Montgomery County	0	0	0	0	0	0	0	0	0	0
		Montour County	0	0	0	0	0	0	0	0	0	0
		Northampton County	0	0	0	0	0	0	0	0	0	0
		Northumberland County	0	0	0	0	0	0	0	0	0	0
		Perry County	0	0	0	0	0	0	0	0	0	0
		Philadelphia County	0	0	0	0	0	0	0	0	0	0
		Pike County	0	0	0	0	0	2	0	0	2	0
		Potter County	0	0	0	0	0	0	0	0	0	0
		Schuylkill County	0	0	0	0	0	0	0	0	0	0
		Snyder County	0	0	0	0	0	0	0	0	0	0
		Somerset County	0	0	0	0	0	0	0	0	0	0
		Sullivan County	0	0	0	0	0	0	0	0	0	0
		Susquehanna County	0	0	0	0	0	0	0	0	0	0
		Tioga County	0	0	0	0	0	0	0	0	0	0
		Union County	0	0	0	0	0	0	0	0	0	0
		Venango County	0	0	0	0	0	0	0	0	0	0
		Warren County	0	0	0	0	0	0	0	0	0	0
		Washington County	0	0	0	0	0	1	0	1	0	0
		Wayne County	0	0	0	0	0	0	0	0	0	0
		Westmoreland County	0	0	0	0	0	1	1	0	0	0
		Wyoming County	0	0	0	0	0	0	0	0	0	0
		York County	0	0	0	0	0	0	0	0	0	0
PENNSYLVANIA- Other Agencies	Allegheny County Port Authority		66	0	0	37	29	111	5	97	9	0
	Allegheny County District Attorney	Criminal Investigation Division	8	0	0	3	5	39	0	39	0	0
	County Detective:	Berks County	5	0	1	0	4	0	0	0	0	0
		Bucks County	3	0	0	0	3	15	0	15	0	1
		Butler County	2	0	0	0	2	0	0	0	0	0
		Chester County	18	0	12	0	6	7	0	7	0	0
		Clinton County	0	0	0	0	0	0	0	0	0	0
		Dauphin County	35	0	2	0	33	45	0	45	0	0
		Lebanon County	23	0	16	0	7	3	0	3	0	0
		Lehigh County	0	0	0	0	0	0	0	0	0	0
		Pike County	0	0	0	0	0	9	0	8	1	0

[1] The FBI does not publish arson data unless it receives data from either the agency or the state for all 12 months of the calendar year.

Table 11. Offenses Known to Law Enforcement, by State and Other Agencies, 2007 *(Contd.)*
(Number.)

State	State/Other Agency	Unit/Office	Violent crime	Murder and non-negligent man-slaughter	Forcible rape	Robbery	Aggra-vated assault	Property crime	Burglary	Larceny-theft	Motor vehicle theft	Arson[1]
		Westmoreland County	4	0	0	0	4	97	0	97	0	0
		York County	3	0	1	0	2	30	0	11	19	0
	Delaware County District Attorney	Criminal Investigation Division	21	0	4	0	17	3	0	2	1	0
	Delaware County Park		8	0	1	1	6	131	1	128	2	0
	Harrisburg International Airport..................................		0	0	0	0	0	24	0	17	7	0
	Tyrone Area School District		0	0	0	0	0	1	0	0	1	0
	Washington County Alternative Education		0	0	0	0	0	0	0	0	0	0
	Wilkes-Barre Area School District		0	0	0	0	0	2	0	2	0	0
RHODE ISLAND-State Agencies	Department of Environmental Management		2	1	0	0	1	24	1	21	2	1
	Rhode Island State Police Headquarters		11	1	5	0	5	37	3	27	7	0
	State Police:............................	Chepachet	5	1	2	0	2	25	2	18	5	0
		Hope Valley	8	0	2	0	6	118	35	75	8	0
		Lincoln	13	0	5	2	6	76	3	38	35	1
		Portsmouth	0	0	0	0	0	5	1	3	1	0
		Wickford	5	0	3	1	1	25	0	23	2	0
SOUTH CAROLINA-State Agencies	Bureau of Protective Services..............................		2	0	0	2	0	52	1	50	1	0
	Department of Disabilities and Special Needs		0	0	0	0	0	0	0	0	0	0
	Department of Mental Health		0	0	0	0	0	2	0	2	0	0
	Department of Natural Resources:	Abbeville County	0	0	0	0	0	0	0	0	0	0
		Aiken County	0	0	0	0	0	0	0	0	0	0
		Allendale County	0	0	0	0	0	0	0	0	0	0
		Anderson County	0	0	0	0	0	0	0	0	0	0
		Bamberg County	0	0	0	0	0	0	0	0	0	0
		Barnwell County	0	0	0	0	0	0	0	0	0	0
		Beaufort County	0	0	0	0	0	0	0	0	0	0
		Berkeley County	0	0	0	0	0	0	0	0	0	0
		Calhoun County	0	0	0	0	0	0	0	0	0	0
		Charleston County	0	0	0	0	0	0	0	0	0	0
		Cherokee County	0	0	0	0	0	0	0	0	0	0
		Chester County	0	0	0	0	0	0	0	0	0	0
		Chesterfield County	0	0	0	0	0	0	0	0	0	0
		Clarendon County	0	0	0	0	0	0	0	0	0	0
		Colleton County	0	0	0	0	0	0	0	0	0	0
		Darlington County	0	0	0	0	0	0	0	0	0	0
		Dillon County	0	0	0	0	0	0	0	0	0	0
		Dorchester County	0	0	0	0	0	0	0	0	0	0
		Edgefield County	0	0	0	0	0	0	0	0	0	0
		Fairfield County	0	0	0	0	0	0	0	0	0	0
		Florence County	0	0	0	0	0	0	0	0	0	0
		Georgetown County	0	0	0	0	0	0	0	0	0	0
		Greenville County	0	0	0	0	0	0	0	0	0	0
		Greenwood County	0	0	0	0	0	0	0	0	0	0
		Hampton County	0	0	0	0	0	0	0	0	0	0
		Horry County	0	0	0	0	0	0	0	0	0	0
		Jasper County	0	0	0	0	0	0	0	0	0	0
		Kershaw County	0	0	0	0	0	0	0	0	0	0
		Lancaster County	0	0	0	0	0	0	0	0	0	0
		Laurens County	0	0	0	0	0	0	0	0	0	0
		Lee County	0	0	0	0	0	0	0	0	0	0
		Lexington County	0	0	0	0	0	0	0	0	0	0
		Marion County	0	0	0	0	0	0	0	0	0	0
		Marlboro County	0	0	0	0	0	0	0	0	0	0
		McCormick County	0	0	0	0	0	0	0	0	0	0
		Newberry County	0	0	0	0	0	0	0	0	0	0
		Oconee County	0	0	0	0	0	0	0	0	0	0
		Orangeburg County	0	0	0	0	0	0	0	0	0	0
		Pickens County	0	0	0	0	0	0	0	0	0	0

[1] The FBI does not publish arson data unless it receives data from either the agency or the state for all 12 months of the calendar year.

Table 11.   Offenses Known to Law Enforcement, by State and Other Agencies, 2007 *(Contd.)*

(Number.)

State	State/Other Agency	Unit/Office	Violent crime	Murder and non-negligent man-slaughter	Forcible rape	Robbery	Aggra-vated assault	Property crime	Burglary	Larceny-theft	Motor vehicle theft	Arson[1]
		Richland County	0	0	0	0	0	0	0	0	0	0
		Saluda County	0	0	0	0	0	0	0	0	0	0
		Spartanburg County	0	0	0	0	0	0	0	0	0	0
		Sumter County	0	0	0	0	0	0	0	0	0	0
		Union County	0	0	0	0	0	0	0	0	0	0
		Williamsburg County	0	0	0	0	0	0	0	0	0	0
		York County	0	0	0	0	0	0	0	0	0	0
	Employment Security Commission............................		0	0	0	0	0	1	0	1	0	0
	Forestry Commission:	Abbeville County	0	0	0	0	0	0	0	0	0	0
		Aiken County	0	0	0	0	0	0	0	0	0	13
		Allendale County	0	0	0	0	0	0	0	0	0	6
		Anderson County	0	0	0	0	0	0	0	0	0	8
		Bamberg County	0	0	0	0	0	0	0	0	0	5
		Barnwell County	0	0	0	0	0	0	0	0	0	9
		Beaufort County	0	0	0	0	0	0	0	0	0	12
		Berkeley County	0	0	0	0	0	0	0	0	0	65
		Calhoun County	0	0	0	0	0	0	0	0	0	0
		Charleston County	0	0	0	0	0	2	0	2	0	14
		Cherokee County	0	0	0	0	0	0	0	0	0	0
		Chester County	0	0	0	0	0	0	0	0	0	0
		Chesterfield County	0	0	0	0	0	4	0	4	0	16
		Clarendon County	0	0	0	0	0	1	0	1	0	25
		Colleton County	0	0	0	0	0	0	0	0	0	19
		Darlington County	0	0	0	0	0	2	0	2	0	1
		Dillon County	0	0	0	0	0	2	0	2	0	0
		Dorchester County	0	0	0	0	0	0	0	0	0	11
		Edgefield County	0	0	0	0	0	0	0	0	0	0
		Fairfield County	0	0	0	0	0	2	0	2	0	1
		Florence County	0	0	0	0	0	1	0	1	0	3
		Georgetown County	0	0	0	0	0	0	0	0	0	0
		Greenville County	0	0	0	0	0	0	0	0	0	4
		Greenwood County	0	0	0	0	0	0	0	0	0	0
		Hampton County	0	0	0	0	0	0	0	0	0	16
		Horry County	0	0	0	0	0	2	0	2	0	18
		Jasper County	0	0	0	0	0	0	0	0	0	26
		Kershaw County	0	0	0	0	0	0	0	0	0	4
		Lancaster County	0	0	0	0	0	1	0	1	0	0
		Laurens County	0	0	0	0	0	0	0	0	0	0
		Lee County	0	0	0	0	0	0	0	0	0	0
		Lexington County	0	0	0	0	0	0	0	0	0	2
		Marion County	0	0	0	0	0	0	0	0	0	1
		Marlboro County	0	0	0	0	0	1	0	1	0	2
		McCormick County	0	0	0	0	0	0	0	0	0	0
		Newberry County	0	0	0	0	0	4	0	4	0	0
		Oconee County	0	0	0	0	0	0	0	0	0	2
		Orangeburg County	0	0	0	0	0	5	0	5	0	26
		Pickens County	0	0	0	0	0	1	0	1	0	2
		Richland County	0	0	0	0	0	1	0	1	0	3
		Saluda County	0	0	0	0	0	0	0	0	0	0
		Spartanburg County	0	0	0	0	0	0	0	0	0	1
		Sumter County	0	0	0	0	0	2	0	2	0	9
		Union County	0	0	0	0	0	0	0	0	0	0
		Williamsburg County	0	0	0	0	0	1	0	1	0	111
		York County	0	0	0	0	0	0	0	0	0	0
	Highway Patrol:......................	Abbeville County	0	0	0	0	0	0	0	0	0	0
		Aiken County	0	0	0	0	0	0	0	0	0	0
		Allendale County	0	0	0	0	0	0	0	0	0	0
		Anderson County	1	0	0	0	1	9	0	4	5	0
		Bamberg County	0	0	0	0	0	0	0	0	0	0
		Barnwell County	0	0	0	0	0	0	0	0	0	0
		Beaufort County	0	0	0	0	0	0	0	0	0	0
		Berkeley County	1	0	0	0	1	0	0	0	0	0
		Calhoun County	0	0	0	0	0	0	0	0	0	0
		Charleston County	0	0	0	0	0	0	0	0	0	0
		Cherokee County	0	0	0	0	0	0	0	0	0	0
		Chester County	0	0	0	0	0	0	0	0	0	0
		Chesterfield County	0	0	0	0	0	0	0	0	0	0
		Clarendon County	0	0	0	0	0	0	0	0	0	0
		Colleton County	0	0	0	0	0	0	0	0	0	0
		Darlington County	0	0	0	0	0	0	0	0	0	0
		Dillon County	0	0	0	0	0	0	0	0	0	0
		Dorchester County	1	0	0	0	1	1	0	0	1	0
		Edgefield County	0	0	0	0	0	0	0	0	0	0

[1] The FBI does not publish arson data unless it receives data from either the agency or the state for all 12 months of the calendar year.

Table 11. Offenses Known to Law Enforcement, by State and Other Agencies, 2007 *(Contd.)*

(Number.)

State	State/Other Agency	Unit/Office	Violent crime	Murder and non-negligent man-slaughter	Forcible rape	Robbery	Aggra-vated assault	Property crime	Burglary	Larceny-theft	Motor vehicle theft	Arson[1]
		Fairfield County	0	0	0	0	0	2	0	0	2	0
		Florence County	0	0	0	0	0	0	0	0	0	0
		Georgetown County	0	0	0	0	0	1	0	0	1	0
		Greenville County	4	0	0	0	4	2	0	1	1	0
		Greenwood County	0	0	0	0	0	0	0	0	0	0
		Hampton County	0	0	0	0	0	0	0	0	0	0
		Horry County	1	0	0	0	1	0	0	0	0	0
		Jasper County	0	0	0	0	0	0	0	0	0	0
		Kershaw County	0	0	0	0	0	0	0	0	0	0
		Lancaster County	0	0	0	0	0	1	0	1	0	0
		Laurens County	0	0	0	0	0	1	0	1	0	0
		Lee County	0	0	0	0	0	0	0	0	0	0
		Lexington County	1	0	0	0	1	1	0	0	1	0
		Marion County	0	0	0	0	0	0	0	0	0	0
		Marlboro County	0	0	0	0	0	0	0	0	0	0
		McCormick County	0	0	0	0	0	0	0	0	0	0
		Newberry County	0	0	0	0	0	1	0	0	1	0
		Oconee County	0	0	0	0	0	1	0	1	0	0
		Orangeburg County	0	0	0	0	0	2	0	0	2	0
		Pickens County	0	0	0	0	0	0	0	0	0	0
		Richland County	0	0	0	0	0	1	0	0	1	0
		Saluda County	0	0	0	0	0	0	0	0	0	0
		Spartanburg County	0	0	0	0	0	1	0	1	0	0
		Sumter County	0	0	0	0	0	1	0	1	0	0
		Union County	0	0	0	0	0	0	0	0	0	0
		Williamsburg County	0	0	0	0	0	0	0	0	0	0
		York County	0	0	0	0	0	1	0	1	0	0
	South Carolina Law Enforcement Division Vehicle Crimes.........................		0	0	0	0	0	0	0	0	0	0
	South Carolina Law Enforcement Division Vice:	Abbeville County	0	0	0	0	0	0	0	0	0	0
		Aiken County	0	0	0	0	0	1	0	1	0	0
		Allendale County	0	0	0	0	0	0	0	0	0	0
		Anderson County	0	0	0	0	0	0	0	0	0	0
		Bamberg County	0	0	0	0	0	0	0	0	0	0
		Barnwell County	0	0	0	0	0	0	0	0	0	0
		Beaufort County	0	0	0	0	0	0	0	0	0	0
		Berkeley County	0	0	0	0	0	0	0	0	0	0
		Calhoun County	0	0	0	0	0	0	0	0	0	0
		Charleston County	0	0	0	0	0	0	0	0	0	0
		Cherokee County	0	0	0	0	0	0	0	0	0	0
		Chester County	0	0	0	0	0	0	0	0	0	0
		Chesterfield County	0	0	0	0	0	0	0	0	0	0
		Clarendon County	0	0	0	0	0	0	0	0	0	0
		Colleton County	0	0	0	0	0	0	0	0	0	0
		Darlington County	0	0	0	0	0	0	0	0	0	0
		Dillon County	0	0	0	0	0	0	0	0	0	0
		Dorchester County	0	0	0	0	0	0	0	0	0	0
		Edgefield County	0	0	0	0	0	0	0	0	0	0
		Fairfield County	0	0	0	0	0	0	0	0	0	0
		Florence County	0	0	0	0	0	0	0	0	0	0
		Georgetown County	0	0	0	0	0	0	0	0	0	0
		Greenville County	0	0	0	0	0	0	0	0	0	0
		Greenwood County	0	0	0	0	0	0	0	0	0	0
		Hampton County	0	0	0	0	0	0	0	0	0	0
		Horry County	0	0	0	0	0	0	0	0	0	0
		Jasper County	0	0	0	0	0	0	0	0	0	0
		Kershaw County	0	0	0	0	0	0	0	0	0	0
		Lancaster County	0	0	0	0	0	0	0	0	0	0
		Laurens County	0	0	0	0	0	0	0	0	0	0
		Lee County	0	0	0	0	0	0	0	0	0	0
		Lexington County	0	0	0	0	0	0	0	0	0	0
		Marion County	0	0	0	0	0	0	0	0	0	0
		Marlboro County	0	0	0	0	0	0	0	0	0	0
		McCormick County	0	0	0	0	0	0	0	0	0	0
		Newberry County	0	0	0	0	0	0	0	0	0	0
		Oconee County	0	0	0	0	0	0	0	0	0	0
		Orangeburg County	0	0	0	0	0	0	0	0	0	0
		Pickens County	0	0	0	0	0	0	0	0	0	0
		Richland County	0	0	0	0	0	0	0	0	0	0
		Saluda County	0	0	0	0	0	0	0	0	0	0

[1] The FBI does not publish arson data unless it receives data from either the agency or the state for all 12 months of the calendar year.

Table 11. Offenses Known to Law Enforcement, by State and Other Agencies, 2007 *(Contd.)*

(Number.)

State	State/Other Agency	Unit/Office	Violent crime	Murder and non-negligent man-slaughter	Forcible rape	Robbery	Aggra-vated assault	Property crime	Burglary	Larceny-theft	Motor vehicle theft	Arson[1]
		Spartanburg County	0	0	0	0	0	0	0	0	0	0
		Sumter County	0	0	0	0	0	0	0	0	0	0
		Union County	0	0	0	0	0	0	0	0	0	0
		Williamsburg County	0	0	0	0	0	0	0	0	0	0
		York County	0	0	0	0	0	0	0	0	0	0
	South Carolina School for the Deaf and Blind............		0	0	0	0	0	1	0	1	0	0
	State Museum		0	0	0	0	0	0	0	0	0	0
	State Ports Authority..............		0	0	0	0	0	1	0	1	0	0
	State Transport Police:	Aiken County	0	0	0	0	0	0	0	0	0	0
		Allendale County	0	0	0	0	0	0	0	0	0	0
		Anderson County	0	0	0	0	0	0	0	0	0	0
		Bamberg County	0	0	0	0	0	0	0	0	0	0
		Barnwell County	0	0	0	0	0	0	0	0	0	0
		Beaufort County	0	0	0	0	0	0	0	0	0	0
		Berkeley County	0	0	0	0	0	0	0	0	0	0
		Charleston County	0	0	0	0	0	0	0	0	0	0
		Cherokee County	0	0	0	0	0	0	0	0	0	0
		Colleton County	0	0	0	0	0	1	0	1	0	0
		Darlington County	0	0	0	0	0	0	0	0	0	0
		Dillon County	0	0	0	0	0	0	0	0	0	0
		Dorchester County	0	0	0	0	0	0	0	0	0	0
		Edgefield County	0	0	0	0	0	0	0	0	0	0
		Fairfield County	0	0	0	0	0	0	0	0	0	0
		Florence County	0	0	0	0	0	0	0	0	0	0
		Georgetown County	0	0	0	0	0	0	0	0	0	0
		Greenville County	0	0	0	0	0	0	0	0	0	0
		Greenwood County	0	0	0	0	0	0	0	0	0	0
		Horry County	0	0	0	0	0	0	0	0	0	0
		Jasper County	0	0	0	0	0	0	0	0	0	0
		Kershaw County	0	0	0	0	0	0	0	0	0	0
		Laurens County	0	0	0	0	0	0	0	0	0	0
		Lee County	0	0	0	0	0	0	0	0	0	0
		Lexington County	0	0	0	0	0	0	0	0	0	0
		Marion County	0	0	0	0	0	0	0	0	0	0
		Marlboro County	0	0	0	0	0	0	0	0	0	0
		Newberry County	0	0	0	0	0	0	0	0	0	0
		Oconee County	0	0	0	0	0	0	0	0	0	0
		Orangeburg County	0	0	0	0	0	0	0	0	0	0
		Richland County	0	0	0	0	0	1	0	0	1	0
		Spartanburg County	0	0	0	0	0	0	0	0	0	0
		Sumter County	0	0	0	0	0	0	0	0	0	0
		Union County	0	0	0	0	0	0	0	0	0	0
		Williamsburg County	0	0	0	0	0	0	0	0	0	0
		York County	0	0	0	0	0	0	0	0	0	0
SOUTH CAROLINA- Other Agencies	United States Department of Energy................................	Savannah River Plant	0	0	0	0	0	34	0	34	0	0
	Charleston County Aviation Authority		0	0	0	0	0	35	0	18	17	0
	Columbia Metropolitan Airport.....................................		0	0	0	0	0	13	0	10	3	0
	Greenville-Spartanburg International Airport		0	0	0	0	0	12	0	5	7	0
	Whitten Center.......................		5	0	0	0	5	14	0	14	0	0
SOUTH DAKOTA- State Agencies	Division of Criminal Investigation		41	6	14	2	19	24	13	6	5	3
TENNESSEE- State Agencies	Alcoholic Beverage Commission...............................		0	0	0	0	0	0	0	0	0	0
	Department of Correction	Internal Affairs	14	0	0	0	14	3	0	3	0	0
	Department of Safety		2	0	0	0	2	21	0	0	21	0
	State Fire Marshal		0	0	0	0	0	0	0	0	0	28
	State Park Rangers:.................	Bicentennial Capitol Mall	1	0	1	0	0	0	0	0	0	0
		Big Hill Pond	0	0	0	0	0	0	0	0	0	0
		Big Ridge	1	0	0	0	1	1	0	1	0	0
		Bledsoe Creek	0	0	0	0	0	0	0	0	0	0
		Booker T. Washington	0	0	0	0	0	2	0	2	0	0
		Burgess Falls Natural Area	0	0	0	0	0	0	0	0	0	0

[1] The FBI does not publish arson data unless it receives data from either the agency or the state for all 12 months of the calendar year.

Table 11. Offenses Known to Law Enforcement, by State and Other Agencies, 2007 *(Contd.)*

(Number.)

State	State/Other Agency	Unit/Office	Violent crime	Murder and non-negligent man-slaughter	Forcible rape	Robbery	Aggra-vated assault	Property crime	Burglary	Larceny-theft	Motor vehicle theft	Arson[1]
		Cedars of Lebanon	0	0	0	0	0	0	0	0	0	0
		Chickasaw	0	0	0	0	0	0	0	0	0	0
		Cove Lake	0	0	0	0	0	1	0	1	0	0
		Cumberland Mountain	0	0	0	0	0	0	0	0	0	0
		Cumberland Trail	0	0	0	0	0	1	0	1	0	0
		David Crockett	1	0	0	0	1	0	0	0	0	0
		David Crockett Birthplace	0	0	0	0	0	0	0	0	0	0
		Dunbar Cave Natural Area	0	0	0	0	0	0	0	0	0	0
		Edgar Evins	0	0	0	0	0	0	0	0	0	0
		Fall Creek Falls	0	0	0	0	0	2	1	0	1	0
		Fort Loudon State Historic Park	0	0	0	0	0	0	0	0	0	0
		Fort Pillow State Historic Park	0	0	0	0	0	0	0	0	0	0
		Frozen Head Natural Area	0	0	0	0	0	0	0	0	0	0
		Harpeth Scenic Rivers	0	0	0	0	0	0	0	0	0	0
		Harrison Bay	1	0	0	0	1	5	1	4	0	0
		Henry Horton	0	0	0	0	0	2	0	2	0	0
		Hiwassee/Ocoee State Scenic Rivers	0	0	0	0	0	1	0	1	0	0
		Indian Mountain	0	0	0	0	0	2	0	2	0	0
		Johnsonville State Historic Park	0	0	0	0	0	0	0	0	0	0
		Long Hunter	0	0	0	0	0	0	0	0	0	0
		Meeman-Shelby Forest	0	0	0	0	0	2	0	2	0	0
		Montgomery Bell	0	0	0	0	0	0	0	0	0	0
		Mousetail Landing	0	0	0	0	0	0	0	0	0	0
		Natchez Trace	0	0	0	0	0	0	0	0	0	0
		Nathan Bedford Forrest	0	0	0	0	0	0	0	0	0	0
		Norris Dam	0	0	0	0	0	2	1	1	0	0
		Old Stone Fort State Archaeological Area	0	0	0	0	0	0	0	0	0	0
		Panther Creek	0	0	0	0	0	0	0	0	0	0
		Paris Landing	0	0	0	0	0	0	0	0	0.	0
		Pickett	0	0	0	0	0	0	0	0	0	0
		Pickwick Landing	0	0	0	0	0	0	0	0	0	0
		Pinson Mounds State Archaeological Park	0	0	0	0	0	0	0	0	0	0
		Radnor Lake Natural Area	0	0	0	0	0	0	0	0	0	0
		Red Clay State Historic Park	0	0	0	0	0	0	0	0	0	0
		Reelfoot Lake	0	0	0	0	0	0	0	0	0	0
		Roan Mountain	0	0	0	0	0	0	0	0	0	0
		Rock Island	0	0	0	0	0	0	0	0	0	0
		Sgt. Alvin C. York	0	0	0	0	0	0	0	0	0	0
		South Cumberland Recreation Area	0	0	0	0	0	2	0	1	1	0
		Standing Stone	0	0	0	0	0	0	0	0	0	0
		Sycamore Shoals State Historic Park	0	0	0	0	0	0	0	0	0	0
		Tim's Ford	0	0	0	0	0	0	0	0	0	0
		T.O. Fuller	0	0	0	0	0	0	0	0	0	0
		Warrior's Path	0	0	0	0	0	4	0	4	0	0
	Tennessee Bureau of Investigation............		1	1	0	0	0	2	1	1	0	0
	TennCare Office of Inspector General...................		0	0	0	0	0	0	0	0	0	0
	Tennessee Department of Revenue............................	Special Investigations Unit	1	0	0	0	1	0	0	0	0	0
	Wildlife Resources Agency:...................................	Region 1	0	0	0	0	0	0	0	0	0	0
		Region 2	0	0	0	0	0	0	0	0	0	0
		Region 3	0	0	0	0	0	0	0	0	0	0
		Region 4	5	0	0	0	5	0	0	0	0	0
TENNESSEE-Other Agencies	Chattanooga Metropolitan Airport................................		1	0	0	1	0	4	0	4	0	0
	Dickinson Parks and Recreation..........................		0	0	0	0	0	1	0	1	0	0

[1] The FBI does not publish arson data unless it receives data from either the agency or the state for all 12 months of the calendar year.

Table 11.   Offenses Known to Law Enforcement, by State and Other Agencies, 2007 *(Contd.)*

(Number.)

State	State/Other Agency	Unit/Office	Violent crime	Murder and non-negligent man-slaughter	Forcible rape	Robbery	Aggra-vated assault	Property crime	Burglary	Larceny-theft	Motor vehicle theft	Arson[1]
	Drug Task Force:	1st Judicial District	0	0	0	0	0	0	0	0	0	0
		2nd Judicial District	2	0	0	0	2	0	0	0	0	0
		3rd Judicial District	0	0	0	0	0	0	0	0	0	0
		4th Judicial District	0	0	0	0	0	1	0	1	0	0
		5th Judicial District	0	0	0	0	0	2	1	1	0	0
		8th Judicial District	0	0	0	0	0	2	0	2	0	0
		9th Judicial District	0	0	0	0	0	0	0	0	0	0
		10th Judicial District	0	0	0	0	0	1	0	1	0	0
		12th Judicial District	1	0	0	0	1	0	0	0	0	0
		13th Judicial District	0	0	0	0	0	0	0	0	0	0
		14th Judicial District	0	0	0	0	0	0	0	0	0	0
		15th Judicial District	0	0	0	0	0	0	0	0	0	0
		17th Judicial District	0	0	0	0	0	0	0	0	0	0
		18th Judicial District	0	0	0	0	0	0	0	0	0	0
		19th Judicial District	0	0	0	0	0	0	0	0	0	0
		21st Judicial District	0	0	0	0	0	0	0	0	0	0
		22nd Judicial District	0	0	0	0	0	0	0	0	0	0
		23rd Judicial District	0	0	0	0	0	0	0	0	0	0
		24th Judicial District	0	0	0	0	0	1	0	1	0	0
		27th Judicial District	2	0	0	0	2	0	0	0	0	0
		31st Judicial District	0	0	0	0	0	1	0	1	0	0
	Knoxville Metropolitan Airport..........................		0	0	0	0	0	18	0	17	1	0
	Memphis International Airport..........................		0	0	0	0	0	180	2	168	10	0
	Metropolitan Board of Parks and Recreation..............	Nashville-Davidson	17	0	0	5	12	180	9	164	7	5
	Nashville International Airport..........................		0	0	0	0	0	46	1	41	4	0
	Smyrna/Rutherford County Airport Authority..................		0	0	0	0	0	3	0	3	0	0
	Tri-Cities Regional Airport..........................		0	0	0	0	0	0	0	0	0	0
	West Tennessee Violent Crime Task Force..................		0	0	0	0	0	0	0	0	0	0
TEXAS- **Other Agencies**	Amarillo International Airport..........................		0	0	0	0	0	2	0	2	0	0
	Cameron County Park Rangers......................		1	0	0	0	1	52	8	43	1	0
	Dallas-Fort Worth International Airport..............		3	0	0	2	1	594	16	523	55	0
	Hospital District:....................	Dallas County	6	0	0	5	1	437	5	423	9	0
		Tarrant County	3	0	0	0	3	139	15	121	3	0
	Houston Metropolitan Transit Authority....................		2	0	0	2	0	16	0	14	2	0
	Independent School District:.	Aldine	0	0	0	0	0	145	27	107	11	1
		Alvin	11	0	1	0	10	127	10	117	0	0
		Angleton	2	0	0	0	2	0	0	0	0	0
		Austin	29	0	1	7	21	600	58	535	7	22
		Bay City	1	0	0	0	1	66	7	59	0	0
		Cedar Hill	5	0	1	0	4	34	2	32	0	1
		Conroe	6	0	0	1	5	208	6	199	3	2
		Corpus Christi	38	0	0	6	32	296	39	255	2	9
		East Central	0	0	0	0	0	6	5	1	0	0
		Ector County	25	0	0	1	24	198	28	170	0	0
		El Paso	21	0	0	1	20	428	33	389	6	0
		Fort Bend	60	0	4	7	49	410	18	389	3	6
		Humble	16	0	5	3	8	97	20	77	0	5
		Judson	0	0	0	0	0	10	0	10	0	0
		Katy	5	0	4	0	1	471	14	453	4	1
		Kaufman	0	0	0	0	0	19	1	18	0	0
		Killeen	2	0	0	1	1	107	3	104	0	2
		Klein	5	0	0	2	3	179	11	166	2	1
		Mexia	3	0	1	1	1	19	2	17	0	1
		Midland	0	0	0	0	0	65	4	61	0	0
		North East	3	0	0	0	3	330	7	323	0	0
		Pasadena	5	0	0	2	3	186	17	160	9	0
		Raymondville	0	0	0	0	0	13	2	11	0	0
		Socorro	5	0	0	0	5	137	4	130	3	0
		Spring	52	0	6	1	45	137	5	128	4	2
		Spring Branch	7	0	1	2	4	92	8	84	0	0
		Taft	1	0	0	0	1	7	2	5	0	0
		United	3	0	0	1	2	78	9	68	1	3

[1] The FBI does not publish arson data unless it receives data from either the agency or the state for all 12 months of the calendar year.

Table 11.   Offenses Known to Law Enforcement, by State and Other Agencies, 2007 *(Contd.)*

(Number.)

State	State/Other Agency	Unit/Office	Violent crime	Murder and non-negligent man-slaughter	Forcible rape	Robbery	Aggra-vated assault	Property crime	Burglary	Larceny-theft	Motor vehicle theft	Arson[1]
UTAH- **State Agencies**	Parks and Recreation.............	11	0	1	0	10	56	2	52	2	0	
UTAH- **Other Agencies**	Cache-Rich Drug Task Force		0	0	0	0	0	3	2	1	0	0
	Davis Metropolitan Narcotics Strike Force.............		0	0	0	0	0	0	0	0	0	0
	Granite School District..........		19	0	0	4	15	110	8	96	6	14
	Utah County Attorney	Investigations Division	0	0	0	0	0	0	0	0	0	0
	Utah County Major Crime Task Force		1	0	0	0	1	3	1	2	0	0
	Utah Transit Authority...........		12	0	0	6	6	74	1	73	0	0
VERMONT- **State Agencies**	Attorney General...................		0	0	0	0	0	15	1	14	0	0
	Fish and Wildlife Department............................	Law Enforcement Division	0	0	0	0	0	4	0	4	0	0
	State Police:............................	Bradford	13	0	2	3	8	248	97	125	26	2
		Brattleboro	20	0	3	2	15	153	61	83	9	1
		Derby	14	0	0	0	14	298	123	157	18	0
		Middlesex	14	0	3	2	9	299	129	170	0	2
		New Haven	5	1	1	0	3	312	117	174	21	2
		Rockingham	14	0	3	0	11	201	84	103	14	4
		Royalton	19	0	6	0	13	245	105	115	25	3
		Rutland	22	0	2	4	16	502	198	272	32	6
		Shaftsbury	18	2	2	0	14	177	73	84	20	0
		St. Albans	35	3	6	3	23	629	178	389	62	10
		St. Johnsbury	24	1	3	2	18	311	98	196	17	9
		Williston	14	1	2	1	10	297	100	184	13	6
	Vermont State Police		0	0	0	0	0	0	0	0	0	0
	Vermont State Police Headquarters..........................	Bureau of Criminal Investigations	0	0	0	0	0	2	0	1	1	0
VIRGINIA- **State Agencies**	Alcoholic Beverage Control Commission		0	0	0	0	0	26	1	25	0	0
	Department of Conservation and Recreation.............................		1	0	0	0	1	20	0	19	1	0
	Southside Virginia Training Center.......................		3	0	2	0	1	28	0	28	0	0
	State Police:............................	Accomack County	3	0	2	1	0	14	1	12	1	0
		Alexandria	1	0	0	0	1	2	0	0	2	0
		Alleghany County	0	0	0	0	0	3	0	3	0	0
		Augusta County	0	0	0	0	0	0	0	0	0	4
		Bedford County	2	0	0	0	2	9	2	5	2	0
		Bland County	0	0	0	0	0	9	0	9	0	0
		Botetourt County	1	0	0	0	1	2	0	2	0	0
		Buchanan County	0	0	0	0	0	0	0	0	0	1
		Campbell County	1	1	0	0	0	1	0	1	0	0
		Caroline County	1	0	0	0	1	44	0	23	21	2
		Carroll County	2	0	1	1	0	13	0	9	4	0
		Charles City County	1	0	0	0	1	5	1	3	1	0
		Charlotte County	0	0	0	0	0	2	0	1	1	0
		Chesterfield County	11	0	0	0	11	17	1	10	6	0
		Colonial Heights	0	0	0	0	0	1	0	1	0	0
		Culpeper County	2	0	0	0	2	3	1	1	1	0
		Dinwiddie County	1	0	0	0	1	10	2	3	5	0
		Fairfax County	10	0	0	0	10	34	0	17	17	0
		Fauquier County	1	0	0	0	1	5	0	5	0	0
		Floyd County	1	0	0	0	1	0	0	0	0	0
		Franklin County	0	0	0	0	0	6	0	2	4	0
		Frederick County	1	0	0	0	1	6	0	4	2	0
		Fredericksburg	0	0	0	0	0	0	0	0	0	0
		Giles County	2	0	0	0	2	8	1	5	2	1
		Gloucester County	2	0	0	0	2	3	0	2	1	0
		Goochland County	0	0	0	0	0	3	0	3	0	0
		Grayson County	1	0	0	0	1	3	0	2	1	0
		Greensville County	0	0	0	0	0	3	0	3	0	0
		Halifax County	1	0	0	0	1	5	0	5	0	0
		Hampton	6	0	0	0	6	4	0	3	1	0
		Hanover County	7	0	2	0	5	4	0	3	1	0
		Harrisonburg	0	0	0	0	0	2	0	1	1	0

[1] The FBI does not publish arson data unless it receives data from either the agency or the state for all 12 months of the calendar year.

Table 11.   Offenses Known to Law Enforcement, by State and Other Agencies, 2007 *(Contd.)*

(Number.)

State	State/Other Agency	Unit/Office	Violent crime	Murder and non-negligent man-slaughter	Forcible rape	Robbery	Aggra-vated assault	Property crime	Burglary	Larceny-theft	Motor vehicle theft	Arson[1]
		Henrico County	1	0	0	1	0	14	1	9	4	0
		Henry County	0	0	0	0	0	5	0	3	2	0
		Isle Of Wight County	1	0	0	0	1	1	0	1	0	0
		Lee County	3	0	1	0	2	7	0	3	4	5
		Loudoun County	3	0	0	0	3	11	0	11	0	0
		Louisa County	1	0	0	0	1	3	1	2	0	1
		Lunenburg County	0	0	0	0	0	1	0	1	0	0
		Madison County	0	0	0	0	0	0	0	0	0	0
		Mecklenburg County	2	0	0	0	2	10	1	5	4	0
		Middlesex County	0	0	0	0	0	0	0	0	0	0
		Montgomery County	31	30	0	0	1	12	0	9	3	0
		New Kent County	2	0	0	0	2	1	0	0	1	0
		Newport News	3	0	0	0	3	5	0	3	2	0
		Norfolk	2	0	0	0	2	6	0	5	1	0
		Northampton County	1	1	0	0	0	7	1	4	2	0
		Orange County	2	0	0	0	2	1	0	0	1	1
		Page County	1	0	0	0	1	3	0	3	0	0
		Patrick County	0	0	0	0	0	2	0	0	2	0
		Pittsylvania County	1	0	0	0	1	30	1	5	24	0
		Powhatan County	8	0	0	0	8	4	0	4	0	1
		Prince William County	10	0	0	1	9	15	1	9	5	0
		Pulaski County	3	0	0	0	3	7	0	7	0	1
		Rappahannock County	0	0	0	0	0	0	0	0	0	2
		Richmond	6	1	0	0	5	12	0	10	2	0
		Richmond County	2	0	2	0	0	1	0	1	0	0
		Roanoke	0	0	0	0	0	2	0	2	0	1
		Roanoke County	0	0	0	0	0	2	0	2	0	0
		Rockbridge County	0	0	0	0	0	17	0	17	0	0
		Rockingham County	0	0	0	0	0	14	0	4	10	0
		Russell County	0	0	0	0	0	3	0	2	1	1
		Scott County	0	0	0	0	0	13	0	9	4	1
		Shenandoah County	4	0	0	0	4	6	0	6	0	0
		Smyth County	4	0	0	1	3	23	1	17	5	1
		Southampton County	0	0	0	0	0	1	0	0	1	0
		Spotsylvania County	1	0	1	0	0	3	0	2	1	0
		Stafford County	0	0	0	0	0	1	0	0	1	0
		Surry County	0	0	0	0	0	3	1	1	1	0
		Sussex County	0	0	0	0	0	3	0	3	0	0
		Virginia Beach	1	0	0	0	1	4	0	4	0	0
		Warren County	0	0	0	0	0	4	0	2	2	0
		Washington County	3	1	0	0	2	16	3	9	4	2
		Winchester	1	0	0	0	1	1	0	1	0	0
		Wise County	3	0	0	0	3	7	1	5	1	3
		Wythe County	1	0	0	0	1	33	0	31	2	2
		York County	0	0	0	0	0	0	0	0	0	0
	Virginia State Capitol		0	0	0	0	0	63	2	61	0	0
VIRGINIA- **Other Agencies**	Norfolk Airport Authority		0	0	0	0	0	57	0	57	0	0
	Port Authority	Norfolk	0	0	0	0	0	1	0	1	0	0
	Reagan National Airport		5	0	0	1	4	487	0	359	128	0
	Richmond International Airport		0	0	0	0	0	44	0	34	10	0
WASHINGTON- **Other Agencies**	Lummi Tribal		44	0	5	6	33	261	76	166	19	6
	Nisqually Tribal		4	0	1	0	3	24	8	13	3	0
	Nooksack Tribal		5	0	0	1	4	61	12	48	1	0
	Port of Seattle		18	0	2	6	10	1,030	43	808	179	0
WEST VIRGINIA- **State Agencies**	Department of Natural Resources:	Barbour County	0	0	0	0	0	0	0	0	0	0
		Berkeley County	0	0	0	0	0	0	0	0	0	0
		Boone County	0	0	0	0	0	0	0	0	0	0
		Braxton County	0	0	0	0	0	0	0	0	0	0
		Brooke County	0	0	0	0	0	0	0	0	0	0
		Cabell County	0	0	0	0	0	0	0	0	0	0
		Calhoun County	0	0	0	0	0	0	0	0	0	0
		Clay County	0	0	0	0	0	0	0	0	0	0
		Doddridge County	0	0	0	0	0	0	0	0	0	0
		Fayette County	0	0	0	0	0	0	0	0	0	0
		Gilmer County	0	0	0	0	0	0	0	0	0	0
		Grant County	0	0	0	0	0	0	0	0	0	0
		Greenbrier County	0	0	0	0	0	0	0	0	0	0
		Hampshire County	0	0	0	0	0	0	0	0	0	0
		Hancock County	0	0	0	0	0	0	0	0	0	0

[1] The FBI does not publish arson data unless it receives data from either the agency or the state for all 12 months of the calendar year.

Table 11.   Offenses Known to Law Enforcement, by State and Other Agencies, 2007 *(Contd.)*

(Number.)

State	State/Other Agency	Unit/Office	Violent crime	Murder and non-negligent man-slaughter	Forcible rape	Robbery	Aggra-vated assault	Property crime	Burglary	Larceny-theft	Motor vehicle theft	Arson[1]
		Hardy County	0	0	0	0	0	0	0	0	0	0
		Harrison County	0	0	0	0	0	0	0	0	0	0
		Jackson County	0	0	0	0	0	0	0	0	0	0
		Jefferson County	0	0	0	0	0	0	0	0	0	0
		Kanawha County	0	0	0	0	0	0	0	0	0	0
		Lewis County	0	0	0	0	0	0	0	0	0	0
		Lincoln County	0	0	0	0	0	0	0	0	0	0
		Logan County	0	0	0	0	0	0	0	0	0	0
		Marion County	0	0	0	0	0	0	0	0	0	0
		Marshall County	0	0	0	0	0	0	0	0	0	0
		Mason County	0	0	0	0	0	0	0	0	0	0
		McDowell County	0	0	0	0	0	0	0	0	0	0
		Mercer County	0	0	0	0	0	0	0	0	0	0
		Mineral County	0	0	0	0	0	0	0	0	0	0
		Mingo County	0	0	0	0	0	0	0	0	0	0
		Monongalia County	0	0	0	0	0	0	0	0	0	0
		Monroe County	0	0	0	0	0	0	0	0	0	0
		Morgan County	0	0	0	0	0	0	0	0	0	0
		Nicholas County	0	0	0	0	0	0	0	0	0	0
		Ohio County	0	0	0	0	0	0	0	0	0	0
		Pendleton County	0	0	0	0	0	0	0	0	0	0
		Pleasants County	0	0	0	0	0	0	0	0	0	0
		Pocahontas County	0	0	0	0	0	0	0	0	0	0
		Preston County	0	0	0	0	0	0	0	0	0	0
		Putnam County	0	0	0	0	0	0	0	0	0	0
		Raleigh County	0	0	0	0	0	0	0	0	0	0
		Randolph County	0	0	0	0	0	0	0	0	0	0
		Ritchie County	0	0	0	0	0	0	0	0	0	0
		Roane County	0	0	0	0	0	0	0	0	0	0
		Summers County	0	0	0	0	0	0	0	0	0	0
		Taylor County	0	0	0	0	0	0	0	0	0	0
		Tucker County	0	0	0	0	0	0	0	0	0	0
		Tyler County	0	0	0	0	0	0	0	0	0	0
		Upshur County	0	0	0	0	0	0	0	0	0	0
		Wayne County	0	0	0	0	0	0	0	0	0	0
		Webster County	0	0	0	0	0	0	0	0	0	0
		Wetzel County	0	0	0	0	0	0	0	0	0	0
		Wirt County	0	0	0	0	0	0	0	0	0	0
		Wood County	0	0	0	0	0	0	0	0	0	0
		Wyoming County	0	0	0	0	0	0	0	0	0	0
	State Fire Marshal:	Boone County	0	0	0	0	0	0	0	0	0	1
		Cabell County	0	0	0	0	0	0	0	0	0	5
		Calhoun County	0	0	0	0	0	0	0	0	0	1
		Clay County	0	0	0	0	0	0	0	0	0	1
		Fayette County	0	0	0	0	0	0	0	0	0	2
		Gilmer County	0	0	0	0	0	0	0	0	0	1
		Harrison County	0	0	0	0	0	0	0	0	0	3
		Jackson County	0	0	0	0	0	0	0	0	0	1
		Kanawha County	0	0	0	0	0	0	0	0	0	2
		Logan County	0	0	0	0	0	0	0	0	0	3
		Marshall County	0	0	0	0	0	0	0	0	0	1
		Mason County	0	0	0	0	0	0	0	0	0	1
		McDowell County	0	0	0	0	0	0	0	0	0	1
		Mercer County	0	0	0	0	0	0	0	0	0	3
		Mineral County	0	0	0	0	0	0	0	0	0	4
		Mingo County	0	0	0	0	0	0	0	0	0	1
		Monongalia County	0	0	0	0	0	0	0	0	0	9
		Nicholas County	0	0	0	0	0	0	0	0	0	2
		Pleasants County	0	0	0	0	0	0	0	0	0	1
		Preston County	0	0	0	0	0	0	0	0	0	1
		Raleigh County	0	0	0	0	0	0	0	0	0	3
		Randolph County	0	0	0	0	0	0	0	0	0	2
		Summers County	0	0	0	0	0	0	0	0	0	2
		Taylor County	0	0	0	0	0	0	0	0	0	1
		Wayne County	0	0	0	0	0	0	0	0	0	2
		Webster County	0	0	0	0	0	0	0	0	0	1
		Wyoming County	0	0	0	0	0	0	0	0	0	1
	State Police:	Beckley	35	0	6	0	29	443	161	251	31	0
		Berkeley Springs	7	0	1	1	5	100	29	58	13	1
		Bridgeport	24	0	5	2	17	184	45	122	17	2
		Buckeye	15	1	0	0	14	123	28	94	1	1
		Buckhannon	2	0	0	0	2	100	18	74	8	1
		Clay	6	0	2	1	3	82	28	43	11	3

[1] The FBI does not publish arson data unless it receives data from either the agency or the state for all 12 months of the calendar year.

Table 11. Offenses Known to Law Enforcement, by State and Other Agencies, 2007 *(Contd.)*

(Number.)

State	State/Other Agency	Unit/Office	Violent crime	Murder and non-negligent man-slaughter	Forcible rape	Robbery	Aggra-vated assault	Property crime	Burglary	Larceny-theft	Motor vehicle theft	Arson[1]
		Danville	31	0	0	1	30	265	57	182	26	5
		Elizabeth	12	0	1	0	11	55	19	29	7	1
		Elkins	26	0	2	5	19	257	58	187	12	1
		Fairmont	11	0	2	0	9	168	34	122	12	0
		Franklin	8	0	5	0	3	27	12	14	1	0
		Gauley Bridge	1	0	0	0	1	41	10	28	3	0
		Gilbert	15	0	1	0	14	81	14	60	7	1
		Glenville	7	0	1	0	6	37	11	21	5	0
		Grafton	1	0	0	0	1	13	6	5	2	0
		Grantsville	13	0	1	0	12	76	19	41	16	6
		Hamlin	69	1	7	0	61	292	93	162	37	3
		Harrisville	11	1	1	0	9	82	25	51	6	3
		Hinton	6	0	1	1	4	56	24	26	6	2
		Hundred	5	0	0	0	5	21	6	10	5	1
		Huntington	15	1	3	0	11	793	114	628	51	1
		Jesse	11	0	1	1	9	119	28	82	9	0
		Kearneysville	33	0	1	1	31	313	61	225	27	1
		Keyser	40	0	1	3	36	228	73	134	21	6
		Kingwood	21	2	4	1	14	128	49	71	8	1
		Lewisburg	10	0	1	0	9	100	27	62	11	0
		Logan	113	0	9	20	84	813	224	506	83	10
		Martinsburg	100	2	6	19	73	663	159	450	54	8
		Moorefield	13	3	2	1	7	59	15	40	4	1
		Morgantown	25	0	3	7	15	596	120	441	35	2
		Moundsville	11	0	2	0	9	39	12	25	2	0
		New Cumberland	3	0	2	0	1	18	2	15	1	0
		Oak Hill	6	0	0	0	6	147	47	83	17	0
		Paden City	11	0	1	0	10	46	7	34	5	1
		Parkersburg	13	0	2	0	11	289	53	216	20	1
		Parsons	6	0	0	0	6	43	11	29	3	1
		Petersburg	6	0	3	0	3	30	9	16	5	0
		Philippi	29	0	1	0	28	79	24	43	12	0
		Point Pleasant	7	0	0	0	7	118	39	55	24	1
		Princeton	25	1	2	0	22	421	116	267	38	1
		Quincy	21	0	0	4	17	268	48	192	28	6
		Rainelle	3	0	0	0	3	68	21	41	6	0
		Richwood	9	0	0	0	9	41	14	26	1	0
		Ripley	12	0	3	1	8	67	12	47	8	0
		Romney	18	0	3	0	15	155	55	81	19	2
		South Charleston	42	0	2	5	35	693	91	544	58	0
		Spencer	5	0	0	0	5	30	12	15	3	4
		St. Marys	0	0	0	0	0	14	1	11	2	1
		Summersville	6	0	2	0	4	57	10	40	7	3
		Sutton	25	0	4	1	20	85	16	58	11	1
		Union	13	3	0	0	10	101	37	51	13	1
		Upperglade	47	0	0	3	44	84	27	50	7	0
		Wayne	49	2	1	5	41	393	102	251	40	3
		Welch	5	0	1	0	4	16	1	15	0	0
		Wellsburg	4	0	1	0	3	10	3	7	0	0
		West Union	1	0	0	0	1	19	12	5	2	0
		Weston	6	1	0	0	5	115	12	93	10	0
		Wheeling	8	1	1	2	4	50	12	35	3	0
		Whitesville	9	0	1	1	7	65	20	43	2	1
		Williamson	51	0	2	4	45	240	47	153	40	1
		Winfield	22	0	3	0	19	238	39	175	24	1
	State Police, Bureau of Criminal Investigation:	Beckley	0	0	0	0	0	1	0	1	0	0
		Bluefield	2	1	0	0	1	0	0	0	0	0
	State Police, Parkway Authority:	Fayette County	0	0	0	0	0	2	0	2	0	0
		Kanawha County	0	0	0	0	0	4	0	4	0	0
		Raleigh County	0	0	0	0	0	9	0	9	0	0
WEST VIRGINIA-Other Agencies	Eastern Panhandle Drug and Violent Crime Task Force		0	0	0	0	0	0	0	0	0	0
	Metropolitan Drug Enforcement Network Team...		0	0	0	0	0	0	0	0	0	0
	Ohio Valley Drug and Violent Crime Task Force.......		0	0	0	0	0	0	0	0	0	0

[1] The FBI does not publish arson data unless it receives data from either the agency or the state for all 12 months of the calendar year.

Table 11. Offenses Known to Law Enforcement, by State and Other Agencies, 2007 *(Contd.)*

(Number.)

State	State/Other Agency	Unit/Office	Violent crime	Murder and non-negligent man-slaughter	Forcible rape	Robbery	Aggra-vated assault	Property crime	Burglary	Larceny-theft	Motor vehicle theft	Arson[1]
	Tri-Lateral Drug Enforcement Network Team............................		0	0	0	0	0	0	0	0	0	0
WISCONSIN-State Agencies	Capitol Police...........................		3	0	0	2	1	103	0	102	1	0
	Department of Natural Resources		0	0	0	0	0	0	0	0	0	0
	Wisconsin State Patrol...........		0	0	0	0	0	0	0	0	0	0
WISCONSIN-Other Agencies	Lac du Flambeau Tribal..........		18	0	6	1	11	347	34	272	41	4
	Menominee Tribal		65	1	13	4	47	148	27	81	40	3
	Oneida Tribal		2	0	1	1	0	149	4	138	7	0
PUERTO RICO AND OTHER OUTLYING AREAS	Puerto Rico		8,942	728	97	5,134	2,983	53,937	17,160	28,955	7,822	
FEDERAL AGENCIES	National Institutes of Health.......................................		0	0	0	0	0	112	1	111	0	0
	United States Department of the Interior:........................	Bureau of Indian Affairs	5,342	125	618	257	4,342	35,072	3,950	10,116	21,006	801
		Bureau of Land Management	9	4	2	0	3	391	13	356	22	54
		Bureau of Reclamation	0	0	0	0	0	8	1	4	3	0
		Fish and Wildlife Service	40	3	2	1	34	388	128	233	27	137
		National Park Service	389	9	49	57	274	3,515	348	2,994	173	125

[1] The FBI does not publish arson data unless it receives data from either the agency or the state for all 12 months of the calendar year.

Table 12. Crime Trends, by Population Group, 2006–2007

(Number, percent change.)

Population group	Year	Violent crime	Murder and non-negligent man-slaughter	Forcible rape	Robbery	Aggra-vated assault	Property crime	Burglary	Larceny-theft	Motor vehicle theft	Arson	Number of agencies	2007 estimated population
TOTAL ALL AGENCIES:	2006	1,320,967	15,972	81,741	423,509	799,745	9,131,100	1,994,361	6,013,629	1,123,110	66,480		
	2007	1,305,814	15,707	78,669	422,184	789,254	8,988,919	1,989,593	5,970,603	1,028,723	62,000	13,468	272,223,974
	Percent change	-1.1	-1.7	-3.8	-0.3	-1.3	-1.6	-0.2	-0.7	-8.4	-6.7		
TOTAL CITIES	2006	1,051,216	12,497	60,518	370,093	608,108	7,142,853	1,466,164	4,777,524	899,165	49,029		
	2007	1,037,212	12,227	57,689	367,678	599,618	7,008,738	1,458,141	4,733,001	817,596	45,930	9,527	182,727,571
	Percent change	-1.3	-2.2	-4.7	-0.7	-1.4	-1.9	-0.5	-0.9	-9.1	-6.3		
GROUP I (250,000 and over)	2006	499,515	6,878	20,314	205,368	266,955	2,470,035	521,783	1,504,248	444,004	19,416		
	2007	486,694	6,509	19,097	201,730	259,358	2,412,156	519,248	1,493,204	399,704	18,020	72	54,390,034
	Percent change	-2.6	-5.4	-6.0	-1.8	-2.8	-2.3	-0.5	-0.7	-10.0	-7.2		
1,000,000 and over (Group I subset)	2006	217,074	3,089	6,739	97,212	110,034	933,153	180,151	579,452	173,550	6,832		
	2007	209,002	2,790	6,203	94,385	105,624	923,358	187,272	579,090	156,996	6,343	10	25,220,230
	Percent change	-3.7	-9.7	-8.0	-2.9	-4.0	-1.0	+4.0	-0.1	-9.5	-7.2		
500,000 to 999,999 (Group I subset)	2006	158,661	2,197	7,188	60,655	88,621	871,317	194,906	521,463	154,948	6,803		
	2007	158,406	2,195	6,876	61,177	88,158	850,503	188,743	523,071	138,689	6,231	24	16,012,700
	Percent change	-0.2	-0.1	-4.3	+0.9	-0.5	-2.4	-3.2	+0.3	-10.5	-8.4		
250,000 to 499,999 (Group I subset)	2006	123,780	1,592	6,387	47,501	68,300	665,565	146,726	403,333	115,506	5,781		
	2007	119,286	1,524	6,018	46,168	65,576	638,295	143,233	391,043	104,019	5,446	38	13,157,104
	Percent change	-3.6	-4.3	-5.8	-2.8	-4.0	-4.1	-2.4	-3.0	-9.9	-5.8		
GROUP II (100,000 to 249,999)	2006	172,672	2,128	10,271	61,369	98,904	1,202,994	254,612	791,870	156,512	7,413		
	2007	171,921	2,164	9,822	61,515	98,420	1,180,160	254,933	780,935	144,292	7,280	182	27,358,620
	Percent change	-0.4	+1.7	-4.4	+0.2	-0.5	-1.9	+0.1	-1.4	-7.8	-1.8		
GROUP III (50,000 to 99,999)	2006	139,544	1,400	9,556	44,967	83,621	1,108,140	231,346	753,096	123,698	7,806		
	2007	138,191	1,447	9,128	45,485	82,131	1,085,205	229,805	743,212	112,188	7,015	434	29,826,593
	Percent change	-1.0	+3.4	-4.5	+1.2	-1.8	-2.1	-0.7	-1.3	-9.3	-10.1		
GROUP IV (25,000 to 49,999)	2006	93,956	864	7,487	27,572	58,033	853,125	168,378	609,597	75,150	5,372		
	2007	93,018	875	7,267	27,578	57,298	839,615	166,475	604,540	68,600	5,102	724	24,939,612
	Percent change	-1.0	+1.3	-2.9	*	-1.3	-1.6	-1.1	-0.8	-8.7	-5.0		
GROUP V (10,000 to 24,999)	2006	78,252	712	6,964	19,463	51,113	798,645	157,439	582,080	59,126	4,624		
	2007	80,169	719	6,679	19,998	52,773	794,856	156,745	583,352	54,759	4,435	1,596	25,359,101
	Percent change	+2.4	+1.0	-4.1	+2.7	+3.2	-0.5	-0.4	+0.2	-7.4	-4.1		
GROUP VI (under 10,000)	2006	67,277	515	5,926	11,354	49,482	709,914	132,606	536,633	40,675	4,398		
	2007	67,219	513	5,696	11,372	49,638	696,746	130,935	527,758	38,053	4,078	6,519	20,853,611
	Percent change	-0.1	-0.4	-3.9	+0.2	+0.3	-1.9	-1.3	-1.7	-6.4	-7.3		
METROPOLITAN COUNTIES	2006	217,441	2,651	15,348	49,418	150,024	1,571,524	393,567	987,794	190,163	13,405		
	2007	214,836	2,662	14,952	50,412	146,810	1,562,763	395,802	988,988	177,973	12,230	1,647	64,261,573
	Percent change	-1.2	+0.4	-2.6	+2.0	-2.1	0.6	+0.6	+0.1	-6.4	-8.8		
NONMETROPOLITAN COUNTIES[1]	2006	52,310	824	5,875	3,998	41,613	416,723	134,630	248,311	33,782	4,046		
	2007	53,766	818	6,028	4,094	42,826	417,418	135,650	248,614	33,154	3,840	2,294	25,234,830
	Percent change	+2.8	-0.7	+2.6	+2.4	+2.9	+0.2	+0.8	+0.1	-1.9	-5.1		
SUBURBAN AREA[2]	2006	361,169	3,903	26,748	88,639	241,879	3,059,794	672,929	2,069,505	317,360	22,403		
	2007	359,085	3,891	26,002	90,090	239,102	3,032,594	673,059	2,065,399	294,136	20,632	7,078	113,965,191
	Percent change	-0.6	-0.3	-2.8	+1.6	-1.1	-0.9	*	-0.2	-7.3	-7.9		

[1] Includes state police agencies that report aggregately for the entire state.

[2] Suburban area includes law enforcement agencies in cities with less than 50,000 inhabitants and county law enforcement agencies that are within a Metropolitan Statistical Area. Suburban area excludes all metropolitan agencies associated with a principal city. The agencies associated with suburban areas also appear in other groups within this table.

* = Less than one-tenth of 1 percent.

Table 13. Crime Trends, by Suburban and Nonsuburban Cities[1] by Population Group, 2006–2007

(Number, percent change.)

Population group		Violent crime	Murder and non-negligent man-slaughter	Forcible rape	Robbery	Aggra-vated assault	Property crime	Burglary	Larceny-theft	Motor vehicle theft	Arson	Number of agencies	2007 estimated population
TOTAL SUBURBAN CITIES:.............	2006	143,728	1,252	11,400	39,221	91,855	1,488,270	279,362	1,081,711	127,197	8,998		
	2007	144,249	1,229	11,050	39,678	92,292	1,469,831	277,257	1,076,411	116,163	8,402	5,431	49,703,618
	Percent change	+0.4	-1.8	-3.1	+1.2	+0.5	-1.2	-0.8	-0.5	-8.7	-6.6		
GROUP IV (25,000 to 49,999).................	2006	54,716	506	3,871	17,171	33,168	526,212	101,450	370,540	54,222	3,138		
	2007	54,689	516	3,911	17,372	32,890	521,796	101,046	371,960	48,790	2,999	534	18,132,178
	Percent change	*	+2.0	+1.0	+1.2	-0.8	-0.8	-0.4	+0.4	-10.0	-4.4		
GROUP V (10,000 to 24,999)	2006	50,374	467	4,197	14,036	31,674	522,422	100,794	376,667	44,961	3,119		
	2007	51,559	451	4,045	14,392	32,671	517,543	99,754	376,435	41,354	2,891	1,187	18,983,351
	Percent change	+2.4	-3.4	-3.6	+2.5	+3.1	-0.9	-1.0	-0.1	-8.0	-7.3		
GROUP VI (under 10,000)	2006	38,638	279	3,332	8,014	27,013	439,636	77,118	334,504	28,014	2,741		
	2007	38,001	262	3,094	7,914	26,731	430,492	76,457	328,016	26,019	2,512	3,710	12,588,089
	Percent change	-1.6	-6.1	-7.1	-1.2	-1.0	-2.1	-0.9	-1.9	-7.1	-8.4		
TOTAL NONSUBURBAN CITIES:.....	2006	95,757	839	8,977	19,168	66,773	873,414	179,061	646,599	47,754	5,396		
	2007	96,157	878	8,592	19,270	67,417	861,386	176,898	639,239	45,249	5,213	3,408	21,448,706
	Percent change	+0.4	+4.6	-4.3	+0.5	+1.0	-1.4	-1.2	-1.1	-5.2	-3.4		
GROUP IV (25,000 to 49,999).................	2006	39,240	358	3,616	10,401	24,865	326,913	66,928	239,057	20,928	2,234		
	2007	38,329	359	3,356	10,206	24,408	317,819	65,429	232,580	19,810	2,103	190	6,807,434
	Percent change	-2.3	+0.3	-7.2	-1.9	-1.8	-2.8	-2.2	-2.7	-5.3	-5.9		
GROUP V (10,000 to 24,999)	2006	27,878	245	2,767	5,427	19,439	276,223	56,645	205,413	14,165	1,505		
	2007	28,610	268	2,634	5,606	20,102	277,313	56,991	206,917	13,405	1,544	409	6,375,750
	Percent change	+2.6	+9.4	-4.8	+3.3	+3.4	+0.4	+0.6	+0.7	-5.4	+2.6		
GROUP VI (under 10,000)	2006	28,639	236	2,594	3,340	22,469	270,278	55,488	202,129	12,661	1,657		
	2007	29,218	251	2,602	3,458	22,907	266,254	54,478	199,742	12,034	1,566	2,809	8,265,522
	Percent change	+2.0	+6.4	+0.3	+3.5	+1.9	-1.5	-1.8	-1.2	-5.0	-5.5		

[1] Suburban cities include law enforcement agencies in cities with less than 50,000 inhabitants that are within a Metropolitan Statistical Area. Suburban cities exclude all metropolitan agencies associated with a principal city. Nonsuburban cities include law enforcement agencies in cities with less than 50,000 inhabitants that are not associated with a Metropolitan Statistical Area.

* = Less than one-tenth of 1 percent.

Table 14. Crime Trends, by Metropolitan and Nonmetropolitan Counties[1] by Population Group, 2006–2007

(Number, percent change.)

Population group	Population range		Violent crime	Murder and non-negligent man-slaughter	Forcible rape	Robbery	Aggra-vated assault	Property crime	Burglary	Larceny-theft	Motor vehicle theft	Arson	Number of agencies	2007 estimated population
METROPOLITAN COUNTIES......	100,000 and over	2006	155,300	1,878	9,342	42,110	101,970	1,050,601	251,325	668,294	130,982	8,602		
		2007	152,999	1,838	9,007	43,267	98,887	1,050,740	256,150	671,329	123,261	7,739	146	38,948,161
		Percent change	-1.5	-2.1	-3.6	2.7	-3	*	1.9	0.5	-5.9	-10		
	25,000 to 99,999	2006	45,436	564	4,360	5,050	35,462	390,918	112,733	244,041	34,144	3,004		
		2007	45,719	606	4,443	5,122	35,548	384,357	110,650	241,899	31,808	2,912	413	21,176,497
		Percent change	0.6	7.4	1.9	1.4	0.2	-1.7	-1.8	-0.9	-6.8	-3.1		
	Under 25,000	2006	16,705	209	1,646	2,258	12,592	130,005	29,509	75,459	25,037	1,799		
		2007	16,118	218	1,502	2,023	12,375	127,666	29,002	75,760	22,904	1,579	1,088	4,136,915
		Percent change	-3.5	4.3	-8.7	-10.4	-1.7	-1.8	-1.7	0.4	-8.5	-12.2		
NONMETROPOLITAN COUNTIES......	25,000 and over	2006	22,254	315	2,186	2,065	17,688	187,556	61,657	111,182	14,717	1,556		
		2007	23,237	312	2,374	2,080	18,471	190,268	63,634	111,945	14,689	1,424	278	11,004,275
		Percent change	4.4	-1	8.6	0.7	4.4	1.4	3.2	0.7	-0.2	-8.5		
	10,000 to 24,999	2006	15,781	237	1,532	999	13,013	124,804	40,955	74,167	9,682	1,205		
		2007	16,103	241	1,465	1,035	13,362	125,168	40,646	75,070	9,452	1,112	550	8,888,530
		Percent change	2	1.7	-4.4	3.6	2.7	0.3	-0.8	1.2	-2.4	-7.7		
	Under 10,000	2006	8,542	154	1,306	352	6,730	64,803	19,981	39,157	5,665	949		
		2007	8,630	130	1,362	351	6,787	63,175	19,237	38,553	5,385	981	1,312	3,794,269
		Percent change	1	-15.6	4.3	-0.3	0.8	-2.5	-3.7	-1.5	-4.9	3.4		

[1] Metropolitan counties include sheriffs and county law enforcement agencies associated with a Metropolitan Statistical Area. Nonmetropolitan counties include sheriffs and county law enforcement agencies that are not associated with a Metropolitan Statistical Area. The offenses from state police agencies are not included in this table.

* = Less than one-tenth of 1 percent.

Table 15. Crime Trends, by Population Group, 2006–2007

(Number, percent change.)

Population group		Forcible rape		Robbery				Aggravated assault			
		Rape by force	Assault to rape-attempts	Firearm	Knife or cutting instrument	Other weapon	Strong-arm	Firearm	Knife or cutting instrument	Other weapon	Hands, fists, feet, etc.
TOTAL ALL AGENCIES:	2006	72,555	6,320	153,984	31,798	33,928	146,375	157,679	136,371	250,473	187,341
	2007	70,136	5,980	156,191	30,287	33,391	145,992	153,326	135,389	245,570	186,367
	Percent change	-3.3	-5.4	+1.4	-4.8	-1.6	-0.3	-2.8	-0.7	-2.0	-0.5
TOTAL CITIES	2006	52,948	4,982	130,348	27,399	28,644	127,837	123,469	106,052	183,171	129,519
	2007	50,664	4,706	131,527	26,017	27,942	127,456	120,054	104,917	180,423	127,496
	Percent change	-4.3	-5.5	+0.9	-5.0	-2.5	-0.3	-2.8	-1.1	-1.5	-1.6
GROUP I (250,000 and over)	2006	16,257	2,067	69,825	12,919	13,113	58,370	62,983	40,841	71,278	32,758
	2007	15,523	1,833	69,576	12,077	12,516	57,673	59,729	39,731	69,491	30,754
	Percent change	-4.5	-11.3	-0.4	-6.5	-4.6	-1.2	-5.2	-2.7	-2.5	-6.1
1,000,000 and over (Group I subset)	2006	4,796	872	26,598	5,530	4,620	21,090	21,050	13,460	21,401	9,770
	2007	4,558	770	25,832	5,266	4,559	21,516	19,444	12,987	19,915	8,559
	Percent change	-5.0	-11.7	-2.9	-4.8	-1.3	+2.0	-7.6	-3.5	-6.9	-12.4
500,000 to 999,999 (Group I subset)	2006	5,672	647	23,396	4,059	4,943	17,175	23,527	14,536	25,784	10,397
	2007	5,483	550	23,818	3,712	4,558	17,163	22,711	14,634	25,816	10,396
	Percent change	-3.3	-15.0	+1.8	-8.5	-7.8	-0.1	-3.5	+0.7	+0.1	*
250,000 to 499,999 (Group I subset)	2006	5,789	548	19,831	3,330	3,550	20,105	18,406	12,845	24,093	12,591
	2007	5,482	513	19,926	3,099	3,399	18,994	17,574	12,110	23,760	11,799
	Percent change	-5.3	-6.4	+0.5	-6.9	-4.3	-5.5	-4.5	-5.7	-1.4	-6.3
GROUP II (100,000 to 249,999)	2006	8,990	745	23,330	4,923	5,195	23,373	21,569	19,002	34,824	16,875
	2007	8,477	810	23,402	4,849	5,157	23,398	21,061	19,149	34,202	17,043
	Percent change	-5.7	+8.7	+0.3	-1.5	-0.7	+0.1	-2.4	+0.8	-1.8	+1.0
GROUP III (50,000 to 99,999)	2006	8,869	651	16,129	4,128	4,497	20,089	16,076	17,155	28,874	21,426
	2007	8,434	671	17,116	3,949	4,278	20,044	15,901	16,509	28,135	21,506
	Percent change	-4.9	+3.1	+6.1	-4.3	-4.9	-0.2	-1.1	-3.8	-2.6	+0.4
GROUP IV (25,000 to 49,999)	2006	6,948	537	9,955	2,645	2,776	12,215	9,766	11,364	19,240	17,663
	2007	6,780	485	9,822	2,384	2,886	12,487	9,474	11,449	19,304	17,064
	Percent change	-2.4	-9.7	-1.3	-9.9	+4.0	+2.2	-3.0	+0.7	+0.3	-3.4
GROUP V (10,000 to 24,999)	2006	6,499	452	7,169	1,799	2,026	8,412	7,368	9,688	15,962	18,042
	2007	6,242	423	7,696	1,747	1,984	8,536	7,909	10,017	16,488	18,355
	Percent change	-4.0	-6.4	+7.4	-2.9	-2.1	+1.5	+7.3	+3.4	+3.3	+1.7
GROUP VI (under 10,000)	2006	5,385	530	3,940	985	1,037	5,378	5,707	8,002	12,993	22,755
	2007	5,208	484	3,915	1,011	1,121	5,318	5,980	8,062	12,803	22,774
	Percent change	-3.3	-8.7	-0.6	+2.6	+8.1	-1.1	+4.8	+0.7	-1.5	+0.1
METROPOLITAN COUNTIES	2006	14,087	990	22,071	3,998	4,706	17,092	27,053	24,404	55,470	41,158
	2007	13,804	920	22,941	3,899	4,885	17,107	26,242	24,327	52,729	41,693
	Percent change	-2.0	-7.1	+3.9	-2.5	+3.8	+0.1	-3.0	-0.3	-4.9	+1.3
NONMETROPOLITAN COUNTIES	2006	5,520	348	1,565	401	578	1,446	7,157	5,915	11,832	16,664
	2007	5,668	354	1,723	371	564	1,429	7,030	6,145	12,418	17,178
	Percent change	+2.7	+1.7	+10.1	-7.5	-2.4	-1.2	-1.8	+3.9	+5.0	+3.1
SUBURBAN AREA[1]	2006	24,644	1,808	36,547	7,503	8,587	34,407	39,968	40,557	84,725	74,630
	2007	24,072	1,683	37,715	7,143	8,781	34,828	39,502	40,702	82,158	74,893
	Percent change	-2.3	-6.9	+3.2	-4.8	+2.3	+1.2	-1.2	+0.4	-3.0	+0.4

[1] Suburban area includes law enforcement agencies in cities with less than 50,000 inhabitants and county law enforcement agencies that are within a Metropolitan Statistical Area. Suburban area excludes all metropolitan agencies associated with a principal city. The agencies associated with suburban areas also appear in other groups within this table.
* = Less than one-tenth of 1 percent.

Table 15. Crime Trends, by Population Group, 2006–2007 *(Contd.)*

(Number, percent change.)

Population group		Burglary			Motor vehicle theft			Arson			Number of agencies	2007 estimated population
		Forcible entry	Unlawful entry	Attempted forcible entry	Autos	Trucks and buses	Other vehicles	Structure	Mobile	Other		
TOTAL ALL AGENCIES:	2006	1,145,764	618,929	124,760	769,813	187,272	89,944	26,729	18,051	18,824		
	2007	1,150,463	612,002	122,461	702,737	174,464	83,013	25,077	16,604	17,264	13,442	255,978,005
	Percent change	+0.4	-1.1	-1.8	-8.7	-6.8	-7.7	-6.2	-8.0	-8.3		
TOTAL CITIES	2006	832,298	445,061	94,861	623,539	145,967	58,721	19,889	12,853	13,532		
	2007	831,876	438,158	94,488	565,557	136,152	52,486	18,912	11,667	12,530	9,507	167,809,773
	Percent change	-0.1	-1.6	-0.4	-9.3	-6.7	-10.6	-4.9	-9.2	-7.4		
GROUP I (250,000 and over)	2006	299,408	120,422	28,833	278,150	82,921	21,584	6,968	6,498	4,051		
	2007	303,405	113,489	28,352	250,106	78,059	17,735	6,456	5,796	3,811	66	41,081,765
	Percent change	+1.3	-5.8	-1.7	-10.1	-5.9	-17.8	-7.3	-10.8	-5.9		
1,000,000 and over (Group I subset)	2006	91,080	35,901	6,880	89,034	38,542	8,210	2,059	2,580	1,481		
	2007	98,510	35,794	7,302	80,390	37,273	7,473	1,931	2,311	1,362	8	14,175,600
	Percent change	+8.2	-0.3	+6.1	-9.7	-3.3	-9.0	-6.2	-10.4	-8.0		
500,000 to 999,999 (Group I subset)	2006	117,184	41,443	13,111	101,952	22,325	8,416	2,418	1,933	1,405		
	2007	113,754	38,226	12,077	89,512	22,164	6,194	2,174	1,692	1,310	21	14,002,903
	Percent change	-2.9	-7.8	-7.9	-12.2	-0.7	-26.4	-10.1	-12.5	-6.8		
250,000 to 499,999 (Group I subset)	2006	91,144	43,078	8,842	87,164	22,054	4,958	2,491	1,985	1,165		
	2007	91,141	39,469	8,973	80,204	18,622	4,068	2,351	1,793	1,139	37	12,903,262
	Percent change	*	-8.4	+1.5	-8.0	-15.6	-18.0	-5.6	-9.7	-2.2		
GROUP II (100,000 to 249,999)	2006	144,190	73,705	17,228	113,561	23,868	9,422	3,084	1,936	1,947		
	2007	143,057	75,968	17,423	103,934	21,906	8,867	3,237	1,789	1,793	173	25,864,109
	Percent change	-0.8	+3.1	+1.1	-8.5	-8.2	-5.9	+5.0	-7.6	-7.9		
GROUP III (50,000 to 99,999)	2006	134,370	79,741	16,478	97,311	17,274	9,536	3,377	1,873	2,443		
	2007	132,918	80,044	16,327	88,044	15,883	8,520	2,944	1,711	2,230	433	29,776,050
	Percent change	-1.1	+0.4	-0.9	-9.5	-8.1	-10.7	-12.8	-8.6	-8.7		
GROUP IV (25,000 to 49,999)	2006	96,714	59,270	12,339	59,353	8,730	7,127	2,174	1,036	2,046		
	2007	95,419	58,053	12,936	53,439	8,473	6,723	2,082	1,029	1,886	723	24,913,403
	Percent change	-1.3	-2.1	+4.8	-10.0	-2.9	-5.7	-4.2	-0.7	-7.8		
GROUP V (10,000 to 24,999)	2006	87,050	59,198	10,735	44,866	8,024	5,869	2,140	868	1,521		
	2007	87,387	58,241	10,641	41,861	7,050	5,557	2,203	771	1,401	1,594	25,323,890
	Percent change	+0.4	-1.6	-0.9	-6.7	-12.1	-5.3	+2.9	-11.2	-7.9		
GROUP VI (under 10,000)	2006	70,566	52,725	9,248	30,298	5,150	5,183	2,146	642	1,524		
	2007	69,690	52,363	8,809	28,173	4,781	5,084	1,990	571	1,409	6,518	20,850,556
	Percent change	-1.2	-0.7	-4.7	-7.0	-7.2	-1.9	-7.3	-11.1	-7.5		
METROPOLITAN COUNTIES	2006	228,287	130,684	23,883	125,115	35,930	24,053	4,868	4,345	4,179		
	2007	233,779	129,224	21,959	116,470	33,131	23,318	4,402	4,103	3,578	1,644	62,976,299
	Percent change	+2.4	-1.1	-8.1	-6.9	-7.8	-3.1	-9.6	-5.6	-14.4		
NONMETROPOLITAN COUNTIES	2006	85,179	43,184	6,016	21,159	5,375	7,170	1,972	853	1,113		
	2007	84,808	44,620	6,014	20,710	5,181	7,209	1,763	834	1,156	2,291	25,191,933
	Percent change	-0.4	+3.3	*	-2.1	-3.6	+0.5	-10.6	-2.2	+3.9		
SUBURBAN AREA[1]	2006	378,881	238,275	44,441	224,516	51,527	36,031	8,721	5,938	7,559		
	2007	384,030	235,030	42,620	206,662	47,547	34,754	8,010	5,577	6,751	7,072	112,636,189
	Percent change	+1.4	-1.4	-4.1	-8.0	-7.7	-3.5	-8.2	-6.1	-10.7		

[1] Suburban area includes law enforcement agencies in cities with less than 50,000 inhabitants and county law enforcement agencies that are within a Metropolitan Statistical Area. Suburban area excludes all metropolitan agencies associated with a principal city. The agencies associated with suburban areas also appear in other groups within this table.

* = Less than one-tenth of 1 percent.

Table 16. Crime Per 100,000 Population, by Population Group, 2007

(Number, rate.)

Population group	Violent crime		Murder and nonnegligent manslaughter		Forcible rape		Robbery		Aggravated assault	
	Number of offenses known	Rate	Number of offenses known	Rate	Number of offenses known	Rate	Number of offenses known	Rate	Number of offenses known	Rate
TOTAL ALL AGENCIES:	1,310,062	484.3	15,872	5.9	81,398	30.1	421,286	155.7	791,506	292.6
TOTAL CITIES	1,042,793	570.5	12,426	6.8	60,193	32.9	366,962	200.7	603,212	330.0
GROUP I (250,000 and over)	482,214	893.8	6,440	11.9	19,577	36.3	198,421	367.8	257,776	477.8
1,000,000 and over (Group I subset)	209,784	831.8	2,790	11.1	6,985	27.7	94,385	374.2	105,624	418.8
500,000 to 999,999 (Group I subset)	158,406	989.3	2,195	13.7	6,876	42.9	61,177	382.1	88,158	550.6
250,000 to 499,999 (Group I subset)	114,024	896.6	1,455	11.4	5,716	44.9	42,859	337.0	63,994	503.2
GROUP II (100,000 to 249,999)	177,852	635.6	2,396	8.6	10,619	37.9	63,376	226.5	101,461	362.6
GROUP III (50,000 to 99,999)	138,044	467.6	1,432	4.9	9,440	32.0	45,208	153.1	81,964	277.6
GROUP IV (25,000 to 49,999)	94,816	377.0	880	3.5	7,571	30.1	27,957	111.2	58,408	232.3
GROUP V (10,000 to 24,999)	81,046	319.5	746	2.9	7,040	27.8	20,306	80.1	52,954	208.8
GROUP VI (under 10,000)	68,821	330.3	532	2.6	5,946	28.5	11,694	56.1	50,649	243.1
METROPOLITAN COUNTIES	213,529	338.4	2,630	4.2	14,870	23.6	50,286	79.7	145,743	231.0
NONMETROPOLITAN COUNTIES[1]	53,740	218.4	816	3.3	6,335	25.7	4,038	16.4	42,551	172.9
SUBURBAN AREA[2]	360,216	318.5	3,871	3.4	26,443	23.4	90,648	80.1	239,254	211.5

Population group	Property crime		Burglary		Larceny-theft		Motor vehicle theft		Number of agencies	2007 estimated population
	Number of offenses known	Rate	Number of offenses known	Rate	Number of offenses known	Rate	Number of offenses known	Rate		
TOTAL ALL AGENCIES:	9,026,804	3,337.0	1,987,601	734.8	6,008,141	2,221.1	1,031,062	381.2	13,424	270,507,141
TOTAL CITIES	7,069,874	3,867.5	1,464,743	801.3	4,782,773	2,616.4	822,358	449.9	9,428	182,801,234
GROUP I (250,000 and over)	2,407,464	4,462.4	511,856	948.8	1,501,615	2,783.3	393,993	730.3	71	53,950,146
1,000,000 and over (Group I subset)	923,358	3,661.2	187,272	742.5	579,090	2,296.1	156,996	622.5	10	25,220,230
500,000 to 999,999 (Group I subset)	868,175	5,421.8	188,743	1,178.7	540,743	3,377.0	138,689	866.1	24	16,012,700
250,000 to 499,999 (Group I subset)	615,931	4,843.3	135,841	1,068.2	381,782	3,002.1	98,308	773.0	37	12,717,216
GROUP II (100,000 to 249,999)	1,218,215	4,353.5	262,786	939.1	802,535	2,868.0	152,894	546.4	186	27,982,204
GROUP III (50,000 to 99,999)	1,074,797	3,640.7	227,456	770.5	735,297	2,490.7	112,044	379.5	429	29,521,792
GROUP IV (25,000 to 49,999)	850,936	3,383.8	168,866	671.5	612,512	2,435.7	69,558	276.6	729	25,147,055
GROUP V (10,000 to 24,999)	807,069	3,181.7	159,940	630.5	592,013	2,333.9	55,116	217.3	1,597	25,366,317
GROUP VI (under 10,000)	711,393	3,414.6	133,839	642.4	538,801	2,586.2	38,753	186.0	6,416	20,833,720
METROPOLITAN COUNTIES	1,544,543	2,447.7	390,058	618.2	978,458	1,550.6	176,027	279.0	1,674	63,100,718
NONMETROPOLITAN COUNTIES[1]	412,387	1,676.0	132,800	539.7	246,910	1,003.5	32,677	132.8	2,322	24,605,189
SUBURBAN AREA[2]	3,039,970	2,687.8	672,268	594.4	2,073,913	1,833.7	293,789	259.8	7,073	113,100,574

[1] Includes state police agencies that report aggregately for the entire state.

[2] Suburban area includes law enforcement agencies in cities with less than 50,000 inhabitants and county law enforcement agencies that are within a Metropolitan Statistical Area. Suburban area excludes all metropolitan agencies associated with a principal city. The agencies associated with suburban areas also appear in other groups within this table.

Table 17.   Crime Per 100,000 Population, by Suburban and Nonsuburban Cities,[1] by Population Group, 2007

(Number, rate.)

Population group	Number of agencies	2007 estimated population	Violent crime		Murder and nonnegligent manslaughter		Forcible rape		Robbery	
			Number of offenses known	Rate	Number of offenses known	Rate	Number of offenses known	Rate	Number of offenses known	Rate
TOTAL SUBURBAN CITIES:....................................	5,399	49,999,856	146,693	293.4	1,241	2.5	11,579	23.2	40,362	80.7
GROUP IV (25,000 to 49,999)................................	543	18,449,735	56,734	307.5	525	2.8	4,200	22.8	17,840	96.7
GROUP V (10,000 to 24,999)	1,188	18,973,554	51,442	271.1	452	2.4	4,154	21.9	14,429	76
GROUP VI (under 10,000)	3,668	12,576,567	38,517	306.3	264	2.1	3,225	25.6	8,093	64.3
TOTAL NONSUBURBAN CITIES:..................................	3,343	21,347,236	97,981	459	917	4.3	8,969	42	19,595	91.8
GROUP IV (25,000 to 49,999)................................	186	6,697,320	38,059	568.3	355	5.3	3,348	50	10,117	151.1
GROUP V (10,000 to 24,999)	409	6,392,763	29,616	463.3	294	4.6	2,898	45.3	5,877	91.9
GROUP VI (under 10,000)	2,748	8,257,153	30,306	367	268	3.2	2,723	33	3,601	43.6

Population group	Aggravated assault		Property crime		Burglary		Larceny-theft		Motor vehicle theft	
	Number of offenses known	Rate	Number of offenses known	Rate	Number of offenses known	Rate	Number of offenses known	Rate	Number of offenses known	Rate
TOTAL SUBURBAN CITIES:....................................	93,511	187	1,495,427	2,990.90	282,210	564.4	1,095,455	2,190.90	117,762	235.5
GROUP IV (25,000 to 49,999)................................	34,169	185.2	536,333	2,907.00	104,167	564.6	382,097	2,071.00	50,069	271.4
GROUP V (10,000 to 24,999)	32,407	170.8	521,278	2,747.40	100,194	528.1	379,765	2,001.50	41,319	217.8
GROUP VI (under 10,000)	26,935	214.2	437,816	3,481.20	77,849	619	333,593	2,652.50	26,374	209.7
TOTAL NONSUBURBAN CITIES:..................................	68,500	320.9	873,971	4,094.10	180,435	845.2	647,871	3,034.90	45,665	213.9
GROUP IV (25,000 to 49,999)................................	24,239	361.9	314,603	4,697.40	64,699	966	230,415	3,440.40	19,489	291
GROUP V (10,000 to 24,999)	20,547	321.4	285,791	4,470.50	59,746	934.6	212,248	3,320.10	13,797	215.8
GROUP VI (under 10,000)	23,714	287.2	273,577	3,313.20	55,990	678.1	205,208	2,485.20	12,379	149.9

[1] Suburban cities include law enforcement agencies in cities with less than 50,000 inhabitants that are within a Metropolitan Statistical Area. Suburban cities exclude all metropolitan agencies associated with a principal city. Nonsuburban cities include law enforcement agencies in cities with less than 50,000 inhabitants that are not associated with a Metropolitan Statistical Area.

Table 18. Crime Per 100,000 Population, by Metropolitan and Nonmetropolitan Counties[1], by Population Group, 2007

(Number, rate.)

Population group	Population range	Violent crime		Murder and nonnegligent manslaughter		Forcible rape		Robbery		Aggravated assault	
		Number of offenses known	Rate	Number of offenses known	Rate	Number of offenses known	Rate	Number of offenses known	Rate	Number of offenses known	Rate
METROPOLITAN COUNTIES...............	100,000 and over	151,320	394.7	1,804	4.7	8,767	22.9	43,001	112.2	97,748	255.0
	25,000 to 99,999	45,085	219.3	595	2.9	4,479	21.8	5,050	24.6	34,961	170.0
	Under 25,000	17,136	407.6	231	5.5	1,636	38.9	2,235	53.2	13,034	310.1
NONMETROPOLITAN COUNTIES...............	25,000 and over	23,104	220.1	295	2.8	2,404	22.9	1,990	19.0	18,415	175.4
	10,000 to 24,999	15,936	180.5	245	2.8	1,649	18.7	1,048	11.9	12,994	147.2
	Under 10,000	8,830	236.8	140	3.8	1,438	38.6	364	9.8	6,888	184.7

Population group	Population range	Property crime		Burglary		Larceny-theft		Motor vehicle theft		Number of agencies	2007 estimated population
		Number of offenses known	Rate	Number of offenses known	Rate	Number of offenses known	Rate	Number of offenses known	Rate		
METROPOLITAN COUNTIES...............	100,000 and over	1,037,241	2,705.7	252,419	658.4	663,226	1,730.1	121,596	317.2	143	38,335,337
	25,000 to 99,999	376,633	1,831.7	107,850	524.5	237,508	1,155.1	31,275	152.1	404	20,561,550
	Under 25,000	130,669	3,108.3	29,789	708.6	77,724	1,848.9	23,156	550.8	1,127	4,203,831
NONMETROPOLITAN COUNTIES...............	25,000 and over	183,457	1,747.5	60,651	577.7	108,796	1,036.3	14,010	133.5	267	10,498,166
	10,000 to 24,999	126,152	1,428.7	40,605	459.9	76,023	861.0	9,524	107.9	545	8,829,893
	Under 10,000	63,389	1,699.7	19,240	515.9	38,668	1,036.8	5,481	147.0	1,357	3,729,374

[1] Metropolitan counties include sheriffs and county law enforcement agencies associated with a Metropolitan Statistical Area. Nonmetropolitan counties include sheriffs and county law enforcement agencies that are not associated with a Metropolitan Statistical Area. The offenses from state police agencies are not included in this table.

Table 19. Crime Per 100,000 Population, Selected Known Offenses, by Population Group, 2007

(Number, rate.)

Population group		Forcible rape		Robbery				Aggravated assault			
		Rape by force	Assault to rape-attempts	Firearm	Knife or cutting instrument	Other weapon	Strong-arm	Firearm	Knife or cutting instrument	Other weapon	Hands, fists, feet, etc.
TOTAL ALL AGENCIES:.....	Number of offenses										
	known	72,559	6,177	158,240	30,689	33,358	147,285	155,963	137,032	249,372	187,366
	Rate	28.4	2.4	61.9	12.0	13.1	57.7	61.1	53.6	97.6	73.3
TOTAL CITIES	Number of offenses										
	known	52,800	4,911	133,664	26,415	27,929	128,705	122,796	106,678	183,793	129,537
	Rate	31.3	2.9	79.2	15.7	16.5	76.3	72.8	63.2	108.9	76.8
GROUP I (250,000 and over)................	Number of offenses										
	known	15,949	1,920	70,146	12,239	12,275	57,919	60,423	40,260	71,094	31,522
	Rate	38.5	4.6	169.3	29.5	29.6	139.8	145.8	97.2	171.6	76.1
1,000,000 and over (Group I subset)...............	Number of offenses										
	known	4,558	770	25,832	5,266	4,559	21,516	19,444	12,987	19,915	8,559
	Rate	32.2	5.4	182.2	37.1	32.2	151.8	137.2	91.6	140.5	60.4
500,000 to 999,999 (Group I subset)...............	Number of offenses										
	known	5,923	615	25,971	3,958	4,781	18,587	23,950	15,538	27,828	11,417
	Rate	40.0	4.2	175.5	26.7	32.3	125.6	161.8	105.0	188.0	77.1
250,000 to 499,999 (Group I subset)...............	Number of offenses										
	known	5,468	535	18,343	3,015	2,935	17,816	17,029	11,735	23,351	11,546
	Rate	43.9	4.3	147.2	24.2	23.5	142.9	136.6	94.2	187.4	92.6
GROUP II (100,000 to 249,999)...................	Number of offenses										
	known	9,096	840	24,751	5,031	5,306	24,284	22,770	19,959	35,053	18,057
	Rate	34.2	3.2	93.1	18.9	20.0	91.4	85.7	75.1	131.9	67.9
GROUP III (50,000 to 99,999)...................	Number of offenses										
	known	8,692	690	16,927	3,901	4,273	19,783	15,837	16,442	28,095	21,373
	Rate	29.5	2.3	57.5	13.3	14.5	67.2	53.8	55.9	95.5	72.6
GROUP IV (25,000 to 49,999)...................	Number of offenses										
	known	7,068	503	9,927	2,435	2,944	12,651	9,603	11,693	19,905	17,207
	Rate	28.1	2.0	39.5	9.7	11.7	50.3	38.2	46.5	79.2	68.4
GROUP V (10,000 to 24,999)...................	Number of offenses										
	known	6,571	446	7,865	1,766	1,990	8,634	8,062	10,128	16,564	18,131
	Rate	25.9	1.8	31.0	7.0	7.9	34.1	31.8	40.0	65.4	71.5
GROUP VI (under 10,000).......................	Number of offenses										
	known	5,424	512	4,048	1,043	1,141	5,434	6,101	8,196	13,082	23,247
	Rate	26.0	2.5	19.4	5.0	5.5	26.1	29.3	39.4	62.8	111.6
METROPOLITAN COUNTIES	Number of offenses										
	known	13,787	919	22,851	3,905	4,880	17,190	26,174	24,239	53,176	40,899
	Rate	22.2	1.5	36.8	6.3	7.9	27.7	42.1	39.0	85.6	65.8
NONMETROPOLITAN COUNTIES	Number of offenses										
	known	5,972	347	1,725	369	549	1,390	6,993	6,115	12,403	16,930
	Rate	24.3	1.4	7.0	1.5	2.2	5.7	28.5	24.9	50.5	68.9
SUBURBAN AREA[1]	Number of offenses										
	known	24,534	1,720	37,873	7,239	8,858	35,164	39,552	40,926	83,329	74,157
	Rate	21.9	1.5	33.8	6.5	7.9	31.4	35.3	36.5	74.3	66.2

[1] Suburban area includes law enforcement agencies in cities with less than 50,000 inhabitants and county law enforcement agencies that are within a Metropolitan Statistical Area. Suburban area excludes all metropolitan agencies associated with a principal city. The agencies associated with suburban areas also appear in other groups within this table.

Table 19.   Crime Per 100,000 Population, Selected Known Offenses, by Population Group, 2007 *(Contd.)*

(Number, rate.)

Population group		Burglary			Motor vehicle theft			Number of agencies	2007 estimated population
		Forcible entry	Unlawful entry	Attempted forcible entry	Autos	Trucks and buses	Other vehicles		
TOTAL ALL AGENCIES:	Number of offenses								
	known	1,161,059	615,925	123,077	714,975	175,948	83,595	13,360	255,465,442
	Rate	454.5	241.1	48.2	279.9	68.9	32.7		
TOTAL CITIES	Number of offenses								
	known	846,982	443,002	95,810	577,830	138,003	53,464	9,406	168,757,929
	Rate	501.9	262.5	56.8	342.4	81.8	31.7		
GROUP I (250,000 and over)	Number of offenses								
	known	307,961	113,670	29,608	250,472	79,167	18,230	66	41,439,145
	Rate	743.2	274.3	71.4	604.4	191.0	44.0		
1,000,000 and over (Group I subset)	Number of offenses								
	known	98,510	35,794	7,302	80,390	37,273	7,473	8	14,175,600
	Rate	694.9	252.5	51.5	567.1	262.9	52.7		
500,000 to 999,999 (Group I subset)	Number of offenses								
	known	123,307	40,743	13,392	95,375	23,428	6,747	22	14,800,171
	Rate	833.1	275.3	90.5	644.4	158.3	45.6		
250,000 to 499,999 (Group I subset)	Number of offenses								
	known	86,144	37,133	8,914	74,707	18,466	4,010	36	12,463,374
	Rate	691.2	297.9	71.5	599.4	148.2	32.2		
GROUP II (100,000 to 249,999).................	Number of offenses								
	known	150,485	78,982	17,500	114,996	22,726	9,291	177	26,581,642
	Rate	566.1	297.1	65.8	432.6	85.5	35.0		
GROUP III (50,000 to 99,999)	Number of offenses								
	known	130,534	79,005	16,171	87,185	15,625	8,375	428	29,424,744
	Rate	443.6	268.5	55.0	296.3	53.1	28.5		
GROUP IV (25,000 to 49,999)	Number of offenses								
	known	96,749	58,990	13,127	54,293	8,513	6,752	729	25,147,055
	Rate	384.7	234.6	52.2	215.9	33.9	26.9		
GROUP V (10,000 to 24,999)	Number of offenses								
	known	89,839	58,886	10,590	42,297	7,065	5,575	1,595	25,341,547
	Rate	354.5	232.4	41.8	166.9	27.9	22.0		
GROUP VI (under 10,000)...........................	Number of offenses								
	known	71,414	53,469	8,814	28,587	4,907	5,241	6,411	20,823,796
	Rate	342.9	256.8	42.3	137.3	23.6	25.2		
METROPOLITAN COUNTIES	Number of offenses								
	known	231,053	128,826	21,708	116,862	32,823	22,937	1,659	62,129,516
	Rate	371.9	207.4	34.9	188.1	52.8	36.9		
NONMETROPOLITAN COUNTIES	Number of offenses								
	known	83,024	44,097	5,559	20,283	5,122	7,194	2,295	24,577,997
	Rate	337.8	179.4	22.6	82.5	20.8	29.3		
SUBURBAN AREA[1]..................................	Number of offenses								
	known	384,243	236,458	42,591	208,236	47,437	34,527	7,054	112,103,749
	Rate	342.8	210.9	38.0	185.8	42.3	30.8		

[1] Suburban area includes law enforcement agencies in cities with less than 50,000 inhabitants and county law enforcement agencies that are within a Metropolitan Statistical Area. Suburban area excludes all metropolitan agencies associated with a principal city. The agencies associated with suburban areas also appear in other groups within this table.

Table 20. Murder, by State and Type of Weapon, 2007

(Number.)

State	Total murders[1]	Total firearms	Handguns	Rifles	Shotguns	Firearms (type unknown)	Knives or cutting instruments	Other weapons	Hands, fists, feet, etc.[2]
Alabama	385	285	262	7	16	0	38	47	15
Alaska	43	21	13	4	3	1	5	5	12
Arizona	464	323	265	35	11	12	44	67	30
Arkansas	191	130	92	7	10	21	20	29	12
California	2,249	1,605	1,374	51	74	106	298	228	118
Colorado	150	85	56	0	2	27	23	25	17
Connecticut	95	57	37	0	4	16	14	20	4
Delaware	37	22	19	0	0	3	6	8	1
Georgia	674	485	401	24	30	30	84	99	6
Hawaii	12	3	3	0	0	0	3	1	5
Idaho	49	25	11	6	1	7	5	14	5
Illinois[3]	463	343	330	4	6	3	53	57	10
Indiana	333	231	160	12	9	50	38	44	20
Iowa	36	12	4	2	1	5	11	8	5
Kansas	104	63	29	5	3	26	12	23	6
Kentucky	196	131	111	5	11	4	19	27	19
Louisiana	577	455	339	31	15	70	45	55	22
Maine	21	9	3	0	1	5	6	4	2
Maryland	553	414	388	9	11	6	53	63	23
Massachusetts	182	114	65	1	3	45	31	23	14
Michigan	672	444	180	29	26	209	64	134	30
Minnesota	107	61	52	7	2	0	15	20	11
Mississippi	152	119	102	5	9	3	15	12	6
Missouri	351	247	92	18	10	127	34	55	15
Montana	14	10	5	0	2	3	2	1	1
Nebraska	22	9	7	0	0	2	2	6	5
Nevada	192	123	92	7	4	20	25	32	12
New Hampshire	11	7	5	0	0	2	2	2	0
New Jersey	380	260	244	1	5	10	46	37	37
New Mexico	148	81	66	10	1	4	20	26	21
New York	800	500	113	12	9	366	142	124	34
North Carolina	555	369	252	17	24	76	63	83	40
North Dakota	12	3	3	0	0	0	1	4	4
Ohio	486	299	187	6	15	91	45	101	41
Oklahoma	222	132	105	9	8	10	35	36	19
Oregon	72	38	15	2	4	17	12	18	4
Pennsylvania	719	527	439	18	10	60	81	88	23
Rhode Island	19	9	3	0	0	6	7	3	0
South Carolina	349	235	144	6	18	67	40	60	14
South Dakota	15	4	2	1	1	0	3	6	2
Tennessee	397	252	190	11	11	40	50	72	23
Texas	1,419	946	727	58	60	101	177	203	93
Utah	58	38	22	0	0	16	5	10	5
Vermont	12	9	5	2	1	1	2	0	1
Virginia	406	287	163	5	10	109	48	51	20
Washington	170	99	78	5	6	10	27	29	15
West Virginia	59	37	18	7	1	11	5	7	10
Wisconsin	182	121	86	9	5	21	18	27	16
Wyoming	16	7	2	2	2	1	2	1	6

[1] Total number of murders for which supplemental homicide data were received.
[2] Pushed is included in hands, fists, feet, etc.
[3] Limited supplemental homicide data were received.

Table 21.   Robbery, by State and Type of Weapon, 2007

(Number.)

State	Total robberies[1]	Firearms	Knives or cutting instruments	Other weapons	Strong-arm	Agency count	Population
Alabama	2,910	1,579	199	245	887	290	2,833,181
Alaska	578	173	64	75	266	32	667,568
Arizona	9,437	4,648	964	888	2,937	77	5,946,033
Arkansas	2,954	1,415	173	291	1,075	233	2,524,285
California	70,202	23,355	6,581	6,547	33,719	715	36,216,791
Colorado	3,392	1,339	311	346	1,396	207	4,691,449
Connecticut	3,101	1,058	348	311	1,384	93	3,116,015
Delaware	1,686	691	122	128	745	53	853,712
District of Columbia[2]	276	62	20	11	183	2	...
Florida	38,073	17,911	2,548	3,437	14,177	590	18,136,624
Georgia	15,430	9,647	676	1,244	3,863	360	7,730,570
Hawaii	943	91	76	63	713	1	905,903
Idaho	229	92	23	32	82	107	1,476,361
Illinois[2]	633	249	43	75	266	1	155,713
Indiana	6,961	3,382	473	492	2,614	266	4,814,390
Iowa	1,277	325	118	159	675	186	2,644,602
Kansas	2,735	1,272	294	255	914	229	2,734,933
Kentucky	3,419	1,384	258	669	1,108	279	3,476,669
Louisiana	5,410	2,980	269	311	1,850	117	3,447,958
Maine	349	73	36	27	213	164	1,317,207
Maryland	9,333	4,346	925	523	3,539	154	4,940,435
Massachusetts	6,355	1,605	1,265	711	2,774	314	5,754,717
Michigan	13,182	6,270	699	1,211	5,002	516	9,463,609
Minnesota	4,647	1,518	294	658	2,177	299	4,808,769
Mississippi	2,162	1,253	109	275	525	99	1,641,272
Missouri	5,351	2,603	358	369	2,021	585	5,361,516
Montana	188	46	24	39	79	87	913,685
Nebraska	1,067	475	100	83	409	214	1,474,140
Nevada	6,930	3,043	618	603	2,666	33	2,546,867
New Hampshire	174	44	24	28	78	131	891,903
New Jersey	12,526	4,032	1,210	824	6,460	513	8,644,483
New Mexico	1,988	908	288	133	659	68	1,519,970
New York	9,236	2,713	1,013	1,122	4,388	634	10,777,671
North Carolina	11,263	6,208	797	974	3,284	322	6,983,777
North Dakota	67	21	4	9	33	60	568,361
Ohio	12,676	4,697	732	1,002	6,245	372	7,489,853
Oklahoma	3,368	1,503	260	311	1,294	285	3,548,670
Oregon	2,816	761	272	273	1,510	150	3,606,874
Pennsylvania	18,907	8,029	1,395	1,170	8,313	998	11,408,646
Rhode Island	545	146	70	70	259	41	790,879
South Carolina	5,748	3,054	477	516	1,701	479	4,075,106
South Dakota	100	25	18	19	38	96	638,914
Tennessee	10,974	6,380	771	1,033	2,790	452	6,001,560
Texas	38,747	17,862	3,628	3,683	13,574	987	23,853,606
Utah	1,401	459	186	163	593	112	2,507,132
Vermont	80	28	10	11	31	78	608,835
Virginia	7,522	4,057	563	734	2,168	339	7,418,848
Washington	5,918	1,336	535	567	3,480	233	6,062,127
West Virginia	753	261	102	89	301	276	1,408,314
Wisconsin	5,470	2,809	332	541	1,788	370	5,548,443
Wyoming	83	22	14	8	39	61	516,496

[1] The number of robberies for which breakdowns by type of weapon were received from agencies that submitted 12 months of data in 2007.

[2] Limited data were received.

... = Not available.

Table 22.   Aggravated Assault, by State and Type of Weapon, 2007

(Number.)

State	Total aggravated assaults[1]	Firearms	Knives or cutting instruments	Other weapons	Personal weapons	Agency count	Population
Alabama	6,538	1,906	945	1,409	2,278	290	2,833,181
Alaska	3,293	589	690	865	1,149	32	667,568
Arizona	16,952	4,863	2,994	5,561	3,534	77	5,946,033
Arkansas	9,803	2,565	1,723	2,501	3,014	233	2,524,285
California	107,899	21,547	17,243	39,473	29,636	715	36,216,791
Colorado	11,013	2,154	2,489	3,041	3,329	207	4,691,449
Connecticut	3,734	467	839	1,349	1,079	93	3,116,015
Delaware	3,833	829	820	1,790	394	53	853,712
District of Columbia[2]	120	11	59	34	16	2	...
Florida	85,228	17,244	15,239	35,435	17,310	590	18,136,624
Georgia	22,569	6,042	4,228	6,207	6,092	360	7,730,570
Hawaii	1,425	114	382	461	468	1	905,903
Idaho	2,695	468	544	899	784	107	1,476,361
Illinois[2]	1,342	595	251	349	147	1	155,713
Indiana	10,047	1,719	1,529	3,246	3,553	266	4,814,390
Iowa	6,141	575	1,136	1,419	3,011	186	2,644,602
Kansas	8,642	2,624	1,737	2,725	1,556	229	2,734,933
Kentucky	5,607	1,152	750	2,380	1,325	279	3,476,669
Louisiana	18,850	4,760	3,047	4,753	6,290	117	3,447,958
Maine	793	44	150	254	345	164	1,317,207
Maryland	15,207	2,216	3,466	5,530	3,995	154	4,940,435
Massachusetts	17,493	1,758	4,083	9,244	2,408	314	5,754,717
Michigan	34,356	8,627	6,278	12,300	7,151	516	9,463,609
Minnesota	7,869	1,369	1,667	2,197	2,636	299	4,808,769
Mississippi	2,582	792	488	613	689	99	1,641,272
Missouri	17,390	3,660	2,401	4,933	6,396	585	5,361,516
Montana	2,160	299	325	678	858	87	913,685
Nebraska	3,337	494	612	1,628	603	214	1,474,140
Nevada	10,987	2,233	2,029	5,027	1,698	33	2,546,867
New Hampshire	713	130	233	171	179	131	891,903
New Jersey	14,565	2,235	3,171	4,538	4,621	513	8,644,483
New Mexico	7,755	1,531	1,391	2,593	2,240	68	1,519,970
New York	17,563	2,328	4,527	5,272	5,436	634	10,777,671
North Carolina	21,146	6,060	4,120	5,891	5,075	322	6,983,777
North Dakota	587	14	82	128	363	60	568,361
Ohio	11,736	2,697	2,454	3,681	2,904	372	7,489,853
Oklahoma	12,458	2,239	1,905	4,640	3,674	285	3,548,670
Oregon	6,176	721	1,045	2,187	2,223	150	3,606,874
Pennsylvania	26,467	5,353	3,903	6,727	10,484	998	11,408,646
Rhode Island	1,060	201	300	443	116	41	790,879
South Carolina	24,362	6,058	4,313	6,935	7,056	479	4,075,106
South Dakota	778	105	270	226	177	96	638,914
Tennessee	32,445	9,645	6,928	12,396	3,476	452	6,001,560
Texas	73,275	17,174	16,829	25,211	14,061	987	23,853,606
Utah	3,635	660	963	1,270	742	112	2,507,132
Vermont	553	69	104	115	265	78	608,835
Virginia	10,639	1,998	2,381	3,469	2,791	339	7,418,848
Washington	12,323	1,914	2,130	4,007	4,272	233	6,062,127
West Virginia	3,227	759	652	828	988	276	1,408,314
Wisconsin	9,394	2,258	1,027	2,041	4,068	370	5,548,443
Wyoming	971	98	160	302	411	61	516,496

[1] The number of aggravated assaults for which breakdowns by type of weapon were received from agencies that submitted 12 months of data in 2007.

[2] Limited data were received.

...= Not available

Table 23.   Offense Analysis, by Classification and Percent Change, 2006–2007

(Number, percent, dollars.)

Classification		Number of offenses 2007	Percent change from 2006	Percent distribution[1]	Average value
Murder		13,296	-0.8	-	-
Forcible rape		71,857	-3.7	-	-
Robbery:	Total	345,200	+0.3	100.0	$1,321
Robbery by location:	Street/highway	151,048	-0.2	43.8	1,113
	Commercial house	48,102	+0.9	13.9	1,499
	Gas or service station	9,125	-5.3	2.6	1,097
	Convenience store	19,336	+0.6	5.6	800
	Residence	52,353	+4.7	15.2	1,516
	Bank	7,175	-5.1	2.1	4,201
	Miscellaneous	58,061	-1.0	16.8	1,391
Burglary:	Total	1,749,497	-0.1	100.0	1,991
Burglary by location:	Residence (dwelling):	1,187,318	+2.2	67.9	1,991
	Residence Night	338,681	+1.3	19.4	1,484
	Residence Day	593,020	+4.1	33.9	2,168
	Residence Unknown	255,617	-0.8	14.6	2,252
	Nonresidence (store, office, etc.):	562,179	-4.5	32.1	1,989
	Nonresidence Night	235,608	-4.5	13.5	1,727
	Nonresidence Day	182,318	-2.8	10.4	1,833
	Nonresidence Unknown	144,253	-6.6	8.2	2,615
Larceny-theft (except motor vehicle theft):	Total	5,268,582	-0.7	100.0	886
Larceny-theft by type:	Pocket-picking	21,984	-3.5	0.4	728
	Purse-snatching	30,526	-7.3	0.6	402
	Shoplifting	785,228	+11.2	14.9	205
	From motor vehicles (except accessories)	1,369,150	-0.8	26.0	722
	Motor vehicle accessories	480,502	-7.0	9.1	554
	Bicycles	179,945	-3.6	3.4	273
	From buildings	632,947	-3.0	12.0	1,263
	From coin-operated machines	24,894	-11.7	0.5	363
	All others	1,743,406	-2.0	33.1	1,357
Larceny-theft by value:	Over $200	2,313,327	+1.8	43.9	1,945
	$50 to $200	1,179,936	-0.9	22.4	110
	Under $50	1,775,319	-3.6	33.7	22
Motor vehicle theft	914,243	-8.1	-	6,755	

[1] Because of rounding, the percentages may not add to 100.0.

Table 24.   Property Stolen and Recovered, by Type and Value, 2007

(Dollars, percent.)

Type of property	Value of property		Percent recovered
	Stolen	Recovered	
Total	$15,028,201,693	$4,326,925,896	28.8
Currency, notes, etc.	1,117,732,026	38,467,308	3.4
Jewelry and precious metals	1,350,982,461	64,264,441	4.8
Clothing and furs	279,002,874	37,687,660	13.5
Locally stolen motor vehicles	6,465,991,690	3,746,211,696	57.9
Office equipment	656,982,032	27,398,814	4.2
Televisions, radios, stereos, etc.	874,806,433	40,065,937	4.6
Firearms	116,746,215	10,151,048	8.7
Household goods	294,237,686	15,220,352	5.2
Consumable goods	130,696,065	12,479,046	9.5
Livestock	27,372,148	2,283,515	8.3
Miscellaneous	3,713,652,063	332,696,079	9.0

SECTION III:
OFFENSES CLEARED

OFFENSES CLEARED

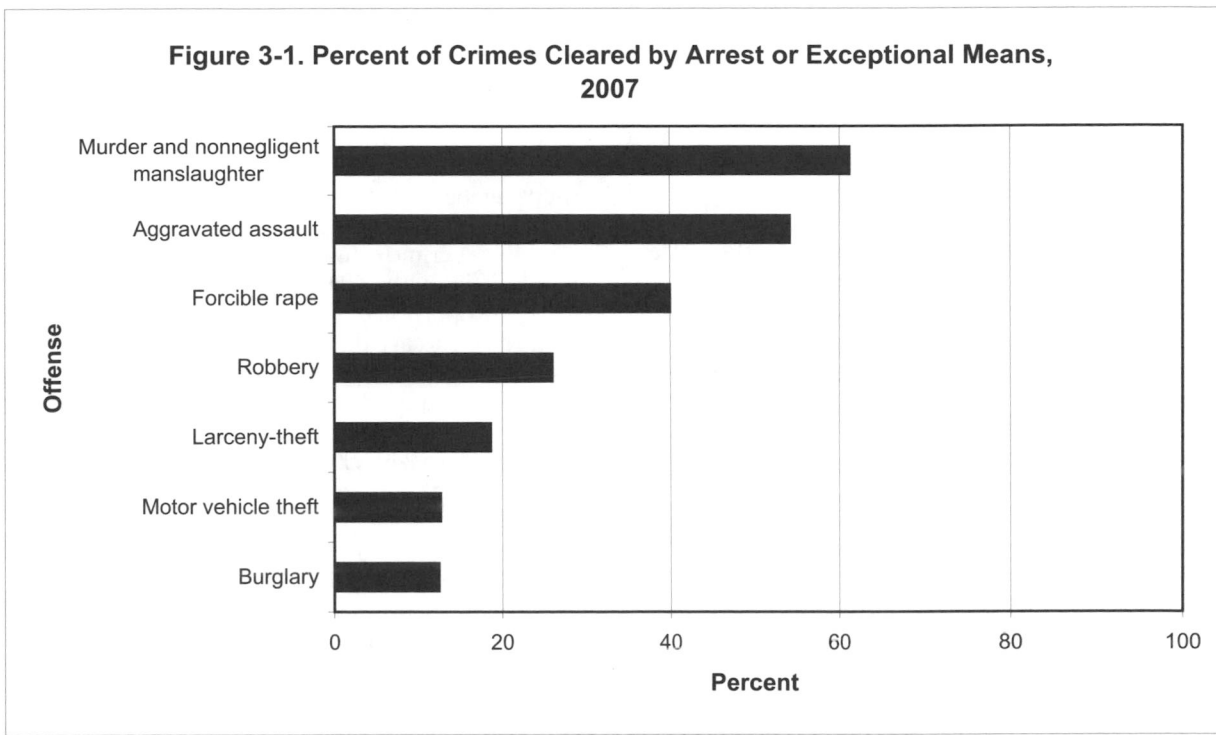

Figure 3-1. Percent of Crimes Cleared by Arrest or Exceptional Means, 2007

Law enforcement agencies that report crime to the Federal Bureau of Investigation (FBI) can clear, or "close," offenses in one of two ways: by arrest or by exceptional means. However, the administrative closing of a case by a local law enforcement agency does not necessarily mean that the agency can clear an offense for UCR purposes. To clear an offense within the program's guidelines, the reporting agency must adhere to certain criteria, which are outlined in this section. (*Note:* The UCR Program does not distinguish between offenses cleared by arrest and those cleared by exceptional means in its data presentations. The distinction is made solely for the purpose of a definition and not for data collection and publication.) See Appendix I for information on the UCR Program's statistical methodology.

Cleared by Arrest

In the UCR Program, a law enforcement agency reports that an offense is cleared by arrest, or solved for crime reporting purposes, when at least one person is arrested, charged with the commission of the offense, and turned over to the court for prosecution (whether following arrest, court summons, or police notice). To qualify as a clearance, *all* of these conditions must be met.

In its calculations, the UCR Program counts the number of offenses that are cleared, not the number of arrestees. Therefore, the arrest of one person may clear several crimes, and the arrest of many persons may clear only one offense. In addition, some clearances recorded by an agency

during a particular calendar year, such as 2007, may pertain to offenses that occurred in previous years.

Cleared by Exceptional Means

In certain situations, elements beyond law enforcement's control prevent the agency from arresting and formally charging the offender. When this occurs, the agency can clear the offense *exceptionally*. There are four UCR Program requirements that law enforcement must meet in order to clear an offense by exceptional means. The agency must have:

• Identified the offender

• Gathered enough evidence to support an arrest, make a charge, and turn over the offender to the court for prosecution

• Identified the offender's exact location so that the suspect could be taken into custody immediately

• Encountered a circumstance outside the control of law enforcement that prohibits the agency from arresting, charging, and prosecuting the offender

Examples of exceptional clearances include, but are not limited to, the death of the offender (e.g., suicide or justifiably killed by a law enforcement officer or a citizen), the victim's refusal to cooperate with the prosecution after the offender has been identified, or the denial of extradition because the offender committed a crime in another jurisdiction and is being prosecuted for that offense. In the UCR Program, the recovery of property does not clear an offense.

National Clearances

A review of the data for 2007 revealed law enforcement agencies in the United States cleared 44.5 percent of violent crimes (murder, forcible rape, robbery, and aggravated assault) and 16.5 percent of property crimes (burglary, larceny-theft, and motor vehicle theft) brought to their attention. In addition, law enforcement cleared 18.0 percent of arson offenses, which are reported in a slightly different manner than the other property crimes. (More details concerning this offense are furnished in the arson text in this section.)

As in most years, law enforcement agencies cleared a higher percentage of violent crimes than property crimes in 2007. As a rule, this long-term trend is attributed to the more vigorous investigative efforts put forth for violent crimes. In addition, violent crimes more often involve victims and/or witnesses who are able to identify the perpetrators.

A breakdown of the clearances for violent crimes for 2007 revealed that the nation's law enforcement agencies cleared 61.2 percent of murder offenses, 54.1 percent of aggravated assault offenses, 40.0 percent of forcible rape offenses, and 25.9 percent of robbery offenses. The data for property crimes showed that agencies cleared 18.6 percent of larceny-theft offenses, 12.6 percent of motor vehicle theft offenses, and 12.4 percent of burglary offenses. (Table 25)

Regional Clearances

The UCR Program divides the nation into four regions: the Northeast, the Midwest, the South, and the West. (See Appendix III for further details.) A review of clearance data for 2007 by region showed that agencies in the Northeast cleared the greatest proportion of their violent crime offenses (49.7 percent). Law enforcement agencies in the South cleared 45.5 percent of their violent crimes, while agencies in the West and Midwest cleared 43.4 percent and 39.2 percent, respectively.

Clearance data for 2007 showed that, among the regions, law enforcement agencies in the Northeast cleared the highest percentage of their property crimes (19.3 percent). Agencies in the South and Midwest cleared 17.1 percent and 16.2 percent, respectively. Agencies in the West cleared 14.5 percent of their property crimes. (Table 26)

Clearances by Population Groups

The UCR Program uses the following population group designations in its data presentations: cities (grouped according to population size) and counties (classified as either metropolitan or nonmetropolitan counties). (A breakdown of these classifications is furnished in Appendix III.)

Cities

In 2007, the clearance data collected showed that law enforcement agencies in the nation's cities cleared 42.5 percent of their violent crime offenses. Among the city population groups, agencies in the smallest cities, those with populations under 10,000 inhabitants, cleared the greatest proportion of their violent crime offenses (56.3 percent), and law enforcement in cities with 250,000 or more inhabitants cleared the smallest proportion of their violent crime offenses (36.5 percent). The clearance data for murder showed that among the city population groups, cities with populations of 10,000 to 24,999 inhabitants cleared the greatest percentage of their murders (71.6 percent). Law enforcement agencies in cities with 100,000 to 249,000 inhabitants cleared the lowest percentage of their murders (57.4 percent).

A further review of the clearance data for 2007 showed that agencies in the nation's cities collectively cleared 16.6 percent of their property crime offenses. Law enforcement in cities with 10,000 to 24,999 inhabitants cleared the highest proportion of the property crimes (20.6 percent) brought to their attention; cities with 500,000 to 999,999 inhabitants cleared the smallest proportion of their property crimes (11.7 percent). (Table 25)

Metropolitan Counties

An examination of clearance data submitted by law enforcement agencies in metropolitan counties in 2007 showed that these agencies cleared 50.3 percent of their violent crime offenses. Of the violent crimes made known to law enforcement agencies, murder offenses had the highest proportion of clearance (60.7 percent). Clearance data also showed that law enforcement agencies in metropolitan counties cleared 16.2 percent of their total property crimes. (Table 25)

Nonmetropolitan Counties

Clearance figures for nonmetropolitan counties showed that these agencies, like their counterparts in metropolitan counties, collectively cleared a greater proportion of their violent crimes than did the nation as a whole in 2007. A further breakdown of the clearance data revealed that agencies in nonmetropolitan counties cleared 57.4 percent of their violent crime offenses. Of the violent crimes known to them, law enforcement in nonmetropolitan counties had the highest number of clearances for murder (70.9 percent). The clearance data collected also showed that law enforcement agencies in nonmetropolitan counties cleared 17.1 percent of their property crime offenses. Among the property crimes known to these agencies, the highest percentage of offenses cleared were for arson and motor vehicle thefts both at 23.7 percent. (Table 25)

Clearances and Juveniles

When an offender under 18 years of age is cited to appear in juvenile court or before other juvenile authorities, the UCR Program considers the incident for which the juvenile is being held responsible to be cleared by arrest, although a physical arrest may not have occurred. In addition, according to program definitions, clearances that include both adult and juvenile offenders are classified as clearances for crimes committed by adults. Therefore, because the clearance percentages for crimes committed by juveniles include only those clearances in which no adults were involved, the figures in this publication should not be used to present a definitive picture of juvenile involvement in crime.

Of the clearances for violent crimes that were reported in the nation in 2007, 12.3 percent involved only juveniles, down from 12.6 percent in 2006. In addition, 18.4 percent of clearances for property crime in 2007 involved only juveniles, down from 19.1 percent in 2006. In 2007, 16.4 percent of all reported robbery clearances involved only juveniles. Arson offenses had the highest percentage of clearances involving only juveniles—39.6 percent—nationally in 2007. (Table 28)

VIOLENT CRIME

National Clearances

In 2007, 44.5 percent of violent crime offenses in the nation was cleared by arrest or exceptional means. Murder had the highest percentage of offenses cleared (61.2 percent). Law enforcement agencies also cleared 54.1 percent of aggravated assaults, 40.0 percent of forcible rapes, and 25.9 percent of robberies. (Table 25)

Regional Clearances

A comparison of clearance data by region showed that law enforcement agencies in the Northeast cleared 49.7 percent of the violent crime reported to them, followed by the South (45.5 percent), the West (43.4 percent), and the Midwest (39.2 percent). For murder, the South cleared 65.3 percent of offenses, followed by the Northeast (49.7 percent), the West (43.4 percent) and the Midwest (39.2 percent each). Forcible rape offenses were cleared 44.3 percent of the time in the South, 44.5 percent of the time in the Northeast, 37.8 percent of the time in the West, and 31.4 percent of the time in the Midwest. For robbery, the Northeast cleared 29.4 percent of offenses, followed by the South (26.2 percent), the West (25.9 percent), and the Midwest (22.1 percent). The Northeast also had the highest proportion of clearances for aggravated assault (62.5 percent), followed by the South (54.3 percent), the West (53.5 percent), and the Midwest (48.6 percent). (Table 26)

Clearances by Population Group

Cities

In the nation's cities, law enforcement agencies collectively cleared 42.5 percent of violent crimes reported to them. Of the population groups with the *city* designation, the nation's smallest cities—those with under 10,000 inhabitants—had the highest percentage of violent crimes cleared (56.3 percent). Cities with 1,000,000 or more inhabitants had the lowest percentage of violent offenses cleared, 34.6 percent. Cities with 10,000 to 24,999 inhabitants cleared the highest percentage of their murder offenses (71.6 percent), while cities with 500,000 to 999,999 inhabitants cleared the lowest percentage of murder offenses (54.6 percent). For forcible rape, cities with 1,000,000 or more inhabitants cleared the largest percentage of offenses at 46.4 percent while cities with 50,000 to 99,999 inhabitants cleared the lowest percentage of offenses at 34.3 percent. Cities with under 10,000 inhabitants cleared the greatest percentage of their robbery offenses at 34.0 percent, and cities with 500,000 to 999,999 inhabitants cleared the lowest percentage of their robbery offenses at 21.4 percent. For aggravated assault, cities with under 10,000 inhabitants cleared the highest proportion of offenses (63.1 percent); cities with 1,000,000 or more inhabitants cleared the lowest percentage of offenses (43.1 percent). (Table 25)

Metropolitan and Nonmetropolitan Counties

Law enforcement agencies in the nation's metropolitan counties cleared 50.3 percent of their violent crimes, with 60.7 percent of murders, 43.5 percent of forcible rapes, 27.5 percent of robberies, and 58.4 percent of aggravated assaults being cleared. Agencies in nonmetropolitan counties cleared 57.4 percent of their violent crime offenses, with 70.9 percent of murders, 44.2 percent of forcible rapes, 39.4 percent of robberies, and 60.7 percent of aggravated assaults being cleared. (Table 25)

Clearances by Classification Group and Type

For forcible rape, by classification group and type, law enforcement agencies cleared 42.6 percent of assault to rape attempts and 38.7 percent of rapes by force in 2007. Cleared robbery offenses included 30.1 percent of offenses involving strong-arm tactics, 28.9 percent of offenses involving knives or other cutting instruments, 20.5 percent of offenses involving firearms, and 27.8 percent of offenses involving other weapons. For aggravated assault, agencies cleared 60.3 percent of offenses involving hands, feet, fists, etc.; 60.9 percent of offenses involving knives or other cutting instruments; 38.8 percent of offenses involving firearms; and 54.2 percent of offenses involving other weapons. (Table 27)

Clearances and Juveniles

When an individual under 18 years of age (a juvenile) is cited to appear before juvenile authorities, the incident is cleared by arrest despite the lack of a physical arrest. In addition, the UCR Program considers any clearance that involves both adults (those age 18 years or over) and juveniles as an adult clearance. Therefore, the juvenile clearance data are limited to those clearances involving juveniles only, and the figures in this publication should not be used to present a definitive picture of juvenile involvement in crime.

In 2007, 12.6 percent of violent crime clearances in the United States exclusively involved juveniles. In the nation's cities, collectively, 12.3 percent of violent crime clearances involved only juveniles, with juveniles in cities exclusively involved in 5.5 percent of murder clearances, 11.1 percent of forcible rape clearances, 16.6 percent of robbery clearances, and 11.6 percent of aggravated assault clearances. Of the nation's city population groups, cities with 50,000 to 99,999 inhabitants had the highest percentage of overall clearances for violent crime only involving juveniles (13.8 percent); cities with 1,000,000 or more inhabitants had the lowest percentage (11.0 percent). Law enforcement agencies in metropolitan counties reported that 12.6 percent of their violent crime clearances—including 6.4 percent of their murder clearances, 13.1 percent of their forcible rape clearances, 16.6 percent of their robbery clearances, and 12.1 percent of their aggravated assault clearances—involved only juveniles. Agencies in nonmetropolitan counties reported that 9.0 percent of their clearances for violent crime involved only juveniles, including 4.4 percent of their murder clearances, 14.4 percent of their forcible rape clearances, 6.9 percent of their robbery clearances, and 8.7 percent of their aggravated assault clearances. (Table 28)

PROPERTY CRIME

National Clearances

Law enforcement agencies throughout the nation collectively cleared 16.5 percent of property crime offenses in 2007, including 12.4 percent of burglary offenses, 18.6 percent of larceny-theft offenses, 12.6 percent of motor vehicle theft offenses, and 18.3 percent of arson offenses. (Table 25)

Regional Clearances

By region in 2007, agencies in the Northeast cleared the highest percentage of property crimes at 19.3 percent, followed by the South at 17.1 percent, the Midwest at 16.2 percent, and the West at 14.5 percent. Agencies in the Northeast also cleared the highest percentage of burglary offenses at 15.0 percent, followed by the South at 13.1 percent, the West at 11.4 percent, and the Midwest at 10.6 percent. For larceny-theft, the Northeast (21.1 percent) was followed by the South (18.8 percent), the Midwest (18.5 percent), and the West (17.0 percent). The South, at 15.3 percent, cleared the greatest percentage of their motor vehicle theft offenses, followed by the Northeast at 15.1 percent, the Midwest at 12.7 percent, and the West at 9.1 percent. The Northeast cleared the greatest percentage of their arson offenses (24.0 percent), followed by the South (20.0 percent), the Midwest (16.3 percent), and the West (15.6 percent). (Table 26)

Clearances by Population Group

Cities

Law enforcement agencies in cities cleared 16.6 percent of property crimes, 11.9 percent of burglaries, 18.9 percent of larceny-thefts, 11.5 percent of motor vehicle thefts, and 17.9 percent of arsons in 2007. (Table 25)

Agencies in cities with populations of 10,000 to 24,999 cleared the largest percentage of their property crimes (20.6 percent), while agencies in cities with populations of 500,000 to 999,999 cleared the smallest percentage of their property crimes (11.7 percent). For burglaries, cities with under 10,000 inhabitants cleared the largest percentage of their offenses, at 16.1 percent, while cities with 1,000,000 or more inhabitants cleared the smallest percentage of their offenses, at 8.0 percent. Cities with 10,000 to 24,999 inhabitants cleared the greatest percentage of their larceny-theft offenses (22.4 percent), and cities with 500,000 to 999,999 inhabitants cleared the lowest percentage of their larceny-theft offenses (13.3 percent). For motor vehicle theft and arson, cities with under 10,000 inhabitants cleared the highest percentages of their offenses, at 23.1 percent and 26.0 percent, respectively; cities with 1,000,000 or more inhabitants cleared the lowest percentages of their offenses, at 9.1 percent and 11.4 percent, respectively. (Table 25)

Metropolitan Counties and Nonmetropolitan Counties

Metropolitan county law enforcement agencies reported that 16.2 percent of their property crimes, 13.3 percent of their burglaries, 17.5 percent of their larceny-thefts, 15.1 percent of their motor vehicle thefts, and 17.9 percent of their arsons were cleared by arrest or exceptional means. Agencies in nonmetropolitan counties reported clearing 17.1 percent of their property crimes, 15.4 percent of their burglaries, 17.1 percent of their larceny-thefts, 23.7 percent of their motor vehicle thefts, and 23.7 percent of their arsons. (Table 25)

Clearances by Classification and Type

For property crime clearances grouped by classification and type, data showed that the highest percentage of burglary clearances in the nation in 2007 (13.9 percent) were of offenses that involved unlawful entry of structures. Law enforcement agencies cleared 11.5 percent of burglaries in which force was used to enter structures and 10.5 percent of attempted burglary offenses. For motor vehicle theft, agencies cleared 12.8 percent of motor vehicle theft offenses involving automobiles and 10.3 percent of motor vehicle theft offenses involving trucks and buses. (Table 27)

In 2007, 22.4 percent of structural arson offenses were cleared by arrest or exceptional means, while 8.6 percent of mobile arson offenses and 20.7 percent of other arson crimes were cleared. (Table 27)

Clearances and Juveniles

When an offender under 18 years of age is cited to appear in juvenile court or before other juvenile authorities, the UCR Program considers the incident for which the juvenile is being held responsible to be cleared by arrest, although a physical arrest may not have occurred. In addition, clearances that include both adult and juvenile offenders are classified as clearances for crimes committed by adults. Thus, juvenile clearance data may not reflect the total involvement of youthful offenders in crime.

Nationally, 18.4 percent of property crime clearances, 16.5 percent of burglary clearances, 19.1 percent of larceny-theft clearances, 15.3 percent of motor vehicle theft clearances, and 39.6 percent of arson clearances nationwide exclusively involved juveniles in 2007. (Table 28) Clearances of juveniles for arson were proportionally higher than those for any other crime.

In cities collectively, 19.0 percent of the clearances for property crime, 16.7 percent of clearances for burglary, 19.8 percent of clearances for larceny-theft, 15.8 percent of clearances for motor vehicle theft, and 41.9 percent of clearances for arson involved juveniles only. Among the population groups labeled *city*, the percentages of clearances involving only juveniles for overall property crime ranged from a low of 14.5 percent in cities with populations of 1,000,000 and over to a high of 21.4 percent in cities with populations of 50,000 to 99,999. Law enforcement in metropolitan counties reported 16.4 percent of property crime clearances, 16.5 percent of burglary clearances, 16.8 percent of larceny-theft clearances, 14.1 percent of motor vehicle theft clearances, and 39.8 percent of arson clearances involved persons under 18 years of age. In nonmetropolitan counties, 13.9 percent of property crime clearances, 14.5 percent of burglary clearances, 13.6 percent of larceny-theft clearances, 13.9 percent of motor vehicle theft clearances, and 19.4 percent of arson clearances involved juveniles exclusively. (Table 28)

Of clearances for structural arsons, 36.2 percent involved only juveniles. Approximately 20.4 percent of clearances for mobile arsons and 51.8 percent of other property type arsons involved only juveniles. (Unpublished Expanded Arson Table 2; see Appendix I for more information)

Table 25.   Percent of Offenses Cleared by Arrest or Exceptional Means, by Population Group, 2007

(Number, percent.)

Population group		Violent crime	Murder and non-negligent man-slaughter	Forcible rape	Robbery	Aggra-vated assault	Property crime	Burglary	Larceny-theft	Motor vehicle theft	Arson[1]	Number of agencies	2007 estimated population
TOTAL ALL AGENCIES:...............................	Offenses known	1,227,330	14,811	78,740	383,749	750,030	8,716,315	1,946,803	5,774,598	994,914	62,248	14,108	262,114,256
	Percent cleared by arrest	44.5	61.2	40.0	25.9	54.1	16.5	12.4	18.6	12.6	18.3		
TOTAL CITIES.................................	Offenses known	958,761	11,354	57,646	330,407	559,354	6,750,388	1,420,331	4,543,080	786,977	45,769	10,006	172,595,675
	Percent cleared by arrest	42.5	60.6	38.6	25.5	52.5	16.6	11.9	18.9	11.5	17.9		
GROUP I (250,000 and over).............	Offenses known	401,518	5,572	18,068	164,288	213,590	2,103,825	469,463	1,270,384	363,978	17,011	69	42,439,501
	Percent cleared by arrest	36.5	58.4	41.2	22.5	46.4	12.6	9.4	14.8	9.3	13.9		
1,000,000 and over (Group I subset)	Offenses known	125,257	1,851	5,328	57,173	60,905	647,572	141,606	380,830	125,136	5,643	8	14,175,600
	Percent cleared by arrest	34.6	62.9	46.4	23.6	43.1	12.1	8.0	14.6	9.1	11.4		
500,000 to 999,999 (Group I subset)	Offenses known	155,793	2,176	6,650	60,234	86,733	813,306	182,966	496,588	133,752	5,824	23	15,106,797
	Percent cleared by arrest	36.9	54.6	39.6	21.4	46.9	11.7	9.1	13.3	9.5	16.8		
250,000 to 499,999 (Group I subset)	Offenses known	120,468	1,545	6,090	46,881	65,952	642,947	144,891	392,966	105,090	5,544	38	13,157,104
	Percent cleared by arrest	38.2	58.3	38.2	22.7	48.7	14.3	11.0	16.8	9.3	13.5		
GROUP II (100,000 to 249,999)	Offenses known	167,798	2,233	9,895	59,741	95,929	1,145,420	248,738	752,558	144,124	7,256	176	26,512,873
	Percent cleared by arrest	41.8	57.4	39.0	25.7	51.7	15.8	11.1	18.4	10.2	17.3		
GROUP III (50,000 to 99,999).............	Offenses known	140,491	1,396	9,334	45,733	84,028	1,098,380	231,520	753,582	113,278	7,166	442	30,409,056
	Percent cleared by arrest	44.3	60.5	34.3	27.7	54.1	18.1	12.8	20.7	11.6	17.2		
GROUP IV (25,000 to 49,999).............	Offenses known	95,890	870	7,550	28,170	59,300	864,244	171,348	622,825	70,071	5,270	744	25,659,304
	Percent cleared by arrest	47.9	68.0	36.1	30.4	57.4	19.0	12.7	21.4	13.7	20.9		
GROUP V (10,000 to 24,999)	Offenses known	83,703	749	6,979	20,728	55,247	817,941	162,736	599,026	56,179	4,628	1,627	25,851,590
	Percent cleared by arrest	51.8	71.6	39.5	32.8	60.2	20.6	14.9	22.4	18.1	23.7		
GROUP VI (under 10,000)	Offenses known	69,361	534	5,820	11,747	51,260	720,578	136,526	544,705	39,347	4,438	6,948	21,723,351
	Percent cleared by arrest	56.3	70.6	39.1	34.0	63.1	19.7	16.1	20.3	23.1	26.0		
METROPOLITAN COUNTIES...	Offenses known	213,587	2,631	14,854	49,200	146,902	1,542,755	390,028	978,492	174,235	12,542	1,722	63,834,694
	Percent cleared by arrest	50.3	60.7	43.5	27.5	58.4	16.2	13.3	17.5	15.1	17.9		
NONMETROPOLITAN COUNTIES...	Offenses known	54,982	826	6,240	4,142	43,774	423,172	136,444	253,026	33,702	3,937	2,380	25,683,887
	Percent cleared by arrest	57.4	70.9	44.2	39.4	60.7	17.1	15.4	17.1	23.7	23.7		
SUBURBAN AREA[2].............................	Offenses known	363,854	3,885	26,392	90,095	243,482	3,059,255	678,307	2,087,106	293,842	21,290	7,394	115,023,793
	Percent cleared by arrest	50.6	62.4	41.6	29.1	59.4	17.6	13.6	19.3	15.2	20.0		

[1] Not all agencies submit reports for arson to the FBI. As a result, the number of reports the FBI uses to compute the percent of offenses cleared for arson is less than the number it uses to compute the percent of offenses cleared for all other offenses.

[2] Suburban area includes law enforcement agencies in cities with less than 50,000 inhabitants and county law enforcement agencies that are within a Metropolitan Statistical Area. Suburban area excludes all metropolitan agencies associated with a principal city. The agencies associated with suburban areas also appear in other groups within this table.

Table 26.   Percent of Offenses Cleared by Arrest or Exceptional Means, by Geographic Division and Region, 2007

(Number, percent.)

Geographic region/division		Violent crime	Murder and non-negligent man-slaughter	Forcible rape	Robbery	Aggra-vated assault	Property crime	Burglary	Larceny-theft	Motor vehicle theft	Arson[1]	Number of agencies	2007 estimated population
TOTAL ALL AGENCIES:	Offenses known	1,227,330	14,811	78,740	383,749	750,030	8,716,315	1,946,803	5,774,598	994,914	62,248	14,108	262,114,256
	Percent cleared by arrest	44.5	61.2	40.0	25.9	54.1	16.5	12.4	18.6	12.6	18.3		
NORTHEAST	Offenses known	147,529	1,717	9,426	51,782	84,604	994,011	198,031	706,050	89,930	6,757	2,979	43,922,345
	Percent cleared by arrest	49.7	60.2	44.5	29.4	62.5	19.3	15.0	21.1	15.1	24.0		
NEW ENGLAND	Offenses known	42,504	336	3,192	11,478	27,498	319,479	66,827	224,014	28,638	1,917	879	13,728,000
	Percent cleared by arrest	47.6	50.9	30.1	25.1	59.0	14.6	11.8	16.0	10.6	20.2		
MIDDLE ATLANTIC	Offenses known	105,025	1,381	6,234	40,304	57,106	674,532	131,204	482,036	61,292	4,840	2,100	30,194,345
	Percent cleared by arrest	50.5	62.5	51.8	30.7	64.1	21.5	16.7	23.4	17.2	25.5		
MIDWEST	Offenses known	189,328	2,208	15,874	57,372	113,874	1,550,436	337,686	1,063,932	148,818	13,210	3,535	47,741,064
	Percent cleared by arrest	39.2	55.7	31.4	22.1	48.6	16.2	10.6	18.5	12.7	16.3		
EAST NORTH CENTRAL	Offenses known	126,607	1,620	11,144	43,706	70,137	985,904	228,496	654,586	102,822	8,992	1,689	29,447,646
	Percent cleared by arrest	34.1	50.5	29.7	20.6	42.8	14.9	9.6	17.3	11.2	15.1		
WEST NORTH CENTRAL	Offenses known	62,721	588	4,730	13,666	43,737	564,532	109,190	409,346	45,996	4,218	1,846	18,293,418
	Percent cleared by arrest	49.5	70.1	35.1	26.6	57.9	18.6	12.7	20.5	16.0	18.6		
SOUTH	Offenses known	575,695	7,311	32,836	171,372	364,176	3,956,202	951,538	2,625,519	379,145	22,959	5,678	103,362,286
	Percent cleared by arrest	45.5	65.3	44.3	26.2	54.3	17.1	13.1	18.8	15.3	20.0		
SOUTH ATLANTIC	Offenses known	318,845	3,970	15,516	99,040	200,319	2,058,093	487,420	1,362,719	207,954	12,286	2,860	55,031,012
	Percent cleared by arrest	47.0	63.5	48.2	26.9	56.5	18.4	14.9	20.0	15.9	20.8		
EAST SOUTH CENTRAL	Offenses known	76,720	979	4,990	21,839	48,912	534,478	135,470	355,143	43,865	2,229	1,140	14,645,882
	Percent cleared by arrest	47.0	63.5	48.2	26.9	56.5	18.4	14.9	20.0	15.9	20.8		
WEST SOUTH CENTRAL	Offenses known	180,130	2,362	12,330	50,493	114,945	1,363,631	328,648	907,657	127,326	8,444	1,678	33,685,392
	Percent cleared by arrest	46.1	64.5	36.5	25.9	55.7	16.8	11.7	18.8	16.5	18.2		
WEST	Offenses known	314,778	3,575	20,604	103,223	187,376	2,215,666	459,548	1,379,097	377,021	19,322	1,916	67,088,561
	Percent cleared by arrest	42.7	68.7	42.4	25.1	49.9	15.2	10.9	17.0	13.9	19.4		
MOUNTAIN	Offenses known	89,648	1,064	7,534	23,737	57,313	715,815	150,033	458,762	107,020	4,900	774	20,440,983
	Percent cleared by arrest	43.4	56.8	37.8	25.9	53.5	14.5	11.4	17.0	9.1	15.6		
PACIFIC	Offenses known	225,130	2,511	13,070	79,486	130,063	1,499,851	309,515	920,335	270,001	14,422	1,142	46,647,578
	Percent cleared by arrest	43.7	60.9	31.6	21.8	54.0	15.1	9.1	18.1	10.5	19.7		
	by arrest	43.3	55.0	41.3	27.1	53.2	14.2	12.5	16.4	8.6	14.2		

[1] Not all agencies submit reports for arson to the FBI. As a result, the number of reports the FBI uses to compute the percent of offenses cleared for arson is less than the number it uses to compute the percent of offenses cleared for all other offenses.

Table 27. Percent of Offenses Cleared by Arrest or Exceptional Means, by Population Group, 2007

(Number, percent.)

Population group		Forcible rape		Robbery				Aggravated assault			
		Rape by force	Assault to rape-attempts	Firearm	Knife or cutting instrument	Other weapon	Strong-arm	Firearm	Knife or cutting instrument	Other weapon	Hands, fists, feet, etc.
TOTAL ALL AGENCIES:......	Offenses known	66,469	5,682	142,220	28,303	30,654	134,480	140,206	123,029	217,114	173,682
	Percent cleared by arrest	38.7	42.6	20.5	28.9	27.8	30.1	38.8	60.9	54.2	60.3
TOTAL CITIES	Offenses known	49,480	4,583	123,394	24,931	26,507	120,224	113,135	98,916	167,085	122,562
	Percent cleared by arrest	37.6	41.8	20.5	28.7	27.7	29.6	36.5	60.2	52.9	59.8
GROUP I (250,000 and over)................	Offenses known	15,451	1,870	68,219	11,801	12,301	56,481	57,741	38,222	67,890	29,610
	Percent cleared by arrest	40.3	41.4	18.5	25.7	23.5	26.4	32.4	56.7	48.8	50.4
1,000,000 and over (Group I subset)...............	Offenses known	4,558	770	25,832	5,266	4,559	21,516	19,444	12,987	19,915	8,559
	Percent cleared by arrest	46.4	46.6	18.4	25.1	25.6	28.9	28.9	52.5	46.9	52.1
500,000 to 999,999 (Group I subset)...............	Offenses known	5,459	604	23,858	3,700	4,497	17,185	21,728	14,226	26,073	10,621
	Percent cleared by arrest	37.9	34.9	17.9	24.5	22.9	23.5	35.4	56.2	47.1	46.5
250,000 to 499,999 (Group I subset)...............	Offenses known	5,434	496	18,529	2,835	3,245	17,780	16,569	11,009	21,902	10,430
	Percent cleared by arrest	37.5	41.1	19.3	28.2	21.3	26.1	32.7	62.1	52.6	52.8
GROUP II (100,000 to 249,999)...............................	Offenses known	8,009	765	21,107	4,456	4,696	21,259	19,520	17,483	29,240	16,012
	Percent cleared by arrest	37.3	45.0	21.1	28.3	28.8	29.9	35.3	61.2	52.1	61.6
GROUP III (50,000 to 99,999)..............................	Offenses known	8,028	625	14,481	3,673	3,802	17,962	13,974	15,027	24,793	19,884
	Percent cleared by arrest	33.2	41.0	21.9	29.7	30.6	31.3	38.4	60.8	55.4	59.6
GROUP IV (25,000 to 49,999)..............................	Offenses known	6,673	450	8,693	2,321	2,767	11,482	8,687	10,844	17,775	16,598
	Percent cleared by arrest	35.3	38.7	24.5	33.0	31.7	33.6	43.4	62.3	56.7	62.6
GROUP V (10,000 to 24,999)..............................	Offenses known	6,166	408	7,133	1,689	1,848	7,950	7,315	9,485	15,126	18,068
	Percent cleared by arrest	39.0	42.6	26.7	37.2	35.7	37.9	47.9	64.3	58.9	64.1
GROUP VI (under 10,000).................................	Offenses known	5,153	465	3,761	991	1,093	5,090	5,898	7,855	12,261	22,390
	Percent cleared by arrest	38.5	41.9	27.4	39.1	35.7	37.2	51.5	66.5	59.9	65.8
METROPOLITAN COUNTIES	Offenses known	11,315	762	17,218	3,036	3,608	12,919	20,399	18,492	38,395	34,559
	Percent cleared by arrest	40.7	47.1	19.1	29.4	27.7	32.8	45.1	63.3	58.1	62.7
NONMETROPOLITAN COUNTIES	Offenses known	5,674	337	1,608	336	539	1,337	6,672	5,621	11,634	16,561
	Percent cleared by arrest	43.7	43.0	36.3	39.3	37.7	41.7	59.7	65.8	59.8	58.9
SUBURBAN AREA[1]	Offenses known	21,341	1,479	30,186	6,172	7,213	28,966	32,177	33,778	64,926	66,615
	Percent cleared by arrest	39.5	45.6	21.1	32.1	30.7	34.6	45.7	64.1	58.8	64.2

[1] Suburban area includes law enforcement agencies in cities with less than 50,000 inhabitants and county law enforcement agencies that are within a Metropolitan Statistical Area. Suburban area excludes all metropolitan agencies associated with a principal city. The agencies associated with suburban areas also appear in other groups within this table.

Table 27.   Percent of Offenses Cleared by Arrest or Exceptional Means, by Population Group, 2007 *(Contd.)*

(Number, percent.)

Population group		Burglary			Motor vehicle theft			Arson[2]			Number of agencies	2007 estimated population
		Forcible entry	Unlawful entry	Attempted forcible entry	Autos	Trucks and buses	Other vehicles	Structure	Mobile	Other		
TOTAL ALL AGENCIES:	Offenses known	1,067,533	566,213	110,793	673,193	157,865	73,848	24,551	16,124	16,959	13,511	242,183,651
	Percent cleared by arrest	11.5	13.9	10.5	12.8	10.3	11.2	22.4	8.6	20.7		
TOTAL CITIES	Offenses known	796,659	416,993	87,395	551,829	127,545	48,183	18,668	11,362	12,449	9,676	161,869,593
	Percent cleared by arrest	11.0	13.7	10.2	12.0	9.3	10.1	22.0	8.1	20.7		
GROUP I (250,000 and over)	Offenses known	295,915	111,067	27,365	245,603	76,346	16,908	6,462	5,582	3,610	63	39,428,308
	Percent cleared by arrest	8.4	10.8	9.3	10.1	7.1	8.1	19.5	5.5	17.6		
1,000,000 and over (Group I subset)	Offenses known	98,510	35,794	7,302	80,390	37,273	7,473	1,931	2,311	1,362	8	14,175,600
	Percent cleared by arrest	7.4	9.2	10.4	11.0	5.3	7.5	18.0	4.8	13.7		
500,000 to 999,999 (Group I subset)	Offenses known	110,828	37,402	12,320	89,303	20,933	5,560	2,261	1,578	1,079	20	13,096,918
	Percent cleared by arrest	8.1	9.7	8.1	9.7	8.7	9.3	21.9	7.2	19.9		
250,000 to 499,999 (Group I subset)	Offenses known	86,577	37,871	7,743	75,910	18,140	3,875	2,270	1,693	1,169	35	12,155,790
	Percent cleared by arrest	10.0	13.4	10.2	9.6	9.0	7.4	18.5	5.0	19.9		
GROUP II (100,000 to 249,999)	Offenses known	133,598	68,286	14,455	102,382	19,229	7,538	3,035	1,694	1,781	158	23,724,578
	Percent cleared by arrest	10.3	13.3	9.9	9.9	9.7	8.4	20.9	7.8	19.5		
GROUP III (50,000 to 99,999)	Offenses known	120,817	74,093	14,859	82,908	13,837	7,458	2,850	1,692	2,229	410	28,281,097
	Percent cleared by arrest	11.9	14.6	10.1	11.6	11.5	9.4	19.3	8.3	19.8		
GROUP IV (25,000 to 49,999)	Offenses known	91,504	56,658	11,820	51,946	7,504	6,276	1,979	1,018	1,952	713	24,562,182
	Percent cleared by arrest	11.9	13.8	10.4	13.6	13.7	11.0	24.2	12.7	21.2		
GROUP V (10,000 to 24,999)	Offenses known	84,652	55,219	10,123	40,975	6,089	5,125	2,143	767	1,447	1,557	24,705,932
	Percent cleared by arrest	14.3	16.1	11.8	19.1	16.3	12.5	25.7	14.9	25.3		
GROUP VI (under 10,000)	Offenses known	70,173	51,670	8,773	28,015	4,540	4,878	2,199	609	1,430	6,775	21,167,496
	Percent cleared by arrest	16.2	16.6	11.8	24.4	21.4	17.2	28.3	17.1	25.9		
METROPOLITAN COUNTIES	Offenses known	189,461	107,197	17,620	100,871	25,474	18,776	4,114	3,931	3,352	1,552	55,508,270
	Percent cleared by arrest	12.3	14.2	10.9	15.0	13.1	11.8	22.6	7.9	20.5		
NONMETROPOLITAN COUNTIES	Offenses known	81,413	42,023	5,778	20,493	4,846	6,889	1,769	831	1,158	2,283	24,805,788
	Percent cleared by arrest	15.3	14.8	12.5	25.0	22.9	17.1	26.8	17.8	21.0		
SUBURBAN AREA[1]	Offenses known	332,281	208,251	37,095	188,486	38,087	29,328	7,578	5,400	6,625	7,008	104,399,866
	Percent cleared by arrest	12.8	14.8	11.0	15.3	13.5	11.9	24.3	9.6	22.0		

[1] Suburban area includes law enforcement agencies in cities with less than 50,000 inhabitants and county law enforcement agencies that are within a Metropolitan Statistical Area. Suburban area excludes all metropolitan agencies associated with a principal city. The agencies associated with suburban areas also appear in other groups within this table.

[2] Not all agencies submit reports for arson to the FBI. As a result, the number of reports the FBI uses to compute the percent of offenses cleared for arson is less than the number it uses to compute the percent of offenses cleared for all other offenses. Agencies must report arson clearances by detailed property classification as specified on the *Monthly Return of Arson Offenses Known to Law Enforcement* to be included in this table; therefore, clearances in this table may differ from other clearance tables.

Table 28.   Number of Offenses Cleared by Arrest or Exceptional Means Involving Persons Under 18 Years of Age, by Population Group, 2006

(Number, percent.)

Population group		Violent crime	Murder and non-negligent man-slaughter	Forcible rape	Robbery	Aggra-vated assault	Property crime	Burglary	Larceny-theft	Motor vehicle theft	Arson[1]	Number of agencies	2007 estimated population
TOTAL ALL AGENCIES:................	Total clearances	465,584	7,794	27,472	84,796	345,522	1,263,199	208,392	946,493	108,314	10,546	13,140	236,796,743
	Percent under 18	12.3	5.6	11.8	16.4	11.5	18.4	16.5	19.1	15.3	39.6		
TOTAL CITIES..................................	Total clearances	358,932	6,036	20,247	74,303	258,346	1,010,257	150,866	777,869	81,522	7,695	9,455	158,743,924
	Percent under 18	12.5	5.5	11.1	16.6	11.6	19.0	16.7	19.8	15.8	41.9		
GROUP I (250,000 and over)........	Total clearances	131,203	2,825	6,989	33,315	88,074	242,879	39,253	172,267	31,359	2,262	62	39,177,864
	Percent under 18	11.2	5.6	8.4	15.9	9.8	16.5	15.0	17.0	15.4	37.3		
1,000,000 and over (Group I subset)	Total clearances	43,355	1,164	2,473	13,472	26,246	78,116	11,288	55,423	11,405	644	8	14,175,600
	Percent under 18	11.0	5.6	7.1	16.2	9.0	14.5	14.8	14.6	13.6	38.0		
500,000 to 999,999 (Group I subset)	Total clearances	46,271	837	2,282	10,239	32,913	82,229	13,575	57,650	11,004	878	20	13,096,918
	Percent under 18	11.5	4.8	9.4	15.9	10.4	16.9	16.3	17.0	17.0	35.4		
250,000 to 499,999 (Group I subset)	Total clearances	41,577	824	2,234	9,604	28,915	82,534	14,390	59,194	8,950	740	34	11,905,346
	Percent under 18	11.1	6.3	8.9	15.5	10.0	17.9	14.0	19.1	15.8	38.8		
GROUP II (100,000 to 249,999)	Total clearances	59,554	1,110	3,265	13,167	42,012	156,678	23,860	120,463	12,355	1,112	156	23,488,164
	Percent under 18	12.7	5.2	12.2	18.4	11.1	21.2	18.8	22.0	17.8	36.9		
GROUP III (50,000 to 99,999)........	Total clearances	54,183	736	2,885	10,847	39,715	177,350	26,401	139,173	11,776	1,147	402	27,807,428
	Percent under 18	13.8	6.4	13.2	17.3	13.1	21.4	16.4	22.8	16.1	49.9		
GROUP IV (25,000 to 49,999)........	Total clearances	41,108	538	2,501	7,509	30,560	150,270	19,581	122,113	8,576	1,040	695	24,027,023
	Percent under 18	13.5	5.6	12.0	17.4	12.8	21.0	17.1	21.9	16.3	42.8		
GROUP V (10,000 to 24,999)	Total clearances	37,909	480	2,496	5,937	28,996	151,921	21,381	121,459	9,081	1,037	1,496	23,778,344
	Percent under 18	12.9	5.4	12.7	14.5	12.7	18.1	17.0	18.6	14.3	47.1		
GROUP VI (under 10,000)	Total clearances	34,975	347	2,111	3,528	28,989	131,159	20,390	102,394	8,375	1,097	6,644	20,465,101
	Percent under 18	13.1	4.6	12.6	15.5	13.0	16.6	17.4	16.6	14.7	42.2		
METROPOLITAN COUNTIES.....................................	Total clearances	78,765	1,258	4,812	9,118	63,577	188,170	38,852	129,647	19,671	1,958	1,479	53,819,257
	Percent under 18	12.6	6.4	13.1	16.6	12.1	16.4	16.5	16.8	14.1	39.8		
NONMETROPOLITAN COUNTIES.....................................	Total clearances	27,887	500	2,413	1,375	23,599	64,772	18,674	38,977	7,121	893	2,206	24,233,562
	Percent under 18	9.0	4.4	14.4	6.9	8.7	13.9	14.5	13.6	13.9	19.4		
SUBURBAN AREA[2].........................	Total clearances	144,646	1,989	8,843	19,890	113,924	447,070	74,616	336,596	35,858	3,862	6,782	101,007,098
	Percent under 18	13.4	6.0	12.7	17.1	13.0	18.1	17.2	18.7	14.2	43.9		

[1] Not all agencies submit reports for arson to the FBI. As a result, the number of reports the FBI uses to compute the percent of offenses cleared for arson is less than the number it uses to compute the percent of offenses cleared for all other offenses.

[2] Suburban area includes law enforcement agencies in cities with less than 50,000 inhabitants and county law enforcement agencies that are within a Metropolitan Statistical Area. Suburban area excludes all metropolitan agencies associated with a principal city. The agencies associated with suburban areas also appear in other groups within this table.

SECTION IV:
PERSONS ARRESTED

PERSONS ARRESTED

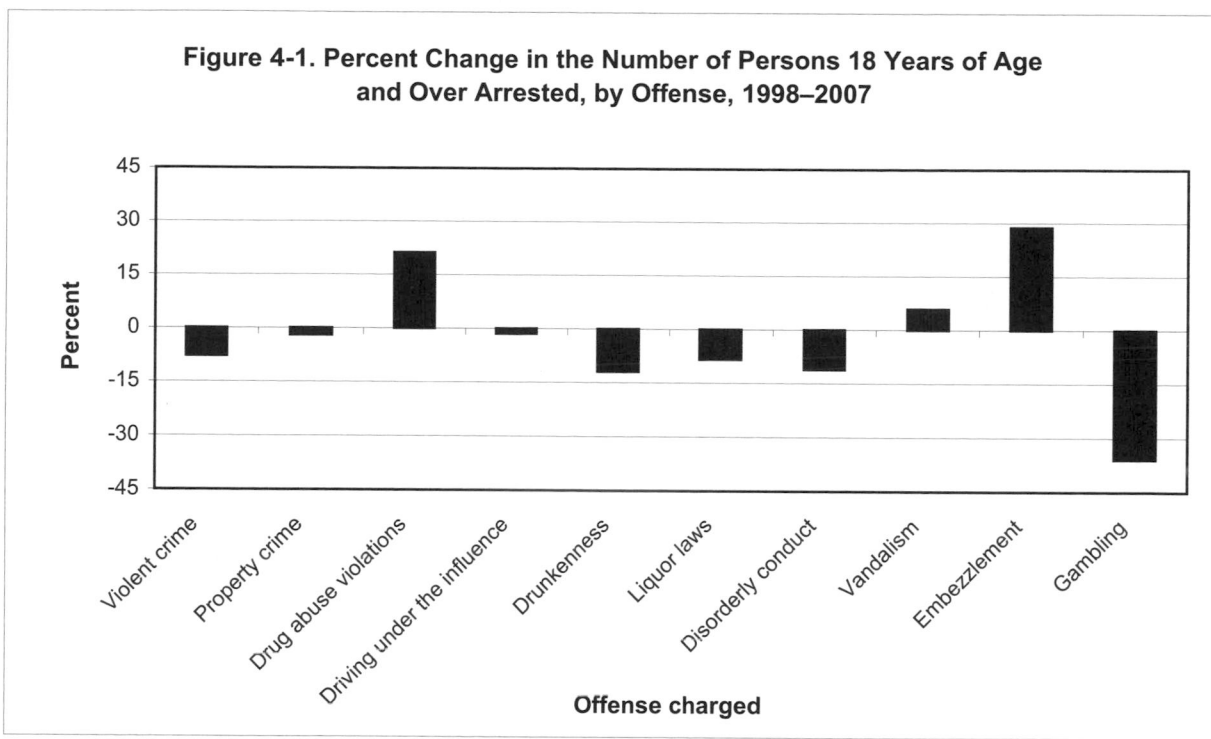

Figure 4-1. Percent Change in the Number of Persons 18 Years of Age and Over Arrested, by Offense, 1998–2007

In the Uniform Crime Reporting (UCR) Program, one arrest is counted for each separate instance in which an individual is arrested, cited, or summoned for criminal acts in Part I and Part II crimes. (See Appendix II for additional information concerning Part I and Part II crimes.) One person may be arrested multiple times during the year; as a result, the arrest figures in this section should not be taken as the total number of individuals arrested. Instead, it provides the number of arrest occurrences reported by law enforcement. Information regarding the UCR Program's statistical methodology and table construction can be found in Appendix I.

National Volume, Trends, and Rates

In 2007, the UCR Program estimated that there were over 14.2 million (14,209,365) arrests in the United States for all criminal offenses (except traffic violations). Law enforcement made an estimated 1,610,088 million arrests (11.3 percent of all arrests) for property crimes and 597,447 arrests (4.2 percent of all arrests) for violent crimes. More arrests were made for drug abuse violations (an estimated 1.8 million arrests and 13.0 percent of all arrests) than for any other offense. (Table 29)

The estimated overall arrest rate of in the nation in 2007 was 4,743.3 arrests per 100,000 inhabitants. Arrests for violent crimes were measured at a rate of 200.2 arrests per 100,000 inhabitants; for property crimes, the arrest rate was 544.1. (Table 30)

A comparison of arrest figures from 2006 to 2007 revealed a 0.3 percent decrease. Arrests for violent crimes decreased 1.1 percent, while arrests for property crimes increased 5.4 percent during the 2-year period. An examination of the 5-year and 10-year arrest trends showed that the total number of arrests in 2007 rose 3.9 percent from the 2003 total. Arrests for violent crimes showed a 0.6 percent increase from 2003 to 2007, while property crimes showed a 0.1 percent increase. In the 10-year trend data (1998 to 2007), the number of arrests showed a steeper decline (3.3 percent). For property crimes, the number of arrests fell 12.5 percent, while arrests for violent crimes fell 8.9 percent. (Tables 32, 34, and 36)

By Age, Sex, and Race

Law enforcement agencies that contributed arrest data to the UCR Program reported information on the age, sex, and race of the persons they arrested. According to the 2007 data, adults accounted for 84.6 percent of arrestees nationally. (Table 38)

A review of arrest data by age from 2006 to 2007 showed that arrests of adults decreased 0.3 percent during this period. Arrests of adults for property crimes increased 5.9 percent, and arrests of adults for violent crimes decreased 0.8 percent over the same time span. The arrest total for juveniles (those under 18 years of age) in 2007 decreased 1.6 percent from the 2006 figure. Over the 2-year period, arrests of juveniles for violent crimes decreased 2.8 percent; juvenile arrests property crimes increased 3.9 percent. (Table 36)

By gender, 75.8 percent of arrests in 2007 were of males. Males accounted for 81.8 percent of the total number of arrestees for violent crimes and 66.6 percent of the total number of arrestees for property crimes. Females accounted for 24.2 percent of all arrestees, 18.2 percent of violent crime arrestees, and 33.4 percent of property crime arrestees. (Table 42)

A review of the 2007 arrest data by race indicated that 69.7 percent of arrestees were White, 28.2 percent were Black, and 2.1 percent were of other races (American Indian or Alaskan Native and Asian or Pacific Islander). Of all arrestees for violent crimes, 58.9 percent were White, 39.0 percent were Black, and 2.1 percent were of other races. Of all arrestees for property crimes, 67.9 percent were White, 29.8 percent were Black, and 2.2 percent were of other races. White adults were most commonly arrested for driving under the influence (916,965 arrests) and drug abuse violations (779,590 arrests). Black adults were most frequently arrested for drug abuse violations (441,711 arrests) and other assaults (simple) (244,808 arrests). (Table 43)

Regional Arrest Rates

The UCR Program divides the United States into four regions: the Northeast, the Midwest, the South, and the West. (Appendix III provides a more information about the regions.)

Law enforcement agencies in the Northeast had an overall arrest rate of 3,711.5 arrests per 100,000 inhabitants, well below the national rate (4,743.3 arrests per 100,000 inhabitants). In this region, the arrest rate for violent crimes was 170.6 arrests per 100,000 inhabitants, and for property crime, the arrest rate was 435.8 arrests per 100,000 inhabitants. In the Midwest, law enforcement agencies reported an arrest rate of 4,842.3 arrests per 100,000 inhabitants. The arrest rate for violent crimes was 154.0 and the arrest rate for property crime was 558.7. Law enforcement agencies in the South, the nation's most populous region, reported an arrest rate of 5,300.8 per 100,000 inhabitants. Arrests for violent crime occurred at a rate of 193.9 arrests per 100,000 residents, and for property crime, the arrest rate was 601.7 arrests per 100,000 inhabitants. In the Western states, law enforcement agencies reported an overall arrest rate of 4,738.0 arrests per 100,000 inhabitants. The region's violent crime arrest rate was 260.4, while its property crime arrest rate was 541.4. (Table 30)

Population Groups: Trends and Rates

The national UCR Program aggregates data by various population groups, which include cities, metropolitan coun-

ties, and nonmetropolitan counties. Definitions of these groups can be found in Appendix III. The total number of arrests in U.S. cities rose 0.3 percent from 2006 to 2007. The number of arrests for property crimes increased 6.7 percent during the 2-year time frame; however, arrests for violent crimes in cities decreased 0.8 percent. (Table 44)

In 2007, law enforcement agencies in cities collectively recorded an arrest rate of 5,187.4 arrests per 100,000 inhabitants. The nation's smallest cities, those with under 10,000 inhabitants, had the highest arrest rate among the city population groups with 6,178.2 arrests per 100,000 inhabitants. Law enforcement agencies in cities with 25,000 to 49,999 inhabitants recorded the lowest rate, 4,605.8. In the nation's metropolitan counties, law enforcement agencies reported an arrest rate of 3,733.8 per 100,000 inhabitants. Agencies in nonmetropolitan counties reported an arrest rate of 3,677.8. (Table 31)

By Age, Sex, and Race

In 2007, law enforcement agencies in the nation's cities reported that 83.2 percent of arrests in their jurisdictions were of adults and 16.8 percent of arrests were of juveniles. Adults accounted for 82.8 percent of arrestees for violent crimes, while juveniles accounted for 17.2 percent. Adults made up 73.2 percent of the arrestees for property crimes, and juveniles accounted for 26.8 percent. Of all arrests in the nation's cities in 2007, 46.1 percent were of individuals under 25 years of age. In metropolitan counties, 39.8 percent of arrests were of individuals under 25 years of age. In nonmetropolitan counties, 37.7 percent of persons arrested were of individuals under 25 years of age. (Tables 46, 47, 53, and 59)

A breakdown of arrests by gender showed that males accounted for 75.5 percent and females accounted for 24.5 percent of arrestees in the nation's cities in 2007. In metropolitan counties, males composed 76.9 percent of arrestees, and in nonmetropolitan counties, males represented 77.0 percent of all arrestees. (Tables 48, 54, and 60)

By race, 67.3 percent of arrestees in the nation's cities in 2007 were White, 30.5 percent were Black, and 2.2 percent were of other races (American Indian or Alaska Native and Asian or Pacific Islander). Whites accounted for 75.4 percent of arrestees in metropolitan counties in 2005, Blacks made up 23.3 percent of arrestees, and persons of other races made up 1.2 percent of the total. In nonmetropolitan counties, Whites made up 82.1 percent of arrestees, Blacks accounted for 14.4 percent of arrestees, and other races made up 3.5 percent of the total. (Tables 49, 55, and 61)

VIOLENT CRIME

Of the estimated 597,447 arrests for violent crime in 2007, 433,945 (72.6 percent) were for aggravated assault, 126,715 (21.2 percent) were for robbery, 23,307 (3.9 percent) were for forcible rape, and 13,480 (2.3 percent) were for murder.

Arrest Trends

A look at 2-year, 5-year, and 10-year trend data showed that the number of arrests for violent crime decreased 1.1 percent from 2006 to 2007, increased 0.6 percent from 2003 to 2007, and declined 8.9 percent from 1998 to 2007. The number of adults arrested for violent crime (arrestees age 18 years and over) decreased 0.8 percent from 2006 to 2007, decreased 0.1 percent from 2003 to 2007, and decreased 7.9 percent from 1998 to 2007. The number of juveniles arrested for violent crime (arrestees under 18 years of age) decreased 2.8 percent from 2006 to 2007, increased 4.6 percent from 2003 to 2007, and decreased 14.1 percent from 1998 to 2007. (Tables 32, 34, and 36)

The trend data for murder showed that the number of arrests for this offense decreased 0.1 percent from 2006 to 2007, increased 2.9 percent from 2003 to 2007, and decreased 11.3 percent from 1998 to 2007. The number of adults arrested for murder declined 0.4 percent from 2006 to 2007, rose 0.9 percent from 2003 to 2007, and fell 9.7 percent from 1998 to 2007. The number of juveniles arrested for murder rose 2.8 percent from 2006 to 2007, rose 25.7 percent from 2003 to 2007, and fell 23.4 percent from 1998 to 2007. (Tables 32, 34, and 36)

For forcible rape, the 2-year trend data showed that arrests declined 4.5 percent from 2006 to 2007, with adult arrests dropping 5.1 percent and juvenile arrests dropping 1.6 percent. The 5-year trend data showed that arrests decreased 12.3 percent from 2003 to 2007; adult arrests decreased 12.2 percent and juvenile arrests declined 12.7 percent during this period. The 10-year trend data showed that forcible rape arrests dropped 23.0 percent from 1998 to 2007, with adult arrests falling 21.1 percent and juvenile arrests falling 31.6 percent. (Tables 32, 34, and 36)

For robbery, the 2-year trend data showed that arrests increased 1.2 percent from 2006 to 2007, with adult arrests rising 2.0 percent and juvenile arrests decreasing 0.9 percent. The 5-year trend data showed that total robbery arrests rose 16.6 percent from 2003 to 2007; adult arrests rose 11.3 percent and juvenile arrests rose 34.6 percent during this period. The 10-year trend data showed that arrests rose 5.9 percent from 1998 to 2007, with adult arrests increasing 5.8 percent and juvenile arrests increasing 6.0 percent. (Tables 32, 34, and 36)

The aggravated assault trend data showed that the number of arrests for this offense fell 1.6 percent from 2006 to 2007, dropped 2.2 percent from 2003 to 2007, and fell 11.5 per-cent from 1998 to 2007. The number of adults arrested for aggravated assault percent decreased 1.3 percent from 2006 to 2007, declined 1.7 percent from 2003 to 2007, and declined 9.8 percent from 1998 to 2007. The number of juveniles arrested for aggravated assault dropped 4.0 percent from 2006 to 2007, fell 5.7 percent from 2003 to 2007, and dropped 21.4 percent from 1998 to 2007. (Tables 32, 34, and 36)

Arrest Rates

Law enforcement agencies throughout the nation reported 200.2 violent crime arrests, 4.5 murder arrests, 7.7 forcible rape arrests, 42.9 robbery arrests, and 145.1 aggravated assault arrests per 100,000 inhabitants in 2007. By region, agencies reported violent crime arrest rates of 170.6 in the Northeast, 154.0 in the Midwest, 193.9 in the South, and 260.4 in the West. The regional murder arrest rates were 3.1 in the Northeast, 3.9 in the Midwest, 5.5 in the South, and 4.7 in the West. For forcible rape, the regional arrest rates were 6.8 in the Northeast, 9.0 in the Midwest, 8.0 in the South, and 7.2 in the West. Regional arrest rates for robbery were 43.8 in the Northeast, 34.9 in the Midwest, 44.2 in the South, and 46.5 in the West. For aggravated assault, the regional arrest rates were 117.0 in the Northeast, 106.2 in the Midwest, 136.1 in the South, and 202.1 in the West. (Table 30)

By population group, law enforcement agencies in the nation's cities collectively reported 225.5 violent crime arrests per 100,000 inhabitants in 2007. In the city population groups, cities with 250,000 or more inhabitants reported the highest violent crime arrest rate (311.8) and cities with 10,000 to 24,999 inhabitants reported the lowest violent crime arrest rate (157.2). Cities reported an overall murder arrest rate of 4.8 per 100,000 inhabitants; cities with 250,000 or more inhabitants had the highest murder arrest rate (8.5) and cities with under 10,000 inhabitants had the lowest murder arrest rate (2.1). The collective city forcible rape arrest rate was 8.2 per 100,000 inhabitants, with the highest rate in cities with 250,000 or more inhabitants (10.3) and the lowest rate in cities with 10,000 to 24,999 inhabitants and 50,000 to 99,999 inhabitants (6.8). The overall robbery arrest rate for cities was 53.0 per 100,000 inhabitants; cities with 250,000 or more inhabitants had the highest robbery arrest rate (87.8) and cities with under 10,000 inhabitants had the lowest robbery arrest rate (21.9). For aggravated assault, the collective city arrest rate was 145.1 per 100,000 inhabitants, with the greatest arrest rate in cities with 250,000 or more inhabitants (205.2) and the lowest arrest rate in cities with 10,000 to 24,999 inhabitants (118.0). (Table 31)

Agencies in metropolitan counties reported a violent crime arrest rate of 153.4 per 100,000 inhabitants, with arrest rates of 4.1 for murder, 6.4 for forcible rape, 24.1 for robbery, and 118.7 for aggravated assault. Agencies in nonmetropolitan counties reported arrest rates of 114.3 for violent crime, 3.0 for murder, 7.5 for forcible rape, 9.3 for robbery, and 94.5 for aggravated assault. (Table 31)

By Age, Sex, and Race

In 2007, most arrestees for violent crime (83.7 percent) were over 18 years of age. By sex, males accounted for 81.8 percent of arrestees for violent crime, 89.8 percent of arrestees for murder, 98.9 percent of arrestees for forcible rape, 88.4 percent of arrestees for robbery, and 78.7 percent of arrestees for aggravated assault. Females accounted for 18.2 percent of violent crime arrestees, 10.2 percent of murder arrestees, 1.1 percent of forcible rape arrestees, 11.6 percent of robbery arrestees, and 21.3 percent of aggravated assault arrestees. (Tables 38 and 42)

By race, 58.9 percent of arrestees for violent crime were White, 39.0 percent were Black, and 2.1 percent were of other races (American Indian or Alaska Native and Asian or Pacific Islander). For murder, 47.6 percent of arrestees were White, 50.4 percent were Black, and 2.0 percent were of other races. For forcible rape, 64.4 percent of arrestees were White, 33.5 percent were Black, and 2.1 percent were of other races. For robbery, 42.0 percent of arrestees were White, 56.7 percent of arrestees were Black, and 1.3 percent were of other races. For aggravated assault, 64.0 percent of arrestees were White, 33.7 percent of arrestees were Black, and 2.3 percent were of other races. (Table 43)

PROPERTY CRIME

Of the estimated 1,610,088 arrests for property crimes in 2007, 1,172,762 (72.8 percent) were for larceny-theft, 303,853 (18.9 percent) were for burglary, 118,231 (7.3 percent) were for motor vehicle theft, and 15,242 (0.9 percent) were for arson. (Table 29)

Arrest Trends

The 2-year, 5-year, and 10-year trend data showed that the number of arrests for property crime increased 5.4 percent from 2006 to 2007, increased 0.1 percent from 2003 to 2007, and declined 12.5 percent from 1998 to 2007. The number of adults arrested for property crime offenses (arrestees age 18 years and over) increased 5.9 percent from 2006 to 2007, increased 4.2 percent from 2003 to 2007, and decreased 2.0 percent from 1998 to 2007. The number of juveniles arrested for property crime (arrestees under 18 years of age) increased 3.9 percent from 2006 to 2007, decreased 9.5 percent from 2003 to 2007, and decreased 32.9 percent from 1998 to 2007. (Tables 32, 34, and 36)

The trend data for burglary showed that the number of arrests for this offense increased 0.7 percent from 2006 to 2007, increased 4.9 percent from 2003 to 2007, and decreased 6.7 percent from 1998 to 2007. The number of adults arrested for burglary rose 1.7 percent from 2006 to 2007, rose 8.2 percent from 2003 to 2007, and rose 6.5 percent from 1998 to 2007. The number of juveniles arrested for burglary declined 1.8 percent from 2006 to 2007, decreased 2.9 percent from 2003 to 2007, and fell 30.3 percent from 1998 to 2007. (Tables 32, 34, and 36)

For larceny-theft, the 2-year trend data showed that arrests increased 8.8 percent from 2006 to 2007, with adult arrests increasing 9.2 percent and juvenile arrests increasing 7.7 percent. The 5-year trend data showed that total larceny-theft arrests increased 1.0 percent from 2003 to 2007; adult arrests increased 5.1 percent and juvenile arrests declined 9.0 percent during this period. The 10-year trend data showed that larceny-theft arrests dropped 12.9 percent from 1998 to 2007, with adult arrests falling 3.6 percent and juvenile arrests falling 32.1 percent. (Tables 32, 34, and 36)

For motor vehicle theft, the 2-year trend data showed that arrests declined 12.7 percent from 2006 to 2007, with adult arrests decreasing 12.2 percent and juvenile arrests decreasing 14.0 percent. The 5-year trend data showed that total motor vehicle theft arrests fell 17.9 percent from 2003 to 2007; adult arrests declined 12.8 percent and juvenile arrests fell 30.3 percent during this period. The 10-year trend data showed that arrests dropped 22.4 percent from 1998 to 2007, with adult arrests falling 7.0 percent and juvenile arrests dropping 48.8 percent. (Tables 32, 34, and 36)

The arson trend data showed that the number of arrests for this offense decreased 5.3 percent from 2006 to 2007, fell 2.7 percent from 2003 to 2007, and fell 9.6 percent from 1998 to 2007. The number of adults arrested for arson fell 2.3 percent from 2006 to 2007, increased 1.9 percent from 2003 to 2007, and increased 1.2 percent from 1998 to 2007. The number of juveniles arrested for arson declined by 8.3 percent from 2006 to 2007, dropped 6.9 percent from 2003 to 2007, and dropped 18.8 percent from 1998 to 2007. (Tables 32, 34, and 36)

Arrest Rates

Law enforcement agencies throughout the nation reported 544.1 property crime arrests, 101.5 burglary arrests, 398.0 larceny-theft arrests, 39.5 motor vehicle theft arrests, and 5.1 arson arrests per 100,000 inhabitants in 2007. By region, agencies reported property crime arrest rates of 435.8 in the Northeast, 558.7 in the Midwest, 601.7 in the South, and 541.4 in the West. The regional burglary arrest rates were 75.8 in the Northeast, 81.9 in the Midwest, 113.4 in the South, and 119.4 in the West. For larceny-theft, the regional arrest rates were 331.5 in the Northeast, 429.0 in the Midwest, 450.7 in the South, and 361.1 in the West. Regional arrest rates for motor vehicle theft were 23.6 in the Northeast, 43.2 in the Midwest, 32.2 in the South, and 55.7 in the West. For arson, the regional arrest rates were 4.9 in the Northeast, 4.6 in the Midwest, 5.4 in the South, and 5.2 in the West. (Table 30)

By population group, law enforcement agencies in the nation's cities collectively reported 642.8 property crime arrests per 100,000 inhabitants in 2007. In the city population groups, cities with 100,000 to 249,999 inhabitants reported the highest property crime arrest rate (704.7) and cities with under 10,000 inhabitants reported the lowest property crime arrest rate (590.6). Cities reported an overall burglary arrest rate of 108.9 per 100,000 inhabitants; cities with 100,000 to 249,999 inhabitants had the highest burglary arrest rate (136.4) and cities with 25,000 to 49,999 inhabitants had the lowest burglary arrest rate (90.8). The collective city larceny-theft arrest rate was 483.7 per 100,000 inhabitants, with the highest rate in cities with 25,000 to 49,999 inhabitants (516.9) and the lowest rate in cities with 250,000 or more inhabitants (442.7). The overall motor vehicle theft arrest rate for cities was 44.8 per 100,000 inhabitants; cities with 250,000 or more inhabitants had the highest motor vehicle theft arrest rate (77.6), and cities with 25,000 to 49,999 inhabitants had the lowest motor vehicle theft arrest rate (25.8). For arson, the collective city arrest rate was 5.3 per 100,000 inhabitants, with the greatest arrest rate in cities with under 10,000 inhabitants (7.1) and the lowest arrest rate in cities with 250,000 or more inhabitants (4.6). (Table 31)

Agencies in metropolitan counties reported a property crime arrest rate of 339.2 per 100,000 inhabitants, with arrest rates of 82.8 for burglary, 222.3 for larceny-theft, 29.4 for motor vehicle theft, and 4.5 for arson. Agencies in non-metropolitan counties reported arrest rates of 262.7 for property crime, 87.4 for burglary, 148.8 for larceny-theft, 22.2 for motor vehicle theft, and 4.3 for arson. (Table 31)

By Age, Sex, and Race

In 2007, most arrestees for property crime (74.0 percent) were over 18 years of age. By sex, males accounted for 66.6 percent of arrestees for property crime, 85.5 percent of arrestees for burglary, 60.0 percent of arrestees for larceny-theft, 82.3 percent of arrestees for motor vehicle theft, and 84.2 percent of arrestees for arson. Females accounted for 33.4 percent of property crime arrestees, 14.5 percent of burglary arrestees, 40.0 percent of larceny-theft arrestees, 17.7 percent of motor vehicle theft arrestees, and 15.8 percent of arson arrestees. (Tables 38 and 42)

By race, 67.9 percent of arrestees for property crime were White, 29.8 percent were Black, and 2.2 percent were of other races (American Indian or Alaska Native and Asian or Pacific Islander). For burglary, 68.5 percent of arrestees were White, 29.8 percent were Black, and 1.7 percent were of other races. For larceny-theft, 68.3 percent of arrestees were White, 29.3 percent were Black, and 2.4 percent were of other races. For motor vehicle theft, 62.2 percent of arrestees were White, 35.8 percent of arrestees were Black, and 2.1 percent were of other races. For arson, 74.6 percent of arrestees were White, 23.4 percent of arrestees were Black, and 1.9 percent were of other races. (Table 43)

Table 29. Estimated Number of Arrests, 2007

(Number.)

Offense4	Arrests
TOTAL[1]	14,209,365
Murder and nonnegligent manslaughter	13,480
Forcible rape	23,307
Robbery	126,715
Aggravated assault	433,945
Burglary	303,853
Larceny-theft	1,172,762
Motor vehicle theft	118,231
Arson	15,242
Violent crime[2]	597,447
Property crime[2]	1,610,088
Other assaults	1,305,693
Forgery and counterfeiting	103,448
Fraud	252,873
Embezzlement	22,381
Stolen property; buying, receiving, possessing	122,061
Vandalism	291,575
Weapons; carrying, possessing, etc.	188,891
Prostitution and commercialized vice	77,607
Sex offenses (except forcible rape and prostitution)	83,979
Drug abuse violations	1,841,182
Gambling	12,161
Offenses against the family and children	122,812
Driving under the influence	1,427,494
Liquor laws	633,654
Drunkenness	589,402
Disorderly conduct	709,105
Vagrancy	33,666
All other offenses	3,931,965
Suspicion	2,176
Curfew and loitering law violations	143,002
Runaways	108,879

[1] Does not include suspicion.

[2] Violent crimes are offenses of murder and nonnegligent manslaughter, forcible rape, robbery, and aggravated assault. Property crimes are offenses of burglary, larceny-theft, motor vehicle theft, and arson.

Table 30. Number and Rate of Arrests, by Geographic Region, 2007

(Number, rate per 100,000.)

Offense charged	United States total (11,936 agencies; population 225,518,634)		Northeast (2,910 agencies; population 43,185,496)		Midwest (3,073 agencies; population 46,018,587)		South (4,229 agencies; population 72,367,116)		West (1,724 agencies; population 63,947,435)	
	Total	Rate	Total	Rate	Total	Rate	Total	Rate	Total	Rate
TOTAL[1]	10,697,033	4,743.3	1,602,821	3,711.5	2,228,363	4,842.3	3,836,036	5,300.8	3,029,813	4,738.0
Murder and nonnegligent manslaughter	10,082	4.5	1,322	3.1	1,778	3.9	3,998	5.5	2,984	4.7
Forcible rape	17,444	7.7	2,916	6.8	4,122	9.0	5,809	8.0	4,597	7.2
Robbery	96,720	42.9	18,923	43.8	16,069	34.9	31,995	44.2	29,733	46.5
Aggravated assault	327,137	145.1	50,507	117.0	48,879	106.2	98,515	136.1	129,236	202.1
Burglary	228,846	101.5	32,730	75.8	37,695	81.9	82,086	113.4	76,335	119.4
Larceny-theft	897,626	398.0	143,144	331.5	197,403	429.0	326,189	450.7	230,890	361.1
Motor vehicle theft	89,022	39.5	10,207	23.6	19,899	43.2	23,285	32.2	35,631	55.7
Arson	11,451	5.1	2,115	4.9	2,114	4.6	3,888	5.4	3,334	5.2
Violent crime[2]	451,383	200.2	73,668	170.6	70,848	154.0	140,317	193.9	166,550	260.4
Property crime[2]	1,226,945	544.1	188,196	435.8	257,111	558.7	435,448	601.7	346,190	541.4
Other assaults	983,964	436.3	160,186	370.9	203,761	442.8	393,556	543.8	226,461	354.1
Forgery and counterfeiting	78,005	34.6	11,871	27.5	12,854	27.9	31,072	42.9	22,208	34.7
Fraud	185,229	82.1	27,206	63.0	33,012	71.7	102,463	141.6	22,548	35.3
Embezzlement	17,015	7.5	2,210	5.1	2,135	4.6	8,684	12.0	3,986	6.2
Stolen property; buying, receiving, possessing	92,215	40.9	16,422	38.0	20,978	45.6	24,383	33.7	30,432	47.6
Vandalism	221,040	98.0	43,359	100.4	46,527	101.1	55,396	76.5	75,758	118.5
Weapons; carrying, possessing, etc.	142,745	63.3	17,808	41.2	26,348	57.3	49,157	67.9	49,432	77.3
Prostitution and commercialized vice	59,390	26.3	7,101	16.4	10,832	23.5	18,727	25.9	22,730	35.5
Sex offenses (except forcible rape and prostitution)	62,756	27.8	10,413	24.1	12,818	27.9	16,249	22.5	23,276	36.4
Drug abuse violations	1,386,394	614.8	219,386	508.0	252,903	549.6	480,863	664.5	433,242	677.5
Gambling	9,152	4.1	714	1.7	4,862	10.6	2,745	3.8	831	1.3
Offenses against the family and children	88,887	39.4	22,294	51.6	23,286	50.6	29,882	41.3	13,425	21.0
Driving under the influence	1,055,981	468.2	141,062	326.6	239,384	520.2	295,549	408.4	379,986	594.2
Liquor laws	478,671	212.3	56,603	131.1	173,406	376.8	112,212	155.1	136,450	213.4
Drunkenness	451,055	200.0	36,111	83.6	36,249	78.8	257,788	356.2	120,907	189.1
Disorderly conduct	540,270	239.6	128,965	298.6	172,039	373.8	162,465	224.5	76,801	120.1
Vagrancy	25,631	11.4	2,962	6.9	4,319	9.4	8,584	11.9	9,766	15.3
All other offenses (except traffic)	2,948,031	1,307.2	398,418	922.6	584,773	1,270.7	1,158,596	1,601.0	806,244	1,260.8
Suspicion	1,589	0.7	172	0.4	209	0.5	1,033	1.4	175	0.3
Curfew and loitering law violations	109,815	48.7	30,338	70.3	19,433	42.2	22,385	30.9	37,659	58.9
Runaways	82,459	36.6	7,528	17.4	20,485	44.5	29,515	40.8	24,931	39.0

[1] Does not include suspicion.

[2] Violent crimes are offenses of murder and nonnegligent manslaughter, forcible rape, robbery, and aggravated assault. Property crimes are offenses of burglary, larceny-theft, motor vehicle theft, and arson.

Table 31.   Number and Rate of Arrests, by Population Group, 2007

(Number, rate per 100,000 population.)

| | Cities | | | | | | | | | |
| Offense charged | Total (11,250 agencies; population 216,686,722) | | Total cities (8,199 cities; population 151,460,208) | | Group I (59 cities, 250,000 and over; population 40,435,530) | | Group II (150 cities, 100,000 to 249,999; population 22,519,131) | | Group III (368 cities, 50,000 to 99,999; population 25,265,390) | |
	Total	Rate	Total	Rate	Total	Rate	Total	Rate	Total	Rate
TOTAL[1]	10,697,033	4,743.3	8,165,997	5,187.4	2,251,897	5,427.1	1,147,663	5,139.3	1,307,595	4,835.1
Murder and nonnegligent manslaughter	10,082	4.5	7,518	4.8	3,514	8.5	1,367	6.1	909	3.4
Forcible rape	17,444	7.7	12,853	8.2	4,266	10.3	1,945	8.7	1,828	6.8
Robbery	96,720	42.9	83,356	53.0	36,439	87.8	14,664	65.7	12,442	46.0
Aggravated assault	327,137	145.1	251,311	159.6	85,151	205.2	41,395	185.4	41,458	153.3
Burglary	228,846	101.5	171,476	108.9	46,126	111.2	30,457	136.4	30,697	113.5
Larceny-theft	897,626	398.0	761,461	483.7	183,677	442.7	114,655	513.4	139,495	515.8
Motor vehicle theft	89,022	39.5	70,482	44.8	32,190	77.6	10,948	49.0	9,221	34.1
Arson	11,451	5.1	8,414	5.3	1,900	4.6	1,297	5.8	1,406	5.2
Violent crime[2]	451,383	200.2	355,038	225.5	129,370	311.8	59,371	265.9	56,637	209.4
Property crime[2]	1,226,945	544.1	1,011,833	642.8	263,893	636.0	157,357	704.7	180,819	668.6
Other assaults	983,964	436.3	751,839	477.6	202,136	487.2	116,244	520.5	122,957	454.7
Forgery and counterfeiting	78,005	34.6	60,078	38.2	16,278	39.2	8,226	36.8	9,719	35.9
Fraud	185,229	82.1	105,543	67.0	17,384	41.9	11,674	52.3	17,369	64.2
Embezzlement	17,015	7.5	13,465	8.6	2,558	6.2	2,884	12.9	2,464	9.1
Stolen property; buying, receiving, possessing	92,215	40.9	71,493	45.4	22,202	53.5	10,002	44.8	12,806	47.4
Vandalism	221,040	98.0	177,716	112.9	44,359	106.9	25,076	112.3	30,065	111.2
Weapons; carrying, possessing, etc.	142,745	63.3	114,494	72.7	44,016	106.1	17,799	79.7	17,052	63.1
Prostitution and commercialized vice	59,390	26.3	56,745	36.0	39,411	95.0	8,150	36.5	4,976	18.4
Sex offenses (except forcible rape and prostitution)	62,756	27.8	45,134	28.7	16,130	38.9	6,151	27.5	7,101	26.3
Drug abuse violations	1,386,394	614.8	1,073,890	682.2	386,211	930.8	157,505	705.3	163,400	604.2
Gambling	9,152	4.1	8,249	5.2	6,571	15.8	565	2.5	265	1.0
Offenses against the family and children	88,887	39.4	40,471	25.7	5,260	12.7	6,132	27.5	7,240	26.8
Driving under the influence	1,055,981	468.2	676,504	429.7	134,078	323.1	80,984	362.6	103,658	383.3
Liquor laws	478,671	212.3	387,504	246.2	61,414	148.0	45,665	204.5	57,947	214.3
Drunkenness	451,055	200.0	392,586	249.4	96,307	232.1	59,509	266.5	67,020	247.8
Disorderly conduct	540,270	239.6	467,398	296.9	110,192	265.6	56,362	252.4	71,853	265.7
Vagrancy	25,631	11.4	22,932	14.6	13,579	32.7	2,500	11.2	2,371	8.8
All other offenses (except traffic)	2,948,031	1,307.2	2,163,947	1,374.6	565,534	1,363.0	295,877	1,325.0	344,965	1,275.6
Suspicion	1,589	0.7	899	0.6	0	0.0	6	0.0	176	0.7
Curfew and loitering law violations	109,815	48.7	105,534	67.0	56,691	136.6	9,446	42.3	13,793	51.0
Runaways	82,459	36.6	63,604	40.4	18,323	44.2	10,184	45.6	13,118	48.5

[1] Does not include suspicion.

[2] Violent crimes are offenses of murder and nonnegligent manslaughter, forcible rape, robbery, and aggravated assault. Property crimes are offenses of burglary, larceny-theft, motor vehicle theft, and arson.

[3] Suburban area includes law enforcement agencies in cities with less than 50,000 inhabitants and county law enforcement agencies that are within a Metropolitan Statistical Area. Suburban area excludes all metropolitan agencies associated with a principal city. The agencies associated with suburban areas also appear in other groups within this table.

Table 31. Number and Rate of Arrests, by Population Group, 2007 *(Contd.)*

(Number, rate per 100,000 population.)

Offense charged	Cities						Counties				Suburban area[3] (6,122 agencies; population 94,714,217)	
	Group IV (654 cities, 25,000 to 49,999; population 22,552,890)		Group V (1,419 cities, 10,000 to 24,999; population 22,395,901)		Group VI (5,549 cities, under 10,000; population 18,291,366)		Metropolitan counties[1] (1,252 agencies; population 45,787,064)		Nonmetropolitan counties (1,799 agencies; population 19,439,450)			
	Total	Rate	Total	Rate	Total	Rate	Total	Rate	Total	Rate	Total	Rate
TOTAL[1]	1,087,187	4,605.8	1,172,238	4,980.9	1,199,417	6,178.2	1,768,264	3,733.8	762,772	3,677.8	4,201,850	4,247.3
Murder and nonnegligent manslaughter	720	3.1	599	2.5	409	2.1	1,944	4.1	620	3.0	3,095	3.1
Forcible rape	1,643	7.0	1,606	6.8	1,565	8.1	3,043	6.4	1,548	7.5	6,302	6.4
Robbery	8,534	36.2	7,024	29.8	4,253	21.9	11,428	24.1	1,936	9.3	27,190	27.5
Aggravated assault	29,713	125.9	27,766	118.0	25,828	133.0	56,233	118.7	19,593	94.5	115,349	116.6
Burglary	21,430	90.8	22,545	95.8	20,221	104.2	39,235	82.8	18,135	87.4	84,443	85.4
Larceny-theft	122,022	516.9	114,446	486.3	87,166	449.0	105,297	222.3	30,868	148.8	340,518	344.2
Motor vehicle theft	6,080	25.8	6,163	26.2	5,880	30.3	13,938	29.4	4,602	22.2	26,932	27.2
Arson	1,126	4.8	1,304	5.5	1,381	7.1	2,153	4.5	884	4.3	4,853	4.9
Violent crime[2]	40,610	172.0	36,995	157.2	32,055	165.1	72,648	153.4	23,697	114.3	151,936	153.6
Property crime[2]	150,658	638.2	144,458	613.8	114,648	590.6	160,623	339.2	54,489	262.7	456,746	461.7
Other assaults	102,647	434.9	105,060	446.4	102,795	529.5	161,719	341.5	70,406	339.5	372,393	376.4
Forgery and counterfeiting	8,242	34.9	9,088	38.6	8,525	43.9	13,104	27.7	4,823	23.3	30,360	30.7
Fraud	15,200	64.4	19,390	82.4	24,526	126.3	51,702	109.2	27,984	134.9	88,486	89.4
Embezzlement	2,267	9.6	2,057	8.7	1,235	6.4	2,635	5.6	915	4.4	6,299	6.4
Stolen property; buying, receiving, possessing	9,715	41.2	9,308	39.6	7,460	38.4	15,625	33.0	5,097	24.6	36,651	37.0
Vandalism	25,749	109.1	26,205	111.3	26,262	135.3	30,259	63.9	13,065	63.0	85,621	86.5
Weapons; carrying, possessing, etc.	12,484	52.9	11,392	48.4	11,751	60.5	21,066	44.5	7,185	34.6	47,877	48.4
Prostitution and commercialized vice	2,742	11.6	917	3.9	549	2.8	2,484	5.2	161	0.8	6,126	6.2
Sex offenses (except forcible rape and prostitution)	5,395	22.9	5,289	22.5	5,068	26.1	12,065	25.5	5,557	26.8	23,328	23.6
Drug abuse violations	120,878	512.1	120,898	513.7	124,998	643.9	222,026	468.8	90,478	436.3	493,774	499.1
Gambling	262	1.1	237	1.0	349	1.8	601	1.3	302	1.5	1,224	1.2
Offenses against the family and children	7,305	30.9	7,524	32.0	7,010	36.1	35,576	75.1	12,840	61.9	50,682	51.2
Driving under the influence	100,210	424.5	122,434	520.2	135,140	696.1	241,360	509.7	138,117	665.9	496,340	501.7
Liquor laws	54,992	233.0	69,557	295.6	97,929	504.4	55,089	116.3	36,078	174.0	196,312	198.4
Drunkenness	53,374	226.1	58,422	248.2	57,954	298.5	40,058	84.6	18,411	88.8	153,383	155.0
Disorderly conduct	62,001	262.7	75,167	319.4	91,823	473.0	49,347	104.2	23,525	113.4	208,355	210.6
Vagrancy	1,960	8.3	948	4.0	1,574	8.1	2,482	5.2	217	1.0	6,001	6.1
All other offenses (except traffic)	293,614	1,243.9	330,320	1,403.6	333,637	1,718.6	558,677	1,179.7	225,407	1,086.8	1,238,040	1,251.4
Suspicion	246	1.0	148	0.6	323	1.7	617	1.3	73	0.4	1,152	1.2
Curfew and loitering law violations	7,969	33.8	8,896	37.8	8,739	45.0	3,873	8.2	408	2.0	22,785	23.0
Runaways	8,913	37.8	7,676	32.6	5,390	27.8	15,245	32.2	3,610	17.4	29,131	29.4

[1] Does not include suspicion.

[2] Violent crimes are offenses of murder and nonnegligent manslaughter, forcible rape, robbery, and aggravated assault. Property crimes are offenses of burglary, larceny-theft, motor vehicle theft, and arson.

[3] Suburban area includes law enforcement agencies in cities with less than 50,000 inhabitants and county law enforcement agencies that are within a Metropolitan Statistical Area. Suburban area excludes all metropolitan agencies associated with a principal city. The agencies associated with suburban areas also appear in other groups within this table.

Table 32.   Ten-Year Arrest Trends, 1998 and 2007

(Number, percent change; 7,946 agencies; 2007 estimated population 171,876,948; 1998 estimated population 154,013,711.)

Offense charged	Number of persons arrested								
	Total all ages			Under 18 years of age			18 years of age and over		
	1998	2007	Percent change	1998	2007	Percent change	1998	2007	Percent change
TOTAL[1]	8,397,065	8,118,197	-3.3	1,527,681	1,215,839	-20.4	6,869,384	6,902,358	+0.5
Murder and nonnegligent manslaughter	8,232	7,301	-11.3	983	753	-23.4	7,249	6,548	-9.7
Forcible rape	17,148	13,212	-23.0	2,975	2,034	-31.6	14,173	11,178	-21.1
Robbery	68,353	72,355	+5.9	18,439	19,550	+6.0	49,914	52,805	+5.8
Aggravated assault	290,851	257,464	-11.5	42,358	33,314	-21.4	248,493	224,150	-9.8
Burglary	195,696	182,552	-6.7	70,171	48,903	-30.3	125,525	133,649	+6.5
Larceny-theft	791,085	689,037	-12.9	258,540	175,561	-32.1	532,545	513,476	-3.6
Motor vehicle theft	80,925	62,766	-22.4	29,882	15,289	-48.8	51,043	47,477	-7.0
Arson	10,055	9,094	-9.6	5,407	4,391	-18.8	4,648	4,703	+1.2
Violent crime[2]	384,584	350,332	-8.9	64,755	55,651	-14.1	319,829	294,681	-7.9
Property crime[2]	1,077,761	943,449	-12.5	364,000	244,144	-32.9	713,761	699,305	-2.0
Other assaults	768,038	754,280	-1.8	138,780	138,795	*	629,258	615,485	-2.2
Forgery and counterfeiting	67,870	58,832	-13.3	4,250	1,699	-60.0	63,620	57,133	-10.2
Fraud	213,800	147,985	-30.8	6,066	4,480	-26.1	207,734	143,505	-30.9
Embezzlement	11,115	14,065	+26.5	1,018	1,072	+5.3	10,097	12,993	+28.7
Stolen property; buying, receiving, possessing	78,371	72,904	-7.0	19,869	13,230	-33.4	58,502	59,674	+2.0
Vandalism	173,617	168,815	-2.8	75,418	64,927	-13.9	98,199	103,888	+5.8
Weapons; carrying, possessing, etc.	109,533	106,080	-3.2	26,395	24,328	-7.8	83,138	81,752	-1.7
Prostitution and commercialized vice	50,082	39,081	-22.0	743	785	+5.7	49,339	38,296	-22.4
Sex offenses (except forcible rape and prostitution)	52,527	45,871	-12.7	9,531	8,106	-15.0	42,996	37,765	-12.2
Drug abuse violations	878,355	1,033,203	+17.6	116,352	109,444	-5.9	762,003	923,759	+21.2
Gambling	5,067	3,289	-35.1	495	360	-27.3	4,572	2,929	-35.9
Offenses against the family and children	85,823	71,305	-16.9	5,765	3,095	-46.3	80,058	68,210	-14.8
Driving under the influence	803,030	788,864	-1.8	11,917	9,867	-17.2	791,113	778,997	-1.5
Liquor laws	375,009	332,231	-11.4	94,257	74,948	-20.5	280,752	257,283	-8.4
Drunkenness	468,796	410,583	-12.4	15,964	11,518	-27.9	452,832	399,065	-11.9
Disorderly conduct	387,534	358,428	-7.5	101,767	104,380	+2.6	285,767	254,048	-11.1
Vagrancy	17,994	16,388	-8.9	1,805	2,719	+50.6	16,189	13,669	-15.6
All other offenses (except traffic)	2,185,863	2,267,145	+3.7	266,238	207,224	-22.2	1,919,625	2,059,921	+7.3
Suspicion	3,463	1,299	-62.5	903	255	-71.8	2,560	1,044	-59.2
Curfew and loitering law violations	104,976	73,217	-30.3	104,976	73,217	-30.3	-	-	-
Runaways	97,320	61,850	-36.4	97,320	61,850	-36.4	-	-	-

[1] Does not include suspicion.

[2] Violent crimes are offenses of murder and nonnegligent manslaughter, forcible rape, robbery, and aggravated assault. Property crimes are offenses of burglary, larceny-theft, motor vehicle theft, and arson.

* = Less than one-tenth of 1 percent.

Table 33. Ten-Year Arrest Trends, by Sex, 1998 and 2007

(7,946 agencies; 2007 estimated population 171,876,948; 1998 estimated population 154,013,711.)

Offense charged	Male						Female					
	Total			Under 18			Total			Under 18		
	1998	2007	Percent change	1998	2007	Percent change	1998	2007	Percent change	1998	2007	Percent change
TOTAL[1]	6,550,864	6,150,145	-6.1	1,114,987	858,746	-23.0	1,846,201	1,968,052	+6.6	412,694	357,093	-13.5
Murder and nonnegligent manslaughter	7,342	6,519	-11.2	898	702	-21.8	890	782	-12.1	85	51	-40.0
Forcible rape	16,942	13,079	-22.8	2,914	2,005	-31.2	206	133	-35.4	61	29	-52.5
Robbery	61,410	64,004	+4.2	16,813	17,654	+5.0	6,943	8,351	+20.3	1,626	1,896	+16.6
Aggravated assault	234,040	202,588	-13.4	33,029	25,602	-22.5	56,811	54,876	-3.4	9,329	7,712	-17.3
Burglary	170,504	154,607	-9.3	62,217	42,872	-31.1	25,192	27,945	+10.9	7,954	6,031	-24.2
Larceny-theft	514,574	413,125	-19.7	169,452	100,042	-41.0	276,511	275,912	-0.2	89,088	75,519	-15.2
Motor vehicle theft	68,494	51,382	-25.0	24,689	12,701	-48.6	12,431	11,384	-8.4	5,193	2,588	-50.2
Arson	8,606	7,685	-10.7	4,832	3,880	-19.7	1,449	1,409	-2.8	575	511	-11.1
Violent crime[2]	319,734	286,190	-10.5	53,654	45,963	-14.3	64,850	64,142	-1.1	11,101	9,688	-12.7
Property crime[2]	762,178	626,799	-17.8	261,190	159,495	-38.9	315,583	316,650	+0.3	102,810	84,649	-17.7
Other assaults	593,042	560,655	-5.5	96,249	91,986	-4.4	174,996	193,625	+10.6	42,531	46,809	+10.1
Forgery and counterfeiting	41,508	36,217	-12.7	2,754	1,146	-58.4	26,362	22,615	-14.2	1,496	553	-63.0
Fraud	114,751	82,340	-28.2	3,969	2,849	-28.2	99,049	65,645	-33.7	2,097	1,631	-22.2
Embezzlement	5,584	6,849	+22.7	575	618	+7.5	5,531	7,216	+30.5	443	454	+2.5
Stolen property; buying, receiving, possessing	66,132	57,865	-12.5	17,289	10,809	-37.5	12,239	15,039	+22.9	2,580	2,421	-6.2
Vandalism	147,331	139,748	-5.1	66,314	56,177	-15.3	26,286	29,067	+10.6	9,104	8,750	-3.9
Weapons; carrying, possessing, etc.	100,973	97,822	-3.1	24,048	21,999	-8.5	8,560	8,258	-3.5	2,347	2,329	-0.8
Prostitution and commercialized vice	20,745	11,485	-44.6	349	170	-51.3	29,337	27,596	-5.9	394	615	+56.1
Sex offenses (except forcible rape and prostitution)	48,658	42,369	-12.9	8,870	7,450	-16.0	3,869	3,502	-9.5	661	656	-0.8
Drug abuse violations	723,435	833,941	+15.3	99,691	91,800	-7.9	154,920	199,262	+28.6	16,661	17,644	+5.9
Gambling	4,568	2,769	-39.4	479	347	-27.6	499	520	+4.2	16	13	-18.8
Offenses against the family and children	67,843	53,754	-20.8	3,648	1,885	-48.3	17,980	17,551	-2.4	2,117	1,210	-42.8
Driving under the influence	676,911	626,371	-7.5	9,849	7,513	-23.7	126,119	162,493	+28.8	2,068	2,354	+13.8
Liquor laws	294,553	242,820	-17.6	66,251	47,505	-28.3	80,456	89,411	+11.1	28,006	27,443	-2.0
Drunkenness	409,100	345,502	-15.5	13,056	8,697	-33.4	59,696	65,081	+9.0	2,908	2,821	-3.0
Disorderly conduct	293,691	261,327	-11.0	72,357	69,051	-4.6	93,843	97,101	+3.5	29,410	35,329	+20.1
Vagrancy	14,281	12,761	-10.6	1,505	1,917	+27.4	3,713	3,627	-2.3	300	802	+167.3
All other offenses (except traffic)	1,732,271	1,744,417	+0.7	199,315	153,225	-23.1	453,592	522,728	+15.2	66,923	53,999	-19.3
Suspicion	2,766	1,031	-62.7	686	189	-72.4	697	268	-61.5	217	66	-69.6
Curfew and loitering law violations	73,163	51,116	-30.1	73,163	51,116	-30.1	31,813	22,101	-30.5	31,813	22,101	-30.5
Runaways	40,412	27,028	-33.1	40,412	27,028	-33.1	56,908	34,822	-38.8	56,908	34,822	-38.8

[1] Does not include suspicion.

[2] Violent crimes are offenses of murder and nonnegligent manslaughter, forcible rape, robbery, and aggravated assault. Property crimes are offenses of burglary, larceny-theft, motor vehicle theft, and arson.

Table 34.   Five-Year Arrest Trends, by Age, 2003 and 2007

(Number, percent change; 9,746 agencies; 2007 estimated population 187,132,870; 2003 estimated population 180,729,448.)

Offense charged	Number of persons arrested								
	Total all ages			Under 18 years of age			18 years of age and over		
	2003	2007	Percent change	2003	2007	Percent change	2003	2007	Percent change
TOTAL[1]	8,480,862	8,814,016	+3.9	1,370,961	1,330,889	-2.9	7,109,901	7,483,127	+5.2
Murder and nonnegligent manslaughter	7,406	7,623	+2.9	599	753	+25.7	6,807	6,870	+0.9
Forcible rape	15,619	13,699	-12.3	2,501	2,183	-12.7	13,118	11,516	-12.2
Robbery	60,487	70,536	+16.6	13,836	18,624	+34.6	46,651	51,912	+11.3
Aggravated assault	275,833	269,706	-2.2	37,231	35,102	-5.7	238,602	234,604	-1.7
Burglary	183,664	192,743	+4.9	54,171	52,595	-2.9	129,493	140,148	+8.2
Larceny-theft	728,039	735,272	+1.0	211,717	192,752	-9.0	516,322	542,520	+5.1
Motor vehicle theft	81,982	67,316	-17.9	23,945	16,679	-30.3	58,037	50,637	-12.8
Arson	10,061	9,792	-2.7	5,255	4,894	-6.9	4,806	4,898	+1.9
Violent crime[2]	359,345	361,564	+0.6	54,167	56,662	+4.6	305,178	304,902	-0.1
Property crime[2]	1,003,746	1,005,123	+0.1	295,088	266,920	-9.5	708,658	738,203	+4.2
Other assaults	783,775	813,015	+3.7	151,619	150,646	-0.6	632,156	662,369	+4.8
Forgery and counterfeiting	72,157	64,027	-11.3	3,045	1,929	-36.7	69,112	62,098	-10.1
Fraud	207,296	167,673	-19.1	5,111	4,819	-5.7	202,185	162,854	-19.5
Embezzlement	11,890	15,151	+27.4	820	1,174	+43.2	11,070	13,977	+26.3
Stolen property; buying, receiving, possessing	83,042	78,750	-5.2	16,004	14,548	-9.1	67,038	64,202	-4.2
Vandalism	173,591	185,412	+6.8	69,445	71,884	+3.5	104,146	113,528	+9.0
Weapons; carrying, possessing, etc.	100,593	113,014	+12.3	23,607	26,345	+11.6	76,986	86,669	+12.6
Prostitution and commercialized vice	34,845	33,421	-4.1	722	728	+0.8	34,123	32,693	-4.2
Sex offenses (except forcible rape and prostitution)	54,249	50,696	-6.5	11,590	9,523	-17.8	42,659	41,173	-3.5
Drug abuse violations	1,002,012	1,097,267	+9.5	117,540	117,686	+0.1	884,472	979,581	+10.8
Gambling	3,512	3,004	-14.5	328	359	+9.5	3,184	2,645	-16.9
Offenses against the family and children	86,404	79,342	-8.2	4,519	3,799	-15.9	81,885	75,543	-7.7
Driving under the influence	888,660	903,244	+1.6	12,825	11,484	-10.5	875,835	891,760	+1.8
Liquor laws	388,033	390,964	+0.8	88,615	90,330	+1.9	299,418	300,634	+0.4
Drunkenness	364,149	408,141	+12.1	11,474	11,819	+3.0	352,675	396,322	+12.4
Disorderly conduct	399,596	418,957	+4.8	123,728	121,975	-1.4	275,868	296,982	+7.7
Vagrancy	17,261	13,061	-24.3	1,332	896	-32.7	15,929	12,165	-23.6
All other offenses (except traffic)	2,312,306	2,483,251	+7.4	244,982	238,424	-2.7	2,067,324	2,244,827	+8.6
Suspicion	1,163	1,423	+22.4	389	292	-24.9	774	1,131	+46.1
Curfew and loitering law violations	57,930	59,686	+3.0	57,930	59,686	+3.0	-	-	-
Runaways	76,470	69,253	-9.4	76,470	69,253	-9.4	-	-	-

[1] Does not include suspicion.

[2] Violent crimes are offenses of murder and nonnegligent manslaughter, forcible rape, robbery, and aggravated assault. Property crimes are offenses of burglary, larceny-theft, motor vehicle theft, and arson.

Table 35. Five-Year Arrest Trends by Age and Sex, 2003 and 2007

(Number, percent change; 9,746 agencies; 2007 estimated population 187,132,870; 2003 estimated population 180,729,44.)

Offense charged	Male						Female					
	Total			Under 18			Total			Under 18		
	2003	2007	Percent change	2003	2007	Percent change	2003	2007	Percent change	2003	2007	Percent change
TOTAL[1]	6,488,366	6,656,579	+2.6	969,405	934,854	-3.6	1,992,496	2,157,437	+8.3	401,556	396,035	-1.4
Murder and nonnegligent manslaughter	6,569	6,805	+3.6	542	690	+27.3	837	818	-2.3	57	63	+10.5
Forcible rape	15,409	13,552	-12.1	2,459	2,143	-12.9	210	147	-30.0	42	40	-4.8
Robbery	54,012	62,432	+15.6	12,591	16,897	+34.2	6,475	8,104	+25.2	1,245	1,727	+38.7
Aggravated assault	218,497	212,486	-2.8	28,506	27,004	-5.3	57,336	57,220	-0.2	8,725	8,098	-7.2
Burglary	157,696	163,537	+3.7	47,626	46,231	-2.9	25,968	29,206	+12.5	6,545	6,364	-2.8
Larceny-theft	456,489	439,829	-3.6	128,945	110,134	-14.6	271,550	295,443	+8.8	82,772	82,618	-0.2
Motor vehicle theft	68,149	55,010	-19.3	19,623	13,718	-30.1	13,833	12,306	-11.0	4,322	2,961	-31.5
Arson	8,550	8,309	-2.8	4,656	4,327	-7.1	1,511	1,483	-1.9	599	567	-5.3
Violent crime[2]	294,487	295,275	+0.3	44,098	46,734	+6.0	64,858	66,289	+2.2	10,069	9,928	-1.4
Property crime[2]	690,884	666,685	-3.5	200,850	174,410	-13.2	312,862	338,438	+8.2	94,238	92,510	-1.8
Other assaults	592,533	604,611	+2.0	102,470	99,858	-2.5	191,242	208,404	+9.0	49,149	50,788	+3.3
Forgery and counterfeiting	42,999	39,268	-8.7	1,969	1,298	-34.1	29,158	24,759	-15.1	1,076	631	-41.4
Fraud	111,771	91,641	-18.0	3,363	3,056	-9.1	95,525	76,032	-20.4	1,748	1,763	+0.9
Embezzlement	5,911	7,360	+24.5	487	685	+40.7	5,979	7,791	+30.3	333	489	+46.8
Stolen property; buying, receiving, possessing	67,850	62,419	-8.0	13,543	11,834	-12.6	15,192	16,331	+7.5	2,461	2,714	+10.3
Vandalism	145,078	153,800	+6.0	59,793	62,173	+4.0	28,513	31,612	+10.9	9,652	9,711	+0.6
Weapons; carrying, possessing, etc.	92,319	104,179	+12.8	21,173	23,896	+12.9	8,274	8,835	+6.8	2,434	2,449	+0.6
Prostitution and commercialized vice	12,546	10,861	-13.4	224	167	-25.4	22,299	22,560	+1.2	498	561	+12.7
Sex offenses (except forcible rape and prostitution)	50,234	46,689	-7.1	10,504	8,617	-18.0	4,015	4,007	-0.2	1,086	906	-16.6
Drug abuse violations	813,481	882,589	+8.5	97,006	97,915	+0.9	188,531	214,678	+13.9	20,534	19,771	-3.7
Gambling	2,913	2,600	-10.7	311	346	+11.3	599	404	-32.6	17	13	-23.5
Offenses against the family and children	66,709	59,557	-10.7	2,753	2,324	-15.6	19,695	19,785	+0.5	1,766	1,475	-16.5
Driving under the influence	724,911	714,625	-1.4	10,213	8,751	-14.3	163,749	188,619	+15.2	2,612	2,733	+4.6
Liquor laws	288,242	281,189	-2.4	57,765	56,562	-2.1	99,791	109,775	+10.0	30,850	33,768	+9.5
Drunkenness	310,909	342,213	+10.1	8,746	8,758	+0.1	53,240	65,928	+23.8	2,728	3,061	+12.2
Disorderly conduct	296,046	305,441	+3.2	85,108	81,550	-4.2	103,550	113,516	+9.6	38,620	40,425	+4.7
Vagrancy	13,380	10,332	-22.8	1,003	697	-30.5	3,881	2,729	-29.7	329	199	-39.5
All other offenses (except traffic)	1,794,343	1,904,256	+6.1	177,206	174,234	-1.7	517,963	578,995	+11.8	67,776	64,190	-5.3
Suspicion	942	1,127	+19.6	298	216	-27.5	221	296	+33.9	91	76	-16.5
Curfew and loitering law violations	39,372	40,403	+2.6	39,372	40,403	+2.6	18,558	19,283	+3.9	18,558	19,283	+3.9
Runaways	31,448	30,586	-2.7	31,448	30,586	-2.7	45,022	38,667	-14.1	45,022	38,667	-14.1

[1] Does not include suspicion.

[2] Violent crimes are offenses of murder and nonnegligent manslaughter, forcible rape, robbery, and aggravated assault. Property crimes are offenses of burglary, larceny-theft, motor vehicle theft, and arson.

Table 36. Current Year Over Previous Year Arrest Trends, 2006–2007

(10,565 agencies; 2007 estimated population 198,239,257; 2006 estimated population 196,944,864)

Offense charged	Number of persons arrested											
	Total all ages			Under 15 years of age			Under 18 years of age			18 years of age and over		
	2006	2007	Percent change	2006	2007	Percent change	2006	2007	Percent change	2006	2007	Percent change
TOTAL[1]	9,373,116	9,347,086	-0.3	429,255	403,797	-5.9	1,459,469	1,435,817	-1.6	7,913,647	7,911,269	*
Murder and nonnegligent manslaughter	8,187	8,177	-0.1	72	85	+18.1	774	796	+2.8	7,413	7,381	-0.4
Forcible rape	15,915	15,195	-4.5	904	840	-7.1	2,451	2,411	-1.6	13,464	12,784	-5.1
Robbery	78,514	79,480	+1.2	4,807	4,418	-8.1	21,144	20,963	-0.9	57,370	58,517	+2.0
Aggravated assault	291,302	286,542	-1.6	12,492	11,666	-6.6	38,728	37,173	-4.0	252,574	249,369	-1.3
Burglary	201,790	203,280	+0.7	17,575	16,256	-7.5	55,398	54,402	-1.8	146,392	148,878	+1.7
Larceny-theft	727,824	791,831	+8.8	64,140	63,628	-0.8	189,735	204,413	+7.7	538,089	587,418	+9.2
Motor vehicle theft	79,906	69,785	-12.7	4,697	3,820	-18.7	19,912	17,134	-14.0	59,994	52,651	-12.2
Arson	11,085	10,500	-5.3	3,176	2,966	-6.6	5,492	5,037	-8.3	5,593	5,463	-2.3
Violent crime[2]	393,918	389,394	-1.1	18,275	17,009	-6.9	63,097	61,343	-2.8	330,821	328,051	-0.8
Property crime[2]	1,020,605	1,075,396	+5.4	89,588	86,670	-3.3	270,537	280,986	+3.9	750,068	794,410	+5.9
Other assaults	857,633	867,481	+1.1	65,105	61,615	-5.4	164,573	159,933	-2.8	693,060	707,548	+2.1
Forgery and counterfeiting	70,985	65,706	-7.4	260	265	+1.9	2,318	2,053	-11.4	68,667	63,653	-7.3
Fraud	196,357	177,389	-9.7	824	783	-5.0	5,237	5,149	-1.7	191,120	172,240	-9.9
Embezzlement	13,996	15,987	+14.2	35	47	+34.3	978	1,226	+25.4	13,018	14,761	+13.4
Stolen property; buying, receiving, possessing	83,112	78,131	-6.0	3,681	3,397	-7.7	14,827	14,177	-4.4	68,285	63,954	-6.3
Vandalism	198,990	195,680	-1.7	32,221	30,603	-5.0	78,352	75,167	-4.1	120,638	120,513	-0.1
Weapons; carrying, possessing, etc.	125,962	118,902	-5.6	10,358	9,000	-13.1	30,169	27,970	-7.3	95,793	90,932	-5.1
Prostitution and commercialized vice	40,109	38,812	-3.2	110	86	-21.8	789	761	-3.5	39,320	38,051	-3.2
Sex offenses (except forcible rape and prostitution)	53,985	51,763	-4.1	4,966	4,765	-4.0	10,432	9,990	-4.2	43,553	41,773	-4.1
Drug abuse violations	1,177,175	1,157,167	-1.7	18,847	18,098	-4.0	123,217	123,590	+0.3	1,053,958	1,033,577	-1.9
Gambling	3,712	3,671	-1.1	90	63	-30.0	471	404	-14.2	3,241	3,267	+0.8
Offenses against the family and children	85,098	83,649	-1.7	1,140	1,201	+5.4	3,628	4,021	+10.8	81,470	79,628	-2.3
Driving under the influence	940,252	947,116	+0.7	381	368	-3.4	12,901	12,113	-6.1	927,351	935,003	+0.8
Liquor laws	425,700	423,246	-0.6	8,693	8,687	-0.1	94,911	95,623	+0.8	330,789	327,623	-1.0
Drunkenness	396,541	422,078	+6.4	1,336	1,319	-1.3	11,848	12,218	+3.1	384,693	409,860	+6.5
Disorderly conduct	472,715	466,953	-1.2	55,368	50,908	-8.1	141,013	133,955	-5.0	331,702	332,998	+0.4
Vagrancy	23,364	20,557	-12.0	1,185	862	-27.3	3,531	2,780	-21.3	19,833	17,777	-10.4
All other offenses (except traffic)	2,629,273	2,590,737	-1.5	67,804	62,371	-8.0	263,006	255,087	-3.0	2,366,267	2,335,650	-1.3
Suspicion	1,457	1,312	-10.0	68	72	+5.9	300	275	-8.3	1,157	1,037	-10.4
Curfew and loitering law violations	91,544	87,226	-4.7	25,454	23,765	-6.6	91,544	87,226	-4.7	-	-	-
Runaways	72,090	70,045	-2.8	23,534	21,915	-6.9	72,090	70,045	-2.8	-	-	-

[1] Does not include suspicion.

[2] Violent crimes are offenses of murder and nonnegligent manslaughter, forcible rape, robbery, and aggravated assault. Property crimes are offenses of burglary, larceny-theft, motor vehicle theft, and arson.

Table 37.   Current Year Over Previous Year Arrest Trends, by Age and Sex, 2006–2007

(Number, percent change; 10,565 agencies; 2007 estimated population 198,239,257; 2006 estimated population 196,944,864.)

Offense charged	Male						Female					
	Total			Under 18			Total			Under 18		
	2006	2007	Percent change	2006	2007	Percent change	2006	2007	Percent change	2006	2007	Percent change
TOTAL[1]	7,117,907	7,055,371	-0.9	1,033,632	1,009,036	-2.4	2,255,209	2,291,715	+1.6	425,837	426,781	+0.2
Murder and nonnegligent manslaughter	7,275	7,320	+0.6	735	737	+0.3	912	857	-6.0	39	59	+51.3
Forcible rape	15,710	15,030	-4.3	2,407	2,364	-1.8	205	165	-19.5	44	47	+6.8
Robbery	69,562	70,271	+1.0	19,175	18,944	-1.2	8,952	9,209	+2.9	1,969	2,019	+2.5
Aggravated assault	230,703	225,270	-2.4	29,683	28,544	-3.8	60,599	61,272	+1.1	9,045	8,629	-4.6
Burglary	171,973	172,858	+0.5	49,001	47,827	-2.4	29,817	30,422	+2.0	6,397	6,575	+2.8
Larceny-theft	451,279	473,191	+4.9	112,067	115,985	+3.5	276,545	318,640	+15.2	77,668	88,428	+13.9
Motor vehicle theft	65,668	57,100	-13.0	16,443	14,122	-14.1	14,238	12,685	-10.9	3,469	3,012	-13.2
Arson	9,228	8,903	-3.5	4,733	4,463	-5.7	1,857	1,597	-14.0	759	574	-24.4
Violent crime[2]	323,250	317,891	-1.7	52,000	50,589	-2.7	70,668	71,503	+1.2	11,097	10,754	-3.1
Property crime[2]	698,148	712,052	+2.0	182,244	182,397	+0.1	322,457	363,344	+12.7	88,293	98,589	+11.7
Other assaults	640,038	645,993	+0.9	108,959	105,906	-2.8	217,595	221,488	+1.8	55,614	54,027	-2.9
Forgery and counterfeiting	42,675	40,028	-6.2	1,535	1,392	-9.3	28,310	25,678	-9.3	783	661	-15.6
Fraud	106,917	97,431	-8.9	3,438	3,279	-4.6	89,440	79,958	-10.6	1,799	1,870	+3.9
Embezzlement	6,548	7,750	+18.4	537	716	+33.3	7,448	8,237	+10.6	441	510	+15.6
Stolen property; buying, receiving, .possessing	67,396	62,948	-6.6	12,657	11,854	-6.3	15,716	15,183	-3.4	2,170	2,323	+7.1
Vandalism	165,478	162,108	-2.0	67,899	64,979	-4.3	33,512	33,572	+0.2	10,453	10,188	-2.5
Weapons; carrying, possessing, etc.	115,669	109,397	-5.4	27,088	25,224	-6.9	10,293	9,505	-7.7	3,081	2,746	-10.9
Prostitution and commercialized vice	14,152	12,339	-12.8	204	176	-13.7	25,957	26,473	+2.0	585	585	0.0
Sex offenses (except forcible rape and prostitution)	50,273	48,184	-4.2	9,455	9,076	-4.0	3,712	3,579	-3.6	977	914	-6.4
Drug abuse violations	948,491	932,383	-1.7	102,450	102,906	+0.4	228,684	224,784	-1.7	20,767	20,684	-0.4
Gambling	3,185	3,041	-4.5	439	387	-11.8	527	630	+19.5	32	17	-46.9
Offenses against the family and children	64,434	62,806	-2.5	2,208	2,464	+11.6	20,664	20,843	+0.9	1,420	1,557	+9.6
Driving under the influence	749,832	749,142	-0.1	9,921	9,207	-7.2	190,420	197,974	+4.0	2,980	2,906	-2.5
Liquor laws	309,821	305,330	-1.4	60,530	59,865	-1.1	115,879	117,916	+1.8	34,381	35,758	+4.0
Drunkenness	334,796	354,052	+5.8	8,859	9,059	+2.3	61,745	68,026	+10.2	2,989	3,159	+5.7
Disorderly conduct	345,354	340,702	-1.3	93,799	89,134	-5.0	127,361	126,251	-0.9	47,214	44,821	-5.1
Vagrancy	17,846	15,660	-12.2	2,426	1,951	-19.6	5,518	4,897	-11.3	1,105	829	-25.0
All other offenses (except traffic)	2,018,548	1,984,428	-1.7	191,928	186,769	-2.7	610,725	606,309	-0.7	71,078	68,318	-3.9
Suspicion	1,153	1,042	-9.6	233	206	-11.6	304	270	-11.2	67	69	+3.0
Curfew and loitering law violations	63,825	60,784	-4.8	63,825	60,784	-4.8	27,719	26,442	-4.6	27,719	26,442	-4.6
Runaways	31,231	30,922	-1.0	31,231	30,922	-1.0	40,859	39,123	-4.2	40,859	39,123	-4.2

[1] Does not include suspicion.

[2] Violent crimes are offenses of murder and nonnegligent manslaughter, forcible rape, robbery, and aggravated assault. Property crimes are offenses of burglary, larceny-theft, motor vehicle theft, and arson.

Table 38. Arrests, Distribution by Age, 2007

(Number, percent; 11,936 agencies; 2007 estimated population 225,518,634)

Offense charged	Total all ages	Ages under 15	Ages under 18	Ages 18 and over	Under 10	10–12	13–14	15	16	17	18	19	20
TOTAL	10,698,310	461,937	1,649,977	9,048,333	13,357	93,571	355,009	326,311	405,753	455,976	509,517	518,623	481,599
Total percent distribution[1]	100.0	4.3	15.4	84.6	0.1	0.9	3.3	3.1	3.8	4.3	4.8	4.8	4.5
Murder and nonnegligent manslaughter	10,082	103	1,011	9,071	1	6	96	131	294	483	736	687	593
Forcible rape	17,132	914	2,633	14,499	8	235	671	447	576	696	829	790	736
Robbery	96,720	5,601	26,324	70,396	72	784	4,745	5,353	7,229	8,141	8,590	7,236	5,620
Aggravated assault	327,137	13,662	43,459	283,678	460	3,320	9,882	8,146	10,231	11,420	12,448	12,564	12,253
Burglary	228,846	18,589	61,695	167,151	631	3,939	14,019	12,580	14,498	16,028	17,104	13,729	11,120
Larceny-theft	897,626	71,314	229,837	667,789	1,804	15,542	53,968	45,808	54,513	58,202	57,221	46,250	37,423
Motor vehicle theft	89,022	4,917	22,266	66,756	33	512	4,372	5,181	6,143	6,025	5,874	4,873	4,070
Arson	11,451	3,204	5,427	6,024	349	1,013	1,842	926	720	577	517	420	312
Violent crime[2]	451,071	20,280	73,427	377,644	541	4,345	15,394	14,077	18,330	20,740	22,603	21,277	19,202
Violent crime percent distribution[1]	100.0	4.5	16.3	83.7	0.1	1.0	3.4	3.1	4.1	4.6	5.0	4.7	4.3
Property crime[2]	1,226,945	98,024	319,225	907,720	2,817	21,006	74,201	64,495	75,874	80,832	80,716	65,272	52,925
Property crime percent distribution[1]	100.0	8.0	26.0	74.0	0.2	1.7	6.0	5.3	6.2	6.6	6.6	5.3	4.3
Other assaults	983,964	70,038	181,378	802,586	2,194	17,638	50,206	35,952	39,029	36,359	32,356	32,319	32,468
Forgery and counterfeiting	78,005	294	2,353	75,652	26	56	212	281	599	1,179	2,538	3,476	3,393
Fraud	185,229	886	5,690	179,539	56	132	698	867	1,464	2,473	4,473	5,865	6,330
Embezzlement	17,015	49	1,288	15,727	6	12	31	58	396	785	1,200	1,192	1,065
Stolen property; buying, receiving, possessing	92,215	4,136	16,889	75,326	79	667	3,390	3,509	4,366	4,878	5,773	5,251	4,481
Vandalism	221,040	34,342	84,744	136,296	1,668	8,647	24,027	16,723	17,187	16,492	13,852	11,560	9,127
Weapons; carrying, possessing, etc.	142,745	10,577	33,187	109,558	438	2,524	7,615	6,251	7,604	8,755	9,517	8,640	7,320
Prostitution and commercialized vice	59,390	147	1,160	58,230	16	14	117	184	315	514	1,890	2,327	2,238
Sex offenses (except forcible rape and prostitution)	62,756	5,574	11,575	51,181	264	1,525	3,785	2,037	1,983	1,981	2,437	2,331	2,056
Drug abuse violations	1,386,394	21,506	147,382	1,239,012	273	2,207	19,026	25,053	40,562	60,261	84,597	84,102	76,405
Gambling	9,152	226	1,584	7,568	7	12	207	283	428	647	705	664	557
Offenses against the family and children	88,887	1,237	4,205	84,682	112	234	891	804	1,026	1,138	1,796	1,909	2,095
Driving under the influence	1,055,981	398	13,497	1,042,484	196	16	186	537	3,169	9,393	23,954	33,125	37,157
Liquor laws	478,671	9,592	106,537	372,134	115	619	8,858	16,210	30,465	50,270	80,215	84,253	69,117
Drunkenness	451,055	1,400	12,966	438,089	75	82	1,243	2,119	3,118	6,329	12,727	14,163	14,210
Disorderly conduct	540,270	57,602	153,293	386,977	1,147	13,136	43,319	31,964	33,452	30,275	24,582	21,580	19,872
Vagrancy	25,631	904	2,924	22,707	15	142	747	766	859	395	1,143	938	770
All other offenses (except traffic)	2,948,031	69,448	284,096	2,663,935	2,244	12,002	55,202	57,709	72,163	84,776	102,335	118,273	120,744
Suspicion	1,589	78	303	1,286	0	15	63	55	104	66	108	106	67
Curfew and loitering law violations	109,815	28,949	109,815	-	456	4,751	23,742	25,435	30,467	24,964	-	-	-
Runaways	82,459	26,250	82,459	-	612	3,789	21,849	20,942	22,793	12,474	-	-	-

[1] Because of rounding, the percentages may not add to 100.0.

[2] Violent crimes are offenses of murder and nonnegligent manslaughter, forcible rape, robbery, and aggravated assault. Property crimes are offenses of burglary, larceny-theft, motor vehicle theft, and arson.

Table 38.   Arrests, Distribution by Age, 2007 *(Contd.)*

(Number, percent; 11,936 agencies; 2007 estimated population 225,518,634)

Offense charged	21	22	23	24	25–29	30–34	35–39	40–44	45–49	50–54	55–59	60–64	65 and over
TOTAL	442,744	410,646	377,997	362,242	1,505,619	1,047,448	972,661	908,080	735,287	424,442	200,498	86,194	64,736
Total percent distribution[1]	4.1	3.8	3.5	3.4	14.1	9.8	9.1	8.5	6.9	4.0	1.9	0.8	0.6
Murder and nonnegligent manslaughter	583	545	473	456	1,758	940	680	558	432	295	175	77	83
Forcible rape	766	590	552	537	2,311	1,883	1,780	1,463	1,047	585	326	151	153
Robbery	4,579	3,881	3,311	3,001	11,175	6,860	5,871	4,865	3,219	1,403	503	178	104
Aggravated assault	12,949	12,208	11,755	11,628	50,759	36,293	32,552	29,840	23,163	13,291	6,317	2,974	2,684
Burglary	9,217	7,870	7,003	6,460	26,124	17,772	16,918	15,073	10,830	5,106	1,855	636	334
Larceny-theft	31,665	27,813	24,783	23,168	98,117	71,066	72,005	68,379	53,626	30,598	14,432	6,128	5,115
Motor vehicle theft	3,674	3,409	3,041	2,967	12,091	8,096	7,217	5,659	3,440	1,471	551	199	124
Arson	282	248	224	184	884	659	606	569	518	290	160	86	65
Violent crime[2]	18,877	17,224	16,091	15,622	66,003	45,976	40,883	36,726	27,861	15,574	7,321	3,380	3,024
Violent crime percent distribution[1]	4.2	3.8	3.6	3.5	14.6	10.2	9.1	8.1	6.2	3.5	1.6	0.7	0.7
Property crime[2]	44,838	39,340	35,051	32,779	137,216	97,593	96,746	89,680	68,414	37,465	16,998	7,049	5,638
Property crime percent distribution[1]	3.7	3.2	2.9	2.7	11.2	8.0	7.9	7.3	5.6	3.1	1.4	0.6	0.5
Other assaults	34,893	34,615	32,942	32,194	142,955	105,901	98,265	88,188	67,702	36,491	16,866	7,634	6,797
Forgery and counterfeiting	3,204	3,182	3,296	3,297	15,085	11,365	9,795	7,708	5,052	2,552	1,079	401	229
Fraud	6,217	6,325	6,217	6,476	31,504	27,390	25,795	21,084	15,204	8,838	4,327	2,074	1,420
Embezzlement	944	875	682	625	2,393	1,721	1,653	1,356	1,037	550	278	101	55
Stolen property; buying, receiving, possessing	3,929	3,599	3,270	3,093	13,060	9,157	8,076	6,909	4,785	2,357	929	390	267
Vandalism	8,739	7,606	6,486	6,026	22,524	13,942	11,605	10,071	7,568	3,890	1,815	774	711
Weapons; carrying, possessing, etc.	7,085	6,514	5,610	5,279	20,033	11,322	8,482	7,015	5,603	3,471	1,911	929	827
Prostitution and commercialized vice	2,309	2,178	2,123	1,955	9,108	7,880	8,597	7,906	5,202	2,528	1,062	462	465
Sex offenses (except forcible rape and prostitution)	1,980	1,817	1,614	1,593	6,935	5,618	6,033	5,821	4,903	3,270	2,024	1,313	1,436
Drug abuse violations	69,504	63,115	57,285	54,075	217,485	136,643	119,766	110,704	88,743	47,922	19,260	6,390	3,016
Gambling	447	415	332	309	1,071	625	489	479	429	329	297	202	218
Offenses against the family and children	2,405	2,430	2,619	2,963	15,258	14,098	13,837	11,516	7,614	3,701	1,421	603	417
Driving under the influence	53,215	52,475	50,092	48,405	190,447	126,294	111,407	104,808	91,814	58,702	32,610	15,920	12,059
Liquor laws	12,190	8,635	6,551	5,676	20,861	14,151	14,771	17,123	17,226	11,407	5,851	2,462	1,645
Drunkenness	21,096	19,512	17,445	16,640	65,982	46,290	46,682	52,731	50,967	33,497	15,716	6,437	3,994
Disorderly conduct	24,730	21,372	18,595	16,960	63,268	39,713	36,652	36,016	30,578	17,797	8,519	3,753	2,990
Vagrancy	800	589	575	557	2,450	2,071	2,662	3,237	3,206	2,060	1,011	412	226
All other offenses (except traffic)	125,274	118,755	111,059	107,666	461,776	329,556	310,342	288,901	231,296	131,986	61,178	25,502	19,292
Suspicion	68	73	62	52	205	142	123	101	83	55	25	6	10
Curfew and loitering law violations	-	-	-	-	-	-	-	-	-	-	-	-	-
Runaways	-	-	-	-	-	-	-	-	-	-	-	-	-

[1] Because of rounding, the percentages may not add to 100.0.

[2] Violent crimes are offenses of murder and nonnegligent manslaughter, forcible rape, robbery, and aggravated assault. Property crimes are offenses of burglary, larceny-theft, motor vehicle theft, and arson.

Table 39.   Male Arrests, Distribution by Age, 2007

(Number, percent; 11,936 agencies; 2007 estimated population 225,518,634.)

Offense charged	Total all ages	Ages under 15	Ages under 18	Ages 18 and over	Under 10	10–12	13–14	15	16	17	18	19	20
TOTAL	8,111,026	319,219	1,164,668	6,946,358	10,792	68,901	239,526	222,121	285,766	337,562	390,495	397,975	371,018
Total percent distribution[1]	100.0	3.9	14.4	85.6	0.1	0.8	3.0	2.7	3.5	4.2	4.8	4.9	4.6
Murder and nonnegligent manslaughter	9,051	94	935	8,116	1	6	87	117	277	447	689	645	549
Forcible rape	16,946	886	2,584	14,362	8	232	646	440	569	689	820	783	725
Robbery	85,544	4,966	23,760	61,784	65	705	4,196	4,815	6,557	7,422	7,830	6,517	5,036
Aggravated assault	257,568	10,356	33,430	224,138	413	2,686	7,257	6,072	7,861	9,141	9,994	10,033	9,642
Burglary	195,550	16,354	54,557	140,993	555	3,463	12,336	11,048	12,914	14,241	15,185	11,917	9,546
Larceny-theft	538,922	42,067	130,539	408,383	1,329	9,818	30,920	25,550	30,161	32,761	33,404	27,269	21,771
Motor vehicle theft	73,241	3,981	18,598	54,643	30	415	3,536	4,281	5,170	5,166	5,079	4,113	3,394
Arson	9,645	2,841	4,782	4,863	324	910	1,607	810	616	515	459	380	270
Violent crime[2]	369,109	16,302	60,709	308,400	487	3,629	12,186	11,444	15,264	17,699	19,333	17,978	15,952
Violent crime percent distribution[1]	100.0	4.4	16.4	83.6	0.1	1.0	3.3	3.1	4.1	4.8	5.2	4.9	4.3
Property crime[2]	817,358	65,243	208,476	608,882	2,238	14,606	48,399	41,689	48,861	52,683	54,127	43,679	34,981
Property crime percent distribution[1]	100.0	8.0	25.5	74.5	0.3	1.8	5.9	5.1	6.0	6.4	6.6	5.3	4.3
Other assaults	735,578	46,909	120,419	615,159	1,817	12,819	32,273	22,927	25,672	24,911	23,030	23,318	23,644
Forgery and counterfeiting	48,220	213	1,612	46,608	18	38	157	196	393	810	1,630	2,131	2,164
Fraud	103,621	554	3,667	99,954	35	70	449	576	962	1,575	2,780	3,520	3,754
Embezzlement	8,256	31	747	7,509	3	8	20	43	229	444	601	579	499
Stolen property; buying, receiving, possessing	73,429	3,257	13,816	59,613	66	499	2,692	2,819	3,634	4,106	4,840	4,258	3,585
Vandalism	183,506	29,612	73,446	110,060	1,472	7,493	20,647	14,642	14,935	14,257	11,911	9,692	7,640
Weapons; carrying, possessing, etc.	131,682	9,314	29,953	101,729	399	2,245	6,670	5,593	6,907	8,139	8,985	8,159	6,915
Prostitution and commercialized vice	18,940	37	251	18,689	6	10	21	30	60	124	280	368	454
Sex offenses (except forcible rape and prostitution)	57,213	5,071	10,450	46,763	232	1,384	3,455	1,809	1,759	1,811	2,151	2,050	1,829
Drug abuse violations	1,125,138	17,169	124,201	1,000,937	223	1,772	15,174	20,737	34,467	51,828	72,350	71,194	64,608
Gambling	8,332	220	1,553	6,779	4	12	204	278	414	641	675	623	501
Offenses against the family and children	66,367	751	2,609	63,758	66	161	524	459	635	764	1,283	1,302	1,405
Driving under the influence	836,671	299	10,233	826,438	153	12	134	386	2,325	7,223	18,800	26,094	29,460
Liquor laws	345,708	4,843	66,676	279,032	80	306	4,457	9,105	18,966	33,762	55,887	60,339	50,430
Drunkenness	378,873	888	9,677	369,196	64	52	772	1,470	2,305	5,014	10,375	11,703	11,912
Disorderly conduct	398,203	37,371	102,371	295,832	923	9,158	27,290	20,474	22,653	21,873	18,510	16,247	15,036
Vagrancy	19,943	596	2,072	17,871	12	95	489	528	629	319	935	757	591
All other offenses (except traffic)	2,271,402	49,492	209,280	2,062,122	1,746	9,082	38,664	40,908	53,210	65,670	81,925	93,898	95,598
Suspicion	1,258	59	231	1,027	0	13	46	41	78	53	87	86	60
Curfew and loitering law violations	76,025	19,187	76,025	-	344	3,359	15,484	17,090	21,537	18,211	-	-	-
Runaways	36,194	11,801	36,194	-	404	2,078	9,319	8,877	9,871	5,645	-	-	-

[1] Because of rounding, the percentages may not add to 100.0.

[2] Violent crimes are offenses of murder and nonnegligent manslaughter, forcible rape, robbery, and aggravated assault. Property crimes are offenses of burglary, larceny-theft, motor vehicle theft, and arson.

Table 39. Male Arrests, Distribution by Age, 2007 *(Contd.)*

(Number, percent; 11,936 agencies; 2007 estimated population 225,518,634.)

Offense charged	21	22	23	24	25–29	30–34	35–39	40–44	45–49	50–54	55–59	60–64	65 and over
TOTAL	344,144	319,136	293,226	280,082	1,159,633	793,373	722,278	678,307	565,921	339,989	165,492	71,613	53,676
Total percent distribution[1]	4.2	3.9	3.6	3.5	14.3	9.8	8.9	8.4	7.0	4.2	2.0	0.9	0.7
Murder and nonnegligent manslaughter	540	494	422	410	1,590	815	590	453	358	259	156	72	74
Forcible rape	757	586	548	533	2,289	1,857	1,770	1,450	1,037	583	322	150	152
Robbery	4,079	3,459	2,937	2,603	9,667	5,835	4,982	4,137	2,775	1,236	441	158	92
Aggravated assault	10,319	9,653	9,305	9,178	40,354	28,464	25,161	22,927	18,137	10,782	5,286	2,574	2,329
Burglary	7,834	6,720	5,894	5,374	21,683	14,515	13,888	12,572	9,170	4,330	1,572	527	266
Larceny-theft	18,794	16,394	14,673	13,566	57,899	42,613	45,116	44,641	35,574	20,372	9,410	3,797	3,090
Motor vehicle theft	3,004	2,771	2,480	2,394	9,684	6,498	5,756	4,595	2,855	1,243	490	179	108
Arson	233	201	187	146	711	516	458	435	395	226	121	70	55
Violent crime[2]	15,695	14,192	13,212	12,724	53,900	36,971	32,503	28,967	22,307	12,860	6,205	2,954	2,647
Violent crime percent distribution[1]	4.3	3.8	3.6	3.4	14.6	10.0	8.8	7.8	6.0	3.5	1.7	0.8	0.7
Property crime[2]	29,865	26,086	23,234	21,480	89,977	64,142	65,218	62,243	47,994	26,171	11,593	4,573	3,519
Property crime percent distribution[1]	3.7	3.2	2.8	2.6	11.0	7.8	8.0	7.6	5.9	3.2	1.4	0.6	0.4
Other assaults	25,725	25,983	24,958	24,555	110,695	82,211	75,325	67,718	53,114	29,260	13,753	6,237	5,633
Forgery and counterfeiting	1,990	2,036	2,083	2,063	9,153	6,798	5,718	4,607	3,244	1,771	758	293	169
Fraud	3,475	3,625	3,486	3,493	16,829	14,118	13,729	11,851	8,969	5,374	2,747	1,325	879
Embezzlement	446	443	334	286	1,097	797	767	670	496	266	141	54	33
Stolen property; buying, receiving, possessing	3,110	2,815	2,536	2,409	10,099	7,061	6,247	5,459	3,864	1,963	798	334	235
Vandalism	7,217	6,180	5,292	4,871	18,017	10,928	8,929	7,704	5,929	3,089	1,443	628	590
Weapons; carrying, possessing, etc.	6,641	6,141	5,273	4,953	18,612	10,397	7,656	6,268	5,081	3,183	1,789	880	796
Prostitution and commercialized vice	540	565	638	637	3,016	2,707	2,599	2,285	1,803	1,224	739	413	421
Sex offenses (except forcible rape and prostitution)	1,781	1,626	1,447	1,408	6,252	5,134	5,462	5,329	4,535	3,081	1,967	1,291	1,420
Drug abuse violations	57,973	52,440	47,409	44,439	177,653	108,754	90,783	82,104	67,822	38,841	16,319	5,560	2,688
Gambling	432	394	317	295	1,022	567	405	389	334	251	232	164	178
Offenses against the family and children	1,658	1,635	1,730	2,020	10,803	10,580	10,637	9,264	6,323	3,116	1,183	487	332
Driving under the influence	41,342	41,030	39,720	38,776	153,903	102,397	87,594	79,618	70,024	46,718	27,102	13,458	10,402
Liquor laws	9,754	6,954	5,333	4,632	16,723	11,260	11,492	13,426	14,194	9,780	5,240	2,154	1,434
Drunkenness	17,875	16,700	14,939	14,319	56,360	39,089	38,059	42,614	42,322	29,196	14,093	5,905	3,735
Disorderly conduct	19,285	16,794	14,585	13,102	48,730	29,602	26,771	26,638	23,560	14,362	7,083	3,083	2,444
Vagrancy	637	476	449	420	1,886	1,517	1,912	2,450	2,597	1,736	923	377	208
All other offenses (except traffic)	98,652	92,957	86,199	83,156	354,755	248,235	230,377	218,622	181,340	107,702	51,363	21,437	15,906
Suspicion	51	64	52	44	151	108	95	81	69	45	21	6	7
Curfew and loitering law violations	-	-	-	-	-	-	-	-	-	-	-	-	-
Runaways	-	-	-	-	-	-	-	-	-	-	-	-	-

[1] Because of rounding, the percentages may not add to 100.0.

[2] Violent crimes are offenses of murder and nonnegligent manslaughter, forcible rape, robbery, and aggravated assault. Property crimes are offenses of burglary, larceny-theft, motor vehicle theft, and arson.

Table 40. Female Arrests, Distribution by Age, 2007

(Number, percent; 11,936 agencies; 2007 estimated population 225,518,634.)

Offense charged	Total all ages	Ages under 15	Ages under 18	Ages 18 and over	Under 10	10–12	13–14	15	16	17	18	19	20
TOTAL	2,587,284	142,718	485,309	2,101,975	2,565	24,670	115,483	104,190	119,987	118,414	119,022	120,648	110,581
Total percent distribution[1]	100.0	5.5	18.8	81.2	0.1	1.0	4.5	4.0	4.6	4.6	4.6	4.7	4.3
Murder and nonnegligent manslaughter	1,031	9	76	955	0	0	9	14	17	36	47	42	44
Forcible rape	186	28	49	137	0	3	25	7	7	7	9	7	11
Robbery	11,176	635	2,564	8,612	7	79	549	538	672	719	760	719	584
Aggravated assault	69,569	3,306	10,029	59,540	47	634	2,625	2,074	2,370	2,279	2,454	2,531	2,611
Burglary	33,296	2,235	7,138	26,158	76	476	1,683	1,532	1,584	1,787	1,919	1,812	1,574
Larceny-theft	358,704	29,247	99,298	259,406	475	5,724	23,048	20,258	24,352	25,441	23,817	18,981	15,652
Motor vehicle theft	15,781	936	3,668	12,113	3	97	836	900	973	859	795	760	676
Arson	1,806	363	645	1,161	25	103	235	116	104	62	58	40	42
Violent crime[2]	81,962	3,978	12,718	69,244	54	716	3,208	2,633	3,066	3,041	3,270	3,299	3,250
Violent crime percent distribution[1]	100.0	4.9	15.5	84.5	0.1	0.9	3.9	3.2	3.7	3.7	4.0	4.0	4.0
Property crime[2]	409,587	32,781	110,749	298,838	579	6,400	25,802	22,806	27,013	28,149	26,589	21,593	17,944
Property crime percent distribution[1]	100.0	8.0	27.0	73.0	0.1	1.6	6.3	5.6	6.6	6.9	6.5	5.3	4.4
Other assaults	248,386	23,129	60,959	187,427	377	4,819	17,933	13,025	13,357	11,448	9,326	9,001	8,824
Forgery and counterfeiting	29,785	81	741	29,044	8	18	55	85	206	369	908	1,345	1,229
Fraud	81,608	332	2,023	79,585	21	62	249	291	502	898	1,693	2,345	2,576
Embezzlement	8,759	18	541	8,218	3	4	11	15	167	341	599	613	566
Stolen property; buying, receiving, possessing	18,786	879	3,073	15,713	13	168	698	690	732	772	933	993	896
Vandalism	37,534	4,730	11,298	26,236	196	1,154	3,380	2,081	2,252	2,235	1,941	1,868	1,487
Weapons; carrying, possessing, etc.	11,063	1,263	3,234	7,829	39	279	945	658	697	616	532	481	405
Prostitution and commercialized vice	40,450	110	909	39,541	10	4	96	154	255	390	1,610	1,959	1,784
Sex offenses (except forcible rape and prostitution)	5,543	503	1,125	4,418	32	141	330	228	224	170	286	281	227
Drug abuse violations	261,256	4,337	23,181	238,075	50	435	3,852	4,316	6,095	8,433	12,247	12,908	11,797
Gambling	820	6	31	789	3	0	3	5	14	6	30	41	56
Offenses against the family and children	22,520	486	1,596	20,924	46	73	367	345	391	374	513	607	690
Driving under the influence	219,310	99	3,264	216,046	43	4	52	151	844	2,170	5,154	7,031	7,697
Liquor laws	132,963	4,749	39,861	93,102	35	313	4,401	7,105	11,499	16,508	24,328	23,914	18,687
Drunkenness	72,182	512	3,289	68,893	11	30	471	649	813	1,315	2,352	2,460	2,298
Disorderly conduct	142,067	20,231	50,922	91,145	224	3,978	16,029	11,490	10,799	8,402	6,072	5,333	4,836
Vagrancy	5,688	308	852	4,836	3	47	258	238	230	76	208	181	179
All other offenses (except traffic)	676,629	19,956	74,816	601,813	498	2,920	16,538	16,801	18,953	19,106	20,410	24,375	25,146
Suspicion	331	19	72	259	0	2	17	14	26	13	21	20	7
Curfew and loitering law violations	33,790	9,762	33,790	-	112	1,392	8,258	8,345	8,930	6,753	-	-	-
Runaways	46,265	14,449	46,265	-	208	1,711	12,530	12,065	12,922	6,829	-	-	-

[1] Because of rounding, the percentages may not add to 100.0.

[2] Violent crimes are offenses of murder and nonnegligent manslaughter, forcible rape, robbery, and aggravated assault. Property crimes are offenses of burglary, larceny-theft, motor vehicle theft, and arson.

Table 40.   Female Arrests, Distribution by Age, 2007 *(Contd.)*

(Number, percent; 11,936 agencies; 2007 estimated population 225,518,634.)

Offense charged	21	22	23	24	25–29	30–34	35–39	40–44	45–49	50–54	55–59	60–64	65 and over
TOTAL	98,600	91,510	84,771	82,160	345,986	254,075	250,383	229,773	169,366	84,453	35,006	14,581	11,060
Total percent distribution[1]	3.8	3.5	3.3	3.2	13.4	9.8	9.7	8.9	6.5	3.3	1.4	0.6	0.4
Murder and nonnegligent manslaughter	43	51	51	46	168	125	90	105	74	36	19	5	9
Forcible rape	9	4	4	4	22	26	10	13	10	2	4	1	1
Robbery	500	422	374	398	1,508	1,025	889	728	444	167	62	20	12
Aggravated assault	2,630	2,555	2,450	2,450	10,405	7,829	7,391	6,913	5,026	2,509	1,031	400	355
Burglary	1,383	1,150	1,109	1,086	4,441	3,257	3,030	2,501	1,660	776	283	109	68
Larceny-theft	12,871	11,419	10,110	9,602	40,218	28,453	26,889	23,738	18,052	10,226	5,022	2,331	2,025
Motor vehicle theft	670	638	561	573	2,407	1,598	1,461	1,064	585	228	61	20	16
Arson	49	47	37	38	173	143	148	134	123	64	39	16	10
Violent crime[2]	3,182	3,032	2,879	2,898	12,103	9,005	8,380	7,759	5,554	2,714	1,116	426	377
Violent crime percent distribution[1]	3.9	3.7	3.5	3.5	14.8	11.0	10.2	9.5	6.8	3.3	1.4	0.5	0.5
Property crime[2]	14,973	13,254	11,817	11,299	47,239	33,451	31,528	27,437	20,420	11,294	5,405	2,476	2,119
Property crime percent distribution[1]	3.7	3.2	2.9	2.8	11.5	8.2	7.7	6.7	5.0	2.8	1.3	0.6	0.5
Other assaults	9,168	8,632	7,984	7,639	32,260	23,690	22,940	20,470	14,588	7,231	3,113	1,397	1,164
Forgery and counterfeiting	1,214	1,146	1,213	1,234	5,932	4,567	4,077	3,101	1,808	781	321	108	60
Fraud	2,742	2,700	2,731	2,983	14,675	13,272	12,066	9,233	6,235	3,464	1,580	749	541
Embezzlement	498	432	348	339	1,296	924	886	686	541	284	137	47	22
Stolen property; buying, receiving, possessing	819	784	734	684	2,961	2,096	1,829	1,450	921	394	131	56	32
Vandalism	1,522	1,426	1,194	1,155	4,507	3,014	2,676	2,367	1,639	801	372	146	121
Weapons; carrying, possessing, etc.	444	373	337	326	1,421	925	826	747	522	288	122	49	31
Prostitution and commercialized vice	1,769	1,613	1,485	1,318	6,092	5,173	5,998	5,621	3,399	1,304	323	49	44
Sex offenses (except forcible rape and prostitution)	199	191	167	185	683	484	571	492	368	189	57	22	16
Drug abuse violations	11,531	10,675	9,876	9,636	39,832	27,889	28,983	28,600	20,921	9,081	2,941	830	328
Gambling	15	21	15	14	49	58	84	90	95	78	65	38	40
Offenses against the family and children	747	795	889	943	4,455	3,518	3,200	2,252	1,291	585	238	116	85
Driving under the influence	11,873	11,445	10,372	9,629	36,544	23,897	23,813	25,190	21,790	11,984	5,508	2,462	1,657
Liquor laws	2,436	1,681	1,218	1,044	4,138	2,891	3,279	3,697	3,032	1,627	611	308	211
Drunkenness	3,221	2,812	2,506	2,321	9,622	7,201	8,623	10,117	8,645	4,301	1,623	532	259
Disorderly conduct	5,445	4,578	4,010	3,858	14,538	10,111	9,881	9,378	7,018	3,435	1,436	670	546
Vagrancy	163	113	126	137	564	554	750	787	609	324	88	35	18
All other offenses (except traffic)	26,622	25,798	24,860	24,510	107,021	81,321	79,965	70,279	49,956	24,284	9,815	4,065	3,386
Suspicion	17	9	10	8	54	34	28	20	14	10	4	0	3
Curfew and loitering law violations	-	-	-	-	-	-	-	-	-	-	-	-	-
Runaways	-	-	-	-	-	-	-	-	-	-	-	-	-

[1] Because of rounding, the percentages may not add to 100.0.

[2] Violent crimes are offenses of murder and nonnegligent manslaughter, forcible rape, robbery, and aggravated assault. Property crimes are offenses of burglary, larceny-theft, motor vehicle theft, and arson.

Table 41. Arrests of Persons Under 15, 18, 21, and 25 Years of Age, 2007

(Number, percent; 11,936 agencies; 2007 estimated population 225,518,634.)

Offense charged	Total all ages	Number of persons arrested				Percent of total all ages			
		Under 15	Under 18	Under 21	Under 25	Under 15	Under 18	Under 21	Under 25
TOTAL	10,698,310	461,937	1,649,977	3,159,716	4,753,345	4.3	15.4	29.5	44.4
Murder and nonnegligent manslaughter	10,082	103	1,011	3,027	5,084	1.0	10.0	30.0	50.4
Forcible rape	17,132	914	2,633	4,988	7,433	5.3	15.4	29.1	43.4
Robbery	96,720	5,601	26,324	47,770	62,542	5.8	27.2	49.4	64.7
Aggravated assault	327,137	13,662	43,459	80,724	129,264	4.2	13.3	24.7	39.5
Burglary	228,846	18,589	61,695	103,648	134,198	8.1	27.0	45.3	58.6
Larceny-theft	897,626	71,314	229,837	370,731	478,160	7.9	25.6	41.3	53.3
Motor vehicle theft	89,022	4,917	22,266	37,083	50,174	5.5	25.0	41.7	56.4
Arson	11,451	3,204	5,427	6,676	7,614	28.0	47.4	58.3	66.5
Violent crime[1]	451,071	20,280	73,427	136,509	204,323	4.5	16.3	30.3	45.3
Property crime[1]	1,226,945	98,024	319,225	518,138	670,146	8.0	26.0	42.2	54.6
Other assaults	983,964	70,038	181,378	278,521	413,165	7.1	18.4	28.3	42.0
Forgery and counterfeiting	78,005	294	2,353	11,760	24,739	0.4	3.0	15.1	31.7
Fraud	185,229	886	5,690	22,358	47,593	0.5	3.1	12.1	25.7
Embezzlement	17,015	49	1,288	4,745	7,871	0.3	7.6	27.9	46.3
Stolen property; buying, receiving, possessing	92,215	4,136	16,889	32,394	46,285	4.5	18.3	35.1	50.2
Vandalism	221,040	34,342	84,744	119,283	148,140	15.5	38.3	54.0	67.0
Weapons; carrying, possessing, etc.	142,745	10,577	33,187	58,664	83,152	7.4	23.2	41.1	58.3
Prostitution and commercialized vice	59,390	147	1,160	7,615	16,180	0.2	2.0	12.8	27.2
Sex offenses (except forcible rape and prostitution)	62,756	5,574	11,575	18,399	25,403	8.9	18.4	29.3	40.5
Drug abuse violations	1,386,394	21,506	147,382	392,486	636,465	1.6	10.6	28.3	45.9
Gambling	9,152	226	1,584	3,510	5,013	2.5	17.3	38.4	54.8
Offenses against the family and children	88,887	1,237	4,205	10,005	20,422	1.4	4.7	11.3	23.0
Driving under the influence	1,055,981	398	13,497	107,733	311,920	*	1.3	10.2	29.5
Liquor laws	478,671	9,592	106,537	340,122	373,174	2.0	22.3	71.1	78.0
Drunkenness	451,055	1,400	12,966	54,066	128,759	0.3	2.9	12.0	28.5
Disorderly conduct	540,270	57,602	153,293	219,327	300,984	10.7	28.4	40.6	55.7
Vagrancy	25,631	904	2,924	5,775	8,296	3.5	11.4	22.5	32.4
All other offenses (except traffic)	2,948,031	69,448	284,096	625,448	1,088,202	2.4	9.6	21.2	36.9
Suspicion	1,589	78	303	584	839	4.9	19.1	36.8	52.8
Curfew and loitering law violations	109,815	28,949	109,815	109,815	109,815	26.4	100.0	100.0	100.0
Runaways	82,459	26,250	82,459	82,459	82,459	31.8	100.0	100.0	100.0

[1] Violent crimes are offenses of murder and nonnegligent manslaughter, forcible rape, robbery, and aggravated assault. Property crimes are offenses of burglary, larceny-theft, motor vehicle theft, and arson.

* = Less than one-tenth of 1 percent.

Table 42. Arrests, Distribution by Sex, 2007

(Number, percent; 11,936 agencies; 2007 estimated population 225,518,634.)

Offense charged	Number of persons arrested			Percent male	Percent female	Percent distribution[1]		
	Total	Male	Female			Total	Male	Female
TOTAL	10,698,310	8,111,026	2,587,284	75.8	24.2	100.0	100.0	100.0
Murder and nonnegligent manslaughter	10,082	9,051	1,031	89.8	10.2	0.1	0.1	*
Forcible rape	17,132	16,946	186	98.9	1.1	0.2	0.2	*
Robbery	96,720	85,544	11,176	88.4	11.6	0.9	1.1	0.4
Aggravated assault	327,137	257,568	69,569	78.7	21.3	3.1	3.2	2.7
Burglary	228,846	195,550	33,296	85.5	14.5	2.1	2.4	1.3
Larceny-theft	897,626	538,922	358,704	60.0	40.0	8.4	6.6	13.9
Motor vehicle theft	89,022	73,241	15,781	82.3	17.7	0.8	0.9	0.6
Arson	11,451	9,645	1,806	84.2	15.8	0.1	0.1	0.1
Violent crime[2]	451,071	369,109	81,962	81.8	18.2	4.2	4.6	3.2
Property crime[2]	1,226,945	817,358	409,587	66.6	33.4	11.5	10.1	15.8
Other assaults	983,964	735,578	248,386	74.8	25.2	9.2	9.1	9.6
Forgery and counterfeiting	78,005	48,220	29,785	61.8	38.2	0.7	0.6	1.2
Fraud	185,229	103,621	81,608	55.9	44.1	1.7	1.3	3.2
Embezzlement	17,015	8,256	8,759	48.5	51.5	0.2	0.1	0.3
Stolen property; buying, receiving, possessing	92,215	73,429	18,786	79.6	20.4	0.9	0.9	0.7
Vandalism	221,040	183,506	37,534	83.0	17.0	2.1	2.3	1.5
Weapons; carrying, possessing, etc.	142,745	131,682	11,063	92.2	7.8	1.3	1.6	0.4
Prostitution and commercialized vice	59,390	18,940	40,450	31.9	68.1	0.6	0.2	1.6
Sex offenses (except forcible rape and prostitution)	62,756	57,213	5,543	91.2	8.8	0.6	0.7	0.2
Drug abuse violations	1,386,394	1,125,138	261,256	81.2	18.8	13.0	13.9	10.1
Gambling	9,152	8,332	820	91.0	9.0	0.1	0.1	*
Offenses against the family and children	88,887	66,367	22,520	74.7	25.3	0.8	0.8	0.9
Driving under the influence	1,055,981	836,671	219,310	79.2	20.8	9.9	10.3	8.5
Liquor laws	478,671	345,708	132,963	72.2	27.8	4.5	4.3	5.1
Drunkenness	451,055	378,873	72,182	84.0	16.0	4.2	4.7	2.8
Disorderly conduct	540,270	398,203	142,067	73.7	26.3	5.1	4.9	5.5
Vagrancy	25,631	19,943	5,688	77.8	22.2	0.2	0.2	0.2
All other offenses (except traffic)	2,948,031	2,271,402	676,629	77.0	23.0	27.6	28.0	26.2
Suspicion	1,589	1,258	331	79.2	20.8	*	*	*
Curfew and loitering law violations	109,815	76,025	33,790	69.2	30.8	1.0	0.9	1.3
Runaways	82,459	36,194	46,265	43.9	56.1	0.8	0.4	1.8

[1] Because of rounding, the percentages may not add to 100.0.

[2] Violent crimes are offenses of murder and nonnegligent manslaughter, forcible rape, robbery, and aggravated assault. Property crimes are offenses of burglary, larceny-theft, motor vehicle theft, and arson.

* = Less than one-tenth of 1 percent.

Table 43. Arrests, Distribution by Race, 2007

(Number, percent; 11,929 agencies; 2007 estimated population 225,477,173.)

Offense charged	Total arrests					Percent distribution[1]					Arrests under 18				
	Total	White	Black	American Indian or Alaskan Native	Asian or Pacific Islander	Total	White	Black	American Indian or Alaskan Native	Asian or Pacific Islander	Total	White	Black	American Indian or Alaskan Native	Asian or Pacific Islander
TOTAL	10,656,710	7,426,278	3,003,060	142,969	84,403	100.0	69.7	28.2	1.3	0.8	1,642,530	1,100,427	505,464	20,504	16,135
Murder and nonnegligent manslaughter	10,067	4,789	5,078	99	101	100.0	47.6	50.4	1.0	1.0	1,011	407	580	15	9
Forcible rape	17,058	10,984	5,708	213	153	100.0	64.4	33.5	1.2	0.9	2,617	1,610	966	24	17
Robbery	96,584	40,573	54,774	602	635	100.0	42.0	56.7	0.6	0.7	26,291	8,119	17,832	122	218
Aggravated assault	326,277	208,762	109,985	4,374	3,156	100.0	64.0	33.7	1.3	1.0	43,322	24,674	17,773	470	405
Burglary	228,346	156,442	68,052	2,191	1,661	100.0	68.5	29.8	1.0	0.7	61,523	40,236	20,176	605	506
Larceny-theft	894,215	610,607	261,730	11,885	9,993	100.0	68.3	29.3	1.3	1.1	228,699	152,143	70,212	2,966	3,378
Motor vehicle theft	88,843	55,229	31,765	1,041	808	100.0	62.2	35.8	1.2	0.9	22,227	12,191	9,426	339	271
Arson	11,400	8,510	2,666	119	105	100.0	74.6	23.4	1.0	0.9	5,397	4,123	1,148	49	77
Violent crime[2]	449,986	265,108	175,545	5,288	4,045	100.0	58.9	39.0	1.2	0.9	73,241	34,810	37,151	631	649
Property crime[2]	1,222,804	830,788	364,213	15,236	12,567	100.0	67.9	29.8	1.2	1.0	317,846	208,693	100,962	3,959	4,232
Other assaults	980,512	641,991	316,217	14,028	8,276	100.0	65.5	32.3	1.4	0.8	180,615	106,119	71,409	1,857	1,230
Forgery and counterfeiting	77,757	54,136	22,460	414	747	100.0	69.6	28.9	0.5	1.0	2,341	1,699	596	21	25
Fraud	184,446	127,377	54,575	1,369	1,125	100.0	69.1	29.6	0.7	0.6	5,649	3,601	1,916	77	55
Embezzlement	16,954	10,813	5,818	95	228	100.0	63.8	34.3	0.6	1.3	1,287	753	498	10	26
Stolen property; buying, receiving, possessing	91,937	57,870	32,570	735	762	100.0	62.9	35.4	0.8	0.8	16,809	9,203	7,302	127	177
Vandalism	220,055	166,201	48,642	3,340	1,872	100.0	75.5	22.1	1.5	0.9	84,298	66,406	16,058	1,062	772
Weapons; carrying, possessing, etc.	142,369	82,311	57,745	1,061	1,252	100.0	57.8	40.6	0.7	0.9	33,040	19,992	12,412	250	386
Prostitution and commercialized vice	59,307	34,190	23,251	550	1,316	100.0	57.6	39.2	0.9	2.2	1,156	473	670	9	4
Sex offenses (except forcible rape and prostitution)	62,586	45,961	15,372	633	620	100.0	73.4	24.6	1.0	1.0	11,526	8,139	3,239	77	71
Drug abuse violations	1,382,783	880,742	485,054	8,872	8,115	100.0	63.7	35.1	0.6	0.6	146,785	101,152	43,343	1,295	995
Gambling	9,141	2,199	6,805	20	117	100.0	24.1	74.4	0.2	1.3	1,584	67	1,511	1	5
Offenses against the family and children	88,437	60,124	26,090	1,686	537	100.0	68.0	29.5	1.9	0.6	4,161	3,029	1,047	60	25
Driving under the influence	1,050,803	929,453	97,472	14,251	9,627	100.0	88.5	9.3	1.4	0.9	13,420	12,498	589	238	95
Liquor laws	474,726	406,221	49,434	14,422	4,649	100.0	85.6	10.4	3.0	1.0	105,799	96,286	5,466	2,965	1,082
Drunkenness	449,117	375,440	62,278	8,891	2,508	100.0	83.6	13.9	2.0	0.6	12,909	11,532	997	277	103
Disorderly conduct	537,809	342,169	183,810	8,376	3,454	100.0	63.6	34.2	1.6	0.6	152,817	87,683	62,490	1,602	1,042
Vagrancy	25,584	15,493	9,474	501	116	100.0	60.6	37.0	2.0	0.5	2,923	2,267	625	19	12
All other offenses (except traffic)	2,936,233	1,969,862	905,656	40,546	20,169	100.0	67.1	30.8	1.4	0.7	282,244	198,916	77,153	3,313	2,862
Suspicion	1,571	904	649	4	14	100.0	57.5	41.3	0.3	0.9	287	184	100	3	0
Curfew and loitering law violations	109,575	69,950	37,532	964	1,129	100.0	63.8	34.3	0.9	1.0	109,575	69,950	37,532	964	1,129
Runaways	82,218	56,975	22,398	1,687	1,158	100.0	69.3	27.2	2.1	1.4	82,218	56,975	22,398	1,687	1,158

[1] Because of rounding, the percentages may not add to 100.0.

[2] Violent crimes are offenses of murder and nonnegligent manslaughter, forcible rape, robbery, and aggravated assault. Property crimes are offenses of burglary, larceny-theft, motor vehicle theft, and arson.

Table 43. Arrests, Distribution by Race, 2007 *(Contd.)*

(Number, percent; 11,929 agencies; 2007 estimated population 225,477,173.)

Offense charged	Percent distribution[1]					Arrests 18 and over					Percent distribution[1]				
	Total	White	Black	American Indian or Alaskan Native	Asian or Pacific Islander	Total	White	Black	American Indian or Alaskan Native	Asian or Pacific Islander	Total	White	Black	American Indian or Alaskan Native	Asian or Pacific Islander
TOTAL	100.0	67.0	30.8	1.2	1.0	9,014,180	6,325,851	2,497,596	122,465	68,268	100.0	70.2	27.7	1.4	0.8
Murder and nonnegligent manslaughter	100.0	40.3	57.4	1.5	0.9	9,056	4,382	4,498	84	92	100.0	48.4	49.7	0.9	1.0
Forcible rape	100.0	61.5	36.9	0.9	0.6	14,441	9,374	4,742	189	136	100.0	64.9	32.8	1.3	0.9
Robbery	100.0	30.9	67.8	0.5	0.8	70,293	32,454	36,942	480	417	100.0	46.2	52.6	0.7	0.6
Aggravated assault	100.0	57.0	41.0	1.1	0.9	282,955	184,088	92,212	3,904	2,751	100.0	65.1	32.6	1.4	1.0
Burglary	100.0	65.4	32.8	1.0	0.8	166,823	116,206	47,876	1,586	1,155	100.0	69.7	28.7	1.0	0.7
Larceny-theft	100.0	66.5	30.7	1.3	1.5	665,516	458,464	191,518	8,919	6,615	100.0	68.9	28.8	1.3	1.0
Motor vehicle theft	100.0	54.8	42.4	1.5	1.2	66,616	43,038	22,339	702	537	100.0	64.6	33.5	1.1	0.8
Arson	100.0	76.4	21.3	0.9	1.4	6,003	4,387	1,518	70	28	100.0	73.1	25.3	1.2	0.5
Violent crime[2]	100.0	47.5	50.7	0.9	0.9	376,745	230,298	138,394	4,657	3,396	100.0	61.1	36.7	1.2	0.9
Property crime[2]	100.0	65.7	31.8	1.2	1.3	904,958	622,095	263,251	11,277	8,335	100.0	68.7	29.1	1.2	0.9
Other assaults	100.0	58.8	39.5	1.0	0.7	799,897	535,872	244,808	12,171	7,046	100.0	67.0	30.6	1.5	0.9
Forgery and counterfeiting	100.0	72.6	25.5	0.9	1.1	75,416	52,437	21,864	393	722	100.0	69.5	29.0	0.5	1.0
Fraud	100.0	63.7	33.9	1.4	1.0	178,797	123,776	52,659	1,292	1,070	100.0	69.2	29.5	0.7	0.6
Embezzlement	100.0	58.5	38.7	0.8	2.0	15,667	10,060	5,320	85	202	100.0	64.2	34.0	0.5	1.3
Stolen property; buying, receiving, possessing	100.0	54.8	43.4	0.8	1.1	75,128	48,667	25,268	608	585	100.0	64.8	33.6	0.8	0.8
Vandalism	100.0	78.8	19.0	1.3	0.9	135,757	99,795	32,584	2,278	1,100	100.0	73.5	24.0	1.7	0.8
Weapons; carrying, possessing, etc.	100.0	60.5	37.6	0.8	1.2	109,329	62,319	45,333	811	866	100.0	57.0	41.5	0.7	0.8
Prostitution and commercialized vice	100.0	40.9	58.0	0.8	0.3	58,151	33,717	22,581	541	1,312	100.0	58.0	38.8	0.9	2.3
Sex offenses (except forcible rape and prostitution)	100.0	70.6	28.1	0.7	0.6	51,060	37,822	12,133	556	549	100.0	74.1	23.8	1.1	1.1
Drug abuse violations	100.0	68.9	29.5	0.9	0.7	1,235,998	779,590	441,711	7,577	7,120	100.0	63.1	35.7	0.6	0.6
Gambling	100.0	4.2	95.4	0.1	0.3	7,557	2,132	5,294	19	112	100.0	28.2	70.1	0.3	1.5
Offenses against the family and children	100.0	72.8	25.2	1.4	0.6	84,276	57,095	25,043	1,626	512	100.0	67.7	29.7	1.9	0.6
Driving under the influence	100.0	93.1	4.4	1.8	0.7	1,037,383	916,955	96,883	14,013	9,532	100.0	88.4	9.3	1.4	0.9
Liquor laws	100.0	91.0	5.2	2.8	1.0	368,927	309,935	43,968	11,457	3,567	100.0	84.0	11.9	3.1	1.0
Drunkenness	100.0	89.3	7.7	2.1	0.8	436,208	363,908	61,281	8,614	2,405	100.0	83.4	14.0	2.0	0.6
Disorderly conduct	100.0	57.4	40.9	1.0	0.7	384,992	254,486	121,320	6,774	2,412	100.0	66.1	31.5	1.8	0.6
Vagrancy	100.0	77.6	21.4	0.7	0.4	22,661	13,226	8,849	482	104	100.0	58.4	39.0	2.1	0.5
All other offenses (except traffic)	100.0	70.5	27.3	1.2	1.0	2,653,989	1,770,946	828,503	37,233	17,307	100.0	66.7	31.2	1.4	0.7
Suspicion	100.0	64.1	34.8	1.0	0.0	1,284	720	549	1	14	100.0	56.1	42.8	0.1	1.1
Curfew and loitering law violations	100.0	63.8	34.3	0.9	1.0	-	-	-	-	-	-	-	-	-	-
Runaways	100.0	69.3	27.2	2.1	1.4	-	-	-	-	-	-	-	-	-	-

[1] Because of rounding, the percentages may not add to 100.0.

[2] Violent crimes are offenses of murder and nonnegligent manslaughter, forcible rape, robbery, and aggravated assault. Property crimes are offenses of burglary, larceny-theft, motor vehicle theft, and arson.

Table 44.   City Arrest Trends, 2006–2007

(Number, percent change; 7,657 agencies; 2007 estimated population 136,244,857; 2006 estimated population 135,060,129.)

Offense charged	Number of persons arrested								
	Total all ages			Under 18 years of age			18 years of age and over		
	2006	2007	Percent change	2006	2007	Percent change	2006	2007	Percent change
TOTAL[1]	6,971,309	6,991,506	+0.3	1,199,377	1,183,685	-1.3	5,771,932	5,807,821	+0.6
Murder and nonnegligent manslaughter	5,912	6,023	+1.9	626	647	+3.4	5,286	5,376	+1.7
Forcible rape	11,252	10,879	-3.3	1,764	1,741	-1.3	9,488	9,138	-3.7
Robbery	67,058	68,278	+1.8	18,695	18,516	-1.0	48,363	49,762	+2.9
Aggravated assault	219,287	215,825	-1.6	30,746	29,415	-4.3	188,541	186,410	-1.1
Burglary	148,496	151,382	+1.9	41,824	41,992	+0.4	106,672	109,390	+2.5
Larceny-theft	608,751	668,752	+9.9	164,204	177,979	+8.4	444,547	490,773	+10.4
Motor vehicle theft	60,054	53,254	-11.3	15,771	13,652	-13.4	44,283	39,602	-10.6
Arson	8,116	7,618	-6.1	4,332	4,009	-7.5	3,784	3,609	-4.6
Violent crime[2]	303,509	301,005	-0.8	51,831	50,319	-2.9	251,678	250,686	-0.4
Property crime[2]	825,417	881,006	+6.7	226,131	237,632	+5.1	599,286	643,374	+7.4
Other assaults	640,884	650,832	+1.6	126,972	122,915	-3.2	513,912	527,917	+2.7
Forgery and counterfeiting	53,569	49,896	-6.9	1,821	1,628	-10.6	51,748	48,268	-6.7
Fraud	107,751	99,086	-8.0	4,167	4,089	-1.9	103,584	94,997	-8.3
Embezzlement	10,886	12,637	+16.1	783	1,027	+31.2	10,103	11,610	+14.9
Stolen property; buying, receiving, possessing	63,909	60,120	-5.9	12,462	12,075	-3.1	51,447	48,045	-6.6
Vandalism	157,126	155,737	-0.9	63,700	61,798	-3.0	93,426	93,939	+0.5
Weapons; carrying, possessing, etc.	100,728	94,540	-6.1	25,162	23,273	-7.5	75,566	71,267	-5.7
Prostitution and commercialized vice	37,600	36,583	-2.7	734	708	-3.5	36,866	35,875	-2.7
Sex offenses (except forcible rape and prostitution)	38,120	35,825	-6.0	7,453	7,043	-5.5	30,667	28,782	-6.1
Drug abuse violations	886,552	877,266	-1.0	98,790	99,763	+1.0	787,762	777,503	-1.3
Gambling	2,642	2,676	+1.3	423	369	-12.8	2,219	2,307	+4.0
Offenses against the family and children	38,976	37,097	-4.8	2,552	2,743	+7.5	36,424	34,354	-5.7
Driving under the influence	589,899	600,193	+1.7	8,625	8,226	-4.6	581,274	591,967	+1.8
Liquor laws	340,168	339,594	-0.2	72,553	74,012	+2.0	267,615	265,582	-0.8
Drunkenness	339,278	362,431	+6.8	10,281	10,643	+3.5	328,997	351,788	+6.9
Disorderly conduct	409,844	403,383	-1.6	123,555	116,810	-5.5	286,289	286,573	+0.1
Vagrancy	20,531	18,178	-11.5	3,257	2,465	-24.3	17,274	15,713	-9.0
All other offenses (except traffic)	1,861,384	1,837,330	-1.3	215,589	210,056	-2.6	1,645,795	1,627,274	-1.1
Suspicion	796	782	-1.8	183	190	+3.8	613	592	-3.4
Curfew and loitering law violations	87,488	82,987	-5.1	87,488	82,987	-5.1	-	-	-
Runaways	55,048	53,104	-3.5	55,048	53,104	-3.5	-	-	-

[1] Does not include suspicion.

[2] Violent crimes are offenses of murder and nonnegligent manslaughter, forcible rape, robbery, and aggravated assault. Property crimes are offenses of burglary, larceny-theft, motor vehicle theft, and arson.

Table 45.   City Arrest Trends, by Age and Sex, 2006–2007

(Number, percent change; 7,657 agencies; 2007 estimated population 136,244,857; 2006 estimated population 135,060,129

Offense charged	Male						Female					
	Total			Under 18			Total			Under 18		
	2006	2007	Percent change	2006	2007	Percent change	2006	2007	Percent change	2006	2007	Percent change
TOTAL[1]	5,267,999	5,246,878	-0.4	846,012	828,251	-2.1	1,703,310	1,744,628	+2.4	353,365	355,434	+0.6
Murder and nonnegligent manslaughter	5,304	5,426	+2.3	600	604	+0.7	608	597	-1.8	26	43	+65.4
Forcible rape	11,124	10,777	-3.1	1,734	1,713	-1.2	128	102	-20.3	30	28	-6.7
Robbery	59,322	60,266	+1.6	16,925	16,707	-1.3	7,736	8,012	+3.6	1,770	1,809	+2.2
Aggravated assault	172,403	168,308	-2.4	23,447	22,430	-4.3	46,884	47,517	+1.4	7,299	6,985	-4.3
Burglary	125,848	127,740	+1.5	36,691	36,600	-0.2	22,648	23,642	+4.4	5,133	5,392	+5.0
Larceny-theft	371,363	392,304	+5.6	95,203	99,044	+4.0	237,388	276,448	+16.5	69,001	78,935	+14.4
Motor vehicle theft	49,379	43,491	-11.9	13,033	11,288	-13.4	10,675	9,763	-8.5	2,738	2,364	-13.7
Arson	6,729	6,460	-4.0	3,725	3,556	-4.5	1,387	1,158	-16.5	607	453	-25.4
Violent crime[2]	248,153	244,777	-1.4	42,706	41,454	-2.9	55,356	56,228	+1.6	9,125	8,865	-2.8
Property crime[2]	553,319	569,995	+3.0	148,652	150,488	+1.2	272,098	311,011	+14.3	77,479	87,144	+12.5
Other assaults	477,648	483,745	+1.3	83,841	80,905	-3.5	163,236	167,087	+2.4	43,131	42,010	-2.6
Forgery and counterfeiting	32,269	30,455	-5.6	1,198	1,090	-9.0	21,300	19,441	-8.7	623	538	-13.6
Fraud	61,383	56,908	-7.3	2,726	2,595	-4.8	46,368	42,178	-9.0	1,441	1,494	+3.7
Embezzlement	5,066	6,116	+20.7	415	588	+41.7	5,820	6,521	+12.0	368	439	+19.3
Stolen property; buying, receiving, possessing	51,671	48,135	-6.8	10,642	10,061	-5.5	12,238	11,985	-2.1	1,820	2,014	+10.7
Vandalism	130,470	128,838	-1.3	55,244	53,498	-3.2	26,656	26,899	+0.9	8,456	8,300	-1.8
Weapons; carrying, possessing, etc.	92,534	87,031	-5.9	22,697	21,017	-7.4	8,194	7,509	-8.4	2,465	2,256	-8.5
Prostitution and commercialized vice	12,972	11,363	-12.4	174	152	-12.6	24,628	25,220	+2.4	560	556	-0.7
Sex offenses (except forcible rape and prostitution)	35,301	33,175	-6.0	6,726	6,331	-5.9	2,819	2,650	-6.0	727	712	-2.1
Drug abuse violations	716,814	709,756	-1.0	82,590	83,501	+1.1	169,738	167,510	-1.3	16,200	16,262	+0.4
Gambling	2,323	2,244	-3.4	395	354	-10.4	319	432	+35.4	28	15	-46.4
Offenses against the family and children	26,062	24,303	-6.7	1,488	1,582	+6.3	12,914	12,794	-0.9	1,064	1,161	+9.1
Driving under the influence	465,504	470,060	+1.0	6,593	6,217	-5.7	124,395	130,133	+4.6	2,032	2,009	-1.1
Liquor laws	247,978	245,365	-1.1	46,412	46,469	+0.1	92,190	94,229	+2.2	26,141	27,543	+5.4
Drunkenness	287,131	304,984	+6.2	7,687	7,907	+2.9	52,147	57,447	+10.2	2,594	2,736	+5.5
Disorderly conduct	298,781	293,872	-1.6	81,737	77,440	-5.3	111,063	109,511	-1.4	41,818	39,370	-5.9
Vagrancy	15,845	13,934	-12.1	2,214	1,735	-21.6	4,686	4,244	-9.4	1,043	730	-30.0
All other offenses (except traffic)	1,422,134	1,400,620	-1.5	157,234	153,665	-2.3	439,250	436,710	-0.6	58,355	56,391	-3.4
Suspicion	628	634	+1.0	144	147	+2.1	168	148	-11.9	39	43	+10.3
Curfew and loitering law violations	61,137	58,032	-5.1	61,137	58,032	-5.1	26,351	24,955	-5.3	26,351	24,955	-5.3
Runaways	23,504	23,170	-1.4	23,504	23,170	-1.4	31,544	29,934	-5.1	31,544	29,934	-5.1

[1] Does not include suspicion.

[2] Violent crimes are offenses of murder and nonnegligent manslaughter, forcible rape, robbery, and aggravated assault. Property crimes are offenses of burglary, larceny-theft, motor vehicle theft, and arson.

Table 46. City Arrests, Distribution by Age, 2007

(Number, percent; 8,693 agencies; 2007 estimated population 157,420,952.)

Offense charged	Total all ages	Ages under 15	Ages under 18	Ages 18 and over	Under 10	10–12	13–14	15	16	17	18	19	20
TOTAL	8,166,688	389,287	1,369,024	6,797,664	10,497	78,530	300,260	274,246	336,034	369,457	401,316	405,761	372,710
Total percent distribution[1]	100.0	4.8	16.8	83.2	0.1	1.0	3.7	3.4	4.1	4.5	4.9	5.0	4.6
Murder and nonnegligent manslaughter	7,518	84	827	6,691	1	3	80	105	235	403	576	550	468
Forcible rape	12,645	690	1,961	10,684	7	181	502	334	428	509	603	582	528
Robbery	83,356	5,025	23,325	60,031	67	704	4,254	4,760	6,443	7,097	7,192	6,146	4,767
Aggravated assault	251,311	11,071	34,901	216,410	350	2,679	8,042	6,632	8,183	9,015	9,634	9,776	9,524
Burglary	171,476	14,885	47,772	123,704	476	3,148	11,261	9,901	11,148	11,838	12,351	9,851	7,843
Larceny-theft	761,461	62,937	200,449	561,012	1,582	13,839	47,516	40,013	47,437	50,062	48,750	39,337	31,614
Motor vehicle theft	70,482	4,088	18,274	52,208	21	414	3,653	4,272	5,040	4,874	4,729	3,910	3,203
Arson	8,414	2,623	4,359	4,055	290	821	1,512	745	559	432	346	272	191
Violent crime[2]	354,830	16,870	61,014	293,816	425	3,567	12,878	11,831	15,289	17,024	18,005	17,054	15,287
Violent crime percent distribution[1]	100.0	4.8	17.2	82.8	0.1	1.0	3.6	3.3	4.3	4.8	5.1	4.8	4.3
Property crime[2]	1,011,833	84,533	270,854	740,979	2,369	18,222	63,942	54,931	64,184	67,206	66,176	53,370	42,851
Property crime percent distribution[1]	100.0	8.4	26.8	73.2	0.2	1.8	6.3	5.4	6.3	6.6	6.5	5.3	4.2
Other assaults	751,839	54,928	140,474	611,365	1,630	13,839	39,459	27,909	29,846	27,791	24,958	25,476	25,597
Forgery and counterfeiting	60,078	212	1,870	58,208	20	36	156	225	500	933	2,000	2,739	2,693
Fraud	105,543	723	4,524	101,019	41	110	572	690	1,163	1,948	3,271	4,031	4,202
Embezzlement	13,465	37	1,085	12,380	6	8	23	45	335	668	999	999	861
Stolen property; buying, receiving, possessing	71,493	3,627	14,340	57,153	71	592	2,964	3,025	3,692	3,996	4,548	4,141	3,467
Vandalism	177,716	28,930	70,064	107,652	1,346	7,257	20,327	13,885	14,034	13,215	11,038	9,223	7,253
Weapons; carrying, possessing, etc.	114,494	8,440	27,336	87,158	279	1,923	6,238	5,163	6,418	7,315	7,948	7,198	6,074
Prostitution and commercialized vice	56,745	137	1,092	55,653	16	13	108	173	295	487	1,816	2,234	2,146
Sex offenses (except forcible rape and prostitution)	45,134	3,958	8,173	36,961	157	1,068	2,733	1,462	1,413	1,340	1,709	1,670	1,443
Drug abuse violations	1,073,890	17,911	120,708	953,182	175	1,814	15,922	21,066	33,565	48,166	66,373	65,398	58,582
Gambling	8,249	218	1,548	6,701	6	12	200	276	415	639	680	639	528
Offenses against the family and children	40,471	832	2,857	37,614	60	163	609	564	685	776	1,140	1,245	1,351
Driving under the influence	676,504	224	9,179	667,325	69	12	143	391	2,156	6,408	16,125	21,936	24,643
Liquor laws	387,504	7,849	83,268	304,236	97	503	7,249	12,936	23,734	38,749	63,707	68,007	56,186
Drunkenness	392,586	1,234	11,399	381,187	69	71	1,094	1,867	2,735	5,563	10,729	12,016	12,081
Disorderly conduct	467,398	50,584	133,198	334,200	903	11,540	38,141	27,777	28,711	26,126	21,327	19,033	17,627
Vagrancy	22,932	843	2,580	20,352	13	138	692	697	751	289	1,040	830	671
All other offenses (except traffic)	2,163,947	58,358	234,105	1,929,842	1,821	9,956	46,581	48,685	59,508	67,554	77,682	88,479	89,128
Suspicion	899	52	218	681	0	11	41	38	80	48	45	43	39
Curfew and loitering law violations	105,534	27,970	105,534	-	440	4,620	22,910	24,517	29,197	23,850	-	-	-
Runaways	63,604	20,817	63,604	-	484	3,055	17,278	16,093	17,328	9,366	-	-	-

[1] Because of rounding, the percentages may not add to 100.0.

[2] Violent crimes are offenses of murder and nonnegligent manslaughter, forcible rape, robbery, and aggravated assault. Property crimes are offenses of burglary, larceny-theft, motor vehicle theft, and arson.

Table 46. City Arrests, Distribution by Age, 2007 *(Contd.)*

(Number, percent; 8,693 agencies; 2007 estimated population 157,420,952.)

Offense charged	21	22	23	24	25–29	30–34	35–39	40–44	45–49	50–54	55–59	60–64	65 and over
TOTAL	340,294	313,154	285,955	272,696	1,121,366	768,297	713,035	671,484	550,292	320,861	150,417	63,256	46,770
Total percent distribution[1]	4.2	3.8	3.5	3.3	13.7	9.4	8.7	8.2	6.7	3.9	1.8	0.8	0.6
Murder and nonnegligent manslaughter	461	400	363	326	1,332	688	479	378	283	192	110	38	47
Forcible rape	574	443	409	401	1,749	1,415	1,302	1,056	771	434	220	100	97
Robbery	3,871	3,306	2,796	2,529	9,515	5,848	5,090	4,261	2,772	1,267	423	157	91
Aggravated assault	10,226	9,487	9,219	9,088	39,284	27,830	24,534	22,343	17,091	9,801	4,598	2,117	1,858
Burglary	6,663	5,758	5,037	4,688	19,068	13,196	12,829	11,636	8,556	4,080	1,430	471	247
Larceny-theft	26,457	23,192	20,644	19,271	81,563	58,953	60,135	57,111	45,701	26,374	12,410	5,166	4,334
Motor vehicle theft	2,941	2,675	2,409	2,357	9,402	6,267	5,605	4,382	2,612	1,096	408	130	82
Arson	197	174	161	141	586	442	423	357	361	190	107	60	47
Violent crime[2]	15,132	13,636	12,787	12,344	51,880	35,781	31,405	28,038	20,917	11,694	5,351	2,412	2,093
Violent crime percent distribution[1]	4.3	3.8	3.6	3.5	14.6	10.1	8.9	7.9	5.9	3.3	1.5	0.7	0.6
Property crime[2]	36,258	31,799	28,251	26,457	110,619	78,858	78,992	73,486	57,230	31,740	14,355	5,827	4,710
Property crime percent distribution[1]	3.6	3.1	2.8	2.6	10.9	7.8	7.8	7.3	5.7	3.1	1.4	0.6	0.5
Other assaults	27,633	27,530	26,016	25,442	111,497	80,643	73,043	64,940	49,889	26,749	12,173	5,209	4,570
Forgery and counterfeiting	2,493	2,486	2,593	2,556	11,668	8,714	7,404	5,776	3,865	1,958	801	304	158
Fraud	3,956	3,951	3,739	3,812	17,805	14,717	13,539	11,334	8,068	4,676	2,209	1,038	671
Embezzlement	782	733	558	519	1,926	1,337	1,225	1,006	697	429	202	72	35
Stolen property; buying, receiving, possessing	3,025	2,758	2,490	2,370	9,776	6,840	6,099	5,158	3,568	1,755	688	288	182
Vandalism	7,061	6,104	5,253	4,857	17,953	10,922	8,960	7,781	5,845	2,988	1,366	556	492
Weapons; carrying, possessing, etc.	5,836	5,327	4,566	4,298	16,125	8,859	6,474	5,265	4,098	2,509	1,345	662	574
Prostitution and commercialized vice	2,204	2,087	2,029	1,867	8,690	7,580	8,229	7,553	4,957	2,409	992	431	429
Sex offenses (except forcible rape and prostitution)	1,434	1,335	1,155	1,183	5,011	4,109	4,327	4,258	3,590	2,418	1,462	883	974
Drug abuse violations	53,241	48,182	43,618	41,163	165,674	104,203	92,446	85,752	68,873	37,343	15,068	4,933	2,333
Gambling	425	389	317	288	968	518	382	377	334	265	235	170	186
Offenses against the family and children	1,461	1,396	1,463	1,580	7,153	5,786	5,332	4,257	2,888	1,476	580	262	244
Driving under the influence	35,356	34,619	32,561	31,557	123,392	80,959	70,424	65,257	56,922	36,419	19,996	9,759	7,400
Liquor laws	10,059	7,085	5,394	4,626	17,082	11,524	12,306	14,567	14,998	10,057	5,139	2,096	1,403
Drunkenness	18,495	17,011	15,154	14,572	57,233	40,143	40,495	45,997	44,671	29,577	13,780	5,724	3,509
Disorderly conduct	22,019	18,954	16,378	14,875	55,059	33,995	31,020	30,274	25,864	15,097	7,199	3,104	2,375
Vagrancy	677	499	486	487	2,085	1,839	2,385	2,929	2,959	1,916	942	396	211
All other offenses (except traffic)	92,705	87,235	81,111	77,816	329,659	230,886	218,482	207,424	170,015	99,358	46,518	19,126	14,218
Suspicion	42	38	36	27	111	84	66	55	44	28	16	4	3
Curfew and loitering law violations	-	-	-	-	-	-	-	-	-	-	-	-	-
Runaways	-	-	-	-	-	-	-	-	-	-	-	-	-

[1] Because of rounding, the percentages may not add to 100.0.

[2] Violent crimes are offenses of murder and nonnegligent manslaughter, forcible rape, robbery, and aggravated assault. Property crimes are offenses of burglary, larceny-theft, motor vehicle theft, and arson.

Table 47.   City Arrests of Persons Under 15, 18, 21, and 25 Years of Age, 2007

(Number, percent; 8,693 agencies; 2007 estimated population 157,420,952.)

Offense charged	Total all ages	Number of persons arrested				Percent of total all ages			
		Under 15	Under 18	Under 21	Under 25	Under 15	Under 18	Under 21	Under 25
TOTAL	8,166,688	389,287	1,369,024	2,548,811	3,760,910	4.8	16.8	31.2	46.1
Murder and nonnegligent manslaughter	7,518	84	827	2,421	3,971	1.1	11.0	32.2	52.8
Forcible rape	12,645	690	1,961	3,674	5,501	5.5	15.5	29.1	43.5
Robbery	83,356	5,025	23,325	41,430	53,932	6.0	28.0	49.7	64.7
Aggravated assault	251,311	11,071	34,901	63,835	101,855	4.4	13.9	25.4	40.5
Burglary	171,476	14,885	47,772	77,817	99,963	8.7	27.9	45.4	58.3
Larceny-theft	761,461	62,937	200,449	320,150	409,714	8.3	26.3	42.0	53.8
Motor vehicle theft	70,482	4,088	18,274	30,116	40,498	5.8	25.9	42.7	57.5
Arson	8,414	2,623	4,359	5,168	5,841	31.2	51.8	61.4	69.4
Violent crime[1]	354,830	16,870	61,014	111,360	165,259	4.8	17.2	31.4	46.6
Property crime[1]	1,011,833	84,533	270,854	433,251	556,016	8.4	26.8	42.8	55.0
Other assaults	751,839	54,928	140,474	216,505	323,126	7.3	18.7	28.8	43.0
Forgery and counterfeiting	60,078	212	1,870	9,302	19,430	0.4	3.1	15.5	32.3
Fraud	105,543	723	4,524	16,028	31,486	0.7	4.3	15.2	29.8
Embezzlement	13,465	37	1,085	3,944	6,536	0.3	8.1	29.3	48.5
Stolen property; buying, receiving, possessing	71,493	3,627	14,340	26,496	37,139	5.1	20.1	37.1	51.9
Vandalism	177,716	28,930	70,064	97,578	120,853	16.3	39.4	54.9	68.0
Weapons; carrying, possessing, etc.	114,494	8,440	27,336	48,556	68,583	7.4	23.9	42.4	59.9
Prostitution and commercialized vice	56,745	137	1,092	7,288	15,475	0.2	1.9	12.8	27.3
Sex offenses (except forcible rape and prostitution)	45,134	3,958	8,173	12,995	18,102	8.8	18.1	28.8	40.1
Drug abuse violations	1,073,890	17,911	120,708	311,061	497,265	1.7	11.2	29.0	46.3
Gambling	8,249	218	1,548	3,395	4,814	2.6	18.8	41.2	58.4
Offenses against the family and children	40,471	832	2,857	6,593	12,493	2.1	7.1	16.3	30.9
Driving under the influence	676,504	224	9,179	71,883	205,976	*	1.4	10.6	30.4
Liquor laws	387,504	7,849	83,268	271,168	298,332	2.0	21.5	70.0	77.0
Drunkenness	392,586	1,234	11,399	46,225	111,457	0.3	2.9	11.8	28.4
Disorderly conduct	467,398	50,584	133,198	191,185	263,411	10.8	28.5	40.9	56.4
Vagrancy	22,932	843	2,580	5,121	7,270	3.7	11.3	22.3	31.7
All other offenses (except traffic)	2,163,947	58,358	234,105	489,394	828,261	2.7	10.8	22.6	38.3
Suspicion	899	52	218	345	488	5.8	24.2	38.4	54.3
Curfew and loitering law violations	105,534	27,970	105,534	105,534	105,534	26.5	100.0	100.0	100.0
Runaways	63,604	20,817	63,604	63,604	63,604	32.7	100.0	100.0	100.0

[1] Violent crimes are offenses of murder and nonnegligent manslaughter, forcible rape, robbery, and aggravated assault. Property crimes are offenses of burglary, larceny-theft, motor vehicle theft, and arson.

* = Less than one-tenth of 1 percent.

Table 48. City Arrests, Distribution by Sex, 2007

(Number, percent; 8,693 agencies; 2007 estimated population 157,420,952.)

Offense charged	Number of persons arrested			Percent male	Percent female	Percent distribution[1]		
	Total	Male	Female			Total	Male	Female
TOTAL	8,166,688	6,163,595	2,003,093	75.5	24.5	100.0	100.0	100.0
Murder and nonnegligent manslaughter	7,518	6,786	732	90.3	9.7	0.1	0.1	*
Forcible rape	12,645	12,528	117	99.1	0.9	0.2	0.2	*
Robbery	83,356	73,615	9,741	88.3	11.7	1.0	1.2	0.5
Aggravated assault	251,311	196,377	54,934	78.1	21.9	3.1	3.2	2.7
Burglary	171,476	145,607	25,869	84.9	15.1	2.1	2.4	1.3
Larceny-theft	761,461	449,564	311,897	59.0	41.0	9.3	7.3	15.6
Motor vehicle theft	70,482	57,982	12,500	82.3	17.7	0.9	0.9	0.6
Arson	8,414	7,091	1,323	84.3	15.7	0.1	0.1	0.1
Violent crime[2]	354,830	289,306	65,524	81.5	18.5	4.3	4.7	3.3
Property crime[2]	1,011,833	660,244	351,589	65.3	34.7	12.4	10.7	17.6
Other assaults	751,839	561,610	190,229	74.7	25.3	9.2	9.1	9.5
Forgery and counterfeiting	60,078	37,288	22,790	62.1	37.9	0.7	0.6	1.1
Fraud	105,543	61,978	43,565	58.7	41.3	1.3	1.0	2.2
Embezzlement	13,465	6,572	6,893	48.8	51.2	0.2	0.1	0.3
Stolen property; buying, receiving, possessing	71,493	56,366	15,127	78.8	21.2	0.9	0.9	0.8
Vandalism	177,716	147,405	30,311	82.9	17.1	2.2	2.4	1.5
Weapons; carrying, possessing, etc.	114,494	105,757	8,737	92.4	7.6	1.4	1.7	0.4
Prostitution and commercialized vice	56,745	17,854	38,891	31.5	68.5	0.7	0.3	1.9
Sex offenses (except forcible rape and prostitution)	45,134	40,618	4,516	90.0	10.0	0.6	0.7	0.2
Drug abuse violations	1,073,890	875,418	198,472	81.5	18.5	13.1	14.2	9.9
Gambling	8,249	7,622	627	92.4	7.6	0.1	0.1	*
Offenses against the family and children	40,471	26,422	14,049	65.3	34.7	0.5	0.4	0.7
Driving under the influence	676,504	531,656	144,848	78.6	21.4	8.3	8.6	7.2
Liquor laws	387,504	280,673	106,831	72.4	27.6	4.7	4.6	5.3
Drunkenness	392,586	330,698	61,888	84.2	15.8	4.8	5.4	3.1
Disorderly conduct	467,398	344,828	122,570	73.8	26.2	5.7	5.6	6.1
Vagrancy	22,932	17,965	4,967	78.3	21.7	0.3	0.3	0.2
All other offenses (except traffic)	2,163,947	1,661,792	502,155	76.8	23.2	26.5	27.0	25.1
Suspicion	899	734	165	81.6	18.4	*	*	*
Curfew and loitering law violations	105,534	73,222	32,312	69.4	30.6	1.3	1.2	1.6
Runaways	63,604	27,567	36,037	43.3	56.7	0.8	0.4	1.8

[1] Because of rounding, the percentages may not add to 100.0.

[2] Violent crimes are offenses of murder and nonnegligent manslaughter, forcible rape, robbery, and aggravated assault. Property crimes are offenses of burglary, larceny-theft, motor vehicle theft, and arson.

* = Less than one-tenth of 1 percent.

Table 49. City Arrests, Distribution by Race, 2007

(Number, percent; 8,686 agencies; 2007 estimated population 157,379,491.)

Offense charged	Total arrests					Percent distribution[1]					Arrests under 18				
	Total	White	Black	American Indian or Alaskan Native	Asian or Pacific Islander	Total	White	Black	American Indian or Alaskan Native	Asian or Pacific Islander	Total	White	Black	American Indian or Alaskan Native	Asian or Pacific Islander
TOTAL	8,134,299	5,473,198	2,481,719	108,271	71,111	100.0	67.3	30.5	1.3	0.9	1,362,556	901,384	430,161	16,440	14,571
Murder and nonnegligent manslaughter	7,505	3,151	4,201	66	87	100.0	42.0	56.0	0.9	1.2	827	315	494	9	9
Forcible rape	12,586	7,510	4,803	147	126	100.0	59.7	38.2	1.2	1.0	1,948	1,112	808	16	12
Robbery	83,230	34,316	47,838	489	587	100.0	41.2	57.5	0.6	0.7	23,293	7,207	15,777	102	207
Aggravated assault	250,587	152,552	92,326	2,974	2,735	100.0	60.9	36.8	1.2	1.1	34,785	19,190	14,899	337	359
Burglary	171,066	111,597	56,693	1,333	1,443	100.0	65.2	33.1	0.8	0.8	47,630	29,990	16,830	368	442
Larceny-theft	758,380	513,012	225,979	10,390	8,999	100.0	67.6	29.8	1.4	1.2	199,402	133,321	60,245	2,707	3,129
Motor vehicle theft	70,337	40,959	27,917	743	718	100.0	58.2	39.7	1.1	1.0	18,242	9,381	8,382	241	238
Arson	8,377	6,066	2,146	77	88	100.0	72.4	25.6	0.9	1.1	4,334	3,287	941	39	67
Violent crime[2]	353,908	197,529	149,168	3,676	3,535	100.0	55.8	42.1	1.0	1.0	60,853	27,824	31,978	464	587
Property crime[2]	1,008,160	671,634	312,735	12,543	11,248	100.0	66.6	31.0	1.2	1.1	269,608	175,979	86,398	3,355	3,876
Other assaults	748,930	468,205	262,874	10,594	7,257	100.0	62.5	35.1	1.4	1.0	139,807	81,410	55,898	1,406	1,093
Forgery and counterfeiting	59,871	40,726	18,198	315	632	100.0	68.0	30.4	0.5	1.1	1,861	1,348	474	15	24
Fraud	104,976	69,289	33,928	882	877	100.0	66.0	32.3	0.8	0.8	4,491	2,738	1,631	70	52
Embezzlement	13,411	8,429	4,693	84	205	100.0	62.9	35.0	0.6	1.5	1,084	655	396	9	24
Stolen property; buying, receiving, possessing	71,264	42,674	27,437	498	655	100.0	59.9	38.5	0.7	0.9	14,271	7,543	6,471	98	159
Vandalism	176,865	130,924	41,660	2,610	1,671	100.0	74.0	23.6	1.5	0.9	69,680	54,674	13,459	842	705
Weapons; carrying, possessing, etc.	114,183	63,339	49,039	717	1,088	100.0	55.5	42.9	0.6	1.0	27,196	16,534	10,157	172	333
Prostitution and commercialized vice	56,665	32,477	22,483	535	1,170	100.0	57.3	39.7	0.9	2.1	1,088	436	639	9	4
Sex offenses (except forcible rape and prostitution)	44,991	31,546	12,496	443	506	100.0	70.1	27.8	1.0	1.1	8,133	5,580	2,448	44	61
Drug abuse violations	1,071,105	646,325	411,972	6,164	6,644	100.0	60.3	38.5	0.6	0.6	120,199	80,559	37,773	1,019	848
Gambling	8,245	1,613	6,516	14	102	100.0	19.6	79.0	0.2	1.2	1,548	56	1,486	1	5
Offenses against the family and children	40,211	28,723	10,310	792	386	100.0	71.4	25.6	2.0	1.0	2,817	2,028	714	55	20
Driving under the influence	673,205	589,540	67,680	9,281	6,704	100.0	87.6	10.1	1.4	1.0	9,130	8,446	455	157	72
Liquor laws	384,375	323,904	43,862	12,602	4,007	100.0	84.3	11.4	3.3	1.0	82,694	74,543	4,776	2,438	937
Drunkenness	390,822	322,964	57,991	7,577	2,290	100.0	82.6	14.8	1.9	0.6	11,345	10,118	905	229	93
Disorderly conduct	465,163	290,450	164,479	7,003	3,231	100.0	62.4	35.4	1.5	0.7	132,762	76,915	53,615	1,254	978
Vagrancy	22,888	13,573	8,711	493	111	100.0	59.3	38.1	2.2	0.5	2,579	1,955	595	19	10
All other offenses (except traffic)	2,155,456	1,389,962	719,763	29,064	16,667	100.0	64.5	33.4	1.3	0.8	232,486	163,093	64,417	2,401	2,575
Suspicion	883	563	306	4	10	100.0	63.8	34.7	0.5	1.1	202	141	58	3	0
Curfew and loitering law violations	105,326	66,446	36,878	914	1,088	100.0	63.1	35.0	0.9	1.0	105,326	66,446	36,878	914	1,088
Runaways	63,396	42,363	18,540	1,466	1,027	100.0	66.8	29.2	2.3	1.6	63,396	42,363	18,540	1,466	1,027

[1] Because of rounding, the percentages may not add to 100.0.

[2] Violent crimes are offenses of murder and nonnegligent manslaughter, forcible rape, robbery, and aggravated assault. Property crimes are offenses of burglary, larceny-theft, motor vehicle theft, and arson.

Table 49. City Arrests, Distribution by Race, 2007 *(Contd.)*

(Number, percent; 8,686 agencies; 2007 estimated population 157,379,491.)

Offense charged	Percent distribution[1]					Arrests 18 years and over					Percent distribution[1]				
	Total	White	Black	American Indian or Alaskan Native	Asian or Pacific Islander	Total	White	Black	American Indian or Alaskan Native	Asian or Pacific Islander	Total	White	Black	American Indian or Alaskan Native	Asian or Pacific Islander
TOTAL	100.0	66.2	31.6	1.2	1.1	6,771,743	4,571,814	2,051,558	91,831	56,540	100.0	67.5	30.3	1.4	0.8
Murder and nonnegligent manslaughter	100.0	38.1	59.7	1.1	1.1	6,678	2,836	3,707	57	78	100.0	42.5	55.5	0.9	1.2
Forcible rape	100.0	57.1	41.5	0.8	0.6	10,638	6,398	3,995	131	114	100.0	60.1	37.6	1.2	1.1
Robbery	100.0	30.9	67.7	0.4	0.9	59,937	27,109	32,061	387	380	100.0	45.2	53.5	0.6	0.6
Aggravated assault	100.0	55.2	42.8	1.0	1.0	215,802	133,362	77,427	2,637	2,376	100.0	61.8	35.9	1.2	1.1
Burglary	100.0	63.0	35.3	0.8	0.9	123,436	81,607	39,863	965	1,001	100.0	66.1	32.3	0.8	0.8
Larceny-theft	100.0	66.9	30.2	1.4	1.6	558,978	379,691	165,734	7,683	5,870	100.0	67.9	29.6	1.4	1.1
Motor vehicle theft	100.0	51.4	45.9	1.3	1.3	52,095	31,578	19,535	502	480	100.0	60.6	37.5	1.0	0.9
Arson	100.0	75.8	21.7	0.9	1.5	4,043	2,779	1,205	38	21	100.0	68.7	29.8	0.9	0.5
Violent crime[2]	100.0	45.7	52.5	0.8	1.0	293,055	169,705	117,190	3,212	2,948	100.0	57.9	40.0	1.1	1.0
Property crime[2]	100.0	65.3	32.0	1.2	1.4	738,552	495,655	226,337	9,188	7,372	100.0	67.1	30.6	1.2	1.0
Other assaults	100.0	58.2	40.0	1.0	0.8	609,123	386,795	206,976	9,188	6,164	100.0	63.5	34.0	1.5	1.0
Forgery and counterfeiting	100.0	72.4	25.5	0.8	1.3	58,010	39,378	17,724	300	608	100.0	67.9	30.6	0.5	1.0
Fraud	100.0	61.0	36.3	1.6	1.2	100,485	66,551	32,297	812	825	100.0	66.2	32.1	0.8	0.8
Embezzlement	100.0	60.4	36.5	0.8	2.2	12,327	7,774	4,297	75	181	100.0	63.1	34.9	0.6	1.5
Stolen property; buying, receiving, possessing	100.0	52.9	45.3	0.7	1.1	56,993	35,131	20,966	400	496	100.0	61.6	36.8	0.7	0.9
Vandalism	100.0	78.5	19.3	1.2	1.0	107,185	76,250	28,201	1,768	966	100.0	71.1	26.3	1.6	0.9
Weapons; carrying, possessing, etc.	100.0	60.8	37.3	0.6	1.2	86,987	46,805	38,882	545	755	100.0	53.8	44.7	0.6	0.9
Prostitution and commercialized vice	100.0	40.1	58.7	0.8	0.4	55,577	32,041	21,844	526	1,166	100.0	57.7	39.3	0.9	2.1
Sex offenses (except forcible rape and prostitution)	100.0	68.6	30.1	0.5	0.8	36,858	25,966	10,048	399	445	100.0	70.4	27.3	1.1	1.2
Drug abuse violations	100.0	67.0	31.4	0.8	0.7	950,906	565,766	374,199	5,145	5,796	100.0	59.5	39.4	0.5	0.6
Gambling	100.0	3.6	96.0	0.1	0.3	6,697	1,557	5,030	13	97	100.0	23.2	75.1	0.2	1.4
Offenses against the family and children	100.0	72.0	25.3	2.0	0.7	37,394	26,695	9,596	737	366	100.0	71.4	25.7	2.0	1.0
Driving under the influence	100.0	92.5	5.0	1.7	0.8	664,075	581,094	67,225	9,124	6,632	100.0	87.5	10.1	1.4	1.0
Liquor laws	100.0	90.1	5.8	2.9	1.1	301,681	249,361	39,086	10,164	3,070	100.0	82.7	13.0	3.4	1.0
Drunkenness	100.0	89.2	8.0	2.0	0.8	379,477	312,846	57,086	7,348	2,197	100.0	82.4	15.0	1.9	0.6
Disorderly conduct	100.0	57.9	40.4	0.9	0.7	332,401	213,535	110,864	5,749	2,253	100.0	64.2	33.4	1.7	0.7
Vagrancy	100.0	75.8	23.1	0.7	0.4	20,309	11,618	8,116	474	101	100.0	57.2	40.0	2.3	0.5
All other offenses (except traffic)	100.0	70.2	27.7	1.0	1.1	1,922,970	1,226,869	655,346	26,663	14,092	100.0	63.8	34.1	1.4	0.7
Suspicion	100.0	69.8	28.7	1.5	0.0	681	422	248	1	10	100.0	62.0	36.4	0.1	1.5
Curfew and loitering law violations	100.0	63.1	35.0	0.9	1.0	-	-	-	-	-	-	-	-	-	-
Runaways	100.0	66.8	29.2	2.3	1.6	-	-	-	-	-	-	-	-	-	-

[1] Because of rounding, the percentages may not add to 100.0.

[2] Violent crimes are offenses of murder and nonnegligent manslaughter, forcible rape, robbery, and aggravated assault. Property crimes are offenses of burglary, larceny-theft, motor vehicle theft, and arson.

Table 50.   Arrest Trends for Metropolitan Counties, 2006–2007

(Number, percent change; 1,182 agencies; 2007 estimated population 42,738,507; 2006 estimated population 42,558,036.)

Offense charged	Number of persons arrested								
	Total all ages			Under 18 years of age			18 years of age and over		
	2006	2007	Percent change	2006	2007	Percent change	2006	2007	Percent change
TOTAL[1]	1,652,713	1,635,770	-1.0	193,773	190,164	-1.9	1,458,940	1,445,606	-0.9
Murder and nonnegligent manslaughter	1,665	1,593	-4.3	128	120	-6.3	1,537	1,473	-4.2
Forcible rape	3,115	2,880	-7.5	454	458	+0.9	2,661	2,422	-9.0
Robbery	9,615	9,477	-1.4	2,253	2,244	-0.4	7,362	7,233	-1.8
Aggravated assault	52,093	51,696	-0.8	6,168	6,097	-1.2	45,925	45,599	-0.7
Burglary	35,482	35,405	-0.2	9,393	8,703	-7.3	26,089	26,702	+2.3
Larceny-theft	89,892	93,965	+4.5	20,747	21,488	+3.6	69,145	72,477	+4.8
Motor vehicle theft	14,722	12,219	-17.0	3,045	2,502	-17.8	11,677	9,717	-16.8
Arson	2,016	2,032	+0.8	864	831	-3.8	1,152	1,201	+4.3
Violent crime[2]	66,488	65,646	-1.3	9,003	8,919	-0.9	57,485	56,727	-1.3
Property crime[2]	142,112	143,621	+1.1	34,049	33,524	-1.5	108,063	110,097	+1.9
Other assaults	147,981	149,632	+1.1	28,769	28,567	-0.7	119,212	121,065	+1.6
Forgery and counterfeiting	12,392	11,449	-7.6	376	319	-15.2	12,016	11,130	-7.4
Fraud	55,780	49,950	-10.5	760	760	0.0	55,020	49,190	-10.6
Embezzlement	2,332	2,601	+11.5	172	183	+6.4	2,160	2,418	+11.9
Stolen property; buying, receiving, possessing	14,571	13,498	-7.4	1,797	1,619	-9.9	12,774	11,879	-7.0
Vandalism	28,762	27,314	-5.0	10,733	9,819	-8.5	18,029	17,495	-3.0
Weapons; carrying, possessing, etc.	18,336	17,755	-3.2	4,153	3,910	-5.9	14,183	13,845	-2.4
Prostitution and commercialized vice	2,315	2,075	-10.4	50	48	-4.0	2,265	2,027	-10.5
Sex offenses (except forcible rape and prostitution)	10,901	10,930	+0.3	2,100	1,994	-5.0	8,801	8,936	+1.5
Drug abuse violations	201,325	196,307	-2.5	18,267	18,303	+0.2	183,058	178,004	-2.8
Gambling	603	607	+0.7	34	28	-17.6	569	579	+1.8
Offenses against the family and children	34,198	34,458	+0.8	746	913	+22.4	33,452	33,545	+0.3
Driving under the influence	226,415	226,355	*	2,314	2,163	-6.5	224,101	224,192	*
Liquor laws	51,692	51,237	-0.9	13,876	13,534	-2.5	37,816	37,703	-0.3
Drunkenness	38,894	40,861	+5.1	1,128	1,110	-1.6	37,766	39,751	+5.3
Disorderly conduct	42,261	42,858	+1.4	12,943	12,824	-0.9	29,318	30,034	+2.4
Vagrancy	2,644	2,185	-17.4	253	307	+21.3	2,391	1,878	-21.5
All other offenses (except traffic)	535,986	529,237	-1.3	35,525	34,126	-3.9	500,461	495,111	-1.1
Suspicion	493	460	-6.7	93	58	-37.6	400	402	+0.5
Curfew and loitering law violations	3,495	3,755	+7.4	3,495	3,755	+7.4	-	-	-
Runaways	13,230	13,439	+1.6	13,230	13,439	+1.6	-	-	-

[1] Does not include suspicion.

[2] Violent crimes are offenses of murder and nonnegligent manslaughter, forcible rape, robbery, and aggravated assault. Property crimes are offenses of burglary, larceny-theft, motor vehicle theft, and arson.

* = Less than one-tenth of 1 percent.

Table 51. Arrest Trends for Metropolitan Counties, by Age and Sex, 2006–2007

(Number, percent change; 1,182 agencies; 2007 estimated population 42,738,507; 2006 estimated population 42,558,036.)

Offense charged	Male						Female					
	Total			Under 18			Total			Under 18		
	2006	2007	Percent change	2006	2007	Percent change	2006	2007	Percent change	2006	2007	Percent change
TOTAL[1]	1,273,780	1,255,778	-1.4	139,487	135,864	-2.6	378,933	379,992	+0.3	54,286	54,300	*
Murder and nonnegligent manslaughter	1,444	1,414	-2.1	119	111	-6.7	221	179	-19.0	9	9	0.0
Forcible rape	3,061	2,843	-7.1	444	448	+0.9	54	37	-31.5	10	10	0.0
Robbery	8,631	8,474	-1.8	2,069	2,054	-0.7	984	1,003	+1.9	184	190	+3.3
Aggravated assault	42,042	41,418	-1.5	4,830	4,768	-1.3	10,051	10,278	+2.3	1,338	1,329	-0.7
Burglary	30,637	30,685	+0.2	8,525	7,838	-8.1	4,845	4,720	-2.6	868	865	-0.3
Larceny-theft	59,114	60,229	+1.9	13,381	13,377	*	30,778	33,736	+9.6	7,366	8,111	+10.1
Motor vehicle theft	12,083	10,061	-16.7	2,539	2,072	-18.4	2,639	2,158	-18.2	506	430	-15.0
Arson	1,693	1,716	+1.4	755	730	-3.3	323	316	-2.2	109	101	-7.3
Violent crime[2]	55,178	54,149	-1.9	7,462	7,381	-1.1	11,310	11,497	+1.7	1,541	1,538	-0.2
Property crime[2]	103,527	102,691	-0.8	25,200	24,017	-4.7	38,585	40,930	+6.1	8,849	9,507	+7.4
Other assaults	110,756	111,799	+0.9	19,173	19,178	*	37,225	37,833	+1.6	9,596	9,389	-2.2
Forgery and counterfeiting	7,552	7,071	-6.4	266	233	-12.4	4,840	4,378	-9.5	110	86	-21.8
Fraud	28,885	26,166	-9.4	509	510	+0.2	26,895	23,784	-11.6	251	250	-0.4
Embezzlement	1,109	1,266	+14.2	109	116	+6.4	1,223	1,335	+9.2	63	67	+6.3
Stolen property; buying, receiving, possessing	11,918	11,102	-6.8	1,517	1,374	-9.4	2,653	2,396	-9.7	280	245	-12.5
Vandalism	24,194	22,747	-6.0	9,305	8,418	-9.5	4,568	4,567	*	1,428	1,401	-1.9
Weapons; carrying, possessing, etc.	16,795	16,319	-2.8	3,624	3,503	-3.3	1,541	1,436	-6.8	529	407	-23.1
Prostitution and commercialized vice	1,067	875	-18.0	26	19	-26.9	1,248	1,200	-3.8	24	29	20.8
Sex offenses (except forcible rape and prostitution)	10,298	10,294	*	1,937	1,869	-3.5	603	636	+5.5	163	125	-23.3
Drug abuse violations	161,193	156,680	-2.8	14,968	15,022	+0.4	40,132	39,627	-1.3	3,299	3,281	-0.5
Gambling	480	492	+2.5	32	27	-15.6	123	115	-6.5	2	1	-50.0
Offenses against the family and children	28,818	28,857	+0.1	479	634	+32.4	5,380	5,601	+4.1	267	279	+4.5
Driving under the influence	183,754	181,806	-1.1	1,812	1,652	-8.8	42,661	44,549	+4.4	502	511	+1.8
Liquor laws	36,947	36,673	-0.7	8,671	8,462	-2.4	14,745	14,564	-1.2	5,205	5,072	-2.6
Drunkenness	32,488	33,685	+3.7	845	810	-4.1	6,406	7,176	+12.0	283	300	+6.0
Disorderly conduct	31,310	31,540	+0.7	8,940	8,636	-3.4	10,951	11,318	+3.4	4,003	4,188	+4.6
Vagrancy	1,848	1,583	-14.3	196	211	+7.7	796	602	-24.4	57	96	+68.4
All other offenses (except traffic)	417,268	411,374	-1.4	26,021	25,183	-3.2	118,718	117,863	-0.7	9,504	8,943	-5.9
Suspicion	384	353	-8.1	69	40	-42.0	109	107	-1.8	24	18	-25.0
Curfew and loitering law violations	2,285	2,444	+7.0	2,285	2,444	+7.0	1,210	1,311	+8.3	1,210	1,311	+8.3
Runaways	6,110	6,165	+0.9	6,110	6,165	+0.9	7,120	7,274	+2.2	7,120	7,274	+2.2

[1] Does not include suspicion.

[2] Violent crimes are offenses of murder and nonnegligent manslaughter, forcible rape, robbery, and aggravated assault. Property crimes are offenses of burglary, larceny-theft, motor vehicle theft, and arson.

* = Less than one-tenth of 1 percent.

Table 52. Arrests in Metropolitan Counties, Distribution by Age, 2007

(Number, percent; 1,311 agencies; 2007 estimated population 47,357,825.)

Offense charged	Total all ages	Ages under 15	Ages under 18	Ages 18 and over	Under 10	10–12	13–14	15	16	17	18	19	20
TOTAL	1,768,840	57,188	213,658	1,555,182	1,857	11,779	43,552	40,820	53,093	62,557	74,393	77,468	74,233
Total percent distribution[1]	100.0	3.2	12.1	87.9	0.1	0.7	2.5	2.3	3.0	3.5	4.2	4.4	4.2
Murder and nonnegligent manslaughter	1,944	13	147	1,797	0	1	12	20	49	65	133	108	91
Forcible rape	3,002	172	470	2,532	1	43	128	76	100	122	150	140	139
Robbery	11,428	556	2,774	8,654	4	78	474	564	718	936	1,216	946	711
Aggravated assault	56,233	2,088	6,795	49,438	91	519	1,478	1,234	1,614	1,859	2,134	2,092	2,037
Burglary	39,235	2,727	9,844	29,391	107	575	2,045	1,961	2,365	2,791	3,185	2,559	2,134
Larceny-theft	105,297	6,931	24,191	81,106	158	1,402	5,371	4,816	5,822	6,622	6,522	5,294	4,352
Motor vehicle theft	13,938	588	2,915	11,023	5	60	523	676	826	825	863	697	669
Arson	2,153	486	874	1,279	43	158	285	160	126	102	109	83	78
Violent crime[2]	72,607	2,829	10,186	62,421	96	641	2,092	1,894	2,481	2,982	3,633	3,286	2,978
Violent crime percent distribution[1]	100.0	3.9	14.0	86.0	0.1	0.9	2.9	2.6	3.4	4.1	5.0	4.5	4.1
Property crime[2]	160,623	10,732	37,824	122,799	313	2,195	8,224	7,613	9,139	10,340	10,679	8,633	7,233
Property crime percent distribution[1]	100.0	6.7	23.5	76.5	0.2	1.4	5.1	4.7	5.7	6.4	6.6	5.4	4.5
Other assaults	161,719	12,145	31,855	129,864	417	3,066	8,662	6,383	7,012	6,315	5,161	4,765	4,656
Forgery and counterfeiting	13,104	70	381	12,723	3	15	52	46	78	187	394	552	508
Fraud	51,702	114	821	50,881	1	18	95	140	213	354	763	1,178	1,349
Embezzlement	2,635	10	186	2,449	0	3	7	12	56	108	180	164	168
Stolen property; buying, receiving, possessing	15,625	407	2,005	13,620	7	60	340	395	521	682	931	796	763
Vandalism	30,259	4,080	10,957	19,302	207	1,031	2,842	2,175	2,351	2,351	1,906	1,532	1,255
Weapons; carrying, possessing, etc.	21,066	1,843	4,963	16,103	133	522	1,188	917	1,017	1,186	1,227	1,140	974
Prostitution and commercialized vice	2,484	9	62	2,422	0	1	8	11	16	26	69	93	88
Sex offenses (except forcible rape and prostitution)	12,065	1,179	2,342	9,723	78	345	756	391	389	383	476	436	406
Drug abuse violations	222,026	2,883	20,759	201,267	28	309	2,546	3,198	5,524	9,154	12,977	13,277	12,523
Gambling	601	6	29	572	0	0	6	5	12	6	9	16	18
Offenses against the family and children	35,576	244	959	34,617	6	36	202	179	279	257	423	423	502
Driving under the influence	241,360	31	2,339	239,021	5	3	23	87	529	1,692	4,751	6,970	7,997
Liquor laws	55,089	1,054	14,452	40,637	7	66	981	2,041	4,213	7,144	10,064	9,964	7,588
Drunkenness	40,058	128	1,094	38,964	5	8	115	180	263	523	1,390	1,503	1,443
Disorderly conduct	49,347	5,361	15,057	34,290	118	1,177	4,066	3,239	3,530	2,927	2,203	1,661	1,457
Vagrancy	2,482	59	334	2,148	2	4	53	66	105	104	96	102	93
All other offenses (except traffic)	558,677	8,660	37,872	520,805	309	1,567	6,784	7,134	9,795	12,283	17,002	20,918	22,207
Suspicion	617	17	63	554	0	4	13	15	17	14	59	59	27
Curfew and loitering law violations	3,873	874	3,873	-	11	119	744	820	1,161	1,018	-	-	-
Runaways	15,245	4,453	15,245	-	111	589	3,753	3,879	4,392	2,521	-	-	-

[1] Because of rounding, the percentages may not add to 100.0.

[2] Violent crimes are offenses of murder and nonnegligent manslaughter, forcible rape, robbery, and aggravated assault. Property crimes are offenses of burglary, larceny-theft, motor vehicle theft, and arson.

Table 52. Arrests in Metropolitan Counties, Distribution by Age, 2007 *(Contd.)*

(Number, percent; 1,311 agencies; 2007 estimated population 47,357,825.)

Offense charged	21	22	23	24	25–29	30–34	35–39	40–44	45–49	50–54	55–59	60–64	65 and over
TOTAL	71,086	67,646	64,001	62,231	266,944	194,245	181,195	165,392	127,216	70,441	32,934	14,780	10,977
Total percent distribution[1]	4.0	3.8	3.6	3.5	15.1	11.0	10.2	9.4	7.2	4.0	1.9	0.8	0.6
Murder and nonnegligent manslaughter	95	118	88	102	324	183	149	132	109	76	37	29	23
Forcible rape	129	96	96	84	371	304	314	288	197	100	55	32	37
Robbery	580	467	413	402	1,376	807	645	510	379	106	68	17	11
Aggravated assault	2,043	2,045	1,838	1,872	8,510	6,216	5,906	5,500	4,366	2,551	1,200	578	550
Burglary	1,681	1,425	1,344	1,194	4,793	3,066	2,775	2,495	1,591	710	278	118	43
Larceny-theft	3,926	3,466	3,081	2,908	12,168	9,063	9,066	8,914	6,165	3,327	1,534	738	582
Motor vehicle theft	544	562	480	473	2,042	1,404	1,229	963	637	284	98	50	28
Arson	55	51	41	34	187	142	117	145	108	66	36	17	10
Violent crime[2]	2,847	2,726	2,435	2,460	10,581	7,510	7,014	6,430	5,051	2,833	1,360	656	621
Violent crime percent distribution[1]	3.9	3.8	3.4	3.4	14.6	10.3	9.7	8.9	7.0	3.9	1.9	0.9	0.9
Property crime[2]	6,206	5,504	4,946	4,609	19,190	13,675	13,187	12,517	8,501	4,387	1,946	923	663
Property crime percent distribution[1]	3.9	3.4	3.1	2.9	11.9	8.5	8.2	7.8	5.3	2.7	1.2	0.6	0.4
Other assaults	5,000	4,837	4,693	4,651	21,229	17,177	17,203	15,826	12,077	6,553	3,085	1,575	1,376
Forgery and counterfeiting	500	518	506	543	2,459	1,918	1,760	1,387	905	444	201	76	52
Fraud	1,437	1,536	1,608	1,734	8,641	8,157	8,045	6,503	4,706	2,718	1,354	680	472
Embezzlement	132	105	100	85	343	289	276	266	158	88	59	22	14
Stolen property; buying, receiving, possessing	670	632	601	532	2,509	1,702	1,462	1,346	907	470	171	75	53
Vandalism	1,093	999	851	755	3,112	2,043	1,857	1,585	1,153	610	276	153	122
Weapons; carrying, possessing, etc.	952	900	782	721	2,904	1,702	1,377	1,193	976	621	341	153	140
Prostitution and commercialized vice	101	86	91	82	401	281	349	333	228	107	62	24	27
Sex offenses (except forcible rape and prostitution)	365	324	304	268	1,341	1,040	1,177	1,075	932	586	378	303	312
Drug abuse violations	11,433	10,453	9,558	8,995	36,333	22,900	19,373	17,911	13,946	7,340	2,884	925	439
Gambling	6	13	8	12	59	68	80	74	70	45	42	24	28
Offenses against the family and children	621	713	816	982	5,818	6,161	6,349	5,492	3,618	1,689	652	260	98
Driving under the influence	11,741	11,802	11,729	11,323	44,717	29,778	26,073	24,362	21,092	13,294	7,349	3,499	2,544
Liquor laws	1,198	868	662	579	2,246	1,567	1,416	1,547	1,334	814	440	228	122
Drunkenness	1,841	1,752	1,560	1,396	5,959	4,178	4,184	4,635	4,347	2,695	1,314	458	309
Disorderly conduct	1,798	1,550	1,468	1,348	5,370	3,705	3,628	3,709	3,043	1,737	849	403	361
Vagrancy	112	83	81	67	337	209	252	284	221	121	62	14	14
All other offenses (except traffic)	23,010	22,213	21,181	21,065	93,308	70,131	66,083	58,875	43,914	23,265	10,101	4,327	3,205
Suspicion	23	32	21	24	87	54	50	42	37	24	8	2	5
Curfew and loitering law violations	-	-	-	-	-	-	-	-	-	-	-	-	-
Runaways	-	-	-	-	-	-	-	-	-	-	-	-	-

[1] Because of rounding, the percentages may not add to 100.0.

[2] Violent crimes are offenses of murder and nonnegligent manslaughter, forcible rape, robbery, and aggravated assault. Property crimes are offenses of burglary, larceny-theft, motor vehicle theft, and arson.

Table 53. Arrests in Metropolitan Counties of Persons Under 15, 18, 21, and 25 Years of Age, 2007

(Number, percent; 1,311 agencies; 2007 estimated population 47,357,825.)

Offense charged	Total all ages	Number of persons arrested				Percent of total all ages			
		Under 15	Under 18	Under 21	Under 25	Under 15	Under 18	Under 21	Under 25
TOTAL	1,768,840	57,188	213,658	439,752	704,716	3.2	12.1	24.9	39.8
Murder and nonnegligent manslaughter	1,944	13	147	479	882	0.7	7.6	24.6	45.4
Forcible rape	3,002	172	470	899	1,304	5.7	15.7	29.9	43.4
Robbery	11,428	556	2,774	5,647	7,509	4.9	24.3	49.4	65.7
Aggravated assault	56,233	2,088	6,795	13,058	20,856	3.7	12.1	23.2	37.1
Burglary	39,235	2,727	9,844	17,722	23,366	7.0	25.1	45.2	59.6
Larceny-theft	105,297	6,931	24,191	40,359	53,740	6.6	23.0	38.3	51.0
Motor vehicle theft	13,938	588	2,915	5,144	7,203	4.2	20.9	36.9	51.7
Arson	2,153	486	874	1,144	1,325	22.6	40.6	53.1	61.5
Violent crime[1]	72,607	2,829	10,186	20,083	30,551	3.9	14.0	27.7	42.1
Property crime[1]	160,623	10,732	37,824	64,369	85,634	6.7	23.5	40.1	53.3
Other assaults	161,719	12,145	31,855	46,437	65,618	7.5	19.7	28.7	40.6
Forgery and counterfeiting	13,104	70	381	1,835	3,902	0.5	2.9	14.0	29.8
Fraud	51,702	114	821	4,111	10,426	0.2	1.6	8.0	20.2
Embezzlement	2,635	10	186	698	1,120	0.4	7.1	26.5	42.5
Stolen property; buying, receiving, possessing	15,625	407	2,005	4,495	6,930	2.6	12.8	28.8	44.4
Vandalism	30,259	4,080	10,957	15,650	19,348	13.5	36.2	51.7	63.9
Weapons; carrying, possessing, etc.	21,066	1,843	4,963	8,304	11,659	8.7	23.6	39.4	55.3
Prostitution and commercialized vice	2,484	9	62	312	672	0.4	2.5	12.6	27.1
Sex offenses (except forcible rape and prostitution)	12,065	1,179	2,342	3,660	4,921	9.8	19.4	30.3	40.8
Drug abuse violations	222,026	2,883	20,759	59,536	99,975	1.3	9.3	26.8	45.0
Gambling	601	6	29	72	111	1.0	4.8	12.0	18.5
Offenses against the family and children	35,576	244	959	2,307	5,439	0.7	2.7	6.5	15.3
Driving under the influence	241,360	31	2,339	22,057	68,652	*	1.0	9.1	28.4
Liquor laws	55,089	1,054	14,452	42,068	45,375	1.9	26.2	76.4	82.4
Drunkenness	40,058	128	1,094	5,430	11,979	0.3	2.7	13.6	29.9
Disorderly conduct	49,347	5,361	15,057	20,378	26,542	10.9	30.5	41.3	53.8
Vagrancy	2,482	59	334	625	968	2.4	13.5	25.2	39.0
All other offenses (except traffic)	558,677	8,660	37,872	97,999	185,468	1.6	6.8	17.5	33.2
Suspicion	617	17	63	208	308	2.8	10.2	33.7	49.9
Curfew and loitering law violations	3,873	874	3,873	3,873	3,873	22.6	100.0	100.0	100.0
Runaways	15,245	4,453	15,245	15,245	15,245	29.2	100.0	100.0	100.0

[1] Violent crimes are offenses of murder and nonnegligent manslaughter, forcible rape, robbery, and aggravated assault. Property crimes are offenses of burglary, larceny-theft, motor vehicle theft, and arson.

* = Less than one-tenth of 1 percent.

Table 54. Arrests in Metropolitan Counties, Distribution by Sex, 2007

(Number, percent; 1,311 agencies; 2007 estimated population 47,357,825.)

Offense charged	Number of persons arrested			Percent male	Percent female	Percent distribution[1]		
	Total	Male	Female			Total	Male	Female
TOTAL	1,768,840	1,359,891	408,949	76.9	23.1	100.0	100.0	100.0
Murder and nonnegligent manslaughter	1,944	1,727	217	88.8	11.2	0.1	0.1	0.1
Forcible rape	3,002	2,967	35	98.8	1.2	0.2	0.2	*
Robbery	11,428	10,210	1,218	89.3	10.7	0.6	0.8	0.3
Aggravated assault	56,233	45,116	11,117	80.2	19.8	3.2	3.3	2.7
Burglary	39,235	34,075	5,160	86.8	13.2	2.2	2.5	1.3
Larceny-theft	105,297	67,300	37,997	63.9	36.1	6.0	4.9	9.3
Motor vehicle theft	13,938	11,475	2,463	82.3	17.7	0.8	0.8	0.6
Arson	2,153	1,808	345	84.0	16.0	0.1	0.1	0.1
Violent crime[2]	72,607	60,020	12,587	82.7	17.3	4.1	4.4	3.1
Property crime[2]	160,623	114,658	45,965	71.4	28.6	9.1	8.4	11.2
Other assaults	161,719	120,932	40,787	74.8	25.2	9.1	8.9	10.0
Forgery and counterfeiting	13,104	8,152	4,952	62.2	37.8	0.7	0.6	1.2
Fraud	51,702	27,296	24,406	52.8	47.2	2.9	2.0	6.0
Embezzlement	2,635	1,295	1,340	49.1	50.9	0.1	0.1	0.3
Stolen property; buying, receiving, possessing	15,625	12,874	2,751	82.4	17.6	0.9	0.9	0.7
Vandalism	30,259	25,225	5,034	83.4	16.6	1.7	1.9	1.2
Weapons; carrying, possessing, etc.	21,066	19,351	1,715	91.9	8.1	1.2	1.4	0.4
Prostitution and commercialized vice	2,484	980	1,504	39.5	60.5	0.1	0.1	0.4
Sex offenses (except forcible rape and prostitution)	12,065	11,354	711	94.1	5.9	0.7	0.8	0.2
Drug abuse violations	222,026	178,181	43,845	80.3	19.7	12.6	13.1	10.7
Gambling	601	485	116	80.7	19.3	*	*	*
Offenses against the family and children	35,576	29,677	5,899	83.4	16.6	2.0	2.2	1.4
Driving under the influence	241,360	193,832	47,528	80.3	19.7	13.6	14.3	11.6
Liquor laws	55,089	39,265	15,824	71.3	28.7	3.1	2.9	3.9
Drunkenness	40,058	33,042	7,016	82.5	17.5	2.3	2.4	1.7
Disorderly conduct	49,347	36,088	13,259	73.1	26.9	2.8	2.7	3.2
Vagrancy	2,482	1,816	666	73.2	26.8	0.1	0.1	0.2
All other offenses (except traffic)	558,677	435,379	123,298	77.9	22.1	31.6	32.0	30.1
Suspicion	617	464	153	75.2	24.8	*	*	*
Curfew and loitering law violations	3,873	2,547	1,326	65.8	34.2	0.2	0.2	0.3
Runaways	15,245	6,978	8,267	45.8	54.2	0.9	0.5	2.0

[1] Because of rounding, the percentages may not add to 100.0.
[2] Violent crimes are offenses of murder and nonnegligent manslaughter, forcible rape, robbery, and aggravated assault. Property crimes are offenses of burglary, larceny-theft, motor vehicle theft, and arson.
* = Less than one-tenth of 1 percent.

Table 55.   Arrests in Metropolitan Counties, Distribution by Race, 2007

(Number, percent; 1,311 agencies; 2007 estimated population 47,357,825.)

Offense charged	Total arrests					Percent distribution[1]					Arrests under 18				
	Total	White	Black	American Indian or Alaskan Native	Asian or Pacific Islander	Total	White	Black	American Indian or Alaskan Native	Asian or Pacific Islander	Total	White	Black	American Indian or Alaskan Native	Asian or Pacific Islander
TOTAL	1,764,034	1,330,691	411,854	11,165	10,324	100.0	75.4	23.3	0.6	0.6	213,114	144,790	65,794	1,157	1,373
Murder and nonnegligent manslaughter	1,944	1,213	713	6	12	100.0	62.4	36.7	0.3	0.6	147	68	79	0	0
Forcible rape	2,993	2,254	688	28	23	100.0	75.3	23.0	0.9	0.8	467	331	133	0	3
Robbery	11,423	5,256	6,076	45	46	100.0	46.0	53.2	0.4	0.4	2,773	823	1,936	3	11
Aggravated assault	56,183	41,486	13,889	434	374	100.0	73.8	24.7	0.8	0.7	6,784	4,262	2,443	37	42
Burglary	39,197	30,024	8,798	198	177	100.0	76.6	22.4	0.5	0.5	9,825	6,875	2,819	70	61
Larceny-theft	105,116	72,312	31,257	621	926	100.0	68.8	29.7	0.6	0.9	24,136	14,490	9,296	108	242
Motor vehicle theft	13,921	10,528	3,233	86	74	100.0	75.6	23.2	0.6	0.5	2,911	1,923	953	13	22
Arson	2,143	1,692	420	17	14	100.0	79.0	19.6	0.8	0.7	870	665	192	5	8
Violent crime[2]	72,543	50,209	21,366	513	455	100.0	69.2	29.5	0.7	0.6	10,171	5,484	4,591	40	56
Property crime[2]	160,377	114,556	43,708	922	1,191	100.0	71.4	27.3	0.6	0.7	37,742	23,953	13,260	196	333
Other assaults	161,435	117,881	41,821	863	870	100.0	73.0	25.9	0.5	0.5	31,806	18,242	13,304	135	125
Forgery and counterfeiting	13,085	9,506	3,427	46	106	100.0	72.6	26.2	0.4	0.8	380	265	113	1	1
Fraud	51,573	36,156	15,017	208	192	100.0	70.1	29.1	0.4	0.4	819	574	239	3	3
Embezzlement	2,632	1,594	1,011	7	20	100.0	60.6	38.4	0.3	0.8	186	85	99	0	2
Stolen property; buying, receiving, possessing	15,605	11,213	4,196	105	91	100.0	71.9	26.9	0.7	0.6	2,001	1,256	718	12	15
Vandalism	30,183	24,292	5,507	213	171	100.0	80.5	18.2	0.7	0.6	10,916	8,520	2,274	61	61
Weapons; carrying, possessing, etc.	21,029	13,592	7,190	113	134	100.0	64.6	34.2	0.5	0.6	4,961	2,858	2,033	20	50
Prostitution and commercialized vice	2,481	1,580	748	8	145	100.0	63.7	30.1	0.3	5.8	62	31	31	0	0
Sex offenses (except forcible rape and prostitution)	12,050	9,624	2,259	69	98	100.0	79.9	18.7	0.6	0.8	2,337	1,655	661	12	9
Drug abuse violations	221,670	162,434	56,975	1,157	1,104	100.0	73.3	25.7	0.5	0.5	20,714	15,603	4,853	124	134
Gambling	594	413	168	3	10	100.0	69.5	28.3	0.5	1.7	29	6	23	0	0
Offenses against the family and children	35,440	22,392	12,773	142	133	100.0	63.2	36.0	0.4	0.4	955	685	264	1	5
Driving under the influence	240,681	215,646	22,044	1,288	1,703	100.0	89.6	9.2	0.5	0.7	2,328	2,218	88	14	8
Liquor laws	54,636	49,345	4,172	646	473	100.0	90.3	7.6	1.2	0.9	14,362	13,541	565	143	113
Drunkenness	39,978	36,392	2,930	483	173	100.0	91.0	7.3	1.2	0.4	1,093	1,000	73	13	7
Disorderly conduct	49,234	33,707	15,049	302	176	100.0	68.5	30.6	0.6	0.4	15,029	7,551	7,370	52	56
Vagrancy	2,481	1,768	705	3	5	100.0	71.3	28.4	0.1	0.2	334	304	28	0	2
All other offenses (except traffic)	556,639	403,400	146,364	3,961	2,914	100.0	72.5	26.3	0.7	0.5	37,755	26,234	11,067	217	237
Suspicion	617	289	324	0	4	100.0	46.8	52.5	0.0	0.6	63	23	40	0	0
Curfew and loitering law violations	3,844	3,158	628	17	41	100.0	82.2	16.3	0.4	1.1	3,844	3,158	628	17	41
Runaways	15,227	11,544	3,472	96	115	100.0	75.8	22.8	0.6	0.8	15,227	11,544	3,472	96	115

[1] Because of rounding, the percentages may not add to 100.0.

[2] Violent crimes are offenses of murder and nonnegligent manslaughter, forcible rape, robbery, and aggravated assault. Property crimes are offenses of burglary, larceny-theft, motor vehicle theft, and arson.

Table 55.   Arrests in Metropolitan Counties, Distribution by Race, 2007 *(Contd.)*

(Number, percent; 1,311 agencies; 2007 estimated population 47,357,825.)

Offense charged	Percent distribution[1]					Arrests under 18					Percent distribution[1]				
	Total	White	Black	American Indian or Alaskan Native	Asian or Pacific Islander	Total	White	Black	American Indian or Alaskan Native	Asian or Pacific Islander	Total	White	Black	American Indian or Alaskan Native	Asian or Pacific Islander
TOTAL	100.0	67.9	30.9	0.5	0.6	1,550,920	1,185,901	346,060	10,008	8,951	100.0	76.5	22.3	0.6	0.6
Murder and nonnegligent manslaughter	100.0	46.3	53.7	0.0	0.0	1,797	1,145	634	6	12	100.0	63.7	35.3	0.3	0.7
Forcible rape	100.0	70.9	28.5	0.0	0.6	2,526	1,923	555	28	20	100.0	76.1	22.0	1.1	0.8
Robbery	100.0	29.7	69.8	0.1	0.4	8,650	4,433	4,140	42	35	100.0	51.2	47.9	0.5	0.4
Aggravated assault	100.0	62.8	36.0	0.5	0.6	49,399	37,224	11,446	397	332	100.0	75.4	23.2	0.8	0.7
Burglary	100.0	70.0	28.7	0.7	0.6	29,372	23,149	5,979	128	116	100.0	78.8	20.4	0.4	0.4
Larceny-theft	100.0	60.0	38.5	0.4	1.0	80,980	57,822	21,961	513	684	100.0	71.4	27.1	0.6	0.8
Motor vehicle theft	100.0	66.1	32.7	0.4	0.8	11,010	8,605	2,280	73	52	100.0	78.2	20.7	0.7	0.5
Arson	100.0	76.4	22.1	0.6	0.9	1,273	1,027	228	12	6	100.0	80.7	17.9	0.9	0.5
Violent crime[2]	100.0	53.9	45.1	0.4	0.6	62,372	44,725	16,775	473	399	100.0	71.7	26.9	0.8	0.6
Property crime[2]	100.0	63.5	35.1	0.5	0.9	122,635	90,603	30,448	726	858	100.0	73.9	24.8	0.6	0.7
Other assaults	100.0	57.4	41.8	0.4	0.4	129,629	99,639	28,517	728	745	100.0	76.9	22.0	0.6	0.6
Forgery and counterfeiting	100.0	69.7	29.7	0.3	0.3	12,705	9,241	3,314	45	105	100.0	72.7	26.1	0.4	0.8
Fraud	100.0	70.1	29.2	0.4	0.4	50,754	35,582	14,778	205	189	100.0	70.1	29.1	0.4	0.4
Embezzlement	100.0	45.7	53.2	0.0	1.1	2,446	1,509	912	7	18	100.0	61.7	37.3	0.3	0.7
Stolen property; buying, receiving, possessing	100.0	62.8	35.9	0.6	0.7	13,604	9,957	3,478	93	76	100.0	73.2	25.6	0.7	0.6
Vandalism	100.0	78.1	20.8	0.6	0.6	19,267	15,772	3,233	152	110	100.0	81.9	16.8	0.8	0.6
Weapons; carrying, possessing, etc.	100.0	57.6	41.0	0.4	1.0	16,068	10,734	5,157	93	84	100.0	66.8	32.1	0.6	0.5
Prostitution and commercialized vice	100.0	50.0	50.0	0.0	0.0	2,419	1,549	717	8	145	100.0	64.0	29.6	0.3	6.0
Sex offenses (except forcible rape and prostitution)	100.0	70.8	28.3	0.5	0.4	9,713	7,969	1,598	57	89	100.0	82.0	16.5	0.6	0.9
Drug abuse violations	100.0	75.3	23.4	0.6	0.6	200,956	146,831	52,122	1,033	970	100.0	73.1	25.9	0.5	0.5
Gambling	100.0	20.7	79.3	0.0	0.0	565	407	145	3	10	100.0	72.0	25.7	0.5	1.8
Offenses against the family and children	100.0	71.7	27.6	0.1	0.5	34,485	21,707	12,509	141	128	100.0	62.9	36.3	0.4	0.4
Driving under the influence	100.0	95.3	3.8	0.6	0.3	238,353	213,428	21,956	1,274	1,695	100.0	89.5	9.2	0.5	0.7
Liquor laws	100.0	94.3	3.9	1.0	0.8	40,274	35,804	3,607	503	360	100.0	88.9	9.0	1.2	0.9
Drunkenness	100.0	91.5	6.7	1.2	0.6	38,885	35,392	2,857	470	166	100.0	91.0	7.3	1.2	0.4
Disorderly conduct	100.0	50.2	49.0	0.3	0.4	34,205	26,156	7,679	250	120	100.0	76.5	22.4	0.7	0.4
Vagrancy	100.0	91.0	8.4	0.0	0.6	2,147	1,464	677	3	3	100.0	68.2	31.5	0.1	0.1
All other offenses (except traffic)	100.0	69.5	29.3	0.6	0.6	518,884	377,166	135,297	3,744	2,677	100.0	72.7	26.1	0.7	0.5
Suspicion	100.0	36.5	63.5	0.0	0.0	554	266	284	0	4	100.0	48.0	51.3	0.0	0.7
Curfew and loitering law violations	100.0	82.2	16.3	0.4	1.1	-	-	-	-	-	-	-	-	-	-
Runaways	100.0	75.8	22.8	0.6	0.8	-	-	-	-	-	-	-	-	-	-

[1] Because of rounding, the percentages may not add to 100.0.

[2] Violent crimes are offenses of murder and nonnegligent manslaughter, forcible rape, robbery, and aggravated assault. Property crimes are offenses of burglary, larceny-theft, motor vehicle theft, and arson.

Table 56.   Arrest Trends for Nonmetropolitan Counties, 2006–2007

(Number, percent change; 1,726 agencies; 2007 estimated population 19,255,893; 2006 estimated population 19,326,699.)

Offense charged	Number of persons arrested								
	Total all ages			Under 18 years of age			18 years of age and over		
	2006	2007	Percent change	2006	2007	Percent change	2006	2007	Percent change
TOTAL[1]	749,094	719,810	-3.9	66,319	61,968	-6.6	682,775	657,842	-3.7
Murder and nonnegligent manslaughter	610	561	-8.0	20	29	+45.0	590	532	-9.8
Forcible rape	1,548	1,436	-7.2	233	212	-9.0	1,315	1,224	-6.9
Robbery	1,841	1,725	-6.3	196	203	+3.6	1,645	1,522	-7.5
Aggravated assault	19,922	19,021	-4.5	1,814	1,661	-8.4	18,108	17,360	-4.1
Burglary	17,812	16,493	-7.4	4,181	3,707	-11.3	13,631	12,786	-6.2
Larceny-theft	29,181	29,114	-0.2	4,784	4,946	+3.4	24,397	24,168	-0.9
Motor vehicle theft	5,130	4,312	-15.9	1,096	980	-10.6	4,034	3,332	-17.4
Arson	953	850	-10.8	296	197	-33.4	657	653	-0.6
Violent crime[2]	23,921	22,743	-4.9	2,263	2,105	-7.0	21,658	20,638	-4.7
Property crime[2]	53,076	50,769	-4.3	10,357	9,830	-5.1	42,719	40,939	-4.2
Other assaults	68,768	67,017	-2.5	8,832	8,451	-4.3	59,936	58,566	-2.3
Forgery and counterfeiting	5,024	4,361	-13.2	121	106	-12.4	4,903	4,255	-13.2
Fraud	32,826	28,353	-13.6	310	300	-3.2	32,516	28,053	-13.7
Embezzlement	778	749	-3.7	23	16	-30.4	755	733	-2.9
Stolen property; buying, receiving, possessing	4,632	4,513	-2.6	568	483	-15.0	4,064	4,030	-0.8
Vandalism	13,102	12,629	-3.6	3,919	3,550	-9.4	9,183	9,079	-1.1
Weapons; carrying, possessing, etc.	6,898	6,607	-4.2	854	787	-7.8	6,044	5,820	-3.7
Prostitution and commercialized vice	194	154	-20.6	5	5	0.0	189	149	-21.2
Sex offenses (except forcible rape and prostitution)	4,964	5,008	+0.9	879	953	+8.4	4,085	4,055	-0.7
Drug abuse violations	89,298	83,594	-6.4	6,160	5,524	-10.3	83,138	78,070	-6.1
Gambling	467	388	-16.9	14	7	-50.0	453	381	-15.9
Offenses against the family and children	11,924	12,094	+1.4	330	365	+10.6	11,594	11,729	+1.2
Driving under the influence	123,938	120,568	-2.7	1,962	1,724	-12.1	121,976	118,844	-2.6
Liquor laws	33,840	32,415	-4.2	8,482	8,077	-4.8	25,358	24,338	-4.0
Drunkenness	18,369	18,786	+2.3	439	465	+5.9	17,930	18,321	+2.2
Disorderly conduct	20,610	20,712	+0.5	4,515	4,321	-4.3	16,095	16,391	+1.8
Vagrancy	189	194	+2.6	21	8	-61.9	168	186	+10.7
All other offenses (except traffic)	231,903	224,170	-3.3	11,892	10,905	-8.3	220,011	213,265	-3.1
Suspicion	168	70	-58.3	24	27	+12.5	144	43	-70.1
Curfew and loitering law violations	561	484	-13.7	561	484	-13.7	-	-	-
Runaways	3,812	3,502	-8.1	3,812	3,502	-8.1	-	-	-

[1] Does not include suspicion.

[2] Violent crimes are offenses of murder and nonnegligent manslaughter, forcible rape, robbery, and aggravated assault. Property crimes are offenses of burglary, larceny-theft, motor vehicle theft, and arson.

Table 57.   Arrest Trends for Nonmetropolitan Counties, by Age and Sex, 2006–2007

(Number, percent; 1,726 agencies; 2007 estimated population 19,255,893; 2006 estimated population 19,326,699.)

Offense charged	Male						Female					
	Total			Under 18			Total			Under 18		
	2006	2007	Percent change	2006	2007	Percent change	2006	2007	Percent change	2006	2007	Percent change
TOTAL[1]	576,128	552,715	-4.1	48,133	44,921	-6.7	172,966	167,095	-3.4	18,186	17,047	-6.3
Murder and nonnegligent manslaughter	527	480	-8.9	16	22	+37.5	83	81	-2.4	4	7	+75.0
Forcible rape	1,525	1,410	-7.5	229	203	-11.4	23	26	+13.0	4	9	+125.0
Robbery	1,609	1,531	-4.8	181	183	+1.1	232	194	-16.4	15	20	+33.3
Aggravated assault	16,258	15,544	-4.4	1,406	1,346	-4.3	3,664	3,477	-5.1	408	315	-22.8
Burglary	15,488	14,433	-6.8	3,785	3,389	-10.5	2,324	2,060	-11.4	396	318	-19.7
Larceny-theft	20,802	20,658	-0.7	3,483	3,564	+2.3	8,379	8,456	+0.9	1,301	1,382	+6.2
Motor vehicle theft	4,206	3,548	-15.6	871	762	-12.5	924	764	-17.3	225	218	-3.1
Arson	806	727	-9.8	253	177	-30.0	147	123	-16.3	43	20	-53.5
Violent crime[2]	19,919	18,965	-4.8	1,832	1,754	-4.3	4,002	3,778	-5.6	431	351	-18.6
Property crime[2]	41,302	39,366	-4.7	8,392	7,892	-6.0	11,774	11,403	-3.2	1,965	1,938	-1.4
Other assaults	51,634	50,449	-2.3	5,945	5,823	-2.1	17,134	16,568	-3.3	2,887	2,628	-9.0
Forgery and counterfeiting	2,854	2,502	-12.3	71	69	-2.8	2,170	1,859	-14.3	50	37	-26.0
Fraud	16,649	14,357	-13.8	203	174	-14.3	16,177	13,996	-13.5	107	126	+17.8
Embezzlement	373	368	-1.3	13	12	-7.7	405	381	-5.9	10	4	-60.0
Stolen property; buying, receiving, possessing	3,807	3,711	-2.5	498	419	-15.9	825	802	-2.8	70	64	-8.6
Vandalism	10,814	10,523	-2.7	3,350	3,063	-8.6	2,288	2,106	-8.0	569	487	-14.4
Weapons; carrying, possessing, etc.	6,340	6,047	-4.6	767	704	-8.2	558	560	+0.4	87	83	-4.6
Prostitution and commercialized vice	113	101	-10.6	4	5	+25.0	81	53	-34.6	1	0	-100.0
Sex offenses (except forcible rape and prostitution)	4,674	4,715	+0.9	792	876	+10.6	290	293	+1.0	87	77	-11.5
Drug abuse violations	70,484	65,947	-6.4	4,892	4,383	-10.4	18,814	17,647	-6.2	1,268	1,141	-10.0
Gambling	382	305	-20.2	12	6	-50.0	85	83	-2.4	2	1	-50.0
Offenses against the family and children	9,554	9,646	+1.0	241	248	+2.9	2,370	2,448	+3.3	89	117	+31.5
Driving under the influence	100,574	97,276	-3.3	1,516	1,338	-11.7	23,364	23,292	-0.3	446	386	-13.5
Liquor laws	24,896	23,292	-6.4	5,447	4,934	-9.4	8,944	9,123	+2.0	3,035	3,143	+3.6
Drunkenness	15,177	15,383	+1.4	327	342	+4.6	3,192	3,403	+6.6	112	123	+9.8
Disorderly conduct	15,263	15,290	+0.2	3,122	3,058	-2.0	5,347	5,422	+1.4	1,393	1,263	-9.3
Vagrancy	153	143	-6.5	16	5	-68.8	36	51	+41.7	5	3	-40.0
All other offenses (except traffic)	179,146	172,434	-3.7	8,673	7,921	-8.7	52,757	51,736	-1.9	3,219	2,984	-7.3
Suspicion	141	55	-61.0	20	19	-5.0	27	15	-44.4	4	8	+100.0
Curfew and loitering law violations	403	308	-23.6	403	308	-23.6	158	176	+11.4	158	176	+11.4
Runaways	1,617	1,587	-1.9	1,617	1,587	-1.9	2,195	1,915	-12.8	2,195	1,915	-12.8

[1] Does not include suspicion.

[2] Violent crimes are offenses of murder and nonnegligent manslaughter, forcible rape, robbery, and aggravated assault. Property crimes are offenses of burglary, larceny-theft, motor vehicle theft, and arson.

Table 58. Arrests in Nonmetropolitan Counties, Distribution by Age, 2007

(Number, percent; 1,932 agencies; 2007 estimated population 20,739,857.)

Offense charged	Total all ages	Ages under 15	Ages under 18	Ages 18 and over	Under 10	10–12	13–14	15	16	17	18	19	20
TOTAL	762,782	15,462	67,295	695,487	1,003	3,262	11,197	11,245	16,626	23,962	33,808	35,394	34,656
Total percent distribution[1]	100.0	2.0	8.8	91.2	0.1	0.4	1.5	1.5	2.2	3.1	4.4	4.6	4.5
Murder and nonnegligent manslaughter	620	6	37	583	0	2	4	6	10	15	27	29	34
Forcible rape	1,485	52	202	1,283	0	11	41	37	48	65	76	68	69
Robbery	1,936	20	225	1,711	1	2	17	29	68	108	182	144	142
Aggravated assault	19,593	503	1,763	17,830	19	122	362	280	434	546	680	696	692
Burglary	18,135	977	4,079	14,056	48	216	713	718	985	1,399	1,568	1,319	1,143
Larceny-theft	30,868	1,446	5,197	25,671	64	301	1,081	979	1,254	1,518	1,949	1,619	1,457
Motor vehicle theft	4,602	241	1,077	3,525	7	38	196	233	277	326	282	266	198
Arson	884	95	194	690	16	34	45	21	35	43	62	65	43
Violent crime[2]	23,634	581	2,227	21,407	20	137	424	352	560	734	965	937	937
Violent crime percent distribution[1]	100.0	2.5	9.4	90.6	0.1	0.6	1.8	1.5	2.4	3.1	4.1	4.0	4.0
Property crime[2]	54,489	2,759	10,547	43,942	135	589	2,035	1,951	2,551	3,286	3,861	3,269	2,841
Property crime percent distribution[1]	100.0	5.1	19.4	80.6	0.2	1.1	3.7	3.6	4.7	6.0	7.1	6.0	5.2
Other assaults	70,406	2,965	9,049	61,357	147	733	2,085	1,660	2,171	2,253	2,237	2,078	2,215
Forgery and counterfeiting	4,823	12	102	4,721	3	5	4	10	21	59	144	185	192
Fraud	27,984	49	345	27,639	14	4	31	37	88	171	439	656	779
Embezzlement	915	2	17	898	0	1	1	1	5	9	21	29	36
Stolen property; buying, receiving, possessing	5,097	102	544	4,553	1	15	86	89	153	200	294	314	251
Vandalism	13,065	1,332	3,723	9,342	115	359	858	663	802	926	908	805	619
Weapons; carrying, possessing, etc.	7,185	294	888	6,297	26	79	189	171	169	254	342	302	272
Prostitution and commercialized vice	161	1	6	155	0	0	1	0	4	1	5	0	4
Sex offenses (except forcible rape and prostitution)	5,557	437	1,060	4,497	29	112	296	184	181	258	252	225	207
Drug abuse violations	90,478	712	5,915	84,563	70	84	558	789	1,473	2,941	5,247	5,427	5,300
Gambling	302	2	7	295	1	0	1	2	1	2	16	9	11
Offenses against the family and children	12,840	161	389	12,451	46	35	80	61	62	105	233	241	242
Driving under the influence	138,117	143	1,979	136,138	122	1	20	59	484	1,293	3,078	4,219	4,517
Liquor laws	36,078	689	8,817	27,261	11	50	628	1,233	2,518	4,377	6,444	6,282	5,343
Drunkenness	18,411	38	473	17,938	1	3	34	72	120	243	608	644	686
Disorderly conduct	23,525	1,657	5,038	18,487	126	419	1,112	948	1,211	1,222	1,052	886	788
Vagrancy	217	2	10	207	0	0	2	3	3	2	7	6	6
All other offenses (except traffic)	225,407	2,430	12,119	213,288	114	479	1,837	1,890	2,860	4,939	7,651	8,876	9,409
Suspicion	73	9	22	51	0	0	9	2	7	4	4	4	1
Curfew and loitering law violations	408	105	408	-	5	12	88	98	109	96	-	-	-
Runaways	3,610	980	3,610	-	17	145	818	970	1,073	587	-	-	-

[1] Because of rounding, the percentages may not add to 100.0.

[2] Violent crimes are offenses of murder and nonnegligent manslaughter, forcible rape, robbery, and aggravated assault. Property crimes are offenses of burglary, larceny-theft, motor vehicle theft, and arson.

Table 58. Arrests in Nonmetropolitan Counties, Distribution by Age, 2007 *(Contd.)*

(Number, percent; 1,932 agencies; 2007 estimated population 20,739,857.)

Offense charged	21	22	23	24	25–29	30–34	35–39	40–44	45–49	50–54	55–59	60–64	65 and over
TOTAL	31,364	29,846	28,041	27,315	117,309	84,906	78,431	71,204	57,779	33,140	17,147	8,158	6,989
Total percent distribution[1]	4.1	3.9	3.7	3.6	15.4	11.1	10.3	9.3	7.6	4.3	2.2	1.1	0.9
Murder and nonnegligent manslaughter	27	27	22	28	102	69	52	48	40	27	28	10	13
Forcible rape	63	51	47	52	191	164	164	119	79	51	51	19	19
Robbery	128	108	102	70	284	205	136	94	68	30	12	4	2
Aggravated assault	680	676	698	668	2,965	2,247	2,112	1,997	1,706	939	519	279	276
Burglary	873	687	622	578	2,263	1,510	1,314	942	683	316	147	47	44
Larceny-theft	1,282	1,155	1,058	989	4,386	3,050	2,804	2,354	1,760	897	488	224	199
Motor vehicle theft	189	172	152	137	647	425	383	314	191	91	45	19	14
Arson	30	23	22	9	111	75	66	67	49	34	17	9	8
Violent crime[2]	898	862	869	818	3,542	2,685	2,464	2,258	1,893	1,047	610	312	310
Violent crime percent distribution[1]	3.8	3.6	3.7	3.5	15.0	11.4	10.4	9.6	8.0	4.4	2.6	1.3	1.3
Property crime[2]	2,374	2,037	1,854	1,713	7,407	5,060	4,567	3,677	2,683	1,338	697	299	265
Property crime percent distribution[1]	4.4	3.7	3.4	3.1	13.6	9.3	8.4	6.7	4.9	2.5	1.3	0.5	0.5
Other assaults	2,260	2,248	2,233	2,101	10,229	8,081	8,019	7,422	5,736	3,189	1,608	850	851
Forgery and counterfeiting	211	178	197	198	958	733	631	545	282	150	77	21	19
Fraud	824	838	870	930	5,058	4,516	4,211	3,247	2,430	1,444	764	356	277
Embezzlement	30	37	24	21	124	95	152	84	182	33	17	7	6
Stolen property; buying, receiving, possessing	234	209	179	191	775	615	515	405	310	132	70	27	32
Vandalism	585	503	382	414	1,459	977	788	705	570	292	173	65	97
Weapons; carrying, possessing, etc.	297	287	262	260	1,004	761	631	557	529	341	225	114	113
Prostitution and commercialized vice	4	5	3	6	17	19	19	20	17	12	8	7	9
Sex offenses (except forcible rape and prostitution)	181	158	155	142	583	469	529	488	381	266	184	127	150
Drug abuse violations	4,830	4,480	4,109	3,917	15,478	9,540	7,947	7,041	5,924	3,239	1,308	532	244
Gambling	16	13	7	9	44	39	27	28	25	19	20	8	4
Offenses against the family and children	323	321	340	401	2,287	2,151	2,156	1,767	1,108	536	189	81	75
Driving under the influence	6,118	6,054	5,802	5,525	22,338	15,557	14,910	15,189	13,800	8,989	5,265	2,662	2,115
Liquor laws	933	682	495	471	1,533	1,060	1,049	1,009	894	536	272	138	120
Drunkenness	760	749	731	672	2,790	1,969	2,003	2,099	1,949	1,225	622	255	176
Disorderly conduct	913	868	749	737	2,839	2,013	2,004	2,033	1,671	963	471	246	254
Vagrancy	11	7	8	3	28	23	25	24	26	23	7	2	1
All other offenses (except traffic)	9,559	9,307	8,767	8,785	38,809	28,539	25,777	22,602	17,367	9,363	4,559	2,049	1,869
Suspicion	3	3	5	1	7	4	7	4	2	3	1	0	2
Curfew and loitering law violations	-	-	-	-	-	-	-	-	-	-	-	-	-
Runaways	-	-	-	-	-	-	-	-	-	-	-	-	-

[1] Because of rounding, the percentages may not add to 100.0.

[2] Violent crimes are offenses of murder and nonnegligent manslaughter, forcible rape, robbery, and aggravated assault. Property crimes are offenses of burglary, larceny-theft, motor vehicle theft, and arson.

Table 59.   Arrests in Nonmetropolitan Counties of Persons Under 15, 18, 21, and 25 Years of Age, 2007

(Number, percent; 1,932 agencies; 2007 estimated population 20,739,857.)

Offense charged	Total all ages	Number of persons arrested				Percent of total all ages			
		Under 15	Under 18	Under 21	Under 25	Under 15	Under 18	Under 21	Under 25
TOTAL	762,782	15,462	67,295	171,153	287,719	2.0	8.8	22.4	37.7
Murder and nonnegligent manslaughter	620	6	37	127	231	1.0	6.0	20.5	37.3
Forcible rape	1,485	52	202	415	628	3.5	13.6	27.9	42.3
Robbery	1,936	20	225	693	1,101	1.0	11.6	35.8	56.9
Aggravated assault	19,593	503	1,763	3,831	6,553	2.6	9.0	19.6	33.4
Burglary	18,135	977	4,079	8,109	10,869	5.4	22.5	44.7	59.9
Larceny-theft	30,868	1,446	5,197	10,222	14,706	4.7	16.8	33.1	47.6
Motor vehicle theft	4,602	241	1,077	1,823	2,473	5.2	23.4	39.6	53.7
Arson	884	95	194	364	448	10.7	21.9	41.2	50.7
Violent crime[1]	23,634	581	2,227	5,066	8,513	2.5	9.4	21.4	36.0
Property crime[1]	54,489	2,759	10,547	20,518	28,496	5.1	19.4	37.7	52.3
Other assaults	70,406	2,965	9,049	15,579	24,421	4.2	12.9	22.1	34.7
Forgery and counterfeiting	4,823	12	102	623	1,407	0.2	2.1	12.9	29.2
Fraud	27,984	49	345	2,219	5,681	0.2	1.2	7.9	20.3
Embezzlement	915	2	17	103	215	0.2	1.9	11.3	23.5
Stolen property; buying, receiving, possessing	5,097	102	544	1,403	2,216	2.0	10.7	27.5	43.5
Vandalism	13,065	1,332	3,723	6,055	7,939	10.2	28.5	46.3	60.8
Weapons; carrying, possessing, etc.	7,185	294	888	1,804	2,910	4.1	12.4	25.1	40.5
Prostitution and commercialized vice	161	1	6	15	33	0.6	3.7	9.3	20.5
Sex offenses (except forcible rape and prostitution)	5,557	437	1,060	1,744	2,380	7.9	19.1	31.4	42.8
Drug abuse violations	90,478	712	5,915	21,889	39,225	0.8	6.5	24.2	43.4
Gambling	302	2	7	43	88	0.7	2.3	14.2	29.1
Offenses against the family and children	12,840	161	389	1,105	2,490	1.3	3.0	8.6	19.4
Driving under the influence	138,117	143	1,979	13,793	37,292	0.1	1.4	10.0	27.0
Liquor laws	36,078	689	8,817	26,886	29,467	1.9	24.4	74.5	81.7
Drunkenness	18,411	38	473	2,411	5,323	0.2	2.6	13.1	28.9
Disorderly conduct	23,525	1,657	5,038	7,764	11,031	7.0	21.4	33.0	46.9
Vagrancy	217	2	10	29	58	0.9	4.6	13.4	26.7
All other offenses (except traffic)	225,407	2,430	12,119	38,055	74,473	1.1	5.4	16.9	33.0
Suspicion	73	9	22	31	43	12.3	30.1	42.5	58.9
Curfew and loitering law violations	408	105	408	408	408	25.7	100.0	100.0	100.0
Runaways	3,610	980	3,610	3,610	3,610	27.1	100.0	100.0	100.0

[1] Violent crimes are offenses of murder and nonnegligent manslaughter, forcible rape, robbery, and aggravated assault. Property crimes are offenses of burglary, larceny-theft, motor vehicle theft, and arson.

Table 60.   Arrests in Nonmetropolitan Counties, Distribution by Sex, 2007

(Number, percent; 1,932 agencies; 2007 estimated population 20,739,857.)

Offense charged	Number of persons arrested			Percent male	Percent female	Percent distribution[1]		
	Total	Male	Female			Total	Male	Female
TOTAL	762,782	587,540	175,242	77.0	23.0	100.0	100.0	100.0
Murder and nonnegligent manslaughter	620	538	82	86.8	13.2	0.1	0.1	*
Forcible rape	1,485	1,451	34	97.7	2.3	0.2	0.2	*
Robbery	1,936	1,719	217	88.8	11.2	0.3	0.3	0.1
Aggravated assault	19,593	16,075	3,518	82.0	18.0	2.6	2.7	2.0
Burglary	18,135	15,868	2,267	87.5	12.5	2.4	2.7	1.3
Larceny-theft	30,868	22,058	8,810	71.5	28.5	4.0	3.8	5.0
Motor vehicle theft	4,602	3,784	818	82.2	17.8	0.6	0.6	0.5
Arson	884	746	138	84.4	15.6	0.1	0.1	0.1
Violent crime[2]	23,634	19,783	3,851	83.7	16.3	3.1	3.4	2.2
Property crime[2]	54,489	42,456	12,033	77.9	22.1	7.1	7.2	6.9
Other assaults	70,406	53,036	17,370	75.3	24.7	9.2	9.0	9.9
Forgery and counterfeiting	4,823	2,780	2,043	57.6	42.4	0.6	0.5	1.2
Fraud	27,984	14,347	13,637	51.3	48.7	3.7	2.4	7.8
Embezzlement	915	389	526	42.5	57.5	0.1	0.1	0.3
Stolen property; buying, receiving, possessing	5,097	4,189	908	82.2	17.8	0.7	0.7	0.5
Vandalism	13,065	10,876	2,189	83.2	16.8	1.7	1.9	1.2
Weapons; carrying, possessing, etc.	7,185	6,574	611	91.5	8.5	0.9	1.1	0.3
Prostitution and commercialized vice	161	106	55	65.8	34.2	*	*	*
Sex offenses (except forcible rape and prostitution)	5,557	5,241	316	94.3	5.7	0.7	0.9	0.2
Drug abuse violations	90,478	71,539	18,939	79.1	20.9	11.9	12.2	10.8
Gambling	302	225	77	74.5	25.5	*	*	*
Offenses against the family and children	12,840	10,268	2,572	80.0	20.0	1.7	1.7	1.5
Driving under the influence	138,117	111,183	26,934	80.5	19.5	18.1	18.9	15.4
Liquor laws	36,078	25,770	10,308	71.4	28.6	4.7	4.4	5.9
Drunkenness	18,411	15,133	3,278	82.2	17.8	2.4	2.6	1.9
Disorderly conduct	23,525	17,287	6,238	73.5	26.5	3.1	2.9	3.6
Vagrancy	217	162	55	74.7	25.3	*	*	*
All other offenses (except traffic)	225,407	174,231	51,176	77.3	22.7	29.6	29.7	29.2
Suspicion	73	60	13	82.2	17.8	*	*	*
Curfew and loitering law violations	408	256	152	62.7	37.3	0.1	*	0.1
Runaways	3,610	1,649	1,961	45.7	54.3	0.5	0.3	1.1

[1] Because of rounding, the percentages may not add to 100.0.

[2] Violent crimes are offenses of murder and nonnegligent manslaughter, forcible rape, robbery, and aggravated assault. Property crimes are offenses of burglary, larceny-theft, motor vehicle theft, and arson.

* = Less than one-tenth of 1 percent.

Table 61.   Arrests in Nonmetropolitan Counties, Distribution by Race, 2007

(Number, percent; 1,932 agencies; 2007 estimated population 20,739,857.)

Offense charged	Total arrests					Percent distribution[1]					Arrests under 18				
	Total	White	Black	American Indian or Alaskan Native	Asian or Pacific Islander	Total	White	Black	American Indian or Alaskan Native	Asian or Pacific Islander	Total	White	Black	American Indian or Alaskan Native	Asian or Pacific Islander
TOTAL	758,377	622,389	109,487	23,533	2,968	100.0	82.1	14.4	3.1	0.4	66,860	54,253	9,509	2,907	191
Murder and nonnegligent manslaughter	618	425	164	27	2	100.0	68.8	26.5	4.4	0.3	37	24	7	6	0
Forcible rape	1,479	1,220	217	38	4	100.0	82.5	14.7	2.6	0.3	202	167	25	8	2
Robbery	1,931	1,001	860	68	2	100.0	51.8	44.5	3.5	0.1	225	89	119	17	0
Aggravated assault	19,507	14,724	3,770	966	47	100.0	75.5	19.3	5.0	0.2	1,753	1,222	431	96	4
Burglary	18,083	14,821	2,561	660	41	100.0	82.0	14.2	3.6	0.2	4,068	3,371	527	167	3
Larceny-theft	30,719	25,283	4,494	874	68	100.0	82.3	14.6	2.8	0.2	5,161	4,332	671	151	7
Motor vehicle theft	4,585	3,742	615	212	16	100.0	81.6	13.4	4.6	0.3	1,074	887	91	85	11
Arson	880	752	100	25	3	100.0	85.5	11.4	2.8	0.3	193	171	15	5	2
Violent crime[2]	23,535	17,370	5,011	1,099	55	100.0	73.8	21.3	4.7	0.2	2,217	1,502	582	127	6
Property crime[2]	54,267	44,598	7,770	1,771	128	100.0	82.2	14.3	3.3	0.2	10,496	8,761	1,304	408	23
Other assaults	70,147	55,905	11,522	2,571	149	100.0	79.7	16.4	3.7	0.2	9,002	6,467	2,207	316	12
Forgery and counterfeiting	4,801	3,904	835	53	9	100.0	81.3	17.4	1.1	0.2	100	86	9	5	0
Fraud	27,897	21,932	5,630	279	56	100.0	78.6	20.2	1.0	0.2	339	289	46	4	0
Embezzlement	911	790	114	4	3	100.0	86.7	12.5	0.4	0.3	17	13	3	1	0
Stolen property; buying, receiving, possessing	5,068	3,983	937	132	16	100.0	78.6	18.5	2.6	0.3	537	404	113	17	3
Vandalism	13,007	10,985	1,475	517	30	100.0	84.5	11.3	4.0	0.2	3,702	3,212	325	159	6
Weapons; carrying, possessing, etc.	7,157	5,380	1,516	231	30	100.0	75.2	21.2	3.2	0.4	883	600	222	58	3
Prostitution and commercialized vice	161	133	20	7	1	100.0	82.6	12.4	4.3	0.6	6	6	0	0	0
Sex offenses (except forcible rape and prostitution)	5,545	4,791	617	121	16	100.0	86.4	11.1	2.2	0.3	1,056	904	130	21	1
Drug abuse violations	90,008	71,983	16,107	1,551	367	100.0	80.0	17.9	1.7	0.4	5,872	4,990	717	152	13
Gambling	302	173	121	3	5	100.0	57.3	40.1	1.0	1.7	7	5	2	0	0
Offenses against the family and children	12,786	9,009	3,007	752	18	100.0	70.5	23.5	5.9	0.1	389	316	69	4	0
Driving under the influence	136,917	124,267	7,748	3,682	1,220	100.0	90.8	5.7	2.7	0.9	1,962	1,834	46	67	15
Liquor laws	35,715	32,972	1,400	1,174	169	100.0	92.3	3.9	3.3	0.5	8,743	8,202	125	384	32
Drunkenness	18,317	16,084	1,357	831	45	100.0	87.8	7.4	4.5	0.2	471	414	19	35	3
Disorderly conduct	23,412	18,012	4,282	1,071	47	100.0	76.9	18.3	4.6	0.2	5,026	3,217	1,505	296	8
Vagrancy	215	152	58	5	0	100.0	70.7	27.0	2.3	0.0	10	8	2	0	0
All other offenses (except traffic)	224,138	176,500	39,529	7,521	588	100.0	78.7	17.6	3.4	0.3	12,003	9,589	1,669	695	50
Suspicion	71	52	19	0	0	100.0	73.2	26.8	0.0	0.0	22	20	2	0	0
Curfew and loitering law violations	405	346	26	33	0	100.0	85.4	6.4	8.1	0.0	405	346	26	33	0
Runaways	3,595	3,068	386	125	16	100.0	85.3	10.7	3.5	0.4	3,595	3,068	386	125	16

[1] Because of rounding, the percentages may not add to 100.0.

[2] Violent crimes are offenses of murder and nonnegligent manslaughter, forcible rape, robbery, and aggravated assault. Property crimes are offenses of burglary, larceny-theft, motor vehicle theft, and arson.

Table 61.   Arrests in Nonmetropolitan Counties, Distribution by Race, 2007 *(Contd.)*

(Number, percent; 1,932 agencies; 2007 estimated population 20,739,857.)

Offense charged	Percent distribution[1]					Arrests under 18					Percent distribution[1]				
	Total	White	Black	American Indian or Alaskan Native	Asian or Pacific Islander	Total	White	Black	American Indian or Alaskan Native	Asian or Pacific Islander	Total	White	Black	American Indian or Alaskan Native	Asian or Pacific Islander
TOTAL	100.0	81.1	14.2	4.3	0.3	691,517	568,136	99,978	20,626	2,777	100.0	82.2	14.5	3.0	0.4
Murder and nonnegligent manslaughter	100.0	64.9	18.9	16.2	0.0	581	401	157	21	2	100.0	69.0	27.0	3.6	0.3
Forcible rape	100.0	82.7	12.4	4.0	1.0	1,277	1,053	192	30	2	100.0	82.5	15.0	2.3	0.2
Robbery	100.0	39.6	52.9	7.6	0.0	1,706	912	741	51	2	100.0	53.5	43.4	3.0	0.1
Aggravated assault	100.0	69.7	24.6	5.5	0.2	17,754	13,502	3,339	870	43	100.0	76.1	18.8	4.9	0.2
Burglary	100.0	82.9	13.0	4.1	0.1	14,015	11,450	2,034	493	38	100.0	81.7	14.5	3.5	0.3
Larceny-theft	100.0	83.9	13.0	2.9	0.1	25,558	20,951	3,823	723	61	100.0	82.0	15.0	2.8	0.2
Motor vehicle theft	100.0	82.6	8.5	7.9	1.0	3,511	2,855	524	127	5	100.0	81.3	14.9	3.6	0.1
Arson	100.0	88.6	7.8	2.6	1.0	687	581	85	20	1	100.0	84.6	12.4	2.9	0.1
Violent crime[2]	100.0	67.7	26.3	5.7	0.3	21,318	15,868	4,429	972	49	100.0	74.4	20.8	4.6	0.2
Property crime[2]	100.0	83.5	12.4	3.9	0.2	43,771	35,837	6,466	1,363	105	100.0	81.9	14.8	3.1	0.2
Other assaults	100.0	71.8	24.5	3.5	0.1	61,145	49,438	9,315	2,255	137	100.0	80.9	15.2	3.7	0.2
Forgery and counterfeiting	100.0	86.0	9.0	5.0	0.0	4,701	3,818	826	48	9	100.0	81.2	17.6	1.0	0.2
Fraud	100.0	85.3	13.6	1.2	0.0	27,558	21,643	5,584	275	56	100.0	78.5	20.3	1.0	0.2
Embezzlement	100.0	76.5	17.6	5.9	0.0	894	777	111	3	3	100.0	86.9	12.4	0.3	0.3
Stolen property; buying, receiving, possessing	100.0	75.2	21.0	3.2	0.6	4,531	3,579	824	115	13	100.0	79.0	18.2	2.5	0.3
Vandalism	100.0	86.8	8.8	4.3	0.2	9,305	7,773	1,150	358	24	100.0	83.5	12.4	3.8	0.3
Weapons; carrying, possessing, etc.	100.0	68.0	25.1	6.6	0.3	6,274	4,780	1,294	173	27	100.0	76.2	20.6	2.8	0.4
Prostitution and commercialized vice	100.0	100.0	0.0	0.0	0.0	155	127	20	7	1	100.0	81.9	12.9	4.5	0.6
Sex offenses (except forcible rape and prostitution)	100.0	85.6	12.3	2.0	0.1	4,489	3,887	487	100	15	100.0	86.6	10.8	2.2	0.3
Drug abuse violations	100.0	85.0	12.2	2.6	0.2	84,136	66,993	15,390	1,399	354	100.0	79.6	18.3	1.7	0.4
Gambling	100.0	71.4	28.6	0.0	0.0	295	168	119	3	5	100.0	56.9	40.3	1.0	1.7
Offenses against the family and children	100.0	81.2	17.7	1.0	0.0	12,397	8,693	2,938	748	18	100.0	70.1	23.7	6.0	0.1
Driving under the influence	100.0	93.5	2.3	3.4	0.8	134,955	122,433	7,702	3,615	1,205	100.0	90.7	5.7	2.7	0.9
Liquor laws	100.0	93.8	1.4	4.4	0.4	26,972	24,770	1,275	790	137	100.0	91.8	4.7	2.9	0.5
Drunkenness	100.0	87.9	4.0	7.4	0.6	17,846	15,670	1,338	796	42	100.0	87.8	7.5	4.5	0.2
Disorderly conduct	100.0	64.0	29.9	5.9	0.2	18,386	14,795	2,777	775	39	100.0	80.5	15.1	4.2	0.2
Vagrancy	100.0	80.0	20.0	0.0	0.0	205	144	56	5	0	100.0	70.2	27.3	2.4	0.0
All other offenses (except traffic)	100.0	79.9	13.9	5.8	0.4	212,135	166,911	37,860	6,826	538	100.0	78.7	17.8	3.2	0.3
Suspicion	100.0	90.9	9.1	0.0	0.0	49	32	17	0	0	100.0	65.3	34.7	0.0	0.0
Curfew and loitering law violations	100.0	85.4	6.4	8.1	0.0	-	-	-	-	-	-	-	-	-	-
Runaways	100.0	85.3	10.7	3.5	0.4	-	-	-	-	-	-	-	-	-	-

[1] Because of rounding, the percentages may not add to 100.0.

[2] Violent crimes are offenses of murder and nonnegligent manslaughter, forcible rape, robbery, and aggravated assault. Property crimes are offenses of burglary, larceny-theft, motor vehicle theft, and arson.

Table 62. Arrest Trends for Suburban Areas,[1] 2006–2007

(Number, percent change; 5,627 agencies; 2007 estimated population 86,451,220; 2006 estimated population 85,771,943.)

Offense charged	Number of persons arrested								
	Total all ages			Under 18 years of age			18 years of age and over		
	2006	2007	Percent change	2006	2007	Percent change	2006	2007	Percent change
TOTAL[2]	3,589,277	3,571,566	-0.5	549,133	537,524	-2.1	3,040,144	3,034,042	-0.2
Murder and nonnegligent manslaughter	2,501	2,404	-3.9	193	199	+3.1	2,308	2,205	-4.5
Forcible rape	5,716	5,409	-5.4	898	902	+0.4	4,818	4,507	-6.5
Robbery	21,736	21,435	-1.4	5,702	5,459	-4.3	16,034	15,976	-0.4
Aggravated assault	99,478	98,278	-1.2	14,136	13,554	-4.1	85,342	84,724	-0.7
Burglary	72,004	71,873	-0.2	20,571	19,529	-5.1	51,433	52,344	+1.8
Larceny-theft	254,739	275,144	+8.0	65,740	69,614	+5.9	188,999	205,530	+8.7
Motor vehicle theft	26,496	22,924	-13.5	6,147	5,301	-13.8	20,349	17,623	-13.4
Arson	4,507	4,239	-5.9	2,332	2,184	-6.3	2,175	2,055	-5.5
Violent crime[3]	129,431	127,526	-1.5	20,929	20,114	-3.9	108,502	107,412	-1.0
Property crime[3]	357,746	374,180	+4.6	94,790	96,628	+1.9	262,956	277,552	+5.6
Other assaults	311,190	313,597	+0.8	66,104	64,258	-2.8	245,086	249,339	+1.7
Forgery and counterfeiting	27,164	24,625	-9.3	953	818	-14.2	26,211	23,807	-9.2
Fraud	94,404	83,694	-11.3	2,014	1,961	-2.6	92,390	81,733	-11.5
Embezzlement	4,922	5,336	+8.4	379	427	+12.7	4,543	4,909	+8.1
Stolen property; buying, receiving, possessing	32,322	30,326	-6.2	5,483	5,427	-1.0	26,839	24,899	-7.2
Vandalism	74,696	72,346	-3.1	31,787	30,163	-5.1	42,909	42,183	-1.7
Weapons; carrying, possessing, etc.	41,086	39,101	-4.8	11,056	9,981	-9.7	30,030	29,120	-3.0
Prostitution and commercialized vice	4,509	4,441	-1.5	109	106	-2.8	4,400	4,335	-1.5
Sex offenses (except forcible rape and prostitution)	20,161	19,900	-1.3	4,215	4,035	-4.3	15,946	15,865	-0.5
Drug abuse violations	424,785	417,756	-1.7	50,137	50,149	*	374,648	367,607	-1.9
Gambling	1,000	1,046	+4.6	131	109	-16.8	869	937	+7.8
Offenses against the family and children	45,128	45,573	+1.0	1,551	1,847	+19.1	43,577	43,726	+0.3
Driving under the influence	434,043	435,750	+0.4	5,640	5,330	-5.5	428,403	430,420	+0.5
Liquor laws	166,320	165,346	-0.6	42,635	41,861	-1.8	123,685	123,485	-0.2
Drunkenness	123,790	130,843	+5.7	5,026	4,959	-1.3	118,764	125,884	+6.0
Disorderly conduct	168,855	168,648	-0.1	56,782	54,124	-4.7	112,073	114,524	+2.2
Vagrancy	5,334	4,272	-19.9	631	582	-7.8	4,703	3,690	-21.5
All other offenses (except traffic)	1,078,610	1,063,577	-1.4	105,000	100,962	-3.8	973,610	962,615	-1.1
Suspicion	936	925	-1.2	166	148	-10.8	770	777	+0.9
Curfew and loitering law violations	19,466	19,748	+1.4	19,466	19,748	+1.4	-	-	-
Runaways	24,315	23,935	-1.6	24,315	23,935	-1.6	-	-	-

[1] Suburban area includes law enforcement agencies in cities with less than 50,000 inhabitants and county law enforcement agencies that are within a Metropolitan Statistical Area. Suburban area excludes all metropolitan agencies associated with a principal city.

[2] Does not include suspicion.

[3] Violent crimes are offenses of murder and nonnegligent manslaughter, forcible rape, robbery, and aggravated assault. Property crimes are offenses of burglary, larceny-theft, motor vehicle theft, and arson.

* = Less than one-tenth of 1 percent.

Table 63.   Arrest Trends for Suburban Areas,[1] by Age and Sex, 2006–2007

(Number, percent change; 5,627 agencies; 2007 estimated population 86,451,220; 2006 estimated population 85,771,943.)

Offense charged	Male						Female					
	Total			Under 18			Total			Under 18		
	2006	2007	Percent change	2006	2007	Percent change	2006	2007	Percent change	2006	2007	Percent change
TOTAL[2]	2,733,568	2,702,863	-1.1	393,703	382,470	-2.9	855,709	868,703	+1.5	155,430	155,054	-0.2
Murder and nonnegligent manslaughter	2,186	2,141	-2.1	184	184	0.0	315	263	-16.5	9	15	+66.7
Forcible rape	5,635	5,353	-5.0	884	886	+0.2	81	56	-30.9	14	16	+14.3
Robbery	19,465	19,039	-2.2	5,233	4,966	-5.1	2,271	2,396	+5.5	469	493	+5.1
Aggravated assault	79,699	78,049	-2.1	10,921	10,513	-3.7	19,779	20,229	+2.3	3,215	3,041	-5.4
Burglary	62,213	62,110	-0.2	18,469	17,480	-5.4	9,791	9,763	-0.3	2,102	2,049	-2.5
Larceny-theft	160,621	167,611	+4.4	40,544	41,559	+2.5	94,118	107,533	+14.3	25,196	28,055	+11.3
Motor vehicle theft	21,692	18,714	-13.7	5,028	4,318	-14.1	4,804	4,210	-12.4	1,119	983	-12.2
Arson	3,811	3,641	-4.5	2,049	1,927	-6.0	696	598	-14.1	283	257	-9.2
Violent crime[3]	106,985	104,582	-2.2	17,222	16,549	-3.9	22,446	22,944	+2.2	3,707	3,565	-3.8
Property crime[3]	248,337	252,076	+1.5	66,090	65,284	-1.2	109,409	122,104	+11.6	28,700	31,344	+9.2
Other assaults	231,700	232,677	+0.4	44,307	43,154	-2.6	79,490	80,920	+1.8	21,797	21,104	-3.2
Forgery and counterfeiting	16,609	15,028	-9.5	659	563	-14.6	10,555	9,597	-9.1	294	255	-13.3
Fraud	50,251	45,021	-10.4	1,330	1,266	-4.8	44,153	38,673	-12.4	684	695	+1.6
Embezzlement	2,318	2,557	+10.3	223	263	17.9	2,604	2,779	+6.7	156	164	+5.1
Stolen property; buying, receiving, possessing	26,089	24,192	-7.3	4,613	4,380	-5.1	6,233	6,134	-1.6	870	1,047	+20.3
Vandalism	63,348	60,766	-4.1	27,803	26,160	-5.9	11,348	11,580	+2.0	3,984	4,003	+0.5
Weapons; carrying, possessing, etc.	37,740	35,967	-4.7	9,878	9,008	-8.8	3,346	3,134	-6.3	1,178	973	-17.4
Prostitution and commercialized vice	1,951	1,785	-8.5	49	33	-32.7	2,558	2,656	+3.8	60	73	+21.7
Sex offenses (except forcible rape and prostitution)	18,981	18,710	-1.4	3,861	3,729	-3.4	1,180	1,190	+0.8	354	306	-13.6
Drug abuse violations	341,172	334,568	-1.9	41,166	41,158	*	83,613	83,188	-0.5	8,971	8,991	+0.2
Gambling	829	866	+4.5	123	100	-18.7	171	180	+5.3	8	9	+12.5
Offenses against the family and children	36,364	36,393	+0.1	941	1,174	+24.8	8,764	9,180	+4.7	610	673	+10.3
Driving under the influence	345,550	343,939	-0.5	4,394	4,064	-7.5	88,493	91,811	+3.7	1,246	1,266	+1.6
Liquor laws	119,305	117,843	-1.2	27,059	26,183	-3.2	47,015	47,503	+1.0	15,576	15,678	+0.7
Drunkenness	102,833	107,768	+4.8	3,637	3,588	-1.3	20,957	23,075	+10.1	1,389	1,371	-1.3
Disorderly conduct	124,529	123,780	-0.6	38,921	36,932	-5.1	44,326	44,868	+1.2	17,861	17,192	-3.7
Vagrancy	4,005	3,301	-17.6	470	431	-8.3	1,329	971	-26.9	161	151	-6.2
All other offenses (except traffic)	830,658	816,767	-1.7	76,943	74,174	-3.6	247,952	246,810	-0.5	28,057	26,788	-4.5
Suspicion	743	734	-1.2	135	113	-16.3	193	191	-1.0	31	35	+12.9
Curfew and loitering law violations	13,129	13,442	+2.4	13,129	13,442	+2.4	6,337	6,306	-0.5	6,337	6,306	-0.5
Runaways	10,885	10,835	-0.5	10,885	10,835	-0.5	13,430	13,100	-2.5	13,430	13,100	-2.5

[1] Suburban area includes law enforcement agencies in cities with less than 50,000 inhabitants and county law enforcement agencies that are within a Metropolitan Statistical Area. Suburban area excludes all metropolitan agencies associated with a principal city.

[2] Does not include suspicion.

[3] Violent crimes are offenses of murder and nonnegligent manslaughter, forcible rape, robbery, and aggravated assault. Property crimes are offenses of burglary, larceny-theft, motor vehicle theft, and arson.

* = Less than one-tenth of 1 percent.

Table 64. Arrests in Suburban Areas,[1] Distribution by Age, 2007

(Number, percent; 6,470 agencies; 2007 estimated population 98,929,880.)

Offense charged	Total all ages	Ages under 15	Ages under 18	Ages 18 and over	Under 10	10–12	13–14	15	16	17	18	19	20
TOTAL	4,202,876	176,348	637,897	3,564,979	5,227	36,390	134,731	124,071	156,036	181,442	213,502	212,741	193,588
Total percent distribution[2]	100.0	4.2	15.2	84.8	0.1	0.9	3.2	3.0	3.7	4.3	5.1	5.1	4.6
Murder and nonnegligent manslaughter	3,095	19	273	2,822	0	2	17	36	89	129	226	181	164
Forcible rape	6,176	338	1,008	5,168	4	80	254	159	228	283	319	303	297
Robbery	27,190	1,414	6,982	20,208	27	197	1,190	1,389	1,858	2,321	2,655	2,157	1,644
Aggravated assault	115,349	4,944	15,968	99,381	203	1,222	3,519	2,989	3,779	4,256	4,676	4,491	4,275
Burglary	84,443	6,705	22,900	61,543	234	1,412	5,059	4,618	5,344	6,233	6,789	5,390	4,375
Larceny-theft	340,518	25,953	86,689	253,829	707	5,387	19,859	17,229	20,696	22,811	22,474	18,037	14,479
Motor vehicle theft	26,932	1,323	6,303	20,629	7	138	1,178	1,533	1,728	1,719	1,701	1,408	1,263
Arson	4,853	1,384	2,422	2,431	120	433	831	434	337	267	241	176	135
Violent crime[3]	151,810	6,715	24,231	127,579	234	1,501	4,980	4,573	5,954	6,989	7,876	7,132	6,380
Violent crime percent distribution[2]	100.0	4.4	16.0	84.0	0.2	1.0	3.3	3.0	3.9	4.6	5.2	4.7	4.2
Property crime[3]	456,746	35,365	118,314	338,432	1,068	7,370	26,927	23,814	28,105	31,030	31,205	25,011	20,252
Property crime percent distribution[2]	100.0	7.7	25.9	74.1	0.2	1.6	5.9	5.2	6.2	6.8	6.8	5.5	4.4
Other assaults	372,393	29,562	76,049	296,344	933	7,614	21,015	15,064	16,446	14,977	12,678	11,990	11,558
Forgery and counterfeiting	30,360	127	1,024	29,336	8	25	94	135	244	518	1,002	1,369	1,323
Fraud	88,486	338	2,293	86,193	16	51	271	351	544	1,060	1,965	2,637	2,839
Embezzlement	6,299	25	466	5,833	1	8	16	32	135	274	432	441	389
Stolen property; buying, receiving, possessing	36,651	1,632	6,629	30,022	22	252	1,358	1,331	1,705	1,961	2,317	2,060	1,830
Vandalism	85,621	13,850	34,818	50,803	639	3,537	9,674	6,847	7,082	7,039	5,998	4,691	3,473
Weapons; carrying, possessing, etc.	47,877	4,394	12,359	35,518	242	1,138	3,014	2,322	2,645	2,998	3,237	2,804	2,351
Prostitution and commercialized vice	6,126	18	137	5,989	0	4	14	23	40	56	189	234	222
Sex offenses (except forcible rape and prostitution)	23,328	2,397	4,885	18,443	140	650	1,607	829	825	834	955	925	795
Drug abuse violations	493,774	8,365	58,272	435,502	99	880	7,386	9,677	15,958	24,272	35,190	33,850	29,394
Gambling	1,224	28	121	1,103	3	2	23	25	40	28	39	42	49
Offenses against the family and children	50,682	608	2,176	48,506	32	121	455	412	578	578	803	841	980
Driving under the influence	496,340	93	6,173	490,167	18	8	67	228	1,389	4,463	11,272	15,511	17,442
Liquor laws	196,312	4,091	49,172	147,140	36	235	3,820	7,353	14,110	23,618	38,014	37,765	29,047
Drunkenness	153,383	582	5,471	147,912	28	26	528	874	1,404	2,611	5,468	5,613	5,283
Disorderly conduct	208,355	23,824	64,485	143,870	434	5,500	17,890	13,520	14,190	12,951	10,415	8,488	7,692
Vagrancy	6,001	145	672	5,329	5	20	120	143	177	207	319	253	190
All other offenses (except traffic)	1,238,040	29,568	118,061	1,119,979	1,000	5,407	23,161	23,449	29,735	35,309	44,047	51,006	52,054
Suspicion	1,152	47	173	979	0	11	36	32	53	41	81	78	45
Curfew and loitering law violations	22,785	5,923	22,785	-	65	849	5,009	5,542	6,457	4,863	-	-	-
Runaways	29,131	8,651	29,131	-	204	1,181	7,266	7,495	8,220	4,765	-	-	-

[1] Suburban area includes law enforcement agencies in cities with less than 50,000 inhabitants and county law enforcement agencies that are within a Metropolitan Statistical Area. Suburban area excludes all metropolitan agencies associated with a principal city.

[2] Because of rounding, the percentages may not add to 100.0.

[3] Violent crimes are offenses of murder and nonnegligent manslaughter, forcible rape, robbery, and aggravated assault. Property crimes are offenses of burglary, larceny-theft, motor vehicle theft, and arson.

Table 64. Arrests in Suburban Areas,[1] Distribution by Age, 2007

(Number, percent; 6,470 agencies; 2007 estimated population 98,929,880.)

Offense charged	21	22	23	24	25–29	30–34	35–39	40–44	45–49	50–54	55–59	60–64	65 and over
TOTAL	176,084	162,926	149,291	143,375	592,511	413,587	384,913	354,557	279,098	156,254	73,521	33,290	25,741
Total percent distribution[2]	4.2	3.9	3.6	3.4	14.1	9.8	9.2	8.4	6.6	3.7	1.7	0.8	0.6
Murder and nonnegligent manslaughter	168	180	129	146	520	292	221	205	157	103	59	42	29
Forcible rape	265	226	203	176	807	645	632	509	361	194	109	56	66
Robbery	1,354	1,128	978	891	3,212	1,885	1,575	1,268	880	349	157	47	28
Aggravated assault	4,487	4,212	3,922	3,902	17,333	12,405	11,576	10,684	8,318	4,737	2,250	1,084	1,029
Burglary	3,540	3,022	2,741	2,417	9,840	6,420	5,931	5,123	3,491	1,566	573	231	94
Larceny-theft	12,368	10,955	9,698	8,959	37,754	27,101	27,179	25,689	19,113	10,682	5,068	2,313	1,960
Motor vehicle theft	1,047	1,053	896	917	3,753	2,563	2,314	1,805	1,113	488	168	86	54
Arson	116	103	81	67	342	269	228	246	185	121	63	32	26
Violent crime[3]	6,274	5,746	5,232	5,115	21,872	15,227	14,004	12,666	9,716	5,383	2,575	1,229	1,152
Violent crime percent distribution[2]	4.1	3.8	3.4	3.4	14.4	10.0	9.2	8.3	6.4	3.5	1.7	0.8	0.8
Property crime[3]	17,071	15,133	13,416	12,360	51,689	36,353	35,652	32,863	23,902	12,857	5,872	2,662	2,134
Property crime percent distribution[2]	3.7	3.3	2.9	2.7	11.3	8.0	7.8	7.2	5.2	2.8	1.3	0.6	0.5
Other assaults	12,419	12,005	11,367	11,347	49,787	38,332	37,641	34,319	26,203	14,042	6,569	3,184	2,903
Forgery and counterfeiting	1,216	1,246	1,229	1,264	5,757	4,325	3,811	3,085	2,028	1,001	426	162	92
Fraud	2,780	2,915	2,871	3,092	14,666	13,226	12,827	10,552	7,566	4,361	2,110	1,058	728
Embezzlement	336	316	249	239	888	635	591	567	340	237	103	45	25
Stolen property; buying, receiving, possessing	1,566	1,405	1,345	1,228	5,227	3,630	3,164	2,787	1,837	960	388	169	109
Vandalism	3,224	2,792	2,312	2,094	7,928	4,879	4,298	3,689	2,782	1,404	613	342	284
Weapons; carrying, possessing, etc.	2,230	2,079	1,756	1,600	6,121	3,559	2,837	2,403	1,988	1,218	680	335	320
Prostitution and commercialized vice	236	208	225	197	972	734	830	795	565	289	138	72	83
Sex offenses (except forcible rape and prostitution)	752	669	579	547	2,492	1,978	2,104	2,055	1,658	1,083	721	522	608
Drug abuse violations	26,003	23,281	20,679	19,312	75,829	46,166	39,488	35,824	27,853	14,361	5,595	1,803	874
Gambling	28	40	29	36	123	134	109	127	107	69	62	63	46
Offenses against the family and children	1,120	1,189	1,342	1,524	8,363	8,270	8,341	7,175	4,770	2,307	904	371	206
Driving under the influence	24,837	24,451	23,587	22,771	88,689	58,699	52,442	50,211	44,075	27,956	15,278	7,446	5,500
Liquor laws	4,733	3,169	2,387	1,962	7,249	4,510	4,303	4,749	4,281	2,627	1,311	617	416
Drunkenness	7,737	7,028	6,066	5,575	22,296	15,289	15,424	17,377	16,502	10,139	4,799	2,026	1,290
Disorderly conduct	9,213	7,789	6,731	6,226	22,580	14,449	13,787	13,435	11,029	6,227	3,046	1,485	1,278
Vagrancy	240	179	162	155	697	530	638	773	599	339	164	45	46
All other offenses (except traffic)	54,019	51,234	47,688	46,687	199,124	142,555	132,524	119,027	91,227	49,351	22,148	9,649	7,639
Suspicion	50	52	39	44	162	107	98	78	70	43	19	5	8
Curfew and loitering law violations	-	-	-	-	-	-	-	-	-	-	-	-	-
Runaways	-	-	-	-	-	-	-	-	-	-	-	-	-

[1] Suburban area includes law enforcement agencies in cities with less than 50,000 inhabitants and county law enforcement agencies that are within a Metropolitan Statistical Area. Suburban area excludes all metropolitan agencies associated with a principal city.

[2] Because of rounding, the percentages may not add to 100.0.

[3] Violent crimes are offenses of murder and nonnegligent manslaughter, forcible rape, robbery, and aggravated assault. Property crimes are offenses of burglary, larceny-theft, motor vehicle theft, and arson.

Table 65. Arrests in Suburban Areas[1] of Persons Under 15, 18, 21, and 25 Years of Age, 2007

(Number, percent; 6,470 agencies; 2007 estimated population 98,929,880.)

Offense charged	Total all ages	Number of persons arrested				Percent of total all ages			
		Under 15	Under 18	Under 21	Under 25	Under 15	Under 18	Under 21	Under 25
TOTAL	4,202,876	176,348	637,897	1,257,728	1,889,404	4.2	15.2	29.9	45.0
Murder and nonnegligent manslaughter	3,095	19	273	844	1,467	0.6	8.8	27.3	47.4
Forcible rape	6,176	338	1,008	1,927	2,797	5.5	16.3	31.2	45.3
Robbery	27,190	1,414	6,982	13,438	17,789	5.2	25.7	49.4	65.4
Aggravated assault	115,349	4,944	15,968	29,410	45,933	4.3	13.8	25.5	39.8
Burglary	84,443	6,705	22,900	39,454	51,174	7.9	27.1	46.7	60.6
Larceny-theft	340,518	25,953	86,689	141,679	183,659	7.6	25.5	41.6	53.9
Motor vehicle theft	26,932	1,323	6,303	10,675	14,588	4.9	23.4	39.6	54.2
Arson	4,853	1,384	2,422	2,974	3,341	28.5	49.9	61.3	68.8
Violent crime[2]	151,810	6,715	24,231	45,619	67,986	4.4	16.0	30.1	44.8
Property crime[2]	456,746	35,365	118,314	194,782	252,762	7.7	25.9	42.6	55.3
Other assaults	372,393	29,562	76,049	112,275	159,413	7.9	20.4	30.1	42.8
Forgery and counterfeiting	30,360	127	1,024	4,718	9,673	0.4	3.4	15.5	31.9
Fraud	88,486	338	2,293	9,734	21,392	0.4	2.6	11.0	24.2
Embezzlement	6,299	25	466	1,728	2,868	0.4	7.4	27.4	45.5
Stolen property; buying, receiving, possessing	36,651	1,632	6,629	12,836	18,380	4.5	18.1	35.0	50.1
Vandalism	85,621	13,850	34,818	48,980	59,402	16.2	40.7	57.2	69.4
Weapons; carrying, possessing, etc.	47,877	4,394	12,359	20,751	28,416	9.2	25.8	43.3	59.4
Prostitution and commercialized vice	6,126	18	137	782	1,648	0.3	2.2	12.8	26.9
Sex offenses (except forcible rape and prostitution)	23,328	2,397	4,885	7,560	10,107	10.3	20.9	32.4	43.3
Drug abuse violations	493,774	8,365	58,272	156,706	245,981	1.7	11.8	31.7	49.8
Gambling	1,224	28	121	251	384	2.3	9.9	20.5	31.4
Offenses against the family and children	50,682	608	2,176	4,800	9,975	1.2	4.3	9.5	19.7
Driving under the influence	496,340	93	6,173	50,398	146,044	*	1.2	10.2	29.4
Liquor laws	196,312	4,091	49,172	153,998	166,249	2.1	25.0	78.4	84.7
Drunkenness	153,383	582	5,471	21,835	48,241	0.4	3.6	14.2	31.5
Disorderly conduct	208,355	23,824	64,485	91,080	121,039	11.4	30.9	43.7	58.1
Vagrancy	6,001	145	672	1,434	2,170	2.4	11.2	23.9	36.2
All other offenses (except traffic)	1,238,040	29,568	118,061	265,168	464,796	2.4	9.5	21.4	37.5
Suspicion	1,152	47	173	377	562	4.1	15.0	32.7	48.8
Curfew and loitering law violations	22,785	5,923	22,785	22,785	22,785	26.0	100.0	100.0	100.0
Runaways	29,131	8,651	29,131	29,131	29,131	29.7	100.0	100.0	100.0

[1] Suburban area includes law enforcement agencies in cities with less than 50,000 inhabitants and county law enforcement agencies that are within a Metropolitan Statistical Area. Suburban area excludes all metropolitan agencies associated with a principal city.

[2] Violent crimes are offenses of murder and nonnegligent manslaughter, forcible rape, robbery, and aggravated assault. Property crimes are offenses of burglary, larceny-theft, motor vehicle theft, and arson.

* = Less than one-tenth of 1 percent.

Table 66.   Arrests in Suburban Areas,[1] Distribution by Sex, 2007

(Number, percent; 6,470 agencies; 2007 estimated population 98,929,880.)

Offense charged	Number of persons arrested			Percent male	Percent female	Percent distribution[2]		
	Total	Male	Female			Total	Male	Female
TOTAL	4,202,876	3,179,537	1,023,339	75.7	24.3	100.0	100.0	100.0
Murder and nonnegligent manslaughter	3,095	2,765	330	89.3	10.7	0.1	0.1	*
Forcible rape	6,176	6,112	64	99.0	1.0	0.1	0.2	*
Robbery	27,190	24,200	2,990	89.0	11.0	0.6	0.8	0.3
Aggravated assault	115,349	91,613	23,736	79.4	20.6	2.7	2.9	2.3
Burglary	84,443	73,177	11,266	86.7	13.3	2.0	2.3	1.1
Larceny-theft	340,518	205,483	135,035	60.3	39.7	8.1	6.5	13.2
Motor vehicle theft	26,932	22,036	4,896	81.8	18.2	0.6	0.7	0.5
Arson	4,853	4,136	717	85.2	14.8	0.1	0.1	0.1
Violent crime[3]	151,810	124,690	27,120	82.1	17.9	3.6	3.9	2.7
Property crime[3]	456,746	304,832	151,914	66.7	33.3	10.9	9.6	14.8
Other assaults	372,393	276,474	95,919	74.2	25.8	8.9	8.7	9.4
Forgery and counterfeiting	30,360	18,504	11,856	60.9	39.1	0.7	0.6	1.2
Fraud	88,486	48,470	40,016	54.8	45.2	2.1	1.5	3.9
Embezzlement	6,299	2,940	3,359	46.7	53.3	0.1	0.1	0.3
Stolen property; buying, receiving, possessing	36,651	29,389	7,262	80.2	19.8	0.9	0.9	0.7
Vandalism	85,621	71,739	13,882	83.8	16.2	2.0	2.3	1.4
Weapons; carrying, possessing, etc.	47,877	44,049	3,828	92.0	8.0	1.1	1.4	0.4
Prostitution and commercialized vice	6,126	2,340	3,786	38.2	61.8	0.1	0.1	0.4
Sex offenses (except forcible rape and prostitution)	23,328	21,899	1,429	93.9	6.1	0.6	0.7	0.1
Drug abuse violations	493,774	396,508	97,266	80.3	19.7	11.7	12.5	9.5
Gambling	1,224	1,026	198	83.8	16.2	*	*	*
Offenses against the family and children	50,682	39,946	10,736	78.8	21.2	1.2	1.3	1.0
Driving under the influence	496,340	391,258	105,082	78.8	21.2	11.8	12.3	10.3
Liquor laws	196,312	140,116	56,196	71.4	28.6	4.7	4.4	5.5
Drunkenness	153,383	126,563	26,820	82.5	17.5	3.6	4.0	2.6
Disorderly conduct	208,355	152,729	55,626	73.3	26.7	5.0	4.8	5.4
Vagrancy	6,001	4,603	1,398	76.7	23.3	0.1	0.1	0.1
All other offenses (except traffic)	1,238,040	951,834	286,206	76.9	23.1	29.5	29.9	28.0
Suspicion	1,152	903	249	78.4	21.6	*	*	*
Curfew and loitering law violations	22,785	15,571	7,214	68.3	31.7	0.5	0.5	0.7
Runaways	29,131	13,154	15,977	45.2	54.8	0.7	0.4	1.6

[1] Suburban area includes law enforcement agencies in cities with less than 50,000 inhabitants and county law enforcement agencies that are within a Metropolitan Statistical Area. Suburban area excludes all metropolitan agencies associated with a principal city.

[2] Because of rounding, the percentages may not add to 100.0.

[3] Violent crimes are offenses of murder and nonnegligent manslaughter, forcible rape, robbery, and aggravated assault. Property crimes are offenses of burglary, larceny-theft, motor vehicle theft, and arson.

* = Less than one-tenth of 1 percent.

Table 67. Arrests in Suburban Areas,[1] Distribution by Race, 2007

(Number, percent; 6,465 agencies; 2007 estimated population 98,904,024.)

Offense charged	Total arrests					Percent distribution[2]					Arrests under 18				
	Total	White	Black	American Indian or Alaskan Native	Asian or Pacific Islander	Total	White	Black	American Indian or Alaskan Native	Asian or Pacific Islander	Total	White	Black	American Indian or Alaskan Native	Asian or Pacific Islander
TOTAL	4,180,882	3,153,313	965,820	31,083	30,666	100.0	75.4	23.1	0.7	0.7	633,624	458,634	165,388	4,064	5,538
Murder and nonnegligent manslaughter	3,093	1,761	1,293	17	22	100.0	56.9	41.8	0.5	0.7	273	114	156	1	2
Forcible rape	6,140	4,491	1,546	54	49	100.0	73.1	25.2	0.9	0.8	997	693	298	0	6
Robbery	27,133	12,831	14,015	113	174	100.0	47.3	51.7	0.4	0.6	6,965	2,355	4,529	16	65
Aggravated assault	114,932	82,096	30,942	977	917	100.0	71.4	26.9	0.9	0.8	15,892	10,049	5,634	97	112
Burglary	84,198	63,205	20,084	414	495	100.0	75.1	23.9	0.5	0.6	22,808	16,177	6,337	125	169
Larceny-theft	338,550	237,701	94,629	2,713	3,507	100.0	70.2	28.0	0.8	1.0	86,044	57,060	27,234	613	1,137
Motor vehicle theft	26,866	19,761	6,734	191	180	100.0	73.6	25.1	0.7	0.7	6,293	4,175	2,018	48	52
Arson	4,815	3,850	903	23	39	100.0	80.0	18.8	0.5	0.8	2,401	1,943	420	6	32
Violent crime[3]	151,298	101,179	47,796	1,161	1,162	100.0	66.9	31.6	0.8	0.8	24,127	13,211	10,617	114	185
Property crime[3]	454,429	324,517	122,350	3,341	4,221	100.0	71.4	26.9	0.7	0.9	117,546	79,355	36,009	792	1,390
Other assaults	370,791	270,425	94,869	2,766	2,731	100.0	72.9	25.6	0.7	0.7	75,625	48,241	26,541	396	447
Forgery and counterfeiting	30,240	21,824	7,993	114	309	100.0	72.2	26.4	0.4	1.0	1,017	766	235	3	13
Fraud	88,111	62,017	25,272	351	471	100.0	70.4	28.7	0.4	0.5	2,276	1,538	709	6	23
Embezzlement	6,271	4,155	2,042	21	53	100.0	66.3	32.6	0.3	0.8	465	274	179	2	10
Stolen property; buying, receiving, possessing	36,468	25,043	10,900	231	294	100.0	68.7	29.9	0.6	0.8	6,577	4,030	2,435	36	76
Vandalism	85,099	68,925	14,955	619	600	100.0	81.0	17.6	0.7	0.7	34,573	28,282	5,817	213	261
Weapons; carrying, possessing, etc.	47,658	31,281	15,717	258	402	100.0	65.6	33.0	0.5	0.8	12,256	8,005	4,052	62	137
Prostitution and commercialized vice	6,111	3,929	1,843	24	315	100.0	64.3	30.2	0.4	5.2	136	72	64	0	0
Sex offenses (except forcible rape and prostitution)	23,248	18,457	4,426	151	214	100.0	79.4	19.0	0.6	0.9	4,861	3,584	1,232	25	20
Drug abuse violations	491,891	363,715	122,828	2,528	2,820	100.0	73.9	25.0	0.5	0.6	57,893	46,006	11,095	348	444
Gambling	1,217	723	462	5	27	100.0	59.4	38.0	0.4	2.2	121	32	87	0	2
Offenses against the family and children	50,404	33,676	16,124	337	267	100.0	66.8	32.0	0.7	0.5	2,158	1,578	559	9	12
Driving under the influence	493,900	442,101	44,050	3,420	4,329	100.0	89.5	8.9	0.7	0.9	6,143	5,800	258	45	40
Liquor laws	194,095	173,504	15,461	2,956	2,174	100.0	89.4	8.0	1.5	1.1	48,773	45,430	2,253	525	565
Drunkenness	152,380	134,730	15,394	1,485	771	100.0	88.4	10.1	1.0	0.5	5,447	5,033	339	41	34
Disorderly conduct	207,112	146,751	57,473	1,562	1,326	100.0	70.9	27.7	0.8	0.6	64,257	40,095	23,442	277	443
Vagrancy	5,991	4,069	1,899	11	12	100.0	67.9	31.7	0.2	0.2	671	556	111	1	3
All other offenses (except traffic)	1,231,344	882,101	332,163	9,332	7,748	100.0	71.6	27.0	0.8	0.6	116,857	87,088	27,984	760	1,025
Suspicion	1,136	600	521	3	12	100.0	52.8	45.9	0.3	1.1	157	67	88	2	0
Curfew and loitering law violations	22,666	17,973	4,433	98	162	100.0	79.3	19.6	0.4	0.7	22,666	17,973	4,433	98	162
Runaways	29,022	21,618	6,849	309	246	100.0	74.5	23.6	1.1	0.8	29,022	21,618	6,849	309	246

[1] Suburban area includes law enforcement agencies in cities with less than 50,000 inhabitants and county law enforcement agencies that are within a Metropolitan Statistical Area. Suburban area excludes all metropolitan agencies associated with a principal city.

[2] Because of rounding, the percentages may not add to 100.0.

[3] Violent crimes are offenses of murder and nonnegligent manslaughter, forcible rape, robbery, and aggravated assault. Property crimes are offenses of burglary, larceny-theft, motor vehicle theft, and arson.

Table 67. Arrests in Suburban Areas,[1] Distribution by Race, 2007 (Contd.)

(Number, percent; 6,465 agencies; 2007 estimated population 98,904,024.)

Offense charged	Percent distribution[2]					Arrests under 18					Percent distribution[2]				
	Total	White	Black	American Indian or Alaskan Native	Asian or Pacific Islander	Total	White	Black	American Indian or Alaskan Native	Asian or Pacific Islander	Total	White	Black	American Indian or Alaskan Native	Asian or Pacific Islander
TOTAL	100.0	72.4	26.1	0.6	0.9	3,547,258	2,694,679	800,432	27,019	25,128	100.0	76.0	22.6	0.8	0.7
Murder and nonnegligent manslaughter	100.0	41.8	57.1	0.4	0.7	2,820	1,647	1,137	16	20	100.0	58.4	40.3	0.6	0.7
Forcible rape	100.0	69.5	29.9	0.0	0.6	5,143	3,798	1,248	54	43	100.0	73.8	24.3	1.0	0.8
Robbery	100.0	33.8	65.0	0.2	0.9	20,168	10,476	9,486	97	109	100.0	51.9	47.0	0.5	0.5
Aggravated assault	100.0	63.2	35.5	0.6	0.7	99,040	72,047	25,308	880	805	100.0	72.7	25.6	0.9	0.8
Burglary	100.0	70.9	27.8	0.5	0.7	61,390	47,028	13,747	289	326	100.0	76.6	22.4	0.5	0.5
Larceny-theft	100.0	66.3	31.7	0.7	1.3	252,506	180,641	67,395	2,100	2,370	100.0	71.5	26.7	0.8	0.9
Motor vehicle theft	100.0	66.3	32.1	0.8	0.8	20,573	15,586	4,716	143	128	100.0	75.8	22.9	0.7	0.6
Arson	100.0	80.9	17.5	0.2	1.3	2,414	1,907	483	17	7	100.0	79.0	20.0	0.7	0.3
Violent crime[3]	100.0	54.8	44.0	0.5	0.8	127,171	87,968	37,179	1,047	977	100.0	69.2	29.2	0.8	0.8
Property crime[3]	100.0	67.5	30.6	0.7	1.2	336,883	245,162	86,341	2,549	2,831	100.0	72.8	25.6	0.8	0.8
Other assaults	100.0	63.8	35.1	0.5	0.6	295,166	222,184	68,328	2,370	2,284	100.0	75.3	23.1	0.8	0.8
Forgery and counterfeiting	100.0	75.3	23.1	0.3	1.3	29,223	21,058	7,758	111	296	100.0	72.1	26.5	0.4	1.0
Fraud	100.0	67.6	31.2	0.3	1.0	85,835	60,479	24,563	345	448	100.0	70.5	28.6	0.4	0.5
Embezzlement	100.0	58.9	38.5	0.4	2.2	5,806	3,881	1,863	19	43	100.0	66.8	32.1	0.3	0.7
Stolen property; buying, receiving, possessing	100.0	61.3	37.0	0.5	1.2	29,891	21,013	8,465	195	218	100.0	70.3	28.3	0.7	0.7
Vandalism	100.0	81.8	16.8	0.6	0.8	50,526	40,643	9,138	406	339	100.0	80.4	18.1	0.8	0.7
Weapons; carrying, possessing, etc.	100.0	65.3	33.1	0.5	1.1	35,402	23,276	11,665	196	265	100.0	65.7	33.0	0.6	0.7
Prostitution and commercialized vice	100.0	52.9	47.1	0.0	0.0	5,975	3,857	1,779	24	315	100.0	64.6	29.8	0.4	5.3
Sex offenses (except forcible rape and prostitution)	100.0	73.7	25.3	0.5	0.4	18,387	14,873	3,194	126	194	100.0	80.9	17.4	0.7	1.1
Drug abuse violations	100.0	79.5	19.2	0.6	0.8	433,998	317,709	111,733	2,180	2,376	100.0	73.2	25.7	0.5	0.5
Gambling	100.0	26.4	71.9	0.0	1.7	1,096	691	375	5	25	100.0	63.0	34.2	0.5	2.3
Offenses against the family and children	100.0	73.1	25.9	0.4	0.6	48,246	32,098	15,565	328	255	100.0	66.5	32.3	0.7	0.5
Driving under the influence	100.0	94.4	4.2	0.7	0.7	487,757	436,301	43,792	3,375	4,289	100.0	89.5	9.0	0.7	0.9
Liquor laws	100.0	93.1	4.6	1.1	1.2	145,322	128,074	13,208	2,431	1,609	100.0	88.1	9.1	1.7	1.1
Drunkenness	100.0	92.4	6.2	0.8	0.6	146,933	129,697	15,055	1,444	737	100.0	88.3	10.2	1.0	0.5
Disorderly conduct	100.0	62.4	36.5	0.4	0.7	142,855	106,656	34,031	1,285	883	100.0	74.7	23.8	0.9	0.6
Vagrancy	100.0	82.9	16.5	0.1	0.4	5,320	3,513	1,788	10	9	100.0	66.0	33.6	0.2	0.2
All other offenses (except traffic)	100.0	74.5	23.9	0.7	0.9	1,114,487	795,013	304,179	8,572	6,723	100.0	71.3	27.3	0.8	0.6
Suspicion	100.0	42.7	56.1	1.3	0.0	979	533	433	1	12	100.0	54.4	44.2	0.1	1.2
Curfew and loitering law violations	100.0	79.3	19.6	0.4	0.7	-	-	-	-	-	-	-	-	-	-
Runaways	100.0	74.5	23.6	1.1	0.8	-	-	-	-	-	-	-	-	-	-

[1] Suburban area includes law enforcement agencies in cities with less than 50,000 inhabitants and county law enforcement agencies that are within a Metropolitan Statistical Area. Suburban area excludes all metropolitan agencies associated with a principal city.

[2] Because of rounding, the percentages may not add to 100.0.

[3] Violent crimes are offenses of murder and nonnegligent manslaughter, forcible rape, robbery, and aggravated assault. Property crimes are offenses of burglary, larceny-theft, motor vehicle theft, and arson.

Table 68.   Police Disposition of Juvenile Offenders Taken into Custody, 2007

(Number, percent.)

Population group		Total[1]	Handled within department and released	Referred to juvenile court jurisdiction	Referred to welfare agency	Referred to other police agency	Referred to criminal or adult court	Number of agencies	2007 estimated population
TOTAL AGENCIES:	Number	663,991	129,404	461,909	2,430	8,141	62,107	5,242	120,286,534
	Percent[2]	100.0	19.5	69.6	0.4	1.2	9.4		
TOTAL CITIES	Number	560,393	117,588	387,512	1,775	7,098	46,420	3,937	87,798,925
	Percent[2]	100.0	21.0	69.2	0.3	1.3	8.3		
GROUP I (250,000 and over)..............................	Number	138,954	41,670	94,226	20	604	2,434	37	25,796,709
	Percent[2]	100.0	30.0	67.8	*	0.4	1.8		
GROUP II (100,000 to 249,999)	Number	82,959	18,009	58,590	378	2,274	3,708	80	12,018,629
	Percent[2]	100.0	21.7	70.6	0.5	2.7	4.5		
GROUP III (50,000 to 99,999)	Number	105,992	19,497	76,429	414	1,295	8,357	234	15,972,903
	Percent[2]	100.0	18.4	72.1	0.4	1.2	7.9		
GROUP IV (25,000 to 49,999)	Number	75,606	12,211	53,794	254	1,671	7,676	360	12,405,704
	Percent[2]	100.0	16.2	71.2	0.3	2.2	10.2		
GROUP V (10,000 to 24,999)	Number	85,504	13,001	59,213	461	688	12,141	793	12,642,471
	Percent[2]	100.0	15.2	69.3	0.5	0.8	14.2		
GROUP VI (under 10,000).................................	Number	71,378	13,200	45,260	248	566	12,104	2,433	8,962,509
	Percent[2]	100.0	18.5	63.4	0.3	0.8	17.0		
METROPOLITAN COUNTIES	Number	81,552	8,543	59,834	493	879	11,803	636	24,275,366
	Percent[2]	100.0	10.5	73.4	0.6	1.1	14.5		
NONMETROPOLITAN COUNTIES......................	Number	22,046	3,273	14,563	162	164	3,884	669	8,212,243
	Percent[2]	100.0	14.8	66.1	0.7	0.7	17.6		
SUBURBAN AREA[3]	Number	288,762	47,148	198,657	1,429	2,557	38,971	3,278	58,405,783
	Percent[2]	100.0	16.3	68.8	0.5	0.9	13.5		

[1] Includes all offenses except traffic and neglect cases.

[2] Because of rounding, the percentages may not add to 100.0.

[3] Suburban area includes law enforcement agencies in cities with less than 50,000 inhabitants and county law enforcement agencies that are within a Metropolitan Statistical Area. Suburban area excludes all metropolitan agencies associated with a principal city. The agencies associated with suburban areas also appear in other groups within this table.

* = Less than one-tenth of 1 percent.

Table 69. Total Arrests, by State, 2007

(Number.)

State		Total all classes[1]	Violent crime[2]	Property crime[2]	Murder and non-negligent man-slaughter	Forcible rape	Robbery	Aggra-vated assault	Burglary	Larceny-theft	Motor vehicle theft	Arson	Other assaults
ALABAMA	Under 18	12,407	697	2,939	35	26	307	329	573	2,221	131	14	1,958
	Total all ages	199,688	6,225	20,812	336	319	1,763	3,807	3,379	16,258	1,068	107	25,034
ALASKA	Under 18	4,161	182	1,287	6	9	24	143	152	1,037	91	7	410
	Total all ages	38,578	1,727	4,247	39	75	160	1,453	470	3,390	357	30	4,098
ARIZONA	Under 18	52,173	1,551	10,518	25	32	422	1,072	1,483	7,915	943	177	4,744
	Total all ages	321,503	8,490	39,236	297	215	1,872	6,106	4,681	30,342	3,924	289	24,597
ARKANSAS	Under 18	8,809	306	2,103	5	12	69	220	491	1,539	68	5	1,035
	Total all ages	101,694	2,937	9,343	60	143	416	2,318	2,064	6,973	274	32	8,162
CALIFORNIA	Under 18	233,558	17,416	45,662	235	239	6,721	10,221	13,908	26,331	4,563	860	22,086
	Total all ages	1,540,894	124,293	165,192	2,022	2,141	21,064	99,066	53,738	87,455	22,458	1,541	90,070
COLORADO[3]	Under 18	43,848	814	7,622	7	60	165	582	785	6,263	370	204	2,243
	Total all ages	225,099	5,741	23,984	109	427	864	4,341	2,644	19,507	1,525	308	15,089
CONNECTICUT	Under 18	18,702	1,028	3,711	3	32	240	753	633	2,721	275	82	3,561
	Total all ages	120,182	5,481	15,546	66	224	1,260	3,931	2,608	11,895	805	238	19,129
DELAWARE	Under 18	7,321	548	1,526	2	34	209	303	290	1,160	42	34	1,617
	Total all ages	41,350	2,857	6,109	23	130	652	2,052	1,027	4,871	147	64	8,491
DISTRICT OF COLUMBIA[3,4]	Under 18	479	66	58	0	0	42	24	1	35	22	0	53
	Total all ages	5,933	123	91	1	0	77	45	1	62	28	0	196
FLORIDA[3,5]	Under 18	120,190	8,833	34,492	121	254	3,051	5,407	8,811	22,575	2,942	164	16,826
	Total all ages	1,126,395	52,291	134,478	902	1,793	11,597	37,999	28,307	94,857	10,874	440	92,738
GEORGIA	Under 18	45,233	2,021	9,225	64	45	748	1,164	2,126	6,341	658	100	6,042
	Total all ages	333,657	12,750	39,586	439	356	3,176	8,779	7,099	29,548	2,337	602	27,667
IDAHO	Under 18	16,035	234	3,018	3	29	19	183	455	2,376	116	71	1,289
	Total all ages	73,896	1,451	6,578	33	114	74	1,230	1,044	5,163	260	111	6,212
ILLINOIS	Under 18	34,250	3,098	5,247	50	74	1,301	1,673	992	2,575	1,647	33	5,748
	Total all ages	191,268	8,779	22,072	372	517	2,890	5,000	2,937	13,895	5,129	111	27,562
INDIANA	Under 18	35,144	1,080	7,798	18	37	318	707	1,001	6,118	603	76	3,272
	Total all ages	215,449	7,402	28,021	223	278	1,897	5,004	3,963	21,803	2,056	199	14,986
IOWA	Under 18	21,362	730	5,266	0	29	97	604	814	4,118	252	82	2,637
	Total all ages	114,816	3,996	13,442	15	115	374	3,492	2,096	10,638	568	140	10,266
KANSAS	Under 18	10,544	341	1,929	7	38	52	244	300	1,511	79	39	1,502
	Total all ages	73,904	2,341	6,170	53	170	292	1,826	1,033	4,639	421	77	10,113
KENTUCKY	Under 18	7,178	315	1,991	2	7	191	115	414	1,471	102	4	563
	Total all ages	63,884	1,807	8,269	33	39	730	1,005	1,628	6,386	242	13	3,108
LOUISIANA	Under 18	24,445	1,100	4,883	23	47	250	780	1,231	3,351	252	49	4,407
	Total all ages	173,584	8,014	22,955	242	324	1,119	6,329	5,103	16,555	1,143	154	21,777
MAINE	Under 18	7,158	86	2,031	0	8	20	58	393	1,522	86	30	870
	Total all ages	57,731	723	7,727	19	71	172	461	1,306	6,064	287	70	7,160
MARYLAND	Under 18	47,646	3,437	11,763	25	52	1,697	1,663	2,390	7,721	1,364	288	8,115
	Total all ages	296,861	12,513	34,595	327	348	4,119	7,719	6,972	23,780	3,365	478	29,922
MASSACHUSETTS	Under 18	18,407	1,897	3,213	5	29	497	1,366	790	2,137	204	82	2,338
	Total all ages	146,284	11,847	17,142	68	305	1,859	9,615	3,707	12,302	995	138	18,796
MICHIGAN	Under 18	41,319	2,431	11,095	26	108	788	1,509	1,741	8,090	1,102	162	4,345
	Total all ages	312,777	14,100	36,575	306	598	2,692	10,504	6,122	26,640	3,464	349	28,988
MINNESOTA[6]	Under 18	49,839	1,234	10,005	7	17	410	800	1,109	8,281	498	117	4,280
	Total all ages	215,671	5,950	27,976	115	125	1,334	4,376	3,521	22,470	1,781	204	19,537
MISSISSIPPI	Under 18	8,454	177	1,577	8	14	72	83	397	1,075	81	24	1,274
	Total all ages	85,271	1,789	8,185	83	135	545	1,026	1,753	5,892	439	101	9,596
MISSOURI	Under 18	40,093	1,431	8,755	19	65	391	956	1,514	6,566	519	156	6,231
	Total all ages	297,234	10,765	35,649	217	461	1,689	8,398	5,734	27,310	2,292	313	30,032
MONTANA	Under 18	6,950	79	1,532	0	2	4	73	98	1,293	105	36	701
	Total all ages	28,136	864	3,983	11	26	47	780	240	3,454	230	59	3,775
NEBRASKA	Under 18	13,708	235	3,100	4	21	77	133	270	2,682	92	56	1,642
	Total all ages	83,957	1,699	8,823	47	135	289	1,228	845	7,493	384	101	8,136
NEVADA	Under 18	21,795	657	3,625	13	24	285	335	686	2,678	195	66	2,048
	Total all ages	167,412	5,595	15,606	151	186	1,739	3,519	2,889	10,747	1,831	139	18,817
NEW HAMPSHIRE	Under 18	6,602	85	687	1	3	12	69	106	535	29	17	802
	Total all ages	38,396	358	2,274	4	30	76	248	333	1,829	82	30	4,337
NEW JERSEY	Under 18	55,824	3,123	8,094	37	56	1,466	1,564	1,568	6,070	246	210	4,425
	Total all ages	383,797	13,680	31,828	269	400	4,065	8,946	5,848	24,672	936	372	26,830
NEW MEXICO	Under 18	10,371	459	1,719	10	17	66	366	241	1,365	94	19	1,202
	Total all ages	78,484	3,396	6,689	74	117	376	2,829	1,001	5,256	389	43	6,856
NEW YORK[3]	Under 18	46,232	3,090	11,478	30	108	1,243	1,709	2,328	8,323	649	178	4,723
	Total all ages	345,251	16,069	52,969	362	715	4,185	10,807	8,283	41,506	2,707	473	33,324
NORTH CAROLINA	Under 18	45,412	2,409	10,847	54	74	915	1,366	3,087	7,282	305	173	7,968
	Total all ages	407,663	19,623	56,115	622	577	4,186	14,238	15,261	38,769	1,668	417	53,785

[1] Does not include traffic arrests.

[2] Violent crimes are offenses of murder and nonnegligent manslaughter, forcible rape, robbery, and aggravated assault. Property crimes are offenses of burglary, larceny-theft, motor vehicle theft, and arson.

[3] See Appendix I for details.

[4] Includes arrests reported by the Metro Transit Police. This agency has no population associated with it.

[5] The arrest category all other offenses also includes the arrest counts for offenses against the family and children, drunkenness, disorderly conduct, vagrancy, suspicion, curfew and loitering law violations, and runaways.

[6] The forcible rape figures for Minnesota include only those provided by the cities of Minneapolis and St. Paul.

Table 69. Total Arrests, by State, 2007 *(Contd.)*

(Number.)

State		Forgery and counterfeiting	Fraud	Embezzlement	Stolen property; buying, receiving, possessing	Vandalism	Weapons; carrying, possessing, etc.	Prostitution and commercialized vice	Sex offenses (except forcible rape and prostitution)	Drug abuse violations	Gambling	Offenses against the family and children	Driving under the influence
ALABAMA	Under 18	33	57	1	207	265	179	1	48	967	3	18	85
	Total all ages	1,892	7,818	61	2,255	2,033	1,467	182	604	17,309	57	1,054	12,857
ALASKA	Under 18	9	7	1	2	259	56	3	33	271	0	6	91
	Total all ages	136	161	8	21	954	402	343	172	1,759	8	332	5,187
ARIZONA	Under 18	74	111	54	159	3,543	570	25	278	5,334	1	318	597
	Total all ages	4,446	1,983	393	1,285	11,573	3,688	1,600	1,695	35,384	1	3,105	38,260
ARKANSAS	Under 18	15	23	1	96	472	124	1	38	791	0	12	138
	Total all ages	811	3,124	19	891	1,336	957	154	154	9,953	3	234	8,892
CALIFORNIA	Under 18	320	597	184	3,301	16,887	8,597	584	2,256	22,047	78	12	1,626
	Total all ages	9,862	10,159	2,268	19,752	34,799	32,513	12,558	15,145	289,449	689	395	204,015
COLORADO[3]	Under 18	51	165	22	150	1,872	645	12	214	3,482	0	75	514
	Total all ages	1,256	2,379	220	1,026	5,796	2,325	668	840	18,290	8	2,745	27,969
CONNECTICUT	Under 18	28	62	10	52	1,006	325	1	134	1,613	4	72	98
	Total all ages	792	1,441	214	450	2,564	1,357	479	564	14,663	25	1,318	8,571
DELAWARE	Under 18	14	107	18	111	376	127	0	40	759	1	4	0
	Total all ages	633	2,061	282	454	1,166	421	188	167	5,744	2	244	229
DISTRICT OF COLUMBIA[3,4]	Under 18	0	1	0	2	14	5	0	0	13	0	0	0
	Total all ages	0	1	0	16	34	29	0	0	77	0	0	23
FLORIDA[3,5]	Under 18	152	746	130	293	2,993	1,959	66	401	14,114	32		466
	Total all ages	5,077	17,277	1,450	2,891	9,152	8,263	6,131	3,706	169,360	297		58,824
GEORGIA	Under 18	121	194	10	666	1,170	1,533	23	615	4,066	9	124	256
	Total all ages	4,634	7,317	332	4,067	3,742	5,528	1,171	3,724	44,019	197	3,482	26,442
IDAHO	Under 18	23	67	21	53	679	182	0	100	901	0	10	263
	Total all ages	255	490	118	245	1,436	571	10	347	5,660	1	584	11,014
ILLINOIS	Under 18	17	95	0	32	1,997	997	58	86	7,298	1,072	8	36
	Total all ages	490	1,318	1	81	5,462	3,736	4,050	1,187	55,125	4,194	435	5,624
INDIANA	Under 18	42	76	3	1,411	1,194	306	15	216	2,510	6	320	217
	Total all ages	1,743	2,067	12	6,374	2,547	1,927	1,861	1,576	22,753	155	1,668	23,463
IOWA	Under 18	44	53	6	70	1,700	126	2	56	1,275	2	9	228
	Total all ages	688	1,023	99	253	3,274	486	149	214	8,825	12	843	13,130
KANSAS	Under 18	11	22	28	39	496	157	1	76	1,079	0	16	226
	Total all ages	446	1,037	170	310	1,745	767	241	283	7,089	0	217	12,080
KENTUCKY	Under 18	15	26	0	235	301	117	1	17	1,249	0	16	32
	Total all ages	625	777	17	876	746	549	766	77	11,883	8	804	3,490
LOUISIANA	Under 18	18	31	23	236	825	342	12	169	1,880	15	176	94
	Total all ages	868	2,086	329	1,575	3,327	2,029	548	1,033	22,964	139	1,745	8,725
MAINE	Under 18	11	21	7	40	492	60	1	63	573	0	5	120
	Total all ages	350	869	57	193	1,535	416	42	256	5,721	2	139	8,097
MARYLAND	Under 18	50	84	54	39	2,214	1,387	18	332	7,474	88	31	290
	Total all ages	1,042	2,329	409	261	4,351	4,271	1,377	1,513	55,155	454	2,255	24,230
MASSACHUSETTS	Under 18	28	45	6	278	930	286	7	97	2,327	0	183	141
	Total all ages	828	1,396	119	1,326	3,380	1,386	1,098	606	20,626	22	1,626	11,746
MICHIGAN	Under 18	33	470	48	505	1,459	965	11	303	3,656	17	19	662
	Total all ages	1,176	6,231	1,249	2,253	3,917	5,086	603	1,094	33,923	159	3,308	40,584
MINNESOTA[6]	Under 18	103	224	4	503	2,082	767	20	313	2,887	4	33	642
	Total all ages	1,994	3,482	24	2,045	4,821	2,375	1,119	1,574	18,814	12	834	31,735
MISSISSIPPI	Under 18	16	51	20	92	218	154	2	33	637	15	127	93
	Total all ages	698	1,267	674	641	1,042	758	110	308	10,289	382	2,248	7,881
MISSOURI	Under 18	63	89	12	489	2,175	540	3	460	3,569	8	108	473
	Total all ages	2,248	3,919	154	2,976	6,169	2,891	320	2,132	32,958	110	3,772	31,633
MONTANA	Under 18	4	18	3	8	470	36	0	24	332	0	20	73
	Total all ages	59	168	28	22	1,054	92	30	66	1,566	0	252	3,264
NEBRASKA	Under 18	21	93	16	152	951	186	1	116	1,095	0	52	268
	Total all ages	520	1,743	102	830	2,519	1,037	182	579	9,816	11	1,507	12,350
NEVADA	Under 18	14	39	54	220	1,167	420	25	128	1,427	9	12	86
	Total all ages	1,329	2,315	544	1,727	2,463	2,389	5,430	1,385	14,444	98	1,650	12,538
NEW HAMPSHIRE	Under 18	4	40	4	107	535	30	0	37	536	0	9	97
	Total all ages	139	877	22	409	1,158	89	27	138	2,570	24	180	4,146
NEW JERSEY	Under 18	71	114	17	1,342	3,436	1,733	17	289	6,448	20	52	347
	Total all ages	1,738	3,681	139	4,567	7,457	5,451	1,706	1,606	52,773	182	14,958	25,031
NEW MEXICO	Under 18	13	38	20	117	427	293	5	17	1,238	1	3	192
	Total all ages	278	453	163	824	856	728	348	147	6,805	1	713	10,006
NEW YORK[3]	Under 18	184	307	144	1,076	4,272	757	8	841	5,958	16	385	364
	Total all ages	4,445	8,474	1,031	5,701	13,408	4,256	1,318	4,344	61,163	163	2,489	28,440
NORTH CAROLINA	Under 18	49	472	97	802	2,276	1,633	8	139	3,855	11	97	408
	Total all ages	2,728	22,278	1,865	5,530	8,594	7,644	1,492	1,478	38,343	159	7,258	26,928

[1] Does not include traffic arrests.

[2] Violent crimes are offenses of murder and nonnegligent manslaughter, forcible rape, robbery, and aggravated assault. Property crimes are offenses of burglary, larceny-theft, motor vehicle theft, and arson.

[3] See Appendix I for details.

[4] Includes arrests reported by the Metro Transit Police. This agency has no population associated with it.

[5] The arrest category *all other offenses* also includes the arrest counts for offenses against the family and children, drunkenness, disorderly conduct, vagrancy, suspicion, curfew and loitering law violations, and runaways.

[6] The forcible rape figures for Minnesota include only those provided by the cities of Minneapolis and St. Paul.

Table 69. Total Arrests, by State, 2007 *(Contd.)*

(Number.)

State		Liquor laws	Drunken-ness[7]	Disorderly conduct	Vagrancy	All other offenses (except traffic)	Suspi-cion	Curfew and loitering law violations	Run-aways	Number of agencies	2007 estimated population
ALABAMA	Under 18	799	92	1,768	21	1,717	0	55	497	287	3,482,050
	Total all ages	6,073	10,584	5,014	421	77,383	1	55	497		
ALASKA	Under 18	277	31	88	0	747	0	11	390	30	654,555
	Total all ages	1,847	129	986	7	15,651	2	11	390		
ARIZONA	Under 18	6,085	0	3,206	42	5,343	0	4,268	5,352	78	5,941,252
	Total all ages	27,405	4	16,750	1,344	90,644	0	4,268	5,352		
ARKANSAS	Under 18	236	264	529	0	1,806	0	528	291	210	1,875,132
	Total all ages	1,369	8,118	2,323	673	41,421	1	528	291		
CALIFORNIA	Under 18	5,579	4,638	11,835	310	44,228	0	21,126	4,189	634	35,715,843
	Total all ages	21,108	112,398	16,604	4,000	350,310	0	21,126	4,189		
COLORADO[3]	Under 18	5,034	3	4,039	15	9,251	3	2,088	5,534	189	4,358,882
	Total all ages	15,943	305	12,287	171	80,426	9	2,088	5,534		
CONNECTICUT	Under 18	310	1	3,404	0	3,221	0	43	18	94	3,243,990
	Total all ages	1,130	3	15,372	36	30,986	0	43	18		
DELAWARE	Under 18	454	23	780	0	695	0	121	0	53	853,712
	Total all ages	2,503	587	2,449	560	6,082	0	121	0		
DISTRICT OF COLUMBIA[3,4]	Under 18	4	0	68	0	195	0	0	0	2	
	Total all ages	1,477	80	204	135	3,447	0	0	0		
FLORIDA[3,5]	Under 18	1,376				37,311				592	18,207,878
	Total all ages	34,898				529,562					
GEORGIA	Under 18	1,173	92	5,414	86	8,964	27	882	2,520	308	5,916,753
	Total all ages	9,954	4,686	24,910	882	104,962	203	882	2,520		
IDAHO	Under 18	1,962	23	618	0	3,724	0	842	2,026	99	1,382,317
	Total all ages	5,946	435	2,447	13	27,215	0	842	2,026		
ILLINOIS	Under 18	417	0	3,390	0	3,808	0	828	18	2	2,980,147
	Total all ages	1,672	0	22,274	73	26,287	0	828	18		
INDIANA	Under 18	2,839	507	2,388	7	6,454	9	1,136	3,338	155	4,535,059
	Total all ages	10,839	17,567	7,908	26	57,936	144	1,136	3,338		
IOWA	Under 18	1,991	374	2,553	0	2,659	0	947	634	180	2,567,706
	Total all ages	8,468	11,940	6,519	27	29,581	0	947	634		
KANSAS	Under 18	1,313	2	636	0	1,185	0	0	1,485	217	1,783,134
	Total all ages	7,066	278	3,565	0	18,501	0	0	1,485		
KENTUCKY	Under 18	96	112	412	0	1,388	0	170	122	11	850,422
	Total all ages	1,038	4,023	1,453	612	22,664	0	170	122		
LOUISIANA	Under 18	315	68	4,048	20	4,324	31	707	721	107	2,617,038
	Total all ages	6,391	3,147	16,257	562	47,624	61	707	721		
MAINE	Under 18	1,111	8	170	0	1,328	0	57	104	163	1,314,909
	Total all ages	4,472	65	1,882	0	17,864	0	57	104		
MARYLAND	Under 18	1,320	1	2,418	27	7,446	86	276	696	154	5,562,657
	Total all ages	6,830	1	7,171	126	106,364	720	276	696		
MASSACHUSETTS	Under 18	1,000	322	1,455	1	3,540	22	7	284	323	5,899,072
	Total all ages	5,209	7,378	8,019	14	33,257	172	7	284		
MICHIGAN	Under 18	4,958	9	1,467	0	6,542	0	976	1,348	513	9,301,438
	Total all ages	22,237	432	9,872	419	98,247	0	976	1,348		
MINNESOTA[6]	Under 18	7,231	0	4,996	14	6,370	0	4,022	4,105	318	5,078,367
	Total all ages	29,932	0	15,158	406	39,756	0	4,022	4,105		
MISSISSIPPI	Under 18	168	99	1,364	3	1,558	4	555	217	79	1,082,611
	Total all ages	2,496	4,897	6,199	69	24,923	47	555	217		
MISSOURI	Under 18	2,690	37	2,192	81	6,822	0	1,200	2,665	580	4,980,958
	Total all ages	14,380	322	13,345	204	99,390	0	1,200	2,665		
MONTANA	Under 18	1,342	0	557	0	828	0	568	355	83	803,145
	Total all ages	5,011	0	2,431	41	4,507	0	568	355		
NEBRASKA	Under 18	2,231	0	871	0	2,076	0	290	312	216	1,506,881
	Total all ages	11,228	0	4,089	44	18,140	0	290	312		
NEVADA	Under 18	2,189	60	972	23	3,565	32	3,572	1,451	30	2,467,618
	Total all ages	9,281	123	3,255	3,873	59,493	34	3,572	1,451		
NEW HAMPSHIRE	Under 18	987	373	159	0	1,832	0	8	270	131	891,903
	Total all ages	4,753	4,333	918	21	11,345	0	8	270		
NEW JERSEY	Under 18	2,863	0	4,763	36	9,120	0	4,872	4,642	539	8,421,399
	Total all ages	7,757	0	22,776	992	151,131	0	4,872	4,642		
NEW MEXICO	Under 18	917	4	777	2	2,423	4	12	488	58	1,391,131
	Total all ages	4,014	607	2,737	14	32,312	37	12	488		
NEW YORK[3]	Under 18	1,089	2	2,544	77	8,917	0	0	0	611	10,520,724
	Total all ages	5,262	2	15,868	1,133	85,392	0	0	0		
NORTH CAROLINA	Under 18	1,307	0	4,939	39	7,554	0	2	500	303	6,998,327
	Total all ages	9,898	0	16,454	382	126,607	0	2	500		

[1] Does not include traffic arrests.

[2] Violent crimes are offenses of murder and nonnegligent manslaughter, forcible rape, robbery, and aggravated assault. Property crimes are offenses of burglary, larceny-theft, motor vehicle theft, and arson.

[3] See Appendix I for details.

[4] Includes arrests reported by the Metro Transit Police. This agency has no population associated with it.

[5] The arrest category *all other offenses* also includes the arrest counts for offenses against the family and children, drunkenness, disorderly conduct, vagrancy, suspicion, curfew and loitering law violations, and runaways.

[6] The forcible rape figures for Minnesota include only those provided by the cities of Minneapolis and St. Paul.

[7] Drunkenness is not considered a crime in some states; therefore, the figures vary widely from state to state.

Table 69. Total Arrests, by State, 2007 (Contd.)

(Number.)

State		Total all classes[1]	Violent crime[2]	Property crime[2]	Murder and non-negligent man-slaughter	Forcible rape	Robbery	Aggra-vated assault	Burglary	Larceny-theft	Motor vehicle theft	Arson	Other assaults
NORTH DAKOTA	Under 18	6,651	47	1,122	2	7	8	30	100	935	73	14	456
	Total all ages	27,359	321	2,517	11	38	33	239	259	2,068	165	25	1,957
OHIO	Under 18	40,970	1,158	7,710	29	132	527	470	1,375	5,784	409	142	6,129
	Total all ages	256,718	6,911	33,375	194	562	2,591	3,564	6,110	25,564	1,399	302	30,211
OKLAHOMA	Under 18	21,357	714	4,512	16	58	179	461	920	3,193	290	109	1,389
	Total all ages	161,719	5,665	15,161	183	319	793	4,370	3,066	10,810	1,010	275	10,302
OREGON	Under 18	30,236	862	6,948	7	31	241	583	848	5,568	349	183	2,324
	Total all ages	147,335	4,938	26,225	82	294	1,173	3,389	2,869	21,006	2,049	301	15,173
PENNSYLVANIA	Under 18	102,497	5,257	13,274	52	216	2,117	2,872	2,464	9,241	1,212	357	8,854
	Total all ages	467,655	24,609	56,190	516	1,094	7,211	15,788	9,722	41,558	4,168	742	45,908
RHODE ISLAND	Under 18	4,149	80	890	2	3	16	59	185	657	27	21	478
	Total all ages	26,966	463	2,700	9	37	71	346	567	1,975	125	33	2,946
SOUTH CAROLINA	Under 18	24,945	1,360	5,180	32	56	291	981	1,332	3,584	188	76	4,236
	Total all ages	213,355	10,681	25,181	302	418	1,705	8,256	5,306	18,615	1,073	187	23,105
SOUTH DAKOTA	Under 18	3,665	42	645	0	8	1	33	61	544	18	22	247
	Total all ages	18,014	265	1,502	8	29	17	211	175	1,244	53	30	1,815
TENNESSEE	Under 18	35,880	1,747	6,576	16	47	543	1,141	1,300	4,742	452	82	5,548
	Total all ages	304,793	13,613	36,353	286	368	2,915	10,044	5,880	27,773	2,501	199	30,507
TEXAS	Under 18	166,976	4,881	28,262	59	302	1,487	3,033	5,277	21,347	1,317	321	20,570
	Total all ages	1,087,325	33,309	119,633	759	1,947	7,593	23,010	18,544	93,431	6,817	841	99,238
UTAH	Under 18	25,789	351	5,513	1	60	71	219	367	4,799	248	99	2,028
	Total all ages	120,167	1,798	15,694	38	195	406	1,159	1,256	13,667	625	146	9,788
VERMONT	Under 18	1,836	42	370	3	4	3	32	101	226	37	6	303
	Total all ages	16,731	438	1,820	9	40	24	365	356	1,343	102	19	1,756
VIRGINIA	Under 18	39,666	1,142	6,137	21	39	508	574	1,226	4,490	218	203	4,885
	Total all ages	313,457	7,229	28,562	267	354	2,057	4,551	4,381	22,858	959	364	36,747
WASHINGTON	Under 18	35,096	1,440	10,234	13	120	524	783	1,662	7,887	491	194	4,571
	Total all ages	248,676	7,616	36,073	115	770	1,915	4,816	5,211	28,673	1,845	344	28,616
WEST VIRGINIA	Under 18	2,347	59	513	1	0	9	49	73	400	29	11	404
	Total all ages	46,835	1,182	4,498	35	32	149	966	622	3,608	214	54	5,919
WISCONSIN	Under 18	105,319	1,818	16,047	33	199	675	911	1,953	12,901	1,067	126	3,988
	Total all ages	421,093	8,007	40,989	217	782	1,971	5,037	4,900	33,639	2,187	263	20,158
WYOMING	Under 18	7,139	70	988	0	3	6	61	84	836	58	10	837
	Total all ages	39,808	641	2,683	13	37	43	548	292	2,230	138	23	3,370

[1] Does not include traffic arrests.

[2] Violent crimes are offenses of murder and nonnegligent manslaughter, forcible rape, robbery, and aggravated assault. Property crimes are offenses of burglary, larceny-theft, motor vehicle theft, and arson.

Table 69.   Total Arrests, by State, 2007 (Contd.)

(Number.)

State		Forgery and counter-feiting	Fraud	Embezzle-ment	Stolen property; buying, receiving, possessing	Vandal-ism	Weapons; carrying, possessing, etc.	Prostitu-tion and commer-cialized vice	Sex offenses (except forcible rape and prosti-tution)	Drug abuse violations	Gamb-ling	Offenses against the family and children	Driving under the influence
NORTH DAKOTA	Under 18	4	33	4	46	309	26	0	17	261	0	86	51
	Total all ages	113	863	28	130	608	114	6	70	1,743	3	168	4,119
OHIO	Under 18	46	159	4	800	1,736	539	3	216	3,186	6	856	206
	Total all ages	1,369	3,373	31	3,972	4,506	2,951	1,472	1,027	34,740	53	7,448	19,155
OKLAHOMA	Under 18	26	55	80	479	511	351	1	71	2,022	1	56	254
	Total all ages	977	2,662	637	2,555	1,553	2,520	434	781	22,319	5	1,072	18,229
OREGON	Under 18	51	86	1	101	2,068	353	23	213	2,259	5	11	194
	Total all ages	1,393	1,768	62	684	5,213	1,889	516	1,270	18,664	7	621	17,096
PENNSYLVANIA	Under 18	97	376	37	693	4,715	1,564	14	557	6,458	22	46	650
	Total all ages	3,356	9,376	448	3,355	12,457	4,569	2,301	2,772	57,305	280	1,102	49,238
RHODE ISLAND	Under 18	8	9	8	55	396	108	0	22	358	0	98	31
	Total all ages	102	678	140	253	955	257	128	74	2,933	16	146	2,131
SOUTH CAROLINA	Under 18	74	111	31	300	1,256	775	2	148	3,260	6	223	92
	Total all ages	2,457	17,664	559	2,489	4,173	2,718	654	671	30,679	192	1,611	11,712
SOUTH DAKOTA	Under 18	6	57	3	25	113	30	0	8	210	0	33	75
	Total all ages	52	610	16	67	301	84	4	41	1,371	0	202	4,203
TENNESSEE	Under 18	80	168	39	63	1,459	760	40	143	3,298	34	30	194
	Total all ages	3,426	9,323	1,155	835	4,478	3,404	2,219	733	38,899	335	1,420	27,178
TEXAS	Under 18	208	368	45	110	5,420	1,673	126	618	15,434	68	23	1,180
	Total all ages	7,843	14,401	427	642	13,282	12,681	8,552	3,878	136,361	695	4,757	88,236
UTAH	Under 18	34	72	1	172	1,795	391	4	326	1,485	2	133	124
	Total all ages	990	1,269	17	869	3,930	1,253	349	865	9,239	3	2,073	7,204
VERMONT	Under 18	4	9	0	30	122	23	0	12	186	0	6	40
	Total all ages	121	414	40	168	445	27	2	53	1,632	0	336	3,662
VIRGINIA	Under 18	53	103	105	216	1,548	689	1	248	2,808	10	30	183
	Total all ages	2,101	8,299	1,817	1,015	4,847	3,892	647	1,019	32,941	113	1,636	24,170
WASHINGTON	Under 18	66	55	14	503	2,414	778	54	195	2,913	0	25	706
	Total all ages	2,111	1,223	158	3,903	6,901	3,448	874	1,187	28,872	10	725	37,317
WEST VIRGINIA	Under 18	4	7	1	20	97	22	0	11	224	0	2	30
	Total all ages	337	1,056	101	281	692	289	233	109	3,928	4	62	6,327
WISCONSIN	Under 18	92	216	27	669	4,315	1,422	27	1,182	4,911	50	190	641
	Total all ages	2,015	7,346	249	1,687	10,658	4,894	825	3,041	25,746	153	2,884	41,308
WYOMING	Under 18	1	7	0	15	310	48	0	20	562	0	25	89
	Total all ages	93	180	7	74	783	134	4	157	3,110	5	230	6,116

Table 69.   Total Arrests, by State, 2007 *(Contd.)*

(Number.)

State		Liquor laws	Drunken-ness[3]	Disorderly conduct	Vagrancy	All other offenses (except traffic)	Suspi-cion	Curfew and loitering law violations	Run-aways	Number of agencies	2007 estimated population
NORTH DAKOTA	Under 18	1,306	3	620	0	1,220	0	318	722	63	562,723
	Total all ages	5,717	713	1,584	4	5,541	0	318	722		
OHIO	Under 18	2,523	72	3,410	9	9,453	11	1,791	947	374	6,848,511
	Total all ages	13,600	4,887	20,922	49	63,863	65	1,791	947		
OKLAHOMA	Under 18	442	964	1,125	0	2,975	0	2,200	3,129	292	3,615,869
	Total all ages	3,295	25,171	3,474	0	39,578	0	2,200	3,129		
OREGON	Under 18	4,846	0	1,447	0	3,566	0	2,735	2,143	145	3,522,777
	Total all ages	17,928	0	7,615	24	21,371	0	2,735	2,143		
PENNSYLVANIA	Under 18	7,610	330	16,677	80	7,713	0	25,321	2,152	930	11,408,646
	Total all ages	26,428	24,316	60,747	764	54,661	0	25,321	2,152		
RHODE ISLAND	Under 18	128	4	709	0	685	0	30	52	41	876,018
	Total all ages	749	9	2,313	0	9,891	0	30	52		
SOUTH CAROLINA	Under 18	902	175	3,002	0	3,227	0	50	535	479	4,179,455
	Total all ages	11,311	10,618	14,808	1,361	40,126	0	50	535		
SOUTH DAKOTA	Under 18	1,219	16	153	0	237	0	254	292	89	388,719
	Total all ages	4,572	105	979	13	1,266	0	254	292		
TENNESSEE	Under 18	1,380	377	4,021	0	5,863	0	1,951	2,109	394	4,848,243
	Total all ages	8,754	21,671	11,774	61	84,595	0	1,951	2,109		
TEXAS	Under 18	5,454	3,369	22,717	1,757	29,922	0	12,203	12,568	941	21,758,415
	Total all ages	29,125	130,622	41,719	2,652	314,501	0	12,203	12,568		
UTAH	Under 18	2,670	236	1,996	200	5,595	0	1,969	692	103	2,316,297
	Total all ages	10,679	4,426	5,101	212	41,746	1	1,969	692		
VERMONT	Under 18	228	4	172	0	279	0	0	6	78	608,835
	Total all ages	843	5	1,070	2	3,891	0	0	6		
VIRGINIA	Under 18	1,825	215	1,978	0	9,314	0	2,620	5,556	334	7,325,924
	Total all ages	10,129	28,899	7,034	78	104,106	0	2,620	5,556		
WASHINGTON	Under 18	4,118	0	757	6	4,395	0	31	1,821	214	4,877,122
	Total all ages	12,918	0	5,136	46	69,690	0	31	1,821		
WEST VIRGINIA	Under 18	174	27	35	0	598	0	65	54	275	1,400,508
	Total all ages	1,569	4,684	1,222	10	14,213	0	65	54		
WISCONSIN	Under 18	10,212	3	19,376	61	27,782	0	7,671	4,619	366	5,484,944
	Total all ages	43,695	5	65,824	3,054	126,265	0	7,671	4,619		
WYOMING	Under 18	1,213	26	278	7	1,642	74	437	490	61	516,496
	Total all ages	4,370	2,480	1,452	21	12,879	92	437	490		

[1] Does not include traffic arrests.

[2] Violent crimes are offenses of murder and nonnegligent manslaughter, forcible rape, robbery, and aggravated assault. Property crimes are offenses of burglary, larceny-theft, motor vehicle theft, and arson.

[3] Drunkenness is not considered a crime in some states; therefore, the figures vary widely from state to state.

[4] See Appendix I for details.

[5] Includes arrests reported by the Metro Transit Police. This agency has no population associated with it.

[6] The arrest category *all other offenses* also includes the arrest counts for offenses against the family and children, drunkenness, disorderly conduct, vagrancy, suspicion, curfew and loitering law violations, and runaways.

[7] The forcible rape figures for Minnesota include only those provided by the cities of Minneapolis and St. Paul.

SECTION V:
LAW ENFORCEMENT PERSONNEL

LAW ENFORCEMENT PERSONNEL

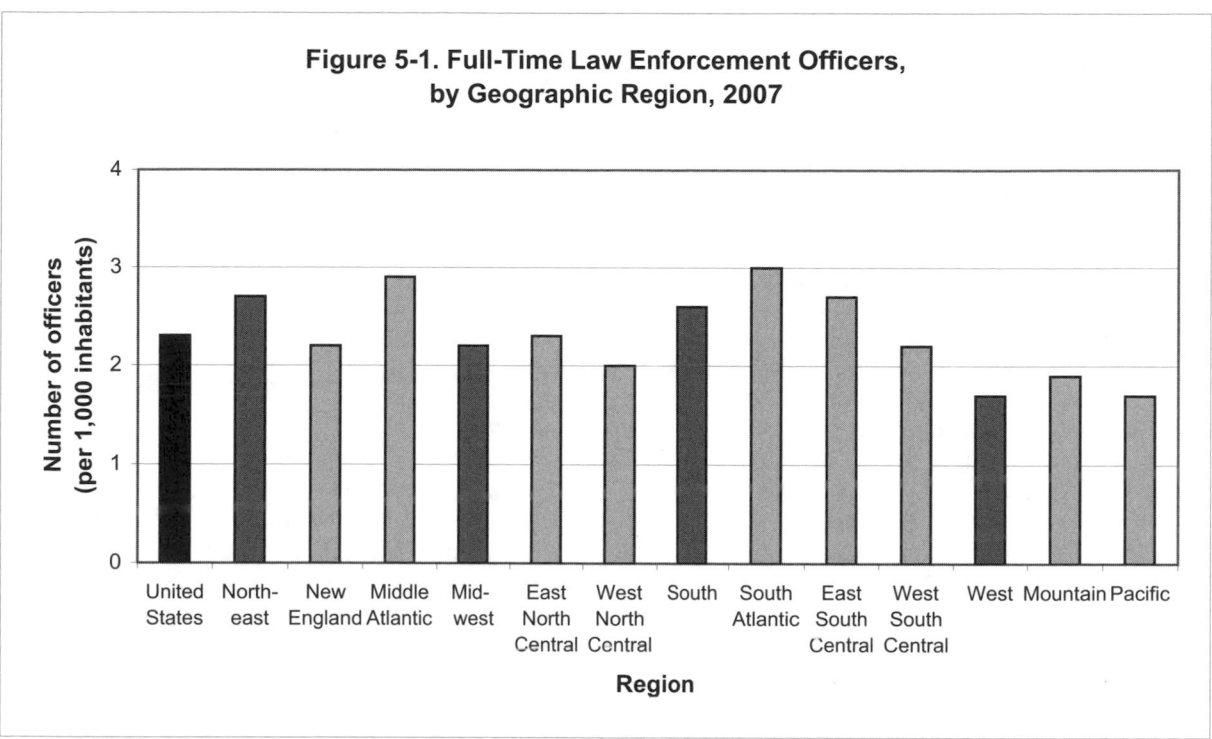

Figure 5-1. Full-Time Law Enforcement Officers,
by Geographic Region, 2007

Because of differing service requirements and functions, caution should be used when drawing comparisons between and among the staffing levels of law enforcement agencies. What follows is not intended as recommended or preferred officer strength; the data should only be used as a guide.

Each year, UCR Program staff ask law enforcement agencies across the United States to report the total number of sworn law enforcement officers and civilians employed in their agencies as of October 31. This section of *Crime in the United States* presents those data as the number and rate of law enforcement officers and civilian employees throughout the United States. In 2007, 14,676 state, city, university and college, metropolitan and nonmetropolitan county, and other law enforcement agencies employed 699,850 sworn officers and 318,104 civilians, who provided law enforcement services to more than 285 million people nationwide. (Table 74)

The data in this section are broken down by geographic region and division, population group, state, city, university and college, metropolitan and nonmetropolitan county, and other law enforcement agencies. (Information about geographic regions and divisions and population groups can be found in Appendix III.) UCR Program staff compute the rate of sworn officers and law enforcement employees by taking the number of employees (sworn officers only or in combination with civilians), dividing by the population for which the agency provides law enforcement service, and multiplying by 1,000.

- Tables 70 and 71 present the number and rate of law enforcement personnel per 1,000 inhabitants collectively employed by agencies, broken down by geographic region and division by population group.

- Tables 72 and 73 provide a count of law enforcement agencies by population group, based on the employment rate ranges for sworn officer and civilian employees per 1,000 inhabitants.

- Table 74 provides the number and percentage of male and female sworn officers and civilian employees by population group.

- Table 75 lists the percentage of full-time civilian law enforcement employees by population group.

- Table 76 breaks down by state the number of sworn law enforcement officers and civilians employed by state law enforcement agencies.

- Tables 78 to 80 list the number of law enforcement employees for cities, universities and colleges, and metropolitan and nonmetropolitan counties.

- Table 81 supplies employee data for those law enforcement agencies that serve the nation's transit systems, parks and forests, schools and school districts, hospitals, etc.

The demographic traits and characteristics of a jurisdiction affect its requirements for law enforcement service. For instance, a village between two large cities may require more law enforcement than a community of the same size with no urban center nearby. A town with legal gambling may have different law enforcement needs than a town near a military base. A city largely made up of college students may have different law enforcement needs than a city whose residents are mainly retirees.

Similarly, the functions of law enforcement agencies are diverse. Employees of these agencies patrol local streets and major highways, protect citizens in the nation's smallest towns and largest cities, and conduct investigations on offenses at the local and state level. State police in one area may enforce traffic laws on state highways and interstates; in another area, they may be responsible for investigating violent crimes. Sheriff's departments may collect tax monies, serve as the enforcement authority for local and state courts, administer jail facilities, or carry out some combination of these duties. This has an impact on an agency's staffing levels.

Because of the differing service requirements and functions, care should be taken when drawing comparisons between and among the staffing levels of law enforcement agencies. The data in this section are not intended as recommended or preferred officer strength; they should be used merely as guides. Adequate staffing levels can be determined only after careful study of the conditions that affect the service requirements in a particular jurisdiction._

Rate

The rate of full-time law enforcement employees (civilian and sworn) per 1,000 inhabitants in the nation for 2007 was 3.6; the rate of sworn officers was 2.4 per 1,000. (Table 74) The UCR Program computes these rates by taking the number of employees, dividing by the population of the agency's jurisdiction, and multiplying by 1,000.

Among the nation's four regions, law enforcement agencies in the Northeast had the highest rate of law enforcement employees in 2007, with 3.5 per 1,000 inhabitants. Agencies in the South had 3.4 law enforcement employees per 1,000 inhabitants, followed by the Midwest (2.7) and the West (2.4). (Table 70)

An examination of the 2007 law enforcement employee data by population group showed that the nation's cities had a collective rate of 3.0 law enforcement employees per 1,000 inhabitants. Cities with under 10,000 inhabitants had the highest rate of law enforcement employees, with 4.3 per 1,000 inhabitants. Cities with 25,000 to 49,999 inhabitants and cities with 50,000 to 99,999 inhabitants had the lowest

rate of law enforcement employees (2.3 per 1,000 in population). The nation's largest cities, those with 250,000 or more inhabitants, averaged 3.8 law enforcement employees for every 1,000 inhabitants. (Table 70)

Sworn Personnel

The UCR Program defines law enforcement officers as individuals who ordinarily carry a firearm and a badge, have full arrest powers, and are paid from government funds set aside specifically for sworn law enforcement representatives.

An analysis of the 2007 data showed that law enforcement agencies in the cities in the Northeast had the highest rate of sworn officers—2.7 per 1,000 inhabitants, followed by the South (2.6), the Midwest (2.2), and the West (1.7). (Table 71)

By population group in 2007, there were 2.3 sworn officers for each 1,000 resident population in the nation's cities collectively. This rate was unchanged from the 2006 data. Cities with under 10,000 inhabitants had the highest rate at 3.3 sworn officers per 1,000 inhabitants. The nation's largest cities, those with 250,000 or more inhabitants, averaged 2.8 officers per 1,000 inhabitants. (Table 71)

Female employees accounted for 61.5 percent of all full-time civilian law enforcement employees in 2007. Males accounted for 88.3 percent of all full-time sworn law enforcement officers in 2007. In cities collectively, 88.2 percent of sworn officers were male. In metropolitan counties, 86.8 percent of officers were male, and in nonmetropolitan counties, 92.6 percent of officers were male. (Table 74)

Civilian Employees

Civilian employees provide a myriad of services to the nation's law enforcement and criminal justice agencies. Among other duties, they dispatch officers, provide administrative and record-keeping support, and query local, state, and national databases.

In 2007, 31.2 percent of all law enforcement employees in the nation were civilians. In cities, civilians made up 23.2 percent of law enforcement agencies employees. Civilians made up 42.4 percent of law enforcement employees in metropolitan counties, 41.0 percent of law enforcement employees in nonmetropolitan counties, and 35.8 percent of law enforcement employees in surburban areas. Of the civilians working in law enforcement agencies throughout the nation, 61.5 percent were female and 38.5 percent were male. (Tables 74 and 75)

Table 70.   Full-Time Law Enforcement Employees,[1] by Geographic Region and Division and Population Group, 2007

(Number, rate per 1,000 population.)

Geographic region/division		Total (11,112 cities; population 192,561,315)	Group I (71 cities, 250,000 and over; population 53,815,350)	Group II (181 cities, 100,000 to 249,999; population 27,270,252)	Group III (441 cities, 50,000 to 99,999; population 30,331,106)	Group IV (806 cities, 25,000 to 49,999; population 27,684,136)	Group V (1,826 cities, 10,000 to 24,999; population 28,984,708)
TOTAL	Number of employees	581,888	203,771	69,425	68,944	64,503	70,372
	Average number of employees per 1,000 inhabitants	3.0	3.8	2.5	2.3	2.3	2.4
NORTHEAST	Number of employees	152,818	67,591	9,718	16,176	19,270	20,427
	Average number of employees per 1,000 inhabitants	3.5	6.1	3.5	2.6	2.4	2.2
NEW ENGLAND	Number of employees	33,940	2,810	4,750	5,945	7,051	7,635
	Average number of employees per 1,000 inhabitants	2.7	4.7	3.3	2.4	2.3	2.2
MIDDLE ATLANTIC	Number of employees	118,878	64,781	4,968	10,231	12,219	12,792
	Average number of employees per 1,000 inhabitants	3.8	6.2	3.6	2.7	2.4	2.2
MIDWEST	Number of employees	121,342	34,569	10,247	15,133	16,740	19,755
	Average number of employees per 1,000 inhabitants	2.7	4.1	2.3	2.0	2.1	2.2
EAST NORTH CENTRAL	Number of employees	88,225	26,860	6,884	10,811	13,252	14,369
	Average number of employees per 1,000 inhabitants	2.8	4.4	2.4	2.2	2.1	2.3
WEST NORTH CENTRAL	Number of employees	33,117	7,709	3,363	4,322	3,488	5,386
	Average number of employees per 1,000 inhabitants	2.5	3.5	2.2	1.7	2.0	2.2
SOUTH	Number of employees	191,213	49,383	30,682	21,858	17,980	23,246
	Average number of employees per 1,000 inhabitants	3.4	3.2	3.0	2.7	2.8	3.0
SOUTH ATLANTIC	Number of employees	91,090	20,922	15,994	11,830	8,959	10,640
	Average number of employees per 1,000 inhabitants	3.9	4.4	3.0	3.0	3.0	3.3
EAST SOUTH CENTRAL	Number of employees	33,105	6,843	4,163	2,324	3,744	5,516
	Average number of employees per 1,000 inhabitants	3.5	2.9	3.4	3.0	2.9	3.1
WEST SOUTH CENTRAL	Number of employees	67,018	21,618	10,525	7,704	5,277	7,090
	Average number of employees per 1,000 inhabitants	2.9	2.6	2.7	2.3	2.5	2.7
WEST	Number of employees	116,515	52,228	18,778	15,777	10,513	6,944
	Average number of employees per 1,000 inhabitants	2.4	2.8	1.9	1.9	2.0	2.1
MOUNTAIN	Number of employees	40,916	18,419	5,759	4,352	4,108	2,546
	Average number of employees per 1,000 inhabitants	2.7	2.9	2.2	2.0	2.2	2.5
PACIFIC	Number of employees	75,599	33,809	13,019	11,425	6,405	4,398
	Average number of employees per 1,000 inhabitants	2.3	2.7	1.8	1.8	1.9	2.0

[1] Full-time law enforcement employees include civilians.

Table 70. Full-Time Law Enforcement Employees,[1] by Geographic Region and Division and Population Group, 2007 *(Contd.)*

(Number, rate per 1,000 population.)

Geographic region/division		Group VI (7,787 cities, under 10,000; population 24,475,763)	Total city agencies	2007 estimated city population	County[2] (3,564 agencies; population 93,305,151)	Total city and county agencies	2007 estimated total agency population	Suburban Area[3] (7,594 agencies; population 121,917,604)
TOTAL	Number of employees	104,873	11,112	192,561,315	436,066	14,676	285,866,466	471,974
	Average number of employees per 1,000 inhabitants	4.3			4.7			3.9
NORTHEAST	Number of employees	19,636	2,493	43,947,553				
	Average number of employees per 1,000 inhabitants	3.5	6.1	3.5	2.6	2.4	2.2	3.0
NEW ENGLAND	Number of employees	5,749	781	12,758,757				
	Average number of employees per 1,000 inhabitants	3.2						
MIDDLE ATLANTIC	Number of employees	13,887	1,712	31,188,796				
	Average number of employees per 1,000 inhabitants	3.0						
MIDWEST	Number of employees	24,898	3,329	44,647,528				
	Average number of employees per 1,000 inhabitants	3.3						
EAST NORTH CENTRAL	Number of employees	16,049	2,105	31,540,465				
	Average number of employees per 1,000 inhabitants	3.2						
WEST NORTH CENTRAL	Number of employees	8,849	1,224	13,107,063				
	Average number of employees per 1,000 inhabitants	3.3						
SOUTH	Number of employees	48,064	3,936	55,919,547				
	Average number of employees per 1,000 inhabitants	6.1						
SOUTH ATLANTIC	Number of employees	22,745	1,657	23,340,872				
	Average number of employees per 1,000 inhabitants	7.5						
EAST SOUTH CENTRAL	Number of employees	10,515	995	9,460,010				
	Average number of employees per 1,000 inhabitants	5.3						
WEST SOUTH CENTRAL	Number of employees	14,804	1,284	23,118,665				
	Average number of employees per 1,000 inhabitants	5.2						
WEST	Number of employees	12,275	1,354	48,046,687				
	Average number of employees per 1,000 inhabitants	4.8						
MOUNTAIN	Number of employees	5,732	587	15,300,745				
	Average number of employees per 1,000 inhabitants	4.5						
PACIFIC	Number of employees	6,543	767	32,745,942				
	Average number of employees per 1,000 inhabitants	2.3	2.7	1.8	1.8	1.9	2.0	5.1

[1] Full-time law enforcement employees include civilians.

[2] The designation county is a combination of both metropolitan and nonmetropolitan counties.

[3] Suburban area includes law enforcement agencies in cities with less than 50,000 inhabitants and county law enforcement agencies that are within a Metropolitan Statistical Area. Suburban area excludes all metropolitan agencies associated with a principal city. The agencies associated with suburban areas also appear in other groups within this table.

Table 71. Full-Time Law Enforcement Officers, by Geographic Region and Division and Population Group, 2007

(Number, rate per 1,000 population.)

Geographic region/division		Total (11,112 cities; population 192,561,315)	Group I (71 cities, 250,000 and over; population 53,815,350)	Group II (181 cities, 100,000 to 249,999; population 27,270,252)	Group III (441 cities, 50,000 to 99,999; population 30,331,106)	Group IV (806 cities, 25,000 to 49,999; population 27,684,136)	Group V (1,826 cities, 10,000 to 24,999; population 28,984,708)
TOTAL	Number of officers	446,669	152,594	52,329	53,271	50,728	56,134
	Average number of officers per 1,000 inhabitants	2.3	2.8	1.9	1.8	1.8	1.9
NORTHEAST	Number of officers	118,485	47,073	8,054	13,486	16,137	17,180
	Average number of officers per 1,000 inhabitants	2.7	4.2	2.9	2.1	2.0	1.9
NEW ENGLAND	Number of officers	27,828	2,170	3,940	5,086	5,869	6,226
	Average number of officers per 1,000 inhabitants	2.2	3.7	2.8	2.1	1.9	1.8
MIDDLE ATLANTIC	Number of officers	90,657	44,903	4,114	8,400	10,268	10,954
	Average number of officers per 1,000 inhabitants	2.9	4.3	3.0	2.2	2.1	1.9
MIDWEST	Number of officers	98,940	29,289	8,270	12,031	13,169	15,782
	Average number of officers per 1,000 inhabitants	2.2	3.5	1.9	1.6	1.7	1.8
EAST NORTH CENTRAL	Number of officers	72,794	23,680	5,609	8,573	10,417	11,469
	Average number of officers per 1,000 inhabitants	2.3	3.9	1.9	1.7	1.7	1.8
WEST NORTH CENTRAL	Number of officers	26,146	5,609	2,661	3,458	2,752	4,313
	Average number of officers per 1,000 inhabitants	2.0	2.5	1.8	1.4	1.6	1.7
SOUTH	Number of officers	145,572	38,120	22,981	16,708	13,910	18,021
	Average number of officers per 1,000 inhabitants	2.6	2.5	2.2	2.1	2.2	2.3
SOUTH ATLANTIC	Number of officers	69,124	15,594	11,874	9,011	7,043	8,413
	Average number of officers per 1,000 inhabitants	3.0	3.3	2.2	2.3	2.4	2.6
EAST SOUTH CENTRAL	Number of officers	25,883	5,569	3,064	1,817	2,963	4,268
	Average number of officers per 1,000 inhabitants	2.7	2.3	2.5	2.3	2.3	2.4
WEST SOUTH CENTRAL	Number of officers	50,565	16,957	8,043	5,880	3,904	5,340
	Average number of officers per 1,000 inhabitants	2.2	2.0	2.1	1.8	1.8	2.0
WEST	Number of officers	83,672	38,112	13,024	11,046	7,512	5,151
	Average number of officers per 1,000 inhabitants	1.7	2.0	1.3	1.3	1.4	1.6
MOUNTAIN	Number of officers	29,295	13,116	4,078	3,107	2,933	1,893
	Average number of officers per 1,000 inhabitants	1.9	2.1	1.6	1.4	1.6	1.8
PACIFIC	Number of officers	54,377	24,996	8,946	7,939	4,579	3,258
	Average number of officers per 1,000 inhabitants	1.7	2.0	1.3	1.3	1.4	1.5

Table 71.   Full-Time Law Enforcement Officers, by Geographic Region and Division and Population Group, 2007
  (Contd.)

(Number, rate per 1,000 population.)

Geographic region/division		Group VI (7,787 cities, under 10,000; population 24,475,763)	Total city agencies	2007 estimated city population	County[1] (3,564 agencies; population 93,305,151)	Total city and county agencies	2007 estimated total agency population	Suburban Area[2] (7,594 agencies; population 121,917,604)
TOTAL	Number of officers	81,613	11,112	192,561,315	253,181	14,676	285,866,466	302,867
	Average number of officers per 1,000 inhabitants	3.3			2.7			2.5
NORTHEAST	Number of officers	16,555	2,493	43,947,553				
	Average number of officers per 1,000 inhabitants	2.6						
NEW ENGLAND	Number of officers	4,537	781	12,758,757				
	Average number of officers per 1,000 inhabitants	2.5						
MIDDLE ATLANTIC	Number of officers	12,018	1,712	31,188,796				
	Average number of officers per 1,000 inhabitants	2.6						
MIDWEST	Number of officers	20,399	3,329	44,647,528				
	Average number of officers per 1,000 inhabitants	2.7						
EAST NORTH CENTRAL	Number of officers	13,046	2,105	31,540,465				
	Average number of officers per 1,000 inhabitants	2.6						
WEST NORTH CENTRAL	Number of officers	7,353	1,224	13,107,063				
	Average number of officers per 1,000 inhabitants	2.8						
SOUTH	Number of officers	35,832	3,936	55,919,547				
	Average number of officers per 1,000 inhabitants	4.6						
SOUTH ATLANTIC	Number of officers	17,189	1,657	23,340,872				
	Average number of officers per 1,000 inhabitants	5.7						
EAST SOUTH CENTRAL	Number of officers	8,202	995	9,460,010				
	Average number of officers per 1,000 inhabitants	4.1						
WEST SOUTH CENTRAL	Number of officers	10,441	1,284	23,118,665				
	Average number of officers per 1,000 inhabitants	3.7						
WEST	Number of officers	8,827	1,354	48,046,687				
	Average number of officers per 1,000 inhabitants	3.4						
MOUNTAIN	Number of officers	4,168	587	15,300,745				
	Average number of officers per 1,000 inhabitants	3.2						
PACIFIC	Number of officers	4,659	767	32,745,942				
	Average number of officers per 1,000 inhabitants	3.6						

[1] The designation county is a combination of both metropolitan and nonmetropolitan counties.

[2] Suburban area includes law enforcement agencies in cities with less than 50,000 inhabitants and county law enforcement agencies that are within a Metropolitan Statistical Area. Suburban area excludes all metropolitan agencies associated with a principal city. The agencies associated with suburban areas also appear in other groups within this table.

Table 72. Full-Time Law Enforcement Employees,[1] by Rate Range, 2007

(Number, rate per 1,000 population.)

Rate range		Total cities[2] (10,153 cities; population 192,561,315)	Group I (71 cities, 250,000 and over; population 53,815,350)	Group II (181 cities, 100,000 to 249,999; population 27,270,252)	Group III (441 cities, 50,000 to 99,999; population 30,331,106)	Group IV (806 cities, 25,000 to 49,999; population 27,684,136)	Group V (1,826 cities, 10,000 to 24,999; population 28,984,708)	Group VI (6,828 cities, under 10,000; population 24,475,763)
.1-.5	Number	111	0	0	2	1	4	104
	Percent	1.1	0.0	0.0	0.5	0.1	0.2	1.5
.6-1.0	Number	464	0	0	4	17	49	394
	Percent	4.6	0.0	0.0	0.9	2.1	2.7	5.8
1.1-1.5	Number	1,103	0	10	55	96	191	751
	Percent	10.9	0.0	5.5	12.5	11.9	10.5	11.0
1.6-2.0	Number	1,893	10	57	141	206	385	1,094
	Percent	18.6	14.1	31.5	32.0	25.6	21.1	16.0
2.1-2.5	Number	2,074	17	46	122	247	481	1,161
	Percent	20.4	23.9	25.4	27.7	30.6	26.3	17.0
2.6-3.0	Number	1,382	19	29	58	108	337	831
	Percent	13.6	26.8	16.0	13.2	13.4	18.5	12.2
3.1-3.5	Number	986	5	20	29	77	193	662
	Percent	9.7	7.0	11.0	6.6	9.6	10.6	9.7
3.6-4.0	Number	605	6	12	13	32	91	451
	Percent	6.0	8.5	6.6	2.9	4.0	5.0	6.6
4.1-4.5	Number	417	3	2	10	14	47	341
	Percent	4.1	4.2	1.1	2.3	1.7	2.6	5.0
4.6-5.0	Number	271	4	4	3	3	23	234
	Percent	2.7	5.6	2.2	0.7	0.4	1.3	3.4
5.1 and over	Number	847	7	1	4	5	25	805
	Percent	8.3	9.9	0.6	0.9	0.6	1.4	11.8
Total cities	Number	10,153	71	181	441	806	1,826	6,828
	Percent[3]	100.0	100.0	100.0	100.0	100.0	100.0	100.0

[1] Full-time law enforcement employees include civilians.
[2] The number of agencies used to compile these figures differs from other tables that include data about law enforcement employees because agencies with no resident population are excluded from this table. These agencies include those associated with universities and colleges and other agencies, as well as some state agencies that have concurrent jurisdiction with other local law enforcement.
[3] Because of rounding, the percentages may not add to 100.0.

Table 73. Full-Time Law Enforcement Officers, by Rate Range, 2007

(Number, rate per 1,000 population.)

Rate range		Total cities[1] (10,153 cities; population 192,561,315)	Group I (71 cities, 250,000 and over; population 53,815,350)	Group II (181 cities, 100,000 to 249,999; population 27,270,252)	Group III (441 cities, 50,000 to 99,999; population 30,331,106)	Group IV (806 cities, 25,000 to 49,999; population 27,684,136)	Group V (1,826 cities, 10,000 to 24,999; population 28,984,708)	Group VI (6,828 cities, under 10,000; population 24,475,763)
.1-.5	Number	128	0	0	2	1	5	120
	Percent	1.3	0.0	0.0	0.5	0.1	0.3	1.8
.6-1.0	Number	646	0	9	35	52	95	455
	Percent	6.4	0.0	5.0	7.9	6.5	5.2	6.7
1.1-1.5	Number	1,892	13	63	147	231	415	1,023
	Percent	18.6	18.3	34.8	33.3	28.7	22.7	15.0
1.6-2.0	Number	2,599	22	51	146	283	631	1,466
	Percent	25.6	31.0	28.2	33.1	35.1	34.6	21.5
2.1-2.5	Number	1,901	14	32	68	136	382	1,269
	Percent	18.7	19.7	17.7	15.4	16.9	20.9	18.6
2.6-3.0	Number	1,053	6	12	21	74	175	765
	Percent	10.4	8.5	6.6	4.8	9.2	9.6	11.2
3.1-3.5	Number	667	7	10	11	20	84	535
	Percent	6.6	9.9	5.5	2.5	2.5	4.6	7.8
3.6-4.0	Number	363	3	3	6	6	22	323
	Percent	3.6	4.2	1.7	1.4	0.7	1.2	4.7
4.1-4.5	Number	239	2	0	4	1	7	225
	Percent	2.4	2.8	0.0	0.9	0.1	0.4	3.3
4.6-5.0	Number	159	3	0	0	0	5	151
	Percent	1.6	4.2	0.0	0.0	0.0	0.3	2.2
5.1 and over	Number	506	1	1	1	2	5	496
	Percent	5.0	1.4	0.6	0.2	0.2	0.3	7.3
Total cities	Number	10,153	71	181	441	806	1,826	6,828
	Percent[2]	100.0	100.0	100.0	100.0	100.0	100.0	100.0

[1] The number of agencies used to compile these figures differs from other tables that include data about law enforcement officers because agencies with no resident population are excluded from this table. These agencies include those associated with universities and colleges and other agencies, as well as some state agencies that have concurrent jurisdiction with other local law enforcement.
[2] Because of rounding, the percentages may not add to 100.0.

Table 74.   Full-Time Law Enforcement Employees, by Population Group, 2007

(Number, percent.)

Population group	Total law enforcement employees	Percent law enforcement employees		Total officers	Percent officers		Total civilians	Percent civilians		Number of agencies	2007 estimated population
		Male	Female		Male	Female		Male	Female		
TOTAL AGENCIES:	1,017,954	72.8	27.2	699,850	88.3	11.7	318,104	38.5	61.5	14,676	285,866,466
TOTAL CITIES	581,888	74.8	25.2	446,669	88.2	11.8	135,219	30.6	69.4	11,112	192,561,315
GROUP I (250,000 and over)	203,771	70.2	29.8	152,594	83.0	17.0	51,177	32.1	67.9	71	53,815,350
1,000,000 and over (Group I subset)	113,693	68.5	31.5	83,852	81.7	18.3	29,841	31.3	68.7	10	25,220,230
500,000 to 999,999 (Group I subset)	51,812	73.2	26.8	40,163	84.0	16.0	11,649	35.9	64.1	23	15,276,719
250,000 to 499,999 (Group I subset)	38,266	71.4	28.6	28,579	85.4	14.6	9,687	30.1	69.9	38	13,318,401
GROUP II (100,000 to 249,999)	69,425	72.9	27.1	52,329	88.0	12.0	17,096	26.5	73.5	181	27,270,252
GROUP III (50,000 to 99,999)	68,944	76.0	24.0	53,271	90.4	9.6	15,673	27.0	73.0	441	30,331,106
GROUP IV (25,000 to 49,999)	64,503	77.9	22.1	50,728	91.4	8.6	13,775	27.9	72.1	806	27,684,136
GROUP V (10,000 to 24,999)	70,372	79.1	20.9	56,134	92.3	7.7	14,238	26.9	73.1	1,826	28,984,708
GROUP VI (under 10,000)	104,873	79.3	20.7	81,613	91.6	8.4	23,260	36.3	63.7	7,787	24,475,763
METROPOLITAN COUNTIES	301,088	69.2	30.8	173,546	86.8	13.2	127,542	45.3	54.7	1,333	65,514,896
NONMETROPOLITAN COUNTIES	134,978	72.0	28.0	79,635	92.6	7.4	55,343	42.3	57.7	2,231	27,790,255
SUBURBAN AREA[1]	471,974	72.5	27.5	302,867	88.8	11.2	169,107	43.3	56.7	7,594	121,917,604

[1] Suburban area includes law enforcement agencies in cities with less than 50,000 inhabitants and county law enforcement agencies that are within a Metropolitan Statistical Area. Suburban area excludes all metropolitan agencies associated with a principal city. The agencies associated with suburban areas also appear in other groups within this table.

Table 75.   Full-Time Civilian Law Enforcement Employees, by Population Group, 2007

(Number, percent.)

Population group	Percent civilian employees	Number of Agencies	2007 estimated population
TOTAL AGENCIES:	31.2	14,676	285,866,466
TOTAL CITIES	23.2	11,112	192,561,315
GROUP I (250,000 and over)	25.1	71	53,815,350
1,000,000 and over (Group I subset)	26.2	10	25,220,230
500,000 to 999,999 (Group I subset)	22.5	23	15,276,719
250,000 to 499,999 (Group I subset)	25.3	38	13,318,401
GROUP II (100,000 to 249,999)	24.6	181	27,270,252
GROUP III (50,000 to 99,999)	22.7	441	30,331,106
GROUP IV (25,000 to 49,999)	21.4	806	27,684,136
GROUP V (10,000 to 24,999)	20.2	1,826	28,984,708
GROUP VI (under 10,000)	22.2	7,787	24,475,763
METROPOLITAN COUNTIES	42.4	1,333	65,514,896
NONMETROPOLITAN COUNTIES	41.0	2,231	27,790,255
SUBURBAN AREA[1]	35.8	7,594	121,917,604

[1] Suburban area includes law enforcement agencies in cities with less than 50,000 inhabitants and county law enforcement agencies that are within a Metropolitan Statistical Area. Suburban area excludes all metropolitan agencies associated with a prin

Table 76. Full-Time State Law Enforcement Employees, by State, 2007

(Number.)

State	Agency	Total law enforcement employees	Total officers		Total civilians	
			Male	Female	Male	Female
ALABAMA	Department of Public Safety	1,385	678	14	193	500
	Other state agencies	236	179	13	7	37
ALASKA	State Troopers	552	319	15	98	120
	Other state agencies	10	5	0	2	3
ARIZONA	Department of Public Safety	2,109	1,146	68	386	509
	Other state agencies	70	29	2	22	17
ARKANSAS	Other state agencies	48	34	3	5	6
CALIFORNIA	Highway Patrol	10,975	6,854	615	1,571	1,935
	Other state agencies	911	655	183	15	58
COLORADO	State Patrol	964	678	48	63	175
	Other state agencies	76	15	2	33	26
CONNECTICUT	State Police	1,821	1,180	82	263	296
	Other state agencies	34	26	1	5	2
DELAWARE	State Police	916	603	74	107	132
	Other state agencies	654	285	94	59	216
FLORIDA	Highway Patrol	2,189	1,457	187	177	368
	Other state agencies	3,206	1,355	171	572	1,108
GEORGIA	Department of Public Safety	1,830	1,030	54	348	398
	Other state agencies	1,178	241	46	340	551
IDAHO	State Police	458	256	12	52	138
ILLINOIS	State Police	4,247	1,858	215	812	1,362
	Other state agencies	419	248	22	90	59
INDIANA	State Police	1,952	1,154	61	310	427
	Other state agencies	7	6	0	0	1
IOWA	Department of Public Safety	981	624	45	134	178
KANSAS	Highway Patrol	846	523	18	113	192
	Other state agencies	549	283	13	98	155
KENTUCKY	State Police	1,753	947	31	398	377
	Other state agencies	571	465	12	46	48
LOUISIANA	State Police	1,708	1,156	49	124	379
	Other state agencies	57	43	3	0	11
MAINE	State Police	545	276	23	130	116
	Other state agencies[1]	78	47	2	18	11
MARYLAND	State Police	2,258	1,339	114	453	352
	Other state agencies	1,642	877	127	307	331
MASSACHUSETTS	State Police	3,006	2,282	192	229	303
MICHIGAN	State Police	2,612	1,531	203	374	504
MINNESOTA	State Patrol	760	475	45	133	107
	Other state agencies	55	10	1	36	8
MISSISSIPPI	Highway Safety Patrol	1,121	552	9	175	385
MISSOURI	State Highway Patrol	2,033	901	31	487	614
	Other state agencies	598	516	36	12	34
MONTANA	Highway Patrol	255	216	12	8	19
	Other state agencies	24	21	0	0	3
NEBRASKA	State Patrol	738	461	29	101	147
NEVADA	Highway Patrol	884	445	48	114	277
	Other state agencies	62	34	2	11	15
NEW HAMPSHIRE	State Police	446	269	26	51	100
	Other state agencies	35	17	4	5	9
NEW JERSEY	State Police	4,514	2,883	115	719	797
	Other state agencies	438	332	29	46	31
	Port Authority of New York and New Jersey[2]	995	830	87	21	57
NEW MEXICO	State Police	650	500	21	39	90
NEW YORK	State Police	6,092	4,499	424	500	669
	Other state agencies	17	14	1	0	2
NORTH CAROLINA	Highway Patrol	2,255	1,684	43	283	245
	Other state agencies	700	496	64	57	83
NORTH DAKOTA	Highway Patrol	187	125	4	27	31
OHIO	Highway Patrol	2,702	1,404	164	514	620
	Other state agencies	474	344	21	38	71
OKLAHOMA	Department of Public Safety	1,463	790	16	282	375
	Other state agencies	66	29	3	21	13
OREGON	State Police	872	483	47	120	222
	Other state agencies	54	31	13	0	10
PENNSYLVANIA	State Police	6,612	4,680	212	765	955
	Other state agencies	389	247	26	95	21

Note: Caution should be used when comparing data from one state to that of another. The responsibilities of the various state police, highway patrol, and department of public safety agencies range from full law enforcement duties to only traffic patrol, which can impact both the level of employment for agencies as well as the ratio of sworn officers to civilians employed. Any valid comparison must take these factors and the other identified variables affecting crime into consideration.

[1] The total employee count includes employees from agencies that are not represented in other law enforcement employee tables.

[2] Data reported are the number of law enforcement employees for the state of New Jersey.

Table 76.   Full-Time State Law Enforcement Employees, by State, 2007 *(Contd.)*

(Number.)

State	Agency	Total law enforcement employees	Total officers		Total civilians	
			Male	Female	Male	Female
RHODE ISLAND................................	State Police	265	196	19	32	18
	Other state agencies	43	31	4	6	2
SOUTH CAROLINA..........................	Highway Patrol	1,125	857	30	88	150
	Other state agencies[1]	1,333	860	158	104	211
SOUTH DAKOTA...............................	Highway Patrol	251	146	2	81	22
	Other state agencies	144	41	3	37	63
TENNESSEE......................................	Department of Safety	1,803	866	40	248	649
	Other state agencies	1,097	586	84	128	299
TEXAS...	Department of Public Safety	7,917	3,286	201	1,516	2,914
UTAH	Highway Patrol	584	454	20	26	84
	Other state agencies	154	135	11	4	4
VERMONT..	State Police	453	285	25	43	100
	Other state agencies	113	90	5	4	14
VIRGINIA	State Police	2,653	1,867	106	211	469
	Other state agencies	538	288	46	88	116
WASHINGTON	State Patrol	2,267	984	80	589	614
WEST VIRGINIA...............................	State Police	993	621	18	129	225
	Other state agencies	194	168	1	2	23
WISCONSIN......................................	State Patrol	666	435	53	80	98
	Other state agencies	267	214	19	14	20
WYOMING	Highway Patrol	346	186	7	66	87

Note: Caution should be used when comparing data from one state to that of another. The responsibilities of the various state police, highway patrol, and department of public safety agencies range from full law enforcement duties to only traffic patrol, which can impact both the level of employment for agencies as well as the ratio of sworn officers to civilians employed. Any valid comparison must take these factors and the other identified variables affecting crime into consideration.

[1] The total employee count includes employees from agencies that are not represented in other law enforcement employee tables.

Table 77.   Full-Time Law Enforcement Employees, by State, 2007

(Number.)

State	Total law enforcement employees	Total officers		Total civilians		Number of agencies	2007 estimated population
		Male	Female	Male	Female		
ALABAMA	16,347	9,919	752	2,048	3,628	363	4,533,379
ALASKA	1,888	1,088	116	235	449	40	681,180
ARIZONA	22,144	11,041	1,313	4,469	5,321	94	6,054,541
ARKANSAS	8,455	5,006	580	1,107	1,762	272	2,832,708
CALIFORNIA	120,976	68,521	9,995	15,269	27,191	459	31,683,834
COLORADO	16,756	9,939	1,448	1,754	3,615	228	4,807,287
CONNECTICUT	9,873	7,262	711	783	1,117	101	3,502,309
DELAWARE	3,125	1,952	284	337	552	53	853,364
DISTRICT OF COLUMBIA	5,021	3,320	982	291	428	3	588,292
FLORIDA	74,562	38,409	6,251	11,046	18,856	461	18,251,243
GEORGIA	28,979	17,594	3,391	2,508	5,486	350	7,708,266
HAWAII	3,678	2,596	285	237	560	4	1,283,388
IDAHO	4,068	2,484	174	424	986	107	1,496,944
ILLINOIS	53,537	31,524	5,778	7,748	8,487	757	12,813,230
INDIANA	16,163	9,944	766	2,460	2,993	242	5,961,949
IOWA	7,812	4,760	394	995	1,663	234	2,976,754
KANSAS	10,532	6,567	654	1,295	2,016	330	2,691,761
KENTUCKY	10,301	7,524	545	844	1,388	377	4,210,320
LOUISIANA	20,981	12,577	2,556	2,018	3,830	185	3,983,159
MAINE	3,012	2,125	136	339	412	132	1,294,381
MARYLAND	20,600	13,396	2,069	1,957	3,178	130	5,439,792
MASSACHUSETTS	20,325	15,479	1,348	1,421	2,077	333	6,366,891
MICHIGAN	26,318	16,835	2,645	2,990	3,848	624	10,018,999
MINNESOTA	13,514	7,676	1,038	1,999	2,801	320	5,065,797
MISSISSIPPI	8,651	4,782	440	1,303	2,126	170	2,375,636
MISSOURI	19,951	12,740	1,382	2,187	3,642	576	5,835,175
MONTANA	2,741	1,625	109	454	553	108	957,619
NEBRASKA	4,621	2,988	361	343	929	158	1,700,074
NEVADA	9,537	5,718	677	747	2,395	37	2,565,382
NEW HAMPSHIRE	3,256	2,287	179	248	542	148	1,167,387
NEW JERSEY	41,672	29,733	2,674	3,395	5,870	529	8,405,701
NEW MEXICO	5,644	3,710	373	499	1,062	95	1,850,280
NEW YORK	86,952	53,742	8,579	8,019	16,612	427	18,883,746
NORTH CAROLINA	30,631	19,098	2,405	3,932	5,196	496	9,036,361
NORTH DAKOTA	1,664	1,090	110	181	283	99	638,897
OHIO	30,950	19,591	2,299	3,547	5,513	625	10,072,335
OKLAHOMA	11,266	6,735	548	1,657	2,326	294	3,617,316
OREGON	10,022	5,349	623	1,680	2,370	202	3,712,636
PENNSYLVANIA	29,582	22,245	2,696	1,771	2,870	997	9,052,251
RHODE ISLAND	3,240	2,392	186	305	357	47	1,057,832
SOUTH CAROLINA	14,999	9,739	1,295	1,384	2,581	379	4,406,102
SOUTH DAKOTA	2,220	1,323	97	346	454	142	792,578
TENNESSEE	24,698	13,898	1,448	4,349	5,003	446	6,150,558
TEXAS	84,403	45,425	5,552	14,424	19,002	995	23,413,736
UTAH	7,827	4,315	315	1,579	1,618	131	2,644,187
VERMONT	1,481	1,019	88	123	251	63	342,945
VIRGINIA	23,306	15,987	2,094	1,444	3,781	280	7,710,724
WASHINGTON	14,637	9,394	973	1,423	2,847	248	6,459,529
WEST VIRGINIA	4,212	3,189	110	351	562	345	1,799,090
WISCONSIN	18,732	11,175	1,795	2,119	3,643	373	5,598,633
WYOMING	2,092	1,280	124	179	509	67	519,988

Table 78. Full-Time Law Enforcement Employees by State by City, 2007

(Number.)

State	City	Population	Total law enforcement employees	Total officers	Total civilians	State	City	Population	Total law enforcement employees	Total officers	Total civilians
ALABAMA	Abbeville	2,955	19	10	9		Douglas	581	4	4	0
	Adamsville	4,771	32	21	11		Dozier	392	1	1	0
	Addison	720	3	3	0		Eclectic	1,148	9	5	4
	Alabaster	28,904	83	68	15		Elba	4,136	21	13	8
	Albertville	19,476	49	39	10		Elberta	591	8	7	1
	Alexander City	15,053	57	42	15		Enterprise	24,035	74	54	20
	Aliceville	2,457	10	6	4		Eufaula	13,272	47	28	19
	Andalusia	8,727	40	30	10		Eutaw	3,001	6	5	1
	Anniston	23,736	118	81	37		Evergreen	3,446	16	15	1
	Arab	7,694	36	25	11		Excel	605	1	1	0
	Ardmore	1,145	11	7	4		Fairfield	11,443	50	37	13
	Argo	1,866	4	3	1		Falkville	1,185	4	4	0
	Ariton	747	2	2	0		Fayette	4,694	14	13	1
	Ashford	1,967	9	5	4		Flomaton	1,541	14	7	7
	Ashland	1,856	11	6	5		Florala	1,904	6	5	1
	Ashville	2,503	5	5	0		Florence	36,784	120	95	25
	Athens	22,295	54	43	11		Foley	13,463	73	47	26
	Atmore	7,452	31	25	6		Fort Payne	13,889	39	35	4
	Attalla	6,426	28	22	6		Frisco City	1,370	3	3	0
	Auburn	53,160	102	97	5		Fultondale	6,948	26	21	5
	Autaugaville	885	2	2	0		Fyffe	1,045	3	3	0
	Baker Hill	318	2	2	0		Gadsden	37,066	124	96	28
	Bay Minette	7,674	32	23	9		Gardendale	13,235	36	26	10
	Bayou La Batre	2,761	18	13	5		Geneva	4,415	16	11	5
	Bear Creek	1,016	1	1	0		Georgiana	1,593	12	9	3
	Berry	1,212	3	3	0		Geraldine	837	3	3	0
	Bessemer	28,217	145	109	36		Glencoe	5,311	10	7	3
	Birmingham	227,686	1,072	773	299		Goodwater	1,542	8	4	4
	Blountsville	1,969	6	6	0		Gordo	1,589	4	4	0
	Boaz	8,175	34	24	10		Grant	692	4	4	0
	Brantley	906	5	4	1		Greensboro	2,579	10	10	0
	Brent	4,328	5	5	0		Greenville	7,067	39	30	9
	Brewton	5,304	31	25	6		Grove Hill	1,373	6	6	0
	Bridgeport	2,698	11	7	4		Guin	2,223	4	4	0
	Brighton	3,358	7	4	3		Gulf Shores	9,486	52	40	12
	Brilliant	732	3	3	0		Guntersville	8,088	42	29	13
	Brookside	1,330	1	1	0		Gurley	850	4	4	0
	Brundidge	2,305	13	8	5		Hackleburg	1,472	4	4	0
	Calera	9,521	30	23	7		Haleyville	4,178	16	11	5
	Camden	2,229	7	6	1		Hamilton	6,478	13	11	2
	Carbon Hill	2,048	11	5	6		Hammondville	545	2	2	0
	Carrollton	953	4	4	0		Hanceville	3,261	13	8	5
	Cedar Bluff	1,580	4	4	0		Harpersville	1,689	8	8	0
	Centre	3,401	10	9	1		Hartford	2,401	15	10	5
	Centreville	2,511	6	6	0		Hartselle	13,650	37	29	8
	Chatom	1,172	6	6	0		Hayneville	1,112	3	3	0
	Cherokee	1,177	3	3	0		Headland	3,864	16	12	4
	Chickasaw	6,000	23	18	5		Heflin	3,439	12	11	1
	Childersburg	4,978	19	14	5		Helena	14,429	26	22	4
	Citronelle	3,716	14	8	6		Henagar	2,560	8	4	4
	Clanton	8,602	25	23	2		Hillsboro	586	1	1	0
	Clayhatchee	494	1	1	0		Hokes Bluff	4,363	7	4	3
	Clayton	1,383	5	5	0		Hollywood	931	1	1	0
	Cleveland	1,405	2	2	0		Homewood	23,602	108	75	33
	Clio	2,209	3	3	0		Hoover	69,527	215	155	60
	Coffeeville	354	1	1	0		Hueytown	15,816	34	29	5
	Collinsville	1,693	9	4	5		Huntsville	169,391	500	386	114
	Columbia	832	2	2	0		Ider	715	5	4	1
	Columbiana	3,809	11	7	4		Irondale	9,471	36	30	6
	Coosada	1,590	3	3	0		Jackson	5,254	23	17	6
	Cordova	2,314	5	4	1		Jacksonville	9,213	30	25	5
	Cottonwood	1,172	2	2	0		Jasper	14,117	67	44	23
	Courtland	760	4	4	0		Jemison	2,593	11	10	1
	Creola	2,084	9	5	4		Killen	1,123	5	5	0
	Cullman	14,914	68	48	20		Kinsey	1,935	2	2	0
	Dadeville	3,239	12	11	1		Kinston	608	1	1	0
	Daleville	4,503	23	17	6		Lafayette	3,054	17	16	1
	Daphne	19,352	71	42	29		Lake View	1,982	5	4	1
	Dauphin Island	1,568	16	10	6		Lanett	7,489	31	28	3
	Decatur	56,019	153	134	19		Leeds	11,169	26	22	4
	Demopolis	7,523	24	21	3		Leesburg	839	2	2	0
	Dora	2,441	6	3	3		Level Plains	1,516	4	4	0
	Dothan	64,931	210	140	70		Lexington	832	1	1	0
	Double Springs	989	5	5	0		Lincoln	5,089	22	17	5

Table 78. Full-Time Law Enforcement Employees by State by City, 2007 *(Contd.)*
(Number.)

State	City	Population	Total law enforcement employees	Total officers	Total civilians	State	City	Population	Total law enforcement employees	Total officers	Total civilians
	Linden	2,326	4	4	0		Sardis City	2,101	4	4	0
	Lineville	2,370	12	8	4		Satsuma	6,032	16	12	4
	Lipscomb	2,265	11	5	6		Scottsboro	14,971	67	44	23
	Littleville	947	5	3	2		Selma	19,101	67	45	22
	Livingston	2,961	11	7	4		Sheffield	9,176	32	27	5
	Louisville	569	3	3	0		Shorter	338	12	4	8
	Loxley	1,587	16	9	7		Silas	487	2	1	1
	Luverne	2,733	14	10	4		Silverhill	704	1	1	0
	Madison	37,994	88	63	25		Sipsey	549	1	1	0
	Maplesville	686	6	6	0		Skyline	842	2	1	1
	Marion	3,373	11	6	5		Slocomb	2,040	7	6	1
	McIntosh	237	8	8	0		Snead	843	4	4	0
	McKenzie	612	1	1	0		Somerville	471	3	3	0
	Midfield	5,196	19	14	5		Southside	8,279	15	10	5
	Midland City	1,839	9	6	3		Spanish Fort	5,619	14	13	1
	Millbrook	16,342	37	28	9		Springville	3,435	13	13	0
	Millport	1,014	1	1	0		Steele	1,186	2	2	0
	Millry	601	3	3	0		Stevenson	2,140	8	4	4
	Mobile	253,842	685	526	159		St. Florian	472	2	2	0
	Monroeville	6,538	28	22	6		Summerdale	701	7	6	1
	Montevallo	5,234	18	14	4		Sylacauga	12,946	48	40	8
	Montgomery	202,062	591	440	151		Sylvania	1,267	3	2	1
	Moody	12,402	19	17	2		Talladega	17,104	48	37	11
	Morris	1,910	9	7	2		Tallassee	5,091	21	15	6
	Moulton	3,262	12	12	0		Tarrant City	6,553	29	23	6
	Mountain Brook	20,952	68	54	14		Thomaston	375	1	1	0
	Mount Vernon	821	6	5	1		Thomasville	4,558	22	17	5
	Muscle Shoals	12,776	43	34	9		Thorsby	2,030	5	5	0
	Napier Field	397	1	1	0		Town Creek	1,202	5	5	0
	New Brockton	1,216	5	4	1		Triana	482	1	1	0
	New Hope	2,709	5	5	0		Trinity	1,907	6	6	0
	New Site	833	2	1	1		Troy	14,056	65	47	18
	Newton	1,663	7	6	1		Trussville	18,401	55	44	11
	Newville	540	4	1	3		Tuscaloosa	83,811	340	265	75
	North Courtland	794	3	2	1		Tuscumbia	8,235	28	21	7
	Northport	22,201	79	60	19		Tuskegee	11,423	34	22	12
	Notasulga	833	8	4	4		Union Springs	4,592	18	11	7
	Oakman	945	1	1	0		Uniontown	1,480	12	8	4
	Odenville	1,238	10	9	1		Valley	8,871	34	23	11
	Ohatchee	1,230	6	6	0		Valley Head	653	3	2	1
	Oneonta	6,860	19	18	1		Vance	656	3	3	0
	Opelika	24,600	94	73	21		Vernon	1,898	7	7	0
	Opp	6,701	28	21	7		Vestavia Hills	31,097	67	65	2
	Orange Beach	5,810	62	40	22		Wadley	647	1	1	0
	Owens Crossroads	1,404	3	3	0		Warrior	2,982	19	13	6
	Oxford	20,396	62	50	12		Weaver	2,620	10	7	3
	Ozark	14,656	39	33	6		Wedowee	821	6	6	0
	Pelham	21,060	81	66	15		West Blocton	1,425	1	1	0
	Pell City	12,256	36	34	2		Wetumpka	7,558	36	28	8
	Phenix City	30,309	105	84	21		Wilton	627	1	1	0
	Phil Campbell	1,046	3	3	0		Winfield	4,711	11	10	1
	Pickensville	646	2	1	1		Woodstock	1,018	4	4	0
	Piedmont	4,998	16	12	4		Woodville	757	2	2	0
	Pinckard	632	2	2	0		York	2,563	12	6	6
	Pine Hill	914	5	5	0	**ALASKA**..................	Anchorage	284,142	529	365	164
	Pleasant Grove	10,323	23	18	5		Bethel	6,488	14	6	8
	Powell	976	3	2	1		Bristol Bay Borough	1,028	9	4	5
	Prattville	31,949	86	75	11		Cordova	2,322	9	3	6
	Priceville	2,503	4	4	0		Craig	1,186	12	5	7
	Prichard	28,087	64	45	19		Dillingham	2,494	21	8	13
	Ragland	2,082	4	3	1		Fairbanks	31,287	48	44	4
	Rainbow City	9,079	31	21	10		Haines	2,260	11	5	6
	Rainsville	4,923	13	9	4		Homer	5,629	21	12	9
	Ranburne	482	2	2	0		Hoonah	724	7	4	3
	Red Bay	3,283	11	7	4		Houston	1,992	4	3	1
	Reform	1,834	4	4	0		Juneau	30,746	79	48	31
	Riverside	1,883	3	3	0		Kenai	7,620	26	17	9
	Roanoke	6,674	29	24	5		Ketchikan	7,384	37	24	13
	Robertsdale	4,976	29	16	13		Klawock	754	2	2	0
	Rockford	396	2	1	1		Kodiak	6,242	33	17	16
	Rogersville	1,190	5	5	0		Kotzebue	3,200	18	9	9
	Russellville	8,842	31	26	5		Nome	3,558	13	7	6
	Samson	2,027	6	4	2		North Pole	1,869	13	12	1
	Saraland	12,839	47	36	11		North Slope Borough	6,569	59	42	17

Table 78.   Full-Time Law Enforcement Employees by State by City, 2007 *(Contd.)*

(Number.)

State	City	Population	Total law enforcement employees	Total officers	Total civilians	State	City	Population	Total law enforcement employees	Total officers	Total civilians
	Palmer	7,931	28	14	14		South Tucson	5,579	23	18	5
	Petersburg	2,890	14	8	6		Springerville	2,002	8	6	2
	Sand Point	915	4	3	1		St. Johns	3,638	12	9	3
	Seldovia	306	1	1	0		Surprise	98,965	154	106	48
	Seward	3,054	22	9	13		Tempe	171,320	511	338	173
	Sitka	8,932	34	18	16		Thatcher	4,285	12	11	1
	Skagway	827	7	3	4		Tolleson	7,121	44	34	10
	Soldotna	4,198	16	14	2		Tucson	523,299	1,452	1,056	396
	St. Paul	431	5	2	3		Wellton	1,898	5	5	0
	Unalaska	4,155	27	14	13		Wickenburg	6,507	22	14	8
	Valdez	3,987	19	10	9		Willcox	3,842	21	10	11
	Wasilla	9,931	49	22	27		Williams	3,255	18	11	7
	Whittier	168	2	2	0		Winslow	10,018	35	26	9
	Wrangell	2,028	12	5	7		Youngtown	5,062	16	14	2
ARIZONA	Apache Junction	30,925	83	49	34		Yuma	88,874	233	156	77
	Avondale	83,487	152	97	55	ARKANSAS	Alma	4,935	17	9	8
	Benson	4,913	25	15	10		Altheimer	1,143	3	3	0
	Bisbee	6,077	23	16	7		Arkadelphia	10,418	28	22	6
	Buckeye	34,618	84	58	26		Arkansas City	538	2	1	1
	Bullhead City	41,209	130	79	51		Ashdown	4,497	12	11	1
	Camp Verde	10,780	35	23	12		Atkins	2,929	7	6	1
	Casa Grande	35,951	105	73	32		Augusta	2,355	7	7	0
	Chandler	250,868	490	314	176		Austin	1,131	3	3	0
	Chino Valley	10,886	39	27	12		Bald Knob	3,364	9	5	4
	Clarkdale	3,904	12	10	2		Barling	4,397	9	9	0
	Clifton	2,285	6	3	3		Bay	1,992	4	3	1
	Colorado City	4,816	11	6	5		Bearden	1,019	2	2	0
	Coolidge	7,875	37	26	11		Beebe	6,062	17	10	7
	Cottonwood	11,455	45	28	17		Benton	27,758	64	55	9
	Douglas	17,077	46	31	15		Bentonville	34,232	79	53	26
	Eagar	4,324	13	8	5		Berryville	5,195	12	10	2
	El Mirage	30,823	28	24	4		Blytheville	16,161	59	42	17
	Eloy	10,795	45	35	10		Bono	1,557	3	3	0
	Flagstaff	58,978	149	98	51		Booneville	4,137	12	8	4
	Florence	16,964	33	21	12		Bradford	839	2	2	0
	Fredonia	1,066	3	3	0		Brinkley	3,368	13	9	4
	Gilbert	206,681	325	221	104		Bryant	14,181	36	28	8
	Glendale	250,444	498	370	128		Bull Shoals	2,124	3	3	0
	Globe	7,097	34	25	9		Cabot	23,366	45	33	12
	Goodyear	53,834	123	89	34		Caddo Valley	622	4	4	0
	Hayden	1,267	6	5	1		Camden	11,812	30	20	10
	Holbrook	5,186	23	16	7		Cammack Village	766	5	4	1
	Huachuca City	1,886	9	4	5		Caraway	1,359	3	3	0
	Jerome	353	4	4	0		Carlisle	2,451	10	6	4
	Kearny	3,000	9	5	4		Cave City	2,074	3	3	0
	Kingman	28,306	81	55	26		Cave Springs	1,583	4	3	1
	Lake Havasu City	58,699	117	89	28		Centerton	7,803	11	10	1
	Mammoth	2,347	10	7	3		Charleston	3,035	3	3	0
	Marana	33,374	103	77	26		Cherokee Village	4,812	7	6	1
	Mesa	454,576	1,324	831	493		Clarendon	1,766	3	3	0
	Miami	1,809	12	8	4		Clarksville	8,553	22	18	4
	Nogales	20,747	81	62	19		Clinton	2,506	8	7	1
	Oro Valley	40,364	128	95	33		Conway	57,245	117	102	15
	Page	6,829	33	23	10		Corning	3,403	11	7	4
	Paradise Valley	14,594	44	34	10		Cotter	1,074	4	3	1
	Parker	3,211	15	13	2		Crossett	5,623	23	14	9
	Patagonia	812	3	3	0		Danville	2,488	6	5	1
	Payson	15,496	47	32	15		Dardanelle	4,431	13	9	4
	Peoria	147,223	261	170	91		Decatur	1,670	7	7	0
	Phoenix	1,541,698	4,284	3,151	1,133		De Queen	5,890	16	13	3
	Pima	1,967	4	4	0		Dermott	3,401	12	7	5
	Pinetop-Lakeside	4,577	24	15	9		Des Arc	1,765	4	4	0
	Prescott	42,674	120	74	46		De Witt	3,354	14	8	6
	Prescott Valley	38,204	85	67	18		Diaz	1,180	2	2	0
	Quartzsite	3,473	13	12	1		Dierks	1,244	3	3	0
	Safford	8,945	25	21	4		Dover	1,388	4	4	0
	Sahuarita	16,011	39	32	7		Dumas	4,725	23	10	13
	San Luis	23,861	47	33	14		Earle	2,835	7	5	2
	Scottsdale	235,243	696	433	263		El Dorado	20,200	65	48	17
	Sedona	11,483	37	28	9		Elkins	2,463	8	8	0
	Show Low	11,588	43	29	14		England	3,049	11	6	5
	Sierra Vista	43,441	92	65	27		Etowah	344	1	1	0
	Snowflake-Taylor	9,448	22	14	8		Eudora	2,493	11	5	6
	Somerton	11,370	27	17	10		Eureka Springs	2,369	16	11	5

Table 78. Full-Time Law Enforcement Employees by State by City, 2007 *(Contd.)*

(Number.)

State	City	Population	Total law enforcement employees	Total officers	Total civilians
	Fairfield Bay	2,527	15	8	7
	Farmington	4,801	8	7	1
	Fayetteville	70,334	182	120	62
	Flippin	1,407	6	6	0
	Fordyce	4,282	11	7	4
	Forrest City	13,699	41	33	8
	Fort Smith	83,860	200	159	41
	Gassville	2,083	4	4	0
	Gentry	2,688	10	8	2
	Glenwood	2,030	3	3	0
	Gosnell	3,692	7	7	0
	Gould	1,171	1	1	0
	Gravette	2,465	8	8	0
	Greenbrier	3,855	14	10	4
	Green Forest	2,876	8	6	2
	Greenland	1,195	4	4	0
	Greenwood	8,404	21	21	0
	Greers Ferry	975	3	2	1
	Gurdon	2,231	4	3	1
	Guy	564	2	1	1
	Hamburg	2,770	6	5	1
	Hampton	1,493	4	4	0
	Hardy	819	3	3	0
	Harrisburg	2,142	4	4	0
	Harrison	13,097	38	28	10
	Hazen	1,502	6	5	1
	Heber Springs	7,156	23	14	9
	Helena-West Helena	12,800	44	31	13
	Highland	1,089	3	3	0
	Hope	10,467	37	26	11
	Horseshoe Bend	2,282	6	6	0
	Hot Springs	38,828	131	98	33
	Hoxie	2,635	6	5	1
	Huntsville	2,406	7	6	1
	Jacksonville	30,565	84	72	12
	Jonesboro	61,199	151	133	18
	Judsonia	2,145	3	2	1
	Keiser	764	1	1	0
	Kensett	1,717	4	4	0
	Lake City	2,022	4	4	0
	Lakeview	832	2	2	0
	Lake Village	2,552	13	8	5
	Leachville	1,813	3	3	0
	Lepanto	2,041	8	4	4
	Lewisville	1,166	2	2	0
	Lincoln	1,988	5	5	0
	Little Flock	3,179	6	6	0
	Little Rock	184,594	643	527	116
	Lonoke	4,651	16	11	5
	Lowell	7,314	22	15	7
	Luxora	1,235	3	3	0
	Magnolia	10,250	28	21	7
	Malvern	9,044	23	20	3
	Mammoth Spring	1,125	2	2	0
	Mansfield	1,126	4	4	0
	Marianna	4,624	16	11	5
	Marion	10,331	22	21	1
	Marked Tree	2,666	12	7	5
	Marmaduke	1,173	4	4	0
	Marvell	1,194	6	3	3
	Maumelle	15,613	36	26	10
	Mayflower	2,022	6	6	0
	McCrory	1,616	5	5	0
	McGehee	4,105	24	9	15
	McRae	695	2	2	0
	Mena	5,632	14	13	1
	Mineral Springs	1,298	3	3	0
	Monette	1,198	3	3	0
	Monticello	9,122	26	21	5
	Morrilton	6,558	32	20	12
	Mountain Home	12,383	34	25	9
	Mountain View	3,079	8	7	1
	Mulberry	1,730	3	3	0
	Murfreesboro	1,666	3	3	0
	Nashville	4,862	16	15	1
	Newport	7,129	23	16	7
	North Little Rock	58,680	214	185	29
	Ola	1,232	3	3	0
	Osceola	7,920	37	23	14
	Ozark	3,587	10	8	2
	Pangburn	671	2	2	0
	Paragould	24,562	49	42	7
	Paris	3,674	14	9	5
	Pea Ridge	4,269	9	9	0
	Perryville	1,450	5	5	0
	Piggott	3,603	9	8	1
	Pine Bluff	51,304	155	129	26
	Plainview	773	1	1	0
	Plummerville	870	4	3	1
	Pocahontas	6,893	14	13	1
	Pottsville	2,528	5	5	0
	Prairie Grove	3,415	9	9	0
	Prescott	4,653	10	9	1
	Quitman	741	4	4	0
	Redfield	1,171	5	4	1
	Rison	1,324	3	3	0
	Rockport	812	6	5	1
	Rogers	54,223	122	87	35
	Rose Bud	453	3	2	1
	Russellville	26,319	58	50	8
	Salem	1,558	3	3	0
	Searcy	21,304	52	36	16
	Sheridan	4,495	29	15	14
	Sherwood	23,703	80	57	23
	Siloam Springs	14,659	47	27	20
	Smackover	1,911	4	4	0
	Springdale	65,695	153	109	44
	Star City	2,253	5	4	1
	Stuttgart	9,197	27	18	9
	Swifton	797	2	1	1
	Texarkana	30,156	122	82	40
	Trumann	6,821	23	16	7
	Tuckerman	1,673	6	5	1
	Van Buren	22,238	57	43	14
	Vilonia	3,085	7	7	0
	Waldron	3,636	10	9	1
	Walnut Ridge	4,631	9	8	1
	Ward	3,659	7	6	1
	Warren	6,182	18	12	6
	Weiner	741	1	1	0
	West Fork	2,259	7	6	1
	West Memphis	28,137	98	80	18
	White Hall	5,196	14	12	2
	Wynne	8,481	18	16	2
CALIFORNIA	Alameda	70,445	142	99	43
	Albany	15,889	34	26	8
	Alhambra	87,729	133	85	48
	Alturas	2,924	7	6	1
	Anaheim	335,133	582	412	170
	Anderson	10,629	31	20	11
	Antioch	101,973	168	118	50
	Arcadia	56,967	99	63	36
	Arcata	16,929	32	23	9
	Arroyo Grande	16,485	36	27	9
	Arvin	15,228	22	16	6
	Atascadero	27,465	42	29	13
	Atherton	7,307	26	21	5
	Atwater	27,762	44	34	10
	Auburn	13,072	34	21	13
	Azusa	47,403	86	62	24
	Bakersfield	318,743	502	340	162
	Baldwin Park	78,943	108	77	31
	Banning	30,163	56	40	16
	Barstow	23,957	52	32	20
	Bear Valley	4,567	16	8	8
	Beaumont	30,093	60	45	15
	Bell	37,420	47	36	11
	Bell Gardens	45,451	72	52	20

Table 78. Full-Time Law Enforcement Employees by State by City, 2007 *(Contd.)*

(Number.)

State	City	Popula-tion	Total law enforce-ment employees	Total officers	Total civilians	State	City	Popula-tion	Total law enforce-ment employees	Total officers	Total civilians
	Belmont	24,605	44	29	15		Fairfield	106,098	197	127	70
	Belvedere	2,065	8	7	1		Farmersville	10,219	17	15	2
	Benicia	26,544	51	33	18		Ferndale	1,398	4	4	0
	Berkeley	101,343	281	168	113		Firebaugh	7,036	16	13	3
	Beverly Hills	35,133	193	130	63		Folsom	68,320	109	78	31
	Bishop	3,566	20	14	6		Fontana	176,490	275	189	86
	Blue Lake	1,110	5	5	0		Fort Bragg	6,780	23	14	9
	Blythe	22,696	40	25	15		Fortuna	11,312	23	14	9
	Brawley	22,666	40	28	12		Foster City	28,958	55	38	17
	Brea	39,041	145	106	39		Fountain Valley	55,973	80	62	18
	Brentwood	52,238	75	61	14		Fowler	5,236	12	10	2
	Brisbane	3,575	21	18	3		Fremont	201,318	292	190	102
	Broadmoor	4,345	11	10	1		Fresno	472,170	1,254	817	437
	Buena Park	79,890	139	93	46		Fullerton	133,855	226	159	67
	Burbank	104,871	246	154	92		Galt	23,967	45	32	13
	Burlingame	27,489	61	42	19		Gardena	59,951	111	85	26
	Calexico	38,928	71	47	24		Garden Grove	166,414	244	165	79
	California City	13,443	22	16	6		Gilroy	49,343	98	60	38
	Calipatria	7,743	6	6	0		Glendale	200,049	376	261	115
	Calistoga	5,217	15	11	4		Glendora	50,495	103	59	44
	Campbell	37,429	64	43	21		Gonzales	8,795	15	14	1
	Capitola	9,432	34	22	12		Grass Valley	12,525	38	28	10
	Carlsbad	95,056	157	112	45		Greenfield	14,484	19	16	3
	Carmel	3,905	21	13	8		Gridley	5,982	21	17	4
	Cathedral City	53,953	87	56	31		Grover Beach	12,761	29	19	10
	Ceres	43,427	66	46	20		Guadalupe	6,621	15	12	3
	Chico	74,288	148	97	51		Gustine	5,243	10	8	2
	Chino	80,699	146	99	47		Half Moon Bay	12,370	23	18	5
	Chowchilla	18,772	27	19	8		Hanford	49,694	65	46	19
	Chula Vista	218,718	352	255	97		Hawthorne	85,609	138	96	42
	City of Angels	3,949	10	9	1		Hayward	140,603	307	194	113
	Claremont	35,250	64	42	22		Healdsburg	10,955	30	18	12
	Clayton	11,252	12	10	2		Hemet	71,825	111	84	27
	Clearlake	15,133	31	22	9		Hercules	25,636	29	26	3
	Cloverdale	8,319	22	13	9		Hermosa Beach	19,676	63	39	24
	Clovis	92,592	160	108	52		Hillsborough	10,697	34	23	11
	Coalinga	17,801	27	18	9		Hollister	35,812	34	28	6
	Colma	1,436	26	19	7		Holtville	5,372	8	7	1
	Colton	51,924	100	71	29		Hughson	6,791	7	6	1
	Colusa	5,901	9	8	1		Huntington Beach	195,067	353	219	134
	Concord	122,202	214	154	60		Huntington Park	62,269	100	63	37
	Corcoran	23,715	27	17	10		Huron	7,301	17	12	5
	Corning	7,348	22	13	9		Imperial	12,506	20	18	2
	Corona	153,518	276	181	95		Indio	81,909	136	85	51
	Coronado	26,888	61	41	20		Inglewood	115,223	268	190	78
	Costa Mesa	109,835	249	163	86		Ione	7,721	6	5	1
	Cotati	7,272	20	13	7		Irvine	201,872	265	173	92
	Covina	47,961	89	59	30		Irwindale	1,474	35	28	7
	Crescent City	7,909	13	13	0		Isleton	800	6	6	0
	Culver City	39,474	155	116	39		Jackson	4,468	12	11	1
	Cypress	47,741	79	57	22		Kensington	5,327	11	10	1
	Daly City	100,632	149	110	39		Kerman	12,795	21	18	3
	Davis	61,238	92	57	35		King City	11,237	22	19	3
	Delano	52,051	64	48	16		Kingsburg	11,483	21	16	5
	Del Rey Oaks	1,545	6	6	0		Laguna Beach	24,215	81	47	34
	Desert Hot Springs	23,890	31	25	6		La Habra	59,290	105	68	37
	Dinuba	19,926	46	37	9		Lakeport	5,291	15	13	2
	Dixon	17,883	31	24	7		Lake Shastina	2,364	5	4	1
	Dos Palos	5,000	9	7	2		La Mesa	52,801	92	62	30
	Downey	109,642	156	106	50		La Palma	15,821	31	24	7
	East Palo Alto	33,210	40	31	9		La Verne	33,549	71	50	21
	El Cajon	91,302	221	139	82		Lemoore	23,461	38	31	7
	El Centro	40,957	72	48	24		Lincoln	47,236	46	36	10
	El Cerrito	22,514	50	41	9		Lindsay	10,925	18	14	4
	Elk Grove	138,103	187	123	64		Livermore	80,253	146	89	57
	El Monte	124,182	224	152	72		Livingston	13,286	29	19	10
	El Segundo	16,533	99	65	34		Lodi	63,218	106	76	30
	Emeryville	9,041	56	39	17		Lompoc	39,697	71	49	22
	Escalon	7,439	15	11	4		Long Beach	473,959	1,377	970	407
	Escondido	133,429	229	164	65		Los Alamitos	11,725	26	22	4
	Etna	785	3	2	1		Los Altos	27,451	46	30	16
	Eureka	25,347	77	44	33		Los Angeles	3,870,487	12,869	9,538	3,331
	Exeter	10,307	18	16	2		Los Banos	36,123	69	47	22
	Fairfax	7,091	16	11	5		Los Gatos	28,320	61	42	19

Table 78.   Full-Time Law Enforcement Employees by State by City, 2007 *(Contd.)*

(Number.)

State	City	Population	Total law enforcement employees	Total officers	Total civilians	State	City	Population	Total law enforcement employees	Total officers	Total civilians
	Madera	56,797	78	58	20		Riverbank	21,096	23	19	4
	Mammoth Lakes	7,449	26	22	4		Riverside	299,312	576	402	174
	Manhattan Beach	37,061	92	58	34		Rocklin	52,328	84	55	29
	Manteca	65,857	101	77	24		Rohnert Park	41,043	101	74	27
	Marina	18,048	40	31	9		Roseville	111,497	198	128	70
	Martinez	35,538	52	39	13		Ross	2,296	8	8	0
	Marysville	11,903	33	22	11		Sacramento	460,546	1,026	712	314
	Maywood	28,796	51	38	13		Salinas	145,251	231	174	57
	Menlo Park	29,867	72	51	21		San Anselmo	11,995	24	18	6
	Merced	78,186	148	107	41		San Bernardino	200,810	499	330	169
	Millbrae	20,425	25	20	5		San Bruno	39,960	61	45	16
	Mill Valley	13,280	28	23	5		San Carlos	26,902	35	28	7
	Milpitas	64,498	113	88	25		Sand City	307	10	9	1
	Modesto	208,067	375	271	104		San Diego	1,261,196	2,675	1,924	751
	Monrovia	38,148	78	54	24		San Fernando	24,189	50	35	15
	Montclair	35,893	84	57	27		San Francisco	733,799	2,679	2,337	342
	Montebello	63,071	119	78	41		San Gabriel	41,186	69	55	14
	Monterey	28,674	68	51	17		Sanger	24,769	37	27	10
	Monterey Park	62,472	113	76	37		San Jose	934,553	1,784	1,396	388
	Moraga	17,034	15	13	2		San Leandro	77,785	139	91	48
	Morgan Hill	36,415	52	35	17		San Luis Obispo	42,781	91	62	29
	Morro Bay	10,100	22	16	6		San Marino	13,112	30	25	5
	Mountain View	69,999	145	98	47		San Mateo	91,441	152	114	38
	Mount Shasta	3,584	14	9	5		San Pablo	31,143	57	56	1
	Murrieta	98,051	117	82	35		San Rafael	55,987	102	73	29
	Napa	75,266	111	69	42		San Ramon	50,295	75	56	19
	National City	61,996	125	91	34		Santa Ana	340,223	666	363	303
	Nevada City	3,014	12	11	1		Santa Barbara	85,142	202	132	70
	Newark	41,781	80	55	25		Santa Clara	109,420	211	137	74
	Newman	10,436	16	13	3		Santa Cruz	54,626	112	85	27
	Newport Beach	80,377	234	145	89		Santa Maria	85,782	154	101	53
	Novato	52,067	79	57	22		Santa Monica	88,584	390	209	181
	Oakdale	19,890	40	27	13		Santa Paula	28,518	45	34	11
	Oakland	396,541	1,078	722	356		Santa Rosa	154,953	255	171	84
	Oceanside	166,424	297	200	97		Sausalito	7,188	23	18	5
	Ontario	175,537	336	231	105		Scotts Valley	11,114	25	19	6
	Orange	135,818	234	162	72		Seal Beach	24,383	41	30	11
	Orland	7,168	14	11	3		Seaside	34,204	60	43	17
	Oroville	13,579	36	21	15		Sebastopol	7,523	22	15	7
	Oxnard	186,367	356	229	127		Selma	23,175	51	35	16
	Pacifica	37,176	52	39	13		Shafter	15,215	30	20	10
	Pacific Grove	14,772	29	22	7		Sierra Madre	11,031	20	15	5
	Palm Springs	48,542	153	89	64		Signal Hill	11,270	48	32	16
	Palo Alto	57,696	153	82	71		Simi Valley	122,677	189	125	64
	Palos Verdes Estates	13,828	34	24	10		Soledad	28,431	27	22	5
	Paradise	26,381	41	26	15		Sonora	4,679	21	17	4
	Parlier	13,391	18	15	3		South Gate	98,701	136	91	45
	Pasadena	145,553	368	246	122		South Lake Tahoe	23,872	56	35	21
	Paso Robles	28,490	53	41	12		South Pasadena	24,967	50	36	14
	Patterson	19,620	22	19	3		South San Francisco	61,458	109	75	34
	Petaluma	54,624	98	68	30		Stallion Springs	1,643	3	3	0
	Piedmont	10,478	28	20	8		St. Helena	5,899	17	13	4
	Pinole	18,844	48	32	16		Stockton	297,170	630	387	243
	Pismo Beach	8,369	32	21	11		Suisun City	27,010	34	23	11
	Pittsburg	63,913	95	70	25		Sunnyvale	130,326	287	223	64
	Placentia	50,428	72	55	17		Susanville	18,192	18	16	2
	Placerville	10,142	30	17	13		Sutter Creek	2,851	8	8	0
	Pleasant Hill	33,233	66	46	20		Taft	9,198	22	13	9
	Pleasanton	66,707	114	84	30		Tiburon	8,721	17	13	4
	Pomona	155,161	325	194	131		Torrance	142,970	324	234	90
	Porterville	46,621	79	58	21		Tracy	84,151	127	87	40
	Port Hueneme	21,804	32	24	8		Trinidad	314	2	2	0
	Red Bluff	14,111	37	24	13		Truckee	16,404	28	24	4
	Redding	91,328	170	117	53		Tulare	53,352	98	68	30
	Redlands	71,358	153	92	61		Tulelake	982	3	3	0
	Redondo Beach	67,909	153	99	54		Turlock	70,386	107	68	39
	Redwood City	73,435	131	96	35		Tustin	69,945	146	94	52
	Reedley	23,098	41	28	13		Twin Cities	21,050	45	34	11
	Rialto	100,451	145	105	40		Ukiah	15,367	39	28	11
	Richmond	102,471	232	161	71		Union City	69,769	108	80	28
	Ridgecrest	26,351	48	35	13		Upland	74,049	120	79	41
	Rio Dell	3,174	8	7	1		Vacaville	93,167	176	111	65
	Rio Vista	7,778	18	14	4		Vallejo	116,763	198	145	53
	Ripon	14,683	36	24	12		Ventura	104,523	182	134	48

Table 78. Full-Time Law Enforcement Employees by State by City, 2007 *(Contd.)*

(Number.)

State	City	Population	Total law enforcement employees	Total officers	Total civilians	State	City	Population	Total law enforcement employees	Total officers	Total civilians
	Vernon	91	69	51	18		Fountain	20,012	53	40	13
	Visalia	116,766	183	128	55		Fowler	1,125	4	3	1
	Walnut Creek	63,568	104	70	34		Fraser/Winter Park	1,621	9	8	1
	Watsonville	49,031	80	60	20		Frederick	8,541	21	18	3
	Weed	3,050	16	10	6		Frisco	2,509	15	13	2
	West Covina	108,097	171	113	58		Fruita	7,115	17	15	2
	Westminster	89,700	142	98	44		Georgetown	1,050	3	3	0
	Westmorland	2,242	5	5	0		Glendale	4,800	36	23	13
	West Sacramento	46,245	106	71	35		Glenwood Springs	8,904	29	23	6
	Wheatland	3,824	6	6	0		Golden	17,244	58	41	17
	Whittier	84,038	179	128	51		Grand Junction	47,235	181	107	74
	Williams	4,895	12	10	2		Greeley	90,707	260	145	115
	Willits	5,051	17	11	6		Green Mountain Falls	794	2	2	0
	Willows	6,304	13	11	2		Greenwood Village	13,744	85	60	25
	Winters	6,817	13	11	2		Gunnison	5,296	28	15	13
	Woodlake	7,435	16	14	2		Haxtun	1,000	2	2	0
	Woodland	51,355	91	65	26		Hayden	1,521	5	5	0
	Yreka	7,536	22	16	6		Holyoke	2,297	4	4	0
	Yuba City	61,881	102	67	35		Hotchkiss	1,099	3	3	0
COLORADO............	Alamosa	8,714	28	24	4		Hugo	757	3	3	0
	Arvada	105,197	221	151	70		Idaho Springs	1,779	9	7	2
	Aspen	5,700	32	22	10		Ignacio	624	7	7	0
	Ault	1,419	6	6	0		Johnstown	9,021	15	13	2
	Aurora	307,621	746	610	136		Kersey	1,421	4	4	0
	Avon	6,517	19	17	2		Kiowa	609	2	2	0
	Basalt	3,093	11	8	3		Kremmling	1,545	5	5	0
	Bayfield	1,823	5	5	0		Lafayette	24,340	46	37	9
	Berthoud	5,142	9	8	1		La Junta	7,198	20	14	6
	Black Hawk	106	36	23	13		Lakeside	19	5	5	0
	Boulder	91,047	252	167	85		Lakewood	139,407	437	300	137
	Breckenridge	2,822	26	23	3		Lamar	8,287	24	19	5
	Brighton	31,215	69	54	15		La Salle	1,927	6	6	0
	Broomfield	46,393	187	107	80		Las Animas	2,503	5	4	1
	Brush	5,216	10	8	2		La Veta	883	5	4	1
	Buena Vista	2,149	8	6	2		Leadville	2,690	9	7	2
	Burlington	3,454	9	8	1		Limon	1,785	6	5	1
	Calhan	865	3	3	0		Littleton	40,343	89	65	24
	Campo	131	1	1	0		Lochbuie	4,390	7	6	1
	Canon City	16,198	47	35	12		Log Lane Village	1,009	2	2	0
	Carbondale	6,128	15	13	2		Lone Tree	9,349	42	38	4
	Castle Rock	43,523	72	53	19		Longmont	84,278	190	136	54
	Cedaredge	2,270	6	4	2		Louisville	18,335	38	33	5
	Centennial	97,746	156	120	36		Loveland	62,586	131	90	41
	Center	2,452	6	5	1		Mancos	1,242	4	3	1
	Central City	514	7	6	1		Manitou Springs	5,085	22	18	4
	Cherry Hills Village	6,218	24	20	4		Manzanola	490	5	4	1
	Collbran	418	2	2	0		Meeker	2,309	3	3	0
	Colorado Springs	374,112	984	669	315		Milliken	6,380	10	9	1
	Columbine Valley	1,274	6	6	0		Minturn	1,141	4	3	1
	Commerce City	42,386	107	83	24		Monte Vista	4,102	15	10	5
	Cortez	8,513	51	28	23		Monument	2,633	17	13	4
	Craig	9,262	29	23	6		Morrison	405	3	2	1
	Crested Butte	1,557	8	6	2		Mountain View	517	7	6	1
	Cripple Creek	1,062	16	12	4		Mount Crested Butte	772	8	7	1
	Dacono	3,865	12	10	2		Nederland	1,323	4	3	1
	De Beque	485	3	3	0		New Castle	3,526	7	6	1
	Del Norte	1,660	6	5	1		Northglenn	33,226	81	67	14
	Delta	8,473	19	14	5		Oak Creek	784	1	1	0
	Denver	573,387	1,917	1,561	356		Olathe	1,739	7	6	1
	Dillon	777	8	7	1		Ouray	908	5	5	0
	Durango	15,785	64	53	11		Pagosa Springs	1,699	10	9	1
	Eagle	5,275	11	10	1		Palisade	2,756	7	6	1
	Eaton	4,281	9	8	1		Palmer Lake	2,306	6	5	1
	Edgewater	5,117	18	15	3		Paonia	1,635	4	4	0
	Elizabeth	1,509	6	5	1		Parachute	1,217	9	7	2
	Empire	332	1	1	0		Parker	44,624	77	54	23
	Englewood	32,362	99	69	30		Platteville	2,646	7	6	1
	Erie	15,759	20	18	2		Pueblo	103,958	246	192	54
	Estes Park	6,078	27	19	8		Rangely	2,089	9	4	5
	Evans	19,420	33	29	4		Ridgway	753	3	3	0
	Firestone	8,463	25	21	4		Rifle	8,699	24	19	5
	Fort Collins	130,935	235	161	74		Rocky Ford	4,096	10	8	2
	Fort Lupton	7,464	23	18	5		Salida	5,394	16	15	1
	Fort Morgan	10,774	34	28	6		Sheridan	5,443	34	25	9

Table 78. Full-Time Law Enforcement Employees by State by City, 2007 *(Contd.)*

(Number.)

State	City	Population	Total law enforcement employees	Total officers	Total civilians	State	City	Population	Total law enforcement employees	Total officers	Total civilians
	Silt	2,516	8	6	2		Norwalk	84,343	186	169	17
	Silverthorne	3,812	19	16	3		Norwich	36,353	99	83	16
	Simla	728	3	3	0		Old Saybrook	10,597	27	19	8
	Snowmass Village	1,732	14	10	4		Orange	13,942	52	41	11
	South Fork	552	3	3	0		Plainfield	15,538	23	18	5
	Springfield	1,323	3	3	0		Plainville	17,294	41	33	8
	Steamboat Springs	9,233	37	23	14		Plymouth	12,225	18	18	0
	Sterling	12,549	25	20	5		Portland	9,707	11	10	1
	Stratton	622	1	1	0		Putnam	9,352	17	14	3
	Telluride	2,274	15	10	5		Redding	8,990	22	16	6
	Thornton	113,289	183	147	36		Ridgefield	24,040	49	43	6
	Trinidad	9,135	31	21	10		Rocky Hill	18,923	43	34	9
	Vail	4,622	56	26	30		Seymour	16,327	39	37	2
	Victor	419	5	4	1		Shelton	40,425	63	54	9
	Walsenburg	3,914	20	11	9		Simsbury	23,674	43	33	10
	Walsh	661	1	1	0		Southington	42,522	78	61	17
	Westminster	106,383	264	178	86		South Windsor	26,214	55	42	13
	Wheat Ridge	30,718	94	69	25		Stamford	119,510	356	293	63
	Wiggins	960	2	2	0		Stonington	18,261	48	36	12
	Windsor	17,031	21	18	3		Stratford	49,440	112	109	3
	Woodland Park	6,747	28	19	9		Suffield	15,334	24	19	5
	Wray	2,156	8	7	1		Thomaston	7,972	16	13	3
	Yuma	3,245	8	7	1		Torrington	35,997	93	79	14
CONNECTICUT.......	Ansonia	18,620	50	43	7		Trumbull	35,055	82	71	11
	Avon	17,526	37	32	5		Vernon	29,843	63	50	13
	Berlin	20,380	51	41	10		Wallingford	44,979	93	72	21
	Bethel	18,670	46	34	12		Waterbury	107,241	361	298	63
	Bloomfield	20,759	57	46	11		Waterford	18,780	50	43	7
	Branford	29,074	63	49	14		Watertown	22,419	47	36	11
	Bridgeport	137,655	528	424	104		West Hartford	60,644	141	122	19
	Bristol	61,292	152	125	27		West Haven	52,770	131	118	13
	Brookfield	16,498	40	30	10		Weston	10,277	16	15	1
	Canton	10,252	20	15	5		Westport	26,704	85	63	22
	Cheshire	28,868	55	44	11		Wethersfield	25,977	58	47	11
	Clinton	13,695	27	24	3		Willimantic	16,272	47	42	5
	Coventry	12,292	19	14	5		Wilton	17,879	48	44	4
	Cromwell	13,612	34	25	9		Winchester	10,888	27	22	5
	Danbury	79,893	153	148	5		Windsor	28,712	63	52	11
	Darien	20,501	57	51	6		Windsor Locks	12,475	30	24	6
	Derby	12,465	34	31	3		Wolcott	16,419	33	24	9
	East Hampton	12,666	17	15	2		Woodbridge	9,261	34	26	8
	East Hartford	48,752	169	133	36	DELAWARE	Bethany Beach	947	10	9	1
	East Haven	28,755	50	47	3		Blades	1,006	3	3	0
	Easton	7,455	18	15	3		Bridgeville	1,597	9	7	2
	East Windsor	10,650	29	22	7		Camden	2,484	16	14	2
	Enfield	45,229	114	95	19		Cheswold	460	5	5	0
	Fairfield	57,889	114	108	6		Clayton	1,438	9	8	1
	Farmington	25,190	59	43	16		Dagsboro	566	2	2	0
	Glastonbury	33,179	75	59	16		Delaware City	1,520	3	2	1
	Granby	11,285	19	14	5		Delmar	1,498	13	12	1
	Greenwich	62,196	176	153	23		Dewey Beach	313	10	8	2
	Groton	9,314	38	29	9		Dover	35,133	121	91	30
	Groton Long Point	669	12	9	3		Elsmere	5,721	11	10	1
	Groton Town	29,377	70	66	4		Felton	857	4	4	0
	Guilford	22,462	42	35	7		Fenwick Island	359	6	5	1
	Hamden	57,982	128	107	21		Georgetown	4,964	22	20	2
	Hartford	124,558	494	411	83		Greenwood	891	2	2	0
	Madison	18,873	36	26	10		Harrington	3,276	11	10	1
	Manchester	55,774	145	113	32		Laurel	3,842	16	15	1
	Meriden	59,607	133	119	14		Lewes	3,137	13	12	1
	Middlebury	7,232	17	11	6		Milford	7,995	38	28	10
	Middletown	47,743	111	98	13		Millsboro	2,532	13	12	1
	Milford	55,404	118	102	16		Milton	1,803	11	10	1
	Monroe	19,599	48	37	11		Newark	30,158	81	65	16
	Naugatuck	31,994	66	54	12		New Castle	4,960	18	16	2
	New Britain	70,630	160	149	11		Newport	1,106	9	8	1
	New Canaan	20,009	52	47	5		Ocean View	1,109	7	6	1
	New Haven	124,034	498	413	85		Rehoboth Beach	1,562	30	19	11
	Newington	29,567	62	49	13		Seaford	7,121	35	26	9
	New London	25,890	94	80	14		Selbyville	1,761	7	6	1
	New Milford	28,890	59	45	14		Smyrna	8,185	28	21	7
	Newtown	27,262	52	45	7		South Bethany	516	6	6	0
	North Branford	14,527	29	23	6		Wilmington	72,842	386	302	84
	North Haven	24,168	57	48	9		Wyoming	1,311	3	3	0

Table 78.   Full-Time Law Enforcement Employees by State by City, 2007 *(Contd.)*

(Number.)

State	City	Population	Total law enforcement employees	Total officers	Total civilians	State	City	Population	Total law enforcement employees	Total officers	Total civilians
DISTRICT OF COLUMBIA	Washington	588,292	4,494	3,907	587		Edgewater	21,898	35	32	3
FLORIDA	Alachua	8,833	27	21	6		Edgewood	2,084	11	10	1
	Altamonte Springs	40,513	125	102	23		El Portal	2,384	10	10	0
	Altha	516	1	1	0		Eustis	18,685	56	42	14
	Apalachicola	2,331	9	8	1		Fellsmere	4,850	9	8	1
	Apopka	36,895	91	81	10		Fernandina Beach	11,423	44	35	9
	Arcadia	7,151	24	19	5		Flagler Beach	2,874	14	12	2
	Astatula	1,747	5	5	0		Florida City	9,704	42	33	9
	Atlantic Beach	13,256	36	24	12		Fort Lauderdale	187,995	644	459	185
	Atlantis	2,131	19	14	5		Fort Meade	5,741	22	15	7
	Auburndale	13,236	45	34	11		Fort Myers	61,810	276	200	76
	Aventura	30,782	111	75	36		Fort Pierce	39,456	140	106	34
	Avon Park	9,135	38	25	13		Fort Walton Beach	19,245	65	52	13
	Bal Harbour Village	3,211	36	28	8		Frostproof	2,915	7	6	1
	Bartow	16,594	69	44	25		Fruitland Park	3,983	13	12	1
	Bay Harbor Island	4,996	29	23	6		Gainesville	108,289	333	263	70
	Belleair	4,149	13	11	2		Golden Beach	893	21	18	3
	Belleair Beach	1,611	3	3	0		Graceville	2,432	8	6	2
	Belleair Bluffs	2,197	3	3	0		Greenacres City	33,042	72	50	22
	Belle Glade	15,231	41	37	4		Green Cove Springs	6,541	23	18	5
	Belleview	4,074	17	15	2		Greensboro	610	1	1	0
	Biscayne Park	3,049	12	11	1		Gretna	1,635	2	2	0
	Blountstown	2,443	12	8	4		Groveland	6,519	32	22	10
	Boca Raton	86,868	269	181	88		Gulf Breeze	6,563	27	19	8
	Bonifay	2,712	6	5	1		Gulfport	12,508	39	29	10
	Bowling Green	2,972	6	6	0		Gulf Stream	751	10	10	0
	Boynton Beach	69,469	222	158	64		Haines City	18,172	63	41	22
	Bradenton	54,253	152	122	30		Hallandale	40,147	129	92	37
	Bradenton Beach	1,557	10	10	0		Hampton	453	3	3	0
	Brooksville	7,651	29	20	9		Havana	1,703	14	10	4
	Bunnell	1,639	16	14	2		Hialeah	215,853	484	363	121
	Bushnell	2,200	10	9	1		Hialeah Gardens	19,705	47	35	12
	Cape Coral	159,936	358	257	101		Highland Beach	4,106	15	14	1
	Carrabelle	1,290	6	6	0		High Springs	4,260	16	11	5
	Casselberry	24,663	68	52	16		Hillsboro Beach	2,357	16	13	3
	Cedar Grove	5,201	5	3	2		Holly Hill	13,510	31	27	4
	Cedar Key	1,008	5	5	0		Hollywood	146,673	497	320	177
	Center Hill	1,009	3	3	0		Holmes Beach	5,086	20	13	7
	Chattahoochee	3,807	11	10	1		Homestead	58,074	149	106	43
	Chiefland	2,133	14	11	3		Howey-in-the-Hills	1,274	6	6	0
	Chipley	3,768	13	12	1		Hypoluxo	2,680	4	4	0
	Clearwater	107,501	365	257	108		Indialantic	2,997	17	11	6
	Clermont	12,385	63	48	15		Indian Creek Village	39	15	11	4
	Clewiston	7,402	25	16	9		Indian Harbour Beach	8,516	26	19	7
	Cocoa	16,704	82	59	23		Indian River Shores	3,488	20	19	1
	Cocoa Beach	12,128	53	35	18		Indian Rocks Beach	5,227	6	6	0
	Coconut Creek	51,033	123	85	38		Indian Shores	4,292	13	11	2
	Coleman	714	2	2	0		Inglis	1,658	6	5	1
	Cooper City	30,182	71	51	20		Interlachen	1,533	3	3	0
	Coral Gables	42,794	257	185	72		Jacksonville	797,350	2,871	1,639	1,232
	Coral Springs	131,307	294	195	99		Jacksonville Beach	21,801	80	59	21
	Cottondale	883	3	3	0		Jasper	1,836	8	7	1
	Crescent City	1,827	7	5	2		Jennings	841	1	1	0
	Crestview	18,753	63	50	13		Juno Beach	3,395	19	14	5
	Cross City	1,838	5	5	0		Jupiter	50,294	141	107	34
	Crystal River	3,590	20	16	4		Jupiter Inlet Colony	392	5	5	0
	Cutler Bay	40,468	43	41	2		Jupiter Island	653	21	16	5
	Dade City	7,079	31	23	8		Kenneth City	4,356	15	13	2
	Dania	29,011	71	63	8		Key Biscayne	9,968	38	27	11
	Davenport	2,056	10	9	1		Key Colony Beach	787	6	6	0
	Davie	87,007	225	164	61		Key West	22,968	126	93	33
	Daytona Beach	64,236	290	229	61		Kissimmee	62,880	207	138	69
	Daytona Beach Shores	5,063	36	25	11		Lady Lake	13,838	42	29	13
	Deerfield Beach	76,469	154	125	29		Lake Alfred	4,280	15	10	5
	De Funiak Springs	4,987	26	20	6		Lake City	12,257	49	37	12
	Deland	26,610	77	57	20		Lake Clarke Shores	3,397	11	11	0
	Delray Beach	65,262	225	151	74		Lake Hamilton	1,440	7	6	1
	Doral	21,356	85	83	2		Lake Helen	2,795	8	7	1
	Dundee	3,148	13	8	5		Lakeland	91,009	344	232	112
	Dunedin	36,702	39	38	1		Lake Mary	15,234	52	37	15
	Dunnellon	2,016	11	9	2		Lake Park	8,919	26	24	2
	Eagle Lake	2,650	6	6	0		Lake Placid	1,867	10	8	2
	Eatonville	2,265	16	14	2		Lake Wales	14,227	48	41	7
							Lake Worth	36,029	120	91	29

Table 78. Full-Time Law Enforcement Employees by State by City, 2007 *(Contd.)*

(Number.)

State	City	Popula-tion	Total law enforce-ment employees	Total officers	Total civilians	State	City	Popula-tion	Total law enforce-ment employees	Total officers	Total civilians
	Lantana	10,475	36	27	9		Panama City Beach	14,755	61	47	14
	Largo	73,789	190	140	50		Parker	4,613	10	9	1
	Lauderdale-by-the-Sea	6,010	27	23	4		Parkland	25,062	31	28	3
	Lauderdale Lakes	32,003	72	57	15		Pembroke Park	4,991	13	13	0
	Lauderhill	59,743	140	117	23		Pembroke Pines	151,817	320	243	77
	Lawtey	692	1	1	0		Pensacola	52,837	198	158	40
	Leesburg	20,401	95	70	25		Perry	6,801	24	22	2
	Lighthouse Point	11,364	42	33	9		Pinellas Park	47,419	124	101	23
	Live Oak	7,100	21	17	4		Plantation	86,346	286	181	105
	Longboat Key	7,387	25	18	7		Plant City	31,985	84	68	16
	Longwood	13,482	46	37	9		Pompano Beach	104,989	297	215	82
	Lynn Haven	16,110	39	28	11		Ponce Inlet	3,294	18	12	6
	Madeira Beach	4,408	6	6	0		Port Orange	56,155	94	80	14
	Madison	3,210	13	12	1		Port Richey	3,421	18	12	6
	Maitland	14,130	51	41	10		Port St. Joe	3,627	12	10	2
	Manalapan	342	12	7	5		Port St. Lucie	154,036	316	242	74
	Mangonia Park	1,259	15	14	1		Punta Gorda	17,552	52	36	16
	Marco Island	16,235	34	32	2		Quincy	6,904	39	26	13
	Margate	56,261	182	114	68		Redington Beaches	1,506	3	3	0
	Marianna	6,293	20	14	6		Riviera Beach	36,795	153	110	43
	Mascotte	5,485	14	13	1		Rockledge	24,910	63	44	19
	Medley	1,043	37	30	7		Royal Palm Beach	32,441	61	57	4
	Melbourne	77,678	234	171	63		Safety Harbor	17,366	10	10	0
	Melbourne Beach	3,208	10	9	1		Sanford	50,757	143	123	20
	Melbourne Village	680	5	5	0		Sanibel	5,777	43	24	19
	Mexico Beach	1,339	7	6	1		Sarasota	52,986	247	192	55
	Miami	410,252	1,381	1,061	320		Satellite Beach	9,987	31	22	9
	Miami Beach	86,742	518	364	154		Sea Ranch Lakes	763	11	7	4
	Miami Gardens	98,762	168	145	23		Sebastian	20,913	55	40	15
	Miami Lakes	22,139	48	46	2		Sebring	10,749	39	33	6
	Miami Shores	9,814	42	32	10		Seminole	19,330	13	13	0
	Miami Springs	12,860	51	41	10		Sewall's Point	2,035	8	8	0
	Milton	8,257	28	21	7		Shalimar	712	4	4	0
	Minneola	9,646	17	16	1		Sneads	1,936	9	5	4
	Miramar	114,029	232	171	61		South Bay	4,667	9	8	1
	Monticello	2,565	12	8	4		South Daytona	13,529	33	25	8
	Mount Dora	11,897	50	36	14		South Miami	11,071	60	51	9
	Mulberry	3,192	77	18	59		South Palm Beach	1,501	10	10	0
	Naples	22,109	118	75	43		South Pasadena	5,634	6	6	0
	Neptune Beach	6,833	26	19	7		Southwest Ranches	7,449	14	14	0
	New Port Richey	17,393	47	36	11		Springfield	8,963	20	14	6
	New Smyrna Beach	23,067	61	51	10		Starke	5,896	28	20	8
	Niceville	12,354	24	19	5		St. Augustine	12,118	61	50	11
	North Bay Village	8,279	35	26	9		St. Augustine Beach	6,001	14	12	2
	North Lauderdale	42,767	65	56	9		St. Cloud	24,791	93	64	29
	North Miami	57,368	165	127	38		St. Pete Beach	10,105	44	31	13
	North Miami Beach	38,790	154	113	41		St. Petersburg	248,069	710	490	220
	North Palm Beach	12,509	42	32	10		Stuart	16,385	64	45	19
	North Port	56,539	111	81	30		Sunny Isles Beach	15,190	59	45	14
	North Redington Beach	1,506	3	3	0		Sunrise	91,480	234	173	61
	Oak Hill	1,596	7	7	0		Surfside	4,599	43	30	13
	Oakland	1,128	10	9	1		Sweetwater	13,436	25	21	4
	Oakland Park	42,486	91	81	10		Tallahassee	159,943	487	358	129
	Ocala	53,490	233	152	81		Tamarac	61,366	84	69	15
	Ocean Ridge	1,678	19	14	5		Tampa	337,220	1,311	983	328
	Ocoee	31,604	88	64	24		Tarpon Springs	23,523	65	48	17
	Okeechobee	6,010	26	20	6		Tavares	13,351	40	29	11
	Oldsmar	13,656	11	11	0		Temple Terrace	22,546	72	50	22
	Opa Locka	15,695	37	24	13		Tequesta	6,018	22	16	6
	Orange City	9,485	25	22	3		Titusville	44,467	127	89	38
	Orange Park	9,108	28	22	6		Treasure Island	7,575	28	20	8
	Orlando	224,417	1,030	739	291		Trenton	1,866	3	2	1
	Ormond Beach	38,792	92	67	25		Umatilla	2,812	10	9	1
	Oviedo	31,269	76	59	17		Valparaiso	6,047	14	10	4
	Pahokee	6,656	17	15	2		Venice	21,329	67	48	19
	Palatka	11,130	43	35	8		Vero Beach	16,840	82	58	24
	Palm Bay	100,666	256	164	92		Village of Pinecrest	19,027	70	51	19
	Palm Beach	9,738	127	73	54		Virginia Gardens	2,221	8	6	2
	Palm Beach Gardens	51,053	147	113	34		Waldo	767	7	6	1
	Palm Beach Shores	1,523	16	11	5		Wauchula	4,517	19	14	5
	Palmetto	14,188	46	35	11		Webster	865	3	3	0
	Palmetto Bay	23,287	41	38	3		Welaka	714	1	1	0
	Palm Springs	15,720	51	39	12		Wellington	57,713	58	54	4
	Panama City	36,840	133	92	41		West Melbourne	16,012	44	32	12

Table 78.　Full-Time Law Enforcement Employees by State by City, 2007 (Contd.)

(Number.)

State	City	Population	Total law enforcement employees	Total officers	Total civilians	State	City	Population	Total law enforcement employees	Total officers	Total civilians
	West Miami	5,725	21	17	4		East Point	42,497	176	124	52
	Weston	68,230	100	70	30		Eatonton	6,727	20	13	7
	West Palm Beach	101,322	409	305	104		Edison	1,232	3	3	0
	West Park	14,917	32	29	3		Elberton	4,655	22	19	3
	White Springs	825	2	2	0		Ellaville	1,824	4	4	0
	Wildwood	3,211	25	18	7		Emerson	1,372	7	7	0
	Williston	2,833	20	12	8		Eton	506	3	3	0
	Wilton Manors	12,937	39	30	9		Euharlee	4,190	12	11	1
	Windermere	2,037	13	12	1		Fairburn	10,369	39	33	6
	Winter Garden	29,284	77	61	16		Fitzgerald	9,152	37	29	8
	Winter Haven	31,556	115	75	40		Folkston	3,248	6	5	1
	Winter Park	28,114	109	87	22		Forest Park	22,174	72	62	10
	Winter Springs	32,817	90	70	20		Forsyth	4,174	25	19	6
	Zephyrhills	12,998	48	34	14		Fort Gaines	1,027	6	6	0
	Zolfo Springs	1,693	4	3	1		Fort Oglethorpe	9,809	34	31	3
GEORGIA	Abbeville	2,604	3	3	0		Fort Valley	8,107	37	33	4
	Adairsville	3,199	12	10	2		Franklin	876	10	8	2
	Alamo	2,756	4	4	0		Gainesville	34,494	123	102	21
	Albany	75,137	212	183	29		Garden City	9,387	43	38	5
	Alma	3,511	12	10	2		Gordon	2,086	11	6	5
	Alpharetta	43,909	142	114	28		Gray	2,222	12	11	1
	Americus	16,448	44	36	8		Greensboro	3,243	21	17	4
	Aragon	1,071	5	4	1		Griffin	23,478	125	97	28
	Athens-Clarke County	113,389	287	227	60		Grovetown	8,476	18	18	0
	Atlanta	497,290	2,177	1,701	476		Guyton	1,906	2	1	1
	Austell	6,976	31	22	9		Hagan	1,057	2	2	0
	Baldwin	2,980	13	9	4		Hahira	2,148	5	4	1
	Ball Ground	910	3	3	0		Hampton	5,167	18	16	2
	Barnesville	5,987	20	17	3		Hapeville	6,149	36	23	13
	Bartow	285	2	1	1		Helen	791	13	10	3
	Baxley	4,444	16	13	3		Hephzibah	4,306	5	5	0
	Bloomingdale	2,644	14	11	3		Hinesville	29,466	99	77	22
	Blythe	802	1	1	0		Hiram	1,959	17	15	2
	Boston	1,448	2	2	0		Hoboken	531	3	2	1
	Bowdon	1,991	12	8	4		Hogansville	2,930	17	11	6
	Bremen	5,622	24	22	2		Holly Springs	6,897	16	16	0
	Buchanan	1,010	10	9	1		Homeland	802	2	2	0
	Buena Vista	1,711	5	5	0		Irwinton	577	2	1	1
	Byron	3,801	21	18	3		Ivey	1,067	2	2	0
	Cairo	9,655	25	22	3		Jackson	4,478	19	14	5
	Calhoun	14,522	49	41	8		Jefferson	6,906	25	21	4
	Camilla	5,599	19	16	3		Kennesaw	32,643	81	50	31
	Carrollton	22,149	75	64	11		Kingsland	12,705	42	39	3
	Cartersville	17,680	57	47	10		LaGrange	27,867	94	80	14
	Cave Spring	1,015	4	4	0		Lake City	2,733	17	16	1
	Centerville	7,123	21	18	3		Lakeland	2,795	9	7	2
	Chamblee	11,038	46	33	13		Lake Park	583	3	2	1
	Chatsworth	4,100	17	14	3		Lawrenceville	29,797	90	71	19
	Chickamauga	2,535	4	4	0		Leesburg	2,939	12	10	2
	Clarkesville	1,646	7	6	1		Lilburn	11,567	36	28	8
	Claxton	2,399	9	8	1		Lincolnton	1,535	5	5	0
	Cleveland	2,535	10	10	0		Lithonia	2,356	9	6	3
	Climax	291	1	1	0		Lookout Mountain	1,561	6	6	0
	Cochran	4,788	17	15	2		Ludowici	1,637	11	7	4
	College Park	20,573	130	102	28		Macon	93,205	376	277	99
	Colquitt	1,918	11	9	2		Madison	3,913	12	11	1
	Columbus	188,944	473	377	96		Manchester	3,808	16	11	5
	Commerce	6,189	32	24	8		Marietta	63,523	166	133	33
	Conyers	12,704	60	46	14		McDonough	18,504	44	40	4
	Coolidge	558	2	2	0		McIntyre	707	5	5	0
	Cornelia	3,822	20	17	3		McRae	4,492	8	7	1
	Covington	14,680	63	54	9		Midway	1,030	3	2	1
	Cumming	6,150	23	17	6		Milledgeville	19,896	62	40	22
	Dalton	33,790	112	94	18		Millen	3,525	8	8	0
	Danielsville	449	2	2	0		Milner	587	1	1	0
	Darien	1,727	5	5	0		Milton	15,464	25	23	2
	Davisboro	1,556	1	1	0		Monroe	12,813	43	37	6
	Dillard	250	3	3	0		Montezuma	3,969	13	11	2
	Donalsonville	2,685	11	8	3		Morrow	5,425	36	32	4
	Doraville	10,364	63	42	21		Moultrie	15,375	42	37	5
	Douglasville	30,422	101	83	18		Mount Airy	680	1	1	0
	Dublin	17,434	57	49	8		Nashville	4,830	15	12	3
	Duluth	26,272	69	53	16		Newton	863	2	2	0
	Eastman	5,524	15	14	1		Ocilla	3,211	13	12	1

Table 78.   Full-Time Law Enforcement Employees by State by City, 2007 *(Contd.)*

(Number.)

State	City	Population	Total law enforcement employees	Total officers	Total civilians	State	City	Population	Total law enforcement employees	Total officers	Total civilians
	Oglethorpe	1,130	5	4	1		Caldwell	38,713	73	58	15
	Oxford	2,480	4	4	0		Cascade	1,018	6	5	1
	Palmetto	5,103	16	14	2		Chubbuck	11,039	31	19	12
	Patterson	678	2	2	0		Coeur d'Alene	42,324	85	67	18
	Peachtree City	35,431	60	56	4		Cottonwood	1,062	1	1	0
	Pelham	3,902	14	13	1		Emmett	6,385	14	13	1
	Pembroke	2,519	9	7	2		Filer	1,919	5	5	0
	Pineview	526	1	1	0		Fruitland	4,603	10	9	1
	Pooler	12,815	32	27	5		Garden City	11,452	35	27	8
	Porterdale	1,784	6	6	0		Gooding	3,267	9	7	2
	Port Wentworth	3,396	26	23	3		Grangeville	3,171	6	6	0
	Powder Springs	15,285	38	32	6		Hagerman	763	2	2	0
	Reidsville	2,458	9	8	1		Hailey	7,984	15	14	1
	Reynolds	1,013	6	6	0		Heyburn	2,749	7	6	1
	Richmond Hill	10,324	34	28	6		Homedale	2,585	6	6	0
	Rincon	7,371	16	14	2		Idaho City	495	1	1	0
	Roberta	771	3	3	0		Idaho Falls	53,049	121	88	33
	Rockmart	4,480	21	19	2		Jerome	8,778	17	15	2
	Rome	36,233	105	91	14		Kamiah	1,150	2	2	0
	Rossville	3,473	11	10	1		Kellogg	2,279	8	7	1
	Roswell	88,879	186	126	60		Ketchum	3,258	25	12	13
	Royston	2,730	24	21	3		Kimberly	2,807	7	7	0
	Sandersville	6,134	22	19	3		Lewiston	31,356	65	45	20
	Sandy Springs	85,830	129	111	18		McCall	2,644	14	11	3
	Savannah-Chatham Metropolitan	208,116	706	516	190		Meridian	64,294	89	70	19
	Senoia	3,213	10	9	1		Montpelier	2,460	3	3	0
	Shiloh	436	1	1	0		Moscow	22,503	41	33	8
	Smithville	974	3	2	1		Mountain Home	11,686	31	23	8
	Smyrna	49,259	129	97	32		Nampa	80,397	173	126	47
	Snellville	20,414	57	47	10		Orofino	3,103	7	6	1
	Statesboro	26,001	76	63	13		Osburn	1,448	2	2	0
	Stone Mountain	7,575	20	19	1		Parma	1,842	4	4	0
	Suwanee	14,959	43	34	9		Payette	7,686	13	11	2
	Sycamore	529	1	1	0		Pinehurst	1,608	4	4	0
	Sylvania	2,522	15	11	4		Pocatello	54,274	127	86	41
	Sylvester	5,874	22	16	6		Ponderay	720	6	5	1
	Tallapoosa	3,157	17	16	1		Post Falls	25,622	56	34	22
	Temple	4,350	11	9	2		Preston	5,147	7	6	1
	Thomaston	9,101	28	24	4		Priest River	1,950	4	4	0
	Thomasville	19,108	65	59	6		Rathdrum	6,551	15	12	3
	Thomson	6,922	16	13	3		Rexburg	28,308	47	35	12
	Tifton	16,803	60	51	9		Rigby	3,332	8	7	1
	Tignall	639	2	1	1		Rupert	5,158	16	15	1
	Toccoa	9,054	31	30	1		Salmon	3,054	8	7	1
	Toomsboro	611	1	1	0		Sandpoint	8,413	26	21	5
	Trion	2,060	9	8	1		Shelley	4,249	8	8	0
	Tunnel Hill	1,095	3	3	0		Soda Springs	3,149	7	6	1
	Tybee Island	3,774	25	17	8		Spirit Lake	1,656	6	5	1
	Tyrone	6,696	17	16	1		St. Anthony	3,383	7	7	0
	Union City	17,217	79	61	18		St. Maries	2,657	5	5	0
	Valdosta	45,712	154	134	20		Sun Valley	1,455	10	9	1
	Vidalia	11,253	38	29	9		Twin Falls	41,236	94	63	31
	Wadley	1,970	8	5	3		Weiser	5,425	15	13	2
	Warm Springs	474	2	1	1		Wendell	2,448	5	4	1
	Warner Robins	60,116	138	104	34		Wilder	1,451	3	3	0
	Warrenton	1,954	8	8	0	ILLINOIS	Abingdon	3,318	4	4	0
	Washington	4,093	16	15	1		Addison	37,143	91	66	25
	Watkinsville	2,810	7	7	0		Albany	914	1	1	0
	Waycross	14,738	68	57	11		Albion	1,834	3	3	0
	West Point	3,349	20	15	5		Aledo	3,626	8	7	1
	Willacoochee	1,519	4	4	0		Algonquin	30,986	54	46	8
	Winder	13,607	43	34	9		Alorton	2,556	12	10	2
	Woodbury	1,075	10	6	4		Alsip	18,833	56	42	14
	Wrens	2,251	14	8	6		Altamont	2,245	6	6	0
	Zebulon	1,230	6	6	0		Alton	29,101	90	66	24
HAWAII	Honolulu	905,903	2,548	2,049	499		Amboy	2,571	3	3	0
IDAHO	Aberdeen	1,805	8	5	3		Anna	5,060	8	8	0
	American Falls	4,244	9	8	1		Annawan	931	1	1	0
	Bellevue	2,238	2	1	1		Antioch	14,308	46	27	19
	Blackfoot	11,084	27	24	3		Arcola	2,641	6	5	1
	Boise	199,104	378	306	72		Arlington Heights	73,802	145	111	34
	Bonners Ferry	2,736	8	8	0		Arthur	2,145	5	5	0
	Buhl	4,028	10	8	2		Ashland	1,342	1	1	0
							Assumption	1,218	1	1	0

Table 78. Full-Time Law Enforcement Employees by State by City, 2007 *(Contd.)*

(Number.)

State	City	Population	Total law enforcement employees	Total officers	Total civilians	State	City	Population	Total law enforcement employees	Total officers	Total civilians
	Athens	1,810	3	3	0		Champaign	74,167	152	121	31
	Atkinson	960	2	2	0		Channahon	14,460	25	21	4
	Atlanta	1,651	1	1	0		Charleston	20,048	34	32	2
	Atwood	1,231	3	3	0		Chatham	10,252	20	15	5
	Auburn	4,234	10	6	4		Chenoa	3,213	3	3	0
	Aurora	174,724	367	289	78		Cherry Valley	2,254	14	14	0
	Aviston	1,707	1	1	0		Chester	7,768	12	9	3
	Bannockburn	1,643	7	7	0		Chicago	2,824,434	14,736	13,671	1,065
	Barrington Hills	4,376	29	19	10		Chicago Heights	30,818	113	84	29
	Barrington-Inverness	17,770	39	32	7		Chicago Ridge	13,459	35	31	4
	Bartlett	40,873	67	50	17		Chillicothe	5,789	13	8	5
	Bartonville	6,121	16	11	5		Christopher	2,841	5	5	0
	Batavia	27,855	52	43	9		Cicero	81,311	165	141	24
	Beardstown	5,936	12	8	4		Clarendon Hills	8,681	16	15	1
	Beckemeyer	1,092	1	1	0		Clinton	7,307	14	13	1
	Bedford Park	537	44	37	7		Coal City	5,422	10	9	1
	Beecher	3,086	10	9	1		Coal Valley	4,029	8	7	1
	Belleville	40,953	101	82	19		Cobden	1,108	3	3	0
	Bellwood	19,163	44	41	3		Colfax	995	1	1	0
	Belvidere	26,404	49	44	5		Collinsville	25,713	55	40	15
	Benld	1,478	4	4	0		Colona	5,277	11	10	1
	Bensenville	20,434	37	29	8		Columbia	9,281	22	15	7
	Benton	6,963	10	9	1		Cordova	697	2	2	0
	Berkeley	4,918	20	16	4		Cortland	3,756	4	4	0
	Berwyn	50,385	134	104	30		Coulterville	1,170	1	1	0
	Bethalto	9,777	22	15	7		Country Club Hills	16,820	48	34	14
	Bloomingdale	21,995	65	48	17		Countryside	5,804	32	26	6
	Bloomington	71,770	164	122	42		Crest Hill	21,759	29	27	2
	Blue Island	22,419	57	40	17		Crestwood	11,155	3	2	1
	Blue Mound	1,030	1	1	0		Crete	9,168	21	19	2
	Bolingbrook	71,959	172	122	50		Creve Coeur	5,204	9	7	2
	Bourbonnais	17,784	28	21	7		Crystal Lake	42,014	72	60	12
	Bradley	14,385	47	33	14		Cuba	1,358	2	2	0
	Braidwood	6,823	19	13	6		Dallas City	996	2	2	0
	Breese	4,348	8	7	1		Danvers	1,131	1	1	0
	Bridgeport	2,139	2	2	0		Danville	32,607	77	62	15
	Bridgeview	14,913	46	44	2		Darien	22,553	55	38	17
	Brighton	2,386	6	4	2		Decatur	76,383	195	162	33
	Broadview	7,695	30	24	6		Deerfield	19,828	52	39	13
	Brookfield	18,144	37	31	6		De Kalb	43,058	77	63	14
	Brooklyn	629	7	6	1		De Pue	1,773	3	3	0
	Buda	575	1	1	0		De Soto	1,568	4	3	1
	Buffalo Grove	43,222	86	71	15		Des Plaines	57,048	125	101	24
	Bull Valley	802	3	3	0		Divernon	1,130	2	2	0
	Bunker Hill	1,774	3	2	1		Dixmoor	3,786	12	7	5
	Burbank	27,634	72	53	19		Dixon	15,258	28	25	3
	Burnham	4,018	14	9	5		Dolton	24,054	58	43	15
	Burr Ridge	11,129	31	27	4		Downers Grove	49,090	111	79	32
	Byron	3,905	8	7	1		Dupo	4,044	7	7	0
	Cahokia	15,302	46	33	13		Du Quoin	6,423	15	11	4
	Cairo	3,166	12	7	5		Durand	1,083	1	1	0
	Calumet City	37,170	118	85	33		Dwight	4,329	10	9	1
	Calumet Park	7,965	30	23	7		Earlville	1,862	3	3	0
	Cambridge	2,099	1	1	0		East Alton	6,536	17	12	5
	Camp Point	1,186	2	2	0		East Carondelet	628	1	1	0
	Canton	14,729	32	23	9		East Dubuque	1,979	7	7	0
	Carbondale	24,760	78	60	18		East Dundee	3,155	15	14	1
	Carlinville	5,713	18	13	5		East Galesburg	787	1	1	0
	Carlyle	3,405	8	7	1		East Hazel Crest	1,550	10	9	1
	Carmi	5,333	10	9	1		East Moline	21,089	48	38	10
	Carol Stream	40,003	85	62	23		East Peoria	22,537	54	40	14
	Carpentersville	38,394	81	67	14		East St. Louis	29,159	85	60	25
	Carrier Mills	1,836	2	2	0		Edwardsville	24,543	52	39	13
	Carrollton	2,452	6	6	0		Effingham	12,454	34	21	13
	Carterville	5,268	7	7	0		Elburn	5,048	10	9	1
	Carthage	2,512	3	3	0		Eldorado	4,398	11	7	4
	Cary	20,301	33	27	6		Elgin	102,960	259	189	70
	Casey	2,950	8	7	1		Elizabeth	666	1	1	0
	Caseyville	4,247	14	10	4		Elk Grove Village	33,512	106	93	13
	Catlin	2,056	1	1	0		Elmhurst	45,545	89	67	22
	Central City	1,333	4	4	0		Elmwood	1,874	1	1	0
	Centralia	13,643	36	27	9		Elmwood Park	24,144	43	36	7
	Centreville	5,748	13	10	3		El Paso	2,798	5	5	0
	Chadwick	478	1	1	0		Elwood	2,412	12	11	1

Table 78. Full-Time Law Enforcement Employees by State by City, 2007 (Contd.)

(Number.)

State	City	Population	Total law enforcement employees	Total officers	Total civilians	State	City	Population	Total law enforcement employees	Total officers	Total civilians
	Energy	1,193	4	4	0		Hickory Hills	13,377	37	29	8
	Erie	1,566	3	3	0		Highland	9,500	28	20	8
	Eureka	5,193	6	6	0		Highland Park	31,797	81	60	21
	Evanston	75,746	217	162	55		Highwood	5,469	14	12	2
	Evergreen Park	19,513	68	56	12		Hillsboro	6,252	8	8	0
	Fairbury	3,837	9	8	1		Hillside	7,619	35	27	8
	Fairfield	5,135	17	13	4		Hinckley	2,049	3	3	0
	Fairmont City	2,277	10	8	2		Hinsdale	18,285	37	27	10
	Fairview	474	1	1	0		Hodgkins	2,038	23	21	2
	Fairview Heights	16,825	50	40	10		Hoffman Estates	52,888	123	104	19
	Farmer City	2,010	6	3	3		Homer	1,127	1	1	0
	Farmington	2,467	5	5	0		Hometown	4,153	5	1	4
	Fisher	1,706	2	2	0		Homewood	18,622	43	38	5
	Flora	4,770	16	11	5		Hoopeston	5,689	16	11	5
	Flossmoor	9,404	24	19	5		Hopedale	918	2	2	0
	Ford Heights	3,230	4	3	1		Huntley	23,778	35	29	6
	Forest Park	15,281	52	38	14		Hutsonville	603	1	1	0
	Forest View	725	11	8	3		Indian Head Park	3,648	11	10	1
	Fox Lake	11,296	31	26	5		Island Lake	8,583	22	16	6
	Fox River Grove	5,147	11	11	0		Itasca	8,468	31	23	8
	Frankfort	18,089	33	29	4		Jacksonville	19,372	50	39	11
	Franklin Park	18,116	56	51	5		Jerome	1,293	8	8	0
	Freeburg	4,208	11	10	1		Jerseyville	8,331	21	15	6
	Freeport	25,092	71	54	17		Johnsburg	6,661	11	10	1
	Fulton	3,855	8	7	1		Johnston City	3,438	3	3	0
	Galena	3,387	12	9	3		Joliet	148,484	389	302	87
	Galesburg	31,470	78	49	29		Jonesboro	1,841	2	2	0
	Galva	2,664	3	3	0		Justice	12,673	32	26	6
	Geneseo	6,523	20	13	7		Kankakee	26,326	88	73	15
	Geneva	24,660	48	37	11		Kenilworth	2,412	14	11	3
	Genoa	4,860	11	10	1		Kewanee	12,505	31	24	7
	Georgetown	3,478	5	5	0		Kildeer	4,153	24	22	2
	Germantown	1,105	1	1	0		Kincaid	1,475	1	1	0
	Gibson City	3,302	11	6	5		Kirkland	1,743	3	3	0
	Gifford	1,018	1	1	0		Knoxville	2,965	5	5	0
	Gilberts	6,621	9	8	1		Lacon	1,878	3	3	0
	Gillespie	3,219	10	7	3		La Grange	15,374	38	29	9
	Gilman	1,771	3	3	0		La Grange Park	12,503	29	23	6
	Girard	2,210	5	5	0		Lake Bluff	6,312	22	16	6
	Glasford	1,026	1	1	0		Lake Forest	21,486	59	41	18
	Glen Carbon	12,629	27	19	8		Lake in the Hills	30,208	57	42	15
	Glencoe	9,044	44	34	10		Lakemoor	5,606	9	9	0
	Glendale Heights	32,400	81	54	27		Lake Villa	9,044	18	17	1
	Glen Ellyn	27,309	46	38	8		Lakewood	3,849	9	8	1
	Glenview	46,790	91	78	13		Lake Zurich	20,673	56	38	18
	Glenwood	8,547	23	22	1		La Moille	754	1	1	0
	Golf	454	4	4	0		Lanark	1,467	2	2	0
	Grafton	727	3	3	0		Lansing	26,923	81	63	18
	Granite City	30,411	67	57	10		La Salle	9,470	29	23	6
	Grant Park	1,627	5	5	0		Lebanon	4,134	12	12	0
	Granville	1,347	2	2	0		Leland	957	1	1	0
	Grayslake	21,799	35	29	6		Leland Grove	1,441	6	6	0
	Grayville	1,605	6	2	4		Lemont	15,812	33	29	4
	Greenfield	1,104	1	1	0		Le Roy	3,450	6	6	0
	Greenup	1,493	4	4	0		Lewistown	2,411	4	4	0
	Greenville	7,144	14	10	4		Lexington	1,872	3	3	0
	Gurnee	31,201	88	61	27		Libertyville	22,120	57	41	16
	Hamilton	2,811	4	4	0		Lincoln	14,747	26	25	1
	Hampshire	4,616	11	11	0		Lincolnshire	7,520	35	24	11
	Hampton	1,792	4	4	0		Lincolnwood	11,888	44	33	11
	Hanover	787	2	2	0		Lindenhurst	14,914	18	16	2
	Hanover Park	37,006	74	52	22		Lisle	23,472	55	42	13
	Harrisburg	9,543	15	14	1		Litchfield	6,770	24	16	8
	Hartford	1,474	5	4	1		Livingston	786	1	1	0
	Harvard	9,947	25	19	6		Lockport	25,368	48	41	7
	Harvey	28,297	89	61	28		Lombard	42,811	90	73	17
	Harwood Heights	8,099	36	26	10		Loves Park	24,280	35	32	3
	Havana	3,399	13	9	4		Ludlow	362	1	1	0
	Hawthorn Woods	8,022	17	16	1		Lynwood	7,927	24	17	7
	Hazel Crest	14,198	34	29	5		Lyons	10,401	34	27	7
	Hebron	1,229	5	5	0		Machesney Park	22,665	25	24	1
	Henry	2,481	4	4	0		Mackinaw	1,674	1	1	0
	Herrin	11,892	23	16	7		Macomb	18,420	29	26	3
	Herscher	1,566	3	3	0		Madison	4,562	15	11	4

Table 78. Full-Time Law Enforcement Employees by State by City, 2007 (Contd.)

(Number.)

State	City	Population	Total law enforcement employees	Total officers	Total civilians	State	City	Population	Total law enforcement employees	Total officers	Total civilians
	Mahomet	6,030	8	7	1		North Chicago	33,823	72	55	17
	Manhattan	6,662	11	10	1		Northfield	5,483	29	20	9
	Manito	1,667	4	4	0		Northlake	11,164	50	34	16
	Manteno	8,597	18	17	1		North Pekin	1,588	2	2	0
	Marengo	7,676	21	16	5		North Riverside	6,270	36	27	9
	Marion	17,459	38	28	10		Oak Brook	8,893	63	40	23
	Marissa	2,008	4	4	0		Oakbrook Terrace	2,440	23	21	2
	Markham	12,196	48	41	7		Oak Forest	27,951	54	42	12
	Maroa	1,548	4	4	0		Oak Lawn	53,571	146	102	44
	Marquette Heights	2,834	5	5	0		Oak Park	49,968	152	122	30
	Marseilles	4,927	13	8	5		Oakwood	1,450	1	1	0
	Marshall	3,721	10	9	1		Oblong	1,543	1	1	0
	Martinsville	1,231	2	2	0		O'Fallon	26,384	62	47	15
	Maryville	7,284	18	13	5		Oglesby	3,641	11	8	3
	Mascoutah	6,278	14	13	1		Okawville	1,341	3	3	0
	Mason City	2,417	5	5	0		Olney	8,396	19	13	6
	Matteson	17,004	47	38	9		Olympia Fields	4,699	21	19	2
	Mattoon	17,219	55	42	13		Oregon	4,189	10	9	1
	Maywood	25,304	71	57	14		Orion	1,710	3	3	0
	McCook	239	21	16	5		Orland Hills	7,377	14	13	1
	McCullom Lake	1,080	2	2	0		Orland Park	56,139	127	97	30
	McHenry	26,526	64	48	16		Oswego	28,794	60	49	11
	McLean	781	1	1	0		Ottawa	19,161	45	34	11
	McLeansboro	2,766	5	5	0		Palatine	67,550	137	110	27
	Melrose Park	22,124	102	73	29		Palestine	1,344	2	2	0
	Mendota	7,044	20	15	5		Palos Heights	12,746	29	27	2
	Meredosia	985	1	1	0		Palos Hills	17,073	35	33	2
	Metamora	3,267	5	5	0		Palos Park	4,753	13	12	1
	Metropolis	6,406	22	17	5		Pana	5,486	12	8	4
	Midlothian	13,751	32	27	5		Paris	8,818	24	18	6
	Milan	5,192	20	15	5		Park City	6,774	12	10	2
	Milledgeville	935	2	2	0		Park Forest	22,763	50	41	9
	Millstadt	3,296	7	7	0		Park Ridge	36,762	72	59	13
	Minier	1,251	2	2	0		Pawnee	2,538	10	6	4
	Minonk	2,170	3	3	0		Paxton	4,547	7	7	0
	Minooka	11,068	20	18	2		Pecatonica	2,218	3	3	0
	Mokena	18,858	35	32	3		Pekin	33,298	63	54	9
	Moline	42,773	110	84	26		Peoria	113,137	288	247	41
	Momence	3,029	9	9	0		Peoria Heights	6,209	16	12	4
	Monee	5,158	12	11	1		Peotone	4,312	11	10	1
	Monmouth	9,060	31	21	10		Peru	9,853	31	24	7
	Montgomery	15,581	31	22	9		Petersburg	2,184	5	5	0
	Monticello	5,374	7	6	1		Phoenix	2,032	3	1	2
	Morris	13,475	35	26	9		Pinckneyville	5,456	8	7	1
	Morrison	4,345	7	7	0		Piper City	744	1	1	0
	Morton	15,826	30	22	8		Pittsfield	4,526	6	6	0
	Morton Grove	22,468	60	46	14		Plainfield	36,144	75	51	24
	Mount Carmel	7,588	17	12	5		Plano	10,164	20	18	2
	Mount Carroll	1,671	3	3	0		Polo	2,513	4	4	0
	Mount Morris	3,100	5	4	1		Pontiac	11,276	25	23	2
	Mount Olive	2,078	5	3	2		Pontoon Beach	6,094	21	15	6
	Mount Prospect	53,849	106	85	21		Port Barrington	1,556	1	1	0
	Mount Pulaski	1,600	2	2	0		Port Byron	1,673	2	2	0
	Mount Sterling	1,941	8	5	3		Posen	4,981	17	15	2
	Mount Vernon	16,417	59	46	13		Potomac	660	1	1	0
	Mount Zion	5,092	11	8	3		Princeton	7,560	17	16	1
	Moweaqua	1,843	2	2	0		Prophetstown	1,943	4	3	1
	Mundelein	33,339	70	52	18		Prospect Heights	16,133	29	26	3
	Murphysboro	8,182	24	17	7		Quincy	39,946	92	76	16
	Naperville	144,933	297	188	109		Rankin	592	1	1	0
	Nashville	3,067	8	7	1		Rantoul	12,224	39	31	8
	Nauvoo	1,177	3	3	0		Raymond	919	1	1	0
	Neoga	1,763	3	3	0		Red Bud	3,586	6	6	0
	New Athens	2,016	5	5	0		Richmond	2,534	5	5	0
	New Baden	3,150	5	5	0		Richton Park	12,992	29	25	4
	New Lenox	25,008	44	40	4		Ridge Farm	867	1	1	0
	Newman	921	1	1	0		Ridgway	880	2	2	0
	Newton	2,988	7	6	1		Riverdale	14,332	46	36	10
	Niles	28,928	74	61	13		River Forest	11,132	34	31	3
	Nokomis	2,301	4	3	1		River Grove	10,088	28	23	5
	Normal	51,458	90	77	13		Riverside	8,329	22	17	5
	Norridge	13,973	54	38	16		Robbins	6,261	14	6	8
	North Aurora	15,603	32	30	2		Robinson	6,398	15	14	1
	Northbrook	34,227	86	61	25		Rochelle	9,818	28	21	7

Table 78.   Full-Time Law Enforcement Employees by State by City, 2007 *(Contd.)*

(Number.)

State	City	Population	Total law enforcement employees	Total officers	Total civilians	State	City	Population	Total law enforcement employees	Total officers	Total civilians
	Rochester	3,109	8	8	0		Tilton	2,807	3	3	0
	Rockdale	2,058	5	5	0		Tinley Park	60,075	104	78	26
	Rock Falls	9,428	24	18	6		Tolono	2,794	4	4	0
	Rockford	155,713	335	304	31		Tremont	2,080	3	3	0
	Rock Island	38,275	113	85	28		Trenton	2,682	5	5	0
	Rockton	5,431	14	13	1		Troy	9,733	24	18	6
	Rolling Meadows	23,547	80	54	26		Tuscola	4,587	8	7	1
	Romeoville	39,718	84	63	21		University Park	8,499	19	16	3
	Roodhouse	2,163	8	4	4		Urbana	38,771	68	55	13
	Roscoe	9,156	17	15	2		Valmeyer	1,203	2	2	0
	Roselle	23,171	52	36	16		Vandalia	6,802	18	13	5
	Rosemont	3,962	96	75	21		Venice	2,417	11	8	3
	Rossville	1,170	2	2	0		Vernon Hills	24,800	69	48	21
	Round Lake	18,722	27	21	6		Vienna	1,335	4	4	0
	Round Lake Beach	28,598	49	39	10		Villa Grove	2,477	5	4	1
	Round Lake Heights	2,581	4	4	0		Villa Park	22,559	53	38	15
	Round Lake Park	6,256	16	14	2		Virden	3,429	10	6	4
	Roxana	1,488	6	5	1		Virginia	1,687	1	1	0
	Royalton	1,180	2	2	0		Wamac	1,284	2	2	0
	Rushville	3,110	4	4	0		Warren	1,398	4	3	1
	Salem	7,500	22	14	8		Warrensburg	1,180	3	3	0
	Sandwich	7,156	19	13	6		Warrenville	13,167	37	30	7
	Sauget	241	15	14	1		Warsaw	1,621	4	3	1
	Sauk Village	10,409	34	25	9		Washburn	1,106	2	2	0
	Savanna	3,225	8	8	0		Washington	13,620	27	20	7
	Schaumburg	72,320	173	125	48		Washington Park	5,639	9	6	3
	Schiller Park	11,432	39	33	6		Waterloo	9,636	15	13	2
	Seneca	2,092	7	3	4		Waterman	1,335	2	2	0
	Sesser	2,144	5	4	1		Watseka	5,525	11	10	1
	Shawneetown	1,339	4	4	0		Wauconda	12,177	39	25	14
	Shelbyville	4,677	8	7	1		Waukegan	92,609	221	164	57
	Sheridan	2,206	3	3	0		Wayne	2,418	4	4	0
	Sherman	3,712	6	6	0		Westchester	15,877	48	35	13
	Shiloh	10,913	17	16	1		West Chicago	27,176	65	48	17
	Shorewood	14,754	30	26	4		West City	748	8	4	4
	Silvis	7,881	21	14	7		West Dundee	8,373	24	21	3
	Skokie	67,148	140	109	31		Western Springs	12,576	29	21	8
	Sleepy Hollow	3,725	7	6	1		West Frankfort	8,321	18	13	5
	Smithton	3,259	5	5	0		Westmont	25,083	57	43	14
	Somonauk	1,622	4	4	0		West Salem	946	1	1	0
	South Barrington	3,986	18	15	3		Westville	3,028	3	3	0
	South Beloit	5,510	16	14	2		Wheaton	54,488	90	69	21
	South Chicago Heights	3,822	12	8	4		Wheeling	36,455	92	64	28
	South Elgin	21,750	43	33	10		White Hall	2,539	8	5	3
	Southern View	1,639	4	4	0		Williamsfield	584	1	1	0
	South Holland	21,256	44	42	2		Williamsville	1,394	2	2	0
	South Jacksonville	3,304	6	5	1		Willowbrook	8,838	30	26	4
	South Pekin	1,215	2	2	0		Willow Springs	6,094	23	17	6
	South Roxana	1,803	5	5	0		Wilmette	26,612	64	46	18
	Sparta	4,330	17	11	6		Wilmington	6,273	20	14	6
	Springfield	117,185	314	267	47		Winchester	1,599	2	2	0
	Spring Grove	5,810	12	10	2		Winfield	10,212	22	20	2
	Spring Valley	5,369	14	11	3		Winnebago	3,153	7	7	0
	St. Anne	1,236	3	3	0		Winnetka	12,433	35	26	9
	Staunton	5,188	10	7	3		Winthrop Harbor	7,289	16	10	6
	St. Charles	33,284	69	55	14		Witt	982	1	1	0
	Steger	10,718	24	17	7		Wonder Lake	3,171	4	3	1
	Sterling	15,284	41	29	12		Wood Dale	13,507	51	34	17
	St. Francisville	748	1	1	0		Woodhull	808	1	1	0
	Stickney	5,813	19	14	5		Woodridge	34,893	79	57	22
	Stockton	1,804	4	4	0		Wood River	10,885	25	19	6
	Stone Park	4,827	23	18	5		Woodstock	23,155	52	40	12
	Stonington	911	1	1	0		Worden	1,023	1	1	0
	Streamwood	37,666	70	58	12		Worth	10,494	26	24	2
	Streator	13,860	32	23	9		Yates City	680	1	1	0
	Sugar Grove	10,111	18	17	1		Yorkville	13,850	34	29	5
	Sullivan	4,345	10	8	2		Zeigler	1,688	4	4	0
	Summit	10,274	37	31	6		Zion	25,176	67	51	16
	Sumner	2,023	2	2	0	INDIANA...............	Albion	2,356	7	6	1
	Swansea	12,832	27	20	7		Alexandria	5,840	17	13	4
	Sycamore	16,910	30	27	3		Anderson	57,189	141	120	21
	Taylorville	11,163	29	24	5		Angola	7,979	21	17	4
	Thomson	531	1	1	0		Attica	3,361	6	6	0
	Thornton	2,408	11	10	1		Auburn	12,902	29	22	7

Table 78.   Full-Time Law Enforcement Employees by State by City, 2007 *(Contd.)*

(Number.)

State	City	Population	Total law enforcement employees	Total officers	Total civilians	State	City	Population	Total law enforcement employees	Total officers	Total civilians
	Austin	4,641	5	5	0		La Porte	21,178	49	40	9
	Avon	10,197	23	21	2		Lawrence	42,196	59	53	6
	Bargersville	2,647	6	6	0		Lawrenceburg	4,783	25	20	5
	Batesville	6,501	16	11	5		Ligonier	4,470	10	9	1
	Bedford	13,557	43	32	11		Linton	5,787	14	10	4
	Beech Grove	13,975	41	30	11		Logansport	18,995	54	44	10
	Berne	4,108	8	7	1		Long Beach	1,544	6	5	1
	Bicknell	3,253	13	7	6		Loogootee	2,661	5	4	1
	Bloomington	68,918	121	86	35		Lowell	8,319	19	14	5
	Bluffton	9,448	31	20	11		Madison	12,657	33	25	8
	Boonville	6,750	15	14	1		Marion	30,288	82	69	13
	Brazil	8,238	16	12	4		Martinsville	11,805	29	20	9
	Bremen	4,719	16	12	4		Merrillville	32,091	62	49	13
	Brownsburg	19,494	44	36	8		Michigan City	32,008	110	92	18
	Burns Harbor	1,060	6	5	1		Mishawaka	49,196	139	102	37
	Carmel	62,037	116	97	19		Mitchell	4,624	10	6	4
	Cedar Lake	10,350	21	16	5		Monticello	5,401	17	12	5
	Charlestown	7,217	20	15	5		Mooresville	11,639	25	19	6
	Chesterfield	2,755	7	6	1		Mount Vernon	7,145	15	14	1
	Chesterton	12,746	26	21	5		Muncie	64,921	117	110	7
	Clarksville	21,295	45	35	10		Munster	22,467	49	38	11
	Clinton	4,896	10	8	2		Nappanee	7,118	22	15	7
	Columbia City	8,227	20	18	2		New Albany	36,840	69	66	3
	Columbus	39,764	84	74	10		New Castle	18,577	38	35	3
	Connersville	14,099	33	32	1		New Chicago	2,012	6	2	4
	Corydon	2,793	7	7	0		New Haven	13,733	28	20	8
	Covington	2,459	6	6	0		New Whiteland	5,658	13	8	5
	Crawfordsville	15,156	46	32	14		Noblesville	41,927	79	67	12
	Crown Point	24,072	51	39	12		North Liberty	1,351	4	4	0
	Culver	1,523	4	4	0		North Manchester	5,887	16	11	5
	Danville	8,033	17	15	2		North Vernon	6,407	20	17	3
	Decatur	9,507	21	17	4		Oakland City	2,584	4	4	0
	Delphi	2,969	11	7	4		Peru	12,677	31	29	2
	Dyer	15,713	34	26	8		Plainfield	25,722	47	42	5
	East Chicago	30,353	132	114	18		Plymouth	11,192	29	24	5
	Edinburgh	4,593	15	10	5		Portage	36,701	74	58	16
	Elkhart	52,779	143	118	25		Portland	6,149	17	13	4
	Elwood	9,013	22	17	5		Prince's Lakes	1,567	3	3	0
	Evansville	114,985	313	279	34		Princeton	8,700	18	17	1
	Fairmount	2,746	9	5	4		Rensselaer	6,276	15	9	6
	Fishers	66,099	89	83	6		Richmond	37,129	89	77	12
	Fort Wayne	248,423	493	457	36		Rochester	6,464	20	14	6
	Fowler	2,254	3	3	0		Roseland	625	4	4	0
	Frankfort	16,431	42	31	11		Rushville	5,570	18	13	5
	Franklin	22,778	56	40	16		Salem	6,558	17	12	5
	Garrett	5,742	16	12	4		Schererville	29,494	61	48	13
	Gary	97,048	321	246	75		Scottsburg	5,982	13	13	0
	Gas City	5,774	14	10	4		Sellersburg	6,163	20	15	5
	Georgetown	2,851	4	4	0		Seymour	19,246	54	39	15
	Goshen	32,210	62	57	5		Shelbyville	18,416	50	38	12
	Greencastle	10,111	18	16	2		South Bend	104,437	335	264	71
	Greendale	4,391	15	11	4		South Whitley	1,865	4	4	0
	Greenfield	17,884	45	35	10		Speedway	12,357	47	34	13
	Greensburg	10,570	27	18	9		St. John	12,237	25	19	6
	Greenwood	46,063	72	50	22		Sullivan	4,481	7	7	0
	Griffith	16,370	40	31	9		Tell City	7,561	19	12	7
	Hagerstown	1,646	5	5	0		Terre Haute	56,946	142	129	13
	Hammond	77,662	261	210	51		Tipton	5,181	14	12	2
	Hartford City	6,493	15	13	2		Union City	3,418	14	8	6
	Hebron	3,634	6	5	1		Valparaiso	29,764	59	48	11
	Highland	22,879	48	39	9		Vincennes	17,905	41	36	5
	Hobart	28,428	72	56	16		Wabash	11,021	33	27	6
	Huntingburg	6,107	11	10	1		Walkerton	2,186	10	6	4
	Huntington	16,767	45	34	11		Warsaw	13,154	42	35	7
	Indianapolis	797,268	1,883	1,605	278		Washington	11,266	25	18	7
	Jasonville	2,497	5	5	0		Waterloo	2,194	7	6	1
	Jasper	14,098	30	21	9		Westfield	14,037	38	33	5
	Jeffersonville	29,412	65	56	9		West Lafayette	29,045	62	46	16
	Kendallville	10,232	27	18	9		West Terre Haute	2,236	9	8	1
	Knox	3,699	7	7	0		Westville	5,194	3	3	0
	Kokomo	45,832	143	107	36		Whiting	4,793	25	18	7
	Kouts	1,829	5	5	0		Winchester	4,705	16	11	5
	Lafayette	61,257	158	122	36		Winona Lake	4,314	5	5	0
	Lake Station	13,401	30	24	6						

Table 78. Full-Time Law Enforcement Employees by State by City, 2007 *(Contd.)*

(Number.)

State	City	Population	Total law enforcement employees	Total officers	Total civilians	State	City	Population	Total law enforcement employees	Total officers	Total civilians
IOWA	Adel	4,135	9	8	1		Marshalltown	25,958	59	43	16
	Albia	3,615	7	6	1		Mason City	27,541	54	49	5
	Algona	5,443	15	10	5		Missouri Valley	2,870	6	6	0
	Altoona	13,882	24	22	2		Monticello	3,738	7	6	1
	Ames	51,622	72	50	22		Mount Pleasant	8,918	15	13	2
	Anamosa	5,675	8	7	1		Mount Vernon	4,210	6	6	0
	Ankeny	40,546	52	43	9		Muscatine	22,705	38	35	3
	Atlantic	6,842	16	14	2		Nevada	6,275	10	9	1
	Audubon	2,166	3	3	0		New Hampton	3,464	7	7	0
	Belle Plaine	2,895	4	4	0		Newton	15,459	30	24	6
	Belmond	2,387	5	5	0		North Liberty	10,826	9	9	0
	Bettendorf	32,501	57	44	13		Norwalk	8,413	13	11	2
	Bloomfield	2,575	5	5	0		Oelwein	6,273	16	11	5
	Boone	12,768	18	17	1		Ogden	2,005	3	3	0
	Burlington	25,258	58	41	17		Onawa	2,838	6	6	0
	Camanche	4,298	7	7	0		Orange City	5,897	7	7	0
	Carlisle	3,599	6	5	1		Osage	3,447	6	6	0
	Carroll	9,976	21	15	6		Osceola	4,782	8	7	1
	Carter Lake	3,304	10	9	1		Oskaloosa	11,033	17	15	2
	Cedar Falls	36,995	45	43	2		Ottumwa	24,822	41	35	6
	Cedar Rapids	124,730	218	187	31		Pella	10,280	20	14	6
	Centerville	5,662	17	12	5		Perry	9,001	19	13	6
	Chariton	4,554	7	6	1		Pleasant Hill	7,458	15	14	1
	Charles City	7,574	20	13	7		Pleasantville	1,622	3	3	0
	Cherokee	4,911	9	8	1		Polk City	3,098	6	6	0
	Clarinda	5,558	13	9	4		Prairie City	1,459	3	3	0
	Clarion	2,796	8	7	1		Rock Rapids	2,579	2	2	0
	Clear Lake	7,848	20	15	5		Rock Valley	3,005	4	4	0
	Clinton	26,937	55	46	9		Sac City	2,157	4	4	0
	Clive	14,231	26	23	3		Sergeant Bluff	4,009	9	8	1
	Coralville	18,496	36	32	4		Sheldon	4,863	7	7	0
	Council Bluffs	60,531	124	106	18		Shenandoah	5,172	9	6	3
	Cresco	3,763	7	7	0		Sioux Center	6,693	7	7	0
	Creston	7,401	16	12	4		Sioux City	82,942	154	126	28
	Davenport	99,631	209	163	46		Spencer	11,015	28	20	8
	Decorah	8,066	19	12	7		Spirit Lake	4,783	10	9	1
	Denison	7,427	17	12	5		St. Ansgar	975	1	1	0
	Des Moines	192,940	498	382	116		State Center	1,356	1	1	0
	De Witt	5,360	10	10	0		Storm Lake	9,855	22	18	4
	Dubuque	57,694	101	95	6		Story City	3,187	5	5	0
	Dyersville	4,186	10	6	4		Tama	2,577	5	5	0
	Eagle Grove	3,424	7	7	0		Tipton	3,103	6	6	0
	Eldora	2,789	4	4	0		Urbandale	38,381	50	46	4
	Eldridge	4,685	7	7	0		Vinton	5,239	8	8	0
	Emmetsburg	3,633	7	6	1		Washington	7,264	11	10	1
	Estherville	6,276	11	11	0		Waterloo	65,607	129	120	9
	Evansdale	4,998	8	7	1		Waukee	11,945	13	12	1
	Fairfield	9,354	19	13	6		Waukon	4,013	6	6	0
	Forest City	4,202	8	8	0		Waverly	9,396	17	16	1
	Fort Dodge	25,330	42	37	5		Webster City	8,004	17	13	4
	Fort Madison	10,841	23	18	5		West Burlington	3,376	9	9	0
	Garner	2,990	5	5	0		West Des Moines	54,988	78	63	15
	Glenwood	5,816	10	9	1		West Liberty	3,695	7	6	1
	Grinnell	9,408	17	15	2		West Union	2,436	1	1	0
	Grundy Center	2,581	3	3	0		Williamsburg	2,831	6	6	0
	Hampton	4,226	12	7	5		Wilton	2,862	4	4	0
	Harlan	5,111	9	8	1		Windsor Heights	4,506	14	13	1
	Hawarden	2,426	4	4	0		Winterset	4,970	8	8	0
	Hiawatha	6,642	12	11	1	KANSAS	Abilene	6,419	16	14	2
	Humboldt	4,379	7	7	0		Alma	754	1	1	0
	Independence	6,118	11	11	0		Altamont	1,060	3	3	0
	Indianola	14,399	21	19	2		Andale	835	2	2	0
	Iowa City	62,700	102	73	29		Andover	9,955	26	19	7
	Iowa Falls	5,040	15	11	4		Anthony	2,217	5	5	0
	Jefferson	4,337	7	7	0		Arkansas City	11,342	34	25	9
	Johnston	15,622	22	21	1		Arma	1,484	5	5	0
	Keokuk	10,585	33	23	10		Atchison	10,138	25	23	2
	Knoxville	7,434	13	11	2		Attica	587	1	1	0
	Le Claire	3,181	7	6	1		Atwood	1,104	2	2	0
	Le Mars	9,375	16	14	2		Augusta	8,715	32	24	8
	Leon	1,923	3	3	0		Baldwin City	4,255	10	9	1
	Manchester	4,958	13	9	4		Basehor	3,742	13	11	2
	Maquoketa	6,006	17	11	6		Baxter Springs	4,164	13	9	4
	Marion	31,772	49	40	9		Bel Aire	6,739	13	12	1

Table 78.   Full-Time Law Enforcement Employees by State by City, 2007 *(Contd.)*

(Number.)

State	City	Popula-tion	Total law enforce-ment employees	Total officers	Total civilians	State	City	Popula-tion	Total law enforce-ment employees	Total officers	Total civilians
	Belle Plaine	1,576	5	5	0		Horton	1,821	10	6	4
	Belleville	1,869	5	5	0		Howard	760	1	1	0
	Beloit	3,591	8	7	1		Hugoton	3,552	8	6	2
	Benton	817	1	1	0		Humboldt	1,891	6	6	0
	Bonner Springs	7,121	27	24	3		Hutchinson	40,941	106	68	38
	Buhler	1,336	3	3	0		Independence	9,229	31	20	11
	Burden	544	1	1	0		Inman	1,189	2	2	0
	Burlingame	1,002	2	2	0		Iola	5,916	26	17	9
	Burrton	897	2	2	0		Junction City	15,727	66	48	18
	Bushton	290	1	1	0		Kansas City	143,371	470	361	109
	Caldwell	1,181	3	3	0		Kechi	1,645	4	3	1
	Canton	800	2	2	0		Kingman	3,072	6	6	0
	Carbondale	1,434	3	3	0		Kinsley	1,458	4	4	0
	Cawker City	457	1	1	0		Kiowa	953	1	1	0
	Cedar Vale	637	1	1	0		La Cygne	1,161	2	2	0
	Chanute	8,822	24	21	3		La Harpe	659	2	2	0
	Chapman	1,262	4	4	0		Lake Quivira	924	3	3	0
	Chase	455	1	1	0		Lansing	10,861	18	16	2
	Cheney	1,973	4	4	0		Larned	3,677	11	8	3
	Cherokee	711	1	1	0		Lawrence	90,044	173	140	33
	Chetopa	1,227	4	4	0		Leavenworth	34,918	83	60	23
	Claflin	641	1	1	0		Leawood	31,121	82	59	23
	Clay Center	4,305	7	6	1		Lenexa	45,059	129	83	46
	Coffeyville	10,280	32	26	6		Liberal	20,477	42	31	11
	Colby	4,854	17	12	5		Lindsborg	3,282	7	6	1
	Coldwater	752	1	1	0		Linn Valley	594	2	2	0
	Columbus	3,216	11	9	2		Little River	526	1	1	0
	Colwich	1,380	2	2	0		Louisburg	3,739	8	8	0
	Concordia	5,229	15	10	5		Lyndon	1,026	2	2	0
	Conway Springs	1,221	2	2	0		Lyons	3,460	8	7	1
	Council Grove	2,273	7	6	1		Marion	1,978	5	5	0
	Derby	21,531	50	36	14		Marysville	3,110	9	8	1
	Dodge City	26,236	61	48	13		McPherson	13,577	31	25	6
	Eastborough	788	7	7	0		Medicine Lodge	2,010	7	6	1
	Edwardsville	4,565	15	14	1		Merriam	10,733	33	28	5
	El Dorado	12,693	27	25	2		Minneapolis	2,021	5	5	0
	Elkhart	1,969	3	3	0		Mission	9,691	32	29	3
	Ellinwood	1,985	5	5	0		Moran	531	1	1	0
	Ellis	1,849	5	5	0		Moundridge	1,635	3	3	0
	Ellsworth	2,869	7	6	1		Mount Hope	853	2	2	0
	Elwood	1,144	5	5	0		Mulberry	566	2	2	0
	Emporia	26,125	64	44	20		Mulvane	5,836	18	12	6
	Enterprise	811	1	1	0		Neodesha	2,635	8	7	1
	Erie	1,146	3	2	1		Newton	18,164	36	32	4
	Eudora	6,323	11	9	2		Nickerson	1,160	4	4	0
	Fairway	3,815	10	9	1		North Newton	1,574	2	2	0
	Florence	633	1	1	0		Norton	2,726	5	5	0
	Fort Scott	7,922	25	19	6		Norwich	505	1	1	0
	Fredonia	2,446	7	6	1		Oakley	1,870	10	5	5
	Frontenac	3,134	9	6	3		Oberlin	1,739	4	4	0
	Galena	3,150	13	7	6		Olathe	117,973	208	163	45
	Galva	804	1	1	0		Osage City	2,936	6	6	0
	Garden City	26,949	75	50	25		Osawatomie	4,578	17	11	6
	Garden Plain	842	2	2	0		Osborne	1,388	4	4	0
	Gardner	16,658	38	35	3		Oswego	1,993	5	5	0
	Garnett	3,272	12	8	4		Ottawa	12,901	31	26	5
	Girard	2,645	7	6	1		Overbrook	962	2	2	0
	Goddard	3,836	7	7	0		Overland Park	169,224	305	252	53
	Goodland	4,289	10	9	1		Oxford	1,092	3	3	0
	Grandview Plaza	995	6	6	0		Paola	5,378	22	16	6
	Great Bend	15,562	32	28	4		Park City	7,603	21	19	2
	Halstead	1,907	6	5	1		Parsons	11,190	32	25	7
	Harper	1,431	3	3	0		Peabody	1,264	3	3	0
	Haven	1,170	3	3	0		Perry	863	1	1	0
	Hays	19,672	49	31	18		Pittsburg	19,104	50	39	11
	Haysville	10,227	31	24	7		Plainville	1,843	5	5	0
	Herington	2,459	5	4	1		Pleasanton	1,367	2	2	0
	Hesston	3,666	7	6	1		Prairie Village	21,312	58	46	12
	Hiawatha	3,207	6	5	1		Pratt	6,389	21	14	7
	Hill City	1,415	4	4	0		Protection	525	1	1	0
	Hillsboro	2,694	5	5	0		Richmond	512	1	1	0
	Hoisington	2,816	9	7	2		Roeland Park	6,916	17	15	2
	Holcomb	1,880	2	1	1		Rolla	431	1	1	0
	Holton	3,364	12	8	4		Rose Hill	4,028	10	9	1

Table 78. Full-Time Law Enforcement Employees by State by City, 2007 *(Contd.)*

(Number.)

State	City	Population	Total law enforcement employees	Total officers	Total civilians	State	City	Population	Total law enforcement employees	Total officers	Total civilians
	Rossville	1,008	3	3	0		Campton	411	1	1	0
	Russell	4,224	9	8	1		Caneyville	663	1	1	0
	Sabetha	2,506	5	5	0		Carlisle	2,133	9	6	3
	Salina	46,180	105	75	30		Carrollton	3,888	10	9	1
	Scott City	3,459	12	7	5		Catlettsburg	1,901	8	8	0
	Scranton	698	1	1	0		Cave City	2,088	7	7	0
	Sedan	1,210	3	3	0		Central City	5,763	12	12	0
	Sedgwick	1,657	2	2	0		Clarkson	839	1	1	0
	Seneca	2,054	6	6	0		Clay	1,176	1	1	0
	Shawnee	60,950	109	89	20		Clay City	1,365	2	2	0
	Silver Lake	1,356	2	2	0		Clinton	1,331	2	2	0
	Smith Center	1,653	3	3	0		Cloverport	1,248	1	1	0
	South Hutchinson	2,477	9	7	2		Cold Spring	5,758	12	11	1
	Spearville	879	1	1	0		Columbia	4,195	10	10	0
	Spring Hill	5,203	13	11	2		Corbin	8,344	29	21	8
	Stafford	1,041	4	4	0		Covington	42,682	130	105	25
	Sterling	2,537	5	5	0		Crab Orchard	873	1	1	0
	St. Francis	1,340	3	3	0		Crescent Springs	3,988	8	8	0
	St. George	514	1	1	0		Crofton	777	1	1	0
	St. John	1,185	4	4	0		Cumberland	2,308	5	5	0
	St. Marys	2,240	5	5	0		Cynthiana	6,291	14	13	1
	Stockton	1,421	5	5	0		Danville	15,377	30	28	2
	Tonganoxie	4,312	11	10	1		Dawson Springs	2,947	8	4	4
	Topeka	121,885	328	277	51		Dayton	5,443	10	9	1
	Towanda	1,371	4	3	1		Earlington	1,593	1	1	0
	Troy	1,018	1	1	0		Eddyville	2,408	6	6	0
	Udall	758	1	1	0		Edgewood	8,789	13	13	0
	Valley Center	6,044	13	9	4		Edmonton	1,624	7	7	0
	Valley Falls	1,182	2	2	0		Elizabethtown	23,547	59	43	16
	Victoria	1,161	2	2	0		Elkhorn City	1,023	3	3	0
	Wa Keeney	1,716	5	5	0		Elkton	1,962	7	7	0
	Wakefield	883	1	1	0		Elsmere	7,848	12	11	1
	Walton	291	1	1	0		Eminence	2,264	7	7	0
	Wamego	4,243	12	7	5		Erlanger	16,986	44	36	8
	Waterville	619	1	1	0		Evarts	1,056	4	4	0
	Wathena	1,297	2	2	0		Falmouth	2,129	8	7	1
	Wellington	7,898	18	16	2		Flatwoods	7,647	11	10	1
	Wellsville	1,694	4	3	1		Fleming-Neon	805	2	2	0
	Westwood	1,832	8	7	1		Flemingsburg	3,105	7	7	0
	Wichita	358,294	836	645	191		Florence	27,405	62	58	4
	Winfield	11,672	29	22	7		Fort Mitchell	7,476	13	13	0
	Yates Center	1,451	3	3	0		Fort Thomas	15,266	22	21	1
KENTUCKY.............	Albany	2,323	9	8	1		Fort Wright	5,379	13	12	1
	Alexandria	7,948	15	13	2		Frankfort	26,984	70	65	5
	Allen	149	1	1	0		Franklin	8,101	23	22	1
	Anchorage	2,804	15	10	5		Fulton	2,435	14	10	4
	Ashland	21,482	56	49	7		Gamaliel	434	1	1	0
	Auburn	1,509	2	2	0		Georgetown	20,997	55	48	7
	Audubon Park	1,568	8	7	1		Glasgow	14,282	45	34	11
	Augusta	1,258	3	3	0		Glencoe	251	1	1	0
	Barbourville	3,561	18	14	4		Graymoor-Devondale	3,008	4	4	0
	Bardstown	11,158	29	23	6		Grayson	3,997	12	12	0
	Bardwell	789	1	1	0		Greensburg	2,408	6	6	0
	Beattyville	1,135	7	5	2		Greenup	1,187	3	3	0
	Beaver Dam	3,181	6	6	0		Greenville	4,258	9	9	0
	Bellefonte	846	4	4	0		Guthrie	1,441	4	4	0
	Bellevue	5,871	11	10	1		Hardinsburg	2,466	4	4	0
	Benham	547	3	3	0		Harlan	1,893	11	9	2
	Benton	4,388	9	7	2		Harrodsburg	8,164	25	15	10
	Berea	13,946	31	28	3		Hartford	2,685	6	6	0
	Bloomfield	887	1	1	0		Hawesville	983	1	1	0
	Booneville	150	2	2	0		Hazard	4,862	27	22	5
	Bowling Green	53,663	136	101	35		Henderson	27,960	67	58	9
	Brandenburg	2,212	5	5	0		Heritage Creek	1,654	9	9	0
	Brooksville	613	1	1	0		Hickman	2,253	3	3	0
	Brownsville	1,045	3	3	0		Highland Heights	5,708	10	10	0
	Burgin	916	1	1	0		Hillview	7,506	13	13	0
	Burkesville	1,730	9	5	4		Hindman	768	2	2	0
	Burnside	681	5	5	0		Hodgenville	2,781	5	5	0
	Butler	648	1	1	0		Hollow Creek	846	1	1	0
	Cadiz	2,604	9	8	1		Hopkinsville	27,197	78	72	6
	Calhoun	803	1	1	0		Hustonville	358	1	1	0
	Campbellsburg	716	1	1	0		Hyden	195	4	4	0
	Campbellsville	10,957	23	21	2		Independence	21,038	30	29	1

Table 78.   Full-Time Law Enforcement Employees by State by City, 2007 *(Contd.)*

(Number.)

State	City	Popula-tion	Total law enforce-ment employees	Total officers	Total civilians	State	City	Popula-tion	Total law enforce-ment employees	Total officers	Total civilians
	Indian Hills	3,149	8	8	0		Princeton	6,402	13	12	1
	Inez	450	2	2	0		Prospect	5,044	10	9	1
	Irvine	2,699	6	6	0		Providence	3,521	5	5	0
	Irvington	1,421	4	4	0		Raceland	2,548	6	6	0
	Jackson	2,401	15	13	2		Radcliff	21,560	53	40	13
	Jamestown	1,738	6	6	0		Ravenna	676	2	2	0
	Jeffersontown	25,837	58	49	9		Richmond	32,017	92	62	30
	Jenkins	2,288	5	5	0		Russell	3,598	12	12	0
	Junction City	2,183	3	3	0		Russell Springs	2,573	9	8	1
	La Center	1,029	3	2	1		Russellville	7,351	21	19	2
	La Grange	6,238	12	12	0		Sadieville	309	1	1	0
	Lakeside Park-Crestview Hills	6,205	10	9	1		Salyersville	1,601	3	3	0
	Lancaster	4,452	9	9	0		Science Hill	658	3	2	1
	Lawrenceburg	9,710	21	13	8		Scottsville	4,567	20	13	7
	Lebanon	5,980	23	15	8		Sebree	1,554	1	1	0
	Lebanon Junction	1,994	5	5	0		Shelbyville	11,101	24	23	1
	Leitchfield	6,561	14	13	1		Shepherdsville	9,123	23	22	1
	Lewisburg	924	1	1	0		Shively	15,621	24	19	5
	Lewisport	1,658	2	2	0		Somerset	12,344	35	32	3
	Lexington	272,815	635	558	77		Southgate	3,291	7	7	0
	Liberty	1,903	5	5	0		Springfield	2,845	13	8	5
	London	7,922	38	35	3		Stanford	3,467	8	8	0
	Lone Oak	437	1	1	0		Stanton	3,153	8	8	0
	Louisa	2,076	6	6	0		St. Matthews	17,676	36	30	6
	Louisville Metro	624,030	1,426	1,179	247		Sturgis	1,967	4	4	0
	Loyall	718	1	1	0		Taylor Mill	6,682	11	10	1
	Ludlow	4,809	11	10	1		Taylorsville	1,226	4	4	0
	Lynch	838	3	3	0		Tompkinsville	2,656	10	8	2
	Lynnview	980	3	3	0		Uniontown	1,046	2	2	0
	Madisonville	19,293	45	37	8		Vanceburg	1,722	6	6	0
	Manchester	1,945	10	10	0		Versailles	7,726	42	41	1
	Marion	3,022	7	5	2		Villa Hills	7,672	9	8	1
	Martin	636	3	3	0		Vine Grove	3,915	7	7	0
	Mayfield	10,326	27	20	7		Warsaw	1,832	6	6	0
	Maysville	9,205	30	23	7		Wayland	292	1	1	0
	McKee	864	3	3	0		West Liberty	3,362	16	8	8
	Middlesboro	10,077	28	24	4		West Point	992	3	3	0
	Millersburg	872	1	1	0		Wilder	3,037	6	6	0
	Monticello	6,120	8	8	0		Williamsburg	5,192	12	12	0
	Morehead	7,575	29	19	10		Williamstown	3,465	7	7	0
	Morganfield	3,365	13	8	5		Wilmore	5,862	10	9	1
	Morgantown	2,538	6	6	0		Winchester	16,515	46	34	12
	Mortons Gap	953	1	1	0		Wingo	600	1	1	0
	Mount Olivet	293	1	1	0		Worthington	1,686	4	4	0
	Mount Sterling	6,569	25	23	2		Wurtland	1,051	1	1	0
	Mount Vernon	2,622	8	8	0	LOUISIANA	Abbeville	11,797	41	33	8
	Mount Washington	12,334	16	15	1		Addis	3,145	9	8	1
	Muldraugh	1,309	3	3	0		Alexandria	45,720	195	162	33
	Munfordville	1,624	3	3	0		Amite	4,278	28	28	0
	Murray	15,811	37	31	6		Baker	13,600	36	34	2
	New Castle	932	1	1	0		Baldwin	2,618	8	7	1
	New Haven	876	1	1	0		Ball	3,727	6	5	1
	Newport	15,540	53	48	5		Basile	2,392	12	7	5
	Nicholasville	25,495	62	54	8		Bastrop	12,249	38	36	2
	Nortonville	1,250	1	1	0		Baton Rouge	228,446	909	632	277
	Oak Grove	7,303	17	14	3		Berwick	4,312	11	11	0
	Olive Hill	1,823	5	5	0		Blanchard	2,468	6	5	1
	Owensboro	55,702	133	102	31		Bogalusa	12,927	59	37	22
	Owenton	1,491	5	4	1		Bossier City	61,993	237	196	41
	Owingsville	1,596	5	5	0		Breaux Bridge	8,047	18	14	4
	Paducah	25,550	84	70	14		Broussard	7,466	24	21	3
	Paintsville	4,176	10	9	1		Brusly	2,130	7	6	1
	Paris	9,329	29	27	2		Church Point	4,734	14	13	1
	Park Hills	2,748	6	6	0		Clarence	493	2	2	0
	Pembroke	754	1	1	0		Clinton	1,907	6	5	1
	Perryville	752	1	1	0		Coushatta	2,166	6	6	0
	Pewee Valley	1,598	1	1	0		Covington	9,745	47	36	11
	Pikeville	6,331	29	21	8		Crowley	13,992	39	32	7
	Pineville	1,997	7	7	0		Delhi	3,013	11	7	4
	Pioneer Village	2,687	5	5	0		Denham Springs	10,552	39	32	7
	Pippa Passes	448	1	1	0		De Quincy	3,192	14	14	0
	Powderly	892	1	1	0		De Ridder	10,143	28	22	6
	Prestonsburg	3,850	17	17	0		Dixie Inn	348	3	3	0
							Elton	1,252	11	7	4

SECTION V: LAW ENFORCEMENT PERSONNEL 417

Table 78. Full-Time Law Enforcement Employees by State by City, 2007 *(Contd.)*

(Number.)

State	City	Popula-tion	Total law enforce-ment employees	Total officers	Total civilians	State	City	Popula-tion	Total law enforce-ment employees	Total officers	Total civilians
	Erath	2,205	14	10	4		Vinton	3,131	13	11	2
	Eunice	11,621	41	30	11		Washington	1,064	7	7	0
	Farmerville	3,567	13	13	0		Westlake	4,526	23	13	10
	Ferriday	3,588	20	13	7		West Monroe	12,989	81	77	4
	Franklin	7,794	25	23	2		Westwego	9,957	44	41	3
	Franklinton	3,723	22	16	6		Winnfield	5,183	23	14	9
	French Settlement	1,100	2	2	0		Youngsville	6,189	9	7	2
	Golden Meadow	2,158	3	3	0		Zachary	13,428	45	42	3
	Gonzales	9,067	36	36	0	MAINE	Ashland	1,460	3	3	0
	Grambling	4,474	14	9	5		Auburn	23,150	54	49	5
	Gramercy	6,946	5	5	0		Augusta	18,572	56	41	15
	Gretna	16,240	114	89	25		Baileyville	1,593	6	6	0
	Hammond	19,190	99	75	24		Bangor	30,940	93	73	20
	Harahan	9,212	27	22	5		Bar Harbor	5,197	13	9	4
	Haughton	2,997	9	7	2		Bath	9,175	22	18	4
	Haynesville	2,492	7	7	0		Belfast	6,866	14	12	2
	Homer	3,472	12	11	1		Berwick	7,603	13	12	1
	Houma	32,597	83	68	15		Bethel	2,671	4	4	0
	Independence	1,826	16	16	0		Biddeford	22,079	72	48	24
	Iowa	2,565	15	10	5		Boothbay Harbor	2,340	7	6	1
	Jackson	3,714	5	5	0		Brewer	9,101	22	20	2
	Jeanerette	6,015	11	11	0		Bridgton	5,325	11	7	4
	Jena	2,850	7	6	1		Brownville	1,306	2	2	0
	Jennings	10,577	36	34	2		Brunswick	22,048	51	36	15
	Kaplan	5,192	21	15	6		Bucksport	4,969	11	7	4
	Kenner	66,473	225	171	54		Buxton	8,284	14	9	5
	Kentwood	2,302	10	9	1		Calais	3,253	12	8	4
	Kinder	2,148	18	12	6		Camden	5,327	13	12	1
	Krotz Springs	1,268	5	3	2		Cape Elizabeth	8,806	17	13	4
	Lafayette	114,212	291	225	66		Caribou	8,279	16	15	1
	Lake Arthur	2,894	10	6	4		Carrabassett Valley	467	1	1	0
	Lake Charles	69,966	181	174	7		Clinton	3,400	3	3	0
	Leesville	5,763	34	29	5		Cumberland	7,728	12	11	1
	Mandeville	12,346	52	37	15		Damariscotta	1,965	6	5	1
	Mansfield	5,466	17	13	4		Dexter	3,720	6	5	1
	Many	2,777	11	9	2		Dixfield	2,564	4	4	0
	Marksville	5,787	22	17	5		Dover-Foxcroft	4,391	5	5	0
	McNary	199	2	1	1		East Millinocket	3,171	4	4	0
	Minden	13,238	30	29	1		Eastport	1,575	4	4	0
	Monroe	51,350	220	175	45		Eliot	6,453	9	8	1
	Moreauville	944	2	2	0		Ellsworth	7,165	19	15	4
	Morgan City	11,802	52	34	18		Fairfield	6,808	13	12	1
	Napoleonville	685	2	1	1		Falmouth	10,591	23	17	6
	Natchitoches	17,680	64	48	16		Farmington	7,603	13	12	1
	Newllano	2,031	11	6	5		Fort Fairfield	3,510	4	4	0
	New Orleans	220,614	1,666	1,416	250		Fort Kent	4,202	8	4	4
	Oakdale	7,997	17	17	0		Freeport	8,190	17	12	5
	Olla	1,352	4	4	0		Fryeburg	3,363	5	5	0
	Opelousas	23,223	65	50	15		Gardiner	6,174	12	10	2
	Patterson	5,223	19	19	0		Gorham	15,593	24	22	2
	Pearl River	2,170	16	10	6		Gouldsboro	2,040	2	2	0
	Pineville	14,540	64	56	8		Greenville	1,759	3	2	1
	Plaquemine	6,627	30	25	5		Hallowell	2,521	5	5	0
	Ponchatoula	6,244	25	20	5		Hampden	6,847	12	11	1
	Port Allen	5,136	24	20	4		Holden	2,961	2	2	0
	Port Barre	2,353	15	8	7		Houlton	6,258	18	13	5
	Port Vincent	552	2	2	0		Jay	4,847	8	7	1
	Rayne	8,628	23	23	0		Kennebunk	11,658	29	21	8
	Richwood	2,090	20	13	7		Kennebunkport	4,070	13	12	1
	Ruston	20,532	48	39	9		Kittery	10,645	27	20	7
	Scott	8,091	22	21	1		Lewiston	35,747	94	81	13
	Shreveport	199,811	679	595	84		Limestone	2,298	3	3	0
	Simmesport	2,228	10	10	0		Lincoln	5,235	5	4	1
	Slidell	28,272	114	88	26		Lisbon	9,474	21	16	5
	Sorrento	1,443	6	5	1		Livermore Falls	3,200	10	6	4
	Sterlington	1,240	9	9	0		Machias	2,191	4	4	0
	St. Gabriel	5,592	13	8	5		Madawaska	4,402	7	6	1
	St. Martinville	7,012	18	13	5		Madison	4,673	7	6	1
	Stonewall	1,927	2	2	0		Mechanic Falls	3,256	5	5	0
	Sulphur	19,362	63	42	21		Mexico	2,932	5	5	0
	Sunset	2,580	12	12	0		Milbridge	1,316	3	3	0
	Thibodaux	14,501	47	38	9		Millinocket	4,927	9	9	0
	Tickfaw	687	8	8	0		Milo	2,414	3	3	0
	Vidalia	4,189	26	20	6		Monmouth	3,849	4	4	0

Table 78. Full-Time Law Enforcement Employees by State by City, 2007 *(Contd.)*

(Number.)

State	City	Population	Total law enforcement employees	Total officers	Total civilians	State	City	Population	Total law enforcement employees	Total officers	Total civilians
	Mount Desert	2,214	10	6	4		Forest Heights	2,656	6	5	1
	Newport	3,106	6	6	0		Frederick	59,731	181	146	35
	North Berwick	4,911	9	8	1		Frostburg	7,809	15	12	3
	Norway	4,846	7	6	1		Fruitland	4,193	17	16	1
	Oakland	6,239	10	9	1		Glenarden	6,340	4	3	1
	Ogunquit	1,295	12	10	2		Greenbelt	22,090	64	53	11
	Old Orchard Beach	9,423	26	18	8		Greensboro	2,016	4	4	0
	Old Town	7,704	16	15	1		Hagerstown	39,263	127	99	28
	Orono	9,737	15	14	1		Hampstead	5,535	10	8	2
	Oxford	3,954	6	5	1		Hancock	1,721	4	3	1
	Paris	5,048	9	8	1		Havre de Grace	12,584	40	31	9
	Phippsburg	2,205	1	1	0		Hurlock	2,015	9	8	1
	Pittsfield	4,296	6	6	0		Hyattsville	15,152	48	37	11
	Portland	62,894	221	163	58		Landover Hills	1,575	4	3	1
	Presque Isle	9,217	23	20	3		La Plata	9,090	13	12	1
	Rangeley	1,168	3	3	0		Laurel	22,086	71	55	16
	Richmond	3,440	5	5	0		Luke	74	1	1	0
	Rockland	7,582	22	19	3		Manchester	3,609	5	5	0
	Rockport	3,590	7	6	1		Morningside	1,305	8	7	1
	Rumford	6,405	15	14	1		Mount Rainier	8,660	19	16	3
	Sabattus	4,702	8	7	1		New Carrollton	12,712	14	12	2
	Saco	18,509	44	32	12		North East	2,856	8	7	1
	Sanford	21,648	53	39	14		Oakland	1,869	7	6	1
	Scarborough	19,187	48	33	15		Ocean City	7,005	131	105	26
	Searsport	2,668	2	2	0		Ocean Pines	11,134	18	13	5
	Skowhegan	8,876	13	13	0		Oxford	735	3	3	0
	South Berwick	7,350	12	8	4		Perryville	3,826	7	5	2
	South Portland	23,836	68	52	16		Pocomoke City	3,863	23	16	7
	Southwest Harbor	1,982	5	5	0		Port Deposit	704	3	3	0
	Swan's Island	311	1	1	0		Preston	647	2	2	0
	Thomaston	4,203	5	5	0		Princess Anne	2,934	13	11	2
	Topsham	10,073	14	13	1		Ridgely	1,485	6	6	0
	Van Buren	2,520	4	4	0		Rising Sun	1,821	6	5	1
	Veazie	1,873	5	5	0		Riverdale Park	6,584	23	17	6
	Waldoboro	5,123	5	4	1		Rock Hall	1,424	4	4	0
	Washburn	1,616	1	1	0		Salisbury	27,727	114	87	27
	Waterville	15,631	40	31	9		Seat Pleasant	5,020	15	14	1
	Wells	10,142	26	20	6		Smithsburg	3,031	4	3	1
	Westbrook	16,188	37	35	2		Snow Hill	2,278	9	8	1
	Wilton	4,210	5	5	0		St. Michaels	1,088	7	6	1
	Windham	16,814	37	26	11		Sykesville	4,499	8	7	1
	Winslow	7,979	10	9	1		Takoma Park	18,539	54	40	14
	Winthrop	6,514	14	9	5		Taneytown	5,533	12	11	1
	Wiscasset	3,904	15	14	1		Thurmont	6,092	11	9	2
	Yarmouth	8,106	20	12	8		Trappe	1,179	1	1	0
	York	13,384	38	27	11		University Park	2,379	8	8	0
MARYLAND	Aberdeen	14,187	54	44	10		Upper Marlboro	681	4	4	0
	Annapolis	36,462	153	108	45		Westernport	1,971	5	4	1
	Baltimore	624,237	3,684	2,963	721		Westminster	18,036	59	45	14
	Baltimore City Sheriff		170	138	32	MASSACHUSETTS	Abington	16,673	30	28	2
	Bel Air	10,074	45	31	14		Acton	20,619	43	33	10
	Berlin	3,812	16	11	5		Acushnet	10,575	21	19	2
	Berwyn Heights	3,045	8	7	1		Adams	8,316	20	16	4
	Bladensburg	7,849	23	17	6		Agawam	28,573	54	46	8
	Boonsboro	3,286	4	4	0		Amesbury	16,551	37	31	6
	Bowie	53,672	29	25	4		Amherst	33,913	53	50	3
	Brunswick	5,282	11	9	2		Andover	33,615	71	52	19
	Cambridge	11,479	65	51	14		Aquinnah	356	4	4	0
	Capitol Heights	4,259	12	8	4		Arlington	40,902	77	61	16
	Centreville	3,099	10	9	1		Ashburnham	6,065	13	9	4
	Chestertown	4,942	14	13	1		Ashby	2,957	6	6	0
	Cheverly	6,614	17	15	2		Ashfield	1,826	2	2	0
	Chevy Chase Village	2,779	16	10	6		Ashland	15,818	31	27	4
	Cottage City	1,166	5	4	1		Athol	11,721	23	18	5
	Crisfield	2,804	14	11	3		Attleboro	43,474	89	76	13
	Cumberland	20,654	53	50	3		Auburn	16,445	45	35	10
	Delmar	2,590	13	12	1		Avon	4,310	19	15	4
	Denton	3,602	13	12	1		Ayer	7,306	22	17	5
	District Heights	6,253	15	12	3		Barnstable	47,342	133	114	19
	Easton	14,249	59	45	14		Barre	5,467	13	9	4
	Edmonston	1,381	7	6	1		Becket	1,804	2	2	0
	Elkton	15,228	40	34	6		Bedford	12,862	36	28	8
	Fairmount Heights	1,554	4	3	1		Belchertown	14,268	22	17	5
	Federalsburg	2,647	12	12	0		Bellingham	15,965	38	30	8

Table 78. Full-Time Law Enforcement Employees by State by City, 2007 *(Contd.)*

(Number.)

State	City	Population	Total law enforcement employees	Total officers	Total civilians	State	City	Population	Total law enforcement employees	Total officers	Total civilians
	Belmont	23,184	60	46	14		Groveland	6,863	13	8	5
	Berkley	6,494	7	6	1		Hadley	4,817	15	11	4
	Berlin	2,771	11	7	4		Halifax	7,834	16	11	5
	Beverly	39,493	72	68	4		Hamilton	8,262	20	15	5
	Billerica	41,568	85	64	21		Hampden	5,349	14	9	5
	Blackstone	9,067	19	16	3		Hanover	14,266	31	28	3
	Bolton	4,517	14	9	5		Hanson	10,054	25	21	4
	Boston	591,855	2,810	2,170	640		Hardwick	2,670	3	3	0
	Bourne	19,308	42	36	6		Harvard	6,062	14	9	5
	Boxborough	5,106	15	10	5		Harwich	12,573	40	34	6
	Boxford	8,155	14	13	1		Hatfield	3,266	1	1	0
	Boylston	4,295	13	10	3		Haverhill	60,308	100	91	9
	Braintree	34,147	84	76	8		Hingham	22,059	53	44	9
	Brewster	10,158	18	15	3		Hinsdale	1,782	1	1	0
	Bridgewater	25,767	36	35	1		Holbrook	10,724	23	22	1
	Brockton	94,180	220	192	28		Holden	16,816	26	23	3
	Brookfield	3,075	3	3	0		Holliston	13,903	25	24	1
	Brookline	54,976	148	125	23		Holyoke	39,769	145	124	21
	Buckland	2,002	2	2	0		Hopedale	6,277	16	12	4
	Burlington	24,978	71	62	9		Hopkinton	14,294	26	21	5
	Cambridge	101,161	294	262	32		Hubbardston	4,494	10	6	4
	Canton	21,890	43	42	1		Hudson	19,595	37	31	6
	Carlisle	4,870	10	10	0		Hull	11,261	33	24	9
	Carver	11,639	21	17	4		Ipswich	13,326	25	24	1
	Charlton	12,765	23	19	4		Kingston	12,581	32	24	8
	Chatham	6,811	27	21	6		Lakeville	10,770	21	16	5
	Chelmsford	33,740	69	53	16		Lancaster	7,043	12	11	1
	Chelsea	32,439	88	82	6		Lanesboro	2,914	6	6	0
	Chicopee	54,414	129	125	4		Lawrence	70,462	179	151	28
	Clinton	14,247	34	29	5		Lee	5,842	12	11	1
	Cohasset	7,213	24	18	6		Leicester	11,077	23	18	5
	Concord	16,766	43	35	8		Lenox	5,169	10	10	0
	Dalton	6,627	12	11	1		Leominster	41,602	90	72	18
	Danvers	25,979	60	47	13		Leverett	1,790	2	2	0
	Dartmouth	31,465	77	63	14		Lexington	30,220	61	47	14
	Dedham	23,653	70	60	10		Lincoln	7,929	19	13	6
	Deerfield	4,763	8	7	1		Littleton	8,713	19	14	5
	Dennis	15,666	50	41	9		Longmeadow	15,465	31	26	5
	Douglas	8,093	20	15	5		Lowell	102,918	308	229	79
	Dover	5,650	16	16	0		Ludlow	22,066	39	34	5
	Dracut	29,444	42	37	5		Lunenburg	10,105	13	13	0
	Dudley	10,951	16	12	4		Lynn	87,817	203	183	20
	Dunstable	3,278	7	7	0		Lynnfield	11,429	24	19	5
	Duxbury	14,659	35	27	8		Malden	55,538	110	103	7
	East Bridgewater	14,077	26	23	3		Manchester-by-the-Sea	5,301	22	16	6
	East Brookfield	2,095	4	4	0		Mansfield	23,175	48	36	12
	Eastham	5,519	21	15	6		Marblehead	20,194	38	29	9
	Easthampton	16,082	32	27	5		Marion	5,313	14	14	0
	East Longmeadow	15,061	24	23	1		Marlborough	38,227	74	63	11
	Easton	23,142	34	30	4		Marshfield	24,915	46	43	3
	Edgartown	3,939	16	15	1		Mattapoisett	6,502	18	18	0
	Egremont	1,364	3	3	0		Maynard	10,150	23	21	2
	Erving	1,574	4	4	0		Medfield	12,299	23	18	5
	Essex	3,328	12	8	4		Medford	55,706	111	107	4
	Everett	36,826	107	97	10		Medway	12,867	20	19	1
	Fairhaven	16,268	38	32	6		Melrose	26,549	44	43	1
	Fall River	91,413	300	244	56		Mendon	5,837	17	13	4
	Falmouth	33,722	71	63	8		Merrimac	6,420	11	7	4
	Fitchburg	40,180	99	90	9		Methuen	44,333	105	88	17
	Foxborough	16,276	35	29	6		Middleboro	21,503	45	41	4
	Framingham	64,482	123	115	8		Middleton	9,562	14	13	1
	Franklin	31,478	57	46	11		Milford	27,635	55	45	10
	Freetown	9,042	18	18	0		Millbury	13,711	24	20	4
	Gardner	20,813	41	31	10		Millis	7,977	18	14	4
	Georgetown	8,210	13	11	2		Millville	2,988	8	5	3
	Gill	1,387	3	3	0		Milton	25,888	61	46	15
	Gloucester	30,597	64	61	3		Monson	8,856	16	12	4
	Goshen	965	3	2	1		Montague	8,359	21	15	6
	Grafton	17,750	23	18	5		Nahant	3,544	13	12	1
	Granby	6,381	13	11	2		Nantucket	10,341	39	34	5
	Granville	1,689	1	1	0		Natick	31,854	65	53	12
	Great Barrington	7,423	14	13	1		Needham	28,343	55	45	10
	Greenfield	17,648	50	35	15		New Bedford	92,373	342	284	58
	Groton	10,737	22	17	5		New Braintree	1,130	1	1	0

Table 78.   Full-Time Law Enforcement Employees by State by City, 2007 *(Contd.)*

(Number.)

State	City	Population	Total law enforcement employees	Total officers	Total civilians	State	City	Population	Total law enforcement employees	Total officers	Total civilians
	Newbury	6,992	16	13	3		Sunderland	3,778	5	5	0
	Newburyport	17,317	33	30	3		Sutton	9,154	20	15	5
	Newton	82,731	195	152	43		Swampscott	14,097	35	33	2
	Norfolk	10,596	19	17	2		Swansea	16,271	37	31	6
	North Adams	13,738	30	25	5		Taunton	56,091	120	115	5
	Northampton	28,550	63	54	9		Templeton	7,812	13	9	4
	North Andover	27,271	51	39	12		Tewksbury	29,450	60	56	4
	North Attleboro	28,095	62	49	13		Tisbury	3,806	12	11	1
	Northborough	14,783	26	20	6		Topsfield	6,128	14	10	4
	Northbridge	14,596	22	17	5		Townsend	9,343	18	16	2
	North Brookfield	4,847	6	6	0		Truro	2,163	17	12	5
	Northfield	3,326	4	3	1		Tyngsboro	11,584	27	21	6
	North Reading	13,970	31	30	1		Upton	6,597	18	13	5
	Norton	19,423	29	28	1		Uxbridge	12,818	23	18	5
	Norwell	10,466	27	18	9		Wakefield	24,557	44	43	1
	Norwood	28,336	69	58	11		Walpole	23,199	44	39	5
	Oak Bluffs	3,768	17	15	2		Waltham	59,425	183	150	33
	Oakham	1,946	3	3	0		Ware	10,031	18	18	0
	Orange	7,762	13	12	1		Wareham	21,472	58	50	8
	Orleans	6,412	28	22	6		Warren	5,141	12	7	5
	Oxford	13,760	25	20	5		Watertown	32,065	81	68	13
	Palmer	12,991	26	20	6		Wayland	12,954	31	22	9
	Paxton	4,591	12	8	4		Webster	16,886	32	28	4
	Peabody	52,194	111	96	15		Wellesley	26,966	54	39	15
	Pembroke	18,932	30	28	2		Wellfleet	2,798	17	13	4
	Pepperell	11,454	19	18	1		Wenham	4,609	11	10	1
	Petersham	1,303	2	2	0		Westborough	18,740	34	28	6
	Phillipston	1,802	2	2	0		West Boylston	7,810	18	13	5
	Pittsfield	43,194	104	84	20		West Bridgewater	6,795	22	21	1
	Plainville	8,162	20	15	5		West Brookfield	3,879	6	6	0
	Plymouth	56,023	119	101	18		Westfield	40,518	91	79	12
	Plympton	2,787	7	7	0		Westford	21,624	46	36	10
	Princeton	3,547	8	5	3		Westminster	7,494	16	12	4
	Provincetown	3,411	25	18	7		West Newbury	4,306	12	6	6
	Quincy	91,382	226	198	28		Weston	11,665	31	25	6
	Randolph	30,233	48	48	0		Westport	15,280	33	29	4
	Raynham	13,975	35	26	9		West Springfield	27,854	92	81	11
	Reading	23,004	51	39	12		West Tisbury	2,673	10	9	1
	Rehoboth	11,551	27	22	5		Westwood	13,790	36	28	8
	Revere	46,658	107	97	10		Weymouth	53,553	113	97	16
	Rochester	5,530	10	10	0		Whitman	14,540	27	26	1
	Rockland	17,914	40	33	7		Wilbraham	14,123	29	28	1
	Rockport	7,677	18	17	1		Williamstown	8,159	16	12	4
	Rowley	5,927	16	14	2		Wilmington	21,545	48	46	2
	Russell	1,750	1	1	0		Winchendon	10,221	17	12	5
	Rutland	7,800	9	8	1		Winchester	21,155	46	38	8
	Salem	41,507	89	84	5		Winthrop	17,056	36	34	2
	Salisbury	8,506	20	14	6		Woburn	36,996	77	71	6
	Sandwich	20,584	35	34	1		Worcester	175,825	513	462	51
	Saugus	27,215	74	54	20		Wrentham	11,225	17	15	2
	Scituate	18,116	35	30	5		Yarmouth	24,304	69	59	10
	Seekonk	13,681	34	32	2	MICHIGAN...............	Adrian	21,612	36	33	3
	Sharon	17,100	31	27	4		Adrian Township	7,241	2	2	0
	Sheffield	3,372	6	6	0		Albion	9,267	29	24	5
	Shelburne	2,045	2	2	0		Algonac	4,585	8	7	1
	Sherborn	4,217	14	14	0		Allegan	4,963	12	11	1
	Shirley	7,661	16	12	4		Allen Park	27,384	51	46	5
	Shrewsbury	33,485	59	45	14		Alma	9,231	14	13	1
	Somerset	18,473	38	32	6		Almont	2,863	8	8	0
	Somerville	74,156	149	127	22		Alpena	10,554	20	18	2
	Southampton	6,010	8	8	0		Ann Arbor	113,011	205	150	55
	Southborough	9,674	21	16	5		Argentine Township	7,328	6	5	1
	Southbridge	17,109	39	36	3		Armada	1,640	2	2	0
	South Hadley	17,011	34	29	5		Auburn	2,058	3	2	1
	Southwick	9,719	20	16	4		Auburn Hills	21,149	69	54	15
	Spencer	12,153	21	17	4		Bad Axe	3,163	9	9	0
	Springfield	151,074	546	450	96		Bancroft	606	1	1	0
	Sterling	7,927	18	13	5		Bangor	1,881	4	4	0
	Stockbridge	2,256	6	6	0		Baraga	1,242	3	3	0
	Stoneham	21,374	41	34	7		Barry Township	3,659	2	2	0
	Stoughton	26,814	59	52	7		Bath Township	11,721	12	11	1
	Stow	6,263	11	11	0		Battle Creek	62,143	133	114	19
	Sturbridge	9,141	23	18	5		Bay City	34,145	66	61	5
	Sudbury	17,061	35	29	6		Beaverton	1,105	1	1	0

Table 78. Full-Time Law Enforcement Employees by State by City, 2007 (Contd.)

(Number.)

State	City	Population	Total law enforcement employees	Total officers	Total civilians
	Belding	5,872	8	7	1
	Bellaire	1,141	3	3	0
	Belleville	3,766	11	9	2
	Bellevue	1,361	2	2	0
	Benton Harbor	10,567	39	30	9
	Benton Township	15,626	33	22	11
	Berkley	14,906	34	28	6
	Berrien Springs-Oronoko Township	9,570	7	6	1
	Beverly Hills	9,955	28	24	4
	Big Rapids	10,536	19	18	1
	Birch Run	1,700	6	5	1
	Birmingham	19,149	51	35	16
	Blackman Township	25,461	29	28	1
	Blissfield	3,251	6	6	0
	Bloomfield Hills	3,818	27	23	4
	Bloomfield Township	41,231	98	75	23
	Bloomingdale	504	1	1	0
	Boyne City	3,193	8	7	1
	Breckenridge	1,303	2	2	0
	Bridgeport Township	11,134	9	8	1
	Bridgman	2,429	4	4	0
	Brighton	7,326	20	18	2
	Bronson	2,294	8	5	3
	Brown City	1,294	2	2	0
	Brownstown Township	30,336	47	36	11
	Buchanan	4,444	10	9	1
	Buena Vista Township	9,631	18	16	2
	Burr Oak	759	1	1	0
	Burton	30,958	47	42	5
	Byron	578	1	1	0
	Cadillac	10,329	18	15	3
	Calumet	797	1	1	0
	Cambridge Township	6,026	3	3	0
	Canton Township	88,126	121	84	37
	Capac	2,308	3	3	0
	Carleton	2,947	4	3	1
	Caro	4,136	9	8	1
	Carrollton Township	6,128	8	7	1
	Carson City	1,209	2	2	0
	Carsonville	486	1	1	0
	Caseville	870	2	2	0
	Caspian	2,082	1	1	0
	Cass City	2,568	4	4	0
	Cassopolis	1,792	5	5	0
	Cedar Springs	3,287	7	7	0
	Center Line	8,209	28	23	5
	Charlevoix	2,692	7	7	0
	Charlotte	9,047	20	19	1
	Cheboygan	5,114	10	9	1
	Chelsea	5,014	11	8	3
	Chesterfield Township	45,849	63	47	16
	Chikaming Township	3,686	6	5	1
	Chocolay Township	5,989	5	4	1
	Clare	3,198	9	8	1
	Clarkston	920	2	2	0
	Clawson	12,175	19	18	1
	Clayton Township	7,885	7	6	1
	Clay Township	9,848	16	12	4
	Clinton	2,439	4	4	0
	Clinton Township	96,948	139	107	32
	Clio	2,606	5	5	0
	Coldwater	10,711	19	18	1
	Coleman	1,252	1	1	0
	Coloma Township	6,662	10	8	2
	Colon	1,173	3	3	0
	Columbia Township	7,734	5	5	0
	Concord	1,110	2	2	0
	Constantine	2,149	6	5	1
	Corunna	3,375	4	3	1
	Covert Township	3,123	6	6	0
	Croswell	2,554	6	6	0
	Crystal Falls	1,636	4	4	0
	Davison	5,294	12	10	2
	Davison Township	18,940	20	18	2
	Dearborn	91,748	220	190	30
	Dearborn Heights	54,901	112	85	27
	Decatur	1,872	4	4	0
	Deckerville	917	1	1	0
	Denmark Township	1,842	1	1	0
	Denton Township	5,649	4	4	0
	Detroit	860,971	3,403	3,037	366
	Dewitt	4,399	7	6	1
	Dewitt Township	13,295	16	15	1
	Douglas	2,209	9	8	1
	Dowagiac	5,913	16	15	1
	Dryden Township	4,773	4	4	0
	Durand	3,836	6	6	0
	East Grand Rapids	10,309	32	29	3
	East Jordan	2,270	6	5	1
	East Lansing	45,979	93	61	32
	Eastpointe	32,797	57	52	5
	East Tawas	2,808	7	6	1
	Eaton Rapids	5,304	11	10	1
	Ecorse	10,450	25	23	2
	Edmore	1,256	1	1	0
	Elk Rapids	1,708	5	5	0
	Elkton	783	2	2	0
	Elsie	989	2	2	0
	Emmett Township	12,048	18	16	2
	Erie Township	4,780	6	5	1
	Escanaba	12,494	46	33	13
	Essexville	3,523	8	8	0
	Evart	1,717	4	4	0
	Farmington	9,930	30	23	7
	Farmington Hills	79,475	169	120	49
	Fenton	12,151	21	16	5
	Ferndale	21,207	54	45	9
	Flat Rock	9,739	31	26	5
	Flint	116,024	321	261	60
	Flint Township	32,626	47	39	8
	Flushing	8,014	14	13	1
	Flushing Township	10,394	11	10	1
	Forsyth Township	4,855	7	6	1
	Fowlerville	3,148	5	5	0
	Frankenmuth	4,777	7	7	0
	Frankfort	1,480	3	3	0
	Franklin	2,977	10	10	0
	Fraser	15,068	52	41	11
	Fremont	4,303	9	8	1
	Frost Township	1,153	1	1	0
	Fruitport	1,080	10	9	1
	Galesburg	1,910	4	3	1
	Garden City	28,282	45	36	9
	Gaylord	3,749	13	11	2
	Genesee Township	23,961	29	25	4
	Gerrish Township	3,198	6	6	0
	Gibraltar	5,300	11	10	1
	Gladstone	5,252	11	10	1
	Gladwin	2,984	5	5	0
	Grand Beach	245	4	4	0
	Grand Blanc	7,749	21	18	3
	Grand Blanc Township	36,319	54	45	9
	Grand Haven	10,478	37	32	5
	Grand Ledge	7,708	16	15	1
	Grand Rapids	192,376	390	320	70
	Grandville	16,838	28	26	2
	Grant	877	1	1	0
	Grayling	1,902	6	6	0
	Green Oak Township	18,279	15	13	2
	Greenville	8,374	21	17	4
	Grosse Ile Township	10,455	25	18	7
	Grosse Pointe	5,289	27	25	2
	Grosse Pointe Farms	9,099	49	35	14
	Grosse Pointe Park	11,606	49	43	6
	Grosse Pointe Shores	2,644	21	18	3
	Grosse Pointe Woods	15,998	46	40	6
	Hamburg Township	22,486	16	15	1

Table 78.   Full-Time Law Enforcement Employees by State by City, 2007 *(Contd.)*

(Number.)

State	City	Population	Total law enforcement employees	Total officers	Total civilians	State	City	Population	Total law enforcement employees	Total officers	Total civilians
	Hampton Township	9,827	11	10	1		Manton	1,201	1	1	0
	Hamtramck	21,448	43	43	0		Marenisco Township	1,822	1	1	0
	Hancock	4,156	7	7	0		Marine City	4,417	6	5	1
	Harbor Beach	1,670	4	4	0		Marion	829	1	1	0
	Harbor Springs	1,575	6	5	1		Marlette	2,047	4	4	0
	Harper Woods	13,284	38	35	3		Marquette	20,467	38	32	6
	Hart	2,004	3	3	0		Marshall	7,244	18	14	4
	Hartford	2,407	5	5	0		Marysville	10,135	17	14	3
	Hastings	7,091	16	14	2		Mason	8,191	14	13	1
	Hazel Park	18,211	40	36	4		Mattawan	2,945	5	5	0
	Hesperia	989	2	2	0		Mayville	1,017	2	2	0
	Hillsdale	7,842	17	15	2		Melvindale	10,469	26	23	3
	Holland	34,137	74	61	13		Memphis	1,123	2	2	0
	Holly	6,410	19	14	5		Mendon	922	2	2	0
	Homer	1,785	2	2	0		Menominee	8,537	15	13	2
	Home Township	1,563	1	1	0		Meridian Township	37,958	51	44	7
	Hopkins	563	2	2	0		Metamora Township	4,796	6	6	0
	Houghton	7,017	8	6	2		Michiana	197	3	3	0
	Howard City	1,615	3	3	0		Midland	41,540	51	48	3
	Howell	9,921	20	18	2		Milan	5,686	12	9	3
	Hudson	2,378	11	10	1		Milford	6,629	27	20	7
	Huntington Woods	5,866	18	17	1		Millington	1,104	1	1	0
	Huron Township	16,354	25	20	5		Monroe	21,787	49	44	5
	Imlay City	3,825	8	7	1		Montague	2,305	5	5	0
	Inkster	28,233	69	59	10		Montrose Township	7,919	9	8	1
	Ionia	12,595	19	17	2		Morenci	2,323	2	2	0
	Iron Mountain	7,963	14	14	0		Morrice	897	2	2	0
	Iron River	3,085	8	7	1		Mount Morris	3,308	7	6	1
	Ironwood	5,506	13	13	0		Mount Morris Township	22,966	35	32	3
	Ishpeming	6,440	11	10	1		Mount Pleasant	26,270	40	32	8
	Ishpeming Township	3,580	1	1	0		Mundy Township	14,577	22	20	2
	Ithaca	3,074	4	4	0		Munising	2,350	5	5	0
	Jackson	34,325	82	62	20		Muskegon	39,562	91	81	10
	Jonesville	2,281	5	5	0		Muskegon Heights	11,698	24	21	3
	Kalamazoo	71,462	299	245	54		Muskegon Township	18,634	16	15	1
	Kalamazoo Township	21,497	38	30	8		Napoleon Township	7,148	2	2	0
	Kalkaska	2,207	5	4	1		Nashville	1,697	2	2	0
	Keego Harbor	2,848	7	6	1		Negaunee	4,429	9	8	1
	Kentwood	46,748	85	69	16		Newaygo	1,670	5	4	1
	Kingsford	5,426	20	20	0		New Baltimore	12,071	21	17	4
	Kingston	436	1	1	0		Newberry	1,538	1	1	0
	Kinross Township	8,060	3	3	0		New Buffalo	2,429	8	7	1
	Laingsburg	1,276	2	2	0		New Haven	5,185	9	8	1
	Lake Angelus	312	5	5	0		Niles	11,491	32	22	10
	Lake Linden	1,050	1	1	0		North Branch	1,009	2	2	0
	Lake Odessa	2,281	4	4	0		Northfield Township	8,383	14	12	2
	Lake Orion	2,759	8	4	4		North Muskegon	3,968	7	7	0
	Lakeview	1,120	2	2	0		Northville	6,202	17	16	1
	L'anse	1,977	4	4	0		Northville Township	26,528	47	33	14
	Lansing	113,643	328	241	87		Norton Shores	23,567	31	29	2
	Lansing Township	7,822	15	14	1		Norvell Township	3,077	2	2	0
	Lapeer	9,372	23	20	3		Norway	2,897	4	4	0
	Lapeer Township	5,214	1	1	0		Novi	55,127	99	70	29
	Lathrup Village	4,112	8	8	0		Oak Park	30,771	77	65	12
	Laurium	2,001	4	4	0		Onaway	934	1	1	0
	Lawton	1,839	6	6	0		Ontwa Township-Edwardsburg	5,930	8	8	0
	Lennon	501	1	1	0		Orchard Lake	2,230	9	8	1
	Leoni Township	13,889	4	3	1		Oscoda Township	7,028	13	12	1
	Leslie	2,328	3	3	0		Otsego	3,900	7	6	1
	Lexington	1,086	3	3	0		Ovid	1,415	3	3	0
	Lincoln Park	37,294	56	47	9		Owosso	15,341	23	21	2
	Lincoln Township	14,496	13	11	2		Oxford	3,583	18	9	9
	Linden	3,560	5	5	0		Parchment	1,778	3	3	0
	Litchfield	1,422	3	3	0		Parma-Sandstone	6,902	2	2	0
	Livonia	96,261	180	146	34		Paw Paw	3,294	11	9	2
	Lowell	4,159	9	7	2		Pentwater	988	3	3	0
	Ludington	8,433	15	14	1		Perry	2,084	7	7	0
	Luna Pier	1,550	3	3	0		Petoskey	6,128	21	19	2
	Mackinac Island	465	7	6	1		Pigeon	1,099	1	1	0
	Mackinaw City	856	6	6	0		Pinckney	2,470	5	5	0
	Madison Heights	29,901	71	57	14		Pinconning	1,327	3	3	0
	Madison Township	7,977	2	2	0		Pittsfield Township	34,615	49	37	12
	Manistee	6,604	15	13	2		Plainwell	3,952	9	8	1
	Manistique	3,399	8	8	0						

Table 78. Full-Time Law Enforcement Employees by State by City, 2007 *(Contd.)*

(Number.)

State	City	Popula-tion	Total law enforce-ment employees	Total officers	Total civilians	State	City	Popula-tion	Total law enforce-ment employees	Total officers	Total civilians
	Pleasant Ridge	2,471	6	6	0		Tecumseh	8,878	16	14	2
	Plymouth	9,046	16	15	1		Thomas Township	12,670	8	7	1
	Plymouth Township	26,751	45	30	15		Three Oaks	1,731	3	3	0
	Pontiac	67,059	155	133	22		Three Rivers	7,245	20	16	4
	Portage	45,287	74	57	17		Tittabawassee Township	9,047	5	5	0
	Port Austin	673	1	1	0		Traverse City	14,406	36	33	3
	Port Huron	31,166	70	51	19		Trenton	19,011	37	36	1
	Portland	3,793	6	6	0		Troy	81,130	184	134	50
	Port Sanilac	637	1	1	0		Tuscarora Township	3,145	8	7	1
	Potterville	2,141	2	2	0		Ubly	796	2	2	0
	Prairieville Township	3,553	3	3	0		Unadilla Township	3,477	2	2	0
	Raisin Township	7,358	3	3	0		Union City	1,737	4	4	0
	Reading	1,096	1	1	0		Utica	5,022	20	16	4
	Redford Township	48,489	81	65	16		Van Buren Township	28,247	51	37	14
	Reed City	2,396	4	4	0		Vassar	2,738	5	5	0
	Reese	1,384	2	2	0		Vernon	813	1	1	0
	Richfield Township, Genesee County	8,874	10	8	2		Vicksburg	2,151	8	7	1
	Richfield Township, Roscommon County	4,249	6	6	0		Walker	23,794	47	38	9
							Walled Lake	6,988	17	14	3
	Richland	733	2	2	0		Warren	134,081	276	233	43
	Richland Township, Saginaw County	4,354	4	4	0		Waterford Township	71,233	99	77	22
	Richmond	5,804	12	9	3		Waterloo Township	3,035	3	3	0
	River Rouge	8,920	24	21	3		Watertown Township	2,222	1	1	0
	Riverview	12,447	31	29	2		Watervliet	1,769	3	3	0
	Rochester	11,360	25	20	5		Wayland	3,906	6	5	1
	Rockford	5,248	12	10	2		Wayne	18,203	48	37	11
	Rockwood	3,349	10	8	2		West Bloomfield Township	64,616	103	79	24
	Rogers City	3,131	8	8	0		West Branch	1,875	6	5	1
	Romeo	3,806	12	8	4		Westland	84,293	127	101	26
	Romulus	24,269	69	54	15		White Cloud	1,421	1	1	0
	Roosevelt Park	3,790	7	6	1		Whitehall	2,819	8	8	0
	Rose City	704	1	1	0		White Lake Township	30,412	37	27	10
	Roseville	47,329	94	84	10		White Pigeon	1,579	4	4	0
	Royal Oak	57,695	104	88	16		Williamston	3,825	9	8	1
	Saginaw	56,989	107	99	8		Wixom	13,572	25	21	4
	Saginaw Township	39,736	52	47	5		Wolverine Lake	4,307	6	6	0
	Saline	8,955	18	13	5		Woodhaven	13,514	34	30	4
	Sandusky	2,676	6	5	1		Woodstock Township	3,723	1	1	0
	Sault Ste. Marie	14,279	27	25	2		Wyandotte	26,290	49	38	11
	Schoolcraft	1,482	3	3	0		Wyoming	70,243	116	87	29
	Scottville	1,263	3	3	0		Yale	1,967	4	4	0
	Sebewaing	1,809	3	3	0		Ypsilanti	21,672	48	39	9
	Shelby	1,981	3	3	0		Zeeland	5,433	10	9	1
	Shelby Township	71,736	92	70	22		Zilwaukee	1,698	2	2	0
	Shepherd	1,347	2	2	0	**MINNESOTA**	Albany	2,072	5	4	1
	Southfield	75,830	188	156	32		Albert Lea	17,663	39	29	10
	Southgate	29,074	48	39	9		Alexandria	11,029	24	19	5
	South Haven	5,182	27	19	8		Annandale	3,114	5	5	0
	South Lyon	11,226	20	18	2		Anoka	17,413	33	26	7
	South Rockwood	1,646	4	4	0		Appleton	1,929	4	4	0
	Sparta	4,007	6	5	1		Apple Valley	50,794	59	50	9
	Spaulding Township	2,248	1	1	0		Aurora	1,720	4	4	0
	Spring Arbor Township	8,495	2	2	0		Austin	23,300	34	31	3
	Springfield	5,137	17	16	1		Avon	1,284	3	3	0
	Spring Lake-Ferrysburg	5,347	10	9	1		Babbitt	1,588	4	4	0
	Springport Township	2,272	2	2	0		Baxter	8,243	16	15	1
	St. Charles	2,107	3	3	0		Bayport	3,266	5	5	0
	St. Clair	5,938	11	10	1		Becker	4,294	6	5	1
	St. Clair Shores	60,900	100	84	16		Belgrade	705	2	2	0
	Sterling Heights	128,555	216	164	52		Belle Plaine	4,998	9	7	2
	St. Ignace	2,324	6	6	0		Bemidji	13,448	34	31	3
	St. Johns	7,329	11	9	2		Benson	3,096	8	7	1
	St. Joseph	8,600	24	18	6		Big Lake	9,852	14	11	3
	St. Joseph Township	9,827	13	12	1		Biwabik	944	3	3	0
	St. Louis	6,463	7	6	1		Blackduck	765	2	2	0
	Stockbridge	1,274	2	2	0		Blaine	56,747	69	57	12
	Sturgis	11,026	23	18	5		Blooming Prairie	1,975	3	3	0
	Sumpter Township	11,811	22	15	7		Bloomington	80,218	147	116	31
	Suttons Bay	591	2	2	0		Blue Earth	3,366	6	6	0
	Swartz Creek	5,394	9	8	1		Brainerd	13,731	33	26	7
	Sylvan Lake	1,654	5	5	0		Breckenridge	3,325	6	6	0
	Taylor	64,048	119	96	23		Brooklyn Center	27,118	55	44	11
							Brooklyn Park	70,112	116	90	26

Table 78. Full-Time Law Enforcement Employees by State by City, 2007 *(Contd.)*

(Number.)

State	City	Population	Total law enforcement employees	Total officers	Total civilians	State	City	Population	Total law enforcement employees	Total officers	Total civilians
	Browns Valley	619	3	3	0		Lino Lakes	20,334	28	25	3
	Brownton	795	2	2	0		Litchfield	6,655	10	9	1
	Buffalo	14,456	22	18	4		Little Falls	8,162	13	11	2
	Burnsville	59,127	81	72	9		Long Prairie	2,877	6	6	0
	Caledonia	2,910	4	4	0		Madison	1,605	3	3	0
	Cambridge	7,687	14	12	2		Mankato	35,331	62	49	13
	Cannon Falls	4,038	11	9	2		Maple Grove	62,145	76	63	13
	Centennial Lakes	11,454	19	17	2		Mapleton	1,633	3	3	0
	Champlin	23,463	30	25	5		Maplewood	35,444	60	54	6
	Chaska	24,764	27	24	3		Marshall	12,410	24	21	3
	Chisholm	4,592	12	11	1		Medina	5,033	11	10	1
	Cloquet	11,523	21	19	2		Melrose	3,146	6	5	1
	Cold Spring	3,726	9	8	1		Mendota Heights	11,318	19	17	2
	Columbia Heights	17,894	29	22	7		Milaca	3,073	7	6	1
	Coon Rapids	62,299	74	64	10		Minneapolis	371,240	1,084	848	236
	Corcoran	5,698	7	7	0		Minnetonka	49,751	74	55	19
	Cottage Grove	33,288	46	39	7		Minnetrista	8,350	14	11	3
	Crookston	7,752	16	14	2		Montevideo	5,305	11	10	1
	Crosby	2,232	9	8	1		Montgomery	3,308	7	6	1
	Crystal	21,325	37	27	10		Moorhead	35,052	62	49	13
	Dawson	1,405	3	3	0		Moose Lake	2,622	4	4	0
	Dayton	4,620	6	5	1		Mora	3,521	8	7	1
	Deephaven-Woodland	4,129	8	7	1		Morris	5,057	10	8	2
	Detroit Lakes	8,111	17	15	2		Mound	9,404	16	13	3
	Dilworth	3,600	7	6	1		Mounds View	11,921	21	19	2
	Duluth	83,932	169	143	26		Mountain Iron	2,902	5	5	0
	Eagan	63,718	82	69	13		Mountain Lake	1,982	4	4	0
	Eagle Lake	2,130	2	2	0		New Brighton	20,644	34	29	5
	East Grand Forks	7,896	24	22	2		New Hope	20,301	36	29	7
	Eden Prairie	61,910	87	65	22		Newport	3,606	8	8	0
	Edina	45,007	68	51	17		New Prague	7,153	11	9	2
	Elk River	23,224	40	30	10		New Richland	1,155	2	2	0
	Elmore	677	1	1	0		New Ulm	13,369	25	22	3
	Ely	3,565	8	7	1		North Branch	10,886	14	12	2
	Eveleth	3,577	11	10	1		Northfield	19,447	26	21	5
	Fairmont	10,337	20	17	3		North Mankato	12,295	13	12	1
	Faribault	22,408	39	30	9		North St. Paul	11,201	17	15	2
	Farmington	19,276	26	23	3		Oakdale	27,306	41	32	9
	Fergus Falls	13,842	29	23	6		Oak Park Heights	4,097	10	9	1
	Floodwood	493	3	3	0		Olivia	2,449	5	5	0
	Forest Lake	17,984	27	24	3		Orono	12,212	22	19	3
	Fridley	26,124	45	39	6		Ortonville	2,003	4	4	0
	Gilbert	1,743	5	5	0		Osakis	1,570	4	3	1
	Glencoe	5,644	11	10	1		Osseo	2,553	6	5	1
	Glenwood	2,553	4	4	0		Owatonna	24,796	37	34	3
	Golden Valley	19,865	36	27	9		Park Rapids	3,577	10	9	1
	Goodview	3,394	4	4	0		Paynesville	2,255	5	4	1
	Grand Rapids	8,297	21	17	4		Plainview	3,306	7	7	0
	Granite Falls	2,961	5	5	0		Plymouth	70,737	82	69	13
	Hallock	1,051	1	1	0		Princeton	4,885	12	10	2
	Hastings	21,839	32	27	5		Prior Lake	23,879	26	23	3
	Hermantown	9,247	15	13	2		Proctor	2,771	8	7	1
	Hibbing	16,198	32	29	3		Ramsey	23,617	27	22	5
	Hokah	582	1	1	0		Red Wing	15,705	33	27	6
	Hopkins	16,613	36	23	13		Redwood Falls	5,155	13	11	2
	Houston	991	1	1	0		Richfield	33,112	60	45	15
	Hoyt Lakes	1,957	5	5	0		Robbinsdale	13,211	26	21	5
	Hutchinson	14,050	34	23	11		Rochester	98,287	177	127	50
	International Falls	6,108	14	13	1		Rogers	6,802	15	13	2
	Inver Grove Heights	34,060	42	34	8		Roseau	2,827	8	7	1
	Jackson	3,429	6	5	1		Rosemount	21,393	24	21	3
	Janesville	2,201	3	3	0		Roseville	31,645	56	49	7
	Jordan	5,550	10	8	2		Sartell	13,816	19	17	2
	Kasson	5,737	9	8	1		Sauk Centre	3,906	7	6	1
	Kimball	691	3	3	0		Sauk Rapids	11,768	15	13	2
	La Crescent	5,106	8	7	1		Savage	28,266	34	29	5
	Lake City	5,409	11	10	1		Shakopee	35,113	53	47	6
	Lake Crystal	2,562	4	4	0		Silver Bay	1,913	5	5	0
	Lakefield	1,687	3	3	0		Silver Lake	814	2	2	0
	Lakes Area	8,333	15	13	2		Slayton	1,907	4	4	0
	Lakeville	54,565	62	52	10		Sleepy Eye	3,463	4	4	0
	Lester Prairie	1,737	3	3	0		South Lake Minnetonka	12,066	16	14	2
	Le Sueur	4,331	8	7	1		South St. Paul	19,188	28	26	2
	Lewiston	1,483	2	2	0		Springfield	2,124	5	5	0

Table 78.   Full-Time Law Enforcement Employees by State by City, 2007 *(Contd.)*

(Number.)

State	City	Population	Total law enforcement employees	Total officers	Total civilians	State	City	Population	Total law enforcement employees	Total officers	Total civilians
	Spring Grove	1,268	2	2	0		Horn Lake	23,125	61	50	11
	Spring Lake Park	6,618	13	11	2		Houston	3,899	12	8	4
	St. Anthony	7,680	24	21	3		Indianola	11,143	29	21	8
	Staples	3,082	6	5	1		Itta Bena	1,917	10	7	3
	St. Charles	3,567	4	4	0		Iuka	2,947	12	9	3
	St. Cloud	67,290	125	96	29		Jackson	175,525	617	429	188
	St. Francis	7,744	11	9	2		Kosciusko	7,325	21	21	0
	Stillwater	18,116	27	23	4		Laurel	18,437	81	59	22
	St. James	4,380	8	7	1		Leakesville	993	2	1	1
	St. Joseph	5,926	9	8	1		Leland	5,008	23	17	6
	St. Louis Park	43,001	68	50	18		Lexington	1,902	10	9	1
	St. Paul	271,662	800	602	198		Louisville	6,671	30	23	7
	St. Paul Park	5,285	9	9	0		Lucedale	3,026	17	11	6
	St. Peter	10,823	19	14	5		Macon	2,792	6	5	1
	Thief River Falls	8,440	18	16	2		Madison	17,554	63	49	14
	Tracy	2,045	4	4	0		Magee	4,314	18	14	4
	Two Harbors	3,435	9	8	1		Magnolia	2,126	4	4	0
	Virginia	8,471	21	20	1		McComb	13,583	62	33	29
	Wabasha	2,587	5	4	1		Mendenhall	2,538	7	4	3
	Wadena	3,981	9	8	1		Meridian	37,954	110	95	15
	Waite Park	6,795	15	12	3		Moorhead	2,440	7	6	1
	Warroad	1,663	14	5	9		Morton	3,421	10	10	0
	Waseca	9,465	16	14	2		Moss Point	14,464	35	25	10
	Wayzata	3,894	12	10	2		Mound Bayou	1,984	8	8	0
	Wells	2,442	4	4	0		Natchez	16,930	73	48	25
	West Hennepin	5,671	11	9	2		New Albany	8,113	26	24	2
	West St. Paul	18,748	32	29	3		Newton	3,698	15	10	5
	Wheaton	1,463	3	3	0		Ocean Springs	17,216	60	48	12
	White Bear Lake	23,486	35	28	7		Okolona	2,891	10	10	0
	Willmar	18,012	37	33	4		Olive Branch	31,223	63	59	4
	Windom	4,327	9	8	1		Oxford	14,362	58	50	8
	Winnebago	1,386	3	3	0		Pascagoula	23,555	86	53	33
	Winona	26,464	43	39	4		Pass Christian	6,041	24	18	6
	Winsted	2,457	3	3	0		Pearl	24,161	66	50	16
	Woodbury	55,376	70	59	11		Pelahatchie	1,494	8	6	2
	Worthington	11,026	32	24	8		Petal	10,302	35	28	7
	Wyoming	3,985	6	6	0		Picayune	11,805	55	37	18
	Zumbrota	3,050	5	5	0		Poplarville	2,781	12	11	1
MISSISSIPPI.............	Aberdeen	6,138	23	19	4		Port Gibson	1,717	11	7	4
	Amory	7,332	28	21	7		Purvis	2,579	12	9	3
	Batesville	7,767	46	37	9		Raymond	1,664	6	6	0
	Bay Springs	2,211	7	7	0		Richland	7,273	47	36	11
	Bay St. Louis	6,399	31	26	5		Ridgeland	21,701	88	58	30
	Booneville	8,669	30	26	4		Ripley	5,680	14	13	1
	Brandon	20,621	56	39	17		Rolling Fork	2,159	7	6	1
	Brookhaven	9,991	33	28	5		Sandersville	808	4	4	0
	Bruce	2,018	7	6	1		Senatobia	6,908	18	15	3
	Byhalia	714	14	8	6		Shaw	2,199	2	2	0
	Canton	12,505	39	29	10		Shelby	2,646	10	6	4
	Charleston	1,969	10	9	1		Starkville	22,663	61	52	9
	Clarksdale	18,650	42	33	9		Stonewall	1,095	2	1	1
	Cleveland	12,500	55	43	12		Summit	1,641	7	7	0
	Clinton	26,349	64	46	18		Sunflower	629	3	3	0
	Collins	2,788	14	10	4		Vaiden	852	2	2	0
	Columbia	6,491	23	23	0		Verona	3,394	7	7	0
	Columbus	23,968	64	53	11		Vicksburg	25,610	90	64	26
	Corinth	14,316	50	39	11		Water Valley	3,849	10	10	0
	De Kalb	900	4	3	1		Waynesboro	5,655	18	13	5
	Drew	2,156	14	9	5		West Point	11,433	33	27	6
	Edwards	1,309	1	1	0		Wiggins	4,774	21	16	5
	Eupora	2,236	9	7	2		Winona	4,740	13	11	2
	Fayette	2,047	9	6	3		Yazoo City	11,761	41	26	15
	Flowood	7,112	56	43	13	MISSOURI.................	Adrian	1,885	3	3	0
	Forest	6,013	19	14	5		Advance	1,214	3	3	0
	Fulton	4,127	11	11	0		Alton	645	2	2	0
	Gloster	1,054	7	5	2		Anderson	1,927	4	4	0
	Greenville	37,326	138	97	41		Appleton City	1,302	2	2	0
	Greenwood	16,538	69	54	15		Arbyrd	496	2	2	0
	Grenada	14,487	48	43	5		Archie	989	3	3	0
	Gulfport	64,455	249	178	71		Arnold	20,831	60	48	12
	Hattiesburg	48,384	194	124	70		Ash Grove	1,502	3	3	0
	Heidelberg	806	6	5	1		Ashland	2,156	5	5	0
	Hernando	11,115	43	33	10		Aurora	7,421	20	13	7
	Holly Springs	7,970	24	18	6		Ava	3,124	12	8	4

Table 78. Full-Time Law Enforcement Employees by State by City, 2007 *(Contd.)*

(Number.)

State	City	Popula-tion	Total law enforce-ment employees	Total officers	Total civilians	State	City	Popula-tion	Total law enforce-ment employees	Total officers	Total civilians
	Ballwin	30,120	68	54	14		Creve Coeur	17,028	61	50	11
	Bates City	237	2	2	0		Crocker	989	3	3	0
	Battlefield	4,148	5	5	0		Crystal City	4,599	21	16	5
	Bella Villa	642	3	3	0		Cuba	3,529	12	11	1
	Belle	1,362	4	3	1		Deepwater	505	1	1	0
	Bellefontaine Neighbors	10,430	32	31	1		Dellwood	4,937	18	17	1
	Bellflower	408	1	1	0		Desloge	5,218	10	10	0
	Bel-Nor	1,496	9	9	0		De Soto	6,579	19	14	5
	Bel-Ridge	2,924	16	15	1		Des Peres	8,626	46	39	7
	Belton	24,492	66	45	21		Dexter	7,658	23	17	6
	Berkeley	9,460	59	47	12		Diamond	881	2	2	0
	Bernie	1,803	9	5	4		Dixon	1,519	7	5	2
	Bethany	3,078	6	6	0		Doniphan	1,935	12	8	4
	Beverly Hills	564	10	4	6		Doolittle	672	1	1	0
	Billings	1,135	4	4	0		Drexel	1,106	2	2	0
	Birch Tree	627	1	1	0		Duenweg	1,213	3	3	0
	Birmingham	216	1	1	0		Duquesne	1,708	5	5	0
	Bismarck	1,569	3	3	0		East Lynne	308	1	1	0
	Bland	566	2	1	1		East Prairie	3,145	7	4	3
	Bloomfield	1,883	3	3	0		Edina	1,131	4	3	1
	Blue Springs	54,718	107	77	30		Edmundson	789	10	9	1
	Bolivar	10,748	24	19	5		Eldon	4,991	13	11	2
	Bonne Terre	7,153	10	10	0		El Dorado Springs	3,811	10	6	4
	Boonville	8,830	28	21	7		Ellington	999	2	2	0
	Bourbon	1,415	7	5	2		Ellisville	9,323	22	21	1
	Bowling Green	5,166	13	8	5		Elsberry	2,601	5	5	0
	Branson	7,496	51	37	14		Eminence	560	1	1	0
	Branson West	514	6	6	0		Eureka	9,287	27	23	4
	Breckenridge Hills	4,525	15	14	1		Everton	321	1	1	0
	Brentwood	7,238	34	27	7		Excelsior Springs	11,747	32	22	10
	Bridgeton	15,120	65	52	13		Exeter	760	1	1	0
	Brookfield	4,371	18	11	7		Fair Grove	1,331	4	4	0
	Brunswick	882	1	1	0		Fair Play	451	1	1	0
	Bucklin	482	1	1	0		Farber	396	1	1	0
	Buckner	2,738	7	6	1		Farmington	15,711	31	23	8
	Buffalo	3,143	9	8	1		Fayette	2,686	8	8	0
	Butler	4,271	16	10	6		Ferguson	21,142	63	54	9
	Butterfield Village	426	1	1	0		Ferrelview	584	1	1	0
	Byrnes Mill	2,912	5	5	0		Festus	11,390	39	28	11
	Cabool	2,150	10	6	4		Florissant	51,025	104	83	21
	California	4,209	7	6	1		Foley	209	1	1	0
	Calverton Park	1,286	6	6	0		Foristell	330	7	7	0
	Camdenton	3,226	16	13	3		Forsyth	1,698	8	7	1
	Cameron	9,015	25	19	6		Fredericktown	4,057	3	3	0
	Canton	2,489	6	5	1		Freeman	611	1	1	0
	Cape Girardeau	36,754	92	76	16		Frontenac	3,531	27	21	6
	Cardwell	739	2	2	0		Fulton	12,311	35	28	7
	Carl Junction	7,071	17	12	5		Galena	529	1	1	0
	Carrollton	3,952	7	7	0		Gallatin	1,761	2	2	0
	Carterville	1,937	6	6	0		Garden City	1,694	3	3	0
	Carthage	13,407	34	26	8		Gerald	1,242	5	5	0
	Caruthersville	6,310	23	20	3		Gladstone	27,686	39	39	0
	Cassville	3,278	12	12	0		Glasgow	1,194	3	3	0
	Center	646	1	1	0		Glendale	5,526	15	12	3
	Centralia	3,593	13	8	5		Goodman	1,265	3	3	0
	Chaffee	2,981	11	6	5		Gower	1,430	3	3	0
	Charlack	1,357	8	8	0		Grain Valley	10,225	21	19	2
	Chesterfield	46,642	95	85	10		Granby	2,259	5	5	0
	Chillicothe	8,700	23	17	6		Grandin	238	1	1	0
	Clarkton	1,262	3	3	0		Grandview	24,322	62	50	12
	Claycomo	1,289	16	12	4		Greenfield	1,286	3	3	0
	Clayton	16,036	57	49	8		Greenwood	4,650	9	9	0
	Cleveland	690	1	1	0		Hallsville	939	2	2	0
	Clever	1,321	3	3	0		Hamilton	1,800	5	4	1
	Cole Camp	1,160	3	3	0		Hannibal	17,612	48	35	13
	Columbia	95,595	179	145	34		Harrisonville	9,935	29	21	8
	Concordia	2,409	6	6	0		Hartville	604	2	2	0
	Conway	786	1	1	0		Hayti	3,007	8	7	1
	Cool Valley	1,014	10	10	0		Hayti Heights	772	3	2	1
	Cooter	430	2	1	1		Hazelwood	25,407	85	67	18
	Cottleville	2,685	10	10	0		Herculaneum	3,306	14	13	1
	Country Club Hills	1,293	10	10	0		Hermann	2,759	12	7	5
	Crane	1,445	3	3	0		Higbee	658	1	1	0
	Crestwood	11,545	36	29	7		Higginsville	4,662	14	8	6

Table 78. Full-Time Law Enforcement Employees by State by City, 2007 (Contd.)

(Number.)

State	City	Population	Total law enforcement employees	Total officers	Total civilians	State	City	Population	Total law enforcement employees	Total officers	Total civilians
	Highlandville	929	3	3	0		Marionville	2,177	5	5	0
	Hillsboro	1,938	8	8	0		Marquand	265	1	1	0
	Hillsdale	1,398	13	12	1		Marshall	12,281	35	22	13
	Holcomb	691	2	2	0		Marshfield	7,173	10	10	0
	Holden	2,525	6	5	1		Marthasville	864	2	2	0
	Hollister	3,797	15	9	6		Maryland Heights	26,221	97	79	18
	Holt	465	2	1	1		Maryville	10,540	33	21	12
	Holts Summit	3,600	9	7	2		Matthews	545	1	1	0
	Houston	2,025	5	5	0		Maysville	1,137	1	1	0
	Humansville	1,008	2	2	0		Memphis	1,995	2	2	0
	Huntsville	1,641	2	2	0		Merriam Woods	1,194	1	1	0
	Hurley	160	2	1	1		Mexico	10,965	37	35	2
	Iberia	684	1	1	0		Milan	1,796	6	5	1
	Independence	108,879	294	204	90		Miller	801	2	2	0
	Indian Point	672	2	1	1		Miner	1,329	11	7	4
	Iron Mountain Lake	707	1	1	0		Moberly	14,023	48	32	16
	Ironton	1,353	4	4	0		Moline Acres	2,540	8	8	0
	Jackson	13,431	30	22	8		Monett	8,851	28	19	9
	JASCO Metropolitan	2,802	5	4	1		Monroe City	2,541	8	7	1
	Jasper	1,046	2	2	0		Montgomery City	2,538	6	6	0
	Jefferson City	39,121	118	87	31		Montrose	434	1	1	0
	Jennings	14,738	47	43	4		Morehouse	935	2	2	0
	Jonesburg	724	1	1	0		Mosby	244	1	1	0
	Joplin	48,261	88	77	11		Moscow Mills	2,460	9	9	0
	Kahoka	2,185	3	3	0		Mound City	1,078	2	2	0
	Kansas City	447,725	2,102	1,409	693		Mountain Grove	4,635	15	10	5
	Kearney	8,262	14	13	1		Mountain View	2,605	9	8	1
	Kennett	10,909	26	21	5		Mount Vernon	4,511	9	9	0
	Keytesville	508	1	1	0		Napoleon	200	2	2	0
	Kimberling City	2,584	9	7	2		Neosho	11,328	30	26	4
	King City	910	1	1	0		Nevada	8,457	30	21	9
	Kirksville	16,934	29	26	3		Newburg	476	1	1	0
	Kirkwood	26,875	65	55	10		New Florence	776	2	2	0
	Knob Noster	3,072	13	7	6		New Franklin	1,107	2	2	0
	Ladue	8,199	35	28	7		New Haven	2,014	6	6	0
	La Grange	934	9	8	1		New London	1,011	2	2	0
	Lake Lotawana	1,945	7	6	1		New Madrid	3,073	7	6	1
	Lake Ozark	2,022	15	9	6		New Melle	286	2	2	0
	Lakeshire	1,297	6	6	0		Niangua	497	1	1	0
	Lake St. Louis	14,325	38	29	9		Nixa	18,220	33	22	11
	Lake Tapawingo	795	1	1	0		Noel	1,562	2	2	0
	Lake Waukomis	900	1	1	0		Norborne	776	1	1	0
	Lake Winnebago	1,130	4	4	0		Normandy	4,946	21	20	1
	Lamar	4,649	12	10	2		North Kansas City	5,619	47	36	11
	La Monte	1,076	2	2	0		Northmoor	403	1	1	0
	Lanagan	440	1	1	0		Northwoods	4,353	28	18	10
	La Plata	1,438	3	3	0		Oak Grove	7,069	16	15	1
	Lathrop	2,357	5	5	0		Oakview Village	389	4	4	0
	La Tour Village	66	1	1	0		Odessa	4,828	12	11	1
	Lauric	719	6	6	0		O'Fallon	76,542	134	105	29
	Lawson	2,407	5	5	0		Olivette	7,439	24	23	1
	Leadington	220	6	5	1		Olympian Village	675	3	3	0
	Leadwood	1,173	4	4	0		Oran	1,259	1	1	0
	Lebanon	13,964	36	27	9		Orrick	848	2	2	0
	Lee's Summit	83,558	169	115	54		Osage Beach	4,554	40	25	15
	Lexington	4,590	11	9	2		Osceola	804	2	2	0
	Liberal	811	1	1	0		Overland	15,783	54	43	11
	Liberty	30,050	55	39	16		Owensville	2,523	8	6	2
	Licking	1,516	4	4	0		Ozark	17,496	37	31	6
	Lilbourn	1,205	2	2	0		Pacific	7,245	23	16	7
	Lincoln	1,107	3	3	0		Pagedale	3,440	16	15	1
	Linn	1,432	4	4	0		Palmyra	3,443	10	6	4
	Linn Creek	301	3	3	0		Park Hills	8,744	13	12	1
	Lockwood	953	2	2	0		Parkville	5,276	16	15	1
	Lone Jack	887	5	5	0		Parma	785	2	2	0
	Louisiana	3,832	13	8	5		Peculiar	4,495	13	11	2
	Lowry City	749	1	1	0		Perry	668	1	1	0
	Macon	5,446	15	13	2		Perryville	8,062	28	26	2
	Malden	4,569	14	10	4		Pevely	4,442	19	13	6
	Manchester	18,769	41	38	3		Piedmont	1,954	7	7	0
	Mansfield	1,359	4	4	0		Pierce City	1,456	4	4	0
	Maplewood	8,701	31	29	2		Pilot Grove	748	1	1	0
	Marble Hill	1,515	4	4	0		Pilot Knob	688	1	1	0
	Marceline	2,331	12	6	6		Pine Lawn	4,038	26	19	7

Table 78. Full-Time Law Enforcement Employees by State by City, 2007 *(Contd.)*

(Number.)

State	City	Population	Total law enforcement employees	Total officers	Total civilians	State	City	Population	Total law enforcement employees	Total officers	Total civilians
	Pineville	878	16	15	1		Town and Country	10,757	40	34	6
	Platte City	4,971	12	11	1		Tracy	210	1	1	0
	Platte Woods	458	2	2	0		Trenton	6,070	18	11	7
	Plattsburg	2,416	6	6	0		Trimble	481	2	2	0
	Pleasant Hill	7,108	16	12	4		Troy	11,674	29	27	2
	Pleasant Hope	590	3	3	0		Truesdale	615	2	1	1
	Pleasant Valley	3,481	13	8	5		Union	9,648	21	19	2
	Polo	607	2	1	1		Unionville	1,959	2	2	0
	Poplar Bluff	17,054	54	43	11		University City	36,743	93	73	20
	Portageville	2,990	14	10	4		Uplands Park	442	6	5	1
	Purdy	1,175	1	1	0		Urbana	435	2	2	0
	Puxico	1,149	2	2	0		Van Buren	819	1	1	0
	Qulin	487	1	1	0		Vandalia	4,099	8	4	4
	Randolph	50	2	2	0		Velda City	1,512	9	7	2
	Raymore	17,439	37	26	11		Verona	726	5	4	1
	Raytown	28,344	71	53	18		Versailles	2,709	10	10	0
	Reeds Spring	720	1	1	0		Viburnum	808	1	1	0
	Republic	11,777	33	23	10		Vienna	643	1	1	0
	Rich Hill	1,510	2	2	0		Vinita Park	1,803	12	11	1
	Richland	1,756	6	5	1		Walnut Grove	641	3	3	0
	Richmond	6,029	19	14	5		Wardell	255	1	1	0
	Richmond Heights	9,179	41	40	1		Warrensburg	18,206	38	33	5
	Riverside	2,961	28	23	5		Warrenton	7,146	20	16	4
	Riverview	2,948	12	11	1		Warsaw	2,273	7	7	0
	Rockaway Beach	586	3	3	0		Warson Woods	1,875	8	7	1
	Rock Hill	4,641	10	9	1		Washburn	480	2	2	0
	Rock Port	1,306	3	3	0		Washington	14,367	31	28	3
	Rogersville	2,647	6	6	0		Waynesville	3,616	9	8	1
	Rolla	18,208	51	31	20		Weatherby Lake	1,856	3	3	0
	Salem	4,860	19	14	5		Webb City	11,142	27	20	7
	Salisbury	1,600	4	3	1		Webster Groves	22,620	41	38	3
	Sarcoxie	1,341	3	3	0		Wellston	2,332	22	16	6
	Savannah	5,118	6	6	0		Wellsville	1,383	3	3	0
	Scott City	4,571	17	12	5		Wentzville	24,137	68	49	19
	Sedalia	20,682	56	44	12		Weston	1,594	4	4	0
	Seligman	924	4	2	2		West Plains	11,673	28	23	5
	Senath	1,626	3	3	0		Wheaton	749	1	1	0
	Seneca	2,277	6	6	0		Willard	3,320	10	9	1
	Seymour	2,025	6	6	0		Willow Springs	2,145	7	6	1
	Shelbina	1,850	4	4	0		Winfield	900	3	3	0
	Shrewsbury	6,290	20	18	2		Winona	1,343	3	3	0
	Sikeston	17,188	75	67	8		Woodson Terrace	4,056	20	17	3
	Silex	288	1	1	0		Wright City	2,837	9	8	1
	Slater	1,911	6	3	3	MONTANA	Baker	1,620	3	3	0
	Smithville	7,777	16	16	0		Belgrade	7,552	15	12	3
	Southwest City	931	4	4	0		Billings	101,342	169	134	35
	Sparta	1,223	1	1	0		Boulder	1,468	2	2	0
	Springfield	150,488	386	311	75		Bozeman	36,158	55	48	7
	St. Ann	12,887	53	39	14		Bridger	749	1	1	0
	St. Charles	63,277	144	109	35		Chinook	1,283	4	4	0
	St. Clair	4,400	15	13	2		Colstrip	2,342	13	6	7
	Steele	2,136	8	8	0		Columbia Falls	4,826	15	9	6
	Steelville	1,454	6	6	0		Columbus	1,954	5	4	1
	Ste. Genevieve	4,479	12	11	1		Conrad	2,556	5	5	0
	Stewartsville	741	1	1	0		Cut Bank	3,182	9	8	1
	St. George	1,222	2	2	0		Dillon	4,029	9	8	1
	St. James	4,110	8	7	1		East Helena	2,108	5	5	0
	St. John	6,444	25	23	2		Ennis	1,029	1	1	0
	St. Joseph	72,424	160	117	43		Eureka	1,030	12	3	9
	St. Louis	348,197	1,967	1,350	617		Fort Benton	1,451	5	4	1
	St. Marys	392	1	1	0		Glasgow	2,926	8	7	1
	Stover	1,045	3	3	0		Glendive	4,606	14	8	6
	St. Peters	55,291	105	86	19		Great Falls	56,159	119	82	37
	Strafford	2,025	8	8	0		Hamilton	4,774	16	15	1
	St. Robert	3,319	27	19	8		Havre	9,414	20	18	2
	Sturgeon	897	2	2	0		Helena	28,128	75	53	22
	Sugar Creek	3,506	21	15	6		Hot Springs	574	1	1	0
	Sullivan	6,698	26	18	8		Joliet	617	1	1	0
	Summersville	562	2	2	0		Kalispell	20,104	46	35	11
	Sunset Hills	8,314	28	21	7		Laurel	6,434	19	12	7
	Sweet Springs	1,527	3	3	0		Lewistown	6,047	20	14	6
	Tarkio	1,823	5	3	2		Libby	2,666	5	5	0
	Thayer	2,166	10	8	2		Livingston	7,307	14	13	1
	Tipton	3,125	3	3	0		Manhattan	1,503	4	3	1

Table 78. Full-Time Law Enforcement Employees by State by City, 2007 (Contd.)

(Number.)

State	City	Population	Total law enforcement employees	Total officers	Total civilians	State	City	Population	Total law enforcement employees	Total officers	Total civilians
	Miles City	8,033	17	16	1		St. Paul	2,263	4	4	0
	Missoula	65,037	121	101	20		Superior	1,845	3	3	0
	Pinesdale	853	3	3	0		Sutton	1,363	2	2	0
	Plains	1,272	3	3	0		Tecumseh	2,059	2	1	1
	Polson	5,082	13	11	2		Tekamah	1,773	2	2	0
	Poplar	900	6	5	1		Valentine	2,694	6	5	1
	Red Lodge	2,494	7	7	0		Valley	1,868	4	4	0
	Ronan City	2,033	4	4	0		Wahoo	4,060	6	6	0
	Sidney	4,761	11	10	1		Wayne	5,136	14	9	5
	Stevensville	1,966	4	3	1		West Point	3,446	7	7	0
	St. Ignatius	830	2	2	0		Wilber	1,804	4	4	0
	Thompson Falls	1,420	4	4	0		Wymore	1,612	3	3	0
	Three Forks	1,865	4	3	1		York	7,921	20	14	6
	Troy	996	4	3	1	NEVADA	Boulder City	15,028	47	34	13
	West Yellowstone	1,240	6	6	0		Carlin	2,121	6	5	1
	Whitefish	8,007	20	15	5		Elko	16,933	46	41	5
	Wolf Point	2,608	8	7	1		Fallon	8,444	34	21	13
NEBRASKA.............	Albion	1,634	3	3	0		Henderson	251,270	528	354	174
	Alliance	8,054	24	17	7		Las Vegas Metropolitan				
	Ashland	2,586	6	5	1		Police Department	1,341,156	4,812	3,214	1,598
	Auburn	3,187	4	4	0		Lovelock	1,886	7	6	1
	Aurora	4,261	8	7	1		Mesquite	15,660	47	32	15
	Bayard	1,143	2	2	0		North Las Vegas	211,419	453	298	155
	Beatrice	12,972	32	21	11		Reno	214,197	451	361	90
	Bellevue	48,067	102	86	16		Sparks	86,884	166	114	52
	Blair	7,962	17	15	2		West Wendover	5,128	21	14	7
	Bridgeport	1,478	3	3	0		Winnemucca	8,051	18	16	2
	Broken Bow	3,235	7	6	1		Yerington	3,947	6	5	1
	Central City	2,839	6	5	1	NEW					
	Chadron	5,158	17	12	5	HAMPSHIRE............	Alexandria	1,524	1	1	0
	Columbus	21,420	46	33	13		Alstead	2,057	2	2	0
	Cozad	4,293	7	7	0		Alton	5,205	13	11	2
	Crete	6,345	18	11	7		Amherst	11,836	19	18	1
	David City	2,520	6	5	1		Andover	2,246	1	1	0
	Emerson	819	2	2	0		Antrim	2,642	4	4	0
	Fairbury	3,969	7	6	1		Ashland	2,029	6	6	0
	Falls City	4,119	12	8	4		Auburn	5,235	9	7	2
	Fremont	25,423	47	38	9		Barnstead	4,719	5	5	0
	Gering	7,677	18	15	3		Barrington	8,384	11	10	1
	Gothenburg	3,748	7	6	1		Bartlett	2,945	5	4	1
	Grand Island	44,812	85	75	10		Bedford	21,389	45	33	12
	Hastings	25,250	52	38	14		Belmont	7,365	19	16	3
	Holdrege	5,281	16	10	6		Bennington	1,488	2	2	0
	Imperial	1,833	4	4	0		Berlin	9,909	30	22	8
	Kearney	29,652	59	47	12		Bethlehem	2,452	4	3	1
	Kimball	2,266	7	6	1		Boscawen	3,930	7	6	1
	La Vista	16,816	35	31	4		Bow	8,250	16	12	4
	Lexington	10,262	17	15	2		Bradford	1,534	3	3	0
	Lincoln	243,243	403	308	95		Brentwood	3,866	6	6	0
	Lyons	887	2	2	0		Bristol	3,145	10	9	1
	Madison	2,279	4	4	0		Campton	3,001	6	5	1
	McCook	7,491	19	15	4		Candia	4,200	7	6	1
	Milford	2,045	5	5	0		Canterbury	2,353	2	2	0
	Minden	2,867	5	5	0		Carroll	752	4	4	0
	Mitchell	1,774	4	4	0		Charlestown	4,987	8	5	3
	Nebraska City	7,106	13	12	1		Chester	4,793	3	2	1
	Neligh	1,505	3	3	0		Claremont	13,291	29	24	5
	Norfolk	23,977	56	36	20		Colebrook	2,406	5	5	0
	North Platte	24,436	67	42	25		Concord	42,638	94	72	22
	Ogallala	4,585	12	11	1		Conway	9,300	29	20	9
	Omaha	431,810	920	755	165		Danville	4,425	5	4	1
	O'Neill	3,391	8	7	1		Deerfield	4,220	9	8	1
	Ord	2,094	3	3	0		Deering	2,070	4	4	0
	Papillion	21,748	37	33	4		Derry	34,118	72	59	13
	Pierce	1,715	3	3	0		Dover	28,661	68	49	19
	Plainview	1,254	4	2	2		Dublin	1,565	4	3	1
	Plattsmouth	7,070	17	15	2		Dunbarton	2,641	3	3	0
	Ralston	6,144	15	13	2		Durham	13,415	21	19	2
	Schuyler	5,194	8	6	2		Enfield	4,890	7	6	1
	Scottsbluff	14,719	37	32	5		Epping	6,263	13	12	1
	Scribner	966	2	2	0		Epsom	4,609	7	6	1
	Seward	6,922	11	9	2		Exeter	14,851	34	24	10
	Sidney	6,386	14	12	2		Farmington	6,688	16	14	2
	South Sioux City	12,139	28	27	1		Fitzwilliam	2,321	3	3	0

Table 78. Full-Time Law Enforcement Employees by State by City, 2007 (*Contd.*)

(Number.)

State	City	Population	Total law enforcement employees	Total officers	Total civilians	State	City	Population	Total law enforcement employees	Total officers	Total civilians
	Franconia	1,052	3	3	0		Sandown	5,873	7	7	0
	Franklin	8,843	22	15	7		Sandwich	1,335	2	2	0
	Freedom	1,469	3	3	0		Seabrook	8,588	32	25	7
	Fremont	4,156	5	4	1		Somersworth	11,815	29	22	7
	Gilford	7,569	23	17	6		Strafford	4,084	4	4	0
	Gilmanton	3,621	6	5	1		Stratham	7,293	11	10	1
	Goffstown	17,810	40	28	12		Sugar Hill	602	2	2	0
	Gorham	2,914	10	7	3		Sunapee	3,398	5	5	0
	Grantham	2,578	4	4	0		Thornton	2,105	5	4	1
	Greenland	3,409	7	7	0		Tilton	3,645	18	17	1
	Hampstead	8,904	7	7	0		Troy	2,098	4	4	0
	Hampton	15,493	41	32	9		Wakefield	5,477	9	8	1
	Hancock	1,824	3	3	0		Walpole	3,713	4	3	1
	Hanover	11,198	35	20	15		Warner	3,021	5	4	1
	Haverhill	4,623	8	7	1		Washington	1,084	1	1	0
	Henniker	5,187	10	8	2		Waterville Valley	271	7	6	1
	Hillsborough	5,539	18	12	6		Weare	9,086	12	11	1
	Hinsdale	4,219	8	7	1		Webster	1,900	3	3	0
	Hooksett	13,705	35	23	12		Wilton	3,946	7	6	1
	Hopkinton	5,651	6	6	0		Winchester	4,330	8	7	1
	Hudson	24,996	60	45	15		Windham	13,283	24	18	6
	Jaffrey	5,729	10	9	1		Wolfeboro	6,710	17	12	5
	Keene	22,693	59	44	15		Woodstock	1,181	5	5	0
	Kingston	6,284	10	9	1	NEW JERSEY............	Aberdeen Township	18,301	41	34	7
	Laconia	17,153	45	35	10		Absecon	8,029	33	26	7
	Lancaster	3,362	8	7	1		Allendale	6,683	20	14	6
	Lebanon	12,589	48	35	13		Allenhurst	698	13	9	4
	Lee	4,481	8	7	1		Allentown	1,839	6	5	1
	Lincoln	1,322	14	9	5		Alpine	2,418	13	13	0
	Lisbon	1,663	4	4	0		Andover Township	6,523	19	13	6
	Litchfield	8,737	12	10	2		Asbury Park	16,473	102	90	12
	Littleton	6,213	13	12	1		Atlantic City	39,781	462	366	96
	Londonderry	25,121	85	69	16		Atlantic Highlands	4,594	20	15	5
	Loudon	5,215	7	6	1		Audubon	8,941	24	22	2
	Madison	2,329	5	4	1		Avalon	2,116	28	20	8
	Manchester	109,873	276	214	62		Avon-by-the-Sea	2,156	12	12	0
	Marlborough	2,107	3	3	0		Barnegat Township	21,098	54	43	11
	Meredith	6,780	17	13	4		Barrington	6,973	16	15	1
	Merrimack	26,847	50	37	13		Bay Head	1,254	9	8	1
	Middleton	1,806	4	4	0		Bayonne	58,583	265	225	40
	Milford	15,271	29	25	4		Beach Haven	1,360	13	10	3
	Milton	4,531	8	7	1		Beachwood	10,696	20	18	2
	Mont Vernon	2,433	3	3	0		Bedminster Township	8,412	19	17	2
	Moultonborough	5,019	15	11	4		Belleville	34,291	114	105	9
	Nashua	87,217	215	162	53		Bellmawr	11,143	26	24	2
	New Boston	5,121	5	4	1		Belmar	5,897	26	21	5
	Newbury	2,129	4	4	0		Belvidere	2,689	7	6	1
	New Durham	2,536	6	5	1		Bergenfield	26,078	51	43	8
	Newfields	1,598	4	4	0		Berkeley Heights Township	13,515	34	27	7
	New Hampton	2,283	5	5	0		Berkeley Township	42,388	95	74	21
	Newington	816	11	10	1		Berlin	7,875	21	20	1
	New Ipswich	5,258	6	5	1		Berlin Township	5,381	22	20	2
	New London	4,510	13	8	5		Bernards Township	27,020	54	39	15
	Newmarket	9,723	20	13	7		Bernardsville	7,654	24	18	6
	Newport	6,570	19	14	5		Beverly	2,639	8	7	1
	Newton	4,544	8	5	3		Blairstown Township	5,956	9	8	1
	Northfield	5,257	11	10	1		Bloomfield	45,171	149	133	16
	North Hampton	4,600	13	12	1		Bloomingdale	7,570	17	16	1
	Northumberland	2,397	4	4	0		Bogota	8,072	21	16	5
	Northwood	4,122	8	7	1		Boonton	8,562	25	21	4
	Nottingham	4,564	7	6	1		Boonton Township	4,377	13	13	0
	Ossipee	4,723	9	8	1		Bordentown	3,935	15	13	2
	Pelham	12,774	26	19	7		Bordentown Township	10,423	28	22	6
	Pembroke	7,466	14	12	2		Bound Brook	10,180	27	22	5
	Peterborough	6,127	13	11	2		Bradley Beach	4,763	20	17	3
	Pittsfield	4,476	9	8	1		Branchburg Township	14,982	28	26	2
	Plaistow	7,702	23	15	8		Brick Township	77,886	176	129	47
	Plymouth	6,406	15	10	5		Bridgeton	24,281	79	62	17
	Portsmouth	20,584	88	66	22		Bridgewater Township	44,620	96	78	18
	Raymond	10,256	25	17	8		Brielle	4,831	15	15	0
	Rindge	6,541	10	8	2		Brigantine	12,829	49	38	11
	Rochester	30,355	73	54	19		Brooklawn	2,284	7	7	0
	Rollinsford	2,627	4	4	0		Buena	3,787	15	9	6
	Rye	5,219	10	9	1						

Table 78. Full-Time Law Enforcement Employees by State by City, 2007 (Contd.)

(Number.)

State	City	Population	Total law enforcement employees	Total officers	Total civilians	State	City	Population	Total law enforcement employees	Total officers	Total civilians
	Burlington	9,672	41	36	5		Fairview	13,568	35	33	2
	Burlington Township	21,691	56	46	10		Fanwood	7,179	22	21	1
	Butler	8,038	17	16	1		Far Hills	924	6	6	0
	Byram Township	8,618	15	14	1		Flemington	4,248	15	14	1
	Caldwell	7,340	21	20	1		Florence Township	11,585	33	27	6
	Camden	78,967	497	410	87		Florham Park	12,549	37	33	4
	Cape May	3,792	30	23	7		Fort Lee	36,844	128	108	20
	Carlstadt	6,010	33	31	2		Franklin	5,187	16	15	1
	Carney's Point Township	7,946	27	22	5		Franklin Lakes	11,290	27	22	5
	Carteret	22,165	72	62	10		Franklin Township, Gloucester County	16,778	33	30	3
	Cedar Grove Township	12,791	33	32	1		Franklin Township, Hunterdon County	3,138	6	6	0
	Chatham	8,353	30	24	6		Franklin Township, Somerset County	60,006	138	118	20
	Chatham Township	10,233	29	24	5		Freehold	11,344	36	28	8
	Cherry Hill Township	71,269	178	140	38		Freehold Township	33,803	86	71	15
	Chesilhurst	1,871	11	10	1		Frenchtown	1,484	2	2	0
	Chester	1,644	9	8	1		Galloway Township	36,045	88	73	15
	Chesterfield Township	6,422	11	10	1		Garfield	29,515	64	57	7
	Chester Township	7,855	17	16	1		Garwood	4,214	20	16	4
	Cinnaminson Township	15,381	37	32	5		Gibbsboro	2,440	7	7	0
	Clark Township	14,585	49	38	11		Glassboro	19,274	51	45	6
	Clayton	7,436	19	17	2		Glen Ridge	6,877	34	28	6
	Clementon	4,900	18	16	2		Glen Rock	11,346	22	21	1
	Cliffside Park	22,868	55	46	9		Gloucester City	11,431	33	30	3
	Clifton	79,253	188	158	30		Gloucester Township	65,396	136	116	20
	Clinton	2,593	10	10	0		Green Brook Township	6,824	28	22	6
	Clinton Township	14,020	27	24	3		Greenwich Township, Gloucester County	4,950	23	18	5
	Closter	8,691	27	22	5		Greenwich Township, Warren County	5,206	13	12	1
	Collingswood	13,899	42	37	5		Guttenberg	10,670	29	22	7
	Colts Neck Township	11,536	23	22	1		Hackensack	43,478	134	110	24
	Cranbury Township	3,882	20	19	1		Hackettstown	9,436	20	19	1
	Cranford Township	22,270	69	52	17		Haddonfield	11,464	25	23	2
	Cresskill	8,400	28	22	6		Haddon Heights	7,332	15	14	1
	Deal	1,039	20	16	4		Haddon Township	14,420	32	30	2
	Delanco Township	4,205	11	10	1		Haledon	8,321	19	17	2
	Delaware Township	4,709	8	7	1		Hamburg	3,538	9	8	1
	Delran Township	17,206	37	32	5		Hamilton Township, Atlantic County	24,315	89	69	20
	Demarest	5,083	14	14	0		Hamilton Township, Mercer County	90,158	213	182	31
	Denville Township	16,597	44	35	9		Hammonton	13,512	42	34	8
	Deptford Township	30,082	75	71	4		Hanover Township	13,676	39	32	7
	Dover	18,306	40	35	5		Harding Township	3,348	15	14	1
	Dumont	17,288	39	31	8		Hardyston Township	8,246	27	21	6
	Dunellen	6,909	22	18	4		Harrington Park	4,894	12	12	0
	Eastampton Township	6,667	18	17	1		Harrison	13,880	72	53	19
	East Brunswick Township	47,438	119	93	26		Harrison Township	11,797	19	18	1
	East Greenwich Township	6,758	22	20	2		Harvey Cedars	387	9	9	0
	East Hanover Township	11,581	41	33	8		Hasbrouck Heights	11,570	34	32	2
	East Newark	2,207	10	7	3		Haworth	3,418	14	13	1
	East Orange	66,949	339	277	62		Hawthorne	18,086	38	34	4
	East Rutherford	8,891	37	33	4		Hazlet Township	20,843	54	46	8
	East Windsor Township	26,807	63	49	14		Helmetta	2,014	3	3	0
	Eatontown	13,960	47	37	10		High Bridge	3,746	7	7	0
	Edgewater	9,585	34	33	1		Highland Park	14,112	37	30	7
	Edgewater Park Township	7,933	15	14	1		Highlands	4,965	17	13	4
	Edison Township	99,082	246	200	46		Hightstown	5,277	19	14	5
	Egg Harbor City	4,434	16	14	2		Hillsborough Township	37,941	70	56	14
	Egg Harbor Township	38,621	127	100	27		Hillsdale	10,008	22	20	2
	Elizabeth	125,621	469	349	120		Hillside Township	21,588	88	73	15
	Elk Township	3,850	11	10	1		Hi-Nella	1,003	5	5	0
	Elmer	1,364	1	1	0		Hoboken	39,676	166	150	16
	Elmwood Park	18,722	45	43	2		Ho-Ho-Kus	4,077	19	16	3
	Emerson	7,286	22	19	3		Holland Township	5,286	7	6	1
	Englewood	27,701	106	81	25		Holmdel Township	16,759	57	43	14
	Englewood Cliffs	5,767	28	27	1		Hopatcong	15,814	39	29	10
	Englishtown	1,833	8	8	0		Hopewell Township	17,888	39	31	8
	Essex Fells	2,062	13	13	0		Howell Township	50,324	111	94	17
	Evesham Township	46,504	82	74	8		Independence Township	5,744	9	8	1
	Ewing Township	36,753	93	79	14		Interlaken	877	5	5	0
	Fairfield Township, Essex County	7,673	48	41	7						
	Fair Haven	5,859	17	13	4						
	Fair Lawn	31,108	78	64	14						

Table 78. Full-Time Law Enforcement Employees by State by City, 2007 *(Contd.)*

(Number.)

State	City	Population	Total law enforcement employees	Total officers	Total civilians	State	City	Population	Total law enforcement employees	Total officers	Total civilians
	Irvington	57,767	220	192	28		Millburn Township	19,068	63	53	10
	Island Heights	1,869	5	5	0		Milltown	7,007	18	15	3
	Jackson Township	52,073	118	89	29		Millville	28,069	94	81	13
	Jamesburg	6,401	18	13	5		Monmouth Beach	3,558	11	10	1
	Jefferson Township	21,866	46	39	7		Monroe Township, Gloucester County	31,793	72	66	6
	Jersey City	240,718	1,080	902	178		Monroe Township, Middlesex County	34,752	66	49	17
	Keansburg	10,526	43	35	8		Montclair	37,144	136	111	25
	Kearny	37,840	128	120	8		Montgomery Township	23,140	41	31	10
	Kenilworth	7,707	31	30	1		Montvale	7,276	24	22	2
	Keyport	7,438	22	17	5		Montville Township	21,347	49	42	7
	Kinnelon	9,638	17	16	1		Moonachie	2,785	22	19	3
	Lacey Township	26,184	61	46	15		Moorestown Township	19,907	49	38	11
	Lake Como	1,744	9	9	0		Morris Plains	5,576	21	17	4
	Lakehurst	2,662	11	9	2		Morristown	18,838	69	61	8
	Lakewood Township	69,298	159	131	28		Morris Township	21,279	52	43	9
	Lambertville	3,791	14	11	3		Mountain Lakes	4,324	17	14	3
	Laurel Springs	1,914	7	7	0		Mountainside	6,615	27	22	5
	Lavallette	2,740	17	12	5		Mount Arlington	5,683	14	13	1
	Lawnside	2,788	9	7	2		Mount Ephraim	4,417	14	13	1
	Lawrence Township, Mercer County	31,939	84	69	15		Mount Holly Township	10,555	28	26	2
	Lebanon Township	6,264	9	8	1		Mount Laurel Township	40,147	88	74	14
	Leonia	8,760	25	19	6		Mount Olive Township	25,950	63	54	9
	Lincoln Park	10,808	32	26	6		Mullica Township	6,053	15	14	1
	Linden	39,697	157	130	27		National Park	3,201	7	7	0
	Lindenwold	17,084	41	38	3		Neptune City	5,127	21	16	5
	Linwood	7,321	24	20	4		Neptune Township	28,038	94	74	20
	Little Egg Harbor Township	20,193	59	47	12		Netcong	3,277	11	9	2
	Little Falls Township	11,777	29	24	5		Newark	280,158	1,623	1,227	396
	Little Ferry	10,668	31	28	3		New Brunswick	49,950	173	142	31
	Little Silver	6,062	21	16	5		Newfield	1,657	6	6	0
	Livingston Township	28,287	92	75	17		New Hanover Township	9,437	2	2	0
	Lodi	24,202	54	43	11		New Milford	16,171	35	32	3
	Logan Township	6,150	23	22	1		New Providence	11,862	30	24	6
	Long Beach Township	3,483	51	40	11		Newton	8,300	35	25	10
	Long Branch	32,171	120	102	18		North Arlington	15,010	39	32	7
	Long Hill Township	8,746	29	26	3		North Bergen Township	56,984	132	116	16
	Longport	1,083	19	14	5		North Brunswick Township	39,676	101	84	17
	Lopatcong Township	8,402	15	14	1		North Caldwell	7,175	22	17	5
	Lower Alloways Creek Township	1,906	18	13	5		Northfield	7,968	21	20	1
	Lower Township	20,693	60	46	14		North Haledon	8,999	23	18	5
	Lumberton Township	12,276	32	28	4		North Hanover Township	7,543	10	9	1
	Lyndhurst Township	19,645	54	48	6		North Plainfield	21,642	53	47	6
	Madison	15,945	41	36	5		Northvale	4,542	16	15	1
	Magnolia	4,360	11	11	0		North Wildwood	4,782	34	27	7
	Mahwah Township	24,451	64	55	9		Norwood	6,239	15	14	1
	Manalapan Township	37,004	81	66	15		Nutley Township	26,891	80	67	13
	Manasquan	6,172	24	18	6		Oakland	13,498	32	26	6
	Manchester Township	41,628	83	66	17		Oaklyn	4,062	13	12	1
	Mansfield Township, Burlinton County	8,011	16	13	3		Ocean City	15,057	74	61	13
	Mansfield Township, Warren County	8,237	16	15	1		Ocean Gate	2,121	5	5	0
	Mantoloking	449	8	7	1		Oceanport	5,726	21	16	5
	Mantua Township	14,908	30	28	2		Ocean Township, Monmouth County	27,362	77	61	16
	Manville	10,435	26	22	4		Ocean Township, Ocean County	8,205	29	18	11
	Maple Shade Township	19,454	45	36	9		Ogdensburg	2,611	7	7	0
	Maplewood Township	22,658	78	64	14		Old Bridge Township	65,370	140	105	35
	Margate City	8,563	47	36	11		Old Tappan	5,986	14	13	1
	Marlboro Township	39,667	98	73	25		Oradell	7,922	24	22	2
	Matawan	8,742	25	23	2		Orange	31,717	130	107	23
	Maywood	9,332	28	24	4		Oxford Township	2,610	5	4	1
	Medford Lakes	4,143	10	9	1		Palisades Park	19,220	38	31	7
	Medford Township	23,295	57	44	13		Palmyra	7,564	18	16	2
	Mendham	5,153	14	12	2		Paramus	26,430	117	93	24
	Mendham Township	5,571	18	15	3		Park Ridge	8,905	19	18	1
	Merchantville	3,789	16	14	2		Parsippany-Troy Hills Township	51,609	126	102	24
	Metuchen	13,157	33	28	5		Passaic	67,673	225	189	36
	Middlesex	13,685	32	30	2		Paterson	148,049	578	494	84
	Middle Township	16,306	65	52	13		Paulsboro	6,035	21	19	2
	Middletown Township	67,279	130	102	28						
	Midland Park	6,875	14	13	1						

Table 78. Full-Time Law Enforcement Employees by State by City, 2007 *(Contd.)*

(Number.)

State	City	Population	Total law enforcement employees	Total officers	Total civilians	State	City	Population	Total law enforcement employees	Total officers	Total civilians
	Peapack and Gladstone	2,469	10	9	1		South Harrison Township	2,943	7	6	1
	Pemberton	1,375	7	6	1		South Orange	16,298	65	57	8
	Pemberton Township	28,703	70	59	11		South Plainfield	22,694	72	56	16
	Pennington	2,676	7	6	1		South River	15,752	38	30	8
	Pennsauken Township	35,286	120	94	26		South Toms River	3,700	13	12	1
	Penns Grove	4,776	21	16	5		Sparta Township	19,262	50	40	10
	Pennsville Township	13,274	26	24	2		Spotswood	8,143	23	19	4
	Pequannock Township	16,248	36	31	5		Springfield	14,652	47	41	6
	Perth Amboy	48,392	149	124	25		Springfield Township	3,554	10	9	1
	Phillipsburg	14,765	38	36	2		Spring Lake	3,460	18	14	4
	Pine Beach	2,023	7	6	1		Spring Lake Heights	5,083	12	12	0
	Pine Hill	11,225	24	22	2		Stafford Township	25,705	85	59	26
	Pine Valley	23	4	4	0		Stanhope	3,650	9	8	1
	Piscataway Township	52,425	112	92	20		Stillwater Township	4,366	6	6	0
	Pitman	9,158	15	14	1		Stone Harbor	1,034	22	16	6
	Plainfield	47,143	181	150	31		Stratford	7,090	16	15	1
	Plainsboro Township	21,119	46	34	12		Summit	21,010	57	48	9
	Pleasantville	18,898	78	64	14		Surf City	1,535	11	11	0
	Plumsted Township	8,086	13	13	0		Swedesboro	2,034	10	9	1
	Pohatcong Township	3,395	16	15	1		Teaneck Township	39,435	119	104	15
	Point Pleasant	19,794	41	33	8		Tenafly	14,326	44	37	7
	Point Pleasant Beach	5,374	32	25	7		Tewksbury Township	6,061	12	11	1
	Pompton Lakes	11,193	30	26	4		Tinton Falls	17,006	41	40	1
	Princeton	13,623	45	34	11		Toms River Township	94,469	195	160	35
	Princeton Township	17,276	40	31	9		Totowa	10,587	31	28	3
	Prospect Park	5,695	16	15	1		Trenton	83,551	414	360	54
	Rahway	27,720	91	80	11		Tuckerton	3,810	10	10	0
	Ramsey	14,710	39	33	6		Union Beach	6,602	20	16	4
	Randolph Township	25,622	51	42	9		Union City	63,647	217	167	50
	Raritan	6,399	24	19	5		Union Township	54,795	191	139	52
	Raritan Township	22,619	38	35	3		Upper Saddle River	8,493	24	18	6
	Readington Township	16,223	25	23	2		Ventnor City	12,508	52	40	12
	Red Bank	11,798	47	41	6		Vernon Township	25,340	44	34	10
	Ridgefield	10,947	31	28	3		Verona	12,880	35	31	4
	Ridgefield Park	12,609	39	30	9		Vineland	58,013	191	155	36
	Ridgewood	24,530	48	43	5		Voorhees Township	29,261	66	51	15
	Ringwood	12,757	28	23	5		Waldwick	9,578	24	19	5
	Riverdale	2,664	22	17	5		Wallington	11,379	23	22	1
	River Edge	10,814	25	21	4		Wall Township	25,882	101	71	30
	Riverside Township	7,915	17	16	1		Wanaque	11,122	27	23	4
	Riverton	2,703	7	6	1		Warren Township	15,746	35	28	7
	River Vale Township	9,708	24	21	3		Washington	6,811	14	13	1
	Rochelle Park Township	6,000	26	21	5		Washington Township, Bergen County	9,627	22	22	0
	Rockaway	6,382	16	15	1		Washington Township, Gloucester County	51,595	92	85	7
	Rockaway Township	25,675	70	58	12		Washington Township, Mercer County	11,853	36	27	9
	Roseland	5,376	33	28	5		Washington Township, Morris County	18,608	46	33	13
	Roselle	21,064	69	59	10		Washington Township, Warren County	6,950	14	13	1
	Roselle Park	13,066	40	34	6		Watchung	6,256	36	29	7
	Roxbury Township	23,698	55	48	7		Waterford Township	10,660	26	24	2
	Rumson	7,162	22	17	5		Wayne Township	54,606	147	119	28
	Runnemede	8,424	22	20	2		Weehawken Township	12,593	63	58	5
	Rutherford	17,792	43	39	4		Wenonah	2,323	7	7	0
	Saddle Brook Township	13,565	36	33	3		Westampton Township	8,732	26	23	3
	Saddle River	3,769	23	18	5		West Amwell Township	2,931	7	6	1
	Salem	5,758	26	23	3		West Caldwell Township	10,749	35	29	6
	Sayreville	42,372	113	90	23		West Deptford Township	21,667	45	40	5
	Scotch Plains Township	23,143	52	45	7		Westfield	29,811	74	59	15
	Sea Bright	1,791	12	11	1		West Long Branch	8,275	24	20	4
	Sea Girt	2,035	16	12	4		West Milford Township	28,019	55	49	6
	Sea Isle City	2,936	33	22	11		West New York	46,193	130	119	11
	Seaside Heights	3,228	33	25	8		West Orange	43,343	135	119	16
	Seaside Park	2,292	20	15	5		West Paterson	11,184	31	26	5
	Secaucus	15,493	71	62	9		Westville	4,438	11	10	1
	Ship Bottom	1,421	12	11	1		West Wildwood	406	7	7	0
	Shrewsbury	3,701	21	16	5		West Windsor Township	26,163	58	47	11
	Somerdale	5,100	15	14	1		Westwood	10,886	31	25	6
	Somers Point	11,522	32	27	5		Wharton	6,183	22	21	1
	Somerville	12,494	39	32	7		Wildwood	5,285	58	46	12
	South Amboy	7,830	35	30	5						
	South Bound Brook	4,504	14	13	1						
	South Brunswick Township	40,390	107	82	25						
	South Hackensack Township	2,303	18	17	1						

Table 78.   Full-Time Law Enforcement Employees by State by City, 2007 *(Contd.)*

(Number.)

State	City	Population	Total law enforcement employees	Total officers	Total civilians	State	City	Population	Total law enforcement employees	Total officers	Total civilians
	Wildwood Crest	3,691	28	21	7		Akron Village	3,015	2	2	0
	Willingboro Township	32,899	85	73	12		Albany	93,916	457	334	123
	Winfield Township	1,479	9	9	0		Alexandria Bay Village	1,083	1	1	0
	Winslow Township	38,441	101	85	16		Alfred Village	4,995	6	6	0
	Woodbine	2,497	2	2	0		Allegany Village	1,795	2	2	0
	Woodbridge Township	98,769	257	205	52		Altamont Village	1,701	1	1	0
	Woodbury	10,364	30	27	3		Amherst Town	111,622	190	146	44
	Woodbury Heights	3,017	8	7	1		Amity Town and				
	Woodcliff Lake	5,927	19	18	1		Belmont Village	2,158	1	1	0
	Wood-Ridge	7,560	27	22	5		Amityville Village	9,412	29	26	3
	Woodstown	3,318	10	9	1		Amsterdam	17,678	38	37	1
	Woolwich Township	8,574	20	19	1		Arcade Village	1,927	6	6	0
	Wyckoff Township	17,091	33	25	8		Ardsley Village	4,943	20	20	0
NEW MEXICO	Alamogordo	36,162	121	74	47		Asharoken Village	635	3	3	0
	Albuquerque	513,124	1,384	986	398		Attica Village	2,464	4	4	0
	Angel Fire	1,115	7	5	2		Auburn	27,662	77	69	8
	Artesia	10,563	46	31	15		Avon Village	2,955	5	5	0
	Aztec	7,154	18	15	3		Baldwinsville Village	7,105	18	15	3
	Bayard	2,371	6	6	0		Ballston Spa Village	5,511	9	5	4
	Belen	7,128	26	20	6		Batavia	15,368	37	31	6
	Bernalillo	7,200	21	18	3		Beacon	14,928	36	34	2
	Bloomfield	7,529	22	17	5		Bedford Town	18,668	50	45	5
	Bosque Farms	3,991	12	11	1		Bethlehem Town	33,057	62	43	19
	Carlsbad	25,360	72	51	21		Binghamton	44,931	154	145	9
	Carrizozo	1,099	4	1	3		Blooming Grove Town	12,396	17	15	2
	Cimarron	848	4	3	1		Bolivar Village	1,126	1	1	0
	Clayton	2,080	16	8	8		Boonville Village	2,074	2	2	0
	Cloudcroft	755	3	3	0		Brant Town	1,849	1	1	0
	Clovis	33,395	79	54	25		Briarcliff Manor				
	Corrales	7,936	21	18	3		Village	8,034	20	20	0
	Cuba	640	5	4	1		Brighton Town	34,335	47	41	6
	Deming	15,449	35	30	5		Brockport Village	8,138	12	11	1
	Dexter	1,243	4	4	0		Bronxville Village	6,477	18	15	3
	Espanola	9,607	28	20	8		Buchanan Village	2,279	6	6	0
	Estancia	1,545	4	3	1		Buffalo	273,832	856	708	148
	Eunice	2,636	12	7	5		Cairo Town	6,689	2	2	0
	Farmington	44,396	165	127	38		Cambridge Village	1,843	6	6	0
	Gallup	19,160	71	50	21		Camden Village	2,288	2	2	0
	Grants	9,000	21	17	4		Camillus Town and				
	Hatch	1,648	9	7	2		Village	23,350	26	24	2
	Hobbs	29,378	117	75	42		Canajoharie Village	2,186	5	5	0
	Hurley	1,363	5	4	1		Canastota Village	4,401	8	7	1
	Jal	2,046	9	5	4		Canton Village	6,100	11	9	2
	Las Cruces	87,958	243	168	75		Carmel Town	34,972	41	35	6
	Las Vegas	13,797	50	33	17		Carthage Village	3,717	5	5	0
	Lordsburg	2,691	12	9	3		Catskill Village	4,337	16	15	1
	Los Alamos	19,088	81	35	46		Cayuga Heights Village	3,670	7	6	1
	Los Lunas	12,022	32	28	4		Cazenovia Village	2,717	6	6	0
	Lovington	9,723	31	23	8		Centre Island Village	437	8	8	0
	Melrose	721	1	1	0		Chatham Village	1,726	4	3	1
	Mesilla	2,198	10	9	1		Cheektowaga Town	79,164	168	127	41
	Milan	2,651	9	5	4		Chester Town	9,929	13	13	0
	Moriarty	1,797	11	10	1		Chester Village	3,616	11	10	1
	Portales	11,334	38	24	14		Chittenango Village	4,936	7	6	1
	Questa	1,908	3	2	1		Cicero Town	28,347	15	14	1
	Raton	6,721	22	15	7		Clarkstown Town	78,909	196	169	27
	Red River	494	9	4	5		Clayton Village	1,839	3	3	0
	Rio Rancho	74,542	190	121	69		Clay Town	54,134	22	17	5
	Roswell	45,581	104	75	29		Clifton Springs Village	2,174	2	2	0
	Ruidoso	9,524	39	25	14		Clyde Village	2,133	5	4	1
	Ruidoso Downs	2,080	14	6	8		Cobleskill Village	4,647	12	12	0
	Santa Clara	1,823	6	6	0		Coeymans Town	7,991	9	6	3
	Santa Rosa	2,450	17	10	7		Cohoes	14,944	48	35	13
	Silver City	9,903	36	31	5		Colchester Town	2,054	2	2	0
	Socorro	8,570	31	20	11		Cold Spring Village	2,008	1	1	0
	Sunland Park	14,364	24	21	3		Colonie Town	77,550	152	108	44
	Taos	5,253	29	22	7		Cooperstown Village	1,911	6	5	1
	Taos Ski Valley	57	3	3	0		Corning	10,428	27	23	4
	Tatum	717	4	2	2		Cornwall-on-Hudson				
	Texico	1,050	3	3	0		Village	3,094	4	4	0
	Truth or Consequences	6,869	16	14	2		Cornwall Town	9,763	15	11	4
	Wagon Mound	350	1	1	0		Cortland	18,382	46	43	3
NEW YORK	Addison Town and						Coxsackie Village	2,835	1	1	0
	Village	2,559	2	2	0		Crawford Town	9,540	14	12	2

Table 78. Full-Time Law Enforcement Employees by State by City, 2007 (Contd.)

(Number.)

State	City	Population	Total law enforcement employees	Total officers	Total civilians	State	City	Population	Total law enforcement employees	Total officers	Total civilians
	Croton-on-Hudson Village	7,938	23	21	2		Herkimer Village	7,117	22	21	1
	Cuba Town	3,364	4	4	0		Highland Falls Village	3,742	15	11	4
	Dansville Village	4,574	9	7	2		Hoosick Falls Village	3,289	5	3	2
	Deerpark Town	8,433	7	7	0		Hornell	8,662	23	22	1
	Delhi Village	2,745	4	4	0		Horseheads Village	6,256	14	12	2
	Depew Village	15,473	36	29	7		Hudson	6,914	32	26	6
	Deposit Village	1,605	3	3	0		Hudson Falls Village	6,752	15	12	3
	Dewitt Town	21,606	40	37	3		Hunter Town	2,756	1	1	0
	Dobbs Ferry Village	11,206	30	28	2		Huntington Bay Village	1,472	6	6	0
	Dolgeville Village	2,060	3	3	0		Hyde Park Town	20,675	17	14	3
	Dryden Village	1,821	7	6	1		Ilion Village	8,187	20	18	2
	Dunkirk	12,190	37	36	1		Inlet Town	389	2	2	0
	East Aurora-Aurora Town	13,611	21	16	5		Irondequoit Town	50,106	69	58	11
	Eastchester Town	18,768	55	48	7		Irvington Village	6,658	24	22	2
	East Fishkill Town	29,535	38	28	10		Ithaca	29,970	86	70	16
	East Greenbush Town	17,159	32	24	8		Jamestown	29,646	74	62	12
	East Hampton Town	19,143	87	61	26		Johnstown	8,489	26	25	1
	East Rochester Village	6,231	8	7	1		Kenmore Village	15,172	24	24	0
	East Syracuse Village	3,029	11	9	2		Kensington Village	1,181	6	6	0
	Eden Town	7,789	5	4	1		Kent Town	14,443	26	21	5
	Ellenville Village	3,914	12	10	2		Kings Point Village	5,204	25	23	2
	Ellicott Town	5,294	13	12	1		Kingston	22,741	85	79	6
	Ellicottville	1,880	3	3	0		Kirkland Town	8,423	6	6	0
	Elmira	29,375	91	78	13		Lackawanna	17,775	67	47	20
	Elmira Heights Village	3,931	10	10	0		Lake Placid Village	2,840	18	14	4
	Elmira Town	5,907	2	2	0		Lake Success Village	2,833	27	23	4
	Elmsford Village	4,772	18	18	0		Lakewood-Busti	7,455	9	9	0
	Endicott Village	12,499	41	37	4		Lancaster Town	23,342	64	49	15
	Evans Town	17,000	31	26	5		Larchmont Village	6,535	32	27	5
	Fairport Village	5,467	11	10	1		Le Roy Village	4,226	12	9	3
	Fallsburg Town	12,082	20	16	4		Lewisboro Town	12,606	2	2	0
	Floral Park Village	15,550	46	34	12		Lewiston Town and Village	16,766	10	9	1
	Florida Village	2,793	1	1	0		Liberty Village	3,973	20	17	3
	Fort Plain Village	2,201	4	4	0		Little Falls	4,952	13	12	1
	Frankfort Village	2,409	1	1	0		Lloyd Harbor Village	3,654	13	12	1
	Franklinville Village	1,741	2	2	0		Lloyd Town	10,771	13	11	2
	Fredonia Village	11,192	19	15	4		Lockport	20,872	49	49	0
	Freeport Village	43,050	102	88	14		Long Beach	35,057	96	76	20
	Freeville Village	505	1	1	0		Lowville Village	3,216	7	7	0
	Fulton City	11,404	37	35	2		Lynbrook Village	19,392	56	48	8
	Garden City Village	21,804	68	55	13		Lyons Village	3,475	12	10	2
	Gates Town	28,396	36	29	7		Macedon Town and Village	8,963	3	3	0
	Geddes Town	10,616	18	16	2		Malone Village	5,879	14	14	0
	Geneseo Village	7,841	8	8	0		Malverne Village	8,725	25	24	1
	Geneva	13,336	38	33	5		Mamaroneck Town	11,470	41	40	1
	Glen Cove	26,406	55	51	4		Mamaroneck Village	18,468	58	52	6
	Glens Falls	14,043	36	31	5		Manlius Town	25,127	45	38	7
	Glenville Town	21,347	36	22	14		Marcellus Village	1,777	1	1	0
	Gloversville	15,146	34	32	2		Marlborough Town	8,351	10	8	2
	Goshen Town	8,608	12	11	1		Massena Village	10,747	26	21	5
	Goshen Village	5,527	19	17	2		Maybrook Village	4,185	2	2	0
	Gouverneur Village	4,088	12	8	4		Mechanicville	4,912	12	11	1
	Granville Village	2,585	6	6	0		Medina Village	6,160	11	10	1
	Great Neck Estates Village	2,711	15	13	2		Menands Village	3,782	12	9	3
	Greece Town	93,123	101	94	7		Middleport Village	1,803	3	3	0
	Greenburgh Town	43,734	142	120	22		Middletown	26,097	89	75	14
	Greene Village	1,683	2	1	1		Mohawk Village	2,523	4	4	0
	Green Island Village	2,591	2	1	1		Monroe Village	8,187	23	18	5
	Greenwich Village	1,858	6	6	0		Montgomery Town	8,921	14	13	1
	Greenwood Lake Village	3,460	8	6	2		Monticello Village	6,654	27	24	3
	Guilderland Town	33,006	50	34	16		Moriah Town	3,547	2	2	0
	Hamburg Town	44,187	76	57	19		Mount Kisco Village	10,505	36	33	3
	Hamburg Village	9,413	17	15	2		Mount Morris Village	2,944	5	5	0
	Hamilton Village	3,787	3	3	0		Mount Pleasant Town	26,693	56	47	9
	Hammondsport Village	697	1	1	0		Mount Vernon	68,380	230	201	29
	Harriman Village	2,274	7	7	0		Newark Village	9,234	17	16	1
	Harrison Town	26,654	92	83	9		New Berlin Town	1,717	1	1	0
	Hastings-on-Hudson Village	7,858	21	21	0		Newburgh	28,340	108	95	13
	Haverstraw Town	24,515	75	71	4		Newburgh Town	30,995	72	59	13
	Hempstead Village	52,430	134	107	27		New Castle Town	17,819	46	42	4
							New Hartford Town and Village	19,586	31	20	11

Table 78.   Full-Time Law Enforcement Employees by State by City, 2007 *(Contd.)*
(Number.)

State	City	Population	Total law enforcement employees	Total officers	Total civilians	State	City	Population	Total law enforcement employees	Total officers	Total civilians
	New Paltz Town and Village	14,121	25	24	1		Shandaken Town	3,113	4	4	0
	New Rochelle	73,603	252	183	69		Shawangunk Town	12,813	5	5	0
	New Windsor Town	25,320	58	46	12		Shelter Island Town	2,471	10	9	1
	New York	8,220,196	53,848	35,404	18,444		Sherrill	3,152	4	4	0
	Niagara Falls	51,897	161	144	17		Sidney Village	3,809	8	8	0
	Niagara Town	8,515	7	6	1		Silver Creek Village	2,842	6	5	1
	Niskayuna Town	21,863	40	29	11		Skaneateles Village	2,585	5	5	0
	Nissequogue Village	1,458	3	3	0		Sleepy Hollow Village	10,262	26	26	0
	North Castle Town	12,317	41	38	3		Solvay Village	6,514	15	13	2
	North Greenbush Town	11,837	19	17	2		Southampton Town	50,284	118	103	15
	Northport Village	7,480	19	15	4		South Glens Falls Village	3,435	6	6	0
	North Syracuse Village	6,668	14	13	1		South Nyack Village	3,358	6	6	0
	North Tonawanda	31,575	58	48	10		Southold Town	19,872	71	52	19
	Norwich	7,183	19	18	1		Spring Valley Village	25,397	66	57	9
	Ocean Beach Village	145	2	2	0		Stony Point Town	15,073	31	30	1
	Ogdensburg	11,213	31	26	5		Suffern Village	10,944	32	27	5
	Ogden Town	19,186	15	12	3		Syracuse	139,880	553	489	64
	Old Brookville Village	2,254	52	40	12		Tarrytown Village	11,525	41	34	7
	Old Westbury Village	5,340	31	26	5		Ticonderoga Town	5,076	10	7	3
	Olean	14,485	33	32	1		Tonawanda	14,971	34	29	5
	Olive Town	4,720	1	1	0		Tonawanda Town	57,312	156	104	52
	Oneida	10,928	27	24	3		Troy	47,776	132	116	16
	Oneonta City	13,239	29	25	4		Tuckahoe Village	6,311	29	26	3
	Orangetown Town	36,171	101	92	9		Tupper Lake Village	3,842	9	9	0
	Orchard Park Town	28,208	38	33	5		Tuxedo Park Village	726	5	2	3
	Ossining Town	5,755	18	18	0		Tuxedo Town	3,033	15	12	3
	Ossining Village	23,514	69	60	9		Ulster Town	12,877	32	28	4
	Oswego City	17,573	57	49	8		Utica	58,888	199	182	17
	Owego Village	3,760	7	7	0		Vernon Village	1,168	1	1	0
	Oxford Village	1,566	1	1	0		Vestal Town	27,403	41	37	4
	Oyster Bay Cove Village	2,248	10	10	0		Walden Village	6,929	16	13	3
	Painted Post Village	1,784	5	5	0		Wallkill Town	27,554	48	41	7
	Palmyra Village	3,475	6	5	1		Walton Village	2,880	7	6	1
	Peekskill	24,910	74	59	15		Wappingers Falls Village	5,181	4	2	2
	Pelham Manor Village	5,420	28	28	0		Washingtonville Village	6,239	18	16	2
	Pelham Village	6,403	30	27	3		Waterford Town and Village	8,660	13	10	3
	Penn Yan Village	5,217	12	11	1		Waterloo Village	5,098	8	7	1
	Perry Village	3,743	5	4	1		Watertown	26,726	77	73	4
	Piermont Village	2,603	8	8	0		Watervliet	9,749	30	26	4
	Plattsburgh City	19,365	54	48	6		Watkins Glen Village	2,092	5	5	0
	Port Chester Village	28,019	65	62	3		Waverly Village	4,442	11	10	1
	Port Dickinson Village	1,605	4	4	0		Wayland Village	1,819	2	2	0
	Port Jervis	9,203	33	32	1		Webster Town and Village	41,471	38	33	5
	Portville Village	973	1	1	0		Wellsville Village	4,877	15	11	4
	Port Washington	18,532	70	63	7		Westfield Village	3,405	5	5	0
	Potsdam Village	9,869	17	14	3		Westhampton Beach Village	1,956	20	18	2
	Poughkeepsie	30,074	141	107	34		West Seneca Town	43,955	80	66	14
	Poughkeepsie Town	44,016	98	87	11		Whitehall Village	2,609	5	5	0
	Pulaski Village	2,323	2	2	0		White Plains	57,638	233	218	15
	Quogue Village	1,125	13	13	0		Whitesboro Village	3,823	8	8	0
	Ramapo Town	76,371	143	119	24		Whitestown Town	9,348	6	6	0
	Rensselaer City	7,822	33	27	6		Windham Town	1,914	3	3	0
	Riverhead Town	35,087	106	84	22		Woodbury Town	10,458	26	22	4
	Rochester	206,686	907	734	173		Woodstock Town	6,214	14	10	4
	Rockville Centre Village	23,952	60	50	10		Yonkers	198,071	722	645	77
	Rome	34,123	82	78	4		Yorktown Town	38,003	65	56	9
	Rosendale Town	6,312	2	1	1		Yorkville Village	2,593	4	4	0
	Rotterdam Town	29,547	61	44	17	**NORTH CAROLINA**..............	Aberdeen	5,337	26	24	2
	Rouses Point Village	2,420	2	2	0		Ahoskie	4,278	22	15	7
	Rye	15,127	44	39	5		Albemarle	15,355	55	49	6
	Rye Brook Village	9,820	29	28	1		Andrews	1,719	6	6	0
	Sag Harbor Village	2,363	12	12	0		Angier	4,288	13	12	1
	Sands Point Village	2,839	21	21	0		Apex	31,816	65	51	14
	Saranac Lake Village	4,895	13	12	1		Archdale	9,474	33	27	6
	Saratoga Springs	28,807	89	71	18		Asheboro	24,399	82	76	6
	Saugerties Town	15,816	21	17	4		Asheville	72,907	250	201	49
	Saugerties Village	3,912	13	12	1		Atlantic Beach	1,839	22	18	4
	Scarsdale Village	17,890	51	45	6		Aulander	869	1	1	0
	Schenectady	61,535	203	158	45		Aurora	581	1	1	0
	Schodack Town	11,374	12	10	2		Ayden	4,852	20	16	4
	Schoharie Village	1,001	1	1	0						
	Scotia Village	8,107	14	13	1						
	Seneca Falls Village	6,791	19	12	7						

Table 78. Full-Time Law Enforcement Employees by State by City, 2007 *(Contd.)*

(Number.)

State	City	Population	Total law enforcement employees	Total officers	Total civilians	State	City	Population	Total law enforcement employees	Total officers	Total civilians
	Badin	1,357	5	5	0		Erwin	4,843	10	9	1
	Bailey	679	3	3	0		Fair Bluff	1,164	3	3	0
	Bald Head Island	295	12	11	1		Fairmont	2,737	15	12	3
	Banner Elk	895	9	8	1		Farmville	4,553	21	16	5
	Beaufort	4,326	17	16	1		Fayetteville	167,157	510	342	168
	Beech Mountain	307	14	10	4		Fletcher	4,662	15	14	1
	Belhaven	1,997	13	9	4		Forest City	7,277	37	31	6
	Belmont	9,005	42	33	9		Four Oaks	1,881	6	6	0
	Benson	3,422	15	14	1		Foxfire Village	477	3	3	0
	Bethel	1,680	5	5	0		Franklin	3,633	19	17	2
	Beulaville	1,117	5	5	0		Franklinton	1,948	10	9	1
	Biltmore Forest	1,527	14	13	1		Fremont	1,428	5	3	2
	Biscoe	1,732	10	9	1		Fuquay-Varina	14,661	34	29	5
	Black Creek	702	3	3	0		Garland	841	2	2	0
	Black Mountain	7,686	22	18	4		Garner	24,547	61	55	6
	Bladenboro	1,701	6	6	0		Garysburg	1,171	2	2	0
	Blowing Rock	1,426	13	9	4		Gaston	910	2	2	0
	Boiling Spring Lakes	4,637	8	7	1		Gastonia	70,127	185	161	24
	Boiling Springs	3,856	8	8	0		Gibsonville	4,627	15	14	1
	Boone	13,283	43	35	8		Glen Alpine	1,074	2	2	0
	Brevard	6,634	28	22	6		Goldsboro	38,053	107	97	10
	Broadway	1,123	4	4	0		Graham	14,275	35	32	3
	Bryson City	1,382	7	6	1		Granite Falls	4,597	15	13	2
	Bunn	402	3	3	0		Granite Quarry	2,243	7	7	0
	Burgaw	3,975	11	10	1		Greensboro	238,122	645	534	111
	Burlington	48,689	144	105	39		Greenville	73,319	206	164	42
	Burnsville	1,652	8	8	0		Grifton	2,174	5	5	0
	Butner	6,520	49	42	7		Hamlet	5,715	23	19	4
	Cameron	301	1	1	0		Havelock	21,839	34	27	7
	Candor	842	6	6	0		Henderson	16,165	56	47	9
	Canton	3,925	18	13	5		Hendersonville	11,863	47	35	12
	Cape Carteret	1,460	7	7	0		Hertford	2,135	7	6	1
	Carolina Beach	5,675	31	28	3		Hickory	41,008	140	114	26
	Carrboro	16,514	38	35	3		Highlands	948	12	11	1
	Carthage	2,036	12	11	1		High Point	99,297	252	216	36
	Cary	114,221	188	150	38		Hillsborough	5,380	29	26	3
	Caswell Beach	490	4	4	0		Holden Beach	863	10	10	0
	Catawba	792	2	2	0		Holly Ridge	727	8	8	0
	Chadbourn	2,071	9	8	1		Holly Springs	18,704	44	36	8
	Chapel Hill	50,198	137	115	22		Hope Mills	12,778	40	30	10
	Charlotte-Mecklenburg[1]	733,291	2,018	1,515	503		Hot Springs	641	1	1	0
	Cherryville	5,533	26	17	9		Hudson	3,075	13	12	1
	China Grove	3,723	12	12	0		Huntersville	41,018	80	71	9
	Chocowinity	730	3	3	0		Indian Beach	96	4	4	0
	Claremont	1,127	9	8	1		Jackson	658	1	1	0
	Clayton	14,843	42	38	4		Jacksonville	70,368	129	109	20
	Cleveland	829	4	4	0		Jefferson	1,368	2	2	0
	Clinton	8,818	34	31	3		Jonesville	2,296	11	10	1
	Clyde	1,295	4	4	0		Kannapolis	40,554	94	71	23
	Columbus	993	6	6	0		Kenansville	902	4	4	0
	Concord	63,284	162	144	18		Kenly	1,894	10	8	2
	Conover	7,183	23	22	1		Kernersville	22,325	81	63	18
	Conway	686	1	1	0		Kill Devil Hills	6,718	31	25	6
	Cooleemee	976	3	3	0		King	6,639	19	17	2
	Cornelius	21,563	52	38	14		Kings Mountain	11,003	39	32	7
	Cramerton	3,050	12	12	0		Kinston	22,568	84	74	10
	Creedmoor	3,472	17	13	4		Kitty Hawk	3,391	16	14	2
	Dallas	3,433	15	11	4		Knightdale	6,530	22	21	1
	Davidson	9,023	19	18	1		Kure Beach	2,441	11	10	1
	Denton	1,483	5	5	0		La Grange	2,782	8	8	0
	Dobson	1,506	5	5	0		Lake Lure	1,022	11	10	1
	Drexel	1,900	5	5	0		Lake Royale		5	5	0
	Dunn	10,072	53	38	15		Lake Waccamaw	1,464	5	5	0
	Durham	211,873	608	474	134		Landis	3,074	11	10	1
	East Bend	672	2	2	0		Laurel Park	2,123	7	7	0
	East Spencer	1,770	5	5	0		Laurinburg	15,743	42	36	6
	Eden	15,608	55	45	10		Leland	4,693	33	30	3
	Edenton	4,988	14	12	2		Lenoir	17,988	68	51	17
	Elizabeth City	19,279	63	48	15		Lexington	20,452	69	55	14
	Elizabethtown	3,841	16	15	1		Liberty	2,743	11	10	1
	Elkin	4,314	20	17	3		Lillington	3,214	13	12	1
	Elon	7,173	16	15	1		Lincolnton	10,646	34	29	5
	Emerald Isle	3,752	21	16	5		Littleton	650	4	4	0
	Enfield	2,345	10	9	1		Locust	2,562	9	8	1

[1] The employee data presented in this table for Charlotte-Mecklenburg represent only Charlotte-Mecklenburg Police Department employees and exclude Mecklenburg County Sheriff's Office employees.

Table 78.   Full-Time Law Enforcement Employees by State by City, 2007 *(Contd.)*

(Number.)

State	City	Population	Total law enforcement employees	Total officers	Total civilians	State	City	Population	Total law enforcement employees	Total officers	Total civilians
	Long View	4,904	15	15	0		Roanoke Rapids	16,407	46	40	6
	Louisburg	3,813	13	12	1		Robbins	1,238	4	4	0
	Lowell	2,706	9	9	0		Robersonville	1,601	7	7	0
	Lumberton	21,983	76	66	10		Rockingham	9,093	40	35	5
	Madison	2,283	13	12	1		Rockwell	1,989	5	5	0
	Maggie Valley	810	9	8	1		Rocky Mount	57,132	188	146	42
	Magnolia	987	2	2	0		Rolesville	1,805	10	10	0
	Maiden	3,366	15	14	1		Roseboro	1,463	5	5	0
	Manteo	1,336	8	7	1		Rose Hill	1,403	4	4	0
	Marion	5,070	27	22	5		Rowland	1,157	6	5	1
	Marshall	837	5	5	0		Roxboro	8,738	37	33	4
	Mars Hill	1,821	5	5	0		Rutherfordton	4,090	15	15	0
	Marshville	3,054	8	8	0		Salisbury	28,449	99	77	22
	Matthews	26,693	67	56	11		Saluda	581	5	5	0
	Maxton	2,666	12	8	4		Sanford	28,413	98	79	19
	Mayodan	2,624	16	14	2		Scotland Neck	2,195	5	4	1
	Maysville	978	2	2	0		Seagrove	262	1	1	0
	McAdenville	643	2	2	0		Selma	6,877	25	23	2
	Mebane	9,555	21	16	5		Seven Devils	160	5	5	0
	Middlesex	856	5	5	0		Shallotte	1,698	16	15	1
	Mint Hill	18,810	30	28	2		Sharpsburg	2,432	7	7	0
	Mocksville	4,568	23	21	2		Shelby	21,437	85	68	17
	Monroe	31,345	93	82	11		Siler City	8,636	26	21	5
	Montreat	710	5	5	0		Smithfield	12,456	41	37	4
	Mooresville	21,143	64	48	16		Southern Pines	12,351	38	29	9
	Morehead City	9,501	44	35	9		Southern Shores	2,708	10	9	1
	Morganton	17,183	94	60	34		Southport	2,960	11	10	1
	Morrisville	14,336	28	26	2		Sparta	1,767	6	6	0
	Mount Airy	8,448	54	42	12		Spencer	3,355	14	13	1
	Mount Gilead	1,406	5	5	0		Spindale	3,916	12	12	0
	Mount Holly	9,811	35	28	7		Spring Hope	1,280	5	5	0
	Mount Olive	4,391	16	15	1		Spring Lake	8,080	26	20	6
	Murfreesboro	2,276	14	9	5		Spruce Pine	1,973	10	10	0
	Murphy	1,573	13	9	4		Stallings	4,201	22	20	2
	Nags Head	3,114	20	18	2		Stanfield	1,113	4	4	0
	Nashville	4,509	15	14	1		Stanley	3,134	15	12	3
	Navassa	1,726	4	4	0		Stantonsburg	707	4	4	0
	New Bern	28,254	127	81	46		Star	814	4	4	0
	Newland	663	5	5	0		Statesville	25,756	87	68	19
	Newport	4,070	9	9	0		Stoneville	986	5	5	0
	Newton	13,211	43	35	8		St. Pauls	2,053	17	12	5
	Norlina	1,026	5	5	0		Sugar Mountain	213	5	5	0
	North Topsail Beach	874	12	11	1		Sunset Beach	2,296	12	12	0
	Northwest	891	2	2	0		Surf City	1,873	19	17	2
	North Wilkesboro	4,195	24	21	3		Swansboro	1,540	8	8	0
	Norwood	2,150	8	7	1		Sylva	2,369	13	12	1
	Oakboro	1,176	4	4	0		Tabor City	2,641	10	9	1
	Oak Island	8,355	30	24	6		Tarboro	10,463	34	28	6
	Ocean Isle Beach	536	13	13	0		Thomasville	26,437	72	64	8
	Old Fort	963	6	5	1		Topsail Beach	577	8	7	1
	Oxford	8,567	38	31	7		Trent Woods	3,889	5	5	0
	Pembroke	2,677	18	14	4		Troutman	1,767	9	9	0
	Pikeville	703	3	3	0		Troy	3,408	10	9	1
	Pilot Mountain	1,276	9	8	1		Tryon	1,745	10	8	2
	Pinebluff	1,352	4	4	0		Valdese	4,525	13	12	1
	Pinehurst	12,132	31	26	5		Vanceboro	830	2	2	0
	Pine Knoll Shores	1,584	10	9	1		Vass	778	3	3	0
	Pine Level	1,480	4	4	0		Wadesboro	5,134	27	22	5
	Pinetops	1,293	7	5	2		Wagram	782	1	1	0
	Pineville	3,826	46	35	11		Wake Forest	24,348	53	45	8
	Pink Hill	535	1	1	0		Wallace	3,603	15	12	3
	Pittsboro	2,537	11	10	1		Walnut Cove	1,613	6	6	0
	Plymouth	3,930	12	12	0		Walnut Creek	850	2	2	0
	Princeton	1,248	3	3	0		Warsaw	3,149	15	11	4
	Raeford	3,646	15	14	1		Washington	10,092	37	29	8
	Raleigh	367,120	848	725	123		Waxhaw	3,505	14	13	1
	Ramseur	1,728	8	8	0		Waynesville	9,436	37	31	6
	Randleman	3,700	14	14	0		Weaverville	2,543	14	13	1
	Ranlo	2,222	7	7	0		Weldon	1,290	7	7	0
	Red Springs	3,518	23	17	6		Wendell	4,867	16	14	2
	Reidsville	14,906	56	46	10		West Jefferson	1,128	6	6	0
	Richlands	835	4	4	0		Whispering Pines	2,138	9	8	1
	Rich Square	996	2	2	0		Whitakers	772	3	3	0
	River Bend	3,086	5	5	0		White Lake	581	6	6	0

Table 78.   Full-Time Law Enforcement Employees by State by City, 2007 *(Contd.)*

(Number.)

State	City	Population	Total law enforcement employees	Total officers	Total civilians	State	City	Population	Total law enforcement employees	Total officers	Total civilians
	Whiteville	5,239	29	25	4		Ashville	3,285	7	7	0
	Wilkesboro	3,193	20	18	2		Athens	20,833	30	23	7
	Williamston	5,531	21	20	1		Aurora	14,512	34	26	8
	Wilmington	96,913	306	254	52		Austintown	35,888	47	38	9
	Wilson	47,727	133	111	22		Avon	17,300	38	30	8
	Wilson's Mills	1,535	3	3	0		Avon Lake	22,725	34	29	5
	Windsor	2,175	8	8	0		Bainbridge Township	11,334	25	17	8
	Wingate	3,876	7	7	0		Baltic	743	1	1	0
	Winston-Salem	198,316	674	500	174		Baltimore	2,948	2	2	0
	Winterville	4,658	21	19	2		Barberton	26,942	54	42	12
	Woodfin	3,335	13	13	0		Barnesville	4,118	11	7	4
	Woodland	776	1	1	0		Batavia	1,691	4	4	0
	Wrightsville Beach	2,573	25	23	2		Bath Township,				
	Yadkinville	2,898	13	12	1		Summit County	10,277	28	20	8
	Yanceyville	2,152	5	5	0		Bay Village	14,828	27	24	3
	Youngsville	738	10	9	1		Bazetta Township	6,124	6	6	0
	Zebulon	4,358	21	20	1		Beach City	1,099	1	1	0
NORTH DAKOTA	Beulah	2,974	6	5	1		Beachwood	11,239	57	43	14
	Bismarck	58,648	117	89	28		Beavercreek	39,552	63	48	15
	Bowman	1,473	3	3	0		Beaver Township	6,176	16	12	4
	Burlington	989	2	2	0		Bedford	13,201	43	33	10
	Cando	1,087	1	1	0		Bedford Heights	10,568	68	33	35
	Carrington	2,131	4	4	0		Bellaire	4,674	11	11	0
	Cavalier	1,404	4	4	0		Bellbrook	6,892	17	12	5
	Crosby	981	2	2	0		Bellefontaine	12,772	30	23	7
	Devils Lake	6,647	18	16	2		Bellevue	7,967	18	14	4
	Dickinson	15,595	44	30	14		Bellville	1,731	6	6	0
	Elgin	576	1	1	0		Belpre	6,518	15	10	5
	Emerado	466	1	1	0		Bentleyville Village	909	3	3	0
	Fargo	89,998	148	130	18		Berea	18,026	39	32	7
	Fessenden	519	1	1	0		Berlin Heights	645	1	1	0
	Grafton	4,118	10	9	1		Bethel	2,608	7	6	1
	Grand Forks	50,477	94	78	16		Bethesda	1,365	1	1	0
	Harvey	1,671	3	3	0		Beverly	1,310	3	3	0
	Hazen	2,303	4	4	0		Bexley	12,161	35	28	7
	Hillsboro	1,502	2	2	0		Blanchester	4,382	7	7	0
	Jamestown	14,696	32	28	4		Blendon Township	7,561	12	11	1
	Lamoure	851	1	1	0		Bluffton	3,992	7	7	0
	Larimore	1,273	2	2	0		Boardman	40,038	69	54	15
	Lincoln	2,548	2	2	0		Bolivar	894	1	1	0
	Linton	1,071	1	1	0		Bowling Green	29,733	58	43	15
	Lisbon	2,185	3	3	0		Bratenahl	1,287	11	10	1
	Mandan	17,521	38	26	12		Brecksville	13,065	36	29	7
	Mayville	1,919	3	3	0		Brewster	2,308	5	5	0
	Minot	34,487	82	60	22		Bridgeport	2,079	7	5	2
	Napoleon	712	1	1	0		Brimfield Township	7,854	13	11	2
	Northwood	853	2	2	0		Broadview Heights	17,798	44	30	14
	Oakes	1,797	3	3	0		Brookfield Township	9,664	10	9	1
	Rolla	1,451	3	3	0		Brooklyn	10,574	41	33	8
	Rugby	2,606	4	4	0		Brooklyn Heights	1,474	17	17	0
	South Heart	294	1	1	0		Brook Park	19,498	55	44	11
	Steele	676	1	1	0		Brookville	5,307	14	11	3
	Thompson	937	1	1	0		Brunswick	35,334	55	40	15
	Valley City	6,325	19	13	6		Bryan	8,327	26	19	7
	Wahpeton	7,850	16	14	2		Buchtel	600	1	1	0
	Watford City	1,371	4	4	0		Buckeye Lake	3,055	3	3	0
	West Fargo	22,462	45	32	13		Bucyrus	12,493	26	20	6
	Williston	12,260	30	22	8		Burton	1,445	3	3	0
	Wishek	962	2	2	0		Butler Township	8,208	16	15	1
OHIO	Aberdeen	1,619	2	2	0		Cadiz	3,379	6	6	0
	Ada	5,881	11	8	3		Caldwell	1,921	2	2	0
	Addyston	932	1	1	0		Cambridge	11,444	29	24	5
	Akron	208,701	519	474	45		Camden	2,248	3	3	0
	Alliance	22,703	51	38	13		Campbell	8,630	14	14	0
	Amberley Village	3,204	20	16	4		Canal Fulton	5,106	9	8	1
	Amelia	3,624	7	6	1		Canfield	7,014	20	15	5
	Amherst	11,850	26	20	6		Canton	78,653	206	168	38
	Ansonia	1,099	2	2	0		Cardington	2,011	4	4	0
	Arcanum	2,002	4	4	0		Carey	3,811	10	6	4
	Archbold	4,530	8	8	0		Carlisle	5,985	8	7	1
	Arlington Heights	790	3	3	0		Carrollton	3,295	7	7	0
	Ashland	21,939	41	29	12		Celina	10,403	22	16	6
	Ashtabula	20,071	37	32	5		Centerville	23,049	52	39	13
							Chagrin Falls	3,701	19	11	8

Table 78. Full-Time Law Enforcement Employees by State by City, 2007 (Contd.)

(Number.)

State	City	Popula-tion	Total law enforce-ment employees	Total officers	Total civilians	State	City	Popula-tion	Total law enforce-ment employees	Total officers	Total civilians
	Champion Township	9,409	8	8	0		Garfield Heights	28,221	80	61	19
	Chardon	5,298	17	11	6		Gates Mills	2,308	15	11	4
	Chester Township	11,061	14	13	1		Geneva	6,413	16	12	4
	Cheviot	7,925	10	10	0		Geneva-on-the-Lake	1,522	5	5	0
	Chillicothe	22,227	53	47	6		Genoa	2,319	5	4	1
	Cincinnati	332,388	1,363	1,107	256		Genoa Township	15,674	27	25	2
	Circleville	13,648	31	24	7		Georgetown	3,624	7	7	0
	Clay Center	309	2	2	0		Germantown	5,126	12	11	1
	Clayton	13,030	15	15	0		German Township, Clark County	7,359	4	4	0
	Clay Township, Ottawa County	2,732	5	5	0		German Township, Montgomery County	3,255	6	6	0
	Cleveland	439,888	2,021	1,655	366		Gibsonburg	2,478	4	4	0
	Cleveland Heights	46,609	121	109	12		Girard	10,306	17	14	3
	Cleves	2,501	4	4	0		Glendale	2,090	7	7	0
	Clinton Township	3,938	9	9	0		Gnadenhutten	1,294	2	2	0
	Clyde	6,172	18	14	4		Golf Manor	3,551	10	9	1
	Coitsville Township	1,654	2	2	0		Goshen Township, Clermont County	16,421	13	12	1
	Coldwater	4,454	6	6	0		Granville	5,306	13	10	3
	Columbiana	5,977	12	12	0		Greenfield	5,172	12	10	2
	Conneaut	12,573	27	20	7		Greenhills	3,619	9	8	1
	Copley Township	14,145	29	22	7		Greenville	12,978	30	23	7
	Cortland	6,508	10	10	0		Greenwich	1,535	4	4	0
	Crestline	5,077	13	9	4		Grove City	32,472	74	58	16
	Creston	2,132	2	1	1		Groveport	5,087	19	18	1
	Cridersville	1,743	3	3	0		Hamilton	62,330	165	139	26
	Crooksville	2,469	6	5	1		Hanging Rock	295	5	5	0
	Cross Creek Township	5,618	3	3	0		Harrison	8,440	23	21	2
	Cuyahoga Falls	50,543	112	93	19		Hartville	2,564	7	7	0
	Danville	1,081	2	2	0		Heath	8,936	23	18	5
	Dayton	155,526	513	390	123		Hebron	2,165	8	7	1
	Deer Park	5,432	14	10	4		Hicksville	3,481	9	8	1
	Defiance	16,159	33	30	3		Highland Heights	8,693	29	22	7
	Delaware	33,177	65	47	18		Highland Hills	1,386	8	7	1
	Delhi Township	29,808	31	29	2		Hilliard	27,186	66	50	16
	Delphos	6,794	18	14	4		Hillsboro	6,736	20	16	4
	Delta	2,936	7	7	0		Hinckley Township	7,833	11	8	3
	Dennison	2,896	4	4	0		Holland	1,274	9	9	0
	Deshler	1,854	3	3	0		Howland Township	16,761	19	18	1
	Dover	12,533	23	22	1		Hubbard	7,871	18	14	4
	Doylestown	2,884	7	6	1		Hubbard Township	5,826	7	6	1
	Dublin	37,326	89	67	22		Huber Heights	37,588	69	53	16
	East Cleveland	24,947	45	40	5		Hudson	23,248	34	27	7
	Eastlake	19,590	46	33	13		Hunting Valley	700	11	11	0
	East Liverpool	12,200	23	18	5		Huron	7,394	18	13	5
	East Palestine	4,775	8	6	2		Independence	6,760	49	35	14
	Eaton	8,213	20	14	6		Indian Hill	5,611	25	20	5
	Edgerton	1,997	3	3	0		Ironton	11,431	19	15	4
	Elida	1,889	2	2	0		Jackson	6,241	23	17	6
	Elmwood Place	2,343	2	2	0		Jackson Township, Mahoning County	2,290	5	5	0
	Elyria	55,697	134	89	45		Jackson Township, Montgomery County	3,820	6	6	0
	Empire	292	2	2	0		Jackson Township, Stark County	39,149	47	39	8
	Englewood	12,844	31	20	11		Jefferson	3,483	6	5	1
	Euclid	48,186	153	95	58		Jewett	788	1	1	0
	Evendale	2,789	21	19	2		Johnstown	4,037	17	12	5
	Fairborn	31,705	59	43	16		Junction City	859	1	1	0
	Fairfax	1,745	9	8	1		Kent	27,921	54	40	14
	Fairfield	42,264	81	61	20		Kenton	8,123	21	16	5
	Fairfield Township	17,093	17	16	1		Kettering	54,254	106	81	25
	Fairlawn	7,138	34	24	10		Kirtland	7,400	14	9	5
	Fairport Harbor	3,225	8	7	1		Kirtland Hills	793	10	9	1
	Fairview Park	16,032	27	26	1		Lagrange	1,986	6	6	0
	Fayette	1,307	1	1	0		Lake Township	7,362	13	12	1
	Findlay	38,038	92	73	19		Lakewood	51,606	112	90	22
	Forest	1,442	2	2	0		Lancaster	36,735	84	65	19
	Forest Park	17,470	43	35	8		Lawrence Township	8,604	6	6	0
	Fort Loramie	1,482	2	2	0		Lebanon	20,828	34	25	9
	Fort Recovery	1,350	2	2	0		Lexington	4,189	13	9	4
	Fort Shawnee	3,741	6	5	1		Liberty Township	12,118	26	21	5
	Franklin	12,868	38	31	7		Lima	37,767	100	79	21
	Frazeysburg	1,315	1	1	0						
	Fredericktown	2,468	4	4	0						
	Fremont	16,885	39	33	6						
	Gahanna	33,140	73	60	13						
	Galion	11,093	20	16	4						

Table 78. Full-Time Law Enforcement Employees by State by City, 2007 *(Contd.)*

(Number.)

State	City	Popula-tion	Total law enforce-ment employees	Total officers	Total civilians	State	City	Popula-tion	Total law enforce-ment employees	Total officers	Total civilians
	Lithopolis	957	3	3	0		Newcomerstown	3,916	13	8	5
	Liverpool Township	4,246	4	4	0		New Concord	2,671	4	4	0
	Lockland	3,271	13	13	0		New Franklin	15,087	16	12	4
	Logan	7,426	18	16	2		New Lebanon	4,150	8	8	0
	London	9,603	23	18	5		New Lexington	4,613	12	8	4
	Lorain	70,861	116	95	21		New London	2,592	4	4	0
	Lordstown	3,611	12	8	4		New Middletown	1,587	3	3	0
	Loudonville	2,995	10	6	4		New Paris	1,524	1	1	0
	Louisville	9,517	12	9	3		New Philadelphia	17,470	26	22	4
	Loveland	11,076	20	18	2		Newton Falls	4,752	8	5	3
	Lowellville	1,166	5	3	2		Newtown	3,966	7	6	1
	Luckey	981	1	1	0		New Vienna	1,401	1	1	0
	Lynchburg	1,427	3	3	0		New Washington	935	2	2	0
	Lyndhurst	14,052	41	31	10		North Baltimore	3,321	5	5	0
	Macedonia	10,595	29	22	7		North Canton	16,761	30	23	7
	Madeira	8,052	13	12	1		North College Hill	9,037	14	14	0
	Madison	3,111	5	5	0		Northfield	3,700	7	7	0
	Madison Township, Franklin County	18,023	19	17	2		North Olmsted	31,854	73	57	16
	Madison Township, Lake County	16,953	17	15	2		North Ridgeville	27,959	47	38	9
	Magnolia	933	3	3	0		North Royalton	29,575	58	37	21
	Mansfield	50,004	132	93	39		Northwood	5,482	28	21	7
	Maple Heights	24,045	51	37	14		Norton	11,551	22	16	6
	Marblehead	847	4	4	0		Norwalk	16,586	32	25	7
	Mariemont	3,011	11	10	1		Norwood	19,255	58	52	6
	Marietta	14,128	37	30	7		Oak Harbor	2,814	6	4	2
	Marion	35,975	80	63	17		Oak Hill	1,642	3	3	0
	Marlboro Township	4,775	4	3	1		Oakwood, Montgomery County	8,532	39	33	6
	Marysville	17,829	37	31	6		Oakwood, Paulding County	561	1	1	0
	Mason	30,640	48	41	7		Oakwood Village	3,625	15	13	2
	Massillon	32,443	50	48	2		Oberlin	8,247	22	17	5
	Maumee	14,024	58	43	15		Olmsted Falls	8,376	16	10	6
	Mayfield Heights	17,941	51	41	10		Ontario	5,301	24	19	5
	Mayfield Village	3,159	24	16	8		Orange Village	3,316	15	14	1
	McArthur	2,074	4	4	0		Oregon	19,074	59	45	14
	McComb	1,653	3	3	0		Orrville	8,451	17	12	5
	McConnelsville	1,726	3	3	0		Orwell	1,501	6	5	1
	Mechanicsburg	1,716	3	3	0		Ottawa	4,438	9	9	0
	Medina Township	8,683	6	6	0		Ottawa Hills	4,628	14	11	3
	Mentor	51,775	119	85	34		Owensville	836	2	2	0
	Mentor-on-the-Lake	8,316	16	11	5		Oxford	22,457	42	27	15
	Miamisburg	19,925	51	40	11		Oxford Township	2,525	3	3	0
	Miami Township	40,056	43	40	3		Painesville	17,975	44	40	4
	Middleburg Heights	15,193	37	31	6		Parma	79,250	143	88	55
	Middlefield	2,437	15	11	4		Parma Heights	20,108	40	33	7
	Middleport	2,506	6	4	2		Pataskala	13,002	20	19	1
	Middletown	51,244	116	80	36		Payne	1,149	1	1	0
	Midvale	596	1	1	0		Peebles	1,865	1	1	0
	Milford	6,323	17	15	2		Peninsula	689	5	5	0
	Millersburg	3,610	10	10	0		Pepper Pike	5,698	26	20	6
	Milton Township	2,892	1	1	0		Perkins Township	12,994	26	19	7
	Minerva	3,967	14	9	5		Perrysburg	16,885	41	32	9
	Minerva Park	1,250	6	6	0		Perrysville	822	2	2	0
	Mingo Junction	3,373	10	10	0		Perry Township, Columbiana County	4,685	6	6	0
	Minster	2,794	6	5	1		Perry Township, Franklin County	3,595	11	10	1
	Mogadore	3,952	8	8	0		Perry Township, Stark County	28,623	28	22	6
	Monroe	14,327	26	20	6		Pickerington	17,854	36	26	10
	Monroeville	1,374	4	4	0		Pierce Township	11,002	16	16	0
	Montgomery	9,819	24	21	3		Piqua	20,875	40	34	6
	Montpelier	4,082	10	9	1		Plain City	3,653	9	9	0
	Montville Township	7,410	11	11	0		Poland Township	11,336	13	11	2
	Moreland Hills	3,121	15	14	1		Poland Village	2,724	6	6	0
	Mount Healthy	6,385	12	11	1		Pomeroy	1,989	12	6	6
	Mount Orab	2,891	9	8	1		Port Clinton	6,246	18	13	5
	Mount Sterling	1,826	10	6	4		Portsmouth	20,030	44	40	4
	Munroe Falls	5,253	8	8	0		Powell	12,527	18	17	1
	Napoleon	9,092	22	16	6		Powhatan Point	1,689	3	3	0
	Navarre	1,424	5	5	0		Racine	755	5	4	1
	Nelsonville	5,441	6	6	0		Ravenna	11,371	32	24	8
	New Albany	6,776	22	16	6		Reading	9,936	24	19	5
	Newark	47,373	94	77	17						
	New Boston	2,161	12	8	4						
	New Bremen	3,001	6	6	0						

Table 78.   Full-Time Law Enforcement Employees by State by City, 2007 *(Contd.)*

(Number.)

State	City	Population	Total law enforcement employees	Total officers	Total civilians	State	City	Population	Total law enforcement employees	Total officers	Total civilians
	Reminderville	2,544	8	8	0		Toronto	5,321	10	10	0
	Reynoldsburg	33,210	67	54	13		Trenton	10,958	18	14	4
	Richfield	3,607	24	17	7		Trotwood	26,266	50	46	4
	Richland Township	8,851	2	2	0		Troy	22,356	46	41	5
	Richmond Heights	10,294	29	22	7		Twinsburg	17,545	47	35	12
	Richwood	2,148	6	6	0		Uhrichsville	5,597	8	8	0
	Rio Grande	871	1	1	0		Union City	1,673	5	5	0
	Rittman	6,291	14	9	5		Uniontown	2,830	9	8	1
	Riverside	22,317	33	32	1		Union Township, Clermont County	43,837	71	55	16
	Roaming Shores Village	1,217	2	2	0		Union Township, Licking County	3,813	3	3	0
	Rockford	1,111	2	2	0		University Heights	12,865	36	30	6
	Russell Township	5,645	8	7	1		Upper Arlington	31,009	61	48	13
	Russia	627	1	1	0		Urbana	11,582	22	22	0
	Sabina	2,855	5	5	0		Utica	2,103	8	3	5
	Sagamore Hills	9,593	12	10	2		Valley View, Cuyahoga County	2,048	20	18	2
	Salem	11,915	25	24	1		Valleyview, Franklin County	557	1	1	0
	Saline Township	1,373	5	5	0		Vandalia	14,171	39	30	9
	Sandusky	25,994	63	53	10		Van Wert	10,381	31	23	8
	Sebring	4,587	10	7	3		Vermilion	10,892	23	18	5
	Senecaville	449	1	1	0		Vienna Township	3,935	1	1	0
	Seven Hills	11,875	20	19	1		Village of Leesburg	1,345	3	3	0
	Seville	2,464	9	8	1		Wadsworth	20,391	39	29	10
	Shadyside	3,517	6	5	1		Waite Hill	554	6	6	0
	Shaker Heights	26,959	96	70	26		Walbridge	3,077	4	4	0
	Sharon Township	2,306	10	10	0		Walton Hills	2,310	20	15	5
	Sharonville	12,762	46	36	10		Wapakoneta	9,583	19	14	5
	Shawnee Hills	567	2	2	0		Warren	44,858	99	81	18
	Shawnee Township	8,641	15	10	5		Warrensville Heights	13,815	43	36	7
	Sheffield Lake	9,049	16	12	4		Warren Township	6,173	8	8	0
	Shelby	9,441	19	15	4		Washington Court House	13,612	28	22	6
	Shreve	1,502	3	3	0		Waterville Township	5,439	4	4	0
	Sidney	20,110	52	40	12		Wauseon	7,390	16	14	2
	Silverton	4,556	13	10	3		Waverly	4,430	17	13	4
	Smith Township	4,969	4	4	0		Waynesville	3,081	4	3	1
	Smithville	1,306	3	3	0		Wellington	4,693	8	6	2
	Solon	22,318	73	46	27		Wellston	5,998	16	12	4
	Somerset	1,575	1	1	0		Wellsville	3,985	7	7	0
	South Charleston	1,808	3	3	0		West Alexandria	1,328	3	3	0
	South Euclid	21,559	52	40	12		West Carrollton	12,897	31	25	6
	South Russell	3,982	8	8	0		West Chester Township	55,216	108	83	25
	South Solon	387	3	3	0		Westerville	34,907	86	72	14
	Spencer	825	2	2	0		Westfield Center	1,160	1	1	0
	Spencerville	2,180	4	4	0		West Jefferson	4,254	13	10	3
	Springboro	17,684	28	22	6		West Lafayette	2,539	4	4	0
	Springdale	9,520	47	38	9		Westlake	30,920	73	52	21
	Springfield	62,426	143	123	20		West Liberty	1,735	2	2	0
	Springfield Township, Hamilton County	35,051	57	50	7		West Union	3,145	6	4	2
	Springfield Township, Mahoning County	6,116	8	8	0		West Unity	1,781	4	4	0
	Springfield Township, Summit County	15,449	18	16	2		Whitehall	17,719	55	43	12
	St. Bernard	4,364	15	14	1		Wickliffe	13,045	39	29	10
	St. Clair Township	7,805	13	13	0		Willard	6,757	17	13	4
	Steubenville	19,107	53	43	10		Williamsburg	2,352	5	5	0
	St. Henry	2,382	2	2	0		Willoughby	22,319	59	44	15
	St. Marys	8,189	19	15	4		Willoughby Hills	8,430	26	19	7
	Stow	34,617	54	44	10		Willowick	13,804	35	25	10
	St. Paris	1,984	4	4	0		Wilmington	12,806	35	24	11
	Strasburg	2,704	4	4	0		Winchester	1,097	1	1	0
	Streetsboro	14,470	34	26	8		Windham	2,711	7	5	2
	Struthers	10,987	19	15	4		Wintersville	3,860	9	8	1
	Sugarcreek	2,167	5	5	0		Woodlawn	2,492	15	15	0
	Sugarcreek Township	6,875	23	16	7		Woodsfield	2,470	6	6	0
	Sunbury	3,346	12	11	1		Woodville	2,002	5	5	0
	Sycamore	875	1	1	0		Wooster	25,914	43	38	5
	Sylvania	19,147	41	34	7		Worthington	12,941	47	34	13
	Sylvania Township	26,380	65	47	18		Wyoming	7,485	17	15	2
	Tallmadge	17,506	37	26	11		Xenia	23,335	70	46	24
	Terrace Park	2,077	7	6	1		Yellow Springs	3,618	9	7	2
	Thornville	1,127	1	1	0		Youngstown	81,521	238	191	47
	Tiffin	17,238	42	29	13		Zanesville	25,332	91	54	37
	Tipp City	9,376	22	19	3						
	Toledo	296,403	805	669	136						

Table 78. Full-Time Law Enforcement Employees by State by City, 2007 (Contd.)

(Number.)

State	City	Population	Total law enforcement employees	Total officers	Total civilians	State	City	Population	Total law enforcement employees	Total officers	Total civilians
OKLAHOMA	Achille	530	5	4	1		Hobart	3,741	15	10	5
	Ada	15,901	40	33	7		Holdenville	5,546	14	9	5
	Altus	19,284	61	43	18		Hollis	2,072	11	6	5
	Alva	4,747	10	8	2		Hominy	3,701	9	6	3
	Anadarko	6,519	21	14	7		Hooker	1,725	4	4	0
	Antlers	2,481	11	6	5		Hugo	5,573	15	13	2
	Apache	1,583	3	3	0		Hulbert	530	3	3	0
	Ardmore	24,663	56	47	9		Hydro	1,034	2	2	0
	Arkoma	2,205	6	3	3		Idabel	6,906	24	18	6
	Atoka	3,044	16	15	1		Jay	3,020	11	7	4
	Bartlesville	34,902	78	53	25		Jenks	14,906	19	13	6
	Beaver	1,378	3	3	0		Jones	2,674	7	7	0
	Beggs	1,374	7	2	5		Kingfisher	4,515	11	9	2
	Bethany	19,456	40	31	9		Kingston	1,561	7	7	0
	Bixby	20,303	34	24	10		Konawa	1,417	5	5	0
	Blackwell	7,134	19	15	4		Krebs	2,137	6	6	0
	Blanchard	6,351	16	13	3		Lawton	86,864	217	162	55
	Boise City	1,284	3	3	0		Lexington	2,071	10	10	0
	Boley	1,086	1	1	0		Lindsay	2,918	12	8	4
	Bristow	4,402	14	10	4		Locust Grove	1,589	9	5	4
	Broken Arrow	89,463	169	122	47		Lone Grove	5,239	8	5	3
	Broken Bow	4,217	18	13	5		Luther	1,098	6	5	1
	Caddo	982	3	3	0		Madill	3,735	12	11	1
	Calera	1,817	8	7	1		Mangum	2,695	10	5	5
	Carnegie	1,589	7	4	3		Mannford	2,787	9	6	3
	Catoosa	6,789	17	16	1		Marietta	2,568	6	4	2
	Chandler	2,876	11	6	5		Marlow	4,564	13	10	3
	Checotah	3,520	13	10	3		Maysville	1,304	3	2	1
	Chelsea	2,269	7	4	3		McAlester	18,414	58	45	13
	Cherokee	1,445	7	3	4		McLoud	4,250	12	6	6
	Chickasha	17,346	38	26	12		Meeker	1,000	4	4	0
	Choctaw	11,009	16	14	2		Miami	13,622	42	30	12
	Chouteau	2,016	8	7	1		Midwest City	55,315	116	90	26
	Claremore	17,519	53	37	16		Minco	1,805	4	4	0
	Clayton	722	6	4	2		Moore	50,548	77	71	6
	Cleveland	3,230	5	5	0		Mooreland	1,229	1	1	0
	Clinton	8,395	25	16	9		Morris	1,323	3	3	0
	Coalgate	1,836	5	5	0		Mountain View	816	2	2	0
	Colbert	1,115	5	5	0		Muldrow	3,216	8	5	3
	Collinsville	4,559	16	11	5		Muskogee	40,113	116	86	30
	Comanche	1,525	4	4	0		Mustang	16,960	26	19	7
	Cordell	2,910	10	7	3		Newcastle	6,880	21	16	5
	Coweta	8,847	23	15	8		Newkirk	2,128	7	6	1
	Crescent	1,356	5	3	2		Nichols Hills	3,981	19	15	4
	Cushing	8,479	22	14	8		Nicoma Park	2,371	6	6	0
	Davenport	893	2	2	0		Noble	5,638	9	6	3
	Davis	2,671	15	10	5		Norman	103,721	184	133	51
	Del City	21,872	31	21	10		Nowata	4,009	8	6	2
	Dewey	3,281	10	8	2		Oilton	1,125	4	4	0
	Drumright	2,890	5	5	0		Okemah	2,965	11	7	4
	Duncan	22,486	48	41	7		Oklahoma City	542,199	1,270	1,023	247
	Durant	15,177	48	35	13		Okmulgee	12,805	36	30	6
	Edmond	77,879	147	116	31		Oologah	1,163	4	4	0
	Elk City	11,079	39	28	11		Owasso	25,974	59	44	15
	El Reno	16,221	43	31	12		Pauls Valley	6,175	21	15	6
	Enid	46,454	108	91	17		Pawhuska	3,481	13	9	4
	Eufaula	2,797	13	10	3		Pawnee	2,222	6	6	0
	Fairfax	1,486	6	3	3		Perkins	2,251	7	7	0
	Fairview	2,592	7	4	3		Perry	5,045	23	15	8
	Fort Gibson	4,328	16	11	5		Piedmont	5,233	12	9	3
	Frederick	4,113	13	12	1		Pocola	4,499	8	5	3
	Geary	1,239	9	5	4		Ponca City	24,548	62	52	10
	Glenpool	9,251	22	15	7		Porum	735	1	1	0
	Goodwell	1,127	3	3	0		Poteau	8,347	32	27	5
	Grove	6,141	26	18	8		Prague	2,153	17	10	7
	Guthrie	11,074	23	18	5		Pryor	9,361	28	20	8
	Guymon	10,721	21	14	7		Purcell	6,026	20	19	1
	Harrah	5,010	8	8	0		Ringling	1,062	1	1	0
	Hartshorne	2,072	5	5	0		Roland	3,216	11	7	4
	Haskell	1,781	6	6	0		Rush Springs	1,349	3	2	1
	Healdton	2,772	8	4	4		Sallisaw	8,842	29	21	8
	Heavener	3,274	13	8	5		Sand Springs	18,362	45	31	14
	Henryetta	6,090	17	12	5		Sapulpa	20,960	60	47	13
	Hinton	2,172	4	4	0		Sayre	2,743	12	7	5

Table 78. Full-Time Law Enforcement Employees by State by City, 2007 *(Contd.)*

(Number.)

State	City	Population	Total law enforcement employees	Total officers	Total civilians	State	City	Population	Total law enforcement employees	Total officers	Total civilians
	Seminole	6,960	15	13	2		Culver	1,064	1	1	0
	Shawnee	30,109	73	54	19		Dallas	15,097	29	18	11
	Skiatook	6,486	22	17	5		Eagle Point	8,547	15	13	2
	Snyder	1,430	3	3	0		Elgin	1,623	3	3	0
	Spencer	3,943	9	8	1		Enterprise	1,736	4	4	0
	Spiro	2,336	4	4	0		Eugene	147,458	292	178	114
	Stigler	2,825	13	9	4		Fairview	9,753	14	13	1
	Stillwater	45,692	106	70	36		Florence	8,250	24	15	9
	Stilwell	3,551	19	13	6		Forest Grove	20,457	30	27	3
	Stratford	1,496	5	3	2		Gearhart	1,117	3	3	0
	Stringtown	413	3	3	0		Gervais	2,451	5	5	0
	Stroud	2,777	14	9	5		Gladstone	12,256	18	16	2
	Sulphur	4,924	15	11	4		Gold Beach	1,909	5	4	1
	Tahlequah	16,491	40	32	8		Grants Pass	30,292	72	44	28
	Talihina	1,250	8	4	4		Gresham	98,089	159	120	39
	Tecumseh	6,723	16	11	5		Hermiston	15,148	34	23	11
	Texhoma	936	2	2	0		Hillsboro	90,439	151	115	36
	The Village	9,719	25	19	6		Hines	1,464	3	3	0
	Tishomingo	3,248	7	6	1		Hood River	6,778	18	15	3
	Tonkawa	3,080	15	10	5		Hubbard	2,624	7	6	1
	Tulsa	381,469	944	836	108		Independence	9,211	16	13	3
	Tushka	363	3	3	0		Jacksonville	2,190	6	5	1
	Tuttle	5,935	14	10	4		John Day	1,555	9	4	5
	Valliant	752	6	4	2		Junction City	5,378	14	8	6
	Vian	1,483	5	4	1		Keizer	35,423	49	41	8
	Vinita	5,982	21	16	5		King City	2,257	5	5	0
	Wagoner	8,043	19	13	6		Klamath Falls	19,817	46	40	6
	Walters	2,548	4	4	0		La Grande	12,288	33	18	15
	Warner	1,447	4	4	0		Lake Oswego	36,917	73	43	30
	Warr Acres	9,384	22	17	5		Lakeview	2,412	6	6	0
	Watonga	5,807	11	8	3		Lebanon	14,620	34	22	12
	Waukomis	1,192	3	3	0		Lincoln City	7,996	34	25	9
	Waurika	1,811	2	2	0		Madras	5,301	11	10	1
	Waynoka	901	3	3	0		Malin	634	2	1	1
	Weatherford	9,951	32	20	12		Manzanita	640	3	3	0
	Weleetka	938	7	3	4		McMinnville	30,980	43	33	10
	Westville	1,687	10	6	4		Medford	71,969	155	103	52
	Wetumka	1,422	5	5	0		Milton-Freewater	6,392	17	11	6
	Wewoka	3,368	12	8	4		Milwaukie	21,060	37	33	4
	Wilburton	2,896	6	5	1		Molalla	7,210	15	12	3
	Wilson	1,627	6	4	2		Monmouth	9,751	15	13	2
	Woodward	12,064	39	24	15		Mount Angel	3,429	8	6	2
	Wright City	803	3	3	0		Myrtle Creek	3,555	9	7	2
	Wynnewood	2,311	5	4	1		Myrtle Point	2,509	6	6	0
	Yale	1,284	5	2	3		Newberg-Dundee	25,209	35	22	13
	Yukon	22,457	46	34	12		Newport	9,953	23	19	4
OREGON...............	Albany	46,999	91	62	29		North Bend	9,892	24	17	7
	Amity	1,462	2	2	0		North Plains	1,833	2	2	0
	Ashland	21,068	34	27	7		Nyssa	3,039	7	7	0
	Astoria	9,935	25	16	9		Oakridge	3,127	11	6	5
	Athena	1,207	2	2	0		Ontario	11,100	29	22	7
	Aumsville	3,378	7	6	1		Oregon City	31,284	41	34	7
	Aurora	1,025	13	12	1		Pendleton	16,620	24	21	3
	Baker City	9,614	18	16	2		Philomath	4,206	10	9	1
	Bandon	2,911	8	7	1		Phoenix	4,416	11	9	2
	Beaverton	91,184	158	128	30		Pilot Rock	1,511	2	2	0
	Bend	75,185	113	88	25		Portland	538,133	1,259	989	270
	Black Butte		7	6	1		Prairie City	936	1	1	0
	Boardman	3,094	7	6	1		Prineville	9,583	30	20	10
	Brookings	6,476	20	13	7		Rainier	1,852	7	6	1
	Burns	2,702	4	4	0		Redmond	24,095	51	36	15
	Canby	15,725	30	25	5		Reedsport	4,352	15	10	5
	Cannon Beach	1,740	9	8	1		Rockaway Beach	1,346	3	3	0
	Carlton	1,523	3	3	0		Rogue River	1,943	5	4	1
	Central Point	16,701	28	22	6		Roseburg	21,128	42	37	5
	Clatskanie	1,663	6	5	1		Salem	154,484	308	196	112
	Coburg	1,011	4	4	0		Sandy	8,770	15	12	3
	Columbia City	1,965	1	1	0		Scappoose	6,222	12	11	1
	Condon	684	2	1	1		Seaside	6,229	29	21	8
	Coos Bay	16,096	35	24	11		Shady Cove	2,293	4	4	0
	Coquille	4,250	8	7	1		Sherwood	17,957	24	21	3
	Cornelius	11,498	15	14	1		Silverton	9,200	18	16	2
	Corvallis	49,870	80	53	27		Springfield	56,201	110	70	40
	Cottage Grove	8,921	24	17	7		Stanfield	1,964	4	4	0

Table 78.   Full-Time Law Enforcement Employees by State by City, 2007 *(Contd.)*

(Number.)

State	City	Popula-tion	Total law enforce-ment employees	Total officers	Total civilians	State	City	Popula-tion	Total law enforce-ment employees	Total officers	Total civilians
	Stayton	7,385	18	15	3		Bethlehem	72,908	174	151	23
	St. Helens	12,708	22	20	2		Bethlehem Township	23,960	36	34	2
	Sunriver		12	11	1		Biglerville	1,167	2	2	0
	Sutherlin	7,396	17	15	2		Birdsboro	5,224	8	7	1
	Sweet Home	8,659	23	17	6		Birmingham Township	4,273	4	4	0
	Talent	6,150	8	7	1		Blairsville	3,421	5	5	0
	The Dalles	11,900	22	20	2		Blair Township	4,739	4	4	0
	Tigard	50,087	80	64	16		Blakely	6,782	3	3	0
	Tillamook	4,435	13	10	3		Blawnox	1,446	3	3	0
	Toledo	3,398	13	8	5		Bloomsburg Town	12,959	21	15	6
	Troutdale	15,212	26	22	4		Boyertown	3,961	8	7	1
	Tualatin	26,712	44	36	8		Brackenridge	3,239	4	4	0
	Turner	1,689	3	3	0		Bradford	8,501	22	22	0
	Umatilla	5,397	10	8	2		Bradford Township	4,763	5	5	0
	Vernonia	2,319	5	5	0		Brandywine Regional	10,045	17	16	1
	Warrenton	4,438	9	8	1		Brecknock Township,				
	West Linn	25,636	36	30	6		Berks County	4,935	6	6	0
	Winston	4,803	8	7	1		Brentwood	9,574	16	14	2
	Woodburn	22,399	41	32	9		Briar Creek Township	3,062	8	8	0
	Yamhill	850	3	3	0		Bridgeport	4,404	10	9	1
PENNSYLVANIA	Abington Township	54,413	121	91	30		Bridgeville	4,898	10	9	1
	Adams Township,						Bridgewater	891	2	2	0
	Butler County	8,963	5	5	0		Brighton Township	7,996	6	6	0
	Adams Township,						Bristol	9,747	17	15	2
	Cambria County	6,113	3	3	0		Bristol Township	54,096	87	74	13
	Akron	4,013	5	5	0		Brockway	2,080	2	2	0
	Albion	1,540	1	1	0		Brookhaven	7,805	9	8	1
	Alburtis	2,393	4	4	0		Brookville	4,037	7	6	1
	Aldan	4,277	4	4	0		Brownsville	2,653	1	1	0
	Aliquippa	10,854	18	18	0		Buckingham Township	19,293	23	21	2
	Allegheny Township,						Buffalo Township	7,318	5	5	0
	Blair County	6,907	6	5	1		Burgettstown	1,497	1	1	0
	Allegheny Township,						Bushkill Township	8,136	12	10	2
	Westmoreland County	8,177	9	8	1		Butler	14,258	24	23	1
	Allentown	107,397	265	188	77		Butler Township,				
	Altoona	46,609	82	74	8		Butler County	16,894	23	21	2
	Ambler	6,248	15	13	2		Butler Township,				
	Amity Township	11,838	13	12	1		Luzerne County	9,116	10	9	1
	Annville Township	4,717	6	5	1		Butler Township,				
	Archbald	6,422	3	3	0		Schuykill County	5,751	5	5	0
	Arnold	5,301	12	11	1		Caernarvon Township,				
	Ashland	3,121	5	5	0		Berks County	3,615	10	9	1
	Ashley	2,691	2	2	0		California	6,065	8	7	1
	Ashville	262	1	1	0		Caln Township	12,283	22	20	2
	Aspinwall	2,720	5	4	1		Cambria Township	6,199	4	4	0
	Aston Township	16,853	18	16	2		Cambridge Springs	2,260	3	3	0
	Athens	3,272	7	6	1		Camp Hill	7,384	11	10	1
	Athens Township	5,100	10	9	1		Canonsburg	8,856	16	15	1
	Auburn	805	1	1	0		Carbondale	9,256	11	11	0
	Avalon	4,837	6	6	0		Carlisle	18,317	37	32	5
	Avonmore Boro	775	1	1	0		Carnegie	8,001	14	12	2
	Baldwin Borough	18,440	28	26	2		Carrolltown	977	1	1	0
	Baldwin Township	2,048	5	5	0		Carroll Township,				
	Bally	1,112	2	2	0		York County	5,383	11	11	0
	Bangor	5,282	10	9	1		Carroll Valley	3,574	5	4	1
	Barrett Township	4,387	7	7	0		Castle Shannon	8,099	13	12	1
	Beaver	4,447	9	8	1		Catasauqua	6,562	9	8	1
	Beaver Falls	9,189	19	18	1		Catawissa	1,544	3	3	0
	Bedford	3,011	4	4	0		Cecil Township	10,456	17	16	1
	Bedminster Township	5,681	7	6	1		Center Township	11,804	26	26	0
	Bell Acres	1,383	4	4	0		Centerville	3,242	2	2	0
	Bellefonte	6,096	12	10	2		Central Berks Regional	7,489	13	12	1
	Bellevue	8,023	17	14	3		Chalfont	4,243	7	6	1
	Bellwood	1,890	2	2	0		Charleroi	5,781	8	6	2
	Ben Avon	1,754	11	10	1		Chartiers Township	7,239	11	11	0
	Bensalem Township	58,788	125	95	30		Cheltenham Township	36,403	92	81	11
	Berks-Lehigh Regional	28,142	28	27	1		Chester	36,799	108	100	8
	Berlin	2,105	2	2	0		Chester Township	4,594	11	10	1
	Bern Township	7,165	13	13	0		Cheswick	1,751	3	3	0
	Berwick	10,246	16	15	1		Chippewa Township	9,815	8	7	1
	Bessemer	1,106	1	1	0		Churchill	3,267	11	11	0
	Bethel Park	31,669	44	38	6		Clarion	5,141	9	8	1
	Bethel Township,						Claysville	682	2	2	0
	Berks County	4,543	2	2	0		Clay Township	5,766	4	4	0

Table 78. Full-Time Law Enforcement Employees by State by City, 2007 *(Contd.)*

(Number.)

State	City	Population	Total law enforcement employees	Total officers	Total civilians	State	City	Population	Total law enforcement employees	Total officers	Total civilians
	Clearfield	6,240	7	7	0		East Cocalico Township	10,398	23	21	2
	Cleona	2,104	4	4	0		East Conemaugh	1,186	2	2	0
	Clifton Heights	6,586	10	9	1		East Coventry Township	6,236	8	7	1
	Clymer	1,448	1	1	0		East Deer Township	1,338	1	1	0
	Coal Township	10,277	13	12	1		East Earl Township	6,311	7	7	0
	Cochranton	1,079	1	1	0		Eastern Adams Regional	9,083	9	9	0
	Colebrookdale District	6,462	11	10	1		East Fallowfield Township	7,343	8	7	1
	Collegeville	5,011	9	8	1		East Franklin Township	3,981	4	2	2
	Collier Township	6,235	16	15	1		East Hempfield Township	23,212	33	29	4
	Collingdale	8,440	10	8	2		East Lampeter Township	14,910	43	39	4
	Colonial Regional	19,420	26	24	2		East Lansdowne	2,495	5	3	2
	Columbia	10,034	22	19	3		East McKeesport	2,816	2	2	0
	Colwyn	2,375	3	3	0		East Norriton Township	13,485	31	28	3
	Conemaugh Township, Cambria County	2,507	2	2	0		East Pennsboro Township	19,894	20	19	1
	Conemaugh Township, Somerset County	7,310	8	8	0		East Penn Township	2,716	1	1	0
	Conewago Township, Adams County	6,184	9	8	1		East Pikeland Township	6,849	10	8	2
	Conewango Township	3,647	4	4	0		Easttown Township	10,503	15	14	1
	Conneaut Lake Regional	3,539	3	3	0		East Vincent Township	6,589	8	8	0
	Conoy Township	3,288	14	13	1		East Washington	1,877	1	1	0
	Conshohocken	8,629	21	19	2		East Whiteland Township	10,632	21	19	2
	Conyngham	1,844	2	2	0		Ebensburg	2,880	4	4	0
	Coopersburg	2,573	7	7	0		Economy	9,192	13	12	1
	Coplay	3,381	4	4	0		Eddystone	2,361	10	9	1
	Coraopolis	5,610	12	9	3		Edgewood	3,018	12	10	2
	Cornwall	3,460	9	8	1		Edgeworth	1,582	6	4	2
	Corry	6,451	16	12	4		Edinboro	6,646	7	7	0
	Coudersport	2,484	4	4	0		Edwardsville	4,688	4	4	0
	Covington Township	2,154	2	2	0		Elizabeth	1,468	2	2	0
	Crafton	6,138	10	9	1		Elizabethtown	11,900	18	16	2
	Cranberry Township	28,084	32	28	4		Elizabeth Township	12,837	14	13	1
	Crescent Township	2,823	3	3	0		Elkland	1,685	1	1	0
	Cresson	1,507	1	1	0		Ellwood City	8,064	12	11	1
	Cresson Township	4,239	4	3	1		Emlenton Borough	743	2	2	0
	Croyle Township	2,262	1	1	0		Emmaus	11,414	17	15	2
	Cumberland Township, Adams County	6,377	6	6	0		Emporium	2,270	2	2	0
	Cumberland Township, Greene County	6,492	3	3	0		Ephrata	13,067	35	30	5
	Cumru Township	17,595	28	25	3		Erie	101,812	204	167	37
	Curwensville	2,505	3	3	0		Etna	3,578	8	7	1
	Dale	1,384	2	2	0		Evans City	1,933	2	2	0
	Dallas	2,493	4	4	0		Everett	1,869	4	4	0
	Dallas Township	8,424	7	7	0		Exeter	5,995	5	4	1
	Danville	4,530	10	9	1		Exeter Township, Berks County	27,080	34	32	2
	Darby Township	9,615	12	12	0		Exeter Township, Luzerne County	2,557	2	2	0
	Decatur Township	3,089	1	1	0		Fairfield	518	5	4	1
	Delmont	2,473	4	4	0		Fairview Township, Luzerne County	4,321	5	5	0
	Derry	2,822	2	2	0		Fairview Township, York County	16,630	18	16	2
	Derry Township, Dauphin County	21,923	42	35	7		Fallowfield Township	4,242	2	2	0
	Dickson City	5,916	7	7	0		Falls Township, Bucks County	34,033	58	51	7
	Donegal Township	2,574	2	2	0		Fawn Township	2,324	3	3	0
	Donora	5,317	20	20	0		Ferguson Township	16,302	18	16	2
	Dormont	8,467	16	15	1		Ferndale	1,685	1	1	0
	Douglass Township, Berks County	3,545	2	2	0		Findlay Township	5,053	23	16	7
	Downingtown	7,924	19	16	3		Fleetwood	4,029	6	6	0
	Doylestown	8,208	21	16	5		Folcroft	6,878	9	9	0
	Doylestown Township	18,847	24	22	2		Ford City	3,190	3	3	0
	Dublin Borough	2,182	2	2	0		Forest City	1,765	2	2	0
	Du Bois	7,757	13	13	0		Forest Hills	6,271	12	11	1
	Duncannon	1,503	2	2	0		Forks Township	14,452	19	18	1
	Duncansville	1,181	2	2	0		Forty Fort	4,273	2	2	0
	Dunmore	13,884	17	17	0		Foster Township	4,304	4	4	0
	Dupont	2,601	1	1	0		Fountain Hill	4,602	9	9	0
	Duquesne	6,705	16	15	1		Fox Chapel	5,144	10	10	0
	East Bangor	1,041	1	1	0		Frackville	4,115	4	4	0
	East Berlin	1,451	1	1	0						
	East Brady	998	1	1	0						
	East Buffalo Township	5,939	8	8	0						

Table 78.   Full-Time Law Enforcement Employees by State by City, 2007 *(Contd.)*

(Number.)

State	City	Population	Total law enforcement employees	Total officers	Total civilians	State	City	Population	Total law enforcement employees	Total officers	Total civilians
	Franconia Township	12,623	14	13	1		Jackson Township, Cambria County	4,783	2	2	0
	Franklin Park	11,908	12	11	1		Jackson Township, Luzerne County	4,597	4	4	0
	Franklin Township, Beaver County	4,330	2	2	0		Jeannette	10,021	15	14	1
	Franklin Township, Carbon County	4,873	4	4	0		Jefferson Hills Borough	9,614	21	16	5
	Freedom	1,624	2	2	0		Jenkins Township	4,951	2	2	0
	Freedom Township	3,191	1	1	0		Jermyn	2,230	1	1	0
	Freeland	3,411	2	2	0		Jersey Shore	4,360	8	7	1
	Freemansburg	2,007	4	4	0		Jim Thorpe	4,898	6	6	0
	Freeport	1,818	2	2	0		Johnsonburg	2,747	2	2	0
	Galeton	1,263	1	1	0		Johnstown	23,609	52	46	6
	Gallitzin	1,908	2	2	0		Kane	3,828	5	5	0
	Gettysburg	8,194	13	11	2		Kennedy Township	9,313	15	11	4
	Gilberton	828	2	1	1		Kennett Square	5,294	15	12	3
	Gilpin Township	2,534	1	1	0		Kidder Township	1,386	10	10	0
	Girard	2,991	4	4	0		Kilbuck Township	662	4	3	1
	Glenolden	7,261	10	9	1		Kingston	13,036	25	19	6
	Granville Township	4,915	7	6	1		Kingston Township	7,069	11	11	0
	Greencastle	4,036	2	2	0		Kiskiminetas Township	4,801	1	1	0
	Greenfield Township, Blair County	3,779	2	2	0		Kline Township	1,491	1	1	0
	Greensburg	15,567	38	28	10		Knox	1,110	3	3	0
	Green Tree	4,353	12	11	1		Koppel	788	1	1	0
	Greenville	6,263	10	9	1		Kulpmont	2,771	1	1	0
	Greenwood Township	2,046	1	1	0		Kutztown	5,075	13	11	2
	Grove City	7,644	9	8	1		Laflin Borough	1,503	3	3	0
	Hamburg	4,209	5	4	1		Lake City	2,985	3	3	0
	Hamiltonban Township	2,739	1	1	0		Lancaster	54,562	219	167	52
	Hampden Township	26,612	24	24	0		Lancaster Township, Butler County	2,574	2	2	0
	Hanover Township, Luzerne County	11,060	15	15	0		Lansdale	15,669	25	19	6
	Hanover Township, Washington County	2,752	9	3	6		Lansdowne	10,720	19	16	3
	Harmar Township	3,018	7	7	0		Lansford	4,180	3	3	0
	Harmony Township	3,111	5	5	0		Larksville	4,474	4	4	0
	Harrisburg	46,924	230	179	51		Latrobe	8,504	14	13	1
	Harrison Township	10,016	21	18	3		Laureldale	3,783	5	5	0
	Hastings	1,312	1	1	0		Lawrence Park Township	3,778	8	7	1
	Hatboro	7,177	17	14	3		Lawrence Township, Clearfield County	7,613	9	8	1
	Hatfield Township	20,241	30	25	5		Lebanon	24,144	54	47	7
	Haverford Township	48,434	81	69	12		Leetsdale	1,122	4	4	0
	Hegins Township	3,377	2	2	0		Leet Township	1,510	10	5	5
	Heidelberg	1,149	3	3	0		Lehighton	5,489	10	9	1
	Heidelberg Township, Berks County	1,774	1	1	0		Lehigh Township, Northampton County	10,831	13	12	1
	Heidelberg Township, Lebanon County	4,113	2	2	0		Lehman Township	3,308	2	2	0
	Hellam Township	9,139	8	8	0		Lewisburg	5,572	10	8	2
	Hellertown	5,620	11	10	1		Liberty Township, Adams County	1,298	1	1	0
	Hemlock Township	2,214	6	6	0		Ligonier	1,633	3	3	0
	Hermitage	16,576	32	29	3		Ligonier Township	6,784	3	3	0
	Highspire	2,585	6	6	0		Limerick Township	17,087	17	16	1
	Hilltown Township	13,175	21	18	3		Lincoln	1,125	1	1	0
	Hollidaysburg	5,563	11	8	3		Linesville	1,110	1	1	0
	Homestead	3,476	11	11	0		Lititz	9,029	16	13	3
	Honesdale	4,795	9	9	0		Littlestown	4,187	8	8	0
	Hooversville	718	1	1	0		Locust Township	2,518	5	5	0
	Hopewell Township	12,511	14	13	1		Logan Township	11,887	18	16	2
	Horsham Township	24,947	49	40	9		Lower Burrell	12,315	16	16	0
	Hummelstown	4,386	6	6	0		Lower Chichester Township	3,458	4	4	0
	Huntingdon	6,815	13	12	1		Lower Frederick Township	4,858	3	3	0
	Independence Township, Beaver County	2,736	4	4	0		Lower Gwynedd Township	11,368	19	18	1
	Indiana	14,792	29	22	7		Lower Heidelberg Township	5,282	9	8	1
	Indiana Township	6,947	9	9	0		Lower Makefield Township	32,550	40	36	4
	Industry	1,821	1	1	0		Lower Merion Township	57,691	158	139	19
	Ingram	3,389	4	4	0		Lower Milford Township	3,919	1	1	0
	Irwin	4,116	4	4	0						
	Ivyland	882	2	2	0						
	Jackson Township, Butler County	3,841	9	7	2						

Table 78. Full-Time Law Enforcement Employees by State by City, 2007 *(Contd.)*

(Number.)

State	City	Population	Total law enforcement employees	Total officers	Total civilians	State	City	Population	Total law enforcement employees	Total officers	Total civilians
	Lower Moreland Township	11,894	27	22	5		Milton	6,377	10	9	1
	Lower Paxton Township	44,961	67	60	7		Minersville	4,264	6	6	0
	Lower Pottsgrove Township	12,240	18	16	2		Mohnton	3,111	4	4	0
	Lower Providence Township	26,047	35	30	5		Monaca	5,833	7	7	0
	Lower Salford Township	14,419	21	19	2		Monessen	8,159	12	12	0
	Lower Saucon Township	11,360	16	14	2		Monongahela	4,468	10	8	2
	Lower Southampton Township	19,189	33	30	3		Monroeville	27,659	55	51	4
	Lower Swatara Township	8,364	11	10	1		Montgomery	5,078	3	3	0
	Lower Windsor Township	7,847	11	10	1		Montgomery Township	24,419	44	35	9
	Luzerne Township	6,739	1	1	0		Montoursville	4,630	6	6	0
	Lykens	1,834	3	3	0		Moon Township	22,623	36	30	6
	Macungie	3,132	5	5	0		Moore Township	9,502	7	6	1
	Mahanoy City	4,361	4	4	0		Moosic	5,793	9	9	0
	Mahanoy Township	3,592	1	1	0		Morris-Cooper Regional	5,725	1	1	0
	Mahoning Township, Carbon County	4,336	5	5	0		Morrisville	9,706	12	11	1
	Mahoning Township, Montour County	4,262	7	6	1		Morton	2,649	5	4	1
	Malvern	3,115	6	5	1		Moscow	1,953	3	3	0
	Manheim	4,626	8	7	1		Mount Carmel	5,914	9	9	0
	Manheim Township	36,069	69	54	15		Mount Carmel Township	2,586	5	5	0
	Manor	2,867	3	3	0		Mount Joy	7,097	12	12	0
	Manor Township, Lancaster County	18,683	22	20	2		Mount Lebanon	30,543	53	44	9
	Mansfield	3,245	5	5	0		Mount Oliver	3,681	8	8	0
	Marietta	2,587	14	13	1		Mount Pleasant	4,453	3	3	0
	Marion Township, Beaver County	889	2	2	0		Mount Union	2,356	4	4	0
	Marion Township, Berks County	1,659	3	3	0		Muhlenberg Township	18,334	29	27	2
	Marlborough Township	3,280	4	4	0		Muncy	2,486	3	3	0
	Marple Township	23,579	38	33	5		Munhall	11,239	26	22	4
	Martinsburg	2,139	2	2	0		Murrysville	19,565	26	21	5
	Marysville	2,454	1	1	0		Nanticoke	10,261	14	13	1
	Masontown	3,424	5	5	0		Narberth	4,079	7	7	0
	Matamoras	2,669	2	2	0		Nazareth Area	6,061	6	5	1
	Mayfield	1,702	1	1	0		Neshannock Township	9,369	7	7	0
	McAdoo	2,103	1	1	0		Nether Providence Township	13,257	18	16	2
	McCandless	27,339	29	27	2		Newberry Township	15,563	18	16	2
	McKeesport	22,190	54	51	3		New Bethlehem	998	1	1	0
	McKees Rocks	6,042	10	9	1		New Brighton	9,493	12	9	3
	McSherrystown	2,841	5	5	0		New Britain	2,292	6	5	1
	Meadville	13,385	26	22	4		New Britain Township	10,795	14	12	2
	Mechanicsburg	8,771	17	16	1		New Castle	24,514	37	35	2
	Media	5,445	24	16	8		New Castle Township	392	1	1	0
	Mercer	2,253	4	4	0		New Garden Township	11,699	11	10	1
	Mercersburg	1,556	2	2	0		New Hanover Township	9,267	11	10	1
	Meyersdale	2,302	1	1	0		New Holland	5,152	13	12	1
	Middleburg	1,345	3	2	1		New Hope	2,296	11	9	2
	Middlesex Township, Butler County	5,564	3	3	0		New Kensington	13,833	29	23	6
	Middletown	8,806	16	15	1		Newport	1,465	2	2	0
	Middletown Township	47,710	60	53	7		New Sewickley Township	7,722	10	9	1
	Midland	2,898	5	5	0		Newton Township	2,763	1	1	0
	Mifflin	622	1	1	0		Newtown	2,247	5	5	0
	Mifflinburg	3,564	8	7	1		Newtown Township, Bucks County	19,234	32	28	4
	Mifflin County Regional	26,255	27	25	2		Newtown Township, Delaware County	11,894	18	16	2
	Mifflin Township	2,266	10	10	0		Newville	1,313	2	2	0
	Milford	2,945	2	2	0		New Wilmington	2,396	4	4	0
	Millbourne	911	1	1	0		Norristown	30,205	78	64	14
	Millcreek Township, Erie County	52,592	77	59	18		Northampton	9,818	14	12	2
	Millcreek Township, Lebanon County	3,147	3	3	0		Northampton Township	41,293	49	43	6
	Millersburg	2,454	4	4	0		North Belle Vernon	1,987	3	2	1
	Millersville	7,204	14	12	2		North Catasauqua	2,861	5	5	0
	Millvale	3,675	5	5	0		North Charleroi	1,327	1	1	0
	Millville	950	1	1	0		North Cornwall Township	6,526	10	8	2
							North Coventry Township	7,698	13	12	1
							North East, Erie County	4,268	9	8	1
							Northeastern Regional	11,000	11	10	1
							Northern Berks Regional	12,351	15	14	1
							Northern Cambria Borough	3,970	5	5	0
							Northern Regional	27,442	30	28	2
							Northern York Regional	63,294	50	46	4

Table 78. Full-Time Law Enforcement Employees by State by City, 2007 *(Contd.)*

(Number.)

State	City	Population	Total law enforcement employees	Total officers	Total civilians	State	City	Population	Total law enforcement employees	Total officers	Total civilians
	North Fayette Township	12,998	25	20	5		Pocono Mountain				
	North Franklin Township	4,681	6	6	0		Regional	35,733	34	29	5
	North Huntingdon						Pocono Township	11,468	17	17	0
	Township	29,478	36	29	7		Point Township	3,827	5	5	0
	North Lebanon Township	10,896	11	10	1		Polk	1,000	2	2	0
	North Londonderry						Portage	2,631	2	2	0
	Township	6,939	9	8	1		Port Allegany	2,228	3	3	0
	North Middleton						Port Carbon	1,887	2	2	0
	Township	10,946	9	8	1		Port Vue	3,865	4	4	0
	North Sewickley						Pottstown	21,346	60	46	14
	Township	5,729	42	40	2		Prospect Park	6,402	9	9	0
	North Strabane						Punxsutawney	6,046	12	9	3
	Township	12,176	20	19	1		Pymatuning Township	3,644	4	4	0
	Northumberland	3,517	5	5	0		Quakertown	8,745	23	15	8
	North Versailles						Quarryville	2,150	3	3	0
	Township	12,280	23	19	4		Raccoon Township	3,277	4	4	0
	North Wales	3,248	5	4	1		Radnor Township	31,098	57	47	10
	Northwest Lancaster						Ralpho Township	3,909	5	5	0
	County Regional	18,083	16	15	1		Rankin	2,116	1	1	0
	Northwest Lawrence						Reading	81,168	233	206	27
	County Regional	6,759	2	2	0		Redstone Township	6,106	4	4	0
	Norwegian Township	2,148	1	1	0		Reserve Township	3,544	6	6	0
	Norwood	5,813	7	7	0		Reynoldsville	2,582	2	2	0
	Oakmont	6,451	7	7	0		Rice Township	2,826	4	4	0
	O'Hara Township	9,537	16	15	1		Richland Township,				
	Ohioville	3,654	2	2	0		Bucks County	13,027	13	12	1
	Oil City	10,762	23	18	5		Richland Township,				
	Old Forge	8,540	5	5	0		Cambria County	12,623	20	19	1
	Old Lycoming Township	5,317	11	10	1		Ridgway	4,194	4	4	0
	Oley Township	3,672	6	6	0		Ridley Park	7,029	14	10	4
	Olyphant	4,899	5	5	0		Ridley Township	30,055	37	32	5
	Orangeville Area	1,651	1	1	0		Riverside	1,795	3	3	0
	Orwigsburg	2,969	3	3	0		Roaring Brook				
	Overfield Township	1,559	3	3	0		Township	1,759	2	2	0
	Oxford	4,738	12	11	1		Roaring Spring	2,280	2	2	0
	Paint Township	3,210	5	4	1		Robesonia	2,074	2	2	0
	Palmerton	5,261	10	9	1		Robeson Township	7,619	6	5	1
	Palmyra	6,944	10	9	1		Robinson Township,				
	Parkesburg	3,455	11	10	1		Allegheny County	13,585	26	21	5
	Parks Township	2,609	2	2	0		Rochester	3,717	11	9	2
	Patterson Area	3,617	4	4	0		Rochester Township	2,917	4	4	0
	Patton	1,883	2	2	0		Rockledge	2,497	5	5	0
	Patton Township	12,839	19	17	2		Roseto	1,655	2	2	0
	Paxtang	1,480	3	3	0		Rosslyn Farms	425	2	2	0
	Pen Argyl	3,667	5	5	0		Ross Township	30,522	40	40	0
	Penbrook	2,891	6	6	0		Rostraver Township	11,749	15	14	1
	Penn Hills	43,955	58	53	5		Rush Township	3,567	3	3	0
	Pennridge Regional	10,414	23	15	8		Rye Township	2,511	1	1	0
	Penn Township,						Sadsbury Township,				
	Butler County	5,246	4	3	1		Chester County	3,439	2	2	0
	Penn Township,						Salem Township,				
	Lancaster County	8,201	10	9	1		Luzerne County	4,133	3	3	0
	Penn Township,						Salisbury Township	14,006	14	12	2
	Perry County	3,222	6	5	1		Sandy Lake	708	1	1	0
	Penn Township,						Sandy Township	11,602	10	9	1
	Westmoreland County	20,476	23	21	2		Saxonburg	1,635	2	2	0
	Penn Township,						Saxton	761	1	1	0
	York County	16,010	23	21	2		Sayre	5,554	14	14	0
	Pequea Township	4,492	9	9	0		Schuylkill Haven	5,198	8	8	0
	Perkasie	8,709	20	18	2		Schuylkill Township,				
	Perryopolis	1,735	2	2	0		Chester County	7,811	12	10	2
	Peters Township	20,264	23	21	2		Scottdale	4,488	7	7	0
	Philadelphia	1,435,533	7,542	6,714	828		Scott Township,				
	Phoenixville	15,962	26	25	1		Allegheny County	15,908	23	22	1
	Pine Creek Township	3,179	1	1	0		Scott Township,				
	Pittsburgh	312,179	912	850	62		Columbia County	4,976	6	6	0
	Pittston	7,600	10	10	0		Scott Township,				
	Plainfield Township	6,142	13	12	1		Lackawanna County	4,932	4	4	0
	Plains Township	10,403	17	16	1		Scranton	72,444	170	150	20
	Pleasant Hills	7,767	17	15	2		Selinsgrove	5,339	6	5	1
	Plum	26,209	37	30	7		Seven Springs	119	7	6	1
	Plumstead Township	11,978	17	15	2		Seward	458	1	1	0
	Plymouth Township,						Sewickley	3,584	13	12	1
	Montgomery County	16,260	57	47	10		Sewickley Heights	919	5	3	2

Table 78.   Full-Time Law Enforcement Employees by State by City, 2007 *(Contd.)*

(Number.)

State	City	Population	Total law enforcement employees	Total officers	Total civilians	State	City	Population	Total law enforcement employees	Total officers	Total civilians
	Shaler Township	28,042	27	26	1		Spring Township, Centre County	6,720	7	6	1
	Shamokin	7,396	18	13	5		State College	52,047	78	65	13
	Shamokin Dam	1,451	3	3	0		St. Clair Boro	3,052	6	6	0
	Sharon	15,150	33	28	5		Steelton	5,576	9	8	1
	Sharon Hill	5,326	8	7	1		Stewartstown	2,047	6	5	1
	Sharpsburg	3,281	4	4	0		St. Marys City	13,614	15	14	1
	Sharpsville	4,186	6	5	1		Stoneboro	1,038	1	1	0
	Sheffield Township	2,232	2	2	0		Stonycreek Township	2,959	2	2	0
	Shenandoah	5,199	8	7	1		Stowe Township	6,110	8	7	1
	Shenango Township, Lawrence County	7,680	6	6	0		Strasburg	2,734	4	4	0
	Shillington	5,047	8	8	0		Stroud Area Regional	35,211	58	53	5
	Shippensburg	5,604	9	8	1		Sugarcreek	5,033	6	6	0
	Shippingport	223	2	2	0		Sugarloaf Township, Luzerne County	3,975	5	4	1
	Shiremanstown	1,471	2	2	0		Summerhill Township	2,618	3	3	0
	Shohola Township	2,479	1	1	0		Summit Hill	2,996	3	3	0
	Silver Lake Township	1,772	2	2	0		Summit Township	2,278	2	2	0
	Silver Spring Township	13,052	13	12	1		Sunbury	9,855	14	12	2
	Sinking Spring	3,641	5	5	0		Susquehanna Regional	6,533	14	13	1
	Slatington	4,420	7	7	0		Susquehanna Township, Dauphin County	22,905	42	40	2
	Slippery Rock	3,248	4	4	0		Swarthmore	6,148	9	9	0
	Smethport	1,593	2	2	0		Swatara Township	22,281	42	40	2
	Smith Township	4,508	1	1	0		Sweden Township	741	1	1	0
	Solebury Township	9,007	15	13	2		Swissvale	8,811	14	14	0
	Somerset	6,428	7	6	1		Swoyersville	7,649	7	7	0
	Souderton	6,623	6	6	0		Tamaqua	6,633	10	9	1
	South Abington Township	9,646	12	10	2		Tarentum	4,558	8	7	1
	South Annville Township	3,171	2	2	0		Taylor	6,177	7	7	0
	South Beaver Township	2,875	4	4	0		Telford	4,629	7	6	1
	South Buffalo Township	2,811	2	2	0		Throop	3,996	5	5	0
	South Centre Township	1,917	10	10	0		Tidioute	732	1	1	0
	South Coatesville	1,075	1	1	0		Tinicum Township, Bucks County	4,265	5	5	0
	Southern Regional Lancaster County	3,825	9	9	0		Tinicum Township, Delaware County	4,226	17	15	2
	Southern Regional York County	9,873	12	11	1		Titusville	5,759	16	16	0
	South Fayette Township	13,174	18	17	1		Towamencin Township	17,812	34	22	12
	South Fork	1,046	1	1	0		Towanda	2,885	6	6	0
	South Greensburg	2,226	2	2	0		Trainer	1,847	6	6	0
	South Heidelberg Township	7,146	6	6	0		Tredyffrin Township	29,002	60	51	9
	South Lebanon Township	8,622	8	7	1		Troy	1,479	3	3	0
	South Londonderry Township	7,124	7	6	1		Tullytown	1,981	7	6	1
	South Park Township	13,953	18	17	1		Tulpehocken Township	3,588	3	3	0
	South Pymatuning Township	2,841	2	2	0		Tunkhannock	1,801	5	5	0
	South Waverly	980	3	3	0		Tunkhannock Township, Wyoming County	4,332	4	4	0
	Southwestern Regional	17,840	14	13	1		Turtle Creek	5,569	7	6	1
	Southwest Greensburg	2,241	2	2	0		Ulster Township	1,299	1	1	0
	Southwest Mercer County Regional	11,421	21	20	1		Union City	3,348	3	3	0
	Southwest Regional	2,180	3	2	1		Uniontown	11,774	16	16	0
	South Whitehall Township	19,486	40	37	3		Union Township, Lawrence County	5,102	2	2	0
	South Williamsport	6,064	10	9	1		Upland	2,965	1	1	0
	Spring City	3,410	4	3	1		Upper Burrell Township	2,166	3	2	1
	Springdale	3,507	2	2	0		Upper Chichester Township	17,623	25	23	2
	Springdale Township	1,655	2	2	0		Upper Darby Township	79,020	139	126	13
	Springettsbury Township	24,663	33	30	3		Upper Gwynedd Township	15,870	23	20	3
	Springfield Township, Bucks County	5,099	2	2	0		Upper Makefield Township	8,668	17	16	1
	Springfield Township, Delaware County	22,935	40	34	6		Upper Merion Township	26,680	81	62	19
	Springfield Township, Montgomery County	19,003	29	28	1		Upper Moreland Township	24,398	50	39	11
	Spring Garden Township	11,876	20	18	2		Upper Nazareth Township	5,669	4	3	1
	Spring Township, Berks County	26,659	30	29	1		Upper Perkiomen	6,464	9	8	1
							Upper Pottsgrove Township	5,161	12	11	1
							Upper Providence Township, Delaware County	11,232	13	12	1

Table 78. Full-Time Law Enforcement Employees by State by City, 2007 *(Contd.)*

(Number.)

State	City	Population	Total law enforcement employees	Total officers	Total civilians
	Upper Providence Township, Montgomery County	19,373	23	21	2
	Upper Saucon Township	14,725	19	18	1
	Upper Southampton Township	15,404	25	22	3
	Upper St. Clair Township	18,927	35	28	7
	Upper Uwchlan Township	10,022	10	10	0
	Upper Yoder Township	5,580	13	13	0
	Uwchlan Township	18,689	24	22	2
	Valley Township	6,445	4	4	0
	Vandergrift	5,088	8	8	0
	Vernon Township	5,398	5	4	1
	Verona	2,857	5	4	1
	Walnutport	2,170	4	4	0
	Warminster Township	33,777	54	48	6
	Warren	9,519	20	14	6
	Warrington Township	23,208	31	28	3
	Warwick Township, Bucks County	15,086	19	17	2
	Warwick Township, Lancaster County	17,362	17	15	2
	Washington, Washington County	14,710	33	31	2
	Washington Township, Fayette County	4,186	3	3	0
	Washington Township, Northampton County	4,898	4	4	0
	Washington Township, Westmoreland County	7,476	7	7	0
	Watsontown	2,100	5	5	0
	Waynesboro	9,755	21	19	2
	Waynesburg	4,169	10	8	2
	Weatherly	2,608	4	4	0
	Wellsboro	3,293	6	6	0
	Wernersville	2,504	2	2	0
	Wesleyville	3,386	11	10	1
	West Alexander	304	2	2	0
	West Brandywine Township	7,756	8	7	1
	West Caln Township	8,237	1	1	0
	West Chester	18,276	58	47	11
	West Conshohocken	1,505	10	9	1
	West Deer Township	12,002	12	11	1
	West Earl Township	7,465	6	6	0
	West Fallowfield Township	2,615	1	1	0
	Westfall Township	2,933	5	5	0
	West Goshen Township	21,255	29	24	5
	West Grove Borough	2,712	3	3	0
	West Hazleton	3,334	1	1	0
	West Hempfield Township	16,026	21	19	2
	West Hills Regional	10,863	12	11	1
	West Homestead	2,008	18	7	11
	West Lampeter Township	15,539	16	15	1
	West Lebanon Township	840	11	10	1
	West Manchester Township	18,181	29	26	3
	West Manheim Township	7,178	8	8	0
	West Mead Township	5,119	2	2	0
	West Mifflin	20,757	42	37	5
	West Norriton Township	14,642	32	27	5
	West Penn Township	4,233	3	3	0
	West Pikeland Township	4,113	4	4	0
	West Pike Run	1,848	1	1	0
	West Pittston	4,883	4	4	0
	West Pottsgrove Township	3,801	9	9	0
	West Reading	4,086	18	16	2
	West Sadsbury Township	2,512	4	3	1
	West Salem Township	3,389	10	9	1
	West Shore Regional	6,619	11	9	2
	Westtown-East Goshen Regional	31,691	32	30	2
	West View	6,704	12	8	4
	West Vincent Township	4,180	4	4	0
	West Whiteland Township	18,480	30	28	2
	West Wyoming	2,698	2	2	0
	West York	4,219	8	8	0
	Whitehall	13,439	25	20	5
	Whitehall Township	26,917	59	50	9
	White Haven Borough	1,153	2	2	0
	Whitemarsh Township	17,422	39	32	7
	White Oak	8,064	12	11	1
	White Township	1,334	4	4	0
	Whitpain Township	18,799	38	31	7
	Wiconisco Township	1,102	1	1	0
	Wilkes-Barre	41,050	95	87	8
	Wilkes-Barre Township	3,060	18	16	2
	Wilkinsburg	17,583	27	24	3
	Wilkins Township	6,453	12	12	0
	Williamsburg	1,260	2	2	0
	Williamsport	29,701	57	53	4
	Willistown Township	10,861	18	16	2
	Windber	4,043	3	2	1
	Wyoming	3,020	5	5	0
	Wyomissing	10,464	27	22	5
	Yeadon	11,440	16	14	2
	York	40,339	114	100	14
	York Area Regional	57,252	53	48	5
	Youngsville	1,689	2	2	0
	Zelienople	4,008	10	9	1
RHODE ISLAND	Barrington	16,414	30	23	7
	Bristol	24,274	51	40	11
	Burrillville	16,392	36	26	10
	Central Falls	18,818	54	44	10
	Charlestown	8,131	26	21	5
	Coventry	34,353	73	60	13
	Cranston	80,724	180	148	32
	Cumberland	34,027	58	47	11
	East Greenwich	13,338	43	34	9
	East Providence	48,668	123	105	18
	Foster	4,467	13	7	6
	Glocester	10,498	22	16	6
	Hopkinton	7,976	23	16	7
	Jamestown	5,484	19	15	4
	Johnston	28,585	94	75	19
	Lincoln	21,855	44	36	8
	Little Compton	3,510	14	10	4
	Middletown	16,278	41	37	4
	Narragansett	16,552	52	41	11
	Newport	24,192	105	85	20
	New Shoreham	1,023	9	5	4
	North Kingstown	26,475	62	50	12
	North Providence	32,685	94	71	23
	North Smithfield	11,183	26	21	5
	Pawtucket	72,319	183	147	36
	Portsmouth	16,853	34	31	3
	Providence	173,719	576	484	92
	Richmond	7,665	18	13	5
	Scituate	10,814	25	18	7
	Smithfield	21,495	55	41	14
	South Kingstown	29,172	73	55	18
	Tiverton	15,074	40	28	12
	Warren	11,089	27	22	5
	Warwick	85,139	228	177	51
	Westerly	23,197	62	51	11
	West Greenwich	6,371	17	11	6
	West Warwick	29,293	73	60	13
	Woonsocket	43,529	117	100	17
SOUTH CAROLINA	Abbeville	5,659	24	21	3
	Aiken	29,256	125	83	42

Table 78. Full-Time Law Enforcement Employees by State by City, 2007 *(Contd.)*

(Number.)

State	City	Population	Total law enforcement employees	Total officers	Total civilians	State	City	Population	Total law enforcement employees	Total officers	Total civilians
	Allendale	3,781	10	9	1		Harleyville	694	4	4	0
	Anderson	26,326	124	91	33		Hartsville	7,460	33	30	3
	Andrews	3,017	9	8	1		Hemingway	513	5	3	2
	Atlantic Beach	385	5	5	0		Holly Hill	1,346	8	8	0
	Aynor	580	6	5	1		Honea Path	3,628	14	14	0
	Bamberg	3,480	12	10	2		Inman	1,942	8	8	0
	Barnwell	4,847	18	16	2		Irmo	11,364	25	22	3
	Batesburg-Leesville	5,620	22	17	5		Isle of Palms	4,653	30	20	10
	Beaufort	11,960	53	48	5		Iva	1,188	6	5	1
	Belton	4,607	14	12	2		Jackson	1,650	4	4	0
	Bennettsville	10,898	37	34	3		Jamestown	96	3	2	1
	Bethune	367	1	1	0		Johnsonville	1,461	5	4	1
	Bishopville	3,945	15	13	2		Johnston	2,339	7	7	0
	Blacksburg	1,899	11	11	0		Jonesville	914	4	4	0
	Blackville	2,888	9	7	2		Kingstree	3,317	21	19	2
	Bluffton	3,791	33	29	4		Lake City	6,693	25	18	7
	Bonneau	338	2	2	0		Lake View	789	4	4	0
	Bowman	1,163	3	3	0		Lamar	1,001	4	4	0
	Branchville	1,037	5	4	1		Lancaster	8,393	43	34	9
	Brunson	576	3	2	1		Landrum	2,554	10	9	1
	Burnettown	2,670	2	2	0		Lane	533	1	1	0
	Calhoun Falls	2,231	8	8	0		Latta	1,501	11	10	1
	Camden	7,071	30	26	4		Laurens	9,841	37	30	7
	Cameron	416	1	1	0		Lexington	14,715	42	39	3
	Campobello	584	5	5	0		Liberty	3,034	17	11	6
	Cayce	12,659	74	61	13		Loris	2,322	12	8	4
	Central	4,147	11	10	1		Lyman	2,812	8	7	1
	Chapin	698	7	5	2		Lynchburg	579	4	4	0
	Charleston	109,382	513	368	145		Manning	4,016	17	15	2
	Cheraw	5,417	27	21	6		Marion	6,949	26	22	4
	Chesnee	1,057	5	5	0		Mauldin	20,494	50	39	11
	Chester	6,074	31	24	7		McBee	713	2	1	1
	Chesterfield	1,321	6	5	1		McColl	2,368	4	4	0
	Clemson	12,532	36	27	9		McCormick	2,712	7	7	0
	Clinton	9,018	36	34	2		Moncks Corner	6,645	28	25	3
	Clio	740	4	3	1		Mount Pleasant	60,746	175	137	38
	Clover	4,493	17	13	4		Mullins	4,820	22	21	1
	Columbia	120,549	360	320	40		Myrtle Beach	29,361	229	179	50
	Conway	14,285	63	49	14		Newberry	10,927	33	30	3
	Cottageville	699	5	4	1		New Ellenton	2,251	6	6	0
	Coward	674	2	2	0		Nichols	404	3	3	0
	Cowpens	2,364	5	5	0		Ninety Six	1,920	5	5	0
	Darlington	6,525	27	24	3		North	778	3	3	0
	Denmark	3,052	12	10	2		North Augusta	20,270	62	51	11
	Dillon	6,382	22	18	4		North Charleston	88,431	388	291	97
	Due West	1,286	5	5	0		North Myrtle Beach	15,577	121	95	26
	Duncan	3,020	14	14	0		Norway	363	2	1	1
	Easley	19,372	55	43	12		Orangeburg	13,674	94	70	24
	Edgefield	4,529	9	9	0		Pacolet	2,756	4	4	0
	Edisto Beach	724	6	6	0		Pageland	2,539	15	10	5
	Ehrhardt	561	3	2	1		Pamplico	1,152	4	4	0
	Elgin	1,080	6	5	1		Pawleys Island	143	7	6	1
	Elloree	698	3	3	0		Pelion	599	3	3	0
	Estill	2,381	8	5	3		Pickens	2,990	14	13	1
	Eutawville	329	3	3	0		Pine Ridge	1,760	3	2	1
	Fairfax	3,167	7	6	1		Port Royal	9,959	21	20	1
	Florence	31,377	124	100	24		Prosperity	1,072	6	4	2
	Folly Beach	2,339	19	13	6		Ridgeland	2,640	15	14	1
	Forest Acres	9,818	34	27	7		Ridgeville	2,075	3	2	1
	Fort Lawn	816	4	4	0		Rock Hill	63,388	160	118	42
	Fort Mill	8,709	37	31	6		Salem	132	2	2	0
	Fountain Inn	7,261	28	21	7		Salley	415	1	1	0
	Gaffney	12,945	44	40	4		Saluda	2,979	10	10	0
	Gaston	1,405	2	2	0		Santee	714	5	1	4
	Georgetown	8,668	38	29	9		Scranton	998	2	2	0
	Goose Creek	32,139	73	53	20		Seneca	8,076	42	31	11
	Great Falls	2,052	7	6	1		Simpsonville	16,211	49	39	10
	Greeleyville	410	3	3	0		Society Hill	696	4	4	0
	Greenville	57,595	215	171	44		South Congaree	2,413	7	7	0
	Greenwood	22,428	56	49	7		Spartanburg	38,388	147	121	26
	Greer	23,224	67	51	16		Springdale	2,956	10	10	0
	Hampton	2,780	8	8	0		Springfield	483	1	1	0
	Hanahan	13,983	38	30	8		St. George	2,124	11	10	1
	Hardeeville	1,857	17	15	2		St. Matthews	1,995	6	6	0

Table 78. Full-Time Law Enforcement Employees by State by City, 2007 (Contd.)

(Number.)

State	City	Popula-tion	Total law enforce-ment employees	Total officers	Total civilians	State	City	Popula-tion	Total law enforce-ment employees	Total officers	Total civilians
	St. Stephen	1,702	6	6	0		Mitchell	14,894	36	27	9
	Sullivans Island	1,868	7	6	1		Mobridge	3,188	13	7	6
	Summerton	1,047	10	9	1		New Effington	225	1	1	0
	Summerville	43,985	97	77	20		North Sioux City	2,545	7	6	1
	Sumter	38,955	160	111	49		Parkston	1,506	2	2	0
	Surfside Beach	4,846	24	18	6		Philip	728	2	2	0
	Swansea	784	5	4	1		Pierre	14,124	38	25	13
	Tega Cay	4,612	20	16	4		Platte	1,317	2	2	0
	Timmonsville	2,384	9	7	2		Rapid City	63,162	134	107	27
	Travelers Rest	4,396	21	15	6		Rosholt	437	1	1	0
	Turbeville	721	3	3	0		Scotland	816	1	1	0
	Union	8,167	39	37	2		Selby	674	1	1	0
	Vance	199	1	1	0		Sioux Falls	144,985	253	216	37
	Varnville	2,035	8	8	0		Sisseton	2,515	7	7	0
	Wagener	878	3	3	0		Spearfish	9,796	26	18	8
	Walhalla	3,689	15	14	1		Springfield	1,510	2	2	0
	Walterboro	5,601	31	24	7		Sturgis	6,090	19	16	3
	Ware Shoals	2,359	9	7	2		Tea	2,922	3	3	0
	Wellford	2,315	8	7	1		Tripp	643	1	1	0
	West Columbia	13,729	61	50	11		Tyndall	1,135	2	2	0
	Westminster	2,675	9	9	0		Vermillion	9,810	17	16	1
	West Pelzer	905	3	3	0		Viborg	793	1	1	0
	Whitmire	1,543	6	4	2		Wagner	1,596	3	3	0
	Williamston	3,914	16	13	3		Watertown	20,568	49	35	14
	Williston	3,239	10	9	1		Webster	1,732	5	5	0
	Winnsboro	3,637	27	26	1		Whitewood	810	2	2	0
	Woodruff	4,076	14	12	2		Winner	2,892	9	8	1
	Yemassee	857	7	7	0		Worthing	858	1	1	0
	York	7,537	32	25	7		Yankton	13,805	37	26	11
SOUTH						TENNESSEE	Adamsville	2,122	9	6	3
DAKOTA	Aberdeen	23,992	46	38	8		Alamo	2,349	4	4	0
	Alcester	890	2	2	0		Alcoa	8,544	48	41	7
	Armour	693	1	1	0		Alexandria	870	3	3	0
	Avon	536	1	1	0		Algood	3,293	12	11	1
	Belle Fourche	4,769	11	10	1		Ardmore	1,142	11	6	5
	Beresford	2,069	8	4	4		Ashland City	4,696	14	13	1
	Box Elder	3,112	9	7	2		Athens	14,183	29	27	2
	Brandon	7,956	12	11	1		Atoka	6,868	17	16	1
	Brookings	18,805	35	28	7		Baileyton	501	2	2	0
	Burke	590	1	1	0		Bartlett	47,333	143	111	32
	Canton	3,237	5	5	0		Baxter	1,367	5	5	0
	Centerville	856	1	1	0		Bean Station	3,043	6	6	0
	Chamberlain	2,241	5	5	0		Belle Meade	3,170	19	15	4
	Clark	1,128	2	2	0		Bells	2,275	5	5	0
	Corsica	601	2	2	0		Benton	1,080	7	7	0
	Deadwood	1,269	14	11	3		Berry Hill	690	17	13	4
	Eagle Butte	950	2	2	0		Bethel Springs	786	1	1	0
	Elk Point	1,885	4	4	0		Big Sandy	515	2	2	0
	Estelline	668	1	1	0		Blaine	1,751	4	3	1
	Eureka	952	1	1	0		Bluff City	1,629	10	10	0
	Faith	456	2	1	1		Bolivar	5,617	25	19	6
	Flandreau	2,306	7	6	1		Bradford	1,063	2	2	0
	Freeman	1,178	2	2	0		Brentwood	35,019	70	57	13
	Gettysburg	1,130	2	2	0		Brighton	2,664	6	6	0
	Gregory	1,218	3	3	0		Bristol	25,346	86	65	21
	Groton	1,370	3	3	0		Brownsville	10,539	35	30	5
	Highmore	767	1	1	0		Bruceton	1,469	4	4	0
	Hot Springs	4,095	7	6	1		Burns	1,411	3	3	0
	Hoven	421	1	1	0		Calhoun	522	4	4	0
	Huron	10,779	32	25	7		Camden	3,693	19	14	5
	Jefferson	593	2	2	0		Carthage	2,234	11	7	4
	Kadoka	673	1	1	0		Caryville	2,400	6	6	0
	Kimball	678	1	1	0		Celina	1,380	11	5	6
	Lead	2,837	6	5	1		Centerville	4,018	21	13	8
	Lemmon	1,205	3	3	0		Chapel Hill	1,285	5	5	0
	Lennox	2,154	4	4	0		Charleston	654	3	3	0
	Leola	394	1	1	0		Chattanooga	155,043	615	421	194
	Madison	6,221	12	11	1		Church Hill	6,644	11	10	1
	Martin	1,029	4	4	0		Clarksville	114,582	286	233	53
	McIntosh	212	1	1	0		Cleveland	38,808	102	90	12
	McLaughlin	755	2	1	1		Clifton	2,684	6	6	0
	Menno	675	1	1	0		Clinton	9,516	27	25	2
	Milbank	3,257	6	6	0		Collegedale	7,423	22	21	1
	Miller	1,343	3	3	0		Collierville	39,569	120	87	33

Table 78.   Full-Time Law Enforcement Employees by State by City, 2007 *(Contd.)*

(Number.)

State	City	Population	Total law enforcement employees	Total officers	Total civilians	State	City	Population	Total law enforcement employees	Total officers	Total civilians
	Collinwood	1,038	3	3	0		Kingston	5,588	13	12	1
	Columbia	33,897	88	77	11		Kingston Springs	2,945	6	5	1
	Cookeville	28,691	90	69	21		Knoxville	183,319	482	382	100
	Coopertown	3,324	10	9	1		Lafayette	4,289	22	15	7
	Copperhill	465	2	2	0		La Follette	8,212	27	21	6
	Cornersville	948	3	3	0		La Grange	146	1	1	0
	Covington	9,193	33	32	1		Lake City	1,856	10	7	3
	Cowan	1,758	6	6	0		Lakewood	2,403	3	3	0
	Cross Plains	1,602	3	3	0		La Vergne	28,719	62	45	17
	Crossville	11,111	43	39	4		Lawrenceburg	10,826	40	34	6
	Crump	1,457	4	3	1		Lebanon	24,219	86	71	15
	Cumberland City	321	3	3	0		Lenoir City	7,835	22	21	1
	Dandridge	2,497	10	9	1		Lewisburg	10,866	35	25	10
	Dayton	6,686	19	17	2		Lexington	7,829	28	24	4
	Decatur	1,468	3	3	0		Livingston	3,518	18	12	6
	Decaturville	825	1	1	0		Lookout Mountain	1,865	20	16	4
	Decherd	2,164	11	10	1		Loretto	1,707	3	3	0
	Dickson	13,171	47	42	5		Loudon	4,915	16	15	1
	Dover	1,550	6	6	0		Madisonville	4,542	16	14	2
	Dresden	2,629	9	8	1		Manchester	9,858	39	32	7
	Dunlap	4,891	12	11	1		Martin	10,043	32	26	6
	Dyer	2,422	6	6	0		Maryville	26,941	59	52	7
	Dyersburg	17,391	68	57	11		Mason	1,174	7	6	1
	East Ridge	19,641	45	32	13		Maynardville	1,940	4	4	0
	Elizabethton	13,917	39	35	4		McEwen	1,681	5	4	1
	Elkton	500	2	2	0		McKenzie	5,438	20	15	5
	Englewood	1,722	6	6	0		McMinnville	13,378	40	36	4
	Erin	1,453	5	4	1		Medina	1,609	10	10	0
	Erwin	5,802	12	12	0		Memphis	669,264	2,529	2,056	473
	Estill Springs	2,285	6	6	0		Middleton	623	4	4	0
	Ethridge	555	1	1	0		Milan	7,885	33	27	6
	Etowah	3,775	14	10	4		Millersville	6,365	15	11	4
	Fairview	7,712	17	16	1		Millington	10,323	48	37	11
	Fayetteville	7,104	24	22	2		Minor Hill	450	1	1	0
	Franklin	57,489	148	125	23		Monteagle	1,209	12	5	7
	Friendship	602	1	1	0		Monterey	2,856	8	8	0
	Gainesboro	845	4	4	0		Morristown	27,147	86	80	6
	Gallatin	28,419	79	60	19		Moscow	571	5	5	0
	Gallaway	715	9	8	1		Mountain City	2,389	10	10	0
	Gates	852	2	2	0		Mount Carmel	5,436	7	7	0
	Gatlinburg	5,165	55	45	10		Mount Juliet	20,259	53	39	14
	Germantown	37,450	108	86	22		Mount Pleasant	4,442	12	11	1
	Gibson	406	3	3	0		Munford	6,268	15	14	1
	Gleason	1,402	5	5	0		Murfreesboro	96,264	234	186	48
	Goodlettsville	15,854	55	40	15		Nashville	564,169	1,568	1,250	318
	Gordonsville	1,320	5	5	0		Newbern	3,134	19	13	6
	Grand Junction	312	2	2	0		New Hope	1,025	1	1	0
	Graysville	1,438	4	4	0		New Johnsonville	1,993	4	4	0
	Greenbrier	6,434	13	12	1		New Market	1,327	5	4	1
	Greeneville	15,558	47	45	2		Newport	7,406	31	27	4
	Greenfield	2,028	8	7	1		New Tazewell	2,896	11	11	0
	Halls	2,201	10	10	0		Niota	805	3	3	0
	Harriman	6,714	23	22	1		Nolensville	2,643	6	6	0
	Henderson	6,290	15	14	1		Norris	1,468	7	7	0
	Hendersonville	46,989	95	71	24		Oakland	3,821	19	16	3
	Henning	1,290	1	1	0		Oak Ridge	27,682	67	53	14
	Henry	545	1	1	0		Obion	1,100	4	4	0
	Hohenwald	3,832	15	14	1		Oliver Springs	3,322	14	10	4
	Hollow Rock	943	2	2	0		Oneida	3,685	20	15	5
	Hornbeak	425	1	1	0		Paris	10,014	37	26	11
	Humboldt	9,213	30	24	6		Parsons	2,377	7	7	0
	Huntingdon	4,163	16	12	4		Petersburg	603	2	2	0
	Huntland	882	4	4	0		Pigeon Forge	6,019	64	52	12
	Jacksboro	2,055	6	6	0		Pikeville	1,890	3	3	0
	Jackson	63,125	229	188	41		Piperton	1,001	11	9	2
	Jamestown	1,907	9	9	0		Pittman Center	622	2	2	0
	Jasper	3,086	8	8	0		Pleasant View	3,822	5	5	0
	Jefferson City	8,055	21	19	2		Portland	11,060	32	26	6
	Jellico	2,546	6	6	0		Powells Crossroads	1,216	1	1	0
	Johnson City	60,488	175	146	29		Pulaski	7,869	28	25	3
	Jonesborough	4,803	20	15	5		Puryear	678	2	2	0
	Kenton	1,306	5	5	0		Red Bank	11,526	24	22	2
	Kimball	1,380	9	9	0		Red Boiling Springs	1,072	5	5	0
	Kingsport	44,079	146	104	42		Ridgely	1,513	6	5	1

Table 78.   Full-Time Law Enforcement Employees by State by City, 2007 *(Contd.)*

(Number.)

State	City	Population	Total law enforcement employees	Total officers	Total civilians	State	City	Population	Total law enforcement employees	Total officers	Total civilians
	Ridgetop	1,705	7	6	1		Anthony	4,155	14	13	1
	Ripley	7,705	33	26	7		Anton	1,153	1	1	0
	Rockwood	5,453	16	15	1		Aransas Pass	9,082	28	22	6
	Rogersville	4,327	19	14	5		Arcola	1,292	7	6	1
	Rossville	514	4	4	0		Argyle	3,291	10	9	1
	Rutherford	1,236	4	4	0		Arlington	372,073	759	584	175
	Rutledge	1,282	6	4	2		Arp	945	4	4	0
	Savannah	7,281	27	16	11		Athens	12,742	33	25	8
	Scotts Hill	913	2	2	0		Atlanta	5,606	19	15	4
	Selmer	4,724	19	18	1		Austin	716,817	1,995	1,418	577
	Sevierville	16,070	65	51	14		Azle	10,973	31	24	7
	Sewanee	2,555	13	9	4		Baird	1,668	2	2	0
	Sharon	908	1	1	0		Balch Springs	19,852	54	37	17
	Shelbyville	19,586	52	41	11		Balcones Heights	2,969	22	17	5
	Signal Mountain	7,063	16	15	1		Ballinger	3,875	7	6	1
	Smithville	4,227	11	10	1		Bangs	1,636	4	4	0
	Smyrna	35,664	99	78	21		Bastrop	7,966	21	18	3
	Sneedville	1,309	1	1	0		Bay City	18,211	52	36	16
	Soddy-Daisy	12,098	30	24	6		Bayou Vista	1,717	5	5	0
	Somerville	2,949	11	11	0		Baytown	69,040	179	129	50
	South Carthage	1,301	4	4	0		Beaumont	109,345	303	236	67
	South Fulton	2,446	7	6	1		Bedford	48,974	135	82	53
	South Pittsburg	3,113	8	8	0		Bee Cave	2,464	11	10	1
	Sparta	4,839	16	15	1		Beeville	13,721	23	18	5
	Spencer	1,683	3	3	0		Bellaire	17,879	56	42	14
	Spring City	2,018	7	7	0		Bellmead	9,573	25	17	8
	Springfield	16,844	55	38	17		Bellville	4,416	11	10	1
	Spring Hill	23,774	46	34	12		Belton	16,191	35	27	8
	St. Joseph	859	1	1	0		Benbrook	22,618	48	37	11
	Surgoinsville	1,777	3	2	1		Bertram	1,378	2	2	0
	Sweetwater	6,419	20	18	2		Beverly Hills	2,046	10	6	4
	Tazewell	2,158	6	6	0		Big Sandy	1,360	5	4	1
	Tellico Plains	955	3	3	0		Big Spring	24,099	58	37	21
	Tiptonville	3,998	5	5	0		Bishop	3,199	8	4	4
	Townsend	262	4	4	0		Blanco	1,641	4	4	0
	Tracy City	1,685	5	5	0		Bloomburg	368	1	1	0
	Trenton	4,538	24	18	6		Blue Mound	2,354	11	7	4
	Trezevant	889	1	1	0		Boerne	9,090	42	26	16
	Trimble	727	2	2	0		Bogata	1,318	3	3	0
	Troy	1,241	4	4	0		Bonham	10,756	25	17	8
	Tullahoma	19,036	42	37	5		Borger	13,128	36	26	10
	Tusculum	2,260	2	2	0		Bovina	1,790	2	2	0
	Union City	10,772	44	36	8		Bowie	5,591	21	14	7
	Vonore	1,483	11	10	1		Brady	5,382	17	9	8
	Wartburg	912	4	4	0		Brazoria	2,998	12	7	5
	Watertown	1,408	4	4	0		Breckenridge	5,647	17	12	5
	Waverly	4,215	14	13	1		Bremond	895	2	2	0
	Waynesboro	2,146	8	8	0		Brenham	14,887	32	29	3
	Westmoreland	2,195	10	6	4		Bridge City	8,735	18	13	5
	White Bluff	2,473	3	3	0		Bridgeport	5,966	24	16	8
	White House	9,464	26	18	8		Brookshire	3,734	14	10	4
	White Pine	2,099	9	8	1		Brookside Village	2,005	5	5	0
	Whiteville	4,480	8	8	0		Brownfield	9,110	24	16	8
	Whitwell	1,589	8	5	3		Brownsville	177,090	307	231	76
	Winchester	7,911	25	24	1		Brownwood	19,820	54	35	19
	Winfield	999	3	3	0		Bruceville-Eddy	1,535	3	3	0
	Woodbury	2,554	9	8	1		Bryan	67,484	156	121	35
TEXAS.....................	Abernathy	2,748	4	4	0		Bullard	1,741	6	5	1
	Abilene	114,644	232	163	69		Bulverde	4,662	12	12	0
	Addison	13,764	79	58	21		Burkburnett	10,203	24	19	5
	Alamo	16,496	37	28	9		Burleson	33,383	71	52	19
	Alamo Heights	7,087	30	19	11		Burnet	5,779	13	11	2
	Alice	19,850	45	36	9		Cactus	2,679	6	5	1
	Allen	78,630	140	99	41		Caddo Mills	1,218	3	3	0
	Alpine	6,056	17	10	7		Caldwell	3,807	14	13	1
	Alto	1,152	4	4	0		Calvert	1,401	4	4	0
	Alton	7,793	16	12	4		Cameron	5,883	13	8	5
	Alvarado	4,200	21	15	6		Caney City	260	3	3	0
	Alvin	22,542	74	47	27		Canton	3,688	18	13	5
	Amarillo	187,234	413	303	110		Canyon	13,644	23	20	3
	Andrews	9,541	25	16	9		Carrollton	123,324	232	165	67
	Angleton	18,811	49	37	12		Carthage	6,598	21	14	7
	Anna	1,811	8	8	0		Castle Hills	4,148	26	20	6
	Anson	2,364	2	2	0		Castroville	3,080	11	9	2

Table 78. Full-Time Law Enforcement Employees by State by City, 2007 (Contd.)

(Number.)

State	City	Population	Total law enforcement employees	Total officers	Total civilians	State	City	Population	Total law enforcement employees	Total officers	Total civilians
	Cedar Hill	44,629	86	66	20		El Campo	10,799	37	26	11
	Cedar Park	57,286	84	59	25		Electra	2,854	12	7	5
	Celina	4,789	7	7	0		Elgin	9,951	25	20	5
	Center	5,823	23	15	8		El Paso	616,029	1,446	1,106	340
	Childress	6,631	13	8	5		Elsa	6,758	14	9	5
	Chillicothe	721	2	2	0		Ennis	19,520	40	34	6
	Cibolo	11,960	19	17	2		Euless	52,899	121	80	41
	Cisco	3,777	9	7	2		Everman	5,739	16	11	5
	Clarksville	3,582	9	9	0		Fairfield	3,612	12	12	0
	Cleburne	30,174	69	53	16		Fair Oaks Ranch	6,082	14	14	0
	Cleveland	8,081	33	23	10		Falfurrias	5,042	11	10	1
	Clifton	3,654	7	6	1		Farmers Branch	26,455	104	72	32
	Clint	990	1	1	0		Farmersville	3,481	8	7	1
	Clute	10,781	37	27	10		Ferris	2,414	13	9	4
	Clyde	3,744	8	7	1		Flatonia	1,423	4	4	0
	Cockrell Hill	4,291	18	13	5		Florence	1,133	3	3	0
	Coffee City	209	2	2	0		Floresville	7,463	16	15	1
	Coleman	4,832	14	8	6		Flower Mound	68,191	107	69	38
	College Station	74,997	154	108	46		Floydada	3,214	6	6	0
	Colleyville	23,773	46	36	10		Forest Hill	13,771	35	26	9
	Collinsville	1,528	2	2	0		Forney	14,020	33	21	12
	Colorado City	3,918	11	7	4		Fort Stockton	7,350	29	20	9
	Columbus	3,930	11	10	1		Fort Worth	670,693	1,792	1,412	380
	Comanche	4,308	8	7	1		Frankston	1,276	4	4	0
	Combes	2,892	7	6	1		Fredericksburg	11,004	33	29	4
	Commerce	9,692	21	18	3		Freeport	12,588	42	30	12
	Conroe	51,582	139	105	34		Freer	3,022	10	6	4
	Converse	14,323	43	31	12		Friendswood	34,140	72	54	18
	Coppell	39,572	72	56	16		Friona	3,698	10	6	4
	Copperas Cove	29,706	63	46	17		Frisco	90,674	169	121	48
	Corrigan	1,975	9	6	3		Gainesville	16,710	52	39	13
	Corsicana	26,696	51	39	12		Galena Park	10,177	24	19	5
	Cottonwood Shores	1,166	2	2	0		Galveston	57,590	209	160	49
	Crane	3,028	10	6	4		Ganado	1,848	3	3	0
	Crockett	6,960	16	14	2		Garland	218,236	444	318	126
	Crowell	1,055	1	1	0		Gatesville	15,450	23	16	7
	Crowley	11,618	31	24	7		Georgetown	44,834	94	66	28
	Crystal City	7,388	14	9	5		Giddings	5,517	18	13	5
	Cuero	6,642	14	13	1		Gilmer	5,191	22	18	4
	Cuney	150	2	1	1		Gladewater	6,355	20	14	6
	Daingerfield	2,462	7	7	0		Glenn Heights	10,739	24	17	7
	Dalhart	6,990	18	15	3		Godley	1,011	4	4	0
	Dallas	1,239,104	3,816	3,212	604		Gonzales	7,534	23	17	6
	Dalworthington Gardens	2,408	18	14	4		Gorman	1,248	3	3	0
	Danbury	1,683	3	3	0		Graham	8,689	23	21	2
	Dayton	7,377	20	15	5		Granbury	8,040	37	32	5
	Decatur	6,402	27	20	7		Grand Prairie	157,913	322	221	101
	Deer Park	29,971	74	54	20		Grand Saline	3,296	7	7	0
	De Kalb	1,795	6	6	0		Granger	1,359	4	4	0
	Del Rio	36,864	87	63	24		Granite Shoals	2,794	9	7	2
	Denison	24,130	59	45	14		Grapeland	1,400	3	2	1
	Denton	113,936	205	153	52		Grapevine	49,498	122	89	33
	Denver City	4,012	14	8	6		Greenville	26,130	68	48	20
	DeSoto	47,253	92	69	23		Gregory	2,261	4	4	0
	Devine	4,531	10	8	2		Groesbeck	4,368	8	8	0
	Diboll	5,512	20	14	6		Groves	14,610	22	20	2
	Dickinson	18,151	40	30	10		Gun Barrel City	6,168	21	15	6
	Dilley	4,142	6	6	0		Hale Center	2,176	3	3	0
	Dimmitt	3,815	8	6	2		Hallettsville	2,532	7	6	1
	Donna	16,662	33	23	10		Hallsville	2,984	4	4	0
	Double Oak	3,199	6	6	0		Haltom City	40,114	93	70	23
	Driscoll	818	3	2	1		Hamlin	1,954	8	4	4
	Dublin	3,674	12	9	3		Harker Heights	23,726	52	44	8
	Dumas	14,084	28	24	4		Harlingen	64,984	153	120	33
	Duncanville	35,512	70	58	12		Haskell	2,683	4	4	0
	Eagle Lake	3,732	9	8	1		Hawk Cove	617	1	1	0
	Eagle Pass	26,974	77	62	15		Hawkins	1,520	5	5	0
	Early	2,821	8	7	1		Hawley	592	2	2	0
	Earth	1,046	2	2	0		Hearne	4,751	16	10	6
	Eastland	3,915	11	9	2		Heath	7,263	19	18	1
	Eden	2,386	3	3	0		Hedwig Village	2,317	22	17	5
	Edgewood	1,478	5	4	1		Helotes	6,826	20	18	2
	Edinburg	69,708	154	111	43		Hemphill	1,070	3	3	0
	Edna	5,854	11	9	2		Hempstead	7,188	17	15	2

Table 78. Full-Time Law Enforcement Employees by State by City, 2007 *(Contd.)*

(Number.)

State	City	Population	Total law enforcement employees	Total officers	Total civilians	State	City	Population	Total law enforcement employees	Total officers	Total civilians
	Henderson	11,633	42	30	12		Laguna Vista	3,068	7	7	0
	Hereford	14,528	29	23	6		La Joya	4,833	16	12	4
	Hewitt	13,522	31	22	9		Lake Dallas	7,423	20	13	7
	Hickory Creek	3,553	10	10	0		Lake Jackson	27,788	58	43	15
	Hidalgo	12,008	52	38	14		Lakeside	1,279	4	4	0
	Highland Park	9,062	67	53	14		Lakeview	6,477	16	12	4
	Highland Village	16,298	34	26	8		Lakeway	9,774	34	27	7
	Hill Country Village	1,083	12	12	0		Lake Worth	4,732	35	27	8
	Hillsboro	9,161	33	23	10		La Marque	14,081	38	28	10
	Hitchcock	7,389	16	12	4		Lamesa	9,167	21	14	7
	Holliday	1,821	3	3	0		Lampasas	7,973	24	17	7
	Hollywood Park	3,276	12	11	1		Lancaster	35,090	71	56	15
	Hondo	9,089	22	19	3		La Porte	34,165	97	70	27
	Hooks	2,934	6	6	0		Laredo	221,253	494	416	78
	Horizon City	11,855	10	9	1		La Vernia	1,203	6	5	1
	Horseshoe Bay	3,822	14	13	1		La Villa	1,477	5	5	0
	Houston	2,169,544	6,338	4,892	1,446		Lavon	424	9	8	1
	Howe	2,749	7	7	0		League City	68,743	119	89	30
	Hubbard	1,706	4	4	0		Leander	23,175	37	27	10
	Hudson	4,191	5	3	2		Leon Valley	9,876	30	22	8
	Hudson Oaks	1,944	12	12	0		Levelland	12,653	31	21	10
	Humble	14,977	74	56	18		Lewisville	97,184	183	136	47
	Huntington	2,099	5	5	0		Lexington	1,265	4	4	0
	Huntsville	37,906	56	49	7		Liberty	8,474	28	17	11
	Hurst	38,452	113	70	43		Lindale	4,503	22	17	5
	Hutchins	3,039	20	16	4		Linden	2,181	6	5	1
	Hutto	12,635	22	17	5		Little Elm	26,824	34	29	5
	Idalou	2,052	4	4	0		Littlefield	6,213	21	13	8
	Ingleside	9,355	19	12	7		Live Oak	12,117	44	30	14
	Ingram	1,886	6	5	1		Livingston	6,567	23	16	7
	Iowa Park	6,100	16	11	5		Llano	3,326	10	8	2
	Irving	196,676	456	319	137		Lockhart	13,946	27	20	7
	Italy	2,124	6	5	1		Lockney	1,802	3	3	0
	Itasca	1,655	6	6	0		Lone Star	1,597	6	5	1
	Jacinto City	9,890	24	19	5		Longview	77,003	217	162	55
	Jacksboro	4,653	13	7	6		Lorena	1,656	7	6	1
	Jacksonville	14,481	34	24	10		Lorenzo	1,241	2	2	0
	Jamaica Beach	1,127	5	5	0		Los Fresnos	5,465	19	13	6
	Jarrell	1,439	3	2	1		Lubbock	213,988	521	365	156
	Jasper	7,435	31	23	8		Lufkin	33,997	95	73	22
	Jefferson	1,991	8	7	1		Luling	5,442	24	15	9
	Jersey Village	7,176	33	23	10		Lumberton	9,853	18	15	3
	Johnson City	1,581	4	4	0		Lytle	2,733	5	5	0
	Jones Creek	2,120	4	3	1		Madisonville	4,349	9	8	1
	Jonestown	2,192	9	8	1		Magnolia	1,288	11	10	1
	Joshua	5,731	14	13	1		Malakoff	2,374	5	5	0
	Jourdanton	4,445	9	9	0		Manor	2,993	16	14	2
	Junction	2,647	4	4	0		Mansfield	43,901	195	77	118
	Karnes City	3,399	7	6	1		Manvel	4,912	13	8	5
	Katy	13,830	58	41	17		Marble Falls	7,562	36	24	12
	Kaufman	8,294	24	18	6		Marfa	1,903	4	4	0
	Keene	6,301	13	9	4		Marion	1,135	5	3	2
	Keller	38,439	78	49	29		Marlin	6,097	19	13	6
	Kemah	2,497	23	19	4		Marshall	23,978	65	49	16
	Kemp	1,309	3	3	0		Mart	2,517	3	3	0
	Kempner	1,190	1	1	0		Martindale	1,117	5	5	0
	Kenedy	3,363	8	7	1		Mathis	5,486	17	10	7
	Kennedale	6,848	28	21	7		McAllen	129,455	396	263	133
	Kerens	1,844	3	3	0		McGregor	4,862	19	12	7
	Kermit	5,144	16	10	6		McKinney	118,113	191	149	42
	Kerrville	22,636	66	50	16		Meadows Place	6,919	15	14	1
	Kilgore	12,152	41	31	10		Melissa	3,395	9	8	1
	Killeen	104,188	246	198	48		Memorial Villages	11,714	37	31	6
	Kingsville	24,235	67	52	15		Memphis	2,363	4	3	1
	Kirby	8,560	17	13	4		Mercedes	14,879	36	30	6
	Kirbyville	2,020	6	6	0		Meridian	1,510	2	2	0
	Knox City	1,043	3	3	0		Merkel	2,587	4	4	0
	Kountze	2,172	7	6	1		Mesquite	132,399	294	222	72
	Kress	779	1	1	0		Mexia	6,726	22	15	7
	Kyle	24,778	27	18	9		Midland	103,118	208	161	47
	Lacy-Lakeview	5,761	21	13	8		Midlothian	15,600	35	26	9
	La Feria	6,890	17	13	4		Milford	748	5	5	0
	Lago Vista	5,986	20	14	6		Mineola	5,172	14	12	2
	La Grange	4,669	9	9	0		Mineral Wells	17,083	36	28	8

Table 78. Full-Time Law Enforcement Employees by State by City, 2007 *(Contd.)*

(Number.)

State	City	Population	Total law enforcement employees	Total officers	Total civilians	State	City	Population	Total law enforcement employees	Total officers	Total civilians
	Mission	66,216	161	115	46		Primera	3,356	7	6	1
	Missouri City	77,166	98	74	24		Princeton	5,057	13	13	0
	Monahans	6,340	16	11	5		Progreso	5,375	9	9	0
	Mont Belvieu	2,645	14	9	5		Prosper	5,828	10	9	1
	Montgomery	593	8	8	0		Queen City	1,577	5	5	0
	Morgans Point Resort	4,291	8	7	1		Quinlan	1,466	3	3	0
	Mount Pleasant	15,360	36	26	10		Quitman	2,273	6	6	0
	Muleshoe	4,481	14	8	6		Ranger	2,516	4	4	0
	Munday	1,291	1	1	0		Ransom Canyon	1,079	3	3	0
	Murphy	15,497	27	19	8		Raymondville	9,554	20	13	7
	Mustang Ridge	931	3	3	0		Red Oak	8,538	28	21	7
	Nacogdoches	31,300	73	58	15		Refugio	2,760	11	8	3
	Nash	2,426	10	9	1		Reno	3,073	5	4	1
	Nassau Bay	4,040	13	12	1		Richardson	100,933	239	144	95
	Navasota	7,464	25	16	9		Richland Hills	8,067	26	18	8
	Nederland	16,325	33	21	12		Richmond	13,979	41	31	10
	Needville	3,585	4	4	0		Richwood	3,389	8	7	1
	New Boston	4,630	13	9	4		Riesel	1,012	3	3	0
	New Braunfels	51,860	107	82	25		Rio Grande City	14,098	32	23	9
	New Deal	726	3	2	1		Rising Star	834	1	1	0
	Nocona	3,291	9	6	3		River Oaks	6,914	24	18	6
	Nolanville	2,393	8	8	0		Roanoke	3,758	36	27	9
	Northlake	1,109	7	7	0		Robinson	10,011	28	20	8
	North Richland Hills	63,270	161	114	47		Robstown	12,361	31	22	9
	Oak Ridge	258	2	2	0		Rockdale	6,066	16	10	6
	Oak Ridge North	3,422	14	14	0		Rockport	9,464	24	22	2
	Odessa	95,839	190	145	45		Rockwall	34,872	77	62	15
	O'Donnell	966	1	1	0		Roma	11,394	36	27	9
	Olmos Park	2,298	12	12	0		Roman Forest	3,788	6	6	0
	Olney	3,328	7	3	4		Roscoe	1,260	1	1	0
	Olton	2,232	2	2	0		Rosebud	1,365	3	3	0
	Onalaska	1,564	6	6	0		Rose City	514	2	1	1
	Orange	17,793	54	41	13		Rosenberg	33,131	79	58	21
	Ore City	1,169	4	4	0		Round Rock	97,727	179	132	47
	Overton	2,337	7	4	3		Rowlett	56,432	106	77	29
	Ovilla	3,925	10	9	1		Royse City	8,086	20	17	3
	Oyster Creek	1,236	9	5	4		Rusk	5,173	13	11	2
	Paducah	1,286	6	1	5		Sabinal	1,672	4	4	0
	Palacios	5,158	12	8	4		Sachse	19,028	34	23	11
	Palestine	18,250	41	32	9		Saginaw	19,818	41	35	6
	Palmer	2,200	10	9	1		Salado	1,926	4	4	0
	Pampa	16,998	36	24	12		San Angelo	88,285	166	138	28
	Panhandle	2,619	4	4	0		San Antonio	1,316,882	2,773	2,132	641
	Pantego	2,344	14	11	3		San Augustine	2,429	7	6	1
	Paris	26,583	82	63	19		San Diego	4,520	6	5	1
	Parker	2,781	7	7	0		Sanger	7,391	13	13	0
	Pasadena	145,235	337	252	85		San Juan	33,213	47	37	10
	Pearland	73,190	135	105	30		San Marcos	48,979	119	87	32
	Pearsall	7,779	12	10	2		San Saba	2,548	5	4	1
	Pecos	7,946	39	17	22		Sansom Park Village	4,140	17	12	5
	Pelican Bay	1,609	4	4	0		Santa Anna	1,034	2	2	0
	Penitas	1,189	11	4	7		Santa Fe	10,735	25	18	7
	Perryton	8,305	14	7	7		Santa Rosa	2,995	8	8	0
	Pflugerville	32,157	76	58	18		Schertz	29,519	63	43	20
	Pharr	63,666	159	115	44		Seabrook	11,448	36	30	6
	Pilot Point	4,293	9	9	0		Seadrift	1,433	2	2	0
	Pinehurst	2,202	10	6	4		Seagoville	11,452	27	18	9
	Pineland	907	2	2	0		Seagraves	2,360	3	3	0
	Pittsburg	4,648	12	10	2		Sealy	6,267	16	14	2
	Plainview	22,054	42	34	8		Seguin	25,203	63	48	15
	Plano	259,771	485	342	143		Selma	3,219	26	23	3
	Pleasanton	9,742	22	17	5		Seminole	6,105	12	11	1
	Point Comfort	726	1	1	0		Seven Points	1,274	12	8	4
	Ponder	1,114	1	1	0		Seymour	2,639	10	7	3
	Port Aransas	3,812	26	18	8		Shallowater	2,227	5	5	0
	Port Arthur	55,481	142	111	31		Shamrock	1,834	6	2	4
	Port Isabel	5,433	24	19	5		Shavano Park	3,138	14	13	1
	Portland	16,645	33	22	11		Shenandoah	1,954	28	25	3
	Port Lavaca	11,658	24	18	6		Sherman	37,985	82	59	23
	Port Neches	12,803	21	18	3		Silsbee	6,844	21	16	5
	Poteet	3,719	5	5	0		Sinton	5,491	10	9	1
	Pottsboro	2,130	6	6	0		Slaton	5,642	15	9	6
	Premont	2,822	4	4	0		Smithville	4,543	16	10	6
	Presidio	4,939	5	4	1		Snyder	10,549	21	19	2

Table 78. Full-Time Law Enforcement Employees by State by City, 2007 (Contd.)

(Number.)

State	City	Population	Total law enforcement employees	Total officers	Total civilians	State	City	Population	Total law enforcement employees	Total officers	Total civilians
	Socorro	31,588	37	27	10		West Orange	3,935	10	9	1
	Somerset	1,832	3	3	0		Westover Hills	689	14	11	3
	Somerville	1,723	4	4	0		West Tawakoni	1,773	7	7	0
	Sonora	3,081	6	4	2		West University Place	15,249	28	20	8
	Sour Lake	1,748	6	6	0		Westworth	3,079	20	15	5
	South Houston	16,348	32	24	8		Wharton	9,355	32	24	8
	Southlake	26,367	53	48	5		Whitehouse	7,556	23	16	7
	South Padre Island	2,747	34	25	9		White Oak	6,350	18	14	4
	Southside Place	1,636	11	7	4		Whitesboro	4,054	12	7	5
	Spearman	2,911	2	2	0		White Settlement	16,106	44	32	12
	Springtown	2,905	15	11	4		Whitney	2,101	13	7	6
	Spring Valley	3,717	22	17	5		Wichita Falls	98,717	261	182	79
	Spur	996	2	2	0		Willis	4,298	16	14	2
	Stafford	20,460	57	42	15		Willow Park	4,057	14	10	4
	Stamford	3,175	8	6	2		Wills Point	3,940	11	9	2
	Stanton	2,229	5	5	0		Wilmer	3,616	18	12	6
	Stephenville	16,219	47	33	14		Windcrest	5,156	21	14	7
	Stratford	1,878	4	3	1		Wink	878	1	1	0
	Sudan	1,020	1	1	0		Winnsboro	3,901	13	9	4
	Sugar Land	82,402	165	119	46		Winters	2,630	5	5	0
	Sullivan City	4,466	11	8	3		Wolfforth	3,281	10	9	1
	Sulphur Springs	15,396	40	29	11		Woodville	2,281	10	9	1
	Sunrise Beach Village	757	1	1	0		Woodway	8,693	33	24	9
	Sunset Valley	798	11	11	0		Wortham	1,076	3	3	0
	Surfside Beach	880	7	6	1		Wylie	36,386	45	40	5
	Sweeny	3,613	7	7	0		Yoakum	5,659	13	6	7
	Sweetwater	10,519	26	21	5		Yorktown	2,222	4	4	0
	Taft	3,435	4	4	0	UTAH	Alpine/Highland	24,586	21	19	2
	Tahoka	2,691	4	4	0		Alta	364	8	4	4
	Tatum	1,198	3	3	0		American Fork/				
	Taylor	15,597	36	25	11		Cedar Hills	35,945	38	33	5
	Teague	4,785	10	8	2		Blanding	3,161	6	5	1
	Temple	55,057	152	125	27		Bountiful	41,132	50	36	14
	Terrell	19,302	49	35	14		Brian Head	117	5	5	0
	Terrell Hills	5,136	13	13	0		Brigham City	18,609	29	23	6
	Texarkana	36,237	101	90	11		Cedar City	26,479	41	34	7
	Texas City	45,574	104	84	20		Centerville	15,140	20	17	3
	The Colony	42,563	72	49	23		Clearfield	27,419	40	27	13
	Thrall	874	3	3	0		Clinton	19,882	17	16	1
	Three Rivers	1,707	7	6	1		Draper	38,875	41	34	7
	Tioga	924	3	3	0		East Carbon	1,266	3	3	0
	Tolar	684	1	1	0		Ephraim	5,163	5	5	0
	Tomball	10,176	50	37	13		Fairview	1,161	1	1	0
	Tool	2,495	11	7	4		Farmington	16,078	16	13	3
	Trinity	2,762	10	6	4		Garland	2,001	4	4	0
	Trophy Club	7,836	15	14	1		Grantsville	8,329	11	9	2
	Troup	2,101	8	7	1		Gunnison	2,768	2	2	0
	Troy	1,344	4	4	0		Harrisville	5,514	9	8	1
	Tulia	4,664	13	7	6		Heber	10,155	16	14	2
	Tye	1,114	4	4	0		Helper	1,869	6	6	0
	Tyler	95,596	227	179	48		Hildale	1,958	11	6	5
	Universal City	18,238	36	28	8		Hurricane	12,749	22	17	5
	University Park	24,300	61	40	21		Ivins	7,663	12	8	4
	Uvalde	16,594	49	36	13		Kamas	1,520	2	2	0
	Van	2,632	7	6	1		Kanab	3,781	9	7	2
	Van Alstyne	2,948	14	9	5		Kaysville	24,050	22	20	2
	Vernon	11,161	25	18	7		La Verkin	4,260	6	5	1
	Victoria	62,404	128	97	31		Layton	63,284	107	81	26
	Vidor	11,158	31	23	8		Lehi	39,483	37	34	3
	Waco	122,514	313	236	77		Logan	48,403	92	62	30
	Waelder	1,018	3	3	0		Mantua	766	1	1	0
	Wake Village	5,528	7	6	1		Mapleton	7,363	8	7	1
	Waller	2,034	8	7	1		Midvale	27,275	54	45	9
	Wallis	1,298	3	3	0		Minersville	852	1	1	0
	Watauga	23,931	48	33	15		Moab	4,886	19	14	5
	Waxahachie	27,500	63	49	14		Monticello	1,918	5	4	1
	Weatherford	25,500	80	57	23		Moroni	1,272	1	1	0
	Webster	10,070	65	48	17		Mount Pleasant	2,698	5	5	0
	Weimar	2,031	7	6	1		Murray	44,748	95	75	20
	Wells	803	1	1	0		Naples	1,533	8	7	1
	Weslaco	32,707	96	66	30		Nephi	5,276	11	9	2
	West	2,693	6	6	0		North Ogden	17,050	19	16	3
	West Columbia	4,216	14	8	6		North Park	10,615	10	9	1
	West Lake Hills	3,044	19	13	6		North Salt Lake	12,070	16	14	2
							Ogden	78,160	158	130	28

Table 78. Full-Time Law Enforcement Employees by State by City, 2007 *(Contd.)*

(Number.)

State	City	Population	Total law enforcement employees	Total officers	Total civilians	State	City	Population	Total law enforcement employees	Total officers	Total civilians
	Orem	91,816	122	88	34		St. Johnsbury	7,553	17	11	6
	Park City	8,132	38	29	9		Stowe	4,822	14	13	1
	Parowan	2,545	4	3	1		Swanton	6,508	5	4	1
	Payson	17,378	18	16	2		Thetford	2,836	2	2	0
	Perry	3,579	9	8	1		Vergennes	2,747	5	5	0
	Pleasant Grove/Lindon	41,890	37	29	8		Vernon	2,072	3	3	0
	Pleasant View	6,607	9	8	1		Waterbury	5,290	4	4	0
	Price	7,954	20	17	3		Weathersfield	2,868	1	1	0
	Provo	115,264	142	94	48		Williston	8,363	16	14	2
	Richfield	7,139	15	13	2		Windsor	3,687	7	5	2
	Riverdale	8,023	22	18	4		Winhall	786	7	6	1
	Roosevelt	4,740	12	11	1		Winooski	6,284	25	17	8
	Roy	35,366	43	38	5		Woodstock	3,174	6	5	1
	Salem	5,790	10	9	1	VIRGINIA	Abingdon	7,953	25	23	2
	Salina	2,399	6	5	1		Alexandria	137,812	440	319	121
	Salt Lake City	178,449	575	425	150		Altavista	3,379	11	11	0
	Sandy	94,975	141	117	24		Amherst	2,221	5	5	0
	Santaquin/Genola	8,367	10	10	0		Appalachia	1,751	6	6	0
	Saratoga Springs	12,315	18	15	3		Ashland	7,111	25	21	4
	Smithfield	7,484	9	8	1		Bedford	6,216	31	27	4
	South Jordan	46,571	56	49	7		Berryville	3,216	8	7	1
	South Ogden	15,473	30	25	5		Big Stone Gap	5,689	20	18	2
	South Salt Lake	21,262	74	57	17		Blacksburg	39,250	74	59	15
	Spanish Fork	28,950	31	28	3		Blackstone	3,526	17	12	5
	Springville	26,883	34	25	9		Bluefield	5,213	21	16	5
	St. George	70,579	140	101	39		Boykins	611	1	1	0
	Stockton	593	1	1	0		Bridgewater	5,431	9	9	0
	Sunset	4,870	9	8	1		Bristol	17,484	75	53	22
	Syracuse	21,544	22	19	3		Broadway	3,016	4	4	0
	Taylorsville City	57,944	61	56	5		Brookneal	1,252	3	3	0
	Tooele	30,019	37	32	5		Buena Vista	6,456	16	14	2
	Tremonton	6,383	13	10	3		Burkeville	470	1	1	0
	Vernal	8,231	26	21	5		Cape Charles	1,530	5	5	0
	Washington	16,607	18	16	2		Cedar Bluff	1,064	3	3	0
	Wellington	1,558	4	4	0		Charlottesville	40,265	136	109	27
	Wendover	1,643	3	3	0		Chase City	2,343	11	9	2
	West Bountiful	5,287	11	10	1		Chatham	1,278	4	4	0
	West Jordan	96,681	128	96	32		Chesapeake	223,093	512	370	142
	West Valley	121,447	212	169	43		Chilhowie	1,771	6	6	0
	Willard	1,681	2	2	0		Chincoteague	4,379	14	10	4
	Woods Cross	8,440	13	11	2		Christiansburg	17,983	65	49	16
VERMONT	Barre	9,050	25	18	7		Clarksville	1,269	9	8	1
	Barre Town	8,146	8	7	1		Clifton Forge	4,008	15	10	5
	Bellows Falls	2,957	12	6	6		Clinchco	408	1	1	0
	Bennington	15,297	33	26	7		Clintwood	1,513	4	4	0
	Berlin	2,875	8	7	1		Coeburn	1,996	8	7	1
	Brandon	3,926	7	6	1		Colonial Beach	3,733	17	12	5
	Brattleboro	11,706	33	22	11		Colonial Heights	17,747	49	45	4
	Bristol	3,814	4	4	0		Courtland	1,259	3	1	2
	Burlington	38,153	129	97	32		Covington	6,027	25	14	11
	Castleton	4,384	3	3	0		Crewe	2,266	5	5	0
	Chester	3,092	5	4	1		Culpeper	13,574	50	41	9
	Colchester	17,201	34	27	7		Damascus	1,086	5	5	0
	Dover	1,448	4	3	1		Danville	45,114	137	129	8
	Essex	19,350	33	27	6		Dayton	1,347	9	8	1
	Fair Haven	2,963	3	3	0		Dublin	2,206	10	9	1
	Hardwick	3,271	8	7	1		Dumfries	4,795	15	13	2
	Hartford	10,892	26	19	7		Edinburg	877	2	2	0
	Hinesburg	4,552	4	4	0		Elkton	2,597	7	6	1
	Ludlow	2,736	9	5	4		Emporia	5,607	36	26	10
	Manchester	4,366	12	8	4		Exmore	1,381	7	7	0
	Middlebury	8,194	16	14	2		Fairfax City	22,484	79	57	22
	Milton	10,469	14	13	1		Falls Church	10,831	43	33	10
	Montpelier	7,944	23	15	8		Farmville	6,908	28	27	1
	Morristown	5,606	11	11	0		Franklin	8,856	36	24	12
	Newport	5,329	12	10	2		Fredericksburg	21,521	97	70	27
	Northfield	5,813	8	7	1		Fries	557	1	1	0
	Norwich	3,551	6	5	1		Front Royal	14,700	48	37	11
	Randolph	5,124	5	5	0		Galax	6,643	40	24	16
	Richmond	4,128	4	4	0		Gate City	2,081	6	6	0
	Rutland	19,626	49	40	9		Glade Spring	1,544	2	2	0
	South Burlington	17,333	46	38	8		Glasgow	1,011	1	1	0
	Springfield	8,752	20	15	5		Glen Lyn	167	1	1	0
	St. Albans	7,374	22	14	8		Gordonsville	1,684	6	6	0

Table 78.   Full-Time Law Enforcement Employees by State by City, 2007 *(Contd.)*

(Number.)

State	City	Population	Total law enforcement employees	Total officers	Total civilians	State	City	Population	Total law enforcement employees	Total officers	Total civilians
	Gretna	1,204	4	4	0		Tazewell	4,369	13	11	2
	Grottoes	2,178	5	5	0		Timberville	1,705	3	3	0
	Grundy	975	6	6	0		Victoria	1,783	6	5	1
	Halifax	1,272	5	5	0		Vienna	14,923	50	41	9
	Hampton	144,490	400	281	119		Vinton	7,924	35	25	10
	Harrisonburg	40,869	95	80	15		Virginia Beach	435,943	962	800	162
	Haymarket	1,290	6	5	1		Warrenton	9,064	22	19	3
	Haysi	179	2	2	0		Warsaw	1,364	3	3	0
	Herndon	21,892	72	56	16		Waverly	2,194	12	7	5
	Hillsville	2,691	12	11	1		Waynesboro	21,681	56	48	8
	Honaker	909	5	3	2		Weber City	1,349	4	4	0
	Hopewell	22,741	69	53	16		West Point	3,133	9	8	1
	Hurt	1,226	2	2	0		Williamsburg	11,740	53	37	16
	Independence	901	2	2	0		Winchester	25,443	82	68	14
	Jonesville	981	4	4	0		Wise	3,256	14	13	1
	Kenbridge	1,315	8	8	0		Woodstock	4,303	17	16	1
	Kilmarnock	1,195	6	6	0		Wytheville	8,184	40	28	12
	La Crosse	595	4	4	0	WASHINGTON	Aberdeen	16,382	49	37	12
	Lawrenceville	1,139	5	5	0		Airway Heights	4,794	14	13	1
	Lebanon	3,185	12	11	1		Algona	2,726	8	6	2
	Leesburg	38,931	83	65	18		Anacortes	16,948	33	25	8
	Lexington	6,711	19	17	2		Arlington	16,736	34	28	6
	Louisa	1,557	5	5	0		Asotin	1,130	3	3	0
	Luray	4,879	14	11	3		Auburn	49,710	119	88	31
	Lynchburg	67,932	217	150	67		Bainbridge Island	22,442	25	21	4
	Manassas	36,735	120	93	27		Battle Ground	14,149	31	25	6
	Manassas Park	11,816	41	32	9		Bellevue	118,984	250	171	79
	Marion	6,100	18	16	2		Bellingham	76,290	161	111	50
	Martinsville	14,856	57	50	7		Black Diamond	3,948	13	12	1
	McKenney	483	1	1	0		Blaine	4,622	16	13	3
	Middleburg	954	4	4	0		Bonney Lake	15,737	33	28	5
	Middletown	1,137	2	2	0		Bothell	31,521	81	55	26
	Mount Jackson	1,799	4	4	0		Bremerton	35,068	81	66	15
	Narrows	2,189	4	4	0		Brewster	2,124	8	6	2
	New Market	1,863	5	5	0		Brier	6,382	9	7	2
	Newport News	177,550	541	394	147		Buckley	5,514	9	9	0
	Norfolk	227,903	837	714	123		Burien	31,035	33	32	1
	Norton	3,602	24	18	6		Burlington	8,921	29	24	5
	Occoquan	817	2	2	0		Camas	18,256	32	26	6
	Onancock	1,437	3	3	0		Castle Rock	2,147	6	5	1
	Onley	490	5	5	0		Centralia	15,708	38	31	7
	Orange	4,597	18	15	3		Chehalis	7,249	23	18	5
	Parksley	822	3	3	0		Cheney	10,597	20	14	6
	Pearisburg	2,805	8	7	1		Chewelah	2,334	6	5	1
	Pembroke	1,190	2	2	0		Clarkston	7,231	14	13	1
	Pennington Gap	1,753	6	6	0		Cle Elum	3,330	9	7	2
	Petersburg	32,210	137	105	32		Clyde Hill	2,997	10	9	1
	Pocahontas	428	1	1	0		Colfax	2,675	6	6	0
	Poquoson	11,939	25	21	4		College Place	9,148	13	10	3
	Portsmouth	101,284	338	245	93		Colton	358	1	1	0
	Pound	1,082	4	4	0		Colville	5,055	13	11	2
	Pulaski	9,006	33	24	9		Connell	2,987	7	7	0
	Purcellville	5,048	14	13	1		Cosmopolis	1,692	6	5	1
	Quantico	634	3	2	1		Coulee City	648	1	1	0
	Radford	14,317	44	33	11		Coulee Dam	1,083	7	7	0
	Rich Creek	692	2	1	1		Coupeville	1,857	4	4	0
	Richlands	4,083	25	19	6		Covington	18,072	11	11	0
	Richmond	191,785	930	702	228		Des Moines	28,907	49	36	13
	Roanoke	90,894	305	251	54		Dupont	6,831	11	10	1
	Rocky Mount	4,568	18	16	2		Duvall	6,064	18	16	2
	Rural Retreat	1,357	1	1	0		East Wenatchee	9,013	23	20	3
	Salem	24,774	91	64	27		Eatonville	2,455	6	5	1
	Saltville	2,256	7	6	1		Edgewood	9,860	8	8	0
	Shenandoah	1,873	5	5	0		Edmonds	40,218	64	54	10
	Smithfield	7,098	26	22	4		Ellensburg	17,033	31	23	8
	South Boston	8,007	29	27	2		Elma	3,177	8	7	1
	South Hill	4,618	22	20	2		Enumclaw	10,966	28	16	12
	Stanley	1,336	3	3	0		Ephrata	7,361	17	14	3
	Staunton	23,210	69	53	16		Everett	98,845	240	196	44
	Stephens City	1,463	3	3	0		Everson	2,031	6	6	0
	St. Paul	971	4	4	0		Federal Way	84,026	159	128	31
	Strasburg	4,348	22	20	2		Ferndale	10,559	21	18	3
	Suffolk	83,631	235	174	61		Fife	6,746	49	28	21
	Tappahannock	2,158	12	11	1		Fircrest	6,318	11	10	1

Table 78. Full-Time Law Enforcement Employees by State by City, 2007 *(Contd.)*

(Number.)

State	City	Population	Total law enforcement employees	Total officers	Total civilians	State	City	Population	Total law enforcement employees	Total officers	Total civilians
	Forks	3,249	14	7	7		Quincy	5,659	13	11	2
	Garfield	604	1	1	0		Raymond	2,976	7	6	1
	Gig Harbor	6,691	19	16	3		Reardan	610	1	1	0
	Goldendale	3,758	10	9	1		Redmond	49,195	113	77	36
	Grand Coulee	1,950	7	7	0		Renton	59,656	140	98	42
	Grandview	9,222	24	18	6		Republic	985	3	3	0
	Granger	2,892	9	7	2		Richland	45,555	64	54	10
	Granite Falls	2,972	7	6	1		Ridgefield	4,023	7	6	1
	Hoquiam	9,058	20	18	2		Ritzville	1,714	4	4	0
	Issaquah	19,193	54	32	22		Rosalia	571	1	1	0
	Kalama	2,077	5	5	0		Roy	834	4	4	0
	Kelso	12,156	32	28	4		Royal City	1,990	3	3	0
	Kenmore	20,167	12	12	0		Ruston	882	4	4	0
	Kennewick	63,147	106	87	19		Sammamish	35,327	22	22	0
	Kent	83,929	176	126	50		Sea Tac	25,320	41	38	3
	Kettle Falls	1,621	5	4	1		Seattle	585,118	1,775	1,273	502
	Kirkland	46,686	105	66	39		Sedro Woolley	10,643	20	15	5
	Kittitas	1,194	3	3	0		Selah	7,037	15	13	2
	La Center	1,944	10	9	1		Sequim	5,898	24	21	3
	Lacey	36,037	60	48	12		Shelton	9,352	34	20	14
	Lake Forest Park	12,506	26	21	5		Shoreline	52,189	50	48	2
	Lake Stevens	8,238	27	22	5		Snohomish	8,838	25	21	4
	Lakewood	57,465	131	105	26		Snoqualmie	8,403	14	11	3
	Langley	1,035	4	4	0		Soap Lake	1,884	4	4	0
	Liberty Lake	6,399	9	9	0		South Bend	1,840	4	3	1
	Long Beach	1,400	7	6	1		Spokane	198,272	391	282	109
	Longview	37,068	64	53	11		Spokane Valley	83,928	102	101	1
	Lynden	11,159	18	14	4		Springdale	288	1	1	0
	Lynnwood	33,663	103	71	32		Stanwood	5,685	13	11	2
	Mabton	2,071	4	4	0		Steilacoom	6,159	12	11	1
	Malden	191	1	1	0		Sultan	4,215	6	6	0
	Maple Valley	16,798	10	10	0		Sumas	1,157	6	6	0
	Marysville	32,623	76	49	27		Sumner	9,601	38	18	20
	Mattawa	3,302	2	2	0		Sunnyside	14,931	44	25	19
	McCleary	1,589	4	4	0		Tacoma	196,909	413	361	52
	Medical Lake	4,493	8	7	1		Tenino	2,251	6	5	1
	Medina	3,561	10	8	2		Tieton	1,185	2	2	0
	Mercer Island	23,671	34	30	4		Toledo	686	2	2	0
	Mill Creek	15,843	26	22	4		Tonasket	960	5	4	1
	Milton	6,836	12	11	1		Toppenish	9,213	19	12	7
	Monroe	16,505	48	35	13		Tukwila	17,103	81	67	14
	Montesano	3,556	10	8	2		Tumwater	13,695	30	25	5
	Morton	1,102	4	3	1		Twisp	913	3	2	1
	Moses Lake	17,561	38	30	8		Union Gap	5,702	22	18	4
	Mossyrock	512	1	1	0		University Place	30,699	25	24	1
	Mountlake Terrace	20,193	42	31	11		Vader	622	1	1	0
	Mount Vernon	30,521	52	42	10		Vancouver	161,092	235	202	33
	Moxee	2,044	4	4	0		Walla Walla	31,002	73	44	29
	Mukilteo	20,642	29	25	4		Wapato	4,609	21	12	9
	Napavine	1,499	4	3	1		Warden	2,645	5	4	1
	Newcastle	9,867	7	7	0		Washougal	11,769	22	20	2
	Normandy Park	6,207	15	13	2		Wenatchee	30,179	52	41	11
	North Bend	4,605	1	1	0		Westport	2,554	9	7	2
	North Bonneville	775	1	1	0		West Richland	10,477	17	14	3
	Oakesdale	379	1	1	0		White Salmon	2,373	5	5	0
	Oak Harbor	23,168	40	27	13		Wilbur	891	2	2	0
	Ocean Shores	4,785	16	14	2		Winlock	1,233	2	2	0
	Odessa	931	2	2	0		Winthrop	374	3	3	0
	Olympia	44,946	97	69	28		Woodinville	10,143	10	10	0
	Omak	4,745	13	11	2		Woodland	4,691	12	10	2
	Oroville	1,588	6	5	1		Yakima	82,951	174	129	45
	Orting	5,727	9	9	0		Yelm	5,359	16	14	2
	Othello	6,357	22	16	6		Zillah	2,679	8	7	1
	Pacific	5,910	12	9	3	WEST VIRGINIA.....	Alderson	1,081	1	1	0
	Palouse	905	2	2	0		Anawalt	240	1	1	0
	Pasco	52,761	75	64	11		Anmoore	786	2	2	0
	Pe Ell	690	1	1	0		Athens	1,177	1	1	0
	Port Angeles	19,064	56	32	24		Barboursville	3,276	19	17	2
	Port Orchard	8,026	21	19	2		Barrackville	1,294	1	1	0
	Port Townsend	9,248	20	16	4		Beckley	16,774	57	39	18
	Poulsbo	7,919	20	17	3		Belington	1,831	2	2	0
	Prosser	5,150	19	11	8		Belle	1,166	4	4	0
	Pullman	25,408	39	28	11		Benwood	1,463	5	5	0
	Puyallup	37,078	74	52	22		Berkeley Springs	698	3	3	0

Table 78. Full-Time Law Enforcement Employees by State by City, 2007 *(Contd.)*

(Number.)

State	City	Population	Total law enforcement employees	Total officers	Total civilians	State	City	Population	Total law enforcement employees	Total officers	Total civilians
	Bethlehem	2,506	5	4	1		Moundsville	9,385	20	16	4
	Bluefield	11,000	31	22	9		Mount Hope	1,386	5	4	1
	Bradshaw	256	3	3	0		Mullens	1,612	3	3	0
	Bramwell	407	1	1	0		New Cumberland	1,021	2	2	0
	Bridgeport	7,806	23	21	2		New Haven	1,523	1	1	0
	Buckhannon	5,551	9	8	1		New Martinsville	5,604	15	11	4
	Burnsville	470	1	1	0		Nitro	6,723	17	16	1
	Cameron	1,110	1	1	0		Northfork	437	3	3	0
	Capon Bridge	250	2	2	0		Nutter Fort	1,640	5	5	0
	Cedar Grove	809	2	2	0		Oak Hill	7,230	15	13	2
	Ceredo	1,607	9	6	3		Oceana	1,445	5	5	0
	Chapmanville	1,132	6	6	0		Paden City	2,659	4	3	1
	Charleston	50,510	208	180	28		Parkersburg	31,562	70	60	10
	Charles Town	4,013	20	17	3		Paw Paw	503	1	1	0
	Chesapeake	1,550	2	2	0		Pennsboro	1,199	3	1	2
	Chester	2,371	5	5	0		Petersburg	2,734	1	1	0
	Clarksburg	16,420	45	38	7		Peterstown	493	1	1	0
	Clendenin	1,044	3	3	0		Philippi	2,821	6	6	0
	Danville	538	3	3	0		Piedmont	925	1	1	0
	Delbarton	437	3	3	0		Pineville	664	3	3	0
	Dunbar	7,612	16	13	3		Point Pleasant	4,459	11	10	1
	East Bank	886	3	3	0		Pratt	529	2	2	0
	Elkins	7,050	11	8	3		Princeton	6,178	24	20	4
	Fairmont	19,127	40	34	6		Rainelle	1,489	1	1	0
	Farmington	388	1	1	0		Ranson	4,067	16	15	1
	Fayetteville	2,641	12	10	2		Ravenswood	3,992	11	10	1
	Follansbee	2,893	7	7	0		Reedsville	534	1	1	0
	Fort Gay	809	2	2	0		Richwood	2,340	5	5	0
	Gary	771	1	1	0		Ridgeley	690	3	3	0
	Gassaway	879	1	1	0		Ripley	3,272	10	9	1
	Gauley Bridge	694	5	4	1		Rivesville	915	1	1	0
	Gilbert	396	5	4	1		Romney	1,975	4	3	1
	Glasgow	739	2	2	0		Ronceverte	1,523	6	5	1
	Glen Dale	1,443	8	5	3		Rowlesburg	622	1	1	0
	Glenville	1,470	4	3	1		Salem	2,046	3	3	0
	Grafton	5,372	8	7	1		Shepherdstown	1,168	6	4	2
	Grantsville	542	1	1	0		Shinnston	2,238	6	6	0
	Grant Town	640	1	1	0		Sistersville	1,479	3	3	0
	Granville	780	11	10	1		Smithers	849	5	4	1
	Hamlin	1,093	2	1	1		Sophia	1,242	4	4	0
	Harpers Ferry/Bolivar	1,413	4	3	1		South Charleston	12,468	28	25	3
	Harrisville	1,880	1	1	0		Spencer	2,242	7	7	0
	Hartford City	515	1	1	0		St. Albans	10,999	25	21	4
	Henderson	311	1	1	0		Star City	1,404	6	5	1
	Hinton	2,622	9	8	1		St. Marys	1,913	4	4	0
	Huntington	48,669	94	88	6		Stonewood	1,861	1	1	0
	Hurricane	6,179	16	14	2		Summersville	3,366	17	15	2
	Iaeger	303	1	1	0		Sutton	987	2	1	1
	Kenova	3,325	11	7	4		Sylvester	567	2	2	0
	Kermit	225	2	2	0		Terra Alta	1,517	1	1	0
	Keyser	5,331	17	12	5		Vienna	10,667	21	17	4
	Keystone	381	1	1	0		Wardensville	246	2	1	1
	Kimball	349	3	3	0		Wayne	1,141	2	1	1
	Kingwood	2,957	5	5	0		Webster Springs	769	2	2	0
	Lewisburg	3,554	13	11	2		Weirton	19,095	38	34	4
	Logan	1,525	11	8	3		Welch	2,283	8	7	1
	Lumberport	975	2	2	0		Wellsburg	2,648	7	6	1
	Mabscott	1,344	5	4	1		West Logan	394	1	1	0
	Madison	2,610	6	5	1		Weston	4,215	8	7	1
	Man	705	4	4	0		Westover	3,922	9	9	0
	Mannington	2,080	4	4	0		West Union	806	1	1	0
	Marlinton	1,241	1	1	0		Wheeling	29,057	82	80	2
	Marmet	1,610	5	5	0		White Sulphur Springs	2,323	8	7	1
	Martinsburg	16,610	54	44	10		Whitesville	510	2	1	1
	Mason	1,044	4	4	0		Williamson	3,128	9	8	1
	Masontown	656	1	1	0		Williamstown	2,975	5	4	1
	Matewan	497	1	1	0		Winfield	2,060	4	4	0
	Matoaka	302	2	2	0	**WISCONSIN**.............	Albany	1,119	3	3	0
	McMechen	1,780	2	2	0		Algoma	3,228	6	6	0
	Milton	2,377	6	5	1		Altoona	6,377	12	11	1
	Monongah	911	1	1	0		Amery	2,846	8	7	1
	Montgomery	1,925	7	6	1		Antigo	8,225	19	16	3
	Moorefield	2,432	6	6	0		Appleton	70,169	136	109	27
	Morgantown	28,951	69	59	10		Arcadia	2,329	5	5	0

Table 78. Full-Time Law Enforcement Employees by State by City, 2007 *(Contd.)*

(Number.)

State	City	Popula-tion	Total law enforce-ment employees	Total officers	Total civilians	State	City	Popula-tion	Total law enforce-ment employees	Total officers	Total civilians
	Ashland	8,147	21	19	2		Fond du Lac	42,349	69	64	5
	Ashwaubenon	17,033	61	48	13		Fontana	1,890	7	6	1
	Bangor	1,343	3	3	0		Fort Atkinson	12,023	27	20	7
	Baraboo	11,015	31	27	4		Fox Lake	1,486	4	3	1
	Barron	3,145	7	7	0		Fox Point	6,663	18	17	1
	Bayfield	579	3	3	0		Fox Valley	17,525	29	26	3
	Bayside	4,216	21	14	7		Franklin	34,449	76	59	17
	Beaver Dam	15,551	34	29	5		Frederic	1,220	2	2	0
	Belleville	2,246	5	5	0		Geneva Town	4,726	8	6	2
	Beloit	36,424	99	76	23		Genoa City	2,911	5	4	1
	Beloit Town	7,475	15	13	2		Germantown	19,491	42	31	11
	Berlin	5,197	13	12	1		Glendale	12,736	50	46	4
	Black River Falls	3,456	8	7	1		Grafton	11,712	27	20	7
	Blair	1,276	3	3	0		Grand Chute	20,793	32	28	4
	Bloomer	3,378	12	7	5		Grand Rapids	7,741	6	4	2
	Bloomfield	5,990	8	7	1		Grantsburg	1,445	3	3	0
	Boscobel	3,185	6	6	0		Green Bay	100,010	225	180	45
	Brillion	2,857	8	7	1		Greendale	13,708	37	29	8
	Brodhead	3,089	12	8	4		Greenfield	35,435	79	57	22
	Brookfield	39,738	82	64	18		Green Lake	1,158	4	4	0
	Brookfield Township	6,243	13	12	1		Hales Corners	7,538	20	16	4
	Brown Deer	11,507	34	29	5		Hartford	13,611	29	25	4
	Burlington	10,599	27	21	6		Hartland	8,793	18	16	2
	Burlington Town	6,552	10	9	1		Hayward	2,330	8	7	1
	Butler	1,806	9	8	1		Hazel Green	1,134	2	2	0
	Caledonia	25,682	44	34	10		Hillsboro	1,283	3	3	0
	Campbellsport	1,929	3	2	1		Hobart-Lawrence	9,725	4	3	1
	Campbell Township	4,437	5	5	0		Holmen	7,512	9	8	1
	Cedarburg	11,216	29	20	9		Horicon	3,640	10	8	2
	Chenequa	590	7	6	1		Hortonville	2,774	6	5	1
	Chetek	2,177	6	5	1		Hudson	12,408	22	19	3
	Chilton	3,635	6	6	0		Hurley	1,623	6	6	0
	Chippewa Falls	13,158	30	24	6		Independence	1,243	2	2	0
	Cleveland	1,401	3	2	1		Iron Ridge	990	1	1	0
	Clinton	2,261	6	6	0		Jackson	6,248	12	11	1
	Clintonville	4,435	15	11	4		Janesville	63,383	115	104	11
	Colby-Abbotsford	3,649	7	6	1		Jefferson	7,773	17	14	3
	Columbus	5,068	15	10	5		Juneau	2,654	5	4	1
	Combined Locks	3,121	5	5	0		Kaukauna	15,405	27	25	2
	Cornell	1,424	3	3	0		Kenosha	96,996	196	185	11
	Cottage Grove	5,530	13	12	1		Kewaskum	4,070	9	8	1
	Crandon	1,880	4	3	1		Kewaunee	2,877	6	6	0
	Cross Plains	3,541	6	5	1		Kiel	3,518	8	7	1
	Cuba City	2,052	5	4	1		Kohler	1,992	8	7	1
	Cudahy	17,998	39	27	12		La Crosse	50,032	115	94	21
	Cumberland	2,299	5	5	0		Ladysmith	3,594	11	10	1
	Darien	1,609	7	6	1		Lake Delton	2,973	17	16	1
	Darlington	2,328	5	5	0		Lake Geneva	8,209	29	21	8
	Deerfield	2,290	4	4	0		Lake Hallie	5,959	6	5	1
	DeForest	8,845	19	16	3		Lake Mills	5,483	11	11	0
	Delafield	6,975	16	15	1		Lancaster	3,869	8	8	0
	Delavan	8,450	23	17	6		Lodi	2,947	6	5	1
	Delavan Town	4,906	9	9	0		Luxemburg	2,286	2	2	0
	Denmark	2,124	2	2	0		Madison	225,370	501	410	91
	De Pere	22,781	36	31	5		Manitowoc	33,541	75	65	10
	Dodgeville	4,577	11	10	1		Maple Bluff	1,286	5	5	0
	Durand	1,867	4	4	0		Marathon City	1,562	9	8	1
	Eagle River	1,579	6	6	0		Marinette	10,906	28	23	5
	Eagle Village	1,838	2	2	0		Marion	1,232	3	3	0
	East Troy	4,276	9	7	2		Markesan	1,332	4	3	1
	Eau Claire	63,472	129	99	30		Marshall Village	3,604	9	8	1
	Edgar	1,490	1	1	0		Marshfield	19,175	46	38	8
	Edgerton	5,230	11	10	1		Mauston	4,329	8	8	0
	Eleva	656	1	1	0		Mayville	5,430	12	10	2
	Elkhart Lake	1,153	3	3	0		McFarland	7,663	15	13	2
	Elkhorn	9,354	19	16	3		Medford	4,108	9	8	1
	Elk Mound	805	1	1	0		Menasha	16,756	36	30	6
	Ellsworth	3,112	6	6	0		Menomonee Falls	34,612	81	58	23
	Elm Grove	6,064	25	17	8		Menomonie	15,367	33	27	6
	Elroy	1,487	3	3	0		Mequon	23,736	46	37	9
	Evansville	5,023	10	9	1		Merrill	9,860	24	21	3
	Everest	15,771	28	25	3		Middleton	16,710	40	31	9
	Fennimore	2,255	5	5	0		Milton	5,800	10	8	2
	Fitchburg	22,793	53	41	12		Milwaukee	572,938	2,649	1,936	713

Table 78.   Full-Time Law Enforcement Employees by State by City, 2007 *(Contd.)*

(Number.)

State	City	Population	Total law enforcement employees	Total officers	Total civilians	State	City	Population	Total law enforcement employees	Total officers	Total civilians
	Mineral Point	2,562	6	6	0		South Milwaukee	20,641	39	33	6
	Minocqua	5,026	12	8	4		Sparta	9,070	19	17	2
	Mishicot	1,397	1	1	0		Spencer	1,846	3	3	0
	Mondovi	2,638	4	4	0		Spooner	2,577	7	6	1
	Monona	7,924	25	19	6		Spring Green	1,439	4	3	1
	Monroe	10,563	35	26	9		Stanley	3,676	4	4	0
	Mosinee	4,078	8	7	1		St. Croix Falls	2,192	5	5	0
	Mount Horeb	6,674	19	17	2		Stevens Point	24,333	58	45	13
	Mount Pleasant	26,237	52	40	12		St. Francis	8,899	26	21	5
	Mukwonago	6,890	21	14	7		Stoughton	12,572	25	19	6
	Muskego	22,961	46	36	10		Strum	1,038	2	2	0
	Neenah	24,871	48	37	11		Sturgeon Bay	9,129	22	21	1
	Neillsville	2,615	7	6	1		Sturtevant	6,626	9	8	1
	New Berlin	39,350	92	73	19		Summit	5,155	8	8	0
	New Glarus	2,064	5	5	0		Sun Prairie	27,366	68	45	23
	New Holstein	3,166	8	7	1		Superior	26,896	63	57	6
	New Lisbon	2,592	5	4	1		Theresa	1,326	2	2	0
	New London	7,008	18	16	2		Thiensville	3,258	8	7	1
	New Richmond	8,200	17	16	1		Three Lakes	2,266	4	4	0
	Niagara	1,766	4	4	0		Tomah	8,764	21	19	2
	North Fond du Lac	4,959	14	12	2		Tomahawk	3,708	8	7	1
	North Hudson	3,800	6	5	1		Town of East Troy	3,936	6	6	0
	Oak Creek	32,896	80	58	22		Town of Madison	5,828	18	16	2
	Oconomowoc	14,414	28	22	6		Town of Menasha	17,192	33	26	7
	Oconomowoc Town	8,196	14	12	2		Trempealeau	1,532	2	2	0
	Oconto	4,713	8	8	0		Twin Lakes	5,580	18	12	6
	Oconto Falls	2,854	5	5	0		Two Rivers	11,916	30	27	3
	Omro	3,316	7	6	1		Valders	987	1	1	0
	Onalaska	16,377	29	26	3		Verona	10,525	17	15	2
	Oregon	9,006	17	15	2		Viroqua	4,378	10	8	2
	Osceola	2,719	7	6	1		Walworth	2,669	7	6	1
	Oshkosh	64,183	110	92	18		Washburn	2,125	5	5	0
	Osseo	1,637	4	4	0		Waterloo	3,252	8	7	1
	Palmyra	1,751	3	3	0		Watertown	23,334	53	39	14
	Park Falls	2,425	8	7	1		Waukesha	68,162	147	111	36
	Pepin	929	1	1	0		Waunakee	10,894	18	16	2
	Peshtigo	3,276	7	6	1		Waupaca	5,833	15	14	1
	Pewaukee	12,939	29	26	3		Waupun	10,668	20	18	2
	Pewaukee Village	9,125	19	17	2		Wausau	38,405	76	69	7
	Phillips	1,530	5	5	0		Wautoma	2,088	6	5	1
	Platteville	9,711	26	20	6		Wauwatosa	44,463	120	91	29
	Pleasant Prairie	19,426	28	26	2		West Allis	58,366	156	133	23
	Plover	11,495	21	18	3		West Bend	30,070	74	55	19
	Plymouth	8,333	16	16	0		Westby	2,166	3	3	0
	Portage	9,789	30	22	8		West Milwaukee	3,977	20	17	3
	Port Washington	11,115	24	19	5		West Salem	4,725	7	6	1
	Poynette	2,579	6	5	1		Whitefish Bay	13,450	29	24	5
	Prairie du Chien	5,708	18	15	3		Whitehall	1,620	4	4	0
	Prescott	4,058	9	8	1		Whitewater	14,147	33	23	10
	Princeton	1,448	3	3	0		Williams Bay	2,687	7	6	1
	Pulaski	3,528	6	6	0		Winneconne	2,490	6	5	1
	Racine	79,285	256	196	60		Wisconsin Dells	2,538	17	12	5
	Readstown	384	1	1	0		Wisconsin Rapids	17,633	43	38	5
	Reedsburg	8,629	27	18	9	WYOMING...............	Woodruff	2,036	6	5	1
	Rhinelander	7,786	19	16	3		Afton	1,817	5	5	0
	Rice Lake	8,422	21	20	1		Baggs	370	2	2	0
	Richland Center	5,145	13	11	2		Basin	1,242	4	4	0
	Ripon	7,286	20	14	6		Buffalo	4,566	21	12	9
	River Falls	13,803	24	22	2		Casper	52,434	102	86	16
	River Hills	1,614	12	12	0		Cheyenne	55,604	127	103	24
	Rome Town	3,015	8	7	1		Cody	9,266	23	20	3
	Rothschild	5,232	12	10	2		Cokeville	480	2	2	0
	Sauk Prairie	4,225	14	12	2		Diamondville	678	4	3	1
	Saukville	4,334	13	11	2		Douglas	5,691	23	16	7
	Seymour	3,411	6	5	1		Evanston	11,585	35	29	6
	Shawano	8,790	20	18	2		Evansville	2,321	11	9	2
	Sheboygan	48,291	119	81	38		Gillette	24,438	74	46	28
	Sheboygan Falls	7,795	15	13	2		Glenrock	2,393	12	7	5
	Shorewood	13,185	30	25	5		Green River	11,957	40	30	10
	Shorewood Hills	1,629	7	6	1		Greybull	1,754	6	5	1
	Silver Lake	2,530	5	4	1		Guernsey	1,118	2	2	0
	Siren	842	3	3	0		Hanna	855	5	2	3
	Slinger	4,476	9	8	1		Hulett	447	1	1	0
	Somerset	2,365	7	6	1		Jackson	9,292	35	23	12

Table 78. Full-Time Law Enforcement Employees by State by City, 2007 *(Contd.)*

(Number.)

State	City	Popula-tion	Total law enforce-ment employees	Total officers	Total civilians	State	City	Popula-tion	Total law enforce-ment employees	Total officers	Total civilians
	Kemmerer	2,508	9	8	1		Rawlins	8,572	36	23	13
	La Barge	441	2	1	1		Riverton	9,795	40	27	13
	Lander	7,066	21	20	1		Rock Springs	19,432	64	44	20
	Laramie	25,504	79	49	30		Saratoga	1,721	10	5	5
	Lovell	2,279	9	6	3		Sheridan	16,507	50	28	22
	Lusk	1,316	4	4	0		Sundance	1,199	4	4	0
	Mills	2,926	13	11	2		Thermopolis	2,912	14	8	6
	Moorcroft	861	5	4	1		Torrington	5,446	21	15	6
	Newcastle	3,275	14	7	7		Wheatland	3,426	9	8	1
	Pine Bluffs	1,142	6	2	4		Worland	4,857	10	10	0
	Powell	5,388	24	17	7						

Table 79.   Full-Time Law Enforcement Employees, by State by University and College, 2007

(Number.)

State	University/College	Campus	Student enrollment[1]	Total law enforcement employees	Total officers	Total civilians
ALABAMA................................	Alabama A&M University		6,076	30	17	13
	Alabama State University		5,565	40	30	10
	Auburn University	Montgomery	5,079	22	13	9
	Calhoun Community College[2]			6	4	2
	George C. Wallace State Community College		3,420	3	3	0
	Jacksonville State University		8,957	15	11	4
	Talladega College		425	8	6	2
	Troy University		27,938	13	11	2
	University of Alabama:	Birmingham	16,561	154	67	87
		Huntsville	7,091	16	12	4
		Tuscaloosa	23,838	68	58	10
	University of Montevallo		2,895	15	9	6
	University of North Alabama		6,810	14	12	2
	University of South Alabama		13,090	47	27	20
	University of West Alabama		3,633	9	6	3
ALASKA....................................	University of Alaska:	Anchorage	16,163	21	14	7
		Fairbanks	8,340	18	11	7
ARIZONA.................................	Arizona State University	Main Campus	51,234	112	65	47
	Arizona Western College		6,579	11	6	5
	Central Arizona College		6,471	10	7	3
	Northern Arizona University		20,555	23	15	8
	Pima Community College		32,532	34	26	8
	Yavapai College		9,305	9	8	1
ARKANSAS...............................	Arkansas State University:	Beebe	4,073	4	3	1
		Jonesboro	10,949	21	17	4
	Arkansas Tech University		7,038	11	9	2
	Henderson State University		3,664	8	7	1
	Northwest Arkansas Community College		5,732	10	6	4
	Southern Arkansas University		3,113	7	6	1
	University of Arkansas:	Fayetteville	17,926	41	33	8
		Little Rock	11,905	39	27	12
		Medical Sciences	2,435	49	41	8
		Monticello	3,179	7	6	1
		Pine Bluff	3,128	17	12	5
	University of Central Arkansas		12,330	34	25	9
CALIFORNIA	Allan Hancock College		12,321	20	5	15
	California State Polytechnic University:	Pomona	20,510	32	20	12
		San Luis Obispo	18,722	35	17	18
	California State University:	Bakersfield	7,711	15	11	4
		Channel Islands	3,123	19	14	5
		Chico	16,250	29	19	10
		Dominguez Hills	12,068	22	16	6
		East Bay	12,706	28	13	15
		Fresno	22,098	26	18	8
		Fullerton	35,921	32	24	8
		Long Beach	35,574	45	24	21
		Los Angeles	20,565	36	20	16
		Monterey Bay	3,818	16	14	2
		Northridge	34,560	39	25	14
		Sacramento	28,529	31	22	9
		San Bernardino	16,479	20	11	9
		San Jose[2]		55	28	27
		San Marcos	8,734	22	14	8
		Stanislaus	8,374	22	11	11
	College of the Sequoias		9,959	5	4	1
	Contra Costa Community College		6,870	34	23	11
	Cuesta College		10,578	7	6	1
	El Camino College		23,488	21	15	6
	Foothill-De Anza College		39,874	21	11	10
	Fresno Community College		22,040	18	15	3
	Humboldt State University		7,435	19	11	8
	Marin Community College		6,512	7	6	1
	Pasadena Community College		25,873	11	6	5
	Riverside Community College		29,486	22	16	6
	San Bernardino Community College		12,090	15	10	5
	San Diego State University		33,441	47	26	21
	San Francisco State University		29,628	50	27	23
	San Jose/Evergreen Community College		18,164	14	6	8
	Santa Rosa Junior College		24,806	26	13	13
	Solano Community College		10,900	6	4	2
	Sonoma State University		8,274	17	10	7
	University of California:	Berkeley	33,920	129	77	52
		Davis	29,628	71	41	30
		Hastings College of Law	1,272	12	12	0
		Irvine	25,230	43	30	13

[1] The student enrollment figures provided by the United States Department of Education are for the 2006 school year, the most recent available. The enrollment figures include full-time and part-time students.

[2] Student enrollment figures were not available.

Table 79. Full-Time Law Enforcement Employees, by State by University and College, 2007 *(Contd.)*

(Number.)

State	University/College	Campus	Student enrollment[1]	Total law enforcement employees	Total officers	Total civilians
		Los Angeles	36,611	92	55	37
		Merced	1,286	16	9	7
		Riverside	16,875	36	26	10
		San Diego	26,247	64	36	28
		San Francisco	2,943	107	34	73
		Santa Barbara	21,082	44	31	13
		Santa Cruz	15,364	46	19	27
	Ventura County Community College		11,757	29	13	16
	West Valley-Mission College		18,740	12	8	4
COLORADO	Adams State College		8,442	6	5	1
	Arapahoe Community College		6,918	11	8	3
	Auraria Higher Education Center[2]			37	23	14
	Colorado School of Mines		4,357	9	8	1
	Colorado State University	Fort Collins	27,636	69	42	27
	Fort Lewis College		3,905	10	8	2
	Pikes Peak Community College		10,526	15	13	2
	Red Rocks Community College		6,727	1	1	0
	University of Colorado:	Boulder	31,665	52	40	12
		Colorado Springs	8,647	23	15	8
		Health Sciences Center[2]		5	5	0
		Health Sciences Center, Fitzsimons Campus[2]		56	21	35
CONNECTICUT	Central Connecticut State University		12,144	28	22	6
	Eastern Connecticut State University		5,239	25	18	7
	Southern Connecticut State University		12,326	33	26	7
	University of Connecticut:	Health Center[2]		21	13	8
		Storrs, Avery Point, and Hartford[2]		80	68	12
	Western Connecticut State University		6,086	27	16	11
	Yale University		11,415	96	82	14
DELAWARE	Delaware State University		3,690	31	10	21
	University of Delaware		20,380	68	36	32
FLORIDA	Florida A&M University		11,907	56	34	22
	Florida Atlantic University		25,325	48	37	11
	Florida Gulf Coast University		8,279	21	14	7
	Florida International University		37,997	56	39	17
	Florida State University:	Panama City[2]		6	5	1
		Tallahassee	39,973	74	57	17
	New College of Florida		746	20	13	7
	Pensacola Junior College		10,208	17	12	5
	Santa Fe Community College		14,012	22	16	6
	Tallahassee Community College		12,732	19	9	10
	University of Central Florida		46,646	91	60	31
	University of Florida		50,912	150	83	67
	University of North Florida		15,954	37	28	9
	University of South Florida:	St. Petersburg[2]		15	9	6
		Tampa	43,636	53	40	13
	University of West Florida		9,819	31	21	10
GEORGIA	Abraham Baldwin Agricultural College		3,574	15	14	1
	Albany State University		3,927	28	16	12
	Armstrong Atlantic State University		6,713	12	8	4
	Berry College		1,841	16	13	3
	Clark Atlanta University		4,514	38	13	25
	Clayton College and State University		6,081	21	12	9
	Columbus State University		7,587	29	22	7
	Dalton State College		4,348	9	8	1
	Emory University		12,338	60	41	19
	Georgia College and State University		6,040	22	16	6
	Georgia Military College[2]			4	2	2
	Georgia Perimeter College		19,955	81	35	46
	Georgia Southern University		16,425	29	25	4
	Georgia State University		26,135	109	69	40
	Kennesaw State University		19,844	43	23	20
	Medical College of Georgia		2,227	45	34	11
	Mercer University		7,049	36	27	9
	Morehouse College		2,933	38	15	23
	Morris-Brown College[2]			7	3	4
	North Georgia College and State University		4,922	12	9	3
	Piedmont College		2,118	8	2	6
	Savannah State University		3,241	24	10	14
	South Georgia College		1,465	6	6	0
	University of Georgia		33,959	93	72	21
	University of West Georgia		10,160	44	17	27

[1] The student enrollment figures provided by the United States Department of Education are for the 2006 school year, the most recent available. The enrollment figures include full-time and part-time students.

[2] Student enrollment figures were not available.

Table 79. Full-Time Law Enforcement Employees, by State by University and College, 2007 *(Contd.)*

(Number.)

State	University/College	Campus	Student enrollment[1]	Total law enforcement employees	Total officers	Total civilians
	Valdosta State University		10,888	28	20	8
	Wesleyan College		632	4	4	0
	Young Harris College		604	2	2	0
ILLINOIS	Black Hawk College		6,151	10	9	1
	Chicago State University		7,035	35	25	10
	College of DuPage		26,032	20	15	5
	College of Lake County		15,558	20	12	8
	Eastern Illinois University		12,349	23	20	3
	Governors State University		5,382	9	7	2
	Illinois State University		20,521	24	19	5
	John A. Logan College		7,364	8	7	1
	Joliet Junior College		12,924	19	10	9
	Loyola University of Chicago		15,194	59	35	24
	Moraine Valley Community College		15,693	16	10	6
	Morton College		5,049	4	2	2
	Northeastern Illinois University		12,056	25	18	7
	Northern Illinois University		25,313	57	36	21
	Northwestern University:	Chicago[2]		16	12	4
		Evanston[2]		67	30	37
	Oakton Community College		10,597	11	10	1
	Parkland College		9,336	18	13	5
	Rock Valley College		8,011	14	11	3
	Southern Illinois University:	Carbondale	21,003	45	34	11
		Edwardsville	13,449	40	31	9
		School of Medicine[2]		14	2	12
	South Suburban College		7,160	14	10	4
	Triton College		15,738	15	10	5
	University of Illinois:	Chicago	24,644	124	72	52
		Springfield	4,761	21	15	6
		Urbana	42,738	68	53	15
	Waubonsee College		8,843	4	4	0
	Western Illinois University		13,602	31	26	5
	William Rainey Harper College		15,053	16	11	5
INDIANA	Ball State University		20,030	32	25	7
	Indiana State University		10,568	34	25	9
	Indiana University:	Bloomington	38,247	53	43	10
		Gary	4,819	14	11	3
		Indianapolis[2]		44	29	15
		New Albany	6,183	10	8	2
	Marian College		1,796	7	5	2
	Purdue University		40,609	50	40	10
IOWA	Iowa State University		25,462	33	28	5
	University of Iowa		28,816	55	33	22
	University of Northern Iowa		12,327	23	17	6
KANSAS	Emporia State University		6,473	9	9	0
	Fort Hays State University		9,122	10	8	2
	Kansas State University		23,141	34	20	14
	Pittsburg State University		6,859	16	13	3
	University of Kansas:	Main Campus	26,773	46	28	18
		Medical Center	2,150	59	31	28
	Washburn University		7,153	18	13	5
	Wichita State University		13,964	33	24	9
KENTUCKY	Eastern Kentucky University		15,763	38	24	14
	Kentucky State University		2,498	8	4	4
	Morehead State University		8,958	27	16	11
	Murray State University		10,298	21	14	7
	Northern Kentucky University		14,617	24	18	6
	University of Louisville		20,785	60	27	33
	Western Kentucky University		18,660	36	25	11
LOUISIANA	Delgado Community College		11,916	32	21	11
	Grambling State University		5,065	25	13	12
	Louisiana State University:	Baton Rouge[2]		64	61	3
		Health Sciences Center, New Orleans	2,199	30	30	0
		Health Sciences Center, Shreveport	768	65	45	20
		Shreveport	4,023	11	10	1
	McNeese State University		8,327	18	14	4
	Nicholls State University		6,804	13	8	5
	Northwestern State University		9,431	19	15	4
	Southeastern Louisiana University		15,106	35	26	9
	Southern University and A&M College:	Baton Rouge	8,624	51	31	20
		New Orleans	2,197	9	8	1
	Tulane University		10,237	48	37	11

[1] The student enrollment figures provided by the United States Department of Education are for the 2006 school year, the most recent available. The enrollment figures include full-time and part-time students.
[2] Student enrollment figures were not available.

Table 79. Full-Time Law Enforcement Employees, by State by University and College, 2007 *(Contd.)*

(Number.)

State	University/College	Campus	Student enrollment[1]	Total law enforcement employees	Total officers	Total civilians
	University of Louisiana:	Lafayette	16,302	25	21	4
		Monroe	8,576	28	21	7
	University of New Orleans		11,747	26	23	3
MAINE...............	University of Maine:	Farmington	2,421	5	4	1
		Orono	11,797	33	20	13
	University of Southern Maine		10,478	27	15	12
MARYLAND..........	Bowie State University		5,291	29	15	14
	Coppin State University		4,104	21	14	7
	Frostburg State University		4,910	20	16	4
	Morgan State University		6,705	55	35	20
	Salisbury University		7,383	20	16	4
	St. Mary's College		1,957	13	1	12
	Towson University		18,921	59	39	20
	University of Baltimore		4,948	30	12	18
	University of Maryland:	Baltimore City	5,636	138	55	83
		Baltimore County	11,798	33	24	9
		College Park	35,102	120	81	39
		Eastern Shore	4,130	16	9	7
MASSACHUSETTS..........	Assumption College		2,792	23	14	9
	Bentley College		5,555	35	25	10
	Boston College		14,661	70	53	17
	Boston University		31,574	62	50	12
	Brandeis University		5,313	23	19	4
	Bridgewater State College		9,655	26	21	5
	Bristol Community College		6,927	8	6	2
	Clark University		3,071	14	12	2
	Dean College		1,315	12	7	5
	Fitchburg State College		5,508	16	13	3
	Framingham State College		5,836	17	13	4
	Harvard University		25,778	96	71	25
	Lasell College		1,275	13	13	0
	Massachusetts College of Art		2,286	21	8	13
	Massachusetts College of Liberal Arts		1,805	21	18	3
	Massachusetts Institute of Technology		10,253	58	55	3
	Massasoit Community College		6,975	14	11	3
	Merrimack College		2,282	16	12	4
	Mount Holyoke College		2,153	24	16	8
	Northeastern University		23,411	76	53	23
	North Shore Community College		6,910	21	19	2
	Quinsigamond Community College		6,022	12	12	0
	Salem State College		10,230	28	25	3
	Springfield College		4,994	31	13	18
	Tufts University:	Medford	9,638	64	42	22
		Worcester[2]		21	16	5
	University of Massachusetts:	Amherst	25,593	76	60	16
		Dartmouth	8,756	40	23	17
		Harbor Campus, Boston	12,362	31	24	7
		Medical Center, Worcester	1,020	30	21	9
	Wellesley College		2,370	20	15	5
	Wentworth Institute of Technology		3,613	18	12	6
	Western New England College		3,653	25	16	9
	Westfield State College		5,426	18	15	3
MICHIGAN..............	Central Michigan University		26,710	30	21	9
	Delta College		10,149	11	8	3
	Eastern Michigan University		22,950	28	22	6
	Ferris State University		12,574	18	13	5
	Grand Rapids Community College		15,224	14	11	3
	Grand Valley State University		23,295	20	16	4
	Lansing Community College		20,394	17	15	2
	Macomb Community College		21,131	37	30	7
	Michigan State University		45,520	107	70	37
	Michigan Technological University		6,546	12	9	3
	Mott Community College		10,038	7	3	4
	Northern Michigan University		9,689	26	22	4
	Oakland Community College		24,123	27	25	2
	Oakland University		17,737	23	18	5
	Saginaw Valley State University		9,543	10	8	2
	University of Michigan:	Ann Arbor	40,025	89	54	35
		Dearborn	8,342	4	4	0
		Flint	6,527	20	6	14
	Western Michigan University		24,841	64	27	37
MINNESOTA..........	University of Minnesota:	Duluth	11,190	10	9	1
		Morris	1,747	6	3	3
		Twin Cities	50,402	62	45	17

[1] The student enrollment figures provided by the United States Department of Education are for the 2006 school year, the most recent available. The enrollment figures include full-time and part-time students.

[2] Student enrollment figures were not available.

Table 79.   Full-Time Law Enforcement Employees, by State by University and College, 2007 *(Contd.)*

(Number.)

State	University/College	Campus	Student enrollment[1]	Total law enforcement employees	Total officers	Total civilians
MISSISSIPPI	Coahoma Community College		1,838	9	8	1
	Itawamba Community College		5,213	10	9	1
	Jackson State University		8,256	61	43	18
	Mississippi State University		16,206	33	27	6
	University of Mississippi:	Medical Center	1,598	80	56	24
		Oxford	15,220	42	24	18
MISSOURI	Lincoln University		3,224	12	9	3
	Mineral Area College		2,926	8	7	1
	Missouri Western State University		5,276	13	10	3
	Northwest Missouri State University		6,242	12	10	2
	Southeast Missouri State University		10,454	26	18	8
	St. Louis Community College	Meramec	10,887	11	9	2
	Truman State University		5,820	10	9	1
	University of Central Missouri		10,711	22	18	4
	University of Missouri:	Columbia	28,184	45	30	15
		Kansas City	14,213	42	27	15
		Rolla	5,858	19	8	11
		St. Louis	15,528	22	18	4
	Washington University		13,355	39	26	13
MONTANA	Montana State University		12,052	28	14	14
	University of Montana		13,925	22	12	10
NEBRASKA	University of Nebraska:	Kearney	6,468	7	7	0
		Lincoln	22,106	39	29	10
NEVADA	Truckee Meadows Community College		11,556	10	5	5
	University of Nevada:	Las Vegas	27,912	54	37	17
		Reno	16,663	33	27	6
NEW JERSEY	Brookdale Community College		13,745	22	14	8
	Essex County College		10,972	47	16	31
	Kean University of New Jersey		13,050	45	22	23
	Middlesex County College		11,990	16	11	5
	Monmouth University		6,399	37	20	17
	Montclair State University		16,076	42	26	16
	New Jersey Institute of Technology		8,209	57	26	31
	Richard Stockton College		7,212	28	19	9
	Rowan University		9,578	45	14	31
	Rutgers University:	Camden	5,165	37	17	20
		Newark	10,203	38	29	9
		New Brunswick	34,392	88	48	40
	Stevens Institute of Technology		4,829	20	12	8
	The College of New Jersey		6,934	24	16	8
	University of Medicine and Dentistry:	Camden[2]		21	20	1
		Newark	5,677	146	48	98
		Piscataway[2]		42	30	12
	William Paterson University		10,599	42	28	14
NEW MEXICO	Eastern New Mexico University		4,122	10	9	1
	New Mexico Highlands University		3,747	13	3	10
	New Mexico State University		16,415	27	15	12
	University of New Mexico		25,721	52	30	22
NEW YORK	Cornell University		19,639	61	47	14
	Ithaca College		6,409	27	17	10
	State University of New York:	Albany	17,434	69	37	32
		Albany (Plaza)[2]		15	15	0
		Binghamton	14,373	42	30	12
		Buffalo	27,823	69	63	6
		Downstate Medical Center[2]		123	33	90
		Maritime College	1,324	10	6	4
		Stony Brook[2]		138	58	80
	State University of New York Agricultural and Technical College:	Alfred	3,201	15	10	5
		Canton	2,584	11	10	1
		Cobleskill	2,508	11	10	1
		Farmingdale[2]		26	16	10
		Morrisville[2]		12	11	1
	State University of New York College:	Brockport	8,312	19	17	2
		Buffalo	11,220	33	31	2
		Cortland	6,995	23	19	4
		Environmental Science and Forestry	2,069	13	11	2
		Fredonia	5,406	16	15	1
		Geneseo	5,530	21	16	5
		New Paltz	7,699	26	23	3
		Old Westbury	3,450	24	20	4
		Oneonta	5,786	27	17	10

[1] The student enrollment figures provided by the United States Department of Education are for the 2006 school year, the most recent available. The enrollment figures include full-time and part-time students.

[2] Student enrollment figures were not available.

Table 79.   Full-Time Law Enforcement Employees, by State by University and College, 2007 *(Contd.)*

(Number.)

State	University/College	Campus	Student enrollment[1]	Total law enforcement employees	Total officers	Total civilians
		Optometry	302	16	6	10
		Plattsburgh	6,217	20	15	5
		Potsdam	4,332	14	11	3
		Utica-Rome[2]		13	9	4
NORTH CAROLINA	Appalachian State University		15,117	34	21	13
	Belmont Abbey College		1,110	6	6	0
	Davidson College		1,667	6	5	1
	Duke University		13,373	155	52	103
	Elizabeth City State University		2,681	10	6	4
	Elon University		5,230	15	14	1
	Fayetteville State University		6,301	25	16	9
	Methodist College		2,116	7	7	0
	North Carolina Agricultural and Technical State University		11,098	52	23	29
	North Carolina Central University		8,675	42	25	17
	North Carolina School of the Arts		845	14	13	1
	North Carolina State University	Raleigh	31,130	61	47	14
	Saint Augustine's College		1,247	27	8	19
	University of North Carolina:	Asheville	3,639	21	13	8
		Chapel Hill	27,717	76	49	27
		Charlotte	21,519	36	26	10
		Greensboro	16,872	49	31	18
		Pembroke	5,827	15	13	2
		Wilmington	12,098	39	27	12
	Wake Forest University		6,739	41	16	25
	Western Carolina University		8,861	20	16	4
	Winston-Salem State University		5,650	33	18	15
NORTH DAKOTA	North Dakota State College of Science		2,493	3	3	0
	North Dakota State University		12,258	14	9	5
	University of North Dakota		12,834	14	11	3
OHIO	Bowling Green State University		19,108	31	24	7
	Central State University		1,766	13	12	1
	Cleveland State University		14,807	30	21	9
	Columbus State Community College		22,745	32	16	16
	Cuyahoga Community College		24,289	32	26	6
	Hocking College		4,600	6	6	0
	Kent State University		22,697	33	26	7
	Lakeland Community College		8,649	13	9	4
	Marietta College		1,522	8	7	1
	Miami University		16,329	38	28	10
	Ohio State University		51,818	96	46	50
	Ohio University		20,610	28	21	7
	Sinclair Community College		19,103	26	22	4
	University of Akron		21,882	39	32	7
	University of Cincinnati		28,327	112	60	52
	Wilberforce University		863	4	4	0
	Wright State University		16,088	28	20	8
	Youngstown State University		13,273	25	21	4
OKLAHOMA	Cameron University		5,737	11	11	0
	East Central University		4,453	5	5	0
	Murray State College		2,232	1	1	0
	Northeastern Oklahoma A&M College		1,923	9	7	2
	Northeastern State University		9,417	19	17	2
	Oklahoma State University:	Main Campus	23,499	39	31	8
		Okmulgee	3,255	6	6	0
		Tulsa[2]		7	5	2
	Rogers State University		3,955	4	4	0
	Seminole State College		2,038	3	3	0
	Southeastern Oklahoma State University		3,830	8	7	1
	Southwestern Oklahoma State University		5,122	8	6	2
	Tulsa Community College		16,632	15	9	6
	University of Central Oklahoma		15,588	20	15	5
	University of Oklahoma:	Health Sciences Center	3,790	56	45	11
		Norman	25,923	69	35	34
PENNSYLVANIA	California University		7,720	15	13	2
	Cheyney University		1,667	19	18	1
	Clarion University		6,563	14	10	4
	Dickinson College		2,400	16	10	6
	East Stroudsburg University		7,013	17	14	3
	Edinboro University		7,579	15	14	1
	Elizabethtown College		2,329	17	11	6
	Indiana University		14,248	32	23	9
	Kutztown University		10,193	23	16	7
	Lehigh University		6,858	30	20	10

[1] The student enrollment figures provided by the United States Department of Education are for the 2006 school year, the most recent available. The enrollment figures include full-time and part-time students.
[2] Student enrollment figures were not available.

Table 79.   Full-Time Law Enforcement Employees, by State by University and College, 2007 *(Contd.)*

(Number.)

State	University/College	Campus	Student enrollment[1]	Total law enforcement employees	Total officers	Total civilians
	Lock Haven University		5,175	12	10	2
	Millersville University		8,194	18	14	4
	Moravian College		1,965	12	7	5
	Pennsylvania State University:	Altoona	3,837	9	8	1
		Beaver	730	5	5	0
		Behrend	3,839	10	6	4
		Berks	2,660	9	8	1
		Harrisburg	3,799	8	6	2
		Hazelton	1,143	4	4	0
		McKeesport[2]		5	3	2
		Mont Alto	1,032	4	4	0
		University Park	42,914	65	45	20
	Shippensburg University		7,516	20	17	3
	Slippery Rock University		8,230	17	14	3
	University of Pittsburgh:	Bradford	1,333	6	5	1
		Pittsburgh	26,860	127	73	54
	West Chester University		12,879	35	19	16
RHODE ISLAND	Brown University		8,125	67	33	34
	University of Rhode Island		15,062	45	24	21
SOUTH CAROLINA	Benedict College		2,531	27	24	3
	Bob Jones University[2]			4	4	0
	Clemson University		17,309	51	34	17
	Coastal Carolina University		8,049	77	26	51
	College of Charleston		11,218	60	31	29
	Columbia College		1,446	13	11	2
	Denmark Technical College		1,377	4	4	0
	Erskine College		924	2	2	0
	Francis Marion University		4,075	13	12	1
	Lander University		2,682	11	9	2
	Medical University of South Carolina		2,498	69	49	20
	Midlands Technical College		10,849	6	6	0
	Presbyterian College		1,224	9	7	2
	South Carolina State University		4,384	38	17	21
	Spartanburg Methodist College		779	4	4	0
	The Citadel		3,306	14	13	1
	Trident Technical College		11,808	23	20	3
	University of South Carolina:	Aiken	3,380	9	9	0
		Columbia	27,390	81	57	24
		Upstate	4,608	11	10	1
	Winthrop University		6,292	22	15	7
SOUTH DAKOTA	South Dakota State University		11,303	18	12	6
TENNESSEE.............................	Austin Peay State University		9,207	20	9	11
	Christian Brothers University		1,779	15	8	7
	East Tennessee State University		12,390	26	19	7
	Middle Tennessee State University		22,863	35	28	7
	Northeast State Technical Community College		5,145	5	5	0
	Southwest Tennessee Community College		11,446	28	23	5
	Tennessee State University		9,038	48	31	17
	Tennessee Technological University		9,733	22	15	7
	University of Memphis		20,562	35	30	5
	University of Tennessee:	Chattanooga	8,923	23	14	9
		Knoxville	28,901	75	51	24
		Martin	6,888	16	12	4
		Memphis[2]		40	24	16
	Vanderbilt University		11,607	109	79	30
	Volunteer State Community College		7,370	6	5	1
	Walters State Community College		5,738	7	7	0
TEXAS	Abilene Christian University		4,777	11	10	1
	Alamo Community College District[2]			73	52	21
	Alvin Community College		3,996	11	9	2
	Amarillo College		10,356	16	14	2
	Angelo State University		6,265	16	12	4
	Austin College		1,354	8	7	1
	Baylor Health Care System[2]			166	55	111
	Baylor University	Waco	14,040	30	24	6
	Central Texas College		17,726	10	9	1
	College of the Mainland		3,834	7	6	1
	Eastfield College		12,015	12	10	2
	El Paso Community College		26,105	42	35	7
	Grayson County College		3,720	4	4	0
	Hardin-Simmons University		2,367	7	6	1
	Houston Baptist University		2,143	18	12	6
	Lamar University	Beaumont	9,906	29	14	15
	Laredo Community College		8,152	22	21	1

[1] The student enrollment figures provided by the United States Department of Education are for the 2006 school year, the most recent available. The enrollment figures include full-time and part-time students.

[2] Student enrollment figures were not available.

Table 79. Full-Time Law Enforcement Employees, by State by University and College, 2007 *(Contd.)*

(Number.)

State	University/College	Campus	Student enrollment[1]	Total law enforcement employees	Total officers	Total civilians
	McLennan Community College		7,794	16	6	10
	Midwestern State University		6,042	13	8	5
	Mountain View College		7,022	13	13	0
	North Lake College		9,397	14	13	1
	Paris Junior College		4,331	3	3	0
	Rice University		5,024	38	28	10
	Richland College		14,555	18	17	1
	Southern Methodist University		10,941	29	22	7
	South Plains College		9,045	6	6	0
	Southwestern University		1,277	7	6	1
	Stephen F. Austin State University		11,756	39	22	17
	St. Mary's University		3,904	14	12	2
	St. Thomas University		3,524	12	2	10
	Sul Ross State University		2,773	9	7	2
	Tarleton State University		9,464	14	11	3
	Texas A&M International University		4,917	20	13	7
	Texas A&M University:	College Station	45,380	121	58	63
		Commerce	8,471	25	15	10
		Corpus Christi	8,585	24	14	10
		Galveston	1,553	8	7	1
		Kingsville	6,728	19	14	5
	Texas Christian University		8,865	35	22	13
	Texas Southern University		11,224	60	39	21
	Texas State Technical College:	Harlingen	4,281	13	9	4
		Marshall	626	4	4	0
		Waco	4,209	14	12	2
	Texas State University	San Marcos	27,485	70	31	39
	Texas Technological University	Lubbock	27,996	81	49	32
	Texas Woman's University		11,832	35	15	20
	Trinity University		2,698	28	14	14
	Tyler Junior College		9,423	12	5	7
	University of Houston:	Central Campus	34,334	99	41	58
		Clearlake	7,706	23	13	10
		Downtown Campus	11,449	30	18	12
	University of Mary Hardin-Baylor		2,735	9	9	0
	University of North Texas:	Denton	33,395	77	43	34
		Health Science Center	1,129	19	9	10
	University of Texas:	Arlington	24,825	102	32	70
		Austin	49,697	136	60	76
		Brownsville	15,688	37	17	20
		Dallas	14,523	40	21	19
		El Paso	19,842	50	21	29
		Health Science Center, San Antonio	2,874	111	32	79
		Health Science Center, Tyler[2]		21	5	16
		Houston[2]		326	91	235
		Medical Branch	2,255	86	43	43
		Pan American	17,337	29	8	21
		Permian Basin	3,462	12	5	7
		San Antonio	28,379	97	48	49
		Southwestern Medical School	2,434	112	37	75
		Tyler	5,926	18	10	8
	Western Texas College		1,974	1	1	0
	West Texas A&M University		7,412	14	10	4
UTAH............................	Brigham Young University		34,185	40	29	11
	College of Eastern Utah		2,262	1	1	0
	Southern Utah University		7,029	5	4	1
	University of Utah		30,511	96	29	67
	Utah State University		14,444	18	12	6
	Utah Valley State College		23,305	10	8	2
	Weber State University		18,303	11	10	1
VERMONT.............................	University of Vermont		11,870	35	21	14
VIRGINIA	Christopher Newport University		4,793	21	16	5
	College of William and Mary		7,709	23	18	5
	Emory and Henry College		1,051	4	2	2
	Ferrum College		1,060	7	7	0
	George Mason University		29,889	61	43	18
	Hampton University		6,152	36	21	15
	James Madison University		17,393	32	24	8
	J. Sargeant Reynolds Community College		12,213	14	8	6
	Longwood College		4,479	20	15	5
	Norfolk State University		6,238	41	25	16
	Northern Virginia Community College		38,166	34	33	1
	Old Dominion University		21,625	55	46	9

[1] The student enrollment figures provided by the United States Department of Education are for the 2006 school year, the most recent available. The enrollment figures include full-time and part-time students.

[2] Student enrollment figures were not available.

Table 79.   Full-Time Law Enforcement Employees, by State by University and College, 2007 *(Contd.)*

(Number.)

State	University/College	Campus	Student enrollment[1]	Total law enforcement employees	Total officers	Total civilians
	Radford University		9,220	26	20	6
	Thomas Nelson Community College		9,718	16	11	5
	University of Mary Washington		4,862	20	11	9
	University of Richmond		4,496	32	18	14
	University of Virginia		24,068	117	55	62
	University of Virginia's College at Wise		2,043	9	8	1
	Virginia Commonwealth University		30,189	171	78	93
	Virginia Military Institute		1,397	7	7	0
	Virginia Polytechnic Institute and State University		28,470	62	40	22
	Virginia State University		4,872	37	21	16
	Virginia Western Community College		8,365	6	6	0
WASHINGTON	Central Washington University		10,688	19	13	6
	Eastern Washington University		11,161	13	12	1
	Evergreen State College		4,416	16	10	6
	University of Washington		39,524	60	44	16
	Washington State University:	Pullman	23,655	18	15	3
		Vancouver[2]		3	2	1
	Western Washington University		14,035	21	15	6
WEST VIRGINIA	Bluefield State College		1,923	1	1	0
	Concord University		2,787	9	6	3
	Fairmont State University		4,611	7	4	3
	Glenville State College		1,381	6	2	4
	Marshall University		13,936	23	22	1
	Potomac State College		1,485	6	5	1
	Shepherd University		4,091	9	8	1
	West Liberty State College		2,268	4	4	0
	West Virginia State University		3,502	11	9	2
	West Virginia Tech		1,472	7	7	0
	West Virginia University		27,115	58	51	7
WISCONSIN	University of Wisconsin:	Eau Claire	10,766	11	10	1
		Green Bay	5,690	12	5	7
		La Crosse	9,849	9	7	2
		Madison	41,028	109	61	48
		Milwaukee	28,309	42	31	11
		Oshkosh	12,530	11	9	2
		Parkside	5,007	13	8	5
		Platteville	6,813	8	7	1
		Stevens Point	9,048	8	3	5
		Stout	8,372	10	9	1
		Superior	2,924	8	1	7
		Whitewater	10,502	12	11	1
WYOMING	Sheridan College		3,066	2	2	0
	University of Wyoming		13,203	24	13	11

[1] The student enrollment figures provided by the United States Department of Education are for the 2006 school year, the most recent available. The enrollment figures include full-time and part-time students.

[2] Student enrollment figures were not available.

Table 80. Full-Time Law Enforcement Employees, by State by Metropolitan and Nonmetropolitan Counties, 2007

(Number.)

State	County	Total law enforcement employees	Total officers	Total civilians	State	County	Total law enforcement employees	Total officers	Total civilians
ALABAMA- Metropolitan Counties......	Autauga	24	22	2	**ARIZONA- Nonmetropolitan Counties**......	Cochise	196	88	108
	Bibb	12	11	1		Gila	130	41	89
	Blount	78	48	30		Greenlee	35	17	18
	Calhoun	83	40	43		La Paz	94	36	58
	Chilton	56	27	29		Navajo	131	45	86
	Colbert	54	30	24	**ARKANSAS- Metropolitan Counties**......				
	Elmore	79	32	47		Benton	190	102	88
	Etowah	151	59	92		Cleveland	12	8	4
	Geneva	25	11	14		Craighead	42	30	12
	Greene	25	8	17		Crawford	56	23	33
	Hale	8	6	2		Crittenden	136	31	105
	Henry	13	11	2		Faulkner	143	54	89
	Houston	82	52	30		Franklin	18	9	9
	Jefferson	704	550	154		Garland	117	43	74
	Lauderdale	42	33	9		Grant	15	13	2
	Lawrence	41	22	19		Jefferson	52	46	6
	Lee	146	61	85		Lincoln	22	10	12
	Limestone	97	39	58		Lonoke	40	24	16
	Lowndes	41	12	29		Madison	16	8	8
	Madison	281	106	175		Miller	62	25	37
	Mobile	535	163	372		Perry	14	8	6
	Montgomery	163	121	42		Poinsett	42	13	29
	Morgan	174	49	125		Pulaski	438	321	117
	Russell	90	32	58		Saline	82	40	42
	Shelby	191	110	81		Sebastian	132	39	93
	St. Clair	45	39	6		Washington	282	127	155
	Tuscaloosa	191	92	99	**ARKANSAS- Nonmetropolitan Counties**......				
	Walker	64	31	33		Arkansas	50	12	38
ALABAMA- Nonmetropolitan Counties......						Ashley	45	19	26
	Baldwin	240	85	155		Baxter	48	32	16
	Bullock	14	6	8		Boone	38	22	16
	Butler	12	10	2		Bradley	5	4	1
	Chambers	55	23	32		Calhoun	12	6	6
	Cherokee	40	18	22		Carroll	20	17	3
	Clarke	33	14	19		Chicot	7	6	1
	Clay	29	10	19		Clark	25	13	12
	Cleburne	25	9	16		Clay	19	8	11
	Coffee	47	21	26		Cleburne	36	22	14
	Conecuh	30	6	24		Columbia	35	15	20
	Coosa	22	9	13		Conway	32	15	17
	Covington	27	25	2		Cross	29	16	13
	Crenshaw	11	10	1		Dallas	29	6	23
	Cullman	126	73	53		Desha	8	7	1
	Dale	24	19	5		Drew	23	10	13
	Dallas	50	24	26		Fulton	14	7	7
	De Kalb	88	38	50		Greene	46	12	34
	Escambia	55	20	35		Hempstead	49	18	31
	Fayette	16	11	5		Hot Spring	24	22	2
	Jackson	76	28	48		Howard	21	10	11
	Lamar	21	8	13		Independence	75	47	28
	Macon	37	18	19		Izard	26	13	13
	Marengo	27	13	14		Jackson	21	12	9
	Marion	25	12	13		Johnson	32	13	19
	Marshall	73	30	43		Lafayette	16	7	9
	Monroe	56	20	36		Lawrence	23	12	11
	Perry	14	7	7		Lee	7	5	2
	Pickens	25	7	18		Little River	19	8	11
	Pike	30	16	14		Logan	23	11	12
	Randolph	11	11	0		Marion	22	13	9
	Talladega	98	40	58		Mississippi	81	28	53
	Tallapoosa	54	26	28		Monroe	9	3	6
	Washington	16	6	10		Montgomery	16	8	8
	Wilcox	27	9	18		Nevada	17	6	11
	Winston	23	10	13		Newton	12	8	4
ARIZONA- Metropolitan Counties......						Ouachita	32	19	13
	Coconino	264	69	195		Phillips	17	14	3
	Maricopa	3,498	763	2,735		Pike	14	7	7
	Mohave	254	94	160		Polk	25	11	14
	Pima	1,450	538	912		Pope	88	34	54
	Yavapai	401	132	269		Prairie	17	7	10
	Yuma	305	68	237		Randolph	11	9	2

Table 80. Full-Time Law Enforcement Employees, by State by Metropolitan and Nonmetropolitan Counties, 2007 *(Contd.)*

(Number.)

State	County	Total law enforcement employees	Total officers	Total civilians	State	County	Total law enforcement employees	Total officers	Total civilians
	Scott	15	8	7	**COLORADO-**				
	Searcy	13	7	6	**Metropolitan**				
	Sevier	22	11	11	**Counties**..............	Adams	505	350	155
	Sharp	28	11	17		Arapahoe	487	300	187
	St. Francis	37	14	23		Boulder	336	220	116
	Stone	24	8	16		Clear Creek	54	21	33
	Union	60	27	33		Douglas	398	274	124
	Van Buren	27	14	13		El Paso	618	403	215
	White	84	37	47		Gilpin	41	26	15
	Woodruff	16	6	10		Jefferson	780	542	238
	Yell	20	14	6		Larimer	415	180	235
CALIFORNIA-						Mesa	240	168	72
Metropolitan						Park	83	32	51
Counties..............	Alameda	1,612	967	645		Pueblo	291	131	160
	Butte	280	112	168		Teller	88	61	27
	Contra Costa	1,005	674	331		Weld	296	86	210
	El Dorado	372	196	176	**COLORADO-**				
	Fresno	1,197	487	710	**Nonmetropolitan**				
	Imperial	261	177	84	**Counties**..............	Alamosa	36	21	15
	Kern	1,083	476	607		Archuleta	45	14	31
	Kings	221	81	140		Baca	9	3	6
	Los Angeles	15,651	9,278	6,373		Bent	7	6	1
	Madera	110	76	34		Chaffee	40	17	23
	Marin	316	209	107		Cheyenne	9	5	4
	Merced	255	199	56		Conejos	22	7	15
	Monterey	431	317	114		Costilla	9	5	4
	Napa	123	93	30		Crowley	11	7	4
	Orange	3,555	1,753	1,802		Custer	17	7	10
	Placer	441	259	182		Delta	56	25	31
	Riverside	3,640	1,965	1,675		Dolores	7	5	2
	Sacramento	2,296	1,419	877		Eagle	63	53	10
	San Benito	67	32	35		Fremont	87	33	54
	San Bernardino	3,378	1,783	1,595		Garfield	112	40	72
	San Diego	3,791	2,191	1,600		Grand	49	19	30
	San Francisco	1,005	831	174		Gunnison	26	12	14
	San Joaquin	737	296	441		Hinsdale	5	4	1
	San Luis Obispo	383	162	221		Huerfano	21	9	12
	San Mateo	633	433	200		Jackson	7	4	3
	Santa Barbara	688	309	379		Kiowa	5	4	1
	Santa Clara	692	517	175		Kit Carson	20	6	14
	Santa Cruz	312	137	175		Lake	18	9	9
	Shasta	237	147	90		La Plata	114	86	28
	Solano	480	118	362		Las Animas	37	14	23
	Sonoma	729	534	195		Lincoln	21	5	16
	Stanislaus	616	233	383		Logan	50	21	29
	Sutter	129	100	29		Mineral	4	3	1
	Tulare	711	450	261		Moffat	37	17	20
	Ventura	1,224	748	476		Montezuma	61	24	37
	Yolo	260	87	173		Montrose	99	49	50
	Yuba	174	137	37		Morgan	56	28	28
CALIFORNIA-						Otero	20	12	8
Nonmetropolitan						Ouray	8	8	0
Counties..............	Alpine	20	15	5		Phillips	4	3	1
	Amador	88	45	43		Pitkin	27	25	2
	Calaveras	111	64	47		Prowers	31	11	20
	Colusa	59	31	28		Rio Blanco	29	15	14
	Del Norte	62	32	30		Rio Grande	29	8	21
	Glenn	68	29	39		Routt	44	23	21
	Humboldt	216	164	52		Saguache	19	8	11
	Inyo	70	51	19		San Juan	4	3	1
	Lake	150	57	93		San Miguel	37	33	4
	Lassen	91	69	22		Sedgwick	9	5	4
	Mariposa	75	60	15		Summit	76	56	20
	Mendocino	163	127	36		Washington	47	15	32
	Modoc	26	22	4		Yuma	19	7	12
	Mono	43	26	17	**DELAWARE-**				
	Nevada	191	71	120	**Metropolitan**				
	Plumas	73	38	35	**Counties**..............	New Castle County Police			
	Sierra	15	11	4		Department	450	336	114
	Siskiyou	131	99	32	**FLORIDA-**				
	Tehama	105	72	33	**Metropolitan**				
	Trinity	41	20	21	**Counties**..............	Alachua	755	257	498
	Tuolumne	128	60	68		Baker	88	45	43

Table 80.   Full-Time Law Enforcement Employees, by State by Metropolitan and Nonmetropolitan Counties, 2007 *(Contd.)*

(Number.)

State	County	Total law enforcement employees	Total officers	Total civilians	State	County	Total law enforcement employees	Total officers	Total civilians
	Bay	278	211	67		Bryan	42	37	5
	Brevard	1,117	483	634		Butts	84	35	49
	Broward	1,818	461	1,357		Carroll	184	105	79
	Charlotte	613	283	330		Catoosa	134	68	66
	Clay	545	273	272		Chatham	428	344	84
	Collier	1,314	847	467		Clarke	138	113	25
	Escambia	1,092	400	692		Clayton County Police Department	375	344	31
	Flagler	174	121	53		Cobb County Police Department	726	589	137
	Gadsden	82	56	26		Coweta	197	130	67
	Gilchrist	56	29	27		Crawford	33	16	17
	Hernando	384	249	135		DeKalb County Police Department	1,476	966	510
	Hillsborough	3,400	1,223	2,177		Dougherty County Police Department	53	43	10
	Indian River	495	201	294		Douglas	311	226	85
	Jefferson	48	21	27		Fayette	221	143	78
	Lake	714	343	371		Floyd	143	73	70
	Lee	924	554	370		Forsyth	341	291	50
	Leon	346	238	108		Fulton	1,277	1,101	176
	Manatee	691	443	248		Fulton County Police Department	214	182	32
	Marion	894	399	495		Glynn County Police Department	128	114	14
	Martin	541	272	269		Gwinnett County Police Department	939	659	280
	Miami-Dade	4,538	3,118	1,420		Hall	433	370	63
	Nassau	204	102	102		Heard	37	20	17
	Okaloosa	366	260	106		Henry	220	210	10
	Orange	2,008	1,355	653		Jasper	35	20	15
	Osceola	559	381	178		Jones	72	39	33
	Palm Beach	2,948	1,219	1,729		Lamar	51	22	29
	Pasco	1,114	484	630		Lee	66	37	29
	Pinellas	1,297	718	579		Liberty	119	64	55
	Polk	1,555	627	928		Long	15	14	1
	Santa Rosa	314	188	126		Lowndes	229	206	23
	Sarasota	933	419	514		McDuffie	48	15	33
	Seminole	1,028	400	628		McIntosh	53	29	24
	St. Johns	567	279	288		Meriwether	46	29	17
	St. Lucie	636	267	369		Monroe	119	58	61
	Volusia	742	456	286		Murray	63	39	24
	Wakulla	159	73	86		Muscogee	417	309	108
FLORIDA- Nonmetropolitan Counties..........						Newton	213	118	95
	Bradford	66	25	41		Oglethorpe	23	17	6
	Calhoun	22	15	7		Paulding	193	154	39
	Citrus	321	208	113		Pickens	77	63	14
	Columbia	189	90	99		Rockdale	209	194	15
	DeSoto	113	55	58		Spalding	175	144	31
	Dixie	62	27	35		Twiggs	40	24	16
	Franklin	83	64	19		Walker	102	74	28
	Glades	44	30	14		Whitfield	189	161	28
	Gulf	41	27	14	**GEORGIA- Nonmetropolitan Counties**..........				
	Hamilton	57	16	41		Appling	45	14	31
	Hardee	92	46	46		Atkinson	11	9	2
	Hendry	90	58	32		Bacon	23	9	14
	Highlands	314	121	193		Baldwin	110	66	44
	Holmes	23	17	6		Banks	55	32	23
	Jackson	76	57	19		Ben Hill	54	27	27
	Lafayette	11	10	1		Berrien	33	14	19
	Levy	150	73	77		Bleckley	26	14	12
	Liberty	30	14	16		Calhoun	15	6	9
	Madison	42	28	14		Camden	138	102	36
	Monroe	497	218	279		Charlton	28	27	1
	Okeechobee	202	90	112		Chattooga	42	42	0
	Putnam	218	108	110		Cook	48	19	29
	Sumter	198	115	83		Crisp	54	49	5
	Suwannee	101	58	43		Dooly	66	21	45
	Taylor	48	35	13		Early	51	28	23
	Union	15	9	6		Elbert	31	29	2
	Walton	206	160	46		Fannin	44	26	18
	Washington	75	37	38		Franklin	33	24	9
GEORGIA- Metropolitan Counties..........						Gilmer	93	53	40
	Augusta-Richmond	682	616	66		Gordon	86	60	26
	Baker	3	3	0		Grady	19	15	4
	Barrow	169	121	48		Greene	57	35	22
	Bibb	314	274	40		Habersham	33	27	6
	Brantley	23	16	7		Hancock	41	28	13
	Brooks	40	19	21					

Table 80. Full-Time Law Enforcement Employees, by State by Metropolitan and Nonmetropolitan Counties, 2007 *(Contd.)*

(Number.)

State	County	Total law enforcement employees	Total officers	Total civilians	State	County	Total law enforcement employees	Total officers	Total civilians
	Hart	43	26	17		Lincoln	8	6	2
	Irwin	20	13	7		Madison	34	22	12
	Jenkins	9	3	6		Minidoka	27	16	11
	Laurens	103	59	44		Oneida	10	6	4
	Lumpkin	75	42	33		Payette	32	18	14
	Macon	20	9	11		Shoshone	28	16	12
	Miller	26	12	14		Teton	15	8	7
	Mitchell	52	24	28		Twin Falls	62	39	23
	Peach	60	30	30		Valley	31	16	15
	Polk County Police Department	35	33	2		Washington	17	12	5
	Pulaski	24	12	12	**ILLINOIS-**				
	Putnam	56	30	26	**Metropolitan**				
	Seminole	20	11	9	**Counties**	Bond	19	11	8
	Stephens	50	44	6		Boone	94	33	61
	Sumter	92	43	49		Calhoun	11	6	5
	Taliaferro	14	8	6		Champaign	152	130	22
	Tattnall	36	16	20		Clinton	35	16	19
	Taylor	21	20	1		Cook	6,979	2,390	4,589
	Tift	104	57	47		De Kalb	96	40	56
	Towns	19	17	2		Du Page	516	395	121
	Treutlen	19	11	8		Ford	23	7	16
	Troup	119	66	53		Grundy	62	30	32
	Upson	71	33	38		Henry	74	23	51
	Ware	117	38	79		Jersey	27	14	13
	Washington	33	28	5		Kane	293	93	200
	Webster	5	4	1		Kankakee	204	64	140
	Wheeler	8	4	4		Kendall	106	50	56
	White	60	38	22		Lake	468	176	292
	Wilcox	13	9	4		Macon	160	50	110
	Wilkes	22	13	9		Macoupin	48	44	4
	Wilkinson	23	13	10		Madison	174	82	92
HAWAII-						Marshall	16	7	9
Nonmetropolitan						McHenry	379	107	272
Counties	Hawaii Police Department	543	397	146		McLean	135	55	80
	Kauai Police Department	169	124	45		Menard	15	8	7
	Maui Police Department	418	311	107		Mercer	30	12	18
IDAHO-						Monroe	35	15	20
Metropolitan						Peoria	268	64	204
Counties	Ada	388	142	246		Piatt	30	10	20
	Bannock	62	29	33		Rock Island	154	64	90
	Boise	14	12	2		Sangamon	227	75	152
	Bonneville	84	57	27		Stark	12	4	8
	Canyon	143	75	68		St. Clair	176	162	14
	Franklin	15	12	3		Tazewell	108	41	67
	Gem	21	11	10		Vermilion	82	31	51
	Jefferson	32	18	14		Will	550	255	295
	Kootenai	144	80	64		Winnebago	390	109	281
	Nez Perce	38	22	16		Woodford	40	37	3
	Owyhee	19	11	8	**ILLINOIS-**				
	Power	17	9	8	**Nonmetropolitan**				
IDAHO-					**Counties**	Adams	68	27	41
Nonmetropolitan						Alexander	10	8	2
Counties	Adams	16	10	6		Brown	6	5	1
	Bear Lake	13	5	8		Bureau	34	19	15
	Benewah	18	9	9		Carroll	23	9	14
	Bingham	48	30	18		Cass	8	7	1
	Blaine	26	19	7		Christian	35	17	18
	Bonner	60	41	19		Clark	17	9	8
	Boundary	20	11	9		Clay	17	11	6
	Butte	10	4	6		Coles	48	24	24
	Camas	6	4	2		Crawford	21	9	12
	Caribou	10	8	2		Cumberland	16	6	10
	Cassia	50	32	18		De Witt	38	16	22
	Clark	7	3	4		Douglas	26	10	16
	Clearwater	26	18	8		Edgar	19	8	11
	Custer	15	8	7		Edwards	10	4	6
	Elmore	44	23	21		Effingham	48	20	28
	Fremont	24	16	8		Fayette	29	10	19
	Gooding	17	10	7		Franklin	45	18	27
	Idaho	32	20	12		Fulton	46	19	27
	Jerome	19	15	4		Gallatin	4	4	0
	Latah	37	26	11		Greene	14	6	8
	Lemhi	6	5	1		Hamilton	7	3	4
	Lewis	11	6	5		Hancock	24	9	15

Table 80. Full-Time Law Enforcement Employees, by State by Metropolitan and Nonmetropolitan Counties, 2007 *(Contd.)*

(Number.)

State	County	Total law enforcement employees	Total officers	Total civilians	State	County	Total law enforcement employees	Total officers	Total civilians
	Hardin	2	2	0		Shelby	82	26	56
	Henderson	14	8	6		St. Joseph	288	120	168
	Iroquois	30	18	12		Sullivan	32	10	22
	Jackson	71	25	46		Tippecanoe	147	46	101
	Jasper	19	9	10		Tipton	22	11	11
	Jefferson	51	20	31		Vanderburgh	248	107	141
	Jo Daviess	37	19	18		Vermillion	25	9	16
	Johnson	13	7	6		Warrick	81	37	44
	Knox	54	51	3		Wells	38	15	23
	La Salle	109	46	63	**INDIANA-**				
	Lawrence	17	8	9	**Nonmetropolitan**				
	Lee	41	22	19	**Counties**.....................	Adams	41	16	25
	Livingston	63	30	33		Blackford	32	9	23
	Logan	27	20	7		Clinton	65	19	46
	Marion	35	13	22		Crawford	17	8	9
	Mason	21	9	12		Daviess	62	18	44
	Massac	29	11	18		Decatur	38	11	27
	McDonough	25	13	12		Dubois	33	16	17
	Montgomery	28	14	14		Fayette	11	10	1
	Morgan	42	15	27		Fulton	23	10	13
	Moultrie	24	10	14		Grant	111	45	66
	Ogle	59	27	32		Henry	72	29	43
	Perry	32	26	6		Huntington	40	14	26
	Pike	28	12	16		Jackson	53	16	37
	Pope	3	3	0		Jay	16	11	5
	Pulaski	16	7	9		Jefferson	32	14	18
	Putnam	11	7	4		Knox	38	12	26
	Randolph	27	12	15		Kosciusko	87	36	51
	Richland	23	7	16		Lawrence	64	25	39
	Saline	48	12	36		Marshall	57	20	37
	Schuyler	8	3	5		Martin	15	6	9
	Scott	7	3	4		Miami	32	15	17
	Shelby	24	12	12		Montgomery	55	17	38
	Stephenson	70	29	41		Noble	67	20	47
	Union	16	9	7		Orange	30	9	21
	Wabash	6	4	2		Parke	38	12	26
	Warren	21	11	10		Perry	17	7	10
	Washington	20	7	13		Pike	26	9	17
	Wayne	24	9	15		Pulaski	47	13	34
	White	25	7	18		Randolph	41	15	26
	Whiteside	51	24	27		Ripley	26	9	17
	Williamson	64	35	29		Rush	24	10	14
INDIANA-						Scott	23	11	12
Metropolitan						Spencer	14	13	1
Counties.....................	Allen	348	124	224		Starke	27	13	14
	Bartholomew	70	37	33		Steuben	63	21	42
	Benton	18	6	12		Union	11	6	5
	Boone	61	29	32		Wabash	36	14	22
	Brown	36	13	23		Warren	18	7	11
	Carroll	23	13	10		Wayne	105	68	37
	Clark	116	35	81		White	33	13	20
	Clay	38	11	27	**IOWA-**				
	Dearborn	85	31	54	**Metropolitan**				
	Delaware	108	48	60	**Counties**.....................	Benton	26	12	14
	Elkhart	207	66	141		Black Hawk	132	100	32
	Floyd	90	30	60		Bremer	29	12	17
	Gibson	42	17	25		Dallas	42	17	25
	Greene	37	13	24		Dubuque	81	73	8
	Hamilton	231	60	171		Grundy	15	11	4
	Hancock	82	41	41		Guthrie	11	5	6
	Harrison	69	21	48		Harrison	21	9	12
	Hendricks	102	45	57		Johnson	94	64	30
	Howard	44	35	9		Jones	23	10	13
	Jasper	45	21	24		Linn	169	110	59
	Johnson	123	96	27		Madison	15	7	8
	La Porte	148	57	91		Mills	20	11	9
	Madison	108	51	57		Polk	355	147	208
	Monroe	106	31	75		Pottawattamie	158	47	111
	Newton	42	16	26		Scott	165	45	120
	Ohio	9	9	0		Story	82	31	51
	Porter	147	62	85		Warren	34	23	11
	Posey	13	12	1		Washington	31	18	13
	Putnam	31	15	16		Woodbury	116	32	84

Table 80. Full-Time Law Enforcement Employees, by State by Metropolitan and Nonmetropolitan Counties, 2007 *(Contd.)*

(Number.)

State	County	Total law enforcement employees	Total officers	Total civilians	State	County	Total law enforcement employees	Total officers	Total civilians
IOWA-						Wayne	11	6	5
Nonmetropolitan						Webster	35	19	16
Counties.....................	Adair	8	6	2		Winnebago	9	6	3
	Adams	9	4	5		Winneshiek	23	10	13
	Allamakee	14	8	6		Worth	18	7	11
	Appanoose	14	8	6		Wright	19	7	12
	Audubon	8	5	3	**KANSAS-**				
	Boone	30	11	19	**Metropolitan**				
	Buchanan	18	13	5	**Counties.....................**	Butler	48	44	4
	Buena Vista	17	9	8		Doniphan	11	6	5
	Butler	18	10	8		Douglas	134	81	53
	Calhoun	11	6	5		Franklin	57	27	30
	Carroll	15	9	6		Jackson	25	16	9
	Cass	14	8	6		Jefferson	41	23	18
	Cedar	36	10	26		Johnson	624	501	123
	Cerro Gordo	62	20	42		Leavenworth	101	49	52
	Cherokee	17	6	11		Linn	21	10	11
	Chickasaw	14	8	6		Miami	43	25	18
	Clarke	16	5	11		Osage	43	40	3
	Clay	17	10	7		Sedgwick	504	174	330
	Clayton	26	13	13		Shawnee	143	109	34
	Clinton	40	23	17		Sumner	38	20	18
	Crawford	12	10	2		Wabaunsee	19	6	13
	Davis	13	5	8		Wyandotte	154	124	30
	Decatur	11	6	5	**KANSAS-**				
	Delaware	15	10	5	**Nonmetropolitan**				
	Des Moines	44	21	23	**Counties.....................**	Allen	21	9	12
	Dickinson	21	9	12		Anderson	15	14	1
	Emmet	15	8	7		Atchison	27	11	16
	Fayette	33	9	24		Barber	9	4	5
	Floyd	17	10	7		Barton	39	20	19
	Franklin	11	8	3		Bourbon	8	6	2
	Fremont	18	7	11		Brown	20	8	12
	Greene	15	7	8		Chase	4	4	0
	Hamilton	28	8	20		Chautauqua	13	3	10
	Hancock	8	8	0		Cherokee	31	20	11
	Hardin	29	10	19		Cheyenne	5	4	1
	Henry	26	12	14		Clark	9	4	5
	Howard	14	7	7		Clay	16	7	9
	Humboldt	15	9	6		Cloud	8	7	1
	Ida	16	9	7		Coffey	31	13	18
	Iowa	23	11	12		Comanche	3	3	0
	Jackson	15	9	6		Cowley	22	20	2
	Jasper	45	14	31		Crawford	69	33	36
	Jefferson	27	8	19		Decatur	4	3	1
	Keokuk	7	4	3		Dickinson	27	15	12
	Kossuth	24	9	15		Edwards	8	4	4
	Lee	30	15	15		Elk	10	4	6
	Louisa	22	10	12		Ellis	29	17	12
	Lucas	12	4	8		Ellsworth	15	7	8
	Lyon	28	9	19		Finney	97	40	57
	Mahaska	24	8	16		Ford	56	25	31
	Marion	34	13	21		Geary	64	25	39
	Marshall	56	17	39		Graham	7	3	4
	Mitchell	17	6	11		Grant	16	6	10
	Monona	17	7	10		Gray	17	10	7
	Monroe	13	5	8		Greeley	6	3	3
	Muscatine	22	22	0		Greenwood	25	14	11
	O'Brien	30	11	19		Hamilton	12	6	6
	Osceola	15	9	6		Haskell	16	11	5
	Page	15	8	7		Hodgeman	8	4	4
	Palo Alto	15	8	7		Jewell	8	4	4
	Plymouth	27	10	17		Kearny	20	11	9
	Pocahontas	13	7	6		Kingman	17	7	10
	Poweshiek	19	11	8		Kiowa	14	9	5
	Ringgold	10	6	4		Labette	30	18	12
	Sac	18	7	11		Lane	8	4	4
	Shelby	14	8	6		Lincoln	13	8	5
	Sioux	36	13	23		Logan	4	3	1
	Tama	22	12	10		Lyon	39	26	13
	Taylor	9	5	4		McPherson	34	16	18
	Union	11	5	6		Meade	19	5	14
	Van Buren	10	5	5		Montgomery	32	21	11
	Wapello	39	9	30		Morris	12	7	5

Table 80. Full-Time Law Enforcement Employees, by State by Metropolitan and Nonmetropolitan Counties, 2007 *(Contd.)*

(Number.)

State	County	Total law enforce-ment employees	Total officers	Total civilians	State	County	Total law enforce-ment employees	Total officers	Total civilians
	Morton	10	5	5	**KENTUCKY-**				
	Nemaha	17	8	9	**Nonmetropolitan**				
	Neosho	30	14	16	**Counties**......................	Adair	8	6	2
	Ness	13	7	6		Allen	14	12	2
	Norton	9	4	5		Anderson	15	15	0
	Osborne	13	9	4		Ballard	11	11	0
	Ottawa	8	5	3		Barren	19	15	4
	Pottawatomie	42	26	16		Bath	5	4	1
	Pratt	15	8	7		Bell	23	10	13
	Rawlins	4	3	1		Boyle	10	10	0
	Reno	76	46	30		Breathitt	4	2	2
	Republic	13	7	6		Breckinridge	9	7	2
	Riley County Police Department	178	102	76		Butler	9	5	4
	Rooks	10	5	5		Caldwell	9	7	2
	Rush	8	3	5		Calloway	26	17	9
	Russell	18	9	9		Carlisle	3	2	1
	Saline	97	42	55		Carroll	6	4	2
	Scott	5	5	0		Carter	10	7	3
	Seward	38	11	27		Casey	8	7	1
	Sheridan	8	3	5		Clay	12	10	2
	Sherman	13	5	8		Clinton	5	4	1
	Smith	5	5	0		Crittenden	5	4	1
	Stafford	9	4	5		Cumberland	7	5	2
	Stanton	13	5	8		Elliott	3	2	1
	Stevens	21	10	11		Estill	6	5	1
	Thomas	15	9	6		Fleming	8	8	0
	Trego	4	4	0		Floyd	19	12	7
	Wallace	2	2	0		Franklin	19	18	1
	Washington	6	6	0		Fulton	5	4	1
	Wichita	9	4	5		Garrard	7	7	0
	Wilson	33	11	22		Graves	15	11	4
	Woodson	10	6	4		Grayson	12	9	3
KENTUCKY-						Green	4	4	0
Metropolitan						Harlan	20	12	8
Counties......................	Boone	146	137	9		Harrison	9	9	0
	Bourbon	6	5	1		Hart	7	6	1
	Boyd	26	23	3		Hickman	2	2	0
	Bracken	5	4	1		Hopkins	26	19	7
	Bullitt	47	42	5		Jackson	7	4	3
	Campbell	13	10	3		Johnson	15	11	4
	Campbell County Police					Knott	9	6	3
	Department	29	28	1		Knox	11	8	3
	Christian	30	26	4		Laurel	36	30	6
	Clark	15	12	3		Lawrence	8	5	3
	Daviess	52	38	14		Lee	1	1	0
	Edmonson	6	4	2		Leslie	5	4	1
	Fayette	77	43	34		Letcher	14	13	1
	Gallatin	6	6	0		Lewis	7	5	2
	Gallatin County Police Depart					Lincoln	11	9	2
	ment	1	1	0		Livingston	8	8	0
	Grant	19	17	2		Logan	17	16	1
	Greenup	15	14	1		Lyon	5	5	0
	Hancock	7	6	1		Madison	24	18	6
	Hardin	40	33	7		Magoffin	4	3	1
	Henderson	36	20	16		Marion	7	6	1
	Henry	6	5	1		Marshall	18	17	1
	Jefferson	282	234	48		Martin	7	5	2
	Jessamine	30	22	8		Mason	12	10	2
	Kenton	41	34	7		McCracken	41	37	4
	Kenton County Police Department	55	33	22		McCreary	4	2	2
	Larue	4	4	0		Menifee	4	4	0
	McLean	10	8	2		Mercer	10	9	1
	Meade	10	7	3		Metcalfe	5	4	1
	Nelson	28	21	7		Monroe	6	4	2
	Oldham	17	15	2		Montgomery	16	14	2
	Oldham County Police Department	35	32	3		Morgan	4	2	2
	Pendleton	7	6	1		Muhlenberg	13	12	1
	Scott	34	34	0		Nicholas	4	2	2
	Shelby	25	24	1		Ohio	23	19	4
	Spencer	7	6	1		Owen	7	5	2
	Trimble	4	3	1		Owsley	4	3	1
	Warren	62	42	20		Perry	16	10	6
	Webster	8	6	2		Pike	20	10	10
	Woodford	9	9	0		Powell	6	4	2

Table 80.   Full-Time Law Enforcement Employees, by State by Metropolitan and Nonmetropolitan Counties, 2007 *(Contd.)*

(Number.)

State	County	Total law enforcement employees	Total officers	Total civilians	State	County	Total law enforcement employees	Total officers	Total civilians
	Pulaski	39	31	8	**MAINE-**				
	Robertson	1	1	0	**Metropolitan**				
	Rockcastle	5	4	1	**Counties......................**	Androscoggin	25	17	8
	Rowan	13	10	3		Cumberland	57	51	6
	Russell	11	10	1		Penobscot	28	24	4
	Simpson	15	12	3		Sagadahoc	31	28	3
	Taylor	12	10	2		York	29	25	4
	Todd	4	3	1	**MAINE-**				
	Union	9	8	1	**Nonmetropolitan**				
	Washington	6	6	0	**Counties......................**	Aroostook	22	16	6
	Wayne	10	9	1		Franklin	26	15	11
	Whitley	14	11	3		Hancock	19	17	2
	Wolfe	3	2	1		Kennebec	46	39	7
LOUISIANA-						Knox	19	18	1
Metropolitan						Oxford	17	16	1
Counties......................	Ascension	250	216	34		Piscataquis	19	8	11
	Bossier	346	288	58		Somerset	17	15	2
	Caddo	640	432	208		Waldo	18	16	2
	Calcasieu	793	417	376		Washington	22	12	10
	Cameron	68	44	24	**MARYLAND-**				
	East Baton Rouge	803	688	115	**Metropolitan**				
	East Feliciana	65	19	46	**Counties......................**	Allegany	25	23	2
	Grant	65	23	42		Anne Arundel	92	67	25
	Iberville	131	77	54		Anne Arundel County Police			
	Jefferson	1,393	900	493		Department	863	640	223
	Lafourche	316	255	61		Baltimore County	94	79	15
	Livingston	207	207	0		Baltimore County Police Department	2,236	1,882	354
	Ouachita	358	358	0		Calvert	122	102	20
	Plaquemines	185	102	83		Carroll	92	63	29
	Pointe Coupee	84	36	48		Cecil	81	70	11
	Rapides	476	363	113		Charles	430	279	151
	St. Bernard	219	194	25		Frederick	243	186	57
	St. Charles	352	253	99		Harford	344	285	59
	St. Helena	47	15	32		Howard	70	42	28
	St. John the Baptist	216	185	31		Howard County Police Department	551	400	151
	St. Martin	231	114	117		Montgomery	167	141	26
	St. Tammany	667	265	402		Montgomery County Police			
	Terrebonne	295	108	187		Department	1,656	1,235	421
	Union	45	31	14		Prince George's	347	246	101
	West Baton Rouge	165	122	43		Prince George's County Police			
	West Feliciana	105	81	24		Department	1,824	1,561	263
LOUISIANA-						Queen Anne's	49	46	3
Nonmetropolitan						Somerset	24	21	3
Counties......................	Acadia	111	111	0		Washington	225	93	132
	Assumption	76	45	31		Wicomico	109	86	23
	Beauregard	70	49	21	**MARYLAND-**				
	Bienville	54	45	9	**Nonmetropolitan**				
	Caldwell	35	35	0	**Counties......................**	Caroline	31	27	4
	Catahoula	112	16	96		Dorchester	37	33	4
	Claiborne	37	37	0		Garrett	55	30	25
	Concordia	250	239	11		Kent	25	22	3
	East Carroll	215	18	197		St. Mary's	231	127	104
	Evangeline	53	17	36		Talbot	28	25	3
	Jackson	92	26	66		Worcester	59	46	13
	Jefferson Davis	48	37	11	**MICHIGAN-**				
	La Salle	39	22	17	**Metropolitan**				
	Lincoln	61	40	21	**Counties......................**	Barry	49	31	18
	Morehouse	158	37	121		Bay	80	35	45
	Natchitoches	78	58	20		Berrien	166	74	92
	Red River	39	30	9		Calhoun	182	81	101
	Sabine	71	71	0		Cass	70	34	36
	St. James	92	68	24		Clinton	59	25	34
	St. Landry	218	152	66		Eaton	136	72	64
	St. Mary	185	165	20		Genesee	253	144	109
	Tangipahoa	262	198	64		Ingham	205	119	86
	Tensas	141	31	110		Ionia	51	22	29
	Vermilion	124	67	57		Jackson	137	52	85
	Vernon	140	105	35		Kalamazoo	205	161	44
	Washington	137	137	0		Kent	543	207	336
	Webster	145	50	95		Lapeer	82	46	36
	West Carroll	20	20	0		Livingston	130	74	56
	Winn	40	16	24		Macomb	502	250	252
						Monroe	203	96	107
						Muskegon	120	51	69
						Newaygo	64	27	37
						Oakland	1,062	866	196
						Ottawa	224	126	98

Table 80. Full-Time Law Enforcement Employees, by State by Metropolitan and Nonmetropolitan Counties, 2007 *(Contd.)*

(Number.)

State	County	Total law enforcement employees	Total officers	Total civilians	State	County	Total law enforcement employees	Total officers	Total civilians
	Saginaw	128	69	59		Hennepin	799	334	465
	St. Clair	163	56	107		Houston	24	12	12
	Van Buren	87	44	43		Isanti	60	19	41
	Washtenaw	158	128	30		Olmsted	143	56	87
	Wayne	1,332	1,017	315		Polk	26	21	5
MICHIGAN-						Ramsey	397	244	153
Nonmetropolitan						Scott	122	36	86
Counties......	Alcona	24	13	11		Sherburne	265	63	202
	Alger	13	10	3		Stearns	173	62	111
	Allegan	104	58	46		St. Louis	236	95	141
	Alpena	26	13	13		Wabasha	34	19	15
	Antrim	45	18	27		Washington	230	91	139
	Arenac	18	10	8		Wright	168	133	35
	Baraga	13	6	7	**MINNESOTA-**				
	Benzie	41	12	29	**Nonmetropolitan**				
	Branch	49	25	24	**Counties**......	Aitkin	48	19	29
	Charlevoix	24	18	6		Becker	57	22	35
	Cheboygan	34	16	18		Beltrami	82	34	48
	Chippewa	20	16	4		Big Stone	8	5	3
	Clare	23	19	4		Blue Earth	76	24	52
	Crawford	27	15	12		Brown	36	10	26
	Delta	32	16	16		Cass	64	38	26
	Dickinson	22	13	9		Chippewa	18	8	10
	Emmet	46	24	22		Clearwater	20	10	10
	Gladwin	38	16	22		Cook	17	12	5
	Gogebic	20	13	7		Cottonwood	20	9	11
	Grand Traverse	127	66	61		Crow Wing	123	43	80
	Gratiot	35	19	16		Douglas	72	23	49
	Hillsdale	45	29	16		Faribault	22	9	13
	Houghton	20	20	0		Fillmore	30	18	12
	Huron	37	22	15		Freeborn	51	19	32
	Iosco	22	6	16		Goodhue	106	39	67
	Iron	21	8	13		Grant	10	6	4
	Isabella	52	25	27		Hubbard	37	14	23
	Kalkaska	36	19	17		Itasca	72	60	12
	Keweenaw	7	6	1		Jackson	19	8	11
	Lake	64	15	49		Kanabec	32	14	18
	Leelanau	21	20	1		Kandiyohi	113	34	79
	Lenawee	106	49	57		Kittson	10	5	5
	Luce	4	3	1		Koochiching	17	10	7
	Mackinac	19	7	12		Lac Qui Parle	9	7	2
	Manistee	30	14	16		Lake	27	16	11
	Marquette	51	22	29		Lake of the Woods	9	5	4
	Mason	39	20	19		Le Sueur	29	17	12
	Mecosta	48	23	25		Lincoln	10	4	6
	Menominee	13	13	0		Lyon	36	13	23
	Midland	59	37	22		Mahnomen	19	12	7
	Missaukee	27	12	15		Marshall	17	11	6
	Montcalm	60	28	32		Martin	29	10	19
	Montmorency	26	11	15		McLeod	58	25	33
	Oceana	36	21	15		Meeker	41	16	25
	Ogemaw	26	16	10		Mille Lacs	66	25	41
	Ontonagon	12	9	3		Morrison	59	19	40
	Osceola	38	20	18		Mower	47	19	28
	Oscoda	17	11	6		Murray	13	9	4
	Otsego	23	11	12		Nicollet	29	11	18
	Presque Isle	26	14	12		Nobles	34	11	23
	Roscommon	41	27	14		Norman	8	5	3
	Sanilac	30	26	4		Otter Tail	81	34	47
	Schoolcraft	12	4	8		Pennington	27	6	21
	Shiawassee	70	33	37		Pine	82	28	54
	St. Joseph	50	24	26		Pipestone	22	12	10
	Tuscola	46	26	20		Pope	14	7	7
	Wexford	50	24	26		Red Lake	10	6	4
MINNESOTA-						Redwood	23	10	13
Metropolitan						Renville	17	11	6
Counties......	Anoka	238	125	113		Rice	49	24	25
	Benton	69	25	44		Rock	16	11	5
	Carlton	47	20	27		Roseau	24	13	11
	Carver	149	79	70		Sibley	23	11	12
	Chisago	84	41	43		Steele	24	18	6
	Clay	65	32	33		Stevens	12	6	6
	Dakota	187	75	112		Swift	13	6	7
	Dodge	32	22	10		Todd	31	14	17

Table 80. Full-Time Law Enforcement Employees, by State by Metropolitan and Nonmetropolitan Counties, 2007 *(Contd.)*

(Number.)

State	County	Total law enforcement employees	Total officers	Total civilians	State	County	Total law enforcement employees	Total officers	Total civilians
	Traverse	11	5	6		Yalobusha	12	7	5
	Wadena	18	7	11		Yazoo	14	12	2
	Waseca	27	12	15	**MISSOURI-**				
	Watonwan	21	9	12	**Metropolitan**				
	Wilkin	16	6	10	**Counties.....................**	Andrew	13	10	3
	Winona	53	16	37		Bates	30	10	20
	Yellow Medicine	21	8	13		Boone	75	58	17
MISSISSIPPI-						Buchanan	104	72	32
Metropolitan						Caldwell	52	9	43
Counties.....................	DeSoto	204	80	124		Callaway	26	24	2
	George	28	17	11		Cass	88	71	17
	Hancock	51	47	4		Christian	78	51	27
	Harrison	395	152	243		Clay	182	106	76
	Hinds	430	114	316		Clinton	21	14	7
	Lamar	72	38	34		Cole	46	34	12
	Madison	115	50	65		Dallas	19	16	3
	Marshall	50	26	24		De Kalb	9	5	4
	Perry	18	10	8		Franklin	121	100	21
	Rankin	156	80	76		Greene	247	124	123
	Simpson	36	27	9		Howard	7	6	1
	Stone	21	19	2		Jackson	119	86	33
	Tate	33	17	16		Jasper	144	92	52
	Tunica	139	67	72		Jefferson	215	144	71
MISSISSIPPI-						Lafayette	34	30	4
Nonmetropolitan						Lincoln	97	61	36
Counties.....................	Adams	57	29	28		McDonald	30	26	4
	Attala	13	8	5		Moniteau	8	5	3
	Benton	16	5	11		Newton	63	37	26
	Bolivar	92	23	69		Osage	11	7	4
	Calhoun	10	5	5		Platte	110	75	35
	Chickasaw	27	13	14		Polk	35	23	12
	Choctaw	6	6	0		Ray	29	13	16
	Claiborne	29	13	16		St. Charles	220	151	69
	Clarke	20	9	11		St. Louis County Police Department	982	741	241
	Clay	34	8	26		Warren	57	52	5
	Coahoma	16	15	1		Washington	37	24	13
	Greene	7	4	3		Webster	20	18	2
	Grenada	14	11	3	**MISSOURI-**				
	Holmes	12	12	0	**Nonmetropolitan**				
	Humphreys	13	6	7	**Counties.....................**	Adair	28	10	18
	Issaquena	4	4	0		Atchison	9	4	5
	Jasper	27	21	6		Audrain	39	29	10
	Jefferson	51	11	40		Barry	40	21	19
	Jefferson Davis	11	10	1		Barton	18	8	10
	Kemper	17	7	10		Benton	22	15	7
	Lafayette	29	26	3		Bollinger	15	9	6
	Lauderdale	115	55	60		Butler	36	17	19
	Leake	16	14	2		Camden	51	36	15
	Lee	125	44	81		Cape Girardeau	66	40	26
	Leflore	30	19	11		Carroll	14	8	6
	Lincoln	49	21	28		Carter	8	3	5
	Lowndes	49	41	8		Cedar	18	12	6
	Marion	25	12	13		Chariton	12	9	3
	Monroe	42	14	28		Clark	11	5	6
	Montgomery	7	6	1		Cooper	9	8	1
	Neshoba	15	14	1		Crawford	36	25	11
	Newton	18	9	9		Dade	8	5	3
	Noxubee	10	4	6		Daviess	5	4	1
	Oktibbeha	28	25	3		Dent	19	14	5
	Panola	67	26	41		Douglas	10	6	4
	Pearl River	128	48	80		Dunklin	10	8	2
	Pike	48	27	21		Gasconade	12	11	1
	Prentiss	29	13	16		Gentry	6	6	0
	Scott	24	16	8		Grundy	10	5	5
	Smith	16	10	6		Harrison	11	5	6
	Tallahatchie	26	11	15		Henry	25	19	6
	Tippah	16	8	8		Hickory	12	7	5
	Tishomingo	20	11	9		Holt	9	3	6
	Union	37	16	21		Howell	42	29	13
	Walthall	21	11	10		Iron	10	6	4
	Warren	66	42	24		Johnson	44	37	7
	Washington	53	29	24		Knox	5	2	3
	Wayne	18	8	10		Laclede	21	20	1
	Winston	8	7	1		Lawrence	33	23	10

Table 80. Full-Time Law Enforcement Employees, by State by Metropolitan and Nonmetropolitan Counties, 2007 *(Contd.)*

(Number.)

State	County	Total law enforcement employees	Total officers	Total civilians	State	County	Total law enforcement employees	Total officers	Total civilians
	Lewis	11	5	6		Judith Basin	5	4	1
	Linn	6	5	1		Lake	49	21	28
	Livingston	16	9	7		Lewis and Clark	59	40	19
	Macon	14	11	3		Liberty	4	4	0
	Madison	11	9	2		Lincoln	36	19	17
	Maries	11	7	4		Madison	15	9	6
	Marion	37	16	21		McCone	4	4	0
	Mercer	8	3	5		Meagher	4	4	0
	Miller	16	14	2		Mineral	24	12	12
	Mississippi	14	10	4		Musselshell	6	6	0
	Monroe	8	8	0		Park	16	15	1
	Montgomery	16	15	1		Petroleum	1	1	0
	Morgan	46	26	20		Phillips	7	6	1
	New Madrid	25	13	12		Pondera	10	8	2
	Nodaway	12	10	2		Powder River	7	3	4
	Oregon	10	6	4		Powell	10	10	0
	Ozark	17	8	9		Prairie	3	3	0
	Pemiscot	41	18	23		Ravalli	60	30	30
	Perry	28	17	11		Richland	15	8	7
	Pettis	48	23	25		Roosevelt	14	11	3
	Phelps	62	27	35		Rosebud	25	13	12
	Pike	30	10	20		Sanders	26	12	14
	Pulaski	29	20	9		Sheridan	7	4	3
	Putnam	4	3	1		Silver Bow	93	44	49
	Ralls	8	7	1		Stillwater	9	7	2
	Randolph	37	23	14		Sweet Grass	5	5	0
	Reynolds	11	7	4		Teton	15	8	7
	Ripley	12	10	2		Toole	13	12	1
	Saline	31	18	13		Treasure	2	2	0
	Schuyler	8	3	5		Valley	17	8	9
	Scotland	6	3	3		Wheatland	12	5	7
	Scott	42	21	21		Wibaux	2	2	0
	Shannon	8	4	4	**NEBRASKA-**				
	Shelby	10	5	5	**Metropolitan**				
	St. Clair	66	20	46	**Counties......................**	Dakota	16	14	2
	Ste. Genevieve	52	38	14		Dixon	12	7	5
	St. Francois	72	60	12		Douglas	198	131	67
	Stoddard	20	10	10		Lancaster	93	77	16
	Stone	54	41	13		Sarpy	193	128	65
	Sullivan	5	4	1		Saunders	18	11	7
	Taney	74	39	35		Seward	13	12	1
	Texas	14	7	7	**NEBRASKA-**				
	Vernon	21	10	11	**Nonmetropolitan**				
	Wayne	11	6	5	**Counties......................**	Adams	18	16	2
	Worth	4	3	1		Antelope	11	6	5
	Wright	14	8	6		Arthur	1	1	0
MONTANA-						Banner	1	1	0
Metropolitan						Blaine	1	1	0
Counties......................	Carbon	8	8	0		Boone	12	5	7
	Cascade	130	37	93		Box Butte	16	4	12
	Missoula	174	50	124		Boyd	2	2	0
	Yellowstone	129	53	76		Brown	9	5	4
MONTANA-						Buffalo	43	25	18
Nonmetropolitan						Burt	8	4	4
Counties......................	Beaverhead	16	7	9		Butler	22	7	15
	Big Horn	15	12	3		Cedar	9	4	5
	Blaine	21	8	13		Chase	8	4	4
	Broadwater	22	9	13		Cherry	11	5	6
	Carter	3	3	0		Cheyenne	18	7	11
	Chouteau	15	9	6		Colfax	9	7	2
	Custer	7	6	1		Cuming	6	5	1
	Daniels	8	3	5		Custer	7	6	1
	Dawson	18	6	12		Dawes	10	3	7
	Deer Lodge	33	19	14		Deuel	5	4	1
	Fallon	6	3	3		Dundy	7	3	4
	Fergus	19	8	11		Fillmore	12	7	5
	Flathead	122	52	70		Franklin	7	3	4
	Gallatin	92	52	40		Frontier	8	5	3
	Garfield	5	4	1		Furnas	14	9	5
	Glacier	17	11	6		Garden	8	4	4
	Golden Valley	2	2	0		Garfield	2	2	0
	Granite	11	5	6		Gosper	5	4	1
	Hill	15	13	2		Greeley	3	2	1
	Jefferson	22	12	10		Hall	36	29	7

Table 80. Full-Time Law Enforcement Employees, by State by Metropolitan and Nonmetropolitan Counties, 2007 *(Contd.)*

(Number.)

State	County	Total law enforcement employees	Total officers	Total civilians	State	County	Total law enforcement employees	Total officers	Total civilians
	Hamilton	17	8	9	**NEW HAMPSHIRE-Nonmetropolitan Counties**......................				
	Harlan	8	4	4		Carroll	25	14	11
	Hayes	2	2	0		Cheshire	18	10	8
	Hitchcock	7	4	3		Merrimack	27	16	11
	Holt	6	5	1	**NEW JERSEY-Metropolitan Counties**......................				
	Hooker	1	1	0		Atlantic	131	102	29
	Howard	13	6	7		Bergen	545	456	89
	Jefferson	8	7	1		Bergen County Police Department	175	90	85
	Johnson	9	4	5		Burlington	88	72	16
	Kearney	11	7	4		Camden	172	149	23
	Keith	15	8	7		Cape May	146	126	20
	Keya Paha	2	2	0		Cumberland	58	51	7
	Kimball	9	3	6		Essex	506	432	74
	Knox	12	5	7		Gloucester	89	76	13
	Lincoln	43	23	20		Hudson	273	179	94
	Logan	1	1	0		Hunterdon	31	26	5
	Loup	1	1	0		Mercer	179	140	39
	Madison	18	15	3		Middlesex	228	187	41
	McPherson	1	1	0		Monmouth	696	488	208
	Merrick	11	6	5		Morris	353	270	83
	Morrill	9	4	5		Ocean	245	136	109
	Nance	10	6	4		Passaic	821	653	168
	Nemaha	5	5	0		Salem	179	155	24
	Nuckolls	7	4	3		Somerset	227	185	42
	Otoe	26	14	12		Sussex	146	122	24
	Pawnee	4	3	1		Union	213	169	44
	Perkins	7	4	3		Warren	19	16	3
	Phelps	25	6	19	**NEW MEXICO-Metropolitan Counties**......................				
	Pierce	7	3	4		Bernalillo	335	263	72
	Platte	61	18	43		Dona Ana	209	131	78
	Polk	11	7	4		Sandoval	58	50	8
	Red Willow	7	5	2		San Juan	112	87	25
	Richardson	10	6	4		Santa Fe	97	75	22
	Rock	8	3	5		Torrance	15	12	3
	Saline	15	10	5		Valencia	49	36	13
	Scotts Bluff	26	18	8	**NEW MEXICO-Nonmetropolitan Counties**......................				
	Sheridan	7	6	1		Catron	11	6	5
	Sherman	5	4	1		Chaves	53	42	11
	Sioux	1	1	0		Cibola	18	13	5
	Stanton	8	7	1		Colfax	10	8	2
	Thayer	11	7	4		Curry	18	15	3
	Thomas	1	1	0		De Baca	2	2	0
	Valley	6	3	3		Eddy	54	47	7
	Wayne	6	5	1		Grant	39	36	3
	Webster	10	7	3		Lea	53	38	15
	Wheeler	1	1	0		Lincoln	25	16	9
	York	23	9	14		Luna	33	30	3
NEVADA-Metropolitan Counties..................						McKinley	44	32	12
	Carson City	141	95	46		Mora	8	6	2
	Storey	27	24	3		Otero	45	31	14
	Washoe	732	438	294		Quay	9	8	1
NEVADA-Nonmetropolitan Counties......................						Rio Arriba	24	18	6
	Churchill	49	40	9		Roosevelt	16	13	3
	Douglas	121	107	14		Sierra	13	11	2
	Elko	70	55	15		Socorro	13	10	3
	Esmeralda	14	10	4		Taos	23	17	6
	Eureka	20	10	10		Union	4	3	1
	Humboldt	51	35	16	**NEW YORK-Metropolitan Counties**......................				
	Lander	31	17	14		Albany	172	131	41
	Lincoln	32	26	6		Broome	72	54	18
	Lyon	111	78	33		Chemung	43	37	6
	Mineral	24	18	6		Dutchess	135	112	23
	Nye	147	104	43		Erie	170	142	28
	Pershing	19	12	7		Herkimer	11	7	4
	White Pine	31	25	6		Livingston	66	46	20
NEW HAMPSHIRE-Metropolitan Counties......................						Madison	40	33	7
	Rockingham	48	25	23		Monroe	332	279	53
						Nassau	3,413	2,594	819

Table 80.   Full-Time Law Enforcement Employees, by State by Metropolitan and Nonmetropolitan Counties, 2007 *(Contd.)*

(Number.)

State	County	Total law enforcement employees	Total officers	Total civilians	State	County	Total law enforcement employees	Total officers	Total civilians
	Niagara	136	104	32		Mecklenburg[1]	1,176	300	876
	Oneida	89	89	0		Nash	129	75	54
	Onondaga	287	238	49		New Hanover	391	275	116
	Ontario	109	72	37		Onslow	147	104	43
	Orange	105	93	12		Orange	140	82	58
	Orleans	41	27	14		Pender	83	49	34
	Oswego	67	57	10		Person	42	40	2
	Rensselaer	38	33	5		Pitt	269	119	150
	Rockland	107	76	31		Randolph	218	155	63
	Saratoga	146	110	36		Rockingham	138	95	43
	Schenectady	20	14	6		Stokes	61	40	21
	Schoharie	30	15	15		Union	231	165	66
	Suffolk	393	255	138		Wake	780	346	434
	Suffolk County Police Department	3,227	2,642	585		Wayne	143	80	63
	Tioga	56	37	19		Yadkin	58	35	23
	Tompkins	40	36	4	**NORTH**				
	Ulster	77	56	21	**CAROLINA-**				
	Warren	109	73	36	**Nonmetropolitan**				
	Washington	37	31	6	**Counties**......................	Alleghany	27	12	15
	Wayne	64	52	12		Ashe	42	24	18
	Westchester Public Safety	335	264	71		Avery	32	24	8
NEW YORK-						Beaufort	69	45	24
Nonmetropolitan						Bertie	23	17	6
Counties......................	Cattaraugus	76	57	19		Bladen	74	48	26
	Cayuga	48	41	7		Camden	18	17	1
	Chautauqua	122	77	45		Carteret	87	44	43
	Chenango	30	24	6		Caswell	49	26	23
	Clinton	20	20	0		Cherokee	44	24	20
	Columbia	54	43	11		Chowan	39	18	21
	Cortland	54	33	21		Clay	24	15	9
	Delaware	27	15	12		Cleveland	126	83	43
	Essex	27	25	2		Columbus	109	59	50
	Franklin	11	3	8		Craven	120	60	60
	Fulton	50	32	18		Dare	140	62	78
	Genesee	74	48	26		Davidson	192	128	64
	Jefferson	54	45	9		Duplin	80	60	20
	Lewis	29	17	12		Gates	12	11	1
	Montgomery	42	21	21		Graham	23	14	9
	Otsego	25	20	5		Granville	84	45	39
	Seneca	34	28	6		Halifax	75	49	26
	Steuben	50	40	10		Harnett	161	104	57
	St. Lawrence	42	37	5		Hertford	63	31	32
	Sullivan	77	48	29		Hyde	18	13	5
	Wyoming	41	30	11		Iredell	220	156	64
	Yates	44	33	11		Jackson	71	46	25
NORTH						Jones	17	8	9
CAROLINA-						Lee	74	43	31
Metropolitan						Lenoir	98	61	37
Counties......................	Alamance	210	108	102		Lincoln	155	89	66
	Alexander	48	29	19		Macon	64	45	19
	Anson	32	28	4		Martin	32	30	2
	Brunswick	159	108	51		McDowell	61	38	23
	Buncombe	355	225	130		Mitchell	16	14	2
	Burke	109	82	27		Montgomery	44	32	12
	Cabarrus	192	174	18		Moore	113	74	39
	Caldwell	105	55	50		Northampton	42	26	16
	Catawba	169	119	50		Pamlico	15	13	2
	Chatham	92	73	19		Pasquotank	50	43	7
	Cumberland	538	304	234		Perquimans	13	11	2
	Currituck	58	55	3		Polk	33	24	9
	Davie	70	42	28		Richmond	62	54	8
	Durham	428	158	270		Robeson	206	98	108
	Edgecombe	123	51	72		Rowan	171	121	50
	Forsyth	280	222	58		Rutherford	116	70	46
	Franklin	58	53	5		Sampson	120	72	48
	Gaston	208	118	90		Scotland	61	38	23
	Gaston County Police Department	204	127	77		Stanly	78	43	35
	Greene	32	24	8		Surry	95	68	27
	Guilford	521	245	276		Swain	30	16	14
	Haywood	88	50	38		Transylvania	63	48	15
	Henderson	178	124	54		Tyrrell	15	8	7
	Hoke	79	48	31		Vance	92	40	52
	Johnston	187	107	80		Warren	58	28	30
	Madison	31	19	12		Washington	43	24	19

[1] The employee data presented in this table for Mecklenburg represent only Mecklenburg County Sheriff's Office employees and exclude Charlotte-Mecklenburg Police Department employees.

Table 80. Full-Time Law Enforcement Employees, by State by Metropolitan and Nonmetropolitan Counties, 2007 *(Contd.)*

(Number.)

State	County	Total law enforce-ment employees	Total officers	Total civilians	State	County	Total law enforce-ment employees	Total officers	Total civilians
	Watauga	77	38	39		Fairfield	134	100	34
	Wilkes	110	67	43		Franklin	844	625	219
	Wilson	134	83	51		Fulton	31	20	11
	Yancey	23	12	11		Geauga	122	53	69
NORTH DAKOTA-						Greene	159	102	57
Metropolitan						Hamilton	1,043	302	741
Counties......	Burleigh	76	44	32		Jefferson	81	36	45
	Cass	129	67	62		Lake	223	58	165
	Grand Forks	32	26	6		Lawrence	43	35	8
	Morton	31	18	13		Licking	192	137	55
NORTH DAKOTA-						Lorain	240	77	163
Nonmetropolitan						Lucas	540	261	279
Counties......	Adams	4	4	0		Madison	35	30	5
	Barnes	14	5	9		Mahoning	307	290	17
	Benson	4	4	0		Medina	87	66	21
	Billings	4	4	0		Miami	140	53	87
	Bottineau	13	9	4		Morrow	57	23	34
	Bowman	3	3	0		Ottawa	62	23	39
	Burke	5	4	1		Pickaway	83	37	46
	Cavalier	11	5	6		Portage	128	53	75
	Dickey	6	5	1		Preble	62	19	43
	Divide	3	3	0		Richland	116	52	64
	Dunn	5	4	1		Stark	249	143	106
	Eddy	4	4	0		Summit	491	395	96
	Emmons	4	3	1		Trumbull	118	39	79
	Foster	4	3	1		Warren	180	95	85
	Golden Valley	5	4	1		Washington	85	46	39
	Grant	3	3	0	**OHIO-**				
	Griggs	4	4	0	**Nonmetropolitan**				
	Hettinger	3	3	0	**Counties**......	Adams	31	23	8
	Kidder	3	2	1		Ashland	76	53	23
	Lamoure	5	4	1		Ashtabula	80	42	38
	Logan	2	2	0		Athens	28	24	4
	McHenry	5	4	1		Auglaize	56	22	34
	McIntosh	3	3	0		Champaign	24	22	2
	McKenzie	9	5	4		Clinton	71	39	32
	McLean	28	21	7		Crawford	59	17	42
	Mercer	24	13	11		Darke	68	40	28
	Mountrail	11	6	5		Defiance	38	22	16
	Nelson	4	3	1		Fayette	39	25	14
	Oliver	4	3	1		Gallia	33	23	10
	Pembina	14	8	6		Guernsey	43	21	22
	Pierce	7	3	4		Hancock	86	37	49
	Ramsey	7	6	1		Hardin	27	24	3
	Ransom	6	5	1		Harrison	19	14	5
	Renville	5	5	0		Henry	21	20	1
	Richland	25	16	9		Highland	56	56	0
	Rolette	18	8	10		Hocking	24	20	4
	Sargent	4	3	1		Holmes	51	34	17
	Sheridan	2	2	0		Huron	70	30	40
	Sioux	1	1	0		Jackson	19	15	4
	Slope	1	1	0		Logan	115	40	75
	Stark	14	11	3		Marion	41	29	12
	Steele	3	3	0		Meigs	17	13	4
	Stutsman	11	9	2		Mercer	50	35	15
	Towner	3	2	1		Monroe	20	17	3
	Traill	10	5	5		Morgan	16	13	3
	Walsh	16	11	5		Muskingum	121	80	41
	Ward	42	21	21		Noble	18	5	13
	Wells	3	3	0		Paulding	34	15	19
	Williams	28	16	12		Perry	16	11	5
OHIO-						Pike	13	11	2
Metropolitan						Putnam	51	31	20
Counties......	Allen	160	75	85		Ross	103	56	47
	Belmont	57	50	7		Scioto	82	52	30
	Brown	32	27	5		Seneca	82	35	47
	Butler	347	170	177		Shelby	69	33	36
	Carroll	23	15	8		Tuscarawas	104	31	73
	Clark	161	133	28		Van Wert	26	20	6
	Clermont	196	87	109		Vinton	15	10	5
	Delaware	179	79	100		Wayne	84	70	14
	Erie	74	36	38		Williams	27	23	4
						Wyandot	25	13	12

Table 80. Full-Time Law Enforcement Employees, by State by Metropolitan and Nonmetropolitan Counties, 2007 *(Contd.)*

(Number.)

State	County	Total law enforce-ment employees	Total officers	Total civilians	State	County	Total law enforce-ment employees	Total officers	Total civilians
OKLAHOMA-						Texas	35	10	25
Metropolitan						Tillman	20	6	14
Counties......................	Canadian	57	32	25		Washington	39	17	22
	Cleveland	102	43	59		Washita	16	7	9
	Comanche	36	27	9		Woods	10	5	5
	Creek	71	35	36		Woodward	17	10	7
	Grady	20	13	7	**OREGON-**				
	Le Flore	19	13	6	**Metropolitan**				
	Lincoln	36	12	24	**Counties**......................	Benton	96	90	6
	Logan	45	15	30		Clackamas	315	214	101
	McClain	26	14	12		Columbia	38	15	23
	Oklahoma	721	182	539		Deschutes	188	80	108
	Okmulgee	13	12	1		Jackson	163	117	46
	Osage	62	35	27		Lane	367	75	292
	Pawnee	19	9	10		Marion	340	94	246
	Rogers	37	28	9		Multnomah	815	86	729
	Sequoyah	20	15	5		Polk	66	54	12
	Tulsa	504	184	320		Washington	520	220	300
	Wagoner	52	18	34		Yamhill	96	45	51
OKLAHOMA-					**OREGON-**				
Nonmetropolitan					**Nonmetropolitan**				
Counties......................	Adair	31	9	22	**Counties**......................	Baker	26	11	15
	Alfalfa	9	4	5		Clatsop	57	26	31
	Atoka	14	8	6		Coos	80	20	60
	Beaver	13	7	6		Crook	29	16	13
	Beckham	31	9	22		Curry	33	13	20
	Blaine	16	7	9		Douglas	144	112	32
	Bryan	41	15	26		Gilliam	6	5	1
	Caddo	28	16	12		Grant	18	4	14
	Carter	58	19	39		Harney	20	6	14
	Cherokee	24	19	5		Hood River	35	18	17
	Choctaw	15	6	9		Jefferson	49	17	32
	Cimarron	8	4	4		Josephine	88	34	54
	Coal	12	7	5		Klamath	70	33	37
	Cotton	12	6	6		Lake	8	7	1
	Craig	27	10	17		Lincoln	87	27	60
	Custer	24	8	16		Linn	140	69	71
	Delaware	35	19	16		Malheur	47	19	28
	Dewey	11	4	7		Morrow	27	27	0
	Ellis	14	5	9		Sherman	6	5	1
	Garfield	55	20	35		Tillamook	60	56	4
	Garvin	25	12	13		Umatilla	74	49	25
	Grant	11	5	6		Union	11	9	2
	Greer	6	3	3		Wallowa	12	7	5
	Harmon	3	3	0		Wasco	29	15	14
	Harper	10	6	4		Wheeler	14	5	9
	Haskell	16	6	10	**PENNSYLVANIA-**				
	Hughes	10	5	5	**Metropolitan**				
	Jackson	38	12	26	**Counties**......................	Allegheny	180	149	31
	Jefferson	13	4	9		Allegheny County Police			
	Johnston	24	7	17		Department	269	213	56
	Kay	33	12	21		Beaver	29	23	6
	Kingfisher	14	7	7		Cumberland	31	26	5
	Kiowa	17	15	2		Lycoming	16	11	5
	Latimer	18	8	10		Montgomery	123	103	20
	Love	16	6	10		Pike	21	17	4
	Major	9	6	3		Washington	31	27	4
	Marshall	22	6	16		Westmoreland	61	53	8
	Mayes	40	18	22		York	106	95	11
	McCurtain	19	17	2	**PENNSYLVANIA-**				
	McIntosh	25	16	9	**Nonmetropolitan**				
	Murray	11	5	6	**Counties**......................	Adams	9	8	1
	Muskogee	31	28	3		Bradford	11	9	2
	Noble	11	5	6		Clarion	1	1	0
	Nowata	22	10	12		Elk	6	5	1
	Okfuskee	13	9	4		Greene	7	6	1
	Ottawa	35	15	20		Jefferson	3	2	1
	Payne	56	25	31		Snyder	5	5	0
	Pittsburg	15	14	1		Warren	45	18	27
	Pontotoc	13	11	2	**SOUTH**				
	Pottawatomie	24	19	5	**CAROLINA-**				
	Pushmataha	21	7	14	**Metropolitan**				
	Roger Mills	13	8	5	**Counties**......................	Aiken	229	120	109
	Seminole	20	11	9		Anderson	254	175	79
	Stephens	14	11	3		Berkeley	200	129	71

Table 80. Full-Time Law Enforcement Employees, by State by Metropolitan and Nonmetropolitan Counties, 2007 *(Contd.)*

(Number.)

State	County	Total law enforcement employees	Total officers	Total civilians	State	County	Total law enforcement employees	Total officers	Total civilians
	Calhoun	24	21	3		Corson	3	2	1
	Charleston	655	252	403		Custer	12	11	1
	Darlington	114	63	51		Davison	25	6	19
	Dorchester	194	101	93		Day	6	3	3
	Edgefield	59	30	29		Deuel	8	4	4
	Fairfield	51	45	6		Dewey	3	2	1
	Florence	230	115	115		Douglas	2	2	0
	Greenville	452	362	90		Edmunds	4	4	0
	Horry	226	170	56		Fall River	15	5	10
	Horry County Police Department	277	255	22		Faulk	9	3	6
	Kershaw	69	59	10		Grant	4	3	1
	Laurens	97	61	36		Gregory	4	3	1
	Lexington	353	229	124		Haakon	2	2	0
	Pickens	131	94	37		Hamlin	4	4	0
	Richland	519	477	42		Hand	2	1	1
	Saluda	55	21	34		Hanson	2	2	0
	Spartanburg	323	294	29		Harding	3	2	1
	Sumter	129	117	12		Hughes	24	6	18
	York	282	143	139		Hutchinson	3	3	0
SOUTH CAROLINA-						Hyde	1	1	0
Nonmetropolitan						Jackson	2	2	0
Counties......	Abbeville	52	28	24		Jerauld	2	2	0
	Allendale	14	12	2		Jones	2	2	0
	Bamberg	16	13	3		Kingsbury	6	5	1
	Barnwell	45	26	19		Lake	10	5	5
	Beaufort	225	200	25		Lawrence	46	18	28
	Cherokee	92	45	47		Lyman	4	3	1
	Chester	80	45	35		Marshall	11	6	5
	Chesterfield	64	42	22		McPherson	1	1	0
	Clarendon	62	46	16		Mellette	6	4	2
	Colleton	135	66	69		Miner	4	3	1
	Dillon	80	31	49		Moody	9	4	5
	Georgetown	126	76	50		Perkins	4	3	1
	Greenwood	116	70	46		Potter	3	2	1
	Hampton	24	21	3		Roberts	15	4	11
	Jasper	34	29	5		Sanborn	3	2	1
	Lancaster	124	78	46		Shannon	1	1	0
	Lee	34	29	5		Spink	13	8	5
	Marion	45	39	6		Stanley	6	5	1
	Marlboro	29	25	4		Sully	3	3	0
	McCormick	32	12	20		Todd	1	1	0
	Newberry	93	49	44		Tripp	7	6	1
	Oconee	136	77	59		Walworth	10	2	8
	Orangeburg	113	84	29		Yankton	10	9	1
	Union	50	28	22		Ziebach	2	2	0
	Williamsburg	65	32	33	**TENNESSEE-**				
SOUTH					**Metropolitan**				
DAKOTA-					**Counties**......	Anderson	131	47	84
Metropolitan						Blount	266	228	38
Counties......	Lincoln	16	15	1		Bradley	198	99	99
	McCook	7	6	1		Cannon	26	10	16
	Meade	46	18	28		Carter	74	38	36
	Minnehaha	181	78	103		Cheatham	71	32	39
	Pennington	93	65	28		Chester	30	13	17
	Turner	9	7	2		Dickson	122	51	71
	Union	25	5	20		Fayette	66	33	33
SOUTH						Grainger	43	18	25
DAKOTA-						Hamblen	68	32	36
Nonmetropolitan						Hamilton	378	150	228
Counties......	Aurora	4	3	1		Hartsville-Trousdale	31	17	14
	Beadle	26	7	19		Hawkins	39	36	3
	Bennett	4	3	1		Hickman	42	25	17
	Bon Homme	8	3	5		Jefferson	83	34	49
	Brookings	20	12	8		Knox	939	380	559
	Brown	48	14	34		Loudon	61	40	21
	Brule	9	4	5		Macon	59	28	31
	Buffalo	1	1	0		Madison	212	63	149
	Butte	13	5	8		Marion	40	18	22
	Campbell	2	2	0		Montgomery	303	82	221
	Charles Mix	11	5	6		Polk	42	17	25
	Clark	2	2	0		Robertson	100	43	57
	Clay	10	7	3		Rutherford	394	187	207
	Codington	10	7	3		Sequatchie	36	17	19
						Shelby	1,781	531	1,250

Table 80. Full-Time Law Enforcement Employees, by State by Metropolitan and Nonmetropolitan Counties, 2007 *(Contd.)*

(Number.)

State	County	Total law enforcement employees	Total officers	Total civilians	State	County	Total law enforcement employees	Total officers	Total civilians
	Smith	37	15	22		Austin	53	33	20
	Stewart	36	15	21		Bandera	48	27	21
	Sullivan	249	105	144		Bastrop	136	53	83
	Sumner	234	70	164		Bell	260	92	168
	Tipton	72	40	32		Bexar	1,734	504	1,230
	Unicoi	39	19	20		Bowie	46	40	6
	Union	28	15	13		Brazoria	337	158	179
	Washington	170	79	91		Burleson	30	13	17
	Williamson	209	112	97		Caldwell	80	24	56
	Wilson	217	83	134		Calhoun	66	27	39
TENNESSEE-Nonmetropolitan Counties......						Callahan	11	5	6
	Bedford	81	30	51		Cameron	378	98	280
	Benton	38	17	21		Carson	14	6	8
	Bledsoe	12	7	5		Chambers	84	42	42
	Campbell	64	37	27		Clay	19	11	8
	Carroll	34	18	16		Collin	470	141	329
	Claiborne	67	22	45		Comal	216	106	110
	Clay	21	10	11		Coryell	59	22	37
	Cocke	65	32	33		Crosby	17	5	12
	Coffee	70	38	32		Dallas	2,040	445	1,595
	Crockett	30	12	18		Delta	19	10	9
	Cumberland	89	44	45		Denton	542	197	345
	Decatur	20	12	8		Ector	181	90	91
	DeKalb	37	15	22		Ellis	214	79	135
	Dyer	65	24	41		El Paso	1,025	251	774
	Fentress	28	17	11		Fort Bend	580	386	194
	Franklin	51	30	21		Galveston	395	229	166
	Gibson	75	31	44		Goliad	23	12	11
	Giles	58	25	33		Grayson	133	58	75
	Greene	157	62	95		Gregg	232	89	143
	Grundy	22	12	10		Guadalupe	199	67	132
	Hancock	40	14	26		Hardin	62	34	28
	Hardeman	42	22	20		Harris	3,666	2,349	1,317
	Hardin	43	16	27		Hays	257	118	139
	Haywood	47	19	28		Hidalgo	746	257	489
	Henderson	35	23	12		Hunt	114	41	73
	Henry	63	31	32		Irion	8	3	5
	Houston	22	10	12		Jefferson	392	138	254
	Humphreys	29	16	13		Johnson	247	88	159
	Jackson	33	13	20		Jones	26	9	17
	Johnson	43	15	28		Kaufman	241	83	158
	Lake	17	6	11		Kendall	66	42	24
	Lauderdale	58	23	35		Lampasas	32	18	14
	Lawrence	69	41	28		Liberty	63	45	18
	Lewis	28	13	15		Lubbock	297	138	159
	Lincoln	55	25	30		McLennan	307	103	204
	Marshall	49	22	27		Medina	58	22	36
	Maury	130	69	61		Midland	168	83	85
	McMinn	73	36	37		Montgomery	609	343	266
	McNairy	36	15	21		Nueces	302	85	217
	Meigs	28	11	17		Orange	133	60	73
	Monroe	71	36	35		Parker	108	81	27
	Moore	25	13	12		Potter	201	97	104
	Morgan	39	14	25		Randall	156	71	85
	Obion	38	26	12		Robertson	29	11	18
	Overton	54	24	30		Rockwall	104	42	62
	Perry	31	13	18		Rusk	66	38	28
	Pickett	15	10	5		San Jacinto	39	17	22
	Putnam	124	58	66		San Patricio	87	42	45
	Rhea	85	33	52		Tarrant	1,375	467	908
	Roane	71	27	44		Taylor	170	74	96
	Scott	42	21	21		Tom Green	162	54	108
	Sevier	144	84	60		Travis	1,427	738	689
	Van Buren	17	7	10		Upshur	71	34	37
	Warren	78	37	41		Victoria	183	69	114
	Wayne	44	17	27		Waller	65	33	32
	Weakley	42	21	21		Wichita	181	39	142
	White	54	25	29		Williamson	467	196	271
TEXAS-Metropolitan Counties......						Wilson	70	26	44
	Aransas	58	22	36		Wise	109	51	58
	Archer	9	7	2	TEXAS-Nonmetropolitan Counties......				
	Armstrong	6	2	4		Anderson	80	34	46
	Atascosa	72	27	45		Andrews	29	11	18
						Angelina	60	46	14

Table 80. Full-Time Law Enforcement Employees, by State by Metropolitan and Nonmetropolitan Counties, 2007 *(Contd.)*

(Number.)

State	County	Total law enforcement employees	Total officers	Total civilians	State	County	Total law enforcement employees	Total officers	Total civilians
	Bailey	23	4	19		Jackson	31	15	16
	Baylor	7	2	5		Jasper	44	15	29
	Bee	45	22	23		Jeff Davis	3	3	0
	Blanco	18	10	8		Jim Hogg	40	20	20
	Borden	3	2	1		Jim Wells	61	28	33
	Bosque	38	19	19		Karnes	18	9	9
	Brewster	19	12	7		Kenedy	16	10	6
	Briscoe	4	3	1		Kent	5	2	3
	Brooks	166	15	151		Kerr	94	43	51
	Brown	64	25	39		Kimble	15	10	5
	Burnet	84	51	33		King	2	2	0
	Camp	17	6	11		Kinney	15	6	9
	Cass	43	17	26		Kleberg	64	22	42
	Castro	19	10	9		Knox	8	3	5
	Cherokee	68	28	40		Lamar	78	27	51
	Childress	15	5	10		Lamb	31	13	18
	Cochran	13	7	6		La Salle	36	11	25
	Coke	6	4	2		Lavaca	28	11	17
	Coleman	12	6	6		Lee	16	10	6
	Collingsworth	11	4	7		Leon	40	21	19
	Colorado	42	18	24		Limestone	54	19	35
	Comanche	29	11	18		Lipscomb	9	5	4
	Concho	11	5	6		Live Oak	28	11	17
	Cooke	74	22	52		Llano	47	25	22
	Cottle	2	2	0		Loving	3	2	1
	Crane	11	7	4		Lynn	19	7	12
	Crockett	18	13	5		Madison	25	9	16
	Culberson	13	7	6		Marion	15	14	1
	Dallam	26	4	22		Martin	9	4	5
	Dawson	17	6	11		Mason	8	4	4
	Deaf Smith	34	12	22		Matagorda	69	39	30
	Dewitt	29	11	18		Maverick	101	49	52
	Dickens	6	2	4		McCulloch	12	6	6
	Dimmit	26	9	17		McMullen	4	3	1
	Donley	9	5	4		Menard	10	6	4
	Duval	44	24	20		Milam	42	10	32
	Eastland	27	9	18		Mills	9	6	3
	Edwards	10	4	6		Mitchell	10	5	5
	Erath	53	22	31		Montague	25	8	17
	Falls	11	6	5		Moore	49	17	32
	Fannin	44	24	20		Morris	24	10	14
	Fayette	39	19	20		Motley	1	1	0
	Fisher	9	5	4		Nacogdoches	96	38	58
	Floyd	7	3	4		Navarro	119	61	58
	Foard	3	2	1		Newton	21	13	8
	Franklin	23	9	14		Nolan	24	11	13
	Freestone	39	16	23		Ochiltree	19	8	11
	Frio	21	12	9		Oldham	11	6	5
	Gaines	23	12	11		Palo Pinto	47	20	27
	Garza	15	9	6		Panola	41	26	15
	Gillespie	35	20	15		Parmer	19	6	13
	Glasscock	5	3	2		Pecos	28	14	14
	Gonzales	46	17	29		Polk	82	46	36
	Gray	41	14	27		Presidio	28	5	23
	Grimes	51	25	26		Rains	20	9	11
	Hale	67	25	42		Reagan	21	8	13
	Hall	9	3	6		Real	8	3	5
	Hamilton	26	14	12		Red River	34	16	18
	Hansford	10	5	5		Reeves	385	18	367
	Hardeman	13	8	5		Refugio	38	12	26
	Harrison	84	43	41		Roberts	6	5	1
	Hartley	5	5	0		Runnels	25	7	18
	Haskell	8	3	5		Sabine	18	8	10
	Hemphill	17	10	7		San Augustine	16	6	10
	Henderson	140	73	67		San Saba	9	4	5
	Hill	70	31	39		Schleicher	11	5	6
	Hockley	26	10	16		Scurry	23	10	13
	Hood	117	39	78		Shackelford	14	5	9
	Hopkins	55	26	29		Shelby	31	14	17
	Houston	38	21	17		Sherman	9	4	5
	Howard	29	13	16		Somervell	39	20	19
	Hudspeth	39	15	24		Starr	105	35	70
	Hutchinson	29	11	18		Stephens	12	7	5
	Jack	34	11	23		Sterling	4	4	0

Table 80.   Full-Time Law Enforcement Employees, by State by Metropolitan and Nonmetropolitan Counties, 2007 *(Contd.)*

(Number.)

State	County	Total law enforcement employees	Total officers	Total civilians	State	County	Total law enforcement employees	Total officers	Total civilians
	Stonewall	7	2	5	**VIRGINIA-**				
	Sutton	14	5	9	**Metropolitan**				
	Swisher	8	3	5	**Counties**......	Albemarle County Police Department	148	120	28
	Terrell	11	4	7		Amelia	20	12	8
	Terry	38	10	28		Amherst	66	60	6
	Throckmorton	6	2	4		Appomattox	33	30	3
	Titus	56	22	34		Arlington County Police Department	448	361	87
	Tyler	29	16	13		Bedford	76	74	2
	Upton	24	10	14		Botetourt	116	95	21
	Uvalde	35	16	19		Campbell	60	57	3
	Val Verde	47	33	14		Caroline	67	48	19
	Van Zandt	67	26	41		Charles City	19	10	9
	Walker	67	32	35		Chesterfield County Police Department	566	462	104
	Ward	34	12	22		Clarke	28	17	11
	Washington	58	34	24		Craig	13	8	5
	Wharton	70	39	31		Cumberland	22	15	7
	Wheeler	10	5	5		Dinwiddie	48	40	8
	Wilbarger	18	7	11		Fairfax County Police Department	1,733	1,454	279
	Willacy	37	14	23		Fauquier	120	104	16
	Winkler	29	11	18		Fluvanna	38	25	13
	Wood	62	25	37		Franklin	95	76	19
	Yoakum	20	9	11		Frederick	118	106	12
	Young	32	12	20		Giles	33	22	11
	Zapata	106	45	61		Gloucester	117	95	22
	Zavala	30	13	17		Goochland	34	27	7
UTAH-						Greene	31	23	8
Metropolitan						Hanover	219	201	18
Counties......	Cache	147	114	33		Henrico County Police Department	737	551	186
	Davis	292	96	196		Isle of Wight	45	38	7
	Juab	25	23	2		James City County Police			
	Morgan	15	12	3		Department	97	92	5
	Salt Lake	1,202	347	855		King and Queen	17	10	7
	Summit	100	49	51		King William	34	22	12
	Tooele	91	30	61		Loudoun	541	448	93
	Utah	398	127	271		Louisa	58	45	13
	Washington	156	45	111		Mathews	19	12	7
	Weber	365	94	271		Montgomery	123	108	15
UTAH-						Nelson	20	16	4
Nonmetropolitan						New Kent	39	28	11
Counties......	Beaver	60	16	44		Pittsylvania	127	69	58
	Box Elder	77	27	50		Powhatan	50	34	16
	Carbon	45	22	23		Prince George County Police			
	Daggett	25	8	17		Department	70	54	16
	Duchesne	45	18	27		Prince William County Police			
	Emery	41	24	17		Department	632	512	120
	Garfield	27	6	21		Pulaski	52	42	10
	Grand	32	15	17		Roanoke County Police			
	Iron	78	31	47		Department	149	137	12
	Kane	27	12	15		Rockingham	166	55	111
	Millard	55	39	16		Scott	33	24	9
	Piute	3	3	0		Spotsylvania	179	142	37
	Rich	10	4	6		Stafford	202	137	65
	San Juan	36	14	22		Surry	22	13	9
	Sanpete	25	20	5		Sussex	45	40	5
	Sevier	61	31	30		Warren	89	41	48
	Uintah	49	21	28		Washington	70	52	18
	Wasatch	42	18	24		York	105	98	7
	Wayne	6	6	0	**VIRGINIA-**				
VERMONT-					**Nonmetropolitan**				
Metropolitan					**Counties**......	Accomack	68	61	7
Counties......	Franklin	24	15	9		Alleghany	59	43	16
VERMONT-						Augusta	80	68	12
Nonmetropolitan						Bath	18	13	5
Counties......	Addison	16	9	7		Bland	18	10	8
	Bennington	15	12	3		Brunswick	47	35	12
	Caledonia	5	4	1		Buchanan	44	31	13
	Essex	2	1	1		Buckingham	26	18	8
	Orange	2	2	0		Carroll	35	29	6
	Orleans	6	4	2		Charlotte	37	34	3
	Rutland	22	18	4		Culpeper	94	78	16
	Washington	11	9	2		Dickenson	28	21	7
	Windham	16	12	4		Essex	20	20	0
	Windsor	13	11	2		Floyd	27	17	10
						Grayson	24	18	6

Table 80. Full-Time Law Enforcement Employees, by State by Metropolitan and Nonmetropolitan Counties, 2007 *(Contd.)*

(Number.)

State	County	Total law enforcement employees	Total officers	Total civilians	State	County	Total law enforcement employees	Total officers	Total civilians
	Greensville	34	24	10	WEST VIRGINIA- Metropolitan Counties......				
	Halifax	43	35	8		Berkeley	83	57	26
	Henry	123	109	14		Boone	25	22	3
	Highland	11	6	5		Brooke	26	16	10
	King George	45	30	15		Cabell	48	41	7
	Lancaster	32	27	5		Clay	6	5	1
	Lee	36	36	0		Hampshire	16	14	2
	Lunenburg	21	14	7		Hancock	29	24	5
	Madison	28	17	11		Jefferson	32	27	5
	Mecklenburg	50	48	2		Kanawha	122	93	29
	Middlesex	21	15	6		Lincoln	8	8	0
	Northampton	81	66	15		Marshall	27	24	3
	Northumberland	27	16	11		Mineral	14	11	3
	Nottoway	23	14	9		Monongalia	60	33	27
	Orange	44	34	10		Morgan	10	9	1
	Page	53	47	6		Ohio	28	27	1
	Patrick	48	34	14		Pleasants	7	6	1
	Prince Edward	28	28	0		Preston	20	15	5
	Rappahannock	23	23	0		Putnam	44	37	7
	Richmond	20	12	8		Wayne	24	19	5
	Rockbridge	36	28	8		Wirt	2	2	0
	Russell	51	33	18		Wood	71	37	34
	Shenandoah	74	65	9	WEST VIRGINIA- Nonmetropolitan Counties......				
	Smyth	46	46	0		Barbour	7	5	2
	Southampton	76	66	10		Braxton	9	8	1
	Tazewell	54	47	7		Calhoun	6	3	3
	Westmoreland	30	21	9		Doddridge	5	5	0
	Wise	63	60	3		Fayette	31	26	5
	Wythe	46	39	7		Gilmer	5	5	0
WASHINGTON- Metropolitan Counties......	Asotin	11	9	2		Grant	8	8	0
	Benton	65	53	12		Greenbrier	36	30	6
	Chelan	72	59	13		Hardy	10	8	2
	Clark	224	144	80		Harrison	43	41	2
	Cowlitz	60	46	14		Jackson	22	15	7
	Douglas	36	29	7		Lewis	15	13	2
	Franklin	29	27	2		Logan	37	20	17
	King	811	500	311		Marion	39	28	11
	Kitsap	161	125	36		Mason	22	16	6
	Pierce	385	326	59		McDowell	16	16	0
	Skagit	113	57	56		Mercer	36	27	9
	Skamania	27	23	4		Mingo	21	18	3
	Snohomish	336	273	63		Monroe	6	6	0
	Spokane	193	137	56		Nicholas	25	21	4
	Thurston	115	88	27		Pendleton	4	4	0
	Whatcom	101	83	18		Pocahontas	12	7	5
	Yakima	103	69	34		Raleigh	61	45	16
WASHINGTON- Nonmetropolitan Counties......	Adams	21	18	3		Randolph	10	9	1
	Clallam	45	35	10		Ritchie	8	6	2
	Columbia	13	9	4		Roane	6	5	1
	Ferry	17	9	8		Summers	7	6	1
	Garfield	12	7	5		Taylor	14	7	7
	Grant	62	48	14		Tucker	6	4	2
	Grays Harbor	78	41	37		Tyler	11	5	6
	Island	50	42	8		Upshur	12	10	2
	Jefferson	48	22	26		Webster	4	4	0
	Kittitas	37	30	7		Wetzel	9	9	0
	Klickitat	51	33	18		Wyoming	19	18	1
	Lewis	60	42	18	WISCONSIN- Metropolitan Counties......	Brown	307	147	160
	Lincoln	30	17	13		Calumet	54	22	32
	Mason	61	44	17		Chippewa	72	58	14
	Okanogan	35	30	5		Columbia	95	46	49
	Pacific	19	13	6		Dane	536	442	94
	Pend Oreille	35	18	17		Douglas	87	31	56
	San Juan	33	18	15		Eau Claire	82	45	37
	Stevens	33	29	4		Fond du Lac	120	56	64
	Wahkiakum	11	9	2		Iowa	40	28	12
	Walla Walla	31	26	5		Kenosha	343	105	238
	Whitman	22	18	4		Kewaunee	36	34	2

Table 80.   Full-Time Law Enforcement Employees, by State by Metropolitan and Nonmetropolitan Counties, 2007 *(Contd.)*

(Number.)

State	County	Total law enforce-ment employees	Total officers	Total civilians	State	County	Total law enforce-ment employees	Total officers	Total civilians
	La Crosse	106	45	61		Pepin	17	7	10
	Marathon	181	72	109		Polk	84	37	47
	Milwaukee	883	516	367		Portage	88	46	42
	Oconto	68	30	38		Price	22	20	2
	Outagamie	203	81	122		Richland	33	33	0
	Ozaukee	103	82	21		Rusk	33	29	4
	Pierce	47	45	2		Sauk	153	115	38
	Racine	257	158	99		Sawyer	56	38	18
	Rock	187	91	96		Shawano	119	49	70
	Sheboygan	176	74	102		Taylor	41	19	22
	St. Croix	105	63	42		Trempealeau	46	44	2
	Washington	167	64	103		Vernon	54	36	18
	Waukesha	382	170	212		Vilas	70	33	37
	Winnebago	181	123	58		Walworth	229	93	136
WISCONSIN-						Washburn	40	22	18
Nonmetropolitan						Waupaca	108	47	61
Counties......	Adams	66	31	35		Waushara	67	26	41
	Ashland	45	25	20		Wood	79	53	26
	Barron	80	51	29	**WYOMING-**				
	Bayfield	46	26	20	**Metropolitan**				
	Buffalo	22	12	10	**Counties**......	Laramie	86	47	39
	Burnett	59	32	27		Natrona	56	45	11
	Clark	50	47	3	**WYOMING-**				
	Crawford	33	32	1	**Nonmetropolitan**				
	Dodge	179	77	102	**Counties**......	Albany	24	18	6
	Door	68	52	16		Big Horn	9	8	1
	Dunn	55	29	26		Campbell	61	45	16
	Florence	18	11	7		Carbon	26	17	9
	Forest	37	17	20		Converse	20	11	9
	Grant	52	30	22		Crook	14	7	7
	Green	54	31	23		Fremont	36	32	4
	Green Lake	42	18	24		Goshen	12	10	2
	Iron	18	10	8		Hot Springs	9	7	2
	Jackson	48	22	26		Johnson	13	12	1
	Jefferson	127	102	25		Lincoln	19	16	3
	Juneau	59	48	11		Niobrara	17	4	13
	Lafayette	32	20	12		Park	57	20	37
	Langlade	40	16	24		Platte	11	8	3
	Lincoln	56	29	27		Sheridan	26	20	6
	Manitowoc	97	57	40		Sublette	51	35	16
	Marinette	75	30	45		Sweetwater	100	67	33
	Marquette	43	23	20		Teton	41	22	19
	Menominee	14	11	3		Uinta	36	22	14
	Monroe	39	22	17		Washakie	9	8	1
	Oneida	83	35	48		Weston	9	7	2

Table 81. Full-Time Law Enforcement Employees, by State and Other Agencies, 2007

(Number.)

State	State/Other Agency	Unit/Office	Total law enforcement employees	Total officers	Total civilians
ALABAMA-State Agencies...............	Alabama Alcoholic Beverage Control Board		128	105	23
	Alabama Conservation Department Marine Police		71	58	13
	Alabama Department of Mental Health		4	3	1
	Alabama Public Service Commission Enforcement Division		7	7	0
	State Capitol Police		26	19	7
ALABAMA-Other Agencies	22nd Judicial Circuit Drug Task Force		6	5	1
	24th Judicial Circuit Drug and Violent Crime Task Force		5	4	1
	City of Montgomery, Housing Authority Investigative Unit		1	1	0
ALASKA-State Agencies	Alcohol Beverage Control Board		10	5	5
ALASKA-Other Agencies	Anchorage International Airport		57	55	2
	Fairbanks International Airport		25	23	2
ARIZONA-State Agencies.................	Arizona State Capitol		70	31	39
ARKANSAS-State Agencies..............	Camp Robinson		26	18	8
	State Capitol Police		22	19	3
CALIFORNIA-State Agencies	Atascadero State Hospital		124	111	13
	California State Fair		9	4	5
	Department of Parks and Recreation	Capital	676	625	51
	Napa State Hospital		102	98	4
CALIFORNIA-Other Agencies..........	East Bay Regional Parks	Alameda County	75	54	21
	Fontana Unified School District		20	12	8
	Grant Joint Union High School		27	21	6
	Monterey Peninsula Airport		7	6	1
	Port of San Diego Harbor		166	138	28
	San Bernardino Unified School District		80	26	54
	San Francisco Bay Area Rapid Transit	Contra Costa County	281	196	85
	Stockton Unified School District		25	19	6
COLORADO-State Agencies	Colorado Mental Health Institute		76	17	59
COLORADO-Other Agencies...........	Two Rivers Drug Enforcement Team		7	6	1
CONNECTICUT-State Agencies	State Capitol Police		34	27	7
DELAWARE-State Agencies..............	Attorney General:	Kent County	59	35	24
		New Castle County	274	136	138
		Sussex County	51	24	27
	Division of Alcohol and Tobacco Enforcement		18	15	3
	Environmental Control		12	10	2
	Fish and Wildlife		35	30	5
	Office of Narcotics and Dangerous Drugs		5	5	0
	Park Rangers		20	20	0
	River and Bay Authority		63	47	16
	State Capitol Police		61	38	23
	State Fire Marshal		56	19	37
DELAWARE-Other Agencies	Amtrak Police		25	11	14
	Drug Enforcement Administration	Wilmington Resident Office	11	8	3
	Wilmington Fire Department		12	12	0
DISTRICT OF COLUMBIA-Other Agencies	Metro Transit Police		501	369	132
	National Zoological Park		26	26	0
FLORIDA-State Agencies.................	Capitol Police		80	57	23
	Department of Environmental Protection, Division of Law Enforcement:	Alachua County	6	6	0
		Bay County	8	8	0
		Brevard County	5	5	0
		Broward County	4	4	0
		Charlotte County	1	1	0
		Citrus County	1	1	0
		Collier County	2	2	0
		Columbia County	1	1	0
		Duval County	13	10	3
		Escambia County	5	3	2
		Franklin County	1	1	0
		Hernando County	1	1	0
		Hillsborough County	14	9	5
		Jackson County	1	1	0
		Lake County	1	1	0
		Lee County	7	6	1
		Leon County	40	13	27
		Levy County	2	2	0
		Manatee County	2	2	0
		Marion County	2	2	0
		Martin County	1	1	0
		Miami-Dade County	10	10	0
		Monroe County	8	7	1
		Nassau County	1	1	0
		Orange County	11	8	3

Table 81. Full-Time Law Enforcement Employees, by State and Other Agencies, 2007 *(Contd.)*

(Number.)

State	State/Other Agency	Unit/Office	Total law enforcement employees	Total officers	Total civilians
		Palm Beach County	8	4	4
		Pinellas County	3	3	0
		Sarasota County	1	1	0
		Seminole County	3	3	0
		St. Johns County	1	1	0
		St. Lucie County	2	2	0
		Volusia County	7	7	0
		Wakulla County	1	1	0
		Walton County	2	2	0
	Department of Insurance:	Broward County	20	15	5
		Duval County	10	9	1
		Escambia County	9	7	2
		Hillsborough County	14	11	3
		Lee County	6	4	2
		Miami-Dade County	25	19	6
		Orange County	14	11	3
		Palm Beach County	20	16	4
		Pinellas County	10	8	2
	Department of Law Enforcement:	Duval County, Jacksonville	146	43	109
		Escambia County, Pensacola	78	23	55
		Hillsborough County, Tampa	197	59	138
		Lee County, Fort Myers	83	28	55
		Leon County, Tallahassee	976	168	808
		Miami-Dade County, Miami	183	101	82
		Orange County, Orlando	199	55	144
	Florida Game Commission		824	656	168
	State Fire Marshal		118	96	22
	State Treasurer's Office	Division of Insurance Fraud	18	10	8
FLORIDA-Other Agencies	Duval County Schools		26	11	15
	Florida School for the Deaf and Blind		18	9	9
	Fort Lauderdale Airport		142	92	50
	Jacksonville Airport Authority		45	35	10
	Lee County Port Authority		68	40	28
	Melbourne International Airport		13	12	1
	Miami-Dade County Public Schools		267	216	51
	Miccosukee Tribal		63	43	20
	Palm Beach County School District		239	165	74
	Port Everglades		166	64	102
	Sarasota-Bradenton International Airport		13	13	0
	Seminole Tribal		211	156	55
	St. Petersburg-Clearwater International Airport		7	7	0
	Tampa International Airport		157	66	91
	Volusia County Beach Management		65	61	4
GEORGIA-State Agencies	Atlanta State Farmers Market		17	17	0
	Georgia Bureau of Investigation	Headquarters	863	148	715
	Georgia Department of Transportation	Office of Investigations	3	3	0
	Georgia Public Safety Training Center		159	20	139
	Georgia World Congress		65	30	35
	Ports Authority	Savannah	71	69	2
GEORGIA-Other Agencies	Augusta Board of Education		39	37	2
	Chatham County Board of Education		43	34	9
	Cobb County Board of Education		40	37	3
	Forsyth County Fire Investigation Unit		2	2	0
	Fulton County Marshal		74	57	17
	Fulton County School System		62	60	2
	Gwinnett County Public Schools		24	20	4
	Metropolitan Atlanta Rapid Transit Authority		353	300	53
	Muscogee City Marshal		18	16	2
	Stone Mountain Park		26	22	4
ILLINOIS-State Agencies	Illinois Commerce Commission		14	7	7
	Illinois Department of Natural Resources		177	161	16
	Secretary of State Police	District 3	228	102	126
ILLINOIS-Other Agencies	Burlington Northern Santa Fe Railroad		21	17	4
	Capitol Airport Authority		4	4	0
	Chicago Fire Department	Arson Investigations	13	3	10
	Cook County Forest Preserve		106	101	5
	Crystal Lake Park District		3	3	0
	CSX Transportation		20	20	0
	Decatur Park District		5	5	0
	Du Page County Forest Preserve		29	25	4
	Elgin, Joliet and Eastern Railway		6	6	0
	John H. Stroger Hospital		53	48	5
	Lake County Forest Preserve		19	17	2
	Norfolk Southern Railway		52	51	1
	Pekin Park District		1	1	0
	Rockford Park District		17	16	1

Table 81. Full-Time Law Enforcement Employees, by State and Other Agencies, 2007

(Number.)

State	State/Other Agency	Unit/Office	Total law enforcement employees	Total officers	Total civilians
	Springfield Park District		7	5	2
	Will County Forest Preserve		12	12	0
INDIANA-State Agencies	Northern Indiana Commuter Transportation District		7	6	1
INDIANA-Other Agencies.................	St. Joseph County Airport Authority		17	17	0
KANSAS-State Agencies	Kansas Alcoholic Beverage Control		35	21	14
	Kansas Bureau of Investigation		264	84	180
	Kansas Department of Wildlife and Parks		172	171	1
	Kansas Lottery Security Division		9	5	4
	Kansas Racing Commission	Security Division	39	7	32
	Securities Office	Investigation Section	30	8	22
KANSAS-Other Agencies...................	Blue Valley School District		6	6	0
	Iowa Tribal		10	10	0
	Johnson County Park		18	17	1
	Kickapoo Tribal		13	7	6
	Metropolitan Topeka Airport Authority		25	21	4
	Shawnee Mission Public Schools		11	11	0
	Topeka Fire Department	Arson Investigation	3	3	0
	Unified School District:	Auburn-Washburn	5	1	4
		Bluestem	1	1	0
		Goddard	4	4	0
		Maize	4	3	1
		Topeka	14	13	1
	Wyandotte County Parks and Recreation		13	13	0
KENTUCKY-State Agencies...............	Alcohol Beverage Control		41	37	4
	Fish and Wildlife Enforcement		166	157	9
	Kentucky Horse Park		8	8	0
	Motor Vehicle Enforcement		244	168	76
	Park Security		70	70	0
	South Central Kentucky Drug Task Force		6	5	1
	Unlawful Narcotics Investigation	Treatment and Education	36	32	4
KENTUCKY-Other Agencies	Barren County Drug Task Force		2	1	1
	Buffalo Trace-Gateway Narcotics Task Force		3	3	0
	Cincinnati-Northern Kentucky International Airport		66	51	15
	Clark County School System		2	2	0
	Daniel Boone National Forest		12	11	1
	Fayette County Schools		30	26	4
	Greater Hardin County Narcotics Task Force		9	8	1
	Jefferson County Board of Education		26	19	7
	Lake Cumberland Area Drug Enforcement Task Force		8	7	1
	Lexington Bluegrass Airport		28	20	8
	Louisville Regional Airport Authority		38	38	0
	McCracken County Public Schools		4	4	0
	Nicholas County Schools		1	1	0
	Northern Kentucky Narcotics Enforcement Unit		3	2	1
	Pennyrile Narcotics Task Force		14	11	3
LOUISIANA-State Agencies	Department of Public Safety	State Capitol Detail	51	41	10
	Tensas Basin Levee District		6	5	1
MAINE-State Agencies........................	Drug Enforcement Agency	Lincoln County	31	29	2
MARYLAND-State Agencies	Comptroller of the Treasury	Field Enforcement Division	49	21	28
	Department of Public Safety and Correctional Services	Internal Investigations Unit	22	17	5
	General Services:	Annapolis, Anne Arundel County	76	38	38
		Baltimore City	105	43	62
	Natural Resources Police		512	269	243
	Rosewood		6	6	0
	Springfield Hospital		13	4	9
	State Fire Marshal		70	40	30
	Transit Administration		199	142	57
	Transportation Authority		590	424	166
MARYLAND-Other Agencies	Maryland-National Capital Park Police:	Montgomery County	118	94	24
		Prince George's County	123	90	33
MICHIGAN-Other Agencies	Bishop International Airport		7	7	0
	Capitol Region Airport Authority		26	16	10
	Huron-Clinton Metropolitan Authority:	Hudson Mills Metropark	4	4	0
		Kensington Metropark	10	10	0
		Lower Huron Metropark	10	10	0
		Stony Creek Metropark	11	11	0
	Wayne County Airport		135	123	12
MINNESOTA-State Agencies............	Capitol Security	St. Paul	55	11	44
MINNESOTA-Other Agencies	Minneapolis-St. Paul International Airport		117	81	36
	Three Rivers Park District		44	26	18
MISSOURI-State Agencies	Capitol Police		38	31	7
	Department of Conservation		212	198	14
	Division of Alcohol and Tobacco Control		45	41	4

Table 81. Full-Time Law Enforcement Employees, by State and Other Agencies, 2007 *(Contd.)*

(Number.)

State	State/Other Agency	Unit/Office	Total law enforcement employees	Total officers	Total civilians
	Gaming Commission	Enforcement Division	112	110	2
	State Fire Marshal		22	20	2
	State Park Rangers		51	50	1
	State Water Patrol		118	102	16
MISSOURI-Other Agencies...............	Bootheel Drug Task Force		6	6	0
	Clay County Drug Task Force		5	5	0
	Clay County Park Authority		7	7	0
	Jackson County Drug Task Force		4	2	2
	Jackson County Park Rangers		16	14	2
	Lambert-St. Louis International Airport		101	87	14
	St. Charles County Park Rangers		12	12	0
	St. Peters Ranger Division		5	5	0
MONTANA-State Agencies...............	Gambling Investigations Bureau		24	21	3
NEVADA-State Agencies..................	Taxicab Authority		62	36	26
NEVADA-Other Agencies.................	Clark County School District		190	150	40
	Washoe County School District		42	38	4
NEW HAMPSHIRE-					
State Agencies......................................	Liquor Commission		35	21	14
NEW JERSEY-State Agencies...........	Department of Human Services		141	133	8
	Human Services	Woodland Township	4	4	0
	Hunterdon Developmental Center		7	7	0
	New Jersey Transit Police		261	194	67
	Palisades Interstate Parkway		25	23	2
NEW JERSEY-Other Agencies	Park Police:	Camden County	21	20	1
		Morris County	34	33	1
		Union County	368	319	49
	Prosecutor:	Atlantic County	167	72	95
		Bergen County	252	170	82
		Burlington County	148	86	62
		Camden County	246	165	81
		Cape May County	75	33	42
		Cumberland County	96	33	63
		Essex County	443	305	138
		Gloucester County	95	35	60
		Hudson County	223	99	124
		Hunterdon County	56	23	33
		Mercer County	165	105	60
		Middlesex County	202	81	121
		Monmouth County	274	79	195
		Morris County	155	69	86
		Ocean County	170	77	93
		Passaic County	224	93	131
		Salem County	45	17	28
		Somerset County	118	50	68
		Sussex County	52	33	19
		Union County	251	78	173
		Warren County	57	18	39
NEW MEXICO-Other Agencies	Acoma Tribal		19	13	6
	Laguna Tribal		40	20	20
	Zuni Tribal		27	16	11
NEW YORK-State Agencies..............	State Park	Taconic Region	17	15	2
NEW YORK-Other Agencies.............	New York City Metropolitan Transportation Authority		726	676	50
	Onondaga County Parks		1	1	0
	Suffolk County Parks		43	40	3
NORTH CAROLINA-					
State Agencies......................................	Caswell Center Hospital		4	4	0
	Department of Human Resources		11	9	2
	Department of Wildlife		231	209	22
	Division of Alcohol Law Enforcement		133	113	20
	Dorthea Dix Hospital		14	6	8
	North Carolina Arboretum		4	4	0
	State Capitol Police		75	57	18
	State Fairgrounds		5	1	4
	State Park Rangers:	Carolina Beach	5	3	2
		Cliffs of the Neuse	3	2	1
		Crowders Mountain	8	6	2
		Dismal Swamp	6	2	4
		Elk Knob	5	3	2
		Eno River	10	6	4
		Falls Lake Recreation Area	20	18	2
		Fort Macon	6	5	1
		Goose Creek	2	2	0
		Gorges	3	3	0
		Hammocks Beach	5	4	1
		Hanging Rock	8	6	2

Table 81.   Full-Time Law Enforcement Employees, by State and Other Agencies, 2007 *(Contd.)*

(Number.)

State	State/Other Agency	Unit/Office	Total law enforcement employees	Total officers	Total civilians
		Jockey's Ridge	7	4	3
		Jones Lake	8	5	3
		Jordan Lake State Recreation Area	18	14	4
		Kerr Lake	14	12	2
		Lake James	5	2	3
		Lake Norman	8	4	4
		Lake Waccamaw	5	1	4
		Lumber River	5	5	0
		Medoc Mountain	2	2	0
		Merchants Millpond	4	4	0
		Morrow Mountain	8	5	3
		Mt. Mitchell	5	3	2
		New River-Mount Jefferson	9	7	2
		Pettigrew	3	3	0
		Pilot Mountain	8	4	4
		Raven Rock	4	3	1
		Singletary Lake	5	2	3
		South Mountains	13	7	6
		Stone Mountain	7	7	0
		Weymouth Woods Sandhills Nature Preserve	4	3	1
NORTH CAROLINA- **Other Agencies**	Asheville Regional Airport		17	12	5
	Durham County Alcohol Beverage Control Law Enforcement Office		3	3	0
	Nash County Alcohol Beverage Control Enforcement		2	2	0
	Piedmont Triad International Airport		27	19	8
	Raleigh-Durham International Airport		33	30	3
	Triad Alcohol Beverage Control Law Enforcement		7	6	1
	Wilmington International Airport		14	10	4
OHIO-State Agencies	Ohio Department of Natural Resources		459	350	109
OHIO-Other Agencies	Cleveland Lakefront State Parks		15	15	0
	Butler County Metroparks		3	3	0
	Cedar Point		12	12	0
	Cleveland Metropolitan Park District		82	71	11
	Columbus and Franklin County Metropolitan Park District		31	31	0
	Delaware County Preservation Parks		5	5	0
	Greater Cleveland Regional Transit Authority		103	89	14
	Hamilton County Park District		34	31	3
	Johnny Appleseed Metropolitan Park District		8	8	0
	Lake Metroparks		14	12	2
	Lorain County Metropolitan Park District		14	14	0
	Port Columbus International Airport		61	44	17
	Sandusky County Park District		5	5	0
	Toledo-Lucas County Port Authority		11	11	0
	Toledo Metropolitan Park District		25	25	0
	Wood County Park District		6	6	0
OKLAHOMA-State Agencies	Capitol Park Police		66	32	34
OKLAHOMA-Other Agencies	Jenks Public Schools		7	6	1
	Madill Public Schools		1	1	0
	McAlester Public Schools		2	2	0
	Norman Public Schools		4	4	0
	Putnam City Campus		12	8	4
OREGON-State Agencies	Liquor Commission:	Benton County	1	1	0
		Clatsop County	2	1	1
		Coos County	2	1	1
		Douglas County	2	1	1
		Jackson County	7	6	1
		Klamath County	1	1	0
		Lane County	5	4	1
		Lincoln County	2	1	1
		Malheur County	1	1	0
		Marion County	5	4	1
		Multnomah County	22	19	3
		Umatilla County	2	2	0
		Washington County	2	2	0
OREGON-Other Agencies	Port of Portland		66	53	13
PENNSYLVANIA- **State Agencies**	Bureau of Forestry:	Beaver County	1	1	0
		Bedford County	1	1	0
		Berks County	1	1	0
		Blair County	1	1	0
		Bradford County	1	1	0

Table 81.   Full-Time Law Enforcement Employees, by State and Other Agencies, 2007 *(Contd.)*

(Number.)

State	State/Other Agency	Unit/Office	Total law enforcement employees	Total officers	Total civilians
		Bucks County	1	1	0
		Cambria County	1	1	0
		Carbon County	1	1	0
		Centre County	1	1	0
		Chester County	1	1	0
		Clarion County	1	1	0
		Clearfield County	1	1	0
		Clinton County	1	1	0
		Cumberland County	1	1	0
		Dauphin County	1	1	0
		Elk County	1	1	0
		Fayette County	1	1	0
		Franklin County	1	1	0
		Fulton County	1	1	0
		Huntingdon County	1	1	0
		Indiana County	1	1	0
		Jefferson County	1	1	0
		Lackawanna County	1	1	0
		Lancaster County	1	1	0
		Lehigh County	1	1	0
		Luzerne County	1	1	0
		Mckean County	1	1	0
		Northampton County	1	1	0
		Northumberland County	1	1	0
		Perry County	1	1	0
		Pike County	1	1	0
		Potter County	1	1	0
		Schuylkill County	1	1	0
		Somerset County	1	1	0
		Susquehanna County	1	1	0
		Wayne County	1	1	0
		York County	1	1	0
	Bureau of Narcotics:	Adams County	17	14	3
		Chester County	28	2	26
		Delaware County	28	2	26
		Erie County	15	12	3
		Forest County	13	11	2
		Lehigh County	18	15	3
		Luzerne County	19	15	4
		Philadelphia County	28	2	26
		Westmoreland County	30	23	7
	Department of Environmental Resources		12	5	7
	State Capitol Police		141	132	9
	State Park Police	Pymatuning	3	3	0
PENNSYLVANIA- **Other Agencies**	Allegheny County District Attorney	Criminal Investigation Division	27	24	3
	Allegheny County Port Authority		56	41	15
	Altoona Hospital		19	18	1
	Bangor Area School District		3	3	0
	Canadian Pacific Railway		2	2	0
	County Detective:	Berks County	34	34	0
		Bucks County	20	16	4
		Butler County	3	3	0
		Chester County	24	21	3
		Dauphin County	13	10	3
		Lebanon County	7	6	1
		Lehigh County	14	13	1
		Pike County	2	2	0
		Schuylkill County	7	7	0
		Westmoreland County	57	15	42
		York County	11	10	1
	Delaware County District Attorney	Criminal Investigation Division	38	32	6
	Delaware County Park		60	59	1
	Erie City School District		2	2	0
	Harrisburg International Airport		25	14	11
	Tyrone Area School District		1	1	0
	Uniontown Hospital		11	11	0
	Washington County Alternative Education		1	1	0
	Westmoreland County Park		21	21	0
	Wilkes-Barre Area School District		4	4	0
RHODE ISLAND- **State Agencies**	Department of Environmental Management		43	35	8
SOUTH CAROLINA- **State Agencies**	Bureau of Protective Services		77	71	6
	Department of Mental Health		115	70	45

Table 81. Full-Time Law Enforcement Employees, by State and Other Agencies, 2007 *(Contd.)*

(Number.)

State	State/Other Agency	Unit/Office	Total law enforcement employees	Total officers	Total civilians
	Department of Natural Resources:	Abbeville County	3	3	0
		Aiken County	4	4	0
		Allendale County	3	3	0
		Anderson County	4	4	0
		Bamberg County	3	3	0
		Barnwell County	4	4	0
		Beaufort County	8	8	0
		Berkeley County	8	8	0
		Calhoun County	3	3	0
		Charleston County	27	27	0
		Cherokee County	4	4	0
		Chester County	3	3	0
		Chesterfield County	3	3	0
		Clarendon County	6	6	0
		Colleton County	6	6	0
		Darlington County	4	4	0
		Dillon County	2	2	0
		Dorchester County	6	6	0
		Edgefield County	3	3	0
		Fairfield County	3	3	0
		Florence County	4	4	0
		Georgetown County	9	9	0
		Greenville County	4	4	0
		Greenwood County	5	5	0
		Hampton County	4	4	0
		Horry County	9	9	0
		Jasper County	3	3	0
		Kershaw County	5	5	0
		Lancaster County	3	3	0
		Laurens County	4	4	0
		Lee County	2	2	0
		Lexington County	4	4	0
		Marion County	3	3	0
		Marlboro County	4	4	0
		McCormick County	5	5	0
		Newberry County	5	5	0
		Oconee County	5	5	0
		Orangeburg County	5	5	0
		Pickens County	5	5	0
		Richland County	32	32	0
		Saluda County	4	4	0
		Spartanburg County	5	5	0
		Sumter County	4	4	0
		Union County	3	3	0
		Williamsburg County	6	6	0
		York County	4	4	0
	Employment Security Commission		4	4	0
	Forestry Commission:	Bamberg County	1	1	0
		Barnwell County	1	1	0
		Beaufort County	1	1	0
		Berkeley County	1	1	0
		Calhoun County	1	1	0
		Charleston County	1	1	0
		Chesterfield County	3	3	0
		Colleton County	1	1	0
		Darlington County	1	1	0
		Fairfield County	1	1	0
		Florence County	1	1	0
		Greenville County	2	2	0
		Hampton County	2	2	0
		Horry County	2	2	0
		Kershaw County	3	3	0
		Lexington County	2	2	0
		Oconee County	1	1	0
		Orangeburg County	1	1	0
		Pickens County	2	2	0
		Richland County	1	1	0
		Sumter County	3	3	0
		Williamsburg County	2	2	0
	South Carolina School for the Deaf and Blind		1	1	0
	State Museum		4	3	1
	State Ports Authority		81	39	42
	State Transport Police:	Abbeville County	12	12	0
		Aiken County	49	31	18
		Allendale County	11	11	0
		Anderson County	19	16	3

Table 81. Full-Time Law Enforcement Employees, by State and Other Agencies, 2007 *(Contd.)*

(Number.)

State	State/Other Agency	Unit/Office	Total law enforcement employees	Total officers	Total civilians
		Berkeley County	18	15	3
		Cherokee County	11	11	0
		Darlington County	13	13	0
	United States Department of Energy	Savannah River Plant	59	47	12
SOUTH CAROLINA-Other Agencies......................................	Charleston County Aviation Authority		40	29	11
	Columbia Metropolitan Airport		25	20	5
	Greenville-Spartanburg International Airport		21	16	5
	Whitten Center		2	2	0
SOUTH DAKOTA-State Agencies......................................	Division of Criminal Investigation		144	44	100
TENNESSEE-State Agencies..............	Alcoholic Beverage Commission		61	36	25
	Department of Correction	Internal Affairs	13	9	4
	State Fire Marshal		30	25	5
	State Park Rangers:	Bicentennial Capitol Mall	7	5	2
		Big Hill Pond	5	3	2
		Big Ridge	9	4	5
		Bledsoe Creek	2	2	0
		Booker T. Washington	3	3	0
		Burgess Falls Natural Area	2	2	0
		Cedars of Lebanon	4	4	0
		Chickasaw	4	4	0
		Cove Lake	13	4	9
		Cumberland Mountain	4	4	0
		Cumberland Trail	5	5	0
		David Crockett	4	4	0
		David Crockett Birthplace	3	3	0
		Dunbar Cave Natural Area	4	3	1
		Edgar Evins	4	4	0
		Fall Creek Falls	8	8	0
		Fort Loudon State Historic Park	5	4	1
		Fort Pillow State Historic Park	2	2	0
		Frozen Head Natural Area	6	3	3
		Harpeth Scenic Rivers	3	3	0
		Harrison Bay	5	5	0
		Henry Horton	4	4	0
		Hiwassee/Ocoee State Scenic Rivers	8	6	2
		Indian Mountain	2	2	0
		Johnsonville State Historic Park	1	1	0
		Long Hunter	3	3	0
		Meeman-Shelby Forest	6	6	0
		Montgomery Bell	4	4	0
		Mousetail Landing	3	3	0
		Natchez Trace	5	5	0
		Nathan Bedford Forrest	3	3	0
		Norris Dam	4	4	0
		Old Stone Fort State Archaeological Area	4	4	0
		Panther Creek	3	3	0
		Paris Landing	6	6	0
		Pickett	4	4	0
		Pickwick Landing	5	5	0
		Pinson Mounds State Archaeological Park	2	2	0
		Radnor Lake Natural Area	8	6	2
		Red Clay State Historic Park	2	2	0
		Reelfoot Lake	4	4	0
		Roan Mountain	4	4	0
		Rock Island	4	4	0
		Sgt. Alvin C. York	1	1	0
		South Cumberland Recreation Area	6	6	0
		Standing Stone	4	4	0
		Sycamore Shoals State Historic Park	2	2	0
		Tim's Ford	4	4	0
		T.O. Fuller	3	3	0
		Warrior's Path	4	4	0
	TennCare Office of Inspector General		59	17	42
	Tennessee Bureau of Investigation		474	181	293
	Tennessee Department of Revenue	Special Investigations Unit	54	30	24
	Wildlife Resources Agency:	Region 1	40	40	0
		Region 2	63	56	7
		Region 3	43	43	0
		Region 4	45	45	0
TENNESSEE-Other Agencies............	Chattanooga Metropolitan Airport		10	10	0
	Dickson Parks and Recreation		8	3	5
	Drug Task Force:	3rd Judicial District	7	6	1
		4th Judicial District	2	1	1
		5th Judicial District	5	4	1

Table 81. Full-Time Law Enforcement Employees, by State and Other Agencies, 2007 *(Contd.)*

(Number.)

State	State/Other Agency	Unit/Office	Total law enforcement employees	Total officers	Total civilians
		8th Judicial District	2	1	1
		9th Judicial District	1	1	0
		10th Judicial District	14	12	2
		12th Judicial District	3	2	1
		13th Judicial District	2	1	1
		14th Judicial District	2	2	0
		17th Judicial District	6	5	1
		18th Judicial District	8	7	1
		19th Judicial District	6	5	1
		21st Judicial District	12	10	2
		22nd Judicial District	3	3	0
		23rd Judicial District	8	7	1
		25th Judicial District	1	1	0
	Knoxville Metropolitan Airport		43	27	16
	Memphis International Airport		62	49	13
	Metropolitan Board of Parks and Recreation	Nashville-Davidson	26	25	1
	Nashville International Airport		95	67	28
	Smyrna/Rutherford County Airport Authority		4	4	0
	Tri-Cities Regional Airport		17	16	1
	West Tennessee Violent Crime Task Force		7	6	1
TEXAS-Other Agencies	Amarillo International Airport		15	15	0
	Cameron County Park Rangers		11	11	0
	Dallas-Fort Worth International Airport		369	253	116
	Hospital District:	Dallas County	77	49	28
		Tarrant County	53	35	18
	Houston Metropolitan Transit Authority		267	205	62
	Independent School District:	Aldine	45	41	4
		Alvin	22	16	6
		Angleton	4	3	1
		Austin	100	67	33
		Bay City	6	5	1
		Brownsville	124	28	96
		Cedar Hill	16	7	9
		Conroe	60	46	14
		Corpus Christi	54	32	22
		East Central	10	8	2
		Ector County	30	28	2
		El Paso	48	40	8
		Fort Bend	58	49	9
		Hempstead	3	3	0
		Humble	27	21	6
		Judson	22	20	2
		Katy	41	33	8
		Kaufman	5	4	1
		Killeen	12	12	0
		Klein	43	26	17
		Laredo	106	24	82
		Mexia	3	3	0
		Midland	19	10	9
		North East	58	52	6
		Pasadena	38	31	7
		Raymondville	4	4	0
		Socorro	80	28	52
		Spring	40	38	2
		Spring Branch	36	28	8
		Taft	2	2	0
		Tyler	18	13	5
		United	154	53	101
UTAH-State Agencies	Parks and Recreation		83	82	1
	Wildlife Resources		71	64	7
UTAH-Other Agencies	Granite School District		40	17	23
	Utah County Attorney	Investigations Division	7	5	2
	Utah County Major Crime Task Force		1	1	0
	Utah Transit Authority		20	20	0
VERMONT-State Agencies	Attorney General		6	4	2
	Department of Liquor Control	Division of Enforcement and Licensing	22	18	4
	Department of Motor Vehicles		43	33	10
	Fish and Wildlife Department	Law Enforcement Division	42	40	2
VIRGINIA-State Agencies	Alcoholic Beverage Control Commission		170	131	39
	Department of Conservation and Recreation		259	112	147
	Southside Virginia Training Center		21	17	4
	Virginia State Capitol		88	74	14
VIRGINIA-Other Agencies	Chesapeake Bay Bridge-Tunnel		77	38	39
	Norfolk Airport Authority		44	37	7
	Port Authority	Norfolk	88	81	7
	Reagan National Airport		236	172	64
	Richmond International Airport		32	32	0

Table 81. Full-Time Law Enforcement Employees, by State and Other Agencies, 2007 *(Contd.)*

(Number.)

State	State/Other Agency	Unit/Office	Total law enforcement employees	Total officers	Total civilians
WASHINGTON-Other Agencies	Colville Tribal		37	25	12
	Lummi Tribal		20	18	2
	Nisqually Tribal		12	9	3
	Nooksack Tribal		7	6	1
	Port of Seattle		124	100	24
	Skokomish Tribal		10	9	1
	Swinomish Tribal		13	11	2
WEST VIRGINIA-State Agencies......................................	Capitol Protective Services		28	22	6
	Department of Natural Resources:	Barbour County	1	1	0
		Berkeley County	2	2	0
		Boone County	1	1	0
		Braxton County	3	3	0
		Brooke County	1	1	0
		Cabell County	1	1	0
		Calhoun County	1	1	0
		Clay County	2	2	0
		Doddridge County	1	1	0
		Fayette County	2	2	0
		Gilmer County	1	1	0
		Grant County	1	1	0
		Greenbrier County	2	2	0
		Hampshire County	5	4	1
		Hancock County	1	1	0
		Hardy County	1	1	0
		Harrison County	3	3	0
		Jackson County	1	1	0
		Jefferson County	1	1	0
		Kanawha County	14	10	4
		Lewis County	2	2	0
		Lincoln County	2	2	0
		Logan County	2	2	0
		Marion County	6	5	1
		Marshall County	1	1	0
		Mason County	1	1	0
		McDowell County	1	1	0
		Mercer County	2	2	0
		Mineral County	2	2	0
		Mingo County	1	1	0
		Monongalia County	1	1	0
		Monroe County	1	1	0
		Morgan County	1	1	0
		Nicholas County	2	2	0
		Ohio County	1	1	0
		Pendleton County	3	3	0
		Pleasants County	1	1	0
		Pocahontas County	2	2	0
		Preston County	2	2	0
		Putnam County	6	5	1
		Raleigh County	6	6	0
		Randolph County	5	4	1
		Ritchie County	1	1	0
		Roane County	1	1	0
		Summers County	4	3	1
		Taylor County	1	1	0
		Tucker County	2	2	0
		Tyler County	1	1	0
		Upshur County	3	3	0
		Wayne County	2	2	0
		Webster County	3	3	0
		Wetzel County	1	1	0
		Wirt County	1	1	0
		Wood County	7	6	1
		Wyoming County	2	2	0
	State Fire Marshal	Kanawha County	41	32	9
WEST VIRGINIA-Other Agencies......................................	Kanawha County Parks and Recreation		5	5	0
WISCONSIN-State Agencies	Capitol Police		46	41	5
	Department of Natural Resources		221	192	29
WISCONSIN-Other Agencies.............	Lac du Flambeau Tribal		11	9	2
	Menominee Tribal		39	21	18
	Oneida Tribal		21	20	1
PUERTO RICO AND OTHER OUTLYING AREAS	Guam		375	309	66
	Puerto Rico		18,697	17,007	1,690
FEDERAL AGENCY.......................	National Institutes of Health		104	83	21

SECTION VI:
HATE CRIMES

HATE CRIMES

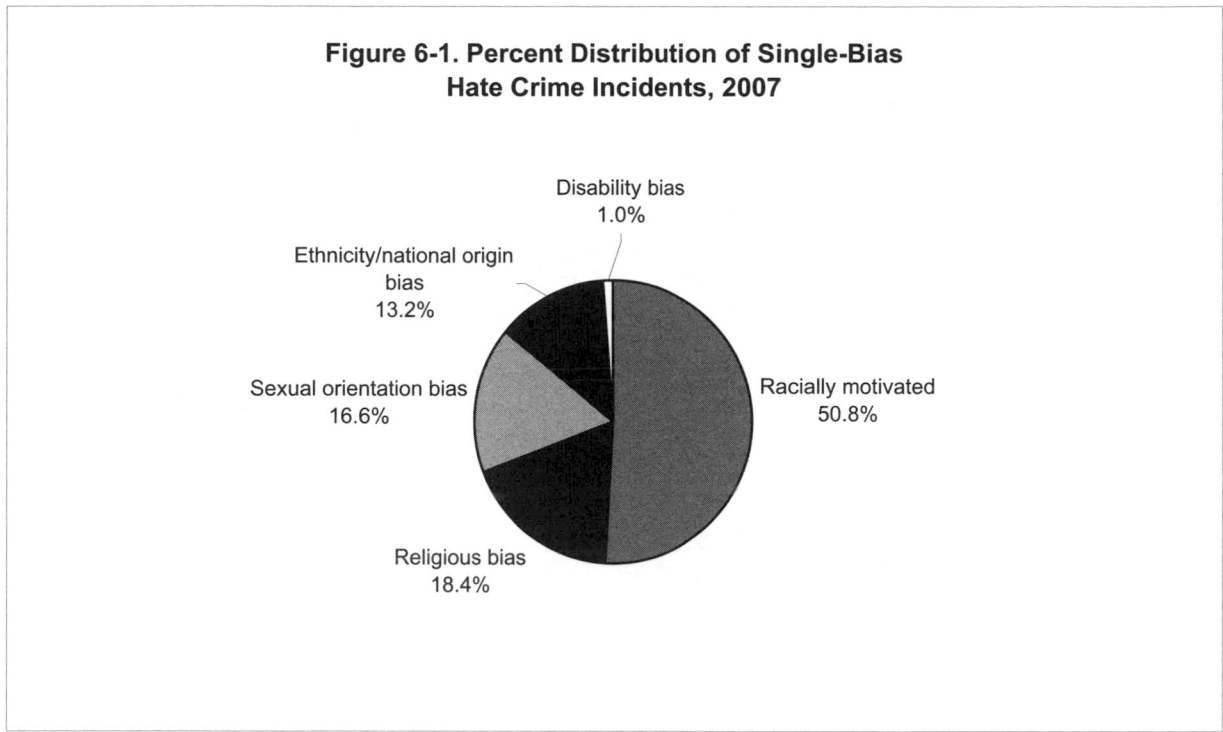

**Figure 6-1. Percent Distribution of Single-Bias
Hate Crime Incidents, 2007**

Disability bias
1.0%

Ethnicity/national origin
bias
13.2%

Sexual orientation bias
16.6%

Racially motivated
50.8%

Religious bias
18.4%

The Federal Bureau of Investigation (FBI) began the procedures for implementing, collecting, and managing hate crime data after Congress passed the Hate Crime Statistics Act in 1990 which required the collection of data "about crimes that manifest evidence of prejudice based on race, religion, sexual orientation, or ethnicity." In 1994, the Hate Crime Statistics Act was amended to include bias against persons with disabilities.

Definition

Hate crimes include any crime motivated by bias against race, religion, sexual orientation, ethnicity/national origin, and/or disability. Because motivation is subjective, it is sometimes difficult to know with certainty whether a crime resulted from the offender's bias. Moreover, the presence of bias alone does not necessarily mean that a crime can be considered a hate crime. Only when law enforcement investigation reveals sufficient evidence to lead a reasonable and prudent person to conclude that the offender's actions were motivated, in whole or in part, by his or her bias, should an incident be reported as a hate crime.

Data Collection

The UCR (Uniform Crime Reporting) Program collects data about both single-bias and multiple-bias hate crimes. A single-bias incident is defined as an incident in which one or more offense types are motivated by the same bias. A multiple-bias incident is defined as an incident in which

more than one offense type occurs and at least two offense types are motivated by different biases.

Agencies that participated in the Hate Crime program in 2007 represented over 260 million inhabitants, or 86.3 percent of the Nation's population, and their jurisdictions covered 49 states and the District of Columbia. The law enforcement agencies that voluntarily participate in the Hate Crime program collect details about an offender's bias motivation associated with 11 offense types already being reported to the UCR Program: murder and nonnegligent manslaughter, forcible rape, aggravated assault, simple assault, and intimidation (crimes against persons); and robbery, burglary, larceny-theft, motor vehicle theft, arson, and destruction/damage/vandalism (crimes against property). The law enforcement agencies that participate in the UCR Program via the National Incident-Based Reporting System (NIBRS) collect data about additional offenses for *crimes against persons* and *crimes against property*. These data appear in the category of other. These agencies also collect hate crime data for the category called *crimes against society*, which includes drug or narcotic offenses, gambling offenses, prostitution offenses, and weapon law violations.

National Volume and Percent Distribution

In 2007, 2,025 law enforcement agencies reported 7,624 hate crime incidents involving 9,006 offenses. Of these, 7,621 were single-bias offenses. An analysis of the single-bias incidents revealed 50.8 percent were racially motivated, 18.4 percent were motivated by religious bias, 16.6 percent resulted from sexual-orientation bias, 13.2 percent were based on an ethnicity/national origin bias and 1.0 percent were prompted by a disability bias. (Table 82)

The majority of the hate crime offenses that were racially motivated resulted from an anti-Black bias (69.3 percent) followed by an anti-White basis (18.4 percent). Bias against people of more than one race accounted for 6.0 percent of offenses while an anti-Asian/Pacific Islander bias accounted for 4.6 percent of racially motivated offenses. (Table 82)

Hate crimes motivated by religious bias accounted for 1,477 offenses reported by law enforcement. A breakdown of these offenses revealed 68.4 percent were motivated by an anti-Jewish bias, 9.0 percent by an anti-Islamic bias, 4.4 percent an anti-Catholic bias, 4.3 percent were anti-multiple religions or groups, 4.0 percent were anti-Protestant, 0.4 percent were anti-Atheism and the remainder of offenses were based on a bias against other religions. (Table 82)

Nearly as many hate crimes were motivated by sexual-orientation as were motivated by religion in 2007. Of the 1,460 offenses based on sexual–orientation, 59.2 percent were classified as having an anti-male homosexual bias, 24.8 percent had an anti-homosexual bias, 12.6 percent had an anti-female homosexual basis, 1.8 percent had an anti-heterosexual bias and 1.6 percent had an anti-bisexual bias. (Table 82)

The vast majority of 1,256 offenses that were committed on the perceived ethnicity or national origin of the victim had an anti-Hispanic basis (61.7 percent). The remaining 38.3 percent were based on a bias against another ethnicity or national origin. (Table 82)

Other hate crimes offenses were committed based on a disability basis. Over 75 percent were classified as anti-mental disability, with the rest being classified as anti-physical disability. (Table 82)

Crimes Against Persons

Law enforcement agencies reported 5,408 hate crimes against persons in 2007. Nearly half of them (47.4 percent) involved intimidation, 31.1 percent involved simple assault, and 20.6 percent involved aggravated assault. In addition, there were 9 murders and 2 forcible rapes. (Table 83)

Crimes Against Property

In 2007, there were 3,579 hate crimes against property. Over 81 percent of offenses involved destruction/damage or vandalism. The remaining 18.6 percent of crimes against property consisted of robbery, burglary, larceny-theft, motor vehicle theft, arson, and other crimes. (Table 83)

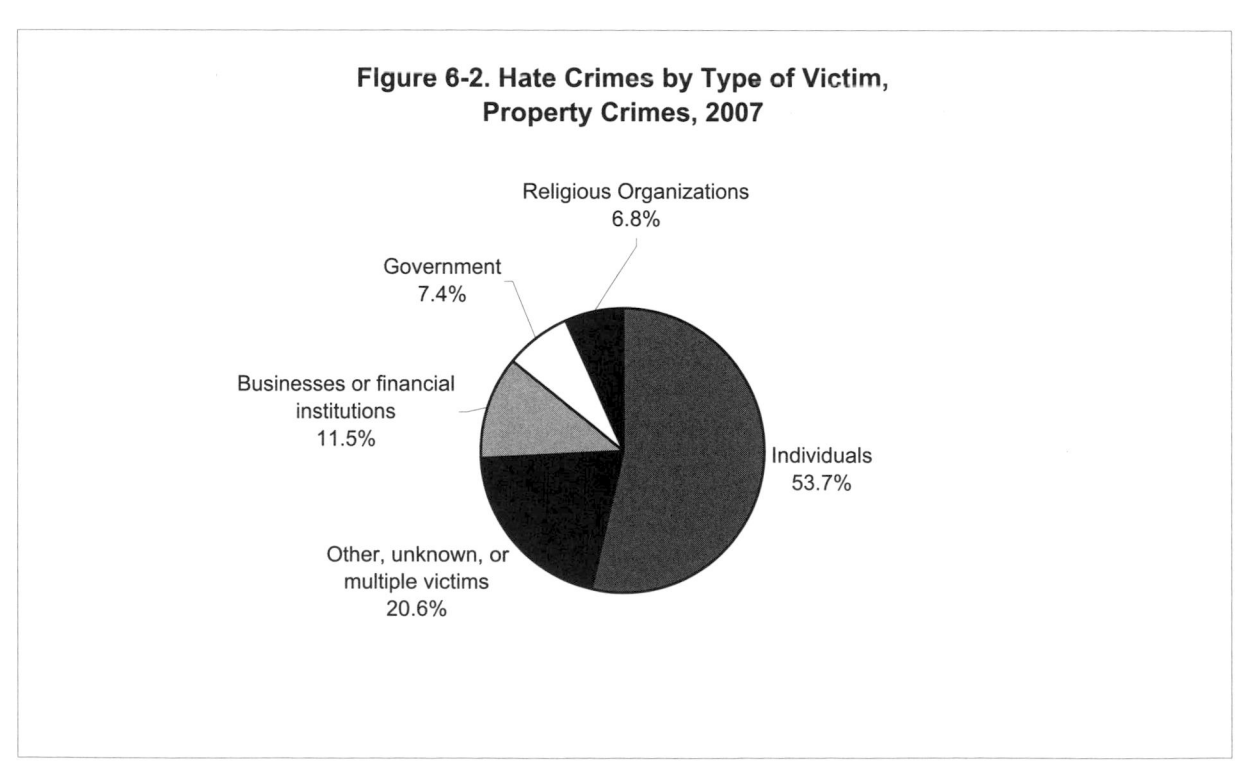

Figure 6-2. Hate Crimes by Type of Victim, Property Crimes, 2007

Religious Organizations 6.8%
Government 7.4%
Businesses or financial institutions 11.5%
Other, unknown, or multiple victims 20.6%
Individuals 53.7%

Table 82. Incidents, Offenses, Victims, and Known Offenders, by Bias Motivation, 2007

(Number.)

Bias motivation	Incidents	Offenses	Victims[1]	Known offenders[2]
TOTAL	7,624	9,006	9,535	6,965
Single-Bias Incidents	7,621	8,999	9,527	6,962
Race:	3,870	4,724	4,956	3,707
Anti-White	749	871	908	828
Anti-Black	2,658	3,275	3,434	2,509
Anti-American Indian/Alaskan Native	61	75	76	63
Anti-Asian/Pacific Islander	188	219	234	165
Anti-Multiple Races, Group	214	284	304	142
Religion:	1,400	1,477	1,628	576
Anti-Jewish	969	1,010	1,127	320
Anti-Catholic	61	65	70	31
Anti-Protestant	57	59	67	22
Anti-Islamic	115	133	142	104
Anti-Other Religion	130	140	148	62
Anti-Multiple Religions, Group	62	64	66	32
Anti-Atheism/Agnosticism/etc.	6	6	8	5
Sexual Orientation:	1,265	1,460	1,512	1,454
Anti-Male Homosexual	772	864	890	923
Anti-Female Homosexual	145	184	197	147
Anti-Homosexual	304	362	375	349
Anti-Heterosexual	22	27	27	19
Anti-Bisexual	22	23	23	16
Ethnicity/National Origin:	1,007	1,256	1,347	1,155
Anti-Hispanic	595	775	830	758
Anti-Other Ethnicity/National Origin	412	481	517	397
Disability:	79	82	84	70
Anti-Physical	20	20	20	27
Anti-Mental	59	62	64	43
Multiple-Bias Incidents[3]	3	7	8	3

[1]The term *victim* may refer to a person, business, institution, or society as a whole.

[2]The term *known offender* does not imply that the identity of the suspect is known, but only that an attribute of the suspect has been identified, which distinguishes him/her from an unknown offender.

[3]In a *multiple-bias incident,* two conditions must be met: (a) more than one offense type must occur in the incident and (b) at least two offense types must be motivated by different biases.

Table 83. Incidents, Offenses, Victims, and Known Offenders, by Offense Type, 2007

(Number.)

Offense type	Incidents[1]	Offenses	Victims[2]	Known offenders[3]
TOTAL	7,624	9,006	9,535	6,965
Crimes against persons:	4,347	5,408	5,408	5,542
Murder and nonnegligent manslaughter	9	9	9	14
Forcible rape	2	2	2	4
Aggravated assault	853	1,116	1,116	1,409
Simple assault	1,410	1,684	1,684	2,052
Intimidation	2,045	2,565	2,565	2,026
Other[4]	28	32	32	37
Crimes against property:	3,579	3,579	4,108	1,826
Robbery	178	178	236	392
Burglary	159	159	193	130
Larceny-theft	221	221	230	126
Motor vehicle theft	22	22	27	4
Arson	40	40	47	33
Destruction/damage/vandalism	2,915	2,915	3,328	1,108
Other[4]	44	44	47	33
Crimes against society[4]	19	19	19	25

[1]The actual number of incidents is 7,624. However, the column figures will not add to the total because incidents may include more than one offense type, and these are counted in each appropriate offense type category.

[2]The term *victim* may refer to a person, business, institution, or society as a whole.

[3]The term *known offender* does not imply that the identity of the suspect is known, but only that an attribute of the suspect has been identified, which distinguishes him/her from an unknown offender. The actual number of known offenders is 6,965. However, the column figures will not add to the total because some offenders are responsible for more than one offense type, and they are, therefore, counted more than once in this table.

[4]Includes additional offenses collected in the NIBRS.

Table 84.   Known Offender's Race, by Offense Type, 2007

(Number.)

Offense type	Total offenses	Known offender's race						Unknown offender
		White	Black	American Indian/ Alaskan Native	Asian/Pacific Islander	Multiple races, group	Unknown race	
TOTAL	9,006	3,802	1,045	75	41	194	600	3,249
Crimes against persons:	5,408	3,191	844	65	33	172	291	812
Murder and nonnegligent manslaughter	9	6	3	0	0	0	0	0
Forcible rape	2	1	1	0	0	0	0	0
Aggravated assault	1,116	752	212	14	11	45	32	50
Simple assault	1,684	974	388	30	15	84	69	124
Intimidation	2,565	1,438	235	21	7	42	188	634
Other[1]	32	20	5	0	0	1	2	4
Crimes against property:	3,579	602	197	10	7	21	307	2,435
Robbery	178	64	85	3	2	6	2	16
Burglary	159	45	12	0	0	1	14	87
Larceny-theft	221	43	29	0	0	2	24	123
Motor vehicle theft	22	1	1	1	0	0	1	18
Arson	40	13	4	0	0	0	3	20
Destruction/damage/vandalism	2,915	417	61	5	4	12	260	2,156
Other[1]	44	19	5	1	1	0	3	15
Crimes against society[1]	19	9	4	0	1	1	2	2

[1]Includes additional offenses collected in the NIBRS.

Table 85. Number of Offenses and Offense Type, by Bias Motivation, 2007

(Number.)

Bias motivation	Total offenses	Crimes against persons						Other[1]
		Murder and nonnegligent manslaughter	Forcible rape	Aggravated assault	Simple assault	Intimidation		
TOTAL	9,006	9	2	1,116	1,684	2,565		32
Single-Bias Incidents	8,999	9	2	1,116	1,683	2,561		32
Race:	4,724	2	1	623	845	1,546		14
Anti-White	871	0	1	107	246	190		8
Anti-Black	3,275	1	0	450	518	1,186		6
Anti-American Indian/Alaskan Native	75	0	0	9	18	22		0
Anti-Asian/Pacific Islander	219	0	0	19	33	79		0
Anti-Multiple Races, Group	284	1	0	38	30	69		0
Religion:	1,477	0	0	44	82	290		5
Anti-Jewish	1,010	0	0	16	42	201		4
Anti-Catholic	65	0	0	0	7	4		0
Anti-Protestant	59	0	0	4	5	3		0
Anti-Islamic	133	0	0	12	21	51		0
Anti-Other Religion	140	0	0	10	5	24		0
Anti-Multiple Religions, Group	64	0	0	1	2	7		1
Anti-Atheism/Agnosticism/etc.	6	0	0	1	0	0		0
Sexual Orientation:	1,460	5	0	242	448	335		9
Anti-Male Homosexual	864	4	0	142	280	203		6
Anti-Female Homosexual	184	0	0	37	48	47		0
Anti-Homosexual	362	1	0	61	104	74		1
Anti-Heterosexual	27	0	0	1	7	8		2
Anti-Bisexual	23	0	0	1	9	3		0
Ethnicity/National Origin:	1,256	2	0	203	292	375		2
Anti-Hispanic	775	2	0	147	172	247		2
Anti-Other Ethnicity/National Origin	481	0	0	56	120	128		0
Disability:	82	0	1	4	16	15		2
Anti-Physical	20	0	0	2	7	7		0
Anti-Mental	62	0	1	2	9	8		2
Multiple-Bias Incidents[2]	7	0	0	0	1	4		0

Bias motivation	Crimes against property							Crimes against society[1]
	Robbery	Burglary	Larceny-theft	Motor vehicle theft	Arson	Destruction/ damage/ vandalism	Other[1]	
TOTAL	178	159	221	22	40	2,915	44	19
Single-Bias Incidents	178	159	221	22	40	2,913	44	19
Race:	67	75	120	16	28	1,361	19	7
Anti-White	39	25	76	4	3	155	15	2
Anti-Black	21	41	26	6	20	992	4	4
Anti-American Indian/Alaskan Native	0	1	10	4	2	9	0	0
Anti-Asian/Pacific Islander	6	5	5	1	0	71	0	0
Anti-Multiple Races, Group	1	3	3	1	3	134	0	1
Religion:	3	36	33	1	3	972	6	2
Anti-Jewish	1	17	6	0	1	718	4	0
Anti-Catholic	0	4	10	0	1	38	1	0
Anti-Protestant	0	2	4	0	0	41	0	0
Anti-Islamic	1	4	3	0	0	41	0	0
Anti-Other Religion	0	6	3	0	1	88	1	2
Anti-Multiple Religions, Group	0	3	7	1	0	42	0	0
Anti-Atheism/Agnosticism/etc.	1	0	0	0	0	4	0	0
Sexual Orientation:	53	16	23	2	3	314	7	3
Anti-Male Homosexual	37	4	9	0	2	173	2	2
Anti-Female Homosexual	2	4	3	1	0	41	1	0
Anti-Homosexual	14	3	6	0	1	93	3	1
Anti-Heterosexual	0	4	1	0	0	3	1	0
Anti-Bisexual	0	1	4	1	0	4	0	0
Ethnicity/National Origin:	53	28	24	3	6	257	6	5
Anti-Hispanic	43	19	11	1	1	123	3	4
Anti-Other Ethnicity/National Origin	10	9	13	2	5	134	3	1
Disability:	2	4	21	0	0	9	6	2
Anti-Physical	0	0	2	0	0	1	1	0
Anti-Mental	2	4	19	0	0	8	5	2
Multiple-Bias Incidents[2]	0	0	0	0	0	2	0	0

[1]Includes additional offenses collected in the NIBRS.

[2]In a *multiple-bias incident*, two conditions must be met: (a) more than one offense type must occur in the incident and (b) at least two offense types must be motivated by different biases.

Table 86. Known Offender's Race, by Bias Motivation, 2007

(Number.)

Bias motivation	Total offenses	Known offender's race						Unknown offender
		White	Black	American Indian/ Alaskan Native	Asian/Pacific Islander	Multipleraces, group	Unknown race	
TOTAL..........	9,006	3,802	1,045	75	41	194	600	3,249
Single-Bias Incidents	8,999	3,799	1,045	75	41	192	600	3,247
Race:	4,724	2,171	500	55	19	118	316	1,545
Anti-White	871	161	394	22	6	21	47	220
Anti-Black	3,275	1,771	79	21	10	67	234	1,093
Anti-American Indian/Alaskan Native...........	75	44	3	7	0	0	4	17
Anti-Asian/Pacific Islander	219	91	18	1	3	11	13	82
Anti-Multiple Races, Group	284	104	6	4	0	19	18	133
Religion:	1,477	295	52	3	6	7	105	1,009
Anti-Jewish	1,010	163	17	0	3	3	68	756
Anti-Catholic	65	10	2	1	0	2	8	42
Anti-Protestant	59	12	3	1	0	0	4	39
Anti-Islamic	133	61	16	1	0	1	10	44
Anti-Other Religion	140	37	7	0	3	0	10	83
Anti-Multiple Religions, Group...........	64	10	6	0	0	1	4	43
Anti-Atheism/Agnosticism/etc.	6	2	1	0	0	0	1	2
Sexual Orientation:	1,460	666	268	9	10	52	92	363
Anti-Male Homosexual...........	864	409	153	6	9	25	56	206
Anti-Female Homosexual...........	184	72	51	1	1	4	11	44
Anti-Homosexual...........	362	170	58	2	0	17	23	92
Anti-Heterosexual...........	27	9	2	0	0	5	0	11
Anti-Bisexual...........	23	6	4	0	0	1	2	10
Ethnicity/National Origin:	1,256	638	212	6	6	14	83	297
Anti-Hispanic	775	405	157	3	2	9	38	161
Anti-Other Ethnicity/National Origin	481	233	55	3	4	5	45	136
Disability:	82	29	13	2	0	1	4	33
Anti-Physical	20	11	5	0	0	0	1	3
Anti-Mental...........	62	18	8	2	0	1	3	30
Multiple-Bias Incidents[1]...........	7	3	0	0	0	2	0	2

[1]In a *multiple-bias incident*, two conditions must be met: (a) more than one offense type must occur in the incident and (b) at least two offense types must be motivated by different biases.

Table 87. Victim Type, by Offense Type, 2007

(Number.)

Offense type	Total offenses	Victim type					Other/ unknown/ multiple
		Individual	Business/ financial institution	Government	Religious organization	Society/ public[1]	
TOTAL..........	9,006	7,330	410	264	245	19	738
Crimes against persons[2]	5,408	5,408	-	-	-	-	-
Crimes against property:	3,579	1,922	410	264	245	0	738
Robbery	178	171	2	0	0	0	5
Burglary	159	103	23	8	9	0	16
Larceny-theft	221	151	58	1	4	0	7
Motor vehicle theft	22	22	0	0	0	0	0
Arson	40	27	3	3	3	0	4
Destruction/damage/vandalism...........	2,915	1,416	315	251	229	0	704
Other[2]...........	44	32	9	1	0	0	2
Crimes against society[2]...........	19	-	-	-	-	19	-

[1]The victim type *society/public* is collected only in the NIBRS.
[2]Includes additional offenses collected in the NIBRS.

Table 88. Number of Victims and Offense Type, by Bias Motivation, 2007

(Number.)

Bias motivation	Total offenses	Crimes against persons					
		Murder and nonnegligent manslaughter	Forcible rape	Aggravated assault	Simple assault	Intimidation	Other[1]
TOTAL..........	9,535	9	2	1,116	1,684	2,565	32
Single-Bias Incidents	9,527	9	2	1,116	1,683	2,561	32 19
Race:	4,956	2	1	623	845	1,546	
Anti-White..........	908	0	1	107	246	190	8
Anti-Black..........	3,434	1	0	450	518	1,186	6
Anti-American Indian/Alaskan Native..........	76	0	0	9	18	22	
Anti-Asian/Pacific Islander..........	234	0	0	19	33	79	0
Anti-Multiple Races, Group..........	304	1	0	38	30	69	0
Religion:	1,628	0	0	44	82	290	5
Anti-Jewish..........	1,127	0	0	16	42	201	4
Anti-Catholic..........	70	0	0	0	7	4	0
Anti-Protestant..........	67	0	0	4	5	3	0
Anti-Islamic..........	142	0	0	12	21	51	0
Anti-Other Religion..........	148	0	0	10	5	24	0
Anti-Multiple Religions, Group..........	66	0	0	1	2	7	1
Anti-Atheism/Agnosticism/etc..........	8	0	0	1	0	0	0
Sexual Orientation:	1,512	5	0	242	448	335	9
Anti-Male Homosexual..........	890	4	0	142	280	203	6
Anti-Female Homosexual..........	197	0	0	37	48	47	0
Anti-Homosexual..........	375	1	0	61	104	74	1
Anti-Heterosexual..........	27	0	0	1	7	8	2
Anti-Bisexual..........	23	0	0	1	9	3	0
Ethnicity/National Origin:	1,347	2	0	203	292	375	2
Anti-Hispanic..........	830	2	0	147	172	247	2
Anti-Other Ethnicity/National Origin..........	517	0	0	56	120	128	0
Disability:	84	0	1	4	16	15	2
Anti-Physical..........	20	0	0	2	7	7	0
Anti-Mental..........	64	0	1	2	9	8	2
Multiple-Bias Incidents[2]..........	8	0	0	0	1	4	0

Bias motivation	Crimes against property							Crimes against society[1]
	Robbery	Burglary	Larceny-theft	Motor vehicle theft	Arson	Destruction/ damage/ vandalism	Other[1]	
TOTAL..........	236	193	230	27	47	3,328	47	19
Single-Bias Incidents	236	193	230	27	47	3,325	47	19
Race:	85	96	125	21	33	1,539	19	7
Anti-White..........	51	28	79	4	3	174	15	2
Anti-Black..........	23	56	27	11	25	1,123	4	4
Anti-American Indian/Alaskan Native..........	0	1	10	4	2	10	0	0
Anti-Asian/Pacific Islander..........	10	8	6	1	0	78	0	0
Anti-Multiple Races, Group..........	1	3	3	1	3	154	0	1
Religion:	3	42	33	1	4	1,116	6	2
Anti-Jewish..........	1	21	6	0	2	830	4	0
Anti-Catholic..........	0	5	10	0	1	42	1	0
Anti-Protestant..........	0	3	4	0	0	48	0	0
Anti-Islamic..........	1	4	3	0	0	50	0	0
Anti-Other Religion..........	0	6	3	0	1	96	1	2
Anti-Multiple Religions, Group..........	0	3	7	1	0	44	0	0
Anti-Atheism/Agnosticism/etc..........	1	0	0	0	0	6	0	0
Sexual Orientation:	61	17	25	2	4	352	9	3
Anti-Male Homosexual..........	43	4	10	0	2	192	2	2
Anti-Female Homosexual..........	2	5	4	1	0	52	1	0
Anti-Homosexual..........	16	3	6	0	2	101	5	1
Anti-Heterosexual..........	0	4	1	0	0	3	1	0
Anti-Bisexual..........	0	1	4	1	0	4	0	0
Ethnicity/National Origin:	84	34	26	3	6	308	7	5
Anti-Hispanic..........	69	25	12	1	1	144	4	4
Anti-Other Ethnicity/National Origin..........	15	9	14	2	5	164	3	1
Disability:	3	4	21	0	0	10	6	2
Anti-Physical..........	0	0	2	0	0	1	1	0
Anti-Mental..........	3	4	19	0	0	9	5	2
Multiple-Bias Incidents[2]..........	0	0	0	0	0	3	0	0

[1]Includes additional offenses collected in the NIBRS.

[2]In a *multiple-bias incident*, two conditions must be met: (a) more than one offense type must occur in the incident and (b) at least two offense types must be motivated by different biases.

Table 89.   Number of Incidents and Victim Type, by Bias Motivation, 2007

(Number.)

Offense type	Total offenses	Victim type					
		Individual	Business/ financial institution	Government	Religious organization	Society/ public[1]	Other/ unknown/ multiple
TOTAL	7,624	5,974	391	253	237	11	758
Single-Bias Incidents	7,621	5,972	391	253	237	11	757
Race	3,870	3,158	218	167	30	5	292
Religion	1,400	665	102	56	201	0	376
Sexual Orientation	1,265	1,169	30	16	2	1	47
Ethnicity/National Origin	1,007	911	34	14	4	3	41
Disability	79	69	7	0	0	2	1
Multiple-Bias Incidents[2]	3	2	0	0	0	0	1

[1]The victim type *society/public* is collected only in the NIBRS.
[2]In a *multiple-bias incident,* two conditions must be met: (a) more than one offense type must occur in the incident and (b) at least two offense types must be motivated by different biases.

Table 90.   Known Offender's[1] Race, 2007

(Number.)

Race	Number
TOTAL	6,965
White	4,378
Black	1,448
American Indian/Alaskan Native	69
Asian/Pacific Islander	50
Multiple Races, Group[2]	339
Unknown Race	681

[1]The term *known offender* does not imply that the identity of the suspect is known, but only that an attribute of the suspect has been identified, which distinguishes him/her from an unknown offender.
[2]The term *multiple races, group* is used to describe a group of offenders of varying races.

Table 91.   Number of Incidents and Bias Motivation, by Location, 2007

(Number.)

Location	Total incidents	Bias motivation					Multiple bias incidents[1]
		Race	Religion	Sexual orientation	Ethnicity/ national origin	Disability	
TOTAL	7,624	3,870	1,400	1,265	1,007	79	3
Air/bus/train terminal	80	45	8	13	12	2	0
Bank/savings and loan	13	5	2	4	2	0	0
Bar/nightclub	149	65	9	53	22	0	0
Church/synagogue/temple	309	43	252	5	9	0	0
Commercial office building	167	91	30	20	26	0	0
Construction site	36	24	8	2	2	0	0
Convenience store	80	40	6	13	21	0	0
Department/discount store	61	41	5	5	10	0	0
Drug store/Dr.'s office/hospital	57	28	15	6	8	0	0
Field/woods	109	55	9	22	22	1	0
Government/public building	119	68	28	12	11	0	0
Grocery/supermarket	57	25	8	7	17	0	0
Highway/road/alley/street	1,438	784	108	302	229	14	1
Hotel/motel/etc.	37	19	4	10	4	0	0
Jail/prison	50	38	1	5	6	0	0
Lake/waterway	11	7	0	3	1	0	0
Liquor store	17	8	1	1	7	0	0
Parking lot/garage	454	231	48	84	87	4	0
Rental storage facility	5	3	1	0	0	1	0
Residence/home	2,329	1,256	363	381	297	30	2
Restaurant	161	88	9	28	33	3	0
School/college	859	468	170	135	81	5	0
Service/gas station	75	37	11	6	17	4	0
Specialty store (TV, fur, etc.)	67	33	11	11	12	0	0
Other/unknown	875	364	291	135	70	15	0
Multiple locations	9	4	2	2	1	0	0

[1]In a *multiple-bias incident,* two conditions must be met: (a) more than one offense type must occur in the incident and (b) at least two offense types must be motivated by different biases.

Table 92. Offense Type, by Participating State, 2007

(Number.)

Participating state	Total offenses	Crimes against persons					Other[1]
		Murder and nonnegligent manslaughter	Forcible rape	Aggravated assault	Simple assault	Intimidation	
TOTAL	9,006	9	2	1,116	1,684	2,565	32
Alabama	6	0	0	1	1	0	0
Alaska	10	0	0	3	5	0	0
Arizona	205	0	0	36	24	68	0
Arkansas	38	0	0	4	10	11	0
California	1,789	2	0	373	313	456	0
Colorado	213	0	0	62	40	70	3
Connecticut	146	0	0	2	20	44	0
Delaware	59	0	0	8	2	15	0
District of Columbia	46	0	0	12	19	6	0
Florida	193	1	0	36	60	28	0
Georgia	14	0	0	3	0	2	0
Idaho	48	0	0	4	12	8	0
Illinois	200	0	0	36	58	34	1
Indiana	48	0	0	0	7	23	0
Iowa	32	0	0	3	9	5	0
Kansas	137	0	0	17	41	27	1
Kentucky	137	0	0	6	3	111	0
Louisiana	34	0	0	8	9	4	0
Maine	82	0	0	3	19	32	1
Maryland	153	0	0	8	12	0	0
Massachusetts	419	0	0	55	78	135	0
Michigan	734	0	0	75	147	263	8
Minnesota	183	0	0	15	41	88	0
Mississippi	0	0	0	0	0	0	0
Missouri	135	0	1	20	42	31	0
Montana	28	0	0	9	6	3	1
Nebraska	48	0	0	0	15	12	0
Nevada	82	0	0	23	16	18	0
New Hampshire	50	0	0	3	5	12	1
New Jersey	773	1	0	13	49	403	0
New Mexico	17	0	0	5	12	0	0
New York	498	1	0	38	62	95	0
North Carolina	85	0	0	10	13	23	0
North Dakota	19	0	0	4	9	0	0
Ohio	373	0	1	9	97	134	4
Oklahoma	37	1	0	3	12	14	0
Oregon	200	0	0	33	39	50	0
Pennsylvania	96	0	0	7	12	25	0
Rhode Island	47	0	0	0	5	2	0
South Carolina	152	1	0	20	39	24	3
South Dakota	39	0	0	4	17	1	0
Tennessee	285	0	0	42	61	65	2
Texas	295	1	0	48	79	57	1
Utah	64	0	0	8	12	6	0
Vermont	21	0	0	2	2	0	0
Virginia	355	0	0	19	68	46	5
Washington	232	0	0	15	42	94	0
West Virginia	47	1	0	4	8	10	0
Wisconsin	79	0	0	6	23	9	1
Wyoming	23	0	0	1	9	1	0

[1]Includes additional offenses collected in the NIBRS.

Table 92. Offense Type, by Participating State, 2007 *(Contd.)*

(Number.)

Participating state	Crimes against property							Crimes against society[1]
	Robbery	Burglary	Larceny-theft	Motor vehicle theft	Arson	Destruction/ damage/ vandalism	Other[1]	
TOTAL	178	159	221	22	40	2,915	44	19
Alabama	0	1	0	0	0	3	0	0
Alaska	0	0	0	0	0	2	0	0
Arizona	4	1	2	0	1	69	0	0
Arkansas	0	1	1	0	0	11	0	0
California	54	30	3	2	6	550	0	0
Colorado	3	3	2	0	1	29	0	0
Connecticut	1	1	3	0	0	75	0	0
Delaware	7	0	0	0	0	26	0	1
District of Columbia	0	1	1	0	0	7	0	0
Florida	4	3	1	0	1	59	0	0
Georgia	1	0	1	0	1	6	0	0
Idaho	0	3	2	0	1	16	1	1
Illinois	5	1	1	0	1	63	0	0
Indiana	0	0	0	0	0	18	0	0
Iowa	1	0	0	0	0	13	0	1
Kansas	2	3	10	1	0	33	1	1
Kentucky	0	2	1	0	0	14	0	0
Louisiana	0	0	7	1	0	5	0	0
Maine	1	0	0	0	0	26	0	0
Maryland	2	0	1	0	3	127	0	0
Massachusetts	7	2	10	0	0	130	2	0
Michigan	10	25	60	5	3	123	12	3
Minnesota	6	1	1	0	0	31	0	0
Mississippi	0	0	0	0	0	0	0	0
Missouri	1	1	0	0	1	38	0	0
Montana	1	0	1	0	0	6	1	0
Nebraska	2	1	2	0	0	14	2	0
Nevada	3	0	0	0	0	22	0	0
New Hampshire	0	1	1	0	0	26	1	0
New Jersey	2	5	1	0	1	298	0	0
New Mexico	0	0	0	0	0	0	0	0
New York	7	5	2	0	1	287	0	0
North Carolina	0	0	0	0	1	38	0	0
North Dakota	0	0	2	1	0	3	0	0
Ohio	7	9	28	1	3	71	7	2
Oklahoma	0	1	0	0	1	5	0	0
Oregon	2	3	1	2	0	70	0	0
Pennsylvania	0	1	0	0	0	51	0	0
Rhode Island	1	12	13	4	0	8	2	0
South Carolina	8	6	11	2	1	34	2	1
South Dakota	0	1	1	0	2	13	0	0
Tennessee	15	10	8	0	4	75	3	0
Texas	4	6	3	0	0	96	0	0
Utah	0	1	4	0	1	28	2	2
Vermont	0	2	0	0	0	14	1	0
Virginia	8	7	21	2	5	162	5	7
Washington	2	4	3	1	1	70	0	0
West Virginia	2	5	7	0	0	8	2	0
Wisconsin	5	0	5	0	0	30	0	0
Wyoming	0	0	0	0	0	12	0	0

[1]Includes additional offenses collected in the NIBRS.

Table 93. Agency Hate Crime Reporting, by State, 2007

Participating state	Number of participating agencies	Population covered	Agencies submitting incident reports	Total number of incidents reported
TOTAL	13,241	260,229,972	2,025	7,624
Alabama	156	2,388,398	5	6
Alaska	1	284,142	1	8
Arizona	78	5,754,940	26	161
Arkansas	265	2,765,195	27	33
California	727	36,553,215	276	1,400
Colorado	213	4,733,294	48	156
Connecticut	101	3,502,309	53	127
Delaware	53	853,712	14	49
District of Columbia	2	588,292	2	41
Florida	490	18,152,012	73	166
Georgia	18	680,591	3	13
Idaho	108	1,497,812	16	38
Illinois	60	4,945,770	45	167
Indiana	127	2,899,537	13	40
Iowa	226	2,951,927	16	27
Kansas	348	2,137,765	45	110
Kentucky	324	3,841,157	23	48
Louisiana	103	2,514,916	14	31
Maine	149	1,317,207	30	72
Maryland	156	5,618,344	25	150
Massachusetts	337	6,272,474	85	353
Michigan	593	9,931,655	185	627
Minnesota	321	5,196,856	47	157
Mississippi	58	704,703	0	0
Missouri	561	5,699,738	39	114
Montana	96	944,103	11	21
Nebraska	162	1,267,389	9	44
Nevada	32	2,526,861	6	63
New Hampshire	143	1,021,621	25	43
New Jersey	512	8,684,873	207	748
New Mexico	48	1,173,881	4	14
New York	273	15,335,616	29	493
North Carolina	369	7,421,793	33	75
North Dakota	77	578,781	10	14
Ohio	534	8,698,569	76	312
Oklahoma	293	3,617,316	26	30
Oregon	239	3,743,591	40	170
Pennsylvania	1,173	12,075,298	24	83
Rhode Island	47	1,057,832	7	47
South Carolina	480	4,407,709	55	127
South Dakota	105	672,329	9	37
Tennessee	461	6,156,260	58	239
Texas	999	23,879,373	60	242
Utah	117	2,619,834	28	55
Vermont	80	610,907	11	21
Virginia	408	7,710,349	83	323
Washington	244	6,437,315	54	195
West Virginia	338	1,686,872	21	44
Wisconsin	374	5,599,350	21	69
Wyoming	62	516,189	7	21

Table 94.   Hate Crime Incidents per Bias Motivation and Quarter by State and Agency, 2007

State	Agency type	Agency name	Number of incidents per bias motivation					Number of incidents per quarter[1]				Popu-lation[2]
			Race	Religion	Sexual orient-ation	Ethnicity	Disability	1st quarter	2nd quarter	3rd quarter	4th quarter	
ALABAMA	Total		5	0	1	0	0					
	Cities		4	0	1	0	0					
		Auburn	1	0	0	0	0	0	1	0	0	53,160
		Hoover	1	0	1	0	0	0	0	0	2	69,527
		Newton	1	0	0	0	0		0		1	1,663
		Tuscaloosa	1	0	0	0	0				1	83,811
	Metropolitan Counties		1	0	0	0	0					
		Tuscaloosa	1	0	0	0	0	0	1			
ALASKA	Total		5	0	2	0	1					
	Cities		5	0	2	0	1					
		Anchorage	5	0	2	0	1	3	3	2	0	284,142
ARIZONA	Total		82	22	27	29	1					
	Cities		73	17	26	24	0					
		Apache Junction	0	1	0	0	0	0	1	0	0	30,925
		Buckeye	0	0	1	1	0	1	0	1	0	34,618
		Chandler	3	0	1	0	0	3	1			250,868
		Chino Valley	1	0	0	0	0	0	1	0		10,886
		Flagstaff	1	0	0	0	0	0	0	1	0	58,978
		Gilbert	4	3	0	0	0	1	4	0	2	206,681
		Glendale	8	2	0	2	0	4	4	3	1	250,444
		Kingman	5	0	0	1	0	3	1	1	1	28,306
		Marana	2	0	0	0	0	0	1	1	0	33,374
		Mesa	4	0	2	3	0	1	3	2	3	454,576
		Paradise Valley	1	0	0	0	0	0	1	0	0	14,594
		Peoria	1	1	0	1	0	0	0	1	2	147,223
		Phoenix	38	9	20	13	0	23	13	27	17	1,541,698
		Prescott Valley	1	0	0	0	0	0	1		0	38,204
		Quartzsite	1	0	0	0	0	1	0	0	0	3,473
		Sedona	0	1	0	0	0	0	0	0	1	11,484
		Show Low	0	0	0	1	0	1	0		0	11,588
		Sierra Vista	1	0	0	0	0	0	0	1		43,441
		Tempe	2	0	1	2	0	1	2	2	0	171,320
		Yuma	0	0	1	0	0	0	0	0	1	88,874
	Universities and Colleges		4	2	1	3	1					
		Arizona State University, Main Campus	0	1	0	0	1	1	0	0	1	51,234
		Northern Arizona University	1	0	1	0	0	1	0	0	1	20,555
		University of Arizona	3	1	0	3	0	5	2	0		36,805
	Metropolitan Counties		4	3	0	2	0					
		Maricopa	2	0	0	0	0	0	0		2	
		Pima	2	3	0	2	0	2	2	1	2	
	Nonmetropolitan Counties		1	0	0	0	0					
		Navajo	1	0	0	0	0	0	0	1	0	
ARKANSAS	Total		21	1	8	3	0					
	Cities		17	0	8	1	0					
		Benton	0	0	1	0	0	0	0	0	1	27,758
		Cherokee Village	0	0	1	0	0	1	0	0	0	4,812
		Crossett	1	0	0	0	0	0	0	0	1	5,623
		De Witt	1	0	0	0	0	0	0	1	0	3,354
		El Dorado	0	0	1	0	0	0	1	0	0	20,200
		Fort Smith	0	0	2	0	0	0	0	2	0	83,860
		Green Forest	2	0	0	0	0	2	0	0	0	2,876
		Hot Springs	1	0	0	0	0	1	0	0	0	38,828
		Jacksonville	2	0	0	1	0	0	1	2	0	30,565
		Jonesboro	1	0	0	0	0	0	0	1	0	61,199
		Lewisville	1	0	0	0	0	0	0	0	1	1,166
		Little Rock	1	0	0	0	0	0	0	0	1	184,594
		Marion	0	0	1	0	0	0	1	0	0	10,331
		Maumelle	1	0	0	0	0	1	0	0	0	15,613
		Morrilton	1	0	0	0	0	1	0	0	0	6,558
		North Little Rock	1	0	0	0	0	1	0	0	0	58,680
		Paragould	0	0	1	0	0	0	0	1	0	24,562
		Sherwood	1	0	1	0	0	0	0	2	0	23,703
		Warren	1	0	0	0	0	0	0	1	0	6,182
		West Memphis	2	0	0	0	0	0	0	2	0	28,137
	Universities and Colleges		1	0	0	0	0					
		University of Central Arkansas	1	0	0	0	0	0	1	0	0	12,330
	Metropolitan Counties		0	1	0	1	0					
		Benton	0	0	0	1	0	0	1	0	0	
		Pulaski	0	1	0	0	0	1	0	0	0	

[1]Agencies published in this table indicated that at least one hate crime incident occurred in their respective jurisdictions during the quarter(s) for which they submitted a report to the Hate Crime program. Blanks indicate quarters for which agencies did not submit reports.
[2]Population figures are published only for the cities. The figures listed for the universities and colleges are student enrollment and were provided by the United States Department of Education for the 2006 school year, the most recent available. The enrollment figures include full-time and part-time students.

Table 94. Hate Crime Incidents per Bias Motivation and Quarter by State and Agency, 2007 *(Contd.)*

State	Agency type	Agency name	Race	Religion	Sexual orient-ation	Ethnicity	Disability	1st quarter	2nd quarter	3rd quarter	4th quarter	Popu-lation[2]
	Nonmetropolitan Counties		3	0	0	1	0					
		Fulton	1	0	0	0	0	0	0	0	1	
		Montgomery	0	0	0	1	0	0	0	0	1	
		Pope	1	0	0	0	0	0	1	0	0	
		Scott	1	0	0	0	0	0	0	1	0	
CALIFORNIA............	**Total**		674	204	263	256	3					
	Cities		566	166	226	225	3					
		Agoura Hills	0	2	0	1	0	1	1	1	0	22,966
		Alameda	1	0	0	0	0	1	0	0	0	70,445
		Aliso Viejo	0	1	0	0	0	0	0	1	0	41,691
		Anaheim	1	0	1	2	0	1	1	0	2	335,133
		Antioch	1	0	0	0	1	0	0	1	1	101,973
		Atascadero	0	1	0	0	0	0	0	1	0	27,465
		Atwater	1	1	0	0	0	0	1	0	1	27,762
		Azusa	1	0	0	0	0	0	0	1	0	47,403
		Bakersfield	1	1	2	0	0	0	2	0	2	318,743
		Belmont	1	0	0	2	0	1	1	0	1	24,605
		Benicia	1	0	0	0	0	0	0	1	0	26,544
		Berkeley	1	0	1	1	0	2	1	0	0	101,343
		Beverly Hills	0	5	0	0	0	1	0	4	0	35,133
		Bishop	0	0	0	1	0	0	1	0	0	3,566
		Brea	1	0	0	0	0	0	0	0	1	39,041
		Brentwood	1	1	0	0	0	1	0	1	0	52,238
		Buena Park	0	0	0	1	0	0	1	0	0	79,890
		Burbank	3	0	1	3	1	4	1	2	1	104,871
		Calabasas	0	1	1	0	0	1	1	0	0	22,693
		Calexico	0	0	1	0	0	0	0	1	0	38,928
		Camarillo	2	0	0	1	0	0	0	1	2	63,238
		Campbell	0	0	1	0	0	0	0	1	0	37,429
		Carson	1	0	0	0	0	1	0	0	0	94,359
		Ceres	1	0	0	1	0	1	0	1	0	43,427
		Cerritos	1	0	0	0	0	1	0	0	0	52,462
		Chico	1	0	2	2	0	2	2	1	0	74,288
		Chino	2	0	1	1	0	0	3	1	0	80,699
		Chula Vista	0	0	2	0	0	1	1	0	0	218,718
		City of Angels	0	1	1	0	0	0	1	1	0	3,949
		Claremont	2	0	0	0	0	2	0	0	0	35,250
		Clayton	1	0	0	0	0	0	0	1	0	11,252
		Clearlake	3	0	0	0	0	0	2	1	0	15,133
		Clovis	5	0	0	2	0	1	1	3	2	92,592
		Compton	5	0	0	3	0	0	2	3	3	95,990
		Concord	2	3	1	1	0	1	3	2	1	122,202
		Corona	0	0	1	0	0	0	0	0	1	153,518
		Coronado	0	0	1	0	0	0	1	0	0	26,888
		Covina	2	0	0	0	0	1	0	1	0	47,961
		Cypress	2	0	0	0	0	0	1	1	0	47,741
		Daly City	1	0	1	0	0	1	1	0	0	100,632
		Dana Point	0	0	0	1	0	0	0	1	0	36,051
		Danville	0	0	0	1	0	0	0	1	0	41,503
		Davis	7	3	0	1	0	0	4	5	2	61,238
		Del Mar	0	1	0	0	0	0	1	0	0	4,365
		Desert Hot Springs	1	0	0	1	0	1	0	1	0	23,890
		Diamond Bar	3	0	1	0	0	0	1	2	1	57,954
		Downey	2	0	1	1	0	1	2	0	1	109,642
		Duarte	3	0	0	1	0	0	0	2	2	22,255
		Dublin	1	0	0	0	0	0	0	0	1	43,751
		El Cajon	1	0	0	0	0	1	0	0	0	91,302
		Elk Grove	2	0	1	0	0	1	2	0	0	138,103
		El Monte	9	1	1	0	0	2	3	4	2	124,182
		El Segundo	1	0	0	0	0	0	0	0	1	16,533
		Encinitas	0	0	1	0	0	1	0	0	0	59,424
		Escondido	2	0	0	0	0	0	0	2	0	133,429
		Eureka	1	0	0	0	0	0	0	1	0	25,347
		Fillmore	1	1	0	0	0	0	0	2	0	15,219
		Folsom	1	0	0	0	0	0	1	0	0	68,320
		Fort Bragg	1	0	0	13	0	0	0	13	1	6,780
		Fountain Valley	2	0	0	0	0	0	0	2	0	55,973
		Fremont	1	1	0	2	0	1	3	0	0	201,318
		Fresno	7	1	1	0	0	1	2	5	1	472,170
		Fullerton	2	0	0	0	0	0	1	0	1	133,855
		Galt	4	0	0	0	0	1	1	2	0	23,967
		Gardena	1	0	0	0	0	1	0	0	0	59,951

[1]Agencies published in this table indicated that at least one hate crime incident occurred in their respective jurisdictions during the quarter(s) for which they submitted a report to the Hate Crime program. Blanks indicate quarters for which agencies did not submit reports.
[2]Population figures are published only for the cities. The figures listed for the universities and colleges are student enrollment and were provided by the United States Department of Education for the 2006 school year, the most recent available. The enrollment figures include full-time and part-time students.

Table 94. Hate Crime Incidents per Bias Motivation and Quarter by State and Agency, 2007 *(Contd.)*

State	Agency type	Agency name	Number of incidents per bias motivation					Number of incidents per quarter[1]				Popu-lation[2]
			Race	Religion	Sexual orient-ation	Ethnicity	Disability	1st quarter	2nd quarter	3rd quarter	4th quarter	
		Garden Grove	2	0	3	4	0	3	3	3	0	166,414
		Gilroy	1	0	0	0	0	0	0	1	0	49,343
		Glendale	3	1	0	4	0	3	3	2	0	200,049
		Glendora	1	0	0	0	0	0	0	0	1	50,495
		Gonzales	0	0	1	0	0	0	1	0	0	8,795
		Grass Valley	1	0	0	0	0	0	0	1	0	12,525
		Hawaiian Gardens	2	0	1	0	0	0	1	2	0	15,510
		Hawthorne	1	0	2	0	0	0	0	2	1	85,609
		Hemet	5	0	1	2	0	1	4	1	2	71,825
		Hercules	1	0	0	0	0	0	1	0	0	25,636
		Hesperia	1	0	0	1	0	1	1	0	0	86,750
		Huntington Beach	4	3	2	0	0	1	1	3	4	195,067
		Huntington Park	1	0	0	1	0	0	0	1	1	62,269
		Inglewood	1	0	0	0	0	0	0	1	0	115,223
		Irvine	0	2	0	0	0	0	0	1	1	201,872
		La Canada Flintridge	2	2	0	0	0	2	1	0	1	21,079
		Lafayette	1	0	0	0	0	0	0	1	0	25,007
		Laguna Hills	1	0	0	0	0	0	1	0	0	32,172
		La Habra	3	0	0	0	0	0	1	0	2	59,290
		Lake Elsinore	1	0	0	2	0	0	2	1	0	47,937
		Lakewood	3	1	0	0	0	0	1	3	0	80,138
		La Mesa	0	1	0	0	0	0	1	0	0	52,801
		La Mirada	1	0	0	1	0	0	1	1	0	50,143
		Lancaster	11	0	2	1	0	5	5	2	2	144,210
		La Puente	1	0	0	0	0	0	1	0	0	41,581
		La Quinta	0	0	2	0	0	0	0	1	1	44,533
		La Verne	1	0	0	0	0	0	0	1	0	33,549
		Lemon Grove	1	0	0	0	0	0	1	0	0	23,721
		Lemoore	0	0	1	0	0	0	0	1	0	23,461
		Livermore	1	1	0	0	0	0	0	1	1	80,253
		Lodi	0	1	0	1	0	1	1	0	0	63,218
		Lomita	1	0	0	0	0	0	0	0	1	20,539
		Long Beach	6	3	3	1	0	6	4	3	0	473,959
		Los Alamitos	2	3	0	0	0	0	2	1	2	11,725
		Los Angeles	132	50	43	54	0	61	72	76	70	3,870,487
		Los Gatos	0	2	0	0	0	0	0	0	2	28,320
		Lynwood	1	0	0	0	0	0	1	0	0	71,216
		Malibu	1	0	0	0	0	0	0	1	0	13,263
		Manhattan Beach	1	2	1	0	0	0	1	2	1	37,061
		Manteca	2	0	0	0	0	1	0	1	0	65,857
		Marina	0	0	1	2	0	1	0	2	0	18,048
		Marysville	1	0	0	0	0	0	0	0	1	11,903
		Menlo Park	1	1	0	0	0	0	1	0	1	29,867
		Millbrae	0	0	0	1	0	0	1	0	0	20,425
		Milpitas	0	0	1	1	0	0	0	2	0	64,498
		Modesto	4	0	4	2	0	0	2	7	1	208,067
		Montclair	0	0	0	1	0	1	0	0	0	35,893
		Monterey	0	0	1	0	0	0	1	0	0	28,674
		Monterey Park	1	0	0	0	0	0	1	0	0	62,472
		Moorpark	0	0	1	1	0	0	0	2	0	36,255
		Moreno Valley	4	0	0	1	0	1	1	1	2	190,248
		Mountain View	0	0	0	1	0	1	0	0	0	69,999
		Murrieta	0	0	1	0	0	1	0	0	0	98,051
		Napa	1	0	1	0	0	0	1	0	1	75,266
		National City	1	0	0	1	0	0	2	0	0	61,996
		Newport Beach	3	0	1	3	0	1	2	0	4	80,377
		Norwalk	5	0	1	0	0	1	1	2	2	105,330
		Novato	2	0	0	2	0	3	0	0	1	52,067
		Oakdale	1	0	0	0	0	1	0	0	0	19,890
		Oakland	5	1	5	4	0	2	4	1	8	396,541
		Oakley	2	0	0	0	0	0	0	1	1	29,302
		Oceanside	10	4	3	3	0	4	7	3	6	166,424
		Ontario	1	1	0	0	0	0	2	0	0	175,537
		Orange	1	1	2	0	0	3	1	0	0	135,818
		Oxnard	1	0	1	1	0	2	1	0	0	186,367
		Pacifica	1	0	2	3	0	2	2	1	1	37,176
		Palmdale	8	2	1	0	0	4	3	0	4	142,122
		Palm Desert	0	3	0	1	0	1	3	0	0	47,903
		Palm Springs	4	0	7	0	0	2	3	1	5	48,542
		Palo Alto	0	2	1	0	0	1	2	0	0	57,696
		Paradise	1	0	0	0	0	1	0	0	0	26,381
		Paramount	1	0	0	0	0	0	0	1	0	56,508

[1]Agencies published in this table indicated that at least one hate crime incident occurred in their respective jurisdictions during the quarter(s) for which they submitted a report to the Hate Crime program. Blanks indicate quarters for which agencies did not submit reports.
[2]Population figures are published only for the cities. The figures listed for the universities and colleges are student enrollment and were provided by the United States Department of Education for the 2006 school year, the most recent available. The enrollment figures include full-time and part-time students.

Table 94.   Hate Crime Incidents per Bias Motivation and Quarter by State and Agency, 2007 *(Contd.)*

State	Agency type	Agency name	Number of incidents per bias motivation					Number of incidents per quarter[1]				Popu-lation[2]
			Race	Religion	Sexual orient-ation	Ethnicity	Disability	1st quarter	2nd quarter	3rd quarter	4th quarter	
		Parlier	0	1	0	0	0	0	1	0	0	13,391
		Pasadena	7	1	3	6	0	4	6	3	4	145,553
		Paso Robles	1	1	0	0	0	1	0	0	1	28,490
		Perris	2	0	0	0	0	1	0	1	0	54,029
		Petaluma	1	0	0	2	0	2	1	0	0	54,624
		Pico Rivera	1	0	0	0	0	0	0	0	1	64,452
		Pinole	2	0	0	0	0	0	0	1	1	18,844
		Placerville	0	0	1	2	0	1	0	1	1	10,142
		Pleasant Hill	1	0	0	1	0	1	1	0	0	33,233
		Pleasanton	1	0	0	0	0	1	0	0	0	66,707
		Pomona	3	0	0	2	0	2	0	1	2	155,161
		Poway	1	0	1	0	0	0	0	1	1	48,105
		Rancho Mirage	0	1	0	0	0	0	0	0	1	17,293
		Rancho Santa Margarita	1	0	0	0	0	1	0	0	0	51,023
		Red Bluff	0	0	1	0	0	1	0	0	0	14,111
		Redding	9	0	5	2	1	5	4	1	7	91,328
		Redlands	1	0	0	0	0	0	0	0	1	71,358
		Redondo Beach	4	0	0	1	0	1	1	1	2	67,909
		Redwood City	2	0	0	0	0	1	0	1	0	73,435
		Rialto	0	1	0	1	0	0	1	0	1	100,451
		Richmond	3	0	2	0	0	2	1	2	0	102,471
		Ridgecrest	0	1	0	0	0	0	1	0	0	26,351
		Riverside	16	0	2	2	0	10	6	4	0	299,312
		Rocklin	1	0	0	0	0	0	0	1	0	52,328
		Rohnert Park	0	1	0	0	0	0	1	0	0	41,043
		Rolling Hills Estates	1	0	0	0	0	0	1	0	0	8,136
		Rosemead	3	0	0	0	0	0	3	0	0	55,187
		Roseville	0	0	1	0	0	0	0	1	0	111,497
		Sacramento	10	2	5	3	0	4	3	8	5	460,546
		Salinas	1	0	1	0	0	0	0	2	0	145,251
		San Bernardino	2	0	2	0	0	0	3	0	1	200,810
		San Bruno	0	0	1	1	0	0	2	0	0	39,960
		San Clemente	0	1	0	1	0	1	1	0	0	62,723
		San Diego	15	5	21	11	0	15	12	15	10	1,261,196
		San Dimas	1	1	0	1	0	3	0	0	0	35,809
		San Francisco	31	9	18	8	0	20	21	12	13	733,799
		San Gabriel	1	1	0	0	0	0	1	0	1	41,186
		San Jacinto	2	1	0	0	0	2	1	0	0	37,056
		San Jose	18	2	9	5	0	10	7	11	6	934,553
		San Juan Capistrano	1	1	0	0	0	0	0	1	1	34,976
		San Leandro	5	1	0	0	0	0	0	2	4	77,785
		San Luis Obispo	3	3	1	3	0	2	4	3	1	42,781
		San Marcos	1	1	0	0	0	1	1	0	0	80,050
		San Mateo	0	2	1	1	0	0	1	2	1	91,441
		San Pablo	1	0	0	0	0	0	0	0	1	31,143
		San Rafael	0	0	1	0	0	0	0	1	0	55,987
		San Ramon	2	0	0	0	0	2	0	0	0	50,295
		Santa Barbara	1	0	0	0	0	1	0	0	0	85,142
		Santa Clarita	1	0	0	0	0	0	0	1	0	170,429
		Santa Cruz	4	2	3	2	0	2	3	4	2	54,626
		Santa Fe Springs	1	0	0	0	0	0	1	0	0	17,207
		Santa Monica	0	0	0	1	0	0	0	1	0	88,584
		Santa Rosa	1	2	1	1	0	3	1	1	0	154,953
		Santee	3	0	0	0	0	1	0	1	1	52,465
		Scotts Valley	0	0	2	1	0	0	1	0	2	11,114
		Seaside	0	0	1	0	0	0	1	0	0	34,204
		Sebastopol	1	0	0	0	0	0	1	0	0	7,523
		Signal Hill	0	0	2	0	0	0	0	1	1	11,270
		Solana Beach	0	1	0	0	0	0	0	0	1	12,601
		Soledad	1	0	1	0	0	0	0	2	0	28,431
		Sonora	1	0	0	0	0	0	0	1	0	4,679
		South Gate	2	0	0	0	0	0	1	0	1	98,701
		South Lake Tahoe	0	0	0	1	0	0	0	1	0	23,872
		South San Francisco	1	0	0	0	0	0	1	0	0	61,458
		Stanton	1	0	0	2	0	1	0	2	0	37,666
		Stockton	5	0	1	4	0	2	2	2	4	297,170
		Sunnyvale	0	0	0	1	0	0	1	0	0	130,326
		Taft	0	0	0	1	0	0	0	0	1	9,198
		Temecula	3	2	0	1	0	0	2	2	2	93,665
		Temple City	1	0	0	0	0	0	1	0	0	38,546
		Thousand Oaks	1	3	0	2	0	1	1	2	2	125,196
		Torrance	3	0	0	0	0	1	1	1	0	142,970

[1]Agencies published in this table indicated that at least one hate crime incident occurred in their respective jurisdictions during the quarter(s) for which they submitted a report to the Hate Crime program. Blanks indicate quarters for which agencies did not submit reports.
[2]Population figures are published only for the cities. The figures listed for the universities and colleges are student enrollment and were provided by the United States Department of Education for the 2006 school year, the most recent available. The enrollment figures include full-time and part-time students.

Table 94. Hate Crime Incidents per Bias Motivation and Quarter by State and Agency, 2007 *(Contd.)*

State	Agency type	Agency name	Number of incidents per bias motivation					Number of incidents per quarter[1]				Population[2]
			Race	Religion	Sexual orientation	Ethnicity	Disability	1st quarter	2nd quarter	3rd quarter	4th quarter	
		Turlock	0	0	1	1	0	2	0	0	0	70,386
		Tustin	0	0	1	0	0	0	0	1	0	69,945
		Union City	5	0	2	0	0	1	5	1	0	69,769
		Upland	2	0	0	1	0	2	1	0	0	74,049
		Vacaville	3	0	1	1	0	1	4	0	0	93,167
		Ventura	0	0	1	2	0	3	0	0	0	104,523
		Visalia	1	0	1	0	0	0	0	2	0	116,766
		Vista	2	0	0	1	0	0	2	0	1	89,851
		Walnut	1	0	0	0	0	0	1	0	0	31,470
		Walnut Creek	1	2	0	1	0	0	1	2	1	63,568
		Watsonville	0	0	1	0	0	0	0	1	0	49,031
		West Covina	3	2	0	0	0	1	1	2	1	108,097
		West Hollywood	0	2	7	1	0	1	1	7	1	36,604
		West Sacramento	1	0	0	1	0	1	1	0	0	46,245
		Whittier	2	0	1	0	0	2	0	0	1	84,038
		Woodland	0	0	2	1	0	0	2	1	0	51,355
		Yorba Linda	0	0	0	1	0	0	0	1	0	66,252
		Yuba City	5	1	1	1	0	2	3	1	2	61,881
	Universities and Colleges		18	11	8	4	0					
		California State University:										
		Bakersfield	1	0	0	0	0	1	0	0	0	7,711
		Dominguez Hills	0	1	0	0	0	1	0	0	0	12,068
		Fresno	1	0	0	0	0	0	1	0	0	22,098
		Fullerton	1	0	0	0	0	0	0	0	1	35,921
		Monterey Bay	0	0	1	0	0	0	0	0	1	3,818
		Northridge	1	0	1	1	0	1	1	0	1	34,560
		Sacramento	0	0	1	1	0	1	0	1	0	28,529
		San Bernardino	0	0	1	0	0	0	1	0	0	16,479
		Fresno Community College	1	0	0	0	0	0	0	1	0	22,040
		Humboldt State University	2	0	0	0	0	2	0	0	0	7,435
		San Francisco State University	2	3	0	0	0	0	1	4	0	29,628
		Santa Rosa Junior College	0	0	0	1	0	0	0	0	1	24,806
		Solano Community College	1	1	0	0	0	2	0	0	0	10,900
		University of California:										
		Berkeley	0	1	2	0	0	1	1	1	0	33,920
		Davis	2	0	1	1	0	1	0	1	2	29,628
		Los Angeles	1	0	0	0	0	1	0	0	0	36,611
		Riverside	0	2	0	0	0	0	1	1	0	16,875
		Santa Cruz	5	3	1	0	0	7	1	1	0	15,364
	Metropolitan Counties		79	27	22	22	0					
		Contra Costa	0	0	1	0	0	0	0	1	0	
		Imperial	1	0	0	0	0	0	0	0	1	
		Kern	4	0	1	2	0	0	2	3	2	
		Los Angeles	35	11	5	7	0	12	18	16	12	
		Marin	0	1	1	0	0	1	1	0	0	
		Merced	0	1	0	0	0	0	0	1	0	
		Orange	3	1	1	0	0	1	2	2	0	
		Riverside	8	5	1	2	0	3	5	3	5	
		Sacramento	8	0	5	5	0	7	6	2	3	
		San Diego	13	3	4	3	0	10	2	8	3	
		San Luis Obispo	0	1	0	0	0	0	0	1	0	
		Santa Clara	0	0	1	1	0	1	1	0	0	
		Santa Cruz	1	1	2	0	0	1	2	1	0	
		Shasta	0	1	0	0	0	1	0	0	0	
		Sonoma	1	0	0	1	0	0	2	0	0	
		Stanislaus	2	0	0	1	0	0	1	1	1	
		Ventura	0	2	0	0	0	0	0	2	0	
		Yuba	3	0	0	0	0	1	0	2	0	
	Nonmetropolitan Counties		7	0	5	3	0					
		Amador	2	0	0	2	0	1	0	2	1	
		Calaveras	1	0	0	0	0	0	0	1	0	
		Colusa	0	0	1	0	0	0	0	1	0	
		Glenn	1	0	0	1	0	1	0	0	1	
		Inyo	0	0	1	0	0	0	1	0	0	
		Lake	1	0	2	0	0	1	0	1	1	
		Lassen	1	0	0	0	0	1	0	0	0	
		Mendocino	1	0	0	0	0	0	0	1	0	
		Tuolumne	0	0	1	0	0	1	0	0	0	

[1]Agencies published in this table indicated that at least one hate crime incident occurred in their respective jurisdictions during the quarter(s) for which they submitted a report to the Hate Crime program. Blanks indicate quarters for which agencies did not submit reports.

[2]Population figures are published only for the cities. The figures listed for the universities and colleges are student enrollment and were provided by the United States Department of Education for the 2006 school year, the most recent available. The enrollment figures include full-time and part-time students.

Table 94. Hate Crime Incidents per Bias Motivation and Quarter by State and Agency, 2007 *(Contd.)*

State	Agency type	Agency name	Number of incidents per bias motivation					Number of incidents per quarter[1]				Popu-lation[2]
			Race	Religion	Sexual orient-ation	Ethnicity	Disability	1st quarter	2nd quarter	3rd quarter	4th quarter	
	State Police Agencies		1	0	0	0	0					
		Highway Patrol, San Bernardino County	1	0	0	0	0	1	0	0	0	
	Other Agencies		3	0	2	2	0					
		Department of Parks and Recreation, Gold Fields District	0	0	1	0	0	0	0	1	0	
		East Bay Regional Parks, Contra Costa County	0	0	1	0	0	0	1	0	0	
		Los Angeles Transportation Services Bureau	3	0	0	2	0	2	2	1	0	
COLORADO...............	**Total**		75	14	32	34	1					
	Cities		58	9	26	27	1					
		Arvada	2	1	2	0	0	0	2	2	1	105,197
		Aurora	3	0	1	1	0	0	2	2	1	307,621
		Berthoud	1	0	0	0	0	1	0	0	0	5,142
		Boulder	4	3	3	0	0	3	0	6	1	91,047
		Castle Rock	0	0	1	0	0	0	0	1	0	43,523
		Centennial	3	1	0	0	0	0	1	2	1	97,746
		Colorado Springs	3	0	3	1	0	2	2	2	1	374,112
		Commerce City	0	0	1	0	0	0	1	0	0	42,386
		Cortez	1	0	0	0	0	0	1	0	0	8,513
		Craig	1	0	1	3	0	0	3	0	2	9,262
		Denver	13	2	5	4	0	1	7	10	6	573,387
		Englewood	1	0	0	3	0	1	0	2	1	32,362
		Evans	0	0	0	1	0	0	1	0	0	19,420
		Fort Collins	5	0	2	1	0	0	2	4	2	130,935
		Fort Lupton	0	0	1	0	0	1	0	0	0	7,464
		Glendale	0	0	0	1	0	0	0	1	0	4,800
		Glenwood Springs	0	0	0	2	0	0	0	2	0	8,904
		Grand Junction	3	0	0	1	0	0	2	2	0	47,235
		Greeley	1	0	1	1	0	0	1	0	2	90,707
		Gunnison	1	1	0	0	0	0	0	1	1	5,296
		Johnstown	1	0	0	0	0	1	0	0	0	9,021
		Kersey	1	0	0	0	0	1	0	0	0	1,421
		Lafayette	0	0	1	1	0	1	0	0	1	24,340
		Lakewood	1	0	0	3	0	1	1	1	1	139,407
		Littleton	0	0	0	0	1	0	1	0	0	40,343
		Lone Tree	1	0	0	0	0	0	0	0	1	9,349
		Louisville	1	0	0	0	0	1	0	0	0	18,335
		Loveland	0	1	1	1	0	0	0	3	0	62,586
		New Castle	2	0	0	1	0	0	1	2	0	3,526
		Steamboat Springs	5	0	0	2	0	0	1	5	1	9,233
		Sterling	0	0	1	0	0	1	0	0	0	12,549
		Telluride	1	0	1	0	0	0	1	1	0	2,274
		Thornton	1	0	0	0	0	0	1	0	0	113,289
		Trinidad	1	0	0	0	0	0	0	1	0	9,135
		Walsenburg	0	0	1	0	0	1	0	0	0	3,914
		Wheat Ridge	1	0	0	0	0	1	0	0	0	30,718
	Universities and Colleges		3	1	0	0	0					
		Auraria Higher Education Center[3]	1	0	0	0	0	0	0	0	1	
		Colorado State University, Fort Collins	2	1	0	0	0	2	0	0	1	27,636
	Metropolitan Counties		11	4	5	5	0					
		Adams	0	0	0	1	0	0	1	0	0	
		Arapahoe	4	3	0	2	0	2	3	3	1	
		Douglas	1	0	0	1	0	2	0	0	0	
		Gilpin	0	0	1	0	0	0	0	0	1	
		Jefferson	0	0	2	0	0	0	0	1	1	
		Mesa	5	0	1	1	0	1	1	3	2	
		Weld	1	1	1	0	0	0	1	2	0	
	Nonmetropolitan Counties		1	0	1	2	0					
		Garfield	1	0	1	1	0	0	1	0	2	
		Routt	0	0	0	1	0	0	0	1	0	
	Other Agencies		2	0	0	0	0					
		Colorado Mental Health Institute	2	0	0	0	0	0	2	0	0	
CONNECTICUT..........	**Total**		66	31	18	11	1					
	Cities		57	29	12	10	1					
		Bloomfield	1	0	1	0	0	0	0	1	1	20,759
		Branford	0	1	0	0	0	0	0	1	0	29,074

[1]Agencies published in this table indicated that at least one hate crime incident occurred in their respective jurisdictions during the quarter(s) for which they submitted a report to the Hate Crime program. Blanks indicate quarters for which agencies did not submit reports.

[2]Population figures are published only for the cities. The figures listed for the universities and colleges are student enrollment and were provided by the United States Department of Education for the 2006 school year, the most recent available. The enrollment figures include full-time and part-time students.

[3]Student enrollment figures were not available.

Table 94.   Hate Crime Incidents per Bias Motivation and Quarter by State and Agency, 2007 *(Contd.)*

State	Agency type	Agency name	Number of incidents per bias motivation					Number of incidents per quarter[1]				Popu-lation[2]
			Race	Religion	Sexual orient-ation	Ethnicity	Disability	1st quarter	2nd quarter	3rd quarter	4th quarter	
		Bridgeport	1	0	1	0	0	1	0	1	0	137,655
		Bristol	1	0	0	1	0	0	1	0	1	61,292
		Clinton	2	0	1	0	1	0	1	1	2	13,695
		Derby	1	0	0	0	0	0	1	0	0	12,465
		East Hartford	1	0	0	1	0	0	0	1	1	48,752
		Enfield	2	0	0	0	0	0	1	1	0	45,229
		Farmington	2	0	0	0	0	1	1	0	0	25,190
		Glastonbury	0	2	0	0	0	0	0	2	0	33,179
		Greenwich	1	1	0	0	0	0	2	0	0	62,196
		Groton	1	0	0	0	0	0	1	0	0	9,314
		Groton Town	2	1	0	0	0	0	1	2	0	29,377
		Guilford	0	0	1	1	0	1	0	1	0	22,462
		Hamden	1	0	0	0	0	1	0	0	0	57,982
		Hartford	2	0	0	0	0	1	0	1	0	124,558
		Madison	1	0	0	1	0	0	1	0	1	18,873
		Manchester	0	0	1	0	0	0	0	1	0	55,774
		Middletown	0	0	1	0	0	0	0	1	0	47,743
		Milford	1	0	1	0	0	0	0	0	2	55,404
		Monroe	0	2	0	0	0	1	1	0	0	19,599
		Naugatuck	5	0	0	1	0	0	1	1	4	31,994
		New Britain	1	0	0	0	0	0	0	1	0	70,630
		New Haven	0	1	0	1	0			2		124,034
		New Milford	2	1	0	1	0	1	2	0	1	28,890
		Norwalk	3	0	0	0	0	0	2	0	1	84,343
		Norwich	3	0	0	0	0	1	1	0	1	36,353
		Orange	2	0	1	0	0	0	0	0	3	13,942
		Plainfield	1	0	0	0	0	0	0	0	1	15,538
		Plymouth	3	0	0	0	0	0	1	1	1	12,225
		Seymour	0	1	0	0	0	0	0	0	1	16,327
		Shelton	0	2	0	0	0	0	1	0	1	40,425
		Southington	1	0	0	1	0	0	1	0	1	42,522
		South Windsor	1	0	0	0	0	0	0	1	0	26,214
		Stamford	2	0	0	0	0	1	0	1	0	119,510
		Stratford	2	6	0	0	0	4	1	1	2	49,440
		Suffield	1	1	0	0	0	0	1	1	0	15,334
		Torrington	0	1	1	0	0	0	1	1	0	35,997
		Trumbull	2	0	0	1	0	1	2	0	0	35,055
		Vernon	1	0	0	0	0	0	0	1	0	29,843
		Wallingford	0	1	0	0	0	0	1	0	0	44,979
		Waterford	0	0	1	0	0	0	0	0	1	18,780
		West Hartford	1	2	2	0	0	2	0	2	1	60,644
		Weston	0	1	0	0	0	0	1	0	0	10,277
		Westport	3	2	0	0	0	0	0	4	1	26,704
		Wilton	0	3	0	1	0	0	3	1	0	17,879
		Winchester	1	0	0	0	0	0	0	0	1	10,888
		Windsor Locks	2	0	0	0	0	1	1	0	0	12,475
	Universities and Colleges		6	1	5	0	0					
		Eastern Connecticut State University	0	0	2	0	0	0	0	2	0	5,239
		University of Connecticut: Health Center[3]	1	0	0	0	0	1	0	0	0	
		Storrs, Avery Point, and Hartford[3]	4	1	3	0	0	5	0	0	3	
		Western Connecticut State University	1	0	0	0	0	1	0	0	0	6,086
	State Police Agencies		3	1	1	1	0					
		Connecticut State Police	3	1	1	1	0	2	0	0	4	
DELAWARE	**Total**		27	6	7	9	0					
	Cities		6	1	1	8	0					
		Dewey Beach	1	0	1	0	0	0	0	2	0	313
		Elsmere	1	0	0	0	0	0	1	0	0	5,721
		Georgetown	0	0	0	7	0	2	1	0	4	4,964
		Harrington	1	0	0	0	0	0	0	1	0	3,276
		Laurel	0	0	0	1	0	0	0	0	1	3,842
		Milford	2	0	0	0	0	0	1	0	1	7,995
		Newark	0	1	0	0	0	1	0	0	0	30,158
		Wilmington	1	0	0	0	0	0	0	0	1	72,842
	Universities and Colleges		3	0	2	1	0					
		University of Delaware	3	0	2	1	0	4	0	2	0	20,380
	Metropolitan Counties		6	2	1	0	0					
		New Castle County Police Department	6	2	1	0	0	3	2	1	3	

[1]Agencies published in this table indicated that at least one hate crime incident occurred in their respective jurisdictions during the quarter(s) for which they submitted a report to the Hate Crime program. Blanks indicate quarters for which agencies did not submit reports.
[2]Population figures are published only for the cities. The figures listed for the universities and colleges are student enrollment and were provided by the United States Department of Education for the 2006 school year, the most recent available. The enrollment figures include full-time and part-time students.
[3]Student enrollment figures were not available.

Table 94.   Hate Crime Incidents per Bias Motivation and Quarter by State and Agency, 2007 *(Contd.)*

State	Agency type	Agency name	Number of incidents per bias motivation					Number of incidents per quarter[1]				Popu-lation[2]
			Race	Religion	Sexual orient-ation	Ethnicity	Disability	1st quarter	2nd quarter	3rd quarter	4th quarter	
	State Police Agencies		12	3	2	0	0					
		State Police:										
		Kent County	5	2	0	0	0	0	0	2	5	
		New Castle County	4	1	2	0	0	2	1	3	1	
		Sussex County	3	0	0	0	0	0	0	2	1	
	Other Agencies		0	0	1	0	0					
		Park Rangers	0	0	1	0	0	0	0	1	0	
DISTRICT OF COLUMBIA	**Total**		3	7	29	2	0					
	Cities		3	6	26	2	0					
		Washington	3	6	26	2	0	11	8	11	7	588,292
	Other Agencies		0	1	3	0	0					
		Metro Transit Police	0	1	3	0	0	1	3	0	0	
FLORIDA	**Total**		86	26	25	29	0					
	Cities		52	16	15	16	0					
		Altamonte Springs	1	0	0	0	0	0	0	1	0	40,513
		Aventura	0	1	0	0	0	1	0	0	0	30,782
		Boca Raton	0	0	0	2	0	0	1	1	0	86,868
		Cape Coral	1	1	1	2	0	1	1	3	0	159,936
		Casselberry	0	0	0	1	0	0	0	1	0	24,663
		Cocoa	0	0	1	0	0	0	0	0	1	16,704
		Coconut Creek	2	0	0	0	0	0	0	0	2	51,033
		Coral Gables	2	0	2	0	0	1	1	0	2	42,794
		Coral Springs	1	0	0	0	0	0	0	0	1	131,307
		Crystal River	1	0	0	0	0	0	0	0	1	3,590
		Dania	1	0	0	0	0	0	1	0	0	29,011
		Delray Beach	1	2	0	0	0	2	0	1	0	65,262
		Fort Lauderdale	2	1	1	0	0	0	1	1	2	187,995
		Gainesville	6	0	0	0	0	0	3	3	0	108,289
		Hallandale	2	0	0	0	0	0	0	2	0	40,147
		Homestead	1	0	0	0	0	1	0	0	0	58,074
		Jacksonville	1	0	0	0	0	0	1	0	0	797,350
		Jupiter	0	0	0	1	0	0	0	1	0	50,294
		Lake Clarke Shores	0	1	0	0	0	1	0	0	0	3,397
		Lakeland	0	0	0	1	0	0	0	0	1	91,009
		Largo	0	0	0	1	0	0	0	0	1	73,789
		Leesburg	1	0	0	0	0	0	0	1	0	20,401
		Longwood	0	0	0	2	0	0	2	0	0	13,482
		Melbourne	5	2	1	1	0	2	4	1	2	77,678
		Miami Beach	0	2	1	2	0	1	1	2	1	86,742
		Miramar	2	0	0	0	0	0	1	0	1	114,029
		New Smyrna Beach	0	0	1	0	0	0	0	1	0	23,067
		North Miami	0	0	1	0	0	1	0	0	0	57,368
		North Port	2	0	0	1	0	1	1	1	0	56,539
		Oakland Park	0	0	1	0	0	1	0	0	0	42,486
		Ocoee	1	0	0	0	0	0	0	0	1	31,604
		Oviedo	0	0	1	0	0	0	0	0	1	31,269
		Palm Bay	1	0	0	0	0	0	0	1	0	100,666
		Panama City	2	0	1	0	0	1	0	2	0	36,840
		Pensacola	2	0	0	0	0	0	0	1	1	52,837
		Port Orange	0	0	0	1	0	1	0	0	0	56,155
		Port St. Lucie	1	0	1	1	0	0	1	2	0	154,036
		Sunny Isles Beach	0	1	0	0	0	0	0	0	1	15,190
		Tampa	8	4	1	0	0	4	4	4	1	337,220
		Tarpon Springs	1	0	0	0	0	1	0	0	0	23,523
		Venice	2	0	0	0	0	1	0	1	0	21,329
		Wellington	0	1	0	0	0	1	0	0	0	57,713
		Wilton Manors	0	0	1	0	0	0	0	1	0	12,937
		Winter Garden	1	0	0	0	0	0	1	0	0	29,284
		Winter Park	1	0	0	0	0	1	0	0	0	28,114
	Universities and Colleges		3	1	0	0	0					
		Florida Atlantic University	0	1	0	0	0	1	0	0	0	25,325
		University of Central Florida	1	0	0	0	0	1	0	0	0	46,646
		University of West Florida	2	0	0	0	0	1	0	1	0	9,819
	Metropolitan Counties		30	8	9	12	0					
		Alachua	1	0	0	0	0	0	0	1	0	
		Bay	2	1	0	0	0	0	1	2	0	
		Brevard	1	0	0	1	0	2	0	0	0	
		Broward	0	1	0	0	0	0	1	0	0	
		Charlotte	1	0	0	0	0	1	0	0	0	

[1] Agencies published in this table indicated that at least one hate crime incident occurred in their respective jurisdictions during the quarter(s) for which they submitted a report to the Hate Crime program. Blanks indicate quarters for which agencies did not submit reports.

[2] Population figures are published only for the cities. The figures listed for the universities and colleges are student enrollment and were provided by the United States Department of Education for the 2006 school year, the most recent available. The enrollment figures include full-time and part-time students.

Table 94. Hate Crime Incidents per Bias Motivation and Quarter by State and Agency, 2007 *(Contd.)*

State	Agency type	Agency name	Number of incidents per bias motivation					Number of incidents per quarter[1]				Popu-lation[2]
			Race	Religion	Sexual orient-ation	Ethnicity	Disability	1st quarter	2nd quarter	3rd quarter	4th quarter	
		Clay	3	0	1	1	0	2	1	2	0	
		Collier	4	2	0	1	0	1	4	1	1	
		Escambia	3	0	1	0	0	3	0	1	0	
		Flagler	3	2	0	0	0	3	1	1	0	
		Hernando	2	0	0	0	0	0	1	0	1	
		Hillsborough	1	1	1	1	0	1	1	2	0	
		Indian River	1	0	1	1	0	0	2	1	0	
		Lake	1	0	0	0	0	0	0	1	0	
		Lee	1	0	1	4	0	3	3	0	0	
		Manatee	0	0	1	0	0	1	0	0	0	
		Orange	0	0	1	1	0	0	0	1	1	
		Osceola	0	0	0	1	0	0	1	0	0	
		Palm Beach	1	1	0	0	0	0	1	1	0	
		Pinellas	0	0	0	1	0	0	1	0	0	
		Polk	0	0	1	0	0	1	0	0	0	
		Santa Rosa	4	0	1	0	0	1	2	0	2	
		Volusia	1	0	0	0	0	0	1	0	0	
	Nonmetropolitan Counties		0	1	1	1	0					
		DeSoto	0	0	0	1	0	0	0	1	0	
		Monroe	0	1	1	0	0	0	1	0	1	
	Other Agencies		1	0	0	0	0					
		Lee County Port Authority	1	0	0	0	0	0	0	1	0	
GEORGIA	Total		3	0	6	4	0					
	Cities		1	0	6	4	0					
		Atlanta	0	0	6	1	0	3	3	0	1	497,290
		Norcross	1	0	0	3	0	3	1	0		10,378
	Metropolitan Counties		2	0	0	0	0					
		Catoosa	2	0	0	0	0		2			
IDAHO	Total		18	6	7	7	0					
	Cities		16	5	7	7	0					
		Bellevue	1	0	0	1	0	2	0	0	0	2,238
		Boise	4	3	1	2	0	1	3	1	5	199,104
		Coeur d'Alene	2	0	1	1	0	1	2	1	0	42,324
		Hailey	2	0	0	0	0	0	2	0	0	7,984
		Idaho Falls	1	0	2	1	0	1	2	1	0	53,049
		Jerome	1	0	0	0	0	0	0	0	1	8,778
		Lewiston	2	0	0	0	0	0	0	2	0	31,356
		Nampa	0	1	2	1	0	0	2	1	1	80,397
		Pocatello	1	0	0	0	0	0	1	0	0	54,274
		Rexburg	0	0	0	1	0	1	0	0	0	28,308
		Spirit Lake	0	1	0	0	0	0	1	0	0	1,656
		Sun Valley	1	0	1	0	0	0	2	0	0	1,455
		Twin Falls	1	0	0	0	0	1	0	0	0	41,236
	Metropolitan Counties		2	1	0	0	0					
		Ada	1	0	0	0	0	0	0	0	1	
		Bonneville	0	1	0	0	0	0	0	0	1	
		Kootenai	1	0	0	0	0	0	1	0	0	
ILLINOIS	Total		94	21	29	21	2					
	Cities		86	21	27	18	2					
		Alton	1	0	0	0	0			1		29,101
		Aurora	8	0	1	3	0	4	1	5	2	174,724
		Beecher	0	0	0	0	1		1			3,086
		Bloomington	3	1	1	1	0	1	2	1	2	71,770
		Carpentersville	1	0	0	0	0			1		38,394
		Chicago	15	8	12	1	1	8	10	14	5	2,824,434
		Columbia	1	0	0	0	0				1	9,281
		Crest Hill	1	0	0	0	0	1				21,759
		Decatur	6	1	2	0	0	2	5	1	1	76,383
		Downers Grove	1	1	0	0	0		1		1	49,090
		Elgin	0	1	0	0	0	0	0	0	1	102,960
		Elwood	1	0	0	0	0				1	2,412
		Evanston	2	1	0	0	0	1	0	2		75,746
		Granite City	2	0	0	0	0		1		1	30,411
		La Grange	1	1	0	0	0		1		1	15,374
		Lombard	2	0	0	0	0				2	42,811
		Marion	3	0	0	0	0			2	1	17,459
		McHenry	0	0	0	1	0			1		26,526
		Naperville	3	0	0	0	0	0	0	0	3	144,933
		Normal	1	0	0	0	0	0	0	1	0	51,458
		Oak Brook	0	0	1	0	0			1		8,893
		Oak Park	1	0	0	0	0				1	49,968

[1]Agencies published in this table indicated that at least one hate crime incident occurred in their respective jurisdictions during the quarter(s) for which they submitted a report to the Hate Crime program. Blanks indicate quarters for which agencies did not submit reports.

[2]Population figures are published only for the cities. The figures listed for the universities and colleges are student enrollment and were provided by the United States Department of Education for the 2006 school year, the most recent available. The enrollment figures include full-time and part-time students.

Table 94. Hate Crime Incidents per Bias Motivation and Quarter by State and Agency, 2007 *(Contd.)*

State	Agency type	Agency name	Number of incidents per bias motivation					Number of incidents per quarter[1]				Popu-lation[2]
			Race	Religion	Sexual orient-ation	Ethnicity	Disability	1st quarter	2nd quarter	3rd quarter	4th quarter	
		Palatine	0	2	0	0	0	2			1	67,550
		Paris	1	0	0	0	0				1	8,818
		Park Ridge	0	1	0	0	0			1		36,762
		Pekin	2	0	0	0	0			2		33,298
		Peoria	3	0	2	1	0	2	3	0	1	113,137
		Rockdale	1	0	0	0	0	1				2,058
		Rockford	7	1	5	4	0	4	2	5	6	155,713
		Rock Island	1	0	0	0	0				1	38,275
		Round Lake	1	0	0	0	0		1			18,722
		Rushville	1	0	0	0	0	0		1		3,110
		Schaumburg	1	0	0	1	0			1	1	72,320
		Skokie	1	2	1	1	0	2	0	3		67,148
		Springfield	12	0	1	4	0	4	3	8	2	117,185
		Urbana	1	0	1	1	0	1		2		38,771
		West Chicago	0	1	0	0	0			1		27,176
		Westmont	1	0	0	0	0				1	25,083
	Universities and Colleges		5	0	2	1	0					
		Eastern Illinois University	1	0	0	0	0		1			12,349
		Northern Illinois University	4	0	0	0	0	1		2	1	25,313
		Northwestern University, Evanston[3]	0	0	1	0	0				1	
		University of Illinois, Urbana	0	0	0	1	0	1				42,738
		Western Illinois University	0	0	1	0	0				1	13,602
	Metropolitan Counties		3	0	0	2	0					
		Du Page	0	0	0	2	0			1	1	
		Peoria	3	0	0	0	0		1	1	1	
INDIANA	**Total**		25	9	3	3	0					
	Cities		23	8	1	3	0					
		Angola	0	1	0	0	0	1	0			7,979
		Bloomington[4]	13	4	0	0	0	2	6	3	6	68,918
		Clarksville	2	0	0	0	0	1	0	0	1	21,295
		Columbus	1	2	0	1	0	2	1		1	39,764
		Evansville	2	0	0	0	0	0	2	0	0	114,985
		Fishers	2	1	0	0	0	1	1	1	0	66,099
		Fort Wayne	1	0	1	0	0	1	1	0	0	248,423
		Greenwood	0	0	0	1	0	0	1	0	0	46,063
		Munster	2	0	0	0	0	0	0	1	1	22,467
		Seymour	0	0	0	1	0	1		0	0	19,246
	Universities and Colleges		1	1	2	0	0					
		Ball State University	0	0	1	0	0	0	0	1	0	20,030
		Purdue University	1	1	1	0	0	0	3	0	0	40,609
	Metropolitan Counties		1	0	0	0	0					
		Elkhart	1	0	0	0	0	0	1	0	0	
IOWA	**Total**		16	1	5	5	0					
	Cities		14	0	4	4	0					
		Cedar Falls	0	0	1	0	0	0	0	0	1	36,995
		Coralville	1	0	0	0	0	0	0	1	0	18,496
		Council Bluffs	3	0	0	0	0	0	0	2	1	60,531
		Davenport	0	0	2	0	0	2	0	0	0	99,631
		Decorah	0	0	0	1	0	0	0	1	0	8,066
		Des Moines	1	0	0	1	0	1	0	1	0	192,948
		Dubuque	3	0	0	0	0	0	1	1	1	57,694
		Fort Dodge	1	0	0	0	0	0	1	0	0	25,330
		Keokuk	4	0	0	0	0	0	0	4		10,585
		Marion	1	0	0	0	0	0	1	0	0	31,772
		Ottumwa	0	0	0	1	0	0	0	1	0	24,822
		Perry	0	0	1	0	0	1	0	0	0	9,001
		Sioux City	0	0	0	1	0	0	1	0	0	82,942
	Universities and Colleges		1	1	1	1	0					
		Iowa State University	0	0	0	1	0	0	0	1	0	25,462
		University of Iowa	1	1	1	0	0	1	2	0	0	28,816
	Metropolitan Counties		1	0	0	0	0					
		Polk	1	0	0	0	0		0	1	0	
KANSAS	**Total**		63	13	19	15	0					
	Cities		47	12	16	14	0					
		Andover	1	0	0	0	0	0	0	1	0	9,955
		Augusta	1	0	0	0	0	0	0	1	0	8,715
		Chanute	0	0	1	0	0	0	0	1	0	8,822
		Coffeyville	1	0	0	0	0	0	0	0	1	10,280

[1]Agencies published in this table indicated that at least one hate crime incident occurred in their respective jurisdictions during the quarter(s) for which they submitted a report to the Hate Crime program. Blanks indicate quarters for which agencies did not submit reports.
[2]Population figures are published only for the cities. The figures listed for the universities and colleges are student enrollment and were provided by the United States Department of Education for the 2006 school year, the most recent available. The enrollment figures include full-time and part-time students.
[4]Includes one incident reported with more than one bias motivation.

Table 94. Hate Crime Incidents per Bias Motivation and Quarter by State and Agency, 2007 *(Contd.)*

State	Agency type	Agency name	Number of incidents per bias motivation					Number of incidents per quarter[1]				Population[2]
			Race	Religion	Sexual orient-ation	Ethnicity	Disability	1st quarter	2nd quarter	3rd quarter	4th quarter	
		Columbus	1	0	0	0	0	0	0	1	0	3,216
		Concordia	1	1	0	0	0	1	1	0	0	5,229
		Edwardsville	0	0	0	1	0	0	1	0	0	4,565
		El Dorado	1	0	0	0	0	1	0	0	0	12,693
		Emporia	1	1	1	3	0	2	1	1	2	26,125
		Garden City	0	0	1	0	0	1	0	0	0	26,949
		Grandview Plaza	1	0	0	0	0	0	1	0	0	995
		Hays	1	0	0	1	0	0	1	1	0	19,672
		Haysville	1	0	0	0	0	0	1	0	0	10,227
		Hutchinson	2	1	0	0	0	0	1	1	1	40,941
		Independence	1	0	0	0	0	0	1	0	0	9,229
		Iola	0	0	1	0	0	0	0	1	0	5,916
		Lansing	1	1	0	1	0	1	1	0	1	10,861
		Lawrence	1	1	1	0	0	0	2	0	1	90,044
		Leavenworth	2	0	2	0	0	1	2	1	0	34,918
		Lenexa	0	0	1	0	0	0	0	1	0	45,059
		Osage City	1	0	0	0	0	0	1	0	0	2,936
		Ottawa	1	0	0	0	0	0	0	1	0	12,901
		Paola	1	0	0	0	0	1	0	0	0	5,378
		Parsons	1	0	0	2	0	0	1	2	0	11,190
		Pittsburg	1	0	0	1	0	1	0	1	0	19,104
		Pratt	2	1	0	0	0	1	2	0	0	6,389
		Salina	5	5	2	1	0	5	2	3	3	46,180
		Shawnee	0	0	0	1	0	1	0	0	0	60,950
		Spring Hill	1	0	0	0	0	0	0	0	1	5,203
		Valley Center	1	0	0	0	0	0	1	0	0	6,044
		Valley Falls	0	0	1	0	0	0	1	0	0	1,182
		Wichita	16	1	5	3	0	5	5	7	8	358,294
	Universities and Colleges		1	0	1	0	0					
		Pittsburg State University	1	0	0	0	0	1	0	0	0	6,859
		University of Kansas, Main Campus	0	0	1	0	0	0	0	0	1	26,773
	Metropolitan Counties		2	0	1	0	0					
		Miami	1	0	0	0	0	0	1	0	0	
		Shawnee	1	0	1	0	0	1	0	0	1	
	Nonmetropolitan Counties		11	1	1	1	0					
		Cowley	0	1	0	0	0	1	0	0	0	
		Finney	1	0	1	0	0	0	1	0	1	
		Kearny	1	0	0	0	0	0	1	0	0	
		Lyon	1	0	0	0	0	0	0	0	1	
		Montgomery	2	0	0	0	0	0	1	1	0	
		Riley County Police Department	6	0	0	0	0	4	1	1	0	
		Stevens	0	0	0	1	0	1	0	0	0	
	Other Agencies		2	0	0	0	0					
		Kansas Bureau of Investigation	1	0	0	0	0	0	1	0	0	
		Unified School District, Auburn-Washburn	1	0	0	0	0	1				
KENTUCKY................	**Total**		30	6	9	3	0					
	Cities		18	6	9	3	0					
		Anchorage	1	0	0	0	0	0	1	0	0	2,804
		Ashland	1	0	0	0	0	0	0	1		21,482
		Bellevue	1	0	0	0	0	0	1	0		5,871
		Bowling Green	1	0	2	0	0	0	2	0	1	53,663
		Covington	3	1	0	0	0	0		4		42,682
		Elsmere	1	0	0	0	0	0	1	0	0	7,848
		Henderson	0	0	1	0	0	1		0		27,960
		Lexington	3	1	2	1	0	1		5	1	272,815
		Louisville Metro	1	0	1	0	0	1	1		0	624,030
		Mount Sterling	1	0	0	0	0	0	0	1	0	6,569
		Murray	1	2	1	0	0	0	3	0	1	15,811
		Newport	2	0	0	0	0	0	1	0	1	15,540
		Paducah	0	1	1	0	0	0	2	0	0	25,550
		Paris	0	0	0	1	0	0	1	0		9,329
		Richmond	1	0	0	0	0	0	1	0	0	32,017
		St. Matthews	0	1	0	0	0	1	0	0	0	17,676
		Versailles	1	0	1	1	0	0	3	0	0	7,726
	Universities and Colleges		2	0	0	0	0					
		University of Kentucky	2	0	0	0	0			1	1	26,382
	Metropolitan Counties		7	0	0	0	0					
		Boone	2	0	0	0	0	0	1	0	1	
		Daviess	4	0	0	0	0	0	0	3	1	
		Kenton County Police Department	1	0	0	0	0		0	1	0	

[1]Agencies published in this table indicated that at least one hate crime incident occurred in their respective jurisdictions during the quarter(s) for which they submitted a report to the Hate Crime program. Blanks indicate quarters for which agencies did not submit reports.

[2]Population figures are published only for the cities. The figures listed for the universities and colleges are student enrollment and were provided by the United States Department of Education for the 2006 school year, the most recent available. The enrollment figures include full-time and part-time students.

Table 94.   Hate Crime Incidents per Bias Motivation and Quarter by State and Agency, 2007 *(Contd.)*

State	Agency type	Agency name	Number of incidents per bias motivation					Number of incidents per quarter[1]				Popu-lation[2]
			Race	Religion	Sexual orient-ation	Ethnicity	Disability	1st quarter	2nd quarter	3rd quarter	4th quarter	
	State Police Agencies		2	0	0	0	0					
		State Police	2	0	0	0	0	0	1	0	1	
	Other Agencies		1	0	0	0	0					
		Jefferson County Board of Education	1	0	0	0	0	0	0	1	0	
LOUISIANA	**Total**		22	4	2	3	0					
	Cities		13	2	1	2	0					
		Alexandria	1	0	0	0	0	0	0	1	0	45,720
		De Quincy	1	0	0	0	0	0	1	0	0	3,192
		Jennings	0	0	0	1	0	1	0	0	0	10,577
		Kentwood	2	0	0	0	0	0	0	2	0	2,302
		Mamou	7	0	0	0	0	0	0	0	7	3,443
		New Orleans	1	2	0	1	0	1	1	1	1	220,614
		Port Allen	1	0	1	0	0	1	1	0	0	5,136
	Metropolitan Counties		8	2	0	1	0					
		Bossier	1	1	0	0	0	0	0	1	1	
		Caddo	2	0	0	0	0	2	0	0	0	
		East Baton Rouge	1	0	0	0	0			1		
		Jefferson	1	0	0	0	0		1			
		Rapides	0	1	0	1	0	0	0	1	1	
		West Feliciana	3	0	0	0	0	0	2	0	1	
	Nonmetropolitan Counties		1	0	1	0	0					
		East Carroll	1	0	1	0	0	1	0	1	0	
MAINE	**Total**		39	7	21	5	0					
	Cities		32	7	13	5	0					
		Augusta	7	0	3	1	0	3	6	2	0	18,572
		Baileyville	1	0	0	0	0	0	0	1	0	1,593
		Bangor	5	1	0	1	0	3	1	3	0	30,940
		Bar Harbor	2	0	0	0	0	0	2	0	0	5,197
		Biddeford	0	1	0	0	0	1	0	0	0	22,079
		Calais	1	0	1	0	0	0	0	1	1	3,253
		Dixfield	1	0	0	0	0	0	0	1	0	2,564
		Eliot	0	0	1	0	0	1	0	0	0	6,453
		Gorham	1	0	0	0	0	0	1	0	0	15,593
		Kennebunk	0	0	1	0	0	0	0	1	0	11,658
		Lewiston	3	1	1	0	0	1	2	2	0	35,747
		Mechanic Falls	0	1	0	0	0	1	0	0	0	3,256
		Milo	1	0	0	0	0	1	0	0	0	2,414
		Ogunquit	0	1	0	0	0	0	0	1	0	1,295
		Old Orchard Beach	1	1	0	1	0	0	1	2	0	9,423
		Old Town	1	0	0	0	0	0	0	1	0	7,704
		Orono	0	0	1	0	0	0	0	0	1	9,737
		Portland	3	1	2	2	0	4	2	1	1	62,894
		Sabattus	0	0	1	0	0	0	0	1	0	4,702
		Sanford	1	0	0	0	0	0	1	0	0	21,648
		South Portland	2	0	2	0	0	1	0	2	1	23,836
		Waterville	1	0	0	0	0	0	0	0	1	15,631
		York	1	0	0	0	0	0	0	0	1	13,384
	Universities and Colleges		1	0	5	0	0					
		University of Southern Maine	1	0	5	0	0	2	1	0	3	10,478
	Metropolitan Counties		4	0	2	0	0					
		Cumberland	2	0	1	0	0	0	1	1	1	
		Penobscot	1	0	1	0	0	1	0	1	0	
		York	1	0	0	0	0	0	0	0	1	
	Nonmetropolitan Counties		2	0	0	0	0					
		Oxford	1	0	0	0	0	0	0	1	0	
		Waldo	1	0	0	0	0	0	0	1	0	
	State Police Agencies		0	0	1	0	0					
		State Police, Kennebec County	0	0	1	0	0	0	1	0	0	
MARYLAND	**Total**		82	40	19	9	0					
	Cities		8	4	2	2	0					
		Annapolis	1	0	0	1	0	2	0	0	0	36,462
		Baltimore	3	3	2	0	0	0	2	4	2	624,237
		Bel Air	1	0	0	0	0	0	0	0	1	10,074
		Cambridge	2	0	0	1	0	0	3	0	0	11,479
		Chestertown	1	0	0	0	0	0	0	1	0	4,942
		Frederick	0	1	0	0	0	0	0	0	1	59,731
	Universities and Colleges		9	1	2	0	0					
		Frostburg State University	4	0	0	0	0	0	1	2	1	4,910

[1]Agencies published in this table indicated that at least one hate crime incident occurred in their respective jurisdictions during the quarter(s) for which they submitted a report to the Hate Crime program. Blanks indicate quarters for which agencies did not submit reports.

[2]Population figures are published only for the cities. The figures listed for the universities and colleges are student enrollment and were provided by the United States Department of Education for the 2006 school year, the most recent available. The enrollment figures include full-time and part-time students.

Table 94. Hate Crime Incidents per Bias Motivation and Quarter by State and Agency, 2007 (Contd.)

State	Agency type	Agency name	Number of incidents per bias motivation					Number of incidents per quarter[1]				Popu-lation[2]
			Race	Religion	Sexual orient-ation	Ethnicity	Disability	1st quarter	2nd quarter	3rd quarter	4th quarter	
		St. Mary's College	2	0	0	0	0	1	0	1	0	1,957
		Towson University	2	1	2	0	0	0	1	0	4	18,921
		University of Maryland, College Park	1	0	0	0	0	0	1	0	0	35,102
	Metropolitan Counties		57	32	15	6	0					
		Anne Arundel County Police Department	2	0	0	0	0	2	0	0	0	
		Baltimore County Police Department	8	5	5	2	0	5	4	6	5	
		Carroll	1	1	0	0	0	0	0	2	0	
		Cecil	1	0	0	0	0	0	1	0	0	
		Frederick	2	0	1	0	0	0	1	2	0	
		Harford	3	0	0	0	0	0	0	1	2	
		Howard County Police Department	21	10	5	3	0	5	9	10	15	
		Montgomery County Police Department	12	16	0	1	0	14	2	6	7	
		Prince George's County Police Department	7	0	4	0	0	0	5	2	4	
	State Police Agencies		5	2	0	1	0					
		State Police:										
		Carroll County	4	1	0	0	0	0	2	2	1	
		Cecil County	1	0	0	0	0	0	1	0	0	
		Wicomico County	0	0	0	1	0	1	0	0	0	
		Worcester County	0	1	0	0	0	0	1	0	0	
	Other Agencies		3	1	0	0	0					
		Maryland-National Capital Park Police, Prince George's County	1	1	0	0	0	0	2	0	0	
		State Fire Marshal	2	0	0	0	0	0	0	2	0	
MASSACHUSETTS....	**Total**		171	58	80	42	2					
	Cities		156	53	72	40	2					
		Acton	2	1	1	0	0	0	1	2	1	20,619
		Amherst	0	0	1	0	0	0	1	0	0	33,913
		Andover	0	1	0	0	0	0	1	0	0	33,615
		Arlington	5	1	0	1	0	0	3	3	1	40,902
		Ashby	0	2	0	0	0	0	0	2	0	2,957
		Attleboro	0	1	0	0	0	1	0	0	0	43,474
		Auburn	0	1	0	0	0	1	0	0	0	16,445
		Ayer	1	0	0	0	0	0	1	0	0	7,306
		Barnstable	2	1	0	0	0	1	2	0	0	47,342
		Bellingham	1	0	0	0	0	0	1	0	0	15,965
		Belmont	2	0	0	1	0	0	2	1	0	23,184
		Beverly	1	0	1	0	0	0	0	2	0	39,493
		Billerica	1	0	0	0	0	1	0	0	0	41,568
		Boston	73	22	49	20	0	32	45	40	47	591,855
		Brockton	5	0	1	0	0	3	0	2	1	94,180
		Brookline	2	0	0	0	0	0	0	2	0	54,976
		Burlington	1	0	0	0	0	0	0	0	1	24,978
		Cambridge	5	3	2	0	0	3	1	3	3	101,161
		Carver	1	0	0	0	0	0	0	0	1	11,639
		Chelmsford	0	0	1	1	1	0	0	0	3	33,740
		Dalton	2	0	0	0	0	0	2	0	0	6,627
		Danvers	0	1	0	0	0	0	0	0	1	25,979
		Dartmouth	0	2	1	0	0	0	1	2	0	31,465
		Dennis	0	1	0	0	0	0	0	1	0	15,666
		Douglas	1	0	0	0	0	1	0	0	0	8,093
		Egremont	1	0	0	0	0			1		1,364
		Everett	5	0	1	2	0	1	2	4	1	36,826
		Falmouth	2	0	3	0	0	0	2	2	1	33,722
		Greenfield	2	0	0	1	0	2	0	0	1	17,648
		Hamilton	1	0	1	0	0	0	0	2	0	8,262
		Haverhill	1	0	0	1	0	1	1	0	0	60,308
		Lancaster	0	0	0	1	0	0	0	1	0	7,043
		Lexington	1	0	0	0	0	1	0	0	0	30,220
		Lowell	0	0	2	1	0		3	0		102,918
		Lynn	1	0	0	0	0	0	0	0	1	87,817
		Malden	3	0	0	2	0	1	1	3	0	55,538
		Mansfield	0	1	0	0	0	0	0	0	1	23,175
		Medford	1	0	0	0	0			1		55,706
		Middleboro	1	1	0	0	0	1	0	1	0	21,503
		Milford	0	0	0	1	0	0	1	0	0	27,635
		Milton	0	1	0	0	0		1			25,888

[1]Agencies published in this table indicated that at least one hate crime incident occurred in their respective jurisdictions during the quarter(s) for which they submitted a report to the Hate Crime program. Blanks indicate quarters for which agencies did not submit reports.
[2]Population figures are published only for the cities. The figures listed for the universities and colleges are student enrollment and were provided by the United States Department of Education for the 2006 school year, the most recent available. The enrollment figures include full-time and part-time students.

Table 94. Hate Crime Incidents per Bias Motivation and Quarter by State and Agency, 2007 *(Contd.)*

State	Agency type	Agency name	Number of incidents per bias motivation					Number of incidents per quarter[1]				Popu-lation[2]
			Race	Religion	Sexual orient-ation	Ethnicity	Disability	1st quarter	2nd quarter	3rd quarter	4th quarter	
		Monson	1	0	0	0	0	0	0	1	0	8,856
		New Bedford	2	0	2	0	0	1	1	2	0	92,373
		Newton	0	1	1	0	1	0	1	1	1	82,731
		Northampton	0	0	1	0	0	1	0	0	0	28,550
		North Attleboro	3	0	0	0	0	0	1	0	2	28,095
		Oxford	1	0	0	0	0	0	0	0	1	13,760
		Palmer	2	1	0	0	0	0	1	1	1	12,991
		Peabody	0	1	0	0	0	0	1	0	0	52,194
		Pittsfield	1	0	0	0	0	0	0	1	0	43,194
		Plainville	2	0	0	0	0	1	0	1	0	8,162
		Plymouth	1	0	0	0	0	0	0	1	0	56,023
		Quincy	5	1	0	0	0	2	2	0	2	91,382
		Randolph	2	0	0	0	0	0	2	0	0	30,233
		Revere	2	1	2	6	0	4	4	2	1	46,658
		Rochester	0	0	0	1	0	0	1	0	0	5,530
		Salem	2	1	1	0	0		0	3	1	41,507
		Scituate	0	0	1	0	0	0	1	0	0	18,116
		Sharon	0	1	0	0	0	1	0	0	0	17,100
		Somerville	1	0	0	0	0	0	0	0	1	74,156
		Southborough	1	0	0	1	0	0	1	1	0	9,674
		Springfield	2	0	0	0	0	0	0	0	2	151,074
		Sunderland	1	0	0	0	0	1	0	0	0	3,778
		Uxbridge	1	0	0	0	0	0	0	1	0	12,818
		Waltham	1	0	0	0	0	0	0	0	1	59,425
		West Boylston	0	1	0	0	0	0	0	0	1	7,810
		West Springfield	0	4	0	0	0	0	0	4	0	27,854
		Winchester	1	0	0	0	0	0	0	1	0	21,155
		Winthrop	0	1	0	0	0	0	0	1	0	17,056
	Universities and Colleges		13	5	8	1	0					
		Assumption College	1	0	0	0	0	0	0	0	1	2,792
		Bentley College	1	0	0	0	0			1		5,555
		Boston College	1	0	0	0	0	1		0		14,661
		Boston University	1	0	0	0	0	1	0	0	0	31,574
		Clark University	0	0	1	0	0	1				3,071
		Dean College	0	0	2	0	0	2				1,315
		Emerson College	0	0	1	0	0		1			4,324
		Framingham State College	0	0	1	0	0		1			5,836
		Harvard University	1	1	0	0	0		1	1		25,778
		Massachusetts Institute of Technology	2	0	0	0	0	1	1	0	0	10,253
		Northeastern University	3	2	0	1	0	1	1		4	23,411
		University of Massachusetts:										
		Amherst	3	1	2	0	0	1	1	2	2	25,593
		Harbor Campus, Boston	0	1	0	0	0	1	0	0	0	12,362
		Westfield State College	0	0	1	0	0	0	0	0	1	5,426
	Other Agencies		2	0	0	1	0					
		Massachusetts Bay Transportation Authority:										
		Middlesex County	1	0	0	1	0	1			1	
		Suffolk County	1	0	0	0	0		1			
MICHIGAN..............	**Total**		425	73	73	53	4					
	Cities		381	61	56	47	4					
		Adrian	5	2	1	0	0	2	2	2	2	21,612
		Albion	1	0	0	0	0	0	1	0	0	9,267
		Ann Arbor	5	0	8	2	1	1	5	5	5	113,011
		Argentine Township	1	0	0	0	0	0	0	0	1	7,328
		Auburn Hills	1	0	0	0	0	0	0	0	1	21,149
		Bay City	1	0	0	0	0	0	1	0	0	34,145
		Benton Harbor	4	0	0	0	0	0	4	0	0	10,567
		Benton Township	11	0	0	0	0	1	5	3	2	15,626
		Berkley	0	1	0	0	0	0	1	0	0	14,906
		Berrien Springs-Oronoko Township	1	0	0	0	0	0	0	0	1	9,570
		Birmingham	1	4	0	0	0	2	0	2	1	19,149
		Blissfield	0	0	0	1	0	0	1	0	0	3,251
		Bloomfield Township	2	0	0	0	0	1	0	0	1	41,231
		Bridgman	1	0	0	0	0	0	0	1	0	2,429
		Brighton	3	3	0	0	0	2	0	2	2	7,326
		Buchanan	11	0	0	0	0	1	3	5	2	4,444
		Burton	10	0	0	0	0	2	1	3	4	30,958
		Cadillac	1	0	0	0	0	1	0	0	0	10,329

[1]Agencies published in this table indicated that at least one hate crime incident occurred in their respective jurisdictions during the quarter(s) for which they submitted a report to the Hate Crime program. Blanks indicate quarters for which agencies did not submit reports.

[2]Population figures are published only for the cities. The figures listed for the universities and colleges are student enrollment and were provided by the United States Department of Education for the 2006 school year, the most recent available. The enrollment figures include full-time and part-time students.

Table 94. Hate Crime Incidents per Bias Motivation and Quarter by State and Agency, 2007 *(Contd.)*

State	Agency type	Agency name	Number of incidents per bias motivation					Number of incidents per quarter[1]				Popu-lation[2]
			Race	Religion	Sexual orient-ation	Ethnicity	Disability	1st quarter	2nd quarter	3rd quarter	4th quarter	
		Canton Township	3	0	0	0	0	1	0	2	0	88,126
		Capac	1	0	0	0	0	0	0	0	1	2,308
		Carleton	1	0	0	0	0	0	0	0	1	2,947
		Center Line	1	0	0	0	0	0	1	0	0	8,209
		Chelsea	1	0	0	0	0	0	0	1	0	5,014
		Chesterfield Township	5	1	1	0	0	4	2	0	1	45,849
		Chikaming Township	1	0	0	1	0	1	1	0	0	3,686
		Clare	1	1	0	0	1	1	1	1	0	3,198
		Clawson	1	0	1	0	0	1	0	1	0	12,175
		Clinton Township	5	1	2	2	1	0	3	6	2	96,948
		Clio	1	0	0	0	0	0	0	0	1	2,606
		Coloma Township	1	1	0	0	0	0	0	1	1	6,662
		Constantine	1	0	0	0	0	1	0	0	0	2,149
		Croswell	1	0	0	0	0	1	0	0	0	2,554
		Dearborn	10	4	1	4	0	4	10	3	2	91,748
		Dearborn Heights	1	0	1	0	0	0	0	2	0	54,901
		Detroit	28	9	6	5	0	13	10	14	11	860,971
		Douglas	1	0	1	1	0	0	1	0	2	2,209
		Eastpointe	9	1	0	1	0	0	6	3	2	32,797
		Eaton Rapids	1	0	0	0	0	0	1	0	0	5,304
		Eau Claire	1	0	0	0	0	0	0	0	1	632
		Elk Rapids	1	0	0	0	0	1	0	0	0	1,708
		Emmett Township	3	0	0	1	0	1	3	0	0	12,048
		Escanaba	0	0	1	0	0	0	1	0	0	12,494
		Essexville	2	0	0	0	0	0	0	0	2	3,523
		Farmington	0	1	0	0	0	0	1	0	0	9,930
		Farmington Hills	1	2	0	0	0	1	1	1	0	79,475
		Ferndale	3	1	1	0	0	0	4	1	0	21,207
		Flint	23	2	8	1	0	4	10	7	13	116,024
		Fowlerville	1	0	0	0	0	0	1	0	0	3,148
		Fraser	1	0	0	0	0	0	1	0	0	15,068
		Fremont	3	0	0	0	0	1	0	0	2	4,303
		Garden City	5	2	0	0	0	1	4	2	0	28,282
		Genesee Township	9	0	0	1	0	0	4	2	4	23,961
		Gibraltar	0	0	1	0	0	0	0	0	1	5,300
		Gladstone	1	0	0	0	0	0	1	0	0	5,252
		Grand Blanc	1	0	0	0	0	0	0	0	1	7,749
		Grand Blanc Township	1	0	0	1	0	0	1	1	0	36,319
		Grand Ledge	1	0	1	0	0	0	1	1	0	7,708
		Grand Rapids	10	0	2	0	0	0	1	6	5	192,376
		Grant	0	0	0	1	0	0	0	0	1	877
		Green Oak Township	2	0	0	0	0	0	1	1	0	18,279
		Greenville	11	0	0	0	0	2	4	4	1	8,374
		Grosse Pointe Woods	1	0	0	0	0	0	0	1	0	15,998
		Hamburg Township	1	0	0	0	0	0	0	0	1	22,486
		Hampton Township	1	0	0	0	0	1	0	0	0	9,827
		Hamtramck	6	0	0	1	0	2	3	2	0	21,448
		Hancock	0	1	0	0	0	0	1	0	0	4,156
		Hartford	1	0	0	0	0	0	0	1	0	2,407
		Hastings	2	0	1	0	0	0	1	1	1	7,091
		Hillsdale	1	0	0	0	0	0	1	0	0	7,842
		Holland	2	0	1	0	0	1	1	0	1	34,137
		Hudson	2	0	0	0	0	0	1	1	0	2,378
		Inkster	5	0	2	0	0	0	5	2	0	28,233
		Ionia	1	0	0	0	0	0	0	1	0	12,595
		Jonesville	1	0	0	0	0	0	1	0	0	2,281
		Kalamazoo	1	0	0	0	0	0	0	1	0	71,462
		Kalkaska	1	0	0	0	0	1	0	0	0	2,207
		Kentwood	5	0	0	0	0	2	1	1	1	46,748
		Laingsburg	0	0	0	1	0	0	0	1	0	1,276
		Lake Odessa	1	0	0	0	0	0	0	0	1	2,281
		Lansing	2	2	2	2	1	3	4	1	1	113,643
		Lincoln Township	1	0	0	0	0	0	1	0	0	14,496
		Livonia	3	1	0	0	0	1	0	1	2	96,261
		Luna Pier	1	0	0	0	0	0	1	0	0	1,550
		Mackinac Island	0	0	1	0	0	0	0	0	1	465
		Madison Heights	1	0	0	0	0	0	0	0	1	29,901
		Madison Township	1	0	0	0	0	0	1	0	0	7,977
		Marshall	0	0	2	0	0	0	2	0	0	7,244
		Mason	1	0	0	0	0	0	1	0	0	8,191
		Meridian Township	1	0	0	0	0	0	1	0	0	37,958
		Milan	1	0	0	0	0	0	0	1	0	5,686

[1]Agencies published in this table indicated that at least one hate crime incident occurred in their respective jurisdictions during the quarter(s) for which they submitted a report to the Hate Crime program. Blanks indicate quarters for which agencies did not submit reports.

[2]Population figures are published only for the cities. The figures listed for the universities and colleges are student enrollment and were provided by the United States Department of Education for the 2006 school year, the most recent available. The enrollment figures include full-time and part-time students.

Table 94. Hate Crime Incidents per Bias Motivation and Quarter by State and Agency, 2007 *(Contd.)*

State	Agency type	Agency name	Number of incidents per bias motivation					Number of incidents per quarter[1]				Popu-lation[2]
			Race	Religion	Sexual orient-ation	Ethnicity	Disability	1st quarter	2nd quarter	3rd quarter	4th quarter	
		Monroe	3	0	0	0	0	0	1	1	1	21,787
		Mount Morris	1	0	0	0	0	0	1	0	0	3,308
		Mount Morris Township	2	0	0	0	0	0	0	1	1	22,966
		Mount Pleasant	1	1	0	1	0	0	1	1	1	26,270
		Mundy Township	2	1	0	0	0	0	0	2	1	14,577
		Muskegon	3	0	0	1	0	1	1	1	1	39,562
		Muskegon Heights	2	0	0	0	0	0	1	1	0	11,698
		New Baltimore	1	0	0	0	0	1	0	0	0	12,071
		New Buffalo	2	0	0	0	0	2	0	0	0	2,429
		Niles	5	0	0	0	0	1	2	1	1	11,491
		Northville	0	0	0	1	0	0	0	1	0	6,202
		Northville Township	3	0	0	0	0	0	2	0	1	26,528
		Norton Shores	1	0	0	0	0	0	1	0	0	23,567
		Oak Park	1	3	0	1	0	2	2	1	0	30,771
		Ontwa Township-Edwardsburg	1	0	0	0	0	0	1	0	0	5,930
		Oscoda Township	2	0	0	0	0	0	1	1	0	7,028
		Parchment	1	0	0	0	0	1	0	0	0	1,778
		Plymouth	0	1	1	0	0	1	1	0	0	9,046
		Plymouth Township	2	1	0	0	0	0	1	1	1	26,751
		Pontiac	2	0	0	0	0	0	1	0	1	67,059
		Portage	3	0	0	2	0	0	1	0	4	45,287
		Port Huron	4	0	0	0	0	2	1	0	1	31,166
		Raisin Township	0	0	0	2	0	0	2	0	0	7,358
		Richfield Township, Roscommon County	1	0	0	0	0	0	1	0	0	4,249
		Riverview	1	0	0	1	0	1	0	0	1	12,447
		Rochester	2	0	0	0	0	0	1	1	0	11,360
		Romulus	1	1	2	0	0	2	2	0	0	24,269
		Roseville	1	1	0	0	0	1	1	0	0	47,329
		Royal Oak	1	0	1	1	0	2	1	0	0	57,695
		Saginaw	3	0	0	0	0	1	2	0	0	56,989
		Saginaw Township	2	0	0	0	0	1	1	0	0	39,736
		Saline	4	0	0	0	0	2	2	0	0	8,955
		Sandusky	1	0	0	0	0	0	0	1	0	2,676
		Scottville	1	0	0	0	0	0	0	1	0	1,263
		Shelby Township	2	2	0	1	0	0	2	1	2	71,736
		Southfield[4]	2	1	0	2	0	0	0	4	0	75,830
		South Lyon	1	0	0	0	0	0	0	1	0	11,226
		Sparta	4	0	0	0	0	0	3	1	0	4,007
		St. Clair Shores	5	1	0	0	0	1	1	4	0	60,900
		Sterling Heights	1	0	0	1	0	0	0	0	2	128,555
		St. Joseph Township	1	0	0	0	0	0	0	1	0	9,827
		Sturgis	0	0	0	2	0	0	1	1	0	11,026
		Swartz Creek	2	1	0	0	0	0	2	1	0	5,394
		Taylor	13	0	1	0	0	5	2	4	3	64,048
		Tecumseh	3	0	0	0	0	1	2	0	0	8,878
		Thomas Township	1	0	0	0	0	0	0	0	1	12,670
		Troy	3	0	0	0	0	0	2	1	0	81,130
		Van Buren Township	1	0	0	1	0	0	1	0	1	28,247
		Vassar	3	0	0	0	0	0	3	0	0	2,738
		Warren	6	2	3	4	0	3	3	7	2	134,081
		Waterford Township	2	0	1	0	0	0	0	1	2	71,233
		Wayne	0	0	1	0	0	0	1	0	0	18,203
		West Bloomfield Township	1	3	0	0	0	0	2	1	1	64,616
		Westland	4	1	1	0	0	2	2	2	0	84,293
		White Cloud	2	0	0	0	0	0	2	0	0	1,421
		White Lake Township	3	0	0	0	0	2	0	1	0	30,412
		Williamston	1	0	0	0	0	0	0	1	0	3,825
		Wixom	1	1	0	0	0	0	1	0	1	13,572
		Wyoming	1	0	0	0	0	0	0	0	1	70,243
		Ypsilanti	1	0	0	0	0	1	0	0	0	21,672
	Universities and Colleges		7	3	6	0	0					
		Central Michigan University	1	0	0	0	0	0	1	0	0	26,710
		Delta College	0	1	0	0	0	0	1	0	0	10,149
		Eastern Michigan University	0	0	1	0	0	0	0	1	0	22,950
		Lansing Community College	0	0	1	0	0	0	0	1	0	20,394
		Oakland Community College	1	0	0	0	0	0	1	0	0	24,123

[1]Agencies published in this table indicated that at least one hate crime incident occurred in their respective jurisdictions during the quarter(s) for which they submitted a report to the Hate Crime program. Blanks indicate quarters for which agencies did not submit reports.

[2]Population figures are published only for the cities. The figures listed for the universities and colleges are student enrollment and were provided by the United States Department of Education for the 2006 school year, the most recent available. The enrollment figures include full-time and part-time students.

[4]Includes one incident reported with more than one bias motivation.

Table 94. Hate Crime Incidents per Bias Motivation and Quarter by State and Agency, 2007 *(Contd.)*

State	Agency type	Agency name	Number of incidents per bias motivation					Number of incidents per quarter[1]				Popu-lation[2]
			Race	Religion	Sexual orient-ation	Ethnicity	Disability	1st quarter	2nd quarter	3rd quarter	4th quarter	
		Oakland University	2	1	1	0	0	2	0	0	2	17,737
		University of Michigan, Ann Arbor	3	1	3	0	0	4	1	0	2	40,025
	Metropolitan Counties		25	3	6	2	0					
		Cass	0	1	0	0	0	0	0	0	1	
		Eaton	1	0	0	0	0	0	0	1	0	
		Ingham	1	0	1	0	0	1	0	0	1	
		Kent	2	0	0	0	0	1	1	0	0	
		Livingston	1	0	0	0	0	0	0	1	0	
		Macomb	8	1	2	1	0	3	5	1	3	
		Monroe	1	0	1	0	0	0	0	2	0	
		Newaygo	2	0	0	0	0	1	1	0	0	
		Oakland	3	0	0	0	0	0	0	1	2	
		Ottawa	2	0	0	0	0	1	1	0	0	
		Saginaw	2	1	0	1	0	0	2	1	1	
		St. Clair	2	0	2	0	0	3	0	1	0	
	Nonmetropolitan Counties		6	3	5	3	0					
		Arenac	1	0	0	0	0	0	1	0	0	
		Baraga	0	1	0	0	0	0	1	0	0	
		Crawford	0	0	1	0	0	1	0	0	0	
		Grand Traverse	2	0	1	1	0	2	2	0	0	
		Keweenaw	1	0	0	0	0	0	0	1	0	
		Mason	1	0	0	0	0	0	1	0	0	
		Mecosta	1	0	0	0	0	0	0	0	1	
		Montcalm	0	0	0	1	0	0	0	1	0	
		Ogemaw	0	0	1	0	0	1	0	0	0	
		Tuscola	0	2	1	1	0	0	2	2	0	
		Wexford	0	0	1	0	0	0	0	1	0	
	State Police Agencies		4	0	0	0	0					
		State Police:										
		Berrien County	1	0	0	0	0	0	1	0	0	
		Isabella County	1	0	0	0	0	1	0	0	0	
		Kalamazoo County	2	0	0	0	0	0	0	1	1	
	Other Agencies		2	3	0	1	0					
		Huron-Clinton Metropolitan Authority, Stony Creek Metropark	1	1	0	1	0	0	3	0	0	
		Wayne County Airport	1	2	0	0	0	2	1	0	0	
MINNESOTA	**Total**		78	18	27	32	2					
	Cities		73	16	25	32	2					
		Anoka	0	0	0	1	0	0	0	1	0	17,413
		Bemidji	3	0	0	0	0	1	0	2	0	13,448
		Blaine	0	0	0	1	0	0	0	1	0	56,747
		Bloomington	2	0	0	1	0	1	1	0	1	80,218
		Brooklyn Center	0	0	0	1	0	1	0	0	0	27,118
		Brooklyn Park	8	1	0	2	0	1	5	2	3	70,112
		Burnsville	2	0	0	0	0	0	0	1	1	59,127
		Coon Rapids	1	0	0	1	0	0	2	0	0	62,299
		Cottage Grove	1	0	0	0	0	0	1	0	0	33,288
		Eagan	1	1	0	0	0	0	0	0	2	63,718
		Eden Prairie	1	0	0	1	0	0	1	0	1	61,910
		Edina	1	1	0	0	0	1	0	0	1	45,007
		Elk River	4	0	0	1	0	0	2	3	0	23,224
		Forest Lake	1	0	0	1	0	2	0	0	0	17,984
		Hibbing	1	0	0	0	0	0	0	1	0	16,198
		Lakes Area	1	0	0	0	0	0	0	0	1	8,333
		Lakeville	0	1	1	0	0	0	1	1	0	54,565
		Mankato	1	0	0	1	0	0	1	1	0	35,331
		Maplewood	1	0	0	0	0	0	0	1	0	35,444
		Marshall	0	0	0	1	0	0	1	0	0	12,410
		Minneapolis	16	4	16	8	1	9	12	12	12	371,240
		Minnetonka	0	1	0	0	0	0	0	0	1	49,751
		Montevideo	1	0	0	0	0	0	1	0	0	5,305
		Moorhead	0	0	1	0	0	0	1	0	0	35,052
		Mora	1	0	0	0	0	1	0	0	0	3,521
		New Hope	0	0	0	1	0	0	0	1	0	20,301
		Northfield	1	0	0	0	0	1	0	0	0	19,447
		North St. Paul	0	0	1	0	0	1	0	0	0	11,201
		Oakdale	0	0	1	0	0	0	0	0	1	27,306
		Plymouth	0	0	0	1	0	1	0	0	0	70,737
		Red Wing	3	1	0	1	0	1	3	0	1	15,705
		Rochester	2	0	1	0	0	0	2	1	0	98,287

[1]Agencies published in this table indicated that at least one hate crime incident occurred in their respective jurisdictions during the quarter(s) for which they submitted a report to the Hate Crime program. Blanks indicate quarters for which agencies did not submit reports.

[2]Population figures are published only for the cities. The figures listed for the universities and colleges are student enrollment and were provided by the United States Department of Education for the 2006 school year, the most recent available. The enrollment figures include full-time and part-time students.

Table 94. Hate Crime Incidents per Bias Motivation and Quarter by State and Agency, 2007 *(Contd.)*

State	Agency type	Agency name	Number of incidents per bias motivation					Number of incidents per quarter[1]				Population[2]
			Race	Religion	Sexual orient-ation	Ethnicity	Disability	1st quarter	2nd quarter	3rd quarter	4th quarter	
		Roseville	0	1	0	0	0	0	0	0	1	31,645
		Savage	2	0	0	0	0	0	2	0	0	28,266
		St. Cloud	2	1	1	3	0	1	2	1	3	67,290
		Stillwater	1	0	0	0	0	1	0	0	0	18,116
		St. Louis Park	2	1	0	0	1	2	0	0	2	43,001
		St. Paul	4	3	3	6	0	1	5	5	5	271,662
		Wheaton	1	0	0	0	0	0	0	1	0	1,463
		White Bear Lake	5	0	0	0	0	2	1	2	0	23,486
		Willmar	1	0	0	0	0	1	0	0	0	18,012
		Woodbury	2	0	0	0	0	0	0	1	1	55,376
	Universities and Colleges		0	1	0	0	0					
		University of Minnesota, Twin Cities	0	1	0	0	0	0	0	1	0	50,402
	Metropolitan Counties		0	0	1	0	0					
		Carver	0	0	1	0	0	0	0	1	0	
	Nonmetropolitan Counties		5	1	1	0	0					
		Beltrami	3	1	1	0	0	0	1	2	2	
		Douglas	1	0	0	0	0	0	0	1	0	
		McLeod	1	0	0	0	0	0	1	0	0	
MISSOURI..................	Total		82	12	9	10	1					
	Cities		70	10	7	7	1					
		Aurora	1	0	0	0	0	0	1	0		7,421
		Blue Springs	1	1	0	0	0	0	1	0	1	54,718
		Bourbon	1	0	0	0	0	0	0	1	0	1,415
		Cameron	2	0	0	0	0	1	0	1	0	9,015
		Chillicothe	1	0	0	0	0	0	1	0	0	8,700
		Dixon	1	0	0	0	0	0	0	0	1	1,519
		Eldon	1	0	0	0	0	0	1	0	0	4,991
		Excelsior Springs	1	0	0	0	0	0	1	0	0	11,747
		Gladstone	1	0	0	0	0	0	0	0	1	27,686
		Grain Valley	1	0	0	1	0	0	1	0	1	10,225
		Grandview	1	0	0	0	0	0	0	0	1	24,322
		Hamilton	0	0	0	1	0	0	1	0	0	1,800
		Holden	1	0	0	0	0	0	0	0	1	2,525
		Independence	8	1	0	2	0	1	2	7	1	108,879
		Jefferson City	0	0	1	0	0	0	1	0	0	39,121
		Kansas City	4	0	0	0	0	2	0	2	0	447,725
		Kirksville	2	0	0	0	0	1	0	1	0	16,934
		Lee's Summit	3	2	1	1	0	2	2	1	2	83,558
		Marble Hill	1	0	0	0	0	1	0	0	0	1,515
		Marshall	1	0	0	0	0	0	1	0	0	12,281
		Monroe City	1	0	0	0	0	0	0	0	1	2,541
		Nixa	1	0	0	0	0	0	0	0	1	18,220
		O'Fallon	1	0	0	0	0	0	0	1	0	76,542
		Peculiar	1	0	0	0	0	0	0	1	0	4,495
		Richmond	1	0	0	0	0	0	0	0	1	6,029
		Rolla	4	0	2	0	0	0	1	3	2	18,208
		Seneca	1	0	0	0	0	0	0	1	0	2,277
		Sikeston	1	0	0	0	0		1	0	0	17,188
		Springfield	8	3	0	2	1	2	9	3	0	150,488
		St. John	1	1	0	0	0	1	0	0	1	6,444
		St. Louis	16	2	3	0	0	5	6	3	7	348,197
		St. Peters	1	0	0	0	0	1	0	0	0	55,291
		Warrensburg	1	0	0	0	0	0	0	0	1	18,206
	Universities and Colleges		4	2	1	0	0					
		University of Missouri: Columbia	3	2	1	0	0	1	1	1	3	28,184
		Kansas City	1	0	0	0	0	1	0	0	0	14,213
	Metropolitan Counties		8	0	0	3	0					
		St. Charles	4	0	0	1	0	0	2	3	0	
		St. Louis County Police Department	3	0	0	1	0	1	1	2	0	
		Warren	1	0	0	1	0	1	0	1	0	
	Nonmetropolitan Counties		0	0	1	0	0					
		Douglas	0	0	1	0	0	0	0	1	0	
MONTANA..................	Total		7	3	6	4	1					
	Cities		5	1	5	2	1					
		Billings	0	0	0	1	0	0	1	0	0	101,342
		Colstrip	0	0	0	1	0	0	0	0	1	2,342
		Great Falls	1	0	0	0	0	0	0	1	0	56,159
		Havre	0	0	1	0	0	0	0	1	0	9,414
		Helena	3	0	0	0	1	0	0	3	1	28,128
		Missoula	1	1	4	0	0	1	2	2	1	65,037

[1]Agencies published in this table indicated that at least one hate crime incident occurred in their respective jurisdictions during the quarter(s) for which they submitted a report to the Hate Crime program. Blanks indicate quarters for which agencies did not submit reports.

[2]Population figures are published only for the cities. The figures listed for the universities and colleges are student enrollment and were provided by the United States Department of Education for the 2006 school year, the most recent available. The enrollment figures include full-time and part-time students.

Table 94. Hate Crime Incidents per Bias Motivation and Quarter by State and Agency, 2007 *(Contd.)*

State	Agency type	Agency name	Number of incidents per bias motivation					Number of incidents per quarter[1]				Popu-lation[2]
			Race	Religion	Sexual orient-ation	Ethnicity	Disability	1st quarter	2nd quarter	3rd quarter	4th quarter	
	Metropolitan Counties		1	1	1	0	0					
		Missoula	1	1	1	0	0	1	2	0	0	
	Nonmetropolitan Counties		1	1	0	2	0					
		Flathead	0	0	0	1	0	0	1	0	0	
		Lewis and Clark	1	0	0	0	0	0	0	1	0	
		Ravalli	0	1	0	0	0	1	0	0	0	
		Silver Bow	0	0	0	1	0	0	1	0	0	
NEBRASKA..............	Total		26	2	9	7	0					
	Cities		24	2	9	7	0					
		Fairbury	1	0	0	0	0	1	0	0	0	3,969
		Hastings	1	0	1	0	0	0	1	0	1	25,250
		Kearney	4	0	0	1	0	2	1	2	0	29,652
		Lincoln	15	1	5	1	0	11	11			243,243
		Omaha	2	0	2	3	0	1	6			431,810
		Papillion	1	1	0	2	0	0	3	1	0	21,748
		Wahoo	0	0	1	0	0	0	0	0	1	4,060
	Nonmetropolitan Counties		2	0	0	0	0					
		Platte	1	0	0	0	0	0	0	0	1	
		Scotts Bluff	1	0	0	0	0	0	0	1	0	
NEVADA	Total		25	16	8	14	0					
	Cities		21	14	8	14	0					
		Las Vegas Metropolitan Police Department	18	14	6	14	0	13	13	12	14	1,341,156
		North Las Vegas	1	0	1	0	0	2	0	0	0	211,419
		Reno	2	0	1	0	0	0	2	1	0	214,197
	Metropolitan Counties		1	0	0	0	0					
		Washoe	1	0	0	0	0	0	1			
	Nonmetropolitan Counties		2	1	0	0	0					
		Nye	2	1	0	0	0	0	2	1		
	Other Agencies		1	1	0	0	0					
		Washoe County School District	1	1	0	0	0	2				
NEW HAMPSHIRE....	Total		19	11	10	2	1					
	Cities		19	11	10	2	1					
		Auburn	0	0	1	0	0	0	1	0	0	5,235
		Bow	1	0	0	0	0	0	0	0	1	8,250
		Concord	2	1	0	0	0	1	2	0	0	42,638
		Derry	1	0	0	0	0	0	1	0	0	34,118
		Exeter	1	1	0	0	0	0	0	2	0	14,851
		Farmington	1	0	1	0	0	0	0	2	0	6,688
		Hanover	0	0	1	0	0	0	1	0	0	11,198
		Henniker	2	0	0	0	0	0	0	0	2	5,187
		Hudson	0	0	0	1	0	0	1	0	0	24,996
		Keene	0	0	1	1	1	0	3	0	0	22,693
		Laconia	1	1	0	0	0	0	0	2	0	17,153
		Lee	0	0	1	0	0	0	1	0	0	4,481
		Londonderry	0	0	1	0	0	0	0	1	0	25,121
		Loudon	1	0	0	0	0	0	1	0	0	5,215
		Merrimack	3	0	0	0	0	1	0	1	1	26,847
		Milford	0	1	0	0	0	0	0	1	0	15,271
		Nashua	2	1	0	0	0	1	2			87,217
		New Boston	0	1	1	0	0	1	0	1	0	5,121
		Pembroke	0	1	0	0	0	0	0	0	1	7,466
		Pittsfield	0	1	0	0	0	0	0	1	0	4,476
		Portsmouth	1	1	1	0	0	1	2	0	0	20,584
		Rindge	0	0	1	0	0	1	0	0	0	6,541
		Rochester	2	1	1	0	0	2	2	0	0	30,355
		Seabrook	1	0	0	0	0	1	0	0	0	8,588
		Windham	0	1	0	0	0	1	0	0	0	13,283
NEW JERSEY..............	Total		349	245	85	64	5					
	Cities		347	245	85	64	5					
		Aberdeen Township	11	8	10	1	0	4	9	2	15	18,301
		Absecon	1	0	0	0	0	0	0	1	0	8,029
		Allenhurst	1	0	0	0	0	0	0	1	0	698
		Allentown	0	0	1	0	0	1	0	0	0	1,839
		Asbury Park	2	1	2	0	0	1	3	0	1	16,473
		Atlantic City	2	1	0	0	0	1	1	1	0	39,781
		Barnegat Township	7	0	0	0	0	1	1	4	1	21,098
		Bayonne	0	1	1	0	0	0	0	0	2	58,583
		Bedminster Township	0	1	0	0	0	1	0	0	0	8,412
		Belleville	0	1	0	0	0	0	1	0	0	34,291
		Berkeley Township	2	1	0	0	0	0	2	1	0	42,388

[1]Agencies published in this table indicated that at least one hate crime incident occurred in their respective jurisdictions during the quarter(s) for which they submitted a report to the Hate Crime program. Blanks indicate quarters for which agencies did not submit reports.

[2]Population figures are published only for the cities. The figures listed for the universities and colleges are student enrollment and were provided by the United States Department of Education for the 2006 school year, the most recent available. The enrollment figures include full-time and part-time students.

Table 94. Hate Crime Incidents per Bias Motivation and Quarter by State and Agency, 2007 *(Contd.)*

State	Agency type	Agency name	Number of incidents per bias motivation					Number of incidents per quarter[1]				Popu-lation[2]
			Race	Religion	Sexual orient-ation	Ethnicity	Disability	1st quarter	2nd quarter	3rd quarter	4th quarter	
		Berlin Township	1	0	0	0	0	0	0	0	1	5,381
		Bernards Township	1	0	0	0	0	1	0	0	0	27,020
		Bloomfield	1	0	0	0	0	1	0	0	0	45,171
		Bloomingdale	0	0	0	1	0	0	0	1	0	7,570
		Bound Brook	1	0	0	0	0	0	0	0	1	10,180
		Bradley Beach	0	0	1	0	0	0	1	0	0	4,763
		Branchburg Township	0	1	0	0	0	0	0	0	1	14,982
		Bridgewater Township	0	2	0	0	0	1	1	0	0	44,620
		Brigantine	1	1	0	0	0	0	1	1	0	12,829
		Buena	1	0	0	0	0	0	0	0	1	3,787
		Burlington Township	2	0	0	0	0	0	0	1	1	21,691
		Caldwell	2	0	0	0	0	0	0	0	2	7,340
		Camden	1	0	0	0	0	0	0	0	1	78,967
		Carteret	2	0	0	0	0	0	0	2	0	22,165
		Cedar Grove Township	3	1	0	1	0	0	2	0	3	12,791
		Chatham	0	0	1	0	0	0	1	0	0	8,353
		Chatham Township	1	0	0	0	0	0	1	0	0	10,233
		Cherry Hill Township	6	1	0	0	0	3	1	2	1	71,269
		Clifton	1	2	0	0	0	0	0	0	3	79,253
		Clinton Township	4	0	0	0	0	0	1	1	2	14,020
		Collingswood	0	3	0	0	0	0	3	0	0	13,899
		Cranbury Township	0	0	1	0	0	0	1	0	0	3,882
		Cranford Township	1	0	0	0	0	0	0	0	1	22,270
		Delanco Township	0	0	1	0	0	0	0	0	1	4,205
		Denville Township	1	0	0	0	0	1	0	0	0	16,597
		Deptford Township	2	2	1	0	0	2	0	0	3	30,082
		Dumont	0	1	0	0	0	1	0	0	0	17,288
		Dunellen	0	1	0	0	0	0	0	0	1	6,909
		Eastampton Township	1	0	0	0	0	0	0	0	1	6,667
		East Brunswick Township	5	6	0	1	0	0	5	2	5	47,438
		East Greenwich Township	1	0	0	0	0	0	0	1	0	6,758
		East Hanover Township	1	0	0	0	0	0	0	0	1	11,581
		East Orange	0	1	0	0	0	0	0	1	0	66,949
		East Windsor Township	0	0	0	1	0	0	0	1	0	26,807
		Edison Township	8	6	1	2	0	6	3	5	3	99,082
		Egg Harbor Township	1	1	0	0	0	1	1	0	0	38,621
		Elizabeth	0	0	1	2	0	0	1	1	1	125,621
		Englishtown	0	0	0	1	0	1	0	0	0	1,833
		Ewing Township	3	0	1	1	0	1	1	1	2	36,753
		Fair Lawn	2	6	0	0	0	1	1	2	4	31,108
		Fairview	0	0	0	1	0	0	1	0	0	13,568
		Franklin Lakes	2	2	0	1	0	0	3	1	1	11,290
		Franklin Township, Hunterdon County	2	1	0	0	0	0	1	0	2	3,138
		Franklin Township, Somerset County	1	0	0	0	0	1	0	0	0	60,006
		Freehold	4	1	0	0	0	1	2	0	2	11,344
		Freehold Township	5	2	1	0	0	0	3	3	2	33,803
		Galloway Township	2	0	0	1	0	1	2	0	0	36,045
		Glassboro	4	4	0	0	0	3	3	0	2	19,274
		Glen Rock	1	0	0	0	0	0	0	1	0	11,346
		Gloucester Township	6	2	1	0	0	2	2	3	2	65,396
		Hackensack	1	0	0	0	0	0	1	0	0	43,478
		Hackettstown	2	0	0	1	0	0	0	0	3	9,436
		Haddonfield	0	2	0	0	0	2	0	0	0	11,464
		Haddon Township	3	0	0	0	0	0	1	2	0	14,420
		Hamilton Township, Atlantic County	1	2	0	0	0	1	0	1	1	24,315
		Hamilton Township, Mercer County	4	4	1	0	0	2	0	3	4	90,158
		Harding Township	1	1	0	0	0	1	0	0	1	3,348
		Hardyston Township	1	0	0	0	0	0	0	0	1	8,246
		Harrison Township	1	3	1	0	0	1	2	0	2	11,797
		Hawthorne	0	0	1	0	0	1	0	0	0	18,086
		Hazlet Township	2	1	3	2	0	2	5	0	1	20,843
		High Bridge	2	0	0	0	0	1	0	0	1	3,746
		Highland Park	2	1	0	0	0	0	3	0	0	14,112
		Hightstown	0	1	0	1	0	1	0	1	0	5,277
		Hillsborough Township	2	10	0	1	0	1	4	4	4	37,941
		Hoboken	0	1	3	0	0	3	0	1	0	39,676
		Holmdel Township	0	0	0	1	0	0	1	0	0	16,759
		Hopatcong	3	0	0	0	0	0	3	0	0	15,814

[1]Agencies published in this table indicated that at least one hate crime incident occurred in their respective jurisdictions during the quarter(s) for which they submitted a report to the Hate Crime program. Blanks indicate quarters for which agencies did not submit reports.
[2]Population figures are published only for the cities. The figures listed for the universities and colleges are student enrollment and were provided by the United States Department of Education for the 2006 school year, the most recent available. The enrollment figures include full-time and part-time students.

Table 94. Hate Crime Incidents per Bias Motivation and Quarter by State and Agency, 2007 *(Contd.)*

State	Agency type	Agency name	Number of incidents per bias motivation					Number of incidents per quarter[1]				Popu-lation[2]
			Race	Religion	Sexual orient-ation	Ethnicity	Disability	1st quarter	2nd quarter	3rd quarter	4th quarter	
		Hopewell Township	0	0	0	1	0	0	0	0	1	17,888
		Howell Township	12	5	0	3	2	3	6	8	5	50,324
		Jackson Township	4	3	0	1	0	2	1	4	1	52,073
		Jersey City	9	0	6	0	0	2	4	5	4	240,718
		Keansburg	22	3	5	5	0	8	11	9	7	10,526
		Kinnelon	0	1	0	0	0	0	0	1	0	9,638
		Lacey Township	5	0	0	0	1	5	0	0	1	26,184
		Lakehurst	1	1	0	0	0	0	0	0	2	2,662
		Lakewood Township	12	22	1	1	0	7	11	5	13	69,298
		Lambertville	1	0	0	0	0	0	0	0	1	3,791
		Lawrence Township	5	1	1	1	0	1	2	2	3	31,939
		Lebanon Township	0	1	0	0	0	1	0	0	0	6,264
		Little Egg Harbor Township	3	4	0	3	0	1	2	2	5	20,193
		Little Falls Township	6	7	4	0	0	3	7	2	5	11,777
		Little Ferry	0	0	0	1	0	1	0	0	0	10,668
		Little Silver	0	0	2	1	0	0	1	1	1	6,062
		Lodi	1	0	3	2	0	3	1	2	0	24,202
		Logan Township	1	0	0	0	0	0	0	1	0	6,150
		Long Beach Township	1	0	0	0	0	0	0	1	0	3,483
		Lumberton Township	1	0	0	0	0	0	1	0	0	12,276
		Madison	2	4	0	0	0	0	1	2	3	15,945
		Magnolia	1	0	0	0	0	1	0	0	0	4,360
		Mahwah Township	0	1	0	0	0	0	0	1	0	24,451
		Manalapan Township	3	3	1	1	0	3	1	2	2	37,004
		Manchester Township	2	4	0	0	0	0	0	1	5	41,628
		Maple Shade Township	1	0	0	1	0	1	1	0	0	19,454
		Margate City	0	1	0	0	0	1	0	0	0	8,563
		Marlboro Township	2	6	1	0	0	0	5	3	1	39,667
		Medford Lakes	1	0	0	0	0	0	0	1	0	4,143
		Medford Township	0	1	0	0	0	0	1	0	0	23,295
		Mendham	0	1	0	0	0	0	1	0	0	5,153
		Middle Township	3	5	0	0	0	5	2	1	0	16,306
		Middletown Township	2	0	0	0	0	1	1	0	0	67,279
		Milltown	1	0	0	0	0	0	1	0	0	7,007
		Millville	3	0	0	0	0	3	0	0	0	28,069
		Monroe Township, Gloucester County	6	1	0	1	0	2	2	4	0	31,793
		Monroe Township, Middlesex County	2	5	0	0	0	0	0	3	4	34,752
		Montclair	3	2	0	0	0	1	1	3	0	37,144
		Montvale	1	0	0	0	0	0	0	0	1	7,276
		Montville Township	0	1	0	0	0	0	0	1	0	21,347
		Moorestown Township	1	0	0	0	0	0	0	0	1	19,907
		Mount Arlington	1	0	0	0	0	0	0	0	1	5,683
		Mount Holly Township	1	0	0	0	0	0	0	1	0	10,555
		Mount Laurel Township	1	0	0	0	0	0	0	0	1	40,147
		Mount Olive Township	2	2	1	0	0	1	3	1	0	25,950
		National Park	1	0	0	0	0	1	0	0	0	3,201
		Neptune City	0	1	0	0	0	0	0	0	1	5,127
		Neptune Township	4	1	2	0	0	1	0	4	2	28,038
		Newark	1	0	0	0	0	1	0	0	0	280,158
		New Brunswick	1	2	5	0	0	2	5	0	1	49,950
		New Providence	1	0	0	0	0	0	0	0	1	11,862
		Newton	1	0	0	1	0	0	0	0	2	8,300
		North Brunswick Township	2	2	1	0	0	1	0	2	2	39,676
		North Plainfield	0	1	0	0	0	0	1	0	0	21,642
		North Wildwood	0	0	1	0	0	1	0	0	0	4,782
		Norwood	0	2	0	0	0	1	1	0	0	6,239
		Nutley Township	0	0	0	1	0	0	1	0	0	26,891
		Oakland	1	4	0	1	0	1	1	2	2	13,498
		Oaklyn	0	0	1	0	0	0	0	1	0	4,062
		Ocean Gate	1	1	0	0	0	0	1	0	1	2,121
		Ocean Township, Monmouth County	0	1	0	0	0	1	0	0	0	27,362
		Old Bridge Township	0	1	0	0	0	0	1	0	0	65,370
		Oradell	0	0	0	1	0	1	0	0	0	7,922
		Oxford Township	1	0	0	0	0	0	0	0	1	2,610
		Park Ridge	1	0	0	0	0	0	0	0	1	8,905
		Parsippany-Troy Hills Township	2	2	0	2	0	1	0	3	2	51,609

[1]Agencies published in this table indicated that at least one hate crime incident occurred in their respective jurisdictions during the quarter(s) for which they submitted a report to the Hate Crime program. Blanks indicate quarters for which agencies did not submit reports.

[2]Population figures are published only for the cities. The figures listed for the universities and colleges are student enrollment and were provided by the United States Department of Education for the 2006 school year, the most recent available. The enrollment figures include full-time and part-time students.

Table 94. Hate Crime Incidents per Bias Motivation and Quarter by State and Agency, 2007 *(Contd.)*

State	Agency type	Agency name	Number of incidents per bias motivation					Number of incidents per quarter[1]				Popu-lation[2]
			Race	Religion	Sexual orient-ation	Ethnicity	Disability	1st quarter	2nd quarter	3rd quarter	4th quarter	
		Passaic	3	1	0	1	0	3	1	0	1	67,673
		Paulsboro	1	0	0	0	0	1	0	0	0	6,035
		Pennsauken Township	1	0	0	0	0	0	1	0	0	35,286
		Pennsville Township	0	0	0	1	0	0	0	1	0	13,274
		Phillipsburg	1	0	1	0	0	0	1	0	1	14,765
		Pine Hill	2	0	0	0	0	0	0	0	2	11,225
		Piscataway Township	9	2	0	0	0	2	9	0	0	52,425
		Plainfield	0	0	0	1	0	0	0	0	1	47,143
		Plainsboro Township	0	0	0	1	0	0	1	0	0	21,119
		Pohatcong Township	0	0	0	1	0	0	0	1	0	3,395
		Point Pleasant	2	0	0	0	0	0	0	2	0	19,794
		Point Pleasant Beach	3	0	0	1	0	1	1	1	1	5,374
		Princeton	0	0	1	0	0	0	0	1	0	13,623
		Prospect Park	0	0	1	0	0	0	1	0	0	5,695
		Raritan	0	1	0	1	0	0	1	1	0	6,399
		Raritan Township	2	0	0	0	0	0	0	1	1	22,619
		Readington Township	1	0	0	0	0	0	0	0	1	16,223
		Red Bank	1	0	0	0	0	0	1	0	0	11,798
		Ridgewood	0	1	0	0	0	0	0	1	0	24,530
		River Vale Township	0	1	0	0	0	0	1	0	0	9,708
		Rockaway Township	0	1	0	0	0	1	0	0	0	25,675
		Roselle	1	0	0	0	0	0	1	0	0	21,064
		Roxbury Township	1	0	0	0	0	0	0	1	0	23,698
		Runnemede	0	1	0	0	0	0	0	0	1	8,424
		Rutherford	0	0	0	1	0	0	1	0	0	17,792
		Salem	1	0	0	0	0	0	0	0	1	5,758
		Sayreville	2	0	1	0	0	2	1	0	0	42,372
		Sea Bright	1	0	0	0	0	0	0	1	0	1,791
		Somerville	0	2	0	0	0	0	1	0	1	12,494
		South Brunswick Township	5	3	2	1	0	0	3	4	4	40,390
		South Harrison Township	2	1	0	0	0	1	0	0	2	2,943
		South Orange	1	3	0	1	0	0	1	4	0	16,298
		South Plainfield	2	1	0	0	0	1	1	0	1	22,694
		South River	0	0	0	1	0	0	1	0	0	15,752
		Spotswood	2	2	0	0	0	3	0	0	1	8,143
		Springfield	0	2	0	0	0	1	0	1	0	14,652
		Stafford Township	1	0	0	0	0	1	0	0	0	25,705
		Stanhope	1	0	0	0	0	0	1	0	0	3,650
		Teaneck Township	1	6	0	0	0	2	2	2	1	39,435
		Tinton Falls	2	3	1	0	0	0	1	4	1	17,006
		Totowa	0	1	0	0	0	0	0	1	0	10,587
		Trenton	2	0	0	0	0	0	0	0	2	83,551
		Union Beach	0	1	0	0	0	1	0	0	0	6,602
		Union City	0	0	3	0	0	0	1	1	1	63,647
		Union Township	0	2	0	0	0	1	1	0	0	54,795
		Ventnor City	0	0	1	0	0	1	0	0	0	12,508
		Vernon Township	0	0	0	1	0	0	0	1	0	25,340
		Voorhees Township	3	2	0	0	0	0	1	1	3	29,261
		Wallington	0	1	1	0	0	0	2	0	0	11,379
		Wanaque	0	0	0	1	0	0	1	0	0	11,122
		Warren Township	1	2	0	0	0	3	0	0	0	15,746
		Washington	2	1	0	0	0	1	1	1	0	6,811
		Washington Township, Gloucester County	4	4	0	0	0	4	0	2	2	51,595
		Washington Township, Mercer County	0	2	0	1	0	1	1	1	0	11,853
		Washington Township, Morris County	0	1	0	0	0	0	1	0	0	18,608
		West Caldwell Township	1	0	0	0	1	0	1	0	1	10,749
		West Long Branch	1	7	2	0	1	3	2	3	3	8,275
		Winslow Township	10	0	0	1	0	4	1	2	4	38,441
		Woodbridge Township	0	0	0	1	0	0	0	0	1	98,769
		Woodbury	2	0	3	0	0	1	2	1	1	10,364
	State Police Agencies		2	0	0	0	0					
		State Police:										
		Sussex County	1	0	0	0	0	0	1	0	0	
		Warren County	1	0	0	0	0	1	0	0	0	
NEW MEXICO	Total		9	0	1	4	0					
	Cities		8	0	1	4	0					
		Albuquerque	6	0	1	4	0	2	1	6	2	513,124
		Farmington	1	0	0	0	0	0	0	0	1	44,396
		Tularosa	1	0	0	0	0			1		2,803

[1]Agencies published in this table indicated that at least one hate crime incident occurred in their respective jurisdictions during the quarter(s) for which they submitted a report to the Hate Crime program. Blanks indicate quarters for which agencies did not submit reports.
[2]Population figures are published only for the cities. The figures listed for the universities and colleges are student enrollment and were provided by the United States Department of Education for the 2006 school year, the most recent available. The enrollment figures include full-time and part-time students.

Table 94. Hate Crime Incidents per Bias Motivation and Quarter by State and Agency, 2007 *(Contd.)*

State	Agency type	Agency name	Number of incidents per bias motivation					Number of incidents per quarter[1]				Popu-lation[2]
			Race	Religion	Sexual orient-ation	Ethnicity	Disability	1st quarter	2nd quarter	3rd quarter	4th quarter	
NEW YORK	**Metropolitan Counties**		1	0	0	0	0					
		Bernalillo	1	0	0	0	0	0	0	0	1	
	Total		126	271	73	22	1					
	Cities		85	167	61	14	1					
		Ballston Spa Village	1	0	0	0	0	0	0	1	0	5,511
		Binghamton	1	0	0	0	0	0	0	1	0	44,931
		Brockport Village	0	3	0	0	0	0	0	3	0	8,138
		Colonie Town	1	0	0	0	0	0	1	0	0	77,550
		Dobbs Ferry Village	0	0	0	1	0	0	0	1	0	11,206
		Elmira	1	0	0	0	0	0	1	0	0	29,375
		Liberty Village	0	0	0	1	0	1	0	0	0	3,973
		Mount Hope Town	0	1	0	0	0	0	0	1	0	7,581
		New Rochelle	0	0	1	0	0		0	0	1	73,603
		New York	69	161	52	12	1	63	72	61	99	8,220,196
		Poughkeepsie	1	1	2	0	0		2		2	30,074
		Rochester	10	0	5	0	0	2	8	2	3	206,686
		Rotterdam Town	1	0	0	0	0	0	1	0	0	29,547
		Suffern Village	0	1	0	0	0	0	0	0	1	10,944
		Utica	0	0	1	0	0		0	0	1	58,888
	Universities and Colleges		4	1	3	1	0					
		Cornell University	0	0	0	1	0			1		19,639
		State University of New York: Buffalo	1	0	0	0	0				1	27,823
		Maritime College	1	0	0	0	0				1	1,324
		State University of New York Agricultural and Technical College, Alfred	1	0	0	0	0		1			3,201
		State University of New York College: Buffalo	0	0	1	0	0		1			11,220
		Geneseo	1	1	2	0	0	1	1	1	1	5,530
	Metropolitan Counties		37	103	8	7	0					
		Dutchess	1	0	0	0	0		0	1	0	
		Monroe	2	1	0	0	0	1	1	1		
		Nassau	10	50	4	3	0			40	27	
		Niagara	3	1	0	0	0	1	0	1	2	
		Saratoga	4	0	0	0	0	1	2	0	1	
		Suffolk County Police Department	15	51	4	4	0	18	10	16	30	
		Westchester Public Safety	2	0	0	0	0	0	0	1	1	
	Nonmetropolitan Counties		0	0	1	0	0					
		Sullivan	0	0	1	0	0	0	0	0	1	
NORTH CAROLINA	Total		46	6	10	13	0					
	Cities		26	3	7	10	0					
		Albemarle	0	0	0	1	0	0	0	1	0	15,355
		Archdale	0	0	0	1	0	0	0	0	1	9,474
		Cary	1	0	0	0	0	0	1	0	0	114,221
		Charlotte-Mecklenburg	6	1	2	1	0	0	1	6	3	733,291
		Concord	2	0	0	0	0	0	1	1	0	63,284
		Dunn	1	0	0	0	0	0	0	1	0	10,072
		Durham	3	0	1	1	0	2	1	2	0	211,873
		Hickory	1	0	0	0	0	1	0	0	0	41,008
		High Point	1	0	0	1	0	0	0	2	0	99,297
		Lexington	0	0	0	2	0	1	1	0	0	20,452
		Mount Airy	0	0	0	2	0	0	2	0	0	8,448
		Oxford	1	0	0	0	0	0	1	0	0	8,567
		Raleigh	2	2	2	0	0	2	2	1	1	367,120
		Reidsville	1	0	0	0	0	0	1	0	0	14,906
		Roxboro	1	0	0	0	0	1	0	0	0	8,738
		Salisbury	4	0	1	0	0	1	0	1	3	28,449
		Siler City	1	0	0	0	0	0	1	0	0	8,636
		Southern Pines	0	0	1	0	0	1	0	0	0	12,351
		Spruce Pine	0	0	0	1	0	0	0	1	0	1,973
		Washington	1	0	0	0	0	1	0	0	0	10,092
	Universities and Colleges		0	0	1	0	0					
		University of North Carolina, Greensboro	0	0	1	0	0	1	0	0	0	16,872
	Metropolitan Counties		17	1	2	3	0					
		Catawba	0	0	0	1	0	1	0	0	0	
		Chatham	4	0	0	0	0	0	1	2	1	

[1]Agencies published in this table indicated that at least one hate crime incident occurred in their respective jurisdictions during the quarter(s) for which they submitted a report to the Hate Crime program. Blanks indicate quarters for which agencies did not submit reports.

[2]Population figures are published only for the cities. The figures listed for the universities and colleges are student enrollment and were provided by the United States Department of Education for the 2006 school year, the most recent available. The enrollment figures include full-time and part-time students.

Table 94. Hate Crime Incidents per Bias Motivation and Quarter by State and Agency, 2007 *(Contd.)*

State	Agency type	Agency name	Number of incidents per bias motivation					Number of incidents per quarter[1]				Popu-lation[2]
			Race	Religion	Sexual orient-ation	Ethnicity	Disability	1st quarter	2nd quarter	3rd quarter	4th quarter	
		Cumberland	1	0	0	0	0	0	1	0	0	
		Currituck	0	0	1	1	0	0	0	2	0	
		Guilford	2	0	0	1	0	1	1	0	1	
		Johnston	4	0	0	0	0	0	1	3	0	
		New Hanover	5	1	1	0	0	0	1	4	2	
		Rockingham	1	0	0	0	0	0	1	0	0	
	Nonmetropolitan Counties		3	2	0	0	0					
		Caswell	0	1	0	0	0	0	0	0	1	
		Iredell	1	1	0	0	0	0	0	1	1	
		Rutherford	1	0	0	0	0	0	0	1	0	
		Transylvania	1	0	0	0	0	0	0	0	1	
NORTH DAKOTA......	**Total**		12	0	2	0	0					
	Cities		6	0	2	0	0					
		Bismarck	1	0	0	0	0	1	0	0	0	58,648
		Fargo	0	0	1	0	0	0	0	0	1	89,998
		Grafton	2	0	0	0	0	0	1	1	0	4,118
		Jamestown	1	0	1	0	0	0	0	1	1	14,696
		Mandan	2	0	0	0	0	0	1	0	1	17,521
	Metropolitan Counties		3	0	0	0	0					
		Burleigh	1	0	0	0	0	1	0	0	0	
		Morton	2	0	0	0	0	1	0	1	0	
	Nonmetropolitan Counties		3	0	0	0	0					
		Mountrail	1	0	0	0	0	0	1	0	0	
		Stark	1	0	0	0	0	0	1	0	0	
		Walsh	1	0	0	0	0	0	0	1	0	
OHIO	**Total**		161	25	53	43	30					
	Cities		143	23	47	41	20					
		Akron	8	0	2	1	0	1	4	3	3	208,701
		Alliance	1	0	0	0	0	1				22,703
		Amherst	2	2	0	0	0	1	0	3	0	11,850
		Athens	3	0	1	0	0	0	2	2	0	20,833
		Bath Township	2	1	0	0	0	1	2	0	0	10,277
		Beavercreek	0	0	0	1	0	0	1	0	0	39,552
		Blue Ash	1	1	0	0	0	0	0	1	1	11,409
		Boardman	1	0	0	0	0	0	0	1	0	40,038
		Bowling Green	0	0	1	0	0	0	1	0	0	29,733
		Cincinnati	5	0	0	2	0	1	3	0	3	332,388
		Cleveland	16	0	0	2	0	6	6	4	2	439,888
		Columbus	41	11	22	16	4	22	32	30	10	735,981
		Dayton	2	0	1	0	0	1	1	1	0	155,526
		Defiance	0	0	1	0	0	0	0	0	1	16,159
		Fairborn	4	0	0	0	0	0	0	4	0	31,705
		Findlay	2	0	4	3	0	2	1	2	4	38,038
		Fremont	2	0	1	0	0	0	0	3	0	16,885
		Gahanna	3	0	0	0	0	1	2	0	0	33,140
		Galion	1	0	0	0	0	1	0	0	0	11,093
		Garfield Heights	1	2	0	0	0	0	1	2	0	28,221
		Genoa Township	0	0	1	0	0	0	0	1		15,674
		Germantown	1	0	0	0	0	0	0	1	0	5,126
		Granville	1	0	0	0	0	0	0	0	1	5,306
		Grove City	0	0	0	1	0	0	0	0	1	32,472
		Groveport	0	0	0	1	0	0	1	0	0	5,087
		Hamilton	0	0	0	2	0	1	1	0	0	62,330
		Heath	1	0	0	0	0	0	0	1	0	8,936
		Hubbard Township	1	0	0	0	0	0	1	0	0	5,826
		Huber Heights	7	0	0	1	0	2	2	1	3	37,588
		Indian Hill	1	0	0	0	0	0	1	0	0	5,611
		Jackson Township, Stark County	2	0	0	0	0	0	1	1	0	39,149
		Lakewood	1	0	1	0	0	1	0	1	0	51,606
		Lebanon	1	0	0	0	0	0	1	0	0	20,828
		Mansfield	1	0	6	1	0	0	3	1	4	50,004
		Marysville	2	0	0	0	0	0	0	1	1	17,829
		Mason	1	0	1	1	0	0	2	1	0	30,640
		Miami Township	0	1	0	0	0	0	1	0	0	40,056
		Millersburg	0	0	0	1	0	0	1	0	0	3,610
		Niles	2	0	0	1	0	1	0	1	1	19,675
		Norwalk	1	0	0	0	0	0	1	0	0	16,586
		Oregon	0	0	1	0	0	0	0	0	1	19,074
		Orwell	1	0	0	0	0	0	0	1	0	1,501
		Parma	2	0	0	0	0	0	0	0	2	79,250
		Piqua	0	0	2	0	0	0	0	2	0	20,875

[1]Agencies published in this table indicated that at least one hate crime incident occurred in their respective jurisdictions during the quarter(s) for which they submitted a report to the Hate Crime program. Blanks indicate quarters for which agencies did not submit reports.
[2]Population figures are published only for the cities. The figures listed for the universities and colleges are student enrollment and were provided by the United States Department of Education for the 2006 school year, the most recent available. The enrollment figures include full-time and part-time students.

Table 94. Hate Crime Incidents per Bias Motivation and Quarter by State and Agency, 2007 (*Contd.*)

State	Agency type	Agency name	Number of incidents per bias motivation					Number of incidents per quarter[1]				Population[2]
			Race	Religion	Sexual orient-ation	Ethnicity	Disability	1st quarter	2nd quarter	3rd quarter	4th quarter	
		Portsmouth	1	0	0	4	16	2	7	6	6	20,030
		Reynoldsburg	2	0	0	0	0	0	2	0	0	33,210
		South Euclid	0	1	0	0	0	0	0	1	0	21,559
		Springfield Township, Hamilton County	3	0	0	0	0			2	1	35,051
		Stow	1	1	0	0	0	0	1	1	0	34,617
		Union	2	0	0	0	0	0	2	0	0	6,345
		Utica	1	0	0	0	0	0	1	0	0	2,103
		Van Wert	1	0	1	0	0	0	1	1	0	10,381
		West Chester Township	2	0	0	1	0	0	1	0	2	55,216
		Westerville	3	1	0	0	0	1	2	1	0	34,907
		Whitehall	0	0	0	1	0	1	0	0	0	17,719
		Wilmington	0	1	0	0	0	0	0	1	0	12,806
		Wooster	1	0	0	0	0	1	0	0	0	25,914
		Worthington	2	1	0	1	0	0	0	2	2	12,941
		Youngstown	2	0	1	0	0	0	1	2	0	81,521
		Zanesville	1	0	0	0	0	0	0	0	1	25,332
	Universities and Colleges		5	0	0	0	0					
		Ohio State University	4	0	0	0	0	1	2	0	1	51,818
		University of Cincinnati	1	0	0	0	0	0	1		0	28,327
	Metropolitan Counties		7	1	6	1	0					
		Butler	2	0	2	0	0	1	3			
		Clermont	1	0	0	0	0	1	0	0	0	
		Greene	0	0	1	0	0	0	0	1	0	
		Licking	1	0	0	0	0	1	0	0	0	
		Lucas	1	0	2	0	0	1	0	1	1	
		Preble	0	1	1	0	0	0	1	0	1	
		Stark	2	0	0	0	0	0	0	0	2	
		Union	0	0	0	1	0	0	0	1	0	
	Nonmetropolitan Counties		5	1	0	1	10					
		Coshocton	2	1	0	0	0	3	0	0	0	
		Muskingum	1	0	0	0	0		0	1		
		Ross	1	0	0	1	0	1	0	1	0	
		Seneca	0	0	0	0	10	1	7	1	1	
		Wayne	1	0	0	0	0	0	1	0	0	
	Other Agencies		1	0	0	0	0					
		Cleveland Metropolitan Park District	1	0	0	0	0	0	0	1	0	
OKLAHOMA.............	**Total**		22	2	3	3	0					
	Cities		20	2	3	1	0					
		Ada	1	0	0	0	0	0	1	0	0	15,901
		Broken Arrow	0	0	1	0	0	0	0	1	0	89,463
		Catoosa	1	0	0	0	0	0	1	0	0	6,789
		Chickasha	2	0	0	0	0	1	0	1	0	17,346
		Cleveland	1	0	0	0	0	1	0	0	0	3,230
		Cushing	1	0	0	0	0	1	0	0	0	8,479
		Dewey	1	0	0	0	0	0	0	0	1	3,281
		Edmond	0	1	0	0	0	0	0	1	0	77,879
		El Reno	1	0	0	0	0	0	0	1	0	16,221
		Guthrie	1	0	0	0	0	0	0	1	0	11,074
		Hollis	1	0	0	0	0	0	0	1	0	2,072
		Mangum	0	0	1	0	0	0	0	1	0	2,695
		Midwest City	1	1	0	0	0	1	0	1	0	55,315
		Mustang	0	0	1	0	0	0	0	0	1	16,960
		Norman	2	0	0	0	0	0	0	1	1	103,721
		Okemah	1	0	0	0	0	0	0	0	1	2,965
		Pawnee	1	0	0	1	0	1	1	0	0	2,222
		Poteau	1	0	0	0	0	0	1	0	0	8,347
		Sallisaw	1	0	0	0	0	0	0	1	0	8,842
		Snyder	1	0	0	0	0	0	0	1	0	1,430
		Stillwater	1	0	0	0	0	0	0	0	1	45,692
		Stroud	1	0	0	0	0	0	1	0	0	2,777
	Universities and Colleges		0	0	0	1	0					
		Oklahoma State University, Main Campus	0	0	0	1	0	0	0	0	1	23,499
	Metropolitan Counties		1	0	0	0	0					
		Sequoyah	1	0	0	0	0	0	0	0	1	
	Nonmetropolitan Counties		1	0	0	1	0					
		Bryan	1	0	0	0	0	0	0	0	1	
		Harper	0	0	0	1	0	0	0	0	1	
OREGON....................	**Total**		77	28	37	27	1					
	Cities		67	20	34	24	1					
		Albany	1	0	0	0	0	0	1	0	0	46,999
		Ashland	0	0	1	0	0	1	0	0	0	21,068

[1]Agencies published in this table indicated that at least one hate crime incident occurred in their respective jurisdictions during the quarter(s) for which they submitted a report to the Hate Crime program. Blanks indicate quarters for which agencies did not submit reports.

[2]Population figures are published only for the cities. The figures listed for the universities and colleges are student enrollment and were provided by the United States Department of Education for the 2006 school year, the most recent available. The enrollment figures include full-time and part-time students.

Table 94.   Hate Crime Incidents per Bias Motivation and Quarter by State and Agency, 2007 *(Contd.)*

State	Agency type	Agency name	Number of incidents per bias motivation					Number of incidents per quarter[1]				Population[2]
			Race	Religion	Sexual orient-ation	Ethnicity	Disability	1st quarter	2nd quarter	3rd quarter	4th quarter	
		Beaverton	6	1	0	3	0	1	2	6	1	91,184
		Bend	0	0	2	0	0	0	1	1	0	75,185
		Boardman	0	0	1	0	0	0	1	0	0	3,094
		Canby	0	1	0	0	0	0	0	0	1	15,725
		Corvallis	2	0	0	2	0	0	0	2	2	49,870
		Eagle Point	1	0	0	0	0	1	0	0	0	8,547
		Grants Pass	1	0	0	0	0	0	0	0	1	30,292
		Hermiston	1	0	0	0	0	0	0	0	1	15,148
		Keizer	1	1	0	0	0	0	2	0	0	35,423
		La Grande	0	0	0	1	0	0	1	0	0	12,288
		Lincoln City	0	0	0	1	0	0	1	0	0	7,996
		Medford	3	0	0	0	0	1	1	1	0	71,969
		Newberg-Dundee	1	0	0	0	0	0	1	0	0	25,209
		Newport	3	0	0	1	0	0	1	0	3	9,953
		Portland	20	11	22	9	1	24	17	12	10	538,133
		Redmond	2	0	0	0	0	0	1	1	0	24,095
		Rogue River	0	1	0	0	0	0	0	1	0	1,943
		Roseburg	0	0	1	0	0	0	0	0	1	21,128
		Salem	2	0	3	3	0	3	1	2	2	154,484
		Seaside	0	0	0	1	0	0	0	0	1	6,229
		Silverton	0	0	1	0	0	0	0	0	1	9,200
		Springfield	4	0	2	2	0	3	4	1	0	56,201
		Stayton	1	0	0	0	0	1	0	0	0	7,385
		Tigard	16	5	0	0	0	12	2	6	1	50,087
		Tillamook	0	0	0	1	0	0	0	0	1	4,435
		Woodburn	2	0	1	0	0	0	3	0	0	22,399
	Metropolitan Counties		6	5	1	3	0					
		Benton	1	1	1	0	0	2	0	1	0	
		Clackamas	2	1	0	0	0	0	0	2	1	
		Deschutes	0	0	0	1	0	0	0	1	0	
		Jackson	1	1	0	0	0	0	1	1	0	
		Lane	1	1	0	1	0	2	1	0	0	
		Marion	0	1	0	1	0	0	0	0	2	
		Yamhill	1	0	0	0	0	0	0	0	1	
	Nonmetropolitan Counties		3	3	2	0	0					
		Douglas	1	1	1	0	0	0	0	0	3	
		Lincoln	1	2	0	0	0	1	1	0	1	
		Tillamook	0	0	1	0	0	1	0	0	0	
		Umatilla	1	0	0	0	0	1	0	0	0	
	State Police Agencies		1	0	0	0	0					
		State Police, Washington County	1	0	0	0	0	0	0	1	0	
PENNSYLVANIA	**Total**		40	25	13	5	0					
	Cities		35	22	7	5	0					
		Abington Township	6	4	0	0	0	2	2	4	2	54,413
		Bensalem Township	0	0	1	0	0	0	1	0	0	58,788
		Camp Hill	0	1	0	0	0	0	1	0	0	7,384
		Carlisle	2	0	0	0	0	0	0	2	0	18,317
		East Cocalico Township	1	0	0	0	0	0	0	1	0	10,398
		East Hempfield Township	1	0	0	0	0	0	1	0	0	23,212
		Harrisburg	0	0	0	1	0	0	0	1	0	46,924
		Hatfield Township	1	0	0	0	0	0	1	0	0	20,241
		Hopewell Township	1	0	0	0	0	0	0	1		12,511
		Johnstown	1	0	1	0	0	1	1	0	0	23,609
		Lancaster	1	0	0	0	0	0	1			54,562
		Moosic	0	0	1	0	0	0	0	1	0	5,793
		Northern York Regional	1	0	0	0	0	0	1	0	0	63,294
		Philadelphia	12	13	3	0	0	1	7	3	17	1,435,533
		Pittsburgh	6	1	0	2	0	1	0	5	3	312,179
		Springdale	1	0	0	0	0	0	0	1	0	3,507
		Spring Township, Berks County	1	0	0	0	0	0	1	0	0	26,659
		Swatara Township	0	0	1	1	0	0	1	1	0	22,281
		Westtown-East Goshen Regional	0	0	0	1	0	0	0	1	0	31,691
		York Area Regional	0	3	0	0	0	0	0	3	0	57,252
	Universities and Colleges		5	1	5	0	0					
		West Chester University	5	1	5	0	0	3	3	5	0	12,879
	State Police Agencies		0	2	1	0	0					
		State Police:										
		Chester County	0	1	0	0	0	0	0	1		
		Monroe County	0	1	0	0	0		1		0	
		Pike County	0	0	1	0	0	1	0	0	0	

[1] Agencies published in this table indicated that at least one hate crime incident occurred in their respective jurisdictions during the quarter(s) for which they submitted a report to the Hate Crime program. Blanks indicate quarters for which agencies did not submit reports.

[2] Population figures are published only for the cities. The figures listed for the universities and colleges are student enrollment and were provided by the United States Department of Education for the 2006 school year, the most recent available. The enrollment figures include full-time and part-time students.

Table 94.   Hate Crime Incidents per Bias Motivation and Quarter by State and Agency, 2007 *(Contd.)*

State	Agency type	Agency name	Number of incidents per bias motivation					Number of incidents per quarter[1]				Popu-lation[2]
			Race	Religion	Sexual orient-ation	Ethnicity	Disability	1st quarter	2nd quarter	3rd quarter	4th quarter	
RHODE ISLAND........	Total		20	5	9	13	0					
	Cities		19	5	9	13	0					
		East Providence	1	0	0	0	0	0	0	0	1	48,668
		Pawtucket	0	0	1	0	0	0	0	1	0	72,319
		Providence	15	5	8	13	0	7	10	10	14	173,719
		South Kingstown	1	0	0	0	0	1	0	0	0	29,172
		Warwick	1	0	0	0	0	0	1	0	0	85,139
		West Warwick	1	0	0	0	0	1	0	0	0	29,293
	Universities and Colleges		1	0	0	0	0					
		Brown University	1	0	0	0	0	0	0	0	1	8,125
SOUTH CAROLINA..................	Total		72	20	16	16	3					
	Cities		35	5	8	12	0					
		Batesburg-Leesville	1	0	0	0	0	0	0	1	0	5,620
		Beaufort	6	0	0	1	0	2	1	1	3	11,960
		Bennettsville	0	0	1	0	0	0	0	0	1	10,898
		Chapin	0	0	1	0	0	1	0	0	0	698
		Cheraw	2	0	0	0	0	0	0	1	1	5,417
		Clinton	1	0	0	0	0	0	0	1	0	9,018
		Clover	1	0	0	0	0	1	0	0	0	4,493
		Darlington	0	0	0	1	0	0	0	1	0	6,525
		Denmark	1	0	0	0	0	0	0	0	1	3,052
		Florence	3	0	0	0	0	0	0	0	3	31,377
		Goose Creek	0	0	1	0	0	0	1	0	0	32,139
		Great Falls	1	0	0	0	0	0	0	1	0	2,052
		Hanahan	0	0	0	2	0	0	0	2	0	13,983
		Hartsville	0	0	2	0	0	0	0	1	1	7,460
		Hemingway	3	0	0	0	0	0	2	1	0	513
		Lexington	2	0	0	0	0	0	2	0	0	14,715
		Lyman	1	0	0	0	0	1	0	0	0	2,812
		Manning	1	0	0	1	0	0	1	1	0	4,016
		Mount Pleasant	3	1	0	0	0	1	1	1	1	60,746
		Myrtle Beach	1	1	0	2	0	3	1	0	0	29,361
		North Augusta	1	0	0	0	0	0	0	1	0	20,270
		Port Royal	0	0	0	1	0	0	1	0	0	9,959
		Rock Hill	0	0	0	1	0	0	0	1	0	63,388
		Simpsonville	0	0	1	0	0	1	0	0	0	16,211
		Spartanburg	0	0	1	1	0	0	1	0	1	38,388
		Summerville	1	0	0	0	0	0	1	0	0	43,985
		Union	2	0	0	0	0	1	0	0	1	8,167
		Walterboro	1	3	0	2	0	1	3	1	1	5,601
		Westminster	1	0	0	0	0	0	0	1	0	2,675
		York	2	0	1	0	0	0	1	1	1	7,537
	Universities and Colleges		0	0	1	0	0					
		College of Charleston	0	0	1	0	0	1	0	0	0	11,218
	Metropolitan Counties		18	6	3	2	1					
		Aiken	2	0	0	0	0	0	1	0	1	
		Anderson	3	0	0	0	0	0	0	3	0	
		Berkeley	0	0	1	1	0	0	1	0	1	
		Charleston	1	0	0	0	0	0	0	1	0	
		Darlington[4]	4	0	0	1	0	1	2	1	1	
		Greenville	2	3	1	0	0	2	3	1	0	
		Horry County Police Department	1	1	0	0	0	0	0	1	1	
		Kershaw	2	0	0	0	0	1	0	0	1	
		Lexington	1	0	0	0	0	1	0	0	0	
		Richland	0	1	1	0	0	2	0	0	0	
		Saluda	1	0	0	0	0	0	0	1	0	
		Spartanburg	1	1	0	0	1	0	1	1	1	
	Nonmetropolitan Counties		19	9	4	2	2					
		Beaufort	1	0	0	0	0	0	0	0	1	
		Chester	3	8	1	0	0	2	2	1	7	
		Chesterfield	1	0	2	0	0	0	0	3	0	
		Clarendon	0	0	0	1	0	0	1	0	0	
		Colleton	1	1	0	1	0	1	0	1	1	
		Greenwood	1	0	0	0	0	1	0	0	0	
		Hampton	5	0	0	0	0	0	0	0	5	
		Lee	0	0	1	0	2	1	1	1	0	
		Marion	1	0	0	0	0	0	1	0	0	
		Marlboro	1	0	0	0	0	0	1	0	0	
		Oconee	2	0	0	0	0	0	2	0	0	
		Williamsburg	3	0	0	0	0	2	0	1	0	

[1]Agencies published in this table indicated that at least one hate crime incident occurred in their respective jurisdictions during the quarter(s) for which they submitted a report to the Hate Crime program. Blanks indicate quarters for which agencies did not submit reports.
[2]Population figures are published only for the cities. The figures listed for the universities and colleges are student enrollment and were provided by the United States Department of Education for the 2006 school year, the most recent available. The enrollment figures include full-time and part-time students.
[4]Includes one incident reported with more than one bias motivation.

Table 94. Hate Crime Incidents per Bias Motivation and Quarter by State and Agency, 2007 (Contd.)

State	Agency type	Agency name	Number of incidents per bias motivation					Number of incidents per quarter[1]				Popu-lation[2]
			Race	Religion	Sexual orient-ation	Ethnicity	Disability	1st quarter	2nd quarter	3rd quarter	4th quarter	
SOUTH DAKOTA.......	Total		21	6	1	9	0					
	Cities		15	5	0	8	0					
		Aberdeen	1	0	0	0	0	0	0	0	1	23,992
		Martin	1	0	0	0	0	0	0	1	0	1,029
		Pierre	1	0	0	0	0	0	0	1	0	14,124
		Rapid City	3	0	0	0	0	1	1	0	1	63,162
		Sioux Falls	8	5	0	8	0	5	10	2	4	144,985
		Spearfish	1	0	0	0	0	1	0	0	0	9,796
	Metropolitan Counties		6	0	1	1	0					
		Minnehaha	6	0	1	0	0	0	3	3	1	
		Pennington	0	0	0	1	0	1	0	0	0	
	Nonmetropolitan Counties		0	1	0	0	0					
		Butte	0	1	0	0	0	0	0	0	1	
TENNESSEE...............	Total		116	33	49	38	3					
	Cities		89	25	38	32	2					
		Bristol	1	0	0	0	0	0	0	1	0	25,346
		Chattanooga	4	0	1	0	0	2	2	0	1	155,043
		Clarksville	1	2	1	0	0	1	1	1	1	114,582
		Cleveland	6	3	1	1	0	2	4	3	2	38,808
		Collegedale	1	1	0	0	0	0	1	0	1	7,423
		Collierville	1	0	0	0	0	0	0	0	1	39,569
		Collinwood	0	0	0	0	1	0	0	1	0	1,038
		Covington	0	0	1	0	0	0	0	0	1	9,193
		Crossville	0	0	3	1	0	3	1	0	0	11,111
		Dayton	1	0	0	0	0	1	0	0	0	6,686
		Decatur	1	0	0	0	0	0	1	0	0	1,468
		Dickson	0	0	1	0	0	1	0	0	0	13,171
		Dyersburg	1	0	0	0	0	1	0	0	0	17,391
		East Ridge	2	2	0	0	0	1	2	0	1	19,641
		Franklin	1	1	0	1	0	0	1	0	2	57,489
		Gallatin	1	0	0	0	0	0	0	0	1	28,419
		Gibson	1	0	0	0	0	0	0	1	0	406
		Goodlettsville	0	1	0	0	0	0	0	1	0	15,854
		Hendersonville	0	0	1	0	0	1	0	0	0	46,989
		Humboldt	1	0	0	0	0	0	1	0	0	9,213
		Jackson	2	0	2	0	0	1	0	1	2	63,125
		Johnson City	2	0	2	0	0	0	1	2	1	60,488
		Kingsport	2	0	0	0	0	1	0	1	0	44,079
		Knoxville	6	1	1	2	0	1	5	3	1	183,319
		Lexington	2	0	1	0	0	0	1	1	1	7,829
		Maryville	3	0	0	0	0	3	0	0	0	26,941
		Maynardville	1	0	0	0	0	0	0	1	0	1,940
		Memphis	37	8	20	20	1	17	25	30	14	669,264
		Murfreesboro	1	0	0	0	0	1	0	0	0	96,264
		Nashville	1	4	3	4	0	4	3	4	1	564,169
		Oak Ridge	2	0	0	0	0	0	0	0	2	27,682
		Paris	1	0	0	0	0	1	0	0	0	10,014
		Portland	0	0	0	1	0	0	1	0	0	11,060
		Pulaski	1	0	0	0	0	0	1	0	0	7,869
		Red Bank	1	0	0	0	0	0	1	0	0	11,526
		Savannah	1	0	0	0	0	0	1	0	0	7,281
		Signal Mountain	0	1	0	0	0	0	0	1	0	7,063
		Spring Hill	2	1	0	1	0	2	1	0	1	23,774
		Winchester	1	0	0	1	0	1	0	0	1	7,911
	Universities and Colleges		1	1	1	1	0					
		Vanderbilt University	1	1	1	1	0	1	0	2	1	11,607
	Metropolitan Counties		20	5	4	5	1					
		Anderson	1	0	0	0	0	0	0	0	1	
		Blount	2	0	0	1	0	0	1	2	0	
		Bradley	2	0	1	1	0	0	2	2	0	
		Cheatham	2	0	0	0	0	0	2	0	0	
		Dickson	1	1	0	0	0	1	0	1	0	
		Jefferson	2	0	1	2	0	2	3	0	0	
		Knox	2	0	1	0	0	1	0	0	2	
		Montgomery	0	2	1	0	0	0	1	2	0	
		Rutherford	2	0	0	1	0	1	0	1	1	
		Shelby	5	1	0	0	1	2	1	1	3	
		Sullivan	1	1	0	0	0	0	1	0	1	
	Nonmetropolitan Counties		6	2	6	0	0					
		Gibson	2	0	0	0	0	0	0	1	1	
		Lauderdale	1	0	0	0	0	0	0	0	1	
		Marshall	1	0	0	0	0	0	0	1	0	

[1] Agencies published in this table indicated that at least one hate crime incident occurred in their respective jurisdictions during the quarter(s) for which they submitted a report to the Hate Crime program. Blanks indicate quarters for which agencies did not submit reports.

[2] Population figures are published only for the cities. The figures listed for the universities and colleges are student enrollment and were provided by the United States Department of Education for the 2006 school year, the most recent available. The enrollment figures include full-time and part-time students.

Table 94. Hate Crime Incidents per Bias Motivation and Quarter by State and Agency, 2007 *(Contd.)*

State	Agency type	Agency name	Number of incidents per bias motivation					Number of incidents per quarter[1]				Popu-lation[2]
			Race	Religion	Sexual orient-ation	Ethnicity	Disability	1st quarter	2nd quarter	3rd quarter	4th quarter	
		Maury	1	1	1	0	0	0	2	1	0	
		Monroe	1	0	0	0	0	0	1	0	0	
		Sevier	0	1	0	0	0	1	0	0	0	
		Warren	0	0	5	0	0	0	5	0	0	
TEXAS........................	**Total**		130	20	46	46	0					
	Cities		117	17	46	45	0					
		Allen	1	0	0	0	0	0	0	1	0	78,630
		Arlington	5	0	1	0	0	0	2	1	3	372,073
		Austin	3	0	1	2	0	1	1	3	1	716,817
		Bedford	1	0	1	0	0	1	0	0	1	48,974
		Bertram	1	0	0	0	0	1	0	0	0	1,378
		Bonham	1	0	0	0	0	0	1	0	0	10,756
		Bryan	1	0	0	0	0	0	0	0	1	67,484
		Carrollton	1	2	1	1	0	1	3	1	0	123,324
		Cedar Park	4	0	0	0	0	1	1	2	0	57,286
		Copperas Cove	1	0	0	0	0	0	0	1	0	29,706
		Corpus Christi	8	2	3	3	0	2	2	9	3	286,428
		Dallas	14	1	7	1	0	9	5	4	5	1,239,104
		Del Rio	1	0	0	0	0	0	0	0	1	36,864
		Denton	1	0	0	0	0	0	1	0	0	113,936
		El Paso	1	0	2	1	0	2	1	0	1	616,029
		Forney	1	0	0	0	0	0	1	0	0	14,020
		Fort Worth	13	1	0	5	0	3	4	5	7	670,693
		Friendswood	0	0	1	0	0	1	0	0	0	34,140
		Frisco	1	0	0	0	0	0	1	0	0	90,674
		Galveston	0	0	1	0	0	0	1	0	0	57,590
		Garland	9	3	0	1	0	0	6	5	2	218,236
		Haltom City	1	0	0	0	0	0	2	0	0	40,114
		Henderson	0	0	1	0	0	0	0	0	1	11,633
		Houston	12	3	11	10	0	4	16	11	5	2,169,544
		Huntsville	0	0	0	1	0	0	0	1	0	37,906
		Keller	1	1	0	0	0	0	0	1	1	38,439
		Kingsville	0	0	0	1	0	0	0	0	1	24,235
		Leander	2	0	0	0	0	1	0	0	1	23,175
		Longview	7	0	1	3	0	4	1	4	2	77,003
		Mansfield	2	0	0	1	0	0	3	0	0	43,901
		Midland	0	1	1	1	0	0	1	1	1	103,118
		Missouri City	1	0	0	0	0	1	0	0	0	77,166
		New Braunfels	0	0	2	1	0	0	2	1	0	51,860
		North Richland Hills	1	0	0	0	0	0	1	0	0	63,270
		Orange	1	0	0	0	0	0	0	0	1	17,793
		Palestine	0	0	1	0	0	0	1	0	0	18,250
		Plano	3	0	0	2	0	1	1	1	2	259,771
		Richland Hills	0	0	0	1	0	0	1	0	0	8,067
		Rockport	1	0	0	0	0	1	0	0	0	9,464
		Round Rock	1	0	0	1	0	0	0	1	1	97,727
		Rowlett	0	0	0	1	0	0	0	0	1	56,432
		San Antonio	8	0	9	5	0	5	10	4	3	1,316,882
		San Marcos	1	0	1	0	0	0	0	1	1	48,979
		Seguin	1	0	1	0	0	1	0	0	1	25,203
		Tomball	0	0	0	2	0	2	0	0	0	10,176
		Tyler	1	0	0	0	0	0	0	1	0	95,596
		Uvalde	1	0	0	0	0	0	0	0	1	16,594
		Victoria	0	1	0	0	0	0	1	0	0	62,404
		Vidor	3	0	0	0	0	0	1	1	1	11,158
		Waco	1	1	0	0	0	0	0	1	1	122,514
		Wichita Falls	0	1	0	0	0	0	1	0	0	98,717
	Universities and Colleges		2	1	0	0	0					
		Texas Technological University, Lubbock	1	0	0	0	0	1	0	0	0	27,996
		University of Texas, Austin	1	1	0	0	0	1	1	0	0	49,697
	Metropolitan Counties		10	1	0	1	0					
		Harris	7	0	0	1	0	1	1	3	3	
		Kendall	1	0	0	0	0	1	0	0	0	
		McLennan	1	0	0	0	0	0	1	0	0	
		Wichita	1	0	0	0	0	0	1	0	0	
		Williamson	0	1	0	0	0	0	1	0	0	
	Nonmetropolitan Counties		1	0	0	0	0					
		Hood	1	0	0	0	0	0	0	1	0	
	Other Agencies		0	1	0	0	0					
		Independent School District, Austin	0	1	0	0	0	1	0	0	0	

[1]Agencies published in this table indicated that at least one hate crime incident occurred in their respective jurisdictions during the quarter(s) for which they submitted a report to the Hate Crime program. Blanks indicate quarters for which agencies did not submit reports.

[2]Population figures are published only for the cities. The figures listed for the universities and colleges are student enrollment and were provided by the United States Department of Education for the 2006 school year, the most recent available. The enrollment figures include full-time and part-time students.

Table 94. Hate Crime Incidents per Bias Motivation and Quarter by State and Agency, 2007 *(Contd.)*

State	Agency type	Agency name	Number of incidents per bias motivation					Number of incidents per quarter[1]				Popu-lation[2]
			Race	Religion	Sexual orient-ation	Ethnicity	Disability	1st quarter	2nd quarter	3rd quarter	4th quarter	
UTAH	**Total**		19	15	9	12	0					
	Cities		17	12	8	10	0					
		Bountiful	0	0	2	0	0	2	0	0	0	41,132
		Centerville	0	3	0	0	0	1	0	2	0	15,140
		Clearfield	1	0	0	0	0	1	0	0	0	27,419
		Clinton	1	0	0	0	0	0	0	1	0	19,882
		Farmington	1	0	0	0	0	0	0	1	0	16,078
		Ivins	0	0	0	1	0	1	0	0	0	7,663
		Layton	2	0	0	0	0	1	0	1	0	63,284
		Murray	1	0	1	0	0	0	0	1	1	44,748
		North Salt Lake	0	0	1	2	0	0	1	0	2	12,070
		Provo	0	2	0	0	0	0	0	0	2	115,264
		Roosevelt	0	1	0	0	0	0	0	1	0	4,740
		Roy	1	0	0	0	0	1	0	0	0	35,366
		Salt Lake City	0	1	0	0	0	0	0	1	0	178,449
		Sandy	0	1	0	0	0	0	1	0	0	94,975
		South Jordan	1	1	1	1	0	1	2	1	0	46,571
		Springville	1	0	0	0	0	1	0	0	0	26,883
		St. George	1	0	0	0	0	0	1	0	0	70,579
		Taylorsville City	0	0	1	0	0	0	1	0	0	57,944
		Tooele	1	0	0	0	0	0	0	0	1	30,019
		Vernal	0	1	0	0	0	0	0	0	1	8,231
		Washington	0	1	1	1	0	0	3	0	0	16,607
		West Valley	6	1	1	5	0	4	3	5	1	121,447
	Universities and Colleges		0	2	0	0	0					
		Brigham Young University	0	2	0	0	0	1	1	0	0	34,185
	Metropolitan Counties		1	1	1	2	0					
		Davis	0	0	0	1	0	0	0	1	0	
		Salt Lake	1	0	0	1	0	0	0	2	0	
		Tooele	0	0	1	0	0	0	0	0	1	
		Weber	0	1	0	0	0	0	1	0	0	
	Nonmetropolitan Counties		1	0	0	0	0					
		Uintah	1	0	0	0	0		1	0	0	
VERMONT..................	**Total**		9	5	7	0	0					
	Cities		9	4	5	0	0					
		Barre Town	1	0	0	0	0	0	1	0	0	8,146
		Bellows Falls	0	0	1	0	0	0	0	0	1	2,957
		Bennington	1	0	0	0	0	0	0	0	1	15,297
		Burlington	4	3	4	0	0	1	2	0	8	38,153
		Montpelier	0	1	0	0	0	0	0	1	0	7,944
		Rutland	1	0	0	0	0	0	1	0	0	19,626
		South Burlington	1	0	0	0	0	0	0	1	0	17,333
		St. Johnsbury	1	0	0	0	0	0	1	0	0	7,553
	Nonmetropolitan Counties		0	0	1	0	0					
		Orange	0	0	1	0	0	0	0	0	1	
	State Police Agencies		0	1	1	0	0					
		State Police: New Haven	0	1	0	0	0	0	0	1	0	
		St. Albans	0	0	1	0	0	0	0	0	1	
VIRGINIA	**Total**		186	54	34	34	15					
	Cities		92	27	20	16	10					
		Alexandria	0	5	0	0	0	0	1	3	1	137,812
		Berryville	0	1	0	0	0	0	0	0	1	3,216
		Bristol	1	0	0	0	0	0	0	1	0	17,484
		Charlottesville	1	0	1	0	2	1	0	1	2	40,265
		Chesapeake	3	0	1	0	1	0	2	1	2	223,093
		Danville	1	0	0	0	0	0	1	0	0	45,114
		Emporia	2	0	0	0	0	0	0	1	1	5,607
		Exmore	0	1	0	0	0	0	0	1	0	1,381
		Fairfax City	0	0	0	1	0	0	0	0	1	22,484
		Falls Church	1	0	0	0	0	0	0	1	0	10,831
		Fredericksburg	0	0	1	1	0	0	1	0	1	21,521
		Hampton	4	2	0	0	0	2	0	3	1	144,490
		Harrisonburg	0	1	2	0	0	0	1	0	2	40,869
		Herndon	1	0	0	1	0	1	0	0	1	21,892
		Hopewell	1	0	0	0	0	0	0	0	1	22,741
		Lynchburg	3	1	1	0	0	1	2	1	1	67,932
		Manassas	6	0	0	0	0	1	1	3	1	36,735
		Manassas Park	0	0	0	1	0	1	0	0	0	11,816
		Newport News	3	3	2	1	0	4	1	2	2	177,550
		Norfolk	27	5	2	4	1	13	10	11	5	227,903

[1] Agencies published in this table indicated that at least one hate crime incident occurred in their respective jurisdictions during the quarter(s) for which they submitted a report to the Hate Crime program. Blanks indicate quarters for which agencies did not submit reports.

[2] Population figures are published only for the cities. The figures listed for the universities and colleges are student enrollment and were provided by the United States Department of Education for the 2006 school year, the most recent available. The enrollment figures include full-time and part-time students.

Table 94. Hate Crime Incidents per Bias Motivation and Quarter by State and Agency, 2007 *(Contd.)*

State	Agency type	Agency name	Number of incidents per bias motivation					Number of incidents per quarter[1]				Popu-lation[2]
			Race	Religion	Sexual orient-ation	Ethnicity	Disability	1st quarter	2nd quarter	3rd quarter	4th quarter	
		Onancock	0	0	0	0	1	0	0	1	0	1,437
		Onley	0	0	0	1	0	0	0	0	1	490
		Petersburg	0	0	0	0	1	0	0	1	0	32,210
		Portsmouth	7	0	0	1	0	4	1	1	2	101,284
		Pulaski	0	1	0	0	0	0	0	1	0	9,006
		Purcellville	2	0	0	0	0	1	0	0	1	5,048
		Radford	1	0	0	0	0	1	0	0	0	14,317
		Richmond	4	3	4	1	0	3	4	4	1	191,785
		Roanoke	3	0	3	1	0	1	2	3	1	90,894
		Rocky Mount	1	0	0	0	0	0	1	0	0	4,568
		Suffolk	2	0	0	1	2	3	0	1	1	83,631
		Vinton	1	0	0	0	0	1	0	0	0	7,924
		Virginia Beach	15	4	3	2	0	9	3	5	7	435,943
		Waverly	0	0	0	0	1	0	1	0	0	2,194
		Williamsburg	2	0	0	0	0	0	1	0	1	11,740
		Wytheville	0	0	0	0	1	0	0	1	0	8,184
	Universities and Colleges		7	5	1	0	0					
		Ferrum College	1	0	0	0	0	0	0	1	0	1,060
		George Mason University	2	2	0	0	0	0	2	1	1	29,889
		James Madison University	1	0	0	0	0	1	0	0	0	17,393
		Northern Virginia Community College	1	1	0	0	0	0	1	0	1	38,166
		Old Dominion University	1	1	0	0	0	0	0	0	2	21,625
		Radford University	1	0	0	0	0	0	0	0	1	9,220
		Virginia Military Institute	0	1	0	0	0	0	0	1	0	1,397
		Virginia State University	0	0	1	0	0	1	0	0	0	4,872
	Metropolitan Counties		80	20	9	15	0					
		Albemarle County Police Department	4	1	1	2	0	3	2	0	3	
		Amelia	0	0	1	0	0	1	0	0	0	
		Amherst	0	1	0	0	0	0	0	1	0	
		Arlington County Police Department	4	0	1	0	0	1	1	1	2	
		Bedford	3	1	0	0	0	1	1	2	0	
		Campbell	4	1	0	1	0	1	2	2	1	
		Chesterfield County Police Department	9	4	0	0	0	4	3	2	4	
		Fairfax County Police Department	9	4	1	1	0	6	4	3	2	
		Fauquier	4	1	0	0	0	1	0	1	3	
		Fluvanna	1	0	1	1	0	0	2	1	0	
		Frederick	0	0	0	1	0	0	0	0	1	
		Gloucester	1	0	0	0	0	0	1	0	0	
		Greene	1	1	1	2	0	2	1	2	0	
		Henrico County Police Department	9	2	0	3	0	4	4	1	5	
		James City County Police Department	3	0	0	0	0	1	1	0	1	
		King and Queen	1	0	0	0	0	0	0	1	0	
		Loudoun	13	1	2	2	0	4	4	5	5	
		Montgomery	3	0	0	0	0	0	1	1	1	
		New Kent	2	0	0	1	0	0	0	2	1	
		Prince George County Police Department	3	0	0	0	0	0	2	1	0	
		Prince William County Police Department	1	0	0	1	0	0	2	0	0	
		Roanoke County Police Department	1	2	1	0	0	0	1	1	2	
		Spotsylvania	2	0	0	0	0	0	1	1	0	
		Washington	2	1	0	0	0	2	0	0	1	
	Nonmetropolitan Counties		5	1	4	2	5					
		Augusta	2	0	0	0	0	0	0	2	0	
		Buckingham	0	0	0	1	0	0	0	0	1	
		Floyd	0	0	0	0	1	1	0	0	0	
		Greensville	0	0	0	0	2	1	0	1	0	
		King George	1	0	0	0	0	1	0	0	0	
		Madison	2	0	0	1	0	1	0	0	2	
		Mecklenburg	0	1	0	0	0	0	0	0	1	
		Northumberland	0	0	0	0	1	0	0	0	1	
		Rappahannock	0	0	1	0	0	0	0	0	1	
		Rockbridge	0	0	0	0	1	0	0	0	1	
		Tazewell	0	0	1	0	0	0	0	1	0	
		Westmoreland	0	0	2	0	0	2	0	0	0	

[1]Agencies published in this table indicated that at least one hate crime incident occurred in their respective jurisdictions during the quarter(s) for which they submitted a report to the Hate Crime program. Blanks indicate quarters for which agencies did not submit reports.

[2]Population figures are published only for the cities. The figures listed for the universities and colleges are student enrollment and were provided by the United States Department of Education for the 2006 school year, the most recent available. The enrollment figures include full-time and part-time students.

Table 94.   Hate Crime Incidents per Bias Motivation and Quarter by State and Agency, 2007 *(Contd.)*

State	Agency type	Agency name	Number of incidents per bias motivation					Number of incidents per quarter[1]				Popu-lation[2]
			Race	Religion	Sexual orient-ation	Ethnicity	Disability	1st quarter	2nd quarter	3rd quarter	4th quarter	
	State Police Agencies		0	1	0	0	0					
		State Police, Washington County	0	1	0	0	0	0	1	0	0	
	Other Agencies		2	0	0	1	0					
		Reagan National Airport	1	0	0	0	0	0	0	1	0	
		Virginia State Capitol	1	0	0	1	0	0	0	1	1	
WASHINGTON	**Total**		104	17	39	34	1					
	Cities		79	12	34	23	1					
		Arlington	1	0	0	0	0	0	0	1	0	16,736
		Auburn	1	0	0	0	0	1	0	0	0	49,710
		Battle Ground	0	0	0	1	0	0	0	0	1	14,149
		Bremerton	1	0	1	0	0	0	0	2	0	35,068
		Burien	0	1	1	0	0	1	1	0	0	31,035
		Clarkston	0	0	0	1	0	0	0	0	1	7,231
		Covington	4	0	0	0	0	0	1	2	1	18,072
		Ellensburg	2	0	0	0	0	0	1	1	0	17,033
		Everett	1	1	1	0	0	1	0	0	2	98,845
		Federal Way	0	0	1	0	0	0	1	0	0	84,026
		Kenmore	0	0	0	1	0	0	0	0	1	20,167
		Kennewick	0	0	1	2	0		1	1	1	63,147
		Kent	2	1	0	0	0	0	2	1	0	83,929
		Lakewood	3	0	0	0	0	2	1	0	0	57,465
		Longview	1	0	0	0	0	0	1	0	0	37,068
		Maple Valley	2	0	1	0	0	0	1	2	0	16,798
		Mercer Island	0	1	0	0	0	0	0	0	1	23,671
		Mill Creek	1	0	0	0	0	0	1	0	0	15,843
		Milton	1	0	0	0	0	0	0	1	0	6,836
		Newcastle	1	0	0	0	0	0	0	1	0	9,867
		North Bend	0	0	0	1	0	1	0	0	0	4,605
		Oak Harbor	1	1	0	0	0	0	1	0	1	23,168
		Olympia	0	0	0	2	0	0	0	2	0	44,946
		Port Angeles	0	0	1	0	0	0	0	1	0	19,064
		Port Orchard	1	0	0	0	0	1	0	0	0	8,026
		Pullman	4	0	1	0	0	0	4	0	1	25,408
		Redmond	1	1	1	0	0	0	1	1	1	49,195
		Renton	1	0	0	0	0	0	1	0	0	59,656
		Richland	1	0	0	1	0	0	0	1	1	45,555
		Sammamish	0	1	0	0	0	0	0	0	1	35,327
		SeaTac	0	1	0	0	0	0	0	0	1	25,320
		Seattle	14	0	11	3	0	5	5	10	8	585,118
		Selah	0	0	1	0	0	0	0	1	0	7,037
		Sequim	1	1	0	0	0	1	0	1	0	5,898
		Shoreline	1	0	0	2	0	1	1	1	0	52,189
		Spokane	10	2	6	4	1	7	8	5	3	198,272
		Spokane Valley	1	0	0	0	0	1	0	0	0	83,928
		Tacoma	10	0	5	2	0	2	1	9	5	196,909
		Tukwila	1	0	0	0	0	0	1	0	0	17,103
		University Place	1	0	0	0	0	0	0	0	1	30,699
		Vancouver	6	0	0	2	0	0	4	3	1	161,092
		Walla Walla	1	0	0	0	0	0	1	0	0	31,002
		Washougal	0	0	1	0	0	1	0	0	0	11,769
		Yakima	3	1	1	1	0	1	2	1	2	82,951
	Universities and Colleges		0	0	0	4	0					
		Eastern Washington University	0	0	0	4	0	4	0	0	0	11,161
	Metropolitan Counties		23	3	3	7	0					
		Chelan	0	0	0	1	0	0	0	1	0	
		Clark	3	0	0	1	0	1	1	0	2	
		King	12	2	1	3	0	4	5	4	5	
		Kitsap	4	0	1	2	0	1	1	4	1	
		Pierce	1	1	0	0	0	1	0	0	1	
		Snohomish	2	0	1	0	0	2	1			
		Yakima	1	0	0	0	0	0	0	1	0	
	Nonmetropolitan Counties		0	1	2	0	0					
		Clallam	0	1	2	0	0	1	2	0	0	
	Other Agencies		2	1	0	0	0					
		Port of Seattle	2	1	0	0	0	1	0	1	1	
WEST VIRGINIA........	**Total**		31	2	10	1	0					
	Cities		24	1	4	1	0					
		Beckley	1	0	0	0	0	0	0	0	1	16,774
		Charleston	3	0	1	0	0	0	0	2	2	50,510
		Clarksburg	2	0	0	1	0	0	1	2	0	16,420

[1]Agencies published in this table indicated that at least one hate crime incident occurred in their respective jurisdictions during the quarter(s) for which they submitted a report to the Hate Crime program. Blanks indicate quarters for which agencies did not submit reports.

[2]Population figures are published only for the cities. The figures listed for the universities and colleges are student enrollment and were provided by the United States Department of Education for the 2006 school year, the most recent available. The enrollment figures include full-time and part-time students.

Table 94. Hate Crime Incidents per Bias Motivation and Quarter by State and Agency, 2007 *(Contd.)*

State	Agency type	Agency name	Number of incidents per bias motivation					Number of incidents per quarter[1]				Popu-lation[2]
			Race	Religion	Sexual orient-ation	Ethnicity	Disability	1st quarter	2nd quarter	3rd quarter	4th quarter	
		Huntington	9	0	2	0	0	5	4	1	1	48,669
		Morgantown	1	1	0	0	0	0	0	0	2	28,951
		Nitro	0	0	1	0	0	0	0	1	0	6,723
		Princeton	1	0	0	0	0	0	1	0	0	6,178
		South Charleston	4	0	0	0	0	1	2	0	1	12,468
		Spencer	1	0	0	0	0	1	0	0	0	2,242
		Weirton	1	0	0	0	0	0	1	0	0	19,095
		Wheeling	1	0	0	0	0	1	0	0	0	29,057
	Universities and Colleges		1	0	0	0	0					
		West Virginia State University	1	0	0	0	0	0	0	0	1	3,502
	Metropolitan Counties		4	0	5	0	0					
		Berkeley	1	0	3	0	0	1	0	2	1	
		Brooke	2	0	0	0	0	0	0	2	0	
		Kanawha	0	0	1	0	0	0	0	0	1	
		Marshall	1	0	0	0	0	0	0	0	1	
		Monongalia	0	0	1	0	0	0	0	1	0	
	Nonmetropolitan Counties		1	0	0	0	0					
		Fayette	1	0	0	0	0	0	0	0	1	
	State Police Agencies		1	1	0	0	0					
		State Police:										
		Keyser	1	0	0	0	0	0	0	1	0	
		Romney	0	1	0	0	0	0	1	0	0	
	Other Agencies		0	0	1	0	0					
		Harrison County Drug and Violent Crime Task Force	0	0	1	0	0	0	1	0	0	
WISCONSIN	**Total**		43	6	9	11	0					
	Cities		38	5	8	10	0					
		Appleton	2	0	0	0	0	0	0	0	2	70,169
		Darlington	0	0	1	0	0	0	1	0	0	2,328
		Fitchburg	0	0	0	1	0	0	0	1	0	22,793
		Fond du Lac	3	1	0	0	0	1	2	1	0	42,349
		Janesville	1	0	1	0	0	0	0	2	0	63,383
		Luxemburg	1	0	0	0	0	0	0	1	0	2,286
		Madison	1	0	0	0	0	0	0	1	0	225,370
		Milwaukee	21	0	4	1	0	5	3	12	6	572,938
		New Berlin	0	2	1	0	0	0	2	1	0	39,350
		New London	0	0	0	1	0	0	1	0	0	7,008
		Oak Creek	6	1	0	6	0	1	1	1	10	32,896
		Rhinelander	0	1	0	0	0	0	0	0	1	7,786
		Sheboygan	1	0	1	0	0	1	0	0	1	48,291
		Town of Madison	1	0	0	0	0	1	0	0	0	5,828
		Watertown	1	0	0	0	0	0	0	1	0	23,334
		Waukesha	0	0	0	1	0	0	1	0	0	68,162
	Universities and Colleges		3	0	0	1	0					
		University of Wisconsin, Platteville	3	0	0	1	0	0	0	0	4	6,813
	Metropolitan Counties		1	0	1	0	0					
		Dane	1	0	0	0	0	1	0	0	0	
		Eau Claire	0	0	1	0	0	0	0	1	0	
	Nonmetropolitan Counties		0	1	0	0	0					
		Oneida	0	1	0	0	0	0	1	0	0	
	Other Agencies–Tribal		1	0	0	0	0					
		Lac du Flambeau Tribal	1	0	0	0	0	0	0	1	0	
WYOMING	**Total**		10	5	5	1	0					
	Cities		10	5	5	1	0					
		Casper	6	5	1	0	0	10	0	2	0	52,434
		Cheyenne	1	0	1	0	0	0	1	0	1	55,604
		Cody	0	0	1	0	0	0	1	0	0	9,266
		Gillette	2	0	0	1	0	0	0	0	3	24,438
		Lusk	1	0	0	0	0	0	0	0	1	1,316
		Riverton	0	0	1	0	0	0	0	0	1	9,795
		Rock Springs	0	0	1	0	0	0	0	1	0	19,432

[1]Agencies published in this table indicated that at least one hate crime incident occurred in their respective jurisdictions during the quarter(s) for which they submitted a report to the Hate Crime program. Blanks indicate quarters for which agencies did not submit reports.
[2]Population figures are published only for the cities. The figures listed for the universities and colleges are student enrollment and were provided by the United States Department of Education for the 2006 school year, the most recent available. The enrollment figures include full-time and part-time students.

Table 95. Hate Crime Zero Data Submitted per Quarter, by State and Agency, 2007

(Number.)

State	Agency type	Agency name	1st quarter	2nd quarter	3rd quarter	4th quarter	Population[2]
ALABAMA	Cities	Alabaster		0			28,904
		Albertville			0		19,476
		Aliceville			0	0	2,457
		Andalusia				0	8,727
		Arab		0	0	0	7,694
		Ashford	0	0	0	0	1,967
		Atmore	0	0	0	0	7,452
		Attalla	0	0	0	0	6,426
		Autaugaville	0	0			885
		Bayou La Batre	0	0			2,761
		Bear Creek				0	1,016
		Berry		0	0	0	1,212
		Boaz	0	0	0	0	8,175
		Brent	0	0			4,328
		Brewton	0	0			5,304
		Brilliant		0	0		732
		Brookside		0	0		1,330
		Carbon Hill				0	2,048
		Centre			0		3,411
		Childersburg	0	0	0	0	4,978
		Clanton	0	0	0		8,602
		Clayton	0	0			1,383
		Cleveland	0	0			1,405
		Clio		0	0	0	2,209
		Coffeeville	0	0	0	0	354
		Collinsville		0			1,693
		Columbia	0	0			832
		Coosada		0			1,590
		Crossville		0			1,463
		Cullman				0	14,914
		Daleville		0			4,503
		Daphne		0	0	0	19,352
		Decatur		0			56,019
		Dora		0			2,441
		Dothan	0	0	0	0	64,931
		Enterprise	0			0	24,035
		Eufaula		0			13,272
		Eutaw	0	0	0		3,001
		Fairfield	0	0	0	0	11,443
		Fairhope		0	0	0	16,735
		Falkville	0	0	0		1,185
		Fayette		0			4,694
		Florala	0	0			1,904
		Florence		0	0	0	36,784
		Fort Payne	0	0			13,889
		Fyffe	0	0			1,045
		Gadsden	0	0	0	0	37,066
		Geneva				0	4,415
		Glencoe			0	0	5,311
		Gordo		0	0	0	1,589
		Greensboro	0	0	0	0	2,579
		Greenville	0	0	0	0	7,067
		Guin			0		2,223
		Gulf Shores	0	0	0	0	9,486
		Guntersville	0	0	0	0	8,088
		Gurley	0	0	0		850
		Hackleburg	0	0	0	0	1,472
		Hamilton	0	0	0	0	6,478
		Hanceville		0			3,261
		Hartford	0	0	0	0	2,401
		Helena	0	0	0		14,429
		Hokes Bluff		0			4,363
		Homewood	0	0	0		23,602
		Huntsville	0	0	0	0	169,391
		Irondale	0	0	0	0	9,471
		Jasper		0	0	0	14,117
		Kimberly	0	0			2,592
		Lafayette	0	0	0	0	3,054
		Level Plains	0	0	0	0	1,516
		Lincoln	0	0			5,089
		Loxley		0	0	0	1,587
		Madison	0	0	0	0	37,994
		Maplesville	0	0			686
		Midland City				0	1,839
		Mobile		0			253,842
		Montevallo	0	0	0	0	5,234
		Moundville	0	0			2,399
		Muscle Shoals	0	0	0	0	12,776
		Myrtlewood	0	0	0	0	134
		New Hope		0	0	0	2,709
		Northport	0	0	0	0	22,201
		Ohatchee	0	0			1,230
		Oneonta		0			6,860
		Opelika		0			24,600
		Opp		0	0	0	6,701
		Owens Crossroads	0		0		1,404
		Oxford		0			20,396
		Ozark			0	0	14,656
		Pelham		0	0	0	21,060
		Pell City		0		0	12,256
		Pennington				0	327
		Phil Campbell			0	0	1,046
		Pickensville			0	0	646
		Pine Hill	0	0	0		914
		Pleasant Grove	0	0			10,323
		Priceville		0			2,503
		Rainbow City	0	0	0	0	9,079
		Rainsville	0	0	0		4,923
		Red Bay	0	0	0		3,283
		Roanoke	0	0	0	0	6,674
		Robertsdale	0	0			4,976
		Russellville			0		8,842
		Samson			0	0	2,027
		Scottsboro			0	0	14,971
		Selma		0			19,101
		Sheffield		0			9,176
		Silas	0	0			487
		Spanish Fort			0		5,619
		Summerdale	0	0	0	0	701
		Tallassee	0	0			5,091
		Tarrant	0	0	0	0	6,553
		Thomaston	0	0	0	0	375
		Thomasville	0	0	0		4,558
		Thorsby		0			2,030
		Triana	0	0	0	0	482
		Trussville		0			18,401
		Valley	0	0	0	0	8,871
		Vestavia Hills	0	0			31,097
		Wetumpka		0			7,558
	Universities and Colleges	Alabama A&M University		0			6,076
		Auburn University, Montgomery	0				5,079
		George C. Wallace State Community College	0	0			3,420
		Jacksonville State University		0	0	0	8,957
		University of Alabama, Birmingham	0	0			16,561
		University of Montevallo	0	0			2,895
		University of North Alabama	0	0			6,810
	Metropolitan Counties	Autauga	0	0			
		Bibb		0			
		Colbert	0	0			
		Elmore		0			
		Geneva				0	
		Henry		0			
		Houston	0	0			
		Jefferson	0	0	0	0	

[1] Agencies published in this table indicated that no hate crimes occurred in their jurisdictions during the quarter(s) for which they submitted reports to the Hate Crime program. Blanks indicate quarters for which agencies did not submit reports.
[2] Population figures are published only for the cities. The figures listed for the universities and colleges are student enrollment and were provided by the United States Department of Education for the 2006 school year, the most recent available. The enrollment figures include full-time and part-time students.

Table 95. Hate Crime Zero Data Submitted per Quarter, by State and Agency, 2007 *(Contd.)*

(Number.)

State	Agency type	Agency name	Zero data per quarter[1] 1st quarter	2nd quarter	3rd quarter	4th quarter	Population[2]
		Lawrence		0			
		Mobile			0	0	
		Shelby			0	0	
		Walker	0	0			
	Nonmetropolitan Counties	Butler	0	0			
		Cleburne		0	0	0	
		Coffee	0	0	0	0	
		Escambia	0	0			
		Jackson	0	0			
		Lamar		0			
		Perry			0		
		Pickens	0	0			
		Pike	0	0	0	0	
		Sumter		0			
		Tallapoosa	0	0	0	0	
		Washington	0	0	0		
	Other Agencies	24th Judicial Circuit Drug and Violent Crime Task Force	0	0	0	0	
ARIZONA	Cities	Benson		0	0	0	4,913
		Bisbee	0	0	0	0	6,077
		Camp Verde	0	0	0	0	10,780
		Clarkdale	0				3,904
		Clifton	0	0	0	0	2,285
		Coolidge		0	0	0	7,875
		Cottonwood	0	0	0	0	11,455
		Douglas				0	17,077
		Eagar	0	0	0		4,324
		Eloy	0	0	0	0	10,795
		Fredonia		0	0	0	1,066
		Globe	0	0	0	0	7,097
		Goodyear	0	0	0	0	53,834
		Hayden	0	0	0	0	1,267
		Holbrook	0	0	0	0	5,186
		Huachuca City	0	0	0	0	1,886
		Kearny	0	0	0	0	3,000
		Lake Havasu City		0	0	0	58,699
		Mammoth	0		0	0	2,347
		Miami	0	0	0	0	1,809
		Nogales	0	0	0	0	20,747
		Parker		0	0	0	3,211
		Payson	0				15,496
		Pima	0	0	0	0	1,967
		Prescott	0	0	0	0	42,674
		Safford	0	0	0	0	8,945
		Snowflake-Taylor	0	0	0	0	9,448
		Somerton	0	0	0	0	11,370
		South Tucson	0	0	0	0	5,579
		Springerville	0	0	0	0	2,002
		Surprise	0	0	0	0	98,965
		Thatcher	0	0	0	0	4,285
		Tucson	0				523,299
		Wellton	0	0	0	0	1,898
		Wickenburg	0	0	0	0	6,507
		Willcox	0	0	0	0	3,842
		Winslow				0	10,018
		Youngtown		0	0	0	5,062
	Universities and Colleges	Central Arizona College	0	0	0	0	6,471
		Pima Community College	0	0	0	0	32,532
		Yavapai College	0	0	0	0	9,305

State	Agency type	Agency name	Zero data per quarter[1] 1st quarter	2nd quarter	3rd quarter	4th quarter	Population[2]
	Metropolitan Counties	Coconino	0	0	0	0	
		Mohave	0	0	0	0	
		Pinal	0	0	0	0	
		Yavapai	0	0	0	0	
		Yuma	0	0	0	0	
	Nonmetropolitan Counties	Apache	0	0	0	0	
		Cochise	0	0	0	0	
		Gila	0	0	0	0	
		La Paz	0	0	0	0	
		Santa Cruz	0	0			
	State Police Agencies	Arizona Department of Public Safety	0	0	0	0	
ARKANSAS ...	Cities	Alma			0	0	4,935
		Altheimer	0	0	0	0	1,143
		Arkadelphia	0	0	0	0	10,418
		Arkansas City	0	0	0	0	538
		Ashdown	0	0	0	0	4,497
		Atkins	0	0	0	0	2,929
		Augusta	0	0	0	0	2,355
		Austin	0	0	0	0	1,131
		Bald Knob	0	0	0	0	3,364
		Barling	0	0	0	0	4,397
		Bay	0	0	0	0	1,992
		Bearden	0	0	0	0	1,019
		Beebe	0	0	0	0	6,062
		Bentonville	0	0	0	0	34,232
		Berryville	0	0	0	0	5,195
		Blytheville	0	0	0	0	16,161
		Bono	0	0	0	0	1,557
		Booneville	0	0	0	0	4,137
		Bradford	0	0	0	0	839
		Brinkley	0	0	0	0	3,368
		Bryant	0	0	0	0	14,181
		Bull Shoals	0	0	0	0	2,124
		Cabot	0	0	0	0	23,366
		Caddo Valley	0	0	0	0	622
		Camden	0	0	0	0	11,812
		Cammack Village	0	0	0	0	766
		Caraway	0	0	0	0	1,359
		Carlisle	0	0	0	0	2,451
		Cave City	0	0	0	0	2,074
		Cave Springs	0	0	0	0	1,583
		Centerton	0	0	0	0	7,803
		Charleston	0	0	0	0	3,035
		Clarendon	0	0	0	0	1,766
		Clarksville	0	0	0	0	8,553
		Clinton	0	0	0	0	2,506
		Conway	0	0	0	0	57,245
		Corning	0	0	0	0	3,403
		Cotter	0	0	0	0	1,074
		Danville	0	0	0	0	2,488
		Dardanelle	0	0	0	0	4,431
		Decatur	0	0	0	0	1,670
		De Queen	0	0	0	0	5,890
		Dermott	0	0			3,401
		Des Arc	0	0	0	0	1,765
		Diaz	0	0	0	0	1,180
		Dierks	0	0	0	0	1,244
		Dover	0	0	0	0	1,388
		Dumas	0	0	0	0	4,725
		Earle	0	0	0	0	2,835
		Elkins	0	0	0	0	2,463
		England	0	0	0	0	3,049
		Etowah	0	0	0	0	344

[1]Agencies published in this table indicated that no hate crimes occurred in their jurisdictions during the quarter(s) for which they submitted reports to the Hate Crime program. Blanks indicate quarters for which agencies did not submit reports.

[2]Population figures are published only for the cities. The figures listed for the universities and colleges are student enrollment and were provided by the United States Department of Education for the 2006 school year, the most recent available. The enrollment figures include full-time and part-time students.

Table 95. Hate Crime Zero Data Submitted per Quarter, by State and Agency, 2007 *(Contd.)*

(Number.)

State	Agency type	Agency name	1st quarter	2nd quarter	3rd quarter	4th quarter	Population[2]
		Eudora	0	0	0	0	2,493
		Eureka Springs	0	0	0	0	2,369
		Fairfield Bay	0	0	0	0	2,527
		Farmington	0	0	0	0	4,801
		Fayetteville	0	0	0	0	70,334
		Flippin	0	0	0	0	1,407
		Fordyce	0	0	0	0	4,282
		Forrest City	0	0	0	0	13,699
		Gassville	0	0	0	0	2,083
		Gentry	0	0	0	0	2,688
		Glenwood	0	0	0		2,030
		Gosnell					3,692
		Gould	0		0	0	1,171
		Gravette	0	0	0	0	2,465
		Greenbrier	0	0	0	0	3,855
		Greenland	0	0	0	0	1,195
		Greenwood	0	0	0	0	8,404
		Greers Ferry	0	0	0	0	975
		Gurdon	0	0	0	0	2,231
		Guy	0	0	0		564
		Hamburg	0	0	0	0	2,770
		Hampton	0	0	0	0	1,493
		Hardy	0	0	0	0	819
		Harrisburg	0	0	0	0	2,142
		Harrison	0	0	0	0	13,097
		Hazen	0	0	0	0	1,502
		Heber Springs	0	0	0	0	7,156
		Helena-West Helena	0	0	0	0	12,800
		Highfill		0	0	0	613
		Highland	0	0	0	0	1,089
		Hope	0	0	0	0	10,467
		Horseshoe Bend	0	0	0	0	2,282
		Hoxie	0	0	0	0	2,635
		Judsonia	0	0	0	0	2,145
		Keiser	0	0	0	0	764
		Kensett	0	0	0	0	1,717
		Lake City	0	0	0	0	2,022
		Lakeview	0	0	0	0	832
		Lake Village	0	0	0	0	2,552
		Leachville	0	0	0	0	1,813
		Lepanto	0	0	0	0	2,041
		Lincoln	0	0	0	0	1,988
		Little Flock	0	0	0	0	3,179
		Lonoke	0	0	0	0	4,651
		Lowell	0	0	0	0	7,314
		Luxora	0	0	0	0	1,235
		Magnolia	0	0	0	0	10,250
		Malvern	0	0	0	0	9,044
		Mammoth Spring	0	0	0	0	1,125
		Mansfield	0	0			1,126
		Marianna	0	0	0	0	4,624
		Marked Tree	0	0	0	0	2,666
		Marmaduke	0	0	0	0	1,173
		Marvell	0	0			1,194
		Mayflower			0	0	2,022
		McCrory	0	0	0	0	1,616
		McGehee	0	0	0	0	4,105
		McRae	0	0	0	0	695
		Mena	0	0	0	0	5,632
		Mineral Springs	0	0	0	0	1,298
		Monette	0	0	0	0	1,198
		Monticello	0	0	0	0	9,122
		Mountain Home	0	0	0	0	12,383
		Mountain View	0	0	0	0	3,079
		Mulberry	0	0	0	0	1,730
		Murfreesboro	0	0	0	0	1,666
		Nashville	0	0	0	0	4,862
		Newport	0	0	0	0	7,129
		Ola	0	0	0	0	1,232
		Osceola	0	0	0	0	7,920
		Ozark	0	0	0	0	3,587
		Pangburn	0	0	0	0	671
		Paris	0	0	0	0	3,674
		Pea Ridge	0	0	0	0	4,269
		Piggott	0	0	0	0	3,603
		Pine Bluff	0	0	0	0	51,304
		Plummerville	0	0	0	0	870
		Pocahontas	0	0	0	0	6,893
		Pottsville	0	0	0	0	2,528
		Prairie Grove	0	0	0	0	3,415
		Prescott	0	0	0	0	4,653
		Quitman	0	0	0	0	741
		Redfield	0	0	0	0	1,171
		Rison	0	0	0	0	1,324
		Rogers	0	0	0	0	54,223
		Rose Bud	0	0	0	0	453
		Russellville	0	0	0	0	26,319
		Salem	0	0	0	0	1,558
		Searcy	0	0	0	0	21,304
		Sheridan	0	0	0	0	4,495
		Siloam Springs	0	0	0	0	14,659
		Springdale	0	0	0	0	65,695
		Star City	0	0	0	0	2,253
		Stuttgart	0	0	0	0	9,197
		Sulphur Springs	0	0	0	0	676
		Swifton	0	0	0	0	797
		Texarkana	0	0	0	0	30,156
		Trumann	0	0	0	0	6,821
		Tuckerman	0	0	0	0	1,673
		Van Buren	0	0	0	0	22,238
		Vilonia	0	0	0	0	3,085
		Waldron	0	0	0	0	3,636
		Walnut Ridge	0	0	0	0	4,631
		Ward	0	0	0	0	3,659
		Weiner	0	0	0	0	741
		West Fork	0	0	0	0	2,259
		White Hall	0	0	0	0	5,196
		Wynne	0	0	0	0	8,481
	Universities and Colleges	Arkansas State University: Beebe	0	0	0	0	4,073
		Arkansas State University: Jonesboro	0	0	0	0	10,949
		Arkansas Tech University	0	0	0	0	7,038
		Henderson State University	0	0	0	0	3,664
		Northwest Arkansas Community College	0	0	0	0	5,732
		Southern Arkansas University	0	0	0	0	3,113
		University of Arkansas: Fayetteville	0	0	0	0	17,926
		University of Arkansas: Little Rock	0	0	0	0	11,905
		University of Arkansas: Medical Sciences	0	0	0	0	2,435
		University of Arkansas: Monticello	0	0	0	0	3,179
		University of Arkansas: Pine Bluff	0	0	0	0	3,128
	Metropolitan Counties	Cleveland	0	0	0	0	
		Craighead	0	0	0	0	
		Crittenden	0	0	0	0	
		Faulkner	0	0	0	0	
		Franklin	0	0	0	0	
		Garland	0	0	0	0	
		Grant	0	0	0	0	
		Jefferson	0	0	0	0	
		Lincoln	0	0	0	0	
		Lonoke	0	0	0	0	
		Madison	0	0	0		
		Miller	0	0			

[1] Agencies published in this table indicated that no hate crimes occurred in their jurisdictions during the quarter(s) for which they submitted reports to the Hate Crime program. Blanks indicate quarters for which agencies did not submit reports.

[2] Population figures are published only for the cities. The figures listed for the universities and colleges are student enrollment and were provided by the United States Department of Education for the 2006 school year, the most recent available. The enrollment figures include full-time and part-time students.

Table 95. Hate Crime Zero Data Submitted per Quarter, by State and Agency, 2007 *(Contd.)*

(Number.)

State	Agency type	Agency name	1st quarter	2nd quarter	3rd quarter	4th quarter	Population[2]
		Perry	0	0	0	0	
		Poinsett	0	0	0	0	
		Saline	0	0	0	0	
		Sebastian	0	0	0	0	
		Washington	0	0	0	0	
	Nonmetro-politan Counties	Arkansas	0	0	0	0	
		Ashley	0	0	0	0	
		Baxter	0	0	0	0	
		Boone	0	0	0	0	
		Bradley	0	0	0	0	
		Calhoun	0	0	0	0	
		Carroll	0	0	0	0	
		Chicot	0	0	0	0	
		Clark	0	0	0	0	
		Clay	0	0	0	0	
		Cleburne	0	0	0	0	
		Columbia	0	0	0	0	
		Cross	0	0	0	0	
		Dallas	0	0	0		
		Desha	0	0			
		Drew	0	0	0	0	
		Greene	0	0	0	0	
		Hempstead	0	0	0	0	
		Hot Spring	0	0	0	0	
		Howard	0	0	0	0	
		Independence	0	0	0	0	
		Izard	0	0	0	0	
		Jackson	0	0	0	0	
		Johnson	0	0	0	0	
		Lafayette	0	0	0	0	
		Lawrence	0	0	0	0	
		Lee	0	0	0	0	
		Little River	0	0	0	0	
		Logan	0	0	0	0	
		Marion	0	0	0	0	
		Mississippi	0	0	0	0	
		Monroe	0	0	0	0	
		Nevada	0	0	0	0	
		Ouachita	0	0	0	0	
		Pike	0				
		Polk	0	0	0	0	
		Prairie	0	0	0	0	
		Randolph	0	0	0	0	
		Searcy	0	0	0	0	
		Sevier	0	0	0	0	
		Sharp	0				
		St. Francis	0	0	0	0	
		Stone	0	0	0	0	
		Union	0	0	0	0	
		Van Buren	0	0	0	0	
		White	0	0	0	0	
		Woodruff	0	0	0	0	
		Yell	0	0	0	0	
	Other Agencies	Camp Robinson	0	0	0	0	
		State Capitol Police	0	0	0	0	
CALIFORNIA.	Cities	Adelanto	0	0	0	0	28,719
		Albany	0	0	0	0	15,889
		Alhambra	0	0	0	0	87,729
		Alturas	0	0	0	0	2,924
		American Canyon	0	0	0	0	17,053
		Anderson	0	0	0	0	10,629
		Apple Valley	0	0	0	0	71,211
		Arcadia	0	0	0	0	56,967
		Arcata	0	0	0	0	16,929
		Arroyo Grande	0	0	0	0	16,485
		Artesia	0	0	0	0	16,607
		Arvin	0	0	0	0	15,228
		Atherton	0	0	0	0	7,307
		Auburn	0	0	0	0	13,072
		Avalon	0	0	0	0	3,325

State	Agency type	Agency name	1st quarter	2nd quarter	3rd quarter	4th quarter	Population[2]
		Avenal	0	0	0	0	17,175
		Baldwin Park	0	0	0	0	78,943
		Banning	0	0	0	0	30,163
		Barstow	0	0	0	0	23,957
		Bear Valley	0	0	0	0	4,567
		Beaumont	0	0	0	0	30,093
		Bell	0	0	0	0	37,420
		Bellflower	0	0	0	0	74,544
		Bell Gardens	0	0	0	0	45,451
		Belvedere	0	0	0	0	2,065
		Big Bear Lake	0	0	0	0	6,276
		Biggs	0	0	0	0	1,802
		Blue Lake	0	0	0	0	1,110
		Blythe	0	0	0	0	22,696
		Bradbury	0	0	0	0	1,067
		Brawley	0	0	0	0	22,666
		Brisbane	0	0	0	0	3,575
		Broadmoor	0	0	0	0	4,345
		Buellton	0	0	0	0	4,345
		Burlingame	0	0	0	0	27,489
		California City	0	0	0	0	13,443
		Calimesa	0	0	0	0	7,528
		Calipatria	0	0	0	0	7,743
		Calistoga	0	0	0	0	5,217
		Canyon Lake	0	0	0	0	11,544
		Capitola	0	0	0	0	9,432
		Carlsbad	0	0	0	0	95,056
		Carmel	0	0	0	0	3,905
		Carpinteria	0	0	0	0	13,392
		Cathedral City	0	0	0	0	53,953
		Chino Hills	0	0	0	0	76,484
		Chowchilla	0	0	0	0	18,772
		Cloverdale	0	0	0	0	8,319
		Coachella	0	0	0	0	38,604
		Coalinga	0	0	0	0	17,801
		Colma	0	0	0	0	1,436
		Colton	0	0	0	0	51,924
		Colusa	0	0	0	0	5,901
		Commerce	0	0	0	0	13,672
		Corcoran	0	0	0	0	23,715
		Corning	0	0	0	0	7,348
		Costa Mesa	0	0	0	0	109,835
		Cotati	0	0	0	0	7,272
		Crescent City	0	0	0	0	7,909
		Cudahy	0	0	0	0	24,953
		Culver City	0	0	0	0	39,474
		Cupertino	0	0	0	0	53,002
		Delano	0	0	0	0	52,051
		Del Rey Oaks	0	0	0	0	1,545
		Dinuba	0	0	0	0	19,926
		Dixon	0	0	0	0	17,883
		Dorris	0	0	0	0	851
		Dos Palos	0	0	0	0	5,000
		Dunsmuir	0	0	0	0	1,824
		East Palo Alto	0	0	0	0	33,210
		El Centro	0	0	0	0	40,957
		El Cerrito	0	0	0	0	22,514
		Emeryville	0	0	0	0	9,041
		Escalon	0	0	0	0	7,439
		Etna	0	0	0	0	785
		Exeter	0	0	0	0	10,307
		Fairfax	0	0	0	0	7,091
		Fairfield	0	0	0	0	106,098
		Farmersville	0	0	0	0	10,219
		Ferndale	0	0	0	0	1,398
		Firebaugh	0	0	0	0	7,036
		Fontana	0	0	0	0	176,490
		Fort Jones	0	0	0	0	659
		Fortuna	0	0	0	0	11,312
		Foster City	0	0	0	0	28,958
		Fowler	0	0	0	0	5,236
		Goleta	0	0	0	0	29,243
		Grand Terrace	0	0	0	0	12,334
		Greenfield	0	0	0	0	14,484
		Gridley	0	0	0	0	5,982

[1]Agencies published in this table indicated that no hate crimes occurred in their jurisdictions during the quarter(s) for which they submitted reports to the Hate Crime program. Blanks indicate quarters for which agencies did not submit reports.

[2]Population figures are published only for the cities. The figures listed for the universities and colleges are student enrollment and were provided by the United States Department of Education for the 2006 school year, the most recent available. The enrollment figures include full-time and part-time students.

Table 95. Hate Crime Zero Data Submitted per Quarter, by State and Agency, 2007 *(Contd.)*

(Number.)

State	Agency type	Agency name	1st quarter	2nd quarter	3rd quarter	4th quarter	Population[2]	State	Agency type	Agency name	1st quarter	2nd quarter	3rd quarter	4th quarter	Population[2]
		Grover Beach	0	0	0	0	12,761			Patterson	0	0	0	0	19,620
		Guadalupe	0	0	0	0	6,621			Piedmont	0	0	0	0	10,478
		Gustine	0	0	0	0	5,243			Pismo Beach	0	0	0	0	8,369
		Half Moon Bay	0	0	0	0	12,370			Pittsburg	0	0	0	0	63,913
		Hanford	0	0	0	0	49,694			Placentia	0	0	0	0	50,428
		Hayward	0	0	0	0	140,603			Porterville	0	0	0	0	46,621
		Healdsburg	0	0	0	0	10,955			Port Hueneme	0	0	0	0	21,804
		Hermosa Beach	0	0	0	0	19,676			Rancho Cucamonga	0	0	0	0	177,683
		Hidden Hills	0	0	0	0	2,060			Rancho Palos Verdes	0	0	0	0	41,845
		Highland	0	0	0	0	52,582			Reedley	0	0	0	0	23,098
		Hillsborough	0	0	0	0	10,697			Rio Dell	0	0	0	0	3,174
		Hollister	0	0	0	0	35,812			Rio Vista	0	0	0	0	7,778
		Holtville	0	0	0	0	5,372			Ripon	0	0	0	0	14,683
		Hughson	0	0	0	0	6,791			Riverbank	0	0	0	0	21,096
		Huron	0	0	0	0	7,301			Rolling Hills	0	0	0	0	1,941
		Imperial	0	0	0	0	12,506			Ross	0	0	0	0	2,296
		Imperial Beach	0	0	0	0	26,013			San Anselmo	0	0	0	0	11,995
		Indian Wells	0	0	0	0	5,175			San Carlos	0	0	0	0	26,902
		Indio	0	0	0	0	81,909			Sand City	0	0	0	0	307
		Industry	0	0	0	0	906			San Fernando	0	0	0	0	24,189
		Ione	0	0	0	0	7,721			Sanger	0	0	0	0	24,769
		Irwindale	0	0	0	0	1,474			San Marino	0	0	0	0	13,112
		Isleton	0	0	0	0	800			Santa Ana	0	0	0	0	340,223
		Jackson	0	0	0	0	4,468			Santa Clara	0	0	0	0	109,420
		Kensington	0	0	0	0	5,327			Santa Maria	0	0	0	0	85,782
		Kerman	0	0	0	0	12,795			Santa Paula	0	0	0	0	28,518
		King City	0	0	0	0	11,237			Saratoga	0	0	0	0	30,067
		Kingsburg	0	0	0	0	11,483			Sausalito	0	0	0	0	7,188
		Laguna Beach	0	0	0	0	24,215			Seal Beach	0	0	0	0	24,383
		Laguna Niguel	0	0	0	0	65,044			Selma	0	0	0	0	23,175
		Laguna Woods	0	0	0	0	18,313			Shafter	0	0	0	0	15,215
		La Habra Heights	0	0	0	0	6,004			Sierra Madre	0	0	0	0	11,031
		Lake Forest	0	0	0	0	76,359			Simi Valley	0	0	0	0	122,677
		Lakeport	0	0	0	0	5,291			Solvang	0	0	0	0	5,091
		Lake Shastina	0	0	0	0	2,364			Sonoma	0	0	0	0	9,981
		La Palma	0	0	0	0	15,821			South El Monte	0	0	0	0	21,696
		Lawndale	0	0	0	0	32,052			South Pasadena	0	0	0	0	24,967
		Lincoln	0	0	0	0	47,236			Stallion Springs	0	0	0	0	1,643
		Lindsay	0	0	0	0	10,925			St. Helena	0	0	0	0	5,899
		Livingston	0	0	0	0	13,286			Suisun City	0	0	0	0	27,010
		Loma Linda	0	0	0	0	21,641			Susanville	0	0	0	0	18,192
		Lompoc	0	0	0	0	39,697			Sutter Creek	0	0	0	0	2,851
		Los Altos	0	0	0	0	27,451			Tiburon	0	0	0	0	8,721
		Los Altos Hills	0	0	0	0	8,341			Tracy	0	0	0	0	84,151
		Los Banos	0	0	0	0	36,123			Trinidad	0	0	0	0	314
		Madera	0	0	0	0	56,797			Truckee	0	0	0	0	16,404
		Mammoth Lakes	0	0	0	0	7,449			Tulare	0	0	0	0	53,352
		Martinez	0	0	0	0	35,538			Tulelake	0	0	0	0	982
		Maywood	0	0	0	0	28,796			Twentynine Palms	0	0	0	0	30,832
		Merced	0	0	0	0	78,186			Twin Cities	0	0	0	0	21,050
		Mill Valley	0	0	0	0	13,280			Ukiah	0	0	0	0	15,367
		Mission Viejo	0	0	0	0	95,095			Vallejo	0	0	0	0	116,763
		Monrovia	0	0	0	0	38,148			Vernon	0	0	0	0	91
		Montague	0	0	0	0	1,485			Victorville	0	0	0	0	104,872
		Montebello	0	0	0	0	63,071			Villa Park	0	0	0	0	6,028
		Monte Sereno	0	0	0	0	3,539			Waterford	0	0	0	0	9,120
		Moraga	0	0	0	0	17,034			Weed	0	0	0	0	3,050
		Morgan Hill	0	0	0	0	36,415			Westlake Village	0	0	0	0	8,613
		Morro Bay	0	0	0	0	10,100			Westminster	0	0	0	0	89,700
		Mount Shasta	0	0	0	0	3,584			Westmorland	0	0	0	0	2,242
		Needles	0	0	0	0	5,397			Wheatland	0	0	0	0	3,824
		Nevada City	0	0	0	0	3,014			Williams	0	0	0	0	4,895
		Newark	0	0	0	0	41,781			Willits	0	0	0	0	5,051
		Newman	0	0	0	0	10,436			Willows	0	0	0	0	6,304
		Norco	0	0	0	0	27,469			Windsor	0	0	0	0	25,633
		Ojai	0	0	0	0	7,861			Winters	0	0	0	0	6,817
		Orinda	0	0	0	0	18,449			Woodlake	0	0	0	0	7,435
		Orland	0	0	0	0	7,168			Yountville	0	0	0	0	3,312
		Oroville	0	0	0	0	13,579			Yreka	0	0	0	0	7,536
		Pacific Grove	0	0	0	0	14,772			Yucaipa	0	0	0	0	51,624
		Palos Verdes Estates	0	0	0	0	13,828			Yucca Valley	0	0	0	0	20,865

[1] Agencies published in this table indicated that no hate crimes occurred in their jurisdictions during the quarter(s) for which they submitted reports to the Hate Crime program. Blanks indicate quarters for which agencies did not submit reports.

[2] Population figures are published only for the cities. The figures listed for the universities and colleges are student enrollment and were provided by the United States Department of Education for the 2006 school year, the most recent available. The enrollment figures include full-time and part-time students.

Table 95. Hate Crime Zero Data Submitted per Quarter, by State and Agency, 2007 (Contd.)

(Number.)

State	Agency type	Agency name	Zero data per quarter[1]				Population[2]
			1st quarter	2nd quarter	3rd quarter	4th quarter	
	Universities and Colleges	Allan Hancock College	0	0	0	0	12,321
		California State Polytechnic University:					
		Pomona	0	0	0	0	20,510
		San Luis Obispo	0	0	0	0	18,722
		California State University:					
		Channel Islands	0	0	0	0	3,123
		Chico	0	0	0	0	16,250
		East Bay	0	0	0	0	12,706
		Long Beach	0	0	0	0	35,574
		Los Angeles	0	0	0	0	20,565
		San Jose[3]	0	0	0	0	
		San Marcos	0	0	0	0	8,734
		Stanislaus	0	0	0	0	8,374
		College of the Sequoias	0	0	0	0	9,959
		Contra Costa Community College	0	0	0	0	6,870
		Cuesta College	0	0	0	0	10,578
		El Camino College	0	0	0	0	23,488
		Foothill-De Anza College	0	0	0	0	39,874
		Marin Community College	0	0	0	0	6,512
		Pasadena Community College	0	0	0	0	25,873
		Reedley Community College	0	0	0	0	11,782
		Riverside Community College	0	0	0	0	29,486
		San Bernardino Community College	0	0	0	0	12,090
		San Diego State University	0	0	0	0	33,441
		San Jose-Evergreen Community College	0	0	0	0	18,164
		Sonoma State University	0	0	0	0	8,274
		University of California:					
		Hastings College of Law	0	0	0	0	1,272
		Irvine	0	0	0	0	25,230
		Medical Center, Sacramento[3]	0	0	0	0	
		Merced	0	0	0	0	1,286
		San Diego	0	0	0	0	26,247
		San Francisco	0	0	0	0	2,943
		Santa Barbara	0	0	0	0	21,082
		Ventura County Community College District	0	0	0	0	11,757
		West Valley-Mission College	0	0	0	0	18,740
	Metropolitan Counties	Alameda	0	0	0	0	
		Butte	0	0	0	0	
		El Dorado	0	0	0	0	
		Fresno	0	0	0	0	
		Kings	0	0	0	0	
		Madera	0	0	0	0	
		Monterey	0	0	0	0	
		Napa	0	0	0	0	
		Placer	0	0	0	0	
		San Benito	0	0	0	0	
		San Bernardino	0	0	0	0	
		San Joaquin	0	0	0	0	
		San Mateo	0	0	0	0	
		Santa Barbara	0	0	0	0	
		Solano	0	0	0	0	
		Sutter	0	0	0	0	
		Tulare	0	0	0	0	
		Yolo	0	0	0	0	
	Nonmetropolitan Counties	Alpine	0	0	0	0	
		Del Norte	0	0	0	0	
		Humboldt	0	0	0	0	
		Mariposa	0	0	0	0	
		Modoc	0	0	0	0	
		Mono	0	0	0	0	
		Nevada	0	0	0	0	
		Plumas	0	0	0	0	
		Sierra	0	0	0	0	
		Siskiyou	0	0	0	0	
		Tehama	0	0	0	0	
		Trinity	0	0	0	0	
	State Police Agencies	Highway Patrol:					
		Alameda County	0	0	0	0	
		Alpine County	0	0	0	0	
		Amador County	0	0	0	0	
		Butte County	0	0	0	0	
		Calaveras County	0	0	0	0	
		Colusa County	0	0	0	0	
		Contra Costa County	0	0	0	0	
		Del Norte County		0	0	0	
		El Dorado County	0	0	0	0	
		Fresno County	0	0	0	0	
		Glenn County	0	0	0	0	
		Humboldt County	0	0	0	0	
		Imperial County	0	0	0	0	
		Inyo County	0	0	0	0	
		Kern County	0	0	0	0	
		Kings County	0	0	0	0	
		Lake County	0	0	0	0	
		Lassen County	0	0	0	0	
		Los Angeles County		0	0	0	
		Madera County	0	0	0	0	
		Marin County	0	0	0	0	
		Mariposa County	0	0	0	0	
		Mendocino County	0	0	0	0	
		Merced County	0	0	0	0	
		Modoc County	0	0	0	0	
		Mono County	0	0	0		
		Monterey County	0	0	0	0	
		Napa County	0	0	0	0	
		Nevada County	0	0	0	0	
		Orange County	0	0	0	0	
		Placer County	0	0	0	0	
		Plumas County	0	0	0	0	
		Riverside County	0	0	0	0	

[1]Agencies published in this table indicated that no hate crimes occurred in their jurisdictions during the quarter(s) for which they submitted reports to the Hate Crime program. Blanks indicate quarters for which agencies did not submit reports.

[2]Population figures are published only for the cities. The figures listed for the universities and colleges are student enrollment and were provided by the United States Department of Education for the 2006 school year, the most recent available. The enrollment figures include full-time and part-time students.

[3]Student enrollment figures were not available.

Table 95. Hate Crime Zero Data Submitted per Quarter, by State and Agency, 2007 *(Contd.)*

(Number.)

State	Agency type	Agency name	Zero data per quarter[1]				Popu-lation[2]
			1st quarter	2nd quarter	3rd quarter	4th quarter	
		Sacramento County	0	0	0	0	
		San Benito County	0	0	0	0	
		San Diego County	0	0	0	0	
		San Francisco County	0	0	0	0	
		San Joaquin County	0	0	0	0	
		San Luis Obispo County	0	0	0	0	
		San Mateo County	0	0	0	0	
		Santa Barbara County	0	0	0	0	
		Santa Clara County	0	0	0	0	
		Santa Cruz County	0	0	0	0	
		Shasta County	0	0	0	0	
		Sierra County	0	0	0	0	
		Siskiyou County	0	0	0	0	
		Solano County	0	0	0	0	
		Sonoma County	0	0	0	0	
		Stanislaus County	0	0	0	0	
		Sutter County	0	0	0	0	
		Tehama County	0	0	0	0	
		Trinity County	0	0	0	0	
		Tulare County	0	0	0	0	
		Tuolumne County	0	0	0	0	
		Ventura County	0	0	0	0	
		Yolo County	0	0	0	0	
		Yuba County	0	0	0	0	
	Other Agencies	Agnews Developmental Center	0	0	0	0	
		Atascadero State Hospital	0	0	0	0	
		California State Fair	0	0	0	0	
		Department of Parks and Recreation:					
		Angeles	0	0	0	0	
		Bay Area	0	0	0	0	
		Calaveras County	0	0	0	0	
		Capital	0	0	0	0	
		Channel Coast	0	0	0	0	
		Colorado	0	0	0	0	
		Four Rivers District	0	0	0	0	
		Hollister Hills	0	0	0	0	
		Hungry Valley	0	0	0	0	
		Inland Empire	0	0	0	0	
		Marin County	0	0	0	0	
		Mendocino Headquarters	0	0	0	0	
		Monterey County	0	0	0	0	
		North Coast Redwoods	0	0	0	0	
		Northern Buttes	0	0	0	0	
		Oceano Dunes	0	0	0	0	
		Ocotillo Wells	0	0	0	0	
		Orange Coast	0	0	0	0	
		Russian River	0	0	0	0	
		San Diego Coast	0	0	0	0	
		San Joaquin	0	0	0	0	
		San Luis Obispo Coast	0	0	0	0	
		Santa Cruz Mountains	0	0	0	0	
		Sierra	0	0	0	0	
		Silverado	0	0	0	0	
		Twin Cities	0	0	0	0	
		East Bay Municipal Utility	0	0	0	0	
		East Bay Regional Parks, Alameda County	0	0	0	0	
		Fairview Developmental Center	0	0	0	0	
		Fontana Unified School District	0	0	0	0	
		Grant Joint Union High School	0	0	0	0	
		Lanterman State Hospital	0	0	0	0	
		Los Angeles County Metropolitan Transportation Authority	0	0	0	0	
		Monterey Peninsula Airport	0	0	0	0	
		Napa State Hospital	0	0	0	0	
		Porterville Developmental Center	0	0	0	0	
		Port of San Diego Harbor	0	0	0	0	
		San Bernardino Unified School District	0	0	0	0	
		San Francisco Bay Area Rapid Transit:					
		Alameda County	0	0	0	0	
		Contra Costa County	0	0	0	0	
		San Francisco County	0	0	0	0	
		San Mateo County	0	0	0	0	
		Santa Clara Transit District	0	0	0	0	
		Sonoma Developmental Center	0	0	0	0	
		Stockton Unified School District	0	0	0	0	
		Union Pacific Railroad:					
		Alameda County	0	0	0	0	
		Amador County	0	0	0	0	
		Butte County	0	0	0	0	
		Calaveras County	0	0	0	0	
		Colusa County	0	0	0	0	
		Contra Costa County	0	0	0	0	
		El Dorado County	0	0	0	0	
		Fresno County	0	0	0	0	

[1] Agencies published in this table indicated that no hate crimes occurred in their jurisdictions during the quarter(s) for which they submitted reports to the Hate Crime program. Blanks indicate quarters for which agencies did not submit reports.

[2] Population figures are published only for the cities. The figures listed for the universities and colleges are student enrollment and were provided by the United States Department of Education for the 2006 school year, the most recent available. The enrollment figures include full-time and part-time students.

Table 95. Hate Crime Zero Data Submitted per Quarter, by State and Agency, 2007 (Contd.)

(Number.)

State	Agency type	Agency name	1st quarter	2nd quarter	3rd quarter	4th quarter	Population[2]
		Glenn County	0	0	0	0	
		Humboldt County	0	0	0	0	
		Imperial County	0	0	0	0	
		Inyo County	0	0	0	0	
		Kern County	0	0	0	0	
		Kings County	0	0	0	0	
		Lassen County	0	0	0	0	
		Los Angeles County	0	0	0	0	
		Madera County	0	0	0	0	
		Marin County	0	0	0	0	
		Mendocino County	0	0	0	0	
		Merced County	0	0	0	0	
		Modoc County	0	0	0	0	
		Monterey County	0	0	0	0	
		Napa County	0	0	0	0	
		Nevada County	0	0	0	0	
		Orange County	0	0	0	0	
		Placer County	0	0	0	0	
		Plumas County	0	0	0	0	
		Riverside County	0	0	0	0	
		Sacramento County	0	0	0	0	
		San Benito County	0	0	0	0	
		San Bernardino County	0	0	0	0	
		San Francisco County	0	0	0	0	
		San Joaquin County	0	0	0	0	
		San Luis Obispo County	0	0	0	0	
		San Mateo County	0	0	0	0	
		Santa Barbara County	0	0	0	0	
		Santa Clara County	0	0	0	0	
		Santa Cruz County	0	0	0	0	
		Shasta County	0	0	0	0	
		Sierra County	0	0	0	0	
		Siskiyou County	0	0	0	0	
		Solano County	0	0	0	0	
		Sonoma County	0	0	0	0	
		Stanislaus County	0	0	0	0	
		Sutter County	0	0	0	0	
		Tehama County	0	0	0	0	
		Trinity County	0	0	0	0	
		Tulare County	0	0	0	0	
		Ventura County	0	0	0	0	
		Yolo County	0	0	0	0	
		Yuba County	0	0	0	0	
COLORADO..	Cities	Alamosa	0	0	0	0	8,714
		Aspen	0	0	0	0	5,700
		Ault	0	0	0	0	1,419
		Avon	0	0	0	0	6,517
		Basalt	0	0	0	0	3,093
		Bayfield	0	0	0	0	1,823
		Black Hawk	0	0	0	0	106
		Bow Mar	0	0	0	0	807
		Breckenridge	0	0	0	0	2,822
		Brighton	0	0	0	0	31,215
		Broomfield	0	0	0	0	46,393
		Brush	0	0	0	0	5,216
		Buena Vista	0	0	0	0	2,149
		Burlington	0	0	0	0	3,454
		Campo	0	0	0	0	131

State	Agency type	Agency name	1st quarter	2nd quarter	3rd quarter	4th quarter	Population[2]
		Canon City	0	0	0	0	16,198
		Carbondale	0	0	0	0	6,128
		Cedaredge	0	0	0	0	2,270
		Center	0	0	0	0	2,452
		Central City	0	0	0	0	514
		Cherry Hills Village	0	0	0	0	6,218
		Columbine Valley	0	0	0	0	1,274
		Crested Butte	0	0	0	0	1,557
		Cripple Creek	0	0	0	0	1,062
		Dacono	0	0	0	0	3,865
		De Beque	0	0	0	0	485
		Delta	0	0	0	0	8,473
		Dillon	0	0	0	0	777
		Durango	0	0	0	0	15,785
		Eagle	0	0	0	0	5,275
		Eaton	0	0	0	0	4,281
		Edgewater	0	0	0	0	5,117
		Elizabeth	0	0	0	0	1,509
		Erie	0	0	0	0	15,759
		Estes Park	0	0	0	0	6,078
		Federal Heights	0	0	0	0	11,697
		Firestone	0	0	0	0	8,463
		Florence	0	0	0	0	3,692
		Fort Morgan	0	0	0	0	10,774
		Fountain	0	0	0	0	20,012
		Fraser-Winter Park	0	0	0	0	1,621
		Frederick	0	0	0	0	8,541
		Frisco	0	0	0	0	2,509
		Fruita	0	0	0	0	7,115
		Golden	0	0	0	0	17,244
		Green Mountain Falls	0	0	0	0	794
		Greenwood Village	0	0	0	0	13,744
		Haxtun	0	0	0	0	1,000
		Hayden	0	0	0	0	1,521
		Holyoke	0	0	0	0	2,297
		Hotchkiss	0	0	0	0	1,099
		Idaho Springs	0	0	0	0	1,779
		Ignacio	0	0	0	0	624
		Kiowa	0	0	0	0	609
		La Junta	0	0	0	0	7,198
		Lakeside	0	0	0	0	19
		Lamar	0	0	0	0	8,287
		La Salle	0	0	0	0	1,927
		Las Animas	0	0	0	0	2,503
		La Veta	0	0	0	0	883
		Leadville	0	0	0	0	2,690
		Limon	0	0	0	0	1,785
		Log Lane Village	0	0	0	0	1,009
		Mancos	0	0	0	0	1,242
		Manitou Springs	0	0	0	0	5,085
		Meeker	0	0	0	0	2,309
		Milliken	0	0	0	0	6,380
		Minturn	0	0	0	0	1,141
		Monte Vista	0	0	0	0	4,102
		Montrose	0	0	0	0	17,024
		Monument	0	0	0	0	2,633
		Morrison	0	0	0	0	405
		Mountain View	0	0	0	0	517
		Mount Crested Butte	0	0	0	0	772
		Nederland	0	0	0	0	1,323
		Northglenn	0	0	0	0	33,226
		Olathe	0	0	0	0	1,739
		Pagosa Springs	0	0	0	0	1,699
		Palisade	0	0	0	0	2,756
		Parachute	0	0	0	0	1,217
		Parker	0	0	0	0	44,624
		Platteville	0	0	0	0	2,646

[1]Agencies published in this table indicated that no hate crimes occurred in their jurisdictions during the quarter(s) for which they submitted reports to the Hate Crime program. Blanks indicate quarters for which agencies did not submit reports.

[2]Population figures are published only for the cities. The figures listed for the universities and colleges are student enrollment and were provided by the United States Department of Education for the 2006 school year, the most recent available. The enrollment figures include full-time and part-time students.

Table 95. Hate Crime Zero Data Submitted per Quarter, by State and Agency, 2007 (Contd.)

(Number.)

State	Agency type	Agency name	1st quarter	2nd quarter	3rd quarter	4th quarter	Population[2]
		Pueblo	0	0	0	0	103,958
		Rangely	0	0	0	0	2,089
		Rocky Ford	0	0	0	0	4,096
		Salida	0	0	0	0	5,394
		Sheridan	0	0	0	0	5,443
		Silt	0	0	0	0	2,516
		Silverthorne	0	0	0	0	3,812
		Snowmass Village	0	0	0	0	1,732
		South Fork	0	0	0	0	552
		Springfield	0	0	0	0	1,323
		Vail	0	0	0	0	4,622
		Victor	0	0	0	0	419
		Walsh	0	0	0	0	661
		Westminster	0	0	0	0	106,383
		Wiggins	0	0	0	0	960
		Windsor	0	0	0	0	17,031
		Woodland Park	0	0	0	0	6,747
		Wray	0	0	0	0	2,156
		Yuma	0	0	0	0	3,245
	Universities and Colleges	Adams State College	0	0	0	0	8,442
		Arapahoe Community College	0	0	0	0	6,918
		Colorado School of Mines	0	0	0	0	4,357
		Colorado State University, Pueblo	0	0	0	0	6,205
		Fort Lewis College	0	0	0	0	3,905
		Pikes Peak Community College	0	0	0	0	10,526
		Red Rocks Community College	0	0	0	0	6,727
		University of Colorado: Boulder	0	0	0	0	31,665
		Colorado Springs	0	0	0	0	8,647
		Health Sciences Center[3]	0	0	0	0	
		Health Sciences Center, Fitzsimons Campus[3]	0	0	0	0	
		University of Northern Colorado	0	0	0	0	13,363
	Metropolitan Counties	Boulder	0	0	0	0	
		Clear Creek	0	0	0	0	
		Elbert	0	0	0	0	
		El Paso	0	0	0	0	
		Larimer	0	0	0	0	
		Park	0	0	0	0	
		Pueblo	0	0	0	0	
		Teller	0	0	0	0	
	Nonmetropolitan Counties	Alamosa	0	0	0	0	
		Archuleta	0	0	0	0	
		Baca	0	0	0	0	
		Bent	0	0	0	0	
		Chaffee	0	0	0	0	
		Cheyenne	0	0	0	0	
		Costilla	0	0	0	0	
		Crowley	0	0	0	0	
		Custer	0	0	0	0	
		Delta	0	0	0	0	
		Dolores	0	0	0	0	

State	Agency type	Agency name	1st quarter	2nd quarter	3rd quarter	4th quarter	Population[2]
		Eagle	0	0	0	0	
		Fremont	0	0	0	0	
		Grand	0	0	0	0	
		Gunnison	0	0	0	0	
		Hinsdale	0	0	0	0	
		Huerfano	0	0	0	0	
		Jackson	0	0	0	0	
		Kiowa	0	0	0	0	
		Lake	0	0	0	0	
		La Plata	0	0	0	0	
		Las Animas	0	0	0	0	
		Logan	0	0	0	0	
		Mineral	0	0	0	0	
		Moffat	0	0	0	0	
		Montezuma	0	0	0	0	
		Montrose	0	0	0	0	
		Morgan	0	0	0	0	
		Otero	0	0	0		
		Ouray	0	0	0	0	
		Phillips	0	0	0	0	
		Pitkin	0	0	0	0	
		Prowers	0	0	0	0	
		Rio Blanco	0	0	0	0	
		Rio Grande	0	0	0	0	
		Saguache	0	0	0	0	
		San Juan	0	0	0	0	
		San Miguel	0	0	0	0	
		Sedgwick	0	0	0	0	
		Summit	0	0	0	0	
		Washington	0	0	0	0	
		Yuma	0	0	0	0	
	State Police Agencies	Colorado State Patrol	0	0	0	0	
	Other Agencies	Two Rivers Drug Enforcement Team	0	0	0	0	
CONNECTICUT	Cities	Ansonia	0	0	0	0	18,620
		Avon	0	0	0	0	17,526
		Berlin	0	0	0	0	20,380
		Bethel	0	0	0	0	18,670
		Brookfield	0	0	0	0	16,498
		Canton	0	0	0	0	10,252
		Cheshire	0	0	0	0	28,868
		Coventry	0	0	0	0	12,292
		Cromwell	0	0	0	0	13,612
		Danbury	0	0	0	0	79,893
		Darien	0	0	0	0	20,501
		East Hampton	0	0	0	0	12,666
		East Haven	0	0	0	0	28,755
		Easton	0	0	0	0	7,455
		East Windsor	0	0	0	0	10,650
		Fairfield	0	0	0	0	57,889
		Granby	0	0	0	0	11,285
		Groton Long Point	0	0	0	0	669
		Meriden	0	0	0	0	59,607
		Middlebury	0	0	0	0	7,232
		New Canaan	0	0	0	0	20,009
		Newington	0	0	0	0	29,567
		New London	0	0	0	0	25,890
		Newtown	0	0	0	0	27,262
		North Branford	0	0	0	0	14,527
		North Haven	0	0	0	0	24,168
		Old Saybrook	0	0	0	0	10,597
		Plainville	0	0	0	0	17,294
		Portland	0	0	0	0	9,707
		Putnam	0	0	0	0	9,352
		Redding	0	0	0	0	8,990
		Ridgefield	0	0	0	0	24,040
		Rocky Hill	0	0	0	0	18,923

[1]Agencies published in this table indicated that no hate crimes occurred in their jurisdictions during the quarter(s) for which they submitted reports to the Hate Crime program. Blanks indicate quarters for which agencies did not submit reports.
[2]Population figures are published only for the cities. The figures listed for the universities and colleges are student enrollment and were provided by the United States Department of Education for the 2006 school year, the most recent available. The enrollment figures include full-time and part-time students.
[3]Student enrollment figures were not available.

Table 95. Hate Crime Zero Data Submitted per Quarter, by State and Agency, 2007 (Contd.)

(Number.)

State	Agency type	Agency name	1st quarter	2nd quarter	3rd quarter	4th quarter	Population[2]
		Simsbury	0	0	0	0	23,674
		Stonington	0	0	0	0	18,261
		Thomaston	0	0			7,972
		Waterbury	0	0	0	0	107,241
		Watertown	0	0	0	0	22,419
		West Haven	0	0	0	0	52,770
		Wethersfield	0	0	0	0	25,977
		Willimantic	0	0	0	0	16,272
		Windsor	0	0	0	0	28,712
		Wolcott	0	0	0	0	16,419
		Woodbridge	0	0	0	0	9,261
	Universities and Colleges	Central Connecticut State University	0	0	0	0	12,144
		Southern Connecticut State University	0	0	0	0	12,326
		Yale University	0	0	0	0	11,415
	Other Agencies	State Capitol Police	0	0	0	0	
DELAWARE	Cities	Bethany Beach	0	0	0	0	947
		Blades	0	0	0	0	1,006
		Bridgeville	0	0	0	0	1,597
		Camden	0	0	0	0	2,484
		Cheswold	0	0	0	0	460
		Clayton	0	0	0	0	1,438
		Dagsboro	0	0	0	0	566
		Delaware City	0	0	0	0	1,520
		Delmar	0	0	0	0	1,498
		Dover	0	0	0	0	35,133
		Ellendale	0	0	0	0	348
		Felton	0	0	0	0	857
		Fenwick Island	0	0	0	0	359
		Greenwood	0	0	0	0	891
		Lewes	0	0	0	0	3,137
		Millsboro	0	0	0	0	2,532
		Milton	0	0	0	0	1,803
		New Castle	0	0	0	0	4,960
		Newport	0	0	0	0	1,106
		Ocean View	0	0	0	0	1,109
		Rehoboth Beach	0	0	0	0	1,562
		Seaford	0	0	0	0	7,121
		Selbyville	0	0	0	0	1,761
		Smyrna	0	0	0	0	8,185
		South Bethany	0	0	0	0	516
		Wyoming	0	0	0	0	1,311
	Universities and Colleges	Delaware State University	0	0	0	0	3,690
	Other Agencies	Amtrak Police	0	0	0	0	
		Attorney General: Kent County	0	0	0	0	
		New Castle County	0	0	0	0	
		Sussex County	0	0	0	0	
		Division of Alcohol and Tobacco Enforcement	0	0	0	0	
		Drug Enforcement Administration, Wilmington Resident Office	0	0	0	0	
		Environmental Control Fish and Wildlife	0	0	0	0	
		River and Bay Authority	0	0	0	0	
		State Capitol Police	0	0	0	0	
		State Fire Marshal	0	0	0	0	
		Wilmington Fire Department	0	0	0	0	
FLORIDA	Cities	Alachua	0	0	0	0	8,833
		Altha	0	0	0	0	516
		Apalachicola	0	0	0	0	2,331
		Apopka	0	0	0	0	36,895
		Arcadia	0	0	0	0	7,151
		Astatula	0	0	0	0	1,747
		Atlantic Beach	0	0	0	0	13,256
		Atlantis	0	0	0	0	2,131
		Auburndale	0	0	0	0	13,236
		Avon Park	0	0	0	0	9,135
		Bal Harbour Village	0	0	0	0	3,211
		Bartow	0	0	0	0	16,594
		Bay Harbor Island	0	0	0	0	4,996
		Belleair	0	0	0	0	4,149
		Belleair Beach	0	0	0	0	1,611
		Belleair Bluffs	0	0	0	0	2,197
		Belle Glade	0	0	0	0	15,231
		Belleview	0	0	0	0	4,074
		Biscayne Park	0	0	0	0	3,049
		Blountstown	0	0	0	0	2,443
		Bonifay	0	0	0	0	2,712
		Bowling Green	0	0	0	0	2,972
		Boynton Beach	0	0	0	0	69,469
		Bradenton	0	0	0	0	54,253
		Bradenton Beach	0	0	0	0	1,557
		Brooksville	0	0	0	0	7,651
		Bunnell	0	0	0	0	1,639
		Bushnell	0	0	0	0	2,200
		Carrabelle	0	0	0	0	1,290
		Cedar Grove	0	0	0	0	5,201
		Cedar Key	0	0	0	0	1,008
		Center Hill	0	0	0	0	1,009
		Chattahoochee	0	0	0	0	3,807
		Chiefland	0	0	0	0	2,133
		Chipley	0	0	0	0	3,768
		Clearwater	0	0	0	0	107,501
		Clermont	0	0	0	0	12,385
		Clewiston	0	0	0	0	7,402
		Cocoa Beach	0	0	0	0	12,128
		Coleman	0	0	0	0	714
		Cooper City	0	0	0	0	30,182
		Cottondale	0	0	0	0	883
		Crescent City	0	0	0	0	1,827
		Crestview	0	0	0	0	18,753
		Cross City	0	0	0	0	1,838
		Dade City	0	0	0	0	7,079
		Davenport	0	0	0	0	2,056
		Davie	0	0	0	0	87,007
		Daytona Beach	0	0	0	0	64,236
		Daytona Beach Shores	0	0	0	0	5,063
		Deerfield Beach	0	0	0	0	76,469
		De Funiak Springs	0	0	0	0	4,987
		Deland	0	0	0	0	26,610
		Doral	0	0	0	0	21,356
		Dundee	0	0	0	0	3,148
		Dunedin	0	0	0	0	36,702
		Dunnellon	0	0	0	0	2,016
		Eagle Lake	0	0	0	0	2,650
		Eatonville	0	0	0	0	2,265
		Edgewater	0	0	0	0	21,898
		Edgewood	0	0	0	0	2,084
		El Portal	0	0	0	0	2,384

[1]Agencies published in this table indicated that no hate crimes occurred in their jurisdictions during the quarter(s) for which they submitted reports to the Hate Crime program. Blanks indicate quarters for which agencies did not submit reports.

[2]Population figures are published only for the cities. The figures listed for the universities and colleges are student enrollment and were provided by the United States Department of Education for the 2006 school year, the most recent available. The enrollment figures include full-time and part-time students.

Table 95. Hate Crime Zero Data Submitted per Quarter, by State and Agency, 2007 *(Contd.)*

(Number.)

State	Agency type	Agency name	1st quarter	2nd quarter	3rd quarter	4th quarter	Population[2]	State	Agency type	Agency name	1st quarter	2nd quarter	3rd quarter	4th quarter	Population[2]
		Eustis	0	0	0	0	18,685			Lauderdale-by-the-Sea	0	0	0	0	6,010
		Fellsmere	0	0	0	0	4,850			Lauderdale Lakes	0	0	0	0	32,003
		Fernandina Beach	0	0	0	0	11,423			Lauderhill	0	0	0	0	59,743
		Flagler Beach	0	0	0	0	2,874			Lawtey	0	0	0	0	692
		Florida City	0	0	0	0	9,704			Lighthouse Point	0	0	0	0	11,364
		Fort Meade	0	0	0	0	5,741			Live Oak	0	0	0	0	7,100
		Fort Myers	0	0	0	0	61,810			Longboat Key	0	0	0	0	7,387
		Fort Pierce	0	0	0	0	39,456			Lynn Haven	0	0	0	0	16,110
		Fort Walton Beach	0	0	0	0	19,245			Madeira Beach	0	0	0	0	4,408
		Frostproof	0	0	0	0	2,915			Madison	0	0	0	0	3,210
		Fruitland Park	0	0	0	0	3,983			Maitland	0	0	0	0	14,130
		Golden Beach	0	0	0	0	893			Manalapan	0	0	0	0	342
		Graceville	0	0	0	0	2,432			Mangonia Park	0	0	0	0	1,259
		Greenacres City	0	0	0	0	33,042			Marco Island	0	0	0	0	16,235
		Green Cove Springs	0	0	0	0	6,541			Margate	0	0	0	0	56,261
		Greensboro	0	0	0	0	610			Marianna	0	0	0	0	6,293
		Gretna	0	0	0	0	1,635			Mascotte	0	0	0	0	5,485
		Groveland	0	0	0	0	6,519			Medley	0	0	0	0	1,043
		Gulf Breeze	0	0	0	0	6,563			Melbourne Beach	0		0	0	3,208
		Gulfport	0	0	0	0	12,508			Melbourne Village	0	0	0	0	680
		Gulf Stream	0	0	0	0	751			Mexico Beach	0	0	0	0	1,339
		Haines City	0	0	0	0	18,172			Miami	0	0	0	0	410,252
		Hampton	0	0	0	0	453			Miami Gardens	0	0	0	0	98,762
		Havana	0	0	0	0	1,703			Miami Shores	0	0	0	0	9,814
		Hialeah	0	0	0	0	215,853			Miami Springs	0	0	0	0	12,860
		Hialeah Gardens	0	0	0	0	19,705			Milton	0	0	0	0	8,257
		Highland Beach	0	0	0	0	4,106			Minneola	0	0	0	0	9,646
		High Springs	0	0	0	0	4,260			Monticello	0	0	0	0	2,565
		Hillsboro Beach	0	0	0	0	2,357			Mount Dora	0	0	0	0	11,897
		Holly Hill	0	0	0	0	13,510			Mulberry	0	0	0	0	3,192
		Hollywood	0	0	0	0	146,673			Naples	0	0	0	0	22,109
		Holmes Beach	0	0	0	0	5,086			Neptune Beach	0	0	0	0	6,833
		Howey-in-the-Hills	0	0	0	0	1,274			New Port Richey	0	0	0	0	17,393
		Indialantic	0	0	0	0	2,997			Niceville	0	0	0	0	12,354
		Indian Creek Village	0	0	0	0	39			North Bay Village	0	0	0	0	8,279
		Indian Harbour Beach	0	0	0	0	8,516			North Lauderdale	0	0	0	0	42,767
		Indian River Shores	0	0	0	0	3,488			North Miami Beach	0	0	0	0	38,790
		Indian Rocks Beach	0	0	0	0	5,227			North Palm Beach	0	0	0	0	12,509
		Indian Shores	0	0	0	0	4,292			North Redington Beach	0	0	0	0	1,506
		Inglis	0	0	0	0	1,658			Oak Hill	0	0	0	0	1,596
		Interlachen	0	0	0	0	1,533			Oakland	0	0	0	0	1,128
		Jacksonville Beach	0	0	0	0	21,801			Ocala	0	0	0	0	53,490
		Jasper	0	0	0	0	1,836			Ocean Ridge	0	0	0	0	1,678
		Jennings	0	0	0	0	841			Okeechobee	0	0	0	0	6,010
		Juno Beach	0	0	0	0	3,395			Oldsmar	0	0	0	0	13,656
		Jupiter Inlet Colony	0	0	0	0	392			Opa Locka	0	0	0	0	15,695
		Jupiter Island	0	0	0	0	653			Orange City	0	0	0	0	9,485
		Kenneth City	0	0	0	0	4,356			Orange Park	0	0	0	0	9,108
		Key Biscayne	0	0	0	0	9,968			Orlando	0	0	0	0	224,417
		Key Colony Beach	0	0	0	0	787			Ormond Beach	0	0	0	0	38,792
		Key West	0	0	0	0	22,968			Pahokee	0	0	0	0	6,656
		Kissimmee	0	0	0	0	62,880			Palatka	0	0	0	0	11,130
		Lady Lake	0	0	0	0	13,838			Palm Beach	0	0	0	0	9,738
		Lake Alfred	0	0	0	0	4,280			Palm Beach Gardens	0	0	0	0	51,053
		Lake City	0	0	0	0	12,257			Palm Beach Shores	0	0	0	0	1,523
		Lake Hamilton	0	0	0	0	1,440			Palmetto	0	0	0	0	14,188
		Lake Helen	0	0	0	0	2,795			Palmetto Bay	0	0	0	0	23,287
		Lake Mary	0	0	0	0	15,234			Palm Springs	0	0	0	0	15,720
		Lake Park	0	0	0	0	8,919			Panama City Beach	0	0	0	0	14,755
		Lake Placid	0	0	0	0	1,867			Parker	0	0	0	0	4,613
		Lake Wales	0	0	0	0	14,227								
		Lake Worth	0	0	0	0	36,029								
		Lantana	0	0	0	0	10,475								

[1] Agencies published in this table indicated that no hate crimes occurred in their jurisdictions during the quarter(s) for which they submitted reports to the Hate Crime program. Blanks indicate quarters for which agencies did not submit reports.

[2] Population figures are published only for the cities. The figures listed for the universities and colleges are student enrollment and were provided by the United States Department of Education for the 2006 school year, the most recent available. The enrollment figures include full-time and part-time students.

Table 95. Hate Crime Zero Data Submitted per Quarter, by State and Agency, 2007 *(Contd.)*

(Number.)

State	Agency type	Agency name	1st quarter	2nd quarter	3rd quarter	4th quarter	Population[2]
		Parkland	0	0	0	0	25,062
		Pembroke Park	0	0	0	0	4,991
		Pembroke Pines	0	0	0	0	151,817
		Perry	0	0	0	0	6,801
		Pinellas Park	0	0	0	0	47,419
		Plantation	0	0	0	0	86,346
		Plant City	0	0	0	0	31,985
		Pompano Beach	0	0	0	0	104,989
		Ponce Inlet	0	0	0	0	3,294
		Port Richey	0	0	0	0	3,421
		Port St. Joe	0	0	0	0	3,627
		Punta Gorda	0	0	0	0	17,552
		Quincy	0	0	0	0	6,904
		Redington Beaches	0	0	0	0	1,506
		Riviera Beach	0	0	0	0	36,795
		Rockledge	0	0	0	0	24,910
		Royal Palm Beach	0	0	0	0	32,441
		Safety Harbor	0	0	0	0	17,366
		Sanford	0	0	0	0	50,757
		Sanibel	0	0	0	0	5,777
		Sarasota	0	0	0	0	52,986
		Satellite Beach	0	0	0	0	9,987
		Sea Ranch Lakes	0	0	0	0	763
		Sebastian	0	0	0	0	20,913
		Sebring	0	0	0	0	10,749
		Seminole	0	0	0	0	19,330
		Sewall's Point	0	0	0	0	2,035
		Shalimar	0	0	0	0	712
		Sneads	0	0	0	0	1,936
		South Bay	0	0	0	0	4,667
		South Daytona	0	0	0	0	13,529
		South Miami	0	0	0	0	11,071
		South Palm Beach	0	0	0	0	1,501
		South Pasadena	0	0	0	0	5,634
		Southwest Ranches	0	0	0	0	7,449
		Springfield	0	0	0	0	8,963
		Starke	0	0	0	0	5,896
		St. Augustine	0	0	0	0	12,118
		St. Augustine Beach	0	0	0	0	6,001
		St. Cloud	0	0	0	0	24,791
		St. Pete Beach	0	0	0	0	10,105
		St. Petersburg	0	0	0	0	248,069
		Stuart	0	0	0	0	16,385
		Sunrise	0	0	0	0	91,480
		Surfside	0	0	0	0	4,599
		Sweetwater	0	0	0	0	13,436
		Tallahassee	0	0	0	0	159,943
		Tamarac	0	0	0	0	61,366
		Tavares	0	0	0	0	13,351
		Temple Terrace	0	0	0	0	22,546
		Tequesta	0	0	0	0	6,018
		Titusville	0	0	0	0	44,467
		Treasure Island	0	0	0	0	7,575
		Trenton	0	0	0	0	1,866
		Umatilla	0	0	0	0	2,812
		Valparaiso	0	0	0	0	6,047
		Vero Beach	0	0	0	0	16,840
		Virginia Gardens	0	0	0	0	2,221
		Waldo	0	0	0	0	767
		Wauchula	0	0	0	0	4,517
		Webster	0	0	0	0	865
		Welaka	0	0	0	0	714
		West Melbourne	0	0	0	0	16,012
		West Miami	0	0	0	0	5,725
		Weston	0	0	0	0	68,230
		West Palm Beach	0	0	0	0	101,322
		White Springs	0	0	0	0	825
		Wildwood	0	0	0	0	3,211
		Williston	0	0	0	0	2,833
		Windermere	0	0	0	0	2,037
		Winter Haven	0	0	0	0	31,556
		Winter Springs	0	0	0	0	32,817
		Zephyrhills	0	0	0	0	12,998
		Zolfo Springs	0	0	0	0	1,693
	Universities and Colleges	Florida A&M University	0	0	0	0	11,907
		Florida Gulf Coast University	0	0	0	0	8,279
		Florida International University	0	0	0	0	37,997
		Florida State University: Panama City[3]	0	0	0	0	
		Tallahassee	0	0	0	0	39,973
		New College of Florida	0	0	0	0	746
		Pensacola Junior College	0	0	0	0	10,208
		Santa Fe Community College	0	0	0	0	14,012
		Tallahassee Community College	0	0	0	0	12,732
		University of Florida	0	0	0	0	50,912
		University of North Florida	0	0	0	0	15,954
		University of South Florida: St. Petersburg[3]	0	0	0	0	
		Tampa	0	0	0	0	43,636
	Metropolitan Counties	Baker	0	0	0	0	
		Gadsden	0	0	0	0	
		Gilchrist	0	0	0	0	
		Jefferson	0	0	0	0	
		Leon	0	0	0	0	
		Marion	0	0	0	0	
		Martin	0	0	0	0	
		Miami-Dade	0	0	0	0	
		Nassau	0	0	0	0	
		Okaloosa	0	0	0	0	
		Pasco	0	0	0	0	
		Sarasota	0	0	0	0	
		Seminole	0	0	0	0	
		St. Johns	0	0	0	0	
		St. Lucie	0	0	0	0	
		Wakulla	0	0	0	0	
	Nonmetropolitan Counties	Bradford	0	0	0	0	
		Calhoun	0	0	0	0	
		Citrus	0	0	0	0	
		Columbia	0	0	0	0	
		Dixie	0	0	0	0	
		Franklin	0	0	0	0	
		Glades	0	0	0	0	
		Gulf	0	0	0	0	
		Hamilton	0	0	0	0	
		Hardee	0	0	0	0	
		Hendry	0	0	0	0	
		Highlands	0	0	0	0	
		Holmes	0	0	0	0	
		Jackson	0	0	0	0	
		Lafayette	0	0	0	0	
		Levy	0	0	0	0	

[1] Agencies published in this table indicated that no hate crimes occurred in their jurisdictions during the quarter(s) for which they submitted reports to the Hate Crime program. Blanks indicate quarters for which agencies did not submit reports.

[3] Student enrollment figures were not available.

Table 95. Hate Crime Zero Data Submitted per Quarter, by State and Agency, 2007 *(Contd.)*

(Number.)

State	Agency type	Agency name	Zero data per quarter[1]				Popu-lation[2]	State	Agency type	Agency name	Zero data per quarter[1]				Popu-lation[2]
			1st quarter	2nd quarter	3rd quarter	4th quarter					1st quarter	2nd quarter	3rd quarter	4th quarter	
		Liberty	0	0	0	0				Miami-Dade County	0	0	0	0	
		Madison	0	0	0	0				Monroe County	0	0	0	0	
		Okeechobee	0	0	0	0				Nassau County	0	0	0	0	
		Putnam	0	0	0	0				Okaloosa County	0	0	0	0	
		Sumter	0	0	0	0				Okeechobee County	0	0	0	0	
		Suwannee	0	0	0	0				Orange County	0	0	0	0	
		Taylor	0	0	0	0				Osceola County	0	0	0	0	
		Union	0	0	0	0				Pasco County	0	0	0	0	
		Walton	0	0	0	0				Pinellas County	0	0	0	0	
		Washington	0	0	0	0				Polk County	0	0	0	0	
	State Police Agencies	Highway Patrol:								Putnam County	0	0	0	0	
		Alachua County	0	0	0	0				Santa Rosa County	0	0	0	0	
		Baker County	0	0	0	0				Sarasota County	0	0	0	0	
		Bay County	0	0	0	0				Seminole County	0	0	0	0	
		Bradford County	0	0	0	0				St. Johns County	0	0	0	0	
		Brevard County	0	0	0	0				St. Lucie County	0	0	0	0	
		Broward County	0	0	0	0				Sumter County	0	0	0	0	
		Calhoun County	0	0	0	0				Suwannee County	0	0	0	0	
		Charlotte County	0	0	0	0				Taylor County	0	0	0	0	
		Citrus County	0	0	0	0				Union County	0	0	0	0	
		Clay County	0	0	0	0				Volusia County	0	0	0	0	
		Collier County	0	0	0	0				Wakulla County	0	0	0	0	
		Columbia County	0	0	0	0				Walton County	0	0	0	0	
		DeSoto County	0	0	0	0				Washington County	0	0	0	0	
		Dixie County	0	0	0	0			**Other Agencies**	Capitol Police	0	0	0	0	
		Duval County	0	0	0	0				Department of Environmental Protection, Division of Law Enforcement:					
		Escambia County	0	0	0	0				Bay County	0	0	0	0	
		Flagler County	0	0	0	0				Brevard County	0	0	0	0	
		Franklin County	0	0	0	0				Citrus County	0	0	0	0	
		Gadsden County	0	0	0	0				Duval County	0	0	0	0	
		Gilchrist County	0	0	0	0				Escambia County	0	0	0	0	
		Glades County	0	0	0	0				Franklin County	0	0	0	0	
		Gulf County	0	0	0	0				Hillsborough County	0	0	0	0	
		Hamilton County	0	0	0	0				Lee County	0	0	0	0	
		Hardee County	0	0	0	0				Leon County	0	0	0	0	
		Hendry County	0	0	0	0				Miami-Dade County	0	0	0	0	
		Hernando County	0	0	0	0				Monroe County	0	0	0	0	
		Highlands County	0	0	0	0				Palm Beach County	0	0	0	0	
		Hillsborough County	0	0	0	0				Pinellas County	0	0	0	0	
		Holmes County	0	0	0	0				Department of Law Enforcement:					
		Indian River County	0	0	0	0				Duval County, Jacksonville	0	0	0	0	
		Jackson County	0	0	0	0				Escambia County, Pensacola	0	0	0	0	
		Jefferson County	0	0	0	0				Hillsborough County, Tampa	0	0	0	0	
		Lafayette County	0	0	0	0				Lee County, Fort Myers	0	0	0	0	
		Lake County	0	0	0	0				Leon County, Tallahassee	0	0	0	0	
		Lee County	0	0	0	0				Miami-Dade County, Miami	0	0	0	0	
		Leon County	0	0	0	0									
		Levy County	0	0	0	0									
		Liberty County	0	0	0	0									
		Madison County	0	0	0	0									
		Manatee County	0	0	0	0									
		Marion County	0	0	0	0									
		Martin County	0	0	0	0									

[1]Agencies published in this table indicated that no hate crimes occurred in their jurisdictions during the quarter(s) for which they submitted reports to the Hate Crime program. Blanks indicate quarters for which agencies did not submit reports.

[2]Population figures are published only for the cities. The figures listed for the universities and colleges are student enrollment and were provided by the United States Department of Education for the 2006 school year, the most recent available. The enrollment figures include full-time and part-time students.

Table 95. Hate Crime Zero Data Submitted per Quarter, by State and Agency, 2007 (Contd.)

(Number.)

State	Agency type	Agency name	1st quarter	2nd quarter	3rd quarter	4th quarter	Population[2]
		Orange County, Orlando	0	0	0	0	
		Duval County Schools	0	0	0	0	
		Florida Game Commission, Leon County	0	0	0	0	
		Florida School for the Deaf and Blind	0	0	0	0	
		Fort Lauderdale Airport	0	0	0	0	
		Jacksonville Airport Authority	0	0	0	0	
		Melbourne International Airport	0	0	0	0	
		Miami-Dade County Public Schools	0	0	0	0	
		Palm Beach County School District	0	0	0	0	
		Port Everglades	0	0	0	0	
		Sarasota-Bradenton International Airport	0	0	0	0	
		State Fire Marshal	0	0	0	0	
		St. Petersburg-Clearwater International Airport	0	0	0	0	
		Tampa International Airport	0	0	0	0	
		Volusia County Beach Management	0	0	0	0	
	Other Agencies–Tribal	Miccosukee Tribal	0	0	0	0	
		Seminole Tribal	0	0	0	0	
GEORGIA	Cities	Colquitt	0				1,918
		Conyers		0	0		12,704
		Davisboro	0	0			1,556
		Greenville			0		937
		Hapeville	0	0	0	0	6,149
		Royston	0	0	0	0	2,730
	Universities and Colleges	Augusta State University	0				6,552
		Georgia College and State University	0	0	0		6,040
		Georgia Southern University	0	0	0	0	16,425
		North Georgia College and State University	0	0	0	0	4,922
	Metropolitan Counties	Coweta	0				
	Nonmetropolitan Counties	Jeff Davis	0	0		0	
		Schley	0	0	0		
	Other Agencies	Fulton County School System	0	0	0	0	
		Gwinnett County Public Schools	0	0	0	0	
IDAHO	Cities	Aberdeen	0	0	0	0	1,805
		American Falls	0	0	0	0	4,244
		Blackfoot	0	0	0	0	11,084
		Bonners Ferry	0	0	0	0	2,736
		Buhl	0	0	0	0	4,028
		Caldwell	0	0	0	0	38,713
		Cascade	0	0	0	0	1,018
		Challis	0	0	0	0	868
		Chubbuck	0	0	0	0	11,039
		Cottonwood	0	0	0	0	1,062
		Emmett	0	0	0	0	6,385
		Filer	0	0	0	0	1,919
		Fruitland	0	0	0	0	4,603
		Garden City	0	0	0	0	11,452
		Gooding	0	0	0	0	3,267
		Grangeville	0	0	0	0	3,171
		Hagerman	0	0	0	0	763
		Heyburn	0	0	0	0	2,749
		Homedale	0	0	0	0	2,585
		Idaho City	0	0	0	0	495
		Kamiah	0	0	0	0	1,150
		Kellogg	0	0	0	0	2,279
		Ketchum	0	0	0	0	3,258
		Kimberly	0	0	0	0	2,807
		McCall	0	0	0	0	2,644
		Meridian	0	0	0	0	64,294
		Montpelier	0	0	0	0	2,460
		Moscow	0	0	0	0	22,503
		Mountain Home	0	0	0	0	11,686
		Orofino	0	0	0	0	3,103
		Osburn	0	0	0	0	1,448
		Parma	0	0	0	0	1,842
		Payette	0	0	0	0	7,686
		Pinehurst	0	0	0	0	1,608
		Ponderay	0	0	0	0	720
		Post Falls	0	0	0	0	25,622
		Preston	0	0	0	0	5,147
		Priest River	0	0	0	0	1,950
		Rathdrum	0	0	0	0	6,551
		Rigby	0	0	0	0	3,332
		Rupert	0	0	0	0	5,158
		Salmon	0	0	0	0	3,054
		Sandpoint	0	0	0	0	8,413
		Shelley	0	0	0	0	4,249
		Soda Springs	0	0	0	0	3,149
		St. Anthony	0	0	0	0	3,383
		St. Maries	0	0	0	0	2,657
		Weiser	0	0	0	0	5,425
		Wendell	0	0	0	0	2,448
		Wilder	0	0	0	0	1,451
	Metropolitan Counties	Bannock	0	0	0	0	
		Boise	0	0	0	0	
		Canyon	0	0	0	0	
		Franklin	0	0	0	0	
		Gem	0	0	0	0	
		Jefferson	0	0	0	0	
		Nez Perce	0	0	0	0	
		Owyhee	0	0	0	0	
		Power	0	0	0	0	
	Nonmetropolitan Counties	Adams	0	0	0	0	
		Bear Lake	0	0	0	0	
		Benewah	0	0	0	0	
		Bingham	0	0	0	0	
		Blaine	0	0	0	0	
		Bonner	0	0	0	0	
		Boundary	0	0	0	0	
		Butte	0	0	0	0	
		Camas	0	0	0	0	
		Caribou	0	0	0	0	
		Cassia	0	0	0	0	

[1] Agencies published in this table indicated that no hate crimes occurred in their jurisdictions during the quarter(s) for which they submitted reports to the Hate Crime program. Blanks indicate quarters for which agencies did not submit reports.

[2] Population figures are published only for the cities. The figures listed for the universities and colleges are student enrollment and were provided by the United States Department of Education for the 2006 school year, the most recent available. The enrollment figures include full-time and part-time students.

Table 95. Hate Crime Zero Data Submitted per Quarter, by State and Agency, 2007 *(Contd.)*

(Number.)

State	Agency type	Agency name	1st quarter	2nd quarter	3rd quarter	4th quarter	Population[2]
		Clark	0	0	0	0	
		Clearwater	0	0	0	0	
		Custer	0	0	0	0	
		Elmore	0	0	0	0	
		Fremont	0	0	0	0	
		Gooding	0	0	0	0	
		Idaho	0	0	0	0	
		Jerome	0	0	0	0	
		Latah	0	0	0	0	
		Lemhi	0	0	0	0	
		Lewis	0	0	0	0	
		Lincoln	0	0	0	0	
		Madison	0	0	0	0	
		Minidoka	0	0	0	0	
		Oneida	0	0	0	0	
		Payette	0	0	0	0	
		Shoshone	0	0	0	0	
		Teton	0	0	0	0	
		Twin Falls	0	0	0	0	
		Valley	0	0	0	0	
		Washington	0	0	0	0	
	State Police Agencies	Idaho State Police	0	0	0	0	
ILLINOIS	Cities	Argenta				0	831
		Colfax				0	995
		Danvers	0	0	0	0	1,131
		East Dubuque	0	0	0	0	1,979
		Fulton	0	0	0	0	3,855
		Gibson City	0	0	0	0	3,302
		Hinsdale	0	0	0	0	18,285
		Holiday Hills	0	0	0	0	813
		Itasca	0	0	0	0	8,468
		Mokena	0	0	0	0	18,885
		Pawnee	0	0	0	0	2,538
		Rockton	0	0	0	0	5,431
		South Beloit			0		5,510
		Wood Dale	0	0	0	0	13,507
	Metropolitan Counties	McLean	0	0	0	0	
INDIANA	Cities	Alexandria	0	0	0	0	5,840
		Anderson	0	0	0	0	57,189
		Bargersville	0	0	0	0	2,647
		Beech Grove	0	0	0	0	13,975
		Bluffton	0	0	0	0	9,448
		Boonville	0	0	0	0	6,750
		Brazil	0	0			8,238
		Bremen	0	0	0	0	4,719
		Brownsburg	0		0	0	19,494
		Burns Harbor	0		0	0	1,060
		Carmel	0	0	0	0	62,037
		Cedar Lake			0		10,350
		Charlestown	0	0	0	0	7,217
		Chesterfield	0	0	0	0	2,755
		Columbia City	0	0	0		8,227
		Corydon	0		0	0	2,793
		Crawfordsville	0	0	0	0	15,156
		Danville	0	0		0	8,033
		Decatur	0	0	0	0	9,507
		Delphi	0	0	0	0	2,969
		East Chicago	0	0	0	0	30,353
		Edinburgh		0	0	0	4,593
		Elwood	0	0	0	0	9,013
		Fairmount	0	0	0	0	2,746
		Frankfort	0	0			16,431
		Franklin	0	0	0	0	22,778
		Gas City	0	0	0		5,774
		Georgetown	0		0		2,851
		Goshen	0	0	0	0	32,210
		Greensburg	0	0	0		10,570
		Hagerstown	0	0	0	0	1,646
		Hammond		0	0		77,662
		Hartford City	0		0	0	6,493
		Hebron			0	0	3,634
		Highland	0	0	0	0	22,879
		Hobart	0	0	0	0	28,428
		Huntington	0	0	0		16,767
		Jasper	0	0		0	14,098
		Knox	0	0		0	3,699
		Lafayette	0		0		61,257
		Ligonier	0	0	0	0	4,470
		Logansport	0		0		18,995
		Lowell	0	0	0	0	8,319
		Martinsville	0		0		11,805
		Merrillville			0	0	32,091
		Mishawaka	0	0		0	49,196
		Monticello	0	0	0		5,401
		Mooresville	0	0		0	11,639
		Nappanee	0	0	0	0	7,118
		New Albany	0	0	0	0	36,840
		New Castle	0	0		0	18,577
		New Whiteland	0	0	0	0	5,658
		Noblesville	0	0	0		41,927
		North Vernon	0		0	0	6,407
		Plainfield	0	0	0	0	25,722
		Plymouth			0	0	11,192
		Portland	0	0	0	0	6,149
		Princeton	0	0			8,700
		Rensselaer	0	0			6,276
		Richmond	0	0		0	37,129
		Roseland	0	0			625
		Rushville	0	0	0	0	5,570
		Salem	0	0		0	6,558
		Schererville	0	0	0	0	29,494
		Scottsburg	0	0	0	0	5,982
		South Whitley			0		1,865
		Sullivan	0	0	0	0	4,481
		Tell City	0	0	0	0	7,561
		Terre Haute	0	0	0		56,946
		Tipton	0	0	0	0	5,181
		Vincennes	0	0	0	0	17,905
		Wabash	0	0	0	0	11,021
		Walkerton	0	0	0	0	2,186
		Warsaw	0	0	0	0	13,154
		West Lafayette	0	0	0	0	29,045
		Westville				0	5,194
		Winchester	0	0		0	4,705
		Winona Lake	0	0	0	0	4,314
	Universities and Colleges	Indiana State University	0	0	0	0	10,568
		Indiana University:					
		Gary	0	0		0	4,819
		Indianapolis[3]	0	0	0	0	
		New Albany			0	0	6,183
	Metropolitan Counties	Bartholomew	0	0	0	0	
		Brown	0	0	0	0	
		Clark				0	
		Floyd		0	0	0	
		Greene	0			0	
		Harrison	0	0		0	
		La Porte		0			
		Monroe	0	0	0	0	
		Newton	0	0	0	0	
		Porter	0	0	0	0	
		Putnam	0	0			
		Shelby	0	0	0	0	
		St. Joseph	0	0	0		
		Tippecanoe	0				
		Tipton	0				
		Warrick	0				
		Wells	0	0	0	0	
	Nonmetropolitan Counties	Blackford	0	0	0	0	
		Cass	0	0			

[1] Agencies published in this table indicated that no hate crimes occurred in their jurisdictions during the quarter(s) for which they submitted reports to the Hate Crime program. Blanks indicate quarters for which agencies did not submit reports.

[2] Population figures are published only for the cities. The figures listed for the universities and colleges are student enrollment and were provided by the United States Department of Education for the 2006 school year, the most recent available. The enrollment figures include full-time and part-time students.

[3] Student enrollment figures were not available.

Table 95. Hate Crime Zero Data Submitted per Quarter, by State and Agency, 2007 *(Contd.)*

(Number.)

State	Agency type	Agency name	Zero data per quarter[1] 1st quarter	2nd quarter	3rd quarter	4th quarter	Popu-lation[2]
		Daviess	0	0	0	0	
		Fulton	0	0	0	0	
		Grant	0	0	0	0	
		Henry	0	0		0	
		Huntington	0	0		0	
		Martin	0	0			
		Noble	0		0	0	
		Parke	0	0	0		
		Pulaski	0	0	0	0	
		Starke	0	0	0	0	
		Steuben	0	0		0	
	Other Agencies	Northern Indiana Commuter Transportation District	0	0	0	0	
		St. Joseph County Airport Authority	0	0		0	
IOWA	Cities	Adel	0	0	0	0	4,135
		Albia	0	0	0	0	3,615
		Algona	0	0	0	0	5,443
		Altoona	0	0	0	0	13,882
		Ames	0	0	0	0	51,622
		Anamosa	0	0	0	0	5,675
		Ankeny	0	0	0	0	40,546
		Atlantic	0	0	0	0	6,842
		Audubon	0	0	0	0	2,166
		Belmond	0	0	0	0	2,387
		Bettendorf	0	0	0	0	32,501
		Bloomfield	0	0	0	0	2,575
		Boone	0	0	0	0	12,768
		Burlington	0	0	0	0	25,258
		Camanche	0	0	0	0	4,298
		Carlisle	0	0	0	0	3,599
		Carroll	0	0	0	0	9,976
		Carter Lake	0	0	0	0	3,304
		Cedar Rapids	0	0	0	0	124,730
		Centerville	0	0	0	0	5,662
		Chariton	0	0	0	0	4,554
		Charles City	0	0	0	0	7,574
		Cherokee	0	0	0	0	4,911
		Clarinda	0	0	0	0	5,558
		Clarion	0	0	0	0	2,796
		Clear Lake	0	0	0	0	7,848
		Clinton	0	0	0	0	26,937
		Clive	0	0	0	0	14,231
		Cresco	0	0	0	0	3,763
		Creston	0	0	0	0	7,401
		Denison	0	0	0	0	7,427
		De Witt	0	0	0	0	5,360
		Dyersville	0	0	0		4,186
		Eagle Grove	0	0		0	3,424
		Eldora	0	0	0	0	2,789
		Eldridge	0	0	0	0	4,685
		Emmetsburg	0	0	0	0	3,633
		Estherville	0	0	0	0	6,276
		Evansdale	0	0	0	0	4,998
		Fairfield	0	0	0	0	9,354
		Forest City	0	0	0	0	4,202
		Fort Madison	0	0	0	0	10,841
		Garner	0	0	0	0	2,990
		Glenwood	0	0	0	0	5,816
		Grinnell	0	0	0	0	9,408
		Grundy Center	0	0	0		2,581
		Hampton	0	0	0	0	4,226
		Harlan	0				5,111
		Hawarden	0	0	0	0	2,426
		Humboldt	0	0	0	0	4,379
		Independence	0	0	0	0	6,118
		Indianola	0	0	0	0	14,399
		Iowa City	0	0	0	0	62,700
		Iowa Falls	0	0	0	0	5,040
		Jefferson	0	0	0	0	4,337
		Johnston	0	0	0	0	15,622
		Knoxville		0			7,434
		Le Claire	0				3,181
		Le Mars	0	0	0	0	9,375
		Leon	0	0	0	0	1,923
		Manchester	0	0	0	0	4,958
		Maquoketa	0	0	0	0	6,006
		Marshalltown	0	0	0	0	25,958
		Mason City	0	0	0	0	27,541
		Missouri Valley	0	0	0		2,870
		Monticello	0	0	0	0	3,738
		Mount Pleasant	0	0	0	0	8,918
		Mount Vernon	0	0	0	0	4,210
		Muscatine	0	0	0	0	22,705
		Nevada	0	0	0	0	6,275
		New Hampton	0	0	0	0	3,464
		Newton	0	0	0	0	15,459
		North Liberty	0	0	0	0	10,826
		Norwalk	0	0	0	0	8,413
		Oelwein	0	0	0	0	6,273
		Ogden	0				2,005
		Onawa			0	0	2,838
		Orange City	0	0	0	0	5,897
		Osage	0	0	0	0	3,447
		Osceola	0	0	0	0	4,782
		Oskaloosa	0	0	0	0	11,033
		Pella	0	0	0	0	10,280
		Pleasant Hill	0	0	0	0	7,458
		Polk City	0	0	0	0	3,098
		Prairie City	0	0	0	0	1,459
		Red Oak	0	0	0	0	5,907
		Rock Valley			0		3,005
		Sac City	0	0	0	0	2,157
		Sergeant Bluff	0	0	0	0	4,009
		Sheldon	0	0	0	0	4,863
		Shenandoah	0	0	0	0	5,172
		Sioux Center	0				6,693
		Spencer	0	0	0	0	11,015
		Spirit Lake	0	0	0	0	4,783
		St. Ansgar	0	0	0	0	975
		State Center	0	0	0	0	1,356
		Storm Lake	0	0	0	0	9,855
		Story City	0	0	0	0	3,187
		Urbandale	0	0	0	0	38,381
		Vinton	0	0	0	0	5,239
		Waterloo	0	0	0	0	65,607
		Waukee	0	0	0	0	11,945
		Waverly	0	0	0	0	9,396
		Webster City	0	0	0	0	8,004
		West Burlington	0	0	0	0	3,376
		West Des Moines	0	0	0	0	54,988
		West Liberty	0	0	0	0	3,695
		West Union	0	0	0	0	2,436
		Williamsburg	0	0	0	0	2,831
		Wilton	0	0	0	0	2,862
		Windsor Heights	0	0	0	0	4,506
		Winterset	0	0	0	0	4,970
	Universities and Colleges	University of Northern Iowa	0	0	0	0	12,327
	Metropolitan Counties	Benton	0	0	0	0	
		Black Hawk	0	0	0	0	
		Bremer	0	0	0	0	
		Dallas	0	0	0	0	
		Dubuque	0	0	0	0	
		Grundy	0	0	0	0	
		Guthrie	0	0	0	0	
		Harrison	0	0	0	0	
		Johnson	0	0	0	0	
		Jones	0	0	0	0	
		Linn	0	0	0	0	
		Madison	0	0	0	0	
		Mills	0	0	0	0	

[1]Agencies published in this table indicated that no hate crimes occurred in their jurisdictions during the quarter(s) for which they submitted reports to the Hate Crime program. Blanks indicate quarters for which agencies did not submit reports.

[2]Population figures are published only for the cities. The figures listed for the universities and colleges are student enrollment and were provided by the United States Department of Education for the 2006 school year, the most recent available. The enrollment figures include full-time and part-time students.

Table 95. Hate Crime Zero Data Submitted per Quarter, by State and Agency, 2007 *(Contd.)*

(Number.)

State	Agency type	Agency name	Zero data per quarter[1] 1st quarter	2nd quarter	3rd quarter	4th quarter	Population[2]
		Pottawattamie	0	0	0	0	
		Scott	0	0	0	0	
		Story	0	0	0	0	
		Warren	0	0	0	0	
		Washington	0	0	0	0	
		Woodbury	0	0	0	0	
	Nonmetropolitan Counties	Adair	0	0	0	0	
		Adams	0	0	0	0	
		Allamakee	0	0	0	0	
		Appanoose	0	0	0	0	
		Audubon	0	0	0	0	
		Boone	0	0	0	0	
		Buchanan	0	0	0	0	
		Buena Vista	0	0	0	0	
		Butler	0	0	0	0	
		Calhoun	0	0	0	0	
		Carroll	0	0	0	0	
		Cass	0	0	0	0	
		Cedar	0	0	0	0	
		Cerro Gordo	0	0	0	0	
		Cherokee	0	0	0	0	
		Chickasaw	0	0	0	0	
		Clarke	0	0	0	0	
		Clay	0	0	0	0	
		Clayton	0	0	0	0	
		Clinton	0	0	0	0	
		Crawford	0	0	0	0	
		Davis	0	0	0	0	
		Decatur	0	0	0	0	
		Delaware	0	0	0	0	
		Des Moines	0	0	0	0	
		Dickinson	0	0	0	0	
		Emmet	0	0	0	0	
		Fayette	0	0	0	0	
		Floyd	0	0	0	0	
		Franklin	0	0	0	0	
		Fremont	0	0			
		Greene			0	0	
		Hamilton	0	0	0	0	
		Hancock	0	0	0	0	
		Hardin	0	0	0	0	
		Henry	0	0	0	0	
		Howard	0	0	0	0	
		Humboldt	0	0	0	0	
		Ida	0	0	0	0	
		Iowa	0	0	0	0	
		Jackson		0	0		
		Jasper	0	0	0	0	
		Jefferson	0	0	0	0	
		Keokuk	0	0	0	0	
		Kossuth	0				
		Lee	0	0	0	0	
		Louisa	0	0	0	0	
		Lucas	0	0	0	0	
		Lyon	0	0	0	0	
		Mahaska	0	0	0	0	
		Marion	0	0	0	0	
		Marshall	0	0	0	0	
		Mitchell	0	0	0	0	
		Monona	0	0	0	0	
		Monroe	0	0	0	0	
		Montgomery	0	0	0	0	
		Muscatine	0	0	0	0	
		O'Brien	0	0	0	0	
		Osceola	0	0	0	0	
		Palo Alto	0	0	0	0	
		Plymouth	0	0	0	0	
		Pocahontas	0	0	0	0	
		Poweshiek	0	0	0		
		Ringgold		0			
		Sac	0	0		0	
		Shelby	0		0	0	
		Sioux	0	0	0	0	
		Tama	0	0	0	0	
		Taylor	0	0	0	0	
		Union	0	0	0	0	
		Van Buren	0	0	0	0	
		Wapello	0	0	0	0	
		Wayne	0	0	0	0	
		Webster	0	0	0	0	
		Winnebago	0	0	0	0	
		Winneshiek	0	0	0	0	
		Worth	0	0	0	0	
		Wright	0	0	0	0	
KANSAS	Cities	Abilene	0	0	0	0	6,419
		Alma	0	0	0	0	754
		Altamont	0	0	0	0	1,060
		Andale	0	0	0	0	835
		Anthony	0	0	0	0	2,217
		Arcadia		0			382
		Arkansas City	0	0	0	0	11,342
		Arma		0	0	0	1,484
		Atchison	0	0	0	0	10,138
		Attica	0	0	0	0	587
		Atwood	0	0	0	0	1,104
		Auburn	0	0	0	0	1,132
		Baldwin City	0	0	0	0	4,255
		Basehor	0	0	0	0	3,742
		Baxter Springs	0	0	0	0	4,164
		Bel Aire	0	0	0	0	6,739
		Belle Plaine	0	0	0	0	1,576
		Beloit	0	0	0	0	3,591
		Benton	0				817
		Blue Rapids	0		0	0	1,035
		Bonner Springs	0	0	0	0	7,121
		Bucklin				0	736
		Burden	0	0	0	0	544
		Burlingame	0				1,002
		Burlington		0	0	0	2,706
		Burns	0	0	0	0	275
		Bushton	0	0	0		290
		Caldwell	0	0	0	0	1,181
		Caney	0	0	0	0	1,976
		Canton	0	0	0	0	800
		Carbondale	0				1,434
		Chapman	0		0	0	1,262
		Chase	0	0	0	0	455
		Cheney	0	0	0	0	1,973
		Cherokee	0			0	711
		Chetopa	0	0	0	0	1,227
		Clay Center	0	0	0	0	4,305
		Clearwater	0	0	0	0	2,299
		Colby	0	0	0	0	4,854
		Coldwater	0	0	0	0	752
		Colwich	0	0	0	0	1,380
		Conway Springs	0	0	0		1,221
		Council Grove	0	0	0	0	2,273
		Derby	0	0	0	0	21,531
		Dodge City	0	0	0	0	26,236
		Eastborough	0	0	0	0	788
		Elkhart	0	0	0	0	1,969
		Ellis	0	0	0	0	1,849
		Ellsworth	0	0	0	0	2,869
		Elwood	0	0	0	0	1,144
		Enterprise	0	0	0		811
		Erie	0	0	0	0	1,146
		Eskridge	0	0	0	0	565
		Eudora	0	0	0	0	6,323
		Fairway	0	0	0	0	3,815
		Florence	0	0	0	0	633
		Fort Scott	0	0	0	0	7,922
		Frankfort		0	0	0	781
		Fredonia	0	0	0	0	2,446
		Frontenac	0	0	0	0	3,134
		Galena	0	0	0	0	3,150
		Garden Plain	0	0	0		842
		Gardner	0	0	0	0	16,658
		Garnett	0	0	0	0	3,272

[1] Agencies published in this table indicated that no hate crimes occurred in their jurisdictions during the quarter(s) for which they submitted reports to the Hate Crime program. Blanks indicate quarters for which agencies did not submit reports.

[2] Population figures are published only for the cities. The figures listed for the universities and colleges are student enrollment and were provided by the United States Department of Education for the 2006 school year, the most recent available. The enrollment figures include full-time and part-time students.

Table 95. Hate Crime Zero Data Submitted per Quarter, by State and Agency, 2007 *(Contd.)*

(Number.)

State	Agency type	Agency name	1st quarter	2nd quarter	3rd quarter	4th quarter	Population[2]
		Girard	0	0	0	0	2,645
		Goddard	0	0	0	0	3,836
		Goodland	0	0	0	0	4,289
		Great Bend	0	0	0	0	15,562
		Halstead	0	0	0	0	1,907
		Harper	0	0	0	0	1,431
		Haven	0	0	0	0	1,170
		Herington	0	0	0	0	2,459
		Hesston	0	0	0	0	3,666
		Hiawatha	0	0	0	0	3,207
		Hill City	0	0	0	0	1,415
		Hillsboro	0	0	0	0	2,694
		Hoisington				0	2,816
		Holcomb	0	0	0		1,880
		Holton	0	0	0	0	3,364
		Holyrood	0	0			448
		Horton	0		0	0	1,821
		Howard		0	0	0	760
		Hoxie	0	0	0	0	1,140
		Hugoton	0	0	0	0	3,552
		Inman	0	0	0	0	1,189
		Junction City	0	0	0	0	15,727
		Kechi	0	0	0	0	1,645
		Kingman	0	0	0	0	3,072
		Kiowa			0		953
		La Crosse	0	0	0	0	1,263
		La Cygne	0	0			1,161
		La Harpe	0	0	0	0	659
		Lake Quivira	0	0	0	0	924
		Larned	0	0	0	0	3,677
		Lebo	0	0	0	0	945
		Leon	0	0			650
		Liberal	0	0	0	0	20,477
		Lindsborg	0	0	0	0	3,282
		Linn Valley	0	0	0	0	594
		Little River	0	0	0	0	526
		Louisburg	0	0	0	0	3,739
		Lyndon	0	0	0	0	1,026
		Lyons	0	0			3,460
		Macksville	0	0	0	0	486
		Maize	0	0	0	0	2,717
		Maple Hill	0	0	0	0	496
		Marion	0	0	0	0	1,978
		Marysville	0	0	0	0	3,110
		McLouth	0	0	0		828
		McPherson	0	0	0	0	13,577
		Meade	0	0	0	0	1,601
		Medicine Lodge		0	0		2,010
		Meriden	0	0	0	0	713
		Minneapolis	0	0	0	0	2,021
		Mission Hills	0	0	0	0	3,514
		Mission Woods				0	158
		Moran	0	0	0	0	531
		Mound City	0	0	0		820
		Moundridge	0	0	0	0	1,635
		Mount Hope	0				853
		Mulberry	0	0	0	0	566
		Mulvane	0	0	0	0	5,836
		Neodesha	0	0	0	0	2,635
		Newton	0	0	0	0	18,164
		Nickerson	0	0	0	0	1,160
		North Newton	0	0	0	0	1,574
		Norton	0	0	0	0	2,726
		Nortonville	0	0	0	0	586
		Norwich	0	0	0	0	505
		Oakley	0	0	0	0	1,870
		Oberlin	0	0	0	0	1,739
		Osawatomie	0	0	0	0	4,578
		Oskaloosa	0	0	0	0	1,123
		Oswego	0	0	0	0	1,993
		Overbrook	0	0	0	0	962
		Oxford	0	0	0	0	1,092
		Park City	0	0	0	0	7,603
		Parker				0	310
		Peabody	0	0	0	0	1,264
		Perry	0	0	0	0	863
		Plainville	0	0	0	0	1,843
		Pleasanton	0	0	0	0	1,367
		Prairie Village	0	0	0		21,312
		Quinter	0			0	815
		Roeland Park	0			0	6,916
		Rolla	0	0	0	0	431
		Rose Hill	0	0	0	0	4,028
		Rossville	0	0	0	0	1,008
		Russell	0	0	0	0	4,224
		Sabetha	0	0	0	0	2,506
		Scott City	0	0	0	0	3,459
		Scranton	0	0	0		698
		Sedan	0				1,210
		Sedgwick	0	0	0	0	1,657
		Seneca	0	0	0	0	2,054
		South Hutchinson	0	0	0	0	2,477
		Stafford	0	0	0	0	1,041
		Sterling	0	0	0	0	2,537
		St. Francis	0	0	0	0	1,340
		St. George	0	0	0	0	514
		St. John	0	0	0	0	1,185
		St. Marys	0	0	0	0	2,240
		Stockton	0	0	0	0	1,421
		Tonganoxie	0	0	0	0	4,312
		Towanda	0	0	0		1,371
		Troy	0	0			1,018
		Udall	0	0	0	0	758
		Ulysses	0	0	0	0	5,620
		Wa Keeney	0	0	0	0	1,716
		Wakefield	0	0	0	0	883
		Walton	0			0	291
		Wamego	0	0	0	0	4,243
		Waterville	0				619
		Wathena	0	0	0	0	1,297
		Waverly				0	553
		Weir	0	0			742
		Wellington	0	0	0	0	7,898
		Wellsville	0	0	0	0	1,694
		West Mineral			0		230
		Westwood	0	0	0	0	1,832
		Wilson	0	0			761
		Winchester	0	0		0	570
		Winfield	0	0	0	0	11,672
		Yates Center	0	0	0	0	1,451
	Universities and Colleges	Emporia State University	0	0	0	0	6,473
		Fort Hays State University	0	0	0	0	9,122
		Kansas City Community College	0	0	0	0	5,547
		Kansas State University	0	0	0	0	23,141
		University of Kansas, Medical Center	0	0	0	0	2,150
		Washburn University	0	0	0	0	7,153
		Wichita State University	0	0	0	0	13,964
	Metropolitan Counties	Butler	0	0	0	0	
		Doniphan	0	0	0	0	
		Douglas	0	0	0	0	
		Franklin	0	0	0	0	
		Harvey	0	0	0	0	
		Jackson	0	0	0	0	
		Jefferson	0	0	0		
		Johnson		0			
		Leavenworth	0	0	0	0	
		Linn	0	0	0	0	

[1]Agencies published in this table indicated that no hate crimes occurred in their jurisdictions during the quarter(s) for which they submitted reports to the Hate Crime program. Blanks indicate quarters for which agencies did not submit reports.

[2]Population figures are published only for the cities. The figures listed for the universities and colleges are student enrollment and were provided by the United States Department of Education for the 2006 school year, the most recent available. The enrollment figures include full-time and part-time students.

Table 95. Hate Crime Zero Data Submitted per Quarter, by State and Agency, 2007 *(Contd.)*

(Number.)

State	Agency type	Agency name	1st quarter	2nd quarter	3rd quarter	4th quarter	Population[2]
		Osage	0	0	0	0	
		Sedgwick	0	0	0	0	
		Sumner	0	0	0	0	
		Wabaunsee	0	0	0		
		Wyandotte				0	
	Nonmetropolitan Counties	Allen	0	0	0	0	
		Anderson	0	0	0	0	
		Atchison	0	0	0	0	
		Barber	0	0	0	0	
		Barton				0	
		Bourbon	0	0	0	0	
		Brown	0	0	0	0	
		Chase	0	0	0	0	
		Chautauqua	0	0	0	0	
		Cherokee	0	0	0	0	
		Cheyenne	0	0	0	0	
		Clark	0	0	0	0	
		Clay	0	0	0	0	
		Cloud	0	0	0	0	
		Coffey	0	0	0	0	
		Crawford	0	0	0	0	
		Decatur	0	0	0	0	
		Dickinson	0	0	0	0	
		Edwards	0	0	0	0	
		Elk	0	0	0	0	
		Ellis	0	0	0	0	
		Ellsworth	0	0	0	0	
		Ford	0	0	0	0	
		Geary	0	0	0	0	
		Gove	0	0	0	0	
		Graham	0	0	0	0	
		Grant	0	0	0	0	
		Gray	0	0	0	0	
		Greeley	0	0	0	0	
		Greenwood	0	0	0	0	
		Harper	0	0	0	0	
		Haskell	0	0	0	0	
		Hodgeman	0	0	0	0	
		Jewell	0	0	0	0	
		Kingman	0	0	0	0	
		Kiowa	0	0	0	0	
		Labette	0	0	0	0	
		Lane	0	0	0	0	
		Lincoln	0	0	0	0	
		Logan	0	0	0	0	
		Marion	0	0	0	0	
		Marshall	0	0	0	0	
		McPherson	0	0	0	0	
		Meade	0				
		Mitchell				0	
		Morris	0	0	0	0	
		Morton	0	0	0	0	
		Nemaha	0	0	0	0	
		Neosho	0	0	0	0	
		Ness	0	0			
		Norton	0	0	0	0	
		Osborne	0	0	0	0	
		Ottawa	0	0	0	0	
		Pawnee	0	0	0	0	
		Phillips	0	0	0	0	
		Pottawatomie	0	0	0	0	
		Pratt	0	0	0	0	
		Rawlins	0	0	0	0	
		Reno	0	0	0	0	
		Republic	0	0	0	0	
		Rice	0	0	0	0	
		Rooks	0	0	0	0	
		Rush	0	0	0	0	
		Russell	0	0	0	0	
		Saline	0	0	0	0	
		Scott	0	0	0	0	
		Seward	0	0	0	0	
		Sheridan	0	0	0		
		Sherman	0	0	0	0	
		Smith	0	0	0	0	
		Stafford	0	0	0	0	
		Stanton	0	0	0	0	
		Thomas	0	0	0	0	
		Trego	0	0	0	0	
		Wallace	0	0	0	0	
		Washington	0	0	0	0	
		Wichita	0	0	0	0	
		Wilson	0	0	0	0	
		Woodson	0	0	0	0	
	State Police Agencies	Kansas Highway Patrol	0	0	0	0	
	Other Agencies	Blue Valley School District	0	0	0	0	
		Johnson County Park	0			0	
		Kansas Alcoholic Beverage Control	0	0	0	0	
		Kansas Department of Wildlife and Parks	0	0	0	0	
		Kansas Lottery Security Division	0	0	0	0	
		Kansas Racing Commission, Security Division	0	0	0	0	
		Metropolitan Topeka Airport Authority	0	0	0	0	
		Securities Office, Investigation Section	0				
		Shawnee Mission Public Schools	0	0	0	0	
		Topeka Fire Department, Arson Investigation	0		0	0	
		Unified School District: Goddard	0	0	0	0	
		Maize	0	0	0	0	
		Topeka	0	0	0	0	
		Wyandotte County Parks and Recreation	0	0	0	0	
	Other Agencies– Tribal	Iowa Tribal	0	0		0	
		Kickapoo Tribal	0	0	0	0	
		Potawatomi Tribal	0	0	0		
KENTUCKY...	Cities	Adairville	0	0	0	0	937
		Albany	0	0	0	0	2,323
		Auburn	0	0	0	0	1,509
		Audubon Park	0	0	0	0	1,568
		Augusta	0	0	0	0	1,258
		Barbourville	0	0	0	0	3,561
		Bardstown	0	0	0	0	11,158
		Beattyville	0	0	0	0	1,135
		Beaver Dam		0			3,181
		Bellefonte		0			846
		Benham		0			547
		Benton	0	0	0	0	4,388
		Berea	0	0	0	0	13,946

[1]Agencies published in this table indicated that no hate crimes occurred in their jurisdictions during the quarter(s) for which they submitted reports to the Hate Crime program. Blanks indicate quarters for which agencies did not submit reports.

[2]Population figures are published only for the cities. The figures listed for the universities and colleges are student enrollment and were provided by the United States Department of Education for the 2006 school year, the most recent available. The enrollment figures include full-time and part-time students.

Table 95. Hate Crime Zero Data Submitted per Quarter, by State and Agency, 2007 *(Contd.)*

(Number.)

State	Agency type	Agency name	Zero data per quarter[1] 1st quarter	2nd quarter	3rd quarter	4th quarter	Popu-lation[2]	State	Agency type	Agency name	Zero data per quarter[1] 1st quarter	2nd quarter	3rd quarter	4th quarter	Popu-lation[2]
		Bloomfield	0	0	0	0	887			Hopkinsville	0	0	0		27,197
		Booneville	0	0			150			Horse Cave		0			2,345
		Brownsville	0	0			1,045			Independence	0	0		0	21,038
		Burkesville	0	0	0	0	1,730			Indian Hills	0	0	0	0	3,149
		Butler	0	0	0	0	648			Inez				0	450
		Cadiz		0	0	0	2,604			Irvine	0	0	0	0	2,699
		Calhoun	0			0	803			Irvington		0			1,421
		Calvert City	0	0	0	0	2,780			Jackson	0		0		2,401
		Campbellsburg	0	0	0	0	716			Jamestown	0	0	0	0	1,738
		Campbellsville		0	0	0	10,957			Jeffersontown	0		0	0	25,837
		Campton	0				411			Jenkins				0	2,288
		Caneyville			0	0	663			La Center	0		0	0	1,029
		Carlisle	0	0	0	0	2,133			La Grange	0	0	0	0	6,238
		Carrollton	0	0	0	0	3,888			Lakeside Park-Crestview Hills	0	0	0	0	6,205
		Catlettsburg	0	0	0		1,901			Lancaster	0	0			4,452
		Cave City	0	0	0	0	2,088			Lawrenceburg	0				9,710
		Central City	0	0	0	0	5,763			Lebanon	0	0	0		5,980
		Clarkson	0	0	0	0	839			Lebanon Junction	0	0	0	0	1,994
		Clinton			0		1,331			Leitchfield	0	0	0	0	6,561
		Cloverport		0	0	0	1,248			Lewisburg	0	0	0	0	924
		Cold Spring	0	0	0		5,758			Lewisport			0		1,658
		Columbia	0	0	0		4,195			Liberty	0	0		0	1,903
		Corbin	0	0		0	8,344			Lone Oak	0		0		437
		Crescent Springs	0	0	0		3,988			Ludlow	0		0		4,809
		Crofton	0	0			777			Lynch		0	0	0	838
		Cynthiana	0	0	0	0	6,291			Lynnview				0	980
		Danville	0		0	0	15,377			Madisonville	0	0	0	0	19,293
		Dawson Springs	0		0	0	2,947			Marion	0	0	0		3,022
		Dayton	0	0		0	5,443			Mayfield		0		0	10,326
		Earlington	0	0		0	1,593			Maysville	0				9,205
		Eddyville	0	0	0		2,408			McKee			0		864
		Edgewood		0	0	0	8,789			Millersburg	0			0	872
		Edmonton	0	0	0	0	1,624			Monticello			0		6,120
		Elizabethtown	0	0	0	0	23,547			Morehead	0	0	0	0	7,575
		Elkhorn City	0	0	0	0	1,023			Morganfield	0	0	0	0	3,365
		Elkton	0	0	0	0	1,962			Morgantown	0	0	0	0	2,538
		Eminence	0	0	0	0	2,264			Mount Olivet	0				293
		Erlanger	0	0	0		16,986			Mount Vernon	0	0			2,622
		Evarts		0	0	0	1,056			Mount Washington	0	0		0	12,334
		Falmouth	0	0	0	0	2,129			Muldraugh	0			0	1,309
		Flatwoods	0	0	0	0	7,647			Munfordville				0	1,624
		Fleming-Neon	0	0	0	0	805			New Castle	0		0	0	932
		Flemingsburg		0	0	0	3,105			New Haven	0		0	0	876
		Florence	0		0	0	27,405			Nicholasville	0	0	0	0	25,495
		Fort Mitchell	0		0	0	7,476			Northfield	0	0		0	1,018
		Fort Thomas	0	0	0	0	15,266			Nortonville	0	0	0	0	1,250
		Fort Wright	0	0	0	0	5,379			Oak Grove	0		0	0	7,303
		Fountain Run			0	0	244			Olive Hill	0	0	0	0	1,823
		Frankfort	0	0	0	0	26,984			Owensboro	0	0	0	0	55,702
		Franklin	0	0	0	0	8,101			Owenton	0				1,491
		Fulton	0	0	0	0	2,435			Owingsville			0	0	1,596
		Gamaliel	0				434			Paintsville	0	0	0		4,176
		Georgetown	0				20,997			Park Hills		0	0	0	2,748
		Glasgow	0	0	0	0	14,282			Pembroke				0	754
		Glencoe	0		0	0	251			Pewee Valley	0				1,598
		Graymoor-Devondale	0		0		3,008			Pikeville	0	0	0	0	6,331
		Grayson	0			0	3,997			Pineville	0	0			1,997
		Greensburg	0	0	0	0	2,408			Pioneer Village			0	0	2,687
		Guthrie		0			1,441			Pleasureville	0	0			894
		Hardinsburg	0		0	0	2,466			Powderly	0	0	0		892
		Harlan			0	0	1,893			Princeton	0	0	0	0	6,402
		Harrodsburg	0	0	0	0	8,164			Prospect	0	0			5,044
		Hartford	0	0			2,685			Raceland		0	0		2,548
		Hawesville	0				983			Radcliff	0	0	0	0	21,560
		Hazard	0	0	0		4,862			Ravenna	0		0		676
		Heritage Creek	0	0	0	0	1,654			Russell			0		3,598
		Highland Heights	0	0	0	0	5,708			Russell Springs	0	0	0		2,573
		Hillview	0	0	0	0	7,506			Russellville	0	0	0	0	7,351
		Hindman	0	0	0	0	768			Sadieville	0	0	0		309
		Hodgenville	0	0	0		2,781			Salyersville		0			1,601
		Hollow Creek		0			846			Scottsville	0	0	0	0	4,567
										Sebree	0	0		0	1,554

[1]Agencies published in this table indicated that no hate crimes occurred in their jurisdictions during the quarter(s) for which they submitted reports to the Hate Crime program. Blanks indicate quarters for which agencies did not submit reports.

[2]Population figures are published only for the cities. The figures listed for the universities and colleges are student enrollment and were provided by the United States Department of Education for the 2006 school year, the most recent available. The enrollment figures include full-time and part-time students.

Table 95. Hate Crime Zero Data Submitted per Quarter, by State and Agency, 2007 *(Contd.)*

(Number.)

State	Agency type	Agency name	Zero data per quarter[1]				Population[2]
			1st quarter	2nd quarter	3rd quarter	4th quarter	
		Shepherdsville	0	0	0	0	9,123
		Shively				0	15,621
		Silver Grove	0	0	0	0	1,158
		Smiths Grove	0	0	0	0	741
		Somerset	0	0	0	0	12,344
		Southgate	0	0	0	0	3,291
		Springfield	0	0	0	0	2,845
		Stamping Ground	0				660
		Stanford	0	0	0	0	3,467
		Stanton	0	0	0	0	3,153
		Sturgis	0	0	0	0	1,967
		Taylor Mill	0	0	0	0	6,682
		Taylorsville	0	0	0		1,226
		Trenton	0	0	0	0	425
		Uniontown		0	0	0	1,046
		Vanceburg	0	0	0	0	1,722
		Villa Hills	0	0	0	0	7,672
		Vine Grove	0	0	0		3,915
		Warsaw		0	0	0	1,832
		West Liberty		0	0	0	3,362
		West Point	0	0	0		992
		Wilder	0	0	0		3,037
		Williamsburg	0	0		0	5,192
		Williamstown	0	0	0	0	3,465
		Wilmore	0	0	0	0	5,862
		Winchester				0	16,515
		Worthington	0	0	0		1,686
	Universities and Colleges	Eastern Kentucky University	0	0	0	0	15,763
		Morehead State University	0	0	0	0	8,958
		Murray State University	0	0	0	0	10,298
		Northern Kentucky University	0	0	0		14,617
		University of Louisville	0	0	0	0	20,785
		Western Kentucky University	0	0	0	0	18,660
	Metropolitan Counties	Bourbon	0	0	0	0	
		Boyd	0	0	0	0	
		Bracken	0	0	0	0	
		Bullitt	0	0	0	0	
		Campbell	0	0	0	0	
		Campbell County Police Department	0	0	0	0	
		Christian	0				
		Clark	0		0	0	
		Fayette	0		0		
		Gallatin County Police Department	0	0	0	0	
		Grant	0	0	0		
		Greenup	0	0	0	0	
		Hardin	0	0	0	0	
		Henderson	0	0	0	0	
		Henry	0	0	0		
		Jefferson	0	0	0	0	
		Jessamine	0	0	0	0	
		Kenton	0	0	0	0	
		McLean	0	0	0	0	
		Meade		0	0	0	
		Nelson	0	0	0	0	
		Oldham	0	0	0		

State	Agency type	Agency name	Zero data per quarter[1]				Population[2]
			1st quarter	2nd quarter	3rd quarter	4th quarter	
		Oldham County Police Department	0	0	0	0	
		Pendleton	0	0	0	0	
		Scott	0			0	
		Shelby		0		0	
		Spencer	0	0	0		
		Trigg	0	0			
		Warren	0	0	0	0	
		Webster	0	0	0	0	
		Woodford	0	0	0	0	
	Nonmetropolitan Counties	Allen	0	0			
		Anderson	0				
		Ballard	0	0	0	0	
		Barren	0	0	0	0	
		Bath	0	0			
		Bell	0		0		
		Boyle	0	0	0	0	
		Breathitt	0				
		Butler	0	0	0	0	
		Caldwell	0	0			
		Calloway	0		0	0	
		Carroll		0	0	0	
		Carter	0	0	0	0	
		Casey		0	0	0	
		Clinton				0	
		Crittenden	0	0	0	0	
		Cumberland	0	0	0	0	
		Elliott	0	0	0		
		Estill	0				
		Fleming	0			0	
		Floyd	0			0	
		Franklin	0	0	0	0	
		Fulton	0	0	0	0	
		Garrard	0	0	0		
		Graves	0	0	0		
		Grayson	0	0	0	0	
		Harlan	0	0	0		
		Harrison		0	0	0	
		Hart	0	0	0	0	
		Hickman	0		0		
		Hopkins		0	0	0	
		Jackson	0	0	0	0	
		Johnson				0	
		Knott	0		0	0	
		Knox	0		0		
		Laurel			0		
		Letcher		0	0		
		Lewis	0		0		
		Lincoln			0		
		Livingston	0	0	0	0	
		Logan	0	0	0	0	
		Lyon	0	0	0	0	
		Madison			0	0	
		Magoffin	0	0	0	0	
		Marion	0	0	0	0	
		Marshall	0	0	0	0	
		McCracken	0		0	0	
		McCreary		0	0		
		Metcalfe	0	0	0		
		Montgomery		0	0		
		Muhlenberg	0	0	0	0	
		Nicholas	0	0			
		Ohio	0	0	0	0	
		Owen	0		0	0	
		Owsley	0	0	0	0	
		Pike	0	0	0	0	
		Powell				0	
		Rockcastle	0	0	0	0	
		Rowan		0	0	0	
		Simpson		0	0	0	
		Taylor	0	0	0	0	

[1] Agencies published in this table indicated that no hate crimes occurred in their jurisdictions during the quarter(s) for which they submitted reports to the Hate Crime program. Blanks indicate quarters for which agencies did not submit reports.

[2] Population figures are published only for the cities. The figures listed for the universities and colleges are student enrollment and were provided by the United States Department of Education for the 2006 school year, the most recent available. The enrollment figures include full-time and part-time students.

Table 95. Hate Crime Zero Data Submitted per Quarter, by State and Agency, 2007 *(Contd.)*

(Number.)

State	Agency type	Agency name	1st quarter	2nd quarter	3rd quarter	4th quarter	Population[2]
		Todd	0		0		
		Union	0	0	0	0	
		Washington	0	0	0		
		Wayne	0	0	0	0	
		Wolfe	0	0	0	0	
	Other Agencies	Alcohol Beverage Control	0				
		Buffalo Trace-Gateway Narcotics Task Force	0	0	0	0	
		Cincinnati-Northern Kentucky International Airport	0	0	0	0	
		Fish and Wildlife Enforcement	0	0	0		
		FIVCO Area Drug Task Force				0	
		Forestry Enforcement	0	0	0		
		Greater Hardin County Narcotics Task Force	0	0	0		
		Kentucky Horse Park	0	0		0	
		Lake Cumberland Area Drug Enforcement Task Force	0	0		0	
		Lexington Bluegrass Airport	0				
		Louisville Regional Airport Authority				0	
		McCracken County Public Schools	0		0	0	
		Motor Vehicle Enforcement	0	0	0		
		Northern Kentucky Narcotics Enforcement Unit	0	0	0	0	
		Pennyrile Narcotics Task Force		0	0	0	
LOUISIANA ..	Cities	Addis	0	0	0	0	3,145
		Baker	0	0	0	0	13,600
		Basile	0	0	0	0	2,392
		Bernice	0	0	0	0	1,677
		Bossier City	0	0	0	0	61,993
		Coushatta	0	0	0	0	2,166
		Covington	0	0	0	0	9,745
		Denham Springs		0	0	0	10,552
		Farmerville	0	0	0	0	3,567
		French Settlement	0	0	0	0	1,100
		Golden Meadow	0	0	0	0	2,158
		Gonzales	0	0	0	0	9,067
		Gramercy	0	0	0	0	6,946
		Gretna	0	0	0	0	16,240
		Harahan	0	0	0	0	9,212
		Haughton	0	0	0	0	2,997
		Homer	0	0	0	0	3,472
		Houma	0	0	0	0	32,597
		Jackson	0		0	0	3,714
		Jeanerette	0	0	0	0	6,015
		Kaplan	0	0			5,192
		Kenner	0	0	0	0	66,473
		Kinder	0	0	0	0	2,148
		Lake Arthur	0	0	0	0	2,894
		Lake Charles	0				69,966
		Leesville	0	0			5,763
		Mandeville			0		12,346
		Mansfield	0	0	0	0	5,466
		Morgan City	0				11,810
		Olla	0	0	0	0	1,352
		Pearl River	0				2,170
		Plaquemine	0	0	0	0	6,627
		Pollock	0	0		0	384
		Ruston	0	0	0	0	20,532
		Sterlington	0	0	0	0	1,240
		Tallulah	0	0	0	0	7,883
		Thibodaux	0	0	0	0	14,501
		Tickfaw	0	0	0	0	687
		Vinton	0	0	0	0	3,131
		Washington	0				1,064
		Westlake	0		0	0	4,526
		West Monroe	0	0	0	0	12,989
		Westwego	0	0	0	0	9,957
		Zachary			0	0	13,428
	Universities and Colleges	Delgado Community College	0	0	0	0	11,916
		Louisiana State University: Baton Rouge[3]	0	0	0	0	
		Eunice	0	0	0	0	2,749
		Shreveport	0	0		0	4,023
		Louisiana Tech University	0	0	0	0	11,203
		McNeese State University	0	0	0	0	8,327
		Nicholls State University	0	0	0	0	6,804
		Northwestern State University	0	0	0	0	9,431
		Southeastern Louisiana University	0	0	0	0	15,106
		Southern University and A&M College, New Orleans	0		0	0	2,197
		Tulane University	0	0	0	0	10,237
		University of Louisiana, Monroe	0		0	0	8,576
		University of New Orleans		0			11,747
	Metropolitan Counties	Ascension	0	0	0	0	
		Cameron	0	0	0	0	
		De Soto	0				
		Grant	0	0	0	0	
		Iberville	0	0	0	0	
		Lafayette	0	0	0	0	
		Livingston	0	0	0		
		Plaquemines	0	0	0	0	
		Pointe Coupee	0	0	0	0	
		St. Bernard	0	0			
		St. Charles	0	0	0	0	
		St. John the Baptist	0	0	0	0	
		St. Martin	0	0			

[1]Agencies published in this table indicated that no hate crimes occurred in their jurisdictions during the quarter(s) for which they submitted reports to the Hate Crime program. Blanks indicate quarters for which agencies did not submit reports.

[3]Student enrollment figures were not available.

Table 95. Hate Crime Zero Data Submitted per Quarter, by State and Agency, 2007 (Contd.)

(Number.)

State	Agency type	Agency name	1st quarter	2nd quarter	3rd quarter	4th quarter	Population[2]
		St. Tammany	0	0	0	0	
		West Baton Rouge	0	0	0	0	
	Nonmetropolitan Counties	Acadia	0	0	0	0	
		Assumption	0				
		Beauregard	0	0	0	0	
		Franklin	0	0	0	0	
		Jackson	0			0	
		Jefferson Davis	0	0	0	0	
		Madison	0	0	0	0	
		Morehouse	0	0	0	0	
		Natchitoches	0	0	0		
		Red River	0			0	
		Sabine	0	0	0	0	
		St. Landry	0	0	0	0	
		Vermilion	0	0	0	0	
		Vernon	0	0	0	0	
		Webster	0				
		West Carroll	0				
	Other Agencies	Department of Public Safety, State Capitol Detail	0	0	0	0	
MAINE	**Cities**	Ashland	0	0	0	0	1,460
		Auburn	0	0	0	0	23,150
		Bath	0	0	0	0	9,175
		Belfast	0	0	0	0	6,866
		Berwick	0	0	0	0	7,603
		Bethel	0	0	0	0	2,671
		Boothbay Harbor	0	0	0	0	2,340
		Brewer	0	0	0	0	9,101
		Bridgton	0	0	0	0	5,325
		Brownville	0	0	0	0	1,306
		Brunswick	0	0	0	0	22,048
		Bucksport	0	0	0	0	4,969
		Buxton	0	0	0	0	8,284
		Camden	0	0	0	0	5,327
		Cape Elizabeth	0	0	0	0	8,806
		Caribou	0	0	0	0	8,279
		Carrabassett Valley	0	0	0	0	467
		Clinton	0	0	0	0	3,400
		Cumberland	0	0	0	0	7,728
		Damariscotta	0	0	0	0	1,965
		Dexter	0	0	0	0	3,720
		Dover-Foxcroft	0	0	0	0	4,391
		East Millinocket	0	0	0	0	3,171
		Eastport	0	0	0	0	1,575
		Ellsworth	0	0	0	0	7,165
		Fairfield	0	0	0	0	6,808
		Falmouth	0	0	0	0	10,591
		Farmington	0	0	0	0	7,603
		Fort Fairfield	0	0	0	0	3,510
		Fort Kent	0	0	0	0	4,202
		Freeport	0	0	0	0	8,190
		Fryeburg	0	0	0	0	3,363
		Gardiner	0	0	0	0	6,174
		Gouldsboro	0	0	0	0	2,040
		Greenville	0	0	0	0	1,759
		Hallowell	0	0	0	0	2,521
		Hampden	0	0	0	0	6,847
		Holden	0	0	0	0	2,961
		Houlton	0	0	0	0	6,258
		Jay	0	0	0	0	4,847
		Kennebunkport	0	0	0	0	4,070
		Kittery	0	0	0	0	10,645
		Limestone	0	0	0	0	2,298
		Lincoln	0	0	0	0	5,235
		Lisbon	0	0	0	0	9,474
		Livermore Falls	0	0	0	0	3,200
		Machias	0	0	0	0	2,191

State	Agency type	Agency name	1st quarter	2nd quarter	3rd quarter	4th quarter	Population[2]
		Madawaska	0	0	0	0	4,402
		Madison	0	0	0	0	4,673
		Mexico	0	0	0	0	2,932
		Milbridge	0	0	0	0	1,316
		Millinocket	0	0	0	0	4,927
		Monmouth	0	0	0	0	3,849
		Mount Desert	0	0	0	0	2,214
		Newport	0	0	0	0	3,106
		North Berwick	0	0	0	0	4,911
		Norway	0	0	0	0	4,846
		Oakland	0	0	0	0	6,239
		Oxford	0	0	0	0	3,954
		Paris	0	0	0	0	5,048
		Phippsburg	0	0	0	0	2,205
		Pittsfield	0	0	0	0	4,296
		Presque Isle	0	0	0	0	9,217
		Rangeley	0	0	0	0	1,168
		Richmond	0	0	0	0	3,440
		Rockland	0	0	0	0	7,582
		Rockport	0	0	0	0	3,590
		Rumford	0	0	0	0	6,405
		Saco	0	0	0	0	18,509
		Scarborough	0	0	0	0	19,187
		Searsport	0	0	0	0	2,668
		Skowhegan	0	0	0	0	8,876
		South Berwick	0	0	0	0	7,350
		Southwest Harbor	0	0	0	0	1,982
		Swan's Island	0	0	0	0	311
		Thomaston	0	0	0	0	4,203
		Topsham	0	0	0	0	10,073
		Van Buren	0	0	0	0	2,520
		Veazie	0	0	0	0	1,873
		Waldoboro	0	0	0	0	5,123
		Washburn	0	0	0	0	1,616
		Wells	0	0	0	0	10,142
		Westbrook	0	0	0	0	16,188
		Wilton	0	0	0	0	4,210
		Windham	0	0	0	0	16,814
		Winslow	0	0	0	0	7,979
		Winter Harbor	0	0	0	0	973
		Winthrop	0	0	0	0	6,514
		Wiscasset	0	0	0	0	3,904
		Yarmouth	0	0	0	0	8,106
	Universities and Colleges	University of Maine:					
		Farmington	0	0	0	0	2,421
		Orono	0	0	0	0	11,797
	Metropolitan Counties	Androscoggin	0	0	0	0	
		Sagadahoc	0	0	0	0	
	Nonmetropolitan Counties	Aroostook	0	0	0	0	
		Franklin	0	0	0	0	
		Hancock	0	0	0	0	
		Kennebec	0	0	0	0	
		Knox	0	0	0	0	
		Lincoln	0	0	0	0	
		Piscataquis	0	0	0	0	
		Somerset	0	0	0	0	
		Washington	0	0	0	0	
	State Police Agencies	Maine State Police, Headquarters		0			
		State Police: Androscoggin County	0	0	0	0	
		Aroostook County	0	0	0	0	
		Cumberland County	0	0	0	0	

[1] Agencies published in this table indicated that no hate crimes occurred in their jurisdictions during the quarter(s) for which they submitted reports to the Hate Crime program. Blanks indicate quarters for which agencies did not submit reports.

[2] Population figures are published only for the cities. The figures listed for the universities and colleges are student enrollment and were provided by the United States Department of Education for the 2006 school year, the most recent available. The enrollment figures include full-time and part-time students.

Table 95. Hate Crime Zero Data Submitted per Quarter, by State and Agency, 2007 *(Contd.)*

(Number.)

State	Agency type	Agency name	1st quarter	2nd quarter	3rd quarter	4th quarter	Population[2]
MARYLAND	Cities	Franklin County	0	0	0	0	
		Hancock County	0	0	0	0	
		Knox County	0	0	0	0	
		Lincoln County	0	0	0	0	
		Oxford County	0	0	0	0	
		Penobscot County	0	0	0	0	
		Piscataquis County	0	0	0	0	
		Sagadahoc County	0	0	0	0	
		Somerset County	0	0	0	0	
		Waldo County	0	0	0	0	
		Washington County	0	0	0	0	
		York County	0	0	0	0	
		Aberdeen	0	0	0	0	14,187
		Baltimore City Sheriff	0	0	0	0	
		Berlin	0	0	0	0	3,812
		Berwyn Heights	0	0	0	0	3,045
		Bladensburg	0	0	0	0	7,849
		Boonsboro	0	0	0	0	3,286
		Bowie			0	0	53,672
		Brunswick	0	0	0	0	5,282
		Capitol Heights	0	0	0	0	4,259
		Centreville	0	0	0	0	3,099
		Cheverly	0	0	0	0	6,614
		Chevy Chase Village			0	0	2,779
		Cottage City	0	0	0	0	1,166
		Crisfield	0	0	0	0	2,804
		Cumberland	0	0	0	0	20,654
		Delmar	0	0	0	0	2,590
		Denton	0	0	0	0	3,602
		District Heights	0	0	0	0	6,253
		Easton	0	0	0	0	14,249
		Edmonston	0	0	0	0	1,381
		Elkton	0	0	0	0	15,228
		Fairmount Heights	0	0	0	0	1,554
		Federalsburg	0	0	0	0	2,647
		Forest Heights	0	0	0	0	2,656
		Frostburg	0	0	0	0	7,809
		Fruitland	0	0	0	0	4,193
		Glenarden	0	0	0	0	6,340
		Greenbelt	0	0	0	0	22,090
		Greensboro	0	0	0	0	2,016
		Hagerstown	0	0	0	0	39,263
		Hampstead	0	0	0	0	5,535
		Hancock	0	0	0	0	1,721
		Havre de Grace	0	0	0	0	12,584
		Hurlock	0	0	0	0	2,015
		Hyattsville	0	0	0	0	15,152
		Landover Hills	0	0	0	0	1,575
		La Plata	0	0	0	0	9,090
		Laurel	0	0	0	0	22,086
		Lonaconing	0	0	0	0	1,137
		Luke	0	0	0	0	74
		Manchester	0	0	0	0	3,609
		Morningside	0	0	0	0	1,305
		Mount Rainier	0	0	0	0	8,660
		New Carrollton	0	0	0	0	12,712
		North Brentwood	0	0		0	482
		North East	0	0	0	0	2,856
		Oakland	0	0	0	0	1,869
		Ocean City	0	0	0	0	7,005
		Ocean Pines	0	0	0	0	11,134
		Oxford	0	0	0	0	735
		Perryville	0	0	0	0	3,826
		Pocomoke City	0	0	0	0	3,863
		Port Deposit	0	0		0	704
		Preston	0	0	0	0	647
		Princess Anne	0	0	0	0	2,934
		Ridgely	0	0	0	0	1,485
		Rising Sun	0	0	0	0	1,821
		Riverdale Park	0	0	0	0	6,584
		Rock Hall	0	0	0	0	1,424
		Salisbury	0	0	0	0	27,727
		Seat Pleasant	0	0	0	0	5,020
		Smithsburg	0	0	0	0	3,031
		Snow Hill	0	0	0	0	2,278
		St. Michaels	0	0	0	0	1,088
		Sykesville	0	0	0	0	4,499
		Takoma Park	0	0	0	0	18,539
		Taneytown	0	0	0	0	5,533
		Thurmont	0	0	0	0	6,092
		Trappe			0	0	1,179
		University Park	0	0	0	0	2,379
		Upper Marlboro	0	0	0	0	681
		Westernport	0	0	0	0	1,971
		Westminster	0	0	0	0	18,036
	Universities and Colleges	Bowie State University	0	0	0	0	5,291
		Coppin State University	0	0	0	0	4,104
		Morgan State University	0	0	0	0	6,705
		Salisbury University	0	0	0	0	7,383
		University of Baltimore	0	0	0	0	4,948
		University of Maryland: Baltimore City	0	0	0	0	5,636
		Baltimore County	0	0	0	0	11,798
		Eastern Shore	0	0	0	0	4,130
	Metropolitan Counties	Allegany	0	0	0	0	
		Anne Arundel	0	0	0	0	
		Baltimore County	0	0	0	0	
		Calvert	0	0	0	0	
		Charles	0	0	0	0	
		Howard	0	0	0	0	
		Montgomery	0	0	0	0	
		Prince George's	0	0	0	0	
		Queen Anne's	0	0	0	0	
		Somerset	0	0	0	0	
		Washington	0	0	0	0	
		Wicomico	0	0	0	0	
	Nonmetropolitan Counties	Caroline	0	0	0	0	
		Dorchester	0	0	0	0	
		Garrett	0	0	0	0	
		Kent	0	0	0	0	
		St. Mary's	0	0	0	0	
		Talbot	0	0	0	0	
		Worcester	0	0	0	0	
	State Police Agencies	Maryland State Police, Headquarters	0	0	0	0	
		State Police: Allegany County	0	0	0	0	
		Anne Arundel County	0	0	0	0	
		Baltimore City	0	0	0	0	
		Baltimore County	0	0	0	0	
		Calvert County	0	0	0	0	
		Caroline County	0	0	0	0	

[1]Agencies published in this table indicated that no hate crimes occurred in their jurisdictions during the quarter(s) for which they submitted reports to the Hate Crime program. Blanks indicate quarters for which agencies did not submit reports.

[2]Population figures are published only for the cities. The figures listed for the universities and colleges are student enrollment and were provided by the United States Department of Education for the 2006 school year, the most recent available. The enrollment figures include full-time and part-time students.

Table 95. Hate Crime Zero Data Submitted per Quarter, by State and Agency, 2007 *(Contd.)*

(Number.)

State	Agency type	Agency name	1st quarter	2nd quarter	3rd quarter	4th quarter	Population[2]
		Charles County	0	0	0	0	
		Dorchester County	0	0	0	0	
		Frederick County	0	0	0	0	
		Garrett County	0	0	0	0	
		Harford County	0	0	0	0	
		Howard County	0	0	0	0	
		Kent County	0	0	0	0	
		Montgomery County	0	0	0	0	
		Prince George's County	0	0	0	0	
		Queen Anne's County	0	0	0	0	
		Somerset County	0	0	0	0	
		St. Mary's County	0	0	0	0	
		Talbot County	0	0	0	0	
		Washington County	0	0	0	0	
	Other Agencies	Comptroller of the Treasury, Field Enforcement Division	0	0	0	0	
		Department of Public Safety and Correctional Services, Internal Investigations Unit	0		0	0	
		General Services: Annapolis, Anne Arundel County	0	0	0	0	
		Baltimore City	0	0	0	0	
		Maryland-National Capital Park Police, Montgomery County	0	0	0	0	
		Natural Resources Police	0	0	0	0	
		Rosewood	0	0	0	0	
		Springfield Hospital	0	0	0	0	
		Transit Administration	0	0	0	0	
		Transportation Authority	0	0	0	0	
MASSACHU- SETTS	**Cities**	Abington	0	0	0	0	16,673
		Acushnet	0	0	0	0	10,575
		Adams	0	0	0	0	8,316
		Agawam	0	0	0	0	28,573
		Amesbury	0	0	0	0	16,551
		Aquinnah				0	356
		Ashburnham	0	0	0	0	6,065
		Ashland	0	0	0	0	15,818
		Athol	0	0	0	0	11,721
		Avon	0	0	0	0	4,310
		Barre	0	0	0	0	5,467
		Becket	0	0	0	0	1,804
		Bedford	0	0	0	0	12,862
		Belchertown	0	0	0	0	14,268
		Berkley	0	0	0	0	6,494
		Berlin	0	0	0	0	2,771
		Blackstone	0	0	0	0	9,067
		Bolton	0	0	0	0	4,517
		Bourne	0	0	0	0	19,308
		Boxborough	0	0	0	0	5,106
		Boxford	0	0	0	0	8,155
		Boylston	0	0	0	0	4,295
		Braintree	0	0	0	0	34,147
		Brewster	0	0	0	0	10,158
		Bridgewater	0	0	0	0	25,767
		Brimfield	0	0	0	0	3,744
		Canton	0		0	0	21,890
		Carlisle		0	0	0	4,870
		Charlemont		0	0	0	1,381
		Charlton	0	0	0	0	12,765
		Chatham	0	0	0	0	6,811
		Chelsea	0	0	0	0	32,439
		Cheshire	0	0	0	0	3,335
		Chicopee	0	0	0	0	54,414
		Clinton	0	0	0	0	14,247
		Cohasset	0	0	0	0	7,213
		Concord	0	0	0	0	16,766
		Dedham	0	0	0	0	23,653
		Deerfield	0	0	0	0	4,763
		Dover	0	0	0	0	5,650
		Dracut	0	0	0	0	29,444
		Dudley	0	0	0	0	10,951
		East Bridgewater	0	0	0	0	14,077
		East Brookfield	0	0	0	0	2,095
		Eastham	0	0	0	0	5,519
		Easthampton	0	0	0	0	16,082
		East Longmeadow	0	0	0	0	15,061
		Easton	0	0	0	0	23,142
		Edgartown			0	0	3,939
		Erving	0	0	0	0	1,574
		Fairhaven	0	0	0	0	16,268
		Fall River	0	0			91,413
		Fitchburg	0	0	0	0	40,180
		Framingham	0	0	0	0	64,482
		Franklin	0	0	0	0	31,478
		Freetown	0	0	0	0	9,042
		Gardner	0	0	0	0	20,813
		Georgetown	0	0	0	0	8,210
		Gloucester	0	0	0	0	30,597
		Goshen	0	0	0	0	965
		Grafton	0	0	0	0	17,750
		Granby	0	0	0	0	6,381
		Great Barrington	0	0	0	0	7,423
		Groton	0	0	0	0	10,737
		Groveland	0	0	0	0	6,863
		Hadley	0	0	0	0	4,817
		Halifax	0	0	0	0	7,834
		Hampden	0	0	0	0	5,349
		Hanover	0	0	0	0	14,266
		Hanson	0	0	0	0	10,054
		Hardwick	0	0	0	0	2,670
		Harvard	0	0	0	0	6,062
		Harwich	0	0	0	0	12,573
		Hatfield	0	0	0	0	3,266
		Hingham	0	0	0	0	22,059
		Hinsdale	0	0	0	0	1,782
		Holden	0	0	0	0	16,816
		Holliston	0	0	0	0	13,903
		Holyoke	0	0	0	0	39,769
		Hopedale	0	0	0	0	6,277
		Hopkinton	0	0	0	0	14,294
		Hubbardston	0	0	0	0	4,494
		Hudson	0	0	0	0	19,595
		Hull	0	0	0	0	11,261
		Ipswich	0	0	0	0	13,326
		Kingston	0	0	0	0	12,581
		Lakeville	0	0	0	0	10,770
		Lawrence	0	0	0	0	70,462
		Lee				0	5,842

[1] Agencies published in this table indicated that no hate crimes occurred in their jurisdictions during the quarter(s) for which they submitted reports to the Hate Crime program. Blanks indicate quarters for which agencies did not submit reports.

[2] Population figures are published only for the cities. The figures listed for the universities and colleges are student enrollment and were provided by the United States Department of Education for the 2006 school year, the most recent available. The enrollment figures include full-time and part-time students.

Table 95. Hate Crime Zero Data Submitted per Quarter, by State and Agency, 2007 (Contd.)

(Number.)

State	Agency type	Agency name	1st quarter	2nd quarter	3rd quarter	4th quarter	Population[2]
		Leicester	0	0	0	0	11,077
		Lenox	0	0	0	0	5,169
		Leominster	0	0	0	0	41,602
		Lincoln	0	0	0	0	7,929
		Littleton	0	0	0	0	8,713
		Longmeadow	0	0	0	0	15,465
		Ludlow	0	0	0	0	22,066
		Lunenburg	0	0	0	0	10,105
		Lynnfield	0	0	0	0	11,429
		Manchester-by-the-Sea			0	0	5,301
		Marblehead	0	0	0	0	20,194
		Marion	0	0	0	0	5,313
		Marlborough	0	0	0	0	38,227
		Marshfield	0	0	0	0	24,915
		Mashpee	0	0	0	0	14,552
		Mattapoisett	0	0	0	0	6,502
		Maynard	0	0	0	0	10,150
		Medfield	0	0	0	0	12,299
		Medway	0	0	0	0	12,867
		Melrose	0	0	0	0	26,549
		Mendon	0	0	0	0	5,837
		Merrimac	0	0	0	0	6,420
		Methuen	0	0	0	0	44,333
		Middleton	0	0	0	0	9,562
		Millbury	0	0	0	0	13,711
		Millis	0	0	0	0	7,977
		Millville	0	0	0	0	2,988
		Montague	0	0	0	0	8,359
		Monterey	0	0	0	0	967
		Nahant	0	0	0	0	3,544
		Natick	0	0	0	0	31,854
		Needham	0	0	0	0	28,343
		Newbury	0	0	0	0	6,992
		Newburyport	0	0	0	0	17,317
		New Salem	0	0	0	0	990
		Norfolk	0	0	0	0	10,596
		North Adams	0	0	0	0	13,738
		North Andover	0	0	0	0	27,271
		Northborough	0	0	0	0	14,783
		Northbridge	0	0	0	0	14,596
		North Brookfield	0	0	0	0	4,847
		North Reading	0	0	0		13,970
		Norton	0	0	0	0	19,423
		Norwell	0	0	0	0	10,466
		Norwood	0	0	0	0	28,336
		Oak Bluffs		0	0	0	3,768
		Oakham	0	0	0	0	1,946
		Orange	0	0	0	0	7,762
		Orleans	0	0	0	0	6,412
		Paxton	0	0	0	0	4,591
		Pembroke	0	0	0	0	18,932
		Pepperell	0	0	0	0	11,454
		Princeton	0	0	0	0	3,547
		Provincetown	0	0	0	0	3,411
		Raynham	0	0	0	0	13,975
		Reading	0	0	0	0	23,004
		Rehoboth	0	0	0	0	11,551
		Rockland	0	0	0	0	17,914
		Rockport	0	0	0	0	7,677
		Rowley	0	0	0	0	5,927
		Royalston	0	0	0	0	1,399
		Rutland	0	0	0	0	7,800
		Salisbury	0	0	0	0	8,506
		Sandwich	0	0	0	0	20,584
		Saugus	0	0	0	0	27,214
		Savoy	0	0	0	0	732
		Seekonk	0	0	0	0	13,681
		Shelburne	0	0	0	0	2,045
		Sherborn	0	0	0	0	4,217
		Shirley	0	0	0	0	7,661
		Shrewsbury	0	0	0	0	33,485
		Somerset	0	0	0	0	18,473

State	Agency type	Agency name	1st quarter	2nd quarter	3rd quarter	4th quarter	Population[2]
		Southampton	0	0	0	0	6,010
		Southbridge	0	0	0	0	17,109
		South Hadley	0	0	0	0	17,011
		Southwick	0	0	0	0	9,719
		Spencer	0	0	0	0	12,153
		Sterling	0	0	0	0	7,927
		Stockbridge	0	0	0	0	2,256
		Stoneham				0	21,374
		Stoughton	0	0	0	0	26,814
		Stow	0	0	0	0	6,263
		Sturbridge	0	0	0	0	9,141
		Sudbury	0	0	0	0	17,061
		Sutton	0	0	0	0	9,154
		Swampscott	0	0	0	0	14,097
		Swansea	0	0	0	0	16,271
		Taunton	0	0	0	0	56,091
		Templeton	0	0	0	0	7,812
		Tewksbury	0	0	0	0	29,450
		Tisbury			0	0	3,806
		Topsfield	0	0	0	0	6,128
		Townsend	0	0	0	0	9,343
		Truro	0	0	0	0	2,163
		Tyngsboro	0	0	0	0	11,584
		Upton	0	0	0	0	6,597
		Wakefield	0	0	0	0	24,557
		Wales	0	0	0	0	1,853
		Walpole	0	0	0	0	23,199
		Ware	0	0	0	0	10,031
		Warren	0	0	0		5,141
		Watertown	0	0	0	0	32,065
		Wayland	0	0	0	0	12,954
		Webster	0	0	0	0	16,886
		Wellesley	0	0	0	0	26,966
		Wellfleet	0	0	0	0	2,798
		Wenham	0	0	0	0	4,609
		Westborough	0	0	0	0	18,740
		West Bridgewater	0	0	0		6,795
		West Brookfield	0	0			3,879
		Westfield	0	0	0	0	40,518
		Westford	0	0	0	0	21,624
		West Newbury	0	0	0	0	4,306
		Weston	0	0	0		11,665
		Westport	0	0	0	0	15,280
		West Tisbury	0	0	0	0	2,673
		Westwood	0	0	0	0	13,790
		Weymouth	0	0	0	0	53,553
		Whately	0	0	0	0	1,578
		Wilbraham	0	0	0	0	14,123
		Williamsburg	0	0	0	0	2,440
		Williamstown	0	0	0	0	8,159
		Winchendon	0	0	0	0	10,221
		Woburn	0	0	0	0	36,996
		Worcester	0	0	0	0	175,825
		Wrentham	0	0	0	0	11,215
		Yarmouth	0	0	0	0	24,304
	Universities and Colleges	Brandeis University	0	0	0	0	5,313
		Bristol Community College	0	0	0	0	6,927
		Fitchburg State College	0	0	0	0	5,508
		Holyoke Community College	0	0	0	0	6,297
		Lasell College	0	0	0	0	1,275
		Massachusetts College of Art	0	0	0	0	2,286
		Massachusetts College of Liberal Arts	0	0	0	0	1,805

[1]Agencies published in this table indicated that no hate crimes occurred in their jurisdictions during the quarter(s) for which they submitted reports to the Hate Crime program. Blanks indicate quarters for which agencies did not submit reports.

[2]Population figures are published only for the cities. The figures listed for the universities and colleges are student enrollment and were provided by the United States Department of Education for the 2006 school year, the most recent available. The enrollment figures include full-time and part-time students.

Table 95. Hate Crime Zero Data Submitted per Quarter, by State and Agency, 2007 *(Contd.)*

(Number.)

State	Agency type	Agency name	1st quarter	2nd quarter	3rd quarter	4th quarter	Population[2]
		Massasoit Community College	0	0	0	0	6,975
		Mount Holyoke College	0	0	0	0	2,153
		North Shore Community College	0	0	0	0	6,910
		Salem State College	0	0	0	0	10,230
		Springfield College	0	0	0	0	4,994
		Tufts University: Medford	0	0	0	0	9,638
		Suffolk[3]	0	0	0	0	
		Worcester[3]	0	0	0	0	
		University of Massachusetts, Dartmouth	0	0	0	0	8,756
		Wellesley College	0	0	0	0	2,370
		Western New England College	0	0	0	0	3,653
	State Police Agencies	State Police:					
		Barnstable County	0	0	0	0	
		Berkshire County	0	0	0	0	
		Bristol County	0	0	0	0	
		Dukes County	0	0	0	0	
		Essex County	0	0	0	0	
		Franklin County	0	0	0	0	
		Hampden County	0	0	0	0	
		Hampshire County	0	0	0	0	
		Middlesex County	0	0	0	0	
		Norfolk County	0	0	0	0	
		Plymouth County	0	0	0	0	
		Suffolk County	0	0	0	0	
		Worcester County	0	0	0	0	
	Other Agencies	Massachusetts Bay Transportation Authority:					
		Bristol County	0	0	0	0	
		Essex County	0	0	0	0	
		Norfolk County	0	0	0	0	
		Plymouth County	0	0	0	0	
		Worcester County	0	0	0	0	
MICHIGAN....	**Cities**	Adrian Township	0	0	0	0	7,241
		Algonac	0	0	0	0	4,585
		Allegan	0	0	0	0	4,963
		Allen Park	0	0	0	0	27,384
		Alma	0	0	0	0	9,231
		Almont	0	0	0	0	2,863
		Alpena	0	0	0	0	10,554
		Armada	0	0	0	0	1,640
		Auburn	0	0	0	0	2,058
		Bad Axe	0	0	0	0	3,163
		Bangor	0	0	0	0	1,881
		Baraga	0	0	0	0	1,242
		Bath Township	0	0	0	0	11,721
		Battle Creek	0	0	0	0	62,143
		Belding	0	0	0	0	5,872
		Belleville	0	0	0	0	3,766
		Beverly Hills	0	0	0	0	9,955
		Big Rapids	0	0	0	0	10,536
		Birch Run	0	0	0	0	1,700
		Blackman Township	0	0	0	0	25,461
		Bloomfield Hills	0	0	0	0	3,818
		Bloomingdale	0	0	0	0	504
		Boyne City	0	0	0	0	3,193
		Breckenridge	0	0	0	0	1,303
		Bridgeport Township	0	0	0	0	11,134
		Bronson	0	0	0	0	2,294
		Brown City	0	0	0	0	1,294
		Brownstown Township	0	0	0	0	30,336
		Buena Vista Township	0	0	0	0	9,631
		Burr Oak	0	0	0	0	759
		Calumet	0	0	0	0	797
		Cambridge Township	0	0	0	0	6,026
		Caro	0	0	0	0	4,136
		Carrollton Township	0	0	0	0	6,128
		Carsonville	0	0	0	0	486
		Caseville	0	0	0		870
		Caspian	0	0	0	0	2,082
		Cass City	0	0	0	0	2,568
		Cassopolis	0	0	0	0	1,792
		Cedar Springs	0	0	0	0	3,287
		Central Lake	0	0	0	0	985
		Charlevoix	0	0	0	0	2,692
		Charlotte	0	0	0	0	9,047
		Cheboygan	0	0	0	0	5,114
		Chocolay Township	0	0	0	0	5,989
		Clarkston	0	0	0	0	920
		Clayton Township	0	0	0	0	7,885
		Clay Township	0	0	0	0	9,848
		Clinton	0	0	0	0	2,439
		Coldwater	0	0	0	0	10,711
		Coleman	0	0	0	0	1,252
		Colon	0	0	0	0	1,173
		Columbia Township	0	0	0	0	7,734
		Concord	0	0		0	1,110
		Corunna	0	0	0	0	3,375
		Covert Township	0	0	0	0	3,123
		Crystal Falls			0	0	1,636
		Davison	0	0	0	0	5,294
		Davison Township	0	0	0	0	18,940
		Decatur	0	0	0	0	1,872
		Denton Township	0	0	0	0	5,649
		Dewitt	0	0	0	0	4,399
		Dewitt Township	0	0	0	0	13,295
		Dowagiac	0	0	0	0	5,913
		Dryden Township	0	0	0	0	4,773
		Durand	0	0	0	0	3,836
		East Grand Rapids	0	0	0	0	10,309
		East Jordan	0	0	0	0	2,270
		East Lansing	0	0	0	0	45,979
		East Tawas	0	0	0	0	2,808
		Edmore	0	0			1,256
		Elkton	0	0	0	0	783
		Erie Township	0	0	0	0	4,780
		Evart	0	0	0	0	1,717

[1] Agencies published in this table indicated that no hate crimes occurred in their jurisdictions during the quarter(s) for which they submitted reports to the Hate Crime program. Blanks indicate quarters for which agencies did not submit reports.

[2] Population figures are published only for the cities. The figures listed for the universities and colleges are student enrollment and were provided by the United States Department of Education for the 2006 school year, the most recent available. The enrollment figures include full-time and part-time students.

[3] Student enrollment figures were not available.

Table 95. Hate Crime Zero Data Submitted per Quarter, by State and Agency, 2007 *(Contd.)*

(Number.)

State	Agency type	Agency name	1st quarter	2nd quarter	3rd quarter	4th quarter	Population[2]
		Fairgrove		0			610
		Fenton	0	0	0	0	12,151
		Flat Rock	0	0	0	0	9,739
		Flint Township	0	0	0	0	32,626
		Flushing	0	0	0	0	8,014
		Flushing Township	0	0	0	0	10,394
		Forsyth Township	0	0	0	0	4,855
		Frankenmuth	0	0	0	0	4,777
		Frankfort	0	0	0	0	1,480
		Franklin	0	0	0	0	2,977
		Frost Township	0		0		1,153
		Fruitport	0	0	0	0	1,080
		Gaylord	0	0	0	0	3,749
		Gerrish Township	0	0	0	0	3,198
		Gladwin	0	0	0	0	2,984
		Grand Beach	0	0	0		245
		Grand Haven	0	0	0		10,478
		Grandville	0	0	0		16,838
		Grayling	0	0	0	0	1,902
		Grosse Ile Township	0	0	0	0	10,455
		Grosse Pointe	0	0	0	0	5,289
		Grosse Pointe Farms	0	0	0	0	9,099
		Grosse Pointe Park	0	0	0	0	11,606
		Grosse Pointe Shores	0	0	0	0	2,644
		Harbor Beach	0	0	0	0	1,670
		Harbor Springs	0	0	0	0	1,575
		Harper Woods	0	0	0	0	13,284
		Hart	0	0	0	0	2,004
		Hazel Park	0	0	0	0	18,211
		Holly	0	0	0	0	6,410
		Homer	0	0	0	0	1,785
		Houghton	0	0	0	0	7,017
		Howard City	0	0	0	0	1,615
		Howell	0	0	0	0	9,921
		Huntington Woods	0	0	0	0	5,866
		Huron Township	0	0	0	0	16,354
		Imlay City	0	0	0	0	3,825
		Iron Mountain	0	0	0	0	7,963
		Iron River	0	0	0	0	3,085
		Ishpeming	0	0	0	0	6,440
		Ishpeming Township	0	0	0	0	3,580
		Ithaca	0	0	0	0	3,074
		Jackson	0	0	0	0	34,325
		Kalamazoo Township	0	0	0	0	21,497
		Keego Harbor	0	0	0	0	2,848
		Kingsford	0	0	0	0	5,426
		Lake Angelus	0	0	0	0	312
		Lake Linden		0	0	0	1,050
		Lake Orion	0	0	0	0	2,759
		Lakeview	0	0	0	0	1,120
		Lansing Township	0				7,822
		Lapeer	0	0	0	0	9,372
		Lapeer Township	0	0	0	0	5,214
		Lathrup Village	0	0	0	0	4,112
		Laurium	0	0	0	0	2,001
		Lawton	0	0	0	0	1,839
		Lennon	0	0	0	0	501
		Leoni Township	0	0	0	0	13,889
		Leslie	0	0	0		2,328
		Lexington	0	0	0		1,086
		Lincoln Park	0	0	0	0	37,294
		Linden	0	0	0	0	3,560
		Litchfield	0	0	0	0	1,422

State	Agency type	Agency name	1st quarter	2nd quarter	3rd quarter	4th quarter	Population[2]
		Lowell	0	0	0	0	4,159
		Ludington	0	0	0	0	8,433
		Mackinaw City	0	0	0	0	856
		Mancelona	0	0	0	0	1,380
		Manistee	0	0	0	0	6,604
		Manton	0				1,201
		Marine City	0	0	0	0	4,417
		Marion	0	0	0		829
		Marlette	0	0	0	0	2,047
		Marquette	0	0	0	0	20,467
		Marysville	0	0	0	0	10,135
		Mattawan	0	0	0	0	2,945
		Melvindale	0	0	0		10,469
		Memphis	0	0	0	0	1,123
		Mendon	0	0	0	0	922
		Menominee	0	0	0	0	8,537
		Metamora Township	0	0	0	0	4,796
		Midland	0	0	0	0	41,540
		Milford	0	0	0	0	6,629
		Montague	0	0	0	0	2,305
		Montrose Township	0	0	0	0	7,919
		Morenci	0	0	0	0	2,323
		Munising	0	0	0	0	2,350
		Muskegon Township	0	0	0		18,634
		Napoleon Township	0	0	0	0	7,148
		Nashville	0	0	0	0	1,697
		Negaunee	0	0	0	0	4,429
		Newaygo	0	0	0	0	1,670
		New Haven	0	0	0	0	5,185
		New Lothrop	0				595
		North Branch	0	0	0	0	1,009
		Northfield Township	0	0	0	0	8,383
		North Muskegon	0	0	0	0	3,968
		Norvell Township	0	0	0	0	3,077
		Norway	0	0	0	0	2,897
		Novi	0	0	0	0	55,127
		Orchard Lake	0	0	0	0	2,230
		Otisville	0				828
		Otsego	0		0	0	3,900
		Ovid	0	0	0	0	1,415
		Owosso	0	0	0	0	15,341
		Oxford	0	0	0	0	3,583
		Parma-Sandstone	0	0	0	0	6,902
		Paw Paw	0	0	0	0	3,294
		Peck	0	0	0	0	580
		Pentwater	0	0	0	0	988
		Perry	0	0	0	0	2,084
		Petoskey	0	0	0	0	6,128
		Pigeon	0	0	0		1,099
		Pinckney	0	0	0	0	2,470
		Pinconning	0	0	0	0	1,327
		Pittsfield Township	0	0	0	0	34,615
		Plainwell	0	0	0	0	3,952
		Pleasant Ridge	0	0	0	0	2,471
		Port Austin	0	0	0	0	673
		Portland	0	0	0	0	3,793
		Prairieville Township	0	0	0	0	3,553
		Reading	0	0	0	0	1,096
		Redford Township	0	0	0	0	48,489
		Reed City	0	0	0	0	2,396
		Reese	0				1,384
		Richfield Township, Genesee County	0	0	0	0	8,874

[1]Agencies published in this table indicated that no hate crimes occurred in their jurisdictions during the quarter(s) for which they submitted reports to the Hate Crime program. Blanks indicate quarters for which agencies did not submit reports.

[2]Population figures are published only for the cities. The figures listed for the universities and colleges are student enrollment and were provided by the United States Department of Education for the 2006 school year, the most recent available. The enrollment figures include full-time and part-time students.

Table 95. Hate Crime Zero Data Submitted per Quarter, by State and Agency, 2007 *(Contd.)*

(Number.)

State	Agency type	Agency name	1st quarter	2nd quarter	3rd quarter	4th quarter	Population[2]	State	Agency type	Agency name	1st quarter	2nd quarter	3rd quarter	4th quarter	Population[2]
		Richland Township, Saginaw County	0	0	0	0	4,354			Macomb Community College	0	0	0	0	21,131
		Richmond	0	0	0	0	5,804			Michigan State University	0	0	0	0	45,520
		Rockford	0	0	0	0	5,248			Michigan Technological University	0	0	0	0	6,546
		Rockwood	0	0	0	0	3,349			Mott Community College	0	0	0	0	10,038
		Rogers City	0	0	0	0	3,131			Northern Michigan University	0	0	0	0	9,689
		Romeo	0	0	0	0	3,806			Saginaw Valley State University	0	0	0	0	9,543
		Roosevelt Park	0	0	0	0	3,790			University of Michigan:					
		Rothbury	0	0	0	0	447			Dearborn	0	0	0	0	8,342
		Sand Lake	0	0	0	0	517			Flint	0	0	0	0	6,527
		Sault Ste. Marie	0	0	0	0	14,279			Western Michigan University	0	0	0	0	24,841
		Schoolcraft	0	0	0	0	1,482		Metropolitan Counties	Barry	0	0	0	0	
		Shepherd	0	0	0		1,347			Bay	0	0	0	0	
		Somerset Township	0	0	0	0	4,767			Berrien	0	0	0	0	
		Southgate	0	0	0	0	29,074			Calhoun	0	0	0	0	
		South Haven	0	0	0	0	5,182			Clinton	0	0	0	0	
		South Rockwood	0	0	0	0	1,646			Genesee	0	0	0	0	
		Spring Arbor Township	0	0	0	0	8,495			Ionia	0	0	0	0	
		Springfield	0	0	0	0	5,137			Jackson	0	0	0	0	
		Spring Lake-Ferrysburg	0	0	0	0	5,347			Kalamazoo	0	0	0	0	
		Standish		0	0	0	2,009			Lapeer	0	0	0	0	
		St. Charles	0	0	0	0	2,107			Muskegon	0	0	0		
		St. Clair	0	0	0	0	5,938			Van Buren	0	0	0	0	
		St. Ignace	0	0	0	0	2,324			Washtenaw	0	0	0	0	
		St. Johns	0	0	0	0	7,329			Wayne	0	0	0	0	
		St. Joseph	0	0	0	0	8,600		Nonmetropolitan Counties	Alcona	0	0	0	0	
		St. Louis	0	0	0	0	6,463			Alger	0	0	0	0	
		Stockbridge	0	0	0	0	1,274			Allegan	0	0	0	0	
		Summit Township	0	0	0	0	22,104			Alpena	0	0	0	0	
		Suttons Bay	0	0	0	0	591			Antrim	0	0	0	0	
		Sylvan Lake	0	0	0	0	1,654			Benzie	0	0	0	0	
		Three Rivers	0	0	0	0	7,245			Branch	0	0	0	0	
		Tittabawassee Township	0	0	0	0	9,047			Charlevoix	0	0	0	0	
		Traverse City	0	0	0	0	14,406			Cheboygan	0	0	0	0	
		Tuscarora Township	0	0	0	0	3,145			Chippewa	0	0	0	0	
		Ubly	0	0	0	0	796			Clare	0	0	0	0	
		Unadilla Township	0	0	0	0	3,477			Delta	0	0	0	0	
		Union City	0	0	0	0	1,737			Dickinson	0	0	0	0	
		Utica	0	0	0	0	5,022			Emmet	0	0	0	0	
		Vernon	0	0	0	0	813			Gladwin	0	0	0	0	
		Vicksburg	0	0	0	0	2,151			Gratiot	0	0	0	0	
		Walker	0	0	0	0	23,794			Hillsdale	0	0	0	0	
		Walled Lake	0	0	0	0	6,988			Houghton	0	0	0	0	
		Waterloo Township	0	0	0	0	3,035			Huron	0	0	0	0	
		Wayland	0	0	0	0	3,906			Iosco	0	0	0	0	
		West Branch	0	0	0	0	1,875			Iron	0	0	0	0	
		Whitehall	0				2,819			Isabella	0	0	0	0	
		White Pigeon	0	0	0	0	1,579			Kalkaska	0	0	0	0	
		Wolverine Lake	0	0	0	0	4,307			Lake	0	0	0	0	
		Woodhaven	0	0	0	0	13,514			Leelanau	0	0	0	0	
		Woodstock Township	0	0	0	0	3,723			Lenawee	0	0	0	0	
		Wyandotte	0	0	0	0	26,290			Luce	0	0	0	0	
		Yale	0	0	0	0	1,967			Mackinac	0	0	0	0	
		Zeeland	0	0	0	0	5,433			Manistee	0	0	0	0	
		Zilwaukee	0	0	0	0	1,698			Marquette	0	0	0	0	
	Universities and Colleges	Ferris State University	0	0	0	0	12,574			Menominee	0	0	0	0	
		Grand Rapids Community College	0	0	0	0	15,224			Midland	0	0	0	0	
		Grand Valley State University	0	0	0	0	23,295			Missaukee	0	0	0	0	
										Montmorency	0	0	0	0	

[1]Agencies published in this table indicated that no hate crimes occurred in their jurisdictions during the quarter(s) for which they submitted reports to the Hate Crime program. Blanks indicate quarters for which agencies did not submit reports.

[2]Population figures are published only for the cities. The figures listed for the universities and colleges are student enrollment and were provided by the United States Department of Education for the 2006 school year, the most recent available. The enrollment figures include full-time and part-time students.

Table 95. Hate Crime Zero Data Submitted per Quarter, by State and Agency, 2007 *(Contd.)*

(Number.)

State	Agency type	Agency name	1st quarter	2nd quarter	3rd quarter	4th quarter	Population[2]
		Oceana	0	0	0	0	
		Ontonagon	0	0	0	0	
		Osceola	0	0	0	0	
		Oscoda	0	0	0	0	
		Otsego	0	0	0	0	
		Presque Isle	0	0	0	0	
		Roscommon	0	0	0	0	
		Sanilac	0				
		Schoolcraft		0	0	0	
		Shiawassee	0	0	0	0	
		St. Joseph	0	0	0	0	
	State Police Agencies	State Police:					
		Alcona County	0	0	0	0	
		Alger County	0	0	0	0	
		Allegan County	0	0	0	0	
		Alpena County	0	0	0	0	
		Antrim County	0	0	0	0	
		Arenac County	0	0	0	0	
		Baraga County	0	0	0	0	
		Barry County	0	0	0	0	
		Bay County	0	0	0	0	
		Benzie County	0	0	0	0	
		Branch County	0	0	0	0	
		Calhoun County	0	0	0	0	
		Cass County	0	0	0	0	
		Charlevoix County	0	0	0	0	
		Cheboygan County	0	0	0	0	
		Chippewa County	0	0	0	0	
		Clare County	0	0	0	0	
		Clinton County	0	0	0	0	
		Crawford County	0	0	0	0	
		Delta County	0	0	0	0	
		Dickinson County	0	0	0	0	
		Eaton County	0	0	0	0	
		Emmet County	0	0	0	0	
		Genesee County	0	0	0	0	
		Gladwin County	0	0	0	0	
		Gogebic County	0	0	0	0	
		Grand Traverse County	0	0	0	0	
		Gratiot County	0	0	0	0	
		Hillsdale County	0	0	0	0	
		Houghton County	0	0	0	0	
		Huron County	0	0	0	0	
		Ingham County	0	0	0	0	
		Ionia County	0	0	0	0	
		Iosco County	0	0	0	0	
		Iron County	0	0	0	0	
		Jackson County	0	0	0	0	
		Kalkaska County	0	0	0	0	
		Kent County	0	0	0	0	
		Keweenaw County	0	0	0	0	
		Lake County	0	0	0	0	
		Lapeer County	0	0	0	0	
		Leelanau County	0	0	0	0	
		Lenawee County	0	0	0	0	
		Livingston County	0	0	0	0	
		Luce County	0	0	0	0	
		Mackinac County	0	0	0	0	
		Macomb County	0	0	0	0	
		Manistee County	0	0	0	0	
		Marquette County	0	0	0	0	
		Mason County	0	0	0	0	
		Mecosta County	0	0	0	0	
		Menominee County	0	0	0	0	
		Midland County	0	0	0	0	
		Missaukee County	0	0	0	0	
		Monroe County	0	0	0	0	
		Montcalm County	0	0	0	0	
		Montmorency County	0	0	0	0	
		Muskegon County	0	0	0	0	
		Newaygo County	0	0	0	0	
		Oakland County	0	0	0	0	
		Oceana County	0	0	0	0	
		Ogemaw County	0	0	0	0	
		Ontonagon County	0	0	0	0	
		Osceola County	0	0	0	0	
		Oscoda County	0	0	0	0	
		Otsego County	0	0	0	0	
		Ottawa County	0	0	0	0	
		Presque Isle County	0	0	0	0	
		Roscommon County	0	0	0	0	
		Saginaw County	0	0	0	0	
		Sanilac County	0	0	0	0	
		Schoolcraft County	0	0	0	0	
		Shiawassee County	0	0	0	0	
		St. Clair County	0	0	0	0	
		St. Joseph County	0	0	0	0	
		Tuscola County	0	0	0	0	
		Van Buren County	0	0	0	0	
		Washtenaw County	0	0	0	0	
		Wayne County	0	0	0	0	
		Wexford County	0	0	0	0	
	Other Agencies	Bishop International Airport	0	0	0	0	
		Huron-Clinton Metropolitan Authority:					
		Hudson Mills Metropark		0	0	0	
		Kensington Metropark	0	0	0	0	
		Lower Huron Metropark	0	0	0	0	
MINNESOTA	**Cities**	Albany	0	0	0	0	2,072
		Albert Lea	0	0	0	0	17,663
		Alexandria	0	0	0	0	11,029
		Andover	0	0	0	0	30,728

[1]Agencies published in this table indicated that no hate crimes occurred in their jurisdictions during the quarter(s) for which they submitted reports to the Hate Crime program. Blanks indicate quarters for which agencies did not submit reports.

[2]Population figures are published only for the cities. The figures listed for the universities and colleges are student enrollment and were provided by the United States Department of Education for the 2006 school year, the most recent available. The enrollment figures include full-time and part-time students.

Table 95. Hate Crime Zero Data Submitted per Quarter, by State and Agency, 2007 *(Contd.)*

(Number.)

State	Agency type	Agency name	Zero data per quarter[1]				Popu-lation[2]	State	Agency type	Agency name	Zero data per quarter[1]				Popu-lation[2]
			1st quarter	2nd quarter	3rd quarter	4th quarter					1st quarter	2nd quarter	3rd quarter	4th quarter	
		Annandale	0	0	0	0	3,114			Houston	0	0	0	0	991
		Appleton	0	0	0	0	1,929			Hoyt Lakes	0	0	0	0	1,957
		Apple Valley	0	0	0	0	50,794			Hutchinson	0	0	0	0	14,050
		Arden Hills	0	0	0	0	9,852			International Falls	0	0	0	0	6,108
		Aurora	0	0	0	0	1,720			Inver Grove Heights	0	0	0	0	34,060
		Austin	0	0	0	0	23,300			Jackson	0	0	0	0	3,429
		Avon	0	0	0	0	1,284			Janesville	0	0	0	0	2,201
		Babbitt	0	0	0	0	1,588			Jordan	0	0	0	0	5,550
		Baxter	0	0	0	0	8,243			Kasson	0	0	0	0	5,737
		Bayport	0	0	0	0	3,266			Kimball	0	0	0	0	691
		Becker	0	0	0	0	4,294			La Crescent	0	0	0	0	5,106
		Belgrade	0	0	0	0	705			Lake City	0	0	0	0	5,409
		Belle Plaine	0	0	0	0	4,998			Lake Crystal	0	0	0	0	2,562
		Benson	0	0	0	0	3,096			Lakefield	0	0	0	0	1,687
		Big Lake	0	0	0	0	9,852			Lauderdale	0	0	0	0	2,169
		Biwabik	0	0	0	0	944			Lester Prairie	0	0	0	0	1,737
		Blooming Prairie	0	0	0	0	1,975			Le Sueur	0	0	0	0	4,331
		Blue Earth	0	0	0	0	3,366			Lewiston	0	0	0	0	1,483
		Brainerd	0	0	0	0	13,731			Lino Lakes	0	0	0	0	20,334
		Breckenridge	0	0	0	0	3,325			Litchfield	0	0	0	0	6,655
		Browns Valley	0	0	0	0	619			Little Canada	0	0	0	0	9,491
		Brownton	0	0	0	0	795			Little Falls	0	0	0	0	8,162
		Buffalo	0	0	0	0	14,456			Long Prairie	0	0	0	0	2,877
		Caledonia	0	0	0	0	2,910			Madison	0	0	0	0	1,605
		Cambridge	0	0	0	0	7,687			Maple Grove	0	0	0	0	62,145
		Cannon Falls	0	0	0	0	4,038			Mapleton	0	0	0	0	1,633
		Centennial Lakes	0	0	0	0	11,454			Medina	0	0	0	0	5,033
		Champlin	0	0	0	0	23,463			Melrose	0	0	0	0	3,146
		Chaska	0	0	0	0	24,764			Mendota Heights	0	0	0	0	11,318
		Chisholm	0	0	0	0	4,592			Milaca	0	0	0	0	3,073
		Cloquet	0	0	0	0	11,523			Minnetrista	0	0	0	0	8,350
		Cold Spring	0	0	0	0	3,726			Montgomery	0	0	0	0	3,308
		Columbia Heights	0	0	0	0	17,894			Moose Lake	0	0	0	0	2,622
		Corcoran	0	0	0	0	5,698			Morris	0	0	0	0	5,057
		Crookston	0	0	0	0	7,752			Mound	0	0	0	0	9,404
		Crosby	0	0	0	0	2,232			Mounds View	0	0	0	0	11,921
		Crystal	0	0	0	0	21,325			Mountain Iron	0	0	0	0	2,902
		Dawson	0	0	0	0	1,405			Mountain Lake	0	0	0	0	1,982
		Dayton	0	0	0	0	4,620			New Brighton	0	0	0	0	20,644
		Deephaven-Woodland	0	0	0	0	4,129			Newport	0	0	0	0	3,606
		Detroit Lakes	0	0	0	0	8,111			New Prague	0	0	0	0	7,153
		Dilworth	0	0	0	0	3,600			New Richland	0	0	0	0	1,155
		Duluth	0	0	0	0	83,932			New Ulm	0	0	0	0	13,369
		Eagle Lake	0	0	0	0	2,130			North Branch	0	0	0	0	10,886
		East Bethel	0	0	0	0	12,267			North Mankato	0	0	0	0	12,295
		East Grand Forks	0	0	0	0	7,896			North Oaks	0	0	0	0	4,194
		Elmore	0	0	0	0	677			Oak Park Heights	0	0	0	0	4,097
		Ely	0	0	0	0	3,565			Olivia	0	0	0	0	2,449
		Eveleth	0	0	0	0	3,577			Orono	0	0	0	0	12,212
		Fairmont	0	0	0	0	10,337			Ortonville	0	0	0	0	2,003
		Falcon Heights	0	0	0	0	5,417			Osakis	0	0	0	0	1,570
		Faribault	0	0	0	0	22,408			Osseo	0	0	0	0	2,553
		Farmington	0	0	0	0	19,276			Owatonna	0	0	0	0	24,796
		Fergus Falls	0	0	0	0	13,842			Park Rapids	0	0	0	0	3,577
		Floodwood	0	0	0	0	493			Paynesville	0	0	0	0	2,255
		Fridley	0	0	0	0	26,124			Plainview	0	0	0	0	3,306
		Gilbert	0	0	0	0	1,743			Princeton	0	0	0	0	4,885
		Glencoe	0	0	0	0	5,644			Prior Lake	0	0	0	0	23,879
		Glenwood	0	0	0	0	2,553			Proctor	0	0	0	0	2,771
		Golden Valley	0	0	0	0	19,865			Ramsey	0	0	0	0	23,617
		Goodview	0	0	0	0	3,394			Redwood Falls	0	0	0	0	5,155
		Grand Rapids	0	0	0	0	8,297			Richfield	0	0	0	0	33,112
		Granite Falls	0	0	0	0	2,961			Richmond	0	0	0	0	1,264
		Hallock	0	0	0	0	1,051			Robbinsdale	0	0	0	0	13,211
		Ham Lake	0	0	0	0	15,235			Rogers	0	0	0	0	6,802
		Hastings	0	0	0	0	21,839			Roseau	0	0	0	0	2,827
		Hermantown	0	0	0	0	9,247			Rosemount	0	0	0	0	21,393
		Hilltop	0	0	0	0	749			Sartell	0	0	0	0	13,816
		Hokah	0	0	0	0	582			Sauk Centre	0	0	0	0	3,906
		Hopkins	0	0	0	0	16,613			Sauk Rapids	0	0	0	0	11,768
										Shakopee	0	0	0	0	35,113

[1]Agencies published in this table indicated that no hate crimes occurred in their jurisdictions during the quarter(s) for which they submitted reports to the Hate Crime program. Blanks indicate quarters for which agencies did not submit reports.

[2]Population figures are published only for the cities. The figures listed for the universities and colleges are student enrollment and were provided by the United States Department of Education for the 2006 school year, the most recent available. The enrollment figures include full-time and part-time students.

Table 95. Hate Crime Zero Data Submitted per Quarter, by State and Agency, 2007 *(Contd.)*

(Number.)

State	Agency type	Agency name	1st quarter	2nd quarter	3rd quarter	4th quarter	Population[2]
		Shoreview	0	0	0	0	26,860
		Silver Bay	0	0	0	0	1,913
		Silver Lake	0	0	0	0	814
		Slayton	0	0	0	0	1,907
		Sleepy Eye	0	0	0	0	3,463
		South Eastern Faribault County	0	0	0	0	1,151
		South Lake Minnetonka	0	0	0	0	12,066
		South St. Paul	0	0	0	0	19,188
		Springfield	0	0	0	0	2,124
		Spring Grove	0	0	0	0	1,268
		Spring Lake Park	0	0	0	0	6,618
		St. Anthony	0	0	0	0	7,680
		Staples	0	0	0	0	3,082
		St. Charles	0	0	0	0	3,567
		St. Francis	0	0	0	0	7,744
		St. James	0	0	0	0	4,380
		St. Joseph	0	0	0	0	5,926
		St. Paul Park	0	0	0	0	5,285
		St. Peter	0	0	0	0	10,823
		Thief River Falls	0	0	0	0	8,440
		Tracy	0	0	0	0	2,045
		Two Harbors	0	0	0	0	3,435
		Vadnais Heights	0	0	0	0	12,447
		Virginia	0	0	0	0	8,471
		Wabasha	0	0	0	0	2,587
		Wadena	0	0	0	0	3,981
		Waite Park	0	0	0	0	6,795
		Warroad	0	0	0	0	1,663
		Waseca	0	0	0	0	9,465
		Wayzata	0	0	0	0	3,894
		Wells	0	0	0	0	2,442
		West Hennepin	0	0	0	0	5,671
		West St. Paul	0	0	0	0	18,748
		Windom	0	0	0	0	4,327
		Winnebago	0	0	0	0	1,386
		Winona	0	0	0	0	26,464
		Winsted	0	0	0	0	2,457
		Worthington	0	0	0	0	11,026
		Wyoming	0	0	0	0	3,985
		Zumbrota	0	0	0	0	3,050
	Universities and Colleges	University of Minnesota:					
		Duluth	0	0	0	0	11,190
		Morris	0	0	0	0	1,747
	Metropolitan Counties	Anoka	0	0	0	0	
		Benton	0	0	0	0	
		Carlton	0	0	0	0	
		Chisago	0	0	0	0	
		Clay	0	0	0	0	
		Dakota	0	0	0	0	
		Dodge	0	0	0	0	
		Hennepin	0	0	0	0	
		Houston	0	0	0	0	
		Isanti	0	0	0	0	
		Olmsted	0	0	0	0	
		Polk	0	0	0	0	
		Ramsey	0	0	0	0	
		Scott	0	0	0	0	
		Sherburne	0	0	0	0	
		Stearns	0	0	0	0	
		St. Louis	0	0	0	0	
		Wabasha	0	0	0	0	
		Washington	0	0	0	0	
		Wright	0	0	0	0	
	Nonmetropolitan Counties	Aitkin	0	0	0	0	
		Becker	0	0	0	0	
		Big Stone	0	0	0	0	
		Blue Earth	0	0	0	0	
		Brown	0	0	0	0	
		Cass	0	0	0	0	
		Chippewa	0	0	0	0	
		Clearwater	0	0	0	0	
		Cook	0	0	0	0	
		Cottonwood	0	0	0	0	
		Crow Wing	0	0	0	0	
		Faribault	0	0	0	0	
		Fillmore	0	0	0	0	
		Freeborn	0	0	0	0	
		Goodhue	0	0	0	0	
		Grant	0	0	0	0	
		Hubbard	0	0	0	0	
		Itasca	0	0	0	0	
		Jackson	0	0	0	0	
		Kanabec	0	0	0	0	
		Kandiyohi	0	0	0	0	
		Kittson	0	0	0	0	
		Koochiching	0	0	0	0	
		Lac Qui Parle	0	0	0	0	
		Lake	0	0	0	0	
		Lake of the Woods	0	0	0	0	
		Le Sueur	0	0	0	0	
		Lincoln	0	0	0	0	
		Lyon	0	0	0	0	
		Mahnomen	0	0	0	0	
		Marshall	0	0	0	0	
		Martin	0	0	0	0	
		Meeker	0	0	0	0	
		Mille Lacs	0	0	0	0	
		Morrison	0	0	0	0	
		Mower	0	0	0	0	
		Murray	0	0	0	0	
		Nicollet	0	0	0	0	
		Nobles	0	0	0	0	
		Norman	0	0	0	0	
		Otter Tail	0	0	0	0	
		Pennington	0	0	0	0	
		Pine	0	0	0	0	
		Pipestone	0	0	0	0	
		Pope	0	0	0	0	
		Red Lake	0	0	0	0	
		Redwood	0	0	0	0	
		Renville	0	0	0	0	
		Rice	0	0	0	0	
		Rock	0	0	0	0	
		Roseau	0	0	0	0	
		Sibley	0	0	0	0	
		Steele	0	0	0	0	
		Stevens	0	0	0	0	
		Swift	0	0	0	0	
		Todd	0	0	0	0	
		Traverse	0	0	0	0	
		Wadena	0	0	0	0	
		Waseca	0	0	0	0	
		Watonwan	0	0	0	0	
		Wilkin	0	0	0	0	
		Winona	0	0	0	0	
		Yellow Medicine	0	0	0	0	
	State Police Agencies	Minnesota State Patrol	0	0	0	0	
	Other Agencies	Capitol Security, St. Paul	0	0	0	0	

[1] Agencies published in this table indicated that no hate crimes occurred in their jurisdictions during the quarter(s) for which they submitted reports to the Hate Crime program. Blanks indicate quarters for which agencies did not submit reports.

[2] Population figures are published only for the cities. The figures listed for the universities and colleges are student enrollment and were provided by the United States Department of Education for the 2006 school year, the most recent available. The enrollment figures include full-time and part-time students.

Table 95. Hate Crime Zero Data Submitted per Quarter, by State and Agency, 2007 *(Contd.)*

(Number.)

State	Agency type	Agency name	1st quarter	2nd quarter	3rd quarter	4th quarter	Population[2]
		Minneapolis-St. Paul International Airport	0	0	0	0	
		Three Rivers Park District	0	0	0	0	
MISSISSIPPI...	Cities	Aberdeen	0	0	0	0	6,138
		Amory	0	0	0	0	7,332
		Batesville	0	0	0		7,767
		Bay St. Louis	0	0		0	6,399
		Bruce		0			2,018
		Byhalia	0	0	0	0	714
		Clarksdale	0		0	0	18,650
		Columbia	0	0	0	0	6,491
		Columbus	0	0	0	0	23,968
		Edwards		0	0		1,309
		Eupora	0	0	0		2,236
		Flowood	0				7,112
		Fulton		0		0	4,127
		Grenada	0	0	0		14,487
		Heidelberg	0	0	0	0	806
		Hernando	0	0	0	0	11,115
		Horn Lake	0	0	0	0	23,125
		Iuka	0	0	0	0	2,947
		Magee	0	0	0	0	4,314
		Magnolia		0	0		2,126
		McComb		0	0	0	13,583
		New Albany			0		8,113
		Newton	0	0	0		3,698
		Olive Branch				0	31,223
		Oxford	0	0			14,362
		Pascagoula	0	0	0	0	23,555
		Picayune		0	0	0	11,805
		Richland	0	0			7,273
		Rolling Fork	0				2,159
		Shaw	0				2,199
		Starkville	0	0	0	0	22,663
		Tupelo	0				36,142
		Vicksburg	0	0		0	25,610
		Waveland	0		0	0	5,668
		Waynesboro	0	0	0	0	5,655
		West Point	0	0	0	0	11,433
	Universities and Colleges	Coahoma Community College	0	0	0	0	1,838
		Jackson State University		0	0	0	8,256
		Mississippi State University	0	0	0	0	16,206
		University of Mississippi, Oxford	0	0		0	15,220
	Metropolitan Counties	Forrest	0				
	Nonmetropolitan Counties	Adams	0	0	0	0	
		Chickasaw	0	0		0	
		Claiborne	0	0	0	0	
		Coahoma	0	0	0	0	
		Grenada	0	0	0	0	
		Leflore	0	0	0	0	
		Lincoln	0	0	0	0	
		Lowndes	0	0	0	0	
		Marion	0		0		
		Oktibbeha	0	0	0	0	
		Panola	0	0	0	0	
		Pontotoc	0				
		Sunflower	0	0	0	0	
		Tippah	0	0	0	0	
		Union	0	0	0	0	
		Warren	0	0	0	0	
		Washington		0		0	

State	Agency type	Agency name	1st quarter	2nd quarter	3rd quarter	4th quarter	Population[2]
MISSOURI......	Cities	Adrian	0	0	0	0	1,885
		Advance	0	0	0	0	1,214
		Alma	0	0	0	0	373
		Alton	0	0	0	0	645
		Anderson	0	0	0	0	1,927
		Appleton City	0	0	0	0	1,302
		Arbyrd	0	0	0		496
		Archie	0	0	0		989
		Arnold	0	0	0	0	20,831
		Ashland	0	0	0	0	2,156
		Auxvasse	0	0	0	0	1,006
		Ava	0	0	0		3,124
		Ballwin	0	0	0	0	30,120
		Bates City	0	0	0	0	237
		Battlefield	0	0	0	0	4,148
		Bella Villa	0	0	0	0	642
		Belle	0	0	0	0	1,362
		Bellefontaine Neighbors	0	0	0	0	10,430
		Bellerive	0	0	0	0	257
		Bel-Nor	0	0	0	0	1,496
		Bel-Ridge	0	0	0	0	2,924
		Belton	0	0	0	0	24,492
		Berkeley	0	0	0	0	9,460
		Bernie					1,803
		Bethany	0		0	0	3,078
		Beverly Hills	0	0		0	564
		Billings	0	0	0	0	1,135
		Birch Tree	0	0	0	0	627
		Birmingham	0	0	0	0	216
		Blackburn		0	0	0	275
		Bloomfield		0	0		1,883
		Bolivar	0	0	0	0	10,748
		Bonne Terre	0	0	0	0	7,153
		Boonville	0	0	0	0	8,830
		Bowling Green	0	0	0	0	5,166
		Branson	0	0	0	0	7,496
		Branson West	0	0	0	0	514
		Braymer	0	0	0	0	963
		Breckenridge Hills	0	0	0	0	4,525
		Brentwood	0	0	0	0	7,238
		Bridgeton	0	0	0	0	15,120
		Brookfield	0	0	0	0	4,371
		Brunswick	0	0	0	0	882
		Bucklin	0	0	0	0	482
		Buckner	0	0	0	0	2,738
		Buffalo	0	0	0	0	3,143
		Bunker	0	0	0	0	437
		Butler	0	0	0	0	4,271
		Butterfield Village	0	0	0	0	426
		Byrnes Mill	0	0	0	0	2,912
		Cabool	0	0	0	0	2,150
		California	0	0	0	0	4,209
		Calverton Park	0	0	0	0	1,286
		Camden Point	0	0	0		558
		Camdenton	0	0	0	0	3,226
		Campbell	0	0	0	0	1,853
		Canton	0	0	0	0	2,489
		Cape Girardeau	0	0	0	0	36,754
		Cardwell	0	0	0		739
		Carl Junction	0	0	0	0	7,071
		Carterville	0	0	0		1,937
		Carthage	0	0	0	0	13,407
		Cassville	0	0	0	0	3,278
		Center	0	0	0	0	646
		Centralia	0	0	0	0	3,593
		Chaffee	0				2,981
		Charlack	0	0	0	0	1,357
		Charleston	0	0	0	0	5,268
		Chesterfield	0	0	0	0	46,642
		Clarkton	0	0	0		1,262
		Claycomo	0	0	0	0	1,289
		Clayton	0	0	0	0	16,036

[1]Agencies published in this table indicated that no hate crimes occurred in their jurisdictions during the quarter(s) for which they submitted reports to the Hate Crime program. Blanks indicate quarters for which agencies did not submit reports.

[2]Population figures are published only for the cities. The figures listed for the universities and colleges are student enrollment and were provided by the United States Department of Education for the 2006 school year, the most recent available. The enrollment figures include full-time and part-time students.

Table 95. Hate Crime Zero Data Submitted per Quarter, by State and Agency, 2007 *(Contd.)*

(Number.)

State	Agency type	Agency name	Zero data per quarter[1] 1st quarter	2nd quarter	3rd quarter	4th quarter	Population[2]
		Cleveland	0	0	0	0	690
		Clever	0	0	0	0	1,321
		Cole Camp	0				1,160
		Columbia	0	0	0	0	95,595
		Concordia	0	0	0	0	2,409
		Conway	0	0	0	0	786
		Cool Valley	0	0	0	0	1,014
		Cooter	0		0	0	430
		Corder	0		0	0	423
		Cottleville	0		0	0	2,685
		Country Club Hills	0	0	0	0	1,293
		Country Club Village	0		0	0	1,977
		Crane	0	0	0	0	1,445
		Crestwood	0	0	0	0	11,545
		Creve Coeur	0	0	0	0	17,028
		Crocker	0	0	0	0	989
		Crystal City	0	0	0	0	4,599
		Cuba	0	0	0		3,529
		Deepwater	0	0	0		505
		Dellwood	0	0	0	0	4,937
		Desloge	0	0	0	0	5,218
		De Soto	0	0	0		6,579
		Des Peres	0	0	0	0	8,626
		Dexter		0		0	7,658
		Doniphan	0	0	0	0	1,935
		Drexel	0	0	0	0	1,106
		Duenweg	0	0	0		1,213
		Duquesne	0	0	0	0	1,708
		East Lynne	0	0		0	308
		Edgerton	0	0		0	550
		Edmundson	0	0	0	0	789
		El Dorado Springs	0	0	0	0	3,811
		Ellington	0	0	0		999
		Ellisville	0	0	0	0	9,323
		Elsberry	0	0	0	0	2,601
		Emma	0	0	0	0	236
		Eureka	0	0	0	0	9,287
		Everton	0	0	0	0	321
		Fair Grove	0	0	0	0	1,331
		Fair Play	0	0		0	451
		Farber	0	0	0		396
		Farmington	0	0	0	0	15,711
		Fayette	0	0	0		2,686
		Ferguson	0	0	0		21,142
		Ferrelview	0	0	0	0	584
		Festus	0	0	0	0	11,390
		Flordell Hills	0	0	0	0	870
		Florissant	0	0	0	0	51,025
		Foley	0	0	0	0	209
		Fordland	0	0	0	0	765
		Foristell	0	0	0		330
		Forsyth	0	0	0	0	1,698
		Fredericktown	0	0	0	0	4,057
		Freeman	0	0	0	0	611
		Frontenac	0	0	0	0	3,531
		Fulton	0	0	0	0	12,311
		Galena	0	0	0	0	529
		Gallatin	0	0	0	0	1,761
		Garden City	0	0	0	0	1,694
		Gerald	0	0	0	0	1,242
		Glasgow	0	0	0	0	1,194
		Glendale	0	0	0	0	5,526
		Glen Echo Park	0	0	0	0	159
		Goodman	0	0	0	0	1,265
		Grandin	0	0	0	0	238
		Greendale	0	0	0		698
		Greenfield	0	0	0	0	1,286
		Greenwood	0	0	0	0	4,650
		Hallsville	0	0	0	0	939
		Hannibal	0	0	0	0	17,612
		Harrisonville	0	0	0	0	9,935
		Hartville	0	0	0	0	604

State	Agency type	Agency name	Zero data per quarter[1] 1st quarter	2nd quarter	3rd quarter	4th quarter	Population[2]
		Hawk Point	0	0	0	0	552
		Hayti Heights	0	0	0		772
		Hazelwood	0	0	0	0	25,407
		Henrietta		0	0	0	442
		Herculaneum	0	0	0	0	3,306
		Hermann	0	0	0	0	2,759
		Higginsville	0	0	0	0	4,662
		High Hill	0	0	0	0	222
		Highlandville	0	0	0	0	929
		Hillsboro	0	0	0	0	1,938
		Holcomb	0	0	0	0	691
		Hollister	0	0	0	0	3,797
		Holts Summit	0	0	0	0	3,600
		Hornersville	0	0	0	0	674
		Houston	0	0	0		2,025
		Humansville	0	0	0	0	1,008
		Huntsville	0	0	0	0	1,641
		Hurley				0	160
		Iberia	0	0	0	0	684
		Indian Point	0	0	0		672
		Iron Mountain Lake	0	0	0	0	707
		Ironton	0	0	0	0	1,353
		Jackson	0	0	0	0	13,431
		JASCO Metropolitan	0	0	0	0	2,802
		Jennings	0	0	0	0	14,738
		Jonesburg	0	0	0	0	724
		Joplin	0	0	0	0	48,261
		Kearney	0		0		8,262
		Kennett	0	0	0	0	10,909
		Keytesville	0	0	0	0	508
		Kimberling City	0	0	0	0	2,584
		King City	0				910
		Kirkwood	0	0	0	0	26,875
		Knob Noster	0	0	0	0	3,072
		Ladue	0	0	0	0	8,199
		La Grange	0	0	0	0	934
		Lake Lotawana	0	0	0		1,945
		Lake Ozark	0	0	0	0	2,022
		Lakeshire	0	0	0	0	1,297
		Lake St. Louis	0	0	0	0	14,325
		Lake Tapawingo	0	0	0	0	795
		Lake Waukomis	0	0	0	0	900
		Lake Winnebago	0	0	0	0	1,130
		Lamar	0	0	0	0	4,649
		La Monte	0	0	0	0	1,076
		Lathrop	0	0	0	0	2,357
		La Tour Village	0	0	0	0	66
		Laurie	0				719
		Lawson		0	0	0	2,407
		Leadington	0	0	0	0	220
		Leadwood	0	0	0		1,173
		Lebanon	0	0	0	0	13,964
		Leeton	0	0	0	0	625
		Lexington	0	0	0	0	4,590
		Liberal	0	0	0	0	811
		Liberty	0	0	0	0	30,050
		Licking	0	0	0	0	1,516
		Lilbourn	0	0	0		1,205
		Lincoln	0	0	0	0	1,107
		Linn	0	0	0	0	1,432
		Linn Creek	0	0	0	0	301
		Lockwood	0	0	0	0	953
		Lone Jack	0	0	0	0	887
		Lowry City	0	0	0	0	749
		Malden	0	0	0	0	4,569
		Manchester	0	0	0	0	18,769
		Mansfield	0	0	0	0	1,359
		Maplewood	0	0	0	0	8,701
		Marceline	0	0	0	0	2,331
		Marionville	0	0	0	0	2,177

[1]Agencies published in this table indicated that no hate crimes occurred in their jurisdictions during the quarter(s) for which they submitted reports to the Hate Crime program. Blanks indicate quarters for which agencies did not submit reports.

[2]Population figures are published only for the cities. The figures listed for the universities and colleges are student enrollment and were provided by the United States Department of Education for the 2006 school year, the most recent available. The enrollment figures include full-time and part-time students.

Table 95. Hate Crime Zero Data Submitted per Quarter, by State and Agency, 2007 *(Contd.)*

(Number.)

State	Agency type	Agency name	1st quarter	2nd quarter	3rd quarter	4th quarter	Population[2]	State	Agency type	Agency name	1st quarter	2nd quarter	3rd quarter	4th quarter	Population[2]
		Marquand	0			0	265			Pilot Knob	0	0	0	0	688
		Marshfield	0	0	0	0	7,173			Pine Lawn	0	0	0		4,038
		Marston	0	0	0	0	549			Pineville	0	0	0	0	878
		Marthasville	0	0	0	0	864			Platte City	0	0	0	0	4,971
		Martinsburg	0	0	0	0	328			Platte Woods	0	0	0	0	458
		Maryland Heights	0	0	0	0	26,221			Plattsburg	0	0	0	0	2,416
		Maryville	0	0	0	0	10,540			Pleasant Hill	0	0	0	0	7,108
		Matthews	0	0	0		545			Pleasant Hope	0	0	0	0	590
		Maysville	0	0	0	0	1,137			Polo	0	0	0	0	607
		Mayview		0	0		292			Poplar Bluff	0	0	0		17,054
		Memphis	0	0	0	0	1,995			Portageville	0	0	0	0	2,990
		Merriam Woods	0	0	0	0	1,194			Purdy	0	0	0	0	1,175
		Mexico	0	0	0	0	10,965			Puxico	0	0	0	0	1,149
		Milan	0	0	0	0	1,796			Randolph	0	0	0	0	50
		Miller	0	0	0	0	801			Raymore	0	0	0	0	17,439
		Miner	0	0	0		1,329			Raytown	0	0	0	0	28,344
		Moberly	0	0	0	0	14,023			Reeds Spring	0	0	0	0	720
		Moline Acres	0	0	0	0	2,540			Republic	0	0	0	0	11,777
		Monett	0	0	0	0	8,851			Rich Hill	0	0	0	0	1,510
		Montgomery City	0	0	0	0	2,538			Richland	0	0	0	0	1,756
		Montrose	0	0	0	0	434			Richmond Heights	0	0	0	0	9,179
		Moscow Mills	0	0	0		2,460			Riverside	0	0	0	0	2,961
		Mound City	0	0	0	0	1,078			Riverview	0	0	0	0	2,948
		Mountain Grove	0	0	0	0	4,635			Rock Hill	0	0	0	0	4,641
		Mountain View	0	0	0	0	2,605			Rock Port	0	0	0	0	1,306
		Mount Vernon	0	0	0	0	4,511			Rogersville	0	0	0	0	2,647
		Napoleon	0	0	0	0	200			Rosebud	0	0	0	0	378
		Neosho	0	0	0	0	11,328			Salem	0	0	0	0	4,860
		Nevada	0	0	0	0	8,457			Salisbury	0	0	0		1,600
		New Bloomfield	0	0	0	0	749			Sarcoxie	0	0			1,341
		Newburg	0	0	0	0	476			Savannah	0	0	0	0	5,118
		New Florence	0	0	0	0	776			Scott City	0				4,571
		New Haven	0	0	0	0	2,014			Sedalia	0	0	0	0	20,682
		New London	0	0	0	0	1,011			Senath	0		0		1,626
		New Madrid	0	0	0	0	3,073			Seymour	0	0	0	0	2,025
		New Melle			0	0	286			Shrewsbury	0	0	0	0	6,290
		Niangua	0	0	0	0	497			Slater	0	0	0	0	1,911
		Noel	0	0	0	0	1,562			Smithville	0	0	0	0	7,777
		Norborne	0	0	0	0	776			Southwest City	0	0	0	0	931
		Normandy	0	0	0	0	4,946			Sparta	0	0	0	0	1,223
		North Kansas City	0	0	0		5,619			St. Ann	0	0	0	0	12,887
		Northmoor	0	0	0	0	403			St. Charles	0	0	0	0	63,277
		Northwoods	0	0		0	4,353			St. Clair	0	0	0	0	4,400
		Norwood				0	583			Steele	0	0	0	0	2,136
		Oak Grove	0	0	0	0	7,069			Steelville	0	0	0	0	1,454
		Oakland	0	0	0	0	1,575			Ste. Genevieve	0	0	0	0	4,479
		Oakview Village		0	0	0	389			Stewartsville	0	0	0	0	741
		Odessa	0	0	0	0	4,828			St. George	0	0	0	0	1,222
		Old Monroe	0	0	0	0	300			St. James	0	0	0	0	4,110
		Olivette	0	0	0	0	7,439			St. Joseph	0	0	0		72,424
		Olympian Village	0	0	0	0	675			St. Marys	0	0	0	0	392
		Oran	0	0	0		1,259			Strafford	0	0	0	0	2,025
		Orrick	0	0	0		848			St. Robert	0	0	0	0	3,319
		Osage Beach	0	0	0	0	4,554			Sturgeon	0	0	0	0	897
		Osceola	0	0	0	0	804			Sugar Creek	0	0	0	0	3,506
		Overland	0	0	0	0	15,783			Sullivan	0	0	0	0	6,698
		Owensville	0	0	0	0	2,523			Summersville	0	0		0	562
		Ozark	0	0	0	0	17,496			Sunset Hills	0	0		0	8,314
		Pacific	0	0	0	0	7,245			Sweet Springs	0	0	0		1,527
		Pagedale	0	0	0	0	3,440			Tarkio	0	0	0	0	1,823
		Parkville	0	0	0	0	5,276			Thayer	0	0	0	0	2,166
		Parma	0	0	0	0	785			Tipton	0	0	0	0	3,125
		Pasadena Park	0	0	0	0	463			Town and Country	0	0	0	0	10,757
		Perry	0	0	0	0	668			Tracy	0	0	0	0	210
		Perryville	0	0	0	0	8,062			Trenton	0	0	0	0	6,070
		Pevely	0	0	0	0	4,442			Trimble	0	0	0	0	481
		Piedmont	0	0	0		1,954			Troy	0	0	0	0	11,674
		Pierce City	0	0	0	0	1,456			Truesdale	0	0	0	0	615
		Pilot Grove	0	0	0	0	748			Union	0	0	0	0	9,648
										Unionville	0	0	0	0	1,959
										University City	0	0	0	0	36,743
										Uplands Park	0	0	0	0	442
										Urbana	0	0	0	0	435

[1]Agencies published in this table indicated that no hate crimes occurred in their jurisdictions during the quarter(s) for which they submitted reports to the Hate Crime program. Blanks indicate quarters for which agencies did not submit reports.

[2]Population figures are published only for the cities. The figures listed for the universities and colleges are student enrollment and were provided by the United States Department of Education for the 2006 school year, the most recent available. The enrollment figures include full-time and part-time students.

Table 95. Hate Crime Zero Data Submitted per Quarter, by State and Agency, 2007 *(Contd.)*

(Number.)

State	Agency type	Agency name	1st quarter	2nd quarter	3rd quarter	4th quarter	Population[2]
		Vandalia	0	0	0	0	4,099
		Velda City	0	0	0	0	1,512
		Velda Village Hills	0	0	0	0	1,047
		Verona	0		0	0	726
		Versailles	0	0			2,709
		Viburnum	0				808
		Vienna	0	0	0	0	643
		Vinita Park	0	0	0	0	1,803
		Wardell	0	0	0	0	255
		Warrenton	0	0	0		7,146
		Warsaw	0	0		0	2,273
		Warson Woods	0	0	0	0	1,875
		Washington	0	0	0	0	14,367
		Waverly	0	0		0	802
		Waynesville	0	0		0	3,616
		Weatherby Lake	0	0	0	0	1,856
		Webb City	0	0	0	0	11,142
		Webster Groves	0	0	0	0	22,620
		Wellington	0		0	0	777
		Wellsville	0	0	0	0	1,383
		Wentzville	0	0	0	0	24,137
		Weston	0	0		0	1,594
		West Plains	0	0	0	0	11,673
		Westwood	0	0	0	0	295
		Wheaton				0	749
		Willard	0	0	0	0	3,320
		Willow Springs	0	0	0	0	2,145
		Winfield	0	0	0	0	900
		Winona	0	0	0		1,343
		Woodson Terrace	0	0	0	0	4,056
		Wright City	0	0	0	0	2,837
	Universities and Colleges	Lincoln University	0	0	0	0	3,224
		Mineral Area College	0	0	0	0	2,926
		Missouri Western State University	0	0	0	0	5,276
		Northwest Missouri State University	0	0	0	0	6,242
		Southeast Missouri State University	0	0	0	0	10,454
		St. Louis Community College, Meramec	0	0	0	0	10,887
		Truman State University	0	0	0	0	5,820
		University of Central Missouri	0	0	0	0	10,711
		University of Missouri:					
		Rolla	0	0	0	0	5,858
		St. Louis	0	0	0	0	15,528
		Washington University	0	0	0	0	13,355
	Metropolitan Counties	Andrew	0	0	0	0	
		Bates	0	0	0	0	
		Boone	0	0	0	0	
		Buchanan	0	0	0	0	
		Caldwell	0	0	0	0	
		Callaway	0	0	0	0	
		Cass	0	0	0	0	
		Christian	0	0	0	0	
		Clay	0	0	0	0	
		Clinton	0	0	0	0	
		Cole	0	0	0	0	
		Dallas	0	0	0	0	

State	Agency type	Agency name	1st quarter	2nd quarter	3rd quarter	4th quarter	Population[2]
		De Kalb	0	0	0	0	
		Franklin	0				
		Greene	0	0	0	0	
		Jackson	0	0	0	0	
		Jasper	0	0	0	0	
		Jefferson	0	0	0	0	
		Lafayette	0	0	0	0	
		Lincoln	0	0	0	0	
		McDonald	0	0	0	0	
		Moniteau	0	0	0	0	
		Newton	0	0	0	0	
		Osage	0	0	0	0	
		Platte	0	0	0	0	
		Polk	0	0	0	0	
		Ray	0	0	0		
		Washington	0	0	0	0	
		Webster				0	
	Nonmetropolitan Counties	Adair	0	0		0	
		Atchison	0	0	0	0	
		Audrain	0	0	0	0	
		Barry	0	0	0	0	
		Barton	0	0	0	0	
		Benton	0	0	0	0	
		Bollinger	0	0	0	0	
		Butler	0	0	0		
		Camden	0	0	0	0	
		Cape Girardeau	0	0	0	0	
		Carroll	0	0	0		
		Carter	0	0	0	0	
		Chariton	0	0	0		
		Cooper	0	0	0	0	
		Crawford	0	0	0	0	
		Dade		0	0	0	
		Daviess	0	0	0	0	
		Dent	0	0	0	0	
		Dunklin	0	0	0	0	
		Gasconade	0	0	0	0	
		Gentry	0	0	0		
		Grundy	0	0	0	0	
		Harrison	0	0	0	0	
		Henry	0	0	0	0	
		Hickory	0	0	0	0	
		Holt	0	0	0		
		Howell	0	0	0	0	
		Iron	0	0	0	0	
		Johnson	0	0	0	0	
		Knox	0	0	0	0	
		Laclede	0	0	0	0	
		Lawrence	0	0	0	0	
		Lewis	0	0	0	0	
		Linn	0	0	0	0	
		Livingston	0	0	0	0	
		Macon	0	0	0	0	
		Maries	0	0	0	0	
		Marion	0	0	0	0	
		Mercer	0	0	0	0	
		Miller	0	0	0	0	
		Monroe	0	0	0	0	
		Montgomery	0	0	0	0	
		Morgan	0	0	0	0	
		New Madrid	0	0	0	0	
		Nodaway	0	0	0	0	
		Ozark	0	0	0	0	
		Pemiscot	0	0	0	0	
		Perry	0	0	0	0	
		Pettis	0	0	0	0	
		Phelps	0	0	0	0	
		Pike	0			0	
		Ralls	0	0	0	0	
		Randolph	0	0	0	0	
		Reynolds	0	0	0		
		Ripley	0	0	0	0	
		Saline	0	0	0	0	

[1] Agencies published in this table indicated that no hate crimes occurred in their jurisdictions during the quarter(s) for which they submitted reports to the Hate Crime program. Blanks indicate quarters for which agencies did not submit reports.

[2] Population figures are published only for the cities. The figures listed for the universities and colleges are student enrollment and were provided by the United States Department of Education for the 2006 school year, the most recent available. The enrollment figures include full-time and part-time students.

Table 95. Hate Crime Zero Data Submitted per Quarter, by State and Agency, 2007 (Contd.)

(Number.)

State	Agency type	Agency name	1st quarter	2nd quarter	3rd quarter	4th quarter	Population[2]
		Scotland	0	0	0	0	
		Scott	0	0	0	0	
		Shannon	0	0	0	0	
		Shelby	0	0	0	0	
		Ste. Genevieve	0	0	0	0	
		St. Francois	0	0	0	0	
		Stoddard	0	0	0		
		Stone	0	0	0	0	
		Sullivan	0	0	0	0	
		Taney	0	0	0	0	
		Texas	0	0	0	0	
		Vernon	0	0	0	0	
		Wayne	0	0	0		
		Wright	0	0	0	0	
	State Police Agencies	State Highway Patrol:					
		Jefferson City	0	0	0	0	
		Kirkwood	0	0	0	0	
		Lee's Summit	0	0	0	0	
		Macon	0	0	0	0	
		Poplar Bluff	0	0	0	0	
		Rolla	0	0	0	0	
		Springfield	0	0	0	0	
		St. Joseph	0	0	0	0	
		Willow Springs	0	0	0	0	
	Other Agencies	Bootheel Drug Task Force	0	0	0	0	
		Capitol Police	0	0	0	0	
		Clay County Drug Task Force	0	0	0	0	
		Clay County Park Authority	0	0	0	0	
		Department of Conservation	0	0	0	0	
		Division of Alcohol and Tobacco Control	0		0	0	
		Gaming Commission, Enforcement Division	0	0	0	0	
		Jackson County Drug Task Force	0	0	0	0	
		Jackson County Park Rangers	0	0	0	0	
		Lambert-St. Louis International Airport	0	0	0	0	
		Platte County Multi-Jurisdictional Enforcement Group	0	0	0	0	
		State Fire Marshal	0	0	0	0	
		State Park Rangers	0	0	0	0	
		State Water Patrol	0	0	0	0	
		St. Charles County Park Rangers	0	0	0	0	
		St. Peters Ranger Division	0	0	0	0	
MONTANA.....	Cities	Baker	0	0	0	0	1,620
		Belgrade	0	0	0	0	7,552
		Boulder	0	0	0	0	1,468
		Bozeman	0	0	0	0	36,158
		Bridger				0	749
		Chinook	0	0	0	0	1,283
		Columbia Falls	0	0	0	0	4,826
		Columbus	0	0	0	0	1,954
		Conrad	0	0	0	0	2,556
		Cut Bank	0	0	0	0	3,182
		Dillon	0	0	0	0	4,029
		East Helena	0	0	0	0	2,108
		Ennis	0	0	0	0	1,029
		Eureka	0	0	0	0	1,030
		Fort Benton	0	0	0	0	1,451
		Glasgow	0	0	0	0	2,926
		Glendive	0	0	0	0	4,606
		Hamilton	0	0	0	0	4,774
		Joliet	0	0	0	0	617
		Kalispell	0	0	0	0	20,104
		Laurel	0	0	0	0	6,434
		Lewistown	0	0	0	0	6,047
		Libby	0	0	0	0	2,666
		Livingston	0	0	0	0	7,307
		Manhattan	0	0	0	0	1,503
		Miles City	0	0	0	0	8,033
		Plains	0	0	0	0	1,272
		Polson	0	0	0	0	5,082
		Poplar	0	0	0	0	900
		Red Lodge	0	0	0	0	2,494
		Ronan City	0	0	0	0	2,033
		Sidney	0			0	4,761
		Stevensville	0		0	0	1,966
		St. Ignatius	0	0	0	0	830
		Thompson Falls	0	0	0	0	1,420
		Three Forks	0	0	0	0	1,865
		Troy	0	0	0	0	996
		West Yellowstone	0	0	0	0	1,240
		Whitefish	0	0	0	0	8,007
		Wolf Point	0				2,608
	Universities and Colleges	Montana State University	0	0	0	0	12,052
	Metropolitan Counties	Carbon	0	0	0	0	
		Cascade	0	0	0	0	
		Yellowstone	0	0	0	0	
	Nonmetropolitan Counties	Beaverhead	0	0	0	0	
		Big Horn	0	0	0	0	
		Blaine	0	0	0	0	
		Broadwater	0	0	0	0	
		Carter	0	0	0	0	
		Chouteau	0	0	0	0	
		Custer	0	0	0	0	
		Dawson	0	0	0	0	
		Deer Lodge	0	0	0	0	
		Fallon	0	0	0	0	
		Fergus	0	0	0	0	
		Gallatin	0	0	0	0	
		Garfield	0	0	0	0	
		Glacier	0	0	0	0	
		Golden Valley	0	0	0	0	
		Granite	0	0	0	0	
		Hill	0	0	0	0	
		Jefferson	0	0	0	0	
		Judith Basin	0	0	0	0	
		Lake	0	0	0	0	
		Lincoln	0	0	0	0	
		Madison	0	0	0	0	
		McCone	0	0	0	0	
		Meagher	0	0	0	0	
		Mineral	0	0	0	0	
		Musselshell	0	0	0	0	
		Park	0	0	0	0	
		Phillips	0	0	0	0	
		Pondera	0	0	0	0	
		Powell	0	0	0	0	

[1] Agencies published in this table indicated that no hate crimes occurred in their jurisdictions during the quarter(s) for which they submitted reports to the Hate Crime program. Blanks indicate quarters for which agencies did not submit reports.

[2] Population figures are published only for the cities. The figures listed for the universities and colleges are student enrollment and were provided by the United States Department of Education for the 2006 school year, the most recent available. The enrollment figures include full-time and part-time students.

Table 95. Hate Crime Zero Data Submitted per Quarter, by State and Agency, 2007 *(Contd.)*

(Number.)

State	Agency type	Agency name	Zero data per quarter[1]				Population[2]	State	Agency type	Agency name	Zero data per quarter[1]				Population[2]
			1st quarter	2nd quarter	3rd quarter	4th quarter					1st quarter	2nd quarter	3rd quarter	4th quarter	
		Roosevelt	0	0	0	0		State Police Agencies		Nebraska State Patrol	0	0	0	0	
		Rosebud	0	0	0	0				State Patrol:					
		Sanders	0	0	0	0				Adams County	0	0	0	0	
		Sheridan	0	0	0	0				Antelope County	0	0	0	0	
		Stillwater	0	0	0	0				Arthur County	0	0	0	0	
		Sweet Grass	0	0	0	0				Banner County	0	0	0	0	
		Teton	0	0	0	0				Blaine County	0	0	0	0	
		Toole	0	0	0	0				Boone County	0	0	0	0	
		Valley	0	0	0	0				Box Butte County	0	0	0	0	
		Wheatland	0	0	0	0				Boyd County	0	0	0	0	
		Wibaux	0	0	0	0				Brown County	0	0	0	0	
NEBRASKA...	Cities	Aurora	0	0	0	0	4,261			Buffalo County	0	0	0	0	
		Beatrice	0	0	0	0	12,972			Burt County	0	0	0	0	
		Bellevue	0	0	0	0	48,067			Butler County	0	0	0	0	
		Blair	0	0	0	0	7,962			Cass County	0	0	0	0	
		Broken Bow	0	0	0	0	3,235			Cedar County	0	0	0	0	
		Central City	0	0	0	0	2,839			Chase County	0	0	0	0	
		Chadron	0	0	0	0	5,158			Cherry County	0	0	0	0	
		Columbus	0	0	0	0	21,420			Cheyenne County	0	0	0	0	
		Cozad	0	0	0	0	4,293			Clay County	0	0	0	0	
		Emerson	0	0	0	0	819			Colfax County	0	0	0	0	
		Fremont	0	0	0	0	25,423			Cuming County	0	0	0	0	
		Gothenburg	0	0	0	0	3,748			Custer County	0	0	0	0	
		Holdrege	0	0	0	0	5,281			Dakota County	0	0	0	0	
		La Vista	0	0	0	0	16,816			Dawes County	0	0	0	0	
		Lexington	0	0	0	0	10,262			Dawson County	0	0	0	0	
		Madison	0	0	0	0	2,279			Deuel County	0	0	0	0	
		McCook	0	0	0	0	7,491			Dixon County	0	0	0	0	
		Minden	0	0	0	0	2,867			Dodge County	0	0	0	0	
		Nebraska City	0	0	0	0	7,106			Douglas County	0	0	0	0	
		Norfolk	0	0	0	0	23,977			Dundy County	0	0	0	0	
		Ogallala	0	0	0	0	4,585			Fillmore County	0	0	0	0	
		Plattsmouth	0	0	0	0	7,070			Franklin County	0	0	0	0	
		Ralston	0	0	0	0	6,144			Frontier County	0	0	0	0	
		Seward	0	0	0	0	6,922			Furnas County	0	0	0	0	
		St. Paul	0	0	0	0	2,263			Gage County	0	0	0	0	
		Valentine	0	0	0	0	2,694			Garden County	0	0	0	0	
		Waterloo	0	0	0		778			Garfield County	0	0	0	0	
		West Point	0	0	0	0	3,446			Gosper County	0	0	0	0	
		Wymore	0	0	0	0	1,612			Grant County	0	0	0	0	
	Metropolitan Counties	Cass	0	0	0	0				Greeley County	0	0	0	0	
		Dixon	0	0	0	0				Hall County	0	0	0	0	
		Sarpy	0	0	0	0				Hamilton County	0	0	0	0	
		Seward	0	0	0	0				Harlan County	0	0	0	0	
	Nonmetropolitan Counties	Adams	0	0	0	0				Hayes County	0	0	0	0	
		Boone	0							Hitchcock County	0	0	0	0	
		Buffalo	0	0	0	0				Holt County	0	0	0	0	
		Cuming	0	0	0	0				Hooker County	0	0	0	0	
		Custer	0	0	0	0				Howard County	0	0	0	0	
		Dawson	0	0	0	0				Jefferson County	0	0	0	0	
		Frontier	0	0	0	0				Johnson County	0	0	0	0	
		Gage	0	0	0	0				Kearney County	0	0	0	0	
		Garden	0	0						Keith County	0	0	0	0	
		Gosper	0	0	0	0				Keya Paha County	0	0	0	0	
		Hall	0	0	0	0				Kimball County	0	0	0	0	
		Hamilton	0	0	0	0				Knox County	0	0	0	0	
		Harlan	0	0	0	0				Lancaster County	0	0	0	0	
		Jefferson	0	0	0	0				Lincoln County	0	0	0	0	
		Kearney	0	0	0	0				Logan County	0	0	0	0	
		Keith	0	0	0	0				Loup County	0	0	0	0	
		Madison	0	0	0	0				Madison County	0	0	0	0	
		Nance	0	0	0	0				McPherson County	0	0	0	0	
		Nemaha	0	0	0	0									
		Perkins	0	0	0	0									
		Phelps	0	0	0	0									
		Polk	0	0	0	0									
		Saline	0	0	0	0									
		Sherman	0	0	0	0									
		Wayne	0	0	0	0									
		York	0	0	0	0									

[1]Agencies published in this table indicated that no hate crimes occurred in their jurisdictions during the quarter(s) for which they submitted reports to the Hate Crime program. Blanks indicate quarters for which agencies did not submit reports.

[2]Population figures are published only for the cities. The figures listed for the universities and colleges are student enrollment and were provided by the United States Department of Education for the 2006 school year, the most recent available. The enrollment figures include full-time and part-time students.

Table 95. Hate Crime Zero Data Submitted per Quarter, by State and Agency, 2007 (Contd.)

(Number.)

State	Agency type	Agency name	1st quarter	2nd quarter	3rd quarter	4th quarter	Population[2]
		Merrick County	0	0	0	0	
		Morrill County	0	0	0	0	
		Nance County	0	0	0	0	
		Nemaha County	0	0	0	0	
		Nuckolls County	0	0	0	0	
		Otoe County	0	0	0	0	
		Pawnee County	0	0	0	0	
		Perkins County	0	0	0	0	
		Phelps County	0	0	0	0	
		Pierce County	0	0	0	0	
		Platte County	0	0	0	0	
		Polk County	0	0	0	0	
		Red Willow County	0	0	0	0	
		Richardson County	0	0	0	0	
		Rock County	0	0	0	0	
		Saline County	0	0	0	0	
		Sarpy County	0	0	0	0	
		Saunders County	0	0	0	0	
		Scotts Bluff County	0	0	0	0	
		Seward County	0	0	0	0	
		Sheridan County	0	0	0	0	
		Sherman County	0	0	0	0	
		Sioux County	0	0	0	0	
		Stanton County	0	0	0	0	
		Thayer County	0	0	0	0	
		Thomas County	0	0	0	0	
		Thurston County	0	0	0	0	
		Valley County	0	0	0	0	
		Washington County	0	0	0	0	
		Wayne County	0	0	0	0	
		Webster County	0	0	0	0	
		Wheeler County	0	0	0	0	
		York County	0	0	0	0	
NEVADA	Cities	Boulder City	0	0			15,028
		Carlin	0	0			2,121
		Elko	0				16,933
		Fallon	0	0			8,444
		Henderson	0	0	0	0	251,270
		Lovelock	0				1,886
		Sparks	0				86,884
		West Wendover	0	0			5,128
		Winnemucca	0	0	0		8,051
		Yerington	0				3,947
	Universities and Colleges	Truckee Meadows Community College	0	0			11,556
		University of Nevada:					
		Las Vegas	0	0			27,912
		Reno	0	0			16,663
	Metropolitan Counties	Carson City	0				
		Storey	0				
	Nonmetropolitan Counties	Churchill	0				
		Douglas	0				
		Esmeralda	0	0			
		Eureka	0				
		Humboldt	0	0	0		
		Lander	0	0			
		Lincoln	0				
		Lyon	0				
		Mineral	0	0	0		
		Pershing	0				
		White Pine	0				
NEW HAMPSHIRE	Cities	Alexandria	0	0	0	0	1,524
		Alstead	0	0	0	0	2,057
		Alton	0	0	0	0	5,205
		Amherst	0	0	0	0	11,836
		Antrim	0	0	0	0	2,642
		Ashland	0	0	0	0	2,029
		Barnstead	0	0	0	0	4,719
		Barrington	0	0	0	0	8,384
		Bartlett	0	0	0	0	2,945
		Bedford	0	0	0	0	21,389
		Belmont	0	0	0	0	7,365
		Bennington	0	0	0	0	1,488
		Berlin	0	0	0	0	9,909
		Bethlehem	0	0	0	0	2,452
		Boscawen	0	0	0	0	3,930
		Bradford	0	0	0	0	1,534
		Brentwood	0	0	0	0	3,866
		Bristol	0	0	0	0	3,145
		Campton	0	0	0	0	3,001
		Candia	0	0	0	0	4,200
		Canterbury	0	0			2,353
		Carroll	0	0	0	0	752
		Charlestown	0	0	0	0	4,987
		Chester	0	0	0	0	4,793
		Claremont	0	0	0	0	13,291
		Colebrook	0	0	0	0	2,406
		Conway	0	0	0	0	9,300
		Dalton	0	0	0	0	907
		Danville	0	0	0	0	4,425
		Deerfield	0	0	0	0	4,220
		Deering	0	0	0	0	2,070
		Dover	0	0	0	0	28,661
		Dublin	0	0	0	0	1,565
		Dunbarton	0	0	0	0	2,641
		Enfield	0	0	0	0	4,890
		Epping	0	0	0	0	6,263
		Epsom	0	0	0	0	4,609
		Fitzwilliam	0	0	0	0	2,321
		Franconia	0	0	0	0	1,052
		Freedom	0	0	0	0	1,469
		Fremont	0	0	0	0	4,156
		Gilford	0	0	0	0	7,569
		Gilmanton	0	0	0	0	3,621
		Goffstown	0	0	0	0	17,810
		Gorham	0	0	0	0	2,914
		Grantham	0	0	0	0	2,578
		Greenland	0	0	0	0	3,409
		Hampstead	0	0	0	0	8,904
		Hampton	0	0	0	0	15,493
		Hancock	0	0	0	0	1,824
		Haverhill	0	0	0	0	4,623
		Hill	0	0	0	0	1,120
		Hillsborough	0	0	0	0	5,539
		Hinsdale	0	0	0	0	4,219
		Hooksett	0	0	0	0	13,705
		Hopkinton	0	0	0	0	5,651
		Jaffrey	0	0	0	0	5,729
		Kingston	0	0	0	0	6,284
		Lancaster	0	0	0	0	3,362
		Lebanon	0	0	0	0	12,589
		Lincoln	0	0	0	0	1,322
		Lisbon	0	0	0	0	1,663
		Litchfield	0	0	0	0	8,737
		Littleton	0	0	0	0	6,213
		Madison	0	0	0	0	2,329
		Marlborough	0	0	0	0	2,107
		Meredith	0	0	0	0	6,780
		Middleton	0	0	0	0	1,806
		Milton	0	0	0	0	4,531
		Mont Vernon	0	0	0	0	2,433

[1]Agencies published in this table indicated that no hate crimes occurred in their jurisdictions during the quarter(s) for which they submitted reports to the Hate Crime program. Blanks indicate quarters for which agencies did not submit reports.

[2]Population figures are published only for the cities. The figures listed for the universities and colleges are student enrollment and were provided by the United States Department of Education for the 2006 school year, the most recent available. The enrollment figures include full-time and part-time students.

Table 95. Hate Crime Zero Data Submitted per Quarter, by State and Agency, 2007 *(Contd.)*

(Number.)

State	Agency type	Agency name	Zero data per quarter[1]				Population[2]
			1st quarter	2nd quarter	3rd quarter	4th quarter	
		Moulton-borough	0	0	0	0	5,019
		Newbury	0	0	0	0	2,129
		New Durham	0	0	0	0	2,536
		Newfields	0	0	0	0	1,598
		New Hampton	0	0	0	0	2,283
		Newington	0	0	0	0	816
		New Ipswich	0	0	0	0	5,258
		New London	0	0	0	0	4,510
		Newmarket	0	0			9,723
		Newport	0	0	0	0	6,570
		Newton	0	0	0	0	4,544
		Northfield	0	0	0	0	5,257
		North Hampton	0	0	0	0	4,600
		Northumberland	0	0	0	0	2,397
		Northwood	0	0	0	0	4,122
		Nottingham	0	0	0	0	4,564
		Ossipee	0	0	0	0	4,723
		Pelham	0	0	0	0	12,774
		Peterborough	0	0	0	0	6,127
		Plaistow	0	0	0	0	7,702
		Plymouth	0	0	0	0	6,406
		Raymond	0	0	0	0	10,256
		Rollinsford	0	0	0	0	2,627
		Rye	0	0	0	0	5,219
		Sandown	0	0	0	0	5,873
		Sandwich	0	0	0	0	1,335
		Somersworth	0	0			11,815
		Strafford	0	0	0	0	4,084
		Stratham	0	0	0	0	7,293
		Sugar Hill	0	0	0	0	602
		Sunapee	0	0	0	0	3,398
		Thornton	0	0	0	0	2,105
		Tilton	0	0	0	0	3,645
		Troy	0	0	0	0	2,098
		Wakefield	0	0	0	0	5,477
		Walpole	0	0			3,713
		Warner	0	0	0	0	3,021
		Washington	0	0	0	0	1,084
		Waterville Valley	0	0	0	0	271
		Webster	0	0	0	0	1,900
		Wilton	0	0	0	0	3,946
		Wolfeboro	0	0	0	0	6,710
		Woodstock	0	0	0	0	1,181
	Metropolitan Counties	Rockingham	0	0	0	0	
	Nonmetropolitan Counties	Carroll	0	0	0	0	
		Cheshire	0	0	0	0	
		Merrimack	0	0	0	0	
	Other Agencies	Liquor Commission	0	0	0	0	
NEW JERSEY	Cities	Allendale	0	0	0	0	6,683
		Alpha	0	0	0	0	2,426
		Alpine	0	0	0	0	2,418
		Andover Township	0	0	0	0	6,523
		Atlantic Highlands	0	0	0	0	4,594
		Audubon	0	0	0	0	8,941
		Audubon Park	0	0	0	0	1,066
		Avalon	0	0	0	0	2,116
		Avon-by-the-Sea	0	0	0	0	2,156
		Barnegat Light	0	0	0	0	829
		Barrington	0	0	0	0	6,973
		Bay Head	0	0	0	0	1,254
		Beach Haven	0	0	0	0	1,360
		Beachwood	0	0	0	0	10,696
		Bellmawr	0	0	0	0	11,143
		Belmar	0	0	0	0	5,897
		Belvidere	0	0	0	0	2,689

State	Agency type	Agency name	Zero data per quarter[1]				Population[2]
			1st quarter	2nd quarter	3rd quarter	4th quarter	
		Bergenfield	0	0	0	0	26,078
		Berkeley Heights Township	0	0	0	0	13,515
		Berlin	0	0	0	0	7,875
		Bernardsville	0	0	0	0	7,654
		Beverly	0	0	0	0	2,639
		Blairstown Township	0	0	0	0	5,956
		Bogota	0	0	0	0	8,072
		Boonton	0	0	0	0	8,562
		Boonton Township	0	0	0	0	4,377
		Bordentown	0	0	0	0	3,935
		Bordentown Township	0	0	0	0	10,423
		Brick Township	0	0	0	0	77,886
		Bridgeton	0	0	0	0	24,281
		Brielle	0	0	0	0	4,831
		Brooklawn	0	0	0	0	2,284
		Burlington	0	0	0	0	9,672
		Butler	0	0	0	0	8,038
		Byram Township	0	0	0	0	8,618
		Cape May	0	0	0	0	3,792
		Cape May Point	0	0	0	0	229
		Carlstadt	0	0	0	0	6,010
		Carney's Point Township	0	0	0	0	7,946
		Chesilhurst	0	0	0	0	1,871
		Chester	0	0	0	0	1,644
		Chesterfield Township	0	0	0	0	6,422
		Chester Township	0	0	0	0	7,855
		Cinnaminson Township	0	0	0	0	15,381
		Clark Township	0	0	0	0	14,585
		Clayton	0	0	0	0	7,436
		Clementon	0	0	0	0	4,900
		Cliffside Park	0	0	0	0	22,868
		Clinton	0	0	0	0	2,593
		Closter	0	0	0	0	8,691
		Colts Neck Township	0	0	0	0	11,536
		Cresskill	0	0	0	0	8,400
		Deal	0	0	0	0	1,039
		Delaware Township	0	0	0	0	4,709
		Delran Township	0	0	0	0	17,206
		Demarest	0	0	0	0	5,083
		Dover	0	0	0	0	18,306
		East Newark	0	0	0	0	2,207
		East Rutherford	0	0	0	0	8,891
		Eatontown	0	0	0	0	13,960
		Edgewater	0	0	0	0	9,585
		Edgewater Park Township	0	0	0	0	7,933
		Egg Harbor City	0	0	0	0	4,434
		Elk Township	0	0	0	0	3,850
		Elmer	0	0	0	0	1,364
		Elmwood Park	0	0	0	0	18,722
		Elsinboro Township	0	0	0	0	1,068
		Emerson	0	0	0	0	7,286
		Englewood	0	0	0	0	27,701
		Englewood Cliffs	0	0	0	0	5,767
		Essex Fells	0	0	0	0	2,062
		Evesham Township	0	0	0	0	46,504

[1]Agencies published in this table indicated that no hate crimes occurred in their jurisdictions during the quarter(s) for which they submitted reports to the Hate Crime program. Blanks indicate quarters for which agencies did not submit reports.

[2]Population figures are published only for the cities. The figures listed for the universities and colleges are student enrollment and were provided by the United States Department of Education for the 2006 school year, the most recent available. The enrollment figures include full-time and part-time students.

Table 95. Hate Crime Zero Data Submitted per Quarter, by State and Agency, 2007 *(Contd.)*

(Number.)

State	Agency type	Agency name	Zero data per quarter[1]				Population[2]
			1st quarter	2nd quarter	3rd quarter	4th quarter	
		Fairfield Township, Essex County	0	0	0	0	7,673
		Fair Haven	0	0	0	0	5,859
		Fanwood	0	0	0	0	7,179
		Far Hills	0	0	0	0	924
		Flemington	0	0	0	0	4,248
		Florence Township	0	0	0	0	11,585
		Florham Park	0	0	0	0	12,549
		Fort Lee	0	0	0	0	36,844
		Franklin	0	0	0	0	5,187
		Franklin Township, Gloucester County	0	0	0	0	16,778
		Frenchtown	0	0	0	0	1,484
		Garfield	0	0	0	0	29,515
		Garwood	0	0	0	0	4,214
		Gibbsboro	0	0	0	0	2,440
		Glen Ridge	0	0	0	0	6,877
		Gloucester City	0	0	0	0	11,431
		Green Brook Township	0	0	0	0	6,824
		Greenwich Township, Gloucester County	0	0	0	0	4,950
		Greenwich Township, Warren County	0	0	0	0	5,206
		Guttenberg	0	0	0	0	10,670
		Haddon Heights	0	0	0	0	7,332
		Haledon	0	0	0	0	8,321
		Hamburg	0	0	0	0	3,538
		Hammonton	0	0	0	0	13,512
		Hanover Township	0	0	0	0	13,676
		Harrington Park	0	0	0	0	4,894
		Harrison	0	0	0	0	13,880
		Harvey Cedars	0	0	0	0	387
		Hasbrouck Heights	0	0	0	0	11,570
		Haworth	0	0	0	0	3,418
		Helmetta	0	0	0	0	2,014
		Highlands	0	0	0	0	4,965
		Hillsdale	0	0	0	0	10,008
		Hillside Township	0	0	0	0	21,588
		Hi-Nella	0	0	0	0	1,003
		Ho-Ho-Kus	0	0	0	0	4,077
		Holland Township	0	0	0	0	5,286
		Hopewell	0	0	0	0	2,013
		Independence Township	0	0	0	0	5,744
		Interlaken	0	0	0	0	877
		Irvington	0	0	0	0	57,767
		Island Heights	0	0	0	0	1,869
		Jamesburg	0	0	0	0	6,401
		Jefferson Township	0	0	0	0	21,866
		Kearny	0	0	0	0	37,840
		Kenilworth	0	0	0	0	7,707
		Keyport	0	0	0	0	7,438
		Lake Como	0	0	0	0	1,744
		Laurel Springs	0	0	0	0	1,914
		Lavallette	0	0	0	0	2,740
		Lawnside	0	0	0	0	2,788
		Leonia	0	0	0	0	8,760
		Lincoln Park	0	0	0	0	10,808
		Linden	0	0	0	0	39,697
		Lindenwold	0	0	0	0	17,084
		Linwood	0	0	0	0	7,321
		Livingston Township	0	0	0	0	28,287
		Loch Arbour	0	0	0	0	273
		Long Branch	0	0	0	0	32,171
		Long Hill Township	0	0	0	0	8,746
		Longport	0	0	0	0	1,083
		Lopatcong Township	0	0	0	0	8,402
		Lower Alloways Creek Township	0	0	0	0	1,906
		Lower Township	0	0	0	0	20,693
		Lyndhurst Township	0	0	0	0	19,645
		Manasquan	0	0	0	0	6,172
		Mansfield Township, Burlington County	0	0	0	0	8,011
		Mansfield Township, Warren County	0	0	0	0	8,237
		Mantoloking	0	0	0	0	449
		Mantua Township	0	0	0	0	14,908
		Manville	0	0	0	0	10,435
		Maplewood Township	0	0	0	0	22,658
		Matawan	0	0	0	0	8,742
		Maywood	0	0	0	0	9,332
		Mendham Township	0	0	0	0	5,571
		Merchantville	0	0	0	0	3,789
		Metuchen	0	0	0	0	13,157
		Middlesex	0	0	0	0	13,685
		Midland Park	0	0	0	0	6,875
		Millburn Township	0	0	0	0	19,068
		Mine Hill Township	0	0		0	3,650
		Monmouth Beach	0	0	0	0	3,558
		Montgomery Township	0	0	0	0	23,140
		Moonachie	0	0	0	0	2,785
		Morris Plains	0	0	0	0	5,576
		Morristown	0	0	0	0	18,838
		Morris Township	0	0	0	0	21,279
		Mountain Lakes	0	0	0	0	4,324
		Mountainside	0	0	0	0	6,615
		Mount Ephraim	0	0	0	0	4,417
		Mullica Township	0	0	0	0	6,053
		Netcong	0	0	0	0	3,277
		Newfield	0	0	0	0	1,657
		New Hanover Township	0	0	0	0	9,437
		New Milford	0	0	0	0	16,171
		North Arlington	0	0	0	0	15,010
		North Bergen Township	0	0	0	0	56,984
		North Caldwell	0	0	0	0	7,175
		Northfield	0	0	0	0	7,968
		North Haledon	0	0	0	0	8,999
		North Hanover Township	0	0	0	0	7,543
		Northvale	0	0	0	0	4,542
		Ocean City	0	0	0	0	15,057
		Oceanport	0	0	0	0	5,726
		Ocean Township, Ocean County	0	0	0	0	8,205

[1]Agencies published in this table indicated that no hate crimes occurred in their jurisdictions during the quarter(s) for which they submitted reports to the Hate Crime program. Blanks indicate quarters for which agencies did not submit reports.

[2]Population figures are published only for the cities. The figures listed for the universities and colleges are student enrollment and were provided by the United States Department of Education for the 2006 school year, the most recent available. The enrollment figures include full-time and part-time students.

Table 95. Hate Crime Zero Data Submitted per Quarter, by State and Agency, 2007 (Contd.)

(Number.)

State	Agency type	Agency name	Zero data per quarter[1]				Popu-lation[2]
			1st quarter	2nd quarter	3rd quarter	4th quarter	
		Ogdensburg	0	0	0	0	2,611
		Old Tappan	0	0	0	0	5,986
		Orange	0	0	0	0	31,717
		Palisades Park	0	0	0	0	19,220
		Palmyra	0	0	0	0	7,564
		Paramus	0	0	0	0	26,430
		Paterson	0	0	0	0	148,049
		Peapack and Gladstone	0	0	0	0	2,469
		Pemberton	0	0	0	0	1,375
		Pemberton Township	0	0	0	0	28,703
		Pennington	0	0	0	0	2,676
		Penns Grove	0	0	0	0	4,776
		Pequannock Township	0	0	0	0	16,248
		Perth Amboy	0	0	0	0	48,392
		Pine Beach	0	0	0	0	2,023
		Pine Valley	0	0	0	0	23
		Pitman	0	0	0	0	9,158
		Pleasantville	0	0	0	0	18,898
		Plumsted Township	0	0	0	0	8,086
		Pompton Lakes	0	0	0	0	11,193
		Princeton Township	0	0	0	0	17,276
		Rahway	0	0	0	0	27,720
		Ramsey	0	0	0	0	14,710
		Randolph Township	0	0	0	0	25,622
		Ridgefield	0	0	0	0	10,947
		Ridgefield Park	0	0	0	0	12,609
		Ringwood	0	0	0	0	12,757
		Riverdale	0	0	0	0	2,664
		River Edge	0	0	0	0	10,814
		Riverside Township	0	0	0	0	7,915
		Riverton	0	0	0	0	2,703
		Rochelle Park Township	0	0	0	0	6,000
		Rockaway	0	0	0	0	6,382
		Rockleigh	0	0	0	0	391
		Roseland	0	0	0	0	5,376
		Roselle Park	0	0	0	0	13,066
		Rumson	0	0	0	0	7,162
		Saddle Brook Township	0	0	0	0	13,565
		Saddle River	0	0	0	0	3,769
		Scotch Plains Township	0	0	0	0	23,143
		Sea Girt	0	0	0	0	2,035
		Sea Isle City	0	0	0	0	2,936
		Seaside Heights	0	0	0	0	3,228
		Seaside Park	0	0	0	0	2,292
		Secaucus	0	0	0	0	15,493
		Ship Bottom	0	0	0	0	1,421
		Shrewsbury	0	0	0	0	3,701
		Somerdale	0	0	0	0	5,100
		Somers Point	0	0	0	0	11,522
		South Amboy	0	0	0	0	7,830
		South Bound Brook	0	0	0	0	4,504
		South Hackensack Township	0	0	0	0	2,303
		South Toms River	0	0	0	0	3,700
		Sparta Township	0	0	0	0	19,262
		Springfield Township	0	0	0	0	3,554
		Spring Lake	0	0	0	0	3,460
		Spring Lake Heights	0	0	0	0	5,083
		Stillwater Township	0	0	0	0	4,366
		Stone Harbor	0	0	0	0	1,034
		Stratford	0	0	0	0	7,090
		Summit	0	0	0	0	21,010
		Surf City	0	0	0	0	1,535
		Swedesboro	0	0	0	0	2,034
		Tavistock	0	0	0	0	26
		Tenafly	0	0	0	0	14,326
		Teterboro	0	0	0	0	18
		Tewksbury Township	0	0	0	0	6,061
		Toms River Township	0	0	0	0	94,469
		Tuckerton	0	0	0	0	3,810
		Upper Saddle River	0	0	0	0	8,493
		Verona	0	0	0	0	12,880
		Vineland	0	0	0	0	58,013
		Waldwick	0	0	0	0	9,578
		Wall Township	0	0	0	0	25,882
		Washington Township, Bergen County	0	0	0	0	9,627
		Washington Township, Warren County	0	0	0	0	6,950
		Watchung	0	0	0	0	6,256
		Waterford Township	0	0	0	0	10,660
		Wayne Township	0	0	0	0	54,606
		Weehawken Township	0	0	0	0	12,593
		Wenonah	0	0	0	0	2,323
		Westampton Township	0	0	0	0	8,732
		West Amwell Township	0	0	0	0	2,931
		West Cape May	0	0	0	0	1,003
		West Deptford Township	0	0	0	0	21,667
		Westfield	0	0	0	0	29,811
		West Milford Township	0	0	0	0	28,019
		West New York	0	0	0	0	46,193
		West Orange	0	0	0	0	43,343
		West Paterson	0	0	0	0	11,184
		Westville	0	0	0	0	4,438
		West Wildwood	0	0	0	0	406
		West Windsor Township	0	0	0	0	26,163
		Westwood	0	0	0	0	10,886
		Wharton	0	0	0	0	6,183
		Wildwood	0	0	0	0	5,285
		Wildwood Crest	0	0	0	0	3,691
		Willingboro Township	0	0	0	0	32,899
		Winfield Township	0	0	0	0	1,479
		Woodbine	0	0	0	0	2,497
		Woodbury Heights	0	0	0	0	3,017
		Woodcliff Lake	0	0	0	0	5,927
		Woodlynne	0	0	0	0	2,706
		Wood-Ridge	0	0	0	0	7,560
		Woodstown	0	0	0	0	3,318
		Woolwich Township	0	0	0	0	8,574
		Wyckoff Township	0	0	0	0	17,091
	State Police Agencies	State Police: Atlantic County	0	0	0	0	
		Bergen County	0	0	0	0	
		Burlington County	0	0	0	0	

[1]Agencies published in this table indicated that no hate crimes occurred in their jurisdictions during the quarter(s) for which they submitted reports to the Hate Crime program. Blanks indicate quarters for which agencies did not submit reports.

[2]Population figures are published only for the cities. The figures listed for the universities and colleges are student enrollment and were provided by the United States Department of Education for the 2006 school year, the most recent available. The enrollment figures include full-time and part-time students.

Table 95. Hate Crime Zero Data Submitted per Quarter, by State and Agency, 2007 (Contd.)

(Number.)

State	Agency type	Agency name	Zero data per quarter[1] 1st quarter	2nd quarter	3rd quarter	4th quarter	Population[2]
		Camden County	0	0	0	0	
		Cape May County	0	0	0	0	
		Cumberland County	0	0	0	0	
		Essex County	0	0	0	0	
		Gloucester County	0	0	0	0	
		Hudson County	0	0	0	0	
		Hunterdon County	0	0	0	0	
		Mercer County	0	0	0	0	
		Middlesex County	0	0	0	0	
		Monmouth County	0	0	0	0	
		Morris County	0	0	0	0	
		Ocean County	0	0	0	0	
		Passaic County	0	0	0	0	
		Salem County	0	0	0	0	
		Somerset County	0	0	0	0	
		Union County	0	0	0	0	
	Other Agencies	Human Services, Woodland Township	0	0	0	0	
		Hunterdon Developmental Center	0	0	0	0	
NEW MEXICO	Cities	Alamogordo	0		0	0	36,162
		Angel Fire		0		0	1,115
		Bayard	0	0	0	0	2,371
		Belen	0	0	0	0	7,128
		Bosque Farms	0	0	0	0	3,991
		Carrizozo	0	0	0	0	1,099
		Corrales	0	0	0	0	7,936
		Cuba	0	0	0	0	640
		Deming	0	0	0	0	15,449
		Dexter	0	0	0	0	1,243
		Eunice	0	0	0	0	2,636
		Hatch		0	0	0	1,648
		Hobbs	0	0	0	0	29,378
		Lordsburg	0	0	0		2,691
		Los Alamos	0	0	0	0	19,088
		Los Lunas	0	0	0	0	12,022
		Lovington	0	0	0	0	9,723
		Melrose	0	0	0		721
		Red River	0				494
		Roswell	0	0	0	0	45,581
		Santa Rosa		0	0		2,450
		Silver City	0	0			9,903
		Socorro	0				8,570
		Springer	0				1,185
		Tatum	0	0	0		717
	Universities and Colleges	Eastern New Mexico University	0	0	0	0	4,122
		University of New Mexico		0	0	0	25,721
	Metropolitan Counties	San Juan	0	0		0	
		Valencia	0	0	0	0	
	Nonmetropolitan Counties	Catron			0		
		Chaves	0	0	0	0	
		Colfax	0	0	0	0	
		Curry			0		
		Eddy	0	0	0	0	
		Hidalgo	0				

State	Agency type	Agency name	Zero data per quarter[1] 1st quarter	2nd quarter	3rd quarter	4th quarter	Population[2]
		Lea		0	0	0	
		Luna	0	0		0	
		McKinley	0	0	0	0	
		Mora	0				
		Quay	0	0	0		
		Rio Arriba	0	0		0	
		Sierra	0	0	0		
		Socorro	0	0			
NEW YORK	Other Agencies– Tribal Cities	Acoma Tribal	0	0	0	0	
		Adams Village	0	0	0	0	1,637
		Addison Town and Village	0			0	2,559
		Akron Village	0	0	0	0	3,015
		Alexandria Bay Village	0	0	0	0	1,083
		Allegany Village	0	0	0	0	1,795
		Amity Town and Belmont Village	0	0	0	0	2,158
		Amityville Village		0			9,412
		Amsterdam	0	0	0	0	17,678
		Arcade Village	0				1,927
		Asharoken Village	0	0	0	0	635
		Attica Village	0	0	0	0	2,464
		Avon Village	0	0	0	0	2,955
		Baldwinsville Village	0	0	0	0	7,105
		Batavia	0	0	0	0	15,368
		Bath Village	0	0	0		5,532
		Beacon	0	0	0	0	14,928
		Bedford Town			0	0	18,668
		Bolivar Village	0	0	0	0	1,126
		Bolton Town	0	0	0	0	2,180
		Boonville Village	0	0	0	0	2,074
		Brewster		0			2,151
		Briarcliff Manor Village		0	0	0	8,034
		Camden Village	0	0	0	0	2,288
		Camillus Town and Village	0	0	0	0	23,350
		Canajoharie Village	0				2,186
		Canisteo Village	0	0	0	0	2,256
		Canton Village	0	0	0		6,100
		Cape Vincent Village	0			0	768
		Carmel Town	0	0	0		34,972
		Carroll Town	0	0	0	0	3,473
		Cattaraugus Village	0	0	0	0	1,006
		Cayuga Heights Village	0	0	0	0	3,670
		Central Square Village			0	0	1,660
		Chatham Village	0	0		0	1,726
		Chester Village				0	3,616
		Chittenango Village	0	0	0	0	4,936
		Cicero Town	0	0	0	0	28,347
		Clayton Village	0	0	0		1,839
		Clay Town				0	54,134
		Clifton Springs Village	0	0	0	0	2,174
		Cobleskill Village	0	0	0	0	4,647
		Cohoes	0	0	0	0	14,944
		Colchester Town	0				2,054

[1]Agencies published in this table indicated that no hate crimes occurred in their jurisdictions during the quarter(s) for which they submitted reports to the Hate Crime program. Blanks indicate quarters for which agencies did not submit reports.

[2]Population figures are published only for the cities. The figures listed for the universities and colleges are student enrollment and were provided by the United States Department of Education for the 2006 school year, the most recent available. The enrollment figures include full-time and part-time students.

Table 95. Hate Crime Zero Data Submitted per Quarter, by State and Agency, 2007 *(Contd.)*

(Number.)

State	Agency type	Agency name	Zero data per quarter[1]				Population[2]	State	Agency type	Agency name	Zero data per quarter[1]				Population[2]
			1st quarter	2nd quarter	3rd quarter	4th quarter					1st quarter	2nd quarter	3rd quarter	4th quarter	
		Cold Spring Village	0	0	0	0	2,008			Huntington Bay Village		0		0	1,472
		Cooperstown Village	0	0	0		1,911			Hyde Park Town			0	0	20,675
		Copake Town		0			3,331			Independence Town	0	0	0	0	1,052
		Corning			0		10,428			Irondequoit Town	0			0	50,106
		Cornwall Town	0				9,763			Irvington Village	0	0	0	0	6,658
		Cortland	0	0	0	0	18,382			Johnson City Village	0		0	0	14,807
		Cuba Town				0	3,364			Johnstown	0	0	0	0	8,489
		Dansville Village			0	0	4,574			Jordan Village	0	0	0	0	1,338
		Delhi Village	0	0	0	0	2,745			Kenmore Village		0	0	0	15,172
		Depew Village	0		0	0	15,473			Kensington Village	0	0	0	0	1,181
		Deposit Village		0			1,605			Kent Town	0	0	0		14,443
		Dewitt Town	0	0	0	0	21,606			Kings Point Village	0	0		0	5,204
		Dexter Village	0	0	0	0	1,119			Kirkland Town	0	0	0	0	8,423
		Dryden Village				0	1,821			Lackawanna	0	0	0	0	17,775
		East Fishkill Town	0	0			29,535			Lake Placid Village	0	0	0	0	2,840
		East Greenbush Town	0	0	0	0	17,159			Larchmont Village	0	0	0	0	6,535
		East Syracuse Village	0	0	0		3,029			Le Roy Village	0	0	0	0	4,226
		Ellenville Village	0	0	0	0	3,914			Little Falls	0	0	0	0	4,952
		Elmira Heights Village	0	0	0	0	3,931			Lloyd Harbor Village	0	0	0	0	3,654
		Evans Town		0	0		17,000			Lockport	0	0	0	0	20,872
		Fairport Village				0	5,467			Malone Village	0	0	0	0	5,879
		Fishkill Town	0		0	0	19,088			Malverne Village	0	0	0	0	8,725
		Fishkill Village	0	0			1,731			Mamaroneck Town	0	0	0	0	11,470
		Floral Park Village			0		15,550			Manchester Village	0	0	0	0	1,434
		Fort Plain Village			0	0	2,201			Manlius Town	0	0		0	25,127
		Franklinville Village	0	0	0	0	1,741			Marlborough Town		0			8,351
		Freeport Village	0				43,050			Maybrook Village	0	0	0	0	4,185
		Freeville Village				0	505			McGraw Village	0	0	0	0	963
		Friendship Town	0	0	0		1,865			Mechanicville	0	0	0	0	4,912
		Garden City Village			0	0	21,804			Middleport Village	0	0	0	0	1,803
		Gates Town	0				28,396			Middletown	0	0	0		26,097
		Germantown Town	0	0	0	0	2,015			Millbrook Village			0	0	1,559
		Glen Park Village	0	0	0	0	491			Moravia Village	0	0	0	0	1,313
		Glens Falls	0	0	0	0	14,043			Mount Kisco Village	0	0		0	10,505
		Gloversville	0	0	0	0	15,146			Nassau Village	0	0	0		1,115
		Goshen Village	0	0	0	0	5,527			New Berlin Town	0	0			1,717
		Gouverneur Village	0	0	0		4,088			Newburgh	0	0			28,340
		Granville Village	0	0	0	0	2,585			Newburgh Town			0	0	30,995
		Great Neck Estates Village	0				2,711			New Windsor Town	0	0	0	0	25,320
		Greece Town		0	0	0	93,123			New York Mills Village	0	0	0	0	3,128
		Greene Village			0	0	1,683			Niskayuna Town	0	0		0	21,863
		Greenwood Lake Village	0	0	0	0	3,460			Nissequogue Village	0	0	0	0	1,458
		Groton Village	0	0	0	0	2,403			North Castle Town	0	0	0	0	12,317
		Guilderland Town	0			0	33,006			North Greenbush Town	0				11,837
		Hancock Village	0	0	0	0	1,111			Northport Village	0	0	0	0	7,480
		Hastings-on-Hudson Village				0	7,858			North Syracuse Village	0	0	0	0	6,668
		Haverstraw Town	0	0	0	0	24,515								
		Homer Village	0	0	0	0	3,265								
		Hoosick Falls Village		0	0	0	3,289								
		Hornell	0			0	8,662								
		Hunter Town	0	0	0	0	2,756								

[1]Agencies published in this table indicated that no hate crimes occurred in their jurisdictions during the quarter(s) for which they submitted reports to the Hate Crime program. Blanks indicate quarters for which agencies did not submit reports.

[2]Population figures are published only for the cities. The figures listed for the universities and colleges are student enrollment and were provided by the United States Department of Education for the 2006 school year, the most recent available. The enrollment figures include full-time and part-time students.

Table 95. Hate Crime Zero Data Submitted per Quarter, by State and Agency, 2007 *(Contd.)*

(Number.)

State	Agency type	Agency name	1st quarter	2nd quarter	3rd quarter	4th quarter	Population[2]
		North Tonawanda	0	0			31,575
		Northville Village	0	0	0	0	1,162
		Old Westbury Village		0	0	0	5,340
		Olean	0	0	0	0	14,485
		Olive Town	0	0		0	4,720
		Oneonta City	0	0	0	0	13,239
		Orchard Park Town	0	0	0	0	28,208
		Oriskany Village	0	0	0	0	1,424
		Ossining Village	0	0	0	0	23,514
		Oswego City	0			0	17,573
		Oxford Village	0		0		1,566
		Oyster Bay Cove Village	0	0	0	0	2,248
		Painted Post Village		0	0	0	1,784
		Penn Yan Village	0	0	0	0	5,217
		Perry Village	0	0	0	0	3,743
		Phelps Village	0	0	0	0	1,931
		Pine Plains Town	0	0	0	0	2,750
		Plattekill Town		0	0		10,993
		Pleasantville Village	0	0	0	0	7,167
		Port Byron Village	0	0			1,257
		Port Chester Village	0	0	0	0	28,019
		Port Dickinson Village	0	0	0	0	1,605
		Port Jervis	0	0	0		9,203
		Portville Village	0	0	0		973
		Port Washington		0	0		18,532
		Pound Ridge Town	0	0	0		5,011
		Pulaski Village	0	0	0	0	2,323
		Quogue Village		0		0	1,125
		Rensselaer City	0	0	0	0	7,822
		Riverhead Town	0	0	0	0	35,087
		Rockville Centre Village	0	0	0		23,952
		Rome	0	0	0	0	34,123
		Rosendale Town	0	0		0	6,312
		Rouses Point Village	0	0	0	0	2,420
		Rye Brook Village	0	0	0	0	9,820
		Sands Point Village	0		0		2,839
		Saratoga Springs		0		0	28,807
		Saugerties Village	0	0	0	0	3,912
		Schenectady	0		0	0	61,535
		Seneca Falls Village	0	0	0	0	6,791
		Shandaken Town				0	3,113
		Shelter Island Town	0			0	2,471
		Sherburne Village	0		0		1,443
		Shortsville Village	0	0	0	0	1,342
		Silver Creek Village	0	0	0	0	2,842
		Skaneateles Village		0		0	2,585
		Sleepy Hollow Village	0	0	0	0	10,262
		Solvay Village	0	0	0	0	6,514
		Southampton Town	0	0	0	0	50,284
		Southampton Village	0	0	0	0	4,091
		Stockport Town	0		0	0	2,882
		Tarrytown Village	0	0	0	0	11,525
		Tonawanda	0		0	0	14,971
		Troy	0	0	0	0	47,776
		Trumansburg Village	0	0	0	0	1,587
		Tuckahoe Village		0	0	0	6,311
		Tuxedo Park Village	0	0	0	0	726
		Ulster Town				0	12,877
		Vestal Town	0	0	0	0	27,403
		Wallkill Town	0	0	0		27,554
		Walton Village	0	0			2,880
		Wappingers Falls Village	0	0	0	0	5,181
		Warsaw Village	0	0	0	0	3,717
		Washingtonville Village	0	0	0	0	6,239
		Waterford Town and Village	0	0	0	0	8,660
		Watertown				0	26,726
		Webster Town and Village	0	0	0	0	41,471
		Weedsport Village	0	0			1,950
		Wellsville Village	0	0	0	0	4,877
		West Carthage Village	0	0			2,126
		Westhampton Beach Village	0	0	0	0	1,956
		West Seneca Town			0	0	43,955
		Whitesboro Village				0	3,823
		Whitestown Town	0	0	0	0	9,348
		Windham Town	0	0	0	0	1,914
		Woodbury Town	0		0		10,458
		Woodridge Village	0	0	0	0	1,085
		Yonkers			0	0	198,071
		Yorkville Village	0	0	0		2,593
	Metro-politan Counties	Albany	0	0	0	0	
		Chemung		0		0	
		Herkimer	0	0	0	0	
		Livingston	0	0	0		
		Madison	0				
		Oneida	0	0	0	0	
		Onondaga	0	0	0	0	
		Ontario		0			
		Orange			0		
		Oswego		0	0	0	
		Putnam	0	0	0	0	
		Rensselaer	0		0	0	
		Schenectady		0	0	0	
		Schoharie	0	0	0	0	
		Suffolk	0	0	0	0	
		Tompkins	0	0	0	0	
		Ulster	0	0	0	0	

[1] Agencies published in this table indicated that no hate crimes occurred in their jurisdictions during the quarter(s) for which they submitted reports to the Hate Crime program. Blanks indicate quarters for which agencies did not submit reports.

[2] Population figures are published only for the cities. The figures listed for the universities and colleges are student enrollment and were provided by the United States Department of Education for the 2006 school year, the most recent available. The enrollment figures include full-time and part-time students.

Table 95. Hate Crime Zero Data Submitted per Quarter, by State and Agency, 2007 (Contd.)

(Number.)

State	Agency type	Agency name	1st quarter	2nd quarter	3rd quarter	4th quarter	Population[2]
NORTH CAROLINA....	Nonmetropolitan Counties	Chenango	0	0	0	0	
		Franklin	0	0	0	0	
		Fulton	0	0	0	0	
		Hamilton	0	0	0	0	
		Montgomery	0	0	0	0	
		Seneca	0	0	0	0	
		Steuben	0	0	0	0	
	Other Agencies	New York City Metropolitan Transportation Authority	0				
	Cities	Aberdeen	0	0	0	0	5,337
		Ahoskie	0	0	0	0	4,278
		Andrews	0	0	0	0	1,719
		Angier	0	0	0	0	4,288
		Apex	0	0	0	0	31,816
		Asheboro	0	0	0	0	24,399
		Atlantic Beach	0	0	0	0	1,839
		Aulander	0	0	0	0	869
		Ayden	0	0	0	0	4,852
		Badin	0	0	0	0	1,357
		Bailey	0	0	0	0	679
		Bald Head Island	0	0	0	0	295
		Banner Elk	0	0	0	0	895
		Beaufort	0	0	0	0	4,326
		Beech Mountain	0	0	0	0	307
		Belhaven	0	0	0	0	1,997
		Belmont	0	0	0	0	9,005
		Benson	0	0	0	0	3,422
		Biltmore Forest	0	0	0	0	1,527
		Biscoe	0	0	0	0	1,732
		Black Mountain	0	0	0	0	7,686
		Bladenboro	0	0	0	0	1,701
		Blowing Rock	0	0	0	0	1,426
		Boiling Springs	0	0	0	0	3,856
		Boone	0	0	0	0	13,283
		Brevard	0	0	0	0	6,634
		Bryson City	0	0	0	0	1,382
		Burgaw	0	0	0	0	3,975
		Burlington	0	0	0	0	48,689
		Burnsville	0	0	0	0	1,652
		Butner	0	0	0	0	6,520
		Cameron	0	0	0	0	301
		Canton	0	0	0	0	3,925
		Carolina Beach	0	0	0	0	5,675
		Carrboro	0	0	0	0	16,514
		Carthage	0	0	0	0	2,036
		Caswell Beach	0	0	0	0	490
		Chadbourn	0	0	0	0	2,071
		Chapel Hill	0	0	0	0	50,198
		Cherryville	0	0	0	0	5,533
		Chocowinity	0	0	0	0	730
		Claremont	0	0	0	0	1,127
		Clayton	0	0	0	0	14,843
		Cleveland	0	0	0	0	829
		Clinton	0	0	0	0	8,818
		Clyde	0	0	0	0	1,295
		Coats	0	0	0	0	2,086
		Conover	0	0	0	0	7,183
		Cornelius	0	0	0	0	21,563
		Cramerton	0	0	0	0	3,050
		Creedmoor	0	0	0	0	3,472
		Dallas	0	0	0	0	3,433
		Davidson	0	0	0	0	9,023
		Drexel	0	0	0	0	1,900
		East Spencer	0	0	0	0	1,770
		Eden	0	0	0	0	15,608
		Edenton	0	0	0	0	4,988
		Elizabeth City	0	0	0	0	19,279
		Elizabethtown	0	0	0	0	3,841
		Elkin	0	0	0	0	4,314
		Elon	0	0	0	0	7,173
		Emerald Isle	0	0	0	0	3,752
		Enfield	0	0	0	0	2,345
		Erwin	0	0	0	0	4,843
		Farmville	0	0	0	0	4,553
		Fletcher	0	0	0	0	4,662
		Franklin	0	0	0	0	3,633
		Fremont	0	0	0	0	1,428
		Fuquay-Varina	0	0	0	0	14,661
		Garner	0	0	0	0	24,547
		Garysburg	0	0	0	0	1,171
		Gastonia	0	0	0	0	70,127
		Gibsonville	0	0	0	0	4,627
		Goldsboro	0	0	0	0	38,053
		Graham	0	0	0	0	14,275
		Granite Falls	0	0	0	0	4,597
		Hamlet	0	0	0	0	5,715
		Havelock	0	0	0	0	21,839
		Henderson	0	0	0	0	16,165
		Hendersonville	0	0	0	0	11,863
		Hertford	0	0	0	0	2,135
		Highlands	0	0	0	0	948
		Hillsborough	0	0	0	0	5,380
		Hobgood	0				382
		Holden Beach	0		0	0	863
		Holly Ridge	0	0	0	0	727
		Hope Mills	0	0	0	0	12,778
		Hudson	0	0	0	0	3,075
		Huntersville	0	0	0	0	41,018
		Indian Beach	0	0	0	0	96
		Jacksonville	0	0	0	0	70,368
		Jefferson	0	0	0	0	1,368
		Jonesville	0	0	0	0	2,296
		Kannapolis	0	0	0	0	40,554
		Kenly	0	0	0	0	1,894
		Kernersville	0	0	0	0	22,325
		Kill Devil Hills	0	0	0	0	6,718
		King	0	0	0	0	6,639
		Kings Mountain	0	0	0	0	11,003
		Kinston	0	0	0	0	22,568
		Kitty Hawk	0	0	0	0	3,391
		Knightdale	0	0	0	0	6,530
		La Grange	0	0	0	0	2,782
		Lake Lure	0	0	0	0	1,022
		Landis	0	0	0	0	3,074
		Laurel Park	0	0	0	0	2,123
		Laurinburg	0	0	0	0	15,743
		Lenoir	0	0	0	0	17,988
		Lillington	0	0	0	0	3,214
		Lincolnton	0	0	0	0	10,646
		Locust	0	0	0	0	2,562
		Long View	0	0	0	0	4,904
		Louisburg	0	0	0	0	3,813
		Lumberton	0	0	0	0	21,983
		Madison	0	0	0	0	2,283
		Maggie Valley	0	0	0	0	810
		Maiden	0	0	0	0	3,366
		Manteo	0	0	0	0	1,336
		Marion	0	0	0	0	5,070
		Marshall	0	0	0	0	837
		Mars Hill	0	0	0	0	1,821
		Marshville	0	0	0	0	3,054
		Matthews	0	0	0	0	26,693
		Maxton	0	0	0	0	2,666
		Mayodan	0	0	0	0	2,624
		Maysville	0	0	0	0	978
		McAdenville	0	0	0	0	643
		Mebane	0	0	0	0	9,555
		Middlesex	0	0	0	0	856
		Mocksville	0	0	0	0	4,568
		Monroe	0	0	0	0	31,345
		Mooresville	0	0	0	0	21,143
		Morehead City	0	0	0	0	9,501
		Morganton	0	0	0	0	17,183
		Morrisville	0	0	0	0	14,336

[1]Agencies published in this table indicated that no hate crimes occurred in their jurisdictions during the quarter(s) for which they submitted reports to the Hate Crime program. Blanks indicate quarters for which agencies did not submit reports.

[2]Population figures are published only for the cities. The figures listed for the universities and colleges are student enrollment and were provided by the United States Department of Education for the 2006 school year, the most recent available. The enrollment figures include full-time and part-time students.

Table 95. Hate Crime Zero Data Submitted per Quarter, by State and Agency, 2007 (Contd.)

(Number.)

State	Agency type	Agency name	1st quarter	2nd quarter	3rd quarter	4th quarter	Population[2]
		Mount Gilead	0	0	0	0	1,406
		Mount Holly	0	0	0	0	9,811
		Murfreesboro	0	0	0	0	2,276
		Murphy	0	0	0	0	1,573
		Nags Head	0	0	0	0	3,114
		Nashville	0	0	0	0	4,509
		New Bern	0	0	0	0	28,254
		Newland	0	0	0	0	663
		Newton	0	0	0	0	13,211
		North Topsail Beach	0	0	0	0	874
		Norwood	0	0	0	0	2,150
		Oakboro	0	0	0	0	1,176
		Ocean Isle Beach	0	0	0	0	536
		Old Fort	0	0	0	0	963
		Pilot Mountain	0	0	0	0	1,276
		Pinebluff	0	0	0	0	1,352
		Pinehurst	0	0	0	0	12,132
		Pinetops	0	0	0	0	1,293
		Pineville	0	0	0	0	3,826
		Pittsboro	0	0	0	0	2,537
		Plymouth	0	0	0	0	3,930
		Ramseur	0	0	0	0	1,728
		Randleman	0	0	0	0	3,700
		Red Springs	0	0	0	0	3,518
		Rich Square	0	0	0	0	996
		Roanoke Rapids	0	0	0	0	16,407
		Robbins	0	0	0	0	1,238
		Robersonville	0	0	0	0	1,601
		Rockingham	0	0	0	0	9,093
		Rockwell	0	0	0	0	1,989
		Rocky Mount	0	0	0	0	57,132
		Rolesville	0	0	0	0	1,805
		Rose Hill	0	0	0	0	1,403
		Rowland	0	0	0	0	1,157
		Rutherfordton	0	0	0	0	4,090
		Saluda	0	0	0	0	581
		Sanford	0	0	0	0	28,413
		Scotland Neck	0	0	0	0	2,195
		Selma	0	0	0	0	6,877
		Sharpsburg	0	0	0	0	2,432
		Shelby	0	0	0	0	21,437
		Smithfield	0	0	0	0	12,456
		Southern Shores	0	0	0	0	2,708
		Spencer	0	0	0	0	3,355
		Spindale	0	0	0	0	3,916
		Spring Hope	0	0	0	0	1,280
		Stallings	0	0	0	0	4,201
		Stanfield	0	0	0	0	1,113
		Stanley	0	0	0	0	3,134
		Star	0	0	0	0	814
		Statesville	0	0	0	0	25,756
		St. Pauls	0	0	0	0	2,053
		Sugar Mountain	0	0	0	0	213
		Sunset Beach	0	0	0	0	2,296
		Surf City	0	0	0	0	1,873
		Sylva	0	0	0	0	2,369
		Tarboro	0	0	0	0	10,463
		Taylorsville	0	0	0	0	1,828
		Thomasville	0	0	0	0	26,437
		Troutman	0	0	0	0	1,767
		Troy	0	0	0	0	3,408
		Tryon	0	0	0	0	1,745
		Valdese	0	0	0	0	4,525
		Vass	0	0	0	0	778
		Wadesboro	0	0	0	0	5,134
		Wake Forest	0	0	0	0	24,348
		Wallace	0	0	0	0	3,603
		Warsaw	0	0	0	0	3,149
		Waxhaw	0	0	0	0	3,505
		Waynesville	0	0	0	0	9,436
		Weaverville	0	0	0	0	2,543
		Wendell	0	0	0	0	4,867
		West Jefferson	0	0	0	0	1,128
		Whispering Pines	0	0	0	0	2,138
		Whiteville	0	0	0	0	5,239
		Wilkesboro	0	0	0	0	3,193
		Williamston	0	0	0	0	5,531
		Wilmington	0	0	0	0	96,913
		Windsor	0	0	0	0	2,175
		Wingate	0	0	0	0	3,876
		Winston-Salem	0	0	0	0	198,316
		Woodfin	0	0	0	0	3,335
		Woodland	0	0	0	0	776
		Wrightsville Beach	0	0	0	0	2,573
		Yadkinville	0	0	0	0	2,898
		Youngsville	0	0	0	0	738
		Zebulon	0	0	0	0	4,358
	Universities and Colleges	Appalachian State University	0	0	0	0	15,117
		Duke University	0	0	0	0	13,373
		East Carolina University	0	0	0	0	24,351
		Elizabeth City State University	0	0	0	0	2,681
		Elon University	0	0	0	0	5,230
		Methodist College	0	0	0	0	2,116
		North Carolina Agricultural and Technical State University	0	0	0	0	11,098
		North Carolina Central University	0	0	0	0	8,675
		North Carolina School of the Arts	0	0	0	0	845
		North Carolina State University, Raleigh	0	0	0	0	31,130
		University of North Carolina: Asheville	0	0	0	0	3,639
		Chapel Hill	0	0	0	0	27,717
		Charlotte	0	0	0	0	21,519
		Pembroke	0	0	0	0	5,827
		Wake Forest University	0	0	0	0	6,739
		Western Carolina University	0	0	0	0	8,861
		Winston-Salem State University	0	0	0	0	5,650
	Metropolitan Counties	Alamance	0	0	0	0	
		Alexander	0	0	0	0	
		Anson	0	0	0	0	
		Brunswick	0	0	0	0	
		Buncombe	0	0	0	0	
		Burke	0	0	0	0	
		Cabarrus	0	0	0	0	
		Davie	0	0	0	0	
		Durham	0	0	0	0	
		Edgecombe	0	0	0	0	
		Franklin	0	0	0	0	
		Gaston	0	0	0	0	
		Gaston County Police Department	0	0	0	0	
		Greene	0	0	0	0	
		Haywood	0	0	0	0	
		Henderson	0	0	0	0	
		Madison	0	0	0	0	

[1] Agencies published in this table indicated that no hate crimes occurred in their jurisdictions during the quarter(s) for which they submitted reports to the Hate Crime program. Blanks indicate quarters for which agencies did not submit reports.

[2] Population figures are published only for the cities. The figures listed for the universities and colleges are student enrollment and were provided by the United States Department of Education for the 2006 school year, the most recent available. The enrollment figures include full-time and part-time students.

Table 95. Hate Crime Zero Data Submitted per Quarter, by State and Agency, 2007 *(Contd.)*

(Number.)

State	Agency type	Agency name	1st quarter	2nd quarter	3rd quarter	4th quarter	Population[2]
		Nash	0	0	0	0	
		Onslow	0	0	0	0	
		Orange	0	0	0	0	
		Pender	0	0	0	0	
		Person	0	0	0	0	
		Pitt	0	0	0	0	
		Randolph	0	0	0	0	
		Stokes	0	0	0	0	
		Union	0	0	0	0	
		Wayne	0	0	0	0	
		Yadkin	0	0	0	0	
	Nonmetropolitan Counties	Alleghany	0	0	0	0	
		Avery	0	0	0	0	
		Beaufort	0	0	0	0	
		Bertie	0	0	0	0	
		Bladen	0	0	0	0	
		Camden	0	0	0	0	
		Carteret	0	0	0	0	
		Cherokee	0	0	0	0	
		Chowan	0	0	0	0	
		Clay	0	0	0	0	
		Columbus	0	0	0	0	
		Craven	0	0	0	0	
		Dare	0	0	0	0	
		Duplin	0	0	0	0	
		Gates	0	0	0	0	
		Graham	0	0	0	0	
		Granville	0	0	0	0	
		Halifax	0	0	0	0	
		Harnett	0	0	0	0	
		Hertford	0	0	0	0	
		Hyde	0	0	0	0	
		Jackson	0	0	0	0	
		Lee	0	0	0	0	
		Lincoln	0	0	0	0	
		Macon	0	0	0	0	
		Martin	0	0	0	0	
		McDowell	0	0	0	0	
		Montgomery	0	0	0	0	
		Moore	0	0	0	0	
		Northampton	0	0	0	0	
		Pamlico	0	0	0	0	
		Pasquotank	0	0	0	0	
		Perquimans	0	0	0	0	
		Polk	0	0	0	0	
		Robeson	0	0	0	0	
		Scotland	0	0	0	0	
		Stanly	0	0	0	0	
		Surry	0	0	0	0	
		Swain	0	0	0	0	
		Tyrrell	0	0	0	0	
		Vance	0	0	0	0	
		Warren	0	0	0	0	
		Watauga	0	0	0	0	
		Wilkes	0	0	0	0	
		Wilson	0	0	0	0	
		Yancey	0	0	0	0	
	Other Agencies	Department of Human Resources	0	0	0	0	
		Department of Wildlife	0	0	0	0	
		Piedmont Triad International Airport	0	0	0	0	
		State Park Rangers: Crowders Mountain	0	0	0	0	
		Dismal Swamp	0	0	0	0	
		Elk Knob	0	0	0	0	
		Eno River	0	0	0	0	
		Goose Creek	0	0	0	0	
		Gorges	0	0	0	0	
		Hanging Rock	0	0	0	0	
		Jockey's Ridge	0	0	0	0	
		Lake James	0	0	0	0	
		Lake Norman	0	0	0	0	
		Medoc Mountain	0	0	0	0	
		Merchants Millpond	0	0	0	0	
		Morrow Mountain	0	0	0	0	
		Mt. Mitchell	0	0	0	0	
		New River-Mount Jefferson	0	0	0	0	
		Pettigrew	0	0	0	0	
		Pilot Mountain	0	0	0	0	
		South Mountains	0	0	0	0	
		Stone Mountain	0	0	0	0	
		Weymouth Woods Sandhills Nature Preserve	0	0	0	0	
NORTH DAKOTA	Cities	Beulah	0	0	0	0	2,974
		Burlington	0	0	0	0	989
		Carrington	0	0	0	0	2,131
		Cavalier	0	0	0	0	1,404
		Emerado	0	0	0	0	466
		Fessenden	0	0	0	0	519
		Grand Forks	0	0	0	0	50,477
		Harvey	0	0	0	0	1,671
		Hillsboro	0	0	0	0	1,502
		Lincoln	0	0	0	0	2,548
		Lisbon	0	0	0	0	2,185
		Mayville	0	0	0	0	1,919
		Minot	0	0	0	0	34,487
		Northwood	0	0	0	0	853
		Portland	0	0	0	0	562
		Rolla	0	0	0	0	1,451
		Rugby	0	0	0	0	2,606
		Steele	0	0	0	0	676
		Thompson	0	0	0	0	937
		Valley City	0	0	0	0	6,325
		Wahpeton	0	0	0	0	7,850
		Watford City	0	0	0	0	1,371
		West Fargo	0	0	0	0	22,462
		Williston	0	0	0	0	12,260
	Universities and Colleges	North Dakota State College of Science	0	0	0	0	2,493
		North Dakota State University	0	0	0	0	12,258
		University of North Dakota	0	0	0	0	12,834
	Metropolitan Counties	Cass	0	0	0	0	
		Grand Forks	0	0	0	0	
	Nonmetropolitan Counties	Adams	0	0	0	0	
		Barnes	0	0	0	0	
		Bottineau	0	0	0	0	
		Bowman	0	0	0	0	
		Burke	0	0	0	0	
		Cavalier	0	0	0	0	
		Dickey	0	0	0	0	
		Dunn	0	0	0	0	
		Eddy	0	0	0	0	
		Emmons	0	0	0	0	
		Foster	0	0	0	0	

[1] Agencies published in this table indicated that no hate crimes occurred in their jurisdictions during the quarter(s) for which they submitted reports to the Hate Crime program. Blanks indicate quarters for which agencies did not submit reports.

[2] Population figures are published only for the cities. The figures listed for the universities and colleges are student enrollment and were provided by the United States Department of Education for the 2006 school year, the most recent available. The enrollment figures include full-time and part-time students.

Table 95. Hate Crime Zero Data Submitted per Quarter, by State and Agency, 2007 *(Contd.)*

(Number.)

State	Agency type	Agency name	1st quarter	2nd quarter	3rd quarter	4th quarter	Population[2]
		Grant	0	0	0		
		Griggs	0	0	0	0	
		Hettinger	0	0	0	0	
		Kidder	0	0	0	0	
		Lamoure	0	0			
		Logan	0	0	0	0	
		McHenry	0	0	0	0	
		McIntosh	0	0	0	0	
		McKenzie	0	0	0	0	
		McLean	0	0	0	0	
		Mercer	0	0	0	0	
		Nelson	0	0	0	0	
		Oliver	0	0	0		
		Pembina	0	0	0	0	
		Pierce	0	0	0	0	
		Renville	0	0	0	0	
		Richland	0	0	0	0	
		Rolette	0	0	0	0	
		Sargent	0	0	0	0	
		Sheridan	0	0	0	0	
		Slope	0	0	0	0	
		Stutsman	0	0	0	0	
		Towner	0	0	0	0	
		Traill	0	0	0	0	
		Ward	0	0	0	0	
		Wells	0	0	0	0	
		Williams	0	0	0	0	
OHIO	Cities	Ada	0	0	0	0	5,881
		Addyston	0				932
		Amberley Village	0	0	0	0	3,204
		Amelia	0	0	0	0	3,624
		Amsterdam				0	551
		Ansonia	0	0	0	0	1,099
		Arcanum	0	0	0	0	2,002
		Archbold	0	0	0	0	4,530
		Ashland	0	0	0	0	21,939
		Ashville	0	0			3,285
		Aurora	0	0	0	0	14,512
		Austintown	0	0	0	0	35,888
		Bainbridge Township	0	0	0		11,334
		Baltimore	0	0	0	0	2,948
		Barnesville	0	0	0	0	4,118
		Barnhill	0	0			379
		Batavia	0	0	0	0	1,691
		Bay View	0	0	0	0	645
		Bay Village	0	0	0	0	14,828
		Bazetta Township		0	0	0	6,124
		Beach City		0	0	0	1,099
		Beachwood	0	0	0		11,239
		Beaver Township	0	0	0	0	6,176
		Bellaire	0	0	0	0	4,674
		Bellbrook	0	0	0	0	6,892
		Bellville	0	0	0	0	1,731
		Berea	0	0	0	0	18,026
		Berlin Heights		0			645
		Bethel	0	0	0	0	2,608
		Bethesda	0	0	0	0	1,365
		Beverly	0	0	0	0	1,310
		Bexley	0			0	12,161
		Blanchester	0	0	0	0	4,382
		Blendon Township	0	0	0	0	7,561
		Bloomville		0	0	0	1,000
		Bratenahl	0	0	0		1,287
		Brecksville	0	0	0	0	13,065
		Bridgeport		0	0	0	2,079
		Brimfield Township	0	0	0	0	7,854
		Broadview Heights	0	0	0	0	17,798
		Brooklyn	0	0			10,574
		Brooklyn Heights				0	1,474
		Brook Park	0	0	0	0	19,498
		Bryan	0	0	0	0	8,327
		Buchtel	0	0			600
		Buckeye Lake	0	0		0	3,055
		Butler	0	0	0	0	896
		Byesville	0	0	0	0	2,571
		Cadiz	0	0	0	0	3,379
		Cairo		0	0	0	506
		Camden	0	0	0	0	2,248
		Campbell	0	0	0	0	8,630
		Canal Fulton	0	0	0	0	5,106
		Canfield	0	0	0	0	7,014
		Cardington	0	0	0	0	2,011
		Carey	0	0	0	0	3,811
		Carlisle	0	0	0		5,985
		Celina	0	0	0	0	10,403
		Centerville	0	0	0	0	23,049
		Chagrin Falls		0			3,701
		Champion Township	0	0	0	0	9,409
		Chesapeake	0	0	0		884
		Cheshire		0			80
		Circleville	0	0	0	0	13,648
		Clay Center			0	0	309
		Clay Township, Ottawa County			0		2,732
		Cleves	0	0	0	0	2,501
		Clinton Township	0	0	0	0	3,938
		Coitsville Township				0	1,654
		Coldwater	0	0	0	0	4,454
		Columbiana	0	0			5,977
		Coolville	0				545
		Cortland		0	0	0	6,508
		Covington	0	0	0	0	2,572
		Craig Beach				0	1,185
		Crestline	0		0	0	5,077
		Creston	0	0	0	0	2,132
		Cridersville	0	0	0	0	1,743
		Crooksville	0	0	0	0	2,469
		Cross Creek Township	0		0		5,618
		Danville	0	0	0	0	1,081
		Deer Park	0	0	0	0	5,432
		Delaware	0	0	0	0	33,177
		Delhi Township	0	0	0	0	29,808
		Delphos	0	0	0	0	6,794
		Delta	0	0	0	0	2,936
		Dennison	0	0	0	0	2,896
		Deshler	0		0		1,854
		Dover	0	0	0	0	12,533
		East Canton		0	0	0	1,611
		Eastlake	0	0	0	0	19,590
		Eaton	0	0	0	0	8,213
		Edgerton	0	0	0	0	1,997
		Elida	0	0	0	0	1,889
		Elmwood Place	0	0	0	0	2,343
		Elyria	0	0	0	0	55,697
		Empire		0			292
		Englewood	0	0	0	0	12,844
		Euclid	0	0	0	0	48,186
		Fairfax	0	0	0	0	1,745
		Fairfield	0		0	0	42,264
		Fairfield Township	0	0	0	0	17,093
		Fairlawn	0	0	0	0	7,138
		Forest	0	0	0	0	1,442
		Forest Park	0	0	0	0	17,470
		Fort Loramie		0			1,482
		Fort Recovery	0		0	0	1,350
		Fort Shawnee	0	0	0	0	3,741
		Frazeysburg	0	0	0	0	1,315

[1]Agencies published in this table indicated that no hate crimes occurred in their jurisdictions during the quarter(s) for which they submitted reports to the Hate Crime program. Blanks indicate quarters for which agencies did not submit reports.

[2]Population figures are published only for the cities. The figures listed for the universities and colleges are student enrollment and were provided by the United States Department of Education for the 2006 school year, the most recent available. The enrollment figures include full-time and part-time students.

Table 95. Hate Crime Zero Data Submitted per Quarter, by State and Agency, 2007 *(Contd.)*

(Number.)

State	Agency type	Agency name	Zero data per quarter[1] 1st quarter	2nd quarter	3rd quarter	4th quarter	Population[2]
		Fredericktown	0	0	0	0	2,468
		Gallipolis	0	0	0	0	4,224
		Gates Mills	0	0	0	0	2,308
		Geneva-on-the-Lake	0	0	0	0	1,522
		Genoa	0	0	0	0	2,319
		Georgetown	0	0	0	0	3,624
		German Township, Clark County	0	0	0	0	7,359
		German Township, Montgomery County	0	0	0	0	3,255
		Gibsonburg		0	0	0	2,478
		Girard				0	10,306
		Glendale	0	0	0	0	2,090
		Gnadenhutten	0	0	0	0	1,294
		Goshen Township, Clermont County	0	0	0	0	16,421
		Goshen Township, Mahoning County	0	0	0	0	3,496
		Grandview Heights	0	0	0	0	6,144
		Greenfield	0	0	0		5,172
		Greenhills	0				3,619
		Greenville	0	0	0	0	12,978
		Greenwich	0	0	0	0	1,535
		Grover Hill		0			374
		Harrison				0	8,440
		Hartville	0	0	0	0	2,564
		Hebron	0	0	0	0	2,165
		Hicksville	0	0	0	0	3,481
		Higginsport	0	0	0	0	295
		Highland Heights	0		0	0	8,693
		Highland Hills	0	0	0	0	1,386
		Hilliard	0	0	0	0	27,186
		Hillsboro	0	0	0	0	6,736
		Holland	0	0	0	0	1,274
		Howland Township	0	0	0	0	16,761
		Hudson	0				23,248
		Huron	0		0		7,394
		Independence	0	0	0	0	6,760
		Ironton	0	0	0	0	11,431
		Jackson	0	0	0	0	6,241
		Jackson Center	0				1,464
		Jackson Township, Mahoning County	0	0	0	0	2,290
		Jackson Township, Montgomery County	0	0	0	0	3,820
		Jefferson	0	0	0	0	3,483
		Jewett	0	0	0		788
		Johnstown	0	0	0	0	4,037
		Junction City	0	0	0	0	859
		Kent	0	0	0	0	27,921
		Kenton	0	0	0	0	8,123
		Kettering	0	0	0	0	54,254
		Kirkersville	0	0	0		542
		Kirtland	0	0	0	0	7,400
		Kirtland Hills	0	0	0	0	793
		Lakemore	0	0	0	0	2,778
		Lake Township	0	0	0	0	7,362
		Lancaster	0	0	0	0	36,735
		Lexington		0	0	0	4,189

State	Agency type	Agency name	Zero data per quarter[1] 1st quarter	2nd quarter	3rd quarter	4th quarter	Population[2]
		Liberty Township	0	0	0	0	12,118
		Lithopolis	0	0	0	0	957
		Liverpool Township	0	0	0	0	4,246
		Lockland	0	0			3,271
		Logan	0	0		0	7,426
		London	0	0	0	0	9,603
		Lorain	0	0	0	0	70,861
		Lordstown	0	0	0	0	3,611
		Loudonville	0	0	0	0	2,995
		Lowellville	0		0	0	1,166
		Luckey	0		0	0	981
		Lynchburg	0		0	0	1,427
		Lyndhurst	0	0	0	0	14,052
		Madeira	0	0	0	0	8,052
		Madison Township, Franklin County			0	0	18,023
		Madison Township, Lake County	0	0	0	0	16,953
		Magnolia	0	0	0	0	933
		Manchester	0	0	0	0	2,125
		Marblehead	0				847
		Mariemont			0	0	3,011
		Marietta		0	0	0	14,128
		Marion	0	0		0	35,975
		Marion Township	0	0	0	0	2,988
		Marshallville	0	0			812
		Martins Ferry					6,764
		Massillon	0		0	0	32,443
		Maumee	0				14,024
		Mayfield Village	0	0	0	0	3,159
		McArthur	0	0	0	0	2,074
		McClure		0			736
		McComb		0	0	0	1,653
		McConnelsville	0	0	0	0	1,726
		Mechanicsburg		0	0		1,716
		Medina Township	0	0	0	0	8,683
		Mentor-on-the-Lake	0	0	0	0	8,316
		Miamisburg	0	0	0		19,925
		Middlefield	0	0	0	0	2,437
		Middletown		0			51,244
		Midvale	0	0	0		596
		Mifflin	0				145
		Milford	0	0	0	0	6,323
		Milton Township	0	0	0	0	2,892
		Mingo Junction	0	0			3,373
		Minster	0	0	0		2,794
		Mogadore	0	0	0	0	3,952
		Monroe	0	0	0	0	14,327
		Monroeville	0	0	0	0	1,374
		Montgomery	0	0	0	0	9,819
		Montpelier	0	0	0	0	4,082
		Montville Township	0	0	0	0	7,410
		Mount Gilead	0	0	0	0	3,532
		Mount Healthy	0	0			6,385
		Mount Orab	0		0	0	2,891
		Mount Pleasant	0				507
		Mount Sterling			0	0	1,826
		Munroe Falls	0	0	0	0	5,253
		Napoleon	0	0	0	0	9,092
		Navarre	0	0	0	0	1,424
		Nelsonville	0	0	0	0	5,441
		New Albany	0	0	0	0	6,776
		Newark	0	0	0	0	47,373
		New Boston	0	0	0	0	2,161
		Newcomerstown	0	0	0	0	3,916

[1]Agencies published in this table indicated that no hate crimes occurred in their jurisdictions during the quarter(s) for which they submitted reports to the Hate Crime program. Blanks indicate quarters for which agencies did not submit reports.

[2]Population figures are published only for the cities. The figures listed for the universities and colleges are student enrollment and were provided by the United States Department of Education for the 2006 school year, the most recent available. The enrollment figures include full-time and part-time students.

Table 95. Hate Crime Zero Data Submitted per Quarter, by State and Agency, 2007 *(Contd.)*

(Number.)

State	Agency type	Agency name	1st quarter	2nd quarter	3rd quarter	4th quarter	Population[2]
		New Concord			0	0	2,671
		New Franklin	0	0	0	0	15,087
		New Knoxville	0			0	909
		New Lebanon	0	0	0	0	4,150
		New Lexington	0	0	0	0	4,613
		New London	0	0	0	0	2,592
		New Madison	0	0	0	0	766
		New Middletown	0	0	0	0	1,587
		New Paris				0	1,524
		New Philadelphia	0	0	0	0	17,470
		New Richmond	0	0			2,524
		New Riegel		0			216
		New Straitsville			0		808
		Newton Township	0	0	0	0	4,440
		Newtown	0	0	0	0	3,966
		North Baltimore	0	0	0		3,321
		North Canton	0	0	0		16,761
		Northfield			0	0	3,700
		North Olmsted	0	0	0	0	31,854
		North Perry			0		965
		North Ridgeville	0	0	0	0	27,959
		Northwood	0	0	0	0	5,482
		Oak Hill		0	0	0	1,642
		Oakwood, Montgomery County			0	0	8,532
		Oakwood, Paulding County			0	0	561
		Oberlin	0	0	0	0	8,247
		Olmsted Falls	0	0	0	0	8,376
		Ontario			0	0	5,301
		Orrville	0	0	0	0	8,451
		Ottawa	0	0	0	0	4,438
		Owensville	0	0	0	0	836
		Oxford Township	0	0	0	0	2,525
		Parma Heights	0	0	0	0	20,108
		Pataskala	0	0	0	0	13,002
		Paulding	0	0	0	0	3,390
		Payne	0	0	0	0	1,149
		Peebles		0	0	0	1,865
		Perkins Township	0	0	0	0	12,994
		Perrysburg	0				16,885
		Perrysville	0	0			822
		Perry Township, Columbiana County	0	0	0	0	4,685
		Perry Township, Franklin County	0	0	0	0	3,595
		Perry Township, Montgomery County	0	0	0	0	3,801
		Perry Township, Stark County	0	0	0	0	28,623
		Pickerington	0	0	0	0	17,854
		Pierce Township	0	0	0	0	11,002
		Plain City	0	0	0	0	3,653
		Plymouth	0	0	0	0	1,849
		Poland Township	0	0	0	0	11,336
		Poland Village	0	0	0	0	2,724
		Port Clinton	0	0	0	0	6,246
		Powell	0	0	0	0	12,527
		Powhatan Point	0	0	0	0	1,689
		Reading	0	0	0	0	9,936
		Reminderville	0	0	0	0	2,544
		Rio Grande	0	0	0	0	871
		Riverside	0	0	0	0	22,317
		Roaming Shores Village	0	0	0	0	1,217
		Rockford	0	0		0	1,111
		Roseville	0				1,918
		Rossford	0	0	0	0	6,349
		Russellville	0	0	0	0	451
		Russia				0	627
		Sabina	0	0	0	0	2,855
		Salem	0				11,915
		Saline Township	0		0	0	1,373
		Sardinia			0	0	869
		Seaman	0	0	0	0	1,091
		Sebring	0	0	0	0	4,587
		Senecaville	0		0		449
		Seven Hills	0	0			11,875
		Seville	0	0	0	0	2,464
		Shadyside	0		0		3,517
		Sharon Township	0	0	0	0	2,306
		Sheffield Lake	0	0	0	0	9,049
		Shelby	0	0	0	0	9,441
		Shreve			0	0	1,502
		Silverton	0	0	0	0	4,556
		Smithville	0	0	0	0	1,306
		Solon	0	0	0	0	22,318
		Somerset	0	0	0	0	1,575
		South Bloomfield	0	0	0		1,704
		South Charleston	0	0	0	0	1,808
		South Russell			0	0	3,982
		South Solon	0	0	0	0	387
		South Vienna	0	0	0	0	501
		South Zanesville	0	0	0	0	2,005
		Spencer	0	0	0	0	825
		Spencerville	0	0	0	0	2,180
		Springboro	0				17,684
		Springfield	0	0	0	0	62,426
		Springfield Township, Mahoning County	0	0	0	0	6,116
		Springfield Township, Summit County	0	0	0	0	15,449
		St. Bernard		0			4,364
		St. Clairsville			0	0	5,079
		St. Clair Township	0	0	0	0	7,805
		St. Henry	0	0	0	0	2,382
		St. Paris	0	0	0	0	1,984
		Strasburg	0	0	0	0	2,704
		Struthers	0	0	0	0	10,987
		Sugarcreek Township	0	0	0	0	6,875
		Sugar Grove	0				439
		Swanton	0	0	0	0	3,712
		Sylvania Township	0	0	0	0	26,380
		Timberlake	0	0	0	0	738
		Tipp City	0	0	0	0	9,376
		Toronto	0	0	0	0	5,321
		Tremont City	0	0	0	0	350
		Twinsburg	0	0	0	0	17,545
		Uhrichsville	0	0	0	0	5,597
		Union City	0	0	0	0	1,673
		Uniontown	0	0	0	0	2,830
		Upper Arlington	0	0	0	0	31,009
		Upper Sandusky			0		6,375
		Vandalia	0	0	0	0	14,171
		Vienna Township	0	0	0	0	3,935

[1] Agencies published in this table indicated that no hate crimes occurred in their jurisdictions during the quarter(s) for which they submitted reports to the Hate Crime program. Blanks indicate quarters for which agencies did not submit reports.

[2] Population figures are published only for the cities. The figures listed for the universities and colleges are student enrollment and were provided by the United States Department of Education for the 2006 school year, the most recent available. The enrollment figures include full-time and part-time students.

Table 95. Hate Crime Zero Data Submitted per Quarter, by State and Agency, 2007 *(Contd.)*

(Number.)

State	Agency type	Agency name	Zero data per quarter[1]				Population[2]
			1st quarter	2nd quarter	3rd quarter	4th quarter	
		Village of Leesburg	0	0	0	0	1,345
		Wadsworth	0	0	0	0	20,391
		Waite Hill	0	0	0	0	554
		Walbridge	0	0	0	0	3,077
		Walton Hills	0	0	0	0	2,310
		Wapakoneta	0	0	0	0	9,583
		Warren	0	0	0	0	44,858
		Warrensville Heights	0	0	0	0	13,815
		Warren Township	0	0	0	0	6,173
		Washington Court House	0	0	0	0	13,612
		Washingtonville	0	0	0	0	762
		Waterville Township	0	0			5,439
		Wauseon	0	0	0	0	7,390
		Waverly	0	0	0	0	4,430
		Waynesburg	0	0	0	0	974
		Wayne Township	0	0			5,541
		Wells Township	0	0	0	0	2,898
		Wellston	0	0	0	0	5,998
		Wellsville	0		0	0	3,985
		West Alexandria	0	0	0	0	1,328
		West Carrollton	0	0	0		12,897
		Westfield Center		0			1,160
		West Jefferson	0	0		0	4,254
		Westlake	0	0	0	0	30,920
		West Liberty	0	0	0	0	1,735
		West Salem	0	0	0	0	1,480
		West Union				0	3,145
		Willard	0	0	0	0	6,757
		Williamsburg	0	0	0	0	2,352
		Willoughby	0	0	0	0	22,319
		Winchester	0	0	0	0	1,097
		Windham	0	0	0	0	2,711
		Wintersville	0	0	0	0	3,860
		Woodlawn	0	0	0	0	2,492
		Wyoming	0	0	0	0	7,485
	Universities and Colleges	Bowling Green State University	0	0	0	0	19,108
		Capital University	0		0	0	3,817
		Central State University	0	0	0	0	1,766
		Cleveland State University	0	0	0	0	14,807
		Columbus State Community College	0	0	0	0	22,745
		Cuyahoga Community College		0	0	0	24,289
		Kent State University	0			0	22,697
		Lakeland Community College	0	0	0	0	8,649
		Marietta College	0	0	0	0	1,522
		Miami University	0	0	0	0	16,329
		Muskingum College	0	0	0	0	2,165
Ohio		Ohio University	0	0	0	0	20,610
		Sinclair Community College	0	0	0	0	19,103
		University of Akron	0	0	0	0	21,882
		Wilberforce University	0	0	0	0	863
		Wright State University	0	0	0	0	16,088
		Youngstown State University	0	0	0	0	13,273
	Metropolitan Counties	Belmont	0	0	0	0	
		Brown	0	0	0	0	
		Carroll	0	0	0	0	
		Clark	0	0	0	0	
		Erie	0	0	0	0	
		Fairfield	0	0	0	0	
		Fulton	0	0	0	0	
		Geauga	0	0	0		
		Hamilton	0	0	0	0	
		Jefferson	0	0	0	0	
		Lawrence	0	0	0	0	
		Lorain	0	0	0	0	
		Medina	0	0	0	0	
		Miami	0	0	0	0	
		Morrow	0	0	0	0	
		Pickaway	0	0	0	0	
		Portage	0	0	0	0	
		Richland	0	0	0	0	
		Summit	0	0	0		
		Trumbull	0	0	0	0	
		Wood	0	0	0	0	
	Nonmetropolitan Counties	Adams	0	0	0	0	
		Ashland	0	0	0	0	
		Auglaize	0				
		Champaign	0	0	0	0	
		Clinton	0	0	0		
		Columbiana	0	0	0	0	
		Crawford	0	0	0	0	
		Darke	0	0	0	0	
		Defiance	0	0	0	0	
		Fayette	0	0	0	0	
		Gallia	0	0	0	0	
		Guernsey	0	0	0	0	
		Hancock	0	0	0	0	
		Hardin	0	0	0	0	
		Harrison	0	0	0	0	
		Henry	0	0	0	0	
		Hocking	0	0	0	0	
		Holmes	0	0	0	0	
		Huron	0	0	0	0	
		Logan	0				
		Marion	0	0	0	0	
		Meigs	0	0	0	0	
		Mercer	0	0	0	0	
		Morgan	0	0	0		
		Noble	0		0		
		Paulding	0	0	0	0	
		Perry	0	0	0	0	
		Pike	0	0	0	0	
		Putnam	0	0	0	0	
		Scioto	0	0	0	0	
		Tuscarawas	0	0	0	0	
		Van Wert	0	0	0	0	
		Williams	0	0	0	0	
	State Police Agencies	Ohio State Highway Patrol	0	0	0	0	

[1]Agencies published in this table indicated that no hate crimes occurred in their jurisdictions during the quarter(s) for which they submitted reports to the Hate Crime program. Blanks indicate quarters for which agencies did not submit reports.

[2]Population figures are published only for the cities. The figures listed for the universities and colleges are student enrollment and were provided by the United States Department of Education for the 2006 school year, the most recent available. The enrollment figures include full-time and part-time students.

Table 95. Hate Crime Zero Data Submitted per Quarter, by State and Agency, 2007 *(Contd.)*

(Number.)

State	Agency type	Agency name	Zero data per quarter[1] 1st quarter	2nd quarter	3rd quarter	4th quarter	Popu-lation[2]
	Other Agencies	Cedar Point		0	0		
		Columbus and Franklin County Metropolitan Park District	0	0	0	0	
		Delaware County Preservation Parks		0	0		
		Erie Metroparks		0			
		Hamilton County Park District	0	0	0		
		Lake Metroparks	0	0	0	0	
		Lorain County Metropolitan Park District	0	0			
		Port Columbus International Airport	0	0	0	0	
		Sandusky County Park District				0	
		Toledo Metropolitan Park District	0	0	0		
OKLAHOMA.	Cities	Achille	0	0	0	0	530
		Altus	0	0	0	0	19,284
		Alva	0	0	0	0	4,747
		Anadarko	0	0	0	0	6,519
		Antlers	0	0	0	0	2,481
		Apache	0	0	0	0	1,583
		Ardmore	0	0	0	0	24,663
		Arkoma	0	0	0	0	2,205
		Atoka	0	0	0	0	3,044
		Bartlesville	0	0	0	0	34,902
		Beaver	0	0	0	0	1,378
		Beggs	0	0	0	0	1,374
		Bethany	0	0	0	0	19,456
		Bixby	0	0	0	0	20,303
		Blackwell	0	0	0	0	7,134
		Blanchard	0	0	0	0	6,351
		Boise City	0	0	0	0	1,284
		Boley	0	0	0	0	1,086
		Bristow	0	0	0	0	4,402
		Broken Bow	0	0	0	0	4,217
		Caddo	0	0	0	0	982
		Calera	0	0	0	0	1,817
		Carnegie	0	0	0	0	1,589
		Chandler	0	0	0	0	2,876
		Checotah	0	0	0	0	3,520
		Chelsea	0	0	0	0	2,269
		Cherokee	0	0	0	0	1,445
		Choctaw	0	0	0	0	11,009
		Chouteau	0	0	0	0	2,016
		Claremore	0	0	0	0	17,519
		Clayton	0	0	0	0	722
		Clinton	0	0	0	0	8,395
		Coalgate	0	0	0	0	1,836
		Colbert	0	0	0	0	1,115
		Collinsville	0	0	0	0	4,559
		Comanche	0	0	0	0	1,525
		Cordell	0	0	0	0	2,910
		Coweta	0	0	0	0	8,847
		Crescent	0	0	0	0	1,356
		Davenport	0	0	0	0	893
		Davis	0	0	0	0	2,671
		Del City	0	0	0	0	21,872
		Drumright	0	0	0	0	2,890
		Duncan	0	0	0	0	22,486
		Durant	0	0	0	0	15,177
		Elk City	0	0	0	0	11,079
		Enid	0	0	0	0	46,454
		Eufaula	0	0	0	0	2,797
		Fairfax	0	0	0	0	1,486
		Fairview	0	0	0	0	2,592
		Fort Gibson	0	0	0	0	4,328
		Frederick	0	0	0	0	4,113
		Geary	0	0	0	0	1,239
		Glenpool	0	0	0	0	9,251
		Goodwell	0	0	0	0	1,127
		Grove	0	0	0	0	6,141
		Guymon	0	0	0	0	10,721
		Harrah	0	0	0	0	5,010
		Hartshorne	0	0	0	0	2,072
		Haskell	0	0	0	0	1,781
		Healdton	0	0	0	0	2,772
		Heavener	0	0	0	0	3,274
		Henryetta	0	0	0	0	6,090
		Hinton	0	0	0	0	2,172
		Hobart	0	0	0	0	3,741
		Holdenville	0	0	0	0	5,546
		Hominy	0	0	0	0	3,701
		Hooker	0	0	0	0	1,725
		Hugo	0	0	0	0	5,573
		Hulbert	0	0	0	0	530
		Hydro	0	0	0	0	1,034
		Idabel	0	0	0	0	6,906
		Jay	0	0	0	0	3,020
		Jenks	0	0	0	0	14,906
		Jones	0	0	0	0	2,674
		Kingfisher	0	0	0	0	4,515
		Kingston	0	0	0	0	1,561
		Konawa	0	0	0	0	1,417
		Krebs	0	0	0	0	2,137
		Lawton	0	0	0	0	86,864
		Lexington	0	0	0	0	2,071
		Lindsay	0	0	0	0	2,918
		Locust Grove	0	0	0	0	1,589
		Lone Grove	0	0	0	0	5,239
		Luther	0	0	0	0	1,098
		Madill	0	0	0	0	3,735
		Mannford	0	0	0	0	2,787
		Marietta	0	0	0	0	2,568
		Marlow	0	0	0	0	4,564
		Maysville	0	0	0	0	1,304
		McAlester	0	0	0	0	18,414
		McLoud	0	0	0	0	4,250
		Meeker	0	0	0	0	1,000
		Miami	0	0	0	0	13,622
		Minco	0	0	0	0	1,805
		Moore	0	0	0	0	50,548
		Mooreland	0	0	0	0	1,229
		Morris	0	0	0	0	1,323
		Mountain View	0	0	0	0	816
		Muldrow	0	0	0	0	3,216
		Muskogee	0	0	0	0	40,113
		Newcastle	0	0	0	0	6,880
		Newkirk	0	0	0	0	2,128
		Nichols Hills	0	0	0	0	3,981
		Nicoma Park	0	0	0	0	2,371
		Noble	0	0	0	0	5,638
		Nowata	0	0	0	0	4,009
		Oilton	0	0	0	0	1,125
		Oklahoma City	0	0	0	0	542,199
		Okmulgee	0	0	0	0	12,805
		Oologah	0	0	0	0	1,163
		Owasso	0	0	0	0	25,974
		Pauls Valley	0	0	0	0	6,175
		Pawhuska	0	0	0	0	3,481
		Perkins	0	0	0	0	2,251
		Perry	0	0	0	0	5,045
		Piedmont	0	0	0	0	5,233
		Pocola	0	0	0	0	4,499
		Ponca City	0	0	0	0	24,548
		Porum	0	0	0	0	735

[1]Agencies published in this table indicated that no hate crimes occurred in their jurisdictions during the quarter(s) for which they submitted reports to the Hate Crime program. Blanks indicate quarters for which agencies did not submit reports.

[2]Population figures are published only for the cities. The figures listed for the universities and colleges are student enrollment and were provided by the United States Department of Education for the 2006 school year, the most recent available. The enrollment figures include full-time and part-time students.

Table 95. Hate Crime Zero Data Submitted per Quarter, by State and Agency, 2007 (Contd.)

(Number.)

State	Agency type	Agency name	1st quarter	2nd quarter	3rd quarter	4th quarter	Population[2]
		Prague	0	0	0	0	2,153
		Pryor	0	0	0	0	9,361
		Purcell	0	0	0	0	6,026
		Ringling	0	0	0	0	1,062
		Roland	0	0	0	0	3,216
		Rush Springs	0	0	0	0	1,349
		Sand Springs	0	0	0	0	18,362
		Sapulpa	0	0	0	0	20,960
		Sayre	0	0	0	0	2,743
		Seminole	0	0	0	0	6,960
		Shawnee	0	0	0	0	30,109
		Skiatook	0	0	0	0	6,486
		Spencer	0	0	0	0	3,943
		Spiro	0	0	0	0	2,336
		Stigler	0	0	0	0	2,825
		Stilwell	0	0	0	0	3,551
		Stratford	0	0	0	0	1,496
		Stringtown	0	0	0	0	413
		Sulphur	0	0	0	0	4,924
		Tahlequah	0	0	0	0	16,491
		Talihina	0	0	0	0	1,250
		Tecumseh	0	0	0	0	6,723
		Texhoma	0	0	0	0	936
		The Village	0	0	0	0	9,719
		Tishomingo	0	0	0	0	3,248
		Tonkawa	0	0	0	0	3,080
		Tulsa	0	0	0	0	381,469
		Tushka	0	0	0	0	363
		Tuttle	0	0	0	0	5,935
		Valliant	0	0	0	0	752
		Vian	0	0	0	0	1,483
		Vinita	0	0	0	0	5,982
		Wagoner	0	0	0	0	8,043
		Walters	0	0	0	0	2,548
		Warner	0	0	0	0	1,447
		Warr Acres	0	0	0	0	9,384
		Watonga	0	0	0	0	5,807
		Waukomis	0	0	0	0	1,192
		Waurika	0	0	0	0	1,811
		Waynoka	0	0	0	0	901
		Weatherford	0	0	0	0	9,951
		Weleetka	0	0	0	0	938
		Westville	0	0	0	0	1,687
		Wetumka	0	0	0	0	1,422
		Wewoka	0	0	0	0	3,368
		Wilburton	0	0	0	0	2,896
		Wilson	0	0	0	0	1,627
		Woodward	0	0	0	0	12,064
		Wright City	0	0	0	0	803
		Wynnewood	0	0	0	0	2,311
		Yale	0	0	0	0	1,284
		Yukon	0	0	0	0	22,457
	Universities and Colleges	Cameron University	0	0	0	0	5,737
		East Central University	0	0	0	0	4,453
		Murray State College	0	0	0	0	2,232
		Northeastern Oklahoma A&M College	0	0	0	0	1,923
		Northeastern State University	0	0	0	0	9,417
		Oklahoma State University: Okmulgee	0	0	0	0	3,255
		Tulsa[3]	0	0	0	0	
		Rogers State University	0	0	0	0	3,955
		Seminole State College	0	0	0	0	2,038
		Southeastern Oklahoma State University	0	0	0	0	3,830
		Southwestern Oklahoma State University	0	0	0	0	5,122
		Tulsa Community College	0	0	0	0	16,632
		University of Central Oklahoma	0	0	0	0	15,588
		University of Oklahoma: Health Sciences Center	0	0	0	0	3,790
		Norman	0	0	0	0	25,923
	Metropolitan Counties	Canadian	0	0	0	0	
		Cleveland	0	0	0	0	
		Comanche	0	0	0	0	
		Creek	0	0	0	0	
		Grady	0	0	0	0	
		Le Flore	0	0	0	0	
		Lincoln	0	0	0	0	
		Logan	0	0	0	0	
		McClain	0	0	0	0	
		Oklahoma	0	0	0	0	
		Okmulgee	0	0	0	0	
		Osage	0	0	0	0	
		Pawnee	0	0	0	0	
		Rogers	0	0	0	0	
		Tulsa	0	0	0	0	
		Wagoner	0	0	0	0	
	Nonmetropolitan Counties	Adair	0	0	0	0	
		Alfalfa	0	0	0	0	
		Atoka	0	0	0	0	
		Beaver	0	0	0	0	
		Beckham	0	0	0	0	
		Blaine	0	0	0	0	
		Caddo	0	0	0	0	
		Carter	0	0	0	0	
		Cherokee	0	0	0	0	
		Choctaw	0	0	0	0	
		Cimarron	0	0	0	0	
		Coal	0	0	0	0	
		Cotton	0	0	0	0	
		Craig	0	0	0	0	
		Custer	0	0	0	0	
		Delaware	0	0	0	0	
		Dewey	0	0	0	0	
		Ellis	0	0	0	0	
		Garfield	0	0	0	0	
		Garvin	0	0	0	0	
		Grant	0	0	0	0	
		Greer	0	0	0	0	
		Harmon	0	0	0	0	
		Haskell	0	0	0	0	
		Hughes	0	0	0	0	
		Jackson	0	0	0	0	
		Jefferson	0	0	0	0	
		Johnston	0	0	0	0	
		Kay	0	0	0	0	
		Kingfisher	0	0	0	0	
		Kiowa	0	0	0	0	
		Latimer	0	0	0	0	
		Love	0	0	0	0	
		Major	0	0	0	0	
		Marshall	0	0	0	0	
		Mayes	0	0	0	0	
		McCurtain	0	0	0	0	
		McIntosh	0	0	0	0	
		Murray	0	0	0	0	
		Muskogee	0	0	0	0	
		Noble	0	0	0	0	

[1]Agencies published in this table indicated that no hate crimes occurred in their jurisdictions during the quarter(s) for which they submitted reports to the Hate Crime program. Blanks indicate quarters for which agencies did not submit reports.

[2]Population figures are published only for the cities. The figures listed for the universities and colleges are student enrollment and were provided by the United States Department of Education for the 2006 school year, the most recent available. The enrollment figures include full-time and part-time students.

[3]Student enrollment figures were not available.

Table 95. Hate Crime Zero Data Submitted per Quarter, by State and Agency, 2007 (Contd.)

(Number.)

State	Agency type	Agency name	Zero data per quarter[1] 1st quarter	2nd quarter	3rd quarter	4th quarter	Population[2]
		Nowata	0	0	0	0	
		Okfuskee	0	0	0	0	
		Ottawa	0	0	0	0	
		Payne	0	0	0	0	
		Pittsburg	0	0	0	0	
		Pontotoc	0	0	0	0	
		Pottawatomie	0	0	0	0	
		Pushmataha	0	0	0	0	
		Roger Mills	0	0	0	0	
		Seminole	0	0	0	0	
		Stephens	0	0	0	0	
		Texas	0	0	0	0	
		Tillman	0	0	0	0	
		Washington	0	0	0	0	
		Washita	0	0	0	0	
		Woods	0	0	0	0	
		Woodward	0	0	0	0	
	Other Agencies	Capitol Park Police	0	0	0	0	
		Jenks Public Schools	0	0	0	0	
		Madill Public Schools	0	0	0	0	
		McAlester Public Schools	0	0	0	0	
		Norman Public Schools	0	0	0	0	
		Putnam City Campus	0	0	0	0	
OREGON	Cities	Amity	0	0	0	0	1,462
		Astoria	0	0	0	0	9,935
		Athena	0	0	0	0	1,207
		Aumsville	0	0	0	0	3,378
		Aurora	0	0	0	0	1,025
		Baker City	0	0	0	0	9,614
		Bandon	0	0	0	0	2,911
		Black Butte	0	0	0	0	
		Brookings	0	0	0	0	6,476
		Burns	0	0	0	0	2,702
		Butte Falls	0	0	0	0	428
		Cannon Beach	0	0	0	0	1,740
		Carlton	0	0	0	0	1,523
		Central Point	0	0	0	0	16,701
		Clatskanie	0	0	0	0	1,663
		Coburg	0	0	0	0	1,011
		Columbia City	0	0	0	0	1,965
		Condon	0	0	0	0	684
		Coos Bay	0	0	0	0	16,096
		Coquille	0	0	0	0	4,250
		Cornelius	0	0	0	0	11,498
		Cottage Grove	0	0	0	0	8,921
		Creswell	0	0	0	0	4,945
		Culver	0	0	0	0	1,064
		Dallas	0	0	0	0	15,097
		Elgin	0	0	0	0	1,623
		Enterprise	0	0	0	0	1,736
		Estacada	0	0	0	0	2,473
		Eugene	0	0	0	0	147,458
		Fairview	0	0	0	0	9,753
		Florence	0	0	0	0	8,250
		Forest Grove	0	0	0	0	20,457
		Gaston	0	0	0	0	803
		Gearhart	0	0	0	0	1,117
		Gervais	0	0	0	0	2,451
		Gladstone	0	0	0	0	12,256
		Gold Beach	0	0	0	0	1,909
		Gresham	0	0	0	0	98,089
		Hillsboro	0	0	0	0	90,439
		Hines	0	0	0	0	1,464
		Hood River	0	0	0	0	6,778
		Hubbard	0	0	0	0	2,624
		Independence	0	0	0	0	9,211
		Jacksonville	0	0	0	0	2,190
		John Day	0	0	0	0	1,555
		Junction City	0	0	0	0	5,378
		King City	0	0	0	0	2,257
		Klamath Falls	0	0	0	0	19,817
		Lake Oswego	0	0	0	0	36,917
		Lakeview	0	0	0	0	2,412
		Lebanon	0	0	0	0	14,620
		Madras	0	0	0	0	5,301
		Malin	0	0	0	0	634
		Manzanita	0	0	0	0	640
		McMinnville	0	0	0	0	30,980
		Milton-Freewater	0	0	0	0	6,392
		Milwaukie	0	0	0	0	21,060
		Molalla	0	0	0	0	7,210
		Monmouth	0	0	0	0	9,751
		Mount Angel	0	0	0	0	3,429
		Myrtle Creek	0	0	0	0	3,555
		Myrtle Point	0	0	0	0	2,509
		North Bend	0	0	0	0	9,892
		North Plains	0	0	0	0	1,833
		Nyssa	0	0	0	0	3,039
		Oakridge	0	0	0	0	3,127
		Ontario	0	0	0	0	11,100
		Oregon City	0	0	0	0	31,284
		Pendleton	0	0	0	0	16,620
		Philomath	0	0	0	0	4,206
		Phoenix	0	0	0	0	4,416
		Pilot Rock	0	0	0	0	1,511
		Powers	0	0	0	0	755
		Prairie City	0	0	0	0	936
		Prineville	0	0	0	0	9,583
		Rainier	0	0	0	0	1,852
		Reedsport	0	0	0	0	4,352
		Rockaway Beach	0	0	0	0	1,346
		Sandy	0	0	0	0	8,770
		Scappoose	0	0	0	0	6,222
		Shady Cove	0	0	0	0	2,293
		Sherwood	0	0	0	0	17,957
		Stanfield	0	0	0	0	1,964
		St. Helens	0	0	0	0	12,708
		Sunriver	0	0	0	0	
		Sutherlin	0	0	0	0	7,396
		Sweet Home	0	0	0	0	8,659
		Talent	0	0	0	0	6,150
		The Dalles	0	0	0	0	11,900
		Toledo	0	0	0	0	3,398
		Troutdale	0	0	0	0	15,212
		Tualatin	0	0	0	0	26,712
		Turner	0	0	0	0	1,689
		Umatilla	0	0	0	0	5,397
		Veneta	0	0	0	0	3,927
		Vernonia	0	0	0	0	2,319
		Warrenton	0	0	0	0	4,438
		West Linn	0	0	0	0	25,636
		Weston	0	0	0	0	708
		Wilsonville	0	0	0	0	16,916
		Winston	0	0	0	0	4,803
		Yamhill	0	0	0	0	850
	Metropolitan Counties	Columbia	0	0	0	0	
		Multnomah	0	0	0	0	
		Polk	0	0	0	0	
		Washington	0	0	0	0	
	Nonmetropolitan Counties	Baker	0	0	0	0	
		Clatsop	0	0	0	0	
		Coos	0	0	0	0	
		Crook	0	0	0	0	
		Curry	0	0	0	0	
		Gilliam	0	0	0	0	
		Grant	0	0	0	0	
		Harney	0	0	0	0	

[1] Agencies published in this table indicated that no hate crimes occurred in their jurisdictions during the quarter(s) for which they submitted reports to the Hate Crime program. Blanks indicate quarters for which agencies did not submit reports.

[2] Population figures are published only for the cities. The figures listed for the universities and colleges are student enrollment and were provided by the United States Department of Education for the 2006 school year, the most recent available. The enrollment figures include full-time and part-time students.

Table 95. Hate Crime Zero Data Submitted per Quarter, by State and Agency, 2007 *(Contd.)*

(Number.)

State	Agency type	Agency name	Zero data per quarter[1]				Population[2]
			1st quarter	2nd quarter	3rd quarter	4th quarter	
		Hood River	0	0	0	0	
		Jefferson	0	0	0	0	
		Josephine	0	0	0	0	
		Klamath	0	0	0	0	
		Lake	0	0	0	0	
		Linn	0	0	0	0	
		Malheur	0	0	0	0	
		Morrow	0	0	0	0	
		Sherman	0	0	0	0	
		Union	0	0	0	0	
		Wallowa	0	0	0	0	
		Wasco	0	0	0	0	
		Wheeler	0	0	0	0	
	State Police Agencies	Oregon State Police, Headquarters	0	0	0	0	
		State Police:					
		Baker County	0	0	0	0	
		Benton County	0	0	0	0	
		Clackamas County	0	0	0	0	
		Clatsop County	0	0	0	0	
		Columbia County	0	0	0	0	
		Coos County	0	0	0	0	
		Crook County	0	0	0	0	
		Curry County	0	0	0	0	
		Deschutes County	0	0	0	0	
		Douglas County	0	0	0	0	
		Gilliam County	0	0	0	0	
		Grant County	0	0	0	0	
		Harney County	0	0	0	0	
		Hood River County	0	0	0	0	
		Jackson County	0	0	0	0	
		Jefferson County	0	0	0	0	
		Josephine County	0	0	0	0	
		Klamath County	0	0	0	0	
		Lake County	0	0	0	0	
		Lane County	0	0	0	0	
		Lincoln County	0	0	0	0	
		Linn County	0	0	0	0	
		Malheur County	0	0	0	0	
		Marion County	0	0	0	0	
		Morrow County	0	0	0	0	
		Multnomah County	0	0	0	0	
		Polk County	0	0	0	0	
		Sherman County	0	0	0	0	
		Tillamook County	0	0	0	0	
		Umatilla County	0	0	0	0	
		Union County	0	0	0	0	
		Wallowa County	0	0	0	0	
		Wasco County	0	0	0	0	
		Wheeler County	0	0	0	0	
		Yamhill County	0	0	0	0	
	Other Agencies	Liquor Commission:					
		Baker County	0	0	0	0	
		Benton County	0	0	0	0	
		Clatsop County	0	0	0	0	
		Columbia County	0	0	0	0	
		Coos County	0	0	0	0	
		Crook County	0	0	0	0	
		Curry County	0	0	0	0	
		Douglas County	0	0	0	0	
		Gilliam County	0	0	0	0	
		Grant County	0	0	0	0	
		Harney County	0	0	0	0	
		Hood River County	0	0	0	0	
		Jackson County	0	0	0	0	
		Jefferson County	0	0	0	0	
		Josephine County	0	0	0	0	
		Klamath County	0	0	0	0	
		Lake County	0	0	0	0	
		Lane County	0	0	0	0	
		Lincoln County	0	0	0	0	
		Linn County	0	0	0	0	
		Malheur County	0	0	0	0	
		Marion County	0	0	0	0	
		Morrow County	0	0	0	0	
		Multnomah County	0	0	0	0	
		Polk County	0	0	0	0	
		Sherman County	0	0	0	0	
		Tillamook County	0	0	0	0	
		Umatilla County	0	0	0	0	
		Union County	0	0	0	0	
		Wallowa County	0	0	0	0	
		Wasco County	0	0	0	0	
		Washington County	0	0	0	0	
		Wheeler County	0	0	0	0	
		Yamhill County	0	0	0	0	
		Port of Portland	0	0	0	0	
	Other Agencies– Tribal	Umatilla Tribal	0	0	0	0	
PENNSYL-VANIA............	**Cities**	Adamstown	0	0	0	0	1,329
		Adams Township, Butler County	0	0	0	0	8,963
		Adams Township, Cambria County	0	0	0	0	6,113
		Akron	0	0	0	0	4,013
		Albion	0	0	0		1,540
		Alburtis	0	0	0		2,393
		Aldan	0	0	0	0	4,277
		Aliquippa	0	0		0	10,854
		Allegheny Township, Blair County	0	0	0	0	6,907
		Allegheny Township, Westmoreland County	0	0	0	0	8,177
		Allentown	0	0	0	0	107,397
		Altoona	0	0	0	0	46,609
		Ambler	0	0	0	0	6,248
		Amity Township	0	0	0	0	11,838
		Annville Township	0		0	0	4,717
		Archbald			0	0	6,422
		Arnold	0	0	0	0	5,301
		Ashland	0	0	0	0	3,121
		Ashley	0	0	0	0	2,691
		Ashville	0	0	0	0	262
		Aspinwall	0	0	0	0	2,720

[1]Agencies published in this table indicated that no hate crimes occurred in their jurisdictions during the quarter(s) for which they submitted reports to the Hate Crime program. Blanks indicate quarters for which agencies did not submit reports.

[2]Population figures are published only for the cities. The figures listed for the universities and colleges are student enrollment and were provided by the United States Department of Education for the 2006 school year, the most recent available. The enrollment figures include full-time and part-time students.

Table 95. Hate Crime Zero Data Submitted per Quarter, by State and Agency, 2007 *(Contd.)*

(Number.)

State	Agency type	Agency name	Zero data per quarter[1] 1st quarter	2nd quarter	3rd quarter	4th quarter	Population[2]
		Aston Township	0	0	0	0	16,853
		Atglen	0	0	0		1,378
		Athens	0	0		0	3,272
		Athens Township	0	0	0	0	5,100
		Auburn	0	0			805
		Avalon	0	0			4,837
		Avondale	0	0	0	0	1,091
		Avonmore Boro	0	0	0	0	775
		Baldwin Borough	0	0	0	0	18,440
		Baldwin Township	0	0	0	0	2,048
		Bally	0	0	0	0	1,112
		Bangor	0	0	0	0	5,282
		Barrett Township	0	0	0	0	4,387
		Beaver	0	0	0	0	4,447
		Beaver Falls	0	0	0	0	9,189
		Bedford	0	0	0	0	3,011
		Bedminster Township	0	0	0	0	5,681
		Bell Acres	0	0	0	0	1,383
		Bellefonte	0	0	0		6,096
		Bellevue	0	0	0		8,023
		Bellwood	0	0	0	0	1,890
		Benton Area		0	0		1,988
		Berks-Lehigh Regional	0	0	0	0	28,142
		Berlin	0	0			2,105
		Bern Township	0	0	0	0	7,165
		Bernville	0	0	0	0	887
		Berwick	0	0	0	0	10,246
		Bessemer	0	0	0	0	1,106
		Bethel Park	0	0	0	0	31,669
		Bethel Township, Armstrong County	0	0	0	0	1,214
		Bethel Township, Berks County	0	0	0		4,543
		Bethel Township, Delaware County	0	0	0	0	10,683
		Bethlehem	0	0	0	0	72,908
		Bethlehem Township	0	0	0	0	23,960
		Biglerville	0	0	0		1,167
		Birdsboro	0	0	0	0	5,224
		Birmingham Township	0	0	0	0	4,273
		Blacklick Township	0	0		0	2,096
		Blairsville	0	0	0	0	3,421
		Blair Township		0			4,739
		Blakely	0	0	0	0	6,782
		Blawnox	0	0	0	0	1,446
		Bloomsburg Town	0	0	0	0	12,959
		Blythe Township	0	0			890
		Bolivar	0	0	0	0	472
		Boyertown	0				3,961
		Brackenridge	0		0	0	3,239
		Braddock Hills	0	0	0	0	1,836
		Bradford	0	0	0	0	8,501
		Bradford Township	0	0	0	0	4,763
		Brandywine Regional	0	0	0	0	10,045
		Brecknock Township, Berks County	0	0	0	0	4,935
		Brentwood	0	0	0	0	9,574
		Briar Creek Township	0	0	0	0	3,062
		Bridgeport	0	0	0	0	4,404
		Bridgeville	0	0	0	0	4,898
		Bridgewater	0	0	0	0	891
		Brighton Township	0	0		0	7,996
		Bristol	0	0	0	0	9,747
		Bristol Township	0	0	0	0	54,096
		Brockway		0	0	0	2,080
		Brookhaven	0	0	0	0	7,805
		Brookville	0	0	0	0	4,037
		Brownsville	0	0	0	0	2,653
		Bryn Athyn	0				1,330
		Buckingham Township	0	0	0	0	19,293
		Buffalo Township	0	0	0	0	7,318
		Burgettstown	0				1,497
		Bushkill Township	0	0	0	0	8,136
		Butler	0	0		0	14,258
		Butler Township, Butler County	0	0	0	0	16,894
		Butler Township, Luzerne County	0	0	0		9,116
		Butler Township, Schuylkill County	0	0	0	0	5,751
		California	0	0	0	0	6,065
		Caln Township	0	0	0	0	12,283
		Cambria Township	0	0	0	0	6,199
		Cambridge Springs	0	0	0	0	2,260
		Canonsburg	0	0			8,856
		Carbondale	0	0		0	9,256
		Carmichaels	0	0			510
		Carnegie	0	0	0	0	8,001
		Carrolltown	0	0	0	0	977
		Carroll Township, Washington County	0				5,524
		Carroll Township, York County	0	0	0	0	5,383
		Carroll Valley	0	0			3,574
		Castle Shannon	0	0	0	0	8,099
		Catasauqua	0	0	0	0	6,562
		Catawissa	0	0	0	0	1,544
		Cecil Township	0	0	0	0	10,456
		Center Township	0	0	0	0	11,804
		Centerville	0	0	0	0	3,242
		Central Berks Regional	0	0	0	0	7,489
		Chalfont	0	0	0	0	4,243
		Chambersburg	0	0	0	0	17,958
		Charleroi	0	0			5,781
		Chartiers Township	0	0		0	7,239
		Cheltenham Township	0	0	0	0	36,403
		Chester	0	0	0		36,799
		Chester Township	0	0	0	0	4,594

[1]Agencies published in this table indicated that no hate crimes occurred in their jurisdictions during the quarter(s) for which they submitted reports to the Hate Crime program. Blanks indicate quarters for which agencies did not submit reports.

[2]Population figures are published only for the cities. The figures listed for the universities and colleges are student enrollment and were provided by the United States Department of Education for the 2006 school year, the most recent available. The enrollment figures include full-time and part-time students.

Table 95. Hate Crime Zero Data Submitted per Quarter, by State and Agency, 2007 *(Contd.)*

(Number.)

State	Agency type	Agency name	Zero data per quarter[1]				Popu-lation[2]	State	Agency type	Agency name	Zero data per quarter[1]				Popu-lation[2]
			1st quarter	2nd quarter	3rd quarter	4th quarter					1st quarter	2nd quarter	3rd quarter	4th quarter	
		Cheswick			0	0	1,751			Darby	0	0	0	0	9,967
		Chippewa Township	0	0	0	0	9,815			Darby Township	0	0	0	0	9,615
		Christiana	0	0	0		1,083			Darlington Township	0	0	0	0	2,040
		Churchill	0	0		0	3,267			Decatur Township	0	0	0	0	3,089
		Clairton	0				7,894			Delaware Water Gap	0	0	0	0	831
		Clarion	0	0	0		5,141			Delmont	0	0	0	0	2,473
		Claysville	0		0	0	682			Denver	0	0	0	0	3,700
		Clay Township	0	0	0	0	5,766			Derry	0	0	0		2,822
		Clearfield	0	0	0	0	6,240			Derry Township, Dauphin County	0	0	0	0	21,923
		Cleona	0	0	0	0	2,104			Dickson City	0	0	0	0	5,916
		Clifton Heights	0	0	0	0	6,586			Donegal Township	0	0	0	0	2,574
		Coal Township	0	0	0	0	10,277			Donora	0	0	0	0	5,317
		Coatesville	0	0	0	0	11,744			Dormont	0	0	0	0	8,467
		Cochranton		0	0		1,079			Douglass Township, Berks County	0	0	0		3,545
		Colebrookdale District	0	0	0	0	6,462			Douglass Township, Montgomery County	0	0	0	0	10,323
		Collegeville	0	0		0	5,011			Downingtown	0	0	0	0	7,924
		Collier Township	0	0	0	0	6,235			Doylestown	0	0	0	0	8,208
		Collingdale	0	0	0	0	8,440			Doylestown Township	0	0	0	0	18,847
		Colonial Regional	0	0	0	0	19,420			Dublin Borough	0	0	0	0	2,182
		Columbia	0	0	0	0	10,034			Du Bois	0	0	0	0	7,757
		Colwyn	0	0	0	0	2,375			Duboistown	0				1,168
		Conemaugh Township, Cambria County	0	0		0	2,507			Dunbar	0	0	0	0	1,157
		Conemaugh Township, Somerset County	0	0	0		7,310			Duncannon	0	0	0	0	1,503
		Conewago Township, Adams County	0	0	0	0	6,184			Duncansville	0	0	0	0	1,181
		Conewango Township	0	0	0	0	3,647			Dunmore	0				13,884
		Conneaut Lake Regional	0	0	0	0	3,539			Dupont	0	0	0	0	2,601
		Connellsville	0	0	0	0	8,526			Duquesne	0	0	0		6,705
		Conoy Township	0	0	0	0	3,288			Earl Township	0	0	0	0	6,918
		Conshohocken	0				8,629			East Bangor	0	0	0		1,041
		Conyngham	0	0	0		1,844			East Berlin	0	0			1,451
		Coopersburg	0	0	0		2,573			East Brady	0	0			998
		Coplay	0	0	0	0	3,381			East Buffalo Township	0	0	0	0	5,939
		Coraopolis	0	0	0	0	5,610			East Conemaugh	0	0	0	0	1,186
		Cornwall	0	0	0	0	3,460			East Coventry Township	0	0	0	0	6,236
		Corry	0	0	0	0	6,451			East Deer Township	0	0	0		1,338
		Covington Township	0	0	0	0	2,154			East Earl Township	0	0			6,311
		Crafton	0	0	0	0	6,138			Eastern Adams Regional	0	0	0	0	9,083
		Cranberry Township	0	0	0	0	28,084			East Fallowfield Township	0	0	0	0	7,343
		Crescent Township		0			2,823			East Franklin Township	0	0		0	3,981
		Cresson	0	0			1,507			East Lampeter Township	0	0	0	0	14,910
		Cresson Township	0	0	0	0	4,239			East Lansdowne	0	0	0	0	2,495
		Croyle Township	0	0	0	0	2,262			East McKeesport	0	0	0	0	2,816
		Cumberland Township, Adams County	0	0		0	6,377			East Norriton Township	0	0	0	0	13,485
		Cumberland Township, Greene County	0	0	0	0	6,492			East Norwegian Township	0	0	0	0	797
		Cumru Township	0	0	0	0	17,595			Easton	0	0	0	0	26,207
		Curwensville	0	0	0	0	2,505			East Pennsboro Township	0	0	0	0	19,894
		Dale	0	0	0	0	1,384								
		Dallas	0	0	0	0	2,493								
		Dallas Township	0	0	0	0	8,424								
		Danville	0	0	0	0	4,530								

[1]Agencies published in this table indicated that no hate crimes occurred in their jurisdictions during the quarter(s) for which they submitted reports to the Hate Crime program. Blanks indicate quarters for which agencies did not submit reports.

[2]Population figures are published only for the cities. The figures listed for the universities and colleges are student enrollment and were provided by the United States Department of Education for the 2006 school year, the most recent available. The enrollment figures include full-time and part-time students.

Table 95. Hate Crime Zero Data Submitted per Quarter, by State and Agency, 2007 *(Contd.)*

(Number.)

State	Agency type	Agency name	Zero data per quarter[1]				Popu-lation[2]
			1st quarter	2nd quarter	3rd quarter	4th quarter	
		East Penn Township	0	0	0		2,716
		East Petersburg	0	0	0	0	4,327
		East Pikeland Township	0	0	0	0	6,849
		East Rochester	0	0	0	0	573
		East Taylor Township	0	0		0	2,571
		Easttown Township	0	0	0	0	10,503
		East Vincent Township	0	0	0	0	6,589
		East Washington	0	0	0	0	1,877
		East Whiteland Township	0	0	0	0	10,632
		Ebensburg	0	0	0	0	2,880
		Economy	0	0	0	0	9,192
		Eddystone	0	0	0	0	2,361
		Edgewood	0	0	0	0	3,018
		Edgeworth	0	0	0	0	1,582
		Edinboro	0	0	0	0	6,646
		Edwardsville	0	0	0	0	4,688
		Elizabethtown	0	0	0	0	11,900
		Elizabeth Township	0	0	0	0	12,837
		Elkland	0	0	0	0	1,685
		Ellwood City	0	0	0	0	8,064
		Emmaus	0	0	0	0	11,414
		Emporium	0	0		0	2,270
		Emsworth	0				2,383
		Ephrata	0	0	0	0	13,067
		Ephrata Township	0	0	0	0	9,557
		Erie	0	0	0	0	101,812
		Etna	0	0	0	0	3,578
		Everett	0	0	0	0	1,869
		Exeter	0	0	0	0	5,995
		Exeter Township, Berks County	0	0	0	0	27,080
		Exeter Township, Luzerne County	0	0		0	2,557
		Fairfield	0				518
		Fairview Township, Luzerne County	0	0	0	0	4,321
		Fairview Township, York County	0	0	0	0	16,630
		Fallowfield Township	0	0	0	0	4,242
		Falls Township, Bucks County	0	0	0	0	34,033
		Fawn Township	0	0	0	0	2,324
		Ferguson Township	0	0	0	0	16,302
		Ferndale	0	0	0	0	1,685
		Findlay Township	0	0	0	0	5,053
		Fleetwood	0	0	0	0	4,029
		Folcroft	0	0	0	0	6,878
		Ford City	0	0	0	0	3,190
		Forest City	0	0	0		1,765
		Forest Hills	0	0	0	0	6,271
		Forks Township	0	0	0	0	14,452
		Forty Fort	0	0	0	0	4,273
		Foster Township	0	0	0	0	4,304
		Fountain Hill	0	0	0		4,602
		Fox Chapel	0	0	0		5,144
		Frackville	0	0		0	4,115
		Franconia Township	0	0	0		12,623
		Franklin	0	0	0	0	6,758
		Franklin Park	0	0	0	0	11,908
		Franklin Township, Beaver County	0	0			4,330
		Franklin Township, Carbon County	0	0	0		4,873
		Freedom	0	0	0	0	1,624
		Freeland	0	0			3,411
		Freemansburg	0	0	0	0	2,007
		Freeport	0	0	0	0	1,818
		Gaines Township	0	0	0	0	569
		Galeton	0	0	0	0	1,263
		Gallitzin	0	0	0	0	1,908
		Gettysburg	0	0	0	0	8,194
		Gilberton	0				828
		Girard	0	0	0	0	2,991
		Glenolden	0	0	0	0	7,261
		Granville Township	0	0	0	0	4,915
		Greencastle	0	0	0	0	4,036
		Greenfield Township, Blair County	0	0	0	0	3,779
		Greensburg	0	0	0	0	15,567
		Green Tree	0	0		0	4,353
		Greenville	0	0	0	0	6,263
		Greenwood Township	0	0	0		2,046
		Grove City	0	0	0	0	7,644
		Halifax Regional	0	0	0	0	4,168
		Hamburg	0	0	0	0	4,209
		Hamiltonban Township	0	0		0	2,739
		Hampden Township	0	0	0	0	26,612
		Hampton Township	0	0	0	0	17,139
		Hanover	0	0	0	0	15,079
		Hanover Township, Luzerne County	0	0	0	0	11,060
		Hanover Township, Washington County	0	0	0	0	2,752
		Harleton	0	0	0	0	265
		Harmar Township	0	0	0	0	3,018
		Harmony Township	0	0	0	0	3,111
		Harrison Township	0	0	0	0	10,016
		Harveys Lake	0	0	0	0	2,903
		Hastings	0	0	0	0	1,312
		Hatboro	0	0	0	0	7,177
		Haverford Township	0	0	0	0	48,434
		Hazleton	0	0	0		21,868
		Heidelberg	0	0	0		1,149
		Heidelberg Township, Berks County	0	0	0		1,774
		Heidelberg Township, Lebanon County	0	0	0	0	4,113
		Hellam Township	0	0	0	0	9,139
		Hellertown	0	0			5,620
		Hemlock Township	0	0	0	0	2,214

[1]Agencies published in this table indicated that no hate crimes occurred in their jurisdictions during the quarter(s) for which they submitted reports to the Hate Crime program. Blanks indicate quarters for which agencies did not submit reports.

[2]Population figures are published only for the cities. The figures listed for the universities and colleges are student enrollment and were provided by the United States Department of Education for the 2006 school year, the most recent available. The enrollment figures include full-time and part-time students.

Table 95. Hate Crime Zero Data Submitted per Quarter, by State and Agency, 2007 (Contd.)

(Number.)

State	Agency type	Agency name	Zero data per quarter[1]				Popu-lation[2]	State	Agency type	Agency name	Zero data per quarter[1]				Popu-lation[2]
			1st quarter	2nd quarter	3rd quarter	4th quarter					1st quarter	2nd quarter	3rd quarter	4th quarter	
		Hempfield Township, Mercer County	0	0	0		3,903			Lancaster Township, Butler County	0	0		0	2,574
		Hermitage	0	0	0	0	16,576			Lancaster Township, Lancaster County	0	0	0	0	14,347
		Hickory Township	0			0	2,294			Lansdale	0	0	0	0	15,669
		Highland Township	0	0	0	0	1,210			Lansdowne	0	0	0	0	10,720
		Highspire	0	0	0	0	2,585			Lansford	0	0	0	0	4,180
		Hilltown Township	0	0	0	0	13,175			Larksville	0			0	4,474
		Hollidaysburg	0	0	0	0	5,563			Latimore-York Springs Regional	0				3,522
		Homestead	0	0	0	0	3,476			Latrobe	0	0	0	0	8,504
		Honesdale	0	0	0	0	4,795			Lawrence Park Township	0	0	0	0	3,778
		Honey Brook Township	0	0	0	0	7,140			Lawrence Township, Clearfield County	0	0	0	0	7,613
		Hooversville	0				718			Lawrence Township, Tioga County	0	0	0	0	1,712
		Horsham Township	0	0	0	0	24,947			Lebanon	0	0	0	0	24,144
		Hughesville	0	0	0	0	2,067			Leetsdale	0	0	0	0	1,122
		Hummelstown		0	0	0	4,386			Leet Township	0	0	0	0	1,510
		Huntingdon	0	0	0	0	6,815			Lehighton	0	0	0	0	5,489
		Independence Township, Beaver County	0	0	0	0	2,736			Lehigh Township, Northampton County	0	0	0	0	10,831
		Indiana	0	0	0	0	14,792			Lehman Township	0	0	0	0	3,308
		Indiana Township	0	0	0	0	6,947			Lewisburg	0	0	0	0	5,572
		Industry	0	0	0	0	1,821			Liberty	0	0	0	0	2,447
		Ingram	0	0	0	0	3,389			Liberty Township, Bedford County	0	0	0	0	1,449
		Irwin	0	0	0	0	4,116			Ligonier	0	0	0	0	1,633
		Ivyland	0	0	0	0	882			Ligonier Township			0	0	6,784
		Jackson Township, Butler County	0	0	0	0	3,841			Limerick Township	0	0	0	0	17,087
		Jackson Township, Cambria County	0	0	0		4,783			Lincoln	0	0	0	0	1,125
		Jackson Township, Luzerne County	0	0	0	0	4,597			Linesville	0		0		1,110
		Jeannette	0	0	0	0	10,021			Lititz	0	0	0	0	9,029
		Jefferson Hills Borough	0	0		0	9,614			Littlestown	0	0	0	0	4,187
		Jenkins Township	0	0	0	0	4,951			Lock Haven	0	0	0	0	8,584
		Jenkintown	0				4,332			Locust Township	0	0	0	0	2,518
		Jermyn	0	0	0	0	2,230			Logan Township	0	0	0	0	11,887
		Jersey Shore	0	0	0	0	4,360			Loretto	0	0	0	0	1,270
		Jim Thorpe	0	0	0	0	4,898			Lower Allen Township	0	0	0		17,701
		Johnsonburg	0	0	0	0	2,747			Lower Burrell	0	0	0	0	12,315
		Juniata Valley Regional	0	0	0		426			Lower Frederick Township	0	0	0	0	4,858
		Kane	0	0	0	0	3,828			Lower Gwynedd Township	0	0	0	0	11,368
		Kennedy Township	0	0	0	0	9,313			Lower Heidelberg Township	0	0	0	0	5,282
		Kennett Square	0	0	0	0	5,294			Lower Makefield Township	0	0	0	0	32,550
		Kidder Township	0	0	0		1,386			Lower Merion Township	0	0	0	0	57,691
		Kingston	0	0	0	0	13,036			Lower Milford Township	0	0	0	0	3,919
		Kingston Township	0	0	0	0	7,069			Lower Moreland Township	0	0	0	0	11,894
		Kiskiminetas Township	0	0	0	0	4,801								
		Kline Township	0	0	0	0	1,491								
		Knox	0	0	0	0	1,110								
		Koppel	0	0	0		788								
		Kulpmont	0	0	0		2,771								
		Kutztown	0	0		0	5,075								
		Laceyville	0	0	0		373								
		Laflin Borough	0	0	0	0	1,503								
		Lake City	0	0	0	0	2,985								
		Lamar Township	0	0	0	0	2,433								

[1]Agencies published in this table indicated that no hate crimes occurred in their jurisdictions during the quarter(s) for which they submitted reports to the Hate Crime program. Blanks indicate quarters for which agencies did not submit reports.

[2]Population figures are published only for the cities. The figures listed for the universities and colleges are student enrollment and were provided by the United States Department of Education for the 2006 school year, the most recent available. The enrollment figures include full-time and part-time students.

Table 95. Hate Crime Zero Data Submitted per Quarter, by State and Agency, 2007 *(Contd.)*

(Number.)

State	Agency type	Agency name	1st quarter	2nd quarter	3rd quarter	4th quarter	Population[2]	State	Agency type	Agency name	1st quarter	2nd quarter	3rd quarter	4th quarter	Population[2]
		Lower Paxton Township	0	0	0	0	44,961			Meyersdale	0	0	0	0	2,302
		Lower Pottsgrove Township	0	0	0	0	12,240			Middleburg	0	0	0	0	1,345
		Lower Providence Township	0	0	0	0	26,047			Middlesex Township, Butler County	0	0	0	0	5,564
		Lower Salford Township	0	0	0	0	14,419			Middlesex Township, Cumberland County	0	0	0	0	6,868
		Lower Saucon Township	0	0		0	11,360			Middletown	0	0	0		8,806
		Lower Southampton Township	0	0	0	0	19,189			Middletown Township	0	0	0	0	47,710
		Lower Swatara Township	0	0	0	0	8,364			Midland	0	0	0	0	2,898
		Lower Windsor Township	0	0	0	0	7,847			Midway	0				934
		Luzerne Township	0	0	0	0	6,739			Mifflin	0				622
		Lykens	0				1,834			Mifflinburg	0	0	0		3,564
		Macungie	0	0			3,132			Mifflin County Regional	0	0	0	0	26,255
		Madison Township	0	0	0	0	1,607			Mifflin Township	0	0	0	0	2,266
		Mahanoy City	0	0	0	0	4,361			Milford	0	0	0	0	2,945
		Mahanoy Township	0	0	0	0	3,592			Millbourne	0	0	0		911
		Mahoning Township, Carbon County	0	0	0	0	4,336			Millcreek Township, Erie County	0	0		0	52,592
		Mahoning Township, Montour County	0	0	0	0	4,262			Millcreek Township, Lebanon County	0				3,147
		Main Township	0	0	0	0	1,305			Millersburg	0	0	0	0	2,454
		Malvern	0	0	0	0	3,115			Millersville	0	0	0	0	7,204
		Manheim	0	0	0	0	4,626			Mill Hall			0		1,468
		Manheim Township	0	0	0	0	36,069			Millvale	0	0			3,675
		Manor		0	0	0	2,867			Millville	0	0	0	0	950
		Manor Township, Armstrong County	0	0	0	0	3,968			Milton	0	0	0	0	6,377
		Manor Township, Lancaster County	0	0	0	0	18,683			Minersville	0	0	0	0	4,264
		Mansfield	0	0	0	0	3,245			Mohnton	0	0	0	0	3,115
		Marietta	0	0	0	0	2,587			Monaca	0	0	0	0	5,833
		Marion Center	0	0	0		422			Monessen	0	0	0	0	8,159
		Marion Township, Berks County	0	0	0	0	1,659			Monongahela	0	0	0	0	4,468
		Marlborough Township	0	0		0	3,280			Monroeville	0	0	0	0	27,659
		Marple Township	0	0	0	0	23,579			Montgomery Township	0	0	0	0	24,419
		Martinsburg		0	0	0	2,139			Montoursville	0	0	0		4,630
		Marysville	0	0	0	0	2,454			Montrose	0	0	0	0	1,570
		Masontown	0	0	0	0	3,424			Moon Township	0	0	0	0	22,623
		Matamoras	0	0	0		2,669			Moore Township	0	0	0	0	9,502
		Mayfield	0	0	0	0	1,702			Morris-Cooper Regional	0				5,725
		McCandless	0	0	0	0	27,339			Morrisville	0	0	0	0	9,706
		McDonald Borough	0				2,135			Morton	0	0	0	0	2,649
		McKeesport	0	0		0	22,190			Moscow	0	0	0	0	1,953
		McKees Rocks	0	0	0		6,042			Mount Carmel	0	0	0	0	5,914
		McSherrystown	0	0	0	0	2,841			Mount Carmel Township	0	0	0	0	2,586
		Meadville	0	0	0	0	13,385			Mount Gretna Borough	0	0	0	0	234
		Mechanicsburg	0	0	0	0	8,771			Mount Jewett	0	0	0	0	1,015
		Media	0	0	0	0	5,445			Mount Joy	0	0	0	0	7,097
		Mercer	0	0	0	0	2,253			Mount Lebanon	0	0	0	0	30,543
		Mercersburg	0	0	0	0	1,556			Mount Oliver	0	0	0	0	3,681
										Mount Union	0				2,356
										Muhlenberg Township	0	0	0	0	18,334
										Muncy	0	0	0	0	2,486
										Munhall	0	0	0	0	11,239
										Murrysville	0	0	0	0	19,565
										Nanticoke	0	0	0	0	10,261
										Narberth	0	0	0	0	4,079
										Nazareth Area	0	0	0	0	6,061
										Nelson Township	0				576
										Neshannock Township	0	0	0	0	9,369

[1]Agencies published in this table indicated that no hate crimes occurred in their jurisdictions during the quarter(s) for which they submitted reports to the Hate Crime program. Blanks indicate quarters for which agencies did not submit reports.

[2]Population figures are published only for the cities. The figures listed for the universities and colleges are student enrollment and were provided by the United States Department of Education for the 2006 school year, the most recent available. The enrollment figures include full-time and part-time students.

Table 95. Hate Crime Zero Data Submitted per Quarter, by State and Agency, 2007 (Contd.)

(Number.)

State	Agency type	Agency name	Zero data per quarter[1]				Popu-lation[2]	State	Agency type	Agency name	Zero data per quarter[1]				Popu-lation[2]
			1st quarter	2nd quarter	3rd quarter	4th quarter					1st quarter	2nd quarter	3rd quarter	4th quarter	
		Nether Providence Township	0	0			13,257			North Huntingdon Township	0	0	0	0	29,478
		Neville Township	0				1,131			North Lebanon Township	0	0	0	0	10,896
		New Berlin	0	0			822			North Londonderry Township	0	0	0	0	6,939
		Newberry Township	0	0	0	0	15,563			North Middleton Township	0	0	0	0	10,946
		New Bethlehem	0	0	0		998			North Sewickley Township	0	0	0	0	5,729
		New Brighton	0	0		0	9,493			North Strabane Township	0	0	0	0	12,176
		New Britain	0	0	0	0	2,292			Northumberland	0	0	0	0	3,517
		New Britain Township	0	0	0		10,795			North Union Township	0	0	0	0	1,248
		New Castle	0	0		0	24,514			North Versailles Township	0	0	0	0	12,280
		New Castle Township	0	0	0	0	392			North Wales	0		0	0	3,248
		New Cumberland	0	0	0		7,084			Northwest Lancaster County Regional	0	0	0	0	18,083
		New Florence	0	0			735			Northwest Lawrence County Regional	0	0	0	0	6,759
		New Garden Township	0	0	0	0	11,699			Norwegian Township	0	0	0		2,148
		New Hanover Township	0	0	0	0	9,267			Norwood	0	0	0	0	5,813
		New Holland	0	0	0	0	5,152			Oakdale	0	0	0	0	1,441
		New Hope	0	0	0	0	2,296			Oakmont	0	0	0		6,451
		New Kensington	0	0	0	0	13,833			O'Hara Township	0	0	0	0	9,537
		Newport	0	0	0	0	1,465			Ohio Township	0				4,041
		New Sewickley Township	0	0	0	0	7,722			Ohioville	0	0	0	0	3,654
		Newton Township	0	0	0	0	2,763			Oil City	0	0	0	0	10,762
		Newtown	0	0	0	0	2,247			Old Forge	0	0	0	0	8,540
		Newtown Township, Bucks County	0	0	0		19,234			Old Lycoming Township	0	0			5,317
		Newtown Township, Delaware County	0	0	0	0	11,894			Oley Township	0	0	0	0	3,672
		Newville	0	0	0	0	1,313			Oliver Township	0	0	0	0	2,068
		New Wilmington	0	0			2,396			Olyphant			0	0	4,899
		Norristown	0	0	0	0	30,205			Orangeville Area		0	0	0	1,651
		Northampton	0	0	0	0	9,818			Orwigsburg	0	0	0	0	2,969
		Northampton Township	0	0	0	0	41,293			Osceola Mills	0	0	0	0	1,170
		North Beaver	0	0			4,025			Overfield Township	0				1,559
		North Belle Vernon	0	0	0	0	1,987			Oxford	0	0	0	0	4,738
		North Buffalo	0	0	0		2,818			Paint Township	0	0	0	0	3,210
		North Catasauqua	0	0	0	0	2,861			Palmerton	0	0	0	0	5,261
		North Charleroi	0	0	0	0	1,327			Palmer Township	0	0	0	0	19,673
		North Cornwall Township	0	0	0	0	6,526			Palmyra	0	0	0	0	6,944
		North Coventry Township	0	0	0	0	7,698			Parkesburg	0	0	0	0	3,455
		North East, Erie County	0	0	0	0	4,268			Parkside	0	0	0	0	2,195
		Northeastern Regional	0	0			11,000			Parks Township	0				2,609
		Northern Berks Regional	0	0	0	0	12,351			Patterson Area	0	0	0	0	3,617
		Northern Cambria Borough	0	0	0	0	3,970			Patton	0	0	0	0	1,883
		Northern Regional	0	0	0	0	27,442			Patton Township	0	0	0	0	12,839
		North Fayette Township	0	0	0	0	12,998			Paxtang	0	0	0	0	1,480
		North Franklin Township	0	0	0	0	4,681			Pen Argyl	0	0	0	0	3,667
										Penbrook	0	0	0	0	2,891
										Penn Hills	0	0	0	0	43,955
										Pennridge Regional	0	0	0	0	10,414
										Penn Township, Butler County	0	0	0	0	5,246

[1]Agencies published in this table indicated that no hate crimes occurred in their jurisdictions during the quarter(s) for which they submitted reports to the Hate Crime program. Blanks indicate quarters for which agencies did not submit reports.

[2]Population figures are published only for the cities. The figures listed for the universities and colleges are student enrollment and were provided by the United States Department of Education for the 2006 school year, the most recent available. The enrollment figures include full-time and part-time students.

Table 95. Hate Crime Zero Data Submitted per Quarter, by State and Agency, 2007 (Contd.)

(Number.)

State	Agency type	Agency name	Zero data per quarter[1]				Popu-lation[2]	State	Agency type	Agency name	Zero data per quarter[1]				Popu-lation[2]
			1st quarter	2nd quarter	3rd quarter	4th quarter					1st quarter	2nd quarter	3rd quarter	4th quarter	
		Penn Township, Lancaster County	0	0	0	0	8,201			Robinson Township, Allegheny County	0	0	0	0	13,585
		Penn Township, Perry County	0	0	0	0	3,222			Robinson Township, Washington County	0	0	0		2,159
		Penn Township, Westmoreland County	0	0	0	0	20,476			Rochester	0	0	0	0	3,717
		Penn Township, York County	0	0	0	0	16,010			Rochester Township	0	0	0	0	2,917
		Pequea Township	0	0	0	0	4,492			Rockledge	0	0	0		2,497
		Perkasie	0	0	0	0	8,709			Roseto	0	0	0	0	1,655
		Perryopolis	0	0	0	0	1,735			Rosslyn Farms	0	0	0	0	425
		Peters Township	0	0	0	0	20,264			Ross Township	0	0	0	0	30,522
		Phoenixville	0	0	0		15,962			Rostraver Township	0	0	0	0	11,749
		Pittston	0	0			7,600			Royersford	0	0	0	0	4,316
		Plainfield Township	0	0			6,142			Rush Township	0	0	0	0	3,567
		Plains Township	0	0	0	0	10,403			Ryan Township	0	0	0	0	2,560
		Pleasant Hills	0	0	0	0	7,767			Rye Township	0	0	0	0	2,511
		Plum	0	0	0	0	26,209			Sadsbury Township, Chester County	0	0	0	0	3,439
		Plumstead Township	0	0	0	0	11,978			Salem Township, Luzerne County	0	0	0	0	4,133
		Plymouth Township, Montgomery County	0	0	0	0	16,260			Salisbury Township	0	0	0	0	14,006
		Pocono Mountain Regional	0		0	0	35,733			Sandy Lake	0	0	0	0	708
		Pocono Township	0	0	0	0	11,468			Sandy Township	0	0	0	0	11,602
		Point Township	0	0	0	0	3,827			Saxonburg	0				1,635
		Polk	0				1,000			Saxton	0	0	0	0	761
		Portage	0	0	0	0	2,631			Sayre	0	0	0	0	5,554
		Port Allegany	0	0	0	0	2,228			Schuylkill Haven	0	0	0	0	5,198
		Port Vue	0	0			3,865			Schuylkill Township, Chester County	0				7,811
		Pottstown	0	0	0	0	21,346			Schuylkill Township, Schuylkill County			0	0	1,101
		Pottsville	0	0	0		14,523			Scottdale	0	0	0	0	4,488
		Prospect Park	0	0	0	0	6,402			Scott Township, Allegheny County	0	0	0	0	15,908
		Punxsutawney	0	0	0	0	6,046			Scott Township, Columbia County	0	0	0	0	4,976
		Pymatuning Township	0	0	0	0	3,644			Scott Township, Lackawanna County	0	0	0	0	4,932
		Quakertown	0	0			8,745			Scranton	0	0	0	0	72,444
		Quarryville	0			0	2,150			Selinsgrove	0	0			5,339
		Raccoon Township	0	0	0	0	3,277			Seven Springs	0	0	0	0	119
		Radnor Township	0	0	0		31,098			Seward	0	0	0	0	458
		Ralpho Township		0			3,909			Sewickley	0	0	0	0	3,584
		Rankin	0	0	0	0	2,116			Sewickley Heights	0	0	0	0	919
		Reading	0	0	0	0	81,168			Shaler Township	0	0	0	0	28,042
		Redstone Township	0	0	0		6,106			Shamokin	0	0	0	0	7,396
		Reynoldsville	0	0	0	0	2,582			Shamokin Dam	0	0	0		1,451
		Rice Township	0	0	0	0	2,826			Sharon	0				15,150
		Richland Township, Bucks County	0	0	0	0	13,027			Sharon Hill	0	0	0	0	5,326
		Richland Township, Cambria County	0	0	0	0	12,623			Sharpsburg	0	0	0	0	3,281
		Ridgway	0	0	0	0	4,194			Sharpsville	0	0	0	0	4,186
		Ridley Park	0	0	0	0	7,029			Shenandoah	0	0	0	0	5,199
		Ridley Township	0	0	0	0	30,055			Shenango Township, Lawrence County	0	0	0	0	7,680
		Riverside	0	0			1,795			Shillington	0	0	0	0	5,047
		Roaring Brook Township	0	0	0	0	1,759			Shippensburg	0	0	0		5,604
		Roaring Spring	0	0	0	0	2,280			Shippingport	0	0	0	0	223
		Robesonia	0	0	0		2,074								
		Robeson Township	0	0	0		7,619								

[1]Agencies published in this table indicated that no hate crimes occurred in their jurisdictions during the quarter(s) for which they submitted reports to the Hate Crime program. Blanks indicate quarters for which agencies did not submit reports.

[2]Population figures are published only for the cities. The figures listed for the universities and colleges are student enrollment and were provided by the United States Department of Education for the 2006 school year, the most recent available. The enrollment figures include full-time and part-time students.

Table 95. Hate Crime Zero Data Submitted per Quarter, by State and Agency, 2007 *(Contd.)*

(Number.)

State	Agency type	Agency name	Zero data per quarter[1]				Popu-lation[2]	State	Agency type	Agency name	Zero data per quarter[1]				Popu-lation[2]
			1st quarter	2nd quarter	3rd quarter	4th quarter					1st quarter	2nd quarter	3rd quarter	4th quarter	
		Shiremanstown	0	0	0	0	1,471			Springfield Township, Bucks County	0	0	0	0	5,099
		Shohola Township	0	0	0	0	2,479			Springfield Township, Delaware County	0	0	0	0	22,935
		Silver Lake Township	0	0		0	1,772			Springfield Township, Montgomery County	0	0	0	0	19,003
		Silver Spring Township	0	0	0		13,052			Spring Garden Township	0	0	0	0	11,876
		Sinking Spring	0	0	0	0	3,641			Spring Township, Centre County	0	0	0	0	6,720
		Slippery Rock	0	0	0	0	3,248			Spring Township, Snyder County	0	0	0	0	1,563
		Smethport	0	0	0	0	1,593			State College	0	0	0		52,047
		Smith Township	0	0			4,508			St. Clair Boro	0	0	0	0	3,052
		Solebury Township	0	0	0	0	9,007			St. Clair Township	0	0	0	0	1,362
		Somerset	0	0	0	0	6,428			Steelton	0	0	0	0	5,576
		Souderton	0	0	0	0	6,623			Stewartstown	0	0	0	0	2,047
		South Abington Township	0	0	0	0	9,646			St. Marys City	0	0	0	0	13,614
		South Beaver Township	0	0	0	0	2,875			Stockertown	0	0	0		773
		South Buffalo Township	0	0	0	0	2,811			Stoneboro	0	0	0	0	1,038
		South Centre Township	0	0	0	0	1,917			Stonycreek Township	0	0	0	0	2,959
		South Coatesville	0	0	0	0	1,075			Stowe Township	0	0	0		6,110
		Southern Regional Lancaster County	0	0	0	0	3,825			Strasburg	0	0	0	0	2,734
		Southern Regional York County	0	0	0	0	9,873			Stroud Area Regional	0	0	0	0	35,211
		South Fayette Township	0	0	0	0	13,174			Sugarcreek	0	0	0	0	5,033
		South Fork	0	0		0	1,046			Sugarloaf Township, Luzerne County	0	0	0	0	3,975
		South Greensburg		0	0	0	2,226			Summerhill Township	0	0	0		2,618
		South Heidelberg Township	0	0	0	0	7,146			Summit Hill	0				2,996
		South Heights	0	0	0	0	501			Summit Township	0	0	0	0	2,278
		South Lebanon Township	0	0	0	0	8,622			Sunbury	0	0	0	0	9,855
		South Londonderry Township	0	0	0	0	7,124			Susquehanna Regional	0	0	0	0	6,533
		South Park Township	0	0	0	0	13,953			Susquehanna Township, Cambria County	0				2,077
		South Pymatuning Township	0	0	0	0	2,841			Susquehanna Township, Dauphin County	0	0	0	0	22,905
		South Strabane Township	0	0	0	0	8,762			Swarthmore	0	0	0	0	6,148
		South Waverly	0	0	0	0	980			Sweden Township	0	0	0	0	741
		Southwestern Regional	0	0	0	0	17,840			Swissvale	0	0	0	0	8,811
		Southwest Greensburg	0	0	0	0	2,241			Swoyersville	0	0	0	0	7,649
		Southwest Mercer County Regional	0	0	0		11,421			Tamaqua	0	0	0	0	6,633
		Southwest Regional	0	0	0	0	2,180			Tarentum	0	0		0	4,558
		South Whitehall Township	0	0	0	0	19,486			Tatamy	0	0		0	1,106
		South Williamsport	0	0	0	0	6,064			Telford	0	0	0	0	4,629
		Spring City	0	0	0	0	3,410			Throop	0	0	0	0	3,996
		Springdale Township	0	0	0	0	1,655			Tidioute	0	0	0	0	732
		Springettsbury Township	0	0	0	0	24,663			Tilden Township		0	0	0	3,825
										Tinicum Township, Bucks County	0	0	0	0	4,265
										Tinicum Township, Delaware County	0	0	0	0	4,226
										Titusville	0	0	0	0	5,759

[1]Agencies published in this table indicated that no hate crimes occurred in their jurisdictions during the quarter(s) for which they submitted reports to the Hate Crime program. Blanks indicate quarters for which agencies did not submit reports.

[2]Population figures are published only for the cities. The figures listed for the universities and colleges are student enrollment and were provided by the United States Department of Education for the 2006 school year, the most recent available. The enrollment figures include full-time and part-time students.

Table 95. Hate Crime Zero Data Submitted per Quarter, by State and Agency, 2007 *(Contd.)*

(Number.)

State	Agency type	Agency name	Zero data per quarter[1]				Popu-lation[2]	State	Agency type	Agency name	Zero data per quarter[1]				Popu-lation[2]
			1st quarter	2nd quarter	3rd quarter	4th quarter					1st quarter	2nd quarter	3rd quarter	4th quarter	
		Towamencin Township	0	0	0	0	17,812			Upper St. Clair Township	0	0	0	0	18,927
		Towanda	0	0	0		2,885			Upper Uwchlan Township	0	0	0	0	10,022
		Trainer	0	0	0		1,847			Upper Yoder Township	0	0	0	0	5,580
		Tredyffrin Township	0	0	0	0	29,002			Uwchlan Township	0	0	0	0	18,689
		Troy	0	0	0	0	1,479			Valley Township	0	0	0	0	6,445
		Tullytown	0	0	0	0	1,981			Vandergrift	0	0			5,088
		Tulpehocken Township	0	0	0	0	3,588			Vandling	0	0	0		705
		Tunkhannock	0	0	0	0	1,801			Vernon Township	0	0	0	0	5,398
		Tunkhannock Township, Wyoming County	0	0	0	0	4,332			Verona	0	0	0	0	2,857
		Turtle Creek	0	0	0	0	5,569			Walnutport	0	0	0	0	2,170
		Ulster Township	0	0	0	0	1,299			Warminster Township	0	0	0	0	33,777
		Union City	0				3,348			Warren	0	0	0	0	9,519
		Uniontown	0	0			11,774			Warrington Township	0	0	0	0	23,208
		Union Township, Lawrence County	0	0	0	0	5,102			Warwick Township, Bucks County	0	0	0	0	15,086
		Union Township, Schuylkill County	0	0			1,338			Warwick Township, Lancaster County	0	0	0	0	17,362
		Upland	0	0	0	0	2,965			Washington, Washington County	0	0	0	0	14,710
		Upper Allen Township	0	0	0	0	17,802			Washington Township, Fayette County	0	0	0	0	4,186
		Upper Burrell Township			0	0	2,166			Washington Township, Franklin County	0	0	0	0	11,942
		Upper Chichester Township	0	0	0	0	17,623			Washington Township, Northampton County	0	0	0	0	4,898
		Upper Darby Township	0	0	0	0	79,020			Washington Township, Westmoreland County	0	0	0	0	7,476
		Upper Dublin Township	0	0	0	0	26,138			Watsontown	0	0	0	0	2,100
		Upper Gwynedd Township	0	0	0	0	15,870			Waynesburg	0	0	0	0	4,169
		Upper Leacock Township	0	0	0	0	8,449			Weatherly	0	0	0	0	2,608
		Upper Makefield Township	0	0	0	0	8,668			Wellsboro	0	0	0	0	3,293
		Upper Merion Township	0	0	0	0	26,680			Wernersville	0	0	0	0	2,504
		Upper Moreland Township	0	0	0	0	24,398			Wesleyville	0	0	0		3,386
		Upper Nazareth Township	0	0	0	0	5,669			West Alexander	0		0	0	304
		Upper Perkiomen	0	0	0	0	6,464			West Brandywine Township	0	0	0	0	7,756
		Upper Pottsgrove Township	0	0	0	0	5,161			West Brownsville	0				1,032
		Upper Providence Township, Delaware County	0	0	0	0	11,232			West Caln Township	0	0	0	0	8,237
		Upper Providence Township, Montgomery County	0	0	0	0	19,373			West Chester	0	0	0	0	18,276
		Upper Saucon Township	0	0	0	0	14,725			West Cocalico Township	0	0	0	0	7,150
		Upper Southampton Township	0	0	0	0	15,404			West Conshohocken	0	0	0		1,505
										West Cornwall Township	0	0	0	0	1,983
										West Deer Township	0	0	0	0	12,002
										West Earl Township	0	0	0	0	7,465
										West Fallowfield Township	0				2,615
										Westfall Township	0	0	0	0	2,933
										Westfield	0	0			1,135

[1]Agencies published in this table indicated that no hate crimes occurred in their jurisdictions during the quarter(s) for which they submitted reports to the Hate Crime program. Blanks indicate quarters for which agencies did not submit reports.

[2]Population figures are published only for the cities. The figures listed for the universities and colleges are student enrollment and were provided by the United States Department of Education for the 2006 school year, the most recent available. The enrollment figures include full-time and part-time students.

Table 95. Hate Crime Zero Data Submitted per Quarter, by State and Agency, 2007 (Contd.)

(Number.)

State	Agency type	Agency name	Zero data per quarter[1]				Popu-lation[2]	State	Agency type	Agency name	Zero data per quarter[1]				Popu-lation[2]
			1st quarter	2nd quarter	3rd quarter	4th quarter					1st quarter	2nd quarter	3rd quarter	4th quarter	
		West Goshen Township	0	0	0	0	21,255			Williamsport	0	0	0	0	29,701
		West Grove Borough		0	0		2,712			Willistown Township	0	0	0	0	10,861
		West Hazleton				0	3,334			Windber	0	0	0	0	4,043
		West Hempfield Township	0	0	0	0	16,026			Wind Gap	0	0	0	0	2,815
		West Hills Regional	0	0	0	0	10,863			Womelsdorf	0	0	0	0	2,823
		West Homestead	0	0	0	0	2,008			Woodward Township	0				2,266
		West Kittanning	0	0	0		1,739			Wright Township	0	0	0	0	5,834
		West Lampeter Township	0	0	0	0	15,539			Wyoming	0	0	0	0	3,020
		West Lebanon Township	0	0	0	0	840			Wyomissing	0	0	0	0	10,464
		West Manchester Township	0	0	0	0	18,181			Yardley	0	0	0	0	2,532
		West Manheim Township	0	0	0	0	7,178			Yeadon	0	0	0	0	11,440
		West Mayfield Borough	0	0			1,098			York	0	0	0	0	40,339
		West Mead Township	0	0	0	0	5,119			Youngsville	0	0	0	0	1,689
		West Norriton Township	0	0	0	0	14,642			Zelienople	0	0	0	0	4,008
		West Nottingham Township	0	0	0	0	2,799		Universities and Colleges	Bloomsburg University	0	0	0	0	8,723
		West Penn Township	0	0		0	4,233			California University	0	0	0	0	7,720
		West Pikeland Township	0	0	0	0	4,113			Cheyney University	0	0	0	0	1,667
		West Pike Run	0	0	0	0	1,848			Clarion University	0		0	0	6,563
		West Pittston				0	4,883			Community College of Beaver County	0				2,516
		West Pottsgrove Township	0	0	0		3,801			Dickinson College	0	0	0	0	2,400
		West Reading	0	0	0	0	4,086			East Stroudsburg University	0	0	0	0	7,013
		West Sadsbury Township	0	0	0	0	2,512			Edinboro University	0	0	0		7,579
		West Salem Township	0	0	0	0	3,389			Elizabethtown College	0	0	0	0	2,329
		West Shore Regional	0	0	0	0	6,619			Indiana University	0	0	0	0	14,248
		West View	0	0	0	0	6,704			Kutztown University	0	0	0	0	10,193
		West Vincent Township	0	0	0	0	4,180			Lehigh University	0	0	0	0	6,858
		West Whiteland Township	0	0	0	0	18,480			Lock Haven University	0	0	0	0	5,175
		West Wyoming	0	0	0	0	2,698			Millersville University	0	0		0	8,194
		West York	0	0	0	0	4,219			Moravian College	0	0	0	0	1,965
		Whitaker Borough	0	0	0		1,224			Pennsylvania State University:					
		Whitehall	0	0		0	13,439			Altoona	0	0	0	0	3,837
		Whitehall Township	0	0	0	0	26,917			Beaver	0	0	0	0	730
		White Haven Borough	0	0	0		1,153			Behrend	0	0	0	0	3,839
		Whitemarsh Township	0	0	0	0	17,422			Berks	0	0	0	0	2,660
		White Township	0	0	0		1,334			Harrisburg	0	0	0	0	3,799
		Whitpain Township	0	0	0	0	18,799			Hazleton	0	0	0	0	1,143
		Wiconisco Township	0	0	0	0	1,102			McKeesport[3]				0	
		Wilkes-Barre	0	0	0	0	41,050			Mont Alto	0	0	0	0	1,032
		Wilkes-Barre Township	0	0	0	0	3,060			University Park	0	0	0		42,914
		Wilkinsburg	0	0	0	0	17,583			Shippensburg University	0	0	0	0	7,516
		Wilkins Township		0	0	0	6,453			Slippery Rock University	0	0	0	0	8,230
		Williamsburg	0	0	0	0	1,260			University of Pittsburgh:					
										Bradford	0	0	0	0	1,333
										Pittsburgh	0		0	0	26,860
									Metro-politan Counties	Allegheny	0	0		0	
										Allegheny County Police Department	0	0	0	0	

[1]Agencies published in this table indicated that no hate crimes occurred in their jurisdictions during the quarter(s) for which they submitted reports to the Hate Crime program. Blanks indicate quarters for which agencies did not submit reports.

[2]Population figures are published only for the cities. The figures listed for the universities and colleges are student enrollment and were provided by the United States Department of Education for the 2006 school year, the most recent available. The enrollment figures include full-time and part-time students.

[3]Student enrollment figures were not available.

Table 95. Hate Crime Zero Data Submitted per Quarter, by State and Agency, 2007 *(Contd.)*

(Number.)

State	Agency type	Agency name	1st quarter	2nd quarter	3rd quarter	4th quarter	Population[2]
		Beaver	0	0	0		
		Centre	0				
		Cumberland	0	0	0	0	
		Lycoming	0	0	0	0	
		Montgomery	0	0	0	0	
		Pike	0	0	0	0	
		Washington	0	0	0	0	
		York	0			0	
	Nonmetropolitan Counties	Adams	0	0	0		
		Bradford	0	0	0	0	
		Clarion	0	0	0		
		Elk	0	0	0	0	
		Greene	0	0	0	0	
		Jefferson	0	0	0		
		Snyder	0	0	0	0	
		Tioga	0	0	0	0	
		Warren	0				
	State Police Agencies	Bureau of Criminal Investigation:					
		Adams County	0	0	0		
		Allegheny County	0	0	0		
		Armstrong County	0	0	0		
		Beaver County	0	0	0		
		Bedford County	0	0	0		
		Berks County	0	0	0		
		Blair County	0	0	0		
		Bradford County	0	0	0		
		Bucks County	0	0	0		
		Butler County	0	0	0		
		Cambria County	0	0	0		
		Cameron County	0	0	0		
		Carbon County	0	0	0		
		Centre County	0	0	0		
		Chester County	0	0	0		
		Clarion County	0	0	0		
		Clearfield County	0	0	0		
		Clinton County	0	0	0		
		Columbia County	0	0	0		
		Crawford County	0	0	0		
		Cumberland County	0	0	0		
		Dauphin County	0	0	0		
		Delaware County	0	0	0		
		Elk County	0	0	0		
		Erie County	0	0	0		
		Fayette County	0	0	0		
		Forest County	0	0	0		
		Franklin County	0	0	0		
		Fulton County	0	0	0		
		Greene County	0	0	0		
		Huntingdon County	0	0	0		
		Indiana County	0	0	0		
		Jefferson County	0	0	0		
		Juniata County	0	0	0		
		Lackawanna County	0	0	0		
		Lancaster County	0	0	0		
		Lawrence County	0	0	0		
		Lebanon County	0	0	0		
		Lehigh County	0	0	0		
		Luzerne County	0	0	0		
		Lycoming County	0	0	0		
		McKean County	0	0	0		
		Mercer County	0	0	0		
		Mifflin County	0	0	0		
		Monroe County	0	0	0		
		Montgomery County	0	0	0		
		Montour County	0	0	0		
		Northhampton County	0	0	0		
		Northumberland County	0	0	0		
		Perry County	0	0	0		
		Philadelphia County	0	0	0		
		Pike County	0	0	0		
		Potter County	0	0	0		
		Schuylkill County	0	0	0		
		Snyder County	0	0	0		
		Somerset County	0	0	0		
		Sullivan County	0	0	0		
		Susquehanna County	0	0	0		
		Tioga County	0	0	0		
		Union County	0	0	0		
		Venango County	0	0	0		
		Warren County	0	0	0		
		Washington County	0	0	0		
		Wayne County	0	0	0		
		Westmoreland County	0	0	0		
		Wyoming County	0	0	0		
		York County	0	0	0		
		State Police:					
		Adams County	0	0	0	0	
		Allegheny County	0	0	0	0	
		Armstrong County	0	0	0	0	
		Beaver County	0	0	0	0	
		Bedford County	0	0	0	0	
		Berks County	0	0	0	0	
		Blair County	0	0	0	0	
		Bradford County	0	0	0	0	
		Bucks County	0	0	0		
		Butler County	0	0	0	0	
		Cambria County	0	0	0	0	
		Cameron County	0	0	0	0	
		Carbon County	0	0	0	0	
		Centre County	0	0	0	0	
		Clarion County	0	0	0	0	
		Clearfield County	0	0	0	0	
		Clinton County	0	0	0	0	
		Columbia County	0	0	0	0	
		Crawford County	0	0	0	0	
		Cumberland County	0	0	0	0	

[1]Agencies published in this table indicated that no hate crimes occurred in their jurisdictions during the quarter(s) for which they submitted reports to the Hate Crime program. Blanks indicate quarters for which agencies did not submit reports.

[2]Population figures are published only for the cities. The figures listed for the universities and colleges are student enrollment and were provided by the United States Department of Education for the 2006 school year, the most recent available. The enrollment figures include full-time and part-time students.

Table 95. Hate Crime Zero Data Submitted per Quarter, by State and Agency, 2007 *(Contd.)*

(Number.)

State	Agency type	Agency name	Zero data per quarter[1] 1st quarter	2nd quarter	3rd quarter	4th quarter	Popu-lation[2]
		Delaware County	0	0	0	0	
		Elizabethville	0	0	0	0	
		Elk County	0	0	0	0	
		Erie County	0	0	0	0	
		Fayette County	0	0	0	0	
		Franklin County	0	0	0	0	
		Fulton County	0	0	0	0	
		Greene County	0	0	0	0	
		Huntingdon County	0	0	0	0	
		Indiana County	0	0	0	0	
		Jefferson County	0	0	0	0	
		Juniata County	0	0	0	0	
		Lackawanna County	0	0	0	0	
		Lancaster County	0	0	0	0	
		Lawrence County	0	0	0	0	
		Lebanon County	0	0	0	0	
		Lehigh County	0	0	0	0	
		Luzerne County	0	0	0	0	
		Lycoming County	0	0	0	0	
		McKean County	0	0	0	0	
		Mercer County	0	0	0	0	
		Mifflin County	0	0	0	0	
		Montour County	0	0	0	0	
		Northampton County	0	0	0	0	
		Northumberland County	0	0	0	0	
		Perry County	0	0	0	0	
		Philadelphia County	0	0	0	0	
		Potter County	0	0	0	0	
		Schuylkill County	0	0	0	0	
		Skippack	0	0	0		
		Snyder County	0	0	0	0	
		Somerset County	0	0	0	0	
		Sullivan County	0	0	0	0	
		Susquehanna County	0	0	0	0	
		Tioga County	0	0	0	0	
		Tionesta	0	0	0	0	
		Union County	0	0	0	0	
		Venango County	0	0	0	0	
		Warren County	0	0	0	0	
		Washington County	0	0	0	0	
		Wayne County	0	0	0		
		Westmoreland County	0	0	0	0	
		Wyoming County	0	0	0	0	
		York County	0	0	0	0	
	Other Agencies	Allegheny County District Attorney, Criminal Investigation Division	0	0	0	0	
		Allegheny County Port Authority	0	0	0	0	
		Altoona Hospital	0				
		Bureau of Narcotics:					
		Adams County	0	0			
		Allegheny County	0	0	0		
		Bedford County	0	0	0		
		Berks County	0				
		Blair County	0	0	0	0	
		Bradford County	0	0	0	0	
		Bucks County	0				
		Cambria County	0	0	0		
		Cameron County	0	0	0		
		Carbon County	0				
		Centre County	0	0	0	0	
		Chester County	0	0	0	0	
		Clearfield County	0	0	0	0	
		Clinton County	0	0	0	0	
		Columbia County	0	0	0	0	
		Crawford County	0	0	0		
		Cumberland County	0	0	0	0	
		Dauphin County	0	0	0	0	
		Delaware County	0	0	0	0	
		Elk County	0	0	0		
		Erie County	0	0	0		
		Fayette County	0	0	0		
		Forest County	0	0	0		
		Greene County	0	0	0		
		Huntingdon County	0	0	0	0	
		Juniata County	0	0	0	0	
		Lackawanna County	0	0	0	0	
		Lehigh County	0				
		Luzerne County	0	0	0	0	
		Lycoming County	0	0	0	0	
		McKean County	0	0	0		
		Mifflin County	0	0	0	0	
		Monroe County	0				
		Montgomery County	0				
		Montour County	0	0	0	0	
		Northampton County	0				
		Northumberland County	0	0	0	0	
		Philadelphia County	0	0	0	0	
		Pike County	0	0	0	0	
		Potter County	0	0	0	0	
		Schuylkill County	0				
		Snyder County	0	0	0	0	
		Somerset County	0	0	0		
		Sullivan County	0	0	0	0	
		Susquehanna County	0	0	0	0	
		Tioga County	0	0	0	0	
		Union County	0	0	0	0	
		Venango County	0	0	0		
		Warren County	0	0	0		

[1]Agencies published in this table indicated that no hate crimes occurred in their jurisdictions during the quarter(s) for which they submitted reports to the Hate Crime program. Blanks indicate quarters for which agencies did not submit reports.

[2]Population figures are published only for the cities. The figures listed for the universities and colleges are student enrollment and were provided by the United States Department of Education for the 2006 school year, the most recent available. The enrollment figures include full-time and part-time students.

Table 95. Hate Crime Zero Data Submitted per Quarter, by State and Agency, 2007 *(Contd.)*

(Number.)

State	Agency type	Agency name	Zero data per quarter[1]				Popu-lation[2]	State	Agency type	Agency name	Zero data per quarter[1]				Popu-lation[2]
			1st quarter	2nd quarter	3rd quarter	4th quarter					1st quarter	2nd quarter	3rd quarter	4th quarter	
		Washington County	0	0	0					Little Compton	0	0	0	0	3,510
		Wayne County	0	0	0	0				Middletown	0	0	0	0	16,278
		Westmoreland County	0	0	0					Narragansett	0	0	0	0	16,552
		Wyoming County	0	0	0	0				Newport	0	0	0	0	24,192
		Canadian Pacific Railway County	0	0	0					New Shoreham	0	0	0	0	1,023
		Detective:								North Kingstown	0	0	0	0	26,475
		Berks County	0	0	0	0				North Providence	0	0	0	0	32,685
		Bucks County	0	0	0	0				North Smithfield	0	0	0	0	11,183
		Butler County	0	0		0				Portsmouth	0	0	0	0	16,853
		Chester County	0	0	0	0				Richmond	0	0	0	0	7,665
		Clinton County	0	0	0	0				Scituate	0	0	0	0	10,814
		Dauphin County	0	0	0	0				Smithfield	0	0	0	0	21,495
		Lebanon County	0	0	0	0				Tiverton	0	0	0	0	15,074
		Lehigh County	0	0	0	0				Warren	0	0	0	0	11,089
		Pike County	0	0	0	0				Westerly	0	0	0	0	23,197
		Schuylkill County		0						West Greenwich	0	0	0	0	6,371
		Westmoreland County	0	0	0	0				Woonsocket	0	0	0	0	43,529
		York County	0	0	0	0			Universities and Colleges	University of Rhode Island	0	0	0	0	15,062
		Delaware County District Attorney, Criminal Investigation Division	0	0	0	0			State Police Agencies	Rhode Island State Police Headquarters	0	0	0	0	
		Delaware County Park Department of Environmental Resources	0	0	0	0				State Police: Chepachet	0	0	0	0	
		Harrisburg International Airport	0	0	0	0				Hope Valley	0	0	0	0	
		State Capitol Police	0	0	0	0				Lincoln	0	0	0	0	
		State Park Police, Pymatuning	0	0	0	0				Portsmouth	0	0	0	0	
		Tyrone Area School District	0	0	0	0				Wickford	0	0	0	0	
		Uniontown Hospital	0	0	0				Other Agencies	Department of Environmental Management	0	0	0	0	
		Washington County Alternative Education	0	0	0	0		SOUTH CAROLINA....	Cities	Abbeville	0	0	0	0	5,659
		Westmoreland County Park	0	0						Aiken	0	0	0	0	29,256
		Wilkes-Barre Area School District	0	0	0	0				Allendale	0	0	0	0	3,781
RHODE ISLAND..........	Cities	Barrington	0	0	0	0	16,414			Anderson	0	0	0	0	26,326
		Bristol	0	0	0	0	24,274			Andrews	0	0	0	0	3,017
		Burrillville	0	0	0	0	16,392			Atlantic Beach	0	0	0	0	385
		Central Falls	0	0	0	0	18,818			Aynor	0	0	0	0	580
		Charlestown	0	0	0	0	8,131			Bamberg	0	0	0	0	3,480
		Coventry	0	0	0	0	34,353			Barnwell	0	0	0	0	4,847
		Cranston	0	0	0	0	80,724			Belton	0	0	0	0	4,607
		Cumberland	0	0	0	0	34,027			Bethune	0	0	0	0	367
		East Greenwich	0	0	0	0	13,338			Bishopville	0	0	0	0	3,945
		Foster	0	0	0	0	4,467			Blacksburg	0	0	0	0	1,899
		Glocester	0	0	0	0	10,498			Blackville	0	0	0	0	2,888
		Hopkinton	0	0	0	0	7,976			Bluffton	0	0	0	0	3,791
		Jamestown	0	0	0	0	5,484			Bonneau	0	0	0	0	338
		Johnston	0	0	0	0	28,585			Bowman	0	0	0	0	1,163
		Lincoln	0	0	0	0	21,855			Branchville	0	0	0	0	1,037
										Brunson	0	0	0	0	576
										Burnettown	0	0	0	0	2,670
										Calhoun Falls	0	0	0	0	2,231
										Camden	0	0	0	0	7,071
										Cameron	0	0	0	0	416
										Campobello	0	0	0	0	584
										Cayce	0	0	0	0	12,659
										Central	0	0	0	0	4,147
										Charleston	0	0	0	0	109,382
										Chesnee	0	0	0	0	1,057
										Chester	0	0	0	0	6,074
										Chesterfield	0	0	0	0	1,321
										Clemson	0	0	0	0	12,532
										Clio	0	0	0	0	740
										Columbia	0	0	0	0	120,549
										Conway	0	0	0	0	14,285
										Cottageville	0	0	0	0	699
										Coward	0	0	0	0	674
										Cowpens	0	0	0	0	2,364

[1]Agencies published in this table indicated that no hate crimes occurred in their jurisdictions during the quarter(s) for which they submitted reports to the Hate Crime program. Blanks indicate quarters for which agencies did not submit reports.

[2]Population figures are published only for the cities. The figures listed for the universities and colleges are student enrollment and were provided by the United States Department of Education for the 2006 school year, the most recent available. The enrollment figures include full-time and part-time students.

Table 95. Hate Crime Zero Data Submitted per Quarter, by State and Agency, 2007 *(Contd.)*

(Number.)

State	Agency type	Agency name	Zero data per quarter[1] 1st quarter	2nd quarter	3rd quarter	4th quarter	Popu-lation[2]
		Dillon	0	0	0	0	6,382
		Due West	0	0	0	0	1,286
		Duncan	0	0	0	0	3,020
		Easley	0	0	0	0	19,372
		Eastover	0	0	0	0	767
		Edgefield	0	0	0	0	4,529
		Edisto Beach	0	0	0	0	724
		Ehrhardt	0	0	0	0	561
		Elgin	0	0	0	0	1,080
		Elloree	0	0	0	0	698
		Estill	0	0	0	0	2,381
		Eutawville	0	0	0	0	329
		Fairfax	0	0	0	0	3,167
		Folly Beach	0	0	0	0	2,339
		Forest Acres	0	0	0	0	9,818
		Fort Lawn	0	0	0	0	816
		Fort Mill	0	0	0	0	8,709
		Fountain Inn	0	0	0	0	7,261
		Gaffney	0	0	0	0	12,945
		Gaston	0	0	0	0	1,405
		Georgetown	0	0	0	0	8,668
		Greeleyville	0	0	0	0	410
		Greenville	0	0	0	0	57,595
		Greenwood	0	0	0	0	22,428
		Greer	0	0	0	0	23,224
		Hampton	0	0	0	0	2,780
		Hardeeville	0	0	0	0	1,857
		Harleyville	0	0	0	0	694
		Holly Hill	0	0	0	0	1,346
		Honea Path	0	0	0	0	3,628
		Inman	0	0	0	0	1,942
		Irmo	0	0	0	0	11,364
		Isle of Palms	0	0	0	0	4,653
		Iva	0	0	0	0	1,188
		Jackson	0	0	0	0	1,650
		Jamestown	0	0	0	0	96
		Johnsonville	0	0	0	0	1,461
		Johnston	0	0	0	0	2,339
		Jonesville	0	0	0	0	914
		Kingstree	0	0	0	0	3,317
		Lake City	0	0	0	0	6,693
		Lake View	0	0	0	0	789
		Lamar	0	0	0	0	1,001
		Lancaster	0	0	0	0	8,393
		Landrum	0	0	0	0	2,554
		Lane	0	0	0	0	533
		Latta	0	0	0	0	1,501
		Laurens	0	0	0	0	9,841
		Liberty	0	0	0	0	3,034
		Lincolnville	0	0	0	0	840
		Loris	0	0	0	0	2,322
		Lynchburg	0	0	0	0	579
		Marion	0	0	0	0	6,949
		Mauldin	0	0	0	0	20,494
		McBee	0	0	0	0	713
		McColl	0	0	0	0	2,368
		McCormick	0	0	0	0	2,712
		Moncks Corner	0	0	0	0	6,645
		Mullins	0	0	0	0	4,820
		Newberry	0	0	0	0	10,927
		New Ellenton	0	0	0	0	2,251
		Nichols	0	0	0	0	404
		Ninety Six	0	0	0	0	1,920
		North	0	0	0	0	778
		North Charleston	0	0	0	0	88,431
		North Myrtle Beach	0	0	0	0	15,577
		Norway	0	0	0	0	363
		Orangeburg	0	0	0	0	13,674
		Pacolet	0	0	0	0	2,756
		Pageland	0	0	0	0	2,539
		Pamplico	0	0	0	0	1,152
		Pawleys Island	0	0	0	0	143
		Pelion	0	0	0	0	599
		Pickens	0	0	0	0	2,990
		Pine Ridge	0	0	0	0	1,760
		Prosperity	0	0	0	0	1,072
		Ridgeland	0	0	0	0	2,640
		Ridgeville	0	0	0	0	2,075
		Salem	0	0	0	0	132
		Salley	0	0	0	0	415
		Saluda	0	0	0	0	2,979
		Santee	0	0	0	0	714
		Scranton	0	0	0	0	998
		Seneca	0	0	0	0	8,076
		Society Hill	0	0	0	0	696
		South Congaree	0	0	0	0	2,413
		Springdale	0	0	0	0	2,956
		Springfield	0	0	0	0	483
		St. George	0	0	0	0	2,124
		St. Matthews	0	0	0	0	1,995
		St. Stephen	0	0	0	0	1,702
		Sullivans Island	0	0	0	0	1,868
		Summerton	0	0	0	0	1,047
		Sumter	0	0	0	0	38,955
		Surfside Beach	0	0	0	0	4,846
		Swansea	0	0	0	0	784
		Tega Cay	0	0	0	0	4,612
		Timmonsville	0	0	0	0	2,384
		Travelers Rest	0	0	0	0	4,396
		Turbeville	0	0	0	0	721
		Vance	0	0	0	0	199
		Varnville	0	0	0	0	2,035
		Wagener	0	0	0	0	878
		Walhalla	0	0	0	0	3,689
		Ware Shoals	0	0	0	0	2,359
		Wellford	0	0	0	0	2,315
		West Columbia	0	0	0	0	13,729
		West Pelzer	0	0	0	0	905
		Whitmire	0	0	0	0	1,543
		Williamston	0	0	0	0	3,914
		Williston	0	0	0	0	3,239
		Winnsboro	0	0	0	0	3,637
		Woodruff	0	0	0	0	4,076
		Yemassee	0	0	0	0	857
	Universities and Colleges	Aiken Technical College	0	0	0	0	2,442
		Benedict College	0	0	0	0	2,531
		Bob Jones University[3]	0	0	0	0	
		Clemson University	0	0	0	0	17,309
		Coastal Carolina University	0	0	0	0	8,049
		Columbia College	0	0	0	0	1,446
		Denmark Technical College	0	0	0	0	1,377
		Erskine College	0	0	0	0	924
		Francis Marion University	0	0	0	0	4,075
		Lander University	0	0	0	0	2,682
		Medical University of South Carolina	0	0	0	0	2,498
		Midlands Technical College	0	0	0	0	10,849
		Presbyterian College	0	0	0	0	1,224
		South Carolina State University	0	0	0	0	4,384

[1]Agencies published in this table indicated that no hate crimes occurred in their jurisdictions during the quarter(s) for which they submitted reports to the Hate Crime program. Blanks indicate quarters for which agencies did not submit reports.

[3]Student enrollment figures were not available.

Table 95. Hate Crime Zero Data Submitted per Quarter, by State and Agency, 2007 (Contd.)

(Number.)

State	Agency type	Agency name	1st quarter	2nd quarter	3rd quarter	4th quarter	Population[2]	State	Agency type	Agency name	1st quarter	2nd quarter	3rd quarter	4th quarter	Population[2]
		Spartanburg Methodist College	0	0	0	0	779			Dorchester County	0	0	0	0	
		The Citadel	0	0	0	0	3,306			Edgefield County	0	0	0	0	
		Trident Technical College	0	0	0	0	11,808			Fairfield County	0	0	0	0	
		University of South Carolina:								Florence County	0	0	0	0	
		Aiken	0	0	0	0	3,380			Georgetown County	0	0	0	0	
		Columbia	0	0	0	0	27,390			Greenville County	0	0	0	0	
		Upstate	0	0	0	0	4,608			Greenwood County	0	0	0	0	
		Winthrop University	0	0	0	0	6,292			Hampton County	0	0	0	0	
	Metropolitan Counties	Calhoun	0	0	0	0				Horry County	0	0	0	0	
		Dorchester	0	0	0	0				Jasper County	0	0	0	0	
		Edgefield	0	0	0	0				Kershaw County	0	0	0	0	
		Fairfield	0	0	0	0				Lancaster County	0	0	0	0	
		Florence	0	0	0	0				Laurens County	0	0	0	0	
		Horry	0	0	0	0				Lee County	0	0	0	0	
		Laurens	0	0	0	0				Lexington County	0	0	0	0	
		Pickens	0	0	0	0				Marion County	0	0	0	0	
		Sumter	0	0	0	0				Marlboro County	0	0	0	0	
		York	0	0	0	0				McCormick County	0	0	0	0	
	Nonmetropolitan Counties	Abbeville	0	0	0	0				Newberry County	0	0	0	0	
		Allendale	0	0	0	0				Oconee County	0	0	0	0	
		Bamberg	0	0	0	0				Orangeburg County	0	0	0	0	
		Barnwell	0	0	0	0				Pickens County	0	0	0	0	
		Cherokee	0	0	0	0				Richland County	0	0	0	0	
		Dillon	0	0	0	0				Saluda County	0	0	0	0	
		Georgetown	0	0	0	0				Spartanburg County	0	0	0	0	
		Jasper	0	0	0	0				Sumter County	0	0	0	0	
		Lancaster	0	0	0	0				Union County	0	0	0	0	
		McCormick	0	0	0	0				Williamsburg County	0	0	0	0	
		Newberry	0	0	0	0				York County	0	0	0	0	
		Orangeburg	0	0	0	0			**Other Agencies**	Bureau of Protective Services	0	0	0	0	
		Union	0	0	0	0				Charleston County Aviation Authority	0	0	0	0	
	State Police Agencies	Highway Patrol:								Columbia Metropolitan Airport	0	0	0	0	
		Abbeville County	0	0	0	0				Department of Mental Health	0	0	0	0	
		Aiken County	0	0	0	0				Department of Natural Resources:					
		Allendale County	0	0	0	0				Abbeville County	0	0	0	0	
		Anderson County	0	0	0	0				Aiken County	0	0	0	0	
		Bamberg County	0	0	0	0				Allendale County	0	0	0	0	
		Barnwell County	0	0	0	0				Anderson County	0	0	0	0	
		Beaufort County	0	0	0	0				Bamberg County	0	0	0	0	
		Berkeley County	0	0	0	0				Barnwell County	0	0	0	0	
		Calhoun County	0	0	0	0									
		Charleston County	0	0	0	0									
		Cherokee County	0	0	0	0									
		Chester County	0	0	0	0									
		Chesterfield County	0	0	0	0									
		Clarendon County	0	0	0	0									
		Colleton County	0	0	0	0									
		Darlington County	0	0	0	0									
		Dillon County	0	0	0	0									

[1] Agencies published in this table indicated that no hate crimes occurred in their jurisdictions during the quarter(s) for which they submitted reports to the Hate Crime program. Blanks indicate quarters for which agencies did not submit reports.

[2] Population figures are published only for the cities. The figures listed for the universities and colleges are student enrollment and were provided by the United States Department of Education for the 2006 school year, the most recent available. The enrollment figures include full-time and part-time students.

Table 95. Hate Crime Zero Data Submitted per Quarter, by State and Agency, 2007 *(Contd.)*

(Number.)

State	Agency type	Agency name	Zero data per quarter[1]				Population[2]
			1st quarter	2nd quarter	3rd quarter	4th quarter	
		Beaufort County	0	0	0	0	
		Berkeley County	0	0	0	0	
		Calhoun County	0	0	0	0	
		Charleston County	0	0	0	0	
		Cherokee County	0	0	0	0	
		Chester County	0	0	0	0	
		Chesterfield County	0	0	0	0	
		Clarendon County	0	0	0	0	
		Colleton County	0	0	0	0	
		Darlington County	0	0	0	0	
		Dillon County	0	0	0	0	
		Dorchester County	0	0	0	0	
		Edgefield County	0	0	0	0	
		Fairfield County	0	0	0	0	
		Florence County	0	0	0	0	
		Georgetown County	0	0	0	0	
		Greenville County	0	0	0	0	
		Greenwood County	0	0	0	0	
		Hampton County	0	0	0	0	
		Horry County	0	0	0	0	
		Jasper County	0	0	0	0	
		Kershaw County	0	0	0	0	
		Lancaster County	0	0	0	0	
		Laurens County	0	0	0	0	
		Lee County	0	0	0	0	
		Lexington County	0	0	0	0	
		Marion County	0	0	0	0	
		Marlboro County	0	0	0	0	
		McCormick County	0	0	0	0	
		Newberry County	0	0	0	0	
		Oconee County	0	0	0	0	
		Orangeburg County	0	0	0	0	
		Pickens County	0	0	0	0	
		Richland County	0	0	0	0	
		Saluda County	0	0	0	0	
		Spartanburg County	0	0	0	0	
		Sumter County	0	0	0	0	
		Union County	0	0	0	0	
		Williamsburg County	0	0	0	0	
		York County	0	0	0	0	
		Employment Security Commission	0	0	0	0	
		Forestry Commission: Abbeville County	0	0	0	0	
		Aiken County	0	0	0	0	

State	Agency type	Agency name	Zero data per quarter[1]				Population[2]
			1st quarter	2nd quarter	3rd quarter	4th quarter	
		Allendale County	0	0	0	0	
		Anderson County	0	0	0	0	
		Bamberg County	0	0	0	0	
		Barnwell County	0	0	0	0	
		Beaufort County	0	0	0	0	
		Berkeley County	0	0	0	0	
		Calhoun County	0	0	0	0	
		Charleston County	0	0	0	0	
		Cherokee County	0	0	0	0	
		Chester County	0	0	0	0	
		Chesterfield County	0	0	0	0	
		Clarendon County	0	0	0	0	
		Colleton County	0	0	0	0	
		Darlington County	0	0	0	0	
		Dillon County	0	0	0	0	
		Dorchester County	0	0	0	0	
		Fairfield County	0	0	0	0	
		Florence County	0	0	0	0	
		Georgetown County	0	0	0	0	
		Greenville County	0	0	0	0	
		Greenwood County	0	0	0	0	
		Hampton County	0	0	0	0	
		Horry County	0	0	0	0	
		Jasper County	0	0	0	0	
		Kershaw County	0	0	0	0	
		Lancaster County	0	0	0	0	
		Laurens County	0	0	0	0	
		Lee County	0	0	0	0	
		Lexington County	0	0	0	0	
		Marion County	0	0	0	0	
		Marlboro County	0	0	0	0	
		Newberry County	0	0	0	0	
		Oconee County	0	0	0	0	
		Orangeburg County	0	0	0	0	
		Pickens County	0	0	0	0	
		Richland County	0	0	0	0	
		Saluda County	0	0	0	0	
		Spartanburg County	0	0	0	0	
		Sumter County	0	0	0	0	
		Union County	0	0	0	0	
		Williamsburg County	0	0	0	0	
		York County	0	0	0	0	
		Greenville-Spartanburg International Airport	0	0	0	0	

[1]Agencies published in this table indicated that no hate crimes occurred in their jurisdictions during the quarter(s) for which they submitted reports to the Hate Crime program. Blanks indicate quarters for which agencies did not submit reports.

[2]Population figures are published only for the cities. The figures listed for the universities and colleges are student enrollment and were provided by the United States Department of Education for the 2006 school year, the most recent available. The enrollment figures include full-time and part-time students.

Table 95. Hate Crime Zero Data Submitted per Quarter, by State and Agency, 2007 *(Contd.)*

(Number.)

State	Agency type	Agency name	Zero data per quarter[1]				Popu-lation[2]
			1st quarter	2nd quarter	3rd quarter	4th quarter	
		South Carolina Law Enforcement Division Vehicle Crimes	0	0	0	0	
		South Carolina Law Enforcement Division Vice:					
		Abbeville County	0	0	0	0	
		Aiken County	0	0	0	0	
		Allendale County	0	0	0	0	
		Anderson County	0	0	0	0	
		Bamberg County	0	0	0	0	
		Barnwell County	0	0	0	0	
		Beaufort County	0	0	0	0	
		Berkeley County	0	0	0	0	
		Calhoun County	0	0	0	0	
		Charleston County	0	0	0	0	
		Cherokee County	0	0	0	0	
		Chester County	0	0	0	0	
		Chesterfield County	0	0	0	0	
		Clarendon County	0	0	0	0	
		Colleton County	0	0	0	0	
		Darlington County	0	0	0	0	
		Dillon County	0	0	0	0	
		Dorchester County	0	0	0	0	
		Edgefield County	0	0	0	0	
		Fairfield County	0	0	0	0	
		Florence County	0	0	0	0	
		Georgetown County	0	0	0	0	
		Greenville County	0	0	0	0	
		Greenwood County	0	0	0	0	
		Hampton County	0	0	0	0	
		Horry County	0	0	0	0	
		Jasper County	0	0	0	0	
		Kershaw County	0	0	0	0	
		Lancaster County	0	0	0	0	
		Laurens County	0	0	0	0	
		Lee County	0	0	0	0	
		Lexington County	0	0	0	0	
		Marion County	0	0	0	0	
		Marlboro County	0	0	0	0	
		McCormick County	0	0	0	0	
		Newberry County	0	0	0	0	
		Oconee County	0	0	0	0	
		Orangeburg County	0	0	0	0	
		Pickens County	0	0	0	0	
		Richland County	0	0	0	0	
		Saluda County	0	0	0	0	
		Spartanburg County	0	0	0	0	
		Sumter County	0	0	0	0	
		Union County	0	0	0	0	
		Williamsburg County	0	0	0	0	
		York County	0	0	0	0	
		South Carolina School for the Deaf and Blind	0	0	0	0	
		State Museum	0	0	0	0	
		State Ports Authority	0	0	0	0	
		State Transport Police:					
		Aiken County	0	0	0	0	
		Allendale County	0	0	0	0	
		Anderson County	0	0	0	0	
		Bamberg County	0	0	0	0	
		Barnwell County	0	0	0	0	
		Beaufort County	0	0	0	0	
		Berkeley County	0	0	0	0	
		Charleston County	0	0	0	0	
		Cherokee County	0	0	0	0	
		Colleton County	0	0	0	0	
		Darlington County	0	0	0	0	
		Dillon County	0	0	0	0	
		Dorchester County	0	0	0	0	
		Edgefield County	0	0	0	0	
		Fairfield County	0	0	0	0	
		Florence County	0	0	0	0	
		Georgetown County	0	0	0	0	
		Greenville County	0	0	0	0	
		Greenwood County	0	0	0	0	
		Horry County	0	0	0	0	
		Jasper County	0	0	0	0	
		Kershaw County	0	0	0	0	
		Laurens County	0	0	0	0	
		Lee County	0	0	0	0	
		Lexington County	0	0	0	0	
		Marion County		0	0	0	
		Marlboro County	0	0	0	0	
		Newberry County	0	0	0	0	
		Oconee County	0	0	0	0	
		Orangeburg County	0	0	0	0	
		Richland County	0	0	0	0	

[1]Agencies published in this table indicated that no hate crimes occurred in their jurisdictions during the quarter(s) for which they submitted reports to the Hate Crime program. Blanks indicate quarters for which agencies did not submit reports.

[2]Population figures are published only for the cities. The figures listed for the universities and colleges are student enrollment and were provided by the United States Department of Education for the 2006 school year, the most recent available. The enrollment figures include full-time and part-time students.

Table 95. Hate Crime Zero Data Submitted per Quarter, by State and Agency, 2007 (Contd.)

(Number.)

State	Agency type	Agency name	Zero data per quarter[1]				Population[2]	State	Agency type	Agency name	Zero data per quarter[1]				Population[2]
			1st quarter	2nd quarter	3rd quarter	4th quarter					1st quarter	2nd quarter	3rd quarter	4th quarter	
		Spartanburg County	0	0	0	0				Bennett	0	0	0	0	
		Sumter County	0	0	0	0				Bon Homme	0	0	0	0	
		Union County	0	0	0	0				Brookings	0	0	0		
		Williamsburg County		0	0	0				Brown	0	0	0	0	
		York County	0	0	0	0				Campbell	0	0	0	0	
		United States Department of Energy, Savannah River Plant	0	0	0	0				Charles Mix	0	0	0	0	
										Clay	0	0	0	0	
										Codington	0	0	0	0	
		Whitten Center	0	0	0	0				Corson	0	0	0	0	
SOUTH DAKOTA	Cities	Armour	0	0	0	0	693			Custer	0	0	0	0	
		Avon	0	0	0	0	536			Davison	0	0	0	0	
		Box Elder	0	0	0	0	3,112			Deuel	0	0	0	0	
		Brandon	0	0	0	0	7,956			Dewey	0	0	0	0	
		Brookings		0	0	0	18,805			Douglas	0	0	0		
		Canton	0	0	0	0	3,237			Edmunds	0	0	0	0	
		Centerville	0	0	0	0	856			Faulk	0	0	0	0	
		Clark	0	0	0	0	1,128			Hamlin	0	0	0	0	
		Colman	0	0	0	0	553			Hand	0	0	0	0	
		Corsica	0	0	0	0	601			Hanson	0	0	0	0	
		Deadwood	0	0	0	0	1,269			Harding	0	0	0	0	
		Eagle Butte	0	0	0	0	950			Hughes	0	0	0	0	
		Estelline	0	0	0	0	668			Hutchinson	0	0	0	0	
		Eureka	0	0	0	0	952			Jerauld	0	0	0	0	
		Faith	0	0	0	0	456			Kingsbury	0	0	0	0	
		Freeman	0	0	0	0	1,178			Lawrence	0	0	0	0	
		Gettysburg	0	0	0	0	1,130			Marshall	0	0	0	0	
		Hot Springs	0	0	0	0	4,095			McPherson	0	0	0	0	
		Irene	0	0	0	0	403			Mellette	0				
		Jefferson	0	0	0	0	593			Miner	0	0	0	0	
		Kadoka	0	0	0	0	673			Moody	0	0	0	0	
		Lead	0	0	0	0	2,837			Perkins	0	0	0	0	
		Lemmon	0	0	0	0	1,205			Potter	0	0	0	0	
		Lennox	0	0	0		2,154			Roberts	0	0	0	0	
		Leola	0	0	0	0	394			Sanborn	0	0	0	0	
		Madison	0	0	0	0	6,221			Spink	0	0	0	0	
		McLaughlin	0	0	0	0	755			Stanley	0	0	0	0	
		Menno	0	0	0	0	675			Sully	0	0	0	0	
		Miller	0	0	0	0	1,343		Other	Tripp	0	0	0	0	
		Mitchell	0	0	0	0	14,894		Agencies	Walworth	0	0	0	0	
		Mobridge	0	0	0	0	3,188			Yankton	0	0	0	0	
		New Effington	0	0	0	0	225			Ziebach	0	0	0	0	
		North Sioux City	0	0	0	0	2,545		Other Agencies	Division of Criminal Investigation	0	0	0	0	
		Parkston	0	0	0	0	1,506	TENNESSEE..	Cities	Adamsville	0	0	0	0	2,122
		Rosholt	0	0	0	0	437			Alamo	0	0	0	0	2,349
		Scotland	0	0	0	0	816			Alcoa	0	0	0	0	8,544
		Springfield	0	0	0	0	1,510			Alexandria	0	0	0	0	870
		Sturgis	0	0	0	0	6,090			Algood	0	0	0	0	3,293
		Tripp	0	0	0	0	643			Ardmore	0	0	0	0	1,142
		Tyndall	0	0	0	0	1,135			Ashland City	0	0	0	0	4,696
		Vermillion	0	0	0	0	9,810			Athens	0	0	0	0	14,183
		Viborg	0	0	0	0	793			Atoka	0	0	0	0	6,868
		Wagner	0	0	0	0	1,596			Baileyton	0	0	0	0	501
		Watertown	0	0	0	0	20,568			Bartlett	0	0	0	0	47,333
		Whitewood	0	0	0	0	810			Baxter	0	0	0	0	1,367
		Winner	0	0	0	0	2,892			Bean Station	0	0	0	0	3,043
		Yankton				0	13,805			Belle Meade	0	0	0	0	3,170
	Universities and Colleges	South Dakota State University	0	0	0	0	11,303			Bells	0	0	0	0	2,275
										Benton	0	0	0	0	1,080
										Berry Hill	0	0	0	0	690
										Bethel Springs	0	0	0	0	786
	Metro- politan Counties	Lincoln	0	0	0	0				Big Sandy	0	0	0	0	515
		McCook	0	0	0	0				Blaine	0	0	0	0	1,751
		Turner	0	0	0	0				Bluff City	0	0	0	0	1,629
		Union	0	0	0	0				Bolivar	0	0	0	0	5,617
										Bradford	0	0	0	0	1,063
	Nonmetro- politan Counties	Aurora	0	0	0	0				Brentwood	0	0	0	0	35,019
										Brighton	0	0	0	0	2,664
										Brownsville	0	0	0	0	10,539
										Bruceton	0	0	0	0	1,469
										Burns	0	0	0	0	1,411
		Beadle	0	0	0	0				Calhoun	0	0	0	0	522
										Camden	0	0	0	0	3,693

[1]Agencies published in this table indicated that no hate crimes occurred in their jurisdictions during the quarter(s) for which they submitted reports to the Hate Crime program. Blanks indicate quarters for which agencies did not submit reports.

[2]Population figures are published only for the cities. The figures listed for the universities and colleges are student enrollment and were provided by the United States Department of Education for the 2006 school year, the most recent available. The enrollment figures include full-time and part-time students.

Table 95. Hate Crime Zero Data Submitted per Quarter, by State and Agency, 2007 (Contd.)

(Number.)

State	Agency type	Agency name	Zero data per quarter[1]				Popu-lation[2]	State	Agency type	Agency name	Zero data per quarter[1]				Popu-lation[2]
			1st quarter	2nd quarter	3rd quarter	4th quarter					1st quarter	2nd quarter	3rd quarter	4th quarter	
		Carthage	0	0	0	0	2,234			Lafayette	0	0	0	0	4,289
		Caryville	0	0	0	0	2,400			La Follette	0	0	0	0	8,212
		Celina	0	0	0	0	1,380			La Grange	0	0	0	0	146
		Centerville	0	0	0	0	4,018			Lake City	0	0	0	0	1,856
		Chapel Hill	0	0	0	0	1,285			Lakewood	0	0	0	0	2,403
		Charleston	0	0	0	0	654			La Vergne	0	0	0	0	28,719
		Church Hill	0	0	0	0	6,644			Lawrenceburg	0	0	0	0	10,826
		Clarksburg	0	0	0	0	374			Lebanon	0	0	0	0	24,219
		Clifton	0	0	0	0	2,684			Lenoir City	0	0	0	0	7,835
		Clinton	0	0	0	0	9,516			Lewisburg	0	0	0	0	10,866
		Columbia	0	0	0	0	33,897			Livingston	0	0	0	0	3,518
		Cookeville	0	0	0	0	28,691			Lookout					
		Coopertown	0	0	0	0	3,324			Mountain	0	0	0	0	1,865
		Copperhill	0	0	0	0	465			Loretto	0	0	0	0	1,707
		Cornersville	0	0	0	0	948			Loudon	0	0	0	0	4,915
		Cowan	0	0	0	0	1,758			Lynnville	0	0	0	0	338
		Cross Plains	0	0	0	0	1,602			Madisonville	0	0	0	0	4,542
		Crump	0	0	0	0	1,457			Manchester	0	0	0	0	9,858
		Cumberland								Martin	0	0	0	0	10,043
		City	0	0	0	0	321			Mason	0	0	0	0	1,174
		Cumberland								Maury City	0	0	0	0	705
		Gap	0	0	0	0	205			McEwen	0	0	0	0	1,681
		Dandridge	0	0	0	0	2,497			McKenzie	0	0	0	0	5,438
		Decaturville	0	0	0	0	825			McMinnville	0	0	0	0	13,378
		Decherd	0	0	0	0	2,164			Medina	0	0	0	0	1,609
		Dover	0	0	0	0	1,550			Middleton	0	0	0	0	623
		Dresden	0	0	0	0	2,629			Milan	0	0	0	0	7,885
		Dunlap	0	0	0	0	4,891			Millersville	0	0	0	0	6,365
		Dyer	0	0	0	0	2,422			Millington	0	0	0	0	10,323
		Eagleville	0	0	0	0	472			Minor Hill	0	0	0	0	450
		Elizabethton	0	0	0	0	13,917			Monteagle	0	0	0	0	1,209
		Elkton	0	0	0	0	500			Monterey	0	0	0	0	2,856
		Englewood	0	0	0	0	1,722			Morristown	0	0	0	0	27,147
		Erin	0	0	0	0	1,453			Moscow	0	0	0	0	571
		Erwin	0	0	0	0	5,802			Mountain City	0	0	0	0	2,389
		Estill Springs	0	0	0	0	2,285			Mount Carmel	0	0	0	0	5,436
		Ethridge	0	0	0	0	555			Mount Juliet	0	0	0	0	20,259
		Etowah	0	0	0	0	3,775			Mount Pleasant	0	0	0	0	4,442
		Fairview	0	0	0	0	7,712			Munford	0	0	0	0	6,268
		Fayetteville	0	0	0	0	7,104			Newbern	0	0	0	0	3,134
		Friendship	0	0	0	0	602			New Hope	0	0	0	0	1,025
		Gadsden	0	0	0	0	547			New					
		Gainesboro	0	0	0	0	845			Johnsonville	0	0	0	0	1,993
		Gallaway	0	0	0	0	715			New Market	0	0	0	0	1,327
		Gates	0	0	0	0	852			Newport	0	0	0	0	7,406
		Gatlinburg	0	0	0	0	5,165			New Tazewell	0	0	0	0	2,896
		Germantown	0	0	0	0	37,450			Niota	0	0	0	0	805
		Gleason	0	0	0	0	1,402			Nolensville	0	0	0	0	2,643
		Gordonsville	0	0	0	0	1,320			Norris	0	0	0	0	1,468
		Grand Junction	0	0	0	0	312			Oakland	0	0	0	0	3,821
		Graysville	0	0	0	0	1,438			Obion	0	0	0	0	1,100
		Greenbrier	0	0	0	0	6,434			Oliver Springs	0	0	0	0	3,322
		Greeneville	0	0	0	0	15,558			Oneida	0	0	0	0	3,685
		Greenfield	0	0	0	0	2,028			Parsons	0	0	0	0	2,377
		Halls	0	0	0	0	2,201			Petersburg	0	0	0	0	603
		Harriman	0	0	0	0	6,714			Pigeon Forge	0	0	0	0	6,019
		Henderson	0	0	0	0	6,290			Pikeville	0	0	0	0	1,890
		Henning	0	0	0	0	1,290			Piperton	0	0	0	0	1,001
		Henry	0	0	0	0	545			Pittman Center	0	0	0	0	622
		Hohenwald	0	0	0	0	3,832			Plainview	0	0	0	0	2,135
		Hollow Rock	0	0	0	0	943			Pleasant View	0	0	0	0	3,822
		Hornbeak	0	0	0	0	425			Powells					
		Huntingdon	0	0	0	0	4,163			Crossroads	0	0	0	0	1,216
		Huntland	0	0	0	0	882			Puryear	0	0	0	0	678
		Jacksboro	0	0	0	0	2,055			Red Boiling					
		Jamestown	0	0	0	0	1,907			Springs	0	0	0	0	1,072
		Jasper	0	0	0	0	3,086			Ridgely	0	0	0	0	1,513
		Jefferson City	0	0	0	0	8,055			Ridgetop	0	0	0	0	1,705
		Jellico	0	0	0	0	2,546			Ripley	0	0	0	0	7,705
		Jonesborough	0	0	0	0	4,803			Rockwood	0	0	0	0	5,453
		Kenton	0	0	0	0	1,306			Rogersville	0	0	0	0	4,327
		Kimball	0	0	0	0	1,380			Rossville	0	0	0	0	514
		Kingston	0	0	0	0	5,588			Rutherford	0	0	0	0	1,236
		Kingston								Rutledge	0	0	0	0	1,282
		Springs	0	0	0	0	2,945			Scotts Hill	0	0	0	0	913

[1]Agencies published in this table indicated that no hate crimes occurred in their jurisdictions during the quarter(s) for which they submitted reports to the Hate Crime program. Blanks indicate quarters for which agencies did not submit reports.

[2]Population figures are published only for the cities. The figures listed for the universities and colleges are student enrollment and were provided by the United States Department of Education for the 2006 school year, the most recent available. The enrollment figures include full-time and part-time students.

Table 95. Hate Crime Zero Data Submitted per Quarter, by State and Agency, 2007 *(Contd.)*

(Number.)

State	Agency type	Agency name	1st quarter	2nd quarter	3rd quarter	4th quarter	Population[2]
		Selmer	0	0	0	0	4,724
		Sevierville	0	0	0	0	16,070
		Sewanee	0	0	0	0	2,555
		Sharon	0	0	0	0	908
		Shelbyville	0	0	0	0	19,586
		Smithville	0	0	0	0	4,227
		Smyrna	0	0	0	0	35,664
		Sneedville	0	0	0	0	1,309
		Soddy-Daisy	0	0	0	0	12,098
		Somerville	0	0	0	0	2,949
		South Carthage	0	0	0	0	1,301
		South Fulton	0	0	0	0	2,446
		South Pittsburg	0	0	0	0	3,113
		Sparta	0	0	0	0	4,839
		Spencer	0	0	0	0	1,683
		Spring City	0	0	0	0	2,018
		Springfield	0	0	0	0	16,844
		St. Joseph	0	0	0	0	859
		Surgoinsville	0	0	0	0	1,777
		Sweetwater	0	0	0	0	6,419
		Tazewell	0	0	0	0	2,158
		Tellico Plains	0	0	0	0	955
		Tiptonville	0	0	0	0	3,998
		Toone	0	0	0	0	356
		Townsend	0	0	0	0	262
		Tracy City	0	0	0	0	1,685
		Trenton	0	0	0	0	4,538
		Trezevant	0	0	0	0	889
		Trimble	0	0	0	0	727
		Troy	0	0	0	0	1,241
		Tullahoma	0	0	0	0	19,036
		Tusculum	0	0	0	0	2,260
		Union City	0	0	0	0	10,772
		Vonore	0	0	0	0	1,483
		Wartburg	0	0	0	0	912
		Wartrace	0	0	0	0	570
		Watertown	0	0	0	0	1,408
		Waverly	0	0	0	0	4,215
		Waynesboro	0	0	0	0	2,146
		Westmoreland	0	0	0	0	2,195
		White Bluff	0	0	0	0	2,473
		White House	0	0	0	0	9,464
		White Pine	0	0	0	0	2,099
		Whiteville	0	0	0	0	4,480
		Whitwell	0	0	0	0	1,589
		Winfield	0	0	0	0	999
		Woodbury	0	0	0	0	2,554
	Universities and Colleges	Austin Peay State University	0	0	0	0	9,207
		Christian Brothers University	0	0	0	0	1,779
		East Tennessee State University	0	0	0	0	12,390
		Middle Tennessee State University	0	0	0	0	22,863
		Northeast State Technical Community College	0	0	0	0	5,145
		Southwest Tennessee Community College	0	0	0	0	11,446
		Tennessee State University	0	0	0	0	9,038
		Tennessee Technological University	0	0	0	0	9,733
		University of Memphis	0	0	0	0	20,562
		University of Tennessee:					
		Chattanooga	0	0	0	0	8,923
		Knoxville	0	0	0	0	28,901
		Martin	0	0	0	0	6,888
		Memphis[3]	0	0	0	0	
		Volunteer State Community College	0	0	0	0	7,370
		Walters State Community College	0	0	0	0	5,738
Metropolitan Counties		Cannon	0	0	0	0	
		Carter	0	0	0	0	
		Chester	0	0	0	0	
		Fayette	0	0	0	0	
		Grainger	0	0	0	0	
		Hamblen	0	0	0	0	
		Hamilton	0	0	0	0	
		Hartsville-Trousdale	0	0	0	0	
		Hawkins	0	0	0	0	
		Hickman	0	0	0	0	
		Loudon	0	0	0	0	
		Macon	0	0	0	0	
		Madison	0	0	0	0	
		Marion	0	0	0	0	
		Polk	0	0	0	0	
		Robertson	0	0	0	0	
		Sequatchie	0	0	0	0	
		Smith	0	0	0	0	
		Stewart	0	0	0	0	
		Sumner	0	0	0	0	
		Tipton	0	0	0	0	
		Unicoi	0	0	0	0	
		Union	0	0	0	0	
		Washington	0	0	0	0	
		Williamson	0	0	0	0	
		Wilson	0	0	0	0	
Nonmetropolitan Counties		Bedford	0	0	0	0	
		Benton	0	0	0	0	
		Bledsoe	0	0	0	0	
		Campbell	0	0	0	0	
		Carroll	0	0	0	0	
		Claiborne	0	0	0	0	
		Clay	0	0	0	0	
		Cocke	0	0	0	0	
		Coffee	0	0	0	0	
		Crockett	0	0	0	0	
		Cumberland	0	0	0	0	
		Decatur	0	0	0	0	
		DeKalb	0	0	0	0	
		Dyer	0	0	0	0	
		Fentress	0	0	0	0	
		Franklin	0	0	0	0	
		Giles	0	0	0	0	
		Greene	0	0	0	0	
		Grundy	0	0	0	0	
		Hancock	0	0	0	0	
		Hardeman	0	0	0	0	
		Hardin	0	0	0	0	
		Haywood	0	0	0	0	
		Henderson	0	0	0	0	
		Henry	0	0	0	0	
		Houston	0	0	0	0	
		Humphreys	0	0	0	0	
		Jackson	0	0	0	0	
		Johnson	0	0	0	0	
		Lake	0	0	0	0	
		Lawrence	0	0	0	0	

[1]Agencies published in this table indicated that no hate crimes occurred in their jurisdictions during the quarter(s) for which they submitted reports to the Hate Crime program. Blanks indicate quarters for which agencies did not submit reports.

[2]Population figures are published only for the cities. The figures listed for the universities and colleges are student enrollment and were provided by the United States Department of Education for the 2006 school year, the most recent available. The enrollment figures include full-time and part-time students.

[3]Student enrollment figures were not available.

Table 95. Hate Crime Zero Data Submitted per Quarter, by State and Agency, 2007 *(Contd.)*

(Number.)

State	Agency type	Agency name	1st quarter	2nd quarter	3rd quarter	4th quarter	Population[2]
		Lewis	0	0	0	0	
		Lincoln	0	0	0	0	
		McMinn	0	0	0	0	
		McNairy	0	0	0	0	
		Meigs	0	0	0	0	
		Moore	0	0	0	0	
		Morgan	0	0	0	0	
		Obion	0	0	0	0	
		Overton	0	0	0	0	
		Perry	0	0	0	0	
		Pickett	0	0	0	0	
		Putnam	0	0	0	0	
		Rhea	0	0	0	0	
		Roane	0	0	0	0	
		Scott	0	0	0	0	
		Van Buren	0	0	0	0	
		Wayne	0	0	0	0	
		Weakley	0	0	0	0	
		White	0	0	0	0	
	State Police Agencies	Department of Safety	0	0	0	0	
	Other Agencies	Alcoholic Beverage Commission	0	0	0	0	
		Chattanooga Metropolitan Airport	0	0	0	0	
		Department of Correction, Internal Affairs	0	0	0	0	
		Dickson Parks and Recreation	0	0	0	0	
		Drug Task Force:					
		1st Judicial District	0	0	0	0	
		2nd Judicial District	0	0	0	0	
		3rd Judicial District	0	0	0	0	
		4th Judicial District	0	0	0	0	
		5th Judicial District	0	0	0	0	
		8th Judicial District	0	0	0	0	
		9th Judicial District	0	0	0	0	
		10th Judicial District	0	0	0	0	
		12th Judicial District	0	0	0	0	
		13th Judicial District	0	0	0	0	
		14th Judicial District	0	0	0	0	
		15th Judicial District	0	0	0	0	
		17th Judicial District	0	0	0	0	
		18th Judicial District	0	0	0	0	
		19th Judicial District	0	0	0	0	
		21st Judicial District	0	0	0	0	
		22nd Judicial District	0	0	0	0	
		23rd Judicial District	0	0	0	0	
		24th Judicial District	0	0	0	0	
		25th Judicial District	0		0	0	
		27th Judicial District	0	0	0	0	
		31st Judicial District	0	0	0	0	
		Knoxville Metropolitan Airport	0	0	0	0	
		Memphis International Airport	0	0	0	0	
		Metropolitan Board of Parks and Recreation, Nashville-Davidson	0	0	0	0	
		Nashville International Airport	0	0	0	0	
		Smyrna-Rutherford County Airport Authority	0	0	0	0	
		State Fire Marshal	0	0	0	0	
		State Park Rangers:					
		Bicentennial Capitol Mall	0	0	0	0	
		Big Hill Pond	0	0	0	0	
		Big Ridge	0	0	0	0	
		Bledsoe Creek	0	0	0	0	
		Booker T. Washington	0	0	0	0	
		Burgess Falls Natural Area	0	0	0	0	
		Cedars of Lebanon	0	0	0	0	
		Chickasaw	0	0	0	0	
		Cove Lake	0	0	0	0	
		Cumberland Mountain	0	0	0	0	
		Cumberland Trail	0	0	0	0	
		David Crockett	0	0	0	0	
		David Crockett Birthplace	0	0	0	0	
		Dunbar Cave Natural Area	0	0	0	0	
		Edgar Evins	0	0	0	0	
		Fall Creek Falls	0	0	0	0	
		Fort Loudon State Historic Park	0	0	0	0	
		Fort Pillow State Historic Park	0	0	0	0	
		Frozen Head Natural Area	0	0	0	0	
		Harpeth Scenic Rivers	0	0	0	0	
		Harrison Bay	0	0	0	0	
		Henry Horton	0	0	0		
		Hiwassee-Ocoee State Scenic Rivers	0	0	0	0	
		Indian Mountain	0	0	0	0	
		Johnsonville State Historic Park	0	0	0	0	
		Long Hunter	0	0	0	0	
		Meeman-Shelby Forest	0	0	0	0	
		Montgomery Bell	0	0	0	0	

[1]Agencies published in this table indicated that no hate crimes occurred in their jurisdictions during the quarter(s) for which they submitted reports to the Hate Crime program. Blanks indicate quarters for which agencies did not submit reports.

[2]Population figures are published only for the cities. The figures listed for the universities and colleges are student enrollment and were provided by the United States Department of Education for the 2006 school year, the most recent available. The enrollment figures include full-time and part-time students.

Table 95. Hate Crime Zero Data Submitted per Quarter, by State and Agency, 2007 (Contd.)

(Number.)

State	Agency type	Agency name	Zero data per quarter[1]				Population[2]
			1st quarter	2nd quarter	3rd quarter	4th quarter	
		Mousetail Landing	0	0	0	0	
		Natchez Trace Nathan Bedford Forrest	0	0	0	0	
		Norris Dam	0	0	0	0	
		Old Stone Fort State Archeological Area	0	0	0	0	
		Panther Creek	0	0	0	0	
		Paris Landing	0	0	0	0	
		Pickett	0	0	0	0	
		Pickwick Landing	0	0	0	0	
		Pinson Mounds State Archeological Park	0	0	0	0	
		Radnor Lake Natural Area	0	0	0	0	
		Red Clay State Historic Park	0	0	0	0	
		Reelfoot Lake	0	0	0	0	
		Roan Mountain	0	0	0	0	
		Rock Island	0	0	0	0	
		Sgt. Alvin C. York	0	0	0	0	
		South Cumberland Recreation Area	0	0	0	0	
		Standing Stone	0	0	0	0	
		Sycamore Shoals State Historic Park	0	0	0	0	
		Tim's Ford	0	0	0	0	
		T.O. Fuller	0	0	0	0	
		Warrior's Path	0	0	0	0	
		TennCare Office of Inspector General	0	0	0	0	
		Tennessee Bureau of Investigation	0	0	0	0	
		Tennessee Department of Revenue, Special Investigations Unit	0	0	0	0	
		Tri-Cities Regional Airport	0	0	0	0	
		West Tennessee Violent Crime Task Force	0	0	0	0	
		Wildlife Resources Agency:					
		Region 1	0	0	0	0	
		Region 2	0	0	0	0	
		Region 3	0	0	0	0	
		Region 4	0	0	0	0	
TEXAS............	Cities	Abernathy	0	0	0	0	2,748
		Abilene	0	0	0	0	114,644
		Addison	0	0	0	0	13,764
		Alamo	0	0	0	0	16,496
		Alamo Heights	0	0	0	0	7,087
		Alice	0	0	0	0	19,850
		Alpine	0	0	0	0	6,056
		Alto	0	0	0	0	1,152
		Alton	0	0	0	0	7,793
		Alvarado	0	0	0	0	4,200

State	Agency type	Agency name	Zero data per quarter[1]				Population[2]
			1st quarter	2nd quarter	3rd quarter	4th quarter	
		Alvin	0	0	0	0	22,542
		Amarillo	0	0	0	0	187,234
		Andrews	0	0	0	0	9,541
		Angleton	0	0	0	0	18,811
		Anna	0	0	0	0	1,811
		Anson	0	0	0	0	2,364
		Anthony	0	0	0	0	4,155
		Anton	0	0	0	0	1,153
		Aransas Pass	0	0	0	0	9,082
		Arcola	0	0	0	0	1,292
		Argyle	0	0	0	0	3,291
		Arp	0	0	0	0	945
		Athens	0	0	0	0	12,742
		Atlanta	0	0	0	0	5,606
		Azle	0	0	0	0	10,973
		Baird	0	0	0	0	1,668
		Balch Springs	0	0	0	0	19,852
		Balcones Heights	0	0	0	0	2,969
		Ballinger	0	0	0	0	3,875
		Bangs	0	0	0	0	1,636
		Bastrop	0	0	0	0	7,966
		Bay City	0	0	0	0	18,211
		Bayou Vista	0	0	0	0	1,717
		Baytown	0	0	0	0	69,040
		Beaumont	0	0	0	0	109,345
		Bee Cave	0	0	0	0	2,464
		Beeville	0	0	0	0	13,721
		Bellaire	0	0	0	0	17,879
		Bellmead	0	0	0	0	9,573
		Bellville	0	0	0	0	4,416
		Belton	0	0	0	0	16,191
		Benbrook	0	0	0	0	22,618
		Beverly Hills	0	0	0	0	2,046
		Big Sandy	0	0	0	0	1,360
		Big Spring	0	0	0	0	24,099
		Bishop	0	0	0	0	3,199
		Blanco	0	0	0	0	1,641
		Bloomburg	0	0	0	0	368
		Blue Mound	0	0	0	0	2,354
		Boerne	0	0	0	0	9,090
		Bogata	0	0	0	0	1,318
		Borger	0	0	0	0	13,128
		Bovina	0	0	0	0	1,790
		Bowie	0	0	0	0	5,591
		Brady	0	0	0	0	5,382
		Brazoria	0	0	0	0	2,998
		Breckenridge	0	0	0	0	5,647
		Bremond	0	0	0	0	895
		Brenham	0	0	0	0	14,887
		Bridge City	0	0	0	0	8,735
		Bridgeport	0	0	0	0	5,966
		Brookshire	0	0	0	0	3,734
		Brookside Village	0	0	0	0	2,005
		Brownfield	0	0	0	0	9,110
		Brownsville	0	0	0	0	177,090
		Brownwood	0	0	0	0	19,820
		Bruceville-Eddy	0	0	0	0	1,535
		Bullard	0	0	0	0	1,741
		Bulverde	0	0	0	0	4,662
		Burkburnett	0	0	0	0	10,203
		Burleson	0	0	0	0	33,383
		Burnet	0	0	0	0	5,779
		Cactus	0	0	0	0	2,679
		Caddo Mills	0	0	0	0	1,218
		Caldwell	0	0	0	0	3,807
		Calvert	0	0	0	0	1,401
		Cameron	0	0	0	0	5,883
		Canton	0	0	0	0	3,688
		Canyon	0	0	0	0	13,644
		Carthage	0	0	0	0	6,598
		Castle Hills	0	0	0	0	4,148
		Castroville	0	0	0	0	3,080

[1]Agencies published in this table indicated that no hate crimes occurred in their jurisdictions during the quarter(s) for which they submitted reports to the Hate Crime program. Blanks indicate quarters for which agencies did not submit reports.

[2]Population figures are published only for the cities. The figures listed for the universities and colleges are student enrollment and were provided by the United States Department of Education for the 2006 school year, the most recent available. The enrollment figures include full-time and part-time students.

Table 95. Hate Crime Zero Data Submitted per Quarter, by State and Agency, 2007 *(Contd.)*

(Number.)

State	Agency type	Agency name	Zero data per quarter[1]				Population[2]	State	Agency type	Agency name	Zero data per quarter[1]				Population[2]
			1st quarter	2nd quarter	3rd quarter	4th quarter					1st quarter	2nd quarter	3rd quarter	4th quarter	
		Cedar Hill	0	0	0	0	44,629			Elgin	0	0	0	0	9,951
		Celina	0	0	0	0	4,789			Elsa	0	0	0	0	6,758
		Center	0	0	0	0	5,823			Ennis	0	0	0	0	19,520
		Childress	0	0	0	0	6,631			Euless	0	0	0	0	52,899
		Chillicothe	0	0	0	0	721			Everman	0	0	0	0	5,739
		Cibolo	0	0	0	0	11,960			Fairfield	0	0	0	0	3,612
		Cisco	0	0	0	0	3,777			Fair Oaks Ranch	0	0	0	0	6,082
		Clarksville	0	0	0	0	3,582			Falfurrias	0	0	0		5,042
		Cleburne	0	0	0	0	30,174			Farmers Branch	0	0	0	0	26,455
		Cleveland	0	0	0	0	8,081			Farmersville	0	0	0	0	3,481
		Clifton	0	0	0	0	3,654			Farwell	0	0	0	0	1,298
		Clint	0	0	0	0	990			Ferris	0	0	0	0	2,414
		Clute	0	0	0	0	10,781			Flatonia	0	0	0	0	1,423
		Clyde	0	0	0	0	3,744			Florence	0	0	0	0	1,133
		Cockrell Hill	0	0	0	0	4,291			Floresville	0	0	0	0	7,463
		Coffee City	0	0	0	0	209			Flower Mound	0	0	0	0	68,191
		Coleman	0	0	0	0	4,832			Floydada	0	0	0	0	3,214
		College Station	0	0	0	0	74,997			Forest Hill	0	0	0	0	13,771
		Colleyville	0	0	0	0	23,743			Fort Stockton	0	0	0	0	7,350
		Collinsville	0	0	0	0	1,528			Frankston	0	0	0	0	1,276
		Colorado City	0	0	0	0	3,918			Fredericksburg	0	0	0	0	11,004
		Columbus	0	0	0	0	3,930			Freeport	0	0	0	0	12,588
		Comanche	0	0	0	0	4,308			Freer	0	0	0	0	3,022
		Combes	0	0	0	0	2,892			Friona	0	0	0	0	3,698
		Commerce	0	0	0	0	9,692			Gainesville	0	0	0	0	16,710
		Conroe	0	0	0	0	51,582			Galena Park	0	0	0	0	10,177
		Converse	0	0	0	0	14,323			Ganado	0	0	0	0	1,848
		Coppell	0	0	0	0	39,572			Gatesville	0	0	0	0	15,450
		Corinth	0	0	0	0	21,054			Georgetown	0	0	0	0	44,834
		Corrigan	0	0	0	0	1,975			Giddings	0	0	0	0	5,517
		Corsicana	0	0	0	0	26,696			Gilmer	0	0	0	0	5,191
		Cottonwood Shores	0				1,166			Gladewater	0	0	0	0	6,355
		Crane	0	0	0	0	3,028			Glenn Heights	0	0	0	0	10,739
		Crockett	0	0	0	0	6,960			Godley	0	0	0	0	1,011
		Crowell	0	0	0	0	1,055			Gonzales	0	0	0	0	7,534
		Crowley	0	0	0	0	11,618			Gorman	0	0	0	0	1,248
		Crystal City	0	0	0	0	7,388			Graham	0	0	0	0	8,689
		Cuero	0	0	0	0	6,642			Granbury	0	0	0	0	8,040
		Daingerfield	0	0	0	0	2,462			Grand Prairie	0	0	0	0	157,913
		Dalhart	0	0	0	0	6,990			Grand Saline	0	0	0	0	3,296
		Dalworthington Gardens	0	0	0	0	2,408			Granger	0	0	0	0	1,359
		Danbury	0	0	0	0	1,683			Granite Shoals	0	0	0	0	2,794
		Dayton	0	0	0	0	7,377			Grapeland	0	0	0	0	1,400
		Decatur	0	0	0	0	6,402			Grapevine	0	0	0	0	49,498
		Deer Park	0	0	0	0	29,971			Greenville	0	0	0	0	26,130
		De Kalb	0	0	0	0	1,795			Gregory	0	0	0	0	2,261
		De Leon	0	0	0	0	2,406			Groesbeck	0	0	0	0	4,368
		Denison	0	0	0	0	24,130			Groves	0	0	0		14,610
		Denver City	0	0	0	0	4,012			Gruver	0	0			1,117
		DeSoto	0	0	0	0	47,253			Gun Barrel City	0	0	0	0	6,168
		Devine	0	0	0	0	4,531			Hale Center	0	0	0	0	2,176
		Diboll	0	0	0	0	5,512			Hallettsville	0	0	0	0	2,532
		Dickinson	0	0	0	0	18,151			Hallsville	0	0	0	0	2,984
		Dilley	0	0	0	0	4,142			Hamlin	0	0	0	0	1,954
		Dimmitt	0	0	0	0	3,815			Harker Heights	0	0	0	0	23,726
		Donna	0	0	0	0	16,662			Harlingen	0	0	0	0	64,984
		Double Oak	0	0	0	0	3,199			Haskell	0	0	0	0	2,683
		Driscoll	0	0	0	0	818			Hawk Cove	0	0	0	0	617
		Dublin	0	0	0	0	3,674			Hawkins	0	0	0	0	1,520
		Dumas	0	0	0	0	14,084			Hawley	0	0	0	0	592
		Duncanville	0	0	0	0	35,512			Hearne	0	0	0	0	4,751
		Eagle Lake	0	0	0	0	3,732			Heath	0	0	0	0	7,263
		Eagle Pass	0	0	0	0	26,974			Hedwig Village	0	0	0	0	2,317
		Early	0	0	0	0	2,821			Helotes	0	0	0	0	6,826
		Eastland	0	0	0	0	3,915			Hemphill	0	0	0	0	1,070
		East Mountain	0	0	0	0	629			Hempstead	0	0	0	0	7,188
		Edcouch	0	0	0	0	4,558			Hereford	0	0	0	0	14,528
		Eden	0	0	0	0	2,386			Hewitt	0	0	0	0	13,522
		Edgewood	0	0	0	0	1,478			Hickory Creek	0	0	0	0	3,553
		Edinburg	0	0	0	0	69,708			Hidalgo	0	0	0	0	12,008
		Edna	0	0	0	0	5,854			Highland Park	0	0	0	0	9,062
		El Campo	0	0	0	0	10,799			Highland Village	0	0	0	0	16,298
		Electra	0	0	0	0	2,854								

[1]Agencies published in this table indicated that no hate crimes occurred in their jurisdictions during the quarter(s) for which they submitted reports to the Hate Crime program. Blanks indicate quarters for which agencies did not submit reports.

[2]Population figures are published only for the cities. The figures listed for the universities and colleges are student enrollment and were provided by the United States Department of Education for the 2006 school year, the most recent available. The enrollment figures include full-time and part-time students.

Table 95. Hate Crime Zero Data Submitted per Quarter, by State and Agency, 2007 *(Contd.)*

(Number.)

State	Agency type	Agency name	1st quarter	2nd quarter	3rd quarter	4th quarter	Population[2]
			Zero data per quarter[1]				
		Hill Country Village	0	0	0	0	1,083
		Hillsboro	0	0	0	0	9,161
		Hitchcock	0	0	0	0	7,389
		Holliday	0	0	0	0	1,821
		Hollywood Park	0	0	0	0	3,276
		Hondo	0	0	0	0	9,089
		Hooks	0	0	0	0	2,934
		Horizon City	0	0	0	0	11,855
		Horseshoe Bay	0	0	0	0	3,822
		Howe	0	0	0	0	2,749
		Hubbard	0	0	0	0	1,706
		Hudson	0	0	0	0	4,191
		Hudson Oaks	0	0	0	0	1,944
		Humble	0	0	0	0	14,977
		Huntington	0	0	0	0	2,099
		Hurst	0	0	0	0	38,452
		Hutchins	0	0	0	0	3,039
		Hutto	0	0	0	0	12,635
		Idalou	0	0	0	0	2,052
		Ingleside	0	0	0	0	9,355
		Ingram	0	0	0	0	1,886
		Iowa Park	0	0	0	0	6,100
		Irving	0	0	0	0	196,676
		Italy	0	0	0	0	2,124
		Itasca	0	0	0	0	1,655
		Jacinto City	0	0	0	0	9,890
		Jacksboro	0	0	0	0	4,653
		Jacksonville	0	0	0	0	14,481
		Jamaica Beach	0	0			1,127
		Jarrell		0	0	0	1,439
		Jasper	0	0	0	0	7,435
		Jefferson	0	0	0	0	1,991
		Jersey Village	0	0	0	0	7,176
		Johnson City	0	0	0	0	1,581
		Jones Creek	0	0	0	0	2,120
		Jonestown	0	0	0	0	2,192
		Joshua	0	0	0		5,731
		Jourdanton	0	0		0	4,445
		Junction	0		0	0	2,647
		Karnes City	0	0	0	0	3,399
		Katy	0	0	0	0	13,830
		Kaufman	0	0	0	0	8,294
		Keene	0	0	0	0	6,301
		Kemah	0	0	0	0	2,497
		Kemp	0	0	0	0	1,309
		Kempner	0	0	0	0	1,190
		Kenedy	0	0	0	0	3,363
		Kennedale	0	0	0	0	6,848
		Kerens	0	0	0	0	1,844
		Kermit	0	0	0	0	5,144
		Kerrville	0	0	0	0	22,636
		Kilgore	0	0	0	0	12,152
		Killeen	0	0	0	0	104,188
		Kirby	0	0	0	0	8,560
		Kirbyville	0	0	0	0	2,020
		Knox City	0	0	0		1,043
		Kountze	0	0	0		2,172
		Kress	0	0	0	0	779
		Kyle	0	0	0	0	24,778
		Lacy-Lakeview	0	0	0	0	5,761
		La Feria	0	0	0	0	6,890
		Lago Vista	0	0	0	0	5,986
		La Grange	0	0	0	0	4,669
		Laguna Vista	0	0	0	0	3,068
		La Joya	0	0	0	0	4,833
		Lake Dallas	0	0	0	0	7,423
		Lake Jackson	0	0	0	0	27,788
		Lakeside	0	0	0	0	1,279
		Lakeview	0	0	0	0	6,477
		Lakeway	0	0	0	0	9,774
		Lake Worth	0	0	0	0	4,732
		La Marque	0	0	0	0	14,081
		Lamesa	0	0	0	0	9,167
		Lampasas	0	0	0	0	7,973
		Lancaster	0	0	0	0	35,090
		La Porte	0	0	0	0	34,165
		Laredo	0	0	0	0	221,253
		La Vernia	0	0	0	0	1,203
		Lavon	0	0	0	0	424
		League City	0	0	0	0	68,743
		Leon Valley	0	0	0	0	9,876
		Levelland	0	0	0	0	12,653
		Lewisville	0	0	0	0	97,184
		Lexington	0	0	0	0	1,265
		Liberty	0	0	0	0	8,474
		Lindale	0	0	0	0	4,503
		Linden	0	0	0	0	2,181
		Little Elm	0	0	0	0	26,824
		Littlefield	0	0	0	0	6,213
		Live Oak	0	0	0	0	12,117
		Livingston	0	0	0	0	6,567
		Llano	0	0	0	0	3,326
		Lockhart	0	0	0	0	13,946
		Lockney	0	0	0	0	1,802
		Lone Star	0	0	0	0	1,597
		Lorena	0	0	0	0	1,656
		Lorenzo	0	0	0	0	1,241
		Los Fresnos	0	0	0	0	5,465
		Lubbock	0	0	0	0	213,988
		Lufkin	0	0	0	0	33,997
		Luling	0	0	0	0	5,442
		Lumberton	0	0	0	0	9,853
		Lytle	0	0	0	0	2,733
		Madisonville	0	0	0	0	4,349
		Magnolia	0	0	0	0	1,288
		Malakoff	0	0	0	0	2,374
		Manor	0	0	0	0	2,993
		Manvel	0	0	0	0	4,912
		Marble Falls	0	0	0	0	7,562
		Marfa	0	0	0	0	1,903
		Marion	0	0	0	0	1,135
		Marlin	0	0	0	0	6,097
		Marshall	0	0	0	0	23,978
		Mart	0	0	0	0	2,517
		Martindale	0	0	0	0	1,117
		Mathis	0	0	0	0	5,486
		McAllen	0	0	0	0	129,455
		McGregor	0	0	0	0	4,862
		McKinney	0	0	0	0	118,113
		Meadows Place	0	0	0	0	6,919
		Melissa	0	0	0	0	3,395
		Memorial Villages	0	0	0	0	11,714
		Memphis	0	0	0	0	2,363
		Mercedes	0	0	0	0	14,879
		Meridian	0	0	0	0	1,510
		Merkel	0	0	0	0	2,587
		Mesquite	0	0	0	0	132,399
		Mexia	0	0	0	0	6,726
		Midlothian	0	0	0	0	15,600
		Milford	0	0	0	0	748
		Mineral Wells	0	0	0	0	17,083
		Mission	0	0	0	0	66,216
		Monahans	0	0	0	0	6,340
		Mont Belvieu	0	0	0	0	2,645
		Montgomery	0	0	0		593
		Morgans Point Resort	0	0	0	0	4,291
		Mount Pleasant	0	0	0	0	15,360
		Muleshoe	0	0	0	0	4,481
		Munday	0	0	0	0	1,291
		Murphy	0	0	0	0	15,497
		Mustang Ridge	0	0	0	0	931
		Nacogdoches	0	0	0	0	31,300
		Nash	0	0	0	0	2,426
		Nassau Bay	0	0	0	0	4,040
		Navasota	0	0	0	0	7,464
		Nederland	0	0	0	0	16,325
		Needville	0	0	0	0	3,585

[1]Agencies published in this table indicated that no hate crimes occurred in their jurisdictions during the quarter(s) for which they submitted reports to the Hate Crime program. Blanks indicate quarters for which agencies did not submit reports.

[2]Population figures are published only for the cities. The figures listed for the universities and colleges are student enrollment and were provided by the United States Department of Education for the 2006 school year, the most recent available. The enrollment figures include full-time and part-time students.

Table 95. Hate Crime Zero Data Submitted per Quarter, by State and Agency, 2007 (Contd.)

(Number.)

State	Agency type	Agency name	Zero data per quarter[1]				Population[2]	State	Agency type	Agency name	Zero data per quarter[1]				Population[2]
			1st quarter	2nd quarter	3rd quarter	4th quarter					1st quarter	2nd quarter	3rd quarter	4th quarter	
		New Boston	0	0	0	0	4,630			Robstown	0	0	0	0	12,361
		New Deal	0	0	0	0	726			Rockdale	0	0	0	0	6,066
		Nocona	0	0	0	0	3,291			Rockwall	0	0	0	0	34,872
		Nolanville	0	0	0	0	2,393			Rollingwood	0	0	0	0	1,363
		Northlake	0	0	0	0	1,109			Roma	0	0	0	0	11,394
		Oak Ridge	0	0	0	0	258			Roman Forest	0	0	0	0	3,788
		Oak Ridge North	0	0	0	0	3,422			Ropesville	0				518
		Odessa	0	0	0	0	95,839			Roscoe	0	0	0	0	1,260
		O'Donnell	0	0	0	0	966			Rosebud	0	0	0	0	1,365
		Olmos Park	0	0	0	0	2,298			Rose City	0	0	0	0	514
		Olney	0	0	0	0	3,328			Rosenberg	0	0	0	0	33,131
		Olton	0	0	0	0	2,232			Royse City	0	0	0	0	8,086
		Onalaska	0	0	0	0	1,564			Runaway Bay	0	0	0	0	1,409
		Orange Grove	0	0	0	0	1,426			Rusk	0	0	0	0	5,173
		Overton	0	0	0	0	2,337			Sabinal	0	0	0	0	1,672
		Ovilla	0	0	0	0	3,925			Sachse	0	0	0	0	19,028
		Oyster Creek	0	0	0	0	1,236			Saginaw	0	0	0	0	19,818
		Paducah	0	0	0	0	1,286			Salado	0	0	0	0	1,926
		Palacios	0	0	0	0	5,158			San Angelo	0	0	0	0	88,285
		Palmer	0	0	0	0	2,200			San Augustine	0	0	0	0	2,429
		Pampa	0	0	0	0	16,998			San Benito	0	0	0	0	25,150
		Panhandle	0	0	0	0	2,619			San Diego	0	0	0	0	4,520
		Pantego	0	0	0	0	2,344			Sanger	0	0	0	0	7,391
		Paris	0	0	0	0	26,583			San Juan	0	0	0	0	33,213
		Parker	0	0	0	0	2,781			San Saba	0	0	0	0	2,548
		Pasadena	0	0	0	0	145,235			Sansom Park Village	0	0	0	0	4,140
		Pearland	0	0	0	0	73,190			Santa Anna	0	0	0	0	1,034
		Pearsall	0	0	0	0	7,779			Santa Fe	0	0	0	0	10,735
		Pecos	0	0	0	0	7,946			Santa Rosa	0	0	0	0	2,995
		Pelican Bay	0	0	0	0	1,609			Schertz	0	0	0	0	29,519
		Penitas	0	0	0	0	1,189			Seabrook	0	0	0	0	11,448
		Perryton	0	0	0	0	8,305			Seadrift	0	0	0	0	1,433
		Pflugerville	0	0	0	0	32,157			Seagoville	0	0	0	0	11,452
		Pharr	0	0	0	0	63,666			Seagraves	0	0	0	0	2,360
		Pilot Point	0	0	0	0	4,293			Sealy	0	0	0	0	6,267
		Pinehurst	0	0	0	0	2,202			Selma	0	0	0	0	3,219
		Pittsburg	0	0	0	0	4,648			Seminole	0	0	0	0	6,105
		Plainview	0	0	0	0	22,054			Seven Points	0	0	0	0	1,274
		Pleasanton	0	0	0	0	9,742			Seymour	0	0	0	0	2,639
		Ponder	0	0	0	0	1,114			Shallowater	0	0	0	0	2,227
		Port Aransas	0	0	0	0	3,812			Shamrock	0	0	0	0	1,834
		Port Arthur	0	0	0	0	55,481			Shavano Park	0	0	0	0	3,138
		Port Isabel	0	0	0	0	5,433			Shenandoah	0	0	0	0	1,954
		Portland	0	0	0	0	16,645			Sherman	0	0	0	0	37,985
		Port Lavaca	0	0	0	0	11,658			Silsbee	0	0	0	0	6,844
		Port Neches	0	0	0	0	12,803			Sinton	0	0	0	0	5,491
		Poteet	0	0	0	0	3,719			Slaton	0	0	0	0	5,642
		Pottsboro	0	0	0	0	2,130			Smithville	0	0	0	0	4,543
		Premont	0	0	0	0	2,822			Snyder	0	0	0	0	10,549
		Presidio	0	0	0	0	4,939			Socorro	0	0	0	0	31,588
		Primera	0	0	0	0	3,356			Somerset	0	0	0	0	1,832
		Princeton	0	0	0	0	5,057			Somerville	0	0	0	0	1,723
		Progreso	0	0	0	0	5,375			Sonora	0	0	0	0	3,081
		Prosper	0	0	0	0	5,828			Sour Lake	0	0	0	0	1,748
		Queen City	0	0	0	0	1,577			South Houston	0	0	0	0	16,348
		Quinlan	0	0	0	0	1,466			Southlake	0	0	0		26,367
		Quitman	0	0	0	0	2,273			South Padre Island	0	0	0	0	2,747
		Ranger	0	0			2,516			Southside Place	0	0	0	0	1,636
		Ransom Canyon	0	0	0	0	1,079			Spearman	0	0	0	0	2,911
		Raymondville	0	0	0	0	9,554			Springtown	0	0	0	0	2,905
		Red Oak	0	0	0	0	8,538			Spring Valley	0	0	0		3,717
		Refugio	0	0	0	0	2,760			Spur	0	0	0	0	996
		Reno	0	0	0	0	3,073			Stafford	0	0	0	0	20,460
		Richardson	0	0	0	0	100,933			Stamford	0	0	0	0	3,175
		Richmond	0	0	0	0	13,979			Stanton	0	0	0	0	2,229
		Richwood	0	0	0	0	3,389			Stephenville	0	0	0	0	16,219
		Riesel	0	0	0	0	1,012			Stratford	0	0	0	0	1,878
		Rio Grande City	0	0	0	0	14,098			Sudan	0	0	0	0	1,020
		Rising Star	0	0	0	0	834			Sugar Land	0	0	0	0	82,402
		River Oaks	0	0	0	0	6,914			Sullivan City	0	0	0	0	4,466
		Roanoke	0	0	0	0	3,758			Sulphur Springs	0	0			15,396
		Robinson	0	0	0	0	10,011			Sunrise Beach Village	0	0	0	0	757

[1]Agencies published in this table indicated that no hate crimes occurred in their jurisdictions during the quarter(s) for which they submitted reports to the Hate Crime program. Blanks indicate quarters for which agencies did not submit reports.

[2]Population figures are published only for the cities. The figures listed for the universities and colleges are student enrollment and were provided by the United States Department of Education for the 2006 school year, the most recent available. The enrollment figures include full-time and part-time students.

Table 95. Hate Crime Zero Data Submitted per Quarter, by State and Agency, 2007 *(Contd.)*

(Number.)

State	Agency type	Agency name	1st quarter	2nd quarter	3rd quarter	4th quarter	Population[2]
		Sunset Valley	0	0	0	0	798
		Surfside Beach	0	0	0	0	880
		Sweeny	0	0	0	0	3,613
		Sweetwater	0	0	0	0	10,519
		Taft	0	0	0	0	3,435
		Tahoka	0	0	0	0	2,691
		Tatum	0	0	0	0	1,198
		Taylor	0	0	0	0	15,597
		Teague	0	0	0	0	4,785
		Temple	0	0	0	0	55,057
		Terrell	0	0	0	0	19,302
		Terrell Hills	0	0	0	0	5,136
		Texarkana	0	0	0	0	36,237
		Texas City	0	0	0	0	45,574
		The Colony	0	0	0	0	42,563
		Thorndale	0	0	0	0	1,335
		Thrall	0	0	0	0	874
		Three Rivers	0	0	0	0	1,707
		Tioga	0	0	0	0	924
		Tolar	0	0	0	0	684
		Tool	0	0	0	0	2,495
		Trinity	0	0	0	0	2,762
		Trophy Club	0	0	0	0	7,836
		Troy	0	0	0	0	1,344
		Tulia	0	0	0	0	4,664
		Tye	0	0	0	0	1,114
		Universal City	0	0	0	0	18,238
		University Park	0	0	0	0	24,300
		Van	0	0	0	0	2,632
		Van Alstyne	0	0	0	0	2,948
		Vernon	0	0	0	0	11,161
		Waelder	0	0	0	0	1,018
		Wake Village	0	0	0	0	5,528
		Waller	0	0	0	0	2,034
		Wallis	0	0	0	0	1,298
		Watauga	0	0	0	0	23,931
		Waxahachie	0	0	0	0	27,500
		Weatherford	0	0	0	0	25,500
		Webster	0	0	0	0	10,070
		Weimar	0	0	0	0	2,031
		Wells	0	0	0	0	803
		Weslaco	0	0	0	0	32,707
		West	0	0	0	0	2,693
		West Columbia	0	0	0	0	4,216
		West Lake Hills	0	0	0	0	3,044
		West Orange	0	0	0	0	3,935
		Westover Hills	0	0	0	0	689
		West Tawakoni	0	0	0	0	1,773
		West University Place	0	0	0	0	15,249
		Westworth	0	0	0	0	3,079
		Wharton	0	0	0	0	9,355
		Whitehouse	0	0	0	0	7,556
		White Oak	0	0	0	0	6,350
		Whitesboro	0	0	0	0	4,054
		White Settlement	0	0	0	0	16,106
		Whitney	0	0	0	0	2,101
		Willis	0	0	0	0	4,298
		Willow Park	0	0	0	0	4,057
		Wills Point	0	0	0	0	3,940
		Wilmer	0	0	0	0	3,616
		Windcrest	0	0	0	0	5,156
		Wink	0	0	0	0	878
		Winnsboro	0	0	0	0	3,901
		Winters	0	0	0	0	2,630
		Wolfforth	0	0	0	0	3,281
		Woodville	0	0	0	0	2,281
		Woodway	0	0	0	0	8,693
		Wortham	0	0	0	0	1,076
		Wylie	0	0	0	0	36,386
		Yoakum	0	0	0	0	5,659
		Yorktown	0	0	0	0	2,222

State	Agency type	Agency name	1st quarter	2nd quarter	3rd quarter	4th quarter	Population[2]
	Universities and Colleges	Abilene Christian University	0	0	0	0	4,777
		Alamo Community College District[3]	0	0	0	0	
		Alvin Community College	0	0	0	0	3,996
		Amarillo College	0	0	0	0	10,356
		Angelo State University	0	0	0	0	6,265
		Austin College	0	0	0	0	1,354
		Baylor Health Care System[3]	0	0	0	0	
		Baylor University, Waco	0	0	0	0	14,040
		Central Texas College	0	0	0	0	17,726
		College of the Mainland	0	0	0	0	3,834
		Eastfield College	0	0	0	0	12,015
		El Paso Community College	0	0	0	0	26,105
		Grayson County College	0	0	0	0	3,720
		Hardin-Simmons University	0	0	0	0	2,367
		Houston Baptist University	0	0	0	0	2,143
		Lamar University, Beaumont	0	0	0	0	9,906
		Laredo Community College	0	0	0	0	8,152
		McLennan Community College	0	0	0	0	7,794
		Midwestern State University	0	0	0	0	6,042
		Mountain View College	0	0	0	0	7,022
		North Lake College	0	0	0	0	9,397
		Paris Junior College	0	0	0	0	4,331
		Prairie View A&M University	0	0	0	0	8,006
		Rice University	0	0	0	0	5,024
		Richland College	0	0	0	0	14,555
		Southern Methodist University	0	0	0	0	10,941
		South Plains College	0	0	0	0	9,045
		Southwestern University	0	0	0	0	1,277
		Stephen F. Austin State University	0	0	0	0	11,756
		St. Mary's University	0	0			3,904
		Sul Ross State University	0	0	0	0	2,773

[1]Agencies published in this table indicated that no hate crimes occurred in their jurisdictions during the quarter(s) for which they submitted reports to the Hate Crime program. Blanks indicate quarters for which agencies did not submit reports.

[2]Population figures are published only for the cities. The figures listed for the universities and colleges are student enrollment and were provided by the United States Department of Education for the 2006 school year, the most recent available. The enrollment figures include full-time and part-time students.

[3]Student enrollment figures were not available.

Table 95. Hate Crime Zero Data Submitted per Quarter, by State and Agency, 2007 *(Contd.)*

(Number.)

State	Agency type	Agency name	1st quarter	2nd quarter	3rd quarter	4th quarter	Population[2]
		Tarleton State University	0	0	0	0	9,464
		Texas A&M International University	0	0	0	0	4,917
		Texas A&M University:					
		College Station	0	0	0	0	45,380
		Commerce	0	0	0	0	8,471
		Corpus Christi	0	0	0	0	8,585
		Galveston	0	0	0	0	1,553
		Kingsville	0	0	0	0	6,728
		Texas Christian University	0	0	0	0	8,865
		Texas Southern University	0	0	0	0	11,224
		Texas State Technical College:					
		Harlingen	0	0	0	0	4,281
		Marshall	0	0	0	0	626
		Waco	0	0	0	0	4,209
		Texas State University, San Marcos	0	0	0	0	27,485
		Texas Woman's University	0	0	0	0	11,832
		Trinity University	0	0	0	0	2,698
		Tyler Junior College	0	0	0	0	9,423
		University of Houston:					
		Central Campus	0	0	0	0	34,334
		Clearlake	0	0	0	0	7,706
		Downtown Campus	0	0	0	0	11,449
		University of Mary Hardin-Baylor	0	0	0	0	2,735
		University of North Texas:					
		Denton	0	0	0	0	33,395
		Health Science Center	0	0	0	0	1,129
		University of Texas:					
		Arlington	0	0	0	0	24,825
		Brownsville	0	0	0	0	15,688
		Dallas	0	0	0	0	14,523
		El Paso	0	0	0	0	19,842
		Health Science Center, San Antonio	0	0	0	0	2,874
		Health Science Center, Tyler[3]	0	0	0	0	
		Houston[3]	0	0	0	0	
		Medical Branch	0	0	0	0	2,255
		Pan American	0	0	0	0	17,337
		Permian Basin	0	0	0	0	3,462
		San Antonio	0	0	0	0	28,379
		Southwestern Medical School	0	0	0	0	2,434
		Tyler	0	0	0	0	5,926
		Western Texas College	0	0	0	0	1,974
		West Texas A&M University	0	0	0	0	7,412
	Metropolitan Counties	Aransas	0	0	0	0	
		Archer	0	0			
		Armstrong	0	0	0	0	

State	Agency type	Agency name	1st quarter	2nd quarter	3rd quarter	4th quarter	Population[2]
		Atascosa	0	0	0	0	
		Austin	0	0	0	0	
		Bandera	0	0	0	0	
		Bastrop	0	0	0	0	
		Bell	0	0	0	0	
		Bexar	0	0	0	0	
		Bowie	0	0	0	0	
		Brazoria	0	0	0	0	
		Brazos	0	0	0	0	
		Burleson	0	0	0	0	
		Caldwell	0	0	0	0	
		Calhoun	0	0	0	0	
		Callahan	0	0	0	0	
		Cameron	0	0	0	0	
		Carson	0	0	0	0	
		Chambers	0	0	0	0	
		Clay	0	0	0	0	
		Collin	0	0	0	0	
		Comal	0	0	0	0	
		Coryell	0	0	0	0	
		Crosby	0	0	0	0	
		Dallas	0	0	0	0	
		Delta	0	0	0	0	
		Denton	0	0	0	0	
		Ector	0	0	0	0	
		Ellis	0	0	0	0	
		El Paso	0	0	0	0	
		Fort Bend	0	0	0	0	
		Galveston	0	0	0	0	
		Goliad	0	0	0	0	
		Grayson	0	0	0	0	
		Gregg	0	0	0	0	
		Guadalupe	0	0	0	0	
		Hardin	0	0	0	0	
		Hays	0	0	0	0	
		Hidalgo	0	0	0	0	
		Hunt	0	0	0	0	
		Irion	0	0	0	0	
		Jefferson	0	0	0	0	
		Johnson	0	0	0	0	
		Jones	0	0	0	0	
		Kaufman	0	0	0	0	
		Lampasas	0	0	0	0	
		Liberty	0	0	0	0	
		Lubbock	0	0	0	0	
		Medina	0	0	0	0	
		Midland	0	0	0	0	
		Montgomery	0	0	0	0	
		Nueces	0	0	0	0	
		Orange	0	0	0	0	
		Parker	0	0	0	0	
		Potter	0	0	0	0	
		Randall	0	0	0	0	
		Robertson	0	0	0	0	
		Rockwall	0	0	0	0	
		Rusk	0	0	0	0	
		San Jacinto	0	0	0	0	
		San Patricio	0	0	0	0	
		Smith	0	0	0	0	
		Tarrant	0	0	0	0	
		Taylor	0	0	0	0	
		Tom Green	0	0	0	0	
		Travis	0	0	0	0	
		Upshur	0	0	0	0	
		Victoria	0	0	0	0	
		Waller	0	0	0	0	
		Webb	0	0	0	0	
		Wilson	0	0	0	0	
		Wise	0	0	0		
	Nonmetropolitan Counties	Anderson	0	0	0	0	
		Andrews	0	0	0	0	
		Angelina	0	0	0	0	
		Bailey	0	0	0	0	

[1]Agencies published in this table indicated that no hate crimes occurred in their jurisdictions during the quarter(s) for which they submitted reports to the Hate Crime program. Blanks indicate quarters for which agencies did not submit reports.

[2]Population figures are published only for the cities. The figures listed for the universities and colleges are student enrollment and were provided by the United States Department of Education for the 2006 school year, the most recent available. The enrollment figures include full-time and part-time students.

[3]Student enrollment figures were not available.

Table 95. Hate Crime Zero Data Submitted per Quarter, by State and Agency, 2007 *(Contd.)*

(Number.)

State	Agency type	Agency name	Zero data per quarter[1]				Population[2]
			1st quarter	2nd quarter	3rd quarter	4th quarter	
		Baylor	0	0	0	0	
		Bee	0	0	0	0	
		Blanco	0	0	0	0	
		Borden	0	0	0	0	
		Bosque	0	0	0	0	
		Brewster	0	0	0	0	
		Briscoe	0	0	0	0	
		Brooks	0	0	0	0	
		Brown	0	0	0	0	
		Burnet	0	0	0	0	
		Camp	0	0	0	0	
		Cass	0	0	0	0	
		Castro	0	0	0	0	
		Cherokee	0	0	0	0	
		Childress	0	0	0	0	
		Cochran	0	0	0	0	
		Coke	0	0	0	0	
		Coleman	0	0	0	0	
		Collingsworth	0	0	0	0	
		Colorado	0	0	0	0	
		Comanche	0	0	0	0	
		Concho	0	0	0	0	
		Cooke	0	0	0	0	
		Cottle	0	0	0	0	
		Crane	0	0	0	0	
		Crockett	0	0	0	0	
		Culberson	0	0	0	0	
		Dallam	0	0	0	0	
		Dawson	0	0	0	0	
		Deaf Smith	0	0	0	0	
		Dewitt	0	0	0	0	
		Dickens	0	0	0	0	
		Dimmit	0	0	0	0	
		Donley	0	0	0	0	
		Duval	0	0	0	0	
		Eastland	0	0	0	0	
		Edwards	0	0	0	0	
		Erath	0	0	0	0	
		Falls	0	0	0	0	
		Fannin	0	0	0	0	
		Fayette	0	0	0	0	
		Fisher	0	0	0	0	
		Floyd	0	0	0	0	
		Foard	0	0	0	0	
		Franklin	0	0	0	0	
		Freestone	0	0	0	0	
		Frio	0	0	0	0	
		Gaines	0	0	0	0	
		Garza	0	0	0	0	
		Gillespie	0	0	0	0	
		Glasscock	0	0	0	0	
		Gonzales	0	0	0	0	
		Gray	0	0	0	0	
		Grimes	0	0	0	0	
		Hale	0	0	0	0	
		Hall	0	0	0	0	
		Hamilton	0	0	0	0	
		Hansford	0	0	0	0	
		Hardeman	0	0	0	0	
		Harrison	0	0	0	0	
		Hartley	0	0	0	0	
		Haskell	0	0	0	0	
		Hemphill	0	0	0	0	
		Henderson	0	0	0	0	
		Hill	0	0	0	0	
		Hockley	0	0	0	0	
		Hopkins	0	0	0	0	
		Houston	0	0	0	0	
		Howard	0	0	0	0	
		Hudspeth	0	0	0	0	
		Hutchinson	0	0	0	0	
		Jack	0	0	0	0	
		Jackson	0	0	0	0	
		Jasper	0	0	0	0	
		Jeff Davis	0	0	0	0	
		Jim Hogg	0	0	0	0	
		Jim Wells	0	0	0	0	
		Karnes	0	0	0	0	
		Kenedy	0	0	0	0	
		Kent	0	0	0	0	
		Kerr	0	0	0	0	
		Kimble	0	0	0	0	
		King	0	0	0	0	
		Kinney	0	0	0	0	
		Kleberg	0	0	0	0	
		Knox	0	0	0	0	
		Lamar	0	0	0	0	
		Lamb	0	0	0	0	
		La Salle	0	0	0	0	
		Lavaca	0	0	0	0	
		Lee	0	0	0	0	
		Leon	0	0	0	0	
		Limestone	0	0	0	0	
		Lipscomb	0	0	0	0	
		Live Oak	0	0	0	0	
		Llano	0	0	0	0	
		Loving	0	0	0	0	
		Lynn	0	0	0	0	
		Madison	0	0	0	0	
		Marion	0	0	0	0	
		Martin	0	0	0	0	
		Mason	0	0	0	0	
		Matagorda	0	0		0	
		Maverick	0	0	0	0	
		McCulloch	0	0	0	0	
		McMullen	0	0	0	0	
		Menard	0	0	0	0	
		Milam	0	0	0	0	
		Mills	0	0	0	0	
		Mitchell	0	0	0	0	
		Montague	0	0	0	0	
		Moore	0	0	0	0	
		Morris	0	0	0	0	
		Motley	0	0	0	0	
		Nacogdoches	0	0	0	0	
		Navarro	0	0	0	0	
		Newton	0	0	0	0	
		Nolan	0	0	0	0	
		Ochiltree	0	0	0	0	
		Oldham	0	0	0	0	
		Palo Pinto	0	0	0	0	
		Panola	0	0	0	0	
		Parmer	0	0	0	0	
		Pecos	0	0	0	0	
		Polk	0	0	0	0	
		Presidio	0	0	0	0	
		Rains	0	0	0	0	
		Reagan	0	0	0	0	
		Real	0	0	0	0	
		Red River	0	0	0	0	
		Reeves	0	0	0	0	
		Refugio	0	0	0	0	
		Roberts	0	0	0	0	
		Runnels	0	0	0	0	
		Sabine	0	0	0	0	
		San Augustine	0	0	0	0	
		San Saba	0	0	0	0	
		Schleicher	0	0	0	0	
		Scurry	0	0	0	0	
		Shackelford	0	0	0	0	
		Shelby	0	0	0	0	
		Sherman	0	0	0	0	
		Somervell	0	0	0	0	
		Starr	0	0	0	0	
		Stephens	0	0	0	0	
		Sterling	0	0	0	0	
		Stonewall	0	0	0	0	
		Sutton	0	0	0	0	
		Swisher	0	0	0	0	
		Terrell	0	0	0	0	

[1]Agencies published in this table indicated that no hate crimes occurred in their jurisdictions during the quarter(s) for which they submitted reports to the Hate Crime program. Blanks indicate quarters for which agencies did not submit reports.

[2]Population figures are published only for the cities. The figures listed for the universities and colleges are student enrollment and were provided by the United States Department of Education for the 2006 school year, the most recent available. The enrollment figures include full-time and part-time students.

Table 95. Hate Crime Zero Data Submitted per Quarter, by State and Agency, 2007 *(Contd.)*

(Number.)

State	Agency type	Agency name	Zero data per quarter[1]				Popu-lation[2]
			1st quarter	2nd quarter	3rd quarter	4th quarter	
		Terry	0	0	0	0	
		Throckmorton	0	0	0	0	
		Titus	0	0	0	0	
		Trinity	0	0	0	0	
		Tyler	0	0	0	0	
		Upton	0	0	0	0	
		Uvalde	0	0	0	0	
		Val Verde	0	0	0	0	
		Van Zandt	0	0	0	0	
		Walker	0	0	0	0	
		Ward	0	0	0	0	
		Washington	0	0	0	0	
		Wharton	0	0	0	0	
		Wheeler	0	0	0	0	
		Wilbarger	0	0	0	0	
		Willacy	0	0	0	0	
		Winkler	0	0	0	0	
		Wood	0	0	0	0	
		Yoakum	0	0	0	0	
		Young	0	0	0	0	
		Zapata	0	0	0	0	
		Zavala	0	0	0	0	
	Other Agencies	Amarillo International Airport	0	0	0	0	
		Cameron County Park Rangers	0	0	0	0	
		Dallas-Fort Worth International Airport	0	0	0	0	
		Department of Public Safety Hospital District:	0	0			
		Dallas County	0	0	0	0	
		Tarrant County	0	0	0	0	
		Houston Metropolitan Transit Authority	0	0	0	0	
		Independent School District:					
		Aldine	0	0	0	0	
		Alvin	0	0	0	0	
		Angleton	0	0	0	0	
		Bay City	0	0	0	0	
		Cedar Hill	0	0	0	0	
		Conroe	0	0	0	0	
		Corpus Christi	0	0	0	0	
		East Central	0	0	0	0	
		Ector County	0	0	0	0	
		El Paso	0	0	0	0	
		Fort Bend	0	0	0	0	
		Humble	0	0	0	0	
		Judson	0	0	0	0	
		Katy	0	0	0	0	
		Kaufman	0	0	0	0	
		Killeen	0	0	0	0	
		Klein	0	0	0	0	
		Mexia	0	0	0	0	
		Midland	0	0	0	0	
		North East	0	0	0	0	
		Pasadena	0	0	0	0	
		Raymondville	0	0	0	0	
		Socorro	0	0	0	0	
		Spring	0	0	0	0	
		Spring Branch	0	0	0	0	
		Taft	0	0	0	0	
		United	0	0	0	0	
UTAH	**Cities**	Alpine-Highland	0	0	0	0	24,586
		American Fork-Cedar Hills	0	0	0	0	35,945
		Blanding	0	0	0	0	3,161
		Brian Head	0	0	0	0	117
		Brigham City	0	0	0	0	18,609
		Cedar City	0	0	0	0	26,479
		Draper	0	0	0	0	38,875
		Garland	0	0	0	0	2,001
		Grantsville	0	0	0	0	8,329
		Gunnison	0	0	0	0	2,768
		Harrisville	0	0	0	0	5,514
		Heber	0	0	0	0	10,155
		Helper	0	0	0	0	1,869
		Hildale	0	0	0	0	1,958
		Hurricane	0	0	0	0	12,749
		Kaysville	0	0	0	0	24,050
		La Verkin	0	0	0	0	4,260
		Leeds	0	0	0	0	731
		Lehi	0	0	0	0	39,483
		Logan	0	0	0	0	48,403
		Mapleton	0	0	0	0	7,363
		Midvale	0	0	0	0	27,275
		Moab	0	0	0	0	4,886
		Monticello	0	0	0	0	1,918
		Naples	0	0	0	0	1,533
		Nephi	0	0	0	0	5,276
		North Ogden	0	0	0	0	17,050
		North Park	0	0	0	0	10,615
		Ogden	0	0	0	0	78,160
		Orem	0	0	0	0	91,816
		Park City	0	0	0	0	8,132
		Parowan	0	0	0	0	2,545
		Payson	0	0	0	0	17,378
		Perry	0	0	0	0	3,579
		Pleasant Grove-Lindon	0	0	0	0	41,890
		Pleasant View	0	0	0	0	6,607
		Price	0	0	0	0	7,954
		Richfield	0	0	0	0	7,139
		Riverdale	0	0	0	0	8,023
		Salem	0	0	0	0	5,790
		Salina	0	0	0	0	2,399
		Santaquin-Genola	0	0	0	0	8,367
		Saratoga Springs			0	0	12,315
		Smithfield	0	0	0	0	7,484
		South Ogden	0	0	0	0	15,473
		South Salt Lake	0	0	0	0	21,262
		Spanish Fork	0	0	0	0	28,950
		Stockton	0	0	0	0	593
		Sunset	0	0	0	0	4,870
		Syracuse	0	0	0	0	21,544
		Tremonton	0	0	0	0	6,383
		West Bountiful	0	0	0	0	5,287
		West Jordan	0	0	0	0	96,681
		Woods Cross	0	0	0	0	8,440
	Universities and Colleges	College of Eastern Utah	0	0	0	0	2,262
		Southern Utah University	0	0	0	0	7,029
		University of Utah	0	0	0	0	30,511
		Utah State University	0	0	0	0	14,444
		Utah Valley State College	0	0	0	0	23,305
		Weber State University	0	0	0	0	18,303
	Metro-politan Counties	Cache	0	0	0	0	
		Juab	0	0	0	0	

[1]Agencies published in this table indicated that no hate crimes occurred in their jurisdictions during the quarter(s) for which they submitted reports to the Hate Crime program. Blanks indicate quarters for which agencies did not submit reports.

[2]Population figures are published only for the cities. The figures listed for the universities and colleges are student enrollment and were provided by the United States Department of Education for the 2006 school year, the most recent available. The enrollment figures include full-time and part-time students.

Table 95. Hate Crime Zero Data Submitted per Quarter, by State and Agency, 2007 *(Contd.)*

(Number.)

State	Agency type	Agency name	1st quarter	2nd quarter	3rd quarter	4th quarter	Population[2]
		Morgan	0	0	0	0	
		Summit	0	0	0	0	
		Utah	0	0	0	0	
		Washington	0	0	0	0	
	Nonmetropolitan Counties	Beaver	0	0	0	0	
		Box Elder	0	0	0	0	
		Carbon	0	0	0	0	
		Daggett	0	0	0	0	
		Duchesne	0	0	0	0	
		Emery	0	0	0	0	
		Garfield	0	0	0	0	
		Grand	0	0	0	0	
		Iron	0	0	0	0	
		Kane	0	0	0	0	
		Millard	0	0	0	0	
		Rich	0	0	0	0	
		San Juan	0	0	0	0	
		Sanpete	0	0	0	0	
		Sevier	0	0	0	0	
		Wasatch	0	0	0	0	
		Wayne	0	0	0	0	
	Other Agencies	Cache-Rich Drug Task Force	0	0	0	0	
		Davis Metropolitan Narcotics Strike Force	0	0	0	0	
		Granite School District	0	0	0	0	
		Utah County Attorney, Investigations Division	0	0	0	0	
		Utah County Major Crime Task Force	0	0	0	0	
		Utah Transit Authority			0	0	
VERMONT	Cities	Barre	0	0	0	0	9,050
		Berlin	0	0	0	0	2,875
		Bradford	0	0	0	0	819
		Brandon	0	0	0	0	3,926
		Brattleboro	0	0	0	0	11,706
		Castleton	0	0	0	0	4,384
		Chester	0	0	0	0	3,092
		Colchester	0	0	0	0	17,201
		Dover	0	0	0	0	1,448
		Essex	0	0	0	0	19,350
		Fair Haven	0	0	0	0	2,963
		Hardwick	0	0	0	0	3,271
		Hartford	0	0	0	0	10,892
		Hinesburg	0	0	0	0	4,552
		Ludlow	0	0	0	0	2,736
		Lyndonville	0	0	0	0	1,238
		Manchester	0	0	0	0	4,366
		Middlebury	0	0	0	0	8,194
		Milton	0	0	0	0	10,469
		Morristown	0	0	0	0	5,606
		Newport	0	0	0	0	5,329
		Northfield	0	0	0	0	5,813
		Norwich	0	0	0	0	3,551
		Randolph	0	0	0	0	5,124
		Richmond	0	0	0	0	4,128
		Shelburne	0	0	0	0	7,071
		Springfield	0	0	0	0	8,752
		St. Albans	0	0	0	0	7,374
		Stowe	0	0	0	0	4,822
		Swanton	0	0	0	0	6,508
		Thetford	0	0	0	0	2,836
		Vergennes	0	0	0	0	2,747
		Vernon	0	0	0	0	2,072
		Waterbury	0	0	0	0	5,290
		Weathersfield	0	0	0	0	2,868
		Williston	0	0	0	0	8,363
		Wilmington	0	0	0	0	2,358
		Windsor	0	0	0	0	3,687
		Winhall	0	0	0	0	786
		Winooski	0	0	0	0	6,284
		Woodstock	0	0	0	0	3,174
	Universities and Colleges	University of Vermont	0	0	0	0	11,870
	Metropolitan Counties	Chittenden	0	0	0	0	
		Franklin	0	0	0	0	
		Grand Isle	0	0	0	0	
	Nonmetropolitan Counties	Addison	0	0	0	0	
		Bennington	0	0	0	0	
		Caledonia	0	0	0	0	
		Lamoille	0	0	0	0	
		Orleans	0	0	0	0	
		Rutland	0	0	0	0	
		Washington	0	0	0	0	
		Windham	0	0	0	0	
		Windsor	0	0	0	0	
	State Police Agencies	State Police: Bradford	0	0	0	0	
		Brattleboro	0	0	0	0	
		Derby	0	0	0	0	
		Middlesex	0	0	0	0	
		Rockingham	0	0	0	0	
		Royalton	0	0	0	0	
		Rutland	0	0	0	0	
		Shaftsbury	0	0	0	0	
		St. Johnsbury	0	0	0	0	
		Williston	0	0	0	0	
		Vermont State Police	0	0	0	0	
		Vermont State Police Headquarters, Bureau of Criminal Investigations	0	0	0	0	
	Other Agencies	Attorney General	0	0	0	0	
		Department of Motor Vehicles	0	0	0	0	
		Fish and Wildlife Department, Law Enforcement Division	0	0	0	0	
VIRGINIA	Cities	Abingdon	0	0	0	0	7,953
		Altavista	0	0	0	0	3,379
		Amherst	0	0	0	0	2,221
		Appalachia	0	0	0	0	1,751
		Ashland	0	0	0	0	7,111
		Bedford	0	0	0	0	6,216
		Big Stone Gap	0	0	0	0	5,689
		Blacksburg	0	0	0	0	39,250
		Blackstone	0	0	0	0	3,526
		Bluefield	0	0	0	0	5,213
		Bowling Green	0	0		0	1,025
		Boykins	0	0	0		611
		Bridgewater	0	0	0	0	5,431
		Broadway	0	0	0	0	3,016
		Brookneal	0	0	0	0	1,252
		Buena Vista	0	0	0	0	6,456
		Burkeville	0	0	0	0	470

[1]Agencies published in this table indicated that no hate crimes occurred in their jurisdictions during the quarter(s) for which they submitted reports to the Hate Crime program. Blanks indicate quarters for which agencies did not submit reports.
[2]Population figures are published only for the cities. The figures listed for the universities and colleges are student enrollment and were provided by the United States Department of Education for the 2006 school year, the most recent available. The enrollment figures include full-time and part-time students.

Table 95. Hate Crime Zero Data Submitted per Quarter, by State and Agency, 2007 *(Contd.)*

(Number.)

State	Agency type	Agency name	1st quarter	2nd quarter	3rd quarter	4th quarter	Population[2]
		Cape Charles	0	0	0	0	1,530
		Cedar Bluff	0	0	0	0	1,064
		Chase City	0	0	0	0	2,343
		Chatham	0	0	0	0	1,278
		Chilhowie	0	0	0	0	1,771
		Chincoteague	0	0	0	0	4,379
		Christiansburg	0	0	0	0	17,983
		Clarksville	0	0	0	0	1,269
		Clifton Forge	0	0	0	0	4,008
		Clinchco	0	0	0	0	408
		Clintwood	0	0	0	0	1,513
		Coeburn	0	0	0	0	1,996
		Colonial Beach	0	0	0	0	3,733
		Colonial Heights	0	0	0	0	17,747
		Covington	0	0	0	0	6,027
		Crewe	0	0	0	0	2,266
		Culpeper	0	0	0	0	13,574
		Damascus	0	0	0	0	1,086
		Dayton	0	0	0	0	1,347
		Dublin	0	0	0	0	2,206
		Dumfries	0	0	0	0	4,795
		Edinburg	0	0	0	0	877
		Elkton	0	0	0	0	2,597
		Farmville	0	0	0	0	6,908
		Franklin	0	0	0	0	8,856
		Fries	0	0	0	0	557
		Front Royal	0	0	0	0	14,700
		Galax	0	0	0	0	6,643
		Gate City	0	0	0	0	2,081
		Glade Spring	0	0	0	0	1,544
		Glasgow	0	0	0	0	1,011
		Glen Lyn	0	0	0	0	167
		Gordonsville	0	0	0	0	1,684
		Gretna	0	0	0	0	1,204
		Grottoes	0	0	0	0	2,178
		Grundy	0	0	0	0	975
		Halifax	0	0	0	0	1,272
		Haymarket	0	0	0	0	1,290
		Haysi	0	0	0	0	179
		Hillsville	0	0	0	0	2,691
		Honaker	0	0	0	0	909
		Hurt	0	0	0	0	1,226
		Independence	0	0	0	0	901
		Jonesville	0	0	0	0	981
		Kenbridge	0	0	0	0	1,315
		Kilmarnock	0	0	0	0	1,195
		La Crosse	0	0	0	0	595
		Lawrenceville	0	0	0	0	1,139
		Lebanon	0	0	0	0	3,185
		Leesburg	0	0	0	0	38,931
		Lexington	0	0	0	0	6,711
		Louisa	0	0	0	0	1,557
		Luray	0	0	0	0	4,879
		Marion	0	0	0	0	6,100
		Martinsville	0	0	0	0	14,856
		Middleburg	0	0	0	0	954
		Middletown	0	0	0	0	1,137
		Mount Jackson	0	0	0	0	1,799
		Narrows	0	0	0	0	2,189
		New Market	0	0	0	0	1,863
		Norton	0	0	0	0	3,602
		Occoquan	0	0	0	0	817
		Orange	0	0	0	0	4,597
		Parksley			0	0	822
		Pearisburg	0	0	0	0	2,805
		Pembroke	0	0	0	0	1,190
		Pennington Gap	0	0	0	0	1,753
		Pocahontas	0	0	0	0	428
		Poquoson	0	0	0	0	11,939
		Pound	0	0	0	0	1,082
		Quantico	0	0	0	0	634
		Rich Creek	0	0	0	0	692
		Richlands	0	0	0	0	4,083
		Rural Retreat	0	0	0	0	1,357
		Salem	0	0	0	0	24,774
		Saltville	0	0	0	0	2,256
		Shenandoah	0	0	0	0	1,873
		Smithfield	0	0	0	0	7,098
		South Boston	0	0	0	0	8,007
		South Hill	0	0	0	0	4,618
		Stanley	0	0	0	0	1,336
		Staunton	0	0	0	0	23,210
		Stephens City	0	0	0	0	1,463
		St. Paul	0	0	0	0	971
		Strasburg	0	0	0	0	4,348
		Tappahannock	0	0	0	0	2,158
		Tazewell	0	0	0	0	4,369
		Timberville	0	0	0	0	1,705
		Victoria	0		0	0	1,783
		Vienna		0	0	0	14,923
		Warrenton	0	0	0	0	9,064
		Warsaw	0	0	0	0	1,364
		Waynesboro	0	0	0	0	21,681
		Weber City	0	0	0	0	1,349
		West Point	0	0	0		3,133
		White Stone				0	342
		Winchester	0	0	0	0	25,443
		Wise	0	0	0	0	3,256
		Woodstock	0	0	0	0	4,303
	Universities and Colleges	Christopher Newport University	0	0	0	0	4,793
		College of William and Mary	0	0	0	0	7,709
		Emory and Henry College	0	0	0	0	1,051
		Hampton University	0	0	0	0	6,152
		J. Sargeant Reynolds Community College	0	0	0		12,213
		Longwood College	0	0	0	0	4,479
		Norfolk State University	0	0	0	0	6,238
		Thomas Nelson Community College	0	0	0	0	9,718
		University of Richmond	0	0	0	0	4,496
		Unversity of Virginia	0	0	0	0	24,068
		University of Virginia's College at Wise	0	0	0	0	2,043
		Virginia Commonwealth University	0	0	0	0	30,189
		Virginia Polytechnic Institute and State University	0	0	0	0	28,470
		Virginia Western Community College	0	0	0	0	8,365
	Metropolitan Counties	Appomattox	0	0	0	0	
		Botetourt	0	0	0	0	
		Caroline	0	0	0	0	
		Charles City	0	0	0	0	
		Clarke	0	0	0	0	
		Craig	0	0	0	0	
		Cumberland	0	0	0	0	

[1] Agencies published in this table indicated that no hate crimes occurred in their jurisdictions during the quarter(s) for which they submitted reports to the Hate Crime program. Blanks indicate quarters for which agencies did not submit reports.

[2] Population figures are published only for the cities. The figures listed for the universities and colleges are student enrollment and were provided by the United States Department of Education for the 2006 school year, the most recent available. The enrollment figures include full-time and part-time students.

Table 95. Hate Crime Zero Data Submitted per Quarter, by State and Agency, 2007 *(Contd.)*

(Number.)

State	Agency type	Agency name	Zero data per quarter[1]				Population[2]
			1st quarter	2nd quarter	3rd quarter	4th quarter	
		Dinwiddie	0	0	0	0	
		Franklin	0	0	0	0	
		Giles	0	0	0	0	
		Goochland	0	0	0	0	
		Hanover	0	0	0	0	
		Isle of Wight	0	0	0	0	
		King William	0	0	0	0	
		Louisa	0	0	0	0	
		Mathews	0	0	0	0	
		Nelson	0	0	0	0	
		Pittsylvania	0	0	0	0	
		Powhatan	0	0	0	0	
		Pulaski	0	0	0	0	
		Rockingham	0	0	0	0	
		Scott	0	0	0	0	
		Stafford	0	0	0	0	
		Surry	0	0	0	0	
		Sussex	0	0	0	0	
		Warren	0	0	0	0	
		York	0	0	0	0	
	Nonmetropolitan Counties	Accomack	0	0	0	0	
		Alleghany	0	0	0	0	
		Bath	0	0	0	0	
		Bland	0	0	0	0	
		Brunswick	0	0	0	0	
		Buchanan	0	0	0	0	
		Carroll	0	0	0	0	
		Charlotte	0	0	0	0	
		Culpeper	0	0	0	0	
		Dickenson	0	0	0	0	
		Essex	0	0	0	0	
		Grayson	0	0	0	0	
		Halifax	0	0	0	0	
		Henry	0	0	0	0	
		Highland	0	0	0	0	
		Lancaster	0	0	0	0	
		Lee	0	0	0	0	
		Lunenburg	0	0	0	0	
		Middlesex	0	0	0	0	
		Northampton	0	0	0	0	
		Nottoway	0	0	0	0	
		Orange	0	0	0	0	
		Page	0	0	0	0	
		Patrick	0	0	0	0	
		Prince Edward	0	0	0	0	
		Richmond	0	0	0	0	
		Russell	0	0	0	0	
		Shenandoah	0	0	0	0	
		Smyth	0	0	0	0	
		Southampton	0	0	0	0	
		Wise	0	0	0	0	
		Wythe	0	0	0	0	
	State Police Agencies	State Police:					
		Accomack County	0	0	0	0	
		Albemarle County	0	0	0	0	
		Alexandria	0	0	0	0	
		Alleghany County	0	0	0	0	
		Amelia County	0	0	0	0	
		Amherst County	0	0	0		
		Appomattox County	0	0	0	0	
		Augusta County	0	0	0	0	
		Bath County	0	0	0	0	
		Bedford		0			
		Bedford County	0	0	0	0	
		Bland County	0	0	0	0	
		Botetourt County	0	0	0	0	
		Bristol	0	0	0	0	
		Brunswick County	0	0	0	0	
		Buchanan County	0	0	0	0	
		Buckingham County	0	0	0	0	
		Buena Vista				0	
		Campbell County	0	0	0	0	
		Caroline County	0	0	0	0	
		Carroll County	0	0	0	0	
		Charles City County	0	0	0	0	
		Charlotte County	0	0	0	0	
		Charlottesville	0		0	0	
		Chesapeake	0	0	0	0	
		Chesterfield County	0	0	0	0	
		Clarke County	0	0	0	0	
		Clifton Forge			0		
		Colonial Heights	0	0	0	0	
		Covington	0	0	0		
		Craig County	0	0	0	0	
		Culpeper County	0	0	0	0	
		Cumberland County	0	0	0	0	
		Danville	0	0	0	0	
		Dickenson County	0	0	0	0	
		Dinwiddie County	0	0	0	0	
		Emporia	0	0	0	0	
		Essex County	0				
		Fairfax City		0	0	0	
		Fairfax County	0	0	0		
		Falls Church				0	
		Fauquier County	0	0	0	0	
		Floyd County	0	0	0	0	
		Fluvanna County	0	0	0	0	
		Franklin				0	
		Franklin County	0	0	0	0	
		Frederick County	0	0	0	0	
		Fredericksburg	0	0	0	0	
		Galax	0	0	0	0	
		Giles County	0	0	0	0	
		Gloucester County	0	0	0	0	
		Goochland County	0	0	0	0	
		Grayson County	0	0	0	0	
		Greene County	0	0	0	0	
		Greensville County	0	0	0	0	
		Halifax County	0	0	0	0	
		Hampton	0	0	0	0	
		Hanover County	0	0	0	0	
		Harrisonburg	0	0	0	0	
		Henrico County	0	0	0	0	
		Henry County	0	0	0	0	
		Highland County	0	0	0		
		Hopewell	0		0	0	

[1] Agencies published in this table indicated that no hate crimes occurred in their jurisdictions during the quarter(s) for which they submitted reports to the Hate Crime program. Blanks indicate quarters for which agencies did not submit reports.

[2] Population figures are published only for the cities. The figures listed for the universities and colleges are student enrollment and were provided by the United States Department of Education for the 2006 school year, the most recent available. The enrollment figures include full-time and part-time students.

Table 95. Hate Crime Zero Data Submitted per Quarter, by State and Agency, 2007 *(Contd.)*

(Number.)

State	Agency type	Agency name	1st quarter	2nd quarter	3rd quarter	4th quarter	Population[2]
		Isle of Wight County	0	0	0	0	
		James City County	0	0	0	0	
		King and Queen County	0	0	0	0	
		King George County	0	0	0	0	
		King William County	0	0		0	
		Lancaster County	0	0	0	0	
		Lee County	0	0	0	0	
		Loudoun County	0	0	0	0	
		Louisa County	0	0	0	0	
		Lunenburg County	0	0	0	0	
		Lynchburg	0	0	0	0	
		Madison County	0	0	0	0	
		Manassas		0			
		Martinsville		0	0	0	
		Mathews County	0	0	0	0	
		Mecklenburg County	0	0	0	0	
		Middlesex County	0	0	0	0	
		Montgomery County	0	0	0	0	
		Nelson County	0	0	0	0	
		New Kent County	0	0	0	0	
		Newport News	0	0	0	0	
		Norfolk	0	0	0	0	
		Northampton County	0	0	0	0	
		Northumberland County	0	0	0	0	
		Nottoway County	0	0	0	0	
		Orange County	0	0	0	0	
		Page County	0	0	0	0	
		Patrick County	0	0	0	0	
		Petersburg	0	0	0	0	
		Pittsylvania County	0	0	0	0	
		Poquoson		0	0	0	
		Portsmouth	0	0	0	0	
		Powhatan County	0	0	0	0	
		Prince Edward County	0	0	0	0	
		Prince George County	0	0	0	0	
		Prince William County	0	0	0	0	
		Pulaski County	0	0	0		
		Radford		0		0	
		Rappahannock County	0	0	0	0	
		Richmond	0	0	0	0	
		Richmond County	0	0	0	0	
		Roanoke	0	0	0	0	
		Roanoke County	0	0	0	0	
		Rockbridge County	0	0	0	0	
		Rockingham County	0	0	0	0	
		Russell County	0	0	0	0	
		Salem	0	0	0	0	
		Scott County	0	0	0	0	
		Shenandoah County	0	0	0	0	
		Smyth County	0	0	0	0	
		Southampton County	0	0	0	0	
		Spotsylvania County	0	0	0	0	
		Stafford County	0	0	0	0	
		Staunton	0	0			
		Suffolk			0	0	
		Surry County	0	0	0	0	
		Sussex County	0	0	0	0	
		Tazewell County	0	0	0	0	
		Virginia Beach	0	0	0	0	
		Warren County	0	0	0		
		Waynesboro	0	0		0	
		Westmoreland County	0		0	0	
		Williamsburg		0	0	0	
		Winchester	0	0	0	0	
		Wise County	0	0	0	0	
		Wythe County	0	0	0	0	
		York County	0	0	0	0	
	Other Agencies	Alcoholic Beverage Control Commission	0	0	0	0	
		Department of Conservation and Recreation	0	0	0	0	
		Norfolk Airport Authority	0	0	0	0	
		Port Authority, Norfolk	0	0	0	0	
		Richmond International Airport	0	0	0	0	
		Southside Virginia Training Center	0	0	0		
WASHINGTON	Cities	Aberdeen	0	0	0	0	16,382
		Airway Heights	0	0	0	0	4,794
		Algona	0	0	0	0	2,726
		Anacortes	0	0	0	0	16,948
		Asotin	0	0	0	0	1,130
		Bainbridge Island	0	0	0	0	22,442
		Bellevue	0	0	0	0	118,984
		Bellingham	0	0	0	0	76,290
		Bingen	0	0	0	0	703
		Black Diamond	0	0	0	0	3,948
		Blaine	0	0	0	0	4,622
		Bonney Lake	0	0	0	0	15,737
		Bothell	0	0	0	0	31,521
		Brewster	0	0	0	0	2,124
		Brier	0	0	0	0	6,382
		Buckley	0	0	0	0	5,514
		Burlington	0	0	0	0	8,921
		Camas	0	0	0	0	18,256
		Carnation	0	0	0	0	1,827
		Castle Rock	0	0	0	0	2,147
		Centralia	0	0	0	0	15,708
		Chehalis	0	0	0	0	7,249
		Cheney	0	0	0	0	10,597
		Chewelah	0	0	0	0	2,334
		Cle Elum	0	0	0	0	3,330
		Clyde Hill	0	0	0	0	2,997
		College Place	0	0	0	0	9,148
		Colville	0	0	0	0	5,055
		Connell	0	0	0	0	2,987
		Cosmopolis	0	0	0	0	1,692

[1] Agencies published in this table indicated that no hate crimes occurred in their jurisdictions during the quarter(s) for which they submitted reports to the Hate Crime program. Blanks indicate quarters for which agencies did not submit reports.

[2] Population figures are published only for the cities. The figures listed for the universities and colleges are student enrollment and were provided by the United States Department of Education for the 2006 school year, the most recent available. The enrollment figures include full-time and part-time students.

Table 95. Hate Crime Zero Data Submitted per Quarter, by State and Agency, 2007 *(Contd.)*

(Number.)

State	Agency type	Agency name	1st quarter	2nd quarter	3rd quarter	4th quarter	Population[2]
		Coulee Dam	0	0	0	0	1,083
		Coupeville	0	0	0	0	1,857
		Des Moines	0	0	0	0	28,907
		Dupont	0	0	0	0	6,831
		Duvall	0	0	0	0	6,064
		East Wenatchee	0	0	0	0	9,013
		Eatonville	0	0	0	0	2,455
		Edgewood	0	0	0	0	9,860
		Edmonds	0	0	0	0	40,218
		Elma	0	0	0	0	3,177
		Enumclaw	0	0	0	0	10,966
		Ephrata	0	0	0	0	7,361
		Everson	0	0	0	0	2,031
		Ferndale	0	0	0	0	10,559
		Fife	0	0	0	0	6,746
		Fircrest	0	0	0	0	6,318
		Forks	0	0	0	0	3,249
		Garfield	0	0	0	0	604
		Gig Harbor	0	0	0	0	6,691
		Goldendale	0	0	0	0	3,758
		Grand Coulee	0	0	0	0	1,950
		Grandview	0	0	0	0	9,222
		Granger	0	0	0	0	2,892
		Granite Falls	0	0	0	0	2,972
		Hoquiam	0	0	0	0	9,058
		Ilwaco	0	0	0	0	1,004
		Issaquah	0	0	0	0	19,193
		Kalama	0	0	0	0	2,077
		Kelso	0	0	0	0	12,156
		Kettle Falls	0	0	0	0	1,621
		Kirkland	0	0	0	0	46,686
		Kittitas	0	0		0	1,194
		La Center	0		0	0	1,944
		Lacey	0	0	0	0	36,037
		Lake Forest Park	0	0	0	0	12,506
		Lake Stevens	0	0	0	0	8,238
		Langley	0	0	0	0	1,035
		Liberty Lake	0	0	0	0	6,399
		Long Beach	0	0	0	0	1,400
		Lynden	0	0	0	0	11,159
		Lynnwood	0	0	0	0	33,663
		Mabton	0	0	0	0	2,071
		Malden	0	0	0	0	191
		Marysville	0	0	0	0	32,623
		McCleary	0	0	0	0	1,589
		Medical Lake	0	0	0	0	4,493
		Medina	0	0	0	0	3,561
		Montesano	0	0	0	0	3,556
		Morton	0	0	0	0	1,102
		Moses Lake	0	0	0	0	17,561
		Mountlake Terrace	0	0	0	0	20,193
		Mount Vernon	0	0	0	0	30,521
		Moxee	0	0	0	0	2,044
		Mukilteo	0	0	0	0	20,642
		Napavine	0	0	0	0	1,499
		Normandy Park	0	0	0	0	6,207
		North Bonneville	0	0	0	0	775
		Oakesdale	0	0	0	0	379
		Oakville	0	0	0	0	730
		Ocean Shores	0	0	0	0	4,785
		Odessa	0	0	0	0	931
		Omak	0	0	0	0	4,745
		Oroville	0	0	0	0	1,588
		Orting	0	0	0	0	5,727
		Othello	0	0	0	0	6,357
		Pacific	0	0	0	0	5,910
		Pasco	0		0	0	52,761
		Pe Ell	0	0	0	0	690
		Port Townsend	0	0	0	0	9,248
		Poulsbo	0	0	0	0	7,919
		Prosser	0	0	0	0	5,150
		Puyallup	0	0	0	0	37,078
		Quincy	0	0	0	0	5,659
		Rainier	0	0	0	0	1,637
		Raymond	0	0	0	0	2,976
		Reardan	0	0	0	0	610
		Republic	0	0	0	0	985
		Ridgefield	0		0	0	4,023
		Ritzville	0	0	0	0	1,714
		Rosalia	0	0	0	0	571
		Roy	0	0	0	0	834
		Royal City	0	0	0	0	1,990
		Ruston	0	0	0	0	882
		Sedro Woolley	0	0	0	0	10,643
		Shelton	0	0	0	0	9,352
		Snohomish	0	0	0	0	8,838
		Snoqualmie	0	0	0	0	8,403
		Soap Lake	0	0	0	0	1,884
		South Bend	0	0	0	0	1,840
		Stanwood	0	0	0	0	5,685
		Steilacoom	0	0	0	0	6,159
		Sultan	0	0	0	0	4,215
		Sumas	0	0	0	0	1,157
		Sumner	0	0	0	0	9,601
		Sunnyside	0	0	0	0	14,931
		Tenino	0	0	0	0	2,251
		Tieton	0	0	0	0	1,185
		Toledo	0	0	0	0	686
		Tonasket	0	0	0	0	960
		Toppenish	0	0	0	0	9,213
		Tumwater	0	0	0	0	13,695
		Twisp		0	0	0	913
		Union Gap	0	0	0	0	5,702
		Vader	0	0	0	0	622
		Wapato	0	0	0	0	4,609
		Wenatchee	0	0	0	0	30,179
		Westport	0	0	0	0	2,554
		West Richland	0	0	0	0	10,477
		White Salmon	0	0	0	0	2,373
		Wilbur	0	0	0	0	891
		Winlock	0	0	0	0	1,233
		Winthrop	0	0	0	0	374
		Woodinville	0	0	0	0	10,143
		Woodland	0	0	0	0	4,691
		Woodway	0	0	0	0	1,390
		Yarrow Point	0	0	0	0	1,039
		Yelm	0	0	0	0	5,359
		Zillah	0	0	0	0	2,679
	Universities and Colleges	Central Washington University	0	0	0	0	10,688
		Evergreen State College	0	0	0	0	4,416
		University of Washington	0	0	0	0	39,524
		Washington State University: Pullman	0	0	0	0	23,655
		Washington State University: Vancouver[3]	0		0	0	
		Western Washington University	0	0	0	0	14,035
	Metropolitan Counties	Asotin	0	0	0	0	
		Benton	0	0	0	0	
		Cowlitz	0	0	0	0	
		Douglas	0	0	0	0	
		Franklin	0	0	0	0	
		Skagit	0	0	0	0	
		Skamania	0	0	0	0	
		Spokane	0	0	0	0	
		Thurston	0	0	0	0	
		Whatcom	0	0	0	0	

[1] Agencies published in this table indicated that no hate crimes occurred in their jurisdictions during the quarter(s) for which they submitted reports to the Hate Crime program. Blanks indicate quarters for which agencies did not submit reports.

[2] Population figures are published only for the cities. The figures listed for the universities and colleges are student enrollment and were provided by the United States Department of Education for the 2006 school year, the most recent available. The enrollment figures include full-time and part-time students.

[3] Student enrollment figures were not available.

Table 95. Hate Crime Zero Data Submitted per Quarter, by State and Agency, 2007 *(Contd.)*

(Number.)

State	Agency type	Agency name	Zero data per quarter[1] 1st quarter	2nd quarter	3rd quarter	4th quarter	Popu-lation[2]
	Nonmetro-politan Counties	Adams	0	0	0	0	
		Columbia	0	0	0	0	
		Ferry	0	0	0	0	
		Garfield	0	0	0	0	
		Grant	0	0	0	0	
		Grays Harbor	0	0	0	0	
		Island	0	0	0	0	
		Jefferson	0	0	0	0	
		Kittitas	0	0	0	0	
		Klickitat	0	0	0	0	
		Lewis	0	0	0	0	
		Lincoln	0	0	0	0	
		Mason	0	0	0	0	
		Okanogan	0	0	0	0	
		Pacific	0	0	0	0	
		Pend Oreille	0	0	0	0	
		San Juan	0	0	0	0	
		Stevens	0	0	0	0	
		Wahkiakum	0	0	0	0	
		Walla Walla	0	0	0	0	
		Whitman	0	0	0	0	
	Other Agencies–Tribal	Colville Tribal	0	0	0	0	
		Lummi Tribal	0	0	0	0	
		Nisqually Tribal	0	0	0	0	
		Nooksack Tribal	0	0	0	0	
		Skokomish Tribal	0	0	0	0	
WEST VIRGINIA	Cities	Ansted	0	0	0	0	1,597
		Barboursville	0	0	0	0	3,276
		Belington	0	0	0	0	1,831
		Benwood	0	0	0	0	1,463
		Bethany	0	0	0	0	977
		Bethlehem	0	0	0	0	2,506
		Bluefield	0	0	0	0	11,000
		Bridgeport	0	0	0	0	7,806
		Buckhannon	0	0	0	0	5,551
		Cameron	0	0	0	0	1,110
		Capon Bridge	0	0	0	0	250
		Ceredo	0	0	0	0	1,607
		Chapmanville	0	0	0	0	1,132
		Charles Town	0	0	0	0	4,013
		Chesapeake	0	0	0	0	1,550
		Chester	0	0	0		2,371
		Clearview	0	0		0	558
		Danville	0		0	0	538
		Dunbar	0	0	0	0	7,612
		Eleanor	0				1,541
		Elkins	0	0	0	0	7,050
		Fairmont	0	0	0	0	19,127
		Fayetteville	0	0	0	0	2,641
		Follansbee	0	0	0	0	2,893
		Fort Gay	0	0	0		809
		Gauley Bridge	0		0	0	694
		Glen Dale	0	0	0	0	1,443
		Glenville	0	0	0	0	1,470
		Grafton	0	0	0	0	5,372
		Hamlin	0	0	0	0	1,093
		Harpers Ferry-Bolivar	0	0	0	0	1,413
		Harrisville	0	0	0	0	1,880
		Hartford City	0	0	0	0	515
		Henderson	0	0	0	0	311
		Hinton	0	0	0	0	2,622
		Hurricane	0	0	0	0	6,179
		Kenova	0	0	0	0	3,325
		Kermit	0	0	0	0	225
		Keyser	0	0	0	0	5,331
		Lewisburg	0	0	0	0	3,554
		Logan	0	0	0	0	1,525

State	Agency type	Agency name	Zero data per quarter[1] 1st quarter	2nd quarter	3rd quarter	4th quarter	Popu-lation[2]
		Mabscott			0		1,344
		Madison	0	0	0	0	2,610
		Man	0	0			705
		Mannington	0	0	0	0	2,080
		Marlinton	0	0	0	0	1,241
		Marmet	0	0	0	0	1,610
		Martinsburg	0	0	0	0	16,610
		Mason	0	0	0	0	1,044
		Masontown	0	0	0	0	656
		Matoaka	0	0	0	0	302
		McMechen	0	0	0	0	1,780
		Milton	0	0	0	0	2,377
		Monongah	0	0	0	0	911
		Montgomery	0	0	0	0	1,925
		Moorefield	0	0	0	0	2,432
		Moundsville	0	0	0	0	9,385
		New Cumberland	0	0	0	0	1,021
		New Haven	0	0	0	0	1,523
		Northfork	0	0	0	0	437
		Nutter Fort	0	0	0	0	1,640
		Oceana	0	0	0	0	1,445
		Paden City	0	0	0	0	2,659
		Parkersburg	0	0	0	0	31,562
		Paw Paw	0	0			503
		Pennsboro	0	0	0		1,199
		Peterstown	0	0	0	0	493
		Philippi	0	0	0		2,821
		Piedmont	0	0	0	0	925
		Poca	0		0	0	1,035
		Point Pleasant	0	0	0	0	4,459
		Ranson	0	0	0	0	4,067
		Ravenswood	0	0	0	0	3,992
		Reedsville	0	0	0	0	534
		Ridgeley	0	0	0	0	690
		Ripley	0	0	0	0	3,272
		Rivesville	0	0	0	0	915
		Romney	0	0	0	0	1,975
		Ronceverte	0	0	0	0	1,523
		Shepherdstown	0	0	0	0	1,168
		Shinnston	0	0			2,238
		Sistersville		0	0	0	1,479
		Sophia	0	0	0	0	1,242
		St. Albans	0	0	0	0	10,999
		Star City	0	0	0	0	1,404
		Stonewood	0	0	0	0	1,861
		Summersville	0	0	0		3,366
		Terra Alta	0	0			1,517
		Triadelphia	0	0	0	0	816
		Vienna	0	0	0	0	10,667
		Wardensville	0	0	0	0	246
		Welch	0	0	0	0	2,283
		West Logan	0	0	0	0	394
		West Milford	0	0	0	0	651
		Weston	0	0	0	0	4,215
		Westover	0	0			3,922
		West Union	0	0	0	0	806
		White Sulphur Springs	0	0	0	0	2,323
		Williamson	0	0	0	0	3,128
		Williamstown	0	0	0	0	2,975
		Winfield	0	0	0	0	2,060
	Universities and Colleges	Concord University	0	0	0	0	2,787
		Fairmont State University	0	0	0	0	4,611
		Glenville State College	0	0	0	0	1,381
		Marshall University	0	0	0	0	13,936
		Potomac State College	0	0	0	0	1,485
		Shepherd University	0	0	0		4,091

[1]Agencies published in this table indicated that no hate crimes occurred in their jurisdictions during the quarter(s) for which they submitted reports to the Hate Crime program. Blanks indicate quarters for which agencies did not submit reports.

[2]Population figures are published only for the cities. The figures listed for the universities and colleges are student enrollment and were provided by the United States Department of Education for the 2006 school year, the most recent available. The enrollment figures include full-time and part-time students.

Table 95. Hate Crime Zero Data Submitted per Quarter, by State and Agency, 2007 *(Contd.)*

(Number.)

State	Agency type	Agency name	1st quarter	2nd quarter	3rd quarter	4th quarter	Population[2]
		West Liberty State College		0		0	2,268
		West Virginia Tech	0	0	0	0	1,472
		West Virginia University	0	0	0	0	27,115
	Metropolitan Counties	Boone	0	0	0	0	
		Cabell	0	0	0	0	
		Hampshire	0	0	0	0	
		Hancock	0	0	0	0	
		Jefferson	0	0	0	0	
		Mineral	0	0	0	0	
		Morgan	0	0	0		
		Ohio				0	
		Pleasants	0	0		0	
		Preston	0				
		Putnam	0		0	0	
		Wayne	0	0	0	0	
		Wirt	0	0	0	0	
		Wood	0	0	0	0	
	Nonmetropolitan Counties	Barbour	0				
		Braxton	0	0	0	0	
		Gilmer	0	0	0	0	
		Grant	0	0	0		
		Greenbrier	0	0	0	0	
		Hardy	0	0	0	0	
		Harrison	0	0	0	0	
		Jackson	0	0	0	0	
		Lewis	0	0	0	0	
		Logan	0	0	0	0	
		Marion	0	0	0	0	
		Mason	0	0	0	0	
		McDowell	0	0	0	0	
		Mercer	0	0	0	0	
		Mingo	0	0	0	0	
		Monroe	0	0	0	0	
		Nicholas	0	0	0	0	
		Pendleton	0	0	0	0	
		Pocahontas	0	0	0	0	
		Raleigh	0	0	0	0	
		Randolph	0	0	0	0	
		Ritchie	0	0	0	0	
		Roane	0	0	0	0	
		Summers	0	0	0	0	
		Taylor	0	0	0	0	
		Tucker	0	0	0	0	
		Tyler	0	0	0	0	
		Upshur	0	0	0	0	
		Wyoming	0	0	0	0	
	State Police Agencies	State Police:					
		Beckley	0	0	0	0	
		Berkeley Springs	0	0	0	0	
		Bridgeport	0	0	0	0	
		Buckeye	0	0	0	0	
		Buckhannon	0	0	0	0	
		Clay	0	0	0	0	
		Danville	0	0	0	0	
		Elizabeth	0	0	0	0	
		Elkins	0	0	0	0	
		Fairmont	0	0	0	0	
		Franklin	0	0	0	0	
		Gauley Bridge	0	0	0	0	
		Gilbert	0	0	0	0	
		Glenville	0	0	0	0	
		Grafton	0	0	0	0	
		Grantsville	0	0	0	0	
		Hamlin	0	0	0	0	
		Harrisville	0	0	0	0	
		Hinton	0	0	0	0	
		Hundred	0	0	0	0	
		Huntington	0	0	0	0	
		Jesse	0	0	0	0	
		Kearneysville	0	0	0	0	
		Kingwood	0	0	0	0	
		Lewisburg	0	0	0	0	
		Logan	0	0	0	0	
		Martinsburg	0	0	0	0	
		Moorefield	0	0	0	0	
		Morgantown	0	0	0	0	
		Moundsville	0	0	0	0	
		New Cumberland	0	0	0	0	
		Oak Hill	0	0	0	0	
		Paden City	0	0	0	0	
		Parkersburg	0	0	0	0	
		Parsons	0	0	0	0	
		Petersburg	0	0	0	0	
		Philippi	0	0	0	0	
		Point Pleasant	0	0	0	0	
		Princeton	0	0	0	0	
		Quincy	0	0	0	0	
		Rainelle	0	0	0	0	
		Richwood	0	0	0	0	
		Ripley	0	0	0	0	
		South Charleston	0	0	0	0	
		Spencer	0	0	0	0	
		St. Marys	0	0	0	0	
		Summersville	0	0	0	0	
		Sutton	0	0	0	0	
		Union	0	0	0	0	
		Upperglade	0	0	0	0	
		Wayne	0	0	0	0	
		Welch	0	0	0	0	
		Wellsburg	0	0	0	0	
		Weston	0	0	0	0	
		West Union	0	0	0	0	
		Wheeling	0	0	0	0	
		Whitesville	0	0	0	0	
		Williamson	0	0	0	0	
		Winfield	0	0	0	0	
		State Police, Bureau of Criminal Investigation:					
		Beckley	0	0	0	0	
		Bluefield	0	0	0	0	
		Buckhannon	0	0	0	0	
		Charleston	0	0	0	0	
		Fairmont	0	0	0	0	
		State Police, Parkway Authority:					
		Fayette County	0	0	0	0	
		Kanawha County	0	0	0	0	
		Mercer County	0	0	0	0	
		Raleigh County	0	0	0	0	
	Other Agencies	Capitol Protective Services	0		0	0	
		Central West Virginia Drug Task Force	0	0	0	0	
		Department of Natural Resources:					
		Barbour County	0	0	0	0	
		Berkeley County	0	0	0	0	
		Boone County	0	0	0	0	
		Braxton County	0	0	0	0	
		Brooke County	0	0	0	0	
		Cabell County	0	0	0	0	

[1]Agencies published in this table indicated that no hate crimes occurred in their jurisdictions during the quarter(s) for which they submitted reports to the Hate Crime program. Blanks indicate quarters for which agencies did not submit reports.

[2]Population figures are published only for the cities. The figures listed for the universities and colleges are student enrollment and were provided by the United States Department of Education for the 2006 school year, the most recent available. The enrollment figures include full-time and part-time students.

Table 95. Hate Crime Zero Data Submitted per Quarter, by State and Agency, 2007 *(Contd.)*

(Number.)

State	Agency type	Agency name	Zero data per quarter[1]				Population[2]
			1st quarter	2nd quarter	3rd quarter	4th quarter	
		Calhoun County	0	0	0	0	
		Clay County	0	0	0	0	
		Fayette County	0	0	0	0	
		Gilmer County	0	0	0	0	
		Grant County	0	0	0	0	
		Greenbrier County	0	0	0	0	
		Hampshire County	0	0	0	0	
		Hancock County	0	0	0	0	
		Hardy County	0	0	0	0	
		Harrison County	0	0	0	0	
		Jackson County	0	0	0	0	
		Jefferson County	0	0	0	0	
		Kanawha County	0	0	0	0	
		Lewis County	0	0	0	0	
		Lincoln County	0	0	0	0	
		Logan County	0	0	0	0	
		Marion County	0	0	0	0	
		Marshall County	0	0	0	0	
		Mason County	0	0	0	0	
		McDowell County	0	0	0	0	
		Mercer County	0	0	0	0	
		Mineral County	0	0	0	0	
		Mingo County	0	0	0	0	
		Monongalia County	0	0	0	0	
		Monroe County	0	0	0	0	
		Morgan County	0	0	0	0	
		Nicholas County	0	0	0	0	
		Ohio County	0	0	0	0	
		Pendleton County	0	0	0	0	
		Pleasants County				0	
		Pocahontas County	0	0	0	0	
		Preston County	0	0	0	0	
		Putnam County	0	0	0	0	
		Raleigh County	0	0	0	0	
		Randolph County	0	0	0	0	
		Ritchie County	0	0	0	0	
		Roane County	0	0	0	0	
		Summers County	0	0	0	0	
		Taylor County	0	0	0	0	
		Tucker County	0	0	0	0	
		Upshur County	0	0	0	0	
		Wayne County	0	0	0	0	
		Webster County	0	0	0	0	
		Wetzel County	0	0	0	0	
		Wirt County	0	0	0	0	
		Wood County	0	0	0	0	
		Wyoming County	0	0	0	0	
		Eastern Panhandle Drug and Violent Crime Task Force	0	0	0	0	
		Greenbrier County Drug and Violent Crime Task Force	0	0	0	0	
		Hancock-Brooke-Weirton Drug Task Force	0	0	0		

State	Agency type	Agency name	Zero data per quarter[1]				Population[2]
			1st quarter	2nd quarter	3rd quarter	4th quarter	
		Huntington Drug and Violent Crime Task Force	0	0	0	0	
		Kanawha County Parks and Recreation	0		0		
		Logan County Drug and Violent Crime Task Force	0	0	0	0	
		Metropolitan Drug Enforcement Network Team	0	0	0	0	
		Mon Valley Drug Task Force	0	0	0	0	
		Ohio Valley Drug and Violent Crime Task Force	0	0	0	0	
		Parkersburg Narcotics and Violent Crime Task Force	0	0			
		Potomac Highlands Drug and Violent Crime Task Force			0	0	
		Southern Regional Drug and Violent Crime Task Force	0				
		State Fire Marshal:					
		Boone County	0	0	0	0	
		Cabell County	0	0	0	0	
		Calhoun County	0	0	0	0	
		Clay County	0	0	0	0	
		Fayette County	0	0	0	0	
		Gilmer County	0	0	0	0	
		Harrison County	0	0	0	0	
		Jackson County	0	0	0	0	
		Kanawha County	0	0	0	0	
		Logan County	0	0	0	0	
		Marshall County	0	0	0	0	
		Mason County	0	0	0	0	
		McDowell County	0	0	0	0	
		Mercer County	0	0	0	0	
		Mineral County	0	0	0	0	
		Mingo County	0	0	0	0	
		Monongalia County	0	0	0	0	
		Nicholas County	0	0	0	0	
		Pleasants County	0	0	0	0	
		Preston County	0	0	0	0	
		Raleigh County	0	0	0	0	
		Randolph County	0	0	0	0	
		Summers County	0	0	0	0	
		Taylor County	0	0	0	0	
		Wayne County	0	0	0	0	
		Webster County	0	0	0	0	
		Wyoming County	0	0	0	0	

[1]Agencies published in this table indicated that no hate crimes occurred in their jurisdictions during the quarter(s) for which they submitted reports to the Hate Crime program. Blanks indicate quarters for which agencies did not submit reports.

[2]Population figures are published only for the cities. The figures listed for the universities and colleges are student enrollment and were provided by the United States Department of Education for the 2006 school year, the most recent available. The enrollment figures include full-time and part-time students.

Table 95. Hate Crime Zero Data Submitted per Quarter, by State and Agency, 2007 *(Contd.)*

(Number.)

State	Agency type	Agency name	1st quarter	2nd quarter	3rd quarter	4th quarter	Population[2]
WISCONSIN...	Cities	Three Rivers Drug and Violent Crime Task Force	0	0	0	0	
		Tri-Lateral Drug Enforcement Network Team	0	0	0	0	
		Albany	0	0	0	0	1,119
		Algoma	0	0	0	0	3,228
		Altoona	0	0	0	0	6,377
		Amery	0	0	0	0	2,846
		Antigo	0	0	0	0	8,225
		Arcadia	0	0	0	0	2,329
		Ashland	0	0	0	0	8,147
		Ashwaubenon	0	0	0	0	17,033
		Bangor	0	0	0	0	1,343
		Baraboo	0	0	0	0	11,015
		Barron	0	0	0	0	3,145
		Bayfield	0	0	0	0	579
		Bayside	0	0	0	0	4,216
		Beaver Dam	0	0	0	0	15,551
		Belleville	0	0	0	0	2,246
		Beloit	0	0	0	0	36,424
		Beloit Town	0	0	0	0	7,475
		Berlin	0	0	0	0	5,197
		Black River Falls	0	0	0	0	3,456
		Blair	0	0	0	0	1,276
		Bloomer	0	0	0	0	3,378
		Bloomfield	0	0	0	0	5,990
		Boscobel	0	0	0	0	3,185
		Brillion	0	0	0	0	2,857
		Brodhead	0	0	0	0	3,089
		Brookfield	0	0	0	0	39,738
		Brookfield Township	0	0	0	0	6,243
		Brown Deer	0	0	0	0	11,507
		Burlington	0	0	0	0	10,599
		Burlington Town	0	0	0	0	6,552
		Butler	0	0	0	0	1,806
		Caledonia	0	0	0	0	25,682
		Campbellsport	0	0	0	0	1,929
		Campbell Township	0	0	0	0	4,437
		Cedarburg	0	0	0	0	11,216
		Chenequa	0	0	0	0	590
		Chetek	0	0	0	0	2,177
		Chilton	0	0	0	0	3,635
		Chippewa Falls	0	0	0	0	13,158
		Cleveland	0	0	0	0	1,401
		Clinton	0	0	0	0	2,261
		Clintonville	0	0	0	0	4,435
		Colby-Abbotsford	0	0	0	0	3,649
		Columbus	0	0	0	0	5,068
		Combined Locks	0	0	0	0	3,121
		Cornell	0	0	0	0	1,424
		Cottage Grove	0	0	0	0	5,530
		Crandon	0	0	0	0	1,880
		Cross Plains	0	0	0	0	3,541
		Cuba City	0	0	0	0	2,052
		Cudahy	0	0	0	0	17,998
		Cumberland	0	0	0	0	2,299
		Dane	0	0	0	0	952
		Darien	0	0	0	0	1,609
		DeForest	0	0	0	0	8,845
		Delafield	0	0	0	0	6,975
		Delavan	0	0	0	0	8,450
		Delavan Town	0	0	0	0	4,906
		Denmark	0	0	0	0	2,124
		De Pere	0	0	0	0	22,781
		Dodgeville	0	0	0	0	4,577
		Durand	0	0	0	0	1,867
		Eagle River	0	0	0	0	1,579
		Eagle Village	0	0	0	0	1,838
		East Troy	0	0	0	0	4,276
		Eau Claire	0	0	0	0	63,472
		Edgar	0	0	0	0	1,490
		Edgerton	0	0	0	0	5,230
		Eleva	0	0	0	0	656
		Elkhart Lake	0	0	0	0	1,153
		Elkhorn	0	0	0	0	9,354
		Elk Mound	0	0	0	0	805
		Ellsworth	0	0	0	0	3,112
		Elm Grove	0	0	0	0	6,064
		Elroy	0	0	0	0	1,487
		Evansville	0	0	0	0	5,023
		Everest	0	0	0	0	15,771
		Fennimore	0	0	0	0	2,255
		Fontana	0	0	0	0	1,890
		Fort Atkinson	0	0	0	0	12,023
		Fox Lake	0	0	0	0	1,486
		Fox Point	0	0	0	0	6,663
		Fox Valley	0	0	0	0	17,525
		Franklin	0	0	0	0	34,449
		Frederic	0	0	0	0	1,220
		Geneva Town	0	0	0	0	4,726
		Genoa City	0	0	0	0	2,911
		Germantown	0	0	0	0	19,491
		Glendale	0	0	0	0	12,736
		Grafton	0	0	0	0	11,712
		Grand Chute	0	0	0	0	20,793
		Grand Rapids	0	0	0	0	7,741
		Grantsburg	0	0	0	0	1,445
		Green Bay	0	0	0	0	100,010
		Greendale	0	0	0	0	13,708
		Greenfield	0	0	0	0	35,435
		Green Lake	0	0	0	0	1,158
		Hales Corners	0	0	0	0	7,538
		Hartford	0	0	0	0	13,611
		Hartland	0	0	0	0	8,793
		Hayward	0	0	0	0	2,330
		Hazel Green	0	0	0	0	1,134
		Hillsboro	0	0	0	0	1,283
		Hobart-Lawrence	0	0	0	0	9,725
		Holmen	0	0	0	0	7,512
		Horicon	0	0	0	0	3,640
		Hortonville	0	0	0	0	2,774
		Hudson	0	0	0	0	12,408
		Hurley	0	0	0	0	1,623
		Independence	0	0	0	0	1,243
		Iron Ridge	0	0	0	0	990
		Jackson	0	0	0	0	6,248
		Jefferson	0	0	0	0	7,773
		Juneau	0	0	0	0	2,654
		Kaukauna	0	0	0	0	15,405
		Kenosha	0	0	0	0	96,996
		Kewaskum	0	0	0	0	4,070
		Kewaunee	0	0	0	0	2,877
		Kiel	0	0	0	0	3,518
		Kohler	0	0	0	0	1,992
		La Crosse	0	0	0	0	50,032
		Ladysmith	0	0	0	0	3,594
		Lake Delton	0	0	0	0	2,973
		Lake Geneva	0	0	0	0	8,209
		Lake Hallie	0	0	0	0	5,959
		Lake Mills	0	0	0	0	5,483
		Lancaster	0	0	0	0	3,869
		Lodi	0	0	0	0	2,947
		Manitowoc	0	0	0	0	33,541
		Maple Bluff	0	0	0	0	1,286
		Marathon City	0	0	0	0	1,562
		Marinette	0	0	0	0	10,906
		Marion	0	0	0	0	1,232
		Markesan	0	0	0	0	1,332
		Marshall Village	0	0	0	0	3,604

[1] Agencies published in this table indicated that no hate crimes occurred in their jurisdictions during the quarter(s) for which they submitted reports to the Hate Crime program. Blanks indicate quarters for which agencies did not submit reports.

[2] Population figures are published only for the cities. The figures listed for the universities and colleges are student enrollment and were provided by the United States Department of Education for the 2006 school year, the most recent available. The enrollment figures include full-time and part-time students.

Table 95. Hate Crime Zero Data Submitted per Quarter, by State and Agency, 2007 *(Contd.)*

(Number.)

State	Agency type	Agency name	1st quarter	2nd quarter	3rd quarter	4th quarter	Population[2]	State	Agency type	Agency name	1st quarter	2nd quarter	3rd quarter	4th quarter	Population[2]
		Marshfield	0	0	0	0	19,175			Rome Town	0	0	0	0	3,015
		Mauston	0	0	0	0	4,329			Rothschild	0	0	0	0	5,232
		Mayville	0	0	0	0	5,430			Sauk Prairie	0	0	0	0	4,225
		McFarland	0	0	0	0	7,663			Saukville	0	0	0	0	4,334
		Medford	0	0	0	0	4,108			Seymour	0	0	0	0	3,411
		Menasha	0	0	0	0	16,756			Shawano	0	0	0	0	8,790
		Menomonee Falls	0	0	0	0	34,612			Sheboygan Falls	0	0	0	0	7,795
		Menomonie	0	0	0	0	15,367			Shorewood	0	0	0	0	13,185
		Mequon	0	0	0	0	23,736			Shorewood Hills	0	0	0	0	1,629
		Merrill	0	0	0	0	9,860			Silver Lake	0	0	0	0	2,530
		Middleton	0	0	0	0	16,710			Siren	0	0	0	0	842
		Milton	0	0	0	0	5,800			Slinger	0	0	0	0	4,476
		Mineral Point	0	0	0	0	2,562			Somerset	0	0	0	0	2,365
		Minocqua	0	0	0	0	5,026			South Milwaukee	0	0	0	0	20,641
		Mishicot	0	0	0	0	1,397			Sparta	0	0	0	0	9,070
		Mondovi	0	0	0	0	2,638			Spencer	0	0	0	0	1,846
		Monona	0	0	0	0	7,924			Spooner	0	0	0	0	2,577
		Monroe	0	0	0	0	10,563			Spring Green	0	0	0	0	1,439
		Mosinee	0	0	0	0	4,078			Stanley	0	0	0	0	3,676
		Mount Horeb	0	0	0	0	6,674			St. Croix Falls	0	0	0	0	2,192
		Mount Pleasant	0	0	0	0	26,237			Stevens Point	0	0	0	0	24,333
		Mukwonago	0	0	0	0	6,890			St. Francis	0	0	0	0	8,899
		Muskego	0	0	0	0	22,961			Stoughton	0	0	0	0	12,572
		Neenah	0	0	0	0	24,871			Strum	0	0	0	0	1,038
		Neillsville	0	0	0	0	2,615			Sturgeon Bay	0	0	0	0	9,129
		New Glarus	0	0	0	0	2,064			Sturtevant	0	0	0	0	6,626
		New Holstein	0	0	0	0	3,166			Summit	0	0	0	0	5,155
		New Lisbon	0	0	0	0	2,592			Sun Prairie	0	0	0	0	27,366
		New Richmond	0	0	0	0	8,200			Superior	0	0	0	0	26,896
		Niagara	0	0	0	0	1,766			Theresa	0	0	0	0	1,326
		North Fond du Lac	0	0	0	0	4,959			Thiensville	0	0	0	0	3,258
		North Hudson	0	0	0	0	3,800			Three Lakes	0	0	0	0	2,266
		North Prairie	0	0	0	0	2,055			Tomah	0	0	0	0	8,764
		Oconomowoc	0	0	0	0	14,414			Tomahawk	0	0	0	0	3,708
		Oconomowoc Town	0	0	0	0	8,196			Town of East Troy	0	0	0	0	3,936
		Oconto	0	0	0	0	4,713			Town of Menasha	0	0	0	0	17,192
		Oconto Falls	0	0	0	0	2,854			Trempealeau	0	0	0	0	1,532
		Omro	0	0	0	0	3,316			Twin Lakes	0	0	0	0	5,580
		Onalaska	0	0	0	0	16,377			Two Rivers	0	0	0	0	11,916
		Oregon	0	0	0	0	9,006			Valders	0	0	0	0	987
		Osceola	0	0	0	0	2,719			Verona	0	0	0	0	10,525
		Oshkosh	0	0	0	0	64,183			Viroqua	0	0	0	0	4,378
		Osseo	0	0	0	0	1,637			Walworth	0	0	0	0	2,669
		Palmyra	0	0	0	0	1,751			Washburn	0	0	0	0	2,125
		Park Falls	0	0	0	0	2,425			Waterloo	0	0	0	0	3,252
		Pepin	0	0	0	0	929			Waunakee	0	0	0	0	10,894
		Peshtigo	0	0	0	0	3,276			Waupaca	0	0	0	0	5,833
		Pewaukee	0	0	0	0	12,939			Waupun	0	0	0	0	10,668
		Pewaukee Village	0	0	0	0	9,125			Wausau	0	0	0	0	38,405
		Phillips	0	0	0	0	1,530			Wautoma	0	0	0	0	2,088
		Platteville	0	0	0	0	9,711			Wauwatosa	0	0	0	0	44,463
		Pleasant Prairie	0	0	0	0	19,426			West Allis	0	0	0	0	58,366
		Plover	0	0	0	0	11,495			West Bend	0	0	0	0	30,070
		Plymouth	0	0	0	0	8,333			Westby	0	0	0	0	2,166
		Portage	0	0	0	0	9,789			West Milwaukee	0	0	0	0	3,977
		Port Washington	0	0	0	0	11,115			West Salem	0	0	0	0	4,725
		Poynette	0	0	0	0	2,579			Whitefish Bay	0	0	0	0	13,450
		Prairie du Chien	0	0	0	0	5,708			Whitehall	0	0	0	0	1,620
		Prescott	0	0	0	0	4,058			Whitewater	0	0	0	0	14,147
		Princeton	0	0	0	0	1,448			Williams Bay	0	0	0	0	2,687
		Pulaski	0	0	0	0	3,528			Winneconne	0	0	0	0	2,490
		Racine	0	0	0	0	79,285			Wisconsin Dells	0	0	0	0	2,538
		Readstown	0	0	0	0	384			Wisconsin Rapids	0	0	0	0	17,633
		Reedsburg	0	0	0	0	8,629			Woodruff	0	0	0	0	2,036
		Rice Lake	0	0	0	0	8,422		**Universities and Colleges**	University of Wisconsin:					
		Richland Center	0	0	0	0	5,145			Eau Claire	0	0	0	0	10,766
		Ripon	0	0	0	0	7,286			Green Bay	0	0	0	0	5,690
		River Falls	0	0	0	0	13,803			La Crosse	0	0	0	0	9,849
		River Hills	0	0	0	0	1,614			Madison	0	0	0	0	41,028
										Milwaukee	0	0	0	0	28,309

[1]Agencies published in this table indicated that no hate crimes occurred in their jurisdictions during the quarter(s) for which they submitted reports to the Hate Crime program. Blanks indicate quarters for which agencies did not submit reports.
[2]Population figures are published only for the cities. The figures listed for the universities and colleges are student enrollment and were provided by the United States Department of Education for the 2006 school year, the most recent available. The enrollment figures include full-time and part-time students.

Table 95. Hate Crime Zero Data Submitted per Quarter, by State and Agency, 2007 *(Contd.)*

(Number.)

State	Agency type	Agency name	1st quarter	2nd quarter	3rd quarter	4th quarter	Population[2]
		Oshkosh	0	0	0	0	12,530
		Parkside	0	0	0	0	5,007
		Stevens Point	0	0	0	0	9,048
		Stout	0	0	0	0	8,372
		Superior	0	0	0	0	2,924
		Whitewater	0	0	0	0	10,502
	Metro-politan Counties	Brown	0	0	0	0	
		Calumet	0	0	0	0	
		Chippewa	0	0	0	0	
		Columbia	0	0	0	0	
		Douglas	0	0	0	0	
		Fond du Lac	0	0	0	0	
		Iowa	0	0	0	0	
		Kenosha	0	0	0	0	
		Kewaunee	0	0	0	0	
		La Crosse	0	0	0	0	
		Marathon	0	0	0	0	
		Milwaukee	0	0	0	0	
		Oconto	0	0	0	0	
		Outagamie	0	0	0	0	
		Ozaukee	0	0	0	0	
		Pierce	0	0	0	0	
		Racine	0	0	0	0	
		Rock	0	0	0	0	
		Sheboygan	0	0	0	0	
		St. Croix	0	0	0	0	
		Washington	0	0	0	0	
		Waukesha	0	0	0	0	
		Winnebago	0	0	0	0	
	Nonmetro-politan Counties	Adams	0	0	0	0	
		Ashland	0	0	0	0	
		Barron	0	0	0	0	
		Bayfield	0	0	0	0	
		Buffalo	0	0	0	0	
		Burnett	0	0	0	0	
		Clark	0	0	0	0	
		Crawford	0	0	0	0	
		Dodge	0	0	0	0	
		Door	0	0	0	0	
		Dunn	0	0	0	0	
		Florence	0	0	0	0	
		Forest	0	0	0	0	
		Grant	0	0	0	0	
		Green	0	0	0	0	
		Green Lake	0	0	0	0	
		Iron	0	0	0	0	
		Jackson	0	0	0	0	
		Jefferson	0	0	0	0	
		Juneau	0	0	0	0	
		Lafayette	0	0	0	0	
		Langlade	0	0	0	0	
		Lincoln	0	0	0	0	
		Manitowoc	0	0	0	0	
		Marinette	0	0	0	0	
		Marquette	0	0	0	0	
		Menominee	0	0	0	0	
		Monroe	0	0	0	0	
		Pepin	0	0	0	0	
		Polk	0	0	0	0	
		Portage	0	0	0	0	
		Price	0	0	0	0	
		Richland	0	0	0	0	
		Rusk	0	0	0	0	
		Sauk	0	0	0	0	
		Sawyer	0	0	0	0	
		Shawano	0	0	0	0	
		Taylor	0	0	0	0	
		Trempealeau	0	0	0	0	
		Vernon	0	0	0	0	
		Vilas	0	0	0	0	
		Walworth	0	0	0	0	
		Washburn	0	0	0	0	
		Waupaca	0	0	0	0	

State	Agency type	Agency name	1st quarter	2nd quarter	3rd quarter	4th quarter	Population[2]
		Waushara	0	0	0	0	
		Wood	0	0	0	0	
	State Police Agencies	Wisconsin State Patrol	0	0	0	0	
	Other Agencies	Capitol Police	0	0	0	0	
		Department of Natural Resources	0	0	0	0	
	Other Agencies– Tribal	Menominee Tribal	0	0	0	0	
		Oneida Tribal	0	0	0	0	
WYOMING.....	Cities	Afton	0	0	0	0	1,817
		Baggs	0				370
		Basin	0	0	0	0	1,242
		Buffalo	0	0	0	0	4,566
		Diamondville	0			0	678
		Douglas	0	0	0	0	5,691
		Evanston	0	0	0	0	11,585
		Evansville	0	0	0	0	2,321
		Glenrock	0	0	0	0	2,393
		Green River	0	0	0	0	11,957
		Hanna	0				855
		Jackson	0		0	0	9,292
		Kemmerer	0	0	0	0	2,508
		La Barge		0			441
		Lander	0	0	0	0	7,066
		Laramie	0	0	0	0	25,504
		Lovell	0	0	0	0	2,279
		Mills	0	0	0	0	2,926
		Moorcroft	0	0	0	0	861
		Newcastle	0	0	0	0	3,275
		Pine Bluffs	0	0	0	0	1,142
		Powell	0	0	0	0	5,388
		Rawlins	0	0	0	0	8,572
		Saratoga	0		0	0	1,721
		Sheridan	0	0	0	0	16,507
		Sundance	0	0	0	0	1,199
		Thermopolis	0	0	0	0	2,912
		Torrington	0	0	0	0	5,446
		Wheatland	0	0	0	0	3,426
		Worland	0	0	0	0	4,857
	Universities and Colleges	Sheridan College	0	0	0	0	3,066
		University of Wyoming	0	0	0	0	13,203
	Metro-politan Counties	Laramie	0	0	0	0	
		Natrona	0	0	0	0	
	Nonmetro-politan Counties	Albany	0	0	0	0	
		Big Horn	0	0	0	0	
		Campbell	0	0	0	0	
		Carbon	0	0	0	0	
		Converse	0	0	0	0	
		Crook	0		0	0	
		Fremont	0				
		Goshen	0	0	0	0	
		Hot Springs	0	0	0	0	
		Johnson	0	0	0	0	
		Lincoln	0	0	0	0	
		Niobrara	0	0	0	0	
		Park	0	0	0	0	
		Platte	0	0	0	0	
		Sheridan	0	0	0	0	
		Sublette	0	0	0	0	
		Sweetwater	0	0	0	0	
		Teton	0	0	0	0	
		Uinta	0	0	0	0	
		Washakie	0	0	0	0	
		Weston	0	0	0	0	

[1]Agencies published in this table indicated that no hate crimes occurred in their jurisdictions during the quarter(s) for which they submitted reports to the Hate Crime program. Blanks indicate quarters for which agencies did not submit reports.

[2]Population figures are published only for the cities. The figures listed for the universities and colleges are student enrollment and were provided by the United States Department of Education for the 2006 school year, the most recent available. The enrollment figures include full-time and part-time students.

APPENDIXES

APPENDIX I. METHODOLOGY

Submitting Uniform Crime Reporting (UCR) Program data to the Federal Bureau of Investigation (FBI) is a collective effort on the part of city, county, state, tribal, and federal law enforcement agencies to present a nationwide view of crime. Law enforcement agencies in 46 states and the District of Columbia voluntarily contribute crime data to the UCR Program through their respective state UCR programs. For those states that do not have a state program, local agencies submit crime statistics directly to the FBI. The state UCR Programs function as liaisons between local agencies and the FBI. Many states have mandatory reporting requirements, and many state programs collect data beyond the scope of the UCR Program to address crime problems specific to their particular jurisdictions. In most cases, state programs also provide direct and frequent service to participating law enforcement agencies, make information readily available for statewide use, and help streamline the national program's operations.

The criteria that have been established for state programs ensure consistency and comparability in the data submitted to the national program, and also ensure regular and timely reporting. These criteria include the following: (1) The state program must conform to the national program's standards, definitions, and required information. (2) The state criminal justice agency must have a proven, effective, statewide program, and must have instituted acceptable quality control procedures. (3) The state crime reporting must cover a percentage of the population at least equal to that covered by the national program through direct reporting. (4) The state program must have adequate field staff assigned to conduct audits and to assist contributing agencies in record-keeping practices and crime-reporting procedures. (5) The state program must provide the FBI with all of the detailed data regularly collected by the FBI from individual agencies that report to the state program in the form of duplicate returns, computer printouts, and/or appropriate electronic media. (6) The state program must have the proven capability (tested over a period of time) to supply all the statistical data required in time to meet the publication deadlines of the national program.

The FBI, in order to fulfill its responsibilities in connection with the UCR Program, continues to edit and review individual agency reports for completeness and quality. National program staff members directly contact individual contributors within the state, when necessary, in connection with crime-reporting matters; staff members also coordinate such contact with the UCR Program. Upon request, they conduct training programs within the state on law enforcement record-keeping and crime-reporting procedures. The FBI conducts an audit of each state's UCR data collection procedures once every three years, in accordance with audit standards established by the federal government. Should circumstances develop in which the state program does not comply with the aforementioned requirements, the national program may institute a direct collection of Uniform Crime Reports from law enforcement agencies within the state.

Reporting Procedures

Based on records of all reports of crime received from victims, officers who discover infractions, and other sources, law enforcement agencies tabulate the number of Part I offenses brought to their attention and submit these data to the FBI every month, either directly or through their state UCR program. Part I offenses include murder, and nonnegligent manslaughter, forcible rape, robbery, aggravated assault, burglary, larceny-theft, motor vehicle theft, and arson. See Appendix II for definitions of these offenses.

Law enforcement's monthly submission to the FBI includes other important information. When, through investigation, an agency determines that complaints of crimes are unfounded or false, it eliminates that offense from its crime tally through an entry on the monthly report. The report also provides the total number of actual Part I offenses, the number of offenses cleared, and the number of clearances that involve only offenders under 18 years of age. (Law enforcement can clear crimes in one of two ways: by the arrest of at least one person who is charged and turned over to the court for prosecution, or by exceptional means, in which when some element beyond law enforcement's control precludes the arrest of a known offender.) Law enforcement agencies also submit monthly to the FBI the value of property stolen and recovered in connection with the offenses and detailed information pertaining to criminal homicide and arson. In addition, the FBI collects supplementary information about offenses, such as the locations of robberies, time of day of burglaries, and other analyses about the offenses.

The expanded homicide data (details about murders such as the age, sex, and race of both the victim and the offender, the weapon used in the homicide, the circumstances surrounding the offense, and the relationship of the victim to the offender) includes the UCR Program's *Supplementary Homicide Reports* (SHRs). SHRs provide information regarding the ages, sexes, and races of murder victims and offenders; the types of weapons used in murders; the victim-to-offender relationships; and the circumstances surrounding the incidents. Law enforcement agencies are asked to complete an SHR for each murder reported to the UCR Program. The UCR Program's expanded homicide data also provide information about jusitfable homicide (the killing of a felon by either a police officer in the line of duty or a private citizen). For more information, see <http://www.fbi.gov/ucr/cius2007/offenses/expanded_information/homicide.html>.

Expanded arson data include details about the types of structures involved in arsons and arson rates per population group. For more information, see <http://www.fbi.gov/ucr/cius2007/offenses/expanded_information/data/arsontable_01.html> and <http://www.fbi.gov/ucr/cius2007/offenses/expanded_information/data/arsontable_02.html>.

The UCR Program also requires law enforcement agencies to report data regarding law enforcement employees. In addition to reporting monthly data on law enforcement officers killed or assaulted, agencies report anually on the number of full-time sworn and civilian law enforcement personnel employed as of October 31 of the reporting year.

At the end of each quarter, law enforcement agencies report summarized data on hate crimes (specific offenses that were motivated by an offender's bias against the perceived race, religion, ethnic origin, sexual orientation, or physical or mental disability). Those agencies participating in the UCR Program's National Incident-Base Reporting System (NIBRS) submit data on hate crimes monthly.

The UCR Program's data collection guidelines stipulate that a hate crime may involve multiple offenses, victims, and offenders within one incident; therefore, the hate crime data collection program is incident-based. According to UCR counting guidelines:

- One offense is counted for each victim in crimes against persons.

- One offense is counted for each offense type in crimes against property.

- One offense is counted for each offense type in crimes against society.

The victim of a hate crime may be an individual, a business, an institution, or society as a whole.

Editing Procedures

The UCR Program thoroughly examines each report it receives for arithmetical accuracy and for deviations in crime data from month to month and from present to past years that may indicate errors. UCR staff members compare an agency's monthly reports with its previous submissions and with reports from similar agencies to identify any unusual fluctuations in the agency's crime count. Large variations in crime levels may indicate modified records procedures, incomplete reporting, or changes in the jurisdiction's geopolitical structure.

Data reliability is a high priority of the national UCR program, which brings any deviations or arithmetical adjustments to the attention of state UCR programs and other submitting agencies. Typically, staff members study the monthly reports to evaluate periodic trends prepared for individual reporting units. Any significant increase or decrease becomes the subject of a special inquiry. Changes in crime reporting procedures or annexations that affect an agency's jurisdiction can influence the level of reported crime. When this occurs, the UCR Program excludes the figures for specific crime categories or totals (if necessary) from the trend tabulations.

To assist contributors in complying with UCR standards, the UCR Program provides training seminars and instructional materials on crime reporting procedures. Throughout the country, the national program maintains liaison with state programs and law enforcement personnel and holds training sessions to explain the purpose of the program, the rules of uniform classification and scoring, and the methods of assembling the information for reporting. When an individual agency has specific problems in compiling its crime statistics and its remedial efforts are unsuccessful, personnel from the FBI's Criminal Justice Information Services Division may visit the contributor to aid in resolving the difficulties.

The final responsibility for data submissions rests with the individual contributing law enforcement agency. Although every effort is made to ensure the validity of the data, accuracy of the statistics depends primarily on the adherence of each contributor to the established standards of reporting.

Population Estimation

For the 2007 population estimates used in this report, the FBI computed individual rates of growth from one year to the next for every city/town and county using 2000 decennial population counts and 2001 through 2006 population estimates from the U.S. Census Bureau. Each agency's rates of growth were averaged; that average was then applied and added to its 2006 Census population estimate to derive the agency's 2007 population estimate.

Population estimates for 2003 are based on the percent change in the state population from the U.S. Census Bureau's 2002 revised estimates and 2003 provisional estimates. Estimates for 1998 are based on the percent change in the state population from the U.S. Census Bureau's 1997 revised estimates and 1998 provisional estimates.

Crime Trends

Trend statistics offer the data user an additional perspective from which to study crime by showing fluctuations from year to year. Percent change tabulations in this publication are computed only for the reporting agencies that provided comparable data for the periods under consideration. The program excludes all figures from the trend calculations, except those received for common months from common agencies. Also excluded are unusual fluctuations that the program determines are the result of variables such as improved records procedures, annexations, etc.

Caution to Users

Data users should exercise care in making any direct comparison between data in this publication and those in prior issues of *Crime in the United States*. Because of differing levels of participation from year to year and reporting problems that require the UCR Program to estimate crime counts for certain contributors, the data are not comparable from year to year.

2007 Arrest Data

Because of changes in local agency reporting practices (updates to the NIBRS), figures are not comparable to previous years' data for Colorado (Denver). Limited arrest data were received from Illinois; i.e., only Chicago and Rockford provided statistics in accordance with UCR guidelines. Except for the cities of Minneapolis and St. Paul, the Minnesota State UCR Program's guidelines for reporting forcible rape arrest counts do not comply with the national UCR Program's guidelines; i.e., Minnesota data include arrests made for forcible rapes of male victims. Therefore, the state forcible rape counts that are published include only the totals received from Minneapolis and St. Paul. For 2007, only arrest totals (with no age or gender breakdowns) are available for Florida. Therefore, Florida arrest totals are included only in Table 69, "Arrests by State, 2007." No 2007 arrest data were received from the District of Columbia's Metropolitan Police Department. The only agency (Metro Transit Police) in the District of Columbia for which 12 months of arrest data were received has no attributable population. No 2007 arrest data were received from Hawaii. However, arrest totals for this state were estimated by the national UCR Program and were included in Table 29 "Estimated Number of Arrests, United States, 2007." No 2007 arrest data were received from the New York City Police Department. However, arrest totals for this area were estimated by the national UCR Program and

were included in Table 29 "Estimated Number of Arrests, United States, 2007."

Offense Estimation

Tables 1 through 5 and Table 7 of this publication contain statistics for the entire United States. Because not all law enforcement agencies provide data for complete reporting periods, the FBI includes estimated crime numbers in these presentations. The FBI estimates data for three areas: Metropolitan Statistical Areas (MSAs), cities outside MSAs, and nonmetropolitan counties. The FBI computes estimates for participating agencies not providing 12 months of complete data. For agencies supplying 3 to 11 months of data, the national UCR Program estimates for the missing data by following a standard estimation procedure using the data provided by the agency. If an agency has supplied less than 3 months of data, the FBI computes estimates by using the known crime figures of similar areas within a state and assigning the same proportion of crime volumes to nonreporting agencies. The estimation process considers the following: population size covered by the agency; type of jurisdiction, e.g., police department versus sheriff's office; and geographic location.

Estimation of State-Level Data

In response to various circumstances, the FBI calculates estimated offense totals for certain states. For example, some states do not provide forcible rape figures in accordance with UCR guidelines. In addition, problems at the state level have, at times, resulted in no useable data. Also, the conversion of the National Incident-Based Reporting System (NIBRS) data to Summary data has contributed to the need for unique estimation procedures. A summary of state-specific and offense-specific estimation procedures follows.

APPENDIX II. DEFINITIONS

The Uniform Crime Reporting (UCR) Program divides offense into two groups. Contributing agencies submit information on the number of Part I offenses known to law enforcement; those offenses cleared by arrest or exceptional means; and the age, sex, and race of persons arrested for each of thse offenses. Contributors provide only arrest data for Part II offenses.

Part I offenses include murder, and nonnegligent manslaughter, forcible rape, robbery, aggravated assault, burglary, larceny-theft, motor vehicle theft, and arson.

Violent crime is composed of four offenses: murder and nonnegligent manslaughter, forcible rape, robbery, and aggravated assault. According to the UCR Program's definition, violent crimes involve force or threat of force.

Criminal homicide—a.) Murder and nonnegligent manslaughter: the willful (nonnegligent) killing of one human being by another. Deaths caused by negligence, attempts to kill, assaults to kill, suicides, and accidental deaths are excluded. The program classifies justifiable homicides separately and limits the definition to (1) the killing of a felon by a law enforcement officer in the line of duty; or (2) the killing of a felon, during the commission of a felony, by a private citizen. b.) Manslaughter by negligence: the killing of another person through gross negligence. Traffic fatalities are excluded.

Forcible rape—The carnal knowledge of a female forcibly and against her will. Assaults and attempts to commit rape by force or threat of force are also included. Statutory rape (no force used—female victim is under the age of consent) and other sex offenses are excluded. Sexual attacks on males are counted as aggravated assaults or sex offenses, depending on the circumstances and the extent of any injuries.

Robbery—The taking or attempted taking of anything of value from the care, custody, or control of a person or persons by force or threat of force or violence and/or by putting the victim in fear.

Aggravated assault—An unlawful attack by one person upon another for the purpose of inflicting severe or aggravated bodily injury. This type of assault usually is accompanied by the use of a weapon or by means likely to produce death or great bodily harm. Attempted aggravated assaults that involve the display of—or threat to use—a gun, knife, or other weapon is included in this crime category because serious personal injury would likely result if the assault were completed. When aggravated assault and larceny-theft occur together, the offense falls under the category of robbery. Simple assaults are excluded.

Property crime includes the offenses of burglary, larceny-theft, motor vehicle theft, and arson. The object of the theft-type offenses is the taking of money or property, but there is no force or threat of force against the victims. The property crime category includes arson because the offense involves the destruction of property; however, arson victims may be subjected to force.

Burglary (breaking or entering)—The unlawful entry of a structure to commit a felony or a theft. The use of force to gain entry need not have occurred. The Program has three subclassifications for burglary: forcible entry, unlawful entry where no force is used, and attempted forcible entry. The UCR definition of "structure" includes, for example, apartment, barn, house trailer or houseboat when used as a permanent dwelling, office, railroad car (but not automobile), stable, and vessel (i.e., ship).

Larceny-theft (except motor vehicle theft)—The unlawful taking, carrying, leading, or riding away of property from the possession or constructive possession of another. Examples are thefts of bicycles or automobile accessories, shoplifting, pocket-picking, or the stealing of any property or article that is not taken by force and violence or by fraud. Attempted larcenies are included. Embezzlement, confidence games, forgery, worthless checks, and the like, are excluded.

Motor vehicle theft—The theft or attempted theft of a motor vehicle. It includes the stealing of automobiles, trucks, buses, motorcycles, snowmobiles, and the like. The taking of a motor vehicle for temporary use by persons having lawful access is excluded from this definition. A motor vehicle is self-propelled and runs on land surface and not on rails. Motorboats, construction equipment, airplanes, and farming equipment are specifically excluded from this category.

Arson—Any willful or malicious burning or attempt to burn, with or without intent to defraud, a dwelling house, public building, motor vehicle, aircraft, personal property of another, and the like. Limited data are available for arson because of limited participation and varying collection procedures by local law enforcement agencies. Arson statistics are included in trend, clearance, and arrest tables throughout *Crime in the United States*, but they are not included in any estimated volume data.

In addition to reporting Part I offenses, law enforcement agencies provide the UCR Program with monthly data on persons arrested for all crimes except traffic violations. These arrest data include the age, sex, and race of arrestees for both Part I and Part II offenses. **Part II** offenses encompass all crimes, except traffic violations, that are not classified as Part I offenses, including:

Other assaults (simple)—Assaults and attempted assaults which are not of an aggravated nature and do not result in serious injury to the victim.

Forgery and counterfeiting—The altering, copying, or imitating of something, without authority or right, with the intent to deceive or defraud by passing the copy or thing altered or imitated as that which is original or genuine; or the selling, buying, or possession of an altered, copied, or imitated thing with the intent to deceive or defraud. Attempts are included.

Fraud—The intentional perversion of the truth for the purpose of inducing another person or other entity in reliance upon it to part with something of value or to surrender a legal right. Fraudulent conversion and obtaining of money or property by false pretenses. Confidence games and bad checks, except forgeries and counterfeiting, are included.

Embezzlement—The unlawful misappropriation or misapplication by an offender to his/her own use or purpose of money, property, or some other thing of value entrusted to his/her care, custody, or control.

Stolen property; buying, receiving, possessing—Buying, receiving, possessing, selling, concealing, or transporting any property with the knowledge that it has been unlawfully taken, as by burglary, embezzlement, fraud, larceny, robbery, etc. Attempts are included.

Vandalism—To willfully or maliciously destroy, injure, disfigure, or deface any public or private property, real or personal, without the consent of the owner or person having custody or control by cutting, tearing, breaking, marking, painting, drawing, covering with filth, or any other such means as may be specified by local law. Attempts are included.

Weapons; carrying, possessing, etc.—The violation of laws or ordinances prohibiting the manufacture, sale, purchase, transportation, possession, concealment, or use of firearms, cutting instruments, explosives, incendiary devices, or other deadly weapons. Attempts are included.

Prostitution and commercialized vice—The unlawful promotion of or participation in sexual activities for profit, including attempts.

Sex offenses (except forcible rape, prostitution, and commercialized vice)—Statutory rape, offenses against chastity, common decency, morals, and the like. Attempts are included.

Drug abuse violations—The violation of laws prohibiting the production, distribution, and/or use of certain controlled substances. The unlawful cultivation, manufacture, distribution, sale, purchase, use, possession, transportation, or importation of any controlled drug or narcotic substance. Arrests for violations of state and local laws, specifically those relating to the unlawful possession, sale, use, growing, manufacturing, and making of narcotic drugs. The following drug categories are specified: opium or cocaine and their derivatives (morphine, heroin, codeine); marijuana; synthetic narcotics/manufactured narcotics that can cause true addiction (demerol, methadone); and dangerous nonnarcotic drugs (barbiturates, benzedrine).

Gambling—To unlawfully bet or wager money or something else of value; assist, promote, or operate a game of chance for money or some other stake; possess or transmit wagering information; manufacture, sell, purchase, possess, or transport gambling equipment, devices, or goods; or tamper with the outcome of a sporting event or contest to gain a gambling advantage.

Offenses against the family and children—Unlawful nonviolent acts by a family member (or legal guardian) that threaten the physical, mental, or economic well-being or morals of another family member and that are not classifiable as other offenses, such as assault or sex offenses. Attempts are included.

Driving under the influence—Driving or operating a motor vehicle or common carrier while mentally or physically impaired as the result of consuming an alcoholic beverage or using a drug or narcotic.

Liquor laws—The violation of state or local laws or ordinances prohibiting the manufacture, sale, purchase, transportation, possession, or use of alcoholic beverages, not including driving under the influence and drunkenness. Federal violations are excluded.

Drunkenness—To drink alcoholic beverages to the extent that one's mental faculties and physical coordination are substantially impaired. Excludes driving under the influence.

Disorderly conduct—Any behavior that tends to disturb the public peace or decorum, scandalize the community, or shock the public sense of morality.

Vagrancy—The violation of a court order, regulation, ordinance, or law requiring the withdrawal of persons from the streets or other specified areas; prohibiting persons from remaining in an area or place in an idle or aimless manner; or prohibiting persons from going from place to place without visible means of support.

All other offenses—All violations of state or local laws not specifically identified as Part I or Part II offenses, except traffic violations.

Suspicion—Arrested for no specific offense and released without formal charges being placed.

Curfew and loitering laws (persons under 18 years of age)—Violations by juveniles of local curfew or loitering ordinances.

Runaways (persons under 18 years of age)—Limited to juveniles taken into protective custody under the provisions of local statutes.

Hate crime—criminal offenses that are motivated, in whole or in part, by the offender's bias against a race, religion, sexual orientation, ethnicity/national origin, or disability and are committed against persons, property, or society.

APPENDIX III. GEOGRAPHIC AREA DEFINITIONS

The UCR Program collects crime data and supplemental information that make it possible to generate a variety of statistical compilations, including data presented by reporting areas. These statistics allow data users to analyze local crime data in conjunction with those for areas of similar geographic location or population size. The reporting areas that the UCR Program uses in its data breakdowns include community types, population groups, and regions and divisions. For community types, the UCR Program considers proximity to metropolitan areas using the designations created by the U.S. Office of Management and Budget (OMB). (Generally, sheriffs, county police, and state police report crimes within counties but outside of cities; local police report crimes within city limits.) The number of inhabitants living in a locale (based on the U.S. Census Bureau's figures) determines the population group into which the program places it. For its geographic breakdowns, the UCR Program divides the United States into regions, divisions, and states.

Regions and Divisions

The map below illustrates the four regions of the United States, along with their nine subdivisions as established by the Census Bureau. The UCR Program uses this widely recognized geographic organization when compiling the nation's crime data. The regions and divisions are as follows:

Northeast

New England—Connecticut, Maine, Massachusetts, New Hampshire, Rhode Island, and Vermont

Middle Atlantic—New York, New Jersey, and Pennsylvania

Midwest

East North Central—Illinois, Indiana, Michigan, Ohio, and Wisconsin

West North Central—Iowa, Kansas, Minnesota, Missouri, Nebraska, North Dakota, and South Dakota

South

South Atlantic—Delaware, District of Columbia, Florida, Georgia, Maryland, North Carolina, South Carolina, Virginia, and West Virginia

East South Central—Alabama, Kentucky, Mississippi, and Tennessee

West South Central—Arkansas, Louisiana, Oklahoma, and Texas

West

Mountain—Arizona, Colorado, Idaho, Montana, Nevada, New Mexico, Utah, and Wyoming

Pacific—Alaska, California, Hawaii, Oregon, and Washington

Community Types

To assist data users who wish to analyze and present uniform statistical data about metropolitan areas, the UCR Program uses reporting units that represent major population centers. The program compiles data for the following three types of communities:

Metropolitan statistical areas (MSAs)—Each MSA contains a principal city or urbanized area with a population of at least 50,000 inhabitants. MSAs include the principal city, the county in which the city is located, and other adjacent counties that have a high degree of economic and social integration with the principal city and county (as defined by the OMB), which is measured through commuting. In the UCR Program, counties within an MSA are considered metropolitan counties. In addition, MSAs may cross state boundaries.

In 2007, approximately 84.2 percent of the nation's population lived in MSAs. Some presentations in this publication refer to Metropolitan Divisions, which are subdivisions of an MSA that consists of a core with "a population of at least 2.5 million persons. A Metropolitan Division consists of one or more main/secondary counties that represent an employment center or centers, plus adjacent counties associated with the main county or counties through commuting ties," (Federal Register 65 [249]). Also, some tables reference suburban areas, which are subdivisions of MSAs that exclude the principal cities but include all the remaining cities (those having fewer than 50,000 inhabitants) and the unincorporated areas of the MSAs.

Because the elements that comprise MSAs, particularly the geographic compositions, are subject to change, the UCR Program discourages data users from making year-to-year comparisons of MSA data.

Cities Outside MSAs—Ordinarily, cities outside MSAs are incorporated areas. In 2007, cities outside MSAs made up 6.2 percent of the nation's population.

Nonmetropolitan Counties Outside MSAs—Most nonmetropolitan counties are composed of unincorporated areas. In 2007, 9.6 percent of the nation's population resided in nonmetropolitan counties.

Metropolitan and nonmetropolitan community types are further illustrated in the following table:

Metropolitan	Nonmetropolitan
Principal cities (50,000+ inhabitants) Suburban cities	Cities outside metropolitan areas
Metropolitan counties	Nonmetropolitan counties

Population Groups

The UCR Program uses the following population group designations:

Population Group	Political Label	Population Range
I	City	250,000 or more
II	City	100,000 to 249,999
III	City	50,000 to 99,999
IV	City	25,000 to 49,999
V	City	10,000 to 24,999
VI	City[1]	Fewer than 10,000
VIII (Nonmetropolitan county)	County[2]	N/A
IX (Metropolitan county)	County[2]	N/A

[1]Includes universities and colleges to which no population is attributed.
[2]Includes state police agencies to which no population is attributed.

Individual law enforcement agencies are the source of UCR data. The number of agencies included in each population group may vary from year to year because of population growth, geopolitical consolidation, municipal incorporation, etc. In noncensus years, the UCR Program estimates population figures for individual jurisdictions. (A more comprehensive explanation of population estimations can be found in Appendix I.)

The categories below show the number of agencies contributing to the UCR Program within each population group for 2007:

Population Group	Number of Agencies	Population Covered
I	73	54,837,759
II	189	28,430,342
III	472	32,458,407
IV	848	29,149,912
V	1,907	30,267,100
VI[1]	9,022	26,467,089
VIII (Nonmetropolitan county)[2]	3,054	30,492,750
IX (Metropolitan county)[2]	2,173	69,517,798
Total	17,738	301,621,157

[1]Includes universities and colleges to which no population is attributed.
[2]Includes state police to which no population is attributed.

APPENDIX IV. THE NATION'S TWO CRIME MEASURES

The Department of Justice administers two statistical programs to measure the magnitude, nature, and impact of crime in the nation: the Uniform Crime Reporting (UCR) Program and the National Crime Victimization Survey (NCVS). Each of these programs produces valuable information about aspects of the nation's crime problem. Because the UCR and NCVS programs are conducted for different purposes, use different methods, and focus on somewhat different aspects of crime, the information they produce together provides a more comprehensive panorama of the nation's crime problem than either could produce alone.

Uniform Crime Reporting (UCR) Program

The UCR Program, administered by the Federal Bureau of Investigation (FBI), was created in 1929 and collects information on the following crimes reported to law enforcement authorities: murder and nonnegligent manslaughter, forcible rape, robbery, aggravated assault, burglary, larceny-theft, motor vehicle theft, and arson. Law enforcement agencies also report arrest data for 21 additional crime categories.

The UCR Program compiles data from monthly law enforcement reports and from individual crime incident records transmitted directly to the FBI or to centralized state agencies that report to the FBI. The program thoroughly examines each report it receives for reasonableness, accuracy, and deviations that may indicate errors. Large variations in crime levels may indicate modified records procedures, incomplete reporting, or changes in a jurisdiction's boundaries. To identify any unusual fluctuations in an agency's crime counts, the program compares monthly reports to previous submissions of the agency and to those for similar agencies.

The FBI annually publishes its findings in a preliminary release in the spring of the following calendar year, followed by a detailed annual report, *Crime in the United States*, issued in the fall. (The printed copy of *Crime in the United States* is now published by Bernan Press.) In addition to crime counts and trends, this report includes data on crimes cleared, persons arrested (age, sex, and race), law enforcement personnel (including the number of sworn officers killed or assaulted), and the characteristics of homicides (including age, sex, and race of victims and offenders; victim-offender relationships; weapons used; and circumstances surrounding the homicides). Other periodic reports are also available from the UCR Program.

The state and local law enforcement agencies participating in the UCR Program are continually converting to the more comprehensive and detailed National Incident-Based Reporting System (NIBRS). The NIBRS provides detailed information about each criminal incident in 22 broad categories of offenses.

The UCR Program presents crime counts for the nation as a whole, as well as for regions, states, counties, cities, towns, tribal law enforcement areas, and colleges and universities. This allows for studies among neighboring jurisdictions and among those with similar populations and other common characteristics.

National Crime Victimization Survey

The NCVS, conducted by the Bureau of Justice Statistics (BJS), began in 1973. It provides a detailed picture of crime incidents, victims, and trends. After a substantial period of research, the BJS completed an intensive methodological redesign of the survey in 1993. It conducted this redesign to improve the questions used to uncover crime, update the survey methods, and broaden the scope of crimes measured. The redesigned survey collects detailed information on the frequency and nature of the crimes of rape, sexual assault, personal robbery, aggravated and simple assault, household burglary, theft, and motor vehicle theft. It does not measure homicide or commercial crimes (such as burglaries of stores).

Twice a year, Census Bureau personnel interview household members in a nationally representative sample of approximately 43,000 households (about 76,000 people). Approximately 150,000 interviews of individuals 12 years of age and over are conducted annually. Households stay in the sample for 3 years, and new households rotate into the sample on an ongoing basis.

The NCVS collects information on crimes suffered by individuals and households, whether or not those crimes were reported to law enforcement. It estimates the proportion of each crime type reported to law enforcement, and it summarizes the reasons that victims give for reporting or not reporting.

The survey provides information about victims (age, sex, race, ethnicity, marital status, income, and educational level); offenders (sex, race, approximate age, and victim-offender relationship); and crimes (time and place of occurrence, use of weapons, nature of injury, and economic consequences). Questions also cover victims' experiences with the criminal justice system, self-protective measures used by victims, and possible substance abuse by offenders. Supplements are added to the survey periodically to obtain detailed information on specific topics, such as school crime.

The BJS published the first data from the redesigned NCVS in a June 1995 bulletin. The publication of NCVS data includes *Criminal Victimization in the United States*, an annual report that covers the broad range of detailed information collected by the NCVS. The bureau also publishes detailed reports on topics such as crime against women, urban crime, and gun use in crime. The National

Archive of Criminal Justice Data at the University of Michigan archives the NCVS data files to help researchers perform independent analyses.

Comparing the UCR Program and the NCVS

Because the BJS designed the NCVS to complement the UCR Program, the two programs share many similarities. As much as their different collection methods permit, the two measure the same subset of serious crimes with the same definitions. Both programs cover rape, robbery, aggravated assault, burglary, theft, and motor vehicle theft; both define rape, robbery, theft, and motor vehicle theft virtually identically. (Although rape is defined analogously, the UCR Program measures the crime against women only, and the NCVS measures it against both sexes.)

There are also significant differences between the two programs. First, the two programs were created to serve different purposes. The UCR Program's primary objective is to provide a reliable set of criminal justice statistics for law enforcement administration, operation, and management. The BJS established the NCVS to provide previously unavailable information about crime (including crime not reported to police), victims, and offenders.

Second, the two programs measure an overlapping but nonidentical set of crimes. The NCVS includes crimes both reported and not reported to law enforcement. The NCVS excludes—but the UCR Program includes—homicide, arson, commercial crimes, and crimes committed against children under 12 years of age. The UCR Program captures crimes reported to law enforcement but collects only arrest data for simple assaults and sexual assaults other than forcible rape.

Third, because of methodology, the NCVS and UCR have different definitions of some crimes. For example, the UCR defines burglary as the unlawful entry or attempted entry of a structure to commit a felony or theft. The NCVS, not wanting to ask victims to ascertain offender motives, defines burglary as the entry or attempted entry of a residence by a person who had no right to be there.

Fourth, for property crimes (burglary, theft, and motor vehicle theft), the two programs calculate crime rates using different bases. The UCR Program rates for these crimes are per capita (number of crimes per 100,000 persons), whereas the NCVS rates for these crimes are per household (number of crimes per 1,000 households). Because the number of households may not grow at the same annual rate as the total population, trend data for rates of property crimes measured by the two programs may not be comparable.

In addition, some differences in the data from the two programs may result from sampling variation in the NCVS and from estimating for nonresponsiveness in the UCR Program. The BJS derives the NCVS estimates from interviewing a sample and are, therefore, subject to a margin of error. The bureau uses rigorous statistical methods to calculate confidence intervals around all survey estimates, and describes trend data in the NCVS reports as genuine only if there is at least a 90-percent certainty that the measured changes are not the result of sampling variation. The UCR Program bases its data on the actual counts of offenses reported by law enforcement agencies. In some circumstances, the UCR Program estimates its data for nonparticipating agencies or those reporting partial data.

Apparent discrepancies between statistics from the two programs can usually be accounted for by their definitional and procedural differences, or resolved by comparing NCVS sampling variations (confidence intervals) of crimes said to have been reported to police with UCR Program statistics.

For most types of crimes measured by both the UCR Program and the NCVS, analysts familiar with the programs can exclude those aspects of crime not common to both from analysis. Resulting long-term trend lines can be brought into close concordance. The impact of such adjustments is most striking for robbery, burglary, and motor vehicle theft, whose definitions most closely coincide.

With robbery, the BJS bases the NCVS victimization rates on only those robberies reported to the police. It is also possible to remove UCR Program robberies of commercial establishments, such as gas stations, convenience stores, and banks, from analysis. When users compare the resulting NCVS police-reported robbery rates and the UCR Program noncommercial robbery rates, the results reveal closely corresponding long-term trends.

Conclusion

Each program has unique strengths. The UCR Program provides a measure of the number of crimes reported to law enforcement agencies throughout the country. The program's Supplementary Homicide Reports provide the most reliable, timely data on the extent and nature of homicides in the nation. The NCVS is the primary source of information on the characteristics of criminal victimization and on the number and types of crimes not reported to law enforcement authorities.

By understanding the strengths and limitations of each program, it is possible to use the UCR Program and NCVS to achieve a greater understanding of crime trends and the nature of crime in the United States. For example, changes in police procedures, shifting attitudes towards crime and police, and other societal changes can affect the extent to which people report and law enforcement agencies record crime. NCVS and UCR Program data can be used in concert to explore why trends in reported and police-recorded crime may differ.

INDEX

INDEX

Offenses known to law enforcement, by state and city, 92
Offenses known to law enforcement, by university and college, 211
Robbery, by state and type of weapon, 300

GUAM
Law enforcement employees, 497

H
HANDGUNS
    see **FIREARMS OFFENSES**
HATE CRIMES
Agency hate crime reporting, by state, 519
Incidents, offenses, victims, and known offenders, by bias motivation, 511
Incidents per bias motivation, by state and agency, 520
Incidents, offenses, victims, and known offenders, by offense type, 511
Known offender's race, 516
Known offender's race, by bias motivation, 514
Known offender's race, by offense type, 512
Number of incidents and bias motivation, by location, 516
Number of incidents and victim type, by bias motivation, 516
Number of offenses and offense type, by bias motivation, 513
Number of victims and offense type, by bias motivation, 515
Offense type, by participating state, 517
Victim type, by offense type, 514
Zero data submitted, by state and agency, 553

HAWAII
Aggravated assault, by state and type of weapon, 301
Arrests, numbers and types of offenses, 377
Crime totals, 33, 41
Law enforcement employees, 393, 395, 396, 467, 476, 497
Murder, by state and type of weapon, 299
Offenses known to law enforcement, by counties, 222
Offenses known to law enforcement, by state and city, 92
Offenses known to law enforcement, by university and college, 211
Robbery, by state and type of weapon, 300

HOMICIDE
Murder and nonnegligent manslaughter
    see **MURDER AND NONNEGLIGENT MANSLAUGHTER**

HOUSEHOLD GOODS
Property stolen and recovered, by type and value, 302

I
IDAHO
Aggravated assault, by state and type of weapon, 301
Arrests, numbers and types of offenses, 377
Crime totals, 33, 41
Hate crime figures, 517–553
Law enforcement employees, 393, 395, 396, 467, 476, 497
Murder, by state and type of weapon, 299
Offenses known to law enforcement, by agencies, 258
Offenses known to law enforcement, by counties, 222
Offenses known to law enforcement, by state and city, 92
Offenses known to law enforcement, by university and college, 211
Robbery, by state and type of weapon, 300

ILLINOIS
Aggravated assault, by state and type of weapon, 301
Arrests, numbers and types of offenses, 377
Crime totals, 33, 41
Hate crime figures, 517–553
Law enforcement employees, 393, 395, 396, 467, 476, 497
Murder, by state and type of weapon, 299
Offenses known to law enforcement, by state and city, 92

Offenses known to law enforcement, by university and college, 211
Robbery, by state and type of weapon, 300

INDIANA
Aggravated assault, by state and type of weapon, 301
Arrests, numbers and types of offenses, 377
Crime totals, 33, 41
Hate crime figures, 517–553
Law enforcement employees, 393, 395, 396, 467, 476, 497
Murder, by state and type of weapon, 299
Offenses known to law enforcement, by agencies, 258
Offenses known to law enforcement, by counties, 222
Offenses known to law enforcement, by state and city, 92
Offenses known to law enforcement, by university and college, 211
Robbery, by state and type of weapon, 300

INTIMIDATION
Hate crimes, by offense type, 511
Hate crimes, number and type by bias motivation, 513
Hate crimes, number of victims, 515
Hate crimes, offender's race by offense type, 512
Hate crimes, state figures, 517

IOWA
Aggravated assault, by state and type of weapon, 301
Arrests, numbers and types of offenses, 377
Crime totals, 33, 41
Hate crime figures, 517–553
Law enforcement employees, 393, 395, 396, 467, 476, 497
Murder, by state and type of weapon, 299
Offenses known to law enforcement, by counties, 222
Offenses known to law enforcement, by state and city, 92
Offenses known to law enforcement, by university and college, 211
Robbery, by state and type of weapon, 300

J
JEWELRY
Property stolen and recovered, by type and value, 302

JUVENILE OFFENDERS
Arrests, by geographic region, 325
Arrests, by population group, 326
Arrests, cities, distribution by age, 346
Arrests, cities, distribution by race, 350
Arrests, cities, distribution by sex, 349
Arrests, cities, persons under 15, 18, 21, and 25, 348
Arrests, counties, persons under 15, 18, 21, and 25, 356, 364
Arrests, disposition of offenders taken into custody, 376
Arrests, distribution by age, 334
Arrests, distribution by race, 342
Arrests, distribution by sex, 341
Arrests, females, distribution by age, 338
Arrests, five-year trends, by age, 330
Arrests, five-year trends, by sex, 331
Arrests, males, distribution by age, 336
Arrests, metropolitan counties, distribution by age, 354
Arrests, metropolitan counties, distribution by race, 358
Arrests, metropolitan counties, distribution by sex, 357
Arrests, metropolitan counties, persons under 15, 18, 21, and 25, 356
Arrests, nonmetropolitan counties, distribution by age, 362
Arrests, nonmetropolitan counties, distribution by race, 366
Arrests, nonmetropolitan counties, distribution by sex, 365
Arrests, nonmetropolitan counties, persons under 15, 18, 21, and 25, 364
Arrests, suburban areas, distribution by age, 370
Arrests, suburban areas, distribution by race, 374
Arrests, suburban areas, distribution by sex, 373

MURDER AND NONNEGLIGENT MANSLAUGHTER (ACTUAL)

MURDER AND NONNEGLIGENT MANSLAUGHTER (ESTIMATED)

N

NATIONAL ORIGIN

NEBRASKA